Why You Need This New Edition

If you are wondering why you should add this new tenth edition of *Literature for Composition* to your personal library, here are 7 good reasons:

1. **Increased Number of Short Stories.** Eighteen stories are new to this edition. Some are by classic authors such as Guy de Maupassant, John Updike, and Jorge Luis Borges, but most are by contemporary writers, including Sherman Alexie, T. Coraghessan Boyle, Ha Jin, and ZZ Packer.

2. **New Essays, Poems, and Plays.** New to the book are essays by noted authors such as Barbara Ehrenreich and Stephen King; poems by contemporary poets such as Joy Harjo, Seamus Heaney, and Kay Ryan; two classic plays (Arthur Miller's *Death of a Salesman* and Sophocles' *Oedipus the King*) and one contemporary one-act play (Billy Goda's *No Crime*).

3. **Two New Thematic Chapters.** "Worlds beyond Worlds" explores a selection of literature concerned with the supernatural, and "All in a Day's Work" offers literature concerned with the challenges of the working world.

4. **New Chapter on Graphic Fiction.** This chapter contains four stories, beginning with a story told in a single panel and ending with Crumb and Mairowitz's graphic version of Kafka's "A Hunger Artist."

5. **New Chapter on Writing as Performance.** Picking up on Robert Frost's comment that "A poem is a performance in words," the chapter extends the idea to fiction, and to the idea that in reading a work of literature the *reader* mentally performs the work.

6. **New Chapter on the Pleasures of Reading and Writing Arguments.** This brief chapter takes a very short story by Bruce Holland, gives a student's responsive jottings and finished essay, and then analyzes the essay, thereby assisting readers to write their own college-level critical analyses.

7. **New Chapter Previews and MyLiteratureLab Connections.** New chapter preview sections preface each chapter in Parts 1–2, providing learning objectives to help you focus on key topics. New MyLiteratureLab boxes appear after any selection that has supporting material available on MyLiteratureLab, making it easier for you to find these rich media resources.

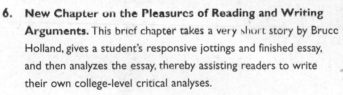

PEARSON

TENTH EDITION

Literature
for Composition

An Introduction to Literature

Sylvan Barnet
Tufts University

William Burto
University of Massachusetts at Lowell

William E. Cain
Wellesley College

PEARSON

Boston Columbus Indianapolis New York San Francisco Upper Saddle River
Amsterdam Cape Town Dubai London Madrid Milan Munich Paris Montréal Toronto
Delhi Mexico City São Paulo Sydney Hong Kong Seoul Singapore Taipei Tokyo

Vice President and Editor in Chief: Joseph P. Terry
Development Editor: Erin Jenkins
Executive Marketing Manager: Joyce Nilsen
Senior Supplements Editor: Donna Campion
Executive Digital Producer: Stefanie Snajder
Content Specialist: Erin Jenkins
Digital Editor: Sara Gordus
Production/Project Manager: Eric Jorgensen
Project Coordination, Text Design, and
    Electronic Page Makeup: Cenveo Publisher Services
Cover Designer/Manager: John Callahan
Cover Image: *Foreshortened View of Christiania,* Henrik Ibsen (1828–1906).
    Watercolor. De Agostini/Lebrecht Music & Arts.
Senior Manufacturing Buyer: Roy L. Pickering, Jr.
Printer/Binder: RRDonnelley/Crawfordsville
Cover Printer: Lehigh-Phoenix Color/Hagerstown
Text Font: Garamond Light

Credits and acknowledgments for works borrowed from other sources and reproduced, with permission, in this textbook appear on the appropriate page within text [or on pages 1428–37.]

Library of Congress Cataloging-in-Publication Data
Literature a for composition : essays, stories, poems, and plays / Sylvan Barnet, Tufts University; William E. Cain, Wellesley College; William Burto; University of Massachusetts at Lowell.—Tenth Edition.
    pages cm
  ISBN 978-0-321-82917-7
  1. College readers. 2. English language--Rhetoric--Problems, exercises, etc. 3. Criticism- -Authorship--Problems, exercises, etc. 4. Academic writing--Problems, exercises, etc. I. Barnet, Sylvan, editor of compilation. II. Burto, William, editor of compilation. III. Cain, William E., 1952- editor of compilation.
  PE1417.L633 2013
  808'.0427--dc23

                                2012045718

Copyright © 2014, 2011, 2007, 2005, 2003 by Sylvan Barnet, William Burto, William E. Cain

10 9 8 7 6 5 4 3 2—DOC—15 14 13

www.pearsonhighered.com

Student ISBN 10: 0-321-82917-4
Student ISBN 13: 978-0-321-82917-7

Contents

CHAPTER 3 The Reader as Writer   **56**

CHAPTER 4 The Pleasures of Reading—and of Writing
                Arguments about Literature   **95**

CHAPTER 8 Arguing an Interpretation   209

CHAPTER 9 Arguing an Evaluation   **276**

CHAPTER **10** Research: Writing with Sources   **306**

PART **II**

*Up Close: Thinking Critically about Literary Works
and Literary Forms*

CHAPTER **11** Critical Thinking: Arguing with Oneself, Asking
                Questions, and Making Comparisons   **316**

CHAPTER **12** A Brief Guide: Writing about Literature   **327**

P A R T   I I I

Standing Back: A Thematic Anthology

CHAPTER **19** Thinking Critically about Poems:
Two Case Studies   550

P A R T   I I I

Standing Back: A Thematic Anthology

CHAPTER **20** The World around Us   587

CHAPTER **21** Journeys 633

CHAPTER 22   Love and Hate   687

CHAPTER 23   Making Men and Women   740

C H A P T E R **24** Innocence and Experience   820

CHAPTER 25 All in a Day's Work   993

CHAPTER 28 Law and Disorder   1299

CHAPTER 29 Worlds beyond Worlds   1372

APPENDIX A Writing about Literature: An Overview
of Critical Strategies   **1393**

APPENDIX B Remarks about Manuscript Form   **1407**

APPENDIX C How Much Do You Know about Citing
Sources? A Quiz with Answers   **1422**

Contents by Genre

Essays

Short Stories

Drama

Poetry

Preface to Instructors

Literature for Composition is based on the assumption that students in composition or literature courses should encounter first-rate writing—not simply competent prose but the powerful reports of experience that have been recorded by highly skilled writers of the past and present, reports of experiences that must be shared.

Our view is not original. A thousand years ago in Japan, Lady Murasaki (978?–1026) wrote a scene in *The Tale of Genji* in which some of her characters talk about reading fiction, and one of them offers his opinion as to why an author writes:

> Again and again writers find something in their experience, or see something in the life around them, that seems so important they cannot bear to let it pass into oblivion. There must never come a time, the writer feels, when people do not know about this.

We assume that you share our belief that the study of such writing offers pleasure (we will talk more about pleasure—both the pleasure of reading and the pleasure of writing—in a few moments) and insight into life and also leads to increased skill in communicating. Here, at the beginning, we want to point out that the skills we emphasize in our discussions of communication are relevant not only to literature courses but to all courses in which students analyze texts or write arguments.

What Is New in the Tenth Edition?

Instructors familiar with earlier editions will notice that we retain our emphasis on critical thinking and argument, but we have made many substitutions in the literary works, most notably by substantially increasing the number of short stories. For the convenience of instructors who have used an earlier edition, we briefly summarize here the major changes:

Increased Number of Short Stories

- A few stories that were not widely taught have been dropped, and eighteen stories are new to this edition. Some are by classic authors such as Guy de Maupassant, Anatole France, and Jorge Luis Borges, but most are by contemporary writers, including Sherman Alexie, T. Coraghessan Boyle, Ha Jin, and ZZ Packer. Several are very short, "flash fiction," so brief that every sentence can be discussed in class.

New Essays, Poems, and Plays

- Essays (for instance, by Stephen King), poems (for instance, by Joy Harjo, Seamus Heaney, and Kay Ryan), and plays (notably *Oedipus the King* and *Death of a Salesman*).

Two New Thematic Chapters

- "All in a Day's Work." Among the sixteen authors represented in this chapter are Barbara Ehrenreich with an essay on her experience in an orientation program at Wal-Mart, Will Eisner with a work of graphic fiction, Gary Snyder and Marge Piercy (with poems), and Arthur Miller's *Death of a Salesman*. An

unusual feature in the chapter is a group of jokes about kinds of work: Students are invited to think about jokes as short stories.
- "Worlds beyond Worlds." The final chapter, offering literature concerned with the supernatural, includes classic popular ballads (for instance, "The Demon Lover," which lies behind Joyce Carol Oates's "Where Are You Going?, Where Have You Been?"), as well as now-classic unrealistic stories such as García Márquez's "A Very Old Man with Enormous Wings."

New Chapter on the Pleasures of Reading and Writing Arguments

- This brief chapter takes a very short story by Bruce Holland, gives a student's responsive jottings and final essay, and then analyzes the essay.

New Chapter on Writing as Performance

- Picking up on Robert Frost's comment that "A poem is a performance in words," the chapter extends the idea to fiction, and also to the idea that in reading a work of literature the reader mentally *performs* the work.

New Chapter on Graphic Fiction

- This chapter contains four stories, beginning with a story told in a single panel, and ending with Crumb and Mairowitz's graphic version of Kafka's "A Hunger Artist." (Another work of graphic fiction appears in a thematic chapter concerned with kinds of work.)

Key Features

Here are the key features of the tenth edition of *Literature for Composition*.

Extensive instruction in composition: Students are guided through the entire process of writing (especially writing arguments), beginning with generating ideas (for instance, by listing or by annotating a text), developing a thesis, supporting the thesis with evidence, and on through the final stages of documenting and editing. Twenty examples of student writing are included; most are prefaced with the students' preliminary notes, and some are annotated or otherwise analyzed.

Strategies for writing effective arguments: The tenth edition focuses on argument and evaluation, not only in the case studies but also in the discussion topics (headed "Joining the Conversation: Critical Thinking and Writing") that follow *every* reading. We emphasize the importance of questioning your own assumptions—a key principle in critical thinking—and we also emphasize the importance of providing evidence in the course of setting forth coherent, readable arguments.

Revised MLA guidelines for papers: The material concerning documentation is in accord with the latest MLA guidelines, as presented in the *MLA Handbook for Writers of Research Papers,* seventh edition (2009).

Wide range of literary selections: The book includes some three hundred selections, ranging from ancient classics such as Sophocles' *Antigone* to works written in the twenty-first century.

Abundant visual material, with suggestions about visual analysis: The book is rich in photographs, paintings, and facsimiles of manuscripts. The images are chosen to enhance the student's understanding of particular works of literature. For example, we include photos of Buffalo Bill and a facsimile of a draft of E. E. Cummings's poem about Buffalo Bill (to our knowledge, never before published in a textbook). Similarly, we include previously unpublished typescript pages of Faulkner's "A Rose for Emily," thereby helping students to think about the kinds of choices and changes that a serious writer makes. And, as we mentioned earlier, this new edition is strong in its representation of graphic fiction.

Introductory genre anthology: After preliminary chapters on getting ideas and thinking critically, students encounter chapters devoted to essays, fiction, drama, and poetry.

Thematic anthology: The chapters in Part 3 are arranged under ten themes: The World around Us, Journeys, Love and Hate, Making Men and Women, Innocence and Experience, All in a Day's Work, Identity in America, American Dreams and Nightmares, Law and Disorder, and Worlds beyond Worlds.

Case studies: The six case studies presented in this book give a variety of perspectives for writing arguments and organizing research: William Faulkner's "A Rose for Emily" (page 249), Flannery O'Connor (page 374), Emily Dickinson (page 550), Comparing Poems and Pictures (page 560), Robert Frost (page 624), and *Hamlet* (page 867).

Extensive material on research and the Internet: Because instructors are increasingly assigning research papers, the tenth edition includes material on short, medium, and long research papers, and it provides up-to-date instruction on evaluating, using, and citing electronic sources.

Words and images: The visual material includes a color insert section, "Word and Image," that presents twelve works of art that are the subjects of poems. Students analyze the poems and paintings and offer evidence to support their arguments. And again, we offer a strong representation of graphic fiction.

Checklists: Seventeen checklists focus on topics such as writing with a computer, revising paragraphs, editing a draft, and using the Internet. Students can use these checklists to become peer readers of their writing.

Organization

Although *Literature for Composition* is in large part an anthology of literature, it offers extensive instruction in writing, especially writing arguments.

Part I, "Getting Started: From Response to Argument," consists of ten chapters with some sixty short works of literature. The aim of all the chapters in this part is to help students read and respond—in writing. Chapter 1 is a crash course, a quick review for students who have already taken a course in composition. The next three chapters discuss annotating, freewriting, and listing, with several examples of students' notes and the essays they developed from those notes. Chapter 4 (new to this edition) emphasizes both pleasure and argument; it includes a mini-story as well as a student's responses and the student's final essay on the story. Chapter 5, "Writing as a Performance" (new to this edition), not only sees a work of literature as a performance (Robert Frost said a poem is "a performance in words") but also sees the *reading*—even the silent reading—of a work as a performance. The chapter concludes with two "txt poms," works that closely resemble what some students write when texting. Chapters 6 and 7 discuss writing explications and analyses; Chapters 8 through 10 cover arguing and research. These chapters include fourteen examples of student writing, most of which are accompanied by the preliminary journal entries or drafts that helped produce them.

Part II, "Up Close: Thinking Critically about Literary Works and Literary Forms," begins with a discussion of critical thinking (Chapter 11). This chapter invites students to use comparison to analyze E. E. Cummings's poem "Buffalo Bill 's." A photograph of Buffalo Bill and Sitting Bull is shown, as is the manuscript draft of the poem. The chapter also includes a very short story by Raymond Carver and Carver's revision of the story. We print the two versions side by side so students can study, line by line, a writer's revising his work. Chapter 12, "A Brief Guide: Writing about Literature," functioning as a preface to the next eight chapters, introduces students to four genres: the essay (Chapter 13), fiction (Chapters 14–16), drama (Chapter 17), and poetry (Chapters 18–19). The chapter on the essay includes two essays, and additional essays appear in the later thematic chapters. For instance, the thematic chapter "All in a Day's Work" includes an essay by Barbara Ehrenreich on orientation sessions for new employees at Wal-Mart. The three chapters on fiction begin with five stories by five authors, followed by a casebook on Flannery O'Connor (two of her stories, and a selection of her remarks about fiction), and conclude with material on graphic fiction (introductory explanations, then four examples). The chapter on drama (17) includes two plays; the two chapters on poetry include twenty-nine poems followed by case studies on Emily Dickinson (ten poems) and on poems about pictures (twelve poems).

In Part II, suggested topics for discussion and examples of student writing (annotations, journal entries, drafts, final essays) help students think critically and develop arguments about the material. Part II, then, offers a small anthology of literature organized by genre, as well as abundant guidance in thinking and writing about literature.

About 150 literary texts appear in Parts I and II; another 160 appear in Part III, "Standing Back: A Thematic Anthology," where the chapters present ten themes: The World around Us, Journeys, Love and Hate, Making Men and Women, Innocence and Experience, All in a Day's Work, Identity in America, American Dreams and Nightmares, Law and Disorder, and Worlds beyond Worlds. Here, as earlier, the essays, stories, plays, and poems are followed by questions to stimulate critical thinking and writing arguments.

The book concludes with three appendixes: "Writing about Literature: An Overview of Critical Strategies," "Remarks about Manuscript Form," and "How Much Do You Know about Citing Sources? A Quiz with Answers." The material on manuscript form may seem to be yet another discussion of writing, and some readers may wonder why it is put at the back of the book. Our explanation is that we see manuscript form as the final packaging of a product that develops during a complicated process, one that begins with reading, responding, and finding a topic, a thesis (supported by evidence), and a voice, not with worrying about the width of margins or the form of citations. The last thing to do in writing an essay, and therefore one of the last things we present in our book, is to set it forth in a pleasing and logical form fit for the reader's consumption. The quiz on plagiarism is a fresh and engaging look at a topic of enormous concern to students and instructors.

Resources for Students and Instructors

For Students

The *new* MyLiteratureLab® is a dynamic interactive online resource designed to accompany *Literature for Composition* and help students in their literature course. The site features an eAnthology with over 200 additional selections, Multimedia Instructional Resources, a Composing space for drafting and revising, and a Gradebook built specifically for courses with a heavy writing component. Longman Lectures—evocative, richly illustrated audio readings—engage students and give advice on how to read, interpret, and write about literary works; they are read by Longman authors. This powerful program also features Diagnostic Tests, Interactive Readings with clickable prompts, film clips of selections in *Literature for Composition,* Writers on Writing (video interviews with distinguished authors and poets that inspire students to explore their creativity), sample student papers, Literature Timelines, and resources for teaching Avoiding Plagiarism. *MyLiteratureLab.com* can be packaged at a nominal cost with most Pearson literature titles. It's the perfect resource for online literature-based composition and introduction to literature courses and can be delivered within Course Compass, Web CT, or Blackboard course management systems.

For Instructors

Instructor's Manual with detailed comments and suggestions for teaching each selection. This important resource, entirely written by the authors of the text, also contains references to critical articles and books that we have found to be the most useful. ISBN 0-321-84213-8.

Penguin Discount Novel Program offers, in cooperation with Penguin Group USA, a variety of Penguin paperbacks at a significant discount of sixty percent off the retail price—when packaged with any Pearson title. To review the list of titles available, visit the Pearson Penguin Group USA Web site at *www.pearsonhighered.com/penguin.*

Video Program is an impressive selection of videotapes that is available to qualified adopters to enrich students' experience of literature. The videos include selections from William Shakespeare, Sylvia Plath, Ezra Pound, and Alice Walker. Contact your Pearson Longman sales representative to see if you qualify.

The Longman Electronic Testbank for Literature features various objective questions on major works of fiction, short fiction, poetry, and drama. With this user-friendly download, instructors choose questions from the electronic testbank and print out the completed test for distribution.

Contact Us

For examination copies of any of these books, CDs, videos, and programs, contact your Pearson Longman sales representative, or write to Literature Marketing Manager, Pearson Education, 51 Madison Avenue, New York, NY 10010. For examination copies only, call (800) 922-0579. To order an examination copy online, go to *http:/www.pearsonhighered.com* or send an e-mail to exam.copies@pearson.

Acknowledgments

We would like to thank the following reviewers, who provided their feedback during the revision of the tenth edition: Cieltia Adams, Bossier Parish Community College; Alexander Ames, Grantham University; Paul Keith Boran, University of Mississippi; Melinda Cianos, Notre Dame of Maryland University; Morgan Cutterini, Itawamba Community College; Shelley Fischer, College of Southern Nevada; Twister Marquiss, Texas State University–San Marcos; Elizabeth Gassel Perkins, Darton College; and Kenneth Poff, St. Philip's College.

   In preparing the first nine editions of *Literature for Composition,* we were indebted to Elizabeth Addison, Jonathan Alexander, James Allen, Kathleen Anderson-Wyman, Larry Armstrong, William D. Atwill, Patricia Baldwin, Mary J. Balkun, Daniel

Barwick, David Beach, Daniel Bender, Billie Bennet, Mary Anne Bernal, Phyllis Betz, Kenneth R. Bishop, Margaret Blayney, Bertha Norman Booker, John P. Boots, Pam Bourgeois, Noelle Brada-Williams, Carol Ann Britt, Jennifer Bruer, Robin W. Bryant, Sharon Buzzard, Kathleen Shine Cain, Diana Cardenas, William Carpenter, Evelyn Cartright, Allan Chavkin, Mike Chu, Alan P. Church, Dennis Ciesielski, Arlene Clift-Pellow, Walter B. Connolly, Stanley Corkin, Linda Cravens, Bruce Danner, Donald A. Daiker, Phebe Davidson, Thomas Deans, Beth DeMeo, John Desjarlais, Emily Dial-Driver, John Dobelbower, Ren Draya, James Dubinsky, Gail Duffy, Bill Elliott, Leonard W. Engel, William Epperson, Gareth Euridge, Martin J. Fertig, Elinor C. Flewellen, Kay Fortson, Marie Foster, Donna Friedman, Larry Frost, Loris Galford, Charlene Gill, Chris Grieco, Esther Godfrey, Dwonna Goldstone, Jessica Beth Gordon, Kim Greenfield, Susan Grimland, Debbie Hanson, Dorothy Hardman, Sandra H. Harris, Syndey Harrison, Sally Harrold, Tom Hayes, Keith Haynes, Michael Hennessey, Mary Herbert, Ana B. Hernandez, Maureen Hoag, Allen Hoey, Diane Houston, Elizabeth Howells, Clayton Hudnall, Joyce A. Ingram, Craig Johnson, Michael Johnson, Angela Jones, Kristianne Kalata, Rodney Keller, Beth Kemper, Glenn Klopfenstein, Alison Kuehner, Donya Lancaster, Theresa René LeBlanc, Regina Lebowitz, Margaret Lindgren, John Loftis, Robert Lynch, Maria Makowiecka, Phil Martin, Kate Massengale, Dennis McDonald, Sara McKnight Boone, Delma McLeod-Porter, Linda McPherson, Bill McWilliams, Martin Meszaros, Zack Miller, JoAnna S. Mink, Dorothy Minor, Wayne Moore, Charles Moran, Patricia G. Morgan, Nancy Morris, Jonathan Morrow, Christina Murphy, Sean Nighbert, Richard Nielson, Torria Norman, David Norlin, Marsha Nourse, John O'Connor, Chris Orchard, Phyllis Orlicek, Eric Otto, Suzanne Owens, Janet Palmer, James R. Payne, Stephanie Pelkowski, Don K. Pierstorff, Gerald Pike, Louis H. Pratt, John Prince, Sharon Prince, Michael Punches, David Raymond, Bruce A. Reid, Thomas Reynolds, Linda Robertson, Lois Sampson, Terry Santos, Daniel Schierenbeck, Sigmar J. Schwarz, Jim Schwartz, Robert Schwegler, Linda Scott, Herbert Shapiro, William Shelley, Janice Slaughter, David Slater, Martha Ann Smith, Tiga Spitsberg, Judith Stanford, Pam Stinson, Darlene Strawser, Geri Strecker, Jim Streeter, Anthony Stubbs, David Sudol, Beverly Swan, Leesther Thomas, Raymond L. Thomas, Susan D. Tilka, Mary Trachsel, Dorothy Trusock, Billie Varnum, John H. Venne, Mickey Wadia, Nancy Walker, Betty Weldon, Patrick White, Jonathon Wild, Bertha Wise, Arthur Wohlgemuth, Cary Wolfe, Sallie Woolf, Linda Woodson, Kathy J. Wright, Rebecca Wright, Carlson Yost, Dennis Young, and Gary Zacharias.

No book of this kind gets done without a great deal of assistance from the publisher. We received insightful editorial guidance from Katharine Glynn and Vivian Garcia, and more recently from Erin Jenkins. Eric Jorgensen (production manager at Pearson) and Barbara Lipson (production coordinator at Cenveo) kept things moving smoothly, and Vernon Nahrgang expertly copyedited the manuscript. Lois Lombardo (project manager at Cenveo) efficiently solved innumerable last-minute problems. Beth Keister handled the difficult job of securing text permissions, and Jorgensen Fernandez the equally difficult job of image permissions.

Bill Cain also thanks his wife, Barbara, and his daughters, Julia and Isabel, for their love and support. If our students had the help that we have had, they would regularly submit A papers.

SYLVAN BARNET
WILLIAM BURTO
WILLIAM E. CAIN

CHAPTER 1

How to Write an Effective Essay: A Crash Course

What is written without effort, in general is read without pleasure.

SAMUEL JOHNSON

Chapter Preview

After reading this chapter you will be able to

- Describe the basic strategy for writing an essay, from choosing a topic to proofreading the final version
- Approach a first draft purposefully
- Revise a draft effectively
- Participate in the peer review process
- Demonstrate your understanding of the writing process by preparing a final version of an essay

Later pages will speak in detail about the writing process; here we offer a brief overview.

The Basic Strategy

Students have assured us that these suggestions are helpful.

- **Choose a topic and a tentative thesis,** an *argument*.
- **Generate ideas,** for instance, by asking yourself questions such as "Why did the author—a woman—tell the story from the point of view of this male character rather than that female character?" and "Does this story give me some insight into life?"
- **Make a tentative outline** of points you plan to make.
- **Rough out a first draft,** working from your outline (don't worry about spelling, punctuation, etc.), but don't hesitate to depart from the outline when new ideas come to you in the process of writing.
- **Make large-scale revisions** in your draft by reorganizing, or by adding details to clarify and support assertions, or by deleting or combining paragraphs.
- **Make small-scale revisions** by revising and editing sentences, checking spelling and grammar.
- **Revise your opening and concluding paragraphs.** Be certain that they are *interesting*, not mere throat-clearing and not mere summary.
- **Have someone read your revised draft** and comment on it.
- **Revise again,** taking into account the reader's suggestions.

- Read this latest version and **make further revisions as needed,** so that your thesis—your argument—is evident.
- **Proofread** your final version.

All writers must work out their own procedures and rituals, but the following basic suggestions will help you write effective essays. They assume that you have annotated the margins of the text and have jotted notes on index cards, but you can easily adapt the principles if you use a laptop. If your paper involves using sources, consult also Chapter 10, "Research: Writing with Sources."

Looking Closely: Approaching a First Draft

- **Look carefully at the work or works you will write about.**
- **Choose a worthwhile and compassable subject,** something that interests you and is not so big that your handling of it must be superficial. As you work, shape your topic, narrowing it, for example, from "Characterization in Updike's 'A & P'" to "Updike's Use of Contrasting Characters in 'A & P.'"
- **Keep your purpose in mind.** Although your instructor may ask you, perhaps as a preliminary writing assignment, to jot down your early responses—your initial experience of the work—it is more likely that he or she will ask you to write an analysis in which you will connect details, draw inferences, and argue that such-and-such is the case. That is, almost surely you will be asked to do more than write a summary or to report your responses; you probably will be expected to support a *thesis*, to make a claim, to offer an *argument*: "The metaphors are chiefly drawn from nature and, broadly speaking, they move from sky and sea to the earth, to human beings, which is to say that they become closer at hand, more immediate, more personal."

Don't expect to have a sound thesis at the very beginning of your work on an essay. The thesis will probably come to you only after you have done some close looking and have stimulated ideas by asking yourself questions. Almost surely you will see that the initial thesis needs to be modified in the light of evidence that you encounter. In short, your thesis will evolve in the course of thinking about what you are looking at.

An essay that evaluates a work will not only offer a value judgment but will also support the judgment with evidence. Even an explication—a sort of line-by-line paraphrase (see Chapter 6)—presents an argument, holding that the work means such-and-such. In thinking about your purpose, remember, too, that your *audience* will in effect determine the amount of detail that you must give. Although your instructor may in reality be your only reader, probably you should imagine that your audience consists of people pretty much like your classmates—intelligent but not especially familiar with the topic on which you have recently become a specialist. In putting yourself into the shoes of your imagined readers, think of reasonable objections the readers might raise, and respond appropriately to these objections.

1. **Keep looking at the literary work you are writing about.** Jot down notes on all relevant matters.
    - You can generate ideas for writing about the issues raised by essays, stories, plays, and poems by asking yourself questions such as those given on pages 342–43, 358–60, 440–41, and 537–38.
    - As you look and think, reflect on your observations and record them.

- When you have an idea, jot it down, perhaps on a post-it note attached to the margin of the book page; don't assume that you will remember it when you begin writing. Many people—if they are not taking notes on a computer—find that 4-by-6-inch index cards are handy for those notes that will not fit in the margins.
- If you do use cards, put only one point on each card, and write a brief caption on the card (e.g., "Significance of title," or "Night = death???" Later you can arrange the cards so that relevant notes are grouped together.

2. **When taking notes from secondary sources, do not simply highlight or photocopy.**
   - Take brief notes, *summarizing* important points and jotting down your own critiques of the material.
   - Read the material analytically, thoughtfully, with an open mind and a questioning spirit.
   - When you read in this attentive and tentatively skeptical way, you will find that the material is valuable not only for what it tells you but also for the ideas that you yourself produce in responding to it.

Writing your paper does not begin when you sit down to write a draft; rather, it begins when you write your first thoughtful notes.

3. **Sort out your notes, putting together what belongs together.** Three separate cards with notes about the texture of the materials of a building, for instance, probably belong together. Reject cards irrelevant to your topic.
4. **Organize your notes into a reasonable sequence.** Your notes contain ideas (or at least facts that you can think about); now the packets of cards have to be put into a coherent sequence. When you have made a tentative arrangement, review it; you may discover a better way to group your notes, and you may even want to add to them. If so, start reorganizing.

A tripartite organization usually works. For this structure, tentatively plan to devote your opening paragraph(s) to a statement of the topic or problem and a proposal of your hypothesis or thesis. The essay can then be shaped into three parts:

- a beginning, in which you identify the work(s) that you will discuss, giving the necessary background and, in a sentence or two, setting forth your underlying argument, your thesis;
- a middle, in which you develop your argument, chiefly by offering evidence and by taking account of possible objections to your argument; and
- a conclusion, in which you wrap things up, perhaps by giving a more general interpretation or by setting your findings in a larger context. (To read more about concluding paragraphs, see pages 7, 17, 175–76, 219, and 439–40.)

In general, organize the material from the simple to the complex in order to ensure intelligibility. For instance, if you are discussing the structure of a poem, it will probably be best to begin with the most obvious points and then to turn to the subtler but perhaps equally important ones. Similarly, if you are comparing two characters, it may be best to move from the most obvious contrasts to the least obvious. When you have arranged your notes into a meaningful sequence, you have begun a key step: dividing your material into paragraphs.

5. **Get it down on paper.** Most essayists find it useful to jot down some sort of **outline,** a map indicating the main idea of each paragraph and, under each main idea, supporting details that give it substance. An outline—not necessarily anything formal, with capital and lowercase letters and Roman and Arabic numerals, but merely key phrases in some sort of order—will help you to overcome the paralysis called "writer's block" that commonly afflicts professional as well as student writers. For an example of a student's rough outline, see the jottings on page 19 that were turned into an essay on page 15.

A page of paper with ideas listed in some sort of sequence, however rough, ought to encourage you. You will discover that you do have something to say. And so, despite the temptation to sharpen another pencil or to have another cup of coffee, follow the advice of Isaac Asimov, author of 225 books: "Sit down and start writing."

If you do not feel that you can work from note cards and a rough outline, try another method: Get something down on paper, writing (preferably on a computer) freely, sloppily, automatically, or whatever, but allowing your ideas about what the work means to you and how it conveys its meaning—rough as your ideas may be—to begin to take visible form. If you are like most people, you cannot do much precise thinking until you have committed to paper at least a rough sketch of your initial ideas. At this stage you are trying to find out what your ideas are, and in the course of getting them down on paper you will find yourself generating new ideas. We *think* with words. Later you can push and polish your ideas into shape, perhaps even deleting all of them and starting over, but it is a lot easier to improve your ideas once you see them in front of you than it is to do the job in your head. On paper, one word leads to another; in your head, one word often blocks another.

You may realize, as you near the end of a sentence, that you no longer believe it. Okay; be glad that your first idea led you to a better one, and pick up your better one and keep going with it. What you are doing, by trial and error, is pushing your way not only toward clear expression but also toward sharper ideas and richer responses.

Revising: Achieving a Readable Draft

Good writing is *re*writing. The evidence? Heavily annotated drafts by Chekhov, Keats, Hemingway, Tolstoy, Woolf—almost any writer you can name. Of course, it is easy enough to spill out words, but, as the dramatist Richard Sheridan said 200 years ago, "Easy writing's curst hard reading." Good writers find writing is difficult because they care; they care about making sense, so they will take time to answer reasonable objections to their arguments and to find the exact words, the words that enable them to say precisely what they mean, so their readers will get it right. And they care about holding a reader's attention; they recognize that part of the job is to be interesting.

1. **Keep looking and thinking,** asking yourself questions and providing tentative answers, searching for additional material that strengthens or weakens your main point, and taking account of it in your outline or draft.

Now is probably the time to think about a title for your essay. It is usually a good idea to let your reader know what your topic is—which works of literature you will discuss—and what your approach will be. For instance, your topic might be Kate Chopin's "Désirée's Baby"—a story about the response to a white woman who gives birth to a black infant—and your approach might be that it is still relevant today. At this stage your title is still tentative, but thinking about that title will help you to organize your thoughts and to determine which of your notes are relevant and which are not. Remember, the title is the first part of the paper that your reader encounters. You will gain the reader's goodwill by providing a helpful, interesting title.

2. **With your outline or draft in front of you, write a more lucid version,** checking your notes for fuller details. If you wrote your draft on a computer, do not revise it by reading the monitor. Print a hard copy and revise it with pen or pencil. You need to read the essay more or less as your instructor will read it. True, the process of revising by hand takes more time than revising on a computer, but time is exactly what you need to devote to the process of revision. When you wrote your first draft, you were eager to find out what you thought, what you knew, what you did not know. Now, in the revising stage, you need to write slowly, thoughtfully. Later you will keyboard the handwritten revisions into the computer.

In revising an early draft it is probably best to start by concentrating on *large-scale revisions*—reorganization, additions (for instance, you may now see that you need to define a term, or to give an example, or to quote further from the work you are discussing). You will probably also make substantial deletions because you now see that some sentences or paragraphs, although interesting, are redundant or irrelevant.

Although it is best to start with large-scale revisions (what teachers of composition somewhat grandly call "global revision"), the truth is that when most writers revise, whether they be experienced or inexperienced, they do not proceed methodically. Rather, they jump around, paying attention to whatever attracts their attention at the moment, like a dog hunting for fleas—and that is not a bad way to proceed. Still, you might at least plan to work in the following sequence:

- **Introductory matters:** Make sure that your title and opening paragraph(s) give your readers an idea of where you will be taking them. Is your thesis evident?
- **Matters of organization:** If some of your material now seems to be in the wrong place, cut and paste. The Golden Rule is "Put together what belongs together." Is your concluding paragraph conclusive without being merely repetitive?
- **Evidence:** Make sure that your assertions are supported by evidence and that the evidence is of varying sorts, ranging from details in the works to quotations from appropriate secondary sources.
- **Counter-evidence:** Consider the objections that a reasonable reader might raise to some or all of your points, and explain why these objections are not substantial.
- **Coherence** in sentences, in paragraphs, and between paragraphs: Usually this is a matter of adding transitional words and phrases (*furthermore, therefore, for instance, on the other hand*).

- **Tone:** Your sentences inevitably convey information not only about your topic but about you yourself. Do the sentences suggest stuffiness? Or are they too informal, too inappropriately casual?
- **Editorial matters:** Check the spelling of any words that you are in doubt about, check the punctuation, and check the form of footnotes and bibliography (list of works cited).

If you find that some of your earlier jottings are no longer relevant, eliminate them; but make sure that your argument flows from one point to the next. It is not enough to keep your thesis in mind; you must keep it in the reader's mind. As you write, your ideas will doubtless become clearer, and some may prove to be poor ideas. (We rarely know exactly what our ideas are until we set them down on paper. As the little girl said, replying to the suggestion that she should think before she speaks, "How do I know what I think until I see what I say?") Not until you have written a draft do you really have a strong sense of what you feel and know, and of how good your essay may be.

If you have not already made an outline at this stage, it is probably advisable to make one in order to ensure that your draft is reasonably organized. Jot down, in sequence, each major point and each subpoint. You may find that some points need amplification, or that a point made on page three really ought to go on page one.

Later you will concern yourself with *small-scale revisions* (polishing sentences, clarifying transitions, varying sentence structure if necessary, checking spelling and documentation).

3. **After a suitable interval, preferably a few days, again revise and edit the draft.** To write a good essay, you must be a good reader of the essay you are writing. (We are not talking at this stage about proofreading or correcting spelling errors). Van Gogh said, "One becomes a painter by painting." Similarly, one becomes a writer by writing—and by rewriting, by revising. In revising their work, writers ask themselves many questions:
   - Do I mean what I say?
   - Do I say what I mean? (Answering this question will generate other questions: Do I need to define my terms? add examples to clarify? reorganize the material so that a reader can grasp it?)

A Rule for Writers: Put yourself in the reader's shoes to make sure not only that the paper has an organization but that the organization will be clear to your reader. If you imagine a classmate as the reader of the draft, you may find that you need to add transition words (*for instance, on the other hand*), clarify definitions, and provide additional supporting evidence.

During this part of the process of writing, read the draft in a skeptical frame of mind. You engaged in critical thinking when you made use of sources; now apply the same questioning spirit to your own writing. In taking account of your doubts, you will probably unify, organize, clarify, and polish the draft.

Reminder: If you have written your draft on a computer do not try to revise it on the monitor. Print the entire draft, and then read it—as your reader will be reading it—page by page, not screen by screen. Almost surely you will detect errors in a hard copy that you miss on the screen. Only by reading the printed copy will you be able to see if, for instance, paragraphs are too long.

After producing a draft that seems good enough to show to someone, writers engage in yet another activity: They edit. **Editing** includes such work as checking the accuracy of quotations by comparing them with the original, checking a dictionary for the spelling of doubtful words, and checking a handbook for doubtful punctuation—for instance, whether a comma or a semicolon is needed in a particular sentence.

✔ CHECKLIST: *Revising a Draft*

Have I asked myself the following questions?

☐ Does the draft fulfill the specifications (e.g., length, scope) of the assignment?

☐ Does the draft have a point, a focus?

☐ Is the title interesting and informative? Does it create a favorable first impression?

☐ Are the early paragraphs engaging, and do they give the reader a fairly good idea of what will follow, perhaps by naming the works of art and the approach?

☐ Are arguable assertions supported with evidence?

☐ Are the readers kept in mind, for instance, by defining terms that they may be unfamiliar with? Are possible objections faced and adequately answered?

☐ If quotations are included, are they introduced rather than just dumped into the essay? Are quotations as brief as possible? Might summaries (properly credited to the sources) be more effective than long quotations?

☐ Are *all* sources cited, including Internet material?

☐ Is the organization clear, reasonable, and effective? (Check by making a quick outline.)

☐ Does the final paragraph nicely round off the paper, or does it merely restate— unnecessarily—the obvious?

☐ Does the paper include whatever visual materials the reader may need to see?

Peer Review

Almost all professional writers get help—from friends, from colleagues, and especially from editors who are paid to go over their manuscripts and call attention to matters that need clarification. If possible, get a fellow student to read your manuscript and give you his or her responses. Do not confuse this sort of help—recommended by all instructors—with plagiarism, which is the unacknowledged use of someone else's words or ideas. Your reader is not rewriting the paper for you, but merely suggesting that (for instance) your title is misleading, that here you need a clear example, there you are excessively repetitive, and so forth. If you are unfamiliar with the process of peer review and uncertain about the nature of plagiarism, we urge you to read the discussions on pages 314–15 and in Appendix C.

If peer review is a part of the writing process in your course, the instructor may distribute a sheet with suggestions and questions. The preceding checklist is an example of such a sheet.

Preparing the Final Version

1. **If you have received comments from a reader, consider them carefully.** Even when you disagree with them, they may alert you to places in your essay that need revision or clarification.

When a friend, a classmate, or another peer reviewer has given you help, acknowledge that person in a footnote or endnote. (If you look at almost any book, you will notice that the author acknowledges the help of friends and colleagues. In your own writing follow this practice.) Here are sample acknowledgments from papers by students:

> I wish to thank Anna Aaron for numerous valuable suggestions.

> I thank Paul Gottsegen for calling my attention to passages that needed clarification, and Jane Leslie for suggesting the comparison between Sammy in Updike's "A & P" and the unnamed narrator in Joyce's "Araby."

2. **Write, type, or print a clean copy,** following the principles concerning margins, pagination, footnotes, and so on, set forth in Appendix B.
3. **If you have borrowed ideas, be sure to give credit,** usually in footnotes, to your sources. Remember that plagiarism is not limited to the unacknowledged borrowing of words; a borrowed idea, even when put into your own words, requires acknowledgment. (On giving credit to sources, see pages 312, 314–15.)
4. **Proofread a hard copy, make corrections as necessary, and reprint.**

All of this adds up to a recipe in a famous Victorian cookbook: "First catch your hare, then cook it."

CHAPTER 2

The Writer as Reader

Interviewer: Did you know as a child you wanted to be a writer?
Toni Morrison: No. I wanted to be a reader.

Chapter Preview

After reading this chapter you will be able to

- Explain the process of reading and responding to literature
- Create an argumentative thesis
- Compare two mini-stories
- Evaluate a student essay

Reading and Responding

Learning to write is in large measure learning to read. The text you should read most carefully is the one you yourself write, an essay—probably an argument defending an interpretation. It may start as a jotting in the margin of a book you are reading or as a note in a journal, and it will go through several drafts before it becomes a finished essay. To produce something that another person will find worth reading, you must read each draft with care, trying to imagine the effect your words are likely to have on your reader. In writing about literature, you will apply some of the same critical skills to your reading; that is, you will examine your responses to what you are reading, and you will try to account for them.

Let's begin by looking at a very short story by Kate Chopin (1851–1904). (Her name is pronounced in the French way, something like "show pan.") Kate O'Flaherty, born into a prosperous family in St. Louis, in 1870 married Oscar Chopin, a French-Creole businessman from Louisiana. They lived in New Orleans, where they had six children. Oscar died of malaria in 1882, and in 1884 Kate returned to St. Louis, where, living with her mother and children, she began to write fiction.

KATE CHOPIN

Ripe Figs

Maman-Nainaine said that when the figs were ripe Babette might go to visit her cousins down on the Bayou-Lafourche where the sugar cane grows. Not that the ripening of figs had the least thing to do with it, but that is the way Maman-Nainaine was.

It seemed to Babette a very long time to wait; for the leaves upon the trees were tender yet, and the figs were like little hard, green marbles.

But warm rains came along and plenty of strong sunshine, and though Maman-Nainaine was as patient as the statue of la Madone, and Babette as restless as a humming-bird, the first thing they both knew it was hot summertime. Every day

9

Babette danced out to where the fig-trees were in a long line against the fence. She walked slowly beneath them, carefully peering between the gnarled, spreading branches. But each time she came disconsolate away again. What she saw there finally was something that made her sing and dance the whole long day.

When Maman-Nainaine sat down in her stately way to breakfast, the following morning, her muslin cap standing like an aureole about her white, placid face, Babette approached. She bore a dainty porcelain platter, which she set down before her godmother. It contained a dozen purple figs, fringed around with their rich, green leaves.

5   "Ah," said Maman-Nainaine arching her eyebrows, "how early the figs have ripened this year!"

"Oh," said Babette. "I think they have ripened very late."

"Babette," continued Maman-Nainaine, as she peeled the very plumpest figs with her pointed silver fruit-knife, "you will carry my love to them all down on Bayou-Lafourche. And tell your Tante Frosine I shall look for her at Toussaint— when the chrysanthemums are in bloom."

[1893]

Reading as Re-creation

If we had been Chopin's contemporaries, we might have read this sketch in *Vogue* in 1893 or in an early collection of her works, *A Night in Acadie* (1897). But since we live more than a century later, we inevitably read "Ripe Figs" in a somewhat different way. And this gets us to an important truth about writing and reading. A writer writes, sets forth his or her meaning, and attempts to guide the reader's responses, as we all do when we write an email home saying that we're thinking of dropping a course or asking for news or money. To this extent, the writer creates the written work and puts a meaning in it.

But the reader, whether reading that written work as a requirement or for recreation, *re-creates* it in terms of his or her own experience and understanding. For instance, if the letter-writer's appeal for money is too indirect, the reader may miss it entirely or may sense it but feel that the need is not urgent. If, on the other hand, the appeal is direct or demanding, the reader may feel imposed upon, even assaulted. "Oh, but I didn't mean it that way," the writer later protests. Nevertheless, that's the way the reader took it. The email is "out there," a physical reality standing between the writer and the reader, but its *meaning* is something both the reader and the writer make.

Since all readers bring themselves to a written work, they each bring something individual. Although many of Chopin's original readers knew that she wrote chiefly about the people of Louisiana, especially Creoles (descendants of the early French and Spanish settlers), Cajuns (descendants of the French whom the British had expelled from Canada in the eighteenth century), African Americans, and mulattoes, those readers must have varied in their attitudes about such people. And many of today's readers do *not* (before they read a work by Chopin) know anything about her subject. Some readers may know where Bayou-Lafourche is, and they may have notions about what it looks like, but most readers will not. Indeed, many readers will not know that a bayou is a sluggish, marshy inlet or outlet of a river or lake.

Moreover, even if a present-day reader in Chicago, Seattle, or Juneau knows what a bayou is, he or she may assume that "Ripe Figs" depicts a way of life still current, whereas a reader from Louisiana may see in the work a lost way of life, a depiction of the good old days (or perhaps the bad old days, depending on the reader's point of view). Much depends, we can say, on the reader's storehouse of experience.

To repeat: Reading is a *re*-creation. An author tries to guide our responses, but inevitably our own experiences, including our ethnic background and education, contribute to our responses. You may find useful a distinction that E. D. Hirsch makes in *Validity in Interpretation* (1967). For Hirsch,

- the *meaning* in a text is the author's intended meaning;
- the *significance* is the particular relevance for each reader.

In this view, when you think about meaning you are thinking about what the author was trying to say and to do—for instance, to take an old theme and treat it in a new way. When you think about significance, you are thinking about what the work does for you—how it enlarges your mind, deepens your understanding of love or grief, offends you by its depiction of women, or produces some other effect.

Collecting Evidence, Making Reasonable Inferences

Does this mean, then, that there is no use talking (or writing) about literature, since all of us perceive it in our individual ways, rather like the seven blind men encountering an elephant in the fable? One man, you will recall, touched the elephant's tail (or was it his trunk?) and said that the elephant is like a snake; another touched the elephant's side and said the elephant is like a wall; a third touched the elephant's leg and said the elephant is like a tree, and so on. This familiar story is usually told to illustrate human limitations, but each of the blind men *did* perceive an aspect of the elephant—an elephant is massive, like a wall or a tree, and an elephant is (in its way) remarkably supple, as you will know if you have given peanuts to one.

As readers we can and should make an effort to understand what an author is getting at. To begin, we should make an effort to understand unfamiliar words. Perhaps we need not look up every word that we don't know, at least on the first reading, but if certain unfamiliar words are repeated and thus seem especially important, we will want to look them up.

It happens that in "Ripe Figs" a French word appears: "*Tante* Frosine" means "*Aunt* Frosine." Fortunately, the meaning of the word is not crucial, and the context probably makes it clear that Frosine is an adult, which is all that we really need to know about her. But a reader who does not know that chrysanthemums bloom in late summer or early autumn will miss part of Chopin's meaning. The point is this: The writer is pitching, and she expects the reader to catch.

On the other hand, although writers tell us a good deal, they cannot tell us everything. We know that Maman-Nainaine is Babette's godmother, but we don't know exactly how old Maman-Nainaine and Babette are. Further, Chopin tells us nothing of Babette's parents. It *sounds* as though Babette and her godmother live alone, but readers' opinions may differ. One reader may argue that Babette's parents must be dead or ill; another may argue that the status of her parents is irrelevant and that what counts is that Babette is supervised by only one person, a mature woman.

In short, a text includes **indeterminacies** (passages that careful readers agree are open to various interpretations) and **gaps** (things left unsaid in the story, such as why a godmother rather than a mother takes care of Babette). As we work our way through a text, we keep reevaluating what we have read, pulling the details together to make sense of them, in a process called **consistency building.**

Whatever the gaps, careful readers will collect evidence and draw many reasonable inferences about Maman-Nainaine. We can list them:

She is older than Babette.
She has a "stately way," and she is "patient as the statue of la Madone."
She has an odd way (is it exasperating, engaging, or a little of each?) of connecting actions with the seasons.
Given this last point, she seems to act slowly, to be very patient.
She is apparently used to being obeyed.

At this point you may want to go back and reread "Ripe Figs" to see what else you can say about Maman-Nainaine.
And now what of Babette?

She is young.
She is active and impatient ("restless as a humming-bird").
She is obedient.

At this point, too, you may want to add to the list.

If you compare your additions with those of a classmate, you may find that the two of you disagree about what may reasonably be inferred from Chopin's words. Suppose, for instance, that your classmate says that although Babette is outwardly obedient, inwardly she probably hates Maman-Nainaine. Would you agree that this is an acceptable inference? If you don't agree, how might you convince your classmate that such a response is not justified? What arguments (supported by what evidence) would you offer? We are speaking here of an activity of mind we call **critical thinking,** a topic to be discussed in the next chapter.

Reading with Pen in Hand

It's probably best to read a work of literature straight through, enjoying it and letting yourself be carried along to the end. But then, when you have an overall view, you'll want to read it again, noticing (for example) how certain innocent-seeming details early in the work prove to be important later.

Perhaps the best way to read attentively is, after a first reading, to mark the text, underlining or highlighting passages that seem especially interesting, and to jot notes or queries in the margins. (*Caution*: Annotate and highlight, but don't get so carried away that you highlight entire pages.)

Recording Your First Responses

Another useful way of getting at the meaning of a work of literature is to jot down your initial responses to it, recording your impressions as they come to you, in any order—almost as though you're talking to yourself. Since no one else is going to read your notes, you can be entirely at ease. You can write in sentences or not; it's up to you.

You can jot down your responses either before or after you annotate the text. Some readers find that annotating a text helps to produce ideas for further jottings; others prefer to jot down a few thoughts immediately after a first reading, and then, stimulated by these thoughts, they reread and annotate the text.

KATE CHOPIN

Ripe Figs

Maman-Nainaine said that when the figs were ripe Babette might go to visit her cousins down on the Bayou-Lafourche where the sugar cane grows. Not that the ripening of figs had the least thing to do with it, but that is the way Maman-Nainaine was.

It seemed to Babette a very long time to wait; for the leaves upon the trees were tender yet, and the figs were like little hard, green marbles.

But warm rains came along and plenty of strong sunshine, and though Maman-Nainaine was as patient as the statue of la Madone, and Babette as restless as a hummingbird, the first thing they both knew it was hot summertime. Every day Babette danced out to where the fig-trees were in a long line against the fence. She walked slowly beneath them, carefully peering between the gnarled, spreading branches. But each time she came disconsolate away again. What she saw there finally was something that made her sing and dance the whole long day.

When Maman-Nainaine sat down in her stately way to breakfast, the following morning, her muslin cap standing like an aureole about her white, placid face, Babette approached. She bore a dainty porcelain platter, which she set down before her godmother. It contained a dozen purple figs, fringed around with their rich, green leaves.

"Ah," said Maman-Nainaine arching her eyebrows, "how early the figs have ripened this year!"

"Oh," said Babette. "I think they have ripened very late."

"Babette," continued Maman-Nainaine, as she peeled the very plumpest figs with her pointed silver fruit-knife, "you will carry my love to them all down on Bayou-Lafourche. And tell your Tante Frosine I shall look for her at Toussaint—when the chrysanthemums are in bloom."

Handwritten annotations:

strange

?

contrast between M-N and B

another contrast ceremonious

Check? this

nice echo

contrast like a song is M-N herself like a plump fig?

time passes fast for M-N slowly for B

B entrusted with a message of love

opens with figs; ends with chrys. (autumn)

fulfillment? Equivalent to figs ripening?

Write whatever comes into your mind, whatever the literary work triggers in your own imagination, whatever you think are the important ideas or values, based on your own experience.

Here is a student's first response to "Ripe Figs":

This is a very short story. I didn't know stories were this short, but I like it because you can get it all quickly and it's no trouble to reread it carefully. The shortness, though, leaves a lot of gaps for the reader to fill in. So much is not said. Your imagination is put to work.

But I can see Maman-N sitting at her table—pleasantly powerful—no one you would want to argue with. She's formal and distant—and definitely has quirks. She wants to postpone Babette's trip, but we don't know why. And you can sense B's frustration.

But maybe she's teaching her that something really good is worth waiting for and that anticipation is as much fun as the trip. Maybe I can develop this idea.

Another thing. I can tell they are not poor—from two things. The pointed silver fruit knife and the porcelain platter, and the fact that Maman sits down to breakfast in a "stately" way. They are the leisure class. But I don't know enough about life on the bayous to go into this. Their life is different from mine; no one I know has that kind of peaceful rural life.

Identifying Your Audience and Purpose

Now suppose that you are beginning the process of writing about "Ripe Figs" for someone else. The first question to ask yourself is: For whom am I writing? That is, who is your *audience*? (You are probably writing because an instructor has asked you to do so, but you must still imagine an audience. Your instructor may tell you, for instance, to write for your classmates, or to write for the best teacher you had in high school.)

- If you are writing for people who are familiar with some of Chopin's work, you won't have to say much about the author.
- If you are writing for an audience that perhaps has never heard of Chopin, you may want to include a brief biographical note of the sort we gave.
- If you are writing for an audience that you believe has read several works by Chopin, you may want to make comparisons, explaining—arguing, really—that "Ripe Figs" resembles or differs from Chopin's other work.

In a sense, your audience is your collaborator; it helps you to decide what you will say. You are also helped by your sense of *purpose*. If your aim is to introduce readers to Chopin, you will make points that reflect this purpose. If your aim is to tell people what you think "Ripe Figs" means to say about human relationships, or about time, you will address that subject. If your aim is to have a little fun and to entertain an audience that is already familiar with "Ripe Figs," you may decide to write a parody (a humorous imitation) of the story.

Your Turn: Arguing a Thesis in an Essay

Let's assume that you want to describe "Ripe Figs" to someone who has not read it. You will briefly summarize the action, such as it is, and will mention where it takes place; tell who the characters are, including what their relationship is; and note what, if anything, happens to them. Beyond that, you'll try to explain as honestly as you can what makes "Ripe Figs" appealing or interesting—or trifling, or boring, or whatever. That is, you will *argue* a thesis, even though you won't want to make so formal a statement as "In this essay I will argue that . . . " or "This essay will attempt to prove that . . . " Your essay will essentially be an argument because (perhaps after a brief summary of the work) you will point to the evidence that has caused you to respond as you did.

A Sample Essay by a Student

Here is an essay that a student, Antonia Tenori, wrote for this assignment.

Tenori 1

Antonia Tenori

Professor Lee

English 102

11 February 2013

Images of Ripening in Kate Chopin's "Ripe Figs"

Very little happens in Kate Chopin's one-page story, "Ripe Figs."
Maman-Nainaine tells her goddaughter Babette that she may "visit her
cousins down on the Bayou-Lafourche" "when the figs were ripe"; the figs
ripen, and Babette is given permission to go. So little happens in "Ripe Figs"
that the story at first appears merely to be a character sketch that illustrates, through Babette and her godmother, the contrast between youth and
age. But by means of the natural imagery of the tale, Chopin suggests more
than this: She asks her readers to see the relationship of human time to
nature's seasons, and she suggests that, try as we may to push the process of
maturity, growth or "ripening" happens in its own time.

The story clearly contrasts the impatience of youth with the patience and
dignity that come with age. Babette, whose name suggests she is still a "little
baby," is "restless as a humming-bird." Each day when she eagerly goes to see if
the figs have ripened, she doesn't simply walk but she dances. By contrast,
Maman-Nainaine has a "stately way," she is "patient as the statue of la Madone,"
and there is an "aureole"—a radiance—"about her white, placid face." The brief
dialog near the end of the story also emphasizes the difference between the two
characters. When the figs finally ripen, Maman-Nainaine is surprised (she arches
her eyebrows), and she exclaims, "how early the figs have ripened this year!"
Babette replies, "I think they have ripened very late."

Chopin is not simply remarking here that time passes slowly for young people, and quickly for old people. She suggests that nature moves at its own pace regardless of human wishes. Babette, young and "tender" as the fig leaves, can't wait to "ripen." Her visit to Bayou-Lafourche is not a mere pleasure trip, but represents her coming into her own season of maturity. Babette's desire to rush this process is tempered by a condition that her godmother sets: Babette must wait until the figs ripen, since everything comes in its own season. Maman-Nainaine recognizes the patterns of the natural world, the rhythms of life. By asking Babette to await the ripening, the young girl is asked to pay attention to the patterns as well.

Chopin further suggests that if we pay attention and wait with patience, the fruits of our own growth will be sweet, plump, and beautiful, like the "dozen purple figs, fringed around with their rich, green leaves," that Babette finally offers her godmother. Chopin uses natural imagery effectively, interweaving the young girl's growth with the rhythms of the seasons. In this way, the reader is connected with both processes in an intimate and inviting way.

[New page]

Work Cited

Chopin, Kate. "Ripe Figs." *Literature for Composition*. Ed. Sylvan Barnet, William Burto, and William E. Cain. 10th ed. New York: Pearson, 2014. 9–10. Print.

The Argument Analyzed

- The title of the essay is informative; it clearly indicates the focus of the analysis. Notice, too, that it is much more interesting than "An Analysis of a Story" or "An Analysis of Kate Chopin's 'Ripe Figs'" or "'Ripe Figs': A Study" or "An Analysis of Imagery." For your own essays, construct titles that inform and interest your reader.
- The first sentence names the author and title being written about. Strictly speaking, this information is redundant, since it appears in the essay's title, but it is customary to give the author's full name and the title of the work early in the essay, and it is essential to give such information when it is not in the title.
- The second sentence offers enough plot summary to enable the reader to follow the discussion. But notice that the essay as a whole is much more than a summary of the plot. Summary here is offered early in order to make the analysis intelligible. Chiefly, the opening paragraph presents one view (the view that Antonia Tenori believes is inadequate); then, after a transitional "but," it offers a second view and presents a thesis—the point that she will argue.

  Perhaps the most common error students make in writing about literature is to confuse a summary of the plot with analysis of the work. A little plot-telling is acceptable, to remind your reader of what happens, but normally your essay will be devoted to setting forth a thesis about a work and supporting that thesis with evidence. Your readers do not want to know what happens in the work; they want to know what you make of the work—how you interpret it, or why you like or dislike it.
- In the second paragraph, Tenori supports her thesis by providing brief quotations. These quotations are not padding; rather, they are evidence supporting her assertion that Chopin "contrasts the impatience of youth with the patience and dignity that come with age."
- In the third paragraph the writer develops her thesis ("Chopin is not simply . . . She suggests . . . ").
- The final paragraph begins with a helpful transition ("Chopin *further* suggests"), offers additional evidence, and ends with a new idea (about the reader's response to the story) that takes the discussion a step further. The essay avoids the deadliest kind of conclusion, a mere summary of the essay ("Thus we have seen," or some such words). Tenori's effective final sentence nicely draws the reader into the essay. (Effective final sentences can be hard to write; we give advice about them on pages 3, 175–76, and 219.)

Antonia Tenori wrote this paper for an assignment in which students were told to write "about 500 words (two double-spaced typed pages)." If the first question to ask is To whom am I writing?, the second question to ask is What is the length of the assignment? The answer to this second question will provide two sorts of guidance: It will give you some sense of how much time you should devote to preparing the paper—an instructor expects you to spend more time on a ten-page paper than on a one-page paper—and it will give you a sense of how much detail you can include. For a short paper—say, one or two pages—you will need to make your main point with directness; you will not have space for lots of details, just those that support the main point. This is what Tenori aims to achieve in her second and third paragraphs, where she highlights the term "ripens" and briefly, but effectively, develops its implications. For a longer paper, three to five pages or more, you can examine the characters, setting, and central themes in depth, and you can focus on more details in the text to strengthen your analysis.

Behind the Scenes: From Early Responses to Final Version

Antonia Tenori's essay is good because it is clear and interesting, and especially because it helps to develop a reader's understanding and enjoyment of Chopin's story. Now let's go backstage, so to speak, to see how this student turned her notes into an effective final draft.

Tenori's Earliest Responses. After reading the story, Tenori annotated it, marking whatever she thought especially noteworthy. She then jotted down ideas in the Notebook application from Circus Ponies Software, although she could just as easily have used several other applications. Is "Ripe Figs" a story, or is it just a character sketch? (She put her responses on a page for that topic.) What contrasts are notable? (She recorded the material on another notebook page.) What words or phrases or images are unusual? (She recorded this material on another notebook page.) A day later, when she returned to work on her paper, stimulated by another reading of "Ripe Figs" and a review of her notes, Tenori made additional jottings.

Organizing Notes. When the time came to turn her notes into a draft essay, she reviewed the notes and added further thoughts. Next, she organized the note pages, putting together into one section the pages about characterization, and into another section the pages about the seasons. Reviewing the notes in each section, on the basis of her review (after making a backup copy), she deleted a few pages that no longer seemed useful and moved an occasional page into a different section (via the Contents view). She then started to think about how she might organize her essay.

As a first step in settling on an organization, she arranged the notebook sections into a sequence that seemed reasonable. It made sense, she thought, to begin with a brief biographical sketch of Chopin, but she soon decided not to include this material because the reader would probably already know it, and in any case it was not relevant to the argument she planned to set forth. She decided to go on to her major points about the story, then to refine some of these points, and finally to offer a conclusion. This organization, she felt, was reasonable and would enable her reader to follow her argument easily.

Preparing a Preliminary Outline. In order to get a clear idea of where she might be going, Tenori then typed an outline, following the sequence of her note packets—the gist of what at this stage seemed to be the organization of her chief points in the OmniOutliner (Omni Group), although she could just as easily have used the Outline view in Microsoft Word or even pen and paper. In short, she prepared a map to confirm that each part of her paper would lead coherently to the next part.

Surveying her outline, Tenori became aware of points that she should have included but had overlooked. Her first outline and the revised version of it follow.

Remember, a tentative outline is not a straitjacket that determines the shape of the final essay. To the contrary, it is a preliminary map that helps the writer to see not only pointless detours that need to be eliminated but also undeveloped areas that need to be worked up. As the two versions of Tenori's outline indicate, drafting her map enabled her to make important changes before writing a first draft.

First Outline	Revised Outline
Bio of Chopin	*Little plot, emph. on contrasting characters*
Plot summary	*Characters related to seasons*
Characterization	*Contrasts*
Babette	*spring vs autumn*
Maman-N	*youth vs maturity*
Contrasts	*impatience vs patience (?)*
Youth: activity, impatient	*Significance, meaning*
Age: stately,"statue"	*Maman-N as teacher*
Differences in perception of nature	*some things can't be hurried*
Point? Meaning?	*implication that B is maturing, can*
	carry message, will become aware of
	the changing seasons, and that there is a
	right time for each action

Writing a Draft. Working from her thoughtfully revised outline, Tenori wrote a first draft, which she then revised. The second draft, when further revised, became the final essay. Microsoft Word, for example, allows you to track the revisions made to a document and look at different versions of a document. However, many writers find comfort in having a printed copy of each draft to go over with a pen; the desired changes can then be made (and kept track of) on the computer.

For more about writing with a computer, see pages 72 and 311.

Other Possibilities for Writing

You might write a paper of a very different sort, based on the same story by Chopin. Consider the following possibilities:

1. Write a sequel, moving from fall to spring.
2. Write a letter from Babette, at Bayou-Lafourche, to Maman-Nainaine.
3. Imagine that Babette is now an old woman, writing her memoirs. What does she say about Maman-Nainaine?
4. Write a narrative based on your own experience of learning a lesson in patience.

Looking Closely at Two Contemporary Mini-Stories: Lydia Davis's "Childcare" and "City People"

LYDIA DAVIS

Lydia Davis, born in 1947 in Northampton, Massachusetts, grew up in New York City and then lived for several years in France and Ireland. She has translated French literature into English and written several books of stories. Among her awards is a MacArthur Fellowship.

Childcare

It's his turn to take care of the baby. He is cross.
    He says, "I never get enough done."
    The baby is in a bad mood, too.
    He gives the baby a bottle of juice and sits him well back in a big armchair.
    He sits himself down in another chair and turns on the television.
    Together they watch *The Odd Couple*.

[2007]

In Davis's *Varieties of Disturbance*, the book from which we reprint "Childcare," the story appears in the middle of a page that is otherwise blank. The very appearance on the page is part of the performance, and it is also part of—dare we say?—the meaning. We see a largely blank page, a bare world, not much to look at, not much to make life rich. What do we know about the inhabitants of this world?

- The unnamed man (he is merely "he") is "cross," and the unnamed baby "is in a bad mood, too."
- The next thing we learn about the man is what we deduce from his statement, "I never get enough done." Ah, he is someone who wants to accomplish something. That sounds admirable.
- But he thinks the temporary job ("it's his turn") of caring for the baby interferes with his unspecified aspirations. That sounds not so nice, and we may wonder, What sort of a guy is this who resents caring for his infant?

"*Once upon a time, they lived happily ever after.*"

The next things we learn dispose us favorably toward the man:

- "He gives the baby a bottle of juice and sits him well back in a big armchair." This business of sitting the child "well back in a big armchair" suggests that the man takes some care to make sure that the child is secure, is safely placed. We like that, we are reassured.
- The man then sits down in another chair and "turns on the television." Television? We might have thought that this man who can "never get enough done" would balance his checkbook, or read the newspaper, or answer a letter, but no, he watches television. That's not a crime, but for a guy who complains that he "can never get enough done," it does seem a bit much.
- The final sentence is, "Together they watch *The Odd Couple*." Surely the thought crosses a reader's mind that these two are themselves an odd couple, and the reader may reasonably conclude that in some ways the man— cross, claiming that he can't get anything done—is as infantile as the baby.

It's a story told very simply, chiefly in simple sentences: "He says," "The baby is," "He gives," etc. Only twice does the author use compound sentences (simple sentences joined by a conjunction, in this case the most childlike of all conjunctions, "and," the language found in Dick and Jane children's books). Not much happens in this very simply told story, but it tells us all that we need to know about the unnamed man. And perhaps it tells us something about life, even about our own lives, such as the disparity between our grand view of ourselves and the simple reality.

Now for a second very short story by Lydia Davis.

City People

They have moved to the country. The country is nice enough: there are quail sitting in the bushes and frogs peeping in the swamps. But they are uneasy. They quarrel more often. They cry, or she cries and he bows his head. He is pale all the time now. She wakes in a panic at night, hearing him sniffle. She wakes in a panic again, hearing a car go up the driveway. In the morning there is sunlight on their faces but mice are chattering in the walls. He hates the mice. The pump breaks. They replace the pump. They poison the mice. Their neighbor's dog barks. It barks and barks. She could poison the dog.

"We're city people," he says, "and there aren't any nice cities to live in."

[2001]

Joining the Conversation: Critical Thinking and Writing

1. What elements of performance—perhaps we can say Davis's craftsmanship—do you see in this tiny narrative?
2. Does the story give at least a tiny glimpse of some aspect of life? Please explain.
3. We are not told *why* these people have moved from the city to the country. Is it reasonable to offer a guess? If you think a reader can plausibly guess why they moved, what, in your view, is the reason for the move?

A Story, with a Student's Notes and Final Essay

RAY BRADBURY

Ray Bradbury (1920–2012) was born in Waukegan, Illinois, and educated there and in Los Angeles. While a high school student he published his first science fiction in the school's magazine, and by 1941 he was publishing professionally. The story printed here is from The Martian Chronicles *(1950), a collection of linked short stories. Among his other works are* Fahrenheit 451 *(1953),* Something Wicked This Way Comes *(1962), and* Death Is a Lonely Business *(1985).*

August 2026: There Will Come Soft Rains

In the living room the voice-clock sang, *Tick-Tock, seven o'clock, time to get up, time to get up, seven o'clock!* as if it were afraid that nobody would. The morning house lay empty. The clock ticked on, repeating and repeating its sounds into the emptiness. *Seven-nine, breakfast time, seven-nine!*

In the kitchen the breakfast stove gave a hissing sigh and ejected from its warm interior eight pieces of perfectly browned toast, eight eggs sunny-side up, sixteen slices of bacon, two coffees, and two cool glasses of milk.

"Today is August 4, 2026," said a second voice from the kitchen ceiling, "in the city of Allendale, California." It repeated the date three times for memory's sake. "Today is Mr. Featherstone's birthday. Today is the anniversary of Tilita's marriage. Insurance is payable, as are the water, gas, and light bills."

Somewhere in the walls, relays clicked, memory tapes glided under electric eyes.

5   *Eight-one, tick-tock, eight-one o'clock, off to school, off to work, run, run, eight-one!* But no doors slammed, no carpets took the soft tread of rubber heels. It was raining outside. The weather box on the front door sang quietly: "Rain, rain, go away; rubbers, raincoats for today. . . ." And the rain tapped on the empty house, echoing.

Outside, the garage chimed and lifted its door to reveal the waiting car. After a long wait the door swung down again.

At eight-thirty the eggs were shriveled and toast was like stone. An aluminum wedge scraped them into the sink, where hot water whirled them down a metal throat which digested and flushed them away to the distant sea. The dirty dishes were dropped into a hot washer and emerged twinkling dry.

Nine-fifteen, sang the clock, *time to clean.*

Out of warrens in the wall, tiny robot mice darted. The rooms were acrawl with the small cleaning animals, all rubber and metal. They thudded against chairs, whirling their mustached runners, kneading the rug nap, sucking gently at hidden dust. Then, like mysterious invaders, they popped into their burrows. Their pink electric eyes faded. The house was clean.

10   *Ten o'clock.* The sun came out from behind the rain. The house stood alone in a city of rubble and ashes. This was the one house left standing. At night the ruined city gave off a radioactive glow which could be seen for miles.

Ten-fifteen. The garden sprinklers whirled up in golden founts, filling the soft morning air with scatterings of brightness. The water pelted windowpanes, running down the charred west side where the house had been burned evenly free of its white paint. The entire west face of the house was black, save for five places. Here the silhouette in paint of a man mowing a lawn. Here, as in a photograph, a woman bent to pick flowers. Still farther over, their images burned on wood in one titanic instant, a small boy, hands flung into the air; higher up, the image of a thrown ball, and opposite him a girl, hands raised to catch a ball which never came down.

The five spots of paint—the man, the woman, the children, the ball—remained. The rest was a thin charcoaled layer.

The gentle sprinkler rain filled the garden with falling light.

Until this day, how well the house had kept its peace. How carefully it had inquired, "Who goes there? What's the password?" and, getting no answer from lonely foxes and whining cats, it had shut up its windows and drawn shades in an old-maidenly preoccupation with self-protection which bordered on a mechanical paranoia.

15 It quivered at each sound, the house did. If a sparrow brushed a window, the shade snapped up. The bird, startled, flew off! No, not even a bird must touch the house!

The house was an altar with ten thousand attendants, big, small, servicing, attending, in choirs. But the gods had gone away, and the ritual of the religion continued senselessly, uselessly.

Twelve noon.

A dog whined, shivering, on the front porch.

The front door recognized the dog voice and opened. The dog, once huge and fleshy, but now gone to bone and covered with sores, moved in and through the house, tracking mud. Behind it whirred angry mice, angry at having to pick up mud, angry at inconvenience.

20 For not a leaf fragment blew under the door but what the wall panels flipped open and the copper scrap rats flashed swiftly out. The offending dust, hair, or paper, seized in miniature steel jaws, was raced back to the burrows. There, down tubes which fed into the cellar, it was dropped into the sighing vent of an incinerator which sat like evil Baal in a dark corner.

The dog ran upstairs, hysterically yelping to each door, at last realizing, as the house realized, that only silence was here.

It sniffed the air and scratched the kitchen door. Behind the door, the stove was making pancakes which filled the house with a rich baked odor and the scent of maple syrup.

The dog frothed at the mouth, lying at the door, sniffing, its eyes turned to fire. It ran wildly in circles, biting at its tail, spun in a frenzy, and died. It lay in the parlor for an hour.

Two o'clock, sang a voice.

25 Delicately sensing decay at last, the regiments of mice hummed out as softly as blown gray leaves in an electrical wind.

Two-fifteen.

The dog was gone.

In the cellar, the incinerator glowed suddenly and a whirl of sparks leaped up the chimney.

Two thirty-five.

30 Bridge tables sprouted from patio walls. Playing cards fluttered onto pads in a shower of pips. Martinis manifested on an oaken bench with egg-salad sandwiches. Music played.

But the tables were silent and the cards untouched.

At four o'clock the tables folded like great butterflies back through the paneled walls. *Four-thirty*.

The nursery walls glowed.

35   Animals took shape: yellow giraffes, blue lions, pink antelopes, lilac panthers cavorting in crystal substance. The walls were glass. They looked out upon color and fantasy. Hidden films clocked through well-oiled sprockets, and the walls lived. The nursery floor was woven to resemble a crisp, cereal meadow. Over this ran aluminum roaches and iron crickets, and in the hot still air butterflies of delicate red tissue wavered among the sharp aroma of animal spoors! There was the sound like a great matted yellow hive of bees within a dark bellows, the lazy bumble of a purring lion. And there was the patter of okapi feet and the murmur of a fresh jungle rain, like other hoofs, falling upon the summer-starched grass. Now the walls dissolved into distances of parched weed, mile on mile, and warm endless sky. The animals drew away into thorn brakes and water holes.

It was the children's hour.

Five o'clock. The bath filled with clear hot water.

Six, seven, eight o'clock. The dinner dishes manipulated like magic tricks, and in the study a *click*. In the metal stand opposite the hearth where a fire now blazed up warmly, a cigar popped out, half an inch of soft gray ash on it, smoking, waiting.

Nine o'clock. The beds warmed their hidden circuits, for nights were cool here.

40 *Nine-five*. A voice spoke from the study ceiling:

"Mrs. McClellan, which poem would you like this evening?"

The house was silent.

The voice said at last, "Since you express no preference, I shall select a poem at random." Quiet music rose to back the voice. "Sara Teasdale. As I recall, your favorite. . . .

There will come soft rains and the smell of the ground,
And swallows circling with their shimmering sound;

And frogs in the pools singing at night,
And wild plum trees in tremulous white;

Robins will wear their feathery fire,
Whistling their whims on a low fence-wire;

And not one will know of the war, not one
Will care at last when it is done.

Not one would mind, neither bird nor tree,
If mankind perished utterly;

And Spring herself, when she woke at dawn
Would scarcely know that we were gone."

45   The fire burned on the stone hearth and the cigar fell away into a mound of quiet ash on its tray. The empty chairs faced each other between the silent walls, and the music played.

At ten o'clock the house began to die.

The wind blew. A falling tree bough crashed through the kitchen window. Cleaning solvent, bottled, shattered over the stove. The room was ablaze in an instant!

"Fire!" screamed a voice. The house lights flashed, water pumps shot water from the ceilings. But the solvent spread on the linoleum, licking, eating, under the kitchen door, while the voices took it up in chorus: "Fire, fire, fire!"

The house tried to save itself. Doors sprang tightly shut, but the windows were broken by the heat and the wind blew and sucked upon the fire.

50 The house gave ground as the fire in ten billion angry sparks moved with flaming ease from room to room and then up the stairs. While scurrying water rats squeaked from the walls, pistoled their water, and ran for more. And the wall sprays let down showers of mechanical rain.

But too late. Somewhere, sighing, a pump shrugged to a stop. The quenching rain ceased. The reserve water supply which had filled baths and washed dishes for many quiet days was gone.

The fire crackled up the stairs. It fed upon Picassos and Matisses in the upper halls, like delicacies, baking off the oily flesh, tenderly crisping the canvases into black shavings.

Now the fire lay in beds, stood in windows, changed the colors of drapes!

And then, reinforcements.

55 From attic trapdoors, blind robot faces peered down with faucet mouths gushing green chemical.

The fire backed off, as even an elephant must at the sight of a dead snake. Now there were twenty snakes whipping over the floor, killing the fire with a clear cold venom of green froth.

But the fire was clever. It had sent flames outside the house, up through the attic to the pumps there. An explosion! The attic brain which directed the pumps was shattered into bronze shrapnel on the beams.

The fire rushed back into every closet and felt of the clothes hung there.

The house shuddered, oak bone on bone, its bared skeleton cringing from the heat, its wire, its nerves revealed as if a surgeon had torn the skin off to let the red veins and capillaries quiver in the scalded air. Help, help! Fire! Run, run! Heat snapped mirrors like the brittle winter ice. And the voices wailed, Fire, fire, run, run, like a tragic nursery rhyme, a dozen voices, high, low, like children dying in a forest, alone, alone. And the voices fading as the wires popped their sheathings like hot chestnuts. One, two, three, four, five voices died.

60 In the nursery the jungle burned. Blue lions roared, purple giraffes bounded off. The panthers ran in circles changing color, and ten million animals, running before the fire, vanished off toward a distant steaming river. . . .

Ten more voices died. In the last instant under the fire avalanche, other choruses, oblivious, could be heard announcing the time, playing music, cutting the lawn by remote-control mower, or setting an umbrella frantically out and in the slamming and opening front door, a thousand things happening, like a clock shop when each clock strikes the hour insanely before or after the other, a scene of maniac confusion, yet unity; singing, screaming, a few last cleaning mice darting bravely out to carry the horrid ashes away! And one voice, with sublime disregard for the situation, read poetry aloud in the fiery study, until all the film spools burned, until all the wires withered and the circuits cracked.

The fire burst the house and let it slam flat down, puffing out skirts of spark and smoke.

In the kitchen, an instant before the rain of fire and timber, the stove could be seen making breakfasts at a psychopathic rate, ten dozen eggs, six loaves of toast, twenty dozen bacon strips, which, eaten by fire, started the stove working again, hysterically hissing!

The crash. The attic smashing into kitchen and parlor. The parlor into cellar, cellar into sub-cellar. Deep freeze, armchair, film tapes, circuits, beds, and all like skeletons thrown in a cluttered mound deep under.

65   Smoke and silence. A great quantity of smoke.

Dawn showed faintly in the east. Among the ruins, one wall stood alone. Within the wall, a last voice said, over and over again and again, even as the sun rose to shine upon the heaped rubble and steam:

"Today is August 5, 2026, today is August 5, 2026, today is . . ."

[1950]

Joining the Conversation: Critical Thinking and Writing

1. What do you know about the family in the story? Does it seem to be a typical family?
2. What does the poem seem to say about the relationship between nature and human beings? In what way, if any, is the poem relevant to the rest of the story?
3. Do you take the story to be mere fantasy, or do you take it to be a comment on our life? Or neither? Explain.
4. Characterize your final response to the story. Does the story create uneasiness, a sense of your own involvement in a sadly deficient society? Or does the story create a sense of satisfaction, a feeling that your own life is superior to the life depicted here?

Student Essay with Preliminary Notes

Here is one student's response to Bradbury's story, preceded by the notes that the student used in preparing a draft. Notice that the final essay does not slavishly follow the notes. For instance, although the student jotted down four possible titles for her essay, none of them is the title that she settled on.

Possible title:
*   *Bradbury's Meaning for us*
*   *Bradbury and Today*
*   *Learning from Literature/Bradbury's Lesson*
*   *Bradbury's Lesson for us*
*   ~~*Begin by quoting first sentence*~~
*   *begin with joke about airline??*
*   ~~*Define science fiction?*~~
*   *technology today–can do almost everything–but is this really LIVING?*
*   *Maybe such a life is a living death. Evidence??*
*   *End essay:*
*   *Does Bradbury show us our future?*
*   *A wake-up call. 2026 is not really very far away*
*   ~~*end with an example of unnecessary technology*~~

Esther Daniels

Professor Izzard

English 101a

14 January 2013

The Lesson of "August 2026"

Before discussing some of the implications of Ray Bradbury's short story "August 2026: There Will Come Soft Rains," I want to tell a little joke. The joke goes like this. Passengers are seated on the latest kind of airplane, a plane that files without a pilot because all of the controls are operated mechanically, and the entire flight has been preprogramed. After all the passengers have boarded the plane, and the door has closed, and the passengers, in accordance with the pre-recorded announcement, have fastened their seat-belts, the plane begins to taxi for a take-off. As the plane moves down the runway, the sound system says, in its flat mechanical voice, "You are now beginning your flight on the most technologically advanced airplane ever designed. There is no pilot or copilot, and there are no flight attendants. Everything has been preprogrammed. The plane will taxi for 60 seconds and then will take off. Nothing can go wrong . . . nothing can go wrong . . . nothing can . . . nothing can . . . nothing can. . . ."

None of us has been on such a plane, but we probably all have had, in a mild way, the sort of experience that the joke implies. We have bought some wonderful gadget—let's say an alarm clock, and we have programmed it according to the complicated instructions, and it has failed to go off the next morning. Apparently we had set it for p.m. instead of a.m., but we still don't see what we did wrong. Or, try as we may we cannot change the margins on the computer. Or the airline has put our luggage on the wrong airplane. Or . . .

None of us wants to give up the wonderful devices we rely on—let's say the automobile, the computer, the iPod. We can even attend an English composition class, and, if we think it is boring, we can silently be exchanging messages with a friend a thousand miles away. Despite these pleasures and these great conveniences, there are times, I think, when most of us must wonder, "Are we really living, or are our machines doing the living for us?" In "August 2026: There Will Come Soft Rains," Ray Bradbury gives us a glimpse—with great exaggeration, of course—of what our lives may seem like in the future. Preprogrammed sounds wake people up, mechanisms prepare food and clean the house, and other mechanisms provide entertainment. If they don't make a choice, a machine chooses something on their behalf. Are the people who are served by these devices happy? We don't know, because there are no people in Bradbury's story. They have all been incinerated, and only their silhouettes survive on the wall of the house. But we, as readers of the story, probably feel that although everything was provided for these people, they could not really have been happy. Things are *too* programmed; the people who lived in this society must have become almost like machines themselves. Probably none of us wants to say that in our own lives we actually want difficulties, but, still, when we read Bradbury's story we probably say that we would not want to live in a society that was as highly programed with labor-saving devices as Bradbury shows.

And yet, that is the way we seem to be going, with faster computers, smarter houses. You can now, from your place of work, phone your home and turn the oven on and set the temperature and the duration, so that when you get home the beef has been roasted to medium-rare.

Bradbury first published the story in 1950, so the story was set seventy-six years in the future. It was set, we can say, at a time when most of his readers would probably not still be alive. But today, 2026 is not all that far from us. Most of us who today are reading this story will still be alive in 2026, unless, as the story warns us, we allow our technology—gadgets that can do just about anything—to blow ourselves up. Bradbury's "August 2026: There Will Come Soft Rains" is a wake-up call, a call that we ought to heed. We have

Daniels 3

somehow let our technical knowledge outrun not only our wisdom but our sense of how to live decent meaningful lives, lives of fun, truly *human* lives, not just lives in which everything is easy, everything is done for us. We are allowing our gadgets to do our living for us—and they may kill us. We are barely living, we are sleep-walking. This cannot go on without some sort of catastrophic ending. To quote the first line of Ray Bradbury's story, it is *"time to get up, time to get up."*

[New page]

Daniels 4

Work Cited

Bradbury, Ray. "August 2026: There Will Come Soft Rains." *Literature for*

   Composition. Ed. Sylvan Barnet, William Burto, and William E. Cain. 10th ed.

   New York: Pearson, 2014. 22-26. Print.

Joining the Conversation: Critical Thinking and Writing

1. Has Esther Daniels done a good job in writing her title and opening paragraph? Please explain.
2. What is Daniels's thesis? Where does she state it?
3. Do you think she has provided sufficient evidence for her thesis?
4. Evaluate the final paragraph. Is it effective?

Stories for Analysis

MICHELE SERROS

Michele Serros, born in Oxnard, California, in 1966, published her first book of poems and stories, Chicana Falsa and Other Stories of Death, Identity and Oxnard, *while she was still a student at Santa Monica City College. We reprint a story from her second book,* How to Be a Chicana Role Model *(2000), which achieved national attention.*

Senior Picture Day

Sometimes I put two different earrings in the same ear. And that's on a day I'm feeling preppy, not really new wave or anything. One time, during a track meet over at Camarillo High, I discovered way too late that I'd forgot to put on deodorant and that was the worst 'cause everyone knows how snooty those girls at Camarillo can be. Hmmm. Actually the worst thing I've ever forgotten to do was take my pill. That happened three mornings in a row and you can bet I was praying for weeks after that.

So many things to remember when you're seventeen years old and your days start at six A.M. and sometimes don't end until five in the afternoon. But today of all days there's one thing I have to remember to do and that's to squeeze my nose. I've been doing it since the seventh grade. Every morning with my thumb and forefinger I squeeze the sides of it, firmly pressing my nostrils as close as they possibly can get near the base. Sometimes while I'm waiting for the tortilla to heat up, or just when I'm brushing my teeth, I squeeze. Nobody ever notices. Nobody ever asks. With all the other shit seniors in high school go through, squeezing my nose is nothing. It's just like some regular early-morning routine, like yawning or wiping the egg from my eyes. Okay, so you might think it's just a total waste of time, but to tell you the truth, I do see the difference. Just last week I lined up all my class pictures and could definitely see the progress. My nose has actually become smaller, narrower. It looks less Indian. *I* look less Indian and you can bet that's the main goal here. Today, when I take my graduation pictures, my nose will look just like Terri's and then I'll have the best picture in the year-book. I think about this as Mrs. Milne's Duster comes honking in the driveway to take me to school.

Terri was my best friend in seventh grade. She came from Washington to Rio Del Valle junior high halfway through October. She was the first girl I knew who had contact lenses and *four* pairs of Chemin de Fers. Can you believe that? She told everyone that her daddy was gonna build 'em a swimming pool for the summer. She told me that I could go over to swim anytime I wanted. But until then, she told me, I could go over and we could play on her dad's CB.[1]

"You dad's really got a CB?" I asked her.

5   "Oh, yeah," she answered, jiggling her locker door. "You can come over and we can make up handles for ourselves and meet lots of guys. Cute ones."

"Whaddaya mean, handles?" I asked.

"Like names, little nicknames. I never use my real name. I'm 'G.G.' when I get on. That stands for Golden Girl. Oh, and you gotta make sure you end every sentence with 'over.' You're like a total nerd if you don't finish with 'over.' I never talk to anyone who doesn't say 'over.' They're the worst."

Nobody's really into citizen band radios anymore. I now see 'em all lined up in pawnshops over on Oxnard Boulevard. But back in the seventh grade, everyone was getting them. They were way better than using a phone 'cause, first of all, there was no phone bill to bust you for talking to boys who lived past the Grade and second, you didn't have your stupid sister yelling at you for tying up the phone line. Most people had CBs in their cars, but Terri's dad had his in the den.

When I showed up at Terri's to check out the CB, her mama was in the front yard planting some purple flowers.

10   "Go on in already." She waved me in. "She's in her father's den."

[1]**CB** Citizens Band (a radio frequency used by the general public to talk to one another over a short distance).

I found Terri just like her mama said. She was already on the CB, looking flustered and sorta excited.

"Hey," I called out to her, and plopped my tote bag on her dad's desk.

She didn't answer but rather motioned to me with her hands to hurry up. Her mouth formed an exaggerated, "Oh, *my* God!" She held out a glass bowl of Pringles and pointed to a glass of Dr Pepper on the desk.

It turned out Terri had found a boy on the CB. An older *interested* one. He was fifteen, a skateboarder, and his handle was Lightning Bolt.

15 "Lightning Bolt," he bragged to Terri. "Like, you know, powerful and fast. That's the way I skate. So," he continued, "where you guys live? Over."

"We live near Malibu." Terri answered. "Between Malibu and Santa Barbara. Over."

"Oh, excuse me, fan-ceee. Over."

"That's right." Terri giggled. "Over."

We actually lived in Oxnard. Really, in El Rio, a flat patch of houses, churches, and schools surrounded by lots of strawberry fields and some new snooty stucco homes surrounded by chainlink. But man, did Terri have this way of making things sound better. I mean, it *was* the truth, geographically, and besides it sounded way more glamorous.

20 I took some Pringles from the bowl and thought we were gonna have this wonderful afternoon of talking and flirting with Lightning Bolt until Terri's dad happened to come home early and found us gabbing in his den.

"What the . . . !" he yelled as soon as he walked in and saw us hunched over his CB. "What do you think this is? Party Central? Get off that thing!" He grabbed the receiver from Terri's hand. "This isn't a toy! It's a tool. A tool for communication, you don't use it just to meet boys!"

"Damn, Dad," Terri complained as she slid off her father's desk. "Don't have a cow." She took my hand and led me to her room. "Come on, let's pick you out a handle."

When we were in her room, I told her I had decided on Cali Girl as my handle.

"You mean, like California?" she asked.

25 "Yeah, sorta."

"But you're Mexican."

"So?"

"So, you look like you're more from Mexico than California."

"What do you mean?"

30 "I mean, California is like, blond girls, you know."

"Yeah, but I *am* Californian. I mean, real Californian. Even my great-grandma was born here."

"It's just that you don't look like you're from California."

"And you're not exactly golden," I snapped.

We decided to talk to Lightning Bolt the next day, Friday, right after school. Terri's dad always came home real late on Fridays, sometimes even early the next Saturday morning. It would be perfect. When I got to her house the garage door was wide open and I went in through the side door. I almost bumped into Terri's mama. She was spraying the house with Pine Scent and offered me some Hi-C.

35 "Help yourself to a Pudding Pop, too," she said before heading into the living room through a mist of aerosol. "They're in the freezer."

Man, Terri's mama made their whole life like an afternoon commercial. Hi-C, Pringles in a bowl, the whole house smelling like a pine forest. Was Terri lucky or what? I grabbed a Pudding Pop out of the freezer and was about to join her when I picked up on her laugh. She was already talking to Lightning Bolt. Dang, she didn't waste time!

"Well, maybe we don't ever want to meet you," I heard Terri flirt with Lightning Bolt. "How do you know we don't already have boyfriends? Over."

"Well, you both sound like foxes. So, uh, what *do* you look like? Over."

"I'm about five-four and have green eyes and ginger-colored hair. Over."

40   Green? Ginger? I always took Terri for having brown eyes and brown hair.

"What about your friend? Over."

"What about her? Over."

Oh, this was about me! I *had* to hear this. Terri knew how to pump up things good. "I mean, what does she look like?" Lightning Bolt asked. "She sounds cute. Over."

45   "Well . . . " I overheard Terri hesitate. "Well, she's real skinny and, uh . . . "

"I like skinny girls!"

"You didn't let me finish!" Terri interrupted. "And you didn't say 'over.' Over."

"Sorry," Lightning Bolt said. "Go ahead and finish. Over."

I tore the wrapper off the Pudding Pop and continued to listen.

50   "Well," Terri continued. "She's also sorta flat-chested, I guess. Over."

What? How could Terri say that?

"Flat-chested? Oh yeah? Over." Lightning Bolt answered.

"Yeah. Over."

Terri paused uncomfortably. It was as if she knew what she was saying was wrong and bad and she should've stopped but couldn't. She was saying things about a friend, things a real friend shouldn't be saying about another friend, but now there was a boy involved and he was interested in that other friend, in me, and her side was losing momentum. She would have to continue to stay ahead.

55   "Yeah, and she also has this, this nose, a nose like . . . like an *Indian*. Over."

"An, Indian?" Lightning Bolt asked. "What do ya mean an Indian? Over."

"You know, *Indian*. Like powwow Indian."

"Really?" Lightning Bolt laughed on the other end. "Like Woo-Woo-Woo Indian?" He clapped his palm over his mouth and wailed. A sound I knew all too well.

"Yeah, just like that!" Terri laughed. "In fact, I think she's gonna pick 'Li'l Squaw' as her handle!"

60   I shut the refrigerator door quietly. I touched the ridge of my nose. I felt the bump my mother had promised me would be less noticeable once my face "filled out." The base of my nose was far from feminine and was broad, like, well, like Uncle Rudy's nose, Grandpa Rudy's nose, and yeah, a little bit of Uncle Vincente's nose, too. Men in my family who looked like Indians and here their Indian noses were lumped together on me, on my face. My nose made me look like I didn't belong, made me look less Californian than my blond counterparts. After hearing Terri and Lightning Bolt laugh, more than anything I hated the men in my family who had given me such a hideous nose.

I grabbed my tote bag and started to leave out through the garage door when Terri's mama called out from the living room. "You're leaving already?" she asked. "I know Terri would love to have you for dinner. Her daddy's working late again."

I didn't answer and I didn't turn around. I just walked out and went home.

And so that's how the squeezing began. I eventually stopped hanging out with Terri and never got a chance to use my handle on her dad's CB. I know it's been almost four years since she said all that stuff about me, about my nose, but man, it still stings.

65   During freshman year I heard that Terri's dad met some lady on the CB and left her mama for this other woman. Can you believe that? Who'd wanna leave a house that smelled like a pine forest and always had Pudding Pops in the freezer?

As Mrs. Milne honks from the driveway impatiently, I grab my books and run down the driveway, squeezing my nose just a little bit more. I do it because today is Senior Picture Day and because I do notice the difference. I might be too skinny. My chest might be too flat. But God forbid I look too Indian.

[2000]

Joining the Conversation: Critical Thinking and Writing

1. How would you characterize the narrator of "Senior Picture Day"? Do you regard her with amusement, pity, contempt, sympathy—or all of the above, or none? Please explain.
2. Briefly recounted within this story about the narrator is another story about Terri's parents. Why do you suppose Serros included this story?
3. If someone asked you to write an essay about your body, would you find the assignment easy or difficult? Please explain.
4. a. Describe the impression that this portrait sculpture (shown below) of the most famous Mayan king, Pakal the Great, makes on you.
   b. When we say that someone is handsome or beautiful or striking-looking, what do we mean? Is this just a strong feeling that we have, or is it a strong feeling that we could explain and support through an argument? Support your answer in an argument of 250–500 words (probably two or three paragraphs).
5. Which statement has the greater effect on you: "That person is very attractive" or "That person is highly intelligent"? Do you think that most people would

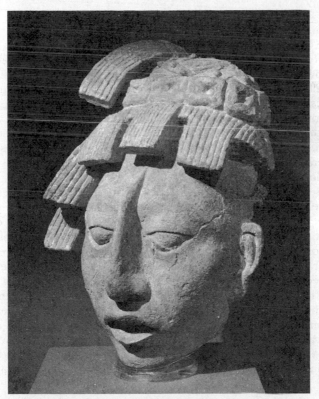

One of the most important Mayan portrait sculptures shows Pakal the Great, with an ample nose. Mayan portrait sculpture (mid-seventh century).

agree with you? Could you present an argument that would convince others to agree with you? What would your argument consist of? What would your evidence be? Set forth your argument in 250–500 words.

GUY DE MAUPASSANT

Born and raised in Normandy, the French novelist and short-story writer Guy de Maupassant (1850–93) studied law in Paris, then served in the Franco-Prussian War. Afterward he worked for a time as a clerk for the government until, with the support of the novelist Gustave Flaubert (a friend of Maupassant's mother) and later Emile Zola, he decided to pursue a career as a writer. Ironic and pointed, detached yet compassionate, Maupassant explores human folly and its grim and comic consequences. His first great success came in April 1880 with the publication of the story "Boule de Suif" ("Ball of Fat"), about a prostitute traveling by coach, with a number of bourgeois companions, through Prussian-occupied France during wartime. Maupassant published six novels, including Bel-Ami *(1885) and* Pierre et Jean *(1888), and a number of collections of stories, before his untimely death from the effects of syphilis, a month short of his forty-third birthday. Like many of his stories, "The Necklace" uses realistic observation and keenly chosen detail to tell its story of a misunderstanding and the years of hard labor that follow from it.*

The Necklace

Translated by Marjorie Laurie

She was one of those pretty and charming girls who are sometimes, as if by a mistake of destiny, born in a family of clerks. She had no dowry, no expectations, no means of being known, understood, loved, wedded by any rich and distinguished man; and she let herself be married to a little clerk at the Ministry of Public Instruction.

She dressed plainly because she could not dress well, but she was as unhappy as though she had really fallen from her proper station, since with women there is neither caste nor rank: and beauty, grace and charm act instead of family and birth. Natural fineness, instinct for what is elegant, suppleness of wit, are the sole hierarchy, and make from women of the people the equals of the very greatest ladies.

She suffered ceaselessly, feeling herself born for all the delicacies and all the luxuries. She suffered from the poverty of her dwelling, from the wretched look of the walls, from the worn-out chairs, from the ugliness of the curtains. All those things, of which another woman of her rank would never even have been conscious, tortured her and made her angry. The sight of the little Breton peasant who did her humble housework aroused in her regrets which were despairing, and distracted dreams. She thought of the silent antechambers hung with Oriental tapestry, lit by tall bronze candelabra, and of the two great footmen in knee breeches who sleep in the big armchairs, made drowsy by the heavy warmth of the hot-air stove. She thought of the long *salons*[1] fitted up with ancient silk, of the delicate furniture carrying priceless curiosities, and of the coquettish perfumed boudoirs made for talks at five o'clock with intimate friends, with men famous and sought after, whom all women envy and whose attention they all desire.

[1] *salons* drawing-rooms.

When she sat down to dinner, before the round table covered with a table-cloth three days old, opposite her husband, who uncovered the soup tureen and declared with an enchanted air, "Ah, the good *pot-au-feu!*[2] I don't know anything better than that," she thought of dainty dinners, of shining silverware, of tapestry which peopled the walls with ancient personages and with strange birds flying in the midst of a fairy forest; and she thought of delicious dishes served on marvelous plates, and of the whispered gallantries which you listen to with a sphinxlike smile, while you are eating the pink flesh of a trout or the wings of a quail.

5   She had no dresses, no jewels, nothing. And she loved nothing but that; she felt made for that. She would so have liked to please, to be envied, to be charming, to be sought after.

She had a friend, a former schoolmate at the convent, who was rich, and whom she did not like to go and see any more, because she suffered so much when she came back.

But one evening, her husband returned home with a triumphant air, and holding a large envelope in his hand.

"There," said he. "Here is something for you."

She tore the paper sharply, and drew out a printed card which bore these words:

10   "The Minister of Public Instruction and Mme. Georges Ramponneau request the honor of M. and Mme. Loisel's company at the palace of the Ministry on Monday evening, January eighteenth."

Instead of being delighted, as her husband hoped, she threw the invitation on the table with disdain, murmuring:

"What do you want me to do with that?"

"But, my dear, I thought you would be glad. You never go out, and this is such a fine opportunity. I had awful trouble to get it. Everyone wants to go; it is very select, and they are not giving many invitations to clerks. The whole official world will be there."

She looked at him with an irritated glance, and said, impatiently:

15   "And what do you want me to put on my back?"

He had not thought of that; he stammered:

"Why, the dress you go to the theater in. It looks very well, to me."

He stopped, distracted, seeing his wife was crying. Two great tears descended slowly from the corners of her eyes toward the corners of her mouth. He stuttered:

"What's the matter? What's the matter?"

20   But, by violent effort, she had conquered her grief, and she replied, with a calm voice, while she wiped her wet cheeks:

"Nothing. Only I have no dress and therefore I can't go to this ball. Give your card to some colleague whose wife is better equipped than I."

He was in despair. He resumed:

"Come, let us see, Mathilde. How much would it cost, a suitable dress, which you could use on other occasions, something very simple?"

She reflected several seconds, making her calculations and wondering also what sum she could ask without drawing on herself an immediate refusal and a frightened exclamation from the economical clerk.

25   Finally, she replied, hesitatingly:

"I don't know exactly, but I think I could manage it with four hundred francs."

He had grown a little pale, because he was laying aside just that amount to buy a gun and treat himself to a little shooting next summer on the plain of Nanterre, with several friends who went to shoot larks down there, of a Sunday.

[2]*pot-au-feu* stew.

But he said:

"All right. I will give you four hundred francs. And try to have a pretty dress."

30   The day of the ball drew near, and Mme. Loisel seemed sad, uneasy, anxious. Her dress was ready, however. Her husband said to her one evening:

"What is the matter? Come, you've been so queer these last three days."

And she answered:

"It annoys me not to have a single jewel, not a single stone, nothing to put on. I shall look like distress. I should almost rather not go at all."

He resumed:

35   "You might wear natural flowers. It's very stylish at this time of the year. For ten francs you can get two or three magnificent roses."

She was not convinced.

"No; there's nothing more humiliating than to look poor among other women who are rich."

But her husband cried:

"How stupid you are! Go look up your friend Mme. Forestier, and ask her to lend you some jewels. You're quite thick enough with her to do that."

40   She uttered a cry of joy:

"It's true. I never thought of it."

The next day she went to her friend and told of her distress.

Mme. Forestier went to a wardrobe with a glass door, took out a large jewel-box, brought it back, opened it, and said to Mme. Loisel:

"Choose, my dear."

45   She saw first of all some bracelets, then a pearl necklace, then a Venetian cross, gold and precious stones of admirable workmanship. She tried on the ornaments before the glass, hesitated, could not make up her mind to part with them, to give them back. She kept asking:

"Haven't you any more?"

"Why, yes. Look. I don't know what you like."

All of a sudden she discovered, in a black satin box, a superb necklace of diamonds, and her heart began to beat with an immoderate desire. Her hands trembled as she took it. She fastened it around her throat, outside her high-necked dress, and remained lost in ecstasy at the sight of herself.

Then she asked, hesitating, filled with anguish:

50   "Can you lend me that, only that?"

"Why, yes, certainly."

She sprang upon the neck of her friend, kissed her passionately, then fled with her treasure.

The day of the ball arrived. Mme. Loisel made a great success. She was prettier than them all, elegant, gracious, smiling, and crazy with joy. All the men looked at her, asked her name, endeavored to be introduced. All the attachés of the Cabinet wanted to waltz with her. She was remarked by the minister himself.

She danced with intoxication, with passion, made drunk by pleasure, forgetting all, in the triumph of her beauty, in the glory of her success, in a sort of cloud of happiness composed of all this homage, of all this admiration, of all these awakened desires, and of that sense of complete victory which is so sweet to a woman's heart.

55   She went away about four o'clock in the morning. Her husband had been sleeping since midnight, in a little deserted anteroom, with three other gentlemen whose wives were having a very good time. He threw over her shoulders the wraps which he had brought, modest wraps of common life, whose poverty contrasted

with the elegance of the ball dress. She felt this, and wanted to escape so as not to be remarked by the other women, who were enveloping themselves in costly furs.

Loisel held her back.

"Wait a bit. You will catch cold outside. I will go and call a cab."

But she did not listen to him, and rapidly descended the stairs. When they were in the street they did not find a carriage; and they began to look for one, shouting after the cabmen whom they saw passing by at a distance.

They went down toward the Seine, in despair, shivering with cold. At last they found on the quay one of those ancient noctambulant coupés which, exactly as if they were ashamed to show their misery during the day, are never seen round Paris until after nightfall.

60 It took them to their door in the Rue des Martyrs, and once more, sadly, they climbed up homeward. All was ended, for her. And as to him, he reflected that he must be at the Ministry at ten o'clock.

She removed the wraps which covered her shoulders, before the glass, so as once more to see herself in all her glory. But suddenly she uttered a cry. She no longer had the necklace around her neck!

Her husband, already half undressed, demanded:

"What is the matter with you?"

She turned madly toward him:

65 "I have—I have—I've lost Mme. Forestier's necklace."

He stood up, distracted.

"What!—how?—impossible!"

And they looked in the folds of her dress, in the folds of her cloak, in her pockets, everywhere. They did not find it.

He asked:

70 "You're sure you had it on when you left the ball?"

"Yes, I felt it in the vestibule of the palace."

"But if you had lost it in the street we should have heard it fall. It must be in the cab."

"Yes. Probably. Did you take his number?"

"No. And you, didn't you notice it?"

75 "No."

They looked, thunderstruck, at one another. At last Loisel put on his clothes.

"I shall go back on foot," said he, "over the whole route which we have taken to see if I can find it."

And he went out. She sat waiting on a chair in her ball dress, without strength to go to bed, overwhelmed, without fire, without a thought.

Her husband came back about seven o'clock. He had found nothing.

80 He went to Police Headquarters, to the newspaper offices, to offer a reward; he went to the cab companies—everywhere, in fact, whither he was urged by the least suspicion of hope.

She waited all day, in the same condition of mad fear before this terrible calamity.

Loisel returned at night with a hollow, pale face; he had discovered nothing.

"You must write to your friend," said he, "that you have broken the clasp of her necklace and that you are having it mended. That will give us time to turn round."

She wrote at his dictation.

85 At the end of a week they had lost all hope.

And Loisel, who had aged five years, declared:

"We must consider how to replace that ornament."

The next day they took the box which had contained it, and they went to the jeweler whose name was found within. He consulted his books.

"It was not I, madame, who sold that necklace; I must simply have furnished the case."

90   Then they went from jeweler to jeweler, searching for a necklace like the other, consulting their memories, sick both of them with chagrin and anguish.

They found, in a shop at the Palais Royal, a string of diamonds which seemed to them exactly like the one they looked for. It was worth forty thousand francs. They could have it for thirty-six.

So they begged the jeweler not to sell it for three days yet. And they made a bargain that he should buy it back for thirty-four thousand francs, in case they found the other one before the end of February.

Loisel possessed eighteen thousand francs which his father had left him. He would borrow the rest.

He did borrow, asking a thousand francs of one, five hundred of another, five louis here, three louis[3] there. He gave notes, took up ruinous obligations, dealt with usurers and all the race of lenders. He compromised all the rest of his life, risked his signature without even knowing if he could meet it; and, frightened by the pains yet to come, by the black misery which was about to fall upon him, by the prospect of all the physical privation and of all the moral tortures which he was to suffer, he went to get the new necklace, putting down upon the merchant's counter thirty-six thousand francs.

95   When Mme. Loisel took back the necklace, Mme. Forestier said to her, with a chilly manner:

"You should have returned it sooner; I might have needed it."

She did not open the case, as her friend had so much feared. If she had detected the substitution, what would she have thought, what would she have said? Would she not have taken Mme. Loisel for a thief?

Mme. Loisel now knew the horrible existence of the needy. She took her part, moreover, all of a sudden, with heroism. That dreadful debt must be paid. She would pay it. They dismissed their servant; they changed their lodgings; they rented a garret under the roof.

She came to know what heavy housework meant and the odious cares of the kitchen. She washed the dishes, using her rosy nails on the greasy pots and pans. She washed the dirty linen, the shirts, and the dishcloths, which she dried upon a line; she carried the slops down to the street every morning, and carried up the water, stopping for breath at every landing. And, dressed like a woman of the people, she went to the fruiterer, the grocer, the butcher, her basket on her arm, bargaining, insulted, defending her miserable money sou by sou.

100   Each month they had to meet some notes, renew others, obtain more time.

Her husband worked in the evening making a fair copy of some tradesman's accounts, and late at night he often copied manuscript for five sous a page.

And this life lasted for ten years.

At the end of ten years, they had paid everything, everything, with the rates of usury, and the accumulations of the compound interest.

Mme. Loisel looked old now. She had become the woman of impoverished households—strong and hard and rough. With frowsy hair, skirts askew, and red hands, she talked loud while washing the floor with great swishes of water. But

---

[3]**louis** a gold coin worth 20 francs.

sometimes, when her husband was at the office, she sat down near the window, and she thought of that gay evening of long ago, of the ball where she had been so beautiful and so fêted.

105 What would have happened if she had not lost that necklace? Who knows? Who knows? How life is strange and changeful! How little a thing is needed for us to be lost or to be saved!

But, one Sunday, having gone to take a walk in the Champs Elysées to refresh herself from the labor of the week, she suddenly perceived a woman who was leading a child. It was Mme. Forestier, still young, still beautiful, still charming.

Mme. Loisel felt moved. Was she going to speak to her? Yes, certainly. And now that she had paid, she was going to tell her all about it. Why not?

She went up.

"Good day, Jeanne."

110 The other, astonished to be familiarly addressed by this plain goodwife, did not recognize her at all, and stammered:

"But—madam!—I do not know—You must be mistaken."

"No. I am Mathilde Loisel."

Her friend uttered a cry.

"Oh, my poor Mathilde! How you are changed!"

115 "Yes, I have had days hard enough, since I have seen you, days wretched enough—and that because of you!"

"Of me! How so?"

"Do you remember that diamond necklace which you lent me to wear at the ministerial ball?"

"Yes. Well?"

"Well, I lost it."

120 "What do you mean? You brought it back."

"I brought you back another just like it. And for this we have been ten years paying. You can understand that it was not easy for us, us who had nothing. At last it is ended, and I am very glad."

Mme. Forestier had stopped.

"You say that you bought a necklace of diamonds to replace mine?"

"Yes. You never noticed it, then! They were very like."

125 And she smiled with a joy which was proud and naïve at once.

Mme. Forestier, strongly moved, took her two hands.

"Oh, my poor Mathilde! Why, my necklace was paste. It was worth at most five hundred francs!"

[1885]

Joining the Conversation: Critical Thinking and Writing

1. What do we learn about Mme. Loisel from the first six paragraphs of the story? What is your response to the narrator's generalizations about women in paragraph 2?

2. Is Maupassant's point that Mme. Loisel is justly punished for her vanity and pride? What about her husband, and the impact of the apparent loss of the necklace on his life?

3. In paragraph 98, as Mme. Loisel decides she must pay the debt, Maupassant writes: "She took her part, moreover, all of a sudden, with heroism." Why the word "heroism"? Isn't this a strange way to characterize Mme. Loisel's behavior?

4. Maupassant, in a discussion of fiction, said that a serious writer's goal

> is not to tell a story to entertain us, or to appeal to our feelings, but to make us think, and to make us understand the hidden meaning of events. By dint of having observed and having meditated, the writer sees the world, facts, people, and things in a distinctive way, a way that is the result of all of his thoughtful observation. It is this personal view of the world that a writer strives to communicate to us. . . . To make the spectacle of life as moving to us as it has been to him, he must bring life before our eyes with scrupulous accuracy. He must construct his work with great skill—his art must seem artless—so that we cannot detect his contrivance or see his intentions.

Among the big ideas in these few sentences are these: (a) The purpose of fiction is "to make us understand the hidden meaning of events"; (b) writers give us a "personal view"; (c) readers should be moved by the story but should not be aware that the artist has imposed a personal view on them. Do you think that "The Necklace" effectively illustrates Maupassant's points? What might be "the hidden meaning of events"? What would you guess is Maupassant's "personal view"? Would you agree that the story is so skillfully constructed that we are unaware of the author's methods and of his intentions?

5. Have you ever done something, tried to make up for it, and then discovered later that you had not done what you thought you did after all? How did this make you feel?

MyLiteratureLab® *For additional resources for "The Necklace," log in to* www.myliteraturelab.com *where you will find a Longman Lecture, Interactive Reading, and Comprehension Quiz, as well as an About the Author for Maupassant (under Student Resources).*

Hautot and His Son

Translated by John Daremo

I

In front of the door of the house—part-farmhouse, part-manorhouse, one of those combined rural dwellings that were once almost manorial and that are now owned by big farmers—the dogs, tied to the apple trees in the courtyard, barked and howled at the game-bags carried by the gamekeeper and the boys. In the large dining room-kitchen, Hautot senior, Hautot junior, M. Bermont the tax-collector, and M. Mondrau the notary, were having a snack and a drink before starting out on the hunt, for it was the opening day of the season.

Hautot senior, proud of everything he owned, was boasting of the game his guests would find on his land. He was a tall Norman, one of those powerful, full-blooded, large-boned men who can lift a cartload of apples onto their shoulders. Half-peasant, half-gentleman, rich, respected, influential, authoritative, he had sent his son, César, to school so that he would be educated, and then pulled him out of secondary school, afraid he might become a fine gentleman, indifferent to the farm.

César Hautot, almost as tall as his father, but thinner, was a good son, docile, content with everything, full of adoration, respect, and deference for the wishes and opinions of Hautot senior.

M. Bermont, the tax-collector, a fat little man whose red cheeks showed thin networks of purple veins like the tributaries and winding courses of rivers on a map, asked: "And hare—are there any hare?"

5   Hautot senior replied, "As many as you want, especially in the Puysatier bottoms."

"Where do we start?" asked the notary, a good-natured fellow, fat and pale, his paunch bulging out of his brand-new, tightly-laced hunting outfit, bought in Rouen last week.

"Why, that way, through the bottoms. We'll drive the partridges into the plain, and then we'll close in on them." Then Hautot senior got up. They all followed suit, took their guns from the corner, checked the locks, stamped their feet to get used to their stiff boots not yet softened by the warmth of their feet. Then they went out; and the dogs, straining at their leashes, let out shrill howls as they pawed the air.

They set out toward the bottoms, a small vale, or rather a large undulating stretch of poor land, which remained uncultivated, furrowed with ravines, overgrown with bracken—an excellent game preserve.

The hunters spread out, Hautot senior keeping to the right, Hautot junior to the left, the two guests in the middle. The gamekeeper and the game-bag carriers followed. Now was that solemn moment when one awaits the first shot, when hearts beat a little faster, while nervous fingers keep feeling for the trigger.

10   Suddenly, the shot went off. Hautot senior had fired. They all stopped and saw a partridge drop from a covey in swift flight and fall into a ravine, disappearing in the thick brushwood. The excited hunter began running, stepping over and yanking at the brambles in his way, and he, in turn, disappeared into the thick brush in search of his game.

Almost immediately, a second shot was heard.

"Ha! ha! the rascal," cried M. Bermont, "he must have routed out a hare in there."

They all waited, their eyes fixed on the heap of branches which their gaze could not penetrate.

The notary, cupping his hands, shouted out: "Did you get them?" Hautot senior didn't answer; then César, turning toward the gamekeeper, said, "Go, give him a hand, Joseph. We have to keep in line. We'll wait here."

15   And old Joseph, a dry, gnarled, old stump of a man, whose every joint was a lump, went off down to the ravine, searching for passable openings with the caution of a fox. Then suddenly, he cried out: "Oh! c'm'ere, c'm'ere, there's been an accident."

They all rushed down and plunged through the brambles. Hautot senior lay on his side unconscious, both hands pressed to his belly. Through his canvas jacket, ripped by the bullet, long streams of blood flowed onto the grass. He had dropped his gun in setting it down to seize the dead partridge, which was just within his reach; it had gone off at the shock, the second discharge ripping open his entrails. They pulled him out of the ditch, undressed him, and saw a ghastly wound through which his intestines protruded. After binding him up as well as they could, they carried him back home and waited for the doctor, who had been sent for, along with a priest.

When the doctor arrived, he shook his head gravely, turned to Hautot junior, who was sitting in a chair, sobbing, and said: "My poor boy, it doesn't look too good."

But when the dressing was finished, the wounded man moved his fingers, opened his mouth, and cast a troubled, haggard look about him; then he seemed to search in his memory, recalling, grasping what had happened, and he murmured: "Good God, I'm finished."

The doctor was holding his hand. "Not at all, not at all. Just a few days' rest and you'll be all right."

20   Hautot continued: "I'm finished! My belly's ripped open! I know it." Then suddenly: "I want to speak to my son, if there's time."

Hautot junior was sobbing despite himself and repeating like a little boy: "Pappa, pappa, poor pappa!"

But his father, in a steadier voice, said: "Come on, stop crying, now's not the time for it. I've something to tell you. Come closer, it won't take long and then I'll feel easier. The rest of you, please give us a minute."

They all went out, leaving the son face to face with the father. As soon as they were alone, he said: "Listen, son, you're twenty-four. I can talk plain to you. And besides, there's not as much mystery about this sort of thing as we make of it. You know, of course, that your mother's been dead for seven years, right? And that I'm no more than forty-five myself, seeing I got married at nineteen. Right?"

The son stammered: "Yes, that's right."

25   "So, your mother's been dead for seven years, and I've stayed a widower. Well, I'm not a man to stay a widower at thirty-seven, right?"

The son answered: "Yes, that's right."

The father, gasping for breath, his face white and drawn with pain, continued: "God, how it hurts. Well, you understand. Man isn't made to live alone, but I wouldn't let anyone take your mother's place, seeing I gave her my word. So . . . you see?"

"Yes, father."

"So, I've kept a girl in Rouen, 18 rue de l'Éperlan, third floor, second door—I'm telling you all this, so don't forget it—and this girl's been as nice as she could be to me, affectionate, devoted, all in all, a real wife, you see? You follow me, my boy?"

30   "Yes, father."

"So, if I move on, I owe her something, but something substantial that'll take care of her. You understand?"

"Yes, father."

"I tell you she's a fine girl, really fine, and if it weren't for you and the memory of your poor mother, and the house where all three of us have lived together, I'd have brought her here. And I'd have married her, too . . . listen . . . listen . . . my boy . . . I could've made a will . . . but I didn't do it . . . I didn't want to . . . some things you don't put down in writing . . . they harm the family too much . . . and then everything gets all tangled up . . . it ruins everyone. Steer clear of legal documents, never use them. If I'm rich it's because I've never used them at all in my whole life. You understand, son?"

"Yes, father."

35   "Now listen . . . listen carefully . . . so I didn't make a will . . . I didn't want to . . . and anyway, I know you, you've got a good heart, you're not stingy, not tight-fisted, I mean. I said to myself that when I was near the end I'd tell you all about it and I'd ask you not to forget the girl:—Caroline Donet, 18 rue de l'Éperlan, third floor, second door, don't forget. And then . . . are you listening? Go there right after I'm gone—and fix it so she won't have any reason to complain about me—You can afford it—You can do it—I'm leaving you enough . . . Listen . . . You won't find her at home every day. She works at Mme. Moreau's, rue Beauvoisine. Go see her on a Thursday. That's the day she expects me. That's been my day for six years. Poor little thing, how she'll cry! . . . I'm telling you all this because I know you so well, my son. Such things aren't let out, not even to the notary or the priest. They're done; everyone knows that, but they're not mentioned, unless they have to be. So there's no outsider in on the secret, only the family, because the family's all one. You understand?"

    "Yes, father."

    "You promise?"

    "Yes, father."

    "You swear?"

40   "Yes, father."

    "I ask you, son, I beg you not to forget. It's important to me."

    "No, father."

    "You'll go there yourself. I want you to make sure of everything."

    "Yes, father."

45   "And then, you'll see . . . you'll see what she'll explain to you. I can't tell you any more myself. You swear?"

    "Yes, father."

    "That's good, son. Kiss me. Good-bye. I'm burning out, I'm sure of it. Tell them to come in."

    Hautot junior kissed his father, moaning as he did so. Then, always obedient, he opened the door, and the priest appeared in a white surplice, carrying the holy oils.

    But the dying man had closed his eyes, and he refused to open them again, he refused to answer, he refused to show, even by a sign, that he understood.

50   Hautot had talked enough; he could not go on. Besides, his heart now felt at ease; he wanted to die in peace. What need was there to confess to God's deputy when he had just confessed to his own son, one of the family.

    He was given the last rites, purified, absolved, surrounded by his kneeling friends and servants, without any expression on his face revealing that he was still alive.

    He died toward midnight, after four hours of shuddering that revealed terrible suffering.

II

The hunting season having opened on Sunday, he was buried on Tuesday. Back home after having accompanied his father to the cemetery, César Hautot spent the rest of the day weeping. He hardly slept at all that night and felt so sad when he awoke that he wondered how he could go on living.

    But all through the day he kept thinking that to obey his father's last wish he would have to go to Rouen the next day and see that girl, Caroline Donet, who lived at 18 rue de l'Éperlan, third floor, second door. Countless times he had repeated the name and address under his breath, as one mutters a prayer, so as not to forget it, and he ended up by muttering it incessantly, unable to stop or to think about anything else, so much were his tongue and mind obsessed by the words.

55   Accordingly, about eight the next morning, he ordered Graindorge to be harnessed to the gig, and set out behind the heavy Norman horse that trotted along the main road from Ainville to Rouen. He wore his black frock coat, his tall silk hat, and his trousers that strapped under his shoes. Under the circumstances, he didn't slip over his fine clothes the blue smock which billows in the wind and protects clothes from dust and stains, and which can be quickly removed on arrival as soon as one has jumped from the carriage.

He got into Rouen just as it struck ten, stopped, as always, at the Hôtel des Bons Enfants, rue des Trois-Mares, endured the embraces of the landlord, his wife, and five sons, who had heard the sad news; then he had to give them the details of the accident, which made him weep; to refuse the helpful offers of all of them, zealous because they knew he was rich; and even to refuse luncheon, which offended them.

Then, having dusted off his hat, brushed his frock coat, and wiped his boots, he set out to find the rue de l'Éperlan, not daring to ask directions of anyone for fear of being recognized and arousing suspicion.

At last, unable to find the place, he caught sight of a priest, and trusting to the professional discretion of the clergy, he asked him. It was only a hundred yards off, just the second street to the right.

Then he hesitated. Up to this moment he had obeyed the dead man's wish like an unthinking animal. Suddenly he felt disturbed, confused, humiliated at the idea of finding himself—him, the son—face to face with this woman who had been his father's mistress. All the morality that lies buried within us, crammed at the bottom of our feelings by centuries of inherited teaching, all he had learned about loose women from his catechism on, the instinctive contempt that every man feels for them, even if he marries one of them, all his narrow peasant propriety—all this worked within him, holding him back, making him blush with shame.

60   But he thought:—"I gave my word to father, I mustn't break it." So he pushed back the half-open door of the house marked number 18, found the dark stairway, went up three flights, saw one door, then a second, found the bell-cord and pulled it.

The tinkle in the neighboring room sent a shiver through his body. The door opened and he found himself face to face with a very well-dressed young woman, with dark hair and a ruddy complexion. She stared at him in astonishment.

He did not know what to say to her, and she, surmising nothing and expecting Hautot senior, did not invite him in. They stared at each other for nearly half a minute. Finally she asked: "Can I help you, sir?"

He mumbled: "I am young Hautot."

She started, turned pale, and stammered out as if she had known him for a long time: "Monsieur César?"

65   "Yes."

"Well?"

"I have something to say to you on my father's behalf."

She exclaimed, "Oh! my God!" and stepped back to let him in. He followed her in and closed the door.

Then he noticed a small boy of four or five, who was playing with a cat. He was sitting on the floor in front of a stove from which rose the steam of food being kept hot.

70   "Sit down," she said. He sat down. She asked: "Well?"

He no longer dared to speak, his eyes fixed on the table in the middle of the room, with three settings, one for a child. He stared at the chair with its back to the fire, at the plate, the napkin, the glasses, the open bottle of red wine and the untouched bottle of white wine. This was his father's chair, with its back to the fire. He was expected. It was his bread he saw—recognized—next to the fork, for the crust had been cut off because of Hautot's bad teeth. Then, looking up he caught sight, on the wall, of his father's picture, the large photograph taken in Paris the year of the Exhibition, the same one that hung over the bed in his room at Ainville.

The young woman asked again: "Well, Monsieur César?"

He looked at her. Her face had darkened with anxiety, and she waited there, her hands trembling with fear.

Now he dared to speak: "Well, mam'zelle, papa died Sunday in opening the hunting season."

75   She was so overwhelmed that she did not move. After several moments of silence, she murmured, almost inaudibly: "Oh! It can't be!"

And suddenly her eyes welled with tears and, raising her hands, she covered her face and began to sob. The little boy turned and, seeing his mother in tears, began to wail. Then, understanding that the stranger was the source of this sudden grief, he rushed at César, seized his trousers with one hand and with the other kept hitting him on the thigh with all his might. César stood there, bewildered, full of pity, between this woman mourning for his father and this child defending its mother. He, too, felt the effect of the emotion, his eyes welling with grief; and, to regain his self-control, he started to talk.

"Yes," he was saying, "the accident happened Sunday morning about eight o'clock. . . ." And he went on to tell the story as if she were listening to him, forgetting no detail, recounting the most trivial points with the peasant's thoroughness. And the little boy kept on hitting him, now kicking his ankles.

When César reached the part where Hautot senior had spoken of her, she heard her name mentioned, uncovered her face, and said: "I'm sorry, I wasn't following you. But I really would like to know. . . . If you don't mind starting all over again."

He started over again in the same words: "The accident happened Sunday morning about eight o'clock. . . ."

80   He told everything, at great length, with short pauses, with full stops, with reflections of his own from time to time. She listened to him intently, perceiving with a woman's sharp sensitivity all the mishaps he was relating, shuddering with horror and exclaiming from time to time: "Oh, my God!" The little boy, believing she had calmed down, had stopped hitting César in order to take his mother's hand, and he, too, was listening as if he understood.

When Hautot junior ended his account, he said: "And now we must settle things according to his wishes. You see, I'm well off; he's left me a good deal of property. I don't want you to have any reason to complain. . . ."

But she broke in abruptly: "Oh! Monsieur César, Monsieur César, not today. I'm too upset. . . . Some other time, some other day. . . . No, not today. . . . If I accept . . . you see . . . it's not for myself . . . no, no, no, I swear. It's for the little boy. The settlement will be for him."

Startled, César guessed, and stammered out: "Then . . . he's his . . . this little boy?"

And Hautot junior stared at his brother with confused emotion, both intense and pained.

85   "Of course," she said.

After a long silence, for she was weeping again, César, quite ill at ease, said: "Well, Mam'zelle Donet, I've got to go. When would you like to talk this over?"

She cried out: "Oh! no, don't go, don't go, don't leave me and Émile all alone. I'll die of sorrow. I've no one anymore, no one but my little boy. Oh! how awful, how awful, Monsieur César. Look, sit down. Talk to me some more. Tell me what he used to do out there all week long."

And César sat down, accustomed to obeying. She drew up another chair for herself, next to his, before the stove where the food was still simmering, put Émile on her lap and asked César a thousand questions about his father, intimate questions about his everyday life, so that César felt without thinking that she had loved his father with all her poor heart.

And, the chain of his thoughts, rather limited in number, brought him back again to the accident and he began to relate it all over again with all the same details.

90   When he said, "He had a hole in his belly you could have put your two fists into," she uttered a sort of cry, and tears welled up in her eyes again. Caught up by her sorrow, César, too, began to weep, and as tears always soften the fibers of the heart, he leaned toward Émile, and kissed him on the forehead.

The mother, recovering her breath, murmured: "Poor little fellow, he's an orphan now."

"So am I," said César.

And they spoke no more.

But suddenly, the practical instinct of a housewife, accustomed to think of everything, revived in the young woman. "Perhaps you've had nothing to eat all morning, Monsieur César?"

95   "No, mam'zelle."

"Oh, you must be hungry. Do have something to eat."

"No, thanks," he said. "I'm not hungry. I've been too upset."

She replied: "In spite of sorrow, we have to go on living. Surely you won't refuse me. And besides, it'll keep you here a bit longer. When you go, I don't know what will become of me."

He yielded, after some further resistance, and sitting with his back to the fire, facing her, he ate a plateful of the tripe which had been crackling in the oven, and drank a glass of red wine. But he would not let her open the bottle of white wine.

100   Several times he wiped the mouth of the little boy, who had smeared gravy all over his chin. As he was getting up to leave, he asked: "When would you like me to come back to talk the matter over, Mam'zelle Donet?"

"If it's all the same to you, next Thursday, Monsieur César. That way I won't lose any time. My Thursdays are always free."

"That's fine for me. Next Thursday."

"Come for lunch, won't you?"

"Oh! I can't make any promises about that."

105   "It's only that we can chat better while eating. And there's more time, too."

"Well, all right. Noon, then."

And he went off, after kissing little Émile again, and shaking hands with Mlle. Donet.

III

The week seemed long to César Hautot. Never before had he been alone, and the isolation seemed unbearable. Until now, he had lived at his father's side, like his shadow, following him to the fields, seeing to it that his father's orders were carried out, and when he would leave him for a short while, he would find him again at dinner. They would spend their evenings smoking their pipes, sitting opposite each other, discussing horses, cows, or sheep; and their morning handshakes seemed to signify their deep family affection.

Now César was alone. He wandered about in the autumn-ploughed lands, still expecting to see the tall, gesticulating figure of his father rise up at the far end of a field. To kill time, he stopped by his neighbors', told the story of the accident to all those who had not heard it, and sometimes told it again to those who had. Then, exhausted by work and by thinking, he would sit down by the roadside and wonder if such a life could go on for very long.

110　　He often thought of Mlle. Donet. He had liked her. He had found her ladylike, gentle, and fine, just as his father had said. Yes, she certainly was a fine person. He was resolved to do the thing handsomely and give her two thousand francs income, settling the capital on the child. He even felt a certain pleasure at the thought of seeing her again the following Thursday and of arranging the whole matter with her. And then the thought of this brother, this little fellow of five, who was his father's son, would bother him, would worry him a little and, at the same time, would give him a warm feeling. He had a kind of family there in that little illegitimate kid who would never bear the Hautot name, a family he could take or leave as he pleased, but which reminded him of his father.

So, when he found himself Thursday morning on the road to Rouen, carried along by the echoing trot of Graindorge, he felt his heart lighter, more at peace than he had felt at any moment since his misfortune.

Entering Mlle. Donet's apartment, he saw the table set as on the previous Thursday, with a single difference that the crust had not been removed from the bread.

He shook hands with the young woman, kissed Émile on both cheeks, and sat down, feeling somewhat at home, but with a heavy heart all the same. Mlle. Donet seemed a little thinner to him, a little paler. She must have cried a lot. She seemed ill at ease in his presence, as if she understood now what she had not realized the week before, under the initial impact of her misfortune, and she now treated him with excessive respect, with stricken humility, and with touching solicitude as if to repay him with attention and devotion for the kindness he had shown her. They spent a long time over lunch, talking about the matter which had brought him here. She didn't want so much money. It was too much, much too much. She earned enough to take care of herself; she only wanted Émile to have a little money he could look forward to when he grew up. But César stood fast, and even added a gift of one thousand francs for her mourning expenses.

When he had finished his coffee, she asked: "Do you smoke?"

115　　"Yes . . . I have my pipe."

He felt his pocket. Damn it, he had forgotten it! He was getting upset about it when she offered him one of his father's pipes, which was kept in the cupboard. He accepted, took it, recognized it, sniffed it, praised its excellence with emotion in his voice, filled it with tobacco, and lit it. Then he set Émile astride his knee and played horse with him while she cleared away the table and set the dirty dishes off on the sideboard to be washed after he had left.

Toward three, he got up regretfully, distressed at the thought of leaving. "Well, Mam'zelle Donet," he said, "I wish you good afternoon. It was a pleasure to see you again."

She stood before him, flushed, very moved, and looked at him while she thought of his father. "Won't we ever see each other again?" she asked.

He replied, simply: "Why, yes, mam'zelle, if you wish."

120   "Certainly, Monsieur César. Would next Thursday suit you?"

"Yes, Mam'zelle Donet."

"You'll come for lunch, of course?"

"Well . . . if you really want me to, I won't say no."

"Then it's settled, Monsieur César, next Thursday, at noon, the same as today."

125   "Thursday noon, Mam'zelle Donet."

[1889]

Joining the Conversation: Critical Thinking and Writing

1. Why does the woman not follow the account of the accident the first time it is related? Why are we told that the son often repeats the story, even to persons who know it?
2. Characterize Hautot senior, and characterize his son César.
3. It has been said that the art of fiction is the art of preparation. Reread the story a couple of times, underlining details that at first seem insignificant but that later are perceived as important.
4. In a long preface to his novel *Pierre and Jean* (1888) Maupassant discusses the business of the writer. In one passage he says:

> To make things seem real on the page consists in giving the complete *illusion* of reality, following the logical order of facts, and not servilely transcribing the pell-mell succession of chronological events in life.
>
> I conclude from this analysis that writers who call themselves realists should more accurately call themselves illusionists.
>
> How childish, moreover, to believe in an absolute reality, since we each carry a personal one in our thoughts and in our senses. Our eyes, our ears, our sense of smell and taste create as many truths as there are individuals. Our minds, diversely impressed by the reception of the senses' information, comprehend, analyze, and judge as if each of us belonged to a separate race.
>
> Thus each of us makes, individually, a personal illusion of the world. . . . It may be a poetic, sentimental, joyful, melancholy, sordid, or dismal one, according to our nature. The writer's goal is to reproduce this illusion of life faithfully, using all the literary techniques at his disposal.

Many readers find Maupassant's "personal illusion of the world" to be, on the whole, cynical and misogynistic. Do you find "Hautot and His Son" cynical and misogynistic? Explain.

T. CORAGHESSAN BOYLE

The son of immigrants from Ireland, T. Coraghessan Boyle (the stress in his middle name is on the second syllable) was born in Peekskill, New York, in 1948. A graduate of the State University of New York, Potsdam, Boyle taught history and English in high school for several years. He then attended the Writers' Workshop at the University of Iowa and went on to receive a PhD in 1977. Boyle has won several awards for his fiction.

Greasy Lake

It's about a mile down on the dark side of Route 88.

—*Bruce Springsteen*

There was a time when courtesy and winning ways went out of style, when it was good to be bad, when you cultivated decadence like a taste. We were all dangerous characters then. We wore torn-up leather jackets, slouched around with toothpicks in our mouths, sniffed glue and ether and what somebody claimed was cocaine. When we wheeled our parents' whining station wagons out into the street we left a patch of rubber half a block long. We drank gin and grape juice, Tango, Thunderbird, and Bali Hai. We were nineteen. We were bad. We read André Gide[1] and struck elaborate poses to show that we didn't give a shit about anything. At night, we went up to Greasy Lake.

Through the center of town, up the strip, past the housing developments and shopping malls, street lights giving way to the thin streaming illumination of the headlights, trees crowding the asphalt in a black unbroken wall: that was the way out to Greasy Lake. The Indians had called it Wakan, a reference to the clarity of its waters. Now it was fetid and murky, the mud banks glittering with broken glass and strewn with beer cans and the charred remains of bonfires. There was a single ravaged island a hundred yards from shore, so stripped of vegetation it looked as if the air force had strafed it. We went up to the lake because everyone went there, because we wanted to snuff the rich scent of possibility on the breeze, watch a girl take off her clothes and plunge into the festering murk, drink beer, smoke pot, howl at the stars, savor the incongruous full-throated roar of rock and roll against the primeval susurrus of frogs and crickets. This was nature.

I was there one night, late, in the company of two dangerous characters. Digby wore a gold star in his right ear and allowed his father to pay his tuition at Cornell; Jeff was thinking of quitting school to become a painter/musician/head-shop proprietor. They were both expert in the social graces, quick with a sneer, able to manage a Ford with lousy shocks over rutted and gutted blacktop road at eighty-five while rolling a joint as compact as a Tootsie Roll Pop stick. They could lounge against a bank of booming speakers and trade "man"s with the best of them or roll out across the dance floor as if their joints worked on bearings. They were slick and quick and they wore their mirror shades at breakfast and dinner, in the shower, in closets and caves. In short, they were bad.

I drove. Digby pounded the dashboard and shouted along with Toots & the Maytals while Jeff hung his head out the window and streaked the side of my mother's Bel Air with vomit. It was early June, the air soft as a hand on your cheek, the third night of summer vacation. The first two nights we'd been out till dawn, looking for something we never found. On this, the third night, we'd cruised the strip sixty-seven times, been in and out of every bar and club we could think of in a twenty-mile radius, stopped twice for bucket chicken and forty-cent hamburgers, debated going to a party at the house of a girl Jeff's sister knew, and chucked two dozen raw eggs at mailboxes and hitchhikers. It was 2:00 A.M.; the bars were closing. There was nothing to do but take a bottle of lemon-flavored gin up to Greasy Lake.

5   The taillights of a single car winked at us as we swung into the dirt lot with its tufts of weed and washboard corrugations; '57 Chevy, mint, metallic blue. On the far side of the lot, like the exoskeleton of some gaunt chrome insect, a chopper

[1]**André Gide** French novelist and critic (1869–1951), much concerned with unconventional behavior.

leaned against its kickstand. And that was it for excitement: some junkie half-wit biker and a car freak pumping his girlfriend. Whatever it was we were looking for, we weren't about to find it at Greasy Lake. Not that night.

But then all of a sudden Digby was fighting for the wheel. "Hey, that's Tony Lovett's car! Hey!" he shouted, while I stabbed at the brake pedal and the Bel Air nosed up to the gleaming bumper of the parked Chevy. Digby leaned on the horn, laughing, and instructed me to put my brights on. I flicked on the brights. This was hilarious. A joke. Tony would experience premature withdrawal and expect to be confronted by grim-looking state troopers with flashlights. We hit the horn, strobed the lights, and then jumped out of the car to press our witty faces to Tony's windows; for all we knew we might even catch a glimpse of some little fox's tit, and then we could slap backs with red-faced Tony, roughhouse a little, and go on to new heights of adventure and daring.

The first mistake, the one that opened the whole floodgate, was losing my grip on the keys. In the excitement, leaping from the car with the gin in one hand and a roach clip in the other, I spilled them in the grass—in the dark, rank, mysterious nighttime grass of Greasy Lake. This was a tactical error, as damaging and irreversible in its way as Westmoreland's decision to dig in at Khe Sanh.[2] I felt it like a jab of intuition, and I stopped there by the open door, peering vaguely into the night that puddled up round my feet.

The second mistake—and this was inextricably bound up with the first was indentifying the car as Tony Lovett's. Even before the very bad character in greasy jeans and engineer boots ripped out of the driver's door, I began to realize that this chrome blue was much lighter than the robin's-egg of Tony's car, and that Tony's car didn't have rear-mounted speakers. Judging from their expressions, Digby and Jeff were privately groping toward the same inevitable and unsettling conclusion as I was.

In any case, there was no reasoning with this bad greasy character—clearly he was a man of action. The first lusty Rockette[3] kick of his steel-toed boot caught me under the chin, chipped my favorite tooth, and left me sprawled in the dirt. Like a fool, I'd gone down on one knee to comb the stiff hacked grass for the keys, my mind making connections in the most dragged out, testudineous[4] way, knowing that things had gone wrong, that I was in a lot of trouble, and that the lost ignition key was my grail[5] and my salvation. The three or four succeeding blows were mainly absorbed by my right buttock and the tough piece of bone at the base of my spine.

10   Meanwhile, Digby vaulted the kissing bumpers and delivered a savage kung-fu blow to the greasy character's collarbone. Digby had just finished a course in martial arts for phys-ed credit and had spent the better part of the past two nights telling us apocryphal tales of Bruce Lee types and of the raw power invested in lightning blows shot from coiled wrists, ankles, and elbows. The greasy character was unimpressed. He merely backed off a step, his face like a Toltec mask, and laid Digby out with a single whistling roundhouse blow . . . but by now Jeff had got into the act, and I was beginning to extricate myself from the dirt, a tinny compound of shock, rage, and impotence wadded in my throat.

[2]**Westmoreland's decision . . . Khe Sanh** General William C. Westmoreland commanded U.S. troops in Vietnam (1964–68). When the North Vietnamese and Viet Cong in 1967 attacked Khe San (or Khesanh), Westmoreland chose to defend an area of little military significance. [3]**Rockette** The Rockettes, a dance troupe at Radio City Music Hall in New York City, were famous for precision and for high kicking   [4]**testudineous** turtle-like (here, slow)   [5]**grail** the holy cup that, according to tradition, Jesus used at the Last Supper. Legend says that the person who finds this object will be saved.

Jeff was on the guy's back, biting at his ear. Digby was on the ground, cursing. I went for the tire iron I kept under the driver's seat. I kept it there because bad characters always keep tire irons under the driver's seat, for just such an occasion as this. Never mind that I hadn't been involved in a fight since sixth grade, when a kid with a sleepy eye and two streams of mucus depending from his nostrils hit me in the knee with a Louisville slugger,[6] never mind that I'd touched the tire iron exactly twice before, to change tires: it was there. And I went for it.

I was terrified. Blood was beating in my ears, my hands were shaking, my heart turning over like a dirtbike in the wrong gear. My antagonist was shirtless, and a single cord of muscle flashed across his chest as he bent forward to peel Jeff from his back like a wet overcoat. "Motherfucker," he spat, over and over, and I was aware in that instant that all four of us—Digby, Jeff, and myself included—were chanting "motherfucker, motherfucker," as if it were a battle cry. (What happened next? the detective asks the murderer from beneath the turned-down brim of his porkpie hat. I don't know, the murderer says, something came over me. Exactly.)

Digby poked the flat of his hand in the bad character's face and I came at him like a kamikaze, mindless, raging, stung with humiliation—the whole thing, from the initial boot in the chin to this murderous primal instant involving no more than sixty hyperventilating, gland-flooding seconds—I came at him and brought the tire iron down across his ear. The effect was instantaneous, astonishing. He was a stunt man and this was Hollywood, he was a big grimacing toothy balloon and I was a man with a straight pin. He collapsed. Wet his pants. Went loose in his boots.

A single second, big as a zeppelin, floated by. We were standing over him in a circle, gritting our teeth, jerking our necks, our limbs and hands and feet twitching with glandular discharges. No one said anything. We just stared down at the guy, the car freak, the lover, the bad greasy character laid low. Digby looked at me; so did Jeff. I was still holding the tire iron, a tuft of hair clinging to the crook like dandelion fluff, like down. Rattled, I dropped it in the dirt, already envisioning the headlines, the pitted faces of the police inquisitors, the gleam of handcuffs, clank of bars, the big black shadows rising from the back of the cell . . . when suddenly a raw torn shriek cut through me like all the juice in all the electric chairs in the country.

15   It was the fox. She was short, barefoot, dressed in panties and a man's shirt. "Animals!" she screamed, running at us with her fists clenched and wisps of blow-dried hair in her face. There was a silver chain round her ankle, and her toenails flashed in the glare of the headlights. I think it was the toenails that did it. Sure, the gin and the cannabis and even the Kentucky Fried may have had a hand in it, but it was the sight of those flaming toes that set us off—the toad emerging from the loaf in *Virgin Spring*,[7] lipstick smeared on a child: she was already tainted. We were on her like Bergman's deranged brothers—see no evil, hear none, speak none—panting, wheezing, tearing at her clothes, grabbing for flesh. We were bad characters, and we were scared and hot and three steps over the line—anything could have happened.

It didn't.

Before we could pin her to the hood of the car, our eyes masked with lust and greed and the purest primal badness, a pair of headlights swung into the lot. There we were, dirty, bloody, guilty, dissociated from humanity and civilization, the first

[6]**Louisville slugger** a brand of baseball bat. [7]***Virgin Spring*** film (1960) by Ingmar Bergman.

of the Ur-crimes[8] behind us, the second in progress, shreds of nylon panty and spandex brassiere dangling from our fingers, our flies open, lips licked—there we were, caught in the spotlight. Nailed.

We bolted. First for the car, and then, realizing we had no way of starting it, for the woods. I thought nothing. I thought escape. The headlights came at me like accusing fingers. I was gone.

Ram-bam-bam, across the parking lot, past the chopper and into the feculent undergrowth at the lake's edge, insects flying up in my face, weeds whipping, frogs and snakes and red-eyed turtles splashing off into the night: I was already ankle-deep in muck and tepid water and still going strong. Behind me, the girl's screams rose in intensity, disconsolate, incriminating, the screams of the Sabine women,[9] the Christian martyrs, Anne Frank[10] dragged from the garret. I kept going, pursued by those cries, imagining cops and bloodhounds. The water was up to my knees when I realized what I was doing: I was going to swim for it. Swim the breadth of Greasy Lake and hide myself in the thick clot of woods on the far side. They'd never find me there!

20   I was breathing in sobs, in gasps. The water lapped at my waist as I looked out over the moon-burnished ripples, the mats of algae that clung to the surface like scabs. Digby and Jeff had vanished. I paused. Listened. The girl was quieter now, screams tapering to sobs, but there were male voices, angry, excited, and the high-pitched ticking of the second car's engine. I waded deeper, stealthy, hunted, the ooze sucking at my sneakers. As I was about to take the plunge—at the very instant I dropped my shoulder for the first slashing stroke—I blundered into something. Something unspeakable, obscene, something soft, wet, moss-grown. A patch of weed? A log? When I reached out to touch it, it gave like a rubber duck, it gave like flesh.

In one of those nasty little epiphanies for which we are prepared by films and TV and childhood visits to the funeral home to ponder the shrunken painted forms of dead grandparents, I understood what it was that bobbed there so inadmissibly in the dark. Understood, and stumbled back in horror and revulsion, my mind yanked in six different directions (I was nineteen, a mere child, an infant, and here in the space of five minutes I'd struck down one greasy character and blundered into the waterlogged carcass of a second), thinking, The keys, the keys, why did I have to go and lose the keys? I stumbled back, but the musk took hold of my feet—a sneaker snagged, balance lost—and suddenly I was pitching face forward into the buoyant black mass, throwing out my hands in desperation while simultaneously conjuring the image of reeking frogs and muskrats revolving in slicks of their own deliquescing juices. AAAAArrrgh! I shot from the water like a torpedo, the dead man rotating to expose a mossy beard and eyes cold as the moon. I must have shouted out, thrashing around in the weeds, because the voices behind me suddenly became animated.

"What was that?"

"It's them, it's them: they tried to, tried to . . . *rape* me!" Sobs.

A man's voice, flat Midwestern accent. "You sons a bitches, we'll kill you!"

25   Frogs, crickets.

Then another voice, harsh, *r*-less, Lower East Side: "Motherfucker!" I recognized the verbal virtuosity of the bad greasy character in the engineer boots. Tooth chipped, sneakers gone, coated in mud and slime and worse, crouching breathless

---

[8]**Ur-crimes** primitive crimes. [9]**Sabine women** women of an ancient tribe in Rome, raped by Romans and carried off to be their wives. [10]**Anne Frank** German Jewish girl (1929–45) who hid from the Nazis in an attic in Amsterdam, but was found and sent to a concentration camp, where she died. Her *Diary* has become famous.

in the weeds waiting to have my ass thoroughly and definitively kicked and fresh from the hideous stinking embrace of a three-days-dead-corpse, I suddenly felt a rush of joy and vindication: the son of a bitch was alive! Just as quickly, my bowels turned to ice. "Come on out of there, you pansy mothers!" the bad greasy character was screaming. He shouted curses till he was out of breath.

The crickets started up again, then the frogs. I held my breath. All at once there was a sound in the reeds, a swishing, a splash: thunk-a-thunk. They were throwing rocks. The frogs fell silent. I cradled my head. Swish; swish, thunk-a-thunk. A wedge of feldspar the size of a cue ball glanced off my knee. I bit my finger.

It was then that they turned to the car. I heard a door slam, a curse, and then the sound of the headlights shattering—almost a good-natured sound, celebratory, like corks popping from the necks of bottles. This was succeeded by the dull booming of the fenders, metal on metal, and then the icy crash of the windshield. I inched forward, elbows and knees, my belly pressed to the muck, thinking of guerrillas and commandos and *The Naked and the Dead.*[11] I parted the weeds and squinted the length of the parking lot.

The second car—it was a Trans-Am—was still running, its high beams washing the scene in a lurid stagy light. Tire iron flailing, the greasy bad character was laying into the side of my mother's Bel Air like an avenging demon, his shadow riding up the trunks of the trees. Whomp. Whomp. Whomp-whomp. The other two guys—blond types, in fraternity jackets—were helping out with tree branches and skull-sized boulders. One of them was gathering up bottles, rocks, muck, candy wrappers, used condoms, pop-tops, and other refuse and pitching it through the window on the driver's side. I could see the fox, a white bulb behind the windshield of the '57 Chevy. "Bobbie," she whined over the thumping, "come *on*." The greasy character paused a moment, took one good swipe at the left taillight, and then heaved the tire iron halfway across the lake. Then he fired up the '57 and was gone.

Blond head nodded at blond head. One said something to the other, too low for me to catch. They were no doubt thinking that in helping to annihilate my mother's car they'd committed a fairly rash act, and thinking too that there were three bad characters connected with that very car watching them from the woods. Perhaps other possibilities occurred to them as well—police, jail cells, justices of the peace, reparations, lawyers, irate parents, fraternal censure. Whatever they were thinking, they suddenly dropped branches, bottles, and rocks and sprang for their car in unison, as if they'd choreographed it. Five seconds. That's all it took. The engine shrieked, the tires squealed, a cloud of dust rose from the rutted lot and then settled back on darkness.

I don't know how long I lay there, the bad breath of decay all around me, my jacket heavy as a bear, the primordial ooze subtly reconstituting itself to accommodate my upper thighs and testicles. My jaws ached, my knee throbbed, my coccyx was on fire. I contemplated suicide, wondered if I'd need bridgework, scraped the recesses of my brain for some sort of excuse to give my parents—a tree had fallen on the car, I was blindsided by a bread truck, hit and run, vandals had got to it while we were playing chess at Digby's. Then I thought of the dead man. He was probably the only person on the planet worse off than I was. I thought about him, fog on the lake, insects chirring eerily, and felt the tug of fear, felt the darkness opening up inside me like a set of jaws. Who was he, I wondered, this victim of time and circumstance bobbing sorrowfully in the lake at my back. The owner of the chopper, no doubt, a bad older character come to this. Shot during a murky drug deal, drowned while drunkenly frolicking in the lake. Another headline. My car was wrecked; he was dead.

[11]*The Naked and the Dead* World War II novel (1948) by Norman Mailer.

When the eastern half of the sky went from black to cobalt and the trees began to separate themselves from the shadows, I pushed myself up from the mud and stepped out into the open. By now the birds had begun to take over for the crickets, and dew lay slick on the leaves. There was a smell in the air, raw and sweet at the same time, the smell of the sun firing buds and opening blossoms. I contemplated the car. It lay there like a wreck along the highway, like a steel sculpture left over from a vanished civilization. Everything was still. This was nature.

I was circling the car, as dazed and bedraggled as the sole survivor of an air blitz, when Digby and Jeff emerged from the trees behind me. Digby's face was crosshatched with smears of dirt; Jeff's jacket was gone and his shirt was torn across the shoulder. They slouched across the lot, looking sheepish, and silently came up beside me to gape at the ravaged automobile. No one said a word. After a while Jeff swung open the driver's door and began to scoop the broken glass and garbage off the seat. I looked at Digby. He shrugged. "At least they didn't slash the tires," he said.

It was true: the tires were intact. There was no windshield, the headlights were staved in, and the body looked as if it had been sledgehammered for a quarter a shot at the county fair, but the tires were inflated to regulation pressure. The car was drivable. In silence, all three of us bent to scrape the mud and shattered glass from the interior. I said nothing about the biker. When we were finished, I reached in my pocket for the keys, experienced a nasty stab of recollection, cursed myself, and turned to search the grass. I spotted them almost immediately, no more than five feet from the open door, glinting like jewels in the first tapering shaft of sunlight. There was no reason to get philosophical about it: I eased into the seat and turned the engine over.

35   It was at that precise moment that the silver Mustang with the flame decals rumbled into the lot. All three of us froze; then Digby and Jeff slid into the car and slammed the door. We watched as the Mustang rocked and bobbed across the ruts and finally jerked to a halt beside the forlorn chopper at the far end of the lot. "Let's go," Digby said. I hesitated, the Bel Air wheezing beneath me.

Two girls emerged from the Mustang. Tight jeans, stiletto heels, hair like frozen fur. They bent over the motorcycle, paced back and forth aimlessly, glanced once or twice at us, and then ambled over to where the reeds sprang up in a green fence round the perimeter of the lake. One of them cupped her hands to her mouth. "Al," she called, "Hey, Al!"

"Come on," Digby hissed. "Let's get out of here."

But it was too late. The second girl was picking her way across the lot, unsteady on her heels, looking up at us and then away. She was older—twenty-five or -six—and as she came closer we could see there was something wrong with her: she was stoned or drunk, lurching now and waving her arms for balance. I gripped the steering wheel as if it were the ejection lever of a flaming jet, and Digby spat out my name, twice, terse and impatient.

"Hi," the girl said.

40   We looked at her like zombies, like war veterans, like deaf-and-dumb pencil peddlers.

She smiled, her lips cracked and dry. "Listen," she said, bending from the waist to look in the window, "you guys seen Al?" Her pupils were pinpoints, her eyes glass. She jerked her neck. "That's his bike over there—Al's. You seen him?"

Al. I didn't know what to say. I wanted to get out of the car and retch, I wanted to go home to my parents' house and crawl into bed. Digby poked me in the ribs. "We haven't seen anybody," I said.

The girl seemed to consider this, reaching out a slim veiny arm to brace herself against the car. "No matter," she said, slurring the *t*'s, "he'll turn up." And then, as if she'd just taken stock of the whole scene—the ravaged car and our battered faces, the desolation of the place—she said: "Hey, you guys look like some pretty bad characters—been fightin', huh?" We stared straight ahead, rigid as catatonics. She was fumbling in her pocket and muttering something. Finally she held out a handful of tablets in glassine wrappers: "Hey, you want to party, you want to do some of these with me and Sarah?"

I just looked at her. I thought I was going to cry. Digby broke the silence. "No, thanks," he said, leaning over me. "Some other time."

45   I put the car in gear and it inched forward with a groan, shaking off pellets of glass like an old dog shedding water after a bath, heaving over the ruts on its worn springs, creeping toward the highway. There was a sheen of sun on the lake. I looked back. The girl was still standing there, watching us, her shoulders slumped, hand outstretched.

[1985]

Joining the Conversation: Critical Thinking and Writing

1. Exactly what does "bad" mean in the first paragraph? Why would some young people think "it was good to be bad"? Notice that the first paragraph ends with a short sentence about Greasy Lake, "This was nature." Is the narrator saying that "bad" behavior is natural?
2. The third paragraph characterizes Digby as "dangerous" and "bad." How dangerous do you think Boyle wants us to think Digby is?
3. Suppose the story had a different title, and Greasy Lake was never mentioned in the story. Would anything be lost? In short, why does Boyle introduce the lake?
4. What do you make of the ending of the story? Why, in your view, do the boys reject the girl's offer?

MyLiteratureLab® *For additional resources for "Greasy Lake," log in to* www.myliteraturelab.com *where you will find a Longman Lecture and Critical Essay, as well as an About the Author and Links for Boyle (under Student Resources).*

CHAPTER 3

The Reader as Writer

All there is to writing is having ideas. To learn to
write is to learn to have ideas.

ROBERT FROST

Chapter Preview

After reading this chapter you will be able to

- Use prewriting strategies to develop a thesis
- Engage effectively in the process of drafting and revising an argument
- Evaluate a student's analysis essay
- Analyze stories

Developing a Thesis, Drafting, and Writing an Argument

Prewriting: Getting Ideas

How do writers "learn to have ideas"? Among the methods are these: reading with a pen or pencil in hand so that you can annotate the text; keeping a journal in which you jot down reflections about your reading; talking with others (including your instructor) about the reading.

Let's take another look at the first of these methods, annotating.

Annotating a Text

In reading, if you own the book don't hesitate to mark it up, indicating (by highlighting or underlining or making marginal notes) what puzzles you, what pleases or interests you, and what displeases or bores you. Later you'll want to think further about these responses, asking yourself, on rereading, whether you still feel that way, and if not, why not; but these first responses will get you started.

Annotations of the sort shown on page 13, which chiefly call attention to contrasts, indicate that the student is thinking about writing an analysis of the story. That is, she is thinking of writing an essay in which she will examine the parts of a literary work either in an effort to see how they relate to each other or in an effort to see how one part relates to the whole.

More about Getting Ideas: A Second Story by Kate Chopin

Let's look at a story that is a little longer than "Ripe Figs," and then we'll discuss how, in addition to annotating it, you might get ideas for writing about it.

The Story of an Hour

Knowing that Mrs. Mallard was afflicted with a heart trouble, great care was taken to break to her as gently as possible the news of her husband's death.

It was her sister Josephine who told her, in broken sentences, veiled hints that revealed in half concealing. Her husband's friend Richards was there, too, near her. It was he who had been in the newspaper office when intelligence of the railroad disaster was received, with Brently Mallard's name leading the list of "killed." He had only taken the time to assure himself of its truth by a second telegram, and had hastened to forestall any less careful, less tender friend in bearing the sad message.

She did not hear the story as many women have heard the same, with a paralyzed inability to accept its significance. She wept at once, with sudden, wild abandonment, in her sister's arms. When the storm of grief had spent itself she went away to her room alone. She would have no one follow her.

There stood, facing the open window, a comfortable, roomy armchair. Into this she sank, pressed down by a physical exhaustion that haunted her body and seemed to reach into her soul.

5   She could see in the open square before her house the tops of trees that were all aquiver with the new spring life. The delicious breath of rain was in the air. In the street below a peddler was crying his wares. The notes of a distant song which some one was singing reached her faintly, and countless sparrows were twittering in the eaves.

There were patches of blue sky showing here and there through the clouds that had met and piled above the other in the west facing her window. She sat with her head thrown back upon the cushion of the chair quite motionless, except when a sob came up into her throat and shook her, as a child who has cried itself to sleep continues to sob in its dreams.

She was young, with a fair, calm face, whose lines bespoke repression and even a certain strength. But now there was a dull stare in her eyes, whose gaze was fixed away off yonder on one of those patches of blue sky. It was not a glance of reflection, but rather indicated a suspension of intelligent thought.

There was something coming to her and she was waiting for it, fearfully. What was it? She did not know; it was too subtle and elusive to name. But she felt it, creeping out of the sky, reaching toward her through the sounds, the scents, the color that filled the air.

Now her bosom rose and fell tumultuously. She was beginning to recognize this thing that was approaching to possess her, and she was striving to beat it back with her will—as powerless as her two white slender hands would have been.

10   When she abandoned herself a little whispered word escaped her slightly parted lips. She said it over and over under her breath: "Free, free, free!" The vacant stare and the look of terror that had followed it went from her eyes. They stayed keen and bright. Her pulses beat fast, and the coursing blood warmed and relaxed every inch of her body.

She did not stop to ask if it were not a monstrous joy that held her. A clear and exalted perception enabled her to dismiss the suggestion as trivial.

She knew that she would weep again when she saw the kind, tender hands folded in death; the face that had never looked save with love upon her, fixed and gray and dead. But she saw beyond that bitter moment a long procession of years to come that would belong to her absolutely. And she opened and spread her arms out to them in welcome.

There would be no one to live for her during those coming years; she would live for herself. There would be no powerful will bending her in that blind persistence with which men and women believe they have a right to impose a private will upon a fellow creature. A kind intention or a cruel intention made the act seem no less a crime as she looked upon it in that brief moment of illumination.

And yet she had loved him—sometimes. Often she had not. What did it matter! What could love, the unsolved mystery, count for in face of this possession of self-assertion which she suddenly recognized as the strongest impulse of her being.

15   "Free! Body and soul free!" she kept whispering.

Josephine was kneeling before the closed door with her lips to the key-hole, imploring for admission. "Louise, open the door! I beg; open the door—you will make yourself ill. What are you doing, Louise? For heaven's sake open the door."

"Go away. I am not making myself ill." No; she was drinking in a very elixir of life through that open window.

Her fancy was running riot along those days ahead of her. Spring days, and summer days, and all sorts of days that would be her own. She breathed a quick prayer that life might be long. It was only yesterday she had thought with a shudder that life might be long.

She arose at length and opened the door to her sister's importunities. There was a feverish triumph in her eyes, and she carried herself unwittingly like a goddess of Victory. She clasped her sister's waist, and together they descended the stairs. Richards stood waiting for them at the bottom.

20   Some one was opening the front door with a latchkey. It was Brently Mallard who entered, a little travel-stained, composedly carrying his gripsack and umbrella. He had been far from the scene of accident, and did not even know there had been one. He stood amazed at Josephine's piercing cry; at Richards' quick motion to screen him from the view of his wife.

But Richards was too late.

When the doctors came they said she had died of heart disease—of joy that kills.

[1894]

MyLiteratureLab® *For additional resources for "The Story of an Hour," log in to* www.myliteraturelab.com *where you will find a Longman Lecture, Comprehension Quiz, Short Evaluation Exercises, Essay Prompts, as well as an About the Author, Bibliography, Links, and Critical Overview for Chopin (under Student Resources).*

Brainstorming Ideas for Writing

Unlike annotating, which consists of making brief notes and small marks on the printed page, "brainstorming"—the free jotting down of ideas—asks that you write down whatever comes to mind, without inhibition. Don't worry about spelling, writing complete sentences, or unifying your thoughts; just let one thought lead to another. Later you can review your jottings, deleting some, connecting those that are related, expanding others, but for now you just want to get going.

Thus you might jot down something about the title:

Title speaks of an hour, and story covers an hour, but maybe takes five minutes to read.

Then, perhaps prompted by "an hour," you might add something to this effect:

Doubt that a woman who got news of the death of her husband could move from grief to joy within an hour.

Your next jotting might have little or nothing to do with this issue; it might simply say

> *Enjoyed "Hour" more than "Ripe Figs" partly because "Hour" is so shocking.*

And then you might ask yourself

> *By shocking, do I mean "improbable," or what? Come to think of it, maybe it's not so improbable. A lot depends on what the marriage was like.*

Focused Freewriting

Focused, or directed, freewriting is a method related to brainstorming that some writers use to uncover ideas. Concentrating on one issue—for instance, a question that strikes them as worth puzzling over (What kind of person is Mrs. Mallard?)—they write at length, nonstop, for perhaps five or ten minutes.

Writers who find freewriting helpful put down everything they can think of that bears on the one issue or question they are examining. They do not stop to evaluate the results or to worry about niceties of sentence structure or spelling. They just pour out their ideas in a steady stream of writing, drawing on whatever associations come to mind. If they pause in their writing, it is only to refer to the text, to search for more detail—perhaps a quotation—that will help them answer their question.

After the freewriting session, these writers reread what they have written, high-lighting or underlining whatever seems to be of value. Of course they find much that is of little or no use, but they usually find that some strong ideas have surfaced and have gotten some development. At this point the writers are often able to make a rough outline and begin a draft.

Here is an example of one student's focused freewriting:

> What do I know about Mrs. Mallard? Let me put everything down here I know about her or can figure out from what Kate Chopin tells me. When she finds herself alone after the death of her husband, she says, "Free. Body and soul free" and before that she said, "Free, free, free" three times. So she has suddenly perceived that she has not been free; she has been under the influence of a "powerful will." In this case it has been her husband, but she says no one, man nor woman, should impose their will on anyone else. So it's not a feminist issue—it's a power issue. No one should push anyone else around is what I guess Chopin means, force someone to do what the other person wants. I used to have a friend that did that to me all the time; he had to run everything. They say that fathers—before the women's movement—used to run things, with the father in charge of all the decisions, so maybe this is an honest reaction to having been pushed around by a husband. I think Mrs. Mallard is a believable character, even if the plot is not all that believable—all those things happening in such quick succession.

Listing

In your preliminary thinking you may find it useful to make lists. In the previous chapter we saw that listing the traits of the two characters was helpful in thinking about Chopin's "Ripe Figs":

> *Maman-Nainaine*
>   *older than Babette*
>   *"stately way"*
>   *"patient as the statue of la Madone"*

connects actions with seasons
expects to be obeyed

Babette
young
active and impatient
obedient

For "The Story of an Hour" you might list Mrs. Mallard's traits; or you might list the stages in her development. Such a list is not the same as a summary of the plot. The list helps the writer to see the sequence of psychological changes.

weeps (when she gets the news)
goes to room, alone
"pressed down by a physical exhaustion"
"dull stare"
"something coming to her"
strives to beat back "this thing"
"Free, free, free!" The "vacant stare went . . . from her eyes"
"A clear and exalted perception"
rejects Josephine
"she was drinking in a very elixir of life"
gets up, opens door, "a feverish triumph in her eyes"
sees B., and dies

Unlike brainstorming and annotating, which let you go in all directions, listing requires that you first make a decision about what you will be listing—traits of character, images, puns, or whatever. Once you make the decision, you can construct a list, and with that list in front of you, you will see patterns that you were not fully conscious of earlier.

Asking Questions

When you feel stuck, ask yourself questions. You'll recall that the assignment on "Ripe Figs" in effect asked that students form questions about the work—for instance, questions about the relationship between the characters—and about their responses to it: "You'll try to explain as honestly as you can what makes 'Ripe Figs' appealing or interesting—or trifling, or boring."

If you are thinking about a work of fiction, ask yourself questions about the plot and the characters—are they believable, are they interesting, and what does it all add up to? What does the story mean to *you*?

One student found it helpful to jot down the following questions:

Plot
    Ending false? Unconvincing? Or prepared for?
Character?
    Mrs. M. unfeeling? Immoral?
    Mrs. M. unbelievable character?
    What might her marriage have been like? Many gaps.
    (Can we tell what her husband was like?)
    "And yet she loved him—sometimes" Fickle? Realistic?
    What is "this thing that was approaching to possess her"?

> *Symbolism*
> *Set on spring day = symbolic of new life?*

You don't have to be as organized as this student. You may begin by jotting down notes and queries about what you like or dislike and about what puzzles or amuses you. What follows are the jottings of another student, Janet Vong. They are in no particular order—the student is brainstorming, putting down whatever occurs to her—though it is obvious that one note sometimes led to the next:

> *Title nothing special. What might be a better title?*
> *Could a woman who loved her husband be so heartless?*
> *Is she heartless? Did she love him?*
> *What are (were) Louise's feelings about her husband?*
> *Did she want too much? What did she want?*
> *Could this story happen today? Feminist interpretation?*
> *Sister (Josephine)—a busybody?*
> *Tricky ending—but maybe it could be true.*
> *"And yet she had loved him—sometimes. Often she had not."*
> *Why does one love someone "sometimes"?*
> *Irony: plot has reversal. Are characters ironic too?*

These jottings helped this reader-writer think about the story, find a special point of interest, and develop a thoughtful argument about it.

Keeping a Journal

A journal is not a diary, a record of what the writer did during the day ("today I read Chopin's 'Hour'"). Rather, a journal is a place to store some of the thoughts you may have inscribed in the margin of the text, such as your initial response to the title of a work or to the ending. It is also a place to jot down further reflections, such as thoughts about what the work means to you, and what was said in the classroom about writing in general or specific works.

You will get value from your journal if you write an entry at least once a week, but you will get much more if you write entries after reading each assignment and after each class meeting. You may, for instance, want to reflect on why your opinion is so different from that of another student, or you may want to apply a concept such as *character* or *irony* or *plausibility* to a story that later you may write about in an essay. Comparisons are especially helpful: How does this work (or this character, or this rhyme scheme) differ from last week's reading?

You might even make an entry in the form of a letter to the author or from one character to another. You might write a dialogue between characters in two works or between two authors, or you might record an experience of your own that is comparable to something in the work.

A student who wrote about "The Story of an Hour" began with the following entry in his journal. In reading this entry, notice that one idea stimulates another. The student was, quite rightly, concerned with getting and exploring ideas, not with writing a unified paragraph.

> *Apparently a "well-made" story, but seems clever rather than moving or real.*
> *Doesn't seem plausible. Mrs. M's change comes out of the blue—maybe some women might respond like this, but probably not most.*

Does literature deal with unusual people, or with usual (typical?) people? Shouldn't it deal with typical? Maybe not. (Anyway, how can I know?) Is "typical" same as "plausible"? Come to think of it, prob. not.

Anyway, whether Mrs. M is typical or not, is her change plausible, believable? Think more about this.

Why did she change? Her husband dominated her life and controlled her actions; he did "impose a private will upon a fellow creature." She calls this a crime, even if well-intentioned. Is it a crime?

Arguing with Yourself: Critical Thinking

In our discussion of annotating, brainstorming, freewriting, listing, asking questions, and keeping a journal, the emphasis has been on responding freely rather than in any systematic or disciplined way. Something strikes us (perhaps an idea, perhaps an uncertainty), and we jot it down. Even before we finish jotting it down we may go on to question it, but at this early stage it is enough to put onto paper some thoughts, rooted in our first responses, and to keep going.

The almost random play of mind in brainstorming and the other activities is a kind of thinking, but the term **critical thinking** (which we addressed briefly in our first chapter) is reserved for something different. When we think critically, we scrutinize our own ideas—for example, by searching out our underlying assumptions or evaluating what we have jotted down as evidence. We have seen examples of this sort of analysis of one's own thinking in the journal entries where a student wrote that literature should probably deal with "typical" people, then wondered if "typical" and "plausible" were the same, and then added "probably not."

Speaking broadly, critical thinking is rational, logical thinking. In thinking critically, writers

- scrutinize their **assumptions;**
- **define** their terms;
- test the **evidence** they have collected and even look for **counterevidence;** and
- revise their **thesis** when necessary, in order to make the argument as complete and convincing as possible.

Let's start with **assumptions.** If I say that a story is weak because it is improbable, I ought to think about my assumption that improbability is a fault. I can begin by asking myself if all good stories—or all the stories that I value highly—are probable. I may recall that among my favorites is *Alice in Wonderland* (or *Gulliver's Travels* or *Animal Farm*)—so I probably have to withdraw my assumption that improbability in itself makes a story less than good. I may go on to refine the idea and decide that improbability is not a fault in satiric stories but is a fault in other kinds, which is not the same as saying bluntly that improbability is a fault.

The second aspect of critical thinking, **definition,** does not refer chiefly to defining technical terms such as "meter" for readers who may be unfamiliar with the language of literary criticism; rather, here we are speaking about the need to define controversial terms. For instance, if you are arguing that a particular story is sentimental, you will have to define what you mean by "sentimental" because the word has several meanings.

The third aspect of critical thinking that we have isolated—testing the **evidence** and searching for **counterevidence** within the work—involves rereading the work to see whether we have overlooked material or taken a detail out of context. If, for instance, we say that in "The Story of an Hour" Josephine is a busybody, we should reexamine the work to make sure that she is indeed meddling needlessly and not offering welcome or necessary assistance. Perhaps the original observation will stand up, but perhaps on rereading the story we may feel, as we examine each of Josephine's actions, that she cannot reasonably be characterized as a busybody.

Different readers may come to different conclusions; the important thing is that all readers subject their initial responses to critical thinking, testing their responses against all of the evidence. Remember, your instructor expects you to hand in an essay that is essentially an **argument,** a paper that advances a thesis of your own, and therefore you will want to revise your thinking if you find counterevidence. Your **thesis** might be that

- the story is improbable, or
- the story is typical of Chopin, or
- the story is anti-woman, or
- the story is a remarkable anticipation of contemporary feminist thinking.

Whatever your thesis, it should be able to withstand scrutiny: That is what a good argument does. You may not convince every reader that you are unquestionably right, but you should make every reader feel that your argument is thoughtful. If you read your notes and then your drafts critically, you will probably write a paper that meets this standard.

One last point, or maybe two: Just as your first jottings probably won't be the products of critical thinking, your first reading of the literary work probably *won't* be a critical reading. It is entirely appropriate to begin by reading simply for enjoyment. After all, we read literature (or listen to music, or go to an art museum, or watch dancers) to derive pleasure. However, in this course you are trying to deepen your understanding of literature, so you are *studying* literature. On subsequent readings, therefore, you will read the work critically, carefully noting the writer's view of human nature and the writer's ways of achieving certain effects.

This business of critical thinking is important. We will return to it on page 213, when we talk about interpretations of literature.

Arguing a Thesis

If you think critically about your early jottings and about the literary work itself, you will probably find that some of your jottings lead to dead ends, but others will lead to further ideas that hold up under scrutiny. What the thesis of your essay will be—the idea that you will assert and *argue* (support with evidence)—is still unclear, but you know that a good essay will need a thesis, a point, an argument. You ought to be able to state your point in a **thesis sentence.**

Consider these candidates for a thesis sentence:

1. Mrs. Mallard dies soon after hearing that her husband has died.

True, but this is not a point that can be argued or even developed. About the most an essayist can do with this sentence is to amplify it by summarizing the plot of the story, a task not worth doing unless the plot is unusually obscure. An essay may include a sentence or two of summary to give readers their bearings, but a summary is not an essay.

2. The story is a libel on women.

Unlike the first statement, this one can be developed into an argument. Probably the writer will try to demonstrate that Mrs. Mallard's behavior is despicable. Whether this point can be argued convincingly is another matter; the thesis may be untenable, but it is a thesis. A second problem, however, is this: Even if the writer demonstrates that Mrs. Mallard's behavior is despicable, he or she will have to go on to demonstrate that the presentation of one despicable woman constitutes a libel on women in general. That's a pretty big order.

3. The story is clever but superficial because it is based on an unreal character.

Here, too, is a thesis—a point of view that can be argued. Whether this thesis is true is another matter. The writer's job will be to support it by presenting evidence. Probably the writer will have no difficulty in finding evidence that the story is "clever"; the difficulty will be in establishing a case that the characterization of Mrs. Mallard is "unreal." The writer will have to set forth some ideas about what makes a character real and then show that Mrs. Mallard is an unreal (unbelievable) figure.

4. The irony of the ending is believable partly because it is consistent with earlier ironies in the story.

The student who wrote the essay that appears on page 69 began by drafting an essay based on the third of these thesis topics, but as she worked on a draft she found that she could not support her assertion that the character was unconvincing. In fact, she came to believe that although Mrs. Mallard's joy was the reverse of what a reader might expect, several early reversals in the story helped to make Mrs. Mallard's shift from grief to joy understandable.

✔ CHECKLIST: *Thesis Sentence*

☐ Does the sentence make a claim rather than merely offer a description?
☐ Is the claim arguable rather than self-evident, universally accepted, or of little interest?
☐ Can evidence be produced to support the claim?
☐ Is the claim narrow enough to be supported convincingly in a paper written within the allotted time and at the assigned length?

Drafting Your Argument

After making notes on your reading and then adding more notes stimulated by your rereading and further thinking, you should be able to formulate a tentative thesis. At this point most writers review their preliminary notes and jot down brief statements of what they think their key points may be. These notes may include quotations of key phrases that the writer thinks will support the thesis.

Having reached this stage in considering irony in "The Story of an Hour," one student made these notes:

title? Ironies in an Hour (?) An Hour of Irony (?) Kate Chopin's Irony (?)
thesis: irony at end is prepared for by earlier ironies
chief irony: Mrs. M. dies just as she is beginning to enjoy life
smaller ironies: *1. "sad message" brings her joy*
                      2. Richards is "too late" at end
                      3. Richards is too early at start

These notes are in effect a very brief **outline.** Some writers at this point like to develop a fuller outline, but most writers begin with only a brief outline, knowing that in the process of developing a draft from their notes additional ideas will arise. For these writers, the time to make a detailed outline is *after* they have written a first or second draft. The outline of the written draft will then help them to make sure that their draft has an adequate organization and that main points are developed.

A Sample Draft: "Ironies in an Hour"

Now for the student's draft—not the first version, but a revised draft with some irrelevancies of the first draft omitted and some evidence added.

The numbers in parentheses refer to the page numbers from which the quotations are drawn, though with so short a work as "The Story of an Hour," page references are hardly necessary. Check with your instructor to find out if you must always give citations. (Detailed information about how to document a paper appears in Appendix B.)

Bridas 1

Jennifer Bridas

Professor Lester

English 1102

22 February 2013

Ironies in an Hour

    After we know how the story turns out, if we reread it we find irony at

the very start, as is true of many other stories. Mrs. Mallard's friends assume,

mistakenly, that Mrs. Mallard was deeply in love with her husband, Brently

Mallard. They take great care to tell her gently of his death. The friends

mean well, and in fact they do well. They bring her an hour of life, an hour

of freedom. They think their news is sad. Mrs. Mallard at first expresses grief

when she hears the news, but soon she finds joy in it. So Richards's "sad

message" (57), though sad in Richards's eyes, is in fact a happy message.

    Among the ironic details is the statement that when Mallard entered

the house, Richards tried to conceal him from Mrs. Mallard, but "Richards was

Bridas 2

too late" (58). This is ironic because earlier Richards "hastened" (57) to

bring his sad message; if he had at the start been "too late" (58), Brently

Mallard would have arrived at home first, and Mrs. Mallard's life would

not have ended an hour later but would simply have gone on as it had

before. Yet another irony at the end of the story is the diagnosis of the

doctors. The doctors say she died of "heart disease—of joy that kills" (58).

In one sense the doctors are right: Mrs. Mallard has experienced a

great joy. But of course the doctors totally misunderstand the joy that

kills her.

    The central irony resides not in the well-intentioned but ironic actions

of Richards, or in the unconsciously ironic words of the doctors, but in her

own life. In a way she has been dead. She "sometimes" (58) loved her

husband, but in a way she has been dead. Now, his apparent death brings her

new life. This new life comes to her at the season of the year when "the tops

of trees . . . were all aquiver with the new spring life" (57). But, ironically,

her new life will last only an hour. She looks forward to "summer days" (58)

but she will not see even the end of this spring day. Her years of marriage

were ironic. They brought her a sort of living death instead of joy. Her new

life is ironic too. It grows out of her moment of grief for her supposedly dead

husband, and her vision of a new life is cut short.

[New page]

Bridas 3

Work Cited

Chopin, Kate. "The Story of an Hour." *Literature for Composition*. Ed. Sylvan

    Barnet, William Burto, and William E. Cain. 10th ed. New York: Pearson,

    2014. 57-58. Print.

Revising an Argument

Jennifer Bridas's draft, although thoughtful and clear, is not yet a finished essay. First, the draft needs a good introductory paragraph, a paragraph that will let the **audience**—the readers—know where the writer will be taking them. (In Chapter 7 we discuss introductory paragraphs.) Doubtless you know from your own experience that readers can follow an argument more easily—and with more pleasure—if early in the discussion the writer tells them what the argument is. (The title, too, can strongly suggest the thesis.) Second, some of the paragraphs could be more effective.

In revising paragraphs—or an entire draft—writers unify, organize, clarify, and polish.

1. **Unity** is achieved partly by eliminating irrelevancies. Notice that in the final version of the essay, which begins on page 69, the writer has deleted "as is true of many other stories."
2. **Organization** is largely a matter of arranging material in a sequence that will assist the reader to grasp the point.
3. **Clarity** is achieved largely by providing concrete details and quotations—evidence—to support generalizations and by providing helpful transitions ("for instance," "furthermore," "on the other hand," "however").
4. **Polish** is small-scale revision, such as deleting unnecessary repetition. In the second paragraph of the draft, the phrase "the doctors" appears four times, but it appears only three times in the final version of the paragraph. Similarly, in polishing, a writer may combine choppy sentences into longer ones and break overly long sentences into shorter ones.

Later, after producing a draft that seems close to a finished essay, writers engage in yet another activity:

5. **Editing** includes checking the accuracy of quotations by comparing them with the original, consulting a dictionary for the spelling of doubtful words, and checking a handbook for appropriate punctuation.

Outlining an Argument

Whether or not you draw up an outline before writing a draft, you will be better able to improve your draft if you prepare an outline of what you have written. (If you write on a word processor, it is even more important that you make an outline of your written draft; otherwise you may find yourself just tapping away, filling screen after screen with loosely structured material.) For each paragraph in your draft, write down the main point of the topic sentence or topic idea. Under each of these sentences, indented, add key words for the idea(s) developed in the paragraph. Thus, in an outline for the first two paragraphs of the draft we have just looked at, you might make these jottings:

> *story ironic from start*
> > *friends think news is sad*
> > *Ms. M. finds joy*
> *some ironic details*
> > *Richards hastened, but "too late"*
> > *doctors right and also wrong*

An outline of what you have written will help you to see whether your draft is adequate in three important ways. The outline will show you:

1. the sequence of major topics,
2. the degree of development of these topics, and
3. the argument, the thesis.

Studying your outline, you may realize that your first major point (probably after an introductory paragraph) would be more effective as your third point, and that your second point needs to be further developed.

An outline of this sort is a short version of your draft, perhaps even containing phrases from the draft. Another sort of outline indicates not what each paragraph says but what each paragraph *does*. Such an outline of the three-paragraph draft of the essay on "The Story of an Hour" might look like this:

1. The action of the friends is ironic.
2. Gives some specific (minor) details about ironies.
3. Explains "central irony."

We ought to see a red flag here. The aim of this sort of outline is to indicate what each paragraph *does*, but the jotting for the first paragraph only summarizes its content. Why? Because the paragraph doesn't *do* anything. It does not clearly introduce a thesis, or define a crucial term, or set the story in the context of Chopin's other work.

An outline indicating the function of each paragraph will force you to see whether your essay has an effective structure. We will see that this student later wrote a new opening paragraph for her essay on "The Story of an Hour."

Soliciting Peer Review, Thinking about Counterarguments

Your instructor may encourage or even require you to discuss your draft with another student or with a small group of students. That is, you may be asked to get a review from your peers. Such a procedure is helpful in several ways. First, it gives the writer a real audience, readers who can point to what pleases or puzzles them, who make suggestions, who may often disagree with the writer or with each other, and who frequently *misread*. Though writers don't always like what they hear about their work, reading and discussing their work with others almost always gives them a fresh perspective on their work, and a fresh perspective can stimulate thoughtful revision. (Having your intentions misread because your writing isn't clear enough can be particularly stimulating.)

Your reviewers may suggest that you have overlooked evidence that works against your interpretation. Obviously you will have to either revise your interpretation or show that in fact the supposed counterevidence really does not weaken your interpretation.

The writer whose work is being reviewed is not the sole beneficiary of a review. When students serve as readers for each other, they become better readers of their own work and consequently better revisers. As we said in Chapter 2, learning to write is in large measure learning to read.

If peer review is a part of the writing process in your course, the instructor may distribute a sheet of questions and suggestions. Here is an example of such a sheet.

QUESTIONS FOR PEER REVIEW   ENGLISH 125A

Read each draft once, quickly. Then read it again, with the following questions in mind.

1. What is the essay's topic? Is it one of the assigned topics, or a variation from it? Does the draft show promise of fulfilling the assignment?
2. Looking at the essay as a whole, what thesis (main idea) is stated or implied? If implied, state it in your own words.
3. Is the thesis plausible? How might the argument be strengthened?
4. Looking at each paragraph separately:
   a. What is the basic point? (If it isn't clear to you, ask for clarification.)
   b. How does the paragraph relate to the essay's main idea or to the previous paragraph?
   c. Should some paragraphs be deleted? Be divided into two or more paragraphs? Be combined? Be put elsewhere? (If you outline the essay by jotting down the main point of each paragraph, it will help you to answer these questions.)
   d. Is each sentence clearly related to the sentence that precedes and to the sentence that follows?
   e. Is each paragraph adequately developed?
   f. Are there sufficient details—perhaps brief, supporting quotations from the text?
5. What are the paper's chief strengths?
6. Make at least two specific suggestions that you think will assist the author to improve the paper.

Final Version of the Sample Essay: "Ironies of Life in Kate Chopin's 'The Story of an Hour'"

Here is the final version of Jennifer Bridas's essay. The essay submitted to the instructor was entirely retyped; but here, so that you can easily see how the draft was revised, we show the draft version with the final changes written in by hand.

Bridas 1

Jennifer Bridas

Professor Lester

English 1102

4 February 2013

Ironies of Life in Kate Chopin's "The Story of an Hour"
~~Ironies in an Hour~~

Despite its title, Kate Chopin's "The Story of an Hour" ironically takes only a few minutes to read. In addition, the story turns out to have an ironic ending, but on rereading it one sees that the irony is not concentrated only in the outcome of the plot—Mrs. Mallard dies just when she is beginning to live—but is also present in many details.

After we know how the story turns out, if we reread it we
find irony at the very start. *Because* ~~as is true of many other stories.~~ Mrs.
and her sister
Mallard's friends assume, mistakenly, that ~~Mrs. Mallard~~ *she* was

deeply in love with her husband, Brently Mallard. They take great
They
care to tell her gently of his death. ~~The friends~~ mean well, and in
ing   *joyous*
fact they *do* well. ~~They~~ bring her an hour of life, an hour of
but it is ironic that   #   True,
freedom. They think their news is sad. Mrs. Mallard at first
(unknown to her friends)
expresses grief when she hears the news, but soon she finds joy in
it. So Richards's "sad message" (57), though sad in Richards's

eyes, is in fact a happy message.
small but significant   *near the end of the story*
Among the ironic details is the statement that when Mallard

entered the house, Richards tried to conceal him from Mrs.
almost at
Mallard, but "Richards was too late" (58). This is ironic because
the start of the story, in the second paragraph,
~~earlier~~ Richards "hastened" (57) to bring his sad message; if he

had at the start been "too late" (58), Brently Mallard would have

arrived at home first, and Mrs. Mallard's life would not have ended

an hour later but would simply have gone on as it had before. Yet

another irony at the end of the story is the diagnosis of the

doctors. The doctors say she died of "heart disease—of joy that
they   *for the last hour*
kills" (58). In one sense ~~the doctors~~ are right: Mrs. Mallard

experienced a great joy. But of course the doctors totally

misunderstand the joy that kills her. *It is not joy at seeing her husband
alive, but her realization that the great joy she
experienced during the last hour is over.*
All of these ironic details add richness to the story, but
The central irony resides not in the well-intentioned but

ironic actions of Richards, or in the unconsciously ironic words of
Mrs. Mallard's
the doctors, but in ~~her~~ own life. ~~In a way she has been dead.~~ She

"sometimes" (58) loved her husband, but in a way she has been

Bridas 3

a body subjected to her husband's will   *Appropriately*

dead./ Now, his apparent death brings her new life. ∧This new

life comes to her at the season of the year when "the tops of

trees . . . were all aquiver with the new spring life" (57). But,

She is "free, free, free"—but only until her husband walks through the

ironically, her new life will last only an hour. ∧She looks   *doorway.*

forward to "summer days" (58) but she will not see even the

If

end of this spring day. ∧Her years of marriage were ironic/,

bringing

~~They brought~~ ∧ her a sort of living death instead of joy/, Her

not only because

new life is ironic too/, ∧It grows out of her moment of grief for

but also because her vision of "a long progression of years"

her supposedly dead husband, ~~and her vision of a new life~~ ∧ is

cut short/ *within an hour on a spring day.*

[New page]

Bridas 4

Work Cited

Chopin, Kate. "The Story of an Hour." *Literature for Composition*. Ed. Sylvan

Barnet, William Burto, and William E. Cain. 10th ed. New York: Pearson,

2014. 57-58. Print.

An Overview of the Final Version

As a review, let's look at several principles illustrated by this essay.

- The **title of the essay** is not merely the title of the work discussed; it should give the reader a clue about the essayist's topic. Because your title will create that crucial first impression, make sure that it is interesting.
- The **opening or introductory paragraph** does not begin with the obvious, "In this story . . ." Rather, by naming the author and the title, it lets the reader know what story is being discussed. It also indicates the writer's *thesis* so readers will know where they are going.
- The **organization** is effective. The smaller ironies are discussed in the second and third paragraphs, the central irony in the last paragraph. The essay does not dwindle or become anticlimactic; the argument builds from the least important to the most important point. Again, if you outline your draft you will see whether it has an effective organization.

- **Brief quotations** are used, both to provide evidence and to let the reader hear—if only fleetingly—Kate Chopin's writing voice.
- The essay is chiefly devoted to **analysis** (*how* the parts relate to each other), not to summary (a restatement of the happenings). The writer, properly assuming that the reader has read the work, does not tell the plot in detail. But, aware that the reader has not memorized the story, the writer gives helpful reminders.
- The **present tense** is used in narrating the action: "Mrs. Mallard dies"; "Mrs. Mallard's friends and relatives all assume."
- Although a **concluding paragraph** is often useful—when it does more than merely summarize—it is not essential in a short analysis. In this essay, the last sentence explains the chief irony and therefore makes an acceptable ending.
- Documentation follows the form set forth in Appendix B.
- If the author has proofread the final version of the paper carefully, it will contain no typographical errors.

Writing on Your Computer

In the preceding chapter we talked about "reading with pen in hand," and we really meant using a pen—or a pencil—in your early stage of interacting with the text, to underline or circle or connect words and phrases. But for recording ideas, or sketching an outline, or drafting an essay, many students use a computer or a word processor. Further, you can receive valuable help from reference books and handbooks on style and usage, from computer programs (which check the spelling and grammar of documents), and from Internet resources. Although no computer program or Internet site can write and revise a paper for you, it can help you to detect mistakes and weak spots in your work that you can then remedy.

✔ **CHECKLIST**: *Writing with a Computer*

Prewriting

☐ Take notes. Try listing, then linking and clustering your ideas. Use an outline if you find it helpful.
☐ Check that your transcriptions are accurate when you quote.
☐ Keep your notes together in one file.
☐ Organize your sources in a bibliography.
☐ *Always back up your material.*
☐ Print out your notes.

Preparing a First Draft

☐ Use your notes—move them around in blocks. Expand on your ideas.
☐ Incorporate notes to yourself in your first draft.
☐ Read your draft on the screen to check for errors.
☐ Print out a copy of your first draft.

Working with Your Draft

☐ Revise your printed draft with pen or pencil. Incorporate these changes into your computer file.
☐ Read your corrected draft on the screen; then print out a fresh copy.
☐ Repeat these steps as many times as necessary.

Responding to Peer Review

☐ Give a copy to a peer for comments and suggestions.
☐ Respond appropriately to your reviewer, making the appropriate changes in your computer file.
☐ Print out your revised version and reread it.

Preparing a Final Copy

☐ If there are only a few changes, make them on your printed copy. Otherwise, incorporate your changes in your computer file and print out a new final copy.

Your Turn: Additional Stories for Analysis

KATE CHOPIN

For biographical information, see page 9.

Désirée's Baby

As the day was pleasant, Madame Valmondé drove over to L'Abri to see Désirée and the baby.

It made her laugh to think of Désirée with a baby. Why, it seemed but yesterday that Désirée was little more than a baby herself; when Monsieur in riding through the gateway of Valmondé had found her lying asleep in the shadow of the big stone pillar.

The little one awoke in his arms and began to cry for "Dada." That was as much as she could do or say. Some people thought she might have strayed there of her own accord, for she was of the toddling age. The prevailing belief was that she had been purposely left by a party of Texans, whose canvas-covered wagon, late in the day, had crossed the ferry that Coton Maïs kept, just below the plantation. In time Madame Valmondé abandoned every speculation but the one that Désirée had been sent to her by a beneficent Providence to be the child of her affection, seeing that she was without child of the flesh. For the girl grew to be beautiful and gentle, affectionate and sincere,—the idol of Valmondé.

It was no wonder, when she stood one day against the stone pillar in whose shadow she had lain asleep, eighteen years before, that Armand Aubigny riding by and seeing her there, had fallen in love with her. That was the way all the Aubignys fell in love, as if struck by a pistol shot. The wonder was that he had not loved her before; for he had known her since his father brought him home from Paris, a boy of eight, after his mother died there. The passion that awoke in him that day, when he saw her at the gate, swept along like an avalanche, or like a prairie fire, or like anything that drives headlong over all obstacles.

5   Monsieur Valmondé grew practical and wanted things well considered: that is, the girl's obscure origin. Armand looked into her eyes and did not care. He was reminded that she was nameless. What did it matter about a name when he could give her one of the oldest and proudest in Louisiana? He ordered the *corbeille*[1] from Paris, and contained himself with what patience he could until it arrived, then they were married.

Madame Valmondé had not seen Désirée and the baby for four weeks. When she reached L'Abri she shuddered at the first sight of it, as she always did. It was a sad looking place, which for many years had not known the gentle presence of a mistress, old Monsieur Aubigny having married and buried his wife in France, and she having loved her own land too well ever to leave it. The roof came down steep and black like a cowl, reaching out beyond the wide galleries that encircled the yellow stuccoed house. Big, solemn oaks grew close to it, and their thick-leaved, far-reaching branches shadowed it like a pall. Young Aubigny's rule was a strict one, too, and under it his negroes had forgotten how to be gay, as they had been during the old master's easy-going and indulgent lifetime.

The young mother was recovering slowly, and lay full length, in her soft white muslins and laces, upon a couch. The baby was beside her, upon her arm, where he had fallen asleep, at her breast. The yellow nurse woman sat beside a window fanning herself.

Madame Valmondé bent her portly figure over Désirée and kissed her, holding her an instant tenderly in her arms. Then she turned to the child.

"This is not the baby!" she exclaimed, in startled tones. French was the language spoken at Valmondé in those days.

10   "I knew you would be astonished," laughed Désirée, "at the way he has grown. The little *cochon de lait!*[2] Look at his legs, mamma, and his hands and fingernails,—real fingernails. Zandrine had to cut them this morning. Isn't it true, Zandrine?"

The woman bowed her turbaned head majestically, "Mais si,[3] Madame."

"And the way he cries," went on Désirée, "is deafening. Armand heard him the other day as far away as La Blanche's cabin."

Madame Valmondé had never removed her eyes from the child. She lifted it and walked with it over to the window that was lightest. She scanned the baby narrowly, then looked as searchingly at Zandrine, whose face was turned to gaze across the fields.

"Yes, the child has grown, has changed," said Madame Valmondé, slowly, as she replaced it beside its mother. "What does Armand say?"

15   Désirée's face became suffused with a glow that was happiness itself.

"Oh, Armand is the proudest father in the parish, I believe, chiefly because it is a boy, to bear his name; though he says not—that he would have loved a girl as well. But I know it isn't true. I know he says that to please me. And mamma," she added, drawing Madame Valmondé's head down to her, and speaking in a whisper, "he hasn't punished one of them—not one of them—since baby is born. Even Négrillon, who pretended to have burnt his leg that he might rest from work—he

---

[1]*corbeille* wedding gifts from the groom to the bride.   [2]*cochon de lait* suckling pig (French).
[3]*Mais si* certainly (French).

only laughed, and said Négrillon was a great scamp. Oh, mamma, I'm so happy; it frightens me."

What Désirée said was true. Marriage, and later the birth of his son had softened Armand Aubigny's imperious and exacting nature greatly. This was what made the gentle Désirée so happy, for she loved him desperately. When he frowned she trembled, but loved him. When he smiled, she asked no greater blessing of God. But Armand's dark, handsome face had not often been disfigured by frowns since the day he fell in love with her.

When the baby was about three months old, Désirée awoke one day to the conviction that there was something in the air menacing her peace. It was at first too subtle to grasp. It had only been a disquieting suggestion; an air of mystery among the blacks; unexpected visits from far-off neighbors who could hardly account for their coming. Then a strange, an awful change in her husband's manner, which she dared not ask him to explain. When he spoke to her, it was with averted eyes, from which the old love-light seemed to have gone out. He absented himself from home; and when there, avoided her presence and that of her child, without excuse. And the very spirit of Satan seemed suddenly to take hold of him in his dealings with the slaves. Désirée was miserable enough to die.

She sat in her room, one hot afternoon, in her *peignoir*, listlessly drawing through her fingers the strands of her long, silky brown hair that hung about her shoulders. The baby, half naked, lay asleep upon her own great mahogany bed, that was like a sumptuous throne, with its satin-lined half-canopy. One of La Blanche's little quadroon boys—half naked too—stood fanning the child slowly with a fan of peacock feathers. Désirée's eyes had been fixed absently and sadly upon the baby, while she was striving to penetrate the threatening mist that she felt closing about her. She looked from her child to the boy who stood beside him, and back again; over and over. "Ah!" It was a cry that she could not help; which she was not conscious of having uttered. The blood turned like ice in her veins, and a clammy moisture gathered upon her face.

20   She tried to speak to the little quadroon boy; but no sound would come, at first. When he heard his name uttered, he looked up, and his mistress was pointing to the door. He laid aside the great, soft fan, and obediently stole away, over the polished floor, on his bare tiptoes.

She stayed motionless, with gaze riveted upon her child, and her face the picture of fright.

Presently her husband entered the room, and without noticing her, went to a table and began to search among some papers which covered it.

"Armand," she called to him, in a voice which must have stabbed him, if he was human. But he did not notice. "Armand," she said again. Then she rose and tottered towards him. "Armand," she panted once more, clutching his arm, "look at our child. What does it mean? tell me."

He coldly but gently loosened her fingers from about his arm and thrust the hand away from him. "Tell me what it means!" she cried despairingly.

25   "It means," he answered lightly, "that the child is not white; it means that you are not white."

A quick conception of all that this accusation meant for her nerved her with unwonted courage to deny it. "It is a lie; it is not true, I am white! Look at my hair, it is brown; and my eyes are gray, Armand, you know they are gray. And my skin is fair," seizing his wrist. "Look at my hand; whiter than yours, Armand," she laughed hysterically.

"As white as La Blanche's," he returned cruelly; and went away leaving her alone with their child.

When she could hold a pen in her hand, she sent a despairing letter to Madame Valmondé.

"My mother, they tell me I am not white. Armand has told me I am not white. For God's sake tell them it is not true. You must know it is not true. I shall die. I must die. I cannot be so unhappy, and live."

30   The answer that came was as brief:

"My own Désirée: Come home to Valmondé; back to your mother who loves you. Come with your child."

When the letter reached Désirée she went with it to her husband's study, and laid it open upon the desk before which he sat. She was like a stone image: silent, white, motionless after she placed it there.

In silence he ran his cold eyes over the written words. He said nothing. "Shall I go, Armand?" she asked in tones sharp with agonized suspense.

"Yes, go."

35   "Do you want me to go?"

"Yes, I want you to go."

He thought Almighty God had dealt cruelly and unjustly with him; and felt, somehow, that he was paying Him back in kind when he stabbed thus into his wife's soul. Moreover he no longer loved her, because of the unconscious injury she had brought upon his home and his name.

She turned away like one stunned by a blow, and walked slowly towards the door, hoping he would call her back.

"Good-by, Armand," she moaned.

40   He did not answer her. That was his last blow at fate.

Désirée went in search of her child. Zandrine was pacing the sombre gallery with it. She took the little one from the nurse's arms with no word of explanation, and descending the steps, walked away, under the live-oak branches.

It was an October afternoon; the sun was just sinking. Out in the still fields the negroes were picking cotton.

Désirée had not changed the thin white garment nor the slippers which she wore. Her hair was uncovered and the sun's rays brought a golden gleam from its brown meshes. She did not take the broad, beaten road which led to the far-off plantation of Valmondé. She walked across a deserted field, where the stubble bruised her tender feet, so delicately shod, and tore her thin gown to shreds.

She disappeared among the reeds and willows that grew thick along the banks of the deep, sluggish bayou; and she did not come back again.

45   Some weeks later there was a curious scene enacted at L'Abri. In the centre of the smoothly swept back yard was a great bonfire. Armand Aubigny sat in the wide hallway that commanded a view of the spectacle; and it was he who dealt out to a half dozen negroes the material which kept this fire ablaze.

A graceful cradle of willow, with all its dainty furbishings, was laid upon the pyre, which had already been fed with the richness of a priceless *layette*. Then there were silk gowns, and velvet and satin ones added to these; laces, too, and embroideries; bonnets and gloves; for the *corbeille* had been of rare quality.

The last thing to go was a tiny bundle of letters; innocent little scribblings that Désirée had sent to him during the days of their espousal. There was the remnant of one back in the drawer from which he took them. But it was not Désirée's; it was part of an old letter from his mother to his father. He read it. She was thanking God for the blessing of her husband's love:—

"But, above all," she wrote, "night and day, I thank the good God for having so arranged our lives that our dear Armand will never know that his mother, who adores him, belongs to the race that is cursed with the brand of slavery."

[1892]

Joining the Conversation: Critical Thinking and Writing

1. Let's start with the ending of "Désirée's Baby." Readers find the ending powerful, but they differ in their interpretations of it. Do you think that when Armand reads the letter he learns something he had never suspected or, instead, something that he had sensed about himself all along? Find evidence in the text to support your view.
2. Describe Désirée's feelings toward Armand. Do you agree with the student who told us, "She makes him into a God"?
3. Chopin writes economically: each word counts, each phrase and sentence is significant. What does she reveal about Armand (and perhaps about the discovery he has made) when she writes, "And the very spirit of Satan seemed suddenly to take hold of him in his dealings with the slaves"?
4. Is this story primarily a character study, or is Chopin seeking to make larger points about race, slavery, and gender?

MyLiteratureLab® *For additional resources for "Désirée's Baby," log in to* www.myliteraturelab.com *where you will find a Longman Lecture and Comprehension Quiz, as well as an About the Author, Bibliography, and Critical Overview for Chopin (under Student Resources).*

A Student's Analysis

Hodges 1

Gus Hodges

Professor Durocher

English 125, section B

16 January 2013

Race and Identity in "Désirée's Baby"

"Désirée's Baby," says the literary scholar Emily Toth, is "a shocking story" that deals with the death of "a beautiful young woman"—the subject that, she notes, Edgar Allan Poe identified as "the perfect subject for poetry" (145). But in my view this story is shocking because it connects sexuality and race. It is not just that Désirée suffers a cruel fate, but that she does so because of her race, or, rather, the race that her husband Armand believes she belongs to. The tragic revelation is that Armand, not Désirée, is the person of mixed blood and thus is the cause or source of the mixed blood of their child.

In a key passage midway through the story, Chopin brings the Désirée/Armand relationship into focus:

> When the baby was about three months old, Désirée awoke one day
> to the conviction that there was something in the air menacing
> her peace. It was at first too subtle to grasp. It had only been
> a disquieting suggestion; an air of mystery among the blacks;
> unexpected visits from far-off neighbors who could hardly account
> for their coming. Then a strange, an awful change in her husband's
> manner, which she dared not ask him to explain. When he spoke to
> her, it was with averted eyes, from which the old love-light seemed
> to have gone out. He absented himself from home; and when there,
> avoided her presence and that of her child, without excuse. And
> the very spirit of Satan seemed suddenly to take hold of him in his
> dealings with the slaves. Désirée was miserable enough to die. (75)

Chopin relates the action from Désirée's point of view—what she is seeing, thinking, feeling, fearing, as she and her husband grow estranged. But, at the same time, Chopin makes the reader aware of Armand. She prompts us to imagine, for ourselves, what might be leading him to shun his wife and child and, furthermore, what might account for his Satan-like treatment of his slaves.

This is a powerful insight on Chopin's part. As the story unfolds, it becomes clear that Armand has turned against Désirée because, to his horror and disgust, he has discovered that she possesses black—that is, "not white"—blood. To him, his family has been made impure, contaminated. He feels betrayed, and he takes out his wrath on his wife and child: he cannot bear to be in their presence. In addition, he unleashes his wrath on his slaves; they become the objects of his fury about his family, which is not what he thought it was.

Chopin is showing the tyranny of male authority and power, but, again, she is relating it to race. Armand becomes abusive—psychologically, emotionally, and physically violent—as a result of his reaction to the presence of blackness in his domestic life. This is intolerable to him, and he drives Désirée and the baby away, as if their disappearance could cancel out all memories of them.

The conclusion of the story is shocking: Armand learns that his child is "not white" not because of Désirée but because of himself. It was his mother who was "cursed with the brand of slavery," and she and her husband (Armand's father) sought to conceal this fact from him. Armand comes to despise his wife and child when he learns—or so it seems—that Désirée is black: this is the explanation that he gives to himself and to Désirée. He loathes himself for making such a marriage in the first place.

I am not sure I can prove this, but I have the feeling that Chopin wants us to perceive an ambiguity in the ending of her story. The meaning on the surface is that when Armand reads his mother's letter, he suddenly realizes what he had never known. But there may be a deeper meaning. Possibly it is the case that now Armand is finding confirmation from his mother of an identity—who he is—that he has known was, or could be, true. Driving away Désirée is, in truth, a desperate effort to cast out the self that is "not white."

The more we delve into "Désirée's Baby," the more it becomes Armand's story: to me, he is its central character. In this respect, it is noteworthy that when the story was first published in a magazine, it was titled "The Father of Désirée's Baby" (Knights xxv). I think that this title is better than the one that Chopin settled on, because it puts the focus on Armand. It could be that

Hodges 4

in the end he learns the truth about who he is. It also could be that in the

end he is forced to see something he might have suspected all along—

something he could not believe ever could be possible.

　　We thus find ourselves asking a two-part question about Armand: What

does he know, and what might he not want to know? Could he really have

been so blind as never to have imagined the possibility that he at last

discovers at the end—that the "not white" blood is his own? Perhaps. To me,

however, it seems just as likely that he suspected this possibility but could

not face it. We do not want to accept the truth about who we might be,

about who we are.

[New page]

Hodges 5

Works Cited

Chopin, Kate. "Désirée's Baby." *Literature for Composition*. Ed. Sylvan Barnet, William

　　Burto, and William E. Cain. 10th ed. New York: Pearson, 2014. 73–77. Print.

Knights, Pamela. "Introduction." *The Awakening, and Other Stories*. New York:

　　Oxford UP, 2000. ix–xliii. Print.

Toth, Emily. *Unveiling Kate Chopin*. Jackson: U of Mississippi, 1999. Print.

Joining the Conversation: Critical Thinking and Writing

1. Has Gus Hodges chosen a good title for his paper?
2. Do you think it is good strategy to begin a paper with a quotation from a secondary source?
3. The student begins his closing paragraph with a question. Is this tactic effective or not?

4. Do you agree with this student's decision to center his paper on a single lengthy quote?
5. Let's now consider the paper as a whole. What is the writer's thesis? Does the writer provide evidence? Does he prove his thesis?
6. If you were to give the writer of this paper one piece of advice for improving his paper, what would it be?
7. Hodges makes an intriguing claim about Armand. Do you agree with him or not? Can you locate evidence in the text to support the student's feeling about what Armand has known, or might have known, all along?
8. Is the final paragraph effective?

KATE CHOPIN

For biographical information, see page 9.

The Storm

I

The leaves were so still that even Bibi thought it was going to rain. Bobinôt, who was accustomed to converse on terms of perfect equality with his little son, called the child's attention to certain sombre clouds that were rolling with sinister intention from the west, accompanied by a sullen, threatening roar. They were at Friedheimer's store and decided to remain there till the storm had passed. They sat within the door on two empty kegs. Bibi was four years old and looked very wise.

"Mama'll be 'fraid, yes," he suggested with blinking eyes.

"She'll shut the house. Maybe she got Sylvie helpin' her this evenin'," Bobinôt responded reassuringly.

"No; she ent got Sylvie. Sylvie was helpin' her yistiday," piped Bibi.

5   Bobinôt arose and going across to the counter purchased a can of shrimps, of which Calixta was very fond. Then he returned to his perch on the keg and sat stolidly holding the can of shrimps while the storm burst. It shook the wooden store and seemed to be ripping great furrows in the distant field. Bibi laid his little hand on his father's knee and was not afraid.

II

Calixta, at home, felt no uneasiness for their safety. She sat at a side window sewing furiously on a sewing machine. She was greatly occupied and did not notice the approaching storm. But she felt very warm and often stopped to mop her face on which the perspiration gathered in beads. She unfastened her white sacque at the throat. It began to grow dark, and suddenly realizing the situation she got up hurriedly and went about closing windows and doors.

Out on the small front gallery[1] she had hung Bobinôt's Sunday clothes to air and she hastened out to gather them before the rain fell. As she stepped outside, Alcée Laballière rode in at the gate. She had not seen him very often since her marriage, and never alone. She stood there with Bobinôt's coat in her hands, and the big rain drops began to fall. Alcée rode his horse under the shelter of a side

[1]**gallery** porch, or passageway along a wall, open to the air but protected by a roof supported by columns.

projection where the chickens had huddled and there were plows and a harrow piled up in the corner.

"May I come and wait on your gallery till the storm is over, Calixta?" he asked.

"Come 'long in, M'sieur Alcée."

His voice and her own startled her as if from a trance, and she seized Bobinôt's vest. Alcée, mounting to the porch, grabbed the trousers and snatched Bibi's braided jacket that was about to be carried away by a sudden gust of wind. He expressed an intention to remain outside, but it was soon apparent that he might as well have been out in the open: the water beat in upon the boards in driving sheets, and he went inside, closing the door after him. It was even necessary to put something beneath the door to keep the water out.

"My! what a rain! It's good two years sence it rain' like that," exclaimed Calixta as she rolled up a piece of bagging and Alcée helped her to thrust it beneath the crack.

She was a little fuller of figure than five years before when she married; but she had lost nothing of her vivacity. Her blue eyes still retained their melting quality; and her yellow hair, dishevelled by the wind and rain, kinked more stubbornly than ever about her ears and temples.

The rain beat upon the low, shingled roof with a force and clatter that threatened to break an entrance and deluge them there. They were in the dining room— the sitting room—the general utility room. Adjoining was her bed room, with Bibi's couch along side her own. The door stood open, and the room with its white, monumental bed, its closed shutters, looked dim and mysterious.

Alcée flung himself into a rocker and Calixta nervously began to gather up from the floor the lengths of a cotton sheet which she had been sewing.

"If this keeps up, *Dieu sait*[2] if the levees goin' to stan' it!" she exclaimed.

"What have you got to do with the levees?"

"I got enough to do! An' there's Bobinôt with Bibi out in that storm—if he only didn' left Friedheimer's!"

"Let us hope, Calixta, that Bobinôt's got sense enough to come in out of a cyclone."

She went and stood at the window with a greatly disturbed look on her face. She wiped the frame that was clouded with moisture. It was stiflingly hot. Alcée got up and joined her at the window, looking over her shoulder. The rain was coming down in sheets obscuring the view of far-off cabins and enveloping the distant wood in a gray mist. The playing of the lightning was incessant. A bolt struck a tall chinaberry tree at the edge of the field. It filled all visible space with a blinding glare and the crash seemed to invade the very boards they stood upon.

Calixta put her hands to her eyes, and with a cry, staggered backward. Alcée's arm encircled her, and for an instant he drew her close and spasmodically to him.

"*Bonté!*"[3] she cried, releasing herself from his encircling arm and retreating from the window, "the house'll go next! If I only knew w'ere Bibi was!" She would not compose herself; she would not be seated. Alcée clasped her shoulders and looked into her face. The contact of her warm, palpitating body when he had unthinkingly drawn her into his arms, had aroused all the old-time infatuation and desire for her flesh.

"Calixta," he said, "don't be frightened. Nothing can happen. The house is too low to be struck, with so many tall trees standing about. There! aren't you going to be quiet? say, aren't you?" He pushed her hair back from her face that was warm and steaming. Her lips were as red and moist as pomegranate seed. Her white neck and a glimpse of her full, firm bosom disturbed him powerfully. As she glanced up at him

[2]***Dieu sait*** God only knows.   [3]***Bonté!*** Heavens!

the fear in her liquid blue eyes had given place to a drowsy gleam that unconsciously betrayed a sensuous desire. He looked down into her eyes and there was nothing for him to do but to gather her lips in a kiss. It reminded him of Assumption.[4]

"Do you remember—in Assumption, Calixta?" he asked in a low voice broken by passion. Oh! she remembered; for in Assumption he had kissed her and kissed and kissed her; until his senses would well nigh fail, and to save her he would resort to a desperate flight. If she was not an immaculate dove in those days, she was still inviolate; a passionate creature whose very defenselessness had made her defense, against which his honor forbade him to prevail. Now—well, now—her lips seemed in a manner free to be tasted, as well as her round, white throat and her whiter breasts.

They did not heed the crashing torrents, and the roar of the elements made her laugh as she lay in his arms. She was a revelation in that dim, mysterious chamber; as white as the couch she lay upon. Her firm, elastic flesh that was knowing for the first time its birthright, was like a creamy lily that the sun invites to contribute its breath and perfume to the undying life of the world.

25 The generous abundance of her passion, without guile or trickery, was like a white flame which penetrated and found response in depths of his own sensuous nature that had never yet been reached.

When he touched her breasts they gave themselves up in quivering ecstasy, inviting his lips. Her mouth was a fountain of delight. And when he possessed her, they seemed to swoon together at the very borderland of life's mystery.

He stayed cushioned upon her, breathless, dazed, enervated, with his heart beating like a hammer upon her. With one hand she clasped his head, her lips lightly touching his forehead. The other hand stroked with a soothing rhythm his muscular shoulders.

The growl of the thunder was distant and passing away. The rain beat softly upon the shingles, inviting them to drowsiness and sleep. But they dared not yield.

The rain was over; and the sun was turning the glistening green world into a place of gems. Calixta, on the gallery, watched Alcée ride away. He turned and smiled at her with a beaming face; and she lifted her pretty chin in the air and laughed aloud.

III

30 Bobinôt and Bibi, trudging home, stopped without at the cistern to make themselves presentable.

"My! Bibi, w'at will yo' mama say! You ought to be ashame'. You oughtn' put on those good pants. Look at 'em! An' that mud on yo' collar! How you got that mud on yo' collar, Bibi? I never saw such a boy!" Bibi was the picture of pathetic resignation. Bobinôt was the embodiment of serious solicitude as he strove to remove from his own person and his son's the signs of their tramp over heavy roads and through wet fields. He scraped the mud off Bibi's bare legs and feet with a stick and carefully removed all traces from his heavy brogans. Then, prepared for the worst—the meeting with an over-scrupulous housewife, they entered cautiously at the back door.

Calixta was preparing supper. She had set the table and was dripping coffee at the hearth. She sprang up as they came in.

"Oh, Bobinôt! You back! My! but I was uneasy. W'ere you been during the rain? An' Bibi? he ain't wet? he ain't hurt?" She had clasped Bibi and was kissing him effusively. Bobinôt's explanations and apologies which he had been composing

---

[4]**Assumption** a parish (i.e., a county) in southeast Louisiana.

all along the way, died on his lips as Calixta felt him to see if he were dry, and seemed to express nothing but satisfaction at their safe return.

"I brought you some shrimps, Calixta," offered Bobinôt, hauling the can from his ample side pocket and laying it on the table.

35   "Shrimps! Oh, Bobinôt! you too good fo' anything!" and she gave him a smacking kiss on the cheek that resounded. "*J'vous reponds,*[5] we'll have a feas' to night! umph-umph!"

Bobinôt and Bibi began to relax and enjoy themselves, and when the three seated themselves at table they laughed much and so loud that anyone might have heard them as far away as Laballière's.

IV

Alcée Laballière wrote to his wife, Clarisse, that night. It was a loving letter, full of tender solicitude. He told her not to hurry back, but if she and the babies liked it at Biloxi, to stay a month longer. He was getting on nicely; and though he missed them, he was willing to bear the separation a while longer—realizing that their health and pleasure were the first things to be considered.

V

As for Clarisse, she was charmed upon receiving her husband's letter. She and the babies were doing well. The society was agreeable; many of her old friends and acquaintances were at the bay. And the first free breath since her marriage seemed to restore the pleasant liberty of her maiden days. Devoted as she was to her husband, their intimate conjugal life was something which she was more than willing to forego for a while.

So the storm passed and everyone was happy.

[1898]

---

[5]*J'vous reponds* Take my word; let me tell you.

Writing about "The Storm"

As we said earlier, what you write will depend on your audience and on your purpose, as well as on your own responses (for instance, pleasure or irritation) to a work. Consider the *differences* among these assignments:

1. Assume that you are trying to describe "The Storm" to someone who has not read it. Briefly summarize the action, then explain why you think "The Storm" is (or is not) worth reading.
2. Assume that your readers are familiar with "The Story of an Hour." Compare the implied attitudes, as you see them, toward marriage in that story and in "The Storm."
3. Write an essay arguing that "The Storm" is (or is not) immoral or (a different thing) amoral. (Because one of her earlier works, *The Awakening*, was widely condemned as sordid, Chopin was unable to find a publisher for "The Storm.")
4. In Part IV we are told that Alcée wrote a letter to Clarisse. Write his letter (500 words). Or write Clarisse's response (500 words).

5. You are writing to a high school teacher to urge that one of the four stories by Chopin be taught in high school. Which one do you recommend, and why?
6. Do you think "The Storm" would make a good film? Why? What devices might you use to turn "Ripe Figs," "The Story of an Hour," or "Désirée's Baby" into an interesting film?

MyLiteratureLab® *For additional resources for "The Storm," log in to* www.myliteraturelab.com *where you will find a Longman Lecture, Interactive Reading, Comprehension Quiz, Short Evaluation Exercises, Essay Prompts (under Student Resources) and a Student Essay (under Composing); you will also find an About the Author, Bibliography, Links, and a Critical Overview for Chopin (under Student Resources).*

ANTON CHEKHOV

Anton Chekhov (1860–1904) was born in Russia, the son of a shopkeeper. While a medical student at Moscow University, Chekhov wrote stories, sketches, and reviews to help support his family and to finance his education. In 1884 he received his medical degree, began to practice medicine, published his first book of stories, and suffered the first of a series of hemorrhages from tuberculosis. In his remaining twenty years, in addition to writing several hundred stories, he wrote plays, half a dozen of which have established themselves as classics. He died from tuberculosis at forty-four.

Misery

Translated by Constance Garnett

"To Whom Shall I Tell My Grief?"

The twilight of evening. Big flakes of wet snow are whirling lazily about the street lamps, which have just been lighted, and lying in a thin soft layer on roofs, horses' backs, shoulders, caps. Iona Potapov, the sledgedriver, is all white like a ghost. He sits on the box without stirring, bent as double as the living body can be bent. If a regular snowdrift fell on him it seems as though even then he would not think it necessary to shake it off. . . . His little mare is white and motionless too. Her stillness, the angularity of her lines, and the stick-like straightness of her legs make her look like a halfpenny gingerbread horse. She is probably lost in thought. Anyone who has been torn away from the plough, from the familiar gray landscapes, and cast into this slough, full of monstrous lights, of unceasing uproar and hurrying people, is bound to think.

It is a long time since Iona and his nag have budged. They came out of the yard before dinner-time and not a single fare yet. But now the shades of evening are falling on the town. The pale light of the street lamps changes to a vivid color, and the bustle of the street grows noisier.

"Sledge to Vyborgskaya!" Iona hears. "Sledge!"

Iona starts, and through his snow-plastered eyelashes sees an officer in a military overcoat with a hood over his head.

5   "To Vyborgskaya," repeats the officer. "Are you asleep? To Vyborgskaya!"

In token of assent Iona gives a tug at the reins which sends cakes of snow flying from the horse's back and shoulders. The officer gets into the sledge.

The sledge-driver clicks to the horse, cranes his neck like a swan, rises in his seat, and more from habit than necessity brandishes his whip. The mare cranes her neck, too, crooks her stick-like legs, and hesitatingly sets off.... .

"Where are you shoving, you devil?" Iona immediately hears shouts from the dark mass shifting to and fro before him. "Where the devil are you going? Keep to the r-right!"

"You don't know how to drive! Keep to the right," says the officer angrily.

A coachman driving a carriage swears at him; a pedestrian crossing the road and brushing the horse's nose with his shoulder looks at him angrily and shakes the snow off his sleeve. Iona fidgets on the box as though he were sitting on thorns, jerks his elbows, and turns his eyes about like one possessed, as though he did not know where he was or why he was there.

10   "What rascals they all are!" says the officer jocosely. "They are simply doing their best to run up against you or fall under the horse's feet. They must be doing it on purpose."

Iona looks at his fare and moves his lips. . . . Apparently he means to say something, but nothing comes out but a sniff.

"What?" inquires the officer.

Iona gives a wry smile, and straining his throat, brings out huskily: "My son . . . , er . . . my son died this week, sir."

"H'm! What did he die of?"

15   Iona turns his whole body round to his fare, and says:

"Who can tell! It must have been from fever. . . . He lay three days in the hospital and then he died. . . . God's will."

"Turn round, you devil!" comes out of the darkness. "Have you gone cracked, you old dog? Look where you are going!"

"Drive on! drive on! . . ." says the officer. "We shan't get there till tomorrow going on like this. Hurry up!"

The sledge-driver cranes his neck again, rises in his seat, and with heavy grace swings his whip. Several times he looks round at the officer, but the latter keeps his eyes shut and is apparently disinclined to listen. Putting his fare down at Vyborgskaya, Iona stops by a restaurant, and again sits huddled up on the box. . . . Again the wet snow paints him and his horse white. One hour passes, and then another. . . .

20   Three young men, two tall and thin, one short and hunchbacked, come up, railing at each other and loudly stamping on the pavement with their galoshes.

"Cabby, to the Police Bridge!" the hunchback cries in a cracked voice. "The three of us, . . . twenty kopecks!"

Iona tugs at the reins and clicks to his horse. Twenty kopecks is not a fair price, but he has no thoughts for that. Whether it is a rouble or whether it is five kopecks does not matter to him now so long as he has a fare. . . . The three young men, shoving each other and using bad language, go up to the sledge, and all three try to sit down at once. The question remains to be settled: Which are to sit down and which one is to stand? After a long altercation, ill-temper, and abuse, they come to the conclusion that the hunchback must stand because he is the shortest.

"Well, drive on," says the hunchback in his cracked voice, settling himself and breathing down Iona's neck. "Cut along! What a cap you've got, my friend! You wouldn't find a worse one in all Petersburg. . . ."

"He-he! . . . he-he! . . ." laughs Iona. "It's nothing to boast of!"

25   "Well, then, nothing to boast of, drive on! Are you going to drive like this all the way? Eh? Shall I give you one in the neck?"

"My head aches," says one of the tall ones. "At the Dukmasovs' yesterday Vaska and I drank four bottles of brandy between us."

"I can't make out why you talk such stuff," says the other tall one angrily. "You lie like a brute."

"Strike me dead, it's the truth! . . ."

"It's about as true as that a louse coughs."

30   "He-he!" grins Iona. "Me-er-ry gentlemen!"

"Tfoo! the devil take you!" cries the hunchback indignantly. "Will you get on, you old plague, or won't you? Is that the way to drive? Give her one with the whip. Hang it all, give it her well."

Iona feels behind his back the jolting person and quivering voice of the hunchback. He hears abuse addressed to him, he sees people, and the feeling of loneliness begins little by little to be less heavy on his heart. The hunchback swears at him, till he chokes over some elaborately whimsical string of epithets and is overpowered by his cough. His tall companions begin talking of a certain Nadyezhda Petrovna. Iona looks round at them. Waiting till there is a brief pause, he looks round once more and says:

"This week . . . er . . . my . . . er . . . son died!"

"We shall all die, . . ." says the hunchback with a sigh, wiping his lips after coughing. "Come, drive on! drive on! My friends, I simply cannot stand crawling like this! When will he get us there?"

35   "Well, you give him a little encouragement . . . one in the neck!"

"Do you hear, you old plague? I'll make you smart. If one stands on ceremony with fellows like you one may as well walk. Do you hear, you old dragon? Or don't you care a hang what we say?"

And Iona hears rather than feels a slap on the back of his neck.

"He-he! . . ." he laughs. "Merry gentlemen . . . God give you health!"

"Cabman, are you married?" asks one of the tall ones.

40   "I? He-he! Me-er-ry gentlemen. The only wife for me now is the damp earth. . . . He-ho-ho! . . . The grave that is! . . . Here my son's dead and I am alive. . . . It's a strange thing, death has come in at the wrong door. . . . Instead of coming for me it went for my son. . . ."

And Iona turns round to tell them how his son died, but at that point the hunchback gives a faint sigh and announces that, thank God! they have arrived at last. After taking his twenty kopecks, Iona gazes for a long while after the revelers, who disappear into a dark entry. Again he is alone and again there is silence for him. . . . The misery which has been for a brief space eased comes back again and tears his heart more cruelly than ever. With a look of anxiety and suffering Iona's eyes stray restlessly among the crowds moving to and fro on both sides of the street: can he not find among those thousands someone who will listen to him? But the crowds flit by heedless of him and his misery. . . . His misery is immense, beyond all bounds. If Iona's heart were to burst and his misery to flow out, it would flood the whole world, it seems, but yet it is not seen. It has found a hiding-place in such an insignificant shell that one would not have found it with a candle by daylight. . . .

Iona sees a house-porter with a parcel and makes up his mind to address him.

"What time will it be, friend?" he asks.

"Going on for ten. . . . Why have you stopped here? Drive on!"

45   Iona drives a few paces away, bends himself double, and gives himself up to his misery. He feels it is no good to appeal to people. But before five minutes have passed he draws himself up, shakes his head as though he feels a sharp pain, and tugs at the reins. . . . He can bear it no longer.

"Back to the yard!" he thinks. "To the yard!"

And his little mare, as though she knew his thoughts, falls to trotting. An hour and a half later Iona is sitting by a big dirty stove. On the stove, on the floor, and on the benches are people snoring. The air is full of smells and stuffiness. Iona looks at the sleeping figures, scratches himself, and regrets that he has come home so early. . . .

"I have not earned enough to pay for the oats, even," he thinks. "That's why I am so miserable. A man who knows how to do his work, . . . who has had enough to eat, and whose horse has had enough to eat, is always at ease. . . ."

In one of the corners a young cabman gets up, clears his throat sleepily, and makes for the waterbucket.

50   "Want a drink?" Iona asks him.

"Seems so."

"May it do you good. . . . But my son is dead, mate. . . . Do you hear? This week in the hospital. . . . It's queer business. . . ."

Iona looks to see the effect produced by his words, but he sees nothing. The young man has covered his head over and is already asleep. The old man sighs and scratches himself. . . . Just as the young man had been thirsty for water, he thirsts for speech. His son will soon have been dead a week, and he has not really talked to anybody yet. . . . He wants to talk of it properly, with deliberation. . . . He wants to tell how his son was taken ill, how he suffered, what he said before he died, how he died. . . . He wants to describe the funeral, and how he went to the hospital to get his son's clothes. He still has his daughter Anisya in the country. . . . And he wants to talk about her too. . . . Yes, he has plenty to talk about now. His listener ought to sigh and exclaim and lament. . . . It would be even better to talk to women. Though they are silly creatures, they blubber at the first word.

"Let's go out and have a look at the mare," Iona thinks. "There is always time for sleep. . . . You'll have sleep enough, no fear. . . ."

55   He puts on his coat and goes into the stables where his mare is standing. He thinks about oats, about hay, about the weather. . . . He cannot think about his son when he is alone. . . . To talk about him with someone is possible, but to think of him and picture him is insufferable anguish. . . .

"Are you munching?" Iona asks his mare, seeing her shining eyes. "There, munch away, munch away. . . . Since we have not earned enough for oats, we will eat hay. . . . Yes, . . . I have grown too old to drive. . . . My son ought to be driving, not I. . . . He was a real coachman. . . . He ought to have lived. . . ."

Iona is silent for a while, and then he goes on:

"That's how it is, old girl. . . . Kuzma Ionitch is gone. . . . He said goodby to me. . . . He went and died for no reason. . . . Now, suppose you had a little colt, and you were mother to that little colt. . . . And all at once that same little colt went and died. . . . You'd be sorry, wouldn't you? . . ."

The little mare munches, listens, and breathes on her master's hands. Iona is carried away and tells her all about it.

[1886]

Joining the Conversation: Critical Thinking and Writing

1. What do you admire or dislike about Chekhov's story? Why? Set forth your response in an argument.

2. Examine in detail your response to the ending and develop an argument about it. Do you think the ending is, in a way, a happy ending? Would you prefer a different ending? For instance, should the story end when the young cabman falls asleep? Or when Iona sets out for the stable? Or can you imagine a better ending? If so, what?

MyLiteratureLab® *For additional resources for Anton Chekov log in to* www.myliteraturelab.com *where you will find an About the Author (under Student Resources).*

V. S. NAIPAUL

V[idiadhar] S[urajprasad] Naipaul was born in 1932 in Trinidad. After completing his early education in Trinidad he emigrated to England and graduated from Oxford in 1954. A prolific novelist and a far-traveler, he writes about the United States, Africa, India—where his grandfather was born—and, especially, about the Caribbean.

The Night Watchman's Occurrence Book

November 21. 10.30 P.M. C. A. Cavander take over duty at C———Hotel all corrected. *Cesar Alwyn Cavander*

7 A M C. A. Cavander hand over duty to Mr Vignales at C———Hotel no report *Cesar Alwyn Cavander*

November 22. 10.30 P.M. C. A. Cavander take over duty at C———Hotel no report. *Cesar Alwyn Cavander*

7 A.M. C. A. Cavander hand over duty to Mr Vignales at C———Hotel all corrected. *Cesar Alwyn Cavander*

This is the third occasion on which I have found C. A. Cavander, Night Watchman, asleep on duty. Last night, at 12.45 A.M., I found him sound asleep in a rocking chair in the hotel lounge. Night Watchman Cavander has therefore been dismissed. Night Watchman Hillyard: This book is to be known in future as "The Night Watchman's Occurrence Book." In it I shall expect to find a detailed account of everything that happens in the hotel tonight. Be warned by the example of ex-Night Watchman Cavander, *W. A. G. Inskip, Manager*

5 Mr Manager, remarks noted. You have no worry where I am concern sir. *Charles Ethelbert Hillyard, Night Watchman*

November 23. 11 P.M. Night Watchman Hillyard take over duty at C———Hotel with one torch light 2 fridge keys and room keys 1, 3, 6, 10 and 13. Also 25 cartoons Carib Beer and 7 cartoons Heineken[1] and 2 cartoons American cigarettes. Beer cartoons intact Bar intact all corrected no report. *Charles Ethelbert Hillyard*

7 A.M. Night Watchman Hillyard hand over duty to Mr Vignales at C———Hotel with one torch light 2 fridge keys and room keys, 1, 3, 6, 10 and 13. 32 cartoons beer. Bar intact all corrected no report. *Charles Ethelbert Hillyard*

Night Watchman Hillyard: Mr Wills complained bitterly to me this morning that last night he was denied entry to the bar by you. I wonder if you know

---

[1]**Heineken** a Dutch beer.

exactly what the purpose of this hotel is. In future all hotel guests are to be allowed entry to the bar at whatever time they choose. It is your duty simply to note what they take. This is one reason why the hotel provides a certain number of beer cartons (please note the spelling of this word). *W. A. G. Inskip*

Mr Manager, remarks noted. I sorry I didnt get the chance to take some education sir. *Chas. Ethelbert Hillyard*

November 24. 11 P.M. N. W. Hillyard take over duty with one Torch, 1 Bar Key, 2 Fridge Keys, 32 cartoons Beer, all intact. 12 Midnight Bar close and Barman left leaving Mr Wills and others in Bar, and they left at 1 A.M. Mr Wills took 16 Carib Beer, Mr Wilson 8, Mr Percy 8. At 2 A.M. Mr Wills come back in the bar and take 4 Carib and some bread, he cut his hand trying to cut the bread, so please dont worry about the stains on the carpet sir. At 6 A.M. Mr Wills come back for some soda water. It didn't have any so he take a ginger beer instead. Sir you see it is my intention to do this job good sir, I cant see how Night Watchman Cavander could fall asleep on this job sir. *Chas. Ethelbert Hillyard*

> You always seems sure of the time, and guests appear to be in the habit of entering the bar on the hour. You will kindly note the exact time. The clock from the kitchen is left on the window near the switches. You can use this clock but you MUST replace it every morning before you go off duty. *W. A. G. Inskip*

Noted. *Chas. Ethelbert Hillyard*

10 *November 25.* Midnight Bar close and 12.23 A.M. Barman left leaving Mr Wills and others in Bar. Mr Owen take 5 bottles Carib, Mr Wilson 6 bottles Heineken, Mr Wills 18 Carib and they left at 2.52 A.M. Nothing unusual. Mr. Wills was helpless, I don't see how anybody could drink so much, eighteen one man alone, this work enough to turn anybody Seventh Day Adventist, and another man come in the bar, I dont know his name, I hear they call him Paul, he assist me because the others couldn't do much, and we take Mr Wills up to his room and take off his boots and slack his other clothes and then we left. Don't know sir if they did take more while I was away, nothing was mark on the Pepsi Cola board, but they was drinking still, it looks as if they come back and take some more, but with Mr Wills I want some extra assistance sir.

Mr Manager, the clock break I find it break when I come back from Mr Wills room sir. It stop 3.19 sir. *Chas. E. Hillyard*

> More than 2 lbs of veal were removed from the Fridge last night, and a cake that was left in the press was cut. It is your duty, Night Watchman Hillyard, to keep an eye on these things. I ought to warn you that I have also asked the Police to check on all employees leaving the hotel, to prevent such occurrences in the future. *W. A. G. Inskip*

Mr Manager, I don't know why people so anxious to blame servants sir. About the cake, the press lock at night and I dont have the key sir, everything safe where I am concern sir. *Chas. Hillyard*

November 26. Midnight Bar close and Barman left. Mr Wills didn't come. I hear he at the American base tonight, all quiet, nothing unusual.

Mr Manager, I request one thing. Please inform the Barman to let me know sir when there is a female guest in the hotel sir. *C. E. Hillyard*

> This morning I received a report from a guest that there were screams in the hotel during the night. You wrote All Quiet. Kindly explain in writing. *W. A. G. Inskip* Write Explanation here:

EXPLANATION. Not long after midnight the telephone ring and a woman ask for Mr Jimminez. I try to tell her where he was but she say she cant hear properly. Fifteen minutes later she came in a car, she was looking vex and sleepy, and I went up to call him. The door was not lock, I went in and touch his foot and call him very soft, and he jump up and begin to shout. When he come to himself he said he had Night Mere, and then he come down and went away with the woman, was not necessary to mention.

15   Mr Manager, I request you again, please inform the Barman to let me know sir when there is a female guest in the Hotel. *C. Hillyard*

November 27. 1 A.M. Bar close, Mr Wills and a American 19 Carib and 2.30 A.M. a Police come and ask for Mr Wills, he say the American report that he was robbed of $200.00¢, he was last drinking at the C———with Mr Wills and others. Mr Wills and the Police ask to open the Bar to search it, I told them I cannot open the Bar for you like that, the Police must come with the Manager. Then the American say it was only joke he was joking, and they try to get the Police to laugh, but the Police looking the way I feeling. Then laughing Mr Wills left in a garage car as he couldn't drive himself and the American was waiting outside and they both fall down as they was getting in the car, and Mr Wills saying any time you want a overdraft you just come to my bank kiddo. The Police left walking by himself. *C. Hillyard*

> Night Watchman Hillyard: "Was not necessary to mention"!! You are not to decide what is necessary to mention in this night watchman's occurrence book. Since when have you become sole owner of the hotel as to determine what is necessary to mention? If the guest did not mention it I would never have known that there were screams in the hotel during the night. Also will you kindly tell me who Mr Jimminez is? And what rooms he occupied or occupies? And by what right? You have been told by me personally that the names of all hotel guests are on the slate next to the light switches. If you find Mr Jimminez's name on this slate, or could give me some information about him, I will be most warmly obliged to you. The lady you ask about is Mrs Roscoc, Room 12, as you very well know. It is your duty to see that guests are not pestered by unauthorized callers. You should give no information about guests to such people, and I would be glad if in future you could direct such callers straight to me. *W. A. G. Inskip*

Sir was what I ask you two times, I dont know what sort of work I take up, I always believe that nightwatchman work is a quiet work and I dont like meddling in white people business, but the gentleman occupy Room 12 also, was there that I went up to call him, I didn't think it necessary to mention because was none of my business sir. *C.E.H.*

November 28. 12 Midnight Bar close and Barman left at 12.20 A.M. leaving Mr Wills and others, and they all left at 1.25 A.M. Mr Wills 8 Carib, Mr Wilson 12, Mr Percy 8, and the man they call Paul 12. Mrs Roscoe join the gentlemen at 12.33 A.M., four gins, everybody calling her Minnie from Trinidad, and then they start singing that song, and some others. Nothing unusual. Afterwards there were mild singing and guitar music in Room 12. A man come in and ask to use the phone at 2.17 A.M. and while he was using it about 7 men come in and wanted to beat him up, so he put down the phone and they all ran away. At 3 A.M. I notice the padlock not on the press, I look inside, no cake, but the padlock was not put on in the first place sir. Mr Wills come down again at 6 A.M. to look for his sweet, he look in the Fridge and did not see any. He took a piece of pineapple. A plate was covered in the Fridge, but it didn't have anything in it. Mr Wills put it out, the cat jump on it and it fall down and break. The garage bulb not burning. *C.E.H.*

> You will please sign your name at the bottom of your report. You are in the habit of writing Nothing Unusual. Please take note and think before making such a statement. I want to know what is meant by nothing unusual. I gather, not from you, needless to say, that the police have fallen into the habit of visiting the hotel at night. I would be most grateful to you if you could find the time to note the times of these visits. *W. A. G. Inskip*

Sir, nothing unusual means everything usual. I dont know, nothing I writing you liking. I dont know what sort of work this night watchman work getting to be, since when people have to start getting Cambridge certificate to get night watchman job, I ain't educated and because of this everybody think they could insult me. *Charles Ethelbert Hillyard*

20   *November 29.* Midnight Bar close and 12.15 Barman left leaving Mr Wills and Mrs Roscoe and others in the Bar. Mr Wills and Mrs Roscoe left at 12.30 A.M. leaving Mr Wilson and the man they call Paul, and they all left at 1.00 A.M. Twenty minutes to 2 Mr Wills and party return and left again at 5 to 3. At 3.45 Mr Wills return and take break and milk and olives and cherries, he ask for nutmeg too, I said we had none, he drink 2 Carib, and left ten minutes later. He also collect Mrs Roscoe bag. All the drinks, except the 2 Carib, was taken by the man they call Paul. I don't know sir I don't like this sort of work, you better hire a night barman. At 5.30 Mrs Roscoe and the man they call Paul come back to the bar, they was having a quarrel, Mr Paul saying you make me sick, Mrs Roscoe saying I feel sick, and then she vomit all over the floor, shouting I didn't want that damned milk. I was cleaning up when Mr Wills come down to ask for soda water, we got to lay in more soda for Mr Wills, but I need extra assistance with Mr Wills Paul and party sir.
The police come at 2, 3.48 and 4.52. They sit down in the bar a long time. Firearms discharge 2 times in the back yard. Detective making inquiries. I dont know sir, I thinking it would be better for me to go back to some other sort of job. At 3 I hear somebody shout Thief, and I see a man running out of the back, and Mr London, Room 9, say he miss 80 cents and a pack of cigarettes which was on his dressing case. I don't know when the people in this place does sleep. *Chas. Ethelbert Hillyard*

> Night Watchman Hillyard: A lot more than 80 cents was stolen. Several rooms were in fact entered during the night, including my own. You are employed to prevent such things occurring. Your interest in the morals of our guests seems to be distracting your attention from your duties. Save your preaching for your roadside prayer meetings. Mr Pick, Room 7, reports that in spite of the most pressing and repeated requests, you did not awaken him at 5. He has missed his plane to British Guiana as a result. No newspapers were delivered to the rooms this morning. I am again notifying you that papers must be handed personally to Doorman Vignales. And the messenger's bicycle, which I must remind you is the property of the hotel, has been damaged. What do you *do* at nights? *W. A. G. Inskip*

Please don't ask me sir.
Relating to the damaged bicycle: I left the bicycle the same place where I meet it, nothing took place so as to damage it. I always take care of all property sir. I don't know how you could think I have time to go out for bicycle rides. About

the papers, sir, the police and them read it and leave them in such a state that I didn't think it would be nice to give them to guests. I wake up Mr Pick, room 7, at 4.50 A.M. 5 A.M. 5.15 A.M. and 5.30. He told me to keep off, he would not get up, and one time he pelt a box of matches at me, matches scatter all over the place. I always do everything to the best of my ability sir but God is my Witness I never find a night watchman work like this, so much writing I dont have time to do anything else, I dont have four hands and six eyes and I want this extra assistance with Mr Wills and party sir. I am a poor man and you could abuse me, but you must not abuse my religion sir because the good Lord sees All and will have His revenge sir, I don't know what sort of work and trouble I land myself in, all I want is a little quiet night work and all I getting is abuse. *Chas. E. Hillyard*

November 30. 12.25 A.M. Bar close and Barman left 1.00 A.M. leaving Mr Wills and party in Bar. Mr Wills take 12 Carib, Mr Wilson 6, Mr Percy 14. Mrs Roscoe five gins. At 1.30 A.M. Mrs Roscoe left and there were a little singing and mild guitar playing in Room 12. Nothing unusual. The police came at 1.35 and sit down in the bar for a time, not drinking, not talking, not doing anything except watching. At 1.45 the man they call Paul come in with Mr McPherson of the SS Naparoni, they was both falling down and laughing whenever anything break and the man they call Paul say Fireworks about to begin tell Minnie Malcolm coming the ship just dock. Mr Wills and party scatter leaving one or two bottles half empty and then the man they call Paul tell me to go up to Room 12 and tell Minnie Roscoe that Malcolm coming. I don't know how people could behave so the thing enough to make anybody turn priest. I notice the padlock on the bar door break off it hanging on only by a little piece of wood. And when I went up to Room 12 and tell Mrs Roscoe that Malcolm coming the ship just dock the woman get sober straight away like she dont want to hear no more guitar music and she asking me where to hide where to go. I dont know, I feel the day of reckoning is at hand, but she not listening to what I saying, she busy straightening up the room one minute packing the next, and then she run out into the corridor and before I could stop she she run straight down the back stairs to the annexe. And then 5 past 2, still in the corridor, I see a big red man running up to me and he sober as a judge and he mad as a drunkard and he asking me where she is where she is. I ask whether he is a authorized caller, he say you don't give me any of that crap now, where she is, where she is. So remembering about the last time Mr Jimminez I direct him to the manager office in the annexe. He hear a little scuffling inside Mr Inskip room and I make out Mr Inskip sleepy voice and Mrs Roscoe voice and the red man run inside and all I hearing for the next five minutes is bam bam bodow bodow bow and this woman screaming. I dont know what sort of work this night watchman getting I want something quiet like the police. In time things quiet down and the red man drag Mrs Roscoe out of the annexe and they take a taxi, and the Police sitting down quiet in the bar. Then Mr Percy and the others come back one by one to the bar and they talking quiet and they not drinking and they left 3 A.M. 3.15 Mr Wills return and take one whisky and 2 Carib. He asked for pineapple or some sweet fruit but it had nothing.

6 A.M. Mr Wills come in the bar looking for soda but it aint have none. We have to get some soda for Mr Wills sir.

25   6.30 A.M. the papers come and I deliver them to Doorman Vignales at 7 A.M. *Chas. Hillyard*

Mr Hillyard: In view of the unfortunate illness of Mr. Inskip, I am temporarily in charge of the hotel. I trust you will continue to make your nightly reports, but I would be glad if you could keep your entries as brief as possible. *Robt. Magnus, Acting Manager*

December 1. 10.30 P.M. C. E. Hillyard take over duty at C———Hotel all corrected 12 Midnight Bar close 2 A.M. Mr Wills 2 Carib, 1 bread 6 A.M. Mr Wills 1 soda 7 A.M. Night Watchman Hillyard hand over duty to Mr Vignales with one torch light 2 Fridge keys and Room Keys 1, 3, 6 and 12. Bar intact all corrected no report. *C.E.H.*

[1967]

Joining the Conversation: Critical Thinking and Writing

1. How many people tell this story? How would you characterize each of them?
2. Is race—or, let's say, the color of the characters—significant in this story? In what ways?
3. Did you enjoy reading this story? Why or why not?
4. Is there a feature of Naipaul's story that you think is especially effective? Be precise, and cite evidence from the text to explain and support your response.
5. How does this story begin? How does it end? What is the relationship between the beginning and the ending?
6. If you were enrolled in a creative-writing course and were given the assignment "Write a story like 'The Night Watchman's Occurrence Book,'" what would be your response? Could you write such a story? What would be the challenges of this assignment? What insights into the process of story writing do you think your instructor might be trying to convey through such an assignment?

CHAPTER 4

The Pleasures of Reading—and of Writing Arguments about Literature

Pleasure is by no means an infallible guide,
but it is the least fallible.

W. H. AUDEN

Chapter Preview

After reading this chapter you will be able to

- Analyze your audience
- Assess a student's work from first response to final draft

"The pleasures of reading," a student may say, are obvious, "but when it comes to talking about the 'pleasures' of writing, surely you must be kidding." Students who make this reply have on their side the authority of many distinguished writers. Edna Ferber said that writing "is a combination of ditch-digging, mountain-climbing, treadmill, and childbirth"; Ernest Hemingway is reported to have said, "There is nothing to writing. All you do is sit down at a typewriter and bleed"; and the novelist William Styron said, "Let's face it, writing is hell."

Every student and every professor understands what these writers are talking about. The bad news is that they are talking about the difficult job of getting down on paper coherent thoughts that are good enough to share with a reader. But there is good news too: All writers know that the very act of writing will stimulate *better* thoughts than those that they began with. Writers—professionals as well as students—put words on paper with the understanding that the process of writing is a method of getting better ideas, a way of shaping the sometimes incoherent stuff that at first drifts through our minds.

For Whom Are You Writing?

You are, first, writing for yourself; you are trying to clarify something. The instructor may have set the problem—let's say (to take a famous example), "Is Hamlet mad or only pretending to be?"—or the problem may be one of your own choosing, even one so broad as "Why do I like (or dislike) this story?" In any event, you look again at the text, thinking, jotting down whatever comes to mind, then perhaps commenting on your notes, amplifying them, perhaps realizing that even though

95

you wrote them only seconds ago you no longer agree with them. In drafting and in revising, you read your own writing with a critical eye; in your effort to get things straight, you are in effect quarreling with yourself, thinking and writing in order to explain something *to yourself.*

But of course you are writing for someone else, too, notably the instructor who will read the essay and probably grade it. **Keep your reader in mind** is good and important advice, but while you are your own first reader, and you will write a thoughtful essay only if you think critically about your own thoughts, notes, and drafts, ultimately you will show your work to someone else. Some other person, or group, will be reading what you write. It is not enough, therefore, to ask, Is this clear to me? You must also ask, Will this be clear to someone who does not share my experiences?

Is your instructor the "someone else" who is the reader? Yes and no. Let's look first at the "no" response:

- No, the instructor is not your reader. Your instructor may specify at the outset, "I am not your reader: Do not try to guess what I am thinking, or what I would like you to say." This makes sense: After all, an instructor will frequently give an assignment that asks a question to which he or she does not know the answer. There may not even be a right answer. Instead, the instructor is curious about how students will respond to the question, what they will say about it, what kind of argument they will present. (Your instructor might even add, "Think of your reader as one of your classmates—not me, but one of them.")
- Yes, the instructor is your reader. At this stage, students are usually just getting to know their classmates, discovering who they are, how they think, their backgrounds, and so on. So you may not yet be clear about what it means to "think of your reader as one of your classmates," and it may be more helpful if the instructor asks you to "think of me as your audience." In this way the student will have someone in mind while writing and revising. And after all, it is the instructor who will read your work, comment on it, and grade it. In this respect, when we propose that you think of your instructor as your audience, we are just being honest about the context in which you are writing.

We may not always have a clear answer to the question, Who is my reader? Ultimately, our goal is to be aware of the question and to think about it. We write in a variety of contexts and situations, and each time we write, we need to reflect on who our reader or readers will be.

The Open Secret of Good Writing

We said that in drafting your essay you quarrel with yourself. It is an open secret of effective writing that good writers are good critics of their own writing. In words attributed to Truman Capote, "Writing is rewriting." When writers reread their own writing, they read in a skeptical spirit, asking themselves

- Have I adequately supported this point?
- Have I considered all the counterevidence?
- Do I really want to say . . . ? Ought I to have said . . . ?
- Come to think of it, isn't there another reason why I think this?

The pleasure you find in writing will come chiefly from your awareness that you are improving your writing, getting better ideas and using words well—a pleasure we all experience when we read something that we enjoy. After revising, and revising again, you can reasonably feel that you have thought about an issue, argued it with yourself, and come to conclusions that you have shared convincingly with your readers.

Let's look now at a story—or is it three stories?—by Bruce Holland Rogers, and then at a student's responses to the writing.

BRUCE HOLLAND ROGERS

Bruce Holland Rogers, an American writer who has won numerous prizes for his short fiction, teaches in the MFA program of Northwest Institute of Literary Arts. In 2001 a film, The Other Side, *was based on his short novel* Lifeboat on a Burning Sea.

The following story consists of three stories, each of which contains sixty-nine words. The form originated with a short-lived Toronto-based magazine, NFC, *which set the limit of sixty-nine words, exclusive of the title. From this limit there somehow evolved the story that consists of three thematically related stories, each of sixty-nine words, a form now known as the three-six-nine.*

Three Soldiers

1. The Hardest Question

My marines bring me questions. "When do we get to shower?" "Sergeant, how do you say 'Good afternoon' again?" "Sarge, where can I get more gun oil?"

I have answers. "Tomorrow, maybe." "*Maysuh alheer.*" "Use mine."

Answering their questions is my job. But when Anaya was shot and bleeding out, he grabbed my arm and said, "Sergeant? Sergeant?" I understood the question, but damn. I didn't have an answer.

2. Foreign War

No U.S. soldier who could see that kid would have shot him. But that's long-range ordnance for you. Calder stood next to me in the street, looking at the pieces. "We've come so far from home," he said, "that we'll never get back."

"You dumbass," I said. But a year later I stood on the tarmac hugging my child, thinking of that kid in pieces, and I wasn't home.

3. Decisions, Decisions

In morning twilight, far away, my men are making up their minds:

What's that guy carrying?
Friend or foe?

I should be there, helping them decide. My wife and my parents do their best to make Christmas dinner conversation around my silence. An hour ago, I was yelling at Angie for turning on the damn news. My father, carving, won't meet my eyes. He says, "White meat, or dark?"

[2004]

Getting Ready to Write: A Student's Response, from Jottings to Finished Essay

Now for the responses to "Three Soldiers" by a student who had been given only the biographical note that appears above the text and the suggestion that students begin by jotting down their first reactions to each story, such as:

- What puzzles you?
- What interests you?
- Are there significant connections among the three stories?

Here is the response of one student, Will Holly.

This business of 69 words seems silly—crazy—to me. I wouldn't want to learn that Shakespeare wrote *Hamlet* because he was challenged to write a play of exactly such-and-such a number of words. Nutty—but I am glad that Rogers *did* write the stories, for whatever reason.

What sort of puzzles me is that I *like* them—even though I ought to be depressed by them—stuff about a soldier dying, a kid blown to pieces, soldiers who can't get over their terrible experiences. Why do we read this stuff, and—maybe a bigger puzzle—why do I like it?

In the first story, exactly what is "the hardest question"? I think the hardest question—not the first three questions but the question hidden in the word "Sergeant?"—the question asked but not asked in words, by the soldier who "was shot and bleeding out" (which I think means he is bleeding to death)—must be, "Why am I dying?" or something close to this. Maybe the question is "Why ME?" but in any case, it is a question about "bleeding out," and this question is a lot harder than "when do we shower" or "how do you say" such-and-such in a foreign language? or "where can I get oil?" Notice that the sergeant does *not* have an answer for *this* question. Sure, we can give answers, but we realize that our answers cannot be adequate to the terrifying occasion.

In the second story, there is no question, but we are still concerned with death in war. A soldier is looking at the "pieces" of a kid who was killed by long-range gunfire. This soldier says, "We've come so far from home that we'll never get back." What does he mean? After all, most of the soldiers *will* actually get back to home. I think he means that we have had an experience—an experience we could not possibly have imagined when we were safe at home, maybe at college or maybe at some job, and now we can never be the same, we can never regain our naivete. We can *literally* go home, but we will be so changed by the experience that everything will look different. And in fact, in the last line of this very short story this soldier *does* get home, and he is hugging his own child, but his thoughts are in the war-zone. So although he is physically home, he is not mentally home.

In the third story the characters are also back home—the soldier is with his parents and his wife—but it is clear that his *mind* is still in the war zone. He is thinking—as any soldier in a combat area would think when he sees a stranger—"What's that guy carrying?" and "Friend or foe?" These questions are different, VERY different—from the trivial question that his father is asking, carving the chicken or turkey at the Christmas dinner, "White meat, or dark?" Again, he is home, but he is so changed from when he was last home that he is not home, he is in another world.

The order of the stories: The first story is set in—well, I don't know where, but I guess maybe Iraq. Certainly in a war zone. The second story, too, is set there, but they talk about home. The third story is set at home—but the soldier is still mentally at war. Further, there is a nice connection between the first and the last stories: The first story pretty much *begins with* a question, and the last story *ends with* a question, so, in a way, the wheel has come full circle. There is a sense of unity, of completion. It's sort of frightening, but, well, one would have to be crazy to think that the experience of war—which can include killing innocent children—is not horrible!

The student ultimately wrote the following short essay.

Holly 1

Will Holly

Professor Cargill

English 101A

28 January 2013

Thinking about Three Soldiers Thinking

On the printed page Bruce Holland Rogers's "Three Soldiers" is three very short stories, and each of the three can stand alone and can be read with interest, but the three really go together and they form a whole that is greater than any of the parts.

All of the stories deal with soldiers who are engaged in killing people—maybe in Vietnam or Iraq, I think but I am not certain, and the exact locale does not really matter. The first story, "The Hardest Question," begins with some trivial questions that soldiers ask a sergeant ("When do we get to shower") but it ends, a few sentences later, with a soldier who is "bleeding out," and whose question—repeated—is only one word long, "Sergeant?" The reader probably is supposed to understand that the soldier is bleeding to death, and the question in his mind is something like, "Sergeant, will I die?" or maybe it is, "Sergeant, why me?" The sergeant can easily answer the earlier questions, about showering, and so forth, but he gives no answer to what the title of the story calls "The Hardest Question."

When readers start to read a story called "The Hardest Question," they probably expect to hear the question stated fully, and they probably also expect some sort of answer to the question. Here, the question is never stated fully—we just get "Sergeant?"—and it certainly isn't answered. Does that mean we are disappointed with the story? No, the story, though painful, is complete. We know there is no satisfactory answer to the question of the soldier who is "bleeding out."

The second story, "Foreign War," is also only a few sentences long. It begins by saying that a soldier is looking at "the pieces" of a "kid" who has been killed by "long-range ordnance." A few sentences later the soldier is home, hugging his own kid, but his mind is back at the scene of the disaster, and he realizes that although he can return home physically, in another sense he can never be back home again, can never return to the place where he had been unaware of such horrors.

The third story, "Decisions," continues this theme of being back home but not being *at home*. The soldier is with his family (wife and parents), and is having Christmas dinner. But when we begin reading the story we do not know that this is the situation. The story begins, "In morning twilight, far away, my men are making up their minds." And then we get two questions, "What's that guy carrying?" and "Friend or foe?" Probably when readers first read these questions they think that even though the speaker says he is "far away" from his men he is still abroad with other soldiers—soldiers who quite naturally are suspicious of some "guy" carrying something—it could be a weapon—and who, seeing a stranger, wonder if it is "Friend or foe?" We then learn where he is physically—although his *mind* is still on the battlefield, where his men are in danger, but he really is safe at home with his family. Here at home the decisions are not the life-and-death decisions of a soldier in combat ("What's that guy carrying?" "Friend or foe?") but are the utterly trivial decisions concerning whether one prefers the white meat or the dark meat of the Christmas bird. Bruce Holland Rogers is probably not saying that we should not express our preferences when it comes to food, but he is saying—or, rather, he is memorably *showing* us—that for someone who has gone through such experiences as seeing a man bleed to death, or seeing the blown-up pieces of a child—to be asked to make "decisions, decisions" about food preferences is almost intolerable.

Holly 3

The three stories are separate and they can be read as separate things, but they are really three parts of one story. The title is "Three Soldiers," so we must assume that the characters in each of the three stories are different, but they really add up to one character, a soldier who has seen the unbearable, and who will carry the memories for the rest of his life, whether he is hugging his child or sitting at a family Christmas dinner. Put this way, the story sounds deeply depressing, and a reader might wonder why Rogers thinks we should read this, but in fact, the story is told so effectively, so vividly, so concisely, so memorably, that it comes across as something that one wants to tell one's friends they must read. It's not that it has an encouraging moral (it doesn't) or a happy ending (it doesn't), but it is told so skillfully— for instance, the first story begins with a question and the last story ends with a question—and it is told with such apparent simplicity and honesty that a reader feels he or she must share it with others.

[New page]

Holly 4

Work Cited

Rogers, Bruce Holland. "Three Soldiers." *Literature for Composition*. Ed. Sylvan

Barnet, William Burto, and William E. Cain. 10th ed. New York: Pearson,

2014. 97. Print.

The Student's Analysis Analyzed

Let's look at this short essay.

- **The title,** though not exceptionally good, is adequate. Will Holly tells us that when he was working on his draft, he was very much taken with his perception that the stories are closely related—for instance, in that questions begin the first story, and a question ends the last story—and he thought he would title his essay "What Goes Around Comes Around." But when he had drafted the essay he realized that this title sounds as though it refers to some aspect of a plot in which a character ends up where he or she started, or gets what he or she deserves, and Holly decided that it wasn't suitable. He then considered "Thinking about 'Three Soldiers'" but soon decided that this title was too vague. Holly says he was getting desperate until at the last minute he realized that he was *thinking* about soldiers who are *thinking*, and he came up with his title, "Thinking about Three Soldiers Thinking." This title is accurate, and it involves a bit of wordplay, so in our view it is appropriate.

- **The opening paragraph** lets the reader know what author and what work(s) will be discussed—always a good idea!—and it makes the interesting claim that the three works are independent yet they also form a unified whole. The reader now expects that the rest of the essay will offer support for this claim.

- **The second and third paragraphs** discuss the first story. They briefly summarize the plot, but they do much more: they *explain* aspects of the story.

- **The fourth paragraph,** devoted to the second story, both summarizes and offers an *interpretation* of the significance of the plot. It tells the reader what the happenings *add up to*. The student is *thinking*, not just retelling what the story clearly says.

- **The fifth paragraph,** devoted to the third story, connects that story with the preceding story ("The third story . . . continues this theme of being back home"), and then reports that here readers probably have to revise their sense of what is going on in the story. It's not that the author of the story was clumsy or careless; rather, Rogers wants to bring us back to the battle-field, so rather than offer an objective view of the setting, he put us in the soldier's *mind*. Again, the essayist is thinking, analyzing, and offering evidence to support a thesis.

- **The final paragraph** begins by reasserting the thesis (the three stories are so connected by theme that they cohere as one story), then it comments on *why* we are not depressed by reading a story (or three stories) on this theme. You may disagree with the author's conclusions, but we think you will agree that the essay goes beyond plot-telling and offers interesting reasons to support its thesis.

Additional Stories for Pleasurable Analysis

JOHN STEINBECK

John Steinbeck (1902–68) was born in Salinas, California, and much of his fiction concerns this landscape and its people. As a young man he worked on ranches, farms, and road gangs and sometimes attended Stanford University—he never graduated—but he wrote whenever he could find the time. His early efforts at writing, however, were uniformly rejected by publishers. Even when he did break into print, he did not achieve much notice for several years: a novel in 1929, a book of stories in 1932, and another novel in 1933 attracted little attention. But the publication of Tortilla Flat *(1935), a novel about Mexican Americans, changed all that. It was followed by other successful novels—*In Dubious Battle *(1936) and* Of Mice and Men *(1937)—and by* The Long Valley *(1938), a collection of stories that included "The Chrysanthemums." His next book,* The Grapes of Wrath *(1939), about dispossessed sharecropper migrants from the Oklahoma dust bowl, was immensely popular and won a Pulitzer Prize. During World War II Steinbeck sent reports from battlefields in Italy and Africa. In 1962 he was awarded the Nobel Prize in Literature.*

The Chrysanthemums

The high grey-flannel fog of winter closed off the Salinas Valley[1] from the sky and from all the rest of the world. On every side it sat like a lid on the mountains and made of the great valley a closed pot. On the broad, level land floor the gang plows bit deep and left the black earth shining like metal where the shares had cut. On the foothill ranches across the Salinas River, the yellow stubble fields seemed to be bathed in pale cold sunshine, but there was no sunshine in the valley now in December. The thick willow scrub along the river flamed with sharp and positive yellow leaves.

It was a time of quiet and of waiting. The air was cold and tender. A light wind blew up from the southwest so that the farmers were mildly hopeful of a good rain before long; but fog and rain do not go together.

Across the river, on Henry Allen's foothill ranch there was little work to be done, for the hay was cut and stored and the orchards were plowed up to receive the rain deeply when it should come. The cattle on the higher slopes were becoming shaggy and rough-coated.

Elisa Allen, working in her flower garden, looked down across the yard and saw Henry, her husband, talking to two men in business suits. The three of them stood by the tractor shed, each man with one foot on the side of the little Fordson[2] They smoked cigarettes and studied the machine as they talked.

5   Elisa watched them for a moment and then went back to her work. She was thirty-five. Her face was lean and strong and her eyes were as clear as water. Her figure looked blocked and heavy in her gardening costume, a man's black hat pulled low down over her eyes, clod-hopper shoes, a figured print dress almost completely covered by a big corduroy apron with four big pockets to hold the snips, the trowel and scratcher, the seeds and the knife she worked with. She wore heavy leather gloves to protect her hands while she worked.

She was cutting down the old year's chrysanthemum stalks with a pair of short and powerful scissors. She looked down toward the men by the tractor shed now and then. Her face was eager and mature and handsome; even her work with the scissors was over-eager, over-powerful. The chrysanthemum stems seemed too small and easy for her energy.

She brushed a cloud of hair out of her eyes with the back of her glove, and left a smudge of earth on her cheek in doing it. Behind her stood the neat white farm house with red geraniums close-banked around it as high as the windows. It was a hard-swept looking little house with hard-polished windows, and a clean mud-mat on the front steps.

Elisa cast another glance toward the tractor shed. The strangers were getting into their Ford coupe. She took off a glove and put her strong fingers down into the forest of new green chrysanthemum sprouts that were growing around the old roots. She spread the leaves and looked down among the close-growing stems. No

[1]**the Salinas Valley** a fertile area in central California. [2]**Fordson** a two-door Ford car.

aphids were there, no sowbugs or snails or cutworms. Her terrier fingers destroyed such pests before they could get started.

Elisa started at the sound of her husband's voice. He had come near quietly, and he leaned over the wire fence that protected her flower garden from cattle and dogs and chickens.

10   "At it again," he said. "You've got a strong new crop coming."

Elisa straightened her back and pulled on the gardening glove again. "Yes. They'll be strong this coming year." In her tone and on her face there was a little smugness.

"You've got a gift with things," Henry observed. "Some of those yellow chrysanthemums you had this year were ten inches across. I wish you'd work out in the orchard and raise some apples that big."

Her eyes sharpened. "Maybe I could do it, too. I've a gift with things, all right. My mother had it. She could stick anything in the ground and make it grow. She said it was having planters' hands that knew how to do it."

"Well, it sure works with flowers," he said.

15   "Henry, who were those men you were talking to?"

"Why, sure, that's what I came to tell you. They were from the Western Meat Company. I sold those thirty head of three-year-old steers. Got nearly my own price, too."

"Good," she said. "Good for you."

"And I thought," he continued, "I thought how it's Saturday afternoon, and we might go into Salinas for dinner at a restaurant, and then to a picture show—to celebrate, you see."

"Good," she repeated. "Oh, yes. That will be good."

20   Henry put on his joking tone. "There's fights tonight. How'd you like to go to the fights?"

"Oh, no," she said breathlessly. "No, I wouldn't like fights."

"Just fooling, Elisa. We'll go to a movie. Let's see. It's two now. I'm going to take Scotty and bring down those steers from the hill. It'll take us maybe two hours. We'll go in town about five and have dinner at the Cominos Hotel. Like that?"

"Of course I'll like it. It's good to eat away from home."

"All right, then. I'll go get up a couple of horses."

25   She said, "I'll have plenty of time to transplant some of these sets, I guess."

She heard her husband calling Scotty down by the barn. And a little later she saw the two men ride up the pale yellow hillside in search of the steers.

There was a little square sandy bed kept for rooting the chrysanthemums. With her trowel she turned the soil over and over, and smoothed it and patted it firm. Then she dug ten parallel trenches to receive the sets. Back at the chrysanthemum bed she pulled out the little crisp shoots, trimmed off the leaves of each one with her scissors and laid it on a small orderly pile.

A squeak of wheels and plod of hoofs came from the road. Elisa looked up. The country road ran along the dense bank of willows and cottonwoods that bordered the river, and up this road came a curious vehicle, curiously drawn. It was an old springwagon, with a round canvas top on it like the cover of a prairie schooner. It was drawn by an old bay horse and a little grey-and-white burro. A big stubble-bearded man sat between the cover flaps and drove the crawling team. Underneath the wagon, between the hind wheels, a lean and rangy mongrel dog walked sedately. Words were painted on the canvas, in clumsy, crooked letters. "Pots, pans, knives, sisors, lawn mores, Fixed." Two rows of articles, and the triumphantly definitive "Fixed" below. The black paint had run down in little sharp points beneath each letter.

Elisa, squatting on the ground, watched to see the crazy, loose-jointed wagon pass by. But it didn't pass. It turned into the farm road in front of her house, crooked old wheels skirling and squeaking. The rangy dog darted from between the wheels and ran ahead. Instantly the two ranch shepherds flew out at him. Then all three stopped, and with stiff and quivering tails, with taut straight legs, with ambassadorial dignity, they slowly circled, sniffing daintily. The caravan pulled up to Elisa's wire fence and stopped. Now the newcomer dog, feeling out-numbered, lowered his tail and retired under the wagon with raised hackles and bared teeth.

30   The man on the wagon seat called out, "That's a bad dog in a fight when he gets started."

Elisa laughed. "I see he is. How soon does he generally get started?"

The man caught up her laughter and echoed it heartily. "Sometimes not for weeks and weeks," he said. He climbed stiffly down, over the wheel. The horse and the donkey drooped like unwatered flowers.

Elisa saw that he was a very big man. Although his hair and beard were greying, he did not look old. His worn black suit was wrinkled and spotted with grease. The laughter had disappeared from his face and eyes the moment his laughing voice ceased. His eyes were dark, and they were full of the brooding that gets in the eyes of teamsters and of sailors. The calloused hands he rested on the wire fence were cracked, and every crack was a black line. He took off his battered hat.

"I'm off my general road, ma'am," he said. "Does this dirt road cut over across the river to the Los Angeles highway?"

35   Elisa stood up and shoved the thick scissors in her apron pocket. "Well, yes, it does, but it winds around and then fords the river. I don't think your team could pull through the sand."

He replied with some asperity. "It might surprise you what them beasts can pull through."

"When they get started?" she asked.

He smiled for a second. "Yes. When they get started."

"Well," said Elisa, "I think you'll save time if you go back to the Salinas road and pick up the highway there."

40   He drew a big finger down the chicken wire and made it sing. "I ain't in any hurry, ma'am. I go from Seattle to San Diego and back every year. Takes all my time. About six months each way. I aim to follow nice weather."

Elisa took off her gloves and stuffed them in the apron pocket with the scissors. She touched the under edge of her man's hat, searching for fugitive hairs. "That sounds like a nice kind of way to live," she said.

He leaned confidentially over the fence. "Maybe you noticed the writing on my wagon. I mend pots and sharpen knives and scissors. You got any of them things to do?"

"Oh, no," she said quickly. "Nothing like that." Her eyes hardened with resistance.

"Scissors is the worst thing," he explained. "Most people just ruin scissors trying to sharpen 'em, but I know how. I got a special tool. It's a little bobbit kind of thing, and patented. But it sure does the trick."

45   "No. My scissors are all sharp."

"All right, then. Take a pot," he continued earnestly, "a bent pot, or a pot with a hole. I can make it like new so you don't have to buy no new ones. That's a saving for you."

"No," she said shortly. "I tell you I have nothing like that for you to do."

His face fell to an exaggerated sadness. His voice took on a whining undertone. "I ain't had a thing to do today. Maybe I won't have no supper tonight. You see I'm off my regular road. I know folks on the highway clear from Seattle to San

Diego. They save their things for me to sharpen up because they know I do it so
good and save them money."

"I'm sorry," Elisa said irritably. "I haven't anything for you to do."

His eyes left her face and fell to searching the ground. They roamed about
until they came to the chrysanthemum bed where she had been working. "What's
them plants, ma'am?"

The irritation and resistance melted from Elisa's face. "Oh, those are chrysanthemums, giant whites and yellows. I raise them every year, bigger than anybody
around here."

"Kind of a long-stemmed flower? Looks like a quick puff of colored smoke?"
he asked.

"That's it. What a nice way to describe them."

"They smell kind of nasty till you get used to them," he said.

"It's a good bitter smell," she retorted, "not nasty at all."

He changed his tone quickly. "I like the smell myself."

"I had ten-inch blooms this year," she said.

The man leaned farther over the fence. "Look. I know a lady down the road
a piece, has got the nicest garden you ever seen. Got nearly every kind of flower
but no chrysanthemums. Last time I was mending a copper-bottom wash-tub for
her (that's a hard job but I do it good), she said to me, 'If you ever run acrost
some nice chrysanthemums I wish you'd try to get me a few seeds.' That's what
she told me."

Elisa's eyes grew alert and eager. "She couldn't have known much about chrysanthemums. You *can* raise them from seed, but it's much easier to root the little
sprouts you see there."

"Oh," he said. "I s'pose I can't take none to her, then."

"Why yes you can," Elisa cried. "I can put some in damp sand, and you can
carry them right along with you. They'll take root in the pot if you keep them
damp. And then she can transplant them."

"She'd sure like to have some, ma'am. You say they're nice ones?"

"Beautiful," she said. "Oh, beautiful." Her eyes shone. She tore off the battered
hat and shook out her dark pretty hair. "I'll put them in a flower pot, and you can
take them right with you. Come into the yard."

While the man came through the picket gate Elisa ran excitedly along the
geranium-bordered path to the back of the house. And she returned carrying a big
red flower pot. The gloves were forgotten now. She kneeled on the ground by the
starting bed and dug up the sandy soil with her fingers and scooped it into the
bright new flower pot. Then she picked up the little pile of shoots she had prepared. With her strong fingers she pressed them into the sand and tamped around
them with her knuckles. The man stood over her. "I'll tell you what to do," she said.
"You remember so you can tell the lady."

"Yes, I'll try to remember."

"Well, look. These will take root in about a month. Then she must set them
out, about a foot apart in good rich earth like this, see?" She lifted a handful of dark
soil for him to look at. "They'll grow fast and tall. Now remember this: In July tell
her to cut them down, about eight inches from the ground."

"Before they bloom?" he asked.

"Yes, before they bloom." Her face was tight with eagerness. "They'll grow
right up again. About the last of September the buds will start."

She stopped and seemed perplexed. "It's the budding that takes the most care,"
she said hesitantly. "I don't know how to tell you." She looked deep into his eyes,

searchingly. Her mouth opened a little, and she seemed to be listening. "I'll try to tell you," she said. "Did you ever hear of planting hands?"

70   "Can't say I have, ma'am."

"Well, I can only tell you what it feels like. It's when you're picking off the buds you don't want. Everything goes right down into your fingertips. You watch your fingers work. They do it themselves. You can feel how it is. They pick and pick the buds. They never make a mistake. They're with the plant. Do you see? Your fingers and the plant. You can feel that, right up your arm. They know. They never make a mistake. You can feel it. When you're like that you can't do anything wrong. Do you see that? Can you understand that?"

She was kneeling on the ground looking up at him. Her breast swelled passionately.

The man's eyes narrowed. He looked away self-consciously. "Maybe I know," he said. "Sometimes in the night in the wagon there—"

Elisa's voice grew husky. She broke in on him, "I've never lived as you do, but I know what you mean. When the night is dark—why, the stars are sharp-pointed, and there's quiet. Why, you rise up and up! Every pointed star gets driven into your body. It's like that. Hot and sharp and—lovely."

75   Kneeling there, her hand went out toward his legs in the greasy black trousers. Her hesitant fingers almost touched the cloth. Then her hand dropped to the ground. She crouched low like a fawning dog.

He said, "It's nice, just like you say. Only when you don't have no dinner, it ain't."

She stood up then, very straight, and her face was ashamed. She held the flower pot out to him and placed it gently in his arms. "Here. Put it in your wagon, on the seat, where you can watch it. Maybe I can find something for you to do."

At the back of the house she dug in the can pile and found two old and battered aluminum saucepans. She carried them back and gave them to him. "Here, maybe you can fix these."

His manner changed. He became professional. "Good as new I can fix them." At the back of his wagon he set a little anvil, and out of an oily tool box dug a small machine hammer. Elisa came through the gate to watch him while he pounded out the dents in the kettles. His mouth grew sure and knowing. At a difficult part of the work he sucked his under-lip.

80   "You sleep right in the wagon?" Elisa asked.

"Right in the wagon, ma'am. Rain or shine I'm dry as a cow in there."

"It must be nice," she said. "It must be very nice. I wish women could do such things."

"It ain't the right kind of a life for a woman."

Her upper lip raised a little, showing her teeth. "How do you know? How can you tell?" she said.

85   "I don't know, ma'am," he protested. "Of course I don't know. Now here's your kettles, done. You don't have to buy no new ones."

"How much?"

"Oh, fifty cents'll do. I keep my prices down and my work good. That's why I have all them satisfied customers up and down the highway."

Elisa brought him a fifty-cent piece from the house and dropped it in his hand. "You might be surprised to have a rival some time. I can sharpen scissors, too. And I can beat the dents out of little pots. I could show you what a woman might do."

He put his hammer back in the oily box and shoved the little anvil out of sight. "It would be a lonely life for a woman, ma'am, and a scarey life, too, with animals creeping under the wagon all night." He climbed over the singletree, steadying himself with a hand on the burro's white rump. He settled himself in the seat, picked up the lines. "Thank you kindly, ma'am," he said. "I'll do like you told me; I'll go back and catch the Salinas road."

90   "Mind," she called, "if you're long in getting there, keep the sand damp."

"Sand, ma'am? . . . Sand? Oh, sure. You mean around the chrysanthemums. Sure I will." He clucked his tongue. The beasts leaned luxuriously into their collars. The mongrel dog took his place between the back wheels. The wagon turned and crawled out the entrance road and back the way it had come, along the river.

Elisa stood in front of her wire fence watching the slow progress of the caravan. Her shoulders were straight, her head thrown back, her eyes half-closed, so that the scene came vaguely into them. Her lips moved silently, forming the words "Good-bye—good-bye." Then she whispered, "That's a bright direction. There's a glowing there." The sound of her whisper startled her. She shook herself free and looked about to see whether anyone had been listening. Only the dogs had heard. They lifted their heads toward her from their sleeping in the dust, and then stretched out their chins and settled asleep again. Elisa turned and ran hurriedly into the house.

In the kitchen she reached behind the stove and felt the water tank. It was full of hot water from the noonday cooking. In the bathroom she tore off her soiled clothes and flung them into the corner. And then she scrubbed herself with a little block of pumice, legs and thighs, loins and chest and arms, until her skin was scratched and red. When she had dried herself she stood in front of a mirror in her bedroom and looked at her body. She tightened her stomach and threw out her chest. She turned and looked over her shoulder at her back.

After a while she began to dress, slowly. She put on her newest underclothing and her nicest stockings and the dress which was the symbol of her prettiness. She worked carefully on her hair, penciled her eyebrows and rouged her lips.

95   Before she was finished she heard the little thunder of hoofs and the shouts of Henry and his helper as they drove the red steers into the corral. She heard the gate bang shut and set herself for Henry's arrival.

His step sounded on the porch. He entered the house calling, "Elisa, where are you?"

"In my room, dressing. I'm not ready. There's hot water for your bath. Hurry up. It's getting late."

When she heard him splashing in the tub, Elisa laid his dark suit on the bed, and shirt and socks and tie beside it. She stood his polished shoes on the floor beside the bed. Then she went to the porch and sat primly and stiffly down. She looked toward the river road where the willow-line was still yellow with frosted leaves so that under the high grey fog they seemed a thin band of sunshine. This was the only color in the grey afternoon. She sat unmoving for a long time. Her eyes blinked rarely.

Henry came banging out of the door shoving his tie inside his vest as he came. Elisa stiffened and her face grew tight. Henry stopped short and looked at her. "Why—why, Elisa. You look so nice!"

100   "Nice? You think I look nice? What do you mean by 'nice'?"

Henry blundered on. "I don't know. I mean you look different, strong and happy."

"I am strong? Yes, strong. What do you mean 'strong'?"

He looked bewildered. "You're playing some kind of a game," he said help-lessly. "It's a kind of a play. You look strong enough to break a calf over your knee, happy enough to eat it like a watermelon."

For a second she lost her rigidity. "Henry! Don't talk like that. You didn't know what you said." She grew complete again. "I'm strong," she boasted. "I never knew before how strong."

105   Henry looked down toward the tractor shed, and when he brought his eyes back to her, they were his own again. "I'll get out the car. You can put on your coat while I'm starting."

    Elisa went into the house. She heard him drive to the gate and idle down his motor, and then she took a long time to put on her hat. She pulled it here and pressed it there. When Henry turned the motor off she slipped into her coat and went out.

    The little roadster bounced along on the dirt road by the river, raising the birds and driving the rabbits into the brush. Two cranes flapped heavily over the willow-line and dropped into the river-bed.

    Far ahead on the road Elisa saw a dark speck. She knew.

    She tried not to look as they passed it, but her eyes would not obey. She whispered to herself sadly, "He might have thrown them off the road. That wouldn't have been much trouble, not very much. But he kept the pot," she explained. "He had to keep the pot. That's why he couldn't get them off the road."

110   The roadster turned a bend and she saw the caravan ahead. She swung full around toward her husband so she could not see the little covered wagon and the mismatched team as the car passed them.

    In a moment it was over. The thing was done. She did not look back.

    She said loudly, to be heard above the motor, "It will be good, tonight, a good dinner."

    "Now you're changed again," Henry complained. He took one hand from the wheel and patted her knee. "I ought to take you in to dinner oftener. It would be good for both of us. We get so heavy out on the ranch."

    "Henry," she asked, "could we have wine at dinner?"

115   "Sure we could. Say! That will be fine."

    She was silent for a while; then she said, "Henry, at those prize fights, do the men hurt each other very much?"

    "Sometimes a little, not often. Why?"

    "Well, I've read how they break noses, and blood runs down their chests. I've read how the fighting gloves get heavy and soggy with blood."

    He looked around at her. "What's the matter, Elisa? I didn't know you read things like that." He brought the car to a stop, then turned to the right over the Salinas River bridge.

120   "Do any women ever go to the fights?" she asked.

    "Oh, sure, some. What's the matter, Elisa? Do you want to go? I don't think you'd like it, but I'll take you if you really want to go."

    She relaxed limply in the seat. "Oh, no. No. I don't want to go. I'm sure I don't." Her face was turned away from him. "It will be enough if we can have wine. It will be plenty." She turned up her coat collar so he could not see that she was crying weakly—like an old woman.

[1937]

Joining the Conversation: Critical Thinking and Writing

1. In the first paragraph of "The Chrysanthemums," the valley, shut off by fog, is said to be "a closed pot." Is this setting significant? Would any other setting do equally well? Why, or why not?

2. What physical descriptions in the story—literal or figurative—suggest that Elisa is frustrated?
3. Describe Elisa and Henry's marriage.
4. In an argument, evaluate the view that Elisa is responsible for her troubles.

MyLiteratureLab° *For additional resources for "The Chrysanthemums," log in to* www.myliteraturelab.com *where you will find a Comprehension Quiz, Short Evaluation Exercises, Essay Prompts, as well as an About the Author, Links, and a Critical Overview for Steinbeck (under Student Resources).*

WILLA CATHER

Willa Cather (1873–1947) was born in Winchester, Virginia. At age nine she moved with her family to the Nebraska prairie town of Red Cloud, which she later used and adapted for the settings, characters, and events in many of her novels and short stories. Cather attended the University of Nebraska, graduating in 1895. She then worked as a journalist and a high school teacher in Pittsburgh and, beginning in 1904, as a member of the editorial staff of McClure's Magazine *in New York City. Her first books were* The Troll Garden *(1905), a collection of stories, and the novel* Alexander's Bridge *(1912); after their publication she resigned her position at McClure's to focus on her writing. Her novels include* O Pioneers! *(1913),* My Ántonia *(1918),* The Song of the Lark *(1915),* The Professor's House *(1925), and* Death Comes for the Archbishop *(1927). Two collections of nonfiction, which give her views on the art of fiction, are* Not Under Forty *(1936) and* On Writing *(1949).*

Cather was proud of, and highly accomplished in her craft. "Writing," she maintained, "ought either to be the manufacture of stories for which there is a market demand—a business as safe and commendable as making soap or breakfast foods—or it should be an art, which is always a search for something for which there is no market demand, something new and untried, where the values are intrinsic and have nothing to do with standardized values."

The story we present here—"A Wagner Matinée,"—was first published in 1904 in the March issue of Everybody's Magazine. *Cather then revised it for publication in her collection* The Troll Garden *(1905). We give both versions here—the revised version first, so that you can read the story as Cather finally envisioned it, and can then go on to see (pages 116–20) a facsimile reproduction of the magazine version of the story. A close reading will let you see Cather at work, making numerous small but extremely important changes. On page 120 we call attention to one of the changes.*

A Wagner Matinée

I received one morning a letter, written in pale ink on glassy, blue-lined note-paper, and bearing the postmark of a little Nebraska village. This communication, worn and rubbed, looking as though it had been carried for some days in a coat pocket that was none too clean, was from my uncle Howard and informed me that his wife had been left a small legacy by a bachelor relative who had recently died, and that it would be necessary for her to go to Boston to attend to the settling of the estate. He requested me to meet her at the station and render her whatever services might be necessary. On examining the date indicated as that of her arrival, I found it no later than to-morrow. He had characteristically delayed writing until, had I been away from home for a day, I must have missed the good woman altogether.

The name of my Aunt Georgiana called up not alone her own figure, at once pathetic and grotesque, but opened before my feet a gulf of recollection so wide and deep that, as the letter dropped from my hand, I felt suddenly a stranger to all the present conditions of my existence, wholly ill at ease and out of place amid the familiar surroundings of my study. I became, in short, the gangling farmer-boy my aunt had known, scourged with chilblains and bashfulness, my hands cracked and sore from the corn husking. I felt the knuckles of my thumb tentatively, as though they were raw again. I sat again before her parlour organ, fumbling the scales with my stiff, red hands, while she, beside me, made canvas mittens for the huskers.

The next morning, after preparing my landlady somewhat, I set out for the station. When the train arrived I had some difficulty in finding my aunt. She was the last of the passengers to alight, and it was not until I got her into the carriage that she seemed really to recognize me. She had come all the way in a day coach; her linen duster had become black with soot and her black bonnet grey with dust during the journey. When we arrived at my boarding-house the landlady put her to bed at once and I did not see her again until the next morning.

Whatever shock Mrs. Springer experienced at my aunt's appearance, she considerately concealed. As for myself, I saw my aunt's misshapen figure with that feeling of awe and respect with which we behold explorers who have left their ears and fingers north of Franz Josef Land, or their health somewhere along the Upper Congo. My Aunt Georgiana had been a music teacher at the Boston Conservatory, somewhere back in the latter sixties. One summer, while visiting in the little village among the Green Mountains where her ancestors had dwelt for generations, she had kindled the callow fancy of the most idle and shiftless of all the village lads, and had conceived for this Howard Carpenter one of those extravagant passions which a handsome country boy of twenty-one sometimes inspires in an angular, spectacled woman of thirty. When she returned to her duties in Boston, Howard followed her, and the upshot of this inexplicable infatuation was that she eloped with him, eluding the reproaches of her family and the criticisms of her friends by going with him to the Nebraska frontier. Carpenter, who, of course, had no money, had taken a homestead in Red Willow County, fifty miles from the railroad. There they had measured off their quarter section themselves by driving across the prairie in a wagon, to the wheel of which they had tied a red cotton handkerchief, and counting off its revolutions. They built a dugout in the red hillside, one of those cave dwellings whose inmates so often reverted to primitive conditions. Their water they got from the lagoons where the buffalo drank, and their slender stock of provisions was always at the mercy of bands of roving Indians. For thirty years my aunt had not been farther than fifty miles from the homestead.

5   But Mrs. Springer knew nothing of all this, and must have been considerably shocked at what was left of my kinswoman. Beneath the soiled linen duster which, on her arrival, was the most conspicuous feature of her costume, she wore a black stuff dress, whose ornamentation showed that she had surrendered herself unquestioningly into the hands of a country dressmaker. My poor aunt's

figure, however, would have presented astonishing difficulties to any dressmaker. Originally stooped, her shoulders were now almost bent together over her sunken chest. She wore no stays, and her gown, which trailed unevenly behind, rose in a sort of peak over her abdomen. She wore ill-fitting false teeth, and her skin was as yellow as a Mongolian's from constant exposure to a pitiless wind and to the alkaline water which hardens the most transparent cuticle into a sort of flexible leather.

I owed to this woman most of the good that ever came my way in my boyhood, and had a reverential affection for her. During the years when I was riding herd for my uncle, my aunt, after cooking the three meals—the first of which was ready at six o'clock in the morning—and putting the six children to bed, would often stand until midnight at her ironing-board, with me at the kitchen table beside her, hearing me recite Latin declensions and conjugations, gently shaking me when my drowsy head sank down over a page of irregular verbs. It was to her, at her ironing or mending, that I read my first Shakspere, and her old text-book on mythology was the first that ever came into my empty hands. She taught me my scales and exercises, too—on the little parlour organ which her husband had bought her after fifteen years, during which she had not so much as seen any instrument, but an accordion that belonged to one of the Norwegian farm-hands. She would sit beside me by the hour, darning and counting, while I struggled with the "Joyous Farmer," but she seldom talked to me about music, and I understood why. She was a pious woman; she had the consolations of religion and, to her at least, her martyrdom was not wholly sordid. Once when I had been doggedly beating out some easy passages from an old score of *Euryanthe* I had found among her music books, she came up to me and, putting her hands over my eyes, gently drew my head back upon her shoulder, saying tremulously, "Don't love it so well, Clark, or it may be taken from you. Oh! dear boy, pray that whatever your sacrifice may be, it be not that."

When my aunt appeared on the morning after her arrival, she was still in a semi-somnambulant state. She seemed not to realize that she was in the city where she had spent her youth, the place longed for hungrily half a lifetime. She had been so wretchedly train-sick throughout the journey that she had no recollection of anything but her discomfort, and, to all intents and purposes, there were but a few hours of nightmare between the farm in Red Willow County and my study on Newbury Street. I had planned a little pleasure for her that afternoon, to repay her for some of the glorious moments she had given me when we used to milk together in the strawthatched cowshed and she, because I was more than usually tired, or because her husband had spoken sharply to me, would tell me of the splendid performance of the *Huguenots* she had seen in Paris, in her youth. At two o'clock the Symphony Orchestra was to give a Wagner programme, and I intended to take my aunt; though, as I conversed with her, I grew doubtful about her enjoyment of it. Indeed, for her own sake, I could only wish her taste for such things quite dead, and the long struggle mercifully ended at last. I suggested our visiting the Conservatory and the Common before lunch, but she seemed altogether too timid to wish to venture out. She questioned me absently about various changes in the city, but she was chiefly concerned that she had forgotten to leave instructions about feeding half-skimmed milk to a certain weakling calf, "old Maggie's calf, you know, Clark," she explained, evidently having forgotten how long I had been away. She was further troubled because she had neglected to tell her daughter about the freshly-opened kit of mackerel in the cellar, which would spoil if it were not used directly.

I asked her whether she had ever heard any of the Wagnerian operas, and found that she had not, though she was perfectly familiar with their respective situations, and had once possessed the piano score of *The Flying Dutchman*. I began to think it would have been best to get her back to Red Willow County without waking her, and regretted having suggested the concert.

From the time we entered the concert hall, however, she was a trifle less passive and inert, and for the first time seemed to perceive her surroundings. I had felt some trepidation lest she might become aware of the absurdities of her attire, or might experience some painful embarrassment at stepping suddenly into the world to which she had been dead for more than a quarter of a century. But, again, I found how superficially I had judged her. She sat looking about her with eyes as impersonal, almost as stony, as those with which the granite Rameses in a museum watches the froth and fret that ebbs and flows about his pedestal—separated from it by the lonely stretch of centuries. I have seen this same aloofness in old miners who drift into the Brown Hotel at Denver, their pockets full of bullion, their linen soiled, their haggard faces unshaven; standing in the thronged corridors as solitary as though they were still in a frozen camp on the Yukon, conscious that certain experiences have isolated them from their fellows by a gulf no haberdasher could bridge.

10   We sat at the extreme left of the first balcony, facing the arc of our own and the balcony above us, veritable hanging gardens, brilliant as tulip beds. The matinée audience was made up chiefly of women. One lost the contour of faces and figures, indeed any effect of line whatever; and there was only the colour of bodices past counting, the shimmer of fabrics soft and firm, silky and sheer; red, mauve, pink, blue, lilac, purple, ecru, rose, yellow, cream, and white, all the colours that an impressionist finds in a sunlit landscape, with here and there the dead shadow of a frock coat. My Aunt Georgiana regarded them as though they had been so many daubs of tube-paint on a palette.

When the musicians came out and took their places, she gave a little stir of anticipation, and looked with quickening interest down over the rail at that invariable grouping, perhaps the first wholly familiar thing that had greeted her eye since she had left old Maggie and her weakling calf. I could feel how all those details sank into her soul, for I had not forgotten how they had sunk into mine when I came fresh from ploughing forever and forever between green aisles of corn, where, as in a treadmill, one might walk from daybreak to dusk without perceiving a shadow of change. The clean profiles of the musicians, the gloss of their linen, the dull black of their coats, the beloved shapes of the instruments, the patches of yellow light thrown by the green shaded lamps on the smooth, varnished bellies of the 'cellos and the bass viols in the rear, the restless, wind-tossed forest of fiddle necks and bows—I recalled how, in the first orchestra I had ever heard, those long bow strokes seemed to draw the heart out of me, as a conjurer's stick reels out yards of paper ribbon from a hat.

The first number was the *Tannhäuser* overture. When the horns drew out the first strain of the Pilgrim's chorus, my Aunt Georgiana clutched my coat sleeve. Then it was I first realized that for her this broke a silence of thirty years; the inconceivable silence of the plains. With the battle between the two motives, with the frenzy of the Venusberg theme and its ripping of strings, there came to me an overwhelming sense of the waste and wear we are so powerless to combat; and I saw again the tall, naked house on the prairie, black and grim as a wooden fortress; the black pond where I had learned to swim, its margin pitted with sun-dried cattle tracks; the rain gullied clay banks about the naked house, the four dwarf ash seedlings where the dishcloths were always hung to dry before the kitchen door. The world there was the flat world of the ancients; to the east, a cornfield that stretched to daybreak; to the west, a corral that reached to sunset; between, the conquests of peace, dearer bought than those of war.

The overture closed, my aunt released my coat sleeve, but she said nothing. She sat staring at the orchestra through a dullness of thirty years, through the films made little by little by each of the three hundred and sixty-five days in every one of them. What, I wondered, did she get from it? She had been a good pianist in her day I knew, and her musical education had been broader than that of most music teachers of a quarter of a century ago. She had often told me of Mozart's operas and Meyerbeer's, and I could remember hearing her sing, years ago, certain melodies of Verdi's. When I had fallen ill with a fever in her house she used to sit by my cot in the evening—when the cool, night wind blew in through the faded mosquito netting tacked over the window and I lay watching a certain bright star that burned red above the cornfield—and sing "Home to our mountains, O, let us return!" in a way fit to break the heart of a Vermont boy near dead of homesickness already.

I watched her closely through the prelude to *Tristan and Isolde,* trying vainly to conjecture what that seething turmoil of strings and winds might mean to her, but she sat mutely staring at the violin bows that drove obliquely downward, like the pelting streaks of rain in a summer shower. Had this music any message for her? Had she enough left to at all comprehend this power which had kindled the world since she had left it? I was in a fever of curiosity, but Aunt Georgiana sat silent upon her peak in Darien. She preserved this utter immobility throughout the number from *The Flying Dutchman,* though her fingers worked mechanically upon her black dress, as though, of themselves, they were recalling the piano score they had once played. Poor old hands! They had been stretched and twisted into mere tentacles to hold and lift and knead with; the palm, unduly swollen, the fingers bent and knotted—on one of them a thin, worn band that had once been a wedding ring. As I pressed and gently quieted one of those groping hands, I remembered with quivering eyelids their services for me in other days.

15   Soon after the tenor began the "Prize Song," I heard a quick drawn breath and turned to my aunt. Her eyes were closed, but the tears were glistening on her cheeks, and I think, in a moment more, they were in my eyes as well. It never really died, then—the soul that can suffer so excruciatingly and so interminably; it withers to the outward eye only; like that strange moss which can lie on a dusty shelf half a century and yet, if placed in water, grows green again. She wept so throughout the development and elaboration of the melody.

During the intermission before the second half of the concert, I questioned my aunt and found that the "Prize Song" was not new to her. Some years before there had drifted to the farm in Red Willow County a young German, a tramp cow-puncher, who had sung in the chorus at Bayreuth, when he was a boy, along with the other peasant boys and girls. Of a Sunday morning he used to sit on his gingham-sheeted bed in the hands' bedroom which opened off the kitchen, cleaning the leather of his boots and saddle, singing the "Prize Song," while my aunt went about her work in the kitchen. She had hovered about him until she had prevailed upon him to join the country church, though his sole fitness for this step, in so far as I could gather, lay in his boyish face and his possession of this divine melody. Shortly afterward he had gone to town on the Fourth of July, been drunk for several days, lost his money at a faro table, ridden a saddled Texas steer on a bet, and disappeared with a fractured collar-bone. All this my aunt told me huskily, wanderingly, as though she were talking in the weak lapses of illness.

"Well, we have come to better things than the old *Trovatore* at any rate, Aunt Georgie?" I queried, with a well meant effort at jocularity.

Her lip quivered and she hastily put her handkerchief up to her mouth. From behind it she murmured, "And you have been hearing this ever since you left me, Clark?" Her question was the gentlest and saddest of reproaches.

The second half of the programme consisted of four numbers from the *Ring,* and closed with Siegfried's funeral march. My aunt wept quietly, but almost continuously, as a shallow vessel overflows in a rain-storm. From time to time her dim eyes looked up at the lights which studded the ceiling, burning softly under their dull glass globes; doubtless they were stars in truth to her. I was still perplexed as to what measure of musical comprehension was left to her, she who had heard nothing but the singing of Gospel Hymns at Methodist services in the square frame school-house on Section Thirteen for so many years. I was wholly unable to gauge how much of it had been dissolved in soapsuds, or worked into bread, or milked into the bottom of a pail.

20 The deluge of sound poured on and on; I never knew what she found in the shining current of it; I never knew how far it bore her, or past what happy islands. From the trembling of her face I could well believe that before the last numbers she had been carried out where the myriad graves are, into the grey, nameless burying grounds of the sea; or into some world of death vaster yet, where, from the beginning of the world, hope has lain down with hope and dream with dream and, renouncing, slept.

The concert was over; the people filed out of the hall chattering and laughing, glad to relax and find the living level again, but my kinswoman made no effort to rise. The harpist slipped its green felt cover over his instrument; the flute-players shook the water from their mouthpieces; the men of the orchestra went out one by one, leaving the stage to the chairs and music stands, empty as a winter cornfield.

I spoke to my aunt. She burst into tears and sobbed pleadingly. "I don't want to go, Clark, I don't want to go!"

I understood. For her, just outside the door of the concert hall, lay the black pond with the cattle-tracked bluffs; the tall, unpainted house, with weather-curled boards; naked as a tower; the crook-backed ash seedlings where the dish-cloths hung to dry; the gaunt, moulting turkeys picking up refuse about the kitchen door.

[1905]

A Wagner Matinée

By WILLA SIBERT CATHER

I RECEIVED one morning a letter written in pale ink, on glassy, blue-lined notepaper, and bearing the postmark of a little Nebraska village. This communication, worn and rubbed, looking as though it had been carried for some days in a coat-pocket that was none too clean, was from my Uncle Howard. It informed me that his wife had been left a small legacy by a bachelor relative who had recently died, and that it had become necessary for her to come to Boston to attend to the settling of the estate. He requested me to meet her at the station, and render her whatever services might prove necessary. On examining the date indicated as that of her arrival, I found it no later than to-morrow. He had characteristically delayed writing until, had I been away from home for a day, I must have missed the good woman altogether.

The name of my Aunt Georgiana called up not alone her own figure, at once pathetic and grotesque, but opened before my feet a gulf of recollections so wide and deep that, as the letter dropped from my hand, I felt suddenly a stranger to all the present conditions of my existence, wholly ill at ease and out of place amid the surroundings of my study. I became, in short, the gangling farmer-boy my aunt had known, scourged with chilblains and bashfulness, my hands cracked and raw from the corn-husking. I felt the knuckles of my thumb tentatively, as though they were raw again. I sat again before her parlor organ, thumbing the scales with my stiff, red hands, while she beside me made canvas mittens for the huskers.

The next morning, after preparing my landlady somewhat, I set out for the station. When the train arrived I had some difficulty in finding my aunt. She was the last of the passengers to alight, and when I got her into the carriage she looked not unlike one of those charred, smoked bodies that firemen lift from the *débris* of a burned building. She had come all the way in a day coach; her linen duster had become black with soot and her black bonnet gray with dust during the journey. When we arrived at my boarding-house the landlady put her to bed at once, and I did not see her again until the next morning.

Whatever shock Mrs. Springer experienced at my aunt's appearance she considerately concealed. Myself, I saw my aunt's misshapen figure with that feeling of awe and respect with which we behold explorers who have left their ears and fingers north of Franz Josef Land, or their health somewhere along the Upper Congo. My Aunt Georgiana had been a music-teacher at the Boston Conservatory, somewhere back in the latter sixties. One summer, which she had spent in the little village in the Green Mountains where her ancestors had dwelt for generations, she had kindled the callow fancy of the most idle and shiftless of all the village lads, and had conceived for this Howard Carpenter one of those absurd and extravagant passions which a handsome country boy of twenty-one sometimes inspires in a plain, angular, spectacled woman of thirty. When she returned to her duties in Boston, Howard followed her; and the upshot of this inexplicable infatuation was that she eloped with him, eluding the reproaches of her family and the criticism of her friends by going with him to the Nebraska frontier. Carpenter, who of course had no money, took a homestead in Red Willow County, fifty miles from the railroad. There they measured off their eighty acres by driving across the prairie in a wagon, to the wheel of which they had tied a red cotton handkerchief, and counting its revolutions. They built a dugout in the red hillside, one of those cave dwellings whose inmates usually reverted to the conditions of primitive savagery. Their water they got from the lagoons where the buffalo drank, and their slender stock of provisions was always at the mercy of bands of roving Indians. For thirty years my aunt had not been farther than fifty miles from the homestead.

But Mrs. Springer knew nothing of all this, and must have been considerably shocked at what was left of my kinswoman. Beneath the soiled linen duster, which on her arrival was the most conspicuous feature of her costume, she wore a black stuff dress whose ornamentation showed that she had surrendered herself unquestioningly into the hands of a country dressmaker. My poor aunt's figure, however, would have presented astonishing difficulties to any dressmaker. Her skin was yellow as a Mongolian's from constant exposure to a pitiless wind, and to the alkaline water, which transforms the most transparent cuticle into a sort of flexible leather. She wore ill-fitting false teeth. The most striking thing about her physiognomy, however, was an incessant twitching of the mouth and eyebrows, a form of nervous disorder resulting from isolation and monotony, and from frequent physical suffering.

In my boyhood this affliction had possessed a sort of horrible fascination for me, of which I was secretly very much ashamed, for in those days I owed to this woman most of the good that ever came my way, and had a reverential affection for her. During the three winters when I was riding herd for my uncle, my aunt, after cooking three meals for half a dozen farm-hands, and putting the six children to bed, would often stand until midnight at her ironing-board, hearing me at the kitchen table beside her recite Latin declensions and conjugations, and gently shaking me when my drowsy head sank down over a page of irregular verbs. It was to her, at her ironing or mending, that I read my first Shakespeare; and her old text-book of mythology was the first that ever came into my empty hands. She taught me my scales and exercises, too, on the little parlor organ which her husband had bought her after fifteen years, during which she had not so much as seen any instrument except an accordion, that belonged to one of the Norwegian farm-hands. She would sit beside me by the hour, darning and counting, while I struggled with the "Harmonious Blacksmith"; but she seldom talked to me about music, and I understood why. She was a pious woman; she had the consolation of religion; and to her at least her martyrdom was not wholly sordid. Once when I had been doggedly beating out some passages from an old score of "Euryanthe" I had found among her music-books, she came up to me and, putting her hands over my eyes, gently drew my head back upon her shoulder, saying tremulously, "Don't love it so well, Clark, or it may be taken from you.

Oh! dear boy, pray that whatever your sacrifice be it is not that."

When my aunt appeared on the morning after her arrival, she was still in a semi-somnambulent state. She seemed not to realize that she was in the city where she had spent her youth, the place longed for hungrily for half a lifetime. She had been so wretchedly trainsick throughout the journey that she had no recollection of anything but her discomfort, and, to all intents and purposes, there were but a few hours of nightmare between the farm in Red Willow County and my study on Newbury Street. I had planned a little pleasure for her that afternoon, to repay her for some of the glorious moments she had given me when we used to milk together in the straw-thatched cow-shed, and she, because I was more than usually tired, or because her husband had spoken sharply to me, would tell me of the splendid performance of Meyerbeer's "Huguenots" she had seen in Paris in her youth. At two o'clock the Boston Symphony Orchestra was to give a Wagner programme, and I intended to take my aunt, though as I conversed with her I grew doubtful about her enjoyment of it. Indeed, for her own sake, I could only wish her taste for such things quite dead, and the long struggle mercifully ended at last. I suggested our visiting the Conservatory and the Common before lunch, but she seemed altogether too timid to wish to venture out. She questioned me absently about various changes in the city, but she was chiefly concerned that she had forgotten to leave instructions about feeding half-skimmed milk to a certain weakling calf, "Old Maggie's calf, you know, Clark," she explained, evidently having forgotten how long I had been away. She was further troubled because she had neglected to tell her daughter about the freshly opened kit of mackerel in the cellar, that would spoil if it were not used directly.

I asked her whether she had ever heard any of the Wagnerian operas, and found that she had not, though she was perfectly familiar with their respective situations and had once possessed the piano score of "The Flying Dutchman." I began to think it would have been best to get her back to Red Willow County without waking her, and regretted having suggested the concert.

From the time we entered the concert-hall, however, she was a trifle less passive and inert, and seemed to begin to perceive her surroundings. I had felt some trepidation lest she might become aware of the absurdities of her attire, or might experience some painful embarrassment at stepping suddenly into the world to which she had been dead for a quarter of a century. But again I found how superficially I had judged her. She sat looking about her with eyes as impersonal, almost as stony, as those with which the granite Rameses in a museum watches the froth and fret that ebbs and flows about his pedestal, separated from it by the lonely stretch of centuries. I have seen this same aloofness in old miners who drift into the Brown Hotel at Denver, their pockets full of bullion, their linen soiled, their haggard faces unshorn, and who stand in the thronged corridors as solitary as though they were still in a frozen camp on the Yukon, or in the yellow blaze of the Arizona desert, conscious that certain experiences have isolated them from their fellows by a gulf no haberdasher could conceal.

The audience was made up chiefly of women. One lost the contour of faces and figures, indeed any effect of line whatever, and there was only the color contrast of bodices past counting, the shimmer and shading of fabrics soft and firm, silky and sheer, resisting and yielding: red, mauve, pink, blue, lilac, purple, écru, rose, yellow, cream, and white, all the colors that an impressionist finds in a sunlit landscape, with here and there the dead black shadow of a frock-coat. My Aunt Georgiana regarded them as though they had been so many daubs of tube paint on a palette.

When the musicians came out and took their places, she gave a little stir of anticipation, and looked with quickening interest down over the rail at that invariable grouping; perhaps the first wholly familiar thing that had greeted her eye since she had left old Maggie and her weakling calf. I could feel how all those details sank into her soul, for I had not forgotten how they had sunk into mine when I came fresh from ploughing forever and forever between green aisles of corn, where, as in a treadmill, one might walk from daybreak to dusk without perceiving a shadow of change in one's environment. I reminded myself of the impression made on me by the clean profiles of the musicians, the gloss of their linen, the dull black of their coats, the beloved shapes of the instruments, the patches of yellow light thrown by the green-shaded stand-lamps on the smooth, varnished bellies of the 'cellos and the bass viols in the rear, the restless,

wind-tossed forest of fiddle necks and bows; I recalled how, in the first orchestra I had ever heard, those long bow strokes seemed to draw the soul out of me, as a conjuror's stick reels out paper ribbon from a hat.

The first number was the Tannhäuser overture. When the violins drew out the first strain of the Pilgrims' chorus, my Aunt Georgiana clutched my coat-sleeve. Then it was that I first realized that for her this singing of basses and stinging frenzy of lighter strings broke a silence of thirty years, the inconceivable silence of the plains. With the battle between the two motifs, with the bitter frenzy of the Venusberg theme and its ripping of strings, came to me an overwhelming sense of the waste and wear we are so powerless to combat. I saw again the tall, naked house on the prairie, black and grim as a wooden fortress; the black pond where I had learned to swim, the rain-gullied clay about the naked house; the four dwarf ash-seedlings on which the dishcloths were always hung to dry before the kitchen door. The world there is the flat world of the ancients; to the east, a cornfield that stretched to daybreak; to the west, a corral that stretched to sunset; between, the sordid conquests of peace, more merciless than those of war.

The overture closed. My aunt released my coat-sleeve, but she said nothing. She sat staring at the orchestra through a dulness of thirty years, through the films made, little by little, by each of the three hundred and sixty-five days in every one of them. What, I wondered, did she get from it? She had been a good pianist in her day, I knew, and her musical education had been broader than that of most music-teachers of a quarter of a century ago. She had often told me of Mozart's operas and Meyerbeer's, and I could remember hearing her sing, years ago, certain melodies of Verdi's. When I had fallen ill with a fever she used to sit by my cot in the evening, while the cool night wind blew in through the faded mosquito-netting tacked over the window, and I lay watching a bright star that burned red above the cornfield, and sing "Home to our mountains, oh, let us return!" in a way fit to break the heart of a Vermont boy near dead of homesickness already.

I watched her closely through the prelude to Tristan and Isolde, trying vainly to conjecture what that warfare of motifs, that seething turmoil of strings and winds, might mean to her. Had this music any message for her? Did or did not a new planet swim into her ken? Wagner had been a sealed book to Americans before the sixties. Had she anything left with which to comprehend this glory that had flashed around the world since she had gone from it? I was in a fever of curiosity, but Aunt Georgiana sat silent upon her peak in Darien. She preserved this utter immobility throughout the numbers from the "Flying Dutchman," though her fingers worked mechanically upon her black dress, as though of themselves they were recalling the piano score they had once played. Poor old hands! They were stretched and pulled and twisted into mere tentacles to hold, and lift, and knead with; the palms unduly swollen, the fingers bent and knotted, on one of them a thin worn band that had once been a wedding-ring. As I pressed and gently quieted one of those groping hands, I remembered, with quivering eyelids, their services for me in other days.

Soon after the tenor began the Prize Song, I heard a quick-drawn breath, and turned to my aunt. Her eyes were closed, but the tears were glistening on her cheeks, and I think in a moment more they were in my eyes as well. It never really dies, then, the soul? It withers to the outward eye only, like that strange moss which can lie on a dusty shelf half a century and yet, if placed in water, grows green again. My aunt wept gently throughout the development and elaboration of the melody.

During the intermission before the second half of the concert, I questioned my aunt and found that the Prize Song was not new to her. Some years before there had drifted to the farm in Red Willow County a young German, a tramp cow-puncher, who had sung in the chorus at Baireuth, when he was a boy, along with the other peasant boys and girls. Of a Sunday morning he used to sit on his blue gingham-sheeted bed in the hands' bedroom, which opened off the kitchen, cleaning the leather of his boots and saddle, and singing the Prize Song, while my aunt went about her work in the kitchen. She had hovered about him until she had prevailed upon him to join the country church, though his sole fitness for this step, so far as I could gather, lay in his boyish face and his possession of this divine melody. Shortly afterward he had gone to town on the Fourth of July, been drunk for several days, lost his money at a faro-table, ridden a saddled

Texas steer on a bet, and disappeared with a fractured collar-bone.

"Well, we have come to better things than the old Trovatore at any rate, Aunt Georgie?" I queried, with well-meant jocularity.

Her lip quivered and she hastily put her handkerchief up to her mouth. From behind it she murmured, "And you've been hearing this ever since you left me, Clark?" Her question was the gentlest and saddest of reproaches.

"But do you get it, Aunt Georgiana, the astonishing structure of it all?" I persisted.

"Who could?" she said, absently; "why should one?"

The second half of the programme consisted of four numbers from the Ring. This was followed by the forest music from Siegfried, and the programme closed with Siegfried's funeral march. My aunt wept quietly, but almost continuously. I was perplexed as to what measure of musical comprehension was left to her, to her who had heard nothing for so many years but the singing of gospel hymns in Methodist services at the square frame school-house on Section Thirteen. I was unable to gauge how much of it had been dissolved in soapsuds, or worked into bread, or milked into the bottom of a pail.

The deluge of sound poured on and on; I never know what she found in the shining current of it; I never knew how far it bore her, or past what happy islands, or under what skies. From the trembling of her face I could well believe that the Siegfried march, at least, carried her out where the myriad graves are, out into the gray, burying-grounds of the sea; or into some world of death vaster yet, where, from the beginning of the world, hope has lain down with hope, and dream with dream and, renouncing, slept.

The concert was over; the people filed out of the hall chattering and laughing, glad to relax and find the living level again, but my kinswoman made no effort to rise. I spoke gently to her. She burst into tears and sobbed pleadingly, "I don't want to go, Clark, I don't want to go!"

I understood. For her, just outside the door of the concert-hall, lay the black pond with the cattle-tracked bluffs, the tall, unpainted house, naked as a tower, with weather-curled boards; the crook-backed ash-seedlings where the dishcloths hung to dry, the gaunt, moulting turkeys picking up refuse about the kitchen door.

Joining the Conversation: Critical Thinking and Writing

1. Look at the third-from-the-last paragraph in the story. When Cather first published "A Wagner Matinée," after the first sentence of this paragraph ("The concert . . . no effort to rise") she went directly to what now begins the next paragraph, "I spoke to my aunt." Do you think the addition in the revised version ("The harpist slipped . . . a winter cornfield") is an improvement or a mistake? Why?

2. How would you characterize Clark? Do you think that he changes during the story? Or, as we go from page to page, do we just get to know him better?

3. In the middle of the story, before Clark and his aunt attend the concert, Clark says that he "began to think it would be best to get her back to Red Willow County without waking her." Does he make a mistake in taking her to the concert? Explain.

4. Has any work of art—for instance, a song, play, painting, or dance—deeply moved you? If so, in an essay of about 500 words describe your emotions during and immediately after the experience. Feel free to extend "art" to include, if you wish, such exhibitions of skill as circus or rodeo acts and athletic contests.

CHAPTER 5

Writing as Performance

True ease in writing comes from art, not chance,
As those move easiest who have learned to dance.

ALEXANDER POPE

Chapter Preview

After reading this chapter you will be able to

- Describe the writer's role as a performer
- Describe the reader's role—your own role—as a performer
- Describe the essayist's role—again, your role—as a performer

---

All of us at times "perform" literary works when we tell stories in public. We read a fairy tale to children, or we tell a joke to a friend. When we were children we recited nursery rhymes, perhaps even *performing* them by bouncing a ball or skipping rope to the accompaniment of lines. Moreover, we sing lullabies, hymns, birthday greetings, and national anthems, and on New Year's Eve we may sing Robert Burns's great poem, "Auld Lang Syne."

The Writer as Performer

When Robert Frost said that a poem is "a performance in words," he was not speaking of poetry recitations, though Frost himself was an expert reciter and apparently a born showman. (If Frost had a weakness as a performer, it was that he insisted on being a soloist and never gave readings with other poets: "I only go / When I'm the show.") When Frost said that a poem was a performance in words he was saying that the *writer* does things with words, more or less as a juggler performs with Indian clubs or balls, as a singer performs with vocal cords and air, and as a dancer or an athlete performs with the body. The poet's materials are words, which the poet manipulates into something attractive and meaningful. Consider a very short poem by Frost.

The Span of Life

The old dog barks backward without getting up.
I can remember when he was a pup.

We will discuss this poem on page 133, but here, keeping in mind our point that a piece of writing is a performance by an author, we want to notice these things:

- The poem is set off on the page by its title (somewhat as a picture is set off by a frame, a sculpture by a pedestal) and the white space around it; it appears, so to speak, in a spotlight.
- The rhyme (up/pup) is a device that distinguishes verse from ordinary prose.
- There is a contrast between the first words ("The old dog") and the last word ("pup").

121

- The use of language is skillful, and not only in finding a rhyme. For instance, in "old dog" the speaker must pause a moment between the two words so that each *d* is sounded separately, and the *k* sounds in *bark* and *back* make the first line (about an old dog) somewhat awkward and creaky, compared to the more speakable—let's say more jingling—second line (about a puppy). Moreover, in the first line, after the opening *The,* the next four syllables are all stressed fairly heavily (*old dog barks back*), and there are stresses on the second syllable of *without,* on the first syllable of *getting,* and on *up,* for a total of seven stresses in ten syllables—very effortful!—whereas in the second line there are at most four stresses: *I, mem* (in *remember*), *he,* and *pup* (*I* probably does not get much emphasis, so there are really only three significant stresses in the second line). Readers may differ about exactly how much stress to put on a given syllable, but surely all readers will agree that the first line is heavier and requires more effort to say than the second, which is sprightlier.
- The two lines strike a balance: The first line describes the dog as it is now, old, and (after a reflective pause that the author forces on the reader by providing a period) the second line describes the speaker's memory of the young dog, leaving us with an implication about our own lives. Thus the first line offers an observation, the second line a meditation.

In this poem Frost offers a comment about life (the title makes this clear). He is not just playing with words. Yet he *is* also playing around or performing with words in this composition. (*Composition,* by the way, comes from the Latin *componere,* "to put together"; all writers—not only poets, but essayists also—put words together in order to interest their readers.) And, having spoken of "playing with words," we should add that the playing is not a free-for-all. It has its rules, such as metrical lines and rhyme schemes. Commenting on rhyme, Frost said it was a sort of game and that all games are inventions that human beings contrive in order to have the fun of doing things the hard way. Frost always used rhyme; he said that to write unrhymed poetry would be like playing tennis with the net down.

The Reader as Performer

We hope we have convinced you, with our brief look at "The Span of Life," that a work of literature is indeed a performance in words. Later in this chapter we will argue that *your own* writings are also performances, admittedly command performances required by your instructors, but here we want to suggest that when you read a work of literature—aloud, or even silently—*you are in a sense performing the work.* Now let's go back and reread "The Span of Life."

> The old dog barks backward without getting up.
> I can remember when he was a pup.

Won't you agree, even if you read the poem silently, that in a sense you *performed* the poem, that to some degree you impersonated Robert Frost in the act of reminiscing about a dog? We might almost say you became, momentarily, an incarnation of Frost reflecting on the experience of seeing an old dog bark without getting up.

Let's turn now to an unusual short story by Jamaica Kincaid. In this story you will hear two voices, one of them that of a mother who is tutoring her adolescent daughter for her coming role as a woman. Kincaid informs us that *benna,* mentioned early in the story, refers to "songs of the sort your parents didn't want you to sing, at first calypso and later rock and roll."

Jamaica Kincaid

Jamaica Kincaid was born in 1949 on the island of Antigua, in the West Indies, at that time a British colony. At the age of seventeen she emigrated to the United States, where she still lives, although most of her writing continues to be set in Antigua.

Girl

Wash the white clothes on Monday and put them on the stone heap; wash the color clothes on Tuesday and put them on the clothesline to dry; don't walk barehead in the hot sun; cook pumpkin fritters in very hot sweet oil; soak your little clothes right after you take them off; when buying cotton to make yourself a nice blouse, be sure that it doesn't have gum on it, because that way it won't hold up well after a wash; soak salt fish overnight before you cook it; is it true that you sing benna in Sunday school?; always eat your food in such a way that it won't turn someone else's stomach; on Sundays try to walk like a lady and not like the slut you are so bent on becoming; don't sing benna in Sunday school; you mustn't speak to wharf-rat boys, not even to give directions; don't eat fruits on the street— flies will follow you; *but I don't sing benna on Sundays at all and never in Sunday school;* this is how to sew on a button; this is how to make a buttonhole for the button you have just sewed on; this is how to hem a dress when you see the hem coming down and so to prevent yourself from looking like the slut I know you are so bent on becoming; this is how you iron your father's khaki shirt so that it doesn't have a crease; this is how you iron your father's khaki pants so that they don't have a crease; this is how you grow okra—far from the house, because okra tree harbors red ants; when you are growing dasheen, make sure it gets plenty of water or else it makes your throat itch when you are eating it; this is how you sweep a corner; this is how you sweep a whole house; this is how you sweep a yard; this is how you smile to someone you don't like too much; this is how you smile to someone you don't like at all; this is how you smile to someone you like completely; this is how you set a table for tea; this is how you set a table for dinner; this is how you set a table for dinner with an important guest; this is how you set a table for lunch; this is how you set a table for breakfast; this is how to behave in the presence of men who don't know you very well, and this way they won't recognize immediately the slut I have warned you against becoming; be sure to wash every day, even if it is with your own spit; don't squat down to play marbles—you are not a boy, you know; don't pick people's flowers—you might catch something; don't throw stones at blackbirds, because it might not be a blackbird at all; this is how to make a bread pudding; this is how to make doukona; this is how to make pepper pot; this is how to make a good medicine for a cold; this is how to make a good medicine to throw away a child before it even becomes a child; this is how to catch a fish; this is how to throw back a fish you don't like, and that way something bad won't fall on you; this is how to bully a man; this is how a man bullies you; this is how to love a man, and if this doesn't work there are other ways, and if they don't work don't feel too bad about giving up; this is how to spit up in the air if you feel like it, and this is how to move quick so that it doesn't fall on you; this is how to make ends meet; always squeeze bread to make sure it's fresh; *but what if the baker won't let me feel the bread?;* you mean to say that after all you are really going to be the kind of woman who the baker won't let near the bread?

[1978]

In our introduction we somewhat misleadingly said that you would hear two voices. Had the two voices shared the space equally, the story would be a very different one—that is, the mother would be a different mother and the girl a different girl. Probably you and your mother are quite different from these two. But didn't you enjoy the experience of reading, hearing, almost uttering, almost *performing* the words of these two distinctive characters? Will you agree that the experience of hearing these characters—the experience of becoming them as you read their lines—is a pleasurable experience that enlarges your view of what life is like?

Joining the Conversation: Critical Thinking and Writing

1. What do you make of the girl's second (and last) line of dialogue in "Girl," and what do you make of the mother's response to it?
2. Try reading a section of "Girl" out loud in a rhythmical pattern, giving the two speakers distinctive voices. Then reread the story, trying to incorporate the rhythms mentally into your reading. How do the rhythms compare with speech rhythms that are familiar to you?

MyLiteratureLab® *For additional resources for "Girl," log in to* www.myliteraturelab.com *where you will find a Longman Lecture and Critical Essay, as well as an About the Author and Links for Kincaid (under Student Resources).*

The Essayist as Performer

We now return to the point that when you write an essay you are, like Robert Frost and Jamaica Kincaid, necessarily performing with words. Probably your essays will consist chiefly of

- analysis and
- argument (you want to persuade your reader that your analysis makes sense)

but your essay will surely also include

- exposition (you may have to define terms or summarize someone else's argument) and
- narration (you may have to summarize a plot)

and you will have to use an appropriate

- style (largely a matter of tone)

In short, in writing any essay, even when your emphasis is largely analytic and argumentative, you will probably use all the devices that all good writers use to hold the attention of readers and to convince readers that you have something to say that is worth hearing. And you *will* have something to offer when you think seriously about both the work you are discussing and the work you are producing, the performance in words that you will submit to your classmates or your instructor. Read each draft in a mildly critical spirit; keep asking yourself if your imagined readers will find it convincing and engaging. Here are some of the questions you will ask yourself:

- Have I defined terms that may be crucial to my analysis (for instance, *immoral, realistic, pathetic, tragic, sentimental*)?
- Have I given just the right amount of evidence (*too little* evidence will leave readers unconvinced; *too much* evidence may bore them)?
- Do transitions take the reader easily from sentence to sentence, from paragraph to paragraph?
- Is my title engaging, does my opening paragraph arouse interest, and does my final paragraph provide an effective ending?
- Is my tone appropriate?

The point about tone is worth further comment. As a writer of arguments, you want your readers to trust you. How do writers gain the trust of readers? Usually by being

- **knowledgeable** (the writer quotes accurately and does not make errors of fact),
- **fair** (the writer does not ignore contrary evidence), and
- **courteous** (the writer conveys an impression of goodwill and does not come across to the reader as a smart-aleck).

A Rule for Writers: When you argue your case—when you hand your reader that script to perform—be sure that you are knowledgeable, fair, and courteous.

This book provides many checklists to help you evaluate and improve your performances—your drafts. (In the index, consult *checklists* for page references.) Remember: You are your own first reader, the first viewer of your performance. Get your act together, and your other readers will thank you for giving them an engaging experience.

ANATOLE FRANCE

Anatole France (1844–1924), French poet, journalist, and novelist, won the Nobel Prize in Literature in 1921. Although he was brought up as a Roman Catholic, his later writings offended the Church and in 1922 it put all of his works on its prohibited books index. He responded by saying that he was honored.

"Our Lady's Juggler" ("Le Jongleur de Nôtre-Dame") is based on a French tale of the early thirteenth century. The story also engendered an opera by Jules Massenet (1902) and several film and television versions, including The Young Juggler *with Tony Curtis.*

Our Lady's Juggler

In the days of King Louis there lived a poor juggler named Barnaby, a native of Compiègne, who wandered from town to town performing feats of strength and skill.

On fair days he would unfold in the public square an old threadbare carpet, and after having attracted children and idlers by some amusing remarks which he had learned from an old juggler, and which he never changed in the slightest, he would assume the strangest postures, and balance a tin plate on the tip of his nose. At first the crowd paid little attention to him but when, with his hands and head on the ground he threw into the air and caught with his feet six copper balls that glittered in the sunlight, or when, throwing himself backward until his neck touched his heels, he made himself into a wheel and in that position juggled a dozen knives, a murmur of admiration came from his audience, and coins rained on his carpet.

Still, Barnaby of Compiègne, like most of those who live a hand-to-mouth existence, had a hard time making a living. Earning his bread by the sweat of his brow, he had more than his share of the miseries we all inherit from the misbehavior of our Father Adam.

Further, he could not work as much as he wanted to, because in order to exhibit his exceptional skill he needed—like the flowering fruit trees—the warmth of the sun and the light of the day. In winter time he was a tree stripped of its leaves, half-dead. The frozen earth was too hard for the juggler. Like the grasshopper in the fable of "The Ant and the Grasshopper," during the bad season he was hungry and cold. But, since he was simple-natured, he endured his suffering in silence.

5   He had never thought much about the origin of wealth or about the inequality of human conditions. He firmly believed that if this world was bad the next must be good, and this faith upheld him. He was not like the clever fools who sell their souls to the devil: He never blasphemed, he lived the life of an honest man, and though he had no wife he did not covet his neighbor's, for woman is the enemy of the strong man, as we learn by the story of Samson which is recorded in the Bible. To tell the truth, his mind did not turn toward the flesh, and it was harder for him to give up drinking than women. He was not a drunkard but he liked to drink when the weather was warm.

He was a good man, a God-fearing man devoted to the Holy Virgin. When he entered a church he always knelt before the image of the Mother of God and addressed her with this prayer: "My Lady, watch over my life until it pleases God that I die, and when I am dead, let me have the joys of Paradise."

One evening after a rainy day, while he walked sad and bent, carrying his juggling balls and his knives wrapped up in his old carpet, looking for a barn where he might sleep, supperless, he saw a monk going in his direction, and respectfully greeted him. Since they were both walking at the same pace, they fell into conversation.

"Friend," said the monk, "why are you dressed all in green? Are you going to play the part of the jester in some seasonal play?"

"No, indeed, father," said Barnaby. "My name is Barnaby, and my business is juggling. It would be the best business in the world if I could eat every day."

10   "Friend Barnaby," the monk replied, "be careful what you say. There is no finer calling than the monastic life. The priest celebrates the praise of God, the Virgin, and the saints; the religious life is a perpetual hymn to the Lord."

Barnaby replied: "Father, I confess I spoke foolishly. My work cannot be compared with yours. There may be some good in dancing and balancing a stick with a coin on top of it on the tip of your nose, but it isn't at all like what you do. Father, I wish I could, like you, sing the Office every day, especially the Office of the Very Holy Virgin. I am devoted to Her. I would gladly give up the trade I'm known for, from Soissons to Beauvais, in more than six hundred cities and villages, in order to enter the monastic life."

The monk was touched by the juggler's simplicity, and because he was not lacking in discernment, he recognized in Barnaby one of those men of good-will of whom Our Lord has said, "Let peace be with them on earth." So he said: "Friend Barnaby, come with me and I will see that you are admitted into the monastery of which I am the Prior. He who led St. Mary of Egypt through the desert put me on your path so that I might lead you to salvation."

Thus did Barnaby become a monk. In the monastery that he entered, the monks magnificently celebrated the cult of the Holy Virgin, each of them vying to bring to her service all the knowledge and skill that God had given him.

As for the Prior, he wrote books setting forth, according to the best scholarship, the virtues of the Mother of God. Brother Maurice beautifully copied these treatises on pages of parchment, and Brother Alexander decorated them with delicate miniature paintings of the Queen of Heaven seated on Solomon's throne, with four lions on guard at her feet. Above the halo that encircled Her head flew seven doves, representing the seven gifts of the Holy Spirit: Fear, Piety, Knowledge, Strength, Judgment, Understanding, and Wisdom. With Her were six virgins with golden hair: Humility, Prudence, Retirement, Submission, Virginity, and Obedience. At Her feet two little naked figures, pure white, stood in a pose of supplication. They were souls imploring—surely not in vain—Her all-powerful intercession for their salvation. On another page Brother Alexander showed Eve in the presence of Mary, so that one could see at the same time the Fall and the Redemption, the wife humiliated and the Virgin exalted. Among the other wonderful pictures in his book were the Well of Living Waters, the Fountain, the Lily, the Moon, the Sun, and the Closed Garden (of which much is said in the Song of Songs), the Gate of Heaven and the City of God. These were all symbols of the Virgin.

15   Brother Marbode, too, was one of the loving children of Mary. He was always carving images of stone, so that his beard, his eyebrows and his hair were white with the stone-dust, and his eyes always swollen and tearful. But he was hardy and happy in his old age, and it was evident that the Queen of Paradise watched over Her child in his declining years. Marbode represented Her seated on a throne, Her forehead encircled by a halo set with pearls. He took great pains to make the folds of Her robe cover the feet of Her of whom the prophet has said, "My beloved is like an enclosed garden."

Sometimes he represented Her as a child full of grace; Her image seemed to say, "Lord, Thou art My Lord!"

In the monastery there were also poets who composed, in Latin, prose writings and hymns in honor of the Most Gracious Virgin Mary; there was even one, from Picardy, who set forth the Miracles of Our Lady in rimed verses in ordinary spoken language.

Seeing so much competition in praise and so rich a harvest of good works, Barnaby grieved for his ignorance and simplicity. "Ah!" he sighed as he walked alone one day in the monastery's garden, "How wretched I am. Unlike my brothers, I can't give worthy praise to the Holy Mother of God, whom I love with all my heart. Oh, I am crude, untalented, and I cannot serve you, Madam. I have no sermons, no fancy writings prepared according to the rules, no fine paintings, no beautifully carved statues, and no poems marching in meter! Ah, I have nothing!"

Thus he lamented and made himself miserable.

20   One evening when, during a free hour, the monks were chatting, he heard one of them tell of a monk who could not recite anything but the Ave Maria. This monk was ridiculed for his ignorance, but after he died five roses flowered from his

mouth, in honor of the five letters in the name Maria. Thus was his holiness manifested.

In listening to this story, Barnaby was again conscious of the Virgin's kindness, but he was not comforted by the example of the happy miracle, because his heart was full of zeal and he longed to celebrate the glory of His Lady in Heaven.

He tried to find a way to do this, but he could not, and each day he became more and more depressed, until one morning he woke up joyfully, ran to the chapel, and stayed there, alone, for more than an hour. He returned to the chapel after dinner, and from that day onward, he went to the chapel every day as soon as it was deserted, spending the time there when the other monks dedicated themselves to study and the arts. He was no longer sad, he no longer sighed. But this unusual behavior aroused the curiosity of the other monks, and they wondered why Brother Barnaby so often engaged in solitary retreat, and the Prior, whose duty it was to know everything that his monks were doing, set out to observe Barnaby. One day, therefore, when Barnaby was alone in the chapel, the Prior entered with two of the oldest brothers in order to see, through cracks in the door, what was going on inside the chapel.

They saw Barnaby before the image of the Holy Virgin, his head on the floor, his feet in the air, juggling six copper balls and a dozen knives. In honor of the Holy Mother he was performing the tricks that in the old days had brought him his fame. Not realizing that this simple man was offering his best talents to the service of the Holy Virgin, the two old brothers cried out against such sacrilege. The Prior knew that Barnaby had a pure soul, but he believed that the man had gone out of his mind. The three began to drag Barnaby from the chapel when they saw the Blessed Virgin slowly descend from the altar and, with a fold of her blue mantle, wipe the sweat that oozed from the juggler's forehead.

Then the Prior, bowing his head down to the marble floor, repeated these words: "Blessed are the pure in heart, for they shall see God."

25   "Amen," echoed the old brothers, and they kissed the ground.

[1892; English version by John Daremo, 2011]

Joining the Conversation: Critical Thinking and Writing

Write a short essay (250–350 words) in which you argue that "Our Lady's Juggler" is or is not worth reading. Whatever your responses are to the story, you may find that you will deepen or broaden them if you consult Chapter 14, "Reading and Writing about Stories," and especially the Checklist: Getting Ideas for Writing about Stories on pages 358–60. Your essay may include a narrative element telling how you revised your initial response when you reread the story, but essentially your essay should be an ***argument*** supported by an analysis and an evaluation.

If your essay is going to persuade a reader, it will have to offer ***reasons*** in support of your position. And almost surely your evaluation will be based on ***assumptions,*** stated or unstated, such as

- "A good story has a **plot** that holds a reader's interest," perhaps because (a) the reader does not know how it will turn out until it ends, but when it does end—usually a conflict is resolved—the ending is satisfying, or because (b) even if the reader knows the ending, he or she enjoys the skill with which the story is told, and
- "The **characters** in a good story are memorable," perhaps in part because the characters are of different types and the contrasts between them are interesting, and
- "The **theme** of the story gives the reader something to think about."

We do *not* say that a good story must have these qualities; we say that when you judge the story, you need to think about what assumptions lie beneath your judgments.

Given the context of this chapter on writing as performance, your essay, like Anatole France's story and Barnaby's juggling, will be a kind of performance that you offer. The need to engage your reader may not mean that you must stand on your head and write with your feet, but it does mean that you need to come up with a title that doesn't just repeat the title of the story, and you need to begin with something more interesting than "This essay will be about a short story by a French writer named Anatole France."

2 Txt Poms

JULIA BIRD

Born and educated in England, Julia Bird entered a poetry contest sponsored by a British publication, The Guardian. *The ground rules: Write a poem limited to the 160 characters of the mobile phone screen. Bird's poem won a Special Prize of £250 (about $400) for what* The Guardian *called "the most creative use of SMS 'shorthand' in a poem."*

14: a txt msg pom.

his is r bunsn brnr b1%,
his hair lyk fe filings
W/ac/dc going thru.
I sit by him in kemistry,
It splits my @oms
wen he :-)s @ me.

Translation
14: a text message poem.
his eyes are bunsen burner blue,
his hair like iron filings
with ac/dc going through.
I sit by him in chemistry,
it splits my atoms
when he smiles at me.

[2001]

Joining the Conversation: Critical Thinking and Writing

1. Do you agree that Bird's work is a "performance"? Why, or why not? The use of *r* for *are* in line 1 is certainly not original, but do you find things in this piece that strike you as highly imaginative and especially entertaining?
2. Is the translation itself something of a performance in words? If you think it is, which performance do you prefer? Why?
3. Imagine that you are the person about whom Julia Bird wrote her poem. Are you pleased, or not? Write a text poem in response.
4. Another text poem follows. Suppose you were the judge in a contest and these two poems were final contenders. Which one would you pick as the winner? Why?

NORMAN SILVER

Norman Silver is the author of two books of poetry: Laugh Out Loud :-D *and* Age, Sex, Location. *This poem is from the first of the two. In Silver's book, the last word of the first line and the capital letters in the ninth line are printed in red.*

txt commandments

1. u shall luv ur mobil fone with all ur hart
2. u & ur fone shall neva b apart
3. u shall nt lust aftr ur neibrs fone nor thiev
4. u shall b prepard @ all times 2 tXt & 2 recv
5. u shall use LOL & othr acronyms in conversatns
6. u shall be zappy with ur ast*r*sks & exc!matns!!
7. u shall abbrevi8 & rite words like theyr sed
8. u shall nt speak 2 sum 1 face2face if u cn msg em insted
9. u shall nt shout with capitls XEPT IN DIRE EMERGNCY +
10. u shall nt consult a ninglish dictnry

[2006]

Joining the Conversation: Critical Thinking and Writing

1. How much depends on *seeing* this poem, as opposed to hearing it read?
2. The use of "u" for "you," "b" for "be," "2" for "to," and "8" for the syllable "ate" (in "abbreviate," in line 7) is not highly original. What *is* original in the poem?

CHAPTER 6

Reading Literature
Closely: Explication

Some books are to be tasted, others to be swallowed, and
some few to be chewed and digested.

FRANCIS BACON

Chapter Preview

After reading this chapter you will be able to

- Define *literature*, its characteristics, and its forms
- Describe close reading
- Write an explication
- Analyze purpose and audience

What Is Literature?

Perhaps the first thing to say is that it is impossible to define *literature* in a way that will satisfy everyone. And perhaps the second thing to say is that in the last twenty years or so, some serious thinkers have argued that it is impossible to set off certain verbal works from all others, and on some basis or other to designate them as literature. For one thing, it is argued, a work is just marks on paper or sounds in the air. The audience (reader or listener) turns these marks or sounds into something with meaning, and different audiences will construct different meanings out of what they read or hear. There are *texts* (birthday cards, sermons, political speeches, magazines, novels that sell by the millions and novels that don't sell at all, poems, popular songs, editorials, and so forth), but there is nothing that should be given the special title of literature.

Although there is something to be said for the idea that *literature* is just an honorific word and not a collection of work embodying eternal truths and eternal beauty, let's make the opposite assumption, at least for a start. Let's assume that certain verbal works are of a distinct sort—whether because the author shapes them, or because a reader perceives them a certain way—and that we can call these works literature. But what are these works like?

Literature and Form

We all know why we value a newspaper or a textbook or an atlas, but why do we value a verbal work that doesn't give us the latest news or important information about business cycles or the names of the capitals of nations? About a thousand years ago a Japanese woman, Shikibu Murasaki, or Lady Murasaki (978?–1026), offered an answer in *The Tale of Genji*, a book often called the world's first novel. During a discussion about reading fiction, one of the characters gives an opinion as to why a writer tells a story:

Again and again writers find something in their experience, or see something in the life around them, that seems so important they cannot bear to let it pass into oblivion. There must never come a time, the writer feels, when people do not know about this.

Literature is about human experiences, but the experiences in literature are not simply the shapeless experiences—the chaotic passing scene—captured by a mindless, unselective video camera. Poets, dramatists, and storytellers find or impose a shape on scenes (for instance, the history of two lovers), giving readers things to value—written or spoken accounts that are memorable not only for their content but also for their *form*—the shape of the speeches, of the scenes, of the plots. (In a little while we will see that form and content are inseparable, but for the moment, for our purposes, we can talk about them separately.)

Because this discussion of literature is brief, we will illustrate the point by looking at one of the briefest literary forms, the proverb. Consider this statement:

A rolling stone gathers no moss.

Now let's compare it with a **paraphrase** (a restatement, a translation into other words):

If a stone is always moving around, vegetation won't have a chance to grow on it.

What makes the original version more powerful, more memorable? Surely much of the answer is that the original is more concrete and its form is more shapely. At the risk of being heavy-handed, we can analyze the shapeliness thus: *Stone* and *moss* (the two nouns in the sentence) each contain one syllable; *rolling* and *gathers* (the two words of motion) each contain two syllables, with the accent on the first syllable. Notice, too, the nice contrast between stone (hard) and moss (soft).

The reader probably *feels* this shapeliness unconsciously rather than perceives it consciously. That is, these connections become apparent when one starts to analyze, but the literary work can have its effect on a reader even before the reader analyzes the work. As T. S. Eliot said in his essay on Dante (1929), "Genuine poetry can communicate before it is understood." Indeed, our *first* reading of a work, when, so to speak, we are all eyes and ears (and the mind is highly receptive rather than sifting for evidence), is sometimes the most important reading. Experience proves that we can feel the effects of a work without yet understanding *how* the effects are achieved.

Most readers will probably agree that

- the words in the proverb are paired interestingly and meaningfully;
- the sentence is not simply information but is also (to quote one of Robert Frost's definitions of literature) "a performance in words";
- what the sentence *is*, we might say, is no less significant than what the sentence *says*;
- the sentence as a whole forms a memorable picture, a small but complete world, hard and soft, inorganic and organic, inert and moving;
- the idea set forth is simple—partly because it is highly focused and therefore it leaves out a lot—but it is also complex;
- by virtue of the contrasts, and, again, even by the pairing of monosyllabic nouns and of disyllabic words of motion, it is unified into a pleasing whole.

For all of its specificity and its compactness—the proverb contains only six words—it expands our minds.

A Brief Exercise: Take a minute to think about some other proverb, for instance, "Look before you leap," "Finders keepers," "Haste makes waste," or "Absence makes the heart grow fonder." Paraphrase it, and then ask yourself why the original is more interesting, more memorable, than your paraphrase.

Form and Meaning

Let's turn now to a work not much longer than a proverb—a very short poem by Robert Frost (1874–1963), a poem that we looked at briefly in the previous chapter.

The Span of Life

The old dog barks backward without getting up.
I can remember when he was a pup.

On page 122 we talked about physically experiencing Frost's "performance in words." We noted that the first line is harder to say than the second line, which more or less rolls off the tongue. Why? Because in the first line we must pause between *old* and *dog,* between *backward* and *without,* and between *without* and *getting*—and in fact between *back* and *ward.* Further, when we read the poem aloud, or with the mind's ear, in the first line we hear four consecutive stresses in "old dog barks back," a noticeable contrast to the rather jingling "when he was a pup" in the second line.

No two readers will read the lines in exactly the same way, but, we argued, it is probably safe to say that most readers will agree that in the first line they may stress fairly heavily seven or eight syllables, whereas in the second line they may stress only three or four:

The óld dóg bárks báckward without gétting úp.
Í can remémber when hé was a púp.

And so we can say that the form (a relatively effortful, hard-to-speak line followed by a bouncy line) shapes and is part of the content (a description of a dog that no longer has the energy or the strength to leap up, followed by a memory of the dog as a puppy).

Thinking further about Frost's poem, we notice something else about the form. The first line is about a dog, but the second line is about a dog *and* a human being ("*I* can remember"). The speaker must be getting on, too. And although nothing is said about the dog as a *symbol* of human life, surely the reader, prompted by the title of the poem, makes a connection between the life span of a dog and that of a human being. Part of what makes the poem effective is that this point is *not* stated explicitly, not belabored. Readers have the pleasure of making the connection for themselves—under Frost's careful guidance.

Everyone knows that puppies are frisky and that old dogs are not—though perhaps not until we encountered this poem did we think twice about the fact that "the old dog barks backward without getting up." Or let's put it this way:

- Many people may have noticed this behavior, but
- perhaps only Frost thought (to use Lady Murasaki's words), "There must never come a time . . . when people do not know about this." And,
- fortunately for all of us, Frost had the ability to put his perception into memorable words.

Part of what makes this poem especially memorable is the *relationship* between the two lines. Neither line in itself is very special, but because of the counterpoint, the whole is more than the sum of the parts. Skill in handling language, obviously, is indispensable if the writer is to produce literature. A person may know a great deal about dogs and may be a great lover of dogs, but knowledge and love are not enough equipment to write even a two-line poem about a dog (or the span of life, or both). Poems, like other kinds of literature, are produced by people who know how to delight us with verbal performances.

We can easily see that Robert Frost's "The Span of Life" is a work of literature—a work that uses language in a special way—if we contrast it with another short work in rhyme:

Thirty days hath September,
April, June, and November;
All the rest have thirty-one
Excepting February alone,
Which has twenty-eight in fine,
Till leap year gives it twenty-nine.

This information is important, but it is only information. The lines rhyme, giving the work some form, but there is nothing very interesting about it. (Perhaps you will want to take issue with this opinion.) The poem is true and therefore useful, but it is not of compelling interest, probably because it only *tells* us facts rather than *shows* or *presents* human experience. We all remember the lines, but they offer neither the pleasure of an insight nor the pleasure of an interesting tune. "Thirty days" has nothing of what the poet Thomas Gray said characterizes literature: "Thoughts that breathe, and words that burn."

Reading in Slow Motion

In this chapter, and in the next, we focus on the skills that careful study of literary language requires. "Close reading" is perhaps the most familiar name for this technique of heightened responsiveness to the words on the page. But another, employed by the literary critics Reuben A. Brower and Richard Poirier, may be even better. They refer to "reading in slow motion." Brower, for example, speaks of "slowing down the process of reading to observe what is happening, in order to attend very closely to the words, their uses, and their meanings." This sort of reading, he explains, involves looking and listening with special alertness, slowly, without rushing or feeling impatient if a work puzzles us at first encounter.[1]

As Brower and Poirier point out, sometimes we are so intrigued or moved by a writer's operations with words that we are led to "slow down" in our reading, lingering over verbal details and vivid images—"a watersmooth-silver / stallion" in Cummings's poem about Buffalo Bill (page 320), or "Babette danced out to where the fig-trees were," in Chopin's "Ripe Figs" (page 9). Or else we find that we want to return to a poem, or to a key section of a story or a scene in a play, to articulate— "slow motion" style—why it has affected us as powerfully as it has.

"Close" or slow-motion reading can help you to understand and enjoy a work that at first seems strange or obscure. When we examine a piece of literature with care and intensity, we are not taking it apart in a destructive way but, instead, are

---

[1]The quotation is taken from Brower's introduction to *In Defense of Reading: A Reader's Approach to Literary Criticism*, ed. Reuben A. Brower and Richard Poirier (1962). See also Brower, *The Fields of Light: An Experiment in Critical Reading* (1951); and Poirier, *Poetry and Pragmatism* (1992).

seeking to satisfy our curiosity about how the writer organized it. And almost always, our increased *understanding* of the work results in increased *enjoyment*. Very few poems have been made worse by close reading, and many have been made better—made, that is, more accessible and interesting, deeper, and more rewarding.

This point is clarified when we recall what it's like to watch a scene from a movie in slow motion, or a TV replay in slow motion of a touchdown run in a football game. In slow-motion film we perceive details we might otherwise have missed—the subtle changes in expression on an actress's face, for example, or the interplay of gestures among performers at a climactic moment in the action. Similarly, seeing a touchdown multiple times in slow motion, and perhaps from a half-dozen camera angles, reveals to us how the play developed, who made the crucial blocks, where the defense failed. The touchdown was exciting when it took place; and it remains exciting—and frequently it becomes more so—when we slow it down in order to study and talk about it.

This chapter deals with explication, and the next with analysis. Both approaches are based on the principle that responding well to literature means

- acquiring the ability to read it closely;
- practicing this skill to become better and better at it;
- explaining and demonstrating in critical essays what we have learned.

But the two terms, while related to one another, differ in their emphasis. An **explication** moves from beginning to end of an entire work (if it is fairly short) or of a section of a work; it is sustained, meticulous, thorough, systematic. An **analysis** builds upon the habits of attention that we have gained from explicating texts and passages of texts.

When we engage in the analysis of literature, we are doing so as part of presenting an argument, a thesis, about a work. What is the central theme in this short story by Welty or that one by Updike? What is the most compelling insight into the nature of love that Adrienne Rich offers in this or that group of poems about men and women? Does Hamlet delay—and if he does, why? To deal with questions like these, we have to read the text closely and study its language carefully, but we must be selective in the pieces of textual evidence that we offer. To be sure, we can explicate a single speech in Hamlet, or an exchange between characters. But it would be a daunting assignment in a short critical essay to explicate an entire scene, and impossible in that space to explicate the entire play from start to finish.

Analysis goes hand in hand with the job of presenting and proving a thesis; it goes hand in hand with explication as well, taking the form of close reading, or reading in slow motion, as its foundation. But rather than say more about analysis here, let's turn to explication first and learn what we can discover about literature through it. As you'll see, one of the things we quickly realize is that close reading of literary works makes us not only better readers but also better writers, attuned more sharply and sensitively to the organization of the language in our own prose.

Explication

A line-by-line or episode-by-episode commentary on what is going on in a text is an explication (literally, an unfolding or spreading out). An explication does not deal with the writer's life and times, and it is not a paraphrase or rewording—though it may include paraphrase. Rather, it is a commentary that reveals your sense of the meaning of the work and its structure. When we explicate a text, we ask questions about the meanings of words, the implications of metaphors and images, the speaker's tone of voice as we initially hear it and it develops and perhaps changes. How is this literary work put together? How did the writer organize it to prompt from me the response I had (and am having) to it? How does it begin, and what happens next, and next after that? And so on, through to the end.

It takes some skill to work your way along in an explication without saying, "In line one . . . In the second line . . . In the third line . . ." This sounds mechanical and formulaic. Make good use of transitional words and phrases so that your commentary will feel to your reader more natural, with a better pace and rhythm. For example: "The speaker begins by suggesting . . . The poem then shifts in direction . . . In the next paragraph, however, the narrator implies . . ."

A Sample Explication

The following short poem is by Langston Hughes (1902–67), an African American writer. For biographical information, see page 343.

Harlem

What happens to a dream deferred?

    Does it dry up
    like a raisin in the sun?
    Or fester like a sore—
    And then run?   5
    Does it stink like rotten meat?
    Or crust and sugar over—
    like a syrupy sweet?

    Maybe it just sags
    like a heavy load.   10

    Or does it explode?

[1951]

Different readers will respond at least somewhat differently to any work. On the other hand, because writers want to communicate, they try to control their readers' responses, and they count on their readers to understand the denotations of words as they understand them. Hughes assumed that his readers knew that Harlem was the site of a large African American community in New York City. A reader who confuses the title of the poem with Haarlem in the Netherlands will wonder what this poem is saying about the tulip-growing center in northern Holland. (Explication is based on the assumption that the poem contains a meaning and that by studying the work thoughtfully we can unfold the meaning or meanings.)

Let's assume that the reader understands Hughes is talking about Harlem, New York, and that the "dream deferred" refers to the unfulfilled hopes of African Americans who live in a society dominated by whites. But Hughes does not say "hopes," he says "dream," and he does not say "unfulfilled," he says "deferred." You might ask yourself exactly what differences there are between these words. Next, after you have read the poem several times, you might think about which expression is better in this context, "unfulfilled hopes" or "dream deferred," and why.

Working toward an Explication

In preparing to write an explication, first type on a computer, or handwrite, the complete text of the work that you will explicate—usually a poem but sometimes a short passage of prose. *Don't* photocopy it; the act of typing or writing it will help you to get into the piece, word by word, comma by comma. Type or write it *double-spaced*, so that you will have room for your annotations as you study the piece. It's advisable to make a few photocopies (or to print a few copies, if you are using a computer) before you start annotating so that if one page gets too cluttered you can continue working on a clean copy. Or you may want to use one copy for a certain kind of annotation—let's say those concerning imagery—and other copies for other kinds of notes—let's say those concerning meter or wordplay. If you are writing on a computer, you can highlight words, boldface them, put them in capitals (for instance, to indicate accented syllables), and so forth.

Let's turn to an explication of the poem, a detailed examination of the whole. Here are the preliminary jottings of a student, Bill Horner.

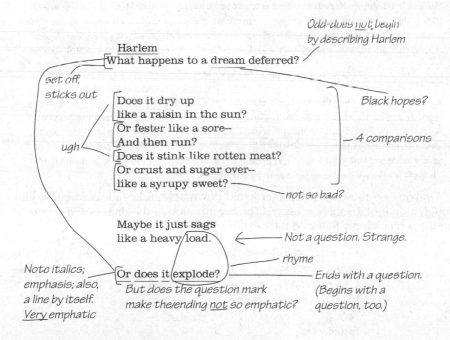

These annotations chiefly get at the structure of the poem, the relationship of its parts. Horner notices that the poem begins with a line set off by itself and ends with a line set off by itself, and he also notices that each of these lines is a question. Further, he indicates that each of these two lines is emphasized in other ways: The first begins farther to the left than any of the other lines—as though the other lines are subheadings or in some way subordinate—and the last is italicized.

Journal Entries: A Reader's Notes on "Harlem"

Bill Horner later wrote these entries in his journal:

Feb. 18. Since the title is "Harlem," it's obvious that the "dream" is by African American people. Also, obvious that Hughes thinks that if the "dream" doesn't become real there may be riots ("explode"). I like "raisin in the sun" (maybe because I like the play), and I like the business about "a syrupy sweet"—much more pleasant than the festering sore and the rotten meat. But if the dream becomes "sweet," what's wrong with that? Why should something "sweet" explode?

Feb. 21. Prof. McCabe said to think of structure or form of a poem as a sort of architecture, a building with a foundation, floors, etc., topped by a roof—but since we read a poem from top to bottom, it's like a building upside down. Title is foundation (even though it's at top); last line is roof, capping the whole. As you read, you add layers. Foundation of "Harlem" is a question (first line). Then, set back a bit from foundation, or built on it by white space, a tall room (7 lines high, with 4 questions); then, on top of this room, another room (lines, statement, not a question). Funny; I thought that in poems all stanzas are the same number of lines. Then—more white space, so another unit— the roof. Man, this roof is going to fall in—"explodes." Not just the roof, maybe the whole house.

Feb. 21, p.m. I get it; one line at start, one line at end; both are questions, but the last sort of says (because it is in italics) that it is the most likely answer to the question of the first line. The last line is also a question, but it's still an answer. The big stanza (7 lines) has 4 questions: 2 lines, 2 lines, 1 line, 2 lines. Maybe the switch to 1 line is to give some variety, so as not to be dull? It's exactly in the middle of the poem. I get the progress from raisin in the sun (dried, but not so terrible), to festering sore and to stinking meat, but I still don't see what's so bad about "a syrupy sweet." Is Hughes saying that after things are very bad they will get better? But why, then, the explosion at the end?

Feb. 23. "Heavy load" and "sags" in next-to-last stanza seem to me to suggest slaves with bales of cotton, or maybe poor cotton pickers dragging big sacks of cotton. Or maybe people doing heavy labor in Harlem. Anyway, very tired. Different from running sore and stinking meat earlier; not disgusting, but pressing down, deadening. Maybe worse than a sore or rotten meat—a hard, hopeless life. And then the last line. Just one line, no fancy (and disgusting) simile. In fact, no simile at all. This is a metaphor, not a simile. Boom! Not just pressed down and tired, like maybe some racist whites think (hope?) blacks will be. Bang! Will there be survivors?

Drawing on these notes, Horner jotted down several key ideas to guide him through a draft of an analysis essay. (The organization of the draft posed no problem; the writer simply followed the organization of the poem.)

> *11 lines; short, but powerful; explosive*
> *Question (first line)*
> *answers (set off by space and also indented)*
> *"raisin in the sun" : shrinking* ⎫
> *"sore"*　　　　　　　　　　　⎬ *disgusting*
> *"rotten meat"*　　　　　　　　⎭
> *"syrupy sweet" : relief from disgusting comparisons*
> *final question (last line): explosion?*
> 　*explosive (powerful) because:*
> 　　*short, condensed, packed*
> 　　*in italics*
> 　　*stands by self—like first line*
> 　　*no fancy comparison; very direct*

A Sample Essay by a Student (Final Version):
"Langston Hughes's 'Harlem'"

Here is Bill Horner's final essay.

Bill Horner

Professor McCabe

English 122

6 February 2013

Langston Hughes's "Harlem"

"Harlem" is a poem that is only eleven lines long, but it is charged

with power. It explodes. Hughes sets the stage, so to speak, by telling us in

the title that he is talking about Harlem, and then he begins by asking,

"What happens to a dream deferred?" The rest of the poem is set off by being

indented, as though it is the answer to his question. This answer is in three

parts (three stanzas, of different lengths).

In a way, it is wrong to speak of the answer, since the rest of the poem

consists of questions, but I think Hughes means that each question (for

instance, does a "deferred" hope "dry up / like a raisin in the sun?") really is an

answer, something that really has happened and that will happen again.

The first question, "Does it dry up / like a raisin in the sun?," is a famous

line. To compare hope to a raisin dried in the sun is to suggest a terrible

shrinking. The next two comparisons are to a "sore" and to "rotten meat."

These comparisons are less clever, but they are very effective because they

are disgusting. Then, maybe because of the disgusting comparisons, he

gives a comparison that is not at all disgusting. In this comparison he says

that maybe the "dream deferred" will "crust over— / like a syrupy sweet."

The seven lines with four comparisons are followed by a stanza of two

lines with just one comparison:

> Maybe it just sags
>
> like a heavy load.

So if we thought that this postponed dream might finally turn into something "sweet," we were kidding ourselves. Hughes comes down to earth, in a short stanza, with an image of a heavy load, which probably also calls to mind images of people bent under heavy loads, maybe of cotton, or maybe just any sort of heavy load carried by African Americans in Harlem and elsewhere.

The opening question ("What happens to a dream deferred?") was followed by four questions in seven lines, but now, with "Maybe it just sags / like a heavy load," we get a statement, as though the poet at last has found an answer. But at the end we get one more question, set off by itself and in italics: "Or does it explode?" This line itself is explosive for three reasons: It is short, it is italicized, and it is a stanza in itself. It's also interesting that this line, unlike the earlier lines, does not use a simile. It uses a metaphor. It's almost as though Hughes is saying, "O.K., we've had enough fancy ways of talking about this terrible situation; here it is, 'boom.'"

[New page]

Work Cited

Hughes, Langston. "Harlem." *Literature for Composition*. Ed. Sylvan Barnet,

    William Burto, and William E. Cain. 10th ed. New York: Pearson, 2014.

    136. Print.

Joining the Conversation: Critical Thinking and Writing

1. Bill Horner's explication suggests that the comparison with "a syrupy sweet" deliberately misleads the reader into thinking the ending will be happy, and it thus serves to make the real ending even more powerful. In class another student

suggested that Hughes may be referring to African Americans who play Uncle Tom, people who adopt a smiling manner in order to cope with an oppressive society. Which explanation do you prefer, and why? What do you think of combining the two?

Does some method or principle help us decide which interpretation is correct? Can we, in fact, talk about a "correct" interpretation, or only about a plausible or implausible interpretation and an interesting or uninteresting interpretation?

2. In *The Collected Poems of Langston Hughes* (1994), the editors title this poem "Harlem." But in the *Selected Poems of Langston Hughes* (1959), published when the poet was still alive, the poem is titled "Dream Deferred." Which title do you think is more effective? Do you interpret the poem differently depending on how it is titled? How might a reader—who knew nothing about Hughes—respond to the poem if he or she came upon it with the title "Dream Deferred"?

MyLiteratureLab® *For additional resources for "Harlem," log in to* www .myliteraturelab.com *where you will find a Longman Lecture, Audio Performance, Comprehension Quiz, Short Evaluation Exercises, and Essay Prompts, as well as an About the Author, Bibliography, Links, and Critical Overview for Hughes (under Student Resources).*

Note: Another explication, of W. B. Yeats's "The Balloon of the Mind," appears in Chapter 18.

Explication as Argument

We have said that an explication unfolds or opens up or interprets a work by calling attention to such things as the speaker's tone of voice and the implications in images. It might seem, then, to be an objective report, the sort of explanatory writing that is called expository rather than argumentative.

But because literature makes considerable use of connotations and symbolic meanings—"A rolling stone gathers no moss" is not essentially a statement about stones and moss but about something else—readers may differ in what they understand words to mean. The writer of an explication not only examines the meanings of specific words and images but also, having come to a conclusion about what the details add up to, argues an interpretation and supports a thesis.

What distinguishes argument from exposition is this: In argument, some statements are offered as *reasons* for others. Because writers of arguments assume that their readers may not at the outset share their views, in their writing they offer evidence to support their assertions.

If you reread Bill Horner's explication of "Harlem," you will notice that in speaking of the line "*Or does it explode?*" Horner says, "This line is explosive for three reasons." He then specifies the three reasons. That is, he argues his case, presenting three pieces of supporting evidence: Hughes's line is short, it is italicized, and it is a stanza in itself.

True, much of Horner's explication is expository writing when he says that the poem consists of "three parts (three stanzas, of different lengths)." There can be little disagreement between writer and reader here—although perhaps a reader might respond, "No, the title is also part of the poem, so the poem consists of four parts."

A reader who is looking for an argument—in the sense of a quarrel, not in the sense of a reasoned discussion—can find it with almost any piece of writing. But, again, our point is that because expository writing does not assume a difference of opinion, it chiefly sets forth information rather than seek to make a case. Argumentative writing, on the other hand, assumes that it must set forth information in a way that persuades the reader of its truth, which means that it must give evidence.

Pure exposition—let's say, information about how to register for classes, or information about what is likely to be on the final examination—is not concerned with persuading readers to accept a thesis. But an explication, even though it might seem only to clarify the meanings of the words in a poem, argues a thesis about the work as a whole.

Notice Bill Horner's opening sentence:

"Harlem" is a poem that is only eleven lines long, but it is charged with power.

What is Horner's thesis? Certainly not that the poem is "only eleven lines long"—a writer hardly needs to argue for this assertion. Rather, Horner's thesis is that the poem "is charged with power." In the rest of the explication he offers evidence that supports this assertion. To persuade us, he points out that certain lines are indented, that certain figures of speech have certain implications, and that the last stanza is italicized and consists of only one line.

You may disagree: You may not think the poem "is charged with power," and you may think that Horner has misread certain lines. We mentioned, in our first topic for "Critical Thinking and Writing," that when Horner offered this interpretation in class, another student saw a different meaning in "syrupy sweet" (line 8). But if you disagree, whether with the reading as a whole or with the interpretation of a single image, it's not enough to assert that you disagree. You will have to offer an argument, which is to say you will have to set forth reasons in your effort to persuade your readers.

Your goal in an explication is to present your insights about aspects of the poem's language. Even more, you want these insights to add up to a whole. When related to one another, they should enable your reader to understand the poem, overall, more clearly, and to enjoy it more fully. Ask yourself, as you study the poem and develop your draft of the paper,

What is my thesis (my central point, my argument)?

This question will help you to make your essay coherent and unified. It is a reminder that an explication is more than a set of observations. The best explications make use of details to teach the reader something new about the poem as a whole.

✔ CHECKLIST: *Drafting an Explication*

Overall Considerations

☐ Does the poem imply a story of some sort, for instance, the speaker's account of a love affair, or of a response to nature? If so, what is its beginning, middle, and end?

☐ If you detect a story in the speaker's mind, a change of mood—for instance, a shift from bitterness that a love affair has ended to hope for its renewal—is this change communicated in part by the connotations of certain words? By syntax? By metrical shifts?

□ Do the details all cohere into a meaningful whole? If so, your explication will largely be an argument on behalf of this thesis.

Detailed Considerations

□ If the poem has a title other than the first line, what are the implications of the title?

□ Are there clusters or patterns of imagery, for instance, religious images, economic images, or images drawn from nature? If so, how do they contribute to the meaning of the poem?

□ Is irony (understatement or overstatement) used? To what effect?

□ How do the connotations of certain words (for instance, *dad* rather than *father*) help to establish the meaning?

□ What are the implications of the syntax—for instance, of notably simple or notably complex sentences? What do such sentences tell us about the speaker?

□ Do metrical variations occur? If so, what is their significance?

□ Do rhyming words have some meaningful connection, as in the clichés *moon* and *June, dove* and *love*?

□ What are the implications of the poem's appearance on the page—for example, of an indented line, or of the stanzaic pattern? (If the poem consists of two stanzas of four lines each, does the second stanza offer a reversal of the first?)

Why Write? Purpose and Audience

In Chapter 2 we discussed audience and purpose, but a few further words may be useful here. People write explications (and other essays on literature) not only to communicate but also to clarify and to account for their responses to material that interests or excites or frustrates them. In putting words on paper you will have to take a second and a third look at what is before you and at what is within you. And so the process of writing is a way of learning. The last word is never said about complex thoughts and feelings, but when we write we hope to make at least a little progress in the difficult but rewarding job of talking about our responses. We learn, and then we hope to interest our reader in what we've learned, because we discovered something that for one reason or another is worth talking about.

When you write, you transform your responses into words that will let your reader share your perceptions, your enthusiasms, and even your doubts. This sharing is, in effect, teaching. Students often think they are writing for the teacher, but this is a misconception. When you write, *you* are the teacher. An essay on literature is an attempt to help someone to see something as you see it.

If you are not writing for the teacher, for whom are you writing? For yourself, of course, but also for others. Occasionally, in an effort to help you develop an awareness that what you write depends partly on your audience, your instructor may specify an audience, suggesting that you write for high school students or for the readers of the *New Yorker* or *Sports Illustrated*. But when an audience is not specified, write for your classmates.

- If you keep your classmates in mind as your audience, you will *not* write, "William Shakespeare, England's most famous playwright," because that remark seems to imply that your reader does not know Shakespeare's nationality or trade.
- On the other hand, you *will* write, "Sei Shōnagon, a lady of the court in medieval Japan," because you can reasonably assume that your classmates do not know who she is.

Your Turn: Poems for Explication

The basic assignment here is to explicate the poems, but your instructor may also ask you to respond to some or all of the questions that follow each poem.

WILLIAM SHAKESPEARE

William Shakespeare (1564–1616), born in Stratford-upon-Avon in England, is chiefly known as a dramatic poet, but he also wrote nondramatic poetry. In 1609 a volume of 154 of his sonnets was published, apparently without his permission. Probably he chose to keep his sonnets unpublished not because he thought that they were of little value but because it was more prestigious to be an amateur (unpublished) poet than a professional (published) poet. Although the sonnets were published in 1609, they were probably written in the mid-1590s, when there was a vogue for sonneteering. A contemporary writer in 1598 said that Shakespeare's "sugared Sonnets [circulate] among his private friends."

Sonnet 73

That time of year thou mayst in me behold
When yellow leaves, or none, or few, do hang
Upon those boughs which shake against the cold,
Bare ruined choirs° where late the sweet birds sang.
In me thou see'st the twilight of such day   5
As after sunset fadeth in the west,
Which by-and-by black night doth take away,
Death's second self that seals up all in rest.
In me thou see'st the glowing of such fire
That on the ashes of his youth doth lie,   10
As the deathbed whereon it must expire,
Consumed with that which it was nourished by.
    This thou perceiv'st, which makes thy love more strong,
    To love that well which thou must leave ere long.

4 choir the part of the church where services are sung.

Joining the Conversation: Critical Thinking and Writing

1. In the first quatrain (the first four lines) to what "time of year" does Shakespeare compare himself? In the second quatrain (lines 5–8) to what does he compare himself? In the third? If the sequence of the three quatrains were reversed, what would be gained or lost?
2. In line 8, what is "Death's second self"? What implications do you perceive in "seals up all in rest," as opposed, for instance, to "brings most welcome rest"?
3. In line 13, exactly what is "This"?
4. In line 14, suppose in place of "To love that well which thou must leave ere long," Shakespeare had written "To love me well whom thou must leave ere long." What if anything would have been gained or lost?
5. What insights into your own feelings and experiences does this poem give you? Please explain, being as specific as you can.

MyLiteratureLab® *For additional resources for Sonnet 73, log in to* www
.myliteraturelab.com *where you will find a Longman Lecture, Interactive Reading,
Comprehension Quiz, Short Evaluation Exercises, and Essay Prompts,
as well as an About the Author, Bibliography, Links, and Critical Overview for
Shakespeare (under Student Resources).*

JOHN DONNE

*John Donne (1572–1631) was born into a Roman Catholic family in England, but
in the 1590s he abandoned that faith. In 1615 he became an Anglican priest and
soon was known as a great preacher. One hundred sixty of his sermons survive,
including one with the famous line "No man is an island, entire of itself; every man
is a piece of the continent, a part of the main; if a clod be washed away by the sea,
Europe is the less . . . ; and therefore never send to know for whom the bell tolls; it
tolls for thee." From 1621 until his death he was dean of St. Paul's Cathedral in
London. His love poems (often bawdy and cynical) are his early work, and his "Holy
Sonnets" (among the greatest religious poems written in English) his later work.*

Holy Sonnet XIV

Batter my heart, three-personed God; for you
As yet but knock, breathe, shine, and seek to mend;
That I may rise and stand, o'erthrow me, and bend
Your force, to break, blow, burn, and make me new.
I, like an usurped town, to another due,   5
Labor to admit you, but oh, to no end.
Reason, your viceroy in me, me should defend,
But is captived, and proves weak or untrue.
Yet dearly I love you, and would be loved fain,
But am betrothed unto your enemy: 10
Divorce me, untie, or break that knot again,

Take me to you, imprison me, for I
Except you enthrall me, never shall be free,
Nor ever chaste, except you ravish me.

[1633]

Joining the Conversation: Critical Thinking and Writing

1. Explain the paradoxes (apparent contradictions) in lines 2, 3, 13, and 14. Explain the double meanings of "enthrall" (line 13) and "ravish" (line 14).
2. In lines 1–4, what is God implicitly compared to (considering especially lines 2 and 4)? How does this comparison lead into the comparison that dominates lines 5–8? What words in lines 9–12 are especially related to the earlier lines?
3. What is gained by piling up verbs in lines 2–4?
4. Are sexual references necessarily irreverent in a religious poem? Present a brief argument in which you say yes, and then another in which you say no. Make each argument as convincing as you can.

MyLiteratureLab® *For additional resources for Holy Sonnet XIV ("Batter my heart"), log in to www.myliteraturelab.com where you will find a Longman Lecture, as well as an About the Author, Bibliography, Links, and Critical Overview for Donne (under Student Resources).*

EMILY BRONTË

Emily Brontë (1818–48) spent most of her short life (she died of tuberculosis) in an English village on the Yorkshire moors. The sister of Charlotte Brontë (author of Jane Eyre*) and of Anne Brontë, Emily is best known for her novel* Wuthering Heights *(1847), but she was a considerable poet, and her first significant publication (1846) was in a volume of poems by the three sisters.*

Spellbound

The night is darkening round me,
The wild winds coldly blow;
But a tyrant spell has bound me
And I cannot, cannot go.

The giant trees are bending   5
Their bare boughs weighed with snow.
And the storm is fast descending,
And yet I cannot go.

Clouds beyond clouds above me,
Wastes beyond wastes below;   10
But nothing drear can move me;
I will not, cannot go.

[1837]

Joining the Conversation: Critical Thinking and Writing

1. What exactly is a "spell," and what does it mean to be "spellbound"?
2. What difference, if any, would it make if the first line said "has darkened" instead of "is darkening"?
3. What difference would it make, if any, if lines 4 and 12 were switched?
4. What does "drear" (line 11) mean? Is this word too unusual? Should the poet have used a more familiar word?
5. Describe the speaker's state of mind. Have you ever experienced anything like this yourself? What was the situation and how did you move beyond it?

LI-YOUNG LEE

Li-Young Lee was born in 1957 in Jakarta, Indonesia, of Chinese parents. In 1964 his family brought him to the United States. He was educated at the University of Pittsburgh, the University of Arizona, and the State University of New York, Brockport. He now lives in Chicago, where he works as an artist.

I Ask My Mother to Sing

She begins, and my grandmother joins her.
Mother and daughter sing like young girls.
If my father were alive, he would play
his accordion and sway like a boat.

I've never been in Peking, or the Summer Palace,   5
nor stood on the great Stone Boat to watch
the rain begin on Kuen Ming Lake, the picnickers
running away in the grass.

But I love to hear it sung;
how the waterlilies fill with rain until   10
they overturn, spilling water into water,
then rock back, and fill with more.

Both women have begun to cry.
But neither stops her song.

[1986]

Joining the Conversation: Critical Thinking and Writing

1. Why might the speaker ask the women to sing?
2. Why do the women cry? Why do they continue to sing?
3. Is this poem simple, or complex? Both? Please point to specific details to support your argument.

RANDALL JARRELL

Randall Jarrell (1914–65)—the accent in Jarrell is on the second syllable—was educated at Vanderbilt, where he majored in psychology. After serving with the air force in World War II as a control tower operator, he taught in several colleges and universities, meanwhile establishing a reputation as a poet and as a literary critic.

The Death of the Ball Turret Gunner

From my mother's sleep I fell into the State,
And I hunched in its belly till my wet fur froze.
Six miles from earth, loosed from its dream of life,
I woke to black flak and the nightmare fighters.
When I died they washed me out of the turret with a hose.

[1955]

Jarrell has furnished an explanatory note: "A ball turret was a plexiglass sphere set into the belly of a B-17 or B-24, and inhabited by two .50 caliber machine-guns and one man, a short small man. When this gunner tracked with his machine-guns a fighter attacking his bomber from below, he revolved with the turret; hunched upside-down in his little sphere, he looked like the fetus in the womb. The fighters which attacked him were armed with cannon firing explosive shells. The hose was a steam hose."

Joining the Conversation: Critical Thinking and Writing

1. What is implied in the first line? In "I woke to . . . nightmare"? Taking account of the title, do you think "wet fur" is literal or metaphoric or both? Do you find the simplicity of the last line anticlimactic? How does it continue the metaphor of birth?
2. Why do you think Jarrell ended each line with punctuation?

MyLiteratureLab® *For additional resources for "The Death of the Ball Turret Gunner," log in to* www.myliteraturelab.com *where you will find a Comprehension Quiz, Short Evaluation Exercises, and Essay Prompts, as well as an About the Author, Links, and Critical Overview for Jarrell (under Student Resources).*

CHAPTER 7

Reading Literature Closely: Analysis

*Until one tries to write about it, the work of art remains a sort
of aesthetic blur. . . . After seeing the work, write about it.
You cannot be satisfied for very long in simply putting down
what you felt. You have to go further.*

ARTHUR DANTO

Chapter Preview

After reading this chapter you will be able to

- Define *analysis* and describe the process for analyzing literary texts
- Analyze literary texts
- Write a summary
- Write a paraphrase
- Write a comparison
- Evaluate literary texts
- Choose a topic and develop an analytic thesis
- Analyze a student's analytical essay from first response to final draft

---

Analysis

Explication is a method used chiefly in the study of fairly short poems or brief extracts from essays, stories, novels, and plays. In writing about works longer than a page or two, a more common approach than explicating is **analyzing** (literally, separating into parts in order to better understand the whole). An analysis of, say, *The Color Purple* may consider the functions of the setting or the uses that certain minor characters serve; an analysis of *Hamlet* may consider the comic passages or the reasons for Hamlet's delay; an analysis of *Death of a Salesman* may consider the depiction of women or the causes of Willy Loman's failure. In effect, an analytic essay usually advances a thesis and offers arguments—reasons, evidence—in support of the thesis.

Most of the writing that you will do in college—not only in your English courses but in courses in history, sociology, economics, fine arts, and philosophy—will involve **analysis,** a method we commonly use in thinking about complex matters and in attempting to account for our responses to them. Watching Venus Williams play tennis, we may admire her serve, or her backhand, or the execution of several brilliant plays, and then think more generally about the concentration and flexibility that allow her to capitalize on her opponent's momentary weakness. And of course when we want to improve our own game, we try to analyze our performance. When writing is our game, we analyze our responses to a work, trying to name them and account for them. We analyze our notes, looking for ideas that connect, searching for significant patterns, and later we analyze our drafts, looking for strengths and weaknesses. Similarly, in peer review we analyze the draft of a fellow student, seeing how the parts (individual words, sentences, whole paragraphs, the tentative title, and so on) relate to one another and fit together as a whole.

To develop an analysis of a work, we tend to formulate questions and then to answer them. We ask a variety of questions:

- What is the function of the setting in this story or play?
- Why has this character been introduced?
- What is the author trying to tell us?
- How exactly can I describe the tone?
- What is the difference in assumptions between this essay and that one?

This book contains an anthology of literary works for you to read, respond to, and then write about, and after most of the works we pose questions about them. We also pose general questions on essays, fiction, drama, and poetry. These questions may stimulate your thinking and thus help you write. Our concern as teachers of writing is not so much with the answers to these questions; we believe and we ask you to believe that there are no "right" answers, only more or less persuasive ones, to most questions about literature—as about life. Our aim is to help you to pose questions that will stimulate your thinking.

Analyzing a Story from the Hebrew Bible: The Judgment of Solomon

A brief analysis of a very short story about King Solomon, from the Hebrew Bible (often called the Old Testament), may be useful here. Because the story is short, the analysis can consider all or almost all of the story's parts, and therefore the analysis can seem relatively complete. ("*Seem* relatively complete" because the analysis will in fact be far from complete, since the number of reasonable things that can be said about a work is almost as great as the number of its readers. And a given reader might, at a later date, offer a different reading from what that reader offers today.)

The following story about King Solomon, customarily called the Judgment of Solomon, appears in the Hebrew Bible, in the latter part of the third chapter of the book called 1 Kings or First Kings, probably written in the mid-sixth century BCE. The translation is from the King James Version of the Bible (1611).

Two expressions in the story need clarification: (1) The woman who "overlaid" her child in her sleep rolled over on the child and suffocated it; and (2) it is said of a woman that her "bowels yearned upon her son," that is, her heart longed for her son. (In Hebrew psychology, the bowels were thought to be the seat of emotion.)

The Judgment of Solomon

Then came there two women, that were harlots, unto the king, and stood before him. And the one woman said, "O my lord, I and this woman dwell in one house, and I was delivered of a child with her in the house. And it came to pass the third day after that I was delivered, that this woman was delivered also: and we were together; there was no stranger in the house, save we two in the house. And this woman's child died in the night; because she overlaid it. And she arose at midnight, and took my son from beside me, while thine handmaid slept, and laid it in her bosom, and laid her dead child in my bosom. And when I rose in the morning to give my child suck, behold, it was dead: but when I considered it in the morning, behold, it was not my son, which I did bear."

And the other woman said, "Nay; but the living is my son, and the dead is thy son." And this said, "No; but the dead is thy son, and the living is my son." Thus they spake before the king.

Then said the king, "The one saith, 'This is my son that liveth, and thy son is dead': and the other saith, 'Nay; but thy son is the dead, and my son is the living.'" And the king said, "Bring me a sword." And they brought a sword before the king. And the king said, "Divide the living child in two, and give half to the one, and half to the other."

Then spake the woman whose the living child was unto the king, for her bowels yearned upon her son, and she said, "O my lord, give her the living child, and in no wise slay it." But the other said, "Let it be neither mine nor thine, but divide it."

5   Then the king answered and said, "Give her the living child, and in no wise slay it: she is the mother thereof."

And all Israel heard of the judgment which the king had judged; and they feared the king, for they saw that the wisdom of God was in him to do judgment.

Analyzing the Story

Let's begin by analyzing the **form** or the shape of the story. One form or shape that we notice is this:

The story moves from a problem to a solution.

We can also say, still speaking of the overall form, that

the story moves from quarreling and talk of death to unity and talk of life.

In short, the story has a happy ending, a form that (because it provides an optimistic view of life and also a sense of completeness) gives most people pleasure.

In thinking about a work of literature, it is always useful to take notice of the basic form of the whole, the overall structural pattern. Doubtless you are already familiar with many basic patterns, for example,

tragedy (joy yielding to sorrow) and
romantic comedy (angry conflict yielding to joyful union).

If you think even briefly about verbal works, you'll notice the structures or patterns that govern songs, episodes in soap operas, political speeches (beginning with the candidate's expression of pleasure at being in Duluth, and ending with "God bless you all"), detective stories, westerns, and so on. And just as viewers of a western film experience one western in the context of others, so readers experience one story in the context of similar stories, and one poem in the context of others.

Looking at its form, we can say that The Judgment of Solomon is a sort of detective story: There is a death, followed by a conflict in the testimony of the witnesses, and then a solution by a shrewd outsider. Consider Solomon's predicament. Ordinarily in literature, characters are sharply defined and individualized, yet the essence of a detective story is that the culprit should *not* be easily recognized as wicked, and here nothing seems to distinguish the two petitioners. Solomon is confronted by "two women, that were harlots." Until late in the story—that is, up to the time Solomon suggests dividing the child—they are described only as "the one woman," "the other woman," "the one," "the other."

Does the story suffer from weak characterization? If we think analytically about this issue, we realize that the point surely is *not* to make each woman distinct. Rather, the point is (until late in the story) to make the women as alike as possible, so that we cannot tell which of the two is speaking the truth. Like Solomon, we have nothing to go on; neither witness is known to be more honest than the other, and there are no other witnesses to support or refute either woman.

Analysis is concerned with

- seeing the relationships between the parts of a work, but it is also concerned with
- taking notice of what is *not* in the work.

A witness would destroy the story, or turn it into an utterly different story. Another thing missing from this story is an explicit editorial comment or interpretation, except for the brief remark at the end that the people "feared the king." If we had read the story in the so-called Geneva Bible (1557–60), which is the translation of the Bible that Shakespeare was familiar with, we would have found a marginal comment: "Her motherly affection herein appeareth that she had rather endure the rigour of the lawe, than see her child cruelly slaine." Would you agree that it is better, at least in this story, for the reader to draw conclusions than for the storyteller explicitly to point them out?

Solomon wisely contrives a situation in which these two claimants, who seem so similar, will reveal their true natures: The mother will reveal her love, and the liar will reveal her hard heart. The early symmetry (the competing identities of the two women) pleases the reader, and so does the device by which we can at last distinguish between the two women.

But even near the end there is a further symmetry. To save the child's life, the true mother gives up her claim, crying out, "Give her the living child, and in no wise slay it." The author (or, rather, the translator who produced this part of the King James Version) takes these very words, with no change whatsoever, and puts them into Solomon's mouth as the king's final judgment. Solomon too says, "Give her the living child, and in no wise slay it," but now the sentence takes on a new meaning. In the first sentence, "her" refers to the liar (the true mother says to give the child to "her"); in Solomon's sentence, "her" refers to the true mother: "Give her the living child. . . ." Surely we take pleasure in the fact that the very words by which the mother renounces her child are the words that (1) reveal to Solomon the truth, and that (2) Solomon uses to restore the child to his mother.

This analysis has talked chiefly about the relations of parts, and it has tried to explain why the two women in this story are *not* distinct until Solomon finds a way to reveal their distinctive natures: If the story is to demonstrate Solomon's wisdom, the women must seem identical until Solomon can show that they differ. But our analysis could have gone into some other topic. Let's consider several possibilities.

A student might begin by asking this question: Although it is important for the women to be highly similar, why are they harlots? (It is too simple to answer that the women in the story are harlots because the author is faithfully reporting a historical episode in Solomon's career. The story is widely recognized as a folktale that is also found in other ancient cultures.) One possible reason for making the women harlots is that the story demands that there be no witnesses; by using harlots, the author disposed of husbands, parents, and siblings who might otherwise be expected to live with the women. A second possible reason is that the author wanted to show that Solomon's justice extended to all, not only to respectable folk. Third, perhaps the author wished to reject or to complicate the stereotype of the harlot as a thoroughly disreputable person. The author rejected or complicated the harlot by introducing another (and truer?) stereotype, the mother motivated by overwhelming maternal love.

Other Topics for Analysis

1. Another kind of analytic essay might go beyond the structure of the individual work, to the relation of the work to some larger whole. For instance, the writer might approach The Judgment of Solomon from the point of view of gender criticism (discussed in Appendix A). In this story, it might be argued, wisdom is an attribute only of a male; women are either deceitful or emotional. From this point the writer might set out to create a research essay on gender in a larger whole, certain books of the Hebrew Bible.

2. We might also analyze the story in the context of other examples of what scholars call Wisdom Literature (the Book of Proverbs and Ecclesiastes, for instance). Notice that Solomon's judgment leads the people to *fear* him—because his wisdom is great, formidable, and God-inspired.

It happens that we do not know who wrote The Judgment of Solomon, but the authors of most later works of literature are known, and therefore some critics seek to analyze a given work within the context of the author's life. Evidence drawn from the author's biography would be used to support an interpretation. For some other critics, the larger context would be the reading process, which includes the psychology of the reader. (Biographical criticism and reader response criticism are discussed in Appendix A.)

3. Still another analysis—again, remember that a work can be analyzed from many points of view—might examine two or more translations of the story. You do not need to know Hebrew in order to compare this early seventeenth century translation with a twentieth-century version such as that of the New Jerusalem Bible or the Revised English Bible. You might argue that one version is, on literary grounds, more effective. Such an essay might include an attempt, by means of a comparison, to analyze the effect of the archaic language of the King James Version. Does the somewhat unfamiliar language turn a reader off, or does it add mystery or dignity or authority to the tale, valuable qualities perhaps not found in the modern version? By the way, in the Revised English Bible, Solomon does *not* exactly repeat the mother's plea. The mother says, "Let her have the baby," and Solomon then says, "Give the living baby to the first woman." In the New Jerusalem Bible, after the mother says, "Let them give her the live child," Solomon says, "Give the live child to the first woman." If you prefer one version to the other two, why not try to analyze the reasons for your preference?

Finally, it should be mentioned that an analysis of the structure of a work, in which the relationships of the parts to the whole are considered, allows the work to be regarded as independent of the external world. If we argue, say, that literature should in all respects reflect life, and we want to analyze the work against reality as we see it, we may find ourselves severely judging The Judgment of Solomon. We might ask if it is likely that a great king would bother to hear the case of two prostitutes quarreling over a child, or if it is likely that the false claimant would really call for the killing of the child. Similarly, to take an absurd example, an analysis of this story in terms of its ability to evoke laughter would be laughable. The point: An analysis will be interesting and useful to a reader only insofar as the aim of the analysis seems reasonable.

Analyzing a Story from the New Testament: The Parable of the Prodigal Son

Let's now look at another brief story from the Bible, this one from the Gospel according to St. Luke, in the New Testament. Luke, the author of the third of the four Gospels, was a second-generation Christian. He was probably a Roman, though some early accounts refer to him as a Syrian; in any case, he wrote in Greek, probably composing the Gospel in about 80–85 CE. In Chapter 15, verses 11–32, Luke reports a story that Jesus told. This story, which occurs only in Luke's Gospel, is of a type called a **parable,** an extremely brief narrative from which a moral may be drawn.

The Parable of the Prodigal Son

And he said, "A certain man had two sons: and the younger of them said to his father, 'Father, give me a portion of goods that falleth to me.' And he divided unto them his living. And not many days after, the younger son gathered all together, and took his journey into a far country, and there wasted his substance with riotous living.

"And when he had spent all, there arose a mighty famine in that land, and he began to be in want. And he went and joined himself to a citizen of that country, and he sent him into his fields to feed swine. And he would fain have filled his belly with the husks that the swine did eat: and no man gave unto him. And when he came to himself, he said, 'How many hired servants of my father's have bread enough and to spare, and I perish with hunger? I will arise and go to my father, and will say unto him, "Father, I have sinned against heaven, and before thee, and am no more worthy to be called thy son: make me as one of thy hired servants."'

"And he arose, and came to his father. But when he was yet a great way off, his father saw him, and had compassion, and ran, and fell on his neck, and kissed him. And the son said unto him, 'Father, I have sinned against heaven, and in thy sight, and am no more worthy to be called thy son.' But the father said to his servants, 'Bring forth the best robe, and put it on him, and put a ring on his hand, and shoes on his feet. And bring hither the fatted calf, and kill it, and let us eat, and be merry. For this my son was dead, and is alive again; he was lost, and is found.' And they began to be merry.

"Now his elder son was in the field, and as he came and drew nigh to the house, he heard music and dancing. And he called one of the servants, and asked what these things meant. And he said unto him 'Thy brother is come, and thy father hath killed the fatted calf, because he hath received him safe and sound.' And he was angry, and would not go in: therefore came his father out, and entreated him. And he answering said to his father 'Lo, these many years do I serve thee, neither transgressed I at any time thy commandment, and yet thou never gavest me a kid, that I might make merry with friends: but as soon as this thy son was come, which hath devoured thy living with harlots, thou hast killed for him the fatted calf.' And he said unto him, 'Son, thou art ever with me, and all that I have is thine. It was meet that we should make merry, and be glad: for this thy brother was dead, and is alive again: and was lost, and is found.'"

Joining the Conversation: Critical Thinking and Writing

1. In talking about The Judgment of Solomon we commented on certain repetitions (e.g., *two* women) and contrasts (e.g., troubled beginning, happy ending), which help to give shape to the story. What parallels or contrasts (or both) do you find in the parable of the prodigal son? What *function* does the older brother serve? If he were omitted, what if anything would be lost? (Characterize him, partly by comparing him with the younger brother and with the father.)

2. Is the father foolish and sentimental? Do you approve or disapprove of his behavior at the end? In a short argumentative essay (250–500 words) support your thesis.

3. Jesus told the story, so it must have had a meaning consistent with his other teachings. Christians customarily interpret the story as meaning that God (like the father in the parable) rejoices in the return of a sinner. What meaning, if any, can it have for readers who are not Christians? Explain.

4. Does this parable present an argument? Can you offer a counterargument to the parable?

Summary

At this point we want to distinguish clearly between *analysis* and *summary*. A summary is a synopsis of the main points of a work; a summary of a work of literature usually gives the gist of the plot. It lets the reader know that X happened, then Y happened, then Z happened, but it does *not* concern itself, for instance, with evaluating whether the happenings are plausible. Normally in your analytic/argumentative essays you will not summarize because you can assume that your readers are familiar with the works you are discussing, but if, for instance, you are comparing an assigned text with another text that your readers probably don't know, you may want to offer a summary in order to help them follow the argument that you will be developing.

Consider this summary of Chopin's "The Story of an Hour" (pages 57–58):

> A newspaper office reports that Brently Mallard has been killed in a railroad accident. When the news is gently broken to Mrs. Mallard by her sister Josephine, Mrs. Mallard weeps wildly and then shuts herself up in her room, where she sinks into an armchair. Staring dully through the window, she sees the signs of spring, and then an unnameable sensation possesses her. She tries to reject it but finally abandons herself to it. Renewed, she exults in her freedom, in the thought that at last the days will be her own. She finally comes out of the room, embraces her sister, and descends the stairs. A moment later her husband—who in fact had not been in the accident—enters. Mrs. Mallard dies—of the joy that kills, according to the doctors' diagnosis.

Here are a few principles that govern summaries:

1. A summary is **much briefer than the original.** It is not a paraphrase—a word-by-word translation of someone's words into your own. A paraphrase is usually at least as long as the original, but a summary is rarely longer than one-fourth of the original and is usually much shorter. A novel may be summarized in a few paragraphs, or even in one paragraph.

2. A summary **usually achieves its brevity by omitting almost all of the concrete details of the original** and by omitting minor characters and

episodes. Notice that the summary of "The Story of an Hour" omits the friend of the family, omits specifying the signs of spring, and omits the business of the sister imploring Mrs. Mallard to open the door.

3. A summary is **as accurate as possible,** given the limits of space. It has no value if it misrepresents the point of the original.

4. A summary is **normally written in the present tense.** Thus "A newspaper office reports . . . , Mrs. Mallard weeps. . . ."

5. If the summary is brief (say, fewer than 250 words), it **may be given as a single paragraph.** If you are summarizing a long work, you may feel that a longer summary is needed. In this case your reader will be grateful to you if you divide the summary into paragraphs. As you draft your summary, you may find **natural divisions.** For instance, the scene of the story may change midway, giving you the opportunity to use two paragraphs. Or you may want to summarize a five-act play in five paragraphs.

6. The writer of a summary **need not make the points in the same order as that of the original.** If the writer of an essay has delayed revealing the main point until the end of the essay, the summary may rearrange the order, stating the main point first. Occasionally, if the original author has presented the elements of an argument in a disorderly or confusing sequence, a summary may be written to disengage the author's argument from its confusing structure.

7. Because a summary is clearly a report of someone else's views, it is usually **not necessary to use quotation marks** around key words or phrases from the original. Nor is it necessary to specify "he says" or "she goes on to prove." From the opening sentence of a summary it should be clear that what follows is what the original author says.

Summaries have their place in essays, but remember that a summary is not an analysis; it is only a summary.

Paraphrase

Like a summary, a paraphrase is *not* an analysis. A **paraphrase** is a restatement— a sort of translation in the same language—of material that may in its original form be somewhat obscure to a reader. A native speaker of English will not need a paraphrase of "Thirty days hath September," though a nonnative speaker might be puzzled by two things, the meaning of *hath* and the inverted word order. For such a reader, "September has thirty days" would be a helpful paraphrase.

Although a paraphrase seeks to make clear the basic meaning of the original, if the original is even a little more complex than "Thirty days hath September," the paraphrase will—in the process of clarifying something—lose something because the substitution of one word for another will change the meaning. "Shut up" and "Be quiet" do not say exactly the same thing; the former (in addition to asking for quiet) says that the speaker is rude, or perhaps that the speaker feels little respect for the auditor, but the paraphrase loses all of this.

Still, a paraphrase can be a first step in helping a reader to understand a line that includes an obsolete word or phrase, or a word or phrase that is current only in one region. In a poem by Emily Dickinson (1830–86), the following line appears:

The sun engrossed the East. . . .

"Engrossed" here has (perhaps among other meanings) a special commercial meaning, "to acquire most or all of a commodity; to monopolize the market," so a paraphrase of the line might say

The sun took over all of the east.

It is worth mentioning that you should always have at your elbow a good desk dictionary, such as the current *American Heritage Dictionary of the English Language*. Writers—especially poets—expect you to pay close attention to every word. When a word puzzles you, look it up.

Idioms, as well as words, can puzzle a reader. The Anglo-Irish poet William Butler Yeats (1865–1939) begins one poem with

The friends that have it I do wrong. . . .

Because the idiom "to have it" (meaning "to believe that," "to think that") will be unfamiliar to many American readers today, a discussion of the poem might include a **paraphrase**—a rewording in more familiar language, such as

The friends who think that I am doing the wrong thing. . . .

Perhaps the rest of the poem is immediately clear, but in any case here is the entire poem, followed by a paraphrase:

The friends that have it I do wrong
When ever I remake a song,
Should know what issue is at stake:
It is myself that I remake.

Now for the paraphrase:

The friends who think that I am doing the wrong thing when I revise one of my poems should be informed what the important issue is: I'm not just revising a poem—rather, I am revising myself (my thoughts, feelings).

Here, as with any paraphrase, the meaning is not translated exactly; there is some distortion. If "song" in the original is clarified by "poem" in the paraphrase, it is also altered; the paraphrase loses the sense of lyricism that is implicit in "song." Further, "Should know what issue is at stake" (in the original) is ambiguous. Does "should" mean "ought," as in "You should know better than to speak so rudely," or does it mean "deserve to be informed," as in "You ought to know that I am thinking about quitting"?

Granted that a paraphrase may miss a great deal, a paraphrase often helps you, or your reader, to understand at least the surface meaning, and the act of paraphrasing will usually help you to understand at least some of the implicit meaning. Furthermore, a paraphrase makes you see that the original writer's words (if the work is a good one) are exactly right, better than any words we might substitute. It becomes clear that what is said in the original—not only the rough idea expressed but the precise tone with which it is expressed—is a sharply defined experience.

> For information concerning paraphrase in connection with using secondary sources, see page 312 and also Appendix B.

Comparison: An Analytic Tool

Analysis frequently involves comparing. A few pages ago we asked you to compare the older brother with the younger brother and the father in the parable of the prodigal son. When we compare, we examine things for their resemblances to and differences from other things. Strictly speaking, if you emphasize the differences rather than the similarities, you are contrasting rather than comparing, but we need not preserve this distinction: we can call both processes **comparing.**

Although your instructor may ask you to write a comparison of two works of literature, the *subject* of the essay is the works; comparison is simply an effective analytic technique for showing the qualities in the works. You might compare Chopin's use of nature in "The Story of an Hour" (pages 57-58) with the use of nature in another story, in order to reveal the subtle differences between the stories, but a comparison of works utterly unlike can hardly tell the reader or the writer anything.

Something should be said about organizing a comparison, say between the settings in two stories, between two characters in a novel (or even between a character at the end of a novel and the same character at the beginning), or between the symbolism in two poems. Probably, a student's first thought after making some jottings is to discuss one half of the comparison and then the second half. Instructors and textbooks (though not this one) usually condemn such an organization, arguing that such an essay breaks into two parts and that the second part involves a good deal of repetition of the categories set up in the first part. Often they recommend that students organize their thoughts along these lines:

1. First similarity
   a. First work (or character, or characteristic)
   b. Second work
2. Second similarity
   a. First work
   b. Second work
3. First difference
   a. First work
   b. Second work
4. Second difference
   a. First work
   b. Second work

and so on, for as many additional differences as seem relevant. If you wish to compare *Adventures of Huckleberry Finn* with *The Catcher in the Rye*, you might organize the material thus:

1. First similarity: the narrator and his quest
   a. Huck
   b. Holden
2. Second similarity: the corrupt world surrounding the narrator
   a. Society in *Huck*
   b. Society in *Catcher*
3. First difference: degree to which the narrator fulfills his quest and escapes from society
   a. Huck's plan to "light out" to the frontier
   b. Holden's breakdown

Here is another way to organize a comparison and contrast:

1. First point: the narrator and his quest
   a. Similarities between Huck and Holden
   b. Differences between Huck and Holden

2. Second point: the corrupt world
    a. Similarities between the worlds in *Huck* and *Catcher*
    b. Differences between the worlds in *Huck* and *Catcher*
3. Third point: degree of success
    a. Similarities between Huck and Holden
    b. Differences between Huck and Holden

A comparison need not employ either of these structures. There is even the danger that an essay employing either of them may not come into focus until the essayist stands back from the seven-layer cake and announces in the concluding paragraph that the odd layers taste better. In your preparatory thinking, you may want to make comparisons in pairs:

- good-natured humor: the clown in *Othello*, the clownish grave-digger in *Hamlet*
- social satire: the clown in *Othello*, the grave-digger in *Hamlet*
- relevance to main theme:
- length of role:

But before writing the final version, you must come to some conclusions about what your comparisons add up to.

This final version should not duplicate your thought processes; rather, it should be organized so as to make your point—the thesis—clearly and effectively. After reflection, you may believe that

- although there are superficial similarities between the clown in *Othello* and the clownish grave-digger in *Hamlet*,
- there are essential differences.

In the finished essay, a writer will not want to obscure the main point by jumping back and forth from play to play, working through a series of similarities and differences. It may be better to discuss the clown in *Othello* and then to point out that although the grave-digger in *Hamlet* resembles him in A, B, and C, the grave-digger also has other functions (D, E, and F) and is of greater consequence to *Hamlet* than the clown is to *Othello*. Some repetition in the second half of the essay ("The grave-digger's puns come even faster than the clown's . . .") will bind the two halves into a meaningful whole, making clear the degree of similarity or difference. The point of the essay will not be to list pairs of similarities or differences but to illuminate a work or works by making thoughtful comparisons.

Although in a long essay the writer cannot postpone until page thirty a discussion of the second half of the comparison, in an essay of fewer than ten pages nothing is wrong with setting forth one half of the comparison and then, in light of it, the second half. The essay will break into two unrelated parts if the second half makes no use of the first, or if it fails to modify the first half, but not if the second half looks back to the first half and calls attention to differences that the new material reveals. Students ought to learn how to write an essay with interwoven comparisons, but they ought also to know that a comparison may be written in another, simpler and clearer way.

Finally, a reminder: **The purpose of a comparison is to call attention to the unique features of something by holding it up against something similar but significantly different.** You can compare Macbeth with Banquo (two men who hear a prophecy but who respond differently), or Macbeth with

Lady Macbeth (a husband and wife, both eager to be monarchs but differing in their sense of the consequences), or Hamlet and Holden Caulfield (two people who see themselves as surrounded by a corrupt world), but you can hardly compare Holden with Macbeth or with Lady Macbeth—there simply aren't enough points of resemblance to make it worth your effort to call attention to subtle differences.

When the differences are great and apparent, a comparison is a waste of effort; you will be arguing about something that is not really arguable. ("Blueberries are different from elephants. Blueberries do not have trunks. And elephants do not grow on bushes.") Indeed, a comparison between essentially and evidently unlike things can only obscure, for by making the comparison the writer implies that significant similarities do exist, and readers can only wonder why they do not see them. The essays that do break into two halves are essays that make uninstructive comparisons: the first half tells the reader about five qualities in Alice Walker, the second half tells the reader about five different qualities in Toni Morrison.

A Sample Essay by a Student: "Two New Women"

A student in an introductory class was asked to compare any two of three stories by Kate Chopin ("Ripe Figs," page 9; "The Story of an Hour," page 57; "The Storm," page 81). She settled on "The Story of an Hour" and "The Storm." We print the final version of her essay, preceded by a page of notes (a synthesis of earlier notes) that she prepared shortly before she wrote her first draft.

> Resemblances or differences greater?
> Resemblances
> Theme: release from marital bonds; liberated women
> Setting: nature plays a role in both; springtime in "Hour," storm in "Storm"
> Characterization: in both stories, no villains
> > forces of nature compel;
> > Clarisse presumably happier without husband
> > both seem to emphasize roles of women
>
> Differences
> Ending: "Hour" sad (LM unfulfilled); "Storm" happy; all characters seem content
> But endings different in that "Hour" ends suddenly, surprise; "Storm" not surprising at
> > very end.
>
> Overall view (theme?)
> "Hour" very restricted view; only one person is of much interest (LM); Josephine inter-
> > esting only in terms of LM (contrast).
> In "Storm," Cal. and Alc. interesting; but also interesting are simple Bobinot and even
> > the child, and also even Clarisse, who sort of has the last word
>
> Possible titles
> Two Women
> New Women
> Tragic Louise, Comic Calixta
> Louise, Calixta, and Clarisse

Linda Hernandez

Professor Welsh

English 102

18 January 2013

Two New Women

It is not surprising that two stories by an author somewhat resemble

each other. What is especially interesting about Kate Chopin's "The Story of an

Hour" and "The Storm" is that although they both deal with women who

achieve a sense of new life or growth outside the bonds of marriage, the

stories differ greatly in what we call tone. "The Story of an Hour" is

bittersweet, or perhaps even bitter and tragic, whereas "The Storm" is

romantic and in some ways comic.

The chief similarity is that Louise Mallard in "The Story of an Hour"

and Calixta in "The Storm" both experience valuable, affirming, liberating

sensations that a traditional moral view would condemn. Mrs. Mallard, after

some moments of deep grief, feels a great sense of liberation when she learns of

the death of her husband. She dies almost immediately after this experience, but

even though she is never physically unfaithful to her husband, there is a sort of

mental disloyalty, at least from a traditional point of view. Calixta's disloyalty is

physical, not merely mental. Unlike Louise Mallard, Calixta does go to bed with a

man who is not her husband. But Calixta, as we will see, is treated just about as

sympathetically as is Mrs. Mallard.

Louise Mallard is sympathetic because she does grieve for her

husband, and because Chopin suggests that Mallard's sense of freedom is

natural, something associated with the spring, the "delicious breath of

rain," and "the tops of trees that were all aquiver with the new spring

life" (57). Furthermore, Chopin explicitly says that Mallard loved her

husband. But Chopin also tells us that one aspect of the marriage was a "powerful will bending her" (57). For all of these reasons, then—Mrs. Mallard's genuine grief, the association of her new feeling with the power of nature, and the assertion that Mrs. Mallard loved her husband but was at least in some degree subject to his will—the reader sympathizes with Mrs. Mallard.

In her presentation of Calixta, too, Chopin takes care to make the unfaithful woman a sympathetic figure. As in "The Story of an Hour," nature plays a role. Here, instead of nature or the outside world being a parallel to the woman's emotions, nature in the form of a storm exerts pressure on the woman. We are told that "the water beat in upon the boards in driving sheets" (82), and a bolt of lightning causes Calixta to stagger backward, into Alcée's arms. These forces of outside nature are parallel to a force of nature within Calixta. Chopin tells us that during the sexual union Calixta's "firm, elastic flesh . . . was knowing for the first time its birthright" (83). And in one additional way, too, Chopin guards against the reader's condemning Calixta. We learn, at the end of the story, that Alcée's wife, Clarisse, is quite pleased to be free from her husband for a while:

> And the first free breath since her marriage seemed to restore the
> pleasant liberty of her maiden days. Devoted as she was to her
> husband, their intimate conjugal life was something which she
> was more than willing to forego for a while. (84)

Since Clarisse is portrayed as somewhat pleased to be relieved of her husband for a while, we probably do not see Alcée as a villainous betrayer of his wife. The story seems to end pleasantly, like a comedy, with everybody happy.

In Louise Mallard and in Calixta we see two women who achieve new lives, although in the case of Louise Mallard the reader is surprised to learn in the last sentence that the achievement lasts only a few moments. By "new lives" I mean emancipation from their husbands, but what is especially interesting is that in both cases Chopin guides the reader to feel that

Hernandez 3

although in fact both women behave in ways that would be strongly condemned by the codes of Chopin's day, and even by many people today, neither woman (as Chopin presents her) is blameworthy. Mrs. Mallard is presented almost as a tragic victim, and Calixta is presented almost as a figure in a very pleasant comedy.

[New page]

Hernandez 4

Works Cited

Chopin, Kate. "The Storm." *Literature for Composition*. Ed. Sylvan Barnet, William Burto, and William E. Cain. 10th ed. New York: Pearson, 2013. 81-84. Print.

---. "The Story of an Hour." *Literature for Composition*. Ed. Sylvan Barnet, William Burto, and William E. Cain. 10th ed. New York: Pearson, 2014. 57-58. Print.

Looking at the Essay

A few comments on this student's essay may be useful.

- The title announces the *topic*.
- The first paragraph announces the *thesis*, the point that will be argued.
- The second paragraph begins by getting directly to the point: "The chief similarity is . . . ."
- The third paragraph advances the argument by giving *evidence*, introduced by a word that implies reasoning, "because."
- The writer provides further evidence in the form of short relevant quotations from the story.
- The final paragraph summarizes but does not boringly repeat; i.e., it does not merely say "Thus we see. . . ." Rather, it presents the argument freshly.

Joining the Conversation: Critical Thinking and Writing

We like Linda Hernandez's essay, but perhaps you have a different view. In any case, what grade would you give this essay? Why? Be as specific as possible in calling attention to what you see as its strengths and weaknesses.

✔ CHECKLIST: *Revising a Comparison*

☐ Does it make sense to compare these things? (What question will the comparison help to answer? What do you hope your reader will learn?)
☐ Is the point of the comparison—the reason for making it—clear? Is the point stated in a thesis sentence?
☐ Does the comparison cover all significant similarities and differences?
☐ Is the comparison readable; that is, is it clear and yet not tediously mechanical?
☐ Is the organization used—perhaps treating one text first and then the other, or perhaps shifting back and forth between texts—the best way to make this comparison?
☐ If the essay offers a value judgment, is that judgment fair? Does the essay offer enough evidence to bring a reader into at least partial agreement?

Evaluation in Explication and Analysis

When we evaluate, we say how good, how successful, how worthwhile, something is. If you reread the student essay on "Harlem" (page 139), you'll notice that he implies that the poem is worth reading. He doesn't say "In this excellent poem," but a reader of the essay probably comes away with the impression that the student thinks the poem is excellent. The writer might have included a more explicit evaluation, along these lines:

> In "Harlem," every word counts, and every word is effective. The image of the "heavy load" that "sags" is not as unusual as the image of the raisin in the sun, but it nevertheless is just right, adding a simple, powerful touch just before the explosive ending.

In any case, when an essay argues that the parts fit together effectively, it is almost surely implying a favorable evaluation. But only "*almost* surely." We might argue that the parts fit but that the work is immoral, or trivial, or unpleasant, or untrue to life. Even though it might be granted that the work is carefully constructed, the final evaluation of the work might be low. Evaluations are based on standards. If you offer an evaluation, make certain that your standards are clear to the reader.

Notice in the following three examples of evaluations of J. D. Salinger's *The Catcher in the Rye* that the writers let their readers know what their standards are. Each excerpt is from a review that was published when the book first appeared. In the first, Anne L. Goodman, writing in the *New Republic* (16 July 1951), began by praising Salinger's earlier short stories and then said this about the novel:

> But the book as a whole is disappointing, and not merely because it is a re-working of a theme that one begins to suspect must obsess the author. Holden Caulfield, the main character who tells his own story, is an extraordinary portrait, but there is too much of him. He describes himself early on and, with the sureness of a wire recording, he remains strictly in character throughout.

Goodman then quotes a longish passage from *Catcher* and says,

> In the course of 277 pages the reader wearies of this kind of explicitness, repetition, and adolescence, exactly as one would weary of Holden himself.

Goodman lets us know that, in her opinion, (1) a book ought not simply to repeat a writer's earlier books, and that, again in her opinion, (2) it's not enough to give a highly realistic portrait of a character; if the character is not a sufficiently interesting person, in the long run the book will be dull.

Another reviewer, Virgilia Peterson, writing in the *New York Herald Tribune Book Review* (15 July 1951), found the book realistic in some ways, but unrealistic and therefore defective because its abundant profanity becomes unconvincing:

> There is probably not one phrase in the whole book that Holden Caulfield would not have used upon occasion, but when they are piled upon each other in cumulative monotony, the ear refuses to believe.

Peterson concluded her review, however, by confessing that she did not think she was in a position to evaluate a book about an adolescent, or at least *this* adolescent.

> . . . it would be interesting and highly enlightening to know what Holden Caulfield's contemporaries, male and female, think of him. Their opinion would constitute the real test of Mr. Salinger's validity. The question of authenticity is one to which no parent can really guess the reply.

Here again the standard is clear—authenticity—but the writer confesses that she isn't sure about authenticity in this matter, and she defers to her juniors. Peterson's review is a rare example of an analysis offered by a writer who confesses an inability to evaluate appropriately.

Finally, here is a brief extract from a more favorable review, written by Paul Engle and published in the *Chicago Sunday Tribune Magazine of Books* (15 July 1951):

> The book ends with Holden in a mental institution, for which the earlier events have hardly prepared the reader. But the story is an engaging and believable one for the most part, full of right observations and sharp insight, and a wonderful sort of grasp of how a boy can create his own world of fantasy and live form.

The first sentence implies that a good book prepares the reader for the end, and that in this respect *Catcher* is deficient. The rest of the paragraph sets forth other standards that *Catcher* meets (it is "engaging and believable," "full of right observations and sharp insight"), though one of the standards in Engle's last sentence ("live form") strikes us as obscure.

Choosing a Topic and Developing a Thesis in an Analytic Paper

Because Hughes's "Harlem" is very short, an analysis of it may discuss the entire poem. But a short essay, or even a long one, cannot discuss all aspects of a play or a novel or even a long story. If you are writing about a long work, you'll have to single out an appropriate topic.

What is an appropriate topic? First, it must be a topic that you can work up some interest in, or your writing will be mechanical and dull. (We say "work up some interest" because interest is commonly the result of some effort.) Second, an appropriate topic is compassable—that is, it is something you can cover with reasonable attention to detail in the few pages (and few days) you have to devote to it. If a work is fairly long, almost surely you will write an analysis of some part of it.

Unless you have lots of time for reflection and revision, you cannot write a meaningful essay of 500 words or even 1,000 words on "Shakespeare's *Hamlet*" or "The Fiction of Alice Walker." At that length, you cannot even write on "Character in *Hamlet*" or "Symbolism in Walker's *The Color Purple*." And probably you won't really want to write on such topics anyway; probably *one* character or *one* symbol has caught your interest. Think of something in your annotations or "response" notes (described in Chapter 2) that has caught your attention. Trust your feelings; you are likely onto something interesting.

In Chapter 3 we talked about the value of asking yourself questions. To find an appropriate topic, ask yourself such questions as:

1. *What purpose does this serve?* For instance, why is this scene in the novel or play? Why is there a comic grave-digger in *Hamlet?* Why are these lines unrhymed? Why did the author call the work by this title?
2. *Why do I have this response?* Why do I feel that this work is more profound (or amusing, or puzzling) than that work? How did the author make this character funny or dignified or pathetic? How did the author communicate the idea that this character is a bore without boring me?

The first of these questions, "What purpose does this serve?" requires that you identify yourself with the author, wondering, for example, whether this opening scene is the best possible for this story. The second question, "Why do I have this response?" requires that you trust your feelings. If you are amused or puzzled or annoyed, assume that these responses are appropriate and follow them up, at least until a rereading of the work provides other responses. If you jot down notes reporting your responses and later think about them, you will probably find that you can select a topic.

A third valuable way to find a thesis is to test a published comment against your response to a work. Perhaps somewhere you have seen—say, in a textbook— a statement about the nature of fiction, poetry, or drama. Maybe you have heard that a tragic hero has a "flaw." Don't simply accept the remark. Test it against your reading of the work. And interpret the word *published* broadly. Students and instructors publish their opinions—offer them to a public—when they utter them in class. Think about something said in class; students who pay close attention to what their peers say learn a great deal.

Given an appropriate topic, you will find your essay easier to write and the finished version of it clearer and more persuasive if, at some point in your preparation, in note taking or in writing a first draft, you have converted your topic into a *thesis* (a proposition, a point, an argument) and constructed a *thesis statement* (a sentence stating your overall point).

Let's dwell a moment on the distinction between a topic and a thesis. It may be useful to think of it this way: A topic is a subject (for example, "The role of Providence in *Hamlet*"); to arrive at a thesis, you have to make an arguable assertion (for example, "The role of Providence in *Hamlet* is not obvious, but it is crucial").

Some theses are more promising than others. Consider this thesis:

The role of Providence in *Hamlet* is interesting.

This sentence asserts a thesis, but it is vague and provides little direction, little help in generating ideas and in shaping your essay. Let's try again. It's almost always necessary to try again and again, for the process of writing is in large part a process of trial and error, of generating better and better ideas by evaluating—selecting or rejecting—ideas and options.

> The role of Providence is evident in the Ghost.

This is much better, and it could stimulate ideas for an interesting essay. Let's assume the writer rereads the play, looking for further evidence, and comes to believe that the Ghost is only one of several manifestations of Providence. The writer may stay with the Ghost or may (especially if the paper is long enough to allow for such a thesis to be developed) alter the thesis thus:

> The role of Providence is not confined to the Ghost but is found also in the killing of Polonius, in the surprising appearance of the pirate ship, and in the presence of the poisoned chalice.

Strictly speaking, the thesis here is given in the first part of the sentence ("The role of Providence is not confined to the Ghost"); the rest of the sentence provides an indication of how the argument will be supported.

Every literary work suggests its own topics for analysis to an active reader, and all essayists must set forth their own theses, but if you begin by seeking to examine one of your responses, you will soon be able to stake out a topic and to formulate a thesis.

A suggestion: With two or three other students, formulate a thesis about Kate Chopin's "The Storm" (in Chapter 3). By practicing with a group you will develop a skill that you will use when you have to formulate a thesis on your own.

Analyzing a Story

If a story is short enough, you may be able to examine everything in it that you think is worth commenting on, but even if it is short you may nevertheless decide to focus on one element, such as the setting, or the construction of the plot, or the connection between two characters, or the degree of plausibility. Here is a story by James Thurber (1894–1961), the American humorist. It was first published in 1939.

JAMES THURBER

The Secret Life of Walter Mitty

"We're going through!" The Commander's voice was like thin ice breaking. He wore his full-dress uniform, with the heavily braided white cap pulled down rakishly over one cold gray eye. "We can't make it, sir. It's spoiling for a hurricane, if you ask me." "I'm not asking you, Lieutenant Berg," said the Commander. "Throw on the power lights! Rev her up to 8,500! We're going through!" The pounding of the cylinders increased: ta-pocketa-pocketa-pocketa-*pocketa-pocketa*. The Commander stared at the ice forming on the pilot window. He walked over and twisted a row of complicated dials. "Switch on No. 8 auxiliary!" he shouted. "Switch on No. 8 auxiliary!" repeated Lieutenant Berg. "Full strength in No. 3 turret!" shouted the Commander. "Full strength in No. 3 turret!" The crew, bending to their various tasks in the huge, hurtling eight-engined Navy hydroplane, looked at each other and grinned. "The Old Man'll get us through," they said to one another. "The Old Man ain't afraid of Hell!" . . .

"Not so fast! You're driving too fast!" said Mrs. Mitty. "What are you driving so fast for?"

"Hmm?" said Walter Mitty. He looked at his wife, in the seat beside him, with shocked astonishment. She seemed grossly unfamiliar, like a strange woman who had yelled at him in a crowd. "You were up to fifty-five," she said. "You know I don't like to go more than forty. You were up to fifty-five." Walter Mitty drove on toward Waterbury in silence, the roaring of the SN202 through the worst storm in twenty years of Navy flying fading in the remote, intimate airways of his mind. "You're tensed up again," said Mrs. Mitty. "It's one of your days. I wish you'd let Dr. Renshaw look you over."

Walter Mitty stopped the car in front of the building where his wife went to have her hair done. "Remember to get those overshoes while I'm having my hair done," she said. "I don't need overshoes," said Mitty. She put her mirror back into her bag. "We've been all through that," she said, getting out of the car. "You're not a young man any longer." He raced the engine a little. "Why don't you wear your gloves? Have you lost your gloves?" Walter Mitty reached in a pocket and brought out the gloves. He put them on, but after she had turned and gone into the building and he had driven on to a red light, he took them off again. "Pick it up, brother!" snapped a cop as the light changed, and Mitty hastily pulled on his gloves and lurched ahead. He drove around the streets aimlessly for a time, and then he drove past the hospital on his way to the parking lot.

5   . . . "It's the millionaire banker, Wellington McMillan," said the pretty nurse. "Yes?" said Walter Mitty, removing his gloves slowly. "Who has the case?" "Dr. Renshaw and Dr. Benbow, but there are two specialists here, Dr. Remington from New York and Dr. Pritchard-Mitford from London. He flew over." A door opened down a long, cool corridor and Dr. Renshaw came out. He looked distraught and haggard. "Hello, Mitty," he said. "We're having the devil's own time with McMillan, the millionaire banker and close personal friend of Roosevelt. Obstreosis of the ductal tract. Tertiary. Wish you'd take a look at him." "Glad to," said Mitty.

In the operating room there were whispered introductions: "Dr. Remington, Dr. Mitty, Mr. Pritchard-Mitford, Dr. Mitty." "I've read your book on streptothricosis," said Pritchard-Mitford, shaking hands. "A brilliant performance, sir." "Thank you," said Walter Mitty. "Didn't know you were in the States, Mitty," grumbled Remington. "Coals to Newcastle, bringing Mitford and me up here for a tertiary." "You are very kind," said Mitty. A huge, complicated machine, connected to the operating table, with many tubes and wires, began at this moment to go pocketa-pocketa-pocketa. "The new anesthetizer is giving way!" shouted an interne. "There is no one in the East who knows how to fix it!" "Quiet, man!" said Mitty, in a low, cool voice. He sprang to the machine, which was now going pocketa-pocketa-queep-pocketa-queep. He began fingering delicately a row of glistening dials. "Give me a fountain pen!" he snapped. Someone handed him a fountain pen. He pulled a faulty piston out of the machine and inserted the pen in its place. "That will hold for ten minutes," he said. "Get on with the operation." A nurse hurried over and whispered to Renshaw, and Mitty saw the man turn pale. "Coreopsis has set in," said Renshaw nervously. "If you would take over, Mitty?" Mitty looked at him and at the craven figure of Benbow, who drank, and at the grave, uncertain faces of the two great specialists. "If you wish," he said. They slipped a white gown on him; he adjusted a mask and drew on thin gloves; nurses handed him shining . . .

"Back it up, Mac! Look out for that Buick!" Walter Mitty jammed on the brakes. "Wrong lane, Mac," said the parking-lot attendant, looking at Mitty closely. "Gee. Yeh," muttered Mitty. He began cautiously to back out of the lane marked "Exit Only." "Leave her sit there," said the attendant. "I'll put her away." Mitty got out of the car. "Hey, better leave the key." "Oh," said Mitty, handing the man the ignition key. The attendant vaulted into the car, backed it up with insolent skill, and put it where it belonged.

They're so damn cocky, thought Walter Mitty, walking along Main Street; they think they know everything. Once he had tried to take his chains off, outside New Milford, and he had got them wound around the axles. A man had had to come out in a wrecking car and unwind them, a young, grinning garageman. Since then Mrs. Mitty always made him drive to the garage to have the chains taken off. The next time, he thought, I'll wear my right arm in a sling; they won't grin at me then. I'll have my right arm in a sling and they'll see I couldn't possibly take the chains off myself. He kicked at the slush on the sidewalk. "Overshoes," he said to himself, and he began looking for a shoe store.

When he came out into the street again, with the overshoes in a box under his arm, Walter Mitty began to wonder what the other thing was his wife had told him to get. She had told him, twice, before they set out from their house for Waterbury. In a way he hated these weekly trips to town—he was always getting something wrong. Kleenex, he thought, Squibb's, razor blades? No. Toothpaste, toothbrush, bicarbonate, carborundum, initiative and referendum? He gave it up. But she would remember it. "Where's the what's-its-name?" she would ask. "Don't tell me you forgot the what's-its-name." A newsboy went by shouting something about the Waterbury trial.

10   "Perhaps this will refresh your memory." The District Attorney suddenly thrust a heavy automatic at the quiet figure on the witness stand. "Have you ever seen this before?" Walter Mitty took the gun and examined it expertly. "This is my Webley-Vickers 50.80," he said calmly. An excited buzz ran around the courtroom. The Judge rapped for order. "You are a crack shot with any sort of firearms, I believe?" said the District Attorney, insinuatingly. "Objection!" shouted Mitty's attorney. "We have shown that the defendant could not have fired the shot. We have shown that he wore his right arm in a sling on the night of the fourteenth of July." Walter Mitty raised his hand briefly and the bickering attorneys were stilled. "With any known make of gun," he said evenly, "I could have killed Gregory Fitzhurst at three hundred feet *with my left hand*." Pandemonium broke loose in the courtroom. A woman's scream rose above the bedlam and suddenly a lovely, dark-haired girl was in Walter Mitty's arms. The District Attorney struck at her savagely. Without rising from his chair, Mitty let the man have it on the point of the chin. "You miserable cur!" . . .

"Puppy biscuit," said Walter Mitty. He stopped walking and the buildings of Waterbury rose up out of the misty courtroom and surrounded him again. A woman who was passing laughed. "He said 'Puppy biscuit,'" she said to her companion. "That man said 'Puppy biscuit' to himself." Walter Mitty hurried on. He went into an A. & P., not the first one he came to but a smaller one farther up the street. "I want some biscuit for small, young dogs," he said to the clerk. "Any special brand, sir?" The greatest pistol shot in the world thought a moment. "It says 'Puppies Bark for It' on the box," said Walter Mitty.

His wife would be through at the hairdresser's in fifteen minutes, Mitty saw in looking at his watch, unless they had trouble drying it; sometimes they had trouble drying it. She didn't like to get to the hotel first; she would want him to be there waiting for her as usual. He found a big leather chair in the lobby, facing a window, and he put the overshoes and the puppy biscuit on the floor beside it. He picked up an old copy of *Liberty* and sank down into the chair. "Can Germany Conquer the World through the Air?" Walter Mitty looked at the pictures of bombing planes and of ruined streets.

. . . "The cannonading has got the wind up in young Raleigh, sir," said the sergeant. Captain Mitty looked up at him through tousled hair. "Get him to bed," he said wearily. "With the others. I'll fly alone." "But you can't, sir," said the sergeant anxiously. "It takes two men to handle that bomber and the Archies are pounding hell out of the air. Von Richtman's circus is between here and Saulier." "Somebody's got to get that ammunition dump," said Mitty. "I'm going over. Spot of brandy?" He poured a drink for the sergeant and one for himself. War thundered and whined around the dugout and battered at the door. There was a rending of wood and splinters flew through the room. "A bit of a near thing," said Captain Mitty carelessly. "The box barrage is closing in," said the sergeant. "We only live once, Sergeant," said Mitty, with his faint, fleeting smile. "Or do we?" He poured another brandy and tossed it off. "I never see a man could hold his brandy like you, sir," said the sergeant. "Begging your pardon, sir." Captain Mitty stood up and strapped on his huge Webley-Vickers automatic. "It's forty kilometers through hell, sir," said the sergeant. Mitty finished one last brandy. "After all," he said softly, "what isn't?" The pounding of the cannon increased; there was the rat-tat-tatting of machine guns, and from somewhere came the menacing pocket-pocketa-pocketa of the new flame-throwers. Walter Mitty walked to the door of the dugout humming "Auprès de Ma Blonde." He turned and waved to the sergeant. "Cheerio!" he said. . . . .

Something struck his shoulder. "I've been looking all over this hotel for you," said Mrs. Mitty. "Why do you have to hide in this old chair? How did you expect me to find you?" "Things close in," said Walter Mitty vaguely. "What?" Mrs. Mitty said. "Did you get the what's-its-name? The puppy biscuit? What's in that box?" "Overshoes," said Mitty. "Couldn't you have put them on in the store?" "I was thinking," said Walter Mitty. "Does it ever occur to you that I am sometimes thinking?" She looked at him. "I'm going to take your temperature when I get you home," she said.

15   They went out through the revolving doors that made a faintly derisive whistling sound when you pushed them. It was two blocks to the parking lot. At the drugstore on the corner she said, "Wait here for me. I forgot something. I won't be a minute." She was more than a minute. Walter Mitty lighted a cigarette. It began to rain, rain with sleet in it. He stood up against the wall of the drugstore, smoking. . . . He put his shoulders back and his heels together. "To hell with the handkerchief," said Walter Mitty scornfully. He took one last drag on his cigarette and snapped it away. Then, with that faint, fleeting smile playing about his lips, he faced the firing squad; erect and motionless, proud and disdainful, Walter Mitty the Undefeated, inscrutable to the last.

[1939]

Working toward a Thesis: Journal Entries

Before reading the following journal entries about "The Secret Life of Walter Mitty," write one or two of your own. You may want to think about what (if anything) you found amusing in the story, or about whether the story is dated, or about some aspect of Mitty's character or of his wife's. The choice is yours.

A student wrote the following entry in her journal after the story was discussed in class.

March 21. Funny, I guess, especially the business about him as a doctor performing an operation. And that "pocketa-pocketa," but I don't think that it's as hysterical as everyone else seems to think it is. And how could anyone stand being married to a man like that? In fact, it's a good thing he has her to look after him. He ought to be locked up, driving into the "Exit Only" lane, talking to himself in the street, and having those crazy daydreams. No wonder the woman in the street laughs at him.

March 24. He's certainly a case, and she's not nearly as bad as everyone was saying. So she tells him to put his overshoes on; well, he ought to put them on, since Thurber says there is slush in the street, and he's no kid anymore. About the worst I can say of her is that she seems a little unreasonable in always wanting him to wait for her, rather than sometimes the other way around, but probably she's really telling him not to wander off, because if he ever drifts away there'll be no finding him. The joke, I guess, is that he's supposed to have these daydreams because he's henpecked, and henpecked men are supposed to be funny. Would people find the story just as funny if she had the daydreams, and he bullied her?

Developing the Thesis: Making Lists

In preparation for writing a draft, the same student reread the story and jotted down tentative notes based on her journal and on material that she had highlighted in the text. (At this point you may want to make your own list, based on your notes.)

Mitty helpless:

he <u>needs</u> her
chains on tires
enters Exit Only
~~Waterbury~~
cop tells him to get going
fantasies

wife a nag? → causes his daydreams? Evidence?
makes him get to hotel first
overshoes
backseat driver?

"Does it ever occur to you that I am sometimes thinking?" <u>Is he thinking, or just having dreams?</u>

M. confuses Richthoven with <u>someone called Richtman.</u>

Funny--or anti-woman? Would it be funny if he nagged her, and <u>she</u> had daydreams?

Next, the student wrote a draft; then she revised the draft and submitted the revision (following pages) to classmates for peer review. (The number enclosed within parentheses cites the page number of a quotation.)

Sample Draft by a Student: "Walter Mitty Is No Joke"

Susan Lee

Professor Markus

English 102

15 February 2013

Walter Mitty Is No Joke

James Thurber's "The Secret Life of Walter Mitty" seems to be highly
regarded as a comic story about a man who is so dominated by his wife that
he has to escape through fantasies. In my high school course in English,
everyone found Mitty's dreams and his wife's bullying funny, and everyone
seems to find them funny in college, too. Everyone except me.

If we look closely at the story, we see that Mitty is a pitiful man who
needs to be told what to do. The slightest glimpse of reality sets him off on a
daydream, as when he passes a hospital and immediately begins to imagine
that he is a famous surgeon, or when he hears a newsboy shouting a headline
about a crime and he imagines himself in a courtroom. The point seems to be that
his wife nags him, so he escapes into daydreams. But the fact is that she needs to
keep after him, because he needs someone to tell him what to do. It depends on
what one considers nagging. She tells him he is driving too fast, and (given the
date of the story, 1939) he probably is, since he is going 55 on a slushy or snowy
road. She tells him to wear overshoes, and he probably ought to, since the
weather is bad. He resents all of these orders, but he clearly is incompetent, since
he delays when the traffic light turns from red to green, and he enters an "Exit
Only" lane in a parking lot. We are also told that he cannot put chains on tires.

In fact, he cannot do anything right. All he can do is daydream, and the
dreams, though they *are* funny, are proof of his inability to live in the real
world. When his wife asks him why he did not put the overshoes on in the
store, instead of carrying them in a box, he says, "Does it ever occur to you that
I am sometimes thinking?" (170). But he does not "think," he just daydreams.

Lee 2

Furthermore, he cannot even get things straight in his daydreams, since he gets

everything mixed up, confusing Richthoven with Richtman, for example.

Is "The Secret Life of Walter Mitty" really a funny story about a man

who daydreams because he is henpecked? Probably it is supposed to be so,

but it is also a story about a man who is lucky to have a wife who can put up

with him and keep him from getting killed on the road or lost in town.

[New page]

Lee 3

Work Cited

Thurber, James. "The Secret Life of Walter Mitty." *Literature for Composition.*

Ed. Sylvan Barnet, William Burto, and William E. Cain. 10th ed.

New York: Pearson, 2014. 167-70. Print.

Developing an Argument

Introductory Paragraphs

As the poet Byron said, at the beginning of a long part of a long poem, "Nothing so difficult as a beginning." Woody Allen thinks so, too. In an interview he said that the toughest part of writing is "to go from nothing to the first draft."

We can give two pieces of advice:

1. *The opening paragraph is unimportant.* It's great if you can write a paragraph that will engage your readers and let them know where the essay will be taking them, but if you can't come up with such a paragraph, just put down anything in order to prime the pump.
2. *The opening paragraph is extremely important.* It must engage your readers, and probably by means of a thesis sentence it should let the readers know where the essay will be taking them.

The contradiction here is only apparent, not real. The first point is relevant to the opening paragraph of a *draft*; the second point is relevant to the opening paragraph of the *final version*. Almost all writers—professionals as well as amateurs—find that the first paragraphs in their drafts are false starts. Don't worry about the opening paragraphs of your draft; you'll revise your opening later. (Surprisingly, your first paragraph may often be deleted altogether; your second, you may find, is where your essay truly begins.)

When writing a first draft you merely need something—almost anything—to break the ice. But in your finished paper the opening cannot be mere throat-clearing. The opening must be interesting.

Among the commonest *uninteresting* **openings** are these:

1. A dictionary definition ("Webster says . . . ").
2. A restatement of your title. The title is (let's assume) "Romeo's Maturation," and the first sentence says, "This essay will study Romeo's maturation." True, there is an attempt at a thesis statement here, but there is no information beyond what has already been given in the title. There is no information about you, either—that is, no sense of your response to the topic, as there would be in, say, *"Romeo and Juliet* covers less than one week, but within this short period Romeo is impressively transformed from a somewhat comic infatuated boy to a thoughtful tragic hero."
3. A platitude, such as "Ever since the beginning of time men and women have fallen in love." Such a sentence may be fine if it helps you to start drafting, but because it sounds canned and because it is insufficiently interesting, it should not remain in your final version.

What is left? What *is* a good way for a final version to begin? Your introductory paragraph will be interesting if it gives information, and it will be pleasing if the information provides a focus—that is, if it goes beyond the title to let the reader know exactly what your topic is and where you are headed.

Let's assume that you agree: An opening paragraph should be *interesting* and *focused.* Doubtless you will find your own ways of fulfilling these goals, but you might consider using one of the following time-tested methods.

1. *Establish a connection between life and literature.* We have already suggested that a platitude ("Ever since the beginning of time men and women have fallen in love") makes a poor beginning because it is dull, but you may find another way of relating the work to daily experience. For instance:

   > Doubtless the popularity of *Romeo and Juliet* (the play has been with us for more than four hundred years) is partly due to the fact that it deals with a universal experience. Still, no other play about love is so much a part of our culture that the mere mention of the names of the lovers immediately calls up an image. But when we say that So-and-so is "a regular Romeo," exactly what do we mean? And exactly what sort of lover is Romeo?

2. *Give an overview.* Here is an example:

   > Langston Hughes's "Harlem" is about the destruction of the hopes of African Americans. More precisely, Hughes begins by asking "What happens to a dream deferred?" and then offers several possibilities, the last of which is that it may "explode."

3. *Include a quotation.* The previous example illustrates this approach. Here is another example:

   > One line from Langston Hughes's poem "Harlem" has become famous, "A raisin in the sun," but its fame is, in a sense, accidental; Lorraine Hansberry happened to use it for the title of a play. Doubtless she used it because it is impressive, but in fact the entire poem is worthy of its most famous line.

4. *Use a definition.* We have suggested that a definition introduced by "Webster says . . ." is boring, but consider this approach:

> When we say that a character is the hero of a story, we usually mean that he is the central figure, and we probably imply that he is manly. But in Kafka's "The Metamorphosis" the hero is most unmanly.

5. *Introduce a critical stance.* If your approach is feminist, or psychoanalytic, or Marxist, or whatever, you may want to say so at the start. Here's an example:

> Feminists have called our attention to the unfunny sexism of mother-in-law jokes, comments about women hooking men into marriage, and so forth. We can now see that the stories of James Thurber, long thought to be wholesome fun, are unpleasantly sexist.

We do not say that these are the only ways to begin, and we certainly do not suggest that you pack all five approaches into an opening paragraph. We are saying that after you have done some brainstorming and written some drafts, you may want to think about using one of these methods for your opening paragraph.

An Exercise: Write (either by yourself or in collaboration with one or two other students) an opening paragraph for an essay on one of Kate Chopin's stories and another for an essay on Hughes's "Harlem." (To write a useful opening paragraph, you will first have to settle on the essay's thesis.)

Middle Paragraphs

The middle, or body, of your essay will develop your thesis by offering supporting evidence. Ideas for the body should emerge from the sketchy outline that you made after you reviewed your brainstorming notes or journal.

1. *Be sure that each paragraph makes a specific point.* This point should be sufficiently developed with evidence. (A brief quotation is often the best evidence.)
2. *Be sure that each paragraph is coherent.* Read each sentence, starting with the second sentence, to see how it relates to the preceding sentence. Does it clarify, extend, reinforce, add an example? If you can't find the relationship, the sentence probably does not belong where it is. Rewrite it, move it, or strike it out.
3. *Be sure that the connections between paragraphs are clear.* Transitional words and phrases, such as "Furthermore," "On the other hand," and "In the next stanza," will often give readers all the help they need in seeing how your points are connected.
4. *Be sure that the paragraphs are in the best possible order.* A good way to test the organization is to jot down the topic sentence or topic idea of each paragraph, and then to see if your jottings form a reasonable sequence.

Concluding Paragraphs

Concluding paragraphs, like opening paragraphs, are especially important, if only because they are so conspicuous. Readers often skim first paragraphs and last paragraphs to see if an essay is worth reading. In conclusions, as in openings, say something interesting. It is not interesting to say, "Thus we see that Mrs. Mitty . . ." (and you go on to echo your title or your first sentence).

What to do? When you are revising a draft, you might keep in mind the following widely practiced principles. They are not inflexible rules, but they often work.

1. *Hint that the end is near.* Expressions such as "Finally," "One other point must be discussed," and "In short" alert the reader that the end is near and help to keep the reader from feeling that the essay ends abruptly.
2. *Reassert the thesis, but put it in a slightly new light.* Replace "I have shown that Romeo and Hamlet are similar in some ways" with this:

> These similarities suggest that in some respects Romeo is an early study for Hamlet. Both are young men in love, both seek by the force of their passion to shape the world according to their own desires, and both die in the attempt. But compared with Hamlet, who at the end of the play understands everything that has happened, Romeo dies in happy ignorance; Romeo is spared the pain of knowing that his own actions will destroy Juliet, whereas Hamlet dies with the painful knowledge that his kingdom has been conquered by Norwegian invaders.

3. *Offer an evaluation.* You may find it appropriate to conclude your analysis with an evaluation:

> Romeo is as convincing as he needs to be in a play about young lovers, but from first to last he is a relatively uncomplicated figure, the ardent lover. Hamlet is a lover, but he is also a good deal more, a figure whose complexity reveals a more sophisticated or a more mature author. Only five or six years separate Romeo and Juliet from Hamlet, but one feels that in those few years Shakespeare made a quantum leap in his grasp of human nature.

4. *Include a brief significant quotation from the work.* Here's an example:

> Romeo has won the hearts of audiences for almost four centuries, but, for all his charm, he is in the last analysis concerned only with fulfilling his own passion. Hamlet, on the other hand, at last fulfills not only his own wish but that of the Ghost, his father. "Remember me," the Ghost says, when he first appears to Hamlet and asks for revenge. Throughout the play Hamlet does remember the Ghost, and finally, at the cost of his own life, Hamlet succeeds in avenging his dead father.

Coherence in Paragraphs: Using Transitions

In addition to having a unified point and a reasonable organization, a good paragraph is **coherent;** that is, the connections between ideas in the paragraph are clear. Coherence can often be achieved by inserting the right transitional words or by taking care to repeat key words.

Richard Wagner, commenting on his work as a composer of operas, once said, "The art of composition is the art of transition," for his art moved from note to note, measure to measure, scene to scene. **Transitions** establish connections between ideas; they alert readers to the way in which you are conducting your argument. Here are some of the most common transitional words and phrases.

1. **Amplification or likeness:** similarly, likewise, and, also, again, second, third, in addition, furthermore, moreover, finally
2. **Emphasis:** chiefly, equally, indeed, even more important
3. **Contrast or concession:** but, on the contrary, on the other hand, by contrast, of course, however, still, doubtless, no doubt, nevertheless, granted that, conversely, although, admittedly
4. **Example:** for example, for instance, as an example, specifically, consider as an illustration, that is, such as, like

5. **Consequence or cause and effect:** thus, so, then, it follows, as a result, therefore, hence
6. **Restatement:** in short, that is, in effect, in other words
7. **Place:** in the foreground, further back, in the distance
8. **Time:** afterward, next, then, as soon as, later, until, when, finally, last, at last
9. **Conclusion:** finally, therefore, thus, to sum up

✔ **CHECKLIST**: *Revising Paragraphs*

☐ Does the paragraph *say* anything? Does it have substance, or is it mere padding?

☐ Does the paragraph have a topic sentence? If so, is it in the best place? If the paragraph doesn't have a topic sentence, might adding one improve the paragraph? Or does it have a clear topic idea?

☐ If the paragraph is an opening paragraph, is it interesting enough to attract and hold a reader's attention? If it is a later paragraph, does it clearly evolve from the previous paragraph and lead into the next paragraph?

☐ Does the paragraph contain some principle of development—for instance, from the general to the particular?

☐ Does each sentence clearly follow from the preceding sentence? Have you provided transitional words or cues to guide your reader? Would it be useful to repeat certain key words for clarity?

☐ What is the purpose of the paragraph? Do you want to summarize, tell a story, give an illustration, concede a point, or what? Is your purpose clear to you, and does the paragraph fulfill your purpose?

☐ Is the closing paragraph effective and not a restatement of the obvious?

Review: Writing an Analysis

Each writing assignment will require its own kind of thinking, but here are a few principles that are usually relevant:

1. Assume that your reader has already read the work you are discussing but is not thoroughly familiar with it—and of course does not know what you think and how you feel about the work. Early in your essay name the author, the work, and your thesis.

2. Do not tell the plot (or, at most, summarize it very briefly); instead, tell your reader what the work is about (not what happens, but what the happenings add up to).

3. Whether you are writing about character or plot or meter or anything else, you will probably be telling your reader something about *how* the work functions—that is, how it develops. The stages by which a work advances may sometimes be marked fairly clearly. For instance, a poem of two stanzas may ask a question in the first and give an answer in the second, or it may express a hope in the first and reveal a doubt in the second. Novels are customarily divided into chapters, and even a short story may be printed with numbered parts. Virtually all works are built from parts, whether or not the parts are labeled.

4. In telling the reader how each part leads to the next, or how each part arises from what has come before, you will probably comment on such

things as (in a story) changes in a character's state of mind—marked perhaps by a change in the setting—or (in a poem) changes in the speaker's tone of voice—for instance, from eager to resigned, or from cautious to enthusiastic. Probably you will not only be describing the development of character or tone or plot, but also (and more important) you will advance your own thesis by offering evidence that supports the thesis.

A Note on Technical Terminology

Literature—like the law, medicine, dance, and for that matter, cooking and baseball—has given rise to technical terminology. A cookbook will tell you to boil, or bake, or blend, and it will speak of a "slow" oven (300 degrees), a "moderate" oven (350 degrees), and a "hot" oven (450 degrees). These are technical terms in the world of cookery. In watching a baseball game we find ourselves saying, "I think the hit-and-run is on," or "He'll probably bunt." We use these terms because they convey a good deal in a few words; they are clear and precise. Further, although we don't use them in order to impress our listener, they do indicate that we have more than a superficial acquaintance with the game. That is, the better we know our subject, the more likely we are to use the technical language of the subject. Why? *Because such language enables us to talk precisely and in considerable depth about the subject.* Technical language, unlike jargon (pretentious diction that needlessly complicates or obscures), is illuminating—provided that the reader is familiar with the terms.

   In writing about literature you will, for the most part, use the same language that you use in your other courses, and you will not needlessly introduce the technical vocabulary of literary study—but you *will* use this vocabulary when it enables you to be clear, concise, and accurate.

A Lyric Poem and a Student's Argument

APHRA BEHN

Aphra Behn (1640–89) is regarded as the first English woman to have made a living by writing. Not much is known of her life, but she seems to have married a London merchant of Dutch descent, and after his death to have served as a spy in the Dutch Wars (1665–67). After her return to England she took up playwriting, and she gained fame with The Rover *(1677). Behn also wrote novels, the most important of which is* Oroonoko, or The Royal Slave *(1688), which is among the first works in English to express pity for enslaved Africans.*

Song: Love Armed

Love in fantastic triumph sate,
   Whilst bleeding hearts around him flowed,
For whom fresh pains he did create,
   And strange tyrannic power he showed:
From thy bright eyes he took his fire,   5
   Which round about in sport he hurled;
But 'twas from mine he took desire,
   Enough to undo the amorous world.

From me he took his sighs and tears:
   From thee, his pride and cruelty;   10
From me, his languishments and fears;

And every killing dart from thee.
Thus thou and I the god have armed
    And set him up a deity;
But my poor heart alone is harmed,   15
    Whilst thine the victor is, and free.

[1676]

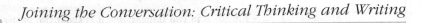

Joining the Conversation: Critical Thinking and Writing

1. The speaker (a man, although the author is a woman) talks of the suffering he is undergoing. Can we nevertheless feel that he enjoys his plight? *Why*, by the way, do we often enjoy songs of unhappy love?
2. The woman ("thee") is said to exhibit "pride and cruelty" (line 10). Is the poem sexist? Is it therefore offensive?
3. Do you suppose that men can enjoy the poem more than women? Set forth your response in a detailed argument.

Journal Entries

The subject is Aphra Behn's "Song: Love Armed." We begin with two entries in a journal kept by a first-year student, Geoffrey Sullivan, and we follow these entries with Sullivan's completed essay.

> October 10. The title "Love Armed" puzzled me at first; funny, I somehow was thinking of the expression "strong armed" and at first I didn't understand that "Love" in this poem is a human—no, not a human, but the god Cupid, who has a human form—and that he is shown as armed, with darts and so forth.
>
> October 13. This god of "Love" is Cupid, and so he is something like what is on a valentine card—Cupid with his bow and arrow. But valentine cards just show cute little Cupids, and in this poem Cupid is a real menace. He causes lots of pain ("bleeding hearts," "tears," "killing dart," etc.). So what is Aphra Behn telling us about the god of love, or love? That love hurts? And she is singing about it! But we do sing songs about how hard life is. But do we sing them when we are really hurting, or only when we are pretty well off and just thinking about being hurt?
>
> When you love someone and they don't return your love, it hurts, but even when love isn't returned it still gives some intense pleasure. Strange, but I think true. I wouldn't say that love always has this two-sided nature, but I do see the idea that love can have two sides, pleasure and pain. And love takes two kinds of people, male and female. Well, for most people, anyway. Maybe there's also something to the idea that "opposites attract." Anyway, Aphra Behn seems to be talking about men vs. women, pain vs. pleasure, power vs. weakness, etc. Pairs, opposites. And in two stanzas (a pair of stanzas?).

A Sample Essay by a Student: "The Double Nature of Love"

The final essay makes use of some, but not of all, of the preliminary jottings, and it includes much that Sullivan did not think of until he reread his jottings, reread the poem, and began drafting the essay.

Geoffrey Sullivan

Professor Morawski

English 2G

31 January 2013

The Double Nature of Love

Aphra Behn's "Love Armed" is in two stanzas, and it is about two people,

"me" and "thee," that is, you and I, the lover and the woman he loves.

I think the speaker is a man, since according to the usual code men are

supposed to be the active lovers and women are the (relatively) passive

people who are loved. In this poem, the beloved—the woman, I think—has

"bright eyes" (line 5) that provide the god of Love with fire, and she also

provides the god with "pride and cruelty" (10). This of course is the way the

man sees it if a woman does not respond to him; if she does not love him in

return, she is (he thinks) arrogant and cruel. What does the man give to

Love? He provides "desire" (7), "sighs and tears" (9), "languishments and

fears" (11). None of this sounds very manly, but the joke is that the god of

love—which means love—can turn a strong man into a crybaby when a

woman does not respond to him.

Although both stanzas are clever *descriptions* of the god of love, the

poem is not just a description. Of course there is not a plot in the way that a

short story has a plot, but there is a sort of a switch at the end, giving the

story something of a plot. The poem is, say, ninety percent expression of

feeling and description of love, but during the course of expressing feelings

and describing love something happens, so there is a tiny *story*. The first

stanza sets the scene ("Love in fantastic triumph sate" [1]) and tells of some

of the things that the speaker and the woman contributed to the god of Love.

The woman's eyes provided Love with fire, and the man's feelings provided

Love with "desire" (7). The second stanza goes on to mention other things

that Love got from the speaker ("sighs and tears," etc. [9]), and other things

Sullivan 2

that Love got from the beloved ("pride and cruelty," etc. [10]), and in line 13
the poet says, "Thus thou and I the god have armed," so the two humans
share something. They have both given Love his weapons. But—and this is
the story I spoke of—the poem ends by emphasizing their difference: Only
the man is "harmed," and the woman is the "victor" because her heart is not
captured, as the man's heart is. In the battle that Love presides over, the
woman is the winner; the man's heart has fallen for the woman, but,
according to the last line, the woman's heart remains "free."

We have all seen the god of Love on valentine cards, a cute little Cupid
armed with a bow and arrow. But despite the bow and arrow that the
Valentine Day Cupid carries, I think that until I read Aphra Behn's "Love
Armed" I had never really thought about Cupid as *powerful* and as capable of
causing real pain. On valentine cards, he is just cute, but when I think about
it, I realize the truth of Aphra Behn's concept of love. Love *is* (or can be)
two-sided, whereas the valentine cards show only the sweet side.

I think it is interesting to notice that although the poem is about the
destructive power of love, it is fun to read. I am not bothered by the fact
that the lover is miserable. Why? I think I enjoy the poem, rather than am
bothered by it, because *he is enjoying his misery*. After all, he is singing
about it, sort of singing in the rain, telling anyone who will listen about how
miserable he is, and he is having a very good time doing it.

[New page]

Sullivan 3

Work Cited

Behn, Aphra. "Love Armed." *Literature for Composition*. Ed. Sylvan Barnet, William
Burto, and William E. Cain. 10th ed. New York: Pearson, 2014. 178-79. Print.

Joining the Conversation: Critical Thinking and Writing

1. What do you think of the essay's title? Is it sufficiently interesting and focused?
2. What are the writer's chief points? Are they clear, and are they adequately developed?
3. Do you think Geoffrey Sullivan is too concerned with himself, and that he loses sight of the poem? Or do you find it interesting that he connects the poem with life?
4. Focus on the writer's use of quotations. Does he effectively introduce and examine quoted lines and phrases?
5. What grade would you give Sullivan's essay? What evidence can you offer to support your evaluation?

✔ **CHECKLIST:** *Editing a Draft*

☐ Is the title of my essay interesting?
☐ Do I identify the subject of my essay (author and title) early?
☐ What is my thesis? Do I state it soon enough (perhaps even in the title) and keep it in view?
☐ Is the organization reasonable? Does each point lead into the next without irrelevancies and without anticlimaxes?
☐ Is each paragraph unified by a topic sentence or a topic idea? Are there adequate transitions from one paragraph to the next?
☐ Are generalizations supported by appropriate evidence, especially by brief quotations from the text?
☐ Is the opening paragraph interesting and, by its end, focused on the topic? Is the final paragraph conclusive without being repetitive?
☐ Is the tone appropriate? No sarcasm, no apologies, no condescension?
☐ If there is a summary, is it as brief as possible, given its purpose?
☐ Are the quotations adequately introduced, and are they accurate? Do they provide evidence and let the reader hear the author's voice, or do they merely add words to the essay?
☐ Is the present tense used to describe what the author does and the action of the work ("Shakespeare *shows*," "Hamlet *dies*")?
☐ Have I kept in mind the needs of my audience, for instance, by defining unfamiliar terms or by briefly summarizing works or opinions with which the reader may be unfamiliar?
☐ Is documentation provided where necessary?
☐ Are the spelling and punctuation correct? Are other mechanical matters (such as margins, spacing, and citations) in correct form? Have I proofread carefully?
☐ Is the paper properly identified—author's name, instructor's name, course number, and date?

Your Turn: Short Stories and Poems for Analysis

EDGAR ALLAN POE

Edgar Allan Poe (1809–49) was the son of traveling actors. His father abandoned the family almost immediately, and his mother died when he was two. The child was adopted—though never legally—by a prosperous merchant and his wife in Richmond. The tensions were great, aggravated by Poe's drinking and heavy gambling, and in 1827 Poe left Richmond for Boston. He wrote, served briefly in the army, attended West Point but left within a year, and became an editor for the remaining eighteen years of his life. It was during these years, too, that he wrote the poems, essays, and fiction— especially detective stories and horror stories—that have made him famous.

The Cask of Amontillado

The thousand injuries of Fortunato I had borne as I best could, but when he ventured upon insult, I vowed revenge. You, who so well know the nature of my soul, will not suppose, however, that I gave utterance to a threat. At *length* I would be avenged; this was a point definitely settled—but the very definitiveness with which it was resolved precluded the idea of risk. I must not only punish, but punish with impunity. A wrong is unredressed when retribution overtakes its redresser. It is equally unredressed when the avenger fails to make himself felt as such to him who has done the wrong.

It must be understood that neither by word nor deed had I given Fortunato cause to doubt my good will. I continued, as was my wont, to smile in his face, and he did not perceive that my smile *now* was at the thought of his immolation.

He had a weak point—this Fortunato—although in other regards he was a man to be respected and even feared. He prided himself on his connoisseurship in wine. Few Italians have the true virtuoso spirit. For the most part their enthusiasm is adopted to suit the time and opportunity to practice imposture upon the British and Austrian *millionaires*. In painting and gemmary Fortunato, like his countrymen, was a quack, but in the matter of old wines he was sincere. In this respect I did not differ from him materially;—I was skillful in the Italian vintages myself, and bought largely whenever I could.

It was about dusk, one evening during the supreme madness of the carnival season, that I encountered my friend. He accosted me with excessive warmth, for he had been drinking much. The man wore motley. He had on a tight-fitting parti-striped dress, and his head was surmounted by the conical cap and bells. I was so pleased to see him, that I thought I should never have done wringing his hand.

5   I said to him—"My dear Fortunato, you are luckily met. How remarkably well you are looking to-day! But I have received a pipe[1] of what passes for Amontillado, and I have my doubts."

"How?" said he, "Amontillado? A pipe? Impossible! And in the middle of the carnival?"

[1]**pipe** wine cask.

"I have my doubts," I replied; "and I was silly enough to pay the full Amontillado price without consulting you in the matter. You were not to be found, and I was fearful of losing a bargain."

"Amontillado!"

"I have my doubts."

10   "Amontillado!"

"And I must satisfy them."

"Amontillado!"

"As you are engaged, I am on my way to Luchesi. If any one has a critical turn, it is he. He will tell me—"

"Luchesi cannot tell Amontillado from Sherry."

15   "And yet some fools will have it that his taste is a match for your own."

"Come, let us go."

"Whither?"

"To your vaults."

"My friend, no; I will not impose upon your good nature. I perceive you have an engagement. Luchesi—"

20   "I have no engagement; come."

"My friend, no. It is not the engagement, but the severe cold with which I perceive you are afflicted. The vaults are insufferably damp. They are encrusted with nitre."

"Let us go, nevertheless. The cold is merely nothing. Amontillado! You have been imposed upon; and as for Luchesi, he cannot distinguish Sherry from Amontillado."

Thus speaking, Fortunato possessed himself of my arm. Putting on a mask of black silk, and drawing a *roquelaure*[2] closely about my person, I suffered him to hurry me to my palazzo.

There were no attendants at home; they had absconded to make merry in honor of the time. I had told them that I should not return until the morning, and had given them explicit orders not to stir from the house. These orders were sufficient, I well knew, to insure their immediate disappearance, one and all, as soon as my back was turned.

25   I took from their sconces two flambeaux, and giving one to Fortunato, bowed him through several suites of rooms to the archway that led into the vaults. I passed down a long and winding staircase, requesting him to be cautious as he followed. We came at length to the foot of the descent, and stood together on the damp ground of the catacombs of the Montresors.

The gait of my friend was unsteady, and the bells upon his cap jingled as he strode.

"The pipe," said he.

"It is farther on," said I; "but observe the white web-work which gleams from these cavern walls."

He turned towards me, and looked into my eyes with two filmy orbs that distilled the rheum of intoxication.

30   "Nitre?" he asked, at length.

"Nitre," I replied. "How long have you had that cough?"

"Ugh! ugh! ugh!—ugh! ugh! ugh!—ugh! ugh! ugh!—ugh! ugh! ugh!—ugh! ugh! ugh!"

My poor friend found it impossible to reply for many minutes.

"It is nothing," he said, at last.

35   "Come," I said, with decision, "we will go back; your health is precious. You are rich, respected, admired, beloved; you are happy, as once I was. You are a man to be missed. For me it is no matter. We will go back; you will be ill, and I cannot be responsible. Besides, there is Luchesi—"

---

[2]***roquelaure*** short cloak.

"Enough," he said; "the cough is a mere nothing: it will not kill me. I shall not die of a cough."

"True—true," I replied; "and, indeed, I had no intention of alarming you unnecessarily—but you should use all proper caution. A draught of this Medoc will defend us from the damps."

Here I knocked off the neck of a bottle which I drew from a long row of its fellows that lay upon the mould.

"Drink," I said, presenting him the wine.

He raised it to his lips with a leer. He paused and nodded to me familiarly, while his bells jingled.

"I drink," he said, "to the buried that repose around us."

"And I to your long life."

He again took my arm, and we proceeded.

"These vaults," he said, "are extensive."

"The Montresors," I replied, "were a great and numerous family."

"I forget your arms."

"A huge human foot d'or, in a field azure; the foot crushes a serpent rampant whose fangs are imbedded in the heel."

"And the motto?"

"*Nemo me impune lacessit.*"[3]

"Good!" he said.

The wine sparkled in his eyes and the bells jingled. My own fancy grew warm with the Medoc. We had passed through walls of piled bones, with casks and puncheons intermingling, into the inmost recesses of the catacombs. I paused again, and this time I made bold to seize Fortunato by an arm above the elbow.

"The nitre!" I said; "see, it increases. It hangs like moss upon the vaults. We are below the river's bed. The drops of moisture tickle among the bones. Come, we will go back ere it is too late. Your cough—"

"It is nothing," he said; "let us go on. But first, another draught of the Medoc."

I broke and reached him a flagon of De Grâve. He emptied it at a breath. His eyes flashed with a fierce light. He laughed and threw the bottle upwards with a gesticulation I did not understand.

I looked at him in surprise. He repeated the movement—a grotesque one.

"You do not comprehend?" he said.

"Not I," I replied.

"Then you are not of the brotherhood."

"How?"

"You are not of the masons."[4]

"Yes, yes," I said, "yes, yes."

"You? Impossible! A mason?"

"A mason," I replied.

"A sign," he said.

"It is this," I answered, producing a trowel from beneath the folds of my *roquelaure.*

"You jest," he exclaimed, recoiling a few paces. "But let us proceed to the Amontillado."

"Be it so," I said, replacing the tool beneath the cloak, and again offering him my arm. He leaned upon it heavily. We continued our route in search of the

---

[3]*Nemo me impune lacessit* No one dare attack me with impunity (the motto of Scotland).

[4]*of the masons* i.e., a member of the Freemasons, an international secret fraternity.

Amontillado. We passed through a range of low arches, descended, passed on, and descending again, arrived at a deep crypt, in which the foulness of the air caused our flambeaux rather to glow than flame.

At the most remote end of the crypt there appeared another less spacious. Its walls had been lined with human remains piled to the vault overhead, in the fashion of the great catacombs of Paris. Three sides of this interior crypt were still ornamented in this manner. From the fourth the bones had been thrown down, and lay promiscuously upon the earth, forming at one point a mound of some size. Within the wall thus exposed by the displacing of the bones, we perceived a still interior recess, in depth about four feet, in width three, in height six or seven. It seemed to have been constructed for no especial use within itself, but formed merely the interval between two of the colossal supports of the roof of the catacombs, and was backed by one of their circumscribing walls of solid granite.

It was in vain that Fortunato, uplifting his dull torch, endeavored to pry into the depths of the recess. Its termination the feeble light did not enable us to see.

70 "Proceed," I said; "herein is the Amontillado. As for Luchesi—"

"He is an ignoramus," interrupted my friend, as he stepped unsteadily forward, while I followed immediately at his heels. In an instant he had reached the extremity of the niche, and finding his progress arrested by the rock, stood stupidly bewildered. A moment more and I had fettered him to the granite. In its surface were two iron staples, distant from each other about two feet, horizontally. From one of these depended a short chain, from the other a padlock. Throwing the links about his waist, it was but the work of a few seconds to secure it. He was too much astounded to resist. Withdrawing the key I stepped back from the recess.

"Pass your hand," I said, "over the wall; you cannot help feeling the nitre. Indeed it is very damp. Once more let me *implore* you to return. No? Then I must positively leave you. But I must first render you all the little attentions in my power."

"The Amontillado!" ejaculated my friend, not yet recovered from his astonishment.

"True," I replied; "the Amontillado."

75 As I said these words I busied myself among the pile of bones of which I have before spoken. Throwing them aside, I soon uncovered a quantity of building-stone and mortar. With these materials and with the aid of my trowel, I began vigorously to wall up the entrance of the niche.

I had scarcely laid the first tier of masonry when I discovered that the intoxication of Fortunato had in a great measure worn off. The earliest indication I had of this was a low moaning cry from the depth of the recess. It was *not* the cry of a drunken man. There was then a long and obstinate silence. I laid the second tier, and the third, and the fourth; and then I heard the furious vibrations of the chain. The noise lasted for several minutes, during which, that I might hearken to it with the more satisfaction, I ceased my labors and sat down upon the bones. When at last the clanking subsided, I resumed the trowel, and finished without interruption the fifth, the sixth, and the seventh tier. The wall was now nearly upon a level with my breast. I again paused, and holding the flambeaux over the masonwork, threw a few feeble rays upon the figure within.

A succession of loud and shrill screams, bursting suddenly from the throat of the chained form, seemed to thrust me violently back. For a brief moment I hesitated—I trembled. Unsheathing my rapier, I began to grope with it about the recess; but the thought of an instant reassured me. I placed my hand upon the solid fabric of the catacombs, and felt satisfied. I reapproached the wall. I replied to the yells of him who clamored. I re-echoed—I aided—I surpassed them in volume and in strength. I did this, and the clamorer grew still.

It was now midnight, and my task was drawing to a close. I had completed the eighth, the ninth, and the tenth tier. I had finished a portion of the last and the eleventh; there remained but a single stone to be fitted and plastered in. I struggled with its weight; I placed it partially in its destined position. But now there came from out the niche a low laugh that erected the hairs upon my head. It was succeeded by a sad voice, which I had difficulty in recognizing as that of the noble Fortunato. The voice said—

"Ha! ha! ha!—he! he! he!—a very good joke indeed—an excellent jest. We will have many a rich laugh about it at the palazzo—he! he! he!—over our wine—he! he! he!"

80   "The Amontillado!" I said.

"He! he! he!—he! he! he!—yes, the Amontillado. But is it not getting late? Will not they be awaiting us at the palazzo, the Lady Fortunato and the rest? Let us be gone."

"Yes," I said, "let us be gone."

"For the love of God, Montresor!"

"Yes," I said, "for the love of God!"

85   But to these words I hearkened in vain for a reply. I grew impatient. I called aloud:

"Fortunato!"

No answer. I called again;

"Fortunato!"

No answer still. I thrust a torch through the remaining aperture and let it fall within. There came forth in return only a jingling of the bells. My heart grew sick— on account of the dampness of the catacombs. I hastened to make an end of my labor. I forced the last stone into its position; I plastered it up. Against the new masonry I reerected the old rampart of bones. For the half of a century no mortal has disturbed them. *In pace requiescat!*[5]

[1846]

---

[5]*In pace requiescat!* May he rest in peace!

Joining the Conversation: Critical Thinking and Writing

1. To whom does Montresor tell his story? The story he tells happened fifty years earlier. Do we have any clue as to why he tells it now?
2. At the end of the story we learn that the murder occurred fifty years ago. Would the story be equally effective if Poe had had Montresor reveal this fact at the outset? Why, or why not?
3. Poe sets Montresor's story at dusk, "during the supreme madness of the carnival season." What is the "carnival season"? (If you are uncertain as to the meaning of "carnival," consult a dictionary.) What details of the story derive from the setting?
4. In the first line Montresor declares, "The thousand injuries of Fortunato I had borne as I best could, but when he ventured upon insult, I vowed revenge." Do we ever learn what those injuries and that insult were? What do we learn about Montresor from this declaration?

5. How does Montresor characterize Fortunato? What details of his portrait unwittingly enlist our sympathy for Fortunato? Does Montresor betray any sympathy for his victim?

6. "The Cask of Amontillado" is sometimes referred to as a "horror tale." Do you think it has anything in common with horror movies? If so, what? (You might begin by making a list of the characteristics of horror movies.) Why do people take pleasure in horror movies? Does this story offer any of the same sorts of pleasure? In any case, why might a reader take pleasure in this story? Set forth your response in an argument of 250–500 words.

7. Construct a definition of madness (you may want to do a little research, but if you make use of your findings, be sure to give credit to your sources) and write an essay of 500–750 words arguing whether or not Montresor is mad. (*Note:* You may want to distinguish between Montresor at the time of the killing and Montresor at the time of narration.)

MyLiteratureLab® *For additional resources for "The Cask of Amontillado," log in to* www.myliteraturelab.com *where you will find a Comprehension Quiz, Short Evaluation Exercises, and Essay Prompts, as well as an About the Author, Bibliography, Links, and Critical Overview for Poe (under Student Resources).*

KATHERINE ANNE PORTER

Katherine Anne Porter (1890–1980) had the curious habit of inventing details in her life, but it is true that she was born in a log cabin in Indian Creek, Texas, that she was originally named Callie Russell Porter, that her mother died when the child was two years old, and that Callie was brought up by her maternal grandmother in Kyle, Texas. She was sent to convent schools, where, in her words, she received a "strangely useless and ornamental education." When she was sixteen she left school, married (and soon divorced), and worked as a reporter, first in Texas and later in Denver and Chicago. She moved around a good deal, both within the United States and abroad; she lived for a while in Mexico, Belgium, Switzerland, France, and Germany.

Even as a child she was interested in writing, but she did not publish her first story until she was thirty-three. She wrote essays and one novel (Ship of Fools), *but she is best known for her stories. Porter's* Collected Stories *won the Pulitzer Prize and the National Book Award in 1965.*

The Jilting of Granny Weatherall

She flicked her wrist neatly out of Doctor Harry's pudgy careful fingers and pulled the sheet up to her chin. The brat ought to be in knee breeches. Doctoring around the country with spectacles on his nose! "Get along now, take your schoolbooks and go. There's nothing wrong with me."

Doctor Harry spread a warm paw like a cushion on her forehead where the forked green vein danced and made her eyelids twitch. "Now, now, be a good girl, and we'll have you up in no time."

"That's no way to speak to a woman nearly eighty years old just because she's down. I'd have you respect your elders, young man."

"Well, Missy, excuse me." Doctor Harry patted her cheek. "But I've got to warn you, haven't I? You're a marvel, but you must be careful or you're going to be good and sorry."

5   "Don't tell me what I'm going to be. I'm on my feet now, morally speaking. It's Cornelia. I had to go to bed to get rid of her."

Her bones felt loose, and floated around in her skin, and Doctor Harry floated like a balloon around the foot of the bed. He floated and pulled down his waistcoat and swung his glasses on a cord. "Well, stay where you are, it certainly can't hurt you."

"Get along and doctor your sick," said Granny Weatherall. "Leave a well woman alone. I'll call for you when I want you. . . . Where were you forty years ago when I pulled through milk-leg and double pneumonia? You weren't even born. Don't let Cornelia lead you on," she shouted, because Doctor Harry appeared to float up to the ceiling and out. "I pay my own bills, and I don't throw my money away on nonsense!"

She meant to wave good-by, but it was too much trouble. Her eyes closed of themselves, it was like a dark curtain drawn around the bed. The pillow rose and floated under her, pleasant as a hammock in a light wind. She listened to the leaves rustling outside the window. No, somebody was swishing newspapers: no, Cornelia and Doctor Harry were whispering together. She leaped broad awake, thinking they whispered in her ear.

"She was *never* like this, never like this!" "Well, what can we expect?" "Yes, eighty years old. . . ."

10   Well, and what if she was? She still had ears. It was like Cornelia to whisper around doors. She always kept things secret in such a public way. She was always being tactful and kind. Cornelia was dutiful; that was the trouble with her. Dutiful and good: "So good and dutiful," said Granny, "that I'd like to spank her." She saw herself spanking Cornelia and making a fine job of it.

"What'd you say, Mother?"

Granny felt her face tying up in hard knots.

"Can't a body think, I'd like to know?"

"I thought you might want something."

15   "I do. I want a lot of things. First off, go away and don't whisper."

She lay and drowsed, hoping in her sleep that the children would keep out and let her rest a minute. It had been a long day. Not that she was tired. It was always pleasant to snatch a minute now and then. There was always so much to be done, let me see: tomorrow.

Tomorrow was far away and there was nothing to trouble about. Things were finished somehow when the time came; thank God there was always a little margin over for peace: then a person could spread out the plan of life and tuck in the edges orderly. It was good to have everything clean and folded away, with the hair brushes and tonic bottles sitting straight on the white embroidered linen: the day started without fuss and the pantry shelves laid out with rows of jelly glasses and brown jugs and white stone-china jars with blue whirligigs and words painted on them: coffee, tea, sugar, ginger, cinnamon, allspice: and the bronze clock with the lion on top nicely dusted off. The dust that lion could collect in twenty-four hours! The box in the attic with all those letters tied up, well, she'd have to go through that tomorrow. All those letters—George's letters and John's letters and her letters to them both— lying around for the children to find afterwards made her uneasy. Yes, that would be tomorrow's business. No use to let them know how silly she had been once.

While she was rummaging around she found death in her mind and it felt clammy and unfamiliar. She had spent so much time preparing for death there was no need for bringing it up again. Let it take care of itself now. When she was sixty she had felt very old, finished, and went around making farewell trips to see her children and grandchildren, with a secret in her mind: This is the very last of your mother, children! Then she made her will and came down with a long fever. That was all just a notion like a lot of other things, but it was lucky too, for she had once for all got over the idea of dying for a long time. Now she couldn't be worried. She hoped she had better sense now. Her father had lived to be one hundred and two years old and had drunk a noggin of strong hot toddy on his last birthday. He told the reporters it was his daily habit, and he owed his long life to that. He had made quite a scandal and was very pleased about it. She believed she'd just plague Cornelia a little.

"Cornelia! Cornelia!" No footsteps, but a sudden hand on her cheek. "Bless you, where have you been?"

20   "Here, Mother."

"Well, Cornelia, I want a noggin of hot toddy."

"Are you cold, darling?"

"I'm chilly, Cornelia. Lying in bed stops the circulation. I must have told you that a thousand times."

Well, she could just hear Cornelia telling her husband that Mother was getting a little childish and they'd have to humor her. The thing that most annoyed her was that Cornelia thought she was deaf, dumb, and blind. Little hasty glances and tiny gestures tossed around her and over her head saying, "Don't cross her, let her have her way, she's eighty years old," and she sitting there as if she lived in a thin glass cage. Sometimes Granny almost made up her mind to pack up and move back to her own house where nobody could remind her every minute that she was old. Wait, wait, Cornelia, till your own children whisper behind your back!

25   In her day she had kept a better house and had got more work done. She wasn't too old yet for Lydia to be driving eighty miles for advice when one of the children jumped the track, and Jimmy still dropped in and talked things over: "Now, Mammy, you've a good business head, I want to know what you think of this? . . . " Old. Cornelia couldn't change the furniture around without asking. Little things, little things! They had been so sweet when they were little. Granny wished the old days were back again with the children young and everything to be done over. It had been a hard pull, but not too much for her. When she thought of all the food she had cooked, and all the clothes she had cut and sewed, and all the gardens she had made—well, the children showed it. There they were, made out of her, and they couldn't get away from that. Sometimes she wanted to see John again and point to them and say, Well, I didn't do so badly, did I? But that would have to wait. That was for tomorrow. She used to think of him as a man, but now all the children were older than their father, and he would be a child beside her if she saw him now. It seemed strange and there was something wrong in the idea. Why, he couldn't possibly recognize her. She had fenced in a hundred acres once, digging the post holes herself and clamping the wires with just a negro boy to help. That changed a woman. John would be looking for a young woman with the peaked Spanish comb in her hair and the painted fan. Digging post holes changed a woman. Riding country roads in the winter when women had their babies was another thing: sitting up nights with sick horses and sick negroes and sick children and hardly ever losing one. John, I hardly ever lost one of them! John would see that in a minute, that would be something he could understand, she wouldn't have to explain anything!

It made her feel like rolling up her sleeves and putting the whole place to rights again. No matter if Cornelia was determined to be everywhere at once, there were a great many things left undone on this place. She would start tomorrow and do them. It was good to be strong enough for everything, even if all you made melted and changed and slipped under your hands, so that by the time you finished you almost forgot what you were working for. What was it I set out to do? she asked herself intently, but she could not remember. A fog rose over the valley, she saw it marching across the creek swallowing the trees and moving up the hill like an army of ghosts. Soon it would be at the near edge of the orchard, and then it was time to go in and light the lamps. Come in, children, don't stay out in the night air.

Lighting the lamps had been beautiful. The children huddled up to her and breathed like little calves waiting at the bars in the twilight. Their eyes followed the match and watched the flame rise and settle in a blue curve, then they moved away from her. The lamp was lit, they didn't have to be scared and hang on to mother any more. Never, never, never more. God, for all my life I thank Thee. Without Thee, my God, I could never have done it. Hail, Mary, full of grace.

I want you to pick all the fruit this year and see that nothing is wasted. There's always someone who can use it. Don't let good things rot for want of using. You waste life when you waste good food. Don't let things get lost. It's bitter to lose things. Now, don't let me get to thinking, not when I am tired and taking a little nap before supper. . . .

The pillow rose about her shoulders and pressed against her heart and the memory was being squeezed out of it: oh, push down that pillow, somebody: it would smother her if she tried to hold it. Such a fresh breeze blowing and such a green day with no threats in it. But he had not come, just the same. What does a woman do when she has put on the white veil and set out the white cake for a man and he doesn't come? She tried to remember. No, I swear he never harmed me but in that. He never harmed me but in that . . . and what if he did? There was the day, the day, but a whirl of dark smoke rose and covered it, crept up and over into the bright field where everything was planted so carefully in orderly rows. That was hell, she knew hell when she saw it. For sixty years she had prayed against remembering him and against losing her soul in the deep pit of hell, and now the two things were mingled in one and the thought of him was a smoky cloud from hell that moved and crept in her head when she had just got rid of Doctor Harry and was trying to rest a minute. Wounded vanity, Ellen, said a sharp voice in the top of her mind. Don't let your wounded vanity get the upper hand of you. Plenty of girls get jilted. You were jilted, weren't you? Then stand up to it. Her eyelids wavered and let in streamers of blue-gray light like tissue paper over her eyes. She must get up and pull the shades down or she'd never sleep. She was in bed again and the shades were not down. How could that happen? Better turn over, hide from the light, sleeping in the light gave you nightmares. "Mother, how do you feel now?" and a stinging wetness on her forehead. But I don't like having my face washed in cold water!

30   Hapsy? George? Lydia? Jimmy? No, Cornelia, and her features were swollen and full of little puddles. "They're coming, darling, they'll all be here soon." Go wash your face, child, you look funny.

Instead of obeying, Cornelia knelt down and put her head on the pillow. She seemed to be talking but there was no sound. "Well, are you tongue-tied? Whose birthday is it? Are you going to give a party?"

Cornelia's mouth moved urgently in strange shapes. "Don't do that, you bother me, daughter."

"Oh, no, Mother. Oh, no. . . ."

Nonsense. It was strange about children. They disputed your every word. "No what, Cornelia?"

35   "Here's Doctor Harry."

"I won't see that boy again. He just left five minutes ago."

"That was this morning, Mother. It's night now. Here's the nurse."

"This is Doctor Harry, Mrs. Weatherall. I never saw you look so young and happy!"

"Ah, I'll never be young again—but I'd be happy if they'd let me lie in peace and get rested."

40   She thought she spoke up loudly, but no one answered. A warm weight on her forehead, a warm bracelet on her wrist, and a breeze went on whispering, trying to tell her something. A shuffle of leaves in the everlasting hand of God. He blew on them and they danced and rattled. "Mother, don't mind, we're going to give you a little hypodermic." "Look here, daughter, how do ants get in this bed? I saw sugar ants yesterday." Did you send for Hapsy too?

It was Hapsy she really wanted. She had to go a long way back through a great many rooms to find Hapsy standing with a baby on her arm. She seemed to herself to be Hapsy also, and the baby on Hapsy's arm was Hapsy and himself and herself, all at once, and there was no surprise in the meeting. Then Hapsy melted from within and turned flimsy as gray gauze and the baby was a gauzy shadow, and Hapsy came up close and said, "I thought you'd never come," and looked at her very searchingly and said, "You haven't changed a bit!" They leaned forward to kiss, when Cornelia began whispering from a long way off, "Oh, is there anything you want to tell me? Is there anything I can do for you?"

Yes, she had changed her mind after sixty years and she would like to see George. I want you to find George. Find him and be sure to tell him I forgot him. I want him to know I had my husband just the same and my children and my house like any other woman. A good house too and a good husband that I loved and fine children out of him. Better than I hoped for even. Tell him I was given back everything he took away and more. Oh, no, oh, God, no, there was something else besides the house and the man and the children. Oh, surely they were not all? What was it? Something not given back. . . . Her breath crowded down under her ribs and grew into a monstrous frightening shape with cutting edges; it bored up into her head, and the agony was unbelievable: Yes, John, get the doctor now, no more talk, my time has come.

When this one was born it should be the last. The last. It should have been born first, for it was the one she had truly wanted. Everything came in good time. Nothing left out, left over. She was strong, in three days she would be as well as ever. Better. A woman needed milk in her to have her full health.

"Mother, do you hear me?"

45   "I've been telling you—"

"Mother, Father Connolly's here."

"I went to Holy Communion only last week. Tell him I'm not so sinful as all that."

"Father just wants to speak to you."

He could speak as much as he pleased. It was like him to drop in and inquire about her soul as if it were a teething baby, and then stay on for a cup of tea and a round of cards and gossip. He always had a funny story of some sort, usually about an Irishman who made his little mistakes and confessed them, and the point lay in some absurd thing he would blurt out in the confessional showing his struggles between native piety and original sin. Granny felt easy about her soul. Cornelia, where are your manners? Give Father Connolly a chair. She had her secret comfortable understanding with a few favorite saints who cleared a straight road to God for her. All as surely signed and sealed as the papers for the new Forty Acres. Forever . . . heirs and assigns forever. Since the day the wedding cake was not cut, but thrown out and wasted. The whole bottom dropped out of the world, and there she was blind and sweating with nothing under her feet and the walls falling away. His hand had caught her under the breast, she had not fallen, there was the freshly polished floor with the green rug on it, just as before. He had cursed like a sailor's parrot and said, "I'll kill him for you." Don't lay a hand on him, for my sake leave something to God. "Now, Ellen, you must believe what I tell you. . . ."

50   So there was nothing, nothing to worry about any more, except sometimes in the night one of the children screamed in a nightmare, and they both hustled out shaking and hunting for the matches and calling, "There, wait a minute, here we are!" John, get the doctor now, Hapsy's time has come. But there was Hapsy standing by the bed in a white cap. "Cornelia, tell Hapsy to take off her cap. I can't see her plain."

Her eyes opened very wide and the room stood out like a picture she had seen somewhere. Dark colors with the shadows rising toward the ceiling in long angles. The tall black dresser gleamed with nothing on it but John's picture, enlarged from a little one, with John's eyes very black when they should have been blue. You never saw him, so how do you know how he looked? But the man insisted the copy was perfect, it was very rich and handsome. For a picture, yes, but it's not my husband. The table by the bed had a linen cover and a candle and a crucifix. The light was blue from Cornelia's silk lampshades. No sort of light at all, just frippery. You had to live forty years with kerosene lamps to appreciate honest electricity. She felt very strong and she saw Doctor Harry with a rosy nimbus around him.

"You look like a saint, Doctor Harry, and I vow that's as near as you'll ever come to it."

"She's saying something."

"I heard you, Cornelia. What's all this carrying on?"

55   "Father Connolly's saying—"

Cornelia's voice staggered and bumped like a cart in a bad road. It rounded corners and turned back again and arrived nowhere. Granny stepped up in the cart very lightly and reached for the reins, but a man sat beside her and she knew him by his hands, driving the cart. She did not look in his face, for she knew without seeing, but looked instead down the road where the trees leaned over and bowed to each other and a thousand birds were singing a Mass. She felt like singing too, but she put her hand in the bosom of her dress and pulled out a rosary, and Father Connolly murmured Latin in a very solemn voice and tickled her feet. My God, will you stop that nonsense? I'm a married woman. What if he did run away and leave me to face the priest by myself? I found another a whole world better. I wouldn't have exchanged my husband for anybody except St. Michael himself, and you may tell him that for me with a thank you in the bargain.

Light flashed on her closed eyelids, and a deep roaring shook her. Cornelia, is that lightning? I hear thunder. There's going to be a storm. Close all the windows. Call the children in. . . . "Mother, here we are, all of us." "Is that you, Hapsy?" "Oh, no, I'm Lydia. We drove as fast as we could." Their faces drifted above her, drifted away. The rosary fell out of her hands and Lydia put it back. Jimmy tried to help, their hands fumbled together, and Granny closed two fingers around Jimmy's thumb. Beads wouldn't do, it must be something alive. She was so amazed her thoughts ran round and round. So, my dear Lord, this is my death and I wasn't even thinking about it. My children have come to see me die. But I can't, it's not time. Oh, I always hated surprises. I wanted to give Cornelia the amethyst set—Cornelia, you're to have the amethyst set, but Hapsy's to wear it when she wants, and, Doctor Harry, do shut up. Nobody sent for you. Oh, my dear Lord, do wait a minute. I meant to do something about the Forty Acres, Jimmy doesn't need it and Lydia will later on, with that worthless husband of hers. I meant to finish the altar cloth and send six bottles of wine to Sister Borgia for her dyspepsia. I want to send six bottles of wine to Sister Borgia, Father Connolly, now don't let me forget.

Cornelia's voice made short turns and tilted over and crashed. "Oh, Mother, oh, Mother, oh, Mother. . . ."

"I'm not going, Cornelia. I'm taken by surprise. I can't go."

60   You'll see Hapsy again. What about her? "I thought you'd never come." Granny made a long journey outward, looking for Hapsy. What if I don't find her? What then? Her heart sank down and down, there was no bottom to death, she couldn't come to the end of it. The blue light from Cornelia's lampshade drew into a tiny point in the center of her brain, it flickered and winked like an eye, quietly it fluttered and dwindled. Granny lay curled down within herself, amazed and watchful, starting at the point of light that was herself; her body was now only a deeper mass of shadow in an endless darkness and this darkness would curl around the light and swallow it up. God, give a sign!

For the second time there was no sign. Again no bridegroom and the priest in the house. She could not remember any other sorrow because this grief wiped them all away. Oh, no, there's nothing more cruel than this—I'll never forgive it. She stretched herself with a deep breath and blew out the light.

[1929]

Joining the Conversation: Critical Thinking and Writing

1. In a paragraph, characterize Granny Weatherall. In another paragraph evaluate her claim that the anguish of the jilting has been compensated for by her subsequent life. Be sure to offer evidence to support your assertions.
2. The final paragraph alludes to Christ's parable of the bridegroom (Matthew 25:1–13). With this allusion in mind, write a paragraph explaining the title of the story.

MyLiteratureLab® *For additional resources for "The Jilting of Granny Weatherall," log in to* www.myliteraturelab.com *where you will find a Video Performance, Comprehension Quiz, Short Evaluation Exercises, and Essay Prompts, as well as an About the Author, Links, and Critical Overview for Porter (under Student Resources).*

JOSÉ ARMAS

Born in 1944, José Armas has been a teacher (at the University of New Mexico and at the University of Albuquerque), publisher, critic, and community organizer. His interest in community affairs won him a fellowship, which in 1974–75 brought him into association with the Urban Planning Department at the Massachusetts Institute of Technology. In 1980 he was awarded a writing fellowship by the National Endowment for the Arts, and he now writes a column on Hispanic affairs for the Albuquerque Journal.

El Tonto del Barrio[1]

Romero Estrado was called "El Cotorro"[2] because he was always whistling and singing. He made nice music even though his songs were spontaneous compositions made up of words with sounds that he liked but which seldom made any sense. But that didn't seem to bother either Romero or anyone else in the Golden Heights Centro where he lived. Not even the kids made fun of him. It just was not permitted.

Romero had a ritual that he followed almost every day. After breakfast he would get his broom and go up and down the main street of the Golden Heights Centro whistling and singing and sweeping the sidewalks for all the businesses. He would sweep in front of the Tortillería America,[3] the XXX Liquor Store, the Tres Milpas[4] Bar run by Tino Gabaldon, Barelas' Barber Shop, the used furniture store owned by Goldstein, El Centro Market of the Avila family, the Model Cities Office, and Lourdes Printing Store. Then, in the afternoons, he would come back and sit in Barelas' Barber Shop and spend the day looking at magazines and watching and waving to the passing people as he sang and composed his songs without a care in the world.

When business was slow, Barelas would let him sit in the barber's chair. Romero loved it. It was a routine that Romero kept every day except Sundays and Mondays when Barelas' Barber Shop was closed. After a period of years, people in the barrio got used to seeing Romero do his little task of sweeping the sidewalks and sitting in Barelas' Barber Shop. If he didn't show up one day someone assumed the responsibility to go to his house to see if he was ill. People would stop to say hello to Romero on the street and although he never initiated a conversation while he was sober, he always smiled and responded cheerfully to everyone. People passing the barber shop in the afternoons made it a point to wave even though they couldn't see him; they knew he was in there and was expecting some salutation.

When he was feeling real good, Romero would sweep in front of the houses on both sides of the block also. He took his job seriously and took great care to sweep cleanly, between the cracks and even between the sides of buildings. The dirt and small scraps went into the gutter. The bottles and bigger pieces of litter were put carefully in cardboard boxes, ready for the garbage man.

5   If he did it the way he wanted, the work took him the whole morning. And always cheerful—always with some song.

Only once did someone call attention to his work. Frank Avila told him in jest that Romero had forgotten to pick up an empty bottle of wine from his door. Romero was so offended and made such a commotion that it got around very quickly that no one should criticize his work. There was, in fact, no reason to.

Although it had been long acknowledged that Romero was a little "touched," he fit very well into the community. He was a respected citizen.

He could be found at the Tres Milpas Bar drinking his occasional beer in the evenings. Romero had a rivalry going with the Ranchera songs on the jukebox. He would try to outsing the songs using the same melody but inserting his own selection of random words. Sometimes, like all people, he would "bust out" and get drunk.

One could always tell when Romero was getting drunk because he would begin telling everyone that he loved them.

10   "I looov youuu," he would sing to someone and offer to compose them a song.

"Ta bueno, Romero. Ta bueno, ya bete,"[5] they would tell him.

---

[1]**El Tonto del Barrio** the barrio dummy (in the United States, a barrio is a Spanish-speaking community) [all notes are by the editors].   [2]**El Cotorro** The Parrot.   [3]**Tortillería America** Tortilla Factory.   [4]**Tres Milpas** Three Cornfields.   [5]**Ta bueno, ya bete** OK, now go away.

Sometimes when he got too drunk he would crap in his pants and then Tino would make him go home.

Romero received some money from Social Security but it wasn't much. None of the merchants gave him any credit because he would always forget to pay his bills. He didn't do it on purpose, he just forgot and spent his money on something else. So instead, the businessmen preferred to do little things for him occasionally. Barelas would trim his hair when things were slow. The Tortillería America would give him menudo[6] and fresh-made tortillas at noon when he was finished with his sweeping. El Centro Market would give him the overripe fruit and broken boxes of food that no one else would buy. Although it was unspoken and unwritten, there was an agreement that existed between Romero and the Golden Heights Centro. Romero kept the sidewalks clean and the barrio looked after him. It was a contract that worked well for a long time.

Then, when Seferino, Barelas' oldest son, graduated from high school he went to work in the barber shop for the summer. Seferino was a conscientious and sensitive young man and it wasn't long before he took notice of Romero and came to feel sorry for him.

15   One day when Romero was in the shop Seferino decided to act.

"Mira, Romero. Yo te doy 50 centavos por cada día que me barres la banqueta. Fifty cents for every day you sweep the sidewalk for us. Qué te parece?"[7]

Romero thought about it carefully.

"Hecho! Done!" he exclaimed. He started for home right away to get his broom.

"Why did you do that for, m'ijo?"[8] asked Barelas.

20   "It don't seem right, Dad. The man works and no one pays him for his work. Everyone should get paid for what they do."

"He don't need no pay. Romero has everything he needs."

"It's not the same, Dad. How would you like to do what he does and be treated the same way? It's degrading the way he has to go around getting scraps and handouts."

"I'm not Romero. Besides you don't know about these things, m'ijo. Romero would be unhappy if his schedule was upset. Right now everyone likes him and takes care of him. He sweeps the sidewalks because he wants something to do, not because he wants money."

"I'll pay him out of my money, don't worry about it then."

25   "The money is not the point. The point is that money will not help Romero. Don't you understand that?"

"Look, Dad. Just put yourself in his place. Would you do it? Would you cut hair for nothing?"

Barelas just knew his son was putting something over on him but he didn't know how to answer. It seemed to make sense the way Seferino explained it. But it still went against his "instinct." On the other hand, Seferino had gone and finished high school. He must know something. There were few kids who had finished high school in the barrio, and fewer who had gone to college. Barelas knew them all. He noted (with some pride) that Seferino was going to be enrolled at Harvard University this year. That must count for something, he thought. Barelas himself had never gone to school. So maybe his son had something there. On the other hand . . . it upset Barelas that he wasn't able to get Seferino to see the issue. How can we be so far apart on something so simple, he thought. But he decided not to say anything else about it.

---

[6]**menudo** tripe soup.   [7]**Qué te parece?** How does that strike you?   [8]**m'ijo** (mi hijo) my son.

Romero came back right away and swept the front of Barelas' shop again and put what little dirt he found into the curb. He swept up the gutter, put the trash in a shoe box and threw it in a garbage can.

Seferino watched with pride as Romero went about his job and when he was finished he went outside and shook Romero's hand. Seferino told him he had done a good job. Romero beamed.

30 Manolo was coming into the shop to get his hair cut as Seferino was giving Romero his wages. He noticed Romero with his broom.

"What's going on?" he asked. Barelas shrugged his shoulders. "Qué tiene Romero?[9] Is he sick or something?"

"No, he's not sick," explained Seferino, who had now come inside. He told Manolo the story.

"We're going to make Romero a businessman," said Seferino. "Do you realize how much money Romero would make if everyone paid him just fifty cents a day? Like my dad says, 'Everyone should be able to keep his dignity, no matter how poor.' And he does a job, you know."

"Well, it makes sense," said Manolo.

35 "Hey, maybe I'll ask people to do that," said Seferino. "That way the poor old man could make a decent wage. Do you want to help, Manolo? You can go with me to ask people to pay him."

"Well," said Manolo as he glanced at Barelas, "I'm not too good at asking people for money."

This did not discourage Seferino. He went out and contacted all the businesses on his own, but no one else wanted to contribute. This didn't discourage Seferino either. He went on giving Romero fifty cents a day.

After a while, Seferino heard that Romero had asked for credit at the grocery store. "See, Dad. What did I tell you? Things are getting better for him already. He's becoming his own man. And look. It's only been a couple of weeks." Barelas did not reply.

But then the next week Romero did not show up to sweep any sidewalks. He was around but he didn't do any work for anybody the entire week. He walked around Golden Heights Centro in his best gray work pants and his slouch hat, looking important and making it a point to walk right past the barber shop every little while.

40 Of course, the people in the Golden Heights Centro noticed the change immediately, and since they saw Romero in the street, they knew he wasn't ill. But the change was clearly disturbing the community. They discussed him in the Tortillería America where people got together for coffee, and at the Tres Milpas Bar. Everywhere the topic of conversation was the great change that had come over Romero. Only Barelas did not talk about it.

The following week Romero came into the barber shop and asked to talk with Seferino in private. Barelas knew immediately something was wrong. Romero never initiated a conversation unless he was drunk.

They went into the back room where Barelas could not hear and then Romero informed Seferino, "I want a raise."

"What? What do you mean, a raise? You haven't been around for a week. You only worked a few weeks and now you want a raise?" Seferino was clearly angry but Romero was calm and insistent.

Romero correctly pointed out that he had been sweeping the sidewalks for a long time. Even before Seferino finished high school.

[9]**Qué tiene Romero?** What's with Romero?

45   "I deserve a raise," he repeated after an eloquent presentation.
          Seferino looked coldly at Romero. It was clearly a stand-off.
          Then Seferino said, "Look, maybe we should forget the whole thing. I was just
trying to help you out and look at what you do."
          Romero held his ground. "I helped you out too. No one told me to do it and
I did it anyway. I helped you many years."
          "Well, let's forget about the whole thing then," said Seferino.
50   "I quit then," said Romero.
          "Quit?" exclaimed Seferino as he laughed at Romero.
          "Quit! I quit!" said Romero as he walked out the front of the shop past Barelas,
who was cutting a customer's hair.
          Seferino came out shaking his head and laughing.
          "Can you imagine that old guy?"
55   Barelas did not seem too amused. He felt he could have predicted that something bad like this would happen.
          Romero began sweeping the sidewalks again the next day with the exception
that when he came to the barber shop he would go around it and continue sweeping the rest of the sidewalks. He did this for the rest of the week. And the following
Tuesday he began sweeping the sidewalk all the way up to the shop and then
pushing the trash to the sidewalk in front of the barber shop. Romero then stopped
coming to the barber shop in the afternoon.
          The barrio buzzed with fact and rumor about Romero. Tino commented that
Romero was not singing anymore. Even if someone offered to buy him a beer he
wouldn't sing. Frank Avila said the neighbors were complaining because he was
leaving his TV on loud the whole day and night. He still greeted people but seldom smiled. He had run up a big bill at the liquor store and when the manager
stopped his credit, he caught Romero stealing bottles of whiskey. He was also
getting careless about his dress. He didn't shave and clean like he used to. Women
complained that he walked around in soiled pants, that he smelled bad. Even one
of the little kids complained that Romero had kicked his puppy, but that seemed
hard to believe.
          Barelas felt terrible. He felt responsible. But he couldn't convince Seferino that
what he had done was wrong. Barelas himself stopped going to the Tres Milpas
Bar after work to avoid hearing about Romero. Once he came across Romero on
the street and Barelas said hello but with a sense of guilt. Romero responded,
avoiding Barelas' eyes and moving past him awkwardly and quickly. Romero's
behavior continued to get erratic and some people started talking about having
Romero committed.
          "You can't do that," said Barelas when he was presented with a petition.
60   "He's flipped," said Tino, who made up part of the delegation circulating the
petition. "No one likes Romero more than I do, you know that Barelas."
          "But he's really crazy," said Frank Avila.
          "He was crazy before. No one noticed," pleaded Barelas.
          "But it was a crazy we could depend on. Now he just wants to sit on the curb
and pull up the women's skirts. It's terrible. The women are going crazy. He's also
running into the street stopping the traffic. You see how he is. What choice do
we have?"
          "It's for his own good," put in one of the workers from the Model Cities Office.
Barelas dismissed them as outsiders. Seferino was there and wanted to say something but a look from Barelas stopped him.

65   "We just can't do that," insisted Barelas. "Let's wait. Maybe he's just going through a cycle. Look. We've had a full moon recently, qué no?[10] That must be it. You know how the moon affects people in his condition."

     "I don't know," said Tino. "What if he hurts. . . ."

     "He's not going to hurt anyone," cut in Barelas.

     "No, Barelas. I was going to say, what if he hurts himself. He has no one at home. I'd say, let him come home with me for a while but you know how stubborn he is. You can't even talk to him any more."

     "He gives everyone the finger when they try to pull him out of the traffic," said Frank Avila. "The cops have missed him, but it won't be long before they see him doing some of his antics and arrest him. Then what? Then the poor guy is in real trouble."

70   "Well, look," said Barelas. "How many names you got on the list?"

     Tino responded slowly, "Well, we sort of wanted you to start off the list."

     "Let's wait a while longer," said Barelas. "I just know that Romero will come around. Let's wait just a while, okay?"

     No one had the heart to fight the issue and so they postponed the petition.

     There was no dramatic change in Romero even though the full moon had completed its cycle. Still, no one initiated the petition again and then in the middle of August Seferino left for Cambridge to look for housing and to register early for school. Suddenly everything began to change again. One day Romero began sweeping the entire sidewalk again. His spirits began to pick up and his strange antics began to disappear.

75   At the Tortillería America the original committee met for coffee and the talk turned to Romero.

     "He's going to be all right now," said a jubilant Barelas. "I guarantee it."

     "Well, don't hold your breath yet," said Tino. "The full moon is coming up again."

     "Yeah," said Frank Avila dejectedly.

     When the next full moon was in force the group was together again drinking coffee and Tino asked, "Well, how's Romero doing?"

80   Barelas smiled and said, "Well. Singing songs like crazy."

[1982]

[10]**qué no?** right?

Joining the Conversation: Critical Thinking and Writing

1. What sort of man do you think Barelas is? In your response take account of the fact that the townspeople "sort of want" Barelas "to start off the list" of petitioners seeking to commit Romero.
2. The narrator, introducing the reader to Seferino, tells us that "Seferino was a conscientious and sensitive young man." Do you agree? Why, or why not? Be sure to support your position with evidence.
3. What do you make of the last line of the story?
4. Do you think this story could take place in almost any community? If you did not grow up in a barrio, could it take place in your community?

LESLIE MARMON SILKO

Leslie Marmon Silko was born in 1948 in Albuquerque, New Mexico, and grew up on the Laguna Pueblo Reservation some fifty miles to the west. Of her family she says,

> *We are mixed blood—Laguna, Mexican, white. . . . All those languages, all those ways of living are combined, and we live somewhere on the fringes of all three. But I don't apologize for this any more—not to whites, not to full bloods—our origin is unlike any other. My poetry, my storytelling rise out of this source.*

After graduating from the University of New Mexico in 1969, Silko entered law school but soon left to become a writer. She taught for two years at Navajo Community College at Many Farms, Arizona, and then went to Alaska for two years where she studied Eskimo-Aleut culture and worked on a novel, Ceremony. *After returning to the Southwest, she taught at the University of Arizona and then at the University of New Mexico.*

In addition to writing stories, a novel, and poems, Silko wrote the screenplay for Marlon Brando's film Black Elk. *In 1981 she was awarded one of the so-called genius grants from the MacArthur Foundation, which supports "exceptionally talented individuals."*

The Man to Send Rain Clouds

One

They found him under a big cottonwood tree. His Levi jacket and pants were faded light-blue so that he had been easy to find. The big cottonwood tree stood apart from a small grove of winterbare cottonwoods which grew in the wide, sandy arroyo. He had been dead for a day or more, and the sheep had wandered and scattered up and down the arroyo. Leon and his brother-in-law, Ken, gathered the sheep and left them in the pen at the sheep camp before they returned to the cottonwood tree. Leon waited under the tree while Ken drove the truck through the deep sand to the edge of the arroyo. He squinted up at the sun and unzipped his jacket—it sure was hot for this time of year. But high and northwest the blue mountains were still deep in snow. Ken came sliding down the low, crumbling bank about fifty yards down, and he was bringing the red blanket.

Before they wrapped the old man, Leon took a piece of string out of his pocket and tied a small gray feather in the old man's long white hair. Ken gave him the paint. Across the brown wrinkled forehead he drew a streak of white and along the high cheekbones he drew a strip of blue paint. He paused and watched Ken throw pinches of corn meal and pollen into the wind that fluttered the small gray feather. Then Leon painted with yellow under the old man's broad nose, and finally, when he had painted green across the chin, he smiled.

"Send us rain clouds, Grandfather." They laid the bundle in the back of the pickup and covered it with a heavy tarp before they started back to the pueblo.

They turned off the highway onto the sandy pueblo road. Not long after they passed the store and post office they saw Father Paul's car coming toward them. When he recognized their faces he slowed his car and waved for them to stop. The young priest rolled down the car window.

5   "Did you find old Teofilo?" he asked loudly.

Leon stopped the truck. "Good morning, Father. We were just out to the sheep camp. Everything is O.K. now."

"Thank God for that. Teofilo is a very old man. You really shouldn't allow him to stay at the sheep camp alone."

"No, he won't do that any more now."

"Well, I'm glad you understand. I hope I'll be seeing you at Mass this week— we missed you last Sunday. See if you can get old Teofilo to come with you." The priest smiled and waved at them as they drove away.

Two

10   Louise and Teresa were waiting. The table was set for lunch, and the coffee was boiling on the black iron stove. Leon looked at Louise and then at Teresa.

"We found him under a cottonwood tree in the big arroyo near sheep camp. I guess he sat down to rest in the shade and never got up again." Leon walked toward the old man's head. The red plaid shawl had been shaken and spread carefully over the bed, and a new brown flannel shirt and pair of stiff new Levis were arranged neatly beside the pillow. Louise held the screen door open while Leon and Ken carried in the red blanket. He looked small and shriveled, and after they dressed him in the new shirt and pants he seemed more shrunken.

It was noontime now because the church bells rang the Angelus.[1] They ate the beans with hot bread, and nobody said anything until after Teresa poured the coffee.

Ken stood up and put on his jacket. "I'll see about the grave-diggers. Only the top layer of soil is frozen. I think it can be ready before dark."

Leon nodded his head and finished his coffee. After Ken had been gone for a while, the neighbors and clanspeople came quietly to embrace Teofilo's family and to leave food on the table because the grave-diggers would come to eat when they were finished.

Three

15   The sky in the west was full of pale-yellow light. Louise stood outside with her hands in the pockets of Leon's green army jacket that was too big for her. The funeral was over, and the old men had taken their candles and medicine bags and were gone. She waited until the body was laid into the pickup before she said anything to Leon. She touched his arm, and he noticed that her hands were still dusty from the corn meal that she had sprinkled around the old man. When she spoke, Leon could not hear her.

"What did you say? I didn't hear you."

"I said that I had been thinking about something."

"About what?"

"About the priest sprinkling holy water for Grandpa. So he won't be thirsty."

20   Leon stared at the new moccasins that Teofilo had made for the ceremonial dances in the summer. They were nearly hidden by the red blanket. It was getting colder, and the wind pushed gray dust down the narrow pueblo road. The sun was approaching the long mesa where it disappeared during the winter. Louise stood

---

[1]**Angelus** a devotional prayer commemorating the Annunciation (the angel Gabriel's announcement delivered to Mary of the Incarnation of God in the human form of Jesus).

there shivering and watching his face. Then he zipped up his jacket and opened the truck door. "I'll see if he's there."

Ken stopped the pickup at the church, and Leon got out; and then Ken drove down the hill to the graveyard where people were waiting. Leon knocked at the old carved door with its symbols of the Lamb. While he waited he looked up at the twin bells from the king of Spain with the last sunlight pouring around them in their tower.

The priest opened the door and smiled when he saw who it was. "Come in! What brings you here this evening?"

The priest walked toward the kitchen, and Leon stood with his cap in his hand, playing with the earflaps and examining the living room—the brown sofa, the green armchair, and the brass lamp that hung down from the ceiling by links of chain. The priest dragged a chair out of the kitchen and offered it to Leon.

"No thank you, Father. I only came to ask you if you would bring your holy water to the graveyard."

25   The priest turned away from Leon and looked out the window at the patio full of shadows and the dining-room windows of the nuns' cloister across the patio. The curtains were heavy, and the light from within faintly penetrated; it was impossible to see the nuns inside eating supper. "Why didn't you tell me he was dead? I could have brought the Last Rites anyway."

Leon smiled. "It wasn't necessary, Father."

The priest stared down at his scuffed brown loafers and the worn hem of his cassock. "For a Christian burial it was necessary."

His voice was distant, and Leon thought that his blue eyes looked tired.

"It's O.K., Father, we just want him to have plenty of water."

30   The priest sank down in the green chair and picked up a glossy missionary magazine. He turned the colored pages full of lepers and pagans without looking at them.

"You know I can't do that, Leon. There should have been the Last Rites and a funeral Mass at the very least."

Leon put on his green cap and pulled the flaps down over his ears. "It's getting late, Father. I've got to go."

When Leon opened the door Father Paul stood up and said, "Wait." He left the room and came back wearing a long brown overcoat. He followed Leon out the door and across the dim churchyard to the adobe steps in front of the church. They both stooped to fit through the low adobe entrance. And when they started down the hill to the graveyard only half of the sun was visible above the mesa.

The priest approached the grave slowly, wondering how they had managed to dig into the frozen ground, and then he remembered that this was New Mexico, and saw the pile of cold loose sand beside the hole. The people stood close to each other with little clouds of steam puffing from their faces. The priest looked at them and saw a pile of jackets, gloves, and scarves in the yellow, dry tumbleweeds that grew in the graveyard. He looked at the red blanket, not sure that Teofilo was so small, wondering if it wasn't some perverse Indian trick—something they did in March to ensure a good harvest—wondering if maybe old Teofilo was actually at sheep camp corraling the sheep for the night. But there he was, facing into a cold dry wind and squinting at the last sunlight, ready to bury a red wool blanket while the faces of the parishioners were in shadow with the last warmth of the sun on their backs.

35   His fingers were stiff, and it took them a long time to twist the lid off the holy water. Drops of water fell on the red blanket and soaked into dark icy

spots. He sprinkled the grave and the water disappeared almost before it touched the dim, cold sand; it reminded him of something—he tried to remember what it was, because he thought if he could remember he might understand this. He sprinkled more water; he shook the container until it was empty, and the water fell through the light from sundown like August rain that fell while the sun was still shining, almost evaporating before it touched the wilted squash flowers.

The wind pulled at the priest's brown Franciscan robe and swirled away the corn meal and pollen that had been sprinkled on the blanket. They lowered the bundle into the ground, and they didn't bother to untie the stiff pieces of new rope that were tied around the ends of the blanket. The sun was gone, and over on the highway the eastbound lane was full of headlights. The priest walked away slowly. Leon watched him climb the hill, and when he had disappeared within the tall, thick walls, Leon turned to look up at the high blue mountains in the deep snow that reflected a faint red light from the west. He felt good because it was finished, and he was happy about the sprinkling of the holy water, now the old man could send them big thunderclouds for sure.

[1969]

Joining the Conversation: Critical Thinking and Writing

1. How would you describe the response of Leon, Ken, Louise, and Teresa to Teofilo's death? To what degree does it resemble or differ from responses to death that you are familiar with?
2. How do the funeral rites resemble or differ from those of your community?
3. How well does Leon understand the priest? How well does the priest understand Leon?
4. At the end of the story we are told that Leon "felt good." Do you assume that the priest also felt good? What evidence supports your view?
5. From what point of view is the story told? Mark the passages where the narrator enters a character's mind, and then explain what, in your opinion, Silko gains (or loses) by doing so.

BILLY COLLINS

Born in New York City in 1941, Collins is a professor of English at Lehman College of the City University of New York. He is the author of several books of poetry and the recipient of numerous awards, including one from the National Endowment for the Arts. Collins's Sailing Alone around the Room: New and Selected Poems *was published in 2001; in the same year, he was appointed poet laureate of the United States.*

Introduction to Poetry

I ask them to take a poem
and hold it up to the light
like a color slide

or press an ear against its hive.

I say drop a mouse into a poem   5
and watch him probe his way out,

or walk inside the poem's room
and feel the walls for a light switch.

I want them to waterski
across the surface of a poem   10
waving at the author's name on the shore.

But all they want to do
is tie the poem to a chair with rope
and torture a confession out of it.

They begin beating it with a hose   15
to find out what it really means.

[1988]

Joining the Conversation: Critical Thinking and Writing

1. Billy Collins has said of this poem, "It's about the teaching of poetry to students." What is Collins recommending? What is he objecting to?
2. One critic has said that "Introduction to Poetry" is a "good poem," but that lines 9–16 "should have come first"—that Collins should first have stated the bad way in which students often react and then he could have come forward with the right way. Prepare an argument in which you agree with this critic's comment, and then prepare an argument in which you disagree. Which of the two arguments do you find more convincing?
3. Which image in the poem do you think is the most effective? Is there an image that you think is not effective, that is confusing or awkward, that you cannot understand?
4. Are the final two stanzas disturbing? Too disturbing? In their tone, are these stanzas similar to or different from the preceding stanzas?
5. If someone asked you What's the best way to teach poetry?, what would be your answer?
6. This is a relatively short poem, just sixteen lines long. Please try to memorize it. Is this hard or easy for you? Does memorizing poems help you to enjoy poetry more? A lot, or a little? Not at all?

MyLiteratureLab° *For additional resources for "Introduction to Poetry," log in to* www.myliteraturelab.com *where you will find Short Evaluation Exercises, as well as an About the Author, Bibliography, Links, and Critical Overview for Collins (under Student Resources).*

ROBERT FROST

Robert Frost (1874–1963) was born in California. After his fa-ther's death in 1885, Frost's mother took the family to New Eng-land, where she taught in high schools in Massachusetts and New Hampshire. Frost studied for part of one term at Dart-mouth College in New Hampshire, then did various jobs (in-cluding teaching), and from 1897 to 1899 was enrolled as a special student at Harvard. He later farmed in New Hampshire, published a few poems in local newspapers, left the farm and taught again, and in 1912 left for England, where he hoped to achieve more popular success as a writer. By 1915 he had won a considerable reputation, and he returned to the United States, settling on a farm in New Hampshire and cultivating the image of the country-wise farmer-poet. In fact he was well read in the classics, in the Bible, and in English and American literature.

Among Frost's many comments about literature, here are three: "Writing is unboring to the extent that it is dramatic"; "Every poem is . . . a figure of the will braving alien entanglements"; and, finally, a poem "begins in delight and ends in wisdom. . . . It runs a course of lucky events, and ends in a clarification of life—not necessarily a great clarification, such as sects and cults are founded on, but in a momentary stay against confusion."

The Road Not Taken

Two roads diverged in a yellow wood,
And sorry I could not travel both
And be one traveler, long I stood
And looked down one as far as I could
To where it bent in the undergrowth;   5

Then took the other, as just as fair,
And having perhaps the better claim,
Because it was grassy and wanted wear;
Though as for that the passing there
Had worn them really about the same,   10

And both that morning equally lay
In leaves no step had trodden black.
Oh, I kept the first for another day!
Yet knowing how way leads on to way,
I doubted if I should ever come back.   15

I shall be telling this with a sigh
Somewhere ages and ages hence:
Two roads diverged in a wood, and I—
I took the one less traveled by,
And that has made all the difference.   20

[1916]

Joining the Conversation: Critical Thinking and Writing

1. If "The Road Not Taken" consisted of only the first and last stanzas, we would probably feel that Frost is talking about a clear-cut choice between two distinctive ways of life—for instance, the life of a poet or the life of a farmer. The poem does not consist only of the first and last stanzas, however. What do the two middle stanzas do? Do they complicate the poem in an interesting way? Or do they make a muddle of it? Please explain.
2. The poem is often interpreted as Frost's statement that he chose the life of a poet. Yet Frost on several occasions said that he was spoofing the indecisiveness of a friend and fellow-poet, Edward Thomas. Given the fact that the middle stanzas suggest that the two roads are pretty much the same, and given the fact that the speaker in the last stanza does seem to playfully mock himself ("I shall be telling this with a sigh / Somewhere ages and ages hence"), do you think that we should or should not take the poem as a serious statement about the decisions we must make? Please explain.

MyLiteratureLab®　*For additional resources for "The Road Not Taken," log in to www .myliteraturelab.com where you will find a Video Performance, Comprehension Quiz, Short Evaluation Exercises, and Critical Essay, as well as an About the Author, Bibliography, Links, and Critical Overview for Frost (under Student Resources).*

ROBERT HERRICK

Robert Herrick (1591–1674) was born in London, the son of a goldsmith. After taking a master's degree at Cambridge, he was ordained in the Church of England, and later he was sent to the country parish of Dean Prior in Devonshire, where he wrote most of his poetry. A loyal supporter of the king, he was expelled in 1647 from his parish by the Puritans, though in 1662 he was restored to Dean Prior.

To the Virgins, to Make Much of Time

Gather ye rosebuds while ye may,
　　Old Time is still a-flying;
And this same flower that smiles today,
　　Tomorrow will be dying.

The glorious lamp of heaven, the sun, 5
　　The higher he's a-getting,
The sooner will his race be run,
　　And nearer he's to setting.

That age is best which is the first,
　　When youth and blood are warmer; 10
But being spent, the worse, and worst
　　Times still succeed the former.

Then be not coy, but use your time;
    And while ye may, go marry;
For having lost but once your prime,   15
    You may for ever tarry.

[1648]

Joining the Conversation: Critical Thinking and Writing

1. Why "rosebuds" rather than "roses" in the first line?
2. What sort of person seems to be speaking? Young or old? How do you know?
3. Doubtless this advice has something to commend it, but it is not the whole truth. Does the value of this poem depend on the soundness of its advice? Explain.
4. Does the poem offer an argument? If so, how is the argument supported? Is it convincing?

MARTÍN ESPADA

Martín Espada was born in Brooklyn in 1957. He received a bachelor's degree from the University of Wisconsin and a law degree from Northeastern University. A poet who publishes regularly, Espada teaches creative writing at the University of Massachusetts–Amherst.

Bully

Boston, Massachusetts, 1987

In the school auditorium,
the Theodore Roosevelt statue
is nostalgic
for the Spanish American War,
each fist lonely for a saber,   5
or the reins of anguish-eyed horses,
or a podium to clatter with speeches
glorying in the malaria of conquest.

But now the Roosevelt school
is pronounced *Hernández*.   10
Puerto Rico has invaded Roosevelt
with its army of Spanish-singing children
in the hallways,
brown children devouring
the stockpiles of the cafeteria,   15
children painting *Taíno* ancestors
that leap naked across murals.

Roosevelt is surrounded
by all the faces
he ever shoved in eugenic spite   20
and cursed as mongrels, skin of one race,
hair and cheekbones of another.

Once Marines tramped
from the newsreel of his imagination;
now children plot to spray graffiti   25
in parrot-brilliant colors across the Victorian mustache
and monocle.

[1990]

Joining the Conversation: Critical Thinking and Writing

1. What was Theodore Roosevelt famous for? If you are not sure, consult an encyclopedia. In the first stanza of "Bully," what words best express Espada's attitude
   toward Roosevelt?
2. In the second stanza, what does Espada mean when he says "Puerto Rico has
   invaded Roosevelt"? What does he mean by an "*army* of Spanish-singing children"? What are the *Taíno?*
3. What does "bully" mean as a noun? As an adjective?
4. Roosevelt was a great believer in America as a "melting pot." What is this theory?
   Do you think there is a great deal to it, something to it, or nothing to it? Why?
5. Here is a quotation from one of Roosevelt's speeches:

   Every immigrant who comes here should be required within five years to learn
   English or leave the country.

   What do you think of this idea? Why? Suppose that for some reason (perhaps
   political, perhaps economic) you decided to spend the rest of your life in, say,
   Argentina, or Germany, or Israel, or Nigeria. Do you think the government
   might reasonably require you to learn the language? Support your response
   with reasons.

CHAPTER 8

Arguing an
Interpretation

Reading furnishes our mind only with materials of knowledge:
It is thinking [that] makes what we read ours.

JOHN LOCKE

Chapter Preview

After reading this chapter you will be able to

- Define *interpretation* and describe the process for interpreting literary texts
- Evaluate your response to literature
- Analyze and evaluate two student interpretations

In Chapter 2 we discussed arguing about meanings or interpretations, and in Chapter 3 we discussed arguing with yourself as a way of developing ideas. In Chapter 11 we will discuss supporting arguments with evidence, but in this and the next two chapters we want to talk about interpretation, assumptions, and evidence.

Interpretation and Meaning

We can define **interpretation** as

- a setting forth of the meaning, or, better,
- a setting forth of one or more of the meanings of a work of literature.

This question of *meaning* versus *meanings* deserves an explanation. Although some critics believe that a work of literature has a single meaning, the meaning it had for the author, most critics hold that a work has several meanings—for instance, the meaning it had for the author, the meaning(s) it had for its first readers (or viewers, if the work is a drama), the meaning(s) it had for later readers, and the meaning(s) it has for us today.

Take *Hamlet* (1600–01), for example. Perhaps this play about a man who has lost his father had a very special meaning for Shakespeare, who had recently lost his own father. Further, Shakespeare had earlier lost a son named Hamnet, a variant spelling of Hamlet. The play, then, may have had important psychological meanings for Shakespeare—but the audience could not have shared (or even known) these meanings.

What *did* the play mean to Shakespeare's audience? Perhaps the original audience of *Hamlet*—people living in a monarchy, presided over by Queen Elizabeth I— were especially concerned with the issue (specifically raised in *Hamlet*) of whether a monarch's subjects ever have the right to overthrow the monarch. But obviously for twenty-first-century Americans the interest in the play lies elsewhere, and the play must mean something else. If we are familiar with Freud, we may see

209

in the play a young man who subconsciously lusts after his mother and seeks to kill his father (in the form of Claudius, Hamlet's uncle). Or we may see the play as being largely about an alienated young man in a bourgeois society. Or—but the interpretations are countless.

Is the Author's Intention a Guide to Meaning?

Shouldn't we be concerned, you might ask, with the *intention* of the author? The question is reasonable, but it presents difficulties, as the members of the Supreme Court find when they try to base their decisions on the original intent of the writers of the Constitution. First, for older works we almost never know what the intention was. Authors did not leave comments about their intentions. We have *Hamlet*, but we do not have any statement of Shakespeare's intention concerning this or any other play. It might be argued that we can deduce Shakespeare's intention from the play itself; but to argue that we should study the play in the light of Shakespeare's intention, and that we can know his intention by studying the play, is to argue in a circle. We can say that Shakespeare must have intended to write a tragedy (if he intended to write a comedy he failed), but we cannot go much further in talking about his intention.

Even if an author has gone on record expressing an intention, we may think twice before accepting the statement as definitive. The author may be speaking facetiously, deceptively, mistakenly, or unconvincingly. For instance, Thomas Mann said, probably sincerely and accurately, that he wrote one of his novels merely in order to entertain his family—but we may nevertheless take the book seriously and find it profound.

What Characterizes a Sound Interpretation?

Even the most vigorous advocates of the idea that meaning is indeterminate do not believe that all interpretations are equally significant. Rather, they believe that an interpretive essay is offered against a background of ideas, shared by essayist and reader, as to what constitutes a *persuasive argument*. Thus, an essay (even if it is characterized as "interpretive free play" or "creative engagement") will have to be

- coherent,
- plausible, and
- rhetorically effective.

The *presentation*—the rhetoric—as well as the interpretation is significant. This means (to repeat a point made in Chapter 3) that the essayist cannot merely set down random expressions of feeling or unsupported opinion. The essayist must, on the contrary, convincingly *argue* a thesis—must point to evidence so that the reader will not only know what the essayist believes but will also understand why he or she believes it.

There are lots of ways of making sense (and even more ways of making nonsense), but one important way of helping readers to see things from your point of view is to do your best to face all the complexities of a work. Put it this way: Some interpretations strike a reader as better than others because they are *more inclusive*, that is, because they *account for more of the details of the work*. The less satisfactory interpretations leave a reader pointing to aspects of the work—to some parts of the whole—and saying, Yes, but your explanation doesn't take account of. . . .

This does not mean that a reader must feel that a persuasive interpretation says the last word about the work. We always realize that a work—if we value it highly— is richer than the discussion; but, again, for us to value an interpretation we must find the interpretation plausible and inclusive.

Interpretation often depends not only on making connections among elements of the work (for instance, among the characters in a story or among the images in a poem), and among the work and other works by the author, but also on making connections between a particular work and a cultural context. The cultural context usually includes other writers and specific works of literature, since any given literary work participates in a tradition. That is, if a work looks toward life, it also looks toward other works. A sonnet is about human experience, but it is also part of a tradition of sonnet-writing. The more works of literature you are familiar with, the better equipped you are to interpret any particular work. Here is how Robert Frost put it, in the preface to *Aforesaid,* a book of verse published in 1954:

> A poem is best read in the light of all the other poems ever written. We read A the better to read B (we have to start somewhere; we may get very little out of A). We read B the better to read C, C the better to read D, D the better to go back and get something more out of A. Progress is not the aim, but circulation. The thing is to get among the poems where they hold each other apart in their places as the stars do.

An Example: Interpreting Pat Mora's "Immigrants"

Let's think about interpreting a short poem by a contemporary poet, Pat Mora.

Immigrants

wrap their babies in the American flag,
feed them mashed hot dogs and apple pie,
name them Bill and Daisy,
buy them blonde dolls that blink
blue eyes or a football and tiny cleats   5
before the baby can even walk,
speak to them in thick English,
   hallo, babee, hallo.
whisper in Spanish or Polish
when the babies sleep, whisper   10
in a dark parent bed, that dark
parent fear, "Will they like
our boy, our girl, our fine american
boy, our fine american girl?"

[1986]

Perhaps most readers will agree that the poem expresses or dramatizes a desire, attributed to "immigrants," that their child grow up in an Anglo mode. (Mora is not saying that *all* immigrants have this desire; she has simply invented one speaker who says such-and-such. *Jones* may say that Mora says all immigrants have this desire, but that is Jones' interpretation.) For this reason the parents call their children Bill and Daisy (rather than, say, José and Juanita) and give them blonde dolls and a football (rather than dark-haired dolls and a soccer ball). Up to this point, the parents seem a bit silly in their mimicking of Anglo ways. But the second part of the poem gives the reader a more interior view of the parents, brings out the fear and hope and worried concern that lies behind their behavior: Some unspecified "they" may not "like / our boy, our girl." Who are "they"? Most readers will probably agree that "they" refers to native-born citizens, especially the blond, blue-eyed "all-American" Anglo types that until recently dominated the establishment in the United States.

We can raise further questions about the interpretation of the poem.

- Exactly what does the poet mean when she says that immigrants "wrap their babies in the American flag"? Are we to take this literally?
- If not, how are we to take it?
- And why in the last two lines is the word "american" not capitalized? Is Mora imitating the non-native speaker's uncertain grasp of English punctuation? (If so, why does Mora capitalize "American" in the first line and "Spanish" and "Polish" later in the poem?) Or is she perhaps implying some mild reservation about becoming 100 percent American, some suggestion that in changing from Spanish or Polish to "american" there is a loss?

A reader might seek out Mora and ask her why she didn't capitalize "american" in the last line, but Mora might not be willing to answer, or she might not give a straight answer, or she might say that she doesn't really know why—it just seemed right when she wrote the poem. Most authors do in fact take this last approach. When they are working as writers, they work by a kind of instinct, a kind of feel for the material. Later they can look critically at their writing, but that's another sort of experience.

To return to our basic question: What characterizes a good interpretation? The short answer is *evidence,* and especially evidence that seems to cover all relevant issues. In an essay it is not enough merely to assert an interpretation. Your readers don't expect you to make an airtight case, but because you are trying to help readers to understand a work—to see a work the way you do—you are obliged to

- offer reasonable supporting evidence, and
- take account of what might be set forth as counterevidence to your thesis.

Of course your essay may originate in an intuition or an emotional response, a sense that the work is about such-and-such, but this intuition or emotion must then be examined, and it must stand a test of reasonableness. Your readers may not be convinced that your interpretation is right or true, but they must feel that the interpretation is plausible and in accord with the details of the work, rather than, say, highly eccentric and irreconcilable with some details.

This book includes several case studies, some of which include essays by critics who advance interpretations. When you read these interpretations, think about *why* you find some interpretations more convincing than others.

Thinking Critically about Responses to Literature

Usually you will begin with a strong *response* to your reading—interest, boredom, bafflement, annoyance, shock, pleasure, or whatever. Then, if you are going to think critically about the work, you will go on to *examine* your response in order to understand it, or to deepen it, or to change it.

How can you change a response? Critical thinking involves seeing an issue from all sides, to as great a degree as possible. As you know, in everyday usage *to criticize* usually means to find fault, but in literary studies the term does not have a negative connotation. Rather, it means "to examine carefully." (The word *criticism* comes from a Greek verb meaning "to distinguish," "to decide," "to judge.") Nevertheless, in one sense the term *critical thinking* does approach the everyday meaning, since critical thinking requires you to take a skeptical view of your response. You will, so to speak, argue with yourself, seeing if your response can stand up to doubts.

Let's say that you have found a story implausible. Question yourself:

- Exactly what is implausible in it?
- Is implausibility always a fault?
- If so, exactly why?

Your answers may deepen your response. Usually, you will find supporting evidence for your response, but in your effort to distinguish and to decide and to judge, try also (if only as an exercise) to find counterevidence. See what can be said against your position. (The best lawyers, it is said, prepare two cases—their own, and the other side's.) As you consider the counterevidence you will sometimes find that it requires you to adjust your thesis. You may even find yourself developing an entirely different response. That's fine, though of course the paper that you ultimately hand in should clearly argue a thesis.

In short, **critical thinking** means examining or exploring one's own responses, by questioning and testing them. Critical thinking is not so much a skill (though it does involve the ability to understand a text) as it is a *habit of mind*, or, rather, several habits, including

- Open-mindedness
- Intellectual curiosity
- Willingness to work

It may involve, too, a willingness to discuss the issues with others and to do research, a topic that will be treated in Chapter 10, on writing a research paper.

✔ **CHECKLIST:** *Writing an Interpretation*

☐ Do I know the work well enough to offer a thoughtful interpretation? Have I looked up the meanings of words that were unfamiliar to me?

(continued)

Writing an Interpretation (continued)

☐ Have I discussed the work with classmates—or at least argued with myself—so that I can reasonably believe that my interpretation makes sense?
☐ What is my thesis, my main point? Can I state it in a sentence?
☐ Have I supported my thesis with evidence, using brief quotations from the text?
☐ Have I taken account of evidence that may seem to contradict my thesis?
☐ Have I kept my audience in mind?
☐ Have I given credit to all sources for borrowed words and also for borrowed ideas? (On avoiding plagiarism, see pages 314–15.)

Two Interpretations by Students

Read Robert Frost's "Stopping by Woods on a Snowy Evening," and then read the first interpretation, written by a first-year student. This interpretation is followed by a discussion that is devoted chiefly to two questions:

- What is the essayist's thesis?
- Does the essayist offer convincing evidence to support the thesis?

A second essay, by another first-year student and offering a different interpretation of the poem, provides further material for you to analyze critically.

ROBERT FROST

For biographical information on Robert Frost, see page 624.

Stopping by Woods on a Snowy Evening

Whose woods these are I think I know.
His house is in the village though;
He will not see me stopping here
To watch his woods fill up with snow.

My little horse must think it queer   5
To stop without a farmhouse near
Between the woods and frozen lake
The darkest evening of the year.

He gives his harness bells a shake
To ask if there is some mistake.   10
The only other sound's the sweep
Of easy wind and downy flake.

The woods are lovely, dark and deep.
But I have promises to keep,
And miles to go before I sleep,   15
And miles to go before I sleep.

[1923]

Manuscript version of Frost's "Stopping by Woods on a Snowy Evening." The first part is lost.

Sample Essay by a Student: "Stopping by Woods—and Going On"

MacDonald 1

Darrel MacDonald

Professor Conner

English 1102

21 December 2012

Stopping by Woods—and Going On

Robert Frost's "Stopping by Woods on a Snowy Evening" is about what the title says it is. It is also about something more than the title says.

When I say it is about what the title says, I mean that the poem really does give us the thoughts of a person who pauses (that is, a person who is "stopping") by woods on a snowy evening. (This person probably is a man, since Robert Frost wrote the poem and nothing in the poem clearly indicates that the speaker is not a man. But, and this point will be important, the speaker perhaps feels that he is not a very masculine man. As we will see, the word "queer" appears in the poem, and, also, the speaker uses the word "lovely," which sounds more like the word a woman would use than a man.) In line 3 the speaker says he is "stopping here," and it is clear that "here" is by woods, since "woods" is mentioned not only in the title but also in the first line of the poem, and again in the second stanza, and still again in the last stanza. It is equally clear that, as the title says, there is snow, and that the time is evening. The speaker mentions "snow" and "downy flake," and he says this is "The darkest evening of the year."

But in what sense is the poem about *more* than the title? The title does not tell us anything about the man who is "stopping by woods," but the poem—the man's meditation—tells us a lot about him. In the first stanza he reveals that he is uneasy at the thought that the owner of the woods may see him stopping by the woods. Maybe he is uneasy because he is trespassing, but the poem does not actually say that he has illegally entered someone else's property. More likely, he feels uneasy, almost ashamed, of watching the "woods fill up with snow." That is, he would not want anyone to see that he actually is enjoying a beautiful aspect of nature and is not hurrying about whatever his real business is in thrifty Yankee style.

The second stanza gives more evidence that he feels guilty about enjoying beauty. He feels so guilty that he even thinks the horse thinks there is something odd about him. In fact, he says that the horse thinks he is "queer," which of course may just mean "odd," but also (as is shown by *The American Heritage Dictionary*) it can mean "gay," "homosexual." A real man, he sort of suggests, would not spend time looking at snow in the woods.

MacDonald 3

So far, then, the speaker in two ways has indicated that he feels insecure, though perhaps he does not realize that he has given himself away. First, he expresses uneasiness that someone might see him watching the woods fill up with snow. Second, he expresses uneasiness when he suggests that even the horse thinks he is strange, maybe even "queer" or unmanly, or at least unbusinesslike. And so in the last stanza, even though he finds the woods beautiful, he decides *not* to stop and to see the woods fill up with snow. And his description of the woods as "lovely"—a woman's word—sounds as though he may be something less than a he-man. He seems to feel ashamed of himself for enjoying the sight of the snowy woods and for seeing them as "lovely," and so he tells himself that he has spent enough time looking at the woods and that he must go on about his business. In fact, he tells himself *twice* that he has business to attend to. Why? Perhaps he is insisting too much. Just as we saw that he was excessively nervous in the first stanza, afraid that someone might see him trespassing and enjoying the beautiful spectacle, now at the end he is again afraid that someone might see him loitering, and so he very firmly, using repetition as a form of emphasis, tries to reassure himself that he is not too much attracted by beauty and is a man of business who keeps his promises.

Frost gives us, then, a man who indeed is seen "stopping by woods on a snowy evening," but a man who, afraid of what society will think of him, is also afraid to "stop" long enough to fully enjoy the sight that attracts him, because he is driven by a sense that he may be seen to be trespassing and also may be thought to be unmanly. So after only a brief stop in the woods he forces himself to go on, a victim (though he probably doesn't know it) of the work ethic and of an over-simple idea of manliness.

[New page]

MacDonald 4

Work Cited

Frost, Robert. "Stopping by Woods on a Snowy Evening." *Literature for Composition.*

Ed. Sylvan Barnet, William Burto, and William E. Cain. 10th ed. New

York: Pearson, 2014. 214. Print.

Let's examine this essay.

The **title** is interesting. It tells the reader which literary work will be discussed ("Stopping by Woods") and it arouses interest, in this case by a sort of wordplay ("Stopping . . . Going On"). A title of this sort is preferable to a title that merely announces the topic, such as "An Analysis of Frost's 'Stopping by Woods'" or "On a Poem by Robert Frost."

The **opening paragraph** helpfully names the exact topic (Robert Frost's poem) and says that the poem is about something more than its title. The writer's thesis presumably will be a fairly specific assertion concerning what else the poem is "about."

The **body of the essay,** beginning with the second paragraph, begins to develop the thesis. (The **thesis** perhaps can be summarized: "The speaker, insecure of his masculinity, feels ashamed that he responds with pleasure to the sight of the snowy woods.") The writer's evidence in the second paragraph is that the word "queer" (a word sometimes used of homosexuals) appears, and that the word "lovely" is "more like the word a woman would use than a man." Readers of MacDonald's essay may at this point be unconvinced by this evidence, but probably they will suspend judgment. In any case, he has offered what he considers to be evidence in support of his thesis.

The next paragraph dwells on what is said to be the speaker's uneasiness, and the following paragraph returns to the word "queer," which, MacDonald correctly says, can mean "gay, homosexual." The question of course is whether *here,* in this poem, the word has this meaning. Do we agree with MacDonald's assertion, in the last sentence of this paragraph, that Frost is suggesting that "A real man . . . wouldn't spend time looking at snow in the woods"?

Clearly this is the way MacDonald takes the poem—but is his response to these lines reasonable? After all, what Frost says is this: "My little horse must think it queer / To stop without a farmhouse near." Is it reasonable to see a reference to homosexuality (rather than merely to oddness) in *this* use of the word "queer"? Hasn't MacDonald offered a response that, so to speak, is private? It is *his* response—but are we likely to share it, to agree that we see it in Frost's poem?

The next paragraph, amplifying the point that the speaker is insecure, offers as evidence the argument that "lovely" is more often a woman's word than a man's. Probably most readers will agree on this point, though many or all might deny that only a gay man would use the word "lovely." And what do you think of MacDonald's assertions that the speaker of the poem "was excessively nervous in the first stanza" and is now "afraid that someone might see him loitering"? In your opinion, does the text lend much support to MacDonald's view?

The **concluding paragraph** effectively reasserts and clarifies MacDonald's thesis, saying that the speaker hesitates to stop and enjoy the woods because "he is driven by a sense that he may be seen to be trespassing and also may be thought to be unmanly."

The big questions, then, are these:

- Is the thesis *argued* rather than merely asserted, and
- Is it argued *convincingly?*

Or, to put it another way,

- Is the evidence adequate?

MacDonald certainly does argue (offer reasons) rather than merely assert, but does he offer enough evidence to make you think that his response is one that you can share? Has he helped you to enjoy the poem by seeing things that you may not have noticed—or has he said things that, however interesting, seem to you not to be in close contact with the poem as you see it?

Here is another interpretation of the same poem.

Sample Essay by a Student: "'Stopping by Woods on a Snowy Evening' as a Short Story"

Fong 1

Sara Fong

Professor Patel

English 102

3 December 2012

"Stopping by Woods on a Snowy Evening" as a Short Story

Robert Frost's "Stopping by Woods on a Snowy Evening" can be read

as a poem about a man who pauses to observe the beauty of nature, and it

can also be read as a poem about a man with a death wish, a man who

seems to long to give himself up completely to nature and thus escape his

responsibilities as a citizen. Much depends, apparently, on what a reader

wants to emphasize. For instance, a reader can emphasize especially

appealing lines about the beauty of nature: "The only other sound's the

sweep / Of easy wind and downy flake," and "The woods are lovely, dark

and deep." On the other hand, a reader can emphasize lines that show the

speaker is fully aware of the responsibilities that most of us agree we have.

For instance, at the very start of the poem he recognizes that the woods are not his but are owned by someone else, and at the end of the poem he recognizes that he has "promises to keep" and that before he sleeps (dies?) he must accomplish many things (go for "miles").

Does a reader have to choose between these two interpretations? I do not think so; to the contrary, I think it makes sense to read the poem as a kind of very short story, with a character whose developing thoughts make up a plot with four stages. In the first stage, the central figure is an ordinary person with rather ordinary thoughts. His very first thought is of the owner of the woods. He knows who the owner is, and since the owner lives in the village, the poet feels safe in trespassing, or at least in watching the woods "fill up with snow." Then, very subtly, the poet begins to tell us that although this seems to be an ordinary person thinking ordinary thoughts, he is a somewhat special person in a special situation. First of all, the horse thinks something is strange. He shakes his bells, wondering why the driver doesn't keep moving, as presumably ordinary drivers would. Second, we are told that this is "The darkest evening of the year." Frost could simply have said that the evening is dark, but he goes out of his way to make the evening a special evening.

We are now through with the first ten lines, and only six lines remain, yet in these six lines the story goes through two additional phases. The first three of these lines ("The only other sound's the sweep / Of easy wind and downy flake" and "The woods are lovely, dark and deep") are probably the most beautiful lines, in the sense that they are the ones that make us say, "I wish I were there," or "I'd love to experience this." We feel that the poet has moved from the ordinary thoughts of the first stanza, about such businesslike things as who owns the woods and where the owner's house is, to less materialistic thoughts, thoughts about the beauty of the nonhuman world of nature. And now, with the three final lines, we get the fourth stage

of the story, the return to the ordinary world of people, the world of "promises."
But this world that we get at the end is not exactly the same as the world we
got at the beginning. The world at the beginning of the poem is a world of
property (who owns the woods, and where the house is), but the world at the
end of the poem is a world of unspecified and rather mysterious responsibilities
("promises to keep," "miles to go before I sleep"). It is almost as though the
poet's experience of the beauty of nature—a beauty that for a moment made
him forget the world of property—has in fact served to sharpen his sense that
human beings have responsibilities. He clearly sees that "The woods are lovely,
dark and deep," and then he says (I add the italics), "*But* I have promises to
keep." The "but" would be logical if after saying that the woods are lovely, dark
and deep, he had said something like "But in the daylight they look different,"
or "But one can freeze to death in them." The logic of what Frost says, however,
is not at all clear: "The woods are lovely, dark and deep, / But I have promises
to keep." What is the logical connection? We have to supply one, something like
"but, *because we are human beings we have responsibilities;* we can refresh
ourselves by perceiving the beauties of nature, and we can even for a moment
get so caught up that we seem to enter an enchanted forest ('the woods are
lovely, dark and deep'), but we cannot forget our responsibilities."

My point is not that Frost ends with an important moral, and it is also not
that we have to choose between saying it is a poem about nature or a poem
about a man with a death wish. Rather, my point is that the poem takes us
through several stages and that, although the poem begins and ends with the
speaker in the woods, the speaker has undergone mental experiences—has, we
might say, gone through a plot with a conflict (the appeal of the snowy woods
versus the call to return to the human world). It is not a matter of good versus
evil and of one side winning. Frost in no way suggests that it is wrong to feel the
beauty of nature—even to the momentary exclusion of all other thoughts. But

Fong 4

the poem is certainly not simply a praise of the beauty of nature. Frost shows us,

in this mini-story or mini-drama, one character who sees the woods as property,

then sees them as a place of almost overwhelming beauty, and then (maybe

refreshed by this experience) rejoins the world of chores and responsibilities.

[New page]

Fong 5

Work Cited

Frost, Robert. "Stopping by Woods on a Snowy Evening." *Literature for*

   Composition. Ed. Sylvan Barnet, William Burto, and William E. Cain. 10th

   ed. New York: Pearson, 2014. 214. Print.

Joining the Conversation: Critical Thinking and Writing

1. What is the thesis of the essay?
2. Does the essayist offer convincing evidence to support the thesis?
3. Do you consider the essay to be well written, poorly written, or something in
    between? On what evidence do you base your opinion?

Your Turn: Poems for Interpretation

ROBERT FROST

*For biographical information on Robert Frost, see page 624. For additional poems
by Frost, see pages 121, 205, 214, 222, 511, 624–29, and 733.*

Mending Wall

Something there is that doesn't love a wall,
That sends the frozen-ground-swell under it,
And spills the upper boulders in the sun;
And makes gaps even two can pass abreast.
The work of hunters is another thing: 5

I have come after them and made repair
Where they have left not one stone on a stone,
But they would have the rabbit out of hiding,
To please the yelping dogs. The gaps I mean,
No one has seen them made or heard them made,   10
But at spring mending-time we find them there.
I let my neighbor know beyond the hill;
And on a day we meet to walk the line
And set the wall between us once again.
We keep the wall between us as we go.   15
To each the boulders that have fallen to each.
And some are loaves and some so nearly balls
We have to use a spell to make them balance:
"Stay where you are until our backs are turned!"
We wear our fingers rough with handling them.   20
Oh, just another kind of outdoor game,
One on a side. It comes to little more:
There where it is we do not need the wall:
He is all pine and I am apple orchard.
My apple trees will never get across   25
And eat the cones under his pines, I tell him.
He only says, "Good fences make good neighbors."
Spring is the mischief in me, and I wonder
If I could put a notion in his head:
"*Why* do they make good neighbors? Isn't it   30
Where there are cows? But here there are no cows.
Before I built a wall I'd ask to know
What I was walling in or walling out,
And to whom I was like to give offense.
Something there is that doesn't love a wall,   35
That wants it down." I could say "Elves" to him,
But it's not elves exactly, and I'd rather
He said it for himself. I see him there
Bringing a stone grasped firmly by the top
In each hand, like an old-stone savage armed.   40
He moves in darkness as it seems to me,
Not of woods only and the shade of trees.
He will not go behind his father's saying,
And he likes having thought of it so well
He says again, "Good fences make good neighbors."   45

[1914]

Joining the Conversation: Critical Thinking and Writing

1. The poem includes a scene, or action, in which the speaker and a neighbor are engaged. Briefly summarize the scene. What indicates that the scene has been enacted before and will be again?
2. Compare and contrast the speaker and the neighbor.

3. Notice that the speaker, not the neighbor, initiates the business of repairing the wall (line 12). Why do you think he does this?

4. Both the speaker and the neighbor repeat themselves; they each make one point twice in identical language. What do they say? And why does Frost allow the neighbor to have the last word?

5. "Something there is that doesn't love a wall" adds up to "Something doesn't love a wall." Or does it? Within the context of the poem, what is the difference between the two statements?

6. Write an essay of 500 words, telling of an experience in which you came to conclude that "good fences make good neighbors." Or tell of an experience that led you to conclude that fences (they can be figurative fences, of course) are "like to give offense" (see lines 32–34).

MyLiteratureLab® *For additional resources for "Mending Wall," log in to www.myliteraturelab.com where you will find a Longman Lecture, Video Performance, Comprehension Quiz, Short Evaluation Exercises, and Essay Prompts, as well as an About the Author, Bibliography, Links, and Critical Overview for Frost (under Student Resources).*

T. S. ELIOT

Thomas Stearns Eliot (1888–1965) was born into a New England family that had moved to St. Louis. He attended a private school in Massachusetts, then graduated from Harvard and did further study in literature and philosophy in France, Germany, and England. In 1914 he began working for Lloyd's Bank in London, and three years later he published his first book of poems (it included "Prufrock"). In 1925 he joined a publishing firm, and in 1927 he became a British citizen and a member of the Church of England. Much of his later poetry, unlike "The Love Song of J. Alfred Prufrock," is highly religious. In 1948 Eliot received the Nobel Prize in Literature.

The Love Song of J. Alfred Prufrock

S'io credesse che mia risposta fosse
A persona che mai tornasse al mondo,
Questa fiamma staria senza piu scosse.
Ma perciocche giammai di questo fondo
Non torno vivo alcun, s'i' odo il vero,
Senza tema d'infama ti rispondo.*

Let us go then, you and I,
When the evening is spread out against the sky

---

*In Dante's *Inferno* 27.61–66, a damned soul who had sought absolution before committing a crime addresses Dante, thinking that his words will never reach the Earth: "If I believed that my answer were to a person who could ever return to the world, this flame would no longer quiver. But because no one ever returned from this depth, if what I hear is true without fear of infamy, I answer you."

Like a patient etherized upon a table;
Let us go, through certain half-deserted streets,
The muttering retreats   5
Of restless nights in one-night cheap hotels
And sawdust restaurants with oyster-shells:
Streets that follow like a tedious argument
Of insidious intent
To lead you to an overwhelming question . . .   10
Oh, do not ask, "What is it?"
Let us go and make our visit.

In the room the women come and go
Talking of Michelangelo.

The yellow fog that rubs its back upon the window-panes,   15
The yellow smoke that rubs its muzzle on the window-panes
Licked its tongue into the corners of the evening,
Lingered upon the pools that stand in drains,
Let fall upon its back the soot that falls from chimneys,
Slipped by the terrace, made a sudden leap,   20
And seeing that it was a soft October night,
Curled once about the house, and fell asleep.

And indeed there will be time
For the yellow smoke that slides along the street,
Rubbing its back upon the window-panes;   25
There will be time, there will be time
To prepare a face to meet the faces that you meet;
There will be time to murder and create,
And time for all the works and days° of hands
That lift and drop a question on your plate;   30
Time for you and time for me,
And time yet for a hundred indecisions,
And for a hundred visions and revisions,
Before the taking of a toast and tea.

In the room the women come and go   35
Talking of Michelangelo.

And indeed there will be time
To wonder, "Do I dare?" and, "Do I dare?"
Time to turn back and descend the stair,
With a bald spot in the middle of my hair—   40
[They will say: "How his hair is growing thin!"]
My morning coat, my collar mounting firmly to the chin,
My necktie rich and modest, but asserted by a simple pin—
[They will say: "But how his arms and legs are thin!"]
Do I dare   45
Disturb the universe?
In a minute there is time
For decisions and revisions which a minute will reverse.

29 works and days "Works and Days" is the title of a poem on farm life by Hesiod (eighth century BCE).

For I have known them all already, known them all:—
Have known the evenings, mornings, afternoons,   50
I have measured out my life with coffee spoons;
I know the voices dying with a dying fall°
Beneath the music from a farther room.
       So how should I presume?

And I have known the eyes already, known them all—   55
The eyes that fix you in a formulated phrase,
And when I am formulated, sprawling on a pin,
When I am pinned and wriggling on the wall,
Then how should I begin
To spit out all the butt-ends of my days and ways?   60
       And how should I presume?

And I have known the arms already, known them all—
Arms that are braceleted and white and bare
[But in the lamplight, downed with light brown hair!]
Is it perfume from a dress   65
That makes me so digress?
Arms that lie along a table, or wrap about a shawl.
       And should I then presume?
       And how should I begin?

                       . . .

Shall I say, I have gone at dusk through narrow streets   70
And watched the smoke that rises from the pipes
Of lonely men in shirt-sleeves, leaning out of windows? . . .

I should have been a pair of ragged claws
Scuttling across the floors of silent seas.
                       . . .

And the afternoon, the evening, sleeps so peacefully!   75
Smoothed by long fingers,
Asleep . . . tired . . . or it malingers,
Stretched on the floor, here beside you and me.
Should I, after tea and cakes and ices,
Have the strength to force the moment to its crisis?   80
But though I have wept and fasted, wept and prayed,
Though I have seen my head [grown slightly bald]
       brought in upon a platter,°
I am no prophet—and here's no great matter;
And I have seen the moment of my greatness flicker,
And I have seen the eternal Footman hold my coat, and snicker,   85
And in short, I was afraid.

And would it have been worth it, after all,
After the cups, the marmalade, the tea,
Among the porcelain, among some talk of you and me,
Would it have been worth while,   90
To have bitten off the matter with a smile,

52 dying fall This line echoes Shakespeare's *Twelfth Night* 1.1.4.   **81–83 But . . . platter**
These lines allude to John the Baptist (see Matthew 14:1–11).

To have squeezed the universe into a ball°
To roll it toward some overwhelming question,
To say: "I am Lazarus,° come from the dead,
Come back to tell you all, I shall tell you all"—   95
If one, settling a pillow by her head,
    Should say: "That is not what I meant at all.
    That is not it, at all."

And would it have been worth it, after all,
Would it have been worth while,   100
After the sunsets and the dooryards and the sprinkled streets,
After the novels, after the teacups, after the skirts that trail along the floor—
And this, and so much more?—
It is impossible to say just what I mean!
But as if a magic lantern threw the nerves in patterns on a screen: 105
Would it have been worth while
If one, settling a pillow or throwing off a shawl,
And turning toward the window, should say:
    "That is not it at all,
    That is not what I meant at all."   110

      . . .

No! I am not Prince Hamlet, nor was meant to be;
Am an attendant lord, one that will do
To swell a progress, start a scene or two,
Advise the prince; no doubt, an easy tool,
Deferential, glad to be of use,   115
Politic, cautious, and meticulous;
Full of high sentence,° but a bit obtuse;
At times, indeed, almost ridiculous—
Almost, at times, the Fool.

I grow old . . . I grow old . . .   120
I shall wear the bottoms of my trousers rolled.

Shall I part my hair behind? Do I dare to eat a peach?
I shall wear white flannel trousers, and walk upon the beach.
I have heard the mermaids singing, each to each.

I do not think that they will sing to me.   125

I have seen them riding seaward on the waves
Combing the white hair of the waves blown back
When the wind blows the water white and black.

We have lingered in the chambers of the sea
By sea-girls wreathed with seaweed red and brown   130
Till human voices wake us, and we drown.

[1910–11]

---

92 To have . . . ball This line echoes lines 41–42 of Marvell's "To His Coy Mistress"
(see page 730).   **94 Lazarus** See Luke 16 and John 11.   **117 full of high sentence**
See Chaucer's description of the Clerk of Oxford in the *Canterbury Tales*. **112–117 Am . . .
obtuse** These lines allude to Polonius and perhaps other figures in *Hamlet*.

Joining the Conversation: Critical Thinking and Writing

1. How does the speaker's name help to characterize him? What suggestions—of class, race, personality—do you find in it? Does the title of this poem strike you as ironic? If so, how or why?
2. What qualities of big-city life are suggested in the poem? How are these qualities linked to the speaker's mood? What other details of the setting—the weather, the time of day—express or reflect his mood? What images do you find especially striking?
3. The speaker's thoughts are represented in a stream-of-consciousness mono-logue, that is, in what appears to be an unedited flow of thought. Nevertheless, they reveal a story. What is the story?
4. In a paragraph, characterize Prufrock as he might be characterized by one of the women in the poem, and then, in a paragraph or two, offer your own charac-terization of him.
5. Consider the possibility that the "you" whom Prufrock is addressing is not a listener but is one aspect of Prufrock, and the "I" is another. Given this pos-sibility, in a paragraph characterize the "you," and in another paragraph charac-terize the "I."
6. Prufrock has gone to a therapist, a psychiatrist, or a member of the clergy for help. Write a 500-word transcript of their session.

MyLiteratureLab® *For additional resources for "The Love Song of J. Alfred Prufrock," log in to* www.myliteraturelab.com *where you will find a Longman Lecture, Student Essay, Comprehension Quiz, Short Evaluation Exercises, and Essay Prompts, as well as an About the Author, Bibliography, Links, and Critical Overview for Eliot (under Student Resources).*

JOHN KEATS

John Keats (1795–1821), son of a London stablekeeper, was taken out of school when he was fifteen and apprenticed to a surgeon and apothecary. In 1816 he was licensed to practice as an apothecary-surgeon, but he almost immediately abandoned medicine and decided to make a career as a poet. His progress was amazing: he published books of poems—to mixed reviews—in 1817, 1818, and 1820, before dying of tuberculosis at the age of twenty-five. Today he is esteemed as one of England's greatest poets.

Ode on a Grecian Urn

I

Thou still unravished bride of quietness,
    Thou foster-child of silence and slow time,
Sylvan historian, who canst thus express
    A flowery tale more sweetly than our rhyme:
What leaf-fringed legend haunts about thy shape   5
    Of deities or mortals, or of both,
        In Tempe or the dales of Arcady?

What men or gods are these? What maidens loth?
What mad pursuit? What struggle to escape?
    What pipes and timbrels? What wild ecstasy?   10

II

Heard melodies are sweet, but those unheard
    Are sweeter; therefore, ye soft pipes, play on;
Not to the sensual° ear, but, more endeared,
    Pipe to the spirit ditties of no tone:
Fair youth, beneath the trees, thou canst not leave   15
    Thy song, nor ever can those trees be bare;
      Bold Lover, never, never canst thou kiss,
Though winning near the goal—yet, do not grieve;
    She cannot fade, though thou hast not thy bliss,
    For ever wilt thou love, and she be fair!   20

III

Ah, happy, happy boughs! that cannot shed
    Your leaves, nor ever bid the Spring adieu;
And, happy melodist, unwearied,
    For ever piping songs for ever new;
More happy love! more happy, happy love!   25
    For ever warm and still to be enjoyed,
      For ever panting, and for ever young;
All breathing human passion far above,
    That leaves a heart high-sorrowful and cloyed,
      A burning forehead, and a parching tongue.   30

IV

Who are these coming to the sacrifice?
    To what green altar, O mysterious priest,
Lead'st thou that heifer lowing at the skies,
    And all her silken flanks with garlands drest?
What little town by river or sea shore,   35
    Or mountain-built with peaceful citadel,
      Is emptied of this folk, this pious morn?
And, little town, thy streets for evermore
    Will silent be; and not a soul to tell
      Why thou art desolate can e'er return.   40

V

O Attic shape! Fair attitude! with brede°
    Of marble men and maidens overwrought,
With forest branches and the trodden weed;
    Thou, silent form, dost tease us out of thought
As doth eternity: Cold Pastoral!   45
When old age shall this generation waste,
      Thou shalt remain, in midst of other woe

13 sensual sensuous. **41** brede design.

Than ours, a friend to man, to whom thou say'st,
"Beauty is truth, truth beauty,"—that is all
    Ye know on earth, and all ye need to know.   50

[1820]

Joining the Conversation: Critical Thinking and Writing

1. In the first stanza Keats calls the urn an "unravished bride of quietness," a "foster-child of silence and slow time," and a "Sylvan historian." Paraphrase each of these terms.
2. How much sense does it make to say that "Heard melodies are sweet, but those unheard / Are sweeter" (lines 11–12)?
3. In the second stanza Keats says that the youth will forever sing, the trees will forever have their foliage, and the woman will forever be beautiful. But what words in the stanza suggest that this scene is not entirely happy? Where else in the poem is it suggested that there are painful aspects to the images on the urn?
4. What arguments can you offer to support the view that "Beauty is truth, truth beauty"?
5. There is much uncertainty about whether everything in the last two lines should be enclosed within quotation marks, or only "Beauty is truth, truth beauty." If only these five words from line 49 should be enclosed within quotation marks, does the speaker address the rest of line 49 and the whole of line 50 to the urn, or to the reader of the poem?

MyLiteratureLab® *For additional resources for "Ode on a Grecian Urn," log in to* www.myliteraturelab.com *where you will find an Audio Performance, Comprehension Quiz, Short Evaluation Exercises, and Essay Prompts, as well as an About the Author, Bibliography, Links, and Critical Overview for Keats (under Student Resources).*

THOMAS HARDY

Thomas Hardy (1840–1928) was born in Dorset, England, the son of a stonemason. Despite great obstacles he studied the classics and architecture, and in 1862 he moved to London to study and practice as an architect. Ill health forced him to return to Dorset, where he continued to work as an architect and to write. Best known for his novels, Hardy ceased writing fiction after the hostile reception of Jude the Obscure *in 1896 and turned to writing lyric poetry.*

The Man He Killed

"Had he and I but met
By some old ancient inn,
We should have sat us down to wet
Right many a nipperkin!°

"But ranged as infantry,   5
And staring face to face,
I shot at him as he at me,
And killed him in his place.

4 nipperkin cup.

"I shot him dead because—
Because he was my foe,
Just so: my foe of course he was;   10
That's clear enough; although

"He thought he'd 'list, perhaps,
Off-hand—just as I—
Was out of work—had sold his traps°—   15
No other reason why.

"Yes; quaint and curious war is!
You shoot a fellow down
You'd treat if met where any bar is,
Or help to half-a-crown."   20

                                                [1902]

15 traps personal belongings.

Joining the Conversation: Critical Thinking and Writing

1. What do we learn about the speaker's life before he enlisted in the infantry? How does his diction characterize him?
2. What is the effect of the series of monosyllables in lines 7 and 8?
3. Consider the punctuation of the third and fourth stanzas. Why are the heavy, frequent pauses appropriate? What question is the speaker trying to answer?
4. In the last stanza, what attitudes toward war does the speaker express? What, from the evidence of this poem, would you infer Hardy's attitude toward war to be? Cite evidence to support your argument.

GWENDOLYN BROOKS

*Gwendolyn Brooks (1917–2000) was born in Topeka, Kansas, but was raised in Chicago's South Side, where she spent most of her life. Brooks taught in several colleges and universities and she wrote a novel (*Maud Martha, *1953) and a memoir (*Report from Part One, *1972), but she is best known as a poet. In 1950, when she won the Pulitzer Prize for Poetry, she became the first African American writer to win a Pulitzer Prize. In 1985 Brooks became Consultant in Poetry to the Library of Congress.*

The Mother

Abortions will not let you forget.
You remember the children you got that you did not get,
The damp small pulps with a little or with no hair,
The singers and workers that never handled the air.
You will never neglect or beat   5

Them, or silence or buy with a sweet.
You will never wind up the sucking-thumb
of scuttle off ghosts that come.
You will never leave them, controlling your luscious sign,
Return for a snack of them, with gobbling mother-eye.   10

I have heard in the voices of the wind the voices of my dim
        killed children.
I have contracted. I have eased
My dim dears at the breasts they could never suck.
I have said, Sweets, if I sinned, if I seized
Your luck   15
And your lives from your unfinished reach,
If I stole your births and your names,
Your straight baby tears and your games,
Your stilted or lovely loves, your tumults, your marriages, aches,
        and your deaths,
If I poisoned the beginnings of your breaths,   20
Believe that even in my deliberateness I was not deliberate,
Though why should I whine,
Whine that the crime was other than mine?—
Since anyhow you are dead
Or rather, or instead,   25
You were never made,
But that too, I am afraid,
Is faulty: oh, what shall I say, how is the truth to be said?
You were born, you had body, you died.
It is just that you never giggled or planned or cried.   30

Believe me, I loved you all.
Believe me, I knew you, though faintly, and I loved, I loved you
All.

                                                            [1945]

Joining the Conversation: Critical Thinking and Writing

1. The first ten lines sound like a chant. What gives them that quality? What makes them nonetheless serious?
2. In lines 20–23 the mother attempts to deny the "crime" but cannot. What is her reasoning here?
3. Do you find the last lines convincing? Explain.

Stories for Interpretation

JOYCE CAROL OATES

Joyce Carol Oates was born in 1938 in Millerport, New York. She won a scholarship to Syracuse University, from which she graduated (Phi Beta Kappa and valedictorian) in 1960. She then did graduate work in English, first at the University of Wisconsin and then at Rice University, but she withdrew from Rice in order to be able to devote more time to writing. Her first collection of stories, By the North Gate, *was published in 1963; since then she has published many books—stories, poems, essays, and novels. She has received many awards, has been elected to the American Academy and Institute of Arts and Letters, and now teaches creative writing at Princeton University.*

Where Are You Going, Where Have You Been?

For Bob Dylan

Her name was Connie. She was fifteen and she had a quick nervous giggling habit of craning her neck to glance into mirrors or checking other people's faces to make sure her own was all right. Her mother, who noticed everything and knew everything and who hadn't much reason any longer to look at her own face, always scolded Connie about it. "Stop gawking at yourself, who are you? You think you're so pretty?" she would say. Connie would raise her eyebrows at these familiar complaints and look right through her mother, into a shadowy vision of herself as she was right at that moment: she knew she was pretty and that was everything. Her mother had been pretty once too, if you could believe those old snapshots in the album, but now her looks were gone and that was why she was always after Connie.

"Why don't you keep your room clean like your sister? How've you got your hair fixed—what the hell stinks? Hair spray? You don't see your sister using that junk."

Her sister June was twenty-four and still lived at home. She was a secretary in the high school Connie attended, and if that wasn't bad enough—with her in the same building—she was so plain and chunky and steady that Connie had to hear her praised all the time by her mother and her mother's sisters. June did this, June did that, she saved money and helped clean the house and cooked and Connie couldn't do a thing, her mind was all filled with trashy daydreams. Their father was away at work most of the time and when he came home he wanted supper and he read the newspaper at supper and after supper he went to bed. He didn't bother talking much to them, but around his bent head Connie's mother kept picking at her until Connie wished her mother was dead and she herself was dead and it was all over. "She makes me want to throw up sometimes," she complained to her friends. She had a high, breathless, amused voice which made everything she said sound a little forced, whether it was sincere or not.

There was one good thing: June went places with girlfriends of hers, girls who were just as plain and steady as she, and so when Connie wanted to do that her mother had no objections. The father of Connie's best girlfriend drove the girls the three miles to town and left them off at a shopping plaza, so that they could walk through the stores or go to a movie, and when he came to pick them up again at eleven he never bothered to ask what they had done.

5   They must have been familiar sights, walking around that shopping plaza in their shorts and flat ballerina slippers that always scuffed the sidewalk, with charm bracelets jingling on their thin wrists; they would lean together to whisper and laugh secretly if someone passed by who amused or interested them. Connie had long dark blond hair that drew anyone's eye to it, and she wore part of it pulled up on her head and puffed out and the rest of it she let fall down her back. She wore a pull-over jersey blouse that looked one way when she was at home and another way when she was away from home. Everything about her had two sides to it, one for home and one for anywhere that was not home: her walk that could be childlike and bobbing, or languid enough to make anyone think she was hearing music in her head, her mouth which was pale and smirking most of the time, but bright and pink on these evenings out, her laugh which was cynical and drawling at home— "Ha, ha, very funny"—but high-pitched and nervous anywhere else, like the jingling of the charms on her bracelet.

Sometimes they did go shopping or to a movie, but sometimes they went across the highway, ducking fast across the busy road, to a drive-in restaurant where older kids hung out. The restaurant was shaped like a big bottle, though squatter than a real bottle, and on its cap was a revolving figure of a grinning boy who held a hamburger aloft. One night in midsummer they ran across, breathless with daring, and right away someone leaned out a car window and invited them over, but it was just a boy from high school they didn't like. It made them feel good to be able to ignore him. They went up through the maze of parked and cruising cars to the bright-lit, fly-infested restaurant, their faces pleased and expectant as if they were entering a sacred building that loomed out of the night to give them what haven and what blessing they yearned for. They sat at the counter and crossed their legs at the ankles, their thin shoulders rigid with excitement, and listened to the music that made everything so good: the music was always in the background like music at a church service, it was something to depend upon.

A boy named Eddie came in to talk with them. He sat backward on his stool, turning himself jerkily around in semicircles and then stopping and turning again, and after a while he asked Connie if she would like something to eat. She said she did and so she tapped her friend's arm on her way out—her friend pulled her face up into a brave droll look—and Connie said she would meet her at eleven, across the way. "I just hate to leave her like that," Connie said earnestly, but the boy said that she wouldn't be alone for long. So they went out to his car and on the way Connie couldn't help but let her eyes wander over the windshields and faces all around her, her face gleaming with a joy that had nothing to do with Eddie or even this place; it might have been the music. She drew her shoulders up and sucked in her breath with the pure pleasure of being alive, and just at that moment she happened to glance at a face just a few feet from hers. It was a boy with shaggy black hair, in a convertible jalopy painted gold. He stared at her and then his lips widened into a grin. Connie slit her eyes at him and turned away, but she couldn't help glancing back and there he was still watching her. He wagged a finger and laughed and said, "Gonna get you, baby," and Connie turned away again without Eddie noticing anything.

She spent three hours with him, at the restaurant where they ate hamburgers and drank Cokes in wax cups that were always sweating, and then down an alley a mile or so away, and when he left her off at five to eleven only the movie house was still open at the plaza. Her girlfriend was there, talking with a boy. When Connie came up the two girls smiled at each other and Connie said, "How was the movie?" and the girl said, "*You* should know." They rode off with the girl's father, sleepy and pleased, and Connie couldn't help but look at the darkened shopping plaza with its big empty parking lot and its signs that were faded and ghostly now, and over at the drive-in restaurant where cars were still circling tirelessly. She couldn't hear the music at this distance.

Next morning June asked her how the movie was and Connie said, "So-so."

10   She and that girl and occasionally another girl went out several times a week that way, and the rest of the time Connie spent around the house—it was summer vacation—getting in her mother's way and thinking, dreaming, about the boys she met. But all the boys fell back and dissolved into a single face that was not even a face, but an idea, a feeling, mixed up with the urgent insistent pounding of the music and the humid night air of July. Connie's mother kept dragging her back to the daylight by finding things for her to do or saying, suddenly, "What's this about the Pettinger girl?"

And Connie would say nervously, "Oh, her. That dope." She always drew thick clear lines between herself and such girls, and her mother was simple and kindly enough to believe her. Her mother was so simple, Connie thought, that it was maybe cruel to fool her so much. Her mother went scuffling around the house in old bedroom slippers and complained over the telephone to one sister about the other, then the other called up and the two of them complained about the third one. If June's name was mentioned her mother's tone was approving, and if Connie's name was mentioned it was disapproving. This did not really mean she disliked Connie and actually Connie thought that her mother preferred her to June because she was prettier, but the two of them kept up a pretense of exasperation, a sense that they were tugging and struggling over something of little value to either of them. Sometimes, over coffee, they were almost friends, but something would come up—some vexation that was like a fly buzzing suddenly around their heads—and their faces went hard with contempt.

One Sunday Connie got up at eleven—none of them bothered with church— and washed her hair so that it could dry all day long, in the sun. Her parents and sister were going to a barbecue at an aunt's house and Connie said no, she wasn't interested, rolling her eyes to let her mother know just what she thought of it. "Stay home alone then," her mother said sharply. Connie sat out back in a lawn chair and watched them drive away, her father quiet and bald, hunched around so that he could back the car out, her mother with a look that was still angry and not at all softened through the windshield, and in the back seat poor old June all dressed up as if she didn't know what a barbecue was, with all the running yelling kids and the flies. Connie sat with her eyes closed in the sun, dreaming and dazed with the warmth about her as if this were a kind of love, the caresses of love, and her mind slipped over onto thoughts of the boy she had been with the night before and how nice he had been, how sweet it always was, not the way someone like June would suppose but sweet, gentle, the way it was in movies and promised in songs; and when she opened her eyes she hardly knew where she was, the back yard ran off into weeds and a fence line of trees and behind it the sky was perfectly blue and still. The asbestos "ranch house" that was now three years old startled her—it looked small. She shook her head as if to get awake.

It was too hot. She went inside the house and turned on the radio to drown out the quiet. She sat on the edge of her bed, barefoot, and listened for an hour and a half to a program called XYZ Sunday Jamboree, record after record of hard, fast, shrieking songs she sang along with, interspersed by exclamations from "Bobby King": "An' look here you girls at Napoleon's—Son and Charley want you to pay real close attention to this song coming up!"

And Connie paid close attention herself, bathed in a glow of slow-pulsed joy that seemed to rise mysteriously out of the music itself and lay languidly about the airless little room, breathed in and breathed out with each gentle rise and fall of her chest.

15   After a while she heard a car coming up the drive. She sat up at once, startled, because it couldn't be her father so soon. The gravel kept crunching all the way in from the road—the driveway was long—and Connie ran to the window. It was a car she didn't know. It was an open jalopy, painted a bright gold that caught the sunlight opaquely. Her heart began to pound and her fingers snatched at her hair, checking it, and she whispered "Christ, Christ," wondering how bad she looked. The car came to a stop at the side door and the horn sounded four short taps as if this were a signal Connie knew.

She went into the kitchen and approached the door slowly, then hung out the screen door, her bare toes curling down off the step. There were two boys in the car and now she recognized the driver: he had shaggy, shabby black hair that looked crazy as a wig and he was grinning at her.

"I ain't late, am I?" he said.

"Who the hell do you think you are?" Connie said.

"Toldja I'd be out, didn't I?"

20   "I don't even know who you are."

She spoke sullenly, careful to show no interest or pleasure, and he spoke in a fast bright monotone. Connie looked past him to the other boy, taking her time. He had fair brown hair, with a lock that fell onto his forehead. His sideburns gave him a fierce, embarrassed look, but so far he hadn't even bothered to glance at her. Both boys wore sunglasses. The driver's glasses were metallic and mirrored everything in miniature.

"You wanta come for a ride?" he said.

Connie smirked and let her hair fall loose over one shoulder.

"Don'tcha like my car? New paint job," he said. "Hey."

25   "What?"

"You're cute."

She pretended to fidget, chasing flies away from the door.

"Don'tcha believe me, or what?" he said.

"Look, I don't even know who you are," Connie said in disgust.

30   "Hey, Ellie's got a radio, see. Mine's broke down." He lifted his friend's arm and showed her the little transistor the boy was holding, and now Connie began to hear the music. It was the same program that was playing inside the house.

"Bobby King?" she said.

"I listen to him all the time. I think he's great."

"He's kind of great." Connie said reluctantly.

"Listen, that guy's *great*. He knows where the action is."

35   Connie blushed a little, because the glasses made it impossible for her to see just what this boy was looking at. She couldn't decide if she liked him or if he was just a jerk, and so she dawdled in the doorway and wouldn't come down or go back inside. She said, "What's all that stuff painted on your car?"

"Can'tcha read it?" He opened the door very carefully, as if he was afraid it might fall off. He slid out just as carefully, planting his feet firmly on the ground, the tiny metallic world in his glasses slowing down like gelatine hardening and in the midst of it Connie's bright green blouse. "This here is my name, to begin with," he said. ARNOLD FRIEND was written in tarlike black letters on the side, with a drawing of a round grinning face that reminded Connie of a pumpkin, except it wore sunglasses. "I wanta introduce myself, I'm Arnold Friend and that's my real name and I'm gonna be your friend, honey, and inside the car's Ellie Oscar, he's kinda shy." Ellie brought his transistor radio up to his shoulder and balanced it there. "Now these numbers are a secret code, honey," Arnold Friend explained. He read off the numbers 33, 19, 17 and raised his eyebrows at her to see what she thought of that, but she didn't think much of it. The left rear fender had been smashed and around it was written, on the gleaming gold background: DONE BY CRAZY WOMAN DRIVER. Connie had to laugh at that. Arnold Friend was pleased at her laughter and looked up at her. "Around the other side's a lot more—you wanta come and see them?"

"No."

"Why not?"

"Why should I?"

40 "Don'tcha wanta see what's on the car? Don'tcha wanta go for a ride?"

"I don't know."

"Why not?"

"I got things to do."

"Like what?"

45 "Things."

He laughed as if she had said something funny. He slapped his thighs. He was standing in a strange way, leaning back against the car as if he were balancing himself. He wasn't tall, only an inch or so taller than she would be if she came down to him. Connie liked the way he was dressed, which was the way all of them dressed: tight faded jeans stuffed into black, scuffed boots, a belt that pulled his waist in and showed how lean he was, and a white pullover shirt that was a little soiled and showed the hard small muscles of his arms and shoulders. He looked as if he probably did hard work, lifting and carrying things. Even his neck looked muscular. And his face was a familiar face, somehow: the jaw and chin and cheeks slightly darkened, because he hadn't shaved for a day or two, and the nose long and hawklike, sniffing as if she were a treat he was going to gobble up and it was all a joke.

"Connie, you ain't telling the truth. This is your day set aside for a ride with me and you know it," he said, still laughing. The way he straightened and recovered from his fit of laughing showed that it had been all fake.

"How do you know what my name is?" she said suspiciously.

"It's Connie."

50 "Maybe and maybe not."

"I know my Connie," he said, wagging his finger. Now she remembered him even better, back at the restaurant, and her cheeks warmed at the thought of how she sucked in her breath just at the moment she passed him—how she must have looked to him. And he had remembered her. "Ellie and I come out here especially for you," he said. "Ellie can sit in back. How about it?"

"Where?"

"Where what?"

"Where're we going?"

55 He looked at her. He took off the sunglasses and she saw how pale the skin around his eyes was, like holes that were not in shadow but instead in light. His eyes were like chips of broken glass that catch the light in an amiable way. He smiled. It was as if the idea of going for a ride somewhere, to some place, was a new idea to him.

"Just for a ride, Connie sweetheart."

"I never said my name was Connie," she said.

"But I know what it is. I know your name and all about you, lots of things," Arnold Friend said. He had not moved yet but stood still leaning back against the side of his jalopy. "I took a special interest in you, such a pretty girl, and found out all about you like I know your parents and sister are gone somewheres and I know where and how long they're going to be gone, and I know who you were with last night, and your best girlfriend's name is Betty. Right?"

He spoke in a simple lilting voice, exactly as if he were reciting the words to a song. His smile assured her that everything was fine. In the car Ellie turned up the volume on his radio and did not bother to look around at them.

60   "Ellie can sit in the back seat," Arnold Friend said. He indicated his friend with a casual jerk of his chin, as if Ellie did not count and she should not bother with him.

"How'd you find out all that stuff?" Connie said.

"Listen: Betty Schultz and Tony Fitch and Jimmy Pettinger and Nancy Pettinger," he said, in a chant. "Raymond Stanley and Bob Hutter—"

"Do you know all those kids?"

"I know everybody."

65   "Look, you're kidding. You're not from around here."

"Sure."

"But—how come we never saw you before?"

"Sure you saw me before," he said. He looked down at his boots, as if he were a little offended. "You just don't remember."

"I guess I'd remember you," Connie said.

70   "Yeah?" He looked up at this, beaming. He was pleased. He began to mark time with the music from Ellie's radio, tapping his fists lightly together. Connie looked away from his smile to the car, which was painted so bright it almost hurt her eyes to look at it. She looked at that name, ARNOLD FRIEND. And up at the front fender was an expression that was familiar—MAN THE FLYING SAUCERS. It was an expression kids had used the year before, but didn't use this year. She looked at it for a while as if the words meant something to her that she did not yet know.

"What're you thinking about? Huh?" Arnold Friend demanded. "Not worried about your hair blowing around in the car, are you?"

"No."

"Think I maybe can't drive good?"

"How do I know?"

75   "You're a hard girl to handle. How come?" he said. "Don't you know I'm your friend? Didn't you see me put my sign in the air when you walked by?"

"What sign?"

"My sign." And he drew an X in the air, leaning out toward her. They were maybe ten feet apart. After his hand fell back to his side the X was still in the air, almost visible. Connie let the screen door close and stood perfectly still inside it, listening to the music from her radio and the boy's blend together. She stared at Arnold Friend. He stood there so stiffly relaxed, pretending to be relaxed, with one hand idly on the door handle as if he were keeping himself up that way and had no intention of ever moving again. She recognized most things about him, the tight jeans that showed his thighs and buttocks and the greasy leather boots and the tight shirt, and even that slippery friendly smile of his, that sleepy dreamy smile that all the boys used to get across ideas they didn't want to put into words. She recognized all this and also the singsong way he talked, slightly mocking, kidding, but serious and a little melancholy, and she recognized the way he tapped one fist against the other in homage to the perpetual music behind him. But all these things did not come together.

She said suddenly, "Hey, how old are you?"

His smile faded. She could see then that he wasn't a kid, he was much older—thirty, maybe more. At this knowledge her heart began to pound faster.

80 "That's a crazy thing to ask. Can'tcha see I'm your own age?"

"Like hell you are."

"Or maybe a coupla years older, I'm eighteen."

"Eighteen?" she said doubtfully.

He grinned to reassure her and lines appeared at the corners of his mouth. His teeth were big and white. He grinned so broadly his eyes became slits and she saw how thick the lashes were, thick and black as if painted with a black tarlike material. Then he seemed to become embarrassed, abruptly, and looked over his shoulder at Ellie. "*Him,* he's crazy," he said. "Ain't he a riot, he's a nut, a real character." Ellie was still listening to the music. His sunglasses told nothing about what he was thinking. He wore a bright orange shirt unbuttoned halfway to show his chest, which was a pale, bluish chest and not muscular like Arnold Friend's. His shirt collar was turned up all around and the very tips of the collar pointed out past his chin as if they were protecting him. He was pressing the transistor radio up against his ear and sat there in a kind of daze, right in the sun.

85 "He's kinda strange," Connie said.

"Hey, she says you're kinda strange! Kinda strange!" Arnold Friend cried. He pounded on the car to get Ellie's attention. Ellie turned for the first time and Connie saw with shock that he wasn't a kid either—he had a fair, hairless face, cheeks reddened slightly as if the veins grew too close to the surface of his skin, the face of a forty-year-old baby. Connie felt a wave of dizziness rise in her at this sight and she stared at him as if waiting for something to change the shock of the moment, make it all right again. Ellie's lips kept shaping words, mumbling along, with the words blasting in his ear.

"Maybe you two better go away," Connie said faintly.

"What? How come?" Arnold Friend cried. "We come out here to take you for a ride. It's Sunday." He had the voice of the man on the radio now. It was the same voice, Connie thought. "Don'tcha know it's Sunday all day and honey, no matter who you were with last night today you're with Arnold Friend and don't you forget it!—Maybe you better step out here," he said, and this last was in a different voice. It was a little flatter, as if the heat was finally getting to him.

"No. I got things to do."

90 "Hey."

"You two better leave."

"We ain't leaving until you come with us."

"Like hell I am—"

"Connie, don't fool around with me. I mean, I mean, don't fool *around,*" he said, shaking his head. He laughed incredulously. He placed his sunglasses on top of his head, carefully, as if he were indeed wearing a wig, and brought the stems down behind his ears. Connie stared at him, another wave of dizziness and fear rising in her so that for a moment he wasn't even in focus but was just a blur, standing there against his gold car, and she had the idea that he had driven up the driveway all right but had come from nowhere before that and belonged nowhere and that everything about him and even about the music that was so familiar to her was only half real.

95 "If my father comes and sees you—"

"He ain't coming. He's at a barbecue."

"How do you know that?"

"Aunt Tillie's. Right now they're—uh—they're drinking. Sitting around," he said vaguely, squinting as if he were staring all the way to town and over to Aunt Tillie's back yard. Then the vision seemed to get clear and he nodded energetically. "Yeah. Sitting around. There's your sister in a blue dress, huh? And high heels, the poor sad bitch—nothing like you, sweetheart! And your mother's helping some fat woman with the corn, they're cleaning the corn—husking the corn—"

"What fat woman?" Connie cried.

100   "How do I know what fat woman. I don't know every goddam fat woman in the world!" Arnold Friend laughed.

"Oh, that's Mrs. Hornby. . . . Who invited her?" Connie said. She felt a little light-headed. Her breath was coming quickly.

"She's too fat. I don't like them fat. I like them the way you are, honey," he said, smiling sleepily at her. They stared at each other for a while, through the screen door. He said softly, "Now what you're going to do is this: you're going to come out that door. You're going to sit up front with me and Ellie's going to sit in the back, the hell with Ellie, right? This isn't Ellie's date. You're my date. I'm your lover, honey."

"What? You're crazy—"

"Yes, I'm your lover. You don't know what that is but you will," he said. "I know that too. I know all about you. But look: it's real nice and you couldn't ask for no-body better than me, or more polite. I always keep my word. I'll tell you how it is, I'm always nice at first, the first time. I'll hold you so tight you won't think you have to try to get away or pretend anything because you'll know you can't. And I'll come inside you where it's all secret and you'll give in to me and you'll love me—"

105   "Shut up! You're crazy!" Connie said. She backed away from the door. She put her hands against her ears as if she'd heard something terrible, something not meant for her. "People don't talk like that, you're crazy," she muttered. Her heart was almost too big now for her chest and its pumping made sweat break out all over her. She looked out to see Arnold Friend pause and then take a step toward the porch lurching. He almost fell. But, like a clever drunken man, he managed to catch his balance. He wobbled in his high boots and grabbed hold of one of the porch posts.

"Honey?" he said. "You still listening?"

"Get the hell out of here!"

"Be nice, honey. Listen."

"I'm going to call the police—"

110   He wobbled again and out of the side of his mouth came a fast spat curse, an aside not meant for her to hear. But even this "Christ!" sounded forced. Then he began to smile again. She watched this smile come, awkward as if he were smiling from inside a mask. His whole face was a mask, she thought wildly, tanned down onto his throat but then running out as if he had plastered makeup on his face but had forgotten about his throat.

"Honey—? Listen, here's how it is. I always tell the truth and I promise you this: I ain't coming in that house after you."

"You better not! I'm going to call the police if you—if you don't—"

"Honey," he said, talking right through her voice, "honey, I'm not coming in there but you are coming out here. You know why?"

She was panting. The kitchen looked like a place she had never seen before, some room she had run inside but which wasn't good enough, wasn't going to help her. The kitchen window had never had a curtain, after three years, and there were dishes in the sink for her to do—probably—and if you ran your hand across the table you'd probably feel something sticky there.

115   "You listening, honey? Hey?"

"—going to call the police—"

"Soon as you touch the phone I don't need to keep my promise and can come inside. You won't want that."

She rushed forward and tried to lock the door. Her fingers were shaking. "But why lock it," Arnold Friend said gently, talking right into her face. "It's just a screen door. It's just nothing." One of his boots was at a strange angle, as if his foot wasn't in it. It pointed out to the left, bent at the ankle. "I mean, anybody can break through a screen door and glass and wood and iron or anything else if he needs to, anybody at all and specially Arnold Friend. If the place got lit up with a fire honey you'd come runnin' out into my arms, right into my arms an' safe at home—like you knew I was your lover and'd stopped fooling around. I don't mind a nice shy girl but I don't like no fooling around." Part of those words were spoken with a slight rhythmic lilt, and Connie somehow recognized them—the echo of a song from last year, about a girl rushing into her boyfriend's arms and coming home again—

Connie stood barefoot on the linoleum floor, staring at him. "What do you want?" she whispered.

120   "I want you," he said.

"What?"

"Seen you that night and thought, that's the one, yes sir. I never needed to look any more."

"But my father's coming back. He's coming to get me. I had to wash my hair first—" She spoke in a dry, rapid voice, hardly raising it for him to hear.

"No, your Daddy is not coming and yes, you had to wash your hair and you washed it for me. It's nice and shining and all for me, I thank you, sweetheart," he said, with a mock bow, but again he almost lost his balance. He had to bend and adjust his boots. Evidently his feet did not go all the way down; the boots must have been stuffed with something so that he would seem taller. Connie stared out at him and behind him Ellie in the car, who seemed to be looking off toward Connie's right into nothing. This Ellie said, pulling the words out of the air one after another as if he were just discovering them, "You want me to pull out the phone?"

125   "Shut your mouth and keep it shut," Arnold Friend said, his face red from bending over or maybe from embarrassment because Connie had seen his boots. "This ain't none of your business."

"What—what are you doing? What do you want?" Connie said. "If I call the police they'll get you, they'll arrest you—"

"Promise was not to come in unless you touch that phone, and I'll keep that promise," he said. He resumed his erect position and tried to force his shoulders back. He sounded like a hero in a movie, declaring something important. He spoke too loudly and it was as if he were speaking to someone behind Connie. "I ain't made plans for coming in that house where I don't belong but just for you to come out to me, the way you should. Don't you know who I am?"

"You're crazy," she whispered. She backed away from the door but did not want to go into another part of the house, as if this would give him permission to come through the door. "What do you . . . You're crazy, you . . ."

"Huh? What're you saying, honey?"

130   Her eyes darted everywhere in the kitchen. She could not remember what it was, this room.

"This is how it is, honey: you come out and we'll drive away, have a nice ride. But if you don't come out we're gonna wait till your people come home and then they're all going to get it."

"You want that telephone pulled out?" Ellie said. He held the radio away from his ear and grimaced, as if without the radio the air was too much for him.

"I toldja shut up, Ellie," Arnold Friend said, "you're deaf, get a hearing aid, right? Fix yourself up. This little girl's no trouble and's gonna be nice to me, so Ellie keep to yourself, this ain't your date—right? Don't hem in on me. Don't hog. Don't crush. Don't bird dog. Don't trail me," he said in a rapid meaningless voice, as if he were running through all the expressions he'd learned but was no longer sure which one of them was in style, then rushing on to new ones, making them up with his eyes closed, "Don't crawl under my fence, don't squeeze in my chipmunk hole, don't sniff my glue, suck my popsicle, keep your own greasy fingers on yourself!" He shaded his eyes and peered in at Connie, who was backed against the kitchen table. "Don't mind him honey he's just a creep. He's a dope. Right? I'm the boy for you and like I said you come out here nice like a lady and give me your hand, and nobody else gets hurt, I mean, your nice old bald-headed daddy and your mummy and your sister in her high heels. Because listen: why bring them in this?"

"Leave me alone," Connie whispered.

135 "Hey, you know that old woman down the road, the one with the chickens and stuff—you know her?"

"She's dead!"

"Dead? What? You know her?" Arnold Friend said.

"She's dead—"

"Don't you like her?"

140 "She's dead—she's—she isn't here any more—"

"But don't you like her, I mean, you got something against her? Some grudge or something?" Then his voice dipped as if he were conscious of a rudeness. He touched the sunglasses perched on top of his head as if to make sure they were still there. "Now you be a good girl."

"What are you going to do?"

"Just two things, or maybe three," Arnold Friend said. "But I promise it won't last long and you'll like me the way you get to like people you're close to. You will. It's all over for you here, so come on out. You don't want your people in any trouble, do you?"

She turned and bumped against a chair or something, hurting her leg, but she ran into the back room and picked up the telephone. Something roared in her ear, a tiny roaring, and she was so sick with fear that she could do nothing but listen to it—the telephone was clammy and very heavy and her fingers groped down to the dial but were too weak to touch it. She began to scream into the phone, into the roaring. She cried out, she cried for her mother, she felt her breath start jerking back and forth in her lungs as if it were something Arnold Friend were stabbing her with again and again with no tenderness. A noisy sorrowful wailing rose all about her and she was locked inside it the way she was locked inside the house.

145 After a while she could hear again. She was sitting on the floor with her wet back against the wall.

Arnold Friend was saying from the door, "That's a good girl. Put the phone back."

She kicked the phone away from her.

"No, honey. Pick it up. Put it back right."

She picked it up and put it back. The dial tone stopped.

150 "That's a good girl. Now come outside."

She was hollow with what had been fear, but what was now just an emptiness. All that screaming had blasted it out of her. She sat, one leg cramped under her, and deep inside her brain was something like a pinpoint of light that kept going and would not let her relax. She thought, I'm not going to see my mother again. She thought, I'm not going to sleep in my bed again. Her bright green blouse was all wet.

Arnold Friend said, in a gentle-loud voice that was like a stage voice, "The place where you came from ain't there any more, and where you had in mind to go is canceled out. This place you are now—inside your daddy's house—is nothing but a cardboard box I can knock down any time. You know that and always did know it. You hear me?"

She thought, I have got to think. I have to know what to do.

"We'll go out to a nice field, out in the country here where it smells so nice and it's sunny," Arnold Friend said. "I'll have my arms tight around you so you won't need to try to get away and I'll show you what love is like, what it does. The hell with this house! It looks solid all right," he said. He ran a fingernail down the screen and the noise did not make Connie shiver, as it would have the day before. "Now put your hand on your heart, honey. Feel that? That feels solid too but we know better, be nice to me, be sweet like you can because what else is there for a girl like you but to be sweet and pretty and give in?—and get away before her people come back?"

155 She felt her pounding heart. Her hand seemed to enclose it. She thought for the first time in her life that it was nothing that was hers, that belonged to her, but just a pounding, living thing inside this body that wasn't really hers either.

"You don't want them to get hurt," Arnold Friend went on. "Now get up, honey. Get up all by yourself."

She stood up.

"Now turn this way. That's right. Come over here to me—Ellie, put that away, didn't I tell you? You dope. You miserable creepy dope," Arnold Friend said. His words were not angry but only part of an incantation. The incantation was kindly. "Now come out through the kitchen to me honey, and let's see a smile, try it, you're a brave sweet little girl and now they're eating corn and hot dogs cooked to bursting over an outdoor fire, and they don't know one thing about you and never did and honey you're better than them because not a one of them would have done this for you."

Connie felt the linoleum under her feet; it was cool. She brushed her hair back out of her eyes. Arnold Friend let go of the post tentatively and opened his arms for her, his elbows pointing in toward each other and his wrists limp, to show that this was an embarrassed embrace and a little mocking, he didn't want to make her self-conscious.

160 She put out her hand against the screen. She watched herself push the door slowly open as if she were safe back somewhere in the other doorway, watching this body and this head of long hair moving out into the sunlight where Arnold Friend waited.

"My sweet little blue-eyed girl," he said, in a half-sung sigh that had nothing to do with her brown eyes but was taken up just the same by the vast sunlit reaches of the land behind him and on all sides of him, so much land that Connie had never seen before and did not recognize except to know that she was going to it.

[1966]

Joining the Conversation: Critical Thinking and Writing

1. Characterize Connie. Do you think the early characterization of Connie prepares us for her later behavior?
2. Construct an argument in response to this question: Is Arnold Friend clairvoyant—definitely, definitely not, maybe?
3. Evaluate the view that Arnold Friend is both Satan and the incarnation of Connie's erotic desires.
4. What do you make of the fact that Oates dedicated the story to Bob Dylan? Is she perhaps contrasting Dylan's music with the escapist (or in some other way unwholesome) music of other popular singers?
5. If you have read Flannery O'Connor's "A Good Man Is Hard to Find" (page 375), compare and contrast Arnold Friend and the Misfit.

MyLiteratureLab® *For additional resources for "Where Are You Going, Where Have You Been?," log in to www.myliteraturelab.com where you will find a Longman Lecture, Comprehension Quiz, and Short Evaluation Exercises, as well as an About the Author, Bibliography, Links, and Critical Overview for Oates (under Student Resources).*

JORGE LUIS BORGES

Jorge Luis Borges (1899–1986), one of the first writers of Spanish to achieve an international reputation, was born in Buenos Aires. His paternal grandfather was English, and Borges learned English before he learned Spanish. When his family went to Geneva before the First World War, he became fluent in German and French. After the war the family spent two years in Spain; in 1921 Borges returned to Argentina and began to write; in 1925 he published his first book, a collection of poems. In 1938 he accepted a post as a municipal librarian in Buenos Aires, but in 1946—by which time Borges's fiction had won him an international reputation—the dictator Juan Perón removed him from the post. In 1955, after Perón was deposed, Borges—already blind from a congenital disease—was made the director of the National Library of Buenos Aires, and in 1956 he was appointed Professor of English Literature at the University of Buenos Aires.

Borges, widely regarded as the greatest contemporary writer in Spanish, is known for his poetry, literary criticism, and especially his highly innovative and immensely influential short fiction. For him, stories are not representations of the surface of life but are re-creations of the cultural myths that human beings have devised.

The Lottery in Babylon

Translated by John M. Fein

Like all men in Babylon, I have been proconsul;[1] like all, a slave. I have also known omnipotence, opprobrium, imprisonment. Look: the index finger on my right hand is missing. Look: through the rip in my cape you can see a vermilion tattoo on my

---

[1] **proconsul** provincial governor.

stomach. It is the second symbol, Beth.[2] This letter, on nights when the moon is full, gives me power over men whose mark is Gimmel, but it subordinates me to the men of Aleph, who on moonless nights owe obedience to those marked with Gimmel. In the half light of dawn, in a cellar, I have cut the jugular vein of sacred bulls before a black stone. During a lunar year I have been declared invisible. I shouted and they did not answer me; I stole bread and they did not behead me. I have known what the Greeks do not know, incertitude. In a bronze chamber, before the silent handkerchief of the strangler, hope has been faithful to me, as has panic in the river of pleasure. Heraclides Ponticus tells with amazement that Pythagoras[3] remembered having been Pyrrhus and before that Euphorbus and before that some other mortal. In order to remember similar vicissitudes I do not need to have recourse to death or even to deception.

I owe this almost atrocious variety to an institution which other republics do not know or which operates in them in an imperfect and secret manner: the lottery. I have not looked into its history; I know that the wise men cannot agree. I know of its powerful purposes what a man who is not versed in astrology can know about the moon. I come from a dizzy land where the lottery is the basis of reality. Until today I have thought as little about it as I have about the conduct of indecipherable divinities or about my heart. Now, far from Babylon and its beloved customs, I think with a certain amount of amazement about the lottery and about the blasphemous conjectures which veiled men murmur in the twilight.

My father used to say that formerly—a matter of centuries, of years?—the lottery in Babylon was a game of plebeian character. He recounted (I don't know whether rightly) that barbers sold, in exchange for copper coins, squares of bone or of parchment adorned with symbols. In broad daylight a drawing took place. Those who won received silver coins without any other test of luck. The system was elementary, as you can see.

Naturally these "lotteries" failed. Their moral virtue was nil. They were not directed at all of man's faculties, but only at hope. In the face of public indifference, the merchants who founded these venal lotteries began to lose money. Someone tried a reform: The interpolation of a few unfavorable tickets in the list of favorable numbers. By means of this reform, the buyers of numbered squares ran the double risk of winning a sum and of paying a fine that could be considerable. This slight danger (for every thirty favorable numbers there was one unlucky one) awoke, as is natural, the interest of the public. The Babylonians threw themselves into the game. Those who did not acquire chances were considered pusillanimous, cowardly. In time, that justified disdain was doubled. Those who did not play were scorned, but also the losers who paid the fine were scorned. The Company (as it came to be known then) had to take care of the winners, who could not cash in their prizes if almost the total amount of the fines was unpaid. It started a lawsuit against the losers. The judge condemned them to pay the original fine and costs or spend several days in jail. All chose jail in order to defraud the Company. The bravado of a few is the source of the omnipotence of the Company and of its metaphysical and ecclesiastical power.

[2]**Beth** the second letter of the Hebrew alphabet. The first and third letters (*aleph* and *gimmel*) are mentioned in the next sentence.   [3]**Pythagoras** Greek philosopher born about 580 BCE. He taught the doctrine of the transmigration of souls, and, according to Heraclides Ponticus (a Roman writer of the first century CE), Pythagoras claimed to remember that he had once been Pyrrhus, king of Epirus, and, before that, Euphorbus, a Trojan slain by Menelaus.

5   A little while afterward the lottery lists omitted the amounts of fines and limited
themselves to publishing the days of imprisonment that each unfavorable number
indicated. That laconic spirit, almost unnoticed at the time, was of capital importance. *It was the first appearance in the lottery of nonmonetary elements.* The success
was tremendous. Urged by the clientele, the Company was obliged to increase the
unfavorable numbers.

Everyone knows that the people of Babylon are fond of logic and even of symmetry. It was illogical for the lucky numbers to be computed in round coins and the
unlucky ones in days and nights of imprisonment. Some moralists reasoned that the
possession of money does not always determine happiness and that other forms of
happiness are perhaps more direct.

Another concern swept the quarters of the poorer classes. The members of
the college of priests multiplied their stakes and enjoyed all the vicissitudes of
terror and hope; the poor (with reasonable or unavoidable envy) knew that
they were excluded from that notoriously delicious rhythm. The just desire that
all, rich and poor, should participate equally in the lottery, inspired an indignant agitation, the memory of which the years have not erased. Some obstinate
people did not understand (or pretended not to understand) that it was a question of a new order, of a necessary historical stage. A slave stole a crimson
ticket, which in the drawing credited him with the burning of his tongue. The
legal code fixed that same penalty for the one who stole a ticket. Some Babylonians argued that he deserved the burning irons in his status of a thief; others, generously, that the executioner should apply it to him because chance
had determined it that way. There were disturbances, there were lamentable
drawings of blood, but the masses of Babylon finally imposed their will against
the opposition of the rich. The people achieved amply its generous purposes.
In the first place, it caused the Company to accept total power. (That unifica-
tion was necessary, given the vastness and complexity of the new operations.)
In the second place, it made the lottery secret, free and general. The merce-
nary sale of chances was abolished. Once initiated in the mysteries of Baal,[4]
every free man automatically participated in the sacred drawings, which took
place in the labyrinths of the god every sixty nights and which determined his
destiny until the next drawing. The consequences were incalculable. A fortunate play could bring about his promotion to the council of wise men or the
imprisonment of an enemy (public or private) or finding, in the peaceful darkness of his room, the woman who begins to excite him and whom he never
expected to see again. A bad play: mutilation, different kinds of infamy, death.
At times one single fact—the vulgar murder of C, the mysterious apotheosis of
B—was the happy solution of thirty or forty drawings. To combine the plays
was difficult, but one must remember that the individuals of the Company
were (and are) omnipotent and astute. In many cases the knowledge that certain happinesses were the simple product of chance would have diminished
their virtue. To avoid that obstacle, the agents of the Company made use of the
power of suggestion and magic. Their steps, their maneuverings, were secret.
To find out about the intimate hopes and terrors of each individual, they
had astrologists and spies. There were certain stone lions, there was a sacred
latrine called Qaphqa, there were fissures in a dusty aqueduct which, according to general opinion, *led to the Company;* malignant or benevolent persons

---

[4]**Baal** a Semitic god.

deposited information in these places. An alphabetical file collected these items of varying truthfulness.

Incredibly, there were complaints. The Company, with its usual discretion, did not answer directly. It preferred to scrawl in the rubbish of a mask factory a brief statement which now figures in the sacred sculptures. This doctrinal item observed that the lottery is an interpolation of chance in the order of the world and that to accept errors is not to contradict chance: it is to corroborate it. It likewise observed that those lions and that sacred receptacle, although not disavowed by the Company (which did not abandon the right to consult them), functioned without official guarantee.

This declaration pacified the public's restlessness. It also produced other effects, perhaps unforeseen by its writer. It deeply modified the spirit and the operations of the Company. I don't have much time left; they tell us that the ship is about to weigh anchor. But I shall try to explain it.

However unlikely it might seem, no one had tried out before then a general theory of chance. Babylonians are not very speculative. They revere the judgments of fate, they deliver to them their lives, their hopes, their panic, but it does not occur to them to investigate fate's labyrinthine laws nor the gyratory spheres which reveal it. Nevertheless, the *unofficial* declaration that I have mentioned inspired many discussions of judicial-mathematical character. From some one of them the following conjecture was born: If the lottery is an intensification of chance, a periodical infusion of chaos in the cosmos, would it not be right for chance to intervene in all stages of the drawing and not in one alone? Is it not ridiculous for chance to dictate someone's death and have the circumstances of that death—secrecy, publicity, the fixed time of an hour or a century—not subject to chance? These just scruples finally caused a considerable reform, whose complexities (aggravated by centuries' practice) only a few specialists understand, but which I shall try to summarize, at least in a symbolic way.

Let us imagine a first drawing, which decrees the death of a man. For its fulfillment one proceeds to another drawing, which proposes (let us say) nine possible executors. Of these executors, four can initiate a third drawing which will tell the name of the executioner, two can replace the adverse order with a fortunate one (finding a treasure, let us say), another will intensify the death penalty (that is, will make it infamous or enrich it with tortures), others can refuse to fulfill it. This is the symbolic scheme. In reality the *number of drawings is infinite*. No decision is final, all branch into others. Ignorant people suppose that infinite drawings require an infinite time; actually it is sufficient for time to be infinitely subdivisible, as the famous parable of the contest which the tortoise teaches. This infinity harmonizes admirably with the sinuous numbers of Chance and with the Celestial Archetype of the Lottery, which the Platonists adore. Some warped echo of our rites seems to have resounded on the Tiber: Ellus Lampridius, in the *Life of Antoninus Heliogabalus,* tells that this emperor wrote on shells the lots that were destined for his guests, so that one received ten pounds of gold and another ten flies, ten dormice, ten bears. It is permissible to recall that Heliogabalus was brought up in Asia Minor, among the priests of the eponymous god.

There are also impersonal drawings, with an indefinite purpose. One decrees that a sapphire of Taprobana be thrown into the waters of the Euphrates; another, that a bird be released from the roof of a tower; another, that each century there be withdrawn (or added) a grain of sand from the innumerable ones on the beach. The consequences are, at times, terrible.

Under the beneficent influence of the Company, our customs are saturated with chance. The buyer of a dozen amphoras[5] of Damascene wine will not be surprised if one of them contains a talisman or a snake. The scribe who writes a contract almost never fails to introduce some erroneous information. I myself, in this hasty declaration, have falsified some splendor, some atrocity. Perhaps, also, some mysterious monotony . . . Our historians, who are the most penetrating on the globe, have invented a method to correct chance. It is well known that the operations of this method are (in general) reliable, although, naturally, they are not divulged without some portion of deceit. Furthermore, there is nothing so contaminated with fiction as the history of the Company. A paleographic document, exhumed in a temple, can be the result of yesterday's lottery or of an age-old lottery. No book is published without some discrepancy in each one of the copies. Scribes take a secret oath to omit, to interpolate, to change. The indirect lie is also cultivated.

The Company, with divine modesty, avoids all publicity. Its agents, as is natural, are secret. The orders which it issues continually (perhaps incessantly) do not differ from those lavished by impostors. Moreover, who can brag about being a mere impostor? The drunkard who improvises an absurd order, the dreamer who awakens suddenly and strangles the woman who sleeps at his side, do they not execute, perhaps, a secret decision of the Company? That silent functioning, comparable to God's, gives rise to all sorts of conjectures. One abominably insinuates that the Company has not existed for centuries and that the sacred disorder of our lives is purely hereditary, traditional. Another judges it eternal and teaches that it will last until the last night, when the last god annihilates the world. Another declares that the Company is omnipotent, but that it only has influence in tiny things: in a bird's call, in the shadings of rust and of dust, in the half dreams of dawn. Another, in the words of masked heresiarchs,[6] *that it has never existed and will not exist.* Another, no less vile, reasons that it is indifferent to affirm or deny the reality of the shadowy corporation, because Babylon is nothing else than an infinite game of chance.

[1941]

---

[5]**amphoras** large jars.   [6]**heresiarchs** founders or chief proponents of a heresy.

Joining the Conversation: Critical Thinking and Writing

1. In the first paragraph of "The Lottery in Babylon," the narrator says, "I have known what the Greeks do not know, incertitude." What does he mean? What forces might operate in a world that does not include "incertitude"? That is, *why* might there be no incertitude?
2. Who is the narrator? What is his tone—objective, despairing, or what? Is the narrator reliable? Where is he?
3. What was the first change introduced into the lottery? Why did it make the lottery more interesting? Do the conditions of the lottery connect with real life? Why, by the way, do people play lotteries in real life?
4. What might "the Company" stand for? Do you think the story is an allegory? If so, what is it an allegory of?

Thinking Critically: Case Study on William Faulkner's
"A Rose for Emily"

Overview of the Case Study

1. In this case study we offer Faulkner's story with the illustrations by Weldon Bailey (1905–45) that accompanied it when it was first published, in 1930, in *Forum* magazine. To the best of our knowledge, these illustrations have never been reproduced after their publication in 1930.
2. We also reproduce four pages of the pre-publication typescript of Faulkner's story. Three of these pages include material that does *not* appear in the published version. The fourth page (in this book on page 261), showing the final paragraph of the story, is rather different from the published version, so it allows the reader to see what is in effect a draft for the published final paragraph.
3. Faulkner served as writer-in-residence at the University of Virginia from 1957 to 1958. In the course of lectures and discussions he occasionally commented on "A Rose for Emily." We reproduce the relevant passages.
4. We include two interpretive essays by first-year students, each accompanied by an outline. These essays are not offered as models to emulate; rather, they are offered as material that can be discussed and evaluated in class.

WILLIAM FAULKNER

William Faulkner (1897–1962) was brought up in Oxford, Mississippi. His great-grandfather had been a Civil War hero, and his father was treasurer of the University of Mississippi in Oxford; the family was no longer rich, but it was still respected. In 1918 he enrolled in the Royal Canadian Air Force, though he never saw overseas service. After the war he returned to Mississippi and went to the university for two years. He then moved to New Orleans, where he became friendly with Sherwood Anderson, who was already an established writer. In New Orleans Faulkner worked for the Times-Picayune; *still later, even after he had established himself as a major novelist with* The Sound and the Fury *(1929), he had to work in Hollywood in order to make ends meet. In 1950 he was awarded the Nobel Prize in Literature.*

A Rose for Emily

I

When Miss Emily Grierson died, our whole town went to her funeral: the men through a sort of respectful affection for a fallen monument, the women mostly out of curiosity to see the inside of her house, which no one save an old Negro man-servant—a combined gardener and cook—had seen in at least ten years.

It was a big, squarish, frame house that had once been white, decorated with cupolas and spires and scrolled balconies in the heavily lightsome style of the sev-enties, set on what had once been our most select street. But garages and cotton gins had encroached and obliterated even the august names of that neighborhood; only Miss Emily's house was left, lifting its stubborn and coquettish decay above the cotton wagons and the gasoline pumps—an eyesore among eyesores. And now Miss Emily had gone to join the representatives of those august names where they lay in the cedar-bemused cemetery among the ranked and anonymous graves of Union and Confederate soldiers who fell at the battle of Jefferson.

Alive, Miss Emily had been a tradition, a duty, and a care; a sort of hereditary obligation upon the town, dating from that day in 1894 when Colonel Sartoris, the mayor—he who fathered the edict that no Negro woman should appear on the streets without an apron—remitted her taxes, the dispensation dating from the death of her father on into perpetuity. Not that Miss Emily would have accepted charity. Colonel Sartoris invented an involved tale to the effect that Miss Emily's father had loaned money to the town, which the town, as a matter of business, preferred this way of repaying. Only a man of Colonel Sartoris' generation and thought could have invented it, and only a woman could have believed it.

When the next generation, with its more modern ideas, became mayors and alder-men, this arrangement created some little dissatisfaction. On the first of the year they mailed her a tax notice. February came, and there was no reply. They wrote her a formal letter, asking her to call at the sheriff's office at her convenience. A week later the mayor wrote her himself, offering to call or to send his car for her, and received in reply a note on paper of an archaic shape, in a thin, flowing calligraphy in faded ink, to the effect that she no longer went out at all. The tax notice was also enclosed, without comment.

5   They called a special meeting of the Board of Aldermen. A deputation waited upon her, knocked at the door through which no visitor had passed since she ceased giving china-painting lessons eight or ten years earlier. They were admitted by the old Negro into a dim hall from which a stairway mounted into still more shadow. It smelled of dust and disuse—a close, dank smell. The Negro led them into the parlor. It was furnished in heavy, leather-covered furniture. When the Negro opened the blinds of one window, they could see that the leather was cracked; and when they sat down, a faint dust rose sluggishly about their thighs, spinning with slow motes in the single sun-ray. On a tarnished gilt easel before the fireplace stood a crayon portrait of Miss Emily's father.

They rose when she entered—a small, fat woman in black, with a thin gold chain descending to her waist and vanishing into her belt, leaning on an ebony cane with a tarnished gold head. Her skeleton was small and spare; perhaps that was why what would have been merely plumpness in another was obesity in her. She looked bloated, like a body long submerged in motionless water, and of that pallid hue. Her eyes, lost in the fatty ridges of her face, looked like two small pieces of coal pressed into a lump of dough as they moved from one face to another while the visitors stated their errand.

She did not ask them to sit. She just stood in the door and listened quietly until the spokesman came to a stumbling halt. Then they could hear the invisible watch ticking at the end of the gold chain.

Her voice was dry and cold. "I have no taxes in Jefferson. Colonel Sartoris explained it to me. Perhaps one of you can gain access to the city records and satisfy yourselves."

"But we have. We are the city authorities, Miss Emily. Didn't you get a notice from the sheriff, signed by him?"

10   "I received a paper, yes," Miss Emily said. "Perhaps he considers himself the sheriff. . . . I have no taxes in Jefferson."

"But there is nothing on the books to show that, you see. We must go by the—"

"See Colonel Sartoris. I have no taxes in Jefferson."

"But, Miss Emily—"

"See Colonel Sartoris." (Colonel Sartoris had been dead almost ten years.) "I have no taxes in Jefferson. Tobe!" The Negro appeared. "Show these gentlemen out."

II

15   So she vanquished them, horse and foot, just as she had vanquished their fathers thirty years before about the smell. That was two years after her father's death and a short time after her sweetheart—the one we believed would marry her—had deserted her. After her father's death she went out very little; after her sweetheart went away, people hardly saw her at all. A few of the ladies had the temerity to call, but were not received, and the only sign of life about the place was the Negro man—a young man then—going in and out with a market basket.

"Just as if a man—any man—could keep a kitchen properly," the ladies said; so they were not surprised when the smell developed. It was another link between the gross, teeming world and the high and mighty Griersons.

A neighbor, a woman, complained to the mayor, Judge Stevens, eighty years old.

"But what will you have me do about it, madam?" he said.

"Why, send her word to stop it," the woman said. "Isn't there a law?"

20   "I'm sure that won't be necessary," Judge Stevens said. "It's probably just a snake or a rat that nigger of hers killed in the yard. I'll speak to him about it."

The next day he received two more complaints, one from a man who came in diffident deprecation. "We really must do something about it, Judge. I'd be the last one in the world to bother Miss Emily, but we've got to do something." That night the Board of Aldermen met—three graybeards and one younger man, a member of the rising generation.

"It's simple enough," he said. "Send her word to have her place cleaned up. Give her a certain time to do it in, and if she don't . . ."

"Dammit, sir," Judge Stevens said, "will you accuse a lady to her face of smelling bad?"

So the next night, after midnight, four men crossed Miss Emily's lawn and slunk about the house like burglars, sniffing along the base of the brickwork and at the cellar openings while one of them performed a regular sowing motion with his hand out of a sack slung from his shoulder. They broke open the cellar door and sprinkled lime there, and in all the outbuildings. As they recrossed the lawn, a window that had been dark was lighted and Miss Emily sat in it, the light behind her, and her upright torso motionless as that of an idol. They crept quietly across the lawn and into the shadow of the locusts that lined the street. After a week or two the smell went away.

25   That was when people had begun to feel really sorry for her. People in our town, remembering how old lady Wyatt, her great-aunt, had gone completely crazy at last, believed that the Griersons held themselves a little too high for what they really were. None of the young men were quite good enough for Miss Emily and such. We had long thought of them as a tableau, Miss Emily a slender figure in white in the background, her father a spraddled silhouette in the foreground, his back to her and clutching a horsewhip, the two of them framed by the back-flung front door. So when she got to be thirty and was still single, we were not pleased exactly, but vindicated; even with insanity in the family she wouldn't have turned down all of her chances if they had really materialized.

When her father died, it got about that the house was all that was left to her; and in a way, people were glad. At last they could pity Miss Emily. Being left alone, and a pauper, she had become humanized. Now she too would know the old thrill and the old despair of a penny more or less.

The day after his death all the ladies prepared to call at the house and offer condolence and aid, as is our custom. Miss Emily met them at the door, dressed as usual and with no trace of grief on her face. She told them that her father was not dead. She did that for three days, with the ministers calling on her, and the doctors, trying to persuade her to let them dispose of the body. Just as they were about to resort to law and force, she broke down, and they buried her father quickly.

We did not say she was crazy then. We believed she had to do that. We remembered all the young men her father had driven away, and we knew that with nothing left, she would have to cling to that which had robbed her, as people will.

III

She was sick for a long time. When we saw her again, her hair was cut short, making her look like a girl, with a vague resemblance to those angels in colored church windows—sort of tragic and serene.

30   The town had just let the contracts for paving the sidewalks, and in the summer after her father's death they began the work. The construction company came with niggers and mules and machinery, and a foreman named Homer Barron, a Yankee—a big, dark, ready man, with a big voice and eyes lighter than his face. The little boys would follow in groups to hear him cuss the niggers, and the niggers singing in time to the rise and fall of picks. Pretty soon he knew everybody in town. Whenever you heard a lot of laughing anywhere about the square, Homer Barron would be in the center of the group. Presently we began to see him and Miss Emily on Sunday afternoons driving in the yellow-wheeled buggy and the matched team of bays from the livery stable.

At first we were glad that Miss Emily would have an interest, because the ladies all said, "Of course a Grierson would not think seriously of a Northerner, a day laborer." But there were still others, older people, who said that even grief could not cause a real lady to forget *noblesse oblige*—without calling it *noblesse oblige*. They just said, "Poor Emily. Her kinfolks should come to her." She had some kin in Alabama; but years ago her father had fallen out with them over the estate of old lady Wyatt, the crazy woman, and there was no communication between the two families. They had not even been represented at the funeral.

And as soon as the old people said, "Poor Emily," the whispering began. "Do you suppose it's really so?" they said to one another. "Of course it is. What else could . . ." This behind their hands; rustling of craned silk and satin behind jalousies closed upon the sun of Sunday afternoon as the thin, swift clop-clop-clop of the matched team passed: "Poor Emily."

She carried her head high enough—even when we believed that she was fallen. It was as if she demanded more than ever the recognition of her dignity as the last Grierson; as if it had wanted that touch of earthiness to reaffirm her imperviousness. Like when she bought the rat poison, the arsenic. That was over a year after they had begun to say "Poor Emily," and while the two female cousins were visiting her.

"I want some poison," she said to the druggist. She was over thirty then, still a slight woman, though thinner than usual, with cold, haughty black eyes in a face the flesh of which was strained across the temples and about the eye-sockets as you imagine a lighthouse-keeper's face ought to look. "I want some poison," she said.

35   "Yes, Miss Emily. What kind? For rats and such? I'd recom—"

"I want the best you have. I don't care what kind."

The druggist named several. "They'll kill anything up to an elephant. But what you want is—"

"Arsenic," Miss Emily said. "Is that a good one?"

"Is . . . arsenic? Yes, ma'am. But what you want—"

40   "I want arsenic."

The druggist looked down at her. She looked back at him, erect, her face like a strained flag. "Why, of course," the druggist said. "If that's what you want. But the law requires you to tell what you are going to use it for."

Miss Emily just stared at him, her head tilted back in order to look him eye to eye, until he looked away and went and got the arsenic and wrapped it up. The Negro delivery boy brought her the package; the druggist didn't come back. When she opened the package at home there was written on the box, under the skull and bones: "For rats."

IV

So the next day we all said, "She will kill herself"; and we said it would be the best thing. When she had first begun to be seen with Homer Barron, we had said, "She will marry him." Then we said, "She will persuade him yet," because Homer himself had remarked—he liked men, and it was known that he drank with the younger men in the Elks' Club—that he was not a marrying man. Later we said, "Poor Emily" behind the jalousies as they passed on Sunday afternoon in the glittering buggy, Miss Emily with her head high and Homer Barron with his hat cocked and a cigar in his teeth, reins and whip in a yellow glove.

Then some of the ladies began to say that it was a disgrace to the town and a bad example to the young people. The men did not want to interfere, but at last the ladies forced the Baptist minister—Miss Emily's people were Episcopal— to call upon her. He would never divulge what happened during that interview, but he refused to go back again. The next Sunday they again drove about the streets, and the following day the minister's wife wrote to Miss Emily's relations in Alabama.

45   So she had blood-kin under her roof again and we sat back to watch developments. At first nothing happened. Then we were sure that they were to be married. We learned that Miss Emily had been to the jeweler's and ordered a man's toilet set in silver, with the letters H. B. on each piece. Two days later we learned that she had bought a complete outfit of men's clothing, including a nightshirt, and we said, "They are married." We were really glad. We were glad because the two female cousins were even more Grierson than Miss Emily had ever been.

So we were not surprised when Homer Barron—the streets had been finished some time since—was gone. We were a little disappointed that there was not a public blowing-off, but we believed that he had gone on to prepare for Miss Emily's coming, or to give her a chance to get rid of the cousins. (By that time it was a cabal, and we were all Miss Emily's allies to help circumvent the cousins.) Sure enough, after another week they departed. And, as we had expected all along, within three days Homer Barron was back in town. A neighbor saw the Negro man admit him at the kitchen door at dusk one evening.

And that was the last we saw of Homer Barron. And of Miss Emily for some time. The Negro man went in and out with the market basket, but the front door remained closed. Now and then we would see her at a window for a moment, as the men did that night when they sprinkled the lime, but for almost six months she did not appear on the streets. Then we knew that this was to be expected too; as if that quality of her father which had thwarted her woman's life so many times had been too virulent and too furious to die.

When we next saw Miss Emily, she had grown fat and her hair was turning gray. During the next few years it grew grayer and grayer until it attained an even pepper-and-salt iron gray, when it ceased turning. Up to the day of her death at seventy-four it was still that vigorous iron-gray, like the hair of an active man.

From that time on her front door remained closed, save for a period of six or seven years, when she was about forty, during which she gave lessons in china-painting. She fitted up a studio in one of the downstairs rooms, where the daughters and grand-daughters of Colonel Sartoris' contemporaries were sent to her with the same regularity and in the same spirit that they were sent to church on Sundays with a twenty-five cent piece for the collection plate. Meanwhile her taxes had been remitted.

50 　　Then the newer generation became the backbone and the spirit of the town, and the painting pupils grew up and fell away and did not send their children to her with boxes of color and tedious brushes and pictures cut from the ladies' magazines. The front door closed upon the last one and remained closed for good. When the town got free postal delivery, Miss Emily alone refused to let them fasten the metal numbers above her door and attach a mailbox to it. She would not listen to them.

　　Daily, monthly, yearly we watched the Negro grow grayer and more stooped, going in and out with the market basket. Each December we sent her a tax notice, which would be returned by the post office a week later, unclaimed. Now and then we would see her in one of the downstairs windows—she had evidently shut up the top floor of the house—like the carven torso of an idol in a niche, looking or not looking at us, we could never tell which. Thus she passed from generation to generation—dear, inescapable, impervious, tranquil, and perverse.

　　And so she died. Fell ill in the house filled with dust and shadows, with only a doddering Negro man to wait on her. We did not even know she was sick; we had long since given up trying to get any information from the Negro. He talked to no one, probably not even to her, for his voice had grown harsh and rusty, as if from disuse.

　　She died in one of the downstairs rooms, in a heavy walnut bed with a curtain, her gray head propped on a pillow yellow and moldy with age and lack of sunlight.

V

The Negro met the first of the ladies at the front door and let them in, with their hushed, sibilant voices and their quick, curious glances, and then he disappeared. He walked right through the house and out the back and was not seen again.

55 　　The two female cousins came at once. They held the funeral on the second day, with the town coming to look at Miss Emily beneath a mass of bought flowers, with the crayon face of her father musing profoundly above the bier and the ladies sibilant and macabre; and the very old men—some in their brushed Confederate uniforms—on the porch and the lawn, talking of Miss Emily as if she had been a contemporary of theirs, believing that they had danced with her and courted her perhaps, confusing time with its mathematical progression, as the old do, to whom all the past is not a diminishing road but, instead, a huge meadow which no winter ever quite touches, divided from the now by the narrow bottle-neck of the most recent decade of years.

　　Already we knew that there was one room in that region above stairs which no one had seen in forty years, and which would have to be forced. They waited until Miss Emily was decently in the ground before they opened it.

　　The violence of breaking down the door seemed to fill this room with pervading dust. A thin, acrid pall as of the tomb seemed to lie everywhere upon this room decked and furnished as for a bridal: upon the valance curtains of faded rose color, upon the rose-shaded lights, upon the dressing table, upon the delicate array of crystal and the man's toilet things backed with tarnished silver, silver so tarnished that the monogram was obscured. Among them lay a collar and tie, as if they had just been removed, which, lifted, left upon the surface a pale crescent in the dust. Upon a chair hung the suit, carefully folded; beneath it the two mute shoes and the discarded socks.

　　The man himself lay in the bed.

For a long while we just stood there, looking down at the profound and flesh-less grin. The body had apparently once lain in the attitude of an embrace, but now the long sleep that outlasts love, that conquers even the grimace of love, had cuck-olded him. What was left of him, rotted beneath what was left of the nightshirt, had become inextricable from the bed in which he lay; and upon him and upon the pillow beside him lay that even coating of the patient and biding dust.

60   Then we noticed that in the second pillow was the indentation of a head. One of us lifted something from it, and leaning forward, that faint and invisible dust dry and acrid in the nostrils, we saw a long strand of iron-gray hair.

[1930]

Joining the Conversation: Critical Thinking and Writing

1. Why does the narrator begin with what is almost the end of the story—the death of Miss Emily—rather than save this information for later? What devices does Faulkner use to hold the reader's interest throughout?
2. In a paragraph, offer a conjecture about Miss Emily's attitudes toward Homer Barron after he was last seen alive.
3. In a paragraph or two, characterize Miss Emily, calling attention not only to her eccentricities or even craziness, but also to what you believe to be her moral values. Do the illustrations affect your response to her and to the story?
4. In paragraph 44 we are told that the Baptist minister "would never divulge what happened" during the interview with Miss Emily. Why do you suppose Faulkner does not narrate or describe the interview? Let's assume that in his first draft of the story he *did* give a paragraph of narration or a short dramatic scene. Write such an episode.
5. Suppose that Homer Barron's remains had been discovered before Miss Emily died, and that she was arrested and charged with murder. You are the prosecutor and you are running for a statewide political office. In 500 words, set forth your argument that—despite the fact that she is a public monument—she should be convicted. Or: You are the defense attorney, also running for office. In 500 words, set forth your defense.
6. Assume that Miss Emily kept a journal—perhaps even from her days as a young girl. Write entries for the journal, giving her thoughts about some of the episodes reported in Faulkner's story.
7. Does "A Rose for Emily" make you want to read more stories by Faulkner? Be as specific as you can in explaining your response.

MyLiteratureLab® *For additional resources for "A Rose for Emily," log in to* www.myliteraturelab.com *where you will find a Longman Lecture, Critical Essay, Comprehension Quiz, Short Evaluation Exercises, and Essay Prompts, as well as an About the Author, Bibliography, Links, and Critical Overview for Faulkner (under Student Resources).*

Typescript Showing Material Deleted from the Published Version

The University of Virginia possesses a pre-publication typescript of "A Rose for Emily." The typescript is of special importance because it includes a passage—omitted from the published version—of extended dialogue between Miss Emily and the African American servant. If you look at paragraph 53 of the published version—it consists of only a single sentence—and compare it with the paragraph just above the middle of the first page that we reprint from the typed version, you will notice that the typescript includes a few additional words at the end of the sentence, and then goes on to give substantial material that Faulkner decided not to publish. This material is on the original typescript pages numbered 13, 14, and 15.

dust and shadows, with only a doddering negro man to wait on
her. We did not even know she was sick; we had long since given up
trying to get any information from the negro. He talked to no
one, probably not even to her, for his voice had grown ~~hard~~
harsh and ~~hot~~ rusty, as though with disuse; the sparse words
which he did speak sounded as though he had learned them that
morning by rote---just enough of them to carry him through
the day.

She died in one of the downstairs rooms, in a heavy
walnut bed with a curtain, her gray head propped on a pillow
yellow and moldy with age and lack of sunlight, her voice
cold and strong to the last.

"But not till I'm gone," she said. "Dont you let a
soul in until I'm gone, do you hear?" Standing beside the bed,
his head in the dim light nimbused by a faint halo of napped,
perfectly white hair, the negro made a brief gesture with his
hand. Miss Emily lay with her eyes open, gazing into the opposite shadows of the room. Upon the coverlet her hands lay on
her breast, gnarled, blue with age, motionless. "Hah," she said.
"Then they can. Let 'em go up there and see what's in that
room. ~~And let them be the last one.~~ Fools. ~~And~~ Let
'em. ~~And let them be the last one~~ Satisfy their minds that
I am crazy. Do you think I am?" The negro made no reply, no
movement. He stood above the bed, ~~stooped like an old~~
~~man~~ motionless, musing: a secret and unfathomable soul behind
the death-mask of an ape and haloed like an angel. "Let 'em
go up there and open that door. And you wont be the last one,

13.

either. Will you?"

"I wont have to," the negro said. "I know what's in that room. I dont have to see."

"Hah," Miss Emily said. "You do, do you. How long have you known?" Again he made that brief sign with his hand. Miss Emily had not turned her head. She stared into the shadows where the high ceiling was lost. "You should be glad. Now you can go to Chicago, like you've been talking about for thirty years. And with what you'll get for the house and furniture.... Colonel Sartoris has the will. He'll see they dont rob you."

"I dont want any house," the negro said.

"You cant help yourself. It's signed and sealed thirty-five years ago. Wasn't that our agreement when I found I couldn't pay you any wages? that you were to have everything that was left if you outlived me, and I was to bury you ~~with~~ in a coffin with your name on a gold plate if I outlived you?" He said nothing. "Wasn't it?" Miss Emily said.

"I was young then. Wanted to be rich. But now I dont want any house."

"Not when you have wanted to go to Chicago for thirty years?" Their breathing was alike: each that harsh, rasping breath of the old, the short inhalations that do not reach the bottom of the lungs: tireless, precarious, on the verge of cessation for all time, as if anything might suffice: a word, a look. "What are you going to do, then?"

"Going to the poorhouse."

"The poorhouse? When I'm trying to fix you so you'll

14.

have neither to worry nor lift your hand as long as you live?

"I dont want nothing," the negro said. "I'm going t.
the poorhouse. I already told them."

"Well," Miss Emily said. She had not moved her head,
not moved at all. "Do you mind telling me why you want to go
to the poorhouse?"

Again he mused. The room was still save for their brea
ing: it was as though they had both quitted all living and all
dying; all the travail of mortality and of breath. "So I can
set on that hill in the sun all day and watch them trains pass.
See them at night too, with the engine puffing and lights in
all the windows.

"Oh," Miss Emily said. Motionless, her knotted hands
lying on the yellowed coverlet beneath her chin and her chin
resting upon her breast, she appeared to muse intently, as
though she were listening to dissolution setting up within her.
"Hah," she said.

Then she died, and the negro met the first of the ladies at the front door and let them in, with their hushed sibilant voices and their quick curious glances, and he went on
to the back and disappeared. He walked right through the house
and out the back and was not seen again.

The two female cousins came at once. They held the
funeral on the second day, with the town coming to look at
Miss Emily beneath a mass of bought flowers, with the crayon
face of her father musing profoundly above the bier and the la-

15.

grin cemented into what had once been a pillow by a substance like
hardened sealing-wax. One side of the covers was flung back, as
though he were preparing to rise; we lifted the covers completely
away, liberating still another sluggish cloud of infinitesimal
dust, invisible and tainted. The body had apparently once lain
in the attitude of an embrace, but now the long sleep that outlasts love, that conquers even the grimace of love, had cuckolded
him: what was left of him lay beneath what was left of the
nightshirt, become inextricable with the bed in which he lay,
and upon him and upon the pillow beside him lay that even coating of the patient and biding dust. /#/ Then we noticed that in
the second pillow was the indentation of a head; one of us
lifted something from it, and leaning forward, that faint and
invisible dust lean and acrid in the nostrils, we saw a long
strand of iron-gray hair.

We also print an unnumbered page of the typescript, showing the very end of the story. The final paragraph of the typed version is, in the published version, reworded and made into two paragraphs.

WILLIAM FAULKNER

Comments on the Story

The following remarks, made on various occasions during Faulkner's stay at the University of Virginia in 1957 and 1958, are derived from Faulkner at the University: Class Conferences at the University of Virginia 1957–58, *edited by Frederick Gwynn and Joseph Blotner.*

Q. Sir, in "A Rose for Emily" is it possible to take Homer Barron and Emily and sort of show that one represents the South and the North? Is there anything on your part there trying to show the North and the South in sort of a battle, maybe Miss Emily representing the South coming out victorious in the rather odd way that she did?

A. That would be only incidental. I think that the writer is too busy trying to create flesh-and-blood people that will stand up and cast a shadow to have time to be conscious of all the symbolism that he may put into what he does or what people may read into it. That if he had time to—that is, if one individual could write the authentic, credible, flesh-and-blood character and at the same time deliver the message, maybe he would, but I don't believe any writer is capable of doing both, that he's got to choose one of the two: either he is delivering a message or he's trying to create flesh-and-blood, living, suffering, anguishing human beings. And as any man works out of his past, since any man—no man is himself, he's the sum of his past, and in a way, if you can accept the term, of his future too. And this struggle between the South and the North could have been a part of my background, my experience, without me knowing it.

[11 March 1957]

Q. Sir, it has been argued that "A Rose for Emily" is a criticism of the North, and others have argued saying that it is a criticism of the South. Now, could this story, shall we say, be more properly classified as a criticism of the times?

A. Now that I don't know, because I was simply trying to write about people. The writer uses environment—what he knows—and if there's a symbolism in which the lover represented the North and the woman who murdered him represents the South, I don't say that's not valid and not there, but it was no intention of the writer to say, Now let's see, I'm going to write a piece in which I will use a symbolism for the North and another symbol for the South, that he was simply writing about people, a story which he thought was tragic and true, because it came out of the human heart, the human aspiration, the human—the conflict of conscience with glands, with the Old Adam. It was a conflict not between the North and the South so much as between, well you might say, God and Satan.

Q. Sir, just a little more on that thing. You say it's a conflict between God and Satan. Well, I don't quite understand what you mean. Who is—did one represent the—

A. The conflict was in Miss Emily, that she knew that you do not murder people. She had been trained that you do not take a lover. You marry, you don't take a lover. She had broken all the laws of her tradition, her background, and she had finally broken the law of God too, which says you do not take human life. And she knew she was doing wrong, and that's why her own life was wrecked. Instead of murdering one lover, and then to go on and take another and when she used him up to murder him, she was expiating her crime.

Q. . . . She did do all the things that she had been taught not to do, and being a sensitive sort of a woman, it was sure to have told on her, but do you think it's fair to feel pity for her, because in a way she made her adjustment, and it seems to have wound up in a happy sort of a way—certainly tragic, but maybe it suited her just fine.

A. Yes, it may have, but then I don't think that one should withhold pity simply because the subject of the pity, object of pity, is pleased and satisfied. I think the pity is in the human striving against its own nature, against its own conscience. That's what deserves the pity. It's not the state of the individual, it's man in conflict with his heart, or with his fellows, or with his environment—that's what deserves the pity. It's not that the man suffered, or that he fell off the house, or was run over by the train. It's that he was—that man is trying to do the best he can with his desires and impulses against his own moral conscience, and the conscience of, the social conscience of his time and his place—the little town he must live in, the family he's a part of.

[13 March 1957]

Q. What is the meaning of the title "A Rose for Emily"?

A. Oh, it's simply the poor woman had had no life at all. Her father had kept her more or less locked up and then she had a lover who was about to quit her, she had to murder him. It was just "A Rose for Emily"—that's all.

[15 April 1957]

Q. I was wondering, one of your short stories, "A Rose for Emily," what ever inspired you to write this story . . . ?

A. That to me was another sad and tragic manifestation of man's condition in which he dreams and hopes, in which he is in conflict with himself or with his environment or with others. In this case there was the young girl with a young girl's normal aspirations to find love and then a husband and a family, who was brow-beaten and kept down by her father, a selfish man who didn't want her to leave home because he wanted a housekeeper, and it was a natural instinct of— repressed which—you can't repress it—you can mash it down but it comes up somewhere else and very likely in a tragic form, and that was simply another manifestation of man's injustice to man, of the poor tragic human being struggling with its own heart, with others, with its environment, for the simple things which all human beings want. In that case it was a young girl that just wanted to be loved and to love and to have a husband and a family.

Q. And that purely came from your imagination?

A. Well, the story did but the condition is there. It exists. I didn't invent that condition, I didn't invent the fact that young girls dream of someone to love and children and a home, but the story of what her own particular tragedy was was invented, yes. . . .

[20 May 1957]

Q. Is "A Rose for Emily" all fiction?

A. Yes sir. Yes sir, that's all fiction, for the reason I said, too. If any time a writer writes anything that seems at all familiar to anybody anywhere, he gets a letter about it, and if they think he's got enough money, he's sued, too, so he's awful careful not to write anything he ever saw himself, or anybody ever told him.

[30 May 1957]

Two Interpretations by Students, with Notes and Outlines

Here we give two essays by students on "A Rose for Emily." Each essay is prefaced by brief notes that the student used as an outline, but you will see that although the notes provided much guidance and doubtless helped the students to get started, in the course of drafting, revising, and revising yet again, each writer did not hesitate to depart from the initial outline.

The point: Most writers jot down notes as ideas occur to them, then they organize the notes into what seems to be a reasonable pattern, and from these organized notes they produce a first draft. But even as they write this first draft, fresh ideas will occur. The organized notes are a help in getting started, but they should not become a straitjacket. After the first draft has been written, writers will revise it and then revise the revision, often in the light of comments made by peer reviewers.

Why did Emily Grierson Kill Homer Barron?

Emily must have a motive; she is like a real person, not a symbol (quote Faulkner)

classroom discussion:

she needs a man (substitute for father)

she feels guilty for having had sex with HB (I kept my mouth shut, but I think my

   point — that HB is gay, and she kills him when she finds out he has been using her as

   a cover for his gay life-style—makes better sense

Evidence:

"he linked men"

Homer = homo

Barron = barren, sterile

advantage of this interpretation:

clear and simple; no phony psychologizing

Freer 1

Sally Freer

Professor Hwang

English 102

10 December 2012

Why Miss Emily Grierson Killed Homer Barron

Classroom discussion of William Faulkner's "A Rose for Emily" concentrated

on two topics: "What is the psychological nature of the woman who murders

Homer Barron?" and "Is the story really about Emily or is it about the Old

South versus the New South, or perhaps about the South versus the North?"

Many years ago someone at the University of Virginia raised this second

issue when he or she asked Faulkner if it is "possible to take Homer

Barron and Emily and sort of show that one represents the South and the North." Faulkner replied:

> That would be only incidental. I think that the writer is too busy trying to create flesh-and-blood people that will stand up and cast a shadow to have time to be conscious of all the symbolism that he may put into what he does or what people may read into it. (Faulkner, "Comments" 262)

Faulkner is not saying that interpretations concerning symbolism are wrong, only that they were not part of his conscious intention, and that he was much more concerned with a story about people than with saying something about the South, Old or New, or about the South and the North. This essay will concentrate on one person, Miss Emily Grierson, not as a symbol but as a, to use Faulkner's own words, "flesh-and-blood" person, and it will offer a reason as to why she killed Homer Barron.

The classroom psychological discussion of why Emily Grierson murdered Homer Barron emphasized Emily's need for a man in her life. In her early years, her father was that man—he had driven away any possible lovers—and when he dies, she tries to retain him by denying that he is dead. She cannot persist in this insane belief, but the need for a man, a substitute for her father, does persist. A man, Homer Barron, arrives, and as we know, Emily kills him and holds on to him by keeping the corpse in a room in her house. Another psychological explanation for the murder claimed that Emily felt guilty for fornicating with Homer Barron, and therefore she murdered the man who led her into sin. The sociological explanations considered the pressures of the Southern code of chivalry, and they were concerned with explaining the story in terms of the Old South (Colonel Sartoris and Emily) versus the New South (the townspeople), and with the culture of the South (represented by Colonel Sartoris and Emily) versus the North (Homer Barron). As we have seen, Faulkner indicated that these social differences were not

obviously in his mind, though of course it is possible that they were in his
subconscious mind.

This essay will concentrate on Miss Emily's reason for murdering Homer
Barron. The reason is not that she had some sort of psychological complex,
and not that she felt guilty because she had sinned by having sex, and it is
not related to any sort of cultural differences between the North and the
South. The essay will offer a simple explanation that seems obvious to me
but it was never raised in class. I will argue, and I will support my thesis
with evidence, that Emily kills Homer Barron when she finds out that he is
gay, when she finds out he is using her only as a cover for his sexual interest
which is in young men, not in women. I am not justifying the murder, but
am merely explaining, without turning to psychology or to some sort of
allegory about the South and the North, *why* she murders him.

What evidence supports the argument that Homer Barron is gay? When
I first read the story, I was immediately struck by this passage: "Homer
himself had remarked—he liked men, and it was known that he drank with
the younger men in the Elks' Club—that he was not a marrying man"
(Faulkner, "A Rose" 254). These words seemed to me to mean exactly what
they say: Homer liked young men and was not the marrying kind, which is to
say that he was gay. Why, then, on Sunday afternoons was he driving around
in a yellow-wheeled buggy with Miss Emily? Because, I argue, he wanted
people to think he was straight. He wanted some sort of cover for his sexual
activity with young men. In the days when Faulkner wrote his stories, unlike
today, a person could not be openly gay. A gay man had to seem to be
sexually interested in women. If he secretly had relationships with other
men, he would cover up his sexual orientation by dating women.

Another passage in the story also provides evidence that Homer
Barron is gay: "The construction company came with niggers and mules
and machinery, and a foreman named Homer Barron, a Yankee . . . " (253).

Notice the foreman's name, Homer Barron. Let's begin with his surname, Barron. The word, in another context, might suggest a member of the aristocracy, a baron, but in the context of the story Homer Barron clearly is not an aristocrat. Faulkner is certainly not suggesting that Homer Barron is in any way noble. "Barron" suggests "barren," not "baron." As a gay man, a man sexually interested in other men, Homer is not going to have children; he is barren. Second, and this point is less obvious but I think it is significant, Homer in this sentence is associated with "mules" and with "machinery," again with things that are not fertile. (Mules, the offspring of female horses and male donkeys, are sterile, infertile.) Finally, though I am less confident about this point, I think that Homer Barron's given name, Homer, perhaps suggests "homosexual." I think that maybe it was commonly pronounced something like "Home uh," which wouldn't be too far from "homo."

If we accept the view that Miss Emily was shocked when she somehow found out that Homer Barron was using her as a cover for his sexual interest in men, we can understand her fury and her motive for murdering him. Faulkner himself said, when he was at the University of Virginia, that Emily "was a young girl that just wanted to be loved and to love and to have a husband and a family" ("Comments" 263). Imagine the shock when she discovered that the man she was going with would not marry her and would never help her to have children. I am not justifying her criminal action, but I do think this interpretation explains Emily's behavior without getting into guesses about her psychologically seeing Homer as a substitute for her father, and without getting into far-fetched interpretations—which Faulkner was not enthusiastic about—that see the story as some sort of allegory of the South and the North rather than a story about "flesh-and-blood people" that Faulkner says he wanted to create.

[New page]

Freer 5

Works Cited

Faulkner, William. "A Rose for Emily." *Literature for Composition*. Ed. Sylvan

Barnet, William Burto, and William E. Cain. 10th ed. New York: Pearson,

2014. 249-56. Print.

---. "Comments on the Story." *Literature for Composition*. Ed. Sylvan Barnet,

William Burto, and William E. Cain. 10th ed. New York: Pearson,

2014. 262-63. Print.

Joining the Conversation: Critical Thinking and Writing

1. What is Sally Freer's thesis in this essay?
2. What evidence does Freer offer in support of her thesis?
3. How convincing do you find the evidence? Please explain.
4. Putting aside the matter of whether the essay is convincing, did you find it clear and interesting? Please explain.
5. What grade would you give the essay? Why?

Our second student essay is concerned not with Emily Grierson's motives but with a technique used by Faulkner. The student in effect asks the question "Who narrates the story of Emily Grierson?" Of course Faulkner *wrote* the story, but he invents a narrator who tells it. The student examines the effects that Faulkner gains by using the particular narrator that he does. (On kinds of narrators, see pages 355–56.)

We begin with the notes that the student used as an outline.

Who tells story of Emily's life? A man?? A woman? Everyone in the town?
Faulkner says the men were "respectful," the women were moved by "curiosity." Sexist?
Druggist had written "for rats." How could narrator know this, if he isn't druggist?
Maybe it doesn't matter! Reader doesn't notice!
Character of narrator:
  sexist?
  decent guy otherwise?
    but sort of glad when he hears she is poor. That's bit nasty—or just human?
    "WE were glad." so, not just him!
Still, he seems understanding

WE UNDERSTAND, THROUGH HIM; we are grateful to him
Does he know TOO MUCH? Is he unpleasantly nosy?
No, or maybe just a bit yes; chiefly, he is pretty much a typical person
The rose is his tribute to Emily

Daremo 1

John Daremo

Prof. Washington

English 100B

12 December 2012

   Insight into Horror: The Role of the Narrator in "A Rose for Emily"

   Who tells the reader the story of Miss Emily Grierson's life? Not the

author William Faulkner, but a narrator whom the author invents. Faulkner's

invented narrator is a member of the community in which Emily lived. This

much is evident from the first sentence of the story:

> When Miss Emily Grierson died, our whole town went to her
>
> funeral: the men through a sort of respectful affection for a fallen
>
> monument, the women mostly out of curiosity to see the inside
>
> of her house, which no one save an old Negro manservant—a
>
> combined gardner and cook—had seen in at least ten years.
>
> (Faulkner, "A Rose" 250)

The words "our whole town" identify the speaker as a member of Miss Emily's

community. True, they do not identify the speaker as anyone very specific—

for instance, a relative or a next-door neighbor or a local clergyman or the

druggist who sold Miss Emily the poison—but they do identify the speaker as

someone knowledgeable about the community. I will argue that the narrator

is not just a character in the story but is essential to *the reader's* understanding

of the story.

   Before continuing to examine the speaker as a member of the community

and also as a guide to the reader, it must be pointed out that the story

---

includes a very few passages that such a narrator could not in fact report.
After all, only Emily herself or possibly the African American servant Tobe
could authoritatively report, "When she opened the package at home there
was written on the box, under the skull and bones: 'For rats'" (253). Here we
have the voice of an omniscient narrator, not the voice of a townsman. And
the narrator could know about the handwriting and the ink of the letter Miss
Emily wrote to the mayor only if the mayor told him, or showed him the
letter—actions not mentioned by the narrator, so, again, the information
about the writing and the ink reveals an omniscient narrator—a departure
from the narrator who tells 99% of the story. But I think readers do not
notice these very few passages unless they are re-reading the story and
looking very closely to characterize the narrator. Significantly, Faulkner
omits from the published version a long passage of dialogue, found in the
typewritten version (Faulkner, "Typescript" 258-60), between the African
American servant (Tobe) and Miss Emily. As Hans H. Skei points out in
Reading Faulkner's Best Short Stories, one reason Faulkner probably omitted
this passage from the published version is that the man who narrates most of
the story could not possibly have been present at this episode (153).
Obviously Faulkner intended the story to be told by a narrator who is *not*
omniscient, and although a very few details are given (such as about Miss
Emily reading the label, and about her handwriting), a reader probably does
not notice that they are inconsistent with a first-person point of view. On
the other hand, a whole scene would certainly be noticed, and such a scene
would violate our sense that a member of the town is narrating the story.

Although one scholar, Michael I. Burdock, says that the narrator is a
woman, Burdock offers no convincing evidence, and I think the first
sentence of the story, with its explanation of the difference between the
concern of the men ("respectful affection") and the concern of the women

("curiosity to see the inside of her house") is the sort of put-down of women that too often characterizes male thinking. One other passage seems to me to clearly indicate that the speaker is a male. In the third paragraph Faulkner tells us, through the narrator, that

> Colonel Sartoris invented an involved tale to the effect that Miss
> Emily's father had loaned money to the town, which the town,
> as a matter of business, preferred this way of repaying. Only a
> man of Colonel Sartoris' generation and thought could have
> invented it, and only a woman could have believed it. (250)

Still, even if we sometimes do hear the voice of a male rather than a female, we can still say that the narrator is more or less the voice of the community as a whole, or in these instances at least the voice of the males of the community, rather than a highly individualized specific character.

What else can we say about the narrator beyond saying that he is a member of the community? In the second paragraph the narrator describes Miss Emily's house, built in a fashionable style in the 1870s on what once was "our most select street" but now "an eyesore among eyesores" (250). The narrator certainly does not hesitate to express opinions, but here the opinion probably reflects the view of the entire community. Certainly we do not say that these words show that the narrator is a specialist in architecture, or that he is abnormally sensitive to beauty and to ugliness.

Throughout the story we get passages such as (to take examples almost at random) "Thus she passed from generation to generation—dear, inescapable, impervious, tranquil, and perverse" (255), and "Two days later we learned that she had bought a complete outfit of men's clothing, including a nightshirt, and we said, 'They are married.' We were really glad" (254). Words such as "dear" and "We were really glad" are enough to disprove Kenneth Payson Kempton's comment that the narrator is an objective reporter (30-31), but we can agree with Kempton's point that the narrator

serves chiefly as a reporter rather than as a highly defined character within

the story. That is, these personal comments do not give the narrator a unique

or distinct personality.

Notice, in fact, that the narrator does not say, "I was glad"; rather, he

says, "We were . . . glad." That is, he speaks not as an individual but in his

role as the voice of the community. Another passage in which he expresses

strong partiality, but, again, as the representative of the entire town, is when

he tells us that when Emily denied for three days that her father was dead,

> We did not say she was crazy then. We believed she had to do that.
>
> We remembered all the young men her father had driven away, and we
>
> knew that with nothing left, she would have to cling to that which
>
> had robbed her, as people will. (252)

Here the narrator is very understanding, but in a few passages he—the

community—is not highly sympathetic to Miss Emily. For example, he says,

"So when she got to be thirty and was still single, we were not pleased exactly,

but vindicated; even with insanity in the family she wouldn't have turned

down all of her chances if they had really materialized" (252). We can say that

the attitude here is not high-minded, but, again, it probably represents a

widespread view rather than an individual view. A passage that closely follows

this one similarly expresses a somewhat unpleasant but common view:

> When her father died, it got about that the house was all that was left
>
> to her; and in a way, people were glad. At last they could pity Miss
>
> Emily. Being left alone, and a pauper, she had become humanized.
>
> Now she too would know the old thrill and the old despair of a penny
>
> more or less. (252)

But even though it is hardly nice to be "glad" that someone has become a

pauper, we can in this instance understand the narrator's feeling, and we can even admire his understanding of *why* he and the rest of the community felt

this way. And perhaps, as readers, we recognize that *we* might feel pretty

much what the community feels.

One objection to the narrator's behavior, not just in this last passage

but throughout the story, is voiced especially strongly by the critic Ruth

Sullivan. Sullivan argues that the narrator knows *too much* about Miss Emily,

that the narrator is in effect a spy concerned with other people's sexuality.

Sullivan, who apparently is a Freudian critic, says that the narrator reveals

"unsavory qualities" (162). Sullivan speaks of the narrator's "aggression and

sadism" (171), and she goes so far as to say that the story is "about types of

perversion—Miss Emily's necrophilia and the narrator's voyeurism—that are

motivated by frustrated sexual needs and by fears about loss of the loved

object" (175). True, Faulkner does have the narrator say such things as "Daily,

monthly, yearly, we watched," but surely it is going too far to see this interest

in an eccentric as a "perversion," especially as a perversion comparable to

necrophilia. And it is going too far to say that the story is *about* the narrator

as well as about Emily. After all, this story is not at all like, say, Edgar Allan

Poe's "The Cask of Amontillado," which certainly *is* about the narrator at least

as much as it is about the nominal subject, a man named Fortunato.

My point thus far is simply this: Although the story is told by a

first-person narrator, the reader's interest is chiefly in the *tale* the narrator

tells—the story about Miss Emily—not in the narrator himself. Further, the

narrator represents the voice of the community, and though on rare occasions

he displays a somewhat unpleasant trait, as when he (and the rest of the

community) is pleased that Miss Emily now knows the importance of every

penny, on the whole (despite Sullivan's view that the narrator is a perverse

voyeur) this narrative voice is chiefly sympathetic to Miss Emily. Even more

important, and indeed the reason that this narrative voice is essential to the story, is the fact that Miss Emily's behavior—murdering Homer Barron and at least once laying next to the corpse—would be horrifying if it were not that the narrator has, by his intelligent and (for the most part) sympathetic comments, helped us to see her as an intelligible, believable character. Faulkner's story is not like, for instance, a ghost story, where the interest is entirely in fantastic happenings, and not in the personality of the central figure. Nor is it—even though the story is partly about a murder and a hidden corpse—like a detective story, where, again, the interest is entirely in the plot: Who did it, and how will the mystery be unraveled? Nor is Miss Emily some sort of stock figure out of a **horror** story, someone whose strange actions hold our attention primarily because they are strange, freakish. The story is *not* just a shocker, a meaningless tale with a surprise ending, a story that can be read only once, for its plot, and then, because the ending is known, cannot interest a reader a second or a third time. On the contrary, the story becomes *more* interesting each time one reads it, *more* a revelation of understandable human behavior.

Nor (except in the most literal sense) are the last words in the final paragraph the last word in the story. At the end, probably many readers briefly wonder why it is called "A Rose for Emily." Faulkner himself, when asked in 1955 in an interview in Japan what the significance of the title was, said that it was "a salute, just as if you were to make a gesture, a salute to anyone; to a woman you would hand a rose, as you would lift a cup of *sake* to a man" (Jelliffe 71). The telling of this tale is itself the rose, the community's tribute. And because the narrator helps *us* to see Emily's humanity beneath her weirdness, *we* become part of the narrator's community. By the end of the story, when the narrator says "we," readers can include themselves in the "we." We, with the narrator's help, see the humanity in a woman whose behavior might seem monstrous to us if the narrator had not guided us.

[New page]

Daremo 7

Works Cited

Burdock, Michael I. "Another View of Faulkner's Narrator in 'A Rose for Emily.'"

University of Mississippi Studies in English 8 (1990): 209-11. *Literature*

Resource Center. Web. 1 Oct. 2012.

Faulkner, William. "A Rose for Emily." *Literature for Composition*. Ed. Sylvan

Barnet, William Burto, and William E. Cain. 10th ed. New York: Pearson,

2014. 249-56. Print.

---. "Typescript Showing Material Deleted from the Published Version."

Literature for Composition. Ed. Sylvan Barnet, William Burto, and William

E. Cain. 10th ed. New York: Pearson, 2014. 257-61. Print.

Jelliffe, Robert A., ed. *Faulkner at Nagano*. Tokyo: Kenkyusha, 1956. Print.

Kempton, Kenneth. *The Short Story*. Cambridge: Harvard UP, 1948. Print.

Skei, Hans H. *Reading Faulkner's Best Short Stories*. Columbia: U of South

Carolina P, 1999. Print.

Sullivan, Ruth K. "The Narrator in 'A Rose for Emily.'" *Journal of Narrative*

Technique 1 (1971): 159-78. Print.

Joining the Conversation: Critical Thinking and Writing

1. What is John Daremo's thesis in this essay?
2. What evidence does Daremo offer in support of his thesis?
3. How convincing do you find the evidence? Please explain.
4. Putting aside the matter of whether the essay is convincing, did you find it clear and interesting? Please explain.
5. What grade would you give the essay? Why?

CHAPTER 9

Arguing an Evaluation

Critics are sentinels in the grand army of letters, stationed at the corners of newspapers and reviews, to challenge every new author.

HENRY WADSWORTH LONGFELLOW

Chapter Preview

After reading this chapter you will be able to

- Define *evaluation* and describe the process for evaluating literary texts
- Explain the concept of critical standards and describe their role in evaluation

Criticism and Evaluation

Although, as we have noted, in ordinary usage *criticism* implies finding fault and therefore implies evaluation—"This story is weak"—in fact most literary criticism is *not* concerned with evaluation. Rather, it is chiefly concerned with *interpretation* (the setting forth of meaning) and with *analysis* (examination of relationships among the parts, or of causes and effects). For instance, an interpretation may argue that in *Death of a Salesman* Willy Loman is the victim of a cruel capitalistic economy, and an analysis may show how the symbolic setting of the play (a stage direction tells us that "towering, angular shapes" surround the salesman's house) contributes to the play's meaning.

In Chapter 6 we asked the question "What is literature?" We saw that an analysis of Robert Frost's "The Span of Life" (page 122) called attention to the contrast between the meter of the first line (relatively uneven or irregular, with an exceptional number of heavy stresses) and the meter of the second (relatively even and jingling). The analysis also called attention to the contrast between the content of the first line (the old dog) and that of the second (the speaker's memory of a young dog):

> The old dog barks backward without getting up.
> I can remember when he was a pup.

In our discussion we did not worry about whether this poem deserved an A, B, or C, nor did we consider whether it was better or worse than some other poem by Frost, or by some other writer. And if you read books and journals devoted to literary study, you will find chiefly discussions of meaning. For the most part, critics assume that the works they are writing about have value and are good enough to merit attention, so critics largely concern themselves with other matters.

Yet some critical writing is indeed concerned with evaluation—with saying that works are good or bad, dated or classic, major or minor. (The language need not be as explicit as these words are: Evaluation can also be conveyed through descriptive words like *moving, successful, effective, important,* or, on the other hand, *tedious, unsuccessful, weak, trivial.*) In reviews of plays, books, musical and dance performances, and films, professional critics usually devote much of their space to evaluating the work or the performance, or both. The reviewer seeks, finally, to tell readers whether to buy a book or a ticket—or to save their money and their time.

In short, although in our independent reading we may read what we like, and we need not argue that one work is better than another, the issue of evaluation is evident àll around us.

Some years ago Steve Moss, a writer, editor, and publisher, began an annual contest in which contestants submitted stories of fifty-five words or fewer (plus a title that could be as long as seven words). Here are three entries that were accepted for publication.[1]

JEFFREY WHITMORE

Bedtime Story

"Careful, honey, it's loaded," he said, re-entering the bedroom.
Her back rested against the headboard. "This for your wife?"
"No. Too chancy. I'm hiring a professional."
"How about me?"
He smirked. "Cute. But who'd be dumb enough to hire a lady hit man?"
She wet her lips, sighting along the barrel.
"Your wife."

All readers will have their own responses to this story, and they will make their own evaluations as to whether it is effective; here we offer the annotations of one of our students.

> **Title:** *Clever: I expected a sort of child's nursery tale, and instead got a story that in part is about adults going to bed sexually—so I did get a "bedtime story" but not what I first expected. Sort of clever.*
>
> **Characterization:** *Only two characters—and a very very short story, so we don't expect elaborate characterization, but the man is neatly shown to be a self-satisfied jerk. He thinks he is smart—"Too chancy. I'm hiring a professional"—and he "smirked" when his girlfriend suggests she might act as a hit-man. He has a conventional superior-male idea that a woman can't do a difficult job—but at the end of the story he knows (if only for a few seconds!!!) better. I think it is a pretty effective story. Certainly it is clever.*

Now for a second story.

DOUGLAS L. HASKINS

Hide and Seek

At last he would really show them. He'd picked the very best place to hide. They'd all say he could play the game better than anyone. When they found him, they'd clap their hands.

The dopes. How dumb can they get? They should have looked here first! It's so obvious.

Here in the abandoned refrigerator.

---

[1] Steve Moss, ed., *The World's Shortest Stories* (Philadelphia: Running Press, 1998).

After reading the preceding short story, another student jotted down these notes:

> *This story is horrible! I guess it is "effective" because it really hits me, hurts me, but it is so cruel. As I understand it, a kid wants to show other kids that he is smart, that "he could play the game better than anyone," so he hides in an abandoned refrigerator—and presumably he dies. What we hear—and I admit this is clever—are the thoughts of the kid before he died—his pitiful attempt to be superior. And I think we also hear, in a way, what is said after the other kids discover his dead body: We "should have looked here first! It's so obvious." Frankly, I don't think a story like this should be published. It is too frightening.*

Finally, a third story from the same collection of stories of fifty-five words or fewer, this time with no comment from a student.

MARK PLANTS
Equal Rites

"Highly irregular," said the priest.

"The diocese allows them," replied one of the men.

Overcoming a visceral dislike of same sex unions, the priest agreed to hold the ceremony quietly. There was a harpist. Both men wore tuxedos.

But the priest, even while donning her vestments, still wondered if she was doing the right thing.

Joining the Conversation: Critical Thinking and Writing

1. If you have anything to add to the two observations by the students who commented on the first two stories, jot down your thoughts—perhaps amplifying their thoughts, or perhaps responding with a very different view.
2. Jot down a few sentences indicating your responses to the third story.
3. Let's assume that you were a judge in a literary competition, and these three stories had been nominated. To which author do you give First Prize? Support your choice in an essay of about 250–500 words. (You will probably devote about one-third of the essay to the two stories that you think are the less successful, and about two-thirds to the story you judge to be the winner.)

Are There Critical Standards?

One approach to evaluating a work of literature, or, indeed, to evaluating anything at all, is to rely on personal taste. This approach is evident in a statement such as "I don't know anything about modern art, but I know what I like." The idea is at least as old as the Roman saying *De gustibus non est disputandum* ("There is no disputing tastes").

If we say "This is a good work" or "This book is greater than that book," are we saying anything beyond "I like this" and "I like this better than that"? Are all expressions of evaluation really nothing more than expressions of taste? Most people believe that if there are such things as works of art, or works of literature, there must be standards by which they can be evaluated, just as most utilitarian things are evaluated by standards. The standards for evaluating a scissors, for instance, are clear: It ought to cut cleanly, it ought not to need frequent sharpening, and it ought to feel comfortable in the hand. We may also want it to look nice (perhaps to be painted—or on the contrary to reveal its stainless steel) and to be inexpensive, rustproof, and so on, but in any case we can easily state our standards. Similarly, there are agreed-upon standards for evaluating figure skating, gymnastics, fluency in language, and so on.

But what are the standards for evaluating literature? In earlier pages we implied one standard: In a good work of literature, all of the parts contribute to the whole, making a unified work. Some people would add that mere unity is not enough; a work of high quality needs not only to be unified but also to be complex. The writer offers a "performance in words" (Frost's words, again), and when we read, we can see if the writer has successfully kept all of the Indian clubs in the air. If, for instance, the stated content of the poem is mournful, yet the meter jingles, we can probably say that the performance is unsuccessful; at least one of the juggler's clubs is clattering on the floor.

Here are standards that are commonly set forth:

- Moral content
- Truth, realism
- Personal taste
- Esthetic qualities, such as unity

Let's look at some of these standards in detail.

Morality and Truth as Standards

"It is always a writer's duty to make the world better." Thus wrote Samuel Johnson, in 1765, in his "Preface to Shakespeare." In this view, morality plays a large role: A story that sympathetically treats lesbian or gay love would, from a traditional Judeo-Christian perspective, probably be regarded as a bad story, or at least not as worthy as a story that celebrates heterosexual married love. On the other hand, a gay or lesbian critic, or anyone not committed to Judeo-Christian values, might regard the story highly because, in such a reader's view, it helps to educate readers and thereby does something "to make the world better."

But there can be complications here. A gay or lesbian story might strike even a reader with traditional values as a work that is effectively told, with believable and memorable characters, whereas a story of heterosexual married love might be unbelievable, awkwardly told, trite, sentimental. (More about sentimentality in a moment.) How much value should we give to the ostensible content of the story, the obvious moral or morality, and how much value should we give to the artistry exhibited in telling the story?

People differ greatly over moral (and religious) issues. Edward Fitzgerald's 1859 translation of *The Rubáiyát of Omar Khayyám* (a twelfth-century Persian poem) suggests that God does not exist, or—perhaps worse—if He does exist, He doesn't care about us. That God does not exist is a view held by many moral people; it is also a view opposed by many moral people. The issue then may become a matter of **truth.** Does the value of the poem depend on which view is right? In fact, does a reader have to subscribe to Fitzgerald's view to enjoy (and to evaluate highly) the following stanza from the poem, in which Fitzgerald suggests that the pleasures of this world are the only paradise that we can experience?

> A book of verses underneath the bough,
> A jug of wine, a loaf of bread—and thou
>   Beside me singing in the wilderness—
> Oh, wilderness were paradise enow!

Some critics can give high value to a literary work only if they share its beliefs, if they think that the work corresponds to reality. They measure the work against their vision of the truth.

Other critics may highly value a work of literature that expresses ideas they do not believe, arguing that literature does not require us to believe in its views. Rather, this theory claims, literature gives a reader a strong sense of *what it feels like* to hold certain views—even though the reader does not share those views. Take, for instance, a lyric poem in which Christina Rossetti (1830–94), a devout Anglican, expresses both spiritual numbness and spiritual hope. Here is one stanza from "A Better Resurrection":

My life is like a broken bowl.
   A broken bowl that cannot hold
One drop of water for my soul
   Or cordial in the searching cold:
Cast in the fire the perished thing:
   Melt and remould it, till it be
A royal cup for Him, my King:
   O Jesus, drink of me.

One need not be an Anglican suffering a crisis to find this poem of considerable interest. It offers insight into a state of mind, and the truth or falsity of religious belief is not at issue. Similarly, we can argue that although *The Divine Comedy* by Dante Alighieri (1265–1321) is deeply a Roman Catholic work, the non-Catholic reader can read it with interest and pleasure because of (for example) its rich portrayal of a wide range of characters, the most famous of whom perhaps are the pathetic lovers Paolo and Francesca. In Dante's view, they are eternally damned because they were unrepentant adulterers, but a reader need not share this belief.

Other Ways of Thinking about Truth and Realism

Other solutions to the problem of whether a reader must share a writer's beliefs have been offered. One extreme view says that beliefs are irrelevant because literature has nothing to do with truth. In this view, a work of art does not correspond to anything "outside" itself, that is, to anything in the real world. If a work of art has any "truth," it is only in the sense of its being internally consistent. Thus Shakespeare's *Macbeth,* like, say, the lullaby "Rock-a-bye Baby," isn't making assertions about reality. *Macbeth* has nothing to do with the history of Scotland, just as (in this view) Shakespeare's *Julius Caesar* has nothing to do with the history of Rome, although Shakespeare borrowed some of his material from history books. These tragedies, like lullabies, are worlds in themselves—not to be judged against historical accounts of Scotland or Rome—and we are interested in the characters in the plays only as they exist *in the plays.* We may require, for instance, that the characters be consistent, believable, and engaging, but we cannot require that they correspond to historical figures.

Literary works are neither true nor false; they are only (when successful) coherent and interesting. The poet William Butler Yeats (1865–1939) perhaps had in mind something along these lines when he said that you can refute a philosopher, but you cannot refute the song of sixpence. And indeed "Sing a song of sixpence, / Pocket full of rye" has endured for a couple of centuries, perhaps partly because it has nothing to do with truth or falsity; it has created its own engaging world.

And yet it's possible to object, offering a commonsense response: Surely when we see a play, or read an engaging work of literature, whether it is old or new, we feel that somehow the work says something about the life around us, the real world. True, some of what we read—let's say, detective fiction—is chiefly fanciful: We read it to test our wits, or to escape, or to kill time. But most literature seems to be connected to life. This commonsense view, that literature is related to life, has an ancient history, and in fact almost everyone in the Western world believed it from the time of the ancient Greeks until the nineteenth century. And many people—including authors and highly skilled readers—still believe it today.

Certainly a good deal of literature, most notably the realistic short story and the novel, is devoted to giving a detailed picture that at least *looks like* the real world. One reason we read the fiction of Kate Chopin is to find out what "the real world" of Creole New Orleans in the late nineteenth century was like—as seen through Chopin's eyes, of course. (You need not be a Marxist to believe, with Karl Marx, that you can learn more about industrial England from the novels of Dickens and Elizabeth Gaskell than from economic treatises.) Writers of stories, novels, and plays are concerned to give plausible, indeed precise and insightful, images of the relationships between people. Writers of lyric poems presumably are specialists in presenting human feelings—the experience of love, for instance, or of the loss of faith. Presumably we are invited to compare the writer's created world to the world that we live in, perhaps to be reminded that our own lives can be richer than they are.

Even when a writer describes an earlier time, the implication is that the description is accurate, and especially that people *did* behave the way the writer says they did—and the way our own daily experience shows us that people do behave. Here is George Eliot at the beginning of her novel *Adam Bede* (1859):

> With a single drop of ink for a mirror, the Egyptian sorcerer undertook to reveal to any chance comer far-reaching visions of the past. This is what I undertake to do for you, reader. With this drop of ink at the end of my pen, I will show you the roomy workshop of Jonathan Burge, carpenter and builder in the village of Hayslope, as it appeared on the 18th of June, in the year of Our Lord, 1799.

Why do novelists like George Eliot give us detailed pictures, and cause us to become deeply involved in the lives of their characters? Another novelist, D. H. Lawrence, offers a relevant comment in the ninth chapter of *Lady Chatterley's Lover* (1928):

> It is the way our sympathy flows and recoils that really determines our lives. And here lies the vast importance of the novel, properly handled. It can inform and lead into new places the flow of our sympathetic consciousness, and it can lead our sympathy away in recoil from things gone dead. Therefore, the novel, properly handled, can reveal the most secret places of life.

In Lawrence's view, we can evaluate a novel in terms of its moral effect on the reader: The good novel, Lawrence claims, leads us into worlds—human relationships— that deserve our attention, and leads us away from "things gone dead," presumably relationships and values—whether political, moral, or religious—that no longer deserve to survive. To be blunt, Lawrence claims that good books improve us. His comment is similar to a more violent comment made by Franz Kafka: "A book must be an ice-axe to break the frozen sea inside us."

Realism is not the writer's only tool. In *Gulliver's Travels* Swift gives us a world of Lilliputians, people about six inches tall. Is his book pure fancy, unrelated to life? Not at all. We perceive that the Lilliputians are (except for their size) pretty much like ourselves, and we realize that their tiny stature is an image of human pettiness, an *un*realistic device that helps us to see the real world more clearly.

The view that we have been talking about—that writers do connect us to the world—does not require realism, but it does assume that writers see, understand, and, through the medium of their writings, give us knowledge, deepen our understanding, and even perhaps improve our character. If, the argument goes, a work distorts reality—let's say because the author sees women superficially—the work is inferior. Some such assumption is found, for instance, in a comment by Elaine Savory Fido, who says that the work of Derek Walcott, a Caribbean poet and dramatist, is successful when Walcott deals with racism and with colonialism but is unsuccessful when he deals with women. "His treatment of women," Fido says in an essay in *Journal of Commonwealth Literature* (1986),

> is full of clichés, stereotypes and negativity. I shall seek to show how some of his worst writing is associated with these portraits of women, which sometimes lead him to the brink of losing verbal control, or give rise to a retreat into abstract, conventional terms which prevent any real treatment of the subject. (109)

We need not be concerned here with whether Fido's evaluations of Walcott's works about women and about colonialism are convincing: What concerns us is her assumption that works can be—should be—evaluated in terms of the keenness of the writer's perception of reality.

Although we need not be concerned with an evaluation, we may wish to be concerned with it—and if so, we will probably find, perhaps to our surprise, that in the very process of arguing our evaluation (perhaps only to ourselves) we are also interpreting and reinterpreting. That is, we find ourselves examining passages closely, from a new point of view, and we may therefore find ourselves seeing them differently, finding new meanings in them.

Your Turn: Poems and Stories for Evaluation

SARAH N. CLEGHORN

Sarah N. Cleghorn (1876–1959) was born in Manchester, Vermont. A Quaker, she was active in pacifist, anti-vivisectionist, and women's suffrage movements. Among her many books are The True Ballad of Glorious Harriet Tubman *(1933) and an autobiography,* Threescore *(1936).*

The Golf Links

The golf links lie so near the mill
    That almost every day
The laboring children can look out
    And see the men at play.

[1917]

Joining the Conversation: Critical Thinking and Writing

1. Check the meanings of "ironic," "satiric," and "sarcastic" in a dictionary, and decide which if any of these words applies well to Cleghorn's poem.
2. The poem was published in 1917, when child labor was common. (Children as young as ten worked as much as fifteen hours a day in mills. In 1916—a year before the poem was published—Congress had passed the Child Labor Act, but

in 1918 the Supreme Court struck down the act, arguing that Congress did not have the right to control labor within a state.) Today, however, child labor in the United States is virtually nonexistent. Is there any point, then, in reading this poem? Set forth your response in a brief argument, perhaps of two paragraphs.

WILFRED OWEN

Wilfred Owen (1893–1918) was born in the county of Shropshire in western England, and he studied at London University. He enlisted in the army at the outbreak of World War I and fought in the Battle of the Somme (July–November 1916) until he was hospitalized with shell shock. After his recuperation in England, he returned to the front only to be killed in action one week before the end of the war (11 November 1918). His collected poems were published posthumously (1 December 1920).

*Dulce et Decorum Est**

Bent double, like old beggars under sacks,
Knock-kneed, coughing like hags, we cursed through sludge,
Till on the haunting flares we turned our backs
And towards our distant rest began to trudge.
Men marched asleep. Many had lost their boots   5
But limped on, blood shod. All went lame; all blind;
Drunk with fatigue; deaf even to the hoots
Of tired, outstripped Five-Nines° that dropped behind.

Gas! Gas! Quick, boys! — An ecstasy of fumbling,
Fitting the clumsy helmets just in time;   10
But someone still was yelling out and stumbling
And flound'ring like a man in fire or lime . . .
Dim, through the misty panes and thick green light,
As under a green sea, I saw him drowning.

In all my dreams, before my helpless sight,   15
He plunges at me, guttering, choking, drowning.

If in some smothering dreams you too could pace
Behind the wagon that we flung him in,
And watch the white eyes writhing in his face,
His hanging face, like a devil's sick of sin;   20
If you could hear, at every jolt, the blood
Come gargling from the froth-corrupted lungs,
Obscene as cancer, bitter as the cud
Of vile, incurable sores on innocent tongues,—
My friend,° you would not tell with such high zest   25
To children ardent for some desperate glory,
The old Lie: Dulce et decorum est
Pro patria mori.

[1917]

*Dulce et Decorum Est From the Latin poet Horace's *Odes* (III:2.13): *Dulce et decorum est pro patria mori*—"It is sweet and honorable to die for your country."   **8 Five-Nines** shells containing poison gas.   **25 My friend** Jessie Pope, author of patriotic verse.

Joining the Conversation: Critical Thinking and Writing

How highly do you rate this poem? Why? Does your knowledge of the fact that Owen died in World War I affect your response toward the poem, especially your sense of its value?

MyLiteratureLab° *For additional resources for "Dulce et Decorum Est," log in to* www.myliteraturelab.com *where you will find a Longman Lecture, Interactive Reading, Comprehension Quiz, Short Evaluation Exercises, and Essay Prompts, as well as an About the Author, Links, and Critical Overview for Owen (under Student Resources).*

Anthem for Doomed Youth

What passing-bells for these who die as cattle?
Only the monstrous anger of the guns.
Only the stuttering rifles' rapid rattle
Can patter out their hasty orisons.
No mockeries for them from prayers or bells,   5
Nor any voice of mourning save the choirs—
The shrill, demented choirs of wailing shells;
And bugles calling for them from sad shires.

What candles may be held to speed° them all?
Not in the hands of boys, but in their eyes   10
Shall shine the holy glimmers of good-byes.
The pallor of girls' brows shall be their pall;
Their flowers the tenderness of patient minds,
And each slow dusk a drawing-down of blinds.

[1920]

9 speed aid.

Joining the Conversation: Critical Thinking and Writing

1. What is an anthem? What words or phrases in this poem might be found in a traditional anthem? What words or phrases would you not expect to find in an anthem?
2. How would you characterize the speaker's state of mind? (Your response will probably require more than one word.)

HENRY REED

Born in Birmingham, England, Henry Reed (1914–86) served in the British army during World War II. Later, in civilian life, he had a distinguished career as a journalist, a translator of French and Italian literature, a writer of radio plays, and a poet.
"Naming of Parts" draws on his experience as a military recruit.

Naming of Parts

Today we have naming of parts. Yesterday,
We had daily cleaning. And tomorrow morning,
We shall have what to do after firing. But today,
Today we have naming of parts. Japonica
Glistens like coral in all of the neighboring gardens,   5
      And today we have naming of parts.

This is the lower sling swivel. And this
Is the upper sling swivel, whose use you will see,
When you are given your slings. And this is the piling swivel,
Which in your case you have not got. The branches   10
Hold in the gardens their silent, eloquent gestures,
      Which in our case we have not got.

This is the safety-catch, which is always released
With an easy flick of the thumb. And please do not let me
See anyone using his finger. You can do it quite easy   15
If you have any strength in your thumb. The blossoms
Are fragile and motionless, never letting anyone see
      Any of them using their finger.

And this you can see is the bolt. The purpose of this
Is to open the breech, as you see. We can slide it   20
Rapidly backwards and forwards: we call this
Easing the spring. And rapidly backwards and forwards
The early bees are assaulting and fumbling the flowers:
      They call it easing the Spring.

They call it easing the Spring: it is perfectly easy   25
If you have any strength in your thumb: like the bolt,
And the breech, and the cocking-piece, and the point of balance,
Which in our case we have not got; and the almond-blossom
Silent in all of the gardens and the bees going backwards and forwards,
For today we have naming of parts.   30

[1942]

Joining the Conversation: Critical Thinking and Writing

1. How many speakers do you hear in the poem? How would you characterize
   each of them?
2. Would you argue that this poem is a better poem than one or the other of the
   two preceding poems? Or is it poorer? Or can't one argue such a topic? Explain.

KATHERINE MANSFIELD

*Katherine Mansfield (1888–1923) was born in New Zealand. In 1902 she went to
London for schooling; in 1906 she returned to New Zealand, but dissatisfied with its*

provincialism, she returned in 1908 to London to become a writer. After a disastrous marriage and a love affair, she went to Germany, where she wrote stories; in 1910 she returned to London, published a book of stories in 1911, and in 1912 met and began living with the writer John Middleton Murry. In 1918, after her first husband at last divorced her, she married Murry. She died of tuberculosis in 1923, a few months after her thirty-fourth birthday.

Mansfield published about seventy stories and left some others unpublished. An early admirer of Chekhov, she read his works in German translations before they were translated into English.

Miss Brill

Although it was so brilliantly fine—the blue sky powdered with gold and great spots of light like white wine splashed over the Jardins Publiques[1]—Miss Brill was glad that she had decided on her fur. The air was motionless, but when you opened your mouth there was just a faint chill, like a chill from a glass of iced water before you sip, and now and again a leaf came drifting—from nowhere, from the sky. Miss Brill put up her hand and touched her fur. Dear little thing! It was nice to feel it again. She had taken it out of its box that afternoon, shaken out the moth-powder, given it a good brush, and rubbed the life back into the dim little eyes. "What has been happening to me?" said the sad little eyes. Oh, how sweet it was to see them snap at her again from the red eiderdown! . . . But the nose, which was of some black composition, wasn't at all firm. It must have had a knock, somehow. Never mind—a little dab of black sealing-wax when the time came—when it was absolutely necessary. . . . Little rogue! Yes, she really felt like that about it. Little rogue biting its tail just by her left ear. She could have taken it off and laid it on her lap and stroked it. She felt a tingling in her hands and arms, but that came from walking, she supposed. And when she breathed, something light and sad—no, not sad, exactly—something gentle seemed to move in her bosom.

There were a number of people out this afternoon, far more than last Sunday. And the band sounded louder and gayer. That was because the Season had begun. For although the band played all year round on Sundays, out of season it was never the same. It was like some one playing with only the family to listen; it didn't care how it played if there weren't any strangers present. Wasn't the conductor wearing a new coat, too? She was sure it was new. He scraped with his foot and flapped his arms like a rooster about to crow, and the bandsmen sitting in the green rotunda blew out their cheeks and glared at the music. Now there came a little "flutey" bit—very pretty!—a little chain of bright drops. She was sure it would be repeated. It was; she lifted her head and smiled.

Only two people shared her "special" seat: a fine old man in a velvet coat, his hands clasped over a huge carved walking-stick, and a big old woman, sitting upright, with a roll of knitting on her embroidered apron. They did not speak. This was disappointing, for Miss Brill always looked forward to the conversation. She had become really quite expert, she thought, at listening as though she didn't listen, at sitting in other people's lives just for a minute while they talked round her.

She glanced, sideways, at the old couple. Perhaps they would go soon. Last Sunday, too, hadn't been as interesting as usual. An Englishman and his wife, he wearing a dreadful Panama hat and she button boots. And she'd gone on the whole time about how she ought to wear spectacles; she knew she needed them; but that it was no good getting any; they'd be sure to break and they'd never keep on. And he'd been so patient. He'd suggested everything—gold rims, the kind that

[1]**Jardins Publiques** Public Gardens (French).

curved round your ears, little pads inside the bridge. No, nothing would please her. "They'll always be sliding down my nose!" Miss Brill had wanted to shake her.

5   The old people sat on the bench, still as statues. Never mind, there was always the crowd to watch. To and fro, in front of the flower-beds and the band rotunda, the couples and groups paraded, stopped to talk, to greet, to buy a handful of flowers from the old beggar who had his tray fixed to the railings. Little children ran among them, swooping and laughing; little boys with big white silk bows under their chins, little girls, little French dolls, dressed up in velvet and lace. And sometimes a tiny staggerer came suddenly rocking into the open from under the trees, stopped, stared, as suddenly sat down "flop," until its small high-stepping mother, like a young hen, rushed scolding to its rescue. Other people sat on the benches and green chairs, but they were nearly always the same, Sunday after Sunday, and— Miss Brill had often noticed—there was something funny about nearly all of them. They were odd, silent, nearly all old, and from the way they stared they looked as though they'd just come from dark little rooms or even—even cupboards!

Behind the rotunda the slender trees with yellow leaves down drooping, and through them just a line of sea, and beyond the blue sky with gold-veined clouds.

Tum-tum-tum tiddle-um! tiddle-um! tum tiddley-um tum ta! blew the band.

Two young girls in red came by and two young soldiers in blue met them, and they laughed and paired and went off arm-in-arm. Two peasant women with funny straw hats passed, gravely, leading beautiful smoke-colored donkeys. A cold, pale nun hurried by. A beautiful woman came along and dropped her bunch of violets, and a little boy ran after to hand them to her, and she took them and threw them away as if they'd been poisoned. Dear me! Miss Brill didn't know whether to admire that or not! And now an ermine toque[2] and a gentleman in grey met just in front of her. He was tall, stiff, dignified, and she was wearing the ermine toque she'd bought when her hair was yellow. Now everything, her hair, her face, even her eyes, was the same color as the shabby ermine, and her hand, in its cleaned glove, lifted to dab her lips, was a tiny yellowish paw. Oh, she was so pleased to see him—delighted! She rather thought they were going to meet that afternoon. She described where she'd been—everywhere, here, there, along by the sea. The day was so charming—didn't he agree? And wouldn't he, perhaps? . . . But he shook his head, lighted a cigarette, slowly breathed a great deep puff into her face, and, even while she was still talking and laughing, flicked the match away and walked on. The ermine toque was alone; she smiled more brightly than ever. But even the band seemed to know what she was feeling and played more softly, played tenderly, and the drum beat, "The Brute! The Brute!" over and over. What would she do? What was going to happen now? But as Miss Brill wondered, the ermine toque turned, raised her hand as though she'd seen some one else, much nicer, just over there, and pattered away. And the band changed again and played more quickly, more gaily than ever, and the old couple on Miss Brill's seat got up and marched away, and such a funny old man with long whiskers hobbled along in time to the music and was nearly knocked over by four girls walking abreast.

Oh, how fascinating it was! How she enjoyed it! How she loved sitting here, watching it all! It was like a play. It was exactly like a play. Who could believe the sky at the back wasn't painted? But it wasn't till a little brown dog trotted on solemn and then slowly trotted off, like a little "theatre" dog, a little dog that had been drugged, that Miss Brill discovered what it was that made it so exciting. They were all on the stage. They weren't only the audience, not only looking on; they were acting. Even she had

---

[2]**toque** a brimless, close-fitting woman's hat.

a part and came every Sunday. No doubt somebody would have noticed if she hadn't been there; she was part of the performance after all. How strange she'd never thought of it like that before! And yet it explained why she made such a point of starting from home at just the same time each week—so as not to be late for the performance—and it also explained why she had quite a queer, shy feeling at telling her English pupils how she spent her Sunday afternoons. No wonder! Miss Brill nearly laughed out loud. She was on the stage. She thought of the old invalid gentleman to whom she read the newspaper four afternoons a week while he slept in the garden. She had got quite used to the frail head on the cotton pillow, the hollowed eyes, the open mouth and the high pinched nose. If he'd been dead she mightn't have noticed for weeks; she wouldn't have minded. But suddenly he knew he was having the paper read to him by an actress! "An actress!" The old head lifted; two points of light quivered in the old eyes. "An actress—are ye?" And Miss Brill smoothed the newspaper as though it were the manuscript of her part and said gently: "Yes, I have been an actress for a long time."

10   The band had been having a rest. Now they started again. And what they played was warm, sunny, yet there was just a faint chill—a something, what was it?—not sadness—no, not sadness—a something that made you want to sing. The tune lifted, lifted, the light shone; and it seemed to Miss Brill that in another moment all of them, all the whole company, would begin singing. The young ones, the laughing ones who were moving together, they would begin, and the men's voices, very resolute and brave, would join them. And then she too, she too, and the others on the benches—they would come in with a kind of accompaniment—something low, that scarcely rose or fell, something so beautiful—moving. . . . And Miss Brill's eyes filled with tears and she looked smiling at all the other members of the company. Yes, we understand, we understand, she thought—though what they understood she didn't know.

Just at that moment a boy and a girl came and sat down where the old couple had been. They were beautifully dressed; they were in love. The hero and heroine, of course, just arrived from his father's yacht. And still soundlessly singing, still with that trembling smile, Miss Brill prepared to listen.

"No, not now," said the girl. "Not here, I can't."

"But why? Because of that stupid old thing at the end there?" asked the boy. "Why does she come here at all—who wants her? Why doesn't she keep her silly old mug at home?"

"It's her fu-fur which is so funny," giggled the girl. "It's exactly like a fried whiting."[3]

15   "Ah, be off with you!" said the boy in an angry whisper. Then: "Tell me, my petite chère[4]—"

"No, not here," said the girl. "Not *yet*."

On her way home she usually bought a slice of honey-cake at the baker's. It was her Sunday treat. Sometimes there was an almond in her slice, sometimes not. It made a great difference. If there was an almond it was like carrying home a tiny present—a surprise—something that might very well not have been there. She hurried on the almond Sundays and struck the match for the kettle in quite a dashing way.

But today she passed the baker's by, climbed the stairs, went into the little dark room—her room like a cupboard—and sat down on the red eiderdown. She sat there for a long time. The box that the fur came out of was on the bed. She unclasped the necklet quickly; quickly, without looking, laid it inside. But when she put the lid on she thought she heard something crying.

[1920]

---

[3]**whiting** a kind of fish.   [4]***petite chère*** darling.

Joining the Conversation: Critical Thinking and Writing

1. Why do you think Mansfield did not give Miss Brill a first name?
2. What would be lost (or gained?) if the first paragraph were omitted?
3. Suppose someone said that the story is about a woman who is justly punished for her pride. What might be your response?

MyLiteratureLab® *For additional resources for "Miss Brill," log in to* www.myliteraturelab.com *where you will find an Interactive Reading, Comprehension Quiz, Short Evaluation Exercises, and Essay Prompts, as well as an About the Author, Links, and Critical Overview for Mansfield (under Student Resources).*

W. SOMERSET MAUGHAM

W(illiam) Somerset Maugham (1874–1965), born in Paris of English origin, grew up in England, where he was trained as a physician but never practiced medicine. Rather, he made his living as a novelist, playwright, and writer of short stories. His best-known novel is Of Human Bondage *(1915). The following story is in fact a speech uttered by a character in one of Maugham's plays,* Sheppey *(1933).*

The Appointment in Samarra

Death speaks: There was a merchant in Bagdad who sent his servant to market to buy provisions and in a little while the servant came back, white and trembling, and said, Master, just now when I was in the marketplace I was jostled by a woman in the crowd and when I turned I saw it was Death that jostled me. She looked at me and made a threatening gesture, now, lend me your horse, and I will ride away from the city and avoid my fate. I will go to Samarra and there Death will not find me. The merchant lent him his horse, and the servant mounted it, and he dug his spurs in its flanks and as fast as the horse could gallop he went. Then the merchant went down to the marketplace and he saw me standing in the crowd and he came to me and said, Why did you make a threatening gesture to my servant when you saw him this morning? That was not a threatening gesture, I said, it was only a start of surprise. I was astonished to see him in Bagdad, for I had an appointment with him tonight in Samarra.

[1933]

Joining the Conversation: Critical Thinking and Writing

1. What would you say the thesis or point or moral of the story is? Do you share this belief?
2. If you don't hold the view expressed in the story, can you still enjoy the story, or at least agree that it is an effectively told story? Offer a short argument explaining your position.

AMBROSE BIERCE

Ambrose Bierce (1842–1914?) was born in Horse Creek, Ohio, but soon his family moved to Indiana, where at the age of nineteen he enlisted in the Union Army. In the next four years he fought in several of the bloodiest battles of the Civil War, was wounded twice, and rose to the rank of lieutenant. After the war he worked as a journalist in San Francisco, England, and again in San Francisco. In 1912 he went to Mexico to cover the Mexican Revolution, but he disappeared there and it is assumed that he died in 1914.

Bierce's literary reputation rests chiefly on one story, reprinted here, but he wrote other stories of interest—some about the supernatural—as well as a witty, cynical book called The Devil's Dictionary. *Sample definition: "Marriage. The state or condition of a community consisting of a master, a mistress, and two slaves, making in all, two."*

An Occurrence at Owl Creek Bridge

1

A man stood upon a railroad bridge in northern Alabama, looking down into the swift water twenty feet below. The man's hands were behind his back, the wrists bound with a cord. A rope closely encircled his neck. It was attached to a stout cross-timber above his head and the slack fell to the level of his knees. Some loose boards laid upon the sleepers[1] supporting the metals of the railway supplied a footing for him and his executioners—two private soldiers of the Federal army, directed by a sergeant who in civil life may have been a deputy sheriff. At a short remove upon the same temporary platform was an officer in the uniform of his rank, armed. He was a captain. A sentinel at each end of the bridge stood with his rifle in the position known as "support," that is to say, vertical in front of the left shoulder, the hammer resting on the forearm thrown straight across the chest—a formal and unnatural position, enforcing an erect carriage of the body. It did not appear to be the duty of these two men to know what was occurring at the center of the bridge; they merely blockaded the two ends of the foot planking that traversed it.

Beyond one of the sentinels nobody was in sight; the railroad ran straight away into a forest for a hundred yards, then, curving, was lost to view. Doubtless there was an outpost farther along. The other bank of the stream was open ground—a gentle acclivity topped with a stockade of vertical tree trunks, loopholed for rifles, with a single embrasure through which protruded the muzzle of a brass cannon commanding the bridge. Midway of the slope between bridge and fort were the spectators—a single company of infantry in line, at "parade rest," the butts of the rifles on the ground, the barrels inclining slightly backward against the right shoulder, the hands crossed upon the stock. A lieutenant stood at the right of the line, the point of his sword upon the ground, his left hand resting upon his right. Excepting the group of four at the center of the bridge, not a man moved. The company faced the bridge, staring stonily, motionless. The sentinels, facing the banks of the stream, might have been statues to adorn the bridge. The captain stood with folded arms, silent, observing the work of his subordinates, but making no sign. Death is a dignitary who when he comes announced is to be received with formal manifestations of respect, even by those most familiar with him. In the code of military etiquette silence and fixity are forms of deference.

---

[1]**sleepers** railroad crossties.

The man who was engaged in being hanged was apparently about thirty-five years of age. He was a civilian, if one might judge from his habit, which was that of a planter. His features were good—a straight nose, firm mouth, broad forehead, from which his long, dark hair was combed straight back, falling behind his ears to the collar of his well-fitting frock-coat. He wore a mustache and pointed beard, but no whiskers; his eyes were large and dark gray, and had a kindly expression which one would hardly have expected in one whose neck was in the hemp. Evidently this was no vulgar assassin. The liberal military code makes provision for hanging many kinds of persons, and gentlemen are not excluded.

The preparations being complete, the two private soldiers stepped aside and each drew away the plank upon which he had been standing. The sergeant turned to the captain, saluted and placed himself immediately behind that officer, who in turn moved apart one pace. These movements left the condemned man and the sergeant standing on the two ends of the same plank, which spanned three of the crossties of the bridge. The end upon which the civilian stood almost, but not quite, reached a fourth. This plank had been held in place by the weight of the captain; it was now held by that of the sergeant. At a signal from the former the latter would step aside, the plank would tilt and the condemned man go down between two ties. The arrangement commended itself to his judgment as simple and effective. His face had not been covered nor his eyes bandaged. He looked a moment at his "unsteadfast footing," then let his gaze wander to the swirling water of the stream racing madly beneath his feet. A piece of dancing driftwood caught his attention and his eyes followed it down the current. How slowly it appeared to move! What a sluggish stream!

5 He closed his eyes in order to fix his last thoughts upon his wife and children. The water, touched to gold by the early sun, the brooding mists under the banks at some distance down the stream, the fort, the soldiers, the piece of drift—all had distracted him. And now he became conscious of a new disturbance. Striking through the thought of his dear ones was a sound which he would neither ignore nor understand, a sharp, distinct, metallic percussion like the stroke of a blacksmith's hammer upon the anvil; it had the same ringing quality. He wondered what it was, and whether immeasurably distant or near by—it seemed both. Its recurrence was regular, but as slow as the tolling of a death knell. He awaited each stroke with impatience and—he knew not why—apprehension. The intervals of silence grew progressively longer; the delays became maddening. With their greater infrequency the sounds increased in strength and sharpness. They hurt his ear like the thrust of a knife; he feared he would shriek. What he heard was the ticking of his watch.

He unclosed his eyes and saw again the water below him. "If I could free my hands," he thought, "I might throw off the noose and spring into the stream. By diving I could evade the bullets and, swimming vigorously, reach the bank, take to the woods and get away home. My home, thank God, is as yet outside their lines; my wife and little ones are still beyond the invader's farthest advance."

As these thoughts, which have here to be set down in words, were flashed into the doomed man's brain rather than evolved from it the captain nodded to the sergeant. The sergeant stepped aside.

2

Peyton Farquhar was a well-to-do planter, of an old and highly respected Alabama family. Being a slave owner and like other slave owners a politician he was naturally an original secessionist and ardently devoted to the Southern cause. Circumstances of an imperious nature, which it is unnecessary to relate here, had prevented him from taking service with the gallant army that had fought the disastrous campaigns ending with the fall of Corinth,[2] and he chafed under the inglorious restraint, longing for the release of his energies, the larger life of the soldier, the opportunity for distinction. That opportunity, he felt, would come, as it comes to all in war time. Meanwhile he did what he could. No service was too humble for him to perform in aid of the South, no adventure too perilous for him to undertake if consistent with the character of a civilian who was at heart a soldier, and who in good faith and without too much qualification assented to at least a part of the frankly villainous dictum that all is fair in love and war.

One evening while Farquhar and his wife were sitting on a rustic bench near the entrance to his grounds, a gray-clad soldier rode up to the gate and asked for a drink of water. Mrs. Farquhar was only too happy to serve him with her own white hands. While she was fetching the water her husband approached the dusty horseman and inquired eagerly for news from the front.

10   "The Yanks are repairing the railroads," said the man, "and are getting ready for another advance. They have reached the Owl Creek bridge, put it in order and built a stockade on the north bank. The commandant has issued an order, which is posted everywhere, declaring that any civilian caught interfering with the railroad, its bridges, tunnels or trains will be summarily hanged. I saw the order."

"How far is it to the Owl Creek bridge?" Farquhar asked.

"About thirty miles."

"Is there no force on this side the creek?"

"Only a picket post half a mile out, on the railroad, and a single sentinel at this end of the bridge."

15   "Suppose a man—a civilian and student of hanging—should elude the picket post and perhaps get the better of the sentinel," said Farquhar, smiling, "what could he accomplish?"

The soldier reflected. "I was there a month ago," he replied, "I observed that the flood of last winter had lodged a great quantity of driftwood against the wooden pier at this end of the bridge. It is now dry and would burn like tow."

The lady had now brought the water, which the soldier drank. He thanked her ceremoniously, bowed to her husband and rode away. An hour later, after nightfall, he repassed the plantation, going northward in the direction from which he had come. He was a Federal scout.

3

As Peyton Farquhar fell straight downward through the bridge he lost consciousness and was as one already dead. From this state he was awakened—ages later, it seemed to him—by the pain of a sharp pressure upon his throat, followed by a sense of suffocation. Keen, poignant agonies seemed to shoot from his neck downward through every fiber of his body and limbs. These pains appeared to flash along well-defined lines of ramification and to beat with an inconceivably rapid periodicity. They seemed like streams of pulsating fire heating him to an intolerable temperature. As to his head, he was conscious of nothing but a feeling of fulness—of congestion. These sensations were unaccompanied by thought. The intellectual part of his nature was already effaced; he had power only to feel, and feeling was torment. He was conscious of motion. Encompassed in a luminous

[2]**Corinth** Corinth, Mississippi, where Confederate forces were defeated, 3–4 October 1862.

cloud, of which he was now merely the fiery heart, without material substance, he swung through unthinkable arcs of oscillation, like a vast pendulum. Then all at once, with terrible suddenness, the light about him shot upward with the noise of a loud plash; a frightful roaring was in his ears, and all was cold and dark. The power of thought was restored; he knew that the rope had broken and he had fallen into the stream. There was no additional strangulation; the noose about his neck was already suffocating him and kept the water from his lungs. To die of hanging at the bottom of a river!—the idea seemed to him ludicrous. He opened his eyes in the darkness and saw above him a gleam of light, but how distant, how inaccessible! He was still sinking, for the light became fainter and fainter until it was a mere glimmer. Then it began to grow and brighten, and he knew that he was rising toward the surface—knew it with reluctance, for he was now very comfortable. "To be hanged and drowned," he thought, "that is not so bad; but I do not wish to be shot. No; I will not be shot; that is not fair."

He was not conscious of an effort, but a sharp pain in his wrist apprised him that he was trying to free his hands. He gave the struggle his attention, as an idler might observe the feat of a juggler, without interest in the outcome. What splendid effort!—what magnificent, what superhuman strength! Ah, that was a fine endeavor! Bravo! The cord fell away; his arms parted and floated upward; the hands dimly seen on each side in the growing light. He watched them with new interest as first one and then the other pounced upon the noose at his neck. They tore it away and thrust it fiercely aside, its undulations resembling those of a water-snake. "Put it back, put it back!" He thought he shouted these words to his hands, for the undoing of the noose had been succeeded by the direst pang that he had yet experienced. His neck ached horribly; his brain was on fire; his heart, which had been fluttering faintly, gave a great leap, trying to force itself out at his mouth. His whole body was racked and wrenched with an insupportable anguish! But his disobedient hands gave no heed to the command. They beat the water vigorously with quick, downward strokes, forcing him to the surface. He felt his head emerge; his eyes were blinded by the sunlight; his chest expanded convulsively, and with a supreme and crowning agony his lungs engulfed a great draught of air, which instantly he expelled in a shriek!

20   He was now in full possession of his physical senses. They were, indeed, preternaturally keen and alert. Something in the awful disturbance of his organic system had so exalted and refined them that they made record of things never before perceived. He felt the ripples upon his face and heard their separate sounds as they struck. He looked at the forest on the bank of the stream, saw the individual trees, the leaves and the veining of each leaf—saw the very insects upon them: the locusts, the brilliant-bodied flies, the gray spiders stretching their webs from twig to twig. He noted the prismatic colors in all the dewdrops upon a million blades of grass. The humming of the gnats that danced above the eddies of the stream, the beating of the dragon-flies' wings, the strokes of water-spider's legs, like oars which had lifted their boat—all these made audible music. A fish slid along beneath his eyes and he heard the rush of its body parting the water.

He had come to the surface facing down the stream; in a moment the visible world seemed to wheel slowly round, himself the pivotal point, and he saw the bridge, the fort, the soldiers upon the bridge, the captain, the sergeant, the two privates, his executioners. They were in silhouette against the blue sky. They shouted and gesticulated, pointing at him. The captain had drawn his pistol, but did not fire; the others were unarmed. Their movements were grotesque and horrible, their forms gigantic.

Suddenly he heard a sharp report and something struck the water smartly within a few inches of his head, spattering his face with spray. He heard a second report, and saw one of the sentinels with his rifle at his shoulder, a light cloud of blue smoke rising from the muzzle. The man in the water saw the eye of the man on the bridge gazing into his own through the sights of the rifle. He observed that it was a gray eye and remembered having read that gray eyes were keenest, and that all famous marksmen had them. Nevertheless, this one had missed.

A counter-swirl had caught Farquhar and turned him half round; he was again looking into the forest on the bank opposite the fort. The sound of a clear, high voice in a monotonous singsong now rang out behind him and came across the water with a distinctness that pierced and subdued all other sounds, even the beating of the ripples in his ears. Although no soldier, he had frequented camps enough to know the dread significance of that deliberate, drawling, aspirated chant; the lieutenant on shore was taking a part in the morning's work. How coldly and pitilessly—with what an even, calm intonation, presaging, and enforcing tranquility in the men—with what accurately measured intervals fell those cruel words:

"Attention, company! . . . Shoulder arms! . . . Ready! . . . Aim! . . . Fire!"

25   Farquhar dived—dived as deeply as he could. The water roared in his ears like the voice of Niagara, yet he heard the dulled thunder of the volley and, rising again toward the surface, met shining bits of metal, singularly flattened, oscillating slowly downward. Some of them touched him on the face and hands, then fell away, continuing their descent. One lodged between his collar and neck; it was uncomfortably warm and he snatched it out.

As he rose to the surface, gasping for breath, he saw that he had been a long time under water; he was perceptibly farther down stream—nearer to safety. The soldiers had almost finished reloading; the metal ramrods flashed all at once in the sunshine as they were drawn from the barrels, turned in the air, and thrust into their sockets. The two sentinels fired again, independently and ineffectually.

The hunted man saw all this over his shoulder; he was now swimming vigorously with the current. His brain was as energetic as his arms and legs; he thought with the rapidity of lightning.

"The officer," he reasoned, "will not make that martinet's error a second time. It is as easy to dodge a volley as a single shot. He has probably already given the command to fire at will. God help me, I cannot dodge them all!"

An appalling plash within two yards of him was followed by a loud, rushing sound, *diminuendo*,[3] which seemed to travel back through the air to the fort and died in an explosion which stirred the very river to its deeps! A rising sheet of water curved over him, fell down upon him, blinded him, strangled him! The cannon had taken a hand in the game. As he shook his head free from the commotion of the smitten water he heard the deflected shot humming through the air ahead, and in an instant it was cracking and smashing the branches in the forest beyond.

30   "They will not do that again," he thought; "the next time they will use a charge of grape.[4] I must keep my eye upon the gun; the smoke will apprise me—the report arrives too late; it lags behind the missile. That is a good gun."

Suddenly he felt himself whirled round and round—spinning like a top. The water, the banks, the forests, the now distant bridge, fort and men—all were commingled and blurred. Objects were represented by their colors only; circular horizontal streaks of color—that was all he saw. He had been caught in a vortex and

---

[3]***Diminuendo*** decreasing in loudness.   [4]**grapeshot** a cluster of small iron balls fired from a cannon.

was being whirled on with a velocity of advance and gyration that made him giddy and sick. In a few moments he was flung upon the gravel at the foot of the left bank of the stream—the southern bank—and behind a projecting point which concealed him from his enemies. The sudden arrest of his motion, the abrasion of one of his hands on the gravel, restored him, and he wept with delight. He dug his fingers into the sand, threw it over himself in handfuls and audibly blessed it. It looked like diamonds, rubies, emeralds; he could think of nothing beautiful which it did not resemble. The trees upon the bank were giant garden plants; he noted a definite order in their arrangement, inhaled the fragrance of their blooms. A strange, roseate light shone through the spaces among their trunks and the wind made in their branches the music of aeolian harps. He had no wish to perfect his escape—was content to remain in that enchanting spot until retaken.

A whiz and rattle of grapeshot among the branches high above his head roused him from his dream. The baffled cannoneer had fired him a random farewell. He sprang to his feet, rushed up the sloping bank, and plunged into the forest.

All that day he traveled, laying his course by the rounding sun. The forest seemed interminable; nowhere did he discover a break in it, not even a woodman's road. He had not known that he lived in so wild a region. There was something uncanny in the revelation.

By nightfall he was fatigued, footsore, famishing. The thought of his wife and children urged him on. At last he found a road which led him in what he knew to be the right direction. It was as wide and straight as a city street, yet it seemed untraveled. No fields bordered it, no dwelling anywhere. Not so much as the barking of a dog suggested human habitation. The black bodies of the trees formed a straight wall on both sides, terminating on the horizon in a point, like a diagram in a lesson in perspective. Overhead, as he looked up through this rift in the wood, shone great golden stars looking unfamiliar and grouped in strange constellations. He was sure they were arranged in some order which had a secret and malign significance. The wood on either side was full of singular noises, among which— once, twice, and again—he distinctly heard whispers in an unknown tongue.

35   His neck was in pain and lifting his hand to it he found it horribly swollen. He knew that it had a circle of black where the rope had bruised it. His eyes felt congested; he could no longer close them. His tongue was swollen with thirst; he relieved its fever by thrusting it forward from between his teeth into the cold air. How softly the turf had carpeted the untraveled avenue—he could no longer feel the roadway beneath his feet!

Doubtless, despite his suffering, he had fallen asleep while walking, for now he sees another scene—perhaps he has merely recovered from a delirium. He stands at the gate of his own home. All is as he left it, and all bright and beautiful in the morning sunshine. He must have traveled the entire night. As he pushes open the gate and passes up the wide white walk, he sees a flutter of female garments; his wife, looking fresh and cool and sweet, steps down from the veranda to meet him. At the bottom of the steps she stands waiting, with a smile of ineffable joy, an attitude of matchless grace and dignity. Ah, how beautiful she is! He springs forward with extended arms. As he is about to clasp her he feels a stunning blow upon the back of the neck; a blinding white light blazes all about him with a sound like the shock of a cannon—then all is darkness and silence!

Peyton Farquhar was dead; his body, with a broken neck, swung gently from side to side beneath the timbers of the Owl Creek bridge.

[1891]

Joining the Conversation: Critical Thinking and Writing

1. Characterize Peyton Farquhar. If you think Bierce makes him sympathetic, consider the *ways* in which Bierce does so.
2. Early in the story the narrator says, "The liberal military code makes provision for hanging many kinds of people, and gentlemen are not excluded." How would you characterize the tone of this sentence? What, if anything, does the sentence contribute to the story?
3. Do you think that Bierce takes sides, suggesting that the North—or the South—is morally superior? What evidence can you offer to support your view?
4. Is the ending a complete surprise? Do some passages in the story suggest—at least on rereading—that perhaps Farquhar has not escaped? If so, point out a few.
5. What do you think of the title of the story? How does it compare with, for example, "Peyton Farquhar," or "Peyton Farquhar's Escape," or "The Hanging at Owl Creek Bridge"?

MyLiteratureLab® *For additional resources for "An Occurrence at Owl Creek Bridge," log in to www.myliteraturelab.com where you will find a Longman Lecture and Video Performance, as well as an About the Author and Links for Bierce (under Student Resources).*

Isabel Allende

Isabel Allende was born in Lima, Peru, in 1942, where her father was stationed as a Chilean diplomat, but she grew up in Chile. When her father's brother, the socialist president of Chile, was murdered in September 1973, Isabel was forced into exile, and she now lives in Marin County, California. In addition to writing several novels, including Eva Luna *(1988), about a half-European and half-Indian orphan who is a storyteller, Allende has written a collection of short fiction,* The Stories of Eva Luna *(1991), from which the following story is reprinted.*

If You Touched My Heart

Translated by Margaret Sayers Peden

Amadeo Peralta was raised in the midst of his father's gang and, like all the men of his family, grew up to be a ruffian. His father believed that school was for sissies you don't need books to get ahead in life, he always said, just balls and quick wits, and that was why he trained his boys to be rough and ready. With time, nevertheless, he realized that the world was changing very rapidly and that his business affairs needed to be more firmly anchored. The era of undisguised plunder had been replaced by one of corruption and bribery; it was time to administer his wealth by using modern criteria, and to improve his image. He called his sons together and assigned them the task of establishing friendships with influential persons and of learning the legal tricks that would allow them to continue to prosper without danger of losing their impunity. He also encouraged them to find sweethearts among the old-line families and in this way see whether they could cleanse the Peralta name of all its stains of mud and blood. By then Amadeo was thirty-two years old; the habit of seducing girls and then abandoning them was deeply ingrained; the idea of marriage was not at all to his liking but he did not dare disobey his father. He began to court the daughter of a wealthy landowner whose family had lived in the same place for six generations. Despite her suitor's murky reputation, the girl accepted, for she was not very attractive and was afraid of ending up an old maid. Then began one of those tedious provincial engagements. Wretched in a white linen suit and polished boots, Amadeo came every day to visit his fiancée beneath the hawk-like eye of his future mother-in-law or some aunt, and while the young lady served coffee and *guayaba* sweets he would peek at his watch, calculating the earliest moment to make his departure.

A few weeks before the wedding, Amadeo Peralta had to make a business trip through the provinces and found himself in Agua Santa, one of those towns where nobody stays and whose name travellers rarely recall. He was walking down a narrow street at the hour of the siesta, cursing the heat and the oppressive, cloying odour of mango marmalade in the air, when he heard a crystalline sound like water purling between stones; it was coming from a modest house with paint flaked by the sun and rain like most of the houses in that town. Through the ornamental iron grille he glimpsed an entryway of dark paving stones and whitewashed walls, then a patio and, beyond, the surprising vision of a young girl sitting cross-legged on the ground and cradling a blond wood psaltery on her knees. For a while he stood and watched her.

"Come here, sweet thing," he called, finally. She looked up, and despite the distance he could see the startled eyes and uncertain smile in a still-childish face. "Come with me," Amadeo asked—implored—in a hoarse voice.

She hesitated. The last notes lingered like a question in the air of the patio. Peralta called again. The girl stood up and walked towards him; he slipped his hand through the iron grille, shot the bolt, opened the gate, and seized her hand, all the while reciting his entire repertoire of seduction: he swore that he had seen her in his dreams, that he had been looking for her all his life, that he could not let her go, and that she was the woman fate had meant for him—all of which he could have omitted because the girl was simple and even though she may have been enchanted by the tone of his voice she did not understand the meaning of his words. Hortensia was her name and she had just turned fifteen, her body was turned for its first embrace, though she was unable to put a name to the restlessness and tremors that shook it. It was so easy for Peralta to lead her to his car and drive to a nearby clearing that an hour later he had completely forgotten her. He did not recognize her even when a week later she suddenly appeared at his house, one hundred and forty kilometres away, wearing a simple yellow cotton dress and canvas espadrilles, her psaltery under her arm, and inflamed with the fever of love.

5   Forty-seven years later, when Hortensia was rescued from the pit in which she had been entombed and newspapermen travelled from every corner of the nation to photograph her, not even she could remember her name or how she had got there.

The reporters accosted Amadeo Peralta: "Why did you keep her locked up like a miserable beast?"

"Because I felt like it," he replied calmly. By then he was eighty, and as lucid as ever; he could not understand this belated outcry over something that had happened so long ago.

He was not inclined to offer explanations. He was a man of authority, a patriarch, a great-grandfather, no one dared look him in the eye; even priests greeted him with bowed head. During the course of his long life he had multiplied the fortune he inherited from his father; he had become the owner of all the land from the ruins of the Spanish fort to the state line, and then had launched himself on a political career that made him the most powerful cacique[1] in the territory. He had married the landowner's ugly daughter and sired nine legitimate descendants with her and an indefinite number of bastards with other women, none of whom he remembered since he had a heart hardened to love. The only woman he could not entirely discard was Hortensia; she stuck in his consciousness like a persistent nightmare. After the brief encounter in the tall grass of an empty lot, he had returned to his home, his work, and his insipid, well-bred fiancée. It was Hortensia who had searched until she found *him;* it was she who had planted herself before him and clung to his shirt with the terrifying submission of a slave. This is a fine kettle of fish, he had thought; here I am about to get married with all this hoopla and to-do, and now this idiot girl turns up on my doorstep. He wanted to get rid of her, and yet when he saw her in her yellow dress, with those entreating eyes, it seemed a waste not to take advantage of the opportunity, and he decided to hide her while he found a solution.

And so, by carelessness, really, Hortensia ended up in the cellar of an old sugar mill that belonged to the Peraltas, where she was to remain for a lifetime. It was a large room, dank, and dark, suffocating in summer and in the dry season often cold at night, furnished with a few sticks of furniture and a straw pallet. Amadeo Peralta never took time to make her more comfortable, despite his occasionally feeding a fantasy of making the girl a concubine from an oriental tale, clad in gauzy robes and surrounded with peacock feathers, brocade tented ceilings, stained-glass lamps, gilded furniture with spiral feet, and thick rugs where he could walk barefoot. He might actually have done it had Hortensia reminded him of his promises, but she was like a wild bird, one of these blind guacharos that live in the depths of caves: all she needed was a little food and water. The yellow dress rotted away and she was left naked.

10   "He loves me; he has always loved me," she declared when she was rescued by neighbours. After being locked up for so many years she had lost the use of words and her voice came out in spurts like the croak of a woman on her deathbed.

For a few weeks, Amadeo had spent a lot of time in the cellar with her, satisfying an appetite he thought insatiable. Fearing that she would be discovered, and jealous even of his own eyes, he did not want to expose her to daylight and allowed only a pale ray to enter through the tiny hole that provided ventilation. In the darkness, they coupled frenziedly, their skin burning and their hearts impatient as carnivorous crabs. In that cavern all odours and tastes were heightened to the extreme. When they touched, each entered the other's being and sank into the other's most secret desires. There, voices resounded in repeated echoes; the walls returned amplified murmurs and kisses. The cellar became a sealed flask in which they wallowed like playful twins swimming in amniotic fluid, two swollen, stupefied foetuses. For days they were lost in an absolute intimacy they confused with love.

When Hortensia fell asleep, her lover went out to look for food and before she awakened returned with renewed energy to resume the cycle of caresses. They should have made love to each other until they died of desire; they should have devoured one another or flamed like mirrored torches, but that was not to be. What happened instead was more predictable and ordinary, much less grandiose. Before a month had passed, Amadeo Peralta tired of the games, which they were beginning to repeat; he sensed the dampness eating into his joints, and he began to feel the attraction of things outside the walls of that grotto. It was time to return to the world of the living and to pick up the reins of his destiny.

[1]**cacique** political boss.

"You wait for me here. I'm going out and get very rich. I'll bring you gifts and dresses and jewels fit for a queen," he told her as he said goodbye.

"I want children," said Hortensia.

15   "Children, no; but you shall have dolls."

In the months that followed, Peralta forgot about the dresses, the jewels, and the dolls. He visited Hortensia when he thought of her, not always to make love, sometimes merely to hear her play some old melody on the psaltery; he liked to watch her bent over the instrument, strumming chords. Sometimes he was in such a rush that he did not even speak; he filled her water jugs, left her a sack filled with provisions, and departed. Once he forgot about her for nine days, and found her on the verge of death; he realized then the need to find someone to help care for his prisoner, because his family, his travels, his business, and his social engagements occupied all his time. He chose a tight-mouthed Indian woman to fill that role. She kept the key to the padlock, and regularly came to clean the cell and scrape away the lichens growing on Hortensia's body like pale delicate flowers almost invisible to the naked eye and redolent of tilled soil and neglected things.

"Weren't you ever sorry for that poor woman?" they asked when they arrested her as well, charging her with complicity in the kidnapping. She refused to answer but stared straight ahead with expressionless eyes and spat a black stream of tobacco.

No, she had felt no pity for her; she believed the woman had a calling to be a slave and was happy being one, or else had been born an idiot and like others in her situation was better locked up than exposed to the jeers and perils of the street. Hortensia had done nothing to change her jailer's opinion; she never exhibited any curiosity about the world, she made no attempt to be outside for fresh air, and she complained about nothing. She never seemed bored; her mind had stopped at some moment in her childhood, and solitude in no way disturbed her. She was, in fact, turning into a subterranean creature. There in her tomb her senses grew sharp and she learned to see the invisible; she was surrounded by hallucinatory spirits who led her by the hand to other universes. She left behind a body huddled in a corner and travelled through starry space like a messenger particle, living in a dark land beyond reason. Had she had a mirror, she would have been terrified by her appearance; as she could not see herself, however, she was not witness to her deterioration: she was unaware of the scales sprouting from her skin, or the silkworms that had spun a nest in her long, tangled hair, or the lead-coloured clouds covering eyes already dead from peering into shadows. She did not feel her ears growing to capture external sounds, even the faintest and most distant, like the laughter of children at school recess, the ice-cream vendor's bell, birds in flight, or the murmuring river. Nor did she realize that her legs, once graceful and firm, were growing twisted as they adjusted to moving in that confined space, to crawling, nor that her toenails were thickening like an animal's hooves, her bones changing into tubes of glass, her belly caving in, and a hump forming on her back. Only her hands, forever occupied with the psaltery, maintained their shape and size, although her fingers had forgotten the melodies they had once known and now extracted from the instrument the unvoiced sob trapped in her breast. From a distance, Hortensia resembled a tragic circus monkey; on closer view, she inspired infinite pity. She was totally ignorant of the malignant transformations taking place; in her mind she held intact the image of herself as the young girl she had last seen reflected in the window of Amadeo Peralta's automobile the day he had driven her to this lair. She believed she was as pretty as ever, and continued to act as if she were; the memory of beauty crouched deep inside her and only if someone approached very close would he have glimpsed it beneath the external façade of a prehistoric dwarf.

All the while, Amadeo Peralta, rich and feared, cast the net of his power across the region. Every Sunday he sat at the head of a long table occupied by his sons and nephews, cronies, and accomplices, and special guests such as politicians and generals whom he treated with a hearty cordiality tinged with sufficient arrogance to remind everyone who was master here. Behind his back, people whispered about his victims, about how many he had ruined or caused to disappear, about bribes to authorities; there was talk that he had made half his fortune from smuggling, but no one was disposed to seek the proof of his transgressions. It was also rumoured that Peralta kept a woman prisoner in a cellar. That aspect of his black deeds was repeated with more conviction even than stories of his crooked dealings; in fact, many people knew about it, and with time it became an open secret.

20   One afternoon on a very hot day, three young boys played hookey from school to swim in the river. They spent a couple of hours splashing around on the muddy bank and then wandered off towards the old Peralta sugar mill that had been closed two generations earlier when cane ceased to be a profitable crop. The mill had the reputation of being haunted; people said you could hear sounds of devils, and many had seen a dishevelled old witch invoking the spirits of dead slaves. Excited by their adventure, the boys crept onto the property and approached the mill. Soon they were daring enough to enter the ruins; they ran through large rooms with thick adobe walls and termite-riddled beams; they picked their way through weeds growing from the floor, mounds of rubbish and dog shit, rotted roof tiles, and snakes' nests. Making jokes to work up their courage, egging each other on, they came to the huge roofless room that contained the ruined sugar presses; here rain and sun had created an impossible garden, and the boys thought they could detect a lingering scent of sugar and sweat. Just as they were growing bolder they heard, clear as a bell, the notes of a monstrous song. Trembling, they almost retreated, but the lure of horror was stronger than their fear, and they huddled there, listening, as the last note drilled into their foreheads. Gradually, they were released from their paralysis; their fear evaporated and they began looking for the source of those weird sounds so different from any music they had ever known. They discovered a small trap door in the floor, closed with a lock they could not open. They rattled the wood planks that sealed the entrance and were struck in the face by an indescribable odour that reminded them of a caged beast. They called but no one answered; they heard only a hoarse panting on the other side. Finally they ran home to shout the news that they had discovered the door to hell.

The children's uproar could not be stilled, and thus the neighbours finally proved what they had suspected for decades. First the boys' mothers came to peer through the cracks in the trap door; they, too, heard the terrible notes of the psaltery, so different from the banal melody that had attracted Amadeo Peralta the day he had paused in a small alley in Agua Santa to dry the sweat from his forehead. The mothers were followed by throngs of curious and, last of all, after a crowd had already gathered, came the police and firemen, who chopped open the door and descended into the hole with their lamps and equipment. In the cave they found a naked creature with flaccid skin hanging in pallid folds; this apparition had tangled grey hair that dragged the floor, and moaned in terror of the noise and light. It was Hortensia, glowing with a mother-of-pearl phosphorescence under the steady beams of the firefighters' lanterns; she was nearly blind, her teeth had rotted away, and her legs were so weak she could barely stand. The only sign of her human origins was the ancient psaltery clasped to her breast.

The news stirred indignation throughout the country. Television screens and newspapers displayed pictures of the woman rescued from the hole where she had spent her life, now, at least, half-clothed in a cloak someone had tossed around her shoulders. In only a few hours, the indifference that had surrounded the prisoner for almost half a century was converted into a passion to avenge and succour her. Neighbours improvised lynch parties for Amadeo Peralta; they stormed his house, dragged him out, and had the Guard not arrived in time, would have torn him limb from limb in the plaza. To assuage their guilt for having ignored Hortensia for so many years, everyone wanted to do something for her. They collected money to provide her a pension, they gathered tons of clothing and medicine she did not need, and several welfare organizations were given the task of scraping the filth from her body, cutting her hair, and outfitting her from head to toe, so she looked like an ordinary old lady. The nuns offered her a bed in a shelter for indigents, and for several months kept her tied up to prevent her from running back to her cellar, until finally she grew accustomed to daylight and resigned to living with other human beings.

Taking advantage of the public furor fanned by the press, Amadeo Peralta's numerous enemies finally gathered courage to launch an attack against him. Authorities who for years had overlooked his abuses fell upon him with the full fury of the law. The story occupied everyone's attention long enough to see the former caudillo[2] in prison, and then faded and died away. Rejected by family and friends, a symbol of all that is abominable and abject, harassed by both jailers and companions-in-misfortune, Peralta spent the rest of his days in prison. He remained in his cell, never venturing into the courtyard with the other inmates. From there, he could hear the sounds from the street.

Every day at ten in the morning, Hortensia, with the faltering step of a madwoman, tottered down to the prison where she handed the guard at the gate a warm saucepan for the prisoner.

25   "He almost never left me hungry," she would tell the guard in an apologetic tone. Then she would sit in the street to play her psaltery, wresting from it moans of agony impossible to bear. In the hope of distracting her or silencing her, some passers-by gave her money.

Crouched on the other side of the wall, Amadeo Peralta heard those sounds that seemed to issue from the depths of the earth and course through every nerve in his body. This daily castigation must mean something, but he could not remember what. From time to time he felt something like a stab of guilt, but immediately his memory failed and images of the past evaporated in a dense mist. He did not know why he was in that tomb, and gradually he forgot the world of light and lost himself in his misfortune.

[1991]

[2]**caudillo** dictator.

Joining the Conversation: Critical Thinking and Writing

1. Imagine that you are coming to this story for the first time. What is your response to the opening paragraph?
2. Now that you have completed your reading of the story, please reread the opening paragraph. What is your response to it?
3. If you were assigned to lead a class discussion of Allende's story and were told by your teacher to focus on a single paragraph, which one would you select and why?
4. A literary scholar has praised "If You Touched My Heart" for its "powerful use of symbolism." Do you agree?

5. Please describe the style of this story. Cite examples from the text to support your response.
6. Sometimes it is said that a good short story has a strong "takeaway point"—that is, that it leaves us with an important insight about or perspective on human experience. In your view, what is the takeaway point of this story?

HELENA MARIA VIRAMONTES

Helena Maria Viramontes was born in East Los Angeles in 1954. After completing her undergraduate studies at Immaculate Heart College, she did graduate work at California State University, Los Angeles, and further work (1979–81) in the MFA Creative Writing Program at the University of California, Irvine. Viramontes has won first prize in several fiction competitions, including the Irvine Chicano Literary Contest. In 1989, the year in which she was awarded a Creative Writing Fellowship from the National Endowment for the Arts, she participated in a "Storytelling for Film" workshop at the Sundance Film Institute.

Viramontes writes chiefly about women whose lives are circumscribed by a patriarchal Latino society. Eight of her stories have been collected in "The Moths" and Other Stories (1985).

The Moths

I was fourteen years old when Abuelita[1] requested my help. And it seemed only fair. Abuelita had pulled me through the rages of scarlet fever by placing, removing and replacing potato slices on the temples of my forehead; she had seen me through several whippings, an arm broken by a dare jump off Tío Enrique's tool-shed, puberty, and my first lie. Really, I told Amá, it was only fair.

Not that I was her favorite granddaughter or anything special. I wasn't even pretty or nice like my older sisters and I just couldn't do the girl things they could do. My hands were too big to handle the fineries of crocheting or embroidery and I always pricked my fingers or knotted my colored threads time and time again while my sisters laughed and called me bull hands with their cute waterlike voices. So I began keeping a piece of jagged brick in my sock to bash my sisters or anyone who called me bull hands. Once, while we all sat in the bedroom, I hit Teresa on the forehead, right above her eyebrow and she ran to Amá with her mouth open, her hand over her eye while blood seeped between her fingers. I was used to the whippings by then.

I wasn't respectful either. I even went so far as to doubt the power of Abuelita's slices, the slices she said absorbed my fever. "You're still alive, aren't you?" Abuelita snapped back, her pasty gray eye beaming at me and burning holes in my suspicions. Regretful that I had let secret questions drop out of my mouth, I couldn't look into her eyes. My hands began to fan out, grow like a liar's nose until they hung by my side like low weights. Abuelita made a balm out of dried moth wings and Vicks and rubbed my hands, shaped them back to size and it was the strangest feeling. Like bones melting. Like sun shining through the darkness of your eyelids. I didn't mind helping Abuelita after that, so Amá would always send me over to her.

In the early afternoon Amá would push her hair back, hand me my sweater and shoes, and tell me to go to Mama Luna's. This was to avoid another fight and another whipping, I knew. I would deliver one last direct shot on Marisela's arm and jump out of our house, the slam of the screen door burying her cries of anger,

[1] **Abuelita** Grandma (Spanish); other Spanish words for relatives mentioned in the story are *Tío,* Uncle, *Amá,* Mother, and *Apá,* Dad.

and I'd gladly go help Abuelita plant her wild lilies or jasmine or heliotrope or cilantro or hierbabuena in red Hills Brothers coffee cans. Abuelita would wait for me at the top step of her porch holding a hammer and nail and empty coffee cans. And although we hardly spoke, hardly looked at each other as we worked over root transplants, I always felt her gray eye on me. It made me feel, in a strange sort of way, safe and guarded and not alone. Like God was supposed to make you feel.

5   On Abuelita's porch, I would puncture holes in the bottom of the coffee cans with a nail and a precise hit of a hammer. This completed, my job was to fill them with red clay mud from beneath her rose bushes, packing it softly, then making a perfect hole, four fingers round, to nest a sprouting avocado pit, or the spidery sweet potatoes that Abuelita rooted in mayonnaise jars with toothpicks and daily water, or prickly chayotes² that produced vines that twisted and wound all over her porch pillars, crawling to the roof, up and over the roof, and down the other side, making her small brick house look like it was cradled within the vines that grew pear-shaped squashes ready for the pick, ready to be steamed with onions and cheese and butter. The roots would burst out of the rusted coffee cans and search for a place to connect. I would then feed the seedlings with water.

But this was a different kind of help, Amá said, because Abuelita was dying. Looking into her gray eye, then into her brown one, the doctor said it was just a matter of days. And so it seemed only fair that these hands she had melted and formed found use in rubbing her caving body with alcohol and marihuana, rubbing her arms and legs, turning her face to the window so that she could watch the Bird of Paradise blooming or smell the scent of clove in the air. I toweled her face frequently and held her hand for hours. Her gray wiry hair hung over the mattress. Since I could remember, she'd kept her long hair in braids. Her mouth was vacant and when she slept, her eyelids never closed all the way. Up close, you could see her gray eye beaming out the window, staring hard as if to remember everything. I never kissed her. I left the window open when I went to the market.

Across the street from Jay's Market there was a chapel. I never knew its denomination, but I went in just the same to search for candles. I sat down on one of the pews because there were none. After I cleaned my fingernails, I looked up at the high ceiling. I had forgotten the vastness of these places, the coolness of the marble pillars and the frozen statues with blank eyes. I was alone. I knew why I had never returned.

That was one of Apá's biggest complaints. He would pound his hands on the table, rocking the sugar dish or spilling a cup of coffee and scream that if I didn't go to mass every Sunday to save my goddamn sinning soul, then I had no reason to go out of the house, period. Punto final.³ He would grab my arm and dig his nails into me to make sure I understood the importance of catechism. Did he make himself clear? Then he strategically directed his anger at Amá for her lousy ways of bringing up daughters, being disrespectful and unbelieving, and my older sisters would pull me aside and tell me if I didn't get to mass right this minute, they were all going to kick the holy shit out of me. Why am I so selfish? Can't you see what it's doing to Amá, you idiot? So I would wash my feet and stuff them in my black Easter shoes that shone with Vaseline, grab a missal and veil, and wave good-bye to Amá.

I would walk slowly down Lorena to First to Evergreen, counting the cracks on the cement. On Evergreen I would turn left and walk to Abuelita's. I liked her porch because it was shielded by the vines of the chayotes and I could get a good look at the people and car traffic on Evergreen without them knowing. I would jump up the porch steps, knock on the screen door as I wiped my feet and call Abuelita? mi Abuelita? As I opened the door and stuck my head in, I would catch the gagging scent of toasting

---

²**chayotes** squashlike fruit.   ³**Punto final** period.

chile on the placa.[4] When I entered the sala,[5] she would greet me from the kitchen, wringing her hands in her apron. I'd sit at the corner of the table to keep from being in her way. The chiles made my eyes water. Am I crying? No, Mama Luna, I'm sure not crying. I don't like going to mass, but my eyes watered anyway, the tears dropping on the tablecloth like candle wax. Abuelita lifted the burnt chiles from the fire and sprinkled water on them until the skins began to separate. Placing them in front of me, she turned to check the menudo.[6] I peeled the skins off and put the flimsy, limp looking green and yellow chiles in the molcajete[7] and began to crush and crush and twist and crush the heart out of the tomato, the clove of garlic, the stupid chiles that made me cry, crushed them until they turned into liquid under my bull hand. With a wooden spoon, I scraped hard to destroy the guilt, and my tears were gone. I put the bowl of chile next to a vase filled with freshly cut roses. Abuelita touched my hand and pointed to the bowl of menudo that steamed in front of me. I spooned some chile into the menudo and rolled a corn tortilla thin with the palms of my hands. As I ate, a fine Sunday breeze entered the kitchen and a rose petal calmly feathered down to the table.

10   I left the chapel without blessing myself and walked to Jay's. Most of the time Jay didn't have much of anything. The tomatoes were always soft and the cans of Campbell soups had rusted spots on them. There was dust on the tops of cereal boxes. I picked up what I needed: rubbing alcohol, five cans of chicken broth, a big bottle of Pine Sol. At first Jay got mad because I thought I had forgotten the money. But it was there all the time, in my back pocket.

When I returned from the market, I heard Amá crying in Abuelita's kitchen. She looked up at me with puffy eyes. I placed the bags of groceries on the table and began putting the cans of soup away. Amá sobbed quietly. I never kissed her. After a while, I patted her on the back for comfort. Finally: "¿Y mi Amá?"[8] she asked in a whisper, then choked again and cried into her apron.

Abuelita fell off the bed twice yesterday, I said, knowing that I shouldn't have said it and wondering why I wanted to say it because it only made Amá cry harder. I guess I became angry and just so tired of the quarrels and beatings and unanswered prayers and my hands just there hanging helplessly by my side. Amá looked at me again, confused, angry, and her eyes were filled with sorrow. I went outside and sat on the porch swing and watched the people pass. I sat there until she left. I dozed off repeating the words to myself like rosary prayers: when do you stop giving when do you start giving when do you . . . and when my hands fell from my lap, I awoke to catch them. The sun was setting, an orange glow, and I knew Abuelita was hungry.

There comes a time when the sun is defiant. Just about the time when moods change, inevitable seasons of a day, transitions from one color to another, that hour or minute or second when the sun is finally defeated, finally sinks into the realization that it cannot with all its power to heal or burn, exist forever, there comes an illumination where the sun and earth meet, a final burst of burning red orange fury reminding us that although endings are inevitable, they are necessary for rebirths, and when that time came, just when I switched on the light in the kitchen to open Abuelita's can of soup, it was probably then that she died.

The room smelled of Pine Sol and vomit and Abuelita had defecated the remains of her cancerous stomach. She had turned to the window and tried to speak, but her mouth remained open and speechless. I heard you, Abuelita, I said, stroking her cheek, I heard you. I opened the windows of the house and let the soup simmer and overboil on the stove. I turned the stove off and poured the soup down the

---

[4]**placa** round cast-iron griddle.   [5]**sala** living room.   [6]**menudo** tripe soup.   [7]**molcajete** mixing vessel, mortar.   [8]**¿Y mi Amá?** And my Mother?

sink. From the cabinet I got a tin basin, filled it with lukewarm water and carried it carefully to the room. I went to the linen closet and took out some modest bleached white towels. With the sacredness of a priest preparing his vestments, I unfolded the towels one by one on my shoulders. I removed the sheets and blankets from her bed and peeled off her thick flannel nightgown. I toweled her puzzled face, stretching out the wrinkles, removing the coils of her neck, toweled her shoulders and breasts. Then I changed the water. I returned to towel the creases of her stretch-marked stomach, her sporadic vaginal hairs, and her sagging thighs. I removed the lint from between her toes and noticed a mapped birthmark on the fold of her buttock. The scars on her back which were as thin as the life lines on the palms of her hands made me realize how little I really knew of Abuelita. I covered her with a thin blanket and went into the bathroom. I washed my hands, and turned on the tub faucets and watched the water pour into the tub with vitality and steam. When it was full, I turned off the water and undressed. Then, I went to get Abuelita.

15   She was not as heavy as I thought and when I carried her in my arms, her body fell into a V, and yet my legs were tired, shaky, and I felt as if the distance between the bedroom and bathroom was miles and years away. Amá, where are you?

I stepped into the bathtub one leg first, then the other. I bent my knees slowly to descend into the water slowly so I wouldn't scald her skin. There, there, Abuelita, I said, cradling her, smoothing her as we descended, I heard you. Her hair fell back and spread across the water like eagle's wings. The water in the tub overflowed and poured onto the tile of the floor. Then the moths came. Small, gray ones that came from her soul and out through her mouth fluttering to light, circling the single dull light bulb of the bathroom. Dying is lonely and I wanted to go to where the moths were, stay with her and plant chayotes whose vines would crawl up her fingers and into the clouds; I wanted to rest my head on her chest with her stroking my hair, telling me about the moths that lay within the soul and slowly eat the spirit up; I wanted to return to the waters of the womb with her so that we would never be alone again. I wanted. I wanted my Amá. I removed a few strands of hair from Abuelita's face and held her small light head within the hollow of my neck. The bathroom was filled with moths, and for the first time in a long time I cried, rocking us, crying for her, for me, for Amá, the sobs emerging from the depths of anguish, the misery of feeling half born, sobbing until finally the sobs rippled into circles and circles of sadness and relief. There, there, I said to Abuelita, rocking us gently, there, there.

[1982]

Joining the Conversation: Critical Thinking and Writing

1. The narrator of "The Moths" says that she was not "pretty or nice," could not "do . . . girl things," and was not "respectful." But what *can* she do, and what *is* she? How, in short, would you characterize her?

2. Elements of the fantastic are evident, notably in the moths at the end. What efforts, if any, does the author exert in order to make the fantastic elements plausible or at least partly acceptable?

3. Why do you suppose the author included the rather extended passages about the sprouting plants and (later) the sun?

4. We can say, on the basis of the description of the bathing of Abuelita in the final paragraph, that the narrator is loving, caring, and grief-stricken. What else, if anything, does this paragraph reveal about the narrator?

CHAPTER 10

Research: Writing with Sources

A problem adequately stated is a problem on its way to being solved.

R. BUCKMINSTER FULLER

Chapter Preview

After reading this chapter you will be able to

- Define *research*
- Identify and assess both print and electronic sources for a research project
- Evaluate sources
- Draft a research essay effectively

What Research Is, and What Research Is Not

Because a research paper requires its writer to collect and interpret evidence, usually including the opinions of earlier investigators, it is sometimes said that a research paper, unlike a critical essay, is not the expression of personal opinion. But such a view is unjust both to criticism and to research. A critical essay, if it is any good (as we have implied in all of our earlier chapters and expressly indicated in Chapters 8 and 9, on interpretation and evaluation), is an *argument* offering evidence that supports opinions, and thus persuades the reader of its objective rightness. And a research paper is in the final analysis largely personal because the author continuously uses his or her own judgment to evaluate the evidence, deciding what is relevant and convincing. A research paper is not the mere presentation of what a dozen scholars have said about a topic; it is a thoughtful evaluation of the available evidence and, consequently, an expression of what the author thinks the evidence adds up to.

The literary critic Kenneth Burke said that when we read and write, we are participating in a "conversation" that has been going on for a long time. A playwright or poet or storyteller wrote a work—a work that itself was a sort of response to life around the author—and then, in the following days or decades or centuries others have commented on the work. And now you have read it: In Burke's term, you are joining the conversation. Your responses (pleasure, bafflement, anger, whatever) are your first comments; then you begin to think seriously about the work, perhaps discussing it with your classmates and the instructor, or with friends and family at home, and now you are going to write about it. In writing about it you will be putting words down onto paper, perhaps in the margin of the book, or typing words onto a screen, and the very act of writing will require you to comment on your own comments—that is, you will revise your words as you go along and after you read each draft.

Your responses will be chiefly to the literary works you are writing about, but you will also respond to what you may have read *about* literature in this book and to what your instructor and your classmates have said, and—this is especially important—you will be responding to *your own* second and third and even fourth thoughts in this unending conversation that you hold with a book and with yourself. The English philosopher John Locke nicely summarizes the relationship between reading and thinking:

> Reading furnishes our mind only with materials of knowledge; it is thinking [that] makes what we read ours.

Note: This chapter is concerned with the use of sources, *not* with the format in which you will document your use of them. For details about *citing* sources consult Appendix B, pages 1407–21. For information about plagiarism, see Appendix C, pages 1422–27.

Primary and Secondary Materials

The materials of literary research can be conveniently divided into two categories, primary and secondary. The *primary materials,* or original works, are the real subject of study; the *secondary materials* are critical and historical accounts written about primary materials. For example, Langston Hughes wrote poems, stories, plays, and essays. For a student of Hughes, those works are the primary materials. (We include several of his works in this book.) If you want to study his ways of representing African American speech, or his representations of whites, or his collaboration with Zora Neale Hurston, you will read the primary material—his own writings (and Hurston's, in the case of the collaborative work). But in an effort to reach a thoughtful understanding of some aspect of his work, you will also want to look at later biographical and critical studies of his works and perhaps also at scholarly writing on such topics as Black English. You may even find yourself reading essays on Black English that do not specifically mention Hughes but that nevertheless may prove helpful.

Similarly, if you are writing about Charlotte Perkins Gilman (we include one of her stories), the primary material includes not only other stories but also her social and political writing. If you are investigating her views of the medical treatment of women, you will want to look not only at the story we reprint ("The Yellow Wallpaper") but also at her autobiography. Further, you will want to look at secondary material such as recent scholarly books and articles on the medical treatment of women in the late nineteenth and early twentieth centuries.

Locating Materials: First Steps

The easiest way to locate articles and books on literature written in a modern language—that is, on a topic other than literature of the ancient world—is to consult the

MLA International Bibliography of Books and Articles in the Modern Languages and Literatures (1922–)

which lists scholarly studies—books as well as articles in academic journals—published in a given year. Many college and university libraries offer the *MLA International Bibliography* as part of their package of online resources for research.

Because your time is limited, you probably cannot read everything published on your topic. At least at the start, therefore, you will use only the last five or ten years of this bibliography. Presumably, any important earlier material will have been incorporated into the more recent studies listed. If, when you come to read the recent studies, you find references to an older article that sounds essential, of course you will read that article too.

Although *MLA International Bibliography* includes works on American literature, when you are doing research on an aspect of American literature you may want to begin with

American Literary Scholarship (1965–)

This annual publication, noted for its broad coverage of articles and books on major and minor American writers, is especially valuable for its frank comments on the material that it lists.

On some recent topics—for instance, the arguments for and against dropping *Adventures of Huckleberry Finn* from high school curricula—there may be few or no books, and there may not even be material in the scholarly journals indexed in *MLA International Bibliography.* Popular magazines, however, such as *Atlantic, Ebony,* and *Newsweek*—unlisted in *MLA*—may include useful material. These magazines, and about 200 others, are indexed in

Readers' Guide to Periodical Literature (1900–)

If you want to write a research paper on the controversy over *Huckleberry Finn*—Mark Twain uses the "N-word"—or on the popular reception given to Kenneth Branagh's films of Shakespeare's *Henry V, Much Ado about Nothing,* and *Hamlet,* you can locate material (for instance, reviews of Branagh's films) through *Readers' Guide.* For that matter, you can also locate reviews of older films, let's say Laurence Olivier's films of Shakespeare's plays, by consulting the volumes for the years in which the films were released.

Other Bibliographic Aids

There are hundreds of guides to publications and to reference works. *The Oxford Companion to African American Literature* (1997), edited by William L. Andrews, Frances Smith Foster, and Trudier Harris, provides detailed entries on authors, literary works, and many literary, historical, and cultural topics and terms, as well as suggestions for further reading. *Reader's Guide to Literature in English* (1996), edited by Mark Hawkins-Dady, is a massive work (nearly 1,000 pages) that gives thorough summaries of recent critical and scholarly writing on English and American authors.

How do you find such books? Two invaluable guides to reference works (that is, to bibliographies and to such helpful compilations as handbooks of mythology, place names, and critical terms) are

James L. Harner, *Literary Research Guide: A Guide to Reference Sources for the Study of Literatures in English and Related Topics,* 5th ed. (2008)

Michael J. Marcuse, *A Reference Guide for English Studies* (1990)

And there are guides to these guides: reference librarians. If you don't know where to turn to find something, turn to the librarian.

Databases

Libraries today subscribe to a number of databases that index authors and subjects in popular and scholarly magazines and in newspapers. Electronic databases have significant advantages. Often it is easier to perform searches using them; and in many cases access to the complete article is just a click away.

One of the most popular databases is *InfoTrac*, which provides access to over 18 million articles. Another excellent research site, to which many libraries subscribe, is the *FirstSearch* database service. *FirstSearch* enables you to find books, articles, theses, films, computer software, and other types of material for just about any field, subject, or topic. Within *FirstSearch*, you will find a number of useful databases and resources. Other popular databases include EBSCO's *Academic Search Premier*, *LexisNexis,* and *JSTOR*.

Make your search as focused as possible: Look for materials that bear on the topic that you are writing about, and, even more, that show a connection to the thesis that you are working to develop. Learn from what you find, but approach it critically: Is this source a good one? What are its strengths, and what are (or might be) its limitations? Keep in mind too that you engage in the process of selecting good sources in order to strengthen *your* topic and thesis. The quotations you present from sources are there to support your ideas and insights. Above all, your reader is interested in what *you* have to say.

A good choice of secondary sources can help you to develop your analysis of a literary work, but remember that it is your point of view that counts. Use sources to help you present your own interpretation more effectively.

Encyclopedias

Encyclopedias can give you the basics about a subject, but they have severe limitations. An encyclopedia may not cover the subject that you are researching or not cover it in adequate depth. Knowledge expands rapidly, and because it does, even a good encyclopedia lags somewhat behind current scholarship. A number of encyclopedias are now online, where updated information and links to reference and research resources are listed. One popular online encyclopedia is *Wikipedia*. But because articles from *Wikipedia* can be edited by anyone with access to the Internet, you must view them cautiously. Unlike traditionally published encyclopedias, there is no scholarly oversight to ensure that the information is accurate. Most instructors will recommend that you avoid the site or use it only for background reading and for the bibliographic references that it provides. Be sure to check with the librarians at your school; they can tell you about the kinds of resources that are available. If your library offers a tutorial on the use of electronic and Internet resources, we recommend that you take it. We take such tutorials with our students every year and are always surprised by the new resources we learn about.

It is helpful to have updated information and links, but only when they are reliable. Remember to be a critical user of reference materials. Not everything is of equal value; we must make good judgments about the sources we consult and whether or not we can depend on them for reliable, accurate information.

The Internet/the Web

Because of the ease of using the Internet, with its access to e-mail, newsgroups, mailing lists, and, especially, sites and links on the Web, many students now make it their first—and unfortunately, too often their *only*—resource for research.

As we noted, all of us must be *critical* users of the materials we find on the Web. The Web is up-to-date *and* out-of-date, helpful *and* disappointing. It can be a researcher's dream come true, but also a source of errors and a time-waster.

Keeping this point in mind, we recommend to students that for each Web site they consult, they should consult at least two print or database sources.

Evaluating Sources on the Web

For sources found through Internet searches, as with print sources, you must evaluate what you have located and gauge how much or how little it will contribute to your literary analysis and argument. In the words of one reference librarian, Joan Stockard (formerly of Wellesley College), "The most serious mistake students make when they use the Internet for research is to assume everything is of equal (and acceptable) quality. They need to establish who wrote the material, the qualifications of the author to write on the topic, whether any bias is likely, how current the information is, and how other resources compare."

✔ **CHECKLIST:** *Using Web Searches*

Focus the topic of your research as precisely as you can before you embark on an Internet search. Lots of surfing and browsing can sometimes turn up good material, but searching the Web without a focus can prove distracting and unproductive. It takes you away from library research (where the results might be better) and from the planning and writing of the paper.

Ask the following questions:

☐ Does this site or page look like it can help me in my assignment?
☐ Whose site or page is this?
☐ Who is the intended audience?
☐ What is the point of view? Are there signs of a specific slant or bias?
☐ How good is the detail, depth, and quality of the material presented?
☐ Is the site well constructed and well organized?
☐ Is the text well written?
☐ Can the information be corroborated or supported by print sources?
☐ When was the site or page made available? Has it been recently revised or updated?
☐ Can the person or institution, company, or agency responsible for this site or page receive e-mail comments, questions, and criticisms?

What Does Your Own Institution Offer?

We'll mention again that many colleges and universities now offer as part of their resources for research a wide range of electronic materials and databases.

At Wellesley College, for example, the library offers a detailed list of research resources, and another listing is arranged according to department and interdisciplinary program. Some of these are open or free sites, available to anyone with a connection to the Internet. But others are by "subscription only," which means that only members of this academic community can access them.

Sign up for a library tutorial at your own school, and browse in and examine both the library's home page and the online catalog's options and directories.

Taking Notes

Let's assume now that you have consulted bibliographies and that you have a fair number of references you must read to find evidence and interpretations of the evidence in support of your thesis. Most researchers find it convenient, when examining bibliographies and the library catalog, to write down each reference on a 3-by-5-inch index card—one title per card. You may wish to record these notes on your computer instead. Either way, in your entries record the author's full name (last name first), the exact title of the book or article, and the name of the journal (with dates and pages). Titles of books and periodicals (publications issued at regular intervals—for example, monthly or four times a year) are italicized, titles of articles and of essays in books are enclosed in quotation marks. It's also a good idea to put the library catalog number on the card to save time if you need to get the item for a second look.

Next, start reading or scanning the materials whose titles you have collected. Some of these items will prove irrelevant or silly; others will be valuable in themselves and for the leads they give you to further references, which you should duly record on your computer or on note cards.

Two Mechanical Aids: The Photocopier and the Computer

Use the **photocopier** to make copies of material from the library (including material that does not circulate) that you know you need, or that you might want to refer to later. But remember that it can be even more efficient to

- read the material in the library,
- select carefully what pertains to the purpose of your research, and
- take your notes on it.

The **computer** is useful not only for drafting and for producing a neat copy, but also in the early stages of research, when you are getting ideas and taking notes. With the help of the computer, you can brainstorm ideas, make connections, organize and reorganize material, and develop (and change) outlines. This file can be a kind of creative "work space" for your research paper.

A Guide to Note-Taking

Some students use note cards, but most now write their notes on a computer, then organize and rearrange this body of material by copying and pasting, moving the notes into a coherent order. (We advise you not to delete material that, when you reread your notes, strikes you as irrelevant. It *probably* is irrelevant; but on the other hand, it may turn out to be valuable after all. Just put unwanted material into a file called "rejects," or some such thing, until you have completed the paper.)

Whichever method you prefer, keep in mind the following:

- **For everything you consult or read in detail, always specify the source,** so that you know exactly from where you have taken a key point or a quotation.
- **Write summaries (abridgments), not paraphrases (restatements).** (See pages 132, 156–57.)
- **Quote sparingly.** This is *your* paper—it will present your thesis, not the thesis, arguments, and analyses of someone else. Quote directly only those passages that are particularly effective, crucial, or memorable. In your finished paper these quotations will provide authority and emphasis.
- **Quote accurately.** After copying a quotation, check your note against the original, correct any misquotation, and then put a checkmark after your quotation to indicate that it is accurate. Verify the page number also, and then put a checkmark on your note after the page number. If a quotation runs from the bottom of, say, page 306 to the top of 307, on your note put a distinguishing mark (for instance two parallel vertical lines after the last word of the first page), so that if you later use only part of the quotation, you will know the page on which it appeared.

  Use an ellipsis (three spaced periods) to indicate the omission of any words within a sentence. If the omitted words are at the end of the quoted sentence, put a period where you end the sentence, then add three spaced periods to indicate the omission:

  > If the . . . words were at the end of the quoted sentence, put a period where you end. . . .

  Use square brackets to indicate your additions to a quotation. Here is an example:

  > "Here is an [uninteresting] example."

- **Never copy a passage by changing an occasional word,** under the impression that you are thereby putting it into your own words. Notes of this sort may find their way into your paper, your reader will sense a style other than yours, and suspicions of plagiarism may follow. (For a detailed discussion of plagiarism, see pages 314–15 and Appendix C.)
- **Comment on your notes** as you work, and later as you reflect on what you have jotted down from the sources. Make a special mark—we recommend using double parentheses ((. . .)) or a different-color to write, for example, "Jones seriously misreads the passage," or "Smith makes a good point but fails to see its implications." As you work, consider it your obligation to *think* about the material, evaluating it and using it as a stimulus to further thought.
- **In the upper corner of each note card, write a brief key**—for example, "Swordplay in *Hamlet*"—so that later you can tell at a glance what is on the note. If you are using a computer file, be sure to also label these files clearly and consistently.

Drafting the Paper

The difficult job of writing up your findings remains, but if you have taken good notes and have put useful headings on each note, you are well on your way.

- **Read through your notes and organize them** into packets of related material. Remove all notes that you now see are irrelevant to your paper. (Put them in that "rejects" file in case you may want them later.) Go through the notes again and again, sorting and resorting, putting together what belongs together.
- Probably you will find that you have to do a little **additional research—** somehow you aren't quite clear about this or that—but after you have done this additional research, you should be able to arrange the packets of notes into a reasonable and consistent sequence. You now have a kind of first draft, or at least a tentative organization for your paper.
- **Beware of the compulsion to include every note in your essay**; that is, beware of telling the reader, "A says . . . ; B says . . . ; C says . . . "
- **You must have a point, a thesis.** Make sure that you state it early and that you keep it evident to your readers.
- **Make sure that the organization is evident to the reader.** When you were doing your research, and even perhaps when you were arranging your notes, you may not have been entirely sure where you where going; but by now, with your notes arranged into what seems to be the right sequence, you think you know what everything adds up to. Doubtless in the process of drafting you will make important changes in your focus, but do not abandon a draft until you think it not only says what you want to say, but says it in what seems to you to be a reasonable order. Your final paper should be a finished piece of work, without the inconsistencies, detours, or dead ends of an early draft. Your readers should feel that they are moving toward a conclusion (by means of your thoughtful evaluation of the evidence) rather than merely reading an anthology of commentary. And so we should get some such structure as

    There are three common views on. . . . The first two are represented by A and B; the third, and by far the most reasonable, is C's view that. . . . A argues . . . but. . . . The second view, B's, is based on . . . but. . . . Although the third view, C's, is not conclusive, still. . . . Moreover, C's point can be strengthened when we consider a piece of evidence that she does not make use of. . . .

- **Preface all or almost all quotations with a lead-in,** such as "X concisely states the common view" or "Z, without offering any proof, asserts that . . ." Let the reader know where you are going, **_how_ the quotation fits into your argument.**

Quotations and summaries are always to be accompanied by judicious analyses of your own. By the end of the paper, your readers have not only read a neatly typed paper (see page 1407–08) and gained an idea of what previous writers have said, but they are also persuaded that under your guidance they have seen the evidence, heard the arguments summarized, and reached a sound conclusion.

A bibliography or list of works consulted (see pages 1411–21) is usually appended to a research paper so that readers may look further into the primary and secondary material if they wish; but if you have done your job well, readers will be content to leave the subject where you left it, grateful that you have set matters straight.

Focus on Primary Sources

Remember that your paper should highlight *primary* sources, the materials that are your real subject, rather than secondary sources, the critical and historical discussion of primary materials. **The paper should be, above all, *your* paper,** a paper in which you present a thesis that you have developed about the literary work or works that you have chosen to examine. By using secondary sources, you enrich your analysis, as you place yourself in the midst of the scholarly community interested in this author or authors, and you make your contribution to the ongoing conversation.

To help you succeed in balancing primary and secondary sources, when you review your draft, mark in red the quotations from and references to primary sources, and then in blue do the same marking for secondary sources. If, when you scan the pages of your paper-in-progress, you see a lot more blue than red, you should change the emphasis, the proportion, to what it should be. Guard against the tendency to rely heavily on the secondary sources you have compiled. **The point of view that counts is your own.**

Avoiding Plagiarism

Honest scholarship requires that you acknowledge your indebtedness for material, not only when you quote directly from a work but also when you appropriate an original idea (an idea that is not common knowledge). Not to acknowledge such borrowing is plagiarism. If in doubt whether to give credit, give credit.

You ought, however, to develop a sense of what is considered **common knowledge.** Definitions in a dictionary can be considered common knowledge, so there is no need to say, "According to Webster, a novel is . . ." (This is weak in three ways: It's unnecessary, it's uninteresting, and it's unclear, since "Webster" appears in the titles of many dictionaries, some good and some bad.) Similarly, the date of first publication of *The Scarlet Letter* (1850) can be considered common knowledge. Few can give it when asked, but it can be found out from innumerable sources, and no one need get the credit for providing you with it. The idea that Hamlet delays is also a matter of common knowledge. But if you are impressed by so-and-so's argument that Claudius has been much maligned, you should give credit to so-and-so.

Suppose that in the course of your research for a paper on Langston Hughes you happen to come across Arnold Rampersad's statement, in an essay in *Voices and Visions* (edited by Helen Vendler), that

> books alone could not save Hughes from loneliness, let alone give him the strength to be a writer. At least one other factor was essential in priming him for creative obsession. In the place in his heart, or psychology, vacated by his parents entered the black masses. (355)

This is an interesting idea, and in the last sentence the shift from heart to psychology is perhaps especially interesting. You certainly *cannot* say—with the implication that the idea and the words are your own—something like

> Hughes let enter into his heart, or his psychology—a place vacated by his parents—the black masses.

Here you are simply lifting Rampersad's ideas and making only tiny changes in the wording. But even a larger change in the wording would be unacceptable unless Rampersad is given credit. Here is a restatement that is an example of plagiarism even though the words differ from Rampersad's:

> Hughes took into himself ordinary black people, thus filling the gap created by his mother and father.

In this version, the writer presents Rampersad's idea as if it were the writer's own—and presents it less effectively than Rampersad does.

What to do? Give Rampersad credit, perhaps along these lines:

> As Arnold Rampersad has said, "in the place in his heart, or his psychology" where his parents had once been, Hughes now substituted ordinary black people (355).

You can use another writer's ideas, and even some of the very words, but you must give credit, and you *must* use quotation marks when you quote.

You can

- give credit and quote directly, or
- give credit and summarize the writer's point, or
- give credit and summarize the point but include—within quotation marks—some phrase you think is especially interesting

---

Reminder: For a review of and guidance in the process of selecting and citing sources, please consult the quiz on plagiarism that we reprint in Appendix C (pages 1422–27).

CHAPTER **11**

Critical Thinking: Arguing with Oneself, Asking Questions, and Making Comparisons

Reading is to the mind what exercise is to the body.

JOSEPH ADDISON AND RICHARD STEELE

Chapter Preview

After reading this chapter you will be able to

- Define *critical thinking*
- Compare and contrast works (for instance, a short story and its revised version)
- Analyze and evaluate evidence
- Analyze a poem

What Is Critical Thinking?

The verb *think* has several meanings, such as *to imagine* ("Think how he'll hit the ceiling when you tell him this"), *to expect or hope* ("I think I'll get the job"), and—the meaning we will chiefly be concerned with—*to consider closely, especially by exercising one's powers of reason* ("I've been thinking about why she did it, and I've come to some conclusions").

When we engage in critical thinking as close consideration, we are keenly aware of what we are doing. We are, for instance, studying an effect and searching for its causes. "This story bores me, but exactly *why* does it bore me?" Is the plot too familiar? Are the characters unrealistic? Is the language trite? Is it so technical that I can't follow it? Does the author use too many words to say too little? Or: "I loved the book but hated the movie. Why?" And again we start to consider the problem closely, probably (again) by examining the parts that make up the whole. And here we are at the heart of *critical thinking*.

The words *critic, critical,* and *criticism* come from the Greek word *krinein,* meaning "to separate." In everyday talk, *to criticize* is to find fault or to judge severely. But in the sense we are concerned with here, *to criticize* is to examine and to judge, not necessarily to find fault.

Having said that critical thinking does not necessarily involve fault-finding, we want to modify that statement. There is one writer whose work you should

(continued)

316

indeed judge severely. The writer is you. When you read a draft of your work, adopt a skeptical spirit. As you read, ask yourself if assertions are supported with sufficient evidence, and ask if other interpretations of the evidence might reasonably be offered. When you engage in this process, you are engaged in critical thinking.

Asking and Answering Questions

Critical thinking is a matter of separating the whole into parts in order to see relationships. If you ask yourself questions about a work—whether the work is something reprinted in this book or something that you have just drafted—you will almost surely set yourself thinking about how the parts relate to each other and to the whole, their context. Here are typical questions:

- What expectations does the title arouse in a reader?
- Does the middle drag?
- Do certain characters or settings seem to be symbolic, suggesting more than themselves?
- Is the end satisfactory, and if so, why? Because it is surprising? Because, on the contrary, foreshadowing causes us to anticipate it, and it therefore fulfills our expectations?

When you ask yourself questions such as these, you will find that you are deepening your understanding of how a work (perhaps an essay, story, poem, or play in this book, perhaps an essay of your own) works.

Because thinking about questions is an excellent way to deepen your understanding, questions follow most of the literature in this book. And frequent check lists are in effect lists of questions for you to ask yourself when you are writing—in order to help you think about your own productions.

A process that is synonymous with critical thinking is **analysis;** this word also comes from a Greek word meaning *to separate into parts*. And because the point of analysis is to understand how things connect, how things work, and because the point of writing an analysis is to share your understanding with your readers, your essay normally will include a **synthesis,** "a putting together." It can almost be said that essays based on critical thinking will propose a **thesis** and then support that thesis by giving **reasons,** or evidence: "X is so, *because. . . .*"

You will probably find, like almost everyone else, that your best arguments come to you when you start to put them into writing, whether with pencil and paper or with a keyboard at a computer. Although our main concern in this book is with writing about literature, and in a moment we will look at a short poem, let's start this chapter by thinking analytically, thinking critically, about a photograph. (Our method will be in accord with Polonius's advice in *Hamlet*: "By indirections find directions out.")

Comparing and Contrasting

The photograph we focus on here, of Sitting Bull and Buffalo Bill, was taken by a Canadian photographer, William Notman (1826–91). Buffalo Bill—William F. Cody—got his name from his activities as a supplier of buffalo meat for workers on the Kansas Pacific Railway, but his fame came chiefly from his exploits as an army scout and a fighter against the Sioux Indians, and later from *Buffalo Bill's Wild West*. *Buffalo Bill's Wild West* was a show (though he never used this word because he insisted that the exhibition recreated recent Western history) consisting of mock battles with Indians, an attack on a stagecoach, and feats of horsemanship and sharpshooting. Sitting Bull, a Sioux chief, had defeated General George Custer at the Battle of Little Bighorn ten years before this picture was taken, but he had fled to Canada soon after the battle. In 1879 he was granted amnesty and returned to the United States, and in 1885 he appeared in *Buffalo Bill's Wild West*. The photograph, titled *Foes in '76, Friends in '85,* was used to publicize the show.

William Notman, *Foes in '76, Friends in '85*. Photograph. The Sioux chief appeared for one season in William F. Cody's show, *Buffalo Bill's Wild West*. Souvenir cards with this picture were sold.

In Chapter 7 we talked about writing a comparison (pages 157–60), and we now want to add a few things. The writer Howard Nemerov once said, "If you really want to see something, look at something else." He was talking about the power of comparison to illuminate. We compare X and Y, not for the sake of making lists of similarities and differences, but for the sake of seeing X (or Y) more clearly. This book offers many writings for you to read with pleasure, and one source of pleasure is understanding. Your understanding of one work may be heightened by thinking about it in comparison with another work. For this reason we offer several *case studies* that present a writer *in depth* and several thematic chapters (one of them on "Love and Hate)," wherein works invite comparison.

Suppose now we want to think about the picture of Sitting Bull and Buffalo Bill, in order to deepen our understanding of it and to share our understanding with others. To say that the photograph's dimensions are such-and-such or even to say that it shows two people is merely to *describe* it, not to think about it. But if we look more closely and compare the two figures, our mind is energized. Comparing greatly stimulates the mind; by comparing X with Y, we notice things that we might otherwise pass over. Suppose we ask these questions:

- What resemblances and differences do we see in the clothes of the two figures?
- What about their facial expressions?
- How do their poses compare?
- Is the setting significant?

As we try to answer these and other questions that come to mind, we may find ourselves jotting down phrases and sentences along these lines:

> *Buffalo Bill is in fancy clothing (shiny boots, a mammoth buckle, a decorated jacket.)*
>
> *BB is striking a pose   very theatrical, his right hand on his heart, his head tilted slightly back, his eyes looking off as though he is gazing into the future. He seems to be working hard to present a grand image of himself.*
>
> *Sitting Bull simply stands there, apparently looking downward. One feels that he is going along with what is expected of him—after all, he had joined the show—but he refuses to make a fool of himself.*
>
> *Sitting Bull lets BB have upper hand (literally—on gun)*
>
> *BB in effect surrounds SB (Bill's right shoulder is behind Sitting Bull and Bill's left leg is in front of him).*

Analyzing and Evaluating Evidence

If we continue to look closely, we will probably notice that the landscape is fake—not the great outdoors but a set, a painted backdrop, and probably a fake grass mat. If we see these things, we may formulate the thesis that Buffalo Bill here is all show biz, and that Sitting Bull retains his dignity. And if in our essay we support these assertions by pointing to **evidence,** we are demonstrating critical thinking.

Here is the final paragraph from an essay that a student wrote on this picture:

> Buffalo Bill is obviously the dominant figure in this photograph, but he is not the outstanding one. His efforts to appear great only serve to make him appear small. His attempt to outshine Sitting Bull strikes us as faintly ridiculous. We do not need nor want to know any more about Buffalo Bill's personality; it is spread before us in the picture. Sitting Bull's inwardness and dignity make him more interesting than Buffalo Bill, and make us wish to prove our intuition and to ascertain that this proud Sioux was a great chief.

We think this analysis is excellent, but when we did research of our own on Buffalo Bill we found that he was more complicated and more interesting than we had at first thought. But this is to get ahead of the story.

Thinking Critically: Arguing with Oneself, Asking Questions, and Comparing— E. E. Cummings's "Buffalo Bill 's"

Let's look now at a short poem by E. E. Cummings, probably written in 1917, the year Buffalo Bill died, but not published until 1920. Cummings did not give it a title, but included it in a group of poems called "Portraits." (In line 6, *pigeons* are clay targets used in skeet shooting or in exhibitions of marksmanship.)

> Buffalo Bill 's
> defunct
>   who used to
>   ride a watersmooth-silver
>   stallion   5
> and break onetwothreefourfive pigeonsjustlikethat
>   Jesus
>
> he was a handsome man
>   and what i want to know is
> how do you like your blueeyed boy   10
> Mister Death

Read the poem, preferably aloud, at least two or three times, and with as open a mind as possible. *Don't* assume that because the photograph shows us a man for whom we probably would not want to work, this poem necessarily conveys the same attitude.

Ultimately you will want to ask your own questions about the poem and arrive at your own responses, but for a start you may find it useful to put down tentative answers to these questions. We say "tentative" answers because when you think about them, you will almost surely begin to question them and thus improve your responses.

1. What is the speaker's attitude toward Buffalo Bill? (How do you know? What *evidence* can you point to?)
2. In line 6, why do you suppose the poet ran the words together?
3. Why do you think Cummings spaced the poem as he does? One student suggested that the lines form an arrowhead pointing to the right. Do you find merit in this suggestion? If not, what better explanation(s) can you offer?
4. What do you make of the address to "Mister Death"? Why "Mister Death" rather than "Mr. Death" or "Death"? If Mister Death could speak, what answer do you think he might give to the speaker's question?
5. What do you make of the use of "defunct" (as opposed to "dead") in line 2?
6. What do you make of "Jesus" in line 7? What is the effect of placing the word on a line by itself? Is Cummings being blasphemous? Is he inviting us to compare Buffalo Bill with Jesus? Again, support your response with *evidence*.
7. Compare the published poem with the manuscript draft. In the manuscript (opposite; for a scholar's transcription of it, see page 322) you will notice

Manuscript of the draft of E. E. Cummings's poem (the final version appears on the following page).

that Cummings wrote, near the start, "with his long hair like reindeer moss streaming from the old stone of his face." These words do not appear in the final version. Do you think Cummings showed good judgment in deleting the line? Explain.

8. Some readers say that Cummings is satirizing Buffalo Bill, others that he is satirizing death. Do you agree with either of these views? Why? (In a sentence or two define *satire*—feel free to consult a dictionary—and perhaps

```
1              buffalo Bill [i̶s̶]'s defunct
2                          smooth silver   break one two three four five   one fell.
3              who used to ride a white̶ horse and shoot̶ pidgens before they fell.
4                                    streaming from
5                                          ̶x̶x̶x̶x̶
6              with his long hair like reindeer moss, i̶n̶ the old stone
7                                          of his face

8                               Buffalo Bill's       - - -
9                                   who used to
10    defunct who          defunct  defunct̶        - - - - -
11    used to ride a smooth        who̶
12    silver stallion      ride a a smooth silver  r - - - - -
13                         [horse̶] stallion and

14                              break
15                         break̶ one̶
16    dead ‖Buffalo          two̶ three̶  one  two  three
17         'd
18  alo Bill who rode a     four  x̶x̶x̶x̶ five
19    smooth silver stallion  pidgens
20    he'd break̶
21  how?     pidgens/    glissando down the (hapy) shouting crowd as he passed
22    break break̶
23              one    two
24                     three four  five  |                 who'd ride smooth
25                                       |                 silver ' stallion
26    pidgens pidgens̶ being with him̶ long        tossed by  glissandoing  do
27      ax                              an indian
28    eighty two̶
29    curls
30    hair like ‖ reindeer                     pidgens̶
31              streaming
32    moss streaming̶      from the             tossed by a Comanche brave
33                        face
34    x̶       old
35  x̶x̶x̶ eighty year stone
36    stone x̶x̶ 80 years̶ x̶x̶x̶ stone
37    his long̶
38         how d'you̶
39    you̶ [like̶] you like [it̶] him   blue boy̶ eye[o̶]d boy
40                     death
41    the brave old
42    boy
43                              he had you always in his | ey[o̶s̶]e |
```

Modern transcription of the draft reproduced on page 321.

give an example of it. By the way, it's possible to satirize the common human fear of death, but can death be satirized? How might that be done? And what would be the point?)

You may want to discuss some or all of these questions, and others that you generate for yourself, with classmates and with your instructor. It will be interesting to see whether differences of opinion can be resolved in discussion, by pointing to evidence.

Finally, after you have thought about these questions, and any others that you may initiate, consider two opinions from published discussions of the poem:

1. Buffalo Bill, in the poem, functions as a destroyer, an agent of death.
2. The picture of Buffalo Bill on his "watersmooth-silver stallion," riding to the center of the tent to accept the adulation of the crowd before his demonstration of crack marksmanship is, I think, acidly ironic.

Do you agree with either statement, or with both? What evidence in the poem can you point to, in order to support or rebut these assertions?

Buffalo Bill on a favorite horse, around 1910.

A Short-Short Story and Its Revised Version

Consider now two versions of a very short story by Raymond Carver. In 1977 he published the first version, "Mine." In 1981 he published a revised version with a new title, "Popular Mechanics," and in 1986 he published the same revised version under yet another title, "Little Things."

Read "Mine," then read "Little Things," and then go back over both, marking differences and jotting down your own responses. To take an obvious point, you may want to jot down your responses to the titles: Do you think the new title is better, or not? Why? Or consider the sentences that end the first paragraph in each version: "It was getting dark, outside and inside," and "But it was getting dark on the inside too." Do you think Carver improved the end of the first paragraph? Why, or why not?

RAYMOND CARVER

For biographical information on Raymond Carver, see page 713.

Mine

During the day the sun had come out and the snow melted into dirty water. Streaks of water ran down from the little, shoulder-high window that faced the back yard. Cars slushed by on the street outside. It was getting dark, outside and inside.

He was in the bedroom pushing clothes into a suitcase when she came to the door.

I'm glad you're leaving. I'm glad you're leaving! she said. Do you hear?

He kept on putting his things into the suitcase and didn't look up.

5   Sonofabitch! I'm so glad you're leaving! She began to cry. You can't even look me in the face, can you? Then she noticed the baby's picture on the bed and picked it up.

He looked at her and she wiped her eyes and stared at him before turning and going back to the living room.

Bring that back.

Just get your things and get out, she said.

He did not answer. He fastened the suitcase, put on his coat, and looked at the bedroom before turning off the light. Then he went out to the living room. She stood in the doorway of the little kitchen, holding the baby.

10   I want the baby, he said.

Are you crazy?

No, but I want the baby. I'll get someone to come by for his things.

You can go to hell! You're not touching this baby.

The baby had begun to cry and she uncovered the blanket from around its head.

15   Oh, oh, she said, looking at the baby.

He moved towards her.

For God's sake! she said. She took a step back into the kitchen.

Little Things

Early that day the weather turned and the snow was melting into dirty water. Streaks of it ran down from the little shoulder-high window that faced the backyard. Cars slushed by on the street outside, where it was getting dark. But it was getting dark on the inside too.

He was in the bedroom pushing clothes into a suitcase when she came to the door.

I'm glad you're leaving! I'm glad you're leaving! she said. Do you hear?

He kept on putting his things into the suitcase.

5   Son a bitch! I'm so glad you're leaving! She began to cry. You can't even look me in the face, can you?

Then she noticed the baby's picture on the bed and picked it up.

He looked at her and she wiped her eyes and stared at him before turning and going back to the living room.

Bring that back, he said.

Just get your things and get out, she said.

10   He did not answer. He fastened the suitcase, put on his coat, looked around the bedroom before turning off the light. Then he went out to the living room.

She stood in the doorway of the little kitchen, holding the baby.

I want the baby, he said.

Are you crazy?

No, but I want the baby. I'll get someone to come by for his things.

15   You're not touching this baby, she said.

The baby had begun to cry and she uncovered the blanket from around his head.

I want the baby.

Get out of here!

20   She turned and tried to hold the baby over in a corner behind the stove as he came up.

He reached across the stove and tightened his hands on the baby.

Let go of him, he said.

Get away, get away! she cried.

The baby was red-faced and screaming. In the scuffle they knocked down a little flower pot that hung behind the stove.

25   He crowded her into the wall then, trying to break her grip, holding onto the baby and pushing his weight against her arm.

Let go of him, he said.

Don't, she said, you're hurting him!

He didn't talk again. The kitchen window gave no light. In the near dark he worked on her fisted fingers with one hand and with the other hand he gripped the screaming baby up under an arm near the shoulder.

She felt her fingers being forced open and the baby going from her. No, she said, just as her hands came loose. She would have it, this baby whose chubby face gazed up at them from the picture on the table. She grabbed for the baby's other arm. She caught the baby around the wrist and leaned back.

30   He would not give. He felt the baby going out of his hands and he pulled back hard. He pulled back very hard.

In this manner they decided the issue.

[1977]

Oh, oh, she said, looking at the baby.

He moved toward her.

For God's sake! she said. She took a step back into the kitchen.

20   I want the baby.

Get out of here!

She turned and tried to hold the baby over in a corner behind the stove.

But he came up. He reached across the stove and tightened his hands on the baby.

Let go of him, he said.

25   Get away, get away! she cried.

The baby was red-faced and screaming. In the scuffle they knocked down a flowerpot that hung behind the stove.

He crowded her into the wall then, trying to break her grip. He held on to the baby and pushed with all his weight.

Let go of him, he said.

Don't, she said. You're hurting the baby, she said.

30   I'm not hurting the baby, he said.

The kitchen window gave no light. In the near-dark he worked on her fisted fingers with one hand and with the other hand he gripped the screaming baby up under an arm near the shoulder.

She felt her fingers being forced open. She felt the baby going from her.

No! she screamed just as her hands came loose.

She would have it, this baby. She grabbed for the baby's other arm. She caught the baby around the wrist and leaned back.

35   But he would not let go. He felt the baby slipping out of his hands and he pulled back very hard.

In this manner, the issue was decided.

[1981]

Your Turn: Writing an Argument about Carver's Two Stories

After annotating the two stories and thinking about your annotations, write a short essay arguing that, on balance, one version is superior to the other. You do not have to believe that every change was an improvement (or a worsening); in fact, you may want to argue that in some ways the earlier version is better and in some ways the later version is better. In any case formulate a thesis sentence—a sentence that tells the reader the gist of your point—and then in 250–500 words support the thesis.

CHAPTER 12

A Brief Guide: Writing about Literature

What can be said at all can be said clearly.

LUDWIG WITTGENSTEIN

Chapter Preview

After reading this chapter you will be able to

- Identify the kinds of writing
- Explain the process of writing an essay

Other chapters in this book offer extended discussions of the points that we make here, but at this stage a concise version of what composition teachers call "the writing process"—especially as it relates to writing arguments—may be welcome. While no single process works for all writers—indeed, most writers use different processes for different kinds of assignments—the following basic advice should help anyone to get going, especially on a short paper that draws chiefly on one's own responses to a work.

Standing Back: Kinds of Writing

Most writing about literature seeks to do one or both of two things:

- **to inform** ("This play was written only five years ago"; "The images of night suggest death.")
- **to persuade** ("This early story is one of her best"; "Despite the widespread view that the images of night suggest death, I will argue that here they do nothing more than indicate a time of day.")

Whether you are primarily concerned with informing or with persuading (and the two purposes are often indistinguishable because writers usually want to persuade readers that their information is significant), you ought to be prompted by a strong interest in a work or a body of work. This interest is usually a highly favorable response to the material (essentially, "That's terrific"), but an unfavorable response ("Awful!") or a sense of bafflement ("Why would anyone care for that?") may also motivate writing. In any case, stimulated by a work, you put words onto paper, perhaps first by jotting down observations in no particular sequence. Later you will organize them for the benefit of an imagined reader, offering what D. H. Lawrence calls "a reasoned account of the feelings" produced by a work. Don't be embarrassed if a work produces strong feelings in you, pleasant or unpleasant.

Most academic writing about literature is chiefly explanatory, or, we can say, *analytic:* It is concerned with examining relationships (for instance, of the parts to the whole within a work, or of historical causes and effects), and indeed your instructors will probably ask you to write papers that are largely analytic. Writing about literature includes a range of kinds of writing:

- **description** ("The story is unusually brief, only a page long"; "The poem consists of four stanzas each of four lines; within each stanza, the first and third lines rhyme, and the second and fourth lines rhyme with a different sound. The rhyme scheme can thus be indicated as *abab*.")
- **analysis** or **explanation of the internal relationships—the structure— of the work** ("The second scene in this play has at least three functions.")
- **personal report,** or what might be called "confession," a report of one's immediate response and perhaps of later responses ("The story reminds me of an experience I had when I was about the age of the central character"). Personal report often implies evaluation.
- **evaluation** ("The story is shocking" or "There is nothing here that holds our interest.") In Appendix A we discuss critical principles that underlie evaluation. Here it is enough to say that the two most common sources for judging are
  1. a spontaneous personal response ("The death of a child is deeply disturbing") and
  2. a principle alleged to be widely held ("A story ought to be unified.")
- **argument**—writing that offers reasons (and the reasons will be supported by *evidence,* notably references to passages from the literary works you are discussing).

Although personal responses can hardly be argued about in rational terms, they can and must be set forth clearly and interestingly so that the reader understands—because the writer points to things in the literary work that evoke the responses—*why* the writer experiences these responses and *why* the writer evaluates the work as he or she does.

Again, your instructors will probably ask you to write papers that are chiefly analytic, though some description, personal report, and evaluation will almost surely be implicit (if not explicit) in your analyses.

Getting Close: Drafting the Essay

Generating Ideas

1. **Consider the writing situation.** Is the specific topic assigned, or do you choose your own topic?
   - If the choice is yours, choose a work you like, but
   - allow plenty of time (you may find, once you get to work, that you want to change your topic).

   How long will the essay be? (Allow an appropriate amount of time.)

   What kinds of sources are you expected to use?
   - Only your own insights, supplemented by conversations with friends, and perhaps familiarity with your textbooks?
   - Some research?
   - Substantial research?

Again, allow the appropriate amount of time.

Who is the audience?
- Classmates?
- The general public (e.g., readers of weekly news magazines)? Awareness of the audience—your imagined readers—will help you to determine the amount of detail you need to provide. Unless you are told otherwise, assume that your classmates are your audience; they are intelligent adults, but they have not thought as deeply as you have about the particular topic you are writing about.

When is the essay due? Allow time
- to write, type, and revise the draft several times,
- to proofread, and
- to check any sources.

2. **Jot down at least a few ideas *before* you write a first draft.** Key phrases will do—and you will probably find that these jottings, this mixture of assertions and questions, will engender further ideas. You can immediately generate ideas by thinking about the impact the work makes on you.
   - *Why* does it please, displease, or even anger you?
   - What relevant assertions have you heard in lectures or read in books—for instance, concerning tragedy or characterization, or concerning the criteria for judging a poem?
   - How convincing *are* these ideas? Now that you are looking closely at a particular work or works, do these criteria really apply without modification? What modifications now suggest themselves? (In your final version, be sure to give credit for any ideas that you borrow.) Writing at this stage is not only the setting forth of ideas; it is largely the *discovering* of ideas you didn't know were in you.

3. **Rearrange these jottings into an outline (i.e., a tentative plan for a draft).** A list of a few phrases indicating the topics you plan to address (e.g., "historical context," "metaphor") and their sequence will help you to get going. Such an outline may follow this pattern:
   - The first paragraph will probably name the writer or writers and the works and will specify the general approach (e.g., biographical or comparative) or scope (an early and a late work by a story-writer) of the paper.
   - Additional jottings, in sequence, will indicate the gist of each paragraph.

4. **Start writing without worrying about mechanical errors.** Yes, you have been putting down words, but your preliminary jottings were what composition instructors call "prewriting." Now you are writing a draft—not yet a first draft but a zero draft, so don't worry about mechanical matters such as spelling and punctuation and stylistic elegance. Such things will be important when you revise and edit, but at the moment you are trying to find out what your ideas are and how much sense they make. Don't be afraid to set forth your hunches. As E. M. Forster put it, "How do I know what I think until I see what I say?" Write in a spirit of confidence, and if you are using a computer, be sure to save your material.

   If you have an outline, begin by following it, but remember, the outline is a helpful guide to get you going; it is not a road map that must be followed. Write freely and get your ideas down on paper or up on the screen. At this stage, you are still wrestling with ideas, trying things out, clarifying things *for yourself,* engaging in a search and discovery operation.

Later you will read and reread with a critical (skeptical) mind, but for now, follow your instincts.

Revising a Draft

1. **Reread and revise your material.** This should preferably happen after an interval of a few hours or even a day. You are now prepared to write a serious draft. Your tentative or working thesis has evolved to a point where you have confidence in it. Revisions will be of two sorts:
   - global (large scale, such as reorganization) and
   - local (the substitution of a precise word for an imprecise one or a spelling correction).

   Generally speaking, begin by making global revisions. You may, for instance, decide that introductory background material is or is not needed, or that background material should be distributed throughout the essay rather than given all at the start, or that you are too colloquial, too chatty (or too formal, too stuffy). But if you spot a spelling error, or realize that a particular word is not the best word, there is no harm in pausing to make a correction.

   Now is the time to ask yourself key questions:
   - What will my audience—my readers—make of this paragraph, this sentence, this word?
   - Does this word need to be defined?
   - Do I offer adequate support for this generalization?
   - Is my point clear, and is it expressed effectively?

   Put yourself in your readers' shoes; ask yourself if they will be aware of where they are going. That is, ask yourself if you have provided transitions or signposts such as "moreover," "on the other hand," and "for example." Yes, your instructor or your section leader is in fact your reader, but do *not* write for this specific person. Invent a friendly but skeptical reader; if you write for this imagined reader, you will have created a silent but helpful collaborator who will tell you that you need a transition or a definition or a concrete example.

2. **Reread and revise the draft again.** Ask yourself what your reader will make of each sentence.

3. **Make certain that the mechanics are according to specifications.** Here you are acting as an *editor.*
   - It is appropriate for an author, in drafting, to be indifferent to mechanical details, but
   - it is appropriate for an editor to be cool, detached, finicky—in short, for the editor to tell the author to come down to earth and to package the essay neatly and correctly.
   - Margins, spacing, page numbering, and labeling of illustrations should follow the instructor's requirements.
   - Documentation should be according to the *MLA Handbook for Writers of Research Papers,* 7th edition, guidelines given in Appendix B.

4. **If possible, get a classmate or a friend to read your essay and to make suggestions.** This representative of your audience will not rewrite the essay for you, but he or she can call your attention to
   - paragraphs that need development,
   - unclear organization,
   - unconvincing arguments,
   - awkward sentences, and
   - errors in punctuation and spelling.
5. **Consider your reader's suggestions and revise where you think necessary.** If your reader finds some terms obscure or an argument unsubstantiated, you will almost surely want to revise, clarifying the terms and providing evidence for the argument. As before, in the process of revising, try to imagine yourself as your hypothetical reader.
6. **Print out a hard copy of the revised draft, read it, and revise again—and again—as needed.**

It all adds up to *seeing* and *saying,* to seeing (discovering) in the works of literature things that you will want to communicate to your reader (this is a matter of getting ideas) and to saying effectively what you want to say. Chapter 2 offers suggestions about getting ideas, about finding things that, once found, you will want to communicate to others, and Chapters 6 and 7 offer suggestions about the art of writing, from developing effective opening and concluding paragraphs to technical matters such as using the accepted forms in documenting print and electronic sources.

✔ CHECKLIST: *Reviewing the Basics*

- ☐ Is my title engaging?
- ☐ Does the introduction provide essential information (author, work, topic, approach of the essay)?
- ☐ Does the paper have a thesis, a point?
- ☐ Do I support my argument with sufficient persuasive detail?
- ☐ Have I kept the needs of my audience in mind—for instance, have I defined unfamiliar terms? Have I recognized possible objections to my thesis, and have I offered adequate counterarguments to these objections?
- ☐ Is the paper organized, and is the organization clear to the reader?
- ☐ Have I set forth my views effectively without talking too much about myself?
- ☐ Does the essay fulfill the assignment (length, scope)?

CHAPTER 13

Reading and Writing about Essays

The best of all ways to make one's reading valuable is to write about it.

RALPH WALDO EMERSON

Chapter Preview

After reading this chapter you will be able to

- Identify the types of essays
- Analyze an essayist's persona (voice, tone)
- Identify (using prewriting) an essay's topic and thesis
- Analyze essays

The word ***essay*** entered the English language in 1597, when Francis Bacon called a small book of ten short prose pieces *Essays*. Bacon borrowed the word from Michel de Montaigne, a French writer who in 1580 had published some short prose pieces under the title *Essais*—that is, "testings," or "attempts," from the French verb *essayer*, "to try." Montaigne's title indicated that his graceful and personal jottings—the fruit of pleasant study and meditation—were not fully thought-out treatises but rather sketches that could be amplified and amended.

If you keep a journal, you are working in Montaigne's tradition. You jot down your tentative thoughts, perhaps your responses to a work of literature, partly to find out what you think and how you feel. Montaigne said, in the preface to his book, "I am myself the subject of my book," and in all probability you are the real subject of your journal. Your entries—your responses to other writers and your reflections on those responses—require you to examine yourself.

Types of Essays

If you have already taken a course in composition (or even if you haven't), you are probably familiar with the chief kinds of essays. Essays are usually classified—roughly, of course—along the following lines: meditation (or speculation or reflection), argument (or persuasion), exposition (or information), narration, and description.

Of these kinds of essays, the **meditative** (or **speculative** or **reflective**) **essay** is the closest to what Montaigne wrote. In a meditative essay, the writer is chiefly concerned with exploring an idea or a feeling. The organization usually seems casual, not a careful and evident structure but a free flow of thought—what the Japanese (who wrote with brush and ink) called "following the brush." The essayist is thinking, but he or she is not especially concerned with arguing a case, or even with being logical. We think along with the essayist, chiefly because we find the writer's tentative thoughts engaging. The writer may in the long run be pressing a point, advancing an argument, but the emphasis is on the free play of mind, not on an orderly and logical analysis.

In the **argumentative** (or **persuasive**) **essay,** the organization probably is apparent, and it is reasonable: The essay may announce a problem, define terms, present and refute solutions that the writer considers to be inadequate, and then, by way of a knockdown ending, offer what the writer believes to be the correct solution.

The **expository essay,** in which the writer is concerned with giving information (for instance, on how to annotate a text, or how to read a poem, or how to use a computer), ordinarily has an equally clear organization. A clear organization is necessary in such an essay because the reader is reading not in order to come into contact with an interesting mind that may keep doubling back on its thinking (as in a meditative essay), and not in order to come to a decision about some controversial issue (as in an argumentative essay), but in order to gain information.

Narrative and **descriptive essays** are usually meditative essays. A narrative essay may recount some happening—often a bit of autobiography—partly to allow the writer and the reader to meditate on it. Similarly, a description, let's say of a spider spinning a web or of children playing in the street, usually turns out to be offered not so much as information—thus it is unlike the account of how to annotate a text—but as something for the writer and reader to enjoy in itself, and perhaps to think further about.

Most essays are not pure specimens of a single type. An informative essay, let's say on how to use a computer, may begin with a paragraph that seeks to persuade you to use a particular model of software. Or it might begin with a very brief narrative, an anecdote of a student who switched from program X to program Y, again in order to persuade the reader to use this software (Y, of course). Similarly, an argument—and probably most of the essays that you write in English courses will be arguments concerning the meaning or structure of a literary work—may include some exposition, such as a brief summary to remind the reader of aspects of the work you will be arguing about.

The Essayist's Persona

Many of the essays that give readers the most pleasure are, like entries in a journal, reflective. An essay of this kind sets forth the writer's attitudes or states of mind—the writer's **persona**—and the reader's interest in the essay is almost entirely in the way the writer sees things. It's not so much *what* the writers see and say as *how* they say what they see. Even in essays that are narrative—essays that recount events, such as a bit of biography—our interest is more in the essayists' *responses* to the events than in the events themselves. When we read an essay, we almost say, "So that's how it feels to be you," and "Tell me more about the way you see things." The bit of history is less important than the memorable presence of the writer.

Voice

When you read an essay in this chapter or in a later one, try to imagine the person who wrote it, the kind of person who seems to be speaking it. Then slowly reread the essay, noticing *how* the writer conveyed this personality or persona or "**voice**" (even while he or she was writing about a topic). The writer's persona may be revealed in part by common or uncommon words, by short or long sentences, by literal or figurative language, or by familiar or erudite examples.

Let's take a simple, familiar example of words that establish a persona. Lincoln begins the *Gettysburg Address* with "Four score and seven years ago. . . ." He might have said "Eighty-seven years ago"—but the language would have lacked the biblical echo, and the persona would then have been that of an ordinary person rather than that of a man who has about him something of the tone of an Old Testament prophet. This religious tone of "four score and seven years" was entirely fitting because

- President Lincoln was speaking at the dedication of a cemetery for "these hallowed dead" and
- he was urging the members of his audience to give all of their energies to ensure that the dead men had not died in vain.

By such devices as the choice of words, the length of sentences, and the sorts of evidence offered, an author can sound to the reader solemn or agitated or witty or genial or severe. If you are familiar with Martin Luther King's *I Have a Dream*, you may recall that he begins the piece (originally it was a speech, delivered at the Lincoln Memorial on the one-hundredth anniversary of Lincoln's Emancipation Proclamation) with these words: "Five score years ago. . . ." King is deliberately echoing Lincoln's words, partly in tribute to Lincoln, but also to help establish himself as the spiritual descendant of Lincoln and, further back, of the founders of the Judeo-Christian tradition.

Tone

Only by reading closely can we hear in the mind's ear the writer's **tone**—friendly, or bitter, or indignant, or ironic (characterized by wry understatement or overstatement). Perhaps you have heard the line from Owen Wister's novel *The Virginian* (1902): "When you call me that, smile!" Words spoken with a smile mean something different from the same words forced through clenched teeth. But while speakers can communicate—or guide the responses of their audience—by body language, gestures, facial expressions, and changes in tone of voice, writers have only words on paper.

As a writer, you are learning control of tone when you learn to take pains in your choice of words, in the way you arrange sentences, and even in the punctuation marks you may find yourself changing in your final draft. These skills will pay off doubly if you apply them to your reading, by putting yourself in the place of the writer whose work you are reading.

As a reader, you must make an effort to "hear" the writer's tone as part of the meaning the words communicate. Skimming is not adequate to that task. Thinking carefully about the works in this book means, first of all, reading them carefully, listening for the sound of the speaking voice, so that you can respond to the persona the author presents.

Consider the following paragraph from the middle of "Black Men and Public Space," a short essay by Brent Staples. Staples is speaking of growing up in a tough neighborhood. Of course the paragraph is only a small example; the tone depends, finally, on the entire essay, which will follow.

As a boy, I saw countless tough guys locked away; I have since buried several, too. They were babies, really—a teenage cousin, a brother of twenty-two, a childhood friend in his mid-twenties—all gone down in episodes of bravado played out in the streets. I came to doubt the virtues of intimidation early on. I chose, perhaps unconsciously, to remain a shadow—timid, but a survivor.

Judging only from these few lines, what sense of Staples do we get? Perhaps you will agree that we can probably say something along these lines:

- He is relatively quiet and gentle. We sense this not simply because he tells us that he was "timid" but because (at least in this passage) he does not raise his voice either in a denunciation of white society for creating a system that produces black violence or in a denunciation of those blacks of his youth who engaged in violence.
- He is perceptive; he sees that the "tough guys," despite the fact that some were in their twenties, were babies; their bravado was infantile and destructive.
- He speaks with authority; he is giving a firsthand report.
- He doesn't claim to be especially shrewd; he modestly says that he may have "unconsciously" adopted the behavior that enabled him to survive.
- In saying that he is a "survivor" he displays a bit of wry humor. The usual image of a survivor is a guy in a Banana Republic outfit gripping a knife, someone who survived a dog-eat-dog world by being tougher than the others. But Staples almost comically says he is a "survivor" who is "timid."

If your responses to the paragraph are somewhat different, jot them down and in a few sentences try to explain them.

Prewriting: Identifying the Topic and Thesis

Although we have emphasized the importance of the essayist's personality, essayists also make a point. They have a thesis or an argument, and an argument implies taking a specific viewpoint about a topic. In reading an essay, then, try to identify the topic. The topic of "Do-It-Yourself Brain Surgery" cannot really be brain surgery; it must be do-it-yourself books, and the attitude will probably be one of amused contempt for such books. Even an essay that is largely narrative, like Brent Staples's, recounting a personal experience or a bit of history, will probably have an attitude toward the event that is being narrated. It is that attitude—the interpretation of the event rather than the event itself—that may be the real topic of the essay.

It's time to look at Staples's essay. Following the essay, you will find a student's outline of it and another student's version of its thesis.

BRENT STAPLES

Brent Staples, born in 1951 in Chester, Pennsylvania, received a bachelor's degree from Widener University in Chester, Pennsylvania, and a PhD from the University of Chicago. After working as a journalist in Chicago, he joined the New York Times in 1985, and he is now on the newspaper's editorial board, where he writes on politics and culture. His essay was first published in Ms. magazine in 1986 and reprinted in a slightly revised form—the form we give here—in Harper's in 1987.

Black Men and Public Space

My first victim was a woman—white, well dressed, probably in her late twenties. I came upon her late one evening on a deserted street in Hyde Park, a relatively affluent neighborhood in an otherwise mean, impoverished section of Chicago. As I swung onto the avenue behind her, there seemed to be a discreet, uninflammatory distance between us. Not so. She cast back a worried glance. To her, the youngish black man—a broad six feet two inches with a beard and billowing hair, both hands shoved into the pockets of a bulky military jacket—seemed menacingly close. After a few more quick glimpses, she picked up her pace and was soon running in earnest. Within seconds, she disappeared into a cross street.

That was more than a decade ago. I was twenty-two years old, a graduate student newly arrived at the University of Chicago. It was in the echo of that terrified woman's footfalls that I first began to know the unwieldy inheritance I'd come into— the ability to alter public space in ugly ways. It was clear that she thought herself the quarry of a mugger, a rapist, or worse. Suffering a bout of insomnia, however, I was stalking sleep, not defenseless wayfarers. As a softy who is scarcely able to take a knife to a raw chicken—let alone hold one to a person's throat—I was surprised, embarrassed, and dismayed all at once. Her flight made me feel like an accomplice in tyranny. It also made it clear that I was indistinguishable from the muggers who occasionally seeped into the area from the surrounding ghetto. That first encounter, and those that followed, signified that a vast, unnerving gulf lay between nighttime pedestrians—particularly women—and me. And I soon gathered that being perceived as dangerous is a hazard in itself. I only needed to turn a corner into a dicey situation, or crowd some frightened, armed person in a foyer somewhere, or make an errant move after being pulled over by a policeman. Where fear and weapons meet—and they often do in urban America—there is always the possibility of death.

In that first year, my first away from my hometown, I was to become thoroughly familiar with the language of fear. At dark, shadowy intersections, I could cross in front of a car stopped at a traffic light and elicit the *thunk,* thunk, thunk, thunk of the driver—black, white, male, or female—hammering down the door locks. On less traveled streets after dark, I grew accustomed to but never comfortable with people crossing to the other side of the street rather than pass me. Then there were the standard unpleasantries with policemen, doormen, bouncers, cabdrivers, and others whose business it is to screen out troublesome individuals *before* there is any nastiness.

I moved to New York nearly two years ago and I have remained an avid night walker. In central Manhattan, the near-constant crowd cover minimizes tense one-on-one street encounters. Elsewhere—in SoHo, for example, where sidewalks are narrow and tightly spaced buildings shut out the sky—things can get very taut indeed.

5   After dark, on the warrenlike streets of Brooklyn where I live, I often see women who fear the worst from me. They seem to have set their faces on neutral, and with their purse straps strung across their chests bandolier-style, they forge ahead as though bracing themselves against being tackled. I understand, of course, that the danger they perceive is not a hallucination. Women are particularly vulnerable to street violence, and young black males are drastically overrepresented among the perpetrators of that violence. Yet these truths are no solace against the kind of alienation that comes of being ever the suspect, a fearsome entity with whom pedestrians avoid making eye contact.

It is not altogether clear to me how I reached the ripe old age of twenty-two without being conscious of the lethality nighttime pedestrians attributed to me. Perhaps it was because in Chester, Pennsylvania, the small, angry industrial town where

I came of age in the 1960s, I was scarcely noticeable against a backdrop of gang warfare, street knifings, and murders. I grew up one of the good boys, had perhaps a half-dozen fistfights. In retrospect, my shyness of combat has clear sources.

As a boy, I saw countless tough guys locked away; I have since buried several, too. They were babies, really—a teenage cousin, a brother of twenty-two, a childhood friend in his mid-twenties—all gone down in episodes of bravado played out in the streets. I came to doubt the virtues of intimidation early on. I chose, perhaps unconsciously, to remain a shadow—timid, but a survivor.

The fearsomeness mistakenly attributed to me in public places often has a perilous flavor. The most frightening of these confusions occurred in the late 1970s and early 1980s, when I worked as a journalist in Chicago. One day, rushing into the office of a magazine I was writing for with a deadline story in hand, I was mistaken for a burglar. The office manager called security and, with an ad hoc posse, pursued me through the labyrinthine halls, nearly to my editor's door. I had no way of proving who I was. I could only move briskly toward the company of someone who knew me.

Another time I was on assignment for a local paper and killing time before an interview. I entered a jewelry store on the city's affluent Near North Side. The proprietor excused herself and returned with an enormous red Doberman pinscher straining at the end of a leash. She stood, the dog extended toward me, silent to my questions, her eyes bulging nearly out of her head. I took a cursory look around, nodded, and bade her good night.

10   Relatively speaking, however, I never fared as badly as another black male journalist. He went to nearby Waukegan, Illinois, a couple of summers ago to work on a story about a murderer who was born there. Mistaking the reporter for the killer, police officers hauled him from his car at gunpoint and but for his press credentials would probably have tried to book him. Such episodes are not uncommon. Black men trade tales like this all the time.

Over the years, I learned to smother the rage I felt at so often being taken for a criminal. Not to do so would surely have led to madness. I now take precautions to make myself less threatening. I move about with care, particularly late in the evening. I give a wide berth to nervous people on subway platforms during the wee hours, particularly when I have exchanged business clothes for jeans. If I happen to be entering a building behind some people who appear skittish, I may walk by, letting them clear the lobby before I return, so as not to seem to be following them. I have been calm and extremely congenial on those rare occasions when I've been pulled over by the police.

And on late-evening constitutionals I employ what has proved to be an excellent tension-reducing measure: I whistle melodies from Beethoven and Vivaldi and the more popular classical composers. Even steely New Yorkers hunching toward nighttime destinations seem to relax, and occasionally they even join in the tune. Virtually everybody seems to sense that a mugger wouldn't be warbling bright, sunny selections from Vivaldi's *Four Seasons*. It is my equivalent of the cowbell that hikers wear when they know they are in bear country.

[1987]

Summary and Analysis

A summary is a condensation or abridgment; it briefly gives the reader the gist of a longer work. It boils down the longer work, resembling the longer work as a bouillon cube resembles a bowl of soup. A summary of Staples's "Black Men and Public

Space" will reduce the essay, perhaps to a paragraph or two or even to a sentence. It will not call attention to Staples's various strategies, and it will not evaluate his views or his skill as a writer; it will merely present the gist of what he says.

If, then, you are asked to write an analysis of something you have read, you should not hand in a summary. On the other hand, a very brief summary may appropriately appear within an analytic essay. Usually the reader will need some information, and the writer of the essay will briefly summarize this information. For example, a student who wrote about Staples's essay is *summarizing* when she writes

Staples says that he is aware that his presence frightens many whites, especially women.

She is summarizing because she is reporting, without comment, what Staples said. On the other hand, she is *analyzing* when she writes

By saying at the outset, "My first victim was a woman—white, well dressed, probably in her late twenties," Staples immediately catches the reader's attention and sets up expectations that will be undermined in the next paragraph.

In this sentence the writer is not reporting *what* Staples said but is explaining *how* he achieved an effect.

In Chapter 7 we discussed principles that govern summaries (see the list on pages 155–56). Here is a summary of our comments on "summary":

A summary is a condensation or abridgment. Its chief characteristics are that (1) it is rarely more than one-fourth as long as the original; (2) its brevity is usually achieved by leaving out most of the concrete details of the original; (3) it is accurate; (4) it may rearrange the organization of the original, especially if a rearrangement will make things clearer; (5) it is normally in the present tense; and (6) quoted words need not be enclosed in quotation marks.

Preparing a Summary

When you want to summarize an essay, you may find that the essay includes its own summary, perhaps at the start or more likely near the end. If it does, you're in luck.

If it doesn't, we suggest that after rereading each paragraph, you jot down a sentence summarizing the gist of the paragraph. (A very long or poorly unified paragraph may require two sentences, but make every effort to boil the paragraph down to a dozen or so words.) A paragraph that consists merely of a transitional sentence or two ("We will now turn to another example") you will lump with the next paragraph. Similarly, a series of very short paragraphs—for instance, three examples, each briefly stated, and all illustrating the same point—you will probably cover with a single sentence. But if a paragraph runs to half a page or more of print, it's probably worth its own sentence of summary. In fact, your author may summarize the paragraph in its opening sentence or in its final sentence.

Here is a student's paragraph-by-paragraph summary of Staples's "Black Men and Public Space." The numbers refer to Staples's paragraphs.

1. "First victim" was a white woman in Chicago, who hurried away.
2. Age 22, he realized—to his surprise and embarrassment—that he (a "youngish black man") could be perceived by strangers as a mugger. And, since his presence created fear, he was in a dangerous situation.

3,4,5. At intersections he heard drivers of cars lock their doors, and elsewhere he sensed hostility of bouncers and others. In NY, lots of tension on narrow sidewalks. Women are esp. afraid of him; he knows why, but that's "no solace."

6. He's not sure why it took him 22 years to see that others fear him, but prob. because in his hometown of Chester, Pa., there was lots of adolescent violence, though he stayed clear of it.

7. As a boy, he saw young toughs killed, and he kept clear, "timid, but a survivor."

8,9,10. Though he is gentle, he looks fearsome. Once, working as a journalist, he was mistaken for a burglar. Another time, in a jewelry store, the clerk brought out a guard dog. Another black journalist was covering a crime, but the police thought the journalist was the killer. Many blacks have had such experiences.

11. He has learned to smother his rage—and he keeps away from nervous people.

12. Walking late at night, he whistles familiar classical music, trying to reassure others that he is not a mugger.

When you have written your sentence summarizing the last paragraph, you may have done enough if the summary is intended simply for your own private use—for example, to help you review material for an examination. But if you are going to use it as the basis of a summary within an essay you are writing, you probably won't want to include a summary longer than three or four sentences, so now your job will be to reduce and combine the sentences you have jotted down. Indeed, you may even want to reduce the summary to a single sentence.

 Joining the Conversation: Critical Thinking and Writing

1. Assuming that you find the sentences summarizing "Black Men and Public Space" acceptable, reduce them to a summary no longer than four readable sentences. Then compare your version with the versions of two other students and, working as a group, produce a summary.

Stating the Thesis of an Essay

Summarizing each stage of an essay (we discuss summarizing on pages 155–56) forces a reader to be attentive and can assist the reader in formulating a **thesis sentence,** a sentence that (in the reader's opinion) sets forth the writer's central point. If an essay is essentially an argument—for example, an argument for or against capital punishment—it will probably include one or more sentences that directly assert the thesis. "Black Men and Public Space," chiefly a narrative essay, is much less evidently an argument, but it does have a point, and some of its sentences come pretty close to summarizing the point. Here are three of those sentences:

> And I soon gathered that being perceived as dangerous is a hazard in itself. (2)
> The fearsomeness mistakenly attributed to me in public places often has a perilous flavor. (8)
> I now take precautions to make myself less threatening. (11)

We asked our students to formulate their own thesis sentence for Staples's essay. One student came up with the following sentence after first drafting a couple of tentative versions and then rereading the essay in order to modify them:

In "Black Men and Public Space" Staples recognizes that because many whites fear a young black man and therefore may do violence to him, he may do well to try to cool the situation by making himself unthreatening.

Notice, again, that a thesis sentence states the *point* of the work. Don't confuse a thesis sentence with a summary of a narrative, such as "Staples at the age of twenty-two came to realize that his presence was threatening to whites, and he has since taken measures to make himself less threatening." This sentence, though true, doesn't clearly get at the point of the essay, the generalization that can be drawn from Staples's example.

Look again at the student's formulation of a thesis sentence (*not* the narrative summary sentence that we have just given). If you don't think that it fairly represents Staples's point, you may want to come up with a sentence that seems more precise to you.

Whether you use the thesis sentence we have quoted or one that you formulate for yourself, you can still disagree strongly with what you take to be Staples's point. Your version of Staples's thesis should accurately reflect your understanding of Staples's point, but you need not agree with the point. You may think that Staples is hypersensitive or (to mention only one other possibility) that he is playing the Uncle Tom.

A thesis sentence—whether the words are your own or the author's—is thus a capsule summary of the argument (not of the narrative) of the work. If you are writing an essay about an essay, you'll probably want to offer a sentence that reminds your reader of the point of the work you are discussing or gives the reader the basis of an unfamiliar work:

Black males, however harmless, are in a perilous situation because whites, especially white women, perceive them as threatening.

Or:

In "Black Men and Public Space" Brent Staples recognizes that because many whites fear young black men and may therefore do violence to them, black men may do well to try to cool the situation by making themselves nonthreatening.

Drafting a Summary

Sometimes a fuller summary statement may be useful. For instance, if you are writing about a complex essay that makes six points, you may help your reader if you briefly restate all six. The length of your summary will depend on your purpose and the needs of your audience.

The following principles may help you to write your summary:

1. After having written sentences that summarize each paragraph or group of paragraphs, formulate the essay's thesis sentence. Formulating the sentence in writing will help you to stay with what you take to be the writer's main point.
2. Write a first draft by turning your summaries of the paragraphs into fewer and better sentences. The student who wrote the paragraph-by-paragraph summary (pages 338–39) of Staples's essay turned her first six sentences (on Staples's first five paragraphs) into this:

Staples's "first victim" was a white woman in Chicago. When she hurried away from him, he realized—to his surprise and embarrassment—that because he was large and black and young he seemed to her to be a mugger. And since his presence created fear, *he* was in a dangerous situation. Other experiences, such as hearing drivers lock their cars when they were waiting at an intersection, have made him aware of the hostility of others. Women are especially afraid of him, and although he knows why, this knowledge is "no solace."

The student turned the remaining sentences of the outline into the following summary:

Oddly, it took him twenty-two years to see that others fear him. Perhaps it took this long because he grew up in a violent neighborhood, though he kept clear, "timid, but a survivor." Because he is black and large, whites regard him as fearsome and treat him accordingly (once a clerk in a jewelry store brought out a guard dog), but other blacks have been treated worse. He has learned to smother his rage, and in order to cool things he tries to reassure nervous people by keeping away from them and (when he is walking late at night) by whistling classical music.

3. Write a lead-in sentence, probably incorporating the thesis sentence. Here is an example:

Brent Staples, in "Black Men and Public Space," tells how his awareness that many white people regarded him as dangerous caused him to realize that *he* was in danger. His implicitly recommended solution is to try to cool the anxiety by adopting non-threatening behavior.

After writing a lead-in, revise the draft of your summary, eliminating needless repetition, providing transitions, and adding whatever you think may be needed to clarify the work for someone who is unfamiliar with it. You may rearrange the points if you think the rearrangement will clarify matters.

4. Edit your draft for errors in grammar, punctuation, and spelling. Read it aloud to test it once more for readability. Sometimes only by reading aloud do writers detect needless repetition or confusing phrases.

Joining the Conversation: Critical Thinking and Writing

1. In a paragraph or two, set forth what you take to be Staples's *purpose* in "Black Men and Public Space." Do you think he was writing chiefly to clarify ideas for himself—for instance, to explore how he came to discover the "alienation that comes of being ever the suspect"? Or writing to assist blacks? Or to assist whites? Or what? (You may conclude that none of these suggestions are relevant.)

2. If you think the essay is effective, in a paragraph or two addressed to your classmates try to account for its effectiveness. Do certain examples strike you as particularly forceful? If so, why? Do certain sentences seem especially memorable? Again, why? For example, if the opening and concluding paragraphs strike you as effective, explain why. On the other hand, if you are unimpressed by part or all of the essay, explain why.

3. The success of a narrative as a piece of writing often depends on the reader's willingness to identify with the narrator. From an examination of "Black Men and Public Space," what explanations can you give for your willingness (or unwillingness) to identify yourself with Staples? (Probably you will want to say something about his persona as you sense it from the essay.) In the course of a 500-word essay explaining your position, very briefly summarize Staples's essay and state his thesis.

4. Have *you* ever unintentionally altered public space? You might recall an experience in which, as a child, your mere presence caused adults to alter their behavior—for instance, to stop quarreling.

After a session of brainstorming in which you produce some possible topics, you'll want to try to settle on one. After you have chosen a topic and produced a first draft, if you are not satisfied with your first paragraph—if you feel that it is not likely to get and hold the reader's attention—you may want to imitate the strategy that Staples adopted for his first paragraph.

5. If you have ever been in the position of one of Staples's "victims," that is, if you have ever shown fear or suspicion of someone who, it turned out, meant you no harm (or if you can imagine being in that position), write an essay from the "victim's" point of view. Explain what happened, what you did and thought. Did you think at the time about the feelings of the person you avoided or fled from? Has reading Staples's essay prompted further reflections on your experience? (Suggested length: 750 words.)

✔ CHECKLIST: *Getting Ideas for Writing about Essays*

Persona and Tone

☐ What sort of *persona* does the writer create? Authoritative? Tentative? Wise-guy? Or what?

☐ How does the writer create this persona? (Does the writer use colloquial language or formal language or technical language? Short sentences or long ones? Personal anecdotes? Quotations from authorities?)

☐ What is the *tone* of the essay? Is it, for example, solemn, or playful? Is the tone consistent? If not, how do the shifts affect your understanding of the writer's point or your identification of the writer's persona? Who is the *audience*?

Kind of Essay

☐ What kind of essay is it? Is it chiefly a presentation of facts (an exposition, a report, a history)? A meditation? Or is it chiefly an argument? If it is an argument, what persuasive devices does the writer use? Logic? Appeals to the emotion? (Probably the essay draws on several kinds of writing, but which kind is it primarily? How are the other kinds related to the main kind?) What is the overall *purpose* of the essay?

☐ What does it seem to add up to? If the essay is chiefly meditative or speculative, how much emphasis is placed on the persona? That is, if the essay is a sort of thinking-out-loud, is your interest chiefly in the announced or ostensible topic, or in the writer's mood and personality? If the essay is chiefly a presentation of facts, does it also have a larger implication? If it narrates a happening (history), does the reader draw an inference—find a meaning—in the happening? If the essay is chiefly an argument, what is the thesis? How is the thesis supported? (Is it supported, for example, by induction, deduction, analogy, or emotional appeal?) Do you accept the assumptions (explicit and implicit)?

Structure

☐ Is the title appropriate? Propose a better title, if possible.

☐ Did the opening paragraph interest you? Why, or why not? Did the essay continue more or less as expected, or did it turn out to be different from what you anticipated?

□ Prepare an outline of the essay. What effect does the writer seem to be aiming at by using this structure?

Value

□ What is especially good (or bad) about the essay? Is it logically persuasive? Or entertaining? Or does it introduce an engaging persona? Or (if it is a narrative) does it tell a story effectively, using (where appropriate) description, dialogue, and commentary, and somehow make you feel that this story is worth reporting?
□ Does the writer seem to hold values that you share? Or cannot share? Explain.
□ Do you think that most readers will share your response, or do you think that for some reason—for example, your age, or your cultural background—your responses are unusual? Explain.

Your Turn: Essays for Analysis

LANGSTON HUGHES

Langston Hughes (1902–67) was born in Joplin, Missouri. He lived part of his youth in Mexico, spent a year at Columbia University, served as a merchant seaman, and worked in a Paris nightclub, where he showed some of his poems to Alain Locke, a strong advocate of African American literature. After returning to the United States, Hughes went on to publish poetry, fiction, plays, essays, and biographies.

Salvation

I was saved from sin when I was going on thirteen. But not really saved. It happened like this. There was a big revival at my Auntie Reed's church. Every night for weeks there had been much preaching, singing, praying, and shouting, and some very hardened sinners had been brought to Christ, and the membership of the church had grown by leaps and bounds. Then just before the revival ended, they held a special meeting for children, "to bring the young lambs to the fold." My aunt spoke of it for days ahead. That night I was escorted to the front row and placed on the mourners' bench with all the other young sinners, who had not yet been brought to Jesus.

My aunt told me that when you were saved you saw a light, and something happened to you inside! And Jesus came into your life! And God was with you from then on! She said you could see and hear and feel Jesus in your soul. I believed her. I had heard a great many old people say the same thing and it seemed to me they ought to know. So I sat there calmly in the hot, crowded church, waiting for Jesus to come to me.

The preacher preached a wonderful rhythmical sermon, all moans and shouts and lonely cries and dire pictures of hell, and then he sang a song about the ninety and nine safe in the fold, but one little lamb was left out in the cold. Then he said: "Won't you come? Won't you come to Jesus? Young lambs, won't you come?" And he held out his arms to all us young sinners there on the mourners' bench. And the little girls cried. And some of them jumped up and went to Jesus right away. But most of us just sat there.

A great many old people came and knelt around us and prayed, old women with jet-black faces and braided hair, old men with work-gnarled hands. And the church sang a song about the lower lights are burning, some poor sinners to be saved. And the whole building rocked with prayer and song.

5   Still I kept waiting to *see* Jesus.

Finally all the young people had gone to the altar and were saved, but one boy and me. He was a rounder's son named Westley. Westley and I were surrounded by sisters and deacons praying. It was very hot in the church, and getting late now. Finally Westley said to me in a whisper: "God damn! I'm tired o' sitting here. Let's get up and be saved." So he got up and was saved.

Then I was left all alone on the mourners' bench. My aunt came and knelt at my knees and cried, while prayers and songs swirled all around me in the little church. The whole congregation prayed for me alone, in a mighty wail of moans and voices. And I kept waiting serenely for Jesus, waiting, waiting—but he didn't come. I wanted to see him, but nothing happened to me. Nothing! I wanted something to happen to me, but nothing happened.

I heard the songs and the minister saying: "Why don't you come? My dear child, why don't you come to Jesus? Jesus is waiting for you. He wants you. Why don't you come? Sister Reed, what is this child's name?"

"Langston," my aunt sobbed.

10   "Langston, why don't you come? Why don't you come and be saved? Oh, Lamb of God! Why don't you come?"

Now it was really getting late. I began to be ashamed of myself, holding everything up so long. I began to wonder what God thought about Westley, who certainly hadn't seen Jesus either, but who was now sitting proudly on the platform, swinging his knickerbockered legs and grinning down at me, surrounded by deacons and old women on their knees praying. God had not struck Westley dead for taking his name in vain or for lying in the temple. So I decided that maybe to save further trouble, I'd better lie, too, and say that Jesus had come, and get up and be saved.

So I got up.

Suddenly the whole room broke into a sea of shouting, as they saw me rise. Waves of rejoicing swept the place. Women leaped in the air. My aunt threw her arms around me. The minister took me by the hand and led me to the platform.

When things quieted down, in a hushed silence, punctuated by a few ecstatic "Amens," all the new young lambs were blessed in the name of God. Then joyous singing filled the room.

15   That night, for the last time in my life but one—for I was a big boy twelve years old—I cried. I cried, in bed alone, and couldn't stop. I buried my head under the quilts, but my aunt heard me. She woke up and told my uncle I was crying because the Holy Ghost had come into my life, and because I had seen Jesus. But I was really crying because I couldn't bear to tell her that I had lied, that I had deceived everybody in the church, and I hadn't seen Jesus, and that now I didn't believe there was a Jesus any more, since he didn't come to help me.

[1940]

Joining the Conversation: Critical Thinking and Writing

1. Do you find "Salvation" amusing, or serious, or both? Explain.
2. How would you characterize the style or voice of the first three sentences? Childlike, or sophisticated, or what? How would you characterize the final sentence? How can you explain the change in style or tone?
3. Why does Hughes bother to tell us, in paragraph 11, that Westley was "swinging his knickerbockered legs and grinning"? Do you think that Westley too may have cried that night? Give your reasons.
4. Is the episode told from the point of view of someone "going on thirteen," or from the point of view of a mature man? Cite evidence to support your position.
5. One of the golden rules of narrative writing is "Show, don't tell." In about 500 words, report an experience—for instance, a death in the family, a severe (perhaps unjust) punishment, or the first day in a new school—that produced strong feelings. Like Hughes, you may want to draw on an experience in which you were subjected to group pressure. Do not explicitly state your feelings; rather, let the reader understand them chiefly through concretely detailed actions. But, like Hughes, you might state your thesis or basic position in your first paragraph and then indicate when and where the experience took place.

LAURA VANDERKAM

Laura Vanderkam wrote this essay a few months after graduating from Princeton University. At the time that it was published she was working as a Collegiate Network intern with the editorial board of USA Today. She is a member of USA Today's Board of Contributors, and her work has appeared in Scientific American, Wired, and other publications.

Hookups Starve the Soul

The scene: my college dorm's basement bathroom on a Sunday morning early in my freshman year. As hungover girls crowded around the sinks, I caught a friend's eye in the mirror. What happened when she left last night's party with a boy neither of us had ever seen before?

"Oh," she said with a knowing look, "we hooked up."

No, not planes refueling in midair. Hookups are when a guy and girl get together for a physical encounter and don't expect anything else. They've all but replaced dating at most colleges, according to a study being released today by the Institute on American Values, a non-partisan family issues think tank. Only half of the women interviewed had been on six or more dates during college; a third had been on no more than two.

As a new college graduate, I can attest to this. I've had as many dates in my first 2 months in the real world as I had during my whole college career.

5   Lest you think college students are all libertines, hooking up doesn't mean having sex, although it can. The term includes all of the bases, and the ambiguity

is intentional. Modest types can imply that less happened than did, and braggarts can hint at hitting a home run. Hookups are defined by alcohol, physical attraction and a lack of expectations in the morning.

While the study found that only 40% of the women interviewed admitted to hooking up, the practice pervades college culture. Dates and, for the most part, love affairs, are passè. Why bother asking someone to dinner when you can meet at a party, down a few drinks and go home together?

I hear the traditionalists clucking. Sex without commitment. Sounds like a male plot, right? But women are going along.

Some blame the sexual revolution. Some blame co-ed dorms and alcohol abuse. I blame something else. Hookups are part of a larger cultural picture. Today's college kids are the first generation to have had their entire childhoods scheduled. To them, dating is simply not a productive use of time.

Author David Brooks used the phrase "Organization Kid" in April's *Atlantic Monthly* to describe what he discovered at my alma mater, Princeton. After a lifetime of shuffling from soccer practice to scout meetings and piano lessons, today's college kids no longer want to spend hours debating the nature of good and evil, he noted. Once obsessed with getting into increasingly selective colleges—and now obsessed with getting great grades and even greater jobs—they no longer have hours to spend wooing a lover.

10   "I was amazed to learn how little dating goes on," Brooks wrote in the magazine. "Students go out in groups, and there is certainly a fair bit of partying on campus, but as one told me, 'People don't have time or energy to put into real relationships.'"

But 20-year-olds still have hormones, so they hook up instead. They stumble home together late Saturday night, roll around in bed, then pass out. The next morning, it's as if nothing happened.

Hookups do satisfy biology, but the emotional detachment doesn't satisfy the soul. And that's the real problem—not the promiscuity, but the lack of meaning.

People who don't bother with love affairs cut themselves off from life's headier emotions. What about Scarlett O'Hara's passion, or Juliet's? What about the mad jealousy of Dostoevsky's Dmitry Karamazov or even the illicit pleasures of Lady Chatterley and her lover? No great art will be inspired by the muse of Milwaukee's Best or a tryst that both parties are trying to forget.

In the same way, the Organization Kid's lack of soul-searching doesn't bode well for future poets and philosophers. Dostoevsky's Ivan wouldn't have had time to dream up the Grand Inquisitor if he spent his youth being carted from one sport to another and his early 20s obsessed with the perfect lab report.

15   Parents want the best for their kids—but some also want the perfect kid. Somewhere along the way to achieving these perfect children through structured activities, overachieving parents stunt the growth of their children's souls. Too much supervision creates kids who'd rather hook up than fall in love, who'd rather get the right answers on tests than ask the larger questions.

It's too late to bring back the dormitory mothers, curfews and traditional morals that forced courtships in the past. But the Organization Kid culture can be changed. If parents stop rigidly scheduling their children's lives, and if they no longer teach that life is only a series of concrete goals to be met and then exceeded, then there will be more real lovers and truth-seekers in the future—and fewer hookups.

[2001]

Joining the Conversation: Critical Thinking and Writing

1. Vanderkam's opening words—"The scene"—is unusual because this sounds like the opening of a play. What other rhetorical devices does Vanderkam use in order to make her essay interesting?
2. In a sentence or two, state Vanderkam's thesis. (Please do not confuse a statement of the thesis—the point, the argument—with a summary of the essay.) Do you agree with her thesis? In whole, in part, or not at all? Whether you agree or disagree, write your own 500-word essay on hookups—or on a related topic, such as college dating.

CHAPTER 14

Reading and Writing about Stories

We tell ourselves stories in order to live.

JOAN DIDION

Stories True and False

The word *story* comes from *history;* the stories that historians, biographers, and journalists narrate are supposed to be true accounts of what happened. The stories of novelists and short-story writers, however, are admittedly untrue; they are "fiction," things made up, imagined, manufactured. As readers, we come to a supposedly true story with expectations different from those we bring to fiction.

Consider the difference between reading a narrative in a newspaper and one in a book of short stories. If, while reading a newspaper, we come across a story of, say, a subway accident, we read it for the information about an actual, relatively unusual event. Anyone hurt? What sort of people? In our neighborhood? Whose fault? When we read a book of fiction, however, we do not expect to encounter literal truths; we read novels and short stories not for facts but for pleasure and for some insight or for a sense of what an aspect of life means to the writer. Consider the following short story by Grace Paley.

GRACE PALEY

Born in New York City, Grace Paley (1922–2007) attended Hunter College and New York University but left without a degree. While raising two children she wrote poetry and then, in the 1950s, turned to writing fiction. Her publications include Collected Stories *(1994).*

Paley's chief subject was the life of little people struggling in the Big City. Of life she said, "How daily life is lived is a mystery to me. You write about what's mysterious to you. What is it like? Why do people do this?" Of the short story she said, "It can be just telling a little tale, or writing a complicated philosophical story. It can be a song, almost."

Samuel

Some boys are very tough. They're afraid of nothing. They are the ones who climb a wall and take a bow at the top. Not only are they brave on the roof, but they make a lot of noise in the darkest part of the cellar where even the super hates to go. They also jiggle and hop on the platform between the locked doors of the subway cars.

Four boys are jiggling on the swaying platform. Their names are Alfred, Calvin, Samuel, and Tom. The men and the women in the cars on either side watch them. They don't like them to jiggle or jump but don't want to interfere. Of course some of the men in the cars were once brave boys like these. One of them had ridden the tail of a speeding truck from New York to Rockaway Beach without getting off, without his sore fingers losing hold. Nothing happened to him then or later. He had made a compact with other boys who preferred to watch: Starting at Eighth Avenue and Fifteenth Street, he would get to some specified place, maybe Twenty-third and the river, by hopping the tops of the moving trucks. This was hard to do when one truck turned a corner in the wrong direction and the nearest truck was a couple of feet too high. He made three or four starts before succeeding. He had gotten his idea from a film at school called *The Romance of Logging*. He had finished high school, married a good friend, was in a responsible job and going to night school.

These two men and others looked at the four boys jumping and jiggling on the platform and thought, It must be fun to ride that way, especially now the weather is nice and we're out of the tunnel and way high over the Bronx. Then they thought, These kids do seem to be acting sort of stupid. They *are* little. Then they thought of some of the brave things they had done when they were boys and jiggling didn't seem so risky.

The ladies in the car became very angry when they looked at the four boys. Most of them brought their brows together and hoped the boys could see their extreme disapproval. One of the ladies wanted to get up and say, Be careful you dumb kids, get off that platform or I'll call a cop. But three of the boys were Negroes and the fourth was something else she couldn't tell for sure. She was afraid they'd be fresh and laugh at her and embarrass her. She wasn't afraid they'd hit her, but she was afraid of embarrassment. Another lady thought, Their mothers never know where they are. It wasn't true in this particular case. Their mothers all knew that they had gone to see the missile exhibit on Fourteenth Street.

5   Out on the platform, whenever the train accelerated, the boys would raise their hands and point them up to the sky to act like rockets going off, then they rat-tat-tatted the shatterproof glass pane like machine guns, although no machine guns had been exhibited.

For some reason known only to the motorman, the train began a sudden slow-down. The lady who was afraid of embarrassment saw the boys jerk forward and backward and grab the swinging guard chains. She had her own boy at home. She stood up with determination and went to the door. She slid it open and said, "You boys will be hurt. You'll be killed. I'm going to call the conductor if you don't just go into the next car and sit down and be quiet."

Two of the boys said, "Yes'm," and acted as though they were about to go. Two of them blinked their eyes a couple of times and pressed their lips together. The train resumed its speed. The door slid shut, parting the lady and the boys. She leaned against the side door because she had to get off at the next stop.

The boys opened their eyes wide at each other and laughed. The lady blushed. The boys looked at her and laughed harder. They began to pound each other's back. Samuel laughed the hardest and pounded Alfred's back until Alfred coughed and the tears came. Alfred held tight to the chain hook. Samuel pounded him even harder when he saw the tears. He said, "Why you bawling? You a baby, huh?" and laughed. One of the men whose boyhood had been more watchful than brave became angry. He stood up straight and looked at the boys for a couple of seconds. Then he walked in a citizenly way to the end of the car, where he pulled the emergency cord. Almost at once, with a terrible hiss, the pressure of air abandoned the brakes and the wheels were caught and held.

People standing in the most secure places fell forward, then backward. Samuel had let go of his hold on the chain so he could pound Tom as well as Alfred. All the passengers in the cars whipped back and forth, but he pitched only forward and fell head first to be crushed and killed between the cars.

10   The train had stopped hard, halfway into the station, and the conductor called at once for the trainmen who knew about this kind of death and how to take the body from the wheels and brakes. There was silence except for passengers from other cars who asked, What happened! What happened! The ladies waited around wondering if he might be an only child. The men recalled other afternoons with very bad endings. The little boys stayed close to each other, leaning and touching shoulders and arms and legs.

When the policeman knocked at the door and told her about it, Samuel's mother began to scream. She screamed all day and moaned all night, though the doctors tried to quiet her with pills.

Oh, oh, she hopelessly cried. She did not know how she could ever find another boy like that one. However, she was a young woman and she became pregnant. Then for a few months she was hopeful. The child born to her was a boy. They brought him to be seen and nursed. She smiled. But immediately she saw that this baby wasn't Samuel. She and her husband together have had other children, but never again will a boy exactly like Samuel be known.

[1968]

Joining the Conversation: Critical Thinking and Writing

1. Paley wrote the story, "Samuel," but an unspecified person *tells* it. Describe the voice of this narrator in the first paragraph. Is the voice neutral and objective, or do you hear in it an attitude, a point of view? If you do hear an attitude, what words or phrases in the story indicate it?

2. What do you know about the setting—the locale—of "Samuel"? What can you infer about the neighborhood?

3. In the fourth paragraph we are told that "three of the boys were Negroes and the fourth was something else." Is race important in this story? Is Samuel "Negro" or "something else"? Does it matter? Respond to these questions in a short argumentative essay.

4. Exactly *why* did a man walk "in a citizenly way to the end of the car, where he pulled the emergency cord"? Do you think the author blames him? What evidence can you offer to support your view? Do *you* blame him? Or do you blame the boys? Or anyone? Explain.

5. The story is called "Samuel," and it is, surely, about him. But what happens after Samuel dies? (You might want to list the events.) What else is the story about?

(You might want to comment on why you believe the items in your list are important.)

6. Can you generalize about what the men think of the jigglers and about what the women think? Is Paley saying something about the sexes? About the attitudes of onlookers in a big city?

Elements of Fiction

You might think about the ways in which "Samuel" differs from a newspaper story of an accident in a subway. (You might even want to write a newspaper version of the happening.) In some ways, Paley's story resembles an account that might appear in a newspaper. Journalists write to give information about

- who,
- what,
- when,
- where, and
- why,

and Paley does provide this material. Thus, the **characters** (Samuel and others) are the journalist's Who; the **plot** (the boys were jiggling on the platform, and when a man pulled the emergency cord one of them was killed) is the What; the **setting** (the subway, presumably in modern times) is the When and the Where; the **motivation** (the irritation of the man who pulls the emergency cord) is the Why.

To write about fiction you would think about these elements of fiction, asking yourself questions about each, both separately and how they work together. Much of the rest of this chapter will be devoted to examining such words as *character* and *plot*, but before you read those pages, consider the questions we've posed about "Samuel" and respond to them. Your responses will teach you a good deal about what fiction is and the ways in which it works.

Plot and Character

In some stories, such as adventure stories, the emphasis is on physical action—wanderings and strange encounters. In Paley's "Samuel," however, although there is a violent death in the subway, the emphasis is on other things: for instance, the contrast between some of the adults, the contrast between uptight adults and energetic children, and the impact of the death on Samuel's mother.

The novelist E. M. Forster, in a short critical study, *Aspects of the Novel* (1927), introduced a distinction between **flat characters** and **round characters.** A *flat character* is relatively simple and usually has only one trait: loving wife (or jealous wife), tyrannical husband (or meek husband), braggart, pedant, hypocrite, or whatever. Thus, in "Samuel" we are told about a man "whose boyhood had been more watchful than brave." This man walks "in a citizenly way" to the end of the subway car, where he pulls the emergency cord. He is, so to speak, the conventional solid citizen. He is flat, or uncomplicated, and that is probably part of what the author is getting at. A *round character*, on the other hand, embodies several or even many traits that cohere to form a complex personality. In a story as short as "Samuel" we can hardly expect to find fully rounded characters, but we can say that, at least by comparison with the "citizenly" man, the man who had once been a wild kid, had gone to night school, and now holds a "responsible job" is relatively round. Paley's story asserts rather than shows the development of the character, but much fiction does show such a development.

Whereas a flat character is usually *static* (at the end of the story the character is pretty much what he or she was at the start), a round character is likely to be *dynamic,* changing considerably as the story progresses.

A frequent assignment in writing courses is to set forth a character sketch describing some person in a story or a novel. In preparing such a sketch, take these points into consideration:

- what the character says (but consider that what he or she says need not be taken at face value; the character may be hypocritical, or self-deceived, or biased—you will have to detect this from the context),
- what the character does,
- what other characters say about the character, and
- what others *do.* (A character who serves as a contrast to another character is called a **foil.**)

A character sketch can be complex and demanding, but usually you will want to do more than write a character sketch. You will probably discuss the character's function, or trace the development of his or her personality, or contrast the character with another. (One of the most difficult topics, the narrator's personality, is discussed later in this chapter under the heading "Narrative Point of View.") In writing on one of these topics you will probably want to keep in mind the four suggestions for getting at a character, but you will also want to go further, relating your findings to matters that we discuss later.

Most discussions of fiction are concerned with happenings and with *why* they happen. Why does Samuel die? Because (to put it too simply) his youthful high spirits clash with the values of a "citizenly" adult. Paley never explicitly says anything like this, but a reader of the story tries to make sense of the details by filling in the gaps.

Things happen, in most good fiction, partly because the people have certain personalities or character traits (moral, intellectual, and emotional qualities) and, given their natures, because they respond plausibly to other personalities. What their names are and what they look like may help you to understand them, but probably the best guide to characters is what they do and what they say. As we get to know more about their drives and goals—and especially about the choices they make—we enjoy seeing the writer complete the portraits, finally presenting us with a coherent and credible picture of people in action.

In this view, plot and character are inseparable. Plot is not simply a series of happenings, but happenings that come out of character, that reveal character, and that influence character. The novelist Henry James put it thus in his essay "The Art of Fiction" (1884): "What is character but the determination of incident? What is incident but the illustration of character?" James goes on: "It is an incident for a woman to stand up with her hand resting on a table and look out at you in a certain way."

Foreshadowing

Although some stories depend heavily on a plot with a surprise ending, other stories prepare the reader to some degree for the outcome. The **foreshadowing** that would eliminate surprise, or greatly reduce it, and destroy a story that has nothing else to offer, is a powerful tool in the hands of a writer of serious fiction. In "Samuel," the reader perhaps senses even in the first paragraph that these "tough" boys who "jiggle and hop on the platform" may be vulnerable, may come to an unfortunate end. When a woman says, "You'll be killed," the reader doesn't yet know if she is right, but a seed has been planted.

Even in such a story as Faulkner's "A Rose for Emily" (page 249), where we are surprised to learn near the end that Miss Emily has slept beside the decaying corpse of her dead lover, from the outset we expect something strange; that is, we are not surprised by the surprise, only by its precise nature. The first sentence of the story tells us that after Miss Emily's funeral (the narrator begins at the end) the townspeople cross her threshold "out of curiosity to see the inside of her house, which no one save an old manservant . . . had seen in at least ten years." As the story progresses, we see Miss Emily prohibiting people from entering the house, we hear that after a certain point no one ever sees Homer Barron again, that "the front door remained closed," and (a few paragraphs before the end of the story) that the townspeople "knew that there was one room in that region above the stairs which no one had seen in forty years." The paragraph preceding the revelation that "the man himself lay in the bed" is devoted to a description of Homer's dust-covered clothing and toilet articles. In short, however much we are unprepared for the precise revelation, we are prepared for some strange thing in the house; and, given Miss Emily's purchase of poison and Homer's disappearance, we have some idea of what will be revealed.

The full meaning of a passage will not become apparent until you have read the entire story. In a sense, a story has at least three lives:

- when we read the story sentence by sentence, trying to turn the sequence of sentences into a consistent whole,
- when we have finished reading the story and we think back on it as a whole, even if we think no more than "That was a waste of time,"
- when we reread a story, knowing even as we read the first line how it will turn out at the end.

Setting and Atmosphere

Foreshadowing normally makes use of **setting.** The setting or environment is not mere geography, not mere locale: It provides an **atmosphere,** an air that the characters breathe, a world in which they move. Narrowly speaking, the setting is the physical surroundings—the furniture, the architecture, the landscape, the climate—and these elements are often highly appropriate to the characters who are associated with them. Thus, in Emily Brontë's *Wuthering Heights* (1847) the passionate Earnshaw family is associated with Wuthering Heights, the storm-exposed moorland, whereas the mild Linton family is associated with Thrushcross Grange in the sheltered valley below.

Broadly speaking, setting includes not only the physical surroundings but also a point (or several points) in time. The background against which we see the characters and the happenings may be specified as morning or evening, spring or fall. In a good story, this temporal setting will probably be highly relevant; it will probably be part of the story's meaning, perhaps providing an ironic contrast to or exerting an influence on the characters.

Symbolism

When we read, we may feel that certain characters and certain things in the story stand for more than themselves, or hint at larger meanings. We feel, that is, that they are **symbolic.** But here we must be careful. How does a reader know that this or that figure or place is symbolic? In Hemingway's "Cat in the Rain" (page 693), is the cat symbolic? Is the innkeeper? Is the rain? Reasonable people may differ in their answers. Again, in Chopin's "The Story of an Hour" (page 57), is the railroad accident a symbol? Is Josephine a symbol? Is the season (springtime) a symbol? Again, reasonable people may differ in their responses.

Let's assume, however, that if writers use symbols, they want readers to perceive—at least faintly—that certain characters or places or seasons or happenings have rich implications, stand for something more than what they are on the surface. How do writers help us to perceive these things? By emphasizing them—for instance, by describing them at some length, or by introducing them at times when they might not seem strictly necessary, or by calling attention to them repeatedly.

Consider Chopin's treatment of the season in which "The Story of an Hour" takes place. The story has to take place at *some* time, but Chopin does not simply say, "On a spring day," or an autumn day, and let things go at that. Rather, she tells us about the sky, the trees, the rain, the twittering sparrows—and all of this in an extremely short story where we might think there is no time for talk about the setting. After all, none of this material is strictly necessary to a story about a woman who has heard that her husband was killed in an accident, who grieves, then recovers, and then dies when he suddenly reappears.

Why, then, does Chopin give such emphasis to the season? Because, we think, she is using the season symbolically. In this story, the spring is not just a bit of detail added for realism. It is rich with suggestions of renewal, of the new life that Louise achieves for a moment. But here, a caution: We think that the spring in this story is symbolic, but this is not to say that whenever spring appears in a story, it stands for renewal, any more than whenever winter appears it always symbolizes death. Nor does it mean that since spring recurs, Louise will be reborn. In short, in *this* story Chopin uses the season to convey specific implications.

Is the railroad accident in "The Story of an Hour" also a symbol? Our answer is no—though we don't expect all readers to agree with us. We think that the railroad accident in "The Story of an Hour" is just a railroad accident. It's our sense that Chopin is *not* using this event to say something about modern travel, or about industrialism. The steam-propelled railroad train could be used, symbolically, to say something about industrialism displacing an agrarian economy, but does Chopin give her train any such suggestion? We don't think so. Had she wished to do so, she would probably have talked about the enormous power of the train, the shriek of its whistle, the smoke pouring out of the smokestack, the intense fire burning in the engine, its indifference as it charged through the countryside, and so forth. Had she done so, the story would be a different story. Or she might have made the train a symbol of fate overriding human desires. But, again in our opinion, Chopin does not endow her train with such suggestions. She gives virtually no emphasis to the train, and so we believe it has virtually no significance for the reader.

What of Chopin's "Ripe Figs" (page 9)? Maman-Nainaine tells Babette that when the figs are ripe Babette can visit her cousins. Maman may merely be setting an arbitrary date, but as we read the story we probably feel—because of the emphasis on the *ripening* of the figs, which occurs in the spring or early summer— that the ripening of the figs in some way suggests the maturing of Babette. If we do get such ideas, we will in effect be saying that the story is not simply an anecdote about an old woman whose behavior is odd. True, the narrator of the story, after telling us of Maman-Nainaine's promise, adds, "Not that the ripening of figs had the least thing to do with it, but that is the way Maman-Nainaine was." The narrator sees nothing special—merely Maman-Nainaine's eccentricity—in the connection between the ripening of the figs and Babette's visit to her cousins. Readers, however, may see more than the narrator sees or says. They may see in Babette a young girl maturing; they may see in Maman-Nainaine an older woman who, almost collaborating with nature, helps Babette to mature.

And here, as we talk about symbolism, we are getting into the theme of the story. An apparently inconsequential and even puzzling action, such as is set forth in "Ripe Figs," may cast a long shadow. As Robert Frost once said,

> There is no story written that has any value at all, however straightforward it looks and free from doubleness, double entendre, that you'd value at all if it didn't have intimations of something more than itself.

The stranger, the more mysterious the story, the more likely we are to suspect some intended significance, but even realistic stories such as Chopin's "The Storm" and "The Story of an Hour" may be rich in suggestions. This is not to say, however, that the suggestions (rather than the details of the surface) are what count. A reader does not discard the richly detailed, highly specific narrative (Mrs. Mallard learned that her husband was dead and reacted in such-and-such a way) in favor of some supposedly universal message or theme that it implies. We do not throw away the specific narrative—the memorable characters or the interesting things that happen in the story—and move on to some "higher truth." Robert Frost went on to say, "The anecdote, the parable, the surface meaning has got to be good and got to be sufficient in itself."

Narrative Point of View

An author must choose a **point of view** (or sometimes, several points of view) from which he or she will narrate the story. The choice will contribute to the total effect of the story.

Narrative points of view can be divided into two sorts: **participant** (or **first-person**) and **nonparticipant** (or **third-person**). That is, the narrator may or may not be a character who participates in the story. Each of these two divisions can be subdivided:

  I. Participant (first-person narrative)
     A. Narrator as a major character
     B. Narrator as a minor character
  II. Nonparticipant (third-person narrative)
     A. Omniscient
     B. Selective omniscient
     C. Objective

PARTICIPANT POINTS OF VIEW   Toni Bambara's "The Lesson" (page 654) begins:

> Back in the days when everyone was old and stupid or young and foolish and me and Sugar were the only ones just right, this lady moved on our block with nappy hair and proper speech and no makeup.

In this story, the narrator is a major character. Bambara is the author, but the narrator—the person who tells us the story—is a young girl who speaks of "me and Sugar," and the story is chiefly about the narrator. We can say, then, that Bambara uses a first-person (or participant) point of view. She has invented a young girl who tells us about the impact a woman in the neighborhood had on her: "[Sugar] can run if she want to and even run faster. But ain't nobody gonna beat me at nuthin." The narrator is a major character. She, and not Bambara, tells the story.

Sometimes a first-person narrator tells a story that focuses on someone other than the narrator; he or she is a minor character, a peripheral witness, for example, to a story about Sally Jones, and we get the story of Sally filtered through, say, the eyes of her friend or brother or cat.

Whether a major or a minor character, a first-person narrator is a particular character who sees things in a particular way. The reader should not assume that the speaker is necessarily a reliable source. Some, in fact, are notably **unreliable narrators**—for instance young children, mentally impaired adults, and psychopaths. A story told by an unreliable narrator, such as a man consumed with vengeful thoughts, depends largely on the reader's perception of the gap between what the narrator says and what the facts presumably are.

NONPARTICIPANT POINTS OF VIEW In a nonparticipant (third-person) point of view, the teller of the tale does not introduce himself or herself as a character. If the point of view is **omniscient,** the narrator relates what he or she wants to relate about the thoughts as well as the deeds of all the characters. The omniscient teller can enter the mind of any character; the first-person narrator can only say, "I was angry" or "Jack seemed angry," but the omniscient teller can say, "Jack was inwardly angry but gave no sign; Jill continued chatting, but she sensed his anger." Thus, in Paley's "Samuel," the narrator tells us that Samuel's mother was "hopeful," but when the new baby was born "immediately she saw that this baby wasn't Samuel."

Furthermore, a distinction can be made between **neutral omniscience** (the narrator recounts deeds and thoughts but does not judge) and **editorial omniscience** (the narrator not only recounts but also judges). An editorially omniscient narrator knows what goes on in the minds of all the characters and might comment approvingly or disapprovingly: "He closed the book, having finished the story, but, poor fellow, he had missed the meaning."

Because a short story can scarcely hope to develop a picture of several minds effectively, authors may prefer to limit their omniscience to the minds of a few of their characters, or even to that of only one of the characters; that is, they may use **selective omniscience** as the point of view. Selective omniscience provides a focus, especially if it is limited to a single character. When thus limited, the author sees one character from both outside and inside, but sees the other characters only from the outside and from the impact they have on the mind of this selected receptor. When selective omniscience attempts to record mental activity ranging from consciousness to the unconscious, from clear perceptions to confused longings, it is sometimes labeled the **stream-of-consciousness** point of view.

Finally, sometimes a third-person narrator does not enter even a single mind but records only what crosses an apparently dispassionate eye and ear. Such a point of view is **objective** (sometimes called the **camera** or **fly-on-the-wall point of view**). The absence of editorializing and of dissection of the mind often produces the effect of a play; we see and hear the characters in action. Much of Chekhov's "Misery" (page 85) is objective, consisting of bits of dialogue that make the story look like a play:

> "My head aches," says one of the tall ones. "At the Dukmasovs' yesterday Vaska and I drank four bottles of brandy between us."
> "I can't make out why you talk such stuff," says the other tall one angrily. "You lie like a brute."
> "Strike me dead, it's the truth! . . ."
> "It's about as true as that a louse coughs."

Style and Point of View

A story told by a first-person narrator will have a distinctive style—let's say the voice of an adolescent boy, or an elderly widow, or a madman. The voice of a third-person narrator—especially the voice of a supposedly objective narrator—will be much less distinctive, but if, especially on rereading, you listen carefully, you will probably hear a distinctive tone. (Look, for instance, at the first paragraph of Grace Paley's "Samuel.") Put it this way: Even a supposedly objective point of view is not purely objective, since it represents the writer's choice of a style, a way of reporting material with an apparently dispassionate voice.

After reading a story, you may want to think about what the story might be like if told from a different point of view. You may find it instructive, for instance, to rewrite "Samuel" from the "citizenly" man's point of view, or "Ripe Figs" from Babette's.

Theme

We distinguish between story (or plot) and theme in fiction. *Story* is concerned with "How does it turn out? What happens?" But **theme** is concerned with "What is it about? What does it add up to? What motif holds the happenings together? What does it make of life, and what wisdom does it offer?" In a good work of fiction, the details add up—in Flannery O'Connor's words, they are "controlled by some overall purpose."

In F. Scott Fitzgerald's *The Great Gatsby,* there are many references to popular music, especially to jazz. These references contribute to our sense of the reality of Fitzgerald's depiction of America in the 1920s, but they do more: They help to comment on the shallowness of the white middle-class characters, and they sometimes (very gently) remind us of an alternative culture. A reader might study Fitzgerald's references to music with an eye toward getting a deeper understanding of what the novel is about.

Suppose we think for a moment about the theme of Paley's "Samuel." Do we sense an "overall purpose" that holds the story together? Different readers will inevitably come up with different readings, that is, with different views of what the story is about. Here is one student's version:

Whites cannot understand the feelings of blacks.

This statement gets at an important element in the story—the conflict between the sober-minded adults and the jiggling boys—but it assumes that all of the adults are white, an inference that cannot be supported by pointing to evidence in the story. Further, we cannot be certain that Samuel is black. And, finally, even if Samuel and his mother are black, surely white readers *do understand his youthful enthusiasm and his mother's inconsolable grief.*

Here is a second statement:

One should not interfere with the actions of others.

Does the story really offer such specific advice? This version of the theme seems to us to reduce the story to a too-simple code of action, a heartless rule of behavior, a rule that seems at odds with the writer's awareness of the mother's enduring grief.

A third version:

Middle-class adults, acting from what seem to them to be the best of motives, may cause irreparable harm and grief.

This last statement seems to us to be one that can be fully supported by checking it against the story, but other equally valid statements can probably be made. How would you put it?

✔ **CHECKLIST**: *Getting Ideas for Writing about Stories*

Here are questions that may help to stimulate ideas about stories. Not every question will be relevant to every story; but if after reading a story and thinking about it, you then run your eye over these questions, you will find questions that help you to think further about the story and to get ideas.

As we have said before, it's best to do your thinking with a pen or pencil in hand. If some of the following questions seem to you to be especially relevant to the story you will be writing about, jot down your initial responses, interrupting your writing only to glance again at the story when you feel the need to check the evidence.

Plot

☐ Does the plot grow out of the characters, or does it depend on chance or coincidence? Did something at first strike you as irrelevant that later you perceived as relevant? Do some parts continue to strike you as irrelevant?

☐ Does surprise play an important role, or does foreshadowing? If surprise is very important, can the story be read a second time with any interest? If so, what gives it this further interest?

☐ What conflicts does the story include? Conflicts of one character against another? Of one character against the setting, or against society? Conflicts within a single character?

☐ Are certain episodes narrated out of chronological order? If so, were you puzzled? Annoyed? On reflection, does the arrangement of episodes seem effective? Why, or why not? Are certain situations repeated? If so, what do you make out of the repetitions?

Character

☐ Which character chiefly engages your interest? Why?

☐ What purposes do minor characters serve? Do you find some who by their similarities and differences help to define each other or help to define the major character? How else is a particular character defined—by his or her words, actions (including thoughts and emotions), dress, setting, narrative point of view? Do certain characters act differently in the same, or in a similar, situation?

☐ How does the author reveal character? By explicit authorial (editorial) comment, for instance by revelation through dialogue? Through depicted action? Through the actions of other characters? How are the author's methods especially suited to the whole of the story?

☐ Is the behavior plausible—that is, are the characters well motivated?

☐ If a character changes, why and how does he or she change? (You may want to jot down each event that influences a change.) Or did you change your attitude toward a character not because the character changes but because you came to know the character better?

☐ Are the characters round or flat? Are they complex or highly typical (for instance, one-dimensional representatives of a social class or age)? Are you chiefly interested in a character's psychology, or does the character strike you as standing for something, such as honesty or the arrogance of power?

☐ How has the author caused you to sympathize with certain characters? How does your response—your sympathy or lack of sympathy—contribute to your judgment of the conflict?

Point of View

☐ Who tells the story? How much does the narrator know? Does the narrator strike you as reliable? What effect is gained by using this narrator?

☐ How does the point of view help shape the theme? After all, the basic story of "Little Red Riding Hood"—what happens—remains unchanged whether told from the wolf's point of view or the girl's, but if we hear the story from the wolf's point of view, we may feel that the story is about terrifying yet pathetic compulsive behavior; if from the girl's point of view, about terrified innocence.

☐ It is sometimes said that the best writers are subversive, forcing readers to see something they do not want to see—something that is true but that violates their comfortable conventional ideas. Does this story oppose comfortable conventional views?

☐ Does the narrator's language help you to construct a picture of the narrator's character, class, attitude, strengths, and limitations? (Jot down some evidence, such as colloquial or formal expressions, ironic comments, figures of speech.) How far can you trust the narrator? Why?

Setting

☐ Do you have a strong sense of the time and place? Is the story very much about, say, New England Puritanism, or race relations in the South in the late nineteenth century, or midwestern urban versus small-town life? If time and place are important, how and at what points in the story has the author conveyed this sense? If you do not strongly feel the setting, do you think the author should have made it more evident?

☐ What is the relation of the setting to the plot and the characters? (For instance, do houses or rooms or their furnishings say something about their residents?) Would anything be lost if the descriptions of the setting were deleted from the story or the setting were changed?

Symbolism

☐ Do certain characters seem to stand for something in addition to themselves? Does the setting—whether a house, a farm, a landscape, a town, a period—have an extra dimension?

☐ If you do believe that the story has symbolic elements, do you think they are adequately integrated within the story, or do they strike you as being too obviously stuck in?

Style

☐ How has the point of view shaped or determined the style?

☐ How would you characterize the style? Simple? Understated? Figurative? Or what, and why?

☐ Do you think that the style is consistent? If it isn't—for instance, if there are shifts from simple sentences to highly complex ones—what do you make of the shifts?

Theme

☐ Is the title informative? What does it mean or suggest? Did its meaning seem to change after you read the story? Does the title help you to formulate a theme? If you had written the story, what title would you give it?

☐ Do certain passages—dialogue or description—seem to you to point especially toward the theme? Do you find certain repetitions of words or pairs of incidents highly suggestive and helpful in directing your thoughts toward stating a theme? Flannery O'Connor, in *Mystery and Manners* (1969), says, "In good fiction, certain of the details will tend to accumulate meaning from the action of the story itself, and when that happens, they become symbolic in the way they work." Does this story work that way?

☐ Is the meaning of the story embodied in the whole story, or does it seem stuck in—for example in certain passages of editorializing?

☐ Suppose someone asked you to state the point—the theme—of the story. Could you? And if you could, would you say that the theme of a particular story reinforces values you hold, or does it to some degree challenge them? Or is the concept of a theme irrelevant to this story?

Your Turn: Stories for Analysis

DIANA CHANG

Diana Chang (1934–), author of several novels and books of poems, taught creative writing at Barnard College. She identifies herself as an American writer whose background is mostly Chinese.

The Oriental Contingent

Connie couldn't remember whose party it was, whose house. She had an impression of kerosene lamps on brown wicker tables, of shapes talking in doorways. It was summer, almost the only time Connie has run into her since, too, and someone was saying, "You must know Lisa Mallory."

"I don't think so."

"She's here. You must know her."

Later in the evening, it was someone else who introduced her to a figure perched on the balustrade of the steps leading to the lawn where more shapes milled. In stretching out a hand to shake Connie's, the figure almost fell off sideways. Connie pushed her back upright onto her perch and, peering, took in the fact that Lisa Mallory had a Chinese face. For a long instant, she felt nonplussed, and was rendered speechless.

5   But Lisa Mallory was filling in the silence. "Well, now, Connie Sung," she said, not enthusiastically but with a kind of sophisticated interest. "I'm not in music

myself, but Paul Wu's my cousin. Guilt by association!" She laughed. "No-tone music, I call his. He studied with John Cage, Varèse,[1] and so forth."

Surprised that Lisa knew she was a violinist, Connie murmured something friendly, wondering if she should simply ask outright, "I'm sure I should know, but what do you do?" but she hesitated, taking in her appearance instead, while Lisa went on with, "It's world class composing. Nothing's wrong with the level. But it's hard going for the layman, believe me."

Lisa Mallory wore a one-of-a-kind kimono dress, but it didn't make her look Japanese at all, and her hair was drawn back tightly in a braid which stood out from close to the top of her head horizontally. You could probably lift her off her feet by grasping it, like the handle of a pot.

"You should give a concert here, Connie," she said, using her first name right away, Connie noticed, like any American. "Lots of culturati around." Even when she wasn't actually speaking, she pursued her own line of thought actively and seemed to find herself mildly amusing.

"I'm new to the area," Connie said, deprecatingly. "I've just been a weekend guest, actually, till a month ago."

10 "It's easy to be part of it. Nothing to it. I should know. You'll see."

"I wish it weren't so dark," Connie found herself saying, waving her hand in front of her eyes as if the night were a veil to brush aside. She recognized in herself that intense need to see, to see into fellow Orientals, to fathom them. So far, Lisa Mallory had not given her enough clues, and the darkness itself seemed to be interfering.

Lisa dropped off her perch. "It's important to be true to oneself," she said. "Keep the modern stuff out of your repertory. Be romantic. Don't look like that! You're best at the romantics. Anyhow, take it from me. I know. And *I* like what I like."

Released by her outspokenness, Connie laughed and asked, "I'm sure I should know, but what is it that you do?" She was certain Lisa would say something like, "I'm with a public relations firm." "I'm in city services."

But she replied, "What do all Chinese excel at?" Not as if she'd asked a rhetorical question, she waited, then answered herself. "Well, aren't we all physicists, musicians, architects, or in software?"

15 At that point a voice broke in, followed by a large body which put his arms around both women, "The Oriental contingent! I've got to break this up."

Turning, Lisa kissed him roundly, and said over her shoulder to Connie, "I'll take him away before he tells us we look alike!"

They melted into the steps below, and Connie, feeling put off balance and somehow slow-witted, was left to think over her new acquaintance.

"Hello, Lisa Mallory," Connie Sung always said on the infrequent occasions when they ran into one another. She always said "Hello, Lisa Mallory," with a shyness she did not understand in herself. It was strange, but they had no mutual friends except for Paul Wu, and Connie had not seen him in ages. Connie had no one of whom to ask her questions. But sometime soon, she'd be told Lisa's maiden name. Sometime she'd simply call her Lisa. Sometime what Lisa did with her life would be answered.

Three, four years passed, with their running into one another at receptions and openings, and still Lisa Mallory remained an enigma. Mildly amused herself,

[1]**John Cage** (1912–92) and **Edgard Varèse** (1883–1965) were important and controversial avante-garde composers.

Connie wondered if other people, as well, found her inscrutable. But none of her American friends (though, of course, Lisa and she were Americans, too, she had to remind herself), none of their Caucasian friends seemed curious about backgrounds. In their accepting way, they did not wonder about Lisa's background, or about Connie's or Paul Wu's. Perhaps they assumed they were all cut from the same cloth. But to Connie, the Orientals she met were unread books, books she never had the right occasion or time to fully pursue.

20   She didn't even see the humor in her situation—it was such an issue with her. The fact was she felt less, much less, sure of herself when she was with real Chinese.

As she was realizing this, the truth suddenly dawned on her. Lisa Mallory never referred to her own background because it was more Chinese than Connie's, and therefore of a higher order. She was tact incarnate. All along, she had been going out of her way not to embarrass Connie. Yes, yes. Her assurance was definitely uppercrust (perhaps her father had been in the diplomatic service), and her offhand didacticness, her lack of self-doubt, was indeed characteristically Chinese-Chinese. Connie was not only impressed by these traits, but also put on the defensive because of them.

Connie let out a sigh—a sigh that follows the solution to a nagging problem . . . Lisa's mysteriousness. But now Connie knew only too clearly that her own background made her decidedly inferior. Her father was a second-generation gynecologist who spoke hardly any Chinese. Yes, inferior and totally without recourse.

Of course, at one of the gatherings, Connie met Bill Mallory, too. He was simply American, maybe Catholic, possibly lapsed. She was not put off balance by him at all. But most of the time he was away on business, and Lisa cropped up at functions as single as Connie.

Then one day, Lisa had a man in tow—wiry and tall, he looked Chinese from the Shantung area, or perhaps from Beijing, and his styled hair made him appear vaguely artistic.

25   "Connie," I'd like you to meet Eric Li. He got out at the beginning of the *detente,* went to Berkeley, and is assimilating a mile-a-minute," Lisa said, with her usual irony. "Bill found him and is grooming him, though he came with his own charisma."

Eric waved her remark aside. "Lisa has missed her calling. She was born to be in PR," he said, with an accent.

"Is that what she does?" Connie put in at once, looking only at him. "Is that her profession?"

"You don't know?" he asked, with surprise.

Though she was greeting someone else, Lisa turned and answered, "I'm a fabrics tycoon, I think I can say without immodesty." She moved away and continued her conversation with the other friend.

30   Behind his hand, he said, playfully, as though letting Connie in on a secret, "Factories in Hongkong and Taipei, and now he's—Bill, that is—is exploring them on the mainland."

"With her fabulous contacts over there!" Connie exclaimed, now seeing it all. "Of course, what a wonderful business combination they must make."

Eric was about to utter something, but stopped, and said flatly, "I have all the mainland contacts, even though I was only twenty when I left, but my parents . . . ."

"How interesting," Connie murmured lamely. "I see," preoccupied as she was with trying to put two and two together.

Lisa was back and said without an introduction, continuing her line of thought, "You two look good together, if I have to say so myself. Why don't you ask him to one of your concerts? And you, Eric, you're in America now, so don't stand on ceremony, or you'll be out in left field." She walked away with someone for another drink.

35   Looking uncomfortable, but recovering himself with a smile, Eric said, "Lisa makes me feel more Chinese than I am becoming—it is her directness, I suspect. In China, we'd say she is too much like a man."

At which Connie found herself saying, "She makes me feel *less* Chinese."

"Less!"

"Less Chinese than she is."

"That is not possible," Eric said, with a shade of contempt—for whom? Lisa or Connie? He barely suppressed a laugh, cold as Chinese laughter could be.

40   Connie blurted out, "I'm a failed Chinese. Yes, and it's to you that I need to say it." She paused and repeated emphatically, "I am a failed Chinese." Her heart was beating quicker, but she was glad to have got that out, a confession and a definition that might begin to free her. "Do you know you make me feel that, too? You've been here only about ten years, right?"

"Right, and I'm thirty-one."

"You know what I think? I think it's harder for a Chinese to do two things."

At that moment, an American moved in closer, looking pleased somehow to be with them.

She continued, "It's harder for us to become American than, say, for a German, and it's also harder not to remain residually Chinese, even if you are third generation."

45   Eric said blandly, "Don't take yourself so seriously. You can't help being an American product."

Trying to be comforting, the American interjected with, "The young lady is not a product, an object. She is a human being, and there is no difference among peoples that I can see."

"I judge myself both as a Chinese and as an American," Connie said.

"You worry too much," Eric said, impatiently. Then he looked around and though she wasn't in sight, he lowered his voice. "She is what she is. I know what she is. But she avoids going to Hongkong. She avoids it."

Connie felt turned around. "Avoids it?"

50   "Bill's in Beijing right now. She's here. How come?"

"I don't know," Connie replied, as though an answer had been required of her.

"She makes up many excuses, reasons. Ask her. Ask her yourself," he said, pointedly.

"Oh, I couldn't do that. By the way, I'm going on a concert tour next year in three cities—Shanghai, Beijing and Nanking," Connie said. "It'll be my first time in China."

"Really! You must be very talented to be touring at your age," he said, genuinely interested for the first time. Because she was going to China, or because she now came across as an over-achiever, even though Chinese American?

55   "I'm just about your age," she said, realizing then that maybe Lisa Mallory had left them alone purposely.

"You could both pass as teenagers!" the American exclaimed.

Two months later, she ran into Lisa again. As usual, Lisa began in the middle of her own thoughts. "Did he call?"

"Who? Oh. No, no."

"Well, it's true he's been in China the last three weeks with Bill. They'll be back this weekend."

60   Connie saw her opportunity. "Are you planning to go to China yourself?"

For the first time, Lisa seemed at a loss for words. She raised her shoulders, then let them drop. Too airily, she said, "You know, there's always Paris. I can't bear not to go to Paris, if I'm to take a trip."

"But you're Chinese. You *have* been to China, you came from China originally, didn't you?"

"I could go to Paris twice a year, I love it so," Lisa said. "And then there's London, Florence, Venice."

"But—but your business contacts?"

65   "*My* contacts? Bill, he's the businessman who makes the contacts. Always has. I take care of the New York office, which is a considerable job. We have a staff of eighty-five."

Connie said, "I told Eric I'll be giving a tour in China. I'm taking Chinese lessons right now."

Lisa Mallory laughed, "Save your time. They'll still be disdainful over there. See, *they* don't care," and she waved her hand at the crowd. "Some of them have been born in Buffalo, too! It's the Chinese you can't fool. They know you're not the genuine article—you and I."

Her face was suddenly heightened in color, and she was breathing as if ready to flee from something. "Yes, you heard right. I was born in Buffalo."

"You were!" Connie exclaimed before she could control her amazement.

70   "Well, what about you?" Lisa retorted. She was actually shaking and trying to hide it by making sudden gestures.

"Westchester."

"But your parents at least were Chinese."

"Well, so were, so are, yours!"

"I was adopted by Americans. My full name is Lisa Warren Mallory."

75   Incredulous, Connie said, "I'm more Chinese than you!"

"Who isn't?" She laughed, unhappily. "Having Chinese parents makes all the difference. We're worlds apart."

"And all the time I thought . . . never mind what I thought."

"You have it over me. It's written all over you. I could tell even in the dark that night."

"Oh, Lisa," Connie said to comfort her, "none of this matters to anybody except us. Really and truly. They're too busy with their own problems."

80   "The only time I feel Chinese is when I'm embarrassed I'm not more Chinese—which is a totally Chinese reflex I'd give anything to be rid of!"

"I know what you mean."

"And as for Eric looking down his nose at me, he's knocking himself out to be so American, *but as a secure Chinese!* What's so genuine about that article?"

Both of them struck their heads laughing, but their eyes were not merry.

"Say it again," Connie asked of her, "say it again that my being more Chinese is written all over me."

85   "Consider it said," Lisa said. "My natural mother happened to be there at the time—I can't help being born in Buffalo."

"I know, I know," Connie said with feeling. "If only you had had some say in the matter."

"It's only Orientals who haunt me!" Lisa stamped her foot. "Only them!"

"I'm so sorry," Connie Sung said, for all of them. "It's all so turned around."

"So I'm made in America, so there!" Lisa Mallory declared, making a sniffing sound, and seemed to be recovering her sangfroid.

90   Connie felt tired—as if she'd traveled—but a lot had been settled on the way.

[1989]

Joining the Conversation: Critical Thinking and Writing

1. In an interview published in 1995, Diana Chang says of "The Oriental Contingent": "[This story] is about two Chinese-American women who meet, each trying to hide from the other that she feels inadequate as a Chinese, not as an American." Please present an argument in support of Chang's comment.

2. One scholar who has written about "The Oriental Contingent" maintains that in it Chang "challenges the myth of authentic Asian-American identity." Another scholar says, to the contrary, that it does not. Construct a good argument for your own interpretation.

3. In her 1995 interview, Chang mentions in passing that as a writer she is interested in the "emotion of thought." What do you think this phrase means? Do you perceive examples of emotion of thought in this story?

GISH JEN

Gish Jen, born in 1955 in Yonkers, New York, and the daughter of Chinese immigrants, was named Lillian Jen by her parents. She disliked the name Lillian, and her school friends created a new name for her, derived from the name of a famous actress of the silent screen—Lillian Gish. Jen graduated from Harvard and, in accordance with her parents' wishes, went to Stanford Business School (MBA, 1980). Then, following her own wishes, Jen went to the University of Iowa, where in 1983 she earned an MFA in the writing program. She has published three novels and a book of short stories, Who's Irish? *We reprint the title story.*

Who's Irish?

In China, people say mixed children are supposed to be smart, and definitely my granddaughter Sophie is smart. But Sophie is wild, Sophie is not like my daughter Natalie, or like me. I am work hard my whole life, and fierce besides. My husband always used to say he is afraid of me, and in our restaurant, busboys and cooks all afraid of me too. Even the gang members come for protection money, they try to talk to my husband. When I am there, they stay away. If they come by mistake, they pretend they are come to eat. They hide behind the menu, they order a lot of food. They talk about their mothers. Oh, my mother have some arthritis, need to take herbal medicine, they say. Oh, my mother getting old, her hair all white now.

I say, Your mother's hair used to be white, but since she dye it, it become black again. Why don't you go home once in a while and take a look? I tell them, Confucius[1] say a filial son knows what color his mother's hair is.

My daughter is fierce too, she is vice president in the bank now. Her new house is big enough for everybody to have their own room, including me. But Sophie take after Natalie's husband's family, their name is Shea. Irish. I always thought Irish people are like Chinese people, work so hard on the railroad, but now I know why the Chinese beat the Irish. Of course, not all Irish are like the Shea family, of course not. My daughter tell me I should not say Irish this, Irish that.

How do you like it when people say the Chinese this, the Chinese that, she say.

You know, the British call the Irish heathen, just like they call the Chinese, she say.

5

---

[1] **Confucius** Chinese religious leader and philosopher (551–479 BCE).

You think the Opium War[2] was bad, how would you like to live right next door to the British, she say.

And that is that. My daughter have a funny habit when she win an argument, she take a sip of something and look away, so the other person is not embarrassed. So I am not embarrassed. I do not call anybody anything either. I just happen to mention about the Shea family, an interesting fact: four brothers in the family, and not one of them work. The mother, Bess, have a job before she got sick, she was executive secretary in a big company. She is handle everything for a big shot, you would be surprised how complicated her job is, not just type this, type that. Now she is a nice woman with a clean house. But her boys, every one of them is on welfare, or so-called severance pay, or so-called disability pay. Something. They say they cannot find work, this is not the economy of the fifties, but I say, Even the black people doing better these days, some of them live so fancy, you'd be surprised. Why the Shea family have so much trouble? They are white people, they speak English. When I come to this country, I have no money and do not speak English. But my husband and I own our restaurant before he die. Free and clear, no mortgage. Of course, I understand I am just lucky, come from a country where the food is popular all over the world. I understand it is not the Shea family's fault they come from a country where everything is boiled. Still, I say.

She's right, we should broaden our horizons, say one brother, Jim, at Thanksgiving. Forget about the car business. Think about egg rolls.

Pad thai, say another brother, Mike. I'm going to make my fortune in pad thai. It's going to be the new pizza.

10   I say, You people too picky about what you sell. Selling egg rolls not good enough for you, but at least my husband and I can say, We made it. What can you say? Tell me. What can you say?

Everybody chew their tough turkey.

I especially cannot understand my daughter's husband John, who has no job but cannot take care of Sophie either. Because he is a man, he say, and that's the end of the sentence.

Plain boiled food, plain boiled thinking. Even his name is plain boiled: John. Maybe because I grew up with black bean sauce and hoisin sauce and garlic sauce, I always feel something is missing when my son-in-law talk.

But, okay: so my son-in-law can be man, I am baby-sitter. Six hours a day, same as the old sitter, crazy Amy, who quit. This is not so easy, now that I am sixty-eight, Chinese age almost seventy. Still, I try. In China, daughter take care of mother. Here it is the other way around. Mother help daughter, mother ask, Anything else I can do? Otherwise daughter complain mother is not supportive. I tell daughter, We do not have this word in Chinese, *supportive*. But my daughter too busy to listen, she has to go to meeting, she has to write memo while her husband go to the gym to be a man. My daughter say otherwise he will be depressed. Seems like all his life he has this trouble, depression.

15   No one wants to hire someone who is depressed, she say. It is important for him to keep his spirits up.

Beautiful wife, beautiful daughter, beautiful house, oven can clean itself automatically. No money left over, because only one income, but lucky enough, got the baby-sitter for free. If John lived in China, he would be very happy. But he is not happy. Even at the gym things go wrong. One day, he pull a muscle. Another day, weight room too crowded. Always something.

---

[2]**Opium War** conflicts, 1839–42 and 1856–60, between China and Great Britain involving the opium trade.

Until finally, hooray, he has a job. Then he feel pressure.

I need to concentrate, he say. I need to focus.

He is going to work for insurance company. Salesman job. A paycheck, he say, and at least he will wear clothes instead of gym shorts. My daughter buy him some special candy bars from the health-food store. They say THINK! on them, and are supposed to help John think.

20 John is a good-looking boy, you have to say that, especially now that he shave so you can see his face.

I am an old man in a young man's game, say John.

I will need a new suit, say John.

This time I am not going to shoot myself in the foot, say John.

Good, I say.

25 She means to be supportive, my daughter say. Don't start the send her back to China thing, because we can't.

Sophie is three years old American age, but already I see her nice Chinese side swallowed up by her wild Shea side. She looks like mostly Chinese. Beautiful black hair, beautiful black eyes. Nose perfect size, not so flat looks like something fell down, not so large looks like some big deal got stuck in wrong face. Everything just right, only her skin is a brown surprise to John's family. So brown, they say. Even John say it. She never goes in the sun, still she is that color, he say. Brown. They say, Nothing the matter with brown. They are just surprised. So brown. Nattie is not that brown, they say. They say, It seems like Sophie should be a color in between Nattie and John. Seems funny, a girl named Sophie Shea be brown. But she is brown, maybe her name should be Sophie Brown. She never go in the sun, still she is that color, they say. Nothing the matter with brown. They are just surprised.

The Shea family talk is like this sometimes, going around and around like a Christmas-tree train.

Maybe John is not her father, I say one day, to stop the train. And sure enough, train wreck. None of the brothers ever say the word *brown* to me again.

Instead, John's mother, Bess, say, I hope you are not offended.

30 She say, I did my best on those boys. But raising four boys with no father is no picnic.

You have a beautiful family, I say.

I'm getting old, she say.

You deserve a rest, I say. Too many boys make you old.

I never had a daughter, she say. You have a daughter.

35 I have a daughter, I say. Chinese people don't think a daughter is so great, but you're right. I have a daughter.

I was never against the marriage, you know, she say. I never thought John was marrying down. I always thought Nattie was just as good as white.

I was never against the marriage either, I say. I just wonder if they look at the whole problem.

Of course you pointed out the problem, you are a mother, she say. And now we both have a granddaughter. A little brown granddaughter, she is so precious to me.

I laugh. A little brown granddaughter, I say. To tell you the truth, I don't know how she came out so brown.

40 We laugh some more. These days Bess need a walker to walk. She take so many pills, she need two glasses of water to get them all down. Her favorite TV show is about bloopers, and she love her bird feeder. All day long, she can watch that bird feeder, like a cat.

I can't wait for her to grow up, Bess say. I could use some female company.
Too many boys, I say.

Boys are fine, she say. But they do surround you after a while.

You should take a break, come live with us, I say. Lots of girls at our house.

Be careful what you offer, say Bess with a wink. Where I come from, people
mean for you to move in when they say a thing like that.

Nothing the matter with Sophie's outside, that's the truth. It is inside that she is like
not any Chinese girl I ever see. We go to the park, and this is what she does. She
stand up in the stroller. She take off all her clothes and throw them in the fountain.

Sophie! I say. Stop!

But she just laugh like a crazy person. Before I take over as baby-sitter, Sophie
has that crazy-person sitter, Amy the guitar player. My daughter thought this Amy
very creative—another word we do not talk about in China. In China, we talk
about whether we have difficulty or no difficulty. We talk about whether life is bitter or not bitter. In America, all day long, people talk about creative. Never mind
that I cannot even look at this Amy, with her shirt so short that her belly button
showing. This Amy think Sophie should love her body. So when Sophie take off
her diaper, Amy laugh. When Sophie run around naked, Amy say she wouldn't
want to wear a diaper either. When Sophie go *shu-shu* in her lap, Amy laugh and
say there are no germs in pee. When Sophie take off her shoes, Amy say bare feet
is best, even the pediatrician say so. That is why Sophie now walk around with no
shoes like a beggar child. Also why Sophie love to take off her clothes.

Turn around! say the boys in the park. Let's see that ass!

Of course, Sophie does not understand. Sophie clap her hands, I am the only
one to say, No! This is not a game.

It has nothing to do with John's family, my daughter say. Amy was too permis-
sive, that's all.

But I think if Sophie was not wild inside, she would not take off her shoes and
clothes to begin with.

You never take off your clothes when you were little, I say. All my Chinese
friends had babies, I never saw one of them act wild like that.

Look, my daughter say. I have a big presentation tomorrow.

John and my daughter agree Sophie is a problem, but they don't know what
to do.

You spank her, she'll stop, I say another day.

But they say, Oh no.

In America, parents not supposed to spank the child.

It gives them low self-esteem, my daughter say. And that leads to problems
later, as I happen to know.

My daughter never have big presentation the next day when the subject of
spanking come up.

I don't want you to touch Sophie, she say. No spanking, period.

Don't tell me what to do, I say.

I'm not telling you what to do, say my daughter. I'm telling you how I feel.

I am not your servant, I say. Don't you dare talk to me like that.

My daughter have another funny habit when she lose an argument. She spread
out all her fingers and look at them, as if she like to make sure they are still there.

My daughter is fierce like me, but she and John think it is better to explain to
Sophie that clothes are a good idea. This is not so hard in the cold weather. In the
warm weather, it is very hard.

Use your words, my daughter say. That's what we tell Sophie. How about if you set a good example.

As if good example mean anything to Sophie. I am so fierce, the gang members who used to come to the restaurant all afraid of me, but Sophie is not afraid.

70   I say, Sophie, if you take off your clothes, no snack.

I say, Sophie, if you take off your clothes, no lunch.

I say, Sophie, if you take off your clothes, no park.

Pretty soon we are stay home all day, and by the end of six hours she still did not have one thing to eat. You never saw a child stubborn like that.

I'm hungry! she cry when my daughter come home.

What's the matter, doesn't your grandmother feed you? My daughter laugh.

75   No! Sophie say. She doesn't feed me anything!

My daughter laugh again. Here you go, she say.

She say to John, Sophie must be growing.

Growing like a weed, I say.

Still Sophie take off her clothes, until one day I spank her. Not too hard, but she cry and cry, and when I tell her if she doesn't put her clothes back on I'll spank her again, she put her clothes back on. Then I tell her she is good girl, and give her some food to eat. The next day we go to the park and, like a nice Chinese girl, she does not take off her clothes.

80   She stop taking off her clothes, I report. Finally!

How did you do it? my daughter ask.

After twenty-eight years experience with you, I guess I learn something, I say.

It must have been a phase, John say, and his voice is suddenly like an expert.

His voice is like an expert about everything these days, now that he carry a leather briefcase, and wear shiny shoes, and can go shopping for a new car. On the company, he say. The company will pay for it, but he will be able to drive it whenever he want.

85   A free car, he say. How do you like that.

It's good to see you in the saddle again, my daughter say. Some of your family patterns are scary.

At least I don't drink, he say. He say, And I'm not the only one with scary family patterns.

That's for sure, say my daughter.

Everyone is happy. Even I am happy, because there is more trouble with Sophie, but now I think I can help her Chinese side fight against her wild side. I teach her to eat food with fork or spoon or chopsticks, she cannot just grab into the middle of a bowl of noodles. I teach her not to play with garbage cans. Sometimes I spank her, but not too often, and not too hard.

90   Still, there are problems. Sophie like to climb everything. If there is a railing, she is never next to it. Always she is on top of it. Also, Sophie like to hit the mommies of her friends. She learn this from her playground best friend, Sinbad, who is four. Sinbad wear army clothes every day and like to ambush his mommy. He is the one who dug a big hole under the play structure, a foxhole he call it, all by himself. Very hardworking. Now he wait in the foxhole with a shovel full of wet sand. When his mommy come, he throw it right at her.

Oh, it's all right, his mommy say. You can't get rid of war games, it's part of their imaginative play. All the boys go through it.

Also, he like to kick his mommy, and one day he tell Sophie to kick his mommy too.

I wish this story is not true.

Kick her, kick her! Sinbad say.

95   Sophie kick her. A little kick, as if she just so happened was swinging her little leg and didn't realize that big mommy leg was in the way. Still I spank Sophie and make Sophie say sorry, and what does the mommy say?

Really, it's all right, she say. It didn't hurt.

After that, Sophie learn she can attack mommies in the playground, and some will say, Stop, but others will say, Oh, she didn't mean it, especially if they realize Sophie will be punished.

This is how, one day, bigger trouble come. The bigger trouble start when Sophie hide in the foxhole with that shovel full of sand. She wait, and when I come look for her, she throw it at me. All over my nice clean clothes.

Did you ever see a Chinese girl act this way?

100   Sophie! I say. Come out of there, say you're sorry.

But she does not come out. Instead, she laugh. Naaah, naah-na, naaa-naaa, she say.

I am not exaggerate: millions of children in China, not one act like this.

Sophie! I say. Now! Come out now!

But she know she is in big trouble. She know if she come out, what will happen next. So she does not come out. I am sixty-eight, Chinese age almost seventy, how can I crawl under there to catch her? Impossible. So I yell, yell, yell, and what happen? Nothing. A Chinese mother would help, but American mothers, they look at you, they shake their head, they go home. And, of course, a Chinese child would give up, but not Sophie.

105   I hate you! she yell. I hate you, Meanie!

Meanie is my new name these days.

Long time this goes on, long long time. The foxhole is deep, you cannot see too much, you don't know where is the bottom. You cannot hear too much either. If she does not yell, you cannot even know she is still there or not. After a while, getting cold out, getting dark out. No one left in the playground, only us.

Sophie, I say. How did you become stubborn like this? I am go home without you now.

I try to use a stick, chase her out of there, and once or twice I hit her, but still she does not come out. So finally I leave. I go outside the gate.

110   Bye-bye! I say. I'm go home now.

But still she does not come out and does not come out. Now it is dinnertime, the sky is black. I think I should maybe go get help, but how can I leave a little girl by herself in the playground? A bad man could come. A rat could come. I go back in to see what is happen to Sophie. What if she have a shovel and is making a tunnel to escape?

Sophie! I say.

No answer.

Sophie!

115   I don't know if she is alive. I don't know if she is fall asleep down there. If she is crying, I cannot hear her.

So I take the stick and poke.

Sophie! I say. I promise I no hit you. If you come out, I give you a lollipop.

No answer. By now I worried. What to do, what to do, what to do? I poke some more, even harder, so that I am poking and poking when my daughter and John suddenly appear.

120   What are you doing? What is going on? say my daughter.

Put down that stick? say my daughter.

You are crazy! say my daughter.

John wiggle under the structure, into the foxhole, to rescue Sophie.

She fell asleep, say John the expert. She's okay. That is one big hole.

Now Sophie is crying and crying.

125   Sophie, my daughter say, hugging her. Are you okay, peanut? Are you okay?

She's just scared, say John.

Are you okay? I say too. I don't know what happen, I say.

She's okay, say John. He is not like my daughter, full of questions. He is full of answers until we get home and can see by the lamplight.

Will you look at her? he yell then. What the hell happened?

130   Bruises all over her brown skin, and a swollen-up eye.

You are crazy! say my daughter. Look at what you did! You are crazy!

I try very hard, I say.

How could you use a stick? I told you to use your words!

She is hard to handle, I say.

135   She's three years old! You cannot use a stick! say my daughter.

She is not like any Chinese girl I ever saw, I say.

I brush some sand off my clothes. Sophie's clothes are dirty too, but at least she has her clothes on.

Has she done this before? ask my daughter. Has she hit you before?

She hits me all the time, Sophie say, eating ice cream.

140   Your family, say John.

Believe me, say my daughter.

A daughter I have, a beautiful daughter. I took care of her when she could not hold her head up. I took care of her before she could argue with me, when she was a little girl with two pigtails, one of them always crooked. I took care of her when we have to escape from China, I took care of her when suddenly we live in a country with cars everywhere, if you are not careful your little girl get run over. When my husband die, I promise him I will keep the family together, even though it was just two of us, hardly a family at all.

But now my daughter take me around to look at apartments. After all, I can cook, I can clean, there's no reason I cannot live by myself, all I need is a telephone. Of course, she is sorry. Sometimes she cry, I am the one to say everything will be okay. She say she have no choice, she doesn't want to end up divorced. I say divorce is terrible, I don't know who invented this terrible idea. Instead of live with a telephone, though, surprise, I come to live with Bess. Imagine that. Bess make an offer and, sure enough, where she come from, people mean for you to move in when they say things like that. A crazy idea, go to live with someone else's family, but she like to have some female company, not like my daughter, who does not believe in company. These days when my daughter visit, she does not bring Sophie. Bess say we should give Nattie time, we will see Sophie again soon. But seems like my daughter have more presentation than ever before, every time she come she have to leave.

I have a family to support, she say, and her voice is heavy, as if soaking wet. I have a young daughter and a depressed husband and no one to turn to.

145   When she say no one to turn to, she mean me.

These days my beautiful daughter is so tired she can just sit there in a chair and fall asleep. John lost his job again, already, but still they rather hire a baby-sitter than ask me to help, even they can't afford it. Of course, the new baby-sitter is much younger, can run around. I don't know if Sophie these days is wild or not wild. She call me Meanie, but she like to kiss me too, sometimes. I remember that every time I see a child on TV. Sophie like to grab my hair, a fistful in each hand, and then kiss me smack on the nose. I never see any other child kiss that way.

The satellite TV has so many channels, more channels than I can count, including a Chinese channel from the Mainland and a Chinese channel from Taiwan, but most of the time I watch bloopers with Bess. Also, I watch the bird feeder—so many, many kinds of birds come. The Shea sons hang around all the time, asking when will I go home, but Bess tell them, Get lost.

She's a permanent resident, say Bess. She isn't going anywhere.

Then she wink at me, and switch the channel with the remote control.

150   Of course, I shouldn't say Irish this, Irish that, especially now I am become honorary Irish myself, according to Bess. Me! Who's Irish? I say, and she laugh. All the same, if I could mention one thing about some of the Irish, not all of them of course, I like to mention this: Their talk just stick. I don't know how Bess Shea learn to use her words, but sometimes I hear what she say a long time later. *Permanent resident. Not going anywhere.* Over and over I hear it, the voice of Bess.

[1998]

Joining the Conversation: Critical Thinking and Writing

1. The word "fierce" is used several times in "Who's Irish?" Please look up the definition of "fierce" in a good dictionary, and explain its significance for your understanding of the story.
2. Does the narrator change as a result of the experiences she describes?
3. Imagine that you have been assigned to teach "Who's Irish?" in a course on creative writing. What features of its style and structure would you highlight for your students?
4. Now that you have read and studied "Who's Irish?," what is your response to Jen's choice of title? If the author asked you to suggest an alternative title, what would it be? Explain in detail why your title would be a good one.
5. Does this story help you to perceive something new about "diversity"? Do you think that "diversity" is an overused term? Why or why not?
6. How would you describe the differences between the generations as they are expressed in Jen's story? Do you think in general that there are significant differences between members of older and younger generations, or would you say that they are exaggerated?
7. Do you believe that sometimes there are good reasons for classifying people by race and ethnicity? What are those reasons? Do you find them convincing? How should we classify "mixed race" persons?

RON WALLACE

Ron Wallace, born in 1945, is the author of numerous books of poems and stories. He is a professor of English and the codirector of the creative writing program at the University of Wisconsin–Madison.

Worry

She worried about people; he worried about things. And between them, that about covered it.

"What would you think of our daughter sleeping around?" she said.

"The porch steps are rotting," he replied. "Someone's going to fall through."

They were lying in bed together, talking. They had been lying in bed together talking these twenty-five years: first, about whether to have children—she wanted to (although there was Down's Syndrome, leukemia, microcephaly, mumps); he didn't (the siding was warped; the roof was going fast)—and then, after their daughter was born, a healthy seven pounds eleven ounces ("She's not eating enough;" "The furnace is failing"), about family matters, mostly ("Her friends are hoodlums, her room is a disaster," "The brakes are squealing, the water heater's rusting out.").

5   Worry grew between them like a son, with his own small insistencies and then more pressing demands. They stroked and coddled him; they set a place for him at the table; they sent him to kindergarten, private school, and college. Because he failed at nearly everything and always returned home, they loved him. After all, he was their son.

"I've been reading her diary. She does drugs. She sleeps around."

"I just don't think I can fix them myself. Where will we find a carpenter?"

And so it went. Their daughter married her high school sweetheart, had a family, and started a health food store in a distant town. Although she recalled her childhood as fondly as anyone—how good her parents had been and how they worried for her, how old and infirm they must be growing, their house going to ruin—she rarely called or visited. She had worries of her own.

[1996]

Joining the Conversation: Critical Thinking and Writing

1. If you found this tiny story of interest, would you say that your interest is chiefly in the characters or in the plot—or can the two not be separated?
2. Suppose you delete the first sentence from the story. Is anything lost? Or suppose you keep the first sentence but delete the three sentences of dialogue that immediately follow it. Again, is anything lost? Of the three versions—the original and the two that we have imagined—which is the best, and why?

CHAPTER 15

Thinking Critically: A Case Study about Flannery O'Connor

A story really isn't any good unless it successfully resists paraphrase,
unless it hangs on and expands in the mind.

FLANNERY O'CONNOR

Chapter Preview

After reading this chapter you will have had a good introduction to thinking analytically about the work of Flannery O'Connor, a major author of the twentieth century.

This case study contains two short stories by O'Connor and several of her writings on literature:

1. "A Good Man Is Hard to Find"
2. "Revelation"
3. Passages from five essays about fiction and a letter on "A Good Man Is Hard to Find"

We also include a page from the manuscript of "A Good Man Is Hard to Find," showing O'Connor's revisions.

 Flannery O'Connor (1925–64)—her first name was Mary but she did not use it—was born in Savannah, Georgia, but spent most of her life in Milledgeville, Georgia, where her family moved when she was twelve. She was educated in parochial schools and at the local college and then went to the School for Writers at the University of Iowa, where she earned an MFA in 1946. For a few months she lived at a writers' colony in Saratoga Springs, New York, and then for a few weeks she lived in New York City, but most of her life was spent in Milledgeville, where she tended her peacocks and wrote stories, novels, essays (posthumously published as Mystery and Manners *[1970]), and letters (posthumously published under the title* The Habit of Being *[1979]).*

In 1951, when she was twenty-five, Flannery O'Connor discovered that she was a victim of lupus erythematosus, an incurable autoimmune disease that had crippled and then killed her father ten years before. She died at the age of thirty-nine. O'Connor faced her illness with stoic courage, Christian fortitude—and tough humor. Here is a glimpse, from one of her letters, of how she dealt with those who pitied her:

> *An old lady got on the elevator behind me and as soon as I turned around she fixed me with a moist gleaming eye and said in a loud voice, "Bless you,*

374

darling!" I felt exactly like the Misfit [in "A Good Man Is Hard to Find"] and I gave her a weakly lethal look, whereupon greatly encouraged she grabbed my arm and whispered (very loud) in my ear, "Remember what they said to John at the gate, darling!" It was not my floor but I got off and I suppose the old lady was astounded at how quick I could get away on crutches. I have a one-legged friend and I asked her what they said to John at the gate. She said she reckoned they said, "The lame shall enter first." This may be because the lame will be able to knock everybody else aside with their crutches.

A devout Catholic, O'Connor forthrightly summarized the relationship between her belief and her writing:

I see from the standpoint of Christian orthodoxy. This means that for me the meaning of life is centered in our Redemption by Christ and what I see in the world I see in its relation to that.

A Good Man Is Hard to Find

The grandmother didn't want to go to Florida. She wanted to visit some of her connections in east Tennessee and she was seizing every chance to change Bailey's mind. Bailey was the son she lived with, her only boy. He was sitting on the edge of his chair at the table, bent over the orange sports section of the *Journal.* "Now look here, Bailey," she said, "see here, read this," and she stood with one hand on her thin hip and the other rattling the newspaper at his bald head. "Here this fellow that calls himself The Misfit is aloose from the Federal Pen and headed toward Florida and you read here what it says he did to these people. Just you read it. I wouldn't take my children in any direction with a criminal like that aloose in it. I couldn't answer to my conscience if I did."

Bailey didn't look up from his reading so she wheeled around then and faced the children's mother, a young woman in slacks, whose face was as broad and innocent as a cabbage and was tied around with a green headkerchief that had two points on the top like rabbit's ears. She was sitting on the sofa, feeding the baby his apricots out of a jar. "The children have been to Florida before," the old lady said. "You all ought to take them somewhere else for a change so they would see different parts of the world and be broad. They never have been to east Tennessee."

The children's mother didn't seem to hear her, but the eight-year-old boy, John Wesley, a stocky child with glasses, said. "If you don't want to go to Florida, why dontcha stay at home?" He and the little girl, June Star, were reading the funny papers on the floor.

"She wouldn't stay at home to be queen for a day," June Star said without raising her yellow head.

5   "Yes, and what would you do if this fellow, The Misfit, caught you?" the grandmother said.

"I'd smack his face," John Wesley said.

"She wouldn't stay at home for a million bucks," June Star said. "Afraid she'd miss something. She has to go everywhere we go."

"All right, Miss," the grandmother said. "Just remember that the next time you want me to curl your hair."

June Star said her hair was naturally curly.

10   The next morning the grandmother was the first one in the car, ready to go. She had her big black valise that looked like the head of a hippopotamus in one corner, and underneath it she was hiding a basket with Pitty Sing, the cat, in it. She didn't

2

~~Of course who~~ *the grandmother* was the first one ready to load up the next morning at six
o'clock. She had Baby Brother's bucking bronco ~~that~~ and ~~haxxxxkixx~~ what she
called her "~~Flee~~" and Pitty Sing, the cat, ~~she~~ *put* ~~he~~ packed in the car before
Boatwrite had a chance to ~~gatxxxxkixgxxxxxix~~ ~~come out of the door with the~~
rest of the luggage out of the hall. They got off at seven-thirty, Boatwrite
and ~~Etry~~ the children's mother in the front and Granny, John Wesley, Baby Brother,
Little Sister Mayy Ann, Pitty Sing, and the bucking bronco in the back.

"Why the hell did you bring that goddam rocking horse?" Boatwrite asked
because as soon as ~~the car began~~ ~~hxxxxx~~ *they went out the door they* ~~his~~ ~~they~~ Baby Brother began to squall to get
on the bucking bronco. "He can't get on that thing in this car and that's final,"
his father who was a stern man said.

"Can we open the lunch now?" Little Sister ~~Maxxxhxx~~ asked. "It'll shut
Baby Brother up. Mamma, can we open up the lunch?"

"No," their grandmother said. *It's only eight-thirty.*

Their mother was ~~xixxx~~ reading SCREEN MOTHERS AND THEIR CHILDREN. "Yeah,
sure," she said without looking up. She was all dressed up today. She had on
a purple silk dress and a hat and ~~gixxxxxxxx~~ *a coral* a choker of pink beads and a new
pocket book, and high heel pumps.

"Let's go through Georgia quick so we won't have to look at it much," John
Wesley said. "~~I want everything in a hurry~~."

"You should see Tennessee," his grandmother said. "Now there is a *beautiful* state."

"Like hell," John Wesley said. "That's just a hillbilly dumping ground."

"Hah," his mother said, and nudged Boatwrite. "Didjer hear that?" *She was from Tennessee*

They ate their lunch and got along fine ~~after that~~ for a while until Pitty
Sing who had been asleep jumped into the front of the car and caused Boatwrite
to swerve to the right into a ditch. Pitty Sing was a large grey-striped cat
with a yellow hind leg and a ~~xxxx~~ *big* soiled white face. Granny thought that she
was the only person in the world that he really loved but he had never ~~really~~ *the truth was*
looked ~~xxxxxxxxxxxxxxxx~~ ~~no~~ farther than her middle and he didn't even
like other cats. He jumped snarling into ~~the front seat and Boatwrite's shoulders~~

Typescript page from "A Good Man Is Hard to Find" with O'Connor's handwritten changes.

intend for the cat to be left alone in the house for three days because he would miss her
too much and she was afraid he might brush against one of the gas burners and accidentally asphyxiate himself. Her son, Bailey, didn't like to arrive at a motel with a cat.

She sat in the middle of the back seat with John Wesley and June Star on either
side of her. Bailey and the children's mother and the baby sat in front and they left
Atlanta at eight forty-five with the mileage on the car at 55890. The grandmother wrote
this down because she thought it would be interesting to say how many miles they had
been when they got back. It took them twenty minutes to reach the outskirts of the city.

The old lady settled herself comfortably, removing her white cotton gloves and
putting them up with her purse on the shelf in front of the back window. The children's

mother still had on slacks and still had her head tied up in a green kerchief, but the grandmother had on a navy blue straw sailor hat with a bunch of white violets on the brim and a navy blue dress with a small white dot in the print. Her collars and cuffs were white organdy trimmed with lace and at her neckline she had pinned a purple spray of cloth violets containing a sachet. In case of an accident, anyone seeing her dead on the highway would know at once that she was a lady.

She said she thought it was going to be a good day for driving, neither too hot nor too cold, and she cautioned Bailey that the speed limit was fifty-five miles an hour and that the patrolmen hid themselves behind bill-boards and small clumps of trees and sped out after you before you had a chance to slow down. She pointed out interesting details of the scenery: Stone Mountain; the blue granite that in some places came up to both sides of the highway; the brilliant red clay banks slightly streaked with purple; and the various crops that made rows of green lacework on the ground. The trees were full of silver-white sunlight and the meanest of them sparkled. The children were reading comic magazines and their mother had gone back to sleep.

"Let's go through Georgia fast so we won't have to look at it much," John Wesley said.

15 "If I were a little boy," said the grandmother, "I wouldn't talk about my native state that way. Tennessee has the mountains and Georgia has the hills."

"Tennessee is just a hillbilly dumping ground," John Wesley said, "and Georgia is a lousy state too."

"You said it," June Star said.

"In my time," said the grandmother, folding her thin veined fingers, "children were more respectful of their native states and their parents and everything else. People did right then. Oh look at the cute little pickaninny!" she said and pointed to a Negro child standing in the door of a shack. "Wouldn't that make a picture, now?" she asked and they all turned and looked at the little Negro out of the back window. He waved.

"He didn't have any britches on," June Star said.

20 "He probably didn't have any," the grandmother explained. "Little niggers in the country don't have things like we do. If I could paint, I'd paint that picture," she said.

The children exchanged comic books.

The grandmother offered to hold the baby and the children's mother passed him over the front seat to her. She set him on her knee and bounced him and told him about the things they were passing. She rolled her eyes and screwed up her mouth and stuck her leathery thin face into his smooth bland one. Occasionally he gave her a faraway smile. They passed a large cotton field with five or six graves fenced in the middle of it, like a small island. "Look at the graveyard!" the grandmother said, pointing it out. "That was the old family burying ground. That belonged to the plantation."

"Where's the plantation?" John Wesley asked.

"Gone With the Wind,"[1] said the grandmother. "Ha. Ha."

25 When the children finished all the comic books they had brought, they opened the lunch and ate it. The grandmother ate a peanut butter sandwich and an olive and would not let the children throw the box and the paper napkins out the window. When there was nothing else to do they played a game by choosing a cloud and making the other two guess what shape it suggested. John Wesley took one

---

[1]*Gone With the Wind* a 1939 film about the plantation South and the Civil War that was adapted from Margaret Mitchell's 1936 novel of the same name.

the shape of a cow and June Star guessed a cow and John Wesley said, no, an automobile, and June Star said he didn't play fair, and they began to slap each other over the grandmother.

The grandmother said she would tell them a story if they would keep quiet. When she told a story, she rolled her eyes and waved her head and was very dramatic. She said once when she was a maiden lady she had been courted by a Mr. Edgar Atkins Teagarden from Jasper, Georgia. She said he was a very good-looking man and a gentleman and that he brought her a watermelon every Saturday afternoon with his initials cut in it, E.A.T. Well, one Saturday, she said, Mr. Teagarden brought the watermelon and there was nobody at home and he left it on the front porch and returned in his buggy to Jasper, but she never got the watermelon, she said, because a nigger boy ate it when he saw the initials, E.A.T.! This story tickled John Wesley's funny bone and he giggled and giggled but June Star didn't think it was any good. She said she wouldn't marry a man that just brought her a watermelon on Saturday. The grandmother said she would have done well to marry Mr. Teagarden because he was a gentleman and had bought Coca-Cola stock when it first came out and that he had died only a few years ago, a very wealthy man.

They stopped at The Tower for barbecued sandwiches. The Tower was a part-stucco and part-wood filling station and dance hall set in a clearing outside of Timothy. A fat man named Red Sammy Butts ran it and there were signs stuck here and there on the building and for miles up and down the highway saying, TRY RED SAMMY'S FAMOUS BARBECUE. NONE LIKE FAMOUS RED SAMMY'S! RED SAM! THE FAT BOY WITH THE HAPPY LAUGH. A VETERAN! RED SAMMY'S YOUR MAN!

Red Sammy was lying on the bare ground outside The Tower with his head under a truck while a gray monkey about a foot high, chained to a small chinaberry tree, chattered nearby. The monkey sprang back into the tree and got on the highest limb as soon as he saw the children jump out of the car and run toward him.

Inside, The Tower was a long dark room with a counter at one end and tables at the other and dancing space in the middle. They all sat down at a broad table next to the nickelodeon and Red Sam's wife, a tall burnt-brown woman with hair and eyes lighter than her skin, came and took their order. The children's mother put a dime in the machine and played "The Tennessee Waltz," and the grandmother said that tune always made her want to dance. She asked Bailey if he would like to dance but he only glared at her. He didn't have a naturally sunny disposition like she did and trips made him nervous. The grandmother's brown eyes were very bright. She swayed her head from side to side and pretended she was dancing in her chair. June Star said play something she could tap to so the children's mother put in another dime and played a fast number and June Star stepped out onto the dance floor and did her tap routine.

30   "Ain't she cute?" Red Sam's wife said, leaning over the counter. "Would you like to come be my little girl?"

"No, I certainly wouldn't," June Star said. "I wouldn't live in a broken-down place like this for a million bucks!" and she ran back to the table.

"Ain't she cute?" the woman repeated, stretching her mouth politely.

"Aren't you ashamed?" hissed the grandmother.

Red Sam came in and told his wife to quit lounging on the counter and hurry with these people's order. His khaki trousers reached just to his hip bones and his stomach hung over them like a sack of meal swaying under his shirt. He came over and sat down at a table nearby and let out a combination sigh and yodel. "You can't win," he said. "You can't win," and he wiped his sweating red face off with a gray handkerchief. "These days you don't know who to trust," he said. "Ain't that the truth?"

35 "People are certainly not nice like they used to be," said the grandmother.

"Two fellers come in here last week," Red Sammy said, "driving a Chrysler. It was an old beat-up car but it was a good one and these boys looked all right to me. Said they worked at the mill and you know I let them fellers charge the gas they bought? Now why did I do that?"

"Because you're a good man!" the grandmother said at once.

"Yes'm, I suppose so," Red Sam said as if he were struck with this answer.

His wife brought the orders, carrying the five plates all at once without a tray, two in each hand and one balanced on her arm. "It isn't a soul in this green world of God's that you can trust," she said. "And I don't count nobody out of that, not nobody," she repeated, looking at Red Sammy.

40 "Did you read about that criminal, The Misfit, that's escaped?" asked the grandmother.

"I wouldn't be a bit surprised if he didn't attack this place right here," said the woman. "If he hears about it being here, I wouldn't be none surprised to see him. If he hears it's two cent in the cash register, I wouldn't be a tall surprised if he . . . "

"That'll do," Red Sam said. "Go bring these people their Co'Colas," and the woman went off to get the rest of the order.

"A good man is hard to find," Red Sammy said. "Everything is getting terrible. I remember the day you could go off and leave your screen door unlatched. Not no more."

He and the grandmother discussed better times. The old lady said that in her opinion Europe was entirely to blame for the way things were now. She said the way Europe acted you would think we were made of money and Red Sam said it was no use talking about it, she was exactly right. The children ran outside into the white sunlight and looked at the monkey in the lacy chinaberry tree. He was busy catching fleas on himself and biting each one carefully between his teeth as if it were a delicacy.

45 They drove off again into the hot afternoon. The grandmother took cat naps and woke up every five minutes with her own snoring. Outside of Toombsboro she woke up and recalled an old plantation that she had visited in this neighborhood once when she was a young lady. She said the house had six white columns across the front and that there was an avenue of oaks leading up to it and two little wooden trellis arbors on either side in front where you sat down with your suitor after a stroll in the garden. She recalled exactly which road to turn off to get to it. She knew that Bailey would not be willing to lose any time looking at an old house, but the more she talked about it, the more she wanted to see it once again and find out if the little twin arbors were still standing. "There was a secret panel in this house," she said craftily, not telling the truth but wishing that she were, "and the story went that all the family silver was hidden in it when Sherman came through but it was never found . . . "

"Hey!" John Wesley said. "Let's go see it! We'll find it! We'll poke all the woodwork and find it! Who lives there? Where do you turn off at? Hey, Pop, can't we turn off there?"

"We never have seen a house with a secret panel!" June Star shrieked. "Let's go to the house with the secret panel! Hey, Pop, can't we go see the house with the secret panel!"

"It's not far from here, I know," the grandmother said. "It wouldn't take over twenty minutes."

Bailey was looking straight ahead. His jaw was as rigid as a horseshoe. "No," he said.

50   The children began to yell and scream that they wanted to see the house with the secret panel. John Wesley kicked the back of the front seat and June Star hung over her mother's shoulder and whined desperately into her ear that they never had any fun even on their vacation, that they could never do what THEY wanted to do. The baby began to scream and John Wesley kicked the back of the seat so hard that his father could feel the blows in his kidney.

"All right!" he shouted and drew the car to a stop at the side of the road. "Will you all shut up? Will you all just shut up for one second? If you don't shut up, we won't go anywhere."

"It would be very educational for them," the grandmother murmured.

"All right," Bailey said, "but get this. This is the only time we're going to stop for anything like this. This is the one and only time."

"The dirt road that you have to turn down is about a mile back," the grandmother directed. "I marked it when we passed."

55   "A dirt road," Bailey groaned.

After they had turned around and were headed toward the dirt road, the grandmother recalled other points about the house, the beautiful glass over the front doorway and the candle lamp in the hall. John Wesley said that the secret panel was probably in the fireplace.

"You can't go inside this house," Bailey said. "You don't know who lives there."

"While you all talk to the people in front, I'll run around behind and get in a window," John Wesley suggested.

"We'll all stay in the car," his mother said.

60   They turned onto the dirt road and the car raced roughly along in a swirl of pink dust. The grandmother recalled the times when there were no paved roads and thirty miles was a day's journey. The dirt road was hilly and there were sudden washes in it and sharp curves on dangerous embankments. All at once they would be on a hill, looking down over the blue tops of trees for miles around, then the next minute, they would be in a red depression with the dust-coated trees looking down on them.

"This place had better turn up in a minute," Bailey said, "or I'm going to turn around."

The road looked as if no one had traveled on it in months.

"It's not much farther," the grandmother said and just as she said it, a horrible thought came to her. The thought was so embarrassing that she turned red in the face and her eyes dilated and her feet jumped up, upsetting her valise in the corner. The instant the valise moved, the newspaper top she had over the basket under it rose with a snarl and Pitty Sing, the cat, sprang onto Bailey's shoulder.

The children were thrown to the floor and their mother, clutching the baby, was thrown out the door onto the ground; the old lady was thrown into the front seat. The car turned over once and landed right-side-up in a gulch on the side of the road. Bailey remained in the driver's seat with the cat—gray-striped with a broad white face and an orange nose—clinging to his neck like a caterpillar.

65   As soon as the children saw they could move their arms and legs, they scrambled out of the car, shouting, "We've had an ACCIDENT!" The grandmother was curled up under the dashboard, hoping she was injured so that Bailey's wrath would not come down on her all at once. The horrible thought she had had before the accident was that the house she had remembered so vividly was not in Georgia but in Tennessee.

Bailey removed the cat from his neck with both hands and flung it out the window against the side of a pine tree. Then he got out of the car and started looking for the children's mother. She was sitting against the side of the red gutted ditch, holding the screaming baby, but she only had a cut down her face and a broken shoulder. "We've had an ACCIDENT!" the children screamed in a frenzy of delight.

"But nobody's killed," June Star said with disappointment as the grandmother limped out of the car, her hat still pinned to her head but the broken front brim standing up at a jaunty angle and the violet spray hanging off the side. They all sat down in the ditch, except the children, to recover from the shock. They were all shaking.

"Maybe a car will come along," said the children's mother hoarsely.

"I believe I have injured an organ," said the grandmother, pressing her side, but no one answered her. Bailey's teeth were clattering. He had on a yellow sport shirt with bright blue parrots designed in it and his face was as yellow as the shirt. The grandmother decided that she would not mention that the house was in Tennessee.

70   The road was about ten feet above and they could see only the tops of the trees on the other side of it. Behind the ditch they were sitting in there were more woods, tall and dark and deep. In a few minutes they saw a car some distance away on top of a hill, coming slowly as if the occupants were watching them. The grandmother stood up and waved both arms dramatically to attract their attention. The car continued to come on slowly, disappeared around a bend and appeared again, moving even slower on top of the hill they had gone over. It was a big black battered hearselike automobile. There were three men in it.

It came to a stop just over them and for some minutes, the driver looked down with a steady expressionless gaze to where they were sitting, and didn't speak. Then he turned his head and muttered something to the other two and they got out. One was a fat boy in black trousers and a red sweat shirt with a silver stallion embossed on the front of it. He moved around on the right side of them and stood staring, his mouth partly open in a kind of loose grin. The other had on khaki pants and a blue striped coat and a gray hat pulled down very low, hiding most of his face. He came around slowly on the left side. Neither spoke.

The driver got out of the car and stood by the side of it, looking down at them. He was an older man than the other two. His hair was just beginning to gray and he wore silver-rimmed spectacles that gave him a scholarly look. He had a long creased face and didn't have on any shirt or undershirt. He had on blue jeans that were too tight for him and was holding a black hat and a gun. The two boys also had guns.

"We've had an ACCIDENT!" the children screamed.

The grandmother had the peculiar feeling that the bespectacled man was someone she knew. His face was as familiar to her as if she had known him all her life but she could not recall who he was. He moved away from the car and began to come down the embankment, placing his feet carefully so that he wouldn't slip. He had on tan and white shoes and no socks, and his ankles were red and thin. "Good afternoon," he said. "I see you all had you a little spill."

75   "We turned over twice!" said the grandmother.

"Oncet," he corrected. "We seen it happen. Try their car and see will it run, Hiram," he said quietly to the boy with the gray hat.

"What you got that gun for?" John Wesley asked. "Whatcha gonna do with that gun?"

"Lady," the man said to the children's mother, "would you mind calling them children to sit down by you? Children make me nervous. I want all you to sit down right together there where you're at."

"What are you telling us what to do for?" June Star asked.

80   Behind them the line of woods gaped like a dark open mouth. "Come here," said their mother.

"Look here now," Bailey began suddenly, "we're in a predicament! We're in . . ."

The grandmother shrieked. She scrambled to her feet and stood staring. "You're The Misfit!" she said. "I recognized you at once!"

"Yes'm," the man said, smiling slightly as if he were pleased in spite of himself to be known, "but it would have been better for all of you, lady, if you hadn't of reckernized me."

Bailey turned his head sharply and said something to his mother that shocked even the children. The old lady began to cry and The Misfit reddened.

85   "Lady," he said, "don't you get upset. Sometimes a man says things he don't mean. I don't reckon he meant to talk to you thataway."

"You wouldn't shoot a lady, would you?" the grandmother said and removed a clean handkerchief from her cuff and began to slap at her eyes with it.

The Misfit pointed the toe of his shoe into the ground and made a little hole and then covered it up again. "I would hate to have to," he said.

"Listen," the grandmother almost screamed, "I know you're a good man. You don't look a bit like you have common blood. I know you must come from nice people!"

"Yes ma'm," he said, "finest people in the world." When he smiled he showed a row of strong white teeth. "God never made a finer woman than my mother and my daddy's heart was pure gold," he said. The boy with the red sweat shirt had come around behind them and was standing with his gun at his hip. The Misfit squatted down on the ground. "Watch them children, Bobby Lee," he said. "You know they make me nervous." He looked at the six of them huddled together in front of him and he seemed to be embarrassed as if he couldn't think of anything to say. "Ain't a cloud in the sky," he remarked, looking up at it. "Don't see no sun but don't see no cloud neither."

90   "Yes, it's a beautiful day," said the grandmother. "Listen," she said, "you shouldn't call yourself The Misfit because I know you're a good man at heart. I can just look at you and tell."

"Hush!" Bailey yelled, "Hush! Everybody shut up and let me handle this!" He was squatting in the position of a runner about to sprint forward but he didn't move.

"I pre-chate that, lady," The Misfit said and drew a little circle in the ground with the butt of his gun.

"It'll take a half a hour to fix this here car," Hiram called, looking over the raised hood of it.

"Well, first you and Bobby Lee get him and that little boy to step over yonder with you," The Misfit said, pointing to Bailey and John Wesley. "The boys want to ask you something," he said to Bailey. "Would you mind stepping back in them woods there with them?"

95   "Listen," Bailey began, "we're in a terrible predicament! Nobody realizes what this is," and his voice cracked. His eyes were as blue and intense as the parrots in his shirt and he remained perfectly still.

The grandmother reached up to adjust her hat brim as if she were going to the woods with him but it came off in her hand. She stood staring at it and after a second she let it fall on the ground. Hiram pulled Bailey up by the arm as if he were assisting an old man. John Wesley caught hold of his father's hand and Bobby Lee followed. They went off toward the woods and just as they reached the dark edge, Bailey turned and supporting himself against a gray naked pine trunk, he shouted, "I'll be back in a minute, Mamma, wait on me!"

"Come back this instant!" his mother shrilled but they all disappeared into the woods.

"Bailey Boy!" the grandmother called in a tragic voice but she found she was looking at The Misfit squatting on the ground in front of her. "I just know you're a good man," she said desperately. "You're not a bit common!"

"Nome, I ain't a good man," The Misfit said after a second as if he had considered her statement carefully, "but I ain't the worst in the world neither. My daddy said I was a different breed of dog from my brothers and sisters. 'You know,' Daddy said, 'It's some that can live their whole life without asking about it and it's others has to know why it is, and this boy is one of the latters. He's going to be into everything!'" He put on his black hat and looked up suddenly and then away deep into the woods as if he were embarrassed again. "I'm sorry I don't have on a shirt before you ladies," he said, hunching his shoulders slightly. "We buried our clothes that we had on when we escaped and we're just making do until we can get better. We borrowed these from some folks we met," he explained.

100 "That's perfectly all right," the grandmother said. "Maybe Bailey has an extra shirt in his suitcase."

"I'll look and see terrectly," The Misfit said.

"Where are they taking him?" the children's mother screamed.

"Daddy was a card himself," The Misfit said. "You couldn't put anything over on him. He never got in trouble with the Authorities though. Just had the knack of handling them."

"You could be honest too if you'd only try," said the grandmother. "Think how wonderful it would be to settle down and live a comfortable life and not have to think about somebody chasing you all the time."

105 The Misfit kept scratching in the ground with the butt of his gun as if he were thinking about it. "Yes'm, somebody is always after you," he murmured.

The grandmother noticed how thin his shoulder blades were just behind his hat because she was standing up looking down on him. "Do you ever pray?" she asked.

He shook his head. All she saw was the black hat wiggle between his shoulder blades. "Nome," he said.

There was a pistol shot from the woods, followed closely by another. Then silence. The old lady's head jerked around. She could hear the wind move through the tree tops like a long satisfied insuck of breath. "Bailey Boy!" she called.

"I was a gospel singer for a while," The Misfit said. "I been most everything. Been in the arm service, both land and sea, at home and abroad, been twict married, been an undertaker, been with the railroads, plowed Mother Earth, been in a tornado, seen a man burnt alive oncet," and he looked up at the children's mother and the little girl who were sitting close together, their faces white and their eyes glassy; "I even seen a woman flogged," he said.

110 "Pray, pray," the grandmother began, "pray, pray. . . ."

"I never was a bad boy that I remember of," The Misfit said in an almost dreamy voice, "but somewheres along the line I done something wrong and got sent to the penitentiary. I was buried alive," and he looked up and held her attention to him by a steady stare.

"That's when you should have started to pray," she said. "What did you do to get sent up to the penitentiary that first time?"

"Turn to the right, it was a wall," The Misfit said, looking up again at the cloudless sky. "Turn to the left, it was a wall. Look up it was a ceiling, look down it was a floor. I forget what I done, lady. I set there and set there, trying to remember what it was I done and I ain't recalled it to this day. Oncet in a while, I would think it was coming to me, but it never come."

"Maybe they put you in by mistake," the old lady said vaguely.

115 "Nome," he said. "It wasn't no mistake. They had the papers on me."

"You must have stolen something," she said.

The Misfit sneered slightly. "Nobody had nothing I wanted," he said. "It was a head-doctor at the penitentiary said what I had done was kill my daddy but I known that for a lie. My daddy died in nineteen ought nineteen of the epidemic flu and I never had a thing to do with it. He was buried in the Mount Hopewell Baptist churchyard and you can go there and see for yourself."

"If you would pray," the old lady said, "Jesus would help you."

"That's right," The Misfit said.

120 "Well then, why don't you pray?" she asked trembling with delight suddenly.

"I don't want no hep," he said. "I'm doing all right by myself."

Bobby Lee and Hiram came ambling back from the woods. Bobby Lee was dragging a yellow shirt with bright blue parrots on it.

"Throw me that shirt, Bobby Lee," The Misfit said. The shirt came flying at him and landed on his shoulder and he put it on. The grandmother couldn't name what the shirt reminded her of. "No, lady," The Misfit said while he was buttoning it up, "I found out the crime don't matter. You can do one thing or you can do another, kill a man or take a tire off his car, because sooner or later you're going to forget what it was you done and just be punished for it."

The children's mother had begun to make heaving noises as if she couldn't get her breath. "Lady," he asked, "would you and that little girl like to step off yonder with Bobby Lee and Hiram and join your husband?"

125 "Yes, thank you," the mother said faintly. Her left arm dangled helplessly and she was holding the baby, who had gone to sleep, in the other. "Hep that lady up, Hiram," The Misfit said as she struggled to climb out of the ditch, "and Bobby Lee, you hold onto that little girl's hand."

"I don't want to hold hands with him," June Star said. "He reminds me of a pig."

The fat boy blushed and laughed and caught her by the arm and pulled her off into the woods after Hiram and her mother.

Alone with The Misfit, the grandmother found that she had lost her voice. There was not a cloud in the sky nor any sun. There was nothing around her but woods. She wanted to tell him that he must pray. She opened and closed her mouth several times before anything came out. Finally she found herself saying, "Jesus, Jesus," meaning, Jesus will help you, but the way she was saying it, it sounded as if she might be cursing.

"Yes'm," The Misfit said as if he agreed. "Jesus thown everything off balance. It was the same case with Him as with me except He hadn't committed any crime and they could prove I had committed one because they had the papers on me. Of course," he said, "they never shown me my papers. That's why I sign myself now. I said long ago, you get you a signature and sign everything you do and keep a copy of it. Then you'll know what you done and you can hold up the crime to the punishment and see do they match and in the end you'll have something to prove you ain't been treated right. I call myself The Misfit," he said, "because I can't make what all I done wrong fit what all I gone through in punishment."

130 There was a piercing scream from the woods, followed closely by a pistol report. "Does it seem right to you, lady, that one is punished a heap and another ain't punished at all?"

"Jesus!" the old lady cried. "You've got good blood! I know you wouldn't shoot a lady! I know you come from nice people! Pray! Jesus, you ought not to shoot a lady. I'll give you all the money I've got!"

"Lady," The Misfit said, looking beyond her far into the woods, "there never was a body that give the undertaker a tip."

There were two more pistol reports and the grandmother raised her head like a parched old turkey hen crying for water and called, "Bailey Boy, Bailey Boy!" as if her heart would break.

"Jesus was the only One that ever raised the dead," The Misfit continued, "and He shouldn't have done it. He thown everything off balance. If He did what He said, then it's nothing for you to do but thow away everything and follow Him, and if He didn't, then it's nothing for you to do but enjoy the few minutes you got left the best way you can—by killing somebody or burning down his house or doing some other meanness to him. No pleasure but meanness," he said and his voice had become almost a snarl.

135   "Maybe He didn't raise the dead," the old lady mumbled, not knowing what she was saying and feeling so dizzy that she sank down in the ditch with her legs twisted under her.

"I wasn't there so I can't say He didn't," The Misfit said. "I wisht I had of been there," he said, hitting the ground with his fist. "It ain't right I wasn't there because if I had of been there I would of known. Listen lady," he said in a high voice, "if I had of been there I would of known and I wouldn't be like I am now." His voice seemed about to crack and the grandmother's head cleared for an instant. She saw the man's face twisted close to her own as if he were going to cry and she murmured, "Why you're one of my babies. You're one of my own children!" She reached out and touched him on the shoulder. The Misfit sprang back as if a snake had bitten him and shot her three times through the chest. Then he put his gun down on the ground and took off his glasses and began to clean them.

Hiram and Bobby Lee returned from the woods and stood over the ditch, looking down at the grandmother who half sat and half lay in a puddle of blood with her legs crossed under her like a child's and her face smiling up at the cloudless sky.

Without his glasses, The Misfit's eyes were red-rimmed and pale and defenseless-looking. "Take her off and thow her where you thown the others," he said, picking up the cat that was rubbing itself against his leg.

"She was a talker, wasn't she?" Bobby Lee said, sliding down the ditch with a yodel.

140   "She would of been a good woman," The Misfit said, "if it had been somebody there to shoot her every minute of her life."

"Some fun!" Bobby Lee said.

"Shut up, Bobby Lee," The Misfit said. "It's no real pleasure in life."

[1953]

Joining the Conversation: Critical Thinking and Writing

1. Explain the significance of the title "A Good Man Is Hard to Find."
2. Interpret and evaluate The Misfit's comment on the grandmother: "She would of been a good woman if it had been somebody there to shoot her every minute of her life."
3. O'Connor reported that once, when she read aloud "A Good Man Is Hard to Find," one of her hearers said that "it was a shame someone with so much talent

should look upon life as a horror story." Two questions: What evidence of O'Connor's "talent" do you see in the story, and does the story suggest that O'Connor looked on life as a horror story?

4. What are the values of the members of the family?

5. Flannery O'Connor, a Roman Catholic, wrote, "I see from the standpoint of Christian orthodoxy. This means that for me the meaning of life is centered in our Redemption by Christ and what I see in the world I see in relation to that." In the light of this statement, and drawing on "A Good Man Is Hard to Find," explain what O'Connor saw in the world.

MyLiteratureLab® *For additional resources for "A Good Man Is Hard to Find," log in to* www.myliteraturelab.com *where you will find a Longman Lecture, Interactive Reading, Comprehension Quiz, Short Evaluation Exercises, and Essay Prompts, as well as an About the Author, Links, and Critical Overview for O'Connor (under Student Resources).*

Revelation

The doctor's waiting room, which was very small, was almost full when the Turpins entered and Mrs. Turpin, who was very large, made it look even smaller by her presence. She stood looming at the head of the magazine table set in the center of it, a living demonstration that the room was inadequate and ridiculous. Her little bright black eyes took in all the patients as she sized up the seating situation. There was one vacant chair and a place on a sofa occupied by a blond child in a dirty blue romper who should have been told to move over and make room for the lady. He was five or six, but Mrs. Turpin saw at once that no one was going to tell him to move over. He was slumped down in the seat, his arms idle at his sides and his eyes idle in his head; his nose ran unchecked.

Mrs. Turpin put a firm hand on Claud's shoulder and said in a voice that included anyone who wanted to listen, "Claud, you sit in that chair there," and gave him a push down into the vacant one. Claud was florid and bald and sturdy, somewhat shorter than Mrs. Turpin, but he sat down as if he were accustomed to doing what she told him to.

Mrs. Turpin remained standing. The only man in the room besides Claud was a lean stringy old fellow with a rusty hand spread out on each knee, whose eyes were closed as if he were asleep or dead or pretending to be so as not to get up and offer her his seat. Her gaze settled agreeably on a well-dressed grey-haired lady whose eyes met hers and whose expression said: If that child belonged to me, he would have some manners and move over—there's plenty of room there for you and him too.

Claud looked up with a sigh and made as if to rise.

5   "Sit down," Mrs. Turpin said. "You know you're not supposed to stand on that leg. He has an ulcer on his leg," she explained.

Claud lifted his foot onto the magazine table and rolled his trouser leg up to reveal a purple swelling on a plump marble-white calf.

"My!" the pleasant lady said. "How did you do that?"

"A cow kicked him," Mrs. Turpin said.

"Goodness!" said the lady.

10   Claud rolled his trouser leg down.

"Maybe the little boy would move over," the lady suggested, but the child did not stir.

"Somebody will be leaving in a minute," Mrs. Turpin said. She could not understand why a doctor—with as much money as they made charging five dollars a day to just stick their head in the hospital door and look at you—couldn't afford a decent-sized waiting room. This one was hardly bigger than a garage. The table was cluttered with limp-looking magazines and at one end of it there was a big green glass ash tray full of cigaret butts and cotton wads with little blood spots on them. If she had had anything to do with the running of the place, that would have been emptied every so often. There were no chairs against the wall at the head of the room. It had a rectangular-shaped panel in it that permitted a view of the office where the nurse came and went and the secretary listened to the radio. A plastic fern in a gold pot sat in the opening and trailed its fronds down almost to the floor. The radio was softly playing gospel music.

Just then the inner door opened and a nurse with the highest stack of yellow hair Mrs. Turpin had ever seen put her face in the crack and called for the next patient. The woman sitting beside Claud grasped the two arms of her chair and hoisted herself up; she pulled her dress free from her legs and lumbered through the door where the nurse had disappeared.

Mrs. Turpin eased into the vacant chair, which held her tight as a corset. "I wish I could reduce," she said, and rolled her eyes and gave a comic sigh.

15   "Oh, *you* aren't fat," the stylish lady said.

"Ooooo I am too," Mrs. Turpin said. "Claud he eats all he wants to and never weighs over one hundred and seventy-five pounds, but me I just look at something good to eat and I gain some weight," and her stomach and shoulders shook with laughter. "You can eat all you want to, can't you, Claud?" she asked, turning to him.

Claud only grinned.

"Well, as long as you have such a good disposition," the stylish lady said, "I don't think it makes a bit of difference what size you are. You just can't beat a good disposition."

Next to her was a fat girl of eighteen or nineteen, scowling into a thick blue book which Mrs. Turpin saw was entitled *Human Development*. The girl raised her head and directed her scowl at Mrs. Turpin as if she did not like her looks. She appeared annoyed that anyone should speak while she tried to read. The poor girl's face was blue with acne and Mrs. Turpin thought how pitiful it was to have a face like that at that age. She gave the girl a friendly smile but the girl only scowled the harder. Mrs. Turpin herself was fat but she had always had good skin, and, though she was forty-seven years old, there was not a wrinkle in her face except around her eyes from laughing too much.

20   Next to the ugly girl was the child, still in exactly the same position, and next to him was a thin leathery old woman in a cotton print dress. She and Claud had three sacks of chicken feed in their pump house that was in the same print. She had seen from the first that the child belonged with the old woman. She could tell by the way they sat—kind of vacant and white-trashy, as if they would sit there until Doomsday if nobody called and told them to get up. And at right angles but next to the well-dressed pleasant lady was a lank-faced woman who was certainly the child's mother. She had on a yellow sweat shirt and wine-colored slacks, both gritty-looking, and the rims of her lips were stained with snuff. Her dirty yellow hair was tied behind with a little piece of red paper ribbon. Worse than niggers any day, Mrs. Turpin thought.

The gospel hymn playing was, "When I looked up and He looked down," and Mrs. Turpin, who knew it, supplied the last line mentally, "And wona these days I know I'll we-era crown."

Without appearing to, Mrs. Turpin always noticed people's feet. The well-dressed lady had on red and grey suede shoes to match her dress. Mrs. Turpin had on her good black patent leather pumps. The ugly girl had on Girl Scout shoes and heavy socks. The old woman had on tennis shoes and the white-trashy mother had on what appeared to be bedroom slippers, black straw with gold braid threaded through them—exactly what you would have expected her to have on.

Sometimes at night when she couldn't go to sleep, Mrs. Turpin would occupy herself with the question of who she would have chosen to be if she couldn't have been herself. If Jesus had said to her before he made her, "There's only two places available for you. You can either be a nigger or white-trash," what would she have said? "Please, Jesus, please," she would have said, "just let me wait until there's another place available," and he would have said, "No, you have to go right now and I have only those two places so make up your mind." She would have wiggled and squirmed and begged and pleaded but it would have been no use and finally she would have said, "All right, make me a nigger then—but that don't mean a trashy one." And he would have made her a neat clean respectable Negro-woman, herself but black.

Next to the child's mother was a red-headed youngish woman, reading one of the magazines and working a piece of chewing gum, hell for leather, as Claud would say. Mrs. Turpin could not see the woman's feet. She was not white-trash, just common. Sometimes Mrs. Turpin occupied herself at night naming the classes of people. On the bottom of the heap were most colored people, not the kind she would have been if she had been one, but most of them; then next to them—not above, just away from—were the white-trash; then above them were the home-owners, and above them the home-and-land owners, to which she and Claud belonged. Above she and Claud were people with a lot of money and much bigger houses and much more land. But here the complexity of it would begin to bear in on her, for some of the people with a lot of money were common and ought to be below she and Claud and some of the people who had good blood had lost their money and had to rent and then there were colored people who owned their homes and land as well. There was a colored dentist in town who had two red Lincolns and a swimming pool and a farm with registered white-face cattle on it. Usually by the time she had fallen asleep all the classes of people were moiling and roiling around in her head, and she would dream they were all crammed in together in a box car, being ridden off to be put in a gas oven.

25   "That's a beautiful clock," she said and nodded to her right. It was a big wall clock, the face encased in a brass sunburst.

"Yes, it's very pretty," the stylish lady said agreeably. "And right on the dot too," she added, glancing at her watch.

The ugly girl beside her cast an eye upward at the clock, smirked, then looked directly at Mrs. Turpin and smirked again. Then she returned her eyes to her book. She was obviously the lady's daughter because, although they didn't look anything alike as to disposition, they both had the same shape of face and the same blue eyes. On the lady they sparkled pleasantly but in the girl's seared face they appeared alternately to smolder and to blaze.

What if Jesus had said, "All right, you can be white-trash or a nigger or ugly"!

Mrs. Turpin felt an awful pity for the girl, though she thought it was one thing to be ugly and another to act ugly.

30   The woman with the snuff-stained lips turned around in her chair and looked up at the clock. Then she turned back and appeared to look a little to the side of Mrs. Turpin. There was a cast in one of her eyes. "You want to know wher you can get one of themther clocks?" she asked in a loud voice.

    "No, I already have a nice clock," Mrs. Turpin said. Once somebody like her got a leg in the conversation, she would be all over it.

    "You can get you one with green stamps," the woman said. "That's most likely wher he got hisn. Save you up enough, you can get you most anything. I got me some joo'ry."

    Ought to have got you a wash rag and some soap, Mrs. Turpin thought.

    "I get contour sheets with mine," the pleasant lady said.

35   The daughter slammed her book shut. She looked straight in front of her, directly through Mrs. Turpin and on through the yellow curtain and the plate glass window which made the wall behind her. The girl's eyes seemed lit all of a sudden with a peculiar light, an unnatural light like night road signs give. Mrs. Turpin turned her head to see if there was anything going on outside that she should see, but she could not see anything. Figures passing cast only a pale shadow through the curtain. There was no reason the girl should single her out for her ugly looks.

    "Miss Finley," the nurse said, cracking the door. The gum chewing woman got up and passed in front of her and Claud and went into the office. She had on red high-heeled shoes.

    Directly across the table, the ugly girl's eyes were fixed on Mrs. Turpin as if she had some very special reason for disliking her.

    "This is wonderful weather, isn't it?" the girl's mother said.

    "It's good weather for cotton if you can get the niggers to pick it," Mrs. Turpin said, "but niggers don't want to pick cotton any more. You can't get the white folks to pick it and now you can't get the niggers—because they got to be right up there with the white folks."

40   "They gonna *try* anyways," the white-trash woman said, leaning forward.

    "Do you have one of those cotton picking machines?" the pleasant lady asked.

    "No," Mrs. Turpin said, "they leave half the cotton in the field. We don't have much cotton anyway. If you want to make it farming now, you have to have a little of everything. We got a couple of acres of cotton and a few hogs and chickens and just enough white-face that Claud can look after them himself."

    "One thang I don't want," the white-trash woman said, wiping her mouth with the back of her hand. "Hogs. Nasty stinking things, a-gruntin and a-rootin all over the place."

    Mrs. Turpin gave her the merest edge of her attention. "Our hogs are not dirty and they don't stink," she said. "They're cleaner than some children I've seen. Their feet never touch the ground. We have a pig-parlor—that's where you raise them on concrete," she explained to the pleasant lady, "and Claud scoots them down with the hose every afternoon and washes off the floor." Cleaner by far than that child right there, she thought. Poor nasty little thing. He had not moved except to put the thumb of his dirty hand into his mouth.

45   The woman turned her face away from Mrs. Turpin. "I know I wouldn't scoot down no hog with no hose," she said to the wall.

    You wouldn't have no hog to scoot down, Mrs. Turpin said to herself.

    "A-gruntin and a-rootin and a-groanin," the woman muttered.

    "We got a little of everything," Mrs. Turpin said to the pleasant lady. "It's no use in having more than you can handle yourself with help like it is. We found enough niggers to pick our cotton this year but Claud he has to go after them and take them home again in the evening. They can't walk that half a mile. No they can't. I tell you," she said and laughed merrily, "I sure am tired of buttering up niggers, but you got to love em if you want em to work for you. When they come in the morning, I run out and I say, 'Hi yawl this morning?' and when Claud drives them off to the field I just wave to beat the band and they just wave back." And she waved her hand rapidly to illustrate.

"Like you read out of the same book," the lady said, showing she understood perfectly.

50   "Child, yes," Mrs. Turpin said. "And when they come in from the field, I run out with a bucket of icewater. That's the way it's going to be from now on," she said. "You may as well face it."

"One thang I know," the white-trash woman said. "Two thangs I ain't going to do: love no niggers or scoot down no hog with no hose." And she let out a bark of contempt.

The look that Mrs. Turpin and the pleasant lady exchanged indicated they both understood that you had to *have* certain things before you could *know* certain things. But every time Mrs. Turpin exchanged a look with the lady, she was aware that the ugly girl's peculiar eyes were still on her, and she had trouble bringing her attention back to the conversation.

"When you got something," she said, "you got to look after it." And when you ain't got a thing but breath and britches, she added to herself, you can afford to come to town every morning and just sit on the Court House coping and spit.

A grotesque revolving shadow passed across the curtain behind her and was thrown palely on the opposite wall. Then a bicycle clattered down against the outside of the building. The door opened and a colored boy glided in with a tray from the drug store. It had two large red and white paper cups on it with tops on them. He was a tall, very black boy in discolored white pants and a green nylon shirt. He was chewing gum slowly as if to music. He set the tray down in the office opening next to the fern and stuck his head through to look for the secretary. She was not in there. He rested his arms on the ledge and waited, his narrow bottom stuck out, swaying slowly to the left and right. He raised a hand over his head and scratched the base of his skull.

55   "You see that button there, boy?" Mrs. Turpin said. "You can punch that and she'll come. She's probably in the back somewhere."

"Is that right?" the boy said agreeably, as if he had never seen the button before. He leaned to the right and put his finger on it. "She sometime out," he said and twisted around to face his audience, his elbows behind him on the counter. The nurse appeared and he twisted back again. She handed him a dollar and he rooted in his pocket and made the change and counted it out to her. She gave him fifteen cents for a tip and he went out with the empty tray. The heavy door swung to slowly and closed at length with the sound of suction. For a moment no one spoke.

"They ought to send all them niggers back to Africa," the white-trash woman said. "That's wher they come from in the first place."

"Oh, I couldn't do without my good colored friends," the pleasant lady said.

"There's a heap of things worse than a nigger," Mrs. Turpin agreed. "It's all kinds of them just like it's all kinds of us."

60   "Yes, and it takes all kinds to make the world go round," the lady said in her musical voice.

As she said it, the raw-complexioned girl snapped her teeth together. Her lower lip turned downwards and inside out, revealing the pale pink inside of her mouth. After a second it rolled back up. It was the ugliest face Mrs. Turpin had ever seen anyone make and for a moment she was certain that the girl had made it at

her. She was looking at her as if she had known and disliked her all her life—all
of Mrs. Turpin's life, it seemed too, not just all the girl's life. Why, girl, I don't even
know you, Mrs. Turpin said silently.

She forced her attention back to the discussion. "It wouldn't be practical to
send them back to Africa," she said. "They wouldn't want to go. They got it too
good here."

"Wouldn't be what they wanted—if I had anythang to do with it," the woman said.

"It wouldn't be a way in the world you could get all the niggers back over
there," Mrs. Turpin said. "They'd be hiding out and lying down and turning sick on
you and wailing and hollering and raring and pitching. It wouldn't be a way in the
world to get them over there."

65   "They got over here," the trashy woman said. "Get back like they got over."

"It wasn't so many of them then," Mrs. Turpin explained.

The woman looked at Mrs. Turpin as if here was an idiot indeed but Mrs. Turpin
was not bothered by the look, considering where it came from.

"Nooo," she said, "they're going to stay here where they can go to New York
and marry white folks and improve their color. That's what they all want to do,
every one of them, improve their color."

"You know what comes of that, don't you?" Claud asked.

70   "No, Claud, what?" Mrs. Turpin said.

Claud's eyes twinkled. "White-faced niggers," he said with never a smile.

Everybody in the office laughed except the white-trash and the ugly girl. The
girl gripped the book in her lap with white fingers. The trashy woman looked
around her from face to face as if she thought they were all idiots. The old woman
in the feed sack dress continued to gaze expressionless across the floor at the high-
top shoes of the man opposite her, the one who had been pretending to be asleep
when the Turpins came in. He was laughing heartily, his hands still spread out on
his knees. The child had fallen to the side and was lying now almost face down in
the old woman's lap.

While they recovered from their laughter, the nasal chorus on the radio kept
the room from silence.

> You go to blank blank
> And I'll go to mine
> But we'll all blank along
> To-geth-ther,
> And all along the blank
> We'll hep each other out
> Smile-ling in any kind of
> Weath-ther!

Mrs. Turpin didn't catch every word but she caught enough to agree with the
spirit of the song and it turned her thoughts sober. To help anybody out that
needed it was her philosophy of life. She never spared herself when she found
somebody in need, whether they were white or black, trash or decent. And of all
she had to be thankful for, she was most thankful that this was so. If Jesus had said,
"You can be high society and have all the money you want and be thin and svelte-
like, but you can't be a good woman with it," she would have had to say, "Well
don't make me that then. Make me a good woman and it don't matter what else,
how fat or how ugly or how poor!" Her heart rose. He had not made her a nigger
or white-trash or ugly! He had made her herself and given her a little of everything.
Jesus, thank you! she said. Thank you thank you thank you! Whenever she counted

her blessings she felt as buoyant as if she weighed one hundred and twenty-five pounds instead of one hundred and eighty.

75   "What's wrong with your little boy?" the pleasant lady asked the white-trashy woman.

"He has a ulcer," the woman said proudly. "He ain't give me a minute's peace since he was born. Him and her are just alike," she said, nodding at the old woman, who was running her leathery fingers through the child's pale hair. "Look like I can't get nothing down them two but Co'Cola and candy."

That's all you try to get down em, Mrs. Turpin said to herself. Too lazy to light the fire. There was nothing you could tell her about people like them that she didn't know already. And it was not just that they didn't have anything. Because if you gave them everything, in two weeks it would all be broken or filthy or they would have chopped it up for lightwood. She knew all this from her own experience. Help them you must, but help them you couldn't.

All at once the ugly girl turned her lips inside out again. Her eyes were fixed like two drills on Mrs. Turpin. This time there was no mistaking that there was something urgent behind them.

Girl, Mrs. Turpin exclaimed silently, I haven't done a thing to you! The girl might be confusing her with somebody else. There was no need to sit by and let herself be intimidated. "You must be in college," she said boldly, looking directly at the girl. "I see you reading a book there."

80   The girl continued to stare and pointedly did not answer.

Her mother blushed at this rudeness. "The lady asked you a question, Mary Grace," she said under her breath.

"I have ears," Mary Grace said.

The poor mother blushed again. "Mary Grace goes to Wellesley College," she explained. She twisted one of the buttons on her dress. "In Massachusetts," she added with a grimace. "And in the summer she just keeps right on studying. Just reads all the time, a real book worm. She's done real well at Wellesley; she's taking English and Math and History and Psychology and Social Studies," she rattled on, "and I think it's too much. I think she ought to get out and have fun."

The girl looked as if she would like to hurl them all through the plate glass window.

85   "Way up north," Mrs. Turpin murmured and thought, well, it hasn't done much for her manners.

"I'd almost rather to have him sick," the white-trash woman said, wrenching the attention back to herself. "He's so mean when he ain't. Look like some children just take natural to meanness. It's some gets bad when they get sick but he was the opposite. Took sick and turned good. He don't give me no trouble now. It's me waitin to see the doctor," she said.

If I was going to send anybody back to Africa, Mrs. Turpin thought, it would be your kind, woman. "Yes, indeed," she said aloud, but looking up at the ceiling, "it's a heap of things worse than a nigger." And dirtier than a hog, she added to herself.

"I think people with bad dispositions are more to be pitied than anyone on earth," the pleasant lady said in a voice that was decidedly thin.

"I thank the Lord he has blessed me with a good one," Mrs. Turpin said. "The day has never dawned that I couldn't find something to laugh at."

90   "Not since she married me anyways," Claud said with a comical straight face.

Everybody laughed except the girl and the white-trash.

Mrs. Turpin's stomach shook. "He's such a caution," she said, "that I can't help but laugh at him."

The girl made a loud ugly noise through her teeth.

Her mother's mouth grew thin and tight. "I think the worst thing in the world," she said, "is an ungrateful person. To have everything and not appreciate it. I know a girl," she said, "who has parents who would give her anything, a little brother who loves her dearly, who is getting a good education, who wears the best clothes, but who can never say a kind word to anyone, who never smiles, who just criticizes and complains all day long."

95   "Is she too old to paddle?" Claud asked.

The girl's face was almost purple.

"Yes," the lady said. "I'm afraid there's nothing to do but leave her to her folly. Some day she'll wake up and it'll be too late."

"It never hurt anyone to smile," Mrs. Turpin said. "It just makes you feel better all over."

"Of course," the lady said sadly, "but there are just some people you can't tell anything to. They can't take criticism."

100   "If it's one thing I am," Mrs. Turpin said with feeling, "it's grateful. When I think who all I could have been besides myself and what all I got, a little of everything, and a good disposition besides, I just feel like shouting, 'Thank you, Jesus, for making everything the way it is!' It could have been different!" For one thing, somebody else could have got Claud. At the thought of this, she was flooded with gratitude and a terrible pang of joy ran through her. "Oh thank you, Jesus, Jesus, thank you!" she cried aloud.

The book struck her directly over her left eye. It struck almost at the same instant that she realized the girl was about to hurl it. Before she could utter a sound, the raw face came crashing across the table toward her, howling. The girl's fingers sank like clamps into the soft flesh of her neck. She heard the mother cry out and Claud shout, "Whoa!" There was an instant when she was certain that she was about to be in an earthquake.

All at once her vision narrowed and she saw everything as if it were happening in a small room far away, or as if she were looking at it through the wrong end of a telescope. Claud's face crumpled and fell out of sight. The nurse ran in, then out, then in again. Then the gangling figure of the doctor rushed out of the inner door. Magazines flew this way and that as the table turned over. The girl fell with a thud and Mrs. Turpin's vision suddenly reversed itself and she saw everything large instead of small. The eyes of the white-trashy woman were staring hugely at the floor. There the girl, held down on one side by the nurse and on the other by her mother, was wrenching and turning in their grasp. The doctor was kneeling astride her, trying to hold her arm down. He managed after a second to sink a long needle into it.

Mrs. Turpin felt entirely hollow except for her heart which swung from side to side as if it were agitated in a great empty drum of flesh.

"Somebody that's not busy call for the ambulance," the doctor said in the off-hand voice young doctors adopt for terrible occasions.

105   Mrs. Turpin could not have moved a finger. The old man who had been sitting next to her skipped nimbly into the office and made the call, for the secretary still seemed to be gone.

"Claud!" Mrs. Turpin called.

He was not in his chair. She knew she must jump up and find him but she felt like someone trying to catch a train in a dream, when everything moves in slow motion and the faster you try to run the slower you go.

"Here I am," a suffocated voice, very unlike Claud's, said.

He was doubled up in the corner on the floor, pale as paper, holding his leg. She wanted to get up and go to him but she could not move. Instead, her gaze was drawn slowly downward to the churning face on the floor, which she could see over the doctor's shoulder.

110   The girl's eyes stopped rolling and focused on her. They seemed a much lighter blue than before, as if a door that had been tightly closed behind them was now open to admit light and air.

Mrs. Turpin's head cleared and her power of motion returned. She leaned forward until she was looking directly into the fierce brilliant eyes. There was no doubt in her mind that the girl did know her, knew her in some intense and personal way, beyond time and place and condition. "What you got to say to me?" she asked hoarsely and held her breath, waiting, as for a revelation.

The girl raised her head. Her gaze locked with Mrs. Turpin's. "Go back to hell where you came from, you old wart hog," she whispered. Her voice was low but clear. Her eyes burned for a moment as if she saw with pleasure that her message had struck its target.

Mrs. Turpin sank back in her chair.

After a moment the girl's eyes closed and she turned her head wearily to the side.

115   The doctor rose and handed the nurse the empty syringe. He leaned over and put both hands for a moment on the mother's shoulders, which were shaking. She was sitting on the floor, her lips pressed together, holding Mary Grace's hand in her lap. The girl's fingers were gripped like a baby's around her thumb. "Go on to the hospital," he said. "I'll call and make the arrangements."

"Now let's see that neck," he said in a jovial voice to Mrs. Turpin. He began to inspect her neck with his first two fingers. Two little moonshaped lines like pink fish bones were indented over her windpipe. There was the beginning of an angry red swelling above her eye. His fingers passed over this also.

"Lea' me be," she said thickly and shook him off. "See about Claud. She kicked him."

"I'll see about him in a minute," he said and felt her pulse. He was a thin gray-haired man, given to pleasantries. "Go home and have yourself a vacation the rest of the day," he said and patted her on the shoulder.

Quit your pattin me, Mrs. Turpin growled to herself.

120   "And put an ice pack over that eye," he said. Then he went and squatted down beside Claud and looked at his leg. After a moment he pulled him up and Claud limped after him into the office.

Until the ambulance came, the only sounds in the room were the tremulous moans of the girl's mother, who continued to sit on the floor. The white-trash woman did not take her eyes off the girl. Mrs. Turpin looked straight ahead at nothing. Presently the ambulance drew up, a long dark shadow, behind the curtain. The attendants came in and set the stretcher down beside the girl and lifted her expertly onto it and carried her out. The nurse helped the mother gather up her things. The shadow of the ambulance moved silently away and the nurse came back in the office.

"That ther girl is going to be a lunatic, ain't she?" the white-trash woman asked the nurse, but the nurse kept on to the back and never answered her.

"Yes, she's going to be a lunatic," the white-trash woman said to the rest of them.

"Po' critter," the old woman murmured. The child's face was still in her lap. His eyes looked idly out over her knees. He had not moved during the disturbance except to draw one leg up under him.

125   "I thank Gawd," the white-trash woman said fervently, "I ain't a lunatic."

Claud came limping out and the Turpins went home.

As their pick-up truck turned into their own dirt road and made the crest of the hill, Mrs. Turpin gripped the window ledge and looked out suspiciously. The land sloped gracefully down through a field dotted with lavender weeds and at the start of the rise their small yellow frame house, with its little flower beds spread out around it like a fancy apron, sat primly in its accustomed place between two giant hickory trees. She would not have been startled to see a burnt wound between two blackened chimneys.

Neither of them felt like eating so they put on their house clothes and lowered the shade in the bedroom and lay down, Claud with his leg on a pillow and herself with a damp washcloth over her eye. The instant she was flat on her back, the image of a razor-backed hog with warts on its face and horns coming out behind its ears snorted into her head. She moaned, a low quiet moan.

"I am not," she said tearfully, "a wart hog. From hell." But the denial had no force. The girl's eyes and her words, even the tone of her voice, low but clear, directed only to her, brooked no repudiation. She had been singled out for the message, though there was trash in the room to whom it might justly have been applied. The full force of this fact struck her only now. There was a woman there who was neglecting her own child but she had been overlooked. The message had been given to Ruby Turpin, a respectable, hard-working, church-going woman. The tears dried. Her eyes began to burn instead with wrath.

130   She rose on her elbow and the washcloth fell into her hand. Claud was lying on his back, snoring. She wanted to tell him what the girl had said. At the same time she did not wish to put the image of herself as a wart hog from hell into his mind.

"Hey, Claud," she muttered and pushed his shoulder.

Claud opened one pale baby blue eye.

She looked into it warily. He did not think about anything. He just went his way.

"Wha, whasit?" he said and closed the eye again.

135   "Nothing," she said. "Does your leg pain you?"

"Hurts like hell," Claud said.

"It'll quit terreckly," she said and lay back down. In a moment Claud was snoring again. For the rest of the afternoon they lay there. Claud slept. She scowled at the ceiling. Occasionally she raised her fist and made a small stabbing motion over her chest as if she was defending her innocence to invisible guests who were like the comforters of Job, reasonable-seeming but wrong.

About five-thirty Claud stirred. "Got to go after those niggers," he sighed, not moving.

She was looking straight up as if there were unintelligible handwriting on the ceiling. The protuberance over her eye had turned a greenish-blue. "Listen here," she said.

140   "What"?

"Kiss me."

Claud leaned over and kissed her loudly on the mouth. He pinched her side and their hands interlocked. Her expression of ferocious concentration did not change. Claud got up, groaning and growling, and limped off. She continued to study the ceiling.

She did not get up until she heard the pick-up truck coming back with the Negroes. Then she rose and thrust her feet in her brown oxfords, which she did not bother to lace, and stumped out onto the back porch and got her red plastic bucket. She emptied a tray of ice cubes into it and filled it half full of water and went out into the back yard. Every afternoon after Claud brought the hands in, one of the boys helped him put out hay and the rest waited in the back of the truck until he was ready to take them home. The truck was parked in the shade under one of the hickory trees.

"Hi yawl this evening?" Mrs. Turpin asked grimly, appearing with the bucket and the dipper. There were three women and a boy in the truck.

145   "Us doin nicely," the oldest woman said. "Hi you doin?" and her gaze stuck immediately on the dark lump on Mrs. Turpin's forehead. "You done fell down, ain't you?" she asked in a solicitous voice. The old woman was dark and almost toothless. She had on an old felt hat of Claud's set back on her head. The other two women were younger and lighter and they both had new bright green sun hats. One of them had hers on her head; the other had taken hers off and the boy was grinning beneath it.

Mrs. Turpin set the bucket down on the floor of the truck. "Yawl hep your-selves," she said. She looked around to make sure Claud had gone. "No. I didn't fall down," she said, folding her arms. "It was something worse than that."

"Ain't nothing bad happen to you!" the old woman said. She said it as if they all knew Mrs. Turpin was protected in some special way by Divine Providence. "You just had you a little fall."

"We were in town at the doctor's office for where the cow kicked Mr. Turpin," Mrs. Turpin said in a flat tone that indicated they could leave off their foolishness. "And there was this girl there. A big fat girl with her face all broke out. I could look at that girl and tell she was peculiar but I couldn't tell how. And me and her mama were just talking and going along and all of a sudden WHAM! She throws this big book she was reading at me and . . . ."

"Naw!" the old woman cried out.

150   "And then she jumps over the table and commences to choke me."

"Naw!" they all exclaimed, "naw!"

"Hi come she do that?" the old woman asked. "What ail her?"

Mrs. Turpin only glared in front of her.

"Somethin ail her," the old woman said.

155   "They carried her off in an ambulance," Mrs. Turpin continued, "but before she went she was rolling on the floor and they were trying to hold her down to give her a shot and she said something to me." She paused. "You know what she said to me?"

"What she say?" they asked.

"She said," Mrs. Turpin began, and stopped, her face very dark and heavy. The sun was getting whiter and whiter, blanching the sky overhead so that the leaves of the hickory tree were black in the face of it. She could not bring forth the words. "Something real ugly," she muttered.

"She sho shouldn't said nothin ugly to you," the old woman said. "You so sweet. You the sweetest lady I know."

"She pretty too," the one with the hat on said.

160   "And stout," the other one said. "I never knowed no sweeter white lady."

"That's the truth befo' Jesus," the old woman said. "Amen! You des as sweet and pretty as you can be."

Mrs. Turpin knew just exactly how much Negro flattery was worth and it added to her rage. "She said," she began again and finished this time with a fierce rush of breath, "that I was an old wart hog from hell."

There was an astounded silence.

"Where she at?" the youngest woman cried in a piercing voice.

165   "Lemme see her. I'll kill her!"

"I'll kill her with you!" the other one cried.

"She b'long in the sylum," the old woman said emphatically. "You the sweetest white lady I know."

"She pretty too," the other two said. "Stout as she can be and sweet. Jesus sat-isfied with her!"

"Deed he is," the old woman declared.

170   Idiots! Mrs. Turpin growled to herself. You could never say anything intelligent to a nigger. You could talk at them but not with them. "Yawl ain't drunk your water," she said shortly. "Leave the bucket in the truck when you're finished with it. I got more to do than just stand around and pass the time of day," and she moved off and into the house.

She stood for a moment in the middle of the kitchen. The dark protuberance over her eye looked like a miniature tornado cloud which might any moment sweep across the horizon of her brow. Her lower lip protruded dangerously. She squared her massive shoulders. Then she marched into the front of the house and out the side door and started down the road to the pig parlor. She had the look of a woman going single-handed, weaponless, into battle.

The sun was a deep yellow now like a harvest moon and was riding westward very fast over the far tree line as if it meant to reach the hogs before she did. The road was rutted and she kicked several good-sized stones out of her path as she strode along. The pig parlor was on a little knoll at the end of a lane that ran off from the side of the barn. It was a square of concrete as large as a small room, with a board fence about four feet high around it. The concrete floor sloped slightly so that the hog wash could drain off into a trench where it was carried to the field for fertilizer. Claud was standing on the outside, on the edge of the concrete, hanging onto the top board, hosing down the floor inside. The hose was connected to the faucet of a water trough nearby.

Mrs. Turpin climbed up beside him and glowered down at the hogs inside. There were seven long-snouted bristly shoats in it—tan with liver-colored spots— and an old sow a few weeks off from farrowing. She was lying on her side grunting. The shoats were running about shaking themselves like idiot children, their little slit pig eyes searching the floor for anything left. She had read that pigs were the most intelligent animal. She doubted it. They were supposed to be smarter than dogs. There had even been a pig astronaut. He had performed his assignment perfectly but died of a heart attack afterwards because they left him in his electric suit, sitting upright throughout his examination when naturally a hog should be on all fours.

A-gruntin and a-rootin and a-groanin.

175   "Gimme that hose," she said, yanking it away from Claud. "Go on and carry them niggers home and then get off that leg."

"You look like you might have swallowed a mad dog," Claud observed, but he got down and limped off. He paid no attention to her humors.

Until he was out of earshot, Mrs. Turpin stood on the side of the pen, holding the hose and pointing the stream of water at the hind quarter of any shoat that looked as if it might try to lie down. When he had had time to get over the hill, she turned her head slightly and her wrathful eyes scanned the path. He was nowhere in sight. She turned back again and seemed to gather herself up. Her shoulders rose and she drew in her breath.

"What do you send me a message like that for?" she said in a low fierce voice, barely above a whisper but with the force of a shout in its concentrated fury. "How am I a hog and me both? How am I saved and from hell too?" Her free fist was knotted and with the other she gripped the hose, blindly pointing the stream of water in and out of the eye of the old sow whose outraged squeal she did not hear.

The pig parlor commanded a view of the back pasture where their twenty beef cows were gathered around the hay-bales Claud and the boy had put out. The freshly cut pasture sloped down to the highway. Across it was their cotton field and beyond that a dark green dusty wood which they owned as well. The sun was behind the wood, very red, looking over the paling of trees like a farmer inspecting his own hogs.

180   "Why me?" she rumbled. "It's no trash around here, black or white, that I haven't given to. And break my back to the bone every day working. And do for the church."

She appeared to be the right size woman to command the arena before her. "How am I a hog?" she demanded. "Exactly how am I like them?" and she jabbed the stream of water at the shoats. "There was plenty of trash there. It didn't have to be me.

"If you like trash better, go get yourself some trash then," she railed. "You could have made me trash. Or a nigger. If trash is what you wanted why didn't you make me trash?" She shook her fist with the hose in it and a watery snake appeared momentarily in the air. "I could quit working and take it easy and be filthy," she growled. "Lounge about the sidewalks all day drinking root beer. Dip snuff and spit in every puddle and have it all over my face. I could be nasty.

"Or you could have made me a nigger. It's too late for me to be a nigger," she said with deep sarcasm, "but I could act like one. Lay down in the middle of the road and stop traffic. Roll on the ground."

In the deepening light everything was taking on a mysterious hue. The pasture was growing a peculiar glassy green and the streak of highway had turned lavender. She braced herself for a final assault and this time her voice rolled out over the pasture. "Go on," she yelled, "call me a hog! Call me a hog again. From hell. Call me a wart hog from hell. Put that bottom rail on top. There'll still be a top and bottom!"

185   A garbled echo returned to her.

A final surge of fury shook her and she roared, "Who do you think you are?"

The color of everything, field and crimson sky, burned for a moment with a transparent intensity. The question carried over the pasture and across the highway and the cotton field and returned to her clearly like an answer from beyond the wood.

She opened her mouth but no sound came out of it.

A tiny truck, Claud's, appeared on the highway, heading rapidly out of sight. Its gears scraped thinly. It looked like a child's toy. At any moment a bigger truck might smash into it and scatter Claud's and the niggers' brains all over the road.

190   Mrs. Turpin stood there, her gaze fixed on the highway, all her muscles rigid, until in five or six minutes the truck reappeared, returning. She waited until it had had time to turn into their own road. Then like a monumental statue coming to life, she bent her head slowly and gazed, as if through the very heart of the mystery, down into the pig parlor at the hogs. They had settled all in one corner around the old sow who was grunting softly. A red glow suffused them. They appeared to pant with a secret life.

Until the sun slipped finally behind the tree line, Mrs. Turpin remained there with her gaze bent to them as if she were absorbing some abysmal life-giving knowledge. At last she lifted her head. There was only a purple streak in the sky, cutting through a field of crimson and leading, like an extension of the highway, into the descending dusk. She raised her hands from the side of the pen in a gesture hieratic and profound. A visionary light settled in her eyes. She saw the streak as a vast swinging bridge extending upward from the earth through a field of living fire. Upon it a vast horde of souls were rumbling toward heaven. There were whole companies of white-trash, clean for the first time in their lives, and bands of black niggers in white robes, and battalions of freaks and lunatics shouting and clapping and leaping like frogs. And bringing up the end of the procession was a tribe of people whom she recognized at once as those who, like herself and Claud, had always had a little of everything and the God-given wit to use it right. She leaned forward to observe them closer. They were marching behind the others with great dignity, accountable as they had always been for good order and common sense and respectable behavior. They alone were on key. Yet she could see by their shocked and altered faces that even their virtues were being burned away. She lowered her hands and gripped the rail of the hog pen, her eyes small but fixed unblinkingly on what lay ahead. In a moment the vision faded but she remained where she was, immobile.

At length she got down and turned off the faucet and made her slow way on the darkening path to the house. In the woods around her the invisible cricket choruses had struck up, but what she heard were the voices of the souls climbing upward into the starry field and shouting hallelujah.

[1964]

Joining the Conversation: Critical Thinking and Writing

1. Why does Mary Grace attack Mrs. Turpin?
2. Characterize Mrs. Turpin before her revelation. Does your attitude toward her change at the end of the story?
3. The two chief settings are a doctor's waiting room and a "pig parlor." Can these settings reasonably be called "symbolic"? If so, symbolic of what?
4. When Mrs. Turpin goes toward the pig parlor, she has "the look of a woman going single-handed, weaponless, into battle." Once there, she dismisses Claud, uses the hose as a weapon against the pigs, and talks to herself "in a low fierce voice." What is she battling, besides the pigs?
5. How does O'Connor explore the issue of race relations?

MyLiteratureLab® *For additional resources for "Revelation," log in to* www.myliteraturelab.com *where you will find Short Evaluation Exercises, as well as an About the Author and Links for O'Connor (under Student Resources).*

Remarks from Essays and Letters

From "The Fiction Writer and His Country"

In the greatest fiction, the writer's moral sense coincides with his dramatic sense, and I see no way for it to do this unless his moral judgment is part of the very act of seeing, and he is free to use it. I have heard it said that belief in Christian dogma is a hindrance to the writer, but I myself have found nothing further from the truth. Actually, it frees the storyteller to observe. It is not a set of rules which fixes what he sees in the world. It affects his writing primarily by guaranteeing his respect for mystery. . . .

When I look at stories I have written I find that they are, for the most part, about people who are poor, who are afflicted in both mind and body, who have little—or at best a distorted—sense of spiritual purpose, and whose actions do not apparently give the reader a great assurance of the joy of life.

Yet how is this? For I am no disbeliever in spiritual purpose and no vague believer. I see from the standpoint of Christian orthodoxy. This means that for me the meaning of life is centered in our Redemption by Christ and what I see in the world I see in its relation to that. . . .

The novelist with Christian concerns will find in modern life distortions which are repugnant to him, and his problem will be to make these appear as distortions to an audience which is used to seeing them as natural; and he may well be forced to take ever more violent means to get his vision across to this hostile audience. When you can assume that your audience holds the same beliefs you do, you can relax a little and use more normal means of talking to it; when you have to assume that it does not, then you have to make your vision apparent by shock—to the hard of hearing you shout, and for the almost-blind you draw large and startling figures.

From "Some Aspects of the Grotesque in Southern Fiction"

If the writer believes that our life is and will remain essentially mysterious, if he looks upon us as beings existing in a created order to whose laws we freely respond, then what he sees on the surface will be of interest to him only as he can go through it into an experience of mystery itself. His kind of fiction will always be pushing its own limits outward toward the limits of mystery, because for this kind of writer, the meaning of a story does not begin except at a depth where adequate motivation and adequate psychology and the various determinations have been exhausted. Such a writer will be interested in what we don't understand rather than in what we do. He will be interested in possibility rather than in probability. He will be interested in characters who are forced out to meet evil and grace and who act on a trust beyond themselves—whether they know very clearly what it is they act upon or not. To the modern mind, this kind of character, and his creator, are typical Don Quixotes, tilting at[1] what is not there.

From "The Nature and Aim of Fiction"

The novel works by a slower accumulation of detail than the short story does. The short story requires more drastic procedures than the novel because more has to be accomplished in less space. The details have to carry more immediate weight. In good fiction, certain of the details will tend to accumulate meaning from the story itself, and when this happens, they become symbolic in their action.

Now the word *symbol* scares a good many people off, just as the word *art* does. They seem to feel that a symbol is some mysterious thing put in arbitrarily by the writer to frighten the common reader—sort of a literary Masonic grip that is only for the initiated. They seem to think that it is a way of saying something that you aren't actually saying, and so if they can be got to read a reputedly symbolic work at all, they approach it as if it were a problem in algebra. Find *x*. And when they do find or think they find this abstraction, *x*, then they go off with an elaborate sense of satisfaction and the notion that they have "understood" the story. Many students confuse the *process* of understanding a thing with understanding it.

I think that for the fiction writer himself, symbols are something he uses simply as a matter of course. You might say that these are details that, while having their essential place in the literal level of the story, operate in depth as well as on the surface, increasing the story in every direction. . . .

[1]**tilting at** "tilting at windmills" is a popular expression that derives from Cervantes's novel *Don Quixote,* published in 1604–05.

People have a habit of saying, "What is the theme of your story?" and they expect you to give them a statement: "The theme of my story is the economic pressure of the machine on the middle class"—or some such absurdity. And when they've got a statement like that, they go off happy and feel it is no longer necessary to read the story.

Some people have the notion that you read the story and then climb out of it into the meaning, but for the fiction writer himself the whole story is the meaning, because it is an experience, not an abstraction.

From "Writing Short Stories"

Being short does not mean being slight. A short story should be long in depth and should give us an experience of meaning. . . .

Meaning is what keeps the short story from being short. I prefer to talk about the meaning in a story rather than the theme of a story. People talk about the theme of a story as if the theme were like the string that a sack of chicken feed is tied with. They think that if you can pick out the theme, the way you pick the right thread in the chicken-feed sack, you can rip the story open and feed the chickens. But this is not the way meaning works in fiction.

When you can state the theme of a story, when you can separate it from the story itself, then you can be sure the story is not a very good one. The meaning of a story has to be embodied in it, has to be made concrete in it. A story is a way to say something that can't be said any other way, and it takes every word in the story to say what the meaning is. You tell a story because a statement would be inadequate. When anybody asks what a story is about, the only proper thing is to tell him to read the story. The meaning of fiction is not abstract meaning but experienced meaning, and the purpose of making statements about the meaning of a story is only to help you to experience that meaning more fully.

On Interpreting "A Good Man Is Hard to Find"

A professor of English had sent O'Connor the following letter: "I am writing as spokesman for three members of our department and some ninety university students in three classes who for a week now have been discussing your story 'A Good Man Is Hard to Find.' We have debated at length several possible interpretations, none of which fully satisfies us. In general we believe that the appearance of the Misfit is not 'real' in the same sense that the incidents of the first half of the story are real. Bailey, we believe, imagines the appearance of the Misfit, whose activities have been called to his attention on the night before the trip and again during the stopover at the roadside restaurant. Bailey, we further believe, identifies himself with the Misfit and so plays two roles in the imaginary last half of the story. But we cannot, after great effort, determine the point at which reality fades into illusion or reverie. Does the accident literally occur, or is it a part of Bailey's dream? Please believe me when I say we are not seeking an easy way out of our difficulty. We admire your story and have examined it with great care, but we are convinced that we are missing something important which you intended for us to grasp. We will all be very grateful if you comment on the interpretation which I have outlined above and if you will give us further comments about your intention in writing 'A Good Man Is Hard to Find.'" She replied:

To a Professor of English

28 March 61

The interpretation of your ninety students and three teachers is fantastic and about as far from my intentions as it could get to be. If it were a legitimate interpretation, the story would be little more than a trick and its interest would be simply for abnormal psychology. I am not interested in abnormal psychology.

There is a change of tension from the first part of the story to the second where the Misfit enters, but this is no lessening of reality. This story is, of course, not meant to be realistic in the sense that it portrays the everyday doings of people in Georgia. It is stylized and its conventions are comic even though its meaning is serious.

Bailey's only importance is as the Grandmother's boy and the driver of the car. It is the Grandmother who first recognizes the Misfit and who is most concerned with him throughout. The story is a duel of sorts between the Grandmother and her superficial beliefs and the Misfit's more profoundly felt involvement with Christ's action which set the world off balance for him.

The meaning of a story should go on expanding for the reader the more he thinks about it, but meaning cannot be captured in an interpretation. If teachers are in the habit of approaching a story as if it were a research problem for which any answer is believable so long as it is not obvious, then I think students will never learn to enjoy fiction. Too much interpretation is certainly worse than too little and where feeling for a story is absent, theory will not supply it.

My tone is not meant to be obnoxious. I am in a state of shock.

"A Reasonable Use of the Unreasonable"

Last fall I received a letter from a student who said she would be "graciously appreciative" if I would tell her "just what enlightenment" I expected her to get from each of my stories. I suspect she had a paper to write. I wrote her back to forget about the enlightenment and just try to enjoy them. I knew that was the most unsatisfactory answer I could have given because, of course, she didn't want to enjoy them, she just wanted to figure them out.

In most English classes the short story has become a kind of literary specimen to be dissected. Every time a story of mine appears in a Freshman anthology, I have a vision of it, with its little organs laid open, like a frog in a bottle.

I realize that a certain amount of this what-is-the-significance has to go on, but I think something has gone wrong in the process when, for so many students, the story becomes simply a problem to be solved, something which you evaporate to get Instant Enlightenment.

A story really isn't any good unless it successfully resists paraphrase, unless it hangs on and expands in the mind. Properly, you analyze to enjoy, but it's equally true that to analyze with any discrimination, you have to have enjoyed already, and I think that the best reason to hear a story read is that it should stimulate that primary enjoyment.

I don't have any pretensions to being an Aeschylus or Sophocles and providing you in this story with a cathartic experience out of your mythic background, though this story I'm going to read certainly calls up a good deal of the South's mythic background, and it should elicit from you a degree of pity and terror, even though its way of being serious is a comic one. I do think, though, that like the Greeks you should know what is going to happen in this story so that any element of suspense in it will be transferred from its surface to its interior.

I would be most happy if you have already read it, happier still if you knew it well, but since experience has taught me to keep my expectations along these lines modest, I'll tell you that this is the story of a family of six which, on its way driving to Florida, gets wiped out by an escaped convict who calls himself the Misfit. The family is made up of the Grandmother and her son, Bailey, and his children, John Wesley and June Star and the baby, and there is also the cat and the children's mother. The cat is named Pitty Sing, and the Grandmother is taking him with them, hidden in a basket.

Now I think it behooves me to try to establish with you the basis on which reason operates in this story. Much of my fiction takes its character from a reasonable use of the unreasonable, though the reasonableness of my use of it may not always be apparent. The assumptions that underlie this use of it, however, are those of the central Christian mysteries. These are assumptions to which a large part of the modern audience takes exception. About this I can only say that there are perhaps other ways than my own in which this story could be read, but none other by which it could have been written. Belief, in my own case anyway, is the engine that makes perception operate.

The heroine of this story, the Grandmother, is in the most significant position life offers the Christian. She is facing death. And to all appearances she, like the rest of us, is not too well prepared for it. She would like to see the event postponed. Indefinitely.

I've talked to a number of teachers who use this story in class and who tell their students that the Grandmother is evil, that in fact, she's a witch, even down to the cat. One of these teachers told me that his students, and particularly his Southern students, resisted this interpretation with a certain bemused vigor, and he didn't understand why. I had to tell him that they resisted it because they all had grandmothers or great-aunts just like her at home, and they knew, from personal experience, that the old lady lacked comprehension, but that she had a good heart. The Southerner is usually tolerant of those weaknesses that proceed from innocence, and he knows that a taste for self-preservation can be readily combined with the missionary spirit.

This same teacher was telling his students that morally the Misfit was several cuts above the Grandmother. He had a really sentimental attachment to the Misfit. But then a prophet gone wrong is almost always more interesting than your grandmother, and you have to let people take their pleasures where they find them.

It is true that the old lady is a hypocritical old soul; her wits are no match for the Misfit's, nor is her capacity for grace equal to his; yet I think the unprejudiced reader will feel that the Grandmother has a special kind of triumph in this story which instinctively we do not allow to someone altogether bad.

I often ask myself what makes a story work, and what makes it hold up as a story, and I have decided that it is probably some action, some gesture of a character that is unlike any other in the story, one which indicates where the real heart of the story lies. This would have to be an action or a gesture which was both totally right and totally unexpected; it would have to be one that was both in character and beyond character; it would have to suggest both the world and eternity. The action or gesture I'm talking about would have to be on the anagogical level, that is, the level which has to do with the Divine life and our participation in it. It would be a gesture that transcended any neat allegory that might have been intended or any pat moral categories a reader could make. It would be a gesture which somehow made contact with mystery.

There is a point in this story where such a gesture occurs. The Grandmother is at last alone, facing the Misfit. Her head clears for an instant and she realizes, even in her limited way, that she is responsible for the man before her and joined to him by ties of kinship which have their roots deep in the mystery she has been merely prattling about so far. And at this point, she does the right thing, she makes the right gesture.

I find that students are often puzzled by what she says and does here, but I think myself that if I took out this gesture and what she says with it, I would have no story. What was left would not be worth your attention. Our age not only does not have a very sharp eye for the almost imperceptible intrusions of grace, it no longer has much feeling for the nature of the violences which precede and follow them. The devil's greatest wile, Baudelaire has said, is to convince us that he does not exist.

I suppose the reasons for the use of so much violence in modern fiction will differ with each writer who uses it, but in my own stories I have found that violence is strangely capable of returning my characters to reality and preparing them to accept their moment of grace. Their heads are so hard that almost nothing else will do the work. This idea, that reality is something to which we must be returned at considerable cost, is one which is seldom understood by the casual reader, but it is one which is implicit in the Christian view of the world.

I don't want to equate the Misfit with the devil. I prefer to think that, however unlikely this may seem, the old lady's gesture, like the mustard-seed, will grow to be a great crow-filled tree in the Misfit's heart, and will be enough of a pain to him there to turn him into the prophet he was meant to become. But that's another story.

This story has been called grotesque, but I prefer to call it literal. A good story is literal in the same sense that a child's drawing is literal. When a child draws, he doesn't intend to distort but to set down exactly what he sees, and as his gaze is direct, he sees the lines that create motion. Now the lines of motion that interest the writer are usually invisible. They are lines of spiritual motion. And in this story you should be on the lookout for such things as the action of grace in the Grandmother's soul, and not for the dead bodies.

We hear many complaints about the prevalence of violence in modern fiction, and it is always assumed that this violence is a bad thing and meant to be an end in itself. With the serious writer, violence is never an end in itself. It is the extreme situation that best reveals what we are essentially, and I believe these are times when writers are more interested in what we are essentially than in the tenor of our daily lives. Violence is a force which can be used for good or evil, and among other things taken by it is the kingdom of heaven. But regardless of what can be taken by it, the man in the violent situation reveals those qualities least dispensable in his personality, those qualities which are all he will have to take into eternity with him; and since the characters in this story are all on the verge of eternity, it is appropriate to think of what they take with them. In any case, I hope that if you consider these points in connection with the story, you will come to see it as something more than an account of a family murdered on the way to Florida.

[1957]

Graphic Fiction

*The world always seems brighter when you've just made
something that wasn't there before.*

NEIL GAIMAN

Chapter Preview

After reading this chapter you will be able to

* Define *visual literacy*
* Demonstrate visual literacy by reading graphic fiction

Letters and Pictures

Literature is, literally speaking, made out of letters ("literature," "literally," "literate," and "letters" all come from a Latin word, *littera,* "letter"). A person who can read letters is literate. Yet today we hear a good deal about "visual literacy," which means the ability to understand visual things. In this usage, "literacy" is metaphoric. You cannot literally (again that word!) read a picture; you can look at it and either understand it or not understand it. In order to help prepare you to read a story that is partly told by means of pictures, we will be talking about achieving visual literacy—that is, achieving the ability to understand pictures, to "read" pictures, specifically pictures that are used to tell stories.

The good news is that if you have spent any time at all looking at comic strips or comic books, you already know a great deal about how to "read" pictures that tell stories.

* You know, for instance, that you should read the pictures and the words from left to right (if you were brought up in China or Japan, you would begin at the right and read the first column downward, then the next column, again reading downward, unless the book were a Western-style book).
* You also know that in the usual comic strip a box represents a particular scene; the next box may show the same characters, but at a later moment in time.
* You know that human actions can be conveyed by showing figures in certain postures (walking, eating, etc.) making certain gestures (pointing, making a fist).
* You know that emotions can be conveyed by facial expressions (think Smiley Face, where two dots and a curve say it all).
* You know that the setting can easily be established (a tree indicates the outdoors, the Capitol indicates Washington, D.C.).
* You know that when a heavy object is shown on the ground with the word "bang" in large thick letters next to it, a character has just dropped the object.

- You know that words enclosed in a circle over a character's head indicate words that the character is speaking.
- You know that a character is cursing or using dirty language when words are represented not by letters but by symbols such as @ and # and !
- You know that when the line that encloses words is scalloped, or looks something like a cloud, the words represent *thoughts* rather than utterances.

In short, you know the conventions that enable you to understand what the cartoonist/storyteller is doing, and you can follow the story, the narrative conveyed by words and pictures. All of which says that you are already visually literate. Yet because you may not have developed the habit of reading images closely and taking in all the subtleties that they may offer, we will talk a bit about reading pictures.

The first thing we want to say is that although in some contexts a picture is worth a thousand words, pictures are not very good at telling *stories*. Think of a familiar story—let's say the story of Cain and Abel, or of Cinderella, or (to take an example in our text) the story of King Solomon and the two women who disputed about who was the mother of an infant. Solomon ordered a servant to bring the sword, and to divide the living child so that each woman could have half. A sword was brought, and (here we give the translated text in the Revised Standard Version of the Bible)

> then the woman whose son was alive said to the king, because her heart yearned for her son, "Oh, no my lord, give her [i.e., the other woman] the living child, and by no means slay it." But the other said, "It shall be neither mine nor yours: divide it." Then the king answered and said, "Give the living child to the first woman, and by no means slay it; she is its mother." (I Kings 3.26–27)

Striking images come to mind when reading this story—for instance, an image of two women quarreling over an infant, an image of a servant entering with a massive sword, and an image of the infant being handed over to one woman. But we think it would be impossible by images alone to tell the story, which essentially causes the reader to draw two conclusions:

- A loving mother will give up a child rather than let it die, and
- Solomon was a wise judge.

Tradition says that in the Middle Ages, when most people were illiterate, pictures such as those in stained glass windows were "the Bible of the people," and these windows did tell stories—but the stories could be understood only if the viewers were already familiar with verbal tellings. Similarly, such narratives as those told on Trajan's Column (built 113 CE, adorned with images of the Roman emperor's victories) and in the Bayeux Tapestry (late eleventh century, showing the French invasion of England) show us lots of energetic figures, but to *understand* what is going on, we must already know the story.

Having made the point that pictures are not very good at telling stories, we now admit that a picture *can* tell a simple story. Look, for instance, at this painting by Grant Wood, *Death on the Ridge Road*. The title—words!—tells you what the picture is about, but even if you found the picture in the attic, with no title affixed, you could infer what is about to happen, what story the picture tells:

Death on the Ridge Road (1935), Grant Wood (American; 1892–1942). Oil on masonite, frame: 39 × 46 1/16 in. (99 × 117 cm) Williams College Museum of Art, Williamstown, MA, Gift of Cole Porter, (47.1.3). Art © Figge Art Museum, successors to the Estate of Nan Wood Graham/Licensed by VAGA, New York, NY.

A big black car, apparently a limousine, is going to collide with a truck.

We think all viewers will agree with this statement, and perhaps we can go a *little* further. (First, let us note that the cars are black, the truck is red, the grass is green, and the sky is darkening.)

- Given the facts that the cars are black—in the context, an ominous color— that the sky shows a storm brewing, that the intersecting diagonals of the limousine and the truck imply conflict, and that the telephone pole appears at an angle, the picture makes the viewer uneasy.
- Apparently the limousine was behind the car that is now at the bottom of the picture; in order to pass the car, the limo must have crossed into the left lane, and it is now cutting to the right in order to return to its proper lane.
- The telephone poles, in this context of vehicles about to collide, we perceive as crosses, and thus they turn the pretty landscape with its winding road into a cemetery.
- The picture may cause us to moralize: "Death comes unexpectedly"; "Even in lovely rural surroundings death can be present."

But even when a viewer has such thoughts—and we think these thoughts are supported by the picture—the picture itself tells only a simple story:

A car, having passed on the left another car, is cutting back to the right and will in a
moment collide with a truck coming over a hill.

The picture does *not* tell us anything about the minds of the people involved in
the accident to come. Conceivably a viewer may conjecture that the driver of the
limousine was impatient, driving behind someone in a dinky car going at 20
miles an hour, and—such is the personality of the rich men who drive big cars,
or of their chauffeurs—this driver confidently and recklessly crossed the dividing
line marked on the road, entered the left lane, zoomed ahead of the slowpoke,
and now (here we return to the facts shown in the picture) is cutting back into
the right-hand lane but is too near the truck to avoid a crash. Clearly this interpretation of the character of the driver cannot be supported by the picture. For
all we know, the smaller car may have stalled in the middle of the road, and the
driver of the limousine—maybe a very cautious woman—was forced to go
around the stalled car.

Joining the Conversation: Two Topics for Creative Writing

1. Write two versions (each about 500–1,000 words) of a story based on Grant
   Wood's painting. In one version, tell the story from the point of view of the
   driver of the car that is being passed. This driver cannot know the exact
   thoughts of the other driver, but he or she can say such things as, "This guy
   was behind me, honking like crazy, so I deliberately slowed down, just to
   teach him a lesson." In the second version, use a *different* point of view—
   perhaps the point of view of the driver of the car that will be struck, or
   perhaps the point of view of a spectator, or, if you wish, an omniscient
   point of view.
2. Grant Wood's most famous painting is *American Gothic,* a picture that
   shows a man and a woman standing in front of their home, a house with
   a window shaped like a gothic (pointed) arch. (You can find the picture on
   the Internet.) Do you see a story, a narrative, a sequence of events, in this
   picture? If so, what is the story? If you do not see a story, invent a very short
   one, a story that might plausibly use this picture as an illustration of some
   episode.

   Now let's look at a picture that is accompanied by words.

Reading an Image: A Short Story
Told in One Panel

TONY CARRILLO

*Tony Carrillo was born and raised in Tempe, Arizona. He conceived F Minus when
he was a sophomore at Arizona State University. The strip is currently syndicated in
more than a hundred newspapers.*

F Minus

ONE DAY, IN A QUIET OFFICE BUILDING SOMEWHERE, A SMALL CALCULATOR SUDDENLY BECAME SELF-AWARE.

IN EIGHT SECONDS, IT PLOTTED THE EXTINCTION OF ALL MANKIND.

THEN THE BATTERY DIED.

TWO WEEKS LATER, IT WAS THROWN AWAY.

Tony Carrillo: "F Minus" © 2007 Tony Carrillo. Reprinted by permission of Universal Uclick for UFS. All rights reserved.

For now, let's pretend that the picture didn't exist and we were given only some text:

> One day, in a quiet office building somewhere, a small calculator suddenly became self-aware.
> In eight seconds, it plotted the extinction of all mankind.
> Then the battery died.
> Two weeks later, it was thrown away.

We don't want to make extravagant claims, but we think this is pretty good as a mini-sci-fi story. We hear much about the possibility that some day there may be machines that "think," and we hear even more about technology getting out of control and destroying its creators. In the words of Elias Canetti, winner of a Nobel Prize in Literature, "The planet's survival has become so uncertain that any effort, any thought that presupposes an assured future amounts to a mad gamble." So the graphic story begins with something fantastic yet something that we hear about and that we can imagine may become real:

> One day, in a quiet office building somewhere, a small calculator suddenly became self-aware.
> In eight seconds, it plotted the extinction of all mankind.

There is an engaging combination of vagueness ("One day," "somewhere") and of the highly specific ("In eight seconds"); that is, things in a leisurely once-upon-a-time land suddenly come down to a matter of seconds. The vague fairy-tale world of "one day" has been transformed into real time, and the "small calculator" is now a big threat. Like all good fiction, each sentence of this tiny story stimulates the reader to wonder, What happens next?

What does happen after the calculator "plotted the extinction of all mankind"? "Then the battery died." Well, that makes sense. We hadn't anticipated this happening, but, again, the happening is a plausible one, and we are relieved, satisfied. In a sense the story is over—the battery is dead, so what more can be said?—but we see additional words:

> Two weeks later, it was thrown away.

We think this ending is masterful. E. M. Forster's comment about a good plot comes to mind:

Shock, followed by the feeling, "Oh, that's all right," is a sign that all is well with plot: characters, to be real, ought to run smoothly, but a plot ought to cause surprise.

It is as if we heard a joke, laughed, and thought we had heard the end of the matter and then the narrator went on to top the joke, giving us an unexpected joke that builds on the first joke, a line that, after we have heard it, seems inevitable. The calculator, once an enormous menace, fails to be of even the slightest significance because—as is entirely natural, if we can speak of naturalness in connection with a mechanical device—the battery dies. The story seems to be over, there is nothing more to say. But there *is* more to say. The battery-dead calculator for two weeks is not even noticed, and then, when presumably it somehow comes to some unspecified person's attention, it is unceremoniously discarded, "thrown away." The way of all flesh.

What is convincing is not simply that A is followed by B and B is followed by C, but that there is a *logic* to the sequence, even (may we say?) a *truth* to the sequence. Notice, too, that the artist-writer does not moralize; rather, it is the reader-viewer who draws conclusions.

The theme is a great one, the humbling of the ambitious. Shakespeare often treated it—for instance, in *Richard II,* where the king meditates on his "state" (i.e., high status, exalted rank) and sees death as an "antic" (buffoon, jester) mocking even a king:

> Within the hollow crown
> That rounds the mortal temples of a king
> Keeps Death his court and there the antic sits,
> Scoffing his state and grinning at his pomp,
> Allowing him a breath, a little scene,
> To monarchize, be feared and kill with looks,
> Infusing him with self and vain conceit,
> As if this flesh which walls about our life,
> Were brass impregnable, and humored thus
> Comes at the last and with a little pin
> Bores through his castle wall, and farewell king!

(3.2.160-70)

Or consider these lines by Shakespeare's later contemporary, James Shirley:

> The glories of our blood and state
> Are shadows, not substantial things;
> There is no armor against fate;
> Death lays his icy hand on kings:
> Scepter and crown
> Must tumble down,
> And in the dust be equal made
> With the poor crooked scythe and spade.

We are not claiming that the story about the calculator is in the same league, but we do find it memorable. We think the *text* of this graphic story makes a pretty good short-short story, even without the picture. Now let's examine the accompanying picture.

We think it is clever, sort of cute. The cartoonist might simply have drawn a calculator, but he brilliantly put two eyes into the liquid crystal display, and thus animated the whole thing. The calculator *does* seem to be aware, doesn't it? So, in our view, the story becomes enriched by the image. We can call this sort of thing "graphic fiction," but, to go back to our earlier point, the truth is that the picture doesn't tell the story. It merely enriches a story that is told in words.

That last sentence is, we admit, unfair. The image doesn't "merely" enrich the words. The picture is literally (that word again!) central to the story. If the story consisted only of text, or if all of the text were written above or below the story, the story would not be as effective. The image is integral.

And that's our point: The best graphic fiction does not merely illustrate the verbal story; rather, the images are inseparable from the words. The story is text-and-image, not just text-adorned-with-image.

A Second Example of Reading Images: A Story Told in Sequential Panels

Let's look now at a somewhat more complex work of graphic fiction, this one consisting of eight panels. The artist-author is Art Spiegelman.

ART SPIEGELMAN

Born in Sweden in 1948, Art Spiegelman was raised in New York City. His two-part graphic story (part novel, part memoir), Maus (1986, 1991), based on his Polish-Jewish parents' experiences during the Holocaust, was awarded a Pulitzer Prize in 1992. A highly inventive fellow, Spiegelman not only cofounded several outlets for comic books but he also created Garbage Candy (edible candy in the shape of garbage, packaged in miniature garbage cans). In 2005 Time magazine included Spiegelman in its list of the 100 most influential people.

If you were explaining "Nature vs. Nurture" to critters from outer space, you might point out the following conventions, going panel by panel:

- Spiegelman sets the scene at the extreme upper left, in the first panel, with some text in a small box. This text-box, providing the reader-viewer with background rather than dialogue, is appropriately distinct in shape from the speech balloons.
- The little girl in the first panel is obviously happy. Her happiness is conveyed not only by the text's expressions of motherly love but also by the expression on her face. The father is also smiling.
- In the second panel the well-intentioned, politically correct father takes the doll from the girl. The girl is puzzled (the balloon says "uk?" and the smile is gone from her face).
- In the third panel, the father is full of enthusiasm—his mouth is open, he has a big smile—and the text conveys his enthusiasm. Additional text, "Skreeee," in different lettering (to indicate it is not human speech) comes out of the fire truck. The father has presumably pushed a button or flicked a switch so that the truck emits a sound. The girl's face and posture show puzzlement.
- The enthusiastic father (still with a big smile) seeks to show the girl how to play. His talk is (how shall we put it?) male talk, loud and aggressive ("Clang! Clang! Clang! Everybody get outa the way!").
- In the fifth panel the father, still teaching his daughter but evidently having a great time, is verging on the maniacal with his toothy grin and his "Vroom! Vroom!" A viewer-reader probably thinks, "Hmmm, boys will be boys"—and may also think, seeing this father's childish enthusiasm, "You can't take the boy out of the man."
- The next panel shows the smiling—and complacent—father handing the truck to the girl, whose face conveys uncertainty.
- The bottom row begins with more uncertainty, indicated by a big question mark over the girl's head. She says nothing—there is no speech balloon—but we know that she is puzzled.
- The final panel shows that the girl has covered half of the fire truck with a blanket—instead of thrusting it crazily around and making loud noises—and the father is reduced to silence. His posture—hands thrust into pockets, head slightly turned down—shows that he has given up his attempt (the "nurture" of the title) to stifle the expression of motherly feelings (the "nature" of the title), and a balloon indicates that he is heaving a sigh of resignation. The sigh is conveyed by enclosing the word "sigh" within elongated dots, indicating he is sighing rather than *saying* "sigh."

If we were to think about the story in terms of the elements of fiction, what might we say? Well, so far as **character** (personality) goes, each of the two figures is relatively simple: The girl is just a girl—at her young age we hardly expect her to be a richly complex figure—and the father is essentially a well-meaning dad who wants his daughter to grow up free from gender stereotypes. Surely that is an admirable ambition. The **plot**—the sequence of happenings—shows his attempt to free her by offering her an alternative, a fire truck instead of a doll. He is apparently rather pleased with his efforts (the seventh panel shows him smiling when his little daughter touches the truck)—but with the final panel, reality breaks in. The girl does not careen around the room shouting "Vroom!" as the father did; rather, her maternal instinct manifests itself even toward the fire truck. But this is not quite the end of the story: At the extreme right side we see the father heaving a sigh, shoulders slumped and hands in pockets: He has been forced to accept reality. Not always a bad thing, really, when you think about it. If we are asked what the **theme** of the story is—i.e., What does the story *add up* to? (which is very different from the plot, which is What *happens* in the story?)— we can say that the theme concerns (as the title of the story indicates) the conflict between Nature and Nurture, or, to put it a bit differently, biology versus socialization. We most emphatically do not wish to say anything like "Spiegelman shows that human nature is unchangeable." For one thing, Spiegelman doesn't "show" us (in the sense of prove or demonstrate) anything. He just drew some pictures and wrote some words; he didn't offer anything that can be called evidence. Even if the pictures represent something that happened in his own family, his graphic report of his experience would not prove that other fathers will have the same experience with their daughters. Spiegelman is entertaining us, not arguing, not preaching. Still, one feels that Spiegelman's story—the happenings that he illustrates, the doings of two figures—are plausible. One thing follows from another:

- The father sees his daughter playing with dolls, and
- being a good father, he wishes to free his daughter from stereotypical limited behavior, so
- he gives his daughter a toy that is usually associated with boys, but
- nature will have its way, and the girl turns the fire truck into an object that allows her to express her maternal instinct.
- Heaving a sigh, the father appears to recognize that his efforts have failed.

You have now instructed your Martian visitors in the language of graphic fiction. Yes, you knew it all along, and maybe the Martian visitors did, too.

WILL EISNER

Born in Brooklyn, New York, Will Eisner (1917–2005) drew cartoons for his high school newspaper and after graduation studied for a year at the Art Students League of New York. He was soon publishing cartoons and comic strips, and he became an important figure in establishing the graphic novel ("sequential art") as a form of fiction. He taught at the School of Visual Arts in New York, and he published two highly informative books derived from his lectures, Comics and Sequential Art *(1985) and* Graphic Storytelling and Visual Narrative *(1996). In* Comics and Sequential Art *Eisner includes a chapter titled "Expressive Anatomy." Among the illustrations in this chapter is "Hamlet on a Rooftop," first published in June 1981. Eisner prefaces the* Hamlet *drawings with the following remark, and then offers a running commentary on the pictures.*

Hamlet on a Rooftop

The Body and the Face

The employment of body posture and facial expression (both having equal attention) is a major undertaking and an area of frequent failure. Properly and skillfully done, it can carry the narrative without resorting to unnecessary props or scenery. The use of expressive anatomy in the absence of words is less demanding because the latitude for the art is wider. Where the words have a depth of meaning and nuance, the task is more difficult.

This represents an example of a classic situation — that of author vs. artist. The artist must decide at the outset what his 'input' shall be; to slavishly make visual that which is in the author's mind or to embark on the raft of the author's words onto a visual sea of his own charting.

HAMLET ON A ROOFTOP

His FATHER IS DEAD,
MYSTERIOUSLY!
HIS MOTHER,
WITHIN BUT A MONTH,
MARRIES HIS UNCLE!
SO SOON?, SO SOON?
CAN THERE BE
ANYTHING OTHER
THAN SOMETHING
ROTTEN HERE?
CAN IT BE
ANYTHING BUT
MURDER!?
WELL, THEN, IF
MURDER IT BE
ALL HE VALUES,
INDEED,
HIS MANHOOD
CRIES OUT
FOR RETRIBUTION
....VENGEANCE ..
TO HONOR
THE FILIAL DUTY
HIS FATHER'S
VOICE DEMANDS
IN THE HOT
CAULDRON
OF HIS MIND!
AYE,
TO PUNISH THEM,
TO
MURDER
HIS MOTHER
AND UNCLE...
AS THEY
LAY
IN VIOLATION
OF HIS CODE!!!
...OR PERHAPS
SOMETHING MORE
UNSPEAKABLE
WITHIN HIM.

YET...
CAN HE FIND
IN HIMSELF
THE CAPACITY
TO COMMIT
SO UNNATURAL
AN ACT
AND IN DOING IT
FORFEIT
THE LOVE OF
OPHELIA,
HIS BETROTHED?
WAIT...
HOLD STILL
FOR A
MOMENT,
CLING
BRIEFLY
TO
A PASSING
RAFT OF REASON
BEFORE
IT LEAVES
THE BRAIN,
BEFORE
SURRENDERING
TO THE
SWIFT RIVER
OF HIS
PASSION,
AND SO
TO BE
CARRIED
OUT
INTO THE
TURGID
SEA
OF VIOLENCE
FROM
WHICH
THERE IS
NO RETURN.

In this experiment, Shakespeare's words are intact. The soliloquy is broken up into balloons at the artist's discretion. The intent here is to permit a meaningful fusing of word, imagery and timing. The result should provide the reader with necessary pauses.

The artist here functions as actor and in the process gives his own meaning to the lines.

A gesture signifying contemplation.

Furniture employed in intimate involvement with the actor gives the 'background' story value because it is part of the action.

Submission . . . to a "heavy" thought.

Here, the postures are more than a classical portrayal of emotions. This man is not the Danish Prince Hamlet! His gestures and postures are derivative of his special background. The question of how he would deliver the standard gesture for self-doubt and internal agony is the artist's real challenge!

WHETHER 'TIS NOBLER
IN THE MIND
TO SUFFER
THE SLINGS AND ARROWS
OF OUTRAGEOUS FORTUNE...

OR...

TO TAKE ARMS
AGAINST A SEA OF TROUBLES,
AND BY OPPOSING
END THEM !

Bravado . . . he envisions himself as challenging the forces of troubles.

Exhaustion — beaten by the enormity of his problems

Seeking comfort he lets his body slide down along the wall

Retreat . . . into his refuge . . . sleep

The language of posture is universal and inter-changeable — the application is not.

Wishing with all his might.

Withdrawing into sleep or oblivion, he assumes an almost fetal posture.

Terror . . . in the realization of his options

Awake
again to the
thoughts
that will not
leave him!

Candor . . .
addressing
the unseen
manipulator
of his fate

Anger . . . now he builds his resolution

Arguing . . . he begins to make a case to buttress growing resolve.

Debating . . . the postures of a courtroom advocate

The use of a long-shot, here is meant to reinforce realism — and in that way try to deal with the problem of putting Shakespeare's language in the mouth of such a man.

Hesitation . . . a recurrence of doubt

This wedding of Shakespearean language with a modern denizen of the ghetto may not be appropriate but the exercise serves to demonstrate the potential of the medium because the emotional content is so universal.

Now let's examine a contemporary graphic treatment of an early twentieth-century short story, Franz Kafka's "A Hunger Artist." In one obvious way the job of the illustrator of a classic text is easier than the job of the creator of an entirely original work, but in another way it is also more difficult because the artist who illustrates a classic is in some sense putting himself or herself up against a classic writer: Reader/viewers will inevitably expect the artist to contribute something to the work, to do more than ride piggyback on the original author.

R. CRUMB AND DAVID ZANE MAIROWITZ

Robert Dennis Crumb, born in Philadelphia in 1943, worked for a while in Cleveland as a designer of greeting cards, then began drawing for underground newspapers. Some of his work is strongly sexual and highly satiric, but he has also drawn R. Crumb's Kafka *(1993), with a text by David Zane Mairowitz, illustrating several works of fiction by the writer Franz Kafka (1883–1924).*

David Zane Mairowitz, born in New York City in 1943, emigrated in 1968 to England, where he works as a freelance writer.

We include here the Crumb and Mairowitz version of Franz Kafka's "A Hunger Artist."

In June 1924, his "phantoms" saw to it — with their
usual irony — that while dying of *starvation*, he
would be correcting the galley-proofs of an
astonishing masterwork called...

THE PERIOD OF FASTING WAS SET BY HIS IMPRESARIO AT FORTY DAYS MAXIMUM, BECAUSE AFTER THAT TIME THE PUBLIC BEGAN TO LOSE INTEREST. SO, ON THE FORTIETH DAY, WITH AN EXCITED CROWD FILLING THE ARENA AND A MILITARY BAND PLAYING, TWO YOUNG LADIES CAME TO LEAD THE HUNGER-ARTIST OUT OF HIS CAGE. WHEN THIS HAPPENED HE ALWAYS PUT UP SOME RESISTANCE...WHY STOP AFTER ONLY FORTY DAYS?!? WHY SHOULD THEY TAKE FROM HIM THE GLORY OF FASTING EVEN LONGER, OF SURPASSING EVEN HIMSELF TO REACH UNIMAGINABLE HEIGHTS, FOR HE SAW HIS ABILITY TO GO ON FASTING AS *UNLIMITED!*

THEN CAME THE FEAST, WITH THE IMPRESARIO TRYING TO SPOONFEED THE NEARLY COMATOSE HUNGER-ARTIST, ALL THE WHILE CHATTING CHEERFULLY IN ORDER TO DISTRACT ATTENTION FROM HIS CONDITION.

AFTER THAT THERE WAS EVEN A TOAST TO THE AUDIENCE, SUPPOSEDLY SUGGESTED BY THE HUNGER-ARTIST HIMSELF IN A WHISPER TO THE IMPRESARIO.

E LIVED THIS WAY FOR MANY YEARS, HONORED BY ALL THE WORLD, YET TROUBLED IN HIS SOUL, DEEPLY FRUSTRATED THAT THEY WOULD NOT ALLOW HIS FASTING TO EXCEED FORTY DAYS. HE SPENT MOST OF HIS TIME IN A GLOOMY MOOD, AND WHEN SOME KIND-HEARTED PERSON WOULD TRY TO EXPLAIN THAT HIS DEPRESSION WAS THE RESULT OF THE FASTING, HE WOULD SOMETIMES FLY INTO A RAGE AND BEGIN RATTLING THE BARS OF HIS CAGE LIKE AN ANIMAL.

S TIME WENT BY PEOPLE BECAME INTERESTED IN OTHER AMUSEMENTS, AND WERE REVOLTED BY PROFESSIONAL FASTING. THE HUNGER-ARTIST COULD NOT CHANGE JOBS, FANATICALLY DEVOTED TO FASTING AS HE WAS. SO, DISCHARGING THE IMPRESARIO, HE HIRED HIMSELF OUT TO A LARGE CIRCUS, WHERE HIS CAGE WAS PUT OUTSIDE, NEAR THOSE OF THE ANIMALS.

CHAPTER 17

Reading and Writing about Plays

I regard the theater as a serious business, one that makes or should make man more human, which is to say, less alone.

ARTHUR MILLER

Chapter Preview

After reading this chapter you will be able to

- Identify and define the types of plays
- Identify and analyze the elements of drama
- Analyze a character
- Evaluate a dramatic production
- Compare filmed plays to stage productions
- Describe the conventions of Greek tragedy

Types of Plays

Most of the world's great plays written before the twentieth century may be regarded as one of two kinds: **tragedy** or **comedy.** Roughly speaking, tragedy dramatizes the conflict between the vitality of the individual life and the laws or limits of life. The tragic hero reaches a height, going beyond the experience of others but at the cost of his or her life. Comedy, on the other hand, dramatizes the vitality of the laws of social life. In comedy, the good life is seen to reside in the shedding of an individualism that isolates, in favor of a union with a genial and enlightened society. These points must be amplified a bit before we go on to the further point that any important play does much more than can be put into such crude formulas.

Tragedy

Tragic heroes usually go beyond the standards to which reasonable people adhere; they do some fearful deed which ultimately destroys them. This deed is often said to be an act of **hubris,** a Greek word meaning something like "overweening pride." It may involve, for instance, violating a taboo, such as that against taking life. But if the hubristic act ultimately destroys the man or woman who performs it, it also shows that person (paradoxically) to be in some way more fully a living being—a person who has experienced life more fully, whether by heroic action or by a capacity for enduring suffering—than the other characters in the play. (If the tragic hero does not die, he or she is usually left in a deathlike state, as is the blind Oedipus in *Oedipus the King.*) In tragedy we see humanity pushed to an extreme;

431

the hero enters a world unknown to most and reveals magnificence. After the hero's departure from the stage, we are left in a world of smaller people.

What has just been said may (or may not) be true of most tragedies, but it is not true of all. If you were writing about a tragedy, you might consider whether the points just made are illustrated in your play. Is Willy Loman, in Arthur Miller's *Death of a Salesman* (page 1044), a tragic figure, or is he merely a pathetic figure? In our first paragraph we said that a tragic figure "reaches a height, going beyond the experience of others but at the cost of his or her life," and in our next paragraph we said that "after the hero's departure from the stage, we are left in a world of smaller people." Do these words apply to *Death of a Salesman?* Or is Biff right when in the second act (page 1103) he says to Willy, "Pop, I'm a dime a dozen, and so are you." If Biff is right, is the play not a tragedy? Or does our statement describing tragedy need to be emended? Is the tragic hero guilty of hubris? Does the hero seem a greater person than the others in the play? An essay examining these questions probably requires not only a character sketch but also comparison with other characters.

Tragedy commonly involves **irony** of two sorts: unconsciously ironic deeds and unconsciously ironic speeches. Ironic deeds have some consequence more or less the reverse of what the doer intends. Macbeth thinks that by killing Duncan he will gain happiness, but he finds that his deed brings him sleepless nights. Brutus thinks that by killing Caesar he will bring liberty to Rome, but his action brings tyranny. In an unconsciously ironic speech, the words mean one thing to the speaker but something more significant to the audience, as when King Duncan, baffled by Cawdor's treason, says

> There's no art
> To find the mind's construction in the face:
> He was a gentleman on whom I built
> An absolute trust.

At this moment Macbeth, whom we have already heard meditating the murder of Duncan, enters. Duncan's words are true, but he does not apply them to Macbeth, as the audience does. A few moments later Duncan praises Macbeth as "a peerless kinsman." Soon Macbeth will indeed become peerless, when he kills Duncan and ascends to the throne.[1] Sophocles' use of ironic deeds and speeches is so pervasive, especially in *Oedipus Rex,* that **Sophoclean irony** has become a critical term.

When a deed backfires or has a reverse effect, such as Macbeth's effort to gain happiness has, we have what Aristotle (the first—and still the greatest—drama critic) called a **peripeteia,** or a **reversal.** A character who comes to perceive what has happened (Macbeth's "I have lived long enough: my way of life / Is fall'n into the sere, the yellow leaf") experiences (in Aristotle's language) an **anagnorisis,** or **recognition.** Strictly speaking, for Aristotle the recognition was a matter of literal identification—for example, the recognition that Oedipus was the son of a man he killed. In *Macbeth,* the recognition in this sense is that Macduff, "from his mother's womb / Untimely ripped," is the man who fits the prophecy that Macbeth can be conquered only by someone not "of woman born." Does Willy Loman in *Death of a Salesman* ever experience a recognition? If not, does this lack of recognition indicate that the play is not a tragedy, or, on the other hand, that the description of tragedy needs to be emended?

---

[1]**Dramatic irony** (ironic deeds, or happenings, and unconsciously ironic speeches) must be distinguished from **verbal irony,** which is produced when the speaker is *conscious* that his words mean something different from what they say. In *Macbeth* Lennox says, "The gracious Duncan / Was pitied of Macbeth. Marry, he was dead! / And the right valiant Banquo walked too late. / . . . / Men must not walk too late." He *says* nothing about Macbeth's having killed Duncan and Banquo, but he *means* that Macbeth has killed them.

In his analysis of drama, Aristotle says that the tragic hero comes to grief through his **hamartia,** a term sometimes translated as **tragic flaw** but perhaps better translated as **tragic error,** since *flaw* implies a moral fault. Thus it is a great error for Hamlet not to inspect the foils at the start of the deadly fencing match with Laertes; had he done so, he would have seen that one of the foils was blunt and one pointed. If we hold to the translation *flaw,* we begin to hunt for a fault in the tragic hero's character; and we say, for instance, that Hamlet is gullible, or some such thing. In doing this, we may diminish or even overlook the hero's grandeur.

Comedy

Although in tragedy the hero usually seems to embody certain values that are supe-rior to those of the surrounding society, in comedy the fullest life is seen to reside *within* enlightened social norms: At the beginning of a comedy we find banished dukes, unhappy lovers, crabby parents, jealous husbands, and harsh laws; but at the end we usually have a unified and genial society, often symbolized by a marriage feast to which everyone, or almost everyone, is invited. Early in *A Midsummer Night's Dream,* for instance, we meet quarreling young lovers and a father who demands that his daughter either marry a man she does not love or enter a convent. Such is the Athenian law. At the end of the play the lovers are properly matched, to everyone's satisfaction.

Speaking broadly, most comedies fall into one of two classes: **satiric comedy** or **romantic comedy.** In satiric comedy, the emphasis is on the obstructionists—the irate fathers, hardheaded businessmen, and other members of the establishment who at the beginning of the play seem to hold all the cards, preventing joy from reigning. They are held up to ridicule because they are repressive monomaniacs enslaved to themselves, acting mechanistically (always irate, always hardheaded) instead of responding genially to the ups and downs of life. The outwitting of these obstructionists, usually by the younger generation, often provides the resolution of the plot. Ben Jonson, Molière, and George Bernard Shaw are in this tradition; their comedy, according to an ancient Roman formula, "chastens morals with ridicule"—that is, it reforms folly or vice by laughing at it. On the other hand, in romantic comedy (think of Shakespeare's *A Midsummer Night's Dream, As You Like It,* and *Twelfth Night*) the emphasis is on a pair or pairs of delightful people who engage our sympathies as they run their obstacle race to the altar. There are obstructionists here too, but the emphasis is on festivity.

In writing about comedy you may be concerned with the function of one scene or character. But whatever your topic, you may find it helpful to begin by trying to decide whether the play is primarily romantic or primarily satiric (or something else). One way of getting at this is to ask yourself to what degree you sympathize with the characters. Do you laugh *with* them, sympathetically, or do you laugh *at* them, regarding them as being at least somewhat contemptible?

Elements of Drama

Theme

If we have read or seen a drama thoughtfully, we ought to be able to formulate its **theme,** its underlying idea—and perhaps we can even go so far as to say its moral attitudes, its view of life, its wisdom. Some critics have argued that the concept of theme is meaningless. They hold that *Macbeth,* for example, gives us only an extremely detailed history of one imaginary man. In this view, *Macbeth* says nothing to you or me; it tells only what happened to an imaginary man. Even *Julius Caesar* says nothing about the historical Julius Caesar or about the nature of Roman politics. Here we can agree; no one would offer Shakespeare's play as evidence of what the historical Caesar said or did. But surely the view that the concept of theme is meaningless, and that a work tells us only about imaginary creatures, is a desperate one. We *can* say that we see in *Julius Caesar* the fall of power, or (thinking of Brutus) the vulnerability of idealism, or some such thing.

To the reply that these are mere truisms, we can counter: Yes, but the truisms are presented in such a way that they take on life and become a part of us rather than remain things of which we say, "I've heard it said, and I guess it's so." The play offers instruction, in a pleasant and persuasive way. And surely we are in no danger of equating the play with the theme that we sense underlies it. We recognize that the play presents the theme with such detail that our statement is only a wedge to help us enter into the play.

Some critics (influenced by Aristotle's statement that a drama is an imitation of an action) use **action** in a sense equivalent to theme. In this sense, the action is the underlying happening—the inner happening—for example, "the enlightenment of a character," or "the coming of unhappiness to a character," or "the finding of the self by self-surrender." It might be said that the theme of *Macbeth* is embodied in words that Macbeth himself utters: "Blood will have blood." This is not to say that these words and no other words embody the theme or the action; it is only to say that these words seem to the writer (and, if the essay is effective, to the reader) to bring us close to the center of the play.

Plot

Plot is variously defined, sometimes as the equivalent of *story* (in this sense a synopsis of *Julius Caesar* has the same plot as *Julius Caesar*), but more often, and more usefully, as the dramatist's particular *arrangement of the story.* Thus, because Shakespeare's *Julius Caesar* begins with a scene dramatizing an encounter between plebeians and tribunes, its plot is different from that of a play on Julius Caesar in which such a scene (not necessary to the story) is omitted.

Handbooks on drama often suggest that a plot (arrangement of happenings) should have a **rising action,** a **climax,** and a **falling action.** This sort of plot can be diagrammed as a pyramid: The tension rises through complications or **crises** to a climax, at which point the climax is the apex, and the tension allegedly slackens as we witness the **dénouement** (literally, *unknotting*). Shakespeare sometimes used a pyramidal structure, placing his climax neatly in the middle of what seems to us to be the third of five acts. In *Hamlet,* the protagonist proves to his own satisfaction Claudius's guilt in 3.2, with the play within the play; but almost immediately he begins to worsen his position by failing to kill Claudius when he is an easy target (3.3) and by contaminating himself with the murder of Polonius (3.4). In *Romeo and Juliet,* the first half shows Romeo winning Juliet; but when in 3.1 he kills her cousin Tybalt, Romeo sets in motion the second half of the play, the losing of Juliet and of his own life.

Of course, no law demands such a structure, and a hunt for the pyramid usually causes the hunter to overlook all the crises but the middle one. William Butler Yeats once suggestively diagrammed a good plot not as a pyramid but as a line moving diagonally upward, punctuated by several crises. Perhaps it is sufficient to say that a good plot has its moments of tension, but their location will vary with the play. They are the product of **conflict**, but it should be noted that not all conflict produces tension; there is conflict but little tension in a baseball game when the home team is ahead 10–0 and a pinch hitter comes to bat in the bottom of the ninth inning with two out and no one on base.

Regardless of how a plot is diagrammed, the **exposition** is that part that tells the audience what it has to know about the past, the **antecedent action.** Two gossiping servants who reveal that after a year away in Paris the young master is coming home tomorrow with a new wife are giving the audience the exposition. But the exposition may also extend far into the play, coming to light in small, explosive revelations.

Exposition has been discussed as though it consists simply of informing the audience about events, but exposition can do much more. It can give us an understanding of the characters who themselves are talking about other characters, it can evoke a mood, and it can generate tension. When we summarize the opening act by treating it as "mere exposition," we are probably losing what is dramatic in it.

Exposition usually includes **foreshadowing.** Details given in the exposition, which we may at first take as mere background, often turn out to be highly relevant to later developments. For instance, in the very short first scene of *Macbeth* the witches introduce the name of Macbeth, but in such words as "Fair is foul" and "when the battle's lost and won" they also give glimpses of what will happen: Macbeth will become foul, and though he will seem to win (he becomes king) he will lose the most important battle. Similarly, during the exposition in the second scene we learn that Macbeth has loyally defeated Cawdor, who betrayed King Duncan, and Macbeth has been given Cawdor's title. Later we will find that, like Cawdor, Macbeth betrays Duncan. That is, in giving us the background about Cawdor, the exposition also tells us (though we don't know it when we first see or read the play) something about what will happen to Macbeth.

In writing about an aspect of plot, you may want to consider the following approaches:

- Is the plot improbable? If so, is the play therefore weak?
- Does a scene that might at first seem unimportant or even irrelevant serve an important function?
- If certain actions that could be shown onstage take place offstage, is there a reason? In *Macbeth*, why do you suppose the murder of Duncan takes place offstage, whereas Banquo and Macduff's family are murdered onstage? Why did Shakespeare prefer not to show us the murder of Duncan? What has he gained? (A good way to approach this sort of question is to think of what your own reaction would be if the action were shown on the stage.)
- If there are several conflicts—for example, between pairs of lovers or between parents and their children and also between the parents themselves—how are these conflicts related? Are they parallel? Or are they contrasting?
- Does the arrangement of scenes have a structure? For instance, do the scenes depict a rise and then a fall?
- Does the plot seem satisfactorily concluded? Are there loose threads? If so, is the apparent lack of a complete resolution a weakness in the play? Or does it serve a function?

Gestures

The language of a play, broadly conceived, includes the **gestures** that the characters make and the settings in which they make them. As Ezra Pound said, "The medium of drama is not words, but persons moving about on a stage using words." Because plays are meant to be seen, you'll want to make every effort to visualize the action when you read a play. Ibsen is getting at something important when he tells us in a stage direction that Nora "walks cautiously over to the door to the study and listens." Her silent actions tell us as much about her as many of her speeches do.

Gesture can be interpreted even more broadly: The mere fact that a character enters, leaves, or does not enter may be highly significant. John Russell Brown comments on the actions and the absence of certain words that in *Hamlet* convey the growing separation between King Claudius and his wife, Gertrude:

> Their first appearance together with a public celebration of marriage is a large and simple visual effect, and Gertrude's close concern for her son suggests a simple, and perhaps unremarkable modification. . . . But Claudius enters without Gertrude for his "Prayer Scene" (3.2) and, for the first time, Gertrude enters without him for the Closet Scene (3.4) and is left alone, again for the first time, when Polonius hides behind the arras. Thereafter earlier accord is revalued by an increasing separation, often poignantly silent and unexpected. When Claudius calls Gertrude to leave with him after Hamlet has dragged off Polonius' body, she makes no reply; twice more he urges her and she is still silent. But he does not remonstrate or question; rather he speaks of his own immediate concerns and, far from supporting her with assurances, becomes more aware of his own fears:
>
> > O, come away!
> > My soul is full of discord and dismay. (4.1.44–45)
>
> Emotion has been so heightened that it is remarkable that they leave together without further words. The audience has been aware of a new distance between Gertrude and Claudius, of her immobility and silence, and of his self-concern, haste, and insistence.[2]

Setting

Drama of the nineteenth and early twentieth centuries (especially the plays of Henrik Ibsen, Anton Chekhov, and George Bernard Shaw) is often thought to be "realistic," but even a realistic playwright or stage designer selects from among many available materials. A **realistic setting** (indication of the **locale**), then, can say a great deal, and it can even serve as a symbol. Over and over again in Ibsen we find the realistic setting of a nineteenth-century drawing room, with its heavy draperies and its bulky furniture, helping to convey his vision of a bourgeois world that oppresses the individual who struggles to affirm other values.

Twentieth-century dramatists are often explicit about the symbolic qualities of the setting. Here is an example from Eugene O'Neill's *Desire under the Elms;* only a part of the initial stage direction is given:

> The house is in good condition but in need of paint. Its walls are a sickly grayish, the green of the shutters faded. Two enormous elms are on each side of the

[2]John Russell Brown, *Shakespeare's Plays in Performance* (New York: St. Martin's, 1967), p. 139.

house. They bend their trailing branches down over the roof. They appear to protect and at the same time subdue. There is a sinister maternity in their aspect, a crushing, jealous absorption. . . . They are like exhausted women resting their sagging breasts and hands and hair on its roof.

Not surprisingly, the action in the play includes deeds of "sinister maternity" (a mother kills her infant) and "jealous absorption."

In *The Glass Menagerie* Tennessee Williams tells us that

the apartment faces an alley and is entered by a fire-escape, a structure whose name is a touch of accidental poetic truth, for all of these huge buildings are always burning with the slow and implacable fires of human desperation.

Death of a Salesman opens with a long stage direction that includes this statement: "Before us is the Salesman's house. We are aware of towering, angular shapes behind it, surrounding it on all sides." Later we will understand that this setting is a way of conveying Willy's sense that he is hemmed in, oppressed.

Characterization and Motivation

Characterization, or personality, is defined, as in fiction (see pages 351–52), by what the characters do (a stage direction tells us that "Nora dances more and more wildly"), by what they say (she asks her husband to play the piano), by what others say about them, and by the setting in which they move. The characters are also defined in part by other characters whom they in some degree resemble or from whom they in some degree differ. Hamlet, Laertes, and Fortinbras have each lost his father, but Hamlet spares the praying King Claudius, whereas Laertes, seeking vengeance on Hamlet for murdering Laertes's father, says he would cut Hamlet's throat in church. Hamlet meditates about the nature of action, but Fortinbras leads the Norwegians in a military campaign and ultimately acquires Denmark.

Other plays also provide examples of **foils,** or characters who set one another off. Macbeth and Banquo both hear prophecies, but they act and react differently; Brutus is one kind of assassin, Cassius another, and Casca still another. Any analysis of a character, then, will probably have to take into account, in some degree, the other characters who help to show what he or she is, and who thus help to set forth his or her **motivation** (grounds for action, inner drives, goals).

Organizing an Analysis of a Character

As you read and reread, you'll annotate the text and jot down (in whatever order they come to you) your thoughts about the character you are studying. Reading with a view toward writing, you'll want to

1. jot down traits ("kind," "forgetful," "enthusiastic");
2. look back at the text for supporting evidence (characteristic actions, brief supporting quotations); and
3. look for counterevidence that may modify your earlier impressions.

Brainstorming leads to an evaluation of your ideas and to a shaping of them. Evaluating and shaping lead to a tentative outline, and a tentative outline leads to the search for supporting evidence—the material that will constitute the body of your essay.

When you set out to write a first draft, review your annotations and notes and see if you can summarize your view of the character in one or two sentences:

> X is . . . .

or

> Although X is . . . , she is also. . . .

That is, try to formulate a thesis sentence or a thesis paragraph, a proposition that you will go on to support.

You want to let your reader know, probably in your first sentence and almost certainly by the end of your first paragraph, which character you are writing about and what your thesis is.

First Draft

Here is the first draft of an **opening paragraph** that identifies the character and sets forth a thesis:

> Romeo is a very interesting character, I think. In the beginning of the play Romeo is very adolescent. Romeo is smitten with puppy love for a woman named Rosaline. He desires to show all of his friends that he knows how a lover is supposed to act. When he sees Juliet he experiences true love. From the point when he sees Juliet he experiences true love, and from this point he steadily matures in *Romeo and Juliet*. He moves from a self-centered man to a man who lives not for himself but only for Juliet.

Revised Draft

Later the student edited the draft. We reprint the original, with the additional editing in handwriting:

> Romeo ~~is a very interesting character, I think. In the beginning~~
> *begins as an*
> ~~of the play Romeo is very~~ adolescent. ~~Romeo is~~ smitten with puppy
> *and a desire*
> love for ~~a woman named~~ Rosaline. ~~He desires~~ to show all of his friends
> *however,*
> that he knows how a lover is supposed to act. When he sees Juliet he
> *and   this*
> experiences true love. From ~~the~~ point ~~when he sees Juliet he~~
>
> ~~experiences true love, and from this point~~ he steadily matures, in
> *moving   adolescent*
> ~~Romeo and Juliet. He moves~~ from a self-centered man to a man who
>
> lives ~~not for himself but~~ only for Juliet.

Here is a revised version of another effective opening paragraph, effective partly because it identifies the character and offers a thesis:

> In the last speech of *Macbeth*, Malcolm characterizes Lady Macbeth as "fiend-like," and indeed she invokes evil spirits and prompts her husband to commit murder. But despite her bold pose, her role in the murder, and her belief that she will be untroubled by guilt, she has a conscience that torments her and that finally drives her to suicide.

She is not a mere heartless villain; she is a human being who is less strong—and more moral—than she thinks she is.

Notice that

- the paragraph quotes a word ("fiend-like") from the text. It happens that the writer goes on to argue that this word is *not* a totally accurate description, but the quotation nevertheless helps to bring the reader into close contact with the subject of the essay.
- in writing about literature we do not ordinarily introduce the thesis formally. We do not, that is, say "In this paper it is my intention to prove that . . ." Such a sentence may be perfectly appropriate in a paper in political science, but in a paper on literature it sounds too stiff.

The body of your essay will be devoted to supporting your thesis. If you have asserted that although Lady Macbeth is cruel and domineering she nevertheless is endowed with a conscience, you will go on in your essay to support those assertions with references to passages that demonstrate them. This does *not* mean that you tell the plot of the whole work; an essay on a character is by no means the same as a summary of the plot. But since you must support your generalizations, you will have to make brief references to specific episodes that reveal her personality, and almost surely you will quote an occasional word or passage.

There are many possible **ways to organize** an essay on a character. Much will depend on your purpose and thesis. For instance,

- you may want to show how the character develops—gains knowledge, or matures, or disintegrates. Or
- you may want to show what the character contributes to the story or play as a whole. Or
- you may want to show that the character is unbelievable.

No single method of organization is always right, but two are common and effective. One is to let the organization of your essay follow closely the sequence of the literary work; that is, you might devote a paragraph to Lady Macbeth as we perceive her in the first act, and then go on to show that her character is later seen to be more complex than it at first appears. Such an essay may trace your changing responses. This does not mean that you need to write five paragraphs, one on her character in each of the five acts. But it does mean that you might begin with Lady Macbeth as you perceive her in, say, the first act, and then go on to the additional revelations of the rest of the play.

A second effective way of organizing an essay on a character is to set forth, early in the essay, the character's chief traits—let's say the chief strengths and two or three weaknesses—and then go on to study each trait. Here the organization would (to maintain the reader's interest) probably begin with the most obvious points and then move on to the less obvious, subtler points. The body of your essay, in any case, will offer evidence that supports your generalizations about the character.

What about a **concluding paragraph?** The concluding paragraph ought *not* to begin with the obviousness of "Thus we see," or "In conclusion," or "I recommend this play because. . . ." In fact, after you have given what you consider a sound sketch of the character, it may be appropriate simply to quit. Especially if your essay has moved from the obvious traits to the more subtle and more important traits, and if your essay is fairly short (say, fewer than 500 words), a reader may not need a conclusion. Further, there is probably no reason to blunt what you have said by adding an unnecessary and merely repetitive summary. But if you do feel that a conclusion is necessary, you may find it effective to write a summary of the character, somewhat as you did in your opening. For the conclusion, relate the character's character to the entire drama—that is, try to give the reader a sense of the role that the character plays.

✔ CHECKLIST: *Ideas for Writing Arguments about Plays*

Plot and Conflict

☐ Does the **exposition** introduce elements that will be ironically fulfilled? During the exposition do you perceive things differently from the way the characters perceive them?

☐ **Are certain happenings or situations recurrent?** If so, what significance do you attach to them?

☐ **If there is more than one plot,** do the plots seem to be related? Is one plot clearly the main plot and another a sort of subplot, a minor variation on the theme?

☐ **Do any scenes strike you as irrelevant?**

☐ **Are certain scenes so strongly foreshadowed that you anticipated them?** If so, did the happenings in those scenes merely fulfill your expectations, or did they also surprise you?

☐ What kinds of **conflict** are there? One character against another, one group against another, one part of a personality against another part in the same person?

☐ **How is the conflict resolved?** By an unambiguous triumph of one side or by a triumph that is in some degree a loss for the triumphant side? Do you find the resolution satisfying, or unsettling, or what? Why?

Character

☐ A dramatic character is not likely to be thoroughly realistic, a copy of someone we might know. Still, **we can ask if the character is consistent and coherent.** We can also ask whether the character is complex or a rather simple representative of some human type.

☐ **How is the character defined?** Consider what the character says and does and what others say about him or her and do to him or her. Also consider other characters who more or less resemble the character in question; the similarities—and the differences—may be significant.

☐ **How trustworthy are the characters when they characterize themselves? When they characterize others?**

☐ **Do characters change** as the play goes on, or do we simply know them better at the end?

☐ What do you make of the **minor characters?** Are they merely necessary to the plot, or are they foils to other characters? Or do they serve some other function?

- ☐ If **a character is tragic,** does the tragedy seem to proceed from a moral flaw, from an intellectual error, from the malice of others, from sheer chance, or from some combination of these factors?
- ☐ **What are the character's goals?** To what degree do you sympathize with them? If a character is comic, do you laugh *with* or *at* the character?
- ☐ **Do you think the characters are adequately motivated?**
- ☐ Is a given character so meditative that you feel he or she is engaged less in a dialogue with others than in a dialogue with the self? If so, do you feel that this character is to some extent a **spokesperson for the author,** commenting not only on the world of the play but also on the outside world?

Nonverbal Language

- ☐ If the playwright does not provide full stage directions, **try to imagine for at least one scene what gestures and tones might accompany each speech.** (The first scene is usually a good one to try your hand at.)
- ☐ **What do you make of the setting?** Does it help to reveal character? Do changes of scene strike you as symbolic? If so, symbolic of what?

Thinking about a Filmed Version of a Play

Although one might at first think that a film version of a play is pretty much the play caught on film, as soon as one realizes that movies use such techniques as close-ups and high and low angle shots (the action is seen from above or below), one realizes that the filmed version of a play can be very different from the stage version, even though in both forms a story is told by means of actors. In Laurence Olivier's *Hamlet* (1944), dreamlike dissolves (the shot fades into the background while a new shot appears to emerge from beneath it) suggest the prince's irresoluteness. Or consider the use of black and white versus color film; Olivier made Shakespeare's *Henry V* (1944) in color but *Hamlet* in black-and-white because, in Olivier's view, color conveyed a splendor appropriate to England's heroic history, whereas black-and-white seemed more suited to somber tragedy.

Filmmakers customarily "open out" plays, giving us skies, beaches, city streets, and so forth. In Olivier's *Hamlet* we get shots of the sea and the sky. The camera descends from a great height just before Hamlet delivers his first soliloquy, and when the Ghost leaves at 1.5.96 the camera soars into the air, as though with the Ghost, and then, from above, the camera shows Hamlet fainting at the battlements. Even when the camera shows us scenes within the palace, it opens out the play by panning and traveling through long empty corridors and over staircases, suggesting Hamlet's irresolute mind. (Kenneth Branagh's film version of *Hamlet* [1996] is very different; for a student's discussion of this film, see the essay by Will Saretta that appears in our casebook on *Hamlet*, page 990.)

In the 1985 filmed (for television) version of *Death of a Salesman*, with Dustin Hoffman, perhaps the most impressive example of opening out the play comes at the very beginning, when the screen credits are given: We read the words while we see Willy, through the windshield of his car, driving home. Other examples of opening out the play show Willy walking the streets, muttering to strangers, and at least one scene shows the outside of Willy's house, with its paint peeling.

The 1987 film version of *The Glass Menagerie*, directed by Paul Newman, may suffer in part because the camera is not adventurous enough. Much of the play is shot in close-up, with the result that this film of Williams's "Memory Play" has a realism, an in-your-face quality that is at odds with the dreaminess and fragility of the play. A stage production—usually set within a proscenium and making use of evidently theatrical lighting—has an illusionary or unrealistic quality appropriate to Williams's play, in which a narrator (Tom) conjures up scenes. Newman gives us almost all of Williams's dialogue, but he loses almost all the magic of the play.

Getting Ready to Write

A mastery of the terminology does not make anyone a perceptive film critic, but it helps writers communicate their perceptions to readers. Probably an essay on a film will not be primarily about the use of establishing shots or wipes; rather, it will be about the reasons why a particular film pleases or displeases, succeeds or fails, seems significant or insignificant; and in discussing these large matters it is sometimes necessary (or at least economical) to use common technical terms. Large matters are often determined in part by such seemingly small matters as the distance of the camera from its subject or the way in which transitions are made, and one may as well use the conventional terms. But a filmmaker's technique and technology alone cannot make a first-rate film. An idea, a personal vision, a theme must be embodied in all that is flashed on the screen.

Writing an essay about a new film—one not yet available for study on DVD—presents difficulties not encountered in writing about stories, plays, or poems. Because we experience film in a darkened room, we cannot easily take notes, and because the film may be shown only once, we cannot always take another look at passages that puzzle us. But when brief notes can be taken in the dark, it is best to amplify them as soon as light is available, while you still know what the scrawls mean. If you can see the film more than once, do so, and if the script has been published, study it. Draft your paper as soon as possible after your first viewing, and then see the film again. You can sometimes check hazy memories of certain scenes and techniques with fellow viewers. But even with multiple viewings and the aid of friends, it is almost impossible to get all the details right; it is best for the writer to be humble and for the reader to be tolerant.

Reminder: For a sample essay by a student, see the essay on Kenneth Branagh's *Hamlet*, which appears on page 990.

✔ CHECKLIST: *Writing about a Filmed Play*

Preliminaries

☐ Is the title of the film the same as the title of the play? If not, what is implied?

Dramatic Adaptations

☐ **Does the film closely follow its original** and neglect the potentialities of the camera? Or does it so revel in cinematic devices that it distorts the original?

☐ **Does the film do violence to the theme of the original?** Is the film better than its source? Are additions or omissions due to the medium or to a crude or faulty interpretation of the original?

Plot and Character

☐ **Can film deal as effectively with inner action**—mental processes—as with external, physical action? In a given film, how is the inner action conveyed? Olivier used voice-over for parts of Hamlet's soliloquies—that is, we hear Hamlet's voice but his lips do not move.

☐ **Are shots and sequences adequately developed,** or do they seem jerky? (A shot may be jerky by being extremely brief or at an odd angle; a sequence may be jerky by using discontinuous images or fast cuts. Sometimes, of course, jerkiness may be desirable.) If such cinematic techniques as wipes, dissolves, and slow motion are used, are they meaningful and effective?

☐ **Are the characters believable?**

☐ **Are the actors appropriately cast?**

Soundtrack

☐ Does the soundtrack offer **more than realistic dialogue?** Is the music appropriate and functional? (Music may, among other things, imitate natural sounds, give a sense of locale or of ethnic group, suggest states of mind, provide ironic commentary, or—by repetition—help establish connections.) Are volume, tempo, and pitch—whether of music or of such sounds as the wind blowing or cars moving—used to stimulate emotions?

Your Turn: Plays for Analysis

Susan Glaspell

Susan Glaspell (1876–1948) was born in Davenport, Iowa, and educated at Drake University in Des Moines. In 1903 she married the novelist, poet, and playwright George Cram Cook and, with Cook and other writers, actors, and artists, in 1915 founded the Provincetown Players, a group that remained vital until 1929. Glaspell wrote Trifles *(1916) for the Provincetown Players, and she also wrote stories, novels, and a biography of her husband. In 1931 she won a Pulitzer Prize for* Alison's House, *a play about the family of a deceased poet who in some ways resembles Emily Dickinson.*

Trifles

SCENE: *The kitchen in the now abandoned farmhouse of* JOHN WRIGHT, *a gloomy kitchen, and left without having been put in order—unwashed pans under the sink, a loaf of bread outside the breadbox, a dish towel on the table—other signs of incompleted work. At the rear the outer door opens, and the* SHERIFF *comes in, followed by the* COUNTY ATTORNEY *and* HALE. *The* SHERIFF *and* HALE *are men in middle life, the* COUNTY ATTORNEY *is a young man; all are much bundled up and go at once to the stove. They are followed by the two women—the* SHERIFF'S WIFE *first; she is a slight wiry woman, a thin nervous face.* MRS. HALE *is larger and would ordinarily be called more comfortable looking, but she is disturbed now and looks fearfully about as she enters. The women have come in slowly and stand close together near the door.*

COUNTY ATTORNEY [*rubbing his hands*]: This feels good. Come up to the fire, ladies.

MRS. PETERS [*after taking a step forward*]: I'm not—cold.

SHERIFF [*unbuttoning his overcoat and stepping away from the stove as if to the beginning of official business*]: Now, Mr. Hale, before we move things about, you explain to Mr. Henderson just what you saw when you came here yesterday morning.

COUNTY ATTORNEY: By the way, has anything been moved? Are things just as you left them yesterday?

SHERIFF [*looking about*]: It's just the same. When it dropped below zero last night, I thought I'd better send Frank out this morning to make a fire for us—no use getting pneumonia with a big case on; but I told him not to touch anything except the stove—and you know Frank.

COUNTY ATTORNEY: Somebody should have been left here yesterday.

SHERIFF: Oh—yesterday. When I had to send Frank to Morris Center for that man who went crazy—I want you to know I had my hands full yesterday. I knew you could get back from Omaha by today, and as long as I went over everything here myself—

COUNTY ATTORNEY: Well, Mr. Hale, tell just what happened when you came here yesterday morning.

HALE: Harry and I had started to town with a load of potatoes. We came along the road from my place; and as I got here, I said, "I'm going to see if I can't get

The original Provincetown players production (1916) of *Trifles.*

John Wright to go in with me on a party telephone." I spoke to Wright about it once before, and he put me off, saying folks talked too much anyway, and all he asked was peace and quiet—I guess you know about how much he talked himself; but I thought maybe if I went to the house and talked about it before his wife, though I said to Harry that I didn't know as what his wife wanted made much difference to John—

COUNTY ATTORNEY: Let's talk about that later, Mr. Hale. I do want to talk about that, but tell now just what happened when you got to the house.

HALE: I didn't hear or see anything; I knocked at the door, and still it was all quiet inside. I knew they must be up, it was past eight o'clock. So I knocked again, and I thought I heard somebody say, "Come in." I wasn't sure, I'm not sure yet, but I opened the door—this door [*indicating the door by which the two women are still standing*], and there in that rocker—[*pointing to it*] sat Mrs. Wright. [*They all look at the rocker.*]

COUNTY ATTORNEY: What—was she doing?

HALE: She was rockin' back and forth. She had her apron in her hand and was kind of—pleating it.

COUNTY ATTORNEY: And how did she—look?

HALE: Well, she looked queer.

COUNTY ATTORNEY: How do you mean—queer?

HALE: Well, as if she didn't know what she was going to do next. And kind of done up.

COUNTY ATTORNEY: How did she seem to feel about your coming?

HALE: Why, I don't think she minded—one way or other. She didn't pay much attention. I said, "How do, Mrs. Wright, it's cold, ain't it?" And she said, "Is it?"—and went on kind of pleating at her apron. Well, I was surprised; she didn't ask me to come up to the stove, or to set down, but just sat there, not even looking at me, so I said, "I want to see John." And then she—laughed. I guess you would call it a laugh. I thought of Harry and the team outside, so I said a little sharp: "Can't I see John?" "No," she says, kind o' dull like. "Ain't he home?" says I. "Yes," says she, "he's home." "Then why can't I see him?" I asked her, out of patience. "'Cause he's dead," says she. "*Dead?*" says I. She just nodded her head, not getting a bit excited, but rockin' back and forth. "Why—where is he?" says I, not knowing what to say. She just pointed upstairs—like that [*himself pointing to the room above*]. I got up, with the idea of going up there. I walked from there to here—then I says, "Why, what did he die of?" "He died of a rope around his neck," says she, and just went on pleatin' at her apron. Well, I went out and called Harry. I thought I might—need help. We went upstairs, and there he was lyin'—

COUNTY ATTORNEY: I think I'd rather have you go into that upstairs, where you can point it all out. Just go on now with the rest of the story.

HALE: Well, my first thought was to get that rope off. I looked . . . [*Stops, his face twitches.*] . . . but Harry, he went up to him, and he said, "No, he's dead all right, and we'd better not touch anything." So we went back downstairs. She was still sitting that same way. "Has anybody been notified?" I asked. "No," says she, unconcerned. "Who did this, Mrs. Wright?" said Harry. He said it businesslike—and she stopped pleatin' of her apron. "I don't know," she says. "You don't *know?*" says Harry. "No," says she. "Weren't you sleepin' in the bed with him?" says Harry. "Yes," says she, "but I was on the inside." "Somebody slipped a rope round his neck and strangled him, and you didn't wake up?" says Harry. "I didn't wake up," she said after him. We must 'a looked as if we didn't see how that could be, for after a minute she said, "I sleep sound." Harry was going to ask her more questions, but I said maybe we ought to let her tell her story first to the coroner, or the sheriff, so Harry went fast as he could to Rivers' place, where there's a telephone.

COUNTY ATTORNEY: And what did Mrs. Wright do when she knew that you had gone for the coroner?

HALE: She moved from that chair to this over here . . . [*Pointing to a small chair in the corner.*] . . . and just sat there with her hands held together and looking down. I got a feeling that I ought to make some conversation, so I said I had come in to see if John wanted to put in a telephone, and at that she started to laugh, and then she stopped and looked at me—scared. [*The* COUNTY ATTORNEY, *who has had his notebook out, makes a note.*] I dunno, maybe it wasn't scared. I wouldn't like to say it was. Soon Harry got back, and then Dr. Lloyd came, and you, Mr. Peters, and so I guess that's all I know that you don't.

COUNTY ATTORNEY [*looking around*]: I guess we'll go upstairs first—and then out to the barn and around there. [*To the* SHERIFF.] You're convinced that there was nothing important here—nothing that would point to any motive?

SHERIFF: Nothing here but kitchen things. [*The* COUNTY ATTORNEY, *after again looking around the kitchen, opens the door of a cupboard closet. He gets up on a chair and looks on a shelf. Pulls his hand away, sticky.*]

COUNTY ATTORNEY: Here's a nice mess. [*The women draw nearer.*]

MRS. PETERS [*to the other woman*]: Oh, her fruit; it did freeze. [*To the* LAWYER.] She worried about that when it turned so cold. She said the fir'd go out and her jars would break.

SHERIFF: Well, can you beat the women! Held for murder and worryin' about her preserves.

COUNTY ATTORNEY: I guess before we're through she may have something more serious than preserves to worry about.

HALE: Well, women are used to worrying over trifles.

    [*The two women move a little closer together.*]

COUNTY ATTORNEY [*with the gallantry of a young politician*]: And yet, for all their worries, what would we do without the ladies? [*The women do not unbend. He goes to the sink, takes a dipperful of water from the pail and, pouring it into a basin, washes his hands. Starts to wipe them on the roller towel, turns it for a cleaner place.*] Dirty towels! [*Kicks his foot against the pans under the sink.*] Not much of a housekeeper, would you say, ladies?

MRS. HALE [*stiffly*]: There's a great deal of work to be done on a farm.

COUNTY ATTORNEY: To be sure. And yet . . . [*With a little bow to her.*] . . . I know there are some Dickson county farmhouses which do not have such roller towels. [*He gives it a pull to expose its full length again.*]

MRS. HALE: Those towels get dirty awful quick. Men's hands aren't always as clean as they might be.

COUNTY ATTORNEY: Ah, loyal to your sex, I see. But you and Mrs. Wright were neighbors. I suppose you were friends, too.

MRS. HALE [*shaking her head*]: I've not seen much of her of late years. I've not been in this house—it's more than a year.

COUNTY ATTORNEY: And why was that? You didn't like her?

MRS. HALE: I liked her all well enough. Farmers' wives have their hands full, Mr. Henderson. And then—

COUNTY ATTORNEY: Yes—?

MRS. HALE [*looking about*]: It never seemed a very cheerful place.

COUNTY ATTORNEY: No—it's not cheerful. I shouldn't say she had the homemaking instinct.

MRS. HALE: Well, I don't know as Wright had, either.

COUNTY ATTORNEY: You mean that they didn't get on very well?

MRS. HALE: No, I don't mean anything. But I don't think a place'd be any cheerfuler for John Wright's being in it.

COUNTY ATTORNEY: I'd like to talk more of that a little later. I want to get the lay of things upstairs now. [*He goes to the left, where three steps lead to a stair door.*]

SHERIFF: I suppose anything Mrs. Peters does'll be all right. She was to take in some clothes for her, you know, and a few little things. We left in such a hurry yesterday.

COUNTY ATTORNEY: Yes, but I would like to see what you take, Mrs. Peters, and keep an eye out for anything that might be of use to us.

MRS. PETERS: Yes, Mr. Henderson.

[*The women listen to the men's steps on the stairs, then look about the kitchen.*]

MRS. HALE: I'd hate to have men coming into my kitchen, snooping around and criticizing. [*She arranges the pans under sink which the* LAWYER *had shoved out of place.*]

MRS. PETERS: Of course it's no more than their duty.

MRS. HALE: Duty's all right, but I guess that deputy sheriff that came out to make the fire might have got a little of this on. [*Gives the roller towel a pull.*] Wish I'd thought of that sooner. Seems mean to talk about her for not having things slicked up when she had to come away in such a hurry.

MRS. PETERS [*who has gone to a small table in the left rear corner of the room, and lifted one end of a towel that covers a pan*]: She had bread set. [*Stands still.*]

MRS. HALE [*eyes fixed on a loaf of bread beside the breadbox, which is on a low shelf at the other side of the room; moves slowly toward it*]: She was going to put this in there. [*Picks up loaf, then abruptly drops it. In a manner of returning to familiar things.*] It's a shame about her fruit. I wonder if it's all gone. [*Gets up on the chair and looks.*] I think there's some here that's all right, Mrs. Peters. Yes— here; [*Holding it toward the window.*] this is cherries, too. [*Looking again.*] I declare I believe that's the only one. [*Gets down, bottle in her hand. Goes to the sink and wipes it off on the outside.*] She'll feel awful bad after all her hard work in the hot weather. I remember the afternoon I put up my cherries last summer. [*She puts the bottle on the big kitchen table, center of the room, front table. With a sigh, is about to sit down in the rocking chair. Before she is seated realizes what chair it is; with a slow look at it, steps back. The chair, which she has touched, rocks back and forth.*]

MRS. PETERS: Well, I must get those things from the front room closet. [*She goes to the door at the right, but after looking into the other room steps back.*] You coming with me, Mrs. Hale? You could help me carry them. [*They go into the other room; reappear,* MRS. PETERS *carrying a dress and skirt,* MRS. HALE *following with a pair of shoes.*]

MRS. PETERS: My, it's cold in there. [*She puts the cloth on the big table, and hurries to the stove.*]

MRS. HALE [*examining the skirt*]: Wright was close. I think maybe that's why she kept so much to herself. She didn't even belong to the Ladies' Aid. I suppose she felt she couldn't do her part, and then you don't enjoy things when you feel shabby. She used to wear pretty clothes and be lively, when she was Minnie Foster, one of the town girls singing in the choir. But that—oh, that was thirty years ago. This all you was to take in?

MRS. PETERS: She said she wanted an apron. Funny thing to want, for there isn't much to get you dirty in jail, goodness knows. But I suppose just to make her feel more natural. She said they was in the top drawer in this cupboard. Yes, here. And then her little shawl that always hung behind the door. [*Opens stair door and looks.*] Yes, here it is. [*Quickly shuts door leading upstairs.*]

MRS. HALE [*abruptly moving toward her*]:   Mrs. Peters?

MRS. PETERS: Yes, Mrs. Hale?

MRS. HALE: Do you think she did it?

MRS. PETERS [*in a frightened voice*]:   Oh, I don't know.

MRS. HALE: Well, I don't think she did. Asking for an apron and her little shawl. Worrying about her fruit.

MRS. PETERS [*starts to speak, glances up, where footsteps are heard in the room above. In a low voice.*]:   Mr. Peters says it looks bad for her. Mr. Henderson is awful sarcastic in speech, and he'll make fun of her sayin' she didn't wake up.

MRS. HALE: Well, I guess John Wright didn't wake when they was slipping that rope under his neck.

MRS. PETERS: No, it's strange. It must have been done awful crafty and still. They say it was such a—funny way to kill a man, rigging it all up like that.

MRS. HALE: That's just what Mr. Hale said. There was a gun in the house. He says that's what he can't understand.

MRS. PETERS: Mr. Henderson said coming out that what was needed for the case was a motive; something to show anger, or—sudden feeling.

MRS. HALE [*who is standing by the table*]:   Well, I don't see any signs of anger around here. [*She puts her hand on the dish towel which lies on the table, stands looking down at the table, one half of which is clean, the other half messy.*] It's wiped here. [*Makes a move as if to finish work, then turns and looks at loaf of bread outside the breadbox. Drops towel. In that voice of coming back to familiar things.*] Wonder how they are finding things upstairs? I hope she had it a little more red-up up there. You know, it seems kind of *sneaking.* Locking her up in town and then coming out here and trying to get her own house to turn against her!

MRS. PETERS: But, Mrs. Hale, the law is the law.

MRS. HALE: I s'pose 'is. [*Unbuttoning her coat.*] Better loosen up your things, Mrs. Peters. You won't feel them when you go out.

[MRS. PETERS *takes off her fur tippet, goes to hang it on hook at the back of room, stands looking at the under part of the small corner table.*]

MRS. PETERS: She was piecing a quilt. [*She brings the large sewing basket, and they look at the bright pieces.*]

MRS. HALE: It's log cabin pattern. Pretty, isn't it? I wonder if she was goin' to quilt or just knot it?

[*Footsteps have been heard coming down the stairs. The* SHERIFF *enters, followed by* HALE *and the* COUNTY ATTORNEY.]

SHERIFF: They wonder if she was going to quilt it or just knot it. [*The men laugh, the women look abashed.*]

COUNTY ATTORNEY [*rubbing his hands over the stove*]:   Frank's fire didn't do much up there, did it? Well, let's go out to the barn and get that cleared up.

[*The men go outside.*]

MRS. HALE [*resentfully*]: I don't know as there's anything so strange, our takin' up our time with little things while we're waiting for them to get the evidence. [*She sits down at the big table, smoothing out a block with decision.*] I don't see as it's anything to laugh about.

MRS. PETERS [*apologetically*]: Of course they've got awful important things on their minds. [*Pulls up a chair and joins* MRS. HALE *at the table.*]

MRS. HALE [*examining another block*]: Mrs. Peters, look at this one. Here, this is the one she was working on, and look at the sewing! All the rest of it has been so nice and even. And look at this! It's all over the place! Why, it looks as if she didn't know what she was about! [*After she has said this, they look at each other, then start to glance back at the door. After an instant* MRS. HALE *has pulled at a knot and ripped the sewing.*]

MRS. PETERS: Oh, what are you doing, Mrs. Hale?

MRS. HALE [*mildly*]: Just pulling out a stitch or two that's not sewed very good. [*Threading a needle.*] Bad sewing always made me fidgety.

MRS. PETERS [*nervously*]: I don't think we ought to touch things.

MRS. HALE: I'll just finish up this end. [*Suddenly stopping and leaning forward.*] Mrs. Peters?

MRS. PETERS: Yes, Mrs. Hale?

MRS. HALE: What do you suppose she was so nervous about?

MRS. PETERS: Oh—I don't know. I don't know as she was nervous. I sometimes sew awful queer when I'm just tired. [MRS. HALE *starts to say something, looks at* MRS. PETERS, *then goes on sewing.*] Well, I must get these things wrapped up. They may be through sooner than we think. [*Putting apron and other things together.*] I wonder where I can find a piece of paper, and string.

MRS. HALE: In that cupboard, maybe.

MRS. PETERS [*looking in cupboard*]: Why, here's a birdcage. [*Holds it up.*] Did she have a bird, Mrs. Hale?

MRS. HALE: Why, I don't know whether she did or not—I've not been here for so long. There was a man around last year selling canaries cheap, but I don't know as she took one; maybe she did. She used to sing real pretty herself.

MRS. PETERS [*glancing around*]: Seems funny to think of a bird here. But she must have had one, or why should she have a cage? I wonder what happened to it?

MRS. HALE: I s'pose maybe the cat got it.

MRS. PETERS: No, she didn't have a cat. She's got that feeling some people have about cats—being afraid of them. My cat got in her room, and she was real upset and asked me to take it out.

MRS. HALE: My sister Bessie was like that. Queer, ain't it?

MRS. PETERS [*examining the cage*]: Why, look at this door. It's broke. One hinge is pulled apart.

MRS. HALE [*looking, too*]: Looks as if someone must have been rough with it.

MRS. PETERS: Why, yes. [*She brings the cage forward and puts it on the table.*]

MRS. HALE: I wish if they're going to find any evidence they'd be about it. I don't like this place.

MRS. PETERS: But I'm awful glad you came with me, Mrs. Hale. It would be lonesome for me sitting here alone.

MRS. HALE: It would, wouldn't it? [*Dropping her sewing.*] But I tell you what I do wish, Mrs. Peters. I wish I had come over sometimes when *she* was here. I— [*Looking around the room.*]—wish I had.

MRS. PETERS: But of course you were awful busy, Mrs. Hale—your house and your children.

MRS. HALE: I could've come. I stayed away because it weren't cheerful—and that's why I ought to have come. I—I've never liked this place. Maybe because it's down in a hollow, and you don't see the road. I dunno what it is, but it's a lonesome place and always was. I wish I had come over to see Minnie Foster sometimes. I can see now—[*Shakes her head.*]

MRS. PETERS: Well, you mustn't reproach yourself, Mrs. Hale. Somehow we just don't see how it is with other folks until—something comes up.

MRS. HALE: Not having children makes less work—but it makes a quiet house, and Wright out to work all day, and no company when he did come in. Did you know John Wright, Mrs. Peters?

MRS. PETERS: Not to know him; I've seen him in town. They say he was a good man.

MRS. HALE: Yes—good; he didn't drink, and kept his word as well as most, I guess, and paid his debts. But he was a hard man, Mrs. Peters. Just to pass the time of day with him. [*Shivers.*] Like a raw wind that gets to the bone. [*Pauses, her eye falling on the cage.*] I should think she would 'a wanted a bird. But what do you suppose went with it?

MRS. PETERS: I don't know, unless it got sick and died. [*She reaches over and swings the broken door, swings it again; both women watch it.*]

MRS. HALE: You weren't raised round here, were you? [MRS. PETERS *shakes her head.*] You didn't know—her?

MRS. PETERS: Not till they brought her yesterday.

MRS. HALE: She—come to think of it, she was kind of like a bird herself—real sweet and pretty, but kind of timid and—fluttery. How—she—did—change. [*Silence; then as if struck by a happy thought and relieved to get back to everyday things.*] Tell you what, Mrs. Peters; why don't you take the quilt in with you? It might take up her mind.

MRS. PETERS: Why, I think that's a real nice idea, Mrs. Hale. There couldn't possibly be any objection to it, could there? Now, just what would I take? I wonder if her patches are in here—and her things. [*They look in the sewing basket.*]

MRS. HALE: Here's some red. I expect this has got sewing things in it. [*Brings out a fancy box.*] What a pretty box. Looks like something somebody would give you. Maybe her scissors are in here. [*Opens box. Suddenly puts her hand to her nose.*] Why—[MRS. PETERS *bends nearer, then turns her face away.*] There's something wrapped up in this piece of silk.

MRS. PETERS: Why, this isn't her scissors.

MRS. HALE [*lifting the silk*]: Oh, Mrs. Peters—it's—[MRS. PETERS *bends closer.*]

MRS. PETERS: It's the bird.

MRS. HALE [*jumping up*]: But, Mrs. Peters—look at it. Its neck! Look at its neck! It's all—other side *to*.

MRS. PETERS: Somebody—wrung—its neck.

[*Their eyes meet. A look of growing comprehension of horror. Steps are heard outside.* MRS. HALE *slips box under quilt pieces, and sinks into her chair. Enter* SHERIFF *and* COUNTY ATTORNEY. MRS. PETERS *rises.*]

COUNTY ATTORNEY [*as one turning from serious things to little pleasantries*]: Well, ladies, have you decided whether she was going to quilt it or knot it?

MRS. PETERS: We think she was going to—knot it.

COUNTY ATTORNEY: Well, that's interesting, I'm sure. [*Seeing the birdcage.*] Has the bird flown?

MRS. HALE [*putting more quilt pieces over the box*]: We think the—cat got it.

COUNTY ATTORNEY [*preoccupied*]: Is there a cat?

[MRS. HALE *glances in a quick covert way at* MRS. PETERS.]

MRS. PETERS: Well, not now. They're superstitious, you know. They leave.

COUNTY ATTORNEY [*to* SHERIFF, *continuing an interrupted conversation*]: No sign at all of anyone having come from the outside. Their own rope. Now let's go up again and go over it piece by piece. [*They start upstairs.*] It would have to have been someone who knew just the—[MRS. PETERS *sits down. The two women sit there not looking at one another, but as if peering into something and at the same time holding back. When they talk now, it is the manner of feeling their way over strange ground, as if afraid of what they are saying, but as if they cannot help saying it.*]

MRS. HALE: She liked the bird. She was going to bury it in that pretty box.

MRS. PETERS [*in a whisper*]: When I was a girl—my kitten—there was a boy took a hatchet, and before my eyes—and before I could get there—[*Covers her face an instant.*] If they hadn't held me back, I would have—[*Catches herself, looks upstairs where steps are heard, falters weakly.*]—hurt him.

MRS. HALE [*with a slow look around her*]: I wonder how it would seem never to have had any children around. [*Pause.*] No, Wright wouldn't like the bird—a thing that sang. She used to sing. He killed that, too.

MRS. PETERS [*moving uneasily*]: We don't know who killed the bird.

MRS. HALE: I knew John Wright.

MRS. PETERS: It was an awful thing was done in this house that night, Mrs. Hale. Killing a man while he slept, slipping a rope around his neck that choked the life out of him.

MRS. HALE: His neck. Choked the life out of him.

[*Her hand goes out and rests on the birdcage.*]

MRS. PETERS [*with a rising voice*]: We don't know who killed him. We don't know.

MRS. HALE [*her own feeling not interrupted*]: If there'd been years and years of nothing, then a bird to sing to you, it would be awful—still, after the bird was still.

MRS. PETERS [*something within her speaking*]: I know what stillness is. When we homesteaded in Dakota, and my first baby died—after he was two years old, and me with no other then—

MRS. HALE [*moving*]: How soon do you suppose they'll be through, looking for the evidence?

MRS. PETERS: I know what stillness is. [*Pulling herself back.*] The law has got to punish crime, Mrs. Hale.

MRS. HALE [*not as if answering that*]: I wish you'd seen Minnie Foster when she wore a white dress with blue ribbons and stood up there in the choir and sang. [*A look around the room.*] Oh, I *wish* I'd come over here once in a while! That was a crime! That was a crime! Who's going to punish that?

MRS. PETERS [*looking upstairs*]: We mustn't—take on.

MRS. HALE: I might have known she needed help! I know how things can be—for women. I tell you, it's queer, Mrs. Peters. We live close together and we live far apart. We all go through the same things—it's all just a different kind of the same thing. [*Brushes her eyes, noticing the bottle of fruit, reaches out for it.*] If I was you, I wouldn't tell her her fruit was gone. Tell her it *ain't*. Tell her it's all right. Take this in to prove it to her. She—she may never know whether it was broke or not.

MRS. PETERS [*takes the bottle, looks about for something to wrap it in; takes petticoat from the clothes brought from the other room, very nervously begins winding this around the bottle. In a false voice*]: My, it's a good thing the men couldn't hear us. Wouldn't they just laugh! Getting all stirred up over a little thing like a—dead canary. As if that could have anything to do with—with—wouldn't they *laugh!*

[*The men are heard coming downstairs.*]

MRS. HALE [*under her breath*]: Maybe they would—maybe they wouldn't.

COUNTY ATTORNEY: No, Peters, it's all perfectly clear except a reason for doing it. But you know juries when it comes to women. If there was some definite thing. Something to show—something to make a story about—a thing that would connect up with this strange way of doing it.

[*The women's eyes meet for an instant. Enter* HALE *from outer door.*]

HALE: Well, I've got the team around. Pretty cold out there.

COUNTY ATTORNEY: I'm going to stay here awhile by myself. [*To the* SHERIFF.] You can send Frank out for me, can't you? I want to go over everything. I'm not satisfied that we can't do better.

SHERIFF: Do you want to see what Mrs. Peters is going to take in?

[*The* LAWYER *goes to the table, picks up the apron, laughs.*]

COUNTY ATTORNEY: Oh I guess they're not very dangerous things the ladies have picked up. [*Moves a few things about, disturbing the quilt pieces which cover the box. Steps back.*] No, Mrs. Peters doesn't need supervising. For that matter, a sheriff's wife is married to the law. Ever think of it that way, Mrs. Peters?

MRS. PETERS: Not—just that way.

SHERIFF [*chuckling*]: Married to the law. [*Moves toward the other room.*] I just want you to come in here a minute, George. We ought to take a look at these windows.

COUNTY ATTORNEY [*scoffingly*]: Oh, windows!

SHERIFF: We'll be right out, Mr. Hale.

[HALE *goes outside. The* SHERIFF *follows the* COUNTY ATTORNEY *into the other room. Then* MRS. HALE *rises, hands tight together, looking intensely at* MRS. PETERS, *whose eyes take a slow turn, finally meeting* MRS. HALE's. *A moment* MRS. HALE *holds her, then her own eyes point the way to where the box is concealed. Suddenly* MRS. PETERS *throws back quilt pieces and tries to put the box in the bag she is wearing. It is too big. She opens box, starts to take the bird out, cannot touch it, goes to pieces, stands there helpless. Sound of a knob turning in the other room.* MRS. HALE *snatches the box and puts it in the pocket of her big coat. Enter* COUNTY ATTORNEY *and* SHERIFF.]

COUNTY ATTORNEY [*facetiously*]: Well, Henry, at least we found out that she was not going to quilt it. She was going to—what is it you call it, ladies?

MRS. HALE [*her hand against her pocket*]: We call it—knot it, Mr. Henderson.

CURTAIN

[1916]

Joining the Conversation: Critical Thinking and Writing

The Play on the Page

1. How would you characterize Mr. Henderson, the county attorney in *Trifles*?
2. In what way or ways are Mrs. Peters and Mrs. Hale different from each other?
3. On page 451, when Mrs. Peters tells of the boy who killed her cat, she says, "If they hadn't held me back, I would have—(*catches herself, looks upstairs where steps are heard, falters weakly.*)—hurt him." What do you think she was about to say before she faltered? Why do you suppose Glaspell included this speech about Mrs. Peters's girlhood?
4. We never see Mrs. Wright on stage. Nevertheless, by the end of *Trifles* we know a great deal about her. Explain both what we know about her—physical characteristics, habits, interests, personality, life before her marriage and after—and *how* we know these things.
5. The title of the play is ironic—the "trifles" are important. What other ironies do you find in the play?
6. Do you think the play is immoral? Explain.
7. Assume that the canary has been found, thereby revealing a possible motive, and that Minnie is indicted for murder. You are the defense attorney. In 500 words set forth your defense. (Take any position you wish. For instance, you may want to argue that she committed justifiable homicide or that—on the basis of her behavior as reported by Mr. Hale—she is innocent by reason of insanity.)
8. Assume that the canary had been found and Minnie Wright convicted. Compose the speech you think she might have delivered before the sentence was given.

The Play on the Stage

9. Describe the setting, indicating what it "says" and what atmosphere it evokes.
10. Several times the men "laugh" or "chuckle." In their contexts, what do these expressions of amusement convey?
11. "*The women's eyes meet for an instant.*" (middle of page 452) What do you think this bit of action "says"? What do you understand by the exchange of glances?

MyLiteratureLab® *For additional resources for* Trifles, *log in to* www .myliteraturelab.com *where you will find a Performance, a Longman Lecture, and a Comprehension Quiz, as well as an About the Author, Bibliography, Links, and Critical Overview for Glaspell (under Student Resources).*

A Modern Comedy

DAVID IVES

David Ives, born in Chicago in 1950, was educated at Northwestern University and at the Yale Drama School. Sure Thing *was first publicly staged in 1988, and later staged with six other one-act plays, grouped under the title* All in the Timing.

Sure Thing

This play is for Jason Buzas

BETTY, *a woman in her late twenties, is reading at a café table. An empty chair is opposite her.* BILL, *same age, enters.*

BILL: Excuse me. Is this chair taken?
BETTY: Excuse me?
BILL: Is this taken?
BETTY: Yes it is.
BILL: Oh. Sorry.
BETTY: Sure thing.

[*A bell rings softly.*]

BILL: Excuse me. Is this chair taken?
BETTY: Excuse me?
BILL: Is this taken?
BETTY: No, but I'm expecting somebody in a minute.
BILL: Oh. Thanks anyway.
BETTY: Sure thing.

[*A bell rings softly.*]

BILL: Excuse me. Is this chair taken?
BETTY: No, but I'm expecting somebody very shortly.
BILL: Would you mind if I sit here till he or she or it comes?
BETTY [*glances at her watch*]: They do seem to be pretty late. . . .
BILL: You never know who you might be turning down.
BETTY: Sorry. Nice try, though.
BILL: Sure thing.

[*Bell.*]

Is this seat taken?
BETTY: No it's not.
BILL: Would you mind if I sit here?
BETTY: Yes I would.
BILL: Oh.

[*Bell.*]

Is this chair taken?
BETTY: No it's not.
BILL: Would you mind if I sit here?
BETTY: No. Go ahead.
BILL: Thanks. [*He sits. She continues reading.*] Everyplace else seems to be taken.
BETTY: Mm-hm.
BILL: Great place.
BETTY: Mm-hm.
BILL: What's the book?
BETTY: I just wanted to read in quiet, if you don't mind.
BILL: No. Sure thing.

[*Bell.*]

Everyplace else seems to be taken.
BETTY: Mm-hm.

BILL: Great place for reading.
BETTY: Yes, I like it.
BILL: What's the book?
BETTY: *The Sound and the Fury.*
BILL: Oh. Hemingway.

[*Bell.*]

What's the book?
BETTY: *The Sound and the Fury.*
BILL: Oh. Faulkner.
BETTY: Have you read it?
BILL: Not . . . actually. I've sure read *about* it, though. It's supposed to be great.
BETTY: It is great.
BILL: I hear it's great. [*Small pause.*] Waiter?

[*Bell.*]

What's the book?
BETTY: *The Sound and the Fury.*
BILL: Oh. Faulkner.
BETTY: Have you read it?
BILL: I'm a Mets fan, myself.

[*Bell.*]

BETTY: Have you read it?
BILL: Yeah, I read it in college.
BETTY: Where was college?
BILL: I went to Oral Roberts University.

[*Bell.*]

BETTY: Where was college?
BILL: I was lying. I never really went to college. I just like to party.

[*Bell.*]

BETTY: Where was college?
BILL: Harvard.
BETTY: Do you like Faulkner?
BILL: I love Faulkner. I spent a whole winter reading him once.
BETTY: I've just started.
BILL: I was so excited after ten pages that I went out and bought everything else
      he wrote. One of the greatest reading experiences of my life. I mean, all that
      incredible psychological understanding. Page after page of gorgeous prose.
      His profound grasp of the mystery of time and human existence. The smells
      of the earth . . . What do you think?
BETTY: I think it's pretty boring.

[*Bell.*]

BILL: What's the book?
BETTY: *The Sound and the Fury.*
BILL: Oh! Faulkner!
BETTY: Do you like Faulkner?
BILL: I love Faulkner.
BETTY: He's incredible.
BILL: I spent a whole winter reading him once.

BETTY: I was so excited after ten pages that I went out and bought everything else he wrote.

BILL: All that incredible psychological understanding.

BETTY: And the prose is so gorgeous.

BILL: And the way he's grasped the mystery of time—

BETTY: —and human existence. I can't believe I've waited this long to read him.

BILL: You never know. You might not have liked him before.

BETTY: That's true.

BILL: You might not have been ready for him. You have to hit these things at the right moment or it's no good.

BETTY: That's happened to me.

BILL: It's all in the timing. [*Small pause.*] My name's Bill, by the way.

BETTY: I'm Betty.

BILL: Hi.

BETTY: Hi. [*Small pause.*]

BILL: Yes I thought reading Faulkner was . . . a great experience.

BETTY: Yes. [*Small pause.*]

BILL: *The Sound and the Fury* . . . [*Another small pause.*]

BETTY: Well. Onwards and upwards. [*She goes back to her book.*]

BILL: Waiter—?

[*Bell.*]

You have to hit these things at the right moment or it's no good.

BETTY: That's happened to me.

BILL: It's all in the timing. My name's Bill, by the way.

BETTY: I'm Betty.

BILL: Hi.

BETTY: Hi.

BILL: Do you come in here a lot?

BETTY: Actually I'm just in town for two days from Pakistan.

BILL: Oh. Pakistan.

[*Bell.*]

My name's Bill, by the way.

BETTY: I'm Betty.

BILL: Hi.

BETTY: Hi.

BILL: Do you come in here a lot?

BETTY: Every once in a while. Do you?

BILL: Not so much anymore. Not as much as I used to. Before my nervous breakdown.

[*Bell.*]

Do you come in here a lot?

BETTY: Why are you asking?

BILL: Just interested.

BETTY: Are you really interested, or do you just want to pick me up?

BILL: No, I'm really interested.

BETTY: Why would you be interested in whether I come in here a lot?

BILL: I'm just . . . getting acquainted.

BETTY: Maybe you're only interested for the sake of making small talk long enough to ask me back to your place to listen to some music, or because you've just rented this great tape for your VCR, or because you've got some terrific unknown Django Reinhardt record, only all you really want to do is fuck—which you won't do very well—after which you'll go into the bathroom and pee very loudly, then pad into the kitchen and get yourself a beer from the refrigerator without asking me whether I'd like anything, and then you'll proceed to lie back down beside me and confess that you've got a girlfriend named Stephanie who's away at medical school in Belgium for a year, and that you've been involved with her—*off and on*—in what you'll call a very "intricate" relationship, for the past *seven* YEARS. None of which *interests* me, mister!

BILL: Okay.

[*Bell.*]

Do you come in here a lot?

BETTY: Every other day, I think.

BILL: I come in here quite a lot and I don't remember seeing you.

BETTY: I guess we must be on different schedules.

BILL: Missed connections.

BETTY: Yes. Different time zones.

BILL: Amazing how you can live right next door to somebody in this town and never even know it.

BETTY: I know.

BILL: City life.

BETTY: It's crazy.

BILL: We probably pass each other in the street every day. Right in front of this place, probably.

BETTY: Yep.

BILL [*looks around*]: Well the waiters here sure seem to be in some different time zone. I can't seem to locate one anywhere . . . . Waiter! [*He looks back.*] So what do you—[*He sees that she's gone back to her book.*]

BETTY: I beg pardon?

BILL: Nothing. Sorry.

[*Bell.*]

BETTY: I guess we must be on different schedules.

BILL: Missed connections.

BETTY: Yes. Different time zones.

BILL: Amazing how you can live right next door to somebody in this town and never even know it.

BETTY: I know.

BILL: City life.

BETTY: It's crazy.

BILL: You weren't waiting for somebody when I came in, were you?

BETTY: Actually I was.

BILL: Oh. Boyfriend?

BETTY: Sort of.

BILL: What's a sort-of boyfriend?

BETTY: My husband.

BILL: Ah-ha.

[*Bell.*]

You weren't waiting for somebody when I came in, were you?

BETTY: Actually I was.

Django Reinhardt: jazz guitarist (1910–1953), famous in Paris in the 1930s.

BILL: Oh. Boyfriend?
BETTY: Sort of.
BILL: What's a sort-of boyfriend?
BETTY: We were meeting here to break up.
BILL: Mm-hm . . .

[*Bell.*]

What's a sort-of boyfriend?
BETTY: My lover. Here she comes right now!

[*Bell.*]

BILL: You weren't waiting for somebody when I came in, were you?
BETTY: No, just reading.
BILL: Sort of a sad occupation for a Friday night, isn't it? Reading here, all by yourself?
BETTY: Do you think so?
BILL: Well sure. I mean, what's a good-looking woman like you doing out alone on a Friday night?
BETTY: Trying to keep away from lines like that.
BILL: No, listen—

[*Bell.*]

You weren't waiting for somebody when I came in, were you?
BETTY: No, just reading.
BILL: Sort of a sad occupation for a Friday night, isn't it? Reading here all by yourself?
BETTY: I guess it is, in a way.
BILL: What's a good-looking woman like you doing out alone on a Friday night anyway? No offense, but . . .
BETTY: I'm out alone on a Friday night for the first time in a very long time.
BILL: Oh.
BETTY: You see, I just recently ended a relationship.
BILL: Oh.
BETTY: Of rather long standing.
BILL: I'm sorry. [*Small pause.*] Well listen, since reading by yourself is such a sad occupation for a Friday night, would you like to go elsewhere?
BETTY: No . . .
BILL: Do something else?
BETTY: No thanks.
BILL: I was headed out to the movies in a while anyway.
BETTY: I don't think so.
BILL: Big chance to let Faulkner catch his breath. All those long sentences get him pretty tired.
BETTY: Thanks anyway.
BILL: Okay.
BETTY: I appreciate the invitation.
BILL: Sure thing.

[*Bell.*]

You weren't waiting for somebody when I came in, were you?
BETTY: No, just reading.
BILL: Sort of a sad occupation for a Friday night, isn't it? Reading here all by yourself?
BETTY: I guess I was trying to think of it as existentially romantic. You know— cappuccino, great literature, rainy night . . .

BILL: That only works in Paris. We *could* hop the late plane to Paris. Get on a Concorde. Find a café . . .

BETTY: I'm a little short on plane fare tonight.

BILL: Darn it, so am I.

BETTY: To tell you the truth, I was headed to the movies after I finished this section. Would you like to come along? Since you can't locate a waiter?

BILL: That's a very nice offer, but . . .

BETTY: Uh-huh. Girlfriend?

BILL: Two, actually. One of them's pregnant, and Stephanie—

[*Bell.*]

BETTY: Girlfriend?

BILL: No, I don't have a girlfriend. Not if you mean the castrating bitch I dumped last night.

[*Bell.*]

BETTY: Girlfriend?

BILL: Sort of. Sort of.

BETTY: What's a sort-of girlfriend?

BILL: My mother.

[*Bell.*]

I just ended a relationship, actually.

BETTY: Oh.

BILL: Of rather long standing.

BETTY: I'm sorry to hear it.

BILL: This is my first night out alone in a long time. I feel a little bit at sea, to tell you the truth.

BETTY: So you didn't stop to talk because you're a Moonie, or you have some weird political affiliation—?

BILL: Nope. Straight-down-the-ticket Republican.

[*Bell.*]

Straight-down the ticket Democrat.

[*Bell.*]

Can I tell you something about politics?

[*Bell.*]

I like to think of myself as a citizen of the universe.

[*Bell.*]

I'm unaffiliated.

BETTY: That's a relief. So am I.

BILL: I vote my beliefs.

BETTY: Labels are not important.

BILL: Labels are not important, exactly. Take me, for example. I mean, what does it matter if I had a two-point at—

[*Bell.*]

three-point at—

[*Bell.*]

four-point at college? Or if I did come from Pittsburgh—

[*Bell.*]

Cleveland—

[*Bell.*]

Westchester County?

BETTY: Sure.

BILL: I believe that a man is what he is.

[*Bell.*]

A person is what he is.

[*Bell.*]

A person is . . . what they are.

BETTY: I think so too.

BILL: So what if I admire Trotsky?

[*Bell.*]

So what if I once had a total-body liposuction?

[*Bell.*]

So what if I don't have a penis?

[*Bell.*]

So what if I spent a year in the Peace Corps? I was acting on my convictions.

BETTY: Sure.

BILL: You just can't hang a sign on a person.

BETTY: Absolutely. I'll bet you're a Scorpio.

[*Many bells ring.*]

Listen, I was headed to the movies after I finished this section. Would you like to come along?

BILL: That sounds like fun. What's playing?

BETTY: A couple of the really early Woody Allen movies.

BILL: Oh.

BETTY: You don't like Woody Allen?

BILL: Sure. I like Woody Allen.

BETTY: But you're not crazy about Woody Allen.

BILL: Those early ones kind of get on my nerves.

BETTY: Uh-huh.

[*Bell.*]

BILL: Y'know I was headed to the—

BETTY [*simultaneously*]: I was thinking about—

BILL: I'm sorry.

BETTY: No, go ahead.

BILL: I was going to say that I was headed to the movies in a little while, and . . .

BETTY: So was I.

BILL: The Woody Allen festival?

BETTY: Just up the street.

BILL: Do you like the early ones?

BETTY: I think anybody who doesn't ought to be run off the planet.

BILL: How many times have you seen *Bananas*?

BETTY: Eight times.

BILL: Twelve. So are you still interested? [*Long pause.*]

BETTY: Do you like Entenmann's crumb cake . . . ?

BILL: Last night I went out at two in the morning to get one. Did you have an Etch-a-Sketch as a child?

BETTY: Yes! And do you like Brussels sprouts? [*Pause.*]

BILL: No, I think they're disgusting.

BETTY: They *are* disgusting!

BILL: Do you still believe in marriage in spite of current sentiments against it?

BETTY: Yes.

BILL: And children?

BETTY: Three of them.

BILL: Two girls and a boy.

BETTY: Harvard, Vassar, and Brown.

BILL: And will you love me?

BETTY: Yes.

BILL: And cherish me forever?

BETTY: Yes.

BILL: Do you still want to go to the movies?

BETTY: Sure thing.

BILL AND BETTY [*together*]: *Waiter!*

>   *BLACKOUT*

[1988]

Joining the Conversation: Critical Thinking and Writing

1. Does *Sure Thing* have a plot? Does it follow the traditional formula of a beginning, a middle, and an end? (The conventional advice to playwrights is, "Get your guy up a tree, throw rocks at him, and get him down.") Is there an ending, a resolution, or do you think the play could go on and on? Please explain.

2. Ives's opening stage direction tells us that the play is set in a café, but no details are given. If you were staging the play, would you provide more than a table and two chairs? Some sort of atmosphere? Why, or why not?

3. Ives's text calls at the end for a blackout—a sudden darkening of the stage. Do you think this ending is preferable to a gradual fading of the lights, or a gradual closing of the curtain? Or, for that matter, why shouldn't the two characters leave some money on the table and walk out together? In short, staying with Ives's dialogue, evaluate other possible endings and present an argument for which one you believe is most effective. Ask yourself, What kind of evidence do I need to make my argument as convincing as possible?

4. If someone were to say to you that the play shows the need for people to keep revising their personalities, to (so to speak) keep reinventing themselves if they wish to function efficiently in the world, what might you reply? What does it mean to say that someone is "reinventing" himself or herself? Is that a desirable thing to do?

5. If someone asked you, What is the meaning of *Sure Thing*? how would you reply? Is there one meaning, or more than one? What is your evidence? Please present your view, and the evidence for it, in the form of a good argument.

6. Write a scene that Ives neglected to include in *Sure Thing*. How does your new scene change the play? In your view, does it make the play better?

7. Prepare an essay of one or two pages that you might send to Ives, in which you argue that his play would benefit from the addition of your new scene.

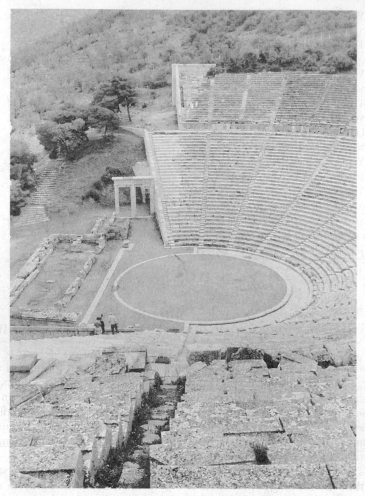

The theater at Epidaurus, located on the Peloponnesus east of Nauplia, Greece.

A Note on Greek Tragedy

Little or nothing is known for certain of the origin of Greek tragedy. The most common hypothesis holds that it developed from improvised speeches during choral dances honoring Dionysus, a Greek nature god associated with spring, fertility, and wine. Thespis (who perhaps never existed) is said to have introduced an actor into these choral performances in the sixth century BCE. Aeschylus (525–456 BCE), Greece's first great writer of tragedies, added the second actor, and Sophocles (496?–406 BCE) added the third actor and fixed the size of the chorus at fifteen. (Because the chorus leader often functioned as an additional actor, and because the actors sometimes doubled in their parts, a Greek tragedy could have more characters than might at first be thought.)

All the extant great Greek tragedy is of the fifth century BCE. It was performed at religious festivals in the winter and early spring, in large outdoor amphitheaters built on hillsides. Some of these theaters were enormous; the one at Epidaurus held about fifteen thousand people. The audience sat in tiers, looking down on the **orchestra** (a place for dancing), with the acting area behind it and the **skene** (the scene building) yet farther back. The scene building served as dressing room, background (suggesting a palace or temple), and place for occasional entrances and exits. Furthermore, this building helped to provide good acoustics, for speech travels well if there is a solid barrier behind the speakers and a hard, smooth surface in front of them, and if the audience sits in tiers. The wall of the scene building provided the barrier; the orchestra provided the surface in front of the actors; and the seats on the hillside fulfilled the third requirement. Moreover, the acoustics were somewhat improved by slightly elevating the actors above the orchestra, but it is not known exactly when this platform was first constructed in front of the scene building.

A tragedy commonly begins with a **prologos (prologue),** during which the exposition is given. Next comes the **párodos,** the chorus's ode of entrance, sung while the chorus marches into the theater through the side aisles and onto the orchestra. The **epeisodion (episode)** is the ensuing scene; it is followed by a **stasimon** (choral song, ode). Usually there are four or five *epeisodia,* alternating with *stasima.* Each of these choral odes has a **strophe** (lines presumably sung while the chorus dances in one direction) and an antistrophe (lines presumably sung while the chorus retraces its steps). Sometimes a third part, an **epode,** concludes an ode. (In addition to odes that are *stasima,* there can be odes within episodes; the fourth episode of *Antigonê* [Chapter 28] contains an ode complete with *epode.*) After the last part of the last ode comes the **exodos,** the epilogue or final scene.

The actors (all male) wore masks, and they seem to have chanted much of the play. Perhaps the total result of combining speech with music and dancing was a sort of music-drama roughly akin to opera with some spoken dialogue, such as Mozart's *The Magic Flute* (1791).

A Greek Tragedy

SOPHOCLES

One of the three great writers of tragedies in ancient Greece, Sophocles (496?–406 BCE) was born in Colonus, near Athens, into a well-to-do family. Well educated, he first won public acclaim as a tragic poet at the age of twenty-seven, in 468 BCE when he defeated Aeschylus in a competition for writing a tragic play. He is said to have written some 120 plays, but only seven tragedies are extant: among them are Oedipus the King, Antigonê, *and* Oedipus at Colonus. *He died, much honored, in his ninetieth year, in Athens, where he had lived his entire life.* Antigonê *appears in our Chapter 28, "Law and Disorder."*

Oedipus the King

Translated by Robert Fagles

CHARACTERS

OEDIPUS, *King of Thebes*
A PRIEST OF ZEUS
CREON, *brother of Jocasta*

Laurence Olivier in *Oedipus Rex*.

A CHORUS *of Theban citizens and their* LEADER
TIRESIAS, *a blind prophet*
JOCASTA, *the queen, wife of Oedipus*
A MESSENGER *from Corinth*
A SHEPHERD
A MESSENGER *from inside the palace*
ANTIGONE, ISMENE, *daughters of Oedipus and Jocasta*
GUARDS *and* ATTENDANTS
PRIESTS *of Thebes*

[TIME AND SCENE: The royal house of Thebes. Double doors dominate the façade; a stone altar stands at the center of the stage.

Many years have passed since OEDIPUS solved the riddle of the Sphinx and ascended the throne of Thebes, and now a plague has struck the city. A procession of priests enters; suppliants, broken and despondent, they carry branches wound in wool and lay them on the altar:

The doors open. GUARDS assemble. OEDIPUS comes forward, majestic but for a telltale limp, and slowly views the condition of his people.]

OEDIPUS. Oh my children, the new blood of ancient Thebes,
    why are you here? Huddling at my altar,
    praying before me, your branches wound in wool.°
    Our city reeks with the smoke of burning incense,
    rings with cries for the Healer° and wailing for the dead.   5
    I thought it wrong, my children, to hear the truth

---

3 branches wound in wool Suppliants laid such offerings on the altar of Apollo, god of healing, until their request was granted. Notice that in line 161 Oedipus tells the suppliants to remove the branches, thus suggesting that he will heal them.   **5 the Healer** Apollo.

from others, messengers. Here I am myself—
you all know me, the world knows my fame:
I am Oedipus.

[*Helping a* PRIEST *to his feet.*]

Speak up, old man. Your years,
your dignity—you should speak for the others.   10
Why here and kneeling, what preys upon you so?
Some sudden fear? some strong desire?
You can trust me. I am ready to help,
I'll do anything. I would be blind to misery
not to pity my people kneeling at my feet.   15

PRIEST. Oh Oedipus, king of the land, our greatest power!
You see us before you now, men of all ages
clinging to your altars. Here are boys,
still too weak to fly from the nest,
and here the old, bowed down with the years,   20
the holy ones—a priest of Zeus° myself—and here
the picked, unmarried men, the young hope of Thebes.
And all the rest, your great family gathers now,
branches wreathed, massing in the squares,
kneeling before the two temples of queen Athena°   25
or the river-shrine where the embers glow and die
and Apollo sees the future in the ashes.°

Our city—
look around you, see with your own eyes—
our ship pitches wildly, cannot lift her head
from the depths, the red waves of death . . .   30
Thebes is dying. A blight on the fresh crops
and the rich pastures, cattle sicken and die,
and the women die in labor, children stillborn,
and the plague, the fiery god of fever hurls down
on the city, his lightning slashing through us—   35
raging plague in all its vengeance, devastating
the house of Cadmus!° And black Death luxuriates
in the raw, wailing miseries of Thebes.
Now we pray to you. You cannot equal the gods,
your children know that, bending at your altar.   40
But we do rate you first of men,
both in the common crises of our lives
and face-to-face encounters with the gods.
You freed us from the Sphinx,° you came to Thebes

---

21 Zeus chief deity on Mt. Olympus, and father of Apollo.   **25 Athena** goddess of wisdom
and protector of cities.   **27 the ashes** Diviners foretold the future by examining the ashes
of burnt offerings.   **37 Cadmus** mythical founder of Thebes.   **44 the Sphinx** a female
monster (body of a lion, wings of a bird, face of a woman) who asked the riddle "What goes
on four legs in the morning, two at noon, and three in the evening?" and who killed those
who could not answer.— When Oedipus responded correctly that man crawls on all fours in
infancy, walks upright in maturity, and uses a staff in old age, the Sphinx destroyed herself.

and cut us loose from the bloody tribute° we had paid   45
that harsh, brutal singer. We taught you nothing,
no skill, no extra knowledge, still you triumphed.
A god was with you, so they say, and we believe it—
you lifted up our lives.

                        So now again,
Oedipus, king, we bend to you, your power—   50
we implore you, all of us on our knees:
find us strength, rescue! Perhaps you've heard
the voice of a god or something from other men,
Oedipus . . . what do you know?
The man of experience—you see it every day—   55
his plans will work in a crisis, his first of all.

Act now—we beg you, best of men, raise up our city!
Act, defend yourself, your former glory!
Your country calls you savior now
for your zeal, your action years ago.   60
Never let us remember of your reign:
you helped us stand, only to fall once more.
Oh raise up our city, set us on our feet.
The omens were good that day you brought us joy—
be the same man today!   65
Rule our land, you know you have the power,
but rule a land of the living, not a wasteland.
Ship and towered city are nothing, stripped of men
alive within it, living all as one.

OEDIPUS.   My children,
I pity you. I see—how could I fail to see   70
what longings bring you here? Well I know
you are sick to death, all of you,
but sick as you are, not one is sick as I.
Your pain strikes each of you alone, each
in the confines of himself, no other. But my spirit   70
grieves for the city, for myself and all of you.
I wasn't asleep, dreaming. You haven't wakened me—
I've wept through the nights, you must know that,
groping, laboring over many paths of thought.
After a painful search I found one cure: 80
I acted at once. I sent Creon,
my wife's own brother, to Delphi°—
Apollo the Prophet's oracle—to learn
what I might do or say to save our city.

Today's the day. When I count the days gone by   85
it torments me . . . what is he doing?
Strange, he's late, he's gone too long.
But once he returns, then, then I'll be a traitor
if I do not do all the god makes clear.

---

45 bloody tribute i.e., the young Thebans who had tried to solve the riddle and had failed.
82 Delphi site of a shrine of Apollo.

PRIEST. Timely words. The men over there   90
    are signaling—Creon's just arriving.
OEDIPUS. [*Sighting* CREON, *then turning to the altar:*]
                            Lord Apollo,
    let him come with a lucky word of rescue,
    shining like his eyes!
PRIEST. Welcome news, I think—he's crowned, look,
    and the laurel wreath is bright with berries.   95
OEDIPUS. We'll soon see. He's close enough to hear—

[*Enter* CREON *from the side; his face is shaded with a wreath.*]

    Creon, prince, my kinsman, what do you bring us?
    What message from the god?
CREON.   Good news.
    I tell you even the hardest things to bear,
    if they should turn out well, all would be well.   100
OEDIPUS. Of course, but what were the god's *words*? There's no hope
    and nothing to fear in what you've said so far.
CREON. If you want my report in the presence of these . . .

[*Pointing to the* PRIESTS *while drawing* OEDIPUS *toward the
palace.*]

    I'm ready now, or we might go inside.
OEDIPUS.   Speak out,
    speak to us all. I grieve for these, my people,   105
    far more than I fear for my own life.
CREON.   Very well,
    I will tell you what I heard from the god.
    Apollo commands us—he was quite clear—
    "Drive the corruption from the land,
    don't harbor it any longer, past all cure,   110
    don't nurse it in your soil—root it out!"
OEDIPUS. How can we cleanse ourselves—what rites?
    What's the source of the trouble?
CREON. Banish the man, or pay back blood with blood.
    Murder sets the plague-storm on the city.
OEDIPUS.   Whose murder?   115
    Whose fate does Apollo bring to light?
CREON.   Our leader,
    my lord, was once a man named Laius,
    before you came and put us straight on course.
OEDIPUS.   I know—
    or so I've heard. I never saw the man myself.
CREON. Well, he was killed, and Apollo commands us now—   120
    he could not be more clear,
    "Pay the killers back—whoever is responsible."
OEDIPUS. Where on earth are they? Where to find it now,
    the trail of the ancient guilt so hard to trace?
CREON. "Here in Thebes," he said.   125
    Whatever is sought for can be caught, you know,
    whatever is neglected slips away.

OEDIPUS.   But where,
in the palace, the fields or foreign soil,
where did Laius meet his bloody death?

CREON. He went to consult an oracle, Apollo said,   130
and he set out and never came home again.

OEDIPUS. No messenger, no fellow-traveler saw what happened?
Someone to cross-examine?

CREON.   No,
they were all killed but one. He escaped,
terrified, he could tell us nothing clearly,   135
nothing of what he saw—just one thing.

OEDIPUS.   What's that?
one thing could hold the key to it all,
a small beginning give us grounds for hope.

CREON. He said thieves attacked them—a whole band,
not single-handed, cut King Laius down.

OEDIPUS.   A thief, so daring,   140
so wild, he'd kill a king? Impossible, unless conspirators paid
him off in Thebes.

CREON. We suspected as much. But with Laius dead
no leader appeared to help us in our troubles.

OEDIPUS. Trouble? Your *king* was murdered—royal blood!   145
What stopped you from tracking down the killer
then and there?

CREON.   The singing, riddling Sphinx.
She . . . persuaded us to let the mystery go
and concentrate on what lay at our feet.

OEDIPUS.   No,
I'll start again—I'll bring it all to light myself!   150
Apollo is right, and so are you, Creon,
to turn our attention back to the murdered man.
Now you have *me* to fight for you, you'll see:
I am the land's avenger by all rights,
and Apollo's champion too.   155
But not to assist some distant kinsman, no,
for my own sake I'll rid us of this corruption.
Whoever killed the king may decide to kill me too,
with the same violent hand—by avenging Laius
I defend myself.

[*To the* PRIESTS.]

                    Quickly, my children.   160
Up from the steps, take up your branches now.

[*To the* GUARDS.]

One of you summon the city here before us,
tell them I'll do everything. God help us,
we will see our triumph—or our fall.

[OEDIPUS *and* CREON *enter the palace, followed by the guards.*]

PRIEST. Rise, my sons. The kindness we came for   165
Oedipus volunteers himself.

Apollo has sent his word, his oracle—
Come down, Apollo, save us, stop the plague.

[*The* PRIESTS *rise, remove their branches and exit to the side. Enter a*
CHORUS, *the citizens of Thebes, who have not heard the news that* CREON
brings. They march around the altar, chanting.]

CHORUS.   Zeus!
Great welcome voice of Zeus,° what do you bring?
What word from the gold vaults of Delphi   170
comes to brilliant Thebes? Racked with terror—
    terror shakes my heart
and I cry your wild cries, Apollo, Healer of Delos°
I worship you in dread . . . what now, what is your price?
some new sacrifice? some ancient rite from the past   175
come round again each spring?—
    what will you bring to birth?
Tell me, child of golden Hope
warm voice that never dies!
You are the first I call, daughter of Zeus   180
deathless Athena—I call your sister Artemis,°
heart of the market place enthroned in glory,
    guardian of our earth—
I call Apollo, Archer astride the thunderheads of heaven—
O triple shield against death, shine before me now!   185
If ever, once in the past, you stopped some ruin
launched against our walls
    you hurled the flame of pain
far, far from Thebes—you gods
come now, come down once more!   190
                              No, no

the miseries numberless, grief on grief, no end—
too much to bear, we are all dying
O my people . . .
    Thebes like a great army dying
and there is no sword of thought to save us, no   195
and the fruits of our famous earth, they will not ripen
no and the women cannot scream their pangs to birth—
screams for the Healer, children dead in the womb
    and life on life goes down
        you can watch them go   200
    like seabirds winging west, outracing the day's fire
down the horizon, irresistibly
        streaking on to the shores of Evening
                          Death

so many deaths, numberless deaths on deaths, no end—
Thebes is dying, look, her children   205

169 welcome voice of Zeus Apollo, son of Zeus, spoke for Zeus.   **173 Delos** sacred island
where Apollo was born.   **181 Artemis** a goddess, sister of Apollo.

stripped of pity . . .
　　generations strewn on the ground
unburied, unwept, the dead spreading death
and the young wives and gray-haired mothers with them
cling to the altars, trailing in from all over the city—　　　　　　　210
Thebes, city of death, one long cortege
　　and the suffering rises
　　　　wails for mercy rise
　　and the wild hymn for the Healer blazes out
clashing with our sobs our cries of mourning—　　　　　　　　215
　　O golden daughter of god,° send rescue
　　radiant as the kindness in your eyes!

Drive him back!—the fever, the god of death
　　that raging god of war
not armored in bronze, not shielded now, he burns me,　　　　220
battle cries in the onslaught burning on—
O rout him from our borders!
Sail him, blast him out to the Sea-queen's chamber
　　the black Atlantic gulfs
　　or the northern harbor, death to all　　　　　　　　　225
where the Thracian surf comes crashing.
Now what the night spares he comes by day and kills—
the god of death.
　　　　　　　O lord of the stormcloud,
you who twirl the lightning, Zeus, Father,
thunder Death to nothing!　　　　　　　　　　　　　230

Apollo, lord of the light, I beg you—
　　whip your longbow's golden cord
showering arrows on our enemies—shafts of power
champions strong before us rushing on!

Artemis, Huntress,　　　　　　　　　　　　　　235
torches flaring over the eastern ridges—
ride Death down in pain!

God of the headdress gleaming gold, I cry to you—
your name and ours are one, Dionysus°—
　　come with your face aflame with wine　　　　　240
　　　　your raving women's cries
your army on the march! Come with the lightning
come with torches blazing, eyes ablaze with glory!
Burn that god of death that all gods hate!

[OEDIPUS *enters from the palace to address the* CHORUS, *as if addressing the
entire city of Thebes.*]

OEDIPUS.　You pray to the gods? Let me grant your prayers.　　245
　　Come, listen to me—do what the plague demands:

---

216 golden daughter of god Athena.　**239 Dionysus** god of wine and fertility. He was
attended by the Maenads (the "raving women" of line 241).

you'll find relief and lift your head from the depths.
I will speak out now as a stranger to the story,
a stranger to the crime. If I'd been present then,
there would have been no mystery, no long hunt   250
without a clue in hand. So now, counted
a native Theban years after the murder,
to all of Thebes I make this proclamation:
if any one of you knows who murdered Laius,
the son of Labdacus, I order him to reveal   255
the whole truth to me. Nothing to fear,
even if he must denounce himself,
let him speak up
and so escape the brunt of the charge—
he will suffer no unbearable punishment,   260
nothing worse than exile, totally unharmed.

[OEDIPUS *pauses, waiting for a reply.*]

                           Next,
if anyone knows the murderer is a stranger,
a man from alien soil, come, speak up.
I will give him a handsome reward, and lay up
gratitude in my heart for him besides.   265

[*Silence again, no reply.*]

But if you keep silent, if anyone panicking,
trying to shield himself or friend or kin,
rejects my offer, then hear what I will do.
I order you, every citizen of the state
where I hold throne and power: banish this man—   270
whoever he may be—never shelter him, never
speak a word to him, never make him partner
to your prayers, your victims burned to the gods.
Never let the holy water touch his hands.
Drive him out, each of you, from every home.   275
He is the plague, the heart of our corruption,
as Apollo's oracle has just revealed to me.
So I honor my obligations:
I fight for the god and for the murdered man.

Now my curse on the murderer. Whoever he is,   280
a lone man unknown in his crime
or one among many, let that man drag out
his life in agony, step by painful step—
I curse myself as well . . . if by any chance
he proves to be an intimate of our house,   285
here at my hearth, with my full knowledge,
may the curse I just called down on him strike me!

These are your orders: perform them to the last.
I command you, for my sake, for Apollo's, for this country
blasted root and branch by the angry heavens.   290
Even if god had never urged you on to act,

how could you leave the crime uncleansed so long?
A man so noble—your king, brought down in blood—
you should have searched. But I am the king now,
I hold the throne that he held then, possess his bed   295
and a wife who shares our seed . . . why, our seed
might be the same, children born of the same mother
might have created blood-bonds between us
if his hope of offspring hadn't met disaster—
but fate swooped at his head and cut him short.   300
So I will fight for him as if he were my father,
stop at nothing, search the world
to lay my hands on the man who shed his blood,
the son of Labdacus descended of Polydorus,
Cadmus of old and Agenor, founder of the line: 305
their power and mine are one.
                                        Oh dear gods,
my curse on those who disobey these orders!
Let no crops grow out of the earth for them—
shrivel their women, kill their sons,
burn them to nothing in this plague   310
that hits us now, or something even worse.
But you, loyal men of Thebes who approve my actions,
may our champion, Justice, may all the gods
be with us, fight beside us to the end!

LEADER. In the grip of your curse, my king, I swear   315
I'm not the murderer, I cannot point him out.
As for the search, Apollo pressed it on us—
he should name the killer.

OEDIPUS.   Quite right,
but to force the gods to act against their will—
no man has the power.

LEADER.   Then if I might mention   320
the next best thing . . .

OEDIPUS.   The third best too—
don't hold back, say it.

LEADER.   I still believe . . .
Lord Tiresias° sees with the eyes of Lord Apollo.
Anyone searching for the truth, my king,
might learn it from the prophet, clear as day.   325

OEDIPUS. I've not been slow with that. On Creon's cue
I sent the escorts, twice, within the hour.
I'm surprised he isn't here.

LEADER.   We need him—
without him we have nothing but old, useless rumors.

OEDIPUS. Which rumors? I'll search out every word.   330

LEADER. Laius was killed, they say, by certain travelers.

OEDIPUS. I know—but no one can find the murderer.

323 Tiresias a blind prophet.

LEADER. If the man has a trace of fear in him
    he won't stay silent long,
    not with your curses ringing in his ears.   335
OEDIPUS. He didn't flinch at murder,
    he'll never flinch at words.

    [*Enter* TIRESIAS, *the blind prophet, led by a boy with escorts in
    attendance. He remains at a distance.*]

LEADER. Here is the one who will convict him, look,
    they bring him on at last, the seer, the man of god.
    The truth lives inside him, him alone.
OEDIPUS.   O Tiresias,   340
    master of all the mysteries of our life,
    all you teach and all you dare not tell,
    signs in the heavens, signs that walk the earth!
    Blind as you are, you can feel all the more
    what sickness haunts our city. You, my lord,   345
    are the one shield, the one savior we can find.

    We asked Apollo—perhaps the messengers
    haven't told you—he sent his answer back:
    "Relief from the plague can only come one way.
    Uncover the murderers of Laius,   350
    put them to death or drive them into exile."
    So I beg you, grudge us nothing now, no voice,
    no message plucked from the birds, the embers
    or the other mantic ways within your grasp.
    Rescue yourself, your city, rescue me—   355
    rescue everything infected by the dead.
    We are in your hands. For a man to help others
    with all his gifts and native strength:
    that is the noblest work.
TIRESIAS.   How terrible—to see the truth
    when the truth is only pain to him who sees!   360
    I knew it well, but I put it from my mind,
    else I never would have come.
OEDIPUS. What's this? Why so grim, so dire?
TIRESIAS. Just send me home. You bear your burdens,
    I'll bear mine. It's better that way,   365
    please believe me.
OEDIPUS.   Strange response . . . unlawful,
    unfriendly too to the state that bred and reared you—
    you withhold the word of god.
TIRESIAS.   I fail to see
    that your own words are so well-timed.
    I'd rather not have the same thing said of me . . .   370
OEDIPUS. For the love of god, don't turn away,
    not if you know something. We beg you,
    all of us on our knees.
TIRESIAS.   None of you knows—
    and I will never reveal my dreadful secrets,
    not to say your own.   375

OEDIPUS. What? You know and you won't tell?
    You're bent on betraying us, destroying Thebes?
TIRESIAS. I'd rather not cause pain for you or me.
    So why this . . . useless interrogation?
    You'll get nothing from me.

OEDIPUS.   Nothing! You,   380
    you scum of the earth, you'd enrage a heart of stone!
    You won't talk? Nothing moves you?
    Out with it, once and for all!
TIRESIAS. You criticize my temper . . . unaware
    of the one *you* live with, you revile me.   385
OEDIPUS. Who could restrain his anger hearing you?
    What outrage—you spurn the city!
TIRESIAS. What will come will come.
    Even if I shroud it all in silence.
OEDIPUS. What will come? You're bound to *tell* me that.   390
TIRESIAS. I'll say no more. Do as you like, build your anger
    to whatever pitch you please, rage your worst—
OEDIPUS. Oh I'll let loose, I have such fury in me—
    now I see it all. You helped hatch the plot,
    you did the work, yes, short of killing him   395
    with your own hands—and given eyes I'd say
    you did the killing single-handed!
TIRESIAS.   Is that so!
    I charge you, then, submit to that decree
    you just laid down: from this day onward
    speak to no one, not these citizens, not myself.   400
    You are the curse, the corruption of the land!
OEDIPUS. You, shameless—
    aren't you appalled to start up such a story?
    You think you can get away with this?
TIRESIAS.   I have already.
    The truth with all its power lives inside me.   405
OEDIPUS. Who primed you for this? Not your prophet's trade.
TIRESIAS. You did, you forced me, twisted it out of me.
OEDIPUS. What? Say it again—I'll understand it better.
TIRESIAS. Didn't you understand, just now?
    Or are you tempting me to talk?   410
OEDIPUS. No, I can't say I grasped your meaning.
    Out with it, again!
TIRESIAS. I say you are the murderer you hunt.
OEDIPUS. That obscenity, twice—by god, you'll pay.
TIRESIAS. Shall I say more, so you can really rage?   415
OEDIPUS. Much as you want. Your words are nothing—futile.
TIRESIAS. You cannot imagine . . . I tell you,
    you and your loved ones live together in infamy,
    you cannot see how far you've gone in guilt.
OEDIPUS. You think you can keep this up and never suffer?   420
TIRESIAS. Indeed, if the truth has any power.

OEDIPUS.   It does
    but not for you, old man. You've lost your power,
    stone-blind, stone-deaf—senses, eyes blind as stone!
TIRESIAS. I pity you, flinging at me the very insults
    each man here will fling at you so soon.
OEDIPUS.   Blind,   425
    lost in the night, endless night that cursed you!
    You can't hurt me or anyone else who sees the light—
    you can never touch me.
TIRESIAS.   True, it is not your fate
    to fall at my hands. Apollo is quite enough,
    and he will take some pains to work this out.   430
OEDIPUS. Creon! Is this conspiracy his or yours?
TIRESIAS. Creon is not your downfall, no, you are your own.
OEDIPUS.   O power—
    wealth and empire, skill outstripping skill
    in the heady rivalries of life,
    what envy lurks inside you! Just for this,   435
    the crown the city gave me—I never sought it,
    they laid it in my hands—for this alone, Creon,
    the soul of trust, my loyal friend from the start
    steals against me . . . so hungry to overthrow me
    he sets this wizard on me, this scheming quack,   440
    this fortune-teller peddling lies, eyes peeled
    for his own profit—seer blind in his craft!

    Come here, you pious fraud. Tell me,
    when did you ever prove yourself a prophet?
    When the Sphinx, that chanting Fury kept her deathwatch here,   445
    why silent then, not a word to set our people free?
    There was a riddle, not for some passer-by to solve—
    it cried out for a prophet. Where were you?
    Did you rise to the crisis? Not a word,
    you and your birds, your gods—nothing.   450
    No, but I came by, Oedipus the ignorant,
    I stopped the Sphinx! With no help from the birds,
    the flight of my own intelligence hit the mark.

    And this is the man you'd try to overthrow?
    You think you'll stand by Creon when he's king?   455
    You and the great mastermind—
    you'll pay in tears, I promise you, for this,
    this witch-hunt. If you didn't look so senile
    the lash would teach you what your scheming means!
LEADER. I would suggest his words were spoken in anger,   460
    Oedipus . . . yours too, and it isn't what we need.
    The best solution to the oracle, the riddle
    posed by god—we should look for that.
TIRESIAS. You are the king no doubt, but in one respect,
    at least, I am your equal: the right to reply.   465
    I claim that privilege too.

I am not your slave. I serve Apollo.
I don't need Creon to speak for me in public.
                                                                So,
    you mock my blindness? Let me tell you this.
    You with your precious eyes,   470
    you're blind to the corruption of your life,
    to the house you live in, those you live with—
    who *are* your parents? Do you know? All unknowing
    you are the scourge of your own flesh and blood,
    the dead below the earth and the living here above,   475
    and the double lash of your mother and your father's curse
    will whip you from this land one day, their footfall
    treading you down in terror, darkness shrouding
    your eyes that now can see the light!
                                                    Soon, soon
    you'll scream aloud—what haven won't reverberate?   480
    What rock of Cithaeron° won't scream back in echo?
    That day you learn the truth about your marriage,
    the wedding-march that sang you into your halls,
    the lusty voyage home to the fatal harbor!
    And a crowd of other horrors you'd never dream   485
    will level you with yourself and all your children.
    There. Now smear us with insults—Creon, myself,
    and every word I've said. No man will ever
    be rooted from the earth as brutally as you.
OEDIPUS. Enough! Such filth from him? Insufferable—   490
    what, still alive? Get out—
    faster, back where you came from—vanish!
TIRESIAS. I would never have come if you hadn't called me here.
OEDIPUS. If I thought you would blurt out such absurdities,
    you'd have died waiting before I'd had you summoned.   495
TIRESIAS. Absurd, am I! To you, not to your parents:
    the ones who bore you found me sane enough.
OEDIPUS. Parents—who? Wait . . . who is my father?
TIRESIAS. This day will bring your birth and your destruction.
OEDIPUS. Riddles—all you can say are riddles, murk and darkness.   500
TIRESIAS. Ah, but aren't you the best man alive at solving riddles?
OEDIPUS. Mock me for that, go on, and you'll reveal my greatness.
TIRESIAS. Your great good fortune, true, it was your ruin.
OEDIPUS. Not if I saved the city—what do I care?
TIRESIAS. Well then, I'll be going.

    [*To his attendant.*]

                                            Take me home, boy.   505
OEDIPUS. Yes, take him away. You're a nuisance here.
    Out of the way, the irritation's gone.

    [*Turning his back on* TIRESIAS, *moving toward the palace.*]

---

481 Cithaeron mountains near Thebes, where Oedipus was abandoned as an infant.

TIRESIAS.   I will go,
    once I have said what I came here to say.
    I'll never shrink from the anger in your eyes—
    you can't destroy me. Listen to me closely: 510
    the man you've sought so long, proclaiming,
    cursing up and down, the murderer of Laius—
    he is here. A stranger,
    you may think, who lives among you,
    he soon will be revealed a native Theban   515
    but he will take no joy in the revelation.
    Blind who now has eyes, beggar who now is rich,
    he will grope his way toward a foreign soil,
    a stick tapping before him step by step.

     [OEDIPUS *enters the palace.*]

    Revealed at last, brother and father both   520
    to the children he embraces; to his mother
    son and husband both—he sowed the loins
    his father sowed, he spilled his father's blood!

    Go in and reflect on that, solve that.
    And if you find I've lied   525
    from this day onward call the prophet blind.

     [TIRESIAS *and the boy exit to the side.*]

CHORUS.   Who—
    who is the man the voice of god denounces
    resounding out of the rocky gorge of Delphi?
       The horror too dark to tell,
    whose ruthless bloody hands have done the work?   530
    His time has come to fly
       to outrace the stallions of the storm
         his feet a streak of speed—
    Cased in armor, Apollo son of the Father
    lunges on him, lightning-bolts afire!   535
    And the grim unerring Furies°
         closing for the kill.
                      Look,
    the word of god has just come blazing
    flashing off Parnassus'° snowy heights!
       That man who left no trace—   540
    after him, hunt him down with all our strength!
    Now under bristling timber
       up through rocks and caves he stalks
         like the wild mountain bull—
    cut off from men, each step an agony, frenzied, racing blind   545
    but he cannot outrace the dread voices of Delphi
    ringing out of the heart of Earth,
    the dark wings beating around him shrieking doom
       the doom that never dies, the terror—

536 Furies avenging deities.   **539 Parnassus** a mountain associated with Apollo.

The skilled prophet scans the birds and shatters me with terror!   550
I can't accept him, can't deny him, don't know what to say,
I'm lost, and the wings of dark foreboding beating—
I cannot see what's come, what's still to come . . .
and what could breed a blood feud between
    Laius' house and the son of Polybus?°   555
I know of nothing, not in the past and not now,
no charge to bring against our king, no cause
to attack his fame that rings throughout Thebes—
    not without proof—not for the ghost of Laius,
    not to avenge a murder gone without a trace.   560

Zeus and Apollo know, they know, the great masters
    of all the dark and depth of human life.
But whether a mere man can know the truth,
whether a seer can fathom more than I—
there is no test, no certain proof   565
    though matching skill for skill
a man can outstrip a rival. No, not till I see
these charges proved will I side with his accusers.
We saw him then, when the she-hawk° swept against him,
saw with our own eyes his skill, his brilliant triumph—   570
    there was the test—he was the joy of Thebes!
    Never will I convict my king, never in my heart.

[*Enter* CREON *from the side.*]

CREON. My fellow-citizens, I hear King Oedipus
levels terrible charges at me. I had to come.
I resent it deeply. If, in the present crisis   575
he thinks he suffers any abuse from me,
anything I've done or said that offers him
the slightest injury, why, I've no desire
to linger out this life, my reputation in ruins.
The damage I'd face from such an accusation   580
is nothing simple. No, there's nothing worse:
branded a traitor in the city, a traitor
to all of you and my good friends.
LEADER.   True,
but a slur might have been forced out of him,
by anger perhaps, not any firm conviction.   585
CREON. The charge was made in public, wasn't it?
I put the prophet up to spreading lies?
LEADER. Such things were said . . .
I don't know with what intent, if any.
CREON. Was his glance steady, his mind right   590
when the charge was brought against me?

---

555 son of Polybus Oedipus is mistakenly thought to be the son of Polybus, King of Corinth.   **569 the she-hawk** the Sphinx.

LEADER. I really couldn't say. I never look
    to judge the ones in power.

    [*The doors open.* OEDIPUS *enters.*]

                  Wait,
    here's Oedipus now.

OEDIPUS.   You—here? You have the gall
    to show your face before the palace gates?   595
    You, plotting to kill me, kill the king—
    I see it all, the marauding thief himself
    scheming to steal my crown and power!
                     Tell me,
    in god's name, what did you take me for,
    coward or fool, when you spun out your plot?   600
    Your treachery—you think I'd never detect it
    creeping against me in the dark? Or sensing it,
    not defend myself? Aren't you the fool,
    you and your high adventure. Lacking numbers,
    powerful friends, out for the big game of empire—   605
    you need riches, armies to bring that quarry down!

CREON. Are you quite finished? It's your turn to listen
    for just as long as you've . . . instructed me.
    Hear me out, then judge me on the facts.

OEDIPUS. You've a wicked way with words, Creon,   610
    but I'll be slow to learn—from you.
    I find you a menace, a great burden to me.

CREON. Just one thing, hear me out in this.

OEDIPUS.   Just one thing,
    don't tell *me* you're not the enemy, the traitor.

CREON. Look, if you think crude, mindless stubbornness   615
    such a gift, you've lost your sense of balance.

OEDIPUS. If you think you can abuse a kinsman,
    then escape the penalty, you're insane.

CREON. Fair enough, I grant you. But this injury
    you say I've done you, what is it?   620

OEDIPUS. Did you induce me, yes or no,
    to send for that sanctimonious prophet?

CREON. I did. And I'd do the same again.

OEDIPUS. All right then, tell me, how long is it now
    since Laius . . .

CREON.   Laius—what did *he* do?

OEDIPUS.   Vanished,   625
    swept from sight, murdered in his tracks.

CREON. The count of the years would run you far back . . .

OEDIPUS. And that far back, was the prophet at his trade?

CREON. Skilled as he is today, and just as honored.

OEDIPUS. Did he ever refer to me then, at that time?

CREON.   No,   630
    never, at least, when I was in his presence.

OEDIPUS. But you did investigate the murder, didn't you?

CREON. We did our best, of course, discovered nothing.

OEDIPUS. But the great seer never accused me then—why not?

CREON. I don't know. And when I don't, *I* keep quiet.   635

OEDIPUS. You do know this, you'd tell it too—
    if you had a shred of decency.

CREON.   What?
    If I know, I won't hold back.

OEDIPUS.   Simply this:
    if the two of you had never put heads together,
    we would never have heard about *my* killing Laius.   640

CREON. If that's what he says . . . well, you know best.
    But now I have a right to learn from you
    as you just learned from me.

OEDIPUS.   Learn your fill,
    you never will convict me of the murder.

CREON. Tell me, you're married to my sister, aren't you?   645

OEDIPUS. A genuine discovery—there's no denying that.

CREON. And you rule the land with her, with equal power?

OEDIPUS. She receives from me whatever she desires.

CREON. And I am the third, all of us are equals?

OEDIPUS. Yes, and it's there you show your stripes—   650
    you betray a kinsman.

CREON.   Not at all.
    Not if you see things calmly, rationally,
    as I do. Look at it this way first:
    who in his right mind would rather rule
    and live in anxiety than sleep in peace?   655
    Particularly if he enjoys the same authority.
    Not I, I'm not the man to yearn for kingship,
    not with a king's power in my hands. Who would?
    Now, as it is, you offer me all I need,
    not a fear in the world. But if I wore the crown . . .   660
    there'd be many painful duties to perform,
    hardly to my taste.
                How could kingship
    please me more than influence, power
    without a qualm? I'm not that deluded yet,
    to reach for anything but privilege outright,   665
    profit free and clear.
    Now all men sing my praises, all salute me,
    now all who request your favors curry mine.
    I am their best hope: success rests in me.
    Why give up that, I ask you, and borrow trouble?   670
    A man of sense, someone who sees things clearly
    would never resort to treason.
    No, I've no lust for conspiracy in me,
    nor could I ever suffer one who does.

    Do you want proof? Go to Delphi yourself,   675
    examine the oracle and see if I've reported

the message word-for-word. This too:
if you detect that I and the clairvoyant
have plotted anything in common, arrest me,
execute me. Not on the strength of one vote,   680
two in this case, mine as well as yours.
But don't convict me on sheer unverified surmise.
How wrong it is to take the good for bad,
purely at random, or take the bad for good.
But reject a friend, a kinsman? I would as soon   685
tear out the life within us, priceless life itself.
You'll learn this well, without fail, in time.
Time alone can bring the just man to light—
the criminal you can spot in one short day.

LEADER.   Good advice,
my lord, for anyone who wants to avoid disaster.   690
Those who jump to conclusions may go wrong.

OEDIPUS.   When my enemy moves against me quickly,
plots in secret, I move quickly too, I must,
I plot and pay him back. Relax my guard a moment,
waiting his next move—he wins his objective,   695
I lose mine.

CREON.   What do you want?
You want me banished?

OEDIPUS.   No, I want you dead.

CREON. Just to show how ugly a grudge can . . .

OEDIPUS.   So,
still stubborn? you don't think I'm serious?

CREON. I think you're insane.

OEDIPUS.   Quite sane—in my behalf.   700

CREON. Not just as much in mine?

OEDIPUS.   You—my mortal enemy?

CREON. What if you're wholly wrong?

OEDIPUS.   No matter—I must rule.

CREON. Not if you rule unjustly.

OEDIPUS.   Hear him, Thebes, my city!

CREON. My city too, not yours alone!

LEADER. Please, my lords.

[*Enter* JOCASTA *from the palace.*]

                              Look, Jocasta's coming,   705
and just in time too. With her help
you must put this fighting of yours to rest.

JOCASTA. Have you no sense? Poor misguided men,
such shouting—why this public outburst?
Aren't you ashamed, with the land so sick,   710
to stir up private quarrels?

[*To* OEDIPUS.]

Into the palace now. And Creon, you go home.
Why make such a furor over nothing?

CREON. My sister, it's dreadful . . . Oedipus, your husband,
    he's bent on a choice of punishments for me,   715
    banishment from the fatherland or death.
OEDIPUS. Precisely. I caught him in the act, Jocasta,
    plotting, about to stab me in the back.
CREON. Never—curse me, let me die and be damned
    if I've done you any wrong you charge me with.   720
JOCASTA. Oh god, believe it, Oedipus,
    honor the solemn oath he swears to heaven.
    Do it for me, for the sake of all your people.

    [*The* CHORUS *begins to chant.*]

CHORUS. Believe it, be sensible
    give way, my king, I beg you!   725
OEDIPUS. What do you want from me, concessions?
CHORUS. Respect him—he's been no fool in the past
    and now he's strong with the oath he swears to god.
OEDIPUS. You know what you're asking?
CHORUS.   I do.
OEDIPUS.   Then out with it!
CHORUS. The man's your friend, your kin, he's under oath—   730
    don't cast him out, disgraced
    branded with guilt on the strength of hearsay only.
OEDIPUS. Know full well, if that is what you want
    you want me dead or banished from the land.
CHORUS.   Never—
    no, by the blazing Sun, first god of the heavens!   735
      Stripped of the gods, stripped of loved ones,
    let me die by inches if that ever crossed my mind.
    But the heart inside me sickens, dies as the land dies
    and now on top of the old griefs you pile this,
    your fury—both of you!
OEDIPUS.   Then let him go,   740
    even if it does lead to my ruin, my death
    or my disgrace, driven from Thebes for life.
    It's you, not him I pity—your words move me.
    He, wherever he goes, my hate goes with him.
CREON. Look at you, sullen in yielding, brutal in your rage—   745
    you'll go too far. It's perfect justice:
    natures like yours are hardest on themselves.
OEDIPUS. Then leave me alone—get out!
CREON.   I'm going.
    You're wrong, so wrong. These men know I'm right.

    [*Exit to the side. The* CHORUS *turns to* JOCASTA.]

CHORUS. Why do you hesitate, my lady   750
    why not help him in?
JOCASTA. Tell me what's happened first.
CHORUS. Loose, ignorant talk started dark suspicions
    and a sense of injustice cut deeply too.
JOCASTA. On both sides?

CHORUS.   Oh yes.

JOCASTA.   What did they say?   755

CHORUS. Enough, please, enough! The land's so racked already
　　or so it seems to me . . .
　　End the trouble here, just where they left it.

OEDIPUS. You see what comes of your good intentions now?
　　And all because you tried to blunt my anger.

CHORUS.   My king,   760
　　I've said it once, I'll say it time and again—
　　I'd be insane, you know it,
　　senseless, ever to turn my back on you.
　　You who set our beloved land—storm-tossed, shattered—
　　straight on course. Now again, good helmsman,   765
　　steer us through the storm!

[*The* CHORUS *draws away, leaving* OEDIPUS *and* JOCASTA *side by side.*]

JOCASTA.   For the love of god,
　　Oedipus, tell me too, what is it?
　　Why this rage? You're so unbending.

OEDIPUS. I will tell you. I respect you, Jocasta,
　　much more than these . . .   770

[*Glancing at the* CHORUS.]

　　Creon's to blame, Creon schemes against me.

JOCASTA. Tell me clearly, how did the quarrel start?

OEDIPUS. He says I murdered Laius—I am guilty.

JOCASTA. How does he know? Some secret knowledge
　　or simple hearsay?

OEDIPUS.   Oh, he sent his prophet in   775
　　to do his dirty work. You know Creon,
　　Creon keeps his own lips clean.

JOCASTA.   A prophet?
　　Well then, free yourself of every charge!
　　Listen to me and learn some peace of mind:
　　no skill in the world,   780
　　nothing human can penetrate the future.
　　Here is proof, quick and to the point.

　　An oracle came to Laius one fine day
　　(I won't say from Apollo himself
　　but his underlings, his priests) and it said   785
　　that doom would strike him down at the hands of a son,
　　our son, to be born of our own flesh and blood. But Laius,
　　so the report goes at least, was killed by strangers,
　　thieves, at a place where three roads meet . . . my son—
　　he wasn't three days old and the boy's father   790
　　fastened his ankles, had a henchman fling him away
　　on a barren, trackless mountain.
　　　　　　　　　　　　There, you see?
　　Apollo brought neither thing to pass. My baby
　　no more murdered his father than Laius suffered—
　　his wildest fear—death at his own son's hands.   795

That's how the seers and all their revelations
mapped out the future. Brush them from your mind.
Whatever the god needs and seeks
he'll bring to light himself, with ease.

OEDIPUS.   Strange,
hearing you just now . . . my mind wandered,   800
my thoughts racing back and forth.

JOCASTA. What do you mean? Why so anxious, startled?

OEDIPUS. I thought I heard you say that Laius
was cut down at a place where three roads meet.

JOCASTA. That was the story. It hasn't died out yet.   805

OEDIPUS. Where did this thing happen? Be precise.

JOCASTA. A place called Phocis, where two branching roads,
one from Daulia, one from Delphi,
come together—a crossroads.

OEDIPUS. When? How long ago?   810

JOCASTA. The heralds no sooner reported Laius dead
than you appeared and they hailed you king of Thebes.

OEDIPUS. My god, my god—what have you planned to do to me?

JOCASTA. What, Oedipus? What haunts you so?

OEDIPUS.   Not yet.
Laius—how did he look? Describe him.   815
Had he reached his prime?

JOCASTA.   He was swarthy,
and the gray had just begun to streak his temples,
and his build . . . wasn't far from yours.

OEDIPUS.   Oh no no,
I think I've just called down a dreadful curse
upon myself—I simply didn't know!   820

JOCASTA. What are you saying? I shudder to look at you.

OEDIPUS. I have a terrible fear the blind seer can see.
I'll know in a moment. One thing more—

JOCASTA.   Anything,
afraid as I am—ask, I'll answer, all I can.

OEDIPUS. Did he go with a light or heavy escort,   825
several men-at-arms, like a lord, a king?

JOCASTA. There were five in the party, a herald among them,
and a single wagon carrying Laius.

OEDIPUS.   Ai—
now I can see it all, clear as day.
Who told you all this at the time, Jocasta?   830

JOCASTA. A servant who reached home, the lone survivor.

OEDIPUS. So, could he still be in the palace—even now?

JOCASTA. No indeed. Soon as he returned from the scene
and saw you on the throne with Laius dead and gone,
he knelt and clutched my hand, pleading with me   835
to send him into the hinterlands, to pasture,
far as possible, out of sight of Thebes.
I sent him away. Slave though he was,
he'd earned that favor—and much more.

OEDIPUS. Can we bring him back, quickly?   840

JOCASTA. Easily. Why do you want him so?

OEDIPUS. I'm afraid,
Jocasta, I have said too much already.
That man—I've got to see him.

JOCASTA. Then he'll come.
But even I have a right, I'd like to think,
to know what's torturing you, my lord.   845

OEDIPUS. And so you shall—I can hold nothing back from you,
now I've reached this pitch of dark foreboding.
Who means more to me than you? Tell me,
whom would I turn toward but you
as I go through all this?   850

My father was Polybus, king of Corinth.
My mother, a Dorian, Merope. And I was held
the prince of the realm among the people there,
till something struck me out of nowhere,
something strange . . . worth remarking perhaps,   855
hardly worth the anxiety I gave it.
Some man at a banquet who had drunk too much
shouted out—he was far gone, mind you—
that I am not my father's son. Fighting words!
I barely restrained myself that day   860
but early the next I went to mother and father,
questioned them closely, and they were enraged
at the accusation and the fool who let it fly.
So as for my parents I was satisfied,
but still this thing kept gnawing at me,   865
the slander spread—I had to make my move.

And so,
unknown to mother and father I set out for Delphi,
and the god Apollo spurned me, sent me away,
denied the facts I came for,
but first he flashed before my eyes a future   870
great with pain, terror, disaster—I can hear him cry,
"You are fated to couple with your mother, you will bring
a breed of children into the light no man can bear to see—
you will kill your father, the one who gave you life!"
I heard all that and ran. I abandoned Corinth,   875
from that day on I gauged its landfall only
by the stars, running, always running
toward some place where I would never see
the shame of all those oracles come true.
And as I fled I reached that very spot   880
where the great king, you say, met his death.
Now, Jocasta, I will tell you all.
Making my way toward this triple crossroad
I began to see a herald, then a brace of colts
drawing a wagon, and mounted on the bench . . . a man,   885
just as you've described him, coming face-to-face,
and the one in the lead and the old man himself

were about to thrust me off the road—brute force—
and the one shouldering me aside, the driver,
I strike him in anger!—and the old man, watching me   890
coming up along his wheels—he brings down
his prod, two prongs straight at my head!
I paid him back with interest!
Short work, by god—with one blow of the staff
in this right hand I knock him out of his high seat,   895
roll him out of the wagon, sprawling headlong—
I killed them all—every mother's son!
Oh, but if there is any blood-tie
between Laius and this stranger . . .
what man alive more miserable than I?   900
More hated by the gods? *I* am the man
no alien, no citizen welcomes to his house,
law forbids it—not a word to me in public,
driven out of every hearth and home.
And all these curses I—no one but I   905
brought down these piling curses on myself!
And you, his wife, I've touched your body with these,
the hands that killed your husband cover you with blood.

Wasn't I born for torment? Look me in the eyes!
I am abomination—heart and soul!   910
I must be exiled, and even in exile
never see my parents, never set foot
on native ground again. Else I am doomed
to couple with my mother and cut my father down . . .
Polybus who reared me, gave me life.

But why, why?   915
Wouldn't a man of judgment say—and wouldn't he be right—
some savage power has brought this down upon my head?

Oh no, not that, you pure and awesome gods,
never let me see that day! Let me slip
from the world of men, vanish without a trace   920
before I see myself stained with such corruption,
stained to the heart.

LEADER. My lord, you fill our hearts with fear.
But at least until you question the witness,
do take hope.

OEDIPUS.   Exactly. He is my last hope—   925
I am waiting for the shepherd. He is crucial.

JOCASTA. And once he appears, what then? Why so urgent?

OEDIPUS. I will tell you. If it turns out that his story
matches yours, I've escaped the worst.

JOCASTA. What did I say? What struck you so?

OEDIPUS.   You said *thieves*—   930
he told you a whole band of them murdered Laius.
So, if he still holds to the same number,
I cannot be the killer. One can't equal many.

But if he refers to one man, one alone,
clearly the scales come down on me: 935
I am guilty.
JOCASTA.   Impossible. Trust me,
I told you precisely what he said,
and he can't retract it now;
the whole city heard it, not just I.
And even if he should vary his first report   940
by one man more or less, still, my lord,
he could never make the murder of Laius
truly fit the prophecy. Apollo was explicit:
my son was doomed to kill my husband . . . my son,
poor defenseless thing, he never had a chance   945
to kill his father. They destroyed him first.

So much for prophecy. It's neither here nor there.
From this day on, I wouldn't look right or left.
OEDIPUS. True, true. Still, that shepherd,
someone fetch him—now!   950
JOCASTA. I'll send at once. But do let's go inside.
I'd never displease you, least of all in this.

[OEDIPUS *and* JOCASTA *enter the palace.*]

CHORUS. Destiny guide me always
Destiny find me filled with reverence
     pure in word and deed.   955
Great laws tower above us, reared on high
born for the brilliant vault of heaven—
     Olympian Sky their only father,
nothing mortal, no man gave them birth,
their memory deathless, never lost in sleep: 960
within them lives a mighty god, the god does not grow old.

Pride breeds the tyrant
violent pride, gorging, crammed to bursting
     with all that is overripe and rich with ruin—
clawing up to the heights, headlong pride   965
crashes down the abyss—sheer doom!
     No footing helps, all foothold lost and gone.
But the healthy strife that makes the city strong—
I pray that god will never end that wrestling:
god, my champion, I will never let you go.   970

But if any man comes striding, high and mighty
     in all he says and does,
no fear of justice, no reverence
for the temples of the gods—
     let a rough doom tear him down,   975
repay his pride, breakneck, ruinous pride!
If he cannot reap his profits fairly
     cannot restrain himself from outrage—
mad, laying hands on the holy things untouchable!

        Can such a man, so desperate, still boast   980
        he can save his life from the flashing bolts of god?
           If all such violence goes with honor now
              why join the sacred dance?

      Never again will I go reverent to Delphi,
          the inviolate heart of Earth   985
      or Apollo's ancient oracle at Abae
      or Olympia of the fires—
         unless these prophecies all come true
      for all mankind to point toward in wonder.
      King of kings, if you deserve your titles   990
      Zeus, remember, never forget!
      You and your deathless, everlasting reign.

        They are dying, the old oracles sent to Laius,
        now our masters strike them off the rolls.
           Nowhere Apollo's golden glory now—   995
              the gods, the gods go down.

[*Enter* JOCASTA *from the palace, carrying a suppliant's branch wound in wool.*]

JOCASTA. Lords of the realm, it occurred to me,
      just now, to visit the temples of the gods,
      so I have my branch in my hand and incense too.

      Oedipus is beside himself. Racked with anguish,   1000
      no longer a man of sense, he won't admit
      the latest prophecies are hollow as the old—
      he's at the mercy of every passing voice
      if the voice tells of terror.
      I urge him gently, nothing seems to help,   1005
      so I turn to you, Apollo, you are nearest.

[*Placing her branch on the altar; while an old herdsman enters from the side, not the one just summoned by the King but an unexpected* MESSENGER *from Corinth.*]

      I come with prayers and offerings . . . I beg you,
      cleanse us, set us free of defilement!
      Look at us, passengers in the grip of fear,
      watching the pilot of the vessel go to pieces.   1010
MESSENGER. [*Approaching* JOCASTA *and the* CHORUS.]
      Strangers, please, I wonder if you could lead us
      to the palace of the king . . . I think it's Oedipus.
      Better, the man himself—you know where he is?
LEADER. This is his palace, stranger. He's inside.
      But here is his queen, his wife and mother   1015
      of his children.
MESSENGER.   Blessings on you, noble queen,
      queen of Oedipus crowned with all your family—
      blessings on you always!
JOCASTA. And the same to you, stranger, you deserve it . . .
      such a greeting. But what have you come for?   1020
      Have you brought us news?

MESSENGER.   Wonderful news—
　　for the house, my lady, for your husband too.
JOCASTA. Really, what? Who sent you?
MESSENGER.   Corinth.
　　I'll give you the message in a moment.
　　You'll be glad of it—how could you help it?—   1025
　　though it costs a little sorrow in the bargain.
JOCASTA. What can it be, with such a double edge?
MESSENGER. The people there, they want to make your Oedipus
　　king of Corinth, so they're saying now.
JOCASTA. Why? Isn't old Polybus still in power?   1030
MESSENGER. No more. Death has got him in the tomb.
JOCASTA. What are you saying? Polybus, dead?—dead?
MESSENGER.   If not,
　　if I'm not telling the truth, strike me dead too.
JOCASTA. [*To a servant.*]
　　Quickly, go to your master, tell him this!
　　You prophecies of the gods, where are you now?   1035
　　This is the man that Oedipus feared for years,
　　he fled him, not to kill him—and now he's dead,
　　quite by chance, a normal, natural death,
　　not murdered by his son.
OEDIPUS. [*Emerging from the palace.*]
　　　　　　　　Dearest,
　　what now? Why call me from the palace?   1040
JOCASTA. [*Bringing the* MESSENGER *closer.*]
　　Listen to *him,* see for yourself what all
　　those awful prophecies of god have come to.
OEDIPUS. And who is he? What can he have for me?
JOCASTA. He's from Corinth, he's come to tell you
　　your father is no more—Polybus—he's dead!   1045
OEDIPUS. [*Wheeling on the* MESSENGER.]
　　What? Let me have it from your lips.
MESSENGER.   Well,
　　if that's what you want first, then here it is:
　　make no mistake, Polybus is dead and gone.
OEDIPUS. How—murder? sickness?—what? what killed him?
MESSENGER. A light tip of the scales put old bones to rest.   1050
OEDIPUS. Sickness then—poor man, it wore him down.
MESSENGER.   That,
　　and the long count of years he'd measured out.
OEDIPUS.   So!
　　Jocasta, why, why look to the Prophet's hearth,
　　the fires of the future? Why scan the birds
　　that scream above our heads? They winged me on   1055
　　to the murder of my father, did they? That was my doom?
　　Well look, he's dead and buried, hidden under the earth,
　　and here I am in Thebes, I never put hand to sword—
　　unless some longing for me wasted him away,
　　then in a sense you'd say I caused his death.   1060
　　But now, all those prophecies I feared—Polybus

packs them off to sleep with him in hell!
They're nothing, worthless.
JOCASTA.   There.
    Didn't I tell you from the start?
OEDIPUS. So you did. I was lost in fear.   1065
JOCASTA. No more, sweep it from your mind forever.
OEDIPUS. But my mother's bed, surely I must fear—
JOCASTA.   Fear?
    What should a man fear? It's all chance,
    chance rules our lives. Not a man on earth
    can see a day ahead, groping through the dark.   1070
    Better to live at random, best we can.
    And as for this marriage with your mother—
    have no fear. Many a man before you,
    in his dreams, has shared his mother's bed.
    Take such things for shadows, nothing at all—   1075
    Live, Oedipus,
    as if there's no tomorrow!
OEDIPUS.   Brave words,
    and you'd persuade me if mother weren't alive.
    But mother lives, so for all your reassurances
    I live in fear, I must.
JOCASTA.   But your father's death,   1080
    that, at least, is a great blessing, joy to the eyes!
OEDIPUS. Great, I know . . . but I fear her—she's still alive.
MESSENGER. Wait, who is this woman, makes you so afraid?
OEDIPUS. Merope, old man. The wife of Polybus.
MESSENGER. The queen? What's there to fear in her?   1085
OEDIPUS. A dreadful prophecy, stranger, sent by the gods.
MESSENGER. Tell me, could you? Unless it's forbidden
    other ears to hear.
OEDIPUS.   Not at all.
    Apollo told me once—it is my fate—
    I must make love with my own mother,   1090
    shed my father's blood with my own hands.
    So for years I've given Corinth a wide berth,
    and it's been my good fortune too. But still,
    to see one's parents and look into their eyes
    is the greatest joy I know.
MESSENGER.   You're afraid of that?   1095
    That kept you out of Corinth?
OEDIPUS.   My *father*, old man—
    so I wouldn't kill my father.
MESSENGER.   So that's it.
    Well then, seeing I came with such good will, my king,
    why don't I rid you of that old worry now?
OEDIPUS. What a rich reward you'd have for that!   1100
MESSENGER. What do you think I came for, majesty?
    So you'd come home and I'd be better off.
OEDIPUS. Never, I will never go near my parents.
MESSENGER. My boy, it's clear, you don't know what you're doing.

OEDIPUS. What do you mean, old man? For god's sake, explain.   1105
MESSENGER. If you ran from *them,* always dodging home . . .
OEDIPUS. Always, terrified Apollo's oracle might come true—
MESSENGER. And you'd be covered with guilt, from both your parents.
OEDIPUS. That's right, old man, that fear is always with me.
MESSENGER. Don't you know? You've really nothing to fear.   1110
OEDIPUS. But why? If I'm their son—Merope, Polybus?
MESSENGER. Polybus was nothing to you, that's why, not in blood.
OEDIPUS. What are you saying—Polybus was not my father?
MESSENGER. No more than I am. He and I are equals.
OEDIPUS.   My father—
    how can my father equal nothing? You're nothing to me!   1115
MESSENGER. Neither was he, no more your father than I am.
OEDIPUS. Then why did he call me his son?
MESSENGER.   You were a gift,
    years ago—know for a fact he took you
    from my hands.
OEDIPUS.   No, from another's hands?
    Then how could he love me so? He loved me, deeply . . .   1120
MESSENGER. True, and his early years without a child
    made him love you all the more.
OEDIPUS.   And you, did you . . .
    buy me? find me by accident?
MESSENGER.   I stumbled on you,
    down the woody flanks of Mount Cithaeron.
OEDIPUS.   So close,
    what were you doing here, just passing through?   1125
MESSENGER. Watching over my flocks, grazing them on the slopes.
OEDIPUS. A herdsman, were you? A vagabond, scraping for wages?
MESSENGER. Your savior too, my son, in your worst hour.
OEDIPUS.   Oh—
    when you picked me up, was I in pain? What exactly?
MESSENGER. Your ankles . . . they tell the story. Look at them.   1130
OEDIPUS. Why remind me of that, that old affliction?
MESSENGER. Your ankles were pinned together. I set you free.
OEDIPUS. That dreadful mark—I've had it from the cradle.
MESSENGER. And you got your name° from that misfortune too,
    the name's still with you.
OEDIPUS.   Dear god, who did it?—   1135
    mother? father? Tell me.
MESSENGER.   I don't know.
    The one who gave you to me, he'd know more.
OEDIPUS. What? You took me from someone else?
    You didn't find me yourself?
MESSENGER.   No sir,
    another shepherd passed you on to me.   1140
OEDIPUS. Who? Do you know? Describe him.

1134 you got your name "Oedipus" means "swollen foot."

MESSENGER. He called himself a servant of . . .
     if I remember rightly—Laius.

     [JOCASTA *turns sharply.*]

OEDIPUS. The king of the land who ruled here long ago?
MESSENGER. That's the one. That herdsman was *his* man.   1145
OEDIPUS. Is he still alive? Can I see him?
MESSENGER. They'd know best, the people of these parts.

     [OEDIPUS *and the* MESSENGER *turn to the* CHORUS.]

OEDIPUS. Does anyone know that herdsman,
     the one he mentioned? Anyone seen him
     in the fields, in the city? Out with it!   1150
     The time has come to reveal this once for all.
LEADER. I think he's the very shepherd you wanted to see,
     a moment ago. But the queen, Jocasta,
     she's the one to say.
OEDIPUS.   Jocasta,
     you remember the man we just sent for?   1155
     Is *that* the one he means?
JOCASTA.   That man . . .
     why ask? Old shepherd, talk, empty nonsense,
     don't give it another thought, don't even think—
OEDIPUS. What—give up now, with a clue like this?
     Fail to solve the mystery of my birth?   1160
     Not for all the world!
JOCASTA.   Stop—in the name of god,
     if you love your own life, call off this search!
     My suffering is enough.
OEDIPUS.   Courage!
     Even if my mother turns out to be a slave,
     and I a slave, three generations back,   1165
     you would not seem common.
JOCASTA.   Oh no,
     listen to me, I beg you, don't do this.
OEDIPUS. Listen to you? No more. I must know it all,
     must see the truth at last.
JOCASTA.   No, please—
     for your sake—I want the best for you!   1170
OEDIPUS. Your best is more than I can bear.
JOCASTA.   You're doomed—
     may you never fathom who you are!
OEDIPUS. [*To a servant.*] Hurry, fetch me the herdsman, now!
     Leave her to glory in her royal birth.
JOCASTA. Aieeeeee—
                         man of agony—   1175
     that is the only name I have for you,
     that, no other—ever, ever, ever!

     [*Flinging through the palace doors. A long, tense silence follows.*]

LEADER. Where's she gone, Oedipus?
    Rushing off, such wild grief . . .
    I'm afraid that from this silence   1180
    something monstrous may come bursting forth.
OEDIPUS. Let it burst! Whatever will, whatever must!
    I must know my birth, no matter how common
    it may be—I must see my origins face-to-face.
    She perhaps, she with her woman's pride   1185
    may well be mortified by my birth,
    but I, I count myself the son of Chance,
    the great goddess, giver of all good things—
    I'll never see myself disgraced. She is my mother!
    And the moons have marked me out, my blood-brothers,   1190
    one moon on the wane, the next moon great with power.
    That is my blood, my nature—I will never betray it,
    never fail to search and learn my birth!
CHORUS. Yes—if I am a true prophet
      if I can grasp the truth,   1195
      by the boundless skies of Olympus,
    at the full moon of tomorrow, Mount Cithaeron
    you will know how Oedipus glories in you—
    you, his birthplace, nurse, his mountain-mother!
    And we will sing you, dancing out your praise—   1200
    you lift our monarch's heart!
      Apollo, Apollo, god of the wild cry
      may our dancing please you!
                Oedipus—
      son, dear child, who bore you?
    Who of the nymphs who seem to live forever   1205
    mated with Pan,° the mountain-striding Father?
    Who was your mother? who, some bride of Apollo
    the god who loves the pastures spreading toward the sun?
      Or was it Hermes, king of the lightning ridges?
    Or Dionysus, lord of frenzy, lord of the barren peaks—   1210
    did he seize you in his hands, dearest of all his lucky finds?—
    found by the nymphs, their warm eyes dancing, gift
    to the lord who loves them dancing out his joy!

[OEDIPUS *strains to see a figure coming from the distance. Attended by palace*
guards, an old SHEPHERD *enters slowly, reluctant to approach the king.*]

OEDIPUS. I never met the man, my friends . . . still,
    if I had to guess, I'd say that's the shepherd,   1215
    the very one we've looked for all along.
    Brothers in old age, two of a kind,
    he and our guest here. At any rate
    the ones who bring him in are my own men,
    I recognize them.

1206 Pan god of shepherds (associated, like Hermes and Dionysus, with wilderness).

[*Turning to the* LEADER.]

But you know more than I,   1220
you should, you've seen the man before.

LEADER. I know him, definitely. One of Laius' men,
a trusty shepherd, if there ever was one.

OEDIPUS. You, I ask you first, stranger,
you from Corinth—is this the one you mean?   1225

MESSENGER. You're looking at him. He's your man.

OEDIPUS. [*To the* SHEPHERD.]
You, old man, come over here—
look at me. Answer all my questions.
Did you ever serve King Laius?

SHEPHERD.   So I did . . .
a slave, not bought on the block though,   1230
born and reared in the palace.

OEDIPUS. Your duties, your kind of work?

SHEPHERD. Herding the flocks, the better part of my life.

OEDIPUS. Where, mostly? Where did you do your grazing?

SHEPHERD.   Well,
Cithaeron sometimes, or the foothills round about.   1235

OEDIPUS. This man—you know him? ever see him there?

SHEPHERD. [*Confused, glancing from the* MESSENGER *to the* KING.]
Doing what?—what man do you mean?

OEDIPUS. [*Pointing to the* MESSENGER.]
This one here—ever have dealings with him?

SHEPHERD. Not so I could say, but give me a chance,
my memory's bad . . .   1240

MESSENGER. No wonder he doesn't know me, master.
But let me refresh his memory for him.
I'm sure he recalls old times we had
on the slopes of Mount Cithaeron;
he and I, grazing our flocks, he with two   1245
and I with one—we both struck up together,
three whole seasons, six months at a stretch
from spring to the rising of Arcturus° in the fall,
then with winter coming on I'd drive my herds
to my own pens, and back he'd go with his   1250
to Laius' folds.

[*To the* SHEPHERD.]

Now that's how it was,
wasn't it—yes or no?

SHEPHERD.   Yes, I suppose . . .
it's all so long ago.

MESSENGER.   Come, tell me,
you gave me a child back then, a boy, remember?
A little fellow to rear, my very own.   1255

1248 Arcturus a star whose rising signaled the end of summer.

SHEPHERD. What? Why rake up that again?

MESSENGER. Look, here he is, my fine old friend—
     the same man who was just a baby then.

SHEPHERD. Damn you, shut your mouth—quiet!

OEDIPUS. Don't lash out at him, old man—   1260
     you need lashing more than he does.

SHEPHERD.   Why,
     master, majesty—what have I done wrong?

OEDIPUS. You won't answer his question about the boy.

SHEPHERD. He's talking nonsense, wasting his breath.

OEDIPUS. So, you won't talk willingly—   1265
     then you'll talk with pain.

[*The guards seize the* SHEPHERD.]

SHEPHERD. No, dear god, don't torture an old man!

OEDIPUS. Twist his arms back, quickly!

SHEPHERD.   God help us, why?—
     what more do you need to know?

OEDIPUS. Did you give him that child? He's asking.   1270

SHEPHERD. I did . . . I wish to god I'd died that day.

OEDIPUS. You've got your wish if you don't tell the truth.

SHEPHERD. The more I tell, the worse the death I'll die.

OEDIPUS. Our friend here wants to stretch things out, does he?

[*Motioning to his men for torture.*]

SHEPHERD. No, no, I gave it to him—I just said so.   1275

OEDIPUS. Where did you get it? Your house? Someone else's?

SHEPHERD. It wasn't mine, no. I got it from . . . someone.

OEDIPUS. Which one of them?

[*Looking at the citizens.*]

                           Whose house?

SHEPHERD.   No—
     god's sake, master, no more questions!

OEDIPUS. You're a dead man if I have to ask again.   1280

SHEPHERD. Then—the child came from the house. . . of Laius.

OEDIPUS. A slave? or born of his own blood?

SHEPHERD.   Oh no,
     I'm right at the edge, the horrible truth—I've got to say it!

OEDIPUS. And I'm at the edge of hearing horrors, yes, but I must hear!

SHEPHERD. All right! His son, they said it was—his son!   1285
     But the one inside, your wife,
     she'd tell it best.

OEDIPUS. My wife—
     she gave it to you?

SHEPHERD. Yes, yes, my king.   1290

OEDIPUS. Why, what for?

SHEPHERD. To kill it.

OEDIPUS. Her own child,
     how could she?

SHEPHERD. She was afraid—   1295
    frightening prophecies.
OEDIPUS. What?
SHEPHERD.   They said—
    he'd kill his parents.
OEDIPUS. But you gave him to this old man—why?
SHEPHERD. I pitied the little baby, master,   1300
    hoped he'd take him off to his own country,
    far away, but he saved him for this, his fate.
    If you are the man he says you are, believe me,
    you were born for pain.
OEDIPUS.   O god—
    all come true, all burst to light!   1305
    O light—now let me look my last on you!
    I stand revealed at last—
    cursed in my birth, cursed in marriage,
    cursed in the lives I cut down with these hands!

[*Rushing through the doors with a great cry. The Corinthian*
MESSENGER, *the* SHEPHERD *and attendants exit slowly to the side.*]

CHORUS. O the generations of men   1310
    the dying generations—adding the total
    of all your lives I find they come to nothing . . .
            does there exist, is there a man on earth
    who seizes more joy than just a dream, a vision?
    And the vision no sooner dawns than dies   1315
    blazing into oblivion.

    You are my great example, you, your life
    your destiny, Oedipus, man of misery—
    I count no man blest.
                    You outranged all men!
        Bending your bow to the breaking-point   1320
    you captured priceless glory, O dear god,
    and the Sphinx came crashing down,
            the virgin, claws hooked
    like a bird of omen singing, shrieking death—
    like a fortress reared in the face of death   1325
    you rose and saved our land.

    From that day on we called you king
    we crowned you with honors, Oedipus, towering over all—
    mighty king of the seven gates of Thebes.

    But now to hear your story—is there a man more   1330
            agonized?
    More wed to pain and frenzy? Not a man on earth,
    the joy of your life ground down to nothing
    O Oedipus, name for the ages—
            one and the same wide harbor served you
                son and father both   1335

son and father came to rest in the same bridal chamber.
How, how could the furrows your father plowed
bear you, your agony, harrowing on
in silence O so long?
                  But now for all your power
Time, all-seeing Time has dragged you to the light,   1340
judged your marriage monstrous from the start—
the son and the father tangling, both one—
O child of Laius, would to god
   I'd never seen you, never never!
     Now I weep like a man who wails the dead   1345
and the dirge comes pouring forth with all my heart!
I tell you the truth, you gave me life
my breath leapt up in you
and now you bring down the night upon my eyes.

[*Enter a* MESSENGER *from the palace.*]

MESSENGER. Men of Thebes, always first in honor,   1350
   what horrors you will hear, what you will see,
   what a heavy weight of sorrow you will shoulder . . .
   if you are true to your birth, if you still have
   some feeling for the royal house of Thebes.
   I tell you neither the waters of the Danube   1355
   nor the Nile can wash this palace clean.
   Such things it hides, it soon will bring to light—
   terrible things, and none done blindly now,
   all done with a will. The pains
   we inflict upon ourselves hurt most of all.   1360
LEADER. God knows we have pains enough already.
   What can you add to them?
MESSENGER. The queen is dead.
LEADER.   Poor lady—how?
MESSENGER. By her own hand. But you are spared the worst,
   you never had to watch . . . I saw it all,   1365
   and with all the memory that's in me
   you will learn what that poor woman suffered.

Once she'd broken in through the gates,
dashing past us, frantic, whipped to fury,
ripping her hair out with both hands—   1370
straight to her rooms she rushed, flinging herself
across the bridal-bed, doors slamming behind her—
once inside, she wailed for Laius, dead so long,
remembering how she bore his child long ago,
the life that rose up to destroy him, leaving   1375
its mother to mother living creatures
with the very son she'd borne.
Oh how she wept, mourning the marriage-bed
where she let loose that double brood—monsters—
husband by her husband, children by her child.
                  And then—   1380

but how she died is more than I can say. Suddenly
Oedipus burst in, screaming, he stunned us so
we couldn't watch her agony to the end,
our eyes were fixed on him. Circling
like a maddened beast, stalking, here, there,   1385
crying out to us—
                    Give him a sword! His wife,
no wife, his mother, where can he find the mother earth
that cropped two crops at once, himself and all his children?
He was raging—one of the dark powers pointing the way,
none of us mortals crowding around him, no,   1390
with a great shattering cry—someone, something leading him on—
he hurled at the twin doors and bending the bolts back
out of their sockets, crashed through the chamber.
And there we saw the woman hanging by the neck,
cradled high in a woven noose, spinning,   1395
swinging back and forth. And when he saw her,
giving a low, wrenching sob that broke our hearts,
slipping the halter from her throat, he eased her down,
in a slow embrace he laid her down, poor thing . . .
then, what came next, what horror we beheld!   1400

He rips off her brooches, the long gold pins
holding her robes—and lifting them high,
looking straight up into the points,
he digs them down the sockets of his eyes, crying, "You,
you'll see no more the pain I suffered, all the pain I caused!   1405
Too long you looked on the ones you never should have seen,
blind to the ones you longed to see, to know! Blind
from this hour on! Blind in the darkness—blind!"
His voice like a dirge, rising, over and over
raising the pins, raking them down his eyes.   1410
And at each stroke blood spurts from the roots,
splashing his beard, a swirl of it, nerves and clots—
black hail of blood pulsing, gushing down.

These are the griefs that burst upon them both,
coupling man and woman. The joy they had so lately,   1415
the fortune of their old ancestral house
was deep joy indeed. Now, in this one day,
wailing, madness and doom, death, disgrace,
all the griefs in the world that you can name,
all are theirs forever.

LEADER.   Oh poor man, the misery—   1420
        has he any rest from pain now?

        [*A voice within, in torment.*]

MESSENGER.   He's shouting,
        "Loose the bolts, someone, show me to all of Thebes!
        My father's murderer, my mother's—"
        No, I can't repeat it, it's unholy.
        Now he'll tear himself from his native earth,   1425

not linger, curse the house with his own curse.
But he needs strength, and a guide to lead him on.
This is sickness more than he can bear.

[*The palace doors open.*]

                              Look,
he'll show you himself. The great doors are opening—
you are about to see a sight, a horror   1430
even his mortal enemy would pity.

[*Enter* OEDIPUS, *blinded, led by a boy. He stands at the palace steps,
as if surveying his people once again.*]

CHORUS.   O the terror—
    the suffering, for all the world to see,
    the worst terror that ever met my eyes.
    What madness swept over you? What god,
    what dark power leapt beyond all bounds,   1435
    beyond belief, to crush your wretched life?—
    godforsaken, cursed by the gods!
    I pity you but I can't bear to look.
    I've much to ask, so much to learn,
    so much fascinates my eyes,   1440
    but you . . . I shudder at the sight.
OEDIPUS.   Oh, Ohh—
    the agony! I am agony—
    where am I going? where on earth?
        where does all this agony hurl me?
    where's my voice?—   1445
        winging, swept away on a dark tide—
    My destiny, my dark power, what a leap you made!
CHORUS. To the depths of terror, too dark to hear, to see.
OEDIPUS. Dark, horror of darkness
    my darkness, drowning, swirling around me   1450
    crashing wave on wave—unspeakable, irresistible
        headwind, fatal harbor! Oh again,
    the misery, all at once, over and over
    the stabbing daggers, stab of memory
    raking me insane.
CHORUS.   No wonder you suffer   1455
    twice over, the pain of your wounds,
    the lasting grief of pain.
OEDIPUS.   Dear friend, still here?
    Standing by me, still with a care for me,
    the blind man? Such compassion,
    loyal to the last. Oh it's you,   1460
    I know you're here, dark as it is
    I'd know you anywhere, your voice—
    it's yours, clearly yours.
CHORUS.   Dreadful, what you've done . . .
    how could you bear it, gouging out your eyes?
    What superhuman power drove you on?   1465

OEDIPUS. Apollo, friends, Apollo—
    he ordained my agonies—these, my pains on pains!
       But the hand that struck my eyes was mine,
       mine alone—no one else—
          I did it all myself!   1470
    What good were eyes to me?
    Nothing I could see could bring me joy.
CHORUS. No, no, exactly as you say.
OEDIPUS.   What can I ever see?
       What love, what call of the heart
    can touch my ears with joy? Nothing, friends.   1475
       Take me away, far, far from Thebes,
          quickly, cast me away, my friends—
    this great murderous ruin, this man cursed to heaven,
       the man the deathless gods hate most of all!
CHORUS. Pitiful, you suffer so, you understand so much . . .   1480
    I wish you'd never known.
OEDIPUS.   Die, die—
    whoever he was that day in the wilds
    who cut my ankles free of the ruthless pins,
       he pulled me clear of death, he saved my life
       for this, this kindness—   1485
          Curse him, kill him!
    If I'd died then, I'd never have dragged myself,
       my loved ones through such hell.
CHORUS. Oh if only . . . would to god.
OEDIPUS.   I'd never have come to this,
       my father's murderer—never been branded   1490
    mother's husband, all men see me now! Now,
       loathed by the gods, son of the mother I defiled
       coupling in my father's bed, spawning lives in the loins
    that spawned my wretched life. What grief can crown this grief?
       It's mine alone, my destiny—I am Oedipus!   1495
CHORUS. How can I say you've chosen for the best?
    Better to die than be alive and blind.
OEDIPUS. What I did was best—don't lecture me,
    no more advice. I, with *my* eyes,
    how could I look my father in the eyes   1500
    when I go down to death? Or mother, so abused . . .
    I have done such things to the two of them,
    crimes too huge for hanging.
                                    Worse yet,
    the sight of my children, born as they were born,
    how could I long to look into their eyes?   1505
    No, not with these eyes of mine, never.
    Not this city either, her high towers,
    the sacred glittering images of her gods—
    I am misery! I, her best son, reared
    as no other son of Thebes was ever reared,   1510
    I've stripped myself, I gave the command myself.
    All men must cast away the great blasphemer,

the curse now brought to light by the gods,
the son of Laius—I, my father's son!

Now I've exposed my guilt, horrendous guilt, 1515
could I train a level glance on you, my countrymen?
Impossible! No, if I could just block off my ears,
the springs of hearing, I would stop at nothing—
I'd wall up my loathsome body like a prison,
blind to the sound of life, not just the sight: 1520
Oblivion—what a blessing . . .
for the mind to dwell a world away from pain.

O Cithaeron, why did you give me shelter?
Why didn't you take me, crush my life out on the spot?
I'd never have revealed my birth to all mankind. 1525

O Polybus, Corinth, the old house of my fathers,
so I believed—what a handsome prince you raised—
under the skin, what sickness to the core.
Look at me! Born of outrage, outrage to the core.
O triple roads—it all comes back, the secret, 1530
dark ravine, and the oaks closing in
where the three roads join . . .
You drank my father's blood, my own blood
spilled by my own hands—you still remember me?
What things you saw me do? Then I came here 1535
and did them all once more!
                                        Marriages! O marriage,
you gave me birth, and once you brought me into the world
you brought my sperm rising back, springing to light
fathers, brothers, sons—one murderous breed—
brides, wives, mothers. The blackest things 1540
a man can do, I have done them all!
                                        No more—
it's wrong to name what's wrong to do. Quickly,
for the love of god, hide me somewhere,
kill me, hurl me into the sea
where you can never look on me again.

[*Beckoning to the* CHORUS *as they shrink away.*]

                                        Closer, 1545
it's all right. Touch the man of grief.
Do. Don't be afraid. My troubles are mine
and I am the only man alive who can sustain them.

[*Enter* CREON *from the palace, attended by palace guards.*]

LEADER. Put your requests to Creon. Here he is,
just when we need him. He'll have a plan, he'll act. 1550
Now that he's the sole defense of the country
in your place.
OEDIPUS.   Oh no, what can I say to him?
How can I ever hope to win his trust?

I wronged him so, just now, in every way.
You must see that—I was so wrong, so wrong.   1555
CREON. I haven't come to mock you, Oedipus,
or to criticize your former failings.

[*Turning to the guards.*]

You there,
have you lost all respect for human feelings?
At least revere the Sun, the holy fire
that keeps us all alive. Never expose a thing   1560
of guilt and holy dread so great it appalls
the earth, the rain from heaven, the light of day!
Get him into the halls—quickly as you can.
Piety demands no less. Kindred alone
should see a kinsman's shame. This is obscene.   1565
OEDIPUS. Please, in god's name . . . you wipe my fears away,
coming so generously to me, the worst of men.
Do one thing more, for your sake, not mine.
CREON. What do you want? Why so insistent?
OEDIPUS. Drive me out of the land at once, far from sight,   1570
where I can never hear a human voice.
CREON. I'd have done that already, I promise you.
First I wanted the god to clarify my duties.
OEDIPUS. The god? His command was clear, every word:
death for the father-killer, the curse—   1575
he said destroy me!
CREON. So he did. Still, in such a crisis
it's better to ask precisely what to do.
OEDIPUS.   So miserable—
you'd consult the god about a man like me?
CREON. By all means. And this time, I assume,   1580
even you will obey the god's decrees.
OEDIPUS.   I will,
I will. And you, I command you—I beg you . . .
the woman inside, bury her as you see fit.
It's the only decent thing,
to give your own the last rites. As for me,   1585
never condemn the city of my fathers
to house my body, not while I'm alive, no,
let me live on the mountains, on Cithaeron,
my favorite haunt, I have made it famous.
Mother and father marked out that rock   1590
to be my everlasting tomb—buried alive.
Let me die there, where they tried to kill me.
Oh but this I know: no sickness can destroy me,
nothing can. I would never have been saved
from death—I have been saved   1595
for something great and terrible, something strange.
Well let my destiny come and take me on its way!
About my children, Creon, the boys at least,
don't burden yourself. They're men,

wherever they go, they'll find the means to live.   1600
But my two daughters, my poor helpless girls,
clustering at our table, never without me
hovering near them . . . whatever I touched,
they always had their share. Take care of them,
I beg you. Wait, better—permit me, would you?   1605
Just to touch them with my hands and take
our fill of tears. Please . . . my king.
Grant it, with all your noble heart.
If I could hold them, just once, I'd think
I had them with me, like the early days   1610
when I could see their eyes.

[ANTIGONE *and* ISMENE, *two small children, are led in from the
palace by a nurse.*]

                    What's that
O god! Do I really hear you sobbing?—
my two children. Creon, you've pitied me?
Sent me my darling girls, my own flesh and blood!
Am I right?

CREON.   Yes, it's my doing.   1615
I know the joy they gave you all these years,
the joy you must feel now.

OEDIPUS.   Bless you, Creon!
May god watch over you for this kindness,
better than he ever guarded me.
                    Children, where are you?
Here, come quickly—

[*Groping for* ANTIGONE *and* ISMENE, *who approach their father
cautiously, then embrace him.*]

                    Come to these hands of mine,   1620
your brother's hands, your own father's hands
that served his once bright eyes so well—
that made them blind. Seeing nothing, children,
knowing nothing, I became your father,
I fathered you in the soil that gave me life.   1625

How I weep for you—I cannot see you now . . .
just thinking of all your days to come, the bitterness,
the life that rough mankind will thrust upon you.
Where are the public gatherings you can join,
the banquets of the clans? Home you'll come,   1630
in tears, cut off from the sight of it all,
the brilliant rites unfinished.
And when you reach perfection, ripe for marriage,
who will he be, my dear ones? Risking all
to shoulder the curse that weighs down my parents,   1635
yes and you too—that wounds us all together.
What more misery could you want?
Your father killed his father, sowed his mother,

one, one and the selfsame womb sprang you—
he cropped the very roots of his existence.   1640

Such disgrace, and you must bear it all!
Who will marry you then? Not a man on earth.
Your doom is clear: you'll wither away to nothing,
single, without a child.

[*Turning to* CREON.]

                    Oh Creon,
you are the only father they have now . . .   1645
we who brought them into the world
are gone, both gone at a stroke—
Don't let them go begging, abandoned,
women without men. Your own flesh and blood!
Never bring them down to the level of my pains.   1650
Pity them. Look at them, so young, so vulnerable,
shorn of everything—you're their only hope.
Promise me, noble Creon, touch my hand!

[*Reaching toward* CREON, *who draws back.*]

You, little ones, if you were old enough
to understand, there is much I'd tell you.   1655
Now, as it is, I'd have you say a prayer.
Pray for life, my children,
live where you are free to grow and season.
Pray god you find a better life than mine,
the father who begot you.

CREON.   Enough.   1660
You've wept enough. Into the palace now.

OEDIPUS. I must, but I find it very hard.

CREON. Time is the great healer, you will see.

OEDIPUS. I am going—you know on what condition?

CREON. Tell me. I'm listening.   1665

OEDIPUS. Drive me out of Thebes, in exile.

CREON. Not I. Only the gods can give you that.

OEDIPUS. Surely the gods hate me so much—

CREON. You'll get your wish at once.

OEDIPUS.   You consent?

CREON. I try to say what I mean; it's my habit.   1670

OEDIPUS. Then take me away. It's time.

CREON. Come along, let go of the children.

OEDIPUS.   No—
don't take them away from me, not now! No no no!

[*Clutching his daughters as the guards wrench them loose and take them
through the palace doors.*]

CREON. Still the king, the master of all things?
No more: here your power ends.   1675
None of your power follows you through life.

[*Exit* OEDIPUS *and* CREON *to the palace. The* CHORUS *comes forward
to address the audience directly.*]

CHORUS. People of Thebes, my countrymen, look on Oedipus.
　　He solved the famous riddle with his brilliance,
　　he rose to power, a man beyond all power.
　　Who could behold his greatness without envy?　　　　　　　　1680
　　Now what a black sea of terror has overwhelmed him.
　　Now as we keep our watch and wait the final day,
　　count no man happy till he dies, free of pain at last.

　　[*Exit in procession.*]

Joining the Conversation: Critical Thinking and Writing

The Play on the Page

1. On the basis of lines 1–149, characterize Oedipus. Does he seem an effective leader? What additional traits are revealed in lines 205–491?
2. In your opinion, how fair is it to say that Oedipus is morally guilty? Does he argue that he is morally innocent because he did not intend to do immoral deeds? Can it be said that he is guilty of *hubris* but that *hubris* (see page 431) has nothing to do with his fall?
3. Oedipus says that he blinds himself in order not to look upon people he should not. What further reasons can be given? Why does he not (like Jocasta) commit suicide?
4. Does the play show the futility of human efforts to act intelligently?
5. In *Oedipus,* do you find the gods evil?
6. Are the choral odes lyrical interludes that serve to separate the scenes, or do they advance the dramatic action?
7. Matthew Arnold said that Sophocles saw life steadily and saw it whole. But in this play is Sophocles facing the facts of life? Or, on the contrary, is he avoiding what we think of as normal life, and presenting a series of unnatural and outrageous coincidences? In either case, do you think the play is relevant today?
8. Can you describe your emotions at the end of the play? Do they include pity for Oedipus? Pity for all human beings, including yourself? Fear that you might be punished for some unintended transgression? Awe, engendered by a perception of the interrelatedness of things? Relief that the story is only a story? Exhilaration? Explain your reaction.

The Play on the Stage

9. During your first consideration of the play, start with a reading of lines 1–149. Choose someone from the group to stand on a chair (Oedipus), two other readers to stand nearby (the Priest and Creon), and several others to kneel or lie on the floor (Theban citizens). After this rough enactment, ask the readers how they felt about their roles. Then discuss the ways a modern staging could create a powerful opening for the play. Some questions to consider: Do the Thebans ever touch Oedipus? Should the actor playing Oedipus make eye contact with anyone on the stage?

10. Originally the Greek chorus chanted and danced. What are your recommendations for a director today? Choose a particular passage from the play to illustrate your ideas.
11. Imagine that you are directing a production of *Oedipus*. Propose a cast for the principal roles, using well-known actors or people from your own circle. Explain the reasons for your choices.
12. What might be gained or lost by performing the play in modern dress? Or is there some period other than ancient Greece—let's say the Victorian period—in which you think the play might be effectively set?
13. Alan MacVey, who directed a production at the University of Iowa, used classical costumes but afterward said that he wished he had used a conference table as the set and had costumed the royalty in "power suits." What is your response to this idea?

MyLiteratureLab® *For additional resources for* Oedipus the King, *log in to* www.myliteraturelab.com *where you will find a Full Length Performance, Longman Lecture, and Comprehension Quiz, as well as an About the Author for Sophocles (under Student Resources).*

CHAPTER 18

Reading and Writing about Poems

*All there is to writing is having ideas. To learn
to write is to learn to have ideas.*

ROBERT FROST

Chapter Preview

After reading this chapter you will be able to

- Identify and analyze the elements of poetry
- Explicate a poem
- Classify types of rhythm

Elements of Poetry

The Speaker and the Poet

The **speaker,** or **voice,** or **mask,** or **persona** (Latin for *mask*) that speaks a poem is not usually identical with the poet who writes it. The author assumes a role, or counterfeits the speech of a person in a particular situation. The nineteenth-century English poet Robert Browning, for instance, in "My Last Duchess" invented a Renaissance Italian duke who, in his palace, talks about his first wife and his art collection with an emissary from a count who is negotiating to offer his daughter in marriage to the duke.

In reading a poem, then, the first and most important question to ask yourself is this: Who is speaking? If an audience and a setting are suggested, keep them in mind, too, although these are not always indicated in a poem. Consider, for example, the following poem.

EMILY DICKINSON

I'm Nobody! Who are you?

I'm Nobody! Who are you?
Are you—Nobody—too?
Then there's a pair of us!
Don't tell! they'd banish us—you know!

How dreary—to be—Somebody!   5
How public—like a Frog—
To tell your name—the livelong June—
To an admiring Bog!

[1861?]

507

We cannot quite say that the speaker is Emily Dickinson, though if we have read a fair number of her poems we can say that the voice in this poem is familiar, and perhaps here we *can* talk of Dickinson rather than of "the speaker of the poem," since this speaker (unlike Browning's Renaissance duke) clearly is not a figure utterly remote from the poet.

Let's consider the sort of person we hear in "I'm Nobody! Who are you?" (Read it aloud, to see if you agree with what we say. In fact, you should test each of our assertions by reading the poem aloud.)

- The voice in the first line is rather like that of a child playing a game with a friend.
- In the second and third lines the speaker sees the reader as a fellow spirit ("Are you—Nobody—too?") and invites the reader to join her ("Then there's a pair of us!"), to form a conspiracy of silence against outsiders ("Don't tell!").

In "they'd banish us," however, we hear a word that a child would not be likely to use, and we probably feel that the speaker is a shy but (with the right companion) playful adult, who here is speaking to an intimate friend, the reader. By means of "banish," a word that brings to mind images of a king's court, the speaker almost comically inflates and thereby makes fun of the "they" who are opposed to "us."

In the second stanza, or we might better say in the space between the two stanzas, the speaker puts aside the childlike manner. In "How dreary," the first words of the second stanza, we hear a sophisticated voice, one might even say a world-weary voice or a voice perhaps with more than a touch of condescension. But since by now we are paired with the speaker in a conspiracy against outsiders, we enjoy the contrast that the speaker makes between the Nobodies and the Somebodies. Who are these Somebodies, these people who would imperiously "banish" the speaker and the friend? What are the Somebodies like?

How dreary—to be—Somebody!
How public—like a Frog—
To tell your name—the livelong June—
To an admiring Bog!

The last two lines do at least two things:

- They amusingly explain to the speaker's new friend (the reader) in what way a Somebody is public (it proclaims its presence all day), and
- they indicate the absurdity of the Somebody-Frog's behavior (the audience is "an admiring Bog").

By the end of the poem we are convinced that it is better to be a Nobody (like Dickinson and the reader?) than a Somebody (a loudmouth).

Dickinson did not always speak in this persona, however. In another poem, "Wild Nights—Wild Nights," probably written in the same year as "I'm Nobody! Who are you?", Dickinson speaks as an impassioned lover, but we need not assume that the beloved is actually in the presence of the lover. Since the second line says, "Were I with Thee," the reader must assume that the person addressed is *not* present. The poem represents a state of mind—a sort of talking to oneself—rather than an address to another person.

Wild Nights—Wild Nights

Wild Nights—Wild Nights,
Were I with Thee
Wild Nights should be
Our luxury

Futile—the Winds 5
To a Heart in port—
Done with the Compass—
Done with the Chart!

Rowing in Eden— 10
Ah, the Sea!
Might I but moor—Tonight—
In Thee.

[c. 1861]

This speaker is passionately in love. The following questions invite you to look more closely at how the speaker of "Wild Nights—Wild Nights" is characterized.

Joining the Conversation: Critical Thinking and Writing

1. How does this poem communicate the speaker's state of mind? For example, in the first stanza (lines 1–4), what—beyond the meaning of the words—is communicated by the repetition of "Wild Nights"? In the last stanza (lines 9–12), what is the tone of "Ah, the Sea"? ("Tone" means something like emotional coloring, as for instance a "businesslike tone," a "bitter tone," or an "eager tone.")
2. Paraphrase (that is, put into your own words) the second stanza. What does this stanza communicate about the speaker's love for the beloved? Compare your paraphrase and the original. What does the form of the original sentences (the *omission*, for instance, of the verbs of lines 5 and 6 and of the subject in lines 7 and 8) communicate?
3. Paraphrase the last stanza. How does "Ah, the Sea!" fit into your paraphrase? If you had trouble fitting it in, do you think the poem would be better off without it? If not, why not?

MyLiteratureLab® *For additional resources for "Wild Nights—Wild Nights," log in to* www.myliteraturelab.com *where you will find a full-length Video Performance, Longman Lecture, Comprehension Quiz, Short Evaluation Questions, and Essay Prompts, as well as an About the Author, Bibliography, Links, and Critical Overview for Dickinson (under Student Resources).*

The voice speaking a poem may have the ring of the author's own voice, and to make a distinction between speaker and author may at times seem perverse. Some poetry (especially contemporary American poetry) is highly autobiographical. Still, even in autobiographical poems it may be convenient to distinguish between author and speaker. The speaker of a given poem is, let's say, Sylvia Plath in her role as parent, or Sylvia Plath in her role as daughter, not simply Sylvia Plath the poet.

The Language of Poetry: Diction and Tone

How is a voice or mask or persona created? From the whole of language, the author consciously or unconsciously selects certain words and grammatical constructions; this selection constitutes the persona's diction. It is, then, partly by the diction that we come to know the speaker of a poem. Just as in life there is a difference between people who speak of a "belly button," a "navel," or an "umbilicus," so in poetry there is a difference between speakers who use one word rather than another. It is also possible that all three of these terms may be part of a given speaker's vocabulary, and the speaker's choice among the three would depend on the situation. That is, in addressing a child, the speaker would probably use the phrase "belly button"; in addressing an adult other than a family member or close friend, the speaker might be more likely to use "navel"; and if the speaker is a physician addressing an audience of physicians, he or she might be most likely to use "umbilicus." But this is only to say, again, that the dramatic situation in which you find yourself helps to define you, helps to establish the particular role that you are playing.

Some words are used in virtually all poems: *I, see, and,* and the like. Still, the grammatical constructions in which they appear may help to define the speaker. In Dickinson's "Wild Nights—Wild Nights," for instance, expressions such as "Were I with Thee" and "Might I" indicate a speaker of an earlier century than ours, and probably an educated speaker.

Speakers have attitudes toward

- themselves,
- their subjects, and
- their audiences,

and, consciously or unconsciously, they choose their words, pitch, and modulation accordingly; all these add up to their tone. In written literature, tone must be detected without the aid of the ear, although it's a good idea to read poetry aloud, trying to find the appropriate tone of voice. The reader must understand by the selection and sequence of words the way the words are meant to sound—playful, angry, confidential, or ironic, for example. The reader must catch what Frost calls "the speaking tone of voice somehow entangled in the words and fastened to the page for the ear of the imagination."

WILLIAM SHAKESPEARE

For biographical information on William Shakespeare, see pages 144 and 878. We print other sonnets on pages 144, 516, and 727.

Sonnet 146

Poor soul, the center of my sinful earth,
[My sinful earth] these rebel pow'rs that thee array,
Why dost thou pine within and suffer dearth,
Painting thy outward walls so costly gay?
Why so large cost,° having so short a lease,   5
Dost thou upon thy fading mansion spend?
Shall worms, inheritors of this excess,
Eat up thy charge? Is this thy body's end?
Then, soul, live thou upon thy servant's loss,
And let that pine to aggravate thy store;   10
Buy terms divine° in selling hours of dross;
Within be fed, without be rich no more.
     So shalt thou feed on Death, that feeds on men,
     And death once dead, there's no more dying then.

[1609]

5 cost expense.   **11 buy terms divine** buy ages of immortality.

Joining the Conversation: Critical Thinking and Writing

1. "My sinful earth," in line 2, is doubtless an error made by the printer of the first edition (1609), who mistakenly repeated the end of the first line. Among suggested replacements are "Thrall to," "Fooled by," "Rebuke," "Leagued with," and "Feeding." If you wish, suggest your own correction. Which do you prefer?
2. In what tone of voice would you speak the first line? The last line? Trace the speaker's shifts in emotion throughout the poem.
3. Is the speaker presenting an argument? What is the argument (if you think there is one)? How does the speaker support it?

Writing about the Speaker

Robert Frost once said:

> Everything written is as good as it is dramatic. . . . [A poem is] heard as sung or spoken by a person in a scene—in a character, in a setting. By whom, where and when is the question. By the dreamer of a better world out in a storm in autumn; by a lover under a window at night.

Suppose, in reading the poem by Frost we reprint below, we try to establish "by whom, where and when" it is spoken. We may not be able to answer all three questions in detail, but let's see what the poem suggests. As you read it, you'll notice—alerted by the quotation marks—that there are *two* speakers; the poem is a tiny drama. Thus, the closing quotation marks at the end of line 9 signal to us that the first speech is finished.

ROBERT FROST

The Telephone

"When I was just as far as I could walk
From here today,
There was an hour
All still
When leaning with my head against a flower   5
I heard you talk.
Don't say I didn't, for I heard you say—
You spoke from that flower on the window sill—
Do you remember what it was you said?"

"First tell me what it was you thought you heard."   10

"Having found the flower and driven a bee away,
I leaned my head,
And holding by the stalk,
I listened and I thought I caught the word—
What was it? Did you call me by my name?   15

Or did you say—
Someone said 'Come'—I heard it as I bowed."

"I may have thought as much, but not aloud."

"Well, so I came."

[1916]

Suppose we ask: Who are these two speakers? What is their relationship? What's going on between them? Where are they? We don't think that these questions can be answered with absolute certainty, but we do think some answers are more probable than others. For instance, line 8 ("You spoke from that flower on the window sill") tells us that the speakers are in a room, probably of a home—rather than, say, in a railroad station—but we cannot say whether the home is a farmhouse, or a house in a village, town, or city, or an apartment.

Let's put the questions (even if they may turn out to be unanswerable) into a more specific form.

Joining the Conversation: Critical Thinking and Writing

1. One speaker speaks lines 1–9, 11–17, and 19. The other speaks lines 10 and 18. Do you think you can tell the gender of each speaker? For sure, probably, or not at all? On what do you base your answer?
2. Try to visualize this miniature drama. In line 7 the first speaker says, "Don't say I didn't, . . . " What happens—what do you see in your mind's eye—after line 6 that causes the speaker to say this?
3. Why do you suppose the speaker of lines 10 and 18 says so little? How would you characterize the tone of these two lines? What sort of relationship do you think exists between the two speakers?
4. How would you characterize the tone of lines 11–17? Of the last line of the poem?

If you haven't jotted down your responses, we suggest that you do so before reading what follows.

Journal Entries

Given questions somewhat like the preceding ones, students were asked to try to identify the speakers by sex, to speculate on their relationship, and then to add whatever they wished to say. One student recorded the following thoughts:

> These two people care about each other—maybe husband and wife, or lovers—and a man is doing most of the talking, though I can't prove it. He has walked as far as possible—that is, as far as possible and still get back on the same day—and he seemed to hear the other person call him. He claims that she spoke to him "from that flower on the window sill," and that's why I think the second person is a woman. She's at home, near the window. Somehow I even imagine she was at the window near the kitchen sink, maybe working while he was out on this long walk.
>
> Then she speaks one line; she won't say if she did or didn't speak. She is very cautious, or suspicious: "First tell me what it was you thought you heard." Maybe she

doesn't want to say something and then have her husband embarrass her by saying, "No, that's not what I thought." Or maybe she just doesn't feel like talking. Then he claims that he heard her speaking through a flower, as though the flower was a telephone, just as though it was hooked up to the flower on the window sill. But at first he won't say what he supposedly heard, or "thought" he heard. Instead, he says that maybe it was someone else: "*Someone* said 'Come.'" Is he teasing her? Pretending that she may have a rival?

Then she speaks—again just one line, saying, "I may have thought as much, but not aloud." She won't admit that she *did* think this thought. And then the man says, "Well, so I came." Just like that; short and sweet. No more fancy talk about flowers as telephones. He somehow (through telepathy?) got the message, and so here he is. He seems like a sensitive guy, playful (the stuff about the flowers as telephones), but also he knows when to stop kidding around.

Another student also identified the couple as a man and woman and thought that this dialogue occurs after a quarrel:

> As the poem goes on, we learn that the man wants to be with the woman, but it starts by telling us that he walked as far away from her as he could. He doesn't say why, but I think from the way the woman speaks later in the poem, they had a fight and he walked out. Then, when he stopped to rest, he thought he heard her voice. He really means that he was thinking of her and he was hoping she was thinking of him. So he returns, and he tells her he heard her calling him, but he pretends he heard her call him through a flower on their window sill. He can't admit that *he* was thinking about her. This seems very realistic to me; when someone feels a bit ashamed, it's sometimes hard to admit that you were wrong, and you want the other person to tell you that things are OK anyhow. And judging from line 7, when he says "Don't say I didn't," it seems that she is going to interrupt him by denying it. She is still angry, or maybe she doesn't want to make up too quickly. But he wants to pretend that *she* called him back. So when he says, "Do you remember what it was you said?" she won't admit that she *was* thinking of him, and she says, "First tell me what it was you thought you heard." She's testing him a little. So he goes on, with the business about flowers as telephones, and he says "someone" called him. He understands that she doesn't want to be pushed into forgiving him, so he backs off. Then she is willing to admit that she did think about him, but still she doesn't quite admit it. She is too proud to say openly that she wants him back but she does say, "I *may* have thought as much, . . . " And then, since they both have preserved their dignity, and also both have admitted that they care about the other, he can say, "Well, so I came."

Joining the Conversation: Critical Thinking and Writing

1. In a paragraph or two, *evaluate* one of these two entries recorded by students. Do you think the comments are weak, plausible, or convincing, and *why* do you think so? Can you offer additional supporting evidence or, on the other hand, counterevidence? You may want to set forth your own scenario.
2. Two small questions: In a sentence or two, offer a suggestion as to why in line 11 Frost wrote, "and driven a bee away." After all, the bee plays no role in the poem. Second, in line 17 Frost has the speaker say, "I heard it as

I bowed." "Bowed" rhymes with "aloud," but let's assume that the need for a rhyme did not dictate the choice of this word. Do you think "I heard it as I bowed" is better than, say, "I heard it as I waited," or "I heard it as I listened"? Why?

3. Write an essay of 500 words either about an uncanny experience of your own or about a quarrel or disagreement that was resolved in a way you had not expected.

Figurative Language

Robert Frost once said, "Poetry provides the one permissible way of saying one thing and meaning another." This is an exaggeration, but it shrewdly suggests the importance of figurative language—saying one thing in terms of something else. Words have their literal meanings, but they can also be used so that something other than the literal meaning is implied. "My love is a rose" is, literally, nonsense, for a person is not a five-petaled, many-stamened plant with a spiny stem. But the suggestions of *rose* (at least for Robert Burns, who compared his beloved to a rose in the line "My love is like a red, red rose") include "delicate beauty," "soft," and "perfumed," and thus the word *rose* can be meaningfully applied—figuratively rather than literally—to "my love." The girl is fragrant; her skin is perhaps like a rose in texture and (in some measure) color; she will not keep her beauty long. The poet, that is, has communicated his perception very precisely.

People who write about poetry have found it convenient to name the various kinds of figurative language. Just as the student of geology employs such special terms as *kames* and *eskers,* the student of literature employs special terms to name things as accurately as possible. The following paragraphs discuss the most common terms.

In a **simile,** items from different classes are explicitly compared by a connective such as *like, as,* or *than,* or by a verb such as *appears* or *seems.* (If the objects compared are from the same class, for example, "Tokyo is like Los Angeles," no simile is present.)

> Float like a butterfly, sting like a bee.
>
> —Muhammad Ali

> It is a beauteous evening, calm and free.
> The holy time is quiet as a Nun,
> Breathless with adoration.
>
> —William Wordsworth

> All of our thoughts will be fairer than doves.
>
> —Elizabeth Bishop

> Seems he a dove? His feathers are but borrowed.
>
> —Shakespeare

A **metaphor** asserts the identity, without a connective such as *like* or a verb such as *appears,* of terms that are literally incompatible.

Umbrellas clothe the beach in every hue.

—Elizabeth Bishop

whirlwind fife-and-drum of the storm bends the salt
marsh grass

—Marianne Moore

Two common types of metaphor have Greek names. In **synecdoche** the whole is replaced by the part, or the part by the whole. For example, *bread* in "Give us this day our daily bread" replaces all sorts of food. In **metonymy** something is named that replaces something closely related to it. For example, James Shirley names certain objects, using them to replace social classes (royalty and the peasantry) to which they are related:

Scepter and crown must tumble down
And in the dust be equal made
With the poor crooked scythe and spade.

The attribution of human feelings or characteristics or abstractions to inanimate objects is called **personification.**

Memory,
that exquisite blunderer.

—Amy Clampitt

There's Wrath who has learnt every trick of guerilla warfare,
The shamming dead, the night-raid, the feinted retreat.

—W. H. Auden

Hope, thou bold taster of delight.

—Richard Crashaw

Crashaw's personification, "Hope, thou bold taster of delight," is also an example of the figure called **apostrophe,** an address to a person or thing not literally listening. Wordsworth begins a sonnet by apostrophizing Milton:

Milton, thou shouldst be living at this hour.

What conclusions can we draw about figurative language? First, figurative language, with its literally incompatible terms, forces the reader to attend to the **connotations** (suggestions, associations) rather than to the **denotations** (dictionary definitions) of one of the terms. Second, although figurative language is said to differ from ordinary speech, it is found in ordinary speech as well as in poetry and other literary forms. "It rained cats and dogs," "War is hell," "Don't be a pig," "Mr. Know-it-all," and other tired figures are part of our daily utterances. But through repeated use, these, and most of the figures we use, have lost whatever impact they once had and are only a shade removed from expressions which, though once figurative, have become literal: the *eye* of a needle, a *branch* office, the *face* of a clock. Third, good figurative language is usually concrete, condensed, and interesting.

We should mention, too, that figurative language is not limited to literary writers; it is used by scientists and social scientists—by almost everyone who is concerned with effective expression. Take, for instance, R. H. Tawney's *Religion and the Rise of Capitalism* (1926), a classic of economics. Among the titles of Tawney's chapters are "The Economic Revolution," "The Puritan Movement," and "The New Medicine for Poverty," all of which include metaphors. (To take only the last: Poverty is seen as a sick person or a disease.) Or take this sentence from Tawney (almost any sentence will serve equally well to reveal his bent for metaphor): "By the end of the sixteenth century the divorce between religious theory and economic realities had long been evident."

Figures are not a fancy way of speaking. Quite the opposite: Writers use figures because they are forceful and exact. Literal language would not only be less interesting, it would also be less precise.

We have already printed two sonnets by Shakespeare; here is a third, but before you read it we might mention that if you have read the other sonnets you may recall that they abound with figurative language. For instance, in Sonnet 73 (page 144), the speaker says that he is aging not by telling us how old he is but by saying

> he is like a tree with "yellow leaves" (we might say, again using a figure of
>   speech, that he is in the autumn of his life),
> he is in his "twilight," and
> he is like a fire that now is merely embers lying on a bed of ashes.

In Sonnet 146 (page 510) he compares his body to "earth" and to a "fading mansion," and he says that the body is the "servant" of the soul—expressions that are figurative, not literal. But in the following poem we see that Shakespeare can also laugh at figurative comparisons. His contemporaries wrote countless sonnets in which they compared their beloved's eyes to the sun, the redness of her lips to coral, her blonde hair to fine gold wire, her red and white complexion to damask roses (or perhaps to a silk called damask—mixed red and white), her breath to perfume, her speech to music, and her gait to that of a goddess (goddesses were said to walk on air, not on earth). Now see how Shakespeare describes his mistress. But first, two cautions: In line 8, "reeks," in "the breath that from my mistress reeks," in Shakespeare's day did not have the strong negative suggestion that it has today; rather, it meant something like "emanates." Second, in the final line, "any she belied with false compare" means "any woman misrepresented by false comparisons."

Sonnet 130

My mistress' eyes are nothing like the sun;
Coral is far more red than her lips' red;
If snow be white, why then her breasts are dun;
If hairs be wires, black wires grow on her head.
I have seen roses damasked, red and white,   5
But no such roses see I in her cheeks;
And in some perfumes is there more delight
Than in the breath that from my mistress reeks.
I love to hear her speak, yet well I know

That music hath a far more pleasing sound;   10
I grant I never saw a goddess go;
My mistress, when she walks, treads on the ground.
And yet, by heaven, I think my love as rare
As any she belied with false compare.

                                                                    [1609]

Joining the Conversation: Critical Thinking and Writing

Shakespeare here seems to ridicule figurative language, yet he uses figurative language in his sonnets and his plays. How can this be explained?

DANA GIOIA

Dana Gioia (pronounced "JOY uh"), born in 1950, is a poet and the author of several books on literature. He has also been a successful businessman and served as Chairman for the National Endowment for the Arts from 2004 to 2009.

Money

> *Money is a kind of poetry.*
>
> —*Wallace Stevens*

Money, the long green,
cash, stash, rhino, jack
or just plain dough.

Chock it up, fork it over,
shell it out. Watch it   5
burn holes through pockets.

To be made of it! To have it
to burn! Greenbacks, double eagles,
megabucks and Ginnie Maes.

It greases the palm, feathers a nest,   10
holds heads above water,
makes both ends meet.

Money breeds money.
Gathering interest, compounding daily.
Always in circulation   15

Money. You don't know where it's been,
but you put it where your mouth is.
And it talks.

                                                                    [1991]

Joining the Conversation: Critical Thinking and Writing

1. Are any of the terms in "Money" unfamiliar to you? If so, check a dictionary, and if you don't find an explanation in a dictionary, turn to other resources—the Internet, and friends and classmates. Do some of the terms come from particular worlds of discourse, for instance banking, or gambling, or drug-dealing?
2. Suppose the last stanza had been placed first. Would the poem be better? Or worse? Why? Argue your case.
3. Write a somewhat comparable poem on a topic of your choice, for instance, students, teachers, athletes, or work.

MyLiteratureLab° *For additional resources for "Money," log in to* www.myliteraturelab.com *where you will find a Video Performance (under Student Resources).*

Although one is almost tempted to say that figurative language is essential to literature, in fact some literature, even some poetry, is not figurative. Consider this short piece.

ROBERT FROST

The Hardship of Accounting

Never ask of money spent
Where the spender thinks it went.
Nobody was ever meant
To remember or invent
What he did with every cent.

[1936]

Joining the Conversation: Critical Thinking and Writing

Do you consider Frost's lines to be a poem? Why, or why not? The lines rhyme, but most people agree that not everything that rhymes is a poem. Consider:

> Thirty days hath September,
> April, June, and November;
> February has twenty-eight alone,
> All the rest have thirty-one,
> Excepting leap year, that's the time
> When February's days are twenty-nine.

Most teachers of literature would agree that although "Thirty days" is verse, it is not poetry. Why? And if "Thirty days" is not poetry, is Frost's "The Hardship of Accounting" poetry? Why or why not?

Imagery and Symbolism

When we read *rose* we may more or less call to mind a picture of a rose, or perhaps we are reminded of the odor or texture of a rose. Whatever in a poem appeals to any of our senses (including sensations of heat as well as of sight, smell, taste, touch, sound) is an image. In short, images are the sensory content of a work, whether literal or figurative. When a poet says "My rose" and is speaking about a rose, we have no figure of speech—though we still have an image. If, however, "My rose" is a shortened form of "My love is a rose," some would say that the poet is using a metaphor; but others would say that because the first term is omitted ("My love is"), the rose is a symbol. A poem about the transience of a rose might compel the reader to feel that the transience of female beauty is the larger theme even though it is never explicitly stated.

Some symbols are **conventional symbols**—people have agreed to accept them as standing for something other than their literal meanings: A poem about the cross would probably be about Christianity; similarly, the rose has long been a symbol for love. In Virginia Woolf's novel *Mrs. Dalloway,* the husband communicates his love by proffering this conventional symbol: "He was holding out flowers— roses, red and white roses. (But he could not bring himself to say he loved her; not in so many words.)" Here is a poem that uses the conventional symbol of the rose.

EDMUND WALLER

Edmund Waller (1606–87), born into a country family of wealth in Bucking-hamshire in England, attended Eton and Cambridge before spending most of his life as a Member of Parliament. When the Puritans came to power, he was imprisoned and eventually banished to France, although he was soon allowed to return to England. When the monarchy was restored, he returned to Parliament.

Song

Go, lovely rose,
Tell her that wastes her time and me,
    That now she knows,
When I resemble her to thee,
    How sweet and fair she seems to be.   5

Tell her that's young,
And shuns to have her graces spied,
    That hadst thou sprung
In deserts where no men abide,
    Thou must have uncommended died.   10

Small is the worth
Of beauty from the light retired:
    Bid her come forth,
Suffer her self to be desired,
    And not blush so to be admired.   15

Then die, that she
The common fate of all things rare
    May read in thee,
How small a part of time they share,
    That are so wondrous sweet and fair.   20

[1645]

Joining the Conversation: Critical Thinking and Writing

1. In the first stanza the poet says that the resemblance between the rose and the woman is that both are "sweet and fair," words that reappear at the end of the poem. In between these two passages, what additional resemblances does the poet find?

2. The poem contains a narrative of the brief life and the imminent death of a rose. In the third stanza, however, the rose is momentarily forgotten while the poet meditates and speaks directly about the woman. If you agree that this third stanza could conceivably stand as an independent poem, explain why it becomes a better poem when placed within the context of the address to the rose.

Let's now look at yet another poem that speaks of a rose, but in a much less traditional way.

WILLIAM BLAKE

The Sick Rose

O Rose, thou art sick.
The invisible worm,
That flies in the night
In the howling storm:

Has found out thy bed   5
Of crimson joy:
And his dark secret love
Does thy life destroy.

[1794]

A reader might perhaps argue that the worm is invisible (line 2) merely because it is hidden within the rose, but an "invisible worm / That flies in the night" is more than a long, slender, soft-bodied, creeping animal; and a rose that has, or is, a "bed / Of crimson joy" is more than a gardener's rose. Blake's worm and rose suggest things beyond themselves—a stranger, more vibrant world than the world we are usually aware of. They are, in short, symbolic, though readers will doubtless differ in their interpretations. Perhaps we find ourselves half thinking, for example, that the worm is male, the rose female, and that the poem is about the violation of virginity. Or that the poem is about the destruction of beauty: Woman's beauty, rooted in joy, is destroyed by a power that feeds on her.

But these interpretations are not fully satisfying: The poem presents a worm and a rose, and yet it is not merely about a worm and a rose. These objects resonate, stimulating our thoughts toward something else, but the something else is elusive. This is not to say, however, that symbols mean whatever any reader says they mean. A reader could scarcely support, we imagine, an interpretation arguing that the poem is about the need to love all aspects of nature. All interpretations are not equally valid; it's the writer's job to offer a reasonably persuasive interpretation.

A symbol, then, is an image so loaded with significance that it is not simply literal, and it does not simply stand for something else; it is both itself *and* something else that it richly suggests, a manifestation of something too complex or too elusive to be otherwise revealed. Blake's poem is about a blighted rose and at the same time about much more. In a symbol, as the nineteenth-century Scottish essayist and historian Thomas Carlyle wrote, "the Infinite is made to blend with the Finite, to stand visible, and as it were, attainable there."

Verbal Irony and Paradox

Among the most common devices in poems is **verbal irony:** The speaker's words mean more or less the opposite of what they seem to say. Sometimes verbal irony takes the form of **overstatement,** or **hyperbole,** as when Lady Macbeth says, while sleepwalking, "All the perfumes of Arabia will not sweeten this little hand." Sometimes it takes the form of **understatement,** as when Andrew Marvell's speaker in "To His Coy Mistress" remarks with cautious wryness, "The grave's a fine and private place, / But none, I think, do there embrace," or when Sylvia Plath sees an intended suicide as "the big strip tease." Speaking broadly, intensely emotional contemporary poems like those of Plath often use irony to undercut—and thus make acceptable—the emotion presented.

Another common device in poems is **paradox:** the assertion of an apparent contradiction, as in Marvell's "am'rous birds of prey" in "To His Coy Mistress." Normally we think of amorous birds as gentle—doves, for example—and not as birds of prey, such as hawks. Another example of an apparent contradiction: In "Auld Lang Syne" there is the paradox that the remembrance of joy evokes sadness.

Structure

The arrangement of the parts, the organization of the entire poem, is its **structure.** Sometimes the poem is divided into blocks of, say, four lines each, but even if the poem is printed as a solid block it probably has some principle of organization. It may move, for example, from sorrow in the first two lines to joy in the next two or from a question in the first three lines to an answer in the last line.

Consider this short poem by an English poet of the seventeenth century.

ROBERT HERRICK

Upon Julia's Clothes

Whenas in silks my Julia goes,
Then, then, methinks, how sweetly flows
That liquefaction of her clothes.

Next, when I cast mine eyes, and see
That brave° vibration, each way free,   5
O how that glittering taketh me!

[1648]

5 brave splendid.

A Sample Essay by a Student: "Herrick's Julia, Julia's Herrick"

One student, Stan Wylie, began thinking about this poem by copying it, double-spaced, and by making notes on his copy:

Upon Julia's Clothes

Whenas in silks my Julia goes, — cool tone?

Then, then, methinks, how sweetly flows

That liquefaction of her clothes.

3

Next, when I cast mine eyes, and see

That brave vibration, each way free,

O how that glittering taketh me!

3

"Then, then" — more excited? Almost at a loss for words?

emotional?

free to do what? free from what?

Wylie got further ideas by thinking about several of the questions that, in the checklist on pages 537–38, we suggest you ask yourself while rereading a poem. Among the questions are these:

- Does the poem proceed in a straightforward way, or at some point or points does the speaker reverse course, altering his or her tone or perception?
- What is the effect on you of the form?

With such questions in mind, Wylie was stimulated to look for some sort of reversal or change in Herrick's poem, and if there is one, how it might be related to the structure. After rereading the poem several times, thinking about it in the light of these questions and perhaps others that came to mind, he produced these notes:

Two stanzas, each of three lines, with the same structure
Basic structure of first stanza: When X (one line), then Y (two lines)
Basic structure of second stanza: Next (one line), then Z (two lines)

When he marked the text, after reading the poem a few times, Wylie noticed that the last line—an exclamation of delight ("O how that glittering taketh me!")—is much more personal than the rest of the poem. A little further thought enabled him to refine this last perception:

Although the pattern of stanzas is repeated, the somewhat analytic, detached tone of the beginning ("Whenas," "Then," "Next") changes to an open, enthusiastic confession of delight in what the poet sees.

Further thinking led to this:

Although the title is "Upon Julia's Clothes," and the first five lines describe Julia's silken dress, the poem finally is not only about Julia's clothing but about the effect of Julia (moving in silk that liquefies or seems to become a liquid) on the poet.

This is a nice observation, but when Wylie looked again at the poem the next day, and started to write about it, he found that he was able to refine his observation.

> Even at the beginning, the speaker is not entirely detached, for he speaks of "*my* Julia."

In writing about Herrick's "Upon Julia's Clothes," Stan Wylie tells us, the thoughts did not come quickly or neatly. After two or three thoughts, he started to write. Only after drafting a paragraph, and rereading the poem, did he notice that the personal element appears not only in the last line ("taketh *me*") but even in the first line ("*my* Julia"). In short, for almost all of us, the only way to get to a good final essay is to read, to think, to jot down ideas, to write a draft, and to revise and revise again. Having gone through such processes, this writer came up with the excellent essay that follows below.

By the way, Wylie did not hit on the final version of his title ("Herrick's Julia, Julia's Herrick") until shortly before he typed his final version. His preliminary title was

Structure and Personality in
Herrick's "Upon Julia's Clothing"

That's a bit heavy-handed, but at least it is focused, as opposed to such an uninformative title as "On a Poem." He soon revised his tentative title to

Julia, Julia's Clothing, and Julia's Poet

That's a good title: It is neat, and it is appropriate because it moves (as the poem and the essay do) from Julia and her clothing to the poet. Of course it doesn't tell the reader exactly what the essay will be about, but it does stimulate the reader's interest. The essayist's final title, however, is even better:

Herrick's Julia, Julia's Herrick

Again, it is neat (the balanced structure, and structure is part of the student's topic), and it moves (as the poem itself moves) from Julia to the poet.

Wylie 1

Stan Wylie

Professor Lloyd

English 112

17 December 2012

Herrick's Julia, Julia's Herrick

Robert Herrick's "Upon Julia's Clothes" begins as a description of Julia's clothing and ends as an expression of the poet's response not just to Julia's clothing but to Julia herself. Despite the apparently objective

Wylie 2

or detached tone of the first stanza and the first two lines of the
second stanza, the poem finally conveys a strong sense of the speaker's
excitement.

The first stanza seems to say, "Whenas" X (one line), "Then" Y
(two lines). The second stanza repeats this basic structure of one line of
assertion and two lines describing the consequence: "Next" (one line),
"then" (two lines). But the logic or coolness of "Whenas," "Then," and
"Next," and of such rather scientific language as "liquefaction" (a more
technical-sounding word than "melting") and "vibration," is undercut by
the breathlessness or excitement of "Then, then" (that is very different
from a simple "Then"). It is also worth mentioning that although there is a
personal rather than a fully detached note even in the first line, in "*my
Julia,*" this expression scarcely reveals much feeling. In fact, it reveals a
touch of male chauvinism, a suggestion that the woman is a possession of
the speaker's. Not until the last line does the speaker reveal that, far from
Julia being his possession, he is possessed by Julia: "O how that glittering
taketh me!" If he begins coolly, objectively, and somewhat complacently,
and uses a structure that suggests a somewhat detached mind, in the
exclamatory "O" he nevertheless at last confesses (to our delight) that he
is enraptured by Julia.

[New page]

Wylie 3

Work Cited

Herrick, Robert. "Upon Julia's Clothes." *Literature for Composition*. Ed. Sylvan
    Barnet, William Burto, and William E. Cain. 10th ed. New York: Pearson,
    2014. 521. Print.

The Argument Analyzed

Other things might be said about this poem. For instance, the writer says nothing about the changes in the basic iambic meter and their contribution to the poem. We have in mind not so much the trochees (a trochee is a metrical foot with a stressed syllable followed by an unstressed one) at the beginning of some lines, which is a fairly routine variation, but the spondees (two consecutive stresses) in "Then, then" and "O how" and the almost-spondees in "Next, when," "each way free," and "that glittering." Also of interest are the two run-on lines (line 2 runs into 3, and 4 runs into 5) introducing related expressions, "That liquefaction" and "that brave vibration."

He also doesn't comment on the *s* and *z* sounds (*Whenas, silk, goes, thinks, sweetly flows*), which presumably imitate the sound of a silk gown in motion, a sound that can be said to resemble the sound of liquid, hence *liquefaction*—though the dress in motion also visually resembles flowing liquid. But the present essay seems excellent to us, and the neglected topics—sound effects in the poem—might be material for another essay.

Explication

As we said in Chapter 6, a line-by-line commentary on a text is an explication (literally, an unfolding or spreading out). Although your explication will for the most part move steadily from the beginning to the end of the selection, try to avoid writing in a rigid, formal manner: "In the first line. . . . In the second line. . . . In the third line. . . ." That is, don't hesitate to vary your language:

> The poem begins. . . . In the next line. . . . The speaker immediately adds. . . .
> He then introduces. . . . The next stanza begins by complicating the tone. . . .

And you can discuss the second line before the first when that seems the best way of handling the passage.

An explication is not a paraphrase (a rewording, a sort of translation)—though it may include paraphrase if a passage in the original seems unclear, perhaps because of an unusual word or an unfamiliar expression. On the whole, however, an explication goes beyond paraphrase, seeking to make explicit what the reader perceives as implicit in the work. It is chiefly concerned with

- connotations of words—for instance, "look" versus "behold";
- implications of syntax—for instance, whether it is notably complex (thereby implying one sort of speaker) or notably simple (implying a very different sort of speaker);
- implications of rhyme—for instance, the implied connection in meaning between "throne" and "alone";
- patterns of imagery—for instance, commercial imagery in a love poem.

As we said in Chapters 6 and 7, explication and analysis are not clearly distinct from each other; it is reasonable to think of explication as a kind of analysis operating on the level of verbal details.

An Example

Let's look at a short poem by the Irish poet William Butler Yeats. The "balloon" in the second line is a dirigible, a blimp.

WILLIAM BUTLER YEATS

The Balloon of the Mind

Hands, do what you're bid:
Bring the balloon of the mind
That bellies and drags in the wind
Into its narrow shed.

[1917]

Annotations and Journal Entries

A student, Tina Washington, began thinking about Yeats's poem by copying it, double-spaced. Then she jotted down her first thoughts:

sounds abrupt

Hands, do what you're bid: —*balloon imagined by the*
                                               mind? Or a mind like *a*
Bring the balloon of the mind   *balloon?*

                                               no real rhymes?
That bellies and drags in the wind

Into its narrow shed.   *line seems to drag—*
                                               it's so long!

Later she wrote some notes in a journal:

I'm still puzzled about the meaning of the words "The balloon of the mind." Does "balloon of the mind" mean a balloon that belongs to the mind, sort of like "a disease of the heart"? If so, it means a balloon that the mind has, a balloon that the mind possesses, I guess by imagining it. Or does it mean that the mind is like a balloon, as when you say "he's a pig of a man," meaning he is like a pig, he is a pig? Can it mean both? What's a balloon that the mind imagines? Something like dreams of fame, wealth? Castles in Spain.

Is Yeats saying that the "hands" have to work hard to make dreams a reality? Maybe. But maybe the idea really is that the mind is like a balloon—hard to keep under control, floating around. Very hard to keep the mind on the job. If the mind is like a balloon, it's hard to get it into the hangar (shed).

"Bellies." Is there such a verb? In this poem it seems to mean something like "puffs out" or "flops around in the wind." Just checked The American Heritage Dictionary, and it says "belly" can be a verb, "to swell out," "to bulge." Well, you learn something every day.

A later entry:

OK; I think the poem is about a writer trying to keep his balloon-like mind from floating around, trying to keep the mind under control, trying to keep it working at the job of writing something, maybe writing something with the "clarity, unity, and coherence" I keep hearing about in this course.

A Sample Essay by a Student: "Explication of W. B. Yeats's 'The Balloon of the Mind'"

Here is Tina Washington's final version of the explication:

Tina Washington

Professor Chase

English 102

14 December 2012

Explication of W. B. Yeats's "The Balloon of the Mind"

Yeats's "Balloon of the Mind" is about writing poetry, specifically about the difficulty of getting one's floating thoughts down in lines on the page. The first line, a short, stern, heavily stressed command to the speaker's hands, perhaps implies by its severe or impatient tone that these hands will be disobedient or inept or careless if not watched closely: the poor bumbling body so often fails to achieve the goals of the mind. The bluntness of the command in the first line is emphasized by the fact that all the subsequent lines have more syllables. Furthermore, the first line is a grammatically complete sentence, whereas the thought of line 2 spills over into the next lines, implying the difficulty of fitting ideas into confining spaces, that is, of getting one's thoughts into order, especially into a coherent poem.

Lines 2 and 3 amplify the metaphor already stated in the title (the product of the mind is an airy but unwieldy balloon), and they also contain a second command, "Bring." Alliteration ties this command, "Bring," to the earlier "bid"; it also ties both of these verbs to their object, "balloon," and to the verb that most effectively describes the balloon, "bellies." In comparison with the abrupt first line of the poem, lines 2 and 3 themselves seem almost swollen, bellying and dragging, an effect aided

Washington 2

by using adjacent unstressed syllables ("of the," "[bell]ies and," "in the") and by using an eye rhyme ("mind" and "wind") rather than an exact rhyme. And then comes the short last line: almost before we could expect it, the cumbersome balloon—here, the idea that is to be packed into the stanza—is successfully lodged in its "narrow shed." Aside from the relatively colorless "into," the only words of more than one syllable in the poem are "balloon," "bellies," and "narrow," and all three emphasize the difficulty of the task. But after "narrow"—the word itself almost looks long and narrow, in this context like a hangar—we get the simplicity of the monosyllable "shed." The difficult job is done, the thought is safely packed away, the poem is completed—but again with an off-rhyme ("bid" and "shed"), for neatness can go only so far when hands and mind and a balloon are involved.

[New page]

Washington 3

Work Cited

Yeats, William Butler. "The Balloon of the Mind." *Literature for Composition.*

Ed. Sylvan Barnet, William Burto, and William E. Cain. 10th ed. New York:

Pearson, 2014. 526. Print.

The reader of an explication needs to see the text, and because the explicated text is usually short, it is advisable to quote it all. (Remember, your imagined audience probably consists of your classmates; even if they have already read the work you are explicating, they have not memorized it, so you helpfully remind them of the work by quoting it.) You can quote the entire text at the outset, or you can quote the first unit (for example, a stanza), then explicate that unit, and then quote the next unit, and so on. And if the poem or passage of prose is longer than, say, six lines, you might number each line at the right for easy reference.

✔ **CHECKLIST**: *Explication*

On pages 142–43 we provided a Checklist on explication. We repeat some of the key points here for your convenience.

Overall Considerations

☐ Does the poem imply a story of some sort—for instance, the speaker's report of a love affair, or a response to nature? If so, what is its beginning, middle, and end?

☐ If you detect a story in the speaker's mind, a change of mood—for instance, a shift from bitterness that a love affair has ended to hope for its renewal—is this change communicated in part by the connotations of certain words? By syntax? By metrical shifts?

Detailed Considerations

☐ If the poem has a title other than the first line, what are the implications of the title?

☐ Are there clusters or patterns of imagery—for instance, religious images, economic images, or images drawn from nature? If so, how do they contribute to the meaning of the poem?

☐ Is irony (understatement or overstatement) used? To what effect?

☐ How do the connotations of certain words (for instance, "dad" rather than "father") help to establish the meaning?

☐ What are the implications of the syntax—for instance, of notably simple or notably complex sentences? What do such sentences tell us about the speaker?

☐ Do metrical variations occur, and if so, what is their significance?

☐ Do rhyming words have some meaningful connection, as in the clichés "moon" and "June," "dove" and "love"?

☐ What are the implications of the appearance of the poem on the page—for example, of an indented line, or of the stanzaic pattern? (For instance, if the poem consists of two stanzas of four lines each, does the second stanza offer a reversal of the first?)

Rhythm and Versification: A Glossary for Reference

Rhythm (most simply, in English poetry, stresses at regular intervals) has a power of its own. A highly pronounced rhythm is common in such forms of poetry as charms, college yells, and lullabies; all of them are aimed at inducing a special effect magically. It is not surprising that *carmen,* the Latin word for poem or song, is also the Latin word for *charm* and the word from which our word *charm* is derived.

In much poetry, rhythm is only half heard, but its presence is suggested by the way poetry is printed. Prose (from Latin *prorsus,* "forward," "straight on") keeps running across the paper until the right-hand margin is reached; then, merely because the paper has given out, the writer or printer starts again at the left, with a small letter. But verse (Latin *versus,* "a turning") often ends well short of the right-hand margin. The next line begins at the left—usually with a capital—not because paper has run out but because the rhythmic pattern begins again. Lines of poetry are continually reminding us that they have a pattern.

Note that a mechanical, unvarying rhythm may be good to put the baby to sleep, but it can be deadly to readers who want to stay awake. Poets vary their rhythm according to their purposes; they ought not to be so regular that they are (in W. H. Auden's words) "accentual pests." In competent hands, rhythm contributes to meaning; it says something. Ezra Pound had a relevant comment: "Rhythm *must* have meaning. It cannot be merely a careless dash off, with no grip and no real hold to the words and sense, a tumty tum tumty tum tum ta."

Consider this description of Hell from John Milton's *Paradise Lost* (stressed syllables are marked by ´, unstressed syllables by �‿:

> Rócks, cáves, lákes, féns, bógs, déns, aňd shádes ǒf déath.

The normal line in *Paradise Lost* is written in iambic feet—alternate unstressed and stressed syllables—but in this line Milton immediately follows one heavy stress with another, helping to communicate the "meaning"—the oppressive monotony of Hell. As a second example, consider the function of the rhythm in two lines by Alexander Pope:

> Whěn Ájǎx stríves soǐe róck's vást wéight ǐo thrów,
> Ťhe líne tóo lábǒrs, aňd ťhe wórds móve slów.

The stressed syllables do not merely alternate with the unstressed ones; rather the great weight of the rock is suggested by three consecutive stressed words, "rock's vast weight," and the great effort involved in moving it is suggested by another three consecutive stresses, "line too labors," and by yet another three, "words move slow." Note also the abundant pauses within the lines. In the first line, for example, unless one's speech is slovenly, one must pause at least slightly after "Ajax," "strives," "rock's," "vast," "weight," and "throw." The grating sounds in "Ajax" and "rock's" do their work, too, and so do the explosive *t*'s.

When Pope wishes to suggest lightness, he reverses his procedure, and he groups *un*stressed syllables:

> Not so, when swift Camilla scours the plain,
> Fliés o'ěr th' ǔnbéndǐng córn, aňd skíms ǎlǒng ťhe máin.

This last line has twelve syllables and is thus longer than the line about Ajax, but the addition of *along* helps to communicate lightness and swiftness because in this line (it can be argued) neither syllable of *along* is strongly stressed. If *along* is omitted, the line still makes grammatical sense and becomes more "regular," but it also becomes less imitative of lightness.

The very regularity of a line may be meaningful too. Shakespeare begins a sonnet thus:

> When Í ďo cóunt ťhe clóck ťhat télls ťhe tíme.

This line about a mechanism runs with appropriate regularity. (It is worth noting, too, that "count the clock" and "tells the time" emphasize the regularity by the repetition of sounds and syntax.) But notice what Shakespeare does in the middle of the next line:

> Aňd sée ťhe bráve dáy súnk ǐn hídeǒus níght.

The technical vocabulary of **prosody** (the study of the principles of verse structure, including meter, rhyme and other sound effects, and stanzaic patterns) is large. An understanding of these terms will not turn you into a poet, but it will enable you to write about some aspects of poetry more efficiently. The chief terms of prosody presented in the sections ahead will provide a good base.

Meter

Most poetry written in English has a pattern of stressed (accented) sounds. This pattern is the **meter** (from the Greek word for "measure"). Strictly speaking, we should not talk of "unstressed" or "unaccented" syllables, since to utter a syllable—however lightly—is to give it some stress. It is a matter of *relative* stress, but the fact is that "unstressed" or "unaccented" are parts of the established terminology of versification.

In a line of poetry, the **foot** is the basic unit of measurement. It is on rare occasions a single stressed syllable; but generally a foot consists of two or three syllables, one of which is stressed. The repetition of feet, then, produces a pattern of stresses throughout the poem.

Two cautions:

- A poem will seldom contain only one kind of foot throughout; significant variations usually occur, but one kind of foot is dominant.
- When reading a poem, we chiefly pay attention to the sense, not to presupposed metrical pattern. By paying attention to the sense, we often find (reading aloud is a great help) that the stress falls on a word that according to the metrical pattern would be unstressed. Or a word that according to the pattern would be stressed may be seen to be unstressed. Furthermore, by reading for sense we find that not all stresses are equally heavy; some are almost as light as unstressed syllables, and sometimes there is a **hovering stress**—that is, the stress is equally distributed over two adjacent syllables. To repeat: We read for sense, allowing the syntax to help indicate the stresses.

METRICAL FEET There are six common types of metrical feet in English poetry:

- **Iamb** (adjective: **iambic**): one unstressed syllable followed by one stressed syllable. The iamb, said to be the most common pattern in English speech, is surely the most common in English poetry. The following example has four iambic feet:

    Mў héart ĭs líke ă síngĭng bírd.

    —Christina Rossetti

- **Trochee (trochaic):** one stressed syllable followed by one unstressed.

    Wé wĕre vérў tírĕd, wé wĕre vérў mérrў

    —Edna St. Vincent Millay

- **Anapest (anapestic):** two unstressed syllables followed by one stressed.

    Thĕre ăre mánў whŏ sáy thăt ă dóg hăs his dáy.

    —Dylan Thomas

- **Dactyl (dactylic):** one stressed syllable followed by two unstressed. This trisyllabic foot, like the anapest, is common in light verse or verse suggesting joy, but its use is not limited to such material, as Longfellow's *Evangeline* shows. Thomas Hood's sentimental "The Bridge of Sighs" begins

> Táke hĕr ŭp ténderly.

- **Spondee (spondaic):** two stressed syllables; most often used as a substitute for an iamb or trochee.

> Smárt lád, tŏ slip bĕtímes áwáy.

—A. E. Housman

- **Pyrrhic:** two unstressed syllables; it is often not considered a legitimate foot in English.

METRICAL LINES A metrical line consists of one or more feet and is named for the number of feet in it. The following names are used:

- **monometer:** one foot
- **dimeter:** two feet
- **trimeter:** three feet
- **tetrameter:** four feet
- **pentameter:** five feet
- **hexameter:** six feet
- **heptameter:** seven feet

A line is scanned for the kind and number of feet in it, and the **scansion** tells you if it is, say, anapestic trimeter (three anapests):

> Ăs Ĭ cáme tŏ thĕ édge ŏf thĕ wóods.

—Robert Frost

Or, in another example, iambic pentameter:

> Thĕ súmmĕr thúndĕr, líke ă wóodĕn béll

—Louise Bogan

A line ending with a stress has a **masculine ending;** a line ending with an extra unstressed syllable has a **feminine ending.** The **caesura** (usually indicated by the symbol / /) is a slight pause within the line. It need not be indicated by punctuation (notice the fourth and fifth lines in the following quotation), and it does not affect the metrical count:

> Awake, my St. John! / / leave all meaner things
> To low ambition, / / and the pride of kings.
> Let us / / (since Life can little more supply
> Than just to look about us / / and to die)
> Expatiate free / / o'er all this scene of Man;
> A mighty maze! / / but not without a plan;
> A wild, / / where weeds and flowers promiscuous shoot;
> Or garden, / / tempting with forbidden fruit.

—Alexander Pope

The varying position of the caesura helps to give Pope's lines an informality that plays against the formality of the pairs of rhyming lines.

An **end-stopped line** concludes with a distinct syntactical pause, but a **run-on line** has its sense carried over into the next line without syntactical pause. (The running-on of a line is called **enjambment.**) In the following passage, only the first is a run-on line:

> Yet if we look more closely we shall find
> Most have the seeds of judgment in their mind:
> Nature affords at least a glimmering light;
> The lines, though touched but faintly, are drawn right.

> —Alexander Pope

Meter produces **rhythm,** recurrences at equal intervals, but rhythm (from a Greek word meaning "flow") is usually applied to larger units than feet. Often it depends most obviously on pauses. Thus, a poem with run-on lines will have a different rhythm from a poem with end-stopped lines, even though both are in the same meter. And prose, though it is unmetrical, can have rhythm, too.

In addition to being affected by syntactical pause, rhythm is affected by pauses attributable to consonant clusters and to the length of words. Polysyllabic words establish a different rhythm from monosyllabic words, even in metrically identical lines. We can say, then, that rhythm is altered by shifts in meter, syntax, and the length and ease of pronunciation. But even with no such shift, even if a line is repeated verbatim, a reader may sense a change in rhythm. The rhythm of the final line of a poem, for example, may well differ from that of the line before, even though in all other respects the lines are identical, as in Frost's "Stopping by Woods on a Snowy Evening" (page 214), which concludes by repeating "And miles to go before I sleep." The reader may simply sense that this final line ought to be spoken, say, more slowly and with more stress on "miles."

Patterns of Sound

Though rhythm is basic to poetry, **rhyme**—the repetition of identical or similar stressed sound or sounds—is not. Rhyme is, presumably, pleasant in itself; it suggests order; and it also may be related to meaning, for it brings two words sharply together, often implying a relationship, as in the now trite *dove* and *love*, or in the more imaginative *throne* and *alone*.

The commonest patterns are:

- **Perfect rhyme** (or **exact rhyme**): differing consonant sounds followed by identical stressed vowel sounds. The following sounds, if any, are identical (*foe—toe; meet—fleet; buffer—rougher*). Notice that perfect rhyme involves identity of sound, not of spelling. *Fix* and *sticks,* like *buffer* and *rougher,* are perfect rhymes.
- **Half-rhyme** (or **off-rhyme**): rhymes in which only the final consonant sounds of the words are identical; the stressed vowel sounds as well as the initial consonant sounds, if any, differ (*soul—oil; mirth—forth; trolley—bully*).
- **Eye rhyme:** sounds that do not in fact rhyme but look as though they would rhyme (*cough—bough*).
- **Masculine rhyme:** Final syllables that are stressed and, after their differing initial consonant sounds, are identical in sound (*stark—mark; support—retort*).
- **Feminine rhyme** (or **double rhyme**): stressed rhyming syllables followed by identical unstressed syllables (*revival—arrival; flatter—batter*). **Triple rhyme** is

a kind of feminine rhyme in which identical stressed vowel sounds are followed by two identical unstressed syllables (*machinery—scenery; tenderly—slenderly*).

- **End rhyme** (or **terminal rhyme**): Rhyming words that occur at the ends of the lines.
- **Internal rhyme:** a type of rhyme in which at least one of the rhyming words occurs within the line (Oscar Wilde's "Each narrow *cell* in which we *dwell*").
- **Alliteration:** sometimes defined as the repetition of initial sounds ("*A*ll the *a*wful *a*uguries," or "*B*ring me my *b*ow of *b*urning gold"), and sometimes as the prominent repetition of a consonant ("a*ft*er life's *f*it*f*ul *f*ever").
- **Assonance:** the repetition, in words of proximity, of identical vowel sounds preceded and followed by differing consonant sounds. Whereas *tide* and *hide* are rhymes, *tide* and *mine* are assonantal.
- **Consonance:** the repetition of identical consonant sounds and differing vowel sounds in words in proximity (*fail—feel; rough—roof; pitter—patter*). Sometimes consonance is more loosely defined merely as the repetition of a consonant (*fail—peel*).
- **Onomatopoeia:** the use of words that imitate sounds, such as *hiss* and *buzz*. There is a mistaken tendency to see onomatopoeia everywhere—for example, in *thunder* and *horror*. Many words sometimes thought to be onomatopoeic are not clearly imitative of the thing they refer to; they merely contain some sounds that, when we know what the word means, seem to have some resemblance to the thing they denote. Tennyson's lines from "Come down, O maid" are usually cited as an example of onomatopoeia:

> The moan of doves in immemorial elms
> And murmuring of innumerable bees.

Stanzaic Patterns

Lines of poetry are commonly arranged in a rhythmical unit called a **stanza** (from an Italian word meaning "room" or "stopping-place"). Usually all the stanzas in a poem have the same rhyme pattern. A stanza is sometimes called a **verse**, though *verse* may also mean a single line of poetry. (In discussing stanzas, rhymes are indicated by identical letters. Thus, *abab* indicates that the first and third lines rhyme with each other, while the second and fourth lines are linked by a different rhyme. An unrhymed line is denoted by *x*.) Common stanzaic forms in English poetry are the following:

- **Couplet:** a stanza of two lines, usually, but not necessarily, with end-rhymes. *Couplet* is also used for a pair of rhyming lines. The **octosyllabic couplet** is iambic or trochaic tetrameter:

> Had we but world enough, and time,
> This coyness, lady, were no crime.

—Andrew Marvell

- **Heroic couplet:** a rhyming couplet of iambic pentameter, often "closed"— that is, containing a complete thought, with a fairly heavy pause at the end of the first line and a still heavier one at the end of the second. Commonly, there is a parallel or an *antithesis* (contrast) within a line or between the two lines. It is called heroic because in England, especially in the eighteenth century, it was much used for heroic (epic) poems.

Some foreign writers, some our own despise;
The ancients only, or the moderns, prize.

—Alexander Pope

- **Triplet** (or **tercet**): a three-line stanza, usually with one rhyme:

Whenas in silks my Julia goes
Then, then, methinks, how sweetly flows
That liquefaction of her clothes.

—Robert Herrick

- **Quatrain:** a four-line stanza, rhymed or unrhymed. The **heroic** (or **elegiac**) **quatrain** is iambic pentameter, rhyming *abab*. That is, the first and third lines rhyme (so they are designated *a*), and the second and fourth lines rhyme (so they are designated *b*).
- **Sonnet:** a fourteen-line poem, predominantly in iambic pentameter. The rhyme is usually according to one of two schemes. The **Italian** (or **Petrarchan**[1]) **sonnet** has two divisions: The first eight lines (rhyming *abba abba*) are the **octave,** and the last six (rhyming *cd cd cd,* or a variant) are the **sestet.** The second kind of sonnet, the **English** (or **Shakespearean**) **sonnet,** is usually arranged into three quatrains and a couplet, rhyming *abab cdcd efef gg.* (For examples, see pages 144, 510, and 516.) In many sonnets there is a marked correspondence between the rhyme scheme and the development of the thought. Thus an Italian sonnet may state a generalization in the octave and a specific example in the sestet. Or an English sonnet may give three examples—one in each quatrain—and draw a conclusion in the couplet.

BILLY COLLINS

Born in New York City in 1941, Collins is a professor of English at Lehman College of the City University of New York. He is the author of many books of poetry and the recipient of numerous awards, including one from the National Endowment for the Arts. Collins's Sailing Alone around the Room: New and Selected Poems *was published in 2001; in the same year, he was appointed poet laureate of the United States.*

The following sonnet uses the Petrarchan form, which consists of an octave and a sestet. Petrarch is additionally present in the poem by the allusion in line 3 to "a little ship on love's storm-tossed seas," because Petrarch compared the hapless lover, denied the favor of his mistress, to a ship in a storm: The lover cannot guide his ship because the North Star is hidden (Petrarch's beloved Laura averts her eyes), and the sails of the ship are agitated by the lover's pitiful sighs. As you will see, Petrarch and Laura explicitly enter the poem in the last three lines.

In line 8 Collins refers to the stations of the cross. In Roman Catholicism, one of the devotions consists of prayers and meditations before each of fourteen crosses or images set up along a path that commemorates the fourteen places at which Jesus halted when, just before the Crucifixion, he was making his way in Jerusalem to Golgotha.

---

[1]So called after Francesco Petrarch (1304–74), the Italian poet who perfected and popularized the form.

Sonnet

All we need is fourteen lines, well, thirteen now,
and after this next one just a dozen
to launch a little ship on love's storm-tossed seas,
then only ten more left like rows of beans.
How easily it goes unless you get Elizabethan   5
and insist the iambic bongos must be played
and rhymes positioned at the ends of lines,
one for every station of the cross.
But hang on here while we make the turn
into the final six where all will be resolved,   10
where longing and heartache will find an end,
where Laura will tell Petrarch to put down his pen,
take off those crazy medieval tights,
blow out the lights, and come at last to bed.

[1999]

Joining the Conversation: Critical Thinking and Writing

1. The headnote explains the stations of the cross (line 8), but what is the point of introducing this image into a sonnet?
2. Normally the "turn" (*volta*) in an Italian sonnet occurs at the beginning of the ninth line; the first eight lines (the octave) establish some sort of problem, and the final six lines (the sestet) respond—for instance—by answering a question, or by introducing a contrasting emotion. In your view, how satisfactorily does Collins handle this form? Support your evaluation with reasons.

Blank Verse and Free Verse

A good deal of English poetry is unrhymed, much of it in **blank verse,** that is, unrhymed iambic pentameter. Introduced into English poetry by Henry Howard, Earl of Surrey, in the middle of the sixteenth century, late in the century it became the standard medium (especially in the hands of Christopher Marlowe and Shakespeare) of English drama. In the seventeenth century, Milton used blank verse for *Paradise Lost,* and it has continued to be used in both dramatic and nondramatic literature. For an example, see the first scene of *Hamlet* (page 878), until the Ghost appears.

The second kind of unrhymed poetry fairly common in English, especially in the twentieth century, is **free verse** (or **vers libre**): rhythmical lines varying in length, adhering to no fixed metrical pattern and usually unrhymed. The pattern is often largely based on repetition and parallel grammatical structure. For examples, see Walt Whitman's "A Noiseless Patient Spider" (page 618) and T. S. Eliot's "The Love Song of J. Alfred Prufrock" (page 224).

✔ **CHECKLIST:** *Getting Ideas for Writing Arguments about Poems*

If you are going to write about a short poem (say, under thirty lines), it's not a bad idea to copy out the poem, writing or typing it double-spaced. By writing it out you will be forced to notice details, down to the punctuation. After you have copied the poem, proofread it carefully against the original. Catching an error—even the addition or omission of a comma—may help you to notice a detail in the original that you might otherwise have overlooked. And now that you have the poem with ample space between the lines, you have a worksheet with room for jottings.

   A good essay is based on a genuine response to a poem; a response may be stimulated in part by first reading the poem aloud and then considering the following questions.

First Response

☐ **What was your response to the poem on first reading?** Did some parts especially please or displease you, or puzzle you? After some study—perhaps checking the meanings of some words in a dictionary and reading the poem several times—did you modify your initial response to the parts and to the whole?

Speaker and Tone

☐ **Who is the speaker?** (Consider age, sex, personality, frame of mind, and tone of voice.) Is the speaker defined precisely (for instance, an older woman speaking to a child), or is the speaker simply a voice meditating? (Jot down your first impressions, then reread the poem and make further jottings, if necessary.)
☐ **Do you think the speaker is fully aware of what he or she is saying,** or does the speaker unconsciously reveal his or her personality and values? What is your attitude toward this speaker?
☐ Is the speaker **narrating or reflecting** on an earlier experience or attitude? If so, does he or she convey a sense of new awareness, such as of regret for innocence lost?

Audience

☐ **To whom is the speaker speaking?** What is the situation (including time and place)? (In some poems, a listener is strongly implied, but in others, especially those in which the speaker is meditating, there may be no audience other than the reader, who "overhears" the speaker.)

Structure and Form

☐ **Does the poem proceed in a straightforward way,** or at some point or points does the speaker reverse course, altering his or her tone or perception? If there is a shift, what do you make of it?
☐ **Is the poem organized into sections?** If so, what are these sections—stanzas, for instance—and how does each section (characterized, perhaps,

(continued)

Getting Ideas for Writing Arguments about Poems (continued)

by a certain tone of voice, or a group of rhymes) grow out of what precedes it?

☐ **What is the effect on you of the form**—say, quatrains (stanzas of four lines) or blank verse (unrhymed lines of ten syllables)? If the sense overflows the form, running without pause from (for example) one quatrain into the next, what effect is created?

Center of Interest and Theme

☐ **What is the poem about?** Is the interest chiefly in a distinctive character, or in meditation? That is, is the poem chiefly psychological or chiefly philosophical?

☐ **Is the theme stated explicitly (directly) or implicitly?** How might you state the theme in a sentence?

Diction

☐ **Do certain words have rich and relevant associations** that relate to other words and help to define the speaker or the theme or both?

☐ **What is the role of figurative language, if any?** Does it help to define the speaker or the theme?

☐ **What do you think is to be taken figuratively or symbolically, and what literally?**

Sound Effects

☐ **What is the role of sound effects,** including repetitions of sound (for instance, alliteration) and of entire words, and shifts in versification?

☐ **If there are off-rhymes** (for instance "dizzy" and "easy," or "home" and "come"), what effect do they have on you? Do they, for instance, add a note of tentativeness or uncertainty?

☐ **If there are unexpected stresses or pauses,** what do they communicate about the speaker's experience? How do they affect you?

Your Turn: Poems about People

ROBERT BROWNING

Born in a suburb of London into a middle-class family, Robert Browning (1812–89) was educated primarily at home, where he read widely. For a while he wrote for the stage, and in 1846 he married Elizabeth Barrett— herself a poet—and lived with her in Italy until her death in 1861. He then returned to England and settled in London with their son. Regarded as one of the most distinguished poets of the Victorian period, he is buried in Westminster Abbey.

My Last Duchess

Ferrara°

That's my last Duchess painted on the wall,
Looking as if she were alive. I call
That piece a wonder, now; Frà Pandolf's° hands
Worked busily a day, and there she stands.
Will't please you sit and look at her? I said   5
"Frà Pandolf" by design, for never read
Strangers like you that pictured countenance,
The depth and passion of its earnest glance,
But to myself they turned (since none puts by
The curtain I have drawn for you, but I)   10
And seemed as they would ask me, if they durst,
How such a glance came there; so, not the first
Are you to turn and ask thus. Sir, 'twas not
Her husband's presence only, called that spot
Of joy into the Duchess' cheek; perhaps   15
Frà Pandolf chanced to say "Her mantle laps
Over my lady's wrist too much," or, "Paint
Must never hope to reproduce the faint
Half-flush that dies along her throat." Such stuff
Was courtesy, she thought, and cause enough   20
For calling up that spot of joy. She had
A heart—how shall I say?—too soon made glad,
Too easily impressed; she liked whate'er
She looked on, and her looks went everywhere.
Sir, 'twas all one! My favor at her breast,   25
The dropping of the daylight in the west,
The bough of cherries some officious fool
Broke in the orchard for her, the white mule
She rode with round the terrace—all and each
Would draw from her alike the approving speech,   30
Or blush, at least. She thanked men—good! but thanked
Somehow—I know not how—as if she ranked
My gift of a nine-hundred-years-old name
With anybody's gift. Who'd stoop to blame
This sort of trifling? Even had you skill   35
In speech—(which I have not)—to make your will
Quite clear to such an one, and say, "Just this
Or that in you disgusts me; here you miss,
Or there exceed the mark"—and if she let
Herself be lessoned so, nor plainly set   40
Her wits to yours, forsooth, and made excuse,
—E'en then would be some stooping; and I choose
Never to stoop. Oh, Sir, she smiled, no doubt,
Whene'er I passed her; but who passed without
Much the same smile? This grew; I gave commands;   45

°**Ferrara** a town in Italy. **3 Frà Pandolf** a fictitious painter.

Then all smiles stopped together. There she stands
As if alive. Will't please you rise? We'll meet
The company below, then. I repeat,
The Count your master's known munificence
Is ample warrant that no just pretense   50
Of mine for dowry will be disallowed;
Though his fair daughter's self, as I avowed
At starting, is my object. Nay, we'll go
Together down, Sir. Notice Neptune, though,
Taming a sea-horse, thought a rarity,   55
Which Claus of Innsbruck° cast in bronze for me!

                                                [1842]

56 Claus of Innsbruck a fictitious sculptor.

Joining the Conversation: Critical Thinking and Writing

1. Who is speaking to whom in "My Last Duchess"? On what occasion?
2. What words or lines especially convey the speaker's arrogance? What is our attitude toward the speaker? Loathing? Fascination? Respect? Explain.
3. The time and place are Renaissance Italy; how do they affect our attitude toward the duke? What would be the effect if the poem were set in the twentieth century?
4. Years after writing this poem, Browning explained that the duke's "commands" (line 45) were "that she should be put to death, or he might have had her shut up in a convent." Should the poem have been more explicit? Does Browning's later uncertainty indicate that the poem is badly thought out? Suppose we did not have Browning's comment on line 45; could the line then mean only that he commanded her to stop smiling and that she obeyed? Explain.
5. Elizabeth Barrett (not yet Mrs. Browning) wrote to Robert Browning that it was not "by the dramatic medium that poets teach most impressively. . . . It is too difficult for the common reader to analyze, and to discern between the vivid and the earnest." She went on, urging him to teach "in the directest and most impressive way, the mask thrown off." What teaching, if any, is in this poem? If there is any teaching here, would it be more impressive if Browning had not used the mask of a Renaissance duke? Explain.
6. You are the envoy, writing to the count, your master, a 500-word report of your interview with the duke. What do you write?
7. You are the envoy, writing to the count, advising—as diplomatically as possible—for or against this marriage. Notice that this exercise, unlike the previous exercise, which calls for a *report,* calls for an *argument.*

MyLiteratureLab® *For additional resources for "My Last Duchess," log in to* www.myliteraturelab.com *where you will find a Performance, Longman Lecture, Critical Essay, Comprehension Quiz, Short Evaluation Exercises, and Essay Prompts, as well as an About the Author, Links, and Critical Overview for Browning (under Student Resources).*

E. E. CUMMINGS

E. E. Cummings was the pen name of Edwin Estlin Cummings (1894–1962), who grew up in Cambridge, Massachusetts, and was graduated from Harvard, where he became interested in modern literature and art, especially in the movements called Cubism and Futurism. His father, a conservative clergyman and a professor at Harvard, seems to have been baffled by the youth's interests, but Cummings's mother encouraged his artistic activities, including his use of unconventional punctuation and capitalization.

Politically liberal in his youth, Cummings became more conservative after a visit to Russia in 1931, but early and late his work emphasizes individuality and freedom of expression.

anyone lived in a pretty how town

anyone lived in a pretty how town
(with up so floating many bells down)
spring summer autumn winter
he sang his didn't he danced his did.

Women and men(both little and small)   5
cared for anyone not at all
they sowed their isn't they reaped their same
sun moon stars rain

children guessed(but only a few
and down they forgot as up they grew   10
autumn winter spring summer)
that noone loved him more by more

when by now and tree by leaf
she laughed his joy she cried his grief
bird by snow and stir by still   15
anyone's any was all to her

someones married their everyones
laughed their cryings and did their dance
(sleep wake hope and then)they
said their nevers they slept their dream   20

stars rain sun moon
(and only the snow can begin to explain
how children are apt to forget to remember
with up so floating many bells down)

one day anyone died i guess   25
(and noone stooped to kiss his face)
busy folk buried them side by side
little by little and was by was

all by all and deep by deep
and more by more they dream their sleep   30
noone and anyone earth by april
wish by spirit and if by yes.

Women and men(both dong and ding)
summer autumn winter spring
reaped their sowing and went their came   35
sun moon stars rain

[1940]

Joining the Conversation: Critical Thinking and Writing

1. Put into normal order (as far as possible) the words of the first two stanzas and then compare your version with Cummings's. What does Cummings gain—or lose?
2. Characterize the "anyone" who "sang his didn't" and "danced his did." In your opinion, how does he differ from the people who "sowed their isn't they reaped their same"?
3. Some readers interpret "anyone died" (line 25) to mean that the child matured and became as dead as the other adults. How, in an argument, might you support or refute this interpretation?

MyLiteratureLab® *For additional resources for "anyone lived in a pretty how town," log in to* www.myliteraturelab.com *where you will find a Performance, Critical Essay, Comprehension Quiz, Short Evaluation Exercises, and Essay Prompts, as well as an About the Author, Bibliography, Links, and Critical Overview for Cummings (under Student Resources).*

SYLVIA PLATH

Sylvia Plath (1932–63) was born in Boston, the daughter of German immigrants. While still an undergraduate at Smith College, she published in Seventeen *and* Mademoiselle, *but her years at college, like her later years, were marked by manic-depressive periods. After graduating from college she went to England to study at Cambridge University, where she met the English poet Ted Hughes, whom she married in 1956. The marriage was unsuccessful, and they separated. One day she committed suicide by turning on the kitchen gas.*

Daddy

You do not do, you do not do
Any more, black shoe
In which I have lived like a foot
For thirty years, poor and white,
Barely daring to breathe or Achoo.   5

Daddy, I have had to kill you.
You died before I had time—
Marble-heavy, a bag full of God,
Ghastly statue with one gray toe
Big as a Frisco seal   10

And a head in the freakish Atlantic
Where it pours bean green over blue
In the waters off beautiful Nauset.
I used to pray to recover you.
Ach, du.°   15

In the German tongue, in the Polish town
Scraped flat by the roller
Of wars, wars, wars.
But the name of the town is common.
My Polack friend   20

Says there are a dozen or two.
So I never could tell where you
Put your foot, your root,
I never could talk to you.
The tongue stuck in my jaw.   25

It stuck in a barb wire snare.
Ich, ich, ich, ich,°
I could hardly speak.
I thought every German was you.
And the language obscene   30

An engine, an engine
Chuffing me off like a Jew.
A Jew to Dachau, Auschwitz, Belsen.°
I began to talk like a Jew.
I think I may well be a Jew.   35

The snows of the Tyrol, the clear beer of Vienna
Are not very pure or true.
With my gypsy ancestress and my weird luck
And my Taroc pack and my Taroc pack
I may be a bit of a Jew.   40

I have always been scared of *you,*
With your Luftwaffe,° your gobbledygoo.
And your neat moustache
And your Aryan eye, bright blue,
Panzer-man,°panzer-man, O You—   45

Not God but a swastika
So black no sky could squeak through.
Every woman adores a Fascist,
The boot in the face, the brute
Brute heart of a brute like you.   50

You stand at the blackboard, daddy,
In the picture I have of you,
A cleft in your chin instead of your foot

---

15 Ach, du O, you (German). **27 Ich, ich, ich, ich** I, I, I, I. **33 Dachau, Auschwitz, Belsen**
concentration camps. **42 Luftwaffe** German air force. **45 Panzer-man** member of a tank crew.

But no less a devil for that, no not
Any less the black man who   55

Bit my pretty red heart in two.
I was ten when they buried you.
At twenty I tried to die
And get back, back, back to you.
I thought even the bones would do   60

But they pulled me out of the sack,
And they stuck me together with glue,
And then I knew what to do.
I made a model of you,
A man in black with a Meinkampf° look   65

And a love of the rack and the screw.
And I said I do, I do.
So daddy, I'm finally through.
The black telephone's off at the root,
The voices just can't worm through.   70

If I've killed one man, I've killed two—
The vampire who said he was you
And drank my blood for a year,
Seven years, if you want to know.
Daddy, you can lie back now.   75

There's a stake in your fat black heart
And the villagers never liked you.
They are dancing and stamping on you.
They always *knew* it was you.
Daddy, daddy, you bastard, I'm through.   80

                                                               [1965]

65 Mein Kampf *My Struggle* (title of Hitler's autobiography).

Joining the Conversation: Critical Thinking and Writing

1. Many readers find in "Daddy" something that reminds them of nursery rhymes.
   If you are among these readers, specify the resemblance(s).
2. Some critics have called parts of the poem "surrealistic." Check a college
   dictionary, and then argue in a paragraph or two why the word is or is not
   appropriate.
3. Is this a poem whose experience a reader can share? Explain.

GWENDOLYN BROOKS

For a biographical note on Gwendolyn Brooks, see page 231.

We Real Cool

The Pool Players.
Seven at the Golden Shovel.

We real cool. We
Left school. We

Lurk late. We
Strike straight. We

Sing sin. We   5
Thin gin. We

Jazz June. We
Die soon.

[1960]

Joining the Conversation: Critical Thinking and Writing

1. What does it mean for the pool players to say that they are "cool," and not just "cool," but "real cool"?
2. Why does Brooks give seven speakers? Why not simply one, as in "I real cool" and so on? Would that have been more focused and thus more effective?
3. The stanzas could have been written:

   We real cool.
   We left school.

   We lurk late.
   We strike straight.

   And so on. What does Brooks gain by organizing the lines as she does?
4. Brooks presents the poem in a first-person plural voice, "we." If someone claimed that Brooks would have made the poem more objective, and hence better, if she had presented it in third-personal plural, "they," what would be your argument in response?
5. One commentary we consulted says that this poem describes "pool-playing gang members at a bar called The Golden Shovel on the South Side of Chicago." Does this specific information add to or detract from your experience of the poem?
6. Is it accurate or is it misleading to say that this poem presents an argument?

MyLiteratureLab® *For additional resources for "We Real Cool," log in to* www.myliteraturelab.com *where you will find a Longman Lecture, Interactive Reading, Comprehension Quiz, Short Evaluation Exercises, and Essay Prompts, as well as an About the Author, Bibliography, Links, and Critical Overview for Brooks (under Student Resources).*

ETHERIDGE KNIGHT

Etheridge Knight, born in Corinth, Mississippi, in 1931, dropped out of school in the eighth grade. He served in the U.S. Army from 1947 to 1951, but after his discharge became addicted to drugs and soon was involved in a life of crime. Arrested for robbery in 1960, Knight began to write poetry while in prison, encouraged by the African American poets Dudley Randall, Sonia Sanchez, and Gwendolyn Brooks. His first book, Poems from Prison, *was published in 1968 by Randall's Broadside Press. Knight was a leading figure in the Black Arts movement of the 1960s and 1970s, a form of radical cultural activity (related to the broader Black Power movement) that promoted "social engagement" as a crucial feature of literary practice. His* Belly Song and Other Poems *(1973) was one of the most influential books of the period for African American writers and critics. Knight died in 1985.*

The following poem was written a year after the assassination of the charismatic African American militant, writer, and orator Malcolm X (nicknamed "Red"). Born in Omaha, Nebraska, in 1925, Malcolm Little moved to Boston in the early 1940s, and there and in New York City he was a drug dealer and a thief. He was arrested in 1946 for armed robbery and spent the next six years in prisons in Massachusetts. While still in prison, he became acquainted with the teachings of Elijah Muhammed, the leader of the Nation of Islam, and he embarked upon an intensive program of self-education, especially in history. Upon his release from prison, Malcolm Little changed his name to Malcolm X, the "X" signifying the name, unknown to him, of his African ancestors who had been sold into slavery. He broke with Elijah Muhammed in 1963 and formed a rival organization, the Muslim Mosque, Inc. He then made a pilgrimage to Mecca, converted to orthodox Islam, and, while remaining a militant black nationalist, stated that he was no longer a racial separatist. In the Audubon Ballroom in Harlem, on February 21, 1965, Malcolm X was murdered by members of the Nation of Islam, though controversy still surrounds the conspiracy that led to his death. Malcolm X's writings and speeches are included in his Autobiography *(as told to Alex Haley, 1964) and* Malcolm X Speaks *(1965).*

For Malcolm, a Year After

Compose for Red a proper verse;
Adhere to foot and strict iamb;
Control the burst of angry words
Or they might boil and break the dam.
Or they might boil and overflow   5
And drench me, drown me, drive me mad.
So swear no oath, so shed no tear,
And sing no song blue Baptist sad.
Evoke no image, stir no flame,
And spin no yarn across the air.   10
Make empty anglo tea lace words—
Make them dead and white and dry bone bare.

Compose a verse for Malcolm man,
And make it rime and make it prim.

The verse will die—as all men do— 15
But not the memory of him!
Death might come singing sweet like C,
Or knocking like the old folk say,
The moon and stars may pass away,
But not the anger of that day. 20

[1966]

Joining the Conversation: Critical Thinking and Writing

1. Knight's poem is both about Malcolm X and about the writing of a poem about him. Why might Knight have wanted to connect the subject of this poem to the act of writing the poem in the first place? Do you think that Knight should have presented a more straightforward tribute?
2. Explain the meaning of line 8. And of line 11. Which line is more effective? Are these lines more or less effective than other lines in the poem?
3. Are the first two lines of the second stanza puzzling? Why the word "prim"?
4. What is the relationship of the fourth line of the second stanza to the final line of the poem?
5. Do you think that Knight's poem remains powerful today? How does a poem keyed to a specific historical event or person retain its power decades after the event or after the person's death? Or is it the case, in your view, that the passing of time always diminishes the impact of a poem like this one?

ANNE SEXTON

Anne Sexton (1928–74) was born in Newton, Massachusetts. She was a member of a well-educated New England family but did not attend college. After the birth of her second child she suffered a mental breakdown, and for much of the rest of her life she was under psychiatric care. Indeed, a psychiatrist encouraged her to write poetry, and she was soon able to publish in national journals such as the New Yorker. *Despite her success, she continued to suffer mentally, and in 1974 she committed suicide.*

Her Kind

I have gone out, a possessed witch,
haunting the black air, braver at night;
dreaming evil, I have done my hitch
over the plain houses, light by light;
lonely thing, twelve-fingered, out of mind. 5
A woman like that is not a woman, quite.
I have been her kind.

I have found the warm caves in the woods,
filled them with skillets, carvings, shelves,
closets, silks, innumerable goods; 10
fixed the suppers for the worms and the elves:

whining, rearranging the disaligned.
A woman like that is misunderstood.
I have been her kind.

I have ridden in your cart, driver,   15
waved my nude arms at villages going by,
learning the last bright routes, survivor
where your flames still bite my thigh
and my ribs crack where your wheels wind.
A woman like that is not ashamed to die.   20
I have been her kind.

[1960]

Joining the Conversation: Critical Thinking and Writing

Whether you are male or female, can you categorically say that you are *not* "her kind"? Explain.

James Wright

James Wright (1927–80) was born in Martins Ferry, Ohio, which provided him with the locale for many of his poems. He is often thought of as a poet of the Midwest, but (as in the example that we give) his poems move beyond the scenery. Wright was educated at Kenyon College in Ohio and at the University of Washington. He wrote several books of poetry and published many translations of European and Latin American poetry.

Lying in a Hammock at William Duffy's Farm in Pine Island, Minnesota

Over my head, I see the bronze butterfly,
Asleep on the black trunk,
Blowing like a leaf in green shadow.
Down the ravine behind the empty house,
The cowbells follow one another   5
Into the distances of the afternoon.
To my right,
In a field of sunlight between two pines,
The droppings of last year's horses
Blaze up into golden stones.   10
I lean back, as the evening darkens and comes on.
A chicken hawk floats over, looking for home.
I have wasted my life.

[1963]

Joining the Conversation: Critical Thinking and Writing

1. How important is it that the poet is "lying in a hammock"? That he is at some place other than his own home?
2. Do you take the last line as a severe self-criticism, or as a joking remark, or as something in between, or what?
3. Imagine yourself lying in a hammock—perhaps you can recall an actual moment in a hammock—or lying in bed, your eye taking in the surroundings. Write a description ending with some sort of judgment or concluding comment, as Wright does. You may want to parody Wright's poem, but you need not. (Keep in mind that the best parodies are written by people who regard the original with affection.)

CHAPTER 19

Thinking Critically about Poems: Two Case Studies

*If I read a book [and] it makes my whole body so cold no fire
ever can warm me I know that is poetry.*

EMILY DICKINSON

Chapter Preview

After reading this chapter you will be able to

- Analyze the work of Emily Dickinson
- Compare poems and pictures

A Case Study about Emily Dickinson

In this case study, we give the texts of ten poems and an essay by a student that focuses on Emily Dickinson's religious poetry.

Dickinson is one of the most important and influential American poets, with an amazing gift for vivid, piercing language and an extraordinary ability to suggest and represent complex movements of thought and feeling. Dickinson is highly engaging and accessible in some poems, and difficult and demanding in many others. She is difficult in large measure because she is unique: No one wrote like this before her, and no one has written like this since. Spending time with Dickinson means rising to a special challenge, and at first this may strike you as a chore or a burden. But in truth it is an intellectual opportunity: Give this poet a chance, and you'll be amply rewarded.

For isn't this, after all, central to our interest in and love of literature? We want to be pushed, provoked, tested, and challenged. When we read Dickinson, it's true that we are often made uncomfortable: She gives immediate kinds of pleasure but also causes in us struggle and strain. She makes us reach and stretch. This is precisely what Dickinson—so innovative and complex and electrifyingly *alive*—sought to achieve in her verse, and this is why we value her. She compels us to think and feel in ways we had not imagined possible.

Yet one of the ironies of Dickinson as a poet, and one of her sources of fascination for us, is that for all her impact, very few of her contemporaries were even aware that she wrote poetry, as the following brief biography indicates.

Except for brief trips in her youth to Boston, Worcester, and Cambridge, a longer visit to Washington and Philadelphia in 1855, and a few weeks in Cambridge in

1864 for treatment of an eye disorder, Emily Dickinson (1830–86) spent her entire life in Amherst, Massachusetts. She was capable of warmth, affection, and playful humor, but, especially as she became older, Dickinson made sure that she alone established (and secured) the terms for interacting with other people. She had no desire for any kind of public life or career; she had no interest in politics or reform movements; and, however fervent her feelings for both men and women may have been, she had no sexual relationship or sustained romance with anyone. She rigorously maintained her privacy in the family home; she dressed in white all the time and only allowed a doctor to examine her as she walked by a door that was open a crack in an adjoining room.

Self-sentenced to confinement in her Amherst house, Dickinson baked bread, spent time in the garden, made brief appearances in this or that room or hallway and then vanished through a door or up a stairway. She sent many heightened, exuberant, often mirthful, and sometimes enigmatic notes and letters, above all to her sister-in-law Sue Gilbert, who lived next door.

Dickinson was complicatedly connected to the members of her family and to a few friends. There was, for example, her ambitious, aloof father, Edward Dickinson, who was an attorney, treasurer of Amherst College, and a one-term U.S. congressman, and her melancholy, detached, but wryly humorous mother, Emily Norcross. There was also the young lawyer B. F. Newton (who gave her a copy of Emerson's poems); the literary journalists and editors Josiah Holland and Samuel Bowles; Charles Wadsworth, a married Presbyterian minister and almost certainly the man, addressed as "Master," to whom Dickinson wrote passionate letters; the radical reformer and essayist Thomas Wentworth Higginson, with whom Dickinson corresponded about her poetry, and who visited her in 1870 (he told his wife, "I never was with anyone who drained my nerve power so much"); and Otis Phillips Lord, a crusty Whig politician and Massachusetts judge, two decades older than Dickinson, with whom she exchanged ardent letters late in her life.

Emotionally and intellectually (she felt special kinship with Shakespeare, Charlotte Brontë, Elizabeth Barrett Browning, and George Eliot), Dickinson was supercharged, as the nearly 1,800 poems she composed—many of which she neatly sewed into booklets and hid away in the drawers of her bureau—demonstrate with a stunning, even shocking, thematic brilliance and technical daring. Extremely condensed in syntax and structure, idiosyncratic in punctuation, and breathtaking in imagery and phrasing, Dickinson's poems (and many of her letters, too) catch our attention immediately.

Only a handful of poems by Dickinson were published in her lifetime, all of them anonymously and probably without her consent. Through her father's friends and acquaintances, and familiar as she was with literary journals and papers, she could have published more, and in her own name, if publication had been a goal. But perhaps Dickinson understood poetry as writing to be done first and foremost for oneself and then in certain instances to be shared with friends and family members, as was the case with the poems she bestowed upon Sue Gilbert. Dickinson saved her poems and assembled many of them into bundles, but, her biographer Alfred Habegger acknowledges, there is not a single "explicit statement as to what the massive project meant to her."

Dickinson made her sister and brother promise that after her death they would burn all of her papers. As instructed, Lavinia proceeded to destroy all of the letters that Dickinson had saved. The poems, which were a revelation to her, she preserved, and many of them were published in the 1890s and in subsequent decades, though in editions that often revised and tampered with the wording and structure of the texts. Modern scholars, led by Thomas H. Johnson and R. W. Franklin, have restored the poems to the versions that Dickinson herself composed.

It is unnerving to realize that we know (and now can read in correct form) Dickinson's thrilling poems because of a broken promise. Possessed as she was with a fierce, ironic intelligence, Dickinson would have understood deeply both the love and betrayal that her sister's act displayed.

In reading the poems below, feel the excitement of and take delight in Dickinson's organizations of language as she explores her major themes and subjects, which include the meaning of death, the nature of identity, the beauty and mystery of nature, the anguish and ecstasy of love, and the majesty of God. But seek too, from poem to poem, to draw and develop for yourself a poetic portrait of Dickinson: What does she sound like? How does her mind work? What makes her so distinctive, so special?

I heard a Fly buzz—when I died—

I heard a Fly buzz—when I died—
The Stillness in the Room
Was like the Stillness in the Air—
Between the Heaves of Storm—

The Eyes around—had wrung them dry—   5
And Breaths were gathering firm
For the last Onset—when the King
Be witnessed—in the Room—

I willed my Keepsakes—Signed away
What portion of me be   10
Assignable—and then it was
There interposed a Fly—

With Blue—uncertain stumbling Buzz—
Between the light—and me—
And then the Windows failed—and then   15
I could not see to see—

[c. 1862]

MyLiteratureLab® *For additional resources for "I heard a Fly buzz—when I died—," log in to* www.myliteraturelab.com *where you will find a Performance, Comprehension Quiz, Short Evaluation Exercises, and Essay Prompts, as well as an About the Author, Bibliography, Links, and Critical Overview for Dickinson (under Student Resources).*

The Soul selects her own Society

The Soul selects her own Society—
Then—shuts the Door—
To her divine Majority—
Present no more—

Unmoved—she notes the Chariots—pausing— 5
At her low Gate—
Unmoved—an Emperor be kneeling
Upon her Mat—

I've known her—from an ample nation—
Choose One— 10
Then—close the Valves° of her attention—
Like Stone—

[1862]

11 Valves the two halves of a hinged door, such as is now found on old telephone booths. Possibly also an allusion to a bivalve, such as an oyster or a clam, having a shell consisting of two hinged parts.

These are the days when Birds come back

These are the days when Birds come back—
A very few—a Bird or two—
To take a backward look.

These are days when skies resume
The old—old sophistries° of June— 5
A blue and gold mistake.

O fraud that cannot cheat the Bee—
Almost thy plausibility
Induces my belief.

Till ranks of seeds their witness bear— 10
And softly thro' the altered air
Hurries a timid leaf.

Oh Sacrament of summer days,
Oh Last Communion in the Haze—
Permit a child to join. 15

Thy sacred emblems to partake—
Thy consecrated bread to take
And thine immortal wine!

[1859]

5 sophistries deceptively subtle arguments.

Papa above!

Papa above!
Regard a Mouse
O'erpowered by the Cat!
Reserve within thy kingdom
A "Mansion" for the Rat!   5

Snug in seraphic Cupboards
To nibble all the day,
While unsuspecting Cycles°
Wheel solemnly away!

[c. 1859]

8 Cycles long periods, eons.

There's a certain Slant of light

There's a certain Slant of light,
Winter Afternoons—
That oppresses, like the Heft°
Of Cathedral Tunes—

Heavenly Hurt, it gives us—   5
We can find no scar,
But internal difference,
Where the Meanings, are—

None may teach it—Any—
'Tis the Seal Despair—   10
An imperial affliction
Sent us of the Air—

When it comes, the Landscape listens—
Shadows—hold their breath—
When it goes, 'tis like the Distance   15
On the look of Death—

[c. 1861]

3 Heft weight.

MyLiteratureLab® *For additional resources for "There's a certain Slant of light," log in to* www.myliteraturelab.com *where you will find a Performance, Comprehension Quiz, Short Evaluation Exercises, and Essay Prompts, as well as an About the Author, Bibliography, Links, and Critical Overview for Dickinson (under Student Resources).*

This World is not Conclusion

This World is not Conclusion.
A Species stands beyond—

Invisible, as Music—
But positive, as Sound—
It beckons, and it baffles—
Philosophy—dont know—
And through a Riddle, at the last—
Sagacity, must go—
To guess it, puzzles scholars—
To gain it, Men have borne
Contempt of Generations
And Crucifixion, shown—
Faith slips—and laughs, and rallies—
Blushes, if any see—
Plucks at a twig of Evidence—
And asks a Vane, the way—
Much Gesture, from the Pulpit—
Strong Hallelujahs roll—
Narcotics cannot still the Tooth
That nibbles at the soul—

5

10

15

20

[c. 1862]

I got so I could hear his name—

I got so I could hear his name—
Without—Tremendous gain—
That Stop-sensation—on my Soul—
And Thunder—in the Room—

I got so I could walk across
That Angle in the floor,
Where he turned so, and I turned—how—
And all our Sinew tore—

I got so I could stir the Box—
In which his letters grew
Without that forcing, in my breath—
As Staples—driven through—

Could dimly recollect a Grace—
I think, they call it "God"—
Renowned to ease Extremity—
When Formula, had failed—

And shape my Hands—
Petition's way,
Tho' ignorant of a word
That Ordination°—utters—

My Business, with the Cloud,
If any Power behind it, be,
Not subject to Despair—

5

10

15

20

20 Ordination the ministry.

It care, in some remoter way,
For so minute affair   25
As Misery—
Itself, too great, for interrupting—more—

                                                                          [1861]

Those—dying, then

Those—dying, then
Knew where they went
They went to God's Right Hand—
The Hand is amputated now
And God cannot be found—   5

The abdication of Belief
Makes the Behavior small—
Better an ignis fatuus°
Than no illume at all—

                                                                          [1882]

8 **ignis fatuus** a phosphorescent light that hovers over swampy ground, hence something
deceptive.

Apparently with no surprise

Apparently with no surprise
To any happy Flower
The Frost beheads it at its play—
In accidental power—
The blonde Assassin passes on—   5
The Sun proceeds unmoved
To measure off another Day
For an Approving God.

                                                                         [c. 1884]

Tell all the Truth but tell it slant

Tell all the Truth but tell it slant—
Success in Circuit lies
Too bright for our infirm Delight
The Truth's superb surprise

As Lightning to the Children eased   5
With explanation kind
The Truth must dazzle gradually
Or every man be blind—

                                                                         [c. 1868]

A Sample Argument by a Student: "Religion and Religious Imagery in Emily Dickinson"

Peter Gottsegen

Professor Diaz

English 150G

7 December 2012

Religion and Religious Imagery in Emily Dickinson

Emily Dickinson was not a preacher but a poet, so if we read her poetry about God we should not be surprised if we do not find a simple, consistent view, or even a clear development from one view—for instance, belief—to another— for instance, loss of faith. Rather, judging from some examples of her poetry, she explored various views, and we should not try to convert this variety into unity.

We can begin by looking at extreme views, first two poems of faith, and then a poem of doubt. One of the poems of faith, "Papa above!" begins with a childlike or almost playful version of the Lord's Prayer. (In Matthew 6:9 Jesus begins a prayer by saying, "Our Father who art in heaven.") I think this poem says that God will see to it that even a mouse or rat will get into heaven, and will remain there for eternity. But Dickinson's God is not always concerned for all of the creatures of the world. In another poem that expresses belief in the existence of God, "Apparently with no surprise," Dickinson describes the frost as beheading a flower—that is, beauty perishes—and she goes on to make the point that this occurs under the eyes of "an Approving God." Here she seems to be saying that evil takes place, and God approves of it. It is important to realize that in this poem Dickinson still says that God exists, even if he is indifferent to suffering.

In another poem, "Those—dying, then," Dickinson expresses doubt that God exists. In olden days, she says, people mistakenly thought that God would protect them, but now, she says, "God cannot be found." She uses a particularly terrifying image to convey the loss of God. In the past, Dickinson says, the faithful went to "God's Right Hand," but, she goes on to say, "The Hand is amputated now. . . ." The faith in God that earlier people had was an illusion, but it was something, and it was "better" than the nothingness we now experience. This nothingness, or something not much more than nothingness, is the subject of "I heard a Fly buzz—when I died." In this poem, the speaker expects "the King" (God) to appear to her as she dies, but all she sees is a fly, and then she hears its buzz. God ("the King") never appears.

Even these few poems show that Dickinson held a variety of views about God and religion, and it is difficult or perhaps impossible for us to say exactly what her religious beliefs were. But what is certain is that religious ideas were so important to her, so much a part of her mind, that even when she was not explicitly writing about the existence of a benevolent God or the absence of God, she used religious imagery—for instance, to describe impressive things in the natural world around her. In "These are the days when Birds come back," she talks about what we call Indian summer, fall days that are like summer days. But the poem is filled with religious words: "belief," "Sacrament," "Communion," "consecrated bread," "immortal wine." The fifth stanza goes like this:

> Oh Sacrament of summer days,
>
> Oh Last Communion in the Haze—
>
> Permit a child to join.

I do not think Dickinson is really talking about traditional religion here. Instead, she is using religious imagery to talk about a particular precious moment in the seasons. As a second example of her use of religious imagery in a poem that is about nature and not about God, we might look at

Gottsegen 3

"There's a certain Slant of light." In this poem she says that on "Winter Afternoons" this particular light has "the Heft / Of Cathedral Tunes." That is, the winter light has the solidity, the feel, the "heft" of religious music. When we see this light, Dickinson says, we are moved, in a way that we are moved by music in church. She is not saying anything here about whether God is benevolent or not, or whether he exists or not. Rather, she is drawing on experiences in church—probably experiences shared by many people even today—to help us to see nature more effectively.

Speaking as someone who was brought up with traditional religious beliefs but who does not go to church now, I can say that Dickinson effectively represents the ideas of a believer and also of a nonbeliever. But what I think is especially impressive is that she sees that someone who no longer is a believer can't help but still think in religious terms when he or she sees something exceptionally beautiful, for instance, on a winter day "a certain Slant of light."

[New page]

Gottsegen 4

Works Cited

Barnet, Sylvan, William Burto, and William E. Cain. *Literature for Composition*.
10th ed. New York: Pearson, 2014. Print.

Dickinson, Emily. "Apparently with no surprise." Barnet, Burto, and Cain 556.

———. "I heard a Fly buzz—when I died." Barnet, Burto, and Cain 552.

———. "Papa above!" Barnet, Burto, and Cain 554.

———. "There's a certain Slant of light." Barnet, Burto, and Cain 554.

———. "These are the days when Birds come back." Barnet, Burto, and Cain 553.

———. "Those—dying, then." Barnet, Burto, and Cain 556.

Joining the Conversation: Critical Thinking and Writing

1. In his essay Peter Gottsegen comments on six poems: "Papa above!" "Apparently with no surprise," "Those—dying, then," "I heard a Fly buzz—when I died," "These are the days when Birds come back," and "There's a certain Slant of light." Read or reread each of these poems to see if you agree with Gottsegen's interpretations of them.
2. Are there other poems in the case study that you think Gottsegen could have used with better effect than some that he did use? Explain.
3. Reread the concluding paragraph. Do you think it is effective? Explain.

A Case Study on Comparing Poems and Pictures

Despite Stéphane Mallarmé's witty remark that poems are not made with ideas but with words, and despite Archibald MacLeish's assertion that "A poem should not mean / But be," poems do include ideas, and they do have meanings. When you read the poems that accompany the paintings in the color insert section that follows (pages 561–84) think about the following questions:

- What is your own first response to the painting? In interpreting the painting, consider the subject matter, the composition (for instance, balanced masses, as opposed to an apparent lack of equilibrium), the technique (for instance, vigorous brush strokes of thick paint, as opposed to thinly applied strokes that leave no trace of the artist's hand), the color, and the title.
- After having read the poem, do you see the painting in a somewhat different way?
- To what extent does the poem illustrate the painting, and to what extent does it depart from the painting and make a very different statement?
- If the painting is based on a poem (see Demuth's painting on page 564), to what extent does the painting capture the poem?
- Beyond their subject matter, what (if anything) do the two works have in common?

Word
and
Image

*Poetry is a
speaking picture,
painting is
silent poetry.*

Simonides

JANE FLANDERS

Jane Flanders, born in Waynesboro, Pennsylvania, in 1940 and educated at Bryn Mawr College and Columbia University, is the author of three books of poems. Among her awards are poetry fellowships from the National Endowment for the Arts and the New York Foundation for the Arts.

Van Gogh's Bed

is orange,
like Cinderella's coach, like
the sun when he looked it
straight in the eye.

is narrow,   5
he slept alone, tossing
between two pillows, while it carried him
bumpily to the ball.

is clumsy,
but friendly. A peasant   10
built the frame; an old wife beat
the mattress till it rose like meringue.

The bedroom of van Gogh at Arles (1889), **Vincent van Gogh** (1853–1890). Oil on canvas. 57.5 × 74 cm. Musée d'Orsay, Paris, France. Erich Lessing/Art Resource, NY.

is empty,
morning light pours in
like wine, melody, fragrance,   15
the memory of happiness

[1985]

Joining the Conversation: Critical Thinking and Writing

Jane Flanders tells us that the poem is indebted not only to the painting but also to two comments in letters that van Gogh wrote to his brother, Theo:

> I can tell you that for my part I will try to keep a straight course, and will paint the most simple, the most common things.
>
> [December 1884]

> My eyes are still tired, but then I had a new idea in my head and here is the sketch of it. . . . It's just simply my bedroom, only here color is to do everything, and giving by its simplification a grander style to things, is to be suggestive here of *rest* or of sleep in general. In a word, to look at the picture ought to rest the brain or rather the imagination.
>
> [September 1888]

1. Does the painting convey "rest" to you? If not, has van Gogh failed to paint a picture of interest? What *does* the picture convey to you?
2. In an earlier version, the last stanza of the poem went thus:

   empty,
   morning light pours in
   like wine; the sheets are what they are,
   casting no shadows.

Which version do you prefer? In an argument of one page, explain why.

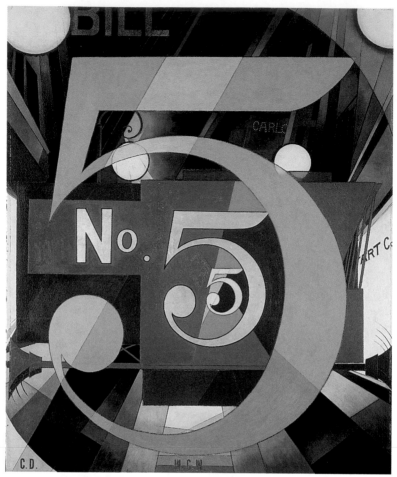

The Figure Five in Gold (1928), **Charles Demuth** (American; 1883–1935). Oil on composition board, 35 1/2" × 30" (90.2 × 76.2 cm). The Metropolitan Museum of Art, The Alfred Stieglitz Collection, 1949 (49.59.1). Photograph © The Metropolitan Museum of Art/Art Resource, NY.

WILLIAM CARLOS WILLIAMS

William Carlos Williams (1883–1963) was the son of an English traveling salesman and a Basque-Jewish woman. The couple met in Puerto Rico and settled in Ruther-ford, New Jersey, where Williams was born. He spent his life there, practicing as a pediatrician and writing poems in the moments between seeing patients who were visiting his office.

In his Autobiography *Williams gives an account of the origin of this poem. He was walking in New York City, on his way to visit a friend:*

> *As I approached his number I heard a great clatter of bells and the roar of a fire engine passing the end of the street down Ninth Avenue. I turned just in time to see a golden 5 on a red background flash by. The impression was*

so sudden and forceful that I took a piece of paper out of my pocket and wrote a short poem about it.

Several years later his friend Charles Demuth (1883–1939), an American painter who has been called a cubist-realist, painted this picture, inspired by the poem. The picture is one of a series of paintings about Demuth's friends.

The Great Figure

Among the rain
and lights
I saw the figure 5
in gold
on a red   5
firetruck
moving
tense
unheeded
to gong clangs   10
siren howls
and wheels rumbling
through the dark city.

[1920]

Joining the Conversation: Critical Thinking and Writing

Williams's draft for the poem runs thus:

Among the rain
and lights
I saw the figure 5
gold on red
moving
to gong clangs
siren howls
and wheels rumbling
tense
unheeded
through the dark city

Do you think the final version is better in all respects, some respects, or no respect? Please present a good argument for your view.

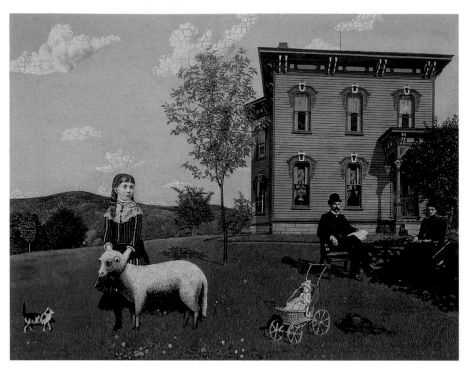

Mourning Picture (1890), **Edwin Romanzo Elmer** (1850–1923). Oil on Canvas, $27^8/_{16}''$ × 36" (70.9 × 91.4 cm). Smith College Museum of Art, Northhampton, Massachusetts. Purchased in 1953.

ADRIENNE RICH

Adrienne Rich (1929–2012) was born in Baltimore, Maryland. She published over sixteen volumes of poetry and five volumes of critical prose. Her most recent books include Tonight No Poetry Will Serve: Poems 2007–2010 *and* Telephone Ringing in the Labyrinth: Poems 2004–2006. A Human Eye: Essays on Art in Society, *appeared in 2009. She edited Muriel Rukeyser's* Selected Poems *for the Library of America. Among numerous other recognitions, she was the 2006 recipient of the National Book Foundation's Medal for Distinguished Contribution to American Letters. Her poetry and essays have been widely translated and published internationally.*

Mourning Picture

*(The picture was painted by Edwin Romanzo Elmer (1850–1923) as a memorial
to his daughter Effie. In the poem, it is the dead girl who speaks.)*

They have carried the mahogany chair and the cane rocker
out under the lilac bush,

and my father and mother darkly sit there, in black clothes.
Our clapboard house stands fast on its hill,
my doll lies in her wicker pram   5
gazing at western Massachusetts.
This was our world.
I could remake each shaft of grass
feeling its rasp on my fingers,
draw out the map of every lilac leaf   10
or the net of veins on my father's
grief-tranced hand.

Out of my head, half-bursting,
still filling, the dream condenses—
shadows, crystals, ceilings, meadows, globes of dew.   15
Under the dull green of the lilacs, out in the light
carving each spoke of the pram, the turned porch-pillars,
under high early-summer clouds,
I am Effie, visible and invisible,
remembering and remembered.   20

They will move from the house,
give the toys and pets away.
Mute and rigid with loss my mother
will ride the train to Baptist Corner,
the silk-spool will run bare.   25
I tell you, the thread that bound us lies
faint as a web in the dew.
Should I make you, world, again,
could I give back the leaf its skeleton, the air
its early-summer cloud, the house   30
its noonday presence, shadowless,
and leave *this* out? I am Effie, you were my dream

[1965]

Two women fixing their hair, from the series "Daily Life of-Women," 1794–95, **Kitagawa Utamaro** (1753–1806). Nishiki-e print, oban format, 38.0 × 25.2 cm. EOI857. Photo: Harry Bréjat. Musée des Arts Asiatiques-Guimet, Paris, France © RMN-Grand Palais/Art Resource, NY.

CATHY SONG

Cathy Song was born in Honolulu in 1952 of a Chinese mother and a Korean father. She holds a bachelor's degree from Wellesley College and a master's degree in creative writing from Boston University. A manuscript that she submitted to the Yale Series of Younger Poets was chosen as the winner and in 1983 was published under the title Picture Bride.

---

*Kitagawa Utamaro (1754–1806) lived in Edo (now called Tokyo). He specialized in designing pictures of courtesans and actors that were then used to make woodblock prints. Brothels and the theater were important parts of what was called the Floating World, that is, the world of transient pleasure.

Beauty and Sadness

for Kitagawa Utamaro

He drew hundreds of women
in studies unfolding
like flowers from a fan.
Teahouse waitresses, actresses,
geishas, courtesans and maids.   5
They arranged themselves
before this quick, nimble man
whose invisible presence
one feels in these prints
is as delicate   10
as the skinlike paper
he used to transfer
and retain their fleeting loveliness.

    Crouching like cats,
they purred amid the layers of   15
   kimono
swirling around them
as though they were bathing
in a mountain pool with irises
growing in the silken sunlit water.
Or poised like porcelain vases,   20
slender, erect and tall; their heavy
brocaded hair was piled high
with sandalwood combs and blossom
   sprigs
poking out like antennae.
They resembled beautiful iridescent   25
   insects,
creatures from a floating world.

    Utamaro absorbed these women
   of Edo
in their moments of melancholy
He captured the wisp of shadows,

the half-draped body   30
emerging from a bath; whatever
skin was exposed
was powdered white as snow.
A private space disclosed.
Portraying another girl   35
catching a glimpse of her own
   vulnerable
face in the mirror, he transposed
the trembling plum lips
like a drop of blood
soaking up the white expanse   40
   of paper.

    At times, indifferent to his
   inconsolable
eye, the women drifted
through the soft gray feathered light,
maintaining stillness, the moments in
   between.
Like the dusty ash-winged moths   45
that cling to the screens in summer
and that the Japanese venerate
as ancestors reincarnated;
Utamaro graced these women with
   immortality
in the thousand sheaves of prints   50
fluttering into the reverent hands of
   keepers:
the dwarfed and bespectacled painter
holding up to a square of sunlight
what he had carried home beneath
   his coat
one afternoon in winter.   55

[1983]

Joining the Conversation: Critical Thinking and Writing

1. In the first stanza the women in Utamaro's prints possess a "fleeting loveliness." What does "fleeting" suggest here? What are Utamaro's characteristics in this stanza?

2. In the second stanza would you say that the women are beautiful, or not? And in the third stanza? What do they look like in each stanza?

3. In the last stanza, in the last few lines, we learn that Utamaro was a "dwarfed and bespectacled painter." We might have learned this earlier in the poem, or not at all. Why does Song wait until this late in the poem to tell us?

The Birth of Venus (1484–86), **Sandro Botticelli.** Tempera on Canvas. 5'9$^7/_8$" × 9'1$^7/_8$" (1.8 × 2.8 m). Galleria degli Uffizi, Florence. SCALA/Art Resource, NY.

MARY JO SALTER

Mary Jo Salter, born in 1954 in Grand Rapids, Michigan, was raised in Detroit and Baltimore and educated at Harvard and at Cambridge University. The author of several books of poetry, Salter has received numerous awards, including a fellowship from the National Endowment for the Arts.

The Rebirth of Venus

He's knelt to fish her face up from the sidewalk
all morning, and at last some shoppers gather
to see it drawn—wide-eyed, and dry as chalk—
whole from the sea of dreams. It's she. None other

than the other one who's copied in the book   5
he copies from, that woman men divined
ages before a painter let them look
into the eyes their eyes had had in mind.

Love's called him too, today, though she has taught
him in her beauty to love best   10
the one who first had formed her from a thought.
One square of pavement, like a headstone (lest

anyone mistake where credit lies),
reads BOTTICELLI, but the long-closed dates
suggest, instead, a view of centuries   15
coming unbracketed, as if the gates

might swing wide to admit, here, in the sun,
one humble man into the pantheon
older and more exalted than her own.
    Slow gods of Art, late into afternoon   20

let there be light: a few of us drop the wish
into his glinting coinbox like a well,
remembering the forecast. Yet he won't rush
her finish, though it means she'll have no shell

to harbor in; it's clear enough the rain   25
will swamp her like a tide, and lion-hearted
he'll set off, black umbrella sprung again,
envisioning faces where the streets have parted.

                                    [1989]

Joining the Conversation: Critical Thinking and Writing

1. In the first stanza, what words suggest that Venus, whose portrait is being drawn on the sidewalk, is born in the sea? What medium is the artist using?
2. What do you think Salter means when she says (lines 6–8) that the sidewalk artist's picture is of "that woman men divined / ages before a painter let them look / into the eyes their eyes had had in mind"?
3. According to the Hebrew Bible, "Let there be light" (line 21) is what God said in Genesis 1:3. In the context of Salter's poem, what do the words mean? Does the poet expect her wish (in line 21) to be granted?
4. If you agree that the poem is lighthearted, what makes it so?
5. Botticelli's painting is a great favorite. Why do you suppose it is so popular?

The Starry Night (1889), **Vincent van Gogh** (1853–1890). Oil on canvas, 29 × 36 1/4"
(73.7 × 92.1 cm). Acquired through the Lillie P. Bliss Bequest. The Museum of Modern Art,
New York, NY, U.S.A. Digital Image ©The Museum of Modern Art/Licensed by SCALA/Art
Resource, NY.

ANNE SEXTON

*Anne Sexton (1928–1974) was born in Newton, Massachusetts. She attended Garland
Junior College, married at twenty, and began a life as a housewife. After a mental
breakdown at the age of twenty-eight, she took up writing poetry on the suggestion of
a therapist. She published eight books of poetry, the third of which won a Pulitzer
Prize. Despite her literary success, her life was deeply troubled, and she attempted
suicide on several occasions. At last she succeeded, by carbon monoxide poisoning.*

The Starry Night

That does not keep me from having a terrible need of—shall I
say the word—religion. Then I go out at night to paint the stars.
—Vincent van Gogh in a letter to his brother

The town does not exist
except where one black-haired tree slips
up like a drowned woman into the hot sky.
The town is silent. The night boils with eleven stars
Oh starry night! This is how   5
I want to die.

It moves. They are all alive.
Even the moon bulges in its orange irons
to push children, like a god, from its eye.
The old unseen serpent swallows up the stars.   10
Oh starry night! This is how
I want to die:

into that rushing beast of the night,
sucked up by that great dragon, to split
from my life with no flag,   15
no belly,
no cry.

[1961]

Joining the Conversation: Critical Thinking and Writing

1. Sexton calls her poem "The Starry Night" and uses an epigraph from van Gogh. In what ways does her poem not describe or evoke van Gogh's painting? In what ways *does* it describe the painting?
2. Does Sexton's poem require a familiarity with Van Gogh's painting in order to be effective? Please argue first that it does, and then that it does not.

Landscape with the Fall of Icarus (c.1560) **Pieter Brueghel, the Elder** (c.1525–1569). Oil on Canvas. Musée d'Art Ancien, Musées Royaux des Beaux-Arts, Brussels, Belgium. SCALA/ Art Resource, NY.

W. H. AUDEN

Wystan Hugh Auden (1907–73) was born in York, England, and educated at Oxford. In the 1930s his left-wing poetry earned him wide acclaim as the leading poet of his generation. He went to Spain during the Spanish Civil War, intending to serve as an ambulance driver for the Republicans in their struggle against fascism, but he was so distressed by the violence of the Republicans that he almost immediately returned to England. In 1939 he came to America, and in 1946 he became a citizen of the United States, though he spent his last years in England. Much of his poetry is characterized by a combination of colloquial diction and technical dexterity.

In the following poem, Auden offers a meditation triggered by a painting in the Museum of Fine Arts in Brussels. The painting, by Pieter Brueghel (c. 1525–69), is based on the legend of Icarus, told by the Roman poet Ovid (43 BCE –17 CE) in his Metamorphoses. *The story goes thus: Daedalus, father of Icarus, was confined with his son on the island of Crete. To escape, Daedalus made wings for himself and Icarus by fastening feathers together with wax; but Icarus flew too near the sun, the wax melted, and Icarus fell into the sea. According to Ovid, the event—a boy falling through the sky—was witnessed with amazement by a plowman, a shepherd, and an angler. In the painting, however, these figures seem to pay no attention to Icarus, who is represented not falling through the sky but already in the water (in the lower right corner, near the ship), with only his lower legs still visible.*

Musée des Beaux Arts

About suffering they were never wrong,
The Old Masters: how well they understood
Its human position; how it takes place
While someone else is eating or opening a window or just walking
    dully along;
How, when the aged are reverently, passionately waiting   5
For the miraculous birth, there always must be
Children who did not specially want it to happen, skating
On a pond at the edge of the wood:
They never forgot
That even the dreadful martyrdom must run its course   10
Anyhow in a corner, some untidy spot
Where the dogs go on with their doggy life and the torturer's horse
Scratches its innocent behind on a tree.

In Brueghel's *Icarus,* for instance: how everything turns away
Quite leisurely from the disaster; the ploughman may   15
Have heard the splash, the forsaken cry,
But for him it was not an important failure; the sun shone
As it had to on the white legs disappearing into the green
Water; and the expensive delicate ship that must have seen
Something amazing, a boy falling out of the sky,   20
Had somewhere to get to and sailed calmly on.

                                       [1938]

Joining the Conversation: Critical Thinking and Writing

1. In your own words sum up what, according to the speaker (in lines 1–13), the Old Masters understood about human suffering. (The Old Masters were the great European painters who worked from about 1500 to about 1750.)
2. Suppose the first lines read:

   > The Old Masters were never wrong about suffering.
   > They understood its human position well.

   What (beside the particular rhymes) would change or be lost?
3. Reread the poem a number of times, jotting down your chief responses after each reading. Then, in connection with a final reading, study your notes, and write an essay of 500 words setting forth the history of your final response to the poem. For example, you may want to report that certain difficulties were soon clarified and that your enjoyment increased. Or, conversely, you may want to report that the poem became less interesting (for reasons you will set forth) the more you studied it. Probably your history will be somewhat more complicated than these simple examples. Try to find a chief pattern in your experience, and shape it into a thesis.
4. Consider a picture, either in a local museum or reproduced in a book, and write a 500-word reflection on it. If the picture is not well known, include a reproduction (a postcard from the museum or a photocopy of a page of a book).

Nude Descending a Staircase, No. 2 (1912), **Marcel Duchamp** (1887–1968). Oil on canvas, $57^7/_8 \times 35^1/_8$ inches (147 × 89.2cm). The Louise and Walter Arensberg Collection, 1950, Philadelphia Museum of Art, Philadelphia, Pennsylvania, U.S.A. Digital Image: The Philadelphia Museum of Art/Art Resource, NY. ©Artists Rights Society, NY.

X. J. Kennedy

X. J. Kennedy was born in New Jersey in 1929. For many years, he taught at Tufts University and is the author of several books of poems, books for children, and college textbooks.

Marcel Duchamp's Nude Descending a Staircase, No. 2 *(1912) was exhibited in 1913 in the Armory Show, an international exhibition held at an armory in New York, and later in Chicago and Boston. The Armory Show gave America its first good look at contemporary European art, including cubism, which had influenced Duchamp's painting.*

Nude Descending a Staircase

Toe upon toe, a snowing flesh,
A gold of lemon, root and rind,
She sifts in sunlight down the stairs
With nothing on. Nor on her mind.

We spy beneath the banister   5
A constant thresh of thigh on thigh—
Her lips imprint the swinging air
That parts to let her parts go by.

One-woman waterfall, she wears
Her slow descent like a long cape   10
And pausing, on the final stair
Collects her motions into shape.

[1961]

Joining the Conversation: Critical Thinking and Writing

1. To what extent does the poem describe the painting? To what extent does it do something else?
2. Some viewers have found Duchamp's painting strange and confusing. Does Kennedy's poem help you to understand Duchamp's style of art? Explain.

American Flamingo, from "The Birds of America," (1827 PL 431), **John James Audubon** (1780–1851). Photo: Bulloz. ©RMN (Institut de France)/Art Resource, NY.

GREG PAPE

Greg Pape was born in 1947 in Eureka, California, and educated at Fresno State College (now California State University, Fresno) and the University of Arizona. The author of several books of poems, he has served as writer-in-residence at several colleges and universities, and now teaches at Northern Arizona University, in Flagstaff.

American Flamingo

I know he shot them to know them.
I did not know the eyes of the flamingo
are blue, a deep live blue.

And the tongue is lined with many small
tongues, thirteen, in the sketch   5
by Audubon,° to function as a sieve.

I knew the long rose-pink neck,
the heavy tricolored down-sweeping bill,
the black primaries.

But I did not know the blue eye   10
drawn so passionately by Audubon
it seems to look out, wary, intense,

---

6 Audubon John James Audubon, American ornithologist and artist (1785–1851), author of the multivolume *Birds of America* (1827–1938).

from the paper it is printed on.
                    —what
Is man but his passion?   15

asked Robert Penn Warren.° In the background
of this sketch, tenderly subtitled *Old Male,*
beneath the over-draping feathered

monument of the body, between the long
flexible neck and the long bony legs   20
covered with pink plates of flesh,

Audubon has given us eight postures,
eight stunning movements in the ongoing
dance of the flamingos.

Once at Hialeah° in late afternoon   25
I watched the satin figures of the jockeys
perched like bright beetles on the backs

of horses pounding down the home
stretch, a few crops whipping
the lathering flanks, the loud flat   30

metallic voice of the announcer fading
as the flamingos, grazing the pond water
at the far end of the infield, rose

in a feathery blush, only a few feet
off the ground, and flew one long   35
clipped-winged ritual lap

in the heavy Miami light, a great
slow swirl of grace from the old world
that made tickets fall from hands,

stilled horses, and drew toasts from the stands   40
as they settled down again
like a rose-colored fog on the pond.

                                                              [1998]

16 Robert Penn Warren American poet, novelist, and literary critic (1905–89).
25 Hialeah city in southeast Florida, site of Hialeah Park racetrack.

Joining the Conversation: Critical Thinking and Writing

1. Why is the speaker preoccupied with the flamingo's eyes?
2. A transition occurs in lines 14–15, with the italicized quotation from Robert Penn Warren. What is the relationship of this to the description of the flamingo (and the speaker's reflections) that precede it?
3. From line 25 to the end, the speaker carefully describes a scene at Hialeah. Take note of the specific details and terms that the speaker presents, and explain how they make the poem both a vivid description and something more than that.

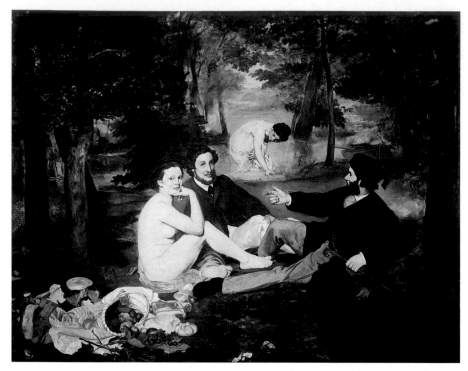

Le Dejeuner sur l'Herbe (*The Luncheon on the Grass*) (1863), **Edouard Manet** (1832–1883). Oil on Canvas. 7' × 8'8" (2.13 × 2.64 m). Musée d'Orsay, Paris. SCALA/Art Resource, NY.

CARL PHILLIPS

Carl Phillips was born in 1959 in Everett, Washington, and was educated at Harvard and at Boston University. African American, gay, a scholar of classical Greek and Latin, and the author of numerous books of poetry, he has taught creative writing at Harvard, and he now teaches English and African American studies at Washington University in St. Louis.

Luncheon on the Grass

They're a curious lot. Manet's scandalous
lunch partners. The two men, lost
in cant and full dress, their legs sprawled
subway-style, as men's legs invariably are, seem
remarkably unruffled, all but oblivious to their nude   5
female companion. Her nudity is puzzling and
correct; clothes for her are surely only needed
to shrug a shoulder out of. She herself appears
baldly there-for-the-ride; her eyes, moving out
toward the viewer, are wide with the most banal,   10
detached surprise, as if to say, "where's
the *real* party?"

Now, in a comparable state of outdoor
undress, I'm beginning to have a fair idea
of what's going on in that scene. Watching   15
you, in clothes, remove one boot to work your
finger toward an itch in your athletic sock,
I look for any similarities between art
and our afternoon here on abandoned
property. The bather in the painting's   20
background, presumably there for a certain
balance of composition, is for us an ungainly,
rusted green dumpster, rising from overgrown
weeds that provide a contrast only remotely
pastoral. We are two to Manet's main group   25
of three, but the hum of the odd car or truck
on the highway below us offers a transient third.
Like the nude, I don't seem especially hungry,
partly because it's difficult eating naked when
everyone else is clothed, partly because   30
you didn't remember I hate chicken salad.
The beer you opened for me sits untouched,
going flat in the sun. I stroke the wet bottle
fitfully, to remind myself just how far
we've come or more probably have always been   35

from the shape of romance. My dear,
this is not art; we're not anywhere close
to Arcadia.°

[1993]

38 Arcadia an ancient region in Greece, traditionally associated in art and literature with the
simple, pastoral life; a Golden Age of unfailing romantic love

Joining the Conversation: Critical Thinking and Writing

1. The author is openly gay. Does knowledge of his sexual orientation affect the
   way in which you read the poem? Explain.
2. Do you agree that the speaker and the partner are "not anywhere close / to Arcadia"?
   Support your argument with evidence.

Girl before a Mirror (Boisgeloup, March 1932), **Pablo Picasso**
(1881–1973). Oil on canvas, 64 × 51 $^1/_4$ in. (162.3 × 130.2 cm). Gift of Mrs.
Simon Guggenheim. (2.1938), The Museum of Modern Art, New York, NY.
Licensed by SCALA/Art Resource, NY. ©Artists Rights Society, NY.

JOHN UPDIKE

*John Updike (1932–2009) grew up in Shillington, Pennsylvania, where his father
was a teacher and his mother was a writer. After receiving a BA from Harvard he
studied drawing at Oxford for a year, but an offer from* The New Yorker *magazine
brought him back to the United States. He at first served as a reporter for the magazine, but soon began contributing poetry, essays, and fiction. He was one of America's most prolific and well-known writers.*

Before the Mirror

How many of us still remember
when Picasso's *Girl Before a Mirror* hung
at the turning of the stairs in the pre-
expansion Museum of Modern Art?

Millions of us, maybe, but we form 5
a dwindling population. Garish
and brush-slashed and yet as balanced
as a cardboard queen in a deck of giant cards,
the painting proclaimed, *Enter here
and abandon preconception.* She bounced 10
the erotic balls of herself back and forth
between reflection and reality.

Now I discover, in the recent retro
spective at the same establishment,
that the dazzling painting dates 15
from March of 1932,
the very month in which I first saw light,
squinting in quick nostalgia for the womb.
Inspecting, I bend closer. The blacks,
the stripy cyanide greens are still uncracked, 20
I note with satisfaction; the cherry reds
and lemon yellows full of childish juice.
No sag, no wrinkle. Fresh as paint. *Back then,*
I reflect, *they knew just how to lay it on.*

[1996]

Joining the Conversation: Critical Thinking and Writing

1. The painting shows a young woman looking into a mirror. In viewing a picture with this subject, what associations might reasonably come to mind? Vanity? Mortality? Or what?
2. The woman (at the left) has two faces, one in profile. Do you think Picasso is showing us two views of the same face, or perhaps two stages in the woman's life? And what of the face in the mirror? Do you think it shows either or both of the faces at the left, or a third face or stage?
3. Why do you suppose the woman is reaching out toward the mirror? (There cannot be any way of proving whatever you or anyone else might offer as an answer, but *why* do you offer the explanation that you do offer?)
4. What do you think the poem is chiefly about? The distinctiveness of modern art (meaning the age of Picasso)? The excellent condition of the picture? The speaker's response to the picture? Explain.
5. The first twelve lines of this poem describe the speaker's thoughts "then," when he first saw *Girl Before a Mirror;* the last twelve lines describe his ideas and feelings "now." In two paragraphs, or in one extended paragraph, write a "Then and Now," describing a picture or a song or a scene—a lake, a house, a kitchen—or a person, then and now.

Two Chained Monkeys (1562), **Pieter Brueghel, the Elder** (c.1525–1569), Oil on oak panel, 20 × 23 cm. bpk, Berlin/Gemaeldegalerie, Staatliche Museen, Berlin, Germany/Photo: Joerg P. Anders/Art Resource, NY.

WISLAWA SZYMBORSKA

Wislawa Szymborska (pronounced "Vislawa Zimborska"; 1923–2012), is one of Poland's leading poets. Her first book published in 1952, she published seven later volumes. Some of her work is available in English, in Sounds, Feelings, Thoughts *(1981). In 1996 she was awarded the Nobel Prize in Literature.*

Brueghel's Two Monkeys

Translated, from the Polish, by Stanislaw Baranczak and Clare Cavanagh.

This is what I see in my dream about final exams:
two monkeys, chained to the floor, sit on the windowsill,
the sky behind them flutters,
the sea is taking its bath.

The exam is History of Mankind.   5
I stammer and hedge.

One monkey stares and listens with mocking disdain,
the other seems to be dreaming away—
but when it's clear I don't know what to say
he prompts me with a gentle   10
clinking of his chain.

[1983]

Joining the Conversation: Critical Thinking and Writing

1. What do we know, or guess, about the speaker from the poem's first line? Are we willing to listen to him (or her)?
2. We are not likely to be examined on "History of Mankind." Why do you suppose the speaker is being quizzed on it? What does the speaker do? (Paraphrase line 6.)
3. In the third stanza the speaker again does not know what to say. Do we know what the question is? Does the prompting (line 10) help?
4. Write a comment, in prose or verse, on Brueghel's painting.

A Sample Argument by a Student

Read (preferably aloud) Anne Sexton's "The Starry Night" (page 573), which was inspired by van Gogh's painting of the same name. Then read the following essay.

Lisa Myers

Professor Peres

English 10G

12 November 2012

Two Ways of Looking at a Starry Night

About a hundred years ago Vincent van Gogh looked up into the sky at night and painted what he saw, or what he felt. We know that he was a very religious man, but even if we had not heard this in an art course or read it in a book we would know it from his painting *The Starry Night*, which shows a glorious heaven, with stars so bright that they all have halos. Furthermore, almost in the lower center of the picture is a church, with its steeple rising above the hills and pointing to the heavens.

Anne Sexton's poem "The Starry Night" is about this painting, and also (we know from the line she quotes above the poem) about van Gogh's religious vision of the stars. But her poem is not about the heavenly comfort that the starry night offered van Gogh. It is a poem about her wish to die. As I understand the poem, she wants to die in a blaze of light, and to become extinct. She says, in the last line of the poem, that she wants to disappear with "no cry," but this seems to me to be very different from anything van Gogh is saying. His picture is about the glorious heavens, not about himself. Or if it is about himself, it is about how wonderful he feels when he sees God's marvelous creation. Van Gogh is concerned with praising God as God expresses himself in nature; Anne Sexton is concerned with expressing her anguish and with her hope that she can find extinction. Sexton's world is not ruled by a benevolent God but

Myers 2

is ruled by an "old unseen serpent." The night is a "rushing beast," presided

over by a "great dragon."

Sexton has responded to the painting in a highly unique way. She is

not trying to put van Gogh's picture into words that he might approve of.

Rather, she has boldly used the picture as a point of departure for her own

word-picture.

[New page]

Myers 3

Works Cited

Sexton, Anne. "The Starry Night." *Literature for Composition.* Ed. Sylvan

   Barnet, William Burto, and William E. Cain. 10th ed. New York: Pearson,

   2014. 573. Print.

Van Gogh, Vincent. *The Starry Night. Literature for Composition.* Ed. Sylvan

   Barnet, William Burto, and William E. Cain. 10th ed. New York: Pearson,

   2014. 572. Print.

Joining the Conversation: Critical Thinking and Writing

1. Do you agree with Lisa Myers's analysis, especially her interpretation of Sexton's poem?
2. Has Myers cited and examined passages from the poem in a convincing way?
3. A general question: Do you think poets are obliged to be faithful to the paintings that they write about, or do poets enjoy the freedom—a kind of poetic license—to interpret a painting just as they choose, doing with it whatever the purpose of the poem requires?

CHAPTER 20

The World around Us

We cannot command nature except by obeying her.
   Francis Bacon

Study nature, love nature, stay close to nature. It will never fail you.
   Frank Lloyd Wright

If a man walks in the woods for love of them half of each day, he is in danger of being regarded as a loafer. But if he spends his days as a speculator, shearing off those woods and making the earth bald before her time, he is deemed an industrious and enterprising citizen.
   Henry David Thoreau

Nature teaches more than she preaches. There are no sermons in stones. It is easier to get a spark out of a stone than a moral.
   John Burroughs

Cats are intended to teach us that not everything in nature has a function.
   Joseph Wood Krutch

It is a wholesome and necessary thing for us to turn again to the earth and in the contemplation of her beauties to know of wonder and humility.
   Rachel Carson

In nature, nothing is perfect and everything is perfect. Trees can be contorted, bent in weird ways, and they're still beautiful.
   Alice Walker

What I see in Nature is a magnificent structure that we can comprehend only very imperfectly, and that must fill a thinking person with a feeling of humility. This is a genuinely religious feeling that has nothing to do with mysticism.
   Albert Einstein

We cannot remember too often that when we observe nature, and especially the ordering of nature, it is always ourselves alone that we are observing.
   G. C. Lichtenberg

We abuse land because we regard it as a commodity belonging to us.
When we see land as a community to which we belong, we may begin to
use it with love and respect.
  Aldo Leopold

Some keep the Sabbath going to Church,
I keep it staying at Home—
With a bobolink for a Chorister,
And an Orchard, for a Dome.
  Emily Dickinson

Nature, red in tooth and claw.
  Alfred, Lord Tennyson

If people think nature is their friend, then they sure don't need an enemy.
  Kurt Vonnegut Jr.

Now, nature, as I am only too well aware, has her enthusiasts, but on the
whole, I am not to be counted among them. To put it rather bluntly, I am
not the type who wants to go back to the land—I am the type who wants
to go back to the hotel.
  Fran Lebowitz

Joining the Conversation: Critical Thinking and Writing

1. Select a quotation that especially appeals to you, and make it the focus of an essay of about 500 words.
2. Take two of the passages—perhaps one that you especially like and one that you think is wrongheaded—and write a dialogue of about 500 words in which the two authors converse or argue. They may each try to convince the other, or they may find that to some degree they share views and they may then work out a statement that both can accept. If you do take the first position— that one writer is on the correct track but the other is utterly mistaken—try to be fair to the view that you think is mistaken. (As an experiment in critical thinking, imagine that you accept it, and make the best case for it that you possibly can.)

ESSAYS

LOUISE ERDRICH

Of American Indian heritage, Louise Erdrich was born in 1954 in Little Falls,
Minnesota. She received her BA degree from Dartmouth in 1976, and her MA in
creative writing from Johns Hopkins in 1979. She has written short stories, essays,
poems, children's books, and novels, including Love Medicine *(1984),* The Beet
Queen *(1986), and, most recently,* Shadow Tag *(2010).*

Ringo's Gold

My parents had a large family to feed on a North Dakota schoolteacher's salary. They taught us to garden, and to relish the unexpected. I once opened our freezer to find a large raccoon, which I don't remember eating. Years later, I asked my father how it had been served. He said, "Ragout, of course." In addition to the raccoon, we ate home-grown asparagus, wild plums, elm-cap mushrooms, venison, head cheese, Old World sausages created by my Old World grandfather (a master butcher), and New World Juneberry preserves and pies from the Ojibwe—or, more correctly, Anishinaabe—side of the family.

Now, in Minneapolis, my sister, my daughters, and I still garden and forage, mainly in our yards, although my mother, exercising her Anishinaabe treaty rights, harvests pembina berries from public parks, where the shrubs are grown as ornamentals. The berries have a musky, sweet flavor and were traditionally pounded into dried buffalo meat to make a portable trail food. I still like them best boiled into a thin sauce and spooned over soft-cooked buffalo roast.

Once, on a glistening spring morning, my sister walked outside to find that a crop of morels had popped out in her front yard. Anointed by the spore gods, she picked in haste, and, unlike lesser mortals, she shared: we had the morels with shallots and quail eggs from the Vietnamese grocery. My yard, meanwhile, was going to the dark side. I had recently added new mulch, from which *Phallus impudicus* sprouted, along with several other devil's-penis varieties of the morel's close relatives: stinkhorns. My garden looked like a male-genital-disease Web site. But once those growths had wilted back into the earth a giant white puffball, lunar and feminine, appeared. *Calvatia gigantea* is a choice eating mushroom, and this one was the size of a toddler's head, with skin as velvety as glove leather. As I reverently sliced it, I was reminded of another puffball I'd found, in a gorge near Ithaca, New York, and decided to prepare for my college friends. They were artists, adventurers, neo-hippies, but apparently they'd never eaten a mushroom plucked from the forest floor. I urged them to tuck in–it was batter-dipped and elegant, I thought—but they stared gravely at their plates. I realized that they were deciding whether to trust me with their lives.

I haven't had a puffball in my yard for two years, and now I wish I'd restrained myself from eating that one. I've learned that, if left to dry, a giant puffball can contain seven trillion spores. I could have had seven trillion puffballs, but all I got this year was oyster mushrooms, which grew on a mulberry-tree stump. My daughter Pallas sliced the creamy mushrooms into thin scimitars and added them to a medley of roasted peppers, which went into a spaghetti sauce she made from the tomatoes that my garden overproduces, along with freshly ground rock salt and basil chopped into uniform shreds. Pallas is a real cook; she has made pasta from scratch since she was twelve. I cook the way I garden—distractedly. But I do have a secret: a substance produced by my ten-year-old daughter's long-haired guinea pig, Ringo. We call it Ringo's Gold. Mixed with his fluffy pine-shaving litter and dumped on the garden all winter, Ringo's harmless, alfalfic crap can make anything grow.

5   Still, the sustenance I get from my yard is largely emotional. I love adding surprises to food, especially my most abundant crops: wild tiger lilies and other flowers that are impossible to kill. This summer, in a burst of creative cookery inspired by Pallas, I began mixing ground chuck with chopped tiger-lily buds. I added crushed nasturtium flowers for their peppery tang, garlic scapes, chive blossoms, marigold, geranium, rose petals, and the leaves and yellow blooms of a weed that my father taught us to eat—we call it sauerkraut plant, because of its pleasantly sour taste. The resulting burger caramelizes deliciously at high heat, maybe owing to the sugar content of the petals.

Although I've found a use for almost everything that appears in my garden, I draw the line at animals. The mulberry stump that grew oyster mushrooms came from a tall white-mulberry tree that used to drop so much fruit that the struggling grass and berry-laden mulch beneath it fermented. The fattest woodchuck I ever saw visited that tarry sixteen-proof sludge every evening one July, at woodchuck cocktail hour. It became my habit to sit on the back steps with my own glass of wine and watch the woodchuck get schnockered. Sometimes he rolled one eye at me, wondering if I was dangerous. I'd lift my glass to him until he tottered away to sleep it off. That eye-roll. Perhaps he sensed what I was thinking. So yard-centric had I become in my eating habits that I was actually imagining what a mulberry-wine-soaked woodchuck might taste like in a stew. Shame on me. It would have been like eating the genial town wino.

Joining the Conversation: Critical Thinking and Writing

1. Do you think that Erdrich begins her essay effectively? Please explain why or why not.
2. What does Erdrich mean in her fifth paragraph when she says, "the sustenance I get from my yard is largely emotional"? What does she mean when she says, "I draw the line at animals"?
3. Do you like to work in a garden? Is someone who works in a garden, close to nature, a better person than someone who does not?
4. If, after reading Erdrich's essay, you could ask her a single question, what would it be?

BILL MCKIBBEN

Bill McKibben, born in California in 1960 and educated at Harvard, became a staff writer for the New Yorker, *then a freelance writer, publishing in numerous magazines including the* New York Review of Books, Rolling Stone, *and the* New Republic. *Among his many books are* The End of Nature *(1989),* The Age of Missing Information *(1992), and* A Year of Living Strenuously *(2000).*

Now or Never

When global warming first emerged as a potential crisis in the late '80s, one academic analyst called it "the public policy problem from hell." The years since have only proven him more astute—15 years into our understanding of climate change, we have yet to figure out how we're going to tackle it. And environmentalists are just as clueless as anyone else: Do we need to work on lifestyles or on lobbying, on politics or on photovoltaics? And is there a difference? How well we handle global warming will determine what kind of century we inhabit—and indeed what kind of planet we leave behind to everyone and everything that follows us down into geologic time. It is *the* environmental question, the one that cuts closest to home and also floats off most easily into the abstract. So far it has been the ultimate "can't get there from here" problem, but the time has come to draw a roadmap—one that may help us deal with the handful of other issues on the list of real, world-shattering problems.

The first thing to know about global warming is this: The science is sound. In 1988, when scientists first testified before Congress about the potential for rapid and destabilizing climate change, they were still describing a hypothesis. It went like this: Every time human beings burn coal, gas, oil, wood or any other carbon-based fuel, they emit large quantities of carbon dioxide. (A car emits its own weight in carbon annually if you drive it the average American distance.) This carbon dioxide accumulates in the atmosphere. It's not a normal pollutant—it doesn't poison you, or change the color of the sunset. But it does have one interesting property: Its molecular structure traps heat near the surface of the planet that would otherwise radiate back out to space. It acts like the panes of glass on a greenhouse.

The hypothesis was that we were putting enough carbon dioxide into the atmosphere to make a difference. The doubters said no—that the earth would compensate for any extra carbon by forming extra clouds and cooling the planet, or through some other feedback mechanism. And so, as scientists will, they went at it. For five years—lavishly funded by governments that wanted to fund research instead of making politically unpopular changes—scientists produced paper after paper. They studied glacial cores and tree rings and old pollen sediments in lake beds to understand past climates; they took temperature measurements on the surface and from space; they refined their computer models and ran them backward in time to see if they worked. By 1995 they had reached a conclusion. That year the Intergovernmental Panel on Climate Change (IPCC), a group of all the world's climatologists assembled under the auspices of the United Nations, announced that human beings were indeed heating up the planet.

The scientists kept up the pace of their research for the next five years, and in the past five months have published a series of massive updates to their findings. These results are uniformly grimmer than even five years before. They include:

- The prediction that humans will likely heat the planet 4 to 6 degrees Fahrenheit in this century, twice as much as earlier forecast, taking global temperatures to a level not seen in millions of years, and never before in human history.
- The worst-case possibility that we will raise the temperature by as much as 11 degrees Fahrenheit, a true science-fiction scenario that no one had seriously envisaged before.
- The near certainty that these temperature increases will lead to rises in sea level of at least a couple of feet.
- The well-documented fear that disease will spread quickly as vectors like mosquitoes expand their range to places that used to be too cool for their survival.

But it isn't just the scientists who are hard at work on this issue. For the past five years, it's almost as if the planet itself has been peer-reviewing their work. We've had the warmest years on record—including 1998, which was warmer than any year for which records exist. And those hot years have shown what even small changes in temperature—barely a degree Fahrenheit averaged globally—can do to the earth's systems.

Consider hydrology, for instance. Warm air holds more water vapor than cold air, so there is an increase in evaporation in dry areas, and hence more drought—something that has been documented on every continent. Once that water is in the atmosphere, it's going to come down somewhere—and indeed we have seen the most dramatic flooding ever recorded in recent years. In 1998, 300 million humans, one in 20 of us, had to leave their homes for a week, a month, a year, forever because of rising waters.

Or look at the planet's cryosphere, its frozen places. Every alpine glacier is in retreat; the snows of Kilimanjaro will have vanished by 2015; and the Arctic ice cap is thinning fast—data collected by U.S. and Soviet nuclear submarines show that it is almost half gone compared with just four decades ago.

In other words, human beings are changing the planet more fundamentally in the course of a couple of decades than in all the time since we climbed down from the trees and began making clever use of our opposable thumbs. There's never been anything like this.

Yet to judge from the political response, this issue ranks well below, say, the estate tax as a cause for alarm and worry. In 1988, there was enough public outcry that George Bush the Elder promised to combat "the greenhouse effect with the White House effect." In 1992, Bill Clinton promised that Americans would emit no more carbon dioxide by 2000 than they had in 1990—and that his administration would do the work of starting to turn around our ocean liner of an economy, laying the foundation for the transition to a world of renewable energy.

10   That didn't happen, of course. Fixated on the economy, Clinton and Gore presided over a decade when Americans, who already emitted a quarter of the world's carbon dioxide, actually managed to increase their total output by 12 percent. Now we have a president who seems unsure whether global warming is real, and far more concerned with increasing power production than with worrying about trifles like the collapse of the globe's terrestrial systems. In November, the hope of global controls on carbon dioxide production essentially collapsed at an international conference in the Hague, when the United States refused to make even modest concessions on its use of fossil fuels, and the rest of the world finally walked away from the table in disgust.

In the face of all this, what is an environmentalist to do? The normal answer, when you're mounting a campaign, is to look for self-interest, to scare people by saying what will happen to us if we don't do something: all the birds will die, the canyon will disappear beneath a reservoir, we will choke to death on smog.

But in the case of global warming, those kind of answers don't exactly do the trick, at least in the time frame we're discussing. At this latitude, climate change will creep up on us. Severe storms have already grown more frequent and more damaging. The seasons are less steady in their progression. Some agriculture is less reliable. But face it: Our economy is so enormous that it handles those kinds of changes in stride. Economists who work on this stuff talk about how it will shave a percentage or two off GNP over the next few decades—not enough to notice in the kind of generalized economic boom they describe. And most of us live lives so divorced from the natural world that we hardly notice the changes anyway. Hotter? Turn up the air conditioning. Stormier? Well, an enormous percentage of Americans commute from remote-controlled garage to office parking garage—they may have gone the last year without getting good and wet in a rainstorm. By the time the magnitude of the change is truly in our faces, it well be too late to do much about it: There's such a lag time with carbon dioxide in the atmosphere that we need to be making the switch to solar and wind and hydrogen right about now. Yesterday, in fact.

So maybe we should think of global warming in a different way—as the great moral crisis of our moment, the equivalent in our time of the civil rights movement of the '60s.

Why a moral question? In the first place, because we've never figured out a more effective way to screw the marginalized and poor of this planet. Having taken their dignity, their resources and their freedom under a variety of other schemes, we now are taking the very physical stability on which they depend for the most bottom-line of existences.

15   Our economy can absorb these changes for a while, but for a moment consider Bangladesh. A river delta that houses 130 million souls in an area the size of

Wisconsin, Bangladesh actually manages food self-sufficiency most years. But in 1998, the sea level in the Bay of Bengal was higher than normal, just the sort of thing we can expect to become more frequent and severe. The waters sweeping down the Ganges and the Brahmaputra from the Himalayas could not drain easily into the ocean—they backed up across the country, forcing most of its inhabitants to spend three months in thigh-deep water. The fall rice crop didn't get planted. We've seen this same kind of disaster in the last few years in Mozambique or Honduras or Venezuela or any of a dozen other wretched spots.

And a moral crisis, too, if you place any value on the rest of creation. Coral reef researchers indicate that these spectacularly intricate ecosystems are also spectacularly vulnerable—rising water temperatures will likely bleach them to extinction by mid-century. In the Arctic, polar bears are 20 percent scrawnier than they were a decade ago: As pack ice melts, so does the opportunity for hunting seals. All in all, this century seems poised to see extinctions at a rate not observed since the last big asteroid slammed into the planet. But this time the asteroid is us.

A moral question, finally, if you think we owe any debt to the future. No one ever has figured out a more thorough-going way to stripmine the present and degrade what comes after. Forget the seventh generation—we're talking 70th generation, and 700th. All the people that will ever be related to you. Ever. No generation yet to come will ever forget us—we are the ones present at the moment when the temperature starts to spike, and so far we have not reacted. If it had been done to us, we would loathe the generation that did it, precisely as we will one day be loathed.

But trying to make a moral campaign is no easy task. In most moral crises, there is a villain—some person or class or institution that must be overcome. Once they're identified, the battle can commence. But you can't really get angry at carbon dioxide, and the people responsible for its production are, well, us. So perhaps we need some symbols to get us started, some places to sharpen the debate and rally ourselves to action. There are plenty to choose from: our taste for ever bigger houses and the heating and cooling bills that come with them; our penchant for jumping on airplanes at the drop of a hat; and so on. But if you wanted one glaring example of our lack of balance, you could do worse than point the finger at sport utility vehicles.

SUVs are more than mere symbol. They are a major part of the problem—one reason we emit so much more carbon dioxide now than we did a decade ago is because our fleet of cars and trucks actually has gotten steadily less fuel efficient for the past 10 years. If you switched today from the average American car to a big SUV, and drove it for just one year, the difference in carbon dioxide that you produced would be the equivalent of opening your refrigerator door and then forgetting to close it for six years. SUVs essentially are machines for burning fossil fuel that just happen to also move you and your stuff around.

20   But what makes them such a perfect symbol is the brute fact that they are simply unnecessary. Go to the parking lot of the nearest suburban supermarket and look around: the only conclusion you can draw is that to reach the grocery, people must drive through three or four raging rivers and up the side of a trackless canyon. These are semi-military machines (some, like the Hummer, are not semi at all), Brinks trucks on a slight diet. They don't keep their occupants safer, they do wreck whatever they plow into—they are the perfect metaphor for a heedless, supersized society. And a gullible one, which has been sold on these vast vehicles partly by the promise that they somehow allow us to commune with nature.

That's why we need a much broader politics than the White House–lobbying that's occupied the big enviros for the past decade, or the mass-market mailing that has been their stock in trade for the past quarter century. We need to take all the brilliant and energetic strategies of local grassroots groups fighting dumps and cleaning up rivers, and we need to make those tactics national and international. So that's why some pastors are starting to talk with their congregations about what car they're going to buy, and why some college seniors are passing around petitions pledging to stay away from the Ford Explorers and Excursions and Extraneouses, and why some few auto dealers have begun to notice informational picketers outside on Saturday mornings urging their customers to think about gas mileage when they go inside.

The point is not that by themselves such actions—any individual actions—will make any real dent in the production of carbon dioxide pouring into our atmosphere. Even if you got 10 percent of Americans really committed to changing energy use, their solar homes wouldn't make much of a dent in our national totals. But 10 percent would be enough to change the politics of the issue, to insure the passage of the laws that would cause us all to shift our habits. And so we need to begin to take an issue that is now the province of technicians and turn it into a political issue—just as bus boycotts began to take the issue of race and make it public, forcing the system to respond. That response is likely to be ugly—there are huge companies with a lot to lose, and many people so tied in to their current ways of life that advocating change smacks of subversion. But this has to become a political issue—and fast. The only way that may happen, short of a hideous drought or monster flood, is if it becomes a personal issue first.

[2001]

Joining the Conversation: Critical Thinking and Writing

1. McKibben argues that global warming constitutes "a moral crisis" (paragraph 13). What reasons does he offer?
2. In paragraphs 19–20 McKibben talks about SUVs, saying that "they are simply unnecessary." Do you agree? If you don't, explain why. And if you do agree, explain why SUVs are popular.
3. What *persona* does McKibben convey in this essay? (On *persona,* see pages 333–35.) Thoughtful? Belligerent? Hysterical? Concerned but eccentric? Support your answer with evidence.
4. McKibben often varies the length of his sentences, sometimes perhaps surprisingly. For instance, in the first paragraph the first sentence contains 24 words, the second 29 words, the third 24, but the fourth—a question—contains only 5 words. What effect does he gain? Take another passage in his essay where there is a sharp contrast, and explain the effect.
5. Now that you have read McKibben's essay, and thought further about it, do you plan to change your behavior in any way? Explain.

STORIES

AESOP

In ancient Greece and Rome many fables were attributed to Aesop, said to have been a Greek slave who lived in the sixth century BCE. In the first of the two that we print here, English versions speak of a grasshopper but in Greek the insect is a cicada.

The Ant and the Grasshopper

One cold winter day an ant was dragging out a grain which he had buried during the winter. A hungry grasshopper asked for a bit of the grain.

"What did you do all summer?" asked the ant.

"I was busy all summer long, singing," replied the grasshopper.

"Well," said the ant, "since you sang all summer, now dance all winter."

The Moral: Negligence leads to hardship.

Joining the Conversation: Critical Thinking and Writing

1. Let's rewrite the ant's final remark, thus: "Well, since you spent the whole summer singing, I guess you'll dance now in the winter." We assume you agree that the original version is more effective. Exactly what makes the original better?
2. Do you think we can draw lessons from nature about how we should behave? Is a significant part of the argument (so to speak) of an Aesop fable that it is "natural," that it shows us "nature's way"? Think of other fables that draw on the nonhuman world, such as "The Fox and the Grapes." (The gist of "The Fox and the Grapes" is this: "A starving fox, seeing bunches of grapes hanging from a vine, but out of reach, went away saying, 'Those grapes aren't ripe, they're sour.'") What do such fables gain by being set in the nonhuman world? Why not just say, "A starving man, seeing bunches of grapes that were out of reach . . . "? Again, what, if anything, is gained by using talking animals? Is the moral enforced by nature?

The North Wind and the Sun

The North Wind and the Sun once got into an argument about which of the two was the most powerful. They agreed that whichever could make a certain traveler take off his overcoat would be declared the winner.

The North Wind was the first to try: He blew as hard as he could, but the harder he blew, the more the traveler buttoned up his coat and held it close to his body by folding his arms across his chest. The wind blew and blew, but finally he was out of breath.

Then it was the Sun's turn. The Sun smiled, sending beams of light that drove away the fog and the mist. He smiled a bit more, and the man unbuttoned his coat and after a little while, feeling pleasantly warm, took off the coat.

The North Wind agreed that the Sun was the winner.

The Moral: Gentleness is more persuasive than violence.

Joining the Conversation: Critical Thinking and Writing

1. Do you think the moral can reasonably be drawn from the story? Do you think the moral is true?
2. Do you think nature can teach us anything about moral behavior? If so, what sorts of things? Be as specific as possible. You may want to cite concrete instances. If you think it cannot teach us anything about morality, explain why you hold this view.

JACK LONDON

Jack London (1876–1916) was born in San Francisco and educated in Oakland High School and the University of California, Berkeley, but his formal education was intermittent. At thirteen or fourteen he was a pirate raiding oyster beds in San Francisco Bay; a little later he worked in a cannery, and at seventeen he joined a sealing expedition to Japan and Siberia. Back in the United States he worked at odd jobs, became a socialist, finished high school in 1895, spent one semester at the University of California, and then was off to the Klondike (age twenty-one) looking—unsuccessfully, it turned out—for gold. He published his first story in 1899, his first collection of stories (The Son of the Wolf) *in 1900, and his first novel* (The Call of the Wild) *in 1903. The novel was an immediate hit. London continued to write, both fiction and journalism, earning over a million dollars from his writing—at that time an astounding amount, especially for a writer.*

To Build a Fire

Day had broken cold and gray, exceedingly cold and gray, when the man turned aside from the main Yukon trail and climbed the high earth-bank, where a dim and little-travelled trail led eastward through the fat spruce timberland. It was a steep bank, and he paused for breath at the top, excusing the act to himself by looking at his watch. It was nine o'clock. There was no sun nor hint of sun, though there was not a cloud in the sky. It was a clear day, and yet there seemed an intangible pall over the face of things, a subtle gloom that made the day dark, and that was due to the absence of sun. This fact did not worry the man. He was used to the lack of sun. It had been days since he had seen the sun, and he knew that a few more days must pass before that cheerful orb, due south, should just peep above the sky line and dip immediately from view.

The man flung a look back along the way he had come. The Yukon[1] lay a mile wide and hidden under three feet of ice. On top of this ice were as many feet of snow. It was all pure white, rolling in gentle undulations where the ice jams of the freeze-up had formed. North and south, as far as his eye could see, it was unbroken white, save for a dark hairline that curved and twisted from around the spruce-covered island to the south, and that curved and twisted away into the north, where it disappeared behind another spruce-covered island. This dark hairline was the trail—the main trail—that led south five hundred miles to the Chilcoot Pass, Dyea, and salt water; and that led north seventy miles to Dawson, and still on to the north a thousand miles to Nulato, and finally to St. Michael, on Bering Sea, a thousand miles and a half a thousand more.

But all this—the mysterious, far-reaching hairline trail, the absence of sun from the sky, the tremendous cold, and the strangeness and weirdness of it all—made no impression on the man. It was not because he was long used to it. He was a newcomer in the land, a *chechaquo,* and this was his first winter. The trouble with him was that he was without imagination. He was quick and alert in the things of life, but only in the things, and not in the significances. Fifty degrees below zero meant eighty-odd degrees of frost. Such fact impressed him as being cold and uncomfortable, and that was all. It did not lead him to meditate upon his frailty as a creature of temperature, and upon man's frailty in general, able only to live within certain narrow limits of heat and cold; and from there on it did not lead him to the

---

[1]**Yukon** a major river in Alaska and western Canada.

conjectural field of immortality and man's place in the universe. Fifty degrees below zero stood for a bite of frost that hurt and that must be guarded against by the use of mittens, ear flaps, warm moccasins, and thick socks. Fifty degrees below zero was to him just precisely fifty degrees below zero. That there should be anything more to it than that was a thought that never entered his head.

As he turned to go on, he spat speculatively. There was a sharp, explosive crackle that startled him. He spat again. And again, in the air, before it could fall to the snow, the spittle crackled. He knew that at fifty below spittle crackled on the snow, but this spittle had crackled in the air. Undoubtedly it was colder than fifty below—how much colder he did not know. But the temperature did not matter. He was bound for the old claim on the left fork of Henderson Creek, where the boys were already. They had come over across the divide from the Indian Creek country, while he had come the roundabout way to take a look at the possibilities of getting out logs in the spring from the islands in the Yukon. He would be in to camp by six o'clock; a bit after dark, it was true, but the boys would be there, a fire would be going, and a hot supper would be ready. As for lunch, he pressed his hand against the protruding bundle under his jacket. It was also under his shirt, wrapped up in a handkerchief and lying against the naked skin. It was the only way to keep the biscuits from freezing. He smiled agreeably to himself as he thought of those biscuits, each cut open and sopped in bacon grease, and each enclosing a generous slice of fried bacon.

5   He plunged in among the big spruce trees. The trail was faint. A foot of snow had fallen since the last sled had passed over, and he was glad he was without a sled, traveling light. In fact, he carried nothing but the lunch wrapped in the handkerchief. He was surprised, however, at the cold. It certainly was cold, he concluded, as he rubbed his numb nose and cheekbones with his mittened hand. He was a warm-whiskered man, but the hair on his face did not protect the high cheekbones and the eager nose that thrust itself aggressively into the frosty air.

At the man's heels trotted a dog, a big native husky, the proper wolf dog, gray-coated and without any visible or temperamental difference from its brother, the wild wolf. The animal was depressed by the tremendous cold. It knew that it was not time for traveling. Its instinct told it a truer tale than was told to the man by the man's judgment. In reality, it was not merely colder than fifty below zero; it was colder than sixty below, than seventy below. It was seventy-five below zero. Since the freezing point is thirty-two above zero, it meant that one hundred and seven degrees of frost obtained. The dog did not know anything about thermometers. Possibly in its brain there was no sharp consciousness of a condition of very cold such as was in the man's brain. But the brute had its instinct. It experienced a vague but menacing apprehension that subdued it and made it slink along at the man's heels, and that made it question eagerly every unwonted movement of the man as if expecting him to go into camp or to seek shelter somewhere and build a fire. The dog had learned fire, and it wanted fire, or else to burrow under the snow and cuddle its warmth away from the air.

The frozen moisture of its breathing had settled on its fur in a fine powder of frost, and especially were its jowls, muzzle, and eyelashes whitened by its crystalled breath. The man's red beard and mustache were likewise frosted, but more solidly, the deposit taking the form of ice and increasing with every warm, moist breath he exhaled. Also, the man was chewing tobacco, and the muzzle of ice held his lips so rigidly that he was unable to clear his chin when he expelled the juice. The result was that a crystal beard of the color and solidity of amber was increasing its length on his chin. If he fell down it would shatter itself, like glass, into brittle fragments. But he did not mind the appendage. It was the penalty all tobacco chewers paid in that country, and he had been out before in two cold snaps. They had not been so cold as this, he knew, but by the spirit thermometer at Sixty Mile he knew they had been registered at fifty below and at fifty-five.

He held on through the level stretch of woods for several miles, crossed a wide flat of nigger heads, and dropped down a bank to the frozen bed of a small stream. This was Henderson Creek, and he knew he was ten miles from the forks. He looked at his watch. It was ten o'clock. He was making four miles an hour, and he calculated that he would arrive at the forks at half-past twelve. He decided to celebrate that event by eating his lunch there.

The dog dropped in again at his heels, with a tail drooping discouragement, as the man swung along the creek bed. The furrow of the old sled trail was plainly visible, but a dozen inches of snow covered the marks of the last runners. In a month no man had come up or down that silent creek. The man held steadily on. He was not much given to thinking, and just then particularly he had nothing to think about save that he would eat lunch at the forks and that at six o'clock he would be in camp with the boys. There was nobody to talk to; and, had there been, speech would have been impossible because of the ice muzzle on his mouth. So he continued monotonously to chew tobacco and to increase the length of his amber beard.

10   Once in a while the thought reiterated itself that it was very cold and that he had never experienced such cold. As he walked along he rubbed his cheekbones and nose with the back of his mittened hand. He did this automatically, now and again changing hands. But, rub as he would, the instant he stopped his cheekbones went numb, and the following instant the end of his nose went numb. He was sure to frost his cheeks; he knew that, and experienced a pang of regret that he had not devised a nose strap of the sort Bud wore in cold snaps. Such a strap passed across the cheeks, as well, and saved them. But it didn't matter much, after all. What were frosted cheeks? A bit painful, that was all; they were never serious.

Empty as the man's mind was of thoughts, he was keenly observant, and he noticed the changes in the creek, the curves and bends and timber jams, and always he sharply noted where he placed his feet. Once, coming around a bend, he shied abruptly, like a startled horse, curved away from the place where he had been walking, and retreated several paces back along the trail. The creek he knew was frozen clear to the bottom—no creek could contain water in that arctic winter—but he knew also that there were springs that bubbled out from the hillsides and ran along under the snow and on top the ice of the creek. He knew that the coldest snaps never froze these springs, and he knew likewise their danger. They were traps. They hid pools of water under the snow that might be three inches deep, or three feet. Sometimes a skin of ice half an inch thick covered them, and in turn was covered by the snow. Sometimes there were alternate layers of water and ice skin, so that when one broke through he kept on breaking through for a while, sometimes wetting himself to the waist.

That was why he had shied in such panic. He had felt the give under his feet and heard the crackle of a snow-hidden ice skin. And to get his feet wet in such a temperature meant trouble and danger. At the very least it meant delay, for he would be forced to stop and build a fire, and under its protection to bare his feet while he dried his socks and moccasins. He stood and studied the creek bed and its banks, and decided that the flow of water came from the right. He reflected awhile, rubbing his nose and cheeks, then skirted to the left, stepping gingerly and testing the footing for each step. Once clear of the danger, he took a fresh chew of tobacco and swung along at his four-mile gait.

In the course of the next two hours he came upon several similar traps. Usually the snow above the hidden pools had a sunken, candied appearance that advertised the danger. Once again, however, he had a close call; and once, suspecting danger, he compelled the dog to go on in front. The dog did not want to go. It hung back until the man shoved it forward, and then it went quickly across the white, unbroken surface. Suddenly it broke through, floundered to one side, and got away to firmer footing. It had wet its forefeet and legs, and almost immediately the water that clung to it turned to ice. It made quick efforts to lick the ice off its legs, then dropped down in the snow and began to bite out the ice that had formed between the toes. This was a matter of instinct. To permit the ice to remain would mean sore feet. It did not know this. It merely obeyed the mysterious prompting that arose from the deep crypts of its being. But the man knew, having achieved a judgment on the subject, and he removed the mitten from his right hand and helped tear out the ice particles. He did not expose his fingers more than a minute, and was astonished at the swift numbness that smote them. It certainly was cold. He pulled on the mitten hastily, and beat the hand savagely across his chest.

At twelve o'clock the day was at its brightest. Yet the sun was too far south on its winter journey to clear the horizon. The bulge of the earth intervened between it and Henderson Creek, where the man walked under a clear sky at noon and cast no shadow. At half-past twelve, to the minute, he arrived at the forks of the creek. He was pleased at the speed he had made. If he kept it up, he would certainly be with the boys by six. He unbuttoned his jacket and shirt and drew forth his lunch. The action consumed no more than a quarter of a minute, yet in that brief moment the numbness laid hold of the exposed fingers. He did not put the mitten on, but, instead, struck the fingers a dozen sharp smashes against his leg. Then he sat down on a snow-covered log to eat. The sting that followed upon the striking of his fingers against his leg ceased so quickly that he was startled. He had had no chance to take a bite of biscuit. He struck the fingers repeatedly and returned them to the mitten, baring the other hand for the purpose of eating. He tried to take a mouthful, but the ice muzzle prevented. He had forgotten to build a fire and thaw out. He chuckled at his foolishness, and as he chuckled he noted the numbness creeping into the exposed fingers. Also, he noted that the stinging which had first come to his toes when he sat down was already passing away. He wondered whether the toes were warm or numb. He moved them inside the moccasins and decided that they were numb.

15   He pulled the mitten on hurriedly and stood up. He was a bit frightened. He stamped up and down until the stinging returned into the feet. It certainly was cold, was his thought. That man from Sulphur Creek had spoken the truth when telling how cold it sometimes got in the country. And he had laughed at him at the time! That showed one must not be too sure of things. There was no mistake about it, it *was* cold. He strode up and down, stamping his feet and threshing his arms, until reassured by the returning warmth. Then he got out matches and proceeded to make a fire. From the undergrowth, where high water of the previous spring had lodged a supply of seasoned twigs, he got his firewood. Working carefully from a small beginning, he soon had a roaring fire, over which he thawed the ice from his face and in the protection of which he ate his biscuits. For the moment the cold of space was outwitted. The dog took satisfaction in the fire, stretching out close enough for warmth and far enough away to escape being singed.

When the man had finished, he filled his pipe and took his comfortable time over a smoke. Then he pulled on his mittens, settled the ear flaps of his cap firmly about his ears, and took the creek trail up the left fork. The dog was disappointed and yearned back toward the fire. This man did not know cold. Possibly all the generations of his ancestry had been ignorant of cold, of real cold, of cold one hundred and seven degrees below freezing point. But the dog knew; all its ancestry knew, and it had inherited the knowledge. And it knew that it was not good to walk abroad in such fearful cold. It was the time to lie snug in a hole in the snow and wait for a curtain of cloud to be drawn across the face of outer space whence this cold came. On the other hand, there was no keen intimacy between the dog and the man. The one was the toil slave of the other, and the only caresses it had ever received were the caresses of the whip lash and of harsh and menacing throat sounds that threatened the whip lash. So the dog made no effort to communicate its apprehension to the man. It was not concerned in the welfare of the man; it was for its own sake that it yearned back toward the fire. But the man whistled, and spoke to it with the sound of whip lashes, and the dog swung in at the man's heels and followed after.

The man took a chew of tobacco and proceeded to start a new amber beard. Also, his moist breath quickly powdered with white his mustache, eyebrows, and lashes. There did not seem to be so many springs on the left fork of the Henderson, and for half an hour the man saw no signs of any. And then it happened. At a place where there were no signs, where the soft, unbroken snow seemed to advertise solidity beneath, the man broke through. It was not deep. He wet himself halfway to the knees before he floundered out to the firm crust.

He was angry, and cursed his luck aloud. He had hoped to get into camp with the boys at six o'clock, and this would delay him an hour, for he would have to build a fire and dry out his footgear. This was imperative at that low temperature— he knew that much; and he turned aside to the bank, which he climbed. On top, tangled in the underbrush about the trunks of several small spruce trees, was a highwater deposit of dry firewood—sticks and twigs, principally, but also larger portions of seasoned branches and fine dry last year's grasses. He threw down several large pieces on top of the snow. This served for a foundation and prevented the young flame from drowning itself in the snow it otherwise would melt. The flame he got by touching a match to a small shred of birch bark that he took from his pocket. This burned even more readily than paper. Placing it on the foundation, he fed the young flame with wisps of dry grass and with the tiniest dry twigs.

He worked slowly and carefully, keenly aware of his danger. Gradually, as the flame grew stronger, he increased the size of the twigs with which he fed it. He squatted in the snow, pulling the twigs out from their entanglement in the brush and feeding directly to the flame. He knew there must be no failure. When it is seventy-five below zero, a man must not fail in his first attempt to build a fire—that is, if his feet are wet. If his feet are dry, and he fails, he can run along the trail for half a mile and restore his circulation. But the circulation of wet and freezing feet cannot be restored by running when it is seventy-five below. No matter how fast he runs, the wet feet will freeze the harder.

20   All this the man knew. The old-timer on Sulphur Creek had told him about it the previous fall, and now he was appreciating the advice. Already all sensation had gone out of his feet. To build the fire he had been forced to remove his mittens, and the fingers had quickly gone numb. His pace of four miles an hour had kept his heart pumping blood to the surface of his body and to all the extremities. But the instant he stopped, the action of the pump eased down. The cold of space smote the unprotected tip of the planet, and he, being on that unprotected tip, received the full force of the blow. The blood of his body recoiled before it. The blood was alive, like the dog, and like the dog it wanted to hide away and cover itself up from the fearful cold. So long as he walked four miles an hour, he pumped that blood, willy-nilly, to the surface; but now it ebbed away and sank down into the recesses of his body. The extremities were the first to feel its absence. His wet feet froze the faster, and his exposed fingers numbed the faster, though they had not yet begun to freeze. Nose and cheeks were already freezing, while the skin of all his body chilled as it lost its blood.

But he was safe. Toes and nose and cheeks would be only touched by the frost, for the fire was beginning to burn with strength. He was feeding it with twigs the size of his finger. In another minute he would be able to feed it with branches the size of his wrist, and then he could remove his wet footgear, and, while it dried, he could keep his naked feet warm by the fire, rubbing them at first, of course, with snow. The fire was a success. He was safe. He remembered the advice of the old-timer on Sulphur Creek, and smiled. The old-timer had been very serious in laying down the law that no man must travel alone in the Klondike after fifty below. Well, here he was; he had had the accident; he was alone; and he had saved himself. Those old-timers were rather womanish, some of them, he thought. All a man had to do was to keep his head, and he was all right. Any man who was a man could travel alone. But it was surprising, the rapidity with which his cheeks and nose were freezing. And he had not thought his fingers could go lifeless in so short a time. Lifeless they were, for he could scarcely make them move together to grip a twig, and they seemed remote from his body and from him. When he touched a twig, he had to look and see whether or not he had hold of it. The wires were pretty well down between him and his finger ends.

All of which counted for little. There was the fire, snapping and crackling and promising life with every dancing flame. He started to untie his moccasins. They were coated with ice; the thick German socks were like sheaths of iron halfway to the knees; and the moccasin strings were like rods of steel all twisted and knotted as by some conflagration. For a moment he tugged with his numb fingers, then, realizing the folly of it, he drew his sheath knife.

But before he could cut the strings, it happened. It was his own fault or, rather, his mistake. He should not have built the fire under the spruce tree. He should have built it in the open. But it had been easier to pull the twigs from the brush and drop them directly on the fire. Now the tree under which he had done this carried a weight of snow on its boughs. No wind had blown for weeks, and each bough was fully freighted. Each time he had pulled a twig he had communicated a slight agitation to the tree—an imperceptible agitation, so far as he was concerned, but an agitation sufficient to bring about the disaster. High up in the tree one bough capsized its load of snow. This fell on the boughs beneath, capsizing them. This process continued, spreading out and involving the whole tree. It grew like an avalanche, and it descended without warning upon the man and the fire, and the fire was blotted out! Where it had burned was a mantle of fresh and disordered snow.

The man was shocked. It was as though he had just heard his own sentence of death. For a moment he sat and stared at the spot where the fire had been. Then he grew very calm. Perhaps the old-timer on Sulphur Creek was right. If he had only had a trail mate he would have been in no danger now. The trail mate could have built the fire. Well, it was up to him to build the fire over again, and this second time there must be no failure. Even if he succeeded, he would most likely lose some toes. His feet must be badly frozen by now, and there would be some time before the second fire was ready.

25   Such were his thoughts, but he did not sit and think them. He was busy all the time they were passing through his mind. He made a new foundation for a fire, this time in the open, where no treacherous tree could blot it out. Next he gathered dry grasses and tiny twigs from the high-water flotsam. He could not bring his fingers together to pull them out, but he was able to gather them by the handful. In this way he got many rotten twigs and bits of green moss that were undesirable, but it was the best he could do. He worked methodically, even collecting an armful of

the larger branches to be used later when the fire gathered strength. And all the while the dog sat and watched him, a certain yearning wistfulness in its eyes, for it looked upon him as the fire provider, and the fire was slow in coming.

When all was ready, the man reached in his pocket for a second piece of birch bark. He knew the bark was there, and, though he could not feel it with his fingers, he could hear its crisp rustling as he fumbled for it. Try as he would, he could not clutch hold of it. And all the time, in his consciousness, was the knowledge that each instant his feet were freezing. This thought tended to put him in a panic, but he fought against it and kept calm. He pulled on his mittens with his teeth, and threshed his arms back and forth, beating his hands with all his might against his sides. He did this sitting down, and he stood up to do it; and all the while the dog sat in the snow, its wolf brush of a tail curled around warmly over its forefeet, its sharp wolf ears pricked forward intently as it watched the man. And the man, as he beat and threshed with his arms and hands, felt a great surge of envy as he regarded the creature that was warm and secure in its natural covering.

After a time he was aware of the first faraway signals of sensation in his beaten fingers. The faint tingling grew stronger till it evolved into a stinging ache that was excruciating, but which the man hailed with satisfaction. He stripped the mitten from his right hand and fetched forth the birch bark. The exposed fingers were quickly going numb again. Next he brought out his bunch of sulphur matches. But the tremendous cold had already driven the life out of his fingers. In his effort to separate one match from the others, the whole bunch fell in the snow. He tried to pick it out of the snow, but failed. The dead fingers could neither touch nor clutch. He was very careful. He drove the thought of his freezing feet, and nose, and cheeks, out of his mind, devoting his whole soul to the matches. He watched, using the sense of vision in place of that of touch, and when he saw his fingers on each side the bunch, he closed them—that is he willed to close them, for the wires were down, and the fingers did not obey. He pulled the mitten on the right hand, and beat it fiercely against his knee. Then, with both mittened hands, he scooped the bunch of matches, along with much snow, into his lap. Yet he was no better off.

After some manipulation he managed to get the bunch between the heels of his mittened hands. In this fashion he carried it to his mouth. The ice crackled and snapped when by a violent effort he opened his mouth. He drew the lower jaw in, curled the upper lip out of the way, scraped the bunch with his upper teeth in order to separate a match. He succeeded in getting one, which he dropped on his lap. He was no better off. He could not pick it up. Then he devised a way. He picked it up in his teeth and scratched it on his leg. Twenty times he scratched before he succeeded in lighting it. As it flamed he held it with his teeth to the birch bark. But the burning brimstone went up his nostrils and into his lungs, causing him to cough spasmodically. The match fell into the snow and went out.

The old-timer on Sulphur Creek was right, he thought in the moment of controlled despair that ensued: after fifty below, a man should travel with a partner. He beat his hands, but failed in exciting any sensation. Suddenly he bared both hands, removing the mittens with his teeth. He caught the whole bunch between the heels of his hands. His arm muscles not being frozen enabled him to press the hand heels tightly against the matches. Then he scratched the bunch along his leg. It flared into flame, seventy sulphur matches at once! There was no wind to blow them out. He kept his head to one side to escape the strangling fumes, and held the blazing bunch to the birch bark. As he so held it, he became aware of sensation in his hand. His flesh was burning. He could smell it. Deep down below the surface he could feel it. The sensation developed into pain that grew acute. And still he endured it, holding the flame of the matches clumsily to the bark that would not light readily because his own burning hands were in the way, absorbing most of the flame.

30   At last, when he could endure no more, he jerked his hands apart. The blazing matches fell sizzling into the snow, but the birch bark was alight. He began laying dry grasses and the tiniest twigs on the flame. He could not pick and choose, for he had to lift the fuel between the heels of his hands. Small pieces of rotten wood and green moss clung to the twigs, and he bit them off as well as he could with his teeth. He cherished the flame carefully and awkwardly. It meant life, and it must not perish. The withdrawal of blood from the surface of his body now made him begin to shiver, and he grew more awkward. A large piece of green moss fell squarely on the little fire. He tried to poke it out with his fingers, but his shivering frame made him poke too far, and he disrupted the nucleus of the little fire, the burning grasses and tiny twigs separating and scattering. He tried to poke them together again, but in spite of the tenseness of the effort, his shivering got away with him, and the twigs were hopelessly scattered. Each twig gushed a puff of smoke and went out. The fire provider had failed. As he looked apathetically about him, his eyes chanced on the dog, sitting across the ruins of the fire from him, in the snow, making restless, hunching, movements, slightly lifting one forefoot and then the other, shifting its weight back and forth on them with wistful eagerness.

      The sight of the dog put a wild idea into his head. He remembered the tale of the man, caught in a blizzard, who killed a steer and crawled inside the carcass, and so was saved. He would kill the dog and bury his hands in the warm body until the numbness went out of them. Then he could build another fire. He spoke to the dog, calling it to him; but in his voice was a strange note of fear that frightened the animal, who had never known the man to speak in such way before. Something was the matter, and its suspicious nature sensed danger—it knew not what danger, but somewhere, somehow, in its brain arose an apprehension of the man. It flattened its ears down at the sound of the man's voice, and its restless, hunching movements and the liftings and shiftings of its forefeet became more pronounced; but it would not come to the man. He got on his hands and knees and crawled toward the dog. This unusual posture again excited suspicion, and the animal sidled mincingly away.

      The man sat up in the snow for a moment and struggled for calmness. Then he pulled on his mittens, by means of his teeth, and got upon his feet. He glanced down at first in order to assure himself that he was really standing up, for the absence of sensation in his feet left him unrelated to the earth. His erect position in itself started to drive the webs of suspicion from the dog's mind; and when he spoke peremptorily, with the sound of whip lashes in his voice, the dog rendered its customary allegiance and came to him. As it came within reaching distance the man lost his control. His arms flashed out to the dog, and he experienced genuine surprise when he discovered that his hands could not clutch, that there was neither bend nor feeling in the fingers. He had forgotten for the moment that they were frozen and that they were freezing more and more. All this happened quickly, and before the animal could get away, he encircled its body with his arms. He sat down in the snow, and in this fashion held the dog, while it snarled and whined and struggled.

      But it was all he could do, hold its body encircled in his arms and sit there. He realized that he could not kill the dog. There was no way to do it. With his helpless hands he could neither draw nor hold his sheath knife nor throttle the animal. He released it, and it plunged wildly away, with tail between its legs, and still snarling. It halted forty feet away and surveyed him curiously, with ears sharply pricked forward.

      The man looked down at his hands in order to locate them, and found them hanging on the ends of his arms. It struck him as curious that one should have to use his eyes in order to find out where his hands were. He began threshing his arms back and forth, beating the mittened hands against his sides. He did this for five minutes, violently, and his heart pumped enough blood up to the surface to put a stop to his shivering. But no sensation was aroused in the hands. He had an impression that they hung like weights on the ends of his arms, but when he tried to run the impression down, he could not find it.

35   A certain fear of death, dull and oppressive, came to him. This fear quickly became poignant as he realized that it was no longer a mere matter of freezing his fingers and toes, or of losing his hands and feet, but that it was a matter of life and death with the chances against him. This threw him into a panic, and he turned and ran up the creek bed along the old, dim trail. The dog joined in behind and kept up with him. He ran blindly, without intention, in fear such as he had never known in his life. Slowly, as he plowed and floundered through the snow, he began to see things again—the banks of the creek, the old timber jams, the leafless aspens, and the sky. The running made him feel better. He did not shiver. Maybe, if he ran on, his feet would thaw out; and, anyway, if he ran far enough, he would reach camp and the boys. Without doubt he would lose some fingers and toes and some of his face; but the boys would take care of him, and save the rest of him when he got there. And at the same time there was another thought in his mind that said he would never get to the camp and the boys; that it was too many miles away, that the freezing had too great a start on him, and that he would soon be stiff and dead. This thought he kept in the background and refused to consider. Sometimes it pushed itself forward and demanded to be heard, but he thrust it back and strove to think of other things.

It struck him as curious that he could run at all on feet so frozen that he could not feel them when they struck the earth and took the weight of his body. He seemed to himself to skim along above the surface, and to have no connection with the earth. Somewhere he had once seen a winged Mercury,[2] and he wondered if Mercury felt as he felt when skimming over the earth.

His theory of running until he reached camp and the boys had one flaw in it: he lacked the endurance. Several times he stumbled, and finally he tottered, crumpled up, and fell. When he tried to rise, he failed. He must sit and rest, he decided, and next time he would merely walk and keep on going. As he sat and regained his breath, he noted that he was feeling quite warm and comfortable. He was not shivering, and it even seemed that a warm glow had come to this chest and trunk. And yet, when he touched his nose or cheeks, there was no sensation. Running would not thaw them out. Nor would it thaw out his hands and feet. Then the thought came to him that the frozen portions of his body must be extending. He tried to keep this thought down, to forget it, to think of something else; he was aware of the panicky feeling that it caused, and he was afraid of the panic. But the thought asserted itself, and persisted, until it produced a vision of his body totally frozen. This was too much, and he made another wild run along the trail. Once he slowed down to a walk, but the thought of the freezing extending itself made him run again.

And all the time the dog ran with him, at his heels. When he fell down a second time, it curled its tail over its forefeet and sat in front of him, facing him, curiously eager and intent. The warmth and security of the animal angered him, and he cursed it till it flattened down its ears appeasingly. This time the shivering came more quickly upon the man. He was losing his battle with the frost. It was creeping into his body from all sides. The thought of it drove him on, but he ran no more than a hundred feet, when he staggered and pitched headlong. It was his last panic. When he had recovered his breath and control, he sat up and entertained in his mind the

---

[2]**winged Mercury** the winged messenger of Roman mythology.

conception of meeting death with dignity. However, the conception did not come to him in such terms. His idea of it was that he had been making a fool of himself, running around like a chicken with its head cut off—such was the simile that occurred to him. Well, he was bound to freeze anyway, and he might as well take it decently. With this new-found peace of mind came the first glimmerings of drowsiness. A good idea, he thought, to sleep off to death. It was like taking an anesthetic. Freezing was not so bad as people thought. There were lots worse ways to die.

He pictured the boys finding his body next day. Suddenly he found himself with them, coming along the trail and looking for himself. And, still with them, he came around a turn in the trail and found himself lying in the snow. He did not belong with himself any more, for even then he was out of himself, standing with the boys and looking at himself in the snow. It certainly was cold, was his thought. When he got back to the States he could tell the folks what real cold was. He drifted on from this to a vision of the old-timer on Sulphur Creek. He could see

40　him quite clearly, warm and comfortable, and smoking a pipe.

"You were right, old hoss; you were right," the man mumbled to the old-timer of Sulphur Creek.

Then the man drowsed off into what seemed to him the most comfortable and satisfying sleep he had ever known. The dog sat facing him and waiting. The brief day drew to a close in a long, slow twilight. There were no signs of a fire to be made, and, besides, never in the dog's experience had it known a man to sit like that in the snow and make no fire. As the twilight drew on, its eager yearning for the fire mastered it, and with a great lifting and shifting of forefeet, it whined softly, then flattened its ears down in anticipation of being chidden by the man. But the man remained silent. Later the dog whined loudly. And still later it crept close to the man and caught the scent of death. This made the animal bristle and back away. A little longer it delayed, howling under the stars that leaped and danced and shone brightly in the cold sky. Then it turned and trotted up the trail in the direction of the camp it knew, where were the other food providers and fire providers.

[1908]

Joining the Conversation: Critical Thinking and Writing

1. In a paragraph, explain the significance of the sentence, "The trouble with him was that he was without imagination" (paragraph 3).
2. In a letter to a young writer, London said: "Don't you tell the reader. . . . But HAVE YOUR CHARACTERS TELL IT BY THEIR DEEDS, ACTIONS, TALK, ETC. . . . The reader . . . doesn't want your dissertations on the subject, . . . your ideas—BUT PUT ALL THOSE THINGS WHICH ARE YOURS INTO THE STORIES." Good advice for a storyteller. Judging from this story, what do you suppose London's "ideas" were? Write a short dissertation—about 250 words—setting forth what you assume was London's view of man and nature.

SARAH ORNE JEWETT

Sarah Orne Jewett (1849–1909) was born and raised in South Berwick, Maine. A sickly girl, Jewett received little formal education, but her father, a doctor, introduced her to British and American fiction. Inspired by the writings of Harriet Beecher Stowe, Jewett determined in her teens to become a writer and began writing sketches and stories about the rural people of her native region. (Although South Berwick in Jewett's day was beginning to become industrialized, it had once been a busy port in a rural setting; Jewett's grandfather had been a sea captain and a leading owner of ships.) When she was twenty, she published her first story in the Atlantic Monthly, *and she continued to publish in national magazines stories about the vanishing era of her childhood.*

A White Heron

I

The woods were already filled with shadows one June evening, just before eight o'clock, though a bright sunset still glimmered faintly among the trunks of the trees. A little girl was driving home her cow, a plodding, dilatory, provoking creature in her behavior, but a valued companion for all that. They were going away from whatever light there was, and striking deep into the woods, but their feet were familiar with the path, and it was no matter whether their eyes could see it or not.

There was hardly a night the summer through when the old cow could be found waiting at the pasture bars; on the contrary, it was her greatest pleasure to hide herself away among the huckleberry bushes, and though she wore a loud bell she had made the discovery that if one stood perfectly still it would not ring. So Sylvia had to hunt for her until she found her, and call Co'! Co'! with never an answering Moo, until her childish patience was quite spent. If the creature had not given good milk and plenty of it, the case would have seemed very different to her owners. Besides, Sylvia had all the time there was, and very little use to make of it. Sometimes in pleasant weather it was a consolation to look upon the cow's pranks as an intelligent attempt to play hide and seek, and as the child had no playmates she lent herself to this amusement with a good deal of zest. Though this chase had been so long that the wary animal herself had given an unusual signal of her whereabouts, Sylvia had only laughed when she came upon Mistress Moolly at the swamp-side, and urged her affectionately homeward with a twig of birch leaves. The old cow was not inclined to wander farther, she even turned in the right direction for once as they left the pasture, and stepped along the road at a good pace. She was quite ready to be milked now, and seldom stopped to browse. Sylvia wondered what her grandmother would say because they were so late. It was a great while since she had left home at half-past five o'clock, but everybody knew the difficulty of making this errand a short one. Mrs. Tilley had chased the hornéd torment too many summer evenings herself to blame any one else for lingering, and was only thankful as she waited that she had Sylvia, nowadays, to give such valuable assistance. The good woman suspected that Sylvia loitered occasionally on her own account; there never was such a child for straying about out-of-doors since the world was made! Everybody said that it was a good change for a little maid who had tried to grow for eight years in a crowded manufacturing town, but as for Sylvia herself, it seemed as if she never had been alive at all before she came to live at the farm. She thought often with wistful compassion of a wretched geranium that belonged to a town neighbor.

"'Afraid of folks,'" old Mrs. Tilley said to herself, with a smile, after she had made the unlikely choice of Sylvia from her daughter's houseful of children, and was returning to the farm. "'Afraid of folks,' they said! I guess she won't be troubled no great with 'em up to the old place!" When they reached the door of the lonely house and stopped to unlock it, and the cat came to purr loudly, and rub against them, a deserted pussy, indeed, but fat with young robins, Sylvia whispered that this was a beautiful place to live in, and she never should wish to go home.

The companions followed the shady wood-road, the cow taking slow steps and the child very fast ones. The cow stopped long at the brook to drink, as if the pasture were not half a swamp, and Sylvia stood still and waited, letting her bare feet cool themselves in the shoal water, while the great twilight moths struck softly against her. She waded on through the brook as the cow moved away, and listened to the thrushes with a heart that beat fast with pleasure. There was a stirring in the great boughs overhead. They were full of little birds and beasts that seemed to be wide awake, and going about their world, or else saying goodnight to each other in sleepy twitters. Sylvia herself felt sleepy as she walked along. However, it was not much farther to the house, and the air was soft and sweet. She was not often in the woods so late as this, and it made her feel as if she were a part of the gray shadows and the moving leaves. She was just thinking how long it seemed since she first came to the farm a year ago, and wondering if everything went on in the noisy town just the same as when she was there; the thought of the great red-faced boy who used to chase and frighten her made her hurry along the path to escape from the shadow of the trees.

5   Suddenly this little woods-girl is horror-stricken to hear a clear whistle not very far away. Not a bird's-whistle, which would have a sort of friendliness, but a boy's whistle, determined, and somewhat aggressive. Sylvia left the cow to whatever sad fate might await her, and stepped discreetly aside into the brushes, but she was just too late. The enemy had discovered her, and called out in a very cheerful and persuasive tone, "Halloa, little girl, how far is it to the road?" and trembling Sylvia answered almost inaudibly, "A good ways."

She did not dare to look boldly at the tall young man, who carried a gun over his shoulder, but she came out of her bush and again followed the cow, while he walked alongside.

"I have been hunting for some birds," the stranger said kindly, "and I have lost my way, and need a friend very much. Don't be afraid," he added gallantly. "Speak up and tell me what your name is, and whether you think I can spend the night at your house, and go out gunning early in the morning."

Sylvia was more alarmed than before. Would not her grandmother consider her much to blame? But who could have foreseen such an accident as this? It did not seem to be her fault, and she hung her head as if the stem of it were broken, but managed to answer "Sylvy," with much effort when her companion again asked her name.

Mrs. Tilley was standing in the doorway when the trio came into view. The cow gave a loud moo by way of explanation.

10   "Yes, you'd better speak up for yourself, you old trial! Where'd she tucked herself away this time, Sylvy?" But Sylvia kept an awed silence; she knew by instinct that her grandmother did not comprehend the gravity of the situation. She must be mistaking the stranger for one of the farmer-lads of the region.

The young man stood his gun beside the door, and dropped a lumpy game-bag beside it; then he bade Mrs. Tilley good-evening, and repeated his wayfarer's story, and asked if he could have a night's lodging.

"Put me anywhere you like," he said. "I must be off early in the morning, before day; but I am very hungry indeed. You can give me some milk at any rate, that's plain."

"Dear sakes, yes," responded the hostess, whose long slumbering hospitality seemed to be easily awakened. "You might fare better if you went out to the main road a mile or so, but you're welcome to what we've got. I'll milk right off, and you make yourself at home. You can sleep on husks or feathers," she proffered graciously. "I raised them all myself. There's good pasturing for geese just below here towards the ma'sh. Now step round and set a plate for the gentleman, Sylvy!" And Sylvia promptly stepped. She was glad to have something to do, and she was hungry herself.

It was a surprise to find so clean and comfortable a little dwelling in this New England wilderness. The young man had known the horrors of its most primitive housekeeping, and the dreary squalor of that level of society which does not rebel at the companionship of hens. This was the best thrift of an old-fashioned farmstead, though on such a small scale that it seemed like a hermitage. He listened eagerly to the old woman's quaint talk, he watched Sylvia's pale face and shining gray eyes with ever growing enthusiasm, and insisted that this was the best supper he had eaten for a month, and afterward the new-made friends sat down in the doorway together while the moon came up.

15   Soon it would be berry-time, and Sylvia was a great help at picking. The cow was a good milker, though a plaguy thing to keep track of, the hostess gossiped frankly, adding presently that she had buried four children, so Sylvia's mother, and a son (who might be dead) in California were all the children she had left. "Dan, my boy, was a great hand to go gunning," she explained sadly. "I never wanted for pa'tridges or gray squer'ls while he was to home. He's been a great wand'rer, I expect, and he's no hand to write letters. There, I don't blame him, I'd ha' seen the world myself if it had been so I could."

"Sylvy takes after him," the grandmother continued affectionately, after a minute's pause. "There ain't a foot o' ground she don't know her way over, and the wild creaturs counts her one o' themselves. Squer'ls she'll tame to come an' feed right out o' her hands, and all sorts o' birds. Last winter she got the jaybirds to bangeing here, and I believe she'd 'a' scanted herself of her own meals to have plenty to throw out amongst 'em, if I hadn't kep' watch. Anything but crows, I tell her, I'm willin' to help support—though Dan he had a tamed one o' them that did seem to have reason same as folks. It was round here a good spell after he went away. Dan an' his father they didn't hitch,—but he never held up his head ag'in after Dan had dared him an' gone off."

The guest did not notice this hint of family sorrows in his eager interest in something else.

"So Sylvy knows all about birds, does she?" he exclaimed, as he looked round at the little girl who sat, very demure but increasingly sleepy, in the moonlight. "I am making a collection of birds myself. I have been at it ever since I was a boy." (Mrs. Tilley smiled.) "There are two or three very rare ones I have been hunting for these five years. I mean to get them on my own ground if they can be found."

"Do you cage 'em up?" asked Mrs. Tilley doubtfully, in response to this enthusiastic announcement.

20   "Oh no, they're stuffed and preserved, dozens and dozens of them," said the ornithologist, "and I have shot or snared every one myself. I caught a glimpse of a white heron a few miles from here on Saturday, and I have followed it in this direction. They have never been found in this district at all. The little white heron, it is," and he turned again to look at Sylvia with the hope of discovering that the rare bird was one of her acquaintances.

But Sylvia was watching a hop-toad in the narrow footpath.

"You would know the heron if you saw it," the stranger continued eagerly. "A queer tall white bird with soft feathers and long thin legs. And it would have a nest perhaps in the top of a high tree, made of sticks, something like a hawk's nest."

Sylvia's heart gave a wild beat; she knew that strange white bird, and had once stolen softly near where it stood in some bright green swamp grass, away over at the other side of the woods. There was an open place where the sunshine always seemed strangely yellow and hot, where tall, nodding rushes grew, and her grandmother had warned her that she might sink in the soft black mud underneath and never be heard of more. Not far beyond were the salt marshes just this side the sea itself, which Sylvia wondered and dreamed much about, but never had seen, whose great voice could sometimes be heard above the noise of the woods on stormy nights.

"I can't think of anything I should like so much as to find that heron's nest," the handsome stranger was saying. "I would give ten dollars to anybody who could show it to me," he added desperately, "and I mean to spend my whole vacation hunting for it if need be. Perhaps it was only migrating, or had been chased out of its own region by some bird of prey."

25   Mrs. Tilley gave amazed attention to all this, but Sylvia still watched the toad, not divining, as she might have done at some calmer time, that the creature wished to get to its hole under the door-step, and was much hindered by the unusual spectators at that hour of the evening. No amount of thought, that night, could decide how many wished-for treasures the ten dollars, so lightly spoken of, would buy.

The next day the young sportsman hovered about the woods, and Sylvia kept him company, having lost her first fear of the friendly lad, who proved to be most kind and sympathetic. He told her many things about the birds and what they knew and where they lived and what they did with themselves. And he gave her a jack-knife, which she thought as great a treasure as if she were a desert-islander. All day long he did not once make her troubled or afraid except when he brought down some unsuspecting singing creature from its bough. Sylvia would have liked him vastly better without his gun: she could not understand why he killed the very birds he seemed to like so much. But as the day waned, Sylvia still watched the young man with loving admiration. She had never seen anybody so charming and delightful; the woman's heart, asleep in the child, was vaguely thrilled by a dream of love. Some premonition of that great power stirred and swayed these young creatures who traversed the solemn woodlands with soft-footed silent care. They stopped to listen to a bird's song; they pressed forward again eagerly, parting the branches—speaking to each other rarely and in whispers; the young man going first and Sylvia following, fascinated, a few steps behind, with her gray eyes dark with excitement.

She grieved because the longed-for white heron was elusive, but she did not lead the guest, she only followed, and there was no such thing as speaking first. The sound of her own unquestioned voice would have terrified her—it was hard enough to answer yes or no when there was need of that. At last evening began to fall, and they drove the cow home together, and Sylvia smiled with pleasure when they came to the place where she heard the whistle and was afraid only the night before.

II

Half a mile from home, at the farther edge of the woods, where the land was highest, a great pine-tree stood, the last of its generation. Whether it was left for a boundary mark, or for what reason, no one could say; the woodchoppers who had felled its mates were dead and gone long ago, and a whole forest of sturdy trees, pines and oaks and maples, had grown again. But the stately head of this old pine towered above them all and made a landmark for sea and shore miles and miles away. Sylvia knew it well. She had always believed that whoever climbed to the top of it could see the ocean; and the little girl had often laid her hand on the great rough trunk and looked up wistfully at those dark boughs that the wind always stirred, no matter how hot and still the air might be below. Now she thought of the tree with a new excitement, for why, if one climbed it at break of day could not one see all the world, and easily discover from whence the white heron flew, and mark the place, and find the hidden nest?

What a spirit of adventure, what wild ambition! What fancied triumph and delight and glory for the later morning when she could make known the secret! It was almost too real and too great for the childish heart to bear.

30   All night the door of the little house stood open and the whippoorwills came and sang upon the very step. The young sportsman and his old hostess were sound asleep, but Sylvia's great design kept her broad awake and watching. She forgot to think of sleep. The short summer night seemed as long as the winter darkness, and at last when the whippoorwills ceased, and she was afraid the morning would after all come too soon, she stole out of the house and followed the pasture path through the woods, hastening toward the open ground beyond, listening with a sense of comfort and companionship to the drowsy twitter of a half-awakened bird, whose perch she had jarred in passing. Alas, if the great wave of human interest which flooded for the first time this dull little life should sweep away the satisfactions of an existence heart to heart with nature and the dumb life of the forest!

There was the huge tree asleep yet in the paling moonlight, and small and silly Sylvia began with utmost bravery to mount to the top of it, with tingling, eager blood coursing the channels of her whole frame, with her bare feet and fingers, that pinched and held like bird's claws to the monstrous ladder reaching up, up, almost to the sky itself. First she must mount the white oak tree that grew alongside, where she was almost lost among the dark branches and the green leaves heavy and wet with dew; a bird fluttered off its nest, and a red squirrel ran to and fro and scolded pettishly at the harmless housebreaker. Sylvia felt her way easily. She had often climbed there, and knew that higher still one of the oak's upper branches chafed against the pine trunk, just where its lower boughs were set close together. There, when she made the dangerous pass from one tree to the other, the great enterprise would really begin.

She crept out along the swaying oak limb at last, and took the daring step across into the old pine-tree. The way was harder than she thought; she must reach far and hold fast, the sharp dry twigs caught and held her and scratched her like angry talons, the pitch made her thin little fingers clumsy and stiff as she went round and round the tree's great stem, higher and higher upward. The sparrows and robins in the woods below were beginning to wake and twitter to the dawn, yet it seemed much lighter there aloft in the pine-tree, and the child knew she must hurry if her project were to be of any use.

The tree seemed to lengthen itself out as she went up, and to reach farther and farther upward. It was like a great main-mast to the voyaging earth; it must truly have been amazed that morning through all its ponderous frame as it felt this determined spark of human spirit wending its way from higher branch to branch. Who knows how steadily the least twigs held themselves to advantage this light, weak creature on her way! The old pine must have loved his new dependent. More than all the hawks, and bats, and moths, and even the sweet voiced thrushes, was the brave, beating heart of the solitary gray-eyed child. And the tree stood still and frowned away the winds that June morning while the dawn grew bright in the east.

Sylvia's face was like a pale star, if one had seen it from the ground, when the last thorny bough was past, and she stood trembling and tired but wholly triumphant, high in the treetop. Yes, there was the sea with the dawning sun making a golden dazzle over it, and toward that glorious east flew two hawks with slow-moving pinions. How low they looked in the air from that height when one had only seen them before far up, and dark against the blue sky. Their gray feathers were as soft as moths; they seemed only a little way from the tree, and Sylvia felt as if she too could go flying away among the clouds. Westward, the woodlands and farms reached miles and miles into the distance; here and there were church steeples, and white villages, truly it was a vast and awesome world!

35   The birds sang louder and louder. At last, the sun came up bewilderingly bright. Sylvia could see the white sails of ships out at sea, and the clouds that were

purple and rose-colored and yellow at first began to fade away. Where was the white heron's nest in the sea of green branches, and was this wonderful sight and pageant of the world the only reward for having climbed to such a giddy height? Now look down again, Sylvia, where the green marsh is set among the shining birches and dark hemlocks; there where you saw the white heron once you will see him again; look, look! a white spot of him like a single floating feather comes up from the dead hemlock and grows larger, and rises, and comes close at last, and goes by the landmark pine with steady sweep of wing and outstretched slender neck and crested head. And wait! wait! do not move a foot or a finger, little girl, do not send an arrow of light and consciousness from your two eager eyes, for the heron has perched on a pine bough not far beyond yours, and cries back to his mate on the nest and plumes his feathers for the new day!

The child gives a long sigh a minute later when a company of shouting cat-birds comes also to the tree, and vexed by their fluttering and lawlessness the solemn heron goes away. She knows his secret now, the wild, light, slender bird that floats and wavers, and goes back like an arrow presently to his home in the green world beneath. Then Sylvia, well satisfied, makes her perilous way down again, not daring to look far below the branch she stands on, ready to cry sometimes because her fingers ache and her lamed feet slip. Wondering over and over again what the stranger would say to her, and what he would think when she told him how to find his way straight to the heron's nest.

"Sylvy, Sylvy!" called the busy old grandmother again and again, but nobody answered, and the small husk bed was empty and Sylvia had disappeared.

The guest waked from a dream, and remembering his day's pleasure hurried to dress himself that might it sooner begin. He was sure from the way the shy little girl looked once or twice yesterday that she had at least seen the white heron, and now she must really be made to tell. Here she comes now, paler than ever, and her worn old frock is torn and tattered, and smeared with pine pitch. The grandmother and the sportsman stand in the door together and question her, and the splendid moment has come to speak of the dead hemlock-tree by the green marsh.

But Sylvia does not speak after all, though the old grandmother fretfully rebukes her, and the young man's kind, appealing eyes are looking straight in her own. He can make them rich with money; he has promised it, and they are poor now. He is so well worth making happy, and he waits to hear the story she can tell.

No, she must keep silence! What is it that suddenly forbids her and makes her dumb? Has she been nine years growing and now, when the great world for the first time puts out a hand to her, must she thrust it aside for a bird's sake? The murmur of the pine's green branches is in her ears, she remembers how the white heron came flying through the golden air and how they watched the sea and the morning together, and Sylvia cannot speak; she cannot tell the heron's secret and give its life away.

Dear loyalty, that suffered a sharp pang as the guest went away disappointed later in the day, that could have served and followed him and loved him as a dog loves! Many a night Sylvia heard the echo of his whistle haunting the pasture path as she came home with the loitering cow. She forgot even her sorrow at the sharp report of his gun and the sight of thrushes and sparrows dropping silent to the ground, their songs hushed and their pretty feathers stained and wet with blood. Were the birds better friends than their hunter might have been,—who can tell? Whatever treasures were lost to her, woodlands and summer-time, remember! Bring your gifts and graces and tell your secrets to this lonely country child!

[1886]

Joining the Conversation: Critical Thinking and Writing

1. What does the name "Sylvia" mean? Why is this name appropriate to the central figure and to the theme of the story?
2. Why does Jewett include the passage about the grandmother's son, Dan? To what extent does Sylvia take after Dan?
3. In 250 words or so, discuss whether or not the final paragraph of "A White Heron" is appropriate and effective.
4. Many fairy tales tell of a hero or heroine who strays (usually into a wood), encounters a villain who seems friendly, passes a test, enters a new world, escapes from the villain, and returns safely home. If you can think of such a fairy tale, perhaps "Little Red Riding Hood" or "Jack and the Beanstalk," write an essay of 750 to 1,000 words, set down its framework, and then see to what extent it corresponds to the framework of "A White Heron."

PATRICIA GRACE

Patricia Grace was born in Wellington, New Zealand, in 1937, of Ngati Raukawa, Ngati Toa, and Te Ati Awa descent. In 1974 she received the first grant awarded to a Maori writer, and in 1975 she became the first Maori woman to publish a book of stories. She is the author of five novels, a play, a book of poems, and several volumes of short stories.

Butterflies

The grandmother plaited her granddaughter's hair and then she said, "Get your lunch. Put it in your bag. Get your apple. You come straight back after school, straight home here. Listen to the teacher," she said. "Do what she say."

Her grandfather was out on the step. He walked down the path with her and out onto the footpath. He said to a neighbor, "Our granddaughter goes to school. She lives with us now."

"She's fine," the neighbor said. "She's terrific with her two plaits in her hair."

"And clever," the grandfather said. "Writes every day in her book."

5   "She's fine," the neighbor said.

The grandfather waited with his granddaughter by the crossing and then he said, "Go to school. Listen to the teacher. Do what she say."

When the granddaughter came home from school her grandfather was hoeing around the cabbages. Her grandmother was picking beans. They stopped their work.

"You bring your book home?" the grandmother asked.

"Yes."

10   "You write your story?"

"Yes."

"What's your story?"

"About the butterflies."

"Get your book then. Read your story."

15   The granddaughter took her book from her schoolbag and opened it.

"I killed all the butterflies," she read. "This is me and this is all the butterflies."

"And your teacher like your story, did she?"

"I don't know."

"What your teacher say?"

20   "She said butterflies are beautiful creatures. They hatch out and fly in the sun. The butterflies visit all the pretty flowers, she said. They lay their eggs and then they die. You don't kill butterflies, that's what she said."

The grandmother and the grandfather were quiet for a long time, and their granddaughter, holding the book, stood quite still in the warm garden.

"Because you see," the grandfather said, "your teacher, she buy all her cabbages from the supermarket and that's why."

[1988]

Joining the Conversation: Critical Thinking and Writing

1. On the basis of the first six paragraphs, how would you characterize the grandparents? How would you characterize the grandfather at the end of the story?
2. Why do you suppose Grace makes the relationship between a girl and her grandparents rather than between the girl and her parents? Or, for that matter, why not a boy and his parents? Would the story have a different feel? Explain.
3. The story is told from an objective point of view. Suppose Grace had told it from the grandfather's point of view. Rewrite the final paragraph, using his point of view, and compare your version with Grace's. Which do you prefer? Why?
4. You are a teacher. You have just read this story and you recognize yourself in it. Record your response in your journal (i.e., record the teacher's response).
5. You are a teacher. A student tells you that this story advocates the use of pesticides. How do you respond?

POEMS

MATTHEW ARNOLD

Matthew Arnold (1822–88) is a central figure in nineteenth-century English literature. After his graduation from Oxford University in 1844, he became an inspector of schools, a post he held nearly his entire life. He is admired both for his poetry and for his influential essays on culture and literature.

In the title of the following sonnet, "Nature" apparently means the world of things other than human beings, a world without human morality.

In Harmony with Nature

To a Preacher

"In Harmony with Nature?" Restless fool,
Who with such heat dost preach what were to thee,
When true, the last impossibility—
To be like Nature strong, like Nature cool!
Know, man hath all which Nature hath, but more,   5
And in that *more* lie all his hopes of good.

Nature is cruel, man is sick of blood;
Nature is stubborn, man would fain adore;

Nature is fickle, man hath need of rest;
Nature forgives no debt, and fears no grave;   10
Man would be mild, and with safe conscience blest.

Man must begin, know this, where Nature ends;
Nature and man can never be fast friends.
Fool, if thou canst not pass her, rest her slave!

[1849]

Joining the Conversation: Critical Thinking and Writing

1. In the first stanza, the speaker is replying to someone, perhaps a preacher, who has espoused the goal of being "in harmony with Nature." Nature is said (line 4) to be "strong" and "cool." Do these adjectives make sense?
2. Having said that nature is strong and cool, Arnold goes on, in lines 5–8, to say that Nature is "cruel" and "stubborn." Is the speaker contradicting himself? Please explain how the first two stanzas do, or do not, fit together.
3. In the remainder of the poem, the speaker objects to the idea of living "in harmony with Nature." Exactly what are the grounds of his objection?
4. Please make your way through the poem, line by line, stating in your own words what the speaker is saying about Nature, and about man. What is the speaker's overall argument?
5. In line 10 Arnold says "Nature forgives no debt." What do you think this means? Do you think that Arnold is establishing a contrast between an amoral Nature and the morality that Jesus preached when he said, in the Lord's Prayer, "Forgive us our debts, as we forgive our debtors" (Matthew 6:12)?
6. What does "harmony" mean? Do you believe we can live "in harmony with Nature"? How would you define "Nature"?
7. Read Whitman's "A Noiseless Patient Spider" (page 618) and then respond to the fourth question that follows Whitman's poem.

THOMAS HARDY

Thomas Hardy (1840–1928) was born near Dorchester, in southwest England, where at fifteen he was apprenticed to an architect. At the age of twenty-one he went to London to practice as an architect, but he soon turned to writing fiction and poetry. Between 1872 and 1896 he achieved fame as a novelist; among his novels are The Return of the Native *(1878) and* Tess of the D'Urbervilles *(1891). After the hostile reception of* Jude the Obscure *(1896) he abandoned writing fiction and concentrated on writing poetry.*

Transformations

Portion of this yew
Is a man my grandsire knew,
Bosomed here at its foot:
This branch may be his wife,

A ruddy human life   5
Now turned to a green shoot.

These grasses must be made
Of her who often prayed,
Last century, for repose;
And the fair girl long ago   10
Whom I often tried to know
May be entering this rose.

So, they are not underground,
But as nerves and veins abound
In the growths of upper air,   15
And they feel the sun and rain,
And the energy again
That made them what they were!

[1917]

Joining the Conversation: Critical Thinking and Writing

1. What is your sense of the speaker's tone in the first stanza? In the last? In lines 7–8 the speaker conjectures that "These grasses must be made / Of her who often prayed." What sort of visual connection is suggested between the grasses and the woman?
2. How might the speaker know that someone "often prayed, / Last century, for repose"?
3. At what stage of life is the speaker? How do you know?
4. What do you think Hardy means by "the energy . . . / That made them what they were"?
5. Do you find the poem far-fetched, or do you feel that the poet has made his assertions plausible? Explain.

JOHN KEATS

John Keats (1795–1821), son of a London stable keeper, was taken out of school when he was fifteen and apprenticed to a surgeon and apothecary. In 1816 he was licensed to practice as an apothecary-surgeon, but he almost immediately abandoned medicine and decided to make a career as a poet. His progress was amazing; he quickly moved from routine verse to major accomplishments, publishing books of poems in 1817, 1818, and 1820, before dying of tuberculosis at the age of twenty-five. Today he is esteemed as one of England's greatest poets.

To Autumn

I

Season of mists and mellow fruitfulness,
    Close bosom-friend of the maturing sun;
Conspiring with him how to load and bless
    With fruit the vines that round the thatch-eaves run;

To bend with apples the mossed cottage trees,   5
    And fill all fruit with ripeness to the core;
To swell the gourd, and plump the hazel shells
    With a sweet kernel; to set budding more,
And still more, later flowers for the bees,
    Until they think warm days will never cease,   10
For summer has o'er-brimmed their clammy cells.

                                    II

Who hath not seen thee oft amid thy store?
    Sometimes whoever seeks abroad may find
Thee sitting careless on a granary floor,
    Thy hair soft-lifted by the winnowing wind;   15
Or on a half-reaped furrow sound asleep,
    Drowsed with the fume of poppies, while thy hook
Spares the next swath and all its twined flowers:
    And sometime like a gleaner thou dost keep
Steady thy laden head across a brook;   20
    Or by a cider-press, with patient look,
Thou watchest the last oozings hours by hours.

                                    III

Where are the songs of Spring? Ay, where are they?
    Think not of them, thou hast thy music too,—
While barred clouds bloom the soft-dying day,   25
    And touch the stubble-plains with rosy hue;
Then in a wailful choir the small gnats mourn
    Among the river sallows, borne aloft
Or sinking as the light wind lives or dies;
    And full-grown lambs loud bleat from hilly bourn;   30
Hedge-crickets sing; and now with treble soft
    The red-breast whistles from a garden-croft;
And gathering swallows twitter in the skies.

                                                              [1819]

Joining the Conversation: Critical Thinking and Writing

1. Please summarize what the speaker is saying in each stanza.
2. A critic who admires Keats has nonetheless said about "To Autumn" that while the poem is "full of gorgeous language," it "lacks a clear point." Do you agree or disagree with this claim?
3. Select a favorite line or lines in "To Autumn." Please explain your choice, and explain how this line or lines fit in the structure of the poem as a whole.
4. If you were assigned to write a poem about one of the four seasons, which one would you choose? Why? Which one offers the most possibilities for poetry?

GERARD MANLEY HOPKINS

Gerard Manley Hopkins (1844–89) was born near London and was educated at Oxford, where he studied the classics. A convert from Anglicanism to Roman Catholicism, he was ordained a Jesuit priest in 1877. After serving as a parish priest and teacher, he was appointed professor of Greek at the Catholic University of Ireland in Dublin.

Hopkins published only a few poems during his lifetime, partly because he believed that the pursuit of literary fame was incompatible with his vocation as a priest, and partly because he was aware that his highly individual style might puzzle readers.

God's Grandeur

The world is charged with the grandeur of God.
   It will flame out, like shining from shook foil;
   It gathers to a greatness, like the ooze of oil
Crushed. Why do men then now not reck his rod?
Generations have trod, have trod, have trod;   5
   And all is seared with trade; bleared, smeared with toil;
   And wears man's smudge and shares man's smell: the soil
Is bare now, nor can foot feel, being shod.

And for all this, nature is never spent;
   There lives the dearest freshness deep down things;   10
And though the last lights off the black West went
   Oh, morning, at the brown brink eastward, springs—
Because the Holy Ghost over the bent
   World broods with warm breast and with ah! bright wings.

[1877]

Joining the Conversation: Critical Thinking and Writing

1. How would you define "charged" in the first line? How does the meaning connect with "flame out," in the next line? The Judeo-Christian tradition, unlike some ancient religions, insists that there are no thunder gods, lightning gods, river gods, and so forth; God is independent of nature, and therefore nature is not to be worshipped. Taking the poem as a whole, do you think Hopkins has slipped into nature-worship? Explain.
2. Hopkins in a letter explained "foil" in the second line thus: "I mean foil in its sense of leaf or tinsel. . . . Shaken goldfoil gives off broad glares like sheet lightning and also, and this is true of nothing else, owing to its zigzag dints and creasings and network of small many cornered facets, a sort of fork lightning too." Suppose Hopkins had not explained it, and a reader thought that "foil" referred to a fencing sword. Might the meaning of the passage—the concept of nature that the line conveys—be equally interesting? How would you characterize Hopkins's view of nature, based on the first two sentences of the poem? ("The ooze of oil / Crushed" probably evokes an image of oil crushed from olives or from seed.)

3. Hopkins was a Roman Catholic priest. Does it therefore make sense to say that in line 6 "man's smudge" probably refers not only to a polluted environment (for instance, from factory smoke) but also to the doctrine of original sin? (If you are unfamiliar with this doctrine, begin by looking up "original sin" in a dictionary.)

4. The poem is a sonnet (14 lines), and, like many (but not all) sonnets, it is constructed with a unit of eight lines (the octave) followed by a unit of six lines (the sestet). What change in voice, in tone, do you hear at the beginning of the sestet? A writing assignment: Is the second part of the sonnet (lines 9–14) more unified or less unified than the first? Probably after writing a first draft you will be able to form a thesis that describes an overall pattern. As you revise your drafts, make sure (a) that the thesis is clear to the reader, and (b) that it is adequately supported by quotations that provide evidence.

5. The Holy Ghost (line 13) is described in Luke 3:22 as descending in the form of a dove. Given this information, explicate the final two lines of the poem.

6. Do you think that a reader has to be a Roman Catholic (as Hopkins was), or at least some sort of believer in the Judeo-Christian God in order to find the poem meaningful? Explain.

WALT WHITMAN

Walt Whitman (1819–92) was born on Long Island, the son of a farmer. The young Whitman taught school and worked as a carpenter, a printer, a newspaper editor, and, during the Civil War, as a volunteer nurse on the Union side. After the war he supported himself by doing secretarial jobs. In Whitman's own day his poetry was highly controversial because of its unusual form (formlessness, many people said) and (though not in the following poem) its abundant erotic implications.

A Noiseless Patient Spider

A noiseless patient spider,
I mark'd where on a little promontory it stood isolated,
Mark'd how to explore the vacant vast surrounding,
It launch'd forth filament, filament, filament, out of itself,
Ever unreeling them, ever tirelessly speeding them.   5

And you O my soul where you stand,
Surrounded, detached, in measureless oceans of space,
Ceaselessly musing, venturing, throwing, seeking the spheres to connect them,
Till the bridge you will need be form'd, till the ductile anchor hold,
Till the gossamer thread you fling catch somewhere, O my soul.   10

[1862–63]

Joining the Conversation: Critical Thinking and Writing

1. How are the suggestions in "launch'd" (line 4) and "unreeling" (line 5) continued in the second stanza?

2. How are the varying lengths of lines 1, 4, and 8 relevant to their ideas?

3. The second stanza is not a complete sentence. Why? The poem is un-rhymed. What effect does the near-rhyme (*hold*—*soul*) in the last two lines have on you?
4. Whitman apparently thinks we can learn something about ourselves by observing nature. Read Matthew Arnold's "In Harmony with Nature" (pages 613–14) and then write a dialogue of about 500 words in which Arnold and Whitman talk about nature.

EMILY DICKINSON

For a biographical note on Emily Dickinson, see pages 550–52.

"Nature" Is What We See

"Nature" is what we see—
The Hill—the Afternoon—
Squirrel—Eclipse—the Bumble bee—
Nay—Nature is Heaven—
Nature is what we hear—   5
The Bobolink—the Sea—
Thunder—the Cricket—
Nay—Nature is Harmony—
Nature is what we know—
Yet have no art to say—   10
So impotent Our Wisdom is
To her Simplicity.

[1863]

Joining the Conversation: Critical Thinking and Writing

1. Why does Dickinson place the word "Nature" in quotation marks?
2. What is the effect of the word "Nay," which Dickinson uses twice?
3. What is the meaning of lines 9–10?
4. What is the meaning of lines 11–12, and what is their relation to the two lines that precede them?
5. The critic Margaret Homans has said: "[The poem] exposes the futility of efforts to master nature by finding linguistic equivalencies for it." Please explain and provide evidence for this interpretation. Do you agree with it?

EMILY DICKINSON

A Narrow Fellow in the Grass

A narrow Fellow in the Grass
Occasionally rides—

You may have met Him—did you not
His notice sudden is—

The Grass divides as with a Comb—   5
A spotted shaft is seen—
And then it closes at your feet
And opens further on—

He likes a Boggy Acre
A Floor too cool for Corn—   10
Yet when a Boy, and Barefoot—
I more than once at Noon
Have passed, I thought, a Whip lash
Unbraiding in the Sun
When stooping to secure it   15
It wrinkled, and was gone—

Several of Nature's People
I know, and they know me—
I feel for them a transport
Of cordiality—   20

But never met this Fellow
Attended, or alone
Without a tighter breathing
And Zero at the Bone—

                                                        [c. 1865]

Joining the Conversation: Critical Thinking and Writing

1. What sorts of things is Dickinson implying by referring to the snake as "a narrow Fellow"?
2. Why does she address the reader in line 3, and then again in line 7? Do you like this effect?
3. How would you reply to someone who says, "I find it confusing that Dickinson presents herself here as a boy."
4. Is this a serious poem, or a humorous one? Please point to evidence in the text to support your view.
5. Please rewrite this poem in prose, and punctuate it as you see fit. What is your response to this prose version?

MyLiteratureLab® *For additional resources for "A narrow Fellow in the Grass," log in to www.myliteraturelab.com where you will find Short Evaluation Exercises, as well as an About the Author, Bibliography, Links, and Critical Overview for Dickinson (under Student Resources).*

JOY HARJO

Joy Harjo, a Creek Indian, was born in Tulsa, Oklahoma, in 1951. She was edu-
cated at the Institute of American Indian Arts in Santa Fe, New Mexico, and at
the University of Iowa Writers' Workshop. She now teaches at the University of
Colorado in Boulder. Her chief books are poetry collections, including The Last
Song *(1975),* What Moon Drove Me to This *(1979),* She Had Some Horses
(1983), and Secrets from the Center of the World *(1989).*

Vision

The rainbow touched down
"somewhere in the Rio Grande,"
we said. And saw the light of it
from your mother's house in Isleta.°
How it curved down between earth   5
and the deepest sky to give us horses
of color

       horses that were within us all of this time
but we didn't see them because   10
we wait for the easiest vision
           to save us.

In Isleta the rainbow was a crack
in the universe. We saw the barest
of all life that is possible.
Bright horses rolled over   15
and over the dusking sky.
I heard the thunder of their beating
hearts. Their lungs hit air
and sang. All the colors of horses
formed the rainbow,   20
          and formed us
watching them.

                                    [1983]

4 Isleta a pueblo in New Mexico.

Joining the Conversation: Critical Thinking and Writing

1. Who are the "we," the "us," referred to in this poem?
2. What main point is the speaker making?
3. Is there anything in this poem that you do not understand or find confusing?
4. Do you like this poem? Yes, no? A lot, a little, not at all?
5. What is the significance of the horses? Would the poem be equally effective, or
   less so, if Harjo had used a different animal?

MARY OLIVER

*Mary Oliver, born in Cleveland in 1935, attended Ohio State University and Vassar College. She is the author of six books of poetry—*American Primitive *received the Pulitzer Prize for Poetry in 1984, and* New and Selected Poems *received a* National Book Award *in 1992—and she has served as a visiting professor or a poet in residence at several colleges.*

Two of her prose comments may be of special interest. Of today's readers she has said, "The question asked today is: What does it mean? Nobody says, how does it feel?" And of her work she has said, "I am trying in my poems to vanish and have the reader be the experiencer. I do not want to be there. It is not even a walk we take together."

The Black Walnut Tree

My mother and I debate:
we could sell
the black walnut tree
to the lumberman,
and pay off the mortgage.   5
Likely some storm anyway
will churn down its dark boughs,
smashing the house. We talk
slowly, two women trying
in a difficult time to be wise.   10
Roots in the cellar drains,
I say, and she replies
that the leaves are getting heavier
every year, and the fruit
harder to gather away.   15
But something brighter than money
moves in our blood—an edge
sharp and quick as a trowel
that wants us to dig and sow.
So we talk, but we don't do   20
anything. That night I dream
of my fathers out of Bohemia
filling the blue fields
of fresh and generous Ohio
with leaves and vines and orchards.   25
What my mother and I both know
is that we'd crawl with shame
in the emptiness we'd made
in our own and our fathers' backyard.
So the black walnut tree   30
swings through another year
of sun and leaping winds,
of leaves and bounding fruit,
and, month after month, the whip-
crack of the mortgage.   35

[1992]

Joining the Conversation: Critical Thinking and Writing

1. Why are the mother and daughter unable to sell the black walnut tree? Do you believe that they should?
2. What is the "something brighter than money" to which the speaker refers in line 16?
3. Do you know what a black walnut tree looks like? Does it matter that Oliver has keyed her poem to this kind of tree, as opposed to some other kind?
4. Please write a response (one page) to someone who says: "These women are too sentimental about Nature; after all, it's just a tree."

KAY RYAN

Kay Ryan, born in San Jose, California, in 1945, holds a bachelor's and a master's degree in English from the University of California, Los Angeles. She has published a number of books of poetry and in 2009 she was appointed the sixteenth Poet Laureate Consultant in Poetry to the Library of Congress.

Turtle

Who would be a turtle who could help it?
A barely mobile hard roll, a four-oared helmet,
she can ill afford the chances she must take
in rowing toward the grasses that she eats.
Her track is graceless, like dragging   5
a packing-case places, and almost any slope
defeats her modest hopes. Even being practical,
she's often stuck up to the axle on her way
to something edible, With everything optimal,
she skirts the ditch which would convert   10
her shell into a serving dish. She lives
below luck-level, never imagining some lottery
will change her load of pottery to wings.
Her only levity is patience,
the sport of truly chastened things.   15

[1994]

Joining the Conversation: Critical Thinking and Writing

1. Elsewhere in this book we say that a poem is (to quote Robert Frost) "a performance in words." In what ways is this poem a "performance"?
2. Does this poem have a point? If so, what is it?
3. Is Ryan saying anything about turtles that is relevant to human beings? If so, what? If not, is there any point to the poem?

Thinking Critically: Case Study about Robert Frost

ROBERT FROST

 Robert Frost (1874–1963) was born in California. After his father's death in 1885, Frost's mother took the family to New England, where she taught in high schools in Massachusetts and New Hampshire. Frost studied for part of one term at Dartmouth College in New Hampshire, then did odd jobs (including teaching), and from 1897 to 1899 was enrolled as a special student at Harvard. He then farmed in New Hampshire, published a few poems in local newspapers, left the farm and taught again, and in 1912 left for England, where he hoped to achieve more popular success as a writer. By 1915 he had won a considerable reputation, and he returned to the United States, settling on a farm in New Hampshire and cultivating the image of the country-wise farmer-poet. In fact he was well read in the classics, the Bible, and English and American literature.

Among Frost's many comments about literature, here are three: "Writing is unboring to the extent that it is dramatic"; "Every poem is . . . a figure of the will braving alien entanglements"; and, finally, a poem "begins in delight and ends in wisdom. . . . It runs a course of lucky events, and ends in a clarification of life—not necessarily a great clarification, such as sects and cults are founded on, but in a momentary stay against confusion."

Here is Frost, in a letter, writing about his own work:

> *You get more credit for thinking if you restate formulae or cite cases that fall in easily under formulae, but all the fun is outside[,] saying things that suggest formulae that won't formulate—that almost but don't quite formulate. I should like to be so subtle at this game as to seem to the casual person altogether obvious. The casual person would assume I meant nothing or else I came near enough meaning something he was familiar with to mean it for all practical purposes. Well, well, well.*

We give six of Frost's poems, and we follow these poems with an essay by Frost on poetry. In the first poem, "The Pasture," the last words of each stanza, "You come too," are an invitation to the reader to join him.

The Pasture

I'm going out to clean the pasture spring;
I'll only stop to rake the leaves away
(And wait to watch the water clear, I may):
I shan't be gone long.—You come too.

I'm going out to fetch the little calf   5
That's standing by the mother. It's so young,
It totters when she licks it with her tongue.
I shan't be gone long.—You come too.

[1914]

Joining the Conversation: Critical Thinking and Writing

1. Would the poem be just as good—maybe better?—if it consisted of only one stanza, either the first or the second? Explain.
2. Although Frost had already published books of poems, after he wrote "The Pasture" he always placed this poem first in any collected edition of his poems. Why do you suppose he did this?

MyLiteratureLab® *For additional resources for "The Pasture," log in to* www .myliteraturelab.com *where you will find a Longman Lecture, as well as an About the Author, Bibliography, Links, and Critical Overview for Frost (under Student Resources).*

Mowing

There was never a sound beside the wood but one,
And that was my long scythe whispering to the ground.
What was it it whispered? I knew not well myself;
Perhaps it was something about the heat of the sun,
Something, perhaps, about the lack of sound—   5
And that was why it whispered and did not speak.
It was no dream of the gift of idle hours,
Or easy gold at the hand of fay or elf:
Anything more than the truth would have seemed too weak
To the earnest love that laid the swale in rows,   10
Not without feeble-pointed spikes of flowers
(Pale orchises), and scared a bright green snake.
The fact is the sweetest dream that labor knows.
My long scythe whispered and left the hay to make.

[1913]

Joining the Conversation: Critical Thinking and Writing

1. What associations come to mind from the title?
2. Please explain the distinction that Frost's speaker makes between whispering and speaking.
3. What is the speaker saying in lines 7–8?
4. Line 13 is well known to many readers. What does it mean? How is this line connected to the meaning of the poem as a whole?
5. Frost was keenly interested in tones of voice—in getting these tones into his poetry. How would you describe the tone or tones of voice in this poem?
6. Frost is a very popular poet, widely read and studied both inside and outside college classrooms. Is this a poem that you like? Please explain.
7. Could you imagine learning "Mowing" by heart? Why might someone want to memorize this poem?

The Wood-Pile

Out walking in the frozen swamp one grey day,
I paused and said, "I will turn back from here.
No, I will go on farther—and we shall see."
The hard snow held me, save where now and then
One foot went through. The view was all in lines   5
Straight up and down of tall slim trees
Too much alike to mark or name a place by
So as to say for certain I was here
Or somewhere else: I was just far from home.
A small bird flew before me. He was careful   10
To put a tree between us when he lighted,
And say no word to tell me who he was
Who was so foolish as to think what *he* thought.
He thought that I was after him for a feather—
The white one in his tail; like one who takes   15
Everything said as personal to himself.
One flight out sideways would have undeceived him.
And then there was a pile of wood for which
I forgot him and let his little fear
Carry him off the way I might have gone,   20
Without so much as wishing him good-night.
He went behind it to make his last stand.
It was a cord of maple, cut and split
And piled—and measured, four by four by eight.
And not another like it could I see.   25
No runner tracks in this year's snow looped near it.
And it was older sure than this year's cutting,
Or even last year's or the year's before.
The wood was grey and the bark warping off it
And the pile somewhat sunken. Clematis   30
Had wound strings round and round it like a bundle.
What held it though on one side was a tree
Still growing, and on one a stake and prop,
These latter about to fall. I thought that only
Someone who lived in turning to fresh tasks   35
Could so forget his handiwork on which
He spent himself, the labour of his axe,
And leave it there far from a useful fireplace
To warm the frozen swamps as best it could
With the slow smokeless burning of decay.   40

[1914]

Joining the Conversation: Critical Thinking and Writing

1. What is the contrast that Frost makes between human beings and nature?
2. What does he say about the relationship between human beings and nature?

The Oven Bird

There is a singer everyone has heard,
Loud, a mid-summer and a mid-wood bird,
Who makes the solid tree trunks sound again.
He says that leaves are old and that for flowers
Mid-summer is to spring as one to ten.   5
He says the early petal-fall is past
When pear and cherry bloom went down in showers
On sunny days a moment overcast;
And comes that other fall we name the fall.
He says the highway dust is over all.
The bird would cease and be as other birds   10
But that he knows in singing not to sing.
The question that he frames in all but words
Is what to make of a diminished thing.

[1916]

Joining the Conversation: Critical Thinking and Writing

1. Does the poem offer anything to a reader who has *not* heard an oven bird? If so, what?
2. Do you have an answer to "The question" raised in the last two lines? If so, what is the answer?

The Need of Being Versed in Country Things

The house had gone to bring again
To the midnight sky a sunset glow.
Now the chimney was all of the house that stood,
Like a pistil after the petals go.

The barn opposed across the way,   5
That would have joined the house in flame
Had it been the will of the wind, was left
To bear forsaken the place's name.

No more it opened with all one end
For teams that came by the stony road   10
To drum on the floor with scurrying hoofs
And brush the mow with the summer load.

The birds that came to it through the air
At broken windows flew out and in,
Their murmur more like the sigh we sigh   15
From too much dwelling on what has been.

Yet for them the lilac renewed its leaf,
And the aged elm, though touched with fire;

And the dry pump flung up an awkward arm;
And the fence post carried a strand of wire.   20

For them there was really nothing sad.
But though they rejoiced in the nest they kept,
One had to be versed in country things
Not to believe the phoebes wept.

[1923]

Joining the Conversation: Critical Thinking and Writing

1. By the end of the second stanza the reader understands that the farmhouse has been destroyed by a fire. Why do you suppose (putting aside the matter of rhyme) in line 2 Frost wrote "a sunset glow" instead of (say) "a burst of flame"? And what is the effect of the simile in line 4? That is, what do these comparisons contribute to the poem? (If you are unsure of the meaning of "pistil," check a dictionary.)

2. In the fifth stanza Frost uses personifications: "the lilac renewed its leaf," and the "pump flung up an awkward arm," and "the fence post carried a strand of wire." What other personifications do you find in the poem? What effect do these personifications have on you? And why do you suppose there are no personifications in the last two lines of the poem?

3. In a sentence or two or three, characterize the speaker. (You can probably characterize him or her by means of an adjective or two or three; use the rest of the allotment to provide evidence, such as brief quotations.)

4. Much of the poem describes a scene, but the speaker also interprets the scene. How would you summarize the interpretation? How might you paraphrase the title? Does the speaker convince you of the "need" to be "versed in country things"?

5. Do you think the poem is sentimental? Or, on the other hand, cynical? Explain.

6. Suppose you were to write a parody of "The Need of Being Versed in Country Things." What scene might you use, or what objects might you personify? (A parody is an amusing imitation of the style of another work, often with an inappropriate subject. Thus, one might parody a sports writer by imitating his or her style, but the subject would not be an athletic event but, say, students engaged in peer review.) Suggestion: consider using your neighborhood or your workplace as a subject.

The Most of It

He thought he kept the universe alone;
For all the voice in answer he could wake
Was but the mocking echo of his own
From some tree-hidden cliff across the lake.
Some morning from the boulder-broken beach   5
He would cry out on life, that what it wants
Is not its own love back in copy speech,
But counter-love, original response.

And nothing ever came of what he cried
Unless it was the embodiment that crashed   10
In the cliff's talus on the other side,
And then in the far distant water splashed,
But after a time allowed for it to swim,
Instead of proving human when it neared
And someone else additional to him,   15
As a great buck it powerfully appeared,
Pushing the crumpled water up ahead,
And landed pouring like a waterfall,
And stumbled through the rocks with horny tread,
And forced the underbrush—and that was all.   20

[1942]

Joining the Conversation: Critical Thinking and Writing

1. How would you characterize the "He" of the first line?
2. Frost does *not* say "a great buck powerfully appeared." Rather, he says, "As a great buck it powerfully appeared." What is going on here?

Design

I found a dimpled spider, fat and white,
On a white heal-all, holding up a moth
Like a white piece of rigid satin cloth—
Assorted characters of death and blight
Mixed ready to begin the morning right,   5
Like the ingredients of a witches' broth—
A snow-drop spider, a flower like a froth,
And dead wings carried like a paper kite.

What had that flower to do with being white,
The wayside blue and innocent heal-all?   10
What brought the kindred spider to that height,
Then steered the white moth thither in the night?
What but design of darkness to appall?—
If design govern in a thing so small.

[1936]

Joining the Conversation: Critical Thinking and Writing

1. Do you find the spider, as described in line 1, cute or disgusting? Why?
2. What is the effect of "If" in the last line?

3. The word *design* can mean "pattern" (as in "a pretty design"), or it can mean "intention," especially an evil intention (as in "He had designs on her"). Does Frost use the word in one sense or in both? Explain.
4. Is Frost offering an argument? If so, what is it?

Robert Frost on Poetry

The Figure a Poem Makes

Abstraction is an old story with the philosophers, but it has been like a new toy in the hands of the artists of our day. Why can't we have any one quality of poetry we choose by itself? We can have in thought. Then it will go hard if we can't in practice. Our lives for it.

Granted no one but a humanist much cares how sound a poem is if it is only *a* sound. The sound is the gold in the ore. Then we will have the sound out alone and dispense with the inessential. We do till we make the discovery that the object in writing poetry is to make all poems sound as different as possible from each other, and the resources for that of vowels, consonants, punctuation, syntax, words, sentences, meter are not enough. We need the help of context—meaning—subject matter. That is the greatest help towards variety. All that can be done with words is soon told. So also with meters—particularly in our language where there are virtually but two, strict iambic and loose iambic. The ancients with many were still poor if they depended on meters for all tune. It is painful to watch our sprung-rhythmists straining at the point of omitting one short from a foot for relief from monotony. The possibilities for tune from the dramatic tones of meaning struck across the rigidity of a limited meter are endless. And we are back in poetry as merely one more art of having something to say, sound or unsound. Probably better if sound, because deeper and from wider experience.

Then there is this wildness whereof it is spoken. Granted again that it has an equal claim with sound to being a poem's better half. If it is a wild tune, it is a poem. Our problem then is, as modern abstractionists, to have the wildness pure: to be wild with nothing to be wild about. We bring up as aberrationists, giving way to undirected associations and kicking ourselves from one chance suggestion to another in all directions as of a hot afternoon in the life of a grasshopper. Theme alone can steady us down. Just as the first mystery was how a poem could have a tune in such a straightness as meter, so the second mystery is how a poem can have wildness and at the same time a subject that shall be fulfilled.

It should be of the pleasure of a poem itself to tell how it can. The figure a poem makes. It begins in delight and ends in wisdom. The figure is the same as for love. No one can really hold that the ecstasy should be static and stand still in one place. It begins in delight, it inclines to the impulse, it assumes direction with the first line laid down, it runs a course of lucky events, and ends in a clarification of life—not necessarily a great clarification, such as sects and cults are founded on, but in a momentary stay against confusion. It has denouement. It has an outcome that though unforeseen was predestined from the first image of the original mood—and indeed from the very mood. It is but a trick poem and no poem at all if the best of it was thought of first and saved for the last. It finds its own name as it goes and discovers the best waiting for it in some final phrase at once wise and sad—the happy-sad blend of the drinking song.

5   No tears in the writer, no tears in the reader. No surprise for the writer, no surprise for the reader. For me the initial delight is in the surprise of remembering something I didn't know I knew. I am in a place, in a situation, as if I had materialized from cloud or risen out of the ground. There is a glad recognition of the long lost and the rest follows. Step by step the wonder of unexpected supply keeps growing. The impressions most useful to my purpose seem always those I was unaware of and so made no note of at the time when taken, and the conclusion is come to that like giants we are always hurling experience ahead of us to pave the future with against the day when we may want to strike a line of purpose across it for somewhere. The line will have the more charm for not being mechanically straight. We enjoy the straight crookedness of a good walking stick. Modern instruments of precision are being used to make things crooked as if by eye and hand in the old days.

I tell how there may be a better wildness of logic than of inconsequence. But the logic is backward, in retrospect, after the act. It must be more felt than seen ahead like prophecy. It must be a revelation, or a series of revelations, as much for the poet as for the reader. For it to be that there must have been the greatest freedom of the material to move about in it and to establish relations in it regardless of time and space, previous relation, and everything but affinity. We prate of freedom. We call our schools free because we are not free to stay away from them till we are sixteen years of age. I have given up my democratic prejudices and now willingly set the lower classes free to be completely taken care of by the upper classes. Political freedom is nothing to me. I bestow it right and left. All I would keep for myself is the freedom of my material—the condition of body and mind now and then to summons aptly from the vast chaos of all I have lived through.

Scholars and artists thrown together are often annoyed at the puzzle of where they differ. Both work from knowledge; but I suspect they differ most importantly in the way their knowledge is come by. Scholars get theirs with conscientious thoroughness along projected lines of logic; poets theirs cavalierly and it happens in and out of books. They stick to nothing deliberately, but let what will stick to them like burrs where they walk in the fields. No acquirement is on assignment, or even self-assignment. Knowledge of the second kind is much more available in the wild free ways of wit and art. A school boy may be defined as one who can tell you what he knows in the order in which he learned it. The artist must value himself as he snatches a thing from some previous order in time and space into a new order with not so much as a ligature clinging to it of the old place where it was organic.

More than once I should have lost my soul to radicalism if it had been the originality it was mistaken for by young converts. Originality and initiative are what I ask for my country. For myself the originality need be no more than the freshness of a poem run in the way I have described: from delight to wisdom. The figure is the same as for love. Like a piece of ice on a hot stove the poem must ride on its own melting. A poem may be worked over once it is in being, but may not be worried into being. Its most precious quality will remain its having run itself and carried away the poet with it. Read it a hundred times: it will forever keep its freshness as a metal keeps its fragrance. It can never lose its sense of a meaning that once unfolded by surprise as it went.

[1939]

Chapter Overview: Looking Backward/Looking Forward

1. Does it make sense for hunters and fishers to say that their activity shows they are lovers of nature? Whatever your personal view, write two essays, each of 500 words, one essay taking one side and the other essay taking the other side.
2. Do you "love nature"? What does it mean to say such a thing?
3. When someone says, "you should take more interest in the world around you," what does this person mean?
4. Could a person live a good life without paying any attention to nature?
5. A well-known contemporary writer who lives in New York City has said, "I hate nature." Please compose a letter of 500–750 words, in which you explain to this writer why she is wrong to feel this way.
6. Would you enjoy living on a farm and making your living from the crops you grew and the animals you raised and cared for?
7. Please describe your most rewarding experience of living or traveling in an unusual natural setting, here or abroad—a setting that you found very different from where you live most of the time.

CHAPTER 21

Journeys

SHORT VIEWS

Here are brief comments about journeys—inner and outer. Read them carefully, then write on one of the topics that appear after the last quotation.

If you don't know where you want to go, any road will take you there.
    Lewis Carroll

They change their clime, not their disposition, who run across the sea.
    Horace

Travel makes a wise man better, but a fool worse.
    Thomas Fuller

Why do you wonder that globe-trotting does not help you, seeing that you always take yourself with you? The reason which set you wandering is ever at your heels.
    Seneca, attributing the line to Socrates

Worth seeing, yes; but not worth going to see.
    Samuel Johnson

We shall not cease from exploration
And the end of all our exploring
Will be to arrive where we started
And know the place for the first time.
    T. S. Eliot

It is easier to sail many thousand miles through cold and storm and cannibals, in a government ship, with five hundred men and boys to assist one, than it is to explore the private sea, the Atlantic and Pacific Ocean of one's being alone. . . .
    Henry David Thoreau

I have traveled a good deal in Concord.
    Henry David Thoreau

*I am not much an advocate for traveling. Who are you that have no task
to keep you at home?*
    Ralph Waldo Emerson

*The whole object of travel is not to set foot on foreign land; it is at last to
set foot on one's own country as a foreign land.*
    G. K. Chesterton

Before taking steps the wise man knows the object and end of his journey.
    W. E. B. Du Bois

*Without stirring abroad
One can know the whole world;
Without looking out of the window
One can see the way of heaven
The further one goes
The less one knows*
        Lao-Tzu (translated by D. C. Lau)

*For my part, I travel not to go anywhere, but to go. I travel for travel's
sake. The great affair is to move; to feel the needs and hitches of our life
more nearly; to come down off this featherbed of civilization, and find
the globe granite underfoot and strewn with cutting flints.*
    Robert Louis Stevenson

*I always think that the most delightful thing about traveling is to always
be running into Americans and to always feel at home.*
    Anita Loos

*Travel spins us round in two ways at once: It shows us the sights and
values and issues that we might ordinarily ignore; but it also, and more
deeply, shows us all the parts of ourselves that might otherwise grow rusty.
For in traveling to a truly foreign place, we inevitably travel to moods
and states of mind and hidden inward passages that we'd otherwise
seldom have cause to visit. . . . Travel, then is a voyage into that famously
subjective zone, the imagination, and what the traveler brings back is—
and has to be—an ineffable compound of himself and the place, what's
really there and what's only in him.*
    Pico Iyer

Because it was there.
    George Mallory (answering the question why he wanted to climb
    Mt. Everest)

Like love, travel makes you innocent again.
    Diane Ackerman

Getting there is half the fun.
  Proverbial

All the way to Heaven is Heaven.
  St. Catherine of Siena

Joining the Conversation: Critical Thinking and Writing

1. Select a quotation that especially appeals to you, and make it the focus of an essay of about 500 words.
2. Take two of the passages—perhaps one that you especially like and one that you think is wrongheaded—and write a dialogue of about 500 words in which the two authors converse or argue. They may each try to convince the other, or they may find that to some degree they share views and they may then work out a statement that both can accept. If you do take the first position—that one writer is on the correct track but the other is utterly mistaken—try to be fair to the view that you think is mistaken. (As an experiment in critical thinking, imagine that you accept it, and make the best case for it that you possibly can.)
3. Emerson says, above, that he is "not much [of] an advocate for traveling." Imagine that you are an advocate *for* traveling, and that Emerson is your reader. List the key points of your argument. Then, working from this list, write an essay of two pages.
4. According to W. E. B. Du Bois, above, before a person travels, he or she should know "the object and end" of the journey. What is Du Bois saying? Do you agree? If Du Bois is right, then why is it said so often that a person should always travel "with an open mind"?
5. Once again, consider Du Bois's observation about travel. Have you ever traveled somewhere when you have known from the start "the object and end"? Please describe this experience. Have you ever traveled somewhere without knowing "the object and end"? Now, describe this experience.
6. Diane Ackerman suggests that travel restores a person's "innocence." What does this mean? Do you believe it? She also connects the experience of travel and love. What is her point? How would her point about travel change if the phrase "like love" were deleted?

ESSAYS

JOAN DIDION

Joan Didion, born in Sacramento in 1934 and educated at the University of California, Berkeley, worked for a while as a features editor at Vogue *but then turned to freelance writing. Among her novels are* Play It as It Lays *(1970),* A Book of Common Prayer *(1977), and* The Last Thing He Wanted *(1996). Collections of her magazine essays include* Slouching towards Bethlehem *(1968), which is the source of the piece we reprint,* The White Album *(1979), and* The Year of Magical Thinking, *which won the National Book Award in 2005.*

On Going Home

I am home for my daughter's first birthday. By "home" I do not mean the house in Los Angeles where my husband and I and the baby live, but the place where my family is, in the Central Valley of California. It is a vital although troublesome distinction. My husband likes my family but is uneasy in their house, because once there I fall into their ways, which are difficult, oblique, deliberately inarticulate, not my husband's ways. We live in dusty houses ("D-U-S-T," he once wrote with his finger on surfaces all over the house, but no one noticed it) filled with mementos quite without value to him (what could the Canton dessert plates mean to him? How could he have known about the assay scales, why should he care if he did know?), and we appear to talk exclusively about people we know who have been committed to mental hospitals, about people we know who have been booked on drunk-driving charges, and about property, particularly about property, land, price per acre and C-2 zoning and assessments, and freeway access. My brother does not understand my husband's inability to perceive the advantage in the rather common real-estate transaction known as "sale-leaseback," and my husband in turn does not understand why so many of the people he hears about in my father's house have recently been committed to mental hospitals or booked on drunk-driving charges. Nor does he understand that when we talk about sale-leasebacks and right-of-way condemnations we are talking in code about the things we like best, the yellow fields and the cottonwoods and the rivers rising and falling and the mountain roads closing when the heavy snow comes in. We miss each other's points, have another drink and regard the fire. My brother refers to my husband, in his presence, as "Joan's husband." Marriage is the classic betrayal.

Or perhaps it is not any more. Sometimes I think that those of us who are now in our thirties were born into the last generation to carry the burden of "home," to find in family life the source of all tension and drama. I had by all objective accounts a "normal" and a "happy" family situation, and yet I was almost thirty years old before I could talk to my family on the telephone without crying after I had hung up. We did not fight. Nothing was wrong. And yet some nameless anxiety colored the emotional charges between me and the place that I came from. The question of whether or not you could go home again was a very real part of the sentimental and largely literary baggage with which we left home in the fifties; I suspect that it is irrelevant to the children born of the fragmentation after World War II. A few weeks ago in a San Francisco bar I saw a pretty young girl on crystal take off her clothes and dance for the cash prize in an "amateur-topless" contest. There was no particular sense of moment about this, none of the effect of romantic degradation, of "dark journey," for which my generation strived so assiduously. What sense could that girl possibly make of, say, *Long Day's Journey into Night*?[1] Who is beside the point?

That I am trapped in this particular irrelevancy is never more apparent to me than when I am home. Paralyzed by the neurotic lassitude engendered by meeting one's past at every turn, around every corner, inside every cupboard, I go aimlessly from room to room. I decide to meet it head-on and clean out a drawer, and I spread the contents on the bed. A bathing suit I wore the summer I was seventeen. A letter of rejection from *The Nation*, an aerial photograph of the site for a shopping center my father did not build in 1954. Three teacups hand-painted with cabbage roses and signed "E.M.," my grandmother's initials. There is no final solution for letters of rejection from *The Nation* and teacups hand-painted in 1900. Nor is there any

---

[1]**Long Days Journey into Night** family drama (written 1941–42, published 1956) by Eugene O'Neill (1888-1953).

answer to snapshots of one's grandfather as a young man on skis, surveying around Donner Pass in the year 1910. I smooth out the snapshot and look into his face, and do and do not see my own. I close the drawer, and have another cup of coffee with my mother. We get along very well, veterans of a guerilla war we never understood.

Days pass. I see no one. I come to dread my husband's evening call, not only because he is full of news of what by now seems to me our remote life in Los Angeles, people he has seen, letters which require attention, but because he asks what I have been doing, suggests uneasily that I get out, drive to San Francisco or Berkeley. Instead I drive across the river to a family graveyard. It has been vandalized since my last visit and the monuments are broken, overturned in the dry grass. Because I once saw a rattlesnake in the grass I stay in the car and listen to a country-and-Western station. Later I drive with my father to a ranch he has in the foothills. The man who runs his cattle on it asks us to the roundup, a week from Sunday, and although I know I will be in Los Angeles I say, in the oblique way my family talks, that I will come. Once home I mention the broken monuments in the graveyard. My mother shrugs.

5   I go to visit my great-aunts. A few of them think now that I am my cousin, or their daughter who died young. We recall an anecdote about a relative last seen in 1948, and they ask if I still like living in New York City. I have lived in Los Angeles for three years, but I say that I do. The baby is offered a horehound drop, and I am slipped a dollar bill "to buy a treat." Questions trail off, answers are abandoned, the baby plays with the dust motes in a shaft of afternoon sun.

It is time for the baby's birthday party: a white cake, strawberry-marshmellow ice cream, a bottle of champagne saved from another party. In the evening, after she has gone to sleep, I kneel beside the crib and touch her face, where it is pressed against the slats, with mine. She is an open and trusting child, unprepared for and unaccustomed to the ambushes of family life, and perhaps it is just as well that I can offer her a little of that life. I would like to give her more. I would like to promise her that she will grow up with a sense of her cousins and of rivers and of her great-grandmother's teacups, would like to pledge her a picnic on a river with fried chicken and her hair uncombed, would like to give her *home* for her birthday, but we live differently now and I can promise her nothing like that. I give her a xylophone and a sundress from Madeira, and promise to tell her a funny story.

[1968]

Joining the Conversation: Critical Thinking and Writing

1. Didion reveals that members of her family are difficult, inarticulate, poor housekeepers, and so forth. Do you find these revelations about her family distasteful? Would you mind seeing in print similarly unflattering things you had written about your own family? How might such revelations be justified? Are they justified in this essay?

2. Summarize the point of the second paragraph. Do you find Didion's speculations about the difference between her generation and succeeding generations meaningful? Are they accurate for your generation?

3. Do you think that growing up necessarily involves estrangement from one's family? Support your thesis with reasons.

MONTESQUIEU (CHARLES DE SECONDAT, BARON DE LA BRÈDE ET DE MONTESQUIEU)

Montesquieu (1689–1755), French jurist, political philosopher, and writer, was born at La Brède, near Bordeaux. Today he is known chiefly for The Spirit of Laws *(1748), a study of three kinds of government (republic, monarchy, despotism), but he achieved fame in his own day with his* Persian Letters *(1721), letters supposedly written by two Persians (and their correspondents) traveling in Europe. Through the device of using narrators who are unsophisticated in European ways—innocent eyes, so to speak—he was able to satirize European social, political, religious, and literary customs. (If you are familiar with the fable of the emperor's clothes, in which a child sees that the emperor is naked, you are familiar with the device of using an innocent to tell the truth.)*

Persian Letters

Translated by J. Robert Loy

Letter 24: Rica to Ibben in Smyrna

We have been in Paris for a month and have been continually in motion. It takes much doing to find a place to live, to meet people to whom you are recommended, and to provide yourself with necessities all at the same time.

Paris is as large as Ispahan.[1] The houses here are so high that you would swear they were all inhabited by astrologers. You can readily understand that a city built up in the air, with six or seven houses built one on top of the other, is an extremely populous city, and that when everyone is down in the streets, there is great confusion.

Perhaps you will not believe this, but for the month I have been here, I have seen nobody walking. There are no people in the world who get so much out of their carcasses as the French: they run; they fly. The slow carriages of Asia, the regular pace of our camels, would make them swoon. As for myself, I am not built that way, and when I go walking, as I do often, without changing my pace, I sometimes fume and rage like a Christian. For, passing over the fact that I am splashed from head to foot, still I cannot forgive the elbowings in my ribs that I collect regularly and periodically. A man walking behind me, passes me and turns me half-around; then another, coming toward me from the opposite direction, briskly puts me back into the position where the first fellow hit me. I have barely made a hundred paces before I am more bruised than if I had gone ten leagues.

Do not expect me to be able just now to talk to you seriously about European usages and customs. I have only a faint idea of them myself and have barely had time to be amazed by them.

5   The King of France is the most powerful prince of Europe. Unlike his neighbor the King of Spain, he has no gold mines. Yet he possesses greater riches, for he draws from the vanity of his subjects a wealth more inexhaustible than mines. He has been known to undertake and wage great wars with no other funds than honorary titles to sell, and by reason of this miracle of human pride, his troops are paid, his fortresses armed, and his navies fitted out.

Moreover, this king is a great magician. He exercises his empire over the very minds of his subjects and makes them think as he likes. If he has only one million

---

[1]**Isphhan** major city in Persia (modern-day Iran).

crowns in his treasury and he needs two million, he has only to convince them that one crown equals two, and they believe him. If he is involved in a war that is difficult in the waging and finds himself short of money, he has only to put into their heads the notion that a slip of paper is money, and they are immediately convinced. He even goes so far as to make them believe that he can cure them of all manner of disease by touching them, so great is his strength and dominion over their minds. . . .

I shall continue to write to you, and I shall teach you things far removed from Persian character and spirit. It is certainly the same earth carrying both countries, but the men of this country where I am and those of the country where you are are quite different.

From Paris, the 4th of the Moon of Rebiab II, 1712

[1721]

Joining the Conversation: Critical Thinking and Writing

1. In the third paragraph Montesquieu's narrator says of his stay in Paris, "I have seen nobody walking. . . . [T]hey run, they fly." He is writing in the eighteenth century, so "they fly" is a figure of speech. (A European friend of ours, visiting Los Angeles, wrote to us that he was the only person walking; everyone else was jogging or roller-blading.) Write your own Persian letter to a fellow-Persian, reporting (as an innocent eye) on the strange behavior that surrounds you in the classroom, the streets, or (drawing on the newspapers and television) the nation. Or you may prefer to take on the persona of some other alleged innocent—for instance, a creature from Mars or an eighteenth-century person, who via a time machine, finds himself or herself in the twenty-first century.

2. Voltaire, Montesquieu's contemporary, said that *Persian Letters* was "a book which anybody might have written easily." Perhaps his thinking was along the lines of Samuel Johnson, who said of Jonathan Swift's *Gulliver's Travels* that once you thought of little people and big people, the rest was easy. If you have written your own Persian letter, evaluate Voltaire's comment.

STORIES

NATHANIEL HAWTHORNE

Nathaniel Hawthorne (1804–64) was born in Salem, Massachusetts, the son of a sea captain. Two of his ancestors were judges; one had persecuted Quakers, and another had served at the Salem witch trials. After graduating from Bowdoin College in Maine, Hawthorne went back to Salem in order to write in relative seclusion. In 1835 he published one of his best stories, "Young Goodman Brown."

From 1839 to 1841 Hawthorne worked in the Boston Customs House and then spent a few months as a member of a communal society, Brook Farm. In 1842 he married and settled with his wife in Concord, Massachusetts, where they became friendly with Emerson and Thoreau. From 1846 to 1849 he was a surveyor at the

Custom-House in Salem; from 1849 to 1850 he wrote The Scarlet Letter, *the book that made him famous. From 1853 to 1857 he served as American consul in Liverpool, England, a plum awarded him in exchange for writing a campaign biography of a former college classmate, President Franklin Pierce. In 1860, after living in England and Italy, he returned to the United States, settling in Concord, Massachusetts.*

In his stories and novels Hawthorne keeps returning to the Puritan past, study-ing guilt, sin, and isolation.

Young Goodman Brown

Young Goodman Brown came forth at sunset into the street at Salem village; but put his head back, after crossing the threshold, to exchange a parting kiss with his young wife. And Faith, as the wife was aptly named, thrust her own pretty head into the street, letting the wind play with the pink ribbons of her cap while she called to Goodman Brown.

"Dearest heart," whispered she, softly and rather sadly, when her lips were close to his ear, "prithee put off your journey until sunrise and sleep in your own bed to-night. A lone woman is troubled with such dreams and such thoughts that she's afeared of herself sometimes. Pray tarry with me this night, dear husband, of all nights in the year."

"My love and my Faith," replied young Goodman Brown, "of all nights in the year, this one night must I tarry away from thee. My journey, as thou callest it, forth and back again, must needs be done 'twixt now and sunrise. What, my sweet, pretty wife, dost thou doubt me already, and we but three months married?"

"Then God bless you!" said Faith, with the pink ribbons; "and may you find all well when you come back."

5   "Amen!" cried Goodman Brown. "Say thy prayers, dear Faith, and go to bed at dusk, and no harm will come to thee."

So they parted; and the young man pursued his way until, being about to turn the corner by the meeting-house, he looked back and saw the head of Faith still peeping after him with a melancholy air, in spite of her pink ribbons.

"Poor little Faith!" thought he, for his heart smote him. "What a wretch am I to leave her on such an errand! She talks of dreams, too. Methought as she spoke there was trouble in her face, as if a dream had warned her what work is to be done to-night. But no, no; 'twould kill her to think it. Well, she's a blessed angel on earth; and after this one night I'll cling to her skirts and follow her to heaven."

With this excellent resolve for the future, Goodman Brown felt himself justified in making more haste on his present evil purpose. He had taken a dreary road, darkened by all the gloomiest trees of the forest, which barely stood aside to let the narrow path creep through, and closed immediately behind. It was all as lonely as could be; and there is this peculiarity in such a solitude, that the traveller knows not who may be concealed by the innumerable trunks and the thick boughs overhead; so that with lonely footsteps he may yet be passing through an unseen multitude.

"There may be a devilish Indian behind every tree," said Goodman Brown to himself; and he glanced fearfully behind him as he added, "What if the devil him-self should be at my very elbow!"

10   His head being turned back, he passed a crook of the road, and, looking for-ward again, beheld the figure of a man, in grave and decent attire, seated at the foot of an old tree. He arose at Goodman Brown's approach and walked onward side by side with him.

"You are late, Goodman Brown," said he. "The clock of the Old South was striking as I came through Boston, and that is full fifteen minutes agone."

"Faith kept me back a while," replied the young man, with a tremor in his voice, caused by the sudden appearance of his companion, though not wholly unexpected.

It was now deep dusk in the forest, and deepest in that part of it where these two were journeying. As nearly as could be discerned, the second traveller was about fifty years old, apparently in the same rank of life as Goodman Brown, and bearing a considerable resemblance to him, though perhaps more in expression than features. Still they might have been taken for father and son. And yet, though the elder person was as simply clad as the younger, and as simple in manner too, he had an indescribable air of one who knew the world, and who would not have felt abashed at the governor's dinner table or in King William's court,[1] were it possible that his affairs should call him thither. But the only thing about him that could be fixed upon as remarkable was his staff, which bore the likeness of a great black snake, so curiously wrought that it might almost be seen to twist and wriggle itself like a living serpent. This, of course, must have been an ocular deception, assisted by the uncertain light.

"Come, Goodman Brown," cried his fellow-traveller, "this is a dull pace for the beginning of a journey. Take my staff, if you are so soon weary."

15 "Friend," said the other, exchanging his slow pace for a full stop, "having kept covenant by meeting thee here, it is my purpose now to return whence I came. I have scruples touching the matter thou wot'st of."

"Sayest thou so?" replied he of the serpent, smiling apart. "Let us walk on, nevertheless, reasoning as we go; and if I convince thee not thou shalt turn back. We are but a little way in the forest yet."

"Too far! too far!" exclaimed the goodman, unconsciously resuming his walk. "My father never went into the woods on such an errand, nor his father before him. We have been a race of honest men and good Christians since the days of the martyrs; and shall I be the first of the name of Brown that ever took this path and kept—"

"Such company, thou wouldst say," observed the elder person, interpreting his pause. "Well said, Goodman Brown! I have been as well acquainted with your family as with ever a one among the Puritans; and that's no trifle to say. I helped your grandfather, the constable, when he lashed the Quaker woman so smartly through the streets of Salem; and it was I that brought your father a pitch-pine knot, kindled at my own hearth, to set fire to an Indian village, in King Philip's war. They were my good friends, both; and many a pleasant walk have we had along this path, and returned merrily after midnight. I would fain be friends with you for their sake."

"If it be as thou sayest," replied Goodman Brown, "I marvel they never spoke of these matters; or, verily, I marvel not, seeing that the least rumor of the sort would have driven them from New England. We are a people of prayer, and good works to boot, and abide no such wickedness."

20 "Wickedness or not," said the traveller with the twisted staff, "I have a very general acquaintance here in New England. The deacons of many a church have drunk the communion wine with me; the selectmen of divers towns make me their chairman; and a majority of the Great and General Court are firm supporters of my interest. The governor and I, too—But these are state secrets."

"Can this be so?" cried Goodman Brown, with a stare of amazement at his undisturbed companion. "Howbeit, I have nothing to do with the governor and

---

[1]**King William's court** refers to the English king who ruled from 1688 to 1694.

council; they have their own ways, and are no rule for a simple husbandman like me. But, were I to go on with thee, how should I meet the eye of that good old man, our minister, at Salem village? Oh, his voice would make me tremble both Sabbath day and lecture day."

Thus far the elder traveller had listened with due gravity; but now burst into a fit of irrepressible mirth, shaking himself so violently that his snake-like staff actually seemed to wriggle in sympathy.

"Ha! ha! ha!" shouted he again and again; then composing himself, "Well, go on, Goodman Brown, go on; but, prithee, don't kill me with laughing."

"Well, then, to end the matter at once," said Goodman Brown, considerably nettled, "there is my wife, Faith. It would break her dear little heart; and I'd rather break my own."

25   "Nay, if that be the case," answered the other, "e'en go thy ways, Goodman Brown. I would not for twenty old women like the one hobbling before us that Faith should come to any harm."

As he spoke he pointed his staff at a female figure on the path, in whom Goodman Brown recognized a very pious and exemplary dame, who had taught him his catechism in youth, and was still his moral and spiritual adviser, jointly with the minister and Deacon Gookin.

"A marvel, truly, that Goody Cloyse should be so far in the wilderness at night-fall," said he. "But with your leave, friend, I shall take a cut through the woods until we have left this Christian woman behind. Being a stranger to you, she might ask whom I was consorting with and whither I was going."

"Be it so," said his fellow-traveller. "Betake you to the woods, and let me keep the path."

Accordingly the young man turned aside, but took care to watch his companion, who advanced softly along the road until he had come within a staff's length of the old dame. She, meanwhile, was making the best of her way, with singular speed for so aged a woman, and mumbling some indistinct words—a prayer, doubtless—as she went. The traveller put forth his staff and touched her withered neck with what seemed the serpent's tail.

30   "The devil!" screamed the pious old lady.

"Then Goody Cloyse knows her old friend?" observed the traveller, confronting her and leaning on his writhing stick.

"Ah, forsooth, and is it your worship indeed?" cried the good dame. "Yea, truly is it, and in the very image of my old gossip, Goodman Brown, the grandfather of the silly fellow that now is. But—would your worship believe it?—my broomstick hath strangely disappeared, stolen, as I suspect, by that unhanged witch, Goody Cory, and that, too, when I was all anointed with the juice of smallage, and cinquefoil, and wolf's bane—"

"Mingled with fine wheat and the fat of a new-born babe," said the shape of old Goodman Brown.

"Ah, your worship knows the recipe," cried the old lady, cackling aloud. "So, as I was saying, being all ready for the meeting, and no horse to ride on, I made up my mind to foot it; for they tell me there is a nice young man to be taken into communion to-night. But now your good worship will lend me your arm, and we shall be there in a twinkling."

35   "That can hardly be," answered her friend. "I may not spare you my arm, Goody Cloyse; but here is my staff, if you will."

So saying, he threw it down at her feet, where, perhaps, it assumed life, being one of the rods which its owner had formerly lent to the Egyptian magi. Of this fact, however, Goodman Brown could not take cognizance. He had cast up his eyes in astonishment, and, looking down again, beheld neither Goody Cloyse nor the serpentine staff, but his fellow-traveller alone, who waited for him as calmly as if nothing had happened.

"That old woman taught me my catechism," said the young man; and there was a world of meaning in this simple comment.

They continued to walk onward, while the elder traveller exhorted his companion to make good speed and persevere in the path, discoursing so aptly that his arguments seemed rather to spring up in the bosom of his auditor than to be suggested by himself. As they went, he plucked a branch of maple to serve for a walking stick, and began to strip it of the twigs and the little boughs, which were wet with evening dew. The moment his fingers touched them they became strangely withered and dried up as with a week's sunshine. Thus the pair proceeded, at a good free pace, until suddenly, in a gloomy hollow of the road, Goodman Brown sat himself down on the stump of a tree and refused to go any farther.

"Friend," said he, stubbornly, "my mind is made up. Not another step will I budge on this errand. What if a wretched old woman do choose to go to the devil when I thought she was going to heaven: is that any reason why I should quit my dear Faith and go after her?"

40 "You will think better of this by and by," said his acquaintance, composedly. "Sit here and rest yourself a while, and when you feel like moving again, there is my staff to help you along."

Without more words, he threw his companion the maple stick, and was as speedily out of sight as if he had vanished into the deepening gloom. The young man sat a few moments by the roadside, applauding himself greatly, and thinking with how clear a conscience he should meet the minister in his morning walk, nor shrink from the eye of good old Deacon Gookin. And what calm sleep would be his that very night, which was to have been spent so wickedly, but so purely and sweetly now, in the arms of Faith! Amidst these pleasant and praiseworthy meditations, Goodman Brown heard the tramp of horses along the road, and deemed it advisable to conceal himself within the verge of the forest, conscious of the guilty purpose that had brought him thither, though now so happily turned from it.

On came the hoof tramps and the voices of the riders, two grave old voices, conversing soberly as they drew near. These mingled sounds appeared to pass along the road, within a few yards of the young man's hiding-place; but, owing doubtless to the depth of the gloom at that particular spot, neither the travellers nor their steeds were visible. Though their figures brushed the small boughs by the wayside, it could not be seen that they intercepted, even for a moment, the faint gleam from the strip of bright sky athwart which they must have passed. Goodman Brown alternately crouched and stood on tiptoe, pulling aside the branches and thrusting forth his head as far as he durst without discerning so much as a shadow. It vexed him the more, because he could have sworn, were such a thing possible, that he recognized the voices of the minister and Deacon Gookin, jogging along quietly, as they were wont to do, when bound to some ordination or ecclesiastical council. While yet within hearing, one of the riders stopped to pluck a switch.

"Of the two, reverend sir," said the voice like the deacon's, "I had rather miss an ordination dinner than to-night's meeting. They tell me that some of our community are to be here from Falmouth and beyond, and others from Connecticut and Rhode Island, besides several of the Indian powwows, who, after their fashion, know almost as much deviltry as the best of us. Moreover, there is a goodly young woman to be taken into communion."

"Mighty well, Deacon Gookin!" replied the solemn old tones of the minister. "Spur up, or we shall be late. Nothing can be done, you know, until I get on the ground."

45   The hoofs clattered again; and the voices, talking so strangely in the empty air, passed on through the forest, where no church had ever been gathered or solitary Christian prayed. Whither, then, could these holy men be journeying so deep into the heathen wilderness? Young Goodman Brown caught hold of a tree for support, being ready to sink down on the ground, faint and overburdened with the heavy sickness of his heart. He looked up to the sky, doubting whether there really was a heaven above him. Yet there was the blue arch, and the stars brightening in it.

"With heaven above and Faith below, I will yet stand firm against the devil!" cried Goodman Brown.

While he still gazed upward into the deep arch of the firmament and had lifted his hands to pray, a cloud, though no wind was stirring, hurried across the zenith and hid the brightening stars. The blue sky was still visible, except directly overhead, where this black mass of cloud was sweeping swiftly northward. Aloft in the air, as if from the depths of the cloud, came a confused and doubtful sound of voices. Once the listener fancied that he could distinguish the accents of towns-people of his own, men and women, both pious and ungodly, many of whom he had met at the communion table, and had seen others rioting at the tavern. The next moment, so indistinct were the sounds, he doubted whether he had heard aught but the murmur of the old forest, whispering without a wind. Then came a stronger swell of those familiar tones, heard daily in the sunshine at Salem village, but never until now from a cloud of night. There was one voice, of a young wom-an, uttering lamentations, yet with an uncertain sorrow, and entreating for some favor, which, perhaps, it would grieve her to obtain; and all the unseen multitude, both saints and sinners, seemed to encourage her onward.

"Faith!" shouted Goodman Brown, in a voice of agony and desperation; and the echoes of the forest mocked him, crying, "Faith! Faith!" as if bewildered wretches were seeking her all through the wilderness.

The cry of grief, rage, and terror was yet piercing the night, when the unhappy husband held his breath for a response. There was a scream, drowned immedi-ately in a louder murmur of voices, fading into far-off laughter, as the dark cloud swept away, leaving the clear and silent sky above Goodman Brown. But some-thing fluttered lightly down through the air and caught on the branch of a tree. The young man seized it, and beheld a pink ribbon.

50   "My Faith is gone!" cried he, after one stupefied moment. "There is no good on earth; and sin is but a name. Come, devil; for to thee is this world given."

And, maddened with despair, so that he laughed loud and long, did Goodman Brown grasp his staff and set forth again, at such a rate that he seemed to fly along the forest path rather than to walk or run. The road grew wilder and drearier and more faintly traced, and vanished at length, leaving him in the heart of the dark wilderness, still rushing onward with the instinct that guides mortal man to evil. The whole forest was peopled with frightful sounds—the creaking of the trees, the howling of wild beasts, and the yell of Indians; while sometimes the wind tolled like a distant church bell, and sometimes gave a broad roar around the traveller, as if all Nature were laughing him to scorn. But he was himself the chief horror of the scene, and shrank not from its other horrors.

"Ha! ha! ha!" roared Goodman Brown when the wind laughed at him. "Let us hear which will laugh loudest. Think not to frighten me with your deviltry. Come witch, come wizard, come Indian powwow, come devil himself, and here comes Goodman Brown. You may as well fear him as he fear you."

In truth, all through the haunted forest there could be nothing more frightful than the figure of Goodman Brown. On he flew among the black pines, brandishing his staff with frenzied gestures, now giving vent to an inspiration of horrid blasphemy, and now shouting forth such laughter as set all the echoes of the forest laughing like demons around him. The fiend in his own shape is less hideous than when he rages in the breast of man. Thus sped the demoniac on his course, until, quivering among the trees, he saw a red light before him, as when the felled trunks and branches of a clearing have been set on fire, and throw up their lurid blaze against the sky, at the hour of midnight. He paused, in a lull of the tempest that had driven him onward, and heard the swell of what seemed a hymn, rolling solemnly from a distance with the weight of many voices. He knew the tune; it was a familiar one in the choir of the village meeting-house. The verse died heavily away, and was lengthened by a chorus, not of human voices, but of all the sounds of the benighted wilderness pealing in awful harmony together. Goodman Brown cried out, and his cry was lost to his own ear by its unison with the cry of the desert.

In the interval of silence he stole forward until the light glared full upon his eyes. At one extremity of an open space, hemmed in by the dark wall of the forest, arose a rock, bearing some rude, natural resemblance either to an altar or a pulpit, and surrounded by four blazing pines, their tops aflame, their stems untouched, like candles at an evening meeting. The mass of foliage that had overgrown the summit of the rock was all on fire, blazing high into the night and fitfully illuminating the whole field. Each pendent twig and leafy festoon was in a blaze. As the red light arose and fell, a numerous congregation alternately shone forth, then disappeared in shadow, and again grew, as it were, out of the darkness, peopling the heart of the solitary woods at once.

55   "A grave and dark-clad company," quoth Goodman Brown.

In truth they were such. Among them, quivering to and fro between gloom and splendor, appeared faces that would be seen next day at the council board of the province, and others which, Sabbath after Sabbath, looked devoutly heavenward, and benignantly over the crowded pews, from the holiest pulpits in the land. Some affirm that the lady of the governor was there. At least three were high dames well known to her, and wives of honored husbands, and widows, a great multitude, and ancient maidens, all of excellent repute, and fair young girls, who trembled lest their mothers should espy them. Either the sudden gleams of light flashing over the obscure field bedazzled Goodman Brown, or he recognized a score of the church members of Salem village famous for their especial sanctity. Good old Deacon Gookin had arrived, and waited at the skirts of that venerable saint, his revered pastor. But, irreverently consorting with these grave, reputable, and pious people, these elders of the church, these chaste dames and dewy virgins, there were men of dissolute lives and women of spotted fame, wretches given over to all mean and filthy vice, and suspected even of horrid crimes. It was strange to see that the good shrank not from the wicked, nor were the sinners abashed by the saints. Scattered also among their pale-faced enemies were the Indian priests, or powwows, who had often scared their native forest with more hideous incantations than any known to English witchcraft.

"But where is Faith?" thought Goodman Brown; and, as hope came into his heart, he trembled.

Another verse of the hymn arose, a slow and mournful strain, such as the pious love, but joined to words which expressed all that our nature can conceive of sin, and darkly hinted at far more. Unfathomable to mere mortals is the lore of fiends. Verse after verse was sung; and still the chorus of the desert swelled between like the deepest tone of a mighty organ; and with the final peal of that dreadful anthem there came a sound, as if the roaring wind, the rushing streams, the howling beasts, and every other voice of the unconcerted wilderness were mingling and according with the voice of guilty man in homage to the prince of all. The four blazing pines threw up a loftier flame, and obscurely discovered shapes and visages of horror on the smoke wreaths above the impious assembly. At the same moment the fire on the rock shot redly forth and formed a glowing arch above its base, where now appeared a figure. With reverence be it spoken, the figure bore no slight similitude, both in garb and manner, to some grave divine of the New England churches.

"Bring forth the converts!" cried a voice that echoed through the field and rolled into the forest.

60   At the word, Goodman Brown stepped forth from the shadow of the trees and approached the congregation, with whom he felt a loathful brotherhood by the sympathy of all that was wicked in his heart. He could have well-nigh sworn that the shape of his own dead father beckoned him to advance, looking downward from a smoke wreath, while a woman, with dim features of despair, threw out her hand to warn him back. Was it his mother? But he had no power to retreat one step, nor to resist, even in thought, when the minister and good old Deacon Gookin seized his arms and led him to the blazing rock. Thither came also the slender form of a veiled female, led between Goody Cloyse, that pious teacher of the catechism, and Martha Carrier, who had received the devil's promise to be queen of hell. A rampant hag was she. And there stood the proselytes beneath the canopy of fire.

"Welcome, my children," said the dark figure, "to the communion of your race. Ye have found thus young your nature and your destiny. My children, look behind you!"

They turned; and flashing forth, as it were, in a sheet of flame, the fiend worshippers were seen; the smile of welcome gleamed darkly on every visage.

"There," resumed the sable form, "are all whom ye have reverenced from youth. Ye deemed them holier than yourselves, and shrank from your own sin, contrasting it with their lives of righteousness and prayerful aspirations heavenward. Yet here are they all in my worshipping assembly. This night it shall be granted you to know their secret deeds: how hoary-bearded elders of the church have whispered wanton words to the young maids of their households; how many a woman, eager for widows' weeds, has given her husband a drink at bedtime and let him sleep his last sleep in her bosom; how beardless youths have made haste to inherit their fathers' wealth; and how fair damsels—blush not, sweet ones—have dug little graves in the garden, and bidden me, the sole guest, to an infant's funeral. By the sympathy of your human hearts for sin ye shall scent out all the places—whether in church, bedchamber, street, field, or forest—where crime has been committed, and shall exult to behold the whole earth one stain of guilt, one mighty blood spot. Far more than this. It shall be yours to penetrate, in every bosom, the deep mystery of sin, the fountain of all wicked arts, and which inexhaustibly supplies more evil impulses than human power—than my power at its utmost—can make manifest in deeds. And now, my children, look upon each other."

They did so; and, by the blaze of the hell-kindled torches, the wretched man beheld his Faith, and the wife her husband, trembling before that unhallowed altar.

65   "Lo, there ye stand, my children," said the figure, in a deep and solemn tone, almost sad with its despairing awfulness, as if his once angelic nature could yet mourn for our miserable race. "Depending upon one another's hearts, ye had still

hoped that virtue were not all a dream. Now are ye undeceived. Evil is the nature of mankind. Evil must be your only happiness. Welcome again, my children, to the communion of your race."

"Welcome," repeated the fiend worshippers, in one cry of despair and triumph.

And there they stood, the only pair, as it seemed, who were yet hesitating on the verge of wickedness in this dark world. A basin was hollowed, naturally, in the rock. Did it contain water, reddened by the lurid light? or was it blood? or, perchance, a liquid flame? Herein did the shape of evil dip his hand and prepare to lay the mark of baptism upon their foreheads, that they might be partakers of the mystery of sin, more conscious of the secret guilt of others, both in deed and thought, than they could now be of their own. The husband cast one look at his pale wife, and Faith at him. What polluted wretches would the next glance show them to each other, shuddering alike at what they disclosed and what they saw!

"Faith! Faith!" cried the husband, "look up to heaven, and resist the wicked one."

Whether Faith obeyed he knew not. Hardly had he spoken when he found himself amid calm night and solitude, listening to a roar of the wind which died heavily away through the forest. He staggered against the rock, and felt it chill and damp; while a hanging twig, that had been all on fire, besprinkled his cheek with the coldest dew.

70 The next morning young Goodman Brown came slowly into the street of Salem village, staring around him like a bewildered man. The good old minister was taking a walk along the graveyard to get an appetite for breakfast and meditate his sermon, and bestowed a blessing, as he passed, on Goodman Brown. He shrank from the venerable saint as if to avoid an anathema. Old Deacon Gookin was at domestic worship, and the holy words of his prayer were heard through the open window. "What God doth the wizard pray to?" quoth Goodman Brown. Goody Cloyse, that excellent old Christian, stood in the early sunshine at her own lattice, catechizing a little girl who had brought her a pint of morning's milk. Goodman Brown snatched away the child as from the grasp of the fiend himself. Turning the corner by the meeting-house, he spied the head of Faith, with the pink ribbons, gazing anxiously forth, and bursting into such joy at sight of him that she skipped along the street and almost kissed her husband before the whole village. But Goodman Brown looked sternly and sadly into her face, and passed on without a greeting.

Had Goodman Brown fallen asleep in the forest and only dreamed a wild dream of a witch-meeting?

Be it so if you will; but alas! it was a dream of evil omen for young Goodman Brown. A stern, a sad, a darkly meditative, a distrustful, if not a desperate man did he become from the night of that fearful dream. On the Sabbath day, when the congregation were singing a holy psalm, he could not listen because an anthem of sin rushed loudly upon his ear and drowned all the blessed strain. When the minister spoke from the pulpit with power and fervid eloquence, and, with his hand on the open Bible, of the sacred truths of our religion, and of saint-like lives and triumphant deaths, and of future bliss or misery unutterable, then did Goodman Brown turn pale, dreading lest the roof should thunder down upon the gray blasphemer and his hearers. Often, awaking suddenly at midnight, he shrank from the bosom of Faith; and at morning or eventide, when the family knelt down at prayer, he scowled and muttered to himself, and gazed sternly at his wife, and turned away. And when he had lived long, and was borne to his grave a hoary corpse, followed by Faith, an aged woman, and children and grandchildren, a goodly procession, besides neighbors not a few, they carved no hopeful verse upon his tombstone, for his dying hour was gloom.

[1835]

Joining the Conversation: Critical Thinking and Writing

1. What do you think Hawthorne gains (or loses) by the last sentence?
2. Evaluate the view that when young Goodman Brown enters the dark forest he is really entering his own evil mind. Why, by the way, does he go into the forest at night? (Hawthorne gives no explicit reason, but you may want to offer a conjecture.)
3. In a sentence or two summarize the plot, and then in another sentence or two state the theme of the story. (On theme, see pages 357–58.)
4. If you have undergone a religious experience, write an essay discussing your condition before, during, and after the experience.

MyLiteratureLab® *For additional resources for "Young Goodman Brown," log in to* www.myliteraturelab.com *where you will find a Longman Lecture, a Comprehension Quiz, and Short Evaluation Exercises, as well as an About the Author, Bibliography, Links, and Critical Overview for Hawthorne (under Student Resources).*

EUDORA WELTY

Eudora Welty (1909–2001) was born in Jackson, Mississippi. Although she earned a bachelor's degree at the University of Wisconsin, and she spent a year studying advertising in New York City at the Columbia University Graduate School of Business, she lived almost all of her life in Jackson.
In the preface to her Collected Stories *she says:*

> *I have been told, both in approval and in accusation, that I seem to love all my characters. What I do in writing of any character is to try to enter into the mind, heart and skin of a human being who is not myself.*

Whether this happens to be a man or a woman, old or young, with skin black or white, the primary challenge lies in making the jump itself. It is the act of a writer's imagination that I set most high.

In addition to writing stories and novels, Welty wrote a book about fiction, The Eye of the Story *(1977), and a memoir,* One Writer's Beginnings *(1984).*

A Worn Path

It was December—a bright frozen day in the early morning. Far out in the country there was an old Negro woman with her head tied in a red rag, coming along a path through the pinewoods. Her name was Phoenix Jackson. She was very old and small and she walked slowly in the dark pine shadows, moving a little from side to side in her steps, with the balanced heaviness and lightness of a pendulum in a grandfather clock. She carried a thin, small cane made from an umbrella, and with this she kept tapping the frozen earth in front of her. This made a grave and persistent noise in the still air, that seemed meditative like the chirping of a solitary little bird.

She wore a dark striped dress reaching down to her shoe tops, and an equally long apron of bleached sugar sacks, with a full pocket: all neat and tidy, but every time she took a step she might have fallen over her shoelaces, which dragged from her unlaced shoes. She looked straight ahead. Her eyes were blue with age. Her skin had a pattern all its own of numberless branching wrinkles and as though a whole little tree stood in the middle of her forehead, but a golden color ran underneath, and the two knobs of her cheeks were illuminated by a yellow burning under the dark. Under the red rag her hair came down on her neck in the frailest of ringlets, still black, and with an odor like copper.

Now and then there was a quivering in the thicket. Old Phoenix said, "Out of my way, all you foxes, owls, beetles, jack rabbits, coons, and wild animals! . . . Keep out from under these feet, little bob-whites. . . . Keep the big wild hogs out of my path. Don't let none of those come running my direction. I got a long way." Under her small black-freckled hand her cane, limber as a buggy whip, would switch at the brush as if to rouse up any hiding things.

On she went. The woods were deep and still. The sun made the pine needles almost too bright to look at, up where the wind rocked. The cones dropped as light as feathers. Down in the hollow was the mourning dove—it was not too late for him.

5   The path ran up a hill. "Seem like there is chains about my feet, time I get this far," she said, in the voice of argument old people keep to use with themselves. "Something always take a hold of me on this hill—pleads I should stay."

After she got to the top she turned and gave a full, severe look behind her where she had come. "Up through pines," she said at length. "Now down through oaks."

Her eyes opened their widest, and she started down gently. But before she got to the bottom of the hill a bush caught her dress.

Her fingers were busy and intent, but her skirts were full and long, so that before she could pull them free in one place they were caught in another. It was not possible to allow the dress to tear. "I in the thorny bush," she said. "Thorns, you doing your appointed work. Never want to let folks pass—no sir. Old eyes thought you was a pretty little *green* bush."

Finally, trembling all over, she stood free, and after a moment dared to stoop for her cane.

10   "Sun so high!" she cried, leaning back and looking, while the thick tears went over her eyes. "The time getting all gone here."

At the foot of this hill was a place where a log was laid across the creek.

"Now comes the trial," said Phoenix.

Putting her right foot out, she mounted the log and shut her eyes. Lifting her skirt, levelling her cane fiercely before her, like a festival figure in some parade, she began to march across. Then she opened her eyes and she was safe on the other side.

"I wasn't as old as I thought," she said.

15   But she sat down to rest. She spread her skirts on the bank around her and folded her hands over her knees. Up above her was a tree in a pearly cloud of mistletoe. She did not dare to close her eyes, and when a little boy brought her a little plate with a slice of marble-cake on it she spoke to him. "That would be acceptable," she said. But when she went to take it there was just her own hand in the air.

So she left that tree, and had to go through a barbed-wire fence. There she had to creep and crawl, spreading her knees and stretching her fingers like a baby trying to climb the steps. But she talked loudly to herself: she could not let her dress be torn now, so late in the day, and she could not pay for having her arm or leg sawed off if she got caught fast where she was.

At last she was safe through the fence and risen up out in the clearing. Big dead trees, like black men with one arm, were standing in the purple stalks of the withered cotton field. There sat a buzzard.

"Who you watching?"

In the furrow she made her way along.

20 "Glad this not the season for bulls," she said, looking sideways, "and the good Lord made his snakes to curl up and sleep in the winter. A pleasure I don't see no two-headed snake coming around that tree, where it come once. It took a while to get by him, back in the summer."

She passed through the old cotton and went into a field of dead corn. It whispered and shook and was taller than her head. "Through the maze now," she said, for there was no path.

Then there was something tall, black, and skinny there, moving before her.

At first she took it for a man. It could have been a man dancing in the field. But she stood still and listened, and it did not make a sound. It was as silent as a ghost.

"Ghost," she said sharply, "who be you the ghost of? For I have heard of nary death close by."

25 But there was no answer—only the ragged dancing in the wind.

She shut her eyes, reached out her hand, and touched a sleeve. She found a coat and inside that an emptiness, cold as ice.

"You scarecrow," she said. Her face lighted. "I ought to be shut up for good," she said with laughter. "My senses is gone, I too old. I the oldest people I ever know. Dance, old scarecrow," she said, "while I dancing with you."

She kicked her foot over the furrow, and with mouth drawn down, shook her head once or twice in a little strutting way. Some husks blew down and whirled in streamers about her skirts.

Then she went on, parting her way from side to side with the cane, through the whispering field. At last she came to the end, to a wagon track where the silver grass blew between the red ruts. The quail were walking around like pullets, seeming all dainty and unseen.

30 "Walk pretty," she said. "This the easy place. This the easy going."

She followed the track, swaying through the quiet bare fields, through the little strings of trees silver in their dead leaves, past cabins silver from weather, with the doors and windows boarded shut, all like old women under a spell sitting there. "I walking in their sleep," she said, nodding her head vigorously.

In a ravine she went where a spring was silently flowing through a hollow log. Old Phoenix bent and drank. "Sweet-gum makes the water sweet," she said, and drank more. "Nobody know who made this well, for it was here when I was born."

The track crossed a swampy part where the moss hung as white as lace from every limb. "Sleep on, alligators, and blow your bubbles." Then the track went into the road.

Deep, deep the road went down between the high green-colored banks. Overhead the live-oaks met, and it was as dark as a cave.

35 A black dog with a lolling tongue came up out of the weeds by the ditch. She was meditating, and not ready, and when he came at her she only hit him a little with her cane. Over she went in the ditch, like a little puff of milk-weed.

Down there, her senses drifted away. A dream visited her, and she reached her hand up, but nothing reached down and gave her a pull. So she lay there and presently went to talking. "Old woman," she said to herself, "that black dog come up out of the weeds to stall you off, and now there he sitting on his fine tail, smiling at you."

A white man finally came along and found her—a hunter, a young man, with his dog on a chain.

"Well, Granny!" he laughed. "What are you doing there?"

"Lying on my back like a June-bug waiting to be turned over, mister," she said, reaching up her hand.

40   He lifted her up, gave her a swing in the air, and set her down. "Anything broken, Granny?"

"No sir, them old dead weeds is springy enough," said Phoenix, when she had got her breath. "I thank you for your trouble."

"Where do you live, Granny?" he asked, while the two dogs were growling at each other.

"Away back yonder, sir, behind the ridge. You can't even see it from here."

"On your way home?"

45   "No, sir, I going to town."

"Why, that's too far! That's as far as I walk when I come out myself, and I get something for my trouble." He patted the stuffed bag he carried, and there hung down a little closed claw. It was one of the bob-whites, with its beak hooked bitterly to show it was dead. "Now you go on home, Granny!"

"I bound to go to town, mister," said Phoenix. "The time come around."

He gave another laugh, filling the whole landscape. "I know you old colored people! Wouldn't miss going to town to see Santa Claus!"

But something held Old Phoenix very still. The deep lines in her face went into a fierce and different radiation. Without warning, she had seen with her own eyes a flashing nickel fall out of the man's pocket onto the ground.

50   "How old are you, Granny?" he was saying.

"There is no telling, mister," she said, "no telling."

Then she gave a little cry and clapped her hands and said, "Git on away from here, dog! Look! Look at that dog!" She laughed as if in admiration. "He ain't scared of nobody. He a big black dog." She whispered, "Sic him!"

"Watch me get rid of that cur," said the man. "Sic him, Pete! Sic him!"

Phoenix heard the dogs fighting, and heard the man running and throwing sticks. She even heard a gunshot. But she was slowly bending forward by that time, further and further forward, the lids stretched down over her eyes, as if she were doing this in her sleep. Her chin was lowered almost to her knees. The yellow palm of her hand came out from the fold of her apron. Her fingers slid down and along the ground under the piece of money with the grace and care they would have in lifting an egg from under a sitting hen. Then she slowly straightened up, she stood erect, and the nickel was in her apron pocket. A bird flew by. Her lips moved. "God watching me the whole time. I come to stealing."

55   The man came back, and his own dog panted about them. "Well, I scared him off that time," he said, and then he laughed and lifted his gun and pointed it at Phoenix.

She stood straight and faced him.

"Doesn't the gun scare you?" he said, still pointing it.

"No, sir, I seen plenty go off closer by, in my day, and for less than what I done," she said, holding utterly still.

He smiled, and shouldered the gun. "Well, Granny," he said, "you must be a hundred years old, and scared of nothing. I'd give you a dime if I had any money with me. But you take my advice and stay home, and nothing will happen to you."

60   "I bound to go on my way, mister," said Phoenix. She inclined her head in the red rag. Then they went in different directions, but she could hear the gun shooting again and again over the hill.

She walked on. The shadows hung from the oak trees to the road like curtains. Then she smelled wood-smoke, and smelled the river, and she saw a steeple and the cabins on their steep steps. Dozens of little black children whirled around her. There ahead was Natchez shining. Bells were ringing. She walked on.

In the paved city it was Christmas time. There were red and green electric lights strung and crisscrossed everywhere, and all turned on in the daytime. Old Phoenix would have been lost if she had not distrusted her eyesight and depended on her feet to know where to take her.

She paused quietly on the sidewalk where people were passing by. A lady came along in the crowd, carrying an armful of red-, green-, and silver-wrapped presents; she gave off perfume like the red roses in hot summer, and Phoenix stopped her.

"Please, missy, will you lace up my shoe?" She held up her foot.

65   "What do you want, Grandma?"

"See my shoe," said Phoenix. "Do all right for out in the country, but wouldn't look right to go in a big building."

"Stand still then, Grandma," said the lady. She put her packages down on the sidewalk beside her and laced and tied both shoes tightly.

"Can't lace 'em with a cane," said Phoenix. "Thank you, missy. I doesn't mind asking a nice lady to tie up my shoe, when I gets out on the street."

Moving slowly and from side to side, she went into the big building and into a tower of steps, where she walked up and around and around until her feet knew to stop.

70   She entered a door, and there she saw nailed up on the wall the document that had been stamped with the gold seal and framed in the gold frame, which matched the dream that was hung up in her head.

"Here I be," she said. There was a fixed and ceremonial stiffness over her body.

"A charity case, I suppose," said an attendant who sat at the desk before her.

But Phoenix only looked above her head. There was sweat on her face, the wrinkles in her skin shone like a bright net.

"Speak up, Grandma," the woman said. "What's your name? We must have your history, you know. Have you been here before? What seems to be the trouble with you?"

75   Old Phoenix only gave a twitch to her face as if a fly were bothering her.

"Are you deaf?" cried the attendant.

But then the nurse came in.

"Oh, that's just old Aunt Phoenix," she said. "She doesn't come for herself—she has a little grandson. She makes these trips just as regular as clockwork. She lives away back off the old Natchez Trace." She bent down. "Well, Aunt Phoenix, why don't you just take a seat? We won't keep you standing after your long trip." She pointed.

The old woman sat down, bolt upright in the chair.

80   "Now, how is the boy?" asked the nurse.

Old Phoenix did not speak.

"I said, how is the boy?"

But Phoenix only waited and stared straight ahead, her face very solemn and withdrawn into rigidity.

"Is his throat any better?" asked the nurse. "Aunt Phoenix, don't you hear me? Is your grandson's throat any better since the last time you came for the medicine?"

85　With her hands on her knees, the old woman waited, silent, erect and motionless, just as if she were in armor.

"You mustn't take up our time this way, Aunt Phoenix," the nurse said. "Tell us quickly about your grandson, and get it over. He isn't dead, is he?"

At last there came a flicker and then a flame of comprehension across her face, and she spoke.

"My grandson. It was my memory had left me. There I sat and forgot why I made my long trip."

"Forgot?" The nurse frowned. "After you came so far?"

90　Then Phoenix was like an old woman begging a dignified forgiveness for waking up frightened in the night. "I never did go to school, I was too old at the Surrender," she said in a soft voice. "I'm an old woman without an education. It was my memory fail me. My little grandson, he is just the same, and I forgot it in the coming."

"Throat never heals, does it?" said the nurse, speaking in a loud, sure voice to Old Phoenix. By now she had a card with something written on it, a little list. "Yes. Swallowed lye. When was it—January—two-three years ago—"

Phoenix spoke unasked now. "No, missy, he not dead, he just the same. Every little while his throat begin to close up again, and he not able to swallow. He not get his breath. He not able to help himself. So the time come around, and I go on another trip for the soothing medicine."

"All right. The doctor said as long as you came to get it, you could have it," said the nurse. "But it's an obstinate case."

"My little grandson, he sit up there in the house all wrapped up, waiting by himself," Phoenix went on. "We is the only two left in the world. He suffer and it don't seem to put him back at all. He got a sweet look. He going to last. He wear a little patch quilt and peep out holding his mouth open like a little bird. I remembers so plain now. I not going to forget him again, no, the whole enduring time. I could tell him from all the others in creation."

95　"All right." The nurse was trying to hush her now. She brought her a bottle of medicine. "Charity," she said, making a check mark in a book.

Old Phoenix held the bottle close to her eyes and then carefully put it into her pocket.

"I thank you," she said.

"It's Christmas time, Grandma," said the attendant. "Could I give you a few pennies out of my purse?"

"Five pennies is a nickel," said Phoenix stiffly.

100　"Here's a nickel," said the attendant.

Phoenix rose carefully and held out her hand. She received the nickel and then fished the other nickel out of her pocket and laid it beside the new one. She stared at her palm closely, with her head on one side.

Then she gave a tap with her cane on the floor.

"This is what come to me to do," she said. "I going to the store and buy my child a little windmill they sells, made out of paper. He going to find it hard to believe there such a thing in the world. I'll march myself back where he waiting, holding it straight up in his hand."

She lifted her free hand, gave a little nod, turned round, and walked out of the doctor's office. Then her slow step began on the stairs, going down.

[1941]

Joining the Conversation: Critical Thinking and Writing

1. If you do not know the legend of the phoenix, look it up in a dictionary or, better, in an encyclopedia. Then carefully reread the story, to learn whether the story in any way connects with the legend.
2. What do you think of the hunter?
3. What would be lost if the episode (with all of its dialogue) of Phoenix falling into the ditch and being helped out of it by the hunter were omitted?
4. Is Christmas a particularly appropriate time in which to set the story? Why or why not?
5. In an argument of no more than one page, explain the significance of the story's title.

TONI CADE BAMBARA

Toni Cade Bambara (1939–95) was born in New York City and grew up in various African American neighborhoods of the city. After studying at the University of Florence in Italy and at City College in New York, where she received a master's degree, she worked for a while as a case investigator for the New York State Welfare Department. Later she directed a recreation program for hospital patients. After her literary reputation became established, she spent most of her time writing, though she also served as writer in residence at Spelman College in Atlanta.

The Lesson

Back in the days when everyone was old and stupid or young and foolish and me and Sugar were the only ones just right, this lady moved on our block with nappy hair and proper speech and no makeup. And quite naturally we laughed at her, laughed the way we did at the junk man who went about his business like he was some big-time president and his sorry-ass horse his secretary. And we kinda hated her too, hated the way we did the winos who cluttered up our parks and pissed on our handball walls and stank up our hallways and stairs so you couldn't halfway play hide-and-seek without a goddamn gas mask. Miss Moore was her name. The only woman on the block with no first name. And she was black as hell, cept for her feet, which were fish-white and spooky. And she was always planning these boring-ass things for us to do, us being my cousin, mostly, who lived on the block cause we all moved North the same time and to the same apartment then spread out gradual to breathe. And our parents would yank our heads into some kinda shape and crisp up our clothes so we'd be presentable for travel with Miss Moore, who always looked like she was going to church, though she never did. Which is just one of the things the grownups talked about when they talked behind her back like a dog. But when she came calling with some sachet she'd sewed up or some gingerbread she'd made or some book, why then they'd all be too embarrassed to turn her down and we'd get handed over all spruced up. She'd been to college and said it was only right that she should take responsibility for the young ones' education, and she not even related by marriage or blood. So they'd go for it. Specially Aunt Gretchen. She was the main gofer in the family. You got some ole dumb shit foolishness you want somebody to go for, you send for Aunt Gretchen. She been screwed into the go-along for so long, it's a blood-deep natural thing with her. Which is how she got saddled with me and Sugar and Junior in the first place while our mothers were in a la-de-da apartment up the block having a good ole time.

So this one day Miss Moore rounds us all up at the mailbox and it's puredee hot and she's knockin herself out about arithmetic. And school suppose to let up in summer I heard, but she don't never let up. And the starch in my pinafore scratching the shit outta me and I'm really hating this nappy-head bitch and her goddamn college degree. I'd much rather go to the pool or to the show where it's cool. So me and Sugar leaning on the mailbox being surly, which is a Miss Moore word. And Flyboy checking out what everybody brought for lunch. And Fat Butt already wasting his peanut-butter-and-jelly sandwich like the pig he is. And Junebug punchin on Q.T.'s arm for potato chips. And Rosie Giraffe shifting from one hip to the other waiting for somebody to step on her foot or ask her if she from Georgia so she can kick ass, preferably Mercedes'. And Miss Moore asking us do we know what money is, like we a bunch of retards. I mean real money, she say, like it's only poker chips or monopoly papers we lay on the grocer. So right away I'm tired of this and say so. And would much rather snatch Sugar and go to the Sunset and terrorize the West Indian kids and take their hair ribbons and their money too. And Miss Moore files that remark away for next week's lesson on brotherhood, I can tell. And finally I say we oughta get to the subway cause it's cooler and besides we might meet some cute boys. Sugar done swiped her mama's lipstick, so we ready.

So we heading down the street and she's boring us silly about what things cost and what our parents make and how much goes for rent and how money ain't divided up right in this country. And then she gets to the part about we all poor and live in the slums, which I don't feature. And I'm ready to speak on that, but she steps out in the street and hails two cabs just like that. Then she hustles half the crew in with her and hands me a five-dollar bill and tells me to calculate 10 percent tip for the driver. And we're off. Me and Sugar and Junebug and Fly-boy hangin out the window and hollering to everybody, putting lipstick on each other cause Flyboy a faggot anyway, and making farts with our sweaty armpits. But I'm mostly trying to figure how to spend this money. But they all fascinated with the meter ticking and Junebug starts laying bets to how much it'll read when Flyboy can't hold his breath no more. Then Sugar lays bets as to how much it'll be when we get there. So I'm stuck. Don't nobody want to go for my plan, which is to jump out at the next light and run off to the first bar-b-que we can find. Then the driver tells us to get the hell out cause we there already. And the meter reads eighty-five cents. And I'm stalling to figure out the tip and Sugar say give him a dime. And I decide he don't need it as bad as I do, so later for him. But then he tries to take off with Junebug foot still in the door so we talk about his mama something ferocious. Then we check out that we on Fifth Avenue and everybody dressed up in stockings. One lady in a fur coat, hot as it is. White folks crazy.

"This is the place," Miss Moore say, presenting it to us in the voice she uses at the museum. "Let's look in the windows before we go in."

5   "Can we steal?" Sugar asks very serious like she's getting the ground rules squared away before she plays. "I beg your pardon," say Miss Moore, and we fall out. So she leads us around the windows of the toy store and me and Sugar

screamin, "This is mine, that's mine, I gotta have that, that was made for me, I was born for that," till Big Butt drowns us out.

"Hey, I'm goin to buy that there."

"That there? You don't even know what it is, stupid."

"I do so," he say punchin on Rosie Giraffe. "It's a microscope."

"Whatcha gonna do with a microscope, fool?"

10   "Look at things."

"Like what, Ronald?" ask Miss Moore. And Big Butt ain't got the first notion. So here go Miss Moore gabbing about the thousands of bacteria in a drop of water and the somethinorother in a speck of blood and the million and one living things in the air around us is invisible to the naked eye. And what she say that for? Junebug go to town on that "naked" and we rolling. Then Miss Moore ask what it cost. So we all jam into the window smudgin it up and the price tag say $300. So then she ask how long'd take for Big Butt and Junebug to save up their allowances. "Too long," I say. "Yeh," adds Sugar, "outgrown it by that time." And Miss Moore say no, you never outgrow learning instruments. "Why, even medical students and interns and," blah, blah, blah. And we ready to choke Big Butt for bringing it up in the first damn place.

"This here costs four hundred eighty dollars," say Rosie Giraffe. So we pile up all over her to see what she pointin out. My eyes tell me it's a chunk of glass cracked with something heavy, and different-color inks dripped into the splits, then the whole thing put into a oven or something. But for $480 it don't make sense.

"That's a paperweight made of semi-precious stones fused together under tremendous pressure," she explains slowly, and her hands doing the mining and all the factory work.

"So what's a paperweight?" asks Rosie Giraffe.

15   "To weigh paper with, dumbbell," say Flyboy, the wise man from the East.

"Not exactly," say Miss Moore, which is what she say when you warm or way off too. "It's to weigh paper down so it won't scatter and make your desk untidy." So right away me and Sugar curtsy to each other and then to Mercedes who is more the tidy type.

"We don't keep paper on top of the desk in my class," say Junebug, figuring Miss Moore crazy or lyin one.

"At home, then," she say. "Don't you have a calendar and a pencil case and a blotter and a letter-opener on your desk at home where you do your homework?" And she know damn well what our homes look like cause she nosys around in them every chance she gets.

"I don't even have a desk," say Junebug. "Do we?"

20   "No. And I don't get no homework neither," says Big Butt.

"And I don't even have a home," say Flyboy like he do at school to keep the white folks off his back and sorry for him. Send this poor kid to camp posters, is his specialty.

"I do," says Mercedes. "I have a box of stationery on my desk and a picture of my cat. My godmother bought the stationery and the desk. There's a big rose on each sheet and the envelopes smell like roses."

"Who wants to know about your smelly-ass stationery," say Rosie Giraffe fore I can get my two cents in.

"It's important to have a work area all your own so that . . ."

25   "Will you look at this sailboat, please," say Flyboy, cuttin her off and pointin to the thing like it was his. So once again we tumble all over each other to gaze at this magnificent thing in the toy store which is just big enough to maybe sail two

kittens across the pond if you strap them to the posts tight. We all start reciting the price tag like we in assembly. "Handcrafted sailboat of fiberglass at one thousand one hundred ninety-five dollars."

"Unbelievable," I hear myself say and am really stunned. I read it again for myself just in case the group recitation put me in a trance. Same thing. For some reason this pisses me off. We look at Miss Moore and she lookin at us, waiting for I dunno what.

"Who'd pay all that when you can buy a sailboat set for a quarter at Pop's, a tube of glue for a dime, and a ball of string for eight cents? It must have a motor and a whole lot else besides," I say. "My sailboat cost me about fifty cents."

"But will it take water?" say Mercedes with her smart ass.

"Took mine to Alley Pond Park once," say Flyboy. "String broke. Lost it. Pity."

30   "Sailed mine in Central Park and it keeled over and sank. Had to ask my father for another dollar."

"And you got the strap," laugh Big Butt. "The jerk didn't even have a string on it. My old man wailed on his behind."

Little Q.T. was staring hard at the sailboat and you could see he wanted it bad. But he too little and somebody'd just take it from him. So what the hell. "This boat for kids, Miss Moore?"

"Parents silly to buy something like that just to get all broke up," say Rosie Giraffe.

"That much money it should last forever," I figure.

35   "My father'd buy it for me if I wanted it."

"Your father, my ass," say Rosie Giraffe getting a chance to finally push Mercedes.

"Must be rich people shop here," say Q.T.

"You are a very bright boy," say Flyboy. "What was your first clue?" And he rap him on the head with the back of his knuckles, since Q.T. the only one he could get away with. Though Q.T. liable to come up behind you years later and get his licks in when you half expect it.

"What I want to know is," I says to Miss Moore though I never talk to her, I wouldn't give the bitch that satisfaction, "is how much a real boat costs? I figure a thousand'd get you a yacht any day."

40   "Why don't you check that out," she says, "and report back to the group?" Which really pains my ass. If you gonna mess up a perfectly good swim day least you could do is have some answers. "Let's go in," she say like she got something up her sleeve. Only she don't lead the way. So me and Sugar turn the corner to where the entrance is, but when we get there I kinda hang back. Not that I'm scared, what's there to be afraid of, just a toy store. But I feel funny, shame. But what I got to be shamed about? Got as much right to go in as anybody. But somehow I can't seem to get hold of the door, so I step away for Sugar to lead. But she hangs back too. And I look at her and she looks at me and this is ridiculous. I mean, damn, I have never ever been shy about doing nothing or going nowhere. But then Mercedes steps up and then Rosie Giraffe and Big Butt crowd in behind and shove, and next thing we all stuffed into the doorway with only Mercedes squeezing past us, smoothing out her jumper and walking right down the aisle. Then the rest of us tumble in like a glued-together jigsaw done all wrong. And people lookin at us. And it's like the time me and Sugar crashed into the Catholic church on a dare. But once we got in there and everything so hushed and holy and the candles and the bowin and the handkerchiefs on all the drooping heads, I just couldn't go through with the plan. Which was for me to run up to the altar and do a tap dance while Sugar played the nose flute and messed around in the holy water.

And Sugar kept givin me the elbow. Then later teased me so bad I tied her up in the shower and turned it on and locked her in. And she'd be there till this day if Aunt Gretchen hadn't finally figured I was lyin about the boarder takin a shower.

Same thing in the store. We all walkin on tiptoe and hardly touchin the games and puzzles and things. And I watched Miss Moore who is steady watchin us like she waitin for a sign. Like Mama Drewery watches the sky and sniffs the air and takes note of just how much slant is in the bird formation. Then me and Sugar bump smack into each other, so busy gazing at the toys, 'specially the sailboat. But we don't laugh and go into our fat-lady bumpstomach routine. We just stare at that price tag. Then Sugar run a finger over the whole boat. And I'm jealous and want to hit her. Maybe not her, but I sure want to punch somebody in the mouth.

"Whatcha bring us here for, Miss Moore?"

"You sound angry, Sylvia. Are you mad about something?" Givin me one of them grins like she tellin a grown-up joke that never turns out to be funny. And she's lookin very closely at me like maybe she plannin to do my portrait from memory. I'm mad, but I won't give her that satisfaction. So I slouch around the store bein very bored and say, "Let's go."

Me and Sugar at the back of the train watchin the tracks whizzin by large then small then gettin gobbled up in the dark. I'm thinkin about this tricky toy I saw in the store. A clown that somersaults on a bar then does chin-ups just cause you yank lightly at his leg. Cost $35. I could see me askin my mother for a $35 birthday clown. "You wanna who that costs what?" she'd say, cocking her head to the side to get a better view of the hole in my head. Thirty-five dollars could buy new bunk beds for Junior and Gretchen's boy. Thirty-five dollars and the whole household could go visit Granddaddy Nelson in the country. Thirty-five dollars would pay for the rent and the piano bill too. Who are these people that spend that much for performing clowns and $1000 for toy sailboats? What kinda work they do and how they live and how come we ain't in on it? Where we are is who we are, Miss Moore always pointin out. But it don't necessarily have to be that way, she always adds then waits for somebody to say that poor people have to wake up and demand their share of the pie and don't none of us know what kind of pie she talkin about in the first damn place. But she ain't so smart cause I still got her four dollars from the taxi and she sure ain't gettin it. Messin up my day with this shit. Sugar nudges me in my pocket and winks.

45   Miss Moore lines us up in front of the mailbox where we started from, seem like years ago, and I got a headache for thinkin so hard. And we lean all over each other so we can hold up under the draggy-ass lecture she always finishes us off with at the end before we thank her for borin us to tears. But she just looks at us like she readin tea leaves. Finally she say, "Well, what do you think of F. A. O. Schwarz?"

Rosie Giraffe mumbles, "White folks crazy."

"I'd like to go there again when I get my birthday money," says Mercedes, and we shove her out the pack so she has to lean on the mailbox by herself.

"I'd like a shower. Tiring day," say Flyboy.

Then Sugar surprises me by sayin, "You know, Miss Moore, I don't think all of us here put together eat in a year what that sailboat costs." And Miss Moore lights up like somebody goosed her. "And?" she say, urging Sugar on. Only I'm standin on her foot so she don't continue.

50   "Imagine for a minute what kind of society it is in which some people can spend on a toy what it would cost to feed a family of six or seven. What do you think?"

"I think," say Sugar pushing me off her feet like she never done before, cause I whip her ass in a minute, "that this is not much of a democracy if you ask me. Equal chance to pursue happiness means an equal crack at the dough, don't it?" Miss Moore is besides herself and I am disgusted with Sugar's treachery. So I stand on her foot one more time to see if she'll shove me. She shuts up, and Miss Moore looks at me, sorrowfully I'm thinkin. And somethin weird is goin on, I can feel it in my chest.

"Anybody else learn anything today?" lookin dead at me. I walk away and Sugar has to run to catch up and don't even seem to notice when I shrug her arm off my shoulder.

"Well, we got four dollars anyway," she says.

"Uh hunh."

55   "We could go to Hascombs and get half a chocolate layer and then go to the Sunset and still have plenty money for potato chips and ice cream sodas."

"Uh hunh."

"Race you to Hascombs," she say.

We start down the block and she gets ahead which is O.K. by me cause I'm going to the West End and then over to the Drive to think this day through. She can run if she want to and even run faster. But ain't nobody gonna beat me at nuthin.

[1972]

Joining the Conversation: Critical Thinking and Writing

1. What is the point of Miss Moore's lesson? Why does Sylvia resist it?
2. Describe the relationship between Sugar and Sylvia. What is Sugar's function in the story?
3. What does the last line of the story suggest?
4. In a paragraph or two, characterize the narrator. Do not summarize the story—assume that your reader is familiar with it—but support your characterization by references to episodes in the story and perhaps by a few brief quotations.

MyLiteratureLab® *For additional resources for "The Lesson," log in to* www.myliteraturelab.com *where you will find a Longman Lecture and Comprehension Quiz, as well as an About the Author, Bibliography, Links, and Critical Overview for Bambara (under Student Resources).*

AMY HEMPEL

Amy Hempel was born in Chicago in 1951. She was educated in California and at Columbia University, and now lives in New York City. She has taught in the writing programs at Bennington College in Vermont and at the New School in New York City.

Today Will Be a Quiet Day

"I think it's the other way around," the boy said. "I think if the quake hit now the *bridge* would collapse and the *ramps* would be left."

He looked at his sister with satisfaction.

"You are just trying to scare your sister," the father said. "You know that is not true."

"No, really," the boy insisted, "and I heard birds in the middle of the night. Isn't that a warning?"

5   The girl gave her brother a toxic look and ate a handful of Raisinets. The three of them were stalled in traffic on the Golden Gate Bridge.

That morning, before waking his children, the father had canceled their music lessons and decided to make a day of it. He wanted to know how they were, is all. Just—how were they. He thought his kids were as self-contained as one of those dogs you sometimes see carrying home its own leash. But you could read things wrong.

Could you ever.

The boy had a friend who jumped from a floor of Langley Porter. The friend had been there for two weeks, mostly playing Ping-Pong. All the friend said the day the boy visited and lost every game was never play Ping-Pong with a mental patient because it's all we do and we'll kill you. That night the friend had cut the red belt he wore in two and left the other half on his bed. That was this time last year when the boy was twelve years old.

You think you're safe, the father thought, but it's thinking you're invisible because you closed your eyes.

10   This day they were headed for Petaluma–the chicken, egg, and arm-wrestling capital of the nation—for lunch. The father had offered to take them to the men's arm-wrestling semifinals. But it was said that arm wrestling wasn't so interesting since the new safety precautions, that hardly anyone broke an arm or a wrist anymore. The best anyone could hope to see would be dislocation, so they said they would rather go to Pete's. Pete's was a gas station turned into a place to eat. The hamburgers there were named after cars, and the gas pumps in front still pumped gas.

"Can I have one?" the boy asked, meaning the Raisinets.

"No," his sister said.

"Can I have two?"

"Neither of you should be eating candy before lunch," the father said. He said it with the good sport of a father who enjoys his kids and gets a kick our of saying Dad things.

15   "You mean dinner," said the girl. "It will be dinner before we get to Pete's."

Only the northbound lanes were stopped. Southbound traffic flashed past at the normal speed.

"Check it out," the boy said from the back seat. "Did you see the bumper sticker on that Porsche? 'If you don't like the way I drive, stay off the sidewalk.'"

He spoke directly to his sister. "I've just solved my Christmas shopping."

"I got the highest score in my class in Driver's Ed," she said.

20   "I thought I would let your sister drive home today," the father said.

From the back seat came sirens, screams for help, and then a dirge.

The girl spoke to her father in a voice rich with complicity. "Don't people make you want to give up?"

"Don't the two of you know any jokes? I haven't laughed all day," the father said.

"Did I tell you the guillotine joke?" the girl said.

25   "He hasn't laughed all day, so you must've," her brother said.

The girl gave her brother a look you could iron clothes with. Then her gaze dropped down. "Oh-oh," she said, "Johnny's out of jail."

Her brother zipped his pants back up. He said, "Tell the joke."

"Two Frenchmen and a Belgian were about to be beheaded," the girl began. "The first Frenchman was led to the block and blindfolded. The executioner let the blade go. But it stopped a quarter inch above the Frenchman's neck. So he was allowed to go free, and ran off shouting 'C'est un miracle! 'C'est un miracle!'"

"It's a miracle," the father said.

30   "Then the second Frenchman was led to the block, and same thing—the blade stopped just before cutting off his head. So *he* got to go free, and ran off shouting, 'C'est un miracle!'

"Finally the Belgian was led to the block. But before they could blindfold him, he looked up, pointed to the top of the guillotine, and cried, 'Voila la difficulté!'"

She doubled over.

"Maybe *I* would be wetting *my* pants if I knew what that meant," the boy said.

"You can't explain after the punch line," the girl said, "and have it still be funny."

35   "There's the problem," said the father.

The waitress handed out menus to the party of three seated in the corner booth of what used to be the lube bay. She told them the specialty of the day was Moroccan chicken.

"That's what I want," the boy said. "Morerotten chicken."

But he changed his order to a Studeburger and fries after his father and sister had ordered.

"So," the father said, "who misses music lessons?"

40   "I'm serious about what I asked you last week," the girl said. "About switching to piano? My teacher says a real flutist only breathes with the stomach, and I can't."

"The real reason she wants to change," said the boy, "is her waist will get two inches bigger when she learns to stomach-breathe. That's what *else* her teacher said."

The boy buttered a piece of sourdough bread and flipped a chunk of cold butter onto his sister's sleeve.

"Jeezo-beezo," the girl said, "why don't they skip the knife and fork and just set his place with a slingshot!"

"Who will ever adopt you if you don't mind your manners?" the father said. "Maybe we could try a little quiet today."

45   "You sound like your tombstone," the girl said. "Remember what you wanted it to say?"

Her brother joined in with his mouth full: "Today will be a quiet day."

"Because it never is with us around," the boy said.

"You guys," said the father.

The waitress brought plates. The father passed sugar to the boy and salt to the girl without being asked. He watched the girl shake out salt onto the fries.

50   "If I had a sore throat, I would gargle with those," he said.

"Looks like she's trying to melt a driveway," the boy offered.

The father watched his children eat. They ate fast. They called it Hoovering. He finished while they sucked at straws in empty drinks.

"Funny," he said thoughtfully, "I'm not hungry anymore."

Every meal ended this way. It was his benediction, one of the Dad things they expected him to say.

55   "That reminds me," the girl said. "Did you feed Rocky before we left?"

"Uh-uh," her brother said. "I fed him yesterday."

"*I* fed him yesterday!" the girl said.

"Okay, we'll compromise," the boy said. "We won't feed the cat today."

"I'd say you are out of bounds on that one," the father said.

60   He meant you could not tease her about animals. Once, during dinner, that cat ran into the dining room shot from guns. He ran around the table at top speed, then spun out on the parquet floor into a leg of the table. He fell over onto his side and made short coughing sounds. "Isn't he smart?" the girl had crooned, kneeling beside him. "He knows he's hurt."

For years, her father had to say that the animals seen on shoulders of roads were napping.

"He never would have not fed Homer," she said to her father.

"Homer was a dog," the boy said. "If I forgot to feed him, he could just go into the hills and bite a deer."

"Or a Campfire Girl selling mints at the front door," their father reminded them.

65   "Homer," the girl sighed. "I hope he likes chasing sheep on that ranch in the mountains."

The boy looked at her, incredulous.

"You *believed* that? You actually *believed* that?"

In her head, a clumsy magician yanked the cloth and the dishes all crashed to the floor. She took air into her lungs until they filled, and then she filled her stomach, too.

"I thought she knew," the boy said.

70   The dog was five years ago.

"The girl's parents insisted," the father said. "It's the law in California."

"Then I hate California," she said. "I hate its guts."

The boy said he would wait for them in the car, and left the table.

"What would help?" the father asked.

75   "For Homer to be alive," she said.

"What would help?"

"Nothing."

"Help."

She pinched a trail of salt on her plate.

80   "A ride," she said. "I'll drive."

The girl started the car and screamed, "Goddammit."

With the power off, the boy had tuned in the Spanish station. Mariachis exploded on ignition.

"Dammit isn't God's last name," the boy said, quoting another bumper sticker.

"Don't people make you want to give up?" the father said.

85   "No talking," the girl said to the rearview mirror, and put the car in gear.

She drove for hours. Through groves of eucalyptus with their damp peeling bark, past acacia bushes with yellow flowers pulsing off their stems. She cut over to the coast route and the stony gray-green tones of Inverness.

"What you'd call scenic," the boy tried.

Otherwise they were quiet.

No one said anything else until the sky started to close, and then it was the boy again, asking shouldn't they be going home.

90   "No, no," the father said, and made a show of looking out the window, up at the sky and back at his watch. "No," he said, "keep driving—it's getting earlier."

But the sky spilled rain, and the girl headed south toward the bridge. She turned on the headlights and the dashboard lit up green. She read off the odometer on the way home: "Twenty-six thousand, three hundred eighty three and eight-tenths miles."

"Today?" the boy said.

The boy got to Rocky first. "Let's play the cat," he said, and carried the Siamese to the upright piano. He sat on the bench holding the cat in his lap and pressed its paws to the keys. Rocky played "Born Free." He tried to twist away.

"Come on, Rocky, ten more minutes and we'll break."

95   "Give him to me," the girl said.

She puckered up and gave the cat a five-lipper.

"Bring the Rock upstairs," the father called. "Bring sleeping bags, too."

Pretty soon three sleeping bags formed a triangle in the master bedroom. The father was the hypotenuse. The girl asked him to brush out her hair, which he did while the boy ate a tangerine, peeling it up close to his face, inhaling the mist. Then he held each segment to the light to find seeds. In his lap, cat paws fluttered like dreaming eyes.

"What are you thinking?" the father asked.

100   "Me?" the girl said. "Fifty-seven T-bird, white with red interior, convertible. I drive it to Texas and wear skirts with rick-rack. I'm changing my name to Ruby," she said, "or else Easy."

The father considered her dream of a checkered future.

"Early ripe, early rot," he warned.

A wet wind slammed the window in its warped sash, and the boy jumped.

"I hate rain," he said. "I hate its guts."

105   The father got up and closed the window tighter against the storm. "It's a real frog-choker," he said.

In darkness, lying still, it was no less camp-like than if they had been under the stars, singing to a stone-ringed fire burned down to embers.

They had already said good-night some minutes earlier when the boy and girl heard their father's voice in the dark.

"Kids, I just remembered—I have some good news and some bad news. Which do you want first?"

It was his daughter who spoke. "Let's get it over with," she said. "Let's get the bad news over with."

110   The father smiled. They are all right, he decided. My kids are as right as this rain. He smiled at the exact spots he knew their heads were turned to his, and doubted he would ever feel—not better, but *more* than he did now.

"I lied," he said. "There is no bad news."

[1986]

Joining the Conversation: Critical Thinking and Writing

1. The story begins with characters in a car on a bridge, talking about the possibility of the bridge's collapsing during an earthquake. A few lines later we read about a boy who committed suicide. Moreover, we are told that the father somehow fears that he may not really know his children. When you began reading the story, did these ominous touches seem to you to be foreshadowing? That is, did they suggest

to you that the story might end unhappily? Or, on the contrary, did you somehow feel, despite these threats, that the story would not end unhappily? Explain.

2. At the beginning of the story, the father says that the boy is trying to "scare" the sister. How would you characterize the relationship between the two children?

3. The mother is never mentioned. Should we have been told if she is dead, or if she has abandoned the family, or whatever? Why do you hold the view that you hold?

4. We are told in paragraph 14 that the father "gets a kick out of saying Dad things" to his children. Try your hand at inventing some "Dad things" that he might have said in this story.

5. The point of the joke about the guillotine is that it doesn't pay to point out the source of difficulties. How does this joke help you to make sense of the story?

JAMES JOYCE

James Joyce (1882–1941) was born into a middle-class family in Dublin, Ireland. His father drank, became increasingly irresponsible and unemployable, and the family sank in the social order. Still, Joyce received a strong classical education at excellent Jesuit schools and at University College, Dublin, where he studied modern languages. In 1902, at the age of twenty, he left Ireland so that he might spend the rest of his life writing about life in Ireland. ("The shortest way to Tara," he said, "is via Holyhead," i.e., the shortest way to the heart of Ireland is to take ship away.) In Trieste, Zurich, and Paris he supported his family in a variety of ways, sometimes teaching English in a Berlitz language school. His fifteen stories, collected under the title of Dubliners, *were written between 1904 and 1907, but he could not get them published until 1914. (The story we present here, "Eveline," comes from* Dubliners.) *Next came a highly autobiographical novel,* A Portrait of the Artist as a Young Man *(1916).* Ulysses *(1922), a complex novel covering eighteen hours in Dublin, was for some years banned by the United States Post Office, though few if any readers today find it offensive. Joyce spent most of the rest of his life working on* Finnegans Wake *(1939).*

Nine years before he succeeded in getting Dubliners *published, Joyce described the manuscript in these terms:*

> *My intention was to write a chapter of the moral history of my country and I chose Dublin for the scene because that city seemed to me the centre of paralysis. . . . I have written it for the most part in a style of scrupulous meanness and with the conviction that he is a very bold man who dares to alter in the presentment, still more to deform, whatever he has seen and heard.*

Eveline

She sat at the window watching the evening invade the avenue. Her head was leaned against the window curtains and in her nostrils was the odor of dusty cretonne. She was tired.

Few people passed. The man out of the last house passed on his way home; she heard his footsteps clacking along the concrete pavement and afterwards crunching on the cinder path before the new red houses. One time there used to be a field there in which they used to play every evening with other people's children. Then a man from Belfast[1] bought the field and built houses in it—not like

---

[1] **a man from Belfast** i.e., a Protestant.

their little brown houses but bright brick houses with shining roofs. The children of the avenue used to play together in that field—the Devines, the Waters, the Dunns, little Keogh the cripple, she and her brothers and sisters. Ernest, however, never played: he was too grown up. Her father used often to hunt them in out of the field with his blackthorn stick; but usually little Keogh used to keep *nix*[2] and call out when he saw her father coming. Still they seemed to have been rather happy then. Her father was not so bad then; and besides, her mother was alive. That was a long time ago; she and her brothers and sisters were all grown up; her mother was dead. Tizzie Dunn was dead, too, and the Waters had gone back to England. Everything changes. Now she was going to go away like the others, to leave her home.

Home! She looked around the room, reviewing all its familiar objects which she had dusted once a week for so many years, wondering where on earth all the dust came from. Perhaps she would never see again those familiar objects from which she had never dreamed of being divided. And yet during all those years she had never found out the name of the priest whose yellowing photograph hung on the wall above the broken harmonium beside the colored print of the promises made to Blessed Margaret Mary Alacoque. He had been a school friend of her father. Whenever he showed the photograph to a visitor her father used to pass it with a casual word:

"He is in Melbourne now."

5   She had consented to go away, to leave her home. Was that wise? She tried to weigh each side of the question. In her home anyway she had shelter and food; she had those whom she had known all her life about her. Of course she had to work hard both in the house and at business. What would they say of her in the Stores when they found out that she had run away with a fellow? Say she was a fool, perhaps; and her place would be filled up by advertisement. Miss Gavan would be glad. She had always had an edge on her, especially whenever there were people listening.

"Miss Hill, don't you see these ladies are waiting?"

"Look lively, Miss Hill, please."

She would not cry many tears at leaving the Stores.

But in her new home, in a distant unknown country, it would not be like that. Then she would be married—she, Eveline. People would treat her with respect then. She would not be treated as her mother had been. Even now, though she was over nineteen, she sometimes felt herself in danger of her father's violence. She knew it was that that had given her the palpitations. When they were growing up he had never gone for her, like he used to go for Harry and Ernest, because she was a girl; but latterly he had begun to threaten her and say what he would do to her only for her dead mother's sake. And now she had nobody to protect her. Ernest was dead and Harry, who was in the church decorating business, was nearly always down somewhere in the country. Besides, the invariable squabble for money on Saturday nights had begun to weary her unspeakably. She always gave her entire wages—seven shillings—and Harry always sent up what he could but the trouble was to get any money from her father. He said she used to squander the money, that she had no head, that he wasn't going to give her his hard-earned money to throw about the streets, and much more, for he was usually fairly bad of a Saturday night. In the end he would give her the money and ask her had she any intention of buying Sunday dinner. Then she had to rush out as quickly as she could and do her marketing, holding her black leather purse tightly in her hand as she elbowed her way through the crowds and returning home late under her load of provisions. She had hard work to keep the house together and to see that the

---

[2]**to keep *nix*** to stand guard.

two young children, who had been left to her charge went to school regularly and got their meals regularly. It was hard work—a hard life—but now that she was about to leave it she did not find it a wholly undesirable life.

10   She was about to explore another life with Frank. Frank was very kind, manly, open-hearted. She was to go away with him by the night-boat to be his wife and to live with him in Buenos Aires where he had a home waiting for her. How well she remembered the first time she had seen him; he was lodging in a house on the main road where she used to visit. It seemed a few weeks ago. He was standing at the gate, his peaked cap pushed back on his head and his hair tumbled forward over a face of bronze. Then they had come to know each other. He used to meet her outside the Stores every evening and see her home. He took her to see *The Bohemian Girl*[3] and she felt elated as she sat in an unaccustomed part of the theater with him. He was awfully fond of music and sang a little. People knew that they were courting and, when he sang about the lass that loves a sailor, she always felt pleasantly confused. He used to call her Poppens out of fun. First of all it had been an excitement for her to have a fellow and then she had begun to like him. He had tales of distant countries. He had started as a deck boy at a pound a month on a ship of the Allan Line going out to Canada. He told her the names of the ships he had been on and the names of the different services. He had sailed through the Straits of Magellan and he told her stories of the terrible Patagonians. He had fallen on his feet in Buenos Aires, he said, and had come over to the old country just for a holiday. Of course, her father had found out the affair and had forbidden her to have anything to say to him.

"I know these sailor chaps," he said.

One day he had quarreled with Frank and after that she had to meet her lover secretly.

The evening deepened in the avenue. The white of two letters in her lap grew indistinct. One was to Harry; the other was to her father. Ernest had been her favorite but she liked Harry too. Her father was becoming old lately, she noticed; he would miss her. Sometimes he could be very nice. Not long before, when she had been laid up for a day, he had read her out a ghost story and made toast for her at the fire. Another day, when their mother was alive, they had all gone for a picnic to the Hill of Howth. She remembered her father putting on her mother's bonnet to make the children laugh.

Her time was running out but she continued to sit by the window, leaning her head against the window curtain, inhaling the odor of dusty cretonne. Down far in the avenue she could hear a street organ playing. She knew the air. Strange that it should come that very night to remind her of the promise to her mother, her promise to keep the home together as long as she could. She remembered the last night of her mother's illness; she was again in the close dark room at the other side of the hall and outside she heard a melancholy air of Italy. The organ player had been ordered to go away and given sixpence. She remembered her father strutting back into the sickroom saying:

15   "Damned Italians! coming over here!"

As she mused the pitiful vision of her mother's life laid its spell on the very quick of her being—that life of commonplace sacrifices closing in final craziness. She trembled as she heard again her mother's voice saying constantly with foolish insistence:

"Derevaun Seraun! Derevaun Seraun!"[4]

---

[3]**The Bohemian Girl** an opera composed by Michael William Balfe with a libretto by Alfred Bunn, first performed in Dublin in 1844.
[4]**Derevaun Seraun** possibly a garbled version of Gaelic for "The end of pleasure is pain," but perhaps meaningless syllables uttered by the dying woman.

She stood up in a sudden impulse of terror. Escape! She must escape! Frank would save her. He would give her life, perhaps love, too. But she wanted to live. Why should she be unhappy? She had a right to happiness. Frank would take her in his arms, fold her in his arms. He would save her.

She stood among the swaying crowd in the station at the North Wall. He held her hand and she knew that he was speaking to her, saying something about the passage over and over again. The station was full of soldiers with brown baggages. Through the wide doors of the sheds she caught a glimpse of the black mass of the boat, lying in beside the quay wall, with illumined portholes. She answered nothing. She felt her cheek pale and cold and, out of a maze of distress, she prayed to God to direct her, to show her what was her duty. The boat blew a long mournful whistle into the mist. If she went, tomorrow she would be on the sea with Frank, steaming towards Buenos Aires. Their passage had been booked. Could she still draw back after all he had done for her? Her distress awoke a nausea in her body and she kept moving her lips in silent, fervent prayer.

20 A bell clanged upon her heart. She felt him seize her hand:

"Come!"

All the seas of the world tumbled about her heart. He was drawing her into them: he would drown her. She gripped with both hands at the iron railing.

"Come!"

No! No! No! It was impossible. Her hands clutched the iron in frenzy. Amid the seas she sent a cry of anguish!

25 "Eveline! Evvy!"

He rushed beyond the barrier and called to her to follow. He was shouted at to go on but he still called to her. She set her white face to him, passive, like a helpless animal. Her eyes gave him no sign of love or farewell or recognition.

[1914]

Joining the Conversation: Critical Thinking and Writing

1. Why, in your opinion, does Eveline not join Frank?
2. What do you think are Eveline's virtues and what are her weaknesses? How sympathetic are you to Eveline?
3. In paragraph 18 Eveline tells herself that "She had a right to happiness." Do we have a right to happiness? If so, where does this right come from? Does it make sense for us to speak of such a right?
4. You are a friend of Eveline's. Write her a letter (500 words) in which you urge her to leave—or to stay.

POEMS

JOHN KEATS

John Keats (1795–1821), son of a London stable keeper, was taken out of school when he was fifteen and apprenticed to a surgeon and apothecary. In 1816 he was licensed to practice as an apothecary-surgeon, but he almost immediately abandoned medicine and decided to make a career as a poet. His progress was amazing;

*he quickly moved from routine verse to major accomplishments, publishing books of
poems in 1817, 1818, and 1820, before dying of tuberculosis at the age of twenty-five.*

On First Looking into Chapman's Homer°

Much have I traveled in the realms of gold,
And many goodly states and kingdoms seen;
Round many western islands have I been
Which bards in fealty to Apollo° hold.
Oft of one wide expanse have I been told   5
That deep-browed Homer ruled as his demesne;°
Yet did I never breathe its pure serene°
Till I heard Chapman speak out loud and bold;
Then felt I like some watcher of the skies
When a new planet swims into his ken;   10
Or like stout Cortez when with eagle eyes
He stared at the Pacific—and all his men
Looked at each other with a wild surmise—
Silent, upon a peak in Darien.

[1816]

°**Chapman's Homer** George Chapman (1559–1634?), Shakespeare's contemporary, is chiefly
known for his translations (from the Greek) of Homer's *Odyssey* and *Iliad*. In lines 11–14 Keats
mistakenly says that Cortés was the first European to see the Pacific, from the heights of Darien,
in Panama. In fact, Balboa was the first.   **4 Apollo** god of poetry.   **6 demesne** domain.
7 serene open space.

Joining the Conversation: Critical Thinking and Writing

1. In line 1, what do you think "realms of gold" stands for? Chapman was an
   Elizabethan; how does this fact add relevance to the metaphor in the first line?
2. Does line 9 introduce a totally new idea, or can you somehow connect it to the
   opening metaphor?
3. Do you like this poem? As specifically as you can, please explain why or why not.

PERCY BYSSHE SHELLEY

*Percy Bysshe Shelley (1792–1822) was born in Sussex in England, the son of a prosper-
ous country squire. Educated at Eton, he went on to Oxford but was expelled for having written a pamphlet supporting a belief in atheism. Like John Keats he was a member
of the second generation of English romantic poets. (The first generation included
Wordsworth and Coleridge.) And like Keats, Shelley died young; he was drowned during a violent storm off the western coast of Italy while sailing with a friend.*

Ozymandias

I met a traveler from an antique land
Who said: Two vast and trunkless legs of stone
Stand in the desert . . . Near them, on the sand,
Half sunk, a shattered visage lies, whose frown,
And wrinkled lip, and sneer of cold command,   5

Tell that its sculptor well those passions read
Which yet survive, stamped on these lifeless things,
The hand that mocked them, and the heart that fed:
And on the pedestal these words appear:
"My name is Ozymandias, king of kings: 10
Look on my works, ye Mighty, and despair!"
Nothing beside remains. Round the decay
Of that colossal wreck, boundless and bare
The lone and level sands stretch far away.

[1817]

Lines 4–8 are somewhat obscure, but the point is that the passions—still evident in the "shattered visage"—survive the sculptor's hand that "mocked"—that is, (1) imitated or copied, (2) derided—them, and the passions also survive the king's heart that had nourished them.

Joining the Conversation: Critical Thinking and Writing

There is an irony of plot here: Ozymandias believed that he created enduring works, but his intentions came to nothing. However, another irony is also present. How are his words, in a way he did not intend, true?

ALFRED, LORD TENNYSON

Alfred, Lord Tennyson (1809–92), the son of an English clergyman, was born in Lincolnshire, where he began writing verse at age five. Educated at Cambridge, he had to leave without a degree when his father died and Alfred had to accept responsibility for bringing up his brothers and sisters. In fact, the family had inherited ample funds, but for some years the money was tied up by litigation. Following Wordsworth's death in 1850, Tennyson was made poet laureate. With his government pension he moved with his family to the Isle of Wight, where he lived in comfort until his death.

Ulysses°

It little profits that an idle king,
By this still hearth, among these barren crags,
Matched with an aged wife, I mete and dole
Unequal laws unto a savage race,
That hoard, and sleep, and feed, and know not me.   5
I cannot rest from travel; I will drink
Life to the lees. All times I have enjoyed
Greatly, have suffered greatly, both with those

°**Ulysses** Odysseus, King of Ithaca, a leader of the Greeks in the Trojan War, famous for his ten years of journeying to remote places.

That loved me, and alone; on shore, and when
Thro' scudding drifts the rainy Hyades   10
Vext the dim sea. I am become a name;
For always roaming with a hungry heart
Much have I seen and known,—cities of men
And manners, climates, councils, governments,
Myself not least, but honored of them all,—   15
And drunk delight of battle with my peers,
Far on the ringing plains of windy Troy.
I am a part of all that I have met;
Yet all experience is an arch wherethro'
Gleams that untravelled world whose margin fades   20
For ever and for ever when I move.
How dull it is to pause, to make an end,
To rust unburnished, not to shine in use!
As tho' to breathe were life! Life piled on life
Were all too little, and of one to me   25
Little remains; but every hour is saved
From that eternal silence, something more,
A bringer of new things; and vile it were
For some three suns to store and hoard myself,
And this gray spirit yearning in desire   30
To follow knowledge like a sinking star
Beyond the utmost bound of human thought.

   This is my son, mine own Telemachus,
To whom I leave the scepter and the isle,—
Well-loved of me, discerning to fulfill   35
This labor, by slow prudence to make mild
A rugged people, and thro' soft degrees
Subdue them to the useful and the good.
Most blameless is he, centered in the sphere
Of common duties, decent not to fail   40
In offices of tenderness, and pay
Meet adoration to my household gods,
When I am gone. He works his work, I mine.

   There lies the port; the vessel puffs her sail;
There gloom the dark, broad seas. My mariners,   45
Souls that have toiled, and wrought, and thought with me,—
That ever with a frolic welcome took
The thunder and the sunshine, and opposed
Free hearts, free foreheads,—you and I are old;
Old age hath yet his honor and his toil.   50
Death closes all; but something ere the end,
Some work of noble note, may yet be done,
Not unbecoming men that strove with Gods.
The lights begin to twinkle from the rocks;
The long day wanes; the slow moon climbs; the deep   55
Moans round with many voices. Come, my friends.
'Tis not too late to seek a newer world.
Push off, and sitting well in order smite
The sounding furrows; for my purpose holds

To sail beyond the sunset, and the baths   60
Of all the western stars, until I die.
It may be that the gulfs will wash us down;
It may be we shall touch the Happy Isles,
And see the great Achilles, whom we knew.
Tho' much is taken, much abides; and tho'   65
We are not now that strength which in old days
Moved earth and heaven, that which we are, we are.
One equal temper of heroic hearts,
Made weak by time and fate, but strong in will
To strive, to seek, to find, and not to yield.   70

[1833]

Joining the Conversation: Critical Thinking and Writing

1. Given the fact that Ulysses is a king and therefore a person with great responsibilities, does such a line as "I cannot rest from travel" (line 6) strike you as
   irresponsible? Explain.
2. It has been said that although at first glance the poem seems optimistic and
   highly positive—the final line is "To strive, to seek, to find, and not to yield"—
   the poem in fact is melancholy and filled with suggestions of death. Your view?
3. Is Tennyson presenting an argument here for how we should live? If so, what is
   your response?

COUNTEE CULLEN

*Countee Cullen (1903–46) was born Countee Porter in New York City, raised by his
grandmother, and then adopted by the Reverend Frederick A Cullen, a Methodist
minister in Harlem. Cullen received a bachelor's degree from New York University
(Phi Beta Kappa) and a master's degree from Harvard. He earned his living as a
high school teacher of French, but his literary gifts were recognized in his own day.*

Incident

(For Eric Walrond)

Once riding in old Baltimore,
  Heart-filled, head-filled with glee,
I saw a Baltimorean
  Keep looking straight at me.

Now I was eight and very small,   5
  And he was no whit bigger,
And so I smiled, but he poked out
  His tongue, and called me, "Nigger."

I saw the whole of Baltimore
  From May until December;   10
Of all the things that happened there
  That's all that I remember.

[1925]

Joining the Conversation: Critical Thinking and Writing

1. How would you define an "incident"? A serious occurrence? A minor occurrence, or what? Think about the word, and then think about Cullen's use of it as a title for the event recorded in this poem. Test out one or two other possible titles as a way of helping yourself to see the strengths or weaknesses of Cullen's title.
2. The dedicatee, Eric Walrond (1898–1966), was an African American essayist and writer of fiction who in an essay, "On Being Black," had described his experiences of racial prejudice. How does the presence of the dedication bear on our response to Cullen's account of the "incident"?
3. What is the tone of the poem? Indifferent? Angry? Or what? What do you think is the speaker's attitude toward the "incident"? What is your attitude?
4. Ezra Pound, poet and critic, once defined literature as "news that *stays* news." What do you think he meant by this? Do you think that the definition fits Cullen's poem?

WILLIAM STAFFORD

William Stafford (1914–93) was born in Hutchinson, Kansas, and was educated at the University of Kansas and the State University of Iowa. A conscientious objector during World War II, he worked for the Brethren Service and the Church World Service. After the war he taught at several universities and then settled at Lewis and Clark College in Portland, Oregon. In addition to several books of poems, Stafford wrote Down in My Heart *(1947), an account of his experiences as a conscientious objector.*

Traveling through the Dark

Traveling through the dark I found a deer
dead on the edge of the Wilson River road.
It is usually best to roll them into the canyon:
the road is narrow; to swerve might make more dead.

By glow of the tail-light I stumbled back of the car   5
and stood by the heap, a doe, a recent killing;
she had stiffened already, almost cold.
I dragged her off; she was large in the belly.

My fingers touching her side brought me the reason—
her side was warm; her fawn lay there waiting,   10
alive, still, never to be born.
Beside that mountain road I hesitated.

The car aimed ahead its lowered parking lights;
under the hood purred the steady engine.
I stood in the glare of the warm exhaust turning red;   15
around our group I could hear the wilderness listen.

I thought hard for us all—my only swerving—
Then pushed her over the edge into the river.

[1960]

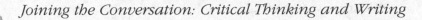

Joining the Conversation: Critical Thinking and Writing

1. Look at the first sentence (the first two lines) and try to recall what your impression of the speaker was, based only on these two lines, or pretend that you have not read the entire poem, and characterize him merely on these two lines. Then take the entire poem into consideration and characterize him.
2. What do you make of the title? Do you think it is a good title for this poem? Explain.

MyLiteratureLab® *For additional resources for "Traveling through the Dark," log in to* www.myliteraturelab.com *where you will find a Comprehension Quiz, as well as an About the Author, Links, and Critical Overview for Stafford (under Student Resources).*

ADRIENNE RICH

Adrienne Rich (1929–2012) was born in Baltimore, Maryland. She published over sixteen volumes of poetry and five volumes of critical prose. Her most recent books include Tonight No Poetry Will Serve: Poems 2007–2010 *and* Telephone Ringing in the Labyrinth: Poems 2004–2006. A Human Eye: Essays on Art in Society, *appeared in 2009. She edited Muriel Rukeyser's Selected Poems for the Library of America. Among numerous other recognitions, she was the 2006 recipient of the National Book Foundation's Medal for Distinguished Contribution to American Letters. Her poetry and essays have been widely translated and published internationally.*

Diving into the Wreck

First having read the book of myths,
and loaded the camera,
and checked the edge of the knife-blade,
I put on
the body-armor of black rubber   5
the absurd flippers
the grave and awkward mask.
I am having to do this
not like Cousteau° with his
assiduous team   10
aboard the sun-flooded schooner
but here alone.

There is a ladder.
The ladder is always there

9 Cousteau Jacques Cousteau (1910–97), French underwater explorer.

hanging innocently   15
close to the side of the schooner.
We know what it is for,
we who have used it.
Otherwise
it's a piece of maritime floss   20
some sundry equipment.

I go down.
Rung after rung and still
the oxygen immerses me
the blue light   25
the clear atoms
of our human air.
I go down.
My flippers cripple me,
I crawl like an insect down the ladder   30
and there is no one
to tell me when the ocean
will begin.

First the air is blue and then
it is bluer and then green and then   35
black I am blacking out and yet
my mask is powerful
it pumps my blood with power
the sea is another story
the sea is not a question of power   40
I have to learn alone
to turn my body without force
in the deep element.

And now: it is easy to forget
what I came for   45
among so many who have always
lived here
swaying their crenellated fans
between the reefs
and besides   50
you breathe differently down here.

I came to explore the wreck.
The words are purposes.
The words are maps.
I came to see the damage that was done   55
and the treasures that prevail.
I stroke the beam of my lamp
slowly along the flank
of something more permanent
than fish or weed   60

the thing I came for:
the wreck and not the story of the wreck
the thing itself and not the myth

the drowned face always staring
toward the sun 65
the evidence of damage
worn by salt and sway into this threadbare beauty
the ribs of the disaster
curving their assertion
among the tentative haunters. 70

This is the place.
And I am here, the mermaid whose dark hair
streams black, the merman in his armored body
We circle silently
about the wreck 75
we dive into the hold.
I am she: I am he

whose drowned face sleeps with open eyes
whose breasts still bear the stress
whose silver, copper, vermeil cargo lies 80
obscurely inside barrels
half-wedged and left to rot
we are the half-destroyed instruments
that once held to a course
the water-eaten log 85
the fouled compass

We are, I am, you are
by cowardice or courage
the one who find our way
back to this scene 90
carrying a knife, a camera
a book of myths
in which
our names do not appear.

[1972]

DEREK WALCOTT

*Derek Walcott, born in 1930 on the Caribbean island of St. Lucia, was award-
ed the Nobel Prize in Literature in 1992. Although in the United States he is
known chiefly as a poet, Walcott is also an important playwright and director
of plays. Much of his work is concerned with his mixed heritage—a black
writer from the Caribbean, whose language is English. Walcott taught for
many years in the Creative Writing Program at Boston University. Walcott's
books include* Collected Poems *(1986) and* Omeros *(1989), a Caribbean epic
that echoes Homer's* Iliad *and* Odyssey *as it explores the Caribbean's past and
present.*

A Far Cry from Africa

A wind is ruffling the tawny pelt
Of Africa. Kikuyu,° quick as flies,
Batten upon the bloodstreams of the veldt.°
Corpses are scattered through a paradise.
Only the worm, colonel of carrion, cries: 5
"Waste no compassion on these separate dead!"
Statistics justify and scholars seize
The salients of colonial policy.
What is that to the white child hacked in bed?
To savages, expendable as Jews?   10

Threshed out by beaters, the long rushes break
In a white dust of ibises whose cries
Have wheeled since civilization's dawn
From the parched river or beast-teeming plain.
The violence of beast on beast is read   15
As natural law, but upright man
Seeks his divinity by inflicting pain.
Delirious as these worried beasts, his wars
Dance to the tightened carcass of a drum,
While he calls courage still that native dread   20
Of the white peace contracted by the dead.

Again brutish necessity wipes its hands
Upon the napkins of a dirty cause, again
A waste of our compassion, as with Spain,°
The gorilla wrestles with the superman.   25

I who am poisoned with the blood of both,
Where shall I turn, divided to the vein?
I who have cursed
The drunken officer of British rule, how choose
Between this Africa and the English tongue I love?   30
Betray them both, or give back what they give?
How can I face such slaughter and be cool?
How can I turn from Africa and live?

[1962]

2 Kikuyu an African tribe that fought against British colonialists. **3 veldt** grassland in southern
Africa. **24 Spain** a reference to the triumph of fascism in Spain after the civil war of 1936–39.

Joining the Conversation: Critical Thinking and Writing

1. Now that you have read the poem, explain the meaning of the title.
2. Do you find the first stanza hard to understand? Why, or why not?
3. Focus on lines 15–17: What is Walcott saying here? Do you think that the poem
   might be even more effective if these lines were placed at the beginning? Or do
   they belong exactly where they are?

4. Imagine that Walcott sent this poem to you with a letter that asked for your response. In a letter ("Dear Mr. Walcott . . .") of one page in length, give your response to the poem.
5. What is the meaning of line 25?
6. Walcott uses the first-person "I" in the final stanza. How would you answer each of the questions he asks in it? Or do you think the point is that these questions cannot be answered?
7. What is your own experience of Africa? Have you lived or traveled there? Would you like to? Has Walcott given you a new perspective on Africa, its history and culture?

SHERMAN ALEXIE

Sherman Alexie, born in 1966 in Spokane, Washington, holds a BA from Washington State University. Author of novels, stories, and poems, and author and director of the highly praised film Smoke Signals *(1998), Alexie was awarded a grant from the National Endowment for the Arts. Of his life and his work he says, "I am a Spokane Coeur d'Alene Indian. . . . I live on the Spokane Indian Reservation. Everything I do now, writing and otherwise, has its origin in that."*

On the Amtrak from Boston to New York City

The white woman across the aisle from me says, "Look,
look at all the history, that house
on the hill there is over two hundred years old,"
as she points out the window past me

into what she has been taught. I have learned   5
little more about American history during my few days
back East than what I expected and far less
of what we should all know of the tribal stories

whose architecture is 15,000 years older
than the corners of the house that sits   10
museumed on the hill. "Walden Pond,"°
the woman on the train asks, "Did you see Walden Pond?"

and I don't have a cruel enough heart to break
her own by telling her there are five Walden Ponds°
on my little reservation out West   15
and at least a hundred more surrounding Spokane,

the city I pretend to call my home. "Listen,"
I could have told her. "I don't give a shit
about Walden. I know the Indians were living stories
around that pond before Walden's grandparents were born   20

and before his grandparents' grandparents were born.
I'm tired of hearing about Don-fucking-Henley° saving it, too,

11 Walden Pond site in Massachusetts where Henry David Thoreau (1817–62) lived from 4 July 1845 to 6 September 1847, and about which he wrote in his most famous book, *Walden* (1854).
22 Don Henley rock singer who was active in preserving Walden from building developers.

because that's redundant. If Don Henley's brothers and sisters
and mothers and fathers hadn't come here in the first place

then nothing would need to be saved."   25
But I didn't say a word to the woman about Walden
Pond because she smiled so much and seemed delighted
that I thought to bring her an orange juice

back from the food car. I respect elders
of every color. All I really did was eat   30
my tasteless sandwich, drink my Diet Pepsi
and nod my head whenever the woman pointed out

another little piece of her country's history
while I, as all Indians have done
since this war began, made plans   35
for what I would do and say the next time

somebody from the enemy thought I was one of their own.

[1993]

Joining the Conversation: Critical Thinking and Writing

1. Characterize the speaker.
2. Take the common idea that "Columbus discovered America." What attitude toward the history of this land and toward Indians is implicit in these words?

WILLIAM BUTLER YEATS

William Butler Yeats (1865–1939) was born in Dublin, Ireland. The early Yeats was much interested in highly lyrical, romantic poetry, often drawing on Irish mythology. The later poems, from about 1910 (and especially after Yeats met Ezra Pound in 1911), are often more colloquial. Although the later poems often employ mythological references too, many believe that these poems are more down-to-earth. Yeats was awarded the Nobel Prize in Literature in 1923.

In the seventh century BCE the ancient Greeks founded the city of Byzantium in Thrace, where Istanbul, Turkey, now stands. (Constantine, the first Christian ruler of the Roman Empire, built a new city there in 330 CE. Named Constantinople, the city served as the capital of the Roman Empire until 1453, when the Turks captured it. In 1930 the name was officially changed to Istanbul.) The capital of the Roman Empire and the "holy city" of the Greek Orthodox Church, Byzantium had two golden ages. The first, in its early centuries, continued the traditions of the antique Greco-Roman world. The second, which is what Yeats had in mind, extended from the mid-ninth to the mid-thirteenth century and was a distinctive blend of classical, Christian, Slavic, and even Islamic culture. This period is noted for mysticism, for the preservation of ancient learning, and for exquisitely refined symbolic art. In short, Byzantium (as Yeats saw it) was wise and passionless. In A Vision, *his prose treatment of his complex mystical system, Yeats says:*

> *I think that in early Byzantium, maybe never before or since in recorded history, religious, aesthetic and practical life were one, that architect and artificers—though not, it may be, poets, for language has been the instrument*

of controversy and must have grown abstract—spoke to the multitude and the few alike. The painter, the mosaic worker, the worker in gold and silver, the illuminator of sacred books, were almost impersonal, almost perhaps without the consciousness of individual design, absorbed in their subject matter and that the vision of the whole people. They could copy out of old Gospel books those pictures that seemed as sacred as the text, and yet weave all into a vast design, the work of many that seemed the work of one, that made building, picture, pattern, metal-work of rail and lamp, seem but a single image.

Sailing to Byzantium

I

That is no country for old men. The young
In one another's arms, birds in the trees
—Those dying generations—at their song,
The salmon-falls, the mackerel-crowded seas,
Fish, flesh, or fowl, commend all summer long   5
Whatever is begotten, born, and dies.
Caught in that sensual music all neglect
Monuments of unaging intellect.

II

An aged man is but a paltry thing,
A tattered coat upon a stick, unless   10
Soul clap its hands and sing, and louder sing
For every tatter in its mortal dress.
Nor is there singing school but studying
Monuments of its own magnificence;
And therefore I have sailed the seas and come   15
To the holy city of Byzantium.

III

O sages standing in God's holy fire
As in the gold mosaic of a wall,
Come from the holy fire, perne° in a gyre,
And be the singing-masters of my soul.   20
Consume my heart away; sick with desire
And fastened to a dying animal
It knows not what it is; and gather me
Into the artifice of eternity.

IV

Once out of nature I shall never take   25
My bodily form from any natural thing,
But such a form as Grecian goldsmiths make
Of hammered gold and gold enameling
To keep a drowsy Emperor awake;
Or set upon a golden bough to sing   30

19 perne whirl down.

To lords and ladies of Byzantium
Of what is past, or passing, or to come.

[1926]

Joining the Conversation: Critical Thinking and Writing

1. What is "that . . . country," mentioned in the first line?
2. By the end of the first stanza, the speaker seems to be dismissing the natural world. Do you agree that even in this stanza, however, he sounds attracted to it?
3. The poem is filled with oppositions—for instance, "old men" versus "the young" (both in line 1), and "birds in the trees" (line 2) versus the mechanical bird in the final stanza. List as many opposites as you see in the poem, and then explain what Yeats is getting at.
4. The first stanza speaks of "monuments of unaging intellect." What might be some examples of these?
5. After reading and rereading this poem, do you think you will—even if only briefly—*act* differently, redirect any of your choices? Support your response with reasons.
6. Have you ever visited any place—perhaps the place where you or your parents or grandparents were born, or perhaps a house of worship, or perhaps a college campus—that you have come to see symbolically, standing for a way of life or for some aspect of life? If so, describe the place and the significance that you give it.

CHRISTINA ROSSETTI

Christina Rossetti (1830–94) was the daughter of an exiled Italian patriot who lived in London and the sister of the poet and painter Dante Gabriel Rossetti. After her father became an invalid, she led an extremely ascetic life, devoting most of her life to doing charitable work. Her first and best-known volume of poetry, Goblin Market and Other Poems, *was published in 1862.*

Uphill

Does the road wind uphill all the way?
   Yes, to the very end.
Will the day's journey take the whole long day?
   From morn to night, my friend.

But is there for the night a resting-place?   5
   A roof for when the slow dark hours begin.
May not the darkness hide it from my face?
   You cannot miss that inn.

Shall I meet other wayfarers at night?
   Those who have gone before.   10
Then must I knock, or call when just in sight?
   They will not keep you standing at that door.

Shall I find comfort, travel-sore and weak?
   Of labor you shall find the sum.
Will there be beds for me and all who seek?   15
   Yea, beds for all who come.

[1858]

Joining the Conversation: Critical Thinking and Writing

1. Suppose someone told you that this poem is about a person preparing to go on a hike. The person is supposedly making inquiries about the road and the possible hotel arrangements. What would you reply?
2. Who is the questioner? A woman? A man? All human beings collectively? "Uphill" does not use quotation marks to distinguish between two speakers. Can one say that in "Uphill" the questioner and the answerer are the same person?
3. Are the answers unambiguously comforting? Or can it, for instance, be argued that the "roof" is (perhaps among other things) the lid of a coffin—hence the questioner will certainly not be kept "standing at that door"? If the poem can be read along these lines, is it chilling rather than comforting?

Emily Dickinson

For a biographical note on Emily Dickinson, see page 550–52.

Because I could not stop for Death

Because I could not stop for Death—
He kindly stopped for me—
The Carriage held but just Ourselves—
And Immortality.

We slowly drove—He knew no haste   5
And I had put away
My labor and my leisure too,
For His Civility—

We passed the School, where Children strove
At Recess—in the Ring—   10
We passed the Fields of Gazing Grain—
We passed the Setting Sun—

Or rather—He passed Us—
The Dews drew quivering and chill—
For only Gossamer, my Gown—   15
My Tippet°—only Tulle°—

We paused before a House that seemed
A Swelling of the Ground—
The Roof was scarcely visible—
The Cornice—in the Ground—   20

Since then—'tis Centuries—and yet
Feels shorter than the Day
I first surmised the Horses' Heads
Were toward Eternity—

[c. 1863]

16 Tippet shawl;   **Tulle** net of silk.

Joining the Conversation: Critical Thinking and Writing

1. Characterize death as it appears in lines 1–8.
2. What is the significance of the details and their arrangement in the third stanza? Why "strove" rather than "played" (line 9)? What meanings does "Ring" (line 10) have? Is "Gazing Grain" better than "Golden Grain"?
3. The "House" in the fifth stanza is a sort of riddle. What is the answer? Does this stanza introduce an aspect of death not present—or present only very faintly— in the rest of the poem? Explain.
4. Evaluate this statement about the poem (from the literary critic Yvor Winters's *In Defense of Reason*): "In so far as it concentrates on the life that is being left behind, it is wholly successful; in so far as it attempts to experience the death to come, it is fraudulent, however exquisitely."

MyLiteratureLab® *For additional resources for "Because I could not stop for Death," log in to* www.myliteraturelab.com *where you will find a Longman Lecture and Comprehension Quiz, as well as an About the Author, Bibliography, Links, and Critical Overview for Dickinson (under Student Resources).*

A. E. HOUSMAN

A. E. Housman (1859–1936) was one of the most distinguished classical scholars of his time. Though he left Oxford without a degree (having failed his examinations), through hard work, discipline, and rigorous study he earned an appointment in 1892 as professor of Latin at University College, London, and in 1911 as professor of Latin at Cambridge and fellow of Trinity College. Only two volumes of Hous-man's poems appeared during his lifetime: A Shropshire Lad *(1896) and* Last Poems *(1922).*

To an Athlete Dying Young

The time you won your town the race
We chaired you through the market-place;
Man and boy stood cheering by,
And home we brought you shoulder-high.

Today, the road all runners come,   5
Shoulder-high we bring you home,
And set you at your threshold down,
Townsman of a stiller town.

Smart lad, to slip betimes away
From fields where glory does not stay   10
And early though the laurel grows
It withers quicker than the rose.

Eyes the shady night has shut
Cannot see the record cut,
And silence sounds no worse than cheers   15
After earth has stopped the ears:

Now you will not swell the rout
Of lads that wore their honours out,
Runners whom renown outran
And the name died before the man.   20

So set, before its echoes fade,
The fleet foot on the sill of shade,
And hold to the low lintel up
The still-defended challenge-cup.

And round that early laurelled head   25
Will flock to gaze the strengthless dead
And find unwithered on its curls
The garland briefer than a girl's.

[1896]

Joining the Conversation: Critical Thinking and Writing

1. When you read this poem out loud, what sorts of things do you hear?
2. Does it seem odd to you that this poem addresses a "you"? Please explain why or why not.
3. A scholar of modern poetry says that while Housman's poem focuses on death, its message ultimately is "upbeat and celebratory." Do you agree?
4. This poem is sometimes termed an elegy, and sometimes termed a dramatic monologue. Which seems the more accurate description to you?
5. Do you find this poem to be sentimental? Is that a bad thing or a good thing, or neither?

MyLiteratureLab® *For additional resources for "To an Athlete Dying Young," log in to* www.myliteraturelab.com *where you will find a Longman Lecture and Short Evaluation Exercises, as well as an About the Author, Bibliography, Links, and Critical Overview for Housman (under Student Resources).*

A Note on Spirituals

We mentioned that the lyric can range from expressions of emotion focused on personal matters to expressions of emotion focused on public matters, and the latter are sometimes characterized as odes or hymns. Among the most memorable hymns produced in the United States are the spirituals, or Sorrow Songs, created by black slaves in the United States, chiefly in the first half of the nineteenth century. The origins of the spirituals are still a matter of some dispute, but most specialists agree that the songs represent a distinctive fusion of African rhythms with European hymns, and of course many of the texts derive ultimately from biblical sources. One of the chief themes is the desire for release, sometimes presented with imagery drawn from ancient Israel. Examples include references to crossing the River Jordan (north of the Sea of Galilee), the release of the Israelites from slavery in Egypt (Exodus), Jonah's release from the whale (Book of Jonah), and Daniel's deliverance from a fiery furnace and from the lions' den (Book of Daniel, chapters 3 and 6).

The texts were collected and published especially in the 1860s, for instance in *Slave Songs of the United States* (1867). These books usually sought to reproduce the singers' pronunciation (for instance *de* for *the*), and we have followed the early texts in the two examples that we give here.

Anonymous

Swing Low, Sweet Chariot

From J. B. T March, *The Story of the Jubilee* Singers, 1881.

"Swing Low, Sweet Chariot" derives its basic images from the geography of ancient Israel (the Jordan River flows north from the Sea of Galilee to the Dead Sea) and from a book in the Hebrew Bible (2 Kings 2.11 reports that Elijah and his friend Elisha were walking by the Jordan, when "there appeared a chariot of fire, and horses of fine, and parted them both asunder, and Elijah went up by a whirlwind into heaven"). There may also be some influence of the New Testament, Luke 16.22, which reports that a rich man named Dives and a poor man were "carried by the angels into Abraham's bosom." Further, the line "I'm sometimes up and sometimes down," from a secular song, "No-body Knows the Trouble I've Seen," often found its way into "Swing Low," as in this version, where the fourth verse goes:

> I'm sometimes up and sometimes down
> But still my soul feels heavenly bound.

Anonymous

Didn't My Lord Deliver Daniel

Didn't my Lord deliver Daniel, deliver Daniel, deliver Daniel,
Didn't my Lord deliver Daniel,
  An' why not every man.
He delivered Daniel from de lion's den,
Jonah from de belly of de whale,   5
An' de Hebrew chillun from de fiery furnace,
An' why not every man.
  Didn't my Lord deliver Daniel, deliver Daniel, deliver Daniel,
  Didn't my Lord deliver Daniel,
    An' why not every man.   10
De moon run down in a purple stream,
De sun forbear to shine,
An' every star disappear,
King Jesus shall-a be mine.   15
  (Refrain)
De win' blows eas' an' de win' blows wes',
It blows like de judgament day,
An' every po' soul dat never did pray
'll be glad to pray dat day.
  (Refrain)   20

I set my foot on de Gospel ship,
And de ship begin to sail.
It landed me over on Canaan's shore,°
An' I'll never come back no mo'.
　(Refrain)   25

24 Canaan's shore Canaan is the ancient name of a territory that included part of what is
now Israel.

Joining the Conversation: Critical Thinking and Writing

We explained that we give the texts of the songs as they were printed in the second
half of the nineteenth century, when an effort to indicate pronunciation was made
(e.g., *chillun* for *children*). If you were printing the songs, would you retain these
attempts to indicate pronunciation? What, if anything, is gained by keeping them?
What, if any, unintentional side effects do you think may be produced?

Chapter Overview: Looking Backward/Looking Forward

1. In a single paragraph, summarize the best, or the worst, consequence of travel.
   Next, try to do the same in just a single sentence.
2. Review the essay that you wrote for the first topic, in defense of travel. What are
   the strengths and weaknesses of your argument? Do you see any weaknesses?
   How might you revise this essay to make it more effective? Do you think you
   should introduce counterarguments into your essay—arguments "on the other
   side" that you could address and try to answer? Or would this prove confusing
   to your reader?
3. When someone says to you that he or she "hates to travel," what is your response? Do you think that such a position can be defended? If you had to argue
   that traveling is a bad idea, what main points would you make? Would you cite
   any of the quotations given at the beginning of this chapter? Which ones? What
   would you gain from such a citation? What, if anything, might you lose?
4. If someone surprised you with the gift of a free trip, what destination would
   excite you the most? Which one would excite you the least?
5. Do you spend much time exploring your own thoughts and feelings? Do you
   set aside a specific time for this? Is there a specific place where it occurs? Is this
   an activity you undertake by yourself, or with someone else, or with some
   group? Describe an occasion when you explored your thoughts and feelings,
   and explain what happened next.

CHAPTER 22

Love and Hate

SHORT VIEWS

Love is a great beautifier.
　　Louisa May Alcott

I do not think that what is called Love at first sight is so great an absurdity as it is sometimes imagined to be. We generally make up our minds beforehand to the sort of person we should like, grave or gay, black, brown, or fair; with golden tresses or raven locks—and when we meet with a complete example of the qualities we admire, the bargain is soon struck.
　　William Hazlitt

For what is love itself, for the one we love best?—an enfolding of immeasurable cares which yet are better than any joys outside our love.
　　George Eliot

We've got this gift of love, but love is like a precious plant. You can't just accept it and leave it in the cupboard or just think it's going to get on by itself. You've got to keep watering it. You've got to really look after it and nurture it.
　　John Lennon

Lovers should also have their days off.
　　Natalie Clifford Barney

In love, there is always one who kisses and one who offers the cheek.
　　French proverb

Love is the word used to label the sexual excitement of the young, the habituation of the middle-aged, and the mutual dependence of the old.
　　John Ciardi

A man falls in love through his eyes, a woman through her ears. What is said to [women] and what they believe about a man's status is usually more important than the superficiality of good looks.
　　Woodrow Wyatt

Now hatred is by far the longest pleasure,
Men love in haste, but they detest at leisure.
　　Lord Byron

687

Men hate more steadily than they love.
    Samuel Johnson

The price of hating other human beings is loving oneself less.
    Eldridge Cleaver

In hatred as in love, we grow like the thing we brood upon. What we loathe, we graft into our very soul.
    Mary Renault

I tell you, there is such a thing as creative hate.
    Willa Cather

Never in this world can hatred be stilled by hatred; it will be stilled only by non-hatred: This is the law Eternal.
    Buddha

Joining the Conversation: Critical Thinking and Writing

1. Select a quotation that especially appeals to you, and make it the focus of an essay of about 500 words.
2. Take two of the passages—perhaps one that you especially like and one that you think is wrongheaded—and write a dialogue of about 500 words in which the two authors converse or argue. They may each try to convince the other, or they may find that to some degree they share views and they may then work out a statement that both can accept. If you do take the first position—that one writer is on the correct track but the other is utterly mistaken—try to be fair to the view that you think is mistaken. (As an experiment in critical thinking, imagine that you accept it, and make the best case for it that you possibly can.)

ESSAY

JUDITH ORTIZ COFER

Born in Puerto Rico in 1952 of a Puerto Rican mother and a United States mainland father who served in the Navy, Judith Ortiz Cofer was educated both in Puerto Rico and on the mainland. After earning a bachelor's and a master's degree in English, she did further graduate work at Oxford and then taught English in Florida. Her publications include books of poetry, a novel, and collections of stories and essays. She is now a professor of English and creative writing at the University of Georgia.

The following selection comes from an autobiography, Silent Dancing *(1990).*

I Fell in Love, or My Hormones Awakened

I fell in love, or my hormones awakened from their long slumber in my body, and suddenly the goal of my days was focused on one thing: to catch a glimpse of my secret love. And it had to remain secret, because I had, of course, in the great tradition of tragic romance, chosen to love a boy who was totally out of my reach. He was not Puerto Rican; he was Italian and rich. He was also an older man. He was a senior at the high school when I came in as a freshman. I first saw him in the hall, leaning casually on a wall that was the border line between girlside and boyside for underclassmen. He looked extraordinarily like a young Marlon Brando[1]—down to the ironic little smile. The total of what I knew about the boy who starred in every one of my awkward fantasies was this: that he was the nephew of the man who owned the supermarket on my block; that he often had parties at his parents' beautiful home in the suburbs which I would hear about; that his family had money (which came to our school in many ways)—and this fact made my knees weak: and that he worked at the store near my apartment building on weekends and in the summer.

My mother could not understand why I became so eager to be the one sent out on her endless errands. I pounced on every opportunity from Friday to late Saturday afternoon to go after eggs, cigarettes, milk (I tried to drink as much of it as possible, although I hated the stuff)—the staple items that she would order from the "American" store.

Week after week I wandered up and down the aisles, taking furtive glances at the stock room in the back, breathlessly hoping to see my prince. Not that I had a plan. I felt like a pilgrim waiting for a glimpse of Mecca. I did not expect him to notice me. It was sweet agony.

One day I did see him. Dressed in a white outfit like a surgeon: white pants and shirt, white cap, and (gross sight, but not to my love-glazed eyes) blood-smeared butcher's apron. He was helping to drag a side of beef into the freezer storage area of the store. I must have stood there like an idiot, because I remember that he did see me, he even spoke to me! I could have died. I think he said, "Excuse me," and smiled vaguely in my direction.

5   After that, I *willed* occasions to go to the supermarket. I watched my mother's pack of cigarettes empty ever so slowly. I wanted her to smoke them fast. I drank milk and forced it on my brother (although a second glass for him had to be bought with my share of Fig Newton cookies which we both liked, but we were restricted to one row each). I gave my cookies up for love, and watched my mother smoke her L&M's with so little enthusiasm that I thought (God, no!) that she might be cutting down on her smoking or maybe even giving up the habit. At this crucial time!

I thought I had kept my lonely romance a secret. Often I cried hot tears on my pillow for the things that kept us apart. In my mind there was no doubt that he would never notice me (and that is why I felt free to stare at him—I was invisible). He could not see me because I was a skinny Puerto Rican girl, a freshman who did not belong to any group he associated with.

At the end of the year I found out that I had not been invisible. I learned one little lesson about human nature—adulation leaves a scent, one that we are all equipped to recognize, and no matter how insignificant the source, we seek it.

[1]**Marlon Brando** charismatic American stage and screen actor (1924–2004)

In June the nuns at our school would always arrange for some cultural extravaganza. In my freshman year it was a Roman banquet. We had been studying Greek drama (as a prelude to church history—it was at a fast clip that we galloped through Sophocles and Euripides toward the early Christian martyrs), and our young, energetic Sister Agnes was in the mood for spectacle. She ordered the entire student body (it was a small group of under 300 students) to have our mothers make us togas out of sheets. She handed out a pattern on mimeo pages fresh out of the machine. I remember the intense smell of the alcohol on the sheets of paper, and how almost everyone in the auditorium brought theirs to their noses and inhaled deeply—mimeographed handouts were the school-day buzz that the new Xerox generation of kids is missing out on. Then, as the last couple of weeks of school dragged on, the city of Paterson becoming a concrete oven, and us wilting in our uncomfortable uniforms, we labored like frantic Roman slaves to build a splendid banquet hall in our small auditorium. Sister Agnes wanted a raised dais where the host and hostess would be regally enthroned.

She had already chosen our Senator and Lady from among our ranks. The Lady was to be a beautiful new student named Sophia, a recent Polish immigrant, whose English was still practically unintelligible, but whose features, classically perfect without a trace of makeup, enthralled us. Everyone talked about her gold hair cascading past her waist, and her voice which could carry a note right up to heaven in choir. The nuns wanted her for God. They kept saying that she had vocation. We just looked at her in awe, and the boys seemed afraid of her. She just smiled and did as she was told. I don't know what she thought of it all. The main privilege of beauty is that others will do almost everything for you, including thinking.

10   Her partner was to be our best basketball player, a tall, red-haired senior whose family sent its many offspring to our school. Together, Sophia and her senator looked like the best combination of immigrant genes our community could produce. It did not occur to me to ask then whether anything but their physical beauty qualified them for the starring roles in our production. I had the highest average in the church history class, but I was given the part of one of many "Roman Citizens." I was to sit in front of the plastic fruit and recite a greeting in Latin along with the rest of the school when our hosts came into the hall and took their places on their throne.

On the night of our banquet, my father escorted me in my toga to the door of our school. I felt foolish in my awkwardly draped sheet (blouse and skirt required underneath). My mother had no great skill as a seamstress. The best she could do was hem a skirt or a pair of pants. That night I would have traded her for a peasant woman with a golden needle. I saw other Roman ladies emerging from their parents' cars looking authentic in sheets of material that folded over their bodies like the garments on a statue by Michelangelo. How did they do it? How was it that I always got it just slightly wrong, and worse, I believed that other people were just too polite to mention it. "The poor little Puerto Rican girl," I could hear them thinking. But in reality, I must have been my worst critic, self-conscious as I was.

Soon, we were all sitting at our circle of tables joined together around the dais. Sophia glittered like a golden statue. Her smile was beatific: a perfect, silent Roman lady. Her "senator" looked uncomfortable, glancing around at his buddies, perhaps waiting for the ridicule that he would surely get in the locker room later. The nuns in their black habits stood in the background watching us. What were they supposed to be, the Fates? Nubian slaves? The dancing girls did their modest little dance to tinny music from their finger cymbals, then the speeches were made. Then the grape juice "wine" was raised in a toast to the Roman Empire we all knew would fall within the week—before finals anyway.

All during the program I had been in a state of controlled hysteria. My secret love sat across the room from me looking supremely bored. I watched his every move, taking him in gluttonously. I relished the shadow of his eyelashes on his ruddy cheeks, his pouty lips smirking sarcastically at the ridiculous sight of our little play. Once he slumped down on his chair, and our sergeant-at-arms nun came over and tapped him sharply on his shoulder. He drew himself up slowly, with disdain. I loved his rebellious spirit. I believed myself still invisible to him in my "nothing" status as I looked upon my beloved. But toward the end of the evening, as we stood chanting our farewells in Latin, he looked straight across the room and into my eyes! How did I survive the killing power of those dark pupils? I trembled in a new way. I was not cold—I was burning! Yet I shook from the inside out, feeling light-headed, dizzy.

The room began to empty and I headed for the girls' lavatory. I wanted to relish the miracle in silence. I did not think for a minute that anything more would follow. I was satisfied with the enormous favor of a look from my beloved. I took my time, knowing that my father would be waiting outside for me, impatient, perhaps glowing in the dark in his phosphorescent white Navy uniform. The others would ride home. I would walk home with my father, both of us in costume. I wanted as few witnesses as possible. When I could no longer hear the crowds in the hallway, I emerged from the bathroom, still under the spell of those mesmerizing eyes.

15   The lights had been turned off in the hallway and all I could see was the lighted stairwell, at the bottom of which a nun would be stationed. My father would be waiting just outside. I nearly screamed when I felt someone grab me by the waist. But my mouth was quickly covered by someone else's mouth. I was being kissed. My first kiss and I could not even tell who it was. I pulled away to see that face not two inches away from mine. It was he. He smiled down at me. Did I have a silly expression on my face? My glasses felt crooked on my nose. I was unable to move or to speak. More gently, he lifted my chin and touched his lips to mine. This time I did not forget to enjoy it. Then, like the phantom lover that he was, he walked away into the darkened corridor and disappeared.

I don't know how long I stood there. My body was changing right there in the hallway of a Catholic school. My cells were tuning up like musicians in an orchestra, and my heart was a chorus. It was an opera I was composing, and I wanted to stand very still and just listen. But, of course, I heard my father's voice talking to the nun. I was in trouble if he had had to ask about me. I hurried down the stairs making up a story on the way about feeling sick. That would explain my flushed face and it would buy me a little privacy when I got home.

The next day Father announced at the breakfast table that he was leaving on a six month tour of Europe with the Navy in a few weeks and that at the end of the school year my mother, my brother, and I would be sent to Puerto Rico to stay for half a year at Mamá's (my mother's mother) house. I was devastated. This was the usual routine for us. We had always gone to Mamá's to stay when Father was away for long periods. But this year it was different for me. I was in love, and . . . my heart knocked against my bony chest at this thought . . . he loved me too? I broke into sobs and left the table.

In the next week I discovered the inexorable truth about parents. They can actually carry on with their plans right through tears, threats, and the awful spectacle of a teenager's broken heart. My father left me to my mother who impassively packed while I explained over and over that I was at a crucial time in my studies and that if I left my entire life would be ruined. All she would say was, "You are an intelligent girl, you'll catch up." Her head was filled with visions of *casa*[2] and family reunions, long gossip sessions with her mamá and sisters. What did she care that I was losing my one chance at true love?

In the meantime I tried desperately to see him. I thought he would look for me too. But the few times I saw him in the hallway, he was always rushing away. It would be long weeks of confusion and pain before I realized that the kiss was nothing but a little trophy for his ego. He had no interest in me other than as his adorer. He was flattered by my silent worship of him, and he had *bestowed* a kiss on me to please himself, and to fan the flames. I learned a lesson about the battle of the sexes then that I have never forgotten: the object is not always to win, but most times simply to keep your opponent (synonymous at times with "the loved one") guessing.

20   But this is too cynical a view to sustain in the face of that overwhelming rush of emotion that is first love. And in thinking back about my own experience with it, I can be objective only to the point where I recall how sweet the anguish was, how caught up in the moment I felt, and how every nerve in my body was involved in this salute to life. Later, much later, after what seemed like an eternity of dragging the weight of unrequited love around with me, I learned to make myself visible and to relish the little battles required to win the greatest prize of all. And much later, I read and understood Camus'[3] statement about the subject that concerns both adolescent and philosopher alike: if love were easy, life would be too simple.

[1990]

[2]*casa* home.   [3]**Albert Camus** (1913–60), French novelist and philosopher.

Joining the Conversation: Critical Thinking and Writing

1. If you agree with us that Cofer's essay is amusing, try to analyze the sources of its humor. Why are some passages funny?
2. In paragraph 9 Cofer says, "The main privilege of beauty is that others will do almost everything for you, including thinking." Do you agree that the beautiful are privileged? If so, draw on your experience (as one of the privileged or the unprivileged) to recount an example or two. By the way, Cofer seems to imply (paragraph 10) that the academically gifted should be privileged, or at least should be recognized as candidates for leading roles (e.g., that of "a perfect,

silent Roman lady") in school productions. Is it any fairer to privilege brains than to privilege beauty? Explain.

3. In her final paragraph Cofer speaks of the experience as a "salute to life." What do you think she means by that?

4. Cofer is describing a state that is (or used to be) called "puppy love." If you have experienced anything like what Cofer experienced, write your own auto-biographical essay. (You can of course amplify or censor as you wish.) If you have experienced a love that you think is more serious, more lasting, write about *that*.

STORIES

ERNEST HEMINGWAY

Ernest Hemingway (1899–1961) was born in Oak Park, Illinois. After graduating from high school in 1917 he worked on the Kansas City Star, *but left to serve as a volunteer ambulance driver in Italy, where he was wounded in action. He returned home, married, and then served as European correspondent for the* Toronto Star, *but he soon focused on fiction. In 1922 he settled in Paris, where he moved in a circle of American expatriates that included Ezra Pound, Gertrude Stein, and F. Scott Fitzgerald. It was in Paris that he wrote stories and novels about what Gertrude Stein called a "lost generation" of rootless Americans in Europe. (For Hemingway's reminiscences of the* Paris years, see his posthumously published A Moveable Feast.) *He served as a journalist during the Spanish Civil War and during World War II, but he was also something of a private soldier.*

After World War II his reputation ebbed, though he was still active as a writer (for instance, he wrote The Old Man and the Sea *in 1952). In 1954 Hemingway was awarded the Nobel Prize in Literature; in 1961, depressed by a sense of failing power, he took his own life.*

Cat in the Rain

There were only two Americans stopping at the hotel. They did not know any of the people they passed on the stairs on their way to and from their room. Their room was on the second floor facing the sea. It also faced the public garden and the war monument. There were big palms and green benches in the public garden. In the good weather there was always an artist with his easel. Artists liked the way the palms grew and the bright colors of the hotels facing the gardens and the sea. Italians came from a long way off to look up at the war monument. It was made of bronze and glistened in the rain. It was raining. The rain dripped from the palm trees. Water stood in pools on the gravel paths. The sea broke in a long line in the rain and slipped back down the beach to come up and break again in a long line in the rain. The motor cars were gone from the square by the war monument. Across the square in the doorway of the café a waiter stood looking out at the empty square.

The American wife stood at the window looking out. Outside right under their window a cat was crouched under one of the dripping green tables. The cat was trying to make herself so compact that she would not be dripped on.

"I'm going down and get that kitty," the American wife said.

"I'll do it," her husband offered from the bed.

5 "No, I'll get it. The poor kitty is out trying to keep dry under a table."

The husband went on reading, lying propped up with the two pillows at the foot of the bed.

"Don't get wet," he said.

The wife went downstairs and the hotel owner stood up and bowed to her as she passed the office. His desk was at the far end of the office. He was an old man and very tall.

"Il piove,"[1] the wife said. She liked the hotel-keeper.

10 "Si, si, Signora, brutto tempo. It is very bad weather."

He stood behind his desk in the far end of the dim room. The wife liked him. She liked the deadly serious way he received any complaints. She liked his dignity. She liked the way he wanted to serve her. She liked the way he felt about being a hotel-keeper. She liked his old, heavy face and big hands.

Liking him she opened the door and looked out. It was raining harder. A man in a rubber cape was crossing the empty square to the café. The cat would be around to the right. Perhaps she could go along under the eaves. As she stood in the doorway an umbrella opened behind her. It was the maid who looked after their room.

"You must not get wet," she smiled, speaking Italian. Of course, the hotel-keeper had sent her.

With the maid holding the umbrella over her, she walked along the gravel path until she was under their window. The table was there, washed bright green in the rain, but the cat was gone. She was suddenly disappointed. The maid looked up at her.

15 "Ha perduto qualque cosa, Signora?"[2]

"There was a cat," said the American girl.

"A cat?"

"Si, il gatto."

"A cat?" the maid laughed. "A cat in the rain?"

20 "Yes," she said, "under the table." Then. "Oh. I wanted it so much. I wanted a kitty."

When she talked English the maid's face tightened.

"Come, Signora," she said. "We must get back inside. You will be wet."

"I suppose so," said the American girl.

They went back along the gravel path and passed in the door. The maid stayed outside to close the umbrella. As the American girl passed the office, the padrone bowed from his desk. Something felt very small and tight inside the girl. The padrone made her feel very small and at the same time really important. She had a momentary feeling of being of supreme importance. She went on up the stairs. She opened the door of the room. George was on the bed, reading.

25 "Did you get the cat?" he asked, putting the book down.

"It was gone."

"Wonder where it went to," he said, resting his eyes from reading.

[1]**Il piove** It's raining (Italian).   [2]**Ha . . . Signora** Have you lost something, Madam?

She sat down on the bed.

"I wanted it so much," she said. "I don't know why I wanted it so much. I wanted that poor kitty. It isn't any fun to be a poor kitty out in the rain."

30   George was reading again.

She went over and sat in front of the mirror of the dressing table looking at herself with the hand glass. She studied her profile, first one side and then the other. Then she studied the back of her head and her neck.

"Don't you think it would be a good idea if I let my hair grow out?" she asked, looking at her profile again.

George looked up and saw the back of her neck, clipped close like a boy's.

"I like it the way it is."

35   "I get so tired of it," she said. "I get so tired of looking like a boy."

George shifted his position in the bed. He hadn't looked away from her since she started to speak.

"You look pretty darn nice," he said.

She laid the mirror down on the dresser and went over to the window and looked out. It was getting dark.

"I want to pull my hair back tight and smooth and make a big knot at the back that I can feel," she said. "I want to have a kitty to sit on my lap and purr when I stroke her."

40   "Yeah?" George said from the bed.

"And I want to eat at a table with my own silver and I want candles. And I want it to be spring and I want to brush my hair out in front of a mirror and I want a kitty and I want some new clothes."

"Oh, shut up and get something to read," George said. He was reading again.

His wife was looking out of the window. It was quite dark now and still raining in the palm trees.

"Anyway, I want a cat," she said, "I want a cat. I want a cat now. If I can't have long hair or any fun, I can have a cat."

45   George was not listening. He was reading his book. His wife looked out of the window where the light had come on in the square.

Someone knocked at the door.

"Avanti,"[3] George said. He looked up from his book.

In the doorway stood the maid. She held a big tortoise-shell cat pressed tight against her and swung down against her body.

"Excuse me," she said, "the padrone asked me to bring this for the Signora."

[1925]

---

[3]**Avanti** Come in.

A Student's Notes and Journal Entries on "Cat in the Rain"

When you read a story—or, perhaps more accurately, when you reread a story before discussing it or writing about it—you'll find it helpful to jot an occasional note (for instance, a brief response or a question) in the margins and to underline or highlight passages that strike you as especially interesting. Here is part of the story, with the annotations of a student, Bill Yanagi.

696   *Chapter 22   Love and Hate*

The cat was trying to make herself so compact that she would not be dripped on.

Is he making a joke? Or maybe he just isn't even thinking about what he is saying?

"I'm going down and get that kitty," the American wife said.

"I'll do it," her husband offered from the bed.

"No, I'll get it. The poor kitty is out trying to keep dry under a table."

The husband <u>went on reading</u>, lying propped up with the two pillows at the foot of the bed.

"Don't get wet," he said.

He doesn't make a move

still doesn't move

---

contrast — with the husband

The wife went downstairs and the <u>hotel owner stood up and bowed to her</u> as she passed the office. His desk was at the far end of the office. He was an old man and very tall.

"Il piove," the wife said. She liked the hotel-keeper.

"Si, si, Signora, brutto tempo. It is very bad weather."

He stood behind his desk in the far end of the dim room. <u>The wife liked him.</u> She liked the deadly serious way he received any complaints. <u>She liked his dignity.</u> She liked the way he wanted to serve her. She liked the way he felt about being a hotel-keeper. She liked his old, heavy face and big hands.

to em-phasize the bad weather??

Liking him she opened the door and looked out. It was raining harder. <u>A man in a rubber cape</u> was crossing the <u>empty square</u> to the café. The cat would be around to the right.

She re-spects him and she is pleased by the atten-tion he shows

Asking Questions about a Story

Everything in a story is presumably important, but if you have read the story once, probably something has especially interested (or puzzled) you, such as the relationship between two people, or the way the end of the story is connected to the beginning. On rereading, then, pen in hand, you'll find yourself noticing things that you missed or didn't find especially significant on your first reading. Now that you know the end of the story, you will read the beginning in a different way.

If your instructor asks you to think about certain questions, you'll keep them in mind while you reread, and you will find ideas coming to you. In "Cat in the Rain," suppose you are asked (or you ask yourself) if the story might just as well be about a dog in the rain. Would anything be lost?

Here are a few questions that you can ask of almost any story. (On pages 358–60, we give a fuller list.) After scanning the questions, you will want to reread the story, pen in hand, and then jot down your responses on a sheet of paper. As you write, it is helpful to go back and reread the story or at least parts of it.

1. *What happens?* In two or three sentences—say 25–50 words—summarize what happens in the story.
2. *What sorts of people are the chief characters?* In "Cat in the Rain" the chief characters are George, George's wife, and the innkeeper (the padrone). Jot down the traits that each seems to possess, and next to each trait briefly give some supporting evidence.

3. *What especially pleased or displeased you in the story?* Devote at least a sentence or two to the end of the story. Do you find the end satisfying? Why or why not?
4. *Have you any thoughts about the title?* If so, what are they? If the story did not have a title, what would you call it?

After you have made your own jottings, compare them with these responses by a student. No two readers will respond in exactly the same way, but all readers can examine their responses and try to account for them, at least in part. If your responses are substantially different, how do you account for the differences?

1. *A summary.* A young wife, stopping with her husband at an Italian hotel, from her room sees a cat in the rain. She goes to get it, but it is gone, and so she returns empty-handed. A moment later the maid knocks at the door, holding a tortoise-shell cat.
2. *The characters: The woman.*
   kind-hearted (pities cat in rain)
   appreciates innkeeper's courtesy ("liked the way he wanted to serve her") and
       admires him ("She liked his dignity")
   unhappy (wants a cat, wants to change her hair, wants to eat at a table with her
       own silver)
   The husband, George.
   not willing to put himself out (says he'll go to garden to get cat but doesn't move)
   doesn't seem very interested in wife (hardly talks to her—he's reading; tells her
       to "shut up")
   but he does say he finds her attractive ("You look pretty darn nice")
   The innkeeper.
   serious, dignified ("She liked the deadly serious way he received any complaints.
       She liked his dignity")
   courteous, helpful (sends maid with umbrella; at end sends maid with cat)
3. *Dislikes and likes.* "Dislikes" is too strong, but I was disappointed that more didn't happen at the end. What is the husband's reaction to the cat? Or his final reaction to his wife? I mean, what did he think about his wife when the maid brings the cat? And, for that matter, what is the wife's reaction? Is she satisfied? Or does she realize that the cat can't really make her happy? Now for the *likes.* (1) I guess I did like the way it turned out; it's sort of a happy ending, I think, since she wants the cat and gets it. (2) I also especially like the innkeeper. Maybe I like him partly because the wife likes him, and if she likes him he must be nice. And he *is* nice— very helpful. And I also like the way Hemingway shows the husband. I don't mean that I like the man himself, but I like the way Hemingway shows he is such a bas- tard—not getting off the bed to get the cat, telling his wife to shut up and read.
   Another thing about him is that the one time he says something nice about her, it's about her hair, and she isn't keen on the way her hair is. She says it makes her look "like a boy," and she is "tired" of looking like a boy. There's something wrong with this marriage. George hardly pays attention to his wife, but he wants her to look like a boy. Maybe the idea is that this macho guy wants to keep her looking like an inferior (immature) version of himself. Anyway, he certainly doesn't seem interested in letting her fulfill herself as a woman.
   I think my feelings add up to this: I like the way Hemingway shows us the rela- tion between the husband and wife (even though the relation is pretty bad), and I like the innkeeper. Even if the relation with the couple ends unhappily, the story has a sort of happy ending, so far as it goes, since the innkeeper does what he can to please his guest: he sends the maid, with the cat. There's really nothing more that he can do.

More about the ending. The more I think about it, the more I feel that the ending is as happy as it can be. George is awful. When his wife says "I want a cat and I want a cat now," Hemingway tells us "George was not listening." And then, a moment later, almost like a good fairy the maid appears and grants the wife's wish.

4. *The title.* I don't suppose that I would have called it "Cat in the Rain," but I don't know what I would have called it. Maybe "An American Couple in Italy." Or maybe "The Innkeeper." I really do think that the innkeeper is very important, even though he only has a few lines. He's very impressive—not only to the girl, but to me (and maybe to all readers), since at the end of the story we see how careful the innkeeper is.

But the more I think about Hemingway's title, the more I think that maybe it also refers to the girl. Like the "poor kitty" in the rain, the wife is in a pretty bad situation. "It isn't any fun to be a poor kitty out in the rain." Of course the woman is indoors, but her husband generates lots of unpleasant weather. She may as well be out in the rain. She says "I want to have a kitty to sit on my lap and purr when I stroke her." This shows that she wants to be affectionate and that she also wants to have someone respond to her affection. She *is* like a cat in the rain.

The responses of this student probably include statements that you want to take issue with. Or perhaps you feel that the student did not even mention some things that you think are important. You may want to make notes and raise some questions in class.

A Sample Essay by a Student: "Hemingway's American Wife"

The responses that we have quoted were written by Bill Yanagi, who later wrote an essay developing one of them. Here is the essay.

Yanagi 1

Bill Yanagi

Professor Costello

English 10B

21 December 2012

Hemingway's American Wife

My title alludes not to any of the four women to whom Hemingway

was married, but to "the American wife" who is twice called by this term in

his short story "Cat in the Rain." We first meet her in the first sentence of

the story ("There were only two Americans stopping at the hotel"), and the

next time she is mentioned (apart from a reference to the wife and her

husband as "they") it is as "the American wife," at the beginning of the

---

second paragraph of the story. The term is used again at the end of the third paragraph.

She is, then, at least in the early part of this story, just an American or an American wife—someone identified only by her nationality and her marital status, but not at all by her personality, her individuality, her inner self. She first becomes something of an individual when she separates herself from her husband by leaving the hotel room and going to look for a cat that she has seen in the garden, in the rain. This act of separation, however, has not the slightest effect on her husband, who "went on reading" (694).

When she returns, without the cat, he puts down his book and speaks to her, but it is obvious that he has no interest in her, beyond as a physical object ("You look pretty darn nice"). This comment is produced when she says she is thinking of letting her hair grow out because she is "so tired of looking like a boy" (695). Why, a reader wonders, does her husband, who has paid almost no attention to her up to now, assure her that she looks "pretty darn nice"? I think it is reasonable to conclude that he *wants* her to look like someone who is not truly a woman, in particular someone who is immature. That she does not feel she has much identity is evident when she continues to talk about letting her hair grow, and she says "I want to pull my hair back tight and smooth and make a big knot at the back that I can feel" (695). Long hair is, or at least was, the traditional sign of a woman; she wants long hair, and at the same time she wants to keep it under her control by tying it in a "big knot," a knot that she can feel, a knot whose presence reminds her, because she can feel it, of her feminine nature.

She goes on to say that she wants to brush her hair "in front of a mirror." That is, she wants to *see* and to feel her femininity, since her husband apparently—so far as we can see in the story, at least—scarcely recognizes it or her. Perhaps her desire for the cat ("I want a cat") is a veiled way of saying that

Yanagi 3

she wants to express her animal nature, and not be simply a neglected woman

who is made by her husband to look like a boy. Hemingway tells us, however,

that when she looked for the cat in the garden she could not find it, a sign,

I think, of her failure to break from the man. At the end of the story the maid

brings her the cat, but a woman cannot just be handed a new nature and

accept it, just like that. She has to find it herself, and in herself, so I think the

story ends with "the American wife" still nothing more than an American wife.

[New page]

Yanagi 4

Work Cited

Hemingway, Ernest. "Cat in the Rain." *Literature for Composition*. Ed. Sylvan

Barnet, William Burto, and William E. Cain. 10th ed. New York: Pearson,

2014. 693-95. Print.

A few comments and questions may be useful.

- Do you find the essay interesting? Explain your response.
- Do you find the essay well written? Explain.
- Do you find the argument convincing? Can you suggest ways of strengthening it, or do you think the argument is mistaken? Carefully reread "Cat in the Rain," taking note of passages that give further support to this student's argument, or that seem to challenge or qualify it.
- We often say that a good critical essay sends us back to the literary work with a fresh point of view. Our rereading differs from our earlier reading. Does this essay change your reading of Hemingway's story?

Joining the Conversation: Critical Thinking and Writing

1. Can we be certain that the cat at the end of the story is the cat that the woman saw in the rain? (When we first hear about the cat in the rain we are not told anything about its color, and at the end of the story we are not told that the tortoise-shell cat is wet.) Does it matter if there are two cats?
2. One student argued that the cat represents the child that the girl wants to have. Do you think there is something to this idea? How might you support or refute it?
3. Consider the following passage:

> As the American girl passed the office, the padrone bowed from his desk. Something felt very small and tight inside the girl. The padrone made her feel very small and at the same time really important. She had a momentary feeling of being of supreme importance.

Do you think there is anything sexual here? And if so, that the passage tells us something about her relations with her husband? Support your view.

4. What do you suppose Hemingway's attitude was toward each of the three chief characters? How might you support your hunch?

5. Hemingway wrote the story in Italy, when his wife Hadley was pregnant. In a letter to F. Scott Fitzgerald he said,

> Cat in the Rain wasn't about Hadley. . . . When I wrote that we were at Rapallo but Hadley was 4 months pregnant with Bumby. The Inn Keeper was the one at Cortina D'Ampezzo. . . . Hadley never made a speech in her life about wanting a baby because she had been told various things by her doctor and I'd—no use going into all that. (*Letters* 180)

According to some biographers, the story shows that Hemingway knew his marriage was going on the rocks (Hemingway and Hadley divorced). Does knowing that Hemingway's marriage turned out unhappily help you to understand the story? Does it make the story more interesting? And do you think that the story tells a biographer something about Hemingway's life?

6. It is sometimes said that a good short story does two things at once: It provides a believable picture of the surface of life, and it illuminates some moral or psychological complexity that we feel is part of the essence of human life. This dual claim may not be true, but for the moment accept it. Do you think that Hemingway's story fulfills either or both of these specifications? Support your view.

A Second Example: An Essay Drawing on Related Material in the Chapter

Another student, Holly Klein, wrote about "Cat in the Rain," but she thought about it partly in terms of a familiar saying, "All the world loves a lover." She also draws on a less familiar quotation; it might have been better to have cited the source of the unfamiliar quotation, but since the words are attributed to an author and are given within quotation marks, there is no problem of plagiarism. Here are her first notes, and the essay that she developed from them.

JOURNAL ENTRIES

"All the world loves a lover? Not necessarily. In real life, few emotions are less sociable than romantic passion." Certainly there's not much romantic passion in this story. But are these people in love?

Is it true that love stories are about people who are happy in love, or are they mostly about people who are unhappy? Many lovers may suffer and some even die (Leonardo DiCaprio in *Titanic*), but aren't they happy anyway? They are happy in their unhappiness. (And Rose—Kate Winslet—survives, happy and unhappy in her love.)

Is "Cat" really a love story anyway? Yes, in the sense it is about people who must at least at some time in the past have been lovers—happy lovers—but who now seem stuck with each other. The wife still seems to be in love, or maybe she is trying to bring a dead love back to life.

Is there something to the idea (as Wilcox says) that "love is a mood" to men but is "life or death" to women? Does this add up to saying that for men, love is something of the moment, and is trivial, but for women it is enduring and important? And do men and women react differently to love stories? Someone in class—and there was plenty of agreement and almost no disagreement—said that *Titanic* is a "woman's picture." But Mark liked it as much as I did. Or at least he said so.

A Sample Essay by a Student: "Hemingway's Unhappy Lovers"

Here is the final version of Holly Klein's essay:

Klein 1

Holly Klein

Professor Chung

English 1102

17 December 2012

Hemingway's Unhappy Lovers

In class someone suggested that *Romeo and Juliet* is not so much

about how happy two people are but about how unhappy they are. This

statement, which at first I thought was ridiculous, now strikes me as true,

or for the most part true. The lovers in *Romeo and Juliet* and in *West Side*

Story, to name only some of the most famous lovers, would not give up

being in love, but during most of the time they are unhappy. I have heard a

saying, "Love means not ever having to say you are sorry," but some of

these lovers, and other lovers in daytime television programs, are always

saying they are sorry, and always feeling sorry for themselves. And we feel

sorry for them. Our interest in them is not in their happiness, but in their

unhappiness.

Certainly in Ernest Hemingway's "Cat in the Rain" the woman is unhappy—

and who would not be unhappy, with a husband like hers? She says she is

going out into the rain to get the cat, and he says "Don't get wet" (694), and

he goes right on reading, obviously uninterested in what his wife is doing, or

in her needs. The wife never explicitly says she is unhappy, but it is obvious

---

that she is. Her husband pays very little attention to her, and then, when he does—he goes so far as to say "You look pretty darn nice"—it is only after she tells him she wants to change her appearance: "I get so tired of looking like a boy." When she adds that she wants to change her hair, his response is, "Yeah?" And a moment later he says, "Oh, shut up and get something to read" (695). I felt like hitting him, and I suddenly realized that, at least for this story, lovers are unhappy. If Hemingway's lovers were happy and spent their time cooing at each other, the story probably would have been boring. What is interesting here is, paradoxically, the man's lack of interest in his wife—he is probably affectionate only when he wants sex—and the woman's basic unhappiness. Her unhappiness is revealed partly by her almost desperate attempt to give affection to the cat, and to receive some affection from it: "I want to have a kitty to sit on my lap and purr when I stroke her" (695). Ella Wheeler Wilcox may be overstating the matter, but, allowing for what is called poetic license, there is something sound in her view that "love is a mood—no more—to man, / And love to a woman is life or death".

Many people probably do not make a distinction between the attitudes of men and women toward love, and they therefore do not distinguish between the responses of men and of women to love stories. I think it is probably true that most love stories are chiefly about unhappiness, but it is probably also true that women in love are more likely than men to express in words their unhappiness. (I think there are psychological or sociological studies that support this view.) In any case, in support of the idea that love stories are chiefly about unhappiness, I can say that "Cat in the Rain" interested me not because the lovers keep expressing their romantic passion but because the man does *not* express his love, and the woman expresses her frustration. In this story about lovers, the man is in bed—but he spends most of his time *reading* in bed, and (as I said) about the best he can say to

Klein 3

the woman is that she looks "pretty darn nice". The wife holds our interest

because she is unhappy, stuck with this guy, and she is so grateful for a kind

word from the hotel-keeper. She does not explicitly say that she is desperately

unhappy, but she does express very vigorously a desire for a life different

from the one she is now living, and we do feel that (at least for her) love is

not just a "mood," as it probably is for the man, but is a matter of "life or

death." She is, so to speak, dying to be loved.

[New page]

Klein 4

Work Cited

Hemingway, Ernest. "Cat in the Rain." *Literature for Composition.* Ed. Sylvan

Barnet, William Burto, and William E. Cain. 10th ed. New York: Pearson,

2014. 693-95. Print.

We can ask of this essay the same questions that we asked of an earlier essay:

- Do you find the essay interesting? Explain your response.
- Do you find the essay well written? Explain.
- Do you find the argument convincing? Can you suggest ways of strengthening it, or do you think the argument is mistaken? Carefully reread "Cat in the Rain," taking note of passages that give further support to this student's argument, or that seem to challenge or qualify it.
- We often say that a good critical essay sends us back to the literary work with a fresh point of view. Our rereading differs from our earlier reading. Does this essay change your reading of Hemingway's story?

We can also ask one additional question:

- Sometimes writers make their essays far too impersonal, removing every trace of the writer as an individual human being, a distinct person. Do you think that this writer goes too far in the other direction, making the essay too personal? If you think that she does, what advice would you give her, to help her strike the right balance?

ZORA NEALE HURSTON

Zora Neale Hurston (1891–1960) was brought up in Eaton-ville, Florida, a town said to be the first all-black self-governing town in the United States. Her mother died in 1904, and when Hurston's father remarried, Hurston felt out of place. In 1914 she joined a traveling theatrical group as a maid, hoping to save money for school. Later, by working at such jobs as mani-curist and waitress, she put herself through college, entering Howard University in 1923. After receiving a scholarship, she transferred in 1926 to Barnard College in New York, where she was the first African American student in the college. After graduating from Barnard in 1928 she taught drama, worked as an editor, and studied anthropology. But when grant money ran out in 1932 she returned to Eatonville to edit the folk material that she had collected during four years of fieldwork, and to do further writing. She published steadily from 1932 to 1938—stories, folklore, and two novels—but she gained very little money. Further-more, although she played a large role in the Harlem Renaissance in the 1930s, she was criticized by Richard Wright and other influential black authors for portraying blacks as stereotypes and for being politically conservative. To many in the 1950s her writing seemed reactionary, almost embarrassing in an age of black protest, and she herself—working as a domestic, a librarian, and a substitute teacher—was almost forgotten. Hurston died in a county welfare home in Florida and is buried in an unmarked grave. But literary scholars now judge her one of the major authors of her era, and her work is widely read and taught.

Sweat

It was eleven o'clock of a Spring night in Florida. It was Sunday. Any other night, Delia Jones would have been in bed for two hours by this time. But she was a washwoman, and Monday morning meant a great deal to her. So she collected the soiled clothes on Saturday when she returned the clean things. Sunday night after church, she sorted them and put the white things to soak. It saved her almost a half day's start. A great hamper in the bedroom held the clothes that she brought home. It was so much neater than a number of bundles lying around.

She squatted in the kitchen floor beside the great pile of clothes, sorting them into small heaps according to color, and humming a song in a mournful key, but wonder-ing through it all where Sykes, her husband, had gone with her horse and buckboard.[1]

Just then something long, round, limp and black fell upon her shoulders and slithered to the floor beside her. A great terror took hold of her. It softened her knees and dried her mouth so that it was a full minute before she could cry out or move. Then she saw that it was the big bull whip her husband liked to carry when he drove.

She lifted her eyes to the door and saw him standing there bent over with laughter at her fright. She screamed at him.

5   "Sykes, what you throw dat whip on me like dat? You know it would skeer me—looks just like a snake, an' you knows how skeered Ah is of snakes."

"Course Ah knowed it! That's how come Ah done it." He slapped his leg with his hand and almost rolled on the ground in his mirth. "If you such a big fool dat you got to have a fit over a earth worm or a string, Ah don't keer how bad Ah skeer you."

---

[1]**buckboard** an open wagon.

"You aint got no business doing it. Gawd knows it's a sin. Some day Ah'm gointuh drop dead from some of yo' foolishness. 'Nother thing, where you been wid mah rig? Ah feeds dat pony. He aint fuh you to be drivin' wid no bull whip."

"Yo sho is one aggravatin' nigger woman!" he declared and stepped into the room. She resumed her work and did not answer him at once. "Ah done tole you time and again to keep them white folks' clothes outa dis house."

He picked up the whip and glared down at her. Delia went on with her work. She went out into the yard and returned with a galvanized tub and set it on the washbench. She saw that Sykes had kicked all of the clothes together again, and now stood in her way truculently, his whole manner hoping, *praying,* for an argument. But she walked calmly around him and commenced to re-sort the things.

10   "Next time, Ah'm gointer to kick 'em outdoors," he threatened as he struck a match along the leg of his corduroy breeches.

Delia never looked up from her work, and her thin, stooped shoulders sagged further.

"Ah aint for no fuss t'night Sykes. Ah just come from taking sacrament at the church house."

He snorted scornfully. "Yeah, you just come from de church house on a Sunday night, but heah you is gone to work on them clothes. You aint nothing but a hypocrite. One of them amen-corner Christians—sing, whoop, shout, then come home and wash white folks clothes on the Sabbath."

He stepped roughly upon the whitest pile of things, kicking them helter-skelter as he crossed the room. His wife gave a little scream of dismay, and quickly gathered them together again.

15   "Sykes, you quit grindin' dirt into these clothes! How can Ah git through by Sat'day if Ah don't start on Sunday?"

"Ah don't keer if you never git through. Anyhow, Ah done promised Gawd and a couple of other men, Ah aint gointer have it in mah house. Don't gimme no lip neither, else Ah'll throw 'em out and put mah fist up side yo' head to boot."

Delia's habitual meekness seemed to slip from her shoulders like a blown scarf. She was on her feet; her poor little body, her bare knuckly hands bravely defying the strapping hulk before her.

"Looka heah, Sykes, you done gone too fur. Ah been married to you fur fifteen years, and Ah been takin' in washin' for fifteen years. Sweat, sweat, sweat! Work and sweat, cry and sweat, pray and sweat!"

"What's that got to do with me?" he asked brutally.

20   "What's it got to do with you, Sykes? Mah tub of suds is filled yo' belly with vittles more times than yo' hands is filled it. Mah sweat is done paid for this house and Ah reckon Ah kin keep on sweatin in it."

She seized the iron skillet from the stove and struck a defensive pose, which act surprised him greatly, coming from her. It cowed him and he did not strike her as he usually did.

"Naw you won't," she panted, "that ole snaggle-toothed black woman you runnin' with aint comin' heah to pile up on *mah* sweat and blood. You aint paid for nothin' on this place, and Ah'm gointer stay right heah till Ah'm toted out foot foremost."

"Well, you better quit gittin' me riled up, else they'll be totin' you out sooner than you expect. Ah'm so tired of you Ah don't know whut to do. Gawd! how Ah hates skinny wimmen!"

A little awed by this new Delia, he sidled out of the door and slammed the back gate after him. He did not say where he had gone, but she knew too well. She knew very well that he would not return until nearly daybreak also. Her work over, she went on to bed but not to sleep at once. Things had come to a pretty pass!

25   She lay awake, gazing upon the debris that cluttered their matrimonial trail. Not an image left standing along the way. Anything like flowers had long ago been drowned in the salty stream that had been pressed from her heart. Her tears, her sweat, her blood. She had brought love to the union and he had brought a longing for the flesh. Two months after the wedding, he had given her the first brutal beating. She had the memory of numerous trips to Orlando with all of his wages when he had returned to her penniless, even before the first year had passed. She was young and soft then, but now she thought of her knotty, muscled limbs, her harsh knuckly hands, and drew herself up into an unhappy little ball in the middle of the big feather bed. Too late now to hope for love, even if it were not Bertha it would be someone else. This case differed from the others only in that she was bolder than the others. Too late for everything except her little home. She had built it for her old days, and planted one by one the trees and flowers there. It was lovely to her, lovely.

Somehow before sleep came, she found herself saying aloud: "Oh well, whatever goes over the Devil's back, is got to come under his belly. Sometime or ruther, Sykes, like everybody else, is gointer reap his sowing." After that she was able to build a spiritual earthworks against her husband. His shells could no longer reach her. *Amen*. She went to sleep and slept until he announced his presence in bed by kicking her feet and rudely snatching the cover away.

"Gimme some kivah heah, an' git yo' damn foots over on yo' own side! Ah oughter mash you in yo' mouf fuh drawing dat skillet on me."

Delia went clear to the rail without answering him. A triumphant indifference to all that he was or did.

The week was as full of work for Delia as all other weeks, and Saturday found her behind her little pony, collecting and delivering clothes.

30   It was a hot, hot day near the end of July. The village men on Joe Clarke's porch even chewed cane listlessly. They did not hurl the cane-knots as usual. They let them dribble over the edge of the porch. Even conversation had collapsed under the heat.

"Heah comes Delia Jones," Jim Merchant said, as the shaggy pony came round the bend of the road toward them. The rusty buckboard was heaped with baskets of crisp, clean laundry.

"Yep," Joe Lindsay agreed, "Hot or col', rain or shine, jes ez reg'lar ez de weeks roll roun' Delia carries 'em an' fetches 'em on Sat'day."

"She better if she wanter eat," said Moss. "Syke Jones aint wuth de shot an' powder hit would tek tuh kill 'em. Not to *bub* he aint."

"He sho' aint," Walter Thomas chimed in. "It's too bad, too, cause she wuz a right pritty lil trick when he got huh. Ah'd uh mah'ied huh mahseft' it' he hadnter beat me to it."

35   Delia nodded briefly at the men as she drove past.

"Too much knockin will ruin *any* 'oman. He done beat huh nough tuh kill three women, let 'lone change they looks," said Elijah Mosely. "How Syke kin stommuck dat big black greasy Mogu[2] he's layin' roun' wid, gits me. Ah swear dat eight-rock couldn't kiss a sardine can Ah done thowed out de back do' 'way las' yeah."

"Aw, she's fat, thass how come. He's allus been crazy 'bout fat women," put in Merchant. "He'd a' been tied up wid one long time ago if he could a' found one tuh have him. Did Ah tell yuh 'bout him come sidlin' roun' *mah* 'wife—bringin' her a basket uh pee-cans outa his yard fuh a present? Yes-sir, mah wife! She tol' him tuh take 'em right straight back home, cause Delia works so hard ovah dat washtub she reckon everything en de place taste lak sweat an' soap-suds. Ah jus' wisht Ah'd a' caught 'im 'roun' dere! Ah'd a' made his hips ketch on fiah down dat shell road."

[2]**Mogu** big person.

"Ah know he done it, too. Ah sees 'im grinnin' at every 'oman dat passes," Walter Thomas said. "But even so, he useter eat some mighty big hunks uh humble pie tuh git dat lil' 'oman he got. She wuz ez pritty ez a speckled pup! Dat wuz fifteen yeahs ago. He useter be so skeered uh losin' huh, she could make him do some parts of a husband's duty. Dey never wuz de same in de mind."

"There oughter be a law about him," said Lindsay. "He aint fit tuh carry guts tuh a bear."

40   Clarke spoke for the first time. "Taint no law on earth dat kin make a man be decent if it aint in 'im. There's plenty men dat takes a wife lak dey do a joint uh sugar-cane. It's round, juicy an' sweet when dey gits it. But dey squeeze an' grind, squeeze an' grind an' wring tell dey wring every drop uh pleasure dat's in 'em out. When dey's satisfied dat dey is wring dry, dey treats 'em jes lak dey do a canechew. Dey thows 'em away. Dey knows whut dey is doin' while dey is at it, an' hates theirselves fuh it but they keeps on hangin' after huh tell she's empty. Den dey hates huh fuh bein' a cane-chew an' in de way."

"We oughter take Syke an' dat stray 'oman uh his'n down in Lake Howell swamp an' lay on de rawhide till they cain't say 'Lawd a' mussy.' He allus wuz uh ovahbearin' niggah, but since dat white 'oman from up north done teached 'im how to run a automobile, he done got too biggety to live—an' we oughter kill 'im," Old Man Anderson advised.

A grunt of approval went around the porch. But the heat was melting their civic virtue and Elijah Moseley began to bait Joe Clarke.

"Come on, Joe, git a melon outa dere an' slice it up for yo' customers. We'se all sufferin' wid de heat. De bear's done got *me!*"

"Thass right. Joe, a watermelon is jes' whut Ah needs tuh cure de eppizudicks."[3] Walter Thomas joined forces with Moseley. "Come on dere, Joe. We all is steady customers an' you aint set us up in a long time. Ah chooses dat long, bowlegged Floridy favorite."

45   "A god, an' be dough. You all gimme twenty cents and slice away," Clarke retorted. "Ah needs a col' slice m'self. Heah, everybody chip in. Ah'll lend y'll mah meat knife."

The money was quickly subscribed and the huge melon brought forth. At that moment, Sykes and Bertha arrived. A determined silence fell on the porch and the melon was put away again.

Merchant snapped down the blade of his jackknife and moved toward the store door.

"Come on in, Joe, an' gimme a slab uh sow belly an' uh pound uh coffee— almost fuhgot 'twas Sat'day. Got to git on home." Most of the men left also.

Just then Delia drove past on her way home, as Sykes was ordering magnificently for Bertha. It pleased him for Delia to see.

50   "Git whutsoever yo' heart desires, Honey. Wait a minute, Joe. Give huh two bottles uh strawberry soda-water, uh quart uh parched groundpeas, an' a block uh chewin' gum."

With all this they left the store, with Sykes reminding Bertha that this was his town and she could have it if she wanted it.

The men returned soon after they left, and held their watermelon feast. "Where did Syke Jones git dat 'oman from nohow?" Lindsay asked.

"Ovah Apopka. Guess dey musta been cleanin' out de town when she lef. She don't look lak a thing but a hunk uh liver wid hair on it."

---

[3]**eppizudicks** i.e., epizootic, an epidemic among animals.

"Well, she sho' kin squall," Dave Carter contributed. "When she gits ready tuh laff, she jes' opens huh mouf an' latches it back tuh de las' notch. No ole grandpa alligator down in Lake Bell aint got nothin' on huh."

55   Bertha had been in town three months now. Sykes was still paying her room rent at Della Lewis'—the only house in town that would have taken her in. Sykes took her frequently to Winter Park to "stomps."[4] He still assured her that he was the swellest man in the state.

"Sho' you kin have dat lil' ole house soon's Ah kin git dat 'oman outa dere. Everything b'longs tuh me an' you sho' kin have it. Ah sho' 'bominates uh skinny 'oman. Lawdy, you sho' is got one portly shape on you! You kin git *anything* you wants. Dis is *mah* town an' you sho' kin have it."

Delia's work-worn knees crawled over the earth in Gethsemane and on the rocks of Calvary[5] many, many times during these months. She avoided the villagers and meeting places in her effort to be blind and deaf. But Bertha nullified this to a degree, by coming to Delia's house to call Sykes out to her at the gate.

Delia and Sykes fought all the time now with no peaceful interludes. They slept and ate in silence. Two or three times Delia had attempted a timid friendliness, but she was repulsed each time. It was plain that the breaches must remain agape.

The sun had burned July to August. The heat streamed down like a million hot arrows, smiting all things living upon the earth. Grass withered, leaves browned, snakes went blind in shedding and men and dogs went mad. Dog days!

60   Delia came home one day and found Sykes there before her. She wondered, but started to go on into the house without speaking, even though he was standing in the kitchen door and she must either stoop under his arm or ask him to move. He made no room for her. She noticed a soap box beside the steps, but paid no particular attention to it, knowing that he must have brought it there. As she was stooping to pass under his outstretched arm, he suddenly pushed her backward, laughingly.

"Look in de box dere Delia. Ah done brung yuh somethin'!"

She nearly fell upon the box in her stumbling, and when she saw what it held, she all but fainted outright.

"Syke! Syke, mah Gawd! You take dat rattlesnake 'way from heah! You *gottuh*. Oh, Jesus, have mussy!"

"Ah aint gut tuh do nuthin' uh de kin'—fact is Ah aint got tuh do nothin' but die. Taint no use uh you puttin' on airs makin' out lak you sceered uh dat snake— he's gointer stay right heah tell he die. He wouldn't bite me cause Ah knows how tuh handle 'im. Nohow he wouldn't risk breakin' out his fangs 'gin *yo'* skinny laigs."

65   "Naw, now Syke, don't keep dat thing 'roun' heah tuh skeer me tuh death. You knows Ah'm even feared uh earth worms. Thass de biggest snake Ah evah did see. Kill 'im Syke, please."

"Doan ast me tuh do nothin 'fuh yuh. Goin' 'roun' tryin' to be so damn aster-perious. Naw, Ah aint gonna kill it. Ah think uh damn sight mo' uh him dan you! Dat's a nice snake an' anybody doan lak 'im kin jes' hit de grit."

The village soon heard that Sykes had the snake, and came to see and ask questions.

"How de hen-fire did you ketch dat six-foot rattler, Syke?" Thomas asked.

---

[4]**stomps** dances. [5]**Gethsemane** the garden where Jesus prayed just before he was betrayed (Matthew 26.36–47); **Calvary** was the hill where he was crucified.

"He's full uh frogs so he caint hardly move, thass how Ah eased up on 'm. But Ah'm a snake charmer an' knows how tuh handle 'em. Shux, dat aint nothin'. Ah could ketch one eve'y day if Ah so wanted tuh."

70   "Whut he needs is a heavy hick'ry club leaned real heavy on his head. Dat's de bes 'way tuh charm a rattlesnake."

"Naw, Walt, y'll jes' don't understand dese diamon' backs lak Ah do," said Sykes in a superior tone of voice.

The village agreed with Walter, but the snake stayed on. His box remained by the kitchen door with its screen wire covering. Two or three days later it had digested its meal of frogs and literally came to life. It rattled at every movement in the kitchen or the yard. One day as Delia came down the kitchen steps she saw his chalky-white fangs curved like scimitars hung in the wire meshes. This time she did not run away with averted eyes as usual. She stood for a long time in the doorway in a red fury that grew bloodier for every second that she regarded the creature that was her torment.

That night she broached the subject as soon as Sykes sat down to the table.

"Syke, Ah wants you tuh take dat snake 'way fum heah. You done starved me an' Ah put up widcher, you done beat me an Ah took dat, but you done kilt all mah insides bringin' dat varmint heah."

75   Sykes poured out a saucer full of coffee and drank it deliberately before he answered her.

"A whole lot Ah keer 'bout how you feels inside uh out. Dat snake aint goin' no damn wheah till Ah gits ready fuh 'im tuh go. So fur as beatin' is concerned, yuh aint took near all dat you gointer take ef yuh stay 'roun' *me*."

Delia pushed back her plate and got up from the table. "Ah hates you. Sykes," she said calmly. "Ah hates you tuh de same degree dat Ah useter love yuh. Ah done took an' took till mah belly is full up tuh mah neck. Dat's de reason Ah got mah letter fum de church an' moved mah membership tuh Woodbridge—so Ah don't haftuh take no sacrament wid yuh. Ah don't wantuh see yuh, 'roun' me atall. Lay 'roun' wid dat 'oman all yuh wants tuh, but gwan 'way fum me an' mah house. Ah hates yuh lak uh suck-egg dog."

Sykes almost let the huge wad of corn bread and collard greens he was chewing fall out of his mouth in amazement. He had a hard time whipping himself to the proper fury to try to answer Delia.

"Well, Ah'm glad you does hate me. Ah'm sho' tiahed uh you hangin' ontuh me. Ah don't want yuh. Look at yuh stringey ole neck! Yo' raw-bony laigs an' arms is enough tuh cut uh man tuh death. You looks jes' lak de devvul's doll-baby tuh *me*. You cain't hate me no worse dan Ah hates you. Ah been hatin' *you* fuh years."

80   "Yo' ole black hide don't look lak nothin' tuh me, but uh passle uh wrinkled up rubber, wid yo' big ole yeahs flappin' on each side lak uh paih uh buzzard wings. Don't think Ah'm gointuh be run 'way fum mah house neither. Ah'm goin' tuh de white folks about *you*, mah young man, de very nex' time you lay yo' han's on me. Mah cup is done run ovah." Delia said this with no signs of fear and Sykes departed from the house, threatening her, but made not the slightest move to carry out any of them.

That night he did not return at all, and the next day being Sunday, Delia was glad that she did not have to quarrel before she hitched up her pony and drove the four miles to Woodbridge.

She stayed to the night service—"love feast"—which was very warm and full of spirit. In the emotional winds her domestic trials were borne far and wide so that she sang as she drove homeward.

> "Jurden water,[6] black an' col'
> Chills de body, not de soul
> An' Ah wantah cross Jurden in uh calm time."

She came from the barn to the kitchen door and stopped.

"Whut's de mattah, ol' satan, you aint kickin' up yo' racket?" She addressed the snake's box. Complete silence. She went on into the house with a new hope in its birth struggles. Perhaps her threat to go to the white folks had frightened Sykes! Perhaps he was sorry! Fifteen years of misery and suppression had brought Delia to the place where she would hope *anything* that looked towards a way over or through her wall of inhibitions.

85   She felt in the match safe behind the stove at once for a match. There was only one there.

"Dat niggah wouldn't fetch nothin heah tuh save his rotten neck, but he kin run thew whut Ah brings quick enough. Now he done toted off nigh on tuh haff uh box uh matches. He done had dat 'oman heah in mah house, too."

Nobody but a woman could tell how she knew this even before she struck the match. But she did and it put her into a new fury.

Presently she brought in the tubs to put the white things to soak. This time she decided she need not bring the hamper out of the bedroom; she would go in there and do the sorting. She picked up the pot-bellied lamp and went in. The room was small and the hamper stood hard by the foot of the white iron bed. She could sit and reach through the bedposts—resting as she worked.

"Ah wantah cross Jurden in uh calm time." She was singing again. The mood of the "love feast" had returned. She threw back the lid of the basket almost gaily. Then, moved by both horror and terror, she sprang back toward the door. *There lay the snake in the basket!* He moved sluggishly at first, but even as she turned round and round, jumped up and down in an insanity of fear, he began to stir vigorously. She saw him pouring his awful beauty from the basket upon the bed, then she seized the lamp and ran as fast as she could to the kitchen. The wind from the open door blew out the light and the darkness added to her terror. She sped to the darkness of the yard, slamming the door after her before she thought to set down the lamp. She did not feel safe even on the ground, so she climbed up in the hay barn.

90   There for an hour or more she lay sprawled upon the hay a gibbering wreck.

Finally she grew quiet, and after that, coherent thought. With this, stalked through her a cold, bloody rage. Hours of this. A period of introspection, a space of retrospection, then a mixture of both. Out of this an awful calm.

"Well, Ah done de bes' Ah could. If things aint right, Gawd knows taint mah fault."

She went to sleep—a twitchy sleep—and woke up to a faint gray sky. There was a loud hollow sound below. She peered out. Sykes was at the wood-pile, demolishing a wire-covered box.

He hurried to the kitchen door, but hung outside there some minutes before he entered, and stood some minutes more inside before he closed it after him.

95   The gray in the sky was spreading. Delia descended without fear now, and crouched beneath the low bedroom window. The drawn shade shut out the dawn, shut in the night. But the thin walls held back no sound.

"Dat ol' scratch is woke up now!" She mused at the tremendous whirr inside, which every woodsman knows, is one of the sound illusions. The rattler is a ventriloquist. His whirr sounds to the right, to the left, straight ahead, behind, close

---

[6]**Jurden** the river Jordan, which the Israelites had to cross in order to reach the Promised Land.

under foot—everywhere but where it is. Woe to him who guesses wrong unless he is prepared to hold up his end of the argument! Sometimes he strikes without rattling at all.

Inside, Sykes heard nothing until he knocked a pot lid off the stove while trying to reach the match safe in the dark. He had emptied his pockets at Bertha's.

The snake seemed to wake up under the stove and Sykes made a quick leap into the bedroom. In spite of the gin he had had, his head was clearing now.

"Mah Gawd!" he chattered. "Ef Ah could only strack uh light!"

100   The rattling ceased for a moment as he stood paralyzed. He waited. It seemed that the snake waited also.

"Oh, fuh de light! Ah thought he'd be too sick"—Sykes was muttering to himself when the whirr began again, closer, right underfoot this time. Long before this, Sykes' ability to think had been flattened down to primitive instinct and he leaped— onto the bed.

Outside Delia heard a cry that might have come from a maddened chimpanzee, a stricken gorilla. All the terror, all the horror, all the rage that man possibly could express, without a recognizable human sound.

A tremendous stir inside there, another series of animal screams, the intermittent whirr of the reptile. The shade torn violently down from the window, letting in the red dawn, a huge brown hand seizing the window stick, great dull blows upon the wooden floor punctuating the gibberish of sound long after the rattle of the snake had abruptly subsided. All this Delia could see and hear from her place beneath the window, and it made her ill. She crept over to the four-o'clocks[7] and stretched herself on the cool earth to recover.

She lay there. "Delia, Delia!" She could hear Sykes calling in a most despairing tone as one who expected no answer. The sun crept on up, and he called. Delia could not move—her legs were gone flabby. She never moved, he called, and the sun kept rising.

105   "Mah Gawd!" She heard him moan. "Mah Gawd fum Heben!" She heard him stumbling about and got up from her flower-bed. The sun was growing warm. As she approached the door she heard him call out hopefully. "Delia, is dat you Ah heah?"

She saw him on his hands and knees as soon as she reached the door. He crept an inch or two toward her—all that he was able, and she saw his horribly swollen neck and his one open eye shining with hope. A surge of pity too strong to support bore her away from that eye that must, could not, fail to see the tubs. He would see the lamp. Orlando with its doctors was too far. She could scarcely reach the Chinaberry tree, where she waited in the growing heat while inside she knew the cold river was creeping up and up to extinguish that eye which must know by now that she knew.

[1926]

[7]**four-o'clocks** flowers that open in the late afternoon.

Joining the Conversation: Critical Thinking and Writing

1. Summarize the relationship of Delia and Sykes before the time of the story.
2. How do the men on Joe Clark's porch further your understanding of Delia and Sykes and of the relationship between the two?

3. To what extent is Delia responsible for Sykes's death? To what extent is Sykes responsible? Do you think that Delia's action (or inaction) at the end of the story is immoral? Why, or why not?

4. To what extent does the relationship between African Americans and whites play a role in the lives of the characters in "Sweat" and in the outcome of the story?

5. Are the African Americans in "Sweat" portrayed stereotypically, as some of Hurston's critics charged? (See the biographical note, page 705.) How, on the evidence available in this story, might Hurston's fiction be defended from that charge?

MyLiteratureLab® *For additional resources for "Sweat," log in to* www.myliteraturelab.com *where you will find a Longman Lecture and an Interactive Reading, as well as an About the Author and Links for Hurston (under Student Resources).*

RAYMOND CARVER

Raymond Carver (1938–88) was born in Clatskanie, a logging town in Oregon. In 1963 he graduated from Humboldt State College in northern California and then did further study at the University of Iowa.

His early years were not easy—he married while still in college, divorced a little later, and sometimes suffered from alcoholism. In his last years he found domestic happiness, but he died of cancer at the age of fifty.

As a young man he wrote poetry while working at odd jobs (janitor, deliveryman, etc.); later he turned to fiction, though he continued to write poetry. Most of Carver's fiction narrates stories about bewildered and sometimes exhausted men and women.

Cathedral

This blind man, an old friend of my wife's, he was on his way to spend the night. His wife had died. So he was visiting the dead wife's relatives in Connecticut. He called my wife from his in-laws'. Arrangements were made. He would come by train, a five-hour trip, and my wife would meet him at the station. She hadn't seen him since she worked for him one summer in Seattle ten years ago. But she and the blind man had kept in touch. They made tapes and mailed them back and forth. I wasn't enthusiastic about his visit. He was no one I knew. And his being blind bothered me. My idea of blindness came from the movies. In the movies, the blind moved slowly and never laughed. Sometimes they were led by seeing-eye dogs. A blind man in my house was not something I looked forward to.

That summer in Seattle she had needed a job. She didn't have any money. The man she was going to marry at the end of the summer was in officers' training school. He didn't have any money, either. But she was in love with the guy, and he was in love with her, etc. She'd seen something in the paper: HELP WANTED—*Reading to Blind Man,* and a telephone number. She phoned and went over, was hired on the spot. She'd worked with this blind man all summer. She read stuff to him, case studies, reports, that sort of thing. She helped him organize his little office in the county social-service department. They'd become good friends, my wife and the blind man. How do I know these things? She told me. And she told me something else. On her last day in the office, the blind man asked if he could touch her face.

She agreed to this. She told me he touched his fingers to every part of her face, her nose—even her neck! She never forgot it. She even tried to write a poem about it. She was always trying to write a poem. She wrote a poem or two every year, usually after something really important had happened to her.

When we first started going out together, she showed me the poem. In the poem, she recalled his fingers and the way they had moved around over her face. In the poem, she talked about what she had felt at the time, about what went through her mind when the blind man touched her nose and lips. I can remember I didn't think much of the poem. Of course, I didn't tell her that. Maybe I just don't understand poetry. I admit it's not the first thing I reach for when I pick up something to read.

Anyway, this man who'd first enjoyed her favors, the officer-to-be, he'd been her childhood sweetheart. So okay. I'm saying that at the end of the summer she let the blind man run his hands over her face, said goodbye to him, married her childhood etc., who was now a commissioned officer, and she moved away from Seattle. But they'd kept in touch, she and the blind man. She made the first contact after a year or so. She called him up one night from an Air Force base in Alabama. She wanted to talk. They talked. He asked her to send a tape and tell him about her life. She did this. She sent the tape. On the tape, she told the blind man about her husband and about their life together in the military. She told the blind man she loved her husband but she didn't like it where they lived and she didn't like it that he was part of the military-industrial thing. She told the blind man she'd written a poem and he was in it. She told him that she was writing a poem about what it was like to be an Air Force officer's wife. The poem wasn't finished yet. She was still writing it. The blind man made a tape. He sent her the tape. She made a tape. This went on for years. My wife's officer was posted to one base and then another. She sent tapes from Moody AFB, McGuire, McConnell, and finally Travis, near Sacramento, where one night she got to feeling lonely and cut off from people she kept losing in that moving-around life. She got to feeling she couldn't go it another step. She went in and swallowed all the pills and capsules in the medicine chest and washed them down with a bottle of gin. Then she got into a hot bath and passed out.

5   But instead of dying, she got sick. She threw up. Her officer—why should he have a name? he was the childhood sweetheart, and what more does he want?—came home from somewhere, found her, and called the ambulance. In time, she put it all on a tape and sent the tape to the blind man. Over the years, she put all kinds of stuff on tapes and sent the tapes off lickety-split. Next to writing a poem every year, I think it was her chief means of recreation. On one tape, she told the blind man she'd decided to live away from her officer for a time. On another tape, she told him about her divorce. She and I began going out, and of course she told her blind man about it. She told him everything, or so it seemed to me. Once she asked me if I'd like to hear the latest tape from the blind man. This was a year ago. I was on the tape, she said. So I said okay, I'd listen to it. I got us drinks and we settled down in the living room. We made ready to listen. First she inserted the tape into the player and adjusted a couple of dials. Then she pushed a lever. The tape squeaked and someone began to talk in this loud voice. She lowered the volume. After a few minutes of harmless chitchat, I heard my own name in the mouth of this stranger, this blind man I didn't even know! And then this: "From all you've said about him, I can only conclude—" But we were interrupted, a knock at the door, something, and we didn't ever get back to the tape. Maybe it was just as well. I'd heard all I wanted to.

Now this same blind man was coming to sleep in my house.

"Maybe I could take him bowling," I said to my wife. She was at the draining board doing scalloped potatoes. She put down the knife she was using and turned around.

"If you love me," she said, "you can do this for me. If you don't love me, okay. But if you had a friend, any friend, and the friend came to visit, I'd make him feel comfortable." She wiped her hands with the dish towel.

"I don't have any blind friends," I said.

"You don't have *any* friends," she said. "Period. Besides," she said, "goddamn it, his wife's just died! Don't you understand that? The man's lost his wife!"

I didn't answer. She'd told me a little about the blind man's wife. Her name was Beulah. Beulah! That's a name for a colored woman.

"Was his wife a Negro?" I asked.

"Are you crazy?" my wife said. "Have you just flipped or something?" She picked up a potato. I saw it hit the floor, then roll under the stove. "What's wrong with you?" she said. "Are you drunk?"

"I'm just asking," I said.

Right then my wife filled me in with more detail than I cared to know. I made a drink and sat at the kitchen table to listen. Pieces of the story began to fall into place.

Beulah had gone to work for the blind man the summer after my wife had stopped working for him. Pretty soon Beulah and the blind man had themselves a church wedding. It was a little wedding—who'd want to go to such a wedding in the first place?—just the two of them, plus the minister and the minister's wife. But it was a church wedding just the same. It was what Beulah had wanted, he'd said. But even then Beulah must have been carrying the cancer in her glands. After they had been inseparable for eight years—my wife's word, *inseparable*—Beulah's health went into a rapid decline. She died in a Seattle hospital room, the blind man sitting beside the bed and holding on to her hand. They'd married, lived and worked together, slept together—had sex, sure—and then the blind man had to bury her. All this without his having ever seen what the goddamned woman looked like. It was beyond my understanding. Hearing this, I felt sorry for the blind man for a little bit. And then I found myself thinking what a pitiful life this woman must have led. Imagine a woman who could never see herself as she was seen in the eyes of her loved one. A woman who could go on day after day and never receive the smallest compliment from her beloved. A woman whose husband could never read the expression on her face, be it misery or something better. Someone who could wear makeup or not—what difference to him? She could, if she wanted, wear green eye-shadow around one eye, a straight pin in her nostril, yellow slacks, and purple shoes, no matter. And then to slip off into death, the blind man's hand on her hand, his blind eyes streaming tears—I'm imagining now—her last thought maybe this: that he never even knew what she looked like, and she on an express to the grave. Robert was left with a small insurance policy and a half of a twenty-peso Mexican coin. The other half of the coin went into the box with her. Pathetic.

So when the time rolled around, my wife went to the depot to pick him up. With nothing to do but wait—sure, I blamed him for that—I was having a drink and watching the TV when I heard the car pull into the drive. I got up from the sofa with my drink and went to the window to have a look.

I saw my wife laughing as she parked the car. I saw her get out of the car and shut the door. She was still wearing a smile. Just amazing. She went around to the other side of the car to where the blind man was already starting to get out. This blind man, feature this, he was wearing a full beard! A beard on a blind man! Too much, I say. The blind man reached into the back seat and dragged out a suitcase. My wife took his arm, shut the car door, and, talking all the way, moved him down the drive and then up the steps to the front porch. I turned off the TV. I finished my drink, rinsed the glass, dried my hands. Then I went to the door.

My wife said, "I want you to meet Robert. Robert, this is my husband. I've told you all about him." She was beaming. She had this blind man by his coat sleeve.

20   The blind man let go of his suitcase and up came his hand. I took it. He squeezed hard, held my hand, and then he let it go.

"I feel like we've already met," he boomed.

"Likewise," I said. I didn't know what else to say. Then I said, "Welcome. I've heard a lot about you." We began to move then, a little group, from the porch into the living room, my wife guiding him by the arm. The blind man was carrying his suitcase in his other hand. My wife said things like, "To your left here, Robert. That's right. Now watch it, there's a chair. That's it. Sit down right here. This is the sofa. We just bought this sofa two weeks ago."

I started to say something about the old sofa. I'd liked that old sofa. But I didn't say anything. Then I wanted to say something else, small-talk, about the scenic ride along the Hudson. How going *to* New York, you should sit on the right-hand side of the train, and coming *from* New York, the left-hand side.

"Did you have a good train ride?" I said. "Which side of the train did you sit on, by the way?"

25   "What a question, which side!" my wife said. "What's it matter which side?" she said.

"I just asked," I said.

"Right side," the blind man said. "I hadn't been on a train in nearly forty years. Not since I was a kid. With my folks. That's been a long time. I'd nearly forgotten the sensation. I have winter in my beard now," he said. "So I've been told, anyway. Do I look distinguished, my dear?" the blind man said to my wife.

"You look distinguished, Robert," she said. "Robert," she said. "Robert, it's just so good to see you."

My wife finally took her eyes off the blind man and looked at me. I had the feeling she didn't like what she saw. I shrugged.

30   I've never met, or personally known, anyone who was blind. This blind man was late forties, a heavy-set, balding man with stooped shoulders, as if he carried a great weight there. He wore brown slacks, brown shoes, a light-brown shirt, a tie, a sports coat. Spiffy. He also had this full beard. But he didn't use a cane and he didn't wear dark glasses. I'd always thought dark glasses were a must for the blind. Fact was, I wished he had a pair. At first glance, his eyes looked like anyone else's eyes. But if you looked close, there was something different about them. Too much white in the iris, for one thing, and the pupils seemed to move around in the sockets without his knowing it or being able to stop it. Creepy. As I stared at his face, I saw the left pupil turn in toward his nose while the other made an effort to keep in one place. But it was only an effort, for that eye was on the roam without his knowing it or wanting it to be.

I said, "Let me get you a drink. What's your pleasure? We have a little of everything. It's one of our pastimes."

"Bub, I'm a Scotch man myself," he said fast enough in this big voice.

"Right," I said. Bub! "Sure you are. I knew it."

He let his fingers touch his suitcase, which was sitting alongside the sofa. He was taking his bearings. I didn't blame him for that.

35   "I'll move that up to your room," my wife said.

"No, that's fine," the blind man said loudly. "It can go up when I go up."

"A little water with the Scotch?" I said.

"Very little," he said.

"I knew it," I said.

40   He said, "Just a tad. The Irish actor, Barry Fitzgerald? I'm like that fellow. When I drink water, Fitzgerald said, I drink water. When I drink whiskey, I drink whiskey." My wife laughed. The blind man brought his hand up under his beard. He lifted his beard slowly and let it drop.

I did the drinks, three big glasses of Scotch with a splash of water in each. Then we made ourselves comfortable and talked about Robert's travels. First the long flight from the West Coast to Connecticut, we covered that. Then from Connecticut up here by train. We had another drink concerning that leg of the trip.

I remembered having read somewhere that the blind didn't smoke because, as speculation had it, they couldn't see the smoke they exhaled. I thought I knew that much and that much only about blind people. But this blind man smoked his cigarette down to the nubbin and then lit another one. This blind man filled his ashtray and my wife emptied it.

When we sat down at the table for dinner, we had another drink. My wife heaped Robert's plate with cube steak, scalloped potatoes, green beans. I buttered him up two slices of bread. I said, "Here's bread and butter for you." I swallowed some of my drink. "Now let us pray," I said, and the blind man lowered his head. My wife looked at me, her mouth agape. "Pray the phone won't ring and the food doesn't get cold," I said.

We dug in. We ate everything there was to eat on the table. We ate like there was no tomorrow. We didn't talk. We ate. We scarfed. We grazed that table. We were into serious eating. The blind man had right away located his foods, he knew just where everything was on his plate. I watched with admiration as he used his knife and fork on the meat. He'd cut two pieces of meat, fork the meat into his mouth, and then go all out for the scalloped potatoes, the beans next, and then he'd tear off a hunk of buttered bread and eat that. He'd follow this up with a big drink of milk. It didn't seem to bother him to use his fingers once in a while, either.

45   We finished everything, including half a strawberry pie. For a few moments, we sat as if stunned. Sweat beaded on our faces. Finally, we got up from the table and left the dirty plates. We didn't look back. We took ourselves into the living room and sank into our places again. Robert and my wife sat on the sofa. I took the big chair. We had us two or three more drinks while they talked about the major things that had come to pass for them in the past ten years. For the most part, I just listened. Now and then I joined in. I didn't want him to think I'd left the room, and I didn't want her to think I was feeling left out. They talked of things that had happened to them—to them!—these past ten years. I waited in vain to hear my name on my wife's sweet lips: "And then my dear husband came into my life"—something like that. But I heard nothing of the sort. More talk of Robert. Robert had done a little of everything, it seemed, a regular blind jack-of-all-trades. But most recently he and his wife had had an Amway distributorship, from which, I gathered, they'd earned their living, such as it was. The blind man was also a ham radio operator. He talked in his loud voice about conversations he'd had with fellow operators in Guam, in the Philippines, in Alaska, and even in Tahiti. He said he'd have a lot of friends there if he ever wanted to go visit those places. From time to time, he'd turn his blind face toward me, put his hand under his beard, ask me something. How long had I been in my present position? (Three years.) Did I like

my work? (I didn't.) Was I going to stay with it? (What were the options?) Finally, when I thought he was beginning to run down, I got up and turned on the TV.

My wife looked at me with irritation. She was heading toward a boil. Then she looked at the blind man and said, "Robert, do you have a TV?"

The blind man said, "My dear, I have two TVs. I have a color set and a black-and-white thing, an old relic. It's funny, but if I turn the TV on, and I'm always turning it on, I turn on the color set. It's funny, don't you think?"

I didn't know what to say to that. I had absolutely nothing to say to that. No opinion. So I watched the news program and tried to listen to what the announcer was saying.

"This is a color TV," the blind man said. "Don't ask me how, but I can tell."

50   "We traded up a while ago," I said.

The blind man had another taste of his drink. He lifted his beard, sniffed it, and let it fall. He leaned forward on the sofa. He positioned his ashtray on the coffee table, then put the lighter to his cigarette. He leaned back on the sofa and crossed his legs at the ankles.

My wife covered her mouth, and then she yawned. She stretched. She said, "I think I'll go upstairs and put on my robe. I think I'll change into something else. Robert, you make yourself comfortable," she said.

"I'm comfortable," the blind man said.

"I want you to feel comfortable in this house," she said.

55   "I am comfortable," the blind man said.

After she'd left the room, he and I listened to the weather report and then to the sports roundup. By that time, she'd been gone so long I didn't know if she was going to come back. I thought she might have gone to bed. I wished she'd come back downstairs. I didn't want to be left alone with a blind man. I asked him if he wanted another drink, and he said sure. Then I asked if he wanted to smoke some dope with me. I said I'd just rolled a number. I hadn't, but I planned to do so in about two shakes.

"I'll try some with you," he said.

"Damn right," I said. "That's the stuff."

I got our drinks and sat down on the sofa with him. Then I rolled us two fat numbers. I lit one and passed it. I brought it to his fingers. He took it and inhaled.

60   "Hold it as long as you can," I said. I could tell he didn't know the first thing.

My wife came back downstairs wearing her pink robe and her pink slippers.

"What do I smell?" she said.

"We thought we'd have us some cannabis," I said.

My wife gave me a savage look. Then she looked at the blind man and said, "Robert, I didn't know you smoked."

65   He said, "I do now, my dear. There's a first time for everything. But I don't feel anything yet."

"This stuff is pretty mellow," I said. "This stuff is mild. It's dope you can reason with," I said. "It doesn't mess you up."

"Not much it doesn't, bub," he said, and laughed.

My wife sat on the sofa between the blind man and me. I passed her the number. She took it and toked and then passed it back to me. "Which way is this going?" she said. Then she said, "I shouldn't be smoking this. I can hardly keep my eyes open as it is. That dinner did me in. I shouldn't have eaten so much."

"It was the strawberry pie," the blind man said. "That's what did it," he said, and he laughed his big laugh. Then he shook his head.

70   "There's more strawberry pie," I said.

"Do you want some more, Robert?" my wife said.

"Maybe in a little while," he said.

We gave our attention to the TV. My wife yawned again. She said, "Your bed is made up when you feel like going to bed, Robert. I know you must have had a long day. When you're ready to go to bed, say so." She pulled his arm. "Robert?"

He came to and said, "I've had a real nice time. This beats tapes, doesn't it?"

75   I said, "Coming at you," and I put the number between his fingers. He inhaled, held the smoke, and then let it go. It was like he'd been doing it since he was nine years old.

"Thanks, bub," he said. "But I think this is all for me. I think I'm beginning to feel it," he said. He held the burning roach out for my wife.

"Same here," she said. "Ditto. Me, too." She took the roach and passed it to me. "I may just sit here for a while between you two guys with my eyes closed. But don't let me bother you, okay? Either one of you. If it bothers you, say so. Otherwise, I may just sit here with my eyes closed until you're ready to go to bed," she said. "Your bed's made up, Robert, when you're ready. It's right next to our room at the top of the stairs. We'll show you up when you're ready. You wake me up now, you guys, if I fall asleep." She said that and then she closed her eyes and went to sleep.

The news program ended. I got up and changed the channel. I sat back down on the sofa. I wished my wife hadn't pooped out. Her head lay across the back of the sofa, her mouth open. She'd turned so that her robe slipped away from her legs, exposing a juicy thigh. I reached to draw her robe back over her, and it was then that I glanced at the blind man. What the hell! I flipped the robe open again.

"You say when you want some strawberry pie," I said.

80   "I will," he said.

I said, "Are you tired? Do you want me to take you up to your bed? Are you ready to hit the hay?"

"Not yet," he said. "No, I'll stay up with you, bub. If that's all right. I'll stay up until you're ready to turn in. We haven't had a chance to talk. Know what I mean? I feel like me and her monopolized the evening." He lifted his beard and he let it fall. He picked up his cigarettes and his lighter.

"That's all right," I said. Then I said, "I'm glad for the company."

And I guess I was. Every night I smoked dope and stayed up as long as I could before I fell asleep. My wife and I hardly ever went to bed at the same time. When I did go to sleep, I had these dreams. Sometimes I'd wake up from one of them, my heart going crazy.

85   Something about the church and the Middle Ages was on the TV. Not your run-of-the-mill TV fare. I wanted to watch something else. I turned to the other channels. But there was nothing on them, either. So I turned back to the first channel and apologized.

"Bub, it's all right," the blind man said. "It's fine with me. Whatever you want to watch is okay. I'm always learning something. Learning never ends. It won't hurt me to learn something tonight. I got ears," he said.

We didn't say anything for a time. He was leaning forward with his head turned at me, his right ear aimed in the direction of the set. Very disconcerting. Now and then his eyelids drooped and then they snapped open again. Now and then he put his fingers into his beard and tugged, like he was thinking about something he was hearing on the television.

On the screen, a group of men wearing cowls was being set upon and tormented by men dressed in skeleton costumes and men dressed as devils. The men dressed as devils wore devil masks, horns, and long tails. This pageant was part of a procession. The Englishman who was narrating the thing said it took place in Spain once a year. I tried to explain to the blind man what was happening.

"Skeletons," he said. "I know about skeletons," he said, and he nodded.

90   The TV showed this one cathedral. Then there was a long, slow look at another one. Finally, the picture switched to the famous one in Paris, with its flying buttresses and its spires reaching up to the clouds. The camera pulled away to show the whole of the cathedral rising above the skyline.

There were times when the Englishman who was telling the thing would shut up, would simply let the camera move around the cathedrals. Or else the camera would tour the countryside, men in fields walking behind oxen. I waited as long as I could. Then I felt I had to say something. I said, "They're showing the outside of this cathedral now. Gargoyles. Little statues carved to look like monsters. Now I guess they're in Italy. Yeah, they're in Italy. There's paintings on the walls of this one church."

"Are those fresco paintings, bub?" he asked, and he sipped from his drink.

I reached for my glass. But it was empty. I tried to remember what I could remember. "You're asking me are those frescoes?" I said. "That's a good question. I don't know."

The camera moved to a cathedral outside Lisbon. The differences in the Portuguese cathedral compared with the French and Italian were not that great. But they were there. Mostly the interior stuff. Then something occurred to me, and I said, "Something has occurred to me. Do you have any idea what a cathedral is? What they look like, that is? Do you follow me? If somebody says cathedral to you, do you have any notion what they're talking about? Do you know the difference between that and a Baptist church, say?"

95   He let the smoke dribble from his mouth. "I know they took hundreds of workers fifty or a hundred years to build," he said. "I just heard the man say that, of course. I know generations of the same families worked on a cathedral. I heard him say that, too. The men who began their life's work on them, they never lived to see the completion of their work. In that wise, bub, they're no different from the rest of us, right?" He laughed. Then his eyelids drooped again. His head nodded. He seemed to be snoozing. Maybe he was imagining himself in Portugal. The TV was showing another cathedral now. This one was in Germany. The Englishman's voice droned on. "Cathedrals," the blind man said. He sat up and rolled his head back and forth. "If you want the truth, bub, that's about all I know. What I just said. What I heard him say. But maybe you could describe one to me? I wish you'd do it. I'd like that. If you want to know, I really don't have a good idea."

I stared hard at the shot of the cathedral on the TV. How could I even begin to describe it? But say my life depended on it. Say my life was being threatened by an insane guy who said I had to do it or else.

I stared some more at the cathedral before the picture flipped off into the countryside. There was no use. I turned to the blind man and said, "To begin with, they're very tall." I was looking around the room for clues. "They reach way up. Up and up. Toward the sky. They're so big, some of them, they have to have these supports. To help hold them up, so to speak. These supports are called buttresses. They remind me of viaducts, for some reason. But maybe you don't know viaducts, either? Sometimes the cathedrals have devils and such carved into the front. Sometimes lords and ladies. Don't ask me why this is," I said.

He was nodding. The whole upper part of his body seemed to be moving back and forth.

"I'm not doing so good, am I?" I said.

100   He stopped nodding and leaned forward on the edge of the sofa. As he listened to me, he was running his fingers through his beard. I wasn't getting through to him, I could see that. But he waited for me to go on just the same. He nodded, like he was trying to encourage me. I tried to think what else to say. "They're really big," I said. "They're massive. They're built of stone. Marble, too, sometimes. In those olden days, when they built cathedrals, men wanted to be close to God. In those olden days, God was an important part of everyone's life. You could tell this from their cathedral-building. I'm sorry," I said, "but it looks like that's the best I can do for you. I'm just no good at it."

"That's all right, bub," the blind man said. "Hey, listen. I hope you don't mind my asking you. Can I ask you something? Let me ask you a simple question, yes or no. I'm just curious and there's no offense. You're my host. But let me ask if you are in any way religious? You don't mind my asking?"

I shook my head. He couldn't see that, though. A wink is the same as a nod to a blind man. "I guess I don't believe in it. In anything. Sometimes it's hard. You know what I'm saying?"

"Sure, I do," he said.

"Right," I said.

105   The Englishman was still holding forth. My wife sighed in her sleep. She drew a long breath and went on with her sleeping.

"You'll have to forgive me," I said. "But I can't tell you what a cathedral looks like. It just isn't in me to do it. I can't do any more than I've done."

The blind man sat very still, his head down, as he listened to me.

I said, "The truth is, cathedrals don't mean anything special to me. Nothing. Cathedrals. They're something to look at on late-night TV. That's all they are."

It was then that the blind man cleared his throat. He brought something up. He took a handkerchief from his back pocket. Then he said, "I get it, bub. It's okay. It happens. Don't worry about it," he said. "Hey, listen to me. Will you do me a favor? I got an idea. Why don't you find us some heavy paper? And a pen. We'll do something. We'll draw one together. Get us a pen and some heavy paper. Go on, bub, get the stuff," he said.

110   So I went upstairs. My legs felt like they didn't have any strength in them. They felt like they did after I'd done some running. In my wife's room, I looked around. I found some ballpoints in a little basket on her table. And then I tried to think where to look for the kind of paper he was talking about.

Downstairs, in the kitchen, I found a shopping bag with onion skins in the bottom of the bag. I emptied the bag and shook it. I brought it into the living room and sat down with it near his legs. I moved some things, smoothed the wrinkles from the bag, spread it out on the coffee table.

The blind man got down from the sofa and sat next to me on the carpet.

He ran his fingers over the paper. He went up and down the sides of the paper. The edges, even the edges. He fingered the corners.

"All right," he said. "All right, let's do her."

115   He found my hand, the hand with the pen. He closed his hand over my hand. "Go ahead, bub, draw," he said. "Draw. You'll see. I'll follow along with you. It'll be okay. Just begin now like I'm telling you. You'll see. Draw," the blind man said.

So I began. First I drew a box that looked like a house. It could have been the house I lived in. Then I put a roof on it. At either end of the roof, I drew spires. Crazy.

"Swell," he said. "Terrific. You're doing fine," he said. "Never thought anything like this could happen in your lifetime, did you, bub? Well, it's a strange life, we all know that. Go on now. Keep it up."

I put in windows with arches. I drew flying buttresses. I hung great doors. I couldn't stop. The TV station went off the air. I put down the pen and closed and opened my fingers. The blind man felt around over the paper. He moved the tips of his fingers over the paper, all over what I had drawn, and he nodded.

"Doing fine," the blind man said.

120   I took up the pen again, and he found my hand. I kept at it. I'm no artist. But I kept drawing just the same.

My wife opened up her eyes and gazed at us. She sat up on the sofa, her robe hanging open. She said, "What are you doing? Tell me, I want to know."

I didn't answer her.

The blind man said, "We're drawing a cathedral. Me and him are working on it. Press hard," he said to me. "That's right. That's good," he said. "Sure. You got it, bub, I can tell. You didn't think you could. But you can, can't you? You're cooking with gas now. You know what I'm saying? We're going to really have us something here in a minute. How's the old arm?" he said. "Put some people in there now. What's a cathedral without people?"

My wife said, "What's going on? Robert, what are you doing? What's going on?"

125   "It's all right," he said to her. "Close your eyes now," the blind man said to me.

I did it. I closed them just like he said.

"Are they closed?" he said. "Don't fudge."

"They're closed," I said.

"Keep them that way," he said. He said, "Don't stop now. Draw."

130   So we kept on with it. His fingers rode my fingers as my hand went over the paper. It was like nothing else in my life up to now.

Then he said, "I think that's it. I think you got it," he said. "Take a look. What do you think?"

But I had my eyes closed. I thought I'd keep them that way for a little longer. I thought it was something I ought to do.

"Well?" he said. "Are you looking?"

My eyes were still closed. I was in my house. I knew that. But I didn't feel like I was inside anything.

135   "It's really something," I said.

[1983]

Joining the Conversation: Critical Thinking and Writing

1. What was your impression of the narrator after reading the first five paragraphs?
2. Why does the narrator feel threatened by the blind man? Has he any reason to feel threatened?
3. What attitude does the narrator reveal in the following passage:

> She'd turned so that her robe slipped away from her legs, exposing a juicy thigh. I reached to draw her robe back over her and it was then that I glanced at the blind man. What the hell! I flipped the robe open again.

4. Why does the narrator not open his eyes at the end of the story?
5. The television program happens to be about cathedrals, but if the point is to get the narrator to draw something while the blind man's hand rests on the narrator's, the program could have been about some other topic—for example, about skyscrapers or about the Statue of Liberty. In a short argument (250 words) explain why you think that a cathedral is or is not a better choice, for Carver's purposes, than these other subjects.
6. In what ways does Carver prepare us for the narrator's final state of mind?

MyLiteratureLab® *For additional resources for "Cathedral," log in to* www .myliteraturelab.com *where you will find a Longman Lecture and Comprehension Quiz, as well as an About the Author, Bibliography, Links, and Critical Overview for Carver (under Student Resources).*

POEMS

ANONYMOUS

Western Wind

Westron° wind, when will thou blow?
The small rain down can rain.
Christ, that my love were in my arms,
And I in my bed again.

[c. 1500]

1 **Westron** western.

Joining the Conversation: Critical Thinking and Writing

1. In "Western Wind," what do you think is the tone of the speaker's voice in the first two lines? Angry? Impatient? Supplicating? Be as precise as possible. What is the tone in the next two lines?
2. In England, the west wind, warmed by the Gulf Stream, rises in the spring. What associations link the wind and rain of lines 1 and 2 with lines 3 and 4?
3. Should we have been told why the lovers are separated? Explain.

CHRISTOPHER MARLOWE

Christopher Marlowe (1564–93), English poet and playwright, was born in the same year as Shakespeare. An early death, in a tavern brawl, cut short what might have been a brilliant career.

Marlowe's "The Passionate Shepherd to His Love" is a pastoral poem; it depicts shepherds and shepherdesses in an idyllic, timeless setting. This poem engendered many imitations and replies, two of which we reprint after Marlowe's.

The Passionate Shepherd to His Love

Come live with me and be my love,
And we will all the pleasures prove,
That valleys, groves, hills, and fields,
Woods or steepy mountain yields.

There we will sit upon the rocks,   5
And see the shepherds feed their flocks,
By shallow rivers to whose falls
Melodious birds sing madrigals.

And I will make thee beds of roses
With a thousand fragrant posies,   10
A cap of flowers, and a kirtle
Embroidered all with leaves of myrtle;

A gown made of the finest wool
Which from our pretty lambs we pull;
Fair lined slippers for the cold,   15
With buckles of the purest gold;

A belt of straw and ivy buds,
With coral clasps and amber studs:
And if these pleasures may thee move,
Come live with me and be my love.   20

The shepherds' swains shall dance and sing
For thy delight each May morning:
If these delights thy mind may move,
Then live with me, and be my love.

[1599–1600]

Joining the Conversation: Critical Thinking and Writing

Read the poem two or three times, preferably aloud. Marlowe's poem is not to be taken seriously as a picture of the pastoral (shepherd) life, but if you have enjoyed the poem, exactly what have you enjoyed?

SIR WALTER RALEIGH

Walter Raleigh (1552–1618) is known chiefly as a soldier and a colonizer—he was the founder of the settlement in Virginia, and he introduced tobacco into Europe—but in his own day he was known also as a poet.

The Nymph's Reply to the Shepherd

If all the world and love were young,
And truth in every shepherd's tongue,
These pretty pleasures might me move,
To live with thee, and be thy love.

Time drives the flocks from field to fold,   5
When rivers rage, and rocks grow cold,
And Philomel° becometh dumb,
The rest complains of cares to come.

The flowers do fade, and wanton fields,
To wayward winter reckoning yields,   10
A honey tongue, a heart of gall,
Is fancy's spring, but sorrow's fall.

Thy gowns, thy shoes, thy beds of roses,
Thy cap, thy kirtle, and thy posies,
Soon break, soon wither, soon forgotten: 15
In folly ripe, in reason rotten.

Thy belt of straw and ivy buds,
Thy coral clasps and amber studs,
All these in me no means can move,
To come to thee, and be thy love.   20

But could youth last, and love still breed,
Had joys no date, nor age no need,
Then these delights my mind might move,
To live with thee and be thy love.

[c. 1600]

7 **Philomel** In Greek mythology, Philomela was a beautiful woman who was raped and later transformed into a chattering sparrow, but in most Roman versions she is transformed into the nightingale, noted for its beautiful song.

Joining the Conversation: Critical Thinking and Writing

1. What is the season in Marlowe's poem? What season(s) does Raleigh envision?
2. Some readers find puns in line 12, in "fancy's spring, but sorrow's fall." How do you paraphrase and interpret the line?
3. How would you describe the tone of the final stanza?
4. Now that you have read Raleigh's poem, reread Marlowe's. Do you now, in the context of Raleigh's poem, enjoy Marlowe's more than before, or less? Why? (You might think of it this way: Does Raleigh's refutation cause you to lose interest in Marlowe's poem?)

John Donne

John Donne (1572–1631) wrote religious poetry as well as love poetry. In the following lyric, he alters Marlowe's pastoral setting to a setting involving people engaged in fishing. The poem thus belongs to a type called piscatory lyric (Latin piscis, "fish"). For a fuller biographical note and another poem by Donne, see page 729.

The Bait

Come live with me, and be my love,
And we will some new pleasures prove
Of golden sands, and crystal brooks,
With silken lines, and silver hooks.

There will the river whispering run   5
Warmed by thy eyes, more than the Sun.
And there th'enamored fish will stay,
Begging themselves they may betray.

When thou wilt swim in that live bath,
Each fish, which every channel hath,   10
Will amorously to thee swim,
Gladder to catch thee, than thou him.

If thou, to be so seen, beest loath,
By Sun, or Moon, thou darknest both,
And if my self have leave to see,   15
I need not their light, having thee.

Let others freeze with angling reeds,
And cut their legs, with shells and weeds,
Or treacherously poor fish beset,
With strangling snare, or windowy net: 20

Let coarse bold hands, from slimy nest
The bedded fish in banks out-wrest,
Or curious traitors, sleavesilk flies
Bewitch poor fishes' wandring eyes.

For thee, thou needst no such deceit,   25
For thou thy self art thine own bait;
That fish, that is not catched thereby,
Alas, is wiser far than I.

                                                           [1633]

Joining the Conversation: Critical Thinking and Writing

1. In Donne's first stanza, which words especially indicate that we are (as in Marlowe's poem) in an idealized world?
2. Which words later in Donne's poem indicate what (for Donne) the real world of fishing is?
3. Paraphrase the last stanza, making it as clear as possible.

WILLIAM SHAKESPEARE

Shakespeare (1564–1616) was born into a middle-class family in Stratford-upon-Avon. Although we have a fair number of records about his life—documents concerning marriage, the birth of children, the purchase of property, and so forth—it is not known exactly why and when he turned to the theater. What we do know, however, is important. He was an actor and a shareholder in a playhouse, and he did write the plays that are attributed to him. The dates of some of the plays can be set precisely, but the dates of some others can be only roughly set from 1599 to 1601. Most of Shakespeare's 154 sonnets were probably written in the late 1590s, but they were not published until 1609.

Sonnet 29

When, in disgrace with Fortune and men's eyes,
I all alone beweep my outcast state,
And trouble deaf heaven with my bootless° cries,
And look upon myself and curse my fate,
Wishing me like to one more rich in hope,   5
Featured like him, like him° with friends possessed,
Desiring this man's art and that man's scope,
With what I most enjoy contented least;
Yet in these thoughts myself almost despising,
Haply° I think on thee, and then my state,   10
Like to the lark at break of day arising
From sullen earth, sings hymns at heaven's gate;
For thy sweet love rememb'red such wealth brings,
That then I scorn to change my state with kings.

[c. 1600]

3 bootless useless. **6 like him, like him** like a second man, like a third man. **10 Haply** perchance.

Joining the Conversation: Critical Thinking and Writing

1. Paraphrase the first eight lines. Then, in a sentence, summarize the speaker's state of mind to this point in the poem.
2. Summarize the speaker's state of mind in lines 9–12. What does "sullen earth" (line 12) suggest to you?
3. Notice that every line in the poem except line 11 ends with a comma or semicolon, indicating a pause. How does the lack of punctuation at the end of line 11 affect your reading of this line and your understanding of the speaker's emotion?
4. In the last two lines of a sonnet Shakespeare often summarizes the preceding lines. In this sonnet, how does the *structure* (the organization) of the summary differ from that of the statement in the first twelve lines? Why? Try reading the last lines as if they were reversed. Thus:

For then I scorn to change my state with kings.
Since thy sweet love rememb'red such wealth brings.

Which version do you like better? What are your reasons?

5. The "thee" of this poem is almost certainly a man, not a woman. Is the "love" of the poem erotic love, or can it be taken as something like brotherly love or even as loving-kindness?

6. Write a paragraph (or a sonnet) describing how thinking of someone you love—or hate—changes your mood.

Sonnet 116

Let me not to the marriage of true minds
Admit impediments; love is not love
Which alters when it alteration finds,
Or bends with the remover to remove.
O, no, it is an ever-fixèd mark°   5
That looks on tempests and is never shaken;
It is the star° to every wand'ring bark,
Whose worth's unknown, although his height be taken.
Love's not Time's fool,° though rosy lips and cheeks
Within his bending sickle's compass° come;   10
Love alters not with his° brief hours and weeks
But bears° it out even to the edge of doom.°
If this be error and upon° me proved,
I never writ, nor no man ever loved.

[c. 1600]

5 ever-fixèd mark seamark, guide to mariners.   **7 the star** the North Star.   **9 fool** plaything.
10 compass range, circle.   **11 his** time's.   **12 bears** survives;   **doom** Judgment Day.
13 upon against.

Joining the Conversation: Critical Thinking and Writing

1. Paraphrase (that is, put into your own words) "Let me not to the marriage of true minds / Admit impediments." Is there more than one appropriate meaning of "Admit"?

2. Notice that the poem celebrates "the marriage of true minds," not bodies. In a sentence or two, using only your own words, summarize Shakespeare's idea of the nature of such love, both what it is and what it is not.

3. Paraphrase lines 13–14. What is the speaker's tone here? Would you say that the tone is different from the tone in the rest of the poem?

4. Write a paragraph or a poem defining either love or hate.

5. Find a definition of love or hate in a popular song. Bring the lyrics to class. Why is this definition a good one?

JOHN DONNE

John Donne (1572–1631), whom we met on page 726, was born into a Roman Catholic family in England, but in the 1590s he abandoned that faith. In 1615 he became an Anglican priest and soon was known as a great preacher. One hundred sixty of his sermons survive, including one with the famous line "No man is an island, entire of itself; every man is a piece of the continent, a part of the main; if a clod be washed away by the sea, Europe is the less. . .; and therefore never send to know for whom the bell tolls; it tolls for thee." From 1621 until his death Donne was dean of St. Paul's Cathedral in London. His love poems (often bawdy and cynical) are said to be his early work, and his "Holy Sonnets" (among the greatest religious poems written in English) his later work.

A Valediction: Forbidding Mourning

As virtuous men pass mildly away,
    And whisper to their souls, to go,
Whilst some of their sad friends do say,
    "The breath goes now," and some say, "No":

So let us melt, and make no noise,   5
    No tear-floods, nor sigh-tempests move;
'Twere profanation of our joys
    To tell the laity our love.

Moving of th' earth° brings harms and fears;
    Men reckon what it did and meant;   10
But trepidation of the spheres,
    Though greater far, is innocent.°

Dull sublunary° lovers' love
    (Whose soul is sense) cannot admit
Absence, because it doth remove   15
    Those things which elemented it.

But we, by a love so much refined
    That our selves know not what it is,
Inter-assurèd of the mind,
    Care less, eyes, lips, and hands to miss.   20

Our two souls therefore, which are one,
    Though I must go, endure not yet
A breach, but an expansion,
    Like gold to airy thinness beat.

If they be two, they are two so   25
    As stiff twin compasses° are two:
Thy soul, the fixed foot, makes no show
    To move, but doth, if the other do.

And though it in the center sit,   30
    Yet when the other far doth roam,

9 Moving of th' earth an earthquake. **11–12 But trepidation . . . innocent** But the movement of the heavenly spheres (in Ptolemaic astronomy), though far greater, is harmless. **13 sublunary** under the moon, i.e., earthly. **26 compasses** i.e., a carpenter's compass.

It leans, and hearkens after it,
    And grows erect as that comes home.

Such wilt thou be to me, who must,
    Like the other foot, obliquely run;
Thy firmness makes my circle just,   35
    And makes me end where I begun.

                                      [1611]

Joining the Conversation: Critical Thinking and Writing

1. The first stanza describes the death of "virtuous men." To what is their death compared in the second stanza?
2. Who is the speaker of this poem? To whom does he speak, and what is the occasion? Explain the title.
3. What is the meaning of "laity" in line 8? What does it imply about the speaker and his beloved?
4. In the fourth stanza the speaker contrasts the love of "dull sublunary lovers" (i.e., ordinary mortals) with the love he and his beloved share. What is the difference?
5. In the figure of the carpenter's or draftsperson's compass (lines 25–36) the speaker offers reasons—some stated clearly, some not so clearly—why he will end where he began. In 250 words explain these reasons.
6. In line 35 Donne speaks of his voyage as a "circle." Explain in a paragraph why the circle is traditionally a symbol of perfection.
7. Write a farewell note—or poem—to someone you love (or hate).

MyLiteratureLab® *For additional resources for "A Valediction: Forbidding Mourning," log in to www.myliteraturelab.com where you will find a Longman Lecture and Short Evaluation Exercises, as well as an About the Author, Bibliography, Links, and Critical Overview for Donne (under Student Resources).*

ANDREW MARVELL

Born in 1621 near Hull in England, Andrew Marvell attended Trinity College, Cambridge, and graduated in 1638. During the Civil War he was tutor to the daughter of Sir Thomas Fairfax in Yorkshire at Nun Appleton House, where most of his best-known poems were written. In 1657 he was appointed assistant to John Milton, the Latin Secretary for the Commonwealth. After the Restoration of the monarchy in 1659 until his death, Marvell represented Hull as a member of Parliament. Most of his poems were not published until after his death in 1678.

To His Coy Mistress

Had we but world enough, and time.
This coyness, lady, were no crime.
We would sit down, and think which way

To walk, and pass our long love's day.
Thou by the Indian Ganges' side   5
Should'st rubies find: I by the tide
Of Humber° would complain.° I would
Love you ten years before the Flood,
And you should, if you please, refuse
Till the conversion of the Jews.°   10
My vegetable° love should grow
Vaster than empires, and more slow.
An hundred years should go to praise
Thine eyes, and on thy forehead gaze:
Two hundred to adore each breast: 15
But thirty thousand to the rest.
An age at least to every part,
And the last age should show your heart.
For, lady, you deserve this state,
Nor would I love at lower rate,   20
     But at my back I always hear
Time's winged chariot hurrying near;
And yonder all before us lie
Deserts of vast eternity.
Thy beauty shall no more be found,   25
Nor in thy marble vault shall sound
My echoing song; then worms shall try
That long preserved virginity,
And your quaint honor turn to dust,
And into ashes all my lust.   30
The grave's a fine and private place,
But none, I think, do there embrace.
     Now therefore, while the youthful hue
Sits on thy skin like morning dew,
And while thy willing soul transpires   35
At every pore with instant fires,
Now let us sport us while we may;
And now, like am'rous birds of prey,
Rather at once our time devour,
Than languish in his slow-chapt° power,   40
Let us roll all our strength, and all
Our sweetness, up into one ball;
And tear our pleasures with rough strife
Thorough° the iron gates of life.
Thus, though we cannot make our sun   45
Stand still, yet we will make him run.

[1641]

---

7 **Humber** river in England;   **complain** write love poems.   10 **conversion of the Jews** It was
believed by Christians that the conversion of the Jews would occur just before the Last Judgment.
11 **vegetable** slowly growing.   40 **slow-chapt** slowly devouring.   44 **Thorough** through.

Joining the Conversation: Critical Thinking and Writing

1. What does "coy" mean in the title, and "coyness" in line 2?
2. Do you think that the speaker's claims in lines 1–20 are so inflated that we detect behind them a playfully ironic tone? Explain. Why does the speaker say in line 8 that he would love "ten years before the Flood," rather than merely "since the Flood"?
3. What do you make of lines 21–24? Why is time behind the speaker, and eternity in front of him? Is this "eternity" the same as the period discussed in lines 1–20? Discuss the change in the speaker's tone after line 20.

EDNA ST. VINCENT MILLAY

Edna St. Vincent Millay (1892–1950) was born in Rockland, Maine. Even as a child she wrote poetry, and by the time she graduated from Vassar College (1917) she had achieved some notice as a poet. Millay settled for a while in Greenwich Village, a center of bohemian activity in New York City, where she wrote, performed in plays, and engaged in feminist causes. In 1923, the year she married, she became the first woman to win the Pulitzer Prize for Poetry. Numerous other awards followed. Though she is best known as a lyric poet—especially as a writer of sonnets—she also wrote political poetry and nature poetry as well as short stories, plays, and a libretto for an opera.

Love Is Not All: It Is Not Meat nor Drink

Love is not all: it is not meat nor drink
Nor slumber nor a roof against the rain;
Nor yet a floating spar to men that sink
And rise and sink and rise and sink again;
Love can not fill the thickened lung with breath,   5
Nor clean the blood, nor set the fractured bone;
Yet many a man is making friends with death
Even as I speak, for lack of love alone.
It well may be that in a difficult hour,
Pinned down by pain and moaning for release,   10
Or nagged by want past resolution's power,
I might be driven to sell your love for peace,
Or trade the memory of this night for food.
It well may be. I do not think I would.

[1931]

Joining the Conversation: Critical Thinking and Writing

1. "Love Is Not All" is a sonnet. Using your own words, briefly summarize the argument of the octet (the first 8 lines). Next, paraphrase the sestet, line by line. On the whole, does the sestet repeat the idea of the octet, or does it add a new idea?
2. Whom did you imagine to be speaking the octet? What does the sestet add to your knowledge of the speaker and the occasion? (And how did you paraphrase line 11?)
3. The first and last lines of the poem consist of words of one syllable, and both lines have a distinct pause in the middle. Do you imagine the lines to be spoken in the same tone of voice? If not, can you describe the difference and account for it?
4. Lines 7 and 8 appear to mean that the absence of love can be a cause of death. To what degree do you believe that to be true?
5. Would you call "Love Is Not All" a love poem? Why or why not? Describe the kind of person who might include the poem in a love letter or valentine, or who would be happy to receive it.
6. One of our friends recited this poem at her wedding. What do you think of that idea?

MyLiteratureLab® *For additional resources for "Love Is Not All," log in to* www
.myliteraturelab.com *where you will find a Performance and a Longman Lecture, as well as an About the Author and Links for Millay (under Student Resources).*

ROBERT FROST

For a biographical note on Robert Frost, see page 624.

The Silken Tent

She is as in a field a silken tent
At midday when a sunny summer breeze
Has dried the dew and all its ropes relent,
So that in guys° it gently sways at ease,
And its supporting central cedar pole,   5
That is its pinnacle to heavenward
And signifies the sureness of the soul,
Seems to owe naught to any single cord,
But strictly held by none, is loosely bound
By countless silken ties of love and thought   10
To everything on earth the compass round,
And only by one's going slightly taut
In the capriciousness of summer air
Is of the slightest bondage made aware.

[1943]

4 guys ropes or lines fixed to the ground to secure a tent or other structure

Page from Frost's notebooks, showing "The Silken Tent."

Joining the Conversation: Critical Thinking and Writing

1. The second line places the scene at "midday" in "summer." In addition to giving us the concreteness of a setting, do these words help to characterize the woman whom the speaker describes? If so, how?
2. The tent is supported by "guys" (not men, but the cords or "ties" of line 10) and by its "central cedar pole." What does Frost tell us about these ties? What does he tell us about the pole?
3. What do you make of lines 12–14?
4. Construct a simile that explains a relationship, and then, in a paragraph, explain how the simile works.

ROBERT PACK

Robert Pack, born in New York City in 1929, was educated at Dartmouth College and Columbia University. The author of many books, he is an emeritus professor at Middlebury College and currently teaches in the University of Montana Honors College as Distinguished Senior Professor.

The Frog Prince

(A Speculation on Grimm's Fairy Tale)

Imagine the princess' surprise!
Who would have thought a frog's cold frame
Could hold the sweet and gentle body
Of a prince? How can I name
The joy she must have felt to learn   5
His transformation was the wonder
Of her touch—that she too, in
Her way, had been transformed under
Those clean sheets? Such powers were
Like nothing she had ever read.   10
And in the morning when her mother
Came and saw them there in bed,
Heard how a frog became a prince;
What was it that her mother said?

[1980]

Joining the Conversation: Critical Thinking and Writing

1. Fairy-tale characters seldom have characteristics that go beyond the legend they are in. What characteristics does Pack give to the princess? How do you understand "she too, in / Her way, had been transformed" (lines 7–8)?
2. And "What was it that her mother said?"
3. Transform a fairy tale that you know by giving one character or two some realistic traits. Retell the story, or one scene from it.

NIKKI GIOVANNI

Nikki Giovanni was born in Knoxville, Tennessee, in 1943 and educated at Fisk University, the University of Pennsylvania School of Social Work, and Columbia University. She has taught at Queens College, Rutgers University, and Ohio State University, and she now teaches at Virginia Tech in Blacksburg, Virginia. Giovanni has published many books of poems, an autobiography (Gemini: An Extended Autobiographical Statement on My First Twenty-Five Years of Being a Black Poet), *a book of essays, and a book consisting of a conversation with James Baldwin (1972).*

Love in Place

I really don't remember falling in love all that much
I remember wanting to bake corn bread and boil a ham and I
certainly remember making lemon pie and when I used to smoke I
stopped in the middle of my day to contemplate

I know I must have fallen in love once because I quit biting   5
my cuticles and my hair is gray and that must indicate
something and I all of a sudden had a deeper appreciation
for Billie Holiday° and Billy Strayhorn° so if it wasn't love I don't
know what it was

I see the old photographs and I am smiling and I'm sure quite   10
happy but what I mostly see is me
through your eyes
and I am still young and slim and very much committed to the
love we still have

[1997]

8 Billie Holiday jazz singer (1915–59);   **Billy Strayhorn** jazz composer and musician (1915–67).

Joining the Conversation: Critical Thinking and Writing

1. What reasons does the speaker offer for supposing that she once fell in love? How seriously does she expect us to take those reasons?
2. Read the poem again, but begin with the third stanza and then read the first and second stanzas. Does it make a difference? If so, what is the difference?
3. In line 14 we learn of the "love we still have." Does "still" refer to the present, or to the time of the "old photographs" (10), as the "still" in line 13 does?
4. Why are two of the lines in the final stanza much shorter than the other three lines?
5. What do you make of the title?
6. In the first line Giovanni speaks of "falling in love," and she returns to the idea in the fifth line. Judging from your own experience (which includes your knowledge of the people around you), is the term "falling in love" apt, or do people

come to love one another in a more gradual fashion than "falling in love" implies? In an essay of 500 words, discuss the similarities and differences between "Love in Place" and the remark by the English essayist William Hazlitt (1778–1830) quoted on page 687.

PLAY

TERRENCE MCNALLY

Terrence McNally, born in 1939 in St. Petersburg, Florida, grew up in Corpus Christi, Texas, and did his undergraduate work at Columbia University. "I'm a gay man who writes plays," he has said, and most of his work concerns gay people—or the responses of straight people to gay people.

We give the original script of Andre's Mother *(1988); McNally later amplified it for a 1990 television broadcast (running time is 58 minutes) that was awarded an Emmy.*

Andre's Mother

CHARACTERS

CAL, a young man
ARTHUR, his father
PENNY, his sister
ANDRE'S MOTHER
Time: *Now*
Place: *New York City, Central Park*

Four people—CAL, ARTHUR, PENNY, *and* ANDRE'S MOTHER—*enter: They are nicely dressed and each carries a white helium-filled balloon on a string.*

CAL: You know what's really terrible? I can't think of anything terrific to say. Goodbye. I love you. I'll miss you. And I'm supposed to be so great with words!
PENNY: What's that over there?
ARTHUR: Ask your brother.
CAL: It's a theatre. An outdoor theatre. They do plays there in the summer. Shakespeare's plays. [*To* ANDRE'S MOTHER.] God, how much he wanted to play Hamlet again. He would have gone to Timbuktu to have another go at that part. The summer he did it in Boston, he was so happy!
PENNY: Cal, I don't think she . . . ! It's not the time. Later.
ARTHUR: Your son was a . . . the Jews have a word for it . . .
PENNY [QUIETLY APPALLED]: Oh my God!
ARTHUR: Mensch, I believe it is, and I think I'm using it right. It means warm, solid, the real thing. Correct me if I'm wrong.
PENNY: Fine, Dad, fine. Just quit while you're ahead.
ARTHUR: I won't say he was like a son to me. Even my son isn't always like a son to me. I mean . . . ! In my clumsy way, I'm trying to say how much I liked Andre. And how much he helped me to know my own boy. Cal was always two handsful but Andre and I could talk about anything under the sun. My wife was very fond of him, too.
PENNY: Cal, I don't understand about the balloons.

CAL: They represent the soul. When you let go, it means you're letting his soul ascend to Heaven. That you're willing to let go. Breaking the last earthly ties.

PENNY: Does the Pope know about this?

ARTHUR: Penny!

PENNY: Andre loved my sense of humor. Listen, you can hear him laughing. [*She lets go of her white balloon.*] So long, you glorious, wonderful, I-know-what-Cal-means-about-words . . . *man!* God forgive me for wishing you were straight every time I laid eyes on you. But if any man was going to have you, I'm glad it was my brother! Look how fast it went up. I bet that means something. Something terrific.

ARTHUR [LETS HIS BALLOON GO]: Good-bye. God speed.

PENNY: Cal?

CAL: I'm not ready yet.

PENNY: Okay. We'll be over there. Come on, Pop, you can buy your little girl a Good Humor.

ARTHUR: They still make Good Humor?

PENNY: Only now they're called Dove Bars and they cost twelve dollars.

[PENNY TAKES ARTHUR OFF. CAL AND ANDRE'S MOTHER *stand with their balloons.*]

CAL: I wish I knew what you were thinking. I think it would help me. You know almost nothing about me and I only know what Andre told me about you. I'd always had it in my mind that one day we would be friends, you and me. But if you didn't know about Andre and me . . . If this hadn't happened, I wonder if he would have ever told you. When he was sick, if I asked him once I asked him a thousand times, tell her. She's your mother. She won't mind. But he was so afraid of hurting you and of your disapproval. I don't know which was worse. [*No response. He sighs.*] God, how many of us live in this city because we don't want to hurt our mothers and live in mortal terror of their disapproval. We lose ourselves here. Our lives aren't furtive, just our feelings toward people like you are! A city of fugitives from our parents' scorn or heartbreak. Sometimes he'd seem a little down and I'd say, "What's the matter, babe?" and this funny sweet, sad smile would cross his face and he'd say, "Just a little homesick, Cal, just a little bit." I always accused him of being a country boy just playing at being a hotshot, sophisticated New Yorker. [*He sighs.*]

    It's bullshit. It's all bullshit. [*Still no response.*]

    Do you remember the comic strip *Little Lulu?* Her mother had no name, she was so remote, so formidable to all the children. She was just Lulu's mother. "Hello, Lulu's Mother," Lulu's friends would say. She was almost anonymous in her remoteness. You remind me of her. Andre's Mother. Let me answer the questions you can't ask and then I'll leave you alone and you won't ever have to see me again. Andre died of AIDS. I don't know how he got it. I tested negative. He died bravely. You would have been proud of him. The only thing that frightened him was you. I'll have everything that was his sent to you. I'll pay for it. There isn't much. You should have come up the summer he played Hamlet. He was magnificent. Yes, I'm bitter. I'm bitter I've lost him. I'm bitter what's happening. I'm bitter even now, after all this, I can't reach you. I'm beginning to feel your disapproval and it's making me ill. [*He looks at his balloon.*] Sorry, old friend. I blew it. [*He lets go of the balloon.*]

    Good night, sweet prince, and flights of angels sing thee to they rest![1] [*Beat.*] Goodbye, Andre's Mother.

---

[1]**Good night . . . rest!** Cal is quoting lines that Hamlet's friend Horatio speaks (5.2.336–37) at the moment of Hamlet's death.

[*He goes.* ANDRE'S MOTHER *stands alone holding her white balloon. Her lips tremble. She looks on the verge of breaking down. She is about to let go of the balloon when she pulls it down to her. She looks at it awhile before she gently kisses it. She lets go of the balloon. She follows it with her eyes as it rises and rises. The lights are beginning to fade.* ANDRE'S MOTHER's *eyes are still on the balloon. The lights fade.*]

[1988]

Joining the Conversation: Critical Thinking and Writing

1. Andre's Mother doesn't speak in the play, but we learn something about her through Cal's words, and something more through the description in the final stage direction. In a paragraph, characterize Andre's Mother.
2. Let's assume that you drafted this play, and now, on rereading it you decide that you want to give Andre's Mother one speech, and one speech only. Write the speech—it can go anywhere in the play that you think best—and then in a brief essay explain why you think the speech is effective.
3. Cal tells Penny that the balloons "represent the soul. When you let go, it means you're letting his soul ascend to Heaven." Is that exactly the way you see the balloons, or would see them if you attended a funeral where white balloons were distributed? Explain.

Chapter Overview: Looking Backward/Looking Forward

1. Do you think it is possible to love many people? Or is love so special that it can only be felt for a few people? Would you go further and say that love—real love, love in the deepest sense—can in truth only be felt for one person in your life?
2. How do we know when we have moved from "liking" someone to "loving" him or her? What are the signs? What is the evidence?
3. What does it mean to say that we have "fallen out of love" with someone? Is this change in us the result of something specific? Or does it, somehow, simply happen? Once you fall out of love, can you ever fall back in, or is that feeling lost forever?
4. Have you ever hated someone? How did this come about? Do you still hate the person, or have your feelings changed?
5. "Love" is a term that is often used in literature courses—love poetry, for instance, or love in the modern novel. What do you imagine a course in literature could teach you about love? Have you read a literary work that made you think and feel differently about love?
6. Do you find it hard to say, "I love you"? Why is that?
7. Do you think that it is a good experience to write about personal feelings, such as love and hate? Would you prefer not to? Would you like to do more of this kind of personal writing in your courses, or less?
8. Are you a religious person? Do you love God? How is this love felt and expressed in your life from day to day?

CHAPTER 23

Making Men and Women

SHORT VIEWS

*The multitude will hardly believe the excessive force of education, and
in the difference of modesty between men and women, ascribe that to
nature which is altogether owing to early instruction. Miss is scarce
three years old, but she's spoke to every day to hide her leg, and rebuked
in good earnest if she shows it, whilst little Master at the same age is bid
to take up his coats and piss like a man.*
> Bernard Mandeville

*We are all androgynous, not only because we are all born of a woman
impregnated by the seed of a man but because each of us, helplessly and
forever, contains the other—male in female, female in male, white in
black and black in white. We are a part of each other. Many of my
countrymen appear to find this fact exceedingly inconvenient and
even unfair, and so, very often, do I. But none of us can do anything
about it.*
> James Baldwin

*In the theory of gender I began from zero. There is no masculine power
or privilege I did not covet. But slowly, step by step, decade by decade,
I was forced to acknowledge that even a woman of abnormal will cannot
escape her hormonal identity.*
> Camille Paglia

*A woman simply is, but a man must become. Masculinity is risky and
elusive. It is achieved by a revolt from woman, and it is confirmed only
by other men.*
> Camille Paglia

One is not born, but rather becomes, a woman.
> Simone de Beauvoir

*There is no female mind. The brain is not an organ of sex. As well speak
of a female liver.*
> Charlotte Perkins Gilman

*Growing up female in America. What a liability! You grew up with your
ears full of cosmetic ads, love songs, advice columns, whoreoscopes,
Hollywood gossip, and moral dilemmas on the level of TV soap operas.
What litanies the advertisers of the good life chanted at you! What
curious catechisms.*
　　Erica Jong

*Men are not to be told anything they might find too painful; the secret
depths of human nature, the sordid physicalities, might overwhelm or
damage them. For instance, men often faint at the sight of their own
blood, to which they are not accustomed. For this reason you should
never stand behind one in the line at the Red Cross donor clinic.*
　　Margaret Atwood

*The true man wants two things: danger and play. For that reason he
wants woman, as the most dangerous plaything.*
　　Friedrich Nietzsche

Joining the Conversation: Critical Thinking and Writing

1. Select a quotation that especially appeals to you, and make it the focus of an
   essay of about 500 words.
2. Take two of the passages—perhaps one that you especially like and one that
   you think is wrongheaded—and write a dialogue of about 500 words in which
   the two authors converse or argue. They may each try to convince the other, or
   they may find that to some degree they share views and they may then work
   out a statement that both can accept. If you do take the first position—that one
   writer is on the correct track but the other is utterly mistaken—try to be fair to the
   view that you think is mistaken. (As an experiment in critical thinking, imagine that
   you accept it, and make the best case for it that you possibly can.)

ESSAYS

STEVEN DOLOFF

*Steven Doloff, a professor of English and Humanities at Pratt Institute, has published
essays on contemporary culture, education, and travel in numerous publications,
including the* New York Times, *the* Boston Globe, *and the* Philadelphia Inquirer.

The Opposite Sex

For just one day, imagine yourself a boy (wow!). A girl (ugh).

Having seen Dustin Hoffman's female impersonation in the movie "Tootsie,"
I decided to give myself some reading over the Christmas recess by assigning
in-class essays to my English composition students on how each would spend a

day as a member of his or her respective opposite sex. From four classes I received approximately 100 essays. The sample, perhaps like the movie, proved both entertaining and annoying in its predictability.

The female students, as a group, took to the subject immediately and with obvious gusto, while the male students tended to wait a while (in several cases half the period), in something of a daze, before starting. The activities hypothetically engaged in by the women, whose ages averaged about 20, generally reflected two areas: envy of men's physical and social privileges, and curiosity regarding men's true feelings concerning women.

In their essays, women jauntily went places *alone,* and sometimes stayed out *all night.* They threw their clothes on the floor and left dishes in the sink. They hung out on the street and sweated happily in a variety of sports from football to weightlifting.

More than a third of them went out to cruise for dates. Appointing themselves in brand names of men's clothing and dousing themselves in men's cologne I have never heard of (I was instructed to read *Gentleman's Quarterly* magazine), they deliberately and aggressively accosted women, *many* women, on the street, in discos, in supermarkets. Others sought out the proverbial locker room for the kinds of bull sessions they hoped would reveal the real nitty-gritty masculine mind at work (on the subject of women).

5   At least two female students in each class spent chunks of their essays under the sheets with imaginary girlfriends, wives or strangers, finding out with a kind of scientific zeal what sex is like as a man.

Some, but not all of the women ended their essays with a formal, almost obligatory sounding statement of preference to be a female, and of gratitude in returning to their correct gender after a day as Mr. Hyde.

The male students, after their initial paralysis wore off, did not write as much as the females. They seemed envious of very little that was female, and curious about nothing. Three or four spent their day as women frantically seeking medical help to turn back into men more quickly. Those who accepted the assignment more seriously, if unenthusiastically, either stayed home and apathetically checked off a list of domestic chores or, more evasively, went off to work in an office and engaged in totally asexual business office routines.

A small percentage of the men ventured into the more feminine pursuits of putting on makeup and going to the beauty parlor. They agreed looking good was important.

If they stayed home as housewives, when their hypothetical husbands returned from work they ate dinner, watched some television and then went right to sleep. If they were businesswomen, they came directly home after work, ate some dinner, watched TV and went right to sleep. A handful actually went out on dates, had dinner in the most expensive restaurants they could cajole their escorts into taking them to, and then, after being taken home, very politely slammed the doors in their escorts' faces and went right to sleep. Not one male student let anybody lay a finger on him/her.

10   Finally, the sense of heartfelt relief at the end of the male students' essays, underscored by the much-repeated fervent anticipation of masculinity returning with the dawn, seemed equivalent to that of jumping up after having been forced to sit on a lit stove.

Granted, my flimsy statistical sample is nothing to go to the Ford Foundation with for research money. But on the other hand, do I really need to prove that young people even now are still burdened with sexist stereotypes and sexist self-images not nearly as vestigial as we would like to think? (One male student rhetorically crumpled up his paper after 10 minutes and growled, "You can't make me write this!") What does that imply about the rest of us? What would *you* do as a member of the opposite sex for a day? This last question is your essay assignment.

[1983]

Joining the Conversation: Critical Thinking and Writing

1. In paragraphs 2–4 Doloff summarizes the essays that the women wrote, and in paragraphs 7–10 the essays that the men wrote. Do you think you would have written something fairly close to the essays he attributes to the persons of your sex? Explain.
2. Do you think Doloff's assignment is a good one? Please argue why or why not.
3. Write an essay that fulfills Doloff's assignment and that honestly represents your thoughts, but that does *not* largely fit the pattern that Doloff finds.

GRETEL EHRLICH

Gretel Ehrlich, born in 1946, was educated at Bennington College, the UCLA Film School, and the New School for Social Research. She has written fiction and poetry, especially about open spaces (she has lived in Wyoming, Colorado, and Greenland), and has received numerous awards. The following selection comes from The Solace of Open Spaces *(1985).*

About Men

When I'm in New York but feeling lonely for Wyoming I look for the Marlboro ads in the subway. What I'm aching to see is horseflesh, the glint of a spur, a line of distant mountains, brimming creeks, and a reminder of the ranchers and cowboys I've ridden with for the last eight years. But the men I see in those posters with their stern, humorless looks remind me of no one I know here. In our hellbent earnestness to romanticize the cowboy we've ironically disesteemed his true character. If he's "strong and silent" it's because there's probably no one to talk to. If he "rides away into the sunset" it's because he's been on horseback since four in the morning moving cattle and he's trying, fifteen hours later, to get home to his family. If he's "a rugged individualist" he's also part of a team: ranch work is teamwork and even the glorified open-range cowboys of the 1880s rode up and down the Chisholm Trail in the company of twenty or thirty other riders. Instead of the macho, trigger-happy man our culture has perversely wanted him to be, the cowboy is more apt to be convivial, quirky, and softhearted. To be "tough" on a ranch has nothing to do with conquests and displays of power. More often than not, circumstances—like the colt he's riding or an unexpected blizzard—are overpowering him. It's not toughness but "toughing it out" that counts. In other words, this macho, cultural artifact the cowboy has become is simply a man who possesses resilience, patience, and an instinct for survival. "Cowboys are just like a pile of rocks—everything happens to them. They get climbed on, kicked, rained and snowed on, scuffed up by wind. Their job is 'just to take it,'" one old-timer told me.

A cowboy is someone who loves his work. Since the hours are long—ten to fifteen hours a day—and the pay is $30 he has to. What's required of him is an odd mixture of physical vigor and maternalism. His part of the beef-raising industry is to birth and nurture calves and take care of their mothers. For the most part his work is done on horseback and in a lifetime he sees and comes to know more animals than people. The iconic myth surrounding him is built on American notions of heroism: the index of a man's value as measured in physical courage. Such ideas have perverted manliness into a self-absorbed race for cheap thrills. In a rancher's world, courage has less to do with facing danger than with acting spontaneously—usually on behalf of an animal or another rider. If a cow is stuck in a boghole he throws a loop around her neck, takes his dally (a half hitch around the saddle horn), and pulls her out with horsepower. If a calf is born sick, he may take her home, warm her in front of the kitchen fire, and massage her legs until dawn. One friend, whose favorite horse was trying to swim a lake with hobbles on, dove under water and cut her legs loose with a knife, then swam her to shore, his arm around her neck lifeguard-style, and saved her from drowning. Because these incidents are usually linked to someone or something outside himself, the westerner's courage is selfless, a form of compassion.

The physical punishment that goes with cowboying is greatly underplayed. Once fear is dispensed with, the threshold of pain rises to meet the demands of the job. When Jane Fonda asked Robert Redford (in the film *Electric Horseman*) if he was sick as he struggled to his feet one morning, he replied, "No, just bent." For once the movies had it right. The cowboys I was sitting with laughed in agreement. Cowboys are rarely complainers; they show their stoicism laughing at themselves.

If a rancher or cowboy has been thought of as a "man's man"—laconic, hard-drinking, inscrutable—there's almost no place in which the balancing act between male and female, manliness and femininity, can be more natural. If he's gruff, handsome, and physically fit on the outside, he's androgynous at the core. Ranchers are midwives, hunters, nurturers, providers, and conservationists all at once. What we've interpreted as toughness—weathered skin, calloused hands, a squint in the eye and a growl in the voice—only masks the tenderness inside. "Now don't go telling me these lambs are cute," one rancher warned me the first day I walked into the football-field-sized lambing sheds. The next thing I knew he was holding a black lamb. "Ain't this little rat good-lookin'?"

5   So many of the men who came to the West were Southerners—men looking for work and a new life after the Civil War—that chivalrousness and strict codes of honor were soon thought of as western traits. There were very few women in Wyoming during territorial days, so when they did arrive (some as mail-order brides from places like Philadelphia) there was a standoffishness between the sexes and a formality that persists now. Ranchers still tip their hats and say, "Howdy, ma'am" instead of shaking hands with me.

Even young cowboys are often evasive with women. It's not that they're Jekyll and Hyde creatures—gentle with animals and rough on women—but rather, that they don't know how to bring their tenderness into the house and lack the vocabulary to express the complexity of what they feel. Dancing wildly all night becomes a metaphor for the explosive emotions pent up inside, and when these are, on occasion, released, they're so battery-charged and potent that one caress of the face or one "I love you" will peal for a long while.

The geographical vastness and the social isolation here make emotional evolution seem impossible. Those contradictions of the heart between respectability, logic, and convention on the one hand, and impulse, passion, and intuition on the other, played out wordlessly against the paradisiacal beauty of the West, give cowboys a wide-eyed but drawn look. Their lips pucker up, not with kisses but with immutability. They may want to break out, staying up all night with a lover just to talk, but they don't know how and can't imagine what the consequences will be. Those rare occasions when they do bare themselves result in confusion. "I feel as if I'd sprained my heart," one friend told me a month after such a meeting.

My friend Ted Hoagland[1] wrote, "No one is as fragile as a woman but no one is as fragile as a man." For all the women here who use "fragileness" to avoid work or as a sexual ploy, there are men who try to hide theirs, all the while clinging to an adolescent dependency on women to cook their meals, wash their clothes, and keep the ranch house warm in winter. But there is true vulnerability in evidence here. Because these men work with animals, not machines or numbers, because they live outside in landscapes of torrential beauty, because they are confined to a place and a routine embellished with awesome variables, because calves die in the arms that pulled others into life, because they go to the mountains as if on a pilgrimage to find out what makes a herd of elk tick, their strength is also a softness, their toughness, a rare delicacy.

[1985]

Joining the Conversation: Critical Thinking and Writing

1. Early on, Ehrlich says: "In our hellbent earnestness to romanticize the cowboy we've ironically disesteemed his true character." What is she saying in this sentence? Do you find the sentence clear, or confusing? Please explain.
2. Later, Ehrlich says that cowboys are not like "Jekyll and Hyde." Identify and explain this reference. Where did you go to find this information?
3. In a paragraph of three or four sentences, summarize the main point that Ehrlich is making. Do you find it hard or easy to write this summary? What does your response suggest to you about Ehrlich's essay as a piece of writing?
4. Would you describe this essay as an "argument"? Or is it something different? After you read the essay, did your understanding of the topic change? In what way?

STORIES

CHARLOTTE PERKINS GILMAN

Charlotte Perkins Gilman (1860–1935) was born in Hartford, Connecticut. Her father deserted the family soon after Charlotte's birth; she was brought up by her mother, who found it difficult to support her family. For a while Charlotte worked as an artist and teacher of art, and in 1884, when she was twenty-four, she married an artist. In 1885 she had a daughter, but soon after the birth of the girl Charlotte had a nervous breakdown. At her husband's urging she spent a month in the sanitarium of Dr. S. Weir Mitchell, a physician who specialized in treating women with nervous disorders. (Mitchell is specifically named in "The

[1]**Ted Hoagland** Edward Hoagland (1932–   ), American essayist and novelist

Yellow Wallpaper.") Because the treatment—isolation and total rest—nearly drove her to insanity, she fled Mitchell and her husband. In California she began a career as a lecturer and writer on feminist topics. (She also supported herself by teaching school and by keeping a boardinghouse.) Among her books are Women and Economics *(1899) and* The Man-Made World *(1911), which have been revived by the feminist movement. In 1900 she married a cousin, George Gilman. From all available evidence, the marriage was successful. Certainly it did not restrict her activities as a feminist. In 1935, suffering from inoperable cancer, she took her own life.*

"The Yellow Wallpaper," written in 1892—that is, written after she had been treated by S. Weir Mitchell for her nervous breakdown—was at first interpreted either as a ghost story or as a Poe-like study of insanity. Only in recent years has it been seen as a feminist story. (One might ask oneself if these interpretations are mutually exclusive.)

The Yellow Wallpaper

It is very seldom that mere ordinary people like John and myself secure ancestral halls for the summer.

A colonial mansion, a hereditary estate. I would say a haunted house, and reach the height of romantic felicity—but that would be asking too much of fate!

Still I will proudly declare that there is something queer about it.

Else, why should it be let so cheaply? And why have stood so long untenanted?

5   John laughs at me, of course, but one expects that in marriage.

John is practical in the extreme. He has no patience with faith, an intense horror of superstition, and he scoffs openly at any talk of things not to be felt and seen and put down in figures.

John is a physician, and *perhaps*—(I would not say it to a living soul, of course, but this is dead paper and a great relief to my mind)—*perhaps* that is one reason I do not get well faster.

You see he does not believe I am sick! And what can one do?

If a physician of high standing, and one's own husband, assures friends and relatives that there is really nothing the matter with one but temporary nervous depression—a slight hysterical tendency—what is one to do?

10   My brother is also a physician, and also of high standing, and he says the same thing.

So I take phosphates or phosphites—whichever it is, and tonics, and journeys, and air, and exercise, and am absolutely forbidden to "work" until I am well again.

Personally, I disagree with their ideas.

Personally, I believe that congenial work, with excitement and change, would do me good.

But what is one to do?

15   I did write for a while in spite of them: but it *does* exhaust me a good deal—having to be so sly about it, or else meet with heavy opposition.

I sometimes fancy that in my condition if I had less opposition and more society and stimulus—but John says the very worst thing I can do is to think about my condition, and I confess it always makes me feel bad.

So I will let it alone and talk about the house.

The most beautiful place! It is quite alone, standing well back from the road, quite three miles from the village. It makes me think of English places that you read about, for there are hedges and walls and gates that lock, and lots of separate little houses for the gardeners and people.

There is a *delicious* garden! I never saw such a garden—large and shady, full of box-bordered paths, and lined with long grape-covered arbors with seats under them. There were greenhouses, too, but they are all broken now.

20 There was some legal trouble. I believe, something about the heirs and co-heirs: anyhow, the place has been empty for years.

That spoils my ghostliness, I am afraid, but I don't care—there is something strange about the house—I can feel it.

I even said so to John one moonlight evening, but he said what I felt was a *draught,* and shut the window.

I get unreasonably angry with John sometimes. I'm sure I never used to be so sensitive. I think it is due to this nervous condition.

But John says if I feel so, I shall neglect proper self-control: so I take pains to control myself—before him, at least, and that makes me very tired.

25 I don't like our room a bit. I wanted one downstairs that opened on the piazza and had roses all over the window, and such pretty old-fashioned chintz hangings! But John would not hear of it.

He said there was only one window and not room for two beds, and no near room for him if he took another.

He is very careful and loving, and hardly lets me stir without special direction.

I have a schedule prescription for each hour in the day: he takes all care from me, and so I feel basely ungrateful not to value it more.

He said we came here solely on my account, that I was to have perfect rest and all the air I could get. "Your exercise depends on your strength, my dear," said he, "and your food somewhat on your appetite; but air you can absorb all the time." So we took the nursery at the top of the house.

30 It is a big, airy room, the whole floor nearly, with windows that look all ways, and air and sunshine galore. It was nursery first and then playroom and gymnasium, I should judge; for the windows are barred for little children, and there are rings and things in the walls.

The paint and paper look as if a boys' school had used it. It is stripped off—the paper—in great patches all around the head of my bed, about as far as I can reach, and in a great place on the other side of the room low down. I never saw a worse paper in my life.

One of those sprawling flamboyant patterns committing every artistic sin.

It is dull enough to confuse the eye in following, pronounced enough to constantly irritate and provoke study, and when you follow the lame uncertain curves for a little distance they suddenly commit suicide—plunge off at outrageous angles, destroy themselves in unheard of contradictions.

The color is repellent, almost revolting: a smouldering unclean yellow, strangely faded by the slow-turning sunlight. It is a dull yet lurid orange in some places, a sickly sulphur tint in others.

35 No wonder the children hated it! I should hate it myself if I had to live in this room long.

There comes John, and I must put this away,—he hates to have me write a word.

We have been here two weeks, and I haven't felt like writing before, since that first day.

I am sitting by the window now, up in this atrocious nursery, and there is nothing to hinder my writing as much as I please, save lack of strength.

John is away all day, and even some nights when his cases are serious.

40   I am glad my case is not serious!

But these nervous troubles are dreadfully depressing.

John does not know how much I really suffer. He knows there is no *reason* to suffer, and that satisfies him.

Of course it is only nervousness. It does weigh on me so not to do my duty in any way!

I meant to be such a help to John, such a real rest and comfort, and here I am a comparative burden already!

45   Nobody would believe what an effort it is to do what little I am able,—to dress and entertain, and order things.

It is fortunate Mary is so good with the baby. Such a dear baby!

And yet I *cannot* be with him, it makes me so nervous.

I suppose John never was nervous in his life. He laughs at me so about this wallpaper!

At first he meant to repaper the room, but afterwards he said that I was letting it get the better of me, and that nothing was worse for a nervous patient than to give way to such fancies.

50   He said that after the wallpaper was changed it would be the heavy bedstead, and then the barred windows, and then that gate at the head of the stairs, and so on.

"You know the place is doing you good," he said, "and really, dear, I don't care to renovate the house just for a three months' rental."

"Then do let us go downstairs," I said, "there are such pretty rooms there."

Then he took me in his arms and called me a blessed little goose, and said he would go down to the cellar, if I wished, and have it whitewashed into the bargain.

But he is right enough about the beds and windows and things.

55   It is an airy and comfortable room as any one need wish, and, of course, I would not be so silly as to make him uncomfortable just for a whim.

I'm really getting quite fond of the big room, all but that horrid paper.

Out of one window I can see the garden, those mysterious deep-shaded arbors, the riotous old-fashioned flowers, and bushes and gnarly trees.

Out of another I get a lovely view of the bay and a little private wharf belonging to the estate. There is a beautiful shaded lane that runs down there from the house. I always fancy I see people walking in these numerous paths and arbors, but John has cautioned me not to give way to fancy in the least. He says that with my imaginative power and habit of story-making, a nervous weakness like mine is sure to lead to all manner of excited fancies, and that I ought to use my will and good sense to check the tendency. So I try.

I think sometimes that if I were only well enough to write a little it would relieve the press of ideas and rest me.

60   But I find I get pretty tired when I try.

It is so discouraging not to have any advice and companionship about my work. When I get really well, John says we will ask Cousin Henry and Julia down for a long visit; but he says he would as soon put fireworks in my pillow-case as to let me have those stimulating people about now.

I wish I could get well faster.

But I must not think about that. This paper looks to me as if it *knew* what a vicious influence it had!

There is a recurrent spot where the pattern lolls like a broken neck and two bulbous eyes stare at you upside down.

65   I get positively angry with the impertinence of it and the everlastingness. Up and down and sideways they crawl, and those absurd, unblinking eyes are everywhere. There is one place where two breadths didn't match, and the eyes go all up and down the line, one a little higher than the other.

I never saw so much expression in an inanimate thing before, and we all know how much expression they have! I used to lie awake as a child and get more entertainment and terror out of blank walls and plain furniture than most children could find in a toystore.

I remember what a kindly wink the knobs of our big, old bureau used to have, and there was one chair that always seemed like a strong friend.

I used to feel that if any of the other things looked too fierce I could always hop into that chair and be safe.

The furniture in this room is no worse than inharmonious, however, for we had to bring it all from downstairs. I suppose when this was used as a playroom they had to take the nursery things out, and no wonder! I never saw such ravages as the children have made here.

70   The wallpaper, as I said before, is torn off in spots, and it sticketh closer than a brother—they must have had perseverance as well as hatred.

Then the floor is scratched and gouged and splintered, the plaster itself is dug out here and there, and this great heavy bed which is all we found in the room, looks as if it had been through the wars.

But I don't mind it a bit—only the paper.

There comes John's sister. Such a dear girl as she is, and so careful of me! I must not let her find me writing.

She is a perfect and enthusiastic housekeeper, and hopes for no better profession. I verily believe she thinks it is the writing which made me sick!

75   But I can write when she is out, and see her a long way off from these windows.

There is one that commands the road, a lovely shaded winding road, and one that just looks off over the country. A lovely country, too, full of great elms and velvet meadows.

This wallpaper has a kind of sub-pattern in a different shade, a particularly irritating one, for you can only see it in certain lights, and not clearly then.

But in the places where it isn't faded and where the sun is just so—I can see a strange, provoking, formless sort of figure, that seems to skulk about behind that silly and conspicuous front design.

There's sister on the stairs!

80   Well, the Fourth of July is over! The people are all gone and I am tired out. John thought it might do me good to see a little company, so we just had mother and Nellie and the children down for a week.

Of course I didn't do a thing. Jennie sees to everything now.

But it tired me all the same.

John says if I don't pick up faster he shall send me to Weir Mitchell in the fall.

But I don't want to go there at all. I had a friend who was in his hands once, and she says he is just like John and my brother, only more so!

85   Besides, it is such an undertaking to go so far.

I don't feel as if it was worthwhile to turn my hand over for anything, and I'm getting dreadfully fretful and querulous.

I cry at nothing, and cry most of the time.

Of course I don't when John is here, or anybody else, but when I am alone.

And I am alone a good deal just now. John is kept in town very often by serious cases, and Jennie is good and lets me alone when I want her to.

90   So I walk a little in the garden or down that lovely lane, sit on the porch under the roses, and lie down up here a good deal.

I'm getting really fond of the room in spite of the wallpaper. Perhaps *because* of the wallpaper.

It dwells in my mind so!

I lie here on this great immovable bed—it is nailed down, I believe—and follow that pattern about by the hour. It is as good as gymnastics, I assure you. I start, we'll say, at the bottom, down in the corner over there where it has not been touched, and I determine for the thousandth time that I *will* follow that pointless pattern to some sort of a conclusion.

I know a little of the principle of design, and I know this thing was not arranged on any laws of radiation, or alternation, or repetition, or symmetry, or anything else that I ever heard of.

95   It is repeated, of course, by the breadths, but not otherwise.

Looked at in one way each breadth stands alone, the bloated curves and flourishes—a kind of "debased Romanesque" with *delirium tremens*—go waddling up and down in isolated columns of fatuity.

But, on the other hand, they connect diagonally, and the sprawling outlines run off in great slanting waves of optic horror, like a lot of wallowing seaweeds in full chase.

The whole thing goes horizontally, too, at least it seems so, and I exhaust myself in trying to distinguish the order of its going in that direction.

They have used a horizontal breadth for a frieze, and that adds wonderfully to the confusion.

100   There is one end of the room where it is almost intact, and there, when the crosslights fade and the low sun shines directly upon it, I can almost fancy radiation after all,—the interminable grotesques seem to form around a common center and rush off in headlong plunges of equal distraction.

It makes me tired to follow it. I will take a nap I guess.

I don't know why I should write this.

I don't want to.

I don't feel able.

105   And I know John would think it absurd. But I *must* say what I feel and think in some way—it is such a relief.

But the effort is getting to be greater than the relief!

Half the time now I am awfully lazy, and lie down ever so much. John says I mustn't lose my strength, and has me take cod liver oil and lots of tonics and things, to say nothing of ale and wine and rare meat.

Dear John! He loves me very dearly, and hates to have me sick. I tried to have a real earnest reasonable talk with him the other day, and tell him how I wish he would let me go and make a visit to Cousin Henry and Julia.

But he said I wasn't able to go, nor able to stand it after I got there: and I did not make out a very good case for myself, for I was crying before I had finished.

110   It is getting to be a great effort for me to think straight. Just this nervous weakness I suppose.

And dear John gathered me up in his arms, and just carried me upstairs and laid me on the bed, and sat by me and read to me till it tired my head.

He said I was his darling and his comfort and all he had, and that I must take care of myself for his sake, and keep well.

He says no one but myself can help me out of it, that I must use my will and self-control and not let any silly fancies run away with me.

There's one comfort, the baby is well and happy, and does not have to occupy this nursery with the horrid wallpaper.

If we had not used it, that blessed child would have! What a fortunate escape! Why, I wouldn't have a child of mine, an impressionable little thing, live in such a room for worlds.

I never thought of it before, but it is lucky that John kept me here after all. I can stand it so much easier than a baby, you see.

Of course I never mention it to them any more—I am too wise,—but I keep watch of it all the same.

There are things in that paper that nobody knows but me, or ever will.

Behind that outside pattern the dim shapes get clearer every day.

It is always the same shape, only very numerous.

And it is like a woman stooping down and creeping about behind that pattern. I don't like it a bit. I wonder—I begin to think—I wish John would take me away from here!

It is so hard to talk with John about my case, because he is so wise, and because he loves me so.

But I tried last night.

It was moonlight. The moon shines in all around just as the sun does.

I hate to see it sometimes, it creeps so slowly, and always comes in by one window or another.

John was asleep and I hated to waken him, so I kept still and watched the moonlight on that undulating wallpaper till I felt creepy.

The faint figure behind seemed to shake the pattern, just as if she wanted to get out.

I got up softly and went to feel and see if the paper *did* move, and when I came back John was awake.

"What is it, little girl?" he said. "Don't go walking about like that—you'll get cold."

I thought it was a good time to talk, so I told him that I really was not gaining here, and that I wished he would take me away.

"Why darling!" said he, "our lease will be up in three weeks, and I can't see how to leave before."

"The repairs are not done at home, and I cannot possibly leave town just now. Of course if you were in any danger, I could and would, but you really are better, dear, whether you can see it or not. I am a doctor, dear, and I know. You are gaining flesh and color, your appetite is better, I feel really much easier about you."

"I don't weigh a bit more," said I, "nor as much: and my appetite may be better in the evening when you are here, but it is worse in the morning when you are away!"

"Bless her little heart!" said he with a big hug, "she shall be as sick as she pleases! But now let's improve the shining hours by going to sleep, and talk about it in the morning!"

"And you won't go away?" I asked gloomily.

"Why, how can I, dear? It is only three weeks more and then we will take a nice little trip of a few days while Jennie is getting the house ready. Really, dear, you are better!"

"Better in body perhaps—" I began, and stopped short, for he sat up straight and looked at me with such a stern, reproachful look that I could not say another word.

"My darling," said he, "I beg of you, for my sake and for our child's sake, as well as for your own, that you will never for one instant let that idea enter your mind! There is nothing so dangerous, so fascinating, to a temperament like yours. It is a false and foolish fancy. Can you not trust me as a physician when I tell you so?"

So of course I said no more on that score, and we went to sleep before long. He thought I was asleep first, but I wasn't and lay there for hours trying to decide whether that front pattern and the back pattern really did move together or separately.

140   On a pattern like this, by daylight, there is a lack of sequence, a defiance of law, that is a constant irritant to a normal mind.

The color is hideous enough, and unreliable enough, and infuriating enough, but the pattern is torturing.

You think you have mastered it, but just as you get well underway in following, it turns a back-somersault and there you are. It slaps you in the face, knocks you down, and tramples upon you. It is like a bad dream.

The outside pattern is a florid arabesque, reminding one of a fungus. If you can imagine a toadstool in joints, an interminable string of toadstools, budding and sprouting in endless convolutions—why, that is something like it.

That is, sometimes!

145   There is one marked peculiarity about this paper, a thing nobody seems to notice but myself, and that is that it changes as the light changes.

When the sun shoots in through the east window—I always watch for that first long, straight ray—it changes so quickly that I never can quite believe it.

That is why I watch it always.

By moonlight—the moon shines in all night when there is a moon—I wouldn't know it was the same paper.

At night in any kind of light, in twilight, candlelight, lamplight, and worst of all by moonlight, it becomes bars! The outside pattern I mean, and the woman behind it is as plain as can be.

150   I didn't realize for a long time what the thing was that showed behind, that dim sub-pattern, but now I am quite sure it is a woman.

By daylight she is subdued, quiet. I fancy it is the pattern that keeps her so still. It is so puzzling. It keeps me quiet by the hour.

I lie down ever so much now. John says it is good for me, and to sleep all I can. Indeed he started the habit by making me lie down for an hour after each meal.

It is a very bad habit I am convinced, for you see I don't sleep.

155   And that cultivates deceit, for I don't tell them I'm awake—O no!

The fact is I am getting a little afraid of John.

He seems very queer sometimes, and even Jennie has an inexplicable look.

It strikes me occasionally, just as a scientific hypothesis—that perhaps it is the paper!

I have watched John when he did not know I was looking, and come into the room suddenly on the most innocent excuses, and I've caught him several times *looking at the paper!* And Jennie too. I caught Jennie with her hand on it once.

160   She didn't know I was in the room, and when I asked her in a quiet, a very quiet voice, with the most restrained manner possible, what she was doing with the paper—she turned around as if she had been caught stealing, and looked quite angry—asked me why I should frighten her so!

    Then she said that the paper stained everything it touched, that she had found yellow smooches on all my clothes and John's, and she wished we would be more careful!

    Did not that sound innocent? But I know she was studying that pattern, and I am determined that nobody shall find it out but myself!

    Life is very much more exciting now than it used to be. You see I have something more to expect, to look forward to, to watch. I really do eat better, and am more quiet than I was.

    John is so pleased to see me improve! He laughed a little the other day, and said I seemed to be flourishing in spite of my wallpaper.

165   I turned it off with a laugh. I had no intention of telling him it was *because* of the wallpaper—he would make fun of me. He might even want to take me away.

    I don't want to leave now until I have found it out. There is a week more, and I think that will be enough.

    I'm feeling ever so much better! I don't sleep much at night, for it is so interesting to watch developments, but I sleep a good deal in the daytime.

    In the daytime it is tiresome and perplexing.

    There are always new shoots on the fungus, and new shades of yellow all over it. I cannot keep count of them, though I have tried conscientiously.

170   It is the strangest yellow, that wallpaper! It makes me think of all the yellow things I ever saw—not beautiful ones like buttercups, but old, foul, bad yellow things.

    But there is something else about that paper—the smell! I noticed it the moment we came into the room, but with so much air and sun it was not bad. Now we have had a week of fog and rain, and whether the windows are open or not, the smell is here.

    It creeps all over the house.

    I find it hovering in the dining-room, skulking in the parlor, hiding in the hall, lying in wait for me on the stairs.

    It gets into my hair.

175   Even when I go to ride, if I turn my head suddenly and surprise it—there is that smell!

    Such a peculiar odor, too! I have spent hours in trying to analyze it, to find what it smelled like.

    It is not bad—at first, and very gentle, but quite the subtlest, most enduring odor I ever met.

    In this damp weather it is awful, I wake up in the night and find it hanging over me.

    It used to disturb me at first. I thought seriously of burning the house—to reach the smell.

180   But now I am used to it. The only thing I can think of that it is like is the *color* of the paper! A yellow smell.

    There is a very funny mark on this wall, low down, near the mopboard. A streak that runs round the room. It goes behind every piece of furniture, except the bed, a long, straight, even *smooch,* as if it had been rubbed over and over.

I wonder how it was done and who did it, and what they did it for. Round and round and round—round and round and round—it makes me dizzy!

I really have discovered something at last.

Through watching so much at night, when it changes so, I have finally found out.

The front pattern *does* move—and no wonder! The woman behind shakes it!

Sometimes I think there are a great many women behind, and sometimes only one, and she crawls around fast, and her crawling shakes it all over.

Then in the very bright spots she keeps still, and in the very shady spots she just takes hold of the bars and shakes them hard.

And she is all the time trying to climb through. But nobody could climb through that pattern—it strangles so: I think that is why it has so many heads.

They get through, and then the pattern strangles them off and turns them upside down, and makes their eyes white!

If those heads were covered or taken off it would not be half so bad.

I think that woman gets out in the daytime!

And I'll tell you why—privately—I've seen her!

I can see her out of every one of my windows!

It is the same woman, I know, for she is always creeping, and most women do not creep by daylight.

I see her in that long shaded lane, creeping up and down. I see her in those dark grape arbors, creeping all round the garden.

I see her on that long road under the trees, creeping along, and when a carriage comes she hides under the blackberry vines.

I don't blame her a bit. It must be very humiliating to be caught creeping by daylight!

I always lock the door when I creep by daylight. I can't do it at night, for I know John would suspect something at once.

And John is so queer now, that I don't want to irritate him. I wish he would take another room! Besides, I don't want anybody to get that woman out at night but myself.

I often wonder if I could see her out of all the windows at once.

But, turn as fast as I can, I can only see out of one at one time. And though I always see her, she *may* be able to creep faster than I can turn!

I have watched her sometimes away off in the open country, creeping as fast as a cloud shadow in a high wind.

If only that top pattern could be gotten off from the under one! I mean to try it, little by little.

I have found out another funny thing, but I shan't tell at this time! It does not do to trust people too much.

There are only two more days to get this paper off, and I believe John is beginning to notice. I don't like the look in his eyes.

And I heard him ask Jennie a lot of professional questions about me. She had a very good report to give.

She said I slept a good deal in the daytime.

John knows I don't sleep very well at night, for all I'm so quiet!

He asked me all sorts of questions, too, and pretended to be very loving and kind.

As if I couldn't see through him!

Still, I don't wonder he acts so, sleeping under this paper for three months.

It only interests me, but I feel sure John and Jennie are secretly affected by it.

Hurrah! This is the last day, but it is enough. John is to stay in town over night, and won't be out until this evening.

Jennie wanted to sleep with me—the sly thing! But I told her I should undoubtedly rest better for a night all alone.

215   That was clever, for really I wasn't alone a bit! As soon as it was moonlight and that poor thing began to crawl and shake the pattern, I got up and ran to help her.

I pulled and she shook, I shook and she pulled, and before morning we had peeled off yards of that paper.

A strip about as high as my head and half round the room.

And then when the sun came and that awful pattern began to laugh at me, I declared I would finish it today!

We go away tomorrow, and they are moving all the furniture down again to leave things as they were before.

220   Jennie looked at the wall in amazement, but I told her merrily that I did it out of pure spite at the vicious thing.

She laughed and said she wouldn't mind doing it herself, but I must not get tired.

How she betrayed herself that time!

But I am here, and no person touches this paper but me—not *alive!*

She tried to get me out of the room—it was too patent! But I said it was so quiet and empty and clean now that I believed I would lie down again and sleep all I could; and not to wake me even for dinner—I would call when I woke.

225   So now she is gone, and the servants are gone, and the things are gone, and there is nothing left but that great bedstead nailed down, with the canvas mattress we found on it.

We shall sleep downstairs tonight, and take the boat home tomorrow.

I quite enjoy the room, now it is bare again.

How those children did tear about here!

This bedstead is fairly gnawed!

230   But I must get to work.

I have locked the door and thrown the key down into the front path.

I don't want to go out, and I don't want to have anybody come in, till John comes.

I want to astonish him.

I've got a rope up here that even Jennie did not find. If that woman does get out, and tries to get away, I can tie her!

235   But I forgot I could not reach far without anything to stand on! This bed will *not* move!

I tried to lift and push it until I was lame, and then I got so angry I bit off a little piece at one corner—but it hurt my teeth.

Then I peeled off all the paper I could reach standing on the floor. It sticks horribly and the pattern just enjoys it! All those strangled heads and bulbous eyes and waddling fungus growths just shriek with derision!

I am getting angry enough to do something desperate. To jump out of the window would be admirable exercise, but the bars are too strong even to try.

Besides I wouldn't do it. Of course not, I know well enough that a step like that is improper and might be misconstrued.

240   I don't like to *look* out of the windows even—there are so many of those creeping women, and they creep so fast.

I wonder if they all come out of that wallpaper as I did?

But I am securely fastened now by my well-hidden rope—you don't get *me* out in the road there!

I suppose I shall have to get back behind the pattern when it comes night, and that is hard!

It is so pleasant to be out in this great room and creep around as I please!

245   I don't want to go outside. I won't, even if Jennie asks me to.

For outside you have to creep on the ground, and everything is green instead of yellow.

But here I can creep smoothly on the floor, and my shoulder just fits in that long smooch around the wall, so I cannot lose my way.

Why there's John at the door!

It is no use, young man, you can't open it!

250   How he does call and pound!

Now he's crying for an axe.

It would be a shame to break down that beautiful door!

"John, dear!" said I in the gentlest voice, "the key is down by the front steps, under a plantain leaf!"

That silenced him for a few moments.

255   Then he said—very quietly indeed, "Open the door, my darling!"

"I can't," said I. "The key is down by the front door under a plantain leaf!"

And then I said it again, several times, very gently and slowly, and said it so often that he had to go and see, and he got it of course, and came in. He stopped short by the door.

"What is the matter?" he cried. "For God's sake, what are you doing!"

I kept on creeping just the same, but I looked at him over my shoulder.

260   "I've got out at last," said I, "in spite of you and Jane. And I've pulled off most of the paper, so you can't put me back!"

Now why should that man have fainted? But he did, and right across my path by the wall, so that I had to creep over him every time!

[1892]

Joining the Conversation: Critical Thinking and Writing

1. Is the narrator insane at the start of "The Yellow Wallpaper," or does she become insane at some point during the narrative? Or can't we be sure? Support your view with evidence from the story.

2. How reliable do you think the narrator's characterization of her husband is? Support your answer with reasons.

3. The narrator says that she cannot get better because her husband is a physician. What do you take this to mean? Do you think the story is about a husband who deliberately drives his wife insane?

4. Is Gilman attacking men in this story? If so, is that a bad thing? If she is not, then what is she doing?

MyLiteratureLab® *For additional resources for "The Yellow Wallpaper," log in to www* *.myliteraturelab.com where you will find a Longman Lecture and Short Evaluation* *Exercises, as well as an About the Author for Gilman (under Student Resources)*

JOHN UPDIKE

John Updike (1932–2009) grew up in Shillington, Pennsylvania, where his father was a teacher and his mother a writer. After receiving a BA in 1954 from Harvard, where he edited the Harvard Lampoon *(for which he both wrote and drew), he studied drawing at Oxford for a year, until an offer from the* New Yorker *brought him back to the United States. He was hired as a reporter for the magazine but soon began contributing poetry, essays, and fiction. In 1957 he left the* New Yorker *in order to write independently full time, though his stories and book reviews appeared regularly in it until his death.*

In 1959 Updike published his first book of stories, The Same Door, *and his first novel,* The Poorhouse Fair; *the next year he published* Rabbit, Run, *a highly successful novel whose protagonist, "Rabbit" Angstrom, reappears in three later novels,* Rabbit Redux *(1971),* Rabbit Is Rich *(1981), and* Rabbit at Rest *(1990). The first and the last Rabbit books each won a Pulitzer Prize.*

Oliver's Evolution

His parents had not meant to abuse him; they had meant to love him, and did love him. But Oliver had come late in their little pack of offspring, at a time when the challenge of child-rearing was wearing thin, and he proved susceptible to mishaps. A big fetus, cramped in his mother's womb, he was born with in-turned feet, and learned to crawl with corrective casts up to his ankles. When they were at last removed, he cried in terror, because he thought those heavy plaster boots scraping and bumping along the floor had been part of himself.

One day in his infancy they found him on their dressing-room floor with a box of mothballs, some of which were wet with saliva; in retrospect they wondered if there had really been a need to rush him to the hospital and have his poor little stomach pumped. His face was gray-green afterwards. The following summer, when he had learned to walk, his parents had unthinkingly swum away off the beach together, striving for romantic harmony the morning after a late party and an alcoholic quarrel, and were quite unaware, until they saw the life-guard racing along the beach, that Oliver had toddled after them and had been floating on his face for what might have been, given a less alert lifeguard a fatal couple of minutes. This time, his face was blue, and he coughed for hours.

He was the least complaining of their children. He did not blame his parents when neither they nor the school authorities detected his "sleepy" right eye in time for therapy, with the result that when he closed that eye everything looked intractably fuzzy. Just the sight of the boy holding a schoolbook at a curious angle to the light made his father want to weep, impotently.

And it happened that he was just the wrong, vulnerable age when his parents went through their separation and divorce. His older brothers were off in boarding school and college, embarked on manhood, free of family. His younger sister was small enough to find the new arrangements—the meals in restaurants with her father, the friendly men who appeared to take her mother out—exciting. But Oliver, at thirteen, felt the weight of the household descend on him; he made his mother's sense of abandonment his own. Again, his father impotently grieved. It was he, and not the boy, who was at fault, really, when the bad grades began to come in from day school, and then from college, and Oliver broke his arm falling down the frat stairs, or leaping, by another account of the confused incident, from a girl's dormitory window. Not one but several family automobiles met a ruinous end with him at the wheel, though with no more injury, as it happened, than contused knees and loosened front teeth. The teeth grew firm again, thank God, for his innocent smile, slowly spreading across his face as the full humor of his newest misadventure dawned, was one of his best features. His teeth were small and round and widely spaced—baby teeth.

5   Then he married, which seemed yet another mishap, to go with the late nights, abandoned jobs, and fallen-through opportunities of his life as a young adult. The girl, Alicia, was as accident-prone as he, given to substance abuse and unwanted pregnancies. Her emotional disturbances left herself and others bruised. By comparison Oliver was solid and surefooted, and she looked up to him. This was the key. What we expect of others, they endeavor to provide. He held on to a job, and she held on to her pregnancies. You should see him now, with their two children, a fair little girl and a dark-haired boy. Oliver has grown broad, and holds the two of them at once. They are birds in a nest. He is a tree, a sheltering boulder. He is a protector of the weak.

[2000]

Joining the Conversation: Critical Thinking and Writing

1. At the end of the fourth paragraph Updike tells us that the mature Oliver's "teeth were small and round and widely spaced—baby teeth." Why do you suppose he gives us this detail?
2. How plausible does Oliver's life seem to you? Explain.
3. The story consists primarily of description and narration, but in the final paragraph Updike—or the narrator—offers a meditative comment: "What we expect of others, they endeavor to provide." Two questions here, which you can argue for or against: Do you think this comment is useful in the story? Second, do you believe this comment by and large is true? Explain.
4. Here is a comment by Garrison Keillor, in his book *Leaving Home* (1987), on parenting:

   > Selective ignorance, a cornerstone of child rearing. You don't put kids under surveillance: it might frighten you. Parents should sit tall in the saddle and look upon their troops with a noble and benevolent and extremely nearsighted gaze.

   Your view? Oliver's parents' view? Oliver's view?

POEMS

Anonymous Nursery Rhyme

Nursery rhymes are of course found in books, but they survive because children find them memorable and pass them on to their playmates and, when they become adults, to their children. Nursery rhymes include lullabies ("Rock-a-by baby, on the tree tops"), counting-out rhymes ("eeny, meeny, miny, mo," "One potato, two potato"), charms ("rain, rain, go away"), short narratives ("Jack and Jill," "Mary had a little lamb"), and they are marked by emphatic rhymes. Scholars believe that perhaps half of the best-loved nursery rhymes of today go back to the eighteenth century, and many to the seventeenth. The earliest printed collections are *Tommy Thumb's Pretty Song Book* (1744) and *Mother Goose's Melody: or Sonnets for the Cradle* (1781).

When you read the following nursery rhyme (or call to mind others that you know), ask yourself this question: Do nursery rhymes indoctrinate children—that is, do they introduce or reinforce attitudes about age, gender, and class? If so, how? And what should be done about it? Explain, using as examples these rhymes or others that you know.

What Are Little Boys Made Of

What are little boys made of, made of?
What are little boys made of?
    Snips and snails
    And puppy-dogs' tails,
That's what little boys are made of.   5

What are little girls made of, made of?
What are little girls made of?
    Sugar and spice
    And all things nice,
That's what little girls are made of.   10

Joining the Conversation: Critical Thinking and Writing

1. Do you imagine that boys like the description of what boys are made of? Do girls like the description of what girls are made of? Or is it only grown-ups who like these descriptions? Explain.
2. A version in 1846 gives two additional stanzas: "What are young men made of? / Sighs and leers and crocodile tears," and "What are young women made of? / Ribbons and laces, and sweet pretty faces." To the best of our knowledge, these two verses are not nearly so widely known as the first two. Why do you think this is so?

ANONYMOUS

The following lines have been attributed to various writers, including the American philosopher William James (1842–1910), but to the best of our knowledge the author is unknown.

Higamus, Hogamus,
Woman's monogamous;
Hogamus, Higamus,
Man is polygamous.

Joining the Conversation: Critical Thinking and Writing

1. If you find these lines engaging, how do you account for their appeal? Does it make any difference—even a tiny difference—if the pairs are reversed; that is, if the first two lines are about men, and the second two about women?

2. The underlying idea largely coincides with the saying, "Men are from Mars, women are from Venus." But consider the four lines of verse: Do you agree that in the form we have just given them, they are more effective than "Men are from Mars, women are from Venus"? And how about "Women are from Venus, men are from Mars"? Admittedly the differences are small, but would you argue that one form is decidedly more effective than the others? How do you explain the greater effectiveness?

DOROTHY PARKER

Dorothy Parker (1893–1967) was born in West End, New Jersey, but brought up in New York City. From 1917 to 1920 she served as drama critic for the magazine Vanity Fair, *where her witty, satiric reviews gained her the reputation of being hard to please. She distinguished between wit and wisecracking: "Wit has truth in it; wisecracking is simply calisthenics with words."*

In addition to essays and stories, Parker wrote light verse, especially about love.

General Review of the Sex Situation

Woman wants monogamy;
Man delights in novelty.
Love is woman's moon and sun;
Man has other forms of fun.

Woman lives but in her lord;   5
Count to ten, and man is bored.
With this the gist and sum of it,
What earthly good can come of it?

[1926]

Joining the Conversation: Critical Thinking and Writing

1. How would you characterize Parker's message? (For instance, is it sad, happy, pitiful?) How would you characterize her tone—her attitude, as you perceive it?
2. How much truth do you think there is in Parker's lines? (Remember: No poem, or, for that matter, no novel—however long—can tell the whole truth about life.) As for truth, how would you compare the validity of the poem's assertion with the following passage, from Barbara Dafoe Whitehead's review (*Times Literary Supplement,* 9 June 1995) of two sociological studies, *The Social Organization of Sexuality: Sexual Practice in the U.S.* and *Sex in America:*

   > Men and women have different sexual interests, stakes and appetites, with men more oriented to the sex act and women more interested in sex as an expression of affiliative and romantic love.

LOUISE BOGAN

Louise Bogan (1897–1970) was born in Maine, but the family moved to Boston, where she attended Girls' Latin School, a school noted for its academic excellence. There she began her career as a poet, publishing not only in school journals but also in the Boston Evening Transcript. *Bogan married early and had a child, but the marriage was unhappy and the couple separated. Her husband died soon after, when Bogan was only twenty-three. She remarried, but this marriage ended in divorce. For most of her life she was an independent single woman, supporting herself by working in bookstores and libraries and by writing reviews of poetry for magazines, including the* Atlantic Monthly *and the* New Yorker. *Most of her poems were written before 1940, and although she achieved considerable fame in her youth she was less visible as a poet in her later years. Today both her poetry and her critical writing are widely admired.*

Women

Women have no wilderness in them,
They are provident instead,
Content in the tight hot cell of their hearts
To eat dusty bread.

They do not see cattle cropping red winter grass,   5
They do not hear
Snow water going down under culverts
Shallow and clear.

They wait, when they should turn to journeys,
They stiffen, when they should bend.   10
They use against themselves that benevolence
To which no man is friend.

They cannot think of so many crops to a field
Or of clean wood cleft by an axe.
Their love is an eager meaninglessness   15
Too tense, or too lax.

They hear in every whisper that speaks to them
A shout and a cry.
As like as not, when they take life over their door-sills
They should let it go by.   20

[1922]

Joining the Conversation: Critical Thinking and Writing

1. Bogan is much admired for her technical skills as a poet. What techniques do you observe in "Women," and how do they work?
2. Bogan writes of women as "they" rather than "we." Try substituting "we" in the poem. What is gained, or lost?
3. Write an imitation of "Women" called "Men." Observe as many of the structural features of the poem (line length, rhyme, metaphor) as you can. What did you learn from this exercise about poetry? About your feelings about men??

Rita Dove

Rita Dove was born in 1952 in Akron, Ohio. After graduating summa cum laude and Phi Beta Kappa from Miami University (Ohio), Dove earned an MFA at the Iowa Writers' Workshop. She has received numerous awards, including fellowships from the Guggenheim Foundation and the National Endowment for the Arts, and a Pulitzer Prize for Poetry. In 1993–95 she served as Poet Laureate of the United States and as Consultant to the Library of Congress, in 1996 she was awarded the National Humanities Medal, and in 2001 she was awarded the Duke Ellington Lifetime Achievement Award. The author of several books of poetry, a book of short stories, a novel, and a book of her laureate lectures, Dove is Commonwealth Professor of English at the University of Virginia in Charlottesville.

Daystar

She wanted a little room for thinking:
but she saw diapers steaming on the line,
a doll slumped behind the door.
So she lugged a chair behind the garage
to sit out the children's naps.   5
Sometimes there were things to watch—
the pinched armor of a vanished cricket,
a floating maple leaf. Other days
she stared until she was assured
when she closed her eyes   10
she'd see only her own vivid blood.

She had an hour, at best, before Liza appeared
pouting from the top of the stairs.
And just *what* was mother doing
out back with the field mice? Why,   15
building a palace. Later
that night when Thomas rolled over and
lurched into her, she would open her eyes
and think of the place that was hers
for an hour—where   20
she was nothing,
pure nothing, in the middle of the day.

[1986]

Joining the Conversation: Critical Thinking and Writing

1. How would you characterize the woman who is the subject of "Daystar"?
2. What do you make of the title?
3. Do you think that women respond to this poem differently than men do? What is your evidence for your view? How would you support it?

THEODORE ROETHKE

Theodore Roethke (1908–63) was born in Saginaw, Michigan, and educated at the University of Michigan and Harvard. From 1947 until his death he taught at the University of Washington in Seattle, where he exerted considerable influence on the next generation of poets. Many of Roethke's best poems are lyrical memories of his childhood.

My Papa's Waltz

The whiskey on your breath
Could make a small boy dizzy;
but I hung on like death:
Such waltzing was not easy.

We romped until the pans   5
Slid from the kitchen shelf;
My mother's countenance
Could not unfrown itself.

The hand that held my wrist
Was battered on one knuckle;   10
At every step you missed
My right ear scraped a buckle.

You beat time on my head
With a palm caked hard by dirt,
Then waltzed me off to bed   15
Still clinging to your shirt.

                                             [1948]

Joining the Conversation: Critical Thinking and Writing

1. Do the syntactical pauses vary much from stanza to stanza? Be specific. Would you say that the rhythm suggests lightness? Why?
2. Does the rhythm parallel or ironically contrast with the episode described? Was the dance a graceful waltz? Explain.
3. What would you say is the function of the stresses in lines 13–14?
4. How different would the poem be if the speaker were female and "girl" instead of "boy" appeared in line 2?

MyLiteratureLab® *For additional resources for "My Papa's Waltz," log in to* www.myliteraturelab.com *where you will find a Longman Lecture and a Comprehension Quiz, as well as an About the Author, Links, and Critical Overview for Roethke (under Student Resources).*

SHARON OLDS

Sharon Olds, born in San Francisco in 1942 and educated at Stanford University and Columbia University, has published many volumes of poetry and received major awards. Olds held the position of New York State Poet from 1998 to 2000, and she currently teaches poetry workshops in the Graduate Creative Writing Program at New York University.

Rites of Passage

As the guests arrive at my son's party
They gather in the living room—
short men, men in first grade
with smooth jaws and chins.
Hands in pockets, they stand around   5
jostling, jockeying for place, small fights
breaking out and calming. One says to another
How old are you? Six. I'm seven. So?
They eye each other, seeing themselves
tiny in the other's pupils. They clear their   10
throats a lot, a room of small bankers,
they fold their arms and frown. *I could beat you
up*, a seven says to a six,
the dark cake, round and heavy as a
turret, behind them on the table. My son,   15
freckles like specks of nutmeg on his cheeks,
chest narrow as the balsa keel of a
model boat, long hands
cool and thin as the day they guided him
out of me, speaks up as a host   20
for the sake of the group.
We could easily kill a two-year-old,
he says in his clear voice. The other
men agree, they clear their throats
like Generals, they relax and get down to   25
playing war, celebrating my son's life.

[1983]

Joining the Conversation: Critical Thinking and Writing

1. Focus on the details that the speaker provides about the boys—how they look, how they speak. What do the details reveal about them?
2. Is the speaker's son the same as or different from the other boys?

3. Some readers find the ironies in this poem (e.g., "short men") to be somewhat comical, while others, noting such phrases as "kill a two-year-old" and "playing war," conclude that the poem as a whole is meant to be upsetting, even frightening. How would you describe the kinds of irony that Olds uses here?

4. An experiment in irony and point of view: Try writing a poem like this one, from the point of view of a father about the birthday party of his son, and then try writing another one, by either a father or a mother, about a daughter's party.

FRANK O'HARA

Frank O'Hara (1926–66) was born in Baltimore and died in a tragic accident—he was run over by a beach vehicle—on Fire Island, New York. O'Hara was not only a prolific writer of verse but also an astute critic of sculpture and painting who worked as an assistant curator at the Museum of Modern Art in New York (on West 53rd Street; see line 16), and as an editor of Art News. *O'Hara's first volume of poetry was* A City Winter, and Other Poems *(1952).* Collected Poems *was issued in 1971, but it was not complete; it has been supplemented by two additional volumes,* Early Poems *(1977) and* Poems Retrieved *(1977).*

Homosexuality

So we are taking off our masks, are we, and keeping
our mouths shut? as if we'd been pierced by a glance!

The song of an old cow is not more full of judgment
than the vapors which escape one's soul when one is sick;

so I pull the shadows around me like a puff   5
and crinkle my eyes as if at the most exquisite moment

of a very long opera, and then we are off!
without reproach and without hope that our delicate feet

will touch the earth again, let alone "very soon."
It is the law of my own voice I shall investigate.   10

I start like ice, my finger to my ear, my ear
to my heart, that proud cur at the garbage can

in the rain. It's wonderful to admire oneself
with complete candor, tallying up the merits of each

of the latrines. 14th Street is drunken and credulous,   15
53rd tries to tremble but is too at rest. The good

love a park and the inept a railway station,
and there are the divine ones who drag themselves up

and down the lengthening shadow of an Abyssinian head
in the dust, trailing their long elegant heels of hot air   20

crying to confuse the brave "It's a summer day,
and I want to be wanted more than anything else in the world."

[1971]

Joining the Conversation: Critical Thinking and Writing

1. Describe your response to the word that O'Hara chooses for his title. In what ways does the poem define and explore the meanings of this word and our responses to it?
2. Characterize the point of view and tone of the speaker. Who is or are the "we" named in line 1?
3. In line 1 the speaker declares that "we are taking off our masks," but then immediately seems to confuse or contradict his point when he says "we" are "keeping / our mouths shut." Explain as clearly as you can what the speaker is suggesting in this first stanza.
4. Some of the language in this poem is ugly or unpleasant—for example, the "cur at the garbage can," "the latrines." What is the purpose of such language? What is its place in the structure of the poem as a whole? Or can one argue that such language has no place in a decent poem?
5. Could O'Hara's poem be reasonably described as an argument on behalf of gays and lesbians? Please explain.

JULIA ALVAREZ

The Latina author Julia Alvarez, born in 1950 in New York of Dominican descent, has written fiction, poetry, and nonfictional prose. Her books include the novel How the Garcia Girls Lost Their Accents *(1991), which tells the story of four sisters and their parents who emigrate from the Dominican Republic to the United States;* Something to Declare: Essays *(1998); and* Homecoming: New and Collected Poems *(1996), which includes her first book,* Homecoming *(1984), as well as more recent work. The following poem is taken from that collection.*

Woman's Work

Who says a woman's work isn't high art?
She'd challenge as she scrubbed the bathroom tiles.
Keep house as if the address were your heart.

We'd clean the whole upstairs before we'd start
downstairs. I'd sigh, hearing my friends outside.   5
Doing her woman's work was a hard art

to practice when the summer sun would bar
the floor I swept till she was satisfied.
She kept me prisoner in her housebound heart.

She'd shine the tines of forks, the wheels of carts,   10
cut lacy lattices for all her pies.
Her woman's work was nothing less than art.

And, I, her masterpiece since I was smart,
was primed, praised, polished, scolded and advised
to keep a house much better than my heart.   15

I did not want to be her counterpart!
I struck out . . . but became my mother's child:
a woman working at home on her art,
housekeeping paper as if it were her heart.

[1996]

Joining the Conversation: Critical Thinking and Writing

1. The poet explores the relationship between mother and daughter through the
   work that each performs. Describe this work, and in particular the lessons that
   the mother teaches through what she does and how she does it.
2. What is the meaning of line 3?
3. How do you interpret the phrase "I struck out"?
4. Do you feel inclined to argue for or against Alvarez's conception of "woman's
   work"? Please explain, and cite evidence from the poem.

MARGE PIERCY

*Marge Piercy, born in Detroit in 1936, was the first member of
her family to attend college. After earning a bachelor's degree
from the University of Michigan in 1957 and a master's degree
from Northwestern University in 1958, she moved to Chicago.
There she worked at odd jobs while writing novels (unpublished) and engaging in action on behalf of women and
African Americans and against the war in Vietnam. In 1970—
the year she moved to Wellfleet, Massachusetts, where she still
lives—she published her first book, a novel. Since then she has
published other novels, short stories, poems, and essays.*

Barbie Doll

This girlchild was born as usual
and presented dolls that did pee-pee
and miniature GE stoves and irons
and wee lipsticks the color of cherry candy.
Then in the magic of puberty, a classmate said: 5
You have a great big nose and fat legs.

She was healthy, tested intelligent,
possessed strong arms and back,
abundant sexual drive and manual dexterity.
She went to and fro apologizing.   10
Everyone saw a fat nose on thick legs.

She was advised to play coy,
exhorted to come on hearty,

exercise, diet, smile and wheedle.
Her good nature wore out   15
like a fan belt.
So she cut off her nose and her legs
and offered them up.

In the casket displayed on satin she lay
with the undertaker's cosmetics painted on,   20
a turned-up putty nose,
dressed in a pink and white nightie.
Doesn't she look pretty? everyone said.
Consummation at last.
To every woman a happy ending.   25

[1969]

Joining the Conversation: Critical Thinking and Writing

1. Why is the poem called "Barbie Doll"?
2. What voice do you hear in lines 1–4? Line 6 is, we are told, the voice of "a class-mate." How do these voices differ? What voice do you hear in the first three lines of the second stanza?
3. Explain in your own words what Piercy is saying about women in this poem. Does her view seem to you fair, slightly exaggerated, or greatly exaggerated? Support your thesis with reasons.

PLAY

HENRIK IBSEN

Henrik Ibsen (1828–1906) was born in Skien, Norway, of wealthy parents who soon after his birth lost their money. Ibsen worked as a pharmacist's apprentice, but at the age of twenty-two he had written his first play, a promising melodrama titled Cataline *(or* Catalina*). He engaged in theater work first in Norway and then in Denmark and Germany. By 1865 his plays had won him a state pension that enabled him to settle in Rome. After writing romantic, historic, and poetic plays, he turned to realistic drama with* The League of Youth *(1869). Among his major realistic "problem plays" are* A Doll's House *(1879),* Ghosts *(1881), and* An Enemy of the People *(1882). In* The Wild Duck *(1884) he moved toward a more symbolic tragicomedy, and his last plays, written in the nineties, are highly symbolic.* Hedda Gabler *(1890) looks backward to the plays of the eighties rather than forward to the plays of the nineties.*

A Doll's House

Translated by R. Farquharson Sharp

CHARACTERS

TORVALD HELMER, *a lawyer and bank manager*
NORA, *his wife*

A Doll's House.

DOCTOR RANK
MRS. CHRISTINE LINDE
NILS KROGSTAD, *a lawyer and bank clerk*
IVAR, BOB, AND EMMY, *the Helmers' three young children*
ANNE, *their nurse*
HELEN, *a housemaid*
A PORTER

The action takes place in HELMER'S *apartment.*

Act 1

SCENE. *A room furnished comfortably and tastefully, but not extravagantly. At the back, a door to the right leads to the entrance hall, another to the left leads to* HELMER'S *study. Between the doors stands a piano. In the middle of the left-hand wall is a door, and beyond it a window. Near the window are a round table, armchairs and a small sofa. In the right-hand wall, at the farther end, another door; and on the same side, nearer the footlights, a stove, two easy chairs and a rocking-chair; between the stove and the door, a small table. Engravings on the walls; a cabinet with china and other small objects; a small book case with well-bound books. The floors are carpeted, and a fire burns in the stove. It is winter.*

A bell rings in the hall; shortly afterwards the door is heard to open. Enter NORA, *humming a tune and in high spirits. She is in outdoor dress and carries a number of parcels; these she lays on the table to the right. She leaves the outer door open after her, and through it is seen a* PORTER *who is carrying a Christmas Tree and a basket, which he gives to the* MAID *who has opened the door.*

NORA: Hide the Christmas Tree carefully, Helen. Be sure the children do not see it till this evening, when it is dressed. [*to the* PORTER, *taking out her purse.*] How much?

PORTER: Sixpence.

NORA: There is a shilling. No, keep the change. [*The* PORTER *thanks her, and goes out.* NORA *shuts the door. She is laughing to herself, as she takes off her hat and coat. She takes a packet of macaroons from her pocket and eats one or two; then goes cautiously to her husband's door and listens.*] Yes, he is in.

[*Still humming, she goes to the table on the right.*]

HELMER [*calls out from his room*]: Is that my little lark twittering out there?

NORA [*busy opening some of the parcels*]: Yes, it is!

HELMER: Is my little squirrel bustling about?

NORA: Yes!

HELMER: When did my squirrel come home?

NORA: Just now. [*puts the bag of macaroons into her pocket and wipes her mouth.*] Come in here, Torvald, and see what I have bought.

HELMER: Don't disturb me. [*A little later, he opens the door and looks into the room, pen in hand.*] Bought, did you say? All these things? Has my little spendthrift been wasting money again?

NORA: Yes, but, Torvald, this year we really can let ourselves go a little. This is the first Christmas that we have not needed to economise.

HELMER: Still, you know, we can't spend money recklessly.

NORA: Yes, Torvald, we may be a wee bit more reckless now, mayn't we? Just a tiny wee bit! You are going to have a big salary and earn lots and lots of money.

HELMER: Yes, after the New Year; but then it will be a whole quarter before the salary is due.

NORA: Pooh! we can borrow till then.

HELMER: Nora! [*goes up to her and takes her playfully by the ear.*] The same little featherhead! Suppose, now, that I borrowed fifty pounds to-day, and you spent it all in the Christmas week, and then on New Year's Eve a slate fell on my head and killed me, and—

NORA [*putting her hands over his mouth*]: Oh! don't say such horrid things.

HELMER: Still, suppose that happened—what then?

NORA: If that were to happen, I don't suppose I should care whether I owed money or not.

HELMER: Yes, but what about the people who had lent it?

NORA: They? Who would bother about them? I should not know who they were.

HELMER: That is like a woman! But seriously, Nora, you know what I think about that. No debt, no borrowing. There can be no freedom or beauty about a home life that depends on borrowing and debt. We two have kept bravely on the straight road so far, and we will go on the same way for the short time longer that there need be any struggle.

NORA [*moving towards the stove*]: As you please, Torvald.

HELMER [*following her*]: Come, come, my little skylark must not droop her wings. What is this! Is my little squirrel out of temper? [*taking out his purse.*] Nora, what do you think I have got here?

NORA [*turning around quickly*]: Money!

HELMER: There you are. [*gives her some money*] Do you think I don't know what a lot is wanted for housekeeping at Christmas-time?

NORA [*counting*]: Ten shillings—a pound—two pounds! Thank you, thank you, Torvald; that will keep me going for a long time.

HELMER: Indeed it must.

NORA: Yes, yes, it will. But come here and let me show you what I have bought. And all so cheap! Look, here is a new suit for Ivar, and a sword; and a horse and a trumpet for Bob; and a doll and dolly's bedstead for Emmy—they are very plain, but anyway she will soon break them in pieces. And here are dress-lengths and handkerchiefs for the maids; old Anne ought really to have something better.

HELMER: And what is in this parcel?

NORA [*crying out*]: No, no! you mustn't see that till this evening.

HELMER: Very well. But now tell me, you extravagant little person, what would you like for yourself?

NORA: For myself? Oh, I am sure I don't want anything.

HELMER: Yes, but you must. Tell me something reasonable that you would particularly like to have.

NORA: No, I really can't think of anything—unless, Torvald—

HELMER: Well?

NORA [*playing with his coat buttons, and without raising her eyes to his*]: If you really want to give me something, you might—you might—

HELMER: Well, out with it!

NORA [*speaking quickly*]: You might give me money, Torvald. Only just as much as you can afford; and then one of these days I will buy something with it.

HELMER: But, Nora—

NORA: Oh, do! dear Torvald; please, please do! Then I will wrap it up in beautiful gilt paper and hang it on the Christmas Tree. Wouldn't that be fun?

HELMER: What are little people called that are always wasting money?

NORA: Spendthrifts—I know. Let us do as you suggest, Torvald, and then I shall have time to think what I am most in want of. That is a very sensible plan, isn't it?

HELMER [*smiling*]: Indeed it is—that is to say, if you were really to save out of the money I give you, and then really buy something for yourself. But if you spend it all on the housekeeping and any number of unnecessary things, then I merely have to pay up again.

NORA: Oh but, Torvald—

HELMER: You can't deny it, my dear little Nora. [*puts his arm round her waist*] It's a sweet little spendthrift, but she uses up a deal of money. One would hardly believe how expensive such little persons are!

NORA: It's a shame to say that. I do really save all I can.

HELMER [*laughing*]: That's very true—all you can. But you can't save anything!

NORA [*smiling quietly and happily*]: You haven't any idea how many expenses we skylarks and squirrels have, Torvald.

HELMER: You are an odd little soul. Very like your father. You always find some new way of wheedling money out of me, and, as soon as you have got it, it seems to melt in your hands. You never know where it has gone. Still, one must take you as you are. It is in the blood; for indeed it is true that you can inherit these things, Nora.

NORA: Ah, I wish I had inherited many of papa's qualities.

HELMER: And I would not wish you to be anything but just what you are, my sweet little skylark. But, do you know, it strikes me that you are looking rather— what shall I say—rather uneasy to-day?

NORA: Do I?

HELMER: You do, really. Look straight at me.

NORA [*looks at him*]: Well?

HELMER [*wagging his finger at her*]: Hasn't Miss Sweet-Tooth been breaking rules in town to-day?

NORA: No; what makes you think that?

HELMER: Hasn't she paid a visit to the confectioner's?

NORA: No, I assure you, Torvald—

HELMER: Not been nibbling sweets?

NORA: No, certainly not.

HELMER: Not even taken a bite at a macaroon or two?

NORA: No, Torvald, I assure you really—

HELMER: There, there, of course I was only joking.

NORA [*going to the table on the right*]: I should not think of going against your wishes.

HELMER: No, I am sure of that! besides, you gave me your word—[*going up to her*] Keep your little Christmas secrets to yourself, my darling. They will all be revealed to-night when the Christmas Tree is lit, no doubt.

NORA: Did you remember to invite Doctor Rank?

HELMER: No. But there is no need; as a matter of course he will come to dinner with us. However, I will ask him when he comes in this morning. I have ordered some good wine. Nora, you can't think how I am looking forward to this evening.

NORA: So am I! And how the children will enjoy themselves, Torvald!

HELMER: It is splendid to feel that one has a perfectly safe appointment, and a big enough income. It's delightful to think of, isn't it?

NORA: It's wonderful!

HELMER: Do you remember last Christmas? For a full three weeks beforehand you shut yourself up every evening till long after midnight, making ornaments for the Christmas Tree and all the other fine things that were to be a surprise to us. It was the dullest three weeks I ever spent!

NORA: I didn't find it dull.

HELMER [*smiling*]: But there was precious little result, Nora.

NORA: Oh, you shouldn't tease me about that again. How could I help the cat's going in and tearing everything to pieces?

HELMER: Of course you couldn't, poor little girl. You had the best of intentions to please us all, and that's the main thing. But it is a good thing that our hard times are over.

NORA: Yes, it is really wonderful.

HELMER: This time I needn't sit here and be dull all alone, and you needn't ruin your dear eyes and your pretty little hands—

NORA [*clapping her hands*]: No, Torvald, I needn't any longer, need I! It's wonderfully lovely to hear you say so! [*taking his arm*] Now I will tell you how I have been thinking we ought to arrange things, Torvald. As soon as Christmas is over—[*A bell rings in the hall.*] There's the bell. [*She tidies the room a little.*] There's someone at the door. What a nuisance!

HELMER: If it is a caller, remember I am not at home.

MAID [*in the doorway*]: A lady to see you, ma'am—a stranger.

NORA: Ask her to come in.

MAID: [*to* HELMER] The doctor came at the same time, sir.

HELMER: Did he go straight into my room?

MAID: Yes sir.

[HELMER *goes into his room. The* MAID *ushers in* MRS. LINDE, *who is in travelling dress, and shuts the door.*]

MRS. LINDE [*in a dejected and timid voice*]: How do you do, Nora?

NORA [*doubtfully*]: How do you do—

MRS. LINDE: You don't recognise me, I suppose.

NORA: No, I don't know—yes, to be sure, I seem to—[*suddenly*] Yes! Christine! Is it really you?

MRS. LINDE: Yes, it is I.

NORA: Christine! To think of my not recognising you! And yet how could I—[*in a gentle voice*] How you have altered, Christine!

MRS. LINDE: Yes, I have indeed. In nine, ten long years—

NORA: Is it so long since we met? I suppose it is. The last eight years have been a happy time for me, I can tell you. And so now you have come into the town, and have taken this long journey in winter—that was plucky of you.

MRS. LINDE: I arrived by steamer this morning.

NORA: To have some fun at Christmas-time, of course. How delightful! We will have such fun together! But take off your things. You are not cold, I hope. [*helps her*] Now we will sit down by the stove, and be cosy. No, take this armchair; I will sit here in the rocking-chair. [*takes her hands*] Now you look like your old self again; it was only the first moment—You are a little paler, Christine, and perhaps a little thinner.

MRS. LINDE: And much, much older, Nora.

NORA: Perhaps a little older; very, very little; certainly not much. [*stops suddenly and speaks seriously*] What a thoughtless creature I am, chattering away like this. My poor, dear Christine, do forgive me.

MRS. LINDE: What do you mean, Nora?

NORA [*gently*]: Poor Christine, you are a widow.

MRS. LINDE: Yes; it is three years ago now.

NORA: Yes, I knew; I saw it in the papers. I assure you, Christine, I meant ever so often to write to you at the time, but I always put it off and something always prevented me.

MRS. LINDE: I quite understand, dear.

NORA: It was very bad of me, Christine. Poor thing, how you must have suffered. And he left you nothing?

MRS. LINDE: No.

NORA: And no children?

MRS. LINDE: No.

NORA: Nothing at all, then?

MRS. LINDE: Not even any sorrow or grief to live upon.

NORA [*looking incredulously at her*]: But, Christine, is that possible?

MRS. LINDE [*smiles sadly and strokes her hair*]: It sometimes happens, Nora.

NORA: So you are quite alone. How dreadfully sad that must be. I have three lovely children. You can't see them just now, for they are out with their nurse. But now you must tell me all about it.

MRS. LINDE: No, no; I want to hear you.

NORA: No, you must begin. I mustn't be selfish to-day; to-day I must only think of your affairs. But there is one thing I must tell you. Do you know we have just had a great piece of good luck?

MRS. LINDE: No, what is it?

NORA: Just fancy, my husband has been made manager of the Bank!

MRS. LINDE: Your husband? What good luck!

NORA: Yes, tremendous! A barrister's profession is such an uncertain thing, especially if he won't undertake unsavoury cases; and naturally Torvald has never been willing to do that, and I quite agree with him. You may imagine how pleased we are! He is to take up his work in the Bank at the New Year, and then he will have a big salary and lots of commissions. For the future we can live quite differently—we can do just as we like. I feel so relieved and so happy, Christine! It will be splendid to have heaps of money and not need to have any anxiety, won't it?

MRS. LINDE: Yes, anyhow I think it would be delightful to have what one needs.

NORA: No, not only what one needs, but heaps and heaps of money.

MRS. LINDE [*smiling*]: Nora, Nora haven't you learnt sense yet? In our schooldays you were a great spendthrift.

NORA [*laughing*]: Yes, that is what Torvald says now. [*wags her finger at her*] But "Nora, Nora" is not so silly as you think. We have not been in a position for me to waste money. We have both had to work.

MRS. LINDE: You too?

NORA: Yes; odds and ends, needlework, crochet-work, embroidery, and that kind of thing. [*dropping her voice*] And other things as well. You know Torvald left his office when we were married? There was no prospect of promotion there, and he had to try and earn more than before. But during the first year he overworked himself dreadfully. You see, he had to make money every way he could, and he worked early and late; but he couldn't stand it, and fell dreadfully ill, and the doctors said it was necessary for him to go south.

MRS. LINDE: You spent a whole year in Italy didn't you?

NORA: Yes. It was no easy matter to get away, I can tell you. It was just as Ivar was born; but naturally we had to go. It was a wonderfully beautiful journey, and it saved Torvald's life. But it cost a tremendous lot of money, Christine.

MRS. LINDE: So I should think.

NORA: It cost about two hundred and fifty pounds. That's a lot, isn't it?

MRS. LINDE: Yes, and in emergencies like that it is lucky to have the money.

NORA: I ought to tell you that we had it from papa.

MRS. LINDE: Oh, I see. It was just about that time that he died, wasn't it?

NORA: Yes; and, just think of it, I couldn't go and nurse him. I was expecting little Ivar's birth every day and I had my poor sick Torvald to look after. My dear, kind father—I never saw him again, Christine. That was the saddest time I have known since our marriage.

MRS. LINDE: I know how fond you were of him. And then you went off to Italy?

NORA: Yes; you see we had money then, and the doctors insisted on our going, so we started a month later.

MRS. LINDE: And your husband came back quite well?

NORA: As sound as a bell!

MRS. LINDE: But—the doctor?

NORA: What doctor?

MRS. LINDE: I thought your maid said the gentleman who arrived here just as I did was the doctor?

NORA: Yes, that was Doctor Rank, but he doesn't come here professionally. He is our greatest friend, and comes in at least once every day. No, Torvald has not had an hour's illness since then, and our children are strong and healthy and so am I. [*jumps up and claps her hands*] Christine! Christine! it's good to be alive and happy!—But how horrid of me; I am talking of nothing but my own affairs. [*sits on a stool near her, and rests her arms on her knees*] You mustn't be angry with me. Tell me, is it really true that you did not love your husband? Why did you marry him?

MRS. LINDE: My mother was alive then, and was bedridden and helpless, and I had to provide for my two younger brothers; so I did not think I was justified in refusing his offer.

NORA: No, perhaps you were quite right. He was rich at that time, then?

MRS. LINDE: I believe he was quite well off. But his business was a precarious one; and, when he died, it all went to pieces and there was nothing left.

NORA: And then?—

MRS. LINDE: Well, I had to turn my hand to anything I could find—first a small shop, then a small school, and so on. The last three years have seemed like one long working-day, with no rest. Now it is at an end, Nora. My poor mother needs me no more, for she is gone; and the boys do not need me either; they have got situations and can shift for themselves.

NORA: What a relief you must feel it—

MRS. LINDE: No, indeed; I only feel my life unspeakably empty. No one to live for any more. [*gets up restlessly*] That was why I could not stand the life in my little backwater any longer. I hope it may be easier here to find something which will busy me and occupy my thoughts. If only I could have the good luck to get some regular work—office work of some kind—

NORA: But, Christine, that is so frightfully tiring, and you look tired out now. You had far better go away to some watering-place.

MRS. LINDE [*walking to the window*]: I have no father to give me money for a journey, Nora.

NORA [*rising*]: Oh, don't be angry with me.

MRS. LINDE [*going up to her*]: It is you that must not be angry with me, dear. The worst of a position like mine is that it makes one so bitter. No one to work for, and yet obliged to be always on the look-out for chances. One must live, and so one becomes selfish. When you told me of the happy turn your fortunes have taken—you will hardly believe it—I was delighted not so much on your account as on my own.

NORA: How do you mean?—Oh, I understand. You mean that perhaps Torvald could get you something to do.

MRS. LINDE: Yes, that was what I was thinking of.

NORA: He must, Christine. Just leave it to me; I will broach the subject very cleverly—I will think of something that will please him very much. It will make me so happy to be of some use to you.

MRS. LINDE: How kind you are, Nora, to be so anxious to help me! It is doubly kind in you, for you know so little of the burdens and troubles of life.

NORA: I—? I know so little of them?

MRS. LINDE [*smiling*]: My dear! Small household cares and that sort of thing!—You are a child, Nora.

NORA [*tosses her head and crosses the stage*]: You ought not to be so superior.

MRS. LINDE: No?

NORA: You are just like the others. They all think that I am incapable of anything really serious—

MRS. LINDE: Come, come—

NORA: —that I have gone through nothing in this world of cares.

MRS. LINDE: But, my dear Nora, you have just told me all your troubles.

NORA: Pooh!—those were trifles. [*lowering her voice*] I have not told you the important thing.

MRS. LINDE: The important thing? What do you mean?

NORA: You look down upon me altogether, Christine—but you ought not to. You are proud, aren't you, of having worked so hard and so long for your mother?

MRS. LINDE: Indeed, I don't look down on any one. But it is true that I am both proud and glad to think that I was privileged to make the end of my mother's life almost free from care.

NORA: And you are proud to think of what you have done for your brothers.

MRS. LINDE: I think I have the right to be.

NORA: I think so, too. But now, listen to this; I too have something to be proud of and glad of.

MRS. LINDE: I have no doubt you have. But what do you refer to?

NORA: Speak low. Suppose Torvald were to hear! He mustn't on any account—no one in the world must know, Christine, except you.

MRS. LINDE: But what is it?

NORA: Come here [*pulls her down on the sofa beside her*] Now I will show you that I too have something to be proud and glad of. It was I who saved Torvald's life.

MRS. LINDE: "Saved"? How?

NORA: I told you about our trip to Italy. Torvald would never have recovered if he had not gone there—

MRS. LINDE: Yes, but your father gave you the necessary funds.

NORA [*smiling*]: Yes, that is what Torvald and all the others think, but—

MRS. LINDE: But—

NORA: Papa didn't give us a shilling. It was I who procured the money.

MRS. LINDE: You? All that large sum?

NORA: Two hundred and fifty pounds. What do you think of that?

MRS. LINDE: But, Nora, how could you possibly do it? Did you win a prize in the Lottery?

NORA [*contemptuously*]: In the Lottery? There would have been no credit in that.

MRS. LINDE: But where did you get it from, then?

NORA [*humming and smiling with an air of mystery*]: Hm, hm! Aha!

MRS. LINDE: Because you couldn't have borrowed it.

NORA: Couldn't I? Why not?

MRS. LINDE: No, a wife cannot borrow without her husband's consent.

NORA [*tossing her head*]: Oh, if it is a wife who has any head for business—a wife who has the wit to be a little bit clever—

MRS. LINDE: I don't understand it at all, Nora.

NORA: There is no need you should. I never said I had borrowed the money. I may have got it some other way. [*lies back on the sofa*] Perhaps I got it from some other admirer. When anyone is as attractive as I am—

MRS. LINDE: You are a mad creature.

NORA: Now, you know you're full of curiosity, Christine.

MRS. LINDE: Listen to me, Nora dear. Haven't you been a little bit imprudent?

NORA [*sits up straight*]: Is it imprudent to save your husband's life?

MRS. LINDE: It seems to me imprudent, without his knowledge, to—

NORA: But it was absolutely necessary that he should not know! My goodness, can't you understand that? It was necessary he should have no idea what a dangerous condition he was in. It was to me that the doctors came and said that his life was in danger, and that the only thing to save him was to live in the south. Do you suppose I didn't try, first of all, to get what I wanted as if it were for myself? I told him how much I should love to travel abroad like other young wives; I tried tears and entreaties with him; I told him that he ought to remember the condition I was in, and that he ought to be kind and indulgent to me; I even hinted that he might raise a loan. That nearly made him angry, Christine. He said I was thoughtless, and that it was his duty as my husband not to indulge me in my whims and caprices—as I believe he called them. Very well I thought, you must be saved—and that was how I came to devise a way out of the difficulty—

MRS. LINDE: And did your husband never get to know from your father that the money had not come from him?

NORA: No, never. Papa died just at that time. I had meant to let him into the secret and beg him never to reveal it. But he was so ill then—alas, there never was any need to tell him.

MRS. LINDE: And since then have you never told your secret to your husband?

NORA: Good Heavens, no! How could you think so? A man who has such strong opinions about these things! And besides, how painful and humiliating it would be for Torvald, with his manly independence, to know that he owed me anything! It would upset our mutual relations altogether; our beautiful happy home would no longer be what it is now.

MRS. LINDE: Do you mean never to tell him about it?

NORA [*meditatively, and with a half smile*]: Yes—some day, perhaps, after many years, when I am no longer as nice-looking as I am now. Don't laugh at me! I mean of course, when Torvald is no longer as devoted to me as he is now; when my dancing and dressing-up and reciting have palled on him; then it may be a good thing to have something in reserve—[*breaking off*] What nonsense! That time will never come. Now, what do you think of my great secret, Christine? Do you still think I am of no use? I can tell you, too, that this affair has caused me a lot of worry. It has been by no means easy for me to meet my engagements punctually. I may tell you that there is something that is called, in business, quarterly interest, and another thing called payment in instalments, and it is always so dreadfully difficult to manage them. I have had to save a little here and there, where I could, you understand. I have not been able to put aside much from my housekeeping money, for Torvald must have a good table. I couldn't let my children be shabbily dressed; I have felt obliged to use up all he gave me for them, the sweet little darlings!

MRS. LINDE: So it has all had to come out of your own necessaries of life, poor Nora?

NORA: Of course. Besides, I was the one responsible for it. Whenever Torvald has given me the money for new dresses and such things, I have never spent more than half of it; I have always bought the simplest and cheapest things. Thank Heaven, any clothes look well on me, and so Torvald has never noticed it. But it was often very hard on me, Christine—because it is delightful to be really well dressed, isn't it?

MRS. LINDE: Quite so.

NORA: Well, then I have found other ways of earning money. Last winter I was lucky enough to get a lot of copying to do; so I locked myself up and sat writing every evening until quite late at night. Many a time I was desperately tired; but all the same it was a tremendous pleasure to sit there working and earning money. It was like being a man.

MRS. LINDE: How much have you been able to pay off in that way?

NORA: I can't tell you exactly. You see, it is very difficult to keep an account of a business matter of that kind. I only know that I have paid every penny that I could scrape together. Many a time I was at my wit's end. [*smiles*] Then I used to sit here and imagine that a rich old gentleman had fallen in love with me—

MRS. LINDE: What! Who was it?

NORA: Be quiet!—that he had died; and that when his will was opened it contained, written in big letters, the instruction: "The lovely Mrs. Nora Helmer is to have all I possess paid over to her at once in cash."

MRS. LINDE: But, my dear Nora—who could the man be?

NORA: Good gracious, can't you understand? There was no old gentleman at all; it
was only something that I used to sit here and imagine, when I couldn't think
of any way of procuring money. But it's all the same now; the tiresome old
person can stay where he is, as far as I am concerned; I don't care about him
or his will either, for I am free from care now. [*jumps up*] My goodness, it's
delightful to think of, Christine! Free from care! To be able to be free from care,
quite free from care; to be able to play and romp with the children; to be able
to keep the house beautifully and have everything just as Torvald likes it! And,
think of it, soon the spring will come and the big blue sky! Perhaps we shall
be able to take a little trip—perhaps I shall see the sea again! Oh, it's a wonderful thing to be alive and be happy. [*A bell is heard in the hall.*]

MRS. LINDE [*rising*]: There is the bell; perhaps I had better go.

NORA: No, don't go; no one will come in here; it is sure to be for Torvald.

SERVANT [*at the hall door*]: Excuse me, ma'am—there is a gentleman to see the master, and as the doctor is with him—

NORA: Who is it?

KROGSTAD [*at the door*]: It is I, Mrs. Helmer. [*Mrs. Linde starts, trembles, and turns
to the window.*]

NORA [*takes a step towards him, and speaks in a strained, low voice*]: You? What is
it? What do you want to see my husband about?

KROGSTAD: Bank business—in a way. I have a small post in the Bank, and I hear
your husband is to be our chief now—

NORA: Then it is—

KROGSTAD: Nothing but dry business matters, Mrs. Helmer; absolutely nothing else.

NORA: Be so good as to go into the study, then. [*She bows indifferently to him and
shuts the door into the hall; then comes back and makes up the fire in the stove.*]

MRS. LINDE: Nora—who was that man?

NORA: A lawyer, of the name of Krogstad.

MRS. LINDE: Then it really was he.

NORA: Do you know the man?

MRS. LINDE: I used to—many years ago. At one time he was a solicitor's clerk in our
town.

NORA: Yes, he was.

MRS. LINDE: He is greatly altered.

NORA: He made a very unhappy marriage.

MRS. LINDE: He is a widower now, isn't he?

NORA: With several children. There now, it is burning up.

[*Shuts the door of the stove and moves the rocking-chair aside.*]

MRS. LINDE: They say he carries on various kinds of business.

NORA: Really! Perhaps he does; I don't know anything about it. But don't let us
think of business; it is so tiresome.

DOCTOR RANK [*comes out of* HELMER'*s study. Before he shuts the door he calls to
him*]: No, my dear fellow, I won't disturb you; I would rather go in to your
wife for a little while. [*shuts the door and sees* MRS. LINDE] I beg your pardon; I
am afraid I am disturbing you too.

NORA: No, not at all. [*introducing him*] Doctor Rank, Mrs. Linde.

RANK: I have often heard Mrs. Linde's name mentioned here. I think I passed you
on the stairs when I arrived, Mrs. Linde?

MRS. LINDE: Yes, I go up very slowly; I can't manage stairs well.

RANK: Ah! some slight internal weakness?

MRS. LINDE: No, the fact is I have been overworking myself.

RANK: Nothing more than that? Then I suppose you have come to town to amuse yourself with our entertainments?

MRS. LINDE: I have come to look for work.

RANK: Is that a good cure for overwork?

MRS. LINDE: One must live, Doctor Rank.

RANK: Yes, the general opinion seems to be that it is necessary.

NORA: Look here, Doctor Rank—you know you want to live.

RANK: Certainly. However wretched I may feel, I want to prolong the agony as long as possible. All my patients are like that. And so are those who are morally diseased; one of them, and a bad case too, is at this very moment with Helmer—

MRS. LINDE [*sadly*]: Ah!

NORA: Whom do you mean?

RANK: A lawyer of the name of Krogstad, a fellow you don't know at all. He suffers from a diseased moral character, Mrs. Helmer; but even he began talking of its being highly important that he should live.

NORA: Did he? What did he want to speak to Torvald about?

RANK: I have no idea; I only heard that it was something about the Bank.

NORA: I didn't know this—what's his name—Krogstad had anything to do with the Bank.

RANK: Yes, he has some sort of appointment there. [*to* MRS. LINDE] I don't know whether you find also in your part of the world that there are certain people who go zealously snuffing about to smell out moral corruption, and, as soon as they have found some, put the person concerned into some lucrative position where they can keep their eye on him. Healthy natures are left out in the cold.

MRS. LINDE: Still I think the sick are those who most need taking care of.

RANK [*shrugging his shoulders*]: Yes, there you are. That is the sentiment that is turning Society into a sickhouse.

[NORA, *who has been absorbed in her thoughts, breaks out into smothered laughter and claps her hands.*]

RANK: Why do you laugh at that? Have you any notion what Society really is?

NORA: What do I care about tiresome Society? I am laughing at something quite different, something extremely amusing. Tell me, Doctor Rank, are all the people who are employed in the Bank dependent on Torvald now?

RANK: Is that what you find so extremely amusing?

NORA [*smiling and humming*]: That's my affair! [*walking about the room*] It's perfectly glorious to think that we have—that Torvald has so much power over so many people. [*takes the packet from her pocket*] Doctor Rank, what do you say to a macaroon?

RANK: What, macaroons? I thought they were forbidden here.

NORA: Yes, but these are some Christine gave me.

MRS. LINDE: What! I?—

NORA: Oh, well, don't be alarmed! You couldn't know that Torvald had forbidden them. I must tell you that he is afraid they will spoil my teeth. But, bah!—once in a way—That's so, isn't it, Doctor Rank? By your leave? [*puts a macaroon into his mouth*] You must have one too, Christine. And I shall have one, just a little one—or at most two. [*walking about*] I am tremendously happy. There is just one thing in the world now that I should dearly love to do.

RANK: Well, what is that?

NORA: It's something I should dearly love to say, if Torvald could hear me.

RANK: Well, why can't you say it?

NORA: No, I daren't; it's so shocking.

MRS. LINDE: Shocking?

RANK: Well, I should not advise you to say it. Still, with us you might. What is it you would so much like to say if Torvald could hear you?

NORA: I should just love to say—Well, I'm damned!

RANK: Are you mad?

MRS. LINDE: Nora, dear—!

RANK: Say it, here he is!

NORA [*hiding the packet*]: Hush! Hush! Hush!

[HELMER *comes out of his room, with his coat over his arm and his hat in his hands.*]

NORA: Well, Torvald dear, have you got rid of him?

HELMER: Yes, he has just gone.

NORA: Let me introduce you—this is Christine, who has come to town.

HELMER: Christine—? Excuse me, but I don't know—

NORA: Mrs. Linde, dear; Christine Linde.

HELMER: Of course. A school friend of my wife's, I presume?

MRS. LINDE: Yes, we have known each other since then.

NORA: And just think, she has taken a long journey in order to see you.

HELMER: What do you mean?

MRS. LINDE: No, really, I—

NORA: Christine is tremendously clever at book-keeping, and she is frightfully anxious to work under some clever man, so as to perfect herself—

HELMER: Very sensible, Mrs. Linde.

NORA: And when she heard you had been appointed manager of the Bank—the news was telegraphed, you know—she travelled here as quick as she could. Torvald, I am sure you will be able to do something for Christine, for my sake, won't you?

HELMER: Well, it is not altogether impossible. I presume you are a widow, Mrs. Linde?

MRS. LINDE: Yes.

HELMER: And have had some experience of book-keeping?

MRS. LINDE: Yes, a fair amount.

HELMER: Ah! well, it's very likely I may be able to find something for you—

NORA [*clapping her hands*]: What did I tell you? What did I tell you?

HELMER: You have just come at a fortunate moment, Mrs. Linde.

MRS. LINDE: How am I to thank you?

HELMER: There is no need. [*puts on his coat*] But to-day you must excuse me—

RANK: Wait a minute; I will come with you.

[*Brings his fur coat from the hall and warms it at the fire.*]

NORA: Don't be long away, Torvald dear.

HELMER: About an hour, not more.

NORA: Are you going too, Christine?

MRS. LINDE [*putting on her cloak*]: Yes, I must go and look for a room.

HELMER: Oh, well then, we can walk down the street together.

NORA [*helping her*]: What a pity it is we are so short of space here: I am afraid it is impossible for us—

MRS. LINDE: Please don't think of it! Good-bye, Nora dear, and many thanks.

NORA: Good-bye for the present. Of course you will come back this evening. And you too, Dr. Rank. What do you say? If you are well enough? Oh, you must be! Wrap yourself up well.

[*They go to the door all talking together. Children's voices are heard on the staircase.*]

NORA: There they are. There they are! [*She runs to open the door. The* NURSE *comes in with the children.*] Come in! Come in! [*stoops and kisses them*] Oh, you sweet blessings! Look at them, Christine! Aren't they darlings?

RANK: Don't let us stand here in the draught.

HELMER: Come along, Mrs. Linde; the place will only be bearable for a mother now!

[RANK, HELMER *and* MRS. LINDE *go downstairs. The* NURSE *comes forward with the children;* NORA *shuts the hall door.*]

NORA: How fresh and well you look! Such red cheeks!—like apples and roses. [*The children all talk at once while she speaks to them.*] Have you had great fun? That's splendid! What, you pulled both Emmy and Bob along on the sledge?— both at once?—that was good. You are a clever boy, Ivar. Let me take her for a little, Anne. My sweet little baby doll! [*takes the baby from the* MAID *and dances it up and down*] Yes, yes, mother will dance with Bob too. What! Have you been snowballing? I wish I had been there too! No, no, I will take their things off, Anne; please let me do it, it is such fun. Go in now, you look half frozen. There is some coffee for you on the stove.

[*The* NURSE *goes into the room on the left.* NORA *takes off the children's things and throws them about, while they all talk to her at once.*]

NORA. Really! Did a big dog run after you? But it didn't bite you? No, dogs don't bite nice little dolly children. You mustn't look at the parcels, Ivar. What are they? Ah, I daresay you would like to know. No, no—it's something nasty! Come, let us have a game! What shall we play at? Hide and Seek? Yes, we'll play Hide and Seek. Bob shall hide first. Must I hide? Very well, I'll hide first.

[*She and the children laugh and shout, and romp in and out of the room; at last* NORA *hides under the table, the children rush in and look for her, but do not see her; they hear her smothered laughter, run to the table, lift up the cloth and find her. Shouts of laughter. She crawls forward and pretends to frighten them. Fresh laughter. Meanwhile there has been a knock at the hall door, but none of them has noticed it. The door is half opened, and* KROGSTAD *appears. He waits a little; the game goes on.*]

KROGSTAD: Excuse me, Mrs. Helmer.

NORA [*with a stifled cry, turns round and gets up on to her knees*]: Ah! what do you want?

KROGSTAD: Excuse me, the outer door was ajar; I suppose someone forgot to shut it.

NORA [*rising*]: My husband is out, Mr. Krogstad.

KROGSTAD: I know that.

NORA: What do you want here, then?

KROGSTAD: A word with you.

NORA: With me?—[*to the children, gently*] Go in to nurse. What? No, the strange man won't do mother any harm. When he has gone we will have another game. [*She takes the children into the room on the left, and shuts the door after them.*] You want to speak to me?

KROGSTAD: Yes, I do.

NORA: To-day? It is not the first of the month yet.

KROGSTAD: No, it is Christmas Eve, and it will depend on yourself what sort of a Christmas you will spend.

NORA: What do you want? To-day it is absolutely impossible for me—

KROGSTAD: We won't talk about that till later on. This is something different. I presume you can give me a moment?

NORA: Yes—yes, I can—although—

KROGSTAD: Good. I was in Olsen's Restaurant and saw your husband going down the street—

NORA: Yes?

KROGSTAD: With a lady.

NORA: What then?

KROGSTAD: May I make so bold as to ask if it was a Mrs. Linde?

NORA: It was.

KROGSTAD: Just arrived in town?

NORA: Yes, to-day.

KROGSTAD: She is a great friend of yours, isn't she?

NORA: She is. But I don't see—

KROGSTAD: I knew her too, once upon a time.

NORA: I am aware of that.

KROGSTAD: Are you? So you know all about it; I thought as much. Then I can ask you, without beating about the bush—is Mrs. Linde to have an appointment in the Bank?

NORA: What right have you to question me, Mr. Krogstad?—You, one of my husband's subordinates! But since you ask, you shall know. Yes, Mrs. Linde *is* to have an appointment. And it was I who pleaded her cause, Mr. Krogstad, let me tell you that.

KROGSTAD: I was right in what I thought, then.

NORA [*walking up and down the stage*]: Sometimes one has a tiny little bit of influence, I should hope. Because one is a woman, it does not necessarily follow that—. When anyone is in a subordinate position, Mr. Krogstad, they should really be careful to avoid offending anyone who—who—

KROGSTAD: Who has influence?

NORA: Exactly.

KROGSTAD [*changing his tone*]: Mrs. Helmer, you will be so good as to use your influence on my behalf.

NORA: What? What do you mean?

KROGSTAD: You will be so kind as to see that I am allowed to keep my subordinate position in the Bank.

NORA: What do you mean by that? Who proposes to take your post away from you?

KROGSTAD: Oh, there is no necessity to keep up the pretence of ignorance. I can quite understand that your friend is not very anxious to expose herself to the chance of rubbing shoulders with me; and I quite understand, too, whom I have to thank for being turned out.

NORA: But I assure you—

KROGSTAD: Very likely; but, to come to the point, the time has come when I should advise you to use your influence to prevent that.

NORA: But, Mr. Krogstad, I *have* no influence.

KROGSTAD: Haven't you? I thought you said yourself just now—

NORA: Naturally I did not mean you to put that construction on it. I! What should make you think I have any influence of that kind with my husband?

KROGSTAD: Oh, I have known your husband from our student days. I don't suppose he is any more unassailable than other husbands.

NORA: If you speak slightingly of my husband, I shall turn you out of the house.

KROGSTAD: You are bold, Mrs. Helmer.

NORA: I am not afraid of you any longer. As soon as the New Year comes, I shall in a very short time be free of the whole thing.

KROGSTAD [*controlling himself*]: Listen to me, Mrs. Helmer. If necessary, I am prepared to fight for my small post in the Bank as if I were fighting for my life.

NORA: So it seems.

KROGSTAD: It is not only for the sake of the money; indeed, that weighs least with me in the matter. There is another reason—well, I may as well tell you. My position is this. I daresay you know, like everybody else, that once, many years ago, I was guilty of an indiscretion.

NORA: I think I have heard something of the kind.

KROGSTAD: The matter never came into court; but every way seemed to be closed to me after that. So I took to the business that you know of. I had to do something; and, honestly, I don't think I've been one of the worst. But now I must cut myself free from all that. My sons are growing up; for their sake I must try and win back as much respect as I can in the town. This post in the Bank was like the first step up for me—and now your husband is going to kick me downstairs again into the mud.

NORA: But you must believe me, Mr. Krogstad; it is not in my power to help you at all.

KROGSTAD: Then it is because you haven't the will; but I have means to compel you.

NORA: You don't mean that you will tell my husband that I owe you money?

KROGSTAD: Hm!—suppose I were to tell him?

NORA: It would be perfectly infamous of you. [*sobbing*] To think of his learning my secret, which has been my joy and pride, in such an ugly, clumsy way—that he should learn it from you! And it would put me in a horribly disagreeable position—

KROGSTAD: Only disagreeable?

NORA [*impetuously*]: Well, do it, then!—and it will be the worse for you. My husband will see for himself what a blackguard you are, and you certainly won't keep your post then.

KROGSTAD: I asked you if it was only a disagreeable scene at home that you were afraid of?

NORA: If my husband does get to know of it, of course he will at once pay you what is still owing, and we shall have nothing more to do with you.

KROGSTAD [*coming a step nearer*]: Listen to me, Mrs. Helmer. Either you have a very bad memory or you know very little of business. I shall be obliged to remind you of a few details.

NORA: What do you mean?

KROGSTAD: When your husband was ill, you came to me to borrow two hundred and fifty pounds.

NORA: I didn't know any one else to go to.

KROGSTAD: I promised to get you that amount—

NORA: Yes, and you did so.

KROGSTAD: I promised to get you that amount, on certain conditions. Your mind was so taken up with your husband's illness, and you were so anxious to get the money for your journey, that you seem to have paid no attention to the conditions of our bargain. Therefore it will not be amiss if I remind you of them. Now, I promised to get the money on the security of a bond which I drew up.

NORA: Yes, and which I signed.

KROGSTAD: Good. But below your signature there were a few lines constituting your father a surety for the money; those lines your father should have signed.

NORA: Should? He did sign them.

KROGSTAD: I had left the date blank; that is to say your father should himself have inserted the date on which he signed the paper. Do you remember that?

NORA: Yes, I think I remember—

KROGSTAD: Then I gave you the bond to send by post to your father. Is that not so?

NORA: Yes.

KROGSTAD: And you naturally did so at once, because five or six days afterwards you brought me the bond with your father's signature. And then I gave you the money.

NORA: Well, haven't I been paying it off regularly?

KROGSTAD: Fairly so, yes. But—to come back to the matter in hand—that must have been a very trying time for you, Mrs. Helmer?

NORA: It was, indeed.

KROGSTAD: Your father was very ill, wasn't he?

NORA: He was very near his end.

KROGSTAD: And died soon afterwards?

NORA: Yes.

KROGSTAD: Tell me, Mrs. Helmer, can you by any chance remember what day your father died?—on what day of the month, I mean.

NORA: Papa died on the 29th of September.

KROGSTAD: That is correct; I have ascertained it for myself. And, as that is so, there is a discrepancy [*taking a paper from his pocket*] which I cannot account for.

NORA: What discrepancy? I don't know—

KROGSTAD: The discrepancy consists, Mrs. Helmer, in the fact that your father signed this bond three days after his death.

NORA: What do you mean? I don't understand—

KROGSTAD: Your father died on the 29th of September. But, look here; your father has dated his signature the 2nd of October. It is a discrepancy, isn't it? [NORA *is silent.*] Can you explain it to me? [NORA *is still silent.*] It is a remarkable thing, too, that the words "2nd of October," as well as the year, are not written in your father's handwriting but in one that I think I know. Well, of course it can be explained; your father may have forgotten to date his signature, and some-one else may have dated it haphazard before they knew of his death. There is no harm in that. It all depends on the signature of the name; and *that* is genuine, I suppose, Mrs. Helmer? It was your father himself who signed his name here?

NORA [*after a short pause, throws her head up and looks defiantly at him*]: No, it was not. It was I that wrote papa's name.

KROGSTAD: Are you aware that is a dangerous confession?

NORA: In what way? You shall have your money soon.

KROGSTAD: Let me ask you a question; why did you not send the paper to your father?

NORA: It was impossible; papa was so ill. If I had asked him for his signature, I should have had to tell him what the money was to be used for; and when he was so ill himself I couldn't tell him that my husband's life was in danger— it was impossible.

KROGSTAD: It would have been better for you if you had given up your trip abroad.

NORA: No, that was impossible. That trip was to save my husband's life; I couldn't give that up.

KROGSTAD: But did it never occur to you that you were committing a fraud on me?

NORA: I couldn't take that into account; I didn't trouble myself about you at all. I couldn't bear you, because you put so many heartless difficulties in my way, although you knew what a dangerous condition my husband was in.

KROGSTAD: Mrs. Helmer, you evidently do not realise clearly what it is that you have been guilty of. But I can assure you that my one false step, which lost me all my reputation, was nothing more or nothing worse than what you have done.

NORA: You? Do you ask me to believe that you were brave enough to run a risk to save your wife's life?

KROGSTAD: The law cares nothing about motives.

NORA: Then it must be a very foolish law.

KROGSTAD: Foolish or not, it is the law by which you will be judged, if I produce this paper in court.

NORA: I don't believe it. Is a daughter not to be allowed to spare her dying father anxiety and care? Is a wife not to be allowed to save her husband's life? I don't know much about law; but I am certain that there must be laws permitting such things as that. Have you no knowledge of such laws—you who are a lawyer? You must be a very poor lawyer, Mr. Krogstad.

KROGSTAD: Maybe. But matters of business—such business as you and I have had together—do you think I don't understand that? Very well. Do as you please. But let me tell you this—if I lose my position a second time, you shall lose yours with me.

[*He bows, and goes out through the hall.*]

NORA [*appears buried in thought for a short time, then tosses her head*]: Nonsense! Trying to frighten me like that!—I am not so silly as he thinks. [*begins to busy herself putting the children's things in order*] And yet—? No, it's impossible! I did it for love's sake.

THE CHILDREN [*in the doorway on the left*]: Mother, the stranger man has gone out through the gate.

NORA: Yes, dears, I know. But, don't tell anyone about the stranger man. Do you hear? Not even papa.

CHILDREN: No, mother; but will you come and play again?

NORA: No, no—not now.

CHILDREN: But, mother, you promised us.

NORA: Yes, but I can't now. Run away in; I have such a lot to do. Run away in, my sweet little darlings. [*She gets them into the room by degrees and shuts the door on them; then sits down on the sofa, takes up a piece of needlework and sews a few stitches, but soon stops.*] No! [*throws down the work, gets up, goes to the hall door and calls out*] Helen! bring the Tree in. [*goes to the table on the left, opens a drawer, and stops again*] No, no! it is quite impossible!

MAID [*coming in with the Tree*]: Where shall I put it, ma'am?

NORA: Here, in the middle of the floor.

MAID: Shall I get you anything else?

NORA: No, thank you. I have all I want.

[*Exit* MAID.]

NORA [*begins dressing the tree*]: A candle here—and flowers here—. The horrible man! It's all nonsense—there's nothing wrong. The Tree shall be splendid! I will do everything I can think of to please you, Torvald!—I will sing for you, dance for you— [HELMER *comes in with some papers under his arm*] Oh! are you back already?

HELMER: Yes. Has anyone been here?

NORA: Here? No.

HELMER: That is strange. I saw Krogstad going out of the gate.

NORA: Did you? Oh yes, I forgot, Krogstad was here for a moment.

HELMER: Nora, I can see from your manner that he has been here begging you to say a good word for him.

NORA: Yes.

HELMER: And you were to appear to do it of your own accord; you were to conceal from me the fact of his having been here; didn't he beg that of you too?

NORA: Yes, Torvald, but—

HELMER: Nora, Nora, and you would be a party to that sort of thing? To have any talk with a man like that, and give him any sort of promise? And to tell me a lie into the bargain?

NORA: A lie—?

HELMER: Didn't you tell me no one had been here? [*shakes his finger at her*] My little song-bird must never do that again. A song-bird must have a clean beak to chirp with—no false notes! [*puts his arm round her waist*] That is so, isn't it? Yes, I am sure it is. [*lets her go*] We will say no more about it. [*sits down by the stove*] How warm and snug it is here!

[*Turns over his papers.*]

NORA [*after a short pause, during which she busies herself with the Christmas Tree*]: Torvald!

HELMER: Yes.

NORA: I am looking forward tremendously to the fancy dress ball at the Stenborgs' the day after to-morrow.

HELMER: And I am tremendously curious to see what you are going to surprise me with.

NORA: It was very silly of me to want to do that.

HELMER: What do you mean?

NORA: I can't hit upon anything that will do; everything I think of seems so silly and insignificant.

HELMER: Does my little Nora acknowledge that at last?

NORA [*standing behind his chair with her arms on the back of it*]: Are you very busy, Torvald?

HELMER: Well—

NORA: What are all those papers?

HELMER: Bank business.

NORA: Already?

HELMER: I have got authority from the retiring manager to undertake the necessary changes in the staff and in the rearrangement of the work; and I must make use of the Christmas week for that, so as to have everything in order for the new year.

NORA: Then that was why this poor Krogstad—

HELMER: Hm!

NORA [*leans against the back of his chair and strokes his hair*]: If you hadn't been so busy I should have asked you a tremendously big favour, Torvald.

HELMER: What is that? Tell me.

NORA: There is no one has such good taste as you. And I do so want to look nice at the fancy-dress ball. Torvald, couldn't you take me in hand and decide what I shall go as, and what sort of a dress I shall wear?

HELMER: Aha! so my obstinate little woman is obliged to get someone to come to her rescue?

NORA: Yes, Torvald, I can't get along a bit without your help.

HELMER: Very well, I will think it over, we shall manage to hit upon something.

NORA: That is nice of you. [*Goes to the Christmas Tree. A short pause.*] How pretty the red flowers look——. But, tell me, was it really something very bad that this Krogstad was guilty of?

HELMER: He forged someone's name. Have you any idea what that means?

NORA: Isn't it possible that he was driven to do it by necessity?

HELMER: Yes; or, as in so many cases, by imprudence. I am not so heartless as to condemn a man altogether because of a single false step of that kind.

NORA: No you wouldn't, would you, Torvald?

HELMER: Many a man has been able to retrieve his character, if he has openly confessed his fault and taken his punishment.

NORA: Punishment—?

HELMER: But Krogstad did nothing of that sort; he got himself out of it by a cunning trick, and that is why he has gone under altogether.

NORA: But do you think it would—?

HELMER: Just think how a guilty man like that has to lie and play the hypocrite with everyone, how he has to wear a mask in the presence of those near and dear to him, even before his own wife and children. And about the children—that is the most terrible part of it all, Nora.

NORA: How?

HELMER: Because such an atmosphere of lies infects and poisons the whole life of a home. Each breath the children take in such a house is full of the germs of evil.

NORA [*coming nearer him*]: Are you sure of that?

HELMER: My dear, I have often seen it in the course of my life as a lawyer. Almost everyone who has gone to the bad early in life has had a deceitful mother.

NORA: Why do you only say—mother?

HELMER: It seems most commonly to be the mother's influence, though naturally a bad father's would have the same result. Every lawyer is familiar with the fact. This Krogstad, now, has been persistently poisoning his own children with lies and dissimulation; that is why I say he has lost all moral character. [*holds out his hands to her*] That is why my sweet little Nora must promise me not to plead his cause. Give me your hand on it. Come, come, what is this? Give me your hand. There now, that's settled. I assure you it would be quite impossible for me to work with him; I literally feel physically ill when I am in the company of such people.

NORA [*takes her hand out of his and goes to the opposite side of the Christmas Tree*]: How hot it is in here; and I have such a lot to do.

HELMER [*getting up and putting his papers in order*]: Yes, and I must try and read through some of these before dinner; and I must think about your costume, too. And it is just possible I may have something ready in gold paper to hang up on the Tree. [*Puts his hand on her head.*] My precious little singing-bird!

[*He goes into his room and shuts the door after him.*]

NORA [*after a pause, whispers*]: No, no—it isn't true. It's impossible; it must be impossible.

[*The* NURSE *opens the door on the left.*]

NURSE: The little ones are begging so hard to be allowed to come in to mamma.

NORA: No, no, no! Don't let them come in to me! You stay with them, Anne.

NURSE: Very well, ma'am.

[*Shuts the door.*]

NORA [*pale with terror*]: Deprave my little children? Poison my home? [*a short pause. Then she tosses her head.*] It's not true. It can't possibly be true.

Act 2

THE SAME SCENE. *The Christmas Tree is in the corner by the piano, stripped of its ornaments and with burnt-down candle-ends on its dishevelled branches.* NORA'*s cloak and hat are lying on the sofa. She is alone in the room, walking about uneasily. She stops by the sofa and takes up her cloak.*

NORA [*drops the cloak*]: Someone is coming now! [*goes to the door and listens*] No—it is no one. Of course, no one will come to-day, Christmas Day—nor tomorrow either. But, perhaps—[*opens the door and looks out*] No, nothing in the letter-box; it is quite empty. [*comes forward*] What rubbish! of course he can't be in earnest about it. Such a thing couldn't happen; it is impossible—I have three little children.

[*Enter the* NURSE *from the room on the left, carrying a big cardboard box.*]

NURSE: At last I have found the box with the fancy dress.

NORA: Thanks; put it on the table.

NURSE [*doing so*]: But it is very much in want of mending.

NORA: I should like to tear it into a hundred thousand pieces.

NURSE: What an idea! It can easily be put in order—just a little patience.

NORA: Yes, I will go and get Mrs. Linde to come and help me with it.

NURSE: What, out again? In this horrible weather? You will catch cold, ma'am, and make yourself ill.

NORA: Well, worse than that might happen. How are the children?

NURSE: The poor little souls are playing with their Christmas presents, but—

NORA: Do they ask much for me?

NURSE: You see, they are so accustomed to have their mamma with them.

NORA: Yes, but, nurse, I shall not be able to be so much with them now as I was before.

NURSE: Oh well, young children easily get accustomed to anything.

NORA: Do you think so? Do you think they would forget their mother if she went away altogether?

NURSE: Good heavens!—went away altogether?

NORA: Nurse, I want you to tell me something I have often wondered about—how could you have the heart to put your own child out among strangers?

NURSE: I was obliged to, if I wanted to be little Nora's nurse.

NORA: Yes, but how could you be willing to do it?

NURSE: What, when I was going to get such a good place by it? A poor girl who has got into trouble should be glad to. Besides, that wicked man didn't do a single thing for me.

NORA: But I suppose your daughter has quite forgotten you.

NURSE: No, indeed she hasn't. She wrote to me when she was confirmed, and when she was married.

NORA [*putting her arms round her neck*]: Dear old Anne, you were a good mother to me when I was little.

NURSE: Little Nora, poor dear, had no other mother but me.

NORA: And if my little ones had no other mother, I am sure you would—What nonsense I am talking! [*opens the box*] Go in to them. Now I must—. You will see tomorrow how charming I shall look.

NURSE: I am sure there will be no one at the ball so charming as you, ma'am.

[*Goes into the room on the left.*]

NORA [*begins to unpack the box, but soon pushes it away from her*]: If only I dared go out. If only no one would come. If only I could be sure nothing would happen here in the meantime. Stuff and nonsense! No one will come. Only I mustn't think about it. I will brush my muff. What, lovely gloves! Out of my thoughts, out of my thoughts! One, two, three, four, five, six—[*Screams.*] Ah! there is someone coming—

[*Makes a movement towards the door, but stands irresolute.*]

[*Enter* MRS. LINDE *from the hall, where she has taken off her cloak and hat.*]

NORA: Oh, it's you, Christine. There is no one else out there, is there? How good of you to come!

MRS. LINDE: I heard you were up asking for me.

NORA: Yes, I was passing by. As a matter of fact, it is something you could help me with. Let us sit down here on the sofa. Look here. To-morrow evening there is to be a fancy-dress ball at the Stenborgs', who live above us; and Torvald wants me to go as a Neapolitan fisher-girl, and dance the Tarantella that I learnt at Capri.

MRS. LINDE: I see; you are going to keep up the character.

NORA: Yes, Torvald wants me to. Look, here is the dress; Torvald had it made for me there, but now it is all so torn, and I haven't any idea

MRS. LINDE: We will easily put that right. It is only some of the trimming come unsewn here and there. Needle and thread? Now then, that's all we want.

NORA: It *is* nice of you.

MRS. LINDE [*sewing*]: So you are going to be dressed up to-morrow, Nora. I will tell you what—I shall come in for a moment and see you in your fine feathers. But I have completely forgotten to thank you for a delightful evening yesterday.

NORA [*gets up, and crosses the stage*]: Well I don't think yesterday was as pleasant as usual. You ought to have come to town a little earlier, Christine. Certainly Torvald does understand how to make a house dainty and attractive.

MRS. LINDE: And so do you, it seems to me; you are not your father's daughter for nothing. But tell me, is Doctor Rank always as depressed as he was yesterday?

NORA: No; yesterday it was very noticeable. I must tell you that he suffers from a very dangerous disease. He has consumption of the spine, poor creature. His father was a horrible man who committed all sorts of excesses; and that is why his son was sickly from childhood, do you understand?

MRS. LINDE [*dropping her sewing*]: But, my dearest Nora, how do you know anything about such things?

NORA [*walking about*]: Pooh! When you have three children, you get visits now and then from—from married women, who know something of medical matters, and they talk about one thing and another.

MRS. LINDE [*goes on sewing. A short silence*]: Does Doctor Rank come here every day?

NORA: Every day regularly. He is Torvald's most intimate friend, and a great friend of mine too. He is just like one of the family.

MRS. LINDE: But tell me this—is he perfectly sincere? I mean, isn't he the kind of man that is very anxious to make himself agreeable?

NORA: Not in the least. What makes you think that?

MRS. LINDE: When you introduced him to me yesterday, he declared he had often heard my name mentioned in this house; but afterwards I noticed that your husband hadn't the slightest idea who I was. So how could Doctor Rank—?

NORA: That is quite right, Christine. Torvald is so absurdly fond of me that he wants me absolutely to himself, as he says. At first he used to seem almost jealous if I mentioned any of the dear folk at home, so naturally I gave up doing so. But I often talk about such things with Doctor Rank, because he likes hearing about them.

MRS. LINDE: Listen to me, Nora. You are still very like a child in many things, and I am older than you in many ways and have a little more experience. Let me tell you this—you ought to make an end of it with Doctor Rank.

NORA: What ought I to make an end of?

MRS. LINDE: Of two things, I think. Yesterday you talked some nonsense about a rich admirer who was to leave you money—

NORA: An admirer who doesn't exist, unfortunately! But what then?

MRS. LINDE: Is Doctor Rank a man of means?

NORA: Yes, he is.

MRS. LINDE: And has no one to provide for?

NORA: No, no one; but—

MRS. LINDE: And comes here every day?

NORA: Yes, I told you so.

MRS. LINDE: But how can this well-bred man be so tactless?

NORA: I don't understand you at all.

MRS. LINDE: Don't prevaricate, Nora. Do you suppose I don't guess who lent you the two hundred and fifty pounds?

NORA: Are you out of your senses? How can you think of such a thing! A friend of ours, who comes here every day! Do you realise what a horribly painful position that would be?

MRS. LINDE: Then it really isn't he?

NORA: No, certainly not. It would never have entered into my head for a moment. Besides, he had no money to lend then; he came into his money afterwards.

MRS. LINDE: Well, I think that was lucky for you, my dear Nora.

NORA: No, it would never have come into my head to ask Doctor Rank. Although I am quite sure that if I had asked him—

MRS. LINDE: But of course you won't.

NORA: Of course not. I have no reason to think it could possibly be necessary. But I am quite sure that if I told Doctor Rank—

MRS. LINDE: Behind your husband's back?

NORA: I *must* make an end of it with the other one, and that will be behind his back too. I *must* make an end of it with him.

MRS. LINDE: Yes, that is what I told you yesterday, but—

NORA [*walking up and down*]: A man can put a thing like that straight much easier than a woman—

MRS. LINDE: One's husband, yes.

NORA: Nonsense! [*standing still*] When you pay off a debt you get your bond back, don't you?

MRS. LINDE: Yes, as a matter of course.

NORA: And can tear it into a hundred thousand pieces, and burn it up—the nasty dirty paper!

MRS. LINDE [*looks hard at her, lays down her sewing and gets up slowly*]: Nora, you are concealing something from me.

NORA: Do I look as if I were?

MRS. LINDE: Something has happened to you since yesterday morning. Nora, what is it?

NORA [*going nearer to her*]: Christine! [*listens*] Hush! there's Torvald come home. Do you mind going in to the children for the present? Torvald can't bear to see dressmaking going on. Let Anne help you.

MRS. LINDE [*gathering some of the things together*]: Certainly—but I am not going away from here till we have had it out with one another.

[*She goes into the room on the left, as* HELMER *comes in from the hall.*]

NORA [*going up to* HELMER]: I have wanted you so much, Torvald dear.

HELMER: Was that the dressmaker?

NORA: No, it was Christine; she is helping me to put my dress in order. You will see I shall look quite smart.

HELMER: Wasn't that a happy thought of mine, now?

NORA: Splendid! But don't you think it is nice of me, too, to do as you wish?

HELMER: Nice?—because you do as your husband wishes? Well, well, you little rogue, I am sure you did not mean it in that way. But I am not going to disturb you; you will want to be trying on your dress, I expect.

NORA: I suppose you are going to work.

HELMER: Yes. [*shows her a bundle of papers*] Look at that. I have just been into the bank. [*Turns to go into his room.*]

NORA: Torvald.

HELMER: Yes.

NORA: If your little squirrel were to ask you for something very, very prettily—?

HELMER: What then?

NORA: Would you do it?

HELMER: I should like to hear what it is, first.

NORA: Your squirrel would run about and do all her tricks if you would be nice, and do what she wants.

HELMER: Speak plainly.

NORA: Your skylark would chirp about in every room, with her song rising and falling—

HELMER: Well, my skylark does that anyhow.

NORA: I would play the fairy and dance for you in the moonlight, Torvald.

HELMER: Nora—you surely don't mean that request you made of me this morning?

NORA [*going near him*]: Yes, Torvald, I beg you so earnestly—

HELMER: Have you really the courage to open up that question again?

NORA: Yes, dear, you *must* do as I ask; you *must* let Krogstad keep his post in the Bank.

HELMER: My dear Nora, it is his post that I have arranged Mrs. Linde shall have.

NORA: Yes, you have been awfully kind about that; but you could just as well dismiss some other clerk instead of Krogstad.

HELMER: This is simply incredible obstinacy! Because you chose to give him a thoughtless promise that you would speak for him, I am expected to—

NORA: That isn't the reason, Torvald. It is for your own sake. This fellow writes in the most scurrilous newspapers; you have told me so yourself. He can do you an unspeakable amount of harm. I am frightened to death of him—

HELMER: Ah, I understand; it is recollections of the past that scare you.

NORA: What do you mean?

HELMER: Naturally you are thinking of your father.

NORA: Yes—yes, of course. Just recall to your mind what these malicious creatures wrote in the papers about papa, and how horribly they slandered him. I believe they would have procured his dismissal if the Department had not sent you over to inquire into it, and if you had not been so kindly disposed and helpful to him.

HELMER: My little Nora, there is an important difference between your father and me. Your father's reputation as a public official was not above suspicion. Mine is, and I hope it will continue to be so, as long as I hold my office.

NORA: You never can tell what mischief these men may contrive. We ought to be so well off, so snug and happy here in our peaceful home, and have no cares— you and I and the children, Torvald! That is why I beg you so earnestly—

HELMER: And it is just by interceding for him that you make it impossible for me to keep him. It is already known at the Bank that I mean to dismiss Krogstad. Is it to get about now that the new manager has changed his mind at his wife's bidding—

NORA: And what if it did?

HELMER: Of course!—if only this obstinate little person can get her way! Do you suppose I am going to make myself ridiculous before my whole staff, to let people think that I am a man to be swayed by all sorts of outside influence? I should very soon feel the consequences of it, I can tell you! And besides, there is one thing that makes it quite impossible for me to have Krogstad in the Bank as long as I am manager.

NORA: Whatever is that?

HELMER: His moral failings I might perhaps have overlooked, if necessary—

NORA: Yes, you could—couldn't you?

HELMER: And I hear he is a good worker, too. But I knew him when we were boys. It was one of those rash friendships that so often prove an incubus in afterlife. I may as well tell you plainly, we were once on very intimate terms with one another. But this tactless fellow lays no restraint on himself when other people are present. On the contrary, he thinks it gives him the right to adopt a familiar tone with me, and every minute it is "I say, Helmer, old fellow!" and that sort of thing. I assure you it is extremely painful for me. He would make my position in the Bank intolerable.

NORA: Torvald, I don't believe you mean that.

HELMER: Don't you? Why not?

NORA: Because it is such a narrow-minded way of looking at things.

HELMER: What are you saying? Narrow-minded? Do you think I am narrow-minded?

NORA: No, just the opposite, dear—and it is exactly for that reason.

HELMER: It's the same thing. You say my point of view is narrow-minded, so I must be so too. Narrow-minded! Very well—I must put an end to this. [*Goes to the hall-door and calls.*] Helen!

NORA: What are you going to do?

HELMER [*looking among his papers*]: Settle it. [*Enter* MAID.] Look here; take this letter and go downstairs with it at once. Find a messenger and tell him to deliver it, and be quick. The address is on it, and here is the money.

MAID: Very well, sir.

[*Exits with the letter.*]

HELMER [*putting his papers together*]: Now then, little Miss Obstinate.

NORA [*breathlessly*]: Torvald—what was that letter?

HELMER: Krogstad's dismissal.

NORA: Call her back, Torvald! There is still time. Oh Torvald, call her back! Do it for my sake—for your own sake—for the children's sake! Do you hear me, Torvald? Call her back!! You don't know what that letter can bring upon us.

HELMER: It's too late.

NORA: Yes, it's too late.

HELMER: My dear Nora, I can forgive the anxiety you are in, although really it is an insult to me. It is, indeed. Isn't it an insult to think that I should be afraid of a starving quill-driver's vengeance? But I forgive you nevertheless, because it is such eloquent witness to your great love for me. [*takes her in his arms*] And that is as it should be, my own darling Nora. Come what will, you may be sure I shall have both courage and strength if they be needed. You will see I am man enough to take everything upon myself.

NORA [*in a horror-stricken voice*]: What do you mean by that?

HELMER: Everything, I say—

NORA [*recovering herself*]: You will never have to do that.

HELMER: That's right. Well, we will share it, Nora, as man and wife should. That is how it shall be. [*caressing her*] Are you content now? There! there!—not these frightened dove's eyes! The whole thing is only the wildest fancy!—Now, you must go and play through the Tarantella and practise with your tambourine. I shall go into the inner office and shut the door, and I shall hear nothing; you can make as much noise as you please. [*turns back at the door*] And when Rank comes, tell him where he will find me.

[*Nods to her, takes his papers and goes into his room, and shuts the door after him*]

NORA [*bewildered with anxiety, stands as if rooted to the spot, and whispers*]: He is capable of doing it. He will do it. He will do it in spite of everything.—No, not that! Never, never! Anything rather than that! Oh, for some help, some way out of it! [*The door-bell rings.*] Doctor Rank! Anything rather than that—anything, whatever it is!

[*She puts her hands over her face, pulls herself together, goes to the door and opens it. RANK is standing without, hanging up his coat. During the following dialogue it begins to grow dark.*]

NORA: Good-day, Doctor Rank. I knew your ring. But you mustn't go in to Torvald now; I think he is busy with something.

RANK: And you?

NORA [*brings him in and shuts the door after him*]: Oh, you know very well I always have time for you.

RANK: Thank you. I shall make use of as much of it as I can.

NORA: What do you mean by that? As much of it as you can?

RANK: Well, does that alarm you?

NORA: It was such a strange way of putting it. Is anything likely to happen?

RANK: Nothing but what I have long been prepared for. But I certainly didn't expect it to happen so soon.

NORA [*gripping him by the arm*]: What have you found out? Doctor Rank, you must tell me.

RANK [*sitting down by the stove*]: It is all up with me. And it can't be helped.

NORA [*with a sigh of relief*]: Is it about yourself?

RANK: Who else? It is no use lying to one's self. I am the most wretched of all my patients, Mrs. Helmer. Lately I have been taking stock of my internal economy. Bankrupt! Probably within a month I shall lie rotting in the churchyard.

NORA: What an ugly thing to say!

RANK: The thing itself is cursedly ugly, and the worst of it is that I shall have to face so much more that is ugly before that. I shall only make one more examination of myself; when I have done that, I shall know pretty certainly when it will be that the horrors of dissolution will begin. There is something I want to tell you. Helmer's refined nature gives him an unconquerable disgust at everything that is ugly; I won't have him in my sick-room.

NORA: Oh, but, Doctor Rank—

RANK: I won't have him there. Not on any account. I bar my door to him. As soon as I am quite certain that the worst has come, I shall send you my card with a black cross on it, and then you will know that the loathsome end has begun.

NORA: You are quite absurd to-day. And I wanted you so much to be in a really good humour.

RANK: With death stalking beside me?—To have to pay this penalty for another man's sin! Is there any justice in that? And in every single family, in one way or another, some such inexorable retribution is being exacted—

NORA [*putting her hands over her ears*]: Rubbish! Do talk of something cheerful.

RANK: Oh, it's a mere laughing matter, the whole thing. My poor innocent spine has to suffer for my father's youthful amusements.

NORA [*sitting at the table on the left*]: I suppose you mean that he was too partial to asparagus and pâté de foie gras, don't you.

RANK: Yes, and to truffles.

NORA: Truffles, yes. And oysters too, I suppose?

RANK: Oysters, of course, that goes without saying.

NORA: And heaps of port and champagne. It is sad that all these nice things should take their revenge on our bones.

RANK: Especially that they should revenge themselves on the unlucky bones of those who have not had the satisfaction of enjoying them.

NORA: Yes, that's the saddest part of it all.

RANK [*with a searching look at her*]: Hm!—

NORA [*after a short pause*]: Why did you smile?

RANK: No, it was you that laughed.

NORA: No, it was you that smiled, Doctor Rank!

RANK [*rising*]: You are a greater rascal than I thought.

NORA: I am in a silly mood to-day.

RANK: So it seems.

NORA [*putting her hands on his shoulders*]: Dear, dear Doctor Rank, death mustn't take you away from Torvald and me.

RANK: It is a loss you would easily recover from. Those who are gone are soon forgotten.

NORA [*looking at him anxiously*]: Do you believe that?

RANK: People form new ties, and then—

NORA: Who will form new ties?

RANK: Both you and Helmer, when I am gone. You yourself are already on the high road to it, I think. What did that Mrs. Linde want here last night?

NORA: Oho!—you don't mean to say you are jealous of poor Christine?

RANK: Yes, I am. She will be my successor in this house. When I am done for, this woman will—

NORA: Hush! don't speak so loud. She is in that room.

RANK: To-day again. There, you see.

NORA: She has only come to sew my dress for me. Bless my soul, how unreasonable you are! [*sits down on the sofa*] Be nice now, Doctor Rank, and tomorrow you will see how beautifully I shall dance, and you can imagine I am doing it all for you—and for Torvald too, of course. [*takes various things out of the box*] Doctor Rank, come and sit down here, and I will show you something.

RANK [*sitting down*]: What is it?

NORA: Just look at those!

RANK: Silk stockings.

NORA: Flesh-coloured. Aren't they lovely? It is so dark here now, but to-morrow—. No, no, no! you must only look at the feet. Oh well, you may have leave to look at the legs too.

RANK: Hm!—

NORA: Why are you looking so critical? Don't you think they will fit me?

RANK: I have no means of forming an opinion about that.

NORA [*looks at him for a moment*]: For shame! [*hits him lightly on the ear with the stockings*] That's to punish you. [*folds them up again*]

RANK: And what other nice things am I to be allowed to see?

NORA: Not a single thing more, for being so naughty. [*She looks among the things, humming to herself.*]

RANK [*after a short silence*]: When I am sitting here, talking to you as intimately as this, I cannot imagine for a moment what would have become of me if I had never come into this house.

NORA [*smiling*]: I believe you do feel thoroughly at home with us.

RANK [*in a lower voice, looking straight in front of him*]: And to be obliged to leave it all—

NORA: Nonsense, you are not going to leave it.

RANK [*as before*]: And not be able to leave behind one the slightest token of one's gratitude, scarcely even a fleeting regret—nothing but an empty place which the first comer can fill as well as any other.

NORA: And if I asked you now for a—? No!

RANK: For what?

NORA: For a big proof of your friendship—

RANK: Yes, yes!

NORA: I mean a tremendously big favour—

RANK: Would you really make me so happy for once?

NORA: Ah, but you don't know what it is yet.

RANK: No—but tell me.

NORA: I really can't, Doctor Rank. It is something out of all reason; it means advice, and help, and a favour—

RANK: The bigger a thing it is the better. I can't conceive what it is you mean. Do tell me. Haven't I your confidence?

NORA: More than anyone else. I know you are my truest and best friend, and so I will tell you what it is. Well, Doctor Rank, it is something you must help me to prevent. You know how devotedly, how inexpressibly deeply Torvald loves me; he would never for a moment hesitate to give his life for me.

RANK [*leaning towards her*]: Nora—do you think he is the only one—?

NORA [*with a slight start*]: The only one—?

RANK: The only one who would gladly give his life for your sake.

NORA [*sadly*]: Is that it?

RANK: I was determined you should know it before I went away, and there will never be a better opportunity than this. Now you know it, Nora. And now you know, too, that you can trust me as you would trust no one else.

NORA [*rises, deliberately and quietly*]:   Let me pass.

RANK [*makes room for her to pass him, but sits still*]:   Nora!

NORA [*at the hall door*]:   Helen, bring in the lamp. [*goes over to the stove*] Dear Doctor Rank, that was really horrid of you.

RANK: To have loved you as much as anyone else does? Was that horrid?

NORA: No, but to go and tell me so. There was really no need—

RANK: What do you mean? Did you know—? [MAID *enters with lamp, puts it down on the table, and goes out.*] Nora—Mrs. Helmer—tell me, had you any idea of this?

NORA: Oh, how do I know whether I had or whether I hadn't? I really can't tell you— To think you could be so clumsy, Doctor Rank! We were getting on so nicely.

RANK: Well, at all events you know now that you can command me, body and soul. So won't you speak out?

NORA [*looking at him*]:   After what happened?

RANK: I beg you to let me know what it is.

NORA: I can't tell you anything now.

RANK: Yes, yes. You mustn't punish me in that way. Let me have permission to do for you whatever a man may do.

NORA: You can do nothing for me now. Besides, I really don't need any help at all. You will find that the whole thing is merely fancy on my part. It really is so— of course it is! [*Sits down in the rocking-chair, and looks at him with a smile*] You are a nice sort of man, Doctor Rank!—don't you feel ashamed of yourself, now the lamp has come?

RANK: Not a bit. But perhaps I had better go—for ever?

NORA: No, indeed, you shall not. Of course you must come here just as before. You know very well Torvald can't do without you.

RANK: Yes, but you?

NORA: Oh, I am always tremendously pleased when you come.

RANK: It is just that, that put me on the wrong track. You are a riddle to me. I have often thought that you would almost as soon be in my company as in Helmer's.

NORA: Yes—you see there are some people one loves best, and others whom one would almost always rather have as companions.

RANK: Yes, there is something in that.

NORA: When I was at home, of course I loved papa best. But I always thought it tremendous fun if I could steal down into the maid's room, because they never moralised at all, and talked to each other about such entertaining things.

RANK: I see—it is *their* place I have taken.

NORA [*jumping up and going to him*]:   Oh, dear, nice Doctor Rank, I never meant that at all. But surely you can understand that being with Torvald is a little like being with papa—

[*Enter* MAID *from the hall*]

MAID: If you please, ma'am. [*whispers and hands her a card*]

NORA [*glancing at the card*]:   Oh! [*puts it in her pocket*]

RANK: Is there anything wrong?

NORA: No, no, not in the least. It is only something—it is my new dress—

RANK: What? Your dress is lying there.

NORA: Oh, yes, that one; but this is another. I ordered it. Torvald mustn't know about it—

RANK: Oho! Then that was the great secret.

NORA: Of course. Just go in to him; he is sitting in the inner room. Keep him as long as—

RANK: Make your mind easy; I won't let him escape. [*goes into* HELMER'S *room*]

NORA [*to the* MAID]: And he is standing waiting in the kitchen?

MAID: Yes; he came up the back stairs.

NORA: But didn't you tell him no one was in?

MAID: Yes, but it was no good.

NORA: He won't go away?

MAID: No; he says he won't until he has seen you, ma'am.

NORA: Well, let him come in—but quietly. Helen, you mustn't say anything about it to anyone. It is a surprise for my husband.

MAID: Yes, ma'am, I quite understand.

[Exit.]

NORA: This dreadful thing is going to happen! It will happen in spite of me! No, no, no, it can't happen—it shan't happen!

[*She bolts the door of* HELMER'S *room. The* MAID *opens the hall door for* KROGSTAD *and shuts it after him. He is wearing a fur coat, high boots and a fur cap.*]

NORA [*advancing towards him*]: Speak low—my husband is at home.

KROGSTAD: No matter about that.

NORA: What do you want of me?

KROGSTAD: An explanation of something.

NORA: Make haste then. What is it?

KROGSTAD: You know, I suppose, that I have got my dismissal.

NORA: I couldn't prevent it, Mr. Krogstad. I fought as hard as I could on your side, but it was no good.

KROGSTAD: Does your husband love you so little, then? He knows that what I can expose you to, and yet he ventures—

NORA: How can you suppose that he has any knowledge of the sort?

KROGSTAD: I didn't suppose so at all. It would not be the least like our dear Torvald Helmer to show so much courage—

NORA: Mr. Krogstad, a little respect for my husband, please.

KROGSTAD: Certainly—all the respect he deserves. But since you have kept the matter so carefully to yourself, I make bold to suppose that you have a little clearer idea, than you had yesterday, of what it actually is that you have done?

NORA: More than you could ever teach me.

KROGSTAD: Yes, such a bad lawyer as I am.

NORA: What is it you want of me?

KROGSTAD: Only to see how you were, Mrs. Helmer. I have been thinking about you all day long. A mere cashier, a quill-driver, a—well, a man like me—even he has a little of what is called feeling, you know.

NORA: Show it, then; think of my little children.

KROGSTAD: Have you and your husband thought of mine? But never mind about that. I only wanted to tell you that you need not take this matter too seriously. In the first place there will be no accusation made on my part.

NORA: No, of course not; I was sure of that.

KROGSTAD: The whole thing can be arranged amicably; there is no reason why anyone should know anything about it. It will remain a secret between us three.

NORA: My husband must never get to know anything about it.

KROGSTAD: How will you be able to prevent it? Am I to understand that you can pay the balance that is owing?

NORA: No, not just at present.

KROGSTAD: Or perhaps that you have some expedient for raising the money soon?

NORA: No expedient that I mean to make use of.

KROGSTAD: Well, in any case, it would have been of no use to you now. If you stood there with ever so much money in your hand, I would never part with your bond.

NORA: Tell me what purpose you mean to put it to.

KROGSTAD: I shall only preserve it—keep it in my possession. No one who is not concerned in the matter shall have the slightest hint of it. So that if the thought of it has driven you to any desperate resolution—

NORA: It has.

KROGSTAD: If you had it in your mind to run away from your home—

NORA: I had.

KROGSTAD: Or even something worse—

NORA: How could you know that?

KROGSTAD: Give up the idea.

NORA: How did you know I had thought of *that?*

KROGSTAD: Most of us think of that at first. I did, too—but I hadn't the courage.

NORA [*faintly*]: No more had I.

KROGSTAD [*in a tone of relief*]: No, that's it, isn't it—you hadn't the courage either?

NORA: No, I haven't—I haven't.

KROGSTAD: Besides, it would have been a great piece of folly. Once the first storm at home is over—. I have a letter for your husband in my pocket.

NORA: Telling him everything?

KROGSTAD: In as lenient a manner as I possibly could.

NORA [*quickly*]: He mustn't get the letter. Tear it up. I will find some means of getting money.

KROGSTAD: Excuse me, Mrs. Helmer, but I think I told you just now—

NORA: I am not speaking of what I owe you. Tell me what sum you are asking my husband for, and I will get the money.

KROGSTAD: I am not asking your husband for a penny.

NORA: What do you want, then?

KROGSTAD: I will tell you. I want to rehabilitate myself, Mrs. Helmer; I want to get on; and in that your husband must help me. For the last year and a half I have not had a hand in anything dishonourable, and all that time I have been struggling in most restricted circumstances. I was content to work my way up step by step. Now I am turned out, and I am not going to be satisfied with merely being taken into favour again. I want to get on, I tell you. I want to get into the Bank again, in a higher position. Your husband must make a place for me—

NORA: That he will never do!

KROGSTAD: He will; I know him; he dare not protest. And as soon as I am in there again with him, then you will see! Within a year I shall be the manager's right hand. It will be Nils Krogstad and not Torvald Helmer who manages the Bank.

NORA: That's a thing you will never see!

KROGSTAD: Do you mean that you will—?

NORA: I have courage enough for it now.

KROGSTAD: Oh, you can't frighten me. A fine, spoilt lady like you—

NORA: You will see, you will see.

KROGSTAD: Under the ice, perhaps? Down into the cold, coal-black water? And then, in the spring, to float up to the surface, all horrible and unrecognisable, with your hair fallen out—

NORA: You can't frighten me.

KROGSTAD: Nor you me. People don't do such things, Mrs. Helmer. Besides, what use would it be? I should have him completely in my power all the same.

NORA: Afterwards? When I am no longer—

KROGSTAD: Have you forgotten that it is I who have the keeping of your reputation? [NORA *stands speechlessly looking at him.*] Well, now, I have warned you. Do not do anything foolish. When Helmer has had my letter, I shall expect a message from him. And be sure you remember that it is your husband himself who has forced me into such ways as this again. I will never forgive him for that. Good-bye, Mrs. Helmer.

[*Exit through the hall*]

NORA [*goes to the hall door, opens it slightly and listens*]: He is going. He is not putting the letter in the box. Oh no, no! that's impossible! [*opens the door by degrees*] What is that? He is standing outside. He is not going downstairs. Is he hesitating? Can he—

[*A letter drops into the box; then* KROGSTAD'S *footsteps are heard, till they die away as he goes downstairs.* NORA *utters a stifled cry and runs across the room to the table by the sofa. A short pause.*]

NORA: In the letter-box. [*steals across to the hall door*] There it lies—Torvald, Torvald, there is no hope for us now!

[MRS. LINDE *comes in from the room on the left, carrying the dress.*]

MRS. LINDE: There, I can't see anything more to mend now. Would you like to try it on—?

NORA [*in a hoarse whisper*]: Christine, come here.

MRS. LINDE [*throwing the dress down on the sofa*]: What is the matter with you? You look so agitated!

NORA: Come here. Do you see that letter? There, look—you can see it through the glass in the letter-box.

MRS. LINDE: Yes, I see it.

NORA: That letter is from Krogstad.

MRS. LINDE: Nora—it was Krogstad who lent you the money!

NORA: Yes, and now Torvald will know all about it.

MRS. LINDE: Believe me, Nora, that's the best thing for both of you.

NORA: You don't know all. I forged a name.

MRS. LINDE: Good heavens—!

NORA: I only want to say this to you, Christine—you must be my witness.

MRS. LINDE: Your witness? What do you mean? What am I to—?

NORA: If I should go out of my mind—and it might easily happen—

MRS. LINDE: Nora!

NORA: Or if anything else should happen to me—anything, for instance, that might prevent my being here—

MRS. LINDE: Nora! Nora! you are quite out of your mind.

NORA: And if it should happen that there were someone who wanted to take all the responsibility, all the blame, you understand—

MRS. LINDE: Yes, yes—but how can you suppose—?

NORA: Then you must be my witness, that it is not true, Christine. I am not out of my mind at all; I am in my right senses now, and I tell you no one else has known anything about it; I, and I alone, did the whole thing. Remember that.

MRS. LINDE: I will, indeed. But I don't understand all this.

NORA: How should you understand it? A wonderful thing is going to happen.

MRS. LINDE: A wonderful thing?

NORA: Yes, a wonderful thing!—But it is so terrible, Christine; it *mustn't* happen, not for all the world.

MRS. LINDE: I will go at once and see Krogstad.

NORA: Don't go to him; he will do you some harm.

MRS. LINDE: There was a time when he would gladly do anything for my sake.

NORA: He?

MRS. LINDE: Where does he live?

NORA: How should I know—? Yes [*feeling in her pocket*] here is his card. But the letter, the letter—!

HELMER [*calls from his room, knocking at the door*]:   Nora!

NORA [*cries out anxiously*]:   Oh, what's that? What do you want?

HELMER: Don't be so frightened. We are not coming in; you have locked the door. Are you trying on your dress?

NORA: Yes, that's it. I look so nice, Torvald.

MRS. LINDE [*who has read the card*]:   I see he lives at the corner here.

NORA: Yes, but it's no use. It is hopeless. The letter is lying there in the box.

MRS. LINDE: And your husband keeps the key?

NORA: Yes, always.

MRS. LINDE: Krogstad must ask for his letter back unread, he must find some pretence—

NORA: But it is just at this time that Torvald generally—

MRS. LINDE: You must delay him. Go in to him in the meantime. I will come back as soon as I can.

[*She goes out hurriedly through the hall door.*]

NORA [*goes to* HELMER's *door, opens it and peeps in*]:   Torvald!

HELMER [*from the inner room*]:   Well? May I venture at last to come into my own room again? Come along, Rank, now you will see—[*halting in the doorway*] But what is this?

NORA: What is what, dear?

HELMER: Rank led me to expect a splendid transformation.

RANK [*in the doorway*]:   I understood so, but evidently I was mistaken.

NORA: Yes, nobody is to have the chance of admiring me in my dress until tomorrow.

HELMER: But, my dear Nora, you look so worn out. Have you been practising too much?

NORA: No, I have not practised at all.

HELMER: But you will need to—

NORA: Yes, indeed I shall, Torvald. But I can't get on a bit without you to help me; I have absolutely forgotten the whole thing.

HELMER: Oh, we will soon work it up again.

NORA: Yes, help me, Torvald. Promise that you will! I am so nervous about it—all the people—. You must give yourself up to me entirely this evening. Not the tiniest bit of business—you mustn't even take a pen in your hand. Will you promise, Torvald dear?

HELMER: I promise. This evening I will be wholly and absolutely at your service, you helpless little mortal. Ah, by the way, first of all I will just—

[*Goes towards the hall door.*]

NORA: What are you going to do there?

HELMER: Only see if any letters have come.

NORA: No, no! don't do that, Torvald!

HELMER: Why not?

NORA: Torvald, please don't. There is nothing there.

HELMER: Well, let me look. [*Turns to go to the letter-box.* NORA, *at the piano, plays the first bars of the Tarantella.* HELMER *stops in the doorway.*] Aha!

NORA: I can't dance to-morrow if I don't practise with you.

HELMER [*going up to her*]: Are you really so afraid of it, dear.

NORA: Yes, so dreadfully afraid of it. Let me practise at once; there is time now, before we go to dinner. Sit down and play for me, Torvald dear; criticise me, and correct me as you play.

HELMER: With great pleasure, if you wish me to.

[*Sits down at the piano.*]

NORA [*takes out of the box a tambourine and a long variegated shawl. She hastily drapes the shawl round her. Then she springs to the front of the stage and calls out*]: Now play for me! I am going to dance!

[HELMER *plays and* NORA *dances.* RANK *stands by the piano behind* HELMER *and looks on.*]

HELMER [*as he plays*]: Slower, slower!

NORA: I can't do it any other way.

HELMER: Not so violently, Nora!

NORA: This is the way.

HELMER [*stops playing*]: No, no—that is not a bit right.

NORA [*laughing and swinging the tambourine*]: Didn't I tell you so?

RANK: Let me play for her.

HELMER [*getting up*]: Yes, do. I can correct her better then.

[RANK *sits down at the piano and plays.* NORA *dances more and more wildly.* HELMER *has taken up a position beside the stove, and during her dance gives her frequent instructions. She does not seem to hear him; her hair comes down and falls over her shoulders; she pays no attention to it, but goes on dancing. Enter* MRS. LINDE.]

MRS. LINDE [*standing as if spell-bound in the doorway*]: Oh!—

NORA [*as she dances*]: Such fun, Christine!

HELMER: My dear darling Nora, you are dancing as if your life depended on it.

NORA: So it does.

HELMER: Stop, Rank; this is sheer madness. Stop, I tell you! [RANK *stops playing, and* NORA *suddenly stands still.* HELMER *goes up to her.*] I could never have believed it. You have forgotten everything I taught you.

NORA [*throwing away the tambourine*]: There, you see.

HELMER: You will want a lot of coaching.

NORA: Yes, you see how much I need it. You must coach me up to the last minute. Promise me that, Torvald!

HELMER: You can depend on me.

NORA: You must not think of anything but me, either to-day or to-morrow; you mustn't open a single letter—not even open the letter-box—

HELMER: Ah, you are still afraid of that fellow—

NORA: Yes, indeed I am.

HELMER: Nora, I can tell from your looks that there is a letter from him lying there.

NORA: I don't know; I think there is; but you must not read anything of that kind now. Nothing horrid must come between us till this is all over.

RANK [*whispers to* HELMER]: You mustn't contradict her.

HELMER [*taking her in his arms*]: The child shall have her way. But to-morrow night, after you have danced—

NORA: Then you will be free.

[MAID *appears in the doorway to the right.*]

MAID: Dinner is served, ma'am.

NORA: We will have champagne, Helen.

MAID: Very good, ma'am.

[*Exit.*]

HELMER: Hullo!—are we going to have a banquet?

NORA: Yes, a champagne banquet till the small hours. [*calls out*] And a few maca-roons, Helen—lots, just for once!

HELMER: Come, come, don't be so wild and nervous. Be my own little skylark, as you used.

NORA: Yes, dear, I will. But go in now, and you too, Doctor Rank. Christine, you must help me to do up my hair.

RANK [*whispers to* HELMER *as they go out*]: I suppose there is nothing—she is not expecting anything?

HELMER: Far from it, my dear fellow; it is simply nothing more than this childish nervousness I was telling you of.

[*They go into the right-hand room.*]

NORA: Well!

MRS. LINDE: Gone out of town.

NORA: I could tell from your face.

MRS. LINDE: He is coming home to-morrow evening. I wrote a note for him.

NORA: You should have let it alone; you must prevent nothing. After all, it is splen-did to be waiting for a wonderful thing to happen.

MRS. LINDE: What is it that you are waiting for?

NORA: Oh, you wouldn't understand. Go in to them, I will come in a moment. [MRS. LINDE *goes into the dining-room.* NORA *stands still for a little while, as if to com-pose herself. Then she looks at her watch.*] Five o'clock. Seven hours till midnight; and then four-and-twenty hours till the next midnight. Then the Tarantella will be over. Twenty-four and seven? Thirty-one hours to live.

HELMER [*from the doorway on the right*]: Where's my little skylark?

NORA [*going to him with her arms outstretched*]: Here she is!

Act 3

THE SAME SCENE. *The table has been placed in the middle of the stage, with chairs round it. A lamp is burning on the table. The door into the hall stands open. Dance music is heard in the room above.* MRS. LINDE *is sitting at the table idly turning over the leaves of a book; she tries to read, but does not seem able to collect her thoughts. Every now and then she listens intently for a sound at the outer door.*

MRS. LINDE [*looking at her watch*]: Not yet—and the time is nearly up. If only he does not—. [*listens again*] Ah, there he is. [*Goes into the hall and opens the outer door carefully. Light footsteps are heard on the stairs. She whispers.*] Come in. There is no one here.

KROGSTAD [*in the doorway*]: I found a note from you at home. What does this mean?

MRS. LINDE: It is absolutely necessary that I should have a talk with you.

KROGSTAD: Really? And is it absolutely necessary that it should be here?

MRS. LINDE: It is impossible where I live; there is no private entrance to my rooms. Come in; we are quite alone. The maid is asleep, and the Helmers are at the dance upstairs.

KROGSTAD [*coming into the room*]: Are the Helmers really at a dance to-night?

MRS. LINDE: Yes, why not?

KROGSTAD: Certainly—why not?

MRS. LINDE: Now, Nils, let us have a talk.

KROGSTAD: Can we two have anything to talk about?

MRS. LINDE: We have a great deal to talk about.

KROGSTAD: I shouldn't have thought so.

MRS. LINDE: No, you have never properly understood me.

KROGSTAD: Was there anything else to understand except what was obvious to all the world—a heartless woman jilts a man when a more lucrative chance turns up?

MRS. LINDE: Do you believe I am as absolutely heartless as all that? And do you believe that I did it with a light heart?

KROGSTAD: Didn't you?

MRS. LINDE: Nils, did you really think that?

KROGSTAD: If it were as you say, why did you write to me as you did at the time?

MRS. LINDE: I could do nothing else. As I had to break with you, it was my duty also to put an end to all that you felt for me.

KROGSTAD [*wringing his hands*]: So that was it, and all this—only for the sake of money!

MRS. LINDE: You must not forget that I had a helpless mother and two little brothers. We couldn't wait for you, Nils, your prospects seemed hopeless then.

KROGSTAD: That may be so, but you had no right to throw me over for anyone else's sake.

MRS. LINDE: Indeed I don't know. Many a time did I ask myself if I had the right to do it.

KROGSTAD [*more gently*]: When I lost you, it was as if all the solid ground went from under my feet. Look at me now—I am a shipwrecked man clinging to a bit of wreckage.

MRS. LINDE: But help may be near.

KROGSTAD: It *was* near; but then you came and stood in my way.

MRS. LINDE: Unintentionally, Nils. It was only to-day that I learnt it was your place I was going to take in the Bank.

KROGSTAD: I believe you, if you say so. But now that you know it, are you not going to give it up to me?

MRS. LINDE: No, because that would not benefit you in the least.

KROGSTAD: Oh, benefit, benefit—I would have done it whether or no.

MRS. LINDE: I have learnt to act prudently. Life, and hard, bitter necessity have taught me that.

KROGSTAD: And life has taught me not to believe in fine speeches.

MRS. LINDE: Then life has taught you something very reasonable. But deeds you must believe in?

KROGSTAD: What do you mean by that?

MRS. LINDE: You said you were like a shipwrecked man clinging to some wreckage.

KROGSTAD: I had good reason to say so.

MRS. LINDE: Well, I am like a shipwrecked woman clinging to some wreckage—no one to mourn for, no one to care for.

KROGSTAD: It was your own choice.

MRS. LINDE: There was no other choice—then.

KROGSTAD: Well, what now?

MRS. LINDE: Nils, how would it be if we two shipwrecked people could join forces?

KROGSTAD: What are you saying?

MRS. LINDE: Two on the same piece of wreckage would stand a better chance than each on their own.

KROGSTAD: Christine!

MRS. LINDE: What do you suppose brought me to town?

KROGSTAD: Do you mean that you gave me a thought?

MRS. LINDE: I could not endure life without work. All my life, as long as I can remember, I have worked, and it has been my greatest and only pleasure. But now I am quite alone in the world—my life is so dreadfully empty and I feel so forsaken. There is not the least pleasure in working for one's self. Nils, give me someone and something to work for.

KROGSTAD: I don't trust that. It is nothing but a woman's overstrained sense of generosity that prompts you to make such an offer of yourself.

MRS. LINDE: Have you ever noticed anything of the sort in me?

KROGSTAD: Could you really do it? Tell me—do you know all about my past life?

MRS. LINDE: Yes.

KROGSTAD: And do you know what they think of me here?

MRS. LINDE: You seemed to me to imply that with me you might have been quite another man.

KROGSTAD: I am certain of it.

MRS. LINDE: Is it too late now?

KROGSTAD: Christine, are you saying this deliberately? Yes, I am sure you are. I see it in your face. Have you really the courage, then—?

MRS. LINDE: I want to be a mother to someone, and your children need a mother. We two need each other. Nils, I have faith in your real character—I can dare anything together with you.

KROGSTAD [*grasps her hands*]: Thanks, thanks, Christine! Now I shall find a way to clear myself in the eyes of the world. Ah, but I forgot—

MRS. LINDE [*listening*]: Hush! The Tarantella! Go, go!

KROGSTAD: Why? What is it?

MRS. LINDE: Do you hear them up there? When that is over, we may expect them back.

KROGSTAD: Yes, yes—I will go. But it is all no use. Of course you are not aware what steps I have taken in the matter of the Helmers.

MRS. LINDE: Yes. I know all about that.

KROGSTAD: And in spite of that have you the courage to—?

MRS. LINDE: I understand very well to what lengths a man like you might be driven by despair.

KROGSTAD: If I could only undo what I have done!

MRS. LINDE: You can. Your letter is lying in the letter-box now.

KROGSTAD: Are you sure of that?

MRS. LINDE: Quite sure, but—

KROGSTAD [*with a searching look at her*]: Is that what it all means?—that you want to save your friend at any cost? Tell me frankly. Is that it?

MRS. LINDE: Nils, a woman who has once sold herself for another's sake, doesn't do it a second time.

KROGSTAD: I will ask for my letter back.

MRS. LINDE: No, no.

KROGSTAD: Yes, of course I will. I will wait here till Helmer comes; I will tell him he must give me my letter back—that it only concerns my dismissal—that he is not to read it—

MRS. LINDE: No, Nils, you must not recall your letter.

KROGSTAD: But, tell me, wasn't it for that very purpose that you asked me to meet you here?

MRS. LINDE: In my first moment of fright, it was. But twenty-four hours have elapsed since then, and in that time I have witnessed incredible things in this house. Helmer must know all about it. This unhappy secret must be disclosed; they must have a complete understanding between them, which is impossible with all this concealment and falsehood going on.

KROGSTAD: Very well, if you will take the responsibility. But there is one thing I can do in any case, and I shall do it at once.

MRS. LINDE [*listening*]: You must be quick and go! The dance is over; we are not safe a moment longer.

KROGSTAD: I will wait for you below.

MRS. LINDE: Yes, do. You must see me back to my door.

KROGSTAD: I have never had such an amazing piece of good fortune in my life.

[*Goes out through the outer door. The door between the room and the hall remains open.*]

MRS. LINDE [*tidying up the room and laying her hat and cloak ready*]: What a difference! what a difference! Someone to work for and live for—a home to bring comfort into. That I will do, indeed. I wish they would be quick and come— [*listens*] Ah, there they are now. I must put on my things.

[*Takes up her hat and cloak.* HELMER'S *and* NORA'S *voices are heard outside; a key is turned, and* HELMER *brings* NORA *almost by force into the hall. She is in an Italian costume with a large black shawl round her; he is in evening dress and a black domino which is flying open.*]

NORA [*hanging back in the doorway, and struggling with him*]: No, no, no!—don't take me in. I want to go upstairs again; I don't want to leave so early.

HELMER: But, my dearest Nora—

NORA: Please, Torvald dear—please, *please*—only an hour more.

HELMER: Not a single minute, my sweet Nora. You know that was our agreement. Come along into the room; you are catching cold standing there.

[*He brings her gently into the room, in spite of her resistance.*]

MRS. LINDE: Good evening.

NORA: Christine!

HELMER: You here, so late, Mrs. Linde?

MRS. LINDE: Yes, you must excuse me; I was so anxious to see Nora in her dress.

NORA: Have you been sitting here waiting for me?

MRS. LINDE: Yes, unfortunately I came too late, you had already gone upstairs; and I thought I couldn't go away without having seen you.

HELMER [*taking off* NORA's *shawl*]: Yes, take a good look at her. I think she is worth looking at. Isn't she charming, Mrs. Linde?

MRS. LINDE: Yes, indeed she is.

HELMER: Doesn't she look remarkably pretty? Everyone thought so at the dance. But she is terribly self-willed, this sweet little person. What are we to do with her? You will hardly believe that I had almost to bring her away by force.

NORA: Torvald, you will repent not having let me stay, even if it were only for half an hour.

HELMER: Listen to her, Mrs. Linde! She had danced her Tarantella, and it had been a tremendous success, as it deserved—although possibly the performance was a trifle too realistic—a little more so, I mean, than was strictly compatible with the limitations of art. But never mind about that! The chief thing is, she had made a success—she had made a tremendous success. Do you think I was going to let her remain there after that, and spoil the effect? No indeed! I took my charming little Capri maiden—my capricious little Capri maiden, I should say—on my arm; took one quick turn round the room; a curtsey on either side, and, as they say in novels, the beautiful apparition disappeared. An exit ought always to be effective, Mrs. Linde; but that is what I cannot make Nora understand. Pooh! this room is hot. [*throws his domino on a chair and opens the door of his room*] Hullo! it's all dark in here. Oh, of course—excuse me—.

[*He goes in and lights some candles.*]

NORA [*in a hurried and breathless whisper*]: Well?

MRS. LINDE [*in a low voice*]: I have had a talk with him.

NORA: Yes, and—

MRS. LINDE: Nora, you must tell your husband all about it.

NORA [*in an expressionless voice*]: I knew it.

MRS. LINDE: You have nothing to be afraid of as far as Krogstad is concerned; but you must tell him.

NORA: I won't tell him.

MRS. LINDE: Then the letter will.

NORA: Thank you, Christine. Now I know what I must do. Hush—!

HELMER [*coming in again*]: Well, Mrs. Linde, have you admired her?

MRS. LINDE: Yes, and now I will say good-night.

HELMER: What, already? Is this yours, this knitting?

MRS. LINDE [*taking it*]: Yes, thank you, I had very nearly forgotten it.

HELMER: So you knit?

MRS. LINDE: Of course.

HELMER: Do you know, you ought to embroider.

MRS. LINDE: Really? Why?

HELMER: Yes, it's far more becoming. Let me show you. You hold the embroidery thus in your left hand, and use the needle with the right—like this—with a long, easy sweep. Do you see?

MRS. LINDE: Yes, perhaps—

HELMER: But in the case of knitting—that can never be anything but ungraceful; look here—the arms close together, the knitting-needles going up and down— it has a sort of Chinese effect—. That was really excellent champagne they gave us.

MRS. LINDE: Well,—good-night, Nora, and don't be self-willed any more.

HELMER: That's right, Mrs. Linde.

MRS. LINDE: Good-night, Mr. Helmer.

HELMER [*accompanying her to the door*]: Good-night, good-night. I hope you will get home all right. I should be very happy to—but you haven't any great distance to go. Good-night, good-night. [*She goes out; he shuts the door after her, and comes in again.*] Ah!—at last we have got rid of her. She is a frightful bore, that woman.

NORA: Aren't you very tired, Torvald?

HELMER: No, not in the least.

NORA: Nor sleepy?

HELMER: Not a bit. On the contrary, I feel extraordinarily lively. And you?—you really look both tired and sleepy.

NORA: Yes, I am very tired. I want to go to sleep at once.

HELMER: There, you see it was quite right of me not to let you stay there any longer.

NORA: Everything you do is quite right, Torvald.

HELMER [*kissing her on the forehead*]: Now my little skylark is speaking reasonably. Did you notice what good spirits Rank was in this evening?

NORA: Really? Was he? I didn't speak to him at all.

HELMER: And I very little, but I have not for a long time seen him in such good form. [*looks for a while at her and then goes nearer to her*] It is delightful to be at home by ourselves again, to be all alone with you—you fascinating, charming little darling!

NORA: Don't look at me like that, Torvald.

HELMER: Why shouldn't I look at my dearest treasure?—at all the beauty that is mine, all my very own?

NORA [*going to the other side of the table*]: You mustn't say things like that to me to-night.

HELMER [*following her*]: You have still got the Tarantella in your blood, I see. And it makes you more captivating than ever. Listen—the guests are beginning to go now. [*in a lower voice*] Nora—soon the whole house will be quiet.

NORA: Yes, I hope so.

HELMER: Yes, my own darling Nora. Do you know, when I am out at a party with you like this, why I speak so little to you, keep away from you, and only send a stolen glance in your direction now and then?—do you know why I do that? It is because I make believe to myself that we are secretly in love, and you are my secretly promised bride, and that no one suspects there is anything between us.

NORA: Yes, yes—I know very well your thoughts are with me all the time.

HELMER: And when we are leaving, and I am putting the shawl over your beautiful young shoulders—on your lovely neck—then I imagine that you are my young bride and that we have just come from the wedding, and I am bringing you for the first time into our home—to be alone with you for the first time—quite alone with my shy little darling! All this evening I have longed for nothing but you. When I watched the seductive figures of the Tarantella, my blood was on fire; I could endure it no longer, and that was why I brought you down so early—

NORA: Go away, Torvald! You must let me go. I won't—

HELMER: What's that? You're joking, my little Nora! You won't—you won't? Am I not your husband—?

[*A knock is heard at the outer door.*]

NORA [*starting*]: Did you hear—?

HELMER [*going into the hall*]: Who is it?

RANK [*outside*]: It is I. May I come in for a moment?

HELMER [*in a fretful whisper*]: Oh, what does he want now? [*aloud*] Wait a minute!
[*unlocks the door*] Come, that's kind of you not to pass by our door.

RANK: I thought I heard your voice, and felt as if I should like to look in. [*with a
swift glance round*] Ah, yes!—these dear familiar rooms. You are very happy
and cosy in here, you two.

HELMER: It seems to me that you looked after yourself pretty well upstairs too.

RANK: Excellently. Why shouldn't I? Why shouldn't one enjoy everything in this
world?—at any rate as much as one can, and as long as one can. The wine was
capital—

HELMER: Especially the champagne.

RANK: So you noticed that too? It is almost incredible how much I managed to put
away!

NORA: Torvald drank a great deal of champagne tonight, too.

RANK: Did he?

NORA: Yes, and he is always in such good spirits afterwards.

RANK: Well, why should one not enjoy a merry evening after a well-spent day?

HELMER: Well spent? I am afraid I can't take credit for that.

RANK [*clapping him on the back*]: But I can, you know!

NORA: Doctor Rank, you must have been occupied with some scientific investiga-
tion to-day.

RANK: Exactly.

HELMER: Just listen!—little Nora talking about scientific investigations!

NORA: And may I congratulate you on the result?

RANK: Indeed you may.

NORA: Was it favourable, then?

RANK: The best possible, for both doctor and patient—certainty.

NORA [*quickly and searchingly*]: Certainty?

RANK: Absolute certainty. So wasn't I entitled to make a merry evening of it after
that?

NORA: Yes, you certainly were, Doctor Rank.

HELMER: I think so too, so long as you don't have to pay for it in the morning.

RANK: Oh well, one can't have anything in this life without paying for it.

NORA: Doctor Rank—are you fond of fancy-dress balls?

RANK: Yes, if there is a fine lot of pretty costumes.

NORA: Tell me—what shall we two wear at the next?

HELMER: Little featherbrain!—are you thinking of the next already?

RANK: We two? Yes, I can tell you. You shall go as a good fairy—

HELMER: Yes, but what do you suggest as an appropriate costume for that?

RANK: Let your wife go dressed just as she is in everyday life.

HELMER: That was really very prettily turned. But can't you tell us what you will be?

RANK: Yes, my dear friend, I have quite made up my mind about that.

HELMER: Well?

RANK: At the next fancy dress ball I shall be invisible.

HELMER: That's a good joke!

RANK: There is a big black hat—have you never heard of hats that make you invisible?
If you put one on, no one can see you.

HELMER [*suppressing a smile*]: Yes, you are quite right.

RANK: But I am clean forgetting what I came for. Helmer, give me a cigar—one of
the dark Havanas.

HELMER: With the greatest pleasure [*offers him his case*].

RANK [*takes a cigar and cuts off the end*]: Thanks.

NORA [*striking a match*]: Let me give you a light.

RANK: Thank you. [*She holds the match for him to light his cigar.*] And now good-bye!

HELMER: Good-bye, good-bye, dear old man!

NORA: Sleep well, Doctor Rank.

RANK: Thank you for that wish.

NORA: Wish me the same.

RANK: You? Well, if you want me to: sleep well! And thanks for the light.

[*He nods to them both and goes out.*]

HELMER [*in a subdued voice*]: He has drunk more than he ought.

NORA [*absently*]: Maybe. [HELMER *takes a bunch of keys out of his pocket and goes into the hall.*] Torvald! what are you going to do there?

HELMER: Empty the letter-box; it is quite full; there will be no room to put the newspaper in to-morrow morning.

NORA: Are you going to work to-night?

HELMER: You know quite well I'm not. What is this? Some one has been at the lock.

NORA: At the lock—?

HELMER: Yes, someone has. What can it mean? I should never have thought the maid—. Here is a broken hairpin. Nora, it is one of yours.

NORA [*quickly*]: Then it must have been the children—

HELMER: Then you must get them out of those ways. There, at last I have got it open. [*Takes out the contents of the letter-box, and calls to the kitchen.*] Helen!— Helen, put out the light over the front door. [*Goes back into the room and shuts the door into the hall. He holds out his hand full of letters.*] Look at that—look what a heap of them there are. [*turning them over*] What on earth is that?

NORA [*at the window*]: The letter—No! Torvald, no!

HELMER: Two cards—of Rank's.

NORA: Of Doctor Rank's?

HELMER [*looking at them*]: Doctor Rank. They were on the top. He must have put them in when he went out.

NORA: Is there anything written on them?

HELMER: There is a black cross over the name. Look there—what an uncomfortable idea! It looks as if he were announcing his own death.

NORA: It is just what he is doing.

HELMER: What? Do you know anything about it? Has he said anything to you?

NORA: Yes. He told me that when the cards came it would be his leave-taking from us. He means to shut himself up and die.

HELMER: My poor old friend. Certainly I knew we should not have him very long with us. But so soon! And so he hides himself away like a wounded animal.

NORA: If it has to happen, it is best it should be without a word—don't you think so, Torvald?

HELMER [*walking up and down*]: He had so grown into our lives. I can't think of him as having gone out of them. He, with his sufferings and his loneliness, was like a cloudy background to our sunlit happiness. Well, perhaps it is best so. For him, anyway. [*standing still*] And perhaps for us too, Nora. We two are thrown quite upon each other now. [*puts his arms round her*] My darling wife, I don't feel as if I could hold you tight enough. Do you know, Nora, I have often wished that you might be threatened by some great danger, so that I might risk my life's blood, and everything, for your sake.

NORA [*disengages herself, and says firmly and decidedly*]: Now you must read your
    letters, Torvald.
HELMER: No, no; not to-night. I want to be with you, my darling wife.
NORA: With the thought of your friend's death—
HELMER: You are right, it has affected us both. Something ugly has come between
    us—the thought of the horrors of death. We must try and rid our minds of that.
    Until then—we will each go to our own room.
NORA [*hanging on his neck*]: Good-night, Torvald—Good-night!
HELMER [*kissing her on the forehead*]: Good-night, my little singing-bird. Sleep
    sound, Nora. Now I will read my letters through.
    [*He takes his letters and goes into his room, shutting the door after him.*]

NORA [*gropes distractedly about, seizes* HELMER's *domino, throws it round her, while
    she says in quick, hoarse, spasmodic whispers*]: Never to see him again. Never!
    Never! [*puts her shawl over her head*] Never to see my children again either—
    never again. Never! Never!—Ah! the icy, black water—the unfathomable
    depths—If only it were over! He has got it now—now he is reading it. Good-
    by, Torvald and my children!

    [*She is about to rush out through the hall, when* HELMER *opens his door hurriedly
and stands with an open letter in his hand.*]

HELMER: Nora!
NORA: Ah!—
HELMER: What is this? Do you know what is in this letter?
NORA: Yes, I know. Let me go! Let me get out!
HELMER [*holding her back*]: Where are you going?
NORA [*trying to get free*]: You shan't save me, Torvald!
HELMER [*reeling*]: True? Is this true, that I read here? Horrible! No, no—it is impos-
    sible that it can be true.
NORA: It is true. I have loved you above everything else in the world.
HELMER: Oh, don't let us have any silly excuses.
NORA [*taking a step towards him*]: Torvald—!
HELMER: Miserable creature—what have you done?
NORA: Let me go. You shall not suffer for my sake. You shall not take it upon
    yourself.
HELMER: No tragedy airs, please. [*locks the hall door*] Here you shall stay and give
    me an explanation. Do you understand what you have done? Answer me? Do
    you understand what you have done?
NORA [*looks steadily at him and says with a growing look of coldness in her face*]: Yes,
    now I am beginning to understand thoroughly.
HELMER [*walking about the room*]: What a horrible awakening! All these eight
    years—she who was my joy and pride—a hypocrite, a liar—worse, worse—
    a criminal! The unutterable ugliness of it all! For shame! For shame! [NORA *is
    silent and looks steadily at him. He stops in front of her.*] I ought to have
    suspected that something of the sort would happen. I ought to have foreseen
    it. All your father's want of principle—be silent!—all your father's want of
    principle has come out in you. No religion, no morality, no sense of duty—.
    How I am punished for having winked at what he did! I did it for your sake,
    and this is how you repay me.
NORA: Yes, that's just it.
HELMER: Now you have destroyed all my happiness. You have ruined all my future.
    It is horrible to think of! I am in the power of an unscrupulous man; he can

do what he likes with me, ask anything he likes of me, give me any orders he pleases— I dare not refuse. And I must sink to such miserable depths because of a thoughtless woman!

NORA: When I am out of the way, you will be free.

HELMER: No fine speeches, please. Your father had always plenty of those ready, too. What good would it be to me if you were out of the way, as you say? Not the slightest. He can make the affair known everywhere; and if he does, I may be falsely suspected of having been a party to your criminal action. Very likely people will think I was behind it all—that it was I who prompted you! And I have to thank you for all this—you whom I have cherished during the whole of our married life. Do you understand now what it is you have done for me?

NORA [*coldly and quietly*]: Yes.

HELMER: It is so incredible that I can't take it in. But we must come to some understanding. Take off that shawl. Take it off, I tell you. I must try and appease him some way or another. The matter must be hushed up at any cost. And as for you and me, it must appear as if everything between us were just as before— but naturally only in the eyes of the world. You will still remain in my house, that is a matter of course. But I shall not allow you to bring up the children; I dare not trust them to you. To think that I should be obliged to say so to one whom I have loved so dearly, and whom I still—. No, that is all over. From this moment happiness is not the question; all that concerns us is to save the remains, the fragments, the appearance—

[*A ring is heard at the front-door bell.*]

HELMER [*with a start*]: What is that? So late! Can the worst—? Can he—? Hide yourself, Nora. Say you are ill.

[NORA *stands motionless.* HELMER *goes and unlocks the hall door.*]

MAID [*half-dressed, comes to the door*]: A letter for the mistress.

HELMER: Give it to me. [*takes the letter, and shuts the door*] Yes, it is from him. You shall not have it; I will read it myself.

NORA: Yes, read it.

HELMER [*standing by the lamp*]: I scarcely have the courage to do it. It may mean ruin for both of us. No, I must know. [*tears open the letter, runs his eye over a few lines, looks at a paper enclosed and gives a shout of joy*] Nora! [*She looks at him questioningly.*] Nora!—No, I must read it once again—. Yes, it is true! I am saved! Nora, I am saved!

NORA: And I?

HELMER: You too, of course; we are both saved, both you and I. Look, he sends you your bond back. He says he regrets and repents—that a happy change in his life—never mind what he says! We are saved, Nora! No one can do anything to you. Oh, Nora, Nora!—no, first I must destroy these hateful things. Let me see—. [*takes a look at the bond*] No, no, I won't look at it. The whole thing shall be nothing but a bad dream to me. [*tears up the bond and both letters, throws them all into the stove, and watches them burn*] There—now it doesn't exist any longer. He says that since Christmas Eve you—. These must have been three dreadful days for you, Nora.

NORA: I have fought a hard fight these three days.

HELMER: And suffered agonies, and seen no way out but—. No, we won't call any of the horrors to mind. We will only shout with joy, and keep saying "It's all over! It's all over!" Listen to me, Nora. You don't seem to realise that it is all over. What is this?—such a cold, set face! My poor little Nora, I quite understand;

you don't feel as if you could believe that I have forgiven you. But it is true, Nora, I swear it; I have forgiven you everything. I know that what you did, you did out of love for me.

NORA: That is true.

HELMER: You have loved me as a wife ought to love her husband. Only you had not sufficient knowledge to judge of the means you used. But do you suppose you are any the less dear to me, because you don't understand how to act on your own responsibility? No, no; only lean on me; I will advise you and direct you. I should not be a man if this womanly helplessness did not just give you a double attractiveness in my eyes. You must not think any more about the hard things I said in my first moment of consternation, when I thought everything was going to overwhelm me. I have forgiven you, Nora; I swear to you I have forgiven you.

NORA: Thank you for your forgiveness.

[*She goes out through the door to the right.*]

HELMER: No, don't go—. [*looks in*] What are you doing in there?

NORA [*from within*]:   Taking off my fancy dress.

HELMER [*standing at the open door*]:   Yes, do. Try and calm yourself, and make your mind easy again, my frightened little singing-bird. Be at rest, and feel secure; I have broad wings to shelter you under. [*walks up and down by the door*] How warm and cosy our home is, Nora. Here is shelter for you; here I will protect you like a hunted dove that I have saved from a hawk's claws. I will bring peace to your poor beating heart. It will come, little by little, Nora, believe me. Tomorrow morning you will look upon it all quite differently; soon everything will be just as it was before. Very soon you won't need me to assure you that I have forgiven you; you will yourself feel the certainty that I have done so. Can you suppose I should ever think of such a thing as repudiating you, or even reproaching you? You have no idea what a true man's heart is like, Nora. There is something so indescribably sweet and satisfying, to a man, in the knowledge that he has forgiven his wife—forgiven her freely, and with all his heart. It seems as if that had made her, as it were, doubly his own; he has given her a new life, so to speak; and she has in a way become both wife and child to him. So you shall be for me after this, my little scared, helpless darling. Have no anxiety about anything, Nora; only be frank and open with me, and I will serve as will and conscience both to you—. What is this? Not gone to bed? Have you changed your things?

NORA [*in everyday dress*]:   Yes, Torvald, I have changed my things now.

HELMER: But what for?—so late as this.

NORA: I shall not sleep to-night.

HELMER: But, my dear Nora—

NORA [*looking at her watch*]:   It is not so very late. Sit down here, Torvald. You and I have much to say to one another.

[*She sits down at one side of the table.*]

HELMER: Nora—what is this?—this cold, set face?

NORA: Sit down. It will take some time; I have a lot to talk over with you.

HELMER [*sits down at the opposite side of the table*]:   You alarm me, Nora!—and I don't understand you.

NORA: No, that is just it. You don't understand me, and I have never understood you either—before to-night. No, you mustn't interrupt me. You must simply listen to what I say. Torvald, this is a settling of accounts.

HELMER: What do you mean by that?

Torvald Helmer (Sam Waterston) begs Nora (Liv Ullmann) to reconsider her decision to leave home in the Joseph Papp New York Shakespeare Festival production (1995) of *A Doll's House* (director, Tormod Skagestad).

NORA [*after a short silence*]: Isn't there one thing that strikes you as strange in our sitting here like this?

HELMER: What is that?

NORA: We have been married now eight years. Does it not occur to you that this is the first time we two, you and I, husband and wife, have had a serious conversation?

HELMER: What do you mean by serious?

NORA: In all these eight years—longer than that—from the very beginning of our acquaintance, we have never exchanged a word on any serious subject.

HELMER: Was it likely that I would be continually and for ever telling you about worries that you could not help me to bear?

NORA: I am not speaking about business matters. I say that we have never sat down in earnest together to try and get at the bottom of anything.

HELMER: But, dearest Nora, would it have been any good to you?

NORA: That is just it; you have never understood me. I have been greatly wronged, Torvald—first by papa and then by you.

HELMER: What! By us two—by us two, who have loved you better than anyone else in the world?

NORA [*shaking her head*]: You have never loved me. You have only thought it pleasant to be in love with me.

HELMER: Nora, what do I hear you saying?

NORA: It is perfectly true, Torvald. When I was at home with papa, he told me his opinion about everything, and so I had the same opinions; and if I differed from him I concealed the fact, because he would not have liked it. He called me his doll-child, and he played with me just as I used to play with my dolls. And when I came to live with you—

HELMER: What sort of an expression is that to use about our marriage?

NORA [*undisturbed*]: I mean that I was simply transferred from papa's hands into yours. You arranged everything according to your own taste, and so I got the same tastes as you—or else I pretended to, I am really not quite sure which— I think sometimes the one and sometimes the other. When I look back on it, it seems to me as if I had been living here like a poor woman—just from hand to mouth. I have existed merely to perform tricks for you, Torvald. But you would have it so. You and papa have committed a great sin against me. It is your fault that I have made nothing of my life.

HELMER: How unreasonable and how ungrateful you are, Nora! Have you not been happy here?

NORA: No, I have never been happy. I thought I was, but it has never really been so.

HELMER: Not—not happy!

NORA: No, only merry. And you have always been so kind to me. But our home has been nothing but a playroom. I have been your doll-wife, just as at home I was papa's doll-child; and here the children have been my dolls. I thought it great fun when you played with me, just as they thought it great fun when I played with them. That is what our marriage has been, Torvald.

HELMER: There is some truth in what you say—exaggerated and strained as your view of it is. But for the future it shall be different. Playtime shall be over, and lesson-time shall begin.

NORA: Whose lessons? Mine, or the children's?

HELMER: Both yours and the children's, my darling Nora.

NORA: Alas, Torvald, you are not the man to educate me into being a proper wife for you.

HELMER: And you can say that!

NORA: And I—how am I fitted to bring up the children?

HELMER: Nora!

NORA: Didn't you say so yourself a little while ago—that you dare not trust me to bring them up?

HELMER: In a moment of anger! Why do you pay any heed to that?

NORA: Indeed, you were perfectly right. I am not fit for the task. There is another task I must undertake first. I must try and educate myself—you are not the man to help me in that. I must do that for myself. And that is why I am going to leave you now.

HELMER [*springing up*]: What do you say?

NORA: I must stand quite alone, if I am to understand myself and everything about me. It is for that reason that I cannot remain with you any longer.

HELMER: Nora! Nora!

NORA: I am going away from here now, at once. I am sure Christine will take me in for the night—

HELMER: You are out of your mind! I won't allow it! I forbid you!

NORA: It is no use forbidding me anything any longer. I will take with me what belongs to myself. I will take nothing from you, either now or later.

HELMER: What sort of madness is this!

NORA: To-morrow I shall go home—I mean, to my old home. It will be easiest for me to find something to do there.

HELMER: You blind, foolish woman!

NORA: I must try and get some sense, Torvald.

HELMER: To desert your home, your husband and your children! And you don't consider what people will say!

NORA: I cannot consider that at all. I only know that it is necessary for me.

HELMER: It's shocking. This is how you would neglect your most sacred duties.

NORA: What do you consider my most sacred duties?

HELMER: Do I need to tell you that? Are they not your duties to your husband and your children?

NORA: I have other duties just as sacred.

HELMER: That you have not. What duties could those be?

NORA: Duties to myself.

HELMER: Before all else, you are a wife and a mother.

NORA: I don't believe that any longer. I believe that before all else I am a reasonable human being, just as you are—or, at all events, that I must try and become one. I know quite well, Torvald, that most people would think you right, and that views of that kind are to be found in books; but I can no longer content myself with what most people say, or with what is found in books. I must think over things for myself and get to understand them.

HELMER: Can you not understand your place in your own home? Have you not a reliable guide in such matters as that? have you no religion?

NORA: I am afraid, Torvald, I do not exactly know what religion is.

HELMER: What are you saying?

NORA: I know nothing but what the clergyman said when I went to be confirmed. He told us that religion was this, and that, and the other. When I am away from all this, and am alone, I will look into that matter too. I will see if what the clergyman said is true, or at all events if it is true for me.

HELMER: This is unheard of in a girl of your age! But if religion cannot lead you aright, let me try and awaken your conscience. I suppose you have some moral sense? Or—answer me—am I to think you have none?

NORA: I assure you, Torvald, that is not an easy question to answer. I really don't know. The thing perplexes me altogether. I only know that you and I look at it in quite a different light. I am learning, too, that the law is quite another thing from what I supposed; but I find it impossible to convince myself that the law is right. According to it a woman has no right to spare her old dying father, or to save her husband's life. I can't believe that.

HELMER: You talk like a child. You don't understand the conditions of the world in which you live.

NORA: No, I don't. But now I am going to try. I am going to see if I can make out who is right, the world or I.

HELMER: You are ill, Nora; you are delirious; I almost think you are out of your mind.

NORA: I have never felt my mind so clear and certain as to-night.

HELMER: And is it with a clear and certain mind that you forsake your husband and your children?

NORA: Yes, it is.

HELMER: Then there is only one possible explanation.

NORA: What is that?

HELMER: You do not love me any more.

NORA: No, that is just it.

HELMER: Nora!—and you can say that?

NORA: It gives me great pain, Torvald, for you have always been so kind to me, but I cannot help it. I do not love you any more.

HELMER [*regaining his composure*]: Is that a clear and certain conviction too?

NORA: Yes, absolutely clear and certain. That is the reason why I will not stay here any longer.

HELMER: And can you tell me what I have done to forfeit your love?

NORA: Yes, indeed I can. It was to-night, when the wonderful thing did not happen; then I saw you were not the man I had thought you.

HELMER: Explain yourself better—I don't understand you.

NORA: I have waited so patiently for eight years; for, goodness knows, I knew very well that wonderful things don't happen every day. Then this horrible misfortune came upon me; and then I felt quite certain that the wonderful thing was going to happen at last. When Krogstad's letter was lying out there, never for a moment did I imagine that you would consent to accept this man's conditions. I was so absolutely certain that you would say to him: Publish the thing to the whole world. And when that was done—

HELMER: Yes, what then?—when I had exposed my wife to shame and disgrace?

NORA: When that was done, I was so absolutely certain, you would come forward and take everything upon yourself, and say: I am the guilty one.

HELMER: Nora—!

NORA: You mean that I would never have accepted such a sacrifice on your part? No, of course not. But what would my assurances have been worth against yours? That was the wonderful thing which I hoped for and feared; and it was to prevent that, that I wanted to kill myself.

HELMER: I would gladly work night and day for you, Nora—bear sorrow and want for your sake. But no man would sacrifice his honour for the one he loves.

NORA: It is a thing hundreds of thousands of women have done.

HELMER: Oh, you think and talk like a heedless child.

NORA: Maybe. But you neither think nor talk like the man I could bind myself to. As soon as your fear was over—and it was not fear for what threatened me, but for what might happen to you—when the whole thing was past, as far as you were concerned it was exactly as if nothing at all had happened. Exactly as before, I was your little skylark, your doll, which you would in future treat with doubly gentle care, because it was so brittle and fragile. [*getting up*] Torvald— it was then it dawned upon me that for eight years I had been living here with a strange man, and had borne him three children—. Oh, I can't bear to think of it! I could tear myself into little bits!

HELMER [*sadly*]: I see, I see. An abyss has opened between us—there is no denying it. But, Nora, would it not be possible to fill it up?

NORA: As I am now, I am no wife for you.

HELMER: I have it in me to become a different man.

NORA: Perhaps—if your doll is taken away from you.

HELMER: But to part!—to part from you! No, no, Nora, I can't understand that idea.

NORA [*going out to the right*]: That makes it all the more certain that it must be done.

[*She comes back with her cloak and hat and a small bag which she puts on a chair by the table.*]

HELMER: Nora, Nora, not now! Wait till to-morrow.

NORA [*putting on her cloak*]: I cannot spend the night in a strange man's room.

HELMER: But can't we live here like brother and sister—?

NORA [*putting on her hat*]: You know very well that would not last long. [*puts the shawl round her*] Good-bye, Torvald. I won't see the little ones. I know they are in better hands than mine. As I am now, I can be of no use to them.

HELMER: But some day, Nora—some day?

NORA: How can I tell? I have no idea what is going to become of me.

HELMER: But you are my wife, whatever becomes of you.

NORA: Listen, Torvald. I have heard that when a wife deserts her husband's house, as I am doing now, he is legally freed from all obligations towards her. In any case I set you free from all your obligations. You are not to feel yourself bound in the slightest way, any more than I shall. There must be perfect freedom on both sides. See here is your ring back. Give me mine.

HELMER: That too?

NORA: That too.

HELMER: Here it is.

NORA: That's right. Now it is all over. I have put the keys here. The maids know all about everything in the house—better than I do. To-morrow, after I have left her, Christine will come here and pack up my own things that I brought with me from home. I will have them sent after me.

HELMER: All over! All over!—Nora, shall you never think of me again?

NORA: I know I shall often think of you and the children and this house.

HELMER: May I write to you, Nora?

NORA: No—never. You must not do that.

HELMER: But at least let me send you—

NORA: Nothing—nothing—

HELMER: Let me help you if you are in want.

NORA: No. I can receive nothing from a stranger.

HELMER: Nora—can I never be anything more than a stranger to you?

NORA [*taking her bag*]: Ah, Torvald, the most wonderful thing of all would have to happen.

HELMER: Tell me what that would be!

NORA: Both you and I would have to be so changed that—. Oh, Torvald, I don't believe any longer in wonderful things happening.

HELMER: But I will believe in it. Tell me? So changed that—?

NORA: That our life together would be a real wedlock. Good-bye.

[*She goes out through the hall.*]

HELMER [*sinks down on a chair at the door and buries his face in his hands*]: Nora! Nora! [*looks round, and rises*] Empty. She is gone. [*A hope flashes across his mind.*] The most wonderful thing of all—?

[*The sound of a door slamming is heard from below.*]

[1879]

Joining the Conversation: Critical Thinking and Writing

1. Near the beginning of the play, how does Mrs. Linde's presence help to define Nora's character? How does Nora's response to Krogstad's entrance tell us something about Nora?

2. What does Dr. Rank contribute to the play? If he were eliminated, what would be lost?

3. Can it be argued that although at the end Nora goes out to achieve self-realization, her abandonment of her children—especially to Torvald's loathsome conventional morality—is a crime?

4. Why does Nora leave the children? She seems to imply, in some passages, that because she forged a signature she is unfit to bring them up. But do you agree with her?

5. Michael Meyer, in his splendid biography *Henrik Ibsen,* says that the play is not so much about women's rights as about "the need of every individual to find out the kind of person he or she really is, and to strive to become that person." What evidence can you offer to support or refute this interpretation?

6. In *The Quintessence of Ibsenism* Bernard Shaw says that Ibsen, reacting against a common theatrical preference for strange situations,

   > saw that . . . the more familiar the situation, the more interesting the play. Shakespeare had put ourselves on the stage but not our situations. Our uncles seldom murder our fathers and . . . marry our mothers. . . . Ibsen . . . gives us not only ourselves, but ourselves in our own situations. The things that happen to his stage figures are things that happen to us. One consequence is that his plays are much more important to us than Shakespeare's. Another is that they are capable both of hurting us cruelly and of filling us with excited hopes of escape from idealistic tyrannies, and with visions of intenser life in the future.

   How much of this do you believe? Support your response with reasons.

MyLiteratureLab® *For additional resources for* A Doll's House, *log in to* www.myliteraturelab.com *where you will find a Longman Lecture and a Comprehension Quiz, as well as an About the Author, Bibliography, Links, and Critical Overview for Ibsen (Under Student Resources).*

Chapter Overview: Looking Backward/Looking Forward

1. Do you think it is beneficial for men and women to be together in the same college classroom? Can you recall a class discussion or debate when you were aware of sharp differences between how women and men were responding to an issue? Are there subjects that you believe are best taught in a single-sex environment?

2. Plays, films, and TV shows often make use of the plot device of a man transformed into a woman, or of a woman who disguises herself as a man, and so

on. Do you think you would gain from such an experience? How long would you like this experience to last?

3. What does it mean to be a feminist? Has feminism gone too far? Can a man be a feminist, or is that impossible?

4. Do you think that men and women should be free to enter into whatever kind of relationship, married or unmarried (that is, living together), gay or straight, they desire? Or is it your view that the government should play a leading role in defining proper and improper relationships?

5. Can you identify a literary work, or a film, that only a man or a woman could understand or appreciate?

6. Who is better at keeping a secret, a man or a woman?

7. Many colleges and universities now offer courses in gay and lesbian literature. Have you taken such a course yourself? What did you learn from it? If you have not taken such a course, do you intend to?

8. If a straight student in a literature course is assigned to write a paper about a book by a gay author, but then tells the teacher that he or she disapproves of homosexuality on religious grounds, should this student be excused from having to do the paper?

CHAPTER 24

Innocence and Experience

SHORT VIEWS

Children, I grant, should be innocent; but when the epithet is applied to men, or women, it is but a civil term for weakness.
Mary Wollstonecraft

People who shut their eyes to reality simply invite their own destruction, and anyone who insists on remaining in a state of innocence long after that innocence is dead turns himself into a monster.
James Baldwin

"Experience iz a good schoolmaster," but reason iz a better one.
Josh Billings

Experience keeps a dear school, but Fools will learn in no other.
Ben Franklin

A moment's insight is sometimes worth a life's experience.
Oliver Wendell Holmes

What is the good of drawing conclusions from experience? I don't deny we sometimes draw the right conclusions, but don't we just as often draw the wrong ones?
G. C. Lichtenberg

The power to guess the unseen from the seen, to trace the implications of things, to judge the whole piece by the pattern, the condition of feeling life in general so completely that you are well on your way to knowing any particular corner of it—this cluster of gifts may almost be said to constitute experience.
Henry James

We should be careful to get out of an experience only the wisdom that is in it—and stop there; lest we be like the cat that sits down on a hot stove-lid. She will never sit down on a hot stove-lid again—and that is well; but also she will never sit down on a cold one anymore.
Mark Twain

Joining the Conversation: Critical Thinking and Writing

1. Select a quotation that especially appeals to you, and make it the focus of an essay of about 500 words.
2. Take two of the passages—perhaps one that you especially like and one that you think is wrongheaded—and write a dialogue of about 500 words in which the two authors converse or argue. They may each try to convince the other, or they may find that to some degree they share views and they may then work out a statement that both can accept. If you do take the first position—that one writer is on the correct track but the other is utterly mistaken—try to be fair to the view that you think is mistaken. (As an experiment in critical thinking, imagine that you accept it, and make the best case for it that you possibly can.)

ESSAY

GEORGE ORWELL

George Orwell (1903–50), an Englishman, adopted this name; he was born Eric Blair, in India. He was educated at Eton, in England, but in 1921 he went to Burma (now Myanmar), where he served for five years as a police officer. He then returned to Europe, doing odd jobs while writing novels and stories. In 1936 he fought in the Spanish Civil War on the side of the Republicans, an experience reported in Homage to Catalonia *(1938). Orwell is best known for his novels* Animal Farm *(1945) and* Nineteen Eighty-Four *(1949).*

Shooting an Elephant

In Moulmein, in Lower Burma, I was hated by large numbers of people—the only time in my life that I have been important enough for this to happen to me. I was sub-divisional police officer of the town, and in an aimless, petty kind of way anti-European feeling was very bitter. No one had the guts to raise a riot, but if a European woman went through the bazaars alone somebody would probably spit betel juice over her dress. As a police officer I was an obvious target and was baited whenever it seemed safe to do so. When a nimble Burman tripped me up on the football field and the referee (another Burman) looked the other way, the crowd yelled with hideous laughter. This happened more than once. In the end the sneering yellow faces of young men that met me everywhere, the insults hooted after me when I was at a safe distance, got badly on my nerves. The young Buddhist priests were the worst of all. There were several thousands of them in the town and none of them seemed to have anything to do except stand on street corners and jeer at Europeans.

All this was perplexing and upsetting. For at that time I had already made up my mind that imperialism was an evil thing and the sooner I chucked up my job and got out of it the better. Theoretically—and secretly, of course—I was all for the Burmese and all against their oppressors, the British. As for the job I was doing, I hated it more bitterly than I can perhaps make clear. In a job like that you see the dirty work of the Empire at close quarters. The wretched prisoners huddling in the stinking cages of the lockups, the grey, cowed faces of the long-term convicts, the scarred buttocks of the men who had been flogged with bamboos—all these oppressed me with an intolerable sense of guilt. But I could get nothing into perspective. I was young and ill-educated and I had had to think out my problems in the utter silence that is imposed on every Englishman in the East. I did not even know that the British Empire is dying, still less did I know that it is a great deal better than the younger empires that are going to supplant it. All I knew was that I was stuck between my hatred of the empire I served and my rage against the evil-spirited little beasts who tried to make my job impossible. With one part of my mind I thought of the British Raj as an unbreakable tyranny, as something clamped down, in *saecula saeculorum,*[1] upon the will of prostrate peoples; with another part I thought that the greatest joy in the world would be to drive a bayonet into a Buddhist priest's guts. Feelings like these are the normal by-products of imperialism; ask any Anglo-Indian official, if you can catch him off duty.

One day something happened which in a roundabout way was enlightening. It was a tiny incident in itself, but it gave me a better glimpse than I had had before of the real nature of imperialism—the real motives for which despotic governments act. Early one morning the sub-inspector at a police station at the other end of the town rang me up on the 'phone and said that an elephant was ravaging the bazaar. Would I please come and do something about it? I did not know what I could do, but I wanted to see what was happening and I got onto a pony and started out. I took my rifle, an old .44 Winchester and much too small to kill an elephant, but I thought the noise might be useful *in terrorem.*[2] Various Burmans stopped me on the way and told me about the elephant's doings. It was not, of course, a wild elephant, but a tame one which had gone "must." It had been chained up, as tame elephants always are when their attack of "must" is due, but on the previous night it had broken its chain and escaped. Its mahout, the only person who could manage it when it was in that state, had set out in pursuit, but had taken the wrong direction and was now twelve hours' journey away, and in the morning the elephant had suddenly reappeared in the town. The Burmese population had no weapons and were quite helpless against it. It had already destroyed somebody's bamboo hut, killed a cow and raided some fruit-stalls and devoured the stock; also it had met the municipal rubbish van and, when the driver jumped out and took to his heels, had turned the van over and inflicted violences upon it.

The Burmese sub-inspector and some Indian constables were waiting for me in the quarter where the elephant had been seen. It was a very poor quarter, a labyrinth of squalid bamboo huts, thatched with palmleaf, winding all over a steep hillside. I remember that it was a cloudy, stuffy morning at the beginning of the rains. We began questioning the people as to where the elephant had gone and, as usual, failed to get any definite information. That is invariably the case in the East; a story always sounds clear enough at a distance, but the nearer you get to the scene of events the vaguer it becomes. Some of the people said that the elephant had gone in one direction, some said that he had gone in another, some professed not even to have heard of any elephant. I had almost made up my mind that the whole story was a pack of lies, when we heard yells a little distance away. There was a loud, scandalized cry of "Go away, child! Go away this instant!" and an old woman with a switch in her hand came round the corner of a hut, violently

---

[1]*Saecula saeculorum* Latin, "For world without end."   [2]*in terrorem* as a warning.

shooing away a crowd of naked children. Some more women followed, clicking their tongues and exclaiming; evidently there was something that the children ought not to have seen. I rounded the hut and saw a man's dead body sprawling in the mud. He was an Indian, a black Dravidian coolie, almost naked, and he could not have been dead many minutes. The people said that the elephant had come suddenly upon him round the corner of the hut, caught him with its trunk, put its foot on his back and ground him into the earth. This was the rainy season and the ground was soft, and his face had scored a trench a foot deep and a couple of yards long. He was lying on his belly with arms crucified and head sharply twisted to one side. His face was coated with mud, the eyes wide open, the teeth bared and grinning with an expression of unendurable agony. (Never tell me, by the way, that the dead look peaceful. Most of the corpses I have seen look devilish.) The friction of the great beast's foot had stripped the skin from his back as neatly as one skins a rabbit. As soon as I saw the dead man I sent an orderly to a friend's house nearby to borrow an elephant rifle. I had already sent back the pony, not wanting it to go mad with fright and throw me if it smelt the elephant.

5   The orderly came back in a few minutes with a rifle and five cartridges, and meanwhile some Burmans had arrived and told us that the elephant was in the paddy fields below, only a few hundred yards away. As I started forward practically the whole population of the quarter flocked out of the houses and followed me. They had seen the rifle and were all shouting excitedly that I was going to shoot the elephant. They had not shown much interest in the elephant when he was merely ravaging their homes, but it was different now that he was going to be shot. It was a bit of fun to them, as it would be to an English crowd; besides they wanted the meat. It made me vaguely uneasy. I had no intention of shooting the elephant— I had merely sent for the rifle to defend myself if necessary—and it is always unnerving to have a crowd following you. I marched down the hill, looking and feeling a fool, with the rifle over my shoulder and an ever-growing army of people jostling at my heels. At the bottom, when you got away from the huts, there was a metalled road and beyond that a miry waste of paddy fields a thousand yards across, not yet ploughed but soggy from the first rains and dotted with coarse grass. The elephant was standing eight yards from the road, his left side towards us. He took not the slightest notice of the crowd's approach. He was tearing up bunches of grass, beating them against his knees to clean them and stuffing them into his mouth.

I had halted on the road. As soon as I saw the elephant I knew with perfect certainty that I ought not to shoot him. It is a serious matter to shoot a working elephant—it is comparable to destroying a huge and costly piece of machinery—and obviously one ought not to do it if it can possibly be avoided. And at that distance, peacefully eating, the elephant looked no more dangerous than a cow. I thought then and I think now that his attack of "must" was already passing off; in which case he would merely wander harmlessly about until the mahout came back and caught him. Moreover, I did not in the least want to shoot him. I decided that I would watch him for a little while to make sure that he did not turn savage again, and then go home.

But at that moment I glanced round at the crowd that had followed me. It was an immense crowd, two thousand at the least and growing every minute. It blocked the road for a long distance on either side. I looked at the sea of yellow faces above the garish clothes—faces all happy and excited over this bit of fun, all certain that the elephant was going to be shot. They were watching me as they would watch a conjurer about to perform a trick. They did not like me, but with the magical rifle in my hands I was momentarily worth watching. And suddenly I realized that I should have to shoot the elephant after all. The people expected it of me and I had got to do it; I could feel their two thousand wills pressing me forward, irresistibly. And it was at this moment, as I stood there with the rifle in my hands, that I first grasped the hollowness, the futility of the white man's dominion in the East. Here was I, the white man with his gun, standing in front of the unarmed native crowd—seemingly the leading actor of the piece; but in reality I was only an absurd puppet pushed to and fro by the will of those yellow faces behind. I perceived in this moment that when the white man turns tyrant it is his own freedom that he destroys. He becomes a sort of hollow, posing dummy, the conventionalized figure of a sahib. For it is the condition of his rule that he shall spend his life in trying to impress the "natives," and so in every crisis he has got to do what the "natives" expect of him. He wears a mask, and his face grows to fit it. I had got to shoot the elephant. I had committed myself to doing it when I sent for the rifle. A sahib has got to act like a sahib; he has got to appear resolute, to know his own mind and do definite things. To come all that way, rifle in hand, with two thousand people marching at my heels, and then to trail feebly away, having done nothing—no, that was impossible. The crowd would laugh at me. And my whole life, every white man's life in the East, was one long struggle not to be laughed at.

But I did not want to shoot the elephant. I watched him beating his bunch of grass against his knees, with that preoccupied grandmotherly air that elephants have. It seemed to me that it would be murder to shoot him. At that age I was not squeamish about killing animals, but I had never shot an elephant and never wanted to. (Somehow it always seems worse to kill a *large* animal.) Besides, there was the beast's owner to be considered. Alive, the elephant was worth at least a hundred pounds; dead, he would only be worth the value of his tusks, five pounds, possibly. But I had got to act quickly. I turned to some experienced-looking Burmans who had been there when we arrived, and asked them how the elephant had been behaving. They all said the same thing; he took no notice of you if you left him alone, but he might charge if you went too close to him.

It was perfectly clear to me what I ought to do. I ought to walk up to within, say, twenty-five yards of the elephant and test his behavior. If he charged, I could shoot; if he took no notice of me, it would be safe to leave him until the mahout came back. But also I knew that I was going to do no such thing. I was a poor shot with a rifle and the ground was soft mud into which one would sink at every step. If the elephant charged and I missed him, I should have about as much chance as a toad under a steam-roller. But even then I was not thinking particularly of my own skin, only of the watchful yellow faces behind. For at that moment, with the crowd watching me, I was not afraid in the ordinary sense, as I would have been if I had been alone. A white man mustn't be frightened in front of "natives"; and so, in general, he isn't frightened. The sole thought in my mind was that if anything went wrong those two thousand Burmans would see me pursued, caught, trampled on and reduced to a grinning corpse like that Indian up the hill. And if that happened it was quite probable that some of them would laugh. That would never do. There was only one alternative. I shoved the cartridges into the magazine and lay down on the road to get a better aim.

10   The crowd grew very still, and a deep, low, happy sigh, as of people who see the theatre curtain go up at last breathed from innumerable throats. They were going to have their bit of fun after all. The rifle was a beautiful German thing with cross-hair sights. I did not then know that in shooting an elephant one would shoot to cut an imaginary bar running from ear-hole to ear-hole. I ought, therefore, as the elephant was sideways on, to have aimed straight at his ear-hole; actually I aimed several inches in front of this, thinking the brain would be further forward.

When I pulled the trigger I did not hear the bang or feel the kick—one never does when a shot goes home—but I heard the devilish roar of glee that went up from the crowd. In that instant, in too short a time, one would have thought, even for the bullet to get there, a mysterious, terrible change had come over the elephant. He neither stirred nor fell, but every line of his body had altered. He looked suddenly stricken, shrunken, immensely old, as though the frightful impact of the bullet had paralysed him without knocking him down. At last, after what seemed a long time—it might have been five seconds, I dare say—he sagged flabbily to his knees. His mouth slobbered. An enormous senility seemed to have settled upon him. One could have imagined him thousands of years old. I fired again into the same spot. At the second shot he did not collapse but climbed with desperate slowness to his feet and stood weakly upright, with legs sagging and head dropping. I fired a third time. That was the shot that did for him. You could see the agony of it jolt his whole body and knock the last remnant of strength from his legs. But in falling he seemed for a moment to rise, for as his hind legs collapsed beneath him he seemed to tower upward like a huge rock toppling, his trunk reaching skywards like a tree. He trumpeted, for the first and only time. And then down he came, his belly towards me, with a crash that seemed to shake the ground even where I lay.

I got up. The Burmans were already racing past me across the mud. It was obvious that the elephant would never rise again, but he was not dead. He was breathing very rhythmically with long rattling gasps, his great mound of a side painfully rising and falling. His mouth was wide open. I could see far down into caverns of pale pink throat. I waited a long time for him to die, but his breathing did not weaken. Finally I fired my two remaining shots into the spot where I thought his heart must be. The thick blood welled out of him like red velvet, but still he did not die. His body did not even jerk when the shots hit him, the tortured breathing continued without a pause. He was dying, very slowly and in great agony, but in some world remote from me where not even a bullet could damage him further. I felt I had got to put an end to that dreadful noise. It seemed dreadful to see the great beast lying there, powerless to move and yet powerless to die, and not even to be able to finish him. I sent back for my small rifle and poured shot after shot into his heart and down his throat. They seemed to make no impression. The tortured gasps continued as steadily as the ticking of a clock.

In the end I could not stand it any longer and went away. I heard later that it took him half an hour to die. Burmans were bringing dahs[3] and baskets even before I left, and I was told they had stripped his body almost to the bones by the afternoon.

Afterwards, of course, there were endless discussions about the shooting of the elephant. The owner was furious, but he was only an Indian and could do nothing. Besides, legally I had done the right thing, for a mad elephant has to be killed, like a mad dog, if its owner fails to control it. Among the Europeans opinion was divided. The older men said I was right, the younger men said it was a damn shame to shoot an elephant for killing a coolie, because an elephant was worth more than any damn Coringhee coolie. And afterwards I was very glad that the coolie had been killed; it put me legally in the right and it gave me a sufficient pretext for shooting the elephant. I often wondered whether any of the others grasped that I had done it solely to avoid looking a fool.

[1936]

---

[3]**dahs** knives.

Joining the Conversation: Critical Thinking and Writing

1. How does Orwell characterize himself at the time of the events he describes? What evidence in the essay suggests that he wrote it some years later?
2. Orwell says the incident was "enlightening." What does he mean? Picking up this clue, state in a sentence or two the thesis or main point of the essay.
3. Compare Orwell's description of the dead coolie (in the fourth paragraph) with his description of the elephant's death (in the eleventh and twelfth paragraphs). Why does Orwell devote more space to the death of the elephant?
4. How would you describe the tone of the last paragraph, particularly of the last two sentences? Do you find the paragraph an effective conclusion to the essay? Explain.

STORIES

HANS CHRISTIAN ANDERSEN

Hans Christian Andersen (1805–75) was born in humble circumstances and apprenticed as a weaver and tailor at the age of eleven. A patron enabled him to return to elementary school, but he was unhappy there, taunted because of his unattractive appearance. In 1829 he published a short story that gained some attention, and in 1835 he published his first book of fairy tales, but the book did not sell widely. A book of travel sketches (1851) did better, and so did his second book of fairy tales (1837). His third book of fairy tales (1845) brought him widespread fame. Among his best-known tales are "The Ugly Duckling," "The Little Mermaid," "The Princess and the Pea," and the one that we present here, "The Emperor's New Clothes."

The Emperor's New Clothes

Many years ago, there was an Emperor, who was so excessively fond of new clothes that he spent all his money in dress. He did not trouble himself in the least about his soldiers; nor did he care to go either to the theatre or the chase, except for the opportunities then afforded him for displaying his new clothes. He had a different suit for each hour of the day; and as of any other king or emperor one is accustomed to say, "He is sitting in council," it was always said of him, "The Emperor is sitting in his wardrobe."

Time passed away merrily in the large town which was his capital; strangers arrived every day at the court. One day two rogues, calling themselves weavers, made their appearance. They gave out that they knew how to weave stuffs of the most beautiful colors and elaborate patterns, the clothes manufactured from which should have the wonderful property of remaining invisible to every one who was unfit for the office he held, or who was extraordinarily simple in character.

"These must, indeed, be splendid clothes!" thought the Emperor. "Had I such a suit, I might at once find out what men in my realm are unfit for their office, and also be able to distinguish the wise from the foolish! This stuff must be woven for me immediately." And he caused large sums of money to be given to both the weavers, in order that they might begin their work directly.

So the two pretended weavers set up two looms, and affected to work very busily, though in reality they did nothing at all. They asked for the most delicate silk and the purest gold thread; put both into their own knapsacks; and then continued their pretended work at the empty looms until late at night.

5 "I should like to know how the weavers are getting on with my cloth," said the emperor to himself, after some little time had elapsed; he was, however, rather embarrassed when he remembered that a simpleton, or one unfit for his office, would be unable to see the manufacture. To be sure, he thought, he had nothing to risk in his own person; but yet he would prefer sending somebody else to bring him intelligence about the weavers, and their work, before he troubled himself in the affair. All the people throughout the city had heard of the wonderful property the cloth was to possess; and all were anxious to learn how wise, or how ignorant, their neighbors might prove to be.

"I will send my faithful old Minister to the weavers," said the Emperor at last, after some deliberation; "he will be best able to see how the cloth looks; for he is a man of sense, and no one can be more suitable for his office than he is."

So the honest old Minister went into the hall, where the knaves were working with all their might at their empty looms. "What can be the meaning of this?" thought the old man, opening his eyes very wide; "I cannot discover the least bit of thread on the looms!" However, he did not express his thoughts aloud.

The impostors requested him very courteously to be so good as to come nearer their looms; and then asked him whether the design pleased him, and whether the colors were not very beautiful; at the same time pointing to the empty frames. The poor old Minister looked and looked; he could not discover anything on the looms, for a very good reason: there was nothing there. "What!" thought he again, "is it possible that I am a simpleton? I have never thought so myself; and, at any rate, if I am so, no one must know it. Can it be that I am unfit for my office? No, that must not be said either. I will never confess that I could not see the stuff."

"Well, Sir Minister!" said one of the knaves, still pretending to work, "you do not say whether the stuff pleases you."

10 "Oh, it is admirable!" replied the old Minister, looking at the loom through his spectacles. "This pattern, and the colors—yes, I will tell the Emperor without delay how very beautiful I think them."

"We shall be much obliged to you," said the impostors, and then they named the different colors and described the patterns of the pretended stuff. The old Minister listened attentively to their words, in order that he might repeat them to the Emperor; and then the knaves asked for more silk and gold, saying that it was necessary to complete what they had begun. However, they put all that was given them into their knapsacks, and continued to work with as much apparent diligence as before at their empty looms.

The Emperor now sent another officer of his court to see how the men were getting on, and to ascertain whether the cloth would soon be ready. It was just the same with this gentleman as with the Minister; he surveyed the looms on all sides, but could see nothing at all but the empty frames.

"Does not the stuff appear as beautiful to you as it did to my Lord the Minister?" asked the impostors of the Emperor's second ambassador; at the same time making the same gestures as before, and talking of the design and colors which were not there.

"I certainly am not stupid!" thought the messenger. "It must be that I am not fit for my good, profitable office! That is very odd; however, no one shall know anything about it." And accordingly he praised the stuff he could not see, and declared that he was delighted with both colors and patterns. "Indeed, please your Imperial Majesty," said he to his sovereign, when he returned, "the cloth which the weavers are preparing is extraordinarily magnificent."

15   The whole city was talking of the splendid cloth which the Emperor had ordered to be woven at his own expense.

And now the Emperor himself wished to see the costly manufacture, whilst it was still on the loom. Accompanied by a select number of officers of the court, among whom were the two honest men who had already admired the cloth, he went to the crafty impostors, who, as soon as they were aware of the Emperor's approach, went on working more diligently than ever; although they still did not pass a single thread through the looms.

"Is not the work absolutely magnificent?" said the two officers of the crown already mentioned. "If your Majesty will only be pleased to look at it! What a splendid design! What glorious colors!" and at the same time they pointed to the empty frames; for they imagined that every one but themselves could see this exquisite piece of workmanship.

"How is this?" said the Emperor to himself; "I can see nothing! This is, indeed, a terrible affair! Am I a simpleton? Or am I unfit to be an Emperor? That would be the worst thing that could happen." "Oh, the cloth is charming!" said he aloud; "it has my entire approbation." And he smiled most graciously, and looked closely at the empty looms; for on no account would he say that he could not see what two of the officers of his court had praised so much. All his retinue now strained their eyes, hoping to discover something on the looms, but they could see no more than the others; nevertheless, they all exclaimed, "Oh! how beautiful!" and advised his Majesty to have some new clothes made from this splendid material for the approaching procession. "Magnificent! charming! excellent!" resounded on all sides; and every one was uncommonly gay. The Emperor shared in the general satisfaction, and presented the impostors with the riband of an order of knighthood to be worn in their buttonholes, and the title of "Gentlemen Weavers."

The rogues sat up the whole of the night before the day on which the procession was to take place, and had sixteen lights burning, so that every one might see how anxious they were to finish the Emperor's new suit. They pretended to roll the cloth off the looms; cut the air with their scissors; and sewed with needles without any thread in them. "See!" cried they at last, "the Emperor's new clothes are ready!"

20   And now the Emperor, with all the grandees of his court, came to the weavers; and the rogues raised their arms, as if in the act of holding something up, saying, "Here are your Majesty's trousers! Here is the scarf! Here is the mantle! The whole suit is as light as a cobweb; one might fancy one has nothing at all on, when dressed in it; that, however, is the great virtue of this delicate cloth."

"Yes, indeed!" said all the courtiers, although not one of them could see anything of this exquisite manufacture.

"If your Imperial Majesty will be graciously pleased to take off your clothes, we will fit on the new suit, in front of the looking-glass."

The Emperor was accordingly undressed, and the rogues pretended to array him in his new suit; the Emperor turning round, from side to side, before the looking-glass.

"How splendid his Majesty looks in his new clothes! and how well they fit!" every one cried out. "What a design! what colors! These are, indeed, royal robes!"

25   "The canopy which is to be borne over your majesty, in the procession, is waiting," announced the Chief Master of the Ceremonies.

"I am quite ready," answered the Emperor. "Do my new clothes fit well?" asked he, turning himself round again before the looking-glass, in order that he might appear to be examining his handsome suit.

The lords of the bed-chamber, who were to carry his Majesty's train, felt about on the ground, as if they were lifting up the ends of the mantle, and pretended to be carrying something; for they would by no means betray anything like simplicity, or unfitness for their office.

So now the Emperor walked under his high canopy in the midst of the procession, through the streets of his capital; and all the people standing by, and those at the windows, cried out, "Oh! How beautiful are our Emperor's new clothes! What a magnificent train there is to the mantle! And how gracefully the scarf hangs!" In short, no one would allow that he could not see these much-admired clothes, because, in doing so, he would have declared himself either a simpleton or unfit for his office. Certainly, none of the Emperor's various suits had ever excited so much admiration as this.

"But the Emperor has nothing at all on!" said a little child. "Listen to the voice of innocence!" exclaimed his father; and what the child had said was whispered from one to another.

30 "But he has nothing at all on!" at last cried out all the people. The Emperor was vexed, for he knew that the people were right; but he thought, "the procession must go on now!" And the lords of the bed-chamber took greater pains than ever to appear holding up a train, although, in reality, there was no train to hold.

[1837]

Joining the Conversation: Critical Thinking and Writing

1. What reason does the emperor give to himself for not being the first to examine the clothes? What is his real reason?
2. Why is it significant that a child rather than an adult is the first to see the truth, that the emperor is naked?
3. In an essay of 500 words, consider whether the story would be better or worse if, after the child's perception, the crowd roared with laughter at the vain and foolish emperor, and the emperor fled in humiliation. Argue for the superiority of the ending you prefer.
4. Drawing on your own experience, set forth and analyze an episode that illustrates the gist of this story; that is, an episode showing the hypocrisy or folly of adults and the insight of a child or adolescent. Your essay should include an analysis of the reasons for the behavior of the adults.

JAMES JOYCE

For a biographical note on James Joyce, see page 664.

Araby

North Richmond Street, being blind,[1] was a quiet street except at the hour when the Christian Brothers' School set the boys free. An uninhabited house of two stories stood at the blind end, detached from its neighbors in a square ground. The other houses of the street, conscious of decent lives within them, gazed at one another with brown imperturbable faces.

[1]**blind** a dead-end street. (All notes are by the editors.)

The former tenant of our house, a priest, had died in the back drawing-room. Air, musty from having long been enclosed, hung in all the rooms, and the waste room behind the kitchen was littered with old useless papers. Among these I found a few papercovered books, the pages of which were curled and damp: *The Abbot,* by Walter Scott, *The Devout Communicant* and *The Memoirs of Vidocq.*[2] I liked the last best because its leaves were yellow. The wild garden behind the house contained a central apple-tree and a few straggling bushes under one of which I found the late tenant's rusty bicycle-pump. He had been a very charitable priest; in his will he had left all his money to institutions and the furniture of his house to his sister.

When the short days of winter came dusk fell before we had well eaten our dinners. When we met in the street the houses had grown sombre. The space of sky above us was the colour of everchanging violet and towards it the lamps of the street lifted their feeble lanterns. The cold air stung us and we played till our bodies glowed. Our shouts echoed in the silent street. The career of our play brought us through the dark muddy lanes behind the houses where we ran the gauntlet of the rough tribes from the cottages, to the back doors of the dark dripping gardens where odours arose from the ashpits, to the dark odorous stables where a coachman smoothed and combed the horse or shook music from the buckled harness. When we returned to the street light from the kitchen windows had filled the areas. If my uncle was seen turning the corner we hid in the shadow until we had seen him safely housed. Or if Mangan's sister came out on the doorstep to call her brother in to his tea we watched her from our shadow peer up and down the street. We waited to see whether she would remain or go in and, if she remained, we left our shadow and walked up to Mangan's steps resignedly. She was waiting for us, her figure defined by the light from the half-opened door. Her brother always teased her before he obeyed and I stood by the railings looking at her. Her dress swung as she moved her body and the soft rope of her hair tossed from side to side.

Every morning I lay on the floor in the front parlour watching her door. The blind was pulled down to within an inch of the sash so that I could not be seen. When she came out on the doorstep my heart leaped. I ran to the hall, seized my books and followed her. I kept her brown figure always in my eye and, when we came near the point at which our ways diverged, I quickened my pace and passed her. This happened morning after morning. I had never spoken to her, except for a few casual words, and yet her name was like a summons to all my foolish blood.

5   Her image accompanied me even in places the most hostile to romance. On Saturday evenings when my aunt went marketing I had to go to carry some of the parcels. We walked through the flaring streets, jostled by drunken men and bargaining women, amid the curses of labourers, the shrill litanies of shop-boys who stood on guard by the barrels of pigs' cheeks, the nasal chanting of street-singers, who sang a *come-all-you* about O'Donovan Rossa,[3] or a ballad about the troubles in our native land. These noises converged in a single sensation of life for me: I imagined that I bore my chalice safely through a throng of foes. Her name sprang to my lips at moments in strange prayers and praises which I myself did not understand. My eyes were often full of tears (I could not tell why) and at times a flood from my heart seemed to pour itself out into my bosom. I thought little of the

---

[2] *The Abbot* one of Scott's popular historical romances (1820);   *The Devout Communicant* a Catholic religious manual published in the eighteenth century;   *The Memoirs of Vidocq* the memoirs of the chief of the French detective force (1829).   [3] *come-all-you* a topical song that began "Come all you gallant Irishmen";   **O'Donovan Rossa** Jeremiah O'Donovan (1831–1915), a popular Irish leader who was jailed by the British for advocating violent rebellion.

future. I did not know whether I would ever speak to her or not or, if I spoke to her, how I could tell her of my confused adoration. But my body was like a harp and her words and gestures were like fingers running upon the wires.

One evening I went into the back drawing-room in which the priest had died. It was a dark rainy evening and there was no sound in the house. Through one of the broken panes I heard the rain impinge upon the earth, the fine incessant needles of water playing in the sodden beds. Some distant lamp or lighted window gleamed below me. I was thankful that I could see so little. All my senses seemed to desire to veil themselves and, feeling that I was about to slip from them, I pressed the palms of my hands together until they trembled, murmuring: *O love! O love!* many times.

At last she spoke to me. When she addressed the first words to me I was so confused that I did not know what to answer. She asked me was I going to Araby.

I forget whether I answered yes or no. It would be a splendid bazaar, she said; she would love to go.

—And why can't you? I asked.

10   While she spoke she turned a silver bracelet round and round her wrist. She could not go, she said, because there would be a retreat that week in her convent. Her brother and two other boys were fighting for their caps and I was alone at the railings. She held one of the spikes, bowing her head towards me. The light from the lamp opposite our door caught the white curve of her neck, lit up her hair that rested there and, falling, lit up the hand upon the railing. It fell over one side of her dress and caught the white border of a petticoat, just visible as she stood at ease.

—It's well for you, she said.

—If I go, I said, I will bring you something.

What innumerable follies laid waste my waking and sleeping thoughts after that evening! I wished to annihilate the tedious intervening days. I chafed against the work of school. At night in my bedroom and by day in the classroom her image came between me and the page I strove to read. The syllables of the word *Araby* were called to me through the silence in which my soul luxuriated and cast an Eastern enchantment over me. I asked for leave to go to the bazaar on Saturday night. My aunt was surprised and hoped it was not some Freemason[4] affair. I answered few questions in class. I watched my master's face pass from amiability to sternness; he hoped I was not beginning to idle. I could not call my wandering thoughts together. I had hardly any patience with the serious work of life which, now that it stood between me and my desire, seemed to me child's play, ugly monotonous child's play.

On Saturday morning I reminded my uncle that I wished to go to the bazaar in the evening. He was fussing at the hallstand, looking for the hat-brush, and answered me curtly:

15   —Yes, boy, I know.

As he was in the hall I could not go into the front parlour and lie at the window. I left the house in bad humour and walked slowly towards the school. The air was pitilessly raw and already my heart misgave me.

When I came home to dinner my uncle had not yet been home. Still it was early. I sat staring at the clock for some time and, when its ticking began to irritate me, I left the room. I mounted the staircase and gained the upper part of the house. The high cold empty gloomy rooms liberated me and I went from room to room singing. From the front window I saw my companions playing below in the street.

[4]**Freemason** Irish Catholics viewed the Masons as their Protestant enemies.

Their cries reached me weakened and indistinct and, leaning my forehead against the cool glass, I looked over at the dark house where she lived. I may have stood there for an hour, seeing nothing but the brown-clad figure cast by my imagination, touched discreetly by the lamplight at the curved neck, at the hand upon the railings and at the border below the dress.

When I came downstairs again I found Mrs Mercer sitting at the fire. She was an old garrulous woman, a pawnbroker's widow, who collected used stamps for some pious purpose. I had to endure the gossip of the tea-table. The meal was prolonged beyond an hour and still my uncle did not come. Mrs Mercer stood up to go: she was sorry she couldn't wait any longer, but it was after eight o'clock and she did not like to be out late, as the night air was bad for her. When she had gone I began to walk up and down the room, clenching my fists. My aunt said:

20   —I'm afraid you may put off your bazaar for this night of Our Lord.

At nine o'clock I heard my uncle's latchkey in the halldoor. I heard him talking to himself and heard the hallstand rocking when it had received the weight of his overcoat. I could interpret these signs. When he was midway through his dinner I asked him to give me the money to go to the bazaar. He had forgotten.

—The people are in bed and after their first sleep now, he said.

I did not smile. My aunt said to him energetically:

—Can't you give him the money and let him go? You've kept him late enough as it is.

My uncle said he was very sorry he had forgotten. He said he believed in the old saying: *All work and no play makes Jack a dull boy.* He asked me where I was going and, when I had told him a second time he asked me did I know *The Arab's Farewell to His Steed.*[5] When I left the kitchen he was about to recite the opening lines of the piece to my aunt.

25   I held a florin tightly in my hand as I strode down Buckingham Street towards the station. The sight of the streets thronged with buyers and glaring with gas recalled to me the purpose of my journey. I took my seat in a third-class carriage of a deserted train. After an intolerable delay the train moved out of the station slowly. It crept onward among ruinous houses and over the twinkling river. At Westland Row Station a crowd of people pressed to the carriage doors; but the porters moved them back, saying that it was a special train for the bazaar. I remained alone in the bare carriage. In a few minutes the train drew up beside an improvised wooden platform. I passed out on to the road and saw by the lighted dial of a clock that it was ten minutes to ten. In front of me was a large building which displayed the magical name.

I could not find any sixpenny entrance and, fearing that the bazaar would be closed, I passed in quickly through a turnstile, handing a shilling to a weary-looking man. I found myself in a big hall girdled at half its height by a gallery. Nearly all the stalls were closed and the greater part of the hall was in darkness. I recognised a silence like that which pervades a church after a service. I walked into the center of the bazaar timidly. A few people were gathered about the stalls which were still open. Before a curtain, over which the words *Café Chantant* were written in coloured lamps, two men were counting money on a salver. I listened to the fall of the coins.

Remembering with difficulty why I had come I went over to one of the stalls and examined porcelain vases and flowered tea-sets. At the door of the stall a young lady was talking and laughing with two young gentlemen. I remarked their English accents and listened vaguely to their conversation.

[5]*The Arab's Farewell to His Steed* "The Arab to His Favorite Steed" was a popular sentimental poem by Caroline Norton (1808–77).

—O, I never said such a thing!

—O, but you did!

30 —O, but I didn't!

—Didn't she say that?

—Yes! I heard her.

—O, there's a . . . fib!

Observing me the young lady came over and asked me did I wish to buy anything. The tone of her voice was not encouraging; she seemed to have spoken to me out of a sense of duty. I looked humbly at the great jars that stood like eastern guards at either side of the dark entrance to the stall and murmured:

35 —No, thank you.

The young lady changed the position of one of the vases and went back to the two young men. They began to talk of the same subject. Once or twice the young lady glanced at me over her shoulder.

I lingered before her stall, though I knew my stay was useless, to make my interest in her wares seem the more real. Then I turned away slowly and walked down the middle of the bazaar. I allowed the two pennies to fall against the sixpence in my pocket. I heard a voice call from one end of the gallery that the light was out. The upper part of the hall was now completely dark.

Gazing up into the darkness I saw myself as a creature driven and derided by vanity; and my eyes burned with anguish and anger.

[1905]

Joining the Conversation: Critical Thinking and Writing

1. Joyce wrote a novel called *A Portrait of the Artist as a Young Man* (1916). Write an essay of about 500 words on "Araby" as a portrait of the artist as a boy.

2. In an essay of about 500 words, consider the role of images of darkness and blindness and what they reveal to us about "Araby" as a story of the fall from innocence into painful awareness.

3. How old, approximately, is the narrator of "Araby" at the time of the experience he describes? How old is he at the time he tells his story? On what evidence do you base your estimates?

4. The boy, apparently an only child, lives with an uncle and aunt rather than with parents. Why do you suppose Joyce put him in this family setting rather than some other?

5. The story is rich in images of religion. This in itself is not surprising, for the story is set in Roman Catholic Ireland, but the religious images are not simply references to religious persons or objects. In an essay of 500 to 750 words, discuss how these images reveal the narrator's state of mind.

HA JIN

Ha Jin is the pseudonym taken by Xuefei Jin, who was born in China in 1945. Once his military service had ended, he studied the English language and then focused on English literature in his undergraduate and graduate work in Chinese universities. He came to the United States in the mid-1980s to attend graduate school at Brandeis University, and later he did advanced work in creative writing at Boston University. Ha Jin has published two books of poetry, three novels, and several collections of short stories, including Ocean of Words *(1996), from which we have taken the story we reprint here, "Love in the Air," and* Under the Red Flag *(1997). He is a professor in the English department at Boston University.*

In an interview in January 2007, Ha Jin spoke about his identity or, rather, identities, as a writer:

> *"Every book is kind of a departure. As a writer, I'm always in the process of becoming. . . . I would be happy to be an Asian-American writer. It's a good thing for me because, as I said, I lived for almost thirty years in China. That's part of my heritage. So the hyphen is good for me, but that also means, eventually, I do want to become an American writer. That identity can only be earned in my case by actual work. If a book or books are valuable to the American experience, then I will be given that identity.*

Love in the Air

After the political study, Chief Jiang turned on both the transmitter and the receiver and started searching for the station of the Regional Headquarters. Half a minute later a resonant signal emerged calling the Fifth Regiment. Kang Wandou, who had served for two years, could tell it was an experienced hand at the opposite end. The dots and dashes were clean and concrete; the pace was fast and steady.

"He's very good," Shi Wei said.

"Of course, Shenyang always has the best hands," Chief Jiang said, returning the call. This was their first direct communication with the Headquarters of Shenyang Military Region. In no time the two stations got in touch. Jiang telegraphed that from now on they would keep twenty-four-hour coverage.

"Understood. So long," Shenyang replied.

5   "So long," Jiang tapped. He turned off the transmitter, but left the receiver on. "Shun Min, it's your turn now. Little Kang will take over in the evening."

"All right." Shun moved his chair close to the machine.

Though the middle-aged chief called him Little Kang, to the other soldiers Kang was Big Kang. His whole person was marked by abnormal largeness except for his voice, which was small and soft. Whenever he spoke, he sounded as though he was mumbling to himself. If his neck were not so long, his comrades would have believed he had suffered from the "big-joint" disease in his childhood. His wrists were thick, and his square thumbs always embarrassed him. But everybody was impressed by the beautiful long lashes above his froggy eyes.

After dinner Kang replaced Shun. The evening shift was not busy. Since all news stations broadcast at dusk and there was too much noise in the air, few telegrams were dispatched or received during these hours. Kang's task was to answer Shenyang's call every hour, and for the rest of the time he had to attend to the receiver in case an emergency arose. Having nothing else to do, he opened the fanlight and watched the night. Gray streaks of clouds were floating rapidly beneath the crescent moon and the glimmering stars. In the air there was a mysterious humming, which seemed to come from the constellations. Except for the swarms of lights in Hutou Town, it was dark everywhere. Even the silhouette of those mountains in Russia had disappeared.

Cold wind kept gushing into the office; Kang closed the fanlight and sat back on the chair. Again, nothing could be seen through the window, on whose frosty panes stretched miniature bushes, hills, caves, coral reefs. He picked up a pencil, turned over a telegram pad, and began drawing pictures. He drew a horse, a cow, a dog, a pig, a rooster, a lamb, a donkey, and a hen leading a flock of chicks.

10   After taps at nine, the quiet grew intolerable. If only he could have something interesting to do. In one of the drawers there was a volume of Chairman Mao's selected works and a copy of Lenin's *What Is to Be Done?*, which Chief Jiang would browse through at night, but these books were too profound for Kang. He missed the picture stories he had read when he was a boy. Those children's books could no longer be found anywhere, because they had been burned at the beginning of the Cultural Revolution. Kang took out his tobacco pouch and rolled a cigarette. Smoking was the only way to prevent himself from dozing off. Then he stretched his legs, rested his feet on the table, and leaned against the back of the chair as if lounging on a sofa. Soon the small office turned foggy.

Shenyang began to call at ten sharp. Kang turned on the transmitter and was ready to reply. It was another radio operator at the other end now. The signal was fluctuating at a much faster speed, approximately 130 numerals a minute. Because of the noise, the dots and the dashes didn't sound very clear, though they were distinguishable.

"Please answer," it ended.

Immediately Kang started to call back. His large hand held the button of the sending key and pounded out the letters one after another. He was a slow hand and could tap only eighty numerals a minute. But his fingers and thumb were powerful—whenever he telegraphed, the key with its heavy steel base would move about on the table. Holding the base with his left hand, he was repeating the reply signal in a resolute manner. His thick wrist was moving up and down while a little red light was flashing nervously at the top of the transmitter.

The operator at the opposite end did not hear Kang and resumed calling. Now there was less noise in the air and the signal became distinct. The call sign, composed of eight letters, was repeated again and again; it formed a crisp tune, flowing around and around. Kang pricked up his ears. This must be the chief of the station. He had never met such an excellent hand. There were automatic machines that could produce 180 numerals a minute clearly, but those dead instruments always sounded monotonous. They didn't have a character. The more you listened to them at night, the more likely you would fall asleep. But this fellow was one of those "machine defeaters."

15   "Please answer," the other side asked again.

Once more Kang went about calling back. Affected by the dexterous hand at the other end, he tried hard to speed up. The chair under his hips creaked while he was struggling with the bakelite key button, which turned slippery in his sweating hand.

Unfortunately this was a bad night. The other side simply could not find him. It called him time and again; Kang replied continually, but they could not get in touch. Forty minutes passed to no avail. By now, the other operator had become impatient. The melodious signal gradually lost its rhythm and flowed so rapidly that the letters were almost indistinguishable. It sounded like raindrops pattering on metal tiles. Patient as he was, Kang began to worry.

Around eleven, the telephone suddenly rang. Kang picked up the receiver and said, "Hello."

"Hello," a tingling female voice said. "This is the Military Region Station. Wake up, comrade. Have you heard me on the machine?"

20   "Ye-yes." Kang paused with surprise, his heart kicking and his throat tightening. Who could imagine a woman would call you on the border at night? "I-I've heard you," he managed to say. "I ne-never dozed off. I've been calling you all the time."

"Sorry, don't take it to heart. I was teasing you. Shall we switch to the second set of frequencies?" She sounded so pleasant.

"All righ-t." His tongue seemed not his own.

"Bye-bye now, meet you on the machine."

"Bye."

25   She hung up. Kang was dazed, still holding the receiver. The sweet voice went on echoing in his ears, "Sorry, don't take it to heart. . . ."

The call sign appeared again. This time it repossessed its elegance and fluency, but to Kang every dot and dash was different now, as though they were tender, meaningful words the young woman sent to him alone.

"Switch frequency please," she ended.

Kang jerked his head and rushed to look for her on the new frequency. Without much effort, he found her again. His body grew tense as he became engrossed in the sways and ripples of the heavenly melody. How wonderful to work with a woman at night. If only she could call him like this for an hour. But she stopped and asked, "Please answer."

Kang's hand began to tremble. It settled on the sending key like a small turtle, shaking out every letter brokenly. He cursed his hand, "Come on, you coward! This is not a battle yet." He wiped his wet forehead with a telegram sheet.

30   What a pity. She heard him in less than a minute and replied promptly: "No business. Meet you at twelve o'clock. So long."

"So long." Kang had to agree, because it was a rule that an operator must never transmit an unnecessary dot or dash. The longer you stayed on the air, the easier it was for the Russians to locate your position.

Kang felt at a loss. He raised his head to look at the clock on the wall—eleven-ten, so he would meet her in fifty minutes. His imagination began to take wing. What was her name? How stupid he was, having forgotten to ask her. How old was she? She sounded so young and must have been around twenty. A good person, no doubt; that pleasant voice was full of good nature. What did she look like? Was she beautiful? Well educated? Intelligent? That voice told everything—all the best a woman could have. But what did she look like exactly? Tall and slim, with large black eyes? Of course he could not find out much about her through only one meeting. It had to take time. He believed that eventually he would get to know her well, because from now on they would meet every night.

The clock moved slowly, as though intending to avoid an ominous ending. Kang kept watching it and longed to arrive at the midnight rendezvous in the twinkling of an eye.

Suddenly somebody knocked at the door. Chief Jiang came in. "You can go to bed now, Kang. I happened to wake up a few minutes earlier tonight." He yawned.

35   Kang stood up and didn't know what to say. He tried to smile, but the effort distorted his face.

"What happened?" the chief asked. "You look as awake as a lynx."

"Nothing, everything is fine." Kang picked up his fur hat; with enormous dismay he slouched out. He forgot to take an apple, which was his night snack.

How could he sleep? Every inch of his skin was affected by a caressing tingle he had never experienced before. At the other side of the room, Shun was snoring and Shi murmured something in his dream.

"I was teasing you. . . ." The voice spoke to Kang again and again. He shut his eyes tight; he shook his head many times in order to get rid of her and go to sleep, but it was no use. She was so close to him, as if sitting right beside his bed in the dark, whispering and smiling.

40   Little by little, he gave up and allowed her to play whatever tricks she wanted to. The most unbearable mystery was what she looked like. He tried to think of all the women he knew, but he could not recall a pretty one. Surely he had aunts and cousins, surely he remembered some girls who had hoed the cornfields and cut millet together with him, but none of them differed much from his male relatives or from the men in his home village. Every one worked like a beast of burden, and none could speak without swearing.

The prettiest women he had ever seen were those female characters in the movie copies of the Revolutionary Model Plays, but most of them were too old, well beyond forty. How about the girl raped by the landlord in *The White-Haired Girl?* Yes, she was a wonderful ballerina, slim and good-looking. How deft her toes were. They capered around as if never touching the ground. She could swing her legs up well beyond her head. And the slender waist, which was full of rebellious spirit. What a wonderful body she had! But did she have a wonderful voice? No one could tell, because she kept quiet in the ballet.

No, she wouldn't do. He would not accept a woman who might lack that charming voice. Besides, that actress had long white hair like an old crone's. She must have been weird, or her hair wouldn't be so silvery.

How about the revolutionary's daughter in *The Story of the Red Lamp?* Well, that was a good one. But did she not seem too young? She was seventeen, old enough to be somebody's wife. A marriageable girl indeed. What he liked most about her was that long glossy braid, which reached her buttocks. But she was too thin and must have been too feeble to work. Her aquiline nose was narrow; that was not a sign of good fortune. Even worse, her voice was sharp. It was all right for singing Peking Opera to a large audience, but who dared to quarrel with a girl like that? In real life, she must have been a "small hot pepper." No, he had to look for another woman.

Now he had it—the female gymnastic athlete he had seen in a documentary film. She performed on the uneven bars. Her body was so supple and powerful that she could stretch, fly, and even somersault in the air. No doubt, that was a healthy energetic woman, not a bourgeois young lady who would fall in a gust of wind. What did she look like? He had not seen her face clearly in the film and could not tell. Then this woman had to go too, at least for the time being.

45   The radiator pipes started clinking and whistling gently. The boiler room pumped steam at four. With dawn approaching, Kang was worried and tried to force himself to sleep. But that voice would not leave him alone. "Wake up, comrade. Have you heard me on the machine? . . ." It sounded even more pleasant and more intimate. You fool, he cursed himself. How stupid you are—bewitched by an unknown voice! Forget it and get some sleep.

Soon he entered another world. He married a young woman who was also a telegrapher. They worked together at the post office in his hometown. They lived in a small house surrounded by a stone wall that had a gate with iron bars. Their garden was filled with vegetables and fruits. The beans were as broad as sickles, and the peaches as fat as babies' faces. Poultry were everywhere, three dozen chickens, twenty ducks, and eight geese. Who was his bride? He didn't know, for he only saw her back, a tall, sturdy young woman with a thick braid.

At breakfast he felt giddy. He could not tell if he had slept at all. Neither was he sure whether the prosperous domestic scene was his dream or his fantasy. How absurd the whole thing was. He had never loved a woman before, but all of a sudden he'd fallen in love with a voice. His first love was an unknown voice. He was scared, because he could not determine whether it was real love or merely a delusion from mental illness. Did people feel this way when they were in love? He felt sick and beside himself. How long would it take for him to grow used to this thing or get over it?

He could not sleep that morning when he was supposed to have a good rest to make up for the previous night and prepare himself for the evening shift. That voice, mixed with the call sign, whispered in his ears constantly. Time and again, he forced himself to think of something else, but he could not summon up anything interesting. He dared not smoke, for fear that Chief Jiang, who slept in the same room, would know he had remained awake for the whole morning.

In the afternoon, during the study of Chairman Mao's "Combat Liberalism," Kang was restless, longing for the arrival of the evening. The words grew blurred before his eyes. When he was asked to read out a page, he managed to accomplish the task with a whistling in his nose. His comrades looked at him strangely. When he finished, Shun said, "Kang, you must have a bad cold."

50   "Yes, it's a bad one." Kang blew his nose with a piece of newspaper. He was both miserable and hopeful. Probably the more he worked with her, the better he would feel. Everything was difficult in the beginning; the end of suffering was happiness. At the moment he must be patient; a few hours later, he would be in a different world.

How ruthless Heaven was. She did not show up in the evening. It was a different operator at the other end. Kang spent the six hours racking his brains about what kind of schedule she had. The following three evenings passed in the same fruitless way. Kang was baffled. Every night he could not help thinking of that mysterious woman—all women—for several hours. In the daytime he was very quiet. Although pining away, he dared not talk to anyone about it. How shameful it would be—to have it known that you were enchanted by a woman about whom you didn't know anything. How silly he was! That woman must have forgotten him like used water. No, she had never bothered about knowing him. How could she, a pretty young woman in the big city and perhaps surrounded by many smart officers in the headquarters, be interested in a soldier like him, who was so dull, so homely, and so rustic? He knew he was the toad that dreamed of eating a swan, but he couldn't help himself.

On Saturday morning, Kang was roused from his catnap by Shi Wei. "Big Kang, come and help your younger brother."

"What's up?"

55   "Too many telegrams this morning, I've been copying for three hours and can't handle it anymore."

"All right, I'm coming." It was almost eleven o'clock anyway. Kang got up and wiped his face with a wet towel.

There she was! He had hardly entered the office when Kang froze stock-still. The pleasant signal, for which he had been yearning for days, was singing proudly as though to a large audience. The dots and dashes sounded like amorous messages inviting him to decode their secret meanings. How magnificent her telegraphic style was in broad daylight. Kang lost himself in an imaginary melody composed of both the electric signal and the tingling voice—"Hello, this is the Military Region Station. Wake up, comrade. Have you heard me on the machine? . . . ."

"What's the matter with you?" Shi rapped him on the shoulder.

"Oh nothing," Kang muttered, moving to the desk. "Never met such a good hand."

60   "True, he has gold fingers."

There was no time to tell Shi that it was she, not he, because the receiver was announcing: "Please ready."

Kang started writing down the numerals rapidly. In the beginning it went well, but soon his attention began to wander. He was distracted by his desire to appreciate the rhythm and the personal touch in the sounds, and he had to drop some numerals now and then. More awful, that voice jumped in to trouble him—"Sorry, don't take it to heart. I was teasing you. . . ."

"Repeat?" she asked, having finished the short telegram.

"Yes, noise," Kang pounded nervously. "Group eight in line four, from group three to eight in line six . . ."

65 Meanwhile, Shi Wei watched him closely. He was surprised to find Kang, a better transcriber than himself, unable to jot down the telegram sent out so clearly. There was no noise at all; why did he tap "noise" as an excuse? Kang was aware of Shi's observing and was sweating all over. He rushed to bring the receiving operation to an end.

"Are you all right?" Shi asked, after Kang signed his name on the telegram.

"I don't know." He felt sick. He got up and hurried out of the office.

Another fruitless evening and another sleepless night. Kang could no longer contain himself. On Sunday evening, he revealed the truth to Shi and Shun, who happened to be in the office.

"Shi Wei, you know, the Shenyang operator with 'gold fingers' is a woman, not a man." He had planned to say a lot, to make a story, but he was bewildered, finding that he completed the project in just one sentence. He blushed to the ears with a strange emotion.

70 "Really?" Shi asked loudly. "No kidding? Why didn't you tell me earlier, Brother Kang?"

Kang smiled. Shun was not sure who they were talking about. "Which one?"

"The best one," Shi said with a thrill in his voice. "I can't believe it. A girl can telegraph so well. Tell me, Big Kang, how did you get to know her?"

"She called me, because she couldn't hear me," he declared proudly.

"What's her name?" Shi asked.

75 "I have no idea. Wish I knew."

"Must be a good girl. I'll go to Shenyang and get her."

"Come on, don't brag," Shun said. "I want to see how you can get her."

"You wait and see."

Kang was shocked that Shi was also interested in her. He regretted telling them the truth. If Shi made a move, Kang would have to give ground. Shi was an excellent basketball player and had in his wallet the pictures of a half dozen young women, who he claimed were all his girlfriends. In addition, his father was a divisional commissar in the navy; Shi had grown up in big cities and knew the world. Most important of all, he spent money like water. How could Kang compete against such a smart, handsome fellow?

80 It was this new development that made him fidgety that evening. He paced up and down in the office, chain-smoking for two hours. Finally, he decided to investigate who she was. He picked up the telephone and called the Shenyang Military Region. It took half an hour for the call to get through.

"Hello, this is Shenyang, can I help you?" an operator asked sleepily.

"Ye-yes," he struggled to say. "I want to speak to—to the wireless station, the one that communicates with Hutou?"

"What's 'Hutou'? A unit's code name?"

"No, it's a county."

85 "Oh, I see. Please tell me the number of the station you want to speak to."

"I don't know the number."

"I can't help you then. We have hundreds of stations, and they are in different cities and mountains. You have to tell me the number. Find the number first, then call back. All right?"

"Uh, all right."

"Bye-bye now."

90   "Bye."

It was so easy to run into a dead end. All the clever questions, which he had prepared to ask the radio operator on duty about that woman, had vanished from his mind. How foolish he was—having never thought there could be more than ten stations in the Regional Headquarters. What was to be done now? Without an address, he could not write to her; even with an address, he didn't know how to compose a love letter. Why was Heaven so merciless? It seemed that the only way to meet her was through the air, but he had not figured out her capricious schedule yet.

It did not make much difference after they rotated the shifts. Now Kang worked afternoons. No matter how exhausted he was when he went to bed at night, he would lie awake for a few hours thinking of one woman after another. His dreams ran wilder. Every night the pillow, which contained his underclothes, moved from beneath his head, little by little, into his arms. He was tormented by endless questions. What was it like to kiss and touch a woman? Did women also have hair on their bodies? Was he a normal man? And could he satisfy a woman? Was he not a neurotic, drenched in sweat and burning away like this in the dark? Could he have children with a woman?

Whenever he woke up from his broken sleep that mysterious voice would greet him, "Wake up, comrade. Have you heard me on the machine? . . ." The sounds grew deeper and deeper into him, as though they were sent out by his own internal organs. During these frantic nights, he discovered that Chief Jiang had to rouse Shi Wei at least three times every night. Shi worked the small hours.

Kang's skull felt numb in the daytime. He was convinced that he was a lunatic. How panicked he was when receiving a telegram, because that melodious signal and that tender voice, again and again, intruded themselves into his brain and forced him to pause in the middle of the transcribing. How good it would be to have peace once more. But peace of mind seemed remote, as though it belonged only to a time that he had outgrown and could never return to. Even the exercises in the mornings became a torture. He used to be able to write down 160 numerals per minute with ease, but now he had to struggle with 110. When they sat together reading documents and newspapers, his comrades often waved their hands before his eyes to test if he could see anything. Somebody would say, "Big Kang, why do you look like you lost your soul?" Another, "What do you see in your trance? A goddess?"

95   On these occasions Kang would let out a sigh. He dared not tell anybody about the ridculous "affair." He was afraid that he would be criticized for having contracted bourgeois liberalism or become a laughingstock.

One morning during the exercises, the telegraphic instructor, Han Jie, looked at Kang's transcription and said under his breath, "No wonder the Confidential Office complained."

Suddenly it dawned on Kang that he had become a nuisance in the Wireless Platoon. A pang seized his heart. No doubt, the confidential officers in the Regimental Headquarters were dissatisfied with his work and had reported him to the company's leaders. It was this stupid "affair" that had reduced him to such a state. He had to find a way to stop it—forget that woman and her bewitching voice— otherwise how could he survive? Although in his heart he knew he had to get rid of her, he didn't know how. Neither did he want to try.

On Thursday evening two weeks later, Chief Jiang held an urgent meeting at the station. Nobody knew what it was about. Kang was scared because he thought it might be about him. The secret would come out sooner or later. Had he babbled it during his sleep at night? He regretted drawing three pictures of women on the back of a telegram pad. Chief Jiang must have seen them. What should he say if the chief questioned him about those drawings?

The meeting had nothing to do with him. When Jiang asked Shi Wei to confess what he had done in the small hours, Kang at last felt relaxed. But like Shun, he was baffled about what had happened. Shi protested that he had not done anything wrong.

100 "You're dishonest, Comrade Shi Wei," the chief said.

"No, no Chief Jiang." Shi looked worried. "I did all the work well."

"You know our Party's policy: Leniency to those who confess, severity to those who refuse. It's up to yourself."

"Why?" Shi seemed puzzled. "This policy applies only to the class enemies. I'm your comrade, am I not?"

"Stop pretending you're innocent. Tell us the truth."

105 "No, I really didn't do anything wrong."

"All right, let me tell you what happened." The chief's voice grew sharper. "You were caught by the monitoring station. You thought you were smart. If you didn't want us to know, you shouldn't have done it in the first place. Look at the report yourself." He tossed the internal bulletin to Shi and handed Shun and Kang each a copy.

The title read: "Radio Operators Proffered Love in the Air." Kang's heart tightened. He turned a page and read "From February 3 on, from 1:00 A.M. to 5:00 A.M., a radio operator in the Fifth regiment and an operator at the 36th station of Shenyang Military Region have developed a love affair in the air. . . ."

Kang was stunned, and his thick lips parted. He could never imagine Shi would make such an unlawful move. A small part of their love talk was transcribed in the report:

I am Shi Wei. Your name?
110 Lili. Where are you from?
Dalian. And you?
Beijing.
Your age?
Twenty-one. And you?
115 Twenty-two. Love your hand.
Why?
It is good.
Why? Not love me?
Yes, I do.
120 !
Love me?
Maybe.
. . . . . .

Kang wanted to cry, but he controlled himself. He saw Shi's face turn pale and sweat break out on his smooth forehead. Meanwhile Shun bit his lower lip, trying hard not to laugh.

125 "Now, what do you want to say?" Jiang asked.

Shi lowered his eyes and remained silent. The chief announced that the Communication Company had decided to suspend Shi Wei from his work during the wait for the final punishment. From now on, Shi had to go to the study room during the day and write out his confession and self-criticism.

Though he was working two more hours a day to cover for Shi, Kang no longer expected to meet Lili, whose family name was not revealed in the bulletin. Obviously she was also suspended from her work and must have been doing the same thing as Shi did every day in the company's study room. But the tune created by her fingers and her charming voice were still with him; actually they hurt him more than before. He tried cursing her and imagining all the bad things that could be attributed to a woman in order to pull her out of himself. He thought of her as a "broken shoe" which was worn by everyone, a bitch that raised her tail to any male dog, a hag who was shunned by all decent men, a White Bone Demon living on innocent blood. Still, he could not get rid of her. Whenever he was receiving a telegram, her voice would break in to catch him. "Sorry, don't take it to heart. I was teasing you. . . ." It was miserable. The misery went so deep that when he spoke to his comrades he often heard himself moaning. He hated his own listless voice.

Shi's punishment was administered a week later. Both Shi Wei and Wang Lili were expelled from the army. This time the woman's full name was given. To Kang's surprise, Shi did not cry and seemed to take it with ease. He ate well and slept well, and went on smoking expensive cigarettes. Kang figured there must have been two reasons why Shi did not care. First, with the help of his father, he would have no problem finding a good job at home; second, the expulsion gave him an opportunity to continue his love affair with Wang Lili, since they were now two grasshoppers tied together by one thread. Lucky for Shi, he didn't lose his military status for nothing. It seemed he would go to Shenyang soon and have a happy time with her.

The station planned to hold a farewell party for Shi Wei. Though it was not an honorable discharge, they had worked with Shi for almost a year and had some good feelings about him. For days Kang had been thinking what souvenir he should give Shi Wei. He finally chose a pair of pillow towels, which cost him four *yuan,* half his monthly pay. In the meantime his scalp remained numb, and he still could not come to himself. Not only did the task of receiving a telegram frighten him, but any telegraphic signal would give him the creeps. He had developed another habit—cursing himself relentlessly for his daydreaming and for having allowed himself to degenerate into a walking corpse for that fickle woman, whose name he would now murmur many times every night.

130   Four older soldiers from the Wireless Platoon were invited to the farewell party. Chief Jiang presented an album to Shi, and Shun gave him a pair of nylon socks. When Kang's pillow towels were displayed, everybody burst out laughing, for on each towel was embroidered a pair of lovely mandarin ducks and a line of red characters. One said: "Happy Life," and the other: "Sweet Dreams." Peanut shells and pear-stones fell on the floor because of the commotion the garish towels caused.

"You must be joking, Big Kang," Shi said, measuring one of the towels against his chest. "You think I'm going home to get married?"

"Why not?" Kang smiled. "Won't you go to Shenyang?"

"For what? I don't know anyone there."

Kang stood up. The floor seemed to be swaying beneath his feet. Tears welled up in his eyes. He picked up a mug and gulped the beer inside, his left hand holding the corner of the desk. He put down the mug, then turned to the door.

135   "Where are you going?" Chief Jiang asked.

Without replying, Kang went out into the open air. He wanted to bolt into the snow and run for hours, until his legs could no longer support him. But he paused. On the drill ground, a dozen soldiers from the Line Construction Platoon were practicing climbing telephone poles without wearing spikes. Behind the brick houses stood the thirty-meter-tall aerial, made of three poles connected to one another, which had been raised for their station by these fellow men. In the northeast, the Wusuli River displayed a series of green, steaming holes along its snow-covered course. On the fields and the slopes of the hills, a curtain of golden sparks, cast by the setting sun, was glittering. The gray forests stretched along the undulating mountain ridges toward the receding horizon. The sky was so high and the land so vast. Kang took a deep breath; a fresh contraction lingered in his chest. For the first time he felt a person was so small.

That evening he wrote a letter to the company's Party branch, imploring the leaders to transfer him to the Line Construction Platoon. He did not give an explicit reason, and merely said that somehow his mind was deteriorating and that he could not operate the telegraphic apparatus anymore. The letter ended as follows:

> If I can no longer serve the Revolutionary Cause and our Motherland with my brain, I can at least work with my hands, which are still young and strong. Please relieve me from the Wireless Platoon.

After writing the letter, he wept, filling his hands with tears. He used to believe that when he was demobilized he could make a decent living by working as a telegrapher at a post office or a train station, but now he had ruined his future. How painful it was to love and then give it up. If only he could forget that woman's voice and her telegraphic style. Whether he could or not, he had to try.

[1996]

Joining the Conversation: Critical Thinking and Writing

1. What is your response to "Love in the Air"? What interests you in it?
2. What do we learn about Kang in the first few pages? In what ways does he change?
3. A literary scholar, commenting on this story, says that it is a "perfect blend of comedy and tragedy." Do you agree?
4. "Love in the Air" is often taught in courses on creative writing, especially when the focus is on how to present "character" in fiction. Why do you think this is the case? What could an aspiring writer learn about "character" by studying Ha Jin's story?
5. Do you think that "Love in the Air" could be made into a good movie? Why or why not? Please explain.

ZZ PACKER

ZZ Packer was born in Chicago, Illinois, in 1973; her given name is Zuwena, *which in Swahili means "good." She received her undergraduate degree from Yale in 1994, and she then pursued graduate study in writing at Johns Hopkins University and the University of Iowa. The recipient of a number of honors and awards for her fiction, Packer has taught at Tulane, the University of Texas, and other institutions. She is best known for her book of stories,* Drinking Coffee Elsewhere *(2003). "Brownies," the story that opens that collection, was first published in 1999.*

Brownies

By our second day at Camp Crescendo, the girls in my Brownie troop had decided to kick the asses of each and every girl in Brownie Troop 909. Troop 909 was doomed from the first day of camp; they were white girls, their complexions a blend of ice cream: strawberry, vanilla. They turtled out from their bus in pairs, their rolled-up sleeping bags chromatized with Disney characters: Sleeping Beauty, Snow White, Mickey Mouse; or the generic ones cheap parents bought: washed-out rainbows, unicorns, curly-eyelashed frogs. Some clutched Igloo coolers and still others held on to stuffed toys like pacifiers, looking all around them like tourists determined to be dazzled.

Our troop was wending its way past their bus, past the ranger station, past the colorful trail guide drawn like a treasure map, locked behind glass.

"Man, did you smell them?" Arnetta said, giving the girls a slow once-over, "They smell like Chihuahuas. *Wet* Chihuahuas." Their troop was still at the entrance, and though we had passed them by yards, Arnetta raised her nose in the air and grimaced.

Arnetta said this from the very rear of the line, far away from Mrs. Margolin, who always strung our troop behind her like a brood of obedient ducklings. Mrs. Margolin even looked like a mother duck—she had hair cropped close to a small ball of a head, almost no neck, and huge, miraculous breasts. She wore enormous belts that looked like the kind that weightlifters wear, except hers would be cheap metallic gold or rabbit fur or covered with gigantic fake sunflowers, and often these belts would become nature lessons in and of themselves. "See," Mrs. Margolin once said to us, pointing to her belt, "this one's made entirely from the feathers of baby pigeons."

5   The belt layered with feathers was uncanny enough, but I was more disturbed by the realization that I had never actually *seen* a baby pigeon. I searched weeks for one, in vain—scampering after pigeons whenever I was downtown with my father.

But nature lessons were not Mrs. Margolin's top priority. She saw the position of troop leader as an evangelical post. Back at the A.M.E. church where our Brownie meetings were held, Mrs. Margolin was especially fond of imparting religious aphorisms by means of acrostics—"Satan" was the "Serpent Always Tempting and Noisome"; she'd refer to the. "Bible" as "Basic Instructions Before Leaving Earth." Whenever she quizzed us on these, expecting to hear the acrostics parroted back to her, only Arnetta's correct replies soared over our vague mumblings. "Jesus?" Mrs. Margolin might ask expectantly, and Arnetta alone would dutifully answer, "Jehovah's Example, Saving Us Sinners."

Arnetta always made a point of listening to Mrs. Margolin's religious talk and giving her what she wanted to hear. Because of this, Arnetta could have blared through a megaphone that the white girls of Troop 909 were "wet Chihuahuas" without so much as a blink from Mrs. Margolin. Once, Arnetta killed the troop goldfish by feeding it a french fry covered in ketchup, and when Mrs. Margolin demanded that she explain what had happened, claimed the goldfish had been eyeing her meal for *hours,* then the fish—giving in to temptation—had leapt up and snatched a whole golden fry from her fingertips.

"*Serious* Chihuahua," Octavia added, and though neither Arnetta nor Octavia could *spell* "Chihuahua," had ever *seen* a Chihuahua, trisyllabic words had gained a sort of exoticism within our fourth-grade set at Woodrow Wilson Elementary. Arnetta and Octavia would flip through the dictionary, determined to work the vulgar-sounding ones like "Djibouti" and "asinine" into conversation.

"*Caucasian* Chihuahuas," Arnetta said.

10   That did it. The girls in my troop turned elastic: Drema and Elise doubled up on one another like inextricably entwined kites; Octavia slapped her belly; Janice jumped straight up in the air, then did it again, as if to slam-dunk her own head.

They could not stop laughing. No one had laughed so hard since a boy named Martez had stuck a pencil in the electric socket and spent the whole day with a strange grin on his face.

"Girls, girls," said our parent helper, Mrs. Hedy. Mrs. Hedy was Octavia's mother, and she wagged her index finger perfunctorily, like a windshield wiper. "Stop it, now. Be good." She said this loud enough to be heard, but lazily, bereft of any feeling or indication that she meant to be obeyed, as though she could say these words again at the exact same pitch if a button somewhere on her were pressed.

But the rest of the girls didn't stop; they only laughed louder. It was the word "Caucasian" that got them all going. One day at school, about a month before the Brownie camping trip, Arnetta turned to a boy wearing impossibly high-ankled floodwater jeans and said, "What are you? *Caucasian?*" The word took off from there, and soon everything was Caucasian. If you ate too fast you ate like a Caucasian, if you ate too slow you ate like a Caucasian. The biggest feat anyone at Woodrow Wilson could do was to jump off the swing in midair, at the highest point in its arc, and if you fell (as I had, more than once) instead of landing on your feet, knees bent Olympic gymnast–style, Arnetta and Octavia were prepared to comment. They'd look at each other with the silence of passengers who'd narrowly escaped an accident, then nod their heads, whispering with solemn horror, *"Caucasian."*

Even the only white kid in our school, Dennis, got in on the Caucasian act. That time when Martez stuck a pencil in the socket, Dennis had pointed and yelled, "That was *so* Caucasian!"

When you lived in the south suburbs of Atlanta, it was easy to forget about whites. Whites were like those baby pigeons: real and existing, but rarely seen or thought about. Everyone had been to Rich's to go clothes shopping, everyone had seen white girls and their mothers coo-cooing over dresses; everyone had gone to the downtown library and seen white businessmen swish by importantly, wrists flexed in front of them to check the time as though they would change from Clark Kent into Superman at any second. But those images were as fleeting as cards shuffled in a deck, whereas the ten white girls behind us—*invaders,* Arnetta would later call them—were instantly real and memorable, with their long, shampoo-commercial hair, straight as spaghetti from the box. This alone was reason for envy and hatred. The only black girl most of us had ever seen with hair that long was Octavia, whose hair hung past her butt like a Hawaiian hula dancer's. The sight of Octavia's mane prompted other girls to listen to her reverentially, as though whatever she had to say would somehow activate their own follicles. For example, when, on the first day of camp, Octavia made as if to speak, and everyone fell silent. "Nobody," Octavia said, "calls us niggers."

15   At the end of that first day, when half of our troop made their way back to the cabin after tag-team restroom visits, Arnetta said she'd heard one of the Troop 909 girls call Daphne a nigger. The other half of the girls and I were helping Mrs. Margolin clean up the pots and pans from the campfire ravioli dinner. When we made our way to the restrooms to wash up and brush our teeth, we met up with Arnetta midway.

"Man, I completely heard the girl," Arnetta reported. "Right, Daphne?"

Daphne hardly ever spoke, but when she did, her voice was petite and tinkly, the voice one might expect from a shiny new earring. She'd written a poem once, for Langston Hughes Day, a poem brimming with all the teacher-winning ingredients—trees and oceans, sunsets and moons—but what cinched the poem for the grown-ups, snatching the win from Octavia's musical ode to Grandmaster Flash and the Furious Five, were Daphne's last lines:

You are my father, the veteran
When you cry in the dark
It rains and rains and rains in my heart

She'd always worn clean, though faded, jumpers and dresses when Chic jeans were the fashion, but when she went up to the dais to receive her prize journal, pages trimmed in gold, she wore a new dress with a velveteen bodice and a taffeta skirt as wide as an umbrella. All the kids clapped, though none of them understood the poem. I'd read encyclopedias the way others read comics, and I didn't get it. But those last lines pricked me, they were so eerie, and as my father and I ate cereal, I'd whisper over my Froot Loops, like a mantra, *"You are my father, the veteran. You are my father, the veteran, the veteran, the veteran,"* until my father, who acted in plays as Caliban and Othello and was not a veteran, marched me up to my teacher one morning and said, "Can you tell me what's wrong with this kid?"

I thought Daphne and I might become friends, but I think she grew spooked by me whispering those lines to her, begging her to tell me what they meant, and I soon understood that two quiet people like us were better off quiet alone.

20   "Daphne? Didn't you hear them call you a nigger?" Arnetta asked, giving Daphne a nudge.

The sun was setting behind the trees, and their leafy tops formed a canopy of black lace for the flame of the sun to pass through. Daphne shrugged her shoulders at first, then slowly nodded her head when Arnetta gave her a hard look.

Twenty minutes later, when my restroom group returned to the cabin, Arnetta was still talking about Troop 909. My restroom group had passed by some of the 909 girls. For the most part, they deferred to us, waving us into the restrooms, letting us go even though they'd gotten there first.

We'd seen them, but from afar, never within their orbit enough to see whether their faces were the way all white girls appeared on TV—ponytailed and full of energy, bubbling over with love and money. All I could see was that some of them rapidly fanned their faces with their hands, though the heat of the day had long passed. A few seemed to be lolling their heads in slow circles, half purposefully, as if exercising the muscles of their necks, half ecstatically, like Stevie Wonder.

"We can't let them get away with that," Arnetta said, dropping her voice to a laryngitic whisper. "We can't let them get away with calling us niggers. I say we teach them a lesson." She sat down cross-legged on a sleeping bag, an embittered Buddha, eyes glimmering acrylic-black. "We can't go telling Mrs. Margolin, either. Mrs. Margolin'll say something about doing unto others and the path of righteousness and all. Forget that shit." She let her eyes flutter irreverently till they half closed, as though ignoring an insult not worth returning. We could all hear Mrs. Margolin outside, gathering the last of the metal campware.

25   Nobody said anything for a while. Usually people were quiet after Arnetta spoke. Her tone had an upholstered confidence that was somehow both regal and vulgar at once. It demanded a few moments of silence in its wake, like the ringing of a church bell or the playing of taps. Sometimes Octavia would ditto or dissent to whatever Arnetta had said, and this was the signal that others could speak. But this time Octavia just swirled a long cord of hair into pretzel shapes.

"Well?" Arnetta said. She looked as if she had discerned the hidden severity of the situation and was waiting for the rest of us to catch up. Everyone looked from Arnetta to Daphne. It was, after all, Daphne who had supposedly been called the name, but Daphne sat on the bare cabin floor, flipping through the pages of the Girl Scout handbook, eyebrows arched in mock wonder, as if the handbook

were a catalogue full of bright and startling foreign costumes. Janice broke the silence. She clapped her hands to broach her idea of a plan.

"They gone be sleeping," she whispered conspiratorially, "then we gone sneak into they cabin, then we'll put daddy longlegs in they sleeping bags. Then they'll wake up. Then we gone beat 'em up till they're as flat as frying pans!" She jammed her fist into the palm of her hand, then made a sizzling sound.

Janice's country accent was laughable, her looks homely, her jumpy acrobatics embarrassing to behold. Arnetta and Octavia volleyed amused, arrogant smiles whenever Janice opened her mouth, but Janice never caught the hint, spoke whenever she wanted, fluttered around Arnetta and Octavia futilely offering her opinions to their departing backs. Whenever Arnetta and Octavia shooed her away, Janice loitered until the two would finally sigh and ask, "What *is* it, Miss Caucausoid? What do you *want?*"

"Shut up, Janice," Octavia said, letting a fingered loop of hair fall to her waist as though just the sound of Janice's voice had ruined the fun of her hair twisting.

30   Janice obeyed, her mouth hung open in a loose grin, unflappable, unhurt.

"All right," Arnetta said, standing up. "We're going to have a secret meeting and talk about what we're going to do."

Everyone gravely nodded her head. The word "secret" had a built-in importance, the modifier form of the word carried more clout than the noun. A secret meant nothing; it was like gossip: just a bit of unpleasant knowledge about someone who happened to be someone other than yourself. A secret *meeting,* or a secret *club* was entirely different.

That was when Arnetta turned to me as though she knew that doing so was both a compliment and a charity.

"Snot, you're not going to be a bitch and tell Mrs. Margolin, are you?"

35   I had been called "Snot" ever since first grade, when I'd sneezed in class and two long ropes of mucus had splattered a nearby girl.

"Hey," I said. "Maybe you didn't hear them right—I mean—"

"Are you gonna tell on us or not?" was all Arnetta wanted to know, and by the time the question was asked, the rest of our Brownie troop looked at me as though they'd already decided their course of action, me being the only impediment.

Camp Crescendo used to double as a high-school-band and field hockey camp until an arcing field hockey ball landed on the clasp of a girl's metal barrette, knifing a skull nerve and paralyzing the right side of her body. The camp closed down for a few years and the girl's teammates built a memorial, filling the spot on which the girl fell with hockey balls, on which they had painted—all in nail polish—get-well tidings, flowers, and hearts. The balls were still stacked there, like a shrine of ostrich eggs embedded in the ground.

On the second day of camp, Troop 909 was dancing around the mound of hockey balls, their limbs jangling awkwardly, their cries like the constant summer squeal of an amusement park. There was a stream that bordered the field hockey lawn, and the girls from my troop settled next to it, scarfing down the last of lunch: sandwiches made from salami and slices of tomato that had gotten waterlogged from the melting ice in the cooler. From the stream bank, Arnetta eyed the Troop 909 girls, scrutinizing their movements to glean inspiration for battle.

40   "Man," Arnetta said, "we could bumrush them right now if that damn lady would *leave.*"

The 909 troop leader was a white woman with the severe pageboy hairdo of an ancient Egyptian. She lay on a picnic blanket, sphinx-like, eating a banana, sometimes holding it out in front of her like a microphone. Beside her sat a girl slowly flapping one hand like a bird with a broken wing. Occasionally, the leader would call out the names of girls who'd attempted leapfrogs and flips, or of girls who yelled too loudly or strayed far from the circle.

"I'm just glad Big Fat Mama's not following us here," Octavia said. "At least we don't have to worry about her." Mrs. Margolin, Octavia assured us, was having her Afternoon Devotional, shrouded in mosquito netting, in a clearing she'd found. Mrs. Hedy was cleaning mud from her espadrilles in the cabin.

"I handled them." Arnetta sucked on her teeth and proudly grinned. "I told her we was going to gather leaves."

"Gather leaves," Octavia said, nodding respectfully. "That's a good one. Especially since they're so mad-crazy about this camping thing." She looked from ground to sky, sky to ground. Her hair hung down her back in two braids like a squaw's. "I mean, I really don't know why it's even called *camping*—all we ever do with Nature is find some twigs and say something like, 'Wow, this fell from a tree.'" She then studied her sandwich. With two disdainful fingers, she picked out a slice of dripping tomato, the sections congealed with red slime. She pitched it into the stream embrowned with dead leaves and the murky effigies of other dead things, but in the opaque water, a group of small silver-brown fish appeared. They surrounded the tomato and nibbled.

45   "Look!" Janice cried. "Fishes! Fishes!" As she scrambled to the edge of the stream to watch, a covey of insects threw up tantrums from the wheatgrass and nettle, a throng of tiny electric machines, all going at once. Octavia sneaked up behind Janice as if to push her in. Daphne and I exchanged terrified looks. It seemed as though only we knew that Octavia was close enough—and bold enough—to actually push Janice into the stream. Janice turned around quickly, but Octavia was already staring serenely into the still water as though she was gathering some sort of courage from it. "What's so funny?" Janice said, eyeing them all suspiciously.

Elise began humming the tune to "Karma Chameleon," all the girls joining in, their hums light and facile. Janice also began to hum, against everyone else, the high-octane opening chords of "Beat It."

"I love me some Michael Jackson," Janice said when she'd finished humming, smacking her lips as though Michael Jackson were a favorite meal. "I *will* marry Michael Jackson."

Before anyone had a chance to impress upon Janice the impossibility of this, Arnetta suddenly rose, made a sun visor of her hand, and watched Troop 909 leave the field hockey lawn.

"Dammit!" she said. "We've got to get them *alone*."

50   "They won't ever be alone," I said. All the rest of the girls looked at me, for I usually kept quiet. If I spoke even a word, I could count on someone calling me Snot. Everyone seemed to think that we could beat up these girls; no one entertained the thought that they might fight *back*. "The only time they'll be unsupervised is in the bathroom."

"Oh shut up, Snot," Octavia said.

But Arnetta slowly nodded her head. "The bathroom," she said.

"The bathroom," she said, again and again. "The bathroom! The bathroom!"

According to Octavia's watch, it took us five minutes to hike to the restrooms, which were midway between our cabin and Troop 909's. Inside, the mirrors above the sinks returned only the vaguest of reflections, as though someone had taken a scouring pad to their surfaces to obscure the shine. Pine needles, leaves, and dirty, flattened wads of chewing gum covered the floor like a mosaic. Webs of hair matted the drain in the middle of the floor. Above the sinks and below the mirrors, stacks of folded white paper towels lay on a long metal counter. Shaggy white balls of paper towels sat on the sinktops in a line like corsages on display A thread of floss snaked from a wad of tissues dotted with the faint red-pink of blood. One of those white girls, I thought, had just lost a tooth.

Though the restroom looked almost the same as it had the night before, it somehow seemed stranger now. We hadn't noticed the wooden rafters coming together in great V's. We were, it seemed, inside a whale, viewing the ribs of the roof of its mouth.

55   "Wow. It's a mess," Elise said.

"You can say that again."

Arnetta leaned against the doorjamb of a restroom stall. "This is where they'll be again," she said. Just seeing the place, just having a plan seemed to satisfy her. "We'll go in and talk to them. You know, 'How you doing? How long'll you be here?' That sort of thing. Then Octavia and I are gonna tell them what happens when they call any one of us a nigger."

"I'm going to say something, too," Janice said.

Arnetta considered this. "Sure," she said. "Of course. Whatever you want."

60   Janice pointed her finger like a gun at Octavia and rehearsed the line she'd thought up, "'We're gonna teach you a *lesson*!' That's what I'm going to say." She narrowed her eyes like a TV mobster. "'We're gonna teach you little girls a lesson!'"

With the back of her hand, Octavia brushed Janice's finger away. "You couldn't teach me to shit in a toilet."

"But," I said, "what if they say, 'We didn't say that? We didn't call anyone an N-I-G-G-E-R.'"

"Snot," Arnetta said, and then sighed. "Don't think. Just fight. If you even know how."

Everyone laughed except Daphne. Arnetta gently laid her hand on Daphne's shoulder. "Daphne. You don't have to fight. We're doing this for you."

65   Daphne walked to the counter, took a clean paper towel, and carefully unfolded it like a map. With it, she began to pick up the trash all around. Everyone watched.

"C'mon," Arnetta said to everyone. "Let's beat it." We all ambled toward the doorway, where the sunshine made one large white rectangle of light. We were immediately blinded, and we shielded our eyes with our hands and our forearms.

"Daphne?" Arnetta asked. "Are you coming?"

We all looked back at the bending girl, the thin of her back hunched like the back of a custodian sweeping a stage, caught in limelight. Stray strands of her hair were lit near-transparent, thin fiber-optic threads. She did not nod yes to the question, nor did she shake her head no. She abided, bent. Then she began again, picking up leaves, wads of paper, the cotton fluff innards from a torn stuffed toy. She did it so methodically, so exquisitely, so humbly, she must have been trained. I thought of those dresses she wore, faded and old, yet so pressed and clean. I then saw the poverty in them; I then could imagine her mother, cleaning the houses of others, returning home, weary.

"I guess she's not coming."

70   We left her and headed back to our cabin, over pine needles and leaves, taking the path full of shade.

"What about our secret meeting?" Elise asked.

Arnetta enunciated her words in a way that defied contradiction: "We just had it."

It was nearing our bedtime, but the sun had not yet set.

"Hey, your mama's coming," Arnetta said to Octavia when she saw Mrs. Hedy walk toward the cabin, sniffling. When Octavia's mother wasn't giving bored, parochial orders, she sniffled continuously, mourning an imminent divorce from her husband. She might begin a sentence, "I don't know what Robert will do when Octavia and I are gone. Who'll buy him cigarettes?" and Octavia would hotly whisper,

"Mama," in a way that meant: Please don't talk about our problems in front of everyone. Please shut up.

75   But when Mrs. Hedy began talking about her husband, thinking about her husband, seeing clouds shaped like the head of her husband, she couldn't be quiet, and no one could dislodge her from the comfort of her own woe. Only one thing could perk her up—Brownie songs. If the girls were quiet, and Mrs. Hedy was in her dopey, sorrowful mood, she would say, "Y'all know I like those songs, girls. Why don't you sing one?" Everyone would groan, except me and Daphne. I, for one, liked some of the songs.

"C'mon, everybody," Octavia said drearily. "She likes the Brownie song best."

We sang, loud enough to reach Mrs. Hedy:

"I've got something in my pocket;
It belongs across my face.
And I keep it very close at hand
    in a most convenient place.
I'm sure you couldn't guess it
If you guessed a long, long while.
So I'll take it out and put it on—
It's a great big Brownie smile!"

The Brownie song was supposed to be sung cheerfully, as though we were elves in a workshop, singing as we merrily cobbled shoes, but everyone except me hated the song so much that they sang it like a maudlin record, played on the most sluggish of rpms.

"That was good," Mrs. Hedy said, closing the cabin door behind her. "Wasn't that nice, Linda?"

80   "Praise God," Mrs. Margolin answered without raising her head from the chore of counting out Popsicle sticks for the next day's craft session.

"Sing another one," Mrs. Hedy said. She said it with a sort of joyful aggression, like a drunk I'd once seen who'd refused to leave a Korean grocery.

"God, Mama, get over it," Octavia whispered in a voice meant only for Arnetta, but Mrs. Hedy heard it and started to leave the cabin.

"Don't go," Arnetta said. She ran after Mrs. Hedy and held her by the arm. "We haven't finished singing." She nudged us with a single look. "Let's sing the 'Friends Song.' For Mrs. Hedy."

Although I liked some of the songs, I hated this one:

Make new friends
But keep the o-old,
One is silver
And the other gold.

85   If most of the girls in the troop could be any type of metal, they'd be bunched-up wads of tinfoil, maybe, or rusty iron nails you had to get tetanus shots for.

"No, no, no," Mrs. Margolin said before anyone could start in on the "Friends Song." "An uplifting song. Something to lift her up and take her mind off all these earthly burdens."

Arnetta and Octavia rolled their eyes. Everyone knew what song Mrs. Margolin was talking about, and no one, no one, wanted to sing it.

"Please, no," a voice called out. "Not 'The Doughnut Song.'"

"Please not 'The Doughnut Song,'" Octavia pleaded.

90   "I'll brush my teeth two times if I don't have to sing 'The Doughnut—'"

"Sing!" Mrs. Margolin demanded.

We sang:

"Life without Jesus is like a do-ough-nut!
Like a do-ooough-nut!
Like a do-ooough-nut!
Life without Jesus is like a do-ough-nut!
There's a hole in the middle of my soul!"

There were other verses, involving other pastries, but we stopped after the first one and cast glances toward Mrs. Margolin to see if we could gain a reprieve. Mrs. Margolin's eyes fluttered blissfully. She was half asleep.

"Awww," Mrs. Hedy said, as though giant Mrs. Margolin were a cute baby, "Mrs. Margolin's had a long day."

95   "Yes indeed," Mrs. Margolin answered. "If you don't mind, I might just go to the lodge where the beds are. I haven't been the same since the operation."

I had not heard of this operation, or when it had occurred, since Mrs. Margolin had never missed the once-a-week Brownie meetings, but I could see from Daphne's face that she was concerned, and I could see that the other girls had decided that Mrs. Margolin's operation must have happened long ago in some remote time unconnected to our own. Nevertheless, they put on sad faces. We had all been taught that adulthood was full of sorrow and pain, taxes and bills, dreaded work and dealings with whites, sickness and death. I tried to do what the others did. I tried to look silent.

"Go right ahead, Linda," Mrs. Hedy said. "I'll watch the girls." Mrs. Hedy seemed to forget about divorce for a moment; she looked at us with dewy eyes, as if we were mysterious, furry creatures. Meanwhile, Mrs. Margolin walked through the maze of sleeping bags until she found her own. She gathered a neat stack of clothes and pajamas slowly, as though doing so was almost painful. She took her toothbrush, her toothpaste, her pillow. "All right!" Mrs. Margolin said, addressing us all from the threshold of the cabin. "Be in bed by nine." She said it with a twinkle in her voice, letting us know she was allowing us to be naughty and stay up till nine-fifteen.

"C'mon everybody," Arnetta said after Mrs. Margolin left. "Time for us to wash up."

Everyone watched Mrs. Hedy closely, wondering whether she would insist on coming with us since it was night, making a fight with Troop 909 nearly impossible. Troop 909 would soon be in the bathroom, washing their faces, brushing their teeth—completely unsuspecting of our ambush.

100   "We won't be long," Arnetta said. "We're old enough to go to the restrooms by ourselves."

Ms. Hedy pursed her lips at this dilemma. "Well, I guess you Brownies are almost Girl Scouts, right?"

"Right!"

"Just one more badge," Drema said.

"And about," Octavia droned, "a million more cookies to sell." Octavia looked at all of us, *Now's our chance,* her face seemed to say, but our chance to do *what,* I didn't exactly know.

105   Finally, Mrs. Hedy walked to the doorway where Octavia stood dutifully waiting to say goodbye but looking bored doing it. Mrs. Hedy held Octavia's chin. "You'll be good?"

"Yes, Mama."

"And remember to pray for me and your father? If I'm asleep when you get back?"

"Yes, Mama."

When the other girls had finished getting their toothbrushes and washcloths and flashlights for the group restroom trip, I was drawing pictures of tiny birds with too many feathers. Daphne was sitting on her sleeping bag, reading.

110   "You're not going to come?" Octavia asked.

Daphne shook her head.

"I'm gonna stay, too," I said. "I'll go to the restroom when Daphne and Mrs. Hedy go."

Arnetta leaned down toward me and whispered so that Mrs. Hedy, who'd taken over Mrs. Margolin's task of counting Popsicle sticks, couldn't hear. "No, Snot. If we get in trouble, you're going to get in trouble with the rest of us."

We made our way through the darkness by flashlight. The tree branches that had shaded us just hours earlier, along the same path, now looked like arms sprouting menacing hands. The stars sprinkled the sky like spilled salt. They seemed fastened to the darkness, high up and holy, their places fixed and definite as we stirred beneath them.

115   Some, like me, were quiet because we were afraid of the dark; others were talking like crazy for the same reason.

"Wow!" Drema said, looking up. "Why are all the stars out here? I never see stars back on Oneida Street."

"It's a camping trip, that's why," Octavia said. "You're supposed to see stars on camping trips."

Janice said, "This place smells like my mother's air freshener."

"These woods are *pine*," Elise said. "Your mother probably uses *pine* air freshener."

120   Janice mouthed an exaggerated "Oh," nodding her head as though she just then understood one of the world's great secrets.

No one talked about fighting. Everyone was afraid enough just walking through the infinite deep of the woods. Even though I didn't fight to fight, was afraid of fighting, I felt I was part of the rest of the troop; like I was defending something. We trudged against the slight incline of the path, Arnetta leading the way.

"You know," I said, "their leader will be there. Or they won't even be there. It's dark already. Last night the sun was still in the sky. I'm sure they're already finished."

Arnetta acted as if she hadn't heard me. I followed her gaze with my flashlight, and that's when I saw the squares of light in the darkness. The bathroom was just ahead.

But the girls were there. We could hear them before we could see them.

125   "Octavia and I will go in first so they'll think there's just two of us, then wait till I say, 'We're gonna teach you a lesson,'" Arnetta said. "Then, bust in. That'll surprise them."

"That's what I was supposed to say," Janice said.

Arnetta went inside, Octavia next to her. Janice followed, and the rest of us waited outside.

They were in there for what seemed like whole minutes, but something was wrong. Arnetta hadn't given the signal yet. I was with the girls outside when I heard one of the Troop 909 girls say, "NO. That did NOT happen!"

That was to be expected, that they'd deny the whole thing. What I hadn't expected was *the voice* in which the denial was said. The girl sounded as though her tongue were caught in her mouth. "That's a BAD word!" the girl continued. "We don't say BAD words!"

130   "Let's go in," Elise said.

"No," Drema said, "I don't want to. What if we get beat up?"

"Snot?" Elise turned to me, her flashlight blinding. It was the first time anyone had asked my opinion, though I knew they were just asking because they were afraid.

"I say we go inside, just to see what's going on."

"But Arnetta didn't give us the signal," Drema said. "She's supposed to say, 'We're gonna teach you a lesson,' and I didn't hear her say it."

135   "C'mon," I said. "Let's just go in."

We went inside. There we found the white girls—about five girls huddled up next to one big girl. I instantly knew she was the owner of the voice we'd heard. Arnetta and Octavia inched toward us as soon as we entered.

"Where's Janice?" Elise asked, then we heard a flush. "Oh."

"I think," Octavia said, whispering to Elise, "they're retarded."

"We ARE NOT retarded!" the big girl said, though it was obvious that she was. That they all were. The girls around her began to whimper.

140   "They're just pretending," Arnetta said, trying to convince herself "I know they are."

Octavia turned to Arnetta. "Arnetta. Let's just leave."

Janice came out of a stall, happy and relieved, then she suddenly remembered her line, pointed to the big girl, and said, "We're gonna teach you a lesson."

"Shut up, Janice," Octavia said, but her heart was not in it. Arnetta's face was set in a lost, deep scowl. Octavia turned to the big girl and said loudly, slowly, as if they were all deaf, "We're going to leave. It was nice meeting you, O.K.? You don't have to tell anyone that we were here. O.K.?"

"Why not?" said the big girl, like a taunt. When she spoke, her lips did not meet, her mouth did not close. Her tongue grazed the roof of her mouth, like a little pink fish. "You'll get in trouble. I know. *I* know."

145   Arnetta got back her old cunning. "If you said anything, then you'd be a tattletale."

The girl looked sad for a moment, then perked up quickly. A flash of genius crossed her face. "I *like* tattletale."

"It's all right, girls. It's gonna be all right!" the 909 troop leader said. All of Troop 909 burst into tears. It was as though someone had instructed them all to cry at once. The troop leader had girls under her arm, and all the rest of the girls crowded about her. It reminded me of a hog I'd seen on a field trip, where all the little hogs gathered about the mother at feeding time, latching onto her teats. The 909 troop leader had come into the bathroom, shortly after the big girl had threatened to tell. Then the ranger came, then, once the ranger had radioed the station, Mrs. Margolin arrived with Daphne in tow.

The ranger had left the restroom area, but everyone else was huddled just outside, swatting mosquitoes.

"Oh. They *will* apologize," Mrs. Margolin said to the 909 troop leader, but she said this so angrily, I knew she was speaking more to us than to the other troop leader. "When their parents find out, every one a them will be on punishment."

150   "It's all right, it's all right," the 909 troop leader reassured Mrs. Margolin. Her voice lilted in the same way it had when addressing the girls. She smiled the whole time she talked. She was like one of those TV-cooking-show women who talk and dice onions and smile all at the same time.

"See. It could have happened. I'm not calling your girls fibbers or anything." She shook her head ferociously from side to side, her Egyptian-style pageboy flapping against her cheeks like heavy drapes. "It *could* have happened. See. Our girls are *not* retarded. They are *delayed* learners." She said this in a syrupy instructional voice, as though our troop might be delayed learners as well. "We're from the Decatur Children's Academy. Many of them just have special needs."

"Now we won't be able to walk to the bathroom by ourselves!" the big girl said.

"Yes you will," the troop leader said, "but maybe we'll wait till we get back to Decatur—"

"I don't want to wait!" the girl said. "I want my Independence badge!"

155   The girls in my troop were entirely speechless. Arnetta looked stoic, as though she were soon to be tortured but was determined not to appear weak. Mrs. Margolin pursed her lips solemnly and said, "Bless them, Lord. Bless them."

In contrast, the Troop 909 leader was full of words and energy. "Some of our girls are echolalic—" She smiled and happily presented one of the girls hanging onto her, but the girl widened her eyes in horror, and violently withdrew herself from the center of attention, sensing she was being sacrificed for the village sins. "Echolalic," the troop leader continued. "That means they will say whatever they hear, like an echo—that's where the word comes from. It comes from 'echo.'" She ducked her head apologetically, "I mean, not all of them have the most *progressive* of parents, so if they heard a bad word, they might have repeated it. But I guarantee it would not have been *intentional*."

Arnetta spoke. "I saw her say the word. I heard her." She pointed to a small girl, smaller than any of us, wearing an oversized T-shirt that read: "Eat Bertha's Mussels."

The troop leader shook her head and smiled, "That's impossible. She doesn't speak. She can, but she doesn't."

Arnetta furrowed her brow. "No. It wasn't her. That's right. It was *her*."

160   The girl Arnetta pointed to grinned as though she'd been paid a compliment. She was the only one from either troop actually wearing a full uniform: the mocha-colored A-line shift, the orange ascot, the sash covered with badges, though all the same one—-the Try-It patch. She took a few steps toward Arnetta and made a grand sweeping gesture toward the sash. "See," she said, full of self-importance, "I'm a Brownie." I had a hard time imagining this girl calling anyone a "nigger"; the girl looked perpetually delighted, as though she would have cuddled up with a grizzly if someone had let her.

On the fourth morning, we boarded the bus to go home.

The previous day had been spent building miniature churches from Popsicle sticks. We hardly left the cabin. Mrs. Margolin and Mrs. Hedy guarded us so closely, almost no one talked for the entire day.

Even on the day of departure from Camp Crescendo, all was serious and silent. The bus ride began quietly enough. Arnetta had to sit beside Mrs. Margolin; Octavia had to sit beside her mother. I sat beside Daphne, who gave me her prize journal without a word of explanation.

"You don't want it?"

165   She shook her head no. It was empty.

Then Mrs. Hedy began to weep. "Octavia," Mrs. Hedy said to her daughter without looking at her, "I'm going to sit with Mrs. Margolin. All right?"

Arnetta exchanged seats with Mrs. Hedy. With the two women up front, Elise felt it safe to speak. "Hey," she said, then she set her face into a placid, vacant stare, trying to imitate that of a Troop 909 girl. Emboldened, Arnetta made a gesture of mock pride toward an imaginary sash, the way the girl in full uniform had done. Then they all made a game of it, trying to do the most exaggerated imitations of the Troop 909 girls, all without speaking, all without laughing loud enough to catch the women's attention.

Daphne looked down at her shoes, white with sneaker polish. I opened the journal she'd given me. I looked out the window, trying to decide what to write, searching for lines, but nothing could compare with what Daphne had written, *"My father, the veteran,"* my favorite line of all time. It replayed itself in my head, and I gave up trying to write.

By then, it seemed that the rest of the troop had given up making fun of the girls in Troop 909. They were now quietly gossiping about who had passed notes to whom in school. For a moment the gossiping fell off, and all I heard was the hum of the bus as we sped down the road and the muffled sounds of Mrs. Hedy and Mrs. Margolin talking about serious things.

170 "You know," Octavia whispered, "why did *we* have to be stuck at a camp with retarded girls? You know?"

"You know why," Arnetta answered. She narrowed her eyes like a cat. "My mama and I were in the mall in Buckhead, and this white lady just kept looking at us. I mean, like we were foreign or something. Like we were from China."

"What did the woman say?" Elise asked.

"Nothing," Arnetta said. "She didn't say nothing."

A few girls quietly nodded their heads.

175 "There was this time," I said, "when my father and I were in the mall and—"

"Oh shut up, Snot," Octavia said.

I stared at Octavia, then rolled my eyes from her to the window. As I watched the trees blur, I wanted nothing more than to be through with it all: the bus ride, the troop, school—all of it. But we were going home. I'd see the same girls in school the next day. We were on a bus, and there was nowhere else to go.

"Go on, Laurel," Daphne said to me. It seemed like the first time she'd spoken the whole trip, and she'd said my name. I turned to her and smiled weakly so as not to cry, hoping she'd remember when I'd tried to be her friend, thinking maybe that her gift of the journal was an invitation of friendship. But she didn't smile back. All she said was, "What happened?"

I studied the girls, waiting for Octavia to tell me to shut up again before I even had a chance to utter another word, but everyone was amazed that Daphne had spoken. The bus was silent. I gathered my voice. "Well," I said. "My father and I were in this mall, but *I* was the one doing the staring." I stopped and glanced from face to face. I continued. "There were these white people dressed like Puritans or something, but they weren't Puritans. They were Mennonites. They're these people who, if you ask them to do a favor, like paint your porch or something, they have to do it. It's in their rules."

180 "That sucks," someone said.

"C'mon," Arnetta said. "You're lying."

"I am not."

"How do you know that's not just some story someone made up?" Elise asked, her head cocked full of daring. "I mean, who's gonna do whatever you ask?"

"It's not made up. I know because when I was looking at them, my father said, 'See those people? If you ask them to do something, they'll do it. Anything you want.'"

185 No one would call anyone's father a liar—then they'd have to fight the person. But Drema parsed her words carefully. "How does your *father* know that's not just some story? Huh?"

"Because," I said, "he went up to the man and asked him would he paint our porch, and the man said yes. It's their religion."

"Man, I'm glad I'm a Baptist," Elise said, shaking her head in sympathy for the Mennonites.

"So did the guy do it?" Drema asked, scooting closer to hear if the story got juicy.

"Yeah," I said. "His whole family was with him. My dad drove them to our house. They all painted our porch. The woman and girl were in bonnets and long, long skirts with buttons up to their necks. The guy wore this weird hat and these huge suspenders."

190   "Why," Arnetta asked archly, as though she didn't believe a word, "would someone pick a *porch?* If they'll do anything, why not make them paint the whole *house?* Why not ask for a hundred bucks?"

I thought about it, and then remembered the words my father had said about them painting our porch, though I had never seemed to think about his words after he'd said them.

"He said," I began, only then understanding the words as they uncoiled from my mouth, "it was the only time he'd have a white man on his knees doing something for a black man for free."

I now understood what he meant, and why he did it, though I didn't like it. When you've been made to feel bad for so long, you jump at the chance to do it to others. I remembered the Mennonites bending the way Daphne had bent when she was cleaning the restroom. I remembered the dark blue of their bonnets, the black of their shoes. They painted the porch as though scrubbing a floor. I was already trembling before Daphne asked quietly, "Did he thank them?"

I looked out the window. I could not tell which were the thoughts and which were the trees. "No," I said, and suddenly knew there was something mean in the world that I could not stop.

195   Arnetta laughed. "If I asked them to take off their long skirts and bonnets and put on some jeans, would they do it?"

And Daphne's voice, quiet, steady: "Maybe they would. Just to be nice."

Joining the Conversation: Critical Thinking and Writing

1. How would you describe the narrator of "Brownies"? Is she someone you could imagine as a friend?
2. Is there anything in Packer's story that you did not understand? Did anything in the story surprise you?
3. The critic Bryan Aubrey has said that "Brownies," while a story with "a serious theme and purpose," also contains "a great deal of humor." Do you agree?
4. What is Packer telling us in this story about race relations and prejudice?
5. In an interview in *Writer's Digest,* 20 July 2011, Packer says, "At some point the writer must ask himself in what way the story—as particular and specific as it hopefully is—is also universal, for all good stories are both particular and universal." What do you see as the "universal" element or theme in "Brownies"?

POEMS

WILLIAM BLAKE

William Blake (1757–1827) was born in London and at fourteen was apprenticed for seven years to an engraver. A Christian visionary poet, he made his living by giving drawing lessons and by illustrating books, including his own Songs of Innocence

(1789) and Songs of Experience *(1794). These two books represent, he said, "two contrary states of the human soul." ("Infant Joy" and "The Echoing Green" come from* Innocence, *"Infant Sorrow" comes from* Experience.*) In 1809 Blake exhibited his art, but the show was a failure. Not until he was in his sixties, when he stopped writing poetry, did he achieve any public recognition—and then it was as a painter.*

"Infant Joy" by William Blake, from *Songs of Innocence.*

Infant Joy

"I have no name,
I am but two days old."
What shall I call thee?
"I happy am,
Joy is my name."

Sweet joy befall thee!
Pretty joy!
Sweet joy but two days old,

Sweet joy I call thee;
Thou dost smile,   10
I sing the while—
Sweet joy befall thee.

[1789]

"Infant Sorrow" by William Blake, from *Songs of Experience*.

Infant Sorrow

My mother groand! my father wept.
Into the dangerous world I leapt,
Helpless, naked, piping loud;
Like a fiend hid in a cloud.

Struggling in my father's hands,   5
Striving against my swadling bands;
Bound and weary I thought best
To sulk upon my mother's breast.

[1794]

Joining the Conversation: Critical Thinking and Writing

1. "Infant Joy" begins "I have no name," but by line 5 the infant says "Joy is my name." What does the mother reply? Does she know the infant's name?

2. In line 9 the mother says, "Sweet joy I call thee." Does the line suggest how the mother has learned the name? What is the child's response?

3. In "Infant Sorrow," why is the infant sorrowful? What does the baby struggle against? Does "Like a fiend" suggest that it is inherently wicked and therefore should be repressed? Or does the adult world wickedly repress energy?

4. Why does the mother groan? Why does the father weep? Is the world "dangerous" to the infant in other than an obviously physical sense? To what degree are its parents its enemies? To what degree does the infant yield to them? In the last line, one might expect a newborn baby to nurse. What does this infant do?

5. Compare "Infant Joy" with "Infant Sorrow." What differences in sound do you hear? In "Infant Sorrow," for instance, look at lines 3, 5, 6, and 7. What repeated sounds do you hear?

6. One scholar has said that each of these poems is a "refutation" of the other one. Do you agree? Please explain.

7. What is your response to Blake's illustrations?

The Echoing Green

The Sun does arise,
And make happy the skies;
The merry bells ring
To welcome the Spring;
The skylark and thrush,   5
The birds of the bush,
Sing louder around
To the bells' cheerful sound,
While our sports shall be seen
On the Echoing Green.   10

Old John, with white hair,
Does laugh away care,
Sitting under the oak,
Among the old folk.
They laugh at our play,   15
And soon they all say:
"Such, such were the joys
When we all, girls and boys,
In our youth time were seen
On the Echoing Green."   20

Till the little ones, weary,
No more can be merry;
The sun does descend,
And our sports have an end.

Round the laps of their mothers   25
Many sisters and brothers,
Like birds in their nest,
Are ready for rest,
And sport no more seen
On the darkening Green.   30

[1789]

Joining the Conversation: Critical Thinking and Writing

1. Who speaks the poem? (Go through the poem, picking up the clues that identify the speaker.)
2. When does the poem begin? And when does it end?
3. What is a "green," and why in this poem does it "echo"?
4. Try writing a piece titled "Such, such were the joys . . ." You may need to pretend to be a bit older than you are, but try to get down what really were the
   joys of your childhood.
5. Please argue why childhood is the best time of our lives. After you have done
   that, argue why it is not.

The Lamb

Little Lamb, who made thee?
  Dost thou know who made thee?
Gave thee life, and bid thee feed
By the stream and o'er the mead;
Gave thee clothing of delight,   5
Softest clothing, wooly, bright;
Gave thee such a tender voice,
Making all the vales rejoice?
  Little Lamb, who made thee?
  Dost thou know who made thee?   10

  Little Lamb, I'll tell thee,
  Little Lamb, I'll tell thee:
He is callèd by thy name,
For he calls himself a Lamb.
He is meek, and he is mild;   15
He became a little child.
I a child, and thou a lamb,
We are callèd by his name.
  Little Lamb, God bless thee!   20
  Little Lamb, God bless thee!

[1789]

The Tyger

Tyger! Tyger! burning bright
In the forests of the night,
What immortal hand or eye
Could frame thy fearful symmetry?

In what distant deeps or skies   5
Burnt the fire of thine eyes?
On what wings dare he aspire?
What the hand dare seize the fire?

And what shoulder, and what art,
Could twist the sinews of thy heart?   10
And, when thy heart began to beat,
What dread hand? and what dread feet?

What the hammer? what the chain?
In what furnace was thy brain?
What the anvil? what dread grasp   15
Dare its deadly terrors clasp?

When the stars threw down their spears,
And watered heaven with their tears,
Did he smile his work to see?
Did he who made the lamb make thee?   20

Tyger! Tyger! burning bright
In the forests of the night,
What immortal hand or eye,
Dare frame thy fearful symmetry?

[1794]

Joining the Conversation: Critical Thinking and Writing

Why does Blake answer his question in "The Lamb" but not in "The Tyger"?

MyLiteratureLab® *For additional resources for "The Tyger," log in to www.myliteraturelab.com where you will find a Video, a Comprehension Quiz, and Short Evaluation Exercises, as well as an About the Author, Critical Overview, and Links for Blake (under Student Resources).*

GERARD MANLEY HOPKINS

Gerard Manley Hopkins (1844–89) was born near London and was educated at Oxford, where he studied the classics. A convert from Anglicanism to Roman Catholicism, he was ordained a Jesuit priest in 1877. After serving as a parish priest and teacher, he was appointed Professor of Greek at the Catholic University of Ireland in Dublin.

Hopkins published only a few poems during his lifetime, partly because he believed that the pursuit of literary fame was incompatible with his vocation as a priest, and partly because he was aware that his highly individual style might puzzle readers.

Spring and Fall

To a Young Child

Márgarét áre you gríeving°
Over Goldengrove unleaving?
Leáves, líke the thíngs of mán, you
With your fresh thoughts care for, can you?
Ah! ás the héart grows older   5
It will come to such sights colder
By and by, nor spare a sigh
Though worlds of wanwood leafmeal lie;
And yet you will weep and know why.
Now no matter, child, the name: 10
Sórrow's spríngs áre the same.
Nor mouth had, no nor mind, expressed
What héart heárd of, ghost° guéssed:
It is the blíght mán was bórn for,
It is Margaret you mourn for.   15
                                                                    [1880]

1 The stress marks in this poem were indicated by Hopkins. **13 ghost** spirit.

Joining the Conversation: Critical Thinking and Writing

1. What is the speaker's age? His tone? What is the relevance of the title to Margaret? What meanings are in "Fall"? Is there more than one meaning to "Spring"? (Notice especially the title and line 11.)
2. What is meant by Margaret's "fresh thoughts" (line 4)? Paraphrase lines 3–4 and lines 12–13.
3. "Wanwood" and "leafmeal" are words coined by Hopkins. What are their suggestions?
4. What does "blight" mean in line 14?
5. Why is it not contradictory for the speaker to say that Margaret weeps for herself (line 15) after saying that she weeps for "Goldengrove unleaving" (line 2)?
6. Do you find this poem to be difficult? Using details from the text, please explain why or why not.

E. E. CUMMINGS

Edwin Estlin Cummings (1894–1962), who used the pen name e. e. cummings, grew up in Cambridge, Massachusetts, and graduated from Harvard, where he became interested in modern literature and art, especially in the movements called Cubism and Futurism. His father, a conservative clergyman and a professor at Harvard, seems to have been baffled by the youth's interests, but Cummings's mother encouraged his artistic activities, including unconventional punctuation.

Politically liberal in his youth, Cummings became more conservative after a visit to Russia in 1931, but early and late his work emphasizes individuality and freedom of expression.

in Just-

in Just-
spring   when the world is mud-
luscious the little
lame baloonman

whistles   far   and wee   5

and eddyandbill come
running from marbles and
piracies and it's
spring

when the world is puddle-wonderful   10

the queer
old baloonman whistles
far   and   wee
and bettyandisbel come dancing

from hop-scotch and jump-rope and   15

it's
spring
and

    the

        goat-footed   20

baloonMan   whistles
far
and
wee

[1920]

Joining the Conversation: Critical Thinking and Writing

1. Why "eddyandbill" and "bettyandisbel" rather than "eddy and bill" and "betty and isabel"? And why not "eddy and betty," and "bill and isabel"?

2. What are some effects that Cummings may be getting at by his unusual arrangement of words on the page? Compare, for instance, the physical appearance of "whistles far and wee" in line 5 with the appearance of the same words in lines 12–13 and 21–24.

3. Because the baloonman is "lame" (line 4) or "goat-footed" (line 20), many readers find an allusion to the Greek god Pan, the goat-footed god of woods, fields, and flocks, and the inventor of a primitive wind instrument consisting of a series

of reeds, "Pan's pipes." (If you are unfamiliar with Pan, consult an encyclopedia or a guide to mythology.) Do you agree that Cummings is alluding to Pan? If so, what is the point of the allusion?

4. A critic has said: "Cummings cares more about words than about their meanings." What is this critic saying? Please argue why you agree or disagree.

LOUISE GLÜCK

Louise Glück was born in 1943 in New York City and attended Sarah Lawrence College and Columbia University. She has taught at Goddard College in Vermont and at Warren Wilson College in North Carolina. Her volume of poems The Triumph of Achilles *(1985) won the National Book Critics Circle Award for poetry. She now teaches creative writing at Yale and Boston University.*

The School Children

The children go forward with their little satchels.
And all morning the mothers have labored
to gather the late apples, red and gold,
like words of another language.

And on the other shore   5
are those who wait behind great desks
to receive these offerings.

How orderly they are—the nails
on which the children hang
their overcoats of blue or yellow wool.   10

And the teachers shall instruct them in silence
and the mothers shall scour the orchards for a way out,
drawing to themselves the gray limbs of the fruit trees
bearing so little ammunition.

[1975]

Joining the Conversation: Critical Thinking and Writing

1. Which words in the poem present a cute picture-postcard view of small children going to school?
2. Which words undercut this happy scene?
3. In the last stanza we read that "the teachers shall instruct" and "the mothers shall scour." What, if anything, is changed if we substitute "will" for "shall"?

4. In this poem about schoolchildren, is the poet herself seeking to teach us something? Explain.

Gretel in Darkness

This is the world we wanted. All who would have seen us dead
Are dead. I hear the witch's cry
Break in the moonlight through a sheet of sugar: God rewards.
Her tongue shrivels into gas. . . .
                              Now, far from women's arms   5
And memory of women, in our father's hut
We sleep, are never hungry.
Why do I not forget?
My father bars the door, bars harm
From this house, and it is years.   10

No one remembers. Even you, my brother,
Summer afternoons you look at me as though you meant
To leave, as though it never happened. But I killed for you.
I see armed firs, the spires of that gleaming kiln come back, come back—
Nights I turn to you to hold me but you are not there.   15
Am I alone? Spies
Hiss in the stillness, Hansel we are there still, and it is real, real,
That black forest, and the fire in earnest.

                                              [1975]

Joining the Conversation: Critical Thinking and Writing

1. How, as the poem develops, is the first sentence of the poem modified? Is this the world "we" wanted? What does Gretel believe that Hansel wants?
2. In stanza 3 Gretel says

> But I killed for you.
> I see . . . the spires of that gleaming kiln come back, come back—

Whether or not you know the story from *Grimm's Fairy Tales,* how do you understand Gretel's plight?
3. Why is the poem called "Gretel in Darkness"? What does the poem seem to tell us about how men and women face danger?

LINDA PASTAN

Linda Pastan was born in New York City in 1932 and educated at Radcliffe College, Simmons College, and Brandeis University. The author of ten books of poems, she has won numerous prizes, including a Pushcart Prize and the 2003 Ruth Lilly Poetry Prize, and she has received a grant from the National Endowment for the Arts.

Ethics

In ethics class so many years ago
our teacher asked this question every fall:
if there were a fire in a museum
which would you save, a Rembrandt painting
or an old woman who hadn't many   5
years left anyhow? Restless on hard chairs
caring little for pictures or old age
we'd opt one year for life, the next for art
and always half-heartedly. Sometimes
the woman borrowed my grandmother's face   10
leaving her usual kitchen to wander
some drafty, half-imagined museum.
One year, feeling clever, I replied
why not let the woman decide herself?
Linda, the teacher would report, eschews   15
the burdens of responsibility.
This fall in a real museum I stand
before a real Rembrandt, old woman,
or nearly so, myself. The colors
within this frame are darker than autumn,   20
darker even than winter—the browns of earth,
though earth's most radiant elements burn
through the canvas. I know now that woman
and painting and season are almost one
and all beyond saving by children.   25

[1980]

Joining the Conversation: Critical Thinking and Writing

1. What do we know about the teacher in the poem? Do you think you would like to take a course with this teacher? Why?
2. Lines 3–6 report a question that a teacher asked. Does the rest of the poem answer the question? If so, what is the answer? If not, what does the rest of the poem do?
3. Do you assume that, for this poem, the responses of younger readers (say, ages 17–22) as a group would differ from those of older readers? If so, set forth your response in a short argumentative essay.
4. Do you think high schools should offer courses in ethics? If so, do you think the question posed by the teacher in the poem is an appropriate question for such a course? And do you think that Pastan's poem suggests that high schools should or should not teach such courses?

<hr />

PLAY

Thinking Critically: Case Study on Writing Arguments about Hamlet

This case study contains (in addition to illustrations of the original texts of *Hamlet*, the Elizabethan theater, and modern productions) the following material:

1. A note on the Elizabethan theater
2. A note on *Hamlet* on the stage
3. A note on the text of *Hamlet*
4. The text of *Hamlet*
5. Anne Barton's general comments on the play
6. Stanley Wells's analysis of the first soliloquy
7. Elaine Showalter's discussion of Ophelia
8. Bernice W. Kliman's review of the BBC TV production of *Hamlet* (1980)
9. A review by student Will Saretta of Kenneth Branagh's *Hamlet*

A Note on the Elizabethan Theater

Shakespeare's theater was wooden, round or polygonal (the Chorus in *Henry V* calls it a "wooden O"). About eight hundred spectators could stand in the yard in front of—and perhaps along the two sides of—the stage that jutted from the rear wall, and another fifteen hundred or so spectators could sit in the three roofed galleries that ringed the stage.

Left, Johannes de Witt, a Continental visitor to London, made a drawing of the Swan Theater in about the year 1596. The original drawing is lost; this is Arend van Buchel's copy of it. *Right,* C. Walter Hodges's drawing (1965) of an Elizabethan playhouse.

That portion of the galleries that was above the rear of the stage was sometimes used by actors. For instance, in *The Tempest,* 3.3, a stage direction following line 17 mentions "Prospero on the top, invisible"—that is, he is imagined to be invisible to the characters in the play.

Entry to the stage was normally gained by doors at the rear, but apparently on rare occasions use was made of a curtained alcove—or perhaps a booth—between the doors, which allowed characters to be "discovered" (revealed) as in the modern proscenium theater, which normally employs a curtain. Such "discovery" scenes are rare.

Although the theater as a whole was unroofed, the stage was protected by a roof, supported by two pillars. They could serve (by an act of imagination) as trees behind which actors might pretend to conceal themselves.

A performance was probably uninterrupted by intermissions or by long pauses for the changing of scenery; a group of characters leaves the stage, another enters, and if the locale has changed the new characters somehow tell us. (Modern editors customarily add indications of locales to help a reader, but it should be remembered that the action on the Elizabethan stage was continuous.)

A Note on *Hamlet* on the Stage

We know that *Hamlet* was popular during Shakespeare's lifetime, but the earliest illustration (1709) showing a scene from the play was engraved more than a century after the play was written, so we know little about what *Hamlet* looked like on Shakespeare's stage. Still, we do have some idea. We know, for instance, that at least in the first scene Hamlet wore black (he speaks of his "inky cloak"), and we know that when the Ghost first appears it is dressed in "the very armor he had on / When he the ambitious Norway combated" (1.1.64–65). We know, too, that when the Ghost appears later, in the Queen's chamber (3.4), he does not wear armor, a sign that his mood is different.

We also have a few tantalizing glimpses of Elizabethan acting. Thus, in the dumb show (pantomime) preceding "The Murder of Gonzago" that the touring players in 3.2 produce for the court, we get this stage direction: "Enter a King and a Queen [very lovingly]; the Queen embracing him, and he her." A little later, when the Queen in this dumb show finds that the King has been poisoned, she "makes passionate action," but then, when the poisoner woos her, "she seems harsh awhile, but in the end accepts love."

We know something, too, of the sound effects. Possibly the play begins with the bell tolling twelve (in 1.1 Bernardo says, "'Tis now struck twelve"), and certainly in the first scene we hear the crowing of a cock, which causes the Ghost to depart. Later we hear the sound of drums, trumpets, and cannon when Claudius drinks toasts, and the play ends with the sound of cannon, when Fortinbras orders the soldiers to pay tribute to the dead Hamlet.

What about costumes? In their own day, Elizabethan plays were staged chiefly in contemporary dress—doublet (close-fitting jacket) and hose (tights) for the men, gowns of various sorts for the women (whose roles were played by boy actors)—though for classical plays such as *Julius Caesar* some attempt was made in the direction of ancient costume, at least for the major characters. The seventeenth and eighteenth centuries, too, staged the plays in the costume of the day, which of course was not Elizabethan. But in much of the nineteenth century, and in the first third of the twentieth, a strong sense that the plays were "Elizabethan" caused producers to use Elizabethan costumes, although these costumes—contemporary when the plays were first performed—now had become historical costume, marking the plays as of an age remote from our own. In 1925 Barry Jackson staged a modern-dress production in London, in an effort to emphasize the play's contemporary relevance. Today, productions tend to be in modern dress in the sense that they avoid Elizabethan costume. Usually, in an effort to add color to the stage as well as some (but not a great) sense of remoteness, they use costumes of the nineteenth century, which allow for splendid gowns and military uniforms with sashes.

Figure 1

Figure 1. "The Murder of Gonzago," in 3.2. Because this episode is a play-within-the-play, Shakespeare uses a distinctive form of verse (pairs of rhyming lines, eight syllables to a line) that sets it off from the language of the rest of the play (chiefly prose, or unrhymed lines of ten syllables). The language, too, is different, for it is conspicuously old-fashioned (the sun is called "Phoebus' cart," the ocean is called "Neptune's salt wash"). In this modern-dress production done at Stratford, England, in 1975, Claudius wore a blue business suit and Fortinbras wore combat gear, but the characters in the play-within-the-play were masked, to emphasize their theatricality.

Figure 2

Figure 2. The "closet" scene, in 3.4. A line in the preceding scene specifically tells us that Hamlet is "going to his mother's closet." (In Elizabethan language, a "closet" is a private room, rather than a public room—for instance, a room in which a monarch might pray, or relax, as opposed to an audience chamber in which he or she would engage in official actions.) In the twentieth century, at least as early as John Gielgud's production in New York in 1935, and probably in response to Freudian interpretations of the play, the Queen's closet has been fitted with a bed on which Hamlet and Gertrude tussle, and indeed the scene is often wrongly called "the bedroom scene." In this 1989 Royal Shakespeare Company production, with Mark Rylance as Hamlet, a ranting Hamlet (at the left) confronts Gertrude. The Ghost, unknown to Gertrude, sits on the bed, presumably seeking to protect her from Hamlet's assault. The setting was not realistic but expressionistic; that is, the curtains stirred and the lighting changed not because a physical wind was blowing or the sources of illumination were changing, but to express the characters' passions.

Figure 3

Figures 3 and (next page) 4. Hamlet meditates on death in the grave yard, in 5.1. Both of these productions used costumes that suggested the late nineteenth century. Kenneth Branagh portrayed Hamlet in 1993 for the Royal Shakespeare Theatre.

In the photograph (page 872) showing Kevin Kline as Hamlet in a New York Shakespeare Festival production, Horatio is played by an African American. Other than plays by black authors, and a very few plays by whites about blacks (such as Eugene O'Neill's *The Emperor Jones*), there are few roles in drama expressly written for blacks. Shakespeare offers only three: Othello, Aaron (a Moor in *Titus Andronicus*), and the Prince of Morocco (in *The Merchant of Venice*). The few black actors who played other Shakespearean roles, such as the great Ira Aldridge who in the nineteenth century was known for his King Lear, performed the roles in whiteface. Since the 1980s, however, directors have engaged in open casting, using blacks (and Asians) in any and all roles without requiring white makeup.

Figure 4

A Note on the Text of *Hamlet*

Shakespeare's *Hamlet* comes to us in three versions. The first, known as the First Quarto (Q1), was published in 1603. It is an illegitimate garbled version, perhaps derived from the memory of the actor who played Marcellus (this part is conspicuously more accurate than the rest of the play) in a short version of the play.

The second printed version (Q2), which appeared in 1604–05, is almost twice as long as Q1; all in all, it is the best text we have, doubtless published (as Q1 was not) with the permission of Shakespeare's theatrical company.

The third printed version, in the First Folio (the collected edition of Shakespeare's plays, published in 1623), is also legitimate, but it seems to be an acting version, for it lacks some two hundred lines of Q2.

On the other hand, the Folio text includes some ninety lines not found in Q2.

Because Q2 is the longest version, giving us more of the play as Shakespeare conceived it than either of the other texts, it serves as the basic version for this text. Unfortunately, the printers of it often worked carelessly: Words and phrases are omitted, there are plain misreadings of what must have been in Shakespeare's manuscript, and speeches are sometimes wrongly assigned. It was therefore necessary to turn to the First Folio for many readings. It has been found useful, also, to divide the play into acts and scenes; these divisions, not found in Q2 (and only a few are found in the Folio), are purely editorial additions, and they are therefore enclosed in square brackets.

We use the text edited by David Bevington.

The Tragedy of Hamlet

And so by continuance, and weakenesse of the braine
Into this frensie, which now possesseth him:
And if this be not true, take this from this.

King Thinke you t'is so?

Cor. How? so my Lord, I would very faine know
That thing that I haue saide t'is so, positiuely,
And it hath fallen out otherwise:
Nay, if circumstances leade me on,
Ile finde it out, if it were hid
As deepe as the centre of the earth.

King. how should wee trie this same?

Cor. Mary my good lord thus,
The Princes walke is here in the galery,
There let *Ofelia,* walke vntill hee comes:
Your selfe and I will stand close in the study,
There shall you heare the effect of all his hart,
And if it proue any otherwise then loue,
Then let my censure faile an other time.

King. see where hee comes poring vppon a booke.

Enter Hamlet.

Cor. Madame, will it please your grace
To leaue vs here?

Que. With all my hart.   *exit.*

Cor. And here *Ofelia,* reade you on this booke,
And walke aloofe, the King shal be vnseene.

Ham. To be, or not to be, I there's the point,
To Die, to sleepe, is that all? I all:
No, to sleepe, to dreame, I mary there it goes,
For in that dreame of death, when wee awake,
And borne before an euerlasting Iudge,
From whence no passenger euer returnd,
The vndiscouered country, at whose sight
The happy smile, and the accursed damn'd.
But for this, the ioyfull hope of this,
Whol'd beare the scornes and flattery of the world,
Scorned by the right rich, the rich cursed of the poore?

                                   The

On this page and on the next, we give the text of "To be or not to be" from the First Quarto (Q1, 1603). On pages 875–76 we give the text from the Second Quarto (Q2, 1604–05), and on page 877 we give a third version, from the First Folio (F1, 1623), beginning at the bottom of the left-hand column.

Prince of Denmarke

The widow being oppreſſed,the orphan wrong'd,
The taſte of hunger, or a tirants raigne,
And thouſand more calamities beſides,
To grunt and ſweate vnder this weary life,
When that he may his full *Quietus* make,
With a bare bodkin, who would this indure,
But for a hope of ſomething after death?
Which puſles the braine, and deth confound the ſence,
Which makes vs rather beare thoſe euilles we haue,
Than flie to others that we know not of.
I that,O this conſcience makes cowardes of vs all,
Lady in thy orizons, be all my ſinnes remembred.

   Ofel. My Lord, I haue ſought opportunitie,which now
I haue,to redeliuer to your worthy handes, a ſmall remembrance, ſuch tokens which I haue receiued of you.

   Ham. Are you faire?

   Ofel. My Lord.

   Ham. Are you honeſt?

   Ofel. What meanes my Lord?

   Ham. That if you be faire and honeſt,
Your beauty ſhould admit no diſcourſe to your honeſty.

   Ofel. My Lord, can beauty haue better priuiledge than
with honeſty?

   Ham. Yea mary may it; for Beauty may transforme
Honeſty, from what ſhe was into a bawd:
Then Honeſty can transſorue Beauty:
This was ſometimes a Paradox,
But now the time giues it ſcope.
I neuer gaue you nothing.

   Ofel. My Lord, you know right well you did,
And with them ſuch earneſt vowes of loue,
As would haue moou'd the ſtonieſt breaſt aliue,
But now too true I finde,
Rich giftes waxe poore, when giuers grow vnkinde.

   Ham. I neuer loued you.

   Ofel. You made me beleeue you did.

              E   *Ham.*

First Quarto continued.

That show of such an exercise may cullour
Your lowlines; we are oft too blame in this,
Tis too much proou'd, that with deuotions visage
And pious action, we doe sugar ore
The deuill himselfe.

  King. O tis too true,
How smart a lash that speech doth giue my conscience.
The harlots cheeke beautied with plastring art,
Is not more ougly to the thing that helps it,
Then is my deede to my most painted word :
O heauy burthen.

Enter Hamlet.

  Pol. I heare him comming, with-draw my Lord.
  Ham. To be, or not to be, that is the question,
Whether tis nobler in the minde to suffer
The slings and arrowes of outragious fortune,
Or to take Armes against a sea of troubles,
And by opposing, end them; to die to sleepe
No more, and by a sleepe, to say we end
The hart-ake, and the thousand naturall shocks
That flesh is heire to; tis a consumation
Deuoutly to be wisht to die to sleepe,
To sleepe, perchance to dreame, I there's the rub,
For in that sleepe of death what dreames may come
When we haue shuffled off this mortall coyle
Must giue vs pause, there's the respect
That makes calamitie of so long life :
For who would beare the whips and scornes of time,
Th'oppressors wrong, the proude mans contumely,
The pangs of despiz'd loue, the lawes delay,
The insolence of office, and the spurnes
That patient merrit of th'vnworthy takes,
When he himselfe might his quietas make
With a bare bodkin; who would fardels beare,
To grunt and sweat vnder a wearie life,
But that the dread of something after death,
The vndiscouer'd country, from whose borne.

G 2

No

On this page and the next we give "To be or not to be," as it appears in the Second Quarto (Q2, 1604–05).

The Tragedie of Hamlet

No trauiler returnes, puzzels the will,
And makes vs rather beare thofe ills we haue,
Then flie to others that we know not of.
Thus confcience dooes make cowards,
And thus the natiue hiew of refolution
Is fickled ore with the pale caft of thought,
And enterprifes of great pitch and moment,
With this regard theyr currents turne awry,
And loofe the name of action. Soft you now,
The faire *Ophelia*, Nimph in thy orizons
Be all my finnes remembred.

   Oph. Good my Lord,
How dooes your honour for this many a day?
   Ham. I humbly thanke you well.
   Oph. My Lord, I haue remembrances of yours
That I haue longed long to redeliuer,
I pray you now receiue them.
   Ham. No, not I, I neuer gaue you ought.
   Oph. My honor'd Lord, you know right well you did,
And with them words of fo fweet breath compofd
As made thefe things more rich, their perfume loft,
Take thefe againe, for to the noble mind
Rich gifts wax poore when giuers prooue vnkind,
There my Lord.
   Ham. Ha, ha, are you honeft.
   Oph. My Lord.
   Ham. Are you faire?
   Oph. What meanes your Lordfhip?
   Ham. That if you be honeft & faire, you fhould admit
no difcourfe to your beautie.
   Oph. Could beauty my Lord haue better comerfe
Then with honeftie?
   Ham. I truly, for the power of beautie will fooner transforme ho-
neftie from what it is to a bawde, then the force of honeftie can tranf-
late beautie into his likenes, this was fometime a paradox, but now the
time giues it proofe, I did loue you once.
   Oph. Indeed my Lord you made me beleeu fo.
   Ham. You fhould not haue beleeu'd me, for vertue cannot fo
euocutat our old ftock, but we fhall relifh of it, I loued you not.

Second Quarto continued.

The Tragedie of Hamlet. 265

With turbulent and dangerous Lunacy.

Rosin. He does confesse he feeles himselfe distracted,
But from what cause he will by no meanes speake.

Guil. Nor do we finde him forward to be sounded,
But with a crafty Madnesse keepes aloofe:
When we would bring him on to some Confession
Of his true state.

Qu. Did he receiue you well?

Rosin. Most like a Gentleman.

Guild. But with much forcing of his disposition.

Rosin. Niggard of question, but of our demands
Most free in his reply.

Qu. Did you assay him to any pastime?

Rosin. Madam, it so fell out, that certaine Players
We ore-wrought on the way: of these we told him,
And there did seeme in him a kinde of ioy
To heare of it: They are about the Court,
And (as I thinke) they haue already order
This night to play before him.

Pol. 'Tis most true:
And he beseech'd me to intreate your Maiesties
To heare, and see the matter.

King. With all my heart, and it doth much content me
To heare him so inclin'd. Good Gentlemen,
Giue him a further edge, and driue his purpose on
To these delights.

Rosin. We shall my Lord.   *Exeunt.*

King. Sweet Gertrude leaue vs too,
For we haue closely sent for *Hamlet* hither,
That he, as 'twere by accident, may there
Affront *Ophelia.* Her Father, and my selfe (lawful espials)
Will so bestow our selues, that seeing vnseene
We may of their encounter frankely iudge,
And gather by him, as he is behaued,
If't be th'affliction of his loue, or no.
That thus he suffers for.

Qu. I shall obey you,
And for your part *Ophelia,* I do wish
That your good Beauties be the happy cause
Of *Hamlets* wildenesse: so shall I hope your Vertues
Will bring him to his wonted way againe,
To both your Honors.

Ophe. Madam, I wish it may.

Pol. *Ophelia,* walke you heere. Gracious so please ye
We will bestow our selues: Reade on this booke,
That shew of such an exercise may colour
Your lonelinesse. We are oft too blame in this,
'Tis too much prou'd, that with Deuotions visage,
And pious Action, we do surge o're
The diuell himselfe.

King. Oh 'tis true:
How smart a lash that speech doth giue my Conscience?
The Harlots Cheeke beautied with plaist'ring Art
Is not more vgly to the thing that helpes it,
Then is my deede, to my most painted word.
Oh heauie burthen!

Pol. I heare him comming, let's withdraw my Lord.
                                                        Exeunt.

Enter Hamlet.

Ham. To be, or not to be, that is the Question:
Whether 'tis Nobler in the minde to suffer
The Slings and Arrowes of outragious Fortune,
Or to take Armes against a Sea of troubles,
And by opposing end them: to dye, to sleepe
No more; and by a sleepe, to say we end
The Heart-ake, and the thousand Naturall shockes

That Flesh is heyre too? 'Tis a consummation
Deuoutly to be wish'd. To dye to sleepe,
To sleepe, perchance to Dreame; I, there's the rub,
For in that sleepe of death, what dreames may come,
When we haue shuffel'd off this mortall coile,
Must giue vs pawse. There's the respect
That makes Calamity of so long life:
For who would beare the Whips and Scornes of time,
The Oppressors wrong, the poore mans Contumely,
The pangs of dispriz'd Loue, the Lawes delay,
The insolence of Office, and the Spurnes
That patient merit of the vnworthy takes,
When he himselfe might his *Quietus* make
With a bare Bodkin? Who would these Fardles beare
To grunt and sweat vnder a weary life,
But that the dread of something after death,
The vndiscouered Countrey, from whose Borne
No Traueller returnes, Puzels the will,
And makes vs rather beare those illes we haue,
Then flye to others that we know not of.
Thus Conscience does make Cowards of vs all,
And thus the Natiue hew of Resolution
Is sicklied o're, with the pale cast of Thought,
And enterprizes of great pith and moment,
With this regard their Currants turne away,
And loose the name of Action. Soft you now,
The faire *Ophelia?* Nimph, in thy Orizons
Be all my sinnes remembred.

Ophe. Good my Lord,
How does your Honor for this many a day?

Ham. I humbly thanke you: well, well, well.

Ophe. My Lord, I haue Remembrances of yours,
That I haue longed long to re-deliuer.
I pray you now, receiue them.

Ham. No, no, I neuer gaue you ought.

Ophe. My honor'd Lord, I know right well you did,
And with them words of so sweet breath compos'd,
As made the things more rich, then perfume left:
Take these againe, for to the Noble minde
Rich gifts wax poore, when giuers proue vnkinde.
There my Lord.

Ham. Ha, ha: Are you honest?

Ophe. My Lord.

Ham. Are you faire?

Ophe. What meanes your Lordship?

Ham. That if you be honest and faire, your Honesty
sho uld admit no discourse to your Beautie.

Ophe. Could Beautie my Lord, haue better Comerce
then your Honestie?

Ham. I trulie: for the power of Beautie, will sooner
transforme Honestie from what it is, to a Bawd, then the
force of Honestie can translate Beautie into his likenesse.
This was sometime a Paradox, but now the time giues it
proofe. I did loue you once.

Ophe. Indeed my Lord, you made me beleeue so.

Ham. You should not haue beleeued me. For vertue
cannot so innocculate our old stocke, but we shall rellish
of it. I loued you not.

Ophe. I was the more deceiued.

Ham. Get thee to a Nunnerie. Why would'st thou
be a breeder of Sinners? I am my selfe indifferent honest,
but yet I could accuse me of such things, that it were better my Mother had not borne me. I am very prowd, re-
uengefull, Ambitious, with more offences at my becke,
then I haue thoughts to put them in imagination, to giue
them shape, or time to acte them in. What should such
                                                           Fel-

"To be or not to be," as given in the First Folio (F1, 1623).

WILLIAM SHAKESPEARE

William Shakespeare (1564–1616) was born in Stratford-on-Avon, England, of middle-class parents. Nothing of interest is known about his early years, but by 1590 he was acting and writing plays in London. By the end of the following decade he had worked in all three Elizabethan dramatic genres—tragedy, comedy, and history. Romeo and Juliet, *for example, was written about 1595, the year of* Richard II. Hamlet *was probably written in 1600–01. Among the plays that followed were* Othello *(1603–04),* King Lear *(1605–06),* Macbeth *(1605–06), and several "romances"—plays that have happy endings but that seem more meditative and closer to tragedy than such comedies as* A Midsummer Night's Dream *(c.1595),* As You Like It *(1598–1600), and* Twelfth Night *(1600–02).*

The Tragedy of Hamlet, Prince of Denmark

DRAMATIS PERSONAE

GHOST *of Hamlet, the former King of Denmark*
CLAUDIUS, *King of Denmark, the former King's brother*
GERTRUDE, *Queen of Denmark, widow of the former King and now wife of Claudius*
HAMLET, *Prince of Denmark, son of the late King and of Gertrude*
POLONIUS, *councillor to the King*
LAERTES, *his son*
OPHELIA, *his daughter*
REYNALDO, *his servant*

HORATIO, *Hamlet's friend and fellow student*

VOLTIMAND,
CORNELIUS,
ROSENCRANTZ,
GUILDENSTERN, } *members of the Danish court*
OSRIC,
A GENTLEMAN,
A LORD,

BERNARDO,
FRANCISCO, } *officers and soldiers on watch*
MARCELLUS,

FORTINBRAS, *Prince of Norway*
CAPTAIN *in his army*
Three or Four PLAYERS, *taking the roles of* PROLOGUE, PLAYER KING, PLAYER QUEEN, and LUCIANUS
Two MESSENGERS
FIRST SAILOR
Two CLOWNS, *a gravedigger and his companion*
PRIEST
FIRST AMBASSADOR *from England*
Lords, Soldiers, Attendants, Guards, other Players, Followers of Laertes, other Sailors, another Ambassador or Ambassadors from England
SCENE: *Denmark*

[1.1]

Enter BERNARDO *and* FRANCISCO, *two sentinels* [*meeting*].

BERNARDO: Who's there?

FRANCISCO: Nay, answer me.° Stand and unfold yourself.°

BERNARDO: Long live the King!

FRANCISCO: Bernardo?

BERNARDO: He.

FRANCISCO: You come most carefully upon your hour.   5

BERNARDO: 'Tis now struck twelve. Get thee to bed, Francisco.

FRANCISCO: For this relief much thanks. 'Tis bitter cold,

    And I am sick at heart.

BERNARDO: Have you had quiet guard?   10

FRANCISCO: Not a mouse stirring.

BERNARDO: Well, good night.

    If you do meet Horatio and Marcellus,

    The rivals° of my watch, bid them make haste.

Enter HORATIO *and* MARCELLUS.

FRANCISCO: I think I hear them.—Stand, ho! Who is there?   10

HORATIO: Friends to this ground.°

MARCELLUS: And liegemen to the Dane.°

FRANCISCO: Give° you good night.

MARCELLUS: O, farewell, honest soldier. Who hath relieved you?

FRANCISCO: Bernardo hath my place. Give you good night.   *Exit* FRANCISCO.   20

MARCELLUS: Holla! Bernardo!

BERNARDO: Say, what, is Horatio there?

HORATIO: A piece of him.

BERNARDO: Welcome, Horatio. Welcome, good Marcellus.

HORATIO: What, has this thing appeared again tonight?   25

BERNARDO: I have seen nothing.

MARCELLUS: Horatio says 'tis but our fantasy,°

    And will not let belief take hold of him

    Touching this dreaded sight twice seen of us.

    Therefore I have entreated him along°   30

    With us to watch° the minutes of this night,

    That if again this apparition come

    He may approve° our eyes and speak to it.

HORATIO: Tush, tush, 'twill not appear.

BERNARDO: Sit down awhile,

    And let us once again assail your ears,   35

    That are so fortified against our story,

    What° we have two nights seen.

Note: Stage directions that are enclosed within square brackets do not appear in the original text. They have been added by the editor.

[1.1] Location: Elsinore castle. A guard platform.   2 me (Francisco emphasizes that *he* is the sentry currently on watch.); **unfold yourself** reveal your identity.   **14 rivals** partners. **16 ground** ground, land.   **17 liegemen to the Dane** men sworn to serve the Danish king. **18 Give** i.e., may God give.   **27 fantasy** imagination.   **30 along** to come along.   **31 watch** keep watch during.   **33 approve** corroborate.   **37 What** with what.

HORATIO: Well, sit we down,
          And let us hear Bernardo speak of this.
BERNARDO: Last night of all,°
          When yond same star that's westward from the pole°   40
          Had made his° course t' illume° that part of heaven
          Where now it burns, Marcellus and myself,
          The bell then beating one—

          Enter GHOST.

MARCELLUS: Peace, break thee off! Look where it comes again!
BERNARDO: In the same figure like the King that's dead.   45
MARCELLUS: Thou art a scholar.° Speak to it, Horatio.
BERNARDO: Looks 'a° not like the King? Mark it, Horatio.
HORATIO: Most like. It harrows me with fear and wonder.
BERNARDO: It would be spoke to.°
MARCELLUS: Speak to it, Horatio.
HORATIO: What art thou that usurp'st° this time of night,   50
          Together with that fair and warlike form
          In which the majesty of buried Denmark°
          Did sometime° march? By heaven, I charge thee, speak!
MARCELLUS: It is offended.
BERNARDO: See, it stalks away.
HORATIO: Stay! Speak, speak! I charge thee, speak!   *Exit* GHOST.   55
MARCELLUS: 'Tis gone and will not answer.
BERNARDO: How now, Horatio? You tremble and look pale.
          Is not this something more than fantasy?
          What think you on 't?°
HORATIO: Before my God, I might not this believe   60
          Without the sensible° and true avouch°
          Of mine own eyes.
MARCELLUS: Is it not like the King?
HORATIO: As thou art to thyself.
          Such was the very armor he had on
          When he the ambitious Norway° combated.   65
          So frowned he once when, in an angry parle,°
          He smote the sledded° Polacks° on the ice.
          'Tis strange.
MARCELLUS: Thus twice before, and jump° at this dead hour,
          With martial stalk° hath he gone by our watch.   70
HORATIO: In what particular thought to work° I know not,
          But in the gross and scope° of mine opinion
          This bodes some strange eruption to our state.

---

39 Last . . . all i.e., this *very* last night (emphatic).   **40 pole** Pole Star, North Star.   **41 his** its;
illume illuminate.   **46 scholar** one learned enough to know how to question a ghost properly.
47 'a he.   **49 It . . . to** (It was commonly believed that a ghost could not speak until spoken to.)
50 usurp'st wrongfully takes over.   **52 buried Denmark** the buried King of Denmark.
53 sometime formerly.   **59 on 't** of it.   **61 sensible** confirmed by the sense;   **avouch** warrant evidence.   **65 Norway** King of Norway.   **66 parle** parley.   **67 sledded** traveling on sleds;
Polacks Poles.   **69 jump** exactly.   **70 stalk** stride.   **71 to work** i.e., to collect my thoughts
and try to understand this.   **72 gross and scope** general drift.

MARCELLUS: Good now,° sit down, and tell me, he that knows,
          Why this same strict and most observant watch   75
          So nightly toils° the subject° of the land,
          And why such daily cast° of brazen cannon
          And foreign mart° for implements of war,
          Why such impress° of shipwrights, whose sore task
          Does not divide the Sunday from the week.   80
          What might be toward,° that this sweaty haste
          Doth make the night joint-laborer with the day?
          Who is 't that can inform me?
HORATIO: That can I;
          At least, the whisper goes so. Our last king,
          Whose image even but now appeared to us,   85
          Was, as you know, by Fortinbras of Norway,
          Thereto pricked on° by a most emulate° pride,°
          Dared to the combat; in which our valiant Hamlet—
          For so this side of our known world° esteemed him—
          Did slay this Fortinbras; who by a sealed° compact   90
          Well ratified by law and heraldry
          Did forfeit, with his life, all those his lands
          Which he stood seized° of, to the conqueror;
          Against the° which a moiety competent°
          Was gagèd° by our king, which had returned°   95
          To the inheritance° of Fortinbras
          Had he been vanquisher, as, by the same cov'nant°
          And carriage of the article designed,°
          His fell to Hamlet. Now, sir, young Fortinbras,
          Of unimprovèd mettle° hot and full,   100
          Hath in the skirts° of Norway here and there
          Sharked up° a list° of lawless resolutes°
          For food and diet° to some enterprise
          That hath a stomach° in 't, which is no other—
          As it doth well appear unto our state—   105
          But to recover of us, by strong hand
          And terms compulsatory, those foresaid lands
          So by his father lost. And this, I take it,
          Is the main motive of our preparations,

---

74 Good now (An expression denoting entreaty or expostulation.)   **76 toils** causes to toil; **subject** subjects.   **77 cast** casting.   **78 mart** buying and selling.   **79 impress** impressment, conscription.   **81 toward** in preparation.   **87 pricked on** incited;   **emulate** emulous, ambitious; **Thereto . . . pride** (refers to old Fortinbras, not the Danish King.)   **89 this . . . world** i.e., all Europe, the Western world.   **90 sealed** certified, confirmed.   **93 seized** possessed. **94 Against the** in return for;   **moiety competent** corresponding portion.   **95 gagèd** engaged, pledged; **had returned** would have passed.   **96 inheritance** possession. **97 cov'nant** i.e., the *sealed compact* on line 90.   **98 carriage . . . designed** carrying out of the article or clause drawn up to cover the point.   **100 unimprovèd mettle** untried, undisciplined spirits.   **101 skirts** outlying regions, outskirts.   **102 Sharked up** gathered up, as a shark takes fish;   **list** i.e., troop; **resolutes** Desperadoes.   **103 For food and diet** i.e., they are to serve as *food,* or "means," *to some enterprises,* also they serve in return for the rations they get.   **104 stomach** (1) a spirit of daring; (2) an appetite that is fed by the *lawless resolutes.*

The source of this our watch, and the chief head° 110
Of this posthaste and rummage° in the land.

BERNARDO: I think it be no other but e'en so.

Well may it sort° that this portentous figure
Comes armèd through our watch so like the King
That was and is the question° of these wars. 115

HORATIO: A mote° it is to trouble the mind's eye.

In the most high and palmy° state of Rome,
A little ere the mightiest Julius fell,
The graves stood tenantless, and the sheeted° dead
Did squeak and gibber in the Roman streets; 120
As° stars with trains° of fire and dews of blood,
Disasters° in the sun; and the moist star°
Upon whose influence Neptune's° empire stands°
Was sick almost to doomsday° with eclipse.
And even the like precurse° of feared events, 125
As harbingers° preceding still° the fates
And prologue to the omen° coming on,
Have heaven and earth together demonstrated
Unto our climatures° and countrymen.

Enter GHOST.

But soft,° behold! Lo, where it comes again! 130
I'll cross° it, though it blast° me. [*It spreads his° arms.*]
    Stay, *illusion!*
If thou hast any sound or use of voice,
Speak to me!
If there be any good thing to be done
That may to thee do ease and grace to me, 135
Speak to me!
If thou art privy to° thy country's fate,
Which, happily,° foreknowing may avoid,
O, speak!
Or if thou hast uphoarded in thy life 140
Extorted treasure in the womb of earth,
For which, they say, you spirits oft walk in death,
Speak of it! [*The cock crows.*] Stay and speak!—Stop it, Marcellus.

MARCELLUS: Shall I strike at it with my partisan?°

HORATIO: Do, if it will not stand.   [*They strike at it.*] 145

BERNARDO: 'Tis here!

HORATIO: 'Tis here!   [*Exit* GHOST.]

---

110 head source. **111 rummage** bustle, commotion. **113 sort** suit. **115 question** focus of
contention. **116 mote** speck of dust. **117 palmy** flourishing. **119 sheeted** shrouded.
121 As (This abrupt transition suggests that matter is possibly omitted between lines 120 and 121.);
trains trails. **122 Disasters** unfavorable signs or aspects; **moist star** i.e., moon, governing tides.
123 Neptune god of the sea; **stands** depends. **124 sick . . . doomsday** (See Matthew 24:29
and Revelation 6:12.) **125 precurse** heralding, foreshadowing. **126 harbingers** forerunners;
still continually. **127 omen** calamitous event. **129 climatures** regions. **130 soft** i.e., enough,
break off. **131 cross** stand in its path, confront; **blast** wither, strike with a curse; **s.d. his** its.
137 privy to in on the secret of. **138 happily** haply, perchance. **144 partisan** long-handled spear.

MARCELLUS: 'Tis gone.
    We do it wrong, being so majestical,
    To offer it the show of violence,   150
    For it is as the air invulnerable,
    And our vain blows malicious mockery.
BERNARDO: It was about to speak when the cock crew.
HORATIO: And then it started like a guilty thing
    Upon a fearful summons. I have heard   155
    The cock, that is the trumpet° to the morn,
    Doth with his lofty and shrill-sounding throat
    Awake the god of day, and at his warning,
    Whether in sea or fire, in earth or air,
    Th' extravagant and erring° spirit hies°   160
    To his confine; and of the truth herein
    This present object made probation.°
MARCELLUS: It faded on the crowing of the cock.
    Some say that ever 'gainst° that season comes
    Wherein our Savior's birth is celebrated,   165
    This bird of dawning singeth all night long,
    And then, they say, no spirit dare stir abroad;
    The nights are wholesome, then no planets strike,°
    No fairy takes,° nor witch hath power to charm,
    So hallowed and so gracious° is that time.   170
HORATIO: So have I heard and do in part believe it.
    But, look, the morn in russet mantle clad
    Walks o'er the dew of yon high eastward hill.
    Break we our watch up, and by my advice
    Let us impart what we have seen tonight   175
    Unto young Hamlet; for upon my life,
    This spirit, dumb to us, will speak to him.
    Do you consent we shall acquaint him with it,
    As needful in our loves, fitting our duty?
MARCELLUS: Let's do 't, I pray, and I this morning know   180
    Where we shall find him most conveniently.   *Exeunt.*

[1.2]

Flourish. Enter CLAUDIUS, *King of Denmark,* GERTRUDE *the Queen,*
[the] Council, as° POLONIUS *and his son* LAERTES, HAMLET, *cum aliis°*
[including VOLTIMAND *and* CORNELIUS].

KING: Though yet of Hamlet our° dear brother's death
    The memory be green, and that it us befitted
    To bear our hearts in grief and our whole kingdom
    To be contracted in one brow of woe,
    Yet so far hath discretion fought with nature   5
    That we with wisest sorrow think on him

---

156 trumpet trumpeter. **160 extravagant and erring** wandering beyond bounds. (The words have similar meaning.); **hies** hastens. **162 probation** proof. **164 'gainst** just before. **168 strike** destroy by evil influence. **169 takes** bewitches. **170 gracious** full of grace. **[1.2] Location:** The castle. **s.d. as** i.e., such as, including; **cum aliis** with others. **1 our** my. (The royal "we"; also in the following lines.)

Together with remembrance of ourselves.
Therefore our sometime° sister, now our queen,
Th' imperial jointress° to this warlike state,
Have we, as 'twere with a defeated joy—   10
With an auspicious and a dropping eye,°
With mirth in funeral and with dirge in marriage,
In equal scale weighing delight and dole°—
Taken to wife: Nor have we herein barred
Your better wisdoms, which have freely gone   15
With this affair along. For all, our thanks.
Now follows that you know° young Fortinbras,
Holding a weak supposal° of our worth,
Or thinking by our late dear brother's death
Our state to be disjoint and out of frame,   20
Co-leaguèd with° this dream of his advantage,°
He hath not failed to pester us with message
Importing° the surrender of those lands
Lost by his father, with all bonds° of law,
To our most valiant brother. So much for him.   25
Now for ourself and for this time of meeting.
Thus much the business is: we have here writ
To Norway, uncle of young Fortinbras—
Who, impotent° and bed-rid, scarcely hears
Of this his nephew's purpose—to suppress   30
His° further gait° herein, in that the levies,
The lists, and full proportions are all made
Out of his subject;° and we here dispatch
You, good Cornelius, and you, Voltimand,
For bearers of this greeting to old Norway,   35
Giving to you no further personal power
To business with the King more than the scope
Of these dilated° articles allow.   [*He gives a paper.*]
Farewell, and let your haste commend your duty.°
CORNELIUS, VOLTIMAND: In that, and all things, will we show our duty.   40
KING: We doubt it nothing.° Heartily farewell.

                        [*Exeunt* VOLTIMAND *and* CORNELIUS.]

And now, Laertes, what's the news with you?
You told us of some suit; what is 't, Laertes?
You cannot speak of reason to the Dane°
And lose your voice.° What wouldst thou beg, Laertes,   45

---

8 sometime former.   **9 jointress** woman possessing property with her husband.   **11 With . . .
eye** with one eye smiling and the other weeping.   **13 dole** grief.   **17 that you know** what you
know already, that; or, that you be informed as follows.   **18 weak supposal** low estimate.
21 Co-leaguèd with joined to, allied with;   **dream . . . advantage** illusory hope of having the
advantage. (His only ally is this hope.)   **23 Importing** pertaining to.   **24 bonds** contracts.
29 impotent helpless.   **31 His** i.e., Fortinbras';   **gait** proceeding.   **31–33 in that . . . subject**
since the levying of troops and supplies is drawn entirely from the King of Norway's own subjects.
38 dilated set out at length.   **39 let . . . duty** let your swift obeying of orders, rather than mere
words, express your dutifulness.   **41 nothing** not at all.   **44 the Dane** the Danish king.
45 lose your voice waste your speech.

That shall not be my offer, not thy asking?
The head is not more native° to the heart,
The hand more instrumental° to the mouth,
Than is the throne of Denmark to thy father.
What wouldst thou have, Laertes?

LAERTES: My dread lord, 50
Your leave and favor° to return to France,
From whence though willingly I came to Denmark
To show my duty in your coronation,
Yet now I must confess, that duty done,
My thoughts and wishes bend again toward France 55
And bow them to your gracious leave and pardon.°

KING: Have you your father's leave? What says Polonius?

POLONIUS: H'ath,° my lord, wrung from me my slow leave
By laborsome petition, and at last
Upon his will I sealed° my hard° consent. 60
I do beseech you, give him leave to go.

KING: Take thy fair hour,° Laertes. Time be thine,
And thy best graces spend it at thy will!°
But now, my cousin° Hamlet, and my son—

HAMLET: A little more than kin, and less than kind.° 65

KING: How is it that the clouds still hang on you?

HAMLET: Not so, my lord. I am too much in the sun.°

QUEEN: Good Hamlet, cast thy nighted color° off,
And let thine eye look like a friend on Denmark.°
Do not forever with thy vailèd lids° 70
Seek for thy noble father in the dust.
Thou know'st 'tis common,° all that lives must die,
Passing through nature to eternity.

HAMLET: Ay, madam, it is common.

QUEEN: If it be,
Why seems it so particular° with thee? 75

HAMLET: Seems, madam? Nay, it is. I know not "seems."
'Tis not alone my inky cloak, good Mother,
Nor customary° suits of solemn black,
Nor windy suspiration° of forced breath,
No, nor the fruitful° river in the eye, 80

---

47 native closely connected, related.   **48 instrumental** serviceable.   **51 leave and favor** kind permission.   **56 bow . . . pardon** entreatingly make a deep bow, asking your permission to depart. **58 H'ath** he has.   **60 sealed** (as if sealing a legal document.);   **hard** reluctant.   **62 Take thy fair hour** enjoy your time of youth. **63 And . . . will** and may your finest qualities guide the way you choose to spend your time.   **64 cousin** any kin not of the immediate family.   **65 A little . . . kind** i.e., closer than an ordinary nephew (since I am stepson), and yet more separated in natural feeling (with pun on *kind* meaning "affectionate" and "natural," "lawful." This line is often read as an aside, but it need not be. The King chooses perhaps not to respond to Hamlet's cryptic and bitter remark.)   **67 the sun** i.e., the sunshine of the King's royal favor (with pun on *son*).   **68 nighted color** (1) mourning garments of black, (2) dark melancholy. **69 Denmark** the King of Denmark.   **70 vailèd lids** lowered eyes.   **72 common** of universal occurrence. (But Hamlet plays on the sense of "vulgar" in line 74.)   **75 particular** personal. **78 customary** (1) socially conventional, (2) habitual with me.   **79 suspiration** sighing. **80 fruitful** abundant.

Nor the dejected havior° of the visage,
Together with all forms, moods,° shapes of grief,
That can denote me truly. These indeed seem,
For they are actions that a man might play.
But I have that within which passes show;   85
These but the trappings and the suits of woe.

KING: 'Tis sweet and commendable in your nature, Hamlet,
To give these mourning duties to your father.
But you must know your father lost a father,
That father lost, lost his, and the survivor bound   90
In filial obligation for some term
To do obsequious° sorrow. But to persever°
In obstinate condolement° is a course
Of impious stubbornness. 'Tis unmanly grief.
It shows a will most incorrect to heaven,   95
A heart unfortified,° a mind impatient,
An understanding simple° and unschooled.
For what we know must be and is as common
As any the most vulgar thing to sense,°
Why should we in our peevish opposition   100
Take it to heart? Fie, 'tis a fault to heaven,
A fault against the dead, a fault to nature,
To reason most absurd, whose common theme
Is death of fathers, and who still° hath cried,
From the first corpse° till he that died today,   105
"This must be so." We pray you, throw to earth
This unprevailing° woe and think of us
As of a father; for let the world take note,
You are the most immediate° to our throne,
And with no less nobility of love   110
Than that which dearest father bears his son
Do I impart toward° you. For° your intent
In going back to school° in Wittenberg,°
It is most retrograde° to our desire,
And we beseech you bend you° to remain   115
Here in the cheer and comfort of our eye,
Our chiefest courtier, cousin, and our son.

QUEEN: Let not thy mother lose her prayers, Hamlet.
I pray thee, stay with us, go not to Wittenberg.

HAMLET: I shall in all my best° obey you, madam.   120

KING: Why, 'tis a loving and a fair reply.
Be as ourself in Denmark. Madam, come.

---

81 havior expression. **82 moods** outward expression of feeling. **92 obsequious** suited to
obsequies or funerals; **persever** persevere. **93 condolement** sorrowing. **96 unfortified** i.e.,
against adversity. **97 simple** ignorant. **99 As . . . sense** as the most ordinary experience.
104 still always. **105 the first corpse** (Abel's.) **107 unprevailing** unavailing, useless.
109 most immediate next in succession. **112 impart toward** i.e., bestow my affection on;
For as for. **113 to school** i.e., to your studies; **Wittenberg** famous German university founded
in 1502. **114 retrograde** contrary. **115 bend you** incline yourself. **120 in all my best** to the
best of my ability.

This gentle and unforced accord of Hamlet
Sits smiling to° my heart, in grace° whereof
No jocund° health that Denmark drinks today   125
But the great cannon to the clouds shall tell,
And the King's rouse° the heaven shall bruit again,°
Respeaking earthly thunder.° Come away.

Flourish. Exeunt all but HAMLET.

HAMLET: O, that this too too sullied° flesh would melt,
Thaw, and resolve itself into a dew!   130
Or that the Everlasting had not fixed
His canon° 'gainst self-slaughter! O God, God,
How weary, stale, flat, and unprofitable
Seem to me all the uses° of this world!
Fie on 't, ah fie! 'Tis an unweeded garden   135
That grows to seed. Things rank and gross in nature
Possess it merely.° That it should come to this!
But two months dead—nay, not so much, not two.
So excellent a king, that was to° this
Hyperion° to a satyr,° so loving to my mother   140
That he might not beteem° the winds of heaven
Visit her face too roughly. Heaven and earth,
Must I remember? Why, she would hang on him
As if increase of appetite had grown
By what it fed on, and yet within a month—   145
Let me not think on 't; frailty, thy name is woman!—
A little month, or ere° those shoes were old
With which she followed my poor father's body,
Like Niobe;° all tears, why she, even she—
O God, a beast, that wants discourse of reason,°   150
Would have mourned longer—married with my uncle,
My father's brother, but no more like my father
Than I to Hercules. Within a month,
Ere yet the salt of most unrighteous tears
Had left the flushing in her gallèd° eyes,   155
She married. O, most wicked speed, to post°
With such dexterity to incestuous° sheets!
It is not, nor it cannot come to good.
But break, my heart, for I must hold my tongue.

124 to i.e., at; **grace** thanksgiving. **125 jocund** merry. **127 rouse** drinking of a draft of liquor;
bruit again loudly echo. **128 thunder** i.e., of trumpet and kettledrum, sounded when the King
drinks; see 1.4.8–12. **129 sullied** defiled. (The early quartos read *sallied;* the Folio, *solid.*)
132 canon law. **134 all the uses** the whole routine. **137 merely** completely. **139 to** in
comparison to. **140 Hyperion** Titan sun-god, father of Helios; **satyr** a lecherous creature of
classical mythology, half-human but with a goat's legs, tail, ears, and horns. **141 beteem** allow.
147 or ere even before. **149 Niobe** Tantalus' daughter, Queen of Thebes, who boasted that
she had more sons and daughters than Leto; for this, Apollo and Artemis, children of Leto, slew
her fourteen children. She was turned by Zeus into a stone that continually dropped tears.
150 wants . . . reason lacks the faculty of reason. **155 gallèd** irritated, inflamed. **156 post** hasten.
157 incestuous (In Shakespeare's day, the marriage of a man like Claudius to his deceased
brother's wife was considered incestuous.)

Enter HORATIO, MARCELLUS *and* BERNARDO.

HORATIO: Hail to your lordship!

HAMLET: I am glad to see you well.   160
    Horatio!—or I do forget myself.

HORATIO: The same, my lord, and your poor servant ever.

HAMLET: Sir, my good friend; I'll change that name° with you.
    And what make you from° Wittenberg, Horatio?
    Marcellus.   165

MARCELLUS: My good lord.

HAMLET: I am very glad to see you. [*To* BERNARDO.] Good even, sir.—
    But what in faith make you from Wittenberg?

HORATIO: A truant disposition, good my lord.

HAMLET: I would not hear your enemy say so,   170
    Nor shall you do my ear that violence
    To make it truster of your own report
    Against yourself. I know you are no truant.
    But what is your affair in Elsinore?
    We'll teach you to drink deep ere you depart.   175

HORATIO: My lord, I came to see your father's funeral.

HAMLET: I prithee, do not mock me, fellow student;
    I think it was to see my mother's wedding.

HORATIO: Indeed, my lord, it followed hard° upon.

HAMLET: Thrift, thrift, Horatio! The funeral baked meats°   180
    Did coldly° furnish forth the marriage tables.
    Would I had met my dearest° foe in heaven
    Or ever° I had seen that day, Horatio!
    My father!—Methinks I see my father.

HORATIO: Where, my lord?

HAMLET: In my mind's eye, Horatio.   185

HORATIO: I saw him once. 'A° was a goodly king.

HAMLET: 'A was a man. Take him for all in all,
    I shall not look upon his like again.

HORATIO: My lord, I think I saw him yesternight.

HAMLET: Saw? Who?   190

HORATIO: My lord, the King your father.

HAMLET: The King my father?

HORATIO: Season your admiration° for a while
    With an attent° ear till I may deliver,
    Upon the witness of these gentlemen,   195
    This marvel to you.

HAMLET: For God's love, let me hear!

HORATIO: Two nights together had these gentlemen,
    Marcellus and Bernardo, on their watch,
    In the dead waste° and middle of the night,
    Been thus encountered. A figure like your father,   200

---

163 change that name i.e., give and receive reciprocally the name of "friend" (rather than talk
of "servant").   **164 make you from** are you doing away from.   **179 hard** close.   **180 baked
meats** meat pies.   **181 coldly** i.e., as cold leftovers.   **182 dearest** closest (and therefore deadliest).
183 Or ever before.   **186 'A** he.   **193 Season your admiration** restrain your astonishment.
194 attent attentive.   **199 dead waste** desolate stillness.

Armèd at point° exactly, cap-à-pie,°
Appears before them, and with solemn march
Goes slow and stately by them. Thrice he walked
By their oppressed and fear-surprisèd eyes
Within his truncheon's° length, whilst they, distilled° 205
Almost to jelly with the act° of fear,
Stand dumb and speak not to him. This to me
In dreadful° secrecy impart they did,
And I with them the third night kept the watch,
Where, as they had delivered, both in time, 210
Form of the thing, each word made true and good,
The apparition comes. I knew your father;
These hands are not more like.

HAMLET: But where was this?

MARCELLUS: My lord, upon the platform where we watch.

HAMLET: Did you not speak to it?

HORATIO: My lord, I did, 215
But answer made it none. Yet once methought
It lifted up its head and did address
Itself to motion, like as it would speak;°
But even then° the morning cock crew loud,
And at the sound it shrunk in haste away 220
And vanished from our sight.

HAMLET: 'Tis very strange.

HORATIO: As I do live, my honored lord, 'tis true,
And we did think it writ down in our duty
To let you know of it.

HAMLET: Indeed, indeed, sirs. But this troubles me. 225
Hold you the watch tonight?

ALL: We do, my lord.

HAMLET: Armed, say you?

ALL: Armed, my lord.

HAMLET: From top to toe?

ALL: My lord, from head to foot. 230

HAMLET: Then saw you not his face?

HORATIO: O, yes, my lord, he wore his beaver° up.

HAMLET: What° looked he, frowningly?

HORATIO: A countenance more in sorrow than in anger.

HAMLET: Pale or red? 235

HORATIO: Nay, very pale.

HAMLET: And fixed his eyes upon you?

HORATIO: Most constantly.

HAMLET: I would I had been there.

HORATIO: It would have much amazed you. 240

HAMLET: Very like, very like. Stayed it long?

---

201 at point correctly in every detail; **cap-à-pie** from head to foot. **205 truncheon** officer's staff;
distilled dissolved. **206 act** action, operation. **208 dreadful** full of dread. **217–18 did . . .
speak** began to move as though it were about to speak. **219 even then** at that very instant.
232 beaver visor on the helmet. **233 What** how.

HORATIO: While one with moderate haste might tell° a hundred.

MARCELLUS, BERNARDO: Longer, longer.

HORATIO: Not when I saw 't.

HAMLET: His beard was grizzled°—no?   245

HORATIO: It was, as I have seen it in his life,
    A sable silvered.°

HAMLET: I will watch tonight.
    Perchance 'twill walk again.

HORATIO: I warrant° it will.

HAMLET: If it assume my noble father's person,
    I'll speak to it though hell itself should gape   250
    And bid me hold my peace. I pray you all,
    If you have hitherto concealed this sight,
    Let it be tenable° in your silence still,
    And whatsoever else shall hap tonight,
    Give it an understanding but no tongue.   255
    I will requite your loves. So, fare you well.
    Upon the platform twixt eleven and twelve
    I'll visit you.

ALL: Our duty to your honor.

HAMLET: Your loves, as mine to you. Farewell.   *Exeunt [all but* HAMLET].
    My father's spirit in arms! All is not well.   260
    I doubt° some foul play. Would the night were come!
    Till then sit still, my soul. Foul deeds will rise,
    Though all the earth o'erwhelm them, to men's eyes.   *Exit.*

[1.3]

Enter LAERTES *and* OPHELIA, *his sister.*

LAERTES: My necessaries are embarked. Farewell.
    And, sister, as the winds give benefit
    And convoy is assistant,° do not sleep
    But let me hear from you.

OPHELIA: Do you doubt that?

LAERTES: For Hamlet, and the trifling of his favor,   5
    Hold it a fashion and a toy in blood,°
    A violet in the youth of primy° nature,
    Forward,° not permanent, sweet, not lasting,
    The perfume and suppliance° of a minute—
    No more.

OPHELIA: No more but so?

LAERTES: Think it no more.   10
    For nature crescent° does not grow alone
    In thews° and bulk, but as this temple° waxes

---

242 tell count.   **245 grizzled** gray.   **247 sable silvered** black mixed with white.   **248 warrant**
assure you.   **253 tenable** held.   **261 doubt** suspect.   **[1.3] Location: Polonius' chambers.**
3 convoy is assistant means of conveyance are available.   **6 toy in blood** passing amorous fancy.
7 primy in its prime, springtime.   **8 Forward** precocious.   **9 suppliance** supply, filler.
11 crescent growing, waxing.   **12 thews** bodily strength;   **temple** i.e., body.

The inward service of the mind and soul
Grows wide withal.° Perhaps he loves you now,
And now no soil° nor cautel° doth besmirch   15
The virtue of his will,° but you must fear,
His greatness weighed,° his will is not his own.
For he himself is subject to his birth.
He may not, as unvalued persons do,
Carve° for himself, for on his choice depends   20
The safety and health of this whole state,
And therefore must his choice be circumscribed
Unto the voice and yielding° of that body
Whereof he is the head. Then if he says he loves you,
It fits your wisdom so far to believe it   25
As he in his particular act and place°
May give his saying deed, which is no further
Than the main voice° of Denmark goes withal.°
Then weigh what loss your honor may sustain
If with too credent° ear you list° his songs,   30
Or lose your heart, or your chaste treasure open
To his unmastered importunity.
Fear it, Ophelia, fear it, my dear sister,
And keep you in the rear of your affection,°
Out of the shot and danger of desire.   35
The chariest° maid is prodigal enough
If she unmask her beauty° to the moon.°
Virtue itself scapes not calumnious strokes.
The canker galls° the infants of the spring
Too oft before their buttons° be disclosed,°   40
And in the morn and liquid dew° of youth
Contagious blastments° are most imminent.
Be wary then, best safety lies in fear,
Youth to itself rebels,° though none else near.

OPHELIA: I shall the effect of this good lesson keep   45
As watchman to my heart. But, good my brother,
Do not, as some ungracious° pastors do,
Show me the steep and thorny way to heaven,
Whiles like a puffed° and reckless libertine
Himself the primrose path of dalliance treads,   50
And recks° not his own rede.°

Enter POLONIUS.

---

14 Grows wide withal grows along with it. **15 soil** blemish; **cautel** deceit. **16 will** desire.
17 His greatness weighed if you take into account his high position. **20 Carve** i.e., choose.
23 voice and yielding assent, approval. **26 in . . . place** in his particular restricted circumstances.
28 main voice general assent; **withal** along with. **30 credent** credulous; **list** listen to.
34 keep . . . affection don't advance as far as your affection might lead you (A military metaphor.)
36 chariest most scrupulously modest. **37 If she unmask her beauty** if she does no more
than show her beauty; **moon** (symbol of chastity.) **39 canker galls** canker-worm destroys.
40 buttons buds; **disclosed** opened. **41 liquid dew** i.e., time when dew is fresh and bright.
42 blastments blights. **44 Youth . . . rebels** youth is inherently rebellious. **47 ungracious**
ungodly. **49 puffed** bloated, or swollen with pride. **51 recks** heeds; **rede** counsel.

LAERTES: O, fear me not.°
             I stay too long. But here my father comes.
             A double° blessing is a double grace;
             Occasion smiles upon a second leave.°
POLONIUS: Yet here, Laertes? Aboard, aboard, for shame!   55
             The wind sits in the shoulder of your sail,
             And you are stayed for. There—my blessing with thee!
             And these few precepts in thy memory
             Look° thou character.° Give thy thoughts no tongue,
             Nor any unproportioned° thought his° act.   60
             Be thou familiar,° but by no means vulgar.°
             Those friends thou hast, and their adoption tried,°
             Grapple them unto thy soul with hoops of steel,
             But do not dull thy palm° with entertainment
             Of each new-hatched, unfledged courage.° Beware   65
             Of entrance to a quarrel, but being in,
             Bear 't that° th' opposèd may beware of thee.
             Give every man thy ear, but few thy voice;
             Take each man's censure,° but reserve thy judgment.
             Costly thy habit° as thy purse can buy,   70
             But not expressed in fancy;° rich, not gaudy,
             For the apparel oft proclaims the man,
             And they in France of the best rank and station
             Are of a most select and generous chief in that.°
             Neither a borrower nor a lender be,   75
             For loan oft loses both itself and friend,
             And borrowing dulleth edge of husbandry.°
             This above all: to thine own self be true,
             And it must follow, as the night the day,
             Thou canst not then be false to any man.   80
             Farewell. My blessing season° this in thee!
LAERTES: Most humbly do I take my leave, my lord.
POLONIUS: The time invests° you. Go, your servants tend.°
LAERTES: Farewell, Ophelia, and remember well
             What I have said to you.   85
OPHELIA: 'Tis in my memory locked,
             And you yourself shall keep the key of it.
LAERTES: Farewell.   *Exit* LAERTES.
POLONIUS: What is 't, Ophelia, he hath said to you?
OPHELIA: So please you, something touching the Lord Hamlet.   90

---

51 fear me not don't worry on my account. **53 double** (Laertes has already bid his father good-bye.)
54 Occasion . . . leave happy is the circumstance that provides a second leave-taking. (The
goddess Occasion, or Opportunity, smiles.) **59 Look** be sure that; **character** inscribe.
60 unproportioned badly calculated, intemperate; **his** its. **61 familiar** sociable; **vulgar** common.
62 and their adoption tried and also their suitability for adoption as friends having been tested.
64 dull thy palm i.e., shake hands so often as to make the gesture meaningless. **65 courage**
young man of spirit. **67 Bear 't that** manage it so that. **69 censure** opinion, judgment.
70 habit clothing. **71 fancy** excessive ornament, decadent fashion. **74 Are . . . that** are of a
most refined and well-bred preeminence in choosing what to wear. **77 husbandry** thrift.
81 season mature. **83 invests** besieges, presses upon; **tend** attend, wait.

POLONIUS: Marry,° well bethought.
　　　　　'Tis told me he hath very oft of late
　　　　　Given private time to you, and you yourself
　　　　　Have of your audience been most free and bounteous.
　　　　　If it be so—as so 'tis put on° me,　　　　　　　　　95
　　　　　And that in way of caution—I must tell you
　　　　　You do not understand yourself so clearly
　　　　　As it behooves° my daughter and your honor.
　　　　　What is between you? Give me up the truth.
OPHELIA: He hath, my lord, of late made many tenders°　　　100
　　　　　Of his affection to me.
POLONIUS: Affection? Pooh! You speak like a green girl,
　　　　　Unsifted° in such perilous circumstance.
　　　　　Do you believe his tenders, as you call them?
OPHELIA: I do not know, my lord, what I should think.　　　105
POLONIUS: Marry, I will teach you. Think yourself a baby
　　　　　That you have ta'en these tenders for true pay
　　　　　Which are not sterling.° Tender° yourself more dearly,
　　　　　Or—not to crack the wind° of the poor phrase,
　　　　　Running it thus—you'll tender me a fool.°　　　　110
OPHELIA: My lord, he hath importuned me with love
　　　　　In honorable fashion.
POLONIUS: Ay, fashion° you may call it. Go to,° go to.
OPHELIA: And hath given countenance° to his speech, my lord,
　　　　　With almost all the holy vows of heaven.°　　　　115
POLONIUS: Ay, springes° to catch woodcocks.° I do know,
　　　　　When the blood burns, how prodigal° the soul
　　　　　Lends the tongue vows. These blazes, daughter,
　　　　　Giving more light than heat, extinct in both
　　　　　Even in their promise as it° is a-making,　　　　120
　　　　　You must not take for fire. From this time
　　　　　Be something° scanter of your maiden presence.
　　　　　Set your entreatments° at a higher rate
　　　　　Than a command to parle.° For Lord Hamlet,
　　　　　Believe so much in him° that he is young,　　　　125
　　　　　And with a larger tether may he walk
　　　　　Than may be given you. In few,° Ophelia,
　　　　　Do not believe his vows, for they are brokers,°

---

91 Marry i.e., by the Virgin Mary. (A mild oath.) **95 put on** impressed on, told to. **98 behooves** befits. **100 tenders** offers. **103 Unsifted** i.e., untried. **108 sterling** legal currency; **Tender** hold, look after, offer. **109 crack the wind** i.e., run it until it is broken-winded. **110 tender me a fool** (1) show yourself to me as a fool, (2) show me up as a fool, (3) present me with a grandchild. (*Fool* was a term of endearment for a child.) **113 fashion** mere form, pretense; **Go to** (an expression of impatience.) **114 countenance** credit, confirmation. **116 springes** snares; **woodcocks** birds easily caught; here used to connote gullibility. **117 prodigal** prodigally. **120 it** i.e., the promise. **122 something** somewhat. **123 entreatments** negotiations for surrender. (A military term.) **124 parle** discuss terms with the enemy. (Polonius urges his daughter, in the metaphor of military language, not to meet with Hamlet and consider giving in to him merely because he requests an interview.) **125 so . . . him** this much concerning him. **127 In few** briefly. **128 brokers** go-betweens, procurers.

Not of that dye° which their investments° show,
But mere implorators° of unholy suits,   130
Breathing° like sanctified and pious bawds,
The better to beguile. This is for all:°
I would not, in plain terms, from this time forth
Have you so slander° any moment° leisure
As to give words or talk with the Lord Hamlet.   135
Look to 't, I charge you. Come your ways.°

OPHELIA: I shall obey, my lord.   *Exeunt.*

[1.4]

Enter HAMLET, HORATIO, *and* MARCELLUS.

HAMLET: The air bites shrewdly,° it is very cold.
HORATIO: It is a nipping and an eager° air.
HAMLET: What hour now?
HORATIO: I think it lacks of° twelve.
MARCELLUS: No, it is struck.
HORATIO: Indeed? I heard it not.
It then draws near the season°   5
Wherein the spirit held his wont° to walk.

A flourish of trumpets, and two pieces° go off [within].

What does this mean, my lord?
HAMLET: The King doth wake° tonight and takes his rouse,°
Keeps wassail,° and the swaggering upspring° reels,°
And as he drains his drafts of Rhenish° down,   10
The kettledrum and trumpet thus bray out
The triumph of his pledge.°
HORATIO: It is a custom?
HAMLET: Ay, marry, is 't,
But to my mind, though I am native here
And to the manner° born, it is a custom   15
More honored in the breach than the observance.°
This heavy-headed revel east and west°
Makes us traduced and taxed of° other nations.
They clepe° us drunkards, and with swinish phrase°
Soil our addition;° and indeed it takes   20
From our achievements, though performed at height,°
The pith and marrow of our attribute.°

---

129 dye color or sort;   **investments** clothes. (The vows are not what they seem.)   **130 mere
implorators** out-and-out solicitors.   **131 Breathing** speaking.   **132 for all** once for all, in sum.
134 slander abuse, misuse;   **moment** moment's.   **136 Come your ways** come along.
[1.4] Location: The guard platform.   1 shrewdly keenly, sharply.   **2 eager** biting.
3 lacks of is just short of.   **5 season** time.   **6 held his wont** was accustomed;   **s.d. pieces** i.e.,
of ordnance, cannon.   **8 wake** stay awake and hold revel;   **takes his rouse** carouses.
9 wassail carousal;   **upspring** wild German dance;   **reels** dances.   **10 Rhenish** Rhine wine.
12 The triumph . . . pledge i.e., his feat in draining the wine in a single draft.   **15 manner**
custom (of drinking).   **16 More . . . observance** better neglected than followed.   **17 east and
west** i.e., everywhere.   **18 taxed of** censured by.   **19 clepe** call;   **with swinish phrase** i.e., by
calling us swine.   **20 addition** reputation.   **21 at height** outstandingly.   **22 The pith . . . attribute** the essence of the reputation that others attribute to us.

So, oft it chances in particular men,
That for° some vicious mole of nature° in them,
As in their birth—wherein they are not guilty,   25
Since nature cannot choose his° origin—
By their o'ergrowth of some complexion,°
Oft breaking down the pales° and forts of reason,
Or by some habit that too much o'erleavens°
The form of plausive° manners, that these men,   30
Carrying, I say, the stamp of one defect,
Being nature's livery° or fortune's star,°
His virtues else,° be they as pure as grace,
As infinite as man may undergo,°
Shall in the general censure° take corruption   35
From that particular fault. The dram of evil
Doth all the noble substance often dout
To his own scandal.°

    Enter GHOST.

HORATIO: Look, my lord, it comes!
HAMLET: Angels and ministers of grace° defend us!
Be thou° a spirit of health° or goblin damned,   40
Bring° with thee airs from heaven or blasts from hell,
Be thy intents° wicked or charitable,
Thou com'st in such a questionable° shape
That I will speak to thee. I'll call thee Hamlet,
King, father, royal Dane. O, answer me!   45
Let me not burst in ignorance, but tell
Why thy canonized° bones, hearsèd° in death,
Have burst their cerements;° why the sepulcher
Wherein we saw thee quietly inurned°
Hath oped his ponderous and marble jaws   50
To cast thee up again. What may this mean,
That thou, dead corpse, again in complete steel,°
Revisits thus the glimpses of the moon,°
Making night hideous, and we fools of nature°
So horridly to shake our disposition°   55

24 for on account of; **mole of nature** natural blemish in one's constitution. **26 his** its. **27 their o'ergrowth . . . complexion** the excessive growth in individuals of some natural trait. **28 pales** palings, fences (as of a fortification). **29 o'erleavens** induces a change throughout (as yeast works in dough). **30 plausive** pleasing. **32 nature's livery** sign of one's servitude to nature; **fortune's star** the destiny that chance brings. **33 His virtues else** i.e., the other qualities of *these men* (line 30). **34 may undergo** can sustain. **35 general censure** general opinion that people have of him. **36–38 The dram . . . scandal** i.e., the small drop of evil blots out or works against the noble substance of the whole and brings it into disrepute. To *dout* is to blot out. (A famous crux.) **39 ministers of grace** messengers of God. **40 Be thou** whether you are; **spirit of health** good angel. **41 Bring** whether you bring. **42 Be thy intents** whether your intentions are. **43 questionable** inviting question. **47 canonized** buried according to the canons of the church; **hearsèd** coffined. **48 cerements** grave clothes. **49 inurned** entombed. **52 complete steel** full armor. **53 glimpses of the moon** pale and uncertain moonlight. **54 fools of nature** mere men, limited to natural knowledge and subject to nature. **55 So . . . disposition** to distress our mental composure so violently.

With thoughts beyond the reaches of our souls?
Say, why is this? Wherefore? What should we do?

[*The* GHOST] *beckons* [HAMLET].

HORATIO: It beckons you to go away with it,
　　　As if it some impartment° did desire
　　　To you alone.

MARCELLUS:　　　　　　Look with what courteous action   60
　　　It wafts you to a more removèd ground.
　　　But do not go with it.

HORATIO:　　　　　　　　No, by no means.

HAMLET: It will not speak. Then I will follow it.

HORATIO: Do not, my lord!

HAMLET:　　　　　　Why, what should be the fear?
　　　I do not set my life at a pin's fee,°   65
　　　And for my soul, what can it do to that,
　　　Being a thing immortal as itself?
　　　It waves me forth again. I'll follow it.

HORATIO: What if it tempt you toward the flood,° my lord,
　　　Or to the dreadful summit of the cliff   70
　　　That beetles o'er° his° base into the sea,
　　　And there assume some other horrible form
　　　Which might deprive your sovereignty of reason°
　　　And draw you into madness? Think of it.
　　　The very place puts toys of desperation,°   75
　　　Without more motive, into every brain
　　　That looks so many fathoms to the sea
　　　And hears it roar beneath.

HAMLET: It wafts me still.—Go on, I'll follow thee.

MARCELLUS: You shall not go, my lord.   [*They try to stop him.*]

HAMLET:　　　　　　　Hold off your hands!   80

HORATIO: Be ruled. You shall not go.

HAMLET:　　　　　　　My fate cries out,°
　　　And makes each petty° artery° in this body
　　　As hardy as the Nemean lion's° nerve.°
　　　Still am I called. Unhand me, gentlemen.
　　　By heaven, I'll make a ghost of him that lets° me!   85
　　　I say, away!—Go on, I'll follow thee.   *Exeunt* GHOST *and* HAMLET.

HORATIO: He waxes desperate with imagination.

MARCELLUS: Let's follow. 'Tis not fit thus to obey him.

HORATIO: Have after.° To what issue° will this come?

MARCELLUS: Something is rotten in the state of Denmark.   90

HORATIO: Heaven will direct it.°

MARCELLUS:　　　　　　Nay, let's follow him.   *Exeunt.*

59 impartment communication. **65 fee** value. **69 flood** sea. **71 beetles o'er** overhangs
threateningly (like bushy eyebrows); **his** its. **73 deprive . . . reason** take away the rule of
reason over your mind. **75 toys of desperation** fancies of desperate acts, i.e., suicide.
81 My fate cries out my destiny summons me. **82 petty** weak; **artery** (through which the
vital spirits were thought to have been conveyed). **83 Nemean lion** one of the monsters slain
by Hercules in his twelve labors; **nerve** sinew. **85 lets** hinders. **89 Have after** let's go after
him; **issue** outcome. **91 it** i.e., the outcome.

[1.5]

Enter GHOST *and* HAMLET.

HAMLET: Whither wilt thou lead me? Speak. I'll go no further.
GHOST: Mark me.
HAMLET: I will.
GHOST: My hour is almost come,
    When I to sulfurous and tormenting flames
    Must render up myself.
HAMLET: Alas, poor ghost!
GHOST: Pity me not, but lend thy serious hearing   5
    To what I shall unfold.
HAMLET: Speak. I am bound° to hear.
GHOST: So art thou to revenge, when thou shalt hear.
HAMLET: What?
GHOST: I am thy father's spirit,   10
    Doomed for a certain term to walk the night,
    And for the day confined to fast° in fires,
    Till the foul crimes° done in my days of nature°
    Are burnt and purged away. But that° I am forbid
    To tell the secrets of my prison house,   15
    I could a tale unfold whose lightest word
    Would harrow up° thy soul, freeze thy young blood,
    Make thy two eyes like stars start from their spheres,°
    Thy knotted and combinèd locks° to part,
    And each particular hair to stand on end   20
    Like quills upon the fretful porcupine.
    But this eternal blazon° must not be
    To ears of flesh and blood. List, list, O, list!
    If thou didst ever thy dear father love—
HAMLET: O God!   25
GHOST: Revenge his foul and most unnatural murder.
HAMLET: Murder?
GHOST: Murder most foul, as in the best° it is,
    But this most foul, strange, and unnatural.
HAMLET: Haste me to know't, that I, with wings as swift   30
    As meditation or the thoughts of love,
    May sweep to my revenge.
GHOST: I find thee apt;
    And duller shouldst thou be° than the fat° weed
    That roots itself in ease on Lethe° wharf,

[1.5] Location: The battlements of the castle.   **7 bound** (1) ready, (2) obligated by duty and fate. (the Ghost, in line 8, answers in the second sense.) **12 fast** do penance by fasting. **13 crimes** Sins; **of nature** as a mortal. **14 But that** were it not that. **17 harrow up** lacerate, tear. **18 spheres** i.e., eye-sockets, here compared to the orbits or transparent revolving spheres in which, according to Ptolemaic astronomy, the heavenly bodies were fixed. **19 knotted . . . locks** hair neatly arranged and confined. **22 eternal blazon** revelation of the secrets of eternity. **28 in the best** even at best. **33 shouldst thou be** you would have to be; **fat** torpid, lethargic. **348 Lethe** the river of forgetfulness in Hades.

35

Wouldst thou not stir in this. Now, Hamlet, hear.
'Tis given out that, sleeping in my orchard,°
A serpent stung me. So the whole ear of Denmark
Is by a forgèd process° of my death
Rankly abused.° But know, thou noble youth,

40

The serpent that did sting thy father's life
Now wears his crown.

HAMLET: O, my prophetic soul! My uncle!

GHOST: Ay, that incestuous, that adulterate° beast,
With witchcraft of his wit, with traitorous gifts°—
O wicked wit and gifts, that have the power

45

So to seduce!—won to his shameful lust
The will of my most seeming-virtuous queen.
O Hamlet, what a falling off was there!
From me, whose love was of that dignity
That it went hand in hand even with the vow°

50

I made to her in marriage, and to decline
Upon a wretch whose natural gifts were poor
To° those of mine!
But virtue, as it° never will be moved,
Though lewdness court it in a shape of heaven,°

55

So lust, though to a radiant angel linked,
Will sate itself in a celestial bed°
And prey on garbage.
But soft, methinks I scent the morning air.
Brief let me be. Sleeping within my orchard,

60

My custom always of the afternoon,
Upon my secure° hour thy uncle stole,
With juice of cursèd hebona° in a vial,
And in the porches of my ears° did pour
The leprous distillment,° whose effect

65

Holds such an enmity with blood of man
That swift as quicksilver it courses through
The natural gates and alleys of the body,
And with a sudden vigor it doth posset°
And curd, like eager° droppings into milk,

70

The thin and wholesome blood. So did it mine,
And a most instant tetter° barked° about,
Most lazar-like,° with vile and loathsome crust,
All my smooth body.

---

36 orchard garden.   **38 forgèd process** falsified account.   **39 abused** deceived.   **43 adulterate** adulterous.   **44 gifts** (1) talents, (2) presents.   **50 even with the vow** with the very vow.
53 To compared to.   **54 virtue, as it** as virtue.   **55 shape of heaven** heavenly form.
57 sate . . . bed cease to find sexual pleasure in a virtuously lawful marriage.   **62 secure** confident, unsuspicious.   **63 hebona** a poison. (The word seems to be a form of *ebony*, though it is thought perhaps to be related to *henbane,* a poison, or to *ebenus,* "yew.")   **64 porches of my ears** ears as a porch or entrance of the body.   **65 leprous distillment** distillation causing leprosylike disfigurement.   **69 posset** coagulate, curdle.   **70 eager** sour, acid.   **72 tetter** eruption of scabs;   **barked** recovered with a rough covering, like bark on a tree.
73 lazar-like leperlike.

Thus was I, sleeping, by a brother's hand   75
Of life, of crown, of queen at once dispatched,°
Cut off even in the blossoms of my sin,
Unhouseled,° disappointed,° unaneled,°
No reckoning° made, but sent to my account
With all my imperfections on my head.   80
O, horrible! O, horrible, most horrible!
If thou hast nature° in thee, bear it not.
Let not the royal bed of Denmark be
A couch for luxury° and damnèd incest.
But, howsoever thou pursues this act,   85
Taint not thy mind nor let thy soul contrive
Against thy mother aught. Leave her to heaven
And to those thorns that in her bosom lodge,
To prick and sting her. Fare thee well at once.
The glowworm shows the matin° to be near,   90
And 'gins to pale his° uneffectual fire.
Adieu, adieu, adieu! Remember me.   [*Exit.*]

HAMLET: O all you host of heaven! O earth! What else?
And shall I couple° hell? O, fie! Hold,° hold, my heart,
And you, my sinews, grow not instant° old,   95
But bear me stiffly up. Remember thee?
Ay, thou poor ghost, whiles memory holds a seat
In this distracted globe.° Remember thee?
Yea, from the table° of my memory
I'll wipe away all trivial fond° records,   100
All saws° of books, all forms,° all pressures° past
That youth and observation copied there,
And thy commandment all alone shall live
Within the book and volume of my brain,
Unmixed with baser matter. Yes, by heaven!   105
O most pernicious woman!
O villain, villain, smiling, damnèd villain!
My tables°—meet it is° I set it down
That one may smile, and smile, and be a villain.
At least I am sure it may be so in Denmark.   [*Writing.*] 110
So uncle, there you are.° Now to my word:
It is "Adieu, adieu! Remember me."
I have sworn 't.

   Enter HORATIO *and* MARCELLUS.

HORATIO: My lord, my lord!
MARCELLUS: Lord Hamlet!   115

---

76 dispatched suddenly deprived. **78 Unhouseled** without having received the Sacrament;
disappointed unready (spiritually) for the last journey; **unaneled** without having received
extreme unction. **79 reckoning** settling of accounts. **82 nature** i.e., the promptings of a son.
84 luxury lechery. **90 matin** morning. **91 his** its. **94 couple** add; **Hold** hold together.
95 instant instantly. **98 globe** (1) head, (2) world. **99 table** tablet, slate. **100 fond** foolish.
101 saws wise sayings; **forms** shapes or images copied onto the slate; general ideas;
pressures impressions stamped. **108 tables** writing tablets; **meet it is** it is fitting.
111 there you are i.e., there, I've written that down against you.

HORATIO: Heavens secure him!°
HAMLET: So be it.
MARCELLUS: Hilo, ho, ho, my lord!
HAMLET: Hillo, ho, ho, boy! Come, bird, come.°
MARCELLUS: How is 't, my noble lord?   120
HORATIO: What news, my lord?
HAMLET: O, wonderful!
HORATIO: Good my lord, tell it.
HAMLET: No, you will reveal it.
HORATIO: Not I, my lord, by heaven.   125
MARCELLUS: Nor I, my lord.
HAMLET: How say you, then, would heart of man once° think it?
    But you'll be secret?
HORATIO, MARCELLUS: Ay, by heaven, my lord.
HAMLET: There's never a villain dwelling in all Denmark
    But he's an arrant° knave.   130
HORATIO: There needs no ghost, my lord, come from the grave
    To tell us this.
HAMLET: Why, right, you are in the right.
    And so, without more circumstance° at all,
    I hold it fit that we shake hands and part,
    You as your business and desire shall point you—   135
    For every man hath business and desire,
    Such as it is—and for my own poor part,
    Look you, I'll go pray.
HORATIO: These are but wild and whirling words, my lord.
HAMLET: I am sorry they offend you, heartily;   140
    Yes, faith, heartily.
HORATIO: There's no offense, my lord.
HAMLET: Yes, by Saint Patrick,° but there is, Horatio,
    And much offense° too. Touching this vision here,
    It is an honest ghost,° that let me tell you.
    For your desire to know what is between us,   145
    O'ermaster 't as you may. And now, good friends,
    As you are friends, scholars, and soldiers,
    Give me one poor request.
HORATIO: What is 't, my lord? We will.
HAMLET: Never make known what you have seen tonight.   150
HORATIO, MARCELLUS: My lord, we will not.
HAMLET: Nay, but swear 't.
HORATIO: In faith, my lord, not I.°
MARCELLUS: Nor I, my lord, in faith.
HAMLET: Upon my sword.°   [*He holds out his sword.*]   155

---

116 secure him keep him safe. **119 Hillo . . . come** (A falconer's call to a hawk in air. Hamlet mocks the halloing as though it were a part of hawking.) **127 once** ever. **130 arrant** thoroughgoing. **133 circumstance** ceremony, elaboration. **142 Saint Patrick** (the keeper of Purgatory and patron saint of all blunders and confusion.) **143 offense** (Hamlet deliberately changes Horatio's "no offense against all decency.") **144 an honest ghost** i.e., a real ghost and not an evil spirit. **153 In faith . . . I** i.e., I swear not to tell what I have seen. (Horatio is not refusing to swear.) **155 sword** i.e., the hilt in the form of a cross.

MARCELLUS: We have sworn, my lord, already.°
HAMLET: Indeed, upon my sword, indeed.
GHOST [*cries under the stage*]: Swear.
HAMLET: Ha, ha, boy, sayst thou so? Art thou there, truepenny?°
    Come on, you hear this fellow in the cellarage.   160
    Consent to swear.
HORATIO: Propose the oath, my lord.
HAMLET: Never to speak of this that you have seen,
    Swear by my sword.
GHOST [*beneath*]: Swear.   [*They swear.*°]
HAMLET: *Hic et ubique?*° Then we'll shift our ground.   165

                  [*He moves to another spot.*]

    Come hither, gentlemen,
    And lay your hands again upon my sword.
    Swear by my sword
    Never to speak of this that you have heard.
GHOST [*beneath*]: Swear by his sword.   [*They swear.*] 170
HAMLET: Well said, old mole. Canst work i' th' earth so fast?
    A worthy pioneer!°—Once more removed, good friends.

                      [*He moves again.*]

HORATIO: O day and night, but this is wondrous strange!
HAMLET: And therefore as a stranger° give it welcome.
    There are more things in heaven and earth, Horatio,   175
    Than are dreamt of in your philosophy.°
    But come;
    Here, as before, never, so help you mercy,°
    How strange or odd soe'er I bear myself—
    As I perchance hereafter shall think meet   180
    To put an antic° disposition on—
    That you, at such times seeing me, never shall,
    With arms encumbered° thus, or this headshake,
    Or by pronouncing of some doubtful phrase
    As "Well, we know," or "We could, an if° we would,"   185
    Or "If we list° to speak," or "There be, an if they might,"°
    Or such ambiguous giving out,° to note°
    That you know aught° of me—this do swear,
    So grace and mercy at your most need help you.
GHOST [*beneath*]: Swear.   [*They swear.*] 190

---

156 We . . . already i.e., we swore in *faith.* **159 truepenny** honest old fellow. **164 s.d. They swear** (seemingly they swear here, and at lines 170 and 190, as they lay their hands on Hamlet's sword. Triple oaths would have particular force; these three oaths deal with what they have seen, what they have heard, and what they promise about Hamlet's *antic disposition.*) **165 *Hic et ubique*** here and everywhere (Latin). **172 pioneer** foot soldier assigned to dig tunnels and excavations. **174 as a stranger** i.e., needing your hospitality. **176 your philosophy** this subject called "natural philosophy" or "science" that people talk about. **178 so help you mercy** as you hope for God's mercy when you are judged. **181 antic** fantastic. **183 encumbered** folded. **185 an if** if. **186 list** wished; **There . . . might** i.e., there are people here (we, in fact) who could tell news if we were at liberty to do so. **187 giving out** intimation; **note** draw attention to the fact. **188 aught** i.e., something secret.

HAMLET: Rest, rest, perturbèd spirit! So, gentlemen,
With all my love I do commend me to you;°
And what so poor a man as Hamlet is
May do t' express his love and friending° to you,
God willing, shall not lack.° Let us go in together,   195
And still° your fingers on your lips, I pray.
The time° is out of joint. O cursèd spite°
That ever I was born to set it right!   [*They wait for him to leave first.*]
Nay, come, let's go together.°   *Exeunt.*

[2.1]

Enter old POLONIUS *with his man* [REYNALDO].

POLONIUS: Give him this money and these notes, Reynaldo.

[He gives money and papers.]

REYNALDO: I will, my lord.
POLONIUS: You shall do marvelous° wisely, good Reynaldo,
Before you visit him, to make inquire°
Of his behavior.
REYNALDO: My lord, I did intend it.   5
POLONIUS: Marry, well said, very well said. Look you, sir,
Inquire me first what Danskers° are in Paris,
And how, and who, what means,° and where they keep,°
What company, at what expense; and finding
By this encompassment° and drift° of question   10
That they do know my son, come you more nearer
Than your particular demands will touch it.°
Take you,° as 'twere, some distant knowledge of him,
As thus, "I know his father and his friends,
And in part him." Do you mark this, Reynaldo?   15
REYNALDO: Ay, very well, my lord.
POLONIUS: "And in part him, but," you may say, "not well.
But if 't be he I mean, he's very wild,
Addicted so and so," and there put on° him
What forgeries° you please—marry, none so rank°   20
As may dishonor him, take heed of that,
But, sir, such wanton,° wild, and usual slips
As are companions noted and most known
To youth and liberty.
REYNALDO: As gaming, my lord.   25
POLONIUS: Ay, or drinking, fencing, swearing,
Quarreling, drabbing°—you may go so far.

192 do . . . you entrust myself to you.   **194 friending** friendliness.
195 lack be lacking. **196 still** always.   **197 The time** the state of affairs;   **spite** i.e., the spite of Fortune.   **199 let's go together** (probably they wait for him to leave first, but he refuses this ceremoniousness.)
[2.1] Location: Polonius' chambers.   3 marvelous marvelously.   **4 inquire** inquiry.
7 Danskers Danes.   **8 what means** what wealth (they have);   **keep** dwell.   **10 encompassment** roundabout talking;   **drift** gradual approach or course.   **11–12 come . . . it** you will find out more this way than by asking pointed questions (*particular demands*).   **13 Take you** assume, pretend.   **19 put on** impute to.   **20 forgeries** invented tales;   **rank** gross.   **22 wanton** sportive, unrestrained.   **27 drabbing** whoring.

REYNALDO: My lord, that would dishonor him.

POLONIUS: Faith, no, as you may season° it in the charge.
    You must not put another scandal on him   30
    That he is open to incontinency;°
    That's not my meaning. But breathe his faults so quaintly°
    That they may seem the taints of liberty,°
    The flash and outbreak of a fiery mind,
    A savageness in unreclaimèd blood,   35
    Of general assault.°

REYNALDO: But, my good lord—

POLONIUS: Wherefore should you do this?

REYNALDO: Ay, my lord, I would know that.

POLONIUS: Marry, sir, here's my drift,   40
    And I believe it is a fetch of warrant.°
    You laying these slight sullies on my son,
    As 'twere a thing a little soiled wi' the working,°
    Mark you,
    Your party in converse,° him you would sound,°   45
    Having ever° seen in the prenominate crimes°
    The youth you breathe° of guilty, be assured
    He closes with you in this consequence:°
    "Good sir," or so, or "friend," or "gentleman,"
    According to the phrase or the addition°   50
    Of man and country.

REYNALDO: Very good, my lord.

POLONIUS: And then, sir, does 'a this—'a does—what was I about to say? By the
    Mass, I was about to say something. Where did I leave?

REYNALDO: At "closes in the consequence."

POLONIUS: At "closes in the consequence," ay, marry.   55
    He closes thus: "I know the gentleman,
    I saw him yesterday," or "th' other day,"
    Or then, or then, with such or such, "and as you say,
    There was 'a gaming," "there o'ertook in 's rouse,"°
    "There falling out° at tennis," or perchance   60
    "I saw him enter such a house of sale,"
    Videlicet° a brothel, or so forth. See you now,
    Your bait of falsehood takes this carp° of truth;
    And thus do we of wisdom and of reach,°
    With windlasses° and with assays of bias,°   65

---

29 season temper, soften. **31 incontinency** habitual sexual excess. **32 quaintly** artfully, subtly.
33 taints of liberty faults resulting from free living. **35–36 A savageness . . . assault** a wildness in untamed youth that assails all indiscriminately. **41 fetch of warrant** legitimate trick.
43 soiled wi' the working soiled by handling while it is being made, i.e., by involvement in
the ways of the world. **45 converse** conversation; **sound** i.e., sound out. **46 Having ever** if
he has ever; **prenominate crimes** before-mentioned offenses. **47 breathe** speak. **48 closes . . .
consequence** takes you into his confidence in some fashion, as follows. **50 addition** title.
59 o'ertook in 's rouse overcome by drink. **60 falling out** quarreling. **62 Videlicet** namely.
63 carp a fish. **64 reach** capacity, ability. **65 windlasses** i.e., circuitous paths. (Literally, circuits
made to head off the game in hunting); **assays of bias** attempts through indirection (like the
curving path of the bowling ball, which is biased or weighted to one side).

By indirections find directions° out.
So by my former lecture and advice
Shall you my son. You have° me, have you not?

REYNALDO: My lord, I have.

POLONIUS: God b'wi'° ye; fare ye well.

REYNALDO: Good my lord.   70

POLONIUS: Observe his inclination in yourself.°

REYNALDO: I shall, my lord.

POLONIUS: And let him ply his music.

REYNALDO: Well, my lord.

POLONIUS: Farewell.   *Exit* REYNALDO.

          Enter OPHELIA.

                    How now, Ophelia, what's the matter?   75

OPHELIA: O my lord, my lord, I have been so affrighted!

POLONIUS: With what, i' the name of God?

OPHELIA: My lord, as I was sewing in my closet,°
Lord Hamlet, with his doublet° all unbraced,°
No hat upon his head, his stockings fouled,   80
Ungartered, and down-gyvèd° to his ankle,
Pale as his shirt, his knees knocking each other,
And with a look so piteous in purport°
As if he had been loosèd out of hell
To speak of horrors—he comes before me.   85

POLONIUS: Mad for thy love?

OPHELIA: My lord, I do not know,
But truly I do fear it.

POLONIUS: What said he?

OPHELIA: He took me by the wrist and held me hard.
Then goes he to the length of all his arm,
And, with his other hand thus o'er his brow   90
He falls to such perusal of my face
As° 'a would draw it. Long stayed he so.
At last, a little shaking of mine arm
And thrice his head thus waving up and down,
He raised a sigh so piteous and profound   95
As it did seem to shatter all his bulk°
And end his being. That done, he lets me go,
And with his head over his shoulder turned
He seemed to find his way without his eyes,
For out o' doors he went without their helps,   100
And to the last bended their light on me.

POLONIUS: Come, go with me. I will go seek the King.
This is the very ecstasy° of love,
Whose violent property° fordoes° itself
And leads the will to desperate undertakings   105

---

66 directions i.e., the way things really are.   **68 have** understand.   **69 b' wi'** be with.   **71 in
yourself** in your own person (as well as by asking questions).   **78 closet** private chamber.
79 doublet close-fitting jacket;   **unbraced** unfastened.   **81 down-gyvèd** fallen to the ankles
(like gyves or fetters).   **83 in purport** in what it expressed.   **92 As** as if (also in line 97).
96 bulk body.   **103 ecstasy** madness.   **104 property** nature;   **fordoes** destroys.

As oft as any passion under heaven
That does afflict our natures. I am sorry.
What, have you given him any hard words of late?
OPHELIA: No, my good lord, but as you did command
I did repel his letters and denied   110
His access to me.
POLONIUS: That hath made him mad.
I am sorry that with better heed and judgment
I had not quoted° him. I feared he did but trifle
And meant to wrack° thee. But beshrew my jealousy!°
By heaven, it is as proper to our age°   115
To cast beyond° ourselves in our opinions
As it is common for the younger sort
To lack discretion. Come, go we to the King.
This must be known,° which, being kept close,° might move
More grief to hide than hate to utter love.°   120
Come.   *Exeunt.*

[2.2]

Flourish. Enter KING *and* QUEEN, ROSENCRANTZ, *and* GUILDENSTERN [*with others*].

KING: Welcome, dear Rosencrantz and Guildenstern.
Moreover that° we much did long to see you,
The need we have to use you did provoke
Our hasty sending. Something have you heard
Of Hamlet's transformation—so call it,   5
Sith nor° th' exterior nor the inward man
Resembles that° it was. What it should be,
More than his father's death, that thus hath put him
So much from th' understanding of himself,
I cannot dream of. I entreat you both   10
That, being of so young days° brought up with him,
And sith so neighbored to° his youth and havior,°
That you vouchsafe your rest° here in our court
Some little time, so by your companies
To draw him on to pleasures, and to gather   15
So much as from occasion° you may glean,
Whether aught to us unknown afflicts him thus
That, opened,° lies within our remedy.

113 quoted observed. **114 wrack** ruin, seduce; **beshrew my jealousy** a plague upon my
suspicious nature. **115 proper . . . age** characteristic of us (old) men. **116 cast beyond** over-
shoot, miscalculate. (A metaphor from hunting.) **119 known** made known (to the King);
close secret. **119–20 might . . . love** i.e., might cause more grief (because of what Hamlet might
do) by hiding the knowledge of Hamlet's strange behavior toward Ophelia than unpleasantness
by telling it. **[2.2] Location: The castle. 2 Moreover that** besides the fact that. **6 Sith nor**
since neither. **7 that** what. **11 of . . . days** From such early youth. **12 And sith so neighbored to** and since you are (or, and since that time you are) intimately acquainted with;
havior demeanor. **13 vouchsafe your rest** please to stay. **16 occasion** opportunity.
18 opened being revealed.

QUEEN: Good gentlemen, he hath much talked of you,
          And sure I am two men there is not living   20
          To whom he more adheres. If it will please you
          To show us so much gentry° and good will
          As to expend your time with us awhile
          For the supply and profit of our hope,°
          Your visitation shall receive such thanks   25
          As fits a king's remembrance.°
ROSENCRANTZ: Both Your Majesties
          Might, by the sovereign power you have of° us,
          Put your dread° pleasures more into command
          Than to entreaty.
GUILDENSTERN: But we both obey,
          And here give up ourselves in the full bent°   30
          To lay our service freely at your feet,
          To be commanded.
KING: Thanks, Rosencrantz and gentle Guildenstern.
QUEEN: Thanks, Guildenstern and gentle Rosencrantz.
          And I beseech you instantly to visit   35
          My too much changèd son. Go, some of you,
          And bring these gentlemen where Hamlet is.
GUILDENSTERN: Heavens make our presence and our practices°
          Pleasant and helpful to him!
QUEEN: Ay, amen!

          Exeunt ROSENCRANTZ *and* GUILDENSTERN [*with some attendants*].

          Enter POLONIUS.

POLONIUS: Th' ambassadors from Norway, my good lord,   40
          Are joyfully returned.
KING: Thou still° hast been the father of good news.
POLONIUS: Have I, my lord? I assure my good liege
          I hold° my duty, as° I hold my soul,
          Both to my God and to my gracious king;   45
          And I do think, or else this brain of mine
          Hunts not the trail of policy° so sure
          As it hath used to do, that I have found
          The very cause of Hamlet's lunacy.
KING: O, speak of that! That do I long to hear.   50
POLONIUS: Give first admittance to th' ambassadors.
          My news shall be the fruit° to that great feast.
KING: Thyself do grace° to them and bring them in.   [*Exit* POLONIUS.]
          He tells me, my dear Gertrude, he hath found
          The head and source of all your son's distemper.   55
QUEEN: I doubt° it is no other but the main,°
          His father's death and our o'erhasty marriage.

---

22 gentry courtesy.   **24 supply . . . hope** aid and furtherance of what we hope for.   **26 As fits . . .
remembrance** as would be a fitting gift of a king who rewards true service.   **27 of** over.
28 dread inspiring awe.   **30 in . . . bent** to the utmost degree of our capacity. (An archery metaphor.)
38 practices doings.   **42 still** always.   **44 hold** maintain; **as** firmly as.   **47 policy** sagacity.
52 fruit dessert.   **53 grace** honor (punning on *grace* said before a *feast,* line 52.)   **56 doubt**
fear, suspect;   **main** chief point, principal concern.

Enter Ambassadors VOLTIMAND *and* CORNELIUS, *with* POLONIUS.

KING: Well, we shall sift him.°—Welcome, my good friends!
　　　Say, Voltimand, what from our brother° Norway?
VOLTIMAND: Most fair return of greetings and desires.°　　　　　　60
　　　Upon our first,° he sent out to suppress
　　　His nephew's levies, which to him appeared
　　　To be a preparation 'gainst the Polack,
　　　But, better looked into, he truly found
　　　It was against Your Highness. Whereat grieved　　　　　　　65
　　　That so his sickness, age, and impotence°
　　　Was falsely borne in hand,° sends out arrests°
　　　On Fortinbras, which he, in brief, obeys,
　　　Receives rebuke from Norway, and in fine°
　　　Makes vow before his uncle never more　　　　　　　　　　70
　　　To give th' assay° of arms against Your Majesty.
　　　Whereon old Norway, overcome with joy,
　　　Gives him three thousand crowns in annual fee
　　　And his commission to employ those soldiers,
　　　So levied as before, against the Polack,　　　　　　　　　75
　　　With an entreaty, herein further shown,　　　　　[*giving a paper*]
　　　That it might please you to give quiet pass
　　　Through your dominions for this enterprise
　　　On such regards of safety and allowance°
　　　As therein are set down.
KING:　　　　　　　　　　　　　It likes° us well,　　　　　　　80
　　　And at our more considered° time we'll read,
　　　Answer, and think upon this business.
　　　Meantime we thank you for your well-took labor.
　　　Go to your rest; at night we'll feast together.
　　　Most welcome home!　　　　　　　　　*Exeunt Ambassadors.*
POLONIUS:　　　　　　　　This business is well ended.　　　85
　　　My liege, and madam, to expostulate°
　　　What majesty should be, what duty is,
　　　Why day is day, night night, and time is time,
　　　Were nothing but to waste night, day, and time.
　　　Therefore, since brevity is the soul of wit,°　　　　　　　90
　　　And tediousness the limbs and outward flourishes,
　　　I will be brief. Your noble son is mad.
　　　Mad call I it, for, to define true madness,
　　　What is't but to be nothing else but mad?
　　　But let that go.
QUEEN:　　　　　　　　More matter, with less art.　　　　　95

---

58 sift him question Polonius closely.　**59 brother** fellow king.　**60 desires** good wishes.
61 Upon our first at our first words on the business.　**66 impotence** helplessness.　**67 borne in
hand** deluded, taken advantage of;　**arrests** orders to desist.　**69 in fine** in conclusion.　**71 give
th' assay** make trial of strength, challenge.　**78 On . . . allowance** i.e., with such considerations
for the safety of Denmark and permission for Fortinbras.　**80 likes** pleases.　**81 considered**
suitable for deliberation.　**86 expostulate** expound, inquire into.　**90 wit** sense or judgment.

POLONIUS: Madam, I swear I use no art at all.
    That he's mad, 'tis true; 'tis true tis pity.
    And pity 'tis 'tis true—a foolish figure,°
    But farewell it, for I will use no art.
    Mad let us grant him, then, and now remains   100
    That we find out the cause of this effect,
    Or rather say, the cause of this defect,
    For this effect defective comes by cause.°
    Thus it remains, and the remainder thus.
    Perpend.°   105
    I have a daughter—have while she is mine—
    Who, in her duty and obedience, mark,
    Hath given me this. Now gather and surmise.°
    [*He reads the letter.*] "To the celestial and my soul's idol, the most   110
    beautified Ophelia"—
    That's an ill phrase, a vile phrase; "beautified" is a vile phrase. But you
    shall hear. Thus: [*He reads.*]   115
    "In her excellent white bosom,° these,° etc."
QUEEN: Came this from Hamlet to her?
POLONIUS: Good madam, stay° awhile, I will be faithful.°   [*He reads.*]

        "Doubt thou the stars are fire,
           Doubt that the sun doth move,
        Doubt° truth to be a liar,
           But never doubt I love.
    O dear Ophelia, I am ill at these numbers.° I have not art to reckon° my
    groans. But that I love thee best, O most best, believe it. Adieu.   120
        Thine evermore, most dear lady, whilst this machine° is to him,
                                      Hamlet."
    This in obedience hath my daughter shown me,
    And, more above,° hath his solicitings,   125
    As they fell out° by° time, by means, and place,
    All given to mine ear.°
KING: But how hath she
    Received his love?
POLONIUS: What do you think of me?
KING: As of a man faithful and honorable.
POLONIUS: I would fain° prove so. But what might you think,   130
    When I had seen this hot love on the wing—
    As I perceived it, I must tell you that,
    Before my daughter told me—what might you,
    Or my dear Majesty your queen here, think,
    If I had played the desk or table book,°   135
    Or given my heart a winking,° mute and dumb,

---

98 figure figure of speech. **103 For . . . cause** i.e., for this defective behavior, his madness, has a cause. **105 Perpend** consider. **108 gather and surmise** draw your own conclusions. **113 In . . . bosom** (The letter is poetically addressed to her heart.); **these** i.e., the letter. **115 stay** wait; **faithful** i.e., in reading the letter accurately. **118 Doubt** suspect. **120 ill . . . numbers** unskilled at writing verses. **121 reckon** (1) count, (2) number metrically, scan. **122 machine** i.e., body. **125 more above** moreover. **126 fell out** occurred; **by** according to. **127 given . . . ear** i.e., told me about. **130 fain** gladly. **135 played . . . table book** i.e., remained shut up, concealing the information. **136 given . . . winking** closed the eyes of my heart to this.

Or looked upon this love with idle sight?°
What might you think? No, I went round° to work,
And my young mistress thus I did bespeak:°
"Lord Hamlet is a prince out of thy star;°   140
This must not be." And then I prescripts° gave her,
That she should lock herself from his resort,°
Admit no messengers, receive no tokens.
Which done, she took the fruits of my advice;
And he, repellèd—a short tale to make—   145
Fell into a sadness, then into a fast,
Thence to a watch,° thence into a weakness,
Thence to a lightness,° and by this declension°
Into the madness wherein now he raves,
And all we° mourn for.

KING [*to the* QUEEN]:   Do you think 'tis this?   150
QUEEN: It may be, very like.
POLONIUS: Hath there been such a time—I would fain know that—
     That I have positively said "'Tis so,"
     When it proved otherwise?
KING: Not that I know.
POLONIUS: Take this from this,° if this be otherwise.   155
     If circumstances lead me, I will find
     Where truth is hid, though it were hid indeed
     Within the center.°
KING: How may we try° it further?
POLONIUS: You know sometimes he walks four hours together
     Here in the lobby.
QUEEN: So he does indeed.   160
POLONIUS: At such a time I'll loose° my daughter to him.
     Be you and I behind an arras° then.
     Mark the encounter. If he love her not
     And be not from his reason fall'n thereon,°
     Let me be no assistant for a state,   165
     But keep a farm and carters.°
KING: We will try it.

     Enter HAMLET [*reading on a book*].

QUEEN: But look where sadly° the poor wretch comes reading.
POLONIUS: Away, I do beseech you both, away.
     I'll board° him presently.° O, give me leave.°

---

137 with idle sight complacently or incomprehendingly.   **138 round** roundly, plainly.
139 bespeak address.   **140 out of thy star** above your sphere, position.   **141 prescripts** orders.
142 his resort his visits.   **147 watch** state of sleeplessness.   **148 lightness** lightheadedness;
declension decline, deterioration (with a pun on the grammatical sense).   **150 all we** all of
us, or, into everything that we.   **155 Take this from this** (The actor probably gestures, indicating that he means his head from his shoulders, or his staff of office or chain from his hands
or neck, or something similar.)   **158 center** middle point of the earth (which is also the center
of the Ptolemaic universe);   **try** test, judge.   **161 loose** (as one might release an animal that
is being mated.)   **162 arras** hanging, tapestry.   **164 thereon** on that account.   **166 carters**
wagon drivers.   **167 sadly** seriously.   **169 board** accost;   **presently** at once;   **give me leave**
i.e., excuse me, leave me alone. (Said to those he hurries offstage, including the King and Queen.)

Exeunt KING *and* QUEEN [*with attendants*].

How does my good Lord Hamlet?   170

HAMLET: Well, God-a-mercy.°

POLONIUS: Do you know me, my lord?

HAMLET: Excellent well. You are a fishmonger.°

POLONIUS: Not I, my lord.

HAMLET: Then I would you were so honest a man.   175

POLONIUS: Honest, my lord?

HAMLET: Ay, sir. To be honest, as this world goes, is to be one man picked out of
ten thousand.

POLONIUS: That's very true, my lord.

HAMLET: For if the sun breed maggots in a dead dog, being a good kissing carrion°—   180
Have you a daughter?

POLONIUS: I have, my lord.

HAMLET: Let her not walk i' the sun.° Conception° is a blessing, but as your daughter may conceive, friend, look to 't.

POLONIUS [*aside*]: How say you by that? Still harping on my daughter. Yet he   185
knew me not at first; 'a° said I was a fishmonger. 'A is far gone. And truly
in my youth I suffered much extremity for love, very near this. I'll speak
to him again.—What do you read, my lord?

HAMLET: Words, words, words.

POLONIUS: What is the matter,° my lord?   190

HAMLET: Between who?

POLONIUS: I mean, the matter that you read, my lord.

HAMLET: Slanders, sir; for the satirical rogue says here that old men have gray
beards, that their faces are wrinkled, their eyes purging° thick amber° and
plum-tree gum, and that they have a plentiful lack of wit,° together with   195
most weak hams. All which, sir, though I most powerfully and potently
believe, yet I hold it not honesty° to have it thus set down, for yourself,
sir, shall grow old° as I am, if like a crab you could go backward.

POLONIUS [*aside*]: Though this be madness, yet there is method in 't.—Will you
walk out of the air,° my lord?   200

HAMLET: Into my grave.

POLONIUS: Indeed, that's out of the air. [Aside.] How pregnant° sometimes his
replies are! A happiness° that often madness hits on, which reason and
sanity could not so prosperously° be delivered of. I will leave him and
suddenly° contrive the means of meeting between him and my daughter.—
My honorable lord, I will most humbly take my leave of you.   205

HAMLET: You cannot, sir, take from me anything that I will more willingly part
withal°—except my life, except my life, except my life.

---

171 God-a-mercy God have mercy, i.e., thank you. **173 fishmonger** fish merchant.
180–81 a good kissing carrion i.e., a good piece of flesh for kissing, or for the sun to kiss.
183 i' the sun in public (with additional implication of the sunshine of princely favors);
Conception (1) understanding, (2) pregnancy. **186 'a** he. **190 matter** substance. (But Hamlet
plays on the sense of "basis for a dispute.") **194 purging** discharging; **amber** i.e., resin, like
the resinous **plum-tree gum.** **195 wit** understanding. **197 honesty** decency, decorum.
198 old as old. **200 out of the air** (The open air was considered dangerous for sick people.)
202 pregnant quick-witted, full of meaning. **203 happiness** felicity of expression.
204 prosperously successfully. **205 suddenly** immediately. **208 withal** with.

Enter GUILDENSTERN *and* ROSENCRANTZ.

POLONIUS: Fare you well, my lord.

HAMLET: These tedious old fools!° 210

POLONIUS: You go to seek the Lord Hamlet. There he is.

ROSENCRANTZ [*to* POLONIUS]: God save you, sir! [*Exit* POLONIUS.]

GUILDENSTERN: My honored lord!

ROSENCRANTZ: My most dear lord!

HAMLET: My excellent good friends! How dost thou, Guildenstern? Ah, Rosencrantz! 215
Good lads, how do you both?

ROSENCRANTZ: As the indifferent° children of the earth.

GUILDENSTERN: Happy in that we are not overhappy.
On Fortune's cap we are not the very button.

HAMLET: Nor the soles of her shoe? 220

ROSENCRANTZ: Neither, my lord.

HAMLET: Then you live about her waist, or in the middle of her favors?°

GUILDENSTERN: Faith, her privates we.°

HAMLET: In the secret parts of Fortune? O, most true, she is a strumpet.°
What news? 225

ROSENCRANTZ: None, my lord, but the world's grown honest.

HAMLET: Then is doomsday near. But your news is not true. Let me question
more in particular. What have you, my good friends, deserved at the
hands of Fortune that she sends you to prison hither?

GUILDENSTERN: Prison, my lord? 230

HAMLET: Denmark's a prison.

ROSENCRANTZ: Then is the world one.

HAMLET: A goodly one, in which there are many confines,° wards,° and dungeons,
Denmark being one o' the worst.

ROSENCRANTZ: We think not so, my lord. 235

HAMLET: Why then 'tis none to you, for there is nothing either good or bad but
thinking makes it so. To me it is a prison.

ROSENCRANTZ: Why then, your ambition makes it one. 'Tis too narrow for your mind.

HAMLET: O God, I could be bounded in a nutshell and count myself a king of
infinite space, were it not that I have bad dreams. 240

GUILDENSTERN: Which dreams indeed are ambition, for the very substance of the
ambitious° is merely the shadow of a dream.

HAMLET: A dream itself is but a shadow.

ROSENCRANTZ: Truly, and I hold ambition of so airy and light a quality that it is 245
but a shadow's shadow.

HAMLET: Then are our beggars bodies,° and our monarchs and outstretched°
heroes the beggars' shadows. Shall we to the court? For, by my fay,°
I cannot reason.

---

210 old fools i.e., old men like Polonius. **217 indifferent** ordinary, at neither extreme of
fortune or misfortune. **222 favors** i.e., sexual favors. **223 her privates we** i.e., (1) we are
sexually intimate with Fortune, the fickle goddess who bestows her favors indiscriminately,
(2) we are her private citizens. **224 strumpet** prostitute. (A common epithet for indiscrimi-
nate Fortune; see line 452.) **233 confines** places of confinement; **wards** cells. **241–42 the
very . . . ambitious** that seemingly very substantial thing that the ambitious pursue.
246 bodies i.e., solid substances rather than shadows (since beggars are not ambitious).
outstretched (1) far-reaching in their ambition, (2) elongated as shadows. **247 fay** faith.

ROSENCRANTZ, GUILDENSTERN: We'll wait upon° you.

HAMLET: No such matter. I will not sort° you with the rest of my servants, for, to   250
speak to you like an honest man, I am most dreadfully attended.° But, in
the beaten way° of friendship, what make° you at Elsinore?

ROSENCRANTZ: To visit you, my lord, no other occasion.

HAMLET: Beggar that I am, I am even poor in thanks; but I thank you, and sure,
dear friends, my thanks are too dear a halfpenny.° Were you not sent for?   255
Is it your own inclining? Is it a free° visitation? Come, come, deal justly
with me. Come, come. Nay, speak.

GUILDENSTERN: What should we say, my lord?

HAMLET: Anything but to the purpose.° You were sent for, and there is a kind of
confession in your looks which your modesties° have not craft enough to   260
color.° I know the good King and Queen have sent for you.

ROSENCRANTZ: To what end, my lord?

HAMLET: That you must teach me. But let me conjure° you, by the rights of our
fellowship, by the consonancy of our youth,° by the obligation of our ever-
preserved love, and by what more dear a better° proposer could charge°   265
you withal, be even° and direct with me whether you were sent for or no.

ROSENCRANTZ [*aside to* GUILDENSTERN]: What say you?

HAMLET [*aside*]: Nay, then, I have an eye of° you.—If you love me, hold not off.°

GUILDENSTERN: My lord, we were sent for.

HAMLET: I will tell you why; so shall my anticipation prevent your discovery,° and   270
your secrecy to the King and Queen molt no feather.° I have of late—
but wherefore I know not—lost all my mirth, forgone all custom of exercises; and indeed it goes so heavily with my disposition that this goodly
frame, the earth, seems to me a sterile promontory; this most excellent
canopy, the air, look you, this brave° o'erhanging firmament, this majes-   275
tical roof fretted° with golden fire, why, it appeareth nothing to me but a
foul and pestilent congregation° of vapors. What a piece of work° is a
man! How noble in reason, how infinite in faculties, in form and moving how
express° and admirable, in action how like an angel, in apprehension° how
like a god! The beauty of the world, the paragon of animals! And yet, to me,   280
what is this quintessence° of dust? Man delights not me—no, nor woman
neither, though by your smiling you seem to say so.

ROSENCRANTZ: My lord, there was no such stuff in my thoughts.

HAMLET: Why did you laugh, then, when I said man delights not me?

---

249 wait upon accompany, attend. (But Hamlet uses the phrase in the sense of providing menial
service.)   **250 sort** class, categorize.   **251 dreadfully attended** waited upon in slovenly fashion.
252 beaten way familiar path, tried-and-true course;   **make** do.   **255 too dear a halfpenny**
(1) too expensive at even a halfpenny, i.e., of little worth, (2) too expensive *by* a halfpenny
in return for worthless kindness.   **256 free** voluntary.   **259 Anything but to the purpose**
anything except a straightforward answer. (Said ironically.)   **260 modesties** sense of shame.
261 color disguise.   **263 conjure** adjure, entreat.   **264 the consonancy of our youth** our
closeness in our younger days.   **265 better** more skillful;   **charge** urge.   **266 even** straight,
honest.   **268 of** on;   **hold not off** don't hold back.   **270 so . . . discovery** in that way my
saying it first will spare you from revealing the truth.   **271 molt no feather** i.e., not diminish
in the least.   **275 brave** splendid.   **276 fretted** adorned (with fretwork, as in a vaulted ceiling).
277 congregation mass;   **piece of work** masterpiece.   **279 express** well-framed, exact,
expressive.   **279–80 apprehension** power of comprehending.   **281 quintessence** the fifth
essence of ancient philosophy, beyond earth, water, air, and fire, supposed to be the substance of the heavenly bodies and to be latent in all things.

ROSENCRANTZ: To think, my lord, if you delight not in man, what Lenten entertain-   285
     ment° the players shall receive from you. We coted° them on the way,
     and hither are they coming to offer you service.

HAMLET: He that plays the king shall be welcome; His Majesty shall have tribute°
     of° me. The adventurous knight shall use his foil and target,° the lover
     shall not sigh gratis,° the humorous man° shall end his part in peace,° the   290
     clown shall make those laugh whose lungs are tickle o' the sear,° and the
     lady shall say her mind freely, or the blank verse shall halt° for 't. What
     players are they?

ROSENCRANTZ: Even those you were wont to take such delight in, the tragedians° of
     the city.   295

HAMLET: How chances it they travel? Their residence,° both in reputation and
     profit, was better both ways.

ROSENCRANTZ: I think their inhibition° comes by the means of the late° innovation.°

HAMLET: Do they hold the same estimation they did when I was in the city? Are
     they so followed?   300

ROSENCRANTZ: No, indeed are they not.

HAMLET: How comes it? Do they grow rusty?

ROSENCRANTZ: Nay, their endeavor keeps° in the wonted° pace. But there is, sir,
     an aerie° of children, little eyases,° that cry out on the top of question°
     and are most tyrannically° clapped for 't. These are now the fashion, and   305
     so berattle° the common stages°—so they call them—that many wearing
     rapiers° are afraid of goose quills° and dare scarce come thither.

HAMLET: What, are they children? Who maintains 'em? How are they escoted?°
     Will they pursue the quality° no longer than they can sing?° Will they not
     say afterwards, if they should grow themselves to common° players—as   310
     it is most like,° if their means are no better°—their writers do them
     wrong to make them exclaim against their own succession?°

ROSENCRANTZ: Faith, there has been much to-do° on both sides, and the nation holds
     it no sin to tar° them to controversy. There was for a while no money bid for
     argument unless the poet and the player went to cuffs in the question.°   315

HAMLET: Is 't possible?

285–86 Lenten entertainment meager reception (appropriate to Lent);   **coted** overtook and
passed by.   **288 tribute** (1) applause, (2) homage paid in money.   **289 of** from;   **foil and
target** sword and shield.   **290 gratis** for nothing;   **humorous man** eccentric character, dominated by one trait or "humor";   **in peace** i.e., with full license.   **291 tickle o' the sear** easy
on the trigger, ready to laugh easily. (A *sear* is part of a gunlock.)   **292 halt** limp.   **294 tragedians**
actors.   **296 residence** remaining in their usual place, i.e., in the city.   **298 inhibition** formal
prohibition (from acting plays in the city);   **late** recent;   **innovation** i.e., the new fashion in
satirical plays performed by boy actors in the "private" theaters; or possibly a political uprising; or the strict limitations set on theaters in London in 1600.   **303 keeps** continues;
wonted usual.   **304 aerie** nest;   **eyases** young hawks;   **cry . . . question** speak shrilly, domi-
nating the controversy (in decrying the public theaters).   **305 tyrannically** outrageously.
306 berattle berate, clamor against;   **common stages** public theaters.   **306–07 many wearing rapiers** i.e., many men of fashion, afraid to patronize the common players for fear of
being satirized by the poets writing for the boy actors;   **goose quills** i.e., pens of satirists.
308 escoted maintained.   **309 quality** (acting) profession;   **no longer . . . sing** i.e., only until
their voices change.   **310 common** regular, adult.   **311 like** likely;   **if . . . better** if they find
no better way to support themselves.   **312 succession** i.e., future careers.   **313 to-do** ado.
314 tar set on (as dogs).   **314–15 There . . . question** i.e., for a while, no money was offered
by the acting companies to playwrights for the plot to a play unless the satirical poets who
wrote for the boys and the adult actors came to blows in the play itself.

GUILDENSTERN: O, there has been much throwing about of brains.

HAMLET: Do the boys carry it away?°

ROSENCRANTZ: Ay, that they do, my lord—Hercules and his load° too.°

HAMLET: It is not very strange; for my uncle is King of Denmark, and those that   320
    would make mouths° at him while my father lived give twenty, forty,
    fifty, a hundred ducats° apiece for his picture in little.° 'Sblood,° there is
    something in this more than natural, if philosophy° could find it out.

                                        A flourish [*of trumpets within*].

GUILDENSTERN: There are the players.

HAMLET: Gentlemen, you are welcome to Elsinore. Your hands, come then.   325
    Th' appurtenance° of welcome is fashion and ceremony. Let me comply°
    with you in this garb,° lest my extent° to the players, which, I tell you,
    must show fairly outwards,° should more appear like entertainment° than
    yours. You are welcome. But my uncle-father and aunt-mother are
    deceived.   330

GUILDENSTERN: In what, my dear lord?

HAMLET: I am but mad north-north-west.° When the wind is southerly I know a
    hawk from a handsaw.°

    Enter POLONIUS.

POLONIUS: Well be with you, gentlemen!

HAMLET: Hark you, Guildenstern, and you too; at each ear a hearer. That great   335
    baby you see there is not yet out of his swaddling clouts.°

ROSENCRANTZ: Haply° he is the second time come to them, for they say an old
    man is twice a child.

HAMLET: I will prophesy he comes to tell me of the players. Mark it.—You say
    right, sir, o' Monday morning, 'twas then indeed.   340

POLONIUS: My lord, I have news to tell you.

HAMLET: My lord, I have news to tell you. When Roscius° was an actor in Rome—

POLONIUS: The actors are come hither, my lord.

HAMLET: Buzz,° buzz!

POLONIUS: Upon my honor—   345

HAMLET: Then came each actor on his ass.

POLONIUS: The best actors in the world, either for tragedy, comedy, history,
    pastoral, pastoral-comical, historical-pastoral, tragical-historical, tragical-
    comical-historical-pastoral, scene individable,° or poem unlimited.°

318 carry it away i.e., win the day.   **319 Hercules . . . load** (thought to be an allusion to the
sign of the Globe Theatre, which was Hercules bearing the world on his shoulders.)
302–19 How . . . load too (The passage, omitted from the early quartos, alludes to the so-called
War of the Theaters, 1599–1602, the rivalry between the children's companies and the adult actors.)
321 mouths faces.   **322 ducats** gold coins;   **in little** in miniature;   **'Sblood** by God's (Christ's)
blood.   **323 philosophy** i.e., scientific inquiry.   **326 appurtenance** proper accompaniment;
comply observe the formalities of courtesy.   **327 garb** i.e., manner;   **my extent** that which I
extend, i.e., my polite behavior.   **328 show fairly outwards** show every evidence of cordiality;
entertainment a (warm) reception.   **332 north-north-west** just off true north, only partly.
333 hawk, handsaw i.e., two very different things, though also perhaps meaning a mattock (or
hack) and carpenter's cutting tools, respectively; also birds, with a play on *hernshaw*, or heron.
336 swaddling clouts cloths in which to wrap a newborn baby.   **337 Haply** perhaps.
342 Roscius a famous Roman actor who died in 62 BCE.   **344 Buzz** (an interjection used to
denote stale news.)   **349 scene individable** a play observing the unity of place; or perhaps
one that is unclassifiable, or performed without intermission;   **poem unlimited** a play disregarding the unities of time and place; one that is all-inclusive.

Seneca° cannot be too heavy, nor Plautus° too light. For the law of writ   350
and the liberty,° these° are the only men.

HAMLET: O Jephthah, judge of Israel,° what a treasure hadst thou!

POLONIUS: What a treasure had he, my lord?

HAMLET: Why,   355

"One fair daughter, and no more,
The which he lovèd passing° well."

POLONIUS [*aside*]: Still on my daughter.

HAMLET: Am I not i' the right, old Jephthah?

POLONIUS: If you call me Jephthah, my lord, I have a daughter that I love   360
passing well.

HAMLET: Nay, that follows not.

POLONIUS: What follows then, my lord?

HAMLET: Why,

"As by lot,° God wot,"°   365
and then, you know,
"It came to pass, as most like° it was"—
the first row° of the pious chanson° will show you more, for look where
my abridgement° comes.

Enter the PLAYERS.

You are welcome, masters; welcome, all. I am glad to see thee well.   370
Welcome, good friends. O, old friend! Why, thy face is valanced° since
I saw thee last. Com'st thou to beard° me in Denmark? What, my young
lady° and mistress! By 'r Lady,° your ladyship is nearer to heaven than
when I saw you last, by the altitude of a chopine.° Pray God your voice,
like a piece of uncurrent° gold, be not cracked within the ring.° Masters,   375
you are all welcome. We'll e'en to 't° like French falconers, fly at anything
we see. We'll have a speech straight.° Come, give us a taste of your
quality.° Come, a passionate speech.

FIRST PLAYER: What speech, my good lord?

HAMLET: I heard thee speak me a speech once, but it was never acted, or if it was,   380
not above once, for the play, I remember, pleased not the million; 'twas
caviar to the general.° But it was—as I received it, and others, whose
judgments in such matters cried in the top of° mine—an excellent play,
well digested° in the scenes, set down with as much modesty° as
cunning.° I remember one said there were no sallets° in the lines to make   385

350 **Seneca** writer of Latin tragedies; **Plautus** writer of Latin comedies. **350–51 law . . .
liberty** dramatic composition both according to the rules and disregarding the rules; **these** i.e.,
the actors. **352 Jephthah . . . Israel** (Jephthah had to sacrifice his daughter; see Judges 11. Hamlet
goes on to quote from a ballad on the theme.) **357 passing** surpassingly. **365 lot** chance;
wot knows. **367 like** likely, probable. **368 row** stanza; **chanson** ballad, song. **369 my
abridgement** something that cuts short my conversation; also, a diversion. **371 valanced**
Fringed (with a beard). **372 beard** confront, challenge (with obvious pun). **372–73 young
lady** i.e., boy playing women's parts; **By 'r Lady** by Our Lady. **374 chopine** thick-soled
shoe of Italian fashion. **375 uncurrent** not passable as lawful coinage; **cracked . . . ring** i.e.,
changed from adolescent to male voice, no longer suitable for women's roles. (Coins featured rings
enclosing the sovereign's head; if the coin was cracked within this ring, it was unfit for currency.)
376 e'en to 't go at it. **377 straight** at once. **378 quality** professional skill. **382 caviar to
the general** caviar to the multitude, i.e., a choice dish too elegant for coarse tastes. **383 cried in
the top of** i.e., spoke with greater authority than. **384 digested** arranged, ordered; **modesty**
moderation, restraint. **385 cunning** skill; **sallets** i.e., something savory, spicy improprieties.

the matter savory, nor no matter in the phrase that might indict° the
author of affectation, but called it an honest method, as wholesome as
sweet, and by very much more handsome° than fine.° One speech in 't I
chiefly loved: 'twas Aeneas' tale to Dido, and thereabout of it especially
when he speaks of Priam's slaughter.° If it live in your memory, begin at   390
this line: let me see, let me see—

"The rugged Pyrrhus,° like th' Hyrcanian beast°"—

'Tis not so. It begins with Pyrrhus:

"The rugged° Pyrrhus, he whose sable° arms,
Black as his purpose, did the night resemble   395
When he lay couchèd° in the ominous horse,°
Hath now this dread and black complexion smeared
With heraldry more dismal.° Head to foot
Now is he total gules,° horridly tricked°
With blood of fathers, mothers, daughters, sons,   400
Baked and impasted° with the parching streets,°
That lend a tyrannous° and a damnèd light
To their lord's° murder. Roasted in wrath and fire,
And thus o'ersizèd° with coagulate gore,
With eyes like carbuncles,° the hellish Pyrrhus   405
Old grandsire Priam seeks."

So proceed you.

POLONIUS: 'Fore God, my lord, well spoken, with good accent and good discretion.
FIRST PLAYER: "Anon he finds him
Striking too short at Greeks. His antique° sword,   410
Rebellious to his arm, lies where it falls,
Repugnant° to command. Unequal matched,
Pyrrhus at Priam drives, in rage strikes wide,
But with the whiff and wind of his fell° sword
Th' unnervèd° father falls. Then senseless Ilium,°   415
Seeming to feel this blow, with flaming top
Stoops to his° base, and with a hideous crash
Takes prisoner Pyrrhus' ear. For, lo! His sword,
Which was declining° on the milky° head

386 indict convict. **388 handsome** well-proportioned; **fine** elaborately ornamented, showy.
390 Priam's slaughter the slaying of the ruler of Troy, when the Greeks finally took the city.
392 Pyrrhus a Greek hero in the Trojan War, also known as Neoptolemus, son of Achilles—
another avenging son; **Hyrcanian beast** i.e., tiger. (On the death of Priam, see Virgil, *Aeneid,*
2.506 ff.; compare the whole speech with Marlowe's *Dido Queen of Carthage,* 2.1.214. ff. On the
Hyrcanian tiger, see *Aeneid,* 4.366–67. Hyrcania is on the Caspian Sea.) **394 rugged** shaggy,
savage; **sable** black (for reasons of camouflage during the episode of the Trojan horse).
396 couchèd concealed; **ominous horse** fateful Trojan horse, by which the Greeks gained
access to Troy. **398 dismal** ill-omened. **399 total gules** entirely red. (A heraldic term);
tricked spotted and smeared. (Heraldic.) **401 impasted** crusted, like a thick paste; **with ...
streets** by the parching heat of the streets (because of the fires everywhere); **402 tyrannous** cruel.
403 their lord's i.e., Priam's. **404 o'ersizèd** covered as with size or glue. **405 carbuncles**
large fiery-red precious stones thought to emit their own light. **410 antique** ancient, long-used.
412 Repugnant disobedient, resistant. **414 fell** cruel. **415 unnervèd** strengthless;
senseless Ilium inanimate citadel of Troy. **417 his** its. **419 declining** descending;
milky white-haired.

Of reverend Priam, seemed i' th' air to stick.   420
So as a painted° tyrant Pyrrhus stood,
And, like a neutral to his will and matter,°
Did nothing.
But as we often see against° some storm
A silence in the heavens, the rack° stand still,   425
The bold winds speechless, and the orb° below
As hush as death, anon the dreadful thunder
Doth rend the region,° so, after Pyrrhus' pause,
A rousèd vengeance sets him new a-work
And never did the Cyclops'° hammers fall   430
On Mars's armor forged for proof eterne°
With less remorse° than Pyrrhus' bleeding sword
Now falls on Priam.
Out, out, thou strumpet Fortune! All you gods
In general synod° take away her power!   435
Break all the spokes and fellies° from her wheel,
And bowl the round nave° down the hill of heaven°
As low as to the fiends!"

POLONIUS: This is too long.

HAMLET: It shall to the barber's with your beard.—Prithee, say on. He's for a jig°   440
or a tale of bawdry, or he sleeps. Say on; come to Hecuba.°

FIRST PLAYER: "But who, ah woe! had° seen the moblèd° queen"—

HAMLET: "The moblèd queen?"

POLONIUS: That's good. "Moblèd queen" is good.

FIRST PLAYER: "Run barefoot up and down, threat'ning the flames°   445
    With bisson rheum,° a clout° upon that head
    Where late° the diadem stood, and, for a robe,
    About her lank and all o'erteemd° loins
    A blanket, in the alarm of fear caught up—
    Who this had seen, with tongue in venom steeped,   450
    'Gainst Fortune's state° would treason have pronounced.°
    But if the gods themselves did see her then
    When she saw Pyrrhus make malicious sport
    In mincing with his sword her husband's limbs,
    The instant burst of clamor that she made,   455
    Unless things mortal move them not at all,
    Would have made milch° the burning eyes of heaven,°
    And passion° in the gods."

421 painted i.e., painted in a picture.   **422 like . . . matter** i.e., as though suspended between his intention and its fulfillment.   **424 against** just before.   **425 rack** mass of clouds.   **426 orb** globe, earth.   **428 region** sky.   **430 Cyclops** giant armor makers in the smithy of Vulcan. **431 proof eterne** eternal resistance to assault.   **432 remorse** pity.   **435 synod** assembly. **436 fellies** pieces of wood forming the rim of a wheel.   **437 nave** hub; **hill of heaven** Mount Olympus.   **440 jig** comic song and dance often given at the end of a play.   **441 Hecuba** wife of Priam.   **442 who . . . had** anyone who had (also in line 469);   **moblèd** muffled.   **445 threat'ning the flames** i.e., weeping hard enough to dampen the flames.   **446 bisson rheum** blinding tears; **clout** cloth.   **447 late** lately.   **448 all o'erteemèd** utterly worn out with bearing children. **451 state** rule, managing;   **pronounced** proclaimed.   **457 milch** milky, moist with tears; **burning eyes of heaven** i.e., heavenly bodies.   **458 passion** overpowering emotion.

POLONIUS: Look whe'er° he has not turned his color and has tears in 's eyes.
    Prithee, no more.   460

HAMLET: 'Tis well; I'll have thee speak out the rest of this soon.—Good my lord, will
    you see the players well bestowed?° Do you hear, let them be well used, for
    they are the abstract° and brief chronicles of the time. After your death you
    were better have a bad epitaph than their ill report while you live.

POLONIUS: My lord, I will use them according to their desert.   465

HAMLET: God's bodikin,° man, much better. Use every man after his desert, and
    who shall scape whipping? Use them after° your own honor and dignity.
    The less they deserve, the more merit is in your bounty. Take them in.

POLONIUS: Come, sirs.   [*Exit.*]

HAMLET: Follow him, friends. We'll hear a play tomorrow. [*As they start to leave,*   470
    HAMLET *detains the* FIRST PLAYER.] Dost thou hear me, old friend? Can you
    play *The Murder of Gonzago?*

FIRST PLAYER: Ay, my lord.

HAMLET: We'll ha 't° tomorrow night. You could, for a need, study° a speech of
    some dozen or sixteen lines which I would set down and insert in 't,   475
    could you not?

FIRST PLAYER: Ay, my lord.

HAMLET: Very well. Follow that lord, and look you mock him not. [*Exeunt* PLAYERS.]
    My good friends, I'll leave you till night. You are welcome to Elsinore.

ROSENCRANTZ: Good my lord!   *Exeunt* [ROSENCRANTZ *and* GUILDENSTERN].   480

HAMLET: Ay, so, goodbye to you.—Now I am alone.
    O, what a rogue and peasant slave am I!
    Is it not monstrous that this player here,
    But° in a fiction, in a dream of passion,
    Could force his soul so to his own conceit°   485
    That from her working° all his visage wanned,°
    Tears in his eyes, distraction in his aspect,°
    A broken voice, and his whole function suiting
    With forms to his conceit?° And all for nothing!
    For Hecuba!   490
    What's Hecuba to him, or he to Hecuba,
    That he should weep for her? What would he do
    Had he the motive and the cue for passion
    That I have? He would drown the stage with tears
    And cleave the general ear° with horrid° speech,   495
    Make mad the guilty and appall° the free,°
    Confound the ignorant,° and amaze° indeed
    The very faculties of eyes and ears. Yet I,
    A dull and muddy-mettled° rascal, peak°

---

459 whe'er whether. **462 bestowed** lodged. **463 abstract** summary account. **466 God's**
bodikin by God's (Christ's) little body, *bodykin*. (Not to be confused with *bodkin,* "dagger.")
467 after according to. **474 ha 't** have it; **study** memorize. **484 But** merely. **485 force . . .**
conceit bring his innermost being so entirely into accord with his conception (of the role).
486 from her working as a result of, or in response to, his soul's activity; **wanned** grew pale.
487 aspect look, glance. **488–89 his whole . . . conceit** all his bodily powers responding
with actions to suit his thought. **495 the general ear** everyone's ear; **horrid** horrible.
496 appall (literally, make pale.); **free** innocent. **497 Confound the ignorant,** i.e., dumb-
found those who know nothing of the crime that has been committed; **amaze** stun.
499 muddy-mettled dull-spirited; **peak** mope, pine.

Like John-a dreams,° unpregnant of° my cause,   500
And can say nothing—no, not for a king
Upon whose property° and most dear life
A damned defeat° was made. Am I a coward?
Who calls me villain? Breaks my pate° across?
Plucks off my beard and blows it in my face?   505
Tweaks me by the nose? Gives me the lie i' the throat°
As deep as to the lungs? Who does me this?
Ha, 'swounds,° I should take it; for it cannot be
But I am pigeon-livered° and lack gall
To make oppression bitter,° or ere this   510
I should ha' fatted all the region kites°
With this slave's offal.° Bloody, bawdy villain!
Remorseless,° treacherous, lecherous, kindless° villain!
O, vengeance!
Why, what an ass am I! This is most brave,°   515
That I, the son of a dear father murdered,
Prompted to my revenge by heaven and hell,
Must like a whore unpack my heart with words
And fall a-cursing, like a very drab,°
A scullion!° Fie upon 't, foh! About,° my brains!   520
Hum, I have heard
That guilty creatures sitting at a play
Have by the very cunning° of the scene°
Been struck so to the soul that presently°
They have proclaimed their malefactions;   525
For murder, though it have no tongue, will speak
With most miraculous organ. I'll have these players
Play something like the murder of my father
Before mine uncle. I'll observe his looks;
I'll tent° him to the quick.° If 'a do blench,°   530
I know my course. The spirit that I have seen
May be the devil, and the devil hath power
T' assume a pleasing shape; yea, and perhaps,
Out of my weakness and my melancholy,
As he is very potent with such spirits,°   535
Abuses° me to damn me. I'll have grounds
More relative° than this. The play's the thing
Wherein I'll catch the conscience of the King.   *Exit.*

---

500 John-a-dreams a sleepy, dreaming idler;   **unpregnant of** not quickened by.   **502 property** i.e., the crown; also character, quality.   **503 damned defeat** damnable act of destruction. **504 pate** head.   **506 Gives . . . throat** calls me an out-and-out liar.   **508 'swounds** by his (Christ's) wounds.   **509 pigeon-livered** (The pigeon or dove was popularly supposed to be mild because it secreted no gall.)   **510 bitter** i.e., bitter to me.   **511 region kites** kites (birds of prey) of the air.   **512 offal** entrails.   **513 Remorseless** pitiless;   **kindless** unnatural.   **515 brave** fine, admirable. (Said ironically.)   **519 drab** whore.   **520 scullion** menial kitchen servant (apt to be foul-mouthed);   **About** about it, to work.   **523 cunning** art, skill;   **scene** dramatic presentation.   **524 presently** at once.   **530 tent** probe;   **the quick** the tender part of a wound, the core;   **blench** quail, flinch.   **535 spirits** humors (of melancholy).   **536 Abuses** deludes. **537 relative** cogent, pertinent.

[3.1]

Enter KING, QUEEN, POLONIUS, OPHELIA, ROSENCRANTZ, GUILDENSTERN, *lords.*

KING: And can you by no drift of conference°
    Get from him why he puts on this confusion,
    Grating so harshly all his days of quiet
    With turbulent and dangerous lunacy?
ROSENCRANTZ: He does confess he feels himself distracted,   5
    But from what cause 'a will by no means speak.
GUILDENSTERN: Nor do we find him forward° to be sounded,°
    But with a crafty madness keeps aloof
    When we would bring him on to some confession
    Of his true state.
QUEEN: Did he receive you well?   10
ROSENCRANTZ: Most like a gentleman.
GUILDENSTERN: But with much forcing of his disposition.°
ROSENCRANTZ: Niggard° of question,° but of our demands
    Most free in his reply.
QUEEN: Did you assay° him
    To any pastime?   15
ROSENCRANTZ: Madam, it so fell out that certain players
    We o'erraught° on the way. Of these we told him,
    And there did seem in him a kind of joy
    To hear of it. They are here about the court,
    And, as I think, they have already order   20
    This night to play before him.
POLONIUS: 'Tis most true,
    And he beseeched me to entreat Your Majesties
    To hear and see the matter.
KING: With all my heart, and it doth much content me
    To hear him so inclined.   25
    Good gentlemen, give him a further edge°
    And drive his purpose into these delights.
ROSENCRANTZ: We shall, my lord.   *Exeunt* ROSENCRANTZ *and* GUILDENSTERN.
KING: Sweet Gertrude, leave us too
    For we have closely° sent for Hamlet hither,
    That he, as 'twere by accident, may here   30
    Affront° Ophelia.
    Her father and myself, lawful espials,°
    Will so bestow ourselves that seeing, unseen,
    We may of their encounter frankly judge,
    And gather by him, as he is behaved,   35
    If't be th' affliction of his love or no
    That thus he suffers for.
QUEEN: I shall obey you.
    And for your part, Ophelia, I do wish

[3.1] Location: The castle. 1 drift of conference directing of conversation. **7 forward**
willing; **sounded** questioned. **12 dispositon** inclination. **13 Niggard** stingy; **question**
conversation. **14 assay** try to win. **17 o'erraught** overtook. **26 edge** incitement.
29 closely privately. **31 Affront** confront, meet. **32 espials** spies.

That your good beauties be the happy cause
Of Hamlet's wildness. So shall I hope your virtues   40
Will bring him to his wonted° way again,
To both your honors.

OPHELIA: Madam, I wish it may.   [*Exit* QUEEN.]

POLONIUS: Ophelia, walk you here.—Gracious,° so please you,
We will bestow° ourselves. [*to* OPHELIA.] Read on this book,

                                         [*giving her a book*]

That show of such an exercise° may color°   45
Your loneliness.° We are oft to blame in this—
'Tis too much proved°—that with devotion's visage
And pious action we do sugar o'er
The devil himself.

KING [*aside*]: O 'tis too true!   50
How smart a lash that speech doth give my conscience!
The harlot's cheek, beautied with plastering art,
Is not more ugly to° the thing° that helps it
Than is my deed to my most painted word.
O heavy burden!   55

POLONIUS: I hear him coming. Let's withdraw, my lord.

                              [*The* KING *and* POLONIUS *withdraw.*°]

Enter HAMLET. [OPHELIA *pretends to read a book.*]

HAMLET: To be, or not to be, that is the question:
Whether 'tis nobler in the mind to suffer
The slings° and arrows of outrageous fortune,
Or to take arms against a sea of troubles   60
And by opposing end them. To die, to sleep—
No more—and by a sleep to say we end
The heartache and the thousand natural shocks
That flesh is heir to. 'Tis a consummation
Devoutly to be wished. To die, to sleep;   65
To sleep, perchance to dream. Ay, there's the rub,°
For in that sleep of death what dreams may come,
When we have shuffled° off this mortal coil,°
Must give us pause. There's the respect°
That makes calamity of so long life.°   70
For who would bear the whips and scorns of time,
Th' oppressor's wrong, the proud man's contumely,°
The pangs of disprized° love, the law's delay,
The insolence of office,° and the spurns°

---

41 wonted accustomed.   **43 Gracious** your Grace (i.e., the King).   **44 bestow** conceal.
45 exercise religious exercise. (The book she reads is one of devotion.);   **color** give a plausible
appearance to.   **46 loneliness** being alone.   **47 too much proved** too often shown to be true,
too often practiced.   **53 to** compared to;   **the thing** i.e., the cosmetic.   **56 s.d. withdraw**
(The King and Polonius may retire behind an arras. The stage directions specify that they
"enter" again near the end of the scene.)   **59 slings** missiles.   **66 rub** (literally, an obstacle
in the game of bowls.)   **68 shuffled** sloughed, cast;   **coil** turmoil.   **69 respect** consideration.
70 of . . . life so long-lived, something we willingly endure for so long (also suggesting that
long life is itself a calamity).   **72 contumely** insolent abuse.   **73 disprized** unvalued.
74 office officialdom;   **spurns** insults.

That patient merit of th' unworthy takes,°   75
When he himself might his quietus° make
With a bare bodkin?° Who would fardels° bear,
To grunt and sweat under a weary life,
But that the dread of something after death,
The undiscovered country from whose bourn°   80
No traveler returns, puzzles the will,
And makes us rather bear those ills we have
Than fly to others that we know not of?
Thus conscience does make cowards of us all;
And thus the native hue° of resolution   85
Is sicklied o'er with the pale cast° of thought,
And enterprises of great pitch° and moment°
With this regard° their currents° turn awry
And lose the name of action.—Soft you° now,
The fair Ophelia. Nymph, in thy orisons°   90
Be all my sins remembered.

OPHELIA: Good my lord,
How does your honor for this many a day?

HAMLET: I humbly thank you; well, well, well.

OPHELIA: My lord, I have remembrances of yours,
That I have longèd long to redeliver.   95
I pray you, now receive them.   [*She offers tokens.*]

HAMLET: No, not I, I never gave you aught.

OPHELIA: My honored lord, you know right well you did,
And with them words of so sweet breath composed
As made the things more rich. Their perfume lost,   100
Take these again, for to the noble mind
Rich gifts wax poor when givers prove unkind.
There, my lord.   [*She gives tokens.*]

HAMLET: Ha, ha! Are you honest?°

OPHELIA: My lord?   105

HAMLET: Are you fair?°

OPHELIA: What means your lordship?

HAMLET: That if you be honest and fair, your honesty° should admit no discourse
to° your beauty.

OPHELIA: Could beauty, my lord, have better commerce° than with honesty?   110

HAMLET: Ay, truly, for the power of beauty will sooner transform honesty from
what it is to a bawd than the force of honesty can translate beauty into
his° likeness. This was sometime° a paradox,° but now the time° gives it
proof. I did love you once.

---

75 of . . . takes receives from unworthy persons.   **76 quietus** acquitance; here, death.   **77 a
bare bodkin** a mere dagger, unsheathed; **fardels** burdens.   **80 bourn** frontier, boundary.
85 native hue natural color, complexion.   **86 cast** tinge, shade of color.   **87 pitch** height
(as of a falcon's flight).   **moment** importance.   **88 regard** respect, consideration;   **currents**
courses.   **89 Soft you** i.e., wait a minute, gently.   **90 orisons** prayers.   **104 honest** (1) truthful,
(2) chaste.   **106 fair** (1) beautiful, (2) just, honorable.   **108 your honesty** your chastity.
108–09 discourse to familiar dealings with.   **110 commerce** dealings, intercourse.
113 his its;   **sometime** formerly;   **a paradox** a view opposite to commonly held opinion;
the time the present age.

OPHELIA: Indeed, my lord, you made me believe so.   115

HAMLET: You should not have believed me, for virtue cannot so inoculate° our
old stock but we shall relish of it.° I loved you not.

OPHELIA: I was the more deceived.

HAMLET: Get thee to a nunnery.° Why wouldst thou be a breeder of sinners? I am
myself indifferent honest,° but yet I could accuse me of such things that it   120
were better my mother had not borne me: I am very proud, revengeful,
ambitious, with more offenses at my beck° than I have thoughts to put them
in, imagination to give them shape, or time to act them in. What should such
fellows as I do crawling between earth and heaven? We are arrant knaves
all; believe none of us. Go thy ways to a nunnery. Where's your father?   125

OPHELIA: At home, my lord.

HAMLET: Let the doors be shut upon him, that he may play the fool nowhere but
in's own house. Farewell.

OPHELIA: O, help him, you sweet heavens!

HAMLET: If thou dost marry, I'll give thee this plague for thy dowry: be thou as   130
chaste as ice, as pure as snow, thou shalt not escape calumny. Get thee
to a nunnery, farewell. Or, if thou wilt needs marry, marry a fool, for
wise men know well enough what monsters° you° make of them. To a
nunnery, go, and quickly too. Farewell.

OPHELIA: Heavenly powers, restore him!   135

HAMLET: I have heard of your paintings too, well enough. God hath given you
one face, and you make yourselves another. You jig,° you amble,° and
you lisp, you nickname God's creatures,° and make your wantonness
your ignorance.° Go to, I'll no more on 't;° it hath made me mad. I say
we will have no more marriage. Those that are married already—all but   140
one—shall live. The rest shall keep as they are. To a nunnery, go.

Exit.

OPHELIA: O, what a noble mind is here o'erthrown!
The courtier's, soldier's, scholar's, eye, tongue, sword,
Th' expectancy° and rose° of the fair state,
The glass of fashion and the mold of form,°   145
Th' observed of all observers,° quite, quite down!
And I, of ladies most deject and wretched,
That sucked the honey of his music° vows,
Now see that noble and most sovereign reason
Like sweet bells jangled out of tune and harsh,   150
That unmatched form and feature of blown° youth
Blasted° with ecstasy.° O, woe is me,
T' have seen what I have seen, see what I see!

---

116 inoculate graft, be engrafted to.   **117 but . . . it** that we do not still have about us a taste
of the old stock, i.e., retain our sinfulness.   **119 nunnery** convent (with possibly an awareness
that the word was also used derisively to denote a brothel).   **120 indifferent honest** reasonably
virtuous.   **122 beck** command.   **133 monsters** (an illusion to the horns of a cuckold.);
you i.e., you women.   **137 jig** dance;   **amble** move coyly.   **138 you nickname . . . creatures**
i.e., you give trendy names to things in place of their god-given names.   **139 make . . . ignorance**
i.e., excuse your affectation on the grounds of pretended ignorance;   **on 't** of it.
144 expectancy hope;   **rose** ornament.   **145 The glass . . . form** the mirror of true fashioning
and the pattern of courtly behavior.   **146 Th' observed . . . observers** i.e., the center of attention and honor in the court.   **148 music** musical, sweetly uttered.   **151 blown** blooming.
152 Blasted withered;   **ecstasy** madness.

Enter KING *and* POLONIUS.

KING: Love? His affections° do not that way tend;
Nor what he spake, though it lacked form a little,   155
Was not like madness. There's something in his soul
O'er which his melancholy sits on brood,°
And I do doubt° the hatch and the disclose°
Will be some danger; which for to prevent,
I have in quick determination   160
Thus set it down:° he shall with speed to England
For the demand of° our neglected tribute.
Haply the seas and countries different
With variable objects° shall expel
This something-settled matter in his heart,°   165
Whereon his brains still° beating puts him thus
From fashion of himself.° What think you on 't?

POLONIUS: It shall do well. But yet do I believe
The origin and commencement of his grief
Sprung from neglected love.—How now, Ophelia?   170
You need not tell us what Lord Hamlet said;
We heard it all.—My lord, do as you please,
But, if you hold it fit, after the play
Let his queen-mother° all alone entreat him
To show his grief. Let her be round° with him;   175
And I'll be placed, so please you, in the ear
Of all their conference. If she find him not,°
To England send him, or confine him where
Your wisdom best shall think.

KING: It shall be so.
Madness in great ones must not unwatched go.   *Exeunt.*   180

[3.2]

Enter HAMLET *and three of the* PLAYERS.

HAMLET: Speak the speech, I pray you, as I pronounced it to you, trippingly on
the tongue. But if you mouth it, as many of our players° do, I had as
lief° the town crier spoke my lines. Nor do not saw the air too much
with your hand, thus, but use all gently; for in the very torrent, tempest,
and, as I may say, whirlwind of your passion, you must acquire and   5
beget a temperance that may give it smoothness. O, it offends me to the
soul to hear a robustious° periwig-pated° fellow tear a passion to tatters,
to very rags, to split the ears of the groundlings,° who for the most part

---

154 affections emotions, feelings. **157 sits on brood** sits like a bird on a nest, about to *hatch*
mischief (line 169). **158 doubt** fear; **disclose** disclosure, hatching. **161 set it down** resolved.
162 For . . . of to demand. **164 variable objects** various sights and surroundings to divert him.
165 This something . . . heart the strange matter settled in his heart. **166 still** continually.
167 From . . . himself out of his natural manner. **174 queen-mother** queen and mother.
175 round blunt. **177 find him not** fails to discover what is troubling him.
[3.2] Location: The castle. **2 our players** players nowadays. **2–3 I had as lief** I would
just as soon. **7 robustious** violent, boisterous; **periwig-pated** wearing a wig.
8 groundlings spectators who paid least and stood in the yard of the theater.

are capable of° nothing but inexplicable dumb shows° and noise. I
would have such a fellow whipped for o'erdoing Termagant.° It out- 10
Herods Herod.° Pray you, avoid it.

FIRST PLAYER: I warrant your honor.

HAMLET: Be not too tame neither, but let your own discretion be your tutor. Suit
the action to the word, the word to the action, with this special observance, that you o'erstep not the modesty° of nature. For anything so o'er- 15
done is from° the purpose of playing, whose end, both at the first and
now, was and is to hold as 't were the mirror up to nature, to show virtue
her feature, scorn° her own image, and the very age and body of the
time° his° form and pressure.° Now this overdone or come tardy off,°
though it makes the unskillful° laugh, cannot but make the judicious 20
grieve, the censure of the which one° must in your allowance° o'erweigh
a whole theater of others. O, there be players that I have seen play, and
heard others praise, and that highly, not to speak it profanely,° that, neither having th' accent of Christians° nor the gait of Christian, pagan, nor
man,° have so strutted and bellowed that I have thought some of nature's 25
journeymen° had made men and not made them well, they imitated humanity so abominably.°

FIRST PLAYER: I hope we have reformed that indifferently° with us, sir.

HAMLET: O, reform it altogether. And let those that play your clowns speak no
more than is set down for them; for there be of them° that will them- 30
selves laugh, to set on some quantity of barren° spectators to laugh too,
though in the meantime some necessary question of the play be then to
be considered. That's villainous, and shows a most pitiful ambition in
the fool that uses it. Go make you ready.   [*Exeunt* PLAYERS.]

Enter POLONIUS, GUILDENSTERN *and* ROSENCRANTZ.

How now, my lord, will the King hear this piece of work? 35

POLONIUS: And the Queen too, and that presently.°

HAMLET: Bid the players make haste.   [*Exit* POLONIUS.]
Will you two help to hasten them?

ROSENCRANTZ: Ay, my lord.   *Exeunt they two.*

HAMLET: What ho, Horatio!

Enter HORATIO.

HORATIO: Here, sweet lord, at your service. 40

9 capable of able to understand;   **dumb shows** mimed performances, often used before Shakespeare's time to precede a play or each act.   **10 Termagant** a supposed deity of the Mohammed-
ans, not found in any English medieval play but elsewhere portrayed as violent and blustering.
11 Herod Herod of Jewry. (A character in *The Slaughter of the Innocents* and other cycle
plays. The part was played with great noise and fury.)   **15 modesty** restraint, moderation.
16 from contrary to.   **18 scorn** i.e., something foolish and deserving of scorn.   **18–19 the
very . . . time** i.e., the present state of affairs;   **his** its;   **pressure** stamp, impressed character;
come tardy off inadequately done.   **20 the unskillful** those lacking in judgment.   **21 the
censure . . . one** the judgment of even one of whom;   **your allowance** your scale of values.
23 not . . . profanely (Hamlet anticipates his idea in lines 25–27 that some men were not
made by God at all.)   **24 Christians** i.e., ordinary decent folk.   **24–25 nor man** i.e., nor any
human being at all.   **26 journeymen** laborers who are not yet masters in their trade.
27 abominably (Shakespeare's usual spelling, *abhominably*, suggests a literal though
etymologically incorrect meaning, "removed from human nature.")   **28 indifferently** tolerably.
30 of them some among them.   **31 barren** i.e., of wit.   **36 presently** at once.

HAMLET: Horatio, thou art e'en as just a man
　　　　As e'er my conversation coped withal.°
HORATIO: O, my dear lord—
HAMLET:　　　　　　　　　Nay, do not think I flatter,
　　　　For what advancement may I hope from thee
　　　　That no revenue hast but thy good spirits　　　　　　　　45
　　　　To feed and clothe thee? Why should the poor be flattered?
　　　　No, let the candied° tongue lick absurd pomp,
　　　　And crook the pregnant° hinges of the knee
　　　　Where thrift° may follow fawning. Dost thou hear?
　　　　Since my dear soul was mistress of her choice　　　　　　50
　　　　And could of men distinguish her election,°
　　　　Sh' hath sealed thee° for herself, for thou hast been
　　　　As one, in suffering all, that suffers nothing,
　　　　A man that Fortune's buffets and rewards
　　　　Hast ta'en with equal thanks; and blest are those　　　　55
　　　　Whose blood° and judgment are so well commeddled°
　　　　That they are not a pipe for Fortune's finger
　　　　To sound what stop° she please. Give me that man
　　　　That is not passion's slave, and I will wear him
　　　　In my heart's core, ay, in my heart of heart,　　　　　　60
　　　　As I do thee.—Something too much of this.—
　　　　There is a play tonight before the King.
　　　　One scene of it comes near the circumstance
　　　　Which I have told thee of my father's death.
　　　　I prithee, when thou seest that act afoot,　　　　　　　　65
　　　　Even with the very comment of thy soul°
　　　　Observe my uncle. If his occulted° guilt
　　　　Do not itself unkennel° in one speech,
　　　　It is a damnéd° ghost that we have seen,
　　　　And my imaginations are as foul　　　　　　　　　　　　70
　　　　As Vulcan's stithy.° Give him heedful note,
　　　　For I mine eyes will rivet to his face,
　　　　And after we will both our judgments join
　　　　In censure of his seeming.°
HORATIO:　　　　　　　　　　Well, my lord.
　　　　If 'a steal aught° the whilst this play is playing　　　　　75
　　　　And scape detecting, I will pay the theft.

　　　　[*Flourish.*] *Enter trumpets and kettledrums,* KING, QUEEN, POLONIUS, OPHELIA,
[ROSENCRANTZ, GUILDENSTERN, *and other lords, with guards carrying torches*].

HAMLET: They are coming to the play. I must be idle.°
　　　　Get you a place.　　　　　　　　[*The* KING, QUEEN, *and courtiers sit.*]

42 my . . . withal my dealings encountered.　**47 candied** sugared, flattering.　**48 pregnant**
compliant.　**49 thrift** profit.　**51 could . . . election** could make distinguishing choices among
persons.　**52 sealed thee** (literally, as one would seal a legal document to mark possession.)
56 blood passion; **commeddled** commingled.　**58 stop** hole in a wind instrument for controlling the sound.　**66 very . . . soul** your most penetrating observation and consideration.
67 occulted hidden.　**68 unkennel** (as one would say of a fox driven from its lair.)
69 damnéd in league with Satan.　**71 stithy** smithy, place of stiths (anvils).　**74 censure of
his seeming** judgment of his appearance or behavior.　**75 If 'a steal aught** if he gets away
with anything.　**77 idle** (1) unoccupied, (2) mad.

KING: How fares our cousin° Hamlet?

HAMLET: Excellent, i' faith, of the chameleon's dish:° I eat the air, promise-   80
crammed. You cannot feed capons° so.

KING: I have nothing with° this answer, Hamlet. These words are not mine.°

HAMLET: No, nor mine now.° [*To* POLONIUS.] My lord, you played once i' th' university, you say?

POLONIUS: That did I, my lord, and was accounted a good actor.   85

HAMLET: What did you enact?

POLONIUS: I did enact Julius Caesar. I was killed i' the Capitol; Brutus killed me.

HAMLET: It was a brute° part° of him to kill so capital a calf° there.—Be the players ready?

ROSENCRANTZ: Ay, my lord. They stay upon° your patience.   90

QUEEN: Come hither, my dear Hamlet, sit by me.

HAMLET: No, good Mother, here's metal° more attractive.

POLONIUS [*to the* KING]: O, ho, do you mark that?

HAMLET: Lady, shall I lie in your lap?   [*Lying down at* OPHELIA'*s feet.*]

OPHELIA: No, my lord.   95

HAMLET: I mean, my head upon your lap?

OPHELIA: Ay, my lord.

HAMLET: Do you think I meant country matters?°

OPHELIA: I think nothing, my lord.

HAMLET: That's a fair thought to lie between maids' legs.   100

OPHELIA: What is, my lord?

HAMLET: Nothing.°

OPHELIA: You are merry, my lord.

HAMLET: Who, I?

OPHELIA: Ay, my lord.   105

HAMLET: O God, your only jig maker.° What should a man do but be merry? For
look you how cheerfully my mother looks, and my father died within 's°
two hours.

OPHELIA: Nay, 'tis twice two months, my lord.

HAMLET: So long? Nay then, let the devil wear black, for I'll have a suit of sables.°   110
O heavens! Die two months ago, and not forgotten yet? Then there's

---

79 cousin i.e., close relative.   **80 chameleon's dish** (Chameleons were supposed to feed on
air. Hamlet deliberately misinterprets the King's *fares* as "feeds." By his phrase *eat the air* he
also plays on the idea of feeding himself with the promise of succession, of being the *heir*.)
81 capons roosters castrated and crammed with feed to make them succulent.   **82 have . . .
with** make nothing of, or gain nothing from;   **are not mine** do not respond to what I asked.
83 nor mine now (once spoken, words are proverbially no longer the speaker's own—and
hence should be uttered warily.)   **88 brute** (the Latin meaning of *brutus*, "stupid," was often
used punningly with the name Brutus.);   **part** (1) deed, (2) role;   **calf** fool.   **90 stay upon**
await.   **92 metal** substance that is *attractive*, i.e., magnetic, but with suggestion also of *mettle*,
"disposition."   **98 country matters** sexual intercourse (making a bawdy pun on the first syllable of *country*).   **102 Nothing** the figure zero or naught, suggesting the female sexual anatomy.
(*Thing* not infrequently has a bawdy connotation of male or female anatomy, and the reference here could be male.)   **106 only jig maker** very best composer of jigs, i.e., pointless
merriment. (Hamlet replies sardonically to Ophelia's observation that he is merry by saying, "If you're looking for someone who is really merry, you've come to the right person.")
107 within 's within this (i.e., these).   **110 suit of sables** garments trimmed with the fur
of the sable and hence suited for a wealthy person, not a mourner (but with a pun on *sable*,
"black," ironically suggesting mourning once again).

hope a great man's memory may outlive his life half a year. But, by 'r
Lady, 'a must build churches, then, or else shall 'a suffer not think-
ing on,° with the hobbyhorse, whose epitaph is
"For O, for O, the hobbyhorse is forgot."°   115

The trumpets sound. Dumb show follows.

Enter a King and a Queen [very lovingly]; the Queen embracing him, and
he her. [She kneels, and makes show of protestation unto him.] He takes her up,
and declines his head upon her neck. He lies him down upon a bank of flowers.
She, seeing him asleep, leaves him. Anon comes in another man, takes off his
crown, kisses it, pours poison in the sleeper's ears, and leaves him. The Queen
returns, finds the King dead, makes passionate action. The Poisoner with some
three or four come in again, seem to condole with her. The dead body is carried
away. The Poisoner woos the Queen with gifts; she seems harsh awhile, but in the
end accepts love.

[Exeunt PLAYERS.]

OPHELIA: What means this, my lord?
HAMLET: Marry, this' miching mallico;° it means mischief.
OPHELIA: Belike° this show imports the argument° of the play.

   Enter PROLOGUE.

HAMLET: We shall know by this fellow. The players cannot keep counsel;° they'll
     tell all.
OPHELIA: Will 'a tell us what this show meant?   120
HAMLET: Ay, or any show that you will show him. Be not you° ashamed to show,
     he'll not shame to tell you what it means.
OPHELIA: You are naught,° you are naught. I'll mark the play.
PROLOGUE: For us, and for our tragedy,   125
     Here stooping° to your clemency,
     We beg your hearing patiently.   [*Exit.*]
HAMLET: Is this a prologue, or the posy of a ring?°
OPHELIA: 'Tis brief, my lord.
HAMLET: As woman's love.   130

   Enter [*two* PLAYERS *as*] *King and Queen.*

PLAYER KING: Full thirty times hath Phoebus' cart° gone round
     Neptune's salt wash° and Tellus'° orbèd ground,
     And thirty dozen moons with borrowed° sheen
     About the world have times twelve thirties been,
     Since love our hearts and Hymen° did our hands   135
     Unite commutual° in most sacred bands.°

113–14 suffer . . . on undergo oblivion.   **115 For . . . forgot** (verse of a song occurring also in
Love's Labour's Lost, 3.1.27–28. The hobbyhorse was a character made up to resemble a horse
and rider, appearing in the morris dance and such May-game sports. This song laments the
disappearance of such customs under pressure from the Puritans.)   **117 this' miching mallico** this is sneaking mischief.   **118 Belike** probably;   **argument** plot.   **119 counsel** secret.
122 Be not you provided you are not.   **124 naught** indecent. (Ophelia is reacting to Hamlet's
pointed remarks about not being ashamed to show all.)   **126 stooping** bowing.
128 posy . . . ring brief motto in verse inscribed in a ring.   **131 Phoebus' cart** the sun-god's
chariot, making its yearly cycle.   **132 salt wash** the sea;   **Tellus** goddess of the earth, of the
orbèd ground.   **133 borrowed** i.e., reflected.   **135 Hymen** god of matrimony.   **136 commutual**
mutually;   **bands** bonds.

PLAYER QUEEN: So many journeys may the sun and moon
      Make us again count o'er ere love be done!
      But, woe is me, you are so sick of late,
      So far from cheer and from your former state,   140
      That I distrust° you. Yet, though I distrust,
      Discomfort° you, my lord, it nothing° must.
      For women's fear and love hold quantity;°
      In neither aught, or in extremity.°
      Now, what my love is, proof° hath made you know,   145
      And as my love is sized,° my fear is so.
      Where love is great, the littlest doubts are fear;
      Where little fears grow great, great love grows there.
PLAYER KING: Faith, I must leave thee, love, and shortly too;
      My operant powers° their functions leave to do.°   150
      And thou shalt live in this fair world behind,°
      Honored, beloved; and haply one as kind
      For husband shalt thou—
PLAYER QUEEN: O, confound the rest!
      Such love must needs be treason in my breast.
      In second husband let me be accurst!   155
      None° wed the second but who° killed the first.
HAMLET: Wormwood,° wormwood.
PLAYER QUEEN: The instances° that second marriage move°
      Are base respects of thrift,° but none of love.
      A second time I kill my husband dead   160
      When second husband kisses me in bed.
PLAYER KING: I do believe you think what now you speak,
      But what we do determine oft we break.
      Purpose is but the slave to memory,°
      Of violent birth, but poor validity,°   165
      Which° now, like fruit unripe, sticks on the tree,
      But fall unshaken when they mellow be.
      Most necessary 'tis that we forget
      To pay ourselves what to ourselves is debt.°
      What to ourselves in passion we propose,   170
      The passion ending, doth the purpose lose.
      The violence of either grief or joy
      Their own enactures° with themselves destroy.
      Where joy most revels, grief doth most lament;
      Grief joys, joy grieves, on slender accident.°   175

141 distrust am anxious about.   **142 Discomfort** distress; **nothing** not at all.   **143 hold quantity** keep proportion with one another.   **144 In . . . extremity** i.e., women fear and love either too little or too much, but the two, fear and love, are equal in either case.   **145 proof** experience.   **146 sized** in size.   **150 operant powers** vital functions; **leave to do** cease to perform.   **151 behind** after I have gone.   **156 None** i.e., let no woman; **but who** except the one who.   **157 Wormwood** i.e., how bitter. (Literally, a bitter-tasting plant.)   **158 instances** motives; **move** motivate.   **159 base . . . thrift** ignoble considerations of material prosperity.   **164 Purpose . . . memory** our good intentions are subject to forgetfulness.   **165 validity** strength, durability.   **166 Which** i.e., purpose.   **168–69 Most . . . debt** it's inevitable that in time we forget the obligations we have imposed on ourselves.   **173 enactures** fulfillments.   **174–75 Where . . . accident** the capacity for extreme joy and grief go together, and often one extreme is instantly changed into its opposite on the slightest provocation.

This world is not for aye,° nor 'tis not strange
That even our loves should with our fortunes change;
For 'tis a question left us yet to prove,
Whether love lead fortune, or else fortune love
The great man down,° you mark his favorite flies;   180
The poor advanced makes friends of enemies.°
And hitherto° doth love on fortune tend;°
For who not needs° shall never lack a friend,
And who in want° a hollow friend doth try°
Directly seasons him° his enemy.   185
But, orderly to end where I begun,
Our wills and fates do so contrary run°
That our devices still° are overthrown;
Our thoughts are ours, their ends° none of our own.
So think thou wilt no second husband wed,   190
But die thy thoughts when thy first lord is dead.

PLAYER QUEEN: Nor° earth to me give food, nor heaven light,
Sport and repose lock from me day and night,°
To desperation turn my trust and hope,
An anchor's cheer° in prison be my scope!°   195
Each opposite that blanks° the face of joy
Meet what I would have well and it destroy!°
Both here and hence° pursue me lasting strife
If, once a widow, ever I be wife!

HAMLET: If she should break it now!   200

PLAYER KING: 'Tis deeply sworn. Sweet, leave me here awhile;
My spirits° grow dull, and fain I would beguile
The tedious day with sleep.

PLAYER QUEEN: Sleep rock thy brain,
And never come mischance between us twain!

[*He sleeps.*] *Exit* [PLAYER QUEEN].

HAMLET: Madam, how like you this play?   205
QUEEN: The lady doth protest too much,° methinks.
HAMLET: O, but she'll keep her word.
KING: Have you heard the argument?° Is there no offense in 't?
HAMLET: No, no, they do but jest,° poison in jest. No offense° i' the world.
KING: What do you call the play?   210

---

176 aye ever.   **180 down** fallen in fortune.   **181 The poor . . . enemies** when one of humble
station is promoted, you see his enemies suddenly becoming his friends.   **182 hitherto** up to
this point in the argument, or, to this extent;   **tend** attend.   **183 who not needs** he who is
not in need (of wealth).   **184 who in want** he who, being in need;   **try** test (his generosity).
185 seasons him ripens him into.   **187 Our . . . run** what we want and what we get go so
contrarily.   **188 devices still** intentions continually.   **189 ends** results.   **192 Nor** let neither.
193 Sport . . . night may day deny me its pastimes and night its repose.   **195 anchor's cheer**
Anchorite's or hermit's fare;   **my scope** the extent of my happiness.   **196 blanks** causes to
blanch or grow pale.   **196–97 Each . . . destroy** may every adverse thing that causes the face
of joy to turn pale meet and destroy everything that I desire to see prosper.   **198 hence** in
the life hereafter.   **202 spirits** vital spirits.   **206 doth . . . much** makes too many promises
and protestations.   **208 argument** plot.   **209 jest** make believe.   **208–09 offense . . . offense**
cause for objection . . . actual injury, crime.

HAMLET: *The Mousetrap*. Marry, how? Tropically.° This play is the image of a murder done in Vienna. Gonzago is the Duke's° name, his wife, Baptista. You shall see anon. 'Tis a knavish piece of work, but what of that? Your Majesty, and we that have free° souls, it touches us not. Let the galled jade° wince, our withers° are unwrung.° 215

Enter LUCIANUS.

This is one Lucianus, nephew to the King.

OPHELIA: You are as good as a chorus,° my lord.

HAMLET: I could interpret° between you and your love, if I could see the puppets dallying.°

OPHELIA: You are keen,° my lord, you are keen. 220

HAMLET: It would cost you a groaning to take off mine edge.

OPHELIA: Still better, and worse.°

HAMLET: So° you mis-take° your husbands. Begin, murder; leave thy damnable faces and begin. Come, the croaking raven doth bellow for revenge.

LUCIANUS: Thoughts black, hands apt, drugs fit, and time agreeing, 225
Confederate season,° else° no creature seeing,°
Thou mixture rank, of midnight weeds collected,
With Hecate's ban° thrice blasted, thrice infected,
Thy natural magic and dire property°
On wholesome life usurp immediately. 230

[He pours the poison into the sleeper's ear.]

HAMLET: 'A poisons him i' the garden for his estate.° His° name's Gonzago. The story is extant, and written in very choice Italian. You shall see anon how the murderer gets the love of Gonzago's wife.

[CLAUDIUS *rises*.]

OPHELIA: The King rises.

HAMLET: What, frighted with false fire?° 235

QUEEN: How fares my lord?

POLONIUS: Give o'er the play.

KING: Give me some light. Away!

POLONIUS: Lights, lights, lights!

Exeunt all but HAMLET *and* HORATIO.

---

211 Tropically figuratively. (The First Quarto reading, *trapically*, suggests a pun on *trap* in *Mousetrap*.)   **212 Duke's** i.e., King's (A slip that may be due to Shakespeare's possible source, the alleged murder of the Duke of Urbino by Luigi Gonzaga in 1538.)   **214 free** guiltless. **214–15 galled jade** horse whose hide is rubbed by saddle or harness.   **215 withers** the part between the horse's shoulder blades; **unwrung** not rubbed sore.   **217 chorus** (In many Elizabethan plays, the forthcoming action was explained by an actor known as the "chorus"; at a puppet show, the actor who spoke the dialogue was known as an "interpreter," as indicated by the lines following.)   **218 interpret** (1) ventriloquize the dialogue, as in a puppet show, (2) act as pander.   **218–19 puppets dallying** (with suggestion of sexual play, continued in *keen*, "sexually aroused," *groaning*, "moaning in pregnancy," and *edge*, "sexual desire" or "impetuosity.")   **220 keen** sharp, bitter.   **222 Still . . . worse** more keen, always *bettering* what other people say with witty wordplay, but at the same time more offensive.   **223 So** even thus (in marriage); **mis-take** take falseheartedly and cheat on. (The marriage vows say "for better, for worse.")   **226 Confederate season** the time and occasion conspiring (to assist the murderer); **else** otherwise; **seeing** seeing me.   **228 Hecate's ban** the curse of Hecate, the goddess of witchcraft.   **229 dire property** baleful quality.   **231 estate** i.e., the kingship; **His** i.e., the King's.   **235 false fire** the blank discharge of a gun loaded with powder but no shot.

HAMLET:

> "Why,° let the strucken deer go weep,   240
>   The hart ungallèd° play.
> For some must watch,° while some must sleep;
>   Thus runs the world away."

> Would not this,° sir, and a forest of feathers°—if the rest of my fortunes   245
> turn Turk with° me—with two Provincial roses° on my razed° shoes, get
> me a fellowship in a cry° of players?°

HORATIO: Half a share.

HAMLET: A whole one, I.

> "For thou dost know, O Damon° dear,   250
>   This realm dismantled° was
> Of Jove himself, and now reigns here
>   A very, very—pajock."°

HORATIO: You might have rhymed.

HAMLET: O good Horatio, I'll take the ghost's word for a thousand pound.
       Didst perceive?   255

HORATIO: Very well, my lord.

HAMLET: Upon the talk of the poisoning?

HORATIO: I did very well note him.

       Enter ROSENCRANTZ *and* GUILDENSTERN.

HAMLET: Aha! Come, some music! Come, the recorders.°

> "For if the King like not the comedy,   260
> Why then, belike, he likes it not, perdy."°

Come, some music.

GUILDENSTERN: Good my lord, vouchsafe me a word with you.

HAMLET: Sir, a whole history.

GUILDENSTERN: The King, sir—   265

HAMLET: Ay, sir, what of him?

GUILDENSTERN: Is in his retirement° marvelous distempered.°

240–43 Why . . . away (probably from an old ballad, with allusion to the popular belief
that a wounded deer retires to weep and die; compare with *As You Like It*, 2.1.33–66.)
241 ungallèd unafflicted.   **242 watch** remain awake.   **243 Thus . . . away** thus the world goes.
244 this i.e., the play;   **feathers** (allusion to the plumes that Elizabethan actors were fond of
wearing.)   **245 turn Turk with** turn renegade against, go back on;   **Provincial roses** rosettes
of ribbon, named for roses grown in a part of France;   **razed** with ornamental slashing.
246 cry pack (of hounds);   **fellowship . . . players** partnership in a theatrical company.
249 Damon the friend of Pythias, as Horatio is friend of Hamlet; or, a traditional pastoral name.
250 dismantled stripped, divested.   **250–52 This realm . . . pajock** i.e., Jove, representing
divine authority and justice, has abandoned this realm to its own devices, leaving in his stead
only a peacock or vain pretender to virtue (though the rhyme-word expected in place of *pajock*
or "peacock" suggests that the realm is now ruled over by an "ass").   **259 recorders** wind
instruments of the flute kind.   **261 perdy** (a corruption of the French *par dieu,* "by God.")
267 retirement withdrawal to his chambers;   **distempered** out of humor. (But Hamlet deliberately plays on the wider application to any illness of mind or body, as in line 298, especially
to drunkenness.)

HAMLET: With drink, sir?

GUILDENSTERN: No, my lord, with choler.°

HAMLET: Your wisdom should show itself more richer to signify this to the doctor, 270
for for me to put him to his purgation° would perhaps plunge him into
more choler.

GUILDENSTERN: Good my lord, put your discourse into some frame° and start° not
so wildly from my affair.

HAMLET: I am tame, sir. Pronounce. 275

GUILDENSTERN: The Queen, your mother, in most great affliction of spirit, hath
sent me to you.

HAMLET: You are welcome.

GUILDENSTERN: Nay, good my lord, this courtesy is not of the right breed.° If it
shall please you to make me a wholesome answer, I will do your 280
mother's commandment; if not, your pardon° and my return shall be the
end of my business.

HAMLET: Sir, I cannot.

ROSENCRANTZ: What, my lord?

HAMLET: Make you a wholesome answer; my wit's diseased. But, sir, such answer 285
as I can make, you shall command, or rather, as you say, my mother.
Therefore no more, but to the matter. My mother, you say—

ROSENCRANTZ: Then thus she says: your behavior hath struck her into amazement
and admiration.°

HAMLET: O wonderful son, that can so stonish a mother! But is there no sequel at 290
the heels of this mother's admiration? Impart.

ROSENCRANTZ: She desires to speak with you in her closet° ere you go to bed.

HAMLET: We shall obey, were she ten times our mother. Have you any further
trade with us?

ROSENCRANTZ: My lord, you once did love me. 295

HAMLET: And do still, by these pickers and stealers.°

ROSENCRANTZ: Good my lord, what is your cause of distemper? You do surely bar
the door upon your own liberty° if you deny° your griefs to your friend.

HAMLET: Sir, I lack advancement.

ROSENCRANTZ: How can that be, when you have the voice of the King himself for 300
your succession in Denmark?

HAMLET: Ay, sir, but "While the grass grows"°—the proverb is something° musty.

Enter the PLAYERS° *with recorders.*

O, the recorders. Let me see one. [*He takes a recorder.*]
To withdraw° with you: why do you go about to recover the wind° of
me, as if you would drive me into a toil?° 305

---

269 choler anger. (But Hamlet takes the word in its more basic humoral sense of "bilious disorder.")
271 purgation (Hamlet hints at something going beyond medical treatment to bloodletting
and the extraction of confession.)   **273 frame** order;   **start** shy or jump away (like a horse;
the opposite of *tame* in line 275).   **279 breed** (1) kind, (2) breeding, manners.   **281 pardon**
permission to depart.   **289 admiration** bewilderment.   **292 closet** private chamber.
296 pickers and stealers i.e., hands. (So called from the catechism, "to keep my hands from
picking and stealing.")   **298 liberty** i.e., being freed from *distemper*, line 297, but perhaps
with a veiled threat as well;   **deny** refuse to share.   **302 While . . . grows** (the rest of the proverb is "the silly horse starves"; Hamlet may not live long enough to succeed to the kingdom.);
something somewhat;   **s.d. Players** actors.   **304 withdraw** speak privately;   **recover the
wind** get to the windward side (thus driving the game into the *toil,* or "net").   **305 toil** snare.

GUILDENSTERN: O, my lord, if my duty be too bold, my love is too unmannerly.°
HAMLET: I do not well understand that.° Will you play upon this pipe?
GUILDENSTERN: My lord, I cannot.
HAMLET: I pray you.
GUILDENSTERN: Believe me, I cannot.   310
HAMLET: I do beseech you.
GUILDENSTERN: I know no touch of it, my lord.
HAMLET: It is as easy as lying. Govern these ventages° with your fingers and
 thumb, give it breath with your mouth, and it will discourse most
 eloquent music. Look you, these are the stops.   315
GUILDENSTERN: But these cannot I command to any utterance of harmony. I have
 not the skill.
HAMLET: Why, look you now, how unworthy a thing you make of me! You would
 play upon me, you would seem to know my stops, you would pluck out
 the heart of my mystery, you would sound° me from my lowest note to   320
 the top of my compass,° and there is much music, excellent voice, in this
 little organ,° yet cannot you make it speak. 'Sblood, do you think I am
 easier to be played on than a pipe? Call me what instrument you will,
 though you can fret° me, you cannot play upon me.

  Enter POLONIUS.

  God bless you, sir!   325
POLONIUS: My lord, the Queen would speak with you, and presently.°
HAMLET: Do you see yonder cloud that's almost in shape of a camel?
POLONIUS: By the Mass and 'tis, like a camel indeed.
HAMLET: Methinks it is like a weasel.
POLONIUS: It is backed like a weasel.
HAMLET: Or like a whale.   330
POLONIUS: Very like a whale.
HAMLET: Then I will come to my mother by and by.° [*Aside.*] They fool me° to
 the top of my bent.°—I will come by and by.
POLONIUS: I will say so.   [*Exit.*]   335
HAMLET: "By and by" is easily said. Leave me, friends.

           [*Exeunt all but* HAMLET.]

 'Tis now the very witching time° of night,
 When churchyards yawn and hell itself breathes out
 Contagion to this world. Now could I drink hot blood
 And do such bitter business as the day   340
 Would quake to look on. Soft, now to my mother.
 O heart, lose not thy nature!° Let not ever
 The soul of Nero° enter this firm bosom.
 Let me be cruel, not unnatural;
 I will speak daggers to her, but use none.   345

---

306 if . . . unmannerly if I am using an unmannerly boldness, it is my love that occasions it.
307 I . . . that i.e., I don't understand how genuine love can be unmannerly.   **313 ventages**
finger-holes or *stops* (line 319) of the recorder.   **320 sound** (1) fathom, (2) produce sound in.
321 compass range (of voice).   **322 organ** musical instrument.   **324 fret** irritate (with a
quibble on *fret*, meaning the piece of wood, gut, or metal that regulates the fingering on an
instrument).   **326 presently** at once.   **333 by and by** quite soon.   **fool me** trifle with me,
humor my fooling.   **334 top of my bent** limit of my ability or endurance. (Literally, the extent to
which a bow may be bent.)   **337 witching time** time when spells are cast and evil is abroad.
342 nature natural feeling.   **343 Nero** murderer of his mother, Agrippina.

My tongue and soul in this be hypocrites:
How in my words soever° she be shent,°
To give them seals° never my soul consent!   *Exit.*

[3.3]

Enter KING, ROSENCRANTZ, *and* GUILDENSTERN.

KING: I like him° not, nor stands it safe with us
    To let his madness range. Therefore prepare you.
    I your commission will forthwith dispatch,°
    And he to England shall along with you.
    The terms of our estate° may not endure   5
    Hazard so near 's as doth hourly grow
    Out of his brows.°
GUILDENSTERN: We will ourselves provide.
    Most holy and religious fear° it is
    To keep those many many bodies safe
    That live and feed upon Your Majesty.   10
ROSENCRANTZ: The single and peculiar° life is bound
    With all the strength and armor of the mind
    To keep itself from noyance,° but much more
    That spirit upon whose weal depends and rests
    The lives of many. The cess° of majesty   15
    Dies not alone, but like a gulf° doth draw
    What's near it with it; or it is a massy° wheel
    Fixed on the summit of the highest mount,
    To whose huge spokes ten thousand lesser things
    Are mortised° and adjoined, which, when it falls,°   20
    Each small annexment, petty consequence,°
    Attends° the boisterous ruin. Never alone
    Did the King sigh, but with a general groan
KING: Arm° you, I pray you, to this speedy voyage,
    For we will fetters put about this fear,   25
    Which now goes too free-footed.
ROSENCRANTZ: We will haste us.
    Exeunt gentlemen [ROSENCRANTZ *and* GUILDENSTERN].

Enter POLONIUS.

POLONIUS: My lord, he's going to his mother's closet.
    Behind the arras° I'll convey myself

---

347 How . . . soever however much by my words; **shent** rebuked. **348 give them seals** i.e.,
confirm them with deeds. **[3.3] Location: The castle. 1 him** i.e., his behavior. **3 dispatch**
prepare, cause to be drawn up. **5 terms of our estate** circumstances of my royal position.
7 Out of his brows i.e., from his brain, in the form of plots and threats. **8 religious fear**
sacred concern. **11 single and peculiar** individual and private. **13 noyance** harm. **15 cess**
decease, cessation. **16 gulf** whirlpool. **17 massy** massive. **20 mortised** fastened (as with
a fitted joint); **when it falls** i.e., when it descends, like the wheel of Fortune, bringing a king
down with it. **21 Each . . . consequence** i.e., every hanger-on and unimportant person or thing
connected with the King. **22 Attends** participates in. **24 Arm** prepare. **28 arras** screen
of tapestry placed around the walls of household apartments. (On the Elizabethan stage, the
arras was presumably over a door or discovery space in the tiring-house facade.)

To hear the process.° I'll warrant she'll tax him home,°
And, as you said—and wisely was it said—   30
'Tis meet° that some more audience than a mother,
Since nature makes them partial, should o'erhear
The speech, of vantage.° Fare you well, my liege.
I'll call upon you ere you go to bed
And tell you what I know.

KING: Thanks, dear my lord.   *Exit* [POLONIUS].   35
O, my offense is rank! It smells to heaven.
It hath the primal eldest curse° upon't,
A brother's murder. Pray can I not,
Though inclination be as sharp as will;°
My stronger guilt defeats my strong intent,   40
And like a man to double business bound°
I stand in pause where I shall first begin,
And both neglect. What if this cursèd hand
Were thicker than itself with brother's blood,
Is there not rain enough in the sweet heavens   45
To wash it white as snow? Whereto serves mercy
But to confront the visage of offense?°
And what's in prayer but this twofold force,
To be forestallèd° ere we come to fall,
Or pardoned being down? Then I'll look up.   50
My fault is past. But O, what form of prayer
Can serve my turn? "Forgive me my foul murder"?
That cannot be, since I am still possessed
Of those effects for which I did the murder:
My crown, mine own ambition, and my Queen.   55
May one be pardoned and retain th' offense?°
In the corrupted currents° of this world
Offense's gilded hand° may shove by° justice,
And oft 'tis seen the wicked prize° itself
Buys out the law. But 'tis not so above.   60
There° is no shuffling,° there the action lies°
In his° true nature, and we ourselves compelled,
Even to the teeth and forehead° of our faults,
To give in° evidence. What then? What rests?°
Try what repentance can. What can it not?   65
Yet what can it, when one cannot repent?
O wretched state, O bosom black as death,

---

29 process proceedings; **tax him home** reprove him severely. **31 meet** fitting. **33 of vantage** from an advantageous place, or, in addition. **37 the primal eldest curse** the curse of Cain, the first murderer; he killed his brother Abel. **39 Though . . . will** though my desire is as strong as my determination. **41 bound** (1) destined, (2) obliged. (The King wants to repent and still enjoy what he has gained.) **46–47 Whereto . . . offense** What function does mercy serve other than to meet sin face to face? **49 forestallèd** prevented (from sinning). **56 th' offense** the thing for which one offended. **57 currents** courses. **58 gilded hand** hand offering gold as a bribe; **shove by** thrust aside. **59 wicked prize** prize won by wickedness. **61 There** i.e., in heaven; **shuffling** escape by trickery; **the action lies** the accusation is made manifest. (A legal metaphor.) **62 his** its. **63 to the teeth and forehead** face to face, concealing nothing. **64 give in** provide; **rests** remains.

limèd° soul that, struggling to be free,
Art more engaged!° Help, angels! Make assay.°
Bow, stubborn knees, and heart with strings of steel,   70
Be soft as sinews of the newborn babe!
All may be well.   *[He kneels.]*

Enter HAMLET.

HAMLET: Now might I do it pat,° now 'a is a-praying;
And now I'll do 't. [*He draws his sword.*] And so 'a goes to heaven,
And so am I revenged. That would be scanned:°   75
A villain kills my father, and for that,
I, his sole son, do this same villain send
To heaven.
Why, this is hire and salary, not revenge.
'A took my father grossly, full of bread,°   80
With all his crimes broad blown,° as flush° as May;
And how his audit° stands who knows save° heaven?
But in our circumstance and course of thought°
'Tis heavy with him. And am I then revenged,
To take him in the purging of his soul   85
When he is fit and seasoned° for his passage?
No!
Up, sword, and know thou a more horrid hent.°
                                                       [He puts up his sword.]
When he is drunk asleep, or in his rage,°
Or in th' incestuous pleasure of his bed,   90
At game,° a-swearing, or about some act
That has no relish° of salvation in 't—
Then trip him, that his heels may kick at heaven,
And that his soul may be as damned and black
As hell, whereto it goes. My mother stays.°   95
This physic° but prolongs thy sickly days.   *Exit.*
KING: My words fly up, my thoughts remain below.
Words without thoughts never to heaven go.   *Exit.*

[3.4]

Enter [QUEEN] GERTRUDE *and* POLONIUS.

POLONIUS: 'A will come straight. Look you lay home° to him.
Tell him his pranks have been too broad° to bear with,

---

68 limèd caught as with birdlime, a sticky substance used to ensnare birds. **69 engaged** entangled; **assay** trial. (Said to himself.) **73 pat** opportunely. **75 would be scanned** needs to be looked into, or, would be interpreted as follows. **80 grossly, full of bread** i.e., enjoying his worldly pleasures rather than fasting. (See Ezekiel 16:49.) **81 crimes broad blown** sins in full bloom; **flush** vigorous. **82 audit** account; **save** except for. **83 in . . . thought** As we see it from our mortal perspective. **86 seasoned** matured, readied. **88 know . . . hent** await to be grasped by me on a more horrid occasion; **hent** act of seizing. **89 drunk . . . rage** dead drunk, or in a fit of sexual passions. **91 game** gambling. **92 relish** trace, savor. **95 stays** awaits (me). **96 physic** purging (by prayer), or, Hamlet's postponement of the killing.
[3.4] Location: The Queen's private chamber. **1 lay home** thrust to the heart, reprove him soundly. **2 broad** unrestrained.

And that Your Grace hath screened and stood between
Much heat° and him. I'll shroud° me even here.
Pray you, be round° with him.

HAMLET [*within*]: Mother, Mother, Mother!   5

QUEEN: I'll warrant you, fear me not.
    Withdraw, I hear him coming.   [POLONIUS *hides behind the arras.*]

    Enter HAMLET.

HAMLET: Now, Mother, what's the matter?

QUEEN: Hamlet, thou hast thy father° much offended.   10

HAMLET: Mother, you have my father much offended.

QUEEN: Come, come, you answer with an idle° tongue.

HAMLET: Go, go, you question with a wicked tongue.

QUEEN: Why, how now, Hamlet?

HAMLET: What's the matter now?

QUEEN: Have you forgot me?°   15

HAMLET: No, by the rood,° not so:
    You are the Queen your husband's brother's wife,
    And—would it were not so!—you are my mother.

QUEEN: Nay, then, I'll set those to you that can speak.°

HAMLET: Come, come, and sit you down; you shall not budge.
    You go not till I set you up a glass   20
    Where you may see the inmost part of you.

QUEEN: What wilt thou do? Thou wilt not murder me?
    Help, ho!

POLONIUS [*behind the arras*]: What ho! Help!

HAMLET [*drawing*]: How now? A rat? Dead for a ducat,° dead!   25

              [*He thrusts his rapier through the arras.*]

POLONIUS [*behind the arras*]: O, I am slain!   [*He falls and dies.*]

QUEEN: O me, what hast thou done?

HAMLET: Nay, I know not. Is it the King?

QUEEN: O, what a rash and bloody deed is this!

HAMLET: A bloody deed—almost as bad, good Mother,
    As kill a King, and marry with his brother.   30

QUEEN: As kill a King!

HAMLET: Ay, lady, it was my word.

      [*He parts the arras and discovers* POLONIUS.]

    Thou wretched, rash, intruding fool, farewell!
    I took thee for thy better. Take thy fortune.
    Thou find'st to be too busy° is some danger.—
    Leave wringing of your hands. Peace, sit you down,   35
    And let me wring your heart, for so I shall,
    If it be made of penetrable stuff,
    If damnèd custom° have not brazed° it so
    That it be proof° and bulwark against sense.°

4 Much heat i.e., the King's anger; **shroud** conceal. (With ironic fitness to Polonius'
imminent death. The word is only in the First Quarto: the Second Quarto and the Folio read
"silence.")   **5 round** blunt.   **10 thy father** i.e., your stepfather, Claudius.   **12 idle** foolish.
15 forgot me i.e., forgotten that I am your mother;   **rood** cross of Christ.   **18 speak** i.e., to
someone so rude.   **25 Dead for a ducat** i.e., I bet a ducat he's dead; or, a ducat is his life's fee.
34 busy nosey.   **38 damnèd custom** habitual wickedness;   **brazed** brazened, hardened.
39 proof armor;   **sense** feeling.

QUEEN: What have I done, that thou dar'st wag thy tongue 40
    In noise so rude against me?

HAMLET: Such an act
    That blurs the grace and blush of modesty,
    Calls virtue hypocrite, takes off the rose
    From the fair forehead of an innocent love
    And sets a blister° there, makes marriage vows 45
    As false as dicers' oaths. O, such a deed
    As from the body of contraction° plucks
    The very soul, and sweet religion makes°
    A rhapsody° of words. Heaven's face does glow
    O'er this solidity and compound mass 50
    With tristful visage, as against the doom,
    Is thought-sick at the act.°

QUEEN: Ay me, what act,
    That roars so loud and thunders in the index?°

HAMLET [*showing her two likenesses*]: Look here upon this picture, and on this,
    The counterfeit presentment° of two brothers. 55
    See what a grace was seated on this brow:
    Hyperion's° curls, the front° of Jove himself,
    An eye like Mars° to threaten and command,
    A station° like the herald Mercury°
    New-lighted° on a heaven-kissing hill— 60
    A combination and a form indeed
    Where every god did seem to set his seal°
    To give the world assurance of a man.
    This was your husband. Look you now what follows:
    Here is your husband, like a mildewed ear,° 65
    Blasting° his wholesome brother. Have you eyes?
    Could you on this fair mountain leave° to feed
    And batten° on this moor?° Ha, have you eyes?
    You cannot call it love, for at your age
    The heyday° in the blood° is tame, it's humble, 70
    And waits upon the judgment, and what judgment
    Would step from this to this? Sense,° sure, you have,
    Else could you not have motion, but sure that sense
    Is apoplexed,° for madness would not err,°
    Nor sense to ecstasy was ne'er so thralled, 75

---

45 sets a blister i.e., brands as a harlot. **47 contraction** the marriage contract. **48 sweet religion makes** i.e., makes marriage vows. **49 rhapsody** senseless string. **49–52 Heaven's . . . act** Heaven's face blushes at this solid world compounded of the various elements, with sorrowful face as though the day of doom were near, and is sick with horror at the deed (i.e., Gertrude's marriage). **54 index** table of contents, prelude or preface. **55 counterfeit presentment** portrayed representation. **57 Hyperion's** the sungod's; **front** brow. **58 Mars** god of war. **59 station** manner of standing; **Mercury** winged messenger of the gods. **60 New-lighted** newly alighted. **62 set his seal** i.e., affix his approval. **65 ear** i.e., of grain. **66 Blasting** blighting. **67 leave** cease. **68 batten** gorge; **moor** barren or marshy ground (suggesting also "dark-skinned"). **70 heyday** state of excitement; **blood** passion. **72 Sense** perception through the five senses (the functions of the middle sensible soul). **74 apoplexed** paralyzed (Hamlet goes on to explain that, without such a paralysis of will, mere madness would not so err, nor would the five senses so enthrall themselves to **ecstasy** or lunacy; even such deranged states of mind would be able to make the obvious choice between Hamlet Senior and Claudius.); **err** so err.

But° it reserved some quantity of choice
To serve in such a difference.° What devil was 't
That thus hath cozened° you at hoodman-blind?°
Eyes without feeling, feeling without sight,
Ears without hands or eyes, smelling sans° all　　　　　　80
Or but a sickly part of one true sense
Could not so mope.° O shame, where is thy blush?
Rebellious hell,
If thou canst mutine° in a matron's bones,
To flaming youth let virtue be as wax　　　　　　　　85
And melt in her own fire.° Proclaim no shame
When the compulsive ardor gives the charge,
Since frost itself as actively doth burn,
And reason panders will.°

QUEEN: O Hamlet, speak no more!　　　　　　　　　　90
Thou turn'st mine eyes into my very soul,
And there I see such black and grainèd° spots
As will not leave their tinct.°

HAMLET:　　　　　　　　　　Nay, but to live
In the rank sweat of an enseamèd° bed,
Stewed° in corruption, honeying and making love　　95
Over the nasty sty!

QUEEN: O, speak to me no more!
These words like daggers enter in my ears.
No more, sweet Hamlet!

HAMLET:　　　　　　　　A murderer and a villain,
A slave that is not twentieth part the tithe°　　　　100
Of your precedent lord,° a vice° of kings,
A cutpurse of the empire and the rule,
That from a shelf the precious diadem stole
And put it in his pocket!

QUEEN: No more!　　　　　　　　　　　　　　105

Enter GHOST [*in his nightgown*].

HAMLET: A king of shreds and patches°—
Save me, and hover o'er me with your wings,
You heavenly guards! What would your gracious figure?

QUEEN: Alas, he's mad!

---

76 But but that.　**77 To . . . difference** to help in making a choice between two such men.
78 cozened cheated;　**hoodman-blind** blindman's buff. (In this game, says Hamlet, the devil
must have pushed Claudius toward Gertrude while she was blindfolded.)　**80 sans** without.
82 mope be dazed, act aimlessly.　**84 mutine** incite mutiny.　**85–86 be as wax . . . fire** melt
like a candle or stick of sealing wax held over the candle flame.　**86–89 Proclaim . . . will** call
it no shameful business when the compelling ardor of youth delivers the attack, i.e., commits
lechery, since the *frost* of advanced age burns with as active a fire of lust and reason perverts
itself by fomenting lust rather than restraining it.　**92 grainèd** dyed in grain, indelible.
93 leave their tinct surrender their color.　**94 enseamèd** saturated in the grease and filth of
passionate lovemaking.　**95 Stewed** soaked, bathed (with a suggestion of "stew," brothel).
100 tithe tenth part.　**101 precedent lord** former husband;　**vice** buffoon. (A reference to the
Vice of the morality plays.)　**106 shreds and patches** i.e., motley, the traditional costume of
the clown or fool.

HAMLET: Do you not come your tardy son to chide,   110
    That, lapsed° in time and passion, lets go by
    Th' important° acting of your dread command?
    O, say!
GHOST: Do not forget. This visitation
    Is but to whet thy almost blunted purpose.   115
    But look, amazement° on thy mother sits.
    O, step between her and her fighting soul!
    Conceit° in weakest bodies strongest works.
    Speak to her, Hamlet.
HAMLET: How is it with you, lady?
QUEEN: Alas, how is 't with you,   120
    That you do bend your eye on vacancy,
    And with th' incorporal° air do hold discourse?
    Forth at your eyes your spirits wildly peep,
    And, as the sleeping soldiers in th' alarm,°
    Your bedded° hair, like life in excrements,°   125
    Start up and stand on end. O gentle son,
    Upon the heat and flame of thy distemper°
    Sprinkle cool patience. Whereon do you look?
HAMLET: On him, on him! Look you how pale he glares!
    His form and cause conjoined,° preaching to stones,   130
    Would make them capable.°—Do not look upon me,
    Lest with this piteous action you convert
    My stern effects.° Then what I have to do
    Will want true color—tears perchance for blood.°
QUEEN: To whom do you speak this?   135
HAMLET: Do you see nothing there?
QUEEN: Nothing at all, yet all that is I see.
HAMLET: Nor did you nothing hear?
QUEEN: No, nothing but ourselves.
HAMLET: Why, look you there, look how it steals away!   140
    My father, in his habit° as° he lived!
    Look where he goes even now out at the portal!   *Exit* GHOST.
QUEEN: This is the very° coinage of your brain.
    This bodiless creation ecstasy
    Is very cunning in.°   145
HAMLET: Ecstasy?
    My pulse as yours doth temperately keep time,
    And makes as healthful music. It is not madness

111 lapsed delaying.   **112 important** importunate, urgent.   **116 amazement** distraction.
118 Conceit imagination.   **122 incorporal** immaterial.   **124 as . . . alarm** like soldiers called
out of sleep by an alarum.   **125 bedded** laid flat;   **like life in excrements** i.e., as though
hair, an outgrowth of the body, had a life of its own. (Hair was thought to be lifeless
because it lacks sensation, and so its standing on end would be unnatural and ominous.)
127 distemper disorder.   **130 His . . . conjoined** his appearance joined to his cause for speaking.
131 capable receptive.   **132–33 convert . . . effects** divert me from my stern duty.   **134 want . . .**
blood lack plausibility so that (with a play on the normal sense of *color*) I shall shed colorless
tears instead of blood.   **141 habit** clothes;   **as** as when.   **143 very** mere.   **144–45 This . . .**
in madness is skillful in creating this kind of hallucination.

That I have uttered. Bring me to the test,
And I the matter will reword,° which madness   150
Would gambol° from. Mother, for love of grace,
Lay not that flattering unction° to your soul
That not your trespass but my madness speaks.
It will but skin° and film the ulcerous place,
Whiles rank corruption, mining° all within,   155
Infects unseen. Confess yourself to heaven,
Repent what's past, avoid what is to come,
And do not spread the compost° on the weeds
To make them ranker. Forgive me this my virtue;°
For in the fatness° of these pursy° times   160
Virtue itself of vice must pardon beg,
Yea, curb° and woo for leave° to do him good.

QUEEN: O Hamlet, thou hast cleft my heart in twain.
HAMLET: O, throw away the worser part of it,
And live the purer with the other half.   165
Good night. But go not to my uncle's bed;
Assume a virtue, if you have it not.
That monster, custom, who all sense doth eat,°
Of habits devil,° is angel yet in this,
That to the use of actions fair and good   170
He likewise gives a frock or livery°
That aptly° is put on. Refrain tonight,
And that shall lend a kind of easiness
To the next abstinence; the next more easy;
For use° almost can change the stamp of nature,°   175
And either° . . . the devil, or throw him out
With wondrous potency. Once more, good night;
And when you are desirous to be blest,
I'll blessing beg of you.° For this same lord,   [*pointing to* POLONIUS.]
I do repent; but heaven hath pleased it so   180
To punish me with this, and this with me,
That I must be their scourge and minister.°
I will bestow° him, and will answer° well
The death I gave him. So, again, good night.
I must be cruel only to be kind.   185

---

150 reword repeat word for word.   **151 gambol** skip away.   **152 unction** ointment.
154 skin grow a skin for.   **155 mining** working under the surface.   **158 compost** manure.
159 this my virtue my virtuous talk in reproving you.   **160 fatness** grossness;   **pursy** flabby,
out of shape.   **162 curb** bow, bend the knee;   **leave** permission.   **168 who . . . eat** which consumes all proper or natural feeling, all sensibility.   **169 Of habits devil** devil-like in prompting
evil habits.   **171 livery** an outer appearance, a customary garb (and hence a predisposition
easily assumed in time of stress).   **172 aptly** readily.   **175 use** habit;   **the stamp of nature**
our inborn traits.   **176 And either** (a defective line, usually emended by inserting the word
master after *either*, following the Fourth Quarto and early editors.)   **178–79 when . . . you**
i.e., when you are ready to be penitent and seek God's blessing, I will ask your blessing as a
dutiful son should.   **182 their scourge and minister** i.e., agent of heavenly retribution.
(By *scourge*, Hamlet also suggests that he himself will eventually suffer punishment in the
process of fulfilling heaven's will.)   **183 bestow** stow, dispose of;   **answer** account or pay for.

This° bad begins, and worse remains behind.°
One word more, good lady.

QUEEN: What shall I do?

HAMLET: Not this by no means that I bid you do:
Let the bloat° King tempt you again to bed,
Pinch wanton° on your cheek, call you his mouse,   190
And let him, for a pair of reechy° kisses,
Or paddling° in your neck with his damned fingers,
Make you to ravel all this matter out°
That I essentially am not in madness,
But mad in craft.° 'Twere good° you let him know,   195
For who that's but a Queen, fair, sober, wise,
Would from a paddock,° from a bat, a gib,°
Such dear concernings° hide? Who would do so?
No, in despite of sense and secrecy,°
Unpeg the basket° on the house's top,   200
Let the birds fly, and like the famous ape,°
To try conclusions,° in the basket creep
And break your own neck down.°

QUEEN: Be thou assured, if words be made of breath,
And breath of life, I have no life to breathe   205
What thou hast said to me.

HAMLET: I must to England. You know that?

QUEEN: Alack,
I had forgot. 'Tis so concluded on.

HAMLET: There's letters sealed, and my two schoolfellows,
Whom I will trust as I will adders fanged,   210
They bear the mandate; they must sweep my way
And marshal me to knavery.° Let it work.°
For 'tis the sport to have the enginer°
Hoist with° his own petard,° and 't shall go hard
But I will° delve one yard below their mines°   215
And blow them at the moon. O, 'tis most sweet
When in one line° two crafts° directly meet.

---

186 This i.e., the killing of Polonius;   **behind** to come.   **189 bloat** bloated.   **190 Pinch wanton**
i.e., leave his love pinches on your cheeks, branding you as wanton.   **191 reechy** dirty, filthy.
192 paddling fingering amorously.   **193 ravel . . . out** unravel, disclose.   **195 in craft** by
cunning;   **good** (said sarcastically; also the following eight lines.)   **197 paddock** toad;
gib tomcat.   **198 dear concernings** important affairs.   **199 sense and secrecy** secrecy that
common sense requires.   **200 Unpeg the basket** open the cage, i.e., let out the secret.
201 famous ape (in a story now lost.)   **202 try conclusions** test the outcome (in which the ape
apparently enters a cage from which birds have been released and then tries to fly out of the
cage as they have done, falling to its death).   **203 down** in the fall; utterly.   **211–12 sweep . . .
knavery** sweep a path before me and conduct me to some *knavery* or treachery prepared
for me;   **work** proceed.   **213 enginer** maker of military contrivances.   **214 Hoist with** blown
up by;   **petard** an explosive used to blow in a door or make a breach.   **214–15 't shall . . .
will** unless luck is against me, I will;   **mines** tunnels used in warfare to undermine the enemy's
emplacements; Hamlet will countermine by going under their mines.   **217 in one line** i.e.,
mines and countermines on a collision course, or the countermines directly below the
mines;   **crafts** acts of guile, plots.

This man shall set me packing.°
I'll lug the guts into the neighbor room.
Mother, good night indeed. This counselor   220
Is now most still, most secret, and most grave,
Who was in life a foolish prating knave.—
Come, sir, to draw toward an end° with you.—
Good night, Mother.

> *Exeunt [separately,* HAMLET *dragging in* POLONIUS].

[4.1]

Enter KING *and* QUEEN,° *with* ROSENCRANTZ *and* GUILDENSTERN.

KING: There's matter° in these sighs, these profound heaves.°
　　　You must translate; 'tis fit we understand them.
　　　Where is your son?
QUEEN: Bestow this place on us a little while.

> [*Exeunt* ROSENCRANTZ *and* GUILDENSTERN.]

　　　Ah, mine own lord, what have I seen tonight!   5
KING: What, Gertrude? How does Hamlet?
QUEEN: Mad as the sea and wind when both contend
　　　Which is the mightier. In his lawless fit,
　　　Behind the arras hearing something stir,
　　　Whips out his rapier, cries, "A rat, a rat!"   10
　　　And in this brainish apprehension° kills
　　　The unseen good old man.
KING:　　　　　　　　　　　　O heavy° deed!
　　　It had been so with us,° had we been there.
　　　His liberty is full of threats to all—
　　　To you yourself, to us, to everyone.   15
　　　Alas, how shall this bloody deed be answered?°
　　　It will be laid to us, whose providence°
　　　Should have kept short,° restrained, and out of haunt°
　　　This mad young man. But so much was our love,
　　　We would not understand what was most fit,   20
　　　But, like the owner of a foul disease,
　　　To keep it from divulging,° let it feed
　　　Even on the pith of life. Where is he gone?
QUEEN: To draw apart the body he hath killed,
　　　O'er whom his very madness, like some ore°   25
　　　Among a mineral° of metals base,
　　　Shows itself pure: 'a weeps for what is done.

218 set me packing set me to making schemes, and set me to lugging (him), and, also, send
me off in a hurry. **223 draw . . . end** finish up (with a pun on *draw*, "pull"). **[4.1] Location:**
The castle. s.d. Enter . . . Queen (Some editors argue that Gertrude never exits in 3.4 and
that the scene is continuous here, as suggested in the Folio, but the Second Quarto marks
an entrance for her and at line 35 Claudius speaks of Gertrude's *closet* as though it were
elsewhere. A short time has elapsed, during which the King has become aware of her highly
wrought emotional state.) **1 matter** significance; **heaves** heavy sighs. **11 brainish appre-**
hension headstrong conception. **12 heavy** grievous. **13 us** i.e., me. (The royal "we"; also
in line 15.) **16 answered** explained. **17 providence** foresight. **18 short** i.e., on a short
tether; **out of haunt** secluded. **22 divulging** becoming evident. **25 ore** vein of gold.
26 mineral mine.

KING: O Gertrude, come away!
  The sun no sooner shall the mountains touch
  But we will ship him hence, and this vile deed   30
  We must with all our majesty and skill
  Both countenance° and excuse.—Ho, Guildenstern!

Enter ROSENCRANTZ *and* GUILDENSTERN.

  Friends both, go join you with some further aid.
  Hamlet in madness hath Polonius slain,
  And from his mother's closet hath he dragged him. 35
  Go seek him out, speak fair, and bring the body
  Into the chapel. I pray you, haste in this.
         [*Exeunt* ROSENCRANTZ *and* GUILDENSTERN.]
  Come, Gertrude, we'll call up our wisest friends
  And let them know both what we mean to do
  And what's untimely done°.   40
  Whose whisper o'er the world's diameter,°
  As level° as the cannon to his blank,°
  Transports his poisoned shot, may miss our name
  And hit the woundless° air. O, come away!
  My soul is full of discord and dismay.   *Exeunt.* 45

[4.2]

Enter HAMLET.

HAMLET: Safely stowed.
ROSENCRANTZ, GUILDENSTERN [*within*]: Hamlet! Lord Hamlet!
HAMLET: But soft, what noise? Who calls on Hamlet? O, here they come.

Enter ROSENCRANTZ *and* GUILDENSTERN.

ROSENCRANTZ: What have you done, my lord, with the dead body?
HAMLET: Compounded it with dust, whereto 'tis kin.   5
ROSENCRANTZ: Tell us where 'tis, that we may take it thence
  And bear it to the chapel.
HAMLET: Do not believe it.
ROSENCRANTZ: Believe what?
HAMLET: That I can keep your counsel and not mine own.° Besides, to be demanded
  of° a sponge, what replication° should be made by the son of a king? 10
ROSENCRANTZ: Take you me for a sponge, my lord?
HAMLET: Ay, sir, that soaks up the King's countenance,° his rewards, his authori-
  ties.° But such officers do the King best service in the end. He keeps
  them, like an ape, an apple, in the corner of his jaw, first mouthed to be 15
  last swallowed. When he needs what you have gleaned, it is but squeezing you, and, sponge, you shall be dry again.

---

32 countenance put the best face on. **40 And . . . done** (a defective line; conjectures as to
the missing words include *So, haply, slander* [Capell and other early editors]; *For, haply,
slander* [Theobald and others]; and *So envious slander* [Jenkins].) **41 diameter** extent from
side to side. **42 As level** with as direct aim; **his blank** its target at point-blank range.
44 woundless invulnerable. **[4.2] Location: The castle.** **10 That . . . own** i.e., that I can follow your advice (by telling where the body is) and still keep my own secret. **10–11 demanded
of** questioned by; **replication** reply. **13 countenance** favor. **13–14 authorities** delegated
power, influence.

ROSENCRANTZ: I understand you not, my lord.

HAMLET: I am glad of it. A knavish speech sleeps in° a foolish ear.

ROSENCRANTZ: My lord, you must tell us where the body is and go with us to the   20
    King.

HAMLET: The body is with the King, but the King is not with the body.°
        The King is a thing—

GUILDENSTERN: A thing, my lord?

HAMLET: Of nothing.° Bring me to him. Hide fox, and all after!°   25

                                                        Exeunt [*running*].

                            [4.3]

    Enter KING, *and two or three.*

KING: I have sent to seek him, and to find the body.
        How dangerous is it that this man goes loose!
        Yet must not we put the strong law on him.
        He's loved of° the distracted° multitude,
        Who like not in their judgment, but their eyes,°   5
        And where 'tis so, th' offender's scourge° is weighed,°
        But never the offense. To bear all smooth and even,°
        This sudden sending him away must seem
        Deliberate pause.° Diseases desperate grown
        By desperate appliance° are relieved,   10
        Or not at all.

    Enter ROSENCRANTZ, GUILDENSTERN, *and all the rest.*

                            How now, what hath befall'n?

ROSENCRANTZ: Where the dead body is bestowed, my lord,
        We cannot get from him.

KING: But where is he?

ROSENCRANTZ: Without, my lord; guarded, to know your pleasure.

KING: Bring him before us.

ROSENCRANTZ: Ho! Bring in the lord.   15

    They enter [*with* HAMLET].

KING: Now, Hamlet, where's Polonius?

HAMLET: At supper.

KING: At supper? Where?

19 sleeps in has no meaning to. **22 The . . . body** (Perhaps alludes to the legal commonplace
of "the king's two bodies," which drew a distinction between the sacred office of kingship
and the particular mortal who possessed it at any given time. Hence, although Claudius'
body is necessarily a part of him, true kingship is not contained in it. Similarly, Claudius will
have Polonius' body when it is found, but there is no kingship in this business either.)
25 Of nothing (1) of no account, (2) lacking the essence of kingship, as in lines 24–25 and note;
Hide . . . after (an old signal cry in the game of hide-and-seek, suggesting that Hamlet now
runs away from them.) **[4.3] Location: The castle. 4 of** by; **distracted** fickle, unstable.
5 Who . . . eyes who choose not by judgment but by appearance. **6 scourge** punishment.
(Literally, blow with a whip.); **weighed** sympathetically considered. **7 To . . . even** to manage
the business in an unprovocative way. **9 Deliberate pause** carefully considered action.
10 appliance remedies.

HAMLET: Not where he eats, but where 'a is eaten. A certain convocation of politic
worms° are e'en° at him. Your worm° is your only emperor for diet.° We 20
fat all creatures else to fat us, and we fat ourselves for maggots. Your fat
king and your lean beggar is but variable service°—two dishes, but to
one table. That's the end.

KING: Alas, alas!

HAMLET: A man may fish with the worm that hath eat° of a king, and eat of the
fish that hath fed of that worm. 25

KING: What dost thou mean by this?

HAMLET: Nothing but to show you how a king may go a progress° through the
guts of a beggar.

KING: Where is Polonius? 30

HAMLET: In heaven. Send thither to see. If your messenger find him not there,
seek him i' th' other place yourself. But if indeed you find him not
within this month, you shall nose him as you go up the stairs into the
lobby.

KING [*to some attendants*]: Go seek him there. 35

HAMLET: 'A will stay till you come. [*Exeunt attendants.*]

KING: Hamlet, this deed, for thine especial safety—
Which we do tender,° as we dearly° grieve
For that which thou hast done—must send thee hence
With fiery quickness. Therefore prepare thyself. 40
The bark° is ready, and the wind at help,
Th' associates tend,° and everything is bent°
For England.

HAMLET: For England!

KING: Ay, Hamlet. 45

HAMLET: Good.

KING: So is it, if thou knew'st our purposes.

HAMLET: I see a cherub° that sees them. But come, for England!
Farewell, dear mother.

KING: Thy loving father, Hamlet. 50

HAMLET: My mother. Father and mother is man and wife, man and wife is one
flesh, and so, my mother. Come, for England! *Exit.*

KING: Follow him at foot;° tempt him with speed aboard.
Delay it not. I'll have him hence tonight.
Away! For everything is sealed and done 55
That else leans on° th' affair. Pray you, make haste.
[*Exeunt all but the* KING.]
And, England,° if my love thou hold'st at aught°—

19–20 politic worms crafty worms (suited to a master spy like Polonius); **e'en** even now;
Your worm your average worm. (Compare *your fat king and your lean beggar* in lines 21–22.);
diet food, eating (with a punning reference to the Diet of Worms, a famous *convocation* held
in 1521). **22 variable service** different courses of a single meal. **25 eat** eaten. (Pronounced *et*.)
28 progress royal journey of state. **38 tender** regard, hold dear; **dearly** intensely. **41 bark**
sailing vessel. **42 tend** wait; **bent** in readiness. **48 cherub** (Cherubim are angels of knowledge. Hamlet hints that both he and heaven are onto Claudius' tricks.) **53 at foot** close behind, at heel. **56 leans on** bears upon, is related to. **57 England** i.e., King of England;
at aught at any value.

As my great power thereof may give thee sense,°
Since yet thy cicatrice° looks raw and red
After the Danish sword, and thy free awe°   60
Pays homage to us—thou mayst not coldly set°
Our sovereign process,° which imports at full,°
By letters congruing° to that effect,
The present° death of Hamlet. Do it, England,
For like the hectic° in my blood he rages,   65
And thou must cure me. Till I know 'tis done,
Howe'er my haps,° my joys were ne'er begun.   *Exit.*

[4.4]

Enter FORTINBRAS *with his army over the stage.*

FORTINBRAS: Go, Captain, from me greet the Danish king.
Tell him that by his license° Fortinbras
Craves the conveyance of° a promised march
Over his kingdom. You know the rendezvous.
If that His Majesty would aught with us,   5
We shall express our duty° in his eye;°
And let him know so.
CAPTAIN: I will do 't, my lord.
FORTINBRAS: Go softly° on.   [*Exeunt all but the* CAPTAIN.]

Enter HAMLET, ROSENCRANTZ, [GUILDENSTERN,] *etc.*

HAMLET: Good sir, whose powers° are these?
CAPTAIN: They are of Norway, sir.   10
HAMLET: How purposed, sir, I pray you?
CAPTAIN: Against some part of Poland.
HAMLET: Who commands them, sir?
CAPTAIN: The nephew to old Norway, Fortinbras.   15
HAMLET: Goes it against the main° of Poland, sir,
Or for some frontier?
CAPTAIN: Truly to speak, and with no addition,°
We go to gain a little patch of ground
That hath in it no profit but the name.   20
To pay° five ducats, five, I would not farm it;°
Nor will it yield to Norway or the Pole
A ranker° rate, should it be sold in fee.°
HAMLET: Why, then the Polack never will defend it.
CAPTAIN: Yes, it is already garrisoned.   25

---

58 As . . . sense for so my great power may give you a just appreciation of the importance of valuing my love.   **59 cicatrice** scar.   **60 free awe** voluntary show of respect.   **61 coldly set** regard with indifference.   **62 process** command; **imports at full** conveys specific directions for. **63 congruing** agreeing.   **64 present** immediate.   **65 hectic** persistent fever.   **67 haps** fortunes. **[4.4] Location: The coast of Denmark.   2 license** permission.   **3 the conveyance of** escort during.   **6 duty** respect; **eye** presence.   **9 softly** slowly, circumspectly.   **10 powers** forces. **16 main** main part.   **18 addition** exaggeration.   **21 To pay** i.e., for a yearly rental of; **farm it** take a lease on it.   **23 ranker** higher; **in fee** fee simple, outright.

HAMLET: Two thousand souls and twenty thousand ducats
Will not debate° the question of this straw.°
This is th' impostume° of much wealth and peace,
That inward breaks, and shows no cause without
Why the man dies. I humbly thank you, sir.   30
CAPTAIN: God b' wi' you, sir.   [*Exit.*]
ROSENCRANTZ: Will 't please you go, my lord?
HAMLET: I'll be with you straight. Go a little before.

[*Exeunt all except* HAMLET.]

How all occasions do inform against° me
And spur my dull revenge! What is a man,   35
If his chief good and market of° his time
Be but to sleep and feed? A beast, no more.
Sure he that made us with such large discourse,°
Looking before and after,° gave us not
That capability and godlike reason   40
To fust° in us unused. Now, whether it be
Bestial oblivion,° or some craven° scruple
Of thinking too precisely° on th' event°—
A thought which, quartered, hath but one part wisdom
And ever three parts coward—I do not know   45
Why yet I live to say "This thing's to do,"
Sith° I have cause, and will, and strength, and means
To do 't. Examples gross° as earth exhort me:
Witness this army of such mass and charge,°
Led by a delicate and tender° prince,   50
Whose spirit with divine ambition puffed
Makes mouths° at the invisible event,°
Exposing what is mortal and unsure
To all that fortune, death, and danger dare,°
Even for an eggshell. Rightly to be great   55
Is not to stir without great argument,
But greatly to find quarrel in a straw
When honor's at the stake.° How stand I, then,
That have a father killed, a mother stained,
Excitements of° my reason and my blood,   60
And let all sleep, while to my shame I see
The imminent death of twenty thousand men
That for a fantasy° and trick° of fame
Go to their graves like beds, fight for a plot°

27 debate . . . straw settle this trifling matter.   **28 impostume** abscess.   **34 inform against**
denounce, betray; take shape against.   **36 market of** profit of, compensation for.   **38 discourse**
power of reasoning.   **39 Looking before and after** able to review past events and anticipate
the future.   **41 fust** grow moldy.   **42 oblivion** forgetfulness;   **craven** cowardly.   **43 precisely**
scrupulously;   **event** outcome.   **47 Sith** since.   **48 gross** obvious.   **49 charge** expense.
50 delicate and tender of fine and youthful qualities.   **52 Makes mouths** makes scornful faces;
invisible event unforeseeable outcome.   **54 dare** could do (to him).   **55–58 Rightly . . . stake**
true greatness does not normally consist of rushing into action over some trivial provocation; however, when one's honor is involved, even a trifling insult requires that one respond greatly (?);
at the stake (A metaphor from gambling or bear-baiting.)   **60 Excitements of** promptings by.
63 fantasy fanciful caprice, illusion;   **trick** trifle, deceit.   **64 plot** plot of ground.

Whereon the numbers cannot try the cause,°   65
Which is not tomb enough and continent°
To hide the slain? O, from this time forth
My thoughts be bloody or be nothing worth!   *Exit.*

[4.5]

Enter HORATIO, [QUEEN] GERTRUDE, *and a* GENTLEMAN.

QUEEN: I will not speak with her.
GENTLEMAN: She is importunate,
    Indeed distract.° Her mood will needs be pitied.
QUEEN: What would she have?
GENTLEMAN: She speaks much of her father, says she hears
    There's tricks° i' the world, and hems,° and beats her heart,°   5
    Spurns enviously at straws,° speaks things in doubt°
    That carry but half sense. Her speech is nothing,
    Yet the unshapèd use° of it doth move
    The hearers to collection;° they yawn° at it,
    And botch° the words up fit to their own thoughts,   10
    Which,° as her winks and nods and gestures yield° them,
    Indeed would make one think there might be thought,°
    Though nothing sure, yet much unhappily.°
HORATIO: 'Twere good she were spoken with, for she may strew
    Dangerous conjectures in ill-breeding° minds.   15
QUEEN: Let her come in.   [*Exit* GENTLEMAN.]
    [*Aside.*] To my sick soul, as sin's true nature is,
    Each toy° seems prologue to some great amiss.°
    So full of artless jealousy is guilt,
    It spills itself in fearing to be spilt.°   20

Enter OPHELIA° [*distracted*].

OPHELIA: Where is the beauteous majesty of Denmark?
QUEEN: How now, Ophelia?
OPHELIA [*she sings*]:

    "How should I your true love know
        From another one?
    By his cockle hat° and staff,   25
        And his sandal shoon."°

QUEEN: Alas, sweet lady, what imports this song?

---

65 Whereon . . . cause on which there is insufficient room for the soldiers needed to engage
in a military contest.   **66 continent** receptacle; container.   **[4.5] Location: The castle.**
2 distract distracted.   **5 tricks** deceptions;   **hems** makes "hmm" sounds;   **heart** i.e., breast.
6 Spurns . . . straws kicks spitefully, takes offense at trifles;   **in doubt** obscurely.   **9 unshapèd
use** incoherent manner.   **9 collection** inference, a guess at some sort of meaning;   **yawn** gape,
wonder; grasp. (The Folio reading, *aim*, is possible.)   **10 botch** patch.   **11 Which** which words;
yield deliver, represent.   **12 thought** intended.   **13 unhappily** unpleasantly near the truth,
shrewdly.   **15 ill-breeding** prone to suspect the worst and to make mischief.   **18 toy** trifle;
amiss calamity.   **19–20 So . . . split** guilt is so full of suspicion that it unskilfully betrays itself
in fearing betrayal.   **s.d. Enter Ophelia** (In the First Quarto, Ophelia enters, "playing on a lute, and
her hair down, singing.")   **25 cockle hat** hat with cockle-shell stuck in it as a sign that the wearer
had been a pilgrim to the shrine of Saint James of Compostela in Spain.   **26 shoon** shoes.

OPHELIA: Say you? Nay, pray you, mark.

> "He is dead and gone, lady,   [*Song.*]
>> He is dead and gone;   30
> At his head a grass-green turf,
>> At his heels a stone."
>
> O, ho!

QUEEN: Nay, but Ophelia—

OPHELIA: Pray you, mark.   [*Sings.*] 35

> "White his shroud as the mountain snow"—
>
> *Enter* KING.

QUEEN: Alas, look here, my lord.

OPHELIA:

> "Larded° with sweet flowers;   [*Song.*]
> Which bewept to the ground did not go
> With true-love showers."°   40

KING: How do you, pretty lady?

OPHELIA: Well, God 'ild° you! They say the owl° was a baker's daughter. Lord, we know what we are, but know not what we may be. God be at your table!

KING: Conceit° upon her father.   45

OPHELIA: Pray let's have no words of this; but when they ask you what it means, say you this:

> "Tomorrow is Saint Valentine's day,   [*Song.*]
>> All in the morning betime,
> And I a maid at your window,   50
>> To be your Valentine.
> Then up he rose, and donned his clothes,
>> And dupped° the chamber door,
> Let in the maid, that out a maid
>> Never departed more."   55

KING: Pretty Ophelia—

OPHELIA: Indeed, la, without an oath, I'll make an end on 't: [*Sings.*]

> "By Gis° and by Saint Charity,
>> Alack, and fie for shame!   60
> Young men will do 't, if they come to 't;
>> By Cock,° they are to blame.
> Quoth she, 'Before you tumbled me,
>> You promised me to wed.'"
>
> He answers:
>
> "'So would I ha' done, by yonder sun,   65
> An° thou hadst not come to my bed.'"

---

38 Larded decorated. **40 showers** i.e., tears. **42 God 'ild** god yield or reward; **owl** (refers to a legend about a baker's daughter who was turned into an owl for being ungenerous when Jesus begged a loaf of bread.) **45 Conceit** brooding. **49 betime** early. **53 dupped** did up, opened. **58 Gis** Jesus. **61 Cock** (a perversion of "God" in oaths; here also with a quibble on the slang word for penis.) **66 An** if.

KING: How long hath she been thus?

OPHELIA: I hope all will be well. We must be patient, but I cannot choose but
    weep to think they would lay him i' the cold ground. My brother shall
    know of it. And so I thank you for your good counsel. Come, my
    coach! Good night, ladies, good night, sweet ladies, good night, good   70
    night.   [*Exit.*]

KING [*to* HORATIO]: Follow her close. Give her good watch, I pray you.

                                                   [*Exit* HORATIO.]

    O, this is the poison of deep grief; it springs
    All from her father's death—and now behold!   75
    O Gertrude, Gertrude,
    When sorrows come, they come not single spies,°
    But in battalions. First, her father slain;
    Next, your son gone, and he most violent author
    Of his own just remove;° the people muddied,°   80
    Thick and unwholesome in their thoughts and whispers
    For good Polonius' death—and we have done but greenly,°
    In hugger-mugger° to inter him; poor Ophelia
    Divided from herself and her fair judgment,
    Without the which we are pictures or mere beasts;   85
    Last, and as much containing° as all these,
    Her brother is in secret come from France,
    Feeds on this wonder, keeps himself in clouds,°
    And wants° not buzzers° to infect his ear
    With pestilent speeches of his father's death,   90
    Wherein necessity,° of matter beggared,°
    Will nothing stick our person to arraign
    In ear and ear.° O my dear Gertrude, this,
    Like to a murdering piece,° in many places
    Gives me superfluous death.°   *A noise within.* 95

QUEEN: Alack, what noise is this?

KING: Attend!°
    Where is my Switzers?° Let them guard the door.

    Enter a MESSENGER.

    What is the matter?

MESSENGER: Save yourself, my lord!
    The ocean, overpeering of his list,°   100
    Eats not the flats° with more impetuous° haste
    Than young Laertes, in a riotous head,°
    O'erbears your officers. The rabble call him lord,

---

77 spies scouts sent in advance of the main force. **80 remove** removal; **muddied** stirred up,
confused. **82 greenly** in an inexperienced way, foolishly. **83 hugger-mugger** secret haste.
86 as much containing as full of serious matter. **88 Feeds . . . clouds** feeds his resentment
or shocked grievance, holds himself inscrutable and aloof amid all this rumor. **89 wants** lacks;
buzzers gossipers, informers. **91 necessity** i.e., the need to invent some plausible explanation;
of matter beggared unprovided with facts. **92–93 Will . . . ear** will not hesitate to accuse my
(royal) person in everybody's ears. **94 murdering piece** cannon loaded so as to scatter its shot.
95 Gives . . . death kills me over and over. **97 Attend** i.e., guard me. **98 Switzers** Swiss
guards, mercenaries. **100 overpeering of his list** overflowing its shore, boundary.
101 flats i.e., flatlands near shore; **impetuous** violent. (Perhaps also with the meaning of
impiteous [*impitious*, Q2], "pitiless.") **102 head** insurrection.

And, as° the world were now but to begin,
Antiquity forgot, custom not known, 105
The ratifiers and props of every word,°
They cry, "Choose we! Laertes shall be king!"
Caps,° hands, and tongues applaud it to the clouds,
"Laertes shall be king, Laertes king!"

QUEEN: How cheerfully on the false trail they cry! *A noise within.* 110
    O, this is counter,° you false Danish dogs!

    Enter LAERTES *with others.*

KING: The doors are broke.

LAERTES: Where is this King?—Sirs, stand you all without.

ALL: No, let's come in.

LAERTES: I pray you, give me leave. 115

ALL: We will, we will.

LAERTES: I thank you. Keep the door. [*Exeunt followers.*] O thou vile king,
    Give me my father!

QUEEN [*restraining him*]: Calmly, good Laertes.

LAERTES: That drop of blood that's calm proclaims me bastard, 120
    Cries cuckold to my father, brands the harlot
    Even here, between° the chaste unsmirchèd brow
    Of my true mother.

KING: What is the cause, Laertes,
    That thy rebellion looks so giantlike?
    Let him go, Gertrude. Do not fear our° person. 125
    There's such divinity doth hedge° a king
    That treason can but peep to what it would,°
    Acts little of his will.° Tell me, Laertes,
    Why thou art thus incensed. Let him go, Gertrude.
    Speak, man.

LAERTES: Where is my father?

KING: Dead. 130

QUEEN: But not by him.

KING: Let him demand his fill.

LAERTES: How came he dead? I'll not be juggled with.°
    To hell, allegiance! Vows, to the blackest devil!
    Conscience and grace, to the profoundest pit!
    I dare damnation. To this point I stand,° 135
    That both the worlds I give to negligence,°
    Let come what comes, only I'll be revenged
    Most throughly° for my father.

KING: Who shall stay you?

---

104 as as if. **106 The ratifiers . . . word** i.e., *antiquity* (or tradition) and *custom* ought to confirm (*ratify*) and underprop our every word or promise. **108 Caps** (The caps are thrown in the air.) **111 counter** (a hunting term, meaning to follow the trail in a direction opposite to that which the game has taken.) **122 between** in the middle of. **125 fear our** fear for my. **126 hedge** protect, as with a surrounding barrier. **127 can . . . would** can only peep furtively, as through a barrier, at what it would intend. **128 Acts . . . will** (but) performs little of what it intends. **132 juggled with** cheated, deceived. **135 To . . . stand** I am resolved in this. **136 both . . . negligence** i.e. both this world and the next are of no consequence to me. **138 throughly** thoroughly.

LAERTES: My will, not all the world's.°   140
          And for° my means, I'll husband them so well
          They shall go far with little.

KING: Good Laertes,
          If you desire to know the certainty
          Of your dear father, is 't writ in your revenge
          That, swoopstake,° you will draw both friend and foe,   145
          Winner and loser?

LAERTES: None but his enemies.

KING: Will you know them, then?

LAERTES: To his good friends thus wide I'll ope my arms,
          And like the kind life-rendering pelican°   150
          Repast° them with my blood.

KING: Why, now you speak
          Like a good child and a true gentleman.
          That I am guiltless of your father's death,
          And am most sensibly° in grief for it,
          It shall as level° to your judgment 'pear   155
          As day does to your eye.   *A noise within.*

LAERTES: How now, what noise is that?
          Enter OPHELIA.

KING: Let her come in.

LAERTES: O heat, dry up my brains! Tears seven times salt
          Burn out the sense and virtue° of mine eye!
          By heaven, thy madness shall be paid with weight°   160
          Till our scale turn the beam.° O rose of May!
          Dear maid, kind sister, sweet Ophelia!
          O heavens, is 't possible a young maid's wits
          Should be as mortal as an old man's life?
          Nature is fine in° love, and where 'tis fine   165
          It sends some precious instance° of itself
          After the thing it loves.°

OPHELIA: *[Song.]*

          "They bore him barefaced on the bier,
              Hey non nonny, nonny, hey nonny,
          And in his grave rained many a tear—"   170

          Fare you well, my dove!

LAERTES: Hadst thou thy wits and didst persuade° revenge,
          It could not move thus.

---

140 My will . . . world's I'll stop (*stay*) when my will is accomplished, not for anyone else's.
141 for as for. **145 swoopstake** i.e., indiscriminately. (Literally, taking all stakes on the gambling table at once. *Draw* is also a gambling term, meaning "taken from.") **150 pelican** (refers to the belief that the female pelican fed its young with its own blood.) **151 Repast** feed.
154 sensibly feelingly. **155 level** plain. **159 virtue** faculty, power. **160 paid with weight** repaid, avenged equally or more. **161 beam** crossbar of a balance. **165 fine in** refined by.
166 instance token. **167 After . . . loves** i.e., into the grave, along with Polonius. **172 persuade** argue cogently for.

OPHELIA: You must sing "A-down a-down," and you "call him a-down-a."°
　　　　O, how the wheel° becomes it! It is the false steward° that stole his
　　　　master's daughter.　　　　　　　　　　　　　　　　　　　　175
LAERTES: This nothing's more than matter.°
OPHELIA: There's rosemary,° that's for remembrance; pray you, love, remember.
　　　　And there is pansies;° that's for thoughts.
LAERTES: A document° in madness, thoughts and remembrance fitted.　　　180
OPHELIA: There's fennel° for you, and columbines.° There's rue° for you, and
　　　　here's some for me; we may call it herb of grace o' Sundays. You must
　　　　wear your rue with a difference.° There's a daisy.° I would give you
　　　　some violets,° but they withered all when my father died. They say 'a
　　　　made a good end—　　　　　　　　　　　　　　　　　　185

　　　[*Sings.*] "For bonny sweet Robin is all my joy."

LAERTES: Thought° and affliction, passion,° hell itself,
　　　　She turns to favor° and to prettiness.
OPHELIA:　　　　　　　　　　　　　　　　　　　　　　[*Song.*]
　　　"And will 'a not come again?　　　　　　　　　　　　190
　　　And will 'a not come again?
　　　　No, no, he is dead.
　　　　Go to thy deathbed,
　　　He never will come again.

　　　"His beard was as white as snow,
　　　All flaxen was his poll.°　　　　　　　　　　　　　195
　　　　He is gone, he is gone,
　　　　And we cast away moan.
　　　God ha' mercy on his soul!"

　　　And of all Christian souls, I pray God. God b' wi' you.
　　　　　　　　　　　　　　　　[*Exit, followed by* GERTRUDE.]
LAERTES: Do you see this, O God?　　　　　　　　　　　　200
KING: Laertes, I must commune with your grief,
　　　　Or you deny me right. Go but apart,
　　　　Make choice of whom° your wisest friends you will,
　　　　And they shall hear and judge twixt you and me.
　　　　If by direct or by collateral hand°　　　　　　　　205
　　　　They find us touched,° we will our kingdom give,

174 You . . . a-down-a (Ophelia assigns the singing of refrains, like her own "Hey non nonny," to others present.) **175 wheel** spinning wheel as accompaniment to the song, or refrain; **false steward** (The story is unknown.) **177 This . . . matter** This seeming nonsense is more eloquent than sane utterance. **178 rosemary** (used as a symbol of remembrance both at weddings and at funerals.) **179 pansies** (emblems of love and courtship; perhaps from French *pensées,* "thoughts.") **180 document** instruction, lesson. **181 fennel** (emblem of flattery.); **columbines** (emblems of unchastity or ingratitude.); **rue** (emblem of repentance—a signification that is evident in its popular name, *herb of grace.*) **183 with a difference** (a device used in heraldry to distinguish one family from another on the coat of arms, here suggesting that Ophelia and the others have different causes of sorrow and repentance; perhaps with a play on *rue* in the sense of "ruth," "pity."); **daisy** (emblem of dissembling, faithlessness.) **184 violets** (emblems of faithfulness.) **187 Thought** melancholy; **passion** suffering. **188 favor** grace, beauty. **195 poll** head. **203 whom** whichever of. **205 collateral hand** indirect agency. **206 us touched** me implicated.

Our crown, our life, and all that we call ours
To you in satisfaction; but if not,
Be you content to lend your patience to us,
And we shall jointly labor with your soul   210
To give it due content.
LAERTES: Let this be so.
His means of death, his obscure funeral—
No trophy,° sword, nor hatchment° o'er his bones,
No noble rite, nor formal ostentation°—
Cry to be heard, as 'twere from heaven to earth,   215
That° I must call 't in question.°
KING: So you shall,
And where th' offense is, let the great ax fall.
I pray you, go with me.

Exeunt.

[4.6]°

Enter HORATIO *and others.*

HORATIO: What are they that would speak with me?
GENTLEMAN: Seafaring men, sir. They say they have letters for you.
HORATIO: Let them come in.

[*Exit* GENTLEMAN.]

I do not know from what part of the world
I should be greeted, if not from Lord Hamlet.   5

Enter Sailors.

FIRST SAILOR: God bless you, sir.
HORATIO: Let him bless thee too.
FIRST SAILOR: 'A shall, sir, an 't° please him. There's a letter for you, sir—it came
    from th' ambassador° that was bound for England—if your name be
    Horatio, as I am let to know it is.   [*He gives a letter.*]   10
HORATIO [*reads*]: "Horatio, when thou shalt have overlooked° this, give these fel-
    lows some means° to the King; they have letters for him. Ere we were
    two days old at sea, a pirate of very warlike appointment° gave us chase.
    Finding ourselves too slow of sail, we put on a compelled valor, and in   15
    the grapple I boarded them. On the instant they got clear of our ship, so
    I alone became their prisoner. They have dealt with me like thieves of
    mercy,° but they knew what they did: I am to do a good turn for them.
    Let the King have the letters I have sent, and repair° thou to me with as
    much speed as thou wouldest fly death. I have words to speak in thine
    ear will make thee dumb, yet are they much too light for the bore° of the   20
    matter. These good fellows will bring thee where I am. Rosencrantz and
    Guildenstern hold their course for England. Of them I have much to tell
    thee. Farewell.

---

213 trophy memorial;   **hatchment** tablet displaying the armorial bearings of a deceased person.
214 ostentation ceremony.   **216 That** so that;   **call 't in question** demand an explanation.
[4.6] Location: The castle.   8 an 't if it.   **9 th' ambassador** (evidently Hamlet. The sailor is
being circumspect.)   **11 overlooked** looked over.   **12 means** means of access.   **13 appointment**
equipage.   **16–17 thieves of mercy** merciful thieves.   **18 repair** come.   **20 bore** caliber, i.e.,
importance.

He that thou knowest thine, Hamlet."
Come, I will give you way° for these your letters,   25
And do 't the speedier that you may direct me
To him from whom you brought them.   *Exeunt.*

[4.7]

Enter KING *and* LAERTES.

KING: Now must your conscience my acquittance seal,°
    And you must put me in your heart for friend,
    Sith° you have heard, and with a knowing ear,
    That he which hath your noble father slain
    Pursued my life.
LAERTES: It well appears. But tell me   5
    Why you proceeded not against these feats°
    So crimeful and so capital° in nature,
    As by your safety, greatness, wisdom, all things else,
    You mainly° were stirred up.
KING: O, for two special reasons,   10
    Which may to you perhaps seem much unsinewed,°
    But yet to me they're strong. The Queen his mother
    Lives almost by his looks, and for myself—
    My virtue or my plague, be it either which—
    She is so conjunctive° to my life and soul   15
    That, as the star moves not but in his° sphere,°
    I could not but by her. The other motive
    Why to a public count° I might not go
    Is the great love the general gender° bear him,
    Who, dipping all his faults in their affection,   20
    Work° like the spring° that turneth wood to stone,
    Convert his gyves° to graces, so that my arrows,
    Too slightly timbered° for so loud° a wind,
    Would have reverted° to my bow again
    But not where I had aimed them.   25
LAERTES: And so have I a noble father lost,
    A sister driven into desperate terms,°
    Whose worth, if praises may go back° again,
    Stood challenger on mount° of all the age
    For her perfections. But my revenge will come.   30
KING: Break not your sleeps for that. You must not think
    That we are made of stuff so flat and dull

---

25 way means of access. **[4.7] Location: The castle.** **1 my acquittance seal** confirm or acknowledge my innocence. **3 Sith** since. **6 feats** acts. **7 capital** punishable by death. **9 mainly** greatly. **11 unsinewed** weak. **15 conjunctive** closely united. (An astronomical metaphor.) **16 his** its; **sphere** one of the hollow spheres in which, according to Ptolematic astronomy, the planets were supposed to move. **18 count** account, reckoning, indictment. **19 general gender** common people. **21 Work** operate, act; **spring** i.e., a spring with such a concentration of lime that it coats a piece of wood with limestone, in effect gilding and petrifying it. **22 gyves** fetters (which, gilded by the people's praise, would look like badges of honor). **23 slightly timbered** light; **loud** (suggesting public outcry on Hamlet's behalf). **24 reverted** returned. **27 terms** state, condition. **28 go back** i.e., recall what she was. **29 on mount** set up on high.

That we can let our beard be shook with danger
And think it pastime. You shortly shall hear more.
I loved your father, and we love ourself;   35
And that, I hope, will teach you to imagine—

Enter a MESSENGER *with letters.*

How now? What news?

MESSENGER: Letters, my lord, from Hamlet:
    This to Your Majesty, this to the queen.   *[He gives letters.]*

KING: From Hamlet? Who brought them?   40

MESSENGER: Sailors, my lord, they say. I saw them not.
    They were given me by Claudio. He received them
    Of him that brought them.

KING: Laertes, you shall hear them.—
    Leave us.   *[Exit* MESSENGER.*]*
    [He reads.] "High and mighty, you shall know I am set naked° on your
    kingdom. Tomorrow shall I beg leave to see your kingly eyes, when I
    shall, first asking your pardon,° thereunto recount the occasion of my
    sudden and more strange return.   Hamlet."   45
    What should this mean? Are all the rest come back?
    Or is it some abuse,° and no such thing?°   50

LAERTES: Know you the hand?

KING: 'Tis Hamlet's character.° "Naked!"
    And in a postscript here he says "alone."
    Can you devise° me?

LAERTES: I am lost in it, my lord. But let him come.
    It warms the very sickness in my heart   55
    That I shall live and tell him to his teeth,
    "Thus didst thou."°

KING: If it be so, Laertes—
    As how should it be so? How otherwise?°—
    Will you be ruled by me?

LAERTES: Ay, my lord,
    So° you will not o'errule me to a peace.   60

KING: To thine own peace. If he be now returned,
    As checking at° his voyage, and that° he means
    No more to undertake it, I will work him
    To an exploit, now ripe in my device,°
    Under the which he shall not choose but fall;   65
    And for his death no wind of blame shall breathe,
    But even his mother shall uncharge the practice°
    And call it accident.

---

45 naked destitute, unarmed, without following. **47 pardon** permission. **50 abuse** deceit;
no such thing not what it appears. **51 character** handwriting. **53 devise** explain to.
57 Thus didst thou i.e., here's for what you did to my father. **58 As . . . otherwise** How can
this (Hamlet's return) be true? Yet how otherwise than true (since we have the evidence of his letter)?
60 So provided that. **62 checking at** i.e., turning aside from (like a falcon leaving the quarry
to fly at a chance bird); **that** if. **64 device** devising, invention. **67 uncharge the practice**
acquit the stratagem of being a plot.

LAERTES: My lord, I will be ruled,
        The rather if you could devise it so
        That I might be the organ.°

KING: It falls right.   70
        You have been talked of since your travel much,
        And that in Hamlet's hearing, for a quality
        Wherein they say you shine. Your sum of parts°
        Did not together pluck such envy from him
        As did that one, and that, in my regard,   75
        Of the unworthiest siege.°

LAERTES: What part is that, my lord?

KING: A very ribbon in the cap of youth,
        Yet needful too, for youth no less becomes°
        The light and careless livery that it wears   80
        Than settled age his sables° and his weeds°
        Importing health and graveness.° Two months since
        Here was a gentleman of Normandy.
        I have seen myself, and served against, the French,
        And they can well° on horseback, but this gallant   85
        Had witchcraft in 't; he grew unto his seat,
        And to such wondrous doing brought his horse
        As had he been incorpsed and demi-natured°
        With the brave beast. So far he topped° my thought
        That I in forgery° of shapes and tricks   90
        Come short of what he did.

LAERTES: A Norman was 't?

KING: A Norman.

LAERTES: Upon my life, Lamord.

KING: The very same.

LAERTES: I know him well. He is the brooch° indeed
        And gem of all the nation.   95

KING: He made confession° of you,
        And gave you such a masterly report
        For art and exercise in your defense,°
        And for your rapier most especial,
        That he cried out 'twould be a sight indeed   100
        If one could match you. Th' escrimers° of their nation,
        He swore, had neither motion, guard, nor eye
        If you opposed them. Sir, this report of his
        Did Hamlet so envenom with his envy
        That he could nothing do but wish and beg   105
        Your sudden° coming o'er, to play° with you.
        Now, out of this—

---

70 organ agent, instrument.   **73 Your . . . parts** i.e., all your other virtues.   **76 unworthiest
siege** least important rank.   **79 no less becomes** is no less suited by.   **81 his sables** its
rich robes furred with sable; **weeds** garments.   **82 Importing . . . graveness** signifying a
concern for health and dignified prosperity; also, giving an impression of comfortable prosperity.

85 can well are skilled.   **88 As . . . demi-natured** as if he had been of one body and nearly of one
nature (like the centaur).   **89 topped** surpassed.   **90 forgery** imagining.   **94 brooch** ornament.
96 confession testimonial, admission of superiority.   **98 For . . . defense** with respect to your skill
and practice with your weapon.   **101 escrimers** fencers.   **106 sudden** immediate; **play** fence.

LAERTES: What out of this, my lord?
KING: Laertes, was your father dear to you?
            Or are you like the painting of a sorrow,
            A face without a heart?
LAERTES: Why ask you this?   110
KING: Not that I think you did not love your father,
            But that I know love is begun by time,°
            And that I see, in passages of proof,°
            Time qualifies° the spark and fire of it.
            There lives within the very flame of love   115
            A kind of wick or snuff° that will abate it,
            And nothing is at a like goodness still,°
            For goodness, growing to a pleurisy,°
            Dies in his own too much.° That° we would do,
            We should do when we would; for this "would" changes   120
            And hath abatements° and delays as many
            As there are tongues, are hands, are accidents,°
            And then this "should" is like a spendthrift sigh,°
            That hurts by easing.° But, to the quick o' th' ulcer:°
            Hamlet comes back. What would you undertake   125
            To show yourself in deed your father's son
            More than in words?
LAERTES: To cut his throat i' the church.
KING: No place, indeed, should murder sanctuarize;°
            Revenge should have no bounds. But good Laertes,
            Will you do this,° keep close within your chamber.   130
            Hamlet returned shall know you are come home.
            We'll put on those shall° praise your excellence
            And set a double varnish on the fame
            The Frenchman gave you, bring you in fine° together,
            And wager on your heads. He, being remiss,°   135
            Most generous,° and free from all contriving,
            Will not peruse the foils, so that with ease,
            Or with a little shuffling, you may choose
            A sword unbated,° and in a pass of practice°
            Requite him for your father.

---

112 begun by time i.e., created by the right circumstance and hence subject to change.
113 passages of proof actual instances that prove it.   **114 qualifies** weakens, moderates.
116 snuff the charred part of a candlewick.   **117 nothing . . . still** nothing remains at a constant level of perfection.   **118 pleurisy** excess, plethora. (Literally, a chest inflammation.)
119 in . . . much of its own excess;   **That** that which.   **121 abatements** diminutions.
122 As . . . accidents as there are tongues to dissuade, hands to prevent, and chance events to intervene.   **123 spendthrift sigh** (an allusion to the belief that sighs draw blood from the heart.)
124 hurts by easing i.e., costs the heart blood and wastes precious opportunity even while it affords emotional relief;   **quick o' th' ulcer** i.e., heart of the matter.   **128 sanctuarize** protect from punishment. (Alludes to the right of sanctuary with which certain religious places were invested.)   **130 Will you do this** if you wish to do this.   **132 put on those shall** arrange for some to.   **134 in fine** finally.   **135 remiss** negligently unsuspicious.   **136 generous** nobleminded.   **139 unbated** not blunted, having no button;   **pass of practice** treacherous thrust.

LAERTES: I will do 't, 140

And for that purpose I'll anoint my sword.
I bought an unction° of a mountebank°
So mortal that, but dip a knife in it,
Where it draws blood no cataplasm° so rare,
Collected from all simples° that have virtue° 145
Under the moon,° can save the thing from death
That is but scratched withal. I'll touch my point
With this contagion, that if I gall° him slightly,
It may be death.

KING: Let's further think of this, 150

Weigh what convenience both of time and means
May fit us to our shape.° If this should fail,
And that our drift look through our bad performance,°
'Twere better not assayed. Therefore this project
Should have a back or second, that might hold 155
If this did blast in proof.° Soft, let me see.
We'll make a solemn wager on your cunnings°—
I ha 't!
When in your motion you are hot and dry—
As° make your bouts more violent to that end— 160
And that he calls for drink, I'll have prepared him
A chalice for the nonce,° whereon but sipping,
If he by chance escape your venomed stuck,°
Our purpose may hold there. [*A cry within.*] But stay, what noise?

Enter QUEEN.

QUEEN: One woe doth tread upon another's heel, 165

So fast they follow. Your sister's drowned, Laertes.

LAERTES: Drowned! O, where?

QUEEN: There is a willow grows askant° the brook,

That shows his hoar leaves° in the glassy stream;
Therewith fantastic garlands did she make 170
Of crowflowers, nettles, daisies, and long purples,°
That liberal° shepherds give a grosser name,°
But our cold° maids do dead men's fingers call them.
There on the pendent° boughs her crownet° weeds
Clamb'ring to hang, an envious sliver° broke, 175
When down her weedy° trophies and herself

---

142 unction ointment; **mountebank** quack doctor. **144 cataplasm** plaster or poultice. **145 simples** herbs; **virtue** potency. **146 Under the moon** i.e., anywhere (with reference perhaps to the belief that herbs gathered at night had a special power). **148 gall** graze, wound. **152 shape** part we propose to act. **153 drift . . . performance** intention should be made visible by our bungling. **156 blast in proof** burst in the test (like a cannon). **157 cunnings** respective skills. **160 As** i.e., and you should. **162 nonce** occasion. **163 stuck** thrust. (From *stoccado,* a fencing term.) **168 askant** aslant. **169 hoar leaves** white or gray undersides of the leaves. **171 long purples** early purple orchids. **172 liberal** free-spoken; **a grosser name** (the testicle-resembling tubers of the orchid, which also in some cases resemble *dead men's fingers,* have earned various slang names like "dogstones" and "cullions.") **173 cold** chaste. **174 pendent** over-hanging; **crownet** made into a chaplet or coronet. **175 envious sliver** malicious branch. **176 weedy** i.e., of plants.

Fell in the weeping brook. Her clothes spread wide,
And mermaidlike awhile they bore her up,
Which time she chanted snatches of old lauds,°
As one incapable of° her own distress,   180
Or like a creature native and endued°
Unto that element. But long it could not be
Till that her garments, heavy with their drink,
Pulled the poor wretch from her melodious lay
To muddy death.

LAERTES: Alas, then she is drowned?   185
QUEEN: Drowned, drowned.
LAERTES: Too much of water hast thou, poor Ophelia,
And therefore I forbid my tears. But yet
It is our trick;° nature her custom holds,
Let shame say what it will. [*He weeps.*] When these are gone,   190
The woman will be out.° Adieu, my lord.
I have a speech of fire that fain would blaze,
But that this folly douts° it.   *Exit.*
KING: Let's follow, Gertrude.
How much I had to do to calm his rage!
Now fear I this will give it start again;   195
Therefore let's follow.   *Exeunt.*

[5.1]

Enter two CLOWNS° [*with spades and mattocks*].

FIRST CLOWN: Is she to be buried in Christian burial, when she willfully seeks her
    own salvation?°
SECOND CLOWN: I tell thee she is; therefore make her grave straight.° The
    crowner° hath sat on her,° and finds it° Christian burial.
FIRST CLOWN: How can that be, unless she drowned herself in her own defense?   5
SECOND CLOWN: Why, 'tis found so.°
FIRST CLOWN: It must be *se offendendo,*° it cannot be else. For here lies the point:
    if I drown myself wittingly, it argues an act, and an act hath three
    branches—it is to act, to do, and to perform. Argal,° she drowned herself
    wittingly.   10
SECOND CLOWN: Nay, but hear you, goodman° delver—
FIRST CLOWN: Give me leave. Here lies the water; good. Here stands the man;
    good. If the man go to this water and drown himself, it is, will he, nill he,°
    he goes, mark you that. But if the water come to him and drown him, he
    drowns not himself. Argal, he that is not guilty of his own death shortens   15
    not his own life.

179 lauds hymns.   **180 incapable of** lacking capacity to apprehend.   **181 endued** adapted by
nature.   **189 It is our trick** i.e., weeping is our natural way (when sad).   **190–91 When . . . out**
When my tears are all shed, the woman in me will be expended, satisfied.   **193 douts** extinguishes.
(The Second Quarto reads "drowns.")   **[5.1] Location: A churchyard.   s.d. Clowns** rustics.
2 salvation (a blunder for "damnation," or perhaps a suggestion that Ophelia was taking her own
shortcut to heaven.)   **3 straight** straightway, immediately. (But with a pun on *strait,* "narrow.")
4 crowner coroner;   **sat on her** conducted an inquest on her case;   **finds it** gives his official
verdict that her means of death was consistent with.   **6 found so** determined so in the coroner's
verdict.   **7 se offendendo** (a comic mistake for *se defendendo,* a term used in verdicts of justifiable
homicide.)   **9 Argal** (corruption of *ergo,* "therefore.")   **11 goodman** (an honorific title often
used with the name of a profession or craft.)   **13 will he, nill he** whether he will or no, willy-nilly.

SECOND CLOWN: But is this law?

FIRST CLOWN: Ay, marry, is 't—crowner's quest° law.

SECOND CLOWN: Will you ha' the truth on 't? If this had not been a gentlewoman, she should have been buried out o' Christian burial.

FIRST CLOWN: Why, there thou sayst.° And the more pity that great folk should have countenance° in this world to drown or hang themselves, more than their even-Christian.° Come, my spade. There is no ancient° gentlemen but gardeners, ditchers, and grave makers. They hold up° Adam's profession.

SECOND CLOWN: Was he a gentleman?

FIRST CLOWN: 'A was the first that ever bore arms.°

SECOND CLOWN: Why, he had none.

FIRST CLOWN: What, art a heathen? How dost thou understand the Scripture? The Scripture says Adam digged. Could he dig without arms?° I'll put another question to thee. If thou answerest me not to the purpose, confess thyself°—

SECOND CLOWN: Go to.

FIRST CLOWN: What is he that builds stronger than either the mason, the shipwright, or the carpenter?

SECOND CLOWN: The gallows maker, for that frame° outlives a thousand tenants.

FIRST CLOWN: I like thy wit well, in good faith. The gallows does well.° But how does it well? It does well to those that do ill. Now thou dost ill to say the gallows is built stronger than the church. Argal, the gallows may do well to thee. To 't again, come.

SECOND CLOWN: "Who builds stronger than a mason, a shipwright, or a carpenter?"

FIRST CLOWN: Ay, tell me that, and unyoke.°

SECOND CLOWN: Marry, now I can tell.

FIRST CLOWN: To 't.

SECOND CLOWN: Mass,° I cannot tell.

Enter HAMLET *and* HORATIO [*at a distance*].

FIRST CLOWN: Cudgel thy brains no more about it, for your dull ass will not mend his pace with beating; and when you are asked this question next, say "a grave maker." The houses he makes lasts till doomsday. Go get thee in and fetch me a stoup° of liquor.

[*Exit* SECOND CLOWN: FIRST CLOWN *digs*.]

Song.

"In youth, when I did love, did love,°

Methought it was very sweet,

To contract—O—the time for—a—my behove,°

O, methought there—a—was nothing—a—meet."°

---

18 quest inquest. **21 there thou sayst** i.e., that's right. **22 countenance** privilege. **23 even-Christian** fellow Christians; **ancient** going back to ancient times. **24 hold up** maintain. **26 bore arms** (to be entitled to bear a coat of arms would make Adam a gentleman, but as one who bore a spade, our common ancestor was an ordinary delver in the earth.) **29 arms** i.e., the arms of the body. **30–31 confess thyself** (the saying continues, "and be hanged.") **35 frame** (1) gallows, (2) structure. **36 does well** (1) is an apt answer, (2) does a good turn. **41 unyoke** i.e., after this great effort, you may unharness the team of your wits. **44 Mass** by the Mass. **48 stoup** two-quart measure. **49 In . . . love** (This and the two following stanzas, with nonsensical variations, are from a poem attributed to Lord Vaux and printed in *Tottel's Miscellany,* 1557. The O and a [for "ah"] seemingly are the grunts of the digger.) **51 To contract . . . behove** i.e., to shorten the time for my own advantage. (Perhaps he means to *prolong* it.) **52 meet** suitable, i.e., more suitable.

HAMLET: Has this fellow no feeling of his business, 'a° sings in gravemaking?

HORATIO: Custom hath made it in him a property of easiness.°

HAMLET: 'Tis e'en so. The hand of little employment hath the daintier sense.°   55

FIRST CLOWN: *Song.*

> "But age with his stealing steps
>   Hath clawed me in his clutch,
> And hath shipped me into the land,°
>   As if I had never been such."   *[He throws up a skull.]*

HAMLET: That skull had a tongue in it and could sing once. How the knave jowls°   60
it to the ground, as if 'twere Cain's jawbone, that did the first murder! This
might be the pate of a politician,° which this ass now o'erreaches,°
one that would circumvent God, might it not?

HORATIO: It might, my lord.

HAMLET: Or of a courtier, which could say, "Good morrow, sweet lord! How dost   65
thou, sweet lord?" This might be my Lord Such-a-one, that praised my
Lord Such-a-one's horse when 'a meant to beg it, might it not?

HORATIO: Ay, my lord.

HAMLET: Why, e'en so, and now my Lady Worm's, chapless,° and knocked about
the mazard° with a sexton's spade. Here's fine revolution,° an° we had   70
the trick to see° 't. Did these bones cost no more the breeding but to°
play at loggets° with them? Mine ache to think on 't.

FIRST CLOWN: *Song.*

> "A pickax and a spade, a spade,
>   For and° a shrouding sheet;
> O, a pit of clay for to be made   75
>   For such a guest is meet."   *[He throws up another skull.]*

HAMLET: There's another. Why may not that be the skull of a lawyer? Where be
his quiddities° now, his quillities,° his cases, his tenures,° and his tricks?
Why does he suffer this mad knave now to knock him about the sconce°
with a dirty shovel, and will not tell him of his action of battery?° Hum,   80
this fellow might be in 's time a great buyer of land, with his statutes, his
recognizances,° his fines, his double° vouchers,° his recoveries.° Is this
the fine of his fines and the recovery of his recoveries, to have his fine

---

53 'a that he.   **54 property of easiness** something he can do easily and indifferently.
55 daintier sense more delicate sense of feeling.   **58 into the land** i.e., toward my grave (?)
(But note the lack of rhyme in *steps, land.*)   **60 jowls** dashes (with a pun on *jowl*, "jawbone").
62 politician schemer, plotter;   **o'erreaches** circumvents, gets the better of (with a quibble
on the literal sense).   **69 chapless** having no lower jaw.   **70 mazard** i.e., head (Literally, a
drinking vessel.);   **revolution** turn of Fortune's wheel, change;   **an** if.   **71 trick to see** knack
of seeing;   **cost . . . to** involve so little expense and care in upbringing that we may.   **72 loggets** a
game in which pieces of hard wood shaped like Indian clubs or bowling pins are thrown to
lie as near as possible to a stake.   **74 For and** and moreover.   **78 quiddities** subtleties,
quibbles. (From Latin *quid*, "a thing.");   **quillities** verbal niceties, subtle distinctions. (Variation
of *quiddities.*);   **tenures** the holding of a piece of property or office, or the conditions or
period of such holding.   **79 sconce** head.   **80 action of battery** lawsuit about physical assault.
81–82 statutes, recognizances legal documents guaranteeing a debt by attaching land
and property.   **82 fines, recoveries** ways of converting entailed estates into "fee simple"
or freehold;   **double** signed by two signatories;   **vouchers** guarantees of the legality of a
title to real estate.

pate full of fine dirt?° Will his vouchers vouch him no more of his pur-
chases, and double ones too, than the length and breadth of a pair of in-   85
dentures?° The very conveyances° of his lands will scarcely lie in this
box,° and must th' inheritor° himself have no more, ha?

HORATIO: Not a jot more, my lord.

HAMLET: Is not parchment made of sheepskins?

HORATIO: Ay, my lord, and of calves' skins too.   90

HAMLET: They are sheep and calves which seek out assurance in that.° I will
speak to this fellow.—Whose grave's this, sirrah?°

FIRST CLOWN: Mine, sir.   [*Sings.*]
"O, pit of clay for to be made
For such a guest is meet."   95

HAMLET: I think it be thine, indeed, for thou liest in 't.

FIRST CLOWN: You lie out on 't, sir, and therefore 'tis not yours. For my part, I do
not lie in 't, yet it is mine.

HAMLET: Thou dost lie in 't, to be in 't and say it is thine. 'Tis for the dead, not for
the quick;° therefore thou liest.   100

FIRST CLOWN: 'Tis a quick lie, sir; 'twill away again from me to you.

HAMLET: What man dost thou dig it for?

FIRST CLOWN: For no man, sir.

HAMLET: What woman, then?

FIRST CLOWN: For none, neither.   105

HAMLET: Who is to be buried in 't?

FIRST CLOWN: One that was a woman, sir, but, rest her soul, she's dead.

HAMLET: How absolute° the knave is! We must speak by the card,° or equivoca-
tion° will undo us. By the Lord, Horatio, this three years I have took°
note of it: the age is grown so picked° that the toe of the peasant comes   110
so near the heel of the courtier, he galls his kibe.°—How long hast thou
been grave maker?

FIRST CLOWN: Of all the days i' the year, I came to 't that day that our last king
Hamlet overcame Fortinbras.

HAMLET: How long is that since?   115

FIRST CLOWN: Cannot you tell that? Every fool can tell that. It was that very day
that young Hamlet was born—he that is mad and sent into England.

HAMLET: Ay, marry, why was he sent into England?

FIRST CLOWN: Why, because 'a was mad. 'A shall recover his wits there, or if 'a do
not, 'tis no great matter there.   120

HAMLET: Why?

FIRST CLOWN: 'Twill not be seen in him there. There the men are as mad as he.

HAMLET: How came he mad?

83–84 fine of his fines . . . fine pate . . . fine dirt end of his legal maneuvers . . . elegant head . . .
minutely sifted dirt.   **85–86 pair of indentures** legal document drawn up in duplicate on a
single sheet and then cut apart on a zigzag line so that each pair was uniquely matched. (Hamlet
may refer to two rows of teeth or dentures.)   **86 conveyances** deeds.   **87 box** (1) deed box,
(2) coffin. ("Skull" has been suggested.); **inheritor** possessor, owner.   **91 assurance in that**
safety in legal parchments.   **92 sirrah** (a term of address to inferiors.)   **100 quick** living.
108 absolute strict, precise; **by the card** i.e., with precision. (Literally, by the mariner's
compass-card, on which the points of the compass were marked.)   **109–10 equivocation**
ambiguity in the use of terms.   **109 took** taken.   **110 picked** refined, fastidious.   **111 galls
his kibe** chafes the courtier's chilblain.

FIRST CLOWN: Very strangely, they say.   125

HAMLET: How strangely?

FIRST CLOWN: Faith, e'en with losing his wits.

HAMLET: Upon what ground?°

FIRST CLOWN: Why, here in Denmark. I have been sexton here, man and boy,
      thirty years.

HAMLET: How long will a man lie i' th' earth ere he rot?   130

FIRST CLOWN: Faith, if 'a be not rotten before 'a die—as we have many pocky°
      corpses nowadays, that will scarce hold the laying in°—'a will last you°
      some eight year or nine year. A tanner will last you nine year.

HAMLET: Why he more than another?

FIRST CLOWN: Why, sir, his hide is so tanned with his trade that 'a will keep out   135
      water a great while, and your water is a sore° decayer of your whoreson°
      dead body. [*He picks up a skull.*] Here's a skull now hath lien you° i' th'
      earth three-and-twenty years.

HAMLET: Whose was it?

FIRST CLOWN: A whoreson mad fellow's it was. Whose do you think it was?   140

HAMLET: Nay, I know not.

FIRST CLOWN: A pestilence on him for a mad rogue! 'A poured a flagon of
      Rhenish° on my head once. This same skull, sir, was, sir, Yorick's skull,
      the King's jester.

HAMLET: This?   145

FIRST CLOWN: E'en that.

HAMLET: Let me see. [*He takes the skull.*] Alas, poor Yorick! I knew him, Horatio, a
      fellow of infinite jest, of most excellent fancy. He hath bore° me on his
      back a thousand times, and now how abhorred in my imagination it is!
      My gorge rises° at it. Here hung those lips that I have kissed I know not   150
      how oft. Where be your gibes now? Your gambols, your songs, your
      flashes of merriment that were wont° to set the table on a roar? Not one
      now, to mock your own grinning?° Quite chopfallen?° Now get you to
      my lady's chamber and tell her, let her paint an inch thick, to this favor°
      she must come. Make her laugh at that. Prithee, Horatio, tell me one thing. 155

HORATIO: What's that, my lord?

HAMLET: Dost thou think Alexander looked o' this fashion i' th' earth?

HORATIO: E'en so.

HAMLET: And smelt so? Pah! [*He throws down the skull.*]

HORATIO: E'en so, my lord.   160

HAMLET: To what base uses we may return, Horatio! Why may not imagination
      trace the noble dust of Alexander till 'a find it stopping a bunghole?°

HORATIO: 'Twere to consider too curiously° to consider so.

---

127 ground cause. (But, in the next line, the gravedigger takes the word in the sense of "land,"
"country.")   **131 pocky** rotten, diseased. (Literally, with the pox, or syphilis.)   **132 hold the
laying in** hold together long enough to be interred;   **last you** last. (*You* is used colloquially
here and in the following lines.)   **136 sore** i.e., terrible, great;   **whoreson** i.e., vile, scurvy.
137 lien you lain. (See the note at line 132.)   **143 Rhenish** Rhine wine.   **148 bore** borne.
150 My gorge rises i.e., I feel nauseated.   **152 were wont** used.   **153 mock your own grinning** mock at the way your skull seems to be grinning (just as you used to mock at yourself
and those who grinned at you);   **chopfallen** (1) lacking the lower jaw, (2) dejected.
154 favor aspect, appearance.   **162 bunghole** hole for filling or emptying a cask.
163 curiously minutely.

HAMLET: No, faith, not a jot, but to follow him thither with modesty° enough, and
likelihood to lead it. As thus: Alexander died, Alexander was buried,
Alexander returneth to dust, the dust is earth, of earth we make loam,° and
why of that loam whereto he was converted might they not stop a beer
barrel?   165

      Imperious° Caesar, dead and turned to clay,
Might stop a hole to keep the wind away.   170
O, that that earth which kept the world in awe
Should patch a wall t' expel the winter's flaw!°

Enter KING, QUEEN, LAERTES, *and the corpse* [*of* OPHELIA, *in procession, with*
PRIEST, *lords, etc.*].

      But soft,° but soft awhile! Here comes the King,
The Queen, the courtiers. Who is this they follow?
And with such maimèd° rites? This doth betoken   175
The corpse they follow did with desperate hand
Fordo° its own life. 'Twas of some estate.°
Couch we° awhile and mark.

[*He and* HORATIO *conceal themselves.* OPHELIA*'s body is taken to the grave.*]

LAERTES: What ceremony else?
HAMLET [*to* HORATIO]: That is Laertes, a very noble youth. Mark.   180
LAERTES: What ceremony else?
PRIEST: Her obsequies have been as far enlarged
      As we have warranty.° Her death was doubtful,
      And but that great command o'ersways the order°
      She should in ground unsanctified been lodged°   185
      Till the last trumpet. For° charitable prayers,
      Shards,° flints, and pebbles should be thrown on her.
      Yet here she is allowed her virgin crants,°
      Her maiden strewments,° and the bringing home
      Of bell and burial.°   190
LAERTES: Must there no more be done?
PRIEST: No more be done.
      We should profane the service of the dead
      To sing a requiem and such rest° to her
      As to peace-parted souls.°
LAERTES: Lay her i' th' earth,
      And from her fair and unpolluted flesh   195
      May violets° spring! I tell thee, churlish priest,

---

164 modesty plausible moderation. **166 loam** mortar consisting chiefly of moistened
clay and straw. **169 Imperious** imperial. **172 flaw** gust of wind. **173 soft** i.e., wait,
be careful. **175 maimèd** mutilated, incomplete. **177 Fordo** destroy; **estate** rank.
178 Couch we let's hide, lie low. **183 warranty** i.e., ecclesiastical authority. **184 great . . .
order** orders from on high overrule the prescribed procedures. **185 She should . . .
lodged** she should have been buried in unsanctified ground. **186 For** in place of. **187 Shards**
broken bits of pottery. **188 crants** garlands betokening maidenhood. **189 strewments** flowers strewn on a coffin. **190 bringing . . . burial** laying the body to rest, to the sound of the bell.
193 such rest i.e., to pray for such rest. **194 peace-parted souls** those who have died at
peace with God. **196 violets** (see 4.5.184 and note.)

A ministering angel shall my sister be
When thou liest howling.°

HAMLET [*to* HORATIO]:   What, the fair Ophelia!

QUEEN [*scattering flowers*]: Sweets to the sweet! Farewell.
I hoped thou shouldst have been my Hamlet's wife.   200
I thought thy bride-bed to have decked, sweet maid,
And not t' have strewed thy grave.

LAERTES: O, treble woe
Fall ten times treble on that cursèd head
Whose wicked deed thy most ingenious sense°
Deprived thee of! Hold off the earth awhile,   205
Till I have caught her once more in mine arms.

[*He leaps into the grave and embraces* OPHELIA.]

Now pile your dust upon the quick and dead,
Till of this flat a mountain you have made
T' o'ertop old Pelion or the skyish head
Of blue Olympus.°

HAMLET [*coming forward*]: What is he whose grief   210
Bears such an emphasis,° whose phrase of sorrow
Conjures the wandering stars° and makes them stand
Like wonder-wounded° hearers? This is I,
Hamlet the Dane.°

LAERTES [*grappling with him*°]: The devil take thy soul!

HAMLET: Thou pray'st not well.   215
I prithee, take thy fingers from my throat,
For though I am not splenitive° and rash,
Yet have I in me something dangerous,
Which let thy wisdom fear. Hold off thy hand.

KING: Pluck them asunder.   220

QUEEN: Hamlet, Hamlet!

ALL: Gentlemen!

HORATIO: Good my lord, be quiet.

[HAMLET *and* LAERTES *are parted.*]

HAMLET: Why, I will fight with him upon this theme
Until my eyelids will no longer wag.°   225

QUEEN: O my son, what theme?

HAMLET: I loved Ophelia. Forty thousand brothers
Could not with all their quantity of love
Make up my sum. What wilt thou do for her?

198 howling i.e., in hell.   **204 ingenious sense** a mind that is quick, alert, of fine qualities.
209–10 Pelion, Olympus sacred mountains in the north of Thessaly; see also *Ossa*, below,
at line 241.   **211 emphasis** i.e., rhetorical and florid emphasis. (*Phrase* has a similar rhetorical connotation.) **212 wandering stars** planets. **213 wonder-wounded** struck with amazement.
214 the Dane (This title normally signifies the King; see 1.1.17 and note.) **s.d. grappling
with him** (The testimony of the First Quarto that "*Hamlet leaps in after Laertes*" and the "Elegy
on Burbage" ("Oft have I seen him leap into the grave") seem to indicate one way in which this
fight was staged; however, the difficulty of fitting two contenders and Ophelia's body into a confined space (probably the trapdoor) suggests to many editors the alternative, that Laertes jumps
out of the grave to attack Hamlet.)   **217 splenitive** quick-tempered.   **225 wag** move. (A fluttering eyelid is a conventional sign that life has not yet gone.)

KING: O, he is mad, Laertes.   230
QUEEN: For love of God, forbear him.°
HAMLET: 'Swounds,° show me what thou'lt do.
      Woo't° weep? Woo't fight? Woo't fast? Woo't tear thyself?
      Woo't drink up° eisel?° Eat a crocodile?°
      I'll do 't. Dost come here to whine?   235
      To outface me with leaping in her grave?
      Be buried quick° with her, and so will I.
      And if thou prate of mountains, let them throw
      Millions of acres on us, till our ground,
      Singeing his pate° against the burning zone,°   240
      Make Ossa° like a wart! Nay, an° thou'lt mouth,°
      I'll rant as well as thou.
QUEEN: This is mere° madness,
      And thus awhile the fit will work on him;
      Anon, as patient as the female dove
      When that her golden couplets° are disclosed,°   245
      His silence will sit drooping.
HAMLET: Hear you, sir,
      What is the reason that you use me thus?
      I loved you ever. But it is no matter.
      Let Hercules himself do what he may,
      The cat will mew, and dog will have his day.°   *Exit* HAMLET.   250
KING: I pray thee, good Horatio, wait upon him.   [*Exit*] HORATIO.
      [*To* LAERTES.] Strengthen your patience in° our last night's speech;
      We'll put the matter to the present push.°—
      Good Gertrude, set some watch over your son.—
      This grave shall have a living° monument.   255
      An hour of quiet° shortly shall we see;
      Till then, in patience our proceeding be.   *Exeunt.*

[5.2]

Enter HAMLET *and* HORATIO.

HAMLET: So much for this, sir; now shall you see the other.°
      You do remember all the circumstance?
HORATIO: Remember it, my lord!

---

231 forbear him leave him alone. **232 'Swounds** by His (Christ's) wounds. **233 Woo't**
wilt thou. **234 drink up** drink deeply; **eisel** vinegar; **crocodile** (Crocodiles were tough and
dangerous, and were supposed to shed hypocritical tears.) **237 quick** alive. **240 his pate**
its head, i.e., top; **burning zone** zone in the celestial sphere containing the sun's orbit, between the tropics of Cancer and Capricorn. **241 Ossa** another mountain in Thessaly. (In their
war against the Olympian gods, the giants attempted to heap Ossa on Pelion to scale Olympus.);
an if; **mouth** i.e., rant. **242 mere** utter. **245 golden couplets** two baby pigeons, covered
with yellow down; **disclosed** hatched. **249–50 Let . . . day** i.e., (1) even Hercules couldn't
stop Laertes' theatrical rant, (2) I, too, will have my turn; i.e., despite any blustering attempts
at interference, every person will sooner or later do what he or she must do. **252 in** i.e., by
recalling. **253 present push** immediate test. **255 living** lasting. (For Laertes' private understanding, Claudius also hints that Hamlet's death will serve as such a monument.)
256 hour of quiet time free of conflict. **[5.2] Location: The castle.** **1 see the other** hear
the other news.

HAMLET: Sir, in my heart there was a kind of fighting
That would not let me sleep. Methought I lay   5
Worse than the mutines° in the bilboes.° Rashly,°
And praised be rashness for it—let us know°
Our indiscretion° sometimes serves us well
When our deep plots do pall,° and that should learn° us
There's a divinity that shapes our ends,   10
Rough-hew° them how we will—
HORATIO: That is most certain.
HAMLET: Up from my cabin,
My sea-gown° scarfed° about me, in the dark
Groped I to find out them,° had my desire,
Fingered° their packet, and in fine° withdrew   15
To mine own room again, making so bold,
My fears forgetting manners, to unseal
Their grand commission; where I found, Horatio—
Ah, royal knavery!—an exact command,
Larded° with many several° sorts of reasons   20
Importing° Denmark's health and England's too,
With, ho! such bugs° and goblins in my life,°
That on the supervise,° no leisure bated,°
No, not to stay° the grinding of the ax,
My head should be struck off.
HORATIO: Is't possible?   25
HAMLET [*giving a document*]:
Here's the commission. Read it at more leisure.
But wilt thou hear now how I did proceed?
HORATIO: I beseech you.
HAMLET: Being thus benetted round with villainies—
Ere I could make a prologue to my brains,   30
They had begun the play°—I sat me down,
Devised a new commission, wrote it fair.°
I once did hold it, as our statists° do,
A baseness° to write fair, and labored much
How to forget that learning; but, sir, now   35
It did me yeoman's° service. Wilt thou know
Th' effect° of what I wrote?
HORATIO: Ay, good my lord.
HAMLET: An earnest conjuration° from the King,
As England was his faithful tributary,

---

6 mutines mutineers;   **bilboes** shackles;   **Rashly** on impulse. (This adverb goes with lines 12 ff.)
7 know acknowledge   **8 indiscretion** lack of foresight and judgment (not an indiscreet act).
9 pall fail, falter, go stale;   **learn** teach.   **11 Rough-hew** shape roughly.   **13 sea-gown** seaman's coat;   **scarfed** loosely wrapped.   **14 them** i.e., Rosencrantz and Guildenstern.
15 Fingered pilfered, pinched;   **in fine** finally, in conclusion.   **20 Larded** garnished;
several different.   **21 Importing** relating to.   **22 bugs** bugbears, hobgoblins;   **in my life** i.e.,
to be feared if I were allowed to live.   **23 supervise** reading;   **leisure bated** delay allowed.
24 stay await.   **30–31 Ere . . . play** before I could consciously turn my brain to the matter, it
had started working on a plan.   **32 fair** in a clear hand.   **33 statists** statesmen.   **34 baseness**
i.e., lower-class trait.   **36 yeoman's** i.e., substantial, faithful, loyal.   **37 effect** purport.
38 conjuration entreaty.

As love between them like the palm° might flourish,   40
As peace should still° her wheaten garland° wear
And stand a comma° 'tween their amities,
And many suchlike "as"es° of great charge,°
That on the view and knowing of these contents,
Without debatement further more or less,   45
He should those bearers put to sudden death,
Not shriving time° allowed.

HORATIO: How was this sealed?

HAMLET: Why, even in that was heaven ordinant.°
I had my father's signet° in my purse,
Which was the model° of that Danish seal;   50
Folded the writ° up in the form of th' other,
Subscribed° it, gave 't th' impression,° placed it safely,
The changeling° never known. Now, the next day
Was our sea fight, and what to this was sequent°
Thou knowest already.   55

HORATIO: So Guildenstern and Rosencrantz go to 't.

HAMLET: Why, man, they did make love to this employment.
They are not near my conscience. Their defeat°
Does by their own insinuation° grow.
'Tis dangerous when the baser° nature comes   60
Between the pass° and fell° incensèd points
Of mighty opposites.°

HORATIO: Why, what a king is this!

HAMLET: Does it not, think thee, stand me now upon°—
He that hath killed my king and whored my mother,
Popped in between th' election° and my hopes,   65
Thrown out his angle° for my proper° life,
And with such cozenage°—is 't not perfect conscience
To quit° him with this arm? And is 't not to be damned
To let this canker° of our nature come
In° further evil?   70

HORATIO: It must be shortly known to him from England
What is the issue of the business there.

HAMLET: It will be short. The interim is mine,
And a man's life's no more than to say "one."°

---

40 palm (an image of health; see Psalm 92:12.) **41 still** always; **wheaten garland** (symbolic of fruitful agriculture, of peace and plenty.) **42 comma** (indicating continuity, link.) **43 "as"es** (1) the "whereases" of a formal document, (2) asses; **charge** (1) import, (2) burden (appropriate to asses). **47 shriving time** time for confession and absolution. **48 ordinant** directing. **49 signet** small seal. **50 model** replica. **51 writ** writing. **52 Subscribed** signed (with forged signature); **impression** i.e., with a wax seal. **53 changeling** i.e., substituted letter. (Literally, a fairy child substituted for a human one.) **54 was sequent** followed. **58 defeat** destruction. **59 insinuation** intrusive intervention, sticking their noses in my business. **60 baser** of lower social station. **61 pass** thrust; **fell** fierce. **62 opposites** antagonists. **63 stand me now upon** become incumbent on me now. **65 election** (The Danish monarch was "elected" by a small number of high-ranking electors.) **66 angle** fishhook; **proper** very. **67 cozenage** trickery. **68 quit** requite, pay back. **69 canker** ulcer. **69–70 come In** grow into. **74 a man's . . .** **"one"** one's whole life occupies such a short time, only as long as it takes to count to 1.

But I am very sorry, good Horatio,   75
That to Laertes I forgot myself,
For by the image of my cause I see
The portraiture of his. I'll court his favors.
But, sure, the bravery° of his grief did put me
Into a tow'ring passion.

HORATIO: Peace, who comes here?   80

Enter a Courtier [OSRIC].

OSRIC: Your lordship is right welcome back to Denmark.

HAMLET: I humbly thank you, sir. [*To* HORATIO.] Dost know this water fly?

HORATIO: No, my good lord.

HAMLET: Thy state is the more gracious, for 'tis a vice to know him. He hath
      much land, and fertile. Let a beast be lord of beasts, and his crib° shall   85
      stand at the King's mess.° 'Tis a chuff,° but, as I say, spacious in the
      possession of dirt.

OSRIC: Sweet lord, if your lordship were at leisure, I should impart a thing to you
      from His Majesty.

HAMLET: I will receive it, sir, with all diligence of spirit.   90
      Put your bonnet° to his° right use; 'tis for the head.

OSRIC: I thank your lordship, it is very hot.

HAMLET: No, believe me, 'tis very cold. The wind is northerly.

OSRIC: It is indifferent° cold, my lord, indeed.

HAMLET: But yet methinks it is very sultry and hot for my complexion.°   95

OSRIC: Exceedingly, my lord. It is very sultry, as 'twere—I cannot tell how.
      My lord, His Majesty bade me signify to you that 'a has laid a great
      wager on your head. Sir, this is the matter—

HAMLET: I beseech you, remember.

      [HAMLET *moves him to put on his hat.*]

OSRIC: Nay, good my lord; for my ease,° in good faith. Sir, here is newly   100
      come to court Laertes—believe me, an absolute° gentleman, full of
      most excellent differences,° of very soft society° and great showing.°
      Indeed, to speak feelingly° of him, he is the card° or calendar° of
      gentry,° for you shall find in him the continent of what part a gentleman
      would see.°   105

HAMLET: Sir, his definement° suffers no perdition° in you,° though I know to
      divide him inventorially° would dozy° th' arithmetic of memory, and yet
      but yaw° neither° in respect of° his quick sail. But, in the verity of

---

79 bravery bravado.   **85 crib** manger.   **85–86 Let . . . mess** i.e., if a man, no matter how beast-
like, is as rich in livestock and possessions as Osric, he may eat at the King's table.   **86 chuff** boor,
churl. (The Second Quarto spelling, *chough,* is a variant spelling that also suggests the meaning here of "chattering jackdaw.")   **91 bonnet** any kind of cap or hat;   **his** its.   **94 indifferent** somewhat.   **95 complexion** temperament.   **100 for my ease** (a conventional reply declining the invitation to put his hat back on.)   **101 absolute** perfect.   **102 differences** special
qualities;   **soft society** agreeable manners;   **great showing** distinguished appearance.
103 feelingly with just perception;   **card** chart, map;   **calendar** guide.   **104 gentry** good
breeding.   **104–05 the continent . . . see** one who contains in him all the qualities a gentleman would like to see. (A *continent* is that which contains.)   **106 definement** definition
(Hamlet proceeds to mock Osric by throwing his lofty diction back at him);   **perdition** loss,
diminution;   **you** your description.   **106–07 divide him inventorially** enumerate his graces;
107 dozy dizzy.   **108 yaw** swing unsteadily off course. (Said of a ship.);   **neither** for all that;
in respect of in comparison with.

extolment,° I take him to be a soul of great article,° and his infusion° of
such dearth and rareness° as, to make true diction° of him, his semblable°
is his mirror and who else would trace° him his umbrage,° nothing more. 110

OSRIC: Your lordship speaks most infallibly of him.

HAMLET: The concernancy,° sir? Why do we wrap the gentleman in our more
rawer breath?°

OSRIC: Sir? 115

HORATIO: Is 't not possible to understand in another tongue?° You will do 't,° sir,
really.

HAMLET: What imports the nomination° of this gentleman?

OSRIC: Of Laertes?

HORATIO [*to* HAMLET]: His purse is empty already; all 's golden words are spent. 120

HAMLET: Of him, sir.

OSRIC: I know you are not ignorant—

HAMLET: I would you did, sir. Yet in faith if you did, it would not much approve°
me. Well, sir?

OSRIC: You are not ignorant of what excellence Laertes is— 125

HAMLET: I dare not confess that, lest I should compare with him in excellence.
But to know a man well were to know himself.°

OSRIC: I mean, sir, for° his weapon; but in the imputation laid on him by them,°
in his meed° he's unfellowed.°

HAMLET: What's his weapon? 130

OSRIC: Rapier and dagger.

HAMLET: That's two of his weapons—but well.°

OSRIC: The King, sir, hath wagered with him six Barbary horses, against the
which he° has impawned,° as I take it, six French rapiers and poniards,°
with their assigns,° as girdle, hangers,° and so,° Three of the carriages,° 135
in faith, are very dear to fancy,° very responsive° to the hilts, most deli-
cate° carriages, and of very liberal conceit.°

HAMLET: What call you the carriages?

HORATIO [*to* HAMLET]: I knew you must be edified by the margent° ere you had 140
done.

OSRIC: The carriages, sir, are the hangers.

108–09 in . . . extolment in true praise (of him).   **109 of great article** one with many
articles in his inventory;   **infusion** essence, character infused into him by nature.
110 dearth and rareness rarity;   **make true diction** speak truly;   **semblable** only true
likeness.   **111 who . . . trace** any other person who would wish to follow;   **umbrage** shadow.
113 concernancy import, relevance.   **114 rawer breath** unrefined speech that can only come
short in praising him.   **116 to understand . . . tongue** i.e., for you, Osric, to understand
when someone else speaks your language. (Horatio twits Osric for not being able to
understand the kind of flowery speech he himself uses, when Hamlet speaks in such a
vein. Alternatively, all this could be said to Hamlet.);   **You will do 't** i.e., you can if you
try, or, you may well have to try (to speak plainly).   **118 nomination** naming.   **123 approve**
commend.   **126–27 I dare . . . himself** I dare not boast of knowing Laertes' excellence lest
I seem to imply a comparable excellence in myself. Certainly, to know another person well,
one must know oneself.   **128 for** i.e., with;   **imputation . . . them** reputation given him by others.
129 meed merit;   **unfellowed** unmatched.   **132 but well** but never mind.   **134 he** i.e., Laertes;
impawned staked, wagered;   **poniards** daggers.   **135 assigns** appurtenances;   **hangers** straps
on the sword belt (*girdle*), from which the sword hung;   **and so** and so on;   **carriages** (an affected way of saying *hangers*, literally, gun carriages.) **136 dear to fancy** delightful to the fancy;
responsive corresponding closely, matching or well adjusted.   **136–37 delicate** (i.e., in
workmanship);   **liberal conceit** elaborate design.   **139 margent** margin of a book, place for
explanatory notes.

HAMLET: The phrase would be more germane to the matter if we could carry a
cannon by our sides; I would it might be hangers till then. But, on: six
Barbary horses against six French swords, their assigns, and three liberal-
conceited carriages; that's the French bet against the Danish. Why is this   145
impawned, as you call it?

OSRIC: The King, sir, hath laid,° sir, that in a dozen passes° between yourself and
him, he shall not exceed you three hits. He hath laid on twelve for nine,
and it would come to immediate trial, if your lordship would vouchsafe
the answer.°   150

HAMLET: How if I answer no?

OSRIC: I mean, my lord, the opposition of your person in trial.

HAMLET: Sir, I will walk here in the hall. If it please His Majesty, it is the breathing
time° of day with me. Let° the foils be brought, the gentleman willing,
and the King hold his purpose. I will win for him an I can; if not, I will   155
gain nothing but my shame and the odd hits.

OSRIC: Shall I deliver you° so?

HAMLET: To this effect, sir—after what flourish your nature will.

OSRIC: I commend° my duty to your lordship.

HAMLET: Yours, yours. [*Exit* OSRIC.] 'A does well to commend it himself; there are   160
no tongues else for 's turn.°

HORATIO: This lapwing° runs away with the shell on his head.

HAMLET: 'A did comply with his dug° before 'a sucked it. Thus has he—and many
more of the same breed that I know the drossy° age dotes on—only got   165
the tune° of the time and, out of an habit of encounter,° a kind of yeasty°
collection,° which carries them through and through the most fanned and
winnowed opinions;° and do° but blow them to their trial, the bubbles
are out.°

Enter a LORD.

LORD: My lord, His Majesty commended him to you by young Osric, who brings
back to him that you attend him in the hall. He sends to know if your   170
pleasure hold to play with Laertes, or that° you will take longer time.

---

147 laid wagered; **passes** bouts. (The odds of the betting are hard to explain. Possibly the
King bets that Hamlet will win at least five out of twelve, at which point Laertes raises the
odds against himself by betting he will win nine.)   **149–50 vouchsafe the answer** be so
good as to accept the challenge. (Hamlet deliberately takes the phrase in its literal sense of
replying.)   **153–54 breathing time** exercise period; **Let** i.e., if. **157 deliver you** report
what you say. **159 commend** commit to your favor. (A conventional salutation, but Hamlet
wryly uses a more literal meaning, "recommend," "praise," in line 160.) **161 for 's turn** for
his purposes, i.e., to do it for him. **162 lapwing** (a proverbial type of youthful forwardness.
Also, a bird that draws intruders away from its nest and was thought to run about with its head
in the shell when newly hatched; a seeming reference to Osric's hat.)   **163 comply . . . dug**
observe ceremonious formality toward his nurse's or mother's teat. **164 drossy** laden with
scum and impurities, frivolous. **165 tune** temper, mood, manner of speech; **an habit of
encounter** a demeanor in conversing (with courtiers of his own kind); **yeasty** frothy.
166 collection i.e., of current phrases. **166–67 carries . . . opinions** sustains them right
through the scrutiny of persons whose opinions are select and refined. (Literally, like grain
separated from its chaff. Osric is both the chaff and the bubbly froth on the surface of the
liquor that is soon blown away.) **167 and do** yet do. **167–68 blow . . . out** test them by
merely blowing on them, and their bubbles burst. **171 that** if.

HAMLET: I am constant to my purposes; they follow the King's pleasure. If his fitness speaks, mine is ready;° now or whensoever, provided I be so able as now.

LORD: The King and Queen and all are coming down.

HAMLET: In happy time.°   175

LORD: The Queen desires you to use some gentle entertainment° to Laertes before you fall to play.

HAMLET: She well instructs me.   [*Exit* LORD.]

HORATIO: You will lose, my lord.

HAMLET: I do not think so. Since he went into France, I have been in continual   180
practice; I shall win at the odds. But thou wouldst not think how ill all's here about my heart; but it is no matter.

HORATIO: Nay, good my lord—

HAMLET: It is but foolery, but it is such a kind of gaingiving° as would perhaps trouble a woman.   185

HORATIO: If your mind dislike anything, obey it. I will forestall their repair° hither and say you are not fit.

HAMLET: Not a whit, we defy augury. There is special providence in the fall of a sparrow. If it be now, 'tis not to come; if it be not to come, it will be now; if it be not now, yet it will come. The readiness is all. Since no man of   190
aught he leaves knows, what is 't to leave betimes? Let be.°

A table prepared. [*Enter*] *trumpets, drums, and officers with cushions;* KING,
QUEEN, [OSRIC,] *and all the state; foils, daggers,* [*and wine borne in,*] *and* LAERTES.

KING: Come, Hamlet, come and take this hand from me.

[*The king puts* LAERTES' *hand into* HAMLET'S.]

HAMLET [*to* LAERTES]: Give me your pardon, sir. I have done you wrong,
But pardon 't as you are a gentleman.
This presence° knows,   195
And you must needs have heard, how I am punished°
With a sore distraction. What I have done
That might your nature, honor, and exception°
Roughly awake, I here proclaim was madness.
Was 't Hamlet wronged Laertes? Never Hamlet.   200
If Hamlet from himself be ta'en away,
And when he's not himself does wrong Laertes,
Then Hamlet does it not, Hamlet denies it.
Who does it, then? His madness. If 't be so,
Hamlet is of the faction° that is wronged;   205
His madness is poor Hamlet's enemy.
Sir, in this audience
Let my disclaiming from a purposed evil
Free me so far in your most generous thoughts

172–73 If . . . ready If he declares his readiness, my convenience waits on his.   **175 In happy
time** (a phrase of courtesy indicating that the time is convenient).   **176 entertainment** greeting.
184 gaingiving misgiving.   **186 repair** coming.   **190–91 Since . . . Let be** Since no one has
knowledge of what he is leaving behind, what does an early death matter after all? Enough; don't
struggle against it.   **195 presence** royal assembly.   **196 punished** afflicted.   **198 exception**
disapproval.   **205 faction** party.

	That I have° shot my arrow o'er the house	210
	And hurt my brother.	
LAERTES:	I am satisfied in nature,°	
	Whose motive° in this case should stir me most	
	To my revenge. But in my terms of honor	
	I stand aloof, and will no reconcilement	
	Till by some elder masters of known honor	215
	I have a voice° and precedent of peace°	
	To keep my name ungored.° But till that time	
	I do receive your offered love like love,	
	And will not wrong it.	
HAMLET:	I embrace it freely,	
	And will this brothers' wager frankly° play.—	220
	Give us the foils. Come on.	
LAERTES:	Come, one for me.	
HAMLET:	I'll be your foil,° Laertes. In mine ignorance	
	Your skill shall, like a star i' the darkest night,	
	Stick fiery off° indeed.	
LAERTES:	You mock me, sir.	
HAMLET:	No, by this hand.	225
KING:	Give them the foils, young Osric. Cousin Hamlet,	
	You know the wager?	
HAMLET:	Very well, my lord.	
	Your Grace has laid the odds o'° the weaker side.	
KING:	I do not fear it; I have seen you both.	
	But since he is bettered,° we have therefore odds.	230
LAERTES:	This is too heavy. Let me see another.	

[He exchanges his foil for another.]

HAMLET: This likes me° well. These foils have all a length?

[They prepare to play.]

OSRIC: Ay, my good lord.

KING: Set me the stoups of wine upon that table.
    If Hamlet give the first or second hit,   235
    Or quit in answer of the third exchange,°
    Let all the battlements their ordnance fire.
    The King shall drink to Hamlet's better breath,°
    And in the cup an union° shall he throw
    Richer than that which four successive kings   240
    In Denmark's crown have worn. Give me the cups,
    And let the kettle° to the trumpet speak,
    The trumpet to the cannoneer without,

---

210 That I have as if I had.   **211 in nature** i.e., as to my personal feelings.   **212 motive** prompting.   **216 voice** authoritative pronouncement;   **of peace** for reconciliation. **217 name ungored** reputation unwounded.   **220 frankly** without ill feeling or the burden of rancor.   **222 foil** thin metal background which sets a jewel off (with pun on the blunted rapier for fencing).   **224 Stick fiery off** stand out brilliantly.   **228 laid the odds o'** bet on, backed.   **230 is bettered** has improved; is the odds-on favorite. (Laertes' handicap is the "three hits" specified in line 148.)   **232 likes me** pleases me.   **236 Or . . . exchange** i.e., or requites Laertes in the third bout for having won the first two.   **238 better breath** improved vigor.   **239 union** pearl. (So called, according to Pliny's *Natural History*, 9, because pearls are *unique*, never identical.)   **242 kettle** kettledrum.

The cannons to the heavens, the heaven to earth,
"Now the King drinks to Hamlet." Come, begin.   *Trumpets the while.*   245
And you, the judges, bear a wary eye.

HAMLET: Come on, sir.

LAERTES: Come, my lord.   [*They play.* HAMLET *scores a hit.*]

HAMLET: One.

LAERTES: No.   250

HAMLET: Judgment.

OSRIC: A hit, a very palpable hit.

Drum, trumpets, and shot. Flourish. A piece goes off.

LAERTES: Well, again.

KING: Stay, give me drink. Hamlet, this pearl is thine.

[*He drinks, and throws a pearl in* HAMLET'*s cup.*]

Here's to thy health. Give him the cup.   255

HAMLET: I'll play this bout first. Set it by awhile.
Come. [*They play.*] Another hit; what say you?

LAERTES: A touch, a touch, I do confess 't.

KING: Our son shall win.

QUEEN: He's fat° and scant of breath.
Here, Hamlet, take my napkin,° rub thy brows.
The Queen carouses° to thy fortune, Hamlet.   260

HAMLET: Good madam!

KING: Gertrude, do not drink.

QUEEN: I will, my lord, I pray you pardon me.   [*She drinks.*]

KING [*aside*]: It is the poisoned cup. It is too late.

HAMLET: I dare not drink yet, madam; by and by.   265

QUEEN: Come, let me wipe thy face.

LAERTES [*to* KING]: My lord, I'll hit him now.

KING: I do not think 't.

LAERTES [*aside*]: And yet it is almost against my conscience.

HAMLET: Come, for the third, Laertes. You do but dally.
I pray you, pass° with your best violence;   270
I am afeard you make a wanton of me.°

LAERTES: Say you so? Come on.   [*They play.*]

OSRIC: Nothing neither way.

LAERTES: Have at you now!

[LAERTES *wounds* HAMLET; *then, in scuffling, they change rapiers,*° *and* HAMLET
wounds LAERTES.]

KING: Part them! They are incensed.

HAMLET: Nay, come, again.   [*The* QUEEN *falls.*]

OSRIC: Look to the Queen there, ho!   275

HORATIO: They bleed on both sides. How is it, my lord?

OSRIC: How is 't, Laertes?

LAERTES: Why, as a woodcock° to mine own springe,° Osric;
I am justly killed with mine own treachery.

---

258 fat not physically fit, out of training.   **259 napkin** handkerchief.   **260 carouses** drinks
a toast.   **270 pass** thrust.   **271 make . . . me** i.e., treat me like a spoiled child, trifle with me.
274 s.d. in scuffling, they change rapiers (This stage direction occurs in the Folio. According to a widespread stage tradition, Hamlet receives a scratch, realizes that Laertes' sword is
unbated, and accordingly forces an exchange.)   **278 woodcock** a bird, a type of stupidity or
as a decoy;   **springe** trap, snare.

HAMLET: How does the Queen?

KING: She swoons to see them bleed.   280

QUEEN: No, no, the drink, the drink—O my dear Hamlet—
    The drink, the drink! I am poisoned.   [*She dies.*]

HAMLET: O villainy! Ho, let the door be locked!
    Treachery! Seek it out.   [LAERTES *falls. Exit* OSRIC.]

LAERTES: It is here, Hamlet. Hamlet, thou art slain.   285
    No med'cine in the world can do thee good;
    In thee there is not half an hour's life.
    The treacherous instrument is in thy hand,
    Unbated° and envenomed. The foul practice°
    Hath turned itself on me. Lo, here I lie,   290
    Never to rise again. Thy mother's poisoned.
    I can no more. The King, the King's to blame.

HAMLET: The point envenomed too? Then, venom, to thy work.

                                    [*He stabs the* KING.]

ALL: Treason! Treason!

KING: O, yet defend me, friends! I am but hurt.   295

HAMLET [*forcing the* KING *to drink*]:
    Here, thou incestuous, murderous, damnèd Dane,
    Drink off this potion. Is thy union° here?
    Follow my mother.   [*The* KING *dies.*]

LAERTES: He is justly served.
    It is a poison tempered° by himself.
    Exchange forgiveness with me, noble Hamlet.   300
    Mine and my father's death come not upon thee,
    Nor thine on me!   [*He dies.*]

HAMLET: Heaven make thee free of it! I follow thee.
    I am dead, Horatio. Wretched Queen, adieu!
    You that look pale and tremble at this chance,°   305
    That are but mutes° or audience to this act,
    Had I but time—as this fell° sergeant,° Death,
    Is strict° in his arrest°—O, I could tell you—
    But let it be. Horatio, I am dead;
    Thou livest. Report me and my cause aright   310
    To the unsatisfied.

HORATIO: Never believe it.
    I am more an antique Roman° than a Dane.
    Here's yet some liquor left.

    [*He attempts to drink from the poisoned cup.* HAMLET *prevents him.*]

HAMLET: As thou'rt a man,
    Give me the cup! Let go! By heaven, I'll ha 't.
    O God, Horatio, what a wounded name,   315

---

289 Unbated not blunted with a button; **practice** plot. **297 union** pearl. (See line 239; with grim puns on the word's other meanings: marriage, shared death.) **299 tempered** mixed. **305 chance** mischance. **306 mutes** silent observers. (Literally, actors with nonspeaking parts.) **307 fell** cruel; **sergeant** sheriff's officer. **308 strict** (1) severely just, (2) unavoidable; **arrest** (1) taking into custody, (2) stopping my speech. **312 Roman** (suicide was an honorable choice for many Romans as an alternative to a dishonorable life.)

Things standing thus unknown, shall I leave behind me!
If thou didst ever hold me in thy heart,
Absent thee from felicity awhile,
And in this harsh world draw thy breath in pain
To tell my story.   *A march afar off* [*and a volley within*].   320
What warlike noise is this?

Enter OSRIC.

OSRIC: Young Fortinbras, with conquest come from Poland,
       To th' ambassadors of England gives
       This warlike volley.
HAMLET: O, I die, Horatio!
       The potent poison quite o'ercrows° my spirit.   325
       I cannot live to hear the news from England,
       But I do prophesy th' election lights
       On Fortinbras. He has my dying voice.°
       So tell him, with th' occurents° more and less
       Which have solicited°—the rest is silence.   [*He dies.*]   330
HORATIO: Now cracks a noble heart. Good night, sweet prince,
       And flights of angels sing thee to thy rest!   [*March within.*]
       Why does the drum come hither?

Enter FORTINBRAS, *with the* [*English*] *Ambassadors* [*with drum, colors, and attendants*].

FORTINBRAS: Where is this sight?
HORATIO: What is it you would see?
       If aught of woe or wonder, cease your search.   335
FORTINBRAS: This quarry° cries on havoc.° O proud Death,
       What feast° is toward° in thine eternal cell,
       That thou so many princes at a shot
       So bloodily hast struck?
FIRST AMBASSADOR.   The sight is dismal,
       And our affairs from England come too late.   340
       The ears are senseless that should give us hearing,
       To tell him his commandment is fulfilled,
       That Rosencrantz and Guildenstern are dead.
       Where should we have our thanks?
HORATIO: Not from his° mouth,
       Had it th' ability of life to thank you.   345
       He never gave commandment for their death.
       But since, so jump° upon this bloody question,°
       You from the Polack wars, and you from England,
       And here arrived, give order that these bodies
       High on a stage° be placèd to the view,   350
       And let me speak to th' yet unknowing world

---

325 o'ercrows triumphs over (like the winner in a cockfight). **328 voice** vote. **329 occurrents** events, incidents. **330 solicited** moved, urged. (Hamlet doesn't finish saying what the events have prompted—presumably, his acts of vengeance, or his reporting of those events to Fortinbras.) **336 quarry** heap of dead; **cries on havoc** proclaims a general slaughter. **337 feast** i.e., Death feasting on those who have fallen; **toward** in preparation. **344 his** i.e., Claudius'. **347 jump** precisely, immediately; **question** dispute, affair. **350 stage** platform.

How these things came about. So shall you hear
Of carnal, bloody, and unnatural acts,
Of accidental judgments,° casual° slaughters,
Of deaths put on° by cunning and forced cause,°   355
And, in this upshot, purposes mistook
Fall'n on th' inventors' heads. All this can I
Truly deliver.

FORTINBRAS: Let us haste to hear it,
And call the noblest to the audience.
For me, with sorrow I embrace my fortune.   360
I have some rights of memory° in this kingdom,
Which now to claim my vantage° doth invite me.

HORATIO: Of that I shall have also cause to speak,
And from his mouth whose voice will draw on more.°
But let this same be presently° performed,   365
Even while men's minds are wild, lest more mischance
On° plots and errors happen.

FORTINBRAS: Let four captains
Bear Hamlet, like a soldier, to the stage,
For he was likely, had he been put on,°
To have proved most royal; and for his passage,°   370
The soldiers' music and the rite of war
Speak° loudly for him.
Take up the bodies. Such a sight as this
Becomes the field,° but here shows much amiss.
Go bid the soldiers shoot.   375

Exeunt [marching, bearing off the dead bodies; a peal of ordnance is shot off].

                                                          [1603]

---

354 judgments retributions; **casual** occurring by chance. **355 put on** instigated; **forced
cause** contrivance. **361 of memory** traditional, remembered, unforgotten. **362 vantage**
favorable opportunity. **364 voice . . . more** vote will influence still others. **365 presently**
immediately. **367 On** on the basis of; on top of. **369 put on** i.e., invested in royal office
and so put to the test. **370 Passage** i.e., from life to death. **372 Speak** let them speak.
374 Becomes the field suits the field of battle.

Joining the Conversation: Critical Thinking and Writing

Act 1

1. The first scene (like many other scenes in this play) is full of expressions of
    uncertainty. What are some of these uncertainties? The Ghost first appears at
    1.1.43. Does his appearance surprise us, or have we been prepared for it? Or is
    there both preparation and surprise? Do the last four speeches of 1.1 help to
    introduce a note of hope? If so, how?

2. Does the King's opening speech in 1.2 reveal him to be an accomplished public speaker—or are lines 10–14 offensive? In his second speech (lines 41–49), what is the effect of naming Laertes four times? Claudius sometimes uses the royal pronouns ("we," "our"), sometimes the more intimate "I" and "my." Study his use of these words in lines 1–4 and in 106–17. What do you think he is getting at?

3. Hamlet's first soliloquy (1.2.129–59) reveals that more than just his father's death distresses him. Be as specific as possible about the causes of Hamlet's anguish here.

4. What traits does Hamlet reveal in his conversation with Horatio (1.2.160–258)?

5. What do you make of Polonius's advice to Laertes (1.3.55–81)? Is it sound? Sound advice, but here uttered by a fool? Ignoble advice? How would one follow the advice of line 78: "to thine own self be true"? In his words to Ophelia in 1.3.102–36, what does Polonius reveal about himself?

6. Can 1.4.17–38 reasonably be taken as a speech on the "tragic flaw"? (On this idea, see page 433.) Or is the passage a much more limited discussion, a comment simply on Danish drinking habits?

7. Hamlet is convinced in 1.5.93–105 that the Ghost has told the truth, indeed, the only important truth. But do we detect in 105–12 a hint of a tone suggesting that Hamlet delights in hating villainy? If so, can it be said that later this delight grows, and that in some scenes (e.g., 3.3) we feel that Hamlet has almost become a diabolic revenger? Explain.

Act 2

1. Characterize Polonius on the basis of 2.1.1–75.

2. In light of what we have seen of Hamlet, is Ophelia's report of his strange behavior when he visits her understandable?

3. Why does 2.2.33–34 seem almost comic? How do these lines help us to form a view about Rosencrantz and Guildenstern?

4. Is "the hellish Pyrrhus" (2.2.405) Hamlet's version of Claudius? Or is he Hamlet, who soon will be responsible for the deaths of Polonius, Rosencrantz and Guildenstern, Claudius, Gertrude, Ophelia, and Laertes? Explain.

5. Is the speech that Hamlet and the First Player recite, with some interruptions (2.2.392–453), an absurdly bombastic speech? If so, why? To distinguish it from the poetry of the play itself? To characterize the bloody deeds that Hamlet cannot descend to?

6. In 2.2.482–520 Hamlet rebukes himself for not acting. Why has he not acted? Because he is a coward (line 503)? Because he has a conscience? Because no action can restore his father and his mother's purity? Because he doubts the Ghost? What reason(s) can you offer?

Act 3

1. What do you make of Hamlet's assertion to Ophelia: "I loved you not" (3.1.117)? Of his characterization of himself as full of "offenses" (3.1.121–25)? Why is Hamlet so harsh to Ophelia?

2. In 3.3.36–72 Claudius's conscience afflicts him. But is he repentant? What makes you say so?

3. Is Hamlet other than abhorrent in 3.3.73–96? Do we want him to kill Claudius at this moment, when Claudius (presumably with his back to Hamlet) is praying? Why?

4. The Ghost speaks of Hamlet's "almost blunted purpose" (3.4.115). Is the accusation fair? Explain.

5. How would you characterize Hamlet in 3.4.209–24?

Act 4

1. Is Gertrude protecting Hamlet when she says he is mad (4.1.7), or does she believe that he is mad? If she believes he is mad, does it follow that she no longer feels ashamed and guilty? Explain.
2. Why should Hamlet hide Polonius's body (in 4.2)? Is he feigning madness? Is he on the edge of madness? Explain.
3. How can we explain Hamlet's willingness to go to England (4.3.52)?
4. Judging from 4.5, what has driven Ophelia mad? Is Laertes heroic, or somewhat foolish? Consider also the way Claudius treats him in 4.7.

Act 5

1. Would anything be lost if the gravediggers in 5.1 were omitted?
2. To what extent do we judge Hamlet severely for sending Rosencrantz and Guildenstern to their deaths, as he reports in 5.2? On the whole, do we think of Hamlet as an intriguer? What other intrigues has he engendered? How successful were they?
3. Does 5.2.188–91 show a paralysis of the will, or a wise recognition that more is needed than mere human scheming? Explain.
4. Does 5.2.274 suggest that Laertes takes advantage of a momentary pause and unfairly stabs Hamlet? Is the exchange of weapons accidental, or does Hamlet (as in Olivier's film version), realizing that he has been betrayed, deliberately take possession of Laertes's deadly weapon?
5. Fortinbras is often cut from the play. How much is lost by the cut? Explain.
6. Fortinbras gives Hamlet a soldier's funeral. Is this ridiculous? Can it fairly be said that, in a sense, Hamlet has been at war? Explain.

General Questions

1. Hamlet in 5.2.10–11 speaks of "a divinity that shapes our ends." To what extent does "divinity" (or Fate or mysterious Chance) play a role in the happenings?
2. How do Laertes, Fortinbras, and Horatio help to define Hamlet for us?
3. T. S. Eliot says (in "Shakespeare and the Stoicism of Seneca") that Hamlet, having made a mess, "dies fairly well pleased with himself." Evaluate.

MyLiteratureLab® *For additional resources for* Hamlet, *log in to* www.myliteraturelab.com *where you will find a Performance and a Longman Lecture, as well as an About the Author, Links, and Critical Overview for Shakespeare (under Student Resources).*

Anne Barton

*The Promulgation of Confusion**

The length of the play suggests that it was never, not even in Shakespeare's time, performed uncut. Other plays by Shakespeare are long; no other violates so strikingly the limits of audience attention, or asks for so much from its leading actor. Like *Titus*, like *The Spanish Tragedy* and that lost source play, the so-called *Ur-Hamlet*, which was probably the work of Kyd, Shakespeare's *Hamlet* is a tragedy of revenge. It concentrates, like them, upon a single, essentially sympathetic hero and it confronts

*The title is the editors'.

precisely the same structural problem: how to linger out his vengeance for the necessary five acts. Kyd's Hieronymo (and probably his Hamlet), Shakespeare's Titus and Hamlet all require proof of the villain's identity before they can act. They are temporarily deflected from their purpose, not only by difficulties of strategy, but by a madness partly assumed and partly real. All make use of some kind of dramatic show to further their intention and all accomplish, in the end, a vengeance which, whatever the original provocation, has by this time become more than a little suspect.

As a tragic predicament, revenge has several inherent advantages. Intrigue and spectacle, madness and violence, are not the only elements native to the genre. The isolation naturally imposed upon the revenger not only encourages introspection, it destroys normal human relationships in a fundamentally tragic way. A detached, satirist's view of the society against which they war almost forces itself upon these characters. Their situation generates a corrosive doubt, reaching out to attack religious, moral and legal institutions. Kyd, Marlowe in *The Jew of Malta,* and the young Shakespeare of *Titus,* had all recognized and explored these inbuilt opportunities, at least to some extent. It was only with *Hamlet,* however, that a dramatist seized upon the form to trigger off an enquiry into the whole basis of human existence. Debate over man's right to encroach upon the prerogative of Heaven by undertaking himself what was properly God's act of retributive justice had been and, in the Jacobean period, would continue to be a feature of revenge tragedy.

. . .

Only *Hamlet* side steps the ethic of revenge entirely. It is one of several great silences at the heart of this play. Deliberately, Shakespeare has shifted attention away from an expected centre, from the problem of whether the prince *ought* to kill Claudius—or even whether in practical terms he *can*—to the far more complicated and subjective issue of whether or not he ultimately *will.* It is not the peculiar status of acts of private vengeance that is under review here, but the validity of all and any human action.

Although other dramatists (Marston, Webster and Tourneur especially) later used *Hamlet* as a spring-board for their own exploration of the revenge form, none of them dared to attempt a focus so wide. The range of the play and, above all, of the role of Hamlet himself, is so great that any performance must necessarily be a matter of selection, of emphases more or less arbitrarily imposed. The impossibility of presenting *Hamlet* whole and uncut is not entirely a feature of its great length. It is also bound up with its inclusiveness, with the fact that Shakespeare seems to have been determined to subject a bewildering number of people, ideas, values, kinds of relationship, emotions and social forms to the distorted but strangely clear scrutiny of a revenger so complicated himself that no attempt to describe, or act, him can be more than partial. Even more than most plays of Shakespeare, *Hamlet* is a warning against the fallacy that any critical interpretation or stage production can be definitive, or even complete.

5   When Hamlet cautioned Rosencrantz and Guildenstern, after the play scene, against the attempt to "pluck out the heart of my mystery . . . sound me from my lowest note to the top of my compass" (3.2.319–21), he also provided a useful counsel for literary critics. The play as a whole is built upon contradiction, upon the promulgation of confusion. Shakespeare gives every indication of having constructed an imaginary Denmark intended to baffle, to resist explanation as stubbornly as those mysterious facts of human existence which it illuminates without rationalizing. A distrust of what might be described as a "play-shaped" view of the world of the falseness of clearly defined moral, theological or formal patterns

imposed upon reality in the interests of art is, I think, characteristic of him throughout his dramatic career. It was to become particularly strong in his Jacobean plays. This antipathy may account, in part, for Shakespeare's apparent suspicion of *tragedy* as a term, and also for the variety and restlessness of his own formal development.

Certainly, the eschatology of *Hamlet* defies explication. The ghost of a murdered king appears from an almost embarrassingly specific Catholic Purgatory, a place of "sulph'rous and tormenting flames" (1.5.3) to which it has been confined "till the foul crimes done in my days of nature / Are burnt and purged away" (1.5.13–14). This spirit urges upon its beloved only son a revenge for which, by immutable Christian law, that son must be damned perpetually—sent not to Purgatory, but to the far greater torments of Hell. Neither Hamlet, the sensible Horatio nor the ghost itself ever remark upon this illogicality. Hamlet's worry is only about the truth of the ghost's accusation. If Claudius is guilty, and the Mouse-trap proves that he is, he must be killed. Not for an instant does Hamlet doubt the justice of such a course, let alone the propriety of a repentant soul spending its time in Purgatory meditating a murder. A similar inconsistency adds complications to what is already, on psychological grounds, a most ambiguous scene in Act 3. Hamlet declines to kill the king at prayers because he fears that Claudius' soul will ascend to Heaven. This, at least, is the reason he gives. He will wait to find his enemy

> drunk asleep, or in his rage,
> Or in th'incestuous pleasure of his bed,
> At game, a-swearing, or about some act
> That has no relish of salvation in't,
> Then trip him that his heels may kick at heaven,
> And that his soul may be as damned and black
> As hell whereto it goes.
>
> (3.3.89–95)

Here, the odd fact that Hamlet never considers that his own soul would be damned irrecoverably by the requirements of such a theology, is cunningly mingled with doubts as to whether he really means what he is saying in this speech, or whether it is a feeble excuse for postponing an explicably distasteful task.

In *Hamlet,* Shakespeare affirms a Christian supernatural in one moment to deny it in the next. The hereafter involves Purgatory, hell fire, and flights of angels. It is also silence, an eternal sleep that has nothing to do with punishment or reward. The prince talks about death as "the undiscovered country, from whose bourn / No traveller returns" (3.1.80–81) out of an anguish of mind created by the return of just such a traveller. A special Providence guides the fall of the sparrow, or at least Hamlet asserts that it does just before the fatal game with the foils in Act 5. He seems to die, however, in the agnostic spirit which, a moment later, prompts Horatio's account of the catastrophe as "accidental judgments, casual slaughters" (5.2.354). These conflicting views follow one another so closely in the action, and they are treated by the dramatist with such a non-committal equality, that it becomes impossible to characterize the supernatural in the play. Although we stumble from time to time over the partially submerged rocks of old beliefs, their presence only makes the obscurity of the total picture more poignant. In effect, Shakespeare has created his own, infinitely more complex version of the divided worlds of [Pickering's] *Horestes* and [Kyd's] *The Spanish Tragedy.* Hamlet's questions, instead of being halted artificially as Hieronymo's were by a tidy, Senecan supernatural visible to us in the audience although not to the hero, grope their way into a darkness without form or limit. Like Pickering, Shakespeare placed his spirit of Revenge inside the play itself, as a character who addresses the protagonist directly. Having done so, he proceeded disconcertingly to associate the ghost with a Christian hereafter, and refused to judge its ethic of blood vengeance. *Hamlet* never explains the nature of that silence towards which the hero moves gradually, away from us, and into which he finally vanishes. This is one reason why the tragedy has a terror, and also a relevance to the world as we know it, lacking in Pickering and Kyd.

More perhaps than any other Shakespearean tragedy, *Hamlet* is a play obsessed with words themselves. It displaces the accustomed centre of earlier revenge drama by subordinating plot for its own sake to a new concern with the mysterious gap between thought and action, between the verbal formulation of intent and its concrete realization. The prince himself is the most articulate of Shakespeare's tragic heroes, but he combines verbal fluency with a curious paralysis of the will. When Claudius asks Laertes in Act 4 what he would do "to show yourself in deed your father's son / More than in words" (4.7.126–27), Laertes replies instantly that, to be avenged, he would be happy to cut Hamlet's throat "i' the church." A demonstration that "in deed more than words" he is his father's son is conspicuously what the Hamlet of "O, what a rogue and peasant slave am I" and "How all occasions do inform against me" has not managed. We may respect him for this failing. Certainly, the sharply contrasted readiness of Laertes to act without thinking is unlovely. The fact remains that Hamlet is a man suffering from a peculiar malaise. In his mind, speech and event, language and its realization have become separate and disjunct. He can initiate action only when he has no time to subject it, first, to words: when he stabs impulsively through the arras and kills Polonius, when he sends Rosencrantz and Guildenstern to death *before* "I could make a prologue to my brains" (5.2.30), boards the pirate ship in the heat of the moment or finally, without premeditation, kills the king. The Norwegian captain tells Hamlet in the fourth scene of Act 4 that Fortinbras is hazarding twenty thousand ducats and an army of two thousand men to gain "a little patch of ground / That hath in it no profit but the name" (4.4.19–20). Fortinbras here, as in other respects, is Hamlet's diametric opposite. He has converted a mere word, a name, into a pretext for action. Hamlet, on the other hand, allows a tangible situation, the fact of a father's murder, to dissolve into words alone.

[1971]

STANLEY WELLS

On the First Soliloquy

More than most plays, *Hamlet* is a series of opportunities for virtuosity. This is true above all of the role of Hamlet himself. "Hamlet," wrote Max Beerbohm, is "a hoop through which every very eminent actor must, sooner or later, jump." There is no wonder that it has been such a favourite part with actors, and even with actresses. The performer has the opportunity to demonstrate a wide range of ability, to be melancholy and gay, charming and cynical, thoughtful and flippant, tender and cruel, calm and impassioned, noble and vindictive, downcast and witty, all within a few hours. He can wear a variety of costumes, he need not disguise good looks, he can demonstrate athletic ability, he has perhaps the longest role in drama—he could scarcely ask for more, except perhaps the opportunity to sing and dance.

And if the role of Hamlet is the greatest reason for the play's popularity with actors, the character of Hamlet is surely the greatest reason for its popularity with audiences. Hamlet is the most sympathetic of tragic heroes. We are drawn to him by his youth, his intelligence, and his vulnerability. As soon as he appears we are conscious of one of the sources of his appeal: his immense capacity for taking life seriously. It may sound like a slightly repellent quality, but I don't mean to imply that he is excessively gloomy or over-earnest. Often he is deeply dejected: but he has good cause. There is nothing exceptional about his emotional reactions except perhaps their intensity. He has a larger-than-life capacity for experience, a fullness of response, a depth of feeling, a vibrancy of living, which mark him out from the ordinary. He is a raw nerve in the court of Denmark, disconcertingly liable to make the instinctive rather than the conditioned response. This cuts him off from those around him, but it puts him into peculiar contact with the audience. And as Hamlet is to the other figures of the play, so his soliloquies are to the role, for in them Shakespeare shows us the raw nerves of Hamlet himself.

The use of soliloquy is one of the most brilliant features of the play, for in these speeches Shakespeare solves a major technical problem in the presentation of his central character. The young man who takes himself seriously, who persists in explaining himself and his problems, is someone we are apt—perhaps too apt—to regard as a bore. We have all had experience of him, and so probably have most of our friends. On the other hand, the desire to know someone to the depths is fundamental to human nature. Here was both a problem and a challenge: how to let Hamlet reveal himself without becoming an almighty bore? Shakespeare found a double solution. First, he caused Hamlet to conduct his deepest self-communings in solitude, so that there is none of the awkwardness associated with the presence of a confidant. And secondly, the soliloquies are written in a style which presents us not with conclusions but with the very processes of Hamlet's mind.

There had been nothing like this in drama before: nothing which, while retaining a verse form, at the same time so vividly revealed what Shakespeare elsewhere calls "the quick forge and working-house of thought" (*Henry the Fifth* [5.Pro.23]). Vocabulary, syntax, and rhythm all contribute to the effect. Consider the second half of Hamlet's first soliloquy, beginning with his contrast between his uncle and his dead father:

> That it should come to this!
> But two months dead—nay, not so much, not two.
> So excellent a king, that was to this
> Hyperion to a satyr, so loving to my mother
> That he might not beteem the winds of heaven
> Visit her face too roughly. Heaven and earth,
> Must I remember? Why, she would hang on him
> As if increase of appetite had grown
> By what it fed on, and yet within a month—
> Let me not think on 't; frailty, thy name is woman!—
> A little month, or ere those shoes were old
> With which she followed my poor father's body,
> Like Niobe, all tears, why she, even she—
> O God, a beast that wants discourse of reason,
> Would have mourned longer—married with my uncle,
> My father's brother, but no more like my father

Than I to Hercules. Within a month,
Ere yet the salt of most unrighteous tears
Had left the flushing of her gallèd eyes,
She married. O, most wicked speed, to post
With such dexterity to incestuous sheets!
It is not, nor it cannot come to good.
But break, my heart, for I must hold my tongue.

(1.2.137–59)

5   The anguish that it causes Hamlet to think of his mother's over-hasty marriage is conveyed as much by the tortured syntax as by direct statement; we share his difficulty as he tries—and fails—to assimilate these unwelcome facts into his consciousness, seeking to bring under emotional control the discordant elements of his disrupted universe: his love of his dead father, his love of his mother combined with disgust at her marriage to the uncle whom he loathes, and the disillusion with womankind that this has provoked in him. The short exclamations interrupting the sentence structure point his horror: the rhythms of ordinary speech within the verse give immediacy to the contrasts in phrases such as "Hyperion to a satyr" and "Than I to Hercules"; and the concreteness of the imagery betrays the effort it costs him to master the unwelcome nature of the facts which it expresses: his mother's haste to marry "or ere those shoes were old / With which she followed my poor father's body"—it is as if only by concentrating on the matter-of-fact, physical aspects of the scene can he bear to contemplate it, or bring it within his belief. He ends on a note of utter helplessness: he alone sees the truth; he knows that his mother's actions, which both he and she see as evil, must bring forth evil; but he, the only emotionally honest person there, cannot express his emotion—except to us.

[1995]

ELAINE SHOWALTER

Representing Ophelia

"Of all the characters in *Hamlet*," Bridget Lyons has pointed out, "Ophelia is most persistently presented in terms of symbolic meanings." Her behavior, her appearance, her gestures, her costume, her props, are freighted with emblematic significance, and for many generations of Shakespearean critics her part in the play has seemed to be primarily iconographic. Ophelia's symbolic meanings, moreover, are specifically feminine. Whereas for Hamlet madness is metaphysical, linked with culture, for Ophelia it is a product of the female body and female nature, perhaps that nature's purest form. On the Elizabethan stage, the conventions of female insanity were sharply defined. Ophelia dresses in white, decks herself with "fantastical garlands" of wild flowers, and enters, according to the stage directions of the "Bad" Quarto, "distracted" playing on a lute with her "hair down singing." Her speeches are marked by extravagant metaphors, lyrical free associations, and "explosive sexual imagery." She sings wistful and bawdy ballads, and ends her life by drowning.

    All of these conventions carry specific messages about femininity and sexuality. Ophelia's virginal and vacant white is contrasted with Hamlet's scholar's garb, his "suits of solemn black." Her flowers suggest the discordant double images of female sexuality as both innocent blossoming and whorish contamination; she is the "green girl" of pastoral, the virginal "Rose of May" and the sexually explicit madwoman who, in giving away her wild flowers and herbs, is symbolically de-flowering herself. The "weedy trophies" and phallic "long purples" which she wears to her death intimate an improper and discordant sexuality that Gertrude's lovely elegy cannot quite obscure. In Elizabethan and Jacobean drama, the stage direction that a woman enters with dishevelled hair indicates that she might either be mad or the victim of a rape; the disordered hair, her offense against decorum, suggests sensuality in each case. The mad Ophelia's bawdy songs and verbal license, while they give her access to "an entirely different range of experience" from what she is allowed as the dutiful daughter, seem to be her one sanctioned form of self-assertion as a woman, quickly followed, as if in retribution, by her death.

Drowning too was associated with the feminine, with female fluidity as op-posed to masculine aridity. In his discussion of the "Ophelia complex," the phe-nomenologist Gaston Bachelard traces the symbolic connections between women, water, and death. Drowning, he suggests, becomes the truly feminine death in the dramas of literature and life, one which is a beautiful immersion and submersion in the female element. Water is the profound and organic symbol of the liquid woman whose eyes are so easily drowned in tears, as her body is the repository of blood, amniotic fluid, and milk. A man contemplating this feminine suicide under-stands it by reaching for what is feminine in himself, like Laertes, by a temporary surrender to his own fluidity—that is, his tears; and he becomes a man again in becoming once more dry—when his tears are stopped.

Clinically speaking, Ophelia's behavior and appearance are characteristic of the malady the Elizabethans would have diagnosed as female love-melancholy, or erotomania. From about 1580, melancholy had become a fashionable disease among young men, especially in London, and Hamlet himself is a prototype of the melancholy hero. Yet the epidemic of melancholy associated with intellectual and imaginative genius "curiously bypassed women." Women's melancholy was seen instead as biological, and emotional in origins.

[1985]

Bernice W. Kliman

The BBC Hamlet: *A Television Production*

With *Hamlet*, the producers of the BBC Shakespeare Plays have finally met the demands of Shakespeare-on-television by choosing a relatively bare set, conceding only a few richly detailed movable panels and props to shape key locales. By avoiding both location and realistic settings, they point up the natural affinity be-tween Shakespeare's stage and the undisguised sound set. This starkness of setting admits poetry, heightened intensity—and "what not that's sweet and happy."

The producers have thus made a valid choice from among television's three faces: one, broadcast films, whether made for television or not, which exploit loca-tion settings, long shots, and all the clichés we associate with movies, including sudden shifts of space and time and full use of distance, from the most extreme long shots to "eyes only" closeups; two, studio-shot television drama with natural-istic settings, such as the hospital corridors and middle-class living rooms of sit-coms and soap operas, mostly in mid- to close-shots, often interspersed, to be sure, with a bit of stock footage of highways and skylines to establish a realistic environment. This second style varies from a close representation of real action to frankly staged action, where canned laughter or even shadowy glimpses of the studio audience can heighten the staged effect. Three, there is bare space with little or no effort made to disguise that this is a televised activity with a television crew out of sight but nearby. News broadcasts, talk shows and some television drama fit into this third category. Because of its patently unrepresentational quality, this last type offers the most freedom in shooting style. To all three kinds of settings we bring particular expectations in response to their conventions.

Shakespeare's plays work best in the last kind of television space, I believe, because it avoids the clash between realism and poetry, between the unity often expected in realistic media and the disunity and ambiguity of many of the plays, especially *Hamlet*. Yet, while closest to the kind of stage Shakespeare wrote for, the bare television set can be stretched through creative camera work. For example, when Hamlet follows the ghost in the BBC play, the two repeatedly walk across the frame and out of it, first from one direction, then from another; framing fosters the illusion of extended space. Freeing this *Hamlet* from location (as in the BBC *As You Like It*) and from realistic sets (as in the BBC *Measure for Measure*— however well those sets worked for that play) allows the play to be as inconsistent as it is, with, as Bernard Beckerman has so brilliantly explained in *Shakespeare at the Globe, 1599–1609,* a rising and falling action in each individual scene rather than through the course of the drama as a whole. It also allows for acting, the bravura kind that Derek Jacobi is so capable of.

Although gradually coalescing like the pointillism of impressionistic paintings into a subtly textured portrait, at first his mannerisms suggesting madness seem excessive. It is to be expected, perhaps, that Hamlet is a bit unhinged after the ghost scene, but Jacobi's rapid, hard blows to his forehead with the flat of his hand as he says "My tables" recall the desperation of Lear's cry: "O, let me not be mad, not mad, sweet heaven." And soon after, following the last couplet of the scene, Hamlet, maniacally playful, widens his eyes and points, pretending to see the ghost again, then guffaws at Marcellus's fears. Even more unsettling is his laughter when he is alone, as while he is saying "The play's the thing / Wherein I'll catch the conscience of the King." More significantly, he breaks up his own "Mousetrap" by getting right into the play, destroying the distance between audience and stage (a very real raked proscenium-arch stage), spoiling it as a test, because Claudius has a right to be incensed at Hamlet's behavior. Of course, Hamlet does so because Claudius never gives himself away, an unusual and provocative but not impossible interpretation. Thus, Claudius can only have the court's sympathy as he calmly calls for light and uses it to examine Hamlet closely. Hamlet, in response, covers his face, then laughs.

5   Hamlet himself thinks he is mad. To Ophelia he says, as if the realization had suddenly struck him, "It *hath* made me mad [emphasis his]" (III.i.139). To his mother he stresses the word "essentially" in "I *essentially* am not in madness" (III. iv.194). That is, in all essential matters he can be considered sane, though mad around the edges. This indeed turns out to be the explanation.

However doubtful about Hamlet's sanity Jacobi's acting leaves us, in this production this question does not seem to make a difference because it does not have a bearing on the tragedy, and this is true at least partly because in each scene on this nonrealistic set we seem to start anew, ready to let Hamlet's behavior tell us if he is mad or not. Moreover, if Hamlet is mad, it is not so totally as to obscure reason or sensibility. Far from it. It is more as if exacerbated reason and sensibility sometimes tip him into madness. This madness is no excuse for action or delay; it is simply part of the suffering that Hamlet is heir to.

Hamlet, then, is left to struggle against himself—surely where Shakespeare intended the struggle to abide. One of the conflicts in this Hamlet results from his affinity, perhaps, more to the bureaucratic Claudius who handles war-scares with diplomacy and who sits at a desk while brooding over his sins than to the warlike King Hamlet who comes in full armor. Hamlet may admire Fortinbras but is himself more like the bookish Horatio. Through nuance of gesture, through body movement, through a face that is indeed a map of all emotions, Jacobi shapes a Hamlet who loves his father too much to disregard his command, yet who cannot hate his step-father enough to attend to it. Because Jacobi conveys so fully Hamlet's aloneness and vulnerability, one could be struck, for the first time, by the ghost's silence about his son. There is no declaration of love, no concern about Hamlet's ascension to the throne. Hamlet is doomed, it seems, to care about those who consistently care more for others than for him.

All of this production's richness and suggestiveness was realized not only because Jacobi is a marvelous actor—as indeed he is—but also because within the set's spareness that acting could unfold, an acting style that subsumes and transcends the "real." This production's space tells us what is possible for television presentations of Shakespeare. The more bare the set, it seems, the more glowing the words, the more immediate our apprehension of the enacted emotion.

[1988]

WILL SARETTA

What follows is an undergraduate's review, published in a college newspaper, of Kenneth Branagh's film version of Hamlet *(1996).*

Branagh's Film of Hamlet

Kenneth Branagh's *Hamlet* opened last night at the Harmon Auditorium, and will be shown again on Wednesday and Thursday at 7:30 p.m. According to the clock the evening will be long—the film runs for four hours, and in addition there is one ten-minute intermission—but you will enjoy every minute of it.

Well, almost every minute. Curiously, the film begins and ends relatively weakly, but most of what occurs in between is good and much of it is wonderful. The beginning is weak because it is too strong; Bernardo, the sentinel, offstage says "Who's there?" but before he gets a reply he crashes onto the screen and knocks Francisco down. The two soldiers grapple, swords flash in the darkness, and Francisco finally says, "Nay, answer me. Stand and unfold yourself." Presumably Branagh wanted to begin with a bang, but here, as often, more is less. A quieter, less physical opening in which Bernardo, coming on duty, hears a noise and demands that the maker of the noise identify himself and Francisco, the sentinel on duty, rightly demands that the newcomer identify *himself,* would catch the uneasiness and the mystery that pervades the play much better than does Branagh's showy beginning.

Similarly, at the end of the film, we get too much. For one thing, shots of Fortinbras's army invading Elsinore alternate with shots of the duel between Hamlet and King Claudius's pawn, Laertes, and they merely distract us from what really counts in this scene, the duel itself, which will result in Hamlet's death but also in Hamlet's successful completion of his mission to avenge his father. Second, at the very end we get shots of Fortinbras's men pulling down a massive statue of Hamlet Senior, probably influenced by television and newspaper shots of statues of Lenin being pulled down when the Soviet Union was dissolved a few years earlier. This is ridiculous; *Hamlet* is not a play about the fall of Communism, or about one form of tyranny replacing another. Shakespeare's *Hamlet* is not about the triumph of Fortinbras. It is about Hamlet's brave and ultimately successful efforts to do what is right, against overwhelming odds, and to offer us the consolation that in a world where death always triumphs there nevertheless is something that can be called nobility.

What, then, is good about the film? First of all, the film gives us the whole play, whereas almost all productions, whether on the stage or in the movie house, give us drastically abbreviated versions. Although less is often more, when it comes to the text of *Hamlet*, more is better, and we should be grateful to Branagh for letting us hear all of the lines. Second, it is very well performed, with only a few exceptions. Jack Lemmon as Marcellus is pretty bad, but fortunately the part is small. Other big-name actors in small parts—Charlton Heston as the Player King, Robin Williams as Osric, and Billy Crystal as the First Grave-digger—are admirable. But of course the success or failure of any production of *Hamlet* will depend chiefly on the actor who plays Hamlet, and to a considerable degree on the actors who play Claudius, Gertrude, Polonius, Ophelia, Laertes, and Horatio. There isn't space here to comment on all of these roles, but let it be said that Branagh's Prince Hamlet is indeed princely, a man who strikes us as having the ability to become a king, not a wimpy whining figure. When at the end Fortinbras says that if Hamlet had lived to become the king, he would "have proved most royal," we believe him. And his adversary, King Claudius, though morally despicable, is a man of great charm and great ability. The two men are indeed "mighty opposites," to use Hamlet's own words.

5   Branagh's decision to set the play in the late nineteenth century rather than in the Elizabethan period of Shakespeare's day and rather than in our own day contributes to this sense of powerful forces at work. If the play were set in Shakespeare's day, the men would wear tights, and if it were set in our day they would wear suits or trousers and sports jackets and sweaters, but in the film all of the men wear military costumes (black for Hamlet, scarlet for Claudius, white for Laertes) and the women wear ball gowns of the Victorian period. Branagh gives us a world that is closer to our own than would Elizabethan costumes, but yet it is, visually at least, also distant enough to convey a sense of grandeur, which modern dress cannot suggest. Of course *Hamlet* can be done in modern dress, just as *Romeo and Juliet* was done, successfully, in the recent film starring Claire Danes and Leonardo DiCaprio, set in a world that seemed to be Miami Beach, but *Romeo and Juliet* is less concerned with heroism and grandeur than *Hamlet* is, so Branagh probably did well to avoid contemporary costumes.

Although Branagh is faithful to the text, in that he gives us the entire text, he knows that a good film cannot be made merely by recording on film a stage production, and so he gives us handsome shots of landscape, and of rich interiors—for instance, a great mirrored hall—that would be beyond the resources of any theatrical production. I have already said that at the end, when Fortinbras's army swarms over the countryside and then invades the castle we get material that is distracting, indeed irrelevant, but there are also a few other distractions. It is all very well to let us *see* the content of long narrative speeches (for instance, when the Player King talks of the fall of Troy and the death of King Priam and the lament of Queen Hecuba, Branagh shows us these things, with John Gielgud as Priam and Judi Dench as Hecuba, performing in pantomime), but there surely is no need for us to see a naked Hamlet and a naked Ophelia in bed, when Polonius is warning Ophelia that Hamlet's talk of love cannot be trusted. Polonius's warning is not so long or so undramatic that we need to be entertained visually with an invention that finds not a word of support in the text. On the contrary, all of Ophelia's lines suggest that she would not be other than a dutiful young woman, obedient to the morals of the times and to her father's authority. Yet another of Branagh's unfortunate inventions is the prostitute who appears in Polonius's bedroom, during Polonius's interview with Reynaldo. A final example of unnecessary spectacle is Hamlet's killing of Claudius: He hurls his rapier the length of the hall, impaling Claudius, and then like some 1930's movie star he swings on the chandelier and drops down on Claudius to finish him off.

But it is wrong to end this review by pointing out faults in Branagh's film of *Hamlet*. There is so much in this film that is exciting, so much that is moving, so much that is . . . , well, so much that is *Hamlet* (which is to say that it is a great experience), that the film must be recommended without reservation. Go to see it. The four hours will fly.

A postscript. It is good to see that Branagh uses color-blind casting. Voltemand, Fortinbras's Captain, and the messenger who announces Laertes's return are all blacks—the messenger is a black woman—although of course medieval Denmark and Elizabethan England, and, for that matter, Victorian England, would not have routinely included blacks. These performers are effective, and it is appropriate that actors of color take their place in the world's greatest play.

[2000]

Chapter Overview: Looking Backward/Looking Forward

1. Sometimes we say a person is "so innocent." Is this a compliment, or a criticism?
2. Was there a moment in your own life when you moved in a significant way from "innocence" to "experience"? How did you feel when this event occurred? How do you feel about it now?
3. Do you think it is possible to know something well even without having direct experience of it? Can someone know what being a parent means, for example, if he or she does not have a child? Can someone comment expertly on baseball without having played on a major-league team?
4. Name and describe some things that you have experienced once, but never want to experience again.
5. Name and describe some things that you have not experienced, but that you hope to experience some day. If you do not experience them, will your life be affected a lot or a little?
6. Name and describe some things that you feel you must experience at some point in your life. Why are these things so important to you?
7. If you could have been present at any historical event, however long ago, what would it be? Why would you want to be there? What would this experience give you that you do not now possess?

CHAPTER 25

All in a Day's Work

SHORT VIEWS

To pay attention, this is our endless and proper work.
    Mary Oliver

Everyone who is prosperous or successful must have dreamed of something. It is not because he is a good worker that he is prosperous, but because he dreamed.
    Lost Star of the Maricopa

Work is effort applied toward some end. The most satisfying work involves directing our efforts towards achieving ends that we ourselves endorse as worthy expressions of our talent and character.
    William J. Bennett

Men for the sake of getting a living forget to live.
    Margaret Fuller

Work expands so as to fill the time available for its completion.
    C. Northcote Parkinson

The possible quantity of play depends on the possible quantity of pay.
    John Ruskin

Find a job you like, and you will never work a day in your life.
    Anonymous

There is as much dignity in tilling a field as in writing a poem.
    Booker T. Washington

Far and away the best prize that life offers is the chance to work hard at work worth doing.
    Theodore Roosevelt

Personally, I have nothing against work, particularly when performed, quietly and unobtrusively, by someone else. I just don't happen to think it's an appropriate subject for an "ethic."
    Barbara Ehrenreich

*Being a professional is doing all the things you love to do on the days
when you don't feel like doing them.*
    Julius Erving

All professions are conspiracies against the laity.
    George Bernard Shaw

ESSAY

BARBARA EHRENREICH

*Barbara Ehrenreich was born in Butte, Montana, in 1941, of
parents whom she characterized as strongly pro-union. The two
family rules, she told an interviewer, were "Never cross a picket-
line and never vote Republican." She did her undergraduate
work (in chemistry) at Reed College, and she earned a PhD (in
cellular biology) at Rockefeller University, but her career has
been as a writer, not a scientist. Ehrenreich has written more
than twenty books, chiefly on social issues.*

    We give an extract from Nickel and Dimed: On (Not) Getting
By in America *(2001). In this book she recounts her experiences
while working during 1998–2000 in minimum-wage jobs as a
waitress, hotel maid, nursing-home aide, house cleaner, and Wal-Mart associate. These
jobs tended to pay about seven or eight dollars an hour, close to the minimum wage
established by the federal government, which at the time was $7.25. In 2012 the mini-
mum hourly wage for non-tip jobs was $7.40, and for jobs that get tips, $3.70. Almost
thirty percent of the workers in the United States earn about eight dollars an hour.*

    *In the following pages, Ehrenreich discusses the orientation procedure at Wal-
Mart. The title of this extract from Ehrenreich's book is our own.*

Wal-Mart Orientation Program

For sheer grandeur, scale, and intimidation value, I doubt if any corporate orientation exceeds that of Wal-Mart. I have been told that the process will take eight
hours, which will include two fifteen-minute breaks and one half-hour break for a
meal, and will be paid for like a regular shift. When I arrive, dressed neatly in khakis
and clean T-shirt, as befits a potential Wal-Mart "associate," I find there are ten new
hires besides myself, mostly young and Caucasian, and a team of three, headed by
Roberta, to do the "orientating." We sit around a long table in the same windowless
room where I was interviewed, each with a thick folder of paperwork in front of
us, and hear Roberta tell once again about raising six children, being a "people
person," discovering that the three principles of Wal-Mart philosophy were the
same as her own, and so on. We begin with a video, about fifteen minutes long,
on the history and philosophy of Wal-Mart, or, as an anthropological observer
might call it, the Cult of Sam. First young Sam Walton, in uniform, comes back from
the war. He starts a store, a sort of five-and-dime; he marries and fathers four attractive children; he receives a Medal of Freedom from President Bush, after which
he promptly dies, making way for the eulogies. But the company goes on, yes
indeed. Here the arc of the story soars upward unstoppably, pausing only to mark
some fresh milestone of corporate expansion. 1992: Wal-Mart becomes the largest

retailer in the world. 1997: Sales top $100 billion. 1998: The number of Wal-Mart associates hits 825,000, making Wal-Mart the largest private employer in the nation. Each landmark date is accompanied by a clip showing throngs of shoppers, swarms of associates, or scenes of handsome new stores and their adjoining parking lots. Over and over we hear in voiceover or see in graphic display the "three principles," which are maddeningly, even defiantly, nonparallel: "respect for the individual, exceeding customers' expectations; strive for excellence."

"Respect for the individual" is where we, the associates, come in, because vast as Wal-Mart is, and tiny as we may be as individuals, everything depends on us. Sam always said, and is shown saying, that "the best ideas come from the associates"—for example, the idea of having a "people greeter," an elderly employee (excuse me, associate) who welcomes each customer as he or she enters the store. Three times during the orientation, which began at three and stretches to nearly eleven, we are reminded that this brainstorm originated in a mere associate, and who knows what revolutions in retailing each one of us may propose? Because our ideas are welcome, more than welcome, and we are to think of our managers not as bosses but as "servant leaders," serving us as well as the customers. Of course, all is not total harmony, in every instance, between associates and their servant-leaders. A video on "associate honesty" shows a cashier being caught on videotape as he pockets some bills from the cash register. Drums beat ominously as he is led away in handcuffs and sentenced to four years.

The theme of covert tensions, overcome by right thinking and positive attitude, continues in the twelve-minute video entitled *You've Picked a Great Place to Work*. Here various associates testify to the "essential feeling of family for which Wal-Mart is so well-known," leading up to the conclusion that we don't need a union. Once, long ago, unions had a place in American society, but they "no longer have much to offer workers," which is why people are leaving them "by the droves." Wal-Mart is booming; unions are declining: judge for yourself. But we are warned that "unions have been targeting Wal-Mart for years." Why? For the dues money of course. Think of what you would lose with a union: first, your dues money, which could be $20 a month "and sometimes much more." Second, you would lose "your voice" because the union would insist on doing your talking for you. Finally, you might lose even your wages and benefits because they would all be "at risk on the bargaining table." You have to wonder—and I imagine some of my teenage fellow orientees may be doing so—why such fiends as these union organizers, such outright extortionists, are allowed to roam free in the land.

There is more, much more than I could ever absorb, even if it were spread out over a semester-long course. On the reasonable assumption that none of us is planning to go home and curl up with the "Wal-Mart Associate Handbook," our trainers start reading it out loud to us, pausing every few paragraphs to ask, "Any questions?" There never are. Barry, the seventeen-year-old to my left, mutters that his "butt hurts." Sonya, the tiny African American woman across from me, seems frozen in terror. I have given up on looking perky and am fighting to keep my eyes open. No nose or other facial jewelry, we learn; earrings must be small and discreet, not dangling; no blue jeans except on Friday, and then you have to pay $1 for the privilege of wearing them. No "grazing," that is, eating from food packages that somehow become open; no "time theft." This last sends me drifting off in a sci-fi direction: *And as the time thieves headed back to the year 3420, loaded with weekends and days off looted from the twenty-first century. . .* Finally, a question. The old guy who is being hired as a people greeter wants to know, "What is time theft?" Answer: Doing anything other than working during company time, anything at all. Theft of *our* time is not, however, an issue. There are stretches amounting to many minutes when all three of our trainers wander off, leaving us to sit there in silence or take the opportunity to squirm. Or our junior trainers go through a section of the handbook, and then Roberta, returning from some other business, goes over the same section again. My eyelids droop and I consider walking out. I have seen time move more swiftly during seven-hour airline delays. In fact, I am getting nostalgic about seven-hour airline delays. At least you can read a book or get up and walk around, take a leak.

5   On breaks, I drink coffee purchased at the Radio Grill, as the in-house fast-food place is called, the real stuff with caffeine, more because I'm concerned about being alert for the late-night drive home than out of any need to absorb all the Wal-Mart trivia coming my way. Now, here's a drug the drug warriors ought to take a little more interest in. Since I don't normally drink it at all—iced tea can usually be counted on for enough of a kick—the coffee has an effect like reagent-grade Dexedrine: my pulse races, my brain overheats, and the result in this instance is a kind of delirium. I find myself overly challenged by the little kindergarten-level tasks we are now given to do, such as affixing my personal bar code to my ID card, then sticking on the punch-out letters to spell my name. The letters keep curling up and sticking to my fingers, so I stop at "Barb," or more precisely, "BARB," drifting off to think of all the people I know who have gentrified their names in recent years—Patsy to Patricia, Dick to Richard, and so forth—while I am going in the other direction. Now we start taking turns going to the computers to begin our CBL, or Computer-Based Learning, and I become transfixed by the HIV-inspired module entitled "Blood-borne Pathogens," on what to do in the event that pools of human blood should show up on the sales floor. All right, you put warning cones around the puddles, don protective gloves, etc., but I can't stop trying to envision the circumstances in which these pools might arise: an associate uprising? a guest riot? I have gone through six modules, three more than we are supposed to do tonight—the rest are to be done in our spare moments over the next few weeks—when one of the trainers gently pries me away from the computer. We are allowed now to leave.

Joining the Conversation: Critical Thinking and Writing

1. What is the affect of putting quotation marks around "associate" and "orientation"?
2. Imagine that you are working for a publisher, as the editor of Ehrenreich's manuscript. Have you any suggestions? (Remember that we are reprinting only an extract, so it is *not* appropriate, for instance, to suggest that she should identify Roberta, who in fact is fully identified earlier in the chapter.)
3. Write a 500–750 word essay on an orientation program—perhaps the one that your college offers to incoming students. Do not be merely descriptive: Let your reader sense your attitude toward the program, but communicate this attitude throughout the essay rather than merely in an opening or concluding paragraph.
4. If you were a manager at Wal-Mart and you had read Ehrenreich's essay, would you be likely to hire her? In a paragraph, explain why or why not. And in another paragraph explain why you would or would not be eager to take a course with Ehrenreich if she were teaching at your college.

Stop Me If You've Heard This One: Jokes about Lines of Work

Jokes as Short Stories

Most jokes are short stories—very short short stories. We are not talking about wise-cracks, such as Groucho Marx's indignant "Those are my principles, and if you don't like, them, I have others," but about the sort of thing that begins "Have you heard the one about the two frat brothers. They were at a party when this nerd walks in. . . ."

The Role of Stereotypes

As the line about "the two frat brothers" suggests, the jokes we are talking about involve particular *kinds of characters*—stereotypes, or something close to stereo-types. A joke about fraternity brothers will probably involve drinking, or dating, or both. In any case, the opening introduces characters, establishes a setting, and generates expectations—just as the opening of any short story generates expectations—and then, at the end of the joke, everything comes together in a surprising but satisfactory way, a way that evokes laughter or at least a smile (unless the teller botches the telling).

Many jokes that were once considered funny are seen today as objectionable. They usually involve racial or ethnic or gender stereotypes: The jokes attribute highly undesirable characteristics to particular races or nationalities or to one sex or the other. Take this last group, jokes based on gender. Probably the large major-ity of such jokes are anti-female, and of course they are usually told by males. (Why is it, by the way, that men tend to tell jokes more than women do, and why is it that most professional comedians are males?) Thus there are, or used to be, countless jokes about dumb blondes, and countless jokes about meddlesome mothers-in law. But when you think about it, some kinds of jokes are largely at the expense of males, notably jokes about jocks (jokes implying that male athletes are not too bright) and jokes about drunks (we don't recall ever hearing a joke about a drunken woman).

Sometimes a joke that seems to be based on a stereotype does not really involve the stereotype. Here is a very short example, in its "dumb blonde" form:

> A blonde goes to the doctor and says, "I hurt everywhere. I hurt here" (she touches her leg), "I hurt here" (she touches her chest), "and I even hurt here" (she touches her ear).
> The doctor says, "You've got a broken finger."

In our experience, the joke is just as funny when the teller begins, "A guy goes to the doctor. . . ." Here is another joke that used to be told about blondes, but we don't see that in any way it depends on sex or hair color, so we switch to "A guy":

> A guy tells a friend, "Last night I felt terrible, and I decided to commit suicide by swallowing a hundred aspirin."
> "What happened?"
> "After I took two aspirin I felt better."

Admittedly, in this version listeners are not quite so explicitly prepared to expect a dumb ending, but—since listeners know from the start that they are hearing a joke—they *do* expect the unexpected, and they get it.

Stereotypes of Professions

We said that jokes involving racial, ethnic, and gender stereotypes are no longer considered funny—except when, in some instances, they are told by a member of the group being laughed at. Jokes about kinds of work, that is, about various professions, probably can still be told, but if you think they should not, well, that's a topic to write about. Our first joke, for instance, is about kinds of doctors, particularly surgeons. It was told to us by a doctor, and we have tested it on half a dozen other doctors, two of whom were surgeons, and they all claimed to find it funny. Your opinion is invited.

Four Doctors Went Hunting

Four doctors went duck hunting—a general practice (GP) physician, a pediatrician, a surgeon, and a pathologist.

After a time, a bird came flying by. The first to react was the GP, who raised his shotgun but then hesitated. "I'm not quite sure it's a duck," he said, "I will have to get a second opinion." And by that time the bird was gone.

Another bird soon appeared, and the pediatrician took aim. She saw that it was indeed a duck, but she thought the duck looked pregnant, and she decided it was inappropriate to shoot such a bird, so she put her gun down, and the duck was soon out of sight.

The next to spot a bird was the surgeon, He blasted at the sky—BOOM!!—blowing the bird to smithereens.

He then lowered his gun and said to the pathologist, "Go see if that was a duck."

Joining the Conversation: Critical Thinking and Writing

1. Is the joke funny? Why, or why not?
2. Is the joke offensive? Why or why not? By the way, do you think there may be some truth—even just a bit of truth—in it? That is, do you think that, very generally speaking, the kind of doctor who becomes a surgeon probably does have a different personality from the kind of doctor who becomes a general practitioner or a pediatrician? If you think there may be some truth in the joke, should that make it less offensive to surgeons?

A Businessman Interviewed Job Candidates

A businessman was interviewing people for a division manager position. He decided to choose the candidate who could answer the question "How much is 2 + 2?"

The engineer pulled out his slide rule, shuffled it back and forth, and finally said, "It lies between 3.98 and 4.02."

The mathematician said, "In two hours I can demonstrate it equals 4 with the following short proof."

The physicist said, "It's in the magnitude of 1×10^1."

The logician paused, thought for a long period, and then said, "This problem is solvable."

The social worker said, "I don't know the answer, but I am glad that we discussed this important question."

The lawyer said, "In the case of Svenson vs. the State, 2 + 2 was declared to be 4."

The trader asked, "Are you buying or selling?"

The accountant looked at the business owner, got out of his chair, went to see if anyone was listening at the door, and closed the drapes. Then he returned to the business owner, leaned across the desk and said in a low voice, "What would you like it to be?"

Joining the Conversation: Critical Thinking and Writing

What's the joke? Is it offensive? Why, or why not?

The Absent-Minded Professor

> *A Neighbor:* Hi, professor, when did you get back? How was your trip?
> *Absent-Minded Professor:* Thank you for asking, I came back yesterday.
> *Neighbor:* Did you come back by train or plane?
> *Absent-Minded Professor:* How do I know? My wife bought the tickets.

Joining the Conversation: Critical Thinking and Writing

1. Why are absent-minded professor jokes thought to be inherently funny? Is this joke at all funny? Explain. If you know an absent-minded professor joke that you think is funny, tell the joke and explain why it is funny.
2. Do you have a favorite joke? If so, write it out, and then briefly explain why it is funny.

An American Businessman in Mexico

An American businessman in Mexico was at the pier of a small coastal village when a small boat with just one fisherman docked. Inside the small boat were several large yellowfin tuna. The American complimented the Mexican on the quality of his fish and asked how long it took to catch them. The Mexican replied, only a little while. The American then asked, why didn't he stay out longer and catch more fish? The Mexican said he had enough to support his family's immediate needs.

The American then asked, but what do you do with the rest of your time?

The Mexican fisherman said, "I sleep late, fish a little, play with my children, take siesta with my wife Maria, stroll into the village each evening where I sip wine and play guitar with my amigos. I have a full and busy life, señor."

The American scoffed, "I am a Wharton MBA and could help you. You should spend more time fishing and with the proceeds, buy a bigger boat. With the proceeds from the bigger boat you could buy several boats. Eventually you would have a fleet of fishing boats. Instead of selling your catch to a middleman you would sell directly to the processor, eventually opening your own cannery. You would control the product, processing, and distribution. You would need to leave this small coastal fishing village and move to Mexico City, then LA, and eventually NYC, where you will run your expanding enterprise."

The Mexican fisherman asked, "But señor, how long will this all take?"

To which the American replied, "Fifteen to twenty years."

"But what then, señor?"

The American laughed and said, "That's the best part. When the time is right you would announce an IPO [Initial Public Offering, i.e., first sale of stock by a private company to the public] and sell your company stock and become very rich. You would make millions."

"Millions, señor? Then what?"

The American said, "Then you would retire. Move to a small coastal fishing village where you would sleep late, fish a little, play with your kids, take siesta with your wife, stroll to the village in the evenings where you could sip wine and play guitar with your amigos."

Joining the Conversation: Critical Thinking and Writing

Would you call this narrative a joke? Why or why not? In any case, do you think it worth appearing in this book? Worth discussing in class?

Two New Yorkers on Vacation
Go Hunting in Maine

Two New Yorkers on vacation are hunting in Maine, when one collapses. He doesn't seem to be breathing, and his eyes are glazed. The other guy whips out his phone and calls emergency services. He gasps, "My friend is dead! What can I do?" The operator, in a soothing voice, says, "Calm down. I can help. First, let's make sure he's dead." There is a silence, then a shot is heard. Back on the phone, the guy says "OK, now what?"

Joining the Conversation: Critical Thinking and Writing

1. Why two New Yorkers in Maine? Why not, say, "A Texan was hunting on his ranch. . . ."?
2. Funny? Too grim to be funny?

The Detective and the Logical Doctor

Sherlock Holmes and Dr. Watson were going camping. They pitched their tent under the stars and went to sleep. Sometime in the middle of the night Holmes woke Watson up and said, "Watson, look up at the stars, and tell me what you see."

Watson replied, "I see millions and millions of stars." Holmes said, "And what do you deduce from that?" Watson replied, "Well, if there are millions of stars, and if even a few of them have planets, it's quite likely there are some planets like earth out there. And if there are a few planets like earth out there, there might also be life."

And Holmes said, "Watson, you idiot, it means that somebody stole our tent."

Joining the Conversation: Critical Thinking and Writing

Funny? How funny? Why?

The Heart Surgeon and the Mechanic

A heart surgeon regularly took her car to a local garage for service, where she usually exchanged friendly banter with the owner, a skilled mechanic.

"So tell me," says the mechanic one day, "I've been wondering about what we both do for a living, and how much more you get paid than me."

"Yes?" says the surgeon.

"Well look at this," says the mechanic, as he worked on a big complicated engine. "I check how it's running, get a sense of what's wrong—I guess you could say I diagnose it!—then turn it off, open it up, fix the valves, and put it all back together so it works good as new. We basically do the same job, don't we? And yet you are paid ten times what I am—how do you explain that?"

The surgeon thought for a moment, smiled, and replied, "Try it with the engine running."

Joining the Conversation: Critical Thinking and Writing

At the heart of the joke is the implication that surgeons *do* deserve to be paid much more than car mechanics. Do you believe they should? Why? For the reason implied in the joke?

The Rich Businessman at the Business School Commencement

At the commencement ceremony of the Harvard Business School, an immensely wealthy alumnus who had made large donations to the school was given an honorary degree and invited to address the graduates and their families, to tell them the secret of his success. (His classmates had been amazed at his success because, to put it bluntly, he had not seemed very bright.)

"Well," he said to the assembled crowd, "I saw this gizmo in China, and I thought it would have terrific sales in the U.S. The Chinese manufacturer sold each one for a dollar, and I bought a zillion, added one dollar to the price of each, selling them in the U.S. for two dollars—and you know, if you sell enough of them, even at this price increase of just one percent, you can make a lot of money."

Joining the Conversation: Critical Thinking and Writing

Funny? How funny? Why?

JACOB GRIMM AND WILHELM GRIMM

The brothers Jacob Grimm (1785–1863) and Wilhelm Grimm (1786–1859) were German scholars who collected folktales, chiefly from peasant women who told the stories to children, though the stories also circulated among adults. The first Grimm collection, Children's and Household Tales *(1812), contained more than 200 stories, including such now-classic tales as "The Frog Prince," "Sleeping Beauty," and "Snow White."*

Short narratives of this sort are commonly called fairy tales. *In fact, relatively few of them include fairies, although almost all of them do include supernatural elements such as talking animals, gnomes, giants, and witches. They also include archetypal human beings such as the beautiful princess, the handsome prince, and the wicked stepmother.*

Mother Holle

Translated by Margaret Taylor

There was once a widow who had two daughters—one of whom was pretty and industrious, whilst the other was ugly and idle. But she was much fonder of the ugly and idle one, because she was her own daughter, and the other, who was a step-daughter, was obliged to do all the work, and be the Cinderella of the house. Every day the poor girl had to sit by a well, in the highway, and spin and spin till her fingers bled.

Now it happened that one day the shuttle was marked with her blood, so she dipped it in the well, to wash the mark off; but it dropped out of her hand and fell to the bottom. She began to weep, and ran to her step-mother and told her of the mishap. But she scolded her sharply, and was so merciless as to say, "Since you have let the shuttle fall in, you must fetch it out again." So the girl went back to the well, and did not know what to do; and in the sorrow of her heart she jumped into the well to get the shuttle. She lost her senses; and when she awoke and came to herself again, she was in a lovely meadow where the sun was shining and many thousands of flowers were growing. Along this meadow she went, and at last came to a baker's oven full of bread, and the bread cried out, "Oh, take me out! take me out! or I shall burn; I have been baked a long time!" So she went up to it, and took out all the loaves one after another with the bread-shovel. After that she went on till she came to a tree covered with apples, which called out to her, "Oh, shake me! shake me! we apples are all ripe!" So she shook the tree till the apples fell like rain, and went on shaking till they were all down, and when she had gathered them into a heap, she went on her way.

At last she came to a little house, out of which an old woman peeped; but she had such large teeth that the girl was frightened, and was about to run away. But the old woman called out to her, "What are you afraid of, dear child? Stay with me; if you will do all the work in the house properly, you shall be the better for it. Only you must take care to make my bed well, and shake it thoroughly till the feathers fly—for then there is snow on the earth. I am Mother Holle.

As the old woman spoke so kindly to her, the girl took courage and agreed to enter her service. She attended to everything to the satisfaction of her mistress, and always shook her bed so vigorously that the feathers flew about like snow-flakes. So she had a pleasant life with her; never an angry word; and boiled or roast meat every day.

5   She stayed some time with Mother Holle, and then she became sad. At first she did not know what was the matter with her, but found at length that it was home-sickness: although she was many thousand times better off here than at home, still she had a longing to be there. At last she said to the old woman, "I have a longing for home; and however well off I am down here, I cannot stay any longer; I must go up again to my own people." Mother Holle said, "I am pleased that you long for your home again, and as you have served me so truly, I myself will take you up again." Thereupon she took her by the hand, and led her to a large door. The door was opened, and just as the maiden was standing beneath the doorway, a heavy shower of golden rain fell, and all the gold remained sticking to her, so that she was completely covered over with it.

"You shall have that because you have been so industrious," said Mother Holle, and at the same time she gave her back the shuttle which she had let fall into the well. Thereupon the door closed, and the maiden found herself up above upon the earth, not far from her mother's house. And as she went into the yard the cock was standing by the well-side, and cried—

> *"Cock-a-doodle-doo!*
> *Your golden girl's come back to you!"*

So she went in to her mother, and as she arrived thus covered with gold, she was well received, both by her and her sister.

The girl told all that had happened to her; and as soon as the mother heard how she had come by so much wealth, she was very anxious to obtain the same good luck for the ugly and lazy daughter. She had to seat herself by the well and spin; and in order that her shuttle might be stained with blood, she stuck her hand into a thorn bush and pricked her finger. Then she threw her shuttle into the well, and jumped in after it.

She came, like the other, to the beautiful meadow and walked along the very same path. When she got to the oven the bread again cried, "Oh, take me out! take me out! or I shall burn; I have been baked a long time!" But the lazy thing answered, "As if I had any wish to make myself dirty?" and on she went. Soon she came to the apple-tree, which cried, "Oh, shake me! shake me! we apples are all ripe!" But she answered, "I like that! one of you might fall on my head," and so went on.

10   When she came to Mother Holle's house she was not afraid, for she had already heard of her big teeth, and she hired herself to her immediately.

The first day she forced herself to work diligently, and obeyed Mother Holle when she told her to do anything, for she was thinking of all the gold that she would give her. But on the second day she began to be lazy, and on the third day still more so, and then she would not get up in the morning at all. Neither did she make Mother Holle's bed as she ought, and did not shake it so as to make the feathers fly up. Mother Holle was soon tired of this, and gave her notice to leave. The lazy girl was willing enough to go, and thought that now the golden rain would come. Mother Holle led her also to the great door; but while she was standing beneath it, instead of the gold a big kettleful of pitch was emptied over her. "That is the reward for your service," said Mother Holle, and shut the door.

So the lazy girl went home; but she was quite covered with pitch, and the cock by the well-side, as soon as he saw her, cried out—

> *"Cock-a-doodle-doo!*
> *Your pitchy girl's come back to you!"*

But the pitch stuck fast to her, and could not be got off as long as she lived.

[1884]

Joining the Conversation: Critical Thinking and Writing

1. In this story, work is associated with goodness, laziness with evil. In short, the story illustrates "the work ethic" (sometimes called "the Protestant work ethic"), which holds that work enhances character and that laziness is morally bad. On the other hand, some people argue that the work ethic is essentially a trick, a con game, by which those in power delude the lower classes into working mindlessly while the rich exploit their loyal service. Your thoughts?

2. We often hear today that youngsters may be damaged by the kinds of stories implicit in computer games that seem to celebrate violence. And we hear that children do not read enough or—if the children are very young—that parents do not read enough to their children. But consider "Mother Holle," a traditional story found in many older books of fairy tales. Can a good argument be made that the tale is based on a vicious idea, the idea that physically attractive people are virtuous (the beautiful daughter is industrious) and unattractive or deformed people are morally deficient (the ugly daughter is indolent). After all, our physical appearances often are beyond our control, and—though good looks have been said to be the EZ Pass of life—surely our degree of attractiveness is not correlated with our morality. Further, the lifetime punishment of the ugly girl ("the pitch stuck fast to her . . . as long as she lived") implies that human beings cannot repent, cannot reform—or, if they can, they nevertheless should be horribly punished for life. Do you think, then, that this fairy tale (and there are many others like it in its implicit morality) may have a destructive effect on children? Or, on balance, do you think this fairy tale may have a beneficial effect on young readers? Please explain.

WILL EISNER

For a biographical note, see page 414

[2003]

Joining the Conversation: Critical Thinking and Writing

1. The last line of this story is something like the punchline of a joke: It conveys the point of all that precedes it, but, alas, most of today's readers are not familiar with the charming illustrations of Ludwig Bemelmans. (Fifty or sixty years ago Bemelmans was widely known, especially for a series of children's books about a girl called Madeline.) If you have no sense of Bemelmans's work, substitute the name of any illustrator whose work you greatly admire—perhaps Walt Disney or Garry Trudeau. Presumably Bemelmans was in fact tubby and balding, as depicted. Would the story be more effective or less effective if he were more like the central character, a tall, goodlooking guy? Explain your answer.

2. In the first drawing we see an older man standing behind the artist. Who do you suppose this person is, and what is his attitude? How do you know? Why does the author/cartoonist include this figure? And why does the author/cartoonist include the second drawing, showing the artist tightening his necktie? How relevant is this image to the rest of the story? In the next image, if you were creating the strip, would you show the artist standing—as Eisner does? Why not seated, with the other passengers?

3. Explain the title of the story.

4. If you were writing this textbook, would you have included this piece? Why, or why not?

DANIEL OROZCO

Daniel Orozco, born in 1957, is known chiefly for his short stories. A professor of creative writing at the University of Idaho, Orozco has received several important awards, including a grant from the National Endowment for the Arts.

Orientation

Those are the offices and these are the cubicles. That's my cubicle there, and this is your cubicle. This is your phone. Never answer your phone. Let the Voicemail System answer it. This is your Voicemail System Manual. There are no personal phone calls allowed. We do, however, allow for emergencies. If you must make an emergency phone call, ask your supervisor first. If you can't find your supervisor, ask Phillip Spiers, who sits over there. He'll check with Clarissa Nicks, who sits over there. If you make an emergency phone call without asking, you may be let go.

These are your in- and out-boxes. All the forms in your in-box must be logged in by the date shown in the upper left-hand corner, initialed by you in the upper right-hand corner, and distributed to the Processing Analyst whose name is numerically coded in the lower left-hand corner. The lower right-hand corner is left blank. Here's your Processing Analyst Numerical Code Index. And here's your Forms Processing Procedures Manual.

You must pace your work. What do I mean? I'm glad you asked that. We pace our work according to the eight-hour workday. If you have twelve hours of work in your in-box, for example, you must compress that work into the eight-hour day.

If you have one hour of work in your in-box, you must expand that work to fill the eight-hour day. That was a good question. Feel free to ask questions. Ask too many questions, however, and you may be let go.

That is our receptionist. She is a temp. We go through receptionists here. They quit with alarming frequency. Be polite and civil to the temps. Learn their names, and invite them to lunch occasionally. But don't get close to them, as it only makes it more difficult when they leave. And they always leave. You can be sure of that.

5   The men's room is over there. The women's room is over there. John LaFountaine, who sits over there, uses the women's room occasionally. He says it is accidental. We know better, but we let it pass. John LaFountaine is harmless, his forays into the forbidden territory of the women's room simply a benign thrill, a faint blip on the dull flat line of his life.

Russell Nash, who sits in the cubicle to your left, is in love with Amanda Pierce, who sits in the cubicle to your right. They ride the same bus together after work. For Amanda Pierce, it is just a tedious bus ride made less tedious by the idle nattering of Russell Nash. But for Russell Nash, it is the highlight of his day. It is the highlight of his life. Russell Nash has put on forty pounds, and grows fatter with each passing month, nibbling on chips and cookies while peeking glumly over the partitions at Amanda Pierce and gorging himself at home on cold pizza and ice cream while watching adult videos on TV.

Amanda Pierce, in the cubicle to your right, has a six-year-old son named Jamie, who is autistic. Her cubicle is plastered from top to bottom with the boy's crayon artwork—sheet after sheet of precisely drawn concentric circles and ellipses, in black and yellow. She rotates them every other Friday. Be sure to comment on them. Amanda Pierce also has a husband, who is a lawyer. He subjects her to an escalating array of painful and humiliating sex games, to which Amanda Pierce reluctantly submits. She comes to work exhausted and freshly wounded each morning, wincing from the abrasions on her breasts, or the bruises on her abdomen, or the second-degree burns on the backs of her thighs.

But we're not supposed to know any of this. Do not let on. If you let on, you may be let go.

Amanda Pierce, who tolerates Russell Nash, is in love with Albert Bosch, whose office is over there. Albert Bosch, who only dimly registers Amanda Pierce's existence, has eyes only for Ellie Tapper, who sits over there. Ellie Tapper, who hates Albert Bosch, would walk through fire for Curtis Lance. But Curtis Lance hates Ellie Tapper. Isn't the world a funny place? Not in the ha-ha sense, of course.

10   Anika Bloom sits in that cubicle. Last year, while reviewing quarterly reports in a meeting with Barry Hacker, Anika Bloom's left palm began to bleed. She fell into a trance, stared into her hand, and told Barry Hacker when and how his wife would die. We laughed it off. She was, after all, a new employee. But Barry Hacker's wife is dead. So unless you want to know exactly when and how you'll die, never talk to Anika Bloom.

Colin Heavey sits in that cubicle over there. He was new once, just like you. We warned him about Anika Bloom. But at last year's Christmas Potluck he felt sorry for her when he saw that no one was talking to her. Colin Heavey brought her a drink. He hasn't been himself since. Colin Heavey is doomed. There's nothing he can do about it, and we are powerless to help him. Stay away from Colin Heavey. Never give any of your work to him. If he asks you to do something, tell him you have to check with me. If he asks again, tell him I haven't gotten back to you.

This is the fire exit. There are several on this floor, and they are marked accordingly. We have a Floor Evacuation Review every three months, and an

Escape Route Quiz once a month. We have our Biannual Fire Drill twice a year, and our Annual Earthquake Drill once a year. These are precautions only. These things never happen.

For your information, we have a comprehensive health plan. Any catastrophic illness, any unforeseen tragedy is completely covered. All dependents are completely covered. Larry Bagdikian, who sits over there, has six daughters. If anything were to happen to any of his girls, or to all of them, if all six were to simultaneously fall victim to illness or injury—stricken with a hideous degenerative muscle disease or some rare toxic blood disorder, sprayed with semiautomatic gunfire while on a class field trip, or attacked in their bunk beds by some prowling nocturnal lunatic—if any of this were to pass, Larry's girls would all be taken care of. Larry Bagdikian would not have to pay one dime. He would have nothing to worry about.

We also have a generous vacation and sick leave policy. We have an excellent disability insurance plan. We have a stable and profitable pension fund. We get group discounts for the symphony, and block seating at the ballpark. We get commuter ticket books for the bridge. We have direct deposit. We are all members of Costco.

15   This is our kitchenette. And this, this is our Mr. Coffee. We have a coffee pool, into which we each pay two dollars a week for coffee, filters, sugar, and Coffee-Mate. If you prefer Cremora or half-and-half to Coffee-Mate, there is a special pool for three dollars a week. If you prefer Sweet 'N Low to sugar, there is a special pool for two-fifty a week. We do not do decaf. You are allowed to join the coffee pool of your choice, but you are not allowed to touch the Mr. Coffee.

This is the microwave oven. You are allowed to *heat* food in the microwave oven. You are not, however, allowed to *cook* food in the microwave oven.

We get one hour for lunch. We also get one fifteen-minute break in the morning, and one fifteen-minute break in the afternoon. Always take your breaks. If you skip a break, it is gone forever. For your information, your break is a privilege, not a right. If you abuse the break policy, we are authorized to rescind your breaks. Lunch, however, is a right, not a privilege. If you abuse the lunch policy, our hands will be tied, and we will be forced to look the other way. We will not enjoy that.

This is the refrigerator. You may put your lunch in it. Barry Hacker, who sits over there, steals food from this refrigerator. His petty theft is an outlet for his grief. Last New Year's Eve, while kissing his wife, a blood vessel burst in her brain. Barry Hacker's wife was two months pregnant at the time, and lingered in a coma for half a year before she died. It was a tragic loss for Barry Hacker. He hasn't been himself since. Barry Hacker's wife was a beautiful woman. She was also completely covered. Barry Hacker did not have to pay one dime. But his dead wife haunts him. She haunts all of us. We have seen her, reflected in the monitors of our computers, moving past our cubicles. We have seen the dim shadow of her face in our photocopies. She pencils herself in the receptionist's appointment book, with the notation To see Barry Hacker. She has left messages in the receptionist's Voicemail box, messages garbled by the electronic chirrups and buzzes in the phone line, her voice echoing from an immense distance within the ambient hum. But the voice is hers. And beneath her voice, beneath the tidal whoosh of static and hiss, the gurgling and crying of a baby can be heard.

In any case, if you bring a lunch, put a little something extra in the bag for Barry Hacker. We have four Barrys in this office. Isn't that a coincidence?

20   This is Matthew Payne's office. He is our Unit Manager, and his door is always closed. We have never seen him, and you will never see him. But he is here. You can be sure of that. He is all around us.

This is the Custodian's Closet. You have no business in the Custodian's Closet.

And this, this is our Supplies Cabinet. If you need supplies, see Curtis Lance. He will log you in on the Supplies Cabinet Authorization Log, then give you a Supplies Authorization Slip. Present your pink copy of the Supplies Authorization Slip to Ellie Tapper. She will log you in on the Supplies Cabinet Key Log, then give you the key. Because the Supplies Cabinet is located outside the Unit Manager's office, you must be very quiet. Gather your supplies quietly. The Supplies Cabinet is divided into four sections. Section One contains letterhead stationery, blank paper and envelopes, memo pads and notepads, and so on. Section Two contains pens and pencils and typewriter and printer ribbons, and the like. In Section Three we have erasers, correction fluids, transparent tapes, glue sticks, et cetera. And in Section Four we have paper clips and push pins and scissors and razor blades. And here are the spare blades for the shredder. Do not touch the shredder, which is located over there. The shredder is of no concern to you.

Gwendolyn Stich sits in that office there. She is crazy about penguins and collects penguin knickknacks: penguin posters and coffee mugs and stationery, penguin stuffed animals, penguin jewelry, penguin sweaters and T-shirts and socks. She has a pair of penguin fuzzy slippers she wears when working late at the office. She has a tape cassette of penguin sounds, which she listens to for relaxation. Her favorite colors are black and white. She has personalized license plates that read PEN GWEN. Every morning, she passes through all the cubicles to wish each of us a *good* morning. She brings Danish on Wednesdays for Hump Day morning break, and doughnuts on Fridays for TGIF afternoon break. She organizes the Annual Christmas Potluck and is in charge of the Birthday List. Gwendolyn Stich's door is always open to all of us. She will always lend an ear, and put in a good word for you; she will always give you a hand, or the shirt off her back, or a shoulder to cry on. Because her door is always open, she hides and cries in a stall in the women's room. And John LaFountaine—who, enthralled when a woman enters, sits quietly in his stall with his knees to his chest—John LaFountaine has heard her vomiting in there. We have come upon Gwendolyn Stich huddled in the stairwell, shivering in the updraft, sipping a Diet Mr. Pibb and hugging her knees. She does not let any of this interfere with her work. If it interfered with her work, she might have to be let go.

Kevin Howard sits in that cubicle over there. He is a serial killer, the one they call the Carpet Cutter, responsible for the mutilations across town. We're not supposed to know that, so do not let on. Don't worry. His compulsion inflicts itself on strangers only, and the routine established is elaborate and unwavering. The victim must be a white male, a young adult no older than thirty, heavyset, with dark hair and eyes, and the like. The victim must be chosen at random, before sunset, from a public place; the victim is followed home and must put up a struggle, et cetera. The carnage inflicted is precise: the angle and direction of the incisions, the layering of skin and muscle tissue, the rearrangement of the visceral organs, and so on. Kevin Howard does not let any of this interfere with his work. He is, in fact, our fastest typist. He types as if he were on fire. He has a secret crush on Gwendolyn Stich and leaves a red-foil-wrapped Hershey's Kiss on her desk every afternoon. But he hates Anika Bloom and keeps well away from her. In his presence, she has uncontrollable fits of shaking and trembling. Her left palm does not stop bleeding.

25   In any case, when Kevin Howard gets caught, act surprised. Say that he seemed like a nice person, a bit of a loner, perhaps, but always quiet and polite.

This is the photocopier room. And this, this is our view. It faces southwest. West is down there, toward the water. North is back there. Because we are on the seventeenth floor, we are afforded a magnificent view. Isn't it beautiful? It over-looks the park, where the tops of those trees are. You can see a segment of the bay between those two buildings there. You can see the sun set in the gap between those two buildings over there. You can see this building reflected in the glass panels of that building across the way. There. See? That's you, waving. And look there. There's Anika Bloom in the kitchenette, waving back.

Enjoy this view while photocopying. If you have problems with the photo-copier, see Russell Nash. If you have any questions, ask your supervisor. If you can't find your supervisor, ask Phillip Spiers. He sits over there. He'll check with Clarissa Nicks. She sits over there. If you can't find them, feel free to ask me. That's my cubicle. I sit in there.

[1994]

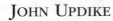

Joining the Conversation: Critical Thinking and Writing

1. How would you characterize the narrator? Thoroughly experienced? Innocent in some ways?
2. Write your own "Orientation" instructions (250–500 words) for someone who is about to take a job that you have had.

JOHN UPDIKE

John Updike (1932–2009) grew up in Shillington, Penn-sylvania, where his father was a teacher and his mother a writer. After receiving a BA degree in 1954 from Har-vard, where he edited the Harvard Lampoon *(for which he both wrote and drew), he studied drawing at Oxford for a year until an offer from the* New Yorker *brought him back to the United States. He was hired as a reporter for the magazine but soon began contributing poetry, essays, and fiction. In 1957 he left the* New Yorker *in order to write independently full-time, though his stories and book reviews appeared regularly in it.*

In 1959 Updike published his first book of stories (The Same Door) *and also his first novel* (The Poorhouse Fair); *the next year he published* Rabbit, Run, *a highly successful novel whose protagonist, "Rabbit" Angstrom, reappears in three later novels:* Rabbit Redux *(1971),* Rabbit Is Rich *(1981), and* Rabbit at Rest *(1990). The first and the last Rabbit books each won a Pulitzer Prize.*

A & P

In walks these three girls in nothing but bathing suits. I'm in the third checkout slot, with my back to the door, so I don't see them until they're over by the bread. The one that caught my eye first was the one in the plaid green two-piece. She was a chunky kid, with a good tan and a sweet broad soft-looking can with those two crescents of white just under it, where the sun never seems to hit, at the top of the backs of her legs. I stood there with my hand on a box of HiHo crackers trying to remember if I rang it up or not. I ring it up again and the customer starts giving me hell. She's one of these cash-register-watchers, a witch about fifty with rouge on her cheekbones and no eyebrows, and I know it made her day to trip me up. She'd been watching cash registers for fifty years and probably never seen a mistake before.

By the time I got her feathers smoothed and her goodies into a bag—she gives me a little snort in passing, if she'd been born at the right time they would have burned her over in Salem—by the time I get her on her way the girls had circled around the bread and were coming back, without a pushcart, back my way along the counters, in the aisle between the checkouts and the Special bins. They didn't even have shoes on. There was this chunky one, with the two-piece—it was bright green and the seams of the bra were still sharp and her belly was still pretty pale so I guessed she just got it (the suit)—there was this one, with one of those chubby berry-faces, the lips all bunched together under her nose, this one, and a tall one, with black hair that hadn't quite frizzed right, and one of these sunburns right across under the eyes, and a chin that was way too long—you know, the kind of girl other girls think is very "striking" and "attractive" but never quite makes it, as they very well know, which is why they like her so much—and then the third one, that wasn't quite so tall. She was the queen. She kind of led them, the other two peeking around and making their shoulders round. She didn't look around, not this queen, she just walked straight on slowly, on these long white prima-donna legs. She came down a little hard on her heels, as if she didn't walk in her bare feet that much, putting down her heels and then letting the weight move along to her toes as if she was testing the floor with every step, putting a little deliberate extra action into it. You never know for sure how girls' minds work (do they really think it's a mind in there or just a little buzz like a bee in a glass jar?) but you got the idea she had talked the other two into coming in here with her, and now she was showing them how to do it, walk slow and hold yourself straight.

She had on a kind of dirty pink—beige maybe, I don't know—bathing suit with a little nubble all over it and, what got me, the straps were down. They were off her shoulders looped loose around the cool tops of her arms, and I guess as a result the suit had slipped on her, so all around the top of the cloth there was this shining rim. If it hadn't been there you wouldn't have known there could have been anything whiter than those shoulders. With the straps pushed off, there was nothing between the top of the suit and the top of her head except just *her*, this clean bare plane of the top of her chest down from the shoulder bones like a dented sheet of metal tilted in the light. I mean, it was more than pretty.

She had sort of oaky hair that the sun and salt had bleached, done up in a bun that was unravelling, and a kind of prim face. Walking into the A & P with your straps down, I suppose it's the only kind of face you *can* have. She held her head so high her neck, coming up out of those white shoulders, looked kind of stretched, but I didn't mind. The longer her neck was, the more of her there was.

5   She must have felt in the corner of her eye me and over my shoulder Stokesie in the second slot watching, but she didn't tip. Not this queen. She kept her eyes moving across the racks, and stopped, and turned so slow it made my stomach rub the inside of my apron, and buzzed to the other two, who kind of huddled against her for relief, and then they all three of them went up the cat and dog food-breakfast cereal-macaroni-rice-raisins-seasonings-spreads-spaghetti-soft drinks-crackers-and-cookies aisle. From the third slot I look straight up this aisle to the meat counter, and I watched them all the way. The fat one with the tan sort of fumbled with the cookies, but on second thought she put the package back. The sheep pushing their carts down the aisle—the girls were walking against the usual traffic (not that we

have one-way signs or anything)—were pretty hilarious. You could see them, when Queenie's white shoulders dawned on them, kind of jerk, or hop, or hiccup, but their eyes snapped back to their own baskets and on they pushed. I bet you could set off dynamite in the A & P and the people would by and large keep reaching and checking oatmeal off their lists and muttering "Let me see, there was a third thing, began with A, asparagus, no, ah, yes, applesauce!" or whatever it is they do mutter. But there was no doubt, this jiggled them. A few house slaves in pin curlers even look around after pushing their carts past to make sure what they had seen was correct.

You know, it's one thing to have a girl in a bathing suit down on the beach, where what with the glare nobody can look at each other much anyway, and another thing in the cool of the A & P, under the fluorescent lights, against all those stacked packages, with her feet paddling along naked over our checker-board green-and-cream, rubber-tile floor.

"Oh, Daddy," Stokesie said beside me. "I feel so faint."

"Darling," I said. "Hold me tight." Stokesie's married, with two babies chalked up on his fuselage already, but as far as I can tell that's the only difference. He's twenty-two, and I was nineteen this April.

"Is it done?" he asks, the responsible married man finding his voice. I forgot to say he thinks he's going to be a manager some sunny day, maybe in 1990 when it's called the Great Alexandrov and Petrooshki Tea Company or something.

10   What he meant was, our town is five miles from a beach, with a big summer colony out on the Point, but we're right in the middle of town, and the women generally put on a shirt or shorts or something before they get out of the car into the street. And anyway these are usually women with six children and varicose veins mapping their legs and nobody, including them, could care less. As I say, we're right in the middle of town, and if you stand at our front doors you can see two banks and the Congregational church and the newspaper store and three real estate offices and about twenty-seven old freeloaders tearing up Central Street because the sewer broke again. It's not as if we're on the Cape; we're north of Boston and there's people in this town haven't seen the ocean for twenty years.

The girls had reached the meat counter and were asking McMahon something. He pointed, they pointed, and they shuffled out of sight behind a pyramid of Diet Delight peaches. All that was left for us to see was old McMahon patting his mouth and looking after them sizing up their joints. Poor kids, I began to feel sorry for them, they couldn't help it.

Now here comes the sad part of the story, at least my family says it's sad, but I don't think it's so sad myself. The store's pretty empty, it being Thursday afternoon, so there was nothing much to do except lean on the register and wait for the girls to show up again. The whole store was like a pinball machine and I didn't know which tunnel they'd come out of. After a while they come around out of the far aisle, around the light bulbs, records at discount of the Caribbean Six or Tony Martin Sings or some such gunk you wonder they waste the wax on, six-packs of candy bars, and plastic toys done up in cellophane that fall apart when a kid looks at them anyway. Around they come, Queenie still leading the way, and holding a little gray jar in her hand. Slots Three through Seven are unmanned and I could see her wondering between Stokes and me, but Stokesie with his usual luck draws an old party in baggy gray pants who stumbles up with four giant cans of pineapple juice (what do these bums *do* with all that pineapple juice? I've often asked myself) so the girls come to me. Queenie puts down the jar and I take it into my fingers icy cold. Kingfish Fancy Herring Snacks in Pure Sour Cream: 49¢. Now her hands are empty, not a ring or a bracelet, bare as God made them, and I wonder where the money's coming from. Still with the prim look she lifts a folded dollar bill out of the hollow at the center of her nubbled pink top. The jar went heavy in my hand. Really, I thought that was so cute.

Then everybody's luck begins to run out. Lengel comes in from haggling with a truck full of cabbages on the lot and is about to scuttle into the door marked MANAGER behind which he hides all day when the girls touch his eye. Lengel's pretty dreary, teaches Sunday school and the rest, but he doesn't miss that much. He comes over and says, "Girls, this isn't the beach."

Queenie blushes, though maybe it's just a brush of sunburn I was noticing for the first time, now that she was so close. "My mother asked me to pick up a jar of herring snacks." Her voice kind of startled me, the way voices do when you see the people first, coming out so flat and dumb yet kind of tony, too, the way it ticked over "pick up" and "snacks." All of a sudden I slid right down her voice into her living room. Her father and the other men were standing around in ice-cream coats and bow ties and the women were in sandals picking up herring snacks on toothpicks off a big glass plate and they were all holding drinks the color of water with olives and sprigs of mint in them. When my parents have somebody over they get lemonade and if it's a real racy affair Schlitz in tall glasses with "They'll Do It Every Time" cartoons stencilled on.

15   "That's all right," Lengel said. "But this isn't the beach." His repeating this struck me as funny, as if it had just occurred to him, and he had been thinking all these years the A & P was a great big dune and he was the head lifeguard. He didn't like my smiling—as I say he doesn't miss much—but he concentrates on giving the girls that sad Sunday-school-superintendent stare.

Queenie's blush was no sunburn now, and the plump one in plaid, that I liked better from the back—a really sweet can—pipes up, "We weren't doing any shopping. We just came in for the one thing."

"That makes no difference," Lengel tells her, and I could see from the way his eyes went that he hadn't noticed she was wearing at two-piece before. "We want you decently dressed when you come in here."

"We *are* decent," Queenie says suddenly, her lower lip pushing, getting sore now that she remembers her place, a place from which the crowd that runs the A & P must look pretty crummy. Fancy Herring Snacks flashed in her very blue eyes.

"Girls, I don't want to argue with you. After this come in here with your shoulders covered. It's our policy." He turns his back. That's policy for you. Policy is what the kingpins want. What the others want is juvenile delinquency.

20   All this while, the customers had been showing up with their carts but, you know, sheep, seeing a scene, they had all bunched up on Stokesie, who shook open a paper bag as gently as peeling a peach, not wanting to miss a word. I could feel in the silence everybody getting nervous, most of all Lengel, who asks me, "Sammy, have you rung up this purchase?"

I thought and said "No" but it wasn't about that I was thinking. I go through the punches, 4, 9, GROC, TOT—it's more complicated than you think and after you do it often enough, it begins to make a little song, that you hear words to, in my case "Hello (*bing*) there, you (*gung*) hap-py *peepul* (*splat*)!"—the *splat* being the drawer flying out. I uncrease the bill, tenderly as you may imagine, it just having come from between the two smoothest scoops of vanilla I had ever known were there, and pass a half and a penny into her narrow pink palm and nestle the herrings in a bag and twist its neck and hand it over, all the time thinking.

The girls, and who'd blame them, are in a hurry to get out, so I say "I quit" to Lengel quick enough for them to hear, hoping they'll stop and watch me, their unsuspected hero. They keep right on going, into the electric eye; the door flies open and they flicker across the lot to their car, Queenie and Plaid and Big Tall Goony-Goony (not that as raw material she was so bad), leaving me with Lengel and a kink in his eyebrow.

"Did you say something, Sammy?"

"I said I quit."

25 "I thought you did."

"You didn't have to embarrass them."

"It was they who were embarrassing us."

I started to say something that came out "Fiddle-de-doo." It's a saying of my grandmother's, and I know she would have been pleased.

"I don't think you know what you're saying," Lengel said.

30 "I know you don't," I said. "But I do." I pull the bow at the back of my apron and start shrugging it off my shoulders. A couple customers that had been heading for my slot begin to knock against each other, like scared pigs in a chute.

Lengel sighs and begins to look very patient and old and gray. He's been a friend of my parents for years. "Sammy, you don't want to do this to your Mom and Dad," he tells me. It's true, I don't. But it seems to me that once you begin a gesture it's fatal not to go through with it. I fold the apron, "Sammy" stitched in red on the pocket, and put it on the counter, and drop the bow tie on top of it. The bow tie is theirs, if you've ever wondered. "You'll feel this for the rest of your life," Lengel says, and I know that's true, too, but remembering how he made that pretty girl blush makes me so scrunchy inside I punch the No Sale tab and the machine whirs "pee-pul" and the drawer splats out. One advantage to this scene taking place in summer, I can follow this up with a clean exit, there's no fumbling around getting your coat and galoshes, I just saunter into the electric eye in my white shirt that my mother ironed the night before, and the door heaves itself open, and outside the sunshine is skating round on the asphalt.

I look around for my girls, but they're gone, of course. There wasn't anybody but some young married screaming with her children about some candy they didn't get by the door of a powder-blue Falcon station wagon. Looking back in the big windows, over the bags of peat moss and aluminum lawn furniture stacked on the pavement, I could see Lengel in my place in the slot, checking the sheep through. His face was dark gray and his back stiff, as if he'd just had an injection of iron, and my stomach kind of fell as I felt how hard the world was going to be to me hereafter.

[1962]

Joining the Conversation: Critical Thinking and Writing

1. In what sort of community is this A & P located? To what extent does this community resemble yours?
2. Do you think Sammy is a male chauvinist pig? Why, or why not? And if you think he is, do you find the story offensive? Again, why or why not? Present your response in the form of a detailed argument.

3. In the last line of the story Sammy says, "I felt how hard the world was going to be to me hereafter." Do you think the world is going to be hard to Sammy? Why, or why not? And if it is hard to him, is this because of a virtue or a weakness in Sammy?

4. Write Lengel's version of the story (500–1000 words) as he might narrate it to his wife during dinner. Or write the story from Queenie's point of view.

5. In speaking of contemporary fiction, Updike said:

> I want stories to startle and engage me within the first few sentences, and in their middle to widen or deepen or sharpen my knowledge of human activity, and to end by giving me a sensation of completed statement.

Let's assume that you share Updike's view of what a story should do. To what extent do you think "A & P" fulfills these demands? (You may want to put your response in the form of a letter to Updike.)

MyLiteratureLab® *For additional resources for "A & P," log in to www.myliteraturelab .com where you will find an Interactive Reading, Comprehension Quiz, Student Essay, and Short Evaluation Exercises, as well as an About the Author, Bibliography, Links, and Critical Overview for Updike (under Student Resources).*

B. TRAVEN

B. Traven (1882–1969), author of The Cotton Pickers *(1925) and* The Treasure of the Sierra Madre *(1927) as well as lesser-known works—all of which originally appeared in German—remains a mysterious figure. The best biography argues that he was christened Hermann Albert Otto Maximilian Wienecke, in Pomerania. His parents were unmarried at the time, so he was given his mother's name; when the parents married he was renamed Otto Feige. He became an actor, but during World War I he edited a journal devoted to peace. After the war he wandered through continental Europe and England, then in 1924 sailed to Mexico, where he took the name B. Traven. He spent the rest of his life in Mexico, using various names, exploring the jungles, and writing. The story we reprint, originally published in German in 1928, appears in* Night Vision and Other Stories.

Assembly Line

Mr. E. L. Winthrop of New York was on vacation in the Republic of Mexico. It wasn't long before he realized that this strange and really wild country had not yet been fully and satisfactorily explored by Rotarians and Lions, who are forever conscious of their glorious mission on earth. Therefore, he considered it his duty as a good American citizen to do his part in correcting this oversight.

In search for opportunities to indulge in his new avocation, he left the beaten track and ventured into regions not especially mentioned, and hence not recommended, by travel agents to foreign tourists. So it happened that one day he found himself in a little, quaint Indian village somewhere in the State of Oaxaca.

Walking along the dusty main street of this pueblecito, which knew nothing of pavements, drainage, plumbing, or of any means of artificial light save candles or pine splinters, he met with an Indian squatting on the earthen-floor front porch of a palm hut, a so-called jacalito.

The Indian was busy making little baskets from bast and from all kinds of fibers gathered by him in the immense tropical bush which surrounded the village on all sides. The material used had not only been well prepared for its purpose but was also richly colored with dyes that the basket-maker himself extracted from various native plants, barks, roots and from certain insects by a process known only to him and the members of his family.

5   His principal business, however, was not producing baskets. He was a peasant who lived on what the small property he possessed—less than fifteen acres of not too fertile soil—would yield, after much sweat and labor and after constantly worrying over the most wanted and best suited distribution of rain, sunshine, and wind and the changing balance of birds and insects beneficial or harmful to his crops. Baskets he made when there was nothing else for him to do in the fields, because he was unable to dawdle. After all, the sale of his baskets, though to a rather limited degree only, added to the small income he received from his little farm.

In spite of being by profession just a plain peasant, it was clearly seen from the small baskets he made that at heart he was an artist, a true and accomplished artist. Each basket looked as if covered all over with the most beautiful sometimes fantastic ornaments, flowers, butterflies, birds, squirrels, antelope, tigers, and a score of other animals of the wilds. Yet, the most amazing thing was that these decorations, all of them symphonies of color, were not painted on the baskets but were instead actually part of the baskets themselves. Bast and fibers dyed in dozens of different colors were so cleverly—one must actually say intrinsically—interwoven that those attractive designs appeared on the inner part of the basket as well as on the outside. Not by painting but by weaving were those highly artistic effects achieved. This performance he accomplished without ever looking at any sketch or pattern. While working on a basket these designs came to light as if by magic, and as long as a basket was not entirely finished one could not perceive what in this case or that the decoration would be like.

People in the market town who bought these baskets would use them for sewing baskets or to decorate tables with or window sills, or to hold little things to keep them from lying around. Women put their jewelry in them or flowers or little dolls. There were in fact a hundred and two ways they might serve certain purposes in a household or in a lady's own room.

Whenever the Indian had finished about twenty of the baskets he took them to town on market day. Sometimes he would already be on his way shortly after midnight because he owned only a burro to ride on, and if the burro had gone astray the day before, as happened frequently, he would have to walk the whole way to town and back again.

At the market he had to pay twenty centavos in taxes to sell his wares. Each basket cost him between twenty and thirty hours of constant work, not counting the time spent gathering bast and fibers, preparing them, making dyes and coloring the bast. All this meant extra time and work. The price he asked for each basket was fifty centavos, the equivalent of about four cents. It seldom happened, however, that a buyer paid outright the full fifty centavos asked—or four reales as the Indian called that money. The prospective buyer started bargaining, telling the Indian that he ought to be ashamed to ask such a sinful price. "Why, the whole dirty thing is nothing but ordinary petate straw which you find in heaps wherever you may look for it; the jungle is packed full of it," the buyer would argue. "Such a little basket, what's it good for anyhow? If I paid you, you thief, ten centavitos for it you should be grateful and kiss my hand. Well, it's your lucky day, I'll be generous this time, I'll pay you twenty, yet not one green centavo more. Take it or run along."

10   So he sold finally for twenty-five centavos, but then the buyer would say, "Now, what do you think of that? I've got only twenty centavos change on me. What can we do about that? If you can change me a twenty-peso bill, all right, you shall have your twenty-five fierros." Of course, the Indian could not change a twenty-peso bill and so the basket went for twenty centavos.

He had little if any knowledge of the outside world or he would have known that what happened to him was happening every hour of every day to every artist all over the world. That knowledge would perhaps have made him very proud; because he would have realized that he belonged to the little army which is the salt of the earth and which keeps culture, urbanity and beauty for their own sake from passing away.

Often it was not possible for him to sell all the baskets he had brought to market, for people here as elsewhere in the world preferred things made by the millions and each so much like the other that you were unable, even with the help of a magnifying glass, to tell which was which and where was the difference between two of the same kind.

Yet he, this craftsman, had in his life made several hundreds of those exquisite baskets, but so far no two of them had he ever turned out alike in design. Each was an individual piece of art and as different from the other as was a Murillo from a Velásquez.

Naturally he did not want to take those baskets which he could not sell at the market place home with him again if he could help it. In such a case he went peddling his products from door to door where he was treated partly as a beggar and partly as a vagrant apparently looking for an opportunity to steal, and he frequently had to swallow all sorts of insults and nasty remarks.

15   Then, after a long run, perhaps a woman would finally stop him, take one of the baskets and offer him ten centavos, which price through talks and talks would perhaps go up to fifteen or even to twenty. Nevertheless, in many instances he would actually get no more than just ten centavos, and the buyer, usually a woman, would grasp that little marvel and right before his eyes throw it carelessly upon the nearest table as if to say, "Well, I take that piece of nonsense only for charity's sake. I know my money is wasted. But then, after all, I'm a Christian and I can't see a poor Indian die of hunger since he has come such a long way from his village." This would remind her of something better and she would hold him and say, "Where are you at home anyway, Indito? What's your pueblo? So, from Huehuetonoc? Now, listen here, Indito, can't you bring me next Saturday two or three turkeys from Huehuetonoc? But they must be heavy and fat and very, very cheap or I won't even touch them. If I wish to pay the regular price I don't need you to bring them. Understand? Hop along, now, Indito."

The Indian squatted on the earthen floor in the portico of his hut, attended to his work and showed no special interest in the curiosity of Mr. Winthrop watching him. He acted almost as if he ignored the presence of the American altogether.

"How much that little basket, friend?" Mr. Winthrop asked when he felt that he at least had to say something as not to appear idiotic.

"Fifty centavitos, patroncito, my good little lordy, four reales," the Indian answered politely.

"All right, sold," Mr. Winthrop blurted out in a tone and with a wide gesture as if he had bought a whole railroad. And examining his buy he added, "I know already who I'll give that pretty little thing to. She'll kiss me for it, sure. Wonder what she'll use it for?"

20   He had expected to hear a price of three or even four pesos. The moment he realized that he had judged the value six times too high, he saw right away what

great business possibilities this miserable Indian village might offer to a dynamic promoter like himself. Without further delay he started exploring those possibilities. "Suppose, my good friend, I buy ten of these little baskets of yours which, as I might as well admit right here and now, have practically no real use whatsoever. Well, as I was saying, if I buy ten, how much would you then charge me apiece?"

The Indian hesitated for a few seconds as if making calculations. Finally he said, "If you buy ten I can let you have them for forty-five centavos each, señorito gentleman."

"All right, amigo. And now, let's suppose I buy from you straight away one hundred of these absolutely useless baskets, how much will cost me each?"

The Indian, never fully looking up to the American standing before him and hardly taking his eyes off his work, said politely and without the slightest trace of enthusiasm in his voice, "In such a case I might not be quite unwilling to sell each for forty centavitos."

Mr. Winthrop bought sixteen baskets, which was all the Indian had in stock.

25   After three weeks' stay in the Republic, Mr. Winthrop was convinced that he knew this country perfectly, that he had seen everything and knew all about the inhabitants, their character and their way of life, and that there was nothing left for him to explore. So he returned to good old Nooyorg and felt happy to be once more in a civilized country, as he expressed it to himself.

One day going out for lunch he passed a confectioner's and, looking at the display in the window, he suddenly remembered the little baskets he had bought in that faraway Indian village.

He hurried home and took all the baskets he still had left to one of the best-known candy-makers in the city.

"I can offer you here," Mr. Winthrop said to the confectioner, "one of the most artistic and at the same time the most original of boxes, if you wish to call them that. These little baskets would be just right for the most expensive chocolates meant for elegant and high-priced gifts. Just have a good look at them, sir, and let me listen."

The confectioner examined the baskets and found them extraordinarily well suited for a certain line in his business. Never before had there been anything like them for originality, prettiness and good taste. He, however, avoided most carefully showing any sign of enthusiasm, for which there would be time enough once he knew the price and whether he could get a whole load exclusively.

30   He shrugged his shoulders and said, "Well, I don't know. If you asked me I'd say it isn't quite what I'm after. However, we might give it a try. It depends, of course, on the price. In our business the package mustn't cost more than what's in it."

"Do I hear an offer?" Mr. Winthrop asked.

"Why don't you tell me in round figures how much you want for them? I'm not good in guessing."

"Well, I'll tell you, Mr. Kemple: since I'm the smart guy who discovered these baskets and since I'm the only Jack who knows where to lay his hands on more, I'm selling to the highest bidder, on an exclusive basis, of course. I'm positive you can see it my way, Mr. Kemple."

"Quite so, and may the best man win," the confectioner said. "I'll talk the matter over with my partners. See me tomorrow same time, please, and I'll let you know how far we might be willing to go."

35   Next day when both gentlemen met again Mr. Kemple said: "Now, to be frank with you, I know art on seeing it, no getting around that. And these baskets are little works of art, they surely are. However, we are no art dealers, you realize that

of course. We've no other use for these pretty little things except as fancy packing for our French pralines made by us. We can't pay for them what we might pay considering them pieces of art. After all to us they're only wrappings. Fine wrappings, perhaps, but nevertheless wrappings. You'll see it our way I hope, Mr.—oh yes, Mr. Winthrop. So, here is our offer, take it or leave it: a dollar and a quarter apiece and not one cent more."

Mr. Winthrop made a gesture as if he had been struck over the head.

The confectioner, misunderstanding this involuntary gesture of Mr. Winthrop, added quickly, "All right, all right, no reason to get excited, no reason at all. Perhaps we can do a trifle better. Let's say one-fifty."

"Make it one-seventy-five," Mr. Winthrop snapped, swallowing his breath while wiping his forehead.

"Sold. One-seventy-five apiece free at port of New York. We pay the customs and you pay the shipping. Right?"

40   "Sold," Mr. Winthrop said also and the deal was closed.

"There is, of course, one condition," the confectioner explained just when Mr. Winthrop was to leave. "One or two hundred won't do for us. It wouldn't pay the trouble and the advertising. I won't consider less than ten thousand, or one thousand dozens if that sounds better in your ears. And they must come in no less than twelve different patterns well assorted. How about that?"

"I can make it sixty different patterns or designs."

"So much the better. And you're sure you can deliver ten thousand let's say early October?"

"Absolutely," Mr. Winthrop avowed and signed the contract.

45   Practically all the way back to Mexico, Mr. Winthrop had a notebook in his left hand and a pencil in his right and he was writing figures, long rows of them, to find out exactly how much richer he would be when this business had been put through.

"Now, let's sum up the whole goddamn thing," he muttered to himself. "Damn it, where is that cursed pencil again? I had it right between my fingers. Ah, there it is. Ten thousand he ordered. Well, well, there we got a clean-cut profit of fifteen thousand four hundred and forty genuine dollars. Sweet smackers. Fifteen grand right into papa's pocket. Come to think of it, that Republic isn't so backward after all."

"Buenas tardes, mi amigo,[1] how are you?" he greeted the Indian whom he found squatting in the porch of his jacalito as if he had never moved from his place since Mr. Winthrop had left for New York.

The Indian rose, took off his hat, bowed politely and said in his soft voice, "Be welcome, patroncito. Thank you, I feel fine, thank you. Muy buenas tardes.[2] This house and all I have is at your kind disposal." He bowed once more, moved his right hand in a gesture of greeting and sat down again. But he excused himself for doing so by saying, "Perdoneme, patroncito, I have to take advantage of the daylight, soon it will be night."

"I've got big business for you, my friend," Mr. Winthrop began.

50   "Good to hear that, señor."

Mr. Winthrop said to himself, "Now, he'll jump up and go wild when he learns what I've got for him." And aloud he said: "Do you think you can make me one thousand of these little baskets?"

"Why not, patroncito? If I can make sixteen, I can make one thousand also."

"That's right, my good man. Can you also make five thousand?"

---

[1]**Buenas . . . amigo** Good afternoon, friend.   [2]**Muy buenas tardes** Very good afternoon.

"Of course, señor. I can make five thousand if I can make one thousand."

"Good. Now, if I should ask you to make me ten thousand, what would you say? And what would be the price of each? You can make ten thousand, can't you?"

"Of course, I can, señor. I can make as many as you wish. You see, I am an expert in this sort of work. No one else in the whole state can make them the way I do."

"That's what I thought and that's exactly why I came to you."

"Thank you for the honor, patroncito."

"Suppose I order you to make me ten thousand of these baskets, how much time do you think you would need to deliver them?"

The Indian, without interrupting his work, cocked his head to one side and then to the other as if he were counting the days or weeks it would cost him to make all these baskets.

After a few minutes he said in a slow voice, "It will take a good long time to make so many baskets, patroncito. You see, the bast and the fibers must be very dry before they can be used properly. Then all during the time they are slowly drying, they must be worked and handled in a very special way so that while drying they won't lose their softness and their flexibility and their natural brilliance. Even when dry they must look fresh. They must never lose their natural properties or they will look just as lifeless and dull as straw. Then while they are drying up I got to get the plants and roots and barks and insects from which I brew the dyes. That takes much time also, believe me. The plants must be gathered when the moon is just right or they won't give the right color. The insects I pick from the plants must also be gathered at the right time and under the right conditions or else they produce no rich colors and are just like dust. But, of course, jefecito,[3] I can make as many of these canastitas[4] as you wish, even as many as three dozens if you want them. Only give me time."

"Three dozens? Three dozens?" Mr. Winthrop yelled, and threw up both arms in desperation. "Three dozens!" he repeated as if he had to say it many times in his own voice so as to understand the real meaning of it, because for a while he thought that he was dreaming. He had expected the Indian to go crazy on hearing that he was to sell ten thousand of his baskets without having to peddle them from door to door and be treated like a dog with a skin disease.

So the American took up the question of price again, by which he hoped to activate the Indian's ambition. "You told me that if I take one hundred baskets you will let me have them for forty centavos apiece. Is that right, my friend?"

"Quite right, jefecito."

"Now," Mr. Winthrop took a deep breath, "now, then, if I ask you to make me one thousand, that is, ten times one hundred baskets, how much will they cost me, each basket?"

That figure was too high for the Indian to grasp. He became slightly confused and for the first time since Mr. Winthrop had arrived he interrupted his work and tried to think it out. Several times he shook his head and looked vaguely around as if for help. Finally he said, "Excuse me, jefecito, little chief, that is by far too much for me to count. Tomorrow, if you will do me the honor, come and see me again and I think I shall have my answer ready for you, patroncito."

When on the next morning Mr. Winthrop came to the hut he found the Indian as usual squatting on the floor under the overhanging palm roof working at his baskets.

"Have you got the price for ten thousand?" he asked the Indian the very moment he saw him, without taking the trouble to say "Good morning!"

---

[3]**jefecito** boss (literally, "little chief").   [4]**canastitas** little baskets.

"Si, patroncito, I have the price ready. You may believe me when I say it has cost me much labor and worry to find out the exact price, because, you see, I do not wish to cheat you out of your honest money."

70 "Skip that, amigo. Come out with the salad. What's the price?" Mr. Winthrop asked nervously.

"The price is well calculated now without any mistake on my side. If I got to make one thousand canastitas each will be three pesos. If I must make five thousand, each will cost nine pesos. And if I have to make ten thousand, in such a case I can't make them for less than fifteen pesos each." Immediately he returned to his work as if he were afraid of losing too much time with such idle talk.

Mr. Winthrop thought that perhaps it was his faulty knowledge of this foreign language that had played a trick on him.

"Did I hear you say fifteen pesos each if I eventually would buy ten thousand?"

"That's exactly and without any mistake what I've said, patroncito," the Indian answered in his soft courteous voice.

75 "But now, see here, my good man, you can't do this to me. I'm your friend and I want to help you get on your feet."

"Yes, patroncito, I know this and I don't doubt any of your words."

"Now, let's be patient and talk this over quietly as man to man. Didn't you tell me that if I would buy one hundred you would sell each for forty centavos?"

"Si, jefecito, that's what I said. If you buy one hundred you can have them for forty centavos apiece, provided that I have one hundred, which I don't."

"Yes, yes, I see that." Mr. Winthrop felt as if he would go insane any minute now. "Yes, so you said. Only what I can't comprehend is why you cannot sell at the same price if you make me ten thousand. I certainly don't wish to chisel on the price. I am not that kind. Only, well, let's see now, if you can sell for forty centavos at all, be it for twenty or fifty or a hundred, I can't quite get the idea why the price has to jump that high if I buy more than a hundred."

80 "Bueno,[5] patroncito, what is there so difficult to understand? It's all very simple. One thousand canastitas cost me a hundred times more work than a dozen. Ten thousand cost me so much time and labor that I could never finish them, not even in a hundred years. For a thousand canastitas I need more bast than for a hundred, and I need more little red beetles and more plants and roots and bark for the dyes. It isn't that you just can walk into the bush and pick all the things you need at your heart's desire. One root with the true violet blue may cost me four or five days until I can find one in the jungle. And have you thought how much time it costs and how much hard work to prepare the bast and fibers? What is more, if I must make so many baskets, who then will look after my corn and my beans and my goats and chase for me occasionally a rabbit for meat on Sunday? If I have no corn, then I have no tortillas to eat, and if I grow no beans, where do I get my frijoles from?"

"But since you'll get so much money from me for your baskets you can buy all the corn and beans in the world and more than you need."

"That's what you think, señorito, little lordy. But you see, it is only the corn I grow myself that I am sure of. Of the corn which others may or may not grow, I cannot be sure to feast upon."

"Haven't you got some relatives here in this village who might help you to make baskets for me?" Mr. Winthrop asked hopefully.

"Practically the whole village is related to me somehow or other. Fact is, I got lots of close relatives in this here place."

[5]**Bueno** well.

85 "Why then can't they cultivate your fields and look after your goats while you make baskets for me? Not only this, they might gather for you the fibers and the colors in the bush and lend you a hand here and there in preparing the material you need for the baskets."

"They might, patroncito, yes, they might. Possible. But then you see who would take care of their fields and cattle if they work for me? And if they help me with the baskets it turns out the same. No one would any longer work his fields properly. In such a case corn and beans would get up so high in price that none of us could buy any and we all would starve to death. Besides, as the price of everything would rise and rise higher still how could I make baskets at forty centavos apiece? A pinch of salt or one green chili would set me back more than I'd collect for one single basket. Now you'll understand, highly estimated caballero and jefecito, why I can't make the baskets any cheaper than fifteen pesos each if I got to make that many."

Mr. Winthrop was hard-boiled, no wonder considering the city he came from. He refused to give up the more than fifteen thousand dollars which at that moment seemed to slip through his fingers like nothing. Being really desperate now, he talked and bargained with the Indian for almost two full hours, trying to make him understand how rich he, the Indian, would become if he would take this greatest opportunity of his life.

The Indian never ceased working on his baskets while he explained his points of view.

"You know, my good man," Mr. Winthrop said, "such a wonderful chance might never again knock on your door, do you realize that? Let me explain to you in ice-cold figures what fortune you might miss if you leave me flat on this deal."

90 He tore out leaf after leaf from his notebook, covered each with figures and still more figures, and while doing so told the peasant he would be the richest man in the whole district.

The Indian without answering watched with a genuine expression of awe as Mr. Winthrop wrote down these long figures, executing complicated multiplications and divisions and subtractions so rapidly that it seemed to him the greatest miracle he had ever seen.

The American, noting this growing interest in the Indian, misjudged the real significance of it. "There you are, my friend," he said. "That's exactly how rich you're going to be. You'll have a bankroll of exactly four thousand pesos. And to show you that I'm a real friend of yours, I'll throw in a bonus. I'll make it a round five thousand pesos, and all in silver."

The Indian, however, had not for one moment thought of four thousand pesos. Such an amount of money had no meaning to him. He had been interested solely in Mr. Winthrop's ability to write figures so rapidly.

"So, what do you say now? Is it a deal or is it? Say yes and you'll get your advance this very minute."

95 "As I have explained before, patroncito, the price is fifteen pesos each."

"But, my good man," Mr. Winthrop shouted at the poor Indian in utter despair, "where have you been all this time? On the moon or where? You are still at the same price as before."

"Yes, I know that, jefecito, my little chief," the Indian answered, entirely unconcerned. "It must be the same price because I cannot make any other one. Besides, señor, there's still another thing which perhaps you don't know. You see, my good lordy and caballero, I've to make these canastitas my own way and with my song in them and with bits of my soul woven into them. If I were to make them in great numbers there would no longer be my soul in each, or my songs. Each would look like the other with no difference whatever and such a thing would slowly eat up my heart. Each has to be another song which I hear in the morning when the sun rises and when the birds begin to chirp and the butterflies come and sit down on my baskets so that I may see a new beauty, because, you see, the butterflies like my baskets and the pretty colors on them, that's why they come and sit down, and I can make my canastitas after them. And now, señor jefecito, if you will kindly excuse me, I have wasted much time already, although it was a pleasure and a great honor to hear the talk of such a distinguished caballero like you. But I'm afraid I've to attend to my work now, for day after tomorrow is market day in town and I got to take my baskets there. Thank you, senor, for your visit. Adiós."

And in this way it happened that American garbage cans escaped the fate of being turned into receptacles for empty, torn, and crumpled little multicolored canastitas into which an Indian of Mexico had woven dreams of his soul, throbs of his heart: his unsung poems.

[1928]

Joining the Conversation: Critical Thinking and Writing

1. Reread the first paragraph of "Assembly Line." Do you recall how you responded to this paragraph when you first read it? If so, what was your response? In any case, what is your response now? Are you amused? Offended? Or what?
2. In paragraph 6 Traven says that the baskets show that "at heart [the peasant] was an artist, a true and accomplished artist." What qualities in a basket might indicate to you that its maker was "a true and accomplished artist"?
3. In paragraph 13 Traven calls the peasant a "craftsman." In ordinary usage, what is the difference between an *artist* and a *craftsman* or *craftsperson*? Explain why you think Traven's peasant is one or the other, or both. In responding to this issue, you may want to make a comparison with the work of some craftsperson or artist you are familiar with.
4. The buyers in Mexico and in New York apparently recognize the exceptional beauty of the baskets, but in other respects these buyers are stupid, crass, imperceptive. Does this characterization strike you as implausible and therefore faulty? Explain.
5. Do you think the American businessman is exploiting the Mexican workers? Support your argument with reasons.
6. Do you take the story to be at least conceivable as a realistic narrative, or is it evidently a fable? Explain. In any case, did you enjoy the story? Why or why not?

LORRIE MOORE

Lorrie Moore, born Marie Lorena Moore in 1957 in Glen Falls, New York, did her undergraduate work at St. Lawrence University and received an MFA from Cornell University. While still an undergraduate she won first prize in the nationwide Seventeen *magazine short story contest (1976), and she has won numerous prizes in recent years. She is the author of stories, novels, and essays. Recent books include* The Collected Stories *(2008) and the novel* A Gate at the Stairs *(2009). We reprint a story from her first collection,* Self-Help *(1985). This story, like most of the stories in* Self-Help, *is written in what Moore in an*

interview (in Contemporary Authors: New Revision Series, *No. 39, 1992) called* "The second person, mock-imperative narrative." *She went on to explain:*

> *Let's see what happens when one eliminates the subject, leaves the verb shivering at the start of a clause; what happens when one appropriates the "how-to" form for a fiction, for an irony, for a "how-not-to." I was interested in whatever tensions resulted when a writer foisted fictional experience off of the "I" of the first person and onto the more generalized "you" of the second—the vernacular "one."*
>
> *The second person stories begin, ostensibly, to tell the generic tale, give the categorical advice, but become so entrenched in their own individuated details that they succeed in telling only their own specific story, suggesting that although life is certainly not jokeless, it probably is remediless.*

How to Become a Writer

First, try to be something, anything, else. A movie star/astronaut. A movie star/missionary. A movie star/kindergarten teacher. President of the World. Fail miserably. It is best if you fail at an early age—say, fourteen. Early, critical disillusionment is necessary so that at fifteen you can write long haiku sequences about thwarted desire. It is a pond, a cherry blossom, a wind brushing against sparrow wing leaving for mountain. Count the syllables. Show it to your mom. She is tough and practical. She has a son in Vietnam and a husband who may be having an affair. She believes in wearing brown because it hides spots. She'll look briefly at your writing, then back up at you with a face blank as a donut. She'll say: "How about emptying the dishwasher?" Look away. Shove the forks in the fork drawer. Accidentally break one of the freebie gas station glasses. This is the required pain and suffering. This is only for starters.

In your high school English class look at Mr. Killian's face. Decide faces are important. Write a villanelle about pores. Struggle. Write a sonnet. Count the syllables: nine, ten, eleven, thirteen. Decide to experiment with fiction. Here you don't have to count syllables. Write a short story about an elderly man and woman who accidentally shoot each other in the head, the result of an inexplicable malfunction of a shotgun which appears mysteriously in their living room one night. Give it to Mr. Killian as your final project. When you get it back, he has written on it: "Some of your images are quite nice, but you have no sense of plot." When you are home, in the privacy of your own room, faintly scrawl in pencil beneath his black-inked comments: "Plots are for dead people, pore-face."

Take all the babysitting jobs you can get. You are great with kids. They love you. You tell them stories about old people who die idiot deaths. You sing them songs like "Blue Bells of Scotland," which is their favorite. And when they are in their pajamas and have finally stopped pinching each other, when they are fast asleep, you read every sex manual in the house, and wonder how on earth anyone could ever do those things with someone they truly loved. Fall asleep in a chair reading Mr. McMurphy's *Playboy*. When the McMurphys come home, they will tap you on the shoulder, look at the magazine in your lap, and grin. You will want to die. They will ask you if Tracey took her medicine all right. Explain, yes, she did, that you promised her a story if she would take it like a big girl and that seemed to work out just fine. "Oh, marvelous," they will exclaim.

Try to smile proudly.

5   Apply to college as a child psychology major.

As a child psychology major, you have some electives. You've always liked birds. Sign up for something called "The Ornithological Field Trip." It meets Tuesdays and Thursdays at two. When you arrive at Room 134 on the first day of class, everyone is sitting around a seminar table talking about metaphors. You've heard of these. After a short, excruciating while, raise your hand and say diffidently, "Excuse me, isn't this Birdwatching One-oh-one?" The class stops and turns to look at you. They seem to all have one face—giant and blank as a vandalized clock. Someone with a beard booms out, "No, this is Creative Writing." Say: "Oh—right," as if perhaps you knew all along. Look down at your schedule. Wonder how the hell you ended up here. The computer, apparently, has made an error. You start to get up to leave and then don't. The lines at the registrar this week are huge. Perhaps you should stick with this mistake. Perhaps your creative writing isn't all that bad. Perhaps it is fate. Perhaps this is what your dad meant when he said, "It's the age of computers, Francie, it's the age of computers."

Decide that you like college life. In your dorm, you meet many nice people. Some are smarter than you. And some, you notice, are dumber than you. You will continue, unfortunately, to view the world in exactly these terms for the rest of your life.

The assignment this week in creative writing is to narrate a violent happening. Turn in a story about driving with your Uncle Gordon and another one about two old people who are accidentally electrocuted when they go to turn on a badly wired desk lamp. The teacher will hand them back to you with comments: "Much of your writing is smooth and energetic. You have, however, a ludicrous notion of plot." Write another story about a man and a woman who, in the very first paragraph, have their lower torsos accidentally blitzed away by dynamite. In the second paragraph, with the insurance money, they buy a frozen yogurt stand together. There are six more paragraphs. You read the whole thing out loud in class. No one likes it. They say your sense of plot is outrageous and incompetent. After class someone asks you if you are crazy.

Decide that perhaps you should stick to comedies. Start dating someone who is funny, someone who has what in high school you called a "really great sense of humor" and what now your creative writing class calls "self-contempt giving rise to comic form." Write down all of his jokes, but don't tell him you are doing this. Make up anagrams of his old girlfriend's name and name all of your socially handicapped characters with them. Tell him his old girlfriend is in all of your stories and then watch how funny he can be, see what a really great sense of humor he can have.

10   Your child psychology advisor tells you you are neglecting courses in your major. What you spend the most time on should be what you're majoring in. Say yes, you understand.

In creative writing seminars over the next two years, everyone continues to smoke cigarettes and ask the same things: "But does it work?" "Why should we care about this character?" "Have you earned this cliché?" These seem like important questions.

On days when it is your turn, you look at the class hopefully as they scour your mimeographs for a plot. They look back up at you, drag deeply, and then smile in a sweet sort of way.

You spend too much time slouched and demoralized. Your boyfriend suggests bicycling. Your roommate suggests a new boyfriend. You are said to be self-mutilating and losing weight, but you continue writing. The only happiness you have is writing something new, in the middle of the night, armpits damp, heart pounding, something no one has yet seen. You have only those brief, fragile, untested moments of exhilaration when you know: you are a genius. Understand what you must do. Switch majors. The kids in your nursery project will be disappointed, but you have a calling, an urge, a delusion, an unfortunate habit. You have, as your mother would say, fallen in with a bad crowd.

Why write? Where does writing come from? These are questions to ask yourself. They are like: Where does dust come from? Or: Why is there war? Or: If there's a God, then why is my brother now a cripple?

15   These are questions that you keep in your wallet, like calling cards. These are questions, your creative writing teacher says, that are good to address in your journals but rarely in your fiction.

The writing professor this fall is stressing the Power of the Imagination. Which means he doesn't want long descriptive stories about your camping trip last July. He wants you to start in a realistic context but then to alter it. Like recombinant DNA. He wants you to let your imagination sail, to let it grow big-bellied in the wind. This is a quote from Shakespeare.

Tell your roommate your great idea, your great exercise of imaginative power: a transformation of Melville to contemporary life. It will be about monomania and the fish-eat-fish world of life insurance in Rochester, New York. The first line will be "Call me Fishmeal," and it will feature a menopausal suburban husband named Richard, who because he is so depressed all the time is called "Mopey Dick" by his witty wife Elaine. Say to your roommate: "Mopey Dick, get it?" Your roommate looks at you, her face blank as a large Kleenex. She comes up to you, like a buddy, and puts an arm around your burdened shoulders. "Listen, Francie," she says, slow as speech therapy. "Let's go out and get a big beer."

The seminar doesn't like this one either. You suspect they are beginning to feel sorry for you. They say: "You have to think about what is happening. Where is the story here?"

The next semester the writing professor is obsessed with writing from personal experience. You must write from what you know, from what has happened to you. He wants deaths, he wants camping trips. Think about what has happened to you. In three years there have been three things: you lost your virginity; your parents got divorced; and your brother came home from a forest ten miles from the Cambodian border with only half a thigh, a permanent smirk nestled into one corner of his mouth.

20   About the first you write: "It created a new space, which hurt and cried in a voice that wasn't mine, 'I'm not the same anymore, but I'll be okay.'"

About the second you write an elaborate story of an old married couple who stumble upon an unknown land mine in their kitchen and accidentally blow themselves up. You call it: "For Better or for Liverwurst."

About the last you write nothing. There are no words for this. Your typewriter hums. You can find no words.

At undergraduate cocktail parties, people say, "Oh, you write? What do you write about?" Your roommate, who has consumed too much wine, too little cheese, and no crackers at all, blurts: "Oh, my god, she always writes about her dumb boyfriend."

Later on in life you will learn that writers are merely open, helpless texts with no real understanding of what they have written and therefore must half-believe anything and everything that is said of them. You, however, have not yet reached this stage of literary criticism. You stiffen and say, "I do not," the same way you said it when someone in the fourth grade accused you of really liking oboe lessons and your parents really weren't just making you take them.

25   Insist you are not very interested in any one subject at all, that you are interested in the music of language, that you are interested in—in—syllables, because they are the atoms of poetry, the cells of the mind, the breath of the soul. Begin to feel woozy. Stare into your plastic wine cup.

"Syllables?" you will hear someone ask, voice trailing off, as they glide slowly toward the reassuring white of the dip.

Begin to wonder what you do write about. Or if you have anything to say. Or if there even is such a thing as a thing to say. Limit these thoughts to no more than ten minutes a day; like sit-ups, they can make you thin.

You will read somewhere that all writing has to do with one's genitals. Don't dwell on this. It will make you nervous.

Your mother will come visit you. She will look at the circles under your eyes and hand you a brown book with a brown briefcase on the cover. It is entitled: *How to Become a Business Executive.* She has also brought the *Names for Baby* encyclopedia you asked for; one of your characters, the aging clown–school teacher, needs a new name. Your mother will shake her head and say: "Francie, Francie, remember when you were going to be a child psychology major?"

30   Say: "Mom, I like to write."

She'll say: "Sure you like to write. Of course. Sure you like to write."

Write a story about a confused music student and title it: "Schubert Was the One with the Glasses, Right?" It's not a big hit, although your roommate likes the part where the two violinists accidentally blow themselves up in a recital room. "I went out with a violinist once," she says, snapping her gum.

Thank god you are taking other courses. You can find sanctuary in nineteenth-century ontological snags and invertebrate courting rituals. Certain globular mollusks have what is called "Sex by the Arm." The male octopus, for instance, loses the end of one arm when placing it inside the female body during intercourse. Marine biologists call it "Seven Heaven." Be glad you know these things. Be glad you are not just a writer. Apply to law school.

From here on in, many things can happen. But the main one will be this: you decide not to go to law school after all, and, instead, you spend a good, big chunk of your adult life telling people how you decided not to go to law school after all. Somehow you end up writing again. Perhaps you go to graduate school. Perhaps you work odd jobs and take writing courses at night. Perhaps you are working on a novel and writing down all the clever remarks and intimate personal confessions you hear during the day. Perhaps you are losing your pals, your acquaintances, your balance.

35   You have broken up with your boyfriend. You now go out with men who, instead of whispering "I love you," shout: "Do it to me, baby." This is good for your writing.

Sooner or later you have a finished manuscript more or less. People look at it in a vaguely troubled sort of way and say, "I'll bet becoming a writer was always a fantasy of yours, wasn't it?" Your lips dry to salt. Say that of all the fantasies possible in the world, you can't imagine being a writer even making the top twenty. Tell them you were going to be a child psychology major. "I bet," they always sigh, "you'd be great with kids." Scowl fiercely. Tell them you're a walking blade.

Quit classes. Quit jobs. Cash in old savings bonds. Now you have time like warts on your hands. Slowly copy all of your friends' addresses into a new address book. Vacuum. Chew cough drops. Keep a folder full of fragments.

An eyelid darkening sideways.
40   *World as conspiracy.*
Possible plot? A woman gets on a bus.
Suppose you threw a love affair and nobody came.

At home drink a lot of coffee. At Howard Johnson's order the cole slaw. Consider how it looks like the soggy confetti of a map: where you've been, where you're going—"You Are Here," says the red star on the back of the menu.

Occasionally a date with a face blank as a sheet of paper asks you whether writers often become discouraged. Say that sometimes they do and sometimes they do. Say it's a lot like having polio.

45   "Interesting," smiles your date, and then he looks down at his arm hairs and starts to smooth them, all, always, in the same direction.

[1985]

Joining the Conversation: Critical Thinking and Writing

1. Do you find this story funny? If so, why? If not, why not?
2. Is Moore satirizing herself? Or amateur writers? Or . . . ?
3. Do you think that being a writer is a real job, real work? Please explain.

POEMS

WILLIAM WORDSWORTH

William Wordsworth (1770–1850), the son of an attorney, grew up in the Lake District of England. After graduating from Cambridge University in 1791, he spent a year in France, falling in love with a French girl, by whom he had a daughter. His enthusiasm for the French Revolution waned, and he returned alone to England where, with the help of a legacy, he devoted his life to poetry. With his friend Samuel Taylor Coleridge, in 1798 he published anonymously a volume of poetry, Lyrical Ballads, *which changed the course of English poetry. In 1799 he and his sister Dorothy settled in Grasmere in the Lake District, where he married and was given the office of distributor of stamps. In 1843 he was appointed poet laureate.*

The Solitary Reaper

Behold her, single in the field,
Yon solitary Highland Lass!
Reaping and singing by herself;
Stop here, or gently pass!
Alone she cuts and binds the grain,   5
And sings a melancholy strain;
O listen! for the vale profound
Is overflowing with the sound.

No Nightingale did ever chant   10
More welcome notes to weary bands

Of travellers in some shady haunt,
Among Arabian sands:
A voice so thrilling ne'er was heard
In spring-time from the Cuckoo-bird,
Breaking the silence of the seas   15
Among the farthest Hebrides.

Will no one tell me what she sings?°—
Perhaps the plaintive numbers flow
For old, unhappy, far-off things,
And battles long ago: 20
Or is it some more humble lay,
Familiar matter of today?
Some natural sorrow, loss, of pain,
That has been, and may be again?

Whate'er the theme, the maiden sang   25
As if her song could have no ending;
I saw her singing at her work,
And o'er the sickle bending;—
I listened, motionless and still;
And, as I mounted up the hill,   30
The music in my heart I bore
Long after it was heard no more.

[1805]

[17]**Will . . . sings?** Wordsworth had read an account of a woman reaping. The author
had specified that the reaper sang in Erse, hence Wordsworth—imagining himself in the
scene—cannot understand the song.

Joining the Conversation: Critical Thinking and Writing

Why do people sometimes sing at their work? And why do people sometimes sing
sad songs?

WALT WHITMAN

For a biographical note, see page 618.

I Hear America Singing

I hear America singing, the varied carols I hear,
Those of mechanics, each one singing his as it should be blithe and strong,
The carpenter singing his as he measures his plank or beam,
The mason singing his as he makes ready for work, or leaves off work,
The boatman singing what belongs to him in his boat, the deckhand singing
    on the steamboat deck,
The shoemaker singing as he sits on his bench, the hatter singing as he stands,

The wood-cutter's song, the ploughboy's on his way in the morning, or at
    noon intermission or at sundown,
The delicious singing of the mother, or of the young wife at work, or of the
    girl sewing or washing,
Each singing what belongs to him or her and to none else,
The day what belongs to the day—at night the party of young fellows, robust,
    friendly,
Singing with open mouths their strong melodious songs.

[1860; rev. 1867]

Joining the Conversation: Critical Thinking and Writing

1. What is Whitman doing in this poem?
2. How are the workers to whom Whitman refers similar to one another? How are
   they different?
3. Does Whitman's poem speak to us today? Explain why it does or does not.
4. Please write your own version of Whitman's poem, with your own choice of
   representative workers.

CARL SANDBURG

*Born in Galesburg, Illinois, Carl Sandburg (1878–1967) was the son of Swedish
immigrants. His first book, a pamphlet of poems,* Reckless Ecstasy, *was published in
1904. His other books include* Chicago Poems *(1916);* Cornhuskers *(1918);* Smoke
and Steel *(1920); and* Slabs of the Sunburnt West *(1922). "Chicago," winner of a
poetry competition in 1910 and later included in* Chicago Poems, *shows his rugged
realism and his tone of uplift.*

Chicago

Hog Butcher for the World,
Tool Maker, Stacker of Wheat,
Player with Railroads and the Nation's Freight Handler;
Stormy, husky, brawling,
City of the Big Shoulders: 5

They tell me you are wicked and I believe them, for I have seen your painted
    women under the gas lamps luring the farm boys.
And they tell me you are crooked and I answer: Yes, it is true I have seen the
    gunman kill and go free to kill again.
And they tell me you are brutal and my reply is: On the faces of women and
    children I have seen the marks of wanton hunger.
And having answered so I turn once more to those who sneer at this my city, and
    I give them back the sneer and say to them:
Come and show me another city with lifted head singing so proud to be alive
    and coarse and strong and cunning.   10
Flinging magnetic curses amid the toil of piling job on job, here is a tall bold
    slugger set vivid against the little soft cities;

Fierce as a dog with tongue lapping for action, cunning as a savage
 pitted against the wilderness,
 Bareheaded,
 Shoveling,
 Wrecking,   15
 Planning,
 Building, breaking, rebuilding,
Under the smoke, dust all over his mouth, laughing with white teeth,
Under the terrible burden of destiny laughing as a young man laughs,
Laughing even as an ignorant fighter laughs who has never lost a battle, 20
Bragging and laughing that under his wrist is the pulse, and under his ribs the
 heart of the people,
      Laughing!
Laughing the stormy, husky, brawling laughter of Youth, half-naked, sweating,
 proud to be Hog Butcher, Tool Maker, Stacker of Wheat, Player with Rail-
 roads and Freight Handler to the Nation.

                    [1914]

Joining the Conversation: Critical Thinking and Writing

1. Please describe how, from the beginning to the end, you would read "Chicago" out loud.
2. In your view, which line or lines in the poem are the most expressive—that express most effectively what Sandburg says that Chicago is?
3. Does Sandburg make Chicago a city where you would like to live?
4. After you have given careful study to Sandburg's poem, write a poem of your own in this style to a city that you know well. If you do not know a city well, write a poem about your hometown instead.

GARY SNYDER

Gary Snyder, born in 1930, grew up on a farm north of Seattle and then in Port-land, Oregon. By the age of fifteen he was deeply concerned with indigenous cul-tures of the American Northwest. He then went to Reed College, working during the summers in logging camps. When he moved to San Francisco he became part of the Beat movement, which included Allen Ginsberg and Jack Kerouac. (He is the hero of Kerouac's novel The Dharma Bums.*) In 1956, in order to deepen his understand-ing of Buddhism, he went to Japan, where he remained for ten years. When he re-turned to the United States he settled with his family in the foothills of the northwest-ern Sierra Nevada. He is the author of several books of poetry, one of which,* Turtle Island *(1974), won the Pulitzer Prize.*

Hay for the Horses

He had driven half the night
From far down San Joaquin
Through Mariposa, up the
Dangerous mountain roads,
And pulled in at eight a.m.   5

With his big truckload of hay
    behind the barn.
With winch and ropes and hooks
We stacked the bales up clean
To splintery redwood rafters   10
High in the dark, flecks of alfalfa
Whirling through shingle-cracks of light,
Itch of haydust in the
    sweaty shirt and shoes.
At lunchtime under Black oak   15
Out in the hot corral,
—The old mare nosing lunchpails,
Grasshoppers crackling in the weeds—
"I'm sixty-eight" he said,
"I first bucked hay when I was seventeen.   20
I thought, that day I started,
I sure would hate to do this all my life.
And dammit, that's just what
I've gone and done."

[1964]

Joining the Conversation: Critical Thinking and Writing

1. The speaker does not explicitly offer his opinion of the man who "had driven half the night," but do the first two sentences (lines 1–14) communicate at least a hint of an attitude?
2. The old man who speaks lines 19–24 sums up his life. He seems to regard it as wasted, but as we hear his words do we hear bitterness? Self-pity? What is our attitude toward him, and how does it compare with that of the speaker of the poem?

ROBERT HAYDEN

Robert Hayden (1913–80) was born in Detroit, Michigan. His parents divorced when he was a child, and he was brought up by a neighboring family, whose name he adopted. In 1942, at the age of twenty-nine, he graduated from Detroit City College (now Wayne State University); he received a master's degree from the University of Michigan. He taught at Fisk University from 1946 to 1969 and after that, for the remainder of his life, at the University of Michigan. In 1979 he was appointed Consultant in Poetry to the Library of Congress, the first African American to hold the post.

Those Winter Sundays

Sundays too my father got up early
and put his clothes on in the blueblack cold,
then with cracked hands that ached

from labor in the weekday weather made
banked fires blaze. No one ever thanked him.   5

I'd wake and hear the cold splintering, breaking.
When the rooms were warm, he'd call,
and slowly I would rise and dress,
fearing the chronic angers of that house.

Speaking indifferently to him,   10
who had driven out the cold
and polished my good shoes as well.
What did I know, what did I know
of love's austere and lonely offices?

[1962]

Joining the Conversation: Critical Thinking and Writing

1. In line 1, what does the word *too* tell us about the father? What does it suggest about the speaker and the implied hearer of the poem?
2. How old do you believe the speaker was at the time he recalls in the second and third stanzas? What details suggest this age?
3. What is the meaning of *offices* in the last line? What does this word suggest that other words Hayden might have chosen do not?
4. What do you take to be the speaker's present attitude toward his father? What circumstances, do you imagine, prompted his memory of "Those Winter Sundays"?
5. In a page or two, try to get down the exact circumstances when you spoke "indifferently," or not at all, to someone who had deserved your gratitude.

SEAMUS HEANEY

Seamus Heaney was born in Belfast, Northern Ireland, in 1939. He grew up on a farm, then went to Queens University in Belfast. Heaney has lectured widely in Ireland, England, and the United States. He taught at Harvard (1985–2006) and was Regius Professor of Poetry at Oxford, a post that was held by Matthew Arnold and W. H. Auden. In addition to writing poetry he has written essays about poetry. In 1995 he was awarded the Nobel Prize in Literature. "Digging," the first poem in his first book, reveals his concern with getting to the bottom of things.

Digging

Between my finger and my thumb
The squat pen rests; snug as a gun.

Under my window, a clean rasping sound
When the spade sinks into gravelly ground:
My father, digging, I look down   5

Till his straining rump among the flowerbeds
Bends low, comes up twenty years away
Stooping in rhythm through potato drills
Where he was digging.

The coarse boot nestled on the lug, the shaft   10
Against the inside knee was levered firmly.
He rooted out tall tops, buried the bright edge deep
To scatter new potatoes that we picked
Loving their cool hardness in our hands.

By God, the old man could handle a spade.   15
Just like his old man.

My grandfather cut more turf in a day
Than any other man on Toner's bog.
Once I carried him milk in a bottle
Corked sloppily with paper. He straightened up   20
To drink it, then fell to right away
Nicking and slicing neatly, heaving sods
Over his shoulder, going down and down
For the good turf. Digging.

The cold smell of potato mould, the squelch and slap   25
Of soggy peat, the curt cuts of an edge
Through living roots awaken in my head.
But I've no spade to follow men like them.

Between my finger and my thumb
The squat pen rests   30
I'll dig with it.

[1966]

Joining the Conversation: Critical Thinking and Writing

1. The poem ends with the speaker saying that he will "dig" with his pen. Given all the preceding lines, what will he dig?
2. The first lines compare the pen with a gun. What implications are suggested by this comparison?

MARGE PIERCY

Marge Piercy, born in Detroit in 1936, was the first member of her family to attend college. After earning a bachelor's degree from the University of Michigan in 1957 and a master's degree from Northwestern University in 1958, she moved to Chicago. There she worked at odd jobs while writing novels (unpublished) and engaging in action on behalf of women and blacks and against the Vietnam War. In 1970—the year she moved to Wellfleet, Massachusetts, where she still lives—she published her first book, a novel. Since then she has published many novels, short stories, poems, and essays.

To be of use

The people I love the best
jump into work head first
without dallying in the shallows
and swim off with sure strokes almost out of sight.
They seem to become natives of that element,   5
the black sleek heads of seals
bouncing like half-submerged balls.

I love people who harness themselves, an ox to a heavy cart,
who pull like water buffalo, with massive patience,
who strain in the mud and the muck to move things forward,   10
who do what has to be done, again and again.

I want to be with people who submerge
in the task, who go into the fields to harvest
and work in a row and pass the bags along,
who are not parlor generals and field deserters   15
but move in a common rhythm
when the food must come in or the fire be put out.

The work of the world is common as mud.
Botched, it smears the hands, crumbles to dust.
But the thing worth doing well done   20
has a shape that satisfies, clean and evident.
Greek amphoras for wine or oil,
Hopi vases that held corn, are put in museums
but you know they were made to be used.
The pitcher cries for water to carry   25
and a person for work that is real.

[1974]

Joining the Conversation: Critical Thinking and Writing

1. Write a short poem—perhaps seven lines, the length of Piercy's first stanza—
   beginning with Piercy's first line, "The people I love the best."

2. Suppose someone argued that Piercy's first stanza is the best, and, moreover, that this stanza can stand by itself. How might you argue that the next three stanzas contribute to the poem, making a better poem than the first stanza by itself?

The Secretary Chant

My hips are a desk,
From my ears hang
chain of paper clips.
Rubber bands form my hair,
My breasts are quills of   5
mimeograph ink.
My feet bear casters,
Buzz. Click.
My head is a badly organized file.
My head is a switchboard   10
where crossed lines crackle.
Press my fingers
and in my eyes appear
credit and debit.
Zing. Tinkle.   15
My navel is a reject button.
From my mouth issue canceled reams.
Swollen, heavy, rectangular
I am about to be delivered
of a baby   20
Xerox machine.
File me under W
because I wonce
was
a woman.   25

[1973]

Joining the Conversation: Critical Thinking and Writing

1. The poem, written in 1973, speaks of mimeograph machines—a tool probably unknown in today's offices. Do you find the poem dated? Please explain.
2. In the third line from the end, Piercy writes "wonce" instead of "once," presumably a playful bit connecting the word with "was" and "woman." Do you take the poem to be a serious social commentary, or chiefly an amusing, witty, playful piece? Or all of the above? Please explain your position.
3. Reread Piercy's poem carefully, noting the devices and techniques that she uses to describe the secretary's chant. Now please try to compose a poem of your own, a "chant" (what, by the way, does this word mean?) by a carpenter, a baseball player, an automobile mechanic, or some other kind of worker. How about a chant by a college student or a college teacher?

JOHN UPDIKE

For a biographical note, see page 1013.

Ex-Basketball Player

Pearl Avenue runs past the high-school lot,
Bends with the trolley tracks, and stops, cut off
Before it has a chance to go two blocks,
At Colonel McComsky Plaza. Berth's Garage
Is on the corner facing west, and there,   5
Most days, you'll find Flick Webb, who helps Berth out.

Flick stands tall among the idiot pumps—
Five on a side, the old bubble-head style,
Their rubber elbows hanging loose and low.
One's nostrils are two S's, and his eyes   10
An E and O. And one is squat, without
A head at all—more of a football type.

Once Flick played for the high-school team, the Wizards.
He was good: in fact, the best. In '46
He bucketed three hundred ninety points,   15
A county record still. The ball loved Flick.
I saw him rack up thirty-eight or forty
In one home game. His hands were like wild birds.

He never learned a trade, he just sells gas,
Checks oil, and changes flats. Once in a while,   20
As a gag, he dribbles an inner tube,
But most of us remember anyway.
His hands are fine and nervous on the lug wrench.
It makes no difference to the lug wrench, though.

Off work, he hangs around Mae's Luncheonette.   25
Grease-gray and kind of coiled, he plays pinball,
Smokes those thin cigars, nurses lemon phosphates.
Flick seldom says a word to Mae, just nods
Beyond her face toward bright applauding tiers
Of Necco Wafers, Nibs, and Juju Beads.   30

[1958]

Joining the Conversation: Critical Thinking and Writing

1. In the first stanza, Updike describes a street—in a sentence that runs the entire length of the stanza. Notice such words as "bends," "stops," "cut off," "Before it has a chance." Does this language, as well as the length of the sentence, evoke in your mind anything in addition to a street? If so, what?

2. What, if anything, does the final stanza contribute to the poem?

PLAYS

JANE MARTIN

Jane Martin has never given an interview and has never been photographed. The name presumably is the pseudonym of a writer who works with the Actors Theatre of Louisville, Kentucky. Rodeo is one of a collection of monologues, Talking With . . . , *first presented at the Actors Theatre during the 1981 Humana Festival of New American Plays. Jane Martin has also written full-length plays.*

Rodeo

A young woman in her late twenties sits working on a piece of tack.[1] Beside her is a Lone Star beer in the can. As the lights come up we hear the last verse of a Tanya Tucker song or some other female country-western vocalist. She is wearing old worn jeans and boots plus a long-sleeved workshirt with the sleeves rolled up. She works until the song is over and then speaks.

BIG EIGHT: Shoot—Rodeo's just goin' to hell in a handbasket. Rodeo used to be somethin'. I loved it. I did. Once Daddy an' a bunch of 'em was foolin' around with some old bronc over to our place and this ol' red nose named Cinch got bucked off and my Daddy hooted and said he had him a nine-year-old girl, namely me, wouldn't have no damn trouble cowboyin' that horse. Well, he put me on up there, stuck that ridin' rein in my hand, gimme a kiss, and said, "Now there's only one thing t' remember Honey Love, if ya fall off you jest don't come home." Well I stayed up. You gotta stay on a bronc eight seconds. Otherwise the ride don't count. So from that day on my daddy called me Big Eight. Heck! That's all the name I got anymore . . . Big Eight.

Used to be fer cowboys, the rodeo did. Do it in some open field, folks would pull their cars and pick-ups round it, sit on the hoods, some ranch hand'd bulldog him some rank steer and everybody'd wave their hats and call him by name. Ride us some buckin' stock, rope a few calves, git throwed off a bull, and then we'd jest git us to a bar and tell each other lies about how good we were.

Used to be a family thing. Wooly Billy Tilson and Tammy Lee had them five kids on the circuit. Three boys, two girls and Wooly and Tammy. Wasn't no two-beer rodeo in Oklahoma didn't have a Tilson entered. Used to call the oldest girl Tits. Tits Tilson. Never seen a girl that top-heavy could ride so well. Said she only fell off when the gravity got her. Cowboys used to say if she landed face down you could plant two young trees in the holes she'd leave. Ha! Tits Tilson.

Used to be people came to a rodeo had a horse of their own back home. Farm people, ranch people—lord, they knew what they were lookin' at. Knew a good ride from a bad ride, *knew* hard from easy. You broke some bones er spent the day eatin' dirt, at least ya got appreciated.

Now they bought the rodeo. Them. Coca-Cola, Pepsi Cola, Marlboro damn cigarettes. You know the ones I mean. Them. Hire some New York faggot t' sit on some ol' stuffed horse in front of a sagebrush photo n' smoke

---

[1] **tack** harness for a horse, including the bridle and saddle.

Margo Martinale, in Jane Martin's *Rodeo,* at the 6th Humana Festival of New American Plays (1981).

that junk. Hell, tobacco wasn't made to smoke, honey, it was made to chew. Lord wanted ya filled up with smoke he would've set ya on fire. Damn it gets me!

There's some guy in a banker's suit runs the rodeo now. Got him a pinky ring and a digital watch, honey. Told us we oughta have a watchamacallit, choriographus or somethin', ol' ballbuster used to be with the Ice damn Capades. Wants us to ride around dressed up like Mickey Mouse, Pluto, crap like that. Told me I had to haul my butt through the barrel race done up like Minnie damn Mouse in a tu-tu. Huh uh, honey! Them people is so screwed-up they probably eat what they run over in the road.

Listen, they got the clowns wearin' Astronaut suits! I ain't lyin'. You know what a rodeo clown does! You go down, fall off whatever—the clown runs in front of the bull so's ya don't git stomped. Pinstripes, he got 'em in space suits tellin' jokes on a microphone. First horse see 'em, done up like the Star Wars went crazy. Best buckin' horse on the circuit, name of Piss 'N' Vinegar, took one look at them clowns, had him a heart attack and died. Cowboy was ridin' him got hisself squashed. Twelve hundred pounds of coronary arrest jes fell right through 'em. Blam! Vio con dios. Crowd thought that was funnier than the astronauts. I swear it won't be long before they're strappin' ice-skates on the ponies. Big crowds now. Ain't hardly no ranch people, no farm people, nobody I know. Buncha disco babies and deevorce lawyers—designer jeans and day-glo Stetsons. Hell, the whole bunch of 'em wears French perfume. Oh it smells like money now! Got it on the cable T and V—hey, you know what, when ya rodeo yer just bound to kick yerself up some dust—well now, seems like that fogs up the ol' TV camera, so they told us a while back that from now on we was gonna ride on some new stuff called Astro-dirt. Dust free. Artificial damn dirt, honey. Lord have mercy.

Banker Suit called me in the other day said "Lurlene . . ." "Hold it," I said. "Who's this Lurlene? Round here they call me Big Eight." "Well, Big Eight," he said, "my name's Wallace." "Well that's a real surprise t' me," I said, "cause aroun' here everybody jes calls you Dumbass." My, he laughed real big, slapped his big ol' desk, an' then he said I wasn't suitable for the rodeo no more. Said they was lookin' fer another type, somethin' a little more in the showgirl line, like the Dallas Cowgirls maybe. Said the ridin' and ropin' wasn't the thing no more. Talked on about floats, costumes, dancin' choreogaphy. If I was a man I woulda pissed on his shoe. Said he'd give me a lifetime pass though. Said I could come to his rodeo any time I wanted.

Rodeo used to be people ridin' horses for the pleasure of people who rode horses—made you feel good about what you could do. Rodeo wasn't worth no money to nobody. Money didn't have nothing to do with it! Used to be seven Tilsons riding in the rodeo. Wouldn't none of 'em dress up like Donald damn Duck so they quit. That there's the law of gravity!

There's a bunch of assholes in this country sneak around until they see ya havin' fun and then they buy the fun and start in sellin' it. See, they figure if ya love it, they can sell it. Well you look out, honey! They want to make them a dollar out of what you love. Dress *you* up like Minnie Mouse. Sell your rodeo. Turn *yer* pleasure into Ice damn Capades. You hear what I'm sayin'? You're jus' merchandise to them, sweetie. You're jus' merchandise to them.

Blackout.

[1981]

Joining the Conversation: Critical Thinking and Writing

1. Try to recall your response to the title and the first paragraph or two of *Rodeo*. Did Big Eight fit your view (perhaps a stereotypical view) of what a cowgirl might sound like?
2. Reread *Rodeo,* this time paying attention not only to what Big Eight says but also to your responses to her. By the end of the play has she become a somewhat more complicated figure than she seems to be after the first paragraph, or does she pretty much seem the same? Do you find that you become increasingly sympathetic? Increasingly unsympathetic? Or does your opinion not change?
3. If you have ever seen a rodeo, do you think Big Eight's characterization is on the mark? Or is she simply bitter because she has been fired?
4. If a local theater group were staging *Rodeo,* presumably with some other short plays, would you go to see it? Why, or why not?

5. If you were directing a production of *Rodeo,* would you keep the actor seated, or would you have her get up, move around the stage, perhaps hang up one piece of tack and take down another? Why?
6. If you were directing *Rodeo,* would you tell Big Eight that her speech is essentially an interior monologue—a soliloquy—or would you tell her that she is speaking directly to the audience—i.e., that the audience is, collectively, a character in the play?
7. The play ends with a stage direction, "Blackout"; that is, the stage suddenly darkens. One director of a recent production, however, chose to end with a "fade out": the illumination decreased slowly by means of dimmers (mechanical devices that regulate the intensity of a lighting unit). If you were directing a production of *Rodeo,* what sort of lighting would you use at the end? Why?

ARTHUR MILLER

Arthur Miller (1915–2005) was born in New York. In 1938 he graduated from the University of Michigan, where he won prizes for drama. Six years later he had his first Broadway production, The Man Who Had All the Luck, *but the play was unlucky and closed after four days. By the time of his first commercial success,* All My Sons *(1947), he had already written several plays. In 1949 he won a Pulitzer Prize for* Death of a Salesman *and achieved an international reputation. Among his other works are an adaptation (1950) of Ibsen's* Enemy of the People *and a play about the Salem witch trials,* The Crucible *(1953), both containing political implications, and* The Misfits *(1961, a screenplay),* After the Fall *(1964), and* Incident at Vichy *(1965).*

Death of a Salesman

Certain Private Conversations in Two Acts and a Requiem

CHARACTERS

WILLY LOMAN
LINDA
BIFF
HAPPY
BERNARD
THE WOMAN
CHARLEY
UNCLE BEN
HOWARD WAGNER
JENNY
STANLEY

Miss Forsythe
Letta

SCENE: The action takes place in WILLY LOMAN's house and yard and in various places he visits in the New York and Boston of today.

Act 1

A melody is heard, played upon a flute. It is small and fine, telling of grass and trees and the horizon. The curtain rises.

Before us is the Salesman's house. We are aware of towering, angular shapes behind it, surrounding it on all sides. Only the blue light of the sky falls upon the house and forestage; the surrounding area shows an angry glow of orange. As more light appears, we see a solid vault of apartment houses around the small, fragile-seeming home. An air of the dream clings to the place, a dream rising out of reality. The kitchen at center seems actual enough, for there is a kitchen table with three chairs, and a refrigerator. But no other fixtures are seen. At the back of the kitchen there is a draped entrance, which leads to the living room. To the right of the kitchen, on a level raised two feet, is a bedroom furnished only with a brass bedstead and a straight chair. On a shelf over the bed a silver athletic trophy stands. A window opens onto the apartment house at the side.

Behind the kitchen, on a level raised six and a half feet, is the boys' bedroom, at present barely visible. Two beds are dimly seen, and at the back of the room a dormer window. (This bedroom is above the unseen living room.) At the left a stairway curves up to it from the kitchen.

The entire setting is wholly or, in some places, partially transparent. The roof-line of the house is one-dimensional; under and over it we see the apartment buildings. Before the house lies an apron, curving beyond the forestage into the orchestra. This forward area serves as the back yard as well as the locale of all WILLY's *imaginings and of his city scenes. Whenever the action is in the present the actors observe the imaginary wall-lines, entering the house only through its door at the left. But in the scenes of the past these boundaries are broken, and characters enter or leave a room by stepping "through" a wall onto the forestage.*

From the right, WILLY LOMAN, *the Salesman, enters, carrying two large sample cases. The flute plays on. He hears but is not aware of it. He is past sixty years of age, dressed quietly. Even as he crosses the stage to the doorway of the house, his exhaustion is apparent. He unlocks the door, comes into the kitchen, and thankfully lets his burden down, feeling the soreness of his palms. A word-sigh escapes his lips—it might be "Oh, boy, oh, boy." He closes the door, then carries his cases out into the living room, through the draped kitchen doorway.*

LINDA, *his wife, has stirred in her bed at the right. She gets out and puts on a robe, listening. Most often jovial, she has developed an iron repression of her exceptions to* WILLY's *behavior—she more than loves him, she admires him, as though his mercurial nature, his temper, his massive dreams and little cruelties, served her only as sharp reminders of the turbulent longings within him, longings which she shares but lacks the temperament to utter and follow to their end.*

Lee J. Cobb as Willy Loman in the 1949 original Broadway production of *Death of a Salesman*.

Dustin Hoffman as Willy Loman, and John Malkovich as Biff, in the 1984 production.

LINDA (*hearing* WILLY *outside the bedroom, calls with some trepidation*): Willy!

WILLY: It's all right. I came back.

LINDA: Why? What happened? (*Slight pause.*) Did something happen, Willy?

WILLY: No, nothing happened.

LINDA: You didn't smash the car, did you?

WILLY (*with casual irritation*): I said nothing happened. Didn't you hear me?

LINDA: Don't you feel well?

WILLY: I'm tired to the death. (*The flute has faded away. He sits on the bed beside her, a little numb.*) I couldn't make it. I just couldn't make it, Linda.

LINDA (*very carefully, delicately*): Where were you all day? You look terrible.

WILLY: I got as far as a little above Yonkers. I stopped for a cup of coffee. Maybe it was the coffee.

LINDA: What?

WILLY (*after a pause*): I suddenly couldn't drive any more. The car kept going off onto the shoulder, y'know?

LINDA (*helpfully*): Oh. Maybe it was the steering again. I don't think Angelo knows the Studebaker.

WILLY: No, it's me, it's me. Suddenly I realize I'm goin' sixty miles an hour and I don't remember the last five minutes. I'm—I can't seem to—keep my mind to it.

LINDA: Maybe it's your glasses. You never went for your new glasses.

WILLY: No, I see everything. I came back ten miles an hour. It took me nearly four hours from Yonkers.

LINDA (*resigned*): Well, you'll just have to take a rest, Willy, you can't continue this way.

WILLY: I just got back from Florida.

LINDA: But you didn't rest your mind. Your mind is overactive, and the mind is what counts, dear.

WILLY: I'll start out in the morning. Maybe I'll feel better in the morning. (*She is taking off his shoes.*) These goddam arch supports are killing me.

LINDA: Take an aspirin. Should I get you an aspirin? It'll soothe you.

WILLY (*with wonder*): I was driving along, you understand? And I was fine. I was even observing the scenery. You can imagine, me looking at scenery, on the road every week of my life. But it's so beautiful up there, Linda, the trees are so thick, and the sun is warm. I opened the windshield and just let the warm air bathe over me. And then all of a sudden I'm goin' off the road! I'm tellin' ya, I absolutely forgot I was driving. If I'd've gone the other way over the white line I might've killed somebody. So I went on again—and five minutes later I'm dreamin' again, and I nearly . . . (*He presses two fingers against his eyes.*) I have such thoughts, I have such strange thoughts.

LINDA: Willy, dear. Talk to them again. There's no reason why you can't work in New York.

WILLY: They don't need me in New York. I'm the New England man. I'm vital in New England.

LINDA: But you're sixty years old. They can't expect you to keep traveling every week.

WILLY: I'll have to send a wire to Portland. I'm supposed to see Brown and Morrison tomorrow morning at ten o'clock to show the line. Goddammit, I could sell them! (*He starts putting on his jacket.*)

LINDA (*taking the jacket from him*): Why don't you go down to the place tomorrow and tell Howard you've simply got to work in New York? You're too accommodating, dear.

WILLY: If old man Wagner was alive I'd a been in charge of New York now! That man was a prince, he was a masterful man. But that boy of his, that Howard, he don't appreciate. When I went north the first time, the Wagner Company didn't know where New England was!

LINDA: Why don't you tell those things to Howard, dear?

WILLY (*encouraged*): I will, I definitely will. Is there any cheese?

LINDA: I'll make you a sandwich.

WILLY: No, go to sleep. I'll take some milk. I'll be up right away. The boys in?

LINDA: They're sleeping. Happy took Biff on a date tonight.

WILLY (*interested*): That so?

LINDA: It was so nice to see them shaving together, one behind the other, in the bathroom. And going out together. You notice? The whole house smells of shaving lotion.

WILLY: Figure it out. Work a lifetime to pay off a house. You finally own it, and there's nobody to live in it.

LINDA: Well, dear, life is a casting off. It's always that way.

WILLY: No, no, some people—some people accomplish something. Did Biff say anything after I went this morning?

LINDA: You shouldn't have criticized him, Willy, especially after he just got off the train. You mustn't lose your temper with him.

WILLY: When the hell did I lose my temper? I simply asked him if he was making any money. Is that a criticism?

LINDA: But, dear, how could he make any money?

WILLY (*worried and angered*): There's such an undercurrent in him. He became a moody man. Did he apologize when I left this morning?

LINDA: He was crestfallen, Willy. You know how he admires you. I think if he finds himself, then you'll both be happier and not fight any more.

WILLY: How can he find himself on a farm? Is that a life? A farm hand? In the beginning, when he was young, I thought, well, a young man, it's good for him to tramp around, take a lot of different jobs. But it's more than ten years now and he has yet to make thirty-five dollars a week!

LINDA: He's finding himself, Willy.

WILLY: Not finding yourself at the age of thirty-four is a disgrace!

LINDA: Shh!

WILLY: The trouble is he's lazy, goddammit!

LINDA: Willy, please!

WILLY: Biff is a lazy bum!

LINDA: They're sleeping. Get something to eat. Go on down.

WILLY: Why did he come home? I would like to know what brought him home.

LINDA: I don't know. I think he's still lost, Willy. I think he's very lost.

WILLY: Biff Loman is lost. In the greatest country in the world a young man with such—personal attractiveness, gets lost. And such a hard worker. There's one thing about Biff—he's not lazy.

LINDA: Never.

WILLY (*with pity and resolve*): I'll see him in the morning; I'll have a nice talk with him. I'll get him a job selling. He could be big in no time. My God! Remember how they used to follow him around in high school? When he smiled at one of them their faces lit up. When he walked down the street . . . (*He loses himself in reminiscences.*)

LINDA (*trying to bring him out of it*): Willy, dear, I got a new kind of American-type cheese today. It's whipped.

WILLY: Why do you get American when I like Swiss?

LINDA: I just thought you'd like a change . . .

WILLY: I don't want a change! I want Swiss cheese. Why am I always being contradicted?

LINDA (*with a covering laugh*): I thought it would be a surprise.

WILLY: Why don't you open a window in here, for God's sake?

LINDA (*with infinite patience*): They're all open, dear.

WILLY: The way they boxed us in here. Bricks and windows, windows and bricks.

LINDA: We should've bought the land next door.

WILLY: The street is lined with cars. There's not a breath of fresh air in the neighborhood. The grass don't grow any more, you can't raise a carrot in the back yard. They should've had a law against apartment houses. Remember those two beautiful elm trees out there? When I and Biff hung the swing between them?

LINDA: Yeah, like being a million miles from the city.

WILLY: They should've arrested the builder for cutting those down. They massacred the neighborhood. (*Lost.*) More and more I think of those days, Linda. This time of year it was lilac and wisteria. And then the peonies would come out, and the daffodils. What fragrance in this room!

LINDA: Well, after all, people had to move somewhere.

WILLY: No, there's more people now.

LINDA: I don't think there's more people. I think . . .

WILLY: There's more people! That's what's ruining this country! Population is getting out of control. The competition is maddening! Smell the stink from that apartment house! And another one on the other side . . . How can they whip cheese?

On WILLY's *last line,* BIFF *and* HAPPY *raise themselves up in their beds, listening.*

LINDA: Go down, try it. And be quiet.

WILLY (*turning to* LINDA, *guiltily*): You're not worried about me, are you, sweetheart?

BIFF: What's the matter?

HAPPY: Listen!

LINDA: You've got too much on the ball to worry about.

WILLY: You're my foundation and my support, Linda.

LINDA: Just try to relax, dear. You make mountains out of molehills.

WILLY: I won't fight with him any more. If he wants to go back to Texas, let him go.

LINDA: He'll find his way.

WILLY: Sure. Certain men just don't get started till later in life. Like Thomas Edison, I think. Or B. F. Goodrich. One of them was deaf. (*He starts for the bedroom doorway.*) I'll put my money on Biff.

LINDA: And Willy—if it's warm Sunday we'll drive in the country. And we'll open the windshield, and take lunch.

WILLY: No, the windshields don't open on the new cars.

LINDA: But you opened it today.

WILLY: Me? I didn't. (*He stops.*) Now isn't that peculiar! Isn't that a remarkable . . . (*He breaks off in amazement and fright as the flute is heard distantly.*)

LINDA: What, darling?

WILLY: That is the most remarkable thing.

LINDA: What, dear?

WILLY: I was thinking of the Chevvy. (*Slight pause.*) Nineteen twenty-eight . . . when I had that red Chevvy . . . (*Breaks off.*) That funny? I coulda sworn I was driving that Chevvy today.

LINDA: Well, that's nothing. Something must've reminded you.

WILLY: Remarkable. Ts. Remember those days? The way Biff used to simonize that car? The dealer refused to believe there was eighty thousand miles on it. (*He shakes his head.*) Heh! (*To Linda.*) Close your eyes, I'll be right up. (*He walks out of the bedroom.*)

HAPPY (*to* BIFF): Jesus, maybe he smashed up the car again!

LINDA (*calling after* WILLY): Be careful on the stairs, dear! The cheese is on the middle shelf. (*She turns, goes over to the bed, takes his jacket, and goes out of the bedroom.*)

Light has risen on the boys' room. Unseen, WILLY *is heard talking to himself; "Eighty thousand miles," and a little laugh.* BIFF *gets out of bed, comes downstage a bit, and stands attentively.* BIFF *is two years older than his brother* HAPPY, *well built, but in these days bears a worn air and seems less self-assured. He has succeeded less, and his dreams are stronger and less acceptable than* HAPPY'*S.* HAPPY *is tall, powerfully made. Sexuality is like a visible color on him, or a scent that many women have discovered. He, like his brother, is lost, but in a different way, for he has never allowed himself to turn his face toward defeat and is thus more confused and hard-skinned, although seemingly more content.*

HAPPY (*getting out of bed*): He's going to get his license taken away if he keeps that up. I'm getting nervous about him, y'know, Biff?

BIFF: His eyes are going.

HAPPY: No, I've driven with him. He sees all right. He just doesn't keep his mind on it. I drove into the city with him last week. He stops at a green light and then it turns red and he goes. (*He laughs.*)

BIFF: Maybe he's color-blind.

HAPPY: Pop? Why he's got the finest eye for color in the business. You know that.

BIFF (*sitting down on his bed*): I'm going to sleep.

HAPPY: You're not still sour on Dad, are you, Biff?

BIFF: He's all right, I guess.

WILLY (*underneath them, in the living room*): Yes, sir, eighty thousand miles— eighty-two thousand!

BIFF: You smoking?

HAPPY (*holding out a pack of cigarettes*): Want one?

BIFF (*taking a cigarette*): I can never sleep when I smell it.

WILLY: What a simonizing job, heh!

HAPPY (*with deep sentiment*): Funny, Biff, y'know? Us sleeping in here again? The old beds. (*He pats his bed affectionately.*) All the talk that went across those beds, huh? Our whole lives.

BIFF: Yeah. Lotta dreams and plans.

HAPPY (*with a deep and masculine laugh*): About five hundred women would like to know what was said in this room. (*They share a soft laugh.*)

BIFF: Remember that big Betsy something—what the hell was her name—over on Bushwick Avenue?

HAPPY (*combing his hair*): With the collie dog!

BIFF: That's the one. I got you in there, remember?

HAPPY: Yeah, that was my first time—I think. Boy, there was a pig. (*They laugh, almost crudely.*) You taught me everything I know about women. Don't forget that.

BIFF: I bet you forgot how bashful you used to be. Especially with girls.

HAPPY: Oh, I still am, Biff.

BIFF: Oh, go on.

HAPPY: I just control it, that's all. I think I got less bashful and you got more so. What happened, Biff? Where's the old humor, the old confidence? (*He shakes* BIFF'S *knee.* BIFF *gets up and moves restlessly about the room.*) What's the matter?

BIFF: Why does Dad mock me all the time?

HAPPY: He's not mocking you, he . . .

BIFF: Everything I say there's a twist of mockery on his face. I can't get near him.

HAPPY: He just wants you to make good, that's all. I wanted to talk to you about Dad for a long time, Biff. Something's—happening to him. He—talks to himself.

BIFF: I noticed that this morning. But he always mumbled.

HAPPY: But not so noticeable. It got so embarrassing I sent him to Florida. And you know something? Most of the time he's talking to you.

BIFF: What's he say about me?

HAPPY: I can't make it out.

BIFF: What's he say about me?

HAPPY: I think the fact that you're not settled, that you're still kind of up in the air . . .

BIFF: There's one or two other things depressing him, Happy.

HAPPY: What do you mean?

BIFF: Never mind. Just don't lay it all to me.

HAPPY: But I think if you just got started—I mean—is there any future for you out there?

BIFF: I tell ya, Hap, I don't know what the future is. I don't know—what I'm supposed to want.

HAPPY: What do you mean?

BIFF: Well, I spent six or seven years after high school trying to work myself up. Shipping clerk, salesman, business of one kind or another. And it's a measly manner of existence. To get on that subway on the hot mornings in summer. To devote your whole life to keeping stock, or making phone calls, or selling or buying. To suffer fifty weeks of the year for the sake of a two-week vacation, when all you really desire is to be outdoors, with your shirt off. And always to have to get ahead of the next fella. And still—that's how you build a future.

HAPPY: Well, you really enjoy it on a farm? Are you content out there?

BIFF (*with rising agitation*): Hap, I've had twenty or thirty different kinds of jobs since I left home before the war, and it always turns out the same. I just realized it lately. In Nebraska when I herded cattle, and the Dakotas, and Arizona, and now in Texas. It's why I came home now, I guess, because I realized it. This farm I work on, it's spring there now, see? And they've got about fifteen new colts. There's nothing more inspiring or—beautiful than the sight of a mare and a new colt. And it's cool there now, see? Texas is cool now, and it's spring. And whenever spring comes to where I am, I suddenly get the feeling, my God, I'm not gettin' anywhere! What the hell am I doing, playing around with horses, twenty-eight dollars a week! I'm thirty-four years old, I oughta be makin' my future. That's when I come running home. And now, I get here, and I don't know what to do with myself. (*After a pause.*) I've always made a point of not wasting my life, and everytime I come back here I know that all I've done is to waste my life.

HAPPY: You're a poet, you know that, Biff? You're a—you're an idealist!

BIFF: No, I'm mixed up very bad. Maybe I oughta get married. Maybe I oughta get stuck into something. Maybe that's my trouble. I'm like a boy. I'm not married, I'm not in business, I just—I'm like a boy. Are you content, Hap? You're a success, aren't you? Are you content?

HAPPY: Hell, no!

BIFF: Why? You're making money, aren't you?

HAPPY (*moving about with energy, expressiveness*): All I can do now is wait for the merchandise manager to die. And suppose I get to be merchandise manager? He's a good friend of mine, and he just built a terrific estate on Long Island. And he lived there about two months and sold it, and now he's building another one. He can't enjoy it once it's finished. And I know that's just what I would do. I don't know what the hell I'm workin' for. Sometimes I sit in my apartment—all alone. And I think of the rent I'm paying. And it's crazy. But then, it's what I always wanted. My own apartment, a car, and plenty of women. And still, goddammit, I'm lonely.

BIFF (*with enthusiasm*): Listen, why don't you come out West with me?

HAPPY: You and I, heh?

BIFF: Sure, maybe we could buy a ranch. Raise cattle, use our muscles. Men built like we are should be working out in the open.

HAPPY (*avidly*): The Loman Brothers, heh?

BIFF (*with vast affection*): Sure, we'd be known all over the counties!

HAPPY (*enthralled*): That's what I dream about, Biff. Sometimes I want to just rip my clothes off in the middle of the store and outbox that goddam merchandise manager. I mean I can outbox, outrun, and outlift anybody in that store, and I have to take orders from those common, petty sons-of-bitches till I can't stand it any more.

BIFF: I'm tellin' you, kid, if you were with me I'd be happy out there.

HAPPY (*enthused*): See, Biff, everybody around me is so false that I'm constantly lowering my ideals . . .

BIFF: Baby, together we'd stand up for one another, we'd have someone to trust.

HAPPY: If I were around you . . .

BIFF: Hap, the trouble is we weren't brought up to grub for money. I don't know how to do it.

HAPPY: Neither can I!

BIFF: Then let's go!

HAPPY: The only thing is—what can you make out there?

BIFF: But look at your friend. Builds an estate and then hasn't the peace of mind to live in it.

HAPPY: Yeah, but when he walks into the store the waves part in front of him. That's fifty-two thousand dollars a year coming through the revolving door, and I got more in my pinky finger than he's got in his head.

BIFF: Yeah, but you just said . . .

HAPPY: I gotta show some of those pompous, self-important executives over there that Hap Loman can make the grade. I want to walk into the store the way he walks in. Then I'll go with you, Biff. We'll be together yet, I swear. But take those two we had tonight. Now weren't they gorgeous creatures?

BIFF: Yeah, yeah, most gorgeous I've had in years.

HAPPY: I get that any time I want, Biff. Whenever I feel disgusted. The only trouble is, it gets like bowling or something. I just keep knockin' them over and it doesn't mean anything. You still run around a lot?

BIFF: Naa. I'd like to find a girl—steady, somebody with substance.

HAPPY: That's what I long for.

BIFF: Go on! You'd never come home.

HAPPY: I would! Somebody with character, with resistance! Like Mom, y'know? You're gonna call me a bastard when I tell you this. That girl Charlotte I was with tonight is engaged to be married in five weeks. (*He tries on his new hat.*)

BIFF: No kiddin'!

HAPPY: Sure, the guy's in line for the vice-presidency of the store. I don't know what gets into me, maybe I just have an over-developed sense of competition or something, but I went and ruined her, and furthermore I can't get rid of her. And he's the third executive I've done that to. Isn't that a crummy characteristic? And to top it all, I go to their weddings! (*Indignantly, but laughing.*) Like I'm not supposed to take bribes. Manufacturers offer me a hundred-dollar bill now and then to throw an order their way. You know how honest I am, but it's like this girl, see. I hate myself for it. Because I don't want the girl, and, still, I take it and—I love it!

BIFF: Let's go to sleep.

HAPPY: I guess we didn't settle anything, heh?

BIFF: I just got one idea that I think I'm going to try.

HAPPY: What's that?

BIFF: Remember Bill Oliver?

HAPPY: Sure, Oliver is very big now. You want to work for him again?

BIFF: No, but when I quit he said something to me. He put his arm on my shoulder, and he said, "Biff, if you ever need anything, come to me."

HAPPY: I remember that. That sounds good.

BIFF: I think I'll go to see him. If I could get ten thousand or even seven or eight thousand dollars I could buy a beautiful ranch.

HAPPY: I bet he'd back you. 'Cause he thought highly of you, Biff. I mean, they all do. You're well liked, Biff. That's why I say to come back here, and we both have the apartment. And I'm tellin' you, Biff, any babe you want . . .

BIFF: No, with a ranch I could do the work I like and still be something. I just wonder though. I wonder if Oliver still thinks I stole that carton of basketballs.

HAPPY: Oh, he probably forgot that long ago. It's almost ten years. You're too sensitive. Anyway, he didn't really fire you.

BIFF: Well, I think he was going to. I think that's why I quit. I was never sure whether he knew or not. I know he thought the world of me, though. I was the only one he'd let lock up the place.

WILLY (*below*): You gonna wash the engine, Biff?

HAPPY: Shh!

BIFF *looks at* HAPPY, *who is gazing down, listening.* WILLY *is mumbling in the parlor.*

HAPPY: You hear that?

They listen. WILLY *laughs warmly.*

BIFF (*growing angry*): Doesn't he know Mom can hear that?

WILLY: Don't get your sweater dirty, Biff!

A look of pain crosses BIFF'S *face.*

HAPPY: Isn't that terrible? Don't leave again, will you? You'll find a job here. You gotta
stick around. I don't know what to do about him, it's getting embarrassing.

WILLY: What a simonizing job!

BIFF: Mom's hearing that!

WILLY: No kiddin', Biff, you got a date? Wonderful!

HAPPY: Go on to sleep. But talk to him in the morning, will you?

BIFF *(reluctantly getting into bed)*: With her in the house. Brother!

HAPPY *(getting into bed)*: I wish you'd have a good talk with him.

The light on their room begins to fade.

BIFF *(to himself in bed)*: That selfish, stupid . . .

HAPPY: Sh . . . Sleep, Biff.

Their light is out. Well before they have finished speaking, WILLY's *form is dimly
seen below in the darkened kitchen. He opens the refrigerator, searches in there,
and takes out a bottle of milk. The apartment houses are fading out, and the
entire house and surroundings become covered with leaves. Music insinuates
itself as the leaves appear.*

WILLY: Just wanna be careful with those girls, Biff, that's all. Don't make any promises. No promises of any kind. Because a girl, y'know, they always believe
what you tell 'em, and you're very young, Biff, you're too young to be talking
seriously to girls.

Light rises on the kitchen. WILLY, *talking, shuts the refrigerator door and comes
downstage to the kitchen table. He pours milk into a glass. He is totally immersed
in himself, smiling faintly.*

WILLY: Too young entirely, Biff. You want to watch your schooling first. Then when
you're all set, there'll be plenty of girls for a boy like you. *(He smiles broadly
at a kitchen chair.)* That so? The girls pay for you? *(He laughs.)* Boy, you must
really be makin' a hit.

WILLY *is gradually addressing—physically—a point offstage, speaking through
the wall of the kitchen, and his voice has been rising in volume to that of a
normal conversation.*

WILLY: I been wondering why you polish the car so careful. Ha! Don't leave the
hubcaps, boys. Get the chamois to the hubcaps. Happy, use newspaper on the
windows, it's the easiest thing. Show him how to do it, Biff! You see, Happy?
Pad it up, use it like a pad. That's it, that's it, good work. You're doin' all right,
Hap. *(He pauses, then nods in approbation for a few seconds, then looks
upward.)* Biff, first thing we gotta do when we get time is clip that big branch
over the house. Afraid it's gonna fall in a storm and hit the roof. Tell you what.
We get a rope and sling her around, and then we climb up there with a couple
of saws and take her down. Soon as you finish the car, boys, I wanna see ya.
I got a surprise for you, boys.

BIFF *(offstage)*: Whatta ya got, Dad?

WILLY: No, you finish first. Never leave a job till you're finished—remember that. *(Looking
toward the "big trees.")* Biff, up in Albany I saw a beautiful hammock. I think I'll
buy it next trip, and we'll hang it right between those two elms. Wouldn't that be
something? Just swingin' there under those branches. Boy, that would be . . .

Young BIFF *and Young* HAPPY *appear from the direction* WILLY *was addressing.*
HAPPY *carries rags and a pail of water.* BIFF, *wearing a sweater with a block "S,"
carries a football.*

BIFF (*pointing in the direction of the car offstage*): How's that, Pop, professional?

WILLY: Terrific. Terrific job, boys. Good work, Biff.

HAPPY: Where's the surprise, Pop?

WILLY: In the back seat of the car.

HAPPY: Boy! (*He runs off.*)

BIFF: What is it, Dad? Tell me, what'd you buy?

WILLY (*laughing, cuffs him*): Never mind, something I want you to have.

BIFF (*turns and starts off*): What is it, Hap?

HAPPY (*offstage*): It's a punching bag!

BIFF: Oh, Pop!

WILLY: It's got Gene Tunney's signature on it!

> HAPPY *runs onstage with a punching bag.*

BIFF: Gee, how'd you know we wanted a punching bag?

WILLY: Well, it's the finest thing for the timing.

HAPPY (*lies down on his back and pedals with his feet*): I'm losing weight, you notice, Pop?

WILLY (*to* HAPPY): Jumping rope is good too.

BIFF: Did you see the new football I got?

WILLY (*examining the ball*): Where'd you get a new ball?

BIFF: The coach told me to practice my passing.

WILLY: That so? And he gave you the ball, heh?

BIFF: Well, I borrowed it from the locker room. (*He laughs confidentially.*)

WILLY (*laughing with him at the theft*): I want you to return that.

HAPPY: I told you he wouldn't like it!

BIFF (*angrily*): Well, I'm bringing it back!

WILLY (*stopping the incipient argument, to* HAPPY): Sure, he's gotta practice with a regulation ball, doesn't he? (*To* BIFF.) *Coach'll probably congratulate you on your initiative!*

BIFF: Oh, he keeps congratulating my initiative all the time, Pop.

WILLY: That's because he likes you. If somebody else took that ball there'd be an uproar. So what's the report, boys, what's the report?

BIFF: Where'd you go this time, Dad? Gee we were lonesome for you.

WILLY (*pleased, puts an arm around each boy and they come down to the apron*): Lonesome, heh?

BIFF: Missed you every minute.

WILLY: Don't say? Tell you a secret, boys. Don't breathe it to a soul. Someday I'll have my own business, and I'll never have to leave home any more.

HAPPY: Like Uncle Charley, heh?

WILLY: Bigger than Uncle Charley! Because Charley is not—liked. He's liked, but he's not—well liked.

BIFF: Where'd you go this time, Dad?

WILLY: Well, I got on the road, and I went north to Providence. Met the Mayor.

BIFF: The Mayor of Providence!

WILLY: He was sitting in the hotel lobby.

BIFF: What'd he say?

WILLY: He said, "Morning!" And I said, "Morning!" And I said, "You got a fine city here, Mayor." And then he had coffee with me. And then I went to Waterbury. Waterbury is a fine city. Big clock city, the famous Waterbury clock. Sold a nice bill there. And then Boston—Boston is the cradle of the Revolution. A fine city. And a couple of other towns in Mass., and on to Portland and Bangor and straight home!

BIFF: Gee, I'd love to go with you sometime, Dad.

WILLY: Soon as summer comes.

HAPPY: Promise?

WILLY: You and Hap and I, and I'll show you all the towns. America is full of beautiful towns and fine, upstanding people. And they know me, boys, they know me up and down New England. The finest people. And when I bring you fellas up, there'll be open sesame for all of us, 'cause one thing, boys: I have friends. I can park my car in any street in New England, and the cops protect it like their own. This summer, heh?

BIFF AND HAPPY (*together*): Yeah! You bet!

WILLY: We'll take our bathing suits.

HAPPY: We'll carry your bags, Pop!

WILLY: Oh, won't that be something! Me comin' into the Boston stores with you boys carryin' my bags. What a sensation!

  BIFF *is prancing around, practicing passing the ball.*

WILLY: You nervous, Biff, about the game?

BIFF: Not if you're gonna be there.

WILLY: What do they say about you in school, now that they made you captain?

HAPPY: There's a crowd of girls behind him everytime the classes change.

BIFF (*taking* WILLY'*s hand*): This Saturday, Pop, this Saturday—just for you, I'm going to break through for a touchdown.

HAPPY: You're supposed to pass.

BIFF: I'm takin' one play for Pop. You watch me, Pop, and when I take off my helmet, that means I'm breakin' out. Then you watch me crash through that line!

WILLY (*kisses* BIFF): Oh, wait'll I tell this in Boston!

  BERNARD *enters in knickers. He is younger than* BIFF, *earnest and loyal, a worried boy.*

BERNARD: Biff, where are you? You're supposed to study with me today.

WILLY: Hey, looka Bernard. What're you lookin' so anemic about, Bernard?

BERNARD: He's gotta study, Uncle Willy. He's got Regents next week.

HAPPY (*tauntingly, spinning* BERNARD *around*): Let's box, Bernard!

BERNARD: Biff! (*He gets away from* HAPPY.) Listen, Biff, I heard Mr. Birnbaum say that if you don't start studyin' math he's gonna flunk you, and you won't graduate. I heard him!

WILLY: You better study with him, Biff. Go ahead now.

BERNARD: I heard him!

BIFF: Oh, Pop, you didn't see my sneakers! (*He holds up a foot for* WILLY *to look at.*)

WILLY: Hey, that's a beautiful job of printing!

BERNARD (*wiping his glasses*): Just because he printed University of Virginia on his sneakers doesn't mean they've got to graduate him, Uncle Willy!

WILLY (*angrily*): What're you talking about? With scholarships to three universities they're gonna flunk him?

BERNARD: But I heard Mr. Birnbaum say . . .

WILLY: Don't be a pest, Bernard! (*To his boys.*) What an anemic!

BERNARD: Okay, I'm waiting for you in my house, Biff.

  BERNARD *goes off. The* LOMANS *laugh.*

WILLY: Bernard is not well liked, is he?

BIFF: He's liked, but he's not well liked.

HAPPY: That's right, Pop.

WILLY: That's just what I mean. Bernard can get the best marks in school, y'understand, but when he gets out in the business world, y'understand, you are going to be five times ahead of him. That's why I thank Almighty God you're both built like Adonises. Because the man who makes an appearance in the business world, the man who creates personal interest, is the man who gets ahead. Be liked and you will never want. You take me, for instance. I never have to wait in line to see a buyer. "Willy Loman is here!" That's all they have to know, and I go right through.

BIFF: Did you knock them dead, Pop?

WILLY: Knocked 'em cold in Providence, slaughtered 'em in Boston.

HAPPY (*on his back, pedaling again*): I'm losing weight, you notice, Pop?

LINDA *enters as of old, a ribbon in her hair, carrying a basket of washing.*

LINDA (*with youthful energy*): Hello, dear!

WILLY: Sweetheart!

LINDA: How'd the Chevvy run?

WILLY: Chevrolet, Linda, is the greatest car ever built. (*To the boys.*) Since when do you let your mother carry wash up the stairs?

BIFF: Grab hold there, boy!

HAPPY: Where to, Mom?

LINDA: Hang them up on the line. And you better go down to your friends, Biff. The cellar is full of boys. They don't know what to do with themselves.

BIFF: Ah, when Pop comes home they can wait!

WILLY (*laughs appreciatively*): You better go down and tell them what to do, Biff.

BIFF: I think I'll have them sweep out the furnace room.

WILLY: Good work, Biff.

BIFF (*goes through wall-line of kitchen to doorway at back and calls down*): Fellas! Everybody sweep out the furnace room! I'll be right down!

VOICES: All right! Okay, Biff.

BIFF: George and Sam and Frank, come out back! We're hangin' up the wash! Come on, Hap, on the double! (*He and* HAPPY *carry out the basket.*)

LINDA: The way they obey him!

WILLY: Well, that's training, the training. I'm tellin' you, I was sellin' thousands and thousands, but I had to come home.

LINDA: Oh, the whole block'll be at that game. Did you sell anything?

WILLY: I did five hundred gross in Providence and seven hundred gross in Boston.

LINDA: No! Wait a minute. I've got a pencil. (*She pulls pencil and paper out of her apron pocket.*) That makes your commission . . . Two hundred—my God! Two hundred and twelve dollars!

WILLY: Well, I didn't figure it yet, but . . .

LINDA: How much did you do?

WILLY: Well, I—I did—about a hundred and eighty gross in Providence. Well, no—it came to—roughly two hundred gross on the whole trip.

LINDA (*without hesitation*): Two hundred gross. That's . . . (*She figures.*)

WILLY: The trouble was that three of the stores were half-closed for inventory in Boston. Otherwise I woulda broke records.

LINDA: Well, it makes seventy dollars and some pennies. That's very good.

WILLY: What do we owe?

LINDA: Well, on the first there's sixteen dollars on the refrigerator . . .

WILLY: Why sixteen?

LINDA: Well, the fan belt broke, so it was a dollar eighty.

WILLY: But it's brand new.

LINDA: Well, the man said that's the way it is. Till they work themselves in, y'know.

They move through the wall-line into the kitchen.

WILLY: I hope we didn't get stuck on that machine.

LINDA: They got the biggest ads of any of them!

WILLY: I know, it's a fine machine. What else?

LINDA: Well, there's nine-sixty for the washing machine. And for the vacuum cleaner there's three and a half due on the fifteenth. Then the roof, you got twenty-one dollars remaining.

WILLY: It don't leak, does it?

LINDA: No, they did a wonderful job. Then you owe Frank for the carburetor.

WILLY: I'm not going to pay that man! That goddam Chevrolet, they ought to prohibit the manufacture of that car!

LINDA: Well, you owe him three and a half. And odds and ends, comes to around a hundred and twenty dollars by the fifteenth.

WILLY: A hundred and twenty dollars! My God, if business don't pick up I don't know what I'm gonna do!

LINDA: Well, next week you'll do better.

WILLY: Oh, I'll knock 'em dead next week. I'll go to Hartford. I'm very well liked in Hartford. You know, the trouble is, Linda, people don't seem to take to me.

They move onto the forestage.

LINDA: Oh, don't be foolish.

WILLY: I know it when I walk in. They seem to laugh at me.

LINDA: Why? Why would they laugh at you? Don't talk that way, Willy.

WILLY *moves to the edge of the stage.* LINDA *goes into the kitchen and starts to darn stockings.*

WILLY: I don't know the reason for it, but they just pass me by. I'm not noticed.

LINDA: But you're doing wonderful, dear. You're making seventy to a hundred dollars a week.

WILLY: But I gotta be at it ten, twelve hours a day. Other men—I don't know—they do it easier. I don't know why—I can't stop myself—I talk too much. A man oughta come in with a few words. One thing about Charley. He's a man of few words, and they respect him.

LINDA: You don't talk too much, you're just lively.

WILLY (*smiling*): Well, I figure, what the hell, life is short, a couple of jokes. (*To himself:*) I joke too much! (*The smile goes.*)

LINDA: Why? You're . . .

WILLY: I'm fat. I'm very—foolish to look at, Linda. I didn't tell you, but Christmas time I happened to be calling on F. H. Stewarts, and a salesman I know, as I was going in to see the buyer I heard him say something about—walrus. And I—I cracked him right across the face. I won't take that. I simply will not take that. But they do laugh at me. I know that.

LINDA: Darling . . .

WILLY: I gotta overcome it. I know I gotta overcome it. I'm not dressing to advantage, maybe.

LINDA: Willy, darling, you're the handsomest man in the world . . .

WILLY: Oh, no, Linda.

LINDA: To me you are. (*Slight pause.*) The handsomest.

From the darkness is heard the laughter of a woman. WILLY *doesn't turn to it, but it continues through* LINDA'*s lines.*

LINDA: And the boys, Willy. Few men are idolized by their children the way you are.

Music is heard as behind a scrim, to the left of the house; THE WOMAN, *dimly seen, is dressing.*

WILLY (*with great feeling*): You're the best there is. Linda, you're a pal, you know that? On the road—on the road I want to grab you sometimes and just kiss the life outa you.

The laughter is loud now, and he moves into a brightening area at the left, where THE WOMAN *has come from behind the scrim and is standing, putting on her hat, looking into a "mirror" and laughing.*

WILLY: 'Cause I get so lonely—especially when business is bad and there's nobody to talk to. I get the feeling that I'll never sell anything again, that I won't make a living for you, or a business, a business for the boys. (*He talks through* THE WOMAN's *subsiding laughter;* THE WOMAN *primps at the "mirror."*) There's so much I want to make for . . .

THE WOMAN: Me? You didn't make me, Willy. I picked you.

WILLY (*pleased*): You picked me?

THE WOMAN (*who is quite proper-looking,* WILLY's *age*): I did. I've been sitting at that desk watching all the salesmen go by, day in, day out. But you've got such a sense of humor, and we do have such a good time together, don't we?

WILLY: Sure, sure. (*He takes her in his arms.*) Why do you have to go now?

THE WOMAN: It's two o'clock . . .

WILLY: No, come on in! (*He pulls her.*)

THE WOMAN: . . . my sisters'll be scandalized. When'll you be back?

WILLY: Oh, two weeks about. Will you come up again?

THE WOMAN: Sure thing. You do make me laugh. It's good for me. (*She squeezes his arm, kisses him.*) And I think you're a wonderful man.

WILLY: You picked me, heh?

THE WOMAN: Sure. Because you're so sweet. And such a kidder.

WILLY: Well, I'll see you next time I'm in Boston.

THE WOMAN: I'll put you right through to the buyers.

WILLY (*slapping her bottom*): Right. Well, bottoms up!

THE WOMAN (*slaps him gently and laughs*): You just kill me, Willy. (*He suddenly grabs her and kisses her roughly.*) You kill me. And thanks for the stockings. I love a lot of stockings. Well, good night.

WILLY: Good night. And keep your pores open!

THE WOMAN: Oh, Willy!

THE WOMAN *bursts out laughing, and* LINDA's *laughter blends in.* THE WOMAN *disappears into the dark. Now the area at the kitchen table brightens.* LINDA *is sitting where she was at the kitchen table, but now is mending a pair of her silk stockings.*

LINDA: You are, Willy. The handsomest man. You've got no reason to feel that . . .

WILLY (*coming out of* THE WOMAN's *dimming area and going over to* LINDA): I'll make it all up to you, Linda, I'll . . .

LINDA: There's nothing to make up, dear. You're doing fine, better than . . .

WILLY (*noticing her mending*): What's that?

LINDA: Just mending my stockings. They're so expensive . . .

WILLY (*angrily, taking them from her*): I won't have you mending stockings in this house! Now throw them out!

LINDA *puts the stockings in her pocket.*

BERNARD (*entering on the run*): Where is he? If he doesn't study!

WILLY (*moving to the forestage, with great agitation*): You'll give him the answers!

BERNARD: I do, but I can't on a Regents! That's a state exam! They're liable to arrest me!

WILLY: Where is he? I'll whip him, I'll whip him!

LINDA: And he'd better give back that football, Willy, it's not nice.

WILLY: Biff! Where is he? Why is he taking everything?

LINDA: He's too rough with the girls, Willy. All the mothers are afraid of him!

WILLY: I'll whip him!

BERNARD: He's driving the car without a license!

THE WOMAN'*s laugh is heard.*

WILLY: Shut up!

LINDA: All the mothers . . .

WILLY: Shut up!

BERNARD (*backing quietly away and out*): Mr. Birnbaum says he's stuck up.

WILLY: Get outa here!

BERNARD: If he doesn't buckle down he'll flunk math! (*He goes off.*)

LINDA: He's right, Willy, you've gotta . . .

WILLY (*exploding at her*): There's nothing the matter with him! You want him to be a worm like Bernard? He's got spirit, personality . . .

As he speaks, LINDA, *almost in tears, exits into the living room.* WILLY *is alone in the kitchen, wilting and staring. The leaves are gone. It is night again, and the apartment houses look down from behind.*

WILLY: Loaded with it. Loaded! What is he stealing? He's giving it back, isn't he? Why is he stealing? What did I tell him? I never in my life told him anything but decent things.

HAPPY *in pajamas has come down the stairs;* WILLY *suddenly becomes aware of* HAPPY'*s presence.*

HAPPY: Let's go now, come on.

WILLY (*sitting down at the kitchen table*): Huh! Why did she have to wax the floors herself? Everytime she waxes the floors she keels over. She knows that!

HAPPY: Shh! Take it easy. What brought you back tonight?

WILLY: I got an awful scare. Nearly hit a kid in Yonkers. God! Why didn't I go to Alaska with my brother Ben that time! Ben! That man was a genius, that man was success incarnate! What a mistake! He begged me to go.

HAPPY: Well, there's no use in . . .

WILLY: You guys! There was a man started with the clothes on his back and ended up with diamond mines!

HAPPY: Boy, someday I'd like to know how he did it.

WILLY: What's the mystery? The man knew what he wanted and went out and got it! Walked into a jungle, and comes out, the age of twenty-one, and he's rich! The world is an oyster, but you don't crack it open on a mattress!

HAPPY: Pop, I told you I'm gonna retire you for life.

WILLY: You'll retire me for life on seventy goddam dollars a week? And your women and your car and your apartment, and you'll retire me for life! Christ's sake, I couldn't get past Yonkers today! Where are you guys, where are you? The woods are burning! I can't drive a car!

CHARLEY *has appeared in the doorway. He is a large man, slow of speech, laconic, immovable. In all he says, despite what he says, there is pity, and, now, trepidation. He has a robe over pajamas, slippers on his feet. He enters the kitchen.*

CHARLEY: Everything all right?

HAPPY: Yeah, Charley, everything's . . .

WILLY: What's the matter?

CHARLEY: I heard some noise. I thought something happened. Can't we do something about the walls? You sneeze in here, and in my house hats blow off.

HAPPY: Let's go to bed, Dad. Come on.

CHARLEY *signals to* HAPPY *to go.*

WILLY: You go ahead, I'm not tired at the moment.

HAPPY (*to* WILLY): Take it easy, huh? (*He exits.*)

WILLY: What're you doin' up?

CHARLEY (*sitting down at the kitchen table opposite* WILLY): Couldn't sleep good. I had a heartburn.

WILLY: Well, you don't know how to eat.

CHARLEY: I eat with my mouth.

WILLY: No, you're ignorant. You gotta know about vitamins and things like that.

CHARLEY: Come on, let's shoot. Tire you out a little.

WILLY (*hesitantly*): All right. You got cards?

CHARLEY (*taking a deck from his pocket*): Yeah, I got them. Someplace. What is it with those vitamins?

WILLY (*dealing*): They build up your bones. Chemistry.

CHARLEY: Yeah, but there's no bones in a heartburn.

WILLY: What are you talkin' about? Do you know the first thing about it?

CHARLEY: Don't get insulted.

WILLY: Don't talk about something you don't know anything about.

They are playing. pause.

CHARLEY: What're you doin' home?

WILLY: A little trouble with the car.

CHARLEY: Oh. (*Pause.*) I'd like to take a trip to California.

WILLY: Don't say.

CHARLEY: You want a job?

WILLY: I got a job, I told you that. (*After a slight pause.*) What the hell are you offering me a job for?

CHARLEY: Don't get insulted.

WILLY: Don't insult me.

CHARLEY: I don't see no sense in it. You don't have to go on this way.

WILLY: I got a good job. (*Slight pause.*) What do you keep comin' in here for?

CHARLEY: You want me to go?

WILLY (*after a pause, withering*): I can't understand it. He's going back to Texas again. What the hell is that?

CHARLEY: Let him go.

WILLY: I got nothin' to give him, Charley, I'm clean, I'm clean.

CHARLEY: He won't starve. None a them starve. Forget about him.

WILLY: Then what have I got to remember?

CHARLEY: You take it too hard. To hell with it. When a deposit bottle is broken you don't get your nickel back.

WILLY: That's easy enough for you to say.

CHARLEY: That ain't easy for me to say.

WILLY: Did you see the ceiling I put up in the living room?

CHARLEY: Yeah, that's a piece of work. To put up a ceiling is a mystery to me. How do you do it?

WILLY: What's the difference?

CHARLEY: Well, talk about it.

WILLY: You gonna put up a ceiling?

CHARLEY: How could I put up a ceiling?

WILLY: Then what the hell are you bothering me for?

CHARLEY: You're insulted again.

WILLY: A man who can't handle tools is not a man. You're disgusting.

CHARLEY: Don't call me disgusting, Willy.

UNCLE BEN, *carrying a valise and an umbrella, enters the forestage from around the right corner of the house. He is a stolid man, in his sixties, with a mustache and an authoritative air. He is utterly certain of his destiny, and there is an aura of far places about him. He enters exactly as* WILLY *speaks.*

WILLY: I'm getting awfully tired, Ben.

BEN*'s music is heard.* BEN *looks around at everything.*

CHARLEY: Good, keep playing; you'll sleep better. Did you call me Ben?

BEN *looks at his watch.*

WILLY: That's funny. For a second there you reminded me of my brother Ben.

BEN: I only have a few minutes. (*He strolls, inspecting the place.* WILLY *and* CHARLEY *continue playing.*)

CHARLEY: You never heard from him again, heh? Since that time?

WILLY: Didn't Linda tell you? Couple of weeks ago we got a letter from his wife in Africa. He died.

CHARLEY: That so.

BEN (*chuckling*): So this is Brooklyn, eh?

CHARLEY: Maybe you're in for some of his money.

WILLY: Naa, he had seven sons. There's just one opportunity I had with that man . . .

BEN: I must make a train, William. There are several properties I'm looking at in Alaska.

WILLY: Sure, sure! If I'd gone with him to Alaska that time, everything would've been totally different.

CHARLEY: Go on, you'd froze to death up there.

WILLY: What're you talking about?

BEN: Opportunity is tremendous in Alaska, William. Surprised you're not up there.

WILLY: Sure, tremendous.

CHARLEY: Heh?

WILLY: There was the only man I ever met who knew the answers.

CHARLEY: Who?

BEN: How are you all?

WILLY (*taking a pot, smiling*): Fine, fine.

CHARLEY: Pretty sharp tonight.

BEN: Is Mother living with you?

WILLY: No, she died a long time ago.

CHARLEY: Who?

BEN: That's too bad. Fine specimen of a lady, Mother.

WILLY (*to* CHARLEY): Heh?

BEN: I'd hoped to see the old girl.

CHARLEY: Who died?

BEN: Heard anything from Father, have you?

WILLY (*unnerved*): What do you mean, who died?

CHARLEY (*taking a pot*): What're you talkin' about?

BEN (*looking at his watch*): William, it's half-past eight!

WILLY (*as though to dispel his confusion he angrily stops* CHARLEY'*s hand*): That's my build!

CHARLEY: I put the ace . . .

WILLY: If you don't know how to play the game I'm not gonna throw my money away on you!

CHARLEY (*rising*): It was my ace, for God's sake!

WILLY: I'm through, I'm through!

BEN: When did Mother die?

WILLY: Long ago. Since the beginning you never knew how to play cards.

CHARLEY (*picks up the cards and goes to the door*): All right! Next time I'll bring a deck with five aces.

WILLY: I don't play that kind of game!

CHARLEY (*turning to him*): You ought to be ashamed of yourself!

WILLY: Yeah?

CHARLEY: Yeah! (*He goes out.*)

WILLY (*slamming the door after him*): Ignoramus!

BEN (*as* WILLY *comes toward him through the wall-line of the kitchen*): So you're William.

WILLY (*shaking* BEN'*s hand*): Ben! I've been waiting for you so long! What's the answer? How did you do it?

BEN: Oh, there's a story in that.

LINDA *enters the forestage, as of old, carrying the wash basket.*

LINDA: Is this Ben?

BEN (*gallantly*): How do you do, my dear.

LINDA: Where've you been all these years? Willy's always wondered why you . . .

WILLY (*pulling* BEN *away from her impatiently*): Where is Dad? Didn't you follow him? How did you get started?

BEN: Well, I don't know how much you remember.

WILLY: Well, I was just a baby, of course, only three or four years old . . .

BEN: Three years and eleven months.

WILLY: What a memory, Ben!

BEN: I have many enterprises, William, and I have never kept books.

WILLY: I remember I was sitting under the wagon in—was it Nebraska?

BEN: It was South Dakota, and I gave you a bunch of wild flowers.

WILLY: I remember you walking away down some open road.

BEN (*laughing*): I was going to find Father in Alaska.

WILLY: Where is he?

BEN: At that age I had a very faulty view of geography, William. I discovered after a few days that I was heading due south, so instead of Alaska, I ended up in Africa.

LINDA: Africa!

WILLY: The Gold Coast!

BEN: Principally diamond mines.

LINDA: Diamond mines!

BEN: Yes, my dear. But I've only a few minutes . . .

WILLY: No! Boys! Boys! (*Young* BIFF *and* HAPPY *appear.*) Listen to this. This is your Uncle Ben, a great man! Tell my boys, Ben!

BEN: Why, boys, when I was seventeen I walked into the jungle, and when I was twenty-one I walked out. (*He laughs.*) And by God I was rich.

WILLY (*to the boys*): You see what I been talking about? The greatest things can happen!

BEN (*glancing at his watch*): I have an appointment in Ketchikan Tuesday week.

WILLY: No, Ben! Please tell about Dad. I want my boys to hear. I want them to know the kind of stock they spring from. All I remember is a man with a big beard, and I was in Mamma's lap, sitting around a fire, and some kind of high music.

BEN: His flute. He played the flute.

WILLY: Sure, the flute, that's right!

New music is heard, a high, rollicking tune.

BEN: Father was a very great and a very wild-hearted man. We would start in Boston, and he'd toss the whole family into the wagon, and then he'd drive the team right across the country; through Ohio, and Indiana, Michigan, Illinois, and all the Western states. And we'd stop in the towns and sell the flutes that he'd made on the way. Great inventor, Father. With one gadget he made more in a week than a man like you could make in a lifetime.

WILLY: That's just the way I'm bringing them up, Ben—rugged, well liked, all-around.

BEN: Yeah? (*To* BIFF.) Hit that, boy—hard as you can. (*He pounds his stomach.*)

BIFF: Oh, no, sir!

BEN (*taking boxing stance*): Come on, get to me! (*He laughs.*)

WILLY: Go to it. Biff! Go ahead, show him!

BIFF: Okay! (*He cocks his fists and starts in.*)

LINDA (*to* WILLY): Why must he fight, dear?

BEN (*sparring with* BIFF): Good boy! Good boy!

WILLY: How's that, Ben, heh?

HAPPY: Give him the left, Biff!

LINDA: Why are you fighting?

BEN: Good boy! (*Suddenly comes in, trips* BIFF, *and stands over him, the point of his umbrella poised over* BIFF*'s eye.*)

LINDA: Look out, Biff!

BIFF: Gee!

BEN (*patting* BIFF*'s knee*): Never fight fair with a stranger, boy. You'll never get out of the jungle that way. (*Taking* LINDA*'s hand and bowing.*) It was an honor and a pleasure to meet you, Linda.

LINDA (*withdrawing her hand coldly, frightened*): Have a nice—trip.

BEN (*to* WILLY): And good luck with your—what do you do?

WILLY: Selling.

BEN: Yes. Well . . . (*He raises his hand in farewell to all.*)

WILLY: No, Ben, I don't want you to think . . . (*He takes* BEN*'s arm to show him.*) It's Brooklyn, I know, but we hunt too.

BEN: Really, now.

WILLY: Oh, sure, there's snakes and rabbits and—that's why I moved out here. Why, Biff can fell any one of these trees in no time! Boys! Go right over to where they're building the apartment house and get some sand. We're gonna rebuild the entire front stoop right now! Watch this, Ben!

BIFF: Yes, sir! On the double, Hap!

HAPPY (*as he and* BIFF *run off*): I lost weight, Pop, you notice?

> CHARLEY *enters in knickers, even before the boys are gone.*

CHARLEY: Listen, if they steal any more from that building the watchman'll put the cops on them!

LINDA (*to* WILLY): Don't let Biff . . .

> BEN *laughs lustily.*

WILLY: You shoulda seen the lumber they brought home last week. At least a dozen six-by-tens worth all kinds a money.

CHARLEY: Listen, if that watchman . . .

WILLY: I gave them hell, understand. But I got a couple of fearless characters there.

CHARLEY: Willy, the jails are full of fearless characters.

BEN (*clapping* WILLY *on the back, with a laugh at* CHARLEY): And the stock exchange, friend!

WILLY (*joining in* BEN'*s laughter*): Where are the rest of your pants?

CHARLEY: My wife bought them.

WILLY: Now all you need is a golf club and you can go upstairs and go to sleep. (*To* BEN.) Great athlete! Between him and his son Bernard they can't hammer a nail!

BERNARD (*rushing in*): The watchman's chasing Biff!

WILLY (*angrily*): Shut up! He's not stealing anything!

LINDA (*alarmed, hurrying off left*): Where is he? Biff, dear! (*She exits.*)

WILLY (*moving toward the left, away from* BEN): There's nothing wrong. What's the matter with you?

BEN: Nervy boy. Good!

WILLY (*laughing*): Oh, nerves of iron, that Biff!

CHARLEY: Don't know what it is. My New England man comes back and he's bleedin', they murdered him up there.

WILLY: It's contacts, Charley, I got important contacts!

CHARLEY (*sarcastically*): Glad to hear it, Willy. Come in later, we'll shoot a little casino. I'll take some of your Portland money. (*He laughs at* WILLY *and exits.*)

WILLY (*turning to* BEN): Business is bad, it's murderous. But not for me, of course.

BEN: I'll stop by on my way back to Africa.

WILLY (*longingly*): Can't you stay a few days? You're just what I need, Ben, because I—I have a fine position here, but I—well, Dad left when I was such a baby and I never had a chance to talk to him and I still feel—kind of temporary about myself.

BEN: I'll be late for my train.

> *They are at opposite ends of the stage.*

WILLY: Ben, my boys—can't we talk? They'd go into the jaws of hell for me, see, but I . . .

BEN: William, you're being first-rate with your boys. Outstanding, manly chaps!

WILLY (*hanging on to his words*): Oh, Ben, that's good to hear! Because sometimes I'm afraid that I'm not teaching them the right kind of—Ben, how should I teach them?

BEN (*giving great weight to each word, and with a certain vicious audacity*): William, when I walked into the jungle, I was seventeen. When I walked out I was twenty-one. And, by God, I was rich! (*He goes off into darkness around the right corner of the house.*)

WILLY: . . . was rich! That's just the spirit I want to imbue them with! To walk into a jungle! I was right! I was right! I was right!

BEN *is gone, but* WILLY *is still speaking to him as* LINDA, *in nightgown and robe, enters the kitchen, glances around for* WILLY, *then goes to the door of the house, looks out and sees him. Comes down to his left. He looks at her.*

LINDA: Willy, dear? Willy?

WILLY: I was right!

LINDA: Did you have some cheese? (*He can't answer.*) It's very late, darling. Come to bed, heh?

WILLY (*looking straight up*): Gotta break your neck to see a star in this yard.

LINDA: You coming in?

WILLY: Whatever happened to that diamond watch fob? Remember? When Ben came from Africa that time? Didn't he give me a watch fob with a diamond in it?

LINDA: You pawned it, dear. Twelve, thirteen years ago. For Biff's radio correspondence course.

WILLY: Gee, that was a beautiful thing. I'll take a walk.

LINDA: But you're in your slippers.

WILLY (*starting to go around the house at the left*): I was right! I was! (*Half to* LINDA, *as he goes, shaking his head.*) What a man! There was a man worth talking to. I was right!

LINDA (*calling after* WILLY): But in your slippers, Willy!

WILLY *is almost gone when* BIFF, *in his pajamas, comes down the stairs and enters the kitchen.*

BIFF: What is he doing out there?

LINDA: Sh!

BIFF: God Almighty, Mom, how long has he been doing this?

LINDA: Don't, he'll hear you.

BIFF: What the hell is the matter with him?

LINDA: It'll pass by morning.

BIFF: Shouldn't we do anything?

LINDA: Oh, my dear, you should do a lot of things, but there's nothing to do, so go to sleep.

HAPPY *comes down the stairs and sits on the steps.*

HAPPY: I never heard him so loud, Mom.

LINDA: Well, come around more often; you'll hear him. (*She sits down at the table and mends the lining of* WILLY's *jacket.*)

BIFF: Why didn't you ever write me about this, Mom?

LINDA: How would I write to you? For over three months you had no address.

BIFF: I was on the move. But you know I thought of you all the time. You know that, don't you, pal?

LINDA: I know, dear, I know. But he likes to have a letter. Just to know that there's still a possibility for better things.

BIFF: He's not like this all the time, is he?

LINDA: It's when you come home he's always the worst.

BIFF: When I come home?

LINDA: When you write you're coming, he's all smiles, and talks about the future, and—he's just wonderful. And then the closer you seem to come, the more shaky he gets, and then, by the time you get here, he's arguing, and he seems angry at you. I think it's just that maybe he can't bring himself to—to open up to you. Why are you so hateful to each other? Why is that?

BIFF (*evasively*): I'm not hateful, Mom.

LINDA: But you no sooner come in the door than you're fighting!

BIFF: I don't know why. I mean to change. I'm tryin', Mom, you understand?

LINDA: Are you home to stay now?

BIFF: I don't know. I want to look around, see what's doin'.

LINDA: Biff, you can't look around all your life, can you?

BIFF: I just can't take hold, Mom. I can't take hold of some kind of a life.

LINDA: Biff, a man is not a bird, to come and go with the spring time.

BIFF: Your hair . . . (*He touches her hair.*) Your hair got so gray.

LINDA: Oh, it's been gray since you were in high school. I just stopped dyeing it, that's all.

BIFF: Dye it again, will ya? I don't want my pal looking old. (*He smiles.*)

LINDA: You're such a boy! You think you can go away for a year and . . . You've got to get it into your head now that one day you'll knock on this door and there'll be strange people here . . .

BIFF: What are you talking about? You're not even sixty, Mom.

LINDA: But what about your father?

BIFF (*lamely*): Well, I meant him too.

HAPPY: He admires Pop.

LINDA: Biff, dear, if you don't have any feeling for him, then you can't have any feeling for me.

BIFF: Sure I can, Mom.

LINDA: No. You can't just come to see me, because I love him. (*With a threat, but only a threat, of tears.*) He's the dearest man in the world to me, and I won't have anyone making him feel unwanted and low and blue. You've got to make up your mind now, darling, there's no leeway any more. Either he's your father and you pay him that respect, or else you're not to come here. I know he's not easy to get along with—nobody knows that better than me—but . . .

WILLY (*from the left, with a laugh*): Hey, hey, Biffo!

BIFF (*starting to go out after* WILLY): What the hell is the matter with him? (HAPPY *stops him.*)

LINDA: Don't—don't go near him!

BIFF: Stop making excuses for him! He always, always wiped the floor with you. Never had an ounce of respect for you.

HAPPY: He's always had respect for . . .

BIFF: What the hell do you know about it?

HAPPY (*surlily*): Just don't call him crazy!

BIFF: He's got no character—Charley wouldn't do this. Not in his own house—spewing out that vomit from his mind.

HAPPY: Charley never had to cope with what he's got to.

BIFF: People are worse off than Willy Loman. Believe me, I've seen them!

LINDA: Then make Charley your father, Biff. You can't do that, can you? I don't say he's a great man. Willy Loman never made a lot of money. His name was never in the paper. He's not the finest character that ever lived. But he's a human being, and a terrible thing is happening to him. So attention must be paid. He's not to be allowed to fall into his grave like an old dog. Attention, attention must be finally paid to such a person. You called him crazy . . .

BIFF: I didn't mean . . .

LINDA: No, a lot of people think he's lost his—balance. But you don't have to be very smart to know what his trouble is. The man is exhausted.

HAPPY: Sure!

LINDA: A small man can be just as exhausted as a great man. He works for a company thirty-six years this March, opens up unheard-of territories to their trademark, and now in his old age they take his salary away.

HAPPY (*indignantly*): I didn't know that, Mom.

LINDA: You never asked, my dear! Now that you get your spending money someplace else you don't trouble your mind with him.

HAPPY: But I gave you money last . . .

LINDA: Christmas time, fifty dollars! To fix the hot water it cost ninety-seven fifty! For five weeks he's been on straight commission, like a beginner, an unknown!

BIFF: Those ungrateful bastards!

LINDA: Are they any worse than his sons? When he brought them business, when he was young, they were glad to see him. But now his old friends, the old buyers that loved him so and always found some order to hand him in a pinch—they're all dead, retired. He used to be able to make six, seven calls a day in Boston. Now he takes his valises out of the car and puts them back and takes them out again and he's exhausted. Instead of walking he talks now. He drives seven hundred miles, and when he gets there no one knows him any more, no one welcomes him. And what goes through a man's mind, driving seven hundred miles home without having earned a cent? Why shouldn't he talk to himself? Why? When he has to go to Charley and borrow fifty dollars a week and pretend to me that it's his pay? How long can that go on? How long? You see what I'm sitting here and waiting for? And you tell me he has no character? The man who never worked a day but for your benefit? When does he get the medal for that? Is this his reward—to turn around at the age of sixty-three and find his sons, who he loved better than his life, one a philandering bum . . .

HAPPY: Mom!

LINDA: That's all you are, my baby! (*To* BIFF.) And you! What happened to the love you had for him? You were such pals! How you used to talk to him on the phone every night! How lonely he was till he could come home to you!

BIFF: All right, Mom. I'll live here in my room, and I'll get a job. I'll keep away from him, that's all.

LINDA: No, Biff. You can't stay here and fight all the time.

BIFF: He threw me out of this house, remember that.

LINDA: Why did he do that? I never knew why.

BIFF: Because I know he's a fake and he doesn't like anybody around who knows!

LINDA: Why a fake? In what way? What do you mean?

BIFF: Just don't lay it all at my feet. It's between me and him—that's all I have to say. I'll chip in from now on. He'll settle for half my paycheck. He'll be all right. I'm going to bed. (*He starts for the stairs.*)

LINDA: He won't be all right.

BIFF (*turning on the stairs, furiously*): I hate this city and I'll stay here. Now what do you want?

LINDA: He's dying, Biff.

HAPPY *turns quickly to her, shocked.*

BIFF (*after a pause*): Why is he dying?

LINDA: He's been trying to kill himself.

BIFF (*with great horror*): How?

LINDA: I live from day to day.

BIFF: What're you talking about?

LINDA: Remember I wrote you that he smashed up the car again? In February?

BIFF: Well?

LINDA: The insurance inspector came. He said that they have evidence. That all these accidents in the last year—weren't—weren't—accidents.

HAPPY: How can they tell that? That's a lie.

LINDA: It seems there's a woman . . . (*She takes a breath as:*)

BIFF (*sharply but contained*): What woman?

LINDA (*simultaneously*): . . . and this woman . . .

LINDA: What?

BIFF: Nothing. Go ahead.

LINDA: What did you say?

BIFF: Nothing. I just said what woman?

HAPPY: What about her?

LINDA: Well, it seems she was walking down the road and saw his car. She says that he wasn't driving fast at all, and that he didn't skid. She says he came to that little bridge, and then deliberately smashed into the railing, and it was only the shallowness of the water that saved him.

BIFF: Oh, no, he probably just fell asleep again.

LINDA: I don't think he fell asleep.

BIFF: Why not?

LINDA: Last month . . . (*With great difficulty.*) Oh, boys, it's so hard to say a thing like this! He's just a big stupid man to you, but I tell you there's more good in him than in many other people. (*She chokes, wipes her eyes.*) I was looking for a fuse. The lights blew out, and I went down the cellar. And behind the fuse box—it happened to fall out—was a length of rubber pipe—just short.

HAPPY: No kidding!

LINDA: There's a little attachment on the end of it. I knew right away. And sure enough, on the bottom of the water heater there's a new little nipple on the gas pipe.

HAPPY (*angrily*): That—jerk

BIFF: Did you have it taken off?

LINDA: I'm—I'm ashamed to. How can I mention it to him? Every day I go down and take away that little rubber pipe. But, when he comes home, I put it back where it was. How can I insult him that way? I don't know what to do. I live from day to day, boys. I tell you, I know every thought in his mind. It sounds so old-fashioned and silly, but I tell you he put his whole life into you and you've turned your backs on him. (*She is bent over in the chair, weeping, her face in her hands.*) Biff, I swear to God! Biff, his life is in your hands!

HAPPY (*to* BIFF): How do you like that damned fool!

BIFF (*kissing her*): All right, pal, all right. It's all settled now. I've been remiss. I know that, Mom. But now I'll stay, and I swear to you, I'll apply myself. (*Kneeling in front of her, in a fever of self-reproach.*) It's just—you see, Mom, I don't fit in business. Not that I won't try. I'll try, and I'll make good.

HAPPY: Sure you will. The trouble with you in business was you never tried to please people.

BIFF: I know, I . . .

HAPPY: Like when you worked for Harrison's. Bob Harrison said you were tops, and then you go and do some damn fool thing like whistling whole songs in the elevator like a comedian.

BIFF (*against* HAPPY): So what? I like to whistle sometimes.

HAPPY: You don't raise a guy to a responsible job who whistles in the elevator!

LINDA: Well, don't argue about it now.

HAPPY: Like when you'd go off and swim in the middle of the day instead of taking the line around.

BIFF (*his resentment rising*): Well, don't you run off? You take off sometimes, don't you? On a nice summer day?

HAPPY: Yeah, but I cover myself!

LINDA: Boys!

HAPPY: If I'm going to take a fade the boss can call any number where I'm supposed to be and they'll swear to him that I just left. I'll tell you something that I hate to say, Biff, but in the business world some of them think you're crazy.

BIFF (*angered*): Screw the business world!

HAPPY: All right, screw it! Great, but cover yourself!

LINDA: Hap, Hap!

BIFF: I don't care what they think! They've laughed at Dad for years, and you know why? Because we don't belong in this nuthouse of a city! We should be mixing cement on some open plain or—or carpenters. A carpenter is allowed to whistle!

WILLY *walks in from the entrance of the house, at left.*

WILLY: Even your grandfather was better than a carpenter. (*Pause. They watch him.*) You never grew up. Bernard does not whistle in the elevator, I assure you.

BIFF (*as though to laugh* WILLY *out of it*): Yeah, but you do, Pop.

WILLY: I never in my life whistled in an elevator! And who in the business world thinks I'm crazy?

BIFF: I didn't mean it like that, Pop. Now don't make a whole thing out of it, will ya?

WILLY: Go back to the West! Be a carpenter, a cowboy, enjoy yourself!

LINDA: Willy, he was just saying . . .

WILLY: I heard what he said!

HAPPY (*trying to quiet* WILLY): Hey, Pop, come on now . . .

WILLY (*continuing over* HAPPY's *line*): They laugh at me, heh? Go to Filene's, go to the Hub, go to Slattery's, Boston. Call out the name Willy Loman and see what happens! Big shot!

BIFF: All right, Pop.

WILLY: Big!

BIFF: All right!

WILLY: Why do you always insult me?

BIFF: I didn't say a word. (*To* LINDA.) Did I say a word?

LINDA: He didn't say anything, Willy.

WILLY (*going to the doorway of the living room*): All right, good night, good night.

LINDA: Willy, dear, he just decided . . .

WILLY (*to* BIFF): If you get tired hanging around tomorrow, paint the ceiling I put up in the living room.

BIFF: I'm leaving early tomorrow.

HAPPY: He's going to see Bill Oliver, Pop.

WILLY (*interestedly*): Oliver? For what?

BIFF (*with reserve, but trying, trying*): He always said he'd stake me. I'd like to go into business, so maybe I can take him up on it.

LINDA: Isn't that wonderful?

WILLY: Don't interrupt. What's wonderful about it? There's fifty men in the City of New York who'd stake him. (*To* BIFF.) Sporting goods?

BIFF: I guess so. I know something about it and . . .

WILLY: He knows something about it! You know sporting goods better than Spalding, for God's sake! How much is he giving you?

BIFF: I don't know, I didn't even see him yet, but . . .

WILLY: Then what're you talkin' about?

BIFF (*getting angry*): Well, all I said was I'm gonna see him, that's all!

WILLY (*turning away*): Ah, you're counting your chickens again.

BIFF (*starting left for the stairs*): Oh, Jesus, I'm going to sleep!

WILLY (*calling after him*): Don't curse in this house!

BIFF (*turning*): Since when did you get so clean?

HAPPY (*trying to stop them*): Wait a . . .

WILLY: Don't use that language to me! I won't have it!

HAPPY (*grabbing* BIFF, *shouts*): Wait a minute! I got an idea. I got a feasible idea. Come here, Biff, let's talk this over now, let's talk some sense here. When I was down in Florida last time, I thought of a great idea to sell sporting goods. It just came back to me. You and I, Biff—we have a line, the Loman Line. We train a couple of weeks, and put on a couple of exhibitions, see?

WILLY: That's an idea!

HAPPY: Wait! We form two basketball teams, see? Two water-polo teams. We play each other. It's a million dollars' worth of publicity. Two brothers, see? The Loman Brothers. Displays in the Royal Palms—all the hotels. And banners over the ring and the basketball court: "Loman Brothers." Baby, we could sell sporting goods!

WILLY: That is a one-million-dollar idea!

LINDA: Marvelous!

BIFF: I'm in great shape as far as that's concerned.

HAPPY: And the beauty of it is, Biff, it wouldn't be like a business. We'd be out playin' ball again.

BIFF (*enthused*): Yeah, that's . . .

WILLY: Million-dollar . . .

HAPPY: And you wouldn't get fed up with it, Biff. It'd be the family again. There'd be the old honor, and comradeship, and if you wanted to go off for a swim or somethin'—well, you'd do it! Without some smart cooky gettin' up ahead of you!

WILLY: Lick the world! You guys together could absolutely lick the civilized world.

BIFF: I'll see Oliver tomorrow. Hap, if we could work that out . . .

LINDA: Maybe things are beginning to . . .

WILLY (*wildly enthused, to* LINDA): Stop interrupting! (*To* BIFF.) But don't wear sport jacket and slacks when you see Oliver.

BIFF: No, I'll . . .

WILLY: A business suit, and talk as little as possible, and don't crack any jokes.

BIFF: He did like me. Always liked me.

LINDA: He loved you!

WILLY (*to* LINDA): Will you stop! (*To* BIFF.) Walk in very serious. You are not applying for a boy's job. Money is to pass. Be quiet, fine, and serious. Everybody likes a kidder, but nobody lends him money.

HAPPY: I'll try to get some myself, Biff. I'm sure I can.

WILLY: I see great things for you kids, I think your troubles are over. But remember, start big and you'll end big. Ask for fifteen. How much you gonna ask for?

BIFF: Gee, I don't know . . .

WILLY: And don't say "Gee." "Gee" is a boy's word. A man walking in for fifteen thousand dollars does not say "Gee!"

BIFF: Ten, I think, would be top though.

WILLY: Don't be so modest. You always started too low. Walk in with a big laugh. Don't look worried. Start off with a couple of your good stories to lighten things up. It's not what you say, it's how you say it—because personality always wins the day.

LINDA: Oliver always thought the highest of him . . .

WILLY: Will you let me talk?

BIFF: Don't yell at her, Pop, will ya?

WILLY (*angrily*): I was talking, wasn't I?

BIFF: I don't like you yelling at her all the time, and I'm tellin' you, that's all.

WILLY: What're you, takin' over this house?

LINDA: Willy . . .

WILLY (*turning to her*): Don't take his side all the time, goddammit!

BIFF (*furiously*): Stop yelling at her!

WILLY (*suddenly pulling on his cheek, beaten down, guilt ridden*): Give my best to Bill Oliver—he may remember me. (*He exits through the living room doorway.*)

LINDA (*her voice subdued*): What'd you have to start that for? (BIFF *turns away.*) You see how sweet he was as soon as you talked hopefully? (*She goes over to* BIFF.) Come up and say good night to him. Don't let him go to bed that way.

HAPPY: Come on, Biff, let's buck him up.

LINDA: Please, dear. Just say good night. It takes so little to make him happy. Come. (*She goes through the living room doorway, calling upstairs from within the living room.*) Your pajamas are hanging in the bathroom, Willy!

HAPPY (*looking toward where* LINDA *went out*): What a woman! They broke the mold when they made her. You know that, Biff.

BIFF: He's off salary. My God, working on commission!

HAPPY: Well, let's face it: he's no hot-shot selling man. Except that sometimes, you have to admit, he's a sweet personality.

BIFF (*deciding*): Lend me ten bucks, will ya? I want to buy some new ties.

HAPPY: I'll take you to a place I know. Beautiful stuff. Wear one of my striped shirts tomorrow.

BIFF: She got gray. Mom got awful old. Gee, I'm gonna go in to Oliver tomorrow and knock him for a . . .

HAPPY: Come on up. Tell that to Dad. Let's give him a whirl. Come on.

BIFF (*steamed up*): You know, with ten thousand bucks, boy!

HAPPY (*as they go into the living room*): That's the talk, Biff, that's the first time I've heard the old confidence out of you! (*From within the living room, fading off*) You're gonna live with me, kid, and any babe you want just say the word . . . (*The last lines are hardly heard. They are mounting the stairs to their parents' bedroom.*)

LINDA (*entering her bedroom and addressing* WILLY, *who is in the bathroom. She is straightening the bed for him*): Can you do anything about the shower? It drips.

WILLY (*from the bathroom*): All of a sudden everything falls to pieces. Goddam plumbing, oughta be sued, those people. I hardly finished putting it in and the thing . . . (*His words rumble off.*)

LINDA: I'm just wondering if Oliver will remember him. You think he might?

WILLY (*coming out of the bathroom in his pajamas*): Remember him? What's the matter with you, you crazy? If he'd've stayed with Oliver he'd be on top by now! Wait'll Oliver gets a look at him. You don't know the average caliber any more. The average young man today— (*he is getting into bed*) —is got a caliber of zero. Greatest thing in the world for him was to bum around.

BIFF *and* HAPPY *enter the bedroom. Slight pause.*

WILLY (*stops short, looking at* BIFF): Glad to hear it, boy.

HAPPY: He wanted to say good night to you, sport.

WILLY (*to* BIFF): Yeah. Knock him dead, boy. What'd you want to tell me?

BIFF: Just take it easy, Pop. Good night. (*He turns to go.*)

WILLY (*unable to resist*): And if anything falls off the desk while you're talking to him—like a package or something—don't you pick it up. They have office boys for that.

LINDA: I'll make a big breakfast . . .

WILLY: Will you let me finish? (*To* BIFF.) Tell him you were in the business in the West. Not farm work.

BIFF: All right, Dad.

LINDA: I think everything . . .

WILLY (*going right through her speech*): And don't undersell yourself. No less than fifteen thousand dollars.

BIFF (*unable to bear him*): Okay. Good night, Mom. (*He starts moving.*)

WILLY: Because you got a greatness in you, Biff, remember that. You got all kinds of greatness . . . (*He lies back, exhausted.* BIFF *walks out.*)

LINDA (*calling after* BIFF): Sleep well, darling!

HAPPY: I'm gonna get married, Mom. I wanted to tell you.

LINDA: Go to sleep, dear.

HAPPY (*going*): I just wanted to tell you.

WILLY: Keep up the good work. (HAPPY *exits.*) God . . . remember that Ebbets Field game? The championship of the city?

LINDA: Just rest. Should I sing to you?

WILLY: Yeah. Sing to me. (LINDA *hums a soft lullaby.*) When that team came out—he was the tallest, remember?

LINDA: Oh, yes. And in gold.

BIFF *enters the darkened kitchen, takes a cigarette, and leaves the house. He comes downstage into a golden pool of light. He smokes, staring at the night.*

WILLY: Like a young god. Hercules—something like that. And the sun, the sun all around him. Remember how he waved to me? Right up from the field, with the representatives of three colleges standing by? And the buyers I brought, and the cheers when he came out—Loman, Loman, Loman! God Almighty, he'll be great yet. A star like that, magnificent, can never really fade away!

The light on WILLY *is fading. The gas heater begins to glow through the kitchen wall, near the stairs, a blue flame beneath red coils.*

LINDA (*timidly*): Willy dear, what has he got against you?

WILLY: I'm so tired. Don't talk any more.

BIFF *slowly returns to the kitchen. He stops, stares toward the heater.*

LINDA: Will you ask Howard to let you work in New York?

WILLY: First thing in the morning. Everything'll be all right.

BIFF *reaches behind the heater and draws out a length of rubber tubing. He is horrified and turns his head toward* WILLY*'s room, still dimly lit, from which the strains of* LINDA*'s desperate but monotonous humming rise.*

WILLY (*staring through the window into the moonlight*): Gee, look at the moon moving between the buildings!

BIFF *wraps the tubing around his hand and quickly goes up the stairs.*

Act 2

Music is heard, gay and bright. The curtain rises as the music fades away. WILLY, *in shirt sleeves, is sitting at the kitchen table, sipping coffee, his hat in his lap.* LINDA *is filling his cup when she can.*

WILLY: Wonderful coffee. Meal in itself.

LINDA: Can I make you some eggs?

WILLY: No. Take a breath.

LINDA: You look so rested, dear.

WILLY: I slept like a dead one. First time in months. Imagine, sleeping till ten on a Tuesday morning. Boys left nice and early, heh?

LINDA: They were out of here by eight o'clock.

WILLY: Good work!

LINDA: It was so thrilling to see them leaving together. I can't get over the shaving lotion in this house!

WILLY (*smiling*): Mmm . . .

LINDA: Biff was very changed this morning. His whole attitude seemed to be hopeful. He couldn't wait to get downtown to see Oliver.

WILLY: He's heading for a change. There's no question, there simply are certain men that take longer to get—solidified. How did he dress?

LINDA: His blue suit. He's so handsome in that suit. He could be a—anything in that suit!

WILLY *gets up from the table.* LINDA *holds his jacket for him.*

WILLY: There's no question, no question at all. Gee, on the way home tonight I'd like to buy some seeds.

LINDA (*laughing*): That'd be wonderful. But not enough sun gets back there. Nothing'll grow any more.

WILLY: You wait, kid, before it's all over we're gonna get a little place out in the country, and I'll raise some vegetables, a couple of chickens . . .

LINDA: You'll do it yet, dear.

WILLY *walks out of his jacket.* LINDA *follows him.*

WILLY: And they'll get married, and come for a weekend. I'd build a little guest house. 'Cause I got so many fine tools, all I'd need would be a little lumber and some peace of mind.

LINDA (*joyfully*): I sewed the lining . . .

WILLY: I could build two guest houses, so they'd both come. Did he decide how much he's going to ask Oliver for?

LINDA (*getting him into the jacket*): He didn't mention it, but I imagine ten or fifteen thousand. You going to talk to Howard today?

WILLY: Yeah. I'll put it to him straight and simple. He'll just have to take me off the road.

LINDA: And Willy, don't forget to ask for a little advance, because we've got the insurance premium. It's the grace period now.

WILLY: That's a hundred . . . ?

LINDA: A hundred and eight, sixty-eight. Because we're a little short again.

WILLY: Why are we short?

LINDA: Well, you had the motor job on the car . . .

WILLY: That goddam Studebaker!

LINDA: And you got one more payment on the refrigerator . . .

WILLY: But it just broke again!

LINDA: Well, it's old, dear.

WILLY: I told you we should've bought a well-advertised machine. Charley bought a General Electric and it's twenty years old and it's still good, that son-of-a-bitch.

LINDA: But, Willy . . .

WILLY: Whoever heard of a Hastings refrigerator? Once in my life I would like to own something outright before it's broken! I'm always in a race with the junk-yard! I just finished paying for the car and it's on its last legs. The refrigerator consumes belts like a goddam maniac. They time those things. They time them so when you finally paid for them, they're used up.

LINDA (*buttoning up his jacket as he unbuttons it*): All told, about two hundred dollars would carry us, dear. But that includes the last payment on the mortgage. After this payment, Willy, the house belongs to us.

WILLY: It's twenty-five years!

LINDA: Biff was nine years old when we bought it.

WILLY: Well, that's a great thing. To weather a twenty-five year mortgage is . . .

LINDA: It's an accomplishment.

WILLY: All the cement, the lumber, the reconstruction I put in this house! There ain't a crack to be found in it any more.

LINDA: Well, it served its purpose.

WILLY: What purpose? Some stranger'll come along, move in, and that's that. If only Biff would take this house, and raise a family . . . (*He starts to go.*) Good-by, I'm late.

LINDA (*suddenly remembering*): Oh, I forgot! You're supposed to meet them for dinner.

WILLY: Me?

LINDA: At Frank's Chop House on Forty-eighth near Sixth Avenue.

WILLY: Is that so! How about you?

LINDA: No, just the three of you. They're gonna blow you to a big meal!

WILLY: Don't say! Who thought of that?

LINDA: Biff came to me this morning, Willy, and he said, "Tell Dad, we want to blow him to a big meal." Be there six o'clock. You and your two boys are going to have dinner.

WILLY: Gee whiz! That's really somethin'. I'm gonna knock Howard for a loop, kid. I'll get an advance, and I'll come home with a New York job. Goddammit, now I'm gonna do it!

LINDA: Oh, that's the spirit, Willy!

WILLY: I will never get behind a wheel the rest of my life!

LINDA: It's changing, Willy, I can feel it changing!

WILLY: Beyond a question. G'by, I'm late. (*He starts to go again.*)

LINDA (*calling after him as she runs to the kitchen table for a handkerchief*): You got your glasses?

WILLY (*feels for them, then comes back in*): Yeah, yeah, got my glasses.

LINDA (*giving him the handkerchief*): And a handkerchief.

WILLY: Yeah, handkerchief.

LINDA: And your saccharine?

WILLY: Yeah, my saccharine.

LINDA: Be careful on the subway stairs.

She kisses him, and a silk stocking is seen hanging from her hand. WILLY *notices it.*

WILLY: Will you stop mending stockings? At least while I'm in the house. It gets me nervous. I can't tell you. Please.

LINDA *hides the stocking in her hand as she follows* WILLY *across the forestage in front of the house.*

LINDA: Remember, Frank's Chop House.

WILLY (*passing the apron*): Maybe beets would grow out there.

LINDA (*laughing*): But you tried so many times.

WILLY: Yeah. Well, don't work hard today. (*He disappears around the right corner of the house.*)

LINDA: Be careful!

As WILLY *vanishes,* LINDA *waves to him. Suddenly the phone rings. She runs across the stage and into the kitchen and lifts it.*

LINDA: Hello? Oh, Biff! I'm so glad you called, I just . . . Yes, sure, I just told him. Yes, he'll be there for dinner at six o'clock, I didn't forget. Listen, I was just dying to tell you. You know that little rubber pipe I told you about? That he connected to the gas heater? I finally decided to go down the cellar this morning and take it away and destroy it. But it's gone! Imagine? He took it away himself, it isn't there! (*She listens.*) When? Oh, then you took it. Oh—nothing, it's just that I'd hoped he'd taken it away himself. Oh, I'm not worried, darling, because this morning he left in such high spirits, it was like the old days! I'm not afraid any more. Did Mr. Oliver see you? . . . Well, you wait there then. And make a nice impression on him, darling. Just don't perspire too much before you see him. And have a nice time with Dad. He may have big news too! . . . That's right, a New York job. And be sweet to him tonight, dear. Be loving to him. Because he's only a little boat looking for a harbor. (*She is trembling with sorrow and joy.*) Oh, that's wonderful, Biff, you'll save his life. Thanks, darling. Just put your arm around him when he comes into the restaurant. Give him a smile. That's the boy . . . Good-by, dear. . . . You got your comb? . . . That's fine. Good-by, Biff dear.

In the middle of her speech, HOWARD WAGNER, *thirty-six, wheels in a small type-writer table on which is a wire-recording machine and proceeds to plug it in. This is on the left forestage. Light slowly fades on* LINDA *as it rises on* HOWARD. HOWARD *is intent on threading the machine and only glances over his shoulder as* WILLY *appears.*

WILLY: Pst! Pst!

HOWARD: Hello, Willy, come in.

WILLY: Like to have a little talk with you, Howard.

HOWARD: Sorry to keep you waiting. I'll be with you in a minute.

WILLY: What's that, Howard?

HOWARD: Didn't you ever see one of these? Wire recorder.

WILLY: Oh. Can we talk a minute?

HOWARD: Records things. Just got delivery yesterday. Been driving me crazy, the most terrific machine I ever saw in my life. I was up all night with it.

WILLY: What do you do with it?

HOWARD: I bought it for dictation, but you can do anything with it. Listen to this. I had it home last night. Listen to what I picked up. The first one is my daughter. Get this. (*He flicks the switch and "Roll out the Barrel" is heard being whistled.*) Listen to that kid whistle.

WILLY: That is lifelike, isn't it?

HOWARD: Seven years old. Get that tone.

WILLY: Ts, ts. Like to ask a little favor if you . . .

The whistling breaks off, and the voice of HOWARD's *daughter is heard.*

HIS DAUGHTER: "Now you, Daddy."

HOWARD: She's crazy for me! (*Again the same song is whistled.*) That's me! Ha! (*He winks.*)

WILLY: You're very good!

The whistling breaks off again. The machine runs silent for a moment.

HOWARD: Sh! Get this now, this is my son.

HIS SON: "The capital of Alabama is Montgomery; the capital of Arizona is Phoenix; the capital of Arkansas is Little Rock; the capital of California is Sacramento . . . " (*and on, and on.*)

HOWARD (*holding up five fingers*): Five years old, Willy!

WILLY: He'll make an announcer some day!

HIS SON (*continuing*): "the capital . . . "

HOWARD: Get that—alphabetical order! (*The machine breaks off suddenly.*) Wait a minute. The maid kicked the plug out.

WILLY: It certainly is a . . .

HOWARD: Sh, for God's sake!

HIS SON: "It's nine o'clock, Bulova watch time. So I have to go to sleep."

WILLY: That really is . . .

HOWARD: Wait a minute! The next is my wife.

They wait.

HOWARD'S VOICE: "Go on, say something." (*Pause.*) "Well, you gonna talk?"

HIS WIFE: "I can't think of anything."

HOWARD'S VOICE: "Well, talk—it's turning."

HIS WIFE (*shyly, beaten*): "Hello." (*Silence.*) "Oh, Howard, I can't talk into this . . . "

HOWARD (*snapping the machine off*): That was my wife.

WILLY: That is a wonderful machine. Can we . . .

HOWARD: I tell you, Willy, I'm gonna take my camera, and my bandsaw, and all my hobbies, and out they go. This is the most fascinating relaxation I ever found.

WILLY: I think I'll get one myself.

HOWARD: Sure, they're only a hundred and a half. You can't do without it. Supposing you wanna hear Jack Benny, see? But you can't be at home at that hour. So you tell the maid to turn the radio on when Jack Benny comes on, and this automatically goes on with the radio . . .

WILLY: And when you come home you . . .

HOWARD: You can come home twelve o'clock, one o'clock, any time you like, and you get yourself a Coke and sit yourself down, throw the switch, and there's Jack Benny's program in the middle of the night!

WILLY: I'm definitely going to get one. Because lots of times I'm on the road, and I think to myself, what I must be missing on the radio!

HOWARD: Don't you have a radio in the car?

WILLY: Well, yeah, but who ever thinks of turning it on?

HOWARD: Say, aren't you supposed to be in Boston?

WILLY: That's what I want to talk to you about, Howard. You got a minute? (*He draws a chair in from the wing.*)

HOWARD: What happened? What're you doing here?

WILLY: Well . . .

HOWARD: You didn't crack up again, did you?

WILLY: Oh, no. No . . .

HOWARD: Geez, you had me worried there for a minute. What's the trouble?

WILLY: Well, tell you the truth, Howard. I've come to the decision that I'd rather not travel any more.

HOWARD: Not travel! Well, what'll you do?

WILLY: Remember, Christmas time, when you had the party here? You said you'd try to think of some spot for me here in town.

HOWARD: With us?

WILLY: Well, sure.

HOWARD: Oh, yeah, yeah. I remember. Well, I couldn't think of anything for you, Willy.

WILLY: I tell ya, Howard. The kids are all grown up, y'know. I don't need much any more. If I could take home—well, sixty-five dollars a week, I could swing it.

HOWARD: Yeah, but Willy, see I . . .

WILLY: I tell ya why, Howard. Speaking frankly and between the two of us, y'know— I'm just a little tired.

HOWARD: Oh, I could understand that, Willy. But you're a road man, Willy, and we do a road business. We've only got a half-dozen salesmen on the floor here.

WILLY: God knows, Howard. I never asked a favor of any man. But I was with the firm when your father used to carry you in here in his arms.

HOWARD: I know that, Willy, but . . .

WILLY: Your father came to me the day you were born and asked me what I thought of the name Howard, may he rest in peace.

HOWARD: I appreciate that, Willy, but there just is no spot here for you. If I had a spot I'd slam you right in, but I just don't have a single solitary spot.

He looks for his lighter. WILLY *has picked it up and gives it to him. Pause.*

WILLY (*with increasing anger*): Howard, all I need to set my table is fifty dollars a week.

HOWARD: But where am I going to put you, kid?

WILLY: Look, it isn't a question of whether I can sell merchandise, is it?

HOWARD: No, but it's business, kid, and everybody's gotta pull his own weight.

WILLY (*desperately*): Just let me tell you a story, Howard . . .

HOWARD: 'Cause you gotta admit, business is business.

WILLY (*angrily*): Business is definitely business, but just listen for a minute. You don't understand this. When I was a boy—eighteen, nineteen—I was already on the road. And there was a question in my mind as to whether selling had a future for me. Because in those days I had a yearning to go to Alaska. See, there were three gold strikes in one month in Alaska, and I felt like going out. Just for the ride, you might say.

HOWARD (*barely interested*): Don't say.

WILLY: Oh, yeah, my father lived many years in Alaska. He was an adventurous man. We've got quite a little streak of self-reliance in our family. I thought I'd go out with my older brother and try to locate him, and maybe settle in the North with the old man. And I was almost decided to go, when I met a sales-man in the Parker House. His name was Dave Singleman. And he was eighty-four years old, and he'd drummed merchandise in thirty-one states. And old Dave, he'd go up to his room, y'understand, put on his green velvet slippers—I'll never forget—and pick up his phone and call the buyers, and without ever leaving his room, at the age of eighty-four, he made his living. And when I saw that, I realized that selling was the greatest career a man could want. 'Cause what could be more satisfying than to be able to go, at the age of eighty-four, into twenty or thirty different cities, and pick up a phone, and be remembered and loved and helped by so many different people? Do you know? when he died—and by the way he died the death of a salesman, in his green velvet slippers in the smoker of the New York, New Haven and Hartford, going into Boston—when he died, hundreds of salesmen and buyers were at his funeral. Things were sad on a lotta trains for months after that. (*He stands up,* HOWARD *has not looked at him.*) In those days there was personality in it, Howard. There was respect, and comradeship, and gratitude in it. Today, it's all cut and dried, and there's no chance for bringing friendship to bear—or personality. You see what I mean? They don't know me any more.

HOWARD (*moving away, to the right*): That's just the thing, Willy.

WILLY: If I had forty dollars a week—that's all I'd need. Forty dollars, Howard.

HOWARD: Kid, I can't take blood from a stone, I . . .

WILLY (*desperation is on him now*): Howard, the year Al Smith was nominated, your father came to me and . . .

HOWARD (*starting to go off*): I've got to see some people, kid.

WILLY (*stopping him*): I'm talking about your father! There were promises made across this desk! You mustn't tell me you've got people to see—I put thirty-four years into this firm, Howard, and now I can't pay my insurance! You can't eat the orange and throw the peel away—a man is not a piece of fruit! (*After a pause.*) Now pay attention. Your father—in 1928 I had a big year. I averaged a hundred and seventy dollars a week in commissions.

HOWARD (*impatiently*): Now, Willy, you never averaged . . .

WILLY (*banging his hand on the desk*): I averaged a hundred and seventy dollars a week in the year of 1928! And your father came to me—or rather, I was in the office here—it was right over this desk—and he put his hand on my shoulder . . .

HOWARD (*getting up*): You'll have to excuse me, Willy, I gotta see some people. Pull yourself together. (*Going out.*) I'll be back in a little while.

On HOWARD'*s exit, the light on his chair grows very bright and strange.*

WILLY: Pull myself together! What the hell did I say to him? My God, I was yelling at him! How could I? (WILLY *breaks off, staring at the light, which occupies the chair, animating it. He approaches this chair, standing across the desk from it.*) Frank, Frank, don't you remember what you told me that time? How you put your hand on my shoulder, and Frank . . . (*He leans on the desk and as he speaks the dead man's name he accidentally switches on the recorder, and instantly*)

HOWARD'S son: ". . . New York is Albany. The capital of Ohio is Cincinnati, the capital of Rhode Island is . . . " (*The recitation continues.*)

WILLY (*leaping away with fright, shouting*): Ha! Howard! Howard! Howard!

HOWARD (*rushing in*): What happened?

WILLY (*pointing at the machine, which continues nasally, childishly, with the capital cities*): Shut it off! Shut it off!

HOWARD (*pulling the plug out*): Look, Willy . . .

WILLY (*pressing his hands to his eyes*): I gotta get myself some coffee. I'll get some coffee . . .

WILLY *starts to walk out.* HOWARD *stops him.*

HOWARD (*rolling up the cord*): Willy, look . . .

WILLY: I'll go to Boston.

HOWARD: Willy, you can't go to Boston for us.

WILLY: Why can't I go?

HOWARD: I don't want you to represent us. I've been meaning to tell you for a long time now.

WILLY: Howard, are you firing me?

HOWARD: I think you need a good long rest, Willy.

WILLY: Howard . . .

HOWARD: And when you feel better, come back, and we'll see if we can work something out.

WILLY: But I gotta earn money, Howard. I'm in no position to . . .

HOWARD: Where are your sons? Why don't your sons give you a hand?

WILLY: They're working on a very big deal.

HOWARD: This is no time for false pride, Willy. You go to your sons and you tell them that you're tired. You've got two great boys, haven't you?

WILLY: Oh, no question, no question, but in the meantime . . .

HOWARD: Then that's that, heh?

WILLY: All right, I'll go to Boston tomorrow.

HOWARD: No, no.

WILLY: I can't throw myself on my sons. I'm not a cripple!

HOWARD: Look, kid, I'm busy this morning.

WILLY (*grasping* HOWARD'S *arm*): Howard, you've got to let me go to Boston!

HOWARD (*hard, keeping himself under control*): I've got a line of people to see this morning. Sit down, take five minutes, and pull yourself together, and then go home, will ya? I need the office, Willy. (*He starts to go, turns, remembering the recorder, starts to push off the table holding the recorder.*) Oh, yeah. Whenever you can this week, stop by and drop off the samples. You'll feel better, Willy, and then come back and we'll talk. Pull yourself together, kid, there's people outside.

HOWARD *exits, pushing the table off left.* WILLY *stares into space, exhausted. Now the music is heard—*BEN'S *music—first distantly, then closer, closer. As* WILLY *speaks,* BEN *enters from the right. He carries valise and umbrella.*

WILLY: Oh, Ben, how did you do it? What is the answer? Did you wind up the Alaska deal already?

BEN: Doesn't take much time if you know what you're doing. Just a short business trip. Boarding ship in an hour. Wanted to say good-by.

WILLY: Ben, I've got to talk to you.

BEN (*glancing at his watch*): Haven't the time, William.

WILLY (*crossing the apron to* BEN): Ben, nothing's working out. I don't know what to do.

BEN: Now, look here, William. I've bought timberland in Alaska and I need a man to look after things for me.

WILLY: God, timberland! Me and my boys in those grand outdoors!

BEN: You've a new continent at your doorstep, William. Get out of these cities, they're full of talk and time payments and courts of law. Screw on your fists and you can fight for a fortune up there.

WILLY: Yes, yes! Linda, Linda!

LINDA *enters as of old, with the wash.*

LINDA: Oh, you're back?

BEN: I haven't much time.

WILLY: No, wait! Linda, he's got a proposition for me in Alaska.

LINDA: But you've got . . . (*To* BEN.) He's got a beautiful job here.

WILLY: But in Alaska, kid, I could . . .

LINDA: You're doing well enough, Willy!

BEN (*To* LINDA): Enough for what, my dear?

LINDA (*frightened of* BEN *and angry at him*): Don't say those things to him! Enough to be happy right here, right now. (*To* WILLY, *while* BEN *laughs.*) Why must everybody conquer the world? You're well liked, and the boys love you, and someday— (*To* BEN)—why, old man Wagner told him just the other day that if he keeps it up he'll be a member of the firm, didn't he, Willy?

WILLY: Sure, sure. I am building something with this firm, Ben, and if a man is building something he must be on the right track, mustn't he?

BEN: What are you building? Lay your hand on it. Where is it?

WILLY (*hesitantly*): That's true, Linda, there's nothing.

LINDA: Why? (*To* BEN.) There's a man eighty-four years old . . .

WILLY: That's right, Ben, that's right. When I look at that man I say, what is there to worry about?

BEN: Bah!

WILLY: It's true, Ben. All he has to do is go into any city, pick up the phone, and he's making his living and you know why?

BEN (*picking up his valise*): I've got to go.

WILLY (*holding* BEN *back*): Look at this boy!

> BIFF, *in his high school sweater, enters carrying suitcase.* HAPPY *carries* BIFF's *shoulder guards, gold helmet, and football pants.*

WILLY: Without a penny to his name, three great universities are begging for him, and from there the sky's the limit, because it's not what you do, Ben. It's who you know and the smile on your face! It's contacts, Ben, contacts! The whole wealth of Alaska passes over the lunch table at the Commodore Hotel, and that's the wonder, the wonder of this country, that a man can end with diamonds here on the basis of being liked! (*He turns to* BIFF.) And that's why when you get out on that field today it's important. Because thousands of people will be rooting for you and loving you. (*To* BEN, *who has again begun to leave.*) And Ben! when he walks into a business office his name will sound out like a bell and all the doors will open to him! I've seen it, Ben, I've seen it a thousand times! You can't feel it with your hand like timber, but it's there!

BEN: Good-by, William.

WILLY: Ben, am I right? Don't you think I'm right? I value your advice.

BEN: There's a new continent at your doorstep, William. You could walk out rich. Rich! (*He is gone.*)

WILLY: We'll do it here, Ben! You hear me? We're gonna do it here!

> *Young* BERNARD *rushes in. The gay music of the Boys is heard.*

BERNARD: Oh, gee, I was afraid you left already!

WILLY: Why? What time is it?

BERNARD: It's half-past one!

WILLY: Well, come on, everybody! Ebbets Field next stop! Where's the pennants? (*He rushes through the wall-line of the kitchen and out into the living room.*)

LINDA (*to* BIFF): Did you pack fresh underwear?

BIFF (*who has been limbering up*): I want to go!

BERNARD: Biff, I'm carrying your helmet, ain't I?

HAPPY: No, I'm carrying the helmet.

BERNARD: Oh, Biff, you promised me.

HAPPY: I'm carrying the helmet.

BERNARD: How am I going to get in the locker room?

LINDA: Let him carry the shoulder guards. (*She puts her coat and hat on in the kitchen.*)

BERNARD: Can I, Biff? 'Cause I told everybody I'm going to be in the locker room.

HAPPY: In Ebbets Field it's the clubhouse.

BERNARD: I meant the clubhouse. Biff!

HAPPY: Biff!

BIFF (*grandly, after a slight pause*): Let him carry the shoulder guards.

HAPPY (*as he gives* BERNARD *the shoulder guards*): Stay close to us now.

> WILLY *rushes in with the pennants.*

WILLY (*handing them out*): Everybody wave when Biff comes out on the field. (HAPPY *and* BERNARD *run off.*) You set now, boy?

> *The music has died away.*

BIFF: Ready to go, Pop. Every muscle is ready.

WILLY (*at the edge of the apron*): You realize what this means?

BIFF: That's right, Pop.

WILLY (*feeling* BIFF's *muscles*): You're comin' home this afternoon captain of the All-Scholastic Championship Team of the City of New York.

BIFF: I got it, Pop. And remember, pal, when I take off my helmet, that touchdown is for you.

WILLY: Let's go! (*He is starting out, with his arm around* BIFF, *when* CHARLEY *enters, as of old, in knickers.*) I got no room for you, Charley.

CHARLEY: Room? For what?

WILLY: In the car.

CHARLEY: You goin' for a ride? I wanted to shoot some casino.

WILLY (*furiously*): Casino! (*Incredulously.*) Don't you realize what today is?

LINDA: Oh, he knows, Willy. He's just kidding you.

WILLY: That's nothing to kid about!

CHARLEY: No, Linda, what's goin' on?

LINDA: He's playing in Ebbets Field.

CHARLEY: Baseball in this weather?

WILLY: Don't talk to him. Come on, come on! (*He is pushing them out.*)

CHARLEY: Wait a minute, didn't you hear the news?

WILLY: What?

CHARLEY: Don't you listen to the radio? Ebbets Field just blew up.

WILLY: You go to hell! (CHARLEY *laughs. Pushing them out.*) Come on, come on! We're late.

CHARLEY (*as they go*): Knock a homer, Biff, knock a homer!

WILLY (*the last to leave, turning to* CHARLEY): I don't think that was funny, Charley. This is the greatest day of his life.

CHARLEY: Willy, when are you going to grow up?

WILLY: Yeah, heh? When this game is over, Charley, you'll be laughing out of the other side of your face. They'll be calling him another Red Grange. Twenty-five thousand a year.

CHARLEY (*kidding*): Is that so?

WILLY: Yeah, that's so.

CHARLEY: Well, then, I'm sorry, Willy. But tell me something.

WILLY: What?

CHARLEY: Who is Red Grange?

WILLY: Put up your hands. Goddam you, put up your hands!

> CHARLEY, *chuckling, shakes his head and walks away, around the left corner of the stage.* WILLY *follows him. The music rises to a mocking frenzy.*

WILLY: Who the hell do you think you are, better than everybody else? You don't know everything, you big, ignorant, stupid . . . Put up your hands!

> *Light rises, on the right side of the forestage, on a small table in the reception room of* CHARLEY's *office. Traffic sounds heard.* BERNARD, *now mature, sits whistling to himself. A pair of tennis rackets and an old overnight bag are on the floor beside him.*

WILLY (*offstage*): What are you walking away for? Don't walk away! If you're going to say something say it to my face! I know you laugh at me behind my back. You'll laugh out of the other side of your goddam face after this game. Touchdown! Touchdown! Eighty thousand people! Touchdown! Right between the goal posts.

> (BERNARD *is a quiet, earnest, but self-assured young man.* WILLY's *voice is coming from right upstage now.* BERNARD *lowers his feet off the table and listens.* JENNY, *his father's secretary, enters.*)

JENNY (*distressed*): Say, Bernard, will you go out in the hall?

BERNARD: What is that noise? Who is it?

JENNY: Mr. Loman. He just got off the elevator.

BERNARD (*getting up*): Who's he arguing with?

JENNY: Nobody. There's nobody with him. I can't deal with him any more, and your father gets all upset every time he comes. I've got a lot of typing to do, and your father's waiting to sign it. Will you see him?

WILLY (*entering*): Touchdown! Touch— (*He sees* JENNY.) Jenny, Jenny, good to see you. How're ya? Workin'? Or still honest?

JENNY: Fine. How've you been feeling?

WILLY: Not much any more, Jenny. Ha, ha! (*He is surprised to see the rackets.*)

BERNARD: Hello, Uncle Willy.

WILLY (*almost shocked*): Bernard! Well, look who's here! (*He comes quickly, guiltily, to* BERNARD *and warmly shakes his hand.*)

BERNARD: How are you? Good to see you.

WILLY: What are you doing here?

BERNARD: Oh, just stopped by to see Pop. Get off my feet till my train leaves. I'm going to Washington in a few minutes.

WILLY: Is he in?

BERNARD: Yes, he's in his office with the accountant. Sit down.

WILLY (*sitting down*): What're you going to do in Washington?

BERNARD: Oh, just a case I've got there, Willy.

WILLY: That so? (*Indicating the rackets.*) You going to play tennis there?

BERNARD: I'm staying with a friend who's got a court.

WILLY: Don't say. His own tennis court. Must be fine people, I bet.

BERNARD: They are, very nice. Dad tells me Biff's in town.

WILLY (*with a big smile*): Yeah, Biff's in. Working on a very big deal, Bernard.

BERNARD: What's Biff doing?

WILLY: Well, he's been doing very big things in the West. But he decided to establish himself here. Very big. We're having dinner. Did I hear your wife had a boy?

BERNARD: That's right. Our second.

WILLY: Two boys! What do you know!

BERNARD: What kind of a deal has Biff got?

WILLY: Well, Bill Oliver—very big sporting-goods man—he wants Biff very badly. Called him in from the West. Long distance, carte blanche, special deliveries. Your friends have their own private tennis court?

BERNARD: You still with the old firm, Willy?

WILLY (*after a pause*): I'm—I'm overjoyed to see how you made the grade, Bernard, overjoyed. It's an encouraging thing to see a young man really— really . . . Looks very good for Biff—very . . . (*He breaks off, then.*) Bernard . . . (*He is so full of emotion, he breaks off again.*)

BERNARD: What is it, Willy?

WILLY (*small and alone*): What—what's the secret?

BERNARD: What secret?

WILLY: How—how did you? Why didn't he ever catch on?

BERNARD: I wouldn't know that, Willy.

WILLY (*confidentially, desperately*): You were his friend, his boyhood friend. There's something I don't understand about it. His life ended after that Ebbets Field game. From the age of seventeen nothing good ever happened to him.

BERNARD: He never trained himself for anything.

WILLY: But he did, he did. After high school he took so many correspondence courses. Radio mechanics; television; God knows what, and never made the slightest mark.

BERNARD (*taking off his glasses*): Willy, do you want to talk candidly?

WILLY (*rising, faces* BERNARD): I regard you as a very brilliant man, Bernard. I value your advice.

BERNARD: Oh, the hell with the advice, Willy. I couldn't advise you. There's just one thing I've always wanted to ask you. When he was supposed to graduate, and the math teacher flunked him . . .

WILLY: Oh, that son-of-a-bitch ruined his life.

BERNARD: Yeah, but, Willy, all he had to do was go to summer school and make up that subject.

WILLY: That's right, that's right.

BERNARD: Did you tell him not to go to summer school?

WILLY: Me? I begged him to go. I ordered him to go!

BERNARD: Then why wouldn't he go?

WILLY: Why? Why! Bernard, that question has been trailing me like a ghost for the last fifteen years. He flunked the subject, and laid down and died like a hammer hit him!

BERNARD: Take it easy, kid.

WILLY: Let me talk to you—I got nobody to talk to. Bernard, Bernard, was it my fault? Y'see? It keeps going around in my mind, maybe I did something to him. I got nothing to give him.

BERNARD: Don't take it so hard.

WILLY: Why did he lay down? What is the story there? You were his friend!

BERNARD: Willy, I remember, it was June, and our grades came out. And he'd flunked math.

WILLY: That son-of-a-bitch!

BERNARD: No, it wasn't right then. Biff just got very angry, I remember, and he was ready to enroll in summer school.

WILLY (*surprised*): He was?

BERNARD: He wasn't beaten by it at all. But then, Willy, he disappeared from the block for almost a month. And I got the idea that he'd gone up to New England to see you. Did he have a talk with you then?

WILLY *stares in silence.*

BERNARD: Willy?

WILLY (*with a strong edge of resentment in his voice*): Yeah, he came to Boston. What about it?

BERNARD: Well, just that when he came back—I'll never forget this, it always mystifies me. Because I'd thought so well of Biff, even though he'd always taken advantage of me. I loved him, Willy, y'know? And he came back after that month and took his sneakers—remember those sneakers with "University of Virginia" printed on them? He was so proud of those, wore them every day. And he took them down in the cellar, and burned them up in the furnace. We had a fist fight. It lasted at least half an hour. Just the two of us, punching each other down the cellar, and crying right through it. I've often thought of how strange it was that I knew he'd given up his life. What happened in Boston, Willy?

WILLY *looks at him as at an intruder.*

BERNARD: I just bring it up because you asked me.

WILLY (*angrily*): Nothing. What do you mean, "What happened?" What's that got to do with anything?

BERNARD: Well, don't get sore.

WILLY: What are you trying to do, blame it on me? If a boy lays down is that my fault?

BERNARD: Now, Willy, don't get . . .

WILLY: Well, don't—don't talk to me that way! What does that mean, "What happened?"

CHARLEY *enters. He is in his vest, and he carries a bottle of bourbon.*

CHARLEY: Hey, you're going to miss that train. (*He waves the bottle.*)

BERNARD: Yeah, I'm going. (*He takes the bottle.*) Thanks, Pop. (*He picks up his rackets and bag.*) Good-by, Willy, and don't worry about it. You know, "If at first you don't succeed . . . "

WILLY: Yes, I believe in that.

BERNARD: But sometimes, Willy, it's better for a man just to walk away.

WILLY: Walk away?

BERNARD: That's right.

WILLY: But if you can't walk away?

BERNARD (*after a slight pause*): I guess that's when it's tough. (*Extending his hand.*) Good-by, Willy.

WILLY (*shaking BERNARD's hand*): Good-by, boy.

CHARLEY (*an arm on BERNARD's shoulder*): How do you like this kid? Gonna argue a case in front of the Supreme Court.

BERNARD (*protesting*): Pop!

WILLY (*genuinely shocked, pained, and happy*): No! The Supreme Court!

BERNARD: I gotta run. 'By, Dad!

CHARLEY: Knock 'em dead, Bernard!

BERNARD *goes off.*

WILLY (*as* CHARLEY *takes out his wallet*): The Supreme Court! And he didn't even mention it!

CHARLEY (*counting out money on the desk*): He don't have to—he's gonna do it.

WILLY: And you never told him what to do, did you? You never took any interest in him.

CHARLEY: My salvation is that I never took any interest in anything. There's some money—fifty dollars. I got an accountant inside.

WILLY: Charley, look . . . (*with difficulty*). I got my insurance to pay. If you can manage it—I need a hundred and ten dollars.

> CHARLEY *doesn't reply for a moment; merely stops moving.*

WILLY: I'd draw it from my bank but Linda would know, and I . . .

CHARLEY: Sit down, Willy.

WILLY (*moving toward the chair*): I'm keeping an account of everything, remember. I'll pay every penny back. (*He sits.*)

CHARLEY: Now listen to me, Willy.

WILLY: I want you to know I appreciate . . .

CHARLEY (*sitting down on the table*): Willy, what're you doin'? What the hell is going on in your head?

WILLY: Why? I'm simply . . .

CHARLEY: I offered you a job. You make fifty dollars a week. And I won't send you on the road.

WILLY: I've got a job.

CHARLEY: Without pay? What kind of a job is a job without pay? (*He rises.*) Now, look, kid, enough is enough. I'm no genius but I know when I'm being insulted.

WILLY: Insulted!

CHARLEY: Why don't you want to work for me?

WILLY: What's the matter with you? I've got a job.

CHARLEY: Then what're you walkin' in here every week for?

WILLY (*getting up*): Well, if you don't want me to walk in here . . .

CHARLEY: I'm offering you a job.

WILLY: I don't want your goddam job!

CHARLEY: When the hell are you going to grow up?

WILLY (*furiously*): You big ignoramus, if you say that to me again I'll rap you one! I don't care how big you are! (*He's ready to fight.*)

> *Pause.*

CHARLEY (*kindly, going to him*): How much do you need, Willy?

WILLY: Charley, I'm strapped. I'm strapped. I don't know what to do. I was just fired.

CHARLEY: Howard fired you?

WILLY: That snotnose. Imagine that? I named him. I named him Howard.

CHARLEY: Willy, when're you gonna realize that them things don't mean anything? You named him Howard, but you can't sell that. The only thing you got in this world is what you can sell. And the funny thing is that you're a salesman, and you don't know that.

WILLY: I've always tried to think otherwise, I guess. I always felt that if a man was impressive, and well liked, that nothing . . .

CHARLEY: Why must everybody like you? Who liked J. P. Morgan? Was he impressive? In a Turkish bath he'd look like a butcher. But with his pockets on he was very well liked. Now listen, Willy, I know you don't like me, and nobody can say I'm in love with you, but I'll give you a job because—just for the hell of it, put it that way. Now what do you say?

WILLY: I—I just can't work for you, Charley.

CHARLEY: What're you, jealous of me?

WILLY: I can't work for you, that's all, don't ask me why.

CHARLEY (*angered, takes out more bills*): You been jealous of me all your life, you damned fool! Here, pay your insurance. (*He puts the money in* WILLY'S *hand.*)

WILLY: I'm keeping strict accounts.

CHARLEY: I've got some work to do. Take care of yourself. And pay your insurance.

WILLY (*moving to the right*): Funny, y'know? After all the highways, and the trains, and the appointments, and the years, you end up worth more dead than alive.

CHARLEY: Willy, nobody's worth nothin' dead. (*After a slight pause.*) Did you hear what I said?

WILLY *stands still, dreaming.*

CHARLEY: Willy!

WILLY: Apologize to Bernard for me when you see him. I didn't mean to argue with him. He's a fine boy. They're all fine boys, and they'll end up big—all of them. Someday they'll all play tennis together. Wish me luck, Charley. He saw Bill Oliver today.

CHARLEY: Good luck.

WILLY (*on the verge of tears*): Charley, you're the only friend I got. Isn't that a remarkable thing? (*He goes out.*)

CHARLEY: Jesus!

CHARLEY *stares after him a moment and follows. All light blacks out. Suddenly raucous music is heard, and a red glow rises behind the screen at right.* STANLEY, *a young waiter, appears, carrying a table, followed by* HAPPY, *who is carrying two chairs.*

STANLEY (*putting the table down*): That's all right, Mr. Loman, I can handle it myself. (*He turns and takes the chairs from* HAPPY *and places them at the table.*)

HAPPY (*glancing around*): Oh, this is better.

STANLEY: Sure, in the front there you're in the middle of all kinds of noise. Whenever you got a party, Mr. Loman, you just tell me and I'll put you back here. Y'know, there's a lotta people they don't like it private, because when they go out they like to see a lotta action around them because they're sick and tired to stay in the house by theirself. But I know you, you ain't from Hackensack. You know what I mean?

HAPPY (*sitting down*): So how's it coming, Stanley?

STANLEY: Ah, it's a dog life. I only wish during the war they'd a took me in the Army. I coulda been dead by now.

HAPPY: My brother's back, Stanley.

STANLEY: Oh, he come back, heh? From the Far West.

HAPPY: Yeah, big cattle man, my brother, so treat him right. And my father's coming too.

STANLEY: Oh, your father too!

HAPPY: You got a couple of nice lobsters?

STANLEY: Hundred percent, big.

HAPPY: I want them with the claws.

STANLEY: Don't worry, I don't give you no mice. (HAPPY *laughs.*) How about some wine? It'll put a head on the meal.

HAPPY: No. You remember, Stanley, that recipe I brought you from overseas? With the champagne in it?

STANLEY: Oh, yeah, sure. I still got it tacked up yet in the kitchen. But that'll have to cost a buck apiece anyways.

HAPPY: That's all right.

STANLEY: What'd you, hit a number or somethin'?

HAPPY: No, it's a little celebration. My brother is—I think he pulled off a big deal today. I think we're going into business together.

STANLEY: Great! That's the best for you. Because a family business, you know what I mean?—that's the best.

HAPPY: That's what I think.

STANLEY: 'Cause what's the difference? Somebody steals? It's in the family. Know what I mean? (*Sotto voce.*) Like this bartender here. The boss is goin' crazy what kinda leak he's got in the cash register. You put it in but it don't come out.

HAPPY (*raising his head*): Sh!

STANLEY: What?

HAPPY: You notice I wasn't lookin' right or left, was I?

STANLEY: No.

HAPPY: And my eyes are closed.

STANLEY: So what's the . . . ?

HAPPY: Strudel's comin'.

STANLEY (*catching on, looks around*): Ah, no, there's no . . .

> He breaks off as a furred, lavishly dressed GIRL enters and sits at the next table. Both follow her with their eyes.

STANLEY: Geez, how'd ya know?

HAPPY: I got radar or something. (*Staring directly at her profile.*) Oooooooo . . . Stanley.

STANLEY: I think that's for you, Mr. Loman.

HAPPY: Look at that mouth. Oh, God. And the binoculars.

STANLEY: Geez, you got a life, Mr. Loman.

HAPPY: Wait on her.

STANLEY (*going to the GIRL's table*): Would you like a menu, ma'am?

GIRL: I'm expecting someone, but I'd like a . . .

HAPPY: Why don't you bring her—excuse me, miss, do you mind? I sell champagne, and I'd like you to try my brand. Bring her a champagne, Stanley.

GIRL: That's awfully nice of you.

HAPPY: Don't mention it. It's all company money. (*He laughs.*)

GIRL: That's a charming product to be selling, isn't it?

HAPPY: Oh, gets to be like everything else. Selling is selling, y'know.

GIRL: I suppose.

HAPPY: You don't happen to sell, do you?

GIRL: No, I don't sell.

HAPPY: Would you object to a compliment from a stranger? You ought to be on a magazine cover.

GIRL (*looking at him a little archly*): I have been.

> STANLEY comes in with a glass of champagne.

HAPPY: What'd I say before, Stanley? You see? She's a cover girl.

STANLEY: Oh, I could see, I could see.

HAPPY (*to the GIRL*): What magazine?

GIRL: Oh, a lot of them. (*She takes the drink.*) Thank you.

HAPPY: You know what they say in France, don't you? "Champagne is the drink of the complexion"—Hya, Biff!

BIFF *has entered and sits with* HAPPY.

BIFF: Hello, kid. Sorry I'm late.

HAPPY: I just got here. Uh, Miss . . . ?

GIRL: Forsythe.

HAPPY: Miss Forsythe, this is my brother.

BIFF: Is Dad here?

HAPPY: His name is Biff. You might've heard of him. Great football player.

GIRL: Really? What team?

HAPPY: Are you familiar with football?

GIRL: No, I'm afraid I'm not.

HAPPY: Biff is quarterback with the New York Giants.

GIRL: Well, that is nice, isn't it? (*She drinks.*)

HAPPY: Good health.

GIRL: I'm happy to meet you.

HAPPY: That's my name. Hap. It's really Harold, but at West Point they called me
   Happy.

GIRL (*now really impressed*): Oh, I see. How do you do? (*She turns her profile.*)

BIFF: Isn't Dad coming?

HAPPY: You want her?

BIFF: Oh, I could never make that.

HAPPY: I remember the time that idea would never come into your head. Where's
   the old confidence, Biff?

BIFF: I just saw Oliver . . .

HAPPY: Wait a minute. I've got to see that old confidence again. Do you want her?
   She's on call.

BIFF: Oh, no. (*He turns to look at the* GIRL.)

HAPPY: I'm telling you. Watch this. (*Turning to the* GIRL.) Honey? (*She turns to him.*)
   Are you busy?

GIRL: Well, I am . . . but I could make a phone call.

HAPPY: Do that, will you, honey? And see if you can get a friend. We'll be here for
   a while. Biff is one of the greatest football players in the country.

GIRL (*standing up*): Well, I'm certainly happy to meet you.

HAPPY: Come back soon.

GIRL: I'll try.

HAPPY: Don't try, honey, try hard.

   The GIRL *exits.* STANLEY *follows, shaking his head in bewildered admiration.*

HAPPY: Isn't that a shame now? A beautiful girl like that? That's why I can't get married. There's not a good woman in a thousand. New York is loaded with them,
   kid!

BIFF: Hap, look . . .

HAPPY: I told you she was on call!

BIFF (*strangely unnerved*): Cut it out, will ya? I want to say something to you.

HAPPY: Did you see Oliver?

BIFF: I saw him all right. Now look, I want to tell Dad a couple of things and I want
   you to help me.

HAPPY: What? Is he going to back you?

BIFF: Are you crazy? You're out of your goddam head, you know that?

HAPPY: Why? What happened?

BIFF (*breathlessly*): I did a terrible thing today, Hap. It's been the strangest day
   I ever went through. I'm all numb, I swear.

HAPPY: You mean he wouldn't see you?

BIFF: Well, I waited six hours for him, see? All day. Kept sending my name in. Even tried to date his secretary so she'd get me to him, but no soap.

HAPPY: Because you're not showin' the old confidence, Biff. He remembered you, didn't he?

BIFF (*stopping* HAPPY *with a gesture*): Finally, about five o'clock, he comes out. Didn't remember who I was or anything. I felt like such an idiot, Hap.

HAPPY: Did you tell him my Florida idea?

BIFF: He walked away. I saw him for one minute. I got so mad I could've torn the walls down! How the hell did I ever get the idea I was a salesman there? I even believed myself that I'd been a salesman for him! And then he gave me one look and—I realized what a ridiculous lie my whole life has been! We've been talking in a dream for fifteen years. I was a shipping clerk.

HAPPY: What'd you do?

BIFF (*with great tension and wonder*): Well, he left, see. And the secretary went out. I was all alone in the waiting room. I don't know what came over me, Hap. The next thing I know I'm in his office—paneled walls, everything. I can't explain it. I—Hap. I took his fountain pen.

HAPPY: Geez, did he catch you?

BIFF: I ran out. I ran down all eleven flights. I ran and ran and ran.

HAPPY: That was an awful dumb—what'd you do that for?

BIFF (*agonized*): I don't know, I just—wanted to take something, I don't know. You gotta help me, Hap. I'm gonna tell Pop.

HAPPY: You crazy? What for?

BIFF: Hap, he's got to understand that I'm not the man somebody lends that kind of money to. He thinks I've been spiting him all these years and it's eating him up.

HAPPY: That's just it. You tell him something nice.

BIFF: I can't.

HAPPY: Say you got a lunch date with Oliver tomorrow.

BIFF: So what do I do tomorrow?

HAPPY: You leave the house tomorrow and come back at night and say Oliver is thinking it over. And he thinks it over for a couple of weeks, and gradually it fades away and nobody's the worse.

BIFF: But it'll go on forever!

HAPPY: Dad is never so happy as when he's looking forward to something!

    WILLY *enters.*

HAPPY: Hello, scout!

WILLY: Gee, I haven't been here in years!

    STANLEY *has followed* WILLY *in and sets a chair for him.* STANLEY *starts off but* HAPPY *stops him.*

HAPPY: Stanley!

    STANLEY *stands by, waiting for an order.*

BIFF (*going to* WILLY *with guilt, as to an invalid*): Sit down, Pop. You want a drink?

WILLY: Sure, I don't mind.

BIFF: Let's get a load on.

WILLY: You look worried.

BIFF: N-no. (*To* STANLEY.) Scotch all around. Make it doubles.

STANLEY: Doubles, right. (*He goes.*)

WILLY: You had a couple already, didn't you?

BIFF: Just a couple, yeah.

WILLY: Well, what happened, boy? (*Nodding affirmatively, with a smile.*) Everything go all right?

BIFF (*takes a breath, then reaches out and grasps* WILLY's *hand*): Pal . . . (*He is smiling bravely, and* WILLY *is smiling too.*) I had an experience today.

HAPPY: Terrific, Pop.

WILLY: That so? What happened?

BIFF (*high, slightly alcoholic, above the earth*): I'm going to tell you everything from first to last. It's been a strange day. (*Silence. He looks around, composes himself as best he can, but his breath keeps breaking the rhythm of his voice.*) I had to wait quite a while for him, and . . .

WILLY: Oliver?

BIFF: Yeah, Oliver. All day, as a matter of cold fact. And a lot of—instances—facts, Pop, facts about my life came back to me. Who was it, Pop? Who ever said I was a salesman with Oliver?

WILLY: Well, you were.

BIFF: No, Dad, I was a shipping clerk.

WILLY: But you were practically . . .

BIFF (*with determination*): Dad, I don't know who said it first, but I was never a salesman for Bill Oliver.

WILLY: What're you talking about?

BIFF: Let's hold on to the facts tonight, Pop. We're not going to get anywhere bullin' around. I was a shipping clerk.

WILLY (*angrily*): All right, now listen to me . . .

BIFF: Why don't you let me finish?

WILLY: I'm not interested in stories about the past or any crap of that kind because the woods are burning, boys, you understand? There's a big blaze going on all around. I was fired today.

BIFF (*shocked*): How could you be?

WILLY: I was fired, and I'm looking for a little good news to tell your mother, because the woman has waited and the woman has suffered. The gist of it is that I haven't got a story left in my head, Biff. So don't give me a lecture about facts and aspects. I am not interested. Now what've you got to say to me?

STANLEY *enters with three drinks. They wait until he leaves.*

WILLY: Did you see Oliver?

BIFF: Jesus, Dad!

WILLY: You mean you didn't go up there?

HAPPY: Sure he went up there.

BIFF: I did. I—saw him. How could they fire you?

WILLY (*on the edge of his chair*): What kind of a welcome did he give you?

BIFF: He won't even let you work on commission?

WILLY: I'm out! (*Driving.*) So tell me, he gave you a warm welcome?

HAPPY: Sure, Pop, sure!

BIFF (*driven*): Well, it was kind of . . .

WILLY: I was wondering if he'd remember you. (*To* HAPPY.) Imagine, man doesn't see him for ten, twelve years and gives him that kind of a welcome!

HAPPY: Damn right!

BIFF (*trying to return to the offensive*): Pop, look . . .

WILLY: You know why he remembered you, don't you? Because you impressed him in those days.

BIFF: Let's talk quietly and get this down to the facts, huh?

WILLY (*as though* BIFF *had been interrupting*): Well, what happened? It's great news, Biff. Did he take you into his office or'd you talk in the waiting room?

BIFF: Well, he came in, see, and . . .

WILLY (*with a big smile*): What'd he say? Betcha he threw his arm around you.

BIFF: Well, he kinda . . .

WILLY: He's a fine man. (*To* HAPPY.) Very hard man to see, y'know.

HAPPY (*agreeing*): Oh, I know.

WILLY (*to* BIFF): Is that where you had the drinks?

BIFF: Yeah, he gave me a couple of—no, no!

HAPPY (*cutting in*): He told him my Florida idea.

WILLY: Don't interrupt. (*To* BIFF.) How'd he react to the Florida idea?

BIFF: Dad, will you give me a minute to explain?

WILLY: I've been waiting for you to explain since I sat down here! What happened? He took you into his office and what?

BIFF: Well—I talked. And—and he listened, see.

WILLY: Famous for the way he listens, y'know. What was his answer?

BIFF: His answer was— (*He breaks off, suddenly angry.*) Dad, you're not letting me tell you what I want to tell you!

WILLY (*accusing, angered*): You didn't see him, did you?

BIFF: I did see him!

WILLY: What'd you insult him or something? You insulted him, didn't you?

BIFF: Listen, will you let me out of it, will you just let me out of it!

HAPPY: What the hell!

WILLY: Tell me what happened!

BIFF (*to* HAPPY): I can't talk to him!

A single trumpet note jars the ear. The light of green leaves stains the house, which holds the air of night and a dream. YOUNG BERNARD *enters and knocks on the door of the house.*

YOUNG BERNARD (*frantically*): Mrs. Loman, Mrs. Loman!

HAPPY: Tell him what happened!

BIFF (*to* HAPPY): Shut up and leave me alone!

WILLY: No, no! You had to go and flunk math!

BIFF: What math? What're you talking about?

YOUNG BERNARD: Mrs. Loman, Mrs. Loman!

LINDA *appears in the house, as of old.*

WILLY (*wildly*): Math, math, math!

BIFF: Take it easy, Pop!

YOUNG BERNARD: Mrs. Loman!

WILLY (*furiously*): If you hadn't flunked you'd've been set by now!

BIFF: Now, look, I'm gonna tell you what happened, and you're going to listen to me.

YOUNG BERNARD: Mrs. Loman!

BIFF: I waited six hours . . .

HAPPY: What the hell are you saying?

BIFF: I kept sending in my name but he wouldn't see me. So finally he . . . (*He continues unheard as light fades low on the restaurant.*)

YOUNG BERNARD: Biff flunked math!

LINDA: No!

YOUNG BERNARD: Birnbaum flunked him! They won't graduate him!

LINDA: But they have to. He's gotta go to the university. Where is he? Biff! Biff!

YOUNG BERNARD: No, he left. He went to Grand Central.

LINDA: Grand—You mean he went to Boston!

YOUNG BERNARD: Is Uncle Willy in Boston?

LINDA: Oh, maybe Willy can talk to the teacher. Oh, the poor, poor boy!

> *Light on house area snaps out.*

BIFF (*at the table, now audible, holding up a gold fountain pen*): . . . so I'm washed up with Oliver, you understand? Are you listening to me?

WILLY (*at a loss*): Yeah, sure. If you hadn't flunked . . .

BIFF: Flunked what? What're you talking about?

WILLY: Don't blame everything on me! I didn't flunk math—you did! What pen?

HAPPY: That was awful dumb, Biff, a pen like that is worth—

WILLY (*seeing the pen for the first time*): You took Oliver's pen?

BIFF (*weakening*): Dad, I just explained it to you.

WILLY: You stole Bill Oliver's fountain pen!

BIFF: I didn't exactly steal it! That's just what I've been explaining to you!

HAPPY: He had it in his hand and just then Oliver walked in, so he got nervous and stuck it in his pocket!

WILLY: My God, Biff!

BIFF: I never intended to do it, Dad!

OPERATOR'S VOICE: Standish Arms, good evening!

WILLY (*shouting*): I'm not in my room!

BIFF (*frightened*): Dad, what's the matter? (*He and* HAPPY *stand up.*)

OPERATOR: Ringing Mr. Loman for you!

WILLY: I'm not there, stop it!

BIFF (*horrified, gets down on one knee before* WILLY): Dad, I'll make good, I'll make good. (WILLY *tries to get to his feet.* BIFF *holds him down.*) Sit down now.

WILLY: No, you're no good, you're no good for anything.

BIFF: I am, Dad, I'll find something else, you understand? Now don't worry about anything. (*He holds up* WILLY'S *face.*) Talk to me, Dad.

OPERATOR: Mr. Loman does not answer. Shall I page him?

WILLY (*attempting to stand, as though to rush and silence the* OPERATOR): No, no, no!

HAPPY: He'll strike something, Pop.

WILLY: No, no . . .

BIFF (*desperately, standing over* WILLY): Pop, listen! Listen to me! I'm telling you something good. Oliver talked to his partner about the Florida idea. You listening? He—he talked to his partner, and he came to me . . . I'm going to be all right, you hear? Dad, listen to me, he said it was just a question of the amount!

WILLY: Then you . . . got it?

HAPPY: He's gonna be terrific, Pop!

WILLY (*trying to stand*): Then you got it, haven't you? You got it! You got it!

BIFF (*agonized, holds* WILLY *down*): No, no. Look, Pop. I'm supposed to have lunch with them tomorrow. I'm just telling you this so you'll know that I can still make an impression, Pop. And I'll make good somewhere, but I can't go tomorrow, see.

WILLY: Why not? You simply . . .

BIFF: But the pen, Pop!

WILLY: You give it to him and tell him it was an oversight!

HAPPY: Sure, have lunch tomorrow!

BIFF: I can't say that . . .

WILLY: You were doing a crossword puzzle and accidentally used his pen!

BIFF: Listen, kid, I took those balls years ago, now I walk in with his fountain pen? That clinches it, don't you see? I can't face him like that! I'll try elsewhere.

PAGE'S VOICE: Paging Mr. Loman!

WILLY: Don't you want to be anything?

BIFF: Pop, how can I go back?

WILLY: You don't want to be anything, is that what's behind it?

BIFF (*now angry at* WILLY *for not crediting his sympathy*): Don't take it that way! You think it was easy walking into that office after what I'd done to him? A team of horses couldn't have dragged me back to Bill Oliver!

WILLY: Then why'd you go?

BIFF: Why did I go? Why did I go! Look at you! Look at what's become of you!

Off left, THE WOMAN *laughs.*

WILLY: Biff, you're going to go to that lunch tomorrow, or . . .

BIFF: I can't go. I've got no appointment!

HAPPY: Biff, for . . . !

WILLY: Are you spiting me?

BIFF: Don't take it that way! Goddammit!

WILLY (*strikes* BIFF *and falters away from the table*): You rotten little louse! Are you spiting me?

THE WOMAN: Someone's at the door, Willy!

BIFF: I'm no good, can't you see what I am?

HAPPY (*separating them*): Hey, you're in a restaurant! Now cut it out, both of you! (*The girls enter.*) Hello, girls, sit down.

THE WOMAN *laughs, off left.*

MISS FORSYTHE: I guess we might as well. This is Letta.

THE WOMAN: Willy, are you going to wake up?

BIFF (*ignoring* WILLY): How're ya, miss, sit down. What do you drink?

MISS FORSYTHE: Letta might not be able to stay long.

LETTA: I gotta get up very early tomorrow. I got jury duty. I'm so excited! Were you fellows ever on a jury?

BIFF: No, but I been in front of them! (*The girls laugh.*) This is my father.

LETTA: Isn't he cute? Sit down with us, Pop.

HAPPY: Sit him down, Biff!

BIFF (*going to him*): Come on, slugger, drink us under the table. To hell with it! Come on, sit down, pal.

On BIFF*'s last insistence,* WILLY *is about to sit.*

THE WOMAN (*now urgently*): Willy, are you going to answer the door!

THE WOMAN*'s call pulls* WILLY *back. He starts right, befuddled.*

BIFF: Hey, where are you going?

WILLY: Open the door.

BIFF: The door?

WILLY: The washroom . . . the door . . . where's the door?

BIFF (*leading* WILLY *to the left*): Just go straight down.

WILLY *moves left.*

THE WOMAN: Willy, Willy, are you going to get up, get up, get up, get up?

WILLY *exits left*.

LETTA: I think it's sweet you bring your daddy along.

MISS FORSYTHE: Oh, he isn't really your father!

BIFF (*at left, turning to her resentfully*): Miss Forsythe, you've just seen a prince walk by. A fine, troubled prince. A hardworking, unappreciated prince. A pal, you understand? A good companion. Always for his boys.

LETTA: That's so sweet.

HAPPY: Well, girls, what's the program? We're wasting time. Come on, Biff. Gather round. Where would you like to go?

BIFF: Why don't you do something for him?

HAPPY: Me!

BIFF: Don't you give a damn for him, Hap?

HAPPY: What're you talking about? I'm the one who . . .

BIFF: I sense it, you don't give a good goddam about him. (*He takes the rolled-up hose from his pocket and puts it on the table in front of* HAPPY.) Look what I found in the cellar, for Christ's sake. How can you bear to let it go on?

HAPPY: Me? Who goes away? Who runs off and . . .

BIFF: Yeah, but he doesn't mean anything to you. You could help him—I can't! Don't you understand what I'm talking about? He's going to kill himself, don't you know that?

HAPPY: Don't I know it! Me!

BIFF: Hap, help him! Jesus . . . help him . . . Help me, help me, I can't bear to look at his face! (*Ready to weep, he hurries out, up right.*)

HAPPY (*starting after him*): Where are you going?

MISS FORSYTHE: What's he so mad about?

HAPPY: Come on, girls, we'll catch up with him.

MISS FORSYTHE (*as* HAPPY *pushes her out*): Say, I don't like that temper of his!

HAPPY: He's just a little overstrung, he'll be all right!

WILLY (*off left, as* THE WOMAN *laughs*): Don't answer! Don't answer!

LETTA: Don't you want to tell your father . . .

HAPPY: No, that's not my father. He's just a guy. Come on, we'll catch Biff, and, honey, we're going to paint this town! Stanley, where's the check! Hey, Stanley!

They exit. STANLEY *looks toward left.*

STANLEY (*calling to* HAPPY *indignantly*): Mr. Loman! Mr. Loman!

STANLEY *picks up a chair and follows them off. Knocking is heard off left.* THE WOMAN *enters, laughing.* WILLY *follows her. She is in a black slip; he is buttoning his shirt. Raw, sensuous music accompanies their speech.*

WILLY: Will you stop laughing? Will you stop?

THE WOMAN: Aren't you going to answer the door? He'll wake the whole hotel.

WILLY: I'm not expecting anybody.

THE WOMAN: Whyn't you have another drink, honey, and stop being so damn self-centered?

WILLY: I'm so lonely.

THE WOMAN: You know you ruined me, Willy? From now on, whenever you come to the office, I'll see that you go right through to the buyers. No waiting at my desk anymore, Willy. You ruined me.

WILLY: That's nice of you to say that.

THE WOMAN: Gee, you are self-centered! Why so sad? You are the saddest, self-centeredest soul I ever did see-saw. (*She laughs. He kisses her.*) Come on inside, drummer boy. It's silly to be dressing in the middle of the night. (*As knocking is heard.*) Aren't you going to answer the door?

WILLY: They're knocking on the wrong door.

THE WOMAN: But I felt the knocking. And he heard us talking in here. Maybe the hotel's on fire!

WILLY (*his terror rising*): It's a mistake.

THE WOMAN: Then tell him to go away!

WILLY: There's nobody there.

THE WOMAN: It's getting on my nerves, Willy. There's somebody standing out there and it's getting on my nerves!

WILLY (*pushing her away from him*): All right, stay in the bathroom here, and don't come out. I think there's a law in Massachusetts about it, so don't come out. It may be that new room clerk. He looked very mean. So don't come out. It's a mistake, there's no fire.

The knocking is heard again. He takes a few steps away from her, and she vanishes into the wing. The light follows him, and now he is facing YOUNG BIFF, *who carries a suitcase.* BIFF *steps toward him. The music is gone.*

BIFF: Why didn't you answer?

WILLY: Biff! What are you doing in Boston?

BIFF: Why didn't you answer? I've been knocking for five minutes, I called you on the phone . . .

WILLY: I just heard you. I was in the bathroom and had the door shut. Did anything happen home?

BIFF: Dad—I let you down.

WILLY: What do you mean?

BIFF: Dad . . .

WILLY: Biffo, what's this about? (*Putting his arm around* BIFF.) Come on, let's go downstairs and get you a malted.

BIFF: Dad, I flunked math.

WILLY: Not for the term?

BIFF: The term. I haven't got enough credits to graduate.

WILLY: You mean to say Bernard wouldn't give you the answers?

BIFF: He did, he tried, but I only got a sixty-one.

WILLY: And they wouldn't give you four points?

BIFF: Birnbaum refused absolutely. I begged him, Pop, but he won't give me those points. You gotta talk to him before they close the school. Because if he saw the kind of man you are, and you just talked to him in your way, I'm sure he'd come through for me. The class came right before practice, see, and I didn't go enough. Would you talk to him? He'd like you, Pop. You know the way you could talk.

WILLY: You're on. We'll drive right back.

BIFF: Oh, Dad, good work! I'm sure he'll change it for you!

WILLY: Go downstairs and tell the clerk I'm checkin' out. Go right down.

BIFF: Yes, sir! See, the reason he hates me, Pop—one day he was late for class so I got up at the blackboard and imitated him. I crossed my eyes and talked with a lithp.

WILLY (*laughing*): You did? The kids like it?

BIFF: They nearly died laughing!

WILLY: Yeah? What'd you do?

BIFF: The thquare root of thixthy twee is . . . (WILLY *bursts out laughing;* BIFF *joins.*) And in the middle of it he walked in!

WILLY *laughs and* THE WOMAN *joins in offstage.*

WILLY (*without hesitation*): Hurry downstairs and . . .

BIFF: Somebody in there?

WILLY: No, that was next door.

THE WOMAN *laughs offstage.*

BIFF: Somebody got in your bathroom!

WILLY: No, it's the next room, there's a party . . .

THE WOMAN (*enters, laughing; she lisps this*): Can I come in? There's something in the bathtub, Willy, and it's moving!

WILLY *looks at* BIFF, *who is staring open-mouthed and horrified at* THE WOMAN.

WILLY: Ah—you better go back to your room. They must be finished painting by now. They're painting her room so I let her take a shower here. Go back, go back . . . (*He pushes her.*)

THE WOMAN (*resisting*): But I've got to get dressed, Willy, I can't . . .

WILLY: Get out of here! Go back, go back . . . (*Suddenly striving for the ordinary.*) This is Miss Francis, Biff, she's a buyer. They're painting her room. Go back, Miss Francis, go back . . .

THE WOMAN: But my clothes, I can't go out naked in the hall!

WILLY (*pushing her offstage*): Get outa here! Go back, go back!

BIFF *slowly sits down on his suitcase as the argument continues offstage.*

THE WOMAN: Where's my stockings? You promised me stockings, Willy!

WILLY: I have no stockings here!

THE WOMAN: You had two boxes of size nine sheers for me, and I want them!

WILLY: Here, for God's sake, will you get outa here!

THE WOMAN (*enters holding a box of stockings*): I just hope there's nobody in the hall. That's all I hope. (*To* BIFF.) Are you football or baseball?

BIFF: Football.

THE WOMAN (*angry, humiliated*): That's me too. G'night. (*She snatches her clothes from* WILLY, *and walks out.*)

WILLY (*after a pause*): Well, better get going. I want to get to the school first thing in the morning. Get my suits out of the closet. I'll get my valise. (BIFF *doesn't move.*) What's the matter! (BIFF *remains motionless, tears falling.*) She's a buyer. Buys for J. H. Simmons. She lives down the hall—they're painting. You don't imagine— (*He breaks off. After a pause.*) Now listen, pal, she's just a buyer. She sees merchandise in her room and they have to keep it looking just so . . . (*Pause. Assuming command.*) All right, get my suits. (BIFF *doesn't move.*) Now stop crying and do as I say. I gave you an order. Biff, I gave you an order! Is that what you do when I give you an order? How dare you cry! (*Putting his arm around* BIFF.) Now look, Biff, when you grow up you'll understand about these things. You mustn't—you mustn't overemphasize a thing like this. I'll see Birnbaum first thing in the morning.

BIFF: Never mind.

WILLY (*getting down beside* BIFF): Never mind! He's going to give you those points. I'll see to it.

BIFF: He wouldn't listen to you.

WILLY: He certainly will listen to me. You need those points for the U. of Virginia.

BIFF: I'm not going there.

WILLY: Heh? If I can't get him to change that mark you'll make it up in summer school. You've got all summer to . . .

BIFF (*his weeping breaking from him*): Dad . . .

WILLY (*infected by it*): Oh, my boy . . .

BIFF: Dad . . .

WILLY: She's nothing to me, Biff. I was lonely, I was terribly lonely.

BIFF: You—you gave her Mama's stockings! (*His tears break through and he rises to go.*)

WILLY (*grabbing for* BIFF): I gave you an order!

BIFF: Don't touch me, you—liar!

WILLY: Apologize for that!

BIFF: You fake! You phony little fake! You fake! (*Overcome, he turns quickly and weeping fully goes out with his suitcase.* WILLY *is left on the floor on his knees.*)

WILLY: I gave you an order! Biff, come back here or I'll beat you! Come back here! I'll whip you!

STANLEY *comes quickly in from the right and stands in front of* WILLY.

WILLY (*shouts at* STANLEY): I gave you an order . . .

STANLEY: Hey, let's pick it up, pick it up, Mr. Loman. (*He helps* WILLY *to his feet.*) Your boys left with the chippies. They said they'll see you home.

A second waiter watches some distance away.

WILLY: But we were supposed to have dinner together.

Music is heard, WILLY *'s theme.*

STANLEY: Can you make it?

WILLY: I'll—sure, I can make it. (*Suddenly concerned about his clothes.*) Do I—I look all right?

STANLEY: Sure, you look all right. (*He flicks a speck off* WILLY*'s lapel.*)

WILLY: Here—here's a dollar.

STANLEY: Oh, your son paid me. It's all right.

WILLY (*putting it in* STANLEY*'s hand*): No, take it. You're a good boy.

STANLEY: Oh, no, you don't have to . . .

WILLY: Here—here's some more, I don't need it any more. (*After a slight pause.*) Tell me—is there a seed store in the neighborhood?

STANLEY: Seeds? You mean like to plant?

As WILLY *turns,* STANLEY *slips the money back into his jacket pocket.*

WILLY: Yes. Carrots, peas . . .

STANLEY: Well, there's hardware stores on Sixth Avenue, but it may be too late now.

WILLY (*anxiously*): Oh, I'd better hurry. I've got to get some seeds. (*He starts off to the right.*) I've got to get some seeds, right away. Nothing's planted. I don't have a thing in the ground.

WILLY *hurries out as the light goes down.* STANLEY *moves over to the right after him, watches him off. The other waiter has been staring at* WILLY.

STANLEY (*to the waiter*): Well, whatta you looking at?

The waiter picks up the chairs and moves off right. STANLEY *takes the table and follows him. The light fades on this area. There is a long pause, the sound of the flute coming over. The light gradually rises on the kitchen, which is empty.* HAPPY *appears at the door of the house, followed by* BIFF. HAPPY *is carrying a large bunch of long-stemmed roses. He enters the kitchen, looks around for* LINDA. *Not seeing her, he turns to* BIFF, *who is just outside the house door, and makes a gesture with his hands, indicating "Not here, I guess." He looks into the living room and freezes. Inside,* LINDA, *unseen, is seated,* WILLY's *coat on her lap. She rises ominously and quietly and moves toward* HAPPY, *who backs up into the kitchen, afraid.*

HAPPY: Hey, what're you doing up? (LINDA *says nothing but moves toward him implacably.*) Where's Pop? (*He keeps backing to the right, and now* LINDA *is in full view in the doorway to the living room.*) Is he sleeping?

LINDA: Where were you?

HAPPY (*trying to laugh it off*): We met two girls, Mom, very fine types. Here, we brought you some flowers. (*Offering them to her.*) Put them in your room, Ma.

She knocks them to the floor at BIFF's *feet. He has now come inside and closed the door behind him. She stares at* BIFF, *silent.*

HAPPY: Now what'd you do that for? Mom, I want you to have some flowers . . .

LINDA (*cutting* HAPPY *off, violently to* BIFF): Don't you care whether he lives or dies?

HAPPY (*going to the stairs*): Come upstairs, Biff.

BIFF (*with a flare of disgust, to* HAPPY): Go away from me! (*To* LINDA.) What do you mean, lives or dies? Nobody's dying around here, pal.

LINDA: Get out of my sight! Get out of here!

BIFF: I wanna see the boss.

LINDA: You're not going near him!

BIFF: Where is he? (*He moves into the living room and* LINDA *follows.*)

LINDA (*shouting after* BIFF): You invite him for dinner. He looks forward to it all day— (BIFF *appears in his parents' bedroom, looks around, and exits*)—and then you desert him there. There's no stranger you'd do that to!

HAPPY: Why? He had a swell time with us. Listen, when I— (LINDA *comes back into the kitchen*)—desert him I hope I don't outlive the day!

LINDA: Get out of here!

HAPPY: Now look, Mom . . .

LINDA: Did you have to go to women tonight? You and your lousy rotten whores!

BIFF *re-enters the kitchen.*

HAPPY: Mom, all we did was follow Biff around trying to cheer him up! (*To* BIFF.) Boy, what a night you gave me!

LINDA: Get out of here, both of you, and don't come back! I don't want you tormenting him any more. Go on now, get your things together! (*To* BIFF.) You can sleep in his apartment. (*She starts to pick up the flowers and stops herself.*) Pick up this stuff, I'm not your maid any more. Pick it up, you bum, you!

HAPPY *turns his back to her in refusal.* BIFF *slowly moves over and gets down on his knees, picking up the flowers.*

LINDA: You're a pair of animals! Not one, not another living soul would have had the cruelty to walk out on that man in a restaurant!

BIFF (*not looking at her*): Is that what he said?

LINDA: He didn't have to say anything. He was so humiliated he nearly limped when he came in.

HAPPY: But, Mom, he had a great time with us . . .

BIFF (*cutting him off violently*): Shut up!

Without another word, HAPPY *goes upstairs.*

LINDA: You! You didn't even go in to see if he was all right!

BIFF (*still on the floor in front of* LINDA, *the flowers in his hand; with self-loathing*): No. Didn't. Didn't do a damned thing. How do you like that, heh? Left him babbling in a toilet.

LINDA: You louse. You . . .

BIFF: Now you hit it on the nose! (*He gets up, throws the flowers in the wastebasket.*) The scum of the earth, and you're looking at him!

LINDA: Get out of here!

BIFF: I gotta talk to the boss, Mom. Where is he?

LINDA: You're not going near him. Get out of this house!

BIFF (*with absolute assurance, determination*): No. We're gonna have an abrupt conversation, him and me.

LINDA: You're not talking to him.

> *Hammering is heard from outside the house, off right.* BIFF *turns toward the noise.*

LINDA (*suddenly pleading*): Will you please leave him alone?

BIFF: What's he doing out there?

LINDA: He's planting the garden!

BIFF (*quietly*): Now? Oh, my God!

> BIFF *moves outside,* LINDA *following. The light dies down on them and comes up on the center of the apron as* WILLY *walks into it. He is carrying a flashlight, a hoe, and a handful of seed packets. He raps the top of the hoe sharply to fix it firmly, and then moves to the left, measuring off the distance with his foot. He holds the flashlight to look at the seed packets, reading off the instructions. He is in the blue of night.*

WILLY: Carrots . . . quarter-inch apart. Rows . . . one-foot rows. (*He measures it off.*) One foot. (*He puts down a package and measures off.*) Beets. (*He puts down another package and measures again.*) Lettuce. (*He reads the package, puts it down.*) One foot— (*He breaks off as* BEN *appears at the right and moves slowly down to him.*) What a proposition, ts, ts. Terrific, terrific. 'Cause she's suffered, Ben, the woman has suffered. You understand me? A man can't go out the way he came in, Ben, a man has got to add up to something. You can't, you can't— (BEN *moves toward him as though to interrupt.*) You gotta consider now. Don't answer so quick. Remember, it's a guaranteed twenty-thousand-dollar proposition. Now look, Ben, I want you to go through the ins and outs of this thing with me. I've got nobody to talk to, Ben, and the woman has suffered, you hear me?

BEN (*standing still, considering*): What's the proposition?

WILLY: It's twenty thousand dollars on the barrelhead. Guaranteed, gilt-edged, you understand?

BEN: You don't want to make a fool of yourself. They might not honor the policy.

WILLY: How can they dare refuse? Didn't I work like a coolie to meet every premium on the nose? And now they don't pay off? Impossible!

BEN: It's called a cowardly thing, William.

WILLY: Why? Does it take more guts to stand here the rest of my life ringing up a zero?

BEN (*yielding*): That's a point, William. (*He moves, thinking, turns.*) And twenty thousand—that is something one can feel with the hand, it is there.

WILLY (*now assured, with rising power*): Oh, Ben, that's the whole beauty of it! I see it like a diamond, shining in the dark, hard and rough, that I can pick up and touch in my hand. Not like—like an appointment! This would not be another damned-fool appointment, Ben, and it changes all the aspects. Because he thinks I'm nothing, see, and so he spites me. But the funeral—.(*Straightening up.*) Ben, that funeral will be massive! They'll come from Maine, Massachusetts, Vermont, New Hampshire! All the old-timers with the strange license plates—that boy will be thunderstruck, Ben, because he never realized—I am known! Rhode Island, New York, New Jersey—I am known, Ben, and he'll see it with his eyes once and for all. He'll see what I am, Ben! He's in for a shock, that boy!

BEN (*coming down to the edge of the garden*): He'll call you a coward.

WILLY (*suddenly fearful*): No, that would be terrible.

BEN: Yes. And a damned fool.

WILLY: No, no, he mustn't, I won't have that! (*He is broken and desperate.*)

BEN: He'll hate you, William.

The gay music of the Boys is heard.

WILLY: Oh, Ben, how do we get back to all the great times? Used to be so full of light, and comradeship, the sleigh-riding in winter, and the ruddiness on his cheeks. And always some kind of good news coming up, always something nice coming up ahead. And never even let me carry the valises in the house, and simonizing, simonizing that little red car! Why, why can't I give him something and not have him hate me?

BEN: Let me think about it. (*He glances at his watch.*) I still have a little time. Remarkable proposition, but you've got to be sure you're not making a fool of yourself.

BEN *drifts off upstage and goes out of sight.* BIFF *comes down from the left.*

WILLY (*suddenly conscious of* BIFF, *turns and looks up at him, then begins picking up the packages of seeds in confusion*): Where the hell is that seed? (*Indignantly.*) You can't see nothing out here! They boxed in the whole goddam neighborhood!

BIFF: There are people all around here. Don't you realize that?

WILLY: I'm busy. Don't bother me.

BIFF (*taking the hoe from* WILLY): I'm saying good-by to you, Pop. (WILLY *looks at him, silent, unable to move.*) I'm not coming back any more.

WILLY: You're not going to see Oliver tomorrow?

BIFF: I've got no appointment, Dad.

WILLY: He put his arm around you, and you've got no appointment?

BIFF: Pop, get this now, will you? Everytime I've left it's been a—fight that sent me out of here. Today I realized something about myself and I tried to explain it to you and I—I think I'm just not smart enough to make any sense out of it for you. To hell with whose fault it is or anything like that. (*He takes* WILLY's *arm.*) Let's just wrap it up, heh? Come on in, we'll tell Mom. (*He gently tries to pull* WILLY *to left.*)

WILLY (*frozen, immobile, with guilt in his voice*): No, I don't want to see her.

BIFF: Come on! (*He pulls again, and* WILLY *tries to pull away.*)

WILLY (*highly nervous*): No, no, I don't want to see her.

BIFF (*tries to look into* WILLY's *face, as if to find the answer there*): Why don't you want to see her?

WILLY (*more harshly now*): Don't bother me, will you?

BIFF: What do you mean, you don't want to see her? You don't want them calling you yellow, do you? This isn't your fault; it's me, I'm a bum. Now come inside! (WILLY *strains to get away.*) Did you hear what I said to you?

WILLY *pulls away and quickly goes by himself into the house.* BIFF *follows.*

LINDA (*to* WILLY): Did you plant, dear?

BIFF (*at the door, to* LINDA): All right, we had it out. I'm going and I'm not writing any more.

LINDA (*going to* WILLY *in the kitchen*): I think that's the best way, dear. 'Cause there's no use drawing it out, you'll just never get along.

WILLY *doesn't respond.*

BIFF: People ask where I am and what I'm doing, you don't know, and you don't care. That way it'll be off your mind and you can start brightening up again. All right? That clears it, doesn't it? (WILLY *is silent, and* BIFF *goes to him.*) You gonna wish me luck, scout? (*He extends his hand.*) What do you say?

LINDA: Shake his hand, Willy.

WILLY (*turning to her, seething with hurt*): There's no necessity—to mention the pen at all, y'know.

BIFF (*gently*): I've got no appointment, Dad.

WILLY (*erupting fiercely*): He put his arm around . . . ?

BIFF: Dad, you're never going to see what I am, so what's the use of arguing? If I strike oil I'll send you a check. Meantime forget I'm alive.

WILLY (*to* LINDA): Spite, see?

BIFF: Shake hands, Dad.

WILLY: Not my hand.

BIFF: I was hoping not to go this way.

WILLY: Well, this is the way you're going. Good-by.

BIFF *looks at him a moment, then turns sharply and goes to the stairs.*

WILLY (*stops him with*): May you rot in hell if you leave this house!

BIFF (*turning*): Exactly what is it that you want from me?

WILLY: I want you to know, on the train, in the mountains, in the valleys, wherever you go, that you cut down your life for spite!

BIFF: No, no.

WILLY: Spite, spite, is the word of your undoing! And when you're down and out, remember what did it. When you're rotting somewhere beside the railroad tracks, remember, and don't you dare blame it on me!

BIFF: I'm not blaming it on you!

WILLY: I won't take the rap for this, you hear?

HAPPY *comes down the stairs and stands on the bottom step, watching.*

BIFF: That's just what I'm telling you!

WILLY (*sinking into a chair at a table, with full accusation*): You're trying to put a knife in me—don't think I don't know what you're doing!

BIFF: All right, phony! Then let's lay it on the line. (*He whips the rubber tube out of his pocket and puts it on the table.*)

HAPPY: You crazy . . .

LINDA: Biff! (*She moves to grab the hose, but* BIFF *holds it down with his hand.*)

BIFF: Leave it there! Don't move it!

WILLY (*not looking at it*): What is that?

BIFF: You know goddam well what that is.

WILLY (*caged, wanting to escape*): I never saw that.

BIFF: You saw it. The mice didn't bring it into the cellar! What is this supposed to do, make a hero out of you? This supposed to make me sorry for you?

WILLY: Never heard of it.

BIFF: There'll be no pity for you, you hear it? No pity!

WILLY (*to* LINDA): You hear the spite!

BIFF: No, you're going to hear the truth—what you are and what I am!

LINDA: Stop it!

WILLY: Spite!

HAPPY (*coming down toward* BIFF): You cut it now!

BIFF (*to* HAPPY): The man don't know who we are! The man is gonna know! (*To* WILLY.) We never told the truth for ten minutes in this house!

HAPPY: We always told the truth!

BIFF (*turning on him*): You big blow, are you the assistant buyer? You're one of the two assistants to the assistant, aren't you?

HAPPY: Well, I'm practically . . .

BIFF: You're practically full of it! We all are! and I'm through with it. (*To* WILLY.) Now hear this, Willy, this is me.

WILLY: I know you!

BIFF: You know why I had no address for three months? I stole a suit in Kansas City and I was in jail. (*To* LINDA, *who is sobbing.*) Stop crying. I'm through with it.

LINDA *turns away from them, her hands covering her face.*

WILLY: I suppose that's my fault!

BIFF: I stole myself out of every good job since high school!

WILLY: And whose fault is that?

BIFF: And I never got anywhere because you blew me so full of hot air I could never stand taking orders from anybody! That's whose fault it is!

WILLY: I hear that!

LINDA: Don't, Biff!

BIFF: It's goddam time you heard that! I had to be boss big shot in two weeks, and I'm through with it!

WILLY: Then hang yourself! For spite, hang yourself!

BIFF: No! Nobody's hanging himself, Willy! I ran down eleven flights with a pen in my hand today. And suddenly I stopped, you hear me? And in the middle of that office building, do you hear this? I stopped in the middle of that building and I saw—the sky. I saw the things that I love in this world. The work and the food and time to sit and smoke. And I looked at the pen and said to myself, what the hell am I grabbing this for? Why am I trying to become what I don't want to be? What am I doing in an office, making a contemptuous, begging fool of myself, when all I want is out there, waiting for me the minute I say I know who I am! Why can't I say that, Willy? (*He tries to make* WILLY *face him, but* WILLY *pulls away and moves to the left.*)

WILLY (*with hatred, threateningly*): The door of your life is wide open!

BIFF: Pop! I'm a dime a dozen, and so are you!

WILLY (*turning on him now in an uncontrolled outburst*): I am not a dime a dozen! I am Willy Loman, and you are Biff Loman!

BIFF *starts for* WILLY, *but is blocked by* HAPPY. *In his fury,* BIFF *seems on the verge of attacking his father.*

BIFF: I am not a leader of men, Willy, and neither are you. You were never anything but a hard-working drummer who landed in the ash can like all the rest of them! I'm one dollar an hour, Willy! I tried seven states and couldn't raise it. A buck an hour! Do you gather my meaning? I'm not bringing home any prizes any more, and you're going to stop waiting for me to bring them home!

WILLY (*directly to* BIFF): You vengeful, spiteful mutt!

> BIFF *breaks from* HAPPY. WILLY, *in fright, starts up the stairs.* BIFF *grabs him.*

BIFF (*at the peak of his fury*): Pop! I'm nothing! I'm nothing, Pop. Can't you understand that? There's no spite in it any more. I'm just what I am, that's all.

> BIFF*'s fury has spent itself and he breaks down, sobbing, holding on to* WILLY, *who dumbly fumbles for* BIFF*'s face.*

WILLY (*astonished*): What're you doing? What're you doing? (*To* LINDA.) Why is he crying?

BIFF (*crying, broken*): Will you let me go, for Christ's sake? Will you take that phony dream and burn it before something happens? (*Struggling to contain himself he pulls away and moves to the stairs.*) I'll go in the morning. Put him— put him to bed. (*Exhausted,* BIFF *moves up the stairs to his room.*)

WILLY (*after a long pause, astonished, elevated*): Isn't that—isn't that remarkable? Biff—he likes me!

LINDA: He loves you, Willy!

HAPPY (*deeply moved*): Always did, Pop.

WILLY: Oh, Biff! (*Staring wildly.*) He cried! Cried to me. (*He is choking with his love, and now cries out his promise.*) That boy—that boy is going to be magnificent!

> BEN *appears in the light just outside the kitchen.*

BEN: Yes, outstanding, with twenty thousand behind him.

LINDA (*sensing the racing of his mind, fearfully, carefully*): Now come to bed, Willy. It's all settled now.

WILLY (*finding it difficult not to rush out of the house*): Yes, we'll sleep. Come on. Go to sleep, Hap.

BEN: And it does take a great kind of a man to crack the jungle.

> *In accents of dread,* BEN*'s idyllic music starts up.*

HAPPY (*his arm around* LINDA): I'm getting married, Pop, don't forget it. I'm changing everything. I'm gonna run that department before the year is up. You'll see, Mom. (*He kisses her.*)

BEN: The jungle is dark but full of diamonds, Willy.

> WILLY *turns, moves, listening to* BEN.

LINDA: Be good. You're both good boys, just act that way, that's all.

HAPPY: 'Night, Pop. (*He goes upstairs.*)

LINDA (*to* WILLY): Come, dear.

BEN (*with greater force*): One must go in to fetch a diamond out.

WILLY (*to* LINDA, *as he moves slowly along the edge of the kitchen, toward the door*): I just want to get settled down, Linda. Let me sit alone for a little.

LINDA (*almost uttering her fear*): I want you upstairs.

WILLY (*taking her in his arms*): In a few minutes, Linda. I couldn't sleep right now. Go on, you look awful tired. (*He kisses her.*)

BEN: Not like an appointment at all. A diamond is rough and hard to the touch.

WILLY: Go on now. I'll be right up.

LINDA: I think this is the only way, Willy.

WILLY: Sure, it's the best thing.

BEN: Best thing!

WILLY: The only way. Everything is gonna be—go on, kid, get to bed. You look so tired.

LINDA: Come right up.

WILLY: Two minutes.

> LINDA *goes into the living room, then reappears in her bedroom.* WILLY *moves just outside the kitchen door.*

WILLY: Loves me. (*Wonderingly.*) Always loved me. Isn't that a remarkable thing? Ben, he'll worship me for it!

BEN (*with promise*): It's dark there, but full of diamonds.

WILLY: Can you imagine that magnificence with twenty thousand dollars in his pocket?

LINDA (*calling from her room*): Willy! Come up!

WILLY (*calling into the kitchen*): Yes! Yes. Coming! It's very smart, you realize that, don't you, sweetheart? Even Ben sees it. I gotta go, baby. 'By! 'By! (*Going over to* BEN, *almost dancing.*) Imagine? When the mail comes he'll be ahead of Bernard again!

BEN: A perfect proposition all around.

WILLY: Did you see how he cried to me? Oh, if I could kiss him, Ben!

BEN: Time, William, time!

WILLY: Oh, Ben, I always knew one way or another we were gonna make it, Biff and I.

BEN (*looking at his watch*): The boat. We'll be late. (*He moves slowly off into the darkness.*)

WILLY (*elegiacally, turning to the house*): Now when you kick off, boy, I want a seventy-yard boot, and get right down the field under the ball, and when you hit, hit low and hit hard, because it's important, boy. (*He swings around and faces the audience.*) There's all kinds of important people in the stands, and the first thing you know . . . (*Suddenly realizing he is alone.*) Ben! Ben, where do I . . . ? (*He makes a sudden movement of search.*) Ben, how do I . . . ?

LINDA (*calling*): Willy, you coming up?

WILLY (*uttering a gasp of fear, whirling about as if to quiet her*): Sh! (*He turns around as if to find his way, sounds, faces, voices, seem to be swarming in upon him and he flicks at them, crying.*) Sh! Sh! (*Suddenly music, faint and high, stops him. It rises in intensity, almost to an unbearable scream. He goes up and down on his toes, and rushes off around the house.*) Shhh!

LINDA: Willy?

> *There is no answer.* LINDA *waits.* BIFF *gets up off his bed. He is still in his clothes.* HAPPY *sits up.* BIFF *stands listening.*

LINDA (*with real fear*): Willy, answer me! Willy!

> *There is the sound of a car starting and moving away at full speed.*

LINDA: No!

BIFF (*rushing down the stairs*): Pop!

> *As the car speeds off the music crashes down in a frenzy of sound, which becomes the soft pulsation of a single cello string.* BIFF *slowly returns to his bedroom. He and* HAPPY *gravely don their jackets.* LINDA *slowly walks out of her room. The music has developed into a dead march. The leaves of day are appearing over everything.* CHARLEY *and* BERNARD, *somberly dressed, appear and knock on the kitchen door.* BIFF *and* HAPPY *slowly descend the stairs to the kitchen as* CHARLEY *and* BERNARD *enter. All stop a moment when* LINDA, *in clothes of mourning, bearing a little bunch of roses, comes through the draped doorway into the kitchen.*

She goes to CHARLEY *and takes his arm. Now all move toward the audience, through the wall-line of the kitchen. At the limit of the apron,* LINDA *lays down the flowers, kneels, and sits back on her heels. All stare down at the grave.*

Requiem

CHARLEY: It's getting dark, Linda.

LINDA *doesn't react. She stares at the grave.*

BIFF: How about it, Mom? Better get some rest, heh? They'll be closing the gate soon.

LINDA *makes no move. Pause.*

HAPPY (*deeply angered*): He had no right to do that. There was no necessity for it. We would've helped him.

CHARLEY (*grunting*): Hmmm.

BIFF: Come along, Mom.

LINDA: Why didn't anybody come?

CHARLEY: It was a very nice funeral.

LINDA: But where are all the people he knew? Maybe they blame him.

CHARLEY: Naa. It's a rough world, Linda. They wouldn't blame him.

LINDA: I can't understand it. At this time especially. First time in thirty-five years we were just about free and clear. He only needed a little salary. He was even finished with the dentist.

CHARLEY: No man only needs a little salary.

LINDA: I can't understand it.

BIFF: There were a lot of nice days. When he'd come home from a trip; or on Sundays, making the stoop; finishing the cellar; putting on the new porch; when he built the extra bathroom; and put up the garage. You know something, Charley, there's more of him in that front stoop than in all the sales he ever made.

CHARLEY: Yeah. He was a happy man with a batch of cement.

LINDA: He was so wonderful with his hands.

BIFF: He had the wrong dreams. All, all, wrong.

HAPPY (*almost ready to fight* BIFF): Don't say that!

BIFF: He never knew who he was.

CHARLEY (*stopping* HAPPY's *movement and reply; to* BIFF): Nobody dast blame this man. You don't understand: Willy was a salesman. And for a salesman, there is no rock bottom to the life. He don't put a bolt to a nut, he don't tell you the law or give you medicine. He's a man way out there in the blue, riding on a smile and a shoeshine. And when they start not smiling back—that's an earthquake. And then you get yourself a couple of spots on your hat, and you're finished. Nobody dast blame this man. A salesman is got to dream, boy. It comes with the territory.

BIFF: Charley, the man didn't know who he was.

HAPPY (*infuriated*): Don't say that!

BIFF: Why don't you come with me, Happy?

HAPPY: I'm not licked that easily. I'm staying right in this city, and I'm gonna beat this racket! (*He looks at* BIFF, *his chin set.*) The Loman Brothers!

BIFF: I know who I am, kid.

HAPPY: All right, boy. I'm gonna show you and everybody else that Willy Loman did not die in vain. He had a good dream. It's the only dream you can have— to come out number-one man. He fought it out here, and this is where I'm gonna win it for him.

BIFF (*with a hopeless glance at* HAPPY, *bends toward his mother*): Let's go, Mom.

LINDA: I'll be with you in a minute. Go on, Charley. (*He hesitates.*) I want to, just for a minute. I never had a chance to say good-by.

CHARLEY *moves away, followed by* HAPPY. BIFF *remains a slight distance up and left of* LINDA. *She sits there, summoning herself. The flute begins, not far away, playing behind her speech.*

LINDA: Forgive me, dear. I can't cry. I don't know what it is, but I can't cry. I don't understand it. Why did you ever do that? Help me, Willy, I can't cry. It seems to me that you're just on another trip. I keep expecting you. Willy, dear, I can't cry. Why did you do it? I search and search and I search, and I can't understand it, Willy. I made the last payment on the house today. Today, dear. And there'll be nobody home. (*A sob rises in her throat.*) We're free and clear. (*Sobbing mournfully, released.*) We're free. (BIFF *comes slowly toward her.*) We're free . . . We're free . . .

BIFF *lifts her to her feet and moves out up right with her in his arms.* LINDA *sobs quietly.* BERNARD *and* CHARLEY *come together and follow them, followed by* HAPPY. *Only the music of the flute is left on the darkening stage as over the house the hard towers of the apartment buildings rise into sharp focus and the curtain falls.*

[1949]

Joining the Conversation: Critical Thinking and Writing

The Play on the Page

1. Arthur Miller said in the *New York Times* (27 February 1949) that tragedy shows man's struggle to secure "his sense of personal dignity" and that "his destruction in the attempt posits a wrong or an evil in his environment." Does this make sense when applied to some earlier tragedy (for example, *Oedipus the King* or *Hamlet*), and does it apply convincingly to *Death of a Salesman*? Is this the tragedy of an individual's own making? Or is society at fault for corrupting and exploiting Willy? Or both?

2. Is Willy pathetic rather than tragic? If pathetic, does this imply that the play is less worthy than if he is tragic?

3. Do you feel that Miller is straining too hard to turn a play about a little man into a big, impressive play? For example, do the musical themes, the unrealistic setting, the appearances of Ben, and the speech at the grave seem out of keeping in a play about the death of a salesman?

4. We don't know what Willy sells, and we don't know whether or not the insurance will be paid after his death. Do you consider these uncertainties to be faults in the play?

5. Is Howard a villain?

6. Characterize Linda.

The Play on the Stage

7. It is sometimes said that in this realistic play that includes symbolic and expressionistic elements, Biff and Happy can be seen as two aspects of Willy. In this view, Biff more or less represents Willy's spiritual needs, and Happy represents his materialism and his sexuality. If you were directing the play, would you

adopt this point of view? Whatever your interpretation, how would you costume the brothers?

8. Although Miller envisioned Willy as a small man (literally small), the role was first performed by Lee J. Cobb, a large man. If you were casting the play, what actor would you select? Why? Whom would you choose for Linda, Biff, Happy, Bernard, and Charley?

9. Select roughly thirty lines of dialogue, and discuss the movements (gestures and blocking) that as a director you would suggest to the performers.

A Context for *Death of a Salesman*

Arthur Miller

The following essay appeared in the New York Times *in 1949, while* Death of a Salesman *was running on Broadway.*

Tragedy and the Common Man

In this age few tragedies are written. It has often been held that the lack is due to a paucity of heroes among us, or else that modern man has had the blood drawn out of his organs of belief by the skepticism of science, and the heroic attack on life cannot feed on an attitude of reserve and circumspection. For one reason or another, we are often held to be below tragedy—or tragedy above us. The inevitable conclusion is, of course, that the tragic mode is archaic, fit only for the very highly placed, the kings or the kingly, and where this admission is not made in so many words it is most often implied.

I believe that the common man is as apt a subject for tragedy in its highest sense as kings were. On the face of it this ought to be obvious in the light of modern psychiatry, which bases its analysis upon classic formulations, such as the Oedipus and Orestes complexes, for instance, which were enacted by royal beings, but which apply to everyone in similar emotional situations.

More simply, when the question of tragedy in art is not at issue, we never hesitate to attribute to the well-placed and the exalted the very same mental processes as the lowly. And finally, if the exaltation of tragic action were truly a property of the high-bred character alone, it is inconceivable that the mass of mankind should cherish tragedy above all other forms, let alone be capable of understanding it.

As a general rule, to which there may be exceptions unknown to me, I think the tragic feeling is evoked in us when we are in the presence of a character who is ready to lay down his life, if need be, to secure one thing—his sense of personal dignity. From Orestes to Hamlet, Medea to Macbeth, the underlying struggle is that of the individual attempting to gain his "rightful" position in his society.

Sometimes he is one who has been displaced from it, sometimes one who seeks to attain it for the first time, but the fateful wound from which the inevitable events spiral is the wound of indignity, and its dominant force is indignation. Tragedy, then, is the consequence of a man's total compulsion to evaluate himself justly.

In the sense of having been initiated by the hero himself, the tale always reveals what has been called his "tragic flaw," a failing that is not peculiar to grand or elevated characters. Nor is it necessarily a weakness. The flaw, or crack in the character, is really nothing—and need be nothing, but his inherent unwillingness to remain passive in the face of what he conceives to be a challenge to his dignity, his image of his rightful status. Only the passive, only those who accept their lot without active retaliation, are "flawless." Most of us are in that category.

But there are among us today, as there always have been, those who act against the scheme of things that degrades them, and in the process of action everything we have accepted out of fear or insensitivity or ignorance is shaken before us and examined, and from this total onslaught by an individual against the seemingly stable cosmos surrounding us—from this total examination of the "unchangeable" environment—comes the terror and the fear that is classically associated with tragedy.

More important, from this total questioning of what has previously been unquestioned, we learn. And such a process is not beyond the common man. In revolutions around the world, these past thirty years, he has demonstrated again and again this inner dynamic of all tragedy.

Insistence upon the rank of the tragic hero, or the so-called nobility of his character, is really but a clinging to the outward forms of tragedy. If rank or nobility of character was indispensable, then it would follow that the problems of those with rank were the particular problems of tragedy. But surely the right of one monarch to capture the domain from another no longer raises our passions, nor are our concepts of justice what they were to the mind of an Elizabethan king.

The quality in such plays that does shake us, however, derives from the underlying fear of being displaced, the disaster inherent in being torn away from our chosen image of what and who we are in this world. Among us today this fear is as strong, and perhaps stronger, than it ever was. In fact, it is the common man who knows this fear best.

Now, if it is true that tragedy is the consequence of a man's total compulsion to evaluate himself justly, his destruction in the attempt posits a wrong or an evil in his environment. And this is precisely the morality of tragedy and its lesson. The discovery of the moral law, which is what the enlightenment of tragedy consists of, is not the discovery of some abstract or metaphysical quantity.

The tragic right is a condition of life, a condition in which the human personality is able to flower and realize itself. The wrong is the condition which suppresses man, perverts the flowing out of his love and creative instinct. Tragedy enlightens—and it must, in that it points the heroic finger at the enemy of man's freedom. The thrust for freedom is the quality in tragedy which exalts. The revolutionary questioning of the stable environment is what terrifies. In no way is the common man debarred from such thoughts or such actions.

Seen in this light, our lack of tragedy may be partially accounted for by the turn which modern literature has taken toward the purely psychiatric view of life, or the purely sociological. If all our miseries, our indignities, are born and bred within our minds, then all action, let alone the heroic action, is obviously impossible.

And if society alone is responsible for the cramping of our lives, then the protagonist must needs be so pure and faultless as to force us to deny his validity as a character. From neither of these views can tragedy derive, simply because neither represents a balanced concept of life. Above all else, tragedy requires the finest appreciation by the writer of cause and effect.

No tragedy can therefore come about when its author fears to question absolutely everything, when he regards any institution, habit or custom as being either everlasting, immutable or inevitable. In the tragic view the need of man to wholly realize himself is the only fixed star, and whatever it is that hedges his nature and lowers it is ripe for attack and examination. Which is not to say that tragedy must preach revolution.

The Greeks could probe the very heavenly origin of their ways and return to confirm the rightness of laws. And Job could face God in anger, demanding his right and end in submission. But for a moment everything is in suspension, nothing is accepted, and in this stretching and tearing apart of the cosmos, in the very action of so doing, the character gains "size," the tragic stature which is spuriously attached to the royal or the highborn in our minds. The commonest of men may take on that stature to the extent of his willingness to throw all he has into the contest, the battle to secure his rightful place in his world.

There is a misconception of tragedy with which I have been struck in review after review, and in many conversations with writers and readers alike. It is the idea that tragedy is of necessity allied to pessimism. Even the dictionary says nothing more about the word than that it means a story with a sad or unhappy ending. This impression is so firmly fixed that I almost hesitate to claim that in truth tragedy implies more optimism in its author than does comedy, and that its final result ought to be the reinforcement of the onlooker's brightest opinions of the human animal.

For, if it is true to say that in essence the tragic hero is intent upon claiming his whole due as a personality, and if this struggle must be total and without reservation, then it automatically demonstrates the indestructible will of man to achieve his humanity.

The possibility of victory must be there in tragedy. Where pathos rules, where pathos is finally derived, a character has fought a battle he could not possibly have won. The pathetic is achieved when the protagonist is, by virtue of his witlessness, his insensitivity or the very air he gives off, incapable of grappling with a much superior force.

Pathos truly is the mode for the pessimist. But tragedy requires a nicer balance between what is possible and what is impossible. And it is curious, although edifying, that the plays we revere, century after century, are the tragedies. In them, and in them alone, lies the belief—optimistic, if you will—in the perfectibility of man.

It is time, I think, that we who are without kings, took up this bright thread of our history and followed it to the only place it can possibly lead in our time—the heart and spirit of the average man.

[1949]

Chapter Overview: Looking Backward/Looking Forward

1. What work, if any, have you done that was rewarding beyond a financial sense? Please explain.
2. What work, if any, have you done that was rewarding *only* financially? Please explain.
3. How important do you think your work will be, to your life as a whole, in the years after your graduation? Would you say that it will matter twenty-five percent, forty percent, or some other figure? What other categories would you include as significant parts of your life, and what percentage would you assign to them?
4. If you think you know what line of work you want to go into after graduation, explain why this line interests you. Because, for instance, you have already done it? Or because a member of your family does it and you esteem this person?
5. Take one of the Short Views (pages 993–94) and, drawing on your own experience, comment on it.
6. Assuming the role of one of the characters in a short story that you have read— for instance, Sammy in Updike's "A & P"—comment on one of the Short Views.

CHAPTER 26

Identity in America

SHORT VIEWS

America is God's crucible, the great melting pot where all the races of
Europe are melting and re-forming.
　　Israel Zangwill

We have room for but one language here and that is the English lan-
guage, for we intend to see that the crucible turns out our people as
Americans, of American nationality and not as dwellers in a polyglot
boarding house, and we have room for but one loyalty and that is a
loyalty to the American people.
　　Theodore Roosevelt

No metaphor can capture completely the complexity of ethnic dynamics
in the U.S. "Melting pot" ignores the persistence and reconfiguration of
ethnicity over the generations. "Mosaic," much more apt for pluralistic
societies such as Kenya or India, is too static a metaphor; it fails to take
into account the easy penetration of many ethnic boundaries. Nor is
"salad bowl" appropriate; the ingredients of a salad bowl are mixed but
do not change. "Rainbow" is a tantalizing metaphor, but rainbows
disappear. "Symphony," like "rainbow," implies near perfect harmony;
both fail to take into account the variety and range of ethnic conflict in
the Untied States.

*　　The most accurately descriptive metaphor, the one that best explains*
the dynamics of ethnicity, is "kaleidoscope." American ethnicity is
kaleidoscopic, i.e., "complex and varied, changing form, pattern, color . . .
continually shifting from one set of relations to another; rapidly chang-
ing." When a kaleidoscope is in motion, the parts give the appearance of
rapid change and extensive variety in color and shape and in their
interrelationships. The viewer sees an endless variety of variegated
patterns, just as takes place on the American ethnic landscape.
　　Lawrence Fuchs

Through our own efforts and concerted good faith in learning to know,
thus to respect, the wonderfully rich and diverse subcommunities of
America, we can establish a new vision of America: a place where
"community" may mean many things, yet retains its deeper spiritual
significance. We may even learn to coincide with the 500th anniversary
of the "discovery" of America by Columbus, that America, in its magnifi-
cent variety, has yet to be discovered.
　　Joyce Carol Oates

It is impossible for a stranger traveling through the United States to tell from the appearance of the people or the country whether he is in Toledo, Ohio, or Portland, Oregon. Ninety million Americans cut their hair in the same way, eat each morning exactly the same breakfast, tie up the small girls' curls with precisely the same kind of ribbon fashioned into bows exactly alike; and in every way all try to look and act as much like all the others as they can.
  Alfred Harmsworth, Lord Northcliffe

Racism is so universal in this country, so wide-spread and deep-seated, that it is invisible because it is so normal.
  Shirley Chisholm

Light came to me when I realized that I did not have to consider any racial group as a whole. God made them duck by duck and that was the only way I could see them.
  Zora Neale Hurston

I have a dream that my four little children will one day live in a nation where they will not be judged by the color of their skin but by the content of their character.
  Martin Luther King Jr.

Joining the Conversation: Critical Thinking and Writing

1. Select a quotation that especially appeals to you, and make it the focus of an essay of about 500 words.
2. Take two of the passages—perhaps one that you especially like and one that you think is wrongheaded—and write a dialogue of about 500 words in which the two authors converse or argue. They may each try to convince the other, or they may find that to some degree they share views and they may then work out a statement that both can accept. If you do take the first position—that one writer is on the correct track but the other is utterly mistaken—try to be fair to the view that you think is mistaken. (As an experiment in critical thinking, imagine that you accept it, and make the best case for it that you possibly can.)

ESSAYS

ANNA LISA RAYA

Anna Lisa Raya, daughter of a second-generation Mexican American father and a Puerto Rican mother, grew up in Los Angeles but went to Columbia University in New York. While an undergraduate at Columbia she wrote and published this essay on identity.

It's Hard Enough Being Me

When I entered college, I *discovered* I was Latina. Until then, I had never questioned who I was or where I was from: My father is a second-generation Mexican-American, born and raised in Los Angeles, and my mother was born in Puerto Rico and raised in Compton, Calif. My home is El Sereno, a predominantly Mexican neighborhood in L.A. Every close friend I have back home is Mexican. So I was always just Mexican. Though sometimes I was just Puerto Rican—like when we would visit Mamo (my grandma) or hang out with my Aunt Titi.

Upon arriving in New York as a first-year student, 3000 miles from home, I not only experienced extreme culture shock, but for the first time I had to define myself according to the broad term "Latina." Although culture shock and identity crisis are common for the newly minted collegian who goes away to school, my experience as a newly minted Latina was, and still is, even more complicating. In El Sereno, I felt like I was part of a majority, whereas at the College I am a minority.

I've discovered that many Latinos like myself have undergone similar experiences. We face discrimination for being a minority in this country while also facing criticism for being "whitewashed" or "sellouts" in the countries of our heritage. But as an ethnic group in college, we are forced to define ourselves according to some vague, generalized Latino experience. This requires us to know our history, our language, our music, and our religion. I can't even be a content "Puerto Mexican" because I have to be a politically-and-socially-aware-Latina-with-a-chip-on-my-shoulder-because-of-how-repressed-I-am-in-this-country.

I am none of the above. I am the quintessential imperfect Latina. I can't dance salsa to save my life, I learned about Montezuma and the Aztecs in sixth grade, and I haven't prayed to the *Virgen de Guadalupe* in years.

5   Apparently I don't even look Latina. I can't count how many times people have just assumed that I'm white or asked me if I'm Asian. True, my friends back home call me *güera* ("whitey") because I have green eyes and pale skin, but that was as bad as it got. I never thought I would wish my skin were a darker shade or my hair a curlier texture, but since I've been in college, I have—many times.

Another thing: my Spanish is terrible. Every time I call home, I berate my mama for not teaching me Spanish when I was a child. In fact, not knowing how to speak the language of my home countries is the biggest problem that I have encountered, as have many Latinos. In Mexico there is a term, *pocha,* which is used by native Mexicans to ridicule Mexican-Americans. It expresses a deep-rooted antagonism and dislike for those of us who were raised on the other side of the border. Our failed attempts to speak pure, Mexican Spanish are largely responsible for the dislike. Other Latin American natives have this same attitude. No matter how well a Latino speaks Spanish, it can never be good enough.

Yet Latinos can't even speak Spanish in the U.S. without running the risk of being called "spic" or "wetback." That is precisely why my mother refused to teach me Spanish when I was a child. The fact that she spoke Spanish was constantly used against her: It prevented her from getting good jobs, and it would have placed me in bilingual education—a construct of the Los Angeles public school system that has proved to be more of a hindrance to intellectual development than a help.

To be fully Latina in college, however, I *must* know Spanish. I must satisfy the equation: Latina [equals] Spanish-speaking.

So I'm stuck in this black hole of an identity crisis, and college isn't making my life any easier, as I thought it would. In high school, I was being prepared for an adulthood in which I would be an individual, in which I wouldn't have to wear a Catholic school uniform anymore. But though I led an anonymous adolescence, I knew who I was. I knew I was different from white, black, or Asian people. I knew there was a language other than English that I could call my own if I only knew how to speak it better. I knew there were historical reasons why I was in this country, distinct reasons that make my existence here easier or more difficult than other people's existence. Ultimately, I was content.

10   Now I feel pushed into a corner, always defining, defending, and proving myself to classmates, professors, or employers. Trying to understand who and why I am, while understanding Plato or Homer, is a lot to ask of myself.

A month ago, I heard three Nuyorican (Puerto Ricans born and raised in New York) writers discuss how New York City has influenced their writing. One problem I have faced as a young writer is finding a voice that is true to my community. I was surprised and reassured to discover that as Latinos, these writers had faced similar pressures and conflicts as myself; some weren't even taught Spanish in childhood. I will never forget the advice that one of them gave me that evening: She said that I need to be true to myself. "Because people will always complain about what you are doing—you're a 'gringa' or a 'spic' no matter what," she explained. "So you might as well do things for yourself and not for them."

I don't know why it has taken 20 years to hear this advice, but I'm going to give it a try. *Soy yo* and no one else. *Punto.*[1]

[1994]

---

[1]*Soy yo . . . Punto* I'm me . . . Period. (Editors' note.)

Joining the Conversation: Critical Thinking and Writing

1. In her first paragraph Raya says that although her parents are American citizens, until she went to New York she "was always just Mexican" or "just Puerto Rican." Why do you suppose she thought this way?

2. In her second paragraph Raya says that in New York she "had to" define herself as "Latina," and in her third paragraph she says that many members of "minority" communities "are forced" to define themselves. In paragraph 10 she says, "Now I feel pushed into a corner, always defining, defending, and proving myself to classmates, professors, or employers. Trying to understand who and why I am, while understanding Plato or Homer, is a lot to ask. . . . ." Is Raya saying that both the majority culture and the minority culture force her to define herself? Drawing on your own experience, give your views on whether it is a good thing or a bad thing (or some of each) to be forced to define oneself in terms of ethnicity.

3. Today the words *Latino* and *Latina* are common, but until perhaps ten years ago Spanish-speaking people from Mexico, Central America, and South America were called *Hispanics* or *Latin Americans.* Do you think these terms are useful, or do you think that the differences between, say, a poor black woman from Cuba and a rich white man from Argentina are so great that it makes very little sense to put them into the same category, whether the category is called *Latino,*

Hispanic, or *Latin American?* Why, incidentally, do you think that *Latino/Latina* is now preferred to *Hispanic?*

4. In paragraph 7 Raya speaks of the Los Angeles bilingual educational program as "a construct of the Los Angeles public school system that has proved to be more of a hindrance to intellectual development than a help." If you have been in a bilingual educational program, evaluate the program. Did it chiefly help you, or chiefly hinder you? Explain.

5. In her last two paragraphs Raya explains that after an acquaintance told her to be true to herself, she concluded, *Soy yo* ("I'm me," or "I'm myself"). You may recall that in *Hamlet* Polonius says to his son Laertes, "This above all: to thine own self be true" (1.3.78). But what does it mean to be true to oneself? Presumably one doesn't behave immorally, but beyond that, what does one do? For instance, if a friend suggested to Raya that she might enjoy (and intellectually profit from) taking a course in Latin American literature, in making a decision, what *self* would she be true to?

6. In your own life, you make many decisions each day. Are many of them based on being true to yourself? Again, putting aside questions concerning immorality, do you think you have a "self" that you are true to? If so, is this self at least in part based on ethnicity?

ANDREW LAM

Born in South Vietnam in 1964, Andrew Lam, essayist and short story writer, is the web editor of the Pacific News Service. We reprint a PNS essay that originally appeared on 7 May 2003.

Who Will Light Incense When Mother's Gone?

My mother turned 70 recently, and though she remains a vivacious woman—her hair is still mostly black and there is a girlish twang in her laughter—mortality nevertheless weighs heavily on her soul. After the gifts were opened and the cake eaten, mother whispered this confidence to her younger sister: "Who will light incense to the dead when we're gone?"

"Honestly, I don't know," my aunt replied. "None of my children will do it, and we can forget the grandchildren. They don't even understand what we are doing. I guess when we're gone, the ritual ends."

Such is the price of living in America. I can't remember the last time I lit incense sticks and talked to my dead ancestors. Having fled so far from Vietnam, I no longer know to whom I should address my prayers or what promises I could possibly make to the long departed.

My mother, on the other hand, lives in America the way she would in Vietnam. Every morning in my parents' suburban home north of San Jose, she climbs a chair and piously lights a few joss sticks for the ancestral altar that sits on top of the living room bookcase. Every morning she talks to ghosts. She mumbles solemn prayers to the spirits of our dead ancestors, asks them for protection.

5   By contrast, on the shelves below stand my older siblings' engineering and business degrees, my own degree in biochemistry, our combined sports trophies and, last but not least, the latest installments of my own unending quest for self-reinvention—plaques and obelisk-shaped crystals—my journalism awards.

What mother's altar and the shelves beneath it seek to tell is the narrative of many an Asian immigrant family's journey to America. The collective, agrarian-based ethos in which ancestor worship is central slowly gives way to the glories of individual ambitions.

At that far end of the Asian immigrant trajectory, however, I cannot help but feel a certain twinge of guilt and regret upon hearing my mother's remark. Once when I was still a rebellious teenager and living at home, Mother asked me to speak more Vietnamese inside the house. "No," I answered in English, "what good is it to speak it? It's not as if I'm going to use it after I move out."

Mother, I remember, had a pained look in her eyes and called me the worst thing she could muster. "You've become a little American now, haven't you? A cowboy."

Vietnamese appropriated the word "cowboy" from the movies to imply selfishness. A cowboy in Vietnamese estimation is a rebel who, as in the spaghetti westerns, leaves town—the communal life—to ride alone into the sunset.

10   America, it had seemed, had stolen my mother's children, especially her youngest and once obedient son. America seduced him with its optimism, twisted his thinking, bent his tongue and dulled his tropic memories. America gave him freeways and fast food and silly cartoons and sitcoms, imbuing him with sappy, happy-ending incitements.

If we have reconciled since then, it does not mean I have become a traditional, incense-lighting Vietnamese son. I visit. I take her to lunch. I come home for important dates—New Year, Thanksgiving, Tet.[1]

But these days in front of the family altar, with all those faded photos of the dead staring down at me, I often feel oddly removed, as if staring at a relic of my distant past. And when, upon my mother's insistence, I light incense, I do not feel as if I am participating in a living tradition so much as pleasing a traditional mother.

We live in two different worlds, Mother and I. Mine is a world of travel and writing and public speaking, of immersing myself in contemporary history. Hers is a world of consulting the Vietnamese horoscope, of attending Buddhist temple on the day of her parents' death anniversaries and of telling and retelling stories of the past.

But on her 70th birthday, having listened to her worries, I have to wonder: What will survive my mother?

15   I wish I could assure my mother that, after she is gone, each morning I would light incense for her and all the ancestor spirits before her, but I can't.

In that odd, contradictory space in which immigrants' children find themselves, I feel strangely comforted when watching my mother's pious gesture each morning in front of the ancestors' altar. She is what connects me and my generation to a traditional past. And essentially, I share her fear that her generation and its memories of the Old World, what preserves us as a community, will fade away like incense smoke. I fear she'll leave me stranded in America, becoming more American than I expected, a lonely cowboy cursed with amnesia.

[2003]

Joining the Conversation: Critical Thinking and Writing

1. What does Andrew Lam mean when he refers to his mother as "a vivacious woman"? What does he mean when he refers to his own "unending quest for

---

[1]**Tet the Vietnamese New Year.**

self-reinvention"? And "collective, agrarian-based ethos": what does this phrase mean?

2. How does Lam's mother feel about America? What about Lam himself: What are his feelings about America?

3. Does this essay give you a new perspective on the immigrant experience, or a familiar one? Do you think Lam intends to show the reader something new? Or does he have a different purpose in mind?

4. Imagine that you know this author, and that, before publishing this essay, he sent it to you and asked for your "response and any suggestions" you might have. Compose a letter of 1–2 pages, beginning "Dear Andrew," in which you reply to him.

STORIES

AMY TAN

Amy Tan was born in Oakland, California, in 1952, of Chinese immigrant parents. When she was eight, she won first prize among elementary students with an essay titled "What the Library Means to Me." She attended Linfield College in Oregon, then transferred to San Jose State University where, while working two part-time jobs, she became an honors student and a President's Scholar. In 1973 she earned a master's degree in linguistics, also at San Jose, and she later enrolled as a doctoral student at the University of California, Berkeley, though she left this program after the murder of a close friend. For the next five years she worked as a language development consultant and a project director, and then she became a freelance business writer. In 1986 she published her first short story; reprinted in Seventeen, it was noticed by an agent who encouraged her to continue writing fiction. In 1989 The Joy Luck Club (a collection of linked short stories, including "Two Kinds") was published. Other books include The Kitchen God's Wife (1991), The Hundred Secret Senses (1995), and The Bonesetter's Daughter (2001). She has also written two books for children, The Moon Lady (1992) and SAGWA The Chinese Siamese Cat (1994).

Two Kinds

My mother believed you could be anything you wanted to be in America. You could open a restaurant. You could work for the government and get good retirement. You could buy a house with almost no money down. You could become rich. You could become instantly famous.

"Of course, you can be prodigy, too," my mother told me when I was nine. "You can be best anything. What does Auntie Lindo know? Her daughter, she is only best tricky."

America was where all my mother's hopes lay. She had come here in 1949 after losing everything in China: her mother and father, her family home, her first husband, and two daughters, twin baby girls. But she never looked back with regret. There were so many ways for things to get better.

We didn't immediately pick the right kind of prodigy. At first my mother thought I could be a Chinese Shirley Temple.[1] We'd watch Shirley's old movies on TV as though they were training films. My mother would poke my arm and say, "*Ni kan.*" —You watch. And I would see Shirley tapping her feet, or singing a sailor song, or pursing her lips into a very round O while saying "Oh, my goodness."

5   "*Ni kan,*" said my mother as Shirley's eyes flooded with tears. "You already know how. Don't need talent for crying!"

Soon after my mother got this idea about Shirley Temple, she took me to a beauty training school in the Mission district and put me in the hands of a student who could barely hold the scissors without shaking. Instead of getting big fat curls, I emerged with an uneven mass of crinkly black fuzz. My mother dragged me off to the bathroom and tried to wet down my hair.

"You look like Negro Chinese," she lamented, as if I had done this on purpose.

The instructor of the beauty training school had to lop off these soggy clumps to make my hair even again. "Peter Pan is very popular these days," the instructor assured my mother. I now had hair the length of a boy's, with straight-across bangs that hung at a slant two inches above my eyebrows. I liked the haircut and it made me actually look forward to my future fame.

In fact, in the beginning, I was just as excited as my mother, maybe even more so. I pictured this prodigy part of me as many different images, trying each one on for size. I was a dainty ballerina girl standing by the curtains, waiting to hear the music that would send me floating on my tiptoes. I was like the Christ child lifted out of the straw manger, crying with holy indignity. I was Cinderella stepping from her pumpkin carriage with sparkly cartoon music filling the air.

10   In all of my imaginings, I was filled with a sense that I would soon become *perfect*. My mother and father would adore me. I would be beyond reproach. I would never feel the need to sulk for anything.

But sometimes the prodigy in me became impatient. "If you don't hurry up and get me out of here, I'm disappearing for good," it warned. "And then you'll always be nothing."

Every night after dinner, my mother and I would sit at the Formica kitchen table. She would present new tests, taking her examples from stories of amazing children she had read in *Ripley's Believe It or Not,* or *Good Housekeeping, Reader's Digest,* and a dozen other magazines she kept in a pile in our bathroom. My mother got these magazines from people whose houses she cleaned. And since she cleaned many houses each week, we had a great assortment. She would look through them all, searching for stories about remarkable children.

The first night she brought out a story about a three-year-old boy who knew the capitals of all the states and even most of the European countries. A teacher was quoted as saying the little boy could also pronounce the names of the foreign cities correctly.

"What's the capital of Finland?" my mother asked me, looking at the magazine story.

15   All I knew was the capital of California, because Sacramento was the name of the street we lived on in Chinatown. "Nairobi!" I guessed, saying the most foreign word I could think of. She checked to see if that was possibly one way to pronounce "Helsinki" before showing me the answer.

The tests got harder—multiplying numbers in my head, finding the queen of hearts in a deck of cards, trying to stand on my head without using my hands, predicting the daily temperatures in Los Angeles, New York, and London.

[1]**Shirley Temple** (1928–), U.S. child movie-star.

One night I had to look at a page from the Bible for three minutes and then report everything I could remember. "Now Jehoshaphat had riches and honor in abundance and . . . that's all I remember, Ma," I said.

And after seeing my mother's disappointed face once again, something inside of me began to die. I hated the tests, the raised hopes and failed expectations. Before going to bed that night, I looked in the mirror above the bathroom sink and when I saw only my face staring back—and that it would always be this ordinary face—I began to cry. Such a sad, ugly girl! I made high-pitched noises like a crazed animal, trying to scratch out the face in the mirror.

And then I saw what seemed to be the prodigy side of me—because I had never seen that face before. I looked at my reflection, blinking so I could see more clearly. The girl staring back at me was angry, powerful. This girl and I were the same. I had new thoughts, willful thoughts, or rather thoughts filled with lots of won'ts. I won't let her change me, I promised myself. I won't be what I'm not.

20   So now on nights when my mother presented her tests, I performed listlessly, my head propped on one arm. I pretended to be bored. And I was. I got so bored I started counting the bellows of the foghorns out on the bay while my mother drilled me in other areas. The sound was comforting and reminded me of the cow jumping over the moon. And the next day, I played a game with myself, seeing if my mother would give up on me before eight bellows. After a while I usually counted only one, maybe two bellows at most. At last she was beginning to give up hope.

Two or three months had gone by without any mention of my being a prodigy again. And then one day my mother was watching *The Ed Sullivan Show*[2] on TV. The TV was old and the sound kept shorting out. Every time my mother got halfway up from the sofa to adjust the set, the sound would go back on and Ed would be talking. As soon as she sat down, Ed would go silent again. She got up, the TV broke into loud piano music. She sat down. Silence. Up and down, back and forth, quiet and loud. It was like a stiff embraceless dance between her and the TV set. Finally she stood by the set with her hand on the sound dial.

She seemed entranced by the music, a little frenzied piano piece with this mesmerizing quality, sort of quick passages and then teasing lilting ones before it returned to the quick playful parts.

"*Ni kan*," my mother said, calling me over with hurried hand gestures, "Look here."

I could see why my mother was fascinated by the music. It was being pounded out by a little Chinese girl, about nine years old, with a Peter Pan haircut. The girl had the sauciness of a Shirley Temple. She was proudly modest like a proper Chinese child. And she also did this fancy sweep of a curtsy, so that the fluffy skirt of her white dress cascaded slowly to the floor like the petals of a large carnation.

25   In spite of these warning signs, I wasn't worried. Our family had no piano and we couldn't afford to buy one, let alone reams of sheet music and piano lessons. So I could be generous in my comments when my mother bad-mouthed the little girl on TV.

"Play note right, but doesn't sound good! No singing sound," my mother complained.

"What are you picking on her for?" I said carelessly. "She's pretty good. Maybe she's not the best, but she's trying hard." I knew almost immediately I would be sorry I said that.

[2]*The Ed Sullivan Show* popular television variety show (1948–71).

"Just like you," she said. "Not the best. Because you not trying." She gave a little huff as she let go of the sound dial and sat down on the sofa.

The little Chinese girl sat down also to play an encore of "Anitra's Dance,"[3] by Grieg. I remember the song, because later on I had to learn how to play it.

30   Three days after watching *The Ed Sullivan Show,* my mother told me what my schedule would be for piano lessons and piano practice. She had talked to Mr. Chong, who lived on the first floor of our apartment building. Mr. Chong was a retired piano teacher and my mother had traded housecleaning services for weekly lessons and a piano for me to practice on every day, two hours a day, from four until six.

When my mother told me this, I felt as though I had been sent to hell. I whined and then kicked my foot a little when I couldn't stand it anymore.

"Why don't you like me the way I am? I'm *not* a genius! I can't play the piano. And even if I could, I wouldn't go on TV if you paid me a million dollars!" I cried.

My mother slapped me. "Who ask you be genius?" she shouted. "Only ask you be your best. For you sake. You think I want you be genius? Hnnh! What for! Who ask you!"

"So ungrateful," I heard her mutter in Chinese. "If she had as much talent as she has temper, she would be famous now."

35   Mr. Chong, whom I secretly nicknamed Old Chong, was very strange, always tapping his fingers to the silent music of an invisible orchestra. He looked ancient in my eyes. He had lost most of the hair on top of his head and he wore thick glasses and had eyes that always looked tired and sleepy. But he must have been younger than I thought, since he lived with his mother and was not yet married.

I met Old Lady Chong once and that was enough. She had this peculiar smell like a baby that had done something in its pants. And her fingers felt like a dead person's, like an old peach I once found in the back of the refrigerator; the skin just slid off the meat when I picked it up.

I soon found out why Old Chong had retired from teaching piano. He was deaf. "Like Beethoven!" he shouted to me. "We're both listening only in our head!" And he would start to conduct his frantic silent sonatas.

Our lessons went like this. He would open the book and point to different things, explaining their purpose: "Key! Treble! Bass! No sharps or flats! So this is C major! Listen now and play after me!"

And then he would play the C scale a few times, a simple chord, and then, as if inspired by an old, unreachable itch, he gradually added more notes and running trills and a pounding bass until the music was really something quite grand.

40   I would play after him, the simple scale, the simple chord, and then I just played some nonsense that sounded like a cat running up and down on top of garbage cans. Old Chong smiled and applauded and then said, "Very good! But now you must learn to keep time!"

So that's how I discovered that Old Chong's eyes were too slow to keep up with the wrong notes I was playing. He went through the motions in half-time. To help me keep rhythm, he stood behind me, pushing down on my right shoulder for every beat. He balanced pennies on top of my wrists so I would keep them still as I slowly played scales and arpeggios. He had me curve my hand around an apple and keep that shape when playing chords. He marched stiffly to show me how to make each finger dance up and down, staccato like an obedient little soldier.

---

[3]**"Anitra's Dance"** a section from the incidental music that Edvard Grieg (1843–1907) wrote for *Peer Gynt,* a play by Henrik Ibsen.

He taught me all these things, and that was how I also learned I could be lazy and get away with mistakes, lots of mistakes. If I hit the wrong notes because I hadn't practiced enough, I never corrected myself. I just kept playing in rhythm. And Old Chong kept conducting his own private reverie.

So maybe I never really gave myself a fair chance. I did pick up the basics pretty quickly, and I might have become a good pianist at that young age. But I was so determined not to try, not to be anybody different that I learned to play only the most ear-splitting preludes, the most discordant hymns.

Over the next year I practiced like this, dutifully in my own way. And then one day I heard my mother and her friend Lindo Jong both talking in a loud bragging tone of voice so others could hear. It was after church, and I was leaning against the brick wall wearing a dress with stiff white petticoats. Auntie Lindo's daughter, Waverly, who was about my age, was standing farther down the wall about five feet away. We had grown up together and shared all the closeness of two sisters squabbling over crayons and dolls. In other words, for the most part, we hated each other. I thought she was snotty. Waverly Jong had gained a certain amount of fame as "Chinatown's Littlest Chinese Chess Champion."

45   "She bring home too many trophy," lamented Auntie Lindo that Sunday. "All day she play chess. All day I have no time do nothing but dust off her winnings." She threw a scolding look at Waverly, who pretended not to see her.

"You lucky you don't have this problem," said Auntie Lindo with a sigh to my mother.

And my mother squared her shoulders and bragged: "Our problem worser than yours. If we ask Jing-mei wash dish, she hear nothing but music. It's like you can't stop this natural talent."

And right then, I was determined to put a stop to her foolish pride.

A few weeks later, Old Chong and my mother conspired to have me play in a talent show which would be held in the church hall. By then, my parents had saved up enough to buy me a secondhand piano, a black Wurlitzer spinet with a scarred bench. It was the showpiece of our living room.

50   For the talent show, I was to play a piece called "Pleading Child" from Schumann's *Scenes from Childhood*.[4] It was a simple, moody piece that sounded more difficult than it was. I was supposed to memorize the whole thing, playing the repeat parts twice to make the piece sound longer. But I dawdled over it, playing a few bars and then cheating, looking up to see what notes followed. I never really listened to what I was playing. I daydreamed about being somewhere else, about being someone else.

The part I liked to practice best was the fancy curtsy: right foot out, touch the rose on the carpet with a pointed foot, sweep to the side, left leg bends, look up and smile.

My parents invited all the couples from the Joy Luck Club to witness my debut. Auntie Lindo and Uncle Tin were there. Waverly and her two older brothers had also come. The first two rows were filled with children both younger and older than I was. The littlest ones got to go first. They recited simple nursery rhymes, squawked out tunes on miniature violins, twirled Hula Hoops, pranced in pink ballet tutus, and when they bowed or curtsied, the audience would sigh in unison, "Awww," and then clap enthusiastically.

---

[4]*Scenes from Childhood* a piano work by Robert Shumann (1810–56) with twelve titled sections and an epilogue.

When my turn came, I was very confident. I remember my childish excitement. It was as if I knew, without a doubt, that the prodigy side of me really did exist. I had no fear whatsoever, no nervousness. I remember thinking to myself, This is it! This is it! I looked out over the audience, at my mother's blank face, my father's yawn, Auntie Lindo's stiff-lipped smile, Waverly's sulky expression. I had on a white dress layered with sheets of lace, and a pink bow in my Peter Pan haircut. As I sat down I envisioned people jumping to their feet and Ed Sullivan rushing up to introduce me to everyone on TV.

And I started to play. It was so beautiful. I was so caught up in how lovely I looked that at first I didn't worry how I would sound. So it was a surprise to me when I hit the first wrong note and I realized something didn't sound quite right. And then I hit another and another followed that. A chill started at the top of my head and began to trickle down. Yet I couldn't stop playing, as though my hands were bewitched. I kept thinking my fingers would adjust themselves back, like a train switching to the right track. I played this strange jumble through two repeats, the sour notes staying with me all the way to the end.

55 When I stood up, I discovered my legs were shaking. Maybe I had just been nervous and the audience, like Old Chong, had seen me go through the right motions and had not heard anything wrong at all. I swept my right foot out, went down on my knee, looked up and smiled. The room was quiet, except for Old Chong, who was beaming and shouting, "Bravo! Bravo! Well done!" But then I saw my mother's face, her stricken face. The audience clapped weakly, and as I walked back to my chair, with my whole face quivering as I tried not to cry, I heard a little boy whisper loudly to his mother, "That was awful," and the mother whispered back, "Well, she certainly tried."

And now I realized how many people were in the audience, the whole world it seemed. I was aware of eyes burning into my back. I felt the shame of my mother and father as they sat stiffly throughout the rest of the show.

We could have escaped during intermission. Pride and some strange sense of honor must have anchored my parents to their chairs. And so we watched it all: the eighteen-year-old boy with a fake moustache who did a magic show and juggled flaming hoops while riding a unicycle. The breasted girl with white makeup who sang from *Madame Butterfly* and got honorable mention. And the eleven-year-old boy who won first prize playing a tricky violin song that sounded like a busy bee.

After the show, the Hsus, the Jongs, and the St. Clairs from the Joy Luck Club, came up to my mother and father.

"Lots of talented kids," Auntie Lindo said vaguely, smiling broadly.

60 "That was somethin' else," said my father, and I wondered if he was referring to me in a humorous way, or whether he even remembered what I had done.

Waverly looked at me and shrugged her shoulders. "You aren't a genius like me," she said matter-of-factly. And if I hadn't felt so bad, I would have pulled her braids and punched her stomach.

But my mother's expression was what devastated me: a quiet, blank look that said she had lost everything. I felt the same way, and it seemed as if everybody were now coming up, like gawkers at the scene of an accident, to see what parts were actually missing. When we got on the bus to go home, my father was humming the busy-bee tune and my mother was silent. I kept thinking she wanted to wait until we got home before shouting at me. But when my father unlocked the door to our apartment, my mother walked in and then went to the back, into the bedroom. No accusations. No blame. And in a way, I felt disappointed. I had been waiting for her to start shouting, so I could shout back and cry and blame her for all my misery.

I assumed my talent-show fiasco meant I never had to play the piano again. But two days later, after school, my mother came out of the kitchen and saw me watching TV.

"Four clock," she reminded me as if it were any other day. I was stunned, as though she were asking me to go through the talent-show torture again. I wedged myself more tightly in front of the TV.

65 "Turn off TV," she called from the kitchen five minutes later.

I didn't budge. And then I decided. I didn't have to do what my mother said anymore. I wasn't her slave. This wasn't China. I had listened to her before and look what happened. She was the stupid one.

She came out from the kitchen and stood in the arched entryway of the living room. "Four clock," she said once again, louder.

"I'm not going to play anymore," I said nonchalantly. "Why should I? I'm not a genius."

She walked over and stood in front of the TV. I saw her chest was heaving up and down in an angry way.

70 "No!" I said, and I now felt stronger, as if my true self had finally emerged. So this was what had been inside me all along.

"No! I won't!" I screamed.

She yanked me by the arm, pulled me off the floor, snapped off the TV. She was frighteningly strong, half pulling, half carrying me toward the piano as I kicked the throw rugs under my feet. She lifted me up and onto the hard bench. I was sobbing by now, looking at her bitterly. Her chest was heaving even more and her mouth was open, smiling crazily as if she were pleased I was crying.

"You want me to be someone that I'm not!" I sobbed. "I'll never be the kind of daughter you want me to be!"

"Only two kinds of daughters," she shouted in Chinese. "Those who are obedient and those who follow their own mind! Only one kind of daughter can live in this house. Obedient daughter!"

75 "Then I wish I wasn't your daughter. I wish you weren't my mother," I shouted. As I said these things I got scared. It felt like worms and toads and slimy things crawling out of my chest, but it also felt good, as if this awful side of me had surfaced, at last.

"Too late change this," said my mother shrilly.

And I could sense her anger rising to its breaking point. I wanted to see it spill over. And that's when I remembered the babies she had lost in China, the ones we never talked about. "Then I wish I'd never been born!" I shouted. "I wish I were dead! Like them."

It was as if I had said the magic words. Alakazam!—and her face went blank, her mouth closed, her arms went slack, and she backed out of the room, stunned, as if she were blowing away like a small brown leaf, thin, brittle, lifeless.

It was not the only disappointment my mother felt in me. In the years that followed, I failed her so many times, each time asserting my own will, my right to fall short of expectations. I didn't get straight As. I didn't become class president. I didn't get into Stanford. I dropped out of college.

80 For unlike my mother, I did not believe I could be anything I wanted to be. I could only be me.

And for all those years, we never talked about the disaster at the recital or my terrible accusations afterward at the piano bench. All of that remained unchecked, like a betrayal that was now unspeakable. So I never found a way to ask her why she had hoped for something so large that failure was inevitable.

And even worse, I never asked her what frightened me the most: Why had she given up hope?

For after our struggle at the piano, she never mentioned my playing again. The lessons stopped. The lid to the piano was closed, shutting out the dust, my misery, and her dreams.

So she surprised me. A few years ago, she offered to give me the piano, for my thirtieth birthday. I had not played in all those years. I saw the offer as a sign of forgiveness, a tremendous burden removed.

85   "Are you sure?" I asked shyly. "I mean, won't you and Dad miss it?"

"No, this your piano," she said firmly. "Always your piano. You only one can play."

"Well, I probably can't play anymore," I said. "It's been years."

"You pick up fast," said my mother, as if she knew this was certain. "You have natural talent. You could been genius if you want to."

"No I couldn't."

90   "You just not trying," said my mother. And she was neither angry nor sad. She said it as if to announce a fact that could never be disproved. "Take it," she said.

But I didn't at first. It was enough that she had offered it to me. And after that, every time I saw it in my parents' living room, standing in front of the bay windows, it made me feel proud, as if it were a shiny trophy I had won back.

Last week I sent a tuner over to my parents' apartment and had the piano reconditioned, for purely sentimental reasons. My mother had died a few months before and I had been getting things in order for my father, a little bit at a time. I put the jewelry in special silk pouches. The sweaters she had knitted in yellow, pink, bright orange—all the colors I hated—I put those in moth-proof boxes. I found some old Chinese silk dresses, the kind with little slits up the sides. I rubbed the old silk against my skin, then wrapped them in tissue and decided to take them home with me.

After I had the piano tuned, I opened the lid and touched the keys. It sounded even richer than I remembered. Really, it was a very good piano. Inside the bench were the same exercise notes with handwritten scales, the same secondhand music books with their covers held together with yellow tape.

I opened up the Schumann book to the dark little piece I had played at the recital. It was on the left-hand side of the page, "Pleading Child." It looked more difficult than I remembered. I played a few bars, surprised at how easily the notes came back to me.

95   And for the first time, or so it seemed, I noticed the piece on the right-hand side. It was called "Perfectly Contented." I tried to play this one as well. It had a lighter melody but the same flowing rhythm and turned out to be quite easy. "Pleading Child" was shorter but slower; "Perfectly Contented" was longer, but faster. And after I played them both a few times, I realized they were two halves of the same song.

[1989]

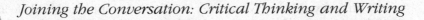

Joining the Conversation: Critical Thinking and Writing

1. Try to recall your responses when you had read just the first three paragraphs. At that point, how did the mother strike you? Now that you have read the entire story, is your view of her different? If so, in what way(s)?
2. When the narrator looks in the mirror, she discovers "the prodigy side," a face she had never seen before. What do you think she is discovering?
3. If you enjoyed "Two Kinds," point out two or three passages that you found particularly engaging, and briefly explain why they appeal to you. Argue someone into sharing your view.
4. Do you think this story is interesting only because it may give a glimpse of life in a Chinese American family? Or do you find it interesting for additional reasons? Explain.
5. Conceivably the story could have ended with the fifth paragraph from the end. What do the last four paragraphs contribute? Argue your case.

MyLiteratureLab® *For additional resources for "Two Kinds," log in to www .myliteraturelab.com where you will find a Longman Lecture and a Comprehension Quiz, as well as an About the Author, Bibliography, Links, and Critical Overview for Tan (under Student Resources).*

ALICE WALKER

Alice Walker was born in 1944 in Eatonton, Georgia, where her parents eked out a living as sharecroppers and dairy farmers; her mother also worked as a domestic. Walker attended Spelman College in Atlanta, and in 1965 she finished her undergraduate work at Sarah Lawrence College near New York City. She then became active in the welfare rights movement in New York and in the voter registration movement in Georgia. Later she taught writing and literature in Mississippi, at Jackson State College and Tougaloo College, and at Wellesley College, the University of Massachusetts, and Yale University.

Walker has written essays, poetry, and fiction. Her best-known novel, The Color Purple *(1982), won a Pulitzer Prize and the National Book Award. She has said that her chief concern is "exploring the oppressions, the insanities, the loyalties, and the triumphs of black women."*

Everyday Use

For your grandmama

I will wait for her in the yard that Maggie and I made so clean and wavy yesterday afternoon. A yard like this is more comfortable than most people know. It is not just a yard. It is like an extended living room. When the hard clay is swept clean as a floor and the fine sand around the edges lined with tiny, irregular grooves, anyone can come and sit and look up into the elm tree and wait for the breezes that never come inside the house.

Maggie will be nervous until after her sister goes: she will stand hopelessly in corners homely and ashamed of the burn scars down her arms and legs, eyeing her sister with a mixture of envy and awe. She thinks her sister had held life always in the palm of one hand, that "no" is a word the world never learned to say to her.

You've no doubt seen those TV shows where the child who has "made it" is confronted, as a surprise, by her own mother and father, tottering in weakly from backstage. (A pleasant surprise, of course: What would they do if parent and child came on the show only to curse out and insult each other?) On TV mother and child embrace and smile into each other's faces. Sometimes the mother and father weep, the child wraps them in her arms and leans across the table to tell how she would not have made it without their help. I have seen these programs.

Sometimes I dream a dream in which Dee and I are suddenly brought together on a TV program of this sort. Out of a dark and soft-seated limousine I am ushered into a bright room filled with many people. There I meet a smiling, gray, sporty man like Johnny Carson[1] who shakes my hand and tells me what a fine girl I have. Then we are on the stage and Dee is embracing me with tears in her eyes. She pins on my dress a large orchid, even though she has told me once that she thinks orchids are tacky flowers.

5   In real life I am a large, big-boned woman with rough, man-working hands. In the winter I wear flannel nightgowns to bed and overalls during the day. I can kill and clean a hog as mercilessly as a man. My fat keeps me hot in zero weather. I can work outside all day, breaking ice to get water for washing. I can eat pork liver cooked over the open fire minutes after it comes steaming from the hog. One winter I knocked a bull calf straight in the brain between the eyes with a sledge hammer and had the meat hung up to chill before nightfall. But of course all this does not show on television. I am the way my daughter would want me to be: a hundred pounds lighter, my skin like an uncooked barley pancake. My hair glistens in the hot bright lights. Johnny Carson has much to do to keep up with my quick and witty tongue.

But that is a mistake. I know even before I wake up. Who ever knew a Johnson with a quick tongue? Who can even imagine me looking a strange white man in the eye? It seems to me I have talked to them always with one foot raised in flight, with my head turned in whichever way is farthest from them. Dee, though. She would always look anyone in the eye. Hesitation was no part of her nature.

"How do I look, Mama?" Maggie says, showing just enough of her thin body enveloped in pink skirt and red blouse for me to know she's there, almost hidden by the door.

"Come out into the yard," I say.

Have you ever seen a lame animal, perhaps a dog run over by some careless person rich enough to own a car, sidle up to someone who is ignorant enough to be kind to him? That is the way my Maggie walks. She has been like this, chin on chest, eyes on ground, feet in shuffle, ever since the fire that burned the other house to the ground.

10   Dee is lighter than Maggie, with nicer hair and a fuller figure. She's a woman now, though sometimes I forget. How long ago was it that the other house burned? Ten, twelve years? Sometimes I can still hear the flames and feel Maggie's arms sticking to me, her hair smoking and her dress falling off her in little black papery flakes. Her eyes seemed stretched open, blazed open by the flames reflected in them. And Dee. I see her standing off under the sweet gum tree she used to dig gum out of; a look of concentration on her face as she watched the last dingy gray board of the house fall in toward the red-hot brick chimney. Why don't you do a dance around the ashes? I'd wanted to ask her. She had hated the house that much.

[1]**Johnny Carson** (1925–2005), U.S. television personality and comedian.

I used to think she hated Maggie, too. But that was before we raised the money, the church and me, to send her to Augusta to school. She used to read to us without pity; forcing words, lies, other folks' habits, whole lives upon us two, sitting trapped and ignorant underneath her voice. She washed us in a river of make-believe, burned us with a lot of knowledge we didn't necessarily need to know. Pressed us to her with the serious way she read, to shove us away at just the moment, like dimwits, we seemed about to understand.

Dee wanted nice things. A yellow organdy dress to wear to her graduation from high school; black pumps to match a green suit she'd made from an old suit somebody gave me. She was determined to stare down any disaster in her efforts. Her eyelids would not flicker for minutes at a time. Often I fought off the temptation to shake her. At sixteen she had a style of her own: and knew what style was.

I never had an education myself. After second grade the school was closed down. Don't ask me why: in 1927 colored asked fewer questions than they do now. Sometimes Maggie reads to me. She stumbles along goodnaturedly but can't see well. She knows she is not bright. Like good looks and money, quickness passed her by. She will marry John Thomas (who has mossy teeth in an earnest face) and then I'll be free to sit here and I guess just sing church songs to myself. Although I never was a good singer. Never could carry a tune. I was always better at a man's job. I used to love to milk till I was hoofed in the side in '49. Cows are soothing and slow and don't bother you, unless you try to milk them the wrong way.

I have deliberately turned my back on the house. It is three rooms, just like the one that burned, except the roof is tin; they don't make shingle roofs any more. There are no real windows, just some holes cut in the sides, like the portholes in a ship, but not round and not square, with rawhide holding the shutters up on the outside. This house is in a pasture, too, like the other one. No doubt when Dee sees it she will want to tear it down. She wrote me once that no matter where we "choose" to live, she will manage to come see us. But she will never bring her friends. Maggie and I thought about this and Maggie asked me, "Mama, when did Dee ever *have* any friends?"

15   She had a few. Furtive boys in pink shirts hanging about on washday after school. Nervous girls who never laughed. Impressed with her they worshiped the well-turned phrase, the cute shape, the scalding humor that erupted like bubbles in lye. She read to them.

When she was courting Jimmy T she didn't have much time to pay to us, but turned all her faultfinding power on him. He *flew* to marry a cheap gal from a family of ignorant flashy people. She hardly had time to recompose herself.

When she comes I will meet—but there they are!

Maggie attempts to make a dash for the house, in her shuffling way, but I stay her with my hand. "Come back here," I say. And she stops and tries to dig a well in the sand with her toe.

It is hard to see them clearly through the strong sun. But even the first glimpse of leg out of the car tells me it is Dee. Her feet were always neat-looking, as if God himself had shaped them with a certain style. From the other side of the car comes a short, stocky man. Hair is all over his head a foot long and hanging from his chin like a kinky mule tail. I hear Maggie suck in her breath. "Uhnnnh," is what it sounds like. Like when you see the wriggling end of a snake just in front of your foot on the road. "Uhnnnh."

20   Dee next. A dress down to the ground, in this hot weather. A dress so loud it hurts my eyes. There are yellows and oranges enough to throw back the light of the sun. I feel my whole face warming from the heat waves it throws out. Earrings, too, gold and hanging down to her shoulders. Bracelets dangling and making noises when she moves her arm up to shake the folds of the dress out of her armpits. The dress is loose and flows, and as she walks closer, I like it. I hear Maggie go "Uhnnnh" again. It is her sister's hair. It stands straight up like the wool on a sheep. It is black as night and around the edges are two long pigtails that rope about like small lizards disappearing behind her ears.

"Wa-su-zo-Tean-o!" she says, coming on in that gliding way the dress makes her move. The short stocky fellow with the hair to his navel is all grinning and he follows up with "Asalamalakim, my mother and sister!" He moves to hug Maggie but she falls back, right up against the back of my chair. I feel her trembling there and when I look up I see the perspiration falling off her chin.

"Don't get up," says Dee. Since I am stout it takes something of a push. You can see me trying to move a second or two before I make it. She turns, showing white heels through her sandals, and goes back to the car. Out she peeks next with a Polaroid. She stoops down quickly and lines up picture after picture of me sitting there in front of the house with Maggie cowering behind me. She never takes a shot without making sure the house is included. When a cow comes nibbling around the edge of the yard she snaps it and me and Maggie *and* the house. Then she puts the Polaroid in the back seat of the car, and comes up and kisses me on the forehead.

Meanwhile Asalamalakim is going through the motions with Maggie's hand. Maggie's hand is as limp as a fish, and probably as cold, despite the sweat, and she keeps trying to pull it back. It looks like Asalamalakim wants to shake hands but wants to do it fancy. Or maybe he don't know how people shake hands. Anyhow, he soon gives up on Maggie.

"Well," I say. "Dee."

25   "No, Mama," she says. "Not 'Dee,' Wangero Leewanika Kemanjo!"

"What happened to 'Dee'?" I wanted to know.

"She's dead," Wangero said. "I couldn't bear it any longer being named after the people who oppress me."

"You know as well as me you was named after your aunt Dicie," I said. Dicie is my sister. She named Dee. We called her "Big Dee" after Dee was born.

"But who was *she* named after?" asked Wangero.

30   "I guess after Grandma Dee," I said.

"And who was she named after?" asked Wangero.

"Her mother," I said, and saw Wangero was getting tired. "That's about as far back as I can trace it," I said. Though, in fact, I probably could have carried it back beyond the Civil War through the branches.

"Well," said Asalamalakim, "there you are."

"Uhnnnh," I heard Maggie say.

35   "There I was not," I said, "before 'Dicie' cropped up in our family, so why should I try to trace it that far back?"

He just stood there grinning, looking down on me like somebody inspecting a Model A car. Every once in a while he and Wangero sent eye signals over my head.

"How do you pronounce this name?" I asked.

"You don't have to call me by it if you don't want to," said Wangero.

"Why shouldn't I?" I asked. "If that's what you want us to call you, we'll call you."

40   "I know it might sound awkward at first," said Wangero.

"I'll get used to it," I said. "Ream it out again."

Well, soon we got the name out of the way. Asalamalakim had a name twice as long and three times as hard. After I tripped over it two or three times he told me to just call him Hakim-a-barber. I wanted to ask him was he a barber, but I didn't really think he was, so I didn't ask.

"You must belong to those beef-cattle peoples down the road," I said. They said "Asalamalakim" when they met you, too, but they didn't shake hands. Always too busy: feeding the cattle, fixing the fences, putting up saltlick shelters, throwing down hay. When the white folks poisoned some of the herd the men stayed up all night with rifles in their hands. I walked a mile and a half just to see the sight.

Hakim-a-barber said, "I accept some of their doctrines, but farming and raising cattle is not my style." (They didn't tell me, and I didn't ask, whether Wangero [Dee] had really gone and married him.)

45   We sat down to eat and right away he said he didn't eat collards and pork was unclean. Wangero, though, went on through the chitlins and corn bread, the greens and everything else. She talked a blue streak over the sweet potatoes. Everything delighted her. Even the fact that we still used the benches her daddy made for the table when we couldn't afford to buy chairs.

"Oh, Mama!" she cried. Then turned to Hakim-a-barber. "I never knew how lovely these benches are. You can feel the rump prints," she said, running her hands underneath her and along the bench. Then she gave a sigh and her hand closed over Grandma Dee's butter dish. "That's it!" she said. "I knew there was something I wanted to ask you if I could have." She jumped up from the table and went over in the corner where the churn stood, the milk in it clabber by now. She looked at the churn and looked at it.

"This churn top is what I need," she said. "Didn't Uncle Buddy whittle it out of a tree you all used to have?"

"Yes," I said.

"Uh huh," she said happily. "And I want the dasher, too."

50   "Uncle Buddy whittle that, too?" asked the barber.

Dee (Wangero) looked up at me.

"Aunt Dee's first husband whittled the dash," said Maggie so low you almost couldn't hear her. "His name was Henry, but they called him Stash."

"Maggie's brain is like an elephant's," Wangero said, laughing. "I can use the churn top as a centerpiece for the alcove table," she said, sliding a plate over the churn, "and I'll think of something artistic to do with the dasher."

When she finished wrapping the dasher the handle stuck out. I took it for a moment in my hands. You didn't even have to look close to see where hands pushing the dasher up and down to make butter had left a kind of sink in the wood. In fact, there were a lot of small sinks; you could see where thumbs and fingers had sunk into the wood. It was beautiful light yellow wood, from a tree that grew in the yard where Big Dee and Stash had lived.

55   After dinner Dee (Wangero) went to the trunk at the foot of my bed and started rifling through it. Maggie hung back in the kitchen over the dishpan. Out came Wangero with two quilts. They had been pieced by Grandma Dee and then Big Dee and me had hung them on the quilt frames on the front porch and quilted them. One was in the Lone Star pattern. The other was Walk Around the Mountain. In both of them were scraps of dresses Grandma Dee had worn fifty and more years ago. Bits and pieces of Grandpa Jarrell's paisley shirts. And one

teeny faded blue piece, about the size of a penny matchbox, that was from Great Grandpa Ezra's uniform that he wore in the Civil War.

"Mama," Wangero said sweet as a bird. "Can I have these old quilts?"

I heard something fall in the kitchen, and a minute later the kitchen door slammed.

"Why don't you take one or two of the others?" I asked. "These old things was just done by me and Big Dee from some tops your grandma pieced before she died."

"No," said Wangero. "I don't want those. They are stitched around the borders by machine."

60   "That'll make them last better," I said.

"That's not the point," said Wangero. "These are all pieces of dresses Grandma used to wear. She did all this stitching by hand. Imagine!" She held the quilts securely in her arms, stroking them.

"Some of the pieces, like those lavender ones, come from old clothes her mother handed down to her," I said, moving up to touch the quilts. Dee (Wangero) moved back just enough so that I couldn't reach the quilts. They already belonged to her.

"Imagine!" she breathed again, clutching them closely to her bosom.

"The truth is," I said, "I promised to give them quilts to Maggie, for when she marries John Thomas."

65   She gasped like a bee had stung her.

"Maggie can't appreciate these quilts!" she said. "She'd probably be backward enough to put them to everyday use."

"I reckon she would," I said. "God knows I been saving 'em for long enough with nobody using 'em. I hope she will!" I didn't want to bring up how I had offered Dee (Wangero) a quilt when she went away to college. Then she had told me they were old-fashioned, out of style.

"But they're *priceless!*" she was saying now, furiously; for she has a temper. "Maggie would put them on the bed and in five years they'd be in rags. Less than that!"

"She can always make some more," I said. "Maggie knows how to quilt."

70   Dee (Wangero) looked at me with hatred. "You just will not understand. The point is these quilts, *these* quilts!"

"Well," I said, stumped. "What would *you* do with them?"

"Hang them," she said. As if that was the only thing you *could* do with quilts.

Maggie by now was standing in the door. I could almost hear the sound her feet made as they scraped over each other.

"She can have them, Mama," she said, like somebody used to never winning anything, or having anything reserved for her. "I can 'member Grandma Dee without the quilts."

75   I looked at her hard. She had filled her bottom lip with checkerberry snuff and it gave her face a kind of dopey, hangdog look. It was Grandma Dee and Big Dee who taught her how to quilt herself. She stood there with her scarred hands hidden in the folds of her skirt. She looked at her sister with something like fear but she wasn't mad at her. This was Maggie's portion. This was the way she knew God to work.

When I looked at her like that something hit me in the top of my head and ran down to the soles of my feet. Just like when I'm in church and the spirit of God touches me and I get happy and shout. I did something I never had done before: hugged Maggie to me, then dragged her on into the room, snatched the quilts out of Miss Wangero's hands and dumped them into Maggie's lap. Maggie just sat there on my bed with her mouth open.

"Take one or two of the others," I said to Dee.

But she turned without a word and went out to Hakim-a-barber.

"You just don't understand," she said, as Maggie and I came out to the car.

80 "What don't I understand?" I wanted to know.

"Your heritage," she said. And then she turned to Maggie, kissed her, and said, "You ought to try to make something of yourself, too, Maggie. It's really a new day for us. But from the way you and Mama still live you'd never know it."

She put on some sunglasses that hid everything above the tip of her nose and her chin.

Maggie smiled; maybe at the sunglasses. But a real smile, not scared. After we watched the car dust settle I asked Maggie to bring me a dip of snuff. And then the two of us sat there just enjoying, until it was time to go in the house and go to bed.

[1973]

Joining the Conversation: Critical Thinking and Writing

1. Alice Walker wrote "Everyday Use," but the story is narrated by one of the characters, Mama. How would you characterize Mama?
2. At the end of the story, Dee tells Maggie, "It's really a new day for us. But from the way you and Mama still live you'd never know it." What does Dee mean? And how do Maggie and Mama respond?
3. In paragraph 76 the narrator says, speaking of Maggie, "When I looked at her like that something hit me in the top of my head and ran down to the soles of my feet." What "hit" Mama? That is, what does she understand at this moment that she had not understood before?
4. In "Everyday Use" why does the family quarrel about who will possess the quilts? Why are the quilts important? What do they symbolize?

MyLiteratureLab° *For additional resources for "Everyday Use," log in to* www.myliteraturelab.com *where you will find a Longman Lecture and a Comprehension Quiz, as well as an About the Author, Bibliography, Links, and Critical Overview for Walker (under Student Resources).*

POEMS

EMMA LAZARUS

Emma Lazarus (1849–87) was of German-Jewish descent on her mother's side, and of Sephardic descent on her father's side. (Sephardic Jews trace their ancestry back to Spain under Moslem rule, before the Jews were expelled by the Christians in 1492.)

In 1883 a committee was formed to raise funds for a pedestal for the largest statue in the world, Liberty Enlightening the People, *to be installed on a small island in New York Harbor. Authors were asked to donate manuscripts that were then auctioned to raise money. Emma Lazarus, keenly aware of ancient persecutions and of contemporary Jewish refugees fleeing Russian persecutions, contributed the following poem. It was read when the statue was unveiled in 1886, and the words of Liberty, spoken in the last five lines, were embossed on a plaque inside the pedestal.*

For the ancients, a colossus was a statue larger than life. The "brazen giant of Greek fame," mentioned in Lazarus's first line, was a statue of the sun god, erected in the harbor of the Greek island of Rhodes, celebrating the island's success in resisting the Macedonians in 305–304 BCE. More than 100 feet tall, it stood in the harbor until it toppled during an earthquake in 225 BCE. In later years its size became mythical; it was said to have straddled the harbor (Lazarus speaks of "limbs astride from land to land"), so that ships supposedly entered the harbor by sailing between its legs.

In Lazarus's poem, the "imprisoned lightning" (line 5) in the torch is electricity. The harbor is said to be "air-bridged" because in 1883, the year of the poem, the Brooklyn Bridge was completed, connecting Brooklyn with New York. (These are the "twin cities" of the poem.)

The New Colossus

Not like the brazen giant of Greek fame,
With conquering limbs astride from land to land;
Here at our sea-washed, sunset gates shall stand
A mighty woman with a torch, whose flame
Is the imprisoned lightning, and her name   5
Mother of Exiles. From her beacon-hand
Glows world-wide welcome; her mild eyes command
The air-bridged harbor that twin cities frame.
"Keep, ancient lands, your storied pomp!" cries she
With silent lips. "Give me your tired, your poor,   10
Your huddled masses yearning to breathe free,
The wretched refuse of your teeming shore.
Send these, the homeless, tempest-tost to me,
I lift my lamp beside the golden door!"

[1883]

Joining the Conversation: Critical Thinking and Writing

1. Does this poem have a message? In a paragraph, please state what this message is.
2. Do you find this poem to be clear, or confusing, or both? Please point to details that are either clear in their meaning or confusing to you.
3. Emma Lazarus uses the word "new" in her title. What is the relationship between the old Colossus and this new one?
4. Have you ever visited the Statue of Liberty? If you have, describe this experience. If you have not, please explain why you have not, and explain too why you do or do not intend to visit this site sometime soon.

5. A prominent historian has said that the Statue of Liberty is the nation's "greatest monument to the true meaning of America." Do you agree with this statement? Please argue for or against it.

THOMAS BAILEY ALDRICH

Thomas Bailey Aldrich (1836–1907) was born in Portsmouth, New Hampshire. He wrote poetry from his youth to his old age, and he also wrote short stories and essays, but his literary career was chiefly that of a journalist and an editor. (One magazine that he edited from 1881 to 1890, Atlantic Monthly, *continues to be important.) As the following poem indicates, Aldrich was deeply conservative. The view that he here expresses is known as Nativism, or the Nativist view, favoring the interests of established inhabitants rather than those of immigrants and newcomers.*

The Unguarded Gates

Wide open and unguarded stand our gates,
And through them press a wild, a motley throng—
Men from the Volga and the Tartar steppes,
Featureless figures of the Hoang-Ho,
Malayan, Scythian, Teuton, Kelt, and Slav,   5
Flying the Old World's poverty and scorn;
These bringing with them unknown gods and rites,
Those tiger passions, here to stretch their claws.
In street and alley what strange tongues are these,
Accents of menace alien to our air,   10
Voices that once the tower of Babel knew!

O, Liberty, white goddess, is it well
To leave the gate unguarded? On thy breast
Fold sorrow's children, soothe the hurts of fate,
Lift the downtrodden, but with the hand of steel   15
Stay those who to thy sacred portals come
To waste the fight of freedom. Have a care
Lest from thy brow the clustered stars be torn
And trampled in the dust. For so of old
The thronging Goth and Vandal trampled Rome,   20
And where the temples of the Caesars stood
The lean wolf unmolested made her lair.

[1885]

Joining the Conversation: Critical Thinking and Writing

1. Using a good dictionary and other reference books or Internet resources, identify the terms in lines 3, 4, 5, 11, 20, and 21.
2. Do you think that this poet is a racist? Please explain.
3. Could someone say, "Aldrich is a racist, but he is making a defensible point"? What is Aldrich's point? In the poem does he argue effectively for it?
4. How would Aldrich respond to Lazarus's poem? How would she respond to him?

JOSEPH BRUCHAC III

Joseph Bruchac III (the name is pronounced "Brewshack") was born in Saratoga Springs, New York, in 1942, and educated at Cornell University, Syracuse University, and Union Graduate School. Like many other Americans, he has a multicultural ethnic heritage, and he includes Native Americans as well as Slovaks among his ancestors. Bruchac, who has taught in Ghana and also in the United States, has chiefly worked as an editor and educator. He lives in Saratoga County, New York.

"Much of my writing and my life," Bruchac says, "relates to the problem of being an American. . . . While in college I was active in Civil Rights work and in the antiwar movement. . . . I went to Africa to teach—but more than that to be taught. It showed me many things. How much we have as Americans and take for granted. How much our eyes refuse to see because they are blinded to everything in a man's face except his color."

Slavic women arrive at Ellis Island in the winter of 1910.

Ellis Island

Beyond the red brick of Ellis Island
where the two Slovak children
who became my grandparents
waited the long days of quarantine,
after leaving the sickness,   5
the old Empires of Europe,
a Circle Line ship slips easily
on its way to the island
of the tall woman, green
as dreams of forests and meadows   10
waiting for those who'd worked
a thousand years
yet never owned their own.

Like millions of others,
I too come to this island, 15
nine decades the answerer
of dreams.
Yet only one part of my blood loves that memory.
Another voice speaks
of native lands 20
within this nation.
Lands invaded
when the earth became owned.
Lands of those who followed
the changing Moon, 25
knowledge of the seasons
in their veins.

[1978]

Joining the Conversation: Critical Thinking and Writing

1. The poet tells of a visit he made to Ellis Island. What did he learn there?
2. Do you think that the poem would be effective if it ended at line 17? If so, effective in what way?
3. How is the effect of the poem changed by lines 18–27?
4. Should every American be required to visit Ellis Island? What would be the benefit of such a requirement?
5. Consider this question, in relation to the poem: Should America be celebrated or criticized? Is Bruchac doing one or the other, or both?

AURORA LEVINS MORALES

Aurora Levins Morales, born in Puerto Rico in 1954, moved to the mainland United States with her family in 1967. She has lived in Chicago and New Hampshire and now lives in the San Francisco Bay Area. A member of the Latina Feminist Group, Levins Morales has published stories, essays, prose poems, and poems.

Child of the Americas

I am a child of the Americas,
a light-skinned mestiza of the Caribbean,
a child of many diaspora,° born into this continent at a crossroads.

3 diaspora literally, "scattering"; the term is used especially to refer to the dispersion of the Jews outside Israel from the sixth century BCE, when they were exiled to Babylonia, to the present time.

I am a U.S. Puerto Rican Jew,
a product of the ghettos of New York I have never known.   5
An immigrant and the daughter and granddaughter of immigrants.
I speak English with passion: it's the tongue of my consciousness,
a flashing knife blade of crystal, my tool, my craft.

I am Caribeña,° island grown. Spanish is in my flesh,
ripples from my tongue, lodges in my hips: 10
the language of garlic and mangoes,
the singing in my poetry, the flying gestures of my hands.

I am of Latinoamerica, rooted in the history of my continent:
I speak from that body.

I am not african. African is in me, but I cannot return.   15
I am not taína.° Taíno is in me, but there is no way back.
I am not european. Europe lives in me, but I have no home there.

I am new. History made me. My first language was spanglish.°
I was born at the crossroads
and I am whole.   20

[1986]

9 Caribeña Caribbean woman.   **16 taína** The Taínos were the Indian tribe native to Puerto
Rico.   **18 spanglish** a mixture of Spanish and English.

Joining the Conversation: Critical Thinking and Writing

1. In the first stanza, Levins Morales speaks of herself as "a child of many diaspora."
   Diaspora often means "a scattering," or "a dispersion of a homogeneous people."
   What does it refer to here?
2. In the second stanza, Levins Morales says that she is "a product of the ghettos
   of New York I have never known." What does she apparently refer to?
3. What attitude does "Child of the Americas" have toward the writer's ethnicity?
   What words or lines particularly communicate it?

GLORIA ANZALDÚA

*Gloria Anzaldúa, a seventh-generation American, was born in
1942 on a ranch settlement in Texas. When she was eleven her
family moved to Hargill, Texas, and in the next few years the
family traveled as migrant workers between Texas and Arkansas.
In 1969 she earned a BA from Pan American University, and
later she earned an MA from the University of Texas at Austin and
did further graduate work at the University of California, Santa
Cruz. Anzaldúa taught at the University of Texas at Austin; San
Francisco State University; Oakes College at the University of
California, Santa Cruz; and Vermont College. She died in 2004.*
    We give a poem from Anzaldúa's Borderlands: La Frontera—
The New Mestiza *(1987), a work that combines seven prose essays with poems. For
Anzaldúa—a woman, a Latina, and a lesbian—the "borderlands" are spiritual as well
as geographic.*

To Live in the Borderlands Means You

To live in the Borderlands means you
    are neither *hispana india negra española*
    ni gabacha,° *eres mestiza, mulata,*° half-breed
    caught in the crossfire between camps
    while carrying all five races on your back   5
    not knowing which side to turn to, run from;

To live in the Borderlands means knowing
    that the *india* in you, betrayed for 500 years,
    is no longer speaking to you,
    that *mexicanas* call you *rajetas,*°   10
    that denying the Anglo inside you
    is as bad as having denied the Indian or Black;

Cuando vives en la frontera°
    people walk through you, the wind steals your voice,
    you're a *burra, buey,*° scapegoat,   15
    forerunner of a new race,
    half and half—both woman and man, neither—
    a new gender;

To live in the Borderlands means to
    put *chile* in the borscht,   20
    eat whole wheat *tortillas,*
    speak Tex-Mex with a Brooklyn accent;
    be stopped by *la migra*° at the border checkpoints;

Living in the Borderlands means you fight hard to
    resist the gold elixer beckoning from the bottle,   25
    the pull of the gun barrel,
    the rope crushing the hollow of your throat;

In the Borderlands
    you are the battleground
    where enemies are kin to each other;   30
    you are at home, a stranger,
    the border disputes have been settled
    the volley of shots have shattered the truce
    you are wounded, lost in action
    dead, fighting back;   35

To live in the Borderlands means
    the mill with the razor white teeth wants to shred off
    your olive-red skin, crush out the kernel, your heart
    pound you pinch you roll you out
    smelling like white bread but dead;   40

2–3 neither . . . *mulata* neither Hispanic Indian black Spanish woman, nor white, you are mixed, a mixed breed.   **3 *gabacha*** a Chicano term for a white woman.   **10 *rajetas*** literally, "split," that is, having betrayed your word (author's note).   **13 *Cuando . . . frontera*** when you live in the borderlands.   **15 *burra, buey*** donkey, oxen (author's note).   **23 *la migra*** immigration officials.

To survive the Borderlands
you must live *sin fronteras*°
be a crossroads.

[1987]

42 sin fronteras without borders.

Joining the Conversation: Critical Thinking and Writing

1. When you first read the title, what was your response to it? After studying the poem, has your understanding of the title changed?
2. What is your response to Anzaldúa's use of Spanish terms? Why might she have wanted this mix of English and Spanish languages?
3. In no more than a paragraph, summarize what it means "to live in the Borderlands."
4. Is the tone of the poem celebratory, despairing, or something else? Does the tone change as the poem unfolds?
5. From your own personal background and experience, do you feel a special connection to Anzaldúa's poem? If you do not have such a background and experience, how does this fact affect your response to the poem?
6. Do some people live more in the Borderlands than do others? Why is that?

JIMMY SANTIAGO BACA

Jimmy Santiago Baca, of Chicano and Apache descent, was born in 1952. When he was two his parents divorced, and a grandparent brought him up until he was five, when he was placed in an orphanage in New Mexico. He ran away when he was eleven, lived on the streets, took drugs, and at the age of twenty was convicted of drug possession. In prison he taught himself to read and write, and he began to compose poetry. A fellow inmate urged him to send some poems to Mother Jones *magazine, and the work was accepted. In 1979 Louisiana State University Press published a book of his poems,* Immigrants in Our Own Land. *He has since published several other books.*

So Mexicans Are Taking Jobs from Americans

O Yes? Do they come on horses
with rifles, and say,
      Ese gringo,° gimmee your job?
And do you, gringo, take off your ring,
drop your wallet into a blanket   5
spread over the ground, and walk away?

3 Ese gringo Hey, whitey.

I hear Mexicans are taking your jobs away.
Do they sneak into town at night,
and as you're walking home with a whore,
do they mug you, a knife at your throat,   10
saying, I want your job?

Even on TV, an asthmatic leader
crawls turtle heavy, leaning on an assistant,
and from a nest of wrinkles on his face,
a tongue paddles through flashing waves   15
of lightbulbs, of cameramen, rasping
"They're taking our jobs away."

Well, I've gone about trying to find them,
asking just where the hell are these fighters.

The rifles I hear sound in the night   20
are white farmers shooting blacks and browns
whose ribs I see jutting out
and starving children,
I see the poor marching for a little work,
I see small white farmers selling out   25
to clean-suited farmers living in New York,
who've never been on a farm,
don't know the look of a hoof or the smell
of a woman's body bending all day long in fields.

I see this, and I hear only a few people   30
got all the money in this world, the rest
count their pennies to buy bread and butter.

Below that cool green sea of money,
millions and millions of people fight to live,
search for pearls in the darkest depths   35
of their dreams, hold their breath for years
trying to cross poverty to just having something.

The children are dead already. We are killing them,
that is what America should be saying;
on TV, in the streets, in offices, should be saying,   40
   "We aren't giving the children a chance to live."

Mexicans are taking our jobs, they say instead.
What they really say is, let them die,
and the children too.

[1979]

Joining the Conversation: Critical Thinking and Writing

1. When you read the title, what was your response to it? What happened to this first response as you read and then reread the poem?
2. To whom is the poem addressed?

3. Is the speaker angry? If so, is the speaker too angry?
4. Please identify and comment on the section of the poem that you think is the most effective. Is the poem effective throughout, or is there a section or sections where, in your view, it is not?
5. One critic, in praise of the poem, has said that in it Baca "uses words as a weapon." Please explain what you think this phrase means. Does it strike you as a good insight about the poem? Please point to evidence in the text to support your argument.
6. Prepare an essay of 1–2 pages in which you argue that Baca's poem should be included on the required reading list for first-year high school students. Then prepare an essay of the same length in which you argue that it should not.

LANGSTON HUGHES

Langston Hughes (1902–67) was born in Joplin, Missouri. He lived part of his youth in Mexico, spent a year at Columbia University, served as a merchant seaman, and worked in a Paris nightclub. Soon he received support from Alain Locke, a strong advocate of African American literature to whom Hughes had shown some of his poems. Hughes went on to publish poetry, fiction, plays, essays, and biographies.

Theme for English B

The instructor said,

> *Go home and write*
> *a page tonight.*
> *And let that page come out of you—*
> *Then, it will be true.*   5

I wonder if it's that simple?
I am twenty-two, colored, born in Winston-Salem.
I went to school there, then Durham, then here
to this college on the hill above Harlem.
I am the only colored student in my class.   10
The steps from the hill lead down into Harlem,
through a park, then I cross St. Nicholas,
Eighth Avenue, Seventh, and I come to the Y,
the Harlem Branch Y, where I take the elevator
up to my room, sit down, and write this page: 15

It's not easy to know what is true for you or me
at twenty-two, my age. But I guess I'm what
I feel and see and hear, Harlem, I hear you:
hear you, hear me—we two—you, me, talk on this page.
(I hear New York, too.) Me—who?   20
Well, I like to eat, sleep, drink, and be in love.
I like to work, read, learn, and understand life.
I like a pipe for a Christmas present,

or records—Bessie,° bop, or Bach.
I guess being colored doesn't make me *not* like   25
the same things other folks like who are other races.
So will my page be colored that I write?
Being me, it will not be white.
But it will be
a part of you, instructor.   30
You are white—
yet a part of me, as I am a part of you.
That's American.
Sometimes perhaps you don't want to be a part of me.
Nor do I often want to be a part of you.   35
But we are, that's true!
As I learn from you,
I guess you learn from me—
although you're older—and white—
and somewhat more free.   40

This is my page for English B.

[1949]

24 **Bessie** Bessie Smith (1898?–1937), African American blues singer.

 Joining the Conversation: Critical Thinking and Writing

1. The teacher instructs the students (line 4) to "let that page come out of you," and adds, "Then, it will be true" (6). Does it follow that what we let "come" out of us is "true"? If you were a student, what would be your response to the teacher's instruction?
2. In lines 21–24 Hughes specifies some of the things he likes—things that many people who are not black doubtless also like. Why, then, does he say (line 28) that his page "will not be white"?
3. Pretend that you are the English B instructor who received Hughes's theme. What comment (about 250 words) do you put at the end of the theme?
4. Aside from the statement that he is a "colored" student (10, 27) from Harlem (9, 11, 14, 18), is there anything particularly African American about this poem? Putting aside these references, might the poem have been written by an Asian American, or (say) an American of Middle Eastern descent?
5. In line 10 the speaker says he is "the only colored student in [his] class." If you have ever been the only student of your race or religion or ethnic background or sex in a group, in an essay of 250–500 words set forth the feelings you had, and the feelings you now have about the experience.

MyLiteratureLab® *For additional resources for "Theme for English B," log in to* www.myliteraturelab.com *where you will find a Comprehension Quiz, as well as an About the Author, Bibliography, Links, and Critical Overview for Hughes (under Student Resources).*

MITSUYE YAMADA

Mitsuye Yamada, the daughter of Japanese immigrants to the United States, was born in Japan in 1923, during her mother's return visit to her native land. Yamada was raised in Seattle, but in 1942 she and her family were incarcerated and then relocated to a camp in Idaho, when Executive Order 9066 gave military authorities the right to remove any and all persons from "military areas." In 1955 she became an American citizen. Later, she became a member of the Asian American Studies Program at the University of California at Irvine. She is the author of poems and stories.

Dorothea Lange, "Grandfather and Grandchildren Awaiting Evacuation Bus."

To the Lady

The one in San Francisco who asked:
Why did the Japanese Americans let
the government put them in
those camps without protest?

Come to think of it I
   should've run off to Canada

5

should've hijacked a plane to Algeria
should've pulled myself up from my
bra straps
and kicked'm in the groin   10
should've bombed a bank
should've tried self-immolation
should've holed myself up in a
woodframe house
and let you watch me   15
burn up on the six o'clock news
should've run howling down the street
naked and assaulted you at breakfast
by AP wirephoto
should've screamed bloody murder   20
like Kitty Genovese°

Then
YOU would've
come to my aid in shining armor
laid yourself across the railroad track   25
marched on Washington
tatooed a Star of David on your arm
written six million enraged
letters to Congress

But we didn't draw the line   30
anywhere
law and order Executive Order 9066°
social order moral order internal order

You let'm
I let'm   35
All are punished.

[1976]

---

21 Kitty Genovese In 1964 Kitty Genovese of Kew Gardens, New York, was stabbed to death when she left her car and walked toward her home. Thirty-eight persons heard her screams, but no one came to her assistance. **32 Executive Order 9066** an authorization, signed in 1941 by President Franklin D. Roosevelt, allowing military authorities to relocate Japanese and Japanese Americans who resided on the Pacific Coast of the United States.

Joining the Conversation: Critical Thinking and Writing

1. Has the lady's question (lines 2–4) ever crossed your mind? If so, what answers did you think of?
2. What, in effect, is the speaker really saying in lines 5–21? And in lines 24–29?
3. Explain the last line.

NILA NORTHSUN

nila northSun was born in 1951 in Schurz, Nevada, of Shoshone-Chippewa stock. She studied at the California State University campuses at Hayward and Humboldt and the University of Montana at Missoula, beginning as a psychology major but switching to art history, specializing in American Indian art. She is a photographer, a teacher, and the author of three books of poetry.

Moving Camp Too Far

i can't speak of
  many moons
  moving camp on travois°
i can't tell of
  the last great battle   5
  counting coup° or
  taking scalp
i don't know what it
  was to hunt buffalo
  or do the ghost dance   10
but
i can see an eagle
  almost extinct
  on slurpee plastic cups
i can travel to powwows   15
  in campers & winnebagos
i can eat buffalo meat
  at the tourist burger stand
i can dance to indian music
  rock-n-roll hey-a-hey-o   20
i can
  & unfortunately
  i do

[1977]

1 travois a frame slung between trailing poles that are pulled by a horse. Plains Indians used the device to transport their goods.   **6 counting coup** recounting one's exploits in battle.

Joining the Conversation: Critical Thinking and Writing

1. What is the speaker's attitude toward the world she has lost? What is her attitude toward herself?
2. The first ten lines are presented in a negative form, and the final ten in a positive form. How would you respond to someone who argued, "This poem is too formulaic"?

PLAYS

LUIS VALDEZ

Luis Valdez was born into a family of migrant farm workers in Delano, California, in 1940. After completing high school he entered San José State College on a scholarship. He wrote his first plays while still an undergraduate, and after receiving his degree (in English and drama) from San José in 1964 he joined the San Francisco Mime Troupe, a left-wing group that performed in parks and streets. Revolutionary in technique as well as in political content, the Mime Troupe rejected the traditional forms of drama and instead drew on the traditions of the circus and the carnival.

In 1965 Valdez returned to Delano, where César Chávez had organized a strike of farm workers and a boycott against grape growers. It was here, under the wing of the United Farm Workers, that he established El Teatro Campesino (the Farm Workers' Theater), which at first specialized in doing short, improvised, satirical skits called actos. *When the teatro moved to Del Rey, California, it expanded its repertoire beyond farm issues, and it became part of a cultural center that gave workshops (in English and Spanish) in such subjects as history, drama, and politics.*

The actos, *performed by amateurs on college campuses and on flatbed trucks and at the edges of vineyards, were highly political. Making use of stereotypes (the boss, the scab), the* actos *sought not to present the individual thoughts of a gifted playwright but to present the social vision of ordinary people—the* pueblo—*though it was acknowledged that in an oppressive society the playwright might have to help guide the people to see their own best interests.*

Valdez moved from actos *to* mitos *(myths)—plays that drew on Aztec mythology, Mexican folklore, and Christianity—and then to* Zoot Suit, *a play that ran for many months in California and that became the first Mexican American play to be produced on Broadway. More recently he wrote and directed a hit movie,* La Bamba, *and in 1991 received an award from the AT&T Foundation for his musical,* Bandido, *presented by El Teatro Campesino. Valdez teaches at California State University, Monterey Bay.*

Los Vendidos was written in 1967, when Ronald Reagan, a conservative Republican, was governor of California.

Los Vendidos[1]

LIST OF CHARACTERS

HONEST SANCHO
SECRETARY
FARM WORKER
JOHNNY
REVOLUCIONARIO
MEXICAN-AMERICAN

SCENE: *Honest Sancho's Used Mexican Lot and Mexican Curio Shop. Three models are on display in Honest* SANCHO'S *shop: to the right, there is a* REVOLUCIONARIO, *complete with sombrero, carrilleras,*[2] *and carabina 30-30. At center, on the floor,*

---

[1]*Los Vendidos* the sellouts.   [2]**carrilleras** cartridge belts.

there is the FARM WORKER *under a broad straw sombrero. At stage left is the* PACHUCO,[3] *filero[4] in hand.*

[*Honest* SANCHO *is moving among his models, dusting them off and preparing for another day of business.*]

SANCHO: Bueno, bueno, mis monos, vamos a ver a quien vendemos ahora, ¿no?[5] [*To audience.*] ¡Quihubo! I'm Honest Sancho and this is my shop. Antes fui contratista pero ahora logré tener mi negocito.[6] All I need now is a customer. [*A bell rings offstage.*] Ay, a customer!

SECRETARY: [*Entering*] Good morning, I'm Miss Jiménez from—

SANCHO: ¡Ah, una chicana! Welcome, welcome Señorita Jiménez.

SECRETARY: [*Anglo pronunciation*] JIM-enez.

SANCHO: ¿Qué?

SECRETARY: My name is Miss JIM-enez. Don't you speak English? What's wrong with you?

SANCHO: Oh, nothing, Señorita JIM-enez. I'm here to help you.

SECRETARY: That's better. As I was starting to say, I'm a secretary from Governor Reagan's office, and we're looking for a Mexican type for the administration.

SANCHO: Well, you come to the right place, lady. This is Honest Sancho's Used Mexican lot, and we got all types here. Any particular type you want?

SECRETARY: Yes, we were looking for somebody suave—

SANCHO: Suave.

SECRETARY: Debonair.

SANCHO: De buen aire.

SECRETARY: Dark.

SANCHO: Prieto.

SECRETARY: But of course not too dark.

SANCHO: No muy prieto.

SECRETARY: Perhaps, beige.

SANCHO: Beige, just the tone. Así como cafecito con leche,[7] ¿no?

SECRETARY: One more thing. He must be hard-working.

SANCHO: That could only be one model. Step right over here to the center of the shop, lady. [*They cross to the* FARM WORKER.] This is our standard farm worker model. As you can see, in the words of our beloved Senator George Murphy, he is "built close to the ground." Also take special notice of his four-ply Goodyear huaraches, made from the rain tire. This wide-brimmed sombrero is an extra added feature—keeps off the sun, rain, and dust.

SECRETARY: Yes, it does look durable.

SANCHO: And our farm worker model is friendly. Muy amable.[8] Watch. [*Snaps his fingers.*]

FARM WORKER [*Lifts up head*]: Buenos días, señorita. [*His head drops.*]

SECRETARY: My, he's friendly.

SANCHO: Didn't I tell you? Loves his patrones! But his most attractive feature is that he's hard working. Let me show you. [*Snaps fingers,* FARM WORKER *stands.*]

FARM WORKER: ¡El jale![9] [*He begins to work.*]

SANCHO: As you can see, he is cutting grapes.

SECRETARY: Oh, I wouldn't know.

---

[3]**Pachuco** an urban tough guy.   [4]**filero** blade.   [5]**Bueno . . . ¿no?** Well, well darlings, let's see who we can sell now, O.K.?   [6]**Antes . . . negocito** I used to be a contractor, but now I've succeeded in having my little business.   [7]**Así . . . leche** like coffee with milk.   [8]**Muy amable** very friendly.   [9]**¡El jale!** the job!

SANCHO: He also picks cotton. [*Snap.* FARM WORKER *begins to pick cotton.*]

SECRETARY: Versatile isn't he?

SANCHO: He also picks melons. [*Snap.* FARM WORKER *picks melons.*] That's his slow speed for late in the season. Here's his fast speed. [*Snap.* FARM WORKER *picks faster.*]

SECRETARY: ¡Chihuahua! . . . I mean, goodness, he sure is a hard worker.

SANCHO [*Pulls the* FARM WORKER *to his feet*]: And that isn't the half of it. Do you see these little holes on his arms that appear to be pores? During those hot sluggish days in the field, when the vines or the branches get so entangled, it's almost impossible to move; these holes emit a certain grease that allow our model to slip and slide right through the crop with no trouble at all.

SECRETARY: Wonderful. But is he economical?

SANCHO: Economical? Señorita, you are looking at the Volkswagen of Mexicans. Pennies a day is all it takes. One plate of beans and tortillas will keep him going all day. That, and chile. Plenty of chile. Chile jalapeños, chile verde, chile colorado. But, of course, if you do give him chile [*Snap.* FARM WORKER *turns left face. Snap.* FARM WORKER *bends over.*] then you have to change his oil filter once a week.

SECRETARY: What about storage?

SANCHO: No problem. You know these new farm labor camps our Honorable Governor Reagan has built out by Parlier or Raisin City? They were designed with our model in mind. Five, six, seven, even ten in one of those shacks will give you no trouble at all. You can also put him in old barns, old cars, river banks. You can even leave him out in the field overnight with no worry!

SECRETARY: Remarkable.

SANCHO: And here's an added feature: Every year at the end of the season, this model goes back to Mexico and doesn't return, automatically, until next Spring.

SECRETARY: How about that. But tell me: does he speak English?

SANCHO: Another outstanding feature is that last year this model was programmed to go out on STRIKE! [*Snap.*]

FARM WORKER: ¡HUELGA! ¡HUELGA! Hermanos, sálganse de esos files.[10] [*Snap. He stops.*]

SECRETARY: No! Oh no, we can't strike in the State Capitol.

SANCHO: Well, he also scabs. [*Snap.*]

FARM WORKER: Me vendo barato, ¿y qué?[11] [*Snap.*]

SECRETARY: That's much better, but you didn't answer my question. Does he speak English?

SANCHO: Bueno . . . no, pero[12] he has other—

SECRETARY: No.

SANCHO: Other features.

SECRETARY: NO! He just won't do!

SANCHO: Okay, okay pues. We have other models.

SECRETARY: I hope so. What we need is something a little more sophisticated.

SANCHO: Sophisti—¿qué?

SECRETARY: An urban model.

SANCHO: Ah, from the city! Step right back. Over here in this corner of the shop is exactly what you're looking for. Introducing our new 1969 JOHNNY PACHUCO

---

[10]**¡HUELGA! . . . files** Strike! Strike! Brothers, leave those rows.   [11]**Me . . . qué?** I come cheap. So what?   [12]**Bueno . . . no, pero** well, no, but.

model! This is our fast-back model. Streamlined. Built for speed, low-riding, city life. Take a look at some of these features. Mag shoes, dual exhausts, green chartreuse paint-job, dark-tint windshield, a little poof on top. Let me just turn him on. [*Snap.* JOHNNY *walks to stage center with a pachuco bounce.*]

SECRETARY: What was that?

SANCHO: That, señorita, was the Chicano shuffle.

SECRETARY: Okay, what does he do?

SANCHO: Anything and everything necessary for city life. For instance, survival: He knife fights. [*Snap.* JOHNNY *pulls out switchblade and swings at* SECRETARY.]

[SECRETARY *screams.*]

SANCHO: He dances. [*Snap.*]

JOHNNY [*Singing*]: "Angel Baby, my Angel Baby . . ." [*Snap.*]

SANCHO: And here's a feature no city model can be without. He gets arrested, but not without resisting, of course. [*Snap.*]

JOHNNY: ¡En la madre, la placa![13] I didn't do it! I didn't do it! [JOHNNY *turns and stands up against an imaginary wall, legs spread out, arms behind his back.*]

SECRETARY: Oh no, we can't have arrests! We must maintain law and order.

SANCHO: But he's bilingual!

SECRETARY: Bilingual?

SANCHO: Simón que yes.[14] He speaks English! Johnny, give us some English. [*Snap.*]

JOHNNY [*Comes downstage*]: Fuck-you!

SECRETARY [*Gasps*]: Oh! I've never been so insulted in my whole life!

SANCHO: Well, he learned it in your school.

SECRETARY: I don't care where he learned it.

SANCHO: But he's economical!

SECRETARY: Economical?

SANCHO: Nickels and dimes. You can keep Johnny running on hamburgers, Taco Bell tacos, Lucky Lager beer, Thunderbird wine, yesca—

SECRETARY: Yesca?

SANCHO: Mota.

SECRETARY: Mota?

SANCHO: Leños[15] . . . Marijuana. [*Snap;* JOHNNY *inhales on an imaginary joint.*]

SECRETARY: That's against the law!

JOHNNY [*Big smile, holding his breath*]: Yeah.

SANCHO: He also sniffs glue. [*Snap.* JOHNNY *inhales glue, big smile.*]

JOHNNY: That's too much man, ése.[16]

SECRETARY: No, Mr. Sancho, I don't think this—

SANCHO: Wait a minute, he has other qualities I know you'll love. For example, an inferiority complex. [*Snap.*]

JOHNNY [*To* SANCHO]: You think you're better than me, huh ése? [*Swings switch-blade.*]

SANCHO: He can also be beaten and he bruises, cut him and he bleeds; kick him and he—[*He beats, bruises and kicks* PACHUCO.] would you like to try it?

SECRETARY: Oh, I couldn't.

SANCHO: Be my guest. He's a great scapegoat.

SECRETARY: No, really.

SANCHO: Please.

SECRETARY: Well, all right. Just once. [*She kicks* PACHUCO.] Oh, he's so soft.

---

[13]¡**En . . . la placa!** Wow, the cops!   [14]**Simón que yes** Yea, sure.   [15]**Leños** joints (marijuana).   [16]**ése** fellow.

SANCHO: Wasn't that good? Try again.

SECRETARY [*Kicks* PACHUCO]: Oh, he's so wonderful! [*She kicks him again.*]

SANCHO: Okay, that's enough, lady. You ruin the merchandise. Yes, our Johnny Pachuco model can give you many hours of pleasure. Why, the L.A.P.D. just bought twenty of these to train their rookie cops on. And talk about maintenance. Señorita, you are looking at an entirely self-supporting machine. You're never going to find our Johnny Pachuco model on the relief rolls. No, sir, this model knows how to liberate.

SECRETARY: Liberate?

SANCHO: He steals. [*Snap.* JOHNNY *rushes the* SECRETARY *and steals her purse.*]

JOHNNY: ¡Dame esa bolsa, vieja![17] [*He grabs the purse and runs. Snap by* SANCHO. *He stops.*]

[SECRETARY *runs after* JOHNNY *and grabs purse away from him, kicking him as she goes.*]

SECRETARY: No, no, no! We can't have any *more* thieves in the State Administration. Put him back.

SANCHO: Okay, we still got other models. Come on, Johnny, we'll sell you to some old lady. [SANCHO *takes* JOHNNY *back to his place.*]

SECRETARY: Mr. Sancho, I don't think you quite understand what we need. What we need is something that will attract the women voters. Something more traditional, more romantic.

SANCHO: Ah, a lover. [*He smiles meaningfully.*] Step right over here, señorita. Introducing our standard Revolucionario and/or Early California Bandit type. As you can see he is well-built, sturdy, durable. This is the International Harvester of Mexicans.

SECRETARY: What does he do?

SANCHO: You name it, he does it. He rides horses, stays in the mountains, crosses deserts, plains, rivers, leads revolutions, follows revolutions, kills, can be killed, serves as a martyr, hero, movie star—did I say movie star? Did you ever see *Viva Zapata? Viva Villa? Villa Rides? Pancho Villa Returns? Pancho Villa Goes Back? Pancho Villa Meets Abbott and Costello*—

SECRETARY: I've never seen any of those.

SANCHO: Well, he was in all of them. Listen to this. [*Snap.*]

REVOLUCIONARIO [*Scream*]: ¡VIVA VILLAAAAA!

SECRETARY: That's awfully loud.

SANCHO: He has a volume control. [*He adjusts volume. Snap.*]

REVOLUCIONARIO [*Mousey voice*]: ¡Viva Villa!

SECRETARY: That's better.

SANCHO: And even if you didn't see him in the movies, perhaps you saw him on TV. He makes commercials. [*Snap.*]

REVOLUCIONARIO: Is there a Frito Bandito in your house?

SECRETARY: Oh yes, I've seen that one!

SANCHO: Another feature about this one is that he is economical. He runs on raw horsemeat and tequila.

SECRETARY: Isn't that rather savage?

SANCHO: Al contrario,[18] it makes him a lover. [*Snap.*]

REVOLUCIONARIO [*To* SECRETARY]: ¡Ay, mamasota, cochota, ven pa'ca![19] [*He grabs* SECRETARY *and folds her back—Latin-Lover style.*]

---

[17]**¡Dame . . . vieja!** Give me that bag, old lady!   [18]**Al contrario** On the contrary.
[19]**¡Ay . . . pa'ca!** Get over here!

SANCHO [*Snap.* REVOLUCIONARIO *goes back upright.*]: Now wasn't that nice?

SECRETARY: Well, it was rather nice.

SANCHO: And finally, there is one outstanding feature about this model I KNOW the ladies are going to love: He's a GENUINE antique! He was made in Mexico in 1910!

SECRETARY: Made in Mexico?

SANCHO: That's right. Once in Tijuana, twice in Guadalajara, three times in
Cuernavaca.

SECRETARY: Mr. Sancho, I thought he was an American product.

SANCHO: No, but—

SECRETARY: No, I'm sorry. We can't buy anything but American-made products. He
just won't do.

SANCHO: But he's an antique!

SECRETARY: I don't care. You still don't understand what we need. It's true we need
Mexican models such as these, but it's more important that he be *American.*

SANCHO: American?

SECRETARY: That's right, and judging from what you've shown me, I don't think you
have what we want. Well, my lunch hour's almost over: I better—

SANCHO: Wait a minute! Mexican but American?

SECRETARY: That's correct.

SANCHO: Mexican but . . . [*A sudden flash.*] AMERICAN! Yeah, I think we've got exactly
what you want. He just came in today! Give me a minute. [*He exits. Talks from
backstage.*] Here he is in the shop. Let me just get some papers off. There. Introducing our new 1970 Mexican-American! Ta-ra-ra-ra-ra-ra-RA-RAAA!

   [SANCHO *brings out the* MEXICAN-AMERICAN *model, a clean-shaven middle-class
type in a business suit, with glasses.*]

SECRETARY [*Impressed*]: Where have you been hiding this one?

SANCHO: He just came in this morning. Ain't he a beauty? Feast your eyes on him!
Sturdy US STEEL frame, streamlined, modern. As a matter of fact, he is built
exactly like our Anglo models except that he comes in a variety of darker
shades: naugahyde, leather, or leatherette.

SECRETARY: Naugahyde.

SANCHO: Well, we'll just write that down. Yes, señorita, this model represents the
apex of American engineering! He is bilingual, college educated, ambitious!
Say the word "acculturate" and he accelerates. He is intelligent, well-mannered,
clean—did I say clean? [*Snap.* MEXICAN-AMERICAN *raises his arm.*] Smell.

SECRETARY [*Smells*]: Old Sobaco, my favorite.

SANCHO [*Snap.* MEXICAN-AMERICAN *turns toward* SANCHO]: Eric! [*To* SECRETARY.] We call
him Eric García. [*To* ERIC.] I want you to meet Miss JIM-enez, Eric.

MEXICAN-AMERICAN: Miss JIM-enez, I am delighted to make your acquaintance. [*He
kisses her hand.*]

SECRETARY: Oh, my, how charming!

SANCHO: Did you feel the suction? He has seven especially engineered suction cups
right behind his lips. He's a charmer all right!

SECRETARY: How about boards? Does he function on boards?

SANCHO: You name them, he is on them. Parole boards, draft boards, school boards,
taco quality control boards, surf boards, two-by-fours.

SECRETARY: Does he function in politics?

SANCHO: Señorita, you are looking at a political MACHINE. Have you ever heard of
the OEO, EOC, COD, WAR ON POVERTY? That's our model! Not only that, he
makes political speeches.

SECRETARY: May I hear one?

SANCHO: With pleasure. [*Snap.*] Eric, give us a speech.

MEXICAN-AMERICAN: Mr. Congressman, Mr. Chairman, members of the board, honored guests, ladies and gentlemen. [SANCHO *and* SECRETARY *applaud.*] Please, please. I come before you as a Mexican-American to tell you about the problems of the Mexican. The problems of the Mexican stem from one thing and one thing alone: He's stupid. He's uneducated. He needs to stay in school. He needs to be ambitious, forward-looking, harder-working. He needs to think American, American, American, AMERICAN, AMERICAN, AMERICAN. GOD BLESS AMERICA! GOD BLESS AMERICA! GOD BLESS AMERICA!! [*He goes out of control.*]

[SANCHO *snaps frantically and the* MEXICAN-AMERICAN *finally slumps forward, bending at the waist.*]

SECRETARY: Oh my, he's patriotic too!

SANCHO: Sí, señorita, he loves his country. Let me just make a little adjustment here. [*Stands* MEXICAN-AMERICAN *up.*]

SECRETARY: What about upkeep? Is he economical?

SANCHO: Well, no, I won't lie to you. The Mexican-American costs a little bit more, but you get what you pay for. He's worth every extra cent. You can keep him running on dry Martinis, Langendorf bread.

SECRETARY: Apple pie?

SANCHO: Only Mom's. Of course, he's also programmed to eat Mexican food on ceremonial functions, but I must warn you: an overdose of beans will plug up his exhaust.

SECRETARY: Fine! There's just one more question: HOW MUCH DO YOU WANT FOR HIM?

SANCHO: Well, I tell you what I'm gonna do. Today and today only, because you've been so sweet, I'm gonna let you steal this model from me! I'm gonna let you drive him off the lot for the simple price of—let's see taxes and license included—$15,000.

SECRETARY: Fifteen thousand DOLLARS? For a MEXICAN!

SANCHO: Mexican? What are you talking, lady? This is a Mexican-AMERICAN! We had to melt down two pachucos, a farm worker and three gabachos[20] to make this model! You want quality, but you gotta pay for it! This is no cheap runabout. He's got class!

SECRETARY: Okay, I'll take him.

SANCHO: You will?

SECRETARY: Here's your money.

SANCHO: You mind if I count it?

SECRETARY: Go right ahead.

SANCHO: Well, you'll get your pink slip in the mail. Oh, do you want me to wrap him up for you? We have a box in the back.

SECRETARY: No, thank you. The Governor is having a luncheon this afternoon, and we need a brown face in the crowd. How do I drive him?

SANCHO: Just snap your fingers. He'll do anything you want.

[SECRETARY *snaps.* MEXICAN-AMERICAN *steps forward.*]

MEXICAN-AMERICAN: RAZA QUERIDA, ¡VAMOS LEVANTANDO ARMAS PARA LIBERARNOS DE ESTOS DESGRACIADOS GABACHOS QUE NOS EXPLOTAN! VAMOS.[21]

[20]**gabachos** whites.   [21]**RAZA . . . VAMOS** Beloved Raza [persons of Mexican descent], let's take up arms to liberate ourselves from those damned whites who exploit us. Let's get going.

SECRETARY: What did he say?

SANCHO: Something about lifting arms, killing white people, etc.

SECRETARY: But he's not supposed to say that!

SANCHO: Look, lady, don't blame me for bugs from the factory. He's your Mexican-American; you bought him, now drive him off the lot!

SECRETARY: But he's broken!

SANCHO: Try snapping another finger.

[SECRETARY *snaps.* MEXICAN-AMERICAN *comes to life again.*]

MEXICAN-AMERICAN: ¡ESTA GRAN HUMANIDAD HA DICHO BASTA! Y SE HA PUESTO EN MARCHA! ¡BASTA! ¡BASTA! ¡VIVA LA RAZA! ¡VIVA LA CAUSA! ¡VIVA LA HUELGA! ¡VIVAN LOS BROWN BERETS! ¡VIVAN LOS ESTUDI-ANTES!²² ¡CHICANO POWER!

[*The* MEXICAN-AMERICAN *turns toward the* SECRETARY, *who gasps and backs up. He keeps turning toward the* PACHUCO, FARM WORKER, *and* REVOLUCIONARIO, *snapping his fingers and turning each of them on, one by one.*]

PACHUCO [*Snap. To* SECRETARY]: I'm going to get you, baby! ¡Viva La Raza!

FARM WORKER [*Snap. To* SECRETARY]: ¡Viva la huelga! ¡Viva la Huelga! ¡VIVA LA HUELGA!

REVOLUCIONARIO [*Snap. To* SECRETARY]: ¡Viva la revolución! ¡VIVA LA REVOLUCIÓN!

[*The three models join together and advance toward the* SECRETARY, *who backs up and runs out of the shop screaming.* SANCHO *is at the other end of the shop holding his money in his hand. All freeze. After a few seconds of silence, the* PACHUCO *moves and stretches, shaking his arms and loosening up. The* FARM WORKER *and* REVOLUCIONARIO *do the same.* SANCHO *stays where he is, frozen to his spot.*]

JOHNNY: Man, that was a long one, ése.²³ [*Others agree with him.*]

FARM WORKER: How did we do?

JOHNNY: Perty good, look at all that lana,²⁴ man! [*He goes over to* SANCHO *and removes the money from his hand.* SANCHO *stays where he is.*]

REVOLUCIONARIO: En la madre, look at all the money.

JOHNNY: We keep this up, we're going to be rich.

FARM WORKER: They think we're machines.

REVOLUCIONARIO: Burros.

JOHNNY: Puppets.

MEXICAN-AMERICAN: The only thing I don't like is—how come I always got to play the godamn Mexican-American?

JOHNNY: That's what you get for finishing high school.

FARM WORKER: How about our wages, ése?

JOHNNY: Here it comes right now. $3,000 for you, $3,000 for you, $3,000 for you, and $3,000 for me. The rest we put back into the business.

MEXICAN-AMERICAN: Too much, man. Heh, where you vatos²⁵ going tonight?

FARM WORKER: I'm going over to Concha's. There's a party.

JOHNNY: Wait a minute, vatos. What about our salesman? I think he needs an oil job.

REVOLUCIONARIO: Leave him to me.

²²**¡ESTA . . . ESTUDIANTES!** This great mass of humanity has said enough! And it has begun to march. Enough! Enough! Long live La Raza! Long live the Cause! Long live the strike! Long live the Brown Berets! Long live the students!   ²³**ése** man.   ²⁴**lana** money.   ²⁵**vatos** guys.

[*The* PACHUCO, FARM WORKER, *and* MEXICAN-AMERICAN *exit, talking loudly about their plans for the night. The* REVOLUCIONARIO *goes over to* SANCHO, *removes his derby hat and cigar, lifts him up and throws him over his shoulder.* SANCHO *hangs loose, lifeless.*]

REVOLUCIONARIO [*To audience*]: He's the best model we got! ¡Ajua!²⁶

[*Exit.*]

THE END

[1967]

²⁶**¡Ajua!** Wow!

Joining the Conversation: Critical Thinking and Writing

1. If you are an Anglo (shorthand for a Caucasian with traditional northern European values), do you find *Los Vendidos* deeply offensive? Why, or why not? If you are a Mexican American, do you find the play entertaining—or do you find parts of it offensive? What might Anglos enjoy in the play, and what might Mexican Americans find offensive? Set forth your views in a detailed argument.
2. What stereotypes of Mexican Americans are presented here? At the end of the play, what image of the Mexican American is presented? How does it compare with the stereotypes?
3. If you are a member of some other minority group, in a few sentences indicate how *Los Vendidos* might be adapted into a play about that group.
4. Putting aside the politics of the play (and your own politics), what do you think are the strengths of *Los Vendidos?* What do you think are its weaknesses?
5. The play was written in 1967. Do you find it dated? If not, why not? Please point to specific passages to support your analysis and argument
6. In 1971 when *Los Vendidos* was produced by El Teatro de la Esperanza, the group altered the ending by having the men decide to use the money to build a community center. Evaluate this ending.
7. When the play was videotaped by KNBC in Los Angeles for broadcast in 1973, Valdez changed the ending. In the revised version we discover that a scientist (played by Valdez) masterminds the operation, placing Mexican American models wherever there are persons of Mexican descent. These models soon will become Chicanos (as opposed to persons with Anglo values) and will aid rather than work against their fellows. Evaluate this ending.
8. In his short essay "The Actos," Valdez says, "Actos: Inspire the audience to social action. Illuminate specific points about social problems. Satirize the opposition. Show or hint at a solution. Express what people are feeling." How many of these things do you think *Los Vendidos* does?
9. Many people assume that politics gets in the way of serious art. That is, they assume that artists ought to be concerned with issues that transcend politics. Does this point make any sense to you? Why, or why not?

LORRAINE HANSBERRY

Lorraine Hansberry (1930–65) was born in Chicago, Illinois, to middle-class black parents who lived on the city's South Side. When she was still a child, her father was barred from purchasing a house in a white neighborhood. He sued and pursued the case all the way to the Supreme Court, which ruled in his favor. Hansberry attended the University of Wisconsin as an undergraduate. Following college, she began a career as a painter, studying at the Art Institute of Chicago and in Mexico before she decided to move to New York to take up her interest in writing. There she wrote for Freedom, *a magazine founded by the great singer-actor turned political activist, Paul Robeson. When her first play,* A Raisin in the Sun, *premiered at the Ethel Barrymore Theater in 1959, it was the first play written by an African American woman to be performed on Broadway. She wrote only one other play,* The Sign in Sidney Brustein's Window *(1965), before she died of cancer at the age of thirty-four. The title of* A Raisin in the Sun *is taken from the poem "A Dream Deferred," by Langston Hughes.*

The 1959 opening night cast for the Broadway production of *A Raisin in the Sun* included Sidney Poitier, Claudia MacNeil, Ruby Dee, Diana Sands, Louis Gossett Jr., Ivan Dixon, Glynn Turman, John Fielder, Lonne Elder III, Ed Hall, and Douglas Turner Ward.

A Raisin in the Sun

CHARACTERS IN ORDER OF APPEARANCE

RUTH YOUNGER, *Walter's wife, about thirty*
TRAVIS YOUNGER, *her son and Walter's*
WALTER LEE YOUNGER, *(Brother) Ruth's husband, mid-thirties*
BENEATHA YOUNGER, *Walter's sister, about twenty*
LENA YOUNGER, *(Mama) mother of Walter and Beneatha*
JOSEPH ASAGAI, *Nigerian, Beneatha's suitor*
GEORGE MURCHISON, *Beneatha's date, wealthy*
KARL LINDNER, *white, chairman of the Clybourne Park New Neighbors Orientation Committee*
BOBO, *one of Walter's business partners*
MOVING MEN

The action of the play is set in Chicago's South Side, sometime between World War II and the present.

ACT I
SCENE 1. *Friday morning*
SCENE 2. *The following morning*

ACT II
SCENE 1. *Later, the same day*
SCENE 2. *Friday night, a few weeks later*
SCENE 3. *Moving day, one week later*

ACT III
An hour later

ACT I

SCENE 1

The Younger living room would be a comfortable and well-ordered room if it were not for a number of indestructible contradictions to this state of being. Its furnishings are typical and undistinguished and their primary feature now is that they have clearly had to accommodate the living of too many people for too many years— and they are tired. Still, we can see that at some time, a time probably no longer remembered by the family (except perhaps for MAMA) the furnishings of this room were actually selected with care and love and even hope—and brought to this apartment and arranged with taste and pride.

That was a long time ago. Now the once loved pattern of the couch upholstery has to fight to show itself from under acres of crocheted doilies and couch covers which have themselves finally come to be more important than the upholstery. And here a table or a chair has been moved to disguise the worn places in the carpet; but the carpet has fought back by showing its weariness, with depressing uniformity, elsewhere on its surface.

Weariness has, in fact, won in this room. Everything has been polished, washed, sat on, used, scrubbed too often. All pretenses but living itself have long since vanished from the very atmosphere of this room.

Moreover, a section of this room, for it is not really a room unto itself, though the landlord's lease would make it seem so, slopes backward to provide a small kitchen area, where the family prepares the meals that are eaten in the living room proper, which must also serve as dining room. The single window that has been provided for these "two" rooms is located in this kitchen area. The sole natural light the family may enjoy in the course of a day is only that which fights its way through this little window.

At left, a door leads to a bedroom which is shared by MAMA *and her daughter,* BENEATHA. *At right, opposite, is a second room (which in the beginning of the life of this apartment was probably a breakfast room) which serves as a bedroom for* WALTER *and his wife,* RUTH.

TIME: *Sometime between World War II and the present.*
PLACE: *Chicago's South Side.*

AT RISE: *It is morning dark in the living room.* TRAVIS *is asleep on the makedown bed at center. An alarm clock sounds from within the bedroom at right, and presently* RUTH *enters from that room and closes the door behind her. She crosses sleepily toward the window. As she passes her sleeping son she reaches down and shakes him a little. At the window she raises the shade and a dusky South Side morning light comes in feebly. She fills a pot with water and puts it on to boil. She calls to the boy, between yawns, in a slightly muffled voice.*

RUTH *is about thirty. We can see that she was a pretty girl, even exceptionally so, but now it is apparent that life has been little that she expected, and disappointment has already begun to hang in her face. In a few years, before thirty-five even, she will be known among her people as a "settled woman."*

She crosses to her son and gives him a good, final, rousing shake.

RUTH: Come on now, boy, it's seven thirty! [*Her son sits up at last, in a stupor of sleepiness.*] I say hurry up, Travis! You ain't the only person in the world got to use a bathroom! [*The child, a sturdy, handsome little boy of ten or eleven, drags himself out of the bed and almost blindly takes his towels and "today's clothes" from drawers and a closet and goes out to the bathroom, which is in an outside hall and which is shared by another family or families on the same floor.* RUTH *crosses to the bedroom door at right and opens it and calls in to her husband.*] Walter Lee! . . . It's after seven thirty! Lemme see you do some waking up in there now! [*She waits.*] You better get up from there, man! It's after seven thirty I tell you. [*She waits again.*] All right, you just go ahead and lay there and next thing you know Travis be finished and Mr. Johnson'll be in there and you'll be fussing and cussing round here like a mad man! And be late too! [*She waits, at the end of patience.*] Walter Lee—it's time for you to get up! [*She waits another second and then starts to go into the bedroom, but is apparently satisfied that her husband has begun to get up. She stops, pulls the door to, and returns to the kitchen area. She wipes her face with a moist cloth and runs her fingers through her sleep-disheveled hair in a vain effort and ties an apron around her housecoat. The bedroom door at right opens and her husband stands in the doorway in his pajamas, which are rumpled and mismated. He is a lean, intense young man in his middle thirties, inclined to quick nervous movements and erratic speech habits—and always in his voice there is a quality of indictment.*]
WALTER: Is he out yet?

RUTH: What you mean *out?* He ain't hardly got in there good yet.

WALTER [*wandering in, still more oriented to sleep than to a new day*]: Well, what was you doing all that yelling for if I can't even get in there yet? [*stopping and thinking*] Check coming today?

RUTH: They *said* Saturday and this is just Friday and I hopes to God you ain't going to get up here first thing this morning and start talking to me 'bout no money—'cause I 'bout don't want to hear it.

WALTER: Something the matter with you this morning?

RUTH: No—I'm just sleepy as the devil. What kind of eggs you want?

WALTER: Not scrambled. [RUTH *starts to scramble eggs.*] Paper come? [RUTH *points impatiently to the rolled up* Tribune *on the table, and he gets it and spreads it out and vaguely reads the front page.*] Set off another bomb yesterday.

RUTH [*maximum indifference*]: Did they?

WALTER [*looking up*]: What's the matter with you?

RUTH: Ain't nothing the matter with me. And don't keep asking me that this morning.

WALTER: Ain't nobody bothering you. [*reading the news of the day absently again*] Say Colonel McCormick is sick.

RUTH [*affecting tea-party interest*]: Is he now? Poor thing.

WALTER [*sighing and looking at his watch*]: Oh, me. [*He waits.*] Now what is that boy doing in that bathroom all this time? He just going to have to start getting up earlier. I can't be being late to work on account of him fooling around in there.

RUTH [*turning on him*]: Oh, no he ain't going to be getting up earlier no such thing! It ain't his fault that he can't get to bed no earlier nights 'cause he got a bunch of crazy good-for-nothing clowns sitting up running their mouths in what is supposed to be his bedroom after ten o'clock at night . . .

WALTER: That's what you mad about, ain't it? The things I want to talk about with my friends just couldn't be important in your mind, could they? [*He rises and finds a cigarette in her handbag on the table and crosses to the little window and looks out, smoking and deeply enjoying this first one.*]

RUTH [*almost matter of factly, a complaint too automatic to deserve emphasis*]: Why you always got to smoke before you eat in the morning?

WALTER [*at the window*]: Just look at 'em down there. . . . Running and racing to work . . . [*He turns and faces his wife and watches her a moment at the stove, and then, suddenly*] You look young this morning, baby.

RUTH [*indifferently*]: Yeah?

WALTER: Just for a second—stirring them eggs. It's gone now—just for a second it was—you looked real young again. [*then, drily*] It's gone now—you look like yourself again.

RUTH: Man, if you don't shut up and leave me alone.

WALTER [*looking out to the street again*]: First thing a man ought to learn in life is not to make love to no colored woman first thing in the morning. You all some evil people at eight o'clock in the morning. [TRAVIS *appears in the hall doorway, almost fully dressed and quite wide awake now, his towels and pajamas across his shoulders. He opens the door and signals for his father to make the bathroom in a hurry.*]

TRAVIS [*watching the bathroom*]: Daddy, come on! [WALTER *gets his bathroom utensils and flies out to the bathroom.*]

RUTH: Sit down and have your breakfast, Travis.

TRAVIS: Mama, this is Friday. [*gleefully*] Check coming tomorrow, huh?

RUTH: You get your mind off money and eat your breakfast.

TRAVIS [*eating*]: This is the morning we supposed to bring the fifty cents to school.

RUTH: Well, I ain't got no fifty cents this morning.

TRAVIS: Teacher say we have to.

RUTH: I don't care what teacher say. I ain't got it. Eat your breakfast, Travis.

TRAVIS: I *am* eating.

RUTH: Hush up now and just eat! [*The boy gives her an exasperated look for her lack of understanding, and eats grudgingly.*]

TRAVIS: You think Grandmama would have it?

RUTH: No! And I want you to stop asking your grandmother for money, you hear me?

TRAVIS [*outraged*]: Gaaaleee! I don't ask her, she just gimme it sometimes!

RUTH: Travis Willard Younger—I got too much on me this morning to be—

TRAVIS: Maybe Daddy—

RUTH: *Travis.* [*The boy hushes abruptly. They are both quiet and tense for several seconds.*]

TRAVIS [*presently*]: Could I maybe go carry some groceries in front of the supermarket for a little while after school then?

RUTH: Just hush, I said. [TRAVIS *jabs his spoon into his cereal bowl viciously, and rests his head in anger upon his fists.*] If you through eating, you can get over there and make up your bed. [*The boy obeys stiffly and crosses the room, almost mechanically, to the bed and more or less carefully folds the covering. He carries the bedding into his mother's room and returns with his books and cap.*]

TRAVIS [*sulking and standing apart from her unnaturally*]: I'm gone.

RUTH [*looking up from the stove to inspect him automatically*]: Come here. [*He crosses to her and she studies his head.*] If you don't take this comb and fix this here head, you better! [TRAVIS *puts down his books with a great sigh of oppression, and crosses to the mirror. His mother mutters under her breath about his "stubbornness."*] 'Bout to march out of here with that head looking just like chickens slept in it! I just don't know where you get your stubborn ways . . . And get your jacket, too. Looks chilly out this morning.

TRAVIS [*with conspicuously brushed hair and jacket*]: I'm gone.

RUTH: Get carfare and milk money—[*waving one finger*]—and not a single penny for no caps, you hear me?

TRAVIS [*with sullen politeness*]: Yes'm. [*He turns in outrage to leave. His mother watches after him as in his frustration he approaches the door almost comically. When she speaks to him, her voice has become a very gentle tease.*]

RUTH [*mocking, as she thinks he would say it*]: Oh, Mama makes me so mad sometimes, I don't know what to do! [*She waits and continues to his back as he stands stock-still in front of the door.*] I wouldn't kiss that woman good-bye for nothing in this world this morning! [*The boy finally turns around and rolls his eyes at her, knowing the mood has changed and he is vindicated; he does not, however, move toward her yet.*] Not for nothing in this world! [*She finally laughs aloud at him and holds out her arms to him and we see that it is a way between them, very old and practiced. He crosses to her and allows her to embrace him warmly but keeps his face fixed with masculine rigidity. She holds him back from her presently and looks at him and runs her fingers over the features of his face. With utter gentleness—*] Now—whose little old angry man are you?

TRAVIS [*The masculinity and gruffness start to fade at last.*]: Aw gaalee—Mama . . .

RUTH [*mimicking*]: Aw—gaaaaalleeeee, Mama! [*She pushes him, with rough playfulness and finality, toward the door.*] Get on out of here or you going to be late.

TRAVIS [*in the face of love, new aggressiveness*]: Mama, could I *please* go carry groceries?

RUTH: Honey, it's starting to get so cold evenings.

WALTER [*coming in from the bathroom and drawing a make-believe gun from a make-believe holster and shooting at his son*]: What is it he wants to do?

RUTH: Go carry groceries after school at the supermarket.

WALTER: Well, let him go . . .

TRAVIS [*quickly, to the ally*]: I *have* to—she won't gimme the fifty cents . . .

WALTER [*to his wife only*]: Why not?

RUTH [*simply, and with flavor*]: 'Cause we don't have it.

WALTER [*to* RUTH *only*]: What you tell the boy things like that for? [*reaching down into his pants with a rather important gesture*] Here, son—[*He hands the boy the coin, but his eyes are directed to his wife's.* TRAVIS *takes the money happily.*]

TRAVIS: Thanks, Daddy. [*He starts out.* RUTH *watches both of them with murder in her eyes.* WALTER *stands and stares back at her with defiance, and suddenly reaches into his pocket again on an afterthought.*]

WALTER [*without even looking at his son, still staring hard at his wife*]: In fact, here's another fifty cents . . . Buy yourself some fruit today—or take a taxicab to school or something!

TRAVIS: Whoopee—[*He leaps up and clasps his father around the middle with his legs, and they face each other in mutual appreciation; slowly* WALTER LEE *peeks around the boy to catch the violent rays from his wife's eyes and draws his head back as if shot.*]

WALTER: You better get down now—and get to school, man.

TRAVIS [*at the door*]: O.K. Good-bye. [*He exits.*]

WALTER [*after him, pointing with pride*]: That's *my* boy. [*She looks at him in disgust and turns back to her work.*] You know what I was thinking 'bout in the bathroom this morning?

RUTH: No.

WALTER: How come you always try to be so pleasant!

RUTH: What is there to be pleasant 'bout!

WALTER: You want to know what I was thinking 'bout in the bathroom or not!

RUTH: I know what you thinking 'bout.

WALTER [*ignoring her*]: 'Bout what me and Willy Harris was talking about last night.

RUTH [*immediately—a refrain*]: Willy Harris is a good-for-nothing loudmouth.

WALTER: Anybody who talks to me has got to be a good-for-nothing loudmouth, ain't he? And what you know about who is just a good-for-nothing loudmouth? Charlie Atkins was just a "good-for-nothing loudmouth" too, wasn't he! When he wanted me to go in the dry-cleaning business with him. And now—he's grossing a hundred thousand a year. A hundred thousand dollars a year! You still call *him* a loudmouth!

RUTH [*bitterly*]: Oh, Walter Lee . . . [*She folds her head on her arms over the table.*]

WALTER [*rising and coming to her and standing over her*]: You tired, ain't you? Tired of everything. Me, the boy, the way we live—this beat-up hole—everything. Ain't you? [*She doesn't look up, doesn't answer.*] So tired—moaning and groaning all the time, but you wouldn't do nothing to help, would you? You couldn't be on my side that long for nothing, could you?

RUTH: Walter, please leave me alone.

WALTER: A man needs for a woman to back him up . . .

RUTH: Walter—

WALTER: Mama would listen to you. You know she listen to you more than she do me and Bennie. She think more of you. All you have to do is just sit down with her when you drinking your coffee one morning and talking 'bout things like you do and—[*He sits down beside her and demonstrates graphically what he thinks her methods and tone should be.*]—you just sip your coffee, see, and say easy like that you been thinking 'bout that deal Walter Lee is so interested in, 'bout the store and all, and sip some more coffee, like what you saying ain't really that important to you—And the next thing you know, she be listening good and asking you questions and when I come home—I can tell her the details. This ain't no fly-by-night proposition, baby. I mean we figured it out, me and Willy and Bobo.

RUTH [*with a frown*]: Bobo?

WALTER: Yeah. You see, this little liquor store we got in mind cost seventy-five thousand and we figured the initial investment on the place be 'bout thirty thousand, see. That be ten thousand each. Course, there's a couple of hundred you got to pay so's you don't spend your life just waiting for them clowns to let your license get approved—

RUTH: You mean graft?

WALTER [*frowning impatiently*]: Don't call it that. See there, that just goes to show you what women understand about the world. Baby, don't *nothing* happen for you in this world 'less you pay *somebody* off!

RUTH: Walter, leave me alone! [*She raises her head and stares at him vigorously— then says, more quietly.*] Eat your eggs, they gonna be cold.

WALTER [*straightening up from her and looking off*]: That's it. There you are. Man say to his woman: I got me a dream. His woman say: Eat your eggs. [*sadly, but gaining in power*] Man say: I got to take hold of this here world, baby! And a woman will say: Eat your eggs and go to work. [*passionately now*] Man say: I got to change my life, I'm choking to death, baby! And his woman say—[*in utter anguish as he brings his fists down on his thighs*]—Your eggs is getting cold!

RUTH [*softly*]: Walter, that ain't none of our money.

WALTER [*not listening at all or even looking at her*]: This morning, I was lookin' in the mirror and thinking about it . . . I'm thirty-five years old; I been married eleven years and I got a boy who sleeps in the living room—[*very, very quietly*]—and all I got to give him is stories about how rich white people live . . .

RUTH: Eat your eggs, Walter.

WALTER: *Damn my eggs . . . damn all the eggs that ever was!*

RUTH: Then go to work.

WALTER [*looking up at her*]: See—I'm trying to talk to you 'bout myself—[*shaking his head with the repetition*]—and all you can say is eat them eggs and go to work.

RUTH [*wearily*]: Honey, you never say nothing new. I listen to you every day, every night and every morning, and you never say nothing new. [*shrugging*] So you would rather *be* Mr. Arnold than be his chauffeur. So—I would *rather* be living in Buckingham Palace.

WALTER: That is just what is wrong with the colored woman in this world . . . Don't understand about building their men up and making 'em feel like they some-body. Like they can do something.

RUTH [*drily, but to hurt*]: There *are* colored men who do things.

WALTER: No thanks to the colored woman.

RUTH: Well, being a colored woman, I guess I can't help myself none. [*She rises and gets the ironing board and sets it up and attacks a huge pile of roughdried clothes, sprinkling them in preparation for the ironing and then rolling them into tight fat balls.*]

WALTER [*mumbling*]: We one group of men tied to a race of women with small minds.

[*His sister* BENEATHA *enters. She is about twenty, as slim and intense as her brother. She is not as pretty as her sister-in-law, but her lean, almost intellectual face has a handsomeness of its own. She wears a bright-red flannel nightie, and her thick hair stands wildly about her head. Her speech is a mixture of many things; it is different from the rest of the family's insofar as education has permeated her sense of English—and perhaps the Midwest rather than the South has finally—at last— won out in her inflection; but not altogether, because over all of it is a soft slurring and transformed use of vowels which is the decided influence of the South Side. She passes through the room without looking at either* RUTH *or* WALTER *and goes to the outside door and looks, a little blindly, out to the bathroom. She sees that it has been lost to the Johnsons. She closes the door with a sleepy vengeance and crosses to the table and sits down a little defeated.*]

BENEATHA: I am going to start timing those people.

WALTER: You should get up earlier.

BENEATHA [*her face in her hands; she is still fighting the urge to go back to bed*]: Really—would you suggest dawn? Where's the paper?

WALTER [*pushing the paper across the table to her as he studies her almost clinically, as though he has never seen her before*]: You a horrible-looking chick at this hour.

BENEATHA [*drily*]: Good morning, everybody.

WALTER [*senselessly*]: How is school coming?

BENEATHA [*in the same spirit*]: Lovely. Lovely. And you know, biology is the greatest. [*looking up at him*] I dissected something that looked just like you yesterday.

WALTER: I just wondered if you've made up your mind and everything.

BENEATHA [*gaining in sharpness and impatience*]: And what did I answer yesterday morning—and the day before that?

RUTH [*from the ironing board, like someone disinterested and old*]: Don't be so nasty, Bennie.

BENEATHA [*still to her brother*]: And the day before that and the day before that!

WALTER [*defensively*]: I'm interested in you. Something wrong with that? Ain't many girls who decide—

WALTER AND BENEATHA [*in unison*]: —"to be a doctor." [*silence*]

WALTER: Have we figured out yet just exactly how much medical school is going to cost?

RUTH: Walter Lee, why don't you leave that girl alone and get out of here to work?

BENEATHA [*exits to the bathroom and bangs on the door*]: Come on out of there, please! [*She comes back into the room.*]

WALTER [*looking at his sister intently*]: You know the check is coming tomorrow.

BENEATHA [*turning on him with a sharpness all her own*]: That money belongs to Mama, Walter and it's for her to decide how she wants to use it. I don't care if she wants to buy a house or a rocket ship or just nail it up somewhere and look at it. It's hers. Not ours—hers.

WALTER [*bitterly*]: Now ain't that fine! You just got your mother's interest at heart, ain't you, girl? You such a nice girl—but if Mama got that money she can always take a few thousand and help you through school too—can't she?

BENEATHA: I have never asked anyone around here to do anything for me!

WALTER: No! And the line between asking and just accepting when the time comes is big and wide—ain't it!

BENEATHA [*with fury*]: What do you want from me, Brother—that I quit school or just drop dead, which!

WALTER: I don't want nothing but for you to stop acting holy 'round here. Me and Ruth done made some sacrifices for you—why can't you do something for the family?

RUTH: Walter, don't be dragging me in it.

WALTER: You are in it—Don't you get up and go work in somebody's kitchen for the last three years to help put clothes on her back?

RUTH: Oh, Walter—that's not fair . . .

WALTER: It ain't that nobody expects you to get on your knees and say thank you, Brother; thank you, Ruth; thank you, Mama—and thank you, Travis, for wearing the same pair of shoes for two semesters—

BENEATHA [*dropping to her knees*]: Well—I do—all right?—thank everybody . . . and forgive me for ever wanting to be anything at all . . . forgive me, forgive me!

RUTH: Please stop it! Your mama'll hear you.

WALTER: Who the hell told you you had to be a doctor? If you so crazy 'bout messing 'round with sick people—then go be a nurse like other women—or just get married and be quiet . . .

BENEATHA: Well—you finally got it said . . . It took you three years but you finally got it said. Walter, give up; leave me alone—it's Mama's money.

WALTER: *He was my father, too!*

BENEATHA: So what? He was mine, too—and Travis' grandfather—but the insurance money belongs to Mama. Picking on me is not going to make her give it to you to invest in any liquor stores—[*under breath, dropping into a chair*]—and I for one say, God bless Mama for that!

WALTER [*to* RUTH]: See—did you hear? Did you hear!

RUTH: Honey, please go to work.

WALTER: Nobody in this house is ever going to understand me.

BENEATHA: Because you're a nut.

WALTER: Who's a nut?

BENEATHA: You—you are a nut. Thee is mad, boy.

WALTER [*looking at his wife and his sister from the door, very sadly*]: The world's most backward race of people, and that's a fact.

BENEATHA [*turning slowly in her chair*]: And then there are all those prophets who would lead us out of the wilderness—[WALTER *slams out of the house.*]—into the swamps!

RUTH: Bennie, why you always gotta be pickin' on your brother? Can't you be a little sweeter sometimes? [*Door opens.* WALTER *walks in.*]

WALTER [*to* RUTH]: I need some money for carfare.

RUTH [*looks at him, then warms; teasing, but tenderly*]: Fifty cents? [*She goes to her bag and gets money.*] Here, take a taxi. [WALTER *exits.* MAMA *enters. She is a woman in her early sixties, full-bodied and strong. She is one of those women of a certain grace and beauty who wear it so unobtrusively that it takes a while to notice. Her dark-brown face is surrounded by the total whiteness of her hair, and, being a woman who has adjusted to many things in life and overcome many more, her face is full of strength. She has, we can see, wit and faith of a kind that keep her eyes lit and full of interest and expectancy. She is, in a word, a beautiful woman. Her bearing is perhaps most like the noble bearing of the*]

*women of the Hereros of Southwest Africa—rather as if she imagines that as she
walks she still bears a basket or a vessel upon her head. Her speech, on the
other hand, is as careless as her carriage is precise—she is inclined to slur
everything—but her voice is perhaps not so much quiet as simply soft.*]

MAMA: Who that 'round here slamming doors at this hour? [*She crosses through the
room, goes to the window, opens it, and brings in a feeble little plant growing
doggedly in a small pot on the window sill. She feels the dirt and puts it back
out.*]

RUTH: That was Walter Lee. He and Bennie was at it again.

MAMA: My children and they tempers. Lord, if this little old plant don't get more sun
that it's been getting it ain't never going to see spring again. [*She turns from
the window.*] What's the matter with you this morning, Ruth? You looks right
peaked. You aiming to iron all them things? Leave some for me. I'll get to 'em
this afternoon. Bennie honey, it's too drafty for you to be sitting 'round half
dressed. Where's your robe?

BENEATHA: In the cleaners.

MAMA: Well, go get mine and put it on.

BENEATHA: I'm not cold, Mama, honest.

MAMA: I know—but you so thin . . .

BENEATHA [*irritably*]: Mama, I'm not cold.

MAMA [*seeing the make-down bed as* TRAVIS *has left it*]: Lord have mercy, look at that
poor bed. Bless his heart—he tries, don't he? [*She moves to the bed* TRAVIS *has
sloppily made up.*]

RUTH: No—he don't half try at all 'cause he knows you going to come along behind
him and fix everything. That's just how come he don't know how to do nothing
right now—you done spoiled that boy so.

MAMA: Well—he's a little boy. Ain't supposed to know 'bout housekeeping. My
baby, that's what he is. What you fix for his breakfast this morning?

RUTH [*angrily*]: I feed my son, Lena!

MAMA: I ain't meddling—[*under breath, busy-bodyish*]: I just noticed all last week
he had cold cereal, and when it starts getting this chilly in the fall a child ought
to have some hot grits or something when he goes out in the cold—

RUTH [*furious*]: I gave him hot oats—is that all right!

MAMA: I ain't meddling. [*pause*] Put a lot of nice butter on it? [RUTH *shoots her an
angry look and does not reply.*] He likes lots of butter.

RUTH [*exasperated*]: Lena—

MAMA [*to* BENEATHA; MAMA *is inclined to wander conversationally sometimes*]: What
was you and your brother fussing 'bout this morning?

BENEATHA: It's not important, Mama. [*She gets up and goes to look out at the bathroom, which is apparently free, and she picks up her towels and rushes out.*]

MAMA: What was they fighting about?

RUTH: Now you know as well as I do.

MAMA [*shaking her head*]: Brother still worrying hisself sick about that money?

RUTH: You know he is.

MAMA: You had breakfast?

RUTH: Some coffee.

MAMA: Girl, you better start eating and looking after yourself better. You almost thin
as Travis.

RUTH: Lena—

MAMA: Uh-hunh?

RUTH: What are you going to do with it?

MAMA: Now don't you start, child. It's too early in the morning to be talking about money. It ain't Christian.

RUTH: It's just that he got his heart set on that store—

MAMA: You mean that liquor store that Willy Harris want him to invest in?

RUTH: Yes—

MAMA: We ain't no business people, Ruth. We just plain working folks.

RUTH: Ain't nobody business people till they go into business. Walter Lee say colored people ain't never going to start getting ahead till they start gambling on some different kinds of things in the world—investments and things.

MAMA: What done got into you, girl? Walter Lee done finally sold you on investing.

RUTH: No. Mama, something is happening between Walter and me. I don't know what it is—but he needs something—something I can't give him any more. He needs this chance, Lena.

MAMA [*frowning deeply*]: But liquor, honey—

RUTH: Well—like Walter say—I spec people going to always be drinking themselves some liquor.

MAMA: Well—whether they drinks it or not ain't none of my business. But whether I go into business selling it to 'em is, and I don't want that on my ledger this late in life. [*stopping suddenly and studying her daughter-in-law*] Ruth Younger, what's the matter with you today? You look like you could fall over right there.

RUTH: I'm tired.

MAMA: Then you better stay home from work today.

RUTH: I can't stay home. She'd be calling up the agency and screaming at them, "My girl didn't come in today—send me somebody! My girl didn't come in!" Oh, she just have a fit . . .

MAMA: Well, let her have it. I'll just call her up and say you got the flu—

RUTH [*laughing*]: Why the flu?

MAMA: 'Cause it sounds respectable to 'em. Something white people get, too. They know 'bout the flu. Otherwise they think you been cut up or something when you tell 'em you sick.

RUTH: I got to go in. We need the money.

MAMA: Somebody would of thought my children done all but starved to death the way they talk about money here late. Child, we got a great big old check coming tomorrow.

RUTH [*sincerely, but also self-righteously*]: Now that's your money. It ain't got nothing to do with me. We all feel like that—Walter and Bennie and me—even Travis.

MAMA [*thoughtfully, and suddenly very far away*]: Ten thousand dollars—

RUTH: Sure is wonderful.

MAMA: Ten thousand dollars.

RUTH: You know what you should do, Miss Lena? You should take yourself a trip somewhere. To Europe or South America or someplace—

MAMA [*throwing up her hands at the thought*]: Oh, child!

RUTH: I'm serious. Just pack up and leave! Go on away and enjoy yourself some. Forget about the family and have yourself a ball for once in your life—

MAMA [*drily*]: You sound like I'm just about ready to die. Who'd go with me? What I look like wandering 'round Europe by myself?

RUTH: Shoot—these here rich white women do it all the time. They don't think nothing of packing up they suitcases and piling on one of them big steamships and—swoosh!—they gone, child.

MAMA: Something always told me I wasn't no rich white woman.

RUTH: Well—what are you going to do with it then?

MAMA: I ain't rightly decided. [*Thinking. She speaks now with emphasis.*] Some of it got to be put away for Beneatha and her schoolin'—and ain't nothing going to touch that part of it. Nothing. [*She waits several seconds, trying to make up her mind about something, and looks at* RUTH *little tentatively before going on.*] Been thinking that we maybe could meet the notes on a little old two-story somewhere, with a yard where Travis could play in the summertime, if we use part of the insurance for a down payment and everybody kind of pitch in. I could maybe take on a little day work again, few days a week—

RUTH [*studying her mother-in-law furtively and concentrating on her ironing, anxious to encourage without seeming to*]: Well, Lord knows, we've put enough rent into this here rat trap to pay for four houses by now . . .

MAMA [*looking up at the words "rat trap" and then looking around and leaning back and sighing—in a suddenly reflective mood*]: "Rat trap"—yes, that's all it is. [*smiling*] I remember just as well the day me and Big Walter moved in here. Hadn't been married but two weeks and wasn't planning on living here no more than a year. [*She shakes her head at the dissolved dream.*] We was going to set away, little by little, don't you know, and buy a little place out in Morgan Park. We had even picked out the house. [*chuckling a little*] Looks right dumpy today. But Lord, child, you should know all the dreams I had 'bout buying that house and fixing it up and making me a little garden in the back—[*She waits and stops smiling.*] And didn't none of it happen [*dropping her hands in a futile gesture*].

RUTH [*keeps her head down, ironing*]: Yes, life can be a barrel of disappointments, sometimes.

MAMA: Honey, Big Walter would come in here some nights back then and slump down on that couch there and just look at the rug, and look at me and look at the rug and then back at me—and I'd know he was down then . . . really down. [*After a second very long and thoughtful pause; she is seeing back to times that only she can see.*] And then, Lord, when I lost that baby—little Claude—I almost thought I was going to lose Big Walter too. Oh, that man grieved hisself! He was one man to love his children.

RUTH: Ain't nothin' can tear at you like losin' your baby.

MAMA: I guess that's how come that man finally worked hisself to death like he done. Likely he was fighting his own war with this here world that took his baby from him.

RUTH: He sure was a fine man, all right. I always liked Mr. Younger.

MAMA: Crazy 'bout his children! God knows there was plenty wrong with Walter Younger—hard-headed, mean, kind of wild with women—plenty wrong with him. But he sure loved his children. Always wanted them to have something— be something. That's where Brother gets all these notions, I reckon. Big Walter used to say, he'd get right wet in the eyes sometimes, lean his head back with the water standing in his eyes and say, "Seem like God didn't see fit to give the black man nothing but dreams—but He did give us children to make them dreams seem worth while." [*She smiles.*] He could talk like that, don't you know.

RUTH: Yes, he sure could. He was a good man, Mr. Younger.

MAMA: Yes, a fine man—just couldn't never catch up with his dreams, that's all. [BENEATHA *comes in, brushing her hair and looking up to the ceiling, where the sound of a vacuum cleaner has started up.*]

BENEATHA: What could be so dirty on that woman's rugs that she has to vacuum them every single day?

RUTH: I wish certain young women 'round here who I could name would take inspiration about certain rugs in a certain apartment I could also mention.

BENEATHA [*shrugging*]: How much cleaning can a house need, for Christ's sakes?

MAMA [*not liking the Lord's name used thus*]: Bennie!

RUTH: Just listen to her—just listen!

BENEATHA: Oh, God!

MAMA: If you use the Lord's name just one more time—

BENEATHA [*a bit of a whine*]: Oh, Mama—

RUTH: Fresh—just fresh as salt, this girl!

BENEATHA [*drily*]: Well—if the salt loses its savor—

MAMA: Now that will do. I just ain't going to have you 'round here reciting the scriptures in vain—you hear me?

BENEATHA: How did I manage to get on everybody's wrong side by just walking into a room?

RUTH: If you weren't so fresh—

BENEATHA: Ruth, I'm twenty years old.

MAMA: What time you be home from school today?

BENEATHA: Kind of late. [*with enthusiasm*] Madeline is going to start my guitar lessons today. [MAMA *and* RUTH *look up with the same expression.*]

MAMA: Your *what* kind of lessons?

BENEATHA: Guitar.

RUTH: Oh, Father!

MAMA: How come you done taken it in your mind to learn to play the guitar?

BENEATHA: I just want to, that's all.

MAMA [*smiling*]: Lord, child, don't you know what to do with yourself? How long it going to be before you get tired of this now—like you got tired of that little play-acting group you joined last year? [*looking at* RUTH] And what was it the year before that?

RUTH: The horseback-riding club for which she bought that fifty-five-dollar riding habit that's been hanging in the closet ever since!

MAMA [*to* BENEATHA]: Why you got to flit so from one thing to another, baby?

BENEATHA [*sharply*]: I just want to learn to play the guitar. Is there anything wrong with that?

MAMA: Ain't nobody trying to stop you. I just wonders sometimes why you has to flit so from one thing to another all the time. You ain't never done nothing with all that camera equipment you brought home—

BENEATHA: I don't flit! I—I experiment with different forms of expression—

RUTH: Like riding a horse?

BENEATHA: —People have to express themselves one way or another.

MAMA: What is it you want to express?

BENEATHA [*angrily*]: Me! [MAMA *and* RUTH *look at each other and burst into raucous laughter*] Don't worry—I don't expect you to understand.

MAMA [*to change the subject*]: Who you going out with tomorrow night?

BENEATHA [*with displeasure*]: George Murchison again.

MAMA [*pleased*]: Oh—you getting a little sweet on him?

RUTH: You ask me, this child ain't sweet on nobody but herself—[*under breath*] Express herself! [*They laugh.*]

BENEATHA: Oh—I like George all right, Mama. I mean I like him enough to go out with him and stuff, but—

RUTH [*for devilment*]: What does and stuff mean?

BENEATHA: Mind your own business.

MAMA: Stop picking at her now, Ruth. [*a thoughtful pause, and then a suspicious sudden look at her daughter as she turns in her chair for emphasis*] What does it mean?

BENEATHA [*wearily*]: Oh, I just mean I couldn't ever really be serious about George. He's—he's so shallow.

RUTH: Shallow—what do you mean he's shallow? He's *Rich!*

MAMA: Hush, Ruth.

BENEATHA: I know he's rich. He knows he's rich, too.

RUTH: Well—what other qualities a man got to have to satisfy you, little girl?

BENEATHA: You wouldn't even begin to understand. Anybody who married Walter could not possibly understand.

MAMA [*outraged*]: What kind of way is that to talk about your brother?

BENEATHA: Brother is a flip—let's face it.

MAMA [*to* RUTH, *helplessly*]: What's a flip?

RUTH [*glad to add kindling*]: She's saying he's crazy.

BENEATHA: Not crazy. Brother isn't really crazy yet—he—he's an elaborate neurotic.

MAMA· Hush your mouth!

BENEATHA: As for George. Well. George looks good—he's got a beautiful car and he takes me to nice places and, as my sister-in-law says, he is probably the richest boy I will ever get to know and I even like him sometimes—but if the Youngers are sitting around waiting to see if their little Bennie is going to tie up the family with the Murchisons, they are wasting their time.

RUTH: You mean you wouldn't marry George Murchison if he asked you someday? That pretty, rich thing? Honey, I knew you was odd—

BENEATHA: No I would not marry him if all I felt for him was what I feel now. Besides, George's family wouldn't really like it.

MAMA: Why not?

BENEATHA: Oh, Mama—The Murchisons are honest-to-God-real-*live*-rich colored people, and the only people in the world who are more snobbish than rich white people are rich colored people. I thought everybody knew that. I've met Mrs. Murchison. She's a scene!

MAMA: You must not dislike people 'cause they well off, honey.

BENEATHA: Why not? It makes just as much sense as disliking people 'cause they are poor, and lots of people do that.

RUTH [*a wisdom-of-the-ages manner; to* MAMA]: Well, she'll get over some of this—

BENEATHA: Get over it? What are you talking about, Ruth? Listen, I'm going to be a doctor. I'm not worried about who I'm going to marry yet—if I ever get married.

MAMA AND RUTH: *If!*

MAMA: Now, Bennie—

BENEATHA: Oh, I probably will . . . but first I'm going to be a doctor, and George, for one, still thinks that's pretty funny. I couldn't be bothered with that. I am going to be a doctor and everybody around here better understand that!

MAMA [*kindly*]: 'Course you going to be a doctor, honey, God willing.

BENEATHA [*drily*]: God hasn't got a thing to do with it.

MAMA: Beneatha—that just wasn't necessary.

BENEATHA: Well—neither is God. I get sick of hearing about God.

MAMA: Beneatha!

BENEATHA: I mean it! I'm just tired of hearing about God all the time. What has He got to do with anything? Does he pay tuition?

MAMA: You 'bout to get your fresh little jaw slapped!

RUTH: That's just what she needs, all right!

BENEATHA: Why? Why can't I say what I want to around here, like everybody else?

MAMA: It don't sound nice for a young girl to say things like that—you wasn't brought up that way. Me and your father went to trouble to get you and Brother to church every Sunday.

BENEATHA: Mama, you don't understand. It's all a matter of ideas, and God is just one idea I don't accept. It's not important. I am not going out and be immoral or commit crimes because I don't believe in God. I don't even think about it. It's just that I get tired of Him getting credit for all the things the human race achieves through its own stubborn effort. There simply is no blasted God—there is only man and it is he who makes miracles! [MAMA *absorbs this speech, studies her daughter and rises slowly and crosses to* BENEATHA *and slaps her powerfully across the face. After, there is only silence and the daughter drops her eyes from her mother's face, and* MAMA *is very tall before her.*]

MAMA: Now—you say after me, in my mother's house there is still God. [*There is a long pause and* BENEATHA *stares at the floor wordlessly.* MAMA *repeats the phrase with precision and cool emotion.*] In my mother's house there is still God.

BENEATHA: In my mother's house there is still God [*a long pause*].

MAMA [*walking away from* BENEATHA, *too disturbed for triumphant posture; stopping and turning back to her daughter*]: There are some ideas we ain't going to have in this house. Not long as I am at the head of this family.

BENEATHA: Yes, ma'am. [MAMA *walks out of the room.*]

RUTH [*almost gently, with profound understanding*]: You think you a woman, Bennie—but you still a little girl. What you did was childish—so you got treated like a child.

BENEATHA: I see. [*quietly*] I also see that everybody thinks it's all right for Mama to be a tyrant. But all the tyranny in the world will never put a God in the heavens! [*She picks up her books and goes out.*]

RUTH [*goes to* MAMA's *door*]: She said she was sorry.

MAMA [*coming out, going to her plant*]: They frightens me, Ruth. My children.

RUTH: You got good children, Lena. They just a little off sometimes—but they're good.

MAMA: No—There's something come down between me and them that don't let us understand each other and I don't know what it is. One done almost lost his mind thinking 'bout money all the time and the other done commence to talk about things I can't seem to understand in no form or fashion. What is it that's changing, Ruth?

RUTH [*soothingly, older than her years*]: Now . . . you taking it all too seriously. You just got strong-willed children and it takes a strong woman like you to keep 'em in hand.

MAMA [*looking at her plant and sprinkling a little water on it*]: They spirited all right, my children. Got to admit they got spirit—Bennie and Walter. Like this little old plant that ain't never had enough sunshine or nothing—and look at it . . . [*She has her back to* RUTH, *who has had to stop ironing and lean against something and put the back of her hand to her forehead.*]

RUTH [*trying to keep* MAMA *from noticing*]: You . . . sure . . . loves that little old thing, don't you? . . .

MAMA: Well, I always wanted me a garden like I used to see sometimes at the back of the houses down home. This plant is close as I ever got to having one. [*She looks out of the window as she replaces the plant.*] Lord, ain't nothing as dreary as the view from this window on a dreary day, is there? Why ain't you singing this morning, Ruth? Sing that "No Ways Tired." That song always lifts me up so—[*She turns at last to see that* RUTH *has slipped quietly into a chair, in a state of semiconsciousness.*] Ruth! Ruth honey—what's the matter with you . . . Ruth!

CURTAIN

SCENE 2

It is the following morning; a Saturday morning, and house cleaning is in progress at the Youngers. Furniture has been shoved hither and yon and MAMA *is giving the kitchen-area walls a washing down.* BENEATHA, *in dungarees, with a handkerchief tied around her face, is spraying insecticide into the cracks in the walls. As they work, the radio is on and a South Side disk jockey program is inappropriately filling the house with a rather exotic saxophone blues.* TRAVIS, *the sole idle one, is leaning on his arms, looking out of the window.*

TRAVIS: Grandmama, that stuff Bennie is using smells awful. Can I go downstairs, please?

MAMA: Did you get all them chores done already? I ain't seen you doing much.

TRAVIS: Yes'm—finished early. Where did Mama go this morning?

MAMA [*looking at* BENEATHA]: She had to go on a little errand.

TRAVIS: Where?

MAMA: To tend to her business.

TRAVIS: Can I go outside then?

MAMA: Oh, I guess so. You better stay right in front of the house, though . . . and keep a good lookout for the postman.

TRAVIS: Yes'm. [*He starts out and decides to give his* AUNT BENEATHA *a good swat on the legs as he passes her*] Leave them poor little old cockroaches alone, they ain't bothering you none. [*He runs as she swings the spray gun at him both viciously and playfully.* WALTER *enters from the bedroom and goes to the phone.*]

MAMA: Look out there, girl, before you be spilling some of that stuff on that child!

TRAVIS [*teasing*]: That's right—look out now! [*He exits.*]

BENEATHA [*drily*]: I can't imagine that it would hurt him—it has never hurt the roaches.

MAMA: Well, little boys' hides ain't as tough as South Side roaches.

WALTER [*into phone*]: Hello—Let me talk to Willy Harris.

MAMA: You better get over there behind the bureau. I seen one marching out of there like Napoleon yesterday.

WALTER: Hello, Willy? It ain't come yet. It'll be here in a few minutes. Did the lawyer give you the papers?

BENEATHA: There's really only one way to get rid of them, Mama—

MAMA: How?

BENEATHA: Set fire to this building.

WALTER: Good. Good. I'll be right over.

BENEATHA: Where did Ruth go, Walter?

WALTER: I don't know. [*He exits abruptly.*]

BENEATHA: Mama, where did Ruth go?

MAMA [*looking at her with meaning*]: To the doctor, I think.

BENEATHA: The doctor? What's the matter? [*They exchange glances.*] You don't think—

MAMA [*with her sense of drama*]: Now I ain't saying what I think. But I ain't never been wrong 'bout a woman neither. [*The phone rings.*]

BENEATHA [*at the phone*]: Hay-lo . . . [*pause, and a moment of recognition*] Well— when did you get back! . . . And how was it? . . . Of course I've missed you— in my way . . . This morning? No . . . house cleaning and all that and Mama hates it if I let people come over when the house is like this . . . You *have?* Well, that's different . . . What is it—Oh, what the hell, come on over . . . Right, see you then. [*She hangs up.*]

MAMA [*who has listened vigorously, as is her habit*]: Who is that you inviting over here with this house looking like this? You ain't got the pride you was born with!

BENEATHA: Asagai doesn't care how houses look, Mama—he's an intellectual.

MAMA: *Who?*

BENEATHA: Asagai—Joseph Asagai. He's an African boy I met on campus. He's been studying in Canada all summer.

MAMA: What's his name?

BENEATHA: Asagai, Joseph. Ah-sah-guy . . . He's from Nigeria.

MAMA: Oh, that's the little country that was founded by slaves way back . . .

BENEATHA: No, Mama—that's Liberia.

MAMA: I don't think I never met no African before.

BENEATHA: Well, do me a favor and don't ask him a whole lot of ignorant questions about Africans. I mean, do they wear clothes and all that—

MAMA: Well, now, I guess if you think we so ignorant 'round here maybe you shouldn't bring your friends here—

BENEATHA: It's just that people ask such crazy things. All anyone seems to know about when it comes to Africa is Tarzan—

MAMA [*indignantly*]: Why should I know anything about Africa?

BENEATHA: Why do you give money at church for the missionary work?

MAMA: Well, that's to help save people.

BENEATHA: You mean save them from *heathenism*—

MAMA [*innocently*]: Yes.

BENEATHA: I'm afraid they need more salvation from the British and the French. [RUTH *comes in forlornly and pulls off her coat with dejection. They both turn to look at her.*]

RUTH [*dispiritedly*]: Well, I guess from all the happy faces—everybody knows.

BENEATHA: You pregnant?

MAMA: Lord have mercy, I sure hope it's a little old girl. Travis ought to have a sister [BENEATHA *and* RUTH *give her a hopeless look for this grandmotherly enthusiasm*].

BENEATHA: How far along are you?

RUTH: Two months.

BENEATHA: Did you mean to? I mean did you plan it or was it an accident?

MAMA: What do you know about planning or not planning?

BENEATHA: Oh, Mama.

RUTH [*wearily*]: She's twenty years old, Lena.

BENEATHA: Did you plan it, Ruth?

RUTH: Mind your own business.

BENEATHA: It is my business—where is he going to live, on the roof? [*There is silence following the remark as the three women react to the sense of it.*] Gee— I didn't mean that, Ruth, honest. Gee, I don't feel like that at all. I—I think it is wonderful.

RUTH [*dully*]: Wonderful.

BENEATHA: Yes—really.

MAMA [*looking at* RUTH, *worried*]: Doctor say everything going to be all right?

RUTH [*far away*]: Yes—she says everything is going to be fine . . .

MAMA [*immediately suspicious*]: "She"—What doctor you went to? [RUTH *folds over, near hysteria.*]

MAMA [*worriedly hovering over* RUTH]: Ruth, honey—what's the matter with you—you sick? [RUTH *has her fists clenched on her thighs and is fighting hard to suppress a scream that seems to be rising in her.*]

BENEATHA: What's the matter with her, Mama?

MAMA [*working her fingers in* RUTH*'s shoulder to relax her*]: She be all right. Women gets right depressed sometimes when they get her way. [*speaking softly, expertly, rapidly*] Now you just relax. That's right . . . just lean back, don't think 'bout nothing at all . . . nothing at all—

RUTH: I'm all right . . . [*The glassy-eyed look melts and then she collapses into a fit of heavy sobbing. The bell rings.*]

BENEATHA: Oh, my God—that must be Asagai.

MAMA [*to* RUTH]: Come on now, honey. You need to lie down and rest awhile . . . then have some nice hot food. [*They exit,* RUTH*'s weight on her mother-in-law.* BENEATHA, *herself profoundly disturbed, opens the door to admit a rather dramatic-looking young man with a large package.*]

ASAGAI: Hello, Alaiyo—

BENEATHA [*holding the door open and regarding him with pleasure*]: Hello . . . [*long pause*] Well—come in. And please excuse everything. My mother was very upset about my letting anyone come here with the place like this.

ASAGAI [*coming into the room*]: You look disturbed too . . . Is something wrong?

BENEATHA [*still at the door, absently*]: Yes . . . we've all got acute ghetto-itus. [*She smiles and comes toward him, finding a cigarette and sitting.*] So—sit down! How was Canada?

ASAGAI [*a sophisticate*]: Canadian.

BENEATHA [*looking at him*]: I'm very glad you are back.

ASAGAI [*looking back at her in turn*]: Are you really?

BENEATHA: Yes—very.

ASAGAI: Why—you were quite glad when I went away. What happened?

BENEATHA: You went away.

ASAGAI: Ahhhhhhhh.

BENEATHA: Before—you wanted to be so serious before there was time.

ASAGAI: How much time must there be before one knows what one feels?

BENEATHA [*stalling this particular conversation; her hands pressed together, in a deliberately childish gesture*]: What did you bring me?

ASAGAI [*handing her the package*]: Open it and see.

BENEATHA [*eagerly opening the package and drawing out some records and the colorful robes of a Nigerian woman*]: Oh, Asagai! . . . You got them for me! . . . How beautiful . . . and the records too! [*She lifts out the robes and runs to the mirror with them and holds the drapery up in front of herself.*]

ASAGAI [*coming to her at the mirror*]: I shall have to teach you how to drape it properly. [*He flings the material about her for the moment and stands back to look at her.*] Ah—Oh-pay-gay-day, oh-gbah-mu-shay. [*a Yoruba exclamation for admiration*] You wear it well . . . very well . . . mutilated hair and all.

BENEATHA [*turning suddenly*]: My hair—what's wrong with my hair?

ASAGAI [*shrugging*]: Were you born with it like that?

BENEATHA [*reaching up to touch it*]: No . . . of course not. [*She looks back to the mirror, disturbed.*]

ASAGAI [*smiling*]: How then?

BENEATHA: You know perfectly well how . . . as crinkly as yours . . . that's how.

ASAGAI: And it is ugly to you that way?

BENEATHA [*quickly*]: Oh, no—not ugly . . . [*more slowly, apologetically*] But it's so hard to manage when it's, well—raw.

ASAGAI: And so to accommodate that—you mutilate it every week?

BENEATHA: It's not mutilation!

ASAGAI [*laughing aloud at her seriousness*]: Oh . . . please! I am only teasing you because you are so very serious about these things. [*He stands back from her and folds his arms across his chest as he watches her pulling at her hair and frowning in the mirror.*] Do you remember the first time you met me at school? . . . [*He laughs.*] You came up to me and said—and I thought you were the most serious little thing I had ever seen—you said: [*He imitates her.*] "Mr. Asagai—I want very much to talk with you. About Africa. You see, Mr. Asagai, I am looking for my *identity!*" [*He laughs.*]

BENEATHA [*turning to him, not laughing*]: Yes—[*Her face is quizzical, profoundly disturbed.*]

ASAGAI [*still teasing and reaching out and taking her face in his hands and turning her profile to him*]: Well . . . it is true that this is not so much a profile of a Hollywood queen as perhaps a queen of the Nile—[*a mock dismissal of the importance of the question*] But what does it matter? Assimilationism is so popular in your country.

BENEATHA [*wheeling, passionately, sharply*]: I am not an assimilationist!

ASAGAI [*the protest hangs in the room for a moment and ASAGAI studies her, his laughter fading*]: Such a serious one. [*There is a pause.*] So—you like the robes? You must take excellent care of them—they are from my sister's personal wardrobe.

BENEATHA [*with incredulity*]: You—you sent all the way home—for me?

ASAGAI [*with charm*]: For you—I would do much more . . . Well, that is what I came for. I must go.

BENEATHA: Will you call me Monday?

ASAGAI: Yes . . . We have a great deal to talk about. I mean about identity and time and all that.

BENEATHA: Time?

ASAGAI: Yes. About how much time one needs to know what one feels.

BENEATHA: You never understood that there is more than one kind of feeling which can exist between a man and a woman—or, at least, there should be.

ASAGAI [*shaking his head negatively but gently*]: No. Between a man and a woman there need be only one kind of feeling. I have that for you . . . Now even . . . right this moment . . .

BENEATHA: I know—and by itself—it won't do. I can find that anywhere.

ASAGAI: For a woman it should be enough.

BENEATHA: I know—because that's what it says in all the novels that men write. But it isn't. Go ahead and laugh—but I'm not interested in being someone's little episode in America or—[*with feminine vengeance*]—one of them! [ASAGAI *has burst into laughter again.*] That's funny as hell, huh!

ASAGAI: It's just that every American girl I have known has said that to me. White—black—in this you are all the same. And the same speech, too!

BENEATHA [*angrily*]: Yuk, yuk, yuk!

ASAGAI: It's how you can be sure that the world's most liberated women are not liberated at all. You all talk about it too much! [MAMA *enters and is immediately all social charm because of the presence of a guest.*]

BENEATHA: Oh—Mama—this is Mr. Asagai.

MAMA: How do you do?

ASAGAI [*total politeness to an elder*]: How do you do, Mrs. Younger. Please forgive me for coming at such an outrageous hour on a Saturday.

MAMA: Well, you are quite welcome. I just hope you understand that our house don't always look like this. [*chatterish*] You must come again. I would love to hear all about—[*not sure of the name*]—your country. I think it's so sad the way our American Negroes don't know nothing about Africa 'cept Tarzan and all that. And all that money they pour into these churches when they ought to be helping you people over there drive out them French and Englishmen done taken away your land. [*The mother flashes a slightly superior look at her daughter upon completion of the recitation.*]

ASAGAI [*taken aback by this sudden and acutely unrelated expression of sympathy*]: Yes . . . yes . . .

MAMA [*smiling at him suddenly and relaxing and looking him over*]: How many miles is it from here to where you come from?

ASAGAI: Many thousands.

MAMA [*looking at him as she would* WALTER]: I bet you don't half look after yourself, being away from your mama either. I spec you better come 'round here from time to time and get yourself some decent home-cooked meals . . .

ASAGAI [*moved*]: Thank you. Thank you very much. [*They are all quiet, then—*] Well . . . I must go. I will call you Monday, Alaiyo.

MAMA: What's that he call you?

ASAGAI: Oh—"Alaiyo." I hope you don't mind. It is what you would call a nickname, I think. It is a Yoruba word. I am a Yoruba.

MAMA [*looking at* BENEATHA]: I—I thought he was from—

ASAGAI [*understanding*]: Nigeria is my country. Yoruba is my tribal origin—

BENEATHA: You didn't tell us what Alaiyo means . . . for all I know, you might be calling me Little Idiot or something . . .

ASAGAI: Well . . . let me see . . . I do not know how just to explain it . . . The sense of a thing can be so different when it changes languages.

BENEATHA: You're evading.

ASAGAI: No—really it is difficult . . . [*thinking*] It means . . . it means One for Whom Bread—Food—Is Not Enough. [*He looks at her.*] Is that all right?

BENEATHA [*understanding, softly*]: Thank you.

MAMA [*looking from one to the other and not understanding any of it*]: Well . . . that's nice . . . You must come see us again—Mr.—

ASAGAI: Ah-sah-guy . . .

MAMA: Yes . . . Do come again.

ASAGAI: Good-bye. [*He exits.*]

MAMA [*after him*]: Lord, that's a pretty thing just went out here! [*insinuatingly, to her daughter*] Yes, I guess I see why we done commence to get so interested in Africa 'round here. Missionaries my aunt Jenny! [*She exits.*]

BENEATHA: Oh, Mama! . . . [*She picks up the Nigerian dress and holds it up to her in front of the mirror again. She sets the headdress on haphazardly and then notices her hair again and clutches at it and then replaces the headdress and frowns at herself. Then she starts to wriggle in front of the mirror as she thinks a Nigerian woman might.* TRAVIS *enters and regards her.*]

TRAVIS: You cracking up?

BENEATHA: Shut up. [*She pulls the headdress off and looks at herself in the mirror and clutches at her hair again and squinches her eyes as if trying to imagine something. Then, suddenly, she gets her raincoat and kerchief and hurriedly prepares for going out.*]

MAMA [*coming back into the room*]: She's resting now. Travis, baby, run next door and ask Miss Johnson to please let me have a little kitchen cleanser. This here can is empty as Jacob's kettle.

TRAVIS: I just came in.

MAMA: Do as you told. [*He exits and she looks at her daughter.*] Where you going?

BENEATHA [*halting at the door*]: To become a queen of the Nile! [*She exits in a breathless blaze of glory.* RUTH *appears in the bedroom doorway.*]

MAMA: Who told you to get up?

RUTH: Ain't nothing wrong with me to be lying in no bed for. Where did Bennie go?

MAMA [*drumming her fingers*]: Far as I could make out—to Egypt. [RUTH *just looks at her.*] What time is it getting to?

RUTH: Ten twenty. And the mailman going to ring that bell this morning just like he done every morning for the last umpteen years. [TRAVIS *comes in with the cleanser can.*]

TRAVIS: She say to tell you that she don't have much.

MAMA [*angrily*]: Lord, some people I could name sure is tight-fisted! [*directing her grandson*] Mark two cans of cleanser down on the list there. If she that hard up for kitchen cleanser, I sure don't want to forget to get her none!

RUTH: Lena—maybe the woman is just short on cleanser—

MAMA [*not listening*]: —Much baking powder as she done borrowed from me all these years, she could of done gone into the baking business! [*The bell sounds suddenly and sharply and all three are stunned—serious and silent— mid-speech. In spite of all the other conversation and distractions of the morning, this is what they have been waiting for, even* TRAVIS, *who looks helplessly from his mother to his grandmother.* RUTH *is the first to come to life again.*]

RUTH [*to* TRAVIS]: Get down them steps, boy! [TRAVIS *snaps to life and flies out to get the mail.*]

MAMA [*her eyes wide, her hand to her breast*]: You mean it done really come?

RUTH [*excited*]: Oh, Miss Lena!

MAMA [*collecting herself*]: Well . . . I don't know what we all so excited about 'round here for. We known it was coming for months.

RUTH: That's a whole lot different from having it come and being able to hold it in your hands . . . a piece of paper worth ten thousand dollars . . . [TRAVIS *bursts back into the room. He holds the envelope high above his head, like a little dancer, his face is radiant and he is breathless. He moves to his grandmother with sudden slow ceremony and puts the envelope into her hands. She accepts it, and then merely holds it and looks at it.*] Come on! Open it . . . Lord have mercy, I wish Walter Lee was here!

TRAVIS: Open it, Grandmama!

MAMA [*staring at it*]: Now you all be quiet. It's just a check.

RUTH: Open it . . .

MAMA [*still staring at it*]: Now don't act silly . . . We ain't never been no people to act silly 'bout no money—

RUTH [*swiftly*]: We ain't never had none before—*open it!* [MAMA *finally makes a good strong tear and pulls out the thin blue slice of paper and inspects it closely. The boy and his mother study it raptly over* MAMA's *shoulders.*]

MAMA: Travis! [*She is counting off with doubt.*] Is that the right number of zeros?

TRAVIS: Yes'm . . . ten thousand dollars. Gaalee, Grandmama, you rich.

MAMA [*She holds the check away from her, still looking at it. Slowly her face sobers into a mask of unhappiness.*]: Ten thousand dollars. [*She hands it to* RUTH.] Put it away somewhere, Ruth. [*She does not look at* RUTH; *her eyes seem to be seeing something somewhere very far off.*] Ten thousand dollars they give you. Ten thousand dollars.

TRAVIS [*to his mother, sincerely*]: What's the matter with Grandmama—don't she want to be rich?

RUTH [*distractedly*]: You go on out and play now, baby. [TRAVIS *exits.* MAMA *starts wiping dishes absently, humming intently to herself.* RUTH *turns to her, with kind exasperation.*] You've gone and got yourself upset.

MAMA [*not looking at her*]: I spec if it wasn't for you all . . . I would just put that money away or give it to the church or something.

RUTH: Now what kind of talk is that. Mr. Younger would just be plain mad if he could hear you talking foolish like that.

MAMA [*stopping and staring off*]: Yes . . . he sure would. [*sighing*] We got enough to do with that money, all right. [*She halts then, and turns and looks at her daughter-in-law hard;* RUTH *avoids her eyes and* MAMA *wipes her hands with finality and starts to speak firmly to* RUTH.] Where did you go today, girl?

RUTH: To the doctor.

MAMA [*impatiently*]: Now, Ruth . . . you know better than that. Old Doctor Jones is strange enough in his way but there ain't nothing 'bout him make somebody slip and call him "she"—like you done this morning.

RUTH: Well, that's what happened—my tongue slipped.

MAMA: You went to see that woman, didn't you?

RUTH [*defensively, giving herself away*]: What woman you talking about?

MAMA [*angrily*]: That woman who— [WALTER *enters in great excitement.*]

WALTER: Did it come?

MAMA [*quietly*]: Can't you give people a Christian greeting before you start asking about money?

WALTER [*to* RUTH]: Did it come? [RUTH *unfolds the check and lays it quietly before him, watching him intently with thoughts of her own.* WALTER *sits down and grasps it close and counts off the zeros.*] Ten thousand dollars—[*He turns suddenly, frantically to his mother and draws some papers out of his breast pocket.*] Mama—look. Old Willy Harris put everything on paper—

MAMA: Son—I think you ought to talk to your wife . . . I'll go on out and leave you alone if you want—

WALTER: I can talk to her later—Mama, look—

MAMA: Son—

WALTER: WILL SOMEBODY PLEASE LISTEN TO ME TODAY!

MAMA [*quietly*]: I don't 'low no yellin' in this house, Walter Lee, and you know it— [WALTER *stares at them in frustration and starts to speak several times.*] And there ain't going to be no investing in no liquor stores. I don't aim to have to speak on that again [*a long pause*].

WALTER: Oh—so you don't aim to have to speak on that again? So you have decided . . . [*crumpling his papers*] Well, *you* tell that to my boy tonight when you put him to sleep on the living-room couch . . . [*turning to* MAMA *and speaking*

directly to her]: Yeah—and tell it to my wife, Mama, tomorrow when she has
to go out of here to look after somebody else's kids. And tell it to *me,* Mama,
every time we need a new pair of curtains and I have to watch *you* go out and
work in somebody's kitchen. Yeah, you tell me then! [WALTER *starts out.*]

RUTH: Where you going?

WALTER: I'm going out!

RUTH: Where?

WALTER: Just out of this house somewhere—

RUTH [*getting her coat*]: I'll come too.

WALTER: I don't want you to come!

RUTH: I got something to talk to you about, Walter.

WALTER: That's too bad.

MAMA [*still quietly*]: Walter Lee—[*She waits and he finally turns and looks at her.*] Sit
   down.

WALTER: I'm a grown man, Mama.

MAMA: Ain't nobody said you wasn't grown. But you still in my house and my presence. And as long as you are—you'll talk to your wife civil. Now sit down.

RUTH [*suddenly*]: Oh, let him go on out and drink himself to death! He makes me
   sick to my stomach! [*She flings her coat against him.*]

WALTER [*violently*]: And you turn mine, too, baby! [RUTH *goes into their bedroom and
   slams the door behind her.*] That was my greatest mistake—

MAMA [*still quietly*]: Walter, what is the matter with you?

WALTER: Matter with me? Ain't nothing the matter with *me!*

MAMA: Yes there is. Something eating you up like a crazy man. Something more
   than me not giving you this money. The past few years I been watching it happen to you. You get all nervous acting and kind of wild in the eyes—[WALTER
   jumps up impatiently at her words.] I said sit there now, I'm talking to you!

WALTER: Mama—I don't need no nagging at me today.

MAMA: Seem like you getting to a place where you always tied up in some kind of
   knot about something. But if anybody ask you 'bout it you just yell at 'em and
   bust out the house and go out and drink somewheres. Walter Lee, people can't
   live with that. Ruth's a good, patient girl in her way—but you getting to be too
   much. Boy, don't make the mistake of driving that girl away from you.

WALTER: Why—what she do for me?

MAMA: She loves you.

WALTER: Mama—I'm going out. I want to go off somewhere and be by myself for a
   while.

MAMA: I'm sorry 'bout your liquor store, son. It just wasn't the thing for us to do.
   That's what I want to tell you about—

WALTER: I got to go out, Mama—[*He rises.*]

MAMA: It's dangerous, son.

WALTER: What's dangerous?

MAMA: When a man goes outside his home to look for peace.

WALTER [*beseechingly*]: Then why can't there never be no peace in this house then?

MAMA: You done found it in some other house?

WALTER: No—there ain't no woman! Why do women always think there's a woman
   somewhere when a man gets restless. [*coming to her*] Mama—Mama—I want
   so many things . . .

MAMA: Yes, son—

WALTER: I want so many things that they are driving me kind of crazy . . . Mama—
   look at me.

MAMA: I'm looking at you. You a good-looking boy. You got a job, a nice wife, a fine boy and—

WALTER: A job. [*looks at her*] Mama, a job? I open and close car doors all day long. I drive a man around in his limousine and I say, "Yes, sir; no, sir; very good, sir; shall I take the Drive, sir?" Mama, that ain't no kind of job . . . that ain't nothing at all. [*very quietly*] Mama, I don't know if I can make you understand.

MAMA: Understand what, baby?

WALTER [*quietly*]: Sometimes it's like I can see the future stretched out in front of me—just plain as day. The future, Mama. Hanging over there at the edge of my days. Just waiting for me—a big, looming blank space—full of *nothing*. Just waiting for *me*. [*pause*] Mama—sometimes when I'm down-town and I pass them cool, quiet-looking restaurants where them white boys are sitting back and talking 'bout things . . . sitting there turning deals worth millions of dollars . . . sometimes I see guys don't look much older than me—

MAMA: Son—how come you talk so much 'bout money?

WALTER [*with immense passion*]: Because it is life, Mama!

MAMA [*quietly*]: Oh—[*very quietly*] So now it's life. Money is life. Once upon a time freedom used to be life—now it's money. I guess the world really do change . . .

WALTER: No—it was always money, Mama. We just didn't know about it.

MAMA: No . . . something has changed. [*She looks at him.*] You something new, boy. In my time we was worried about not being lynched and getting to the North if we could and how to stay alive and still have a pinch of dignity too . . . Now here come you and Beneatha—talking 'bout things we ain't never even thought about hardly, me and your daddy. You ain't satisfied or proud of nothing we done. I mean that you had a home; that we kept you out of trouble till you was grown; that you don't have to ride to work on the back of nobody's streetcar—You my children—but how different we done become.

WALTER: You just don't understand, Mama, you just don't understand.

MAMA: Son—do you know your wife is expecting another baby? [WALTER *stands, stunned, and absorbs what his mother has said.*] That's what she wanted to talk to you about. [WALTER *sinks down into a chair.*] This ain't for me to be telling—but you ought to know. [*She waits*] I think Ruth is thinking 'bout getting rid of that child.

WALTER [*slowly understanding*]: No—no—Ruth wouldn't do that.

MAMA: When the world gets ugly enough—a woman will do anything for her family. *The part that's already living.*

WALTER: You don't know Ruth, Mama, if you think she would do that. [RUTH *opens the bedroom door and stands there a little limp.*]

RUTH [*beaten*]: Yes I would too, Walter, [*pause*] I gave her a five-dollar down payment. [*There is total silence as the man stares at his wife and the mother stares at her son.*]

MAMA [*presently*]: Well—[*tightly*] Well—son, I'm waiting to hear you say something . . . I'm waiting to hear how you be your father's son. Be the man he was . . . [*pause*] Your wife say she going to destroy your child. And I'm waiting to hear you talk like him and say we a people who give children life, not who destroys them—[*She rises.*] I'm waiting to see you stand up and look like your daddy and say we done give up one baby to poverty and that we ain't going to give up nary another one . . . I'm waiting.

WALTER: Ruth—

MAMA: If you a son of mine, tell her! [WALTER *turns, looks at her and can say nothing. She continues, bitterly.*] You . . . you are a disgrace to your father's memory. Somebody get me my hat.

CURTAIN

ACT II

SCENE 1

TIME: *Later the same day.*

AT RISE: RUTH *is ironing again. She has the radio going. Presently* BENEATHA'*s bedroom door opens and* RUTH'*s mouth falls and she puts down the iron in fascination.*

RUTH: What have we got on tonight!

BENEATHA [*emerging grandly from the doorway so that we can see her thoroughly robed in the costume* ASAGAI *brought*]: You are looking at what a well-dressed Nigerian woman wears—[*She parades for* RUTH, *her hair completely hidden by the headdress; she is coquettishly fanning herself with an ornate oriental fan, mistakenly more like Butterfly than any Nigerian that ever was.*] Isn't it beautiful? [*She promenades to the radio and, with an arrogant flourish, turns off the good loud blues that is playing.*] Enough of this assimilationist junk! [RUTH *follows her with her eyes as she goes to the phonograph and puts on a record and turns and waits ceremoniously for the music to come up. Then with a shout*—] OCOMOGOSIAY! [RUTH *jumps. The music comes up, a lovely Nigerian melody.* BENEATHA *listens, enraptured, her eyes far away—"back to the past." She begins to dance.* RUTH *is dumbfounded.*]

RUTH: What kind of dance is that?

BENEATHA: A folk dance.

RUTH [*Pearl Bailey*]: What kind of folks do that, honey?

BENEATHA: It's from Nigeria. It's a dance of welcome.

RUTH: Who you welcoming?

BENEATHA: The men back to the village.

RUTH: Where they been?

BENEATHA: How should I know—out hunting or something. Anyway, they are coming back now. . . .

RUTH: Well, that's good.

BENEATHA [*with the record*]: Alundi, alundi
    Alundi alunya
    Jop pu a jeepua
    Ang gu soooooooooo
    Ai yai yae . . .
    Ayehaye—alundi . . .

[WALTER *comes in during this performance; he has obviously been drinking. He leans against the door heavily and watches his sister, at first with distaste. Then his eyes look off—"back to the past"—as he lifts both his fists to the roof, screaming.*]

WALTER: YEAH . . . AND ETHIOPIA STRETCH FORTH HER HANDS AGAIN! . . .

RUTH [*drily, looking at him*]: Yes—and Africa sure is claiming her own tonight. [*She gives them both up and starts ironing again.*]

WALTER [*all in a drunken, dramatic shout*]: Shut up! . . . I'm digging them drums . . . them drums move me! . . . [*He makes his weaving way to his wife's face and leans in close to her.*] In my heart of hearts—[*He thumps his chest.*]—I am much warrior!

RUTH [*without even looking up*]: In your heart of hearts you are much drunkard.

WALTER [*coming away from her and starting to wander around the room, shouting*]: Me and Jomo . . . [*Intently, in his sister's face. She has stopped dancing to watch him in this unknown mood.*] That's my man, Kenyatta. [*Shouting and thumping his chest.*] FLAMING SPEAR! HOT DAMN! [*He is suddenly in possession of an imaginary spear and actively spearing enemies all over the room.*] OCOMOGOSIAY . . . THE LION IS WAKING . . . OWIMOWEH! [*He pulls his shirt open and leaps up on a table and gestures with his spear. The bell rings. RUTH goes to answer.*]

BENEATHA [*to encourage WALTER, thoroughly caught up with this side of him*]: OCO-MOGOSIAY, FLAMING SPEAR!

WALTER [*On the table, very far gone, his eyes pure glass sheets. He sees what we cannot, that he is a leader of his people, a great chief, a descendant of Chaka, and that the hour to march has come.*]: Listen, my black brothers—

BENEATHA: OCOMOGOSIAY!

WALTER: —Do you hear the waters rushing against the shores of the coast-lands—

BENEATHA: OCOMOGOSIAY!

WALTER: —Do you hear the screeching of the cocks in yonder hills beyond where the chiefs meet in council for the coming of the mighty war—

BENEATHA: OCOMOGOSIAY!

WALTER: —Do you hear the beating of the wings of the birds flying low over the mountains and the low places of our land—[RUTH *opens the door,* GEORGE MURCHISON *enters.*]

BENEATHA: OCOMOGOSIAY!

WALTER: —Do you hear the singing of the women, singing the war songs of our fathers to the babies in the great houses . . . singing the sweet war songs? OH, DO YOU HEAR, MY BLACK BROTHERS?

BENEATHA [*completely gone*]: We hear you, Flaming Spear—

WALTER: Telling us to prepare for the greatness of the time—[*to* GEORGE] Black Brother! [*He extends his hand for the fraternal clasp.*]

GEORGE: Black Brother, hell!

RUTH [*having had enough, and embarrassed for the family*]: Beneatha, you got company—what's the matter with you? Walter Lee Younger, get down off that table and stop acting like a fool . . . [WALTER *comes down off the table suddenly and makes a quick exit to the bathroom.*]

RUTH: He's had a little to drink . . . I don't know what her excuse is.

GEORGE [*to* BENEATHA]: Look honey, we're going *to* the theatre—we're not going to be *in* it . . . so go change, huh?

RUTH: You expect this boy to go out with you looking like that?

BENEATHA [*looking at* GEORGE]: That's up to George. If he's ashamed of his heritage—

GEORGE: Oh, don't be so proud of yourself, Bennie—just because you look eccentric.

BENEATHA: How can something that's natural be eccentric?

GEORGE: That's what being eccentric means—being natural. Get dressed.

BENEATHA: I don't like that, George.

RUTH: Why must you and your brother make an argument out of everything people say?

BENEATHA: Because I hate assimilationist Negroes!

RUTH: Will somebody please tell me what assimila-who-ever means!

GEORGE: Oh, it's just a college girl's way of calling people Uncle Toms—but that isn't what it means at all.

RUTH: Well, what does it mean?

BENEATHA [*cutting* GEORGE *off and staring at him as she replies to* RUTH]: It means someone who is willing to give up his own culture and submerge himself completely in the dominant, and in this case, *oppressive* culture!

GEORGE: Oh, dear, dear, dear! Here we go! A lecture on the African past! On our Great West African Heritage! In one second we will hear all about the great Ashanti empires; the great Songhay civilizations; and the great sculpture of Benin—and then some poetry in the Bantu—and the whole monologue will end with the word *heritage!* [*nastily*] Let's face it, baby, your heritage is nothing but a bunch of raggedy-assed spirituals and some grass huts!

BENEATHA: *Grass huts!* [RUTH *crosses to her and forcibly pushes her toward the bedroom.*] See there . . . you are standing there in your splendid ignorance talking about people who were the first to smelt iron on the face of the earth! [RUTH *is pushing her through the door.*] The Ashanti were performing surgical operations when the English—[RUTH *pulls the door to, with* BENEATHA *on the other side, and smiles graciously at* GEORGE. BENEATHA *opens the door and shouts the end of the sentence defiantly at* GEORGE.]—were still tattooing themselves with blue dragons . . . [*She goes back inside.*]

RUTH: Have a seat, George. [*They both sit.* RUTH *folds her hands rather primly on her lap, determined to demonstrate the civilization of the family.*] Warm, ain't it? I mean for September. [*pause*] Just like they always say about Chicago weather: If it's too hot or cold for you, just wait a minute and it'll change. [*She smiles happily at this cliché of clichés.*] Everybody say it's got to do with them bombs and things they keep setting off. [*pause*] Would you like a nice cold beer?

GEORGE: No, thank you. I don't care for beer. [*He looks at his watch.*] I hope she hurries up.

RUTH: What time is the show?

GEORGE: It's an eight-thirty curtain. That's just Chicago, though. In New York standard curtain time is eight forty. [*He is rather proud of this knowledge.*]

RUTH [*properly appreciating it*]: You get to New York a lot?

GEORGE [*offhand*]: Few times a year.

RUTH: Oh—that's nice. I've never been to New York. [WALTER *enters. We feel he has relieved himself, but the edge of unreality is still with him.*]

WALTER: New York ain't got nothing Chicago ain't. Just a bunch of hustling people all squeezed up together—being "Eastern." [*He turns his face into a screw of displeasure.*]

GEORGE: Oh—you've been?

WALTER: Plenty of times.

RUTH [*shocked at the lie*]: Walter Lee Younger!

WALTER [*staring her down*]: Plenty! [*pause*] What we got to drink in this house? Why don't you offer this man some refreshment. [*to* GEORGE] They don't know how to entertain people in this house, man.

GEORGE: Thank you—I don't really care for anything.

WALTER [*feeling his head; sobriety coming*]: Where's Mama?

RUTH: She ain't come back yet.

WALTER [*looking* MURCHISON *over from head to toe, scrutinizing his carefully casual tweed sports jacket over cashmere V-neck sweater over soft eyelet shirt and tie, and soft slacks, finished off with white buckskin shoes*]: Why all you college boys wear them fairyish-looking white shoes?

RUTH: Walter Lee! [GEORGE MURCHISON *ignores the remark.*]

WALTER [*to* RUTH]: Well, they look crazy as hell—white shoes, cold as it is.

RUTH [*crushed*]: You have to excuse him—

WALTER: No he don't! Excuse me for what? What you always excusing me for! I'll excuse myself when I needs to be excused! [*a pause*] They look as funny as them black knee socks Beneatha wears out of here all the time.

RUTH: It's the college *style*, Walter.

WALTER: Style, hell. She looks like she got burnt legs or something!

RUTH: Oh, Walter—

WALTER [*an irritable mimic*]: Oh, Walter! Oh, Walter! [*to* MURCHISON] How's your old man making out? I understand you all going to buy that big hotel on the Drive?[1] [*He finds a beer in the refrigerator, wanders over to* MURCHISON, *sipping and wiping his lips with the back of his hand, and straddling a chair backwards to talk to the other man.*] Shrewd move. Your old man is all right, man. [*tapping his head and half winking for emphasis*] I mean he knows how to operate. I mean he thinks big, you know what I mean, I mean for a home,[2] you know? But I think he's kind of running out of ideas now. I'd like to talk to him. Listen, man, I got some plans that could turn this city upside down. I mean I think like he does. *Big.* Invest big, gamble big, hell, lose *big* if you have to, you know what I mean. It's hard to find a man on this whole Southside who understands my kind of thinking—you dig? [*He scrutinizes* MURCHISON *again, drinks his beer, squints his eyes and leans in close, confidential, man to man.*] Me and you ought to sit down and talk sometimes, man. Man, I got me some ideas . . .

MURCHISON [*with boredom*]: Yeah—sometimes we'll have to do that, Walter.

WALTER [*understanding the indifference, and offended*]: Yeah—well, when you get the time, man. I know you a busy little boy.

RUTH: Walter, please—

WALTER [*bitterly, hurt*]: I know ain't nothing in this world as busy as you colored college boys with your fraternity pins and white shoes . . .

RUTH [*covering her face with humiliation*]: Oh, Walter Lee—

WALTER: I see you all all the time—with the books tucked under your arms—going to your [*British A—a mimic*] "clahsses." And for what! What the hell you learning over there? Filling up your heads—[*counting off on his fingers*]—with the sociology and the psychology—but they teaching you how to be a man? How to take over and run the world? They teaching you how to run a rubber plantation or a steel mill? Naw—just to talk proper and read books and wear white shoes . . .

GEORGE [*looking at him with distaste, a little above it all*]: You're all wacked up with bitterness, man.

WALTER [*intently, almost quietly, between the teeth, glaring at the boy*]: And you—ain't you bitter, man? Ain't you just about had it yet? Don't you see no stars gleaming that you can't reach out and grab? You happy?—You contented son-of-a-bitch—you happy? You got it made? Bitter? Man, I'm a volcano. Bitter? Here I am a giant—surrounded by ants! Ants who can't even understand what it is the giant is talking about.

RUTH [*passionately and suddenly*]: Oh, Walter—ain't you with nobody!

---

[1]**Drive** Chicago's Outer Drive running along Lake Michigan.   [2]**Home** home-boy; one of us.

WALTER [*violently*]: No! 'Cause ain't nobody with me! Not even my own mother!

RUTH: Walter, that's a terrible thing to say! [BENEATHA *enters, dressed for the evening in a cocktail dress and earrings.*]

GEORGE: Well—hey, you look great.

BENEATHA: Let's go, George. See you all later.

RUTH: Have a nice time.

GEORGE: Thanks. Good night. [*to* WALTER, *sarcastically*] Good night, *Prometheus.* [BENEATHA *and* GEORGE *exit.*]

WALTER [*to* RUTH]: Who is Prometheus?

RUTH: I don't know. Don't worry about it.

WALTER [*in fury, pointing after* GEORGE]: See there—they get to a point where they can't insult you man to man—they got to go talk about something ain't nobody never heard of!

RUTH: How do you know it was an insult? [*to humor him*] Maybe Prometheus is a nice fellow.

WALTER: Prometheus! I bet there ain't even no such thing! I bet that simple-minded clown—

RUTH: Walter—[*She stops what she is doing and looks at him.*]

WALTER [*yelling*]: Don't start!

RUTH: Start what?

WALTER: Your nagging! Where was I? Who was I with? How much money did I spend?

RUTH [*plaintively*]: Walter Lee—why don't we just try to talk about it . . .

WALTER [*not listening*]: I been out talking with people who understand me. People who care about the things I got on my mind.

RUTH [*wearily*]: I guess that means people like Willy Harris.

WALTER: Yes, people like Willy Harris.

RUTH [*with a sudden flash of impatience*]: Why don't you all just hurry up and go into the banking business and stop talking about it!

WALTER: Why? You want to know why? 'Cause we all tied up in a race of people that don't know how to do nothing but moan, pray and have babies! [*The line is too bitter even for him and he looks at her and sits down.*]

RUTH: Oh, Walter . . . [*softly*] Honey, why can't you stop fighting me?

WALTER [*without thinking*]: Who's fighting you? Who even cares about you? [*This line begins the retardation of his mood.*]

RUTH: Well—[*She waits a long time, and then with resignation starts to put away her things.*] I guess I might as well go on to bed . . . [*more or less to herself*] I don't know where we lost it . . . but we have . . . [*Then, to him.*] I—I'm sorry about this new baby, Walter. I guess maybe I better go on and do what I started . . . I guess I just didn't realize how bad things was with us . . . I guess I just didn't really realize—[*She starts out to the bedroom and stops.*] You want some hot milk?

WALTER: Hot milk?

RUTH: Yes—hot milk.

WALTER: Why hot milk?

RUTH: 'Cause after all that liquor you come home with you ought to have something hot in your stomach.

WALTER: I don't want no milk.

RUTH: You want some coffee then?

WALTER: No, I don't want no coffee. I don't want nothing hot to drink. [*almost plaintively*] Why you always trying to give me something to eat?

RUTH [*standing and looking at him helplessly*]: What else can I give you, Walter Lee
   Younger? [*She stands and looks at him and presently turns to go out again. He
   lifts his head and watches her going away from him in a new mood which began to emerge when he asked her, "Who cares about you?"*]

WALTER: It's been rough, ain't it, baby? [*She hears and stops but does not turn around
   and he continues to her back.*] I guess between two people there ain't never as
   much understood as folks generally thinks there is. I mean like between me
   and you—[*She turns to face him.*] How we gets to the place where we scared
   to talk softness to each other. [*He waits, thinking hard himself.*] Why you think
   it got to be like that? [*He is thoughtful, almost as a child would be.*] Ruth, what
   is it gets into people ought to be close?

RUTH: I don't know, honey. I think about it a lot.

WALTER: On account of you and me, you mean? The way things are with us. The
   way something done come down between us.

RUTH: There ain't so much between us, Walter . . . Not when you come to me and
   try to talk to me. Try to be with me . . . a little even.

WALTER [*total honesty*]: Sometimes . . . sometimes . . . I don't even know how to try.

RUTH: Walter—

WALTER: Yes?

RUTH [*coming to him, gently and with misgiving, but coming to him*]: Honey . . . life
   don't have to be like this. I mean sometimes people can do things so
   that things are better . . . You remember how we used to talk when Travis was
   born . . . about the way we were going to live . . . the kind of house . . . [*She
   is stroking his head.*] Well, it's all starting to slip away from us . . . [MAMA *enters,
   and* WALTER *jumps up and shouts at her.*]

WALTER: Mama, where have you been?

MAMA: My—them steps is longer than they used to be. Whew! [*She sits down and
   ignores him.*] How you feeling this evening, Ruth? [RUTH *shrugs, disturbed some
   at having been prematurely interrupted and watching her husband knowingly.*]

WALTER: Mama, where have you been all day?

MAMA [*still ignoring him and leaning on the table and changing to more comfortable shoes*]: Where's Travis?

RUTH: I let him go out earlier and he ain't come back yet. Boy, is he going to
   get it!

WALTER: Mama!

MAMA [*as if she has heard him for the first time*]: Yes, son?

WALTER: Where did you go this afternoon?

MAMA: I went downtown to tend to some business that I had to tend to.

WALTER: What kind of business?

MAMA: You know better than to question me like a child, Brother.

WALTER [*rising and bending over the table*]: Where were you, Mama? [*bringing his
   fists down and shouting*] Mama, you didn't go do something with that insurance money, something crazy? [*The front door opens slowly, interrupting him,
   and* TRAVIS *peeks his head in, less than hopefully.*]

TRAVIS [*to his mother*]: Mama, I—

RUTH: "Mama I" nothing! You're going to get it, boy! Get on in that bedroom and
   get yourself ready!

TRAVIS: But I—

MAMA: Why don't you all never let the child explain hisself.

RUTH: Keep out of it now, Lena. [MAMA *clamps her lips together, and* RUTH *advances
   toward her son menacingly.*]

RUTH: A thousand times I have told you not to go off like that—

MAMA [*holding out her arms to her grandson*]: Well—at least let me tell him something. I want him to be the first one to hear . . . Come here, Travis. [*the boy obeys, gladly*] Travis—[*She takes him by the shoulder and looks into his face.*]—you know that money we got in the mail this morning?

TRAVIS: Yes'm—

MAMA: Well—what you think your grandmama gone and done with that money?

TRAVIS: I don't know, Grandmama.

MAMA [*putting her finger on his nose for emphasis*]: She went out and she bought you a house! [*The explosion comes from* WALTER *at the end of the revelation and he jumps up and turns away from all of them in a fury.* MAMA *continues, to* TRAVIS.] You glad about the house? It's going to be yours when you get to be a man.

TRAVIS: Yeah—I always wanted to live in a house.

MAMA: All right, gimme some sugar then—[TRAVIS *puts his arms around her neck as she watches her son over the boy's shoulder. Then, to* TRAVIS, *after the embrace.*] Now when you say your prayers tonight, you thank God and your grandfather—'cause it was him who give you the house—in his way.

RUTH [*taking the boy from* MAMA *and pushing him toward the bedroom*]: Now you get out of here and get ready for your beating.

TRAVIS: Aw, Mama—

RUTH: Get on in there—[*closing the door behind him and turning radiantly to her mother-in-law*] So you went and did it!

MAMA [*quietly, looking at her son with pain*]: Yes, I did.

RUTH [*raising both arms classically*]: *Praise God!* [*Looks at* WALTER *a moment, who says nothing. She crosses rapidly to her husband.*] Please, honey—let me be glad . . . you be glad too. [*She has laid her hands on his shoulders, but he shakes himself free of her roughly, without turning to face her.*] Oh, Walter . . . a home . . . *a home.* [*She comes back to* MAMA.] Well—where is it? How big is it? How much it going to cost?

MAMA: Well—

RUTH: When we moving?

MAMA [*smiling at her*]: First of the month.

RUTH [*throwing back her head with jubilance*]: *Praise God!*

MAMA [*tentatively, still looking at her son's back turned against her and* RUTH]: It's—it's a nice house too . . . [*She cannot help speaking directly to him. An imploring quality in her voice, her manner, makes her almost like a girl now.*] Three bedrooms—nice big one for you and Ruth . . . Me and Beneatha still have to share our room, but Travis have one of his own—and [*with difficulty*] I figure if the—new baby—is a boy, we could get one of them double-decker outfits . . . And there's a yard with a little patch of dirt where I could maybe get to grow me a few flowers . . . And a nice big basement . . .

RUTH: Walter honey, be glad—

MAMA [*still to his back, fingering things on the table*]: 'Course I don't want to make it sound fancier than it is . . . It's just a plain little old house—but it's made good and solid—and it will be *ours.* Walter Lee—it makes a difference in a man when he can walk on floors that belong to *him* . . .

RUTH: Where is it?

MAMA [*frightened at this telling*]: Well—well—it's out there in Clybourne Park—[RUTH'*s radiance fades abruptly, and* WALTER *finally turns slowly to face his mother with incredulity and hostility.*]

RUTH: Where?

MAMA [*matter-of-factly*]: Four o six Clybourne Street, Clybourne Park.

RUTH: Clybourne Park? Mama, there ain't no colored people living in Clybourne Park.

MAMA [*almost idiotically*]: Well, I guess there's going to be some now.

WALTER [*bitterly*]: So that's the peace and comfort you went out and bought for us today!

MAMA [*raising her eyes to meet his finally*]: Son—I just tried to find the nicest place for the least amount of money for my family.

RUTH [*trying to recover from the shock*]: Well—well—'course I ain't one never been 'fraid of no crackers, mind you—but—well, wasn't there no other houses nowhere?

MAMA: Them houses they put up for colored in them areas way out all seem to cost twice as much as other houses. I did the best I could.

RUTH [*struck senseless with the news, in its various degrees of goodness and trouble, she sits a moment, her fists propping her chin in thought, and then she starts to rise, bringing her fists down with vigor, the radiance spreading from cheek to cheek again*]: Well—well!—All I can say is—if this is my time in life—my time—to say good-bye—[*And she builds with momentum as she starts to circle the room with an exuberant, almost tearfully happy release*]—to these Goddamned cracking walls!—[*she pounds the walls*]—and these marching roaches—[*she wipes at an imaginary army of marching roaches*]—and this cramped little closet which ain't now or never was no kitchen! . . . then I say it loud and good, *Hallelujah! and good-bye misery I don't never want to see your ugly face again! [*She laughs joyously, having practically destroyed the apartment, and flings her arms up and lets them come down happily, slowly, reflectively, over her abdomen, aware for the first time perhaps that the life therein pulses with happiness and not despair.*] Lena?

MAMA [*moved, watching her happiness*]: Yes, honey?

RUTH [*looking off*]: Is there—is there a whole lot of sunlight?

MAMA [*understanding*]: Yes, child, there's a whole lot of sunlight [*long pause*].

RUTH [*collecting herself and going to the door of the room* TRAVIS *is in*]: Well—I guess I better see 'bout Travis. [*to* MAMA] Lord, I sure don't feel like whipping nobody today! [*She exits.*]

MAMA [*the mother and son are left alone now and the mother waits a long time, considering deeply, before she speaks*]: Son—you—you understand what I done, don't you? [WALTER *is silent and sullen.*] I—I just seen my family falling apart today . . . just falling to pieces in front of my eyes . . . We couldn't of gone on like we was today. We was going backwards 'stead of forwards—talking 'bout killing babies and wishing each other was dead . . . When it gets like that in life—you just got to do something different, push on out and do something bigger . . . [*She waits.*] I wish you say something, son . . . I wish you'd say how deep inside you you think I done the right thing—

WALTER [*crossing slowly to his bedroom door and finally turning there and speaking measuredly*]: What you need me to say you done right for? You the head of this family. You run our lives like you want to. It was your money and you did what you wanted with it. So what you need for me to say it was all right for? [*bitterly, to hurt her as deeply as he knows is possible*] So you butchered up a dream of mine—you—who always talking 'bout your children's dreams . . .

MAMA: Walter Lee—[*He just closes the door behind him.* MAMA *sits alone, thinking heavily.*]

CURTAIN

SCENE 2

TIME: *Friday night. A few weeks later.*

AT RISE: *Packing crates mark the intention of the family to move.* BENEATHA *and* GEORGE *come in, presumably from an evening out again.*

GEORGE: O.K. . . . O.K., whatever you say . . . [*They both sit on the couch. He tries to kiss her. She moves away.*] Look, we've had a nice evening; let's not spoil it, huh? . . . [*He again turns her head and tries to nuzzle in and she turns away from him, not with distaste but with momentary lack of interest; in a mood to pursue what they were talking about.*]

BENEATHA: I'm trying to talk to you.

GEORGE: We always talk.

BENEATHA: Yes—and I love to talk.

GEORGE [*exasperated; rising*]:   I know it and I don't mind it sometimes . . . I want you to cut it out, see—The moody stuff, I mean. I don't like it. You're a nice-looking girl . . . all over. That's all you need, honey, forget the atmosphere. Guys aren't going to go for the atmosphere—they're going to go for what they see. Be glad for that. Drop the Garbo routine. It doesn't go with you. As for myself, I want a nice—[*groping*]—simple [*thoughtfully*]—sophisticated girl . . . not a poet—O.K.? [*She rebuffs him again and he starts to leave.*]

BENEATHA: Why are you angry?

GEORGE: Because this is stupid! I don't go out with you to discuss the nature of "quiet desperation" or to hear all about your thoughts—because the world will go on thinking what it thinks regardless—

BENEATHA: Then why read books? Why go to school?

GEORGE [*with artificial patience, counting on his fingers*]:   It's simple. You read books—to learn facts—to get grades—to pass the course—to get a degree. That's all—it has nothing to do with thoughts [*a long pause*].

BENEATHA: I see. [*a longer pause as she looks at him*] Good night, George. [GEORGE *looks at her a little oddly, and starts to exit. He meets* MAMA *coming in.*]

GEORGE: Oh—hello, Mrs. Younger.

MAMA: Hello, George, how you feeling?

GEORGE: Fine—fine, how are you?

MAMA: Oh, a little tired. You know them steps can get you after a day's work. You all have a nice time tonight?

GEORGE: Yes—a fine time. Well, good night.

MAMA: Good night. [*He exits.* MAMA *closes the door behind her.*] Hello, honey. What you sitting like that for?

BENEATHA: I'm just sitting.

MAMA: Didn't you have a nice time?

BENEATHA: No.

MAMA: No? What's the matter?

BENEATHA: Mama, George is a fool—honest. [*She rises.*]

MAMA [*hustling around unloading the packages she has entered with; she stops*]:   Is he, baby?

BENEATHA: Yes. [BENEATHA *makes up* TRAVIS' *bed as she talks.*]

MAMA: You sure?

BENEATHA: Yes.

MAMA: Well—I guess you better not waste your time with no fools. [BENEATHA *looks up at her mother, watching her put groceries in the refrigerator. Finally she gathers up her things and starts into the bedroom. At the door she stops and looks back at her mother.*]

BENEATHA: Mama—

MAMA: Yes, baby—

BENEATHA: Thank you.

MAMA: For what?

BENEATHA: For understanding me this time. [*She exits quickly and the mother stands, smiling a little, looking at the place where* BENEATHA *had stood.* RUTH *enters.*]

RUTH: Now don't you fool with any of this stuff, Lena—

MAMA: Oh, I just thought I'd sort a few things out. [*The phone rings.* RUTH *answers.*]

RUTH [*at the phone*]: Hello—Just a minute. [*goes to door*] Walter, it's Mrs. Arnold. [*Waits. Goes back to the phone. Tense.*] Hello. Yes, this is his wife speaking . . . He's lying down now. Yes . . . well, he'll be in tomorrow. He's been very sick. Yes—I know we should have called, but we were so sure he'd be able to come in today. Yes—yes, I'm very sorry. Yes . . . Thank you very much. [*She hangs up.* WALTER *is standing in the doorway of the bedroom behind her.*] That was Mrs. Arnold.

WALTER [*indifferently*]: Was it?

RUTH: She said if you don't come in tomorrow that they are getting a new man . . .

WALTER: Ain't that sad—ain't that crying sad.

RUTH: She said Mr. Arnold has had to take a cab for three days . . . Walter, you ain't been to work for three days! [*This is a revelation to her.*] Where you been, Walter Lee Younger? [WALTER *looks at her and starts to laugh.*] You're going to lose your job.

WALTER: That's right . . .

RUTH: Oh, Walter, and with your mother working like a dog every day—

WALTER: That's sad too. Everything is sad.

MAMA: What you been doing for these three days, son?

WALTER: Mama—you don't know all the things a man what got leisure can find to do in this city . . . What's this—Friday night? Well—Wednesday I borrowed Willy Harris' car and I went for a drive . . . just me and myself and I drove and drove . . . Way out . . . way past South Chicago, and I parked the car and I sat and looked at the steel mills all day long. I just sat in the car and looked at them big black chimneys for hours. Then I drove back and I went to the Green Hat. [*pause*] And Thursday—Thursday I borrowed the car again and I got in it and I pointed it the other way and I drove the other way—for hours—way, way up to Wisconsin, and I looked at the farms. I just drove and looked at the farms. Then I drove back and I went to the Green Hat. [*pause*] And today—today I didn't get the car. Today I just walked. All over the Southside. And I looked at the Negroes and they looked at me and finally I just sat down on the curb at Thirty-ninth and South Parkway and I just sat there and watched the Negroes go by. And then I went to the Green Hat. You all sad? You all depressed? And you know where I am going right now—[RUTH *goes out quietly.*].

MAMA: Oh, Big Walter, is this the harvest of our days?

WALTER: You know what I like about the Green Hat? [*He turns the radio on and a steamy, deep blues pours into the room.*] I like this little cat they got there who blows a sax . . . He blows. He talks to me. He ain't but 'bout five feet tall and he's got a conked head and his eyes is always closed and he's all music—

MAMA [*rising and getting some papers out of her handbag*]: Walter—

WALTER: And there's this other guy who plays the piano . . . and they got a sound. I mean they can work on some music . . . They got the best little combo in the world in the Green Hat . . . You can just sit there and drink and listen to them three men play and you realize that don't nothing matter worth a damn, but just being there—

MAMA: I've helped do it to you, haven't I, son? Walter, I been wrong.

WALTER: Naw—you ain't never been wrong about nothing, Mama.

MAMA: Listen to me, now. I say I been wrong, son. That I been doing to you what the rest of the world been doing to you. [*She stops and he looks up slowly at her and she meets his eyes pleadingly.*] Walter—what you ain't understood is that I ain't got nothing, don't own nothing, ain't never really wanted nothing that wasn't for you. There ain't nothing as precious to me . . . There ain't nothing worth holding on to, money, dreams, nothing else—if it means—if it means it's going to destroy my boy. [*She puts her papers in front of him and he watches her without speaking or moving.*] I paid the man thirty-five hundred dollars down on the house. That leaves sixty-five hundred dollars. Monday morning I want you to take this money and take three thousand dollars and put it in a savings account for Beneatha's medical schooling. The rest you put in a checking account—with your name on it. And from now on any penny that come out of it or that go in it is for you to look after. For you to decide. [*She drops her hands a little helplessly.*] It ain't much, but it's all I got in the world and I'm putting it in your hands. I'm telling you to be the head of this family from now on like you supposed to be.

WALTER [*stares at the money*]: You trust me like that, Mama?

MAMA: I ain't never stop trusting you. Like I ain't never stop loving you. [*She goes out, and WALTER sits looking at the money on the table as the music continues in its idiom, pulsing in the room. Finally, in a decisive gesture, he gets up, and, in mingled joy and desperation, picks up the money. At the same moment, TRAVIS enters for bed.*]

TRAVIS: What's the matter, Daddy? You drunk?

WALTER [*sweetly, more sweetly than we have ever known him*]: No, Daddy ain't drunk. Daddy ain't going to never be drunk again. . . .

TRAVIS: Well, good night, Daddy. [*The father has come from behind the couch and leans over, embracing his son.*]

WALTER: Son, I feel like talking to you tonight.

TRAVIS: About what?

WALTER: Oh, about a lot of things. About you and what kind of man you going to be when you grow up. . . . Son—son, what do you want to be when you grow up?

TRAVIS: A bus driver.

WALTER [*laughing a little*]: A what? Man, that ain't nothing to want to be!

TRAVIS: Why not?

WALTER: 'Cause, man—it ain't big enough—you know what I mean.

TRAVIS: I don't know then. I can't make up my mind. Sometimes Mama asks me that too. And sometimes when I tell her I just want to be like you— she says she don't want me to be like that and sometimes she says she does . . .

WALTER [*gathering him up in his arms*]: You know what, Travis? In seven years you going to be seventeen years old. And things is going to be very different with us in seven years, Travis. . . . One day when you are seventeen I'll come home—home from my office downtown somewhere—

TRAVIS: You don't work in no office, Daddy.

WALTER: No—but after tonight. After what your daddy gonna do tonight, there's going to be offices—a whole lot of offices. . . .

TRAVIS: What you gonna do tonight, Daddy?

WALTER: You wouldn't understand yet, son, but your daddy's gonna make a transaction . . . a business transaction that's going to change our lives . . . That's how come one day when you 'bout seventeen years old I'll come home and I'll be pretty tired, you know what I mean, after a day of conferences and secretaries getting things wrong the way they do . . . 'cause an executive's life is hell, man—[*The more he talks the farther away he gets.*] And I'll pull the car up on the driveway . . . just a plain black Chrysler, I think, with white walls—no—black tires. More elegant. Rich people don't have to be flashy . . . though I'll have to get something a little sportier for Ruth—maybe a Cadillac convertible to do her shopping in. . . . And I'll come up the steps to the house and the gardener will be clipping away at the hedges and he'll say, "Good evening, Mr. Younger." And I'll say, "Hello, Jefferson, how are you this evening?" And I'll go inside and Ruth will come downstairs and meet me at the door and we'll kiss each other and she'll take my arm and we'll go up to your room to see you sitting on the floor with the catalogues of all the great schools in America around you. . . . All the great schools in the world! And—and I'll say, all right son—it's your seventeenth birthday, what is it you've decided? . . . Just tell me where you want to go to school and you'll go. Just tell me, what it is you want to be—and you'll be it. . . . Whatever you want to be—Yessir! [*He holds his arms open for* TRAVIS.] You just name it, son . . . [TRAVIS *leaps into them*] and I hand you the world! [WALTER'S *voice has risen in pitch and hysterical promise and on the last line he lifts* TRAVIS *high.*]

BLACKOUT

SCENE 3

TIME: *Saturday, moving day, one week later.*

Before the curtain rises, RUTH'S *voice, a strident, dramatic church alto, cuts through the silence.*

It is, in the darkness, a triumphant surge, a penetrating statement of expectation: "Oh, Lord, I don't feel no ways tired! Children, oh, glory hallelujah!"

As the curtain rises we see that RUTH *is alone in the living room, finishing up the family's packing. It is moving day. She is nailing crates and tying cartons.* BENEATHA *enters, carrying a guitar case, and watches her exuberant sister-in-law.*

RUTH: Hey!

BENEATHA [*putting away the case*]: Hi.

RUTH [*pointing at a package*]: Honey—look in that package there and see what I found on sale this morning at the South Center. [RUTH *gets up and moves to the package and draws out some curtains.*] Lookahere—hand-turned hems!

BENEATHA: How do you know the window size out there?

RUTH [*who hadn't thought of that*]: Oh—Well, they bound to fit something in the whole house. Anyhow, they was too good a bargain to pass up. [RUTH *slaps her head, suddenly remembering something.*] Oh, Bennie—I meant to put a special note on that carton over there. That's your mama's good china and she wants 'em to be very careful with it.

BENEATHA: I'll do it. [BENEATHA *finds a piece of paper and starts to draw large letters on it.*]

RUTH: You know what I'm going to do soon as I get in that new house?

BENEATHA: What?

RUTH: Honey—I'm going to run me a tub of water up to here . . . [*with her fingers practically up to her nostrils*] And I'm going to get in it—and I am going to sit . . . and sit . . . and sit in that hot water and the first person who knocks to tell *me* to hurry up and come out—

BENEATHA: Gets shot at sunrise.

RUTH [*laughing happily*]: You said it, sister! [*noticing how large* BENEATHA *is absent-mindedly making the note*] Honey, they ain't going to read that from no airplane.

BENEATHA [*laughing herself*]: I guess I always think things have more emphasis if they are big, somehow.

RUTH [*looking up at her and smiling*]: You and your brother seem to have that as a philosophy of life. Lord, that man—done changed so 'round here. You know— you know what we did last night? Me and Walter Lee?

BENEATHA: What?

RUTH [*smiling to herself*]: We went to the movies. [*looking at* BENEATHA *to see if she understands*] We went to the movies. You know the last time me and Walter went to the movies together?

BENEATHA: No.

RUTH: Me neither. That's how long it been. [*smiling again*] But we went last night. The picture wasn't much good, but that didn't seem to matter. We went—and we held hands.

BENEATHA: Oh, Lord!

RUTH: We held hands—and you know what?

BENEATHA: What?

RUTH: When we come out of the show it was late and dark and all the stores and things was closed up . . . and it was kind of chilly and there wasn't many people on the streets . . . and we was still holding hands, me and Walter.

BENEATHA: You're killing me. [WALTER *enters with a large package. His happiness is deep in him; he cannot keep still with his new-found exuberance. He is singing and wiggling and snapping his fingers. He puts his package in a corner and puts a phonograph record, which he has brought in with him, on the record player. As the music comes up he dances over to* RUTH *and tries to get her to dance with him. She gives in at last to his raunchiness and in a fit of giggling allows herself to be drawn into his mood and together they deliberately bur-lesque an old social dance of their youth.*]

BENEATHA [*regarding them a long time as they dance, then drawing in her breath for a deeply exaggerated comment which she does not particularly mean*]: Talk about—oldddddddddd—fashioneddddddd—Negroes!

WALTER [*stopping momentarily*]: What kind of Negroes? [*He says this in fun. He is not angry with her today, nor with anyone. He starts to dance with his wife again.*]

BENEATHA: Old-fashioned.

WALTER [*as he dances with* RUTH]: You know, when these *New Negroes* have their convention—[*pointing at his sister*]—that is going to be the chairman of the

Committee on Unending Agitation. [*He goes on dancing, then stops.*] Race, race, race! . . . Girl, I do believe you are the first person in the history of the entire human race to successfully brainwash yourself. [BENEATHA *breaks up and he goes on dancing. He stops again, enjoying his tease.*] Damn, even the N double A C P takes a holiday sometimes! [BENEATHA *and* RUTH *laugh. He dances with* RUTH *some more and starts to laugh and stops and pantomimes someone over an operating table.*] I can just see that chick someday looking down at some poor cat on an operating table before she starts to slice him, saying . . . [*pulling his sleeves back maliciously*] "By the way, what are your views on civil rights down there? . . ." [*He laughs at her again and starts to dance happily. The bell sounds.*]

BENEATHA: Sticks and stones may break my bones but . . . words will never hurt me! [BENEATHA *goes to the door and opens it as* WALTER *and* RUTH *go on with the clowning.* BENEATHA *is somewhat surprised to see a quiet-looking middle-aged white man in a business suit holding his hat and a briefcase in his hand and consulting a small piece of paper.*]

MAN: Uh—how do you do, miss. I am looking for a Mrs.—[*He looks at the slip of paper.*] Mrs. Lena Younger?

BENEATHA [*smoothing her hair with slight embarrassment*]: Oh—yes, that's my mother. Excuse me. [*She closes the door and turns to quiet the other two.*] Ruth! Brother! Somebody's here. [*Then she opens the door. The man casts a curious quick glance at all of them.*] Uh—come in please.

MAN [*coming in*]: Thank you.

BENEATHA: My mother isn't here just now. Is it business?

MAN: Yes . . . well, of a sort.

WALTER [*freely, the Man of the House*]: Have a seat. I'm Mrs. Younger's son. I look after most of her business matters. [RUTH *and* BENEATHA *exchange amused glances.*]

MAN [*regarding* WALTER, *and sitting*]: Well—My name is Karl Lindner . . .

WALTER [*stretching out his hand*]: Walter Younger. This is my wife—[RUTH *nods politely.*]—and my sister.

LINDNER: How do you do.

WALTER [*amiably, as he sits himself easily on a chair, leaning with interest forward on his knees and looking expectantly into the newcomer's face*]: What can we do for you, Mr. Lindner!

LINDNER [*some minor shuffling of the hat and briefcase on his knees*]: Well—I am a representative of the Clybourne Park Improvement Association—

WALTER [*pointing*]: Why don't you sit your things on the floor?

LINDNER: Oh—yes. Thank you. [*He slides the briefcase and hat under the chair.*] And as I was saying—I am from the Clybourne Park Improvement Association and we have had it brought to our attention at the last meeting that you people—or at least your mother—has bought a piece of residential property at—[*He digs for the slip of paper again.*]—four o six at Clybourne Street . . .

WALTER: That's right. Care for something to drink? Ruth, get Mr. Lindner a beer.

LINDNER [*upset for some reason*]: Oh—no, really, I mean thank you very much, but no thank you.

RUTH [*innocently*]: Some coffee?

LINDNER: Thank you, nothing at all. [BENEATHA *is watching the man carefully.*]

LINDNER: Well, I don't know how much you folks know about our organization. [*He is a gentle man; thoughtful and somewhat labored in his manner.*] It is one of these community organizations set up to look after—oh, you know, things like block upkeep and special projects and we also have what we call our New Neighbors Orientation Committee . . .

BENEATHA [*drily*]: Yes—and what do they do?

LINDNER [*turning a little to her and then returning the main force to* WALTER]: Well— it's what you might call a sort of welcoming committee, I guess. I mean they, we, I'm the chairman of the committee—go around and see the new people who move into the neighborhood and sort of give them the lowdown on the way we do things out in Clybourne Park.

BENEATHA [*with appreciation of the two meanings, which escape* RUTH *and* WALTER]: Uh-huh.

LINDNER: And we also have the category of what the association calls—[*He looks elsewhere.*]—uh—special community problems . . .

BENEATHA: Yes—and what are some of those?

WALTER: Girl, let the man talk.

LINDNER [*with understated relief*]: Thank you. I would sort of like to explain this thing in my own way. I mean I want to explain to you in a certain way.

WALTER: Go ahead.

LINDNER: Yes. Well. I'm going to try to get right to the point. I'm sure we'll all appreciate that in the long run.

BENEATHA: Yes.

WALTER: Be still now!

LINDNER: Well—

RUTH [*still innocently*]: Would you like another chair—you don't look comfortable.

LINDNER [*more frustrated than annoyed*]: No, thank you very much. Please. Well— to get right to the point I—[*a great breath, and he is off at last*] I am sure you people must be aware of some of the incidents which have happened in various parts of the city when colored people have moved into certain areas— [BENEATHA *exhales heavily and starts tossing a piece of fruit up and down in the air.*] Well—because we have what I think is going to be a unique type of organization in American community life—not only do we deplore that kind of thing—but we are trying to do something about it. [BENEATHA *stops tossing and turns with a new and quizzical interest to the man.*] We feel—[*gaining confidence in his mission because of the interest in the faces of the people he is talking to*]—we feel that most of the trouble in this world, when you come right down to it—[*He hits his knee for emphasis.*]—most of the trouble exists because people just don't sit down and talk to each other.

RUTH [*nodding as she might in church, pleased with the remark*]: You can say that again, mister.

LINDNER [*more encouraged by such affirmation*]: That we don't try hard enough in this world to understand the other fellow's problem. The other guy's point of view.

RUTH: Now that's right. [BENEATHA *and* WALTER *merely watch and listen with genuine interest.*]

LINDNER: Yes—that's the way we feel out in Clybourne Park. And that's why I was elected to come here this afternoon and talk to you people. Friendly like, you know, the way people should talk to each other and see if we couldn't find some way to work this thing out. As I say, the whole business is a matter of caring about the other fellow. Anybody can see that you are a nice family of folks, hard working and honest I'm sure. [BENEATHA *frowns slightly, quizzically, her head tilted regarding him.*] Today everybody knows what it means to be on the outside of *something*. And of course, there is always somebody who is out to take the advantage of people who don't always understand.

WALTER: What do you mean?

LINDNER: Well—you see our community is made of people who've worked hard as the dickens for years to build up that little community. They're not rich and fancy people; just hardworking, honest people who don't really have much but those little homes and a dream of the kind of community they want to raise their children in. Now, I don't say we are perfect and there is a lot wrong in some of the things they want. But you've got to admit that a man, right or wrong, has the right to want to have the neighborhood he lives in a certain kind of way. And at the moment the overwhelming major-ity of our people out there feel that people get along better, take more of a common interest in the life of the community, when they share a common background. I want you to believe me when I tell you that race prejudice simply doesn't enter into it. It is a matter of the people of Clybourne Park believing, rightly or wrongly, as I say, that for the happiness of all con-cerned that our Negro families are happier when they live in their *own* communities.

BENEATHA [*with a grand and bitter gesture*]: This, friends, is the Welcoming Committee!

WALTER [*dumbfounded, looking at* LINDNER]: Is this what you came marching all the way over here to tell us?

LINDNER: Well, now we've been having a fine conversation. I hope you'll hear me all the way through.

WALTER [*tightly*]: Go ahead, man.

LINDNER: You see—in the face of all things I have said, we are prepared to make your family a very generous offer . . .

BENEATHA: Thirty pieces and not a coin less!

WALTER: Yeah?

LINDNER [*putting on his glasses and drawing a form out of the briefcase*]: Our asso-ciation is prepared, through the collective effort of our people, to buy the house from you at a financial gain to your family.

RUTH: Lord have mercy, ain't this the living gall!

WALTER: All right, you through?

LINDNER: Well, I want to give you the exact terms of the financial arrangement—

WALTER: We don't want to hear no exact terms of no arrangements. I want to know if you got any more to tell us 'bout getting together?

LINDNER [*taking off his glasses*]: Well—I don't suppose that you feel . . .

WALTER: Never mind how I feel—you got any more to say 'bout how people ought to sit down and talk to each other? . . . Get out of my house, man. [*He turns his back and walks to the door.*]

LINDNER [*looking around at the hostile faces and reaching and assembling his hat and briefcase*]: Well—I don't understand why you people are reacting this way. What do you think you are going to gain by moving into a neighbor-hood where you just aren't wanted and where some elements—well—people can get awful worked up when they feel that their whole way of life and everything they've ever worked for is threatened.

WALTER: Get out.

LINDNER [*at the door, holding a small card*]: Well—I'm sorry it went like this.

WALTER: Get out.

LINDNER [*almost sadly regarding* WALTER]: You just can't force people to change their hearts, son. [*He turns and put his card on a table and exits.* WALTER *pushes the door to with stinging hatred, and stands looking at it.* RUTH *just sits and* BENEATHA *just stands. They say nothing.* MAMA *and* TRAVIS *enter.*]

MAMA: Well—this all the packing got done since I left out of here this morning. I testify before God that my children got all the energy of the dead. What time the moving men due?

BENEATHA: Four o'clock. You had a caller, Mama. [*She is smiling, teasingly.*]

MAMA: Sure enough—who?

BENEATHA [*her arms folded saucily*]: The Welcoming Committee. [WALTER *and* RUTH *giggle.*]

MAMA [*innocently*]: Who?

BENEATHA: The Welcoming Committee. They said they're sure going to be glad to see you when you get there.

WALTER [*devilishly*]: Yeah, they said they can't hardly wait to see your face. [*laughter*]

MAMA [*sensing their facetiousness*]: What's the matter with you all?

WALTER: Ain't nothing the matter with us. We just telling you 'bout the gentleman who came to see you this afternoon. From the Clybourne Park Improvement Association.

MAMA: What he want?

RUTH [*in the same mood as* BENEATHA *and* WALTER]: To welcome you, honey.

WALTER: He said they can't hardly wait. He said the one thing they don't have, that they just dying to have out there is a fine family of colored people! [*to* RUTH *and* BENEATHA] Ain't that right!

RUTH AND BENEATHA [*mockingly*]: Yeah! He left his card in case—[*They indicate the card, and* MAMA *picks it up and throws it on the floor—understanding and looking off as she draws her chair up to the table on which she has put her plant and some sticks and some cord.*]

MAMA: Father, give us strength. [*knowingly—and without fun*] Did he threaten us?

BENEATHA: Oh—Mama—they don't do it like that any more. He talked Brotherhood. He said everybody ought to learn how to sit down and hate each other with good Christian fellowship. [*She and* WALTER *shake hands to ridicule the remark.*]

MAMA [*sadly*]: Lord, protect us . . .

RUTH: You should hear the money those folks raised to buy the house from us. All we paid and then some.

BENEATHA: What they think we going to do—eat 'em?

RUTH: No, honey, marry 'em.

MAMA [*shaking her head*]: Lord, Lord, Lord . . .

RUTH: Well—that's the way the crackers crumble. Joke.

BENEATHA [*laughingly noticing what her mother is doing*]: Mama, what are you doing?

MAMA: Fixing my plant so it won't get hurt none on the way . . .

BENEATHA: Mama, you going to take that to the new house?

MAMA: Uh-huh—

BENEATHA: That raggedy-looking old thing?

MAMA [*stopping and looking at her*]: It expresses *me*.

RUTH [*with delight, to* BENEATHA]: So there, Miss Thing! [WALTER *comes to* MAMA *suddenly and bends down behind her and squeezes her in his arms with all his strength. She is overwhelmed by the suddenness of it and, though delighted, her manner is like that of* RUTH *with* TRAVIS.]

MAMA: Look out now, boy! You make me mess up my thing here!

WALTER [*his face lit, he slips down on his knees beside her, his arms still about her*]: Mama . . . you know what it means to climb up in the chariot?

MAMA [*gruffly, very happy*]: Get on away from me now . . .

RUTH [*near the gift-wrapped package, trying to catch* WALTER'*s eye*]: Psst—

WALTER: What the old song say, Mama . . .

RUTH: Walter—Now? [*She is pointing at the package.*]

WALTER [*speaking the lines, sweetly, playfully, in his mother's face*]:
I got wings . . . you got wings . . .
All God's children got wings . . .

MAMA: Boy—get out of my face and do some work . . .

WALTER: *When I get to heaven gonna put on my wings,*
Gonna fly all over God's heaven . . .

BENEATHA [*teasingly, from across the room*]: Everybody talking 'bout heaven ain't going there!

WALTER [*to* RUTH, *who is carrying the box across to them*]: I don't know, you think we ought to give her that . . . Seems to me she ain't been very appreciative around here.

MAMA [*eying the box, which is obviously a gift*]: What is that?

WALTER [*taking it from* RUTH *and putting it on the table in front of* MAMA]: Well—what you all think? Should we give it to her?

RUTH: Oh—she was pretty good today.

MAMA: I'll good you—[*She turns her eyes to the box again.*]

BENEATHA: Open it, Mama. [*She stands up, looks at it, turns and looks at all of them, and then presses her hands together and does not open the package.*]

WALTER [*sweetly*]: Open it, Mama. It's for you. [MAMA *looks in his eyes. It is the first present in her life without its being Christmas. Slowly she opens her package and lifts out, one by one, a brand-new sparkling set of gardening tools.* WALTER *continues, prodding.*] Ruth made up the note—read it . . .

MAMA [*picking up the card and adjusting her glasses*]: "To our own Mrs. Miniver— Love from Brother, Ruth and Beneatha." Ain't that lovely . . .

TRAVIS [*tugging at his father's sleeve*]: Daddy, can I give her mine now?

WALTER: All right, son. [TRAVIS *flies to get his gift.*] Travis didn't want to go in with the rest of us, Mama. He got his own. [*somewhat amused*] We don't know what it is . . .

TRAVIS [*racing back in the room with a large hatbox and putting it in front of his grandmother*]: Here!

MAMA: Lord have mercy, baby. You done gone and bought your grandmother a hat?

TRAVIS [*very proud*]: Open it! [*She does and lifts out an elaborate, but very elaborate, wide gardening hat, and all the adults break up at the sight of it.*]

RUTH: Travis, honey, what is that?

TRAVIS [*who thinks it is beautiful and appropriate*]: It's a gardening hat! Like the ladies always have on in the magazines when they work in their gardens.

BENEATHA [*giggling fiercely*]: Travis—we were trying to make Mama Mrs. Miniver— not Scarlett O'Hara!

MAMA [*indignantly*]: What's the matter with you all! This here is a beautiful hat! [*absurdly*] I always wanted me one just like it! [*She pops it on her head to prove it to her grandson, and the hat is ludicrous and considerably oversized.*]

RUTH: Hot dog! Go, Mama!

WALTER [*doubled over with laughter*]: I'm sorry, Mama—but you look like you ready to go out and chop you some cotton sure enough! [*They all laugh except* MAMA, *out of deference to* TRAVIS'*s feelings.*]

MAMA [*gathering the boy up to her*]: Bless your heart—this is the prettiest hat I ever owned—[WALTER, RUTH *and* BENEATHA *chime in—noisily, festively and insincerely congratulating* TRAVIS *on his gift.*] What are we all standing around here for? We ain't finished packin' yet. Bennie, you ain't packed one book. [*The bell rings.*]

BENEATHA: That couldn't be the movers . . . it's not hardly two o'clock yet—[BENEATHA *goes into her room.* MAMA *starts for door.*]

WALTER [*turning, stiffening*]: Wait—wait—I'll get it. [*He stands and looks at the door.*]

MAMA: You expecting company, son?

WALTER [*just looking at the door*]: Yeah—yeah . . . [MAMA *looks at* RUTH, *and they exchange innocent and unfrightened glances.*]

MAMA [*not understanding*]: Well, let them in, son.

BENEATHA [*from her room*]: We need some more string.

MAMA: Travis—you run to the hardware and get me some string cord. [MAMA *goes out and* WALTER *turns and looks at* RUTH. TRAVIS *goes to a dish for money.*]

RUTH: Why don't you answer the door, man?

WALTER [*suddenly bounding across the floor to her*]: 'Cause sometimes it hard to let the future begin! [*stooping down in her face*].

> I got wings! You got wings!
> All God's children got wings!

[*He crosses to the door and throws it open. Standing there is a very slight little man in a not too prosperous business suit and with haunted frightened eyes and a hat pulled down tightly, brim up, around his forehead.* TRAVIS *passes between the men and exits.* WALTER *leans deep in the man's face, still in his jubilance.*]

> When I get to heaven gonna put on my wings,
> Gonna fly all over God's heaven . . .

[*The little man just stares at him*]

Heaven—

[*Suddenly he stops and looks past the little man into the empty hallway.*]

Where's Willy, man?

BOBO: He ain't with me.

WALTER [*not disturbed*]: Oh—come on in. You know my wife.

BOBO [*dumbly, taking off his hat*]: Yes—h'you, Miss Ruth.

RUTH [*quietly, a mood apart from her husband already, seeing* BOBO]: Hello, Bobo.

WALTER: You right on time today . . . Right on time. That's the way! [*He slaps* BOBO *on his back.*] Sit down . . . lemme hear. [RUTH *stands stiffly and quietly in back of them, as though somehow she senses death, her eyes fixed on her husband.*]

BOBO [*his frightened eyes on the floor, his hat in his hands*]: Could I please get a drink of water, before I tell you about it, Walter Lee? [WALTER *does not take his eyes off the man.* RUTH *goes blindly to the tap and gets a glass of water and brings it to* BOBO.]

WALTER: There ain't nothing wrong, is there?

BOBO: Lemme tell you—

WALTER: Man—didn't nothing go wrong?

BOBO: Lemme tell you—Walter Lee. [*Looking at* RUTH *and talking to her more than to* WALTER.] You know how it was. I got to tell you how it was. I mean first I got to tell you how it was all the way . . . I mean about the money I put in, Walter Lee . . .

WALTER [*with taut agitation now*]: What about the money you put in?

BOBO: Well—it wasn't much as we told you—me and Willy—[*He stops.*] I'm sorry, Walter. I got a bad feeling about it. I got a real bad feeling about it . . .

WALTER: Man, what you telling me about all this for? . . . Tell me what happened in Springfield . . .

BOBO: Springfield.

RUTH [*like a dead woman*]: What was supposed to happen in Springfield?

BOBO [*to her*]: This deal that me and Walter went into with Willy—Me and Willy was going to go down to Springfield and spread some money 'round so's we wouldn't have to wait so long for the liquor license . . . That's what we were going to do. Everybody said that was the way you had to do, you understand, Miss Ruth?

WALTER: Man—what happened down there?

BOBO [*a pitiful man, near tears*]: I'm trying to tell you, Walter.

WALTER [*screaming at him suddenly*]: THEN TELL ME, GODDAMMIT . . . WHAT'S THE MATTER WITH YOU?

BOBO: Man . . . I didn't go to no Springfield, yesterday.

WALTER [*halted, life hanging in the moment*]: Why not?

BOBO [*the long way, the hard way to tell*]: 'Cause I didn't have no reasons to . . .

WALTER: Man, what are you talking about!

BOBO: I'm talking about the fact that when I got to the train station yesterday morning—eight o'clock like we planned . . . Man—*Willy didn't never show up.*

WALTER: Why . . . where was he . . . where is he?

BOBO: That's what I'm trying to tell you . . . I don't know . . . I waited six hours . . . I called his house . . . and I waited . . . six hours . . . I waited in that train station six hours . . . [*breaking into tears*] That was all the extra money I had in the world . . . [*looking up at* WALTER *with the tears running down his face*] Man, *Willy is gone.*

WALTER: Gone, what you mean Willy is gone? Gone where? You mean he went by himself. You mean he went off to Springfield by himself—to take care of getting the license—[*turns and looks anxiously at* RUTH] You mean maybe he didn't want too many people in on the business down there? [*looks to* RUTH *again, as before*] You know Willy got his own ways. [*looks back to* BOBO] Maybe you was late yesterday and he just went on down there without you. Maybe—maybe—he's been callin' you at home tryin' to tell you what happened or something. Maybe—maybe—he just got sick. He's somewhere—he's got to be somewhere. We just got to find him—me and you got to find him. [*grabs* BOBO *senselessly by the collar and starts to shake him*] We got to!

BOBO [*in sudden angry, frightened agony*]: What's the matter with you, Walter! *When a cat take off with your money he don't leave you no maps!*

WALTER [*turning madly, as though he is looking for* WILLY *in the very room*]: Willy! . . . Willy . . . don't do it . . . Please don't do it . . . Man, not with that money . . . Man, please, not with that money . . . Oh, God . . . Don't let it be true . . . [*He is wandering around, crying out for* WILLY *and looking for him or perhaps for help from*

God.] Man . . . I trusted you . . . Man, I put my life in your hands . . . [*He starts to crumple down on the floor as* RUTH *just covers her face in horror,* MAMA *opens the door and comes into the room, with* BENEATHA *behind her.*] Man . . . [*He starts to pound the floor with his fists, sobbing wildly.*] That money is made out of my father's flesh . . .

BOBO [*standing over him helplessly*]: I'm sorry, Walter . . . [*Only* WALTER*'s sobs reply.* BOBO *puts on his hat.*] I had my life staked on this deal, too . . . [*He exits.*]

MAMA [*to* WALTER]: Son—[*She goes to him, bends down to him, talks to his bent head.*] Son . . . Is it gone? Son, I gave, you sixty-five hundred dollars. Is it gone? All of it? Beneatha's money too?

WALTER [*lifting his head slowly*]: Mama . . . I never . . . went to the bank at all

MAMA [*not wanting to believe him*]: You mean . . . your sister's school money . . . you used that too . . . Walter? . . .

WALTER: Yessss! . . . All of it . . . It's all gone . . . [*There is total silence.* RUTH *stands with her face covered with her hands;* BENEATHA *leans forlornly against a wall, fingering a piece of red ribbon from the mother's gift.* MAMA *stops and looks at her son without recognition and then, quite without thinking about it, starts to beat him senselessly in the face.* BENEATHA *goes to them and stops it.*]

BENEATHA: Mama! [MAMA *stops and looks at both of her children and rises slowly and wanders vaguely, aimlessly away from them.*]

MAMA: I seen . . . him . . . night after night . . . come in . . . and look at that rug . . . and then look at me . . . the red showing in his eyes . . . the veins moving in his head . . . I seen him grow thin and old before he was forty . . . working and working and working like somebody's old horse . . . killing himself . . . and you—you give it all away in a day . . .

BENEATHA: Mama—

MAMA: Oh, God . . . [*She looks up to Him.*] Look down here—and show me the strength.

BENEATHA: Mama—

MAMA [*folding over*]: Strength . . .

BENEATHA [*plaintively*]: Mama . . .

MAMA: Strength!

CURTAIN

Act III

An hour later.

At curtain, there is a sullen light of gloom in the living room, gray light not unlike that which began the first scene of Act I. At left we can see WALTER *within his room, alone with himself. He is stretched out on the bed, his shirt out and open, his arms under his head. He does not smoke, he does not cry out, he merely lies there, looking up at the ceiling, much as if he were alone in the world.*

In the living room BENEATHA *sits at the table, still surrounded by the now almost ominous packing crates. She sits looking off. We feel that this is a mood struck perhaps an hour before, and it lingers now, full of the empty sound of profound disappointment. We see on a line from her brother's bedroom the sameness of their attitudes. Presently the bell rings and* BENEATHA *rises without ambition or interest in answering. It is* ASAGAI, *smiling broadly, striding into the room with energy and happy expectation and conversation.*

ASAGAI: I came over . . . I had some free time. I thought I might help with the packing. Ah, I like the look of packing crates! A household in preparation for a journey! It depresses some people . . . but for me . . . it is another feeling. Something full of the flow of life, do you understand? Movement, progress . . . It makes me think of Africa.

BENEATHA: Africa!

ASAGAI: What kind of a mood is this? Have I told you how deeply you move me?

BENEATHA: He gave away the money, Asagai . . .

ASAGAI: Who gave away what money?

BENEATHA: The insurance money. My brother gave it away.

ASAGAI: Gave it away?

BENEATHA: He made an investment! With a man even Travis wouldn't have trusted.

ASAGAI: And it's gone?

BENEATHA: Gone!

ASAGAI: I'm very sorry . . . And you, now?

BENEATHA: Me? . . . Me? . . . Me, I'm nothing . . . Me. When I was very small . . . we used to take our sleds out in the wintertime and the only hills we had were the ice-covered stone steps of some houses down the street. And we used to fill them in with snow and make them smooth and slide down them all day . . . and it was very dangerous you know . . . far too steep . . . and sure enough one day a kid named Rufus came down too fast and hit the sidewalk . . . and we saw his face just split open right there in front of us . . . And I remember standing there looking at his bloody open face thinking that was the end of Rufus. But the ambulance came and they took him to the hospital and they fixed the broken bones and they sewed it all up . . . and the next time I saw Rufus he just had a little line down the middle of his face . . . I never got over that . . . [WALTER *sits up, listening on the bed. Throughout this scene it is impor-tant that we feel his reaction at all times, that he visibly respond to the words of his sister and* ASAGAI.]

ASAGAI: What?

BENEATHA: That that was what one person could do for another, fix him up—sew up the problem, make him all right again. That was the most marvelous thing in the world . . . I wanted to do that. I always thought it was the one concrete thing in the world that a human being could do. Fix up the sick, you know— and make them whole again. This was truly being God . . .

ASAGAI: You wanted to be God?

BENEATHA: No—I wanted to cure. It used to be so important to me. I wanted to cure. It used to matter. I used to care. I mean about people and how their bod-ies hurt . . .

ASAGAI: And you've stopped caring?

BENEATHA: Yes—I think so.

ASAGAI: Why? [WALTER *rises, goes to the door of his room and is about to open it, then stops and stands listening, leaning on the door jamb.*]

BENEATHA: Because it doesn't seem deep enough, close enough to what ails man-kind—I mean this thing of sewing up bodies or administering drugs. Don't you understand? It was a child's reaction to the world. I thought that doctors had the secret to all the hurts . . . That's the way a child sees things—or an idealist.

ASAGAI: Children see things very well sometimes—and idealists even better.

BENEATHA: I know that's what you think. Because you are still where I left off—you still care. This is what you see for the world, for Africa. You with the dreams of the future will patch up all Africa—you are going to cure the Great Sore of colonialism with Independence—

ASAGAI: Yes!

BENEATHA: Yes—and you think that one word is the penicillin of the human spirit: "Independence!" But then what?

ASAGAI: That will be the problem for another time. First we must get there.

BENEATHA: And where does it end?

ASAGAI: End? Who even spoke of an end? To life? To living?

BENEATHA: An end to misery!

ASAGAI [*smiling*]: You sound like a French intellectual.

BENEATHA: No! I sound like a human being who just had her future taken right out of her hands! While I was sleeping in my bed in there, things were happening in this world that directly concerned me—and nobody asked me, consulted me—they just went out and did things—and changed my life. Don't you see there isn't any real progress, Asagai, there is only one large circle that we march in, around and around, each of us with our own little picture—in front of us—our own little mirage that we think is the future.

ASAGAI: That is the mistake.

BENEATHA: What?

ASAGAI: What you just said—about the circle. It isn't a circle—it is simply a long line—as in geometry, you know, one that reaches into infinity. And because we cannot see the end—we also cannot see how it changes. And it is very odd but those who see the changes are called "idealists"—and those who cannot, or refuse to think, they are the "realists." It is very strange, and amusing too, I think.

BENEATHA: You—you are almost religious.

ASAGAI: Yes . . . I think I have the religion of doing what is necessary in the world— and of worshipping man—because he is so marvelous, you see.

BENEATHA: Man is foul! And the human race deserves its misery!

ASAGAI: You see: *you* have become the religious one in the old sense. Already, and after such a small defeat, you are worshipping despair.

BENEATHA: From now on, I worship the truth—and the truth is that people are puny, small and selfish . . .

ASAGAI: Truth? Why is it that you despairing ones always think that only you have the truth? I never thought to see *you* like that. You! Your brother made a stupid, childish mistake—and you are grateful to him. So that now you can give up the ailing human race on account of it. You talk about what good is struggle; what good is anything? Where are we all going? And why are we bothering?

BENEATHA: *And you cannot answer it!* All your talk and dreams about Africa and Independence. Independence and then what? What about all the crooks and petty thieves and just plain idiots who will come into power to steal and plunder the same as before—only now they will be black and do it in the name of the new Independence—You cannot answer that.

ASAGAI [*shouting over her*]: *I live the answer!* [*pause*] In my village at home it is the exceptional man who can even read a newspaper . . . or who ever *sees* a book at all. I will go home and much of what I will have to say will seem strange to the people of my village. . . . But I will teach and work and things will happen, slowly and swiftly. At times it will seem that nothing changes at all . . . and then again . . . the sudden dramatic events which make history leap into the future. And then quiet again. Retrogression even. Guns, murder, revolution. And I even will have moments when I wonder if the quiet was not better than all that death and hatred. But I will look about my village at the illiteracy and disease and ignorance and I will not wonder long. And perhaps . . . perhaps I will be a great man . . . I mean perhaps I will hold on to the substance of truth and find my way always with the right course . . . and perhaps for it I will be butchered in my bed some night by the servants of empire . . .

BENEATHA: *The martyr!*

ASAGAI: . . . or perhaps I shall live to be a very old man, respected and es– teemed in my new nation . . . And perhaps I shall hold office and this is what I'm trying to tell you, Alaiyo; perhaps the things I believe now for my country will be wrong and outmoded, and I will not understand and do terrible things to have things my way or merely to keep my power. Don't you see that there will be young men and women, not British soldiers then, but my own black countrymen . . . to step out of the shadows some evening and slit my then useless throat? Don't you see they have always been there . . . that they always will be. And that such a thing as my own death will be an advance? They who might kill me even . . . actually re– plenish me!

BENEATHA: Oh, Asagai, I know all that.

ASAGAI: Good! Then stop moaning and groaning and tell me what you plan to do.

BENEATHA: Do?

ASAGAI: I have a bit of a suggestion.

BENEATHA: What?

ASAGAI [*rather quietly for him*]. That when it is all over—that you come home with me—

BENEATHA [*slapping herself on the forehead with exasperation born of misunder– standing*]. Oh—Asagai—at this moment you decide to be romantic!

ASAGAI [*quickly understanding the misunderstanding*]: My dear, young creature of the New World—I do not mean across the city—I mean across the ocean; home—to Africa.

BENEATHA [*slowly understanding and turning to him with murmured amaze– ment*]: To—to Nigeria?

ASAGAI: Yes! . . . [*smiling and lifting his arms playfully*]. Three hundred years later the African Prince rose up out of the seas and swept the maiden back across the middle passage over which her ancestors had come—

BENEATHA [*unable to play*]: Nigeria?

ASAGAI: Nigeria. Home. [*coming to her with genuine romantic flippancy*] I will show you our mountains and our stars; and give you cool drinks from gourds and teach you the old songs and the ways of our people—and, in time, we will pretend that—[*very softly*]—you have only been away for a day—[*She turns her back to him, thinking. He swings her around and takes her full in his arms in a long embrace which proceeds to passion.*]

BENEATHA [*pulling away*]: You're getting me all mixed up—

ASAGAI: Why?

BENEATHA: Too many things—too many things have happened today. I must sit down and think. I don't know what I feel about anything right this minute. [*She promptly sits down and props her chin on her fist.*]

ASAGAI [*charmed*]: All right, I shall leave you. No—don't get up. [*touching her, gen– tly, sweetly*] Just sit awhile and think . . . Never be afraid to sit awhile and think. [*He goes to door and looks at her.*] How often I have looked at you and said, "Ah—so this is what the New World hath finally wrought . . ." [*He exits.*

BENEATHA *sits on alone. Presently* WALTER *enters from his room and starts to rummage through things, feverishly looking for something. She looks up and turns in her seat.*]

BENEATHA [*hissingly*]: Yes—just look at what the New World hath wrought! . . . Just look! [*She gestures with bitter disgust.*] There he is! *Monsieur le petit bougeois noir*—himself! There he is—Symbol of a Rising Class! Entrepreneur! Titan of the system! [WALTER *ignores her completely and continues frantically and destructively looking for something and hurling things to the floor and tearing things out of their place in his search.* BENEATHA *ignores the eccentricity of his actions and goes on with the monologue of insult.*] Did you dream of yachts on Lake Michigan, Brother? Did you see yourself on that Great Day sitting down at the Conference Table, surrounded by all the mighty bald-headed men in America? All halted, waiting, breathless, waiting for your pronouncements on industry? Waiting for you—Chairman of the Board? [WALTER *finds what he is looking for—a small piece of white paper—and pushes it in his pocket and puts on his coat and rushes out without ever having looked at her. She shouts after him.*] I look at you and I see the final triumph of stupidity in the world! [*The door slams and she returns to just sitting again.* RUTH *comes quickly out of* MAMA'*s room.*]

RUTH: Who was that?

BENEATHA: Your husband.

RUTH: Where did he go?

BENEATHA: Who knows—maybe he has an appointment at U.S. Steel.

RUTH [*anxiously, with frightened eyes*]: You didn't say nothing bad to him, did you?

BENEATHA: Bad? Say anything bad to him? No—I told him he was a sweet boy and full of dreams and everything is strictly peachy keen, as the ofay[3] kids say!

[MAMA *enters from her bedroom. She is lost, vague, trying to catch hold, to make some sense of her former command of the world, but it still eludes her. A sense of waste overwhelms her gait; a measure of apology rides on her shoulders. She goes to her plant, which has remained on the table, looks at it, picks it up and takes it to the window sill and sets it outside, and she stands and looks at it a long moment. Then she closes the window, straightens her body with effort and turns around to her children.*]

MAMA: Well—ain't it a mess in here, though? [*a false cheerfulness, a beginning of something*] I guess we all better stop moping around and get some work done. All this unpacking and everything we got to do. [RUTH *raises her head slowly in response to the sense of the line; and* BENEATHA *in similar manner turns very slowly to look at her mother.*] One of you all better call the moving people and tell 'em not to come.

RUTH: Tell 'em not to come?

MAMA: Of course, baby. Ain't no need in 'em coming all the way here and having to go back. They charges for that too. [*She sits down, fingers to her brow, thinking.*] Lord, ever since I was a little girl, I always remembers people saying, "Lena—Lena Eggleston, you aims too high all the time. You needs to slow down and see life a little more like it is. Just slow down some." That's what they always used to say down home—"Lord, that Lena Eggleston is a high-minded thing. She'll get her due one day!"

RUTH: No, Lena . . .

---

[3]**ofay** White (pig Latin meaning "foe").

MAMA: Me and Big Walter just didn't never learn right.

RUTH: Lena, no! We gotta go. Bennie—tell her . . . [*She rises and crosses to* BENEATHA *with her arms outstretched.* BENEATHA *doesn't respond.*] Tell her we can still move . . . the notes ain't but a hundred and twenty-five a month. We got four grown people in this house—we can work . . .

MAMA [*to herself*]: Just aimed too high all the time—

RUTH [*turning and going to* MAMA *fast—the words pouring out with urgency and desperation*]: Lena—I'll work . . . I'll work twenty hours a day in all the kitchens in Chicago . . . I'll strap my baby on my back if I have to and scrub all the floors in America and wash all the sheets in America if I have to—but we got to move . . . We got to get out of here . . . [MAMA *reaches out absently and pats* RUTH*'s hand.*]

MAMA: No—I sees things differently now. Been thinking 'bout some of the things we could do to fix this place up some. I seen a second-hand bureau over on Maxwell Street just the other day that could fit right there. [*She points to where the new furniture might go.* RUTH *wanders away from her.*] Would need some new handles on it and then a little varnish and then it look like something brand-new. And—we can put up them new curtains in the kitchen . . . Why this place be looking fine. Cheer us all up so that we forget trouble ever came . . . [*to* RUTH] And you could get some nice screens to put up in your room round the baby's bassinet . . . [*She looks at both of them, pleadingly.*] Sometimes you just got to know when to give up some things . . . and hold on to what you got. [WALTER *enters from the outside, looking spent and leaning against the door, his coat hanging from him.*]

MAMA: Where you been, son?

WALTER [*breathing hard*]: Made a call.

MAMA: To who, son?

WALTER: To the Man.

MAMA: What man, baby?

WALTER: The Man, Mama. Don't you know who The Man is?

RUTH: Walter Lee?

WALTER: *The Man.* Like the guys in the street say—*the Man.* Captain Boss—Mistuh Charley . . . Old Captain Please Mr. Bossman . . .

BENEATHA [*suddenly*]: Lindner!

WALTER: That's right! That's good. I told him to come right over.

BENEATHA [*fiercely, understanding*]: For what? What do you want to see him for?

WALTER [*looking at his sister*]: We are going to do business with him.

MAMA: What you talking 'bout, son?

WALTER: Talking 'bout life, Mama. You all always telling me to see life like it is. Well—I laid in there on my back today . . . and I figured it out. Life just like it is. Who gets and who don't get. [*He sits down with his coat on and laughs.*] Mama, you know it's all divided up. Life is. Sure enough. Between the takers and the "tooken." [*He laughs.*] I've figured it out finally. [*He looks around at them.*] Yeah. Some of us always getting "tooken." [*He laughs.*] People like Willy Harris, they don't never get "tooken." And you know why the rest of us do? 'Cause we all mixed up. Mixed up bad. We get to looking 'round for the right and the wrong; and we worry about it and cry about it and stay up nights trying to figure out 'bout the wrong and the right of things all the time . . . And all the time, man, them takers is out there operating, just taking and taking. Willy Harris? Shoot—Willy Harris don't even count. He don't even count in the big scheme of things. But I'll say one thing for old Willy Harris . . . he's taught me something. He's taught me to keep my eye on what counts in this world. Yeah—[*shouting out a little*] Thanks, Willy!

RUTH: What did you call that man for, Walter Lee!

WALTER: Called him to tell him to come on over to the show. Gonna put on a show for the man. Just what he wants to see. You see, Mama, the man came here today and he told us that them people out there where you want us to move—well they so upset they willing to pay us not to move out there. [*He laughs again.*] And—and oh, Mama—you would of been proud of the way me and Ruth and Bennie acted. We told him to get out . . . Lord have mercy! We told the man to get out. Oh, we was some proud folks this afternoon, yeah. [*He lights a cigarette.*] We were still full of that old-time stuff . . .

RUTH [*coming toward him slowly*]: You talking 'bout taking them people's money to keep us from moving in that house?

WALTER: I ain't just talking 'bout it, baby—I'm telling you that's what's going to happen.

BENEATHA: Oh, God! Where is the bottom! Where is the real honest-to-God bottom so he can't go any farther!

WALTER: See—that's the old stuff. You and that boy that was here today. You all want everybody to carry a flag and a spear and sing some marching songs, huh? You wanna spend your life looking into things and trying to find the right and the wrong part, huh? Yeah. You know what's going to happen to that boy someday—he'll find himself sitting in a dungeon, locked in forever—and the takers will have the key! Forget it, baby! There ain't no causes—there ain't nothing but taking in this world, and he who takes most is smartest—and it don't make a damn bit of difference *how*.

MAMA: You making something inside me cry, son. Some awful pain inside me.

WALTER: Don't cry, Mama. Understand. That white man is going to walk in that door able to write checks for more money than we ever had. It's important to him and I'm going to help him . . . I'm going to put on the show, Mama.

MAMA: Son—I come from five generations of people who was slaves and share-croppers—but ain't nobody in my family never let nobody pay 'em no money that was a way of telling us we wasn't fit to walk the earth. We ain't never been that poor. [*raising her eyes and looking at him*] We ain't never been that dead inside.

BENEATHA: Well—we are dead now. All the talk about dreams and sunlight that goes on in this house. All dead.

WALTER: What's the matter with you all! I didn't make this world! It was give to me this way! Hell, yes, I want me some yachts someday! Yes, I want to hang some real pearls 'round my wife's neck. Ain't she supposed to wear no pearls? Somebody tell me—tell me, who decides which women is suppose to wear pearls in this world. I tell you I am a *man*—and I think my wife should wear some pearls in this world! [*This last line hangs a good while and* WALTER *begins to move about the room. The word "Man" has penetrated his consciousness; he mumbles it to himself repeatedly between strange agitated pauses as he moves about.*]

MAMA: Baby, how you going to feel on the inside?

WALTER: Fine! . . . Going to feel fine . . . a man . . .

MAMA: You won't have nothing left then, Walter Lee.

WALTER [*coming to her*]: I'm going to feel fine, Mama. I'm going to look that son-of-a-bitch in the eyes and say—[*He falters.*]—and say, "All right, Mr. Lindner—[*He falters even more.*]—that's your neighborhood out there. You got the right to keep it like you want. You got the right to have it like you want. Just write the check and—the house is yours." And, and I am going to say—[*His voice almost breaks.*] And you—you people just put the money in my hand and you won't have to live next to this bunch of stinking niggers! . . . [*He straightens up and moves away from his mother, walking around the room.*] Maybe—maybe I'll just get down on my black knees . . . [*He does so;* RUTH *and* BENNIE *and* MAMA *watch him in frozen horror.*] Captain, Mistuh, Bossman. [*He starts crying.*] A-hee-hee-hee! [*wringing his hands in profoundly anguished imitation*] Yassss-suh! Great White Father, just gi' ussen de money, fo' God's sake, and we's ain't gwine come out deh and dirty up yo' white folks neighborhood . . . [*He breaks down completely, then gets up and goes into the bedroom.*]

BENEATHA: That is not a man. That is nothing but a toothless rat.

MAMA: Yes—death done come in this here house. [*She is nodding, slowly, reflectively.*] Done come walking in my house. On the lips of my children. You what supposed to be my beginning again. You—what supposed to be my harvest. [*to* BENEATHA] You—you mourning your brother?

BENEATHA: He's no brother of mine.

MAMA: What you say?

BENEATHA: I said that that individual in that room is no brother of mine.

MAMA: That's what I thought you said. You feeling like you better than he is today? [BENEATHA *does not answer.*] Yes? What you tell him a minute ago? That he wasn't a man? Yes? You give him up for me? You done wrote his epitaph too—like the rest of the world? Well, who give you the privilege?

BENEATHA: Be on my side for once! You saw what he just did, Mama! You saw him—down on his knees. Wasn't it you who taught me—to despise any man who would do that? Do what he's going to do.

MAMA: Yes—I taught you that. Me and your daddy. But I thought I taught you something else too . . . I thought I taught you to love him.

BENEATHA: Love him? There is nothing left to love.

MAMA: There is always something left to love. And if you ain't learned that, you ain't learned nothing. [*looking at her*] Have you cried for that boy today? I don't mean for yourself and for the family 'cause we lost the money. I mean for him; what he been through and what it done to him. Child, when do you think is the time to love somebody the most; when they done good and made things easy for everybody? Well then, you ain't through learning—because that ain't the time at all. It's when he's at his lowest and can't believe in hisself 'cause the world done whipped him so. When you starts measuring somebody, measure him right, child, measure him right. Make sure you done taken into account what hills and valleys he come through before he got to wherever he is. [TRAVIS *bursts into the room at the end of the speech, leaving the door open.*]

TRAVIS: Grandmama—the moving men are downstairs! The truck just pulled up.

MAMA [*turning and looking at him*]: Are they, baby? They downstairs? [*She sighs and sits.* LINDNER *appears in the doorway. He peers in and knocks lightly, to gain attention, and comes in. All turn to look at him.*]

LINDNER [*hat and briefcase in hand*]: Uh—hello . . . [RUTH *crosses mechanically to the bedroom door and opens it and lets it swing open freely and slowly as the lights come up on* WALTER *within, still in his coat, sitting at the far corner of the room. He looks up and out through the room to* LINDNER.]

RUTH: He's here. [*A long minute passes and* WALTER *slowly gets up.*]

LINDNER [*coming to the table with efficiency, putting his briefcase on the table and starting to unfold papers and unscrew fountain pens*]: Well, I certainly was

glad to hear from you people. [WALTER *has begun the trek out of the room,
slowly and awkwardly, rather like a small boy, passing the back of his sleeve
across his mouth from time to time.*] Life can really be so much simpler than
people let it be most of the time. Well—with whom do I negotiate? You,
Mrs. Younger, or your son here? [MAMA *sits with her hands folded on her lap and
her eyes closed as* WALTER *advances.* TRAVIS *goes close to* LINDNER *and looks at the
papers curiously.*] Just some official papers, sonny.

RUTH: Travis, you go downstairs.

MAMA [*opening her eyes and looking into* WALTER's]: No. Travis, you stay right here.
And you make him understand what you doing, Walter Lee. You teach him
good. Like Willy Harris taught you. You show where our five generations done
come to. Go ahead, son—

WALTER [*Looks down into his boy's eyes.* TRAVIS *grins at him merrily and* WALTER
draws him beside him with his arm lightly around his shoulders.]: Well, Mr.
Lindner. [BENEATHA *turns away.*] We called you—[*There is a profound, simple groping quality in his speech.*]—because, well, me and my family [*He
looks around and shifts from one foot to the other.*] Well—we are very plain
people . . .

LINDNER: Yes—

WALTER: I mean—I have worked as a chauffeur most of my life—and my wife here,
she does domestic work in people's kitchens. So does my mother. I mean—we
are plain people . . .

LINDNER: Yes, Mr. Younger—

WALTER [*really like a small boy, looking down at his shoes and then up at the
man*]: And—uh—well, my father, well, he was a laborer most of his life.

LINDNER [*absolutely confused*]: Uh, yes—

WALTER [*looking down at his toes once again*]: My father almost beat a man to death
once because this man called him a bad name or something, you know what
I mean?

LINDNER: No, I'm afraid I don't.

WALTER [*finally straightening up*]: Well, what I mean is that we come from people who had a lot of pride. I mean—we are very proud people. And that's
my sister over there and she's going to be a doctor—and we are very
proud—

LINDNER: Well—I am sure that is very nice, but—

WALTER [*starting to cry and facing the man eye to eye*]: What I am telling you is that
we called you over here to tell you that we are very proud and that this is—
this is my son, who makes the sixth generation of our family in this country,
and that we have all thought about your offer and we have decided to move
into our house because my father—my father—he earned it. [MAMA *has her eyes
closed and is rocking back and forth as though she were in church, with her
head nodding the amen yes.*] We don't want to make no trouble for nobody or
fight no causes—but we will try to be good neighbors. That's all we got to say.
[*He looks the man absolutely in the eyes.*] We don't want your money. [*He turns
and walks away from the man.*]

LINDNER [*looking around at all of them*]: I take it then that you have decided to occupy.

BENEATHA: That's what the man said.

LINDNER [*to* MAMA *in her reverie*]: Then I would like to appeal to you, Mrs. Younger.
You are older and wiser and understand things better I am sure . . .

MAMA [*rising*]: I am afraid you don't understand. My son said we was going to move and there ain't nothing left for me to say. [*Shaking her head with double meaning.*] You know how these young folks is nowadays, mister. Can't do a thing with 'em. Good-bye.

LINDNER [*folding up his materials*]: Well—if you are that final about it . . . There is nothing left for me to say. [*He finishes. He is almost ignored by the family, who are concentrating on* WALTER LEE. *At the door* LINDNER *halts and looks around.*] I sure hope you people know what you're doing. [*He shakes his head and exits.*]

RUTH [*looking around and coming to life*]: Well, for God's sake—if the moving men are here—LET'S GET THE HELL OUT OF HERE!

MAMA [*into action*]: Ain't it the truth! Look at all this here mess. Ruth, put Travis' good jacket on him . . . Walter Lee, fix your tie and tuck your shirt in, you look just like somebody's hoodlum. Lord have mercy, where is my plant? [*She flies to get it amid the general bustling of the family, who are deliberately trying to ignore the nobility of the past moment.*] You all start on down . . . Travis child, don't go empty-handed . . . Ruth, where did I put that box with my skillets in it? I want to be in charge of it myself . . . I'm going to make us the biggest dinner we ever ate tonight . . . Beneatha, what's the matter with them stockings? Pull them things up, girl . . . [*The family starts to file out as two moving men appear and begin to carry out the heavier pieces of furniture, bumping into the family as they move about.*]

BENEATHA: Mama, Asagai—asked me to marry him today and go to Africa—

MAMA [*in the middle of her getting-ready activity*]: He did? You ain't old enough to marry nobody—[*Seeing the moving men lifting one of her chairs precariously.*] Darling, that ain't no bale of cotton, please handle it so we can sit in it again. I had that chair twenty five years . . . [*The movers sigh with exasperation and go on with their work.*]

BENEATHA [*girlishly and unreasonably trying to pursue the conversation*]: To go to Africa, Mama—be a doctor in Africa . . .

MAMA [*distracted*]: Yes, baby—

WALTER: Africa! What he want to go to Africa for?

BENEATHA: To practice there . . .

WALTER: Girl, if you don't get all them silly ideas out your head! You better marry yourself a man with some loot . . .

BENEATHA [*angrily, precisely as in the first scene of the play*]: What have you got to do with who I marry!

WALTER: Plenty. Now I think George Murchison—[*He and* BENEATHA *go out yelling at each other vigorously;* BENEATHA *is heard saying that she would not marry* GEORGE MURCHISON *if he were Adam and she were Eve, etc. The anger is loud and real till their voices diminish.* RUTH *stands at the door and turns to* MAMA *and smiles knowingly.*]

MAMA [*fixing her hat at last*]: Yeah—they something all right, my children . . .

RUTH: Yeah—they're something. Let's go, Lena.

MAMA [*stalling, starting to look around at the house*]: Yes—I'm coming. Ruth—

RUTH: Yes?

MAMA [*quietly, woman to woman*]: He finally come into his manhood today, didn't he? Kind of like a rainbow after the rain . . .

RUTH [*biting her lip lest her own pride explode in front of* MAMA]: Yes, Lena. [BENEATHA*'s voice calls for them raucously.*]

MAMA [*waving* RUTH *out vaguely*]: All right, honey—go on down. I be down directly. [RUTH *hesitates, then exits.* MAMA *stands, at last alone in the living room, her plant on the table before her as the lights start to come down. She looks around at all the walls and ceilings and suddenly, despite herself, while the children call below, a great heaving thing rises in her and she puts her fist to her mouth, takes a final desperate look, pulls her coat about her, pats her hat and goes out. The lights dim down. The door opens and she comes back in, grabs her plant, and goes out for the last time.*]

CURTAIN

[1958]

Joining the Conversation: Critical Thinking and Writing

1. On pages 137–41 we discuss Langston Hughes's "Harlem," the poem from which Hansberry chose her title. Please describe why this choice of title is a good one.
2. Imagine that Hansberry has asked your help in selecting a title for her play—and that the title she actually selected, *A Raisin in the Sun,* is not an option. Write a letter to her, of about 1–2 pages, in which you recommend a title of your own choosing based on your reading of the text.
3. A scholar has observed, "the main point of the play is that the characters find they must defer their dreams." Present an argument in which you discuss and provide evidence for this claim.
4. Please list, in two or three sentences each, three key insights that Hansberry offers about race. Describe how you would organize and connect these insights into an effective argument.
5. If you were assigned to give an analysis in class of a crucial passage or scene in the play, which one would you choose? What would be the key questions about it that you would ask the students? What would you be trying to help them discover and understand about Hansberry's work?
6. Mama says, "money is life." What does she mean? Is her view supported by the play as a whole?
7. Consider the phrase "money is life" in a more general sense. In an essay of 1–2 pages, please argue that it is indeed the case that "money is life," and then in a second essay of the same length, argue that it is not.
8. Mama also says: "There is always something left to love." What does she mean by this statement? Does the play as a whole support her view?
9. Commenting on the historical context of *A Raisin the Sun,* a scholar has stated: "The play is best understood in relation to the American civil rights movement of the 1950s and 1960s." Making use of at least three sources, write a 2–3 page essay that summarizes this context for the play. Remember to include a bibliography of the Internet and print sources that you consulted.
10. Another scholar has noted that Hansberry's play "has been translated into over thirty languages on every continent, and has been produced in such diverse countries as the former Czechoslovakia, England, the former Soviet Union, and

France." In your view, what explains this worldwide appeal? Please point to specific passages to support your argument.

11. Do you agree that *A Raisin in the Sun* is not only about race, but also about gender and class? Locate passages in the text that support your response.

12. Are you familiar with the phrase "the American dream"? What does it mean? How does it apply to the characters in this play?

13. Is "the American dream" for these characters the same as or different from what it is for you? Do you expect that you will be able to achieve your dream when you want to, or that you will be obliged to defer it? Please explain as clearly as you can.

14. Why is having a home of one's own so important in this play? Is it important for you as well?

15. Often it is said that each of us—whatever our race, religion, ethnicity, or gender—"wants the same thing in life." Do you agree or disagree? How would you go about developing an argument to explain and support your view? What kinds of evidence would you present?

16. Imagine that you are preparing a new edition of Hansberry's play. Making use of library or Internet sources, locate a photograph or an image of some other kind for the cover of this edition. Please explain your choice. (Be sure to include the image with your essay.)

MyLiteratureLab *For additional resources for* A Raisin in the Sun, *log in to* www.myliteraturelab.com *where you will find a Longman Lecture, Comprehension Quiz, and Short Evaluation Exercise as well as an About the Author and Critical Overview for Hansberry (under Student Resources).*

Chapter Overview: Looking Backward/Looking Forward

1. How would you define patriotism? Stephen Decatur (1779–1820), a heroic officer in the U.S. Navy, once offered a toast, "Our country! In her intercourse with foreign nations may she always be in the right; but our country, right or wrong." Would you say that this toast exemplifies patriotism? In any case, to what degree do you share this sentiment? Do you think it is important for Americans to be patriotic? Please explain.

2. If you are an American, are you proud to be an American? Explain why.

3. If you are not an American, are you thinking about becoming one? Why or why not?

4. Do you feel you are more or less of an "American" than other Americans whom you know, or know about? How does one become a "real" American? Is it just a matter of place of birth, or (for someone coming here from abroad) of place of residence? Have you attended an event, or been part of an experience, when you said to yourself, "This is what it feels like to be an American"?

5. If you are an American who has traveled abroad, where, and in what ways, were you conscious of being an American? More so in some places than in others? If you have traveled abroad at different times, have you found yourself

more conscious now of your American identity than you were in the past? What sorts of interactions and experiences led you to feel this?

6. Sometimes we hear references to the "heartland of America," or the "true America." Are there some parts of the country that are more "American" than others? If this is the case, is it a bad or a good thing?

7. We see, hear, and read a great deal about racial, ethnic, and religious differences, both within the United States and overseas. But isn't it the case that everyone, finally, is the same?

8. A recent survey concluded that "identity" is now the topic studied the most in college and university courses. Do you agree that it should be? Why is this topic receiving so much attention? Are there other topics that you believe are equally important, and maybe even more important? What are they, and what kinds of courses would you design and develop for studying them?

CHAPTER 27

American Dreams
and Nightmares

SHORT VIEWS

The land of the free, and the home of the brave.
    Francis Scott Key

*The Star-Spangled Banner and all its successors have come to embody
our country, what we think of as America. It may not be quite the same
for every one of us who looks at it, but in the end we all pretty much
come out where the framers did. We know we have a country founded on
the then revolutionary idea that all of us are created equal, and equally
entitled to life, liberty, and the pursuit of happiness. . . . You can neither
honor the past, nor imagine the future, without the kind of citizenship
embodied by all our memories of this flag. So as you see this flag and
leave this place, promise yourself that when your great-grandchildren
are here, they will not only be able to see the Star-Spangled Banner, it
will mean just as much to them as it does to you today.*
    William Jefferson Clinton, at the National Museum of American History,
    13 July 1998, standing in front of the Star-Spangled Banner

*I always consider the settlement of America with reverence and wonder,
as the opening of a grand scene and design in providence, for the
illumination of the ignorant and the emancipation of the slavish part of
mankind all over the earth.*
    John Adams

*America is neither free nor brave, but a land of tight, iron-clanking little
wills, everybody trying to put it over everybody else, and a land of men
absolutely devoid of the real courage of trust, trust in life's sacred
spontaneity. They can't trust life until they can control it.*
    D. H. Lawrence

*America is still mostly xenophobic and racist. That's the nature of
America, I think.*
    Jerry Garcia

A man is not expected to love his country, lest he make an ass of himself.
Yet our country, seen through the mists of smog, is curiously lovable, in
somewhat the way an individual who has got himself into an uncon-
scionable scrape seems lovable—or at least deserving of support.
　　E. B. White

Americans are all too soft.
　　Pearl Buck

If American men are obsessed with money, American women are
obsessed with weight. The men talk of gain, the women talk of loss.
　　Marya Mannes

I don't feel we did wrong in taking this great country away from them.
These were great numbers of people who needed new land, and the
Indians were selfishly trying to keep it for themselves.
　　John Wayne

America is the only nation in history which, miraculously, has gone
directly from barbarism to degeneration without the usual interval of
civilization.
　　attributed to Georges Clemenceau

The greatest honor history can bestow is the title of peacemaker. This
honor now beckons America—the chance to help lead the world at last
out of the valley of the turmoil and on to that high ground of peace that
man has dreamed of since the dawn of civilization.
　　Richard M. Nixon

Joining the Conversation: Critical Thinking and Writing

1. Select a quotation that especially appeals to you, and make it the focus of an essay of about 500 words.
2. Take two of the passages—perhaps one that you especially like and one that you think is wrongheaded—and write a dialogue of about 500 words in which the two authors converse or argue. They may each try to convince the other, or they may find that to some degree they share views and they may then work out a statement that both can accept. If you do take the first position—that one writer is on the correct track but the other is utterly mistaken—try to be fair to the view that you think is mistaken. (As an experiment in critical thinking, imagine that you accept it, and make the best case for it that you possibly can.)
3. Imagine you are teaching a class, with this group of quotations as your subject for the day. Which quotation would you choose as your starting point? What would you say about it? What would you do next?

4. In a phrase that is familiar to all of us, Francis Scott Key said that America is "the land of the free, and the home of the brave." What does this phrase mean? What kinds of arguments could you present to support it? Could you imagine counterarguments?

5. Former president Clinton says that American flags "embody our country, what we think of as America." Sometimes American citizens, for instance during the Vietnam War, protest the government's actions by burning the flag. The Supreme Court has protected such action, saying that it is symbolic and is equivalent to speech. Occasionally a bill criminalizing flag-burning is introduced into Congress. Do you think flag-burning should be criminalized? Please explain.

6. Jerry Garcia (1942–95), the rock guitarist and vocalist who was the leader of The Grateful Dead, said that America is "mostly xenophobic and racist." If you had to argue in support of Garcia's claim, what would be your evidence? If you had to argue against this claim, what would be your evidence?

7. E. B. White says that America is "curiously lovable." Why does he use the word "curiously"? Do you think that White explains his point of view clearly? Could someone find what he says to be confusing? Do you? Why is that?

8. Marya Mannes offers a generalization about American men and women. What is your response to what she says? Do you believe that such generalizations illuminate the truth or distort it?

9. Imagine that you are in a debate with John Wayne. He has just begun by making his statement about the Indians, and now it is your turn. What would you say? First, present your reply in a paragraph of five or so sentences. Then, present your reply at greater length, in about a page and a half. Now compare the two versions: Which is more effective and why?

10. The remark attributed to Clemenceau is supposed to be witty, but of course it may also be true—or false. Do you find any truth in it? Please explain.

11. Do you see in the statements by former presidents Adams and Nixon suggestions that can easily lead to the view that it is America's destiny to bring democracy to the rest of the world? Is there, implicit in their remarks, a hint of what Rudyard Kipling called "the white man's burden"?

ESSAYS

CHIEF SEATTLE

Seattle (1786–1866), for whom the city in Washington is named, was a chief of the Suquamish and Duwamish tribes on the coast of the Pacific Northwest region of what is now the United States. There is some uncertainty about exactly when he delivered this speech—perhaps late in 1853, when the white governor of the Washington Territory first visited the territory, or perhaps early in 1855, when Seattle signed the Port Elliott Treaty, which confined the tribes to a reservation.

Seattle spoke little or no English. The speech was given through an interpreter and was transcribed by Henry Smith, who published it in 1887, with a concluding note saying, "The above is but a fragment of his speech." Because Smith's notes are not extant, it is now impossible to know exactly what Seattle said, but one point can be made: The text we print here is based entirely on Smith's version, the only text with any claim to authenticity. Since 1931 Smith's version has occasionally been reprinted with embellishments, the most popular of which is the addition of three sentences at the end: "Dead—did I say? There is no death. Only a change of worlds." Fine words, but they belong to an editor of 1931, not to Seattle.

My People

Yonder sky has wept tears of compassion on our fathers for centuries untold, and which, to us, looks eternal, may change. To-day it is fair, to-morrow it may be overcast with clouds. My words are like the stars that never set. What Seattle says the great chief, Washington, (the Indians in early times thought that Washington was still alive. They knew the name to be that of a president, and when they heard of the president at Washington they mistook the name of the city for the name of the reigning chief. They thought, also, that King George was still England's monarch, because the Hudson Bay traders called themselves "King George men." This innocent deception the company was shrewd enough not to explain away for the Indians had more respect for them than they would have had, had they known England was ruled by a woman. Some of us have learned better.) can rely upon, with as much certainty as our pale-face brothers can rely upon the return of the seasons. The son of the white chief says his father sends us greetings of friendship and good-will. This is kind, for we know he has little need of our friendship in return, because his people are many. They are like the grass that covers the vast prairies, while my people are few, and resemble the scattering trees of a wind-swept plain.

The great, and I presume also good, white chief sends us word that he wants to buy our lands but is willing to allow us to reserve enough to live on comfortably. This indeed appears generous, for the red man no longer has rights that he need respect, and the offer may be wise, also, for we are no longer in need of a great country. There was a time when our people covered the whole land as the waves of a wind-ruffled sea cover its shell-paved floor. But that time has long since passed away with the greatness of tribes almost forgotten. I will not mourn over our untimely decay, nor reproach my pale-face brothers with hastening it, for we, too, may have been somewhat to blame.

When our young men grow angry at some real or imaginary wrong and disfigure their faces with black paint, their hearts, also, are disfigured and turn black, and then their cruelty is relentless and knows no bounds, and our old men are not able to restrain them.

But let us hope that hostilities between the red man and his pale face brothers may never return. We would have everything to lose and nothing to gain.

5   True it is that revenge, with our young braves, is considered gain, even at the cost of their own lives, but old men who stay at home in times of war, and old women who have sons to lose, know better.

Our great father Washington, for I presume he is now our father as well as yours, since George has moved his boundaries to the north; our great and good father, I say, sends us word by his son, who, no doubt, is a great chief among his people, that if we do as he desires, he will protect us. His brave armies will be to us a bristling wall of strength, and his great ships of war will fill our harbors so that our ancient enemies far to the northward, the Simsiams and Hydas, will no longer frighten our women and old men. Then he will be our father and we will be his children. But can this ever be? Your God loves your people and hates mine; he folds his strong arms lovingly around the white man and leads him as a father leads his infant son, but he has forsaken his red children; he makes your people wax strong every day, and soon they will fill the land; while our people are ebbing away like a fast-receding tide, that will never flow again. The white man's God cannot love his red children or he would protect them. They seem to be orphans and can look nowhere for help. How then can we become brothers? How can your father become our father and bring us prosperity and awaken in us dreams of returning greatness?

Your God seems to be partial. He came to the white man. We never saw Him; never even heard His voice; He gave the white man laws but He had no word for His red children whose teeming millions filled this vast continent as the stars fill the firmament. No, we are two distinct races and must ever remain so. There is little in common between us. The ashes of our ancestors are sacred and their final resting place is hallowed ground, while you wander away from the tombs of your fathers seemingly without regret.

Your religion was written on tables of stone by the iron finger of an angry God, lest you might forget it. The red man could never remember nor comprehend it.

Our religion is the traditions of our ancestors, the dreams of our old men, given them by the great Spirit, and the visions of our sachems, and is written in the hearts of our people.

10 Your dead cease to love you and the homes of their nativity as soon as they pass the portals of the tomb. They wander off beyond the stars, are soon forgotten and never return. Our dead never forget the beautiful world that gave them being. They still love its winding rivers, its great mountains and its sequestered vales, and they ever yearn in tenderest affection over the lonely hearted living and often return to visit and comfort them.

Day and night cannot dwell together. The red man has ever fled the approach of the white man, as the changing mists on the mountain side flee before the blazing morning sun.

However, your proposition seems a just one, and I think my folks will accept it and will retire to the reservation you offer them, and we will dwell apart and in peace, for the words of the great white chief seem to be the voice of nature speaking to my people out of the thick darkness that is fast gathering around them like a dense fog floating inward from a midnight sea.

It matters but little where we pass the remainder of our days. They are not many. The Indian's night promises to be dark. No bright star hovers about the horizon. Sad-voiced winds moan in the distance. Some grim Nemesis of our race is on the red man's trail, and wherever he goes he will still hear the sure approaching footsteps of the fell destroyer and prepare to meet his doom, as does the wounded doe that hears the approaching footsteps of the hunter. A few more moons, a few more winters and not one of all the mighty hosts that once filled this broad land or that now roam in fragmentary bands through these vast solitudes will remain to weep over the tombs of a people once as powerful and as hopeful as your own.

But why should we repine? Why should I murmur at the fate of my people? Tribes are made up of individuals and are no better than they. Men come and go like the waves of the sea. A tear, a tamanamus,[1] a dirge, and they are gone from our longing eyes forever. Even the white man, whose God walked and talked with him, as friend to friend, is not exempt from the common destiny. We *may* be brothers after all. We shall see.

[1]**tamanamus** guardian spirit.

15   We will ponder your proposition, and when we have decided we will tell you. But should we accept it, I here and now make this the first condition: That we will not be denied the privilege, without molestation, of visiting at will the graves of our ancestors and friends. Every part of this country is sacred to my people. Every hillside, every valley, every plain and grove has been hallowed by some fond memory or some sad experience of my tribe. Even the rocks that seem to lie dumb as they swelter in the sun along the silent seashore in solemn grandeur thrill with memories of past events connected with the fate of my people, and the very dust under your feet responds more lovingly to our footsteps than to yours, because it is the ashes of our ancestors, and our bare feet are conscious of the sympathetic touch, for the soil is rich with the life of our kindred.

        The sable braves, and fond mothers, and glad-hearted maidens, and the little children who lived and rejoiced here, and whose very names are now forgotten, still love these solitudes, and their deep fastnesses at eventide grow shadowy with the presence of dusky spirits. And when the last red man shall have perished from the earth and his memory among white men shall have become a myth, these shores shall swarm with the invisible dead of my tribe, and when your children's children shall think themselves alone in the field, the shop, upon the highway or in the silence of the woods they will not be alone. In all the earth there is no place dedicated to solitude. At night when the streets of your cities and villages shall be silent, and you think them deserted, they will throng with the returning hosts that once filled and still love this beautiful land. The white man will never be alone. Let him be just and deal kindly with my people, for the dead are not altogether powerless.

                                                                        [c. 1853]

Joining the Conversation: Critical Thinking and Writing

1. In a paragraph explain why Chief Seattle believes white people have a different God from that of American Indians.
2. Chief Seattle says that he thinks the offer of the whites is "fair" and that he thinks his people will accept the offer and retire to the reservation. Judging from his speech, do you think his main reason for approving the proposal is that it is fair?
3. In 250 words explain why Chief Seattle believes that whites and American Indians can never be reconciled, and evaluate his view.
4. Chief Seattle's speech is rich in metaphors and other figures of speech. List three examples. From what areas are most of his figures of speech drawn?

ELIZABETH CADY STANTON

Elizabeth Cady Stanton (1815–1902), a lawyer's daughter and journalist's wife, proposed in 1848 a convention to address the "social, civil, and religious condition and rights of women." Responding to Stanton's call, women from all over the Northeast convened in the village of Seneca Falls, New York. Her Declaration of Sentiments and Resolutions *adopted by the Seneca Falls Convention—but only after vigorous debate and some amendments by others—became the platform for the women's movement in this country.*

Declaration of Sentiments and Resolutions

When, in the course of human events, it becomes necessary for one portion of the family of man to assume among the people of the earth a position different from that which they have hitherto occupied, but one to which the laws of nature and of nature's God entitle them, a decent respect to the opinions of mankind requires that they should declare the causes that impel them to such a course.

We hold these truths to be self-evident: that all men and women are created equal; that they are endowed by their Creator with certain inalienable rights; that among these are life, liberty and the pursuit of happiness; that to secure these rights governments are instituted, deriving their just powers from the consent of the governed. Whenever any form of government becomes destructive of these ends, it is the right of those who suffer from it to refuse allegiance to it, and to insist upon the institution of a new government, laying its foundation on such principles, and organizing its powers in such form, as to them shall seem most likely to effect their safety and happiness. Prudence, indeed, will dictate that governments long established should not be changed for light and transient causes; and accordingly all experience hath shown that mankind are more disposed to suffer, while evils are sufferable, than to right themselves by abolishing the forms to which they were accustomed. But when a long train of abuses and usurpations, pursuing invariably the same object, evinces a design to reduce them under absolute despotism, it is their duty to throw off such government, and to provide new guards for their future security. Such has been the patient sufferance of the women under this government, and such is now the necessity which constrains them to demand the equal station to which they are entitled.

The history of mankind is a history of repeated injuries and usurpations on the part of man toward woman, having in direct object the establishment of an absolute tyranny over her. To prove this, let facts be submitted to a candid world.

He has never permitted her to exercise her inalienable right to the elective franchise.

5   He has compelled her to submit to laws, in the formation of which she had no voice.

He has withheld from her rights which are given to the most ignorant and degraded men—both natives and foreigners.

Having deprived her of this first right of a citizen, the elective franchise, thereby leaving her without representation in the halls of legislation, he has oppressed her on all sides.

He has made her, if married, in the eye of the law, civilly dead.

He has taken from her all right in property, even to the wages she earns.

10   He has made her, morally, an irresponsible being, as she can commit many crimes with impunity, provided they be done in the presence of her husband. In the covenant of marriage, she is compelled to promise obedience to her husband, he becoming to all intents and purposes, her master—the law giving him power to deprive her of her liberty, and to administer chastisement.

He has so framed the laws of divorce, as to what shall be the proper causes, and in case of separation, to whom the guardianship of the children shall be given, as to be wholly regardless of the happiness of women—the law, in all cases, going upon a false supposition of the supremacy of man, and giving all power into his hands.

After depriving her of all rights as a married woman, if single, and the owner of property, he has taxed her to support a government which recognizes her only when her property can be made profitable to it.

He has monopolized nearly all the profitable employments, and from those she is permitted to follow, she receives but a scanty remuneration. He closes against her all the avenues to wealth and distinction which he considers most honorable to himself. As a teacher of theology, medicine, or law, she is not known.

He has denied her the facilities for obtaining a thorough education, all colleges being closed against her.

15　　He allows her in Church, as well as State, but a subordinate position, claiming Apostolic authority for her exclusion from the ministry, and, with some exceptions, from any public participation in the affairs of the Church.

He has created a false public sentiment by giving to the world a different code of morals for men and women, by which moral delinquencies which exclude women from society, are not only tolerated, but deemed of little account in man.

He has usurped the prerogative of Jehovah himself, claiming it as his right to assign for her a sphere of action, when that belongs to her conscience and to her God.

He has endeavored, in every way that he could, to destroy her confidence in her own powers, to lessen her self-respect, and to make her willing to lead a dependent and abject life.

Now, in view of this entire disfranchisement of one-half the people of this country, their social and religious degradation—in view of the unjust laws above mentioned, and because women do feel themselves aggrieved, oppressed, and fraudulently deprived of their most sacred rights, we insist that they have immediate admission to all the rights and privileges which belong to them as citizens of the United States.

20　　In entering upon the great work before us, we anticipate no small amount of misconception, misrepresentation, and ridicule; but we shall use every instrumentality within our power to effect our object. We shall employ agents, circulate tracts, petition the State and National legislatures, and endeavor to enlist the pulpit and the press in our behalf. We hope this Convention will be followed by a series of Conventions embracing every part of the country.

[The following resolutions were discussed by Lucretia Mott, Thomas and Mary Ann McClintock, Amy Post, Catharine A. F. Stebbins, and others, and were adopted:]

Whereas, The great precept of nature is conceded to be, that "man shall pursue his own true and substantial happiness." Blackstone in his Commentaries remarks, that this law of Nature being coeval with mankind, and dictated by God himself, is of course superior in obligation to any other. It is binding over all the globe, in all countries, and at all times; no human laws are of any validity if contrary to this, and such of them as are valid, derive all their force, and all their validity, and all their authority, mediately and immediately, from this original; therefore.

Resolved, That such laws as conflict, in any way, with the true and substantial happiness of woman, are contrary to the great precept of nature and of no validity, for this is "superior in obligation to any other."

Resolved, That all laws which prevent woman from occupying such a station in society as her conscience shall dictate, or which place her in a position inferior to that of man, are contrary to the great precept of nature, and therefore of no force or authority.

Resolved, That woman is man's equal—was intended to be so by the Creator, and the highest good of the race demands that she should be recognized as such.

25　　*Resolved,* That the women of this country ought to be enlightened in regard to the laws under which they live, that they may no longer publish their degradation by declaring themselves satisfied with their present position, nor their ignorance, by asserting that they have all the rights they want.

Resolved, That inasmuch as man, while claiming for himself intellectual superiority, does accord to woman moral superiority, it is preeminently his duty to encourage her to speak and teach, as she has an opportunity, in all religious assemblies.

Resolved, That the same amount of virtue, delicacy, and refinement of behavior that is required of woman in the social state, should also be required of man, and the same transgressions should be visited with equal severity on both man and woman.

Resolved, That the objection of indelicacy and impropriety, which is so often brought against woman when she addresses a public audience, comes with a very ill-grace from those who encourage, by their attendance, her appearance on the stage, in the concert, or in feats of the circus.

Resolved, That woman has too long rested satisfied in the circumscribed limits which corrupt customs and a perverted application of the Scriptures have marked out for her, and that it is time she should move in the enlarged sphere which her great Creator has assigned her.

30   *Resolved,* That it is the duty of the women of this country to secure to themselves their sacred right to the elective franchise.

Resolved, That the equality of human rights results necessarily from the fact of the identity of the race in capabilities and responsibilities.

Resolved, therefore, That, being invested by the Creator with the same capabilities, and the same consciousness of responsibility for their exercise, it is demonstrably the right and duty of woman, equally with man, to promote every righteous cause by every righteous means; and especially in regard to the great subjects of morals and religion, it is self-evidently her right to participate with her brother in teaching them, both in private and in public, by writing and by speaking, by any instrumentalities proper to be used, and in any assemblies proper to be held; and this being a self-evident truth growing out of the divinely implanted principles of human nature, any custom or authority adverse to it, whether modern or wearing the hoary sanction of antiquity, is to be regarded as a self-evident falsehood, and at war with mankind.

[At the last session Lucretia Mott offered and spoke to the following resolution:]

Resolved, That the speedy success of our cause depends upon the zealous and untiring efforts of both men and women, for the overthrow of the monopoly of the pulpit, and for the securing to woman an equal participation with men in the various trades, professions, and commerce.

[1848]

Joining the Conversation: Critical Thinking and Writing

1. Stanton echoes the Declaration of Independence because she wishes to associate her ideas and the movement she supports with a document and a movement that her readers esteem. And of course she must have believed that if readers esteem the Declaration of Independence, they must grant the justice of her goals. Does her strategy work, or does it backfire by making her essay seem strained?

2. When Stanton insists that women have an "inalienable right to the elective franchise" (paragraph 4), what does she mean by "inalienable"?

3. Stanton complains that men have made women, "in the eye of the law, civilly dead" (paragraph 8). What does she mean by "civilly dead"? How is it possible for a person to be biologically alive yet civilly dead?
4. Stanton objects that women are "not known" as teachers of "theology, medicine, or law" (paragraph 13). Is this still true today? Do some research in the library or online, and then write three 100-word biographical sketches, one each on a well-known woman professor of theology, medicine, and law.
5. How might you go about proving (rather than merely asserting) that, as paragraph 24 says, "woman is man's equal—was intended to be so by the Creator"?
6. Stanton's *Declaration* claims that women have "the same capabilities" as men (paragraph 32). Yet in 1848 Stanton and the others at Seneca Falls knew, or should have known, that history recorded no example of an outstanding woman philosopher to compare with Plato or Kant, a great composer to compare with Beethoven or Chopin, a scientist to compare with Galileo or Newton, or a creative mathematician to compare with Euclid or Descartes. Do these facts contradict the Declaration's claim? If not, why not? How else but by different intellectual capabilities do you think such facts are to be explained?
7. Stanton's *Declaration* is about 165 years old. Have all of the issues she raised been satisfactorily resolved? If not, which ones remain?
8. In our society, children have very few rights. For instance, a child cannot decide to drop out of elementary school or high school, and a child cannot decide to leave his or her parents to reside with some other family that he or she finds more compatible. Whatever your view of children's rights, compose the best declaration of the rights of children that you can.

ABRAHAM LINCOLN

Abraham Lincoln (1809–65), sixteenth president of the United States, is not usually thought of as a writer, but his published speeches and writings comprise about 1,078,000 words, the equivalent of about four thousand pages of double-spaced typing. They were all composed without the assistance of a speech writer.

The Gettysburg campaign—a series of battles fought near Gettysburg in south-eastern Pennsylvania—took place in June and July of 1863. Each side lost something like twenty-three thousand men. The battle is regarded as a turning point in the war, but the Confederate army escaped and the war continued until April 1865.

On November 19, 1863, Lincoln delivered this short speech at the dedication of a national cemetery on the battlefield at Gettysburg.

Address at the Dedication of the Gettysburg National Cemetery

Four score and seven years ago our fathers brought forth on this continent, a new nation, conceived in Liberty, and dedicated to the proposition that all men are created equal.

Now we are engaged in a great civil war; testing whether that nation, or any nation so conceived and so dedicated, can long endure. We are met on a great battlefield of that war. We have come to dedicate a portion of that field as a final resting-place for those who here gave their lives that that nation might live. It is altogether fitting and proper that we should do this.

But, in a larger sense, we cannot dedicate—we cannot consecrate—we cannot hallow—this ground. The brave men, living and dead, who struggled here have consecrated it, far above our poor power to add or detract. The world will little note, nor long remember, what we say here, but it can never forget what they did here.

It is for us the living, rather, to be dedicated here to the unfinished work which they who fought here have thus far so nobly advanced. It is rather for us to be here dedicated to the great task remaining before us—that from these honored dead we take increased devotion to that cause for which they gave the last full measure of devotion; that we here highly resolve that these dead shall not have died in vain; that this nation, under God, shall have a new birth of freedom; and that government of the people, by the people, for the people, shall not perish from the earth.

[1863]

Joining the Conversation: Critical Thinking and Writing

1. Why do you suppose Lincoln began by saying "Four score and seven years ago" rather than "Eighty-seven years ago"? By the way, Martin Luther King Jr. began his speech *I Have a Dream* (delivered in 1963 in front of the Lincoln Memorial), "Five score years ago."
2. Some people have objected that (in the final sentence) "government of the people" is the same as "[government] by the people," and the passage is pointlessly redundant. Do you agree? A second question, about "of the people, by the people, for the people": If you were speaking this passage, would you emphasize *of, by,* and *for,* or would you emphasize *people*? Please explain.
3. Do you think that Lincoln says enough in his address about the dead soldiers? Should he have said more about them? How might the family of one of the dead responded to Lincoln's words?
4. What is the "unfinished work" that Lincoln enjoins us to perform? How are we to perform it, and how will we know whether we have done this work successfully or not?

STUDS TERKEL

Studs Terkel (1912–2008) was born Louis Terkel in New York City. After earning a PhD and a law degree from the University of Chicago he worked as a civil servant and an actor before becoming a radio and television broadcaster. Much of his broadcasting work consisted of interviewing people for "Studs' Place," and he later published numerous books of interviews. His American Dreams *presents transcriptions that Terkel recorded. This interview took place in the 1970s, decades before Schwarzenegger served as governor of California.*

Arnold Schwarzenegger's Dream

Call me Arnold.

I was born in a little Austrian town, outside Graz. It was a 300-year-old house.

When I was ten years old, I had the dream of being the best in the world in something. When I was fifteen, I had a dream that I wanted to be the best body builder in the world and the most muscular man. It was not only a dream I dreamed at night. It was also a daydream. It was so much in my mind that I felt it had to become a reality. It took me five years of hard work. Five years later, I turned this dream into reality and became Mr. Universe, the best-built man in the world.

"Winning" is a very important word. There is one that achieves what he wanted to achieve and there are hundreds of thousands that failed. It singles you out: the winner.

5   I came out second three times, but that is not what I call losing. The bottom line for me was: Arnold has to be the winner. I have to win more often the Mr. Universe title than anybody else. I won it five times consecutively. I hold the record as Mr. Olympia, the top professional body-building championship. I won it six times. That's why I retired. There was nobody even close to me. Everybody gave up competing against me. That's what I call a winner.

When I was a small boy, my dream was not to be big physically, but big in a way that everybody listens to me when I talk, that I'm a very important person, that people recognize me and see me as something special. I had a big need for being singled out.

Also my dream was to end up in America. When I was ten years old, I dreamed of being an American. At the time I didn't know much about America, just that it was a wonderful country. I felt it was where I belonged. I didn't like being in a little country like Austria. I did everything possible to get out. I did so in 1968, when I was twenty-one years old.

If I would believe in life after death, I would say my before-life I was living in America. That's why I feel so good here. It is the country where you can turn your dream into reality. Other countries don't have those things. When I came over here to America, I felt I was in heaven. In America, we don't have an obstacle. Nobody's holding you back.

Number One in America pretty much takes care of the rest of the world. You kind of run through the rest of the world like nothing. I'm trying to make people in America aware that they should appreciate what they have here. You have the best tax advantages here and the best prices here and the best products here.

10   One of the things I always had was a business mind. When I was in high school, a majority of my classes were business classes. Economics and accounting and mathematics. When I came over here to this country, I really didn't speak English almost at all. I learned English and then started taking business courses, because that's what America is best known for: business. Turning one dollar into a million dollars in a short period of time. Also when you make money, how do you keep it?

That's one of the most important things when you have money in your hand, how can you keep it? Or make more out of it? Real estate is one of the best ways of doing that. I own apartment buildings, office buildings, and raw land. That's my love, real estate.

I have emotions. But what you do, you keep them cold or you store them away for a time. You must control your emotions, you must have command over yourself. Three, four months before a competition, I could not be interfered by other people's problems. This is sometimes called selfish. It's the only way you can be if you want to achieve something. Any emotional things inside me, I try to keep cold so it doesn't interfere with my training.

Many times things really touched me. I felt them and I felt sensitive about them. But I had to talk myself out of it. I had to suppress those feelings in order to go on. Sport is one of those activities where you really have to concentrate. You must pay attention a hundred percent to the particular thing you're doing. There must be nothing else on your mind. Emotions must not interfere. Otherwise, you're thinking about your girlfriend. You're in love, your positive energies get channeled into another direction rather than going into your weight room or making money.

You have to choose at a very early date what you want: a normal life or to achieve things you want to achieve. I never wanted to win a popularity contest in doing things the way people want me to do it. I went the road I thought was best for me. A few people thought I was cold, selfish. Later they found out that's not the case. After I achieve my goal, I can be Mr. Nice Guy. You know what I mean?

15   California is to me a dreamland. It is the absolute combination of everything I was always looking for. It has all the money in the world there, show business there, wonderful weather there, beautiful country, ocean is there. Snow skiing in the winter, you can go in the desert the same day. You have beautiful-looking people there. They all have a tan.

I believe very strongly in the philosophy of staying hungry. If you have a dream and it becomes a reality, don't stay satisfied with it too long. Make up a new dream and hunt after that one and turn it into reality. When you have that dream achieved, make up a new dream.

I am a strong believer in Western philosophy, the philosophy of success, of progress, of getting rich. The Eastern philosophy is passive, which I believe in maybe three percent of the times, and the ninety-seven percent is Western, conquering and going on. It's a beautiful philosophy, and America should keep it up.

[1980]

Joining the Conversation: Critical Thinking and Writing

1. After saying that America "is the country where you can turn your dream into reality. Other countries don't have those things," Schwarzenegger goes on to say, "In America . . . nobody's holding you back." What do you suppose he means by "those things," and by saying that here "nobody's holding you back"?
2. If you have some firsthand knowledge of another country, in an essay of 250–500 words indicate in what ways that country might differ from America in the matter of allowing individuals to fulfill their dreams. By the way, is it your guess that Schwarzenegger's particular dream ("to be the best body builder in the world") is more easily fulfilled in the United States than elsewhere—say in Canada, or Cuba, or Russia, or Austria? Why?
3. In a paragraph, set forth what you think Schwarzenegger's view of America is.
4. In one paragraph, sketch Schwarzenegger as objectively as possible, as you perceive him in this interview. In a second paragraph, again drawing only on this interview, evaluate him, calling attention to what you think are his strengths and weaknesses.

STORIES

KURT VONNEGUT JR.

Kurt Vonnegut Jr. (1922–2007) was born in Indianapolis and studied biochemistry at Cornell University. He was drafted into the army and was captured by the Germans in the Battle of the Bulge in late 1944. A survivor of the Allied fire-bombing of Dresden in February 1945, along with other prisoners he was required to search for corpses hidden in the rubble. Two months later he was freed. After the war, he studied anthropology at the University of Chicago, then worked as a publicist for General Electric from 1947 until 1950, when he became a full-time writer.

Vonnegut wrote stories, novels, and plays. His two most famous works are probably Cat's Cradle *(1963), which ends with the freezing of the world, and* Slaughterhouse-Five *(1969), which draws on his wartime experience in Dresden.*

Harrison Bergeron

The year was 2081, and everybody was finally equal. They weren't only equal before God and the law. They were equal every which way. Nobody was smarter than anybody else. Nobody was better looking than anybody else. Nobody was stronger or quicker than anybody else. All this equality was due to the 211th, 212th, and 213th Amendments to the Constitution, and to the unceasing vigilance of agents of the United States Handicapper General.

Some things about living still weren't quite right, though. April, for instance, still drove people crazy by not being springtime. And it was in that clammy month that the H-G men took George and Hazel Bergeron's fourteen-year-old son, Harrison, away.

It was tragic, all right, but George and Hazel couldn't think about it very hard. Hazel had a perfectly average intelligence, which meant she couldn't think about anything except in short bursts. And George, while his intelligence was way above normal, had a little mental handicap radio in his ear. He was required by law to wear it at all times. It was tuned to a government transmitter. Every twenty seconds or so, the transmitter would send out some sharp noise to keep people like George from taking unfair advantage of their brains.

George and Hazel were watching television. There were tears on Hazel's cheeks, but she'd forgotten for the moment what they were about.

5   On the television screen, were ballerinas.

A buzzer sounded in George's head. His thoughts fled in panic, like bandits from a burglar alarm.

"That was a real pretty dance, that dance they just did," said Hazel.

"Huh?" said George.

"That dance—it was nice," said Hazel.

10   "Yup," said George. He tried to think a little about the ballerinas. They weren't really very good—no better than anybody else would have been, anyway. They were burdened with sashweights and bags of birdshot, and their faces were masked, so that no one, seeing a free and graceful gesture or a pretty face, would feel like something the cat drug in. George was toying with the vague notion that maybe dancers shouldn't be handicapped. But he didn't get very far with it before another noise in his ear radio scattered his thoughts.

George winced. So did two out of the eight ballerinas.

Hazel saw him wince. Having no mental handicap herself, she had to ask George what the latest sound had been.

"Sounded like somebody hitting a milk bottle with a ball peen hammer," said George.

"I'd think it would be real interesting, hearing all the different sounds," said Hazel, a little envious. "All the things they think up."

15   "Um," said George.

"Only, if I was Handicapper General, you know what I would do?" said Hazel. Hazel, as a matter of fact, bore a strong resemblance to the Handicapper General, a woman named Diana Moon Glampers. "If I was Diana Moon Glampers," said Hazel, "I'd have chimes on Sunday—just chimes. Kind of in honor of religion."

"I could think, if it was just chimes," said George.

"Well—maybe make 'em real loud," said Hazel. "I think I'd make a good Handicapper General."

"Good as anybody else," said George.

20 "Who knows better'n I do what normal is?" said Hazel.

"Right," said George. He began to think glimmeringly about his abnormal son who was now in jail, about Harrison, but a twenty-one-gun salute in his head stopped that.

"Boy!" said Hazel, "that was a doozy, wasn't it?"

It was such a doozy that George was white and trembling, and tears stood on the rims of his red eyes. Two of the eight ballerinas had collapsed to the studio floor, and were holding their temples.

"All of a sudden you look so tired," said Hazel. "Why don't you stretch out on the sofa, so's you can rest your handicap bag on the pillows, honeybunch." She was referring to the forty-seven pounds of birdshot in a canvas bag, which was padlocked around George's neck. "Go on and rest the bag for a little while," she said. "I don't care if you're not equal to me for a while."

25 George weighed the bag with his hands. "I don't mind it," he said. "I don't notice it any more. It's just a part of me."

"You been so tired lately—kind of wore out," said Hazel. "If there was just some way we could make a little hole in the bottom of the bag, and just take out a few of them lead balls. Just a few."

"Two years in prison and two thousand dollars fine for every ball I took out," said George. "I don't call that a bargain."

"If you could just take a few out when you came home from work," said Hazel. "I mean—you don't compete with anybody around here. You just set around."

"If I tried to get away with it," said George, "then other people'd get away with it—and pretty soon we'd be right back to the dark ages again, with everybody competing against everybody else. You wouldn't like that, would you?"

30 "I'd hate it," said Hazel.

"There you are," said George. "The minute people start cheating on laws, what do you think happens to society?"

If Hazel hadn't been able to come up with an answer to this question George couldn't have supplied one. A siren was going off in his head.

"Reckon it'd fall apart," said Hazel.

"What would?" said George blankly.

35 "Society," said Hazel uncertainly. "Wasn't that what you just said?"

"Who knows?" said George.

The television program was suddenly interrupted for a news bulletin. It wasn't clear at first as to what the bulletin was about, since the announcer, like all announcers, had a serious speech impediment. For about half a minute, and in a state of high excitement, the announcer tried to say, "Ladies and gentlemen—"

He finally gave up, handed the bulletin to a ballerina to read.

"That's all right—" Hazel said of the announcer, "he tried. That's the big thing. He tried to do the best he could with what God gave him. He should get a nice raise for trying so hard."

40 "Ladies and gentlemen—" said the ballerina, reading the bulletin. She must have been extraordinarily beautiful, because the mask she wore was hideous. And it was easy to see that she was the strongest and most graceful of all the dancers, for her handicap bags were as big as those worn by two-hundred-pound men.

And she had to apologize at once for her voice, which was a very unfair voice for a woman to use. Her voice was a warm, luminous, timeless melody.

"Excuse me—" she said, and she began again, making her voice absolutely uncompetitive.

"Harrison Bergeron, age fourteen," she said in a grackle squawk, "has just escaped from jail, where he was held on suspicion of plotting to overthrow the government. He is a genius and an athlete, is under-handicapped, and should be regarded as extremely dangerous."

A police photograph of Harrison Bergeron was flashed on the screen upside down, then sideways, upside down again, then right side up. The picture showed the full length of Harrison against a background calibrated in feet and inches. He was exactly seven feet tall.

The rest of Harrison's appearance was Halloween and hardware. Nobody had ever borne heavier handicaps. He had outgrown hindrances faster than the H-G men could think them up. Instead of a little ear radio for a mental handicap, he wore a tremendous pair of earphones, and spectacles with thick wavy lenses. The spectacles were intended to make him not only half blind, but to give him whanging headaches besides.

45   Scrap mental was hung all over him. Ordinarily, there was a certain symmetry, a military neatness to the handicaps issued to strong people, but Harrison looked like a walking junkyard. In the race of life, Harrison carried three hundred pounds.

And to offset his good looks, the H-G men required that he wear at all times a red rubber ball for a nose, keep his eyebrows shaved off, and cover his even white teeth with black caps at snaggle-tooth random.

"If you see this boy," said the ballerina, "do not—I repeat, do not—try to reason with him."

There was the shriek of a door being torn from its hinges.

Screams and barking cries of consternation came from the television set. The photograph of Harrison Bergeron on the screen jumped again and again, as though dancing to the tune of an earthquake.

50   George Bergeron correctly identified the earthquake, and well he might have—for many was the time his own home had danced to the same crashing tune. "My God—" said George, "that must be Harrison!"

The realization was blasted from his mind instantly by the sound of an automobile collision in his head.

When George could open his eyes again, the photograph of Harrison was gone. A living, breathing Harrison filled the screen.

Clanking, clownish, and huge, Harrison stood in the center of the studio. The knob of the uprooted studio door was still in his hand. Ballerinas, technicians, musicians, and announcers cowered on their knees before him, expecting to die.

"I am the Emperor!" cried Harrison. "Do you hear? I am the Emperor! Everybody must do what I say at once!" He stamped his foot and the studio shook.

55   "Even as I stand here—" he bellowed, "crippled, hobbled, sickened—I am a greater ruler than any man who ever lived! Now watch me become what I *can* become!"

Harrison tore the straps of his handicap harness like wet tissue paper, tore straps guaranteed to support five thousand pounds.

Harrison's scrap-iron handicaps crashed to the floor.

Harrison thrust his thumbs under the bar of the padlock that secured his head harness. The bar snapped like celery. Harrison smashed his headphones and spectacles against the wall.

He flung away his rubber-ball nose, revealed a man that would have awed Thor, the god of thunder.

"I shall now select my Empress!" he said, looking down on the cowering people. "Let the first woman who dares rise to her feet claim her mate and her throne!"

A moment passed, and then a ballerina arose, swaying like a willow.

Harrison plucked the mental handicap from her ear, snapped off her physical handicaps with marvelous delicacy. Last of all, he removed her mask.

She was blindingly beautiful.

"Now—" said Harrison, taking her hand, "shall we show the people the meaning of the word dance? Music!" he commanded.

The musicians scrambled back into their chairs, and Harrison stripped them of their handicaps, too. "Play your best," he told them, "and I'll make you barons and dukes and earls."

The music began. It was normal at first—cheap, silly, false. But Harrison snatched two musicians from their chairs, waved them like batons as he sang the music as he wanted it played. He slammed them back into their chairs.

The music began again and was much improved.

Harrison and his Empress merely listened to the music for a while—listened gravely, as though synchronizing their heartbeats with it.

They shifted their weights to their toes.

Harrison placed his big hands on the girl's tiny waist, letting her sense the weightlessness that would soon be hers.

And then, in an explosion of joy and grace, into the air they sprang!

Not only were the laws of the land abandoned, but the law of gravity and the laws of motion as well.

They reeled, whirled, swiveled, flounced, capered, gamboled, and spun.

They leaped like deer on the moon.

The studio ceiling was thirty feet high, but each leap brought the dancers nearer to it.

It became their obvious intention to kiss the ceiling.

They kissed it.

And then, neutralizing gravity with love and pure will, they remained suspended in air inches below the ceiling, and they kissed each other for a long, long time.

It was then that Diana Moon Glampers, the Handicapper General, came into the studio with a double-barreled ten-gauge shotgun. She fired twice, and the Emperor and the Empress were dead before they hit the floor.

Diana Moon Glampers loaded the gun again. She aimed it at the musicians and told them they had ten seconds to get their handicaps back on.

It was then that the Bergerons' television tube burned out.

Hazel turned to comment about the blackout to George. But George had gone out into the kitchen for a can of beer.

George came back in with the beer, paused while a handicap signal shook him up. And then he sat down again. "You been crying?" he said to Hazel.

"Yup," she said.

"What about?" he said.

"I forget," she said. "Something real sad on television."

"What was it?" he said.

"It's all kind of mixed up in my mind," said Hazel.

"Forget sad things," said George.

90   "I always do," said Hazel.

"That's my girl," said George. He winced. There was the sound of a riveting gun in his head.

"Gee—I could tell that one was a doozy," said Hazel.

"You can say that again," said George.

"Gee—" said Hazel, "I could tell that one was a doozy."

[1961]

Joining the Conversation: Critical Thinking and Writing

1. The Declaration of Independence, drafted by Thomas Jefferson, tells us that "all men are created equal." What does this statement mean? Does the society of Harrison Bergeron—a society in which, according to the first sentence of the story, "everybody was finally equal"—show us a society in which Jefferson's words are at last fulfilled? Exactly what are the values of the world in 2081?

2. One sometimes hears that it is the duty of government to equalize society. Hence, for instance, inheritance taxes are sometimes said to be a device employed in an effort to equalize wealth. What forces, if any, can you point to, for example in educational or political systems, that seek to equalize people? If there are such forces at work, do you think they represent unwise and perhaps unlawful government meddling, and are essentially at odds with a basic American idea of rugged individualism and of wholesome competition?

3. Speaking of competition, George says (paragraph 31) to Hazel, "The minute people start cheating on laws, what do you think happens to society?" Hazel replies, "Reckon it'd fall all apart" (33). What do you think that we, as readers, are supposed to make of this statement? In your response—an essay of 500 words—consider the actions of Harrison Bergeron, who declares himself Emperor and who says (54), "Everybody must do what I say at once!" Is Vonnegut suggesting, in George's behavior, that only laws can keep talented individuals from tyrannizing over others?

LANGSTON HUGHES

For a biographical note on Langston Hughes, see page 343.

One Friday Morning

The thrilling news did not come directly to Nancy Lee, but it came in little indirections that finally added themselves up to one tremendous fact: she had won the prize! But being a calm and quiet young lady, she did not say anything, although the whole high school buzzed with rumors, guesses, reportedly authentic announcements on the part of students who had no right to be making announcements at all—since no student really knew yet who had won this year's art scholarship.

But Nancy Lee's drawing was so good, her lines so sure, her colors so bright and harmonious, that certainly no other student in the senior art class at George Washington High was thought to have very much of a chance. Yet you never could tell. Last year nobody had expected Joe Williams to win the Artist Club scholarship with that funny modernistic water color he had done of the high-level bridge. In fact, it was hard to make out there was a bridge until you had looked at the picture a long time. Still, Joe Williams got the prize, was feted by the community's leading painters, club women, and society folks at a big banquet at the Park-Rose Hotel, and was now an award student at the Art School—the city's only art school.

Nancy Lee Johnson was a colored girl, a few years out of the South. But seldom did her high-school classmates think of her as colored. She was smart, pretty, and brown, and fitted in well with the life of the school. She stood high in scholarship, played a swell game of basketball, had taken part in the senior musical in a soft, velvety voice, and had never seemed to intrude or stand out, except in pleasant ways, so it was seldom even mentioned—her color.

Nancy Lee sometimes forgot she was colored herself. She liked her classmates and her school. Particularly she liked her art teacher, Miss Dietrich, the tall red-haired woman who taught her law and order in doing things; and the beauty of working step by step until a job is done; a picture finished; a design created; or a block print carved out of nothing but an idea and a smooth square of linoleum, inked, proofs made, and finally put down on paper—clean, sharp, beautiful, individual, unlike any other in the world, thus making the paper have a meaning nobody else could give it except Nancy Lee. That was the wonderful thing about true creation. You made something nobody else on earth could make—but you.

5   Miss Dietrich was the kind of teacher who brought out the best in her students—but their own best, not anybody else's copied best. For anybody else's best, great though it might be, even Michelangelo's, wasn't enough to please Miss Dietrich, dealing with the creative impulses of young men and women living in an American city in the Middle West, and being American.

Nancy Lee was proud of being American, a Negro American with blood out of Africa a long time ago, too many generations back to count. But her parents had taught her the beauties of Africa, its strength, its song, its mighty rivers, its early smelting of iron, its building of the pyramids, and its ancient and important civilizations. And Miss Dietrich had discovered for her the sharp and humorous lines of African sculpture, Benin, Congo, Makonde. Nancy Lee's father was a mail carrier, her mother a social worker in a city settlement house. Both parents had been to Negro colleges in the South. And her mother had gotten a further degree in social work from a Northern university. Her parents were, like most Americans, simple, ordinary people who had worked hard and steadily for their education. Now they were trying to make it easier for Nancy Lee to achieve learning than it had been for them. They would be very happy when they heard of the award to their daughter—yet Nancy did not tell them. To surprise them would be better. Besides, there had been a promise.

Casually, one day, Miss Dietrich asked Nancy Lee what color frame she thought would be best on her picture. That had been the first inkling.

"Blue," Nancy Lee said. Although the picture had been entered in the Artist Club contest a month ago, Nancy Lee did not hesitate in her choice of a color for the possible frame, since she could still see her picture clearly in her mind's eye— for that picture waiting for the blue frame had come out of her soul, her own life, and had bloomed into miraculous being with Miss Dietrich's help. It was, she knew, the best water color she had painted in her four years as a high-school art student, and she was glad she had made something Miss Dietrich liked well enough to permit her to enter in the contest before she graduated.

It was not a modernistic picture in the sense that you had to look at it a long time to understand what it meant. It was just a simple scene in the city park on a spring day, with the trees still leaflessly lacy against the sky, the new grass fresh and green, a flag on a tall pole in the center, children playing, and an old Negro woman sitting on a bench with her head turned. A lot for one picture, to be sure, but it was not there in heavy and final detail like a calendar. Its charm was that everything was light and airy, happy like spring, with a lot of blue sky; paper-white clouds, and air showing through. You could tell that the old Negro woman was looking at the flag, and that the flag was proud in the spring breeze, and that the breeze helped to make the children's dresses billow as they played.

10   Miss Dietrich had taught Nancy Lee how to paint spring, people, and a breeze on what was only a plain white piece of paper from the supply closet. But Miss Dietrich had not said make it like any other spring-people-breeze ever seen before. She let it remain Nancy Lee's own. That is how the old Negro woman happened to be there looking at the flag—for in her mind the flag, the spring, and the woman formed a kind of triangle holding a dream Nancy Lee wanted to express. White stars on a blue field, spring, children, ever-growing life, and an old woman. Would the judges at the Artist Club like it?

One wet, rainy April afternoon Miss O'Shay, the girls' vice-principal, sent for Nancy Lee to stop by her office as school closed. Pupils without umbrellas or rain-coats were clustered in doorways, hoping to make it home between showers. Outside the skies were gray. Nancy Lee's thoughts were suddenly gray, too.

She did not think she had done anything wrong, yet that tight little knot came in her throat just the same as she approached Miss O'Shay's door. Perhaps she had banged her locker too often and too hard. Perhaps the note in French she had written to Sallie halfway across the study hall just for fun had never gotten to Sallie but into Miss O'Shay's hands instead. Or maybe she was failing in some subject and wouldn't be allowed to graduate. Chemistry! A pang went through the pit of her stomach.

She knocked on Miss O'Shay's door. That familiarly solid and competent voice said, "Come in."

Miss O'Shay had a way of making you feel welcome, even if you came to be expelled.

15   "Sit down, Nancy Lee Johnson," said Miss O'Shay. "I have something to tell you." Nancy Lee sat down. "But I must ask you to promise not to tell anyone yet."

"I won't, Miss O'Shay," Nancy Lee said, wondering what on earth the principal had to say to her.

"You are about to graduate," Miss O'Shay said. "And we shall miss you. You have been an excellent student, Nancy, and you will not be without honors on the senior list, as I am sure you know."

At that point there was a light knock on the door. Miss O'Shay called out, "Come in," and Miss Dietrich entered. "May I be a part of this, too?" she asked, tall and smiling.

"Of course," Miss O'Shay said. "I was just telling Nancy Lee what we thought of her. But I hadn't gotten around to giving her the news. Perhaps, Miss Dietrich, you'd like to tell her yourself."

20   Miss Dietrich was always direct. "Nancy Lee," she said, "your picture has won the Artist Club scholarship."

The slender brown girl's eyes widened, her heart jumped, then her throat tightened again. She tried to smile, but instead tears came to her eyes.

"Dear Nancy Lee," Miss O'Shay said, "we are so happy for you." The elderly white woman took her hand and shook it warmly while Miss Dietrich beamed with pride.

Nancy Lee must have danced all the way home. She never remembered quite how she got there through the rain. She hoped she had been dignified. But certainly she hadn't stopped to tell anybody her secret on the way. Raindrops, smiles, and tears mingled on her brown cheeks. She hoped her mother hadn't yet gotten home and that the house was empty. She wanted to have time to calm down and look natural before she had to see anyone. She didn't want to be bursting with excitement—having a secret to contain.

Miss O'Shay's calling her to the office had been in the nature of a preparation and a warning. The kind, elderly vice-principal said she did not believe in catching young ladies unawares, even with honors, so she wished her to know about the coming award. In making acceptance speeches she wanted her to be calm, prepared, not nervous, overcome, and frightened. So Nancy Lee was asked to think what she would say when the scholarship was conferred upon her a few days hence, both at the Friday morning high-school assembly hour, when the announcement would be made, and at the evening banquet of the Artist Club. Nancy Lee promised the vice-principal to think calmly about what she would say.

25   Miss Dietrich had then asked for some facts about her parents, her background, and her life, since such material would probably be desired for the papers. Nancy Lee had told her how, six years before, they had come up from the Deep South, her father having been successful in achieving a transfer from the one post office to another, a thing he had long sought in order to give Nancy Lee a chance to go to school in the North. Now they lived in a modest Negro neighborhood, went to see the best plays when they came to town, and had been saving to send Nancy Lee to art school, in case she were permitted to enter. But the scholarship would help a great deal, for they were not rich people.

"Now Mother can have a new coat next winter," Nancy Lee thought, "because my tuition will all be covered for the first year. And once in art school, there are other scholarships I can win."

Dreams began to dance through her head, plans and ambitions, beauties she would create for herself, her parents, and the Negro people—for Nancy Lee possessed a deep and reverent race pride. She could see the old woman in her picture (really her grandmother in the South) lifting her head to the bright stars on the flag in the distance. A Negro in America! Often hurt, discriminated against, sometimes lynched—but always there were the stars on the blue body of the flag. Was there any other flag in the world that had so many stars? Nancy Lee thought deeply, but she could remember none in all the encyclopedias or geographies she had ever looked into.

"Hitch your wagon to a star," Nancy Lee thought, dancing home in the rain. "Who were our flag-makers?"

Friday morning came, the morning when the world would know—her high-school world, the newspaper world, her mother and dad. Dad could not be there at the assembly to hear the announcement, nor see her prize picture displayed on the stage, nor to listen to Nancy Lee's little speech of acceptance, but Mother would be able to come, although Mother was much puzzled as to why Nancy Lee was so insistent she be at school on that particular Friday morning.

30   When something is happening, something new and fine, something that will change your very life, it is hard to go to sleep at night for thinking about it, and hard to keep your heart from pounding, or a strange little knot of joy from gathering in your throat. Nancy Lee had taken her bath, brushed her hair until it glowed, and had gone to bed thinking about the next day, the big day, when before three thousand students, she would be the one student honored, her painting the one painting to be acclaimed as the best of the year from all the art classes of the city. Her short speech of gratitude was ready. She went over it in her mind, not word for word

(because she didn't want it to sound as if she had learned it by heart), but she let the thoughts flow simply and sincerely through her consciousness many times.

When the president of the Artist Club presented her with the medal and scroll of the scholarship award, she would say:

"Judges and members of the Artist Club. I want to thank you for this award that means so much to me personally and through me to my people, the colored people of this city, who, sometimes, are discouraged and bewildered, thinking that color and poverty are against them. I accept this award with gratitude and pride, not for myself alone, but for my race that believes in American opportunity and American fairness—and the bright stars in our flag. I thank Miss Dietrich and the teachers who made it possible for me to have the knowledge and training that lie behind this honor you have conferred upon my painting. When I came here from the South a few years ago, I was not sure how you would receive me. You received me well. You have given me a chance and helped me along the road I wanted to follow. I suppose the judges know that every week here at assembly the students of this school pledge allegiance to the flag. I shall try to be worthy of that pledge, and of the help and friendship and understanding of my fellow citizens of whatever race or creed, and of our American dream of 'Liberty and justice for all'!"

That would be her response before the students in the morning. How proud and happy the Negro pupils would be, perhaps almost as proud as they were of the one colored star on the football team. Her mother would probably cry with happiness. Thus Nancy Lee went to sleep dreaming of a wonderful tomorrow.

The bright sunlight of an April morning woke her. There was breakfast with her parents—their half-amused and puzzled faces across the table, wondering what could be this secret that made her eyes so bright. The swift walk to school; the clock in the tower almost nine; hundreds of pupils streaming into the long, rambling old building that was the city's largest high school; the sudden quiet of the homeroom after the bell rang; then the teacher opening her record book to call the roll. But just before she began, she looked across the room until her eyes located Nancy Lee.

35   "Nancy," she said, "Miss O'Shay would like to see you in her office, please."

Nancy Lee rose and went out while the names were being called and the word *present* added its period to each name. Perhaps, Nancy Lee thought, the reporters from the papers had already come. Maybe they wanted to take her picture before assembly, which wasn't until ten o'clock. (Last year they had had the photograph of the winner of the award in the morning papers as soon as the announcement had been made.)

Nancy Lee knocked at Miss O'Shay's door.

"Come in."

The vice-principal stood at her desk. There was no one else in the room. It was very quiet.

40   "Sit down, Nancy Lee," she said. Miss O'Shay did not smile. There was a long pause. The seconds went by slowly. "I do not know how to tell you what I have to say," the elderly woman began, her eyes on the papers on her desk. "I am indignant and ashamed for myself and for this city." Then she lifted her eyes and looked at Nancy Lee in the neat blue dress, sitting there before her. "You are not to receive the scholarship this morning."

Outside in the hall the electric bells announcing the first period rang, loud and interminably long. Miss O'Shay remained silent. To the brown girl there in the chair, the room grew suddenly smaller, smaller, smaller, and there was no air. She could not speak.

Miss O'Shay said, "When the committee learned that you were colored, they changed their plans."

Still Nancy Lee said nothing, for there was no air to give breath to her lungs.

"Here is the letter from the committee, Nancy Lee." Miss O'Shay picked it up and read the final paragraph to her.

45   "'It seems to us wiser to arbitrarily rotate the award among the various high schools of the city from now on. And especially in this case since the student chosen happens to be colored, a circumstance which unfortunately, had we known, might have prevented this embarrassment. But there have never been any Negro students in the local art school, and the presence of one there might create difficulties for all concerned. We have high regard for the quality of Nancy Lee Johnson's talent, but we do not feel it would be fair to honor it with the Artist Club award.'" Miss O'Shay paused. She put the letter down.

"Nancy Lee, I am very sorry to have to give you this message."

"But my speech," Nancy Lee said, "was about. . . ." The words stuck in her throat. ". . . about America. . . ."

Miss O'Shay had risen; she turned her back and stood looking out the window at the spring tulips in the school yard.

"I thought, since the award would be made at assembly right after our oath of allegiance," the words tumbled almost hysterically from Nancy Lee's throat now, "I would put part of the flag salute in my speech. You know, Miss O'Shay, that part about 'liberty and justice for all.'"

50   "I know," said Miss O'Shay, slowly facing the room again. "But America is only what we who believe in it make it. I am Irish. You may not know, Nancy Lee, but years ago we were called the dirty Irish, and mobs rioted against us in the big cities, and we were invited to go back where we came from. But we didn't go. And we didn't give up, because we believed in the American dream, and in our power to make that dream come true. Difficulties, yes. Mountains to climb, yes. Discouragements to face, yes. Democracy to make, yes. That is it, Nancy Lee! We still have in this world of ours democracy to *make*. You and I, Nancy Lee. But the premise and the base are here, the lines of the Declaration of Independence and the words of Lincoln are here, and the stars in our flag. Those who deny you this scholarship do not know the meaning of those stars, but it's up to us to make them know. As a teacher in the public schools of this city, I myself will go before the school board and ask them to remove from our system the offer of any prizes or awards denied to any student because of race or color."

Suddenly Miss O'Shay stopped speaking. Her clear, clear blue eyes looked into those of the girl before her. The woman's eyes were full of strength and courage. "Lift up your head, Nancy Lee, and smile at me."

Miss O'Shay stood against the open window with the green lawn and the tulips beyond, the sunlight tangled in her gray hair, her voice an electric flow of strength to the hurt spirit of Nancy Lee. The Abolitionists who believed in freedom when there was slavery must have been like that. The first white teachers who went into the Deep South to teach the freed slaves must have been like that. All those who stand against ignorance, narrowness, hate, and mud on stars must be like that.

Nancy Lee lifted her head and smiled. The bell for assembly rang. She went through the long hall filled with students, toward the auditorium.

"There will be other awards," Nancy Lee thought. "There're schools in other cities. This won't keep me down. But when I'm a woman, I'll fight to see that these things don't happen to other girls as this has happened to me. And men and women like Miss O'Shay will help me."

55   She took her seat among the seniors. The doors of the auditorium closed. As
the principal came onto the platform, the students rose and turned their eyes to the
flag on the stage.

One hand went to the heart, the other outstretched toward the flag. Three
thousand voices spoke. Among them was the voice of a dark girl whose cheeks
were suddenly wet with tears, ". . . one nation indivisible, with liberty and justice
for all."

"That is the land we must make," she thought.

[1941]

Joining the Conversation: Critical Thinking and Writing

1. The third paragraph begins: "Nancy Lee Johnson was a colored girl. . . ." How
   would your response to the opening of the story change if this paragraph were
   placed at the very beginning?
2. Nancy Lee takes pride in her identity as both a "Negro" and an "American." How
   does she define and understand each of these terms? Does she perceive them
   to be at all at odds with one another? Is she admirable in her convictions, or is
   she simply naive?
3. This is a story about racism, but it is also a study (and an affirmation) of American ideals and principles. What is your response to Miss O'Shay's inspiring
   words to Nancy Lee at the end of the story? What is Nancy Lee's response to
   them, and your response to her? Does Hughes succeed in making us believe in,
   and accept, Nancy Lee's feelings at the conclusion?

WILLIAM CARLOS WILLIAMS

*William Carlos Williams (1883–1963) was the son of an English traveling
salesman and a Basque Jewish woman. The couple met in Puerto Rico and
settled in Rutherford, New Jersey, where Williams was born. He spent his life
there, practicing as a pediatrician and writing poems in the moments between
seeing patients.*

The Use of Force

They were new patients to me, all I had was the name, Olson. Please come down
as soon as you can, my daughter is very sick. When I arrived I was met by the
mother, a big startled looking woman, very clean and apologetic who merely
said, Is this the doctor? and let me in. In the back, she added. You must excuse
us, doctor, we have her in the kitchen where it is warm. It is very damp here
sometimes.

The child was fully dressed and sitting on her father's lap near the kitchen
table. He tried to get up, but I motioned for him not to bother, took off my overcoat and started to look things over. I could see that they were all very nervous,
eyeing me up and down distrustfully. As often, in such cases, they weren't telling
me more than they had to, it was up to me to tell them; that's why they were
spending three dollars on me.

The child was fairly eating me up with her cold, steady eyes, and no expression to her face whatever. She did not move and seemed, inwardly, quiet; an unusually attractive little thing, and as strong as a heifer in appearance. But her face was flushed, she was breathing rapidly, and I realized that she had a high fever. She had magnificent blond hair, in profusion. One of those picture children often reproduced in advertising leaflets and the photogravure sections of the Sunday papers.

She's had a fever for three days, began the father and we don't know what it comes from. My wife has given her things, you know, like people do, but it don't do no good. And there's been a lot of sickness around. So we tho't you'd better look her over and tell us what is the matter.

5   As doctors often do I took a trial shot at it as a point of departure. Has she had a sore throat?

Both parents answered me together, No . . . No, she says her throat don't hurt her.

Does your throat hurt you? added the mother to the child. But the little girl's expression didn't change nor did she move her eyes from my face.

Have you looked?

I tried to, said the mother, but I couldn't see.

10   As it happens we had been having a number of cases of diphtheria in the school to which the child went during that month and we were all, quite apparently, thinking of that, though no one had as yet spoken of the thing.

Well, I said, suppose we take a look at the throat first. I smiled in my best professional manner and asking for the child's first name I said, come on, Mathilda, open your mouth and let's take a look at your throat.

Nothing doing.

Aw, come on, I coaxed, just open your mouth wide and let me take a look. Look, I said opening both hands wide, I haven't anything in my hands. Just open up and let me see.

Such a nice man, put in the mother. Look how kind he is to you. Come on, do what he tells you to, he won't hurt you.

15   At that I ground my teeth in disgust. If only they wouldn't use the word "hurt" I might be able to get somewhere. But I did not allow myself to be hurried or disturbed but speaking quietly and slowly I approached the child again.

As I moved my chair a little nearer suddenly with one catlike movement both her hands clawed instinctively for my eyes and she almost reached them too. In fact she knocked my glasses flying and they fell, though unbroken, several feet away from me on the kitchen floor.

Both the mother and father almost turned themselves inside out in embarrassment and apology. You bad girl, said the mother, taking her and shaking her by one arm. Look what you've done. The nice man . . .

For heaven's sake, I broke in. Don't call me a nice man to her. I'm here to look at her throat on the chance that she might have diphtheria and possibly die of it. But that's nothing to her. Look here, I said to the child, we're going to look at your throat. You're old enough to understand what I'm saying. Will you open it now by yourself or shall we have to open it for you?

Not a move. Even her expression hadn't changed. Her breaths however were coming faster and faster. Then the battle began. I had to do it. I had to have a throat culture for her own protection. But first I told the parents that it was entirely up to them. I explained the danger but said that I would not insist on a throat examination so long as they would take the responsibility.

20   If you don't do what the doctor says you'll have to go to the hospital, the mother admonished her severely.

Oh yeah? I had to smile to myself. After all, I had already fallen in love with the savage brat, the parents were contemptible to me. In the ensuing struggle they grew more and more abject, crushed, exhausted while she surely rose to magnificent heights of insane fury of effort bred of her terror of me.

The father tried his best, and he was a big man but the fact that she was his daughter, his shame at her behavior and his dread of hurting her made him release her just at the critical times when I had almost achieved success, till I wanted to kill him. But his dread also that she might have diphtheria made him tell me to go on, go on though he himself was almost fainting, while the mother moved back and forth behind us raising and lowering her hands in an agony of apprehension.

Put her in front of you on your lap, I ordered, and hold both her wrists.

But as soon as he did the child let out a scream. Don't, you're hurting me. Let go of my hands. Let them go I tell you. Then she shrieked terrifyingly, hysterically. Stop it! Stop it! You're killing me!

25   Do you think she can stand it, doctor! said the mother.

You get out, said the husband to his wife. Do you want her to die of diphtheria? Come on now, hold her, I said.

Then I grasped the child's head with my left hand and tried to get the wooden tongue depressor between her teeth. She fought, with clenched teeth, desperately! But now I also had grown furious—at a child. I tried to hold myself down but I couldn't. I know how to expose a throat for inspection. And I did my best. When finally I got the wooden spatula behind the last teeth and just the point of it into the mouth cavity, she opened up for an instant but before I could see anything she came down again and gripped the wooden blade between her molars. She reduced it to splinters before I could get it out again.

Aren't you ashamed, the mother yelled at her. Aren't you ashamed to act like that in front of the doctor?

30   Get me a smooth-handled spoon of some sort, I told the mother. We're going through with this. The child's mouth was already bleeding. Her tongue was cut and she was screaming in wild hysterical shrieks. Perhaps I should have desisted and come back in an hour or more. No doubt it would have been better. But I have seen at least two children lying dead in bed of neglect in such cases, and feeling that I must get a diagnosis now or never I went at it again. But the worst of it was that I too had got beyond reason. I could have torn the child apart in my own fury and enjoyed it. It was a pleasure to attack her. My face was burning with it.

The damned little brat must be protected against her own idiocy, one says to one's self at such times. Others must be protected against her. It is a social necessity. And all these things are true. But a blind fury, a feeling of adult shame, bred of a longing for muscular release are the operatives. One goes on to the end.

In the final unreasoning assault I overpowered the child's neck and jaws. I forced the heavy silver spoon back of her teeth and down her throat till she gagged. And there it was—both tonsils covered with membrane. She had fought valiantly to keep me from knowing her secret. She had been hiding that sore throat for three days at least and lying to her parents in order to escape just such an outcome as this.

Now truly she was furious. She had been on the defensive before but now she attacked. Tried to get off her father's lap and fly at me while tears of defeat blinded her eyes.

[1938]

Joining the Conversation: Critical Thinking and Writing

1. The characters in "The Use of Force" are the doctor, the girl, and her parents. What can you say about each of them—their characters, their classes—on the basis of the first paragraph? What can you say about the doctor as we perceive him by the end of the fifteenth paragraph?

2. According to popular stereotypes, children are supposed to be nice, sweet, innocent things, and doctors are supposed to be kind, wise, relatively unemotional persons. Do Williams's figures seem to you to be utterly improbable? Explain.

3. The narrator is the doctor, but he occasionally lets us hear other voices. For instance we hear the voice of one of the parents in the second sentence ("Please come down as soon as you can, my daughter is very sick"), the voice of the father in the fourth paragraph ("She's had a fever for three days, began the father and we don't know what it comes from. My wife has given her things, you know, like people do, but it don't do no good"), and the voice of the mother in the fourteenth paragraph ("Such a nice man, put in the mother"). Still, the doctor is the narrator, and we chiefly hear his voice. Now consider the fact that he says such things as "I wanted to kill [the father]" (paragraph 22), "But now I also had grown furious—at a child" (paragraph 28), and "the worst of it was that I too had got beyond reason" (paragraph 30). Can we reasonably say that there are *two* conflicts in the story—the doctor versus the child, and the doctor versus himself, i.e., the doctor as a dispassionate professional, and the doctor as a human being? The first conflict is resolved—the child is defeated—but would you add that the second conflict is never resolved? If you believe it is not resolved, do you think this is a weakness in the story?

4. One of our students, in an analysis of the story, argued that it is really a story about rape, perhaps in the form of a rapist's memoir, written for himself. Her evidence included such passages as "I had already fallen in love with the savage brat" (paragraph 21) and "Will you open it now by yourself or shall we have to open it for you?" (paragraph 18). Do you think the episode describes a rape? What is your evidence?

SHIRLEY JACKSON

Shirley Jackson (1919–65) was born in San Francisco and went to college in New York State, first at the University of Rochester and then at Syracuse University. Although one of her stories was published in The Best American Short Stories 1944, *she did not receive national attention until 1948, when the* New Yorker *published "The Lottery." The magazine later reported that none of its earlier publications had produced so strong a response.*

In 1962 she experienced a breakdown and was unable to write, but she recovered and worked on a new novel. Before completing the book, however, she died of cardiac arrest at the age of forty-six. The book was published posthumously under the title Come Along with Me.

Two of her books, Life among the Savages *(1953) and* Raising Demons *(1957), are engaging self-portraits of a harried mother in a house full of children. But what seems amusing also has its dark underside. After her breakdown Jackson said, "I think all my books laid end to end would be one long documentary of anxiety."*

Her husband, Stanley Edgar Hyman (her college classmate and later a professor of English), said of Jackson, "If she used the resources of supernatural terror, it was to provide metaphors for the all-too-real terrors of the natural."

The Lottery

The morning of June 27th was clear and sunny, with the fresh warmth of a full-summer day; the flowers were blossoming profusely and the grass was richly green. The people of the village began to gather in the square, between the post office and the bank, around ten o'clock; in some towns there were so many people that the lottery took two days and had to be started on June 26th, but in this village, where there were only about three hundred people, the whole lottery took less than two hours, so it could begin at ten o'clock in the morning and still be through in time to allow the villagers to get home for noon dinner.

The children assembled first, of course. School was recently over for the summer, and the feeling of liberty sat uneasily on most of them; they tended to gather together quietly for a while before they broke into boisterous play, and their talk was still of the classroom and the teacher, of books and reprimands. Bobby Martin had already stuffed his pockets full of stones, and the other boys soon followed his example, selecting the smoothest and roundest stones; Bobby and Harry Jones and Dickie Delacroix—the villagers pronounced this name "Dellacroy"—eventually made a great pile of stones in one corner of the square and guarded it against the raids of the other boys. The girls stood aside, talking among themselves, looking over their shoulders at the boys, and the very small children rolled in the dust or clung to the hands of their older brothers or sisters.

Soon the men began to gather, surveying their own children, speaking of planting and rain, tractors and taxes. They stood together, away from the pile of stones in the corner, and their jokes were quiet and they smiled rather than laughed. The women, wearing faded house dresses and sweaters, came shortly after their menfolk. They greeted one another and exchanged bits of gossip as they went to join their husbands. Soon the women, standing by their husbands, began to call to their children, and the children came reluctantly, having to be called four or five times. Bobby Martin ducked under his mother's grasping hand and ran, laughing, back to the pile of stones. His father spoke up sharply, and Bobby came quickly, and took his place between his father and his oldest brother.

The lottery was conducted—as were the square dances, the teenage club, the Halloween program—by Mr. Summers, who had time and energy to devote to civic activities. He was a roundfaced, jovial man and he ran the coal business, and people were sorry for him, because he had no children and his wife was a scold. When he arrived in the square, carrying the black wooden box, there was a murmur of conversation among the villagers and he waved and called, "Little late today, folks." The postmaster, Mr. Graves, followed him, carrying a three-legged stool, and the stool was put in the center of the square and Mr. Summers set the black box down on it. The villagers kept their distance, leaving a space between themselves and the stool, and when Mr. Summers said, "Some of you fellows want to give me a hand?" there was a hesitation before two men, Mr. Martin and his oldest son, Baxter, came forward to hold the box steady on the stool while Mr. Summers stirred up the papers inside it.

5   The original paraphernalia for the lottery had been lost long ago, and the black box now resting on the stool had been put into use even before Old Man Warner, the oldest man in town, was born. Mr. Summers spoke frequently to the

villagers about making a new box, but no one liked to upset even as much tradition as was represented by the black box. There was a story that the present box had been made with some pieces of the box that had preceded it, the one that had been constructed when the first people settled down to make a village here. Every year, after the lottery, Mr. Summers began talking again about a new box, but every year the subject was allowed to fade off without anything's being done. The black box grew shabbier each year; by now it was no longer completely black but splintered badly along one side to show the original wood color, and in some places faded or stained.

Mr. Martin and his oldest son, Baxter, held the black box securely on the stool until Mr. Summers had stirred the papers thoroughly with his hand. Because so much of the ritual had been forgotten or discarded, Mr. Summers had been successful in having slips of paper substituted for the chips of wood that had been used for generations. Chips of wood, Mr. Summers had argued, had been all very well when the village was tiny, but now that the population was more than three hundred and likely to keep on growing, it was necessary to use something that would fit more easily into the black box. The night before the lottery, Mr. Summers and Mr. Graves made up the slips of paper and put them in the box, and it was then taken to the safe of Mr. Summers's coal company and locked up until Mr. Summers was ready to take it to the square next morning. The rest of the year, the box was put away, sometimes one place, sometimes another; it had spent one year in Mr. Graves's barn and another year underfoot in the post office, and sometimes it was set on a shelf in the Martin grocery and left there.

There was a great deal of fussing to be done before Mr. Summers declared the lottery open. There were lists to make up—of heads of families, heads of households in each family, members of each household in each family. There was the proper swearing in of Mr. Summers by the postmaster, as the official of the lottery; at one time, some people remembered, there had been a recital of some sort, performed by the official of the lottery, a perfunctory, tuneless chant that had been rattled off duly each year; some people believed that the official of the lottery used to stand just so when he said or sang it, others believed that he was supposed to walk among the people, but years and years ago this part of the ritual had been allowed to lapse. There had been, also, a ritual salute, which the official of the lottery had had to use in addressing each person who came up to draw from the box, but this also had changed with time, until now it was felt necessary only for the official to speak to each person approaching. Mr. Summers was very good at all this; in his clean white shirt and blue jeans, with one hand resting carelessly on the black box, he seemed very proper and important as he talked interminably to Mr. Graves and the Martins.

Just as Mr. Summers left off talking and turned to the assembled villagers, Mrs. Hutchinson came hurriedly along the path to the square, her sweater thrown over her shoulders, and slid into place in the back of the crowd. "Clean forgot what day it was," she said to Mrs. Delacroix, who stood next to her, and they both laughed softly. "Thought my old man was out back stacking wood," Mrs. Hutchinson went on, "and then I looked out the window and the kids were gone, and then I remembered it was the twenty-seventh and came a-running." She dried her hands on her apron, and Mrs. Delacroix said, "You're in time, though. They're still talking away up there."

Mrs. Hutchinson craned her neck to see through the crowd and found her husband and children standing near the front. She tapped Mrs. Delacroix on the arm as a farewell and began to make her way through the crowd. The people separated good humoredly to let her through, two or three people said, in voices just loud enough to be heard across the crowd, "Here comes your Missus, Hutchinson," and "Bill, she made it after all." Mrs. Hutchinson reached her husband, and Mr. Summers, who had been waiting, said cheerfully, "Thought we were going to have to get on without you, Tessie." Mrs. Hutchinson said, grinning, "Wouldn't have me leave m'dishes in the sink, now would you, Joe?," and soft laughter ran through the crowd as the people stirred back into position after Mrs. Hutchinson's arrival.

10   "Well, now," Mr. Summers said soberly, "guess we better get started, get this over with, so's we can go back to work. Anybody ain't here?"

"Dunbar," several people said. "Dunbar, Dunbar."

Mr. Summers consulted his list. "Clyde Dunbar," he said. "That's right. He's broke his leg, hasn't he? Who's drawing for him?"

"Me, I guess," a woman said, and Mr. Summers turned to look at her. "Wife draws for her husband," Mr. Summers said. "Don't you have a grown boy to do it for you, Janey?" Although Mr. Summers and everyone else in the village knew the answer perfectly well, it was the business of the official of the lottery to ask such questions formally. Mr. Summers waited with an expression of polite interest while Mrs. Dunbar answered.

"Horace's not but sixteen yet," Mrs. Dunbar said regretfully. "Guess I gotta fill in for the old man this year."

15   "Right," Mr. Summers said. He made a note on the list he was holding. Then he asked, "Watson boy drawing this year?"

A tall boy in the crowd raised his hand. "Here," he said. "I'm drawing for m'-mother and me." He blinked his eyes nervously and ducked his head as several voices in the crowd said things like "Good fellow, Jack," and "Glad to see your mother's got a man to do it."

"Well," Mr. Summers said, "guess that's everyone. Old Man Warner make it?"

"Here," a voice said, and Mr. Summers nodded.

A sudden hush fell on the crowd as Mr. Summers cleared his throat and looked at the list. "All ready?" he called. "Now, I'll read the names—heads of families first—and the men come up and take a paper out of the box. Keep the paper folded in your hand without looking at it until everyone has had a turn. Everything clear?"

20   The people had done it so many times that they only half listened to the directions; most of them were quiet, wetting their lips, not looking around. Then Mr. Summers raised one hand high and said, "Adams." A man disengaged himself from the crowd and came forward. "Hi, Steve," Mr. Summers said, and Mr. Adams said, "Hi, Joe." They grinned at one another humorlessly and nervously. Then Mr. Adams reached into the black box and took out a folded paper. He held it firmly by one corner as he turned and went hastily back to his place in the crowd, where he stood a little apart from his family, not looking down at his hand.

"Allen," Mr. Summers said. "Anderson. . . . Bentham."

"Seems like there's no time at all between lotteries any more," Mrs. Delacroix said to Mrs. Graves in the back row. "Seems like we got through with the last one only last week."

"Time sure goes fast," Mrs. Graves said.

"Clark. . . . Delacroix."

25   "There goes my old man," Mrs. Delacroix said. She held her breath while her husband went forward.

"Dunbar," Mr. Summers said, and Mrs. Dunbar went steadily to the box while one of the women said, "Go on, Janey," and another said. "There she goes."

"We're next," Mrs. Graves said. She watched while Mr. Graves came around from the side of the box, greeted Mr. Summers gravely, and selected a slip of paper from the box. By now, all through the crowd there were men holding the small folded papers in their large hands, turning them over and over nervously. Mrs. Dunbar and her two sons stood together. Mrs. Dunbar holding the slip of paper.

"Harburt. . . . Hutchinson."

"Get up there, Bill," Mrs. Hutchinson said, and the people near her laughed.

30   "Jones."

"They do say," Mr. Adams said to Old Man Warner, who stood next to him, "that over in the north village they're talking of giving up the lottery."

Old Man Warner snorted. "Pack of crazy fools," he said. "Listening to the young folks, nothing's good enough for *them*. Next thing you know, they'll be wanting to go back to living in caves, nobody work any more, live *that* way for a while. Used to be a saying about 'Lottery in June, corn be heavy soon.' First thing you know, we'd all be eating stewed chickweed and acorns. There's *always* been a lottery," he added petulantly. "Bad enough to see young Joe Summers up there joking with everybody."

"Some places have already quit lotteries," Mrs. Adams said.

"Nothing but trouble in *that*," Old Man Warner said stoutly. "Pack of young fools."

35   "Martin." And Bobby Martin watched his father go forward. "Overdyke. . . . Percy."

"I wish they'd hurry," Mrs. Dunbar said to her older son. "I wish they'd hurry."

"They're almost through," her son said.

"You get ready to run tell Dad," Mrs. Dunbar said.

Mr. Summers called his own name and then stepped forward precisely and selected a slip from the box. Then he called, "Warner."

40   "Seventy-seventh year I been in the lottery," Old Man Warner said as he went through the crowd. "Seventy-seventh time."

"Watson." The tall boy came awkwardly through the crowd. Someone said, "Don't be nervous, Jack," and Mr. Summers said, "Take your time, son."

"Zanini."

After that, there was a long pause, a breathless pause, until Mr. Summers, holding his slip of paper in the air, said, "All right, fellows." For a minute, no one moved, and then all of the slips of paper were opened. Suddenly, all women began to speak at once, saying, "Who is it?" "Who's got it?" "Is it the Dunbars?" "Is it the Watsons?" Then the voices began to say, "It's Hutchinson. It's Bill." "Bill Hutchinson's got it."

"Go tell your father," Mrs. Dunbar said to her older son.

45   People began to look around to see the Hutchinsons. Bill Hutchinson was standing quiet, staring down at the paper in his hand. Suddenly, Tessie Hutchinson shouted to Mr. Summers, "You didn't give him time enough to take any paper he wanted. I saw you. It wasn't fair!"

"Be a good sport, Tessie," Mrs. Delacroix called, and Mrs. Graves said, "All of us took the same chance."

"Shut up, Tessie," Bill Hutchinson said.

"Well, everyone," Mr. Summers said, "That was done pretty fast, and now we've got to be hurrying a little more to get done in time." He consulted his next list. "Bill," he said, "you draw for the Hutchinson family. You got any other households in the Hutchinsons?"

"There's Don and Eva," Mrs. Hutchinson yelled. "Make *them* take their chance!"

50 "Daughters draw with their husbands' families, Tessie," Mr. Summers said gently. "You know that as well as anyone else."

"It wasn't fair," Tessie said.

"I guess no, Joe," Bill Hutchinson said regretfully. "My daughter draws with her husband's family, that's only fair. And I've got no other family except the kids."

"Then, as far as drawing for families is concerned, it's you," Mr. Summers said in explanation, "and as far as drawing for households is concerned, that's you, too. Right?"

"Right," Bill Hutchinson said.

55 "How many kids, Bill?" Mr. Summers asked formally.

"Three," Bill Hutchinson said. "There's Bill, Jr., and Nancy, and little Dave. And Tessie and me."

"All right, then," Mr. Summers said. "Harry, you got their tickets back?"

Mr. Graves nodded and held up the slips of paper. "Put them in the box, then," Mr. Summers directed. "Take Bill's and put it in."

"I think we ought to start over," Mrs. Hutchinson said, as quietly as she could. "I tell you it wasn't *fair*. You didn't give him time enough to choose. *Everybody* saw that."

60 Mr. Graves had selected the five slips and put them in the box, and he dropped all the papers but those onto the ground, where the breeze caught them and lifted them off.

"Listen, everybody," Mrs. Hutchinson was saying to the people around her.

"Ready, Bill?" Mr. Summers asked, and Bill Hutchinson, with one quick glance around at his wife and children, nodded.

"Remember," Mr. Summers said, "Take the slips and keep them folded until each person has taken one. Harry, you help little Dave." Mr. Graves took the hand of the little boy, who came willingly with him up to the box. "Take a paper out of the box, Davy," Mr. Summers said. Davy put his hand into the box and laughed. "Take just *one* paper," Mr. Summers said. "Harry, you hold it for him." Mr. Graves took the child's hand and removed the folded paper from the tight fist and held it while little Dave stood next to him and looked up at him wonderingly.

"Nancy next," Mr. Summers said. Nancy was twelve, and her school friends breathed heavily as she went forward, switching her skirt, and took a slip daintily from the box. "Bill, Jr.," Mr. Summers said, and Billy, his face red and his feet overlarge, nearly knocked the box over as he got a paper out. "Tessie," Mr. Summers said. She hesitated for a minute, looking around defiantly, and then set her lips and went up to the box. She snatched a paper out and held it behind her.

65 "Bill," Mr. Summers said, and Bill Hutchinson reached into the box and felt around, bringing his hand out at last with the slip of paper in it.

The crowd was quiet. A girl whispered, "I hope it's not Nancy," and the sound of the whisper reached the edges of the crowd.

"It's not the way it used to be," Old Man Warner said clearly. "People ain't the way they used to be."

"All right," Mr. Summers said. "Open the papers. Harry, you open little Dave's."

Mr. Graves opened the slip of paper and there was a general sigh through the crowd as he held it up and everyone could see that it was blank. Nancy and Bill, Jr., opened theirs at the same time, and both beamed and laughed, turning around to the crowd and holding their slips of paper above their heads.

70 "Tessie," Mr. Summers said. There was a pause, and then Mr. Summers looked at Bill Hutchinson, and Bill unfolded his paper and showed it. It was blank.

"It's Tessie," Mr. Summers said, and his voice was hushed. "Show us her paper, Bill."

Bill Hutchinson went over to his wife and forced the slip of paper out of her hand. It had a black spot on it, the black spot Mr. Summers had made the night before with the heavy pencil in the coal-company office. Bill Hutchinson held it up, and there was a stir in the crowd.

"All right, folks," Mr. Summers said, "let's finish quickly."

Although the villagers had forgotten the ritual and lost the original black box, they still remembered to use stones. The pile of stones the boys had made earlier was ready; there were stones on the ground with the blowing scraps of paper that had come out of the box. Mrs. Delacroix selected a stone so large she had to pick it up with both hands and turned to Mrs. Dunbar. "Come on," she said. "Hurry up."

75 Mrs. Dunbar had small stones in both hands, and she said, gasping for breath, "I can't run at all. You'll have to go ahead and I'll catch up with you."

The children had stones already, and someone gave little Davy Hutchinson a few pebbles.

Tessie Hutchinson was in the center of a cleared space by now, and she held her hands out desperately as the villagers moved in on her. "It isn't fair," she said. A stone hit her on the side of the head.

Old Man Warner was saying, "Come on, come on, everyone." Steve Adams was in the front of the crowd of villagers, with Mrs. Graves beside him.

"It isn't fair, it isn't right," Mrs. Hutchinson screamed, and then they were upon her.

[1948]

Joining the Conversation: Critical Thinking and Writing

1. Is "The Lottery" more than a shocker?
2. What is the community's attitude toward tradition?
3. Doubtless a good writer could tell this story effectively from the point of view of a participant, but Jackson chose a nonparticipant point of view. What does she gain?
4. Let's say you were writing this story, and you had decided to write it from Tessie's point of view. What would your first paragraph, or your first 250 words, be?
5. Suppose someone claimed that the story is an attack on religious orthodoxy. What might be your response? (Whether you agree or disagree, set forth your reasons in a thoughtful argument.)

MyLiteratureLab® *For additional resources for "The Lottery," log in to* www .myliteraturelab.com *where you will find a Comprehension Quiz, as well as an About the Author, Links, and Critical Overview for Jackson (under Student Resources).*

GRACE PALEY

Grace Paley (1922–2007) was born in New York City, where she attended Hunter College and New York University but left without a degree. While raising two children she wrote poetry and then, in the 1950s, turned to writing fiction. In 1959 she published her first collection of stories, The Little Disturbances of Man. *The title indicates her chief concern—"little disturbances"; the title of her second collection,* Enormous Changes at the Last Minute *(1974), is similarly revealing.*

Paley's chief subject is the life of little people struggling to live in the big city. Of life she has said, "How daily life is lived is a mystery to me. You write about what's mysterious to you. What is it like? Why do people do this?" Of the short story she has said, "It can be just telling a little tale, or writing a complicated philosophical story. It can be a song, almost."

A Man Told Me the Story of His Life

Vicente said: I wanted to be a doctor. I wanted to be a doctor with my whole heart.

I learned every bone, every organ in the body. What is it for? Why does it work?

The school said to me: Vicente, be an engineer. That would be good. You understand mathematics.

I said to the school: I want to be a doctor. I already know how the organs connect. When something goes wrong, I'll understand how to make repairs.

5　　The school said: Vicente, you will really be an excellent engineer. You show on all the tests what a good engineer you will be. It doesn't show whether you'll be a good doctor.

I said: Oh, I long to be a doctor. I nearly cried. I was seventeen. I said: But perhaps you're right. You're the teacher. You're the principal. I know I'm young.

The school said: And besides, you're going into the Army.

And then I was made a cook. I prepared food for two thousand men.

Now you see me. I have a good job. I have three children. This is my wife, Consuela. Did you know I saved her life?

10　　Look, she suffered pain. The doctor said: What is this? Are you tired? Have you had too much company? How many children? Rest overnight, then tomorrow we'll make tests.

The next morning I called the doctor. I said: She must be operated immediately. I have looked in the book. I see where her pain is. I understand what the pressure is, where it comes from. I see clearly the organ that is making trouble.

The doctor made a test. He said: She must be operated at once. He said to me: Vicente, how did you know?

[1985]

Joining the Conversation: Critical Thinking and Writing

1. If the first two words ("Vicente said") of the first sentence were omitted, the story could be called "The Story of My Life" or even "My Life." What does Paley gain (or lose) by introducing a narrator other than Vicente?
2. Is Vicente characterized, or is he simply (as the title puts it) "a man"?
3. Is Paley saying something about America? If so, *what* is she saying?

TOBIAS WOLFF

For a biographical note, see page 1331.

Bullet in the Brain

Anders couldn't get to the bank until just before it closed, so of course the line was endless and he got stuck behind two women whose loud, stupid conversation put him in a murderous temper. He was never in the best of tempers anyway, Anders—

a book critic known for the weary, elegant savagery with which he dispatched almost everything he reviewed.

With the line still doubled around the rope, one of the tellers stuck a POSITION CLOSED sign in her window and walked to the back of the bank, where she leaned against a desk and began to pass the time with a man shuffling papers. The women in front of Anders broke off their conversation and watched the teller with hatred. "Oh, that's nice," one of them said. She turned to Anders and added, confident of his accord, "One of those little human touches that keep us coming back for more."

Anders had conceived his own towering hatred of the teller, but he immediately turned it on the presumptuous crybaby in front of him. "Damned unfair," he said. "Tragic, really. If they're not chopping off the wrong leg or bombing your ancestral village, they're closing their positions."

She stood her ground. "I didn't say it was tragic," she said. "I just think it's a pretty lousy way to treat your customers."

5   "Unforgivable," Anders said. "Heaven will take note."

She sucked in her cheeks but stared past him and said nothing. Anders saw that her friend was looking in the same direction. And then the tellers stopped what they were doing, the other customers slowly turned, and silence came over the bank. Two men wearing black ski masks and blue business suits were standing to the side of the door. One of them had a pistol pressed against the guard's neck. The guard's eyes were closed, and his lips were moving. The other man had a sawed-off shotgun. "Keep your big mouth shut!" the man with the pistol said, though no one had spoken a word. "One of you tellers hits the alarm, you're all dead meat."

"Oh, bravo," Anders said. "'*Dead meat.*'" He turned to the woman in front of him. "Great script, eh? The stern, brass-knuckled poetry of the dangerous classes."

She looked at him with drowning eyes.

The man with the shotgun pushed the guard to his knees. He handed the shotgun to his partner and yanked the guard's wrists up behind his back and locked them together with a pair of handcuffs. He toppled him onto the floor with a kick between the shoulder blades, then took his shotgun back and went over to the security gate at the end of the counter. He was short and heavy and moved with peculiar slowness. "Buzz him in," his partner said. The man with the shotgun opened the gate and sauntered along the line of tellers, handing each of them a plastic bag. When he came to the empty position he looked over at the man with the pistol, who said, "Whose slot is that?"

10   Anders watched the teller. She put her hand to her throat and turned to the man she'd been talking to. He nodded. "Mine," she said.

"Then get your ugly ass in gear and fill that bag."

"There you go," Anders said to the woman in front of him. "Justice is done."

"Hey! Bright boy! Did I tell you to talk?"

"No," Anders said.

15   "Then shut your trap."

"Did you hear that?" Anders said, "'Bright boy.' Right out of *The Killers*."[1]

"Please, be quiet," the woman said.

"Hey, you deaf or what?" The man with the pistol walked over to Anders and poked the weapon into his gut. "You think I'm playing games?"

"No," Anders said, but the barrel tickled like a stiff finger and he had to fight back the titters. He did this by making himself stare into the man's eyes,

[1]**Bright boy . . . The Killers** a gunman in Ernest Hemingway's short story "The Killers" (1927) uses this term.

which were clearly visible behind the holes in the mask: pale blue and rawly red-rimmed. The man's left eyelid kept twitching. He breathed out a piercing, ammoniac smell that shocked Anders more than anything that had happened, and he was beginning to develop a sense of unease when the man prodded him again with the pistol.

20   "You like me, bright boy?" he said. "You want to suck my dick?"

"No," Anders said.

"Then stop looking at me."

Anders fixed his gaze on the man's shiny wing-tip shoes.

"Not down there. Up there." He stuck the pistol under Anders's chin and pushed it upward until he was looking at the ceiling.

25   Anders had never paid much attention to that part of the bank, a pompous old building with marble floors and counters and gilt scrollwork over the tellers' cages. The domed ceiling had been decorated with mythological figures whose fleshy, toga-draped ugliness Anders had taken in at a glance many years earlier and afterward declined to notice. Now he had no choice but to scrutinize the painter's work. It was even worse than he remembered, and all of it executed with the utmost gravity. The artist had a few tricks up his sleeve and used them again and again—a certain rosy blush on the underside of the clouds, a coy backward glance on the faces of the cupids and fauns. The ceiling was crowded with various dramas, but the one that caught Anders's eye was Zeus and Europa—portrayed, in this rendition, as a bull ogling a cow from behind a haystack. To make the cow sexy, the painter had canted her hips suggestively and given her long, droopy eyelashes through which she gazed back at the bull with sultry welcome. The bull wore a smirk and his eyebrows were arched. If there'd been a caption bubbling out of his mouth, it would have said HUBBA HUBBA.

"What's so funny, bright boy?"

"Nothing."

30   "You think I'm comical? You think I'm some kind of clown?"

"No."

"You think you can fuck with me?"

"No."

"Fuck with me again, you're history. *Capiche?*"[2]

Anders burst out laughing. He covered his mouth with both hands and said, "I'm sorry, I'm sorry," then snorted helplessly through his fingers and said, "*Capiche*—oh, God, *capiche*," and at that the man with the pistol raised the pistol and shot Anders right in the head.

The bullet smashed Anders's skull and plowed through his brain and exited behind his right ear, scattering shards of bone into the cerebral cortex, the corpus callosum, back toward the basal ganglia, and down into the thalamus. But before all this occurred, the first appearance of the bullet in the cerebrum set off a crackling chain of ion transports and neurotransmissions. Because of their peculiar origin these traced a peculiar pattern, flukishly calling to life a summer afternoon some forty years past, and long since lost to memory. After striking the cranium, the bullet was moving at nine hundred feet per second, a pathetically sluggish, glacial pace compared with the synaptic lightning that flashed around it. Once in the brain, that is, the bullet came under the mediation of brain time, which gave

---

[2]Capiche? Get it? (from the Italian verb, capire, "to understand").

Anders plenty of leisure to contemplate the scene that, in a phrase he would have abhorred, "passed before his eyes."

35   It is worth noting what Anders did not remember, given what he did recall. He did not remember his first lover, Sherry, or what he had most madly loved about her, before it came to irritate him—her unembarrassed carnality, and especially the cordial way she had with his unit, which she called Mr. Mole, as in *Uh-oh, looks like Mr. Mole wants to play*. Anders did not remember his wife, whom he had also loved before she exhausted him with her predictability, or his daughter, now a sullen professor of economics at Dartmouth. He did not remember standing just outside his daughter's door as she lectured her bear about his naughtiness and described the appalling punishments Paws would receive unless he changed his ways. He did not remember a single line of the hundreds of poems he had committed to memory in his youth so he could give himself the shivers at will—not "Silent, upon a peak in Darien," or "My God, I heard this day," or "All my pretty ones? Did you say all? O hell-kite! All?"[3] None of these did he remember; not one. Anders did not remember his dying mother saying of his father. "I should have stabbed him in his sleep."

He did not remember Professor Josephs telling his class how Athenian prisoners in Sicily had been released if they could recite Aeschylus,[4] and then reciting Aeschylus himself, right there, in the Greek. Anders did not remember how his eyes had burned at those sounds. He did not remember the surprise of seeing a college classmate's name on the dust jacket of a novel not long after they graduated, or the respect he had felt after reading the book. He did not remember the pleasure of giving respect.

Nor did Anders remember seeing a woman leap to her death from the building opposite his own just days after his daughter was born. He did not remember shouting "Lord have mercy!" He did not remember deliberately crashing his father's car into a tree, or having his ribs kicked in by three policemen at an antiwar rally, or waking himself up with laughter. He did not remember when he began to regard the heap of books on his desk with boredom and dread, or when he grew angry at writers for writing them. He did not remember when everything began to remind him of something else.

This is what he remembered. Heat. A baseball field. Yellow grass, the whir of insects, himself leaning against a tree as the boys of the neighborhood gather for a pickup game. He looks on as the others argue the relative genius of Mantle and Mays. They have been worrying this subject all summer, and it has become tedious to Anders: an oppression, like the heat.

Then the last two boys arrive, Coyle and a cousin of his from Mississippi. Anders has never met Coyle's cousin before and will never see him again. He says hi with the rest but takes no further notice of him until they've chosen sides and someone asks the cousin what position he wants to play. "Shortstop," the boy says. "Short's the best position they is." Anders turns and looks at him. He wants to hear Coyle's cousin repeat what he's just said, though he knows better than to ask. The others

---

[3]**He did not remember . . . O hell-kite! All?"** The first quotation ("Silent . . . Darien") is from John Keats's "On First Looking into Chapman's Homer" (see page 668); the second ("My God") is from George Herbert's poem "Man" (early seventeenth century); the third quotation ("All . . . All?") is from Shakespeare's *Macbeth*, 4.3.217, when Macduff learns that Macbeth has killed Macduff's children.   [4]**Aeschylus** Wolff seems to have made a mistake: Tradition says that some Athenian prisoners in Sicily earned a reprieve by reciting verses from the Greek dramatist Euripides (not, as Wolff says, Aeschylus).

will think he's being a jerk, ragging the kid for his grammar. But that isn't it, not at all—it's that Anders is strangely roused, elated, by those final two words, their pure unexpectedness and their music. He takes the field in a trance, repeating them to himself.

40   The bullet is already in the brain; it won't be outrun forever, or charmed to a halt. In the end it will do its work and leave the troubled skull behind, dragging its comet's tail of memory and hope and talent and love into the marble hall of commerce. That can't be helped. But for now Anders can still make time. Time for the shadows to lengthen on the grass, time for the tethered dog to bark at the flying ball, time for the boy in right field to smack his sweat-blackened mitt and softly chant, *They is, they is, they is.*

[1995]

Joining the Conversation: Critical Thinking and Writing

1. How would you characterize the Anders whom we see in the first part of "Bullet in the Brain" (i.e., up to the place where Wolff indicates a break)? How would you characterize the youthful Anders, the Anders whom we see in the second part of the story?

2. The second part itself can be thought of as having two parts—first, What Anders *did not* remember, and second, What Anders *did* remember. Suppose these two parts (of the second part) had been reversed. What would the story gain or lose?

3. Suppose Wolff showed you the manuscript and said he had not yet chosen a title but he was thinking of the following possibilities, given here in alphabetic order: "Anders," "The Bank Robbery," "Brain Works," "Bullet in the Brain," "Memories," "Shortstop," "They Is." In an argumentative essay of about 500 words, set forth your choice. You may want to devote approximately equal space to your examination of each candidate, or you may want to (for instance) quickly dispose of the two or three that you think are obviously poor choices—but you will have to explain briefly why you think they are poor choices—and then spend more time on the remaining (serious) candidates. In any case, please remember that you are writing an argument. *Optional variation:* In your essay you may want to reject all of these candidates and offer a title of your own invention.

TIM O'BRIEN

Tim O'Brien, born in 1947 in Austin, Minnesota, was drafted into the army in 1968 and served as an infantryman in Vietnam. Drawing on this experience he wrote a memoir, If I Die in a Combat Zone *(1973), in which he explains that he did not believe in the Vietnam War, considered dodging the draft, but, lacking the courage to do so, he served, largely out of fear and embarrassment. A later book, a novel called* Going After Cacciato, *won the National Book Award in 1979.*

"The Things They Carried," first published in 1986, was republished in 1990 as one of a series of interlocking stories in a book titled The Things They Carried. *In one of the stories, "How To Tell a True War Story," he writes,*

A true war story is never moral. It does not instruct, nor encourage virtue, nor suggest models of proper human behavior. . . . If a story seems moral, do not believe it. If at the end of a war story you feel uplifted, or if you feel that some small bit of rectitude has been salvaged from the larger waste, then you have been made the victim of a very old and terrible lie. There is no rectitude whatsoever. There is no virtue. As a first rule of thumb, therefore, you can tell a true war story by its absolute and uncompromising allegiance to obscenity and evil.

The Things They Carried

First Lieutenant Jimmy Cross carried letters from a girl named Martha, a junior at Mount Sebastian College in New Jersey. They were not love letters, but Lieutenant Cross was hoping, so he kept them folded in plastic at the bottom of his rucksack. In the late afternoon, after a day's march, he would dig his foxhole, wash his hands under a canteen, unwrap the letters, hold them with the tips of his fingers, and spend the last hour of light pretending. He would imagine romantic camping trips into the White Mountains in New Hampshire. He would sometimes taste the envelope flaps, knowing her tongue had been there. More than anything, he wanted Martha to love him as he loved her, but the letters were mostly chatty, elusive on the matter of love. She was a virgin, he was almost sure. She was an English major at Mount Sebastian, and she wrote beautifully about her professors and roommates and midterm exams, about her respect for Chaucer and her great affection for Virginia Woolf. She often quoted lines of poetry; she never mentioned the war, except to say, Jimmy, take care of yourself. The letters weighed ten ounces. They were signed "Love, Martha," but Lieutenant Cross understood that Love was only a way of signing and did not mean what he sometimes pretended it meant. At dusk, he would carefully return the letters to his rucksack. Slowly, a bit distracted, he would get up and move among his men, checking the perimeter, then at full dark he would return to his hole and watch the night and wonder if Martha was a virgin.

The things they carried were largely determined by necessity. Among the necessities or near-necessities were P-38 can openers, pocket knives, heat tabs, wrist watches, dog tags, mosquito repellent, chewing gum, candy, cigarettes, salt tablets, packets of Kool-Aid, lighters, matches, sewing kits, Military Payment Certificates, C rations, and two or three canteens of water. Together, these items weighed between fifteen and twenty pounds, depending upon a man's habits or rate of metabolism. Henry Dobbins, who was a big man, carried extra rations; he was especially fond of canned peaches in heavy syrup over pound cake. Dave Jensen, who practiced field hygiene, carried a toothbrush, dental floss, and several hotel-size bars of soap he'd stolen on R&R[1] in Sydney, Australia. Ted Lavender, who was scared, carried tranquilizers until he was shot in the head outside the village of Than Khe in mid-April. By necessity, and because it was SOP,[2] they all carried steel helmets that weighed five pounds including the liner and camouflage cover. They carried the standard fatigue jackets and trousers. Very few carried underwear. On their feet they carried jungle boots—2.1 pounds—and Dave Jensen carried three pairs of socks and a can of Dr. Scholl's foot powder as a precaution against trench foot. Until he was

[1]**R&R** rest and rehabilitation leave.   [2]**SOP** standard operating procedure.

shot, Ted Lavender carried six or seven ounces of premium dope, which for him was a necessity. Mitchell Sanders, the RTO,[3] carried condoms. Norman Bowker carried a diary. Rat Kiley carried comic books. Kiowa, a devout Baptist, carried an illustrated New Testament that had been presented to him by his father, who taught Sunday school in Oklahoma City, Oklahoma. As a hedge against bad times, however, Kiowa also carried his grandmother's distrust of the white man, his grandfather's old hunting hatchet. Necessity dictated. Because the land was mined and booby-trapped, it was SOP for each man to carry a steel-centered, nylon-covered flak jacket, which weighed 6.7 pounds, but which on hot days seemed much heavier. Because you could die so quickly, each man carried at least one large compress bandage, usually in the helmet band for easy access. Because the nights were cold, and because the monsoons were wet, each carried a green plastic poncho that could be used as a raincoat or groundsheet or make-shift tent. With its quilted liner, the poncho weighed almost two pounds, but it was worth every ounce. In April, for instance, when Ted Lavender was shot, they used his poncho to wrap him up, then to carry him across the paddy, then to lift him into the chopper that took him away.

They were called legs or grunts.

To carry something was to "hump" it, as when Lieutenant Jimmy Cross humped his love for Martha up the hills and through the swamps. In its intransitive form, "to hump" meant "to walk," or "to march," but it implied burdens far beyond the in-transitive.

5   Almost everyone humped photographs. In his wallet, Lieutenant Cross carried two photographs of Martha. The first was a Kodachrome snapshot signed "Love," though he knew better. She stood against a brick wall. Her eyes were gray and neutral, her lips slightly open as she stared straight-on at the camera. At night, sometimes, Lieutenant Cross wondered who had taken the picture, because he knew she had boyfriends, because he loved her so much, and because he could see the shadow of the picture taker spreading out against the brick wall. The sec-ond photograph had been clipped from the 1968 Mount Sebastian yearbook. It was an action shot—women's volleyball—and Martha was bent horizontal to the floor, reaching, the palms of her hands in sharp focus, the tongue taut, the expression frank and competitive. There was no visible sweat. She wore white gym shorts. Her legs, he thought, were almost certainly the legs of a virgin, dry and without hair, the left knee cocked and carrying her entire weight, which was just over one hun-dred pounds. Lieutenant Cross remembered touching that left knee. A dark theater, he remembered, and the movie was *Bonnie and Clyde,* and Martha wore a tweed skirt, and during the final scene, when he touched her knee, she turned and looked at him in a sad, sober way that made him pull his hand back, but he would always remember the feel of the tweed skirt and the knee beneath it and the sound of the gunfire that killed Bonnie and Clyde, how embarrassing it was, how slow and oppressive. He remembered kissing her goodnight at the dorm door. Right then, he thought, he should've done something brave. He should've carried her up the stairs to her room and tied her to the bed and touched that left knee all night long. He should've risked it. Whenever he looked at the photographs, he thought of new things he should've done.

What they carried was partly a function of rank, partly of field specialty.

As a first lieutenant and platoon leader, Jimmy Cross carried a compass, maps, code books, binoculars, and a .45-caliber pistol that weighed 2.9 pounds

---

[3]**RTO** radio and telephone operator.

fully loaded. He carried a strobe light and the responsibility for the lives of his men.

As an RTO, Mitchell Sanders carried the PRC-25 radio, a killer, twenty-six pounds with its battery.

As a medic, Rat Kiley carried a canvas satchel filled with morphine and plasma and malaria tablets and surgical tape and comic books and all the things a medic must carry, including M&Ms[4] for especially bad wounds, for a total weight of nearly twenty pounds.

As a big man, therefore a machine gunner, Henry Dobbins carried the M-60, which weighed twenty-three pounds unloaded, but which was almost always loaded. In addition, Dobbins carried between ten and fifteen pounds of ammunition draped in belts across his chest and shoulders.

As PFCs or Spec 4s, most of them were common grunts and carried the standard M-16 gas operated assault rifle. The weapon weighed 7.5 pounds unloaded, 8.2 pounds with its full twenty-round magazine. Depending on numerous factors, such as topography and psychology, the riflemen carried anywhere from twelve to twenty magazines, usually in cloth bandoliers, adding on another 8.4 pounds at minimum, fourteen pounds at maximum. When it was available, they also carried M-16 maintenance gear—rods and steel brushes and swabs and tubes of LSA oil—all of which weighed about a pound. Among the grunts, some carried the M-79 grenade launcher, 5.9 pounds unloaded, a reasonably light weapon except for the ammunition, which was heavy. A single round weighed ten ounces. The typical load was twenty-five rounds. But Ted Lavender, who was scared, carried thirty-four rounds when he was shot and killed outside Than Khe, and he went down under an exceptional burden, more than twenty pounds of ammunition, plus the flak jacket and helmet and rations and water and toilet paper and tranquilizers and all the rest, plus the unweighed fear. He was dead weight. There was no twitching or flopping. Kiowa, who saw it happen, said it was like watching a rock fall, or a big sandbag or something—just boom, then down—not like the movies where the dead guy rolls around and does fancy spins and goes ass over teakettle—not like that, Kiowa said, the poor bastard just flat-fuck fell. Boom. Down. Nothing else. It was a bright morning in mid-April. Lieutenant Cross felt the pain. He blamed himself. They stripped off Lavender's canteens and ammo, all the heavy things, and Rat Kiley said the obvious, the guy's dead, and Mitchell Sanders used his radio to report one U.S. KIA[5] and to request a chopper. Then they wrapped Lavender in his poncho. They carried him out to a dry paddy, established security, and sat smoking the dead man's dope until the chopper came. Lieutenant Cross kept to himself. He pictured Martha's smooth young face, thinking he loved her more than anything, more than his men, and now Ted Lavender was dead because he loved her so much and could not stop thinking about her. When the dust-off arrived, they carried Lavender aboard. Afterward they burned Than Khe. They marched until dusk, then dug their holes, and that night Kiowa kept explaining how you had to be there, how fast it was, how the poor guy just dropped like so much concrete. Boom-down, he said. Like cement.

In addition to the three standard weapons—the M-60, M-16, and M-79—they carried whatever presented itself, or whatever seemed appropriate as a means of killing or staying alive. They carried catch-as-catch-can. At various times, in various situations, they carried M-14s and CAR-15s and Swedish Ks and grease guns and

[4]**M&M** joking term for medical supplies. [5]**KIA** killed in action.

captured AK-47s and Chi-Coms and RPGs and Simonov carbines and black-market
Uzis and .38-caliber Smith & Wesson handguns and 66 mm LAWs and shotguns and
silencers and blackjacks and bayonets and C-4 plastic explosives. Lee Strunk carried
a slingshot; a weapon of last resort, he called it. Mitchell Sanders carried brass knuckles. Kiowa carried his grandfather's feathered hatchet. Every third or fourth man carried
a Claymore antipersonnel mine—3.5 pounds with its firing device. They all carried
fragmentation grenades—fourteen ounces each. They all carried at least one M-18
colored smoke grenade—twenty-four ounces. Some carried CS or tear-gas grenades.
Some carried white-phosphorus grenades. They carried all they could bear, and then
some, including a silent awe for the terrible power of the things they carried.

In the first week of April, before Lavender died, Lieutenant Jimmy Cross received a good-luck charm from Martha. It was a simple pebble, an ounce at most.
Smooth to the touch, it was a milky-white color with flecks of orange and violet,
oval-shaped, like a miniature egg. In the accompanying letter, Martha wrote that
she had found the pebble on the Jersey shoreline, precisely where the land
touched the water at high tide, where things came together but also separated. It
was this separate-but-together quality, she wrote, that had inspired her to pick up
the pebble and to carry it in her breast pocket for several days, where it seemed
weightless, and then to send it through the mail, by air, as a token of her truest
feelings for him. Lieutenant Cross found this romantic. But he wondered what her
truest feelings were, exactly, and what she meant by separate-but-together. He
wondered how the tides and waves had come into play on that afternoon along
the Jersey shoreline when Martha saw the pebble and bent down to rescue it from
geology. He imagined bare feet. Martha was a poet, with the poet's sensibilities,
and her feet would be brown and bare, the toenails unpainted, the eyes chilly and
somber like the ocean in March, and though it was painful, he wondered who had
been with her that afternoon. He imagined a pair of shadows moving along the
strip of sand where things came together but also separated. It was phantom jealousy, he knew, but he couldn't help himself. He loved her so much. On the
march, through the hot days of early April, he carried the pebble in his mouth,
turning it with his tongue, tasting sea salts and moisture. His mind wandered.
He had difficulty keeping his attention on the war. On occasion he would yell at
his men to spread out the column, to keep their eyes open, but then he would
slip away into daydreams, just pretending, walking barefoot along the Jersey
shore, with Martha, carrying nothing. He would feel himself rising. Sun and waves
and gentle winds, all love and lightness.

What they carried varied by mission.

15   When a mission took them to the mountains, they carried mosquito netting,
machetes, canvas tarps, and extra bugjuice.

If a mission seemed especially hazardous, or if it involved a place they knew
to be bad, they carried everything they could. In certain heavily mined AOs,[6]
where the land was dense with Toe Poppers and Bouncing Betties, they took turns
humping a twenty-eight-pound mine detector. With its headphones and big sensing plate, the equipment was a stress on the lower back and shoulders, awkward
to handle, often useless because of the shrapnel in the earth, but they carried it
anyway, partly for safety, partly for the illusion of safety.

---

[6]**AOs** areas of operation.

On ambush, or other night missions, they carried peculiar little odds and ends. Kiowa always took along his New Testament and a pair of moccasins for silence. Dave Jensen carried night-sight vitamins high in carotin. Lee Strunk carried his slingshot; ammo, he claimed, would never be a problem. Rat Kiley carried brandy and M&Ms. Until he was shot, Ted Lavender carried the starlight scope, which weighed 6.3 pounds with its aluminum carrying case. Henry Dobbins carried his girlfriend's panty hose wrapped around his neck as a comforter. They all carried ghosts. When dark came, they would move out single file across the meadows and paddies to their ambush coordinates, where they would quietly set up the Claymores and lie down and spend the night waiting.

Other missions were more complicated and required special equipment. In mid-April, it was their mission to search out and destroy the elaborate tunnel complexes in the Than Khe area south of Chu Lai. To blow the tunnels, they carried one-pound blocks of pentrite high explosives, four blocks to a man, sixty-eight pounds in all. They carried wiring, detonators, and battery-powered clackers. Dave Jensen carried earplugs. Most often, before blowing the tunnels, they were ordered by higher command to search them, which was considered bad news, but by and large they just shrugged and carried out orders. Because he was a big man, Henry Dobbins was excused from tunnel duty. The others would draw numbers. Before Lavender died there were seventeen men in the platoon, and whoever drew the number seventeen would strip off his gear and crawl in headfirst with a flashlight and Lieutenant Cross's .45-caliber pistol. The rest of them would fan out as security. They would sit down or kneel, not facing the hole, listening to the ground beneath them, imagining cobwebs and ghosts, whatever was down there—the tunnel walls squeezing in—how the flashlight seemed impossibly heavy in the hand and how it was tunnel vision in the very strictest sense, compression in all ways, even time, and how you had to wiggle in—ass and elbows—a swallowed-up feeling—and how you found yourself worrying about odd things—will your flashlight go dead? Do rats carry rabies? If you screamed, how far would the sound carry? Would your buddies hear it? Would they have the courage to drag you out? In some respects, though not many, the waiting was worse than the tunnel itself. Imagination was a killer.

On April 16, when Lee Strunk drew the number seventeen, he laughed and muttered something and went down quickly. The morning was hot and very still. Not good, Kiowa said. He looked at the tunnel opening, then out across a dry paddy toward the village of Than Khe. Nothing moved. No clouds or birds or people. As they waited, the men smoked and drank Kool-Aid, not talking much, feeling sympathy for Lee Strunk but also feeling the luck of the draw. You win some, you lose some, said Mitchell Sanders, and sometimes you settle for a rain check. It was a tired line and no one laughed.

20   Henry Dobbins ate a tropical chocolate bar. Ted Lavender popped a tranquilizer and went off to pee.

After five minutes, Lieutenant Jimmy Cross moved to the tunnel, leaned down, and examined the darkness. Trouble, he thought—a cave-in maybe. And then suddenly, without willing it, he was thinking about Martha. The stresses and fractures, the quick collapse, the two of them buried alive under all that weight. Dense, crushing love. Kneeling, watching the hole, he tried to concentrate on Lee Strunk and the war, all the dangers, but his love was too much for him, he felt paralyzed, he wanted to sleep inside her lungs and breathe her blood and be smothered. He wanted her to be a virgin and not a virgin, all at once. He wanted to know her. Intimate secrets—why poetry? Why so sad? Why that grayness in her eyes?

Why so alone? Not lonely, just alone—riding her bike across campus or sitting off by herself in the cafeteria. Even dancing, she danced alone—and it was the aloneness that filled him with love. He remembered telling her that one evening. How she nodded and looked away. And how, later, when he kissed her, she received the kiss without returning it, her eyes wide open, not afraid, not a virgin's eyes, just flat and uninvolved.

Lieutenant Cross gazed at the tunnel. But he was not there. He was buried with Martha under the white sand at the Jersey shore. They were pressed together, and the pebble in his mouth was her tongue. He was smiling. Vaguely, he was aware of how quiet the day was, the sullen paddies, yet he could not bring himself to worry about matters of security. He was beyond that. He was just a kid at war, in love. He was twenty-two years old. He couldn't help it.

A few minutes later Lee Strunk crawled out of the tunnel. He came up grinning, filthy but alive. Lieutenant Cross nodded and closed his eyes while the others clapped Strunk on the back and made jokes about rising from the dead.

Worms, Rat Kiley said. Right out of the grave. Fuckin' zombie.

25   The men laughed. They all felt great relief.

Spook City, said Mitchell Sanders.

Lee Strunk made a funny ghost sound, a kind of moaning, yet very happy, and right then, when Strunk made that high happy moaning sound, when he went *Ah-hooooo*, right then Ted Lavender was shot in the head on his way back from peeing. He lay with his mouth open. The teeth were broken. There was a swollen black bruise under his left eye. The cheekbone was gone. Oh shit, Rat Kiley said, the guy's dead. The guy's dead, he kept saying, which seemed profound—the guy's dead. I mean really.

The things they carried were determined to some extent by superstition. Lieutenant Cross carried his good-luck pebble. Dave Jensen carried a rabbit's foot. Norman Bowker, otherwise a very gentle person, carried a thumb that had been presented to him as a gift by Mitchell Sanders. The thumb was dark brown, rubbery to the touch, and weighed four ounces at most. It had been cut from a VC corpse, a boy of fifteen or sixteen. They'd found him at the bottom of an irrigation ditch, badly burned, flies in his mouth and eyes. They boy wore black shorts and sandals. At the time of his death he had been carrying a pouch of rice, a rifle, and three magazines of ammunition.

You want my opinion, Mitchell Sanders said, there's a definite moral here.

30   He put his hand on the dead boy's wrist. He was quiet for a time, as if counting a pulse, then he patted the stomach, almost affectionately, and used Kiowa's hunting hatchet to remove the thumb.

Henry Dobbins asked what the moral was.

Moral?

You know. *Moral*.

Sanders wrapped the thumb in toilet paper and handed it across to Norman Bowker. There was no blood. Smiling, he kicked the boy's head, watched the flies scatter, and said, It's like with that old TV show—Paladin. Have gun, will travel.

35   Henry Dobbins thought about it.

Yeah, well, he finally said. I don't see no moral.

There it *is*, man.

Fuck off.

They carried USO stationery and pencils and pens. They carried Sterno, safety pins, trip flares, signal flares, spools of wire, razor blades, chewing tobacco, liberated joss sticks and statuettes of the smiling Buddha, candles, grease pencils, *The Stars and Stripes,* fingernail clippers, Psy Ops leaflets, bush hats, bolos, and much more. Twice a week, when the resupply choppers came in, they carried hot chow in green Mermite cans and large canvas bags filled with iced beer and soda pop. They carried plastic water containers, each with a two gallon capacity. Mitchell Sanders carried a set of starched tiger fatigues for special occasions. Henry Dobbins carried Black Flag insecticide. Dave Jensen carried empty sandbags that could be filled at night for added protection. Lee Strunk carried tanning lotion. Some things they carried in common. Taking turns, they carried the big PRC-77 scrambler radio, which weighed thirty pounds with its battery. They shared the weight of memory. They took up what others could no longer bear. Often, they carried each other, the wounded or weak. They carried infections. They carried chess sets, basketballs, Vietnamese-English dictionaries, insignia of rank, Bronze Stars and Purple Hearts, plastic cards imprinted with the Code of Conduct. They carried diseases, among them malaria and dysentery. They carried lice and ringworm and leeches and paddy algae and various rots and molds. They carried the land itself—Vietnam, the place, the soil—a powdery orange-red dust that covered their boots and fatigues and faces. They carried the sky. The whole atmosphere, they carried it, the humidity, the monsoons, the stink of fungus and decay, all of it, they carried gravity. They moved like mules. By daylight they took sniper fire, at night they were mortared, but it was not battle, it was just the endless march, village to village, without purpose, nothing won or lost. They marched for the sake of the march. They plodded along slowly, dumbly, leaning forward against the heat, unthinking, all blood and bone, simple grunts, soldiering with their legs, toiling up the hills and down into the paddies and across the rivers and up again and down, just humping, one step and then the next and then another, but no volition, no will, because it was automatic, it was anatomy, and the war was entirely a matter of posture and carriage, the hump was everything, a kind of inertia, a kind of emptiness, a dullness of desire and intellect and conscience and hope and human sensibility. Their principles were in their feet. Their calculations were biological. They had no sense of strategy or mission. They searched the villages without knowing what to look for, nor caring, kicking over jars of rice, frisking children and old men, blowing tunnels, sometimes setting fires and sometimes not, then forming up and moving on to the next village, then other villages, where it would always be the same. They carried their own lives. The pressures were enormous. In the heat of early afternoon, they would remove their helmets and flak jackets, walking bare, which was dangerous but which helped ease the strain. They would often discard things along the route of march. Purely for comfort, they would throw away rations, blow their Claymores and grenades, no matter, because by nightfall the resupply choppers would arrive with more of the same, then a day or two later still more, fresh watermelons and crates of ammunition and sunglasses and woolen sweaters—the resources were stunning—sparklers for the Fourth of July, colored eggs for Easter. It was the great American war chest—the fruits of sciences, the smokestacks, the canneries, the arsenals at Hartford, the Minnesota forests, the machine shops, the vast fields of corn and wheat—they carried like freight trains; they carried it on their backs and shoulders—and for all the ambiguities of Vietnam, all the mysteries and unknowns, there was at least the single abiding certainty that they would never be at a loss for things to carry.

40   After the chopper took Lavender away, Lieutenant Jimmy Cross led his men into the village of Than Khe. They burned everything. They shot chickens and dogs, they trashed the village well, they called in artillery and watched the wreckage, then they

marched for several hours through the hot afternoon, and then at dusk, while Kiowa explained how Lavender died, Lieutenant Cross found himself trembling.

He tried not to cry. With his entrenching tool, which weighed five pounds, he began digging a hole in the earth.

He felt shame. He hated himself. He had loved Martha more than his men, and as a consequence Lavender was now dead, and this was something he would have to carry like a stone in his stomach for the rest of the war.

All he could do was dig. He used his entrenching tool like an ax, slashing, feeling both love and hate, and then later, when it was full dark, he sat at the bottom of his foxhole and wept. It went on for a long while. In part, he was grieving for Ted Lavender, but mostly it was for Martha, and for himself, because she belonged to another world, which was not quite real, and because she was a junior at Mount Sebastian College in New Jersey, a poet and a virgin and uninvolved, and because he realized she did not love him and never would.

Like cement, Kiowa whispered in the dark. I swear to God—boom-down. Not a word.

45   I've heard this, said Norman Bowker.

A pisser, you know? Still zipping himself up. Zapped while zipping.

All right, fine. That's enough.

Yeah, but you had to see it, the guy just—

I *heard,* man. Cement. So why not shut the fuck *up?*

50   Kiowa shook his head sadly and glanced over at the hole where Lieutenant Jimmy Cross sat watching the night. The air was thick and wet. A warm, dense fog had settled over the paddies and there was the stillness that precedes rain.

After a time Kiowa sighed.

One thing for sure, he said. The lieutenant's in some deep hurt. I mean that crying jag—the way he was carrying on—it wasn't fake or anything, it was real heavy-duty hurt. The man cares.

Sure, Norman Bowker said.

Say what you want, the man does care.

55   We all got problems.

Not Lavender.

No, I guess not, Bowker said. Do me a favor, though.

Shut up?

That's a smart Indian. Shut up.

60   Shrugging, Kiowa pulled off his boots. He wanted to say more, just to lighten up his sleep, but instead he opened his New Testament and arranged it beneath his head as a pillow. The fog made things seem hollow and unattached. He tried not to think about Ted Lavender, but then he was thinking how fast it was, no drama, down and dead, and how it was hard to feel anything except surprise. It seemed unchristian. He wished he could find some great sadness, or even anger, but the emotion wasn't there and he couldn't make it happen. Mostly he felt pleased to be alive. He liked the smell of the New Testament under his cheek, the leather and ink and paper and glue, whatever the chemicals were. He liked hearing the sounds of night. Even his fatigue, it felt fine, the stiff muscles and the prickly awareness of his own body, a floating feeling. He enjoyed not being dead. Lying there, Kiowa admired Lieutenant Jimmy Cross's capacity for grief. He wanted to share the man's pain, he wanted to care as Jimmy Cross cared. And yet when he closed his eyes, all he could think was Boom-down, and all he could feel was the pleasure of having his boots off and the fog curling in around him and damp soil and the Bible smells and the plush comfort of night.

After a moment Norman Bowker sat up in the dark
What the hell, he said. You want to talk, *talk.* Tell it to me.
Forget it.
No, man, go on. One thing I hate, it's a silent Indian.

65   For the most part they carried themselves with poise, a kind of dignity. Now and then, however, there were times of panic, when they squealed or wanted to squeal but couldn't, when they twitched and made moaning sounds and covered their heads and said Dear Jesus and flopped around on the earth and fired their weapons blindly and cringed and sobbed and begged for the noise to stop and went wild and made stupid promises to themselves and to God and to their mothers and fathers, hoping not to die. In different ways, it happened to all of them. Afterward, when the firing ended, they would blink and peek up. They would touch their bodies, feeling shame, then quickly hiding it. They would force themselves to stand. As if in slow motion, frame by frame, the world would take on the old logic—absolute silence, then the wind, then sunlight, then voices. It was the burden of being alive. Awkwardly, the men would reassemble themselves, first in private, then in groups, becoming soldiers again. They would repair the leaks in their eyes. They would check for casualties, call in dust-offs, light cigarettes, try to smile, clear their throats and spit and begin cleaning their weapons. After a time someone would shake his head and say, No lie, I almost shit my pants, and someone else would laugh, which meant it was bad, yes, but the guy had obviously not shit his pants, it wasn't that bad, and in any case nobody would ever do such a thing and then go ahead and talk about it. They would squint into the dense, oppressive sunlight. For a few moments, perhaps, they would fall silent, lighting a joint and tracking its passage from man to man, inhaling, holding in the humiliation. Scary stuff, one of them might say. But then someone else would grin or flick his eyebrows and say, Roger-dodger, almost cut me a new asshole, *almost.*

There were numerous such poses. Some carried themselves with a sort of wistful resignation, others with pride or still soldierly discipline or good humor or macho zeal. They were afraid of dying but they were even more afraid to show it.

They found jokes to tell.

They used a hard vocabulary to contain the terrible softness. *Greased,* they'd say. *Offed, lit up, zapped while zipping.* It wasn't cruelty, just stage presence. They were actors and the war came at them in 3-D. When someone died, it wasn't quite dying, because in a curious way it seemed scripted, and because they had their lines mostly memorized, irony mixed with tragedy, and because they called it by other names, as if to encyst and destroy the reality of death itself. They kicked corpses. They cut off thumbs. They talked grunt lingo. They told stories about Ted Lavender's supply of tranquilizers, how the poor guy didn't feel a thing, how incredibly tranquil he was.

There's a moral here, said Mitchell Sanders.

70   They were waiting for Lavender's chopper, smoking the dead man's dope.

The moral's pretty obvious, Sanders said, and winked. Stay away from drugs. No joke, they'll ruin your day every time.

Cute, said Henry Dobbins.

Mind-blower, get it? Talk about wiggy—nothing left, just blood and brains.

They made themselves laugh.

75   There it is, they'd say, over and over, as if the repetition itself were an act of poise, a balance between crazy and almost crazy, knowing without going. There it

is, which meant be cool, let it ride, because oh yeah, man, you can't change what can't be changed, there it is, there it absolutely and positively and fucking well *is*.

They were tough.

They carried all the emotional baggage of men who might die. Grief, terror, love, longing—these were intangibles, but the intangibles had their own mass and specific gravity, they had tangible weight. They carried shameful memories. They carried the common secret of cowardice barely restrained, the instinct to run or freeze or hide, and in many respects this was the heaviest burden of all, for it could never be put down, it required perfect balance and perfect posture. They carried their reputations. They carried the soldier's greatest fear, which was the fear of blushing. Men killed, and died, because they were embarrassed not to. It was what had brought them to the war in the first place, nothing positive, no dreams of glory or honor, just to avoid the blush of dishonor. They died so as not to die of embarrassment. They crawled into tunnels and walked point and advanced under fire. Each morning, despite the unknowns, they made their legs move. They endured. They kept humping. They did not submit to the obvious alternative, which was simply to close the eyes and fall. So easy, really. Go limp and tumble to the ground and let the muscles unwind and not speak and not budge until your buddies picked you up and lifted you into the chopper that would roar and dip its nose and carry you off to the world. A mere matter of falling, yet no one ever fell. It was not courage, exactly; the object was not valor. Rather, they were too frightened to be cowards.

By and large they carried these things inside, maintaining the masks of composure. They sneered at sick call. They spoke bitterly about guys who had found release by shooting off their own toes or fingers. Pussies, they'd say. Candyasses. It was fierce, mocking talk, with only a trace of envy or awe, but even so, the image played itself out behind their eyes.

They imagined the muzzle against flesh. They imagined the quick, sweet pain, then the evacuation to Japan, then a hospital with warm beds and cute geisha nurses.

80   They dreamed of freedom birds.

At night, on guard, staring into the dark, they were carried away by jumbo jets. They felt the rush of takeoff. *Gone!* they yelled. And then velocity, wings and engines, a smiling stewardess—but it was more than a plane, it was a real bird, a big sleek silver bird with feathers and talons and high screeching. They were flying. The weights fell off, there was nothing to bear. They laughed and held on tight, feeling the cold slap of wind and altitude, soaring, thinking *It's over, I'm gone!*—they were naked, they were light and free—it was all lightness, bright and fast and buoyant, light as light, a helium buzz in the brain, a giddy bubbling in the lungs as they were taken up over the clouds and the war, beyond duty, beyond gravity and mortification and global entanglements—*Sin loi!*[7] They yelled, *I'm sorry, motherfuckers, but I'm out of it, I'm goofed, I'm on a space cruise, I'm gone!*—and it was a restful, disencumbered sensation, just riding the light waves, sailing that big silver freedom bird over the mountains and oceans, over America, over the farms and great sleeping cities and cemeteries and highways and the Golden Arches of McDonald's. It was flight, a kind of fleeing, a kind of falling, falling higher and higher, spinning off the edge of the earth and beyond the sun and through the vast, silent vacuum where there were no burdens and where everything weighed exactly nothing. *Gone!* they screamed, *I'm sorry but I'm gone!*

[7]*Sin loi* sorry.

And so at night, not quite dreaming, they gave themselves over to lightness, they were carried, they were purely borne.

On the morning after Ted Lavender died, First Lieutenant Jimmy Cross crouched at the bottom of his foxhole and burned Martha's letters. Then he burned the two photographs. There was a steady rain falling, which made it difficult, but he used heat tabs and Sterno to build a small fire, screening it with his body, holding the photographs over the tight blue flame with the tips of his fingers.

He realized it was only a gesture. Stupid, he thought. Sentimental, too, but mostly just stupid.

Lavender was dead. You couldn't burn the blame.

85   Besides, the letters were in his head. And even now, without photographs, Lieutenant Cross could see Martha playing volleyball in her white gym shorts and yellow T-shirt. He could see her moving in the rain.

When the fire died out, Lieutenant Cross pulled his poncho over his shoulders and ate breakfast from a can.

There was no great mystery, he decided.

In those burned letters Martha had never mentioned the war, except to say, Jimmy, take care of yourself. She wasn't involved. She signed the letters "Love," but it wasn't love, and all the fine lines and technicalities did not matter.

The morning came up wet and blurry. Everything seemed part of everything else, the fog and Martha and the deepening rain.

90   It was a war, after all.

Half smiling, Lieutenant Jimmy Cross took out his maps. He shook his head hard, as if to clear it, then bent forward and began planning the day's march. In ten minutes, or maybe twenty, he would rouse the men and they would pack up and head west, where the maps showed the country to be green and inviting. They would do what they had always done. The rain might add some weight, but otherwise it would be one more day layered upon all the other days.

He was realistic about it. There was the new hardness in his stomach.

No more fantasies, he told himself.

Henceforth, when he thought about Martha, it would be only to think that she belonged elsewhere. He would shut down the daydreams. This was not Mount Sebastian, it was another world, where there were no pretty poems or midterm exams, a place where men died because of carelessness and gross stupidity. Kiowa was right. Boom-down, and you were dead, never partly dead.

95   Briefly, in the rain, Lieutenant Cross saw Martha's gray eyes gazing back at him.

He understood.

It was very sad, he thought. The things men carried inside. The things men did or felt they had to do.

He almost nodded at her, but didn't.

Instead he went back to his maps. He was now determined to perform his duties firmly and without negligence. It wouldn't help Lavender, he knew that, but from this point on he would comport himself as a soldier. He would dispose of his good-luck pebble. Swallow it, maybe, or use Lee Strunk's slingshot, or just drop it along the trail. On the march he would impose strict field discipline. He would be careful to send out flank security, to prevent straggling or bunching up, to keep his troops moving at the proper pace and at the proper interval. He would insist on clean weapons. He would confiscate the remainder of Lavender's dope. Later in the day, perhaps, he would call the men together and speak to them plainly. He would accept the blame for what had happened to Ted Lavender. He would be a man about it. He would look them in the eyes, keeping his chin level, and he would issue the new SOPs in a calm, impersonal tone of voice, an officer's voice, leaving no room for argument or discussion. Commencing immediately, he'd tell them, they would no longer abandon equipment along the route of march. They would police up their acts. They would get their shit together, and keep it together, and maintain it neatly and in good working order.

He would not tolerate laxity. He would show strength, distancing himself.

100   Among the men there would be grumbling, of course, and maybe worse, because their days would seem longer and their loads heavier, but Lieutenant Cross reminded himself that his obligation was not to be loved but to lead. He would dispense with love; it was not now a factor. And if anyone quarreled or complained, he would simply tighten his lips and arrange his shoulders in the correct command posture. He might give a curt little nod. Or he might not. He might just shrug and say Carry on, then they would saddle up and form into a column and move out toward the villages west of Than Khe.

[1986]

Joining the Conversation: Critical Thinking and Writing

1. What is the point of the insistent repetition of the words "the things they carried"? What sorts of things does Lieutenant Cross carry?
2. We are told that "Kiowa admired Lieutenant Jimmy Cross's capacity for grief" (paragraph 60). But we are also told that although Kiowa "wanted to share the man's pain," he could think only of "Boom-down" and of "the pleasure of having his boots off and the fog curling in around him and damp soil and the Bible smells and the plush comfort of night." What might account for the different responses of the two men?
3. Near the end of the story (paragraph 82), Lieutenant Cross "burned the two photographs." Why does he do this?

MyLiteratureLab® *For additional resources for "The Things They Carried," log in to* www.myliteraturelab.com *where you will find a Longman Lecture and a Comprehension Quiz, as well as an About the Author, Links, and Critical Overview for O'Brien (under Student Resources).*

SHERMAN ALEXIE

Sherman Alexie, born in 1966 in Spokane, Washington, holds a BA from Washington State University. The author of novels, stories, and poems, he adapted a volume of his short stories, The Lone Ranger and Tonto Fistfight in Heaven *(1994), into the film* Smoke Signals *(1998). Of his life and work Alexie has said, "I am a Spokane Coeur d'Alene Indian. . . . everything I do now, writing and otherwise, has its origin in that."*

The Lone Ranger, an immensely popular radio program that began in 1933, successfully made the transition to television (1949–57) and to comic books and films. The chief figure, the Lone Ranger, fought the bad guys of the Old West. He was assisted by the loyal Tonto, an American Indian who played a helpful but decidedly minor role. Tonto's name (it means "stupid" in Spanish, though in fact the character is not stupid) and his primitive English (he said things like "Me help Lone Ranger") make him an unacceptable figure today. Alexie's story never (after its title) mentions either the Lone Ranger or Tonto, nor does a fistfight occur, but a reader of the story presumably keeps in mind the problems that an American Indian faced—and faces—in a white world, a world in which whites and Indians do not easily co-exist, or at least do not co-exist in a Lone Ranger–and–Tonto way.

The Lone Ranger and Tonto Fistfight in Heaven

Too hot to sleep so I walked down to the Third Avenue 7-11 for a Creamsicle and the company of a graveyard-shift cashier. I know that game. I worked graveyard for a Seattle 7-11 and got robbed once too often. The last time the bastard locked me in the cooler. He even took my money and basketball shoes.

The graveyard-shift worker in the Third Avenue 7-11 looked like they all do. Acne scars and a bad haircut, work pants that showed off his white socks, and those cheap black shoes that have no support. My arches still ache from my year at the Seattle 7-11.

"Hello," he asked when I walked into his store. "How you doing?"

I gave him a half-wave as I headed back to the freezer. He looked me over so he could describe me to the police later. I knew the look. One of my old girlfriends said I started to look at her that way, too. She left me not long after that. No, I left her and don't blame her for anything. That's how it happened. When one person starts to look at another like a criminal, then the love is over. It's logical.

5   "I don't trust you," she said to me. "You get too angry."

She was white and I lived with her in Seattle. Some nights we fought so bad that I would just get in my car and drive all night, only stop to fill up on gas. In fact, I worked the graveyard shift to spend as much time away from her as possible. But I learned all about Seattle that way, driving its back ways and dirty alleys.

Sometimes, though, I would forget where I was and get lost. I'd drive for hours, searching for something familiar. Seems like I'd spent my whole life that way, looking for anything I recognized. Once, I ended up in a nice residential neighborhood and somebody must have been worried because the police showed up and pulled me over.

"What are you doing out here?" the police officer asked me as he looked over my license and registration.

"I'm lost."

10   "Well, where are you supposed to be?" he asked me, and I knew there were plenty of places I wanted to be, but none where I was supposed to be.

"I got in a fight with my girlfriend," I said. "I was just driving around, blowing off steam, you know?"

"Well, you should be more careful where you drive," the officer said. "You're making people nervous. You don't fit the profile of the neighborhood."

I wanted to tell him that I didn't really fit the profile of the country but I knew it would just get me into trouble.

"Can I help you?" the 7-11 clerk asked me loudly, searching for some response that would reassure him that I wasn't an armed robber. He knew this dark skin and long, black hair of mine was dangerous. I had potential.

15   "Just getting a Creamsicle," I said after a long interval. It was a sick twist to pull on the guy, but it was late and I was bored. I grabbed my Creamsicle and walked back to the counter slowly, scanned the aisles for effect. I wanted to whistle low and menacingly but I never learned to whistle.

"Pretty hot out tonight?" he asked, that old rhetorical weather bullshit question designed to put us both at ease.

"Hot enough to make you go crazy," I said and smiled. He swallowed hard like a white man does in those situations. I looked him over. Same old green, red, and white 7-11 jacket and thick glasses. But he wasn't ugly, just misplaced and marked by loneliness. If he wasn't working there that night, he'd be at home alone, flipping through channels and wishing he could afford HBO or Showtime.

"Will this be all?" he asked me, in that company effort to make me do some impulse shopping. Like adding a clause onto a treaty. *We'll take Washington and Oregon, and you get six pine trees and a brand-new Chrysler Cordoba.* I knew how to make and break promises.

"No," I said and paused. "Give me a Cherry Slushie, too."

20   "What size?" he asked, relieved.

"Large," I said, and he turned his back to me to make the drink. He realized his mistake but it was too late. He stiffened, ready for the gunshot or the blow behind the ear. When it didn't come, he turned back to me.

"I'm sorry," he said. "What size did you say?"

"Small," I said and changed the story.

"But I thought you said large."

25   "If you knew I wanted a large, then why did you ask me again?" I asked him and laughed. He looked at me, couldn't decide if I was giving him serious shit or just goofing. There was something about him I liked, even if it was three in the morning and he was white.

"Hey," I said. "Forget the Slushie. What I want to know is if you know all the words to the theme from 'The Brady Bunch'?"

He looked at me, confused at first, then laughed.

"Shit," he said. "I was hoping you weren't crazy. You were scaring me."

"Well, I'm going to get crazy if you don't know the words."

30   He laughed loudly then, told me to take the Creamsicle for free. He was the graveyard-shift manager and those little demonstrations of power tickled him. All seventy-five cents of it. I knew how much everything cost.

"Thanks," I said to him and walked out the door. I took my time walking home, let the heat of the night melt the Creamsicle all over my hand. At three in the morning I could act just as young as I wanted to act. There was no one around to ask me to grow up.

In Seattle, I broke lamps. She and I would argue and I'd break a lamp, just pick it up and throw it down. At first she'd buy replacement lamps, expensive and beautiful. But after a while she'd buy lamps from Goodwill or garage sales. Then she just gave up the idea entirely and we'd argue in the dark.

"You're just like your brother," she'd yell. "Drunk all the time and stupid."

"My brother don't drink that much."

35   She and I never tried to hurt each other physically. I did love her, after all, and she loved me. But those arguments were just as damaging as a fist. Words can be like that, you know? Whenever I get into arguments now, I remember her and I also remember Muhammad Ali. He knew the power of his fists but, more importantly, he knew the power of his words, too. Even though he only had an IQ of 80

or so, Ali was a genius. And she was a genius, too. She knew exactly what to say to cause me the most pain.

But don't get me wrong. I walked through that relationship with an executioner's hood. Or more appropriately, with war paint and sharp arrows. She was a kindergarten teacher and I continually insulted her for that.

"Hey, schoolmarm," I asked. "Did your kids teach you anything new today?"

And I always had crazy dreams. I always have had them, but it seemed they became nightmares more often in Seattle.

In one dream, she was a missionary's wife and I was a minor war chief. We fell in love and tried to keep it secret. But the missionary caught us fucking in the barn and shot me. As I lay dying, my tribe learned of the shooting and attacked the whites all across the reservation. I died and my soul drifted above the reservation.

40   Disembodied, I could see everything that was happening. Whites killing Indians and Indians killing whites. At first it was small, just my tribe and the few whites who lived there. But my dream grew, intensified. Other tribes arrived on horseback to continue the slaughter of whites, and the United States Cavalry rode into battle.

The most vivid image of that dream stays with me. Three mounted soldiers played polo with a dead Indian woman's head. When I first dreamed it, I thought it was just a product of my anger and imagination. But since then, I've read similar accounts of that kind of evil in the old West. Even more terrifying, though, is the fact that those kinds of brutal things are happening today in places like El Salvador.

All I know for sure, though, is that I woke from that dream in terror, packed up all my possessions, and left Seattle in the middle of the night.

"I love you," she said as I left her. "And don't ever come back."

I drove through the night, over the Cascades, down into the plains of central Washington, and back home to the Spokane Indian Reservation.

45   When I finished the Creamsicle that the 7-11 clerk gave me, I held the wooden stick up into the air and shouted out very loudly. A couple lights flashed on in windows and a police car cruised by me a few minutes later. I waved to the men in blue and they waved back accidentally. When I got home it was still too hot to sleep so I picked up a week-old newspaper from the floor and read.

There was another civil war, another terrorist bomb exploded, and one more plane crashed and all aboard were presumed dead. The crime rate was rising in every city with populations larger than 100,000, and a farmer in Iowa shot his banker after foreclosure on his 1,000 acres.

A kid from Spokane won the local spelling bee by spelling the word *rhinoceros*.

When I got back to the reservation, my family wasn't surprised to see me. They'd been expecting me back since the day I left for Seattle. There's an old Indian poet who said that Indians can reside in the city, but they can never live there. That's as close to truth as any of us can get.

Mostly I watched television. For weeks I flipped through channels, searched for answers in the game shows and soap operas. My mother would circle the want ads in red and hand the paper to me.

50   "What are you going to do with the rest of your life?" she asked.

"Don't know," I said, and normally, for almost any other Indian in the country, that would have been a perfectly fine answer. But I was special, a former college student, a smart kid. I was one of those Indians who was supposed to make it, to rise above the rest of the reservation like a fucking eagle or something. I was the new kind of warrior.

For a few months I didn't even look at the want ads my mother circled, just left the newspaper where she had set it down. After a while, though, I got tired of television and started to play basketball again. I'd been a good player in high school, nearly great, and almost played at the college I attended for a couple years. But I'd been too out of shape from drinking and sadness to ever be good again. Still, I liked the way the ball felt in my hands and the way my feet felt inside my shoes.

At first I just shot baskets by myself. It was selfish, and I also wanted to learn the game again before I played against anybody else. Since I had been good before and embarrassed fellow tribal members, I knew they would want to take revenge on me. Forget about the cowboys versus Indians business. The most intense competition on any reservation is Indians versus Indians.

But on the night I was ready to play for real, there was this white guy at the gym, playing with all the Indians.

55   "Who is that?" I asked Jimmy Seyler.

"He's the new BIA[1] chief's kid."

"Can he play?"

"Oh, yeah."

And he could play. He played Indian ball, fast and loose, better than all the Indians there.

60   "How long's he been playing here?" I asked.

"Long enough."

I stretched my muscles, and everybody watched me. All these Indians watched one of their old and dusty heroes. Even though I had played most of my ball at the white high school I went to, I was still all Indian, you know? I was Indian when it counted, and this BIA kid needed to be beaten by an Indian, any Indian.

I jumped into the game and played well for a little while. It felt good. I hit a few shots, grabbed a rebound or two, played enough defense to keep the other team honest. Then that white kid took over the game. He was too good. Later, he'd play college ball back East and would nearly make the Knicks team a couple years on. But we didn't know any of that would happen. We just knew he was better that day and every other day.

The next morning I woke up tired and hungry, so I grabbed the want ads, found a job I wanted, and drove to Spokane to get it. I've been working at the high school exchange program ever since, typing and answering phones. Sometimes I wonder if the people on the other end of the line know that I'm Indian and if their voices would change if they did know.

65   One day I picked up the phone and it was her, calling from Seattle.

"I got your number from your mom," she said. "I'm glad you're working."

"Yeah, nothing like a regular paycheck."

"Are you drinking?"

"No, I've been on the wagon for almost a year."

70   "Good."

The connection was good. I could hear her breathing in the spaces between our words. How do you talk to the real person whose ghost has haunted you? How do you tell the difference between the two?

---

[1]**BIA** Bureau of Indian Affairs.

"Listen," I said. "I'm sorry for everything."

"Me, too."

"What's going to happen to us?" I asked her and wished I had the answer for myself.

75 "I don't know," she said. "I want to change the world."

These days, living alone in Spokane, I wish I lived closer to the river, to the falls where ghosts of salmon jump. I wish I could sleep. I put down my paper or book and turn off all the lights, lie quietly in the dark. It may take hours, even years, for me to sleep again. There's nothing surprising or disappointing in that.

I know how all my dreams end anyway.

[1993]

Joining the Conversation: Critical Thinking and Writing

1. Given the fact that neither the Lone Ranger nor Tonto appears in the story, what do you make of the title?
2. Paragraphs 54–63 introduce a white man from the Bureau of Indian Affairs. Why do you suppose Alexie includes this episode in his story?
3. How would you characterize the narrator? How do you think he would characterize himself? (In thinking about these matters you might ask yourself "What are his chief problems?" and "How well does he understand himself and the social world around him?")
4. What do you make of the narrator's statement, in the next-to-last paragraph, that he wishes he "lived closer to the river, to the falls where the ghosts of salmon jump"?
5. Alexie has said that there is "a political purpose" to everything he writes. In your view, does his statement apply to this story? If so, does it increase your enjoyment and your understanding of the story? Or do you think that storytellers—once they have told their story—should let readers draw their own conclusions? In an essay of 250–500 words, offer a comment on Alexie's comment.

AMY STERLING CASIL

Amy Sterling Casil, born in Los Angeles, California, in 1962 and educated at Scripps College and Chapman University, teaches English at Saddleback College in Southern California. Her mother, Sterling Sturtevant, was an Academy Award and Cannes Golden Palm–winning art director who redesigned Mr. Magoo and Charlie Brown, among other well-known characters. Casil has published more than one hundred short stories, three novels, two collections of short fiction and poetry, and a number of nonfiction books. She has twice been nominated for science fiction's Nebula Award.

The following story first appeared in the Magazine of Fantasy & Science Fiction *in 2008. It was inspired by her son Anthony, who was born with Down Syndrome. Casil has said that "every therapy mentioned in the story is currently being developed. The story is fiction; the feelings are real."*

Perfect Stranger

The rain falls in sheets across the yard, another pane of glass beyond our windows.

Would you like it warmer, Mr. Gill?

The house pings once. Twice.

"No," I say. "It's fine the way it is."

5   *Thank you very much*, the house says.

Just like anybody else, the house likes to talk to somebody. I imagined this as a great feature. I'm an ergonomic architect; I designed it.

Denny is asleep in his room. You'd think at fifteen, he'd be too old to take a nap. But he's wiped out after soccer.

Carolyn threw Denny's football out today. The foam rubber football I gave him when he was four years old.

It was old, she said. Falling apart. He didn't want it any more. I thought, if he really doesn't want the football, maybe he could say. I tried asking.

10   But right then, Denny was off to soccer practice, then a study session, then the game. Now, he's sleeping. This is what happens when they're in high school.

Carolyn says I should be proud. Proud he's such an athlete. And a scholar.

And I guess I'm a gentleman.

The rain comes down like liquid leaded glass.

The gardeners have taken the trash all the way to the curb once again.

15   It's a very long way to the end of the driveway.

I return with half of Denny's football.

She must have taken shears to it. A lightning strike of rage flashes. If she were home right now . . .

Your body temperature is lower than normal, Mr. Gill, the house chimes in its chimey voice.

"I've been out in the rain," I mutter.

20   *Would you like some soft, fluffy towels?* the house asks. I want the other half of the football. I'll glue it back together. But I smile and grunt an assent, to which the house responds.

Outside, the rain sleets down, a thousand tiny sticks pattering on a thousand tin drums. Nah, not drums. It's just our solar panels.

Denny was born with HLHS. That's an acronym for hypoplastic left heart syndrome. Hypoplastic left heart syndrome is universally fatal, if left untreated. Even now, there are babies that do not survive, even with full-length clone DNA therapy administered in-utero.

When at five months of pregnancy, Carolyn went for a high-level ultrasound that determined Denny had HLHS, it seemed like the most natural thing in the world to try gene therapy. The doctors explained how the heart healed itself as the baby grew.

It was raining that day.

25   Pouring outside while we listened to the neonatal geneticist explain how the procedure worked. We were so lucky, she said. Before gene therapy, babies like Denny could only survive with full heart transplants. She told us about a doctor that had tried baboon hearts to replace broken baby ones.

Apparently, some parents aborted babies diagnosed with HLHS.

"I'd never accept that," I said.

"What?" Carolyn snapped, her hand over her swollen belly. "You'd rather let my baby suffer?"

I guess I hadn't thought of it that way.

30   The geneticist explained in the past, babies born with this heart defect were simply left to die. Their hearts that barely pumped blood. And they would just fade away.

Maybe that could be less humane than an abortion.

At least that was what we discussed on the way home.

It was a miracle that we had the gene therapy, and that Denny was born whole. And totally healthy.

It was the best moment of my life.

35   The rain rattles the solar panels as I sort pictures on the computer. Denny in his baby swing. Denny playing with blocks.

I should be working. But I can't focus on the Recreation Center today.

There was one of him holding the fuzzy book he got from his grandmother. She was so frightened—my mother—when I told her about Denny's heart problem. She didn't understand gene therapy.

Carolyn got on the phone and explained it to her. When Denny was born perfectly healthy, I don't think any of us gave it much more thought. My mother and Denny sat for hours, reading that little book. *Pat the Bunny.* Her favorite—she insisted on buying it. I have it in my study, in the right drawer of my desk.

At one past garage sale, it had been another item bound for the dumpster.

40   I put the half-football with *Pat the Bunny*.

Denny was about three when he learned to read.

I sorted those pictures, too.

They say a man's not supposed to be interested in pictures. Mementos.

The man lives his life, and the woman saves it.

45   Well, what they say is true and what happens are sometimes two different things.

There was another book Denny liked. *Stan the Hotdog Man.* We read it over and over.

And one day, Denny started talking about Stan. It dawned on me that he was reading.

"Carolyn, come here!" I called.

She came running in from the kitchen, alarmed.

50   "Honey, I think he's reading."

Her face changed. "Horse manure," she said.

"No, really," I said.

Denny then read a whole page of *Stan the Hotdog Man* in his small voice. He beamed proudly up at me.

"See?" I said.

55   "You've read it to him so many times, he's memorized it," she said.

"Oh," I said.

It was some time later when I learned that by memorizing the book, Denny was, indeed, reading. By that time, he was in kindergarten.

I sorted some more of the pictures from later years, and looked pensively out at the rain. Denny was still sleeping.

I think I always hoped that my son would play football.

60   Back before I met Carolyn, I played ball. Played all the way through sophomore year in college. Sidelined by a knee injury. I guess I was a pretty good running back, if a little bit underweight. The guys were all into steroids back in those days. There was no such thing as gene augmentation. All we had were good, old-fashioned workouts and protein shakes.

And maybe a shot in the butt for guys that were really dedicated. Or crazy.

You could blow your heart out on steroids. They made you break out all over. Gave you erectile dysfunction. Made you crazy.

Happened to a lot of my friends. It's a good thing I figured out that trap before I fell into it.

I guess I did try it a few times.

65   Drops of rain dappled the window.

Your heart rate has increased, Mr. Gill, the house chimed. *Your core body temperature has dropped.*

"So turn up the heat," I told the house.

I had to say something. Otherwise, it wouldn't leave me alone.

I folded the blue ribbon neatly into my desk drawer. For math excellence. Why they'd give a math prize to a kid in second grade was beyond me.

70   When Denny hit second grade, his teacher pointed out that he was reading like a pro, but having trouble with his figures.

"I was never too good with math," I told her. Wasn't that great in reading, either, but I didn't feel compelled to share.

"You might want to look into some tutoring," she said.

"He's in second grade!" I said.

Carolyn hushed me. "How far is he behind?" she asked.

75   "Behind?" the teacher asked. "Oh, no—he's not behind."

"Well, there's no reason to worry," I said. "He'll pick it up."

"His times tables," Carolyn said. "Next year he's got to learn the times tables."

"We don't do it that way any more, Mrs. Gill. Each child is tested individually against his or her own standards."

I didn't precisely follow how there could be enough time to set individual standards seeing as the kid had just started second grade.

80   "How far is he behind?" Carolyn asked again.

"He's not behind," the teacher said, a stubborn tone creeping into her voice. "Denny is so bright. I'm sure you'd agree with me that he could do better if he applied himself. That's all I'm trying to say."

"Maybe he just wants to play outside," I said.

"Hush!" Carolyn said. "Gary and I both agree that Denny is bright. And he's got plenty of motivation."

"Well," the teacher said smiling. "Why don't you try that tutoring service, or a math buddy."

85   A math buddy was like an English buddy, or a foreign language buddy. It was a small, silver, pain-in-the-ass robot that could also vacuum the floor. They were notorious for tripping guys foolish enough to buy them for their kids. A guy in Cleveland broke his neck that way.

I was going to be damned if I'd get one. I would have rather gotten Denny another football.

On the way out to the car, Carolyn looked up at me, concern wrinkling her forehead. "He's falling behind in math," she whispered.

"You don't have to whisper," I told her. "Nobody can hear. Besides, the teacher said he's not behind. We can encourage him."

"Encourage him!" Carolyn snapped. "He can do better, and he will."

90   "Well, do you think we should try a tutor?" I asked. The thought of locking Denny inside with some greasy-haired high school math geek made me cringe. But even that was a more appealing choice than bringing a gibbering, tortoise-like "math buddy" into the house, so it could trip me on the stairs and turn me into a paraplegic.

"No," Carolyn said. "Not a tutor."

I felt relieved.

"Have you heard about the new gene therapy?" she asked. "It's just like what they did for Denny's heart defect. Only it can strengthen a child's brain power. I was reading all about it yesterday."

"Oh," I said. I had pretty favorable memories of how they'd fixed Denny's heart. "How does that work?"

95   "Maybe it's like what they did before. Only they inject the new genetic material into someone's brain. Then it makes a few changes and the person gets smarter."

"Oh," I said. I didn't like the thought of anybody injecting anything into Denny's brain. But I'd learned it was best not to interrupt Carolyn when she was thinking like this. Frankly, it was almost always better just to wait things out. Half the time she forgot about this stuff and never mentioned it again.

"If you're concerned about your son's logical and mathematical abilities, I don't think you've got much to worry about with Denny," Dr. Mandel said. "He's a bright, normal boy."

"But his teacher says he's falling behind in math," Carolyn said. "Can't we do something?"

"I'd recommend a math buddy," the doctor said. "My own daughter has one. She's about Denny's age. She used to hate math, and now she loves it."

100   "Doesn't that thing get in your way?" I asked—about the math buddy.

"Thing?" the doctor said, looking puzzled. "Oh!" he said, chuckling. "Yeah, it did trip me up once. I fell right off the deck into the pool."

"There's something I don't like about those little robots," I said. "The teacher also suggested a tutor."

"A wise choice," the doctor said. He started to check his personal assistant, a sure sign our time was up. I started to rise, but Carolyn put her hand on my arm.

"Wait," she said. "Can you explain how the procedure works, doctor?"

105   He paused. I suddenly understood that he was one of those guys who never missed a chance to wow others with his special, technical knowledge.

"Well," he said, smiling. "Years ago, we discovered that viruses could be effective transports to load different types of DNA into human—or any other type—of brains. Now we've identified a specific enzyme or cocktail of enzymes that enhances almost every type of brain function. We load the enzymes into a virus, which then transcribes the DNA, and delivers the desired changes to what we once thought were 'unchangeable' brain cells. I'm sure you've heard of people building up their 'extrasensory perception.'"

Carolyn and I nodded. We'd seen a show about wild-eyed lunatics bending iron and starting fires at a distance the night before.

"It's like an infection," Dr. Mandel said. "But it's one that most people wouldn't mind catching."

"Like a cold?" Carolyn asked.

110   "Exactly!" Dr. Mandel said. "You do understand. Only in this case, the subject catches the cold in their cerebral cortex, and as healing occurs, so do changes for the better."

"Wow," Carolyn said.

"I'm not sure about this," I said.

"Shhh!" she hushed.

"How old is your son?" the doctor asked.

115   "Seven," Carolyn said.

"Ah, the perfect age. Look—" he said, leaning across his shiny titanium desk—everybody who was anybody had one of those a few years back—"It's not cheap. But you could make your son into a math genius if you wanted. He wouldn't feel a thing, and a few days later, his abilities would manifest. They'd grow day by day."

"I don't know," I said. It sounded like mad scientist stuff to me. Weren't they trying these techniques on psychotic murderers? If this was so safe and healthy, I figured we would have heard about it in other areas besides criminal rehabilitation and iron-bending firestarters.

"People are doing it all the time," Dr. Mandel said. "You just don't hear about it on the newslinks because improving kids' test scores isn't nearly as big a story as turning a mass-murderer into Mother Teresa."

Carolyn squeezed my hand under the table. "Doctor, we'd like to try," she said.

120   "I suppose we could—" Dr. Mandel said, voice slightly uncertain.

"Is this necess—"

Carolyn cut me short. "I know he can benefit," she said. "I don't think we mentioned it earlier, but Denny received gene therapy before he was born, to cure a congenital heart defect."

"Oh!" the doctor said. "In that case, he's pre-qualified. Be sure to fill out all the forms, you two. We're conducting multi-treatment longitudinal studies and your son is an ideal candidate."

So, Denny got the blue ribbon in math.

125   He got so into math that he stayed inside almost all the time. He hardly wanted to play with his friends any more. We were supposed to start Pony League football.

But Denny didn't want to play. He didn't want to try for T-Ball, either.

The only thing he'd talk about was math.

One day, Carolyn pointed out that Denny was getting a little chunky.

"He was size eight last month," she said. "Now I've got to buy the next size up."

130   "So? My mom told me I grew three sizes and four inches one summer."

"Your mom said all kinds of things," Carolyn said.

Mom had passed last spring. We used to joke about her seeing Denny through high school. It wasn't meant to be.

"Could you give it a rest, Carolyn?" My wife thought that seven months was long enough. For mourning.

She forged ahead. "Denny's getting fat, Gary. We can't let him get overweight."

135   "So, we'll put him on a diet," I said. I'd been a little chunky when I was his age. When my mom found out how much time I could waste playing video games, she ripped the whole console out of the wall. It was the cold-turkey video game withdrawal method. I lost the weight.

We tried a diet, but Denny was too young to understand why he couldn't eat everything he liked. I wasn't surprised when a couple of frustrating weeks later, Carolyn told me that she'd called Dr. Mandel.

There was of course a gene therapy—the most popular one of all—to deal with unwanted weight gain. This time, the virus carrying altered DNA helped to increase some of the hormones in the brain that controlled appetite and metabolism.

Voila! A thin kid.

That was Denny's third treatment.

140   The rain is imploding on the roof. It's almost in my head.

"Turn up the heat!" I scream.

The house complies. If I didn't know better, I'd almost think that the house was sulking.

After the obesity treatment, Denny started getting into soccer. And discovered his talent for art.

By thirteen, Denny was Dr. Mandel's best patient. He had even been featured on the cover of *Parenting* with two other kids that had been helped by Dr. Mandel's gene practice. It wasn't exactly as if gene therapy was cutting-edge any more. Dr. Mandel was known for his "boutique" practice. That meant that he helped parents with money and fine-edged concerns about their children's growth and well-being.

145   No one really took the dire warnings of the early part of the millennium seriously.

Creating a "master race" and so-on. Well, heck. If a person could get a little bit better in some way, and it wasn't hurting them or anybody else, how did that qualify as a "master race"? People without genetic improvements were never looked down upon.

Sure, it was a generational thing. I mean, there were some skin therapies for people my age and Carolyn's age. And they had learned how to rejuvenate most of the vital organs. When I was young, it was a big deal for anybody to make it to age 100. These days, you had to hit 120 and look really good to get your picture on the newslinks.

It was the kids that benefited. If somebody would have told me back in the day that a Pugsley kid could turn into a hunk in a matter of weeks, or a kid with no chin could suddenly acquire a nice, square one without surgery, I would have laughed out loud. You were what you were born to be.

Up until he was nine or ten, Denny's eyes were kind of a hazel color. Now they were piercing, bright blue. The girls went crazy over his eyes. I mean, the kid was a good-looking fifteen, but—

150   The house chimed. Somebody was calling.

"Gary here," I answered.

"Is Denny home?" came a petite, snippy little voice.

"Yes, but he's sleeping. Tired out after his game." I didn't share that he'd had yet another treatment—this one to deal with a few pimples, of all things. Kids slept a lot after a treatment. Body change and metabolic readjustment, supposedly. Dr. Mandel likened it to "growing pains."

"Oh, well, like we were supposed to be . . . studying . . . for chemistry tonight," the little voice said. After a moment's pause, she added, "This is Candy."

155   "I thought you were Apple," I said. She sounded like the girl Denny had introduced me to named "Apple." Apple was a cheerleader, and—

"No, I'm Candy," she said vehemently. "I don't see how you could confuse us. Apple is completely shallow and self-centered and she can't pass math. I'm the captain of the Debate Team."

"Oh," I said. *Of course* she was Debate Team Captain. "My mistake. Apple calls a lot."

"Oh," Candy said. "I see."

"Denny hardly ever takes her calls," I said. This was utterly untrue, but for some reason, I enjoyed the thought of the little white lie that was involved.

160   "Oh," she said, voice brightening. "Well, just tell Denny that I called.

"Thank you, Mr. Gill." And she broke the connection.

So I went upstairs.

"Hey," I said, waking Denny. "A girl called."

Denny rose, shaking sleep out of his eyes. "Yeah? Who was it, Dad?"

165 "Apple," I said. "Wait—no, Candy."

"Candy," Denny said, smiling slyly. "She likes me, I think."

"She's the jealous type too," I said. "What are you doing to attract all these girls, Denny?"

Denny scooted up in bed and swung his legs to the floor. He started rubbing his shoulder. "Hurt it a little bit in the game," he said.

"How'd it go?"

170 "Not bad," he said. "We won by two goals. I got the last goal."

Of course you did, I thought. I hadn't gone to the game. Somehow, I just hadn't wanted to. It was raining. I said it was crazy to play soccer in the rain. Watching soccer in the rain was even crazier.

I couldn't put my finger on the real reason I hadn't gone to the game.

Carolyn was at work, of course. She had a fulfilling, demanding job at the local art museum. She put together their brochures and maintained their web presence. Everybody says what artistic talent she has. It's really amazing how Denny has the same abilities—maybe even more so. Paintings, drawings, vector art—Denny does it all. He would be taking sculpture, if it didn't conflict with soccer practice.

Denny got up and started to strip off his clothes. He was only fifteen, but his chest and biceps were more muscular than mine. Not just at that age—now.

175 He sprinted into his bathroom and called for the house to turn on the shower.

"Did you order more after-shave, Dad?" he called.

"Yeah," I said. "Yesterday."

"Oh, right," Denny said. "It's all full now—I can see it."

Of course I ordered after-shave. When you work from home, all those little chores seem to fall on you. Tell the house what to cook for dinner, tell it to keep the different meals ready at different times for everyone's schedule, see to it the laundry schedule isn't too full and somebody—namely Denny—isn't going to have to run to a soccer game and play in a dirty jersey. Make sure all the plants are watered and trimmed and the rug is vacuumed and the floor polished and there are no lights out and there—

180 "Hey Dad, what should I do about Candy?" Denny asked from the shower.

"Do about what?"

"She *likes* me, Dad. I like her fine as a friend, but I don't want to get serious. She's just not—"

"What's wrong with her?"

"Nothing," Denny said.

185 "Well, if there's nothing wrong with her, why don't you like her?" I knew perfectly well what he meant, but I was just playing with his mind.

"I mean *like*, Dad. As in . . . you know. . . ."

"You're supposed to be the genius," I said. "I don't know, so explain it to me."

I don't know what I expected to hear. "She's homely, Dad." Or, "She comes on too strong." Or, maybe, "She's pretty nerdy."

"She's a mundane, Dad," Denny said. "I just can't get interested in a girl who's never had any type of modifications."

190 I said, "Oh."

I sat on the bed. I think it was the way he said it.

Denny came out of the shower, a towel wrapped around his Adonis-like frame. "Dad, you know how it is," he said.

"Yeah," I said.

"I mean, look at Apple. She might not be that smart, but she's got a great body. She does a five-minute mile, and her nails are perfect. I know her hair's not real, but what does that matter? It looks great."

195 "Apple's a nice girl," I said.

A long time ago when Denny was a baby, my mother came over and we spent the whole day playing. Building towers of blocks. Reading books. Setting up paper and finger paints on the kitchen table. She baked cookies.

I watched my son and my mother playing together. His hair was light brown and wispy over his hazel eyes. Maybe he looked like an old, balding fat guy, but he was just a baby. There was a funny little cleft in his chin. He was clumsy. We worked with him to use his right hand, then his left. Just letting him experiment. She grabbed his outstretched hands in hers and lifted him up. He giggled and stood and toddled, then soon sat back down.

He was only nine months.

Even a genetically modified baby can't walk at nine months.

200 And it comes to me.

Why I didn't go to the game.

I looked in Denny's eyes a long while. Bright blue, they were. There's been nobody with blue eyes in my family for a long time. Maybe there never were. I can't say those were Carolyn's eyes, either. She has muddy brown eyes, and hates them.

Denny started to laugh, feeling uncomfortable. "Hey, Dad, what are you looking at me like that for?"

I can't reply.

205 "I'm just—you know—" I say, finally. I look over at Denny's artwork.

At the trophies for soccer. Math ribbons. His poster, running for class president last year.

Yeah, he won.

"Your mom threw your little kid football out this morning," I said. "What football?" Denny asked.

It was no big deal, I guess. I really didn't know how to explain.

210 I heard him on the phone after dinner.

Talking up that Apple.

"Yeah, baby. I know it's hard. But everyone's parents are pretty much mundanes. You should see my Dad."

It wasn't like I hadn't had my own rough spots with my Dad. I wanted to run in and grab the vox away from Denny. Yell. Tell her to respect her parents. Tell him.

Denny never knew my father. Carolyn's Dad was an old fart who painted bowls of fruit and sad-eyed clowns.

215 He wasn't a bad guy. He was just kind of . . . distant.

There was no way to make Denny comprehend that my Dad had been a great guy. I mean, I hated Dad when he grounded me. I hated him when he took my car away. I hated him when he flushed my sad little pot stash down the can.

He taught me responsibility. He taught me what it meant to be a man. A mundane.

Hush my feet, I told the house much later that night. The house could do that, you know. Make it quiet to walk, or very noisy. Only the administrator could tell it to do that. I know a lot of parents that use this feature.

I was sleeping in my study again. No. I was lying on the couch in the study, pretending to sleep.

220 It was easier. Carolyn always has some book she's reading or some work she's going over and that light in my eyes drives me crazy.

I was turning the whole thing over in my mind.

All the little treatments. Yeah, it was right to fix Denny's heart.

We had to fix Denny's heart.

Denny was the only son Carolyn and I were ever going to have. I used, back in the day, you know. Stacking. I was juiced up all the time. I thought it made me more of a man.

225   They said it was a minor miracle that Carolyn had gotten pregnant, since I had a sperm count of about 3. Three million particles per ml. And after that, it went down even more. They call that sterile.

She could have left me. Maybe if I had been in her shoes, I would have.

She could have had a lot more kids with a healthy man.

But this was our son. This was Denny.

One time, my Dad was watching me at football practice. I caught a right screen pass we'd been practicing a long time and raced away. My legs were wings. The scrimmagers hurled themselves at me in slow motion. I was flying, the wind whipping through the bars of my helmet. Nobody could touch me.

230   My Dad had this look on his face when he ran out on the field after that scrimmage.

We didn't need to say too much. In fact, we didn't say anything. I was his son, and he was my Dad.

Then it started to rain, and we headed for our car.

I wandered into the kitchen, still remembering.

"Hey house, I'm going to make a sandwich," I whispered. "I want to use the last of that good bread."

235   "Do you want me to slice it?" the house asked.

"No," I said. "You know I cut it myself."

"That's right," the house said. It put the bread and knife out on the counter.

"Mustard?"

"Yes."

240   "Lettuce?"

"No, just bologna."

"Very good," the house said. "Low-fat, high protein."

"Right, house," I said. "Thanks."

I cut the bread for the sandwich. Put mustard on the bread. Slapped down the meat, slapped the whole thing together and stuffed it in my mouth.

245   Then I started upstairs on quiet feet.

"Don't forget to put your knife in the dishwasher," the house said. To some questions, house did not require an immediate answer.

In terms of his eyes, they were blue.

A tear rolls down my mundane cheek.

His chest moves slowly, up and down. His breathing soft, like a cat. Denny stirs. Moans slightly.

250   So they dream.

But what dreams come, I can never know.

There was no such face, ever. Not in my house. Not in my line. None of my father's strength. None of my mother's cleft chin. None of us were ever so broad-shouldered.

None of us were any good at math.

We were good with people. We were fast runners, me and Dad. Denny's a fast runner, too, but different.

255   One time I visited Dad in the care home. Premature Alzheimers, they said. It was the last time he'd know my face. Be able to say my name.

"Carolyn and I are having a baby," I told him. "It's going to be a little boy."

He took my hand.

"I'm so glad, Son," he said, his brown eyes warm and lucid. Knowing me and what I said.

I wonder what it will feel like when I'm an old man. Denny won't come.

260 I can't imagine him ever telling me he's going to have a son.

I dream what it will feel like to look into those ice-blue, strange eyes.

Just one stroke. Quick. Hard.

Down into his changed heart. The heart of a perfect stranger.

Denny turns and sighs.

265 Like a vision, I see my Dad's face. He speaks.

Why did you lose us, Gary? Your Mom—me? For this?

He taught me what it was to be a man.

Outside, the rain falls. It's tapping on the roof like a hundred little cats running up and down.

I listen.

270 Then I turn and go on my quiet feet back down the stairs.

Outside, the rain is a cold curtain of ice knifing my face. I look up, into the clear, black sky. No stars, nothing. Pines shadowed against the midnight fog.

I know if I just look hard enough, I'll find the other half of the football.

Let the sky darken like soot. Let the wind gather.

Let it rain.

For Anthony Sterling Rodgers

[2008]

Joining the Conversation: Critical Thinking and Writing

1. Why is the narrator of "Perfect Stranger" so concerned with retrieving the foam rubber football (paragraphs 8 and 272)?
2. How would you characterize the narrator? How would you characterize the relationship between him and Carolyn, his wife? Suppose Carolyn were the narrator. Write the last paragraph or two or three paragraphs of the story that Carolyn might narrate.
3. Are the treatments given in the story believable? Do you think they are advisable? Are they moral?
4. Do you think we are on the road toward the society that the story depicts? Why, or why not?

RALPH ELLISON

Ralph Ellison (1914–94) was born in Oklahoma City. His father died when Ellison was three, and his mother supported herself and her child by working as a domestic. A trumpeter since boyhood, Ellison studied music at Tuskegee Institute, an historically black college in Alabama founded by Booker T. Washington. In 1936 he dropped out of Tuskegee and went to Harlem to study music composition and the visual arts; there he met Langston Hughes and Richard Wright, who encouraged him to turn to fiction. Ellison published stories and essays, and in 1942 he became the managing editor of Negro Quarterly. *During World War II he served in the Merchant Marine. After the war he returned to writing and later taught in universities.*

"Battle Royal" was first published in 1947 and slightly revised (a transitional paragraph was added at the end of the story) for the opening chapter of Ellison's novel, Invisible Man *(1952), a book cited by* Book-Week *as "the most significant work of fiction written by an American" in the years between 1945 and 1965. In addition to stories and his one novel, Ellison published critical essays, which are brought together in* The Collected Essays of Ralph Ellison *(1995).*

Battle Royal

It goes a long way back, some twenty years. All my life I had been looking for something, and everywhere I turned someone tried to tell me what it was. I accepted their answers too, though they were often in contradiction and even self-contradictory. I was naïve. I was looking for myself and asking everyone except myself questions which I, and only I, could answer. It took me a long time and much painful boomeranging of my expectations to achieve a realization everyone else appears to have been born with: That I am nobody but myself. But first I had to discover that I am an invisible man!

And yet I am no freak of nature, nor of history. I was in the cards, other things having been equal (or unequal) eighty-five years ago. I am not ashamed of my

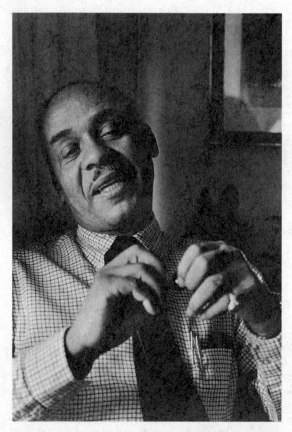

Gordon Parks, *Ralph Ellison.* Parks, an African American photographer with an international reputation, published many books of photographs, including *Camera Portraits,* where this picture appears.

grandparents for having been slaves. I am only ashamed of myself for having at one time been ashamed. About eighty-five years ago they were told that they were free, united with others of our country in everything pertaining to the common good, and, in everything social, separate like the fingers of the hand. And they believed it. They exulted in it. They stayed in their place, worked hard, and brought up my father to do the same. But my grandfather is the one. He was an odd old guy, my grandfather, and I am told I take after him. It was he who caused the trouble. On his deathbed he called my father to him and said, "Son, after I'm gone I want you to keep up the good fight. I never told you, but our life is a war and I have been a traitor all my born days, a spy in the enemy's country ever since I give up my gun back in the Reconstruction. Live with your head in the lion's mouth. I want you to overcome 'em with yeses, undermine 'em with grins, agree 'em to death and destruction, let 'em swoller you till they vomit or bust wide open." They thought the old man had gone out of his mind. He had been the meekest of men. The younger children were rushed from the room, the shades drawn and the flame of the lamp turned so low that it sputtered on the wick like the old man's breathing. "Learn it to the younguns," he whispered fiercely; then he died.

But my folks were more alarmed over his last words than over his dying. It was as though he had not died at all, his words caused so much anxiety. I was warned emphatically to forget what he had said and, indeed, this is the first time it has been mentioned outside the family circle. It had a tremendous effect upon me, however. I could never be sure of what he meant. Grandfather had been a quiet old man who never made any trouble, yet on his deathbed he had called himself a traitor and a spy, and he had spoken of his meekness as a dangerous activity. It became a constant puzzle which lay unanswered in the back of my mind. And whenever things went well for me I remembered my grandfather and felt guilty and uncomfortable. It was as though I was carrying out his advice in spite of myself. And to make it worse, everyone loved me for it. I was praised by the most lily-white men of the town. I was considered an example of desirable conduct—just as my grandfather had been. And what puzzled me was that the old man had defined it as *treachery*. When I was praised for my conduct I felt a guilt that in some way I was doing something that was really against the wishes of the white folks, that if they had understood they would have desired me to act just the opposite, that I should have been sulky and mean, and that that really would have been what they wanted, even though they were fooled and thought they wanted me to act as I did. It made me afraid that some day they would look upon me as a traitor and I would be lost. Still I was more afraid to act any other way because they didn't like that at all. The old man's words were like a curse. On my graduation day I delivered an oration in which I showed that humility was the secret, indeed, the very essence of progress. (Not that I believed this—how could I, remembering my grandfather?—I only believed that it worked.) It was a great success. Everyone praised me and I was invited to give the speech at a gathering of the town's leading white citizens. It was a triumph for our whole community.

It was in the main ballroom of the leading hotel. When I got there I discovered that it was on the occasion of a smoker, and I was told that since I was to be there anyway I might as well take part in the battle royal to be fought by some of my schoolmates as part of the entertainment. The battle royal came first.

5   All of the town's big shots were there in their tuxedoes, wolfing down the buffet foods, drinking beer and whiskey and smoking black cigars. It was a large room with a high ceiling. Chairs were arranged in neat rows around three sides of a portable boxing ring. The fourth side was clear, revealing a gleaming space of

polished floor. I had some misgivings over the battle royal, by the way. Not from a distaste for fighting, but because I didn't care too much for the other fellows who were to take part. They were tough guys who seemed to have no grandfather's curse worrying their minds. No one could mistake their toughness. And besides, I suspected that fighting a battle royal might detract from the dignity of my speech. In those pre-invisible days I visualized myself as a potential Booker T. Washington.[1] But the other fellows didn't care too much for me either, and there were nine of them. I felt superior to them in my way, and I didn't like the manner in which we were all crowded together into the servants' elevator. Nor did they like my being there. In fact, as the warmly lighted floors flashed past the elevator we had words over the fact that I, by taking part in the fight, had knocked one of their friends out of a night's work.

We were led out of the elevator through a rococo hall into an anteroom and told to get into our fighting togs. Each of us was issued a pair of boxing gloves and ushered out into the big mirrored hall, which we entered looking cautiously about us and whispering, lest we might accidentally be heard above the noise of the room. It was foggy with cigar smoke. And already the whiskey was taking effect. I was shocked to see some of the most important men of the town quite tipsy. They were all there—bankers, lawyers, judges, doctors, fire chiefs, teachers, merchants. Even one of the more fashionable pastors. Something we could not see was going on up front. A clarinet was vibrating sensuously and the men were standing up and moving eagerly forward. We were a small tight group, clustered together, our bare upper bodies touching and shining with anticipatory sweat; while up front the big shots were becoming increasingly excited over something we still could not see. Suddenly I heard the school superintendent, who had told me to come, yell. "Bring up the shines, gentlemen! Bring up the little shines!"

We were rushed up to the front of the ballroom, where it smelled even more strongly of tobacco and whiskey. Then we were pushed into place. I almost wet my pants. A sea of faces, some hostile, some amused, ringed around us, and in the center, facing us, stood a magnificent blonde—stark naked. There was dead silence. I felt a blast of cold air chill me. I tried to back away, but they were behind me and around me. Some of the boys stood with lowered heads, trembling. I felt a wave of irrational guilt and fear. My teeth chattered, my skin turned to goose flesh, my knees knocked. Yet I was strongly attracted and looked in spite of myself. Had the price of looking been blindness, I would have looked. The hair was yellow like that of a circus kewpie doll, the face heavily powdered and rouged, as though to form an abstract mask, the eyes hollow and smeared a cool blue, the color of a baboon's butt. I felt a desire to spit upon her as my eyes brushed slowly over her body. Her breasts were firm and round as the domes of East Indian temples, and I stood so close as to see the fine skin texture and beads of pearly perspiration glistening like dew around the pink and erected buds of her nipples. I wanted at one and the same time to run from the room, to sink through the floor, or go to her and cover her from my eyes and the eyes of the others with my body; to feel the soft thighs, to caress her and destroy her, to love her and murder her, to hide from her, and yet to stroke where below the small American flag tattooed upon her belly her thighs formed a capital V. I had a notion that of all in the room she saw only me with her impersonal eyes.

And then she began to dance, a slow sensuous movement; the smoke of a hundred cigars clinging to her like the thinnest of veils. She seemed like a fair bird-girl girdled in veils calling to me from the angry surface of some gray and threatening

---

[1]**Booker T. Washington** (1856–1915), African American educator and leader.

sea. I was transported. Then I became aware of the clarinet playing and the big shots yelling at us. Some threatened us if we looked and others if we did not. On my right I saw one boy faint. And now a man grabbed a silver pitcher from a table and stepped close as he dashed ice water upon him and stood him up and forced two of us to support him as his head hung and moans issued from his thick bluish lips. Another boy began to plead to go home. He was the largest of the group, wearing dark red fighting trunks much too small to conceal the erection which projected from him as though in answer to the insinuating low-registered moans of the clarinet. He tried to hide himself with his boxing gloves.

And all the while the blonde continued dancing, smiling faintly at the big shots who watched her with fascination, and faintly smiling at our fear. I noticed a certain merchant who followed her hungrily, his lips loose and drooling. He was a large man who wore diamond studs in a shirtfront which swelled with the ample paunch underneath, and each time the blonde swayed her undulating hips he ran his hand through the thin hair of his bald head and, with his arms upheld, his posture clumsy like that of an intoxicated panda, wound his belly in a slow and obscene grind. This creature was completely hypnotized. The music had quickened. As the dancer flung herself about with a detached expression on her face, the men began reaching out to touch her. I could see their beefy fingers sink into her soft flesh. Some of the others tried to stop them and she began to move around the floor in graceful circles, as they gave chase, slipping and sliding over the polished floor. It was mad. Chairs went crashing, drinks were spilt, as they ran laughing and howling after her. They caught her just as she reached a door, raised her from the floor, and tossed her as college boys are tossed at a hazing, and above her red, fixed-smiling lips I saw the terror and disgust in her eyes, almost like my own terror and that which I saw in some of the other boys. As I watched, they tossed her twice and her soft breasts seemed to flatten against the air and her legs flung wildly as she spun. Some of the more sober ones helped her to escape. And I started off the floor, heading for the anteroom with the rest of the boys.

10 Some were still crying and in hysteria. But as we tried to leave we were stopped and ordered to get into the ring. There was nothing to do but what we were told. All ten of us climbed under the ropes and allowed ourselves to be blindfolded with broad bands of white cloth. One of the men seemed to feel a bit sympathetic and tried to cheer us up as we stood with our backs against the ropes. Some of us tried to grin. "See that boy over there?" one of the men said. "I want you to run across at the bell and give it to him right in the belly. If you don't get him, I'm going to get you. I don't like his looks." Each of us was told the same. The blindfolds were put on. Yet even then I had been going over my speech. In my mind each word was as bright as flame. I felt the cloth pressed into place, and frowned so that it would be loosened when I relaxed.

But now I felt a sudden fit of blind terror. I was unused to darkness. It was as though I had suddenly found myself in a dark room filled with poisonous cottonmouths. I could hear the bleary voices yelling insistently for the battle royal to begin.

"Get going in there!"

"Let me at that big nigger!"

I strained to pick up the school superintendent's voice, as though to squeeze some security out of that slightly more familiar sound.

15 "Let me at those black sonsabitches!" someone yelled.

"No, Jackson, no!" another voice yelled. "Here, somebody, help me hold Jack."

"I want to get at that ginger-colored nigger. Tear him limb from limb," the first voice yelled.

I stood against the ropes trembling. For in those days I was what they called ginger-colored, and he sounded as though he might crunch me between his teeth like a crisp ginger cookie.

Quite a struggle was going on. Chairs were being kicked about and I could hear voices grunting as with a terrific effort. I wanted to see, to see more desperately than ever before. But the blindfold was as tight as a thick skin-puckering scab and when I raised my gloved hands to push the layers of white aside a voice yelled, "Oh, no you don't, black bastard! Leave that alone!"

20   "Ring the bell before Jackson kills him a coon!" someone boomed in the sudden silence. And I heard the bell clang and the sound of the feet scuffling forward.

A glove smacked against my head. I pivoted, striking out stiffly as someone went past, and felt the jar ripple along the length of my arm to my shoulder. Then it seemed as though all nine of the boys had turned upon me at once. Blows pounded me from all sides while I struck out as best I could. So many blows landed upon me that I wondered if I were not the only blindfolded fighter in the ring, or if the man called Jackson hadn't succeeded in getting me after all.

Blindfolded, I could no longer control my motions. I had no dignity. I stumbled about like a baby or a drunken man. The smoke had become thicker and with each new blow it seemed to sear and further restrict my lungs. My saliva became like hot bitter glue. A glove connected with my head, filling my mouth with warm blood. It was everywhere. I could not tell if the moisture I felt upon my body was sweat or blood. A blow landed hard against the nape of my neck. I felt myself going over, my head hitting the floor. Streaks of blue light filled the black world behind the blindfold. I lay prone, pretending that I was knocked out, but felt myself seized by hands and yanked to my feet. "Get going, black boy! Mix it up!" My arms were like lead, my head smarting from blows. I managed to feel my way to the ropes and held on, trying to catch my breath. A glove landed in my mid-section and I went over again, feeling as though the smoke had become a knife jabbed into my guts. Pushed this way and that by the legs milling around me, I finally pulled erect and discovered that I could see the black, sweat-washed forms weaving in the smoky-blue atmosphere like drunken dancers weaving to the rapid drum-like thuds of blows.

Everyone fought hysterically. It was complete anarchy. Everybody fought everybody else. No group fought together for long. Two, three, four, fought one, then turned to fight each other, were themselves attacked. Blows landed below the belt and in the kidney, with the gloves open as well as closed, and with my eye partly opened now there was not so much terror. I moved carefully, avoiding blows, although not too many to attract attention, fighting from group to group. The boys groped about like blind, cautious crabs crouching to protect their midsections, their heads pulled in short against their shoulders, their arms stretched nervously before them, with their fists testing the smoke-filled air like the knobbed feelers of hypersensitive snails. In one corner I glimpsed a boy violently punching the air and heard him scream in pain as he smashed his hand against a ring post. For a second I saw him bent over holding his hand, then going down as a blow caught his unprotected head. I played one group against the other, slipping and throwing a punch then stepping out of range while pushing the others into the melee to take the blows blindly aimed at me. The smoke was agonizing and there were no rounds, no bells at three minute intervals to relieve our exhaustion. The room spun round me, a swirl of lights, smoke, sweating bodies surrounded by tense white faces. I bled from both nose and mouth, the blood spattering upon my chest.

The men kept yelling, "Slug him, black boy! Knock his guts out!"

25   "Uppercut him! Kill him! Kill that big boy!"

Taking a fake fall, I saw a boy going down heavily beside me as though we were felled by a single blow, saw a sneaker-clad foot shoot into his groin as the two who had knocked him down stumbled upon him. I rolled out of range, feeling a twinge of nausea.

The harder we fought the more threatening the men became. And yet, I had begun to worry about my speech again. How would it go? Would they recognize my ability? What would they give me?

I was fighting automatically and suddenly I noticed that one after another of the boys was leaving the ring. I was surprised, filled with panic, as though I had been left alone with an unknown danger. Then I understood. The boys had arranged it among themselves. It was the custom for the two men left in the ring to slug it out for the winner's prize. I discovered this too late. When the bell sounded two men in tuxedoes leaped into the ring and removed the blindfold. I found myself facing Tatlock, the biggest of the gang. I felt sick at my stomach. Hardly had the bell stopped ringing in my ears than it clanged again and I saw him moving swiftly toward me. Thinking of nothing else to do I hit him smash on the nose. He kept coming, bringing the rank sharp violence of stale sweat. His face was a black blank of a face, only his eyes alive—with hate of me and aglow with a feverish terror from what had happened to us all. I became anxious. I wanted to deliver my speech and he came at me as though he meant to beat it out of me. I smashed him again and again, taking his blows as they came. Then on a sudden impulse I struck him lightly as we clinched, I whispered, "Fake like I knocked you out, you can have the prize."

"I'll break your behind," he whispered hoarsely.

30   "For *them?*"

"For *me*, sonofabitch!"

They were yelling for us to break it up and Tatlock spun me half around with a blow, and as a joggled camera sweeps in a reeling scene, I saw the howling red faces crouching tense beneath the cloud of blue gray smoke. For a moment the world wavered, unraveled, flowed, then my head cleared and Tatlock bounced before me. That fluttering shadow before my eyes was his jabbing left hand. Then falling forward, my head against his damp shoulder, I whispered,

"I'll make it five dollars more."

"Go to hell!"

35   But his muscles relaxed a trifle beneath my pressure and I breathed, "Seven!"

"Give it to your ma," he said, ripping me beneath the heart.

And while I still held him I butted him and moved away. I felt myself bombarded with punches. I fought back with hopeless desperation. I wanted to deliver my speech more than anything else in the world, because I felt that only these men could judge truly my ability, and now this stupid clown was ruining my chances. I began fighting carefully now, moving in to punch him and out again with my greater speed. A lucky blow to his chin and I had him going too—until I heard a loud voice yell, "I got my money on the big boy."

Hearing this, I almost dropped my guard. I was confused: Should I try to win against the voice out there? Would not this go against my speech, and was not this a moment for humility, for nonresistance? A blow to my head as I danced about sent my right eye popping like a jack-in-the-box and settled my dilemma. The room went red as I fell. It was a dream fall, my body languid and fastidious as to where to land, until the floor became impatient and smashed up to meet me.

A moment later I came to. An hypnotic voice said FIVE emphatically. And I lay there, hazily watching a dark red spot of my own blood shaping itself into a butterfly, glistening and soaking into the soiled gray world of the canvas.

When the voice drawled TEN I was lifted up and dragged to a chair. I sat dazed. My eye pained and swelled with each throb of my pounding heart and I wondered if now I would be allowed to speak. I was wringing wet, my mouth still bleeding. We were grouped along the wall now. The other boys ignored me as they congratulated Tatlock and speculated as to how much they would be paid. One boy whimpered over his smashed hand. Looking up front, I saw attendants in white jackets rolling the portable ring away and placing a small square rug in the vacant space surrounded by chairs. Perhaps, I thought, I will stand on the rug to deliver my speech.

40   Then the M.C. called to us, "Come on up here boys and get your money."

We ran forward to where the men laughed and talked in their chairs, waiting. Everyone seemed friendly now.

"There it is on the rug," the man said. I saw the rug covered with coins of all dimensions and a few crumpled bills. But what excited me, scattered here and there, were the gold pieces.

"Boys, it's all yours," the man said. "You get all you grab."

"That's right, Sambo," a blond man said, winking at me confidentially.

45   I trembled with excitement, forgetting my pain. I would get the gold and the bills, I thought. I would use both hands. I would throw my body against the boys nearest me to block them from the gold.

"Get down around the rug now," the man commanded, "and don't anyone touch it until I give the signal."

"This ought to be good," I heard.

As told, we got around the square rug on our knees. Slowly the man raised his freckled hand as we followed it upward with our eyes.

I heard, "These niggers look like they're about to pray!"

50   Then, "Ready," the man said. "Go!"

I lunged for a yellow coin lying on the blue design of the carpet, touching it and sending a surprised shriek to join those rising around me. I tried frantically to remove my hand but could not let go. A hot, violent force tore through my body, shaking me like a wet rat. The rug was electrified. The hair bristled up on my head as I shook myself free. My muscles jumped, my nerves jangled, writhed. But I saw that this was not stopping the other boys. Laughing in fear and embarrassment, some were holding back and scooping up the coins knocked off by the painful contortions of the others. The men roared above us as we struggled.

"Pick it up, goddamnit, pick it up!" someone called like a bass-voiced parrot. "Go on, get it!"

I crawled rapidly around the floor, picking up the coins, trying to avoid the coppers and to get greenbacks and the gold. Ignoring the shock by laughing, as I brushed the coins off quickly, I discovered that I could contain the electricity—a contradiction, but it works. Then the men began to push us onto the rug. Laughing embarrassedly, we struggled out of their hands and kept after the coins. We were all wet and slippery and hard to hold. Suddenly I saw a boy lifted into the air, glistening with sweat like a circus seal, and dropped, his wet back landing flush upon the charged rug, heard him yell and saw him literally dance upon his back, his elbows beating a frenzied tattoo upon the floor, his muscles twitching like the flesh of a horse stung by many flies. When he finally rolled off, his face was gray and no one stopped him when he ran from the floor amid booming laughter.

"Get the money," the M.C. called. "That's good hard American cash!"

55   And we snatched and grabbed, snatched and grabbed. I was careful not to come too close to the rug now, and when I felt the hot whiskey breath descend upon me like a cloud of foul air I reached out and grabbed the leg of a chair. It was occupied and I held on desperately.

"Leggo, nigger! Leggo!"

The huge face wavered down to mine as he tried to push me free. But my body was slippery and he was too drunk. It was Mr. Colcord, who owned a chain of movie houses and "entertainment palaces." Each time he grabbed me I slipped out of his hands. It became a real struggle. I feared the rug more than I did the drunk, so I held on, surprising myself for a moment by trying to topple *him* upon the rug. It was such an enormous idea that I found myself actually carrying it out. I tried not to be obvious, yet when I grabbed his leg, trying to tumble him out of the chair, he raised up roaring with laughter, and, looking at me with soberness dead in the eye, kicked me viciously in the chest. The chair leg flew out of my hand. I felt myself going and rolled. It was as though I had rolled through a bed of hot coals. It seemed a whole century would pass before I would roll free, a century in which I was seared through the deepest levels of my body to the fearful breath within me and the breath seared and heated to the point of explosion. It'll all be over in a flash, I thought as I rolled clear. It'll all be over in a flash.

But not yet, the men on the other side were waiting, red faces swollen as though from apoplexy as they bent forward in their chairs. Seeing their fingers coming toward me I rolled away as a fumbled football rolls off the receiver's fingertips, back into the coals. That time I luckily sent the rug sliding out of place and heard the coins ringing against the floor and the boys scuffling to pick them up and the M.C. calling, "All right, boys, that's all. Go get dressed and get your money."

I was limp as a dish rag. My back felt as though it had been beaten with wires.

60   When we had dressed the M.C. came in and gave us each five dollars, except Tatlock, who got ten for being the last in the ring. Then he told us to leave. I was not to get a chance to deliver my speech, I thought. I was going out into the dim alley in despair when I was stopped and told to go back. I returned to the ballroom, where the men were pushing back their chairs and gathering in groups to talk.

The M.C. knocked on a table for quiet. "Gentlemen," he said, "we almost forgot an important part of the program. A most serious part, gentlemen. This boy was brought here to deliver a speech which he made at his graduation yesterday. . . ."

"Bravo!"

"I'm told that he is the smartest boy we've got out there in Greenwood. I'm told that he knows more big words than a pocket-sized dictionary."

Much applause and laughter.

65   "So now, gentlemen, I want you to give him your attention."

There was still laughter as I faced them, my mouth dry, my eye throbbing. I began slowly, but evidently my throat was tense, because they began shouting, "Louder! Louder!"

"We of the younger generation extol the wisdom of that great leader and educator," I shouted, "who first spoke these flaming words of wisdom: 'A ship lost at sea for many days suddenly sighted a friendly vessel. From the mast of the unfortunate vessel was seen a signal: "Water, water; we die of thirst!" The answer from the friendly vessel came back: "Cast down your bucket where you are." The captain of the distressed vessel, at last heeding the injunction, cast down his bucket, and it came up full of fresh sparkling water from the mouth of the Amazon River.' And like him I say, and in his words, 'To those of my race who depend upon bettering their condition in a foreign land, or who underestimate the importance of cultivating friendly relations with the Southern white man, who is his next-door neighbor, I would say: "Cast down your bucket where you are"—cast it down in making friends in every manly way of the people of all races by whom we are surrounded. . . .'"

I spoke automatically and with such fervor that I did not realize that the men were still talking and laughing until my dry mouth, filling up with blood from the cut, almost strangled me. I coughed, wanting to stop and go to one of the tall brass, sand-filled spittoons to relieve myself, but a few of the men, especially the superintendent, were listening and I was afraid. So I gulped it down, blood, saliva and all, and continued. (What powers of endurance I had during those days! What enthusiasm! What a belief in the rightness of things!) I spoke even louder in spite of the pain. But still they talked and still they laughed, as though deaf with cotton in dirty ears. So I spoke with greater emotional emphasis. I closed my ears and swallowed blood until I was nauseated. The speech seemed a hundred times as long as before, but I could not leave out a single word. All had to be said, each memorized nuance considered, rendered. Nor was that all. Whenever I uttered a word of three or more syllables a group of voices would yell for me to repeat it. I used the phrase "social responsibility" and they yelled:

"What's the word you say, boy?"

70   "Social responsibility," I said.

"What?"

"Social . . ."

"Louder."

". . . responsibility."

75   "More!"

"Respon—"

"Repeat!"

"—sibility."

The room filled with the uproar of laughter until, no doubt, distracted by having to gulp down my blood, I made a mistake and yelled a phrase I had often seen denounced in newspaper editorials, heard debated in private.

80   "Social . . ."

"What?" they yelled.

". . . equality—"

The laughter hung smokelike in the sudden stillness. I opened my eyes, puzzled. Sounds of displeasure filled the room. The M.C. rushed forward. They shouted hostile phrases at me. But I did not understand.

A small dry mustached man in the front row blared out, "Say that slowly, son!"

85   "What sir?"

"What you just said!"

"Social responsibility, sir," I said.

"You weren't being smart, were you, boy?" he said, not unkindly.

"No, sir!"

90   "You sure that about 'equality' was a mistake?"

"Oh, yes, sir," I said. "I was swallowing blood."

"Well, you had better speak more slowly so we can understand. We mean to do right by you, but you've got to know your place at all times. All right, now, go on with your speech."

I was afraid. I wanted to leave but I wanted also to speak and I was afraid they'd snatch me down.

"Thank you, sir," I said, beginning where I had left off, and having them ignore me as before.

95   Yet when I finished there was a thunderous applause. I was surprised to see the superintendent come forth with a package wrapped in white tissue paper, and gesturing for quiet, address the men.

"Gentlemen, you see that I did not overpraise this boy. He makes a good speech and some day he'll lead his people in the proper paths. And I don't have to tell you that that is important in these days and times. This is a good, smart boy, and so to encourage him in the right direction, in the name of the Board of Education I wish to present him a prize in the form of this . . ."

He paused, removing the tissue paper and revealing a gleaming calfskin brief case. ". . . in the form of this first-class article from Shad Whitmore's shop."

"Boy," he said, addressing me, "take this prize and keep it well. Consider it a badge of office. Prize it. Keep developing as you are and some day it will be filled with important papers that will help shape the destiny of your people."

100   I was so moved that I could hardly express my thanks. A rope of bloody saliva forming a shape like an undiscovered continent drooled upon the leather and I wiped it quickly away. I felt an importance that I had never dreamed.

"Open it and see what's inside," I was told.

My fingers a-tremble, I complied, smelling the fresh leather and finding an official-looking document inside. It was a scholarship to the state college for Negroes. My eyes filled with tears and I ran awkwardly off the floor.

I was overjoyed; I did not even mind when I discovered that the gold pieces I had scrambled for were brass pocket tokens advertising a certain make of automobile.

When I reached home everyone was excited. Next day the neighbors came to congratulate me. I even felt safe from grandfather, whose deathbed curse usually spoiled my triumphs. I stood beneath his photograph with my brief case in hand and smiled triumphantly into his stolid black peasant's face. It was a face that fascinated me. The eyes seemed to follow everywhere I went.

105   That night I dreamed I was at a circus with him and that he refused to laugh at the clowns no matter what they did. Then later he told me to open my brief case and read what was inside and I did, finding an official envelope stamped with the state seal; and inside the envelope I found another and another, endlessly, and I thought I would fall of weariness. "Them's years," he said. "Now open that one." And I did and in it I found an engraved document containing a short message in letters of gold. "Read it," my grandfather said. "Out loud."

"To Whom It May Concern," I intoned, "Keep This Nigger-Boy Running."

I awoke with the old man's laughter ringing in my ears.

(It was a dream I was to remember and dream again for many years after. But at the time I had no insight into its meaning. First I had to attend college.)

[1947]

Joining the Conversation: Critical Thinking and Writing

1. Now that you have read the entire story, the opening paragraph of "Battle Royal" may be clearer than it was when you first read it. What does the narrator mean when he declares at the end of this paragraph, "I am an invisible man?" Explain how the events described in the story taught him this painful truth.

2. The narrator says of his grandfather's dying speech, "I could never be sure of what he meant." What do you think the grandfather meant by calling himself a traitor and a spy in the enemy's territory?

3. What is the significance of the scene involving the naked blonde woman? How is this scene related to the narrator's discovery that he is invisible?
4. This story is a powerful, indeed shocking study of racism, but in essays and interviews Ellison often noted that he intended his stories and his novel *Invisible Man* to illuminate "universal truths" about human experience as well. In your view, does "Battle Royal" achieve this goal? What insights does it offer about the nature of self-knowledge and human identity?

POEMS

ROBERT HAYDEN

Robert Hayden (1913–80) was born in Detroit, Michigan. His parents divorced when he was a child, and he was brought up by a neighboring family, whose name he adopted. In 1942, at the age of twenty-nine, he graduated from Detroit City College (now Wayne State University), and he received a master's degree from the University of Michigan. He taught at Fisk University from 1946 to 1969 and after that, for the remainder of his life, at the University of Michigan. In 1979 he was appointed Consultant in Poetry to the Library of Congress, the first African American to hold the post.

Frederick Douglass°

When it is finally ours, this freedom, this liberty, this beautiful
and terrible thing, needful to man as air,
usable as earth; when it belongs at last to all,
when it is truly instinct, brain matter, diastole, systole,
reflex action; when it is finally won; when it is more   5
than the gaudy mumbo jumbo of politicians:
this man, this Douglass, this former slave, this Negro
beaten to his knees, exiled, visioning a world
where none is lonely, none hunted, alien,
this man, superb in love and logic, this man   10
shall be remembered. Oh, not with statues' rhetoric,
not with legends and poems and wreaths of bronze alone,
but with the lives grown out of his life, the lives
fleshing his dream of the beautiful, needful thing.

[1947]

°**Frederick Douglass** (1818–95) Born a slave, Douglass escaped and became an important spokesman for the abolitionist movement and later for civil rights for African Americans.

Joining the Conversation: Critical Thinking and Writing

1. When, according to Hayden, will Douglass "be remembered"? And *how* will he be remembered?
2. "Frederick Douglass" consists of two sentences (or one sentence and a fragment). In what line do you find the subject of the first sentence? What is the main verb (the predicate) and where do you find it? How would you describe the effect of the long delaying of the subject? And of the predicate?

3. Does Hayden assume or seem to predict that there *will* come a time when freedom "is finally ours" (line 1) and "belongs at last to all" (line 3)?
4. Hayden wrote "Frederick Douglass" in 1947. In your opinion are we closer now to Hayden's vision or farther away? (You may find that we are closer in some ways and farther in others.) In your answer—perhaps an essay of 500 words—try to be as specific as possible.
5. "Frederick Douglass" consists of fourteen lines. Is it a sonnet?

LORNA DEE CERVANTES

Lorna Dee Cervantes, born in San Francisco in 1954, founded a press and a poetry magazine, Mango, *chiefly devoted to Chicano literature. In 1978 she received a fellowship from the National Endowment for the Arts, and in 1981 she published her first book of poems. She lives in Boulder, Colorado. "Refugee Ship," originally written in 1974, was revised for the book. We print the revised version.*

Refugee Ship

Like wet cornstarch, I slide
past my grandmother's eyes. Bible
at her side, she removes her glasses.
The pudding thickens.

Mama raised me without language.   5
I'm orphaned from my Spanish name.
The words are foreign, stumbling
on my tongue. I see in the mirror
my reflection: bronzed skin, black hair.

I feel I am a captive   10
aboard the refugee ship.
The ship that will never dock.
El barco que nunca atraca.°

[1981]

13 *El barco que nunca atraca* The ship that never docks.

Joining the Conversation: Critical Thinking and Writing

1. What do you think the speaker in "Refugee Ship" means by the comparison with "wet cornstarch" in line 1? And what do you take her to mean in line 7 when she says, "I'm orphaned from my Spanish name"?
2. Judging from the poem as a whole, why does the speaker feel she is "a captive / aboard the refugee ship"? How would you characterize such feelings?
3. In an earlier version of the poem, instead of "my grandmother's eyes" Cervantes wrote "*mi abuelita's* eyes"; that is, she used the Spanish words for "my grandmother." In line 5 instead of "Mama" she wrote "*mamá*" (again, the Spanish

equivalent), and in line 9 she wrote "brown skin" instead of "bronzed skin." The final line of the original version was not in Spanish but in English, a repetition of the preceding line, which ran thus: "A ship that will never dock." How does each of these changes strike you?

EDWIN ARLINGTON ROBINSON

Edwin Arlington Robinson (1869–1935) grew up in Gardiner, Maine, spent two years at Harvard, and then returned to Maine, where he published his first book of poetry in 1896. Though he received encouragement from neighbors, his finances were precarious, even after President Theodore Roosevelt, having been made aware of the book, secured for him an appointment as customs inspector in New York from 1905 to 1909. Additional books won fame for Robinson, and in 1922 he was awarded the first of three Pulitzer Prizes for poetry that he would win.

Richard Cory

Whenever Richard Cory went down town,
We people on the pavement looked at him:
He was a gentleman from sole to crown,
Clean favored, and imperially slim.

And he was always quietly arrayed,   5
And he was always human when he talked;
But still he fluttered pulses when he said,
"Good-morning," and he glittered when he walked.

And he was rich—yes, richer than a king—
And admirably schooled in every grace: 10
In fine,° we thought that he was everything
To make us wish that we were in his place.

So on we worked, and waited for the light,
And went without the meat, and cursed the bread;
And Richard Cory, one calm summer night,   15
Went home and put a bullet through his head.

[1896]

11 In fine in short.

Joining the Conversation: Critical Thinking and Writing

1. What do you think were Richard Cory's thoughts shortly before he "put a bullet through his head"? In 500 words, set forth his thoughts and actions (what he sees and does). If you wish, you can write in the first person, from Cory's point of view. Further, if you wish, your essay can be in the form of a suicide note.
2. Write a sketch (250–350 words) setting forth your early impression or understanding of someone whose later actions revealed that you had not understood the person.

W. H. AUDEN

*Wystan Hugh Auden (1907–73) was born in York, England, and educated at
Oxford. In the 1930s his left-wing poetry earned him wide acclaim as the leading poet
of his generation. He went to Spain during the Spanish Civil War, intending to serve
as an ambulance driver for the Republicans in their struggle against fascism, but he
was so distressed by the violence of the Republicans that he almost immediately
returned to England. In 1939 he came to America, and in 1946 he became a citizen
of the United States, though he returned to England for his last years. Much of his poetry
is characterized by a combination of colloquial diction and technical dexterity.*

The Unknown Citizen

*(To JS/07/M/378
This Marble Monument
Is Erected by the State)*

He was found by the Bureau of Statistics to be
One against whom there was no official complaint,
And all the reports on his conduct agree
That, in the modern sense of an old-fashioned word, he was a saint,
For in everything he did he served the Greater Community.   5
Except for the War till the day he retired
He worked in a factory and never got fired,
But satisfied his employers, Fudge Motors Inc.
Yet he wasn't a scab or odd in his views,
For his Union reports that he paid his dues,   10
(Our report on his Union shows it was sound)
And our Social Psychology workers found
That he was popular with his mates and liked a drink.
The Press are convinced that he bought a paper every day
And that his reactions to advertisements were normal in every way.   15
Policies taken out in His name prove that he was fully insured,
And his Health-card shows he was once in hospital but left it cured.
Both Producers Research and High-Grade Living declare
He was fully sensible to the advantages of the Installment Plan
And had everything necessary to the Modern Man,   20
A phonograph, radio, a car and a frigidaire.
Our researchers into Public Opinion are content
That he held the proper opinions for the time of year;
When there was peace, he was for peace; when there was war, he went.
He was married and added five children to the population,   25
Which our Eugenist says was the right number for a parent of his generation,
And our teachers report that he never interfered with their education.
Was he free? Was he happy? The question is absurd:
Had anything been wrong, we should certainly have heard.

[1940]

Joining the Conversation: Critical Thinking and Writing

1. What is Auden satirizing in "The Unknown Citizen"? You will want to spend some time thinking about whether Auden is satirizing the speaker, the citizen, conformism, totalitarianism, technology, or what.
2. Write a prose eulogy of 250 words satirizing contemporary conformity, or, if you prefer, contemporary individualism.
3. Was the citizen free? Was he happy? Explain.
4. In a paragraph or two, sketch the values of the speaker of the poem and then sum them up in a sentence or two. Finally, in as much space as you feel you need, judge these values.

ALLEN GINSBERG

Allen Ginsberg (1926–97) was born in Newark, New Jersey, and graduated from Columbia University in 1948. After eight months in Columbia Psychiatric Institute—Ginsberg had pleaded insanity to avoid prosecution when the police discovered that a friend had stored stolen goods in Ginsberg's apartment—he worked at odd jobs and finally left the nine-to-five world for a freer life in San Francisco. In the 1950s he established a reputation as an uninhibited declamatory poet whose chief theme was a celebration of those who were alienated from a repressive America.

A Supermarket in California

What thoughts I have of you tonight, Walt Whitman, for I walked down the sidestreets under the trees with a headache self-conscious looking at the full moon.

In my hungry fatigue, and shopping for images, I went into the neon fruit supermarket, dreaming of your enumerations!

What peaches and what penumbras! Whole families shopping at night! Aisles full of husbands! Wives in the avocados, babies in the tomatoes!—and you, García Lorca,° what were you doing down by the watermelons?

I saw you, Walt Whitman, childless, lonely old grubber, poking among the meats in the refrigerator and eyeing the grocery boys.

I heard you asking questions of each: Who killed the pork chops? What   5
price bananas? Are you my Angel?

I wandered in and out of the brilliant stacks of cans following you, and followed in my imagination by the store detective.

We strode down the open corridors together in our solitary fancy tasting artichokes, possessing every frozen delicacy, and never passing the cashier.

Where are we going, Walt Whitman? The doors close in an hour. Which way does your beard point tonight?

(I touch your book and dream of our odyssey in the supermarket and feel absurd.)

3 García Lorca Federico García Lorca (1899–1936), Spanish poet (and, like Whitman and Ginsberg, a homosexual).

Will we walk all night through solitary streets? The trees add shade to   10
shade, lights out in the houses, we'll both be lonely.

Will we stroll dreaming of the lost America of love past blue automobiles
in driveways, home to our silent cottage?

Ah, dear father, graybeard, lonely old courage-teacher, what America did
you have when Charon quit poling his ferry and you got out on a smoking
bank and stood watching the boat disappear on the black waters of Lethe?°

[1955]

12 Lethe In classical mythology, Charon ferried the souls of the dead across the river Styx
to Hades, where, after drinking from the river Lethe, they forgot the life they had lived.

Joining the Conversation: Critical Thinking and Writing

1. Ginsberg calls his poem "A Supermarket in California." Need the market be in
   California, or can it be anywhere?
2. In the second line, Ginsberg explains why he went into the supermarket. Is the
   explanation clear, or puzzling, or some of each? Explain.
3. In the third line ("What peaches and what penumbras!"), what *is* a penumbra?
   Are the aisles full of them?
4. In line 8 ("Where are we going, Walt Whitman? The doors close in an hour.
   Which way does your beard point tonight?"), is Ginsberg hopeful or not hopeful
   about where he and Walt Whitman will stroll?
5. Read two or three Whitman poems (reprinted elsewhere in this book). In what
   ways does Ginsberg's poem resemble Whitman's poems? In what ways is "A
   Supermarket" pure Ginsberg?

MARGE PIERCY

*Marge Piercy, born in Detroit in 1936, was the first member of her family to attend
college. After earning a bachelor's degree from the University of Michigan in 1957
and a master's degree from Northwestern University in 1958, she moved to Chicago.
There she worked at odd jobs while writing novels (unpublished) and engaging in
action on behalf of women and blacks and against the Vietnam War. In 1970—the
year she moved to Wellfleet, Massachusetts, where she still lives—she published her
first book, a novel. Since then she has published many novels, as well as short stories,
poems, and essays.*

What's That Smell in the Kitchen?

All over America women are burning dinners.
It's lambchops in Peoria; it's haddock
in Providence; it's steak in Chicago;
tofu delight in Big Sur; red
rice and beans in Dallas.   5
All over America women are burning
food they're supposed to bring with calico

smile on platters glittering like wax.
Anger sputters in her brainpan, confined
but spewing out missiles of hot fat.   10
Carbonized despair presses like a clinker
from a barbecue against the back of her eyes.
If she wants to grill anything, it's
her husband spitted over a slow fire.
If she wants to serve him anything   15
it's a dead rat with a bomb in its belly
ticking like the heart of an insomniac.
Her life is cooked and digested,
nothing but leftovers in Tupperware.
Look, she says, once I was roast duck   20
on your platter with parsley but now I am Spam.
Burning dinner is not incompetence but war.

[1982]

Joining the Conversation: Critical Thinking and Writing

1. Suppose a friend told you that she didn't understand lines 20–21. How would
   you paraphrase the lines?
2. Who speaks the title?
3. If a poem begins, "All over America women are . . . ," what words might a
   reader reasonably expect next?
4. Do you take the poem to be chiefly comic? Superficially comic but a work with
   a serious purpose? Or what?

YUSEF KOMUNYAKAA

*Yusef Komunyakaa was born in 1947 in Bogalusa, Louisiana. After graduating
from high school he entered the army and served in Vietnam, where he was awarded the Bronze Star. On his return to the United States he earned a bachelor's degree
at the University of Colorado, and then an MA at Colorado State University and an
MFA in creative writing at the University of California, Irvine. The author of several
books of poetry, Komunyakaa teaches at New York University. "Facing It" is the last
poem in a book of poems about Vietnam,* Dien Cai Dau *(1988). The title of the book
is a slang term for* crazy.

Facing It

My black face fades,
hiding inside the black granite.
I said I wouldn't,
dammit: No tears.
I'm stone. I'm flesh.   5
My clouded reflection eyes me

Vietnam Veterans Memorial, Washington, D.C.

like a bird of prey, the profile of night
slanted against morning. I turn
this way—the stone lets me go.
I turn that way—I'm inside   10
the Vietnam Veterans Memorial
again, depending on the light
to make a difference.
I go down the 58,022 names,
half-expecting to find   15
my own in letters like smoke.
I touch the name Andrew Johnson;
I see the booby trap's white flash.
Names shimmer on a woman's blouse
but when she walks away   20
the names stay on the wall.
Brushstrokes flash, a red bird's
wings cutting across my stare.
The sky. A plane in the sky.
A white vet's image floats   25
closer to me, then his pale eyes
look through mine. I'm a window.
He's lost his right arm
inside the stone. In the black mirror
a woman's trying to erase names: 30
No, she's brushing a boy's hair.

[1988]

Joining the Conversation: Critical Thinking and Writing

1. The poem's title is "Facing It." What is the speaker facing? How would you describe his attitude?
2. Three people, whose names we don't know, briefly appear on the wall. How might we describe their actions? Try to paraphrase: "I'm a window. / He's lost his right arm / inside the stone."
3. At the poem's end, has the speaker "faced it"? What is your evidence?
4. If you have seen the Vietnam Veterans Memorial, describe it and your reaction to it in a paragraph or two. If you haven't seen it, try to describe it from "Facing It" and any written or photographic accounts you have seen.

BILLY COLLINS

"Billy Collins writes lovely poems," the late novelist, critic, and poet John Updike said. "Limpid, gently and consistently startling, more serious than they seem, they describe all the worlds that are and were and some others besides." The recipient of many honors and awards, and a former poet laureate of the United States, Collins was born in New York City in 1941. He has taught at both the City University of New York and Sarah Lawrence College. His Sailing Alone around the Room: New and Selected Poems *was published in 2002.*

Collins wrote the following poem on the first anniversary of the terrorist attack on the World Trade Center, 11 September 2001, which killed about 3,000 people and destroyed the Twin Towers.

The Names

Yesterday, I lay awake in the palm of the night.
A soft rain stole in, unhelped by any breeze,
And when I saw the silver glaze on the windows,
I started with A, with Ackerman, as it happened,
Then Baxter and Calabro,   5
Davis and Eberling, names falling into place
As droplets fell through the dark.

Names printed on the ceiling of the night.
Names slipping around a watery bend.
Twenty-six willows on the banks of a stream.   10

In the morning, I walked out barefoot
Among thousands of flowers
Heavy with dew like the eyes of tears,
And each had a name—
Fiori inscribed on a yellow petal   15
Then Gonzalez and Han, Ishikawa and Jenkins.

Names written in the air
And stitched into the cloth of the day.

A name under a photograph taped to a mailbox.
Monogram on a torn shirt,   20
I see you spelled out on storefront windows
And on the bright unfurled awnings of this city.
I say the syllables as I turn a corner—
Kelly and Lee,
Medina, Nardella, and O'Connor.   25

When I peer in to the woods,
I see a thick tangle where letters are hidden
As in a puzzle concocted for children.
Parker and Quigley in the twigs of an ash,
Rizzo, Schubert, Torres, and Upton,   30
Secrets in the boughs of an ancient maple.

Names written in the pale sky.
Names rising in the updraft amid buildings.
Names silent in stone
Or cried out behind a door.   35
Names blown over the earth and out to sea.

In the evening—weakening light, the last swallows,
A boy on a lake lifts his oars.
A woman by a window puts a match to a candle,
And the names are outlined on the rose clouds—   40
Vanacore and Wallace,
(let X stand, if it can, for the ones unfound)
Then Young and Ziminsky, the final jolt of Z.

Names etched on the head of a pin.
One name spanning a bridge, another undergoing a tunnel.   45
A blue name needled into the skin.
Names of citizens, workers, mothers and fathers,
The bright-eyed daughter, the quick son.
Alphabet of names in a green field.
Names in the small tracks of birds.   50
Names lifted from a hat
Or balanced on the tip of the tongue.
Names wheeled into the dim warehouse of memory.
So many names, there is barely room on the walls of the heart.

[2002]

Joining the Conversation: Critical Thinking and Writing

1. In an interview that appeared several years before "The Names" was published, Collins said of his intention as a poet: "By the end of the poem, the reader should be in a different place from where he started." When you finished reading "The Names," did you find yourself in a "different place"? How would you describe this place?

2. Collins also observed, again in an interview before he wrote "The Names": "Poetry is clearly very serious for me, but without heaviness or a glib sense of

spirituality." Do you perceive a "spiritual" dimension to this poem—one that is not "glib"? What does it mean to say that a poem is "spiritual," that is, creates a spiritual effect? Is this the same thing as saying that a poem is "religious," or is it something different?

3. Many readers have expressed their high regard for "The Names," referring to it as a "great poem." Do you agree? What defines a great poem? Do you think a poet does or does not face a special challenge in trying to write a poem, great or simply good, about the tragedy of 11 September 2001? Please explain.

4. One critic, who otherwise admires Collins's work, has objected to "The Names" for being "too sentimental." How would you define "sentimentality"? (Clarify your definition with an example.) Can you locate evidence in the text that might support the judgment that Collins's poem is sentimental? Are there other passages you could cite and analyze in order to argue against it? And what's the matter with sentimentality? Is sentimentality something that poets should always avoid?

5. How do you feel about your own name? Is it something you give much thought to? Any thought? Why is that? Now that you have read Collins's poem, has your relationship to your own name changed in any way?

MyLiteratureLab® *For additional resources for "The Names," log in to* www .myliteraturelab.com *where you will find a Longman Lecture and a Compre-hension Quiz, as well as an About the Author, Bibliography, Links, and Critical Overview for Collins (under Student Resources).*

GWENDOLYN BROOKS

Gwendolyn Brooks (1917–2000) was born in Topeka, Kansas, but was raised in Chicago's South Side, where she spent most of her life. In 1950, when she won the Pulitzer Prize for Poetry, she became the first African American writer to win a Pulitzer Prize.

The Bean Eaters

They eat beans mostly, this old yellow pair.
Dinner is a casual affair.
Plain chipware on a plain and creaking wood,
Tin flatware.

Two who are Mostly Good.   5
Two who have lived their day,
But keep on putting on their clothes
And putting things away.

And remembering . . .
Remembering, with twinklings and twinges,   10
As they lean over the beans in their rented back room that is full of
    beads and receipts and dolls and clothes, tobacco crumbs, vases
    and fringes.

[1960]

Joining the Conversation: Critical Thinking and Writing

It is often assumed that sentimentality is a fault in literature. First, check the meanings of the word in a dictionary, and then think about that assumption. Second, does the word apply to Brooks's poem, and, if so, is the poem diminished by this quality? Write a paragraph arguing that the poem is or is not sentimental. If you do think it is sentimental, your essay should also face the question of whether sentimentality here is a weakness.

DOROTHY PARKER

For a biographical note on Dorothy Parker, see page 760.

Résumé

Razors pain you;
Rivers are damp;
Acids stain you;
And drugs cause cramp.
Guns aren't lawful;
Nooses give;
Gas smells awful;
You might as well live.

[1926]

Joining the Conversation: Critical Thinking and Writing

1. Exactly what is a *résumé?* How does Parker's *résumé* differ from the usual one?
2. Is the poem amusing? Is it more than amusing, that is, does it offer insight into an interesting state of feeling, or perhaps does it offer a view worth thinking about?

Chapter Overview: Looking Backward/Looking Forward

1. Do you think it is important for Americans to love their country? In what ways would this love be shown?
2. Is it possible to love one's country and, at the same time, to be critical of it? Should love of country be complete and unconditional?
3. If you are not an American, but are, for example, attending school here, what is the relationship between your feelings about the United States and your feelings about your homeland?

4. Do you think Americans are the same as, or different from, people everywhere else? How would you argue that they are the same? How would you argue that they are different? Which argument, in your view, is more convincing?

5. Take any one of the Short Views (pages 1211–12) and write an essay of 500–750 words amplifying the point it makes.

6. In 500 words set forth your idea of the American Dream.

CHAPTER 28

Law and Disorder

SHORT VIEWS

The world is incessantly threatened by two dangers: order and disorder.
   Paul Valéry

Whoever desires to found a state and give it laws, must start with assuming that all men are bad and ever ready to display their vicious nature, whenever they may find occasion for it.
   Niccolò Machiavelli

It is questionable whether, when we break a murderer on the wheel, we aren't lapsing into precisely the mistake of the child who hits the chair he bumps into.
   G. C. Lichtenberg

If a man were permitted to make all the ballads, he need not care who should make the laws of a nation.
   Andrew Fletcher

One law for the ox and the ass is oppression.
   William Blake

The law, in its majestic equality, forbids the rich as well as the poor to sleep under bridges, to beg in the streets, and to steal bread.
   Anatole France

The trouble about fighting for human freedom is that you have to spend much of your life defending sons of bitches; for oppressive laws are always aimed at them originally, and oppression must be stopped in the beginning if it is to be stopped at all.
   H. L. Mencken

Censorship upholds the dignity of the profession, know what I mean?
   Mae West

Joining the Conversation: Critical Thinking and Writing

1. Select a quotation that especially appeals to you, and make it the focus of an essay of about 500 words.
2. Take two of the passages—perhaps one that you especially like and one that you think is wrongheaded—and write a dialogue of about 500 words in which the two authors converse or argue. They may each try to convince the other, or they may find that to some degree they share views and they may then work out a statement that both can accept. If you do take the first position—that one writer is on the correct track but the other is utterly mistaken—try to be fair to the view that you think is mistaken. (As an experiment in critical thinking, imagine that you accept it, and make the best case for it that you possibly can.)
3. Do you agree with the Italian statesman and political philosopher Niccolò Machiavelli (1469–1527) when he says that the lawgiver should assume that people are "bad" and inclined toward "vicious" behavior? Isn't this an extreme overstatement? Machiavelli lived long ago: Do you think his claim held true then, but does not hold true today? Or is it as true today as ever?
4. Identify a law, of some significance, that you believe is unjust. Have you ever been tempted to break this law? If you did, what would your act accomplish?

ESSAYS

MARTIN LUTHER KING JR.

Martin Luther King Jr. (1929–68) was born in Atlanta and educated at Morehouse College, Crozer Theological Seminary, and Boston University. In 1954 he was called to serve as a Baptist minister in Montgomery, Alabama. During the next two years he achieved national fame when, using a policy of nonviolent resistance, he successfully led a boycott of the segregated bus lines in Montgomery. He then organized the Southern Christian Leadership Conference, which furthered the pursuit of civil rights, first in the South and then nationwide. In 1964 he was awarded the Nobel Peace Prize. Four years later he was assassinated in Memphis, Tennessee.

In 1963 Dr. King was arrested in Birmingham, Alabama, for participating in a march for which no parade permit had been issued by the city officials. In jail he wrote a response to a letter, titled "A Call for Unity," that eight local clergymen had published in a newspaper. We print their letter here, and then we follow it with King's response.

April 12, 1963

We the undersigned clergymen are among those who, in January, issued "An Appeal for Law and Order and Common Sense," in dealing with racial problems in Alabama. We expressed understanding that honest convictions in racial matters could properly be pursued in the courts, but urged that decisions of those courts should in the meantime be peacefully obeyed.

Since that time there had been some evidence of increased forebearance and a willingness to face facts. Responsible citizens have undertaken to work on various problems which cause racial friction and unrest. In Birmingham, recent public events have given indication that we all have opportunity for a new constructive and realistic approach to racial problems.

However, we are now confronted by a series of demonstrations by some of our Negro citizens, directed and led in part by outsiders. We recognize the natural impatience of people who feel that their hopes are slow in being realized. But we are convinced that these demonstrations are unwise and untimely.

We agree rather with certain local Negro leadership which has called for honest and open negotiation of racial issues in our area. And we believe this kind of facing of issues can best be accomplished by citizens of our own metropolitan area, white and Negro, meeting with their knowledge and experience of the local situation. All of us need to face that responsibility and find proper channels for its accomplishment.

Just as we formerly pointed out that "hatred and violence have no sanction in our religious and political traditions," we also point out that such actions as incite to hatred and violence, however technically peaceful those actions may be, have not contributed to the resolution of our local problems. We do not believe that these days of new hope are days when extreme measures are justified in Birmingham.

We commend the community as a whole, and the local news media and law enforcement officials in particular, on the calm manner in which these demonstrations have been handled. We urge the public to continue to show restraint should the demonstrations continue, and the law enforcement officials to remain calm and continue to protect our city from violence.

We further strongly urge our own Negro community to withdraw support from these demonstrations, and to unite locally in working peacefully for a better Birmingham. When rights are consistently denied, a cause should be pressed in the courts and in negotiations among local leaders, and not in the streets. We appeal to both our white and Negro citizenry to observe the principles of law and order and common sense.

C.C.J. Carpenter, D.D., L.L.D., Bishop of Alabama; Joseph A. Durick, D.D., Auxiliary Bishop, Diocese of Mobile-Birmingham; Rabbi Milton L. Grafman, Temple Emanu-El, Birmingham, Alabama; Bishop Paul Hardin, Bishop of the Alabama-West Florida Conference of the Methodist Church; Bishop Nolan B. Harmon, Bishop of the North Alabama Conference of the Methodist Church; George M. Murray, D.D., L.L.D., Bishop Coadjutor, Episcopal Diocese of Alabama; Edward V. Ramage, Moderator, Synod of the Alabama Presbyterian Church in the United States; Earl Stallings, Pastor, First Baptist Church, Birmingham, Alabama.

Letter from Birmingham Jail

April 16, 1963

My Dear Fellow Clergymen:

While confined here in the Birmingham city jail, I came across your recent statement calling my present activities "unwise and untimely."[1] Seldom do I pause to answer criticism of my work and ideas. If I sought to answer all the criticisms

---

[1]This response to a published statement by eight fellow clergymen from Alabama (Bishop C.C.J. Carpenter, Bishop Joseph A. Durick, Rabbi Milton L. Grafman, Bishop Paul Hardin, Bishop Nolan B. Harmon, the Reverend George M. Murray, the Reverend Edward V. Ramage, and the Reverend Earl Stallings) was composed under somewhat constricting circumstances. Begun on the margins of the newspaper in which the statement appeared while I was in jail, the letter was continued on scraps of writing paper supplied by a friendly Negro trusty, and concluded on a pad my attorneys were eventually permitted to leave me. Although the text remains in substance unaltered, I have indulged in the author's prerogative of polishing it for publication. [King's note.]

that cross my desk, my secretaries would have little time for anything other than such correspondence in the course of the day, and I would have no time for constructive work. But since I feel that you are men of genuine good will and that your criticisms are sincerely set forth, I want to try to answer your statement in what I hope will be patient and reasonable terms.

I think I should indicate why I am here in Birmingham, since you have been influenced by the view which argues against "outsiders coming in." I have the honor of serving as president of the Southern Christian Leadership Conference, an organization operating in every southern state, with headquarters in Atlanta, Georgia. We have some eighty-five affiliated organizations across the South, and one of them is the Alabama Christian Movement for Human Rights. Frequently we share staff, educational, and financial resources with our affiliates. Several months ago the affiliate here in Birmingham asked us to be on call to engage in a nonviolent direct-action program if such were deemed necessary. We readily consented, and when the hour came we lived up to our promise. So I, along with several members of my staff, am here because I was invited here. I am here because I have organizational ties here.

But more basically, I am in Birmingham because injustice is here. Just as the prophets of the eighth century B.C. left their villages and carried their "thus saith the Lord" far beyond the boundaries of their home towns, and just as the Apostle Paul left his village of Tarsus and carried the gospel of Jesus Christ to the far corners of the Greco-Roman world, so am I compelled to carry the gospel of freedom beyond my own home town. Like Paul, I must constantly respond to the Macedonian call for aid.

Moreover, I am cognizant of the interrelatedness of all communities and states. I cannot sit idly by in Atlanta and not be concerned about what happens in Birmingham. Injustice anywhere is a threat to justice everywhere. We are caught in an inescapable network of mutuality; tied in a single garment of destiny. Whatever affects one directly, affects all indirectly. Never again can we afford to live with the narrow, provincial "outside agitator" idea. Anyone who lives inside the United States can never be considered an outsider anywhere within its bounds.

5   You deplore the demonstrations taking place in Birmingham. But your statement, I am sorry to say, fails to express a similar concern for the conditions that brought about the demonstrations. I am sure that none of you would want to rest content with the superficial kind of social analysis that deals merely with effects and does not grapple with underlying causes. It is unfortunate that demonstrations are taking place in Birmingham, but it is even more unfortunate that the city's white power structure left the Negro community with no alternative.

In any nonviolent campaign there are four basic steps: collection of the facts to determine whether injustices exist; negotiation; self-purification; and direct action. We have gone through all these steps in Birmingham. There can be no gainsaying the fact that racial injustice engulfs this community. Birmingham is probably the most thoroughly segregated city in the United States. Its ugly record of brutality is widely known. Negroes have experienced grossly unjust treatment in the courts. There have been more unsolved bombings of Negro homes and churches in Birmingham than in any other city in the nation. These are the hard, brutal facts of the case. On the basis of these conditions, Negro leaders sought to negotiate with the city fathers. But the latter consistently refused to engage in good-faith negotiation.

Then, last September, came the opportunity to talk with leaders of Birmingham's economic community. In the course of the negotiations, certain promises were made by the merchants—for example, to remove the stores' humiliating racial

Martin Luther King Jr.,
in Birmingham Jail

signs. On the basis of these promises, the Reverend Fred Shuttleworth and the leaders of the Alabama Christian Movement for Human Rights agreed to a moratorium on all demonstrations. As the weeks and months went by, we realized that we were the victims of a broken promise. A few signs, briefly removed, returned; the others remained.

As in so many past experiences, our hopes had been blasted, and the shadow of deep disappointment settled upon us. We had no alternative except to prepare for direct action, whereby we would present our very bodies as a means of laying our case before the conscience of the local and the national community. Mindful of the difficulties involved, we decided to undertake a process of self-purification. We began a series of workshops on nonviolence, and we repeatedly asked ourselves: "Are you able to accept blows without retaliating?" "Are you able to endure the ordeal of jail?" We decided to schedule our direct-action program for the Easter season, realizing that except for Christmas, this is the main shopping period of the year. Knowing that a strong economic-withdrawal program would be the by-product of direct action, we felt that this would be the best time to bring pressure to bear on the merchants for the needed change.

Then it occurred to us that Birmingham's mayoralty election was coming up in March, and we speedily decided to postpone action until after election day. When we discovered that the Commissioner of Public Safety, Eugene "Bull" Connor, had piled up enough votes to be in the run-off, we decided again to postpone action until the day after the run-off so that the demonstrations could not be used to cloud the issues. Like many others, we waited to see Mr. Connor defeated, and to this end we endured postponement after postponement. Having aided in this community need, we felt that our direct-action program could be delayed no longer.

10   You may well ask: "Why direct action? Why sit-ins, marches, and so forth? Isn't negotiation a better path?" You are quite right in calling for negotiation. Indeed, this is the very purpose of direct action. Nonviolent direct action seeks to create such a crisis and foster such a tension that a community which has constantly refused to negotiate is forced to confront the issue. It seeks so to dramatize the issue that it can no longer be ignored. My citing the creation of tension as part of the work of the nonviolent-resister may sound rather shocking. But I must confess that I am not afraid of the word "tension." I have earnestly opposed violent tension, but there is a type of constructive, nonviolent tension which is necessary for growth. Just as Socrates felt that it was necessary to create a tension in the mind so that individuals could rise from the bondage of myths and half-truths to the unfettered realm of creative analysis and objective appraisal, so must we see the need for nonviolent gadflies to create the kind of tension in society that will help men rise from the dark depths of prejudice and racism to the majestic heights of understanding and brotherhood.

The purpose of our direct-action program is to create a situation so crisis-packed that it will inevitably open the door to negotiation. I therefore concur with you in your call for negotiation. Too long has our beloved Southland been bogged down in a tragic effort to live in monologue rather than dialogue.

One of the basic points in your statement is that the action that I and my associates have taken in Birmingham is untimely. Some have asked: "Why didn't you give the new city administration time to act?" The only answer that I can give to this query is that the new Birmingham administration must be prodded about as much as the outgoing one, before it will act. We are sadly mistaken if we feel that the election of Albert Boutwell as mayor will bring the millennium to Birmingham. While Mr. Boutwell is a much more gentle person than Mr. Connor, they are both segregationists, dedicated to maintenance of the status quo. I have hope that Mr. Boutwell will be reasonable enough to see the futility of massive resistance to desegregation. But he will not see this without pressure from devotees of civil rights. My friends, I must say to you that we have not made a single gain in civil rights without determined legal and nonviolent pressure. Lamentably, it is an historical fact that privileged groups seldom give up their privileges voluntarily. Individuals may see the moral light and voluntarily give up their unjust posture; but as Reinhold Niebuhr[2] has reminded us, groups tend to be more immoral than individuals.

We know through painful experience that freedom is never voluntarily given by the oppressor; it must be demanded by the oppressed. Frankly, I have yet to engage in a direct-action campaign that was "well timed" in the view of those who have not suffered unduly from the disease of segregation. For years now I have heard the word "Wait!" It rings in the ear of every Negro with piercing familiarity. This "Wait" has almost always meant "Never." We must come to see, with one of our distinguished jurists, that "justice too long delayed is justice denied."[3]

[2]**Reinhold Niebuhr** Niebuhr (1892–1971) was a minister, political activist, author, and professor at Union Theological Seminary in New York City. [All notes are the editors' unless otherwise specified.] [3]**Justice . . . denied** a quotation attributed to William E. Gladstone (1809–98), British statesman and prime minister.

We have waited for more than 340 years for our constitutional and God-given rights. The nations of Asia and Africa are moving with jetlike speed toward gaining political independence, but we still creep at horse-and-buggy pace toward gaining a cup of coffee at a lunch counter. Perhaps it is easy for those who have never felt the stinging darts of segregation to say, "Wait." But when you have seen vicious mobs lynch your mothers and fathers at will and drown your sisters and brothers at whim; when you have seen hate-filled policemen curse, kick, and even kill your black brothers and sisters; when you see the vast majority of your twenty million Negro brothers smothering in an airtight cage of poverty in the midst of an affluent society; when you suddenly find your tongue twisted and your speech stammering as you seek to explain to your six-year-old daughter why she can't go to the public amusement park that has just been advertised on television, and see tears welling up in her eyes when she is told that Funtown is closed to colored children, and see ominous clouds of inferiority beginning to form in her little mental sky, and see her beginning to distort her personality by developing an unconscious bitterness toward white people; when you have to concoct an answer for a five-year-old son who is asking: "Daddy, why do white people treat colored people so mean?"; when you take a cross-country drive and find it necessary to sleep night after night in the uncomfortable corners of your automobile because no motel will accept you; when you are humiliated day in and day out by nagging signs reading "white" and "colored"; when your first name becomes "nigger," your middle name becomes "boy" (however old you are) and your last name becomes "John," and your wife and mother are never given the respected title "Mrs."; when you are harried by day and haunted by night by the fact that you are a Negro, living constantly at tiptoe stance, never quite knowing what to expect next, and are plagued with inner fears and outer resentments; when you are forever fighting a degenerating sense of "nobodiness"—then you will understand why we find it difficult to wait. There comes a time when the cup of endurance runs over, and men are no longer willing to be plunged into the abyss of despair. I hope, sirs, you can understand our legitimate and unavoidable impatience.

15   You express a great deal of anxiety over our willingness to break laws. This is certainly a legitimate concern. Since we so diligently urge people to obey the Supreme Court's decision of 1954 outlawing segregation in the public schools, at first glance it may seem rather paradoxical for us consciously to break laws. One may well ask: "How can you advocate breaking some laws and obeying others?" The answer lies in the fact that there are two types of laws: just and unjust. I would be the first to advocate obeying just laws. One has not only a legal but a moral responsibility to obey just laws. Conversely, one has a moral responsibility to disobey unjust laws. I would agree with St. Augustine that "an unjust law is no law at all."

Now, what is the difference between the two? How does one determine whether a law is just or unjust? A just law is a man-made code that squares with the moral law or the law of God. An unjust law is a code that is out of harmony with the moral law. To put it in the terms of St. Thomas Aquinas: An unjust law is a human law that is not rooted in eternal law and natural law. Any law that uplifts human personality is just. Any law that degrades human personality is unjust. All segregation statutes are unjust because segregation distorts the soul and damages the personality. It gives the segregator a false sense of superiority and the segregated a false sense of inferiority. Segregation, to use the terminology of the Jewish philosopher Martin Buber,[4] substitutes an "I-it" relationship for an "I-thou" relationship

---

[4]**Martin Buber** Israeli religious philosopher (1878–1965), author of *Land Thou* (1923).

and ends up relegating persons to the status of things. Hence segregation is not only politically, economically, and sociologically unsound, it is morally wrong and sinful. Paul Tillich[5] has said that sin is separation. Is not segregation an existential expression of man's tragic separation, his awful estrangement, his terrible sinfulness? Thus it is that I can urge men to obey the 1954 decision of the Supreme Court, for it is morally right; and I can urge them to disobey segregation ordinances, for they are morally wrong.

Let us consider a more concrete example of just and unjust laws. An unjust law is a code that a numerical or power majority group compels a minority group to obey but does not make binding on itself. This is *difference* made legal. By the same token, a just law is a code that a majority compels a minority to follow and that it is willing to follow itself. This is *sameness* made legal.

Let me give another explanation. A law is unjust if it is inflicted on a minority that, as a result of being denied the right to vote, had no part in enacting or devising the law. Who can say that the legislature of Alabama which set up that state's segregation laws was democratically elected? Throughout Alabama all sorts of devious methods are used to prevent Negroes from becoming registered voters, and there are some counties in which, even though Negroes constitute a majority of the population, not a single Negro is registered. Can any law enacted under such circumstances be considered democratically structured?

Sometimes a law is just on its face and unjust in its application. For instance, I have been arrested on a charge of parading without a permit. Now, there is nothing wrong in having an ordinance which requires a permit for a parade. But such an ordinance becomes unjust when it is used to maintain segregation and to deny citizens the First Amendment privilege of peaceful assembly and protest.

20   I hope you are able to see the distinction I am trying to point out. In no sense do I advocate evading or defying the law, as would the rabid segregationist. That would lead to anarchy. One who breaks an unjust law must do so openly, lovingly, and with a willingness to accept the penalty. I submit that an individual who breaks a law that conscience tells him is unjust, and who willingly accepts the penalty of imprisonment in order to arouse the conscience of the community over its injustice, is in reality expressing the highest respect for law.

Of course, there is nothing new about this kind of civil disobedience. It was evidenced sublimely in the refusal of Shadrach, Meshach, and Abednego to obey the laws of Nebuchadnezzar, on the ground that a higher moral law was at stake. It was practiced superbly by the early Christians, who were willing to face hungry lions and the excruciating pain of chopping blocks rather than submit to certain unjust laws of the Roman Empire. To a degree, academic freedom is a reality today because Socrates practiced civil disobedience. In our own nation, the Boston Tea Party represented a massive act of civil disobedience.

We should never forget that everything Adolf Hitler did in Germany was "legal" and everything the Hungarian freedom fighters did in Hungary was "illegal." It was "illegal" to aid and comfort a Jew in Hitler's Germany. Even so, I am sure that, had I lived in Germany at the time, I would have aided and comforted my Jewish brothers. If today I lived in a Communist country where certain principles dear to the Christian faith are suppressed, I would openly advocate disobeying that country's anti-religious laws.

[5]**Paul Tillich** Tillich (1886–1965), born in Germany, taught theology at several German universities until in 1933 he was dismissed from his post at the University of Frankfurt because of his opposition to the Nazi regime. At the invitation of Reinhold Niebuhr, he came to the United States and taught at Union Theological Seminary.

I must make two honest confessions to you, my Christian and Jewish brothers. First, I must confess that over the past few years I have been gravely disappointed with the white moderate. I have almost reached the regrettable conclusion that the Negro's great stumbling block in his stride toward freedom is not the White Citizen's Counciler or the Ku Klux Klanner, but the white moderate, who is more devoted to "order" than to justice; who prefers a negative peace which is the absence of tension to a positive peace which is the presence of justice; who constantly says: "I agree with you in the goal you seek, but I cannot agree with your methods or direct action"; who paternalistically believes he can set the timetable for another man's freedom; who lives by a mythical concept of time and who constantly advises the Negro to wait for a "more convenient season." Shallow understanding from people of good will is more frustrating than absolute misunderstanding from people of ill will. Lukewarm acceptance is much more bewildering than outright rejection.

I had hoped that the white moderate would understand that law and order exist for the purpose of establishing justice and that when they fail in this purpose they become the dangerously structured dams that block the flow of social progress. I had hoped that the white moderate would understand that the present tension in the South is a necessary phase of the transition from an obnoxious negative peace, in which the Negro passively accepted his unjust plight, to a substantive and positive peace, in which all men will respect the dignity and worth of human personality. Actually, we who engage in nonviolent direct action are not the creators of tension. We merely bring to the surface the hidden tension that is already alive. We bring it out in the open, where it can be seen and dealt with. Like a boil that can never be cured so long as it is covered up but must be opened with all its ugliness to the natural medicines of air and light, injustice must be exposed, with all the tension its exposure creates, to the light of human conscience and the air of national opinion before it can be cured.

25   In your statement you assert that our actions, even though peaceful, must be condemned because they precipitate violence. But is this a logical assertion? Isn't this like condemning a robbed man because his possession of money precipitated the evil act of robbery? Isn't this like condemning Socrates because his unswerving commitment to truth and his philosophical inquiries precipitated the act by the misguided populace in which they made him drink hemlock? Isn't this like condemning Jesus because his unique God-consciousness and never-ceasing devotion to God's will precipitated the evil act of crucifixion? We must come to see that, as the federal courts have consistently affirmed, it is wrong to urge an individual to cease his efforts to gain his basic constitutional rights because the quest may precipitate violence. Society must protect the robbed and punish the robber.

I had also hoped that the white moderate would reject the myth concerning time in relation to the struggle for freedom. I have just received a letter from a white brother in Texas. He writes: "All Christians know that the colored people will receive equal rights eventually, but it is possible that you are in too great a religious hurry. It has taken Christianity almost two thousand years to accomplish what it has. The teachings of Christ take time to come to earth." Such an attitude stems from a tragic misconception of time, from the strangely irrational notion that there is something in the very flow of time that will inevitably cure all ills. Actually, time itself is neutral; it can be used either destructively or constructively. More and more I feel that the people of ill will have used time much more effectively than have the people of good will. We will have to repent in this generation not merely for the hateful words and actions of the bad people but for the appalling silence of the good people. Human progress never rolls in on wheels of inevitability; it comes through the tireless efforts of men willing to be co-workers with God, and without this hard work, time itself becomes an ally of the forces of social stagnation. We must use time creatively, in the knowledge that the time is always ripe to do right. Now is the time to make real the promise of democracy and transform our pending national elegy into a creative psalm of brotherhood. Now is the time to lift our national policy from the quicksand of racial injustice to the solid rock of human dignity.

You speak of our activity in Birmingham as extreme. At first I was rather disappointed that fellow clergymen would see my nonviolent efforts as those of an extremist. I began thinking about the fact that I stand in the middle of two opposing forces in the Negro community. One is a force of complacency, made up in part of Negroes who, as a result of long years of oppression, are so drained of self-respect and a sense of "somebodiness" that they have adjusted to segregation; and in part of a few middle-class Negroes who, because of a degree of academic and economic security and because in some ways they profit by segregation, have become insensitive to the problems of the masses. The other force is one of bitterness and hatred, and it comes perilously close to advocating violence. It is expressed in the various black nationalist groups that are springing up across the nation, the largest and best-known being Elijah Muhammad's Muslim movement. Nourished by the Negro's frustration over the continued existence of racial discrimination, this movement is made up of people who have lost faith in America, who have absolutely repudiated Christianity, and who have concluded that the white man is an incorrigible "devil."

I have tried to stand between these two forces, saying that we need emulate neither the "do-nothingism" of the complacent nor the hatred and despair of the black nationalist. For there is the more excellent way of love and nonviolent protest. I am grateful to God that, through the influence of the Negro church, the way of nonviolence became an integral part of our struggle.

If this philosophy had not emerged, by now many streets of the South should, I am convinced, be flowing with blood. And I am further convinced that if our white brothers dismiss as "rabble-rousers" and "outside agitators" those of us who employ nonviolent direct action, and if they refuse to support our nonviolent efforts, millions of Negroes will, out of frustration and despair, seek solace and security in black-nationalist ideologies—a development that would inevitably lead to a frightening racial nightmare.

30   Oppressed people cannot remain oppressed forever. The yearning for freedom eventually manifests itself, and that is what has happened to the American Negro. Something within has reminded him of his birthright of freedom, and something without has reminded him that it can be gained. Consciously or unconsciously, he has been caught up by the *Zeitgeist*,[6] and with his black brothers of Africa and his brown and yellow brothers of Asia, South America, and the Caribbean, the United States Negro is moving with a sense of great urgency toward the promised land of racial justice. If one recognizes this vital urge that has engulfed the Negro community, one should readily understand why public demonstrations are taking place. The Negro has many pent-up resentments and latent frustrations, and he must release them. So let him march; let him make prayer pilgrimages to the city hall; let him go on freedom rides—and try to understand why he must do so. If his repressed emotions are not released in nonviolent ways, they will seek expression through violence; this is not a threat but a fact of history. So I have not said to my

---

[6]***Zeitgeist*** German for "spirit of the age."

people: "Get rid of your discontent." Rather, I have tried to say that this normal and healthy discontent can be channeled into the creative outlet of nonviolent direct action. And now this approach is being termed extremist.

But though I was initially disappointed at being categorized as an extremist, as I continued to think about the matter I gradually gained a measure of satisfaction from the label. Was not Jesus an extremist for love: "Love your enemies, bless them that curse you, do good to them that hate you, and pray for them which despitefully use you, and persecute you." Was not Amos an extremist for justice: "Let justice roll down like waters and righteousness like an ever-flowing stream." Was not Paul an extremist for the Christian gospel: "I bear in my body the marks of the Lord Jesus." Was not Martin Luther an extremist: "Here I stand; I cannot do otherwise, so help me God." And John Bunyan:[7] "I will stay in jail to the end of my days before I make a butchery of my conscience." And Abraham Lincoln: "This nation cannot survive half slave and half free." And Thomas Jefferson: "We hold these truths to be self-evident, that all men are created equal. . . ." So the question is not whether we will be extremists, but what kind of extremists we will be. Will we be extremists for hate or for love? Will we be extremists for the preservation of injustice or for the extension of justice? In that dramatic scene on Calvary's hill three men were crucified. We must never forget that all three were crucified for the same crime— the crime of extremism. Two were extremists for immorality, and thus fell below their environment. The other, Jesus Christ, was an extremist for love, truth, and goodness, and thereby rose above his environment. Perhaps the South, the nation, and the world are in dire need of creative extremists.

I had hoped that the white moderate would see this need. Perhaps I was too optimistic; perhaps I expected too much. I suppose I should have realized that few members of the oppressor race can understand the deep groans and passionate yearnings of the oppressed race, and still fewer have the vision to see that injustice must be rooted out by strong, persistent, and determined action. I am thankful, however, that some of our white brothers in the South have grasped the meaning of this social revolution and committed themselves to it. They are still all too few in quantity, but they are big in quality. Some—such as Ralph McGill, Lillian Smith, Harry Golden, James McBride Dabbs, Ann Braden, and Sarah Patton Boyle—have written about our struggle in eloquent and prophetic terms. Others have marched with us down nameless streets of the South. They have languished in filthy, roach-infested jails, suffering the abuse and brutality of policemen who view them as "dirty nigger-lovers." Unlike so many of their moderate brothers and sisters, they have recognized the urgency of the moment and sensed the need for powerful "action" antidotes to combat the disease of segregation.

Let me take note of my other major disappointment. I have been so greatly disappointed with the white church and its leadership. Of course, there are some notable exceptions. I am not unmindful of the fact that each of you has taken some significant stands on this issue. I commend you, Reverend Stallings, for your Christian stand on this past Sunday, in welcoming Negroes to your worship service on a nonsegregated basis. I commend the Catholic leaders of this state for integrating Spring Hill College several years ago.

But despite these notable exceptions, I must honestly reiterate that I have been disappointed with the church. I do not say this as one of those negative critics who can always find something wrong with the church. I say this as a minister of the gospel, who

---

[7]**John Bunyan** English writer (1628–88) best known for his *Pilgrim's Progress* (two parts, 1678 and 1684); from 1660 to 1672 he was imprisoned for his political and religious views.

loves the church; who was nurtured in its bosom; who has been sustained by its spiritual blessings and who will remain true to it as long as the cord of life shall lengthen.

35   When I was suddenly catapulted into the leadership of the bus protest in Montgomery, Alabama, a few years ago, I felt we would be supported by the white church. I felt that the white ministers, priests, and rabbis of the South would be among our strongest allies. Instead, some have been outright opponents, refusing to understand the freedom movement and misrepresenting its leaders; all too many others have been more cautious than courageous and have remained silent behind the anesthetizing security of stained-glass windows.

In spite of my shattered dreams, I came to Birmingham with the hope that the white religious leadership of this community would see the justice of our cause and, with deep moral concern, would serve as the channel through which our just grievances could reach the power structure. I had hoped that each of you would understand. But again I have been disappointed.

I have heard numerous southern religious leaders admonish their worshipers to comply with a desegregation decision because it is the law, but I have longed to hear white ministers declare: "Follow this decree because integration is morally right and because the Negro is your brother." In the midst of blatant injustices inflicted upon the Negro, I have watched white churchmen stand on the sideline and mouth pious irrelevancies and sanctimonious trivialities. In the midst of a mighty struggle to rid our nation of racial and economic injustice, I have heard many ministers say: "Those are social issues, with which the gospel has no real concern." And I have watched many churches commit themselves to a completely otherworldly religion which makes a strange, unbiblical distinction between body and soul, between the sacred and the secular.

I have traveled the length and breadth of Alabama, Mississippi, and all the other southern states. On sweltering summer days and crisp autumn mornings I have looked at the South's beautiful churches with their lofty spires pointing heavenward. I have beheld the impressive outlines of her massive religious-education buildings. Over and over I have found myself saying: "What kind of people worship here? Who is their God? Where were their voices when the lips of Governor Barnett dripped with words of interposition and nullification? Where were they when Governor Wallace gave a clarion call for defiance and hatred? Where were their voices of support when bruised and weary Negro men and women decided to rise from the dark dungeons of complacency to the bright hills of creative protest?"

Yes, these questions are still in my mind. In deep disappointment I have wept over the laxity of the church. But be assured that my tears have been tears of love. There can be no deep disappointment where there is not deep love. Yes, I love the church. How could I do otherwise? I am in the rather unique position of being the son, the grandson, and the great-grandson of preachers. Yes, I see the church as the body of Christ. But, Oh! How we have blemished and scarred that body through social neglect and through fear of being nonconformists.

40   There was a time when the church was very powerful—in the time when the early Christians rejoiced at being deemed worthy to suffer for what they believed. In those days the church was not merely a thermometer that recorded the ideas and principles of popular opinion; it was a thermostat that transformed the mores of society. Whenever the early Christians entered a town, the people in power became disturbed and immediately sought to convict the Christians for being "disturbers of the peace" and "outside agitators." But the Christians pressed on, in the conviction that they were "a colony of heaven," called to obey God rather than man. Small in number, they were big in commitment. They were too God-intoxicated to

be "astronomically intimidated." By their effort and example they brought an end to such ancient evils as infanticide and gladiatorial contests.

Things are different now. So often the contemporary church is a weak, ineffectual voice with an uncertain sound. So often it is an archdefender of the status quo. Far from being disturbed by the presence of the church, the power structure of the average community is consoled by the church's silent—and often even vocal—sanction of things as they are.

But the judgment of God is upon the church as never before. If today's church does not recapture the sacrificial spirit of the early church, it will lose its authenticity, forfeit the loyalty of millions, and be dismissed as an irrelevant social club with no meaning for the twentieth century. Every day I meet young people whose disappointment with the church has turned into outright disgust.

Perhaps I have once again been too optimistic. Is organized religion too inextricably bound to the status quo to save our nation and the world? Perhaps I must turn my faith to the inner spiritual church, the church within the church, as the true *ekklesia*[8] and the hope of the world. But again I am thankful to God that some noble souls from the ranks of organized religion have broken loose from the paralyzing chains of conformity and joined us as active partners in the struggle for freedom. They have left their secure congregations and walked the streets of Albany, Georgia, with us. They have gone down the highways of the South on tortuous rides for freedom. Yes, they have gone to jail with us. Some have been dismissed from their churches, have lost the support of their bishops and fellow ministers. But they have acted in the faith that right defeated is stronger than evil triumphant. Their witness has been the spiritual salt that has preserved the true meaning of the gospel in these troubled times. They have carved a tunnel of hope through the dark mountain of disappointment.

I hope the church as a whole will meet the challenge of this decisive hour. But even if the church does not come to the aid of justice, I have no despair about the future. I have no fear about the outcome of our struggle in Birmingham, even if our motives are at present misunderstood. We will reach the goal of freedom in Birmingham and all over the nation, because the goal of America is freedom. Abused and scorned though we may be, our destiny is tied up with America's destiny. Before the pilgrims landed at Plymouth, we were here. Before the pen of Jefferson etched the majestic words of the Declaration of Independence across the pages of history, we were here. For more than two centuries our forebears labored in this country without wages; they made cotton king; they built the homes of their masters while suffering gross injustice and shameful humiliation—and yet out of a bottomless vitality they continue to thrive and develop. If the inexpressible cruelties of slavery could not stop us, the opposition we now face will surely fail. We will win our freedom because the sacred heritage of our nation and the eternal will of God are embodied in our echoing demands.

45   Before closing I feel impelled to mention one other point in your statement that has troubled me profoundly. You warmly commended the Birmingham police force for keeping "order" and "preventing violence." I doubt that you would have so warmly commended the police force if you had seen its dogs sinking their teeth into unarmed, nonviolent Negroes. I doubt that you would so quickly commend the policemen if you were to observe their ugly and inhumane treatment of Negroes here in the city jail; if you were to watch them push and curse old Negro women and young Negro girls; if you were to see them slap and kick old Negro

[8]*ekklesia* the word "church" in the New Testament is translated from the Greek word "ekklesia," from "el" meaning "out" and "kaleo" meaning to "call."

men and young boys; if you were to observe them, as they did on two occasions, refuse to give us food because we wanted to sing our grace together. I cannot join you in your praise of the Birmingham police department.

It is true that the police have exercised a degree of discipline in handling the demonstrators. In this sense they have conducted themselves rather "nonviolently" in public. But for what purpose? To preserve the evil system of segregation. Over the past few years I have consistently preached that nonviolence demands that the means we use must be as pure as the ends we seek. I have tried to make clear that it is wrong to use immoral means to attain moral ends. But now I must affirm that it is just as wrong, or perhaps even more so, to use moral means to preserve immoral ends. Perhaps Mr. Connor and his policemen have been rather nonviolent in public, as was Chief Pritchett in Albany, Georgia, but they used the moral means of nonviolence to maintain the immoral end of racial injustice. As T. S. Eliot has said: "The last temptation is the greatest treason: To do the right deed for the wrong reason."

I wish you had commended the Negro sit-inners and demonstrators of Birmingham for their sublime courage, their willingness to suffer, and their amazing discipline in the midst of great provocation. One day the South will recognize its real heroes. They will be the James Merediths,[9] with the noble sense of purpose that enables them to face jeering and hostile mobs, and with the agonizing loneliness that characterizes the life of the pioneer. They will be old, oppressed, battered Negro women, symbolized in a seventy-two-year-old woman in Montgomery, Alabama, who rose up with a sense of dignity and with her people decided not to ride segregated buses, and who responded with ungrammatical profundity to one who inquired about her weariness: "My feets is tired, but my soul is at rest." They will be the young high school and college students, the young ministers of the gospel and a host of their elders, courageously and nonviolently sitting in at lunch counters and willingly going to jail for conscience' sake. One day the South will know that when these disinherited children of God sat down at lunch counters, they were in reality standing up for what is best in the American dream and for the most sacred values in our Judaeo-Christian heritage, thereby bringing our nation back to those great wells of democracy which were dug deep by the founding fathers in their formulation of the Constitution and the Declaration of Independence.

Never before have I written so long a letter. I'm afraid it is much too long to take your precious time. I can assure you that it would have been much shorter if I had been writing from a comfortable desk, but what else can one do when he is alone in a narrow jail cell, other than write long letters, think long thoughts, and pray long prayers?

If I have said anything in this letter that overstates the truth and indicates an unreasonable impatience, I beg you to forgive me. If I have said anything that understates the truth and indicates my having a patience that allows me to settle for anything less than brotherhood, I beg God to forgive me.

50   I hope this letter finds you strong in the faith. I also hope that circumstances will soon make it possible for me to meet each of you, not as an integrationist or a civil-rights leader but as a fellow clergyman and a Christian brother. Let us all hope that the dark clouds of racial prejudice will soon pass away and the deep fog of misunderstanding will be lifted from our fear-drenched communities, and in some not too distant tomorrow the radiant stars of love and brotherhood will shine over our great nation with all their scintillating beauty.

Yours for the cause of Peace and Brotherhood,

Martin Luther King Jr.

[1963]

[9]**James Meredith** On 1 October 1962, in the face of widespread opposition, James Meredith became the first African American to attend the University of Mississippi.

Joining the Conversation: Critical Thinking and Writing

1. In his first five paragraphs, how does King assure his audience that he is not a meddlesome intruder but a man of good will?
2. In paragraph 3 King refers to Hebrew prophets and to the Apostle Paul, and later (paragraph 10) to Socrates. What is the point of these references?
3. In paragraph 11 what does King mean when he says that "our beloved Southland" has long tried to "live in monologue rather than dialogue"?
4. King begins paragraph 23 with "I must make two honest confessions to you, my Christian and Jewish brothers." What would have been gained or lost if he had used this paragraph as his opening?
5. King's last three paragraphs do not advance his argument. What do they do?
6. Why does King advocate breaking unjust laws "openly, lovingly" (paragraph 20)? What does he mean by these words? What other motives or attitudes do these words rule out?
7. Construct two definitions of "civil disobedience," and explain whether and to what extent it is easier (or harder) to justify civil disobedience, depending on how you have defined the expression.
8. If you feel that you wish to respond to King's letter on some point, write a letter nominally addressed to King. You may, if you wish, adopt the persona of one of the eight clergymen whom King initially addressed.
9. King writes (paragraph 46) that "nonviolence demands that the means we use must be as pure as the ends we seek." How do you think King would evaluate the following acts of civil disobedience: (a) occupying a college administration building in order to protest the administration's unsatisfactory response to a racial incident on campus, or in order to protest the failure of the administration to hire minority persons as staff and faculty, (b) sailing on a collision course with a whaling ship to protest against whaling; (c) trespassing on an abortion clinic to protest abortion? Set down your answer in an essay of 500 words.

STORIES

ELIZABETH BISHOP

Elizabeth Bishop (1911–79) is known chiefly as a poet. Here, however, we give a prose piece. In a letter (3 February 1937) Bishop mentions the act that served as the immediate trigger for the piece, but of course far more experience of life is in the work than the trivial act she specifies: "I once hung [my cat's] artificial mouse on a string to a chairback, without thinking what I had done—it looked very sad."

The Hanging of the Mouse

Early, early in the morning, even before five o'clock, the mouse was brought out, but already there were large crowds. Some of the animals had not gone to bed the night before, but had stayed up later and later; at first because of a vague feeling of celebration, and then, after deciding several times that they might as well wander about the town for an hour more, to conclude the night by arriving at the square in time for the hanging became only sensible. These animals hiccupped a little and had an air of cynical lassitude. Those who had got up out of bed to come also appeared weary and silent, but not so bored.

The mouse was led in by two enormous brown beetles in the traditional picturesque armor of an earlier day. They came on to the square through the small black door and marched between the lines of soldiers standing at attention: straight ahead, to the right, around two sides of the hollow square, to the left, and out into the middle where the gallows stood. Before each turn the beetle on the right glanced quickly at the beetle on the left; their traditional long, long antennae swerved sharply in the direction they were to turn and they did it to perfection. The mouse, of course, who had had no military training and who, at the moment, was crying so hard he could scarcely see where he was going, rather spoiled the precision and snap of the beetles. At each corner he fell slightly forward, and when he was jerked in the right direction his feet became tangled together. The beetles, however, without even looking at him, each time lifted him quickly into the air for a second until his feet were untangled.

At that hour in the morning the mouse's gray clothes were almost indistinguishable from the light. But his whimpering could be heard, and the end of his nose was rose-red from crying so much. The crowd of small animals tipped back their heads and sniffed with pleasure.

A raccoon, wearing the traditional black mask, was the executioner. He was very fastidious and did everything just so. One of his young sons, also wearing a black mask, waited on him with a small basin and a pitcher of water. First he washed his hands and rinsed them carefully; then he washed the rope and rinsed it. At the last minute he again washed his hands and drew on a pair of elegant black kid gloves.

5   A large praying mantis was in charge of the religious end of the ceremonies. He hurried up on the stage after the mouse and his escorts, but once there a fit of nerves seemed to seize him. He glided to the left a few steps, to the right a few steps, lifted his arms gracefully, but could not seem to begin; and it was quite apparent that he would have liked nothing better than to have jumped quickly down and left the whole affair. When his arms were stretched to Heaven his large eyes flashed toward the crowd, and when he looked up, his body was twitching and he moved about in a really pathetic way. He seemed to feel ill at ease with the low characters around him: the beetles, the hangmen, and the criminal mouse. At last he made a great effort to pull himself together and, approaching the mouse, said a few words in a high, incomprehensible voice. The mouse jumped from nervousness, and cried harder than ever.

At this point the spectators would all undoubtedly have burst out laughing, but just then the King's messenger appeared on the balcony above the small black door the mouse and his guards had lately come through. He was a very large, overweight bullfrog, also dressed in the traditional costume and carrying the traditional long scroll that dragged for several feet on the ground and had the real speech, on a little slip of paper, pasted inside it. The scroll and the white plume on his hat made him look comically like something in a nursery tale, but his voice was impressive enough to awe the crowd into polite attention. It was a deep bass: "Glug! Glug! Berrr-up!" No one could understand a word of the mouse's death sentence.

With the help of some pushes and pinches from the beetles, the executioner got the mouse into position. The rope was tied exquisitely behind one of his little round ears. The mouse raised a hand and wiped his nose with it, and most of the crowd interpreted this gesture as a farewell wave and spoke of it for weeks afterwards. The hangman's young son, at a signal from his father, sprang the trap.

"Squee-eek! Squee-eek!" went the mouse.

His whiskers rowed hopelessly round and round in the air a few times and his feet flew up and curled into little balls like young fern-plants.

10   The praying mantis, with an hysterical fling of his long limbs, had disappeared in the crowd. It was all so touching that a cat, who had brought her child in her mouth, shed several large tears. They rolled down on to the child's back and he began to squirm and shriek, so that the mother thought that the sight of the hanging had perhaps been too much for him, but an excellent moral lesson, nevertheless.

[1937]

Joining the Conversation: Critical Thinking and Writing

1. We have several times quoted Robert Frost's observation that a poem (he could have said any work of literature) is "a performance in words." Reread Bishop's first paragraph, and discuss it in terms of "performance." Why, for instance, do you think she repeats the word "early" in the first sentence? In this paragraph notice that Bishop says the animals decided "several times that they might as well wander about the town for an hour more." What do you make of deciding "several times"? And then Bishop says that the idea of concluding the night by "arriving at the square in time for the hanging became only sensible." What do you make of "sensible," especially in the context that immediately follows it: "These animals hiccupped a little and had an air of cynical lassitude." What does "cynical lassitude" mean? How has Bishop juggled her words to convey what you assume is her attitude toward the animals?
2. Would you agree that there are humorous touches in the piece? If so, point them out. If you don't think there is anything humorous in it, point to something that someone might conceivably find amusing, and explain why you do not find it so.
3. Describe your response to the sentence, "The rope was tied exquisitely behind one of his little round ears."
4. In the final paragraph Bishop tells us that the cat believed "the sight of the hanging [provided] . . . an excellent moral lesson. . . ." Do you assume that Bishop agrees? By the way, executions used to be public, partly because it was felt that they served to educate the general public. As the proverb puts it, "Who hangs one corrects a thousand." Do you think Bishop would agree or disagree? Why?

URSULA K. LE GUIN

Ursula K. Le Guin was born in 1929 in Berkeley, California, the daughter of a distinguished mother (Theodora Kroeber, a folklorist) and father (Alfred L. Kroeber, an anthropologist). After graduating from Radcliffe College, she earned a master's degree at Columbia University; in 1952 she held a Fulbright Fellowship for study in Paris, where she met and married Charles Le Guin, a historian. She began writing in earnest while bringing up three children. Although her work is most widely known to fans of science fiction, because it usually has larger moral or political dimensions it interests many readers who normally do not care for sci-fi.

Le Guin has said that she was prompted to write the following story by a remark she encountered in William James's "The Moral Philosopher and the Moral Life." James suggests there that if millions of people could be "kept permanently happy on the one simple condition that a certain lost soul on the far-off edge of things should lead a life of lonely torment," our moral sense "would make us immediately feel" it would be "hideous" to accept such a bargain. This story first appeared in New Dimensions 3 *(1973).*

The Ones Who Walk Away from Omelas

With a clamor of bells that set the swallows soaring, the Festival of Summer came to the city Omelas, bright-towered by the sea. The rigging of the boats in harbor sparkled with flags. In the streets between houses with red roofs and painted walls, between old moss-grown gardens and under avenues of trees, past great parks and public buildings, processions moved. Some were decorous: old people in long stiff robes of mauve and gray, grave master workmen, quiet, merry women carrying their babies and chatting as they walked. In other streets the music beat faster, a shimmering of gong and tambourine, and the people went dancing, the procession was a dance. Children dodged in and out, their high calls rising like the swallows' crossing flights over the music and the singing. All the processions wound towards the north side of the city, where on the great water-meadow called the Green Fields boys and girls, naked in the bright air, with mudstained feet and ankles and long, lithe arms, exercised their restive horses before the race. The horses wore no gear at all but a halter without bit. Their manes were braided with streamers of silver, gold, and green. They flared their nostrils and pranced and boasted to one another; they were vastly excited, the horse being the only animal who has adopted our ceremonies as his own. Far off to the north and west the mountains stood up half encircling Omelas on her bay. The air of morning was so clear that the snow still crowning the Eighteen Peaks burned with white-gold fire across the miles of sunlit air, under the dark blue of the sky. There was just enough wind to make the banners that marked the racecourse snap and flutter now and then. In the silence of the broad green meadows one could hear the music winding through the city streets, farther and nearer and ever approaching, a cheerful faint sweetness of the air that from time to time trembled and gathered together and broke out into the great joyous clanging of the bells.

Joyous! How is one to tell about joy? How describe the citizens of Omelas?

They were not simple folk, you see, though they were happy. But we do not say the words of cheer much any more. All smiles have become archaic. Given a description such as this one tends to make certain assumptions. Given a description such as this one tends to look next for the King, mounted on a splendid stallion and surrounded by his noble knights, or perhaps in a golden litter borne by great-muscled slaves. But there was no king. They did not use swords, or keep slaves. They were not barbarians. I do not know the rules and laws of their society, but I suspect that they were singularly few. As they did without monarchy and slavery, so they also got on without the stock exchange, the advertisement, the secret police, and the bomb. Yet I repeat that these were not simple folk, not dulcet shepherds, noble savages, bland utopians. They were not less complex than us. The trouble is that we have a bad habit, encouraged by pedants and sophisticates, of considering happiness as something rather stupid. Only pain is intellectual, only evil interesting. This is the treason of the artist: a refusal to admit the banality of evil and the terrible boredom of pain. If you can't lick 'em, join 'em. If it hurts, repeat it. But to praise despair is to condemn delight, to embrace violence is to lose hold of everything else. We have almost lost hold, we can no longer describe a happy man, nor make any celebration of joy. How can I tell you about the people of Omelas? They were not naïve and happy children—though their children were, in fact, happy. They were mature, intelligent, passionate adults whose lives were not wretched. O miracle! But I wish I could describe it better. I wish I could convince you. Omelas sounds in my words like a city in a fairy tale, long ago and far away, once upon a time. Perhaps it would be best if you imagined it as your own fancy bids, assuming it will rise to the occasion, for certainly I cannot suit you all. For instance, how about technology? I think that there would be no cars or helicopters in and above the streets; this follows from the fact that the people of Omelas are happy people. Happiness is based on a just discrimination of what is necessary, what is neither necessary nor destructive, and what is destructive. In the middle category, however— that of the unnecessary but undestructive, that of comfort, luxury, exuberance, etc.—they could perfectly well have central heating, subway trains, washing machines, and all kinds of marvelous devices not yet invented here, floating light-sources, fuelless power, a cure for the common cold. Or they could have none of that: it doesn't matter. As you like it. I incline to think that people from towns up and down the coast have been coming in to Omelas during the last days before the Festival on very fast little trains and double-decked trams, and that the train station of Omelas is actually the handsomest building in town, though plainer than the magnificent Farmers' Market. But even granted trains, I fear that Omelas so far strikes some of you as goody-goody. Smiles, bells, parades, horses, bleh. If so, please add an orgy. If an orgy would help, don't hesitate. Let us not, however, have temples from which issue beautiful nude priests and priestesses already half in ecstasy and ready to copulate with any man or woman, lover or stranger, who desires union with the deep godhead of the blood, although that was my first idea. But really it would be better not to have any temples in Omelas—at least, not manned temples. Religion yes, clergy no. Surely the beautiful nudes can just wander about, offering themselves like divine soufflés to the hunger of the needy and the rapture of the flesh. Let them join the processions. Let tambourines be struck above the copulations, and the glory of desire be proclaimed upon the gongs, and (a not unimportant point) let the offspring of these delightful rituals be beloved and looked after by all. One thing I know there is none of in Omelas is guilt. But what else should there be? I thought that first there were no drugs, but that is puritanical. For those who like it, the faint insistent sweetness of *drooz* may perfume the ways of the city, *drooz* which first brings a great lightness and brilliance to the mind and limbs, and then after some hours a dreamy languor, and wonderful visions at last of the very arcana and inmost secrets of the Universe, as well as exciting the pleasure of sex beyond all belief; and it is not habit-forming. For more modest tastes I think there ought to be beer. What else, what else belongs in the joyous city? The sense of victory, surely, the celebration of courage. But as we did without clergy, let us do without soldiers. The joy built upon successful slaughter is not the right kind of joy; it will not do; it is fearful and it is trivial. A boundless and generous contentment, a magnanimous triumph felt not against some outer enemy but in communion with the finest and fairest in the souls of all men everywhere and the splendor of the world's summer: this is what swells the hearts of the people of Omelas, and the victory they celebrate is that of life. I really don't think many of them need to take *drooz*.

Most of the processions have reached the Green Fields by now. A marvelous smell of cooking goes forth from the red and blue tents of the provisioners. The faces of small children are amiably sticky; in the benign grey beard of a man a couple of crumbs of rich pastry are entangled. The youths and girls have mounted their horses and are beginning to group around the starting line of the course. An old woman, small, fat, and laughing, is passing out flowers from a basket, and tall young men wear her flowers in their shining hair. A child of nine or ten sits at the edge of the crowd, alone, playing on a wooden flute. People pause to listen, and they smile, but they do not speak to him, for he never ceases playing and never sees them, his dark eyes wholly rapt in the sweet, thin magic of the tune.

5   He finishes, and slowly lowers his hands holding the wooden flute.

As if that little private silence were the signal, all at once a trumpet sounds from the pavilion near the starting line: imperious, melancholy, piercing. The horses rear on their slender legs, and some of them neigh in answer. Sober-faced, the young riders stroke the horses' necks and soothe them, whispering, "Quiet, quiet, there my beauty, my hope. . . ." They begin to form in rank along the starting line. The crowds along the racecourse are like a field of grass and flowers in the wind. The Festival of Summer has begun.

Do you believe? Do you accept the festival, the city, the joy? No? Then let me describe one more thing.

In a basement under one of the beautiful public buildings of Omelas, or perhaps in the cellar of one of its spacious private homes, there is a room. It has one locked door, and no window. A little light seeps in dustily between cracks in the boards, secondhand from a cobwebbed window somewhere across the cellar. In one corner of the little room a couple of mops, with stiff, clotted, foul-smelling heads, stand near a rusty bucket. The floor is dirt, a little damp to the touch, as cellar dirt usually is. The room is about three paces long and two wide: a mere broom closet or disused tool room. In the room a child is sitting. It could be a boy or a girl. It looks about six, but actually is nearly ten. It is feebleminded. Perhaps it was born defective, or perhaps it has become imbecile through fear, malnutrition, and neglect. It picks its nose and occasionally fumbles vaguely with its toes or genitals, as it sits hunched in the corner farthest from the bucket and the two mops. It is afraid of the mops. It finds them horrible. It shuts its eyes, but it knows the mops are still standing there; and the door is locked; and nobody will come. The door is always locked; and nobody ever comes, except that sometimes—the child has no understanding of time or interval—sometimes the door rattles terribly and opens, and a person, or several people, are there. One of them may come in and kick the child to make it stand up. The others never come close, but peer in at it with frightened, disgusted eyes. The food bowl and the water jug are hastily filled, the door is locked, the eyes disappear. The people at the door never say anything, but the child, who has not always lived in the tool room, and can remember sunlight and its mother's voice, sometimes speaks. "I will be good," it says. "Please let me out. I will be good!" They never answer. The child used to scream for help at night, and cry a good deal, but now it only makes a kind of whining "eh-haa, eh-haa," and it speaks less and less often. It is so thin there are no calves to its legs; its belly protrudes; it lives on a half-bowl of corn meal and grease a day. It is naked. Its buttocks and thighs are a mass of festered sores, as it sits in its own excrement continually.

They all know it is there, all the people of Omelas. Some of them have come to see it, others are content merely to know it is there. They all know that it has to be there. Some of them understand why, and some do not, but they all understand that their happiness, the beauty of their city, the tenderness of their friendships, the health of their children, the wisdom of their scholars, the skill of their makers, even the abundance of their harvest and the kindly weathers of their skies, depend wholly on this child's abominable misery.

10   This is usually explained to children when they are between eight and twelve, whenever they seem capable of understanding; and most of those who come to see the child are young people, though often enough an adult comes, or comes back, to see the child. No matter how well the matter has been explained to them, these young spectators are always shocked and sickened at the sight. They feel disgust, which they had thought themselves superior to. They feel anger, outrage, impotence, despite all the explanations. They would like to do something for the child. But there is nothing they can do. If the child were brought up into the sunlight out of that vile place, if it were cleaned and fed and comforted, that would be a good thing, indeed; but if it were done, in that day and hour all the prosperity and beauty and delight of Omelas would wither and be destroyed. Those are the terms. To exchange all the goodness and grace of every life in Omelas for that single, small improvement: to throw away the happiness of thousands for the chance of the happiness of one: that would be to let guilt within the walls indeed.

The terms are strict and absolute; there may not even be a kind word spoken to the child.

Often the young people go home in tears, or in a tearless rage, when they have seen the child and faced this terrible paradox. They may brood over it for weeks or years. But as time goes on they begin to realize that even if the child could be released, it would not get much good of its freedom: a little vague pleasure of warmth and food, no doubt, but little more. It is too degraded and imbecile to know any real joy. It has been afraid too long ever to be free of fear. Its habits are too uncouth for it to respond to humane treatment. Indeed, after so long it would probably be wretched without walls about it to protect it, and darkness for its eyes, and its own excrement to sit in. Their tears at the bitter injustice dry when they begin to perceive the terrible justice of reality, and to accept it. Yet it is their tears and anger, the trying of their generosity and the acceptance of their helplessness, which are perhaps the true source of the splendor of their lives. Theirs is no vapid, irresponsible happiness. They know that they, like the child, are not free. They know compassion. It is the existence of the child, and their knowledge of its existence, that makes possible the nobility of their architecture, the poignancy of their music, the profundity of their science. It is because of the child that they are so gentle with children. They know that if the wretched one were not there snivelling in the dark, the other one, the flute-player, could make no joyful music as the young riders line up in their beauty for the race in the sunlight of the first morning of summer.

Now do you believe in them? Are they not more credible? But there is one more thing to tell, and this is quite incredible.

At times one of the adolescent girls or boys who go to see the child does not go home to weep or rage, does not, in fact, go home at all. Sometimes also a man or woman much older falls silent for a day or two, and then leaves home. These people go out into the street, and walk down the street alone. They keep walking, and walk straight out of the city of Omelas, through the beautiful gates. They keep walking across the farmlands of Omelas. Each one goes alone, youth or girl, man or woman. Night falls; the traveler must pass down village streets, between the houses with yellow-lit windows, and on out into the darkness of the fields. Each alone, they go west or north, towards the mountains. They go on. They leave Omelas, they walk ahead into the darkness, and they do not come back. The place they go towards is a place even less imaginable to most of us than the city of happiness. I cannot describe it at all. It is possible that it does not exist. But they seem to know where they are going, the ones who walk away from Omelas.

[1973]

Joining the Conversation: Critical Thinking and Writing

1. Summarize the point of "The Ones Who Walk Away from Omelas"—not the plot, but what the story adds up to, what the author is getting at. Next, set forth what you would probably do (and why) if you were born in Omelas.
2. Consider the narrator's assertion (paragraph 3) that happiness "is based on a just discrimination of what is necessary." Please argue for or against this statement.
3. Do you think the story implies a criticism of contemporary American society? Explain.

WILLIAM FAULKNER

For a biographical note on William Faulkner, see page 249.

Barn Burning

The store in which the Justice of the Peace's court was sitting smelled of cheese. The boy, crouched on his nail keg at the back of the crowded room, knew he smelled cheese, and more: from where he sat he could see the ranked shelves close-packed with the solid, squat, dynamic shapes of tin cans whose labels his stomach read, not from the lettering which mean nothing to his mind but from the scarlet devils and the silver curve of fish—this, the cheese which he knew he smelled and the hermetic meat which his intestines believed he smelled coming in intermittent gusts momentary and brief between the other constant one, the smell and sense just a little of fear because mostly of despair and grief, the old fierce pull of blood. He could not see the table where the Justice sat and before which his father and his father's enemy (*our enemy* he thought in that despair; *ourn! mine and hisn both! He's my father!*) stood, but he could hear them, the two of them that is, because his father had said no word yet:

"But what proof have you, Mr. Harris?"

"I told you. The hog got into my corn. I caught it up and sent it back to him. He had no fence that would hold it. I told him so, warned him. The next time I put the hog in my pen. When he came to get it I gave him enough wire to patch up his pen. The next time I put the hog up and kept it. I rode down to his house and saw the wire I gave him still rolled on to the spool in his yard. I told him he could have the hog when he paid me a dollar pound fee. That evening a nigger came with the dollar and got the hog. He was a strange nigger. He said, 'He say to tell you wood and hay kin burn.' I said, 'What?' 'That whut he say to tell you,' the nigger said. 'Wood and hay kin burn.' That night my barn burned. I got the stock out but I lost the barn."

"Where is the nigger? Have you got him?"

5   "He was a strange nigger, I tell you. I don't know what became of him."

"But that's not proof. Don't you see that's not proof?"

"Get that boy up here. He knows." For a moment the boy thought too that the man meant his older brother until Harris said, "Not him. The little one. The boy," and, crouching, small for his age, small and wiry like his father, in patched and faded jeans even too small for him, with straight, uncombed, brown hair and eyes gray and wild as storm scud, he saw the men between himself and the table part and become a lane of grim faces, at the end of which he saw the Justice, a shabby, collarless, graying man in spectacles, beckoning him. He felt no floor under his bare feet; he seemed to walk beneath the palpable weight of the grim turning faces. His father, stiff in his black Sunday coat donned not for the trial but for the moving, did not even look at him. *He aims for me to lie,* he thought, again with that frantic grief and despair. *And I will have to do hit.*

"What's your name, boy?" the Justice said.

"Colonel Sartoris Snopes," the boy whispered.

10   "Hey?" the Justice said. "Talk louder. Colonel Sartoris? I reckon anybody named for Colonel Sartoris in this country can't help but tell the truth, can they?" The boy said nothing. *Enemy! Enemy!* he thought; for a moment he could not even see, could not see that the Justice's face was kindly nor discern that his voice was troubled when he spoke to the man named Harris: "Do you want me to question this boy?" But he could hear, and during those subsequent long seconds while there was absolutely no sound in the crowded little room save that of quiet and intent breathing it was as if he had swung outward at the end of a grape vine, over a ravine, and at the top of the swing had been caught in a prolonged instant of mesmerized gravity, weightless in time.

"No!" Harris said violently, explosively. "Damnation! Send him out of here!" Now time, the fluid world, rushed beneath him again, the voices coming to him again through the smell of cheese and sealed meat, the fear and despair and the old grief of blood:

"This case is closed. I can't find against you, Snopes, but I can give you advice. Leave this country and don't come back to it."

His father spoke for the first time, his voice cold and harsh, level, without emphasis: "I aim to. I don't figure to stay in a country among people who . . ." he said something unprintable and vile, addressed to no one.

"That'll do," the Justice said. "Take your wagon and get out of this country before dark. Case dismissed."

15   His father turned, and he followed the stiff black coat, the wiry figure walking a little stiffly from where a Confederate provost's man's musket ball had taken him in the heel on a stolen horse thirty years ago, followed the two backs now, since his older brother had appeared from somewhere in the crowd, no taller than the father but thicker, chewing tobacco steadily, between the two lines of grim-faced men and out of the store and across the worn gallery and down the sagging steps and among the dogs and half-grown boys in the mild May dust, where as he passed a voice hissed:

"Barn burner!"

Again he could not see, whirling; there was a face in a red haze, moonlike, bigger than the full moon, the owner of it half again his size, he leaping in the red haze toward the face, feeling no blow, feeling no shock when his head struck the earth, scrabbling up and leaping again, feeling no blow this time either and tasting no blood, scrabbling up to see the other boy in full flight and himself already leaping into pursuit as his father's hand jerked him back, the harsh, cold voice speaking above him: "Go get in the wagon."

It stood in a grove of locusts and mulberries across the road. His two hulking sisters in their Sunday dresses and his mother and her sister in calico and sunbonnets were already in it, sitting on and among the sorry residue of the dozen and more movings which even the boy could remember—the battered stove, the broken beds and chairs, the clock inlaid with mother-of-pearl, which would not run, stopped at some fourteen minutes past two o'clock of a dead and forgotten day and time, which had been his mother's dowry. She was crying, though when she saw him she drew her sleeve across her face and began to descend from the wagon. "Get back," the father said.

"He's hurt. I got to get some water and wash his . . ."

20   "Get back in the wagon," his father said. He got in too, over the tail-gate. His father mounted to the seat where the older brother already sat and struck the gaunt mules two savage blows with the peeled willow, but without heat. It was not even sadistic; it was exactly that same quality which in later years would cause his descendants to over-run the engine before putting a motor car into motion, striking and reining back in the same movement. The wagon went on, the store with its quiet crowd of grimly watching men dropped behind; a curve in the road hid it. *Forever* he thought. *Maybe he's done satisfied now, now that he has . . .* stopping himself, not to say it aloud even to himself. His mother's hand touched his shoulder.

"Does hit hurt?" she said.

"Naw," he said. "Hit don't hurt. Lemme be."

"Can't you wipe some of the blood off before hit dries?"

"I'll wash to-night," he said. "Lemme be, I tell you."

25   The wagon went on. He did not know where they were going. None of them ever did or ever asked, because it was always somewhere, always a house of sorts waiting for them a day or two days or even three days away. Likely his father had already arranged to make a crop on another farm before he . . . Again he had to stop himself. He (the father) always did. There was something about his wolflike independence and even courage when the advantage was at least neutral which impressed strangers, as if they got from his latent ravening ferocity not so much a sense of dependability as a feeling that his ferocious conviction in the rightness of his own actions would be of advantage to all whose interest lay with his.

That night they camped, in a grove of oaks and beeches where a spring ran. The nights were still cool and they had a fire against it, of a rail lifted from a nearby fence and cut into lengths—a small fire, neat, niggard almost, a shrewd fire; such fires were his father's habit and custom always, even in freezing weather. Older, the boy might have remarked this and wondered why not a big one; why should not a man who had not only seen the waste and extravagance of war, but who had in his blood an inherent voracious prodigality with material not his own, have burned everything in sight? Then he might have gone a step farther and thought that that was the reason: that niggard blaze was the living fruit of nights passed during those four years in the woods hiding from all men, blue or gray, with his strings of horses (captured horses, he called them). And older still, he might have divined the true reason: that the element of fire spoke to some deep mainspring of his father's being, as the element of steel or of powder spoke to other men, as the one weapon for the preservation of integrity, else breath were not worth the breathing, and hence to be regarded with respect and used with discretion.

But he did not think this now and he had seen those same niggard blazes all his life. He merely ate his supper beside it and was already half asleep over his iron plate when his father called him, and once more he followed the stiff back, the stiff and ruthless limp, up the slope and on to the starlit road where, turning, he could see his father against the stars but without face or depth—a shape black, flat, and bloodless as though cut from tin in the iron folds of the frockcoat which had not been made for him, the voice harsh like tin and without heat like tin:

"You were fixing to tell them. You would have told him." He didn't answer. his father struck him with the flat of his hand on the side of the head, hard but without heat, exactly as he had struck the two mules at the store, exactly as he would strike either of them with any stick in order to kill a horse fly, his voice still without heat or anger: "You're getting to be a man. You got to learn. You got to learn to stick to your own blood or you ain't going to have any blood to stick to you. Do you think either of them, any man there this morning, would? Don't you know all they wanted was a chance to get at me because they knew I had them beat? Eh?" Later, twenty years later, he was to tell himself, "If I had said they wanted only truth, justice, he would have hit me again." But now he said nothing. He was not crying. He just stood there. "Answer me," his father said.

"Yes," he whispered. His father turned.

30   "Get on to bed. We'll be there to-morrow."

To-morrow they were there. In the early afternoon the wagon stopped before a paintless two-room house identical almost with the dozen others it had stopped before even in the boy's ten years, and again, as on the other dozen occasions, his mother and aunt got down and began to unload the wagon, although his two sisters and his father and brother had not moved.

"Likely hit ain't fitten for hawgs," one of the sisters said.

"Nevertheless, fit it will and you'll hog it and like it," his father said. "Get out of them chairs and help your Ma unload."

The two sisters got down, big, bovine, in a flutter of cheap ribbons; one of them drew from the jumbled wagon bed a battered lantern, the other a worn broom. His father handed the reins to the older son and began to climb stiffly over the wheel. "When they get unloaded, take the team to the barn and feed them." Then he said, and at first the boy thought he was still speaking to his brother: "Come with me."

35   "Me?" he said.

"Yes," his father said. "You."

"Abner," his mother said. His father paused and looked back—the harsh level stare beneath the shaggy, graying, irascible brows.

"I reckon I'll have a word with the man that aims to begin to-morrow owning me body and soul for the next eight months."

They went back up the road. A week ago—or before last night, that is—he would have asked where they were going, but not now. His father had struck him before last night but never before had he paused afterward to explain why; it was as if the blow and the following calm, outrageous voice still rang, repercussed, divulging nothing to him save the terrible handicap of being young, the light weight of his few years, just heavy enough to prevent his soaring free of the world as it seemed to be ordered but not heavy enough to keep him footed solid in it, to resist it and try to change the course of its events.

40   Presently he could see the grove of oaks and cedars and the other flowering trees and shrubs where the house would be, though not the house yet. They walked beside a fence massed with honeysuckle and Cherokee roses and came to a gate swinging open between two brick pillars, and now, beyond a sweep of drive, he saw the house for the first time and at that instant he forgot his father and the terror and despair both, and even when he remembered his father again (who had not stopped) the terror and despair did not return. Because, for all the twelve movings, they had sojourned until now in a poor country, a land of small farms and fields and houses, and he had never seen a house like this before. *Hit's big as a courthouse* he thought quietly, with a surge of peace and joy whose reason he could not have thought into words, being too young for that: *They are safe from him. People whose lives are a part of this peace and dignity are beyond his touch, he no more to them than a buzzing wasp: capable of stinging for a little moment but*

that's all; the spell of this peace and dignity rendering even the barns and stable and cribs which belong to it impervious to the puny flames he might contrive . . . this, the peace and joy, ebbing for an instant as he looked again at the stiff black back, the stiff and implacable limp of the figure which was not dwarfed by the house, for the reason that it had never looked big anywhere and which now, against the serene columned backdrop, had more than ever that impervious quality of something cut ruthlessly from tin, depthless, as though, sidewise to the sun, it would cast no shadow. Watching him, the boy remarked the absolutely undeviating course which his father held and saw the stiff foot come squarely down in a pile of fresh droppings where a horse had stood in the drive and which his father could have avoided by a simple change of stride. But it ebbed only for a moment, though he could not have thought this into words either, walking on in the spell of the house, which he could even want but without envy, without sorrow, certainly never with that ravening and jealous rage which unknown to him walked in the ironlike black coat before him: *Maybe he will feel it too. Maybe it will even change him now from what maybe he couldn't help but be.*

They crossed the portico. Now he could hear his father's stiff foot as it came down on the boards with clocklike finality, a sound out of all proportion to the displacement of the body it bore and which was not dwarfed either by the white door before it, as though it had attained to a sort of vicious and ravening minimum not to be dwarfed by anything—the flat, wide, black hat, the formal coat of broadcloth which had once been black but which had now that friction-glazed greenish cast of the bodies of old house flies, the lifted sleeve which was too large, the lifted hand like a curled claw. The door opened so promptly that the boy knew the Negro must have been watching them all the time, an old man with neat grizzled hair, in a linen jacket, who stood barring the door with his body, saying, "Wipe yo foots, white man, fo you come in here. Major ain't home nohow."

"Get out of my way, nigger," his father said, without heat too, flinging the door back and the Negro also and entering, his hat still on his head. And now the boy saw the prints of the stiff foot on the doorjamb and saw them appear on the pale rug behind the machinelike deliberation of the foot which seemed to bear (or transmit) twice the weight which the body compassed. The Negro was shouting "Miss Lula! Miss Lula!" somewhere behind them, then the boy, deluged as though by a warm wave by a suave turn of carpeted stair and a pendant glitter of chandeliers and a mute gleam of gold frames, heard the swift feet and saw her too, a lady—perhaps he had never seen her like before either—in a gray, smooth gown with lace at the throat and an apron tied at the waist and the sleeves turned back, wiping cake or biscuit dough from her hands with a towel as she came up the hall, looking not at his father at all but at the tracks on the blond rug with an expression of incredulous amazement.

"I tried," the Negro cried. "I tole him to . . ."

"Will you please go away?" she said in a shaking voice. "Major de Spain is not at home. Will you please go away?"

45   His father had not spoken again. He did not speak again. He did not even look at her. He just stood stiff in the center of the rug, in his hat, the shaggy iron-gray brows twitching slightly above the pebble-colored eyes as he appeared to examine the house with brief deliberation. Then with the same deliberation he turned; the boy watched him pivot on the good leg and saw the stiff foot drag round the arc of the turning, leaving a final long and fading smear. His father never looked at it, he never once looked down at the rug. The Negro held the door. It closed behind them, upon the hysteric and indistinguishable woman-wail. His father stopped at

the top of the steps and scraped his boot clean on the edge of it. At the gate he stopped again. He stood for a moment, planted stiffly on the stiff foot, looking back at the house. "Pretty and white, ain't it?" he said. "That's sweat. Nigger sweat. Maybe it ain't white enough yet to suit him. Maybe he wants to mix some white sweat with it."

Two hours later the boy was chopping wood behind the house within which his mother and aunt and the two sisters (the mother and aunt, not the two girls, he knew that; even at this distance and muffled by walls the flat loud voices of the two girls emanated an incorrigible idle inertia) were setting up the stove to prepare a meal, when he heard the hooves and saw the linen-clad man on a fine sorrel mare, whom he recognized even before he saw the rolled rug in front of the Negro youth following on a fat bay carriage horse—a suffused, angry face vanishing, still at full gallop, behind the corner of the house where his father and brother were sitting in the two tilted chairs; and a moment later, almost before he could have put the axe down, he heard the hooves again and watched the sorrel mare go back out of the yard, already galloping again. Then his father began to shout one of the sisters' names, who presently emerged backward from the kitchen door dragging the rolled rug along the ground by one end while the other sister walked behind it.

"If you ain't going to tote, go on and set up the wash pot," the first said.

"You, Sarty!" the second shouted. "Set up the wash pot!" His father appeared at the door, framed against that shabbiness, as he had been against that other bland perfection, impervious to either, the mother's anxious face at his shoulder.

"Go on," the father said. "Pick it up." The two sisters stooped, broad, lethargic; stooping, they presented an incredible expanse of pale cloth and a flutter of tawdry ribbons.

50   "If I thought enough of a rug to have to git hit all the way from France I wouldn't keep hit where folks coming in would have to tromp on hit," the first said. They raised the rug.

"Abner," the mother said. "Let me do it."

"You go back and git dinner," his father said. "I'll tend to this."

From the woodpile through the rest of the afternoon the boy watched them, the rug spread flat in the dust beside the bubbling wash-pot, the two sisters stooping over it with that profound and lethargic reluctance, while the father stood over them in turn, implacable and grim, driving them though never raising his voice again. He could smell the harsh homemade lye they were using; he saw his mother come to the door once and look toward them with an expression not anxious now but very like despair; he saw his father turn, and he fell to with the axe and saw from the corner of his eye his father raise from the ground a flattish fragment of field stone and examine it and return to the pot, and this time his mother actually spoke: "Abner. Abner. Please don't. Please, Abner."

Then he was done too. It was dusk; the whippoorwills had already begun. He could smell coffee from the room where they would presently eat the cold food remaining from the midafternoon meal, though when he entered the house he realized they were having coffee again probably because there was a fire on the hearth, before which the rug now lay spread over the backs of the two chairs. The tracks of his father's foot were gone. Where they had been were now long, water-cloudy scoriations resembling the sporadic course of a liliputian[1] mowing machine.

55   It still hung there while they ate the cold food and then went to bed, scattered without order or claim up and down the two rooms, his mother in one bed, where his father would later lie, the older brother in the other, himself, the aunt, and the

[1]**liliputian** trivial or very small, from the imaginary country Liliput, in Jonathan Swift's *Gulliver's Travels* (1726), inhabited by people 6 inches tall.

two sisters on pallets on the floor. But his father was not in bed yet. The last thing the boy remembered was the depthless, harsh silhouette of the hat and coat bending over the rug and it seemed to him that he had not even closed his eyes when the silhouette was standing over him, the fire almost dead behind it, the stiff foot prodding him awake. "Catch up the mule," his father said.

When he returned with the mule his father was standing in the back door, the rolled rug over his shoulder. "Ain't you going to ride?" he said.

"No. Give me your foot."

He bent his knee into his father's hand, the wiry, surprising power flowed smoothly, rising, he rising with it, on to the mule's bare back (they had owned a saddle once; the boy could remember it though not when or where) and with the same effortlessness his father swung the rug up in front of him. Now in the starlight they retraced the afternoon's path, up the dusty road rife with honeysuckle, through the gate and up the black tunnel of the drive to the lightless house, where he sat on the mule and felt the rough warp of the rug drag across his thighs and vanish.

"Don't you want me to help?" he whispered. His father did not answer and now he heard again that stiff foot striking the hollow portico with that wooden and clocklike deliberation, that outrageous overstatement of the weight it carried. The rug, hunched, not flung (the boy could tell that even in the darkness) from his father's shoulder struck the angle of wall and floor with a sound unbelievably loud, thunderous, then the foot again, unhurried and enormous; a light came on in the house and the boy sat, tense, breathing steadily and quietly and just a little fast, though the foot itself did not increase its beat at all, descending the steps now; now the boy could see him.

60   "Don't you want to ride now?" he whispered. "We kin both ride now," the light within the house altering now, flaring up and sinking. *He's coming down the stairs now*, he thought. He had already ridden the mule up beside the horse block; presently his father was up behind him and he doubled the reins over and slashed the mule across the neck, but before the animal could begin to trot the hard, thin arm came round him, the hard, knotted hand jerking the mule back to a walk.

In the first red rays of the sun they were in the lot, putting plow gear on the mules. This time the sorrel mare was in the lot before he heard it at all, the rider collarless and even bareheaded, trembling, speaking in a shaking voice as the woman in the house had done. His father merely looking up once before stooping again to the hame he was buckling, so that the man on the mare spoke to his stooping back:

"You must realize you have ruined that rug. Wasn't there anybody here, any of your women . . ." he ceased, shaking, the boy watching him, the older brother leaning now in the stable door, chewing, blinking slowly and steadily at nothing apparently. "It cost a hundred dollars. But you never had a hundred dollars. You never will. So I'm going to charge you twenty bushels of corn against your crop. I'll add it in your contract and when you come to the commissary you can sign it. That won't keep Mrs. de Spain quiet but maybe it will teach you to wipe your feet off before you enter her house again."

Then he was gone. The boy looked at his father, who still had not spoken or even looked up again, who was now adjusting the loggerhead in the hame.

"Pap," he said. His father looked at him—the inscrutable face, the shaggy brows beneath which the gray eyes glinted coldly. Suddenly the boy went toward him, fast, stopping as suddenly. "You done the best you could!" he cried. "If he wanted hit done different why didn't he wait and tell you how? He won't git no twenty bushels! He won't git none! We'll gether hit and hide hit! I kin watch . . ."

65   "Did you put the cutter back in that straight stock like I told you?"

"No, sir," he said.

"Then go do it."

That was Wednesday. During the rest of that week he worked steadily, at what was within his scope and some which was beyond it, with an industry that did not need to be driven nor even commanded twice; he had this from his mother, with the difference that some at least of what he did he liked to do, such as splitting wood with the half-size axe which his mother and aunt had earned, or saved money somehow, to present him with at Christmas. In company with the two older women (and on one afternoon, even one of the sisters), he built pens for the shoat and the cow which were a part of his father's contract with the landlord, and one afternoon, his father being absent, gone somewhere on one of the mules, he went to the field.

They were running a middle buster now, his brother holding the plow straight while he handled the reins, and walking beside the straining mule, the rich black soil shearing cool and damp against his bare ankles, he thought *Maybe this is the end of it. Maybe even that twenty bushels that seems hard to have to pay for just a rug will be a cheap price for him to stop forever and always from being what he used to be;* thinking, dreaming now, so that his brother had to speak sharply to him to mind the mule: *Maybe he even won't collect the twenty bushels. Maybe it will all add up and balance and vanish—corn, rug, fire; the terror and grief, the being pulled two ways like between two teams of horses—gone, done with for ever and ever.*

70   Then it was Saturday; he looked up from beneath the mule he was harnessing and saw his father in the black coat and hat. "Not that," his father said. "The wagon gear." And then, two hours later, sitting in the wagon bed behind his father and brother on the seat, the wagon accomplished a final curve, and he saw the weathered paintless store with its tattered tobacco- and patent-medicine posters and the tethered wagons and saddle animals below the gallery. He mounted the gnawed steps behind his father and brother, and there again was the lane of quiet, watching faces for the three of them to walk through. He saw the man in spectacles sitting at the plank table and he did not need to be told this was a Justice of the Peace; he sent one glare of fierce, exultant, partisan defiance at the man in collar and cravat now, whom he had seen but twice before in his life, and that on a galloping horse, who now wore on his face an expression not of rage but of amazed unbelief which the boy could not have known was at the incredible circumstance of being sued by one of his own tenants, and came and stood against his father and cried at the Justice: "He ain't done it! He ain't burnt . . ."

"Go back to the wagon," his father said.

"Burnt?" the Justice said. "Do I understand this rug was burned too?"

"Does anybody here claim it was?" his father said. "Go back to the wagon." But he did not, he merely retreated to the rear of the room, crowded as that other had been, but not to sit down this time, instead, to stand pressing among the motionless bodies, listening to the voices:

"And you claim twenty bushels of corn is too high for the damage you did to the rug?"

75   "He brought the rug to me and said he wanted the tracks washed out of it. I washed the tracks out and took the rug back to him."

"But you didn't carry the rug back to him in the same condition it was in before you made the tracks on it."

His father did not answer, and now for perhaps half a minute there was no sound at all save that of breathing, the faint, steady suspiration of complete and intent listening.

"You decline to answer that, Mr. Snopes?" Again his father did not answer. "I'm going to find against you, Mr. Snopes. I'm going to find that you were responsible for the injury to Major de Spain's rug and hold you liable for it. But twenty bushels of corn seems a little high for a man in your circumstances to have to pay. Major de Spain claims it costs a hundred dollars. October corn will be worth about fifty cents. I figure that if Major de Spain can stand a ninety-five-dollar loss on something he paid cash for, you can stand a five-dollar loss you haven't earned yet. I hold you in damages to Major de Spain to the amount of ten bushels of corn over and above your contract with him, to be paid to him out of your crop at gathering time. Court adjourned."

It had taken no time hardly, the morning was but half begun. He thought they would return home and perhaps back to the field, since they were late, far behind all other farmers. But instead his father passed on behind the wagon, merely indicating with his hand for the older brother to follow with it, and crossed the road toward the blacksmith shop opposite, pressing on after his father, overtaking him, speaking, whispering up at the harsh, calm face beneath the weathered hat: "He won't git no ten bushels neither. He won't git one. We'll . . ." until his father glanced for an instant down at him, the face absolutely calm, the grizzled eyebrows tangled above the cold eyes, the voice almost pleasant, almost gentle:

80   "You think so? Well, we'll wait till October anyway."

The matter of the wagon—the setting of a spoke or two and the tightening of the tires—did not take long either, the business of the tires accomplished by driving the wagon into the spring branch behind the shop and letting it stand there, the mules nuzzling into the water from time to time, and the boy on the seat with the idle reins, looking up the slope and through the sooty tunnel of the shed where the slow hammer rang and where his father sat on an upended cypress bolt, easily, either talking or listening, still sitting there when the boy brought the dripping wagon up out of the branch and halted it before the door.

"Take them on to the shade and hitch," his father said. He did so and returned. His father and the smith and a third man squatting on his heels inside the door were talking, about crops and animals; the boy, squatting too in the ammoniac dust and hoof-parings and scales of rust, heard his father tell a long and unhurried story out of the time before the birth of the older brother even when he had been a professional horsetrader. And then his father came up beside him where he stood before a tattered last year's circus poster on the other side of the store, gazing rapt and quiet at the scarlet horses, the incredible poisings and convolutions of tulle and tights and the painted leers of comedians, and said, "It's time to eat."

But not at home. Squatting beside his brother against the front wall, he watched his father emerge from the store and produce from a paper sack a segment of cheese and divide it carefully and deliberately into three with his pocket knife and produce crackers from the same sack. They all three squatted on the gallery and ate, slowly, without talking; then in the store again, they drank from a tin dipper tepid water smelling of the cedar bucket and of living beech trees. And still they did not go home. It was a horse lot this time, a tall rail fence upon and along which men stood and sat and out of which one by one horses were led, to be talked and trotted and then cantered back and forth along the road while the slow swapping and buying went on and the sun began to slant westward, they—the three of them—watching and listening, the older brother with his muddy eyes and his steady, inevitable tobacco, the father commenting now and then on certain of the animals, to no one in particular.

It was after sundown when they reached home. They ate supper by lamplight, then, sitting on the doorstep, the boy watched the night fully accomplish, listening to the whippoorwills and the frogs, when he heard his mother's voice: "Abner! No! No! Oh, God. Oh, God. Abner!" and he rose, whirled, and saw the altered light through the door where a candle stub now burned in a bottle neck on the table and his father, still in the hat and coat, at once formal and burlesque as though dressed carefully for some shabby and ceremonial violence, emptying the reservoir of the lamp back into the five-gallon kerosene can from which it had been filled, while the mother tugged at his arm until he shifted the lamp to the other hand and flung her back, not savagely or viciously, just hard, into the wall, her hands flung out against the wall for balance, her mouth open and in her face the same quality of hopeless despair as had been in her voice. Then his father saw him standing in the door.

85   "Go to the barn and get that can of oil we were oiling the wagon with," he said. The boy did not move. Then he could speak.

"What . . ." he cried. "What are you . . ."

"Go get that oil," his father said. "Go."

Then he was moving, running, outside the house, toward the stable: this the old habit, the old blood which he had not been permitted to choose for himself, which had been bequeathed him willy nilly and which had run for so long (and who knew where, battening on what of outrage and savagery and lust) before it came to him. *I could keep on,* he thought. *I could run on and on and never look back, never need to see his face again. Only I can't. I can't,* the rusted can in his hand now, the liquid sploshing in it as he ran back to the house and into it, into the sound of his mother's weeping in the next room, and handed the can to his father.

"Ain't you going to even send a nigger?" he cried. "At least you sent a nigger before!"

90   This time his father didn't strike him. The hand came even faster than the blow had, the same hand which had set the can on the table with almost excruciating care flashing from the can toward him too quick for him to follow it, gripping him by the back of his shirt and on to tiptoe before he had seen it quit the can, the face stooping at him in breathless and frozen ferocity, the cold, dead voice speaking over him to the older brother who leaned against the table, chewing with that steady, curious, sidewise motion of cows:

"Empty the can into the big one and go on. I'll catch up with you."

"Better tie him up to the bedpost," the brother said.

"Do like I told you," the father said. Then the boy was moving, his bunched shirt and the hard, bony hand between his shoulderblades, his toes just touching the floor, across the room and into the other one, past the sisters sitting with spread heavy thighs in the two chairs over the cold hearth, and to where his mother and aunt sat side by side on the bed, the aunt's arms about his mother's shoulders.

"Hold him," the father said. The aunt made a startled movement. "Not you," the father said. "Lennie. Take hold of him. I want to see you do it." His mother took him by the wrist. "You'll hold him better than that. If he gets loose don't you know what he is going to do? He will go up yonder." He jerked his head toward the road. "Maybe I'd better tie him."

95   "I'll hold him," his mother whispered.

"See you do then." Then his father was gone, the stiff foot heavy and measured upon the boards, ceasing at last.

Then he began to struggle. His mother caught him in both arms, he jerking and wrenching at them. He would be stronger in the end, he knew that. But he had no time to wait for it. "Lemme go!" he cried. "I don't want to have to hit you!"

"Let him go!" the aunt said. "If he don't go, before God, I am going up there myself!"

"Don't you see I can't?" his mother cried. "Sarty! Sarty! No! No! Help me, Lizzie!"

100   Then he was free. His aunt grasped at him but it was too late. He whirled, running, his mother stumbled forward on to her knees behind him, crying to the nearer sister: "Catch him, Net! Catch him!" But that was too late too, the sister (the sisters were twins, born at the same time, yet either of them now gave the impression of being, encompassing as much living meat and volume and weight as any other two of the family) not yet having begun to rise from the chair, her head, face, alone merely turned, presenting to him in the flying instant an astonishing expanse of young female features untroubled by any surprise even, wearing only an expression of bovine interest. Then he was out of the room, out of the house, in the mild dust of the starlit road and the heavy rifeness of honeysuckle, the pale ribbon unspooling with terrific slowness under his running feet, reaching the gate at last and turning in, running, his heart and lungs drumming, on up the drive toward the lighted house, the lighted door. He did not knock, he burst in, sobbing for breath, incapable for the moment of speech; he saw the astonished face of the Negro in the linen jacket without knowing when the Negro had appeared.

"De Spain!" he cried, panted. "Where's . . ." then he saw the white man too emerging from a white door down the hall. "Barn!" he cried. "Barn!"

"What?" the white man said. "Barn?"

"Yes!" the boy cried. "Barn!"

105   "Catch him!" the white man shouted.

But it was too late this time too. The Negro grasped his shirt, but the entire sleeve, rotten with washing, carried away, and he was out that door too and in the drive again, and had actually never ceased to run even while he was screaming into the white man's face.

Behind him the white man was shouting, "My horse! Fetch my horse!" and he thought for an instant of cutting across the park and climbing the fence into the road, but he did not know the park nor how high the vine-massed fence might be and he dared not risk it. So he ran on down the drive, blood and breath roaring; presently he was in the road again though he could not see it. He could not hear either: the galloping mare was almost upon him before he heard her, and even then he held his course, as if the very urgency of his wild grief and need must in a moment more find him wings, waiting until the ultimate instant to hurl himself aside and into the weed-choked roadside ditch as the horse thundered past and on, for an instant in furious silhouette against the stars, the tranquil early summer night sky which, even before the shape of the horse and rider vanished, stained abruptly and violently upward: a long, swirling roar incredible and soundless, blotting the stars, and he springing up and into the road again, running again, knowing it was too late yet still running even after he heard the shot and, an instant later, two shots, pausing now without knowing he had ceased to run, crying "Pap! Pap!", running again before he knew he had begun to run, stumbling, tripping over something and scrabbling up again without ceasing to run, looking backward over his shoulder at the glares as he got up, running on among the invisible trees, panting, sobbing, "Father! Father!"

At midnight he was sitting on the crest of a hill. He did not know it was midnight and he did not know how far he had come. But there was no glare behind him now and he sat now, his back toward what he had called home for four days anyhow, his face toward the dark woods which he would enter when breath was strong again, small, shaking steadily in the chill darkness, hugging himself into the remainder of his thin, rotten shirt, the grief and despair now no longer terror and fear but just grief and despair. *Father. My father,* he thought. "He was brave!" He cried suddenly, aloud but not loud, no more than a whisper: "He was! He was in the war! He was in Colonel Sartoris' cav'ry!" not knowing that his father had gone to that war a private in the fine old European sense, wearing no uniform, admitting the authority of and giving fidelity to no man or army or flag, going to war as Malbrouck himself did: for booty—it meant nothing and less than nothing to him if it were enemy booty or his own.

The slow constellations wheeled on. It would be dawn and then sun-up after a while and he would be hungry. But that would be to-morrow and now he was only cold, and walking would cure that. His breathing was easier now and he decided to get up and go on, and then he found that he had been asleep because he knew it was almost dawn, the night almost over. He could tell that from the whippoorwills. They were everywhere now among the dark trees below him, constant and inflectioned and ceaseless, so that, as the instant for giving over to the day birds drew nearer and nearer, there was no interval at all between them. He got up. He was a little stiff, but walking would cure that too as it would the cold, and soon there would be the sun. He went on down the hill, toward the dark woods within which the liquid silver voices of the birds called unceasing—the rapid and urgent beating of the urgent and quiring heart of the late spring night. He did not look back.

[1939]

Joining the Conversation: Critical Thinking and Writing

1. Discuss "point of view" in this story. Identify passages in the text where we are made aware of the narrator's or a character's point of view.
2. Is Faulkner on Major de Spain's side, or Abner Snopes's, or both, or neither?
3. By the end of the story, how has Sarty changed? Does Faulkner show us this process of change in a convincing way? Do we believe it? In your argument, make sure to cite evidence from the text.
4. While you were reading "Barn Burning," did you feel at any point that you needed "background information" in order to understand and appreciate it? Or do you think that the story itself contains everything you need to know?
5. Many people claim that Faulkner is one of the greatest American writers. Do you think that this story supports such a view? Is this a great story, or a good story?

MyLiteratureLab® *For additional resources for "Barn Burning," log in to www .myliteraturelab.com where you will find a Video and Comprehension Quiz, as well as an About the Author, Bibliography, Links, and Critical Overview for Faulkner (under Student Resources).*

TOBIAS WOLFF

Tobias Wolff was born in Alabama in 1945, but he was raised in the state of Washington. He served for four years in the army (1964–68), including a tour of duty in Vietnam. He graduated from Oxford University in 1972 and then studied creative writing at Stanford. Wolff's first two books were collections of short stories, In the Garden of North American Martyrs *(1981) and* Back in the World *(1985), and both received good reviews, but he achieved greater success and acclaim with the publication of* The Boy's Life *(1989), his memoir of his teenage years. He has also written a memoir of his military service,* In Pharaoh's Army *(1994). The author of many short stories and two novels, his recent publications include* Our Story Begins: New and Selected Stories *(2008). From 1980 to 1997, Wolff taught courses in English and creative writing at Syracuse University, and since then he has taught at Stanford, where he is the Ward W. and Priscilla B. Woods Professor in the School of Humanities and Sciences.*

Powder

Just before Christmas my father took me skiing at Mount Baker. He'd had to fight for the privilege of my company, because my mother was still angry with him for sneaking me into a nightclub during his last visit, to see Thelonius Monk.

He wouldn't give up. He promised, hand on heart, to take good care of me and have me home for dinner on Christmas Eve, and she relented. But as we were checking out of the lodge that morning it began to snow, and in this snow he observed some quality that made it necessary for us to get in one last run. We got in several last runs. He was indifferent to my fretting. Snow whirled around us in bitter, blinding squalls, hissing like sand, and still we skied. As the lift bore us to the peak yet again, my father looked at his watch and said: "Criminey. This'll have to be a fast one."

By now I couldn't see the trail. There was no point in trying. I stuck to him like white on rice and did what he did and somehow made it to the bottom without sailing off a cliff. We returned our skis and my father put chains on the Austin-Healy while I swayed from foot to foot, clapping my mittens and wishing I were home. I could see everything. The green tablecloth, the plates with the holly pattern, the red candles waiting to be lit.

We passed a diner on our way out. "You want some soup?" my father asked. I shook my head. "Buck up," he said. "I'll get you there. Right, doctor?"

5   I was supposed to say, "Right, doctor," but I didn't say anything.

A state trooper waved us down outside the resort. A pair of sawhorses were blocking the road. The trooper came up to our car and bent down to my father's window. His face was bleached by the cold. Snowflakes clung to his eyebrows and to the fur trim of his jacket and cap.

"Don't tell me," my father said.

The trooper told him. The road was closed. It might get cleared, it might not. Storm took everyone by surprise. So much, so fast. Hard to get people moving. Christmas Eve. What can you do?

My father said: "Look. We're talking about four, five inches. I've taken this car through worse than that."

10   The trooper straightened up, boots creaking. His face was out of sight but I could hear him. "The road is closed."

My father sat with both hands on the wheel, rubbing the wood with his thumbs. He looked at the barricade for a long time. He seemed to be trying to master the idea of it. Then he thanked the trooper, and with a weird, old-maidy show of caution turned the car around. "Your mother will never forgive me for this," he said.

"We should have left before," I said. "Doctor."

He didn't speak to me again until we were both in a booth at the diner, waiting for our burgers. "She won't forgive me," he said. "Do you understand? Never."

"I guess," I said, but no guesswork was required; she wouldn't forgive him.

15 "I can't let that happen." He bent toward me. "I'll tell you what I want. I want us to be all together again. Is that what you want?"

"Yes, sir."

He bumped my chin with his knuckles. "That's all I needed to hear."

When we finished eating he went to the pay phone in the back of the dinner, then joined me in the booth again. I figured he'd called my mother, but he didn't give a report. He sipped at his coffee and stared out the window at the empty road. "Come on, come on," he said. A little while later he said, "Come on!" When the trooper's car went past, lights flashing, he got up and dropped some money on the check. "O.K. Vámanos."

The wind had died. The snow was falling straight down, less of it now; lighter. We drove away from the resort, right up to the barricade. "Move it," my father told me. When I looked at him he said, "What are you waiting for?" I got out and dragged one of the sawhorses aside, then put it back after he drove through. He pushed the door open for me. "Now you're an accomplice," he said. "We go down together." He put the car into gear and gave me a look. "Joke, doctor."

20 "Funny, doctor."

Down the first long stretch I watched the road behind us, to see if the trooper was on our tail. The barricade vanished. Then there was nothing but snow: snow on the road, snow kicking up from the chains, snow on the trees, snow in the sky; and our trail in the snow. I faced around and had a shock. The lie of the road behind us had been marked by our own tracks, but there were no tracks ahead of us. My father was breaking virgin snow between a line of tall trees. He was humming "Stars Fell on Alabama." I felt snow brush along the floorboards under my feet. To keep my hands from shaking, I clamped them between my knees.

My father grunted in a thoughtful way and said, "Don't ever try this yourself."

"I won't."

"That's what you say now, but someday you'll get your license and then you'll think you can do anything. Only you won't be able to do this. You need, I don't know—a certain instinct."

25 "Maybe I have it."

"You don't. You have your strong points, but not . . . this. I only mention it, because I don't want you to get the idea this is something just anybody can do. I'm a great driver. That's not a virtue, O.K.? It's just a fact, and one you should be aware of. Of course you have to give the old heap some credit, too—there aren't many cars I'd try this with. Listen!"

I listened. I heard the slap of the chains, the stiff, jerky rasps of the wipers, the purr of the engine. It really did purr. The car was almost new. My father couldn't afford it, and kept promising to sell it, but here it was.

I said, "Where do you think that policeman went to?"

"Are you warm enough?" He reached over and cranked up the blower. Then he turned off the wipers. We didn't need them. The clouds had brightened. A few sparse, feathery flakes drifted into our slipstream and were swept away. We left the trees and entered a broad field of snow that ran level for a while and then tilted sharply downward. Orange stakes had been planted at intervals in two parallel lines and my father steered a course between them, though they were far enough apart to leave considerable doubt in my mind as to where exactly the road lay. He was humming again, doing little scat riffs around the melody.

30   "O.K. then. What are my strong points?"

"Don't get me started," he said. "It'd take all day."

"Oh, right. Name one."

"Easy. You always think ahead."

True. I always thought ahead. I was a boy who kept his clothes on numbered hangers to insure proper rotation. I bothered my teachers for homework assignments far ahead of their due dates so I could make up schedules. I thought ahead, and that was why I knew that there would be other troopers waiting for us at the end of our ride, if we got there. What I did not know was that my father would wheedle and plead his way past them—he didn't sing "O Tannenbaum"[1] but just about—and get me home for dinner, buying a little more time before my mother decided to make the split final. I knew we'd get caught; I was resigned to it. And maybe for this reason I stopped moping and began to enjoy myself.

35   Why not? This was one for the books. Like being in a speedboat, but better. You can't go downhill in a boat. And it was all ours. And it kept coming, the laden trees, the unbroken surface of snow, the sudden white vistas. Here and there I saw hints of the road, ditches, fences, stakes, but not so many that I could have found my way. But then I didn't have to. My father was driving. My father in his 48th year, rumpled, kind, bankrupt of honor, flushed with certainty. He was a great driver. All persuasion, no coercion. Such subtlety at the wheel, such tactful pedalwork. I actually trusted him. And the best was yet to come—the switchbacks and hairpins. Impossible to describe. Except maybe to say this: If you haven't driven fresh powder, you haven't driven.

[1992]

Joining the Conversation: Critical Thinking and Writing

1. How would you characterize the father in "Powder"?
2. How does the boy feel about his father?
3. What argument might you offer to someone who said that this story glorified an irresponsible father?
4. What is the main point of the story? What is your evidence? Or does this story have more than one "main point"? Again, please support your view with evidence.

POEMS

ANONYMOUS

Birmingham Jail was famous, not only in the South but throughout the United States, for many decades before Martin Luther King Jr. was arrested and imprisoned there in 1963. A song called "Birmingham Jail" is at least as old as the early twentieth century (a version was published in 1909), and like many popular ballads it draws on older songs, notably "Down in the Valley," which has been sung at

---

[1]"O Tannenbaum" a German song known in English as "O Christmas Tree."

least since the late nineteenth century. Like all folk songs, "Birmingham Jail" exists in many versions: Singers make small changes within a line, or sometimes drop or add whole verses. For instance, in what may be the most common version, some lines run thus:

> *Send me a letter, send it by mail,*
> *Send it in care of the Birmingham jail.*

But we have also heard

> *Send me a letter, send it by mail,*
> *Back it in care of Birmingham jail.*

and another version sung by Huddie Ledbetter, known as Leadbelly (1888–1949):

> *Send me a letter, send it by mail,*
> *'Dress it all over, that Birmingham jail.*

We print one version as it was actually sung, and then we offer additional stanzas from other versions, that is, from performances by other singers. You can pick and choose and thus create the version that strikes you as most effective. (Inventing new lines and stanzas, or adding lines or stanzas from other ballads, is entirely acceptable.)

Birmingham Jail

Down in the valley, the valley so low,
Put your head out the window, and hear the wind blow.
Hear the wind blow, hear the wind blow,
Put your head out the window, and hear the wind blow.

Write me a letter, send it by mail   5
'Dress it all over, that Birmingham jail.
Birmingham jail, boys, Birmingham jail,
'Dress it all over, that Birmingham jail.

Ty Shek [?] will 'rrest you, bound you over in jail,
Can't get nobody, to go your bail.   10
To go your bail, boys, to go your bail,
Can't get nobody, to go your bail.

Send for your lawyer, come down to your cell,
He swear he can clear you, in spite of all hell.
Spite of all hell, boys, spite of all hell,   15
He swear he can clear you, in spite of all hell.

Get the biggest your money, come back for the rest,
Tell you plead guilty, for he know that is best.
He know that is best, boys, he know that is best,
Tell you plead guilty, he know that is best.   20

Down in the valley, the valley so low,
Put your head out the window, and hear the wind blow.
Hear the wind blow, hear the wind blow,
Put your head out the window, and hear the wind blow.

Joining the Conversation: Critical Thinking and Writing

1. Here are some additional verses, taken from other singers. If you were singing "Birmingham Jail," which verses might you include, and which exclude? Why?

   Writing this letter, containing three lines,
   Answer my question, will you be mine?
   Will you be mine, dear, will you be mine,
   Answer my question, will you be mine?

   The roses are red, and the vi'lets are blue,
   Angels in Heaven sing "I love you."
   Angels in Heaven, Angels in Heaven,
   Angels in Heaven, sing "I love you."

   Roses love sunshine, violets love dew,
   Angels in Heaven know I love you,
   Know I love you, dear, know I love you,
   Angels in Heaven know I love you.

   Go build me a castle, forty feet high,
   So I can see her, as she goes by.
   As she goes by, love, as she goes by,
   So I can see her, as she goes by.

   Bird in a cage, love, bird in a cage,
   Dying for freedom, ever a slave.
   Ever a slave love, ever a slave,
   Dying for freedom, ever a slave.

2. We have never heard a version of "Birmingham Jail" in which the singer tells *why* he is in jail. Other songs talk about gambling debts or drunkenness or disorderly or criminal behavior, but in "Birmingham Jail" no explanation is offered, not even that the singer is unjustly imprisoned. Would the song be better if we were given such information? Why, or why not?

3. How is it that we as readers can feel pleasure in response to a poem that is sorrowful in tone and situation? What kind of pleasure is it? Do we share the speaker's sorrow, or do we remain somewhat at a distance from it?

A. E. HOUSMAN

Alfred Edward Housman (1859–1936) was born near rural Shropshire, England, and educated in classics and philosophy at Oxford University. Although he was a brilliant student, he failed his final examination and he did not receive the academic appointment that he had anticipated. He began working as a civil servant at the British Patent Office, but in his spare time he wrote scholarly articles on Latin literature. These writings in 1892 won him an appointment as Professor of Latin at the University of London. In 1911 he was appointed to Cambridge University. During his lifetime he published (in addition to his scholarly writings) only two thin books of poetry, A Shropshire Lad *(1896) and* Last Poems *(1922), and a highly readable lecture called*

The Name and Nature of Poetry *(1933). After his death a third book of poems,* More Poems *(1936), was published. The best edition of Housman's poems (containing not only the three books of poems already mentioned but also additional poems, fragments, translations, light verse, and Latin verse) is* The Poems of A. E. Housman *(1997), edited by Archie Burnett.*

The usual explanation for Housman's failure at his examination is that he was in a state of shock resulting from his repressed homosexual love for a fellow student. In any case, Housman, like almost all homosexuals of the period, kept his homosexuality a secret. This is not surprising; in England, "unnatural acts" between men were punishable by death until 1885, when the penalty was modified to a maximum of two years at hard labor. (Not until 1967 was homosexual behavior between consenting adults legalized in England.) In the poetry published in Housman's lifetime there is nothing explicitly homosexual, but today readers who are aware of his sexual orientation can easily and reasonably perceive the sexual implications in the voice of the man who believes he is doomed to be an outsider.

The first of the two poems that we print here, "The Carpenter's Son," was written in 1895 and published the next year in A Shropshire Lad. *In this poem Housman sets forth, in nineteenth-century rural imagery, the story of a carpenter's son—Jesus was the son of a carpenter—who is carried in a cart to a gallows, where he will be hanged between two thieves. The youth who speaks the poem differs from his two fellow victims, he says, in that he "dies for love."*

The second poem, "Oh who is that young sinner," was written in August 1895, shortly after Oscar Wilde (1854–1900), the most popular British playwright of the period, was convicted of sodomy and given the maximum prison sentence. Although the poem does not mention homosexuality, Wilde's conviction unquestionably inspired it. Housman never published it, but after Housman died his brother, Laurence Housman, published it in A.E.H.: Some Poems, Some Letters and a Personal Memoir by His Brother *(1936).*

The Carpenter's Son°

"Here the hangman stops his cart:
Now the best of friends must part.
Fare you well, for ill fare I:
Live, lads, and I will die.

"Oh, at home had I but stayed   5
'Prenticed to my father's trade,
Had I stuck to plane and adze,
I had not been lost, my lads.

"Then I might have built perhaps
Gallows-trees for other chaps,   10
Never dangled on my own,
Had I but left ill alone.

"Now, you see, they hang me high,
And the people passing by

°**The Carpenter's Son** The Gospels according to Matthew (13:55) and Mark (6:3) identify Jesus as a carpenter's son. Lines 18–19 in the poem allude to the two thieves between whom Jesus was crucified (Matthew 27:38; Mark 15:27; Luke 23:39–40).

Stop to shake their fists and curse;   15
So 'is come from ill to worse.

"Here hang I, and right and left
Two poor fellows hang for theft:
All the same's the luck we prove,
Though the midmost hangs for love.   20

"Comrades all, that stand and gaze,
Walk henceforth in other ways;
See my neck and save your own:
Comrades all, leave ill alone.

"Make some day a decent end,   25
Shrewder fellows than your friend.
Fare you well, for ill fare I:
Live, lads, and I will die."

                                            [1895]

Joining the Conversation: Critical Thinking and Writing

1. We think you will agree that even separated from the context of the other po-
    ems in *A Shropshire Lad*—a world in which Housman speaks of lads, barns,
    ploughing, country fairs, and so forth—"The Carpenter's Son" evokes a folksy,
    rural nineteenth-century world. What words make it seem to be set in relatively
    modern times, rather than the time of the crucifixion of Jesus? Or put it this way:
    Why does the speaker sound like a youth of the modern world (nineteenth
    century) rather than Jesus?
2. The speaker says that he "hangs for love" but he never amplifies what he means.
    Should he have?
3. Is the poem blasphemous? (If you are not a Christian, try to put yourself into
    the shoes of a Christian while thinking about this question.)

Oh who is that young sinner

Oh who is that young sinner with the handcuffs on his wrists?
And what has he been after that they groan and shake their fists?
And wherefore is he wearing such a conscience-stricken air?
Oh they're taking him to prison for the colour of his hair.

'Tis a shame to human nature, such a head of hair as his;   5
In the good old time 'twas hanging for the colour that it is;
Though hanging isn't bad enough and flaying would be fair
For the nameless and abominable colour of his hair.

Oh a deal of pains he's taken and a pretty price he's paid
To hide his poll° or dye it of a mentionable shade;   10

10 poll the hair-covered back and top of the human head.

But they've pulled the beggar's hat off for the world to see and stare,
And they're haling him to justice for the colour of his hair.

Now 'tis oakum for his fingers° and the treadmill for his feet
And the quarry-gang on Portland in the cold and in the heat,
And between his spells of labour in the time he has to spare   15
He can curse the God that made him for the colour of his hair.

[1895]

13 oakum for his fingers Prisoners sentenced to hard labor had to shred jute, a coarse fiber mixed with tar to make oakum, used for caulking wooden ships. The task bloodied their fingers.

Joining the Conversation: Critical Thinking and Writing

1. Characterize the tone of the speaker in the first two stanzas. He begins by asking a simple question, but what causes him to change to the tone we hear in the second stanza? What is the tone of the last line of the poem?
2. In a draft of the first line, Housman wrote "fellow" but he then replaced it with "sinner." Why do you suppose he made the change?
3. No one in England, or probably anywhere else, is or was put into prison "for the colour of his hair." What is Housman getting at?

CLAUDE McKAY

Born in Jamaica, Claude McKay (1890–1948) wrote his first poems there, in dialect that drew upon the island's folk culture. In 1912 he left Jamaica to pursue a literary career in the United States. McKay attended school and worked at a number of jobs in the 1910s, but above all he continued to write poems, which were well received. During the 1920s, he became part of the Harlem literary and cultural renaissance. A political radical, McKay was also active in left-wing groups and causes; in 1922–23 he traveled to the Soviet Union, where he lectured on politics and literature. McKay's books of poems include Songs of Jamaica *(1912) and* Harlem Shadows *(1922). His most notable novel,* Home to Harlem *(1928), tells the story of an African American soldier who deserts from the army in France and then returns to the United States; it was the first novel by an African American to become a best-seller. McKay's autobiography is* A Long Way from Home *(1937). "If We Must Die," printed here, is McKay's best-known poem. A response to a horrific outbreak of racial violence in the summer of 1919 in Chicago and other major cities, the poem was first published in July of that year in the radical journal* Liberator.

If We Must Die

If we must die, let it not be like hogs
Hunted and penned in an inglorious spot,
While round us bark the mad and hungry dogs,
Making their mock at our accursed lot.
If we must die, O let us nobly die,   5

So that our precious blood may not be shed
In vain: then even the monsters we defy
Shall be constrained to honor us though dead!
O kinsmen! we must meet the common foe!
Though far outnumbered let us show us brave,   10
And for their thousand blows deal one deathblow!
What though before us lies the open grave?
Like men we'll face the murderous, cowardly pack,
Pressed to the wall, dying, but fighting back!

[1919]

Joining the Conversation: Critical Thinking and Writing

1. In line 9, the speaker refers to "the common foe." In what other ways in the poem is this "foe" characterized?
2. We know that "If We Must Die" is a poem about racial violence. How would you interpret the poem if you did not know this?
3. Some would argue that violence should never be the response to injustice, no matter how cruel the injustice might be. Do you believe this yourself? Or can you think of instances where violence might be justified?

JIMMY SANTIAGO BACA

For a biographical note on Jimmy Santiago Baca, see page 1138. Immigrants in Our Own Land, *published in 1979, was Baca's first book, and it includes the poem printed here. Among his other books are* Black Mesa Poems *(1989) and* Healing Earthquakes: Poems *(2001).*

Cloudy Day

It is windy today. A wall of wind crashes against,
windows clunk against, iron frames
as wind swings past broken glass
and seethes, like a frightened cat
in empty spaces of the cellblock.   5

In the exercise yard
we sat huddled in our prison jackets,
on our haunches against the fence,
and the wind carried our words
over the fence,   10
while the vigilant guard on the tower
held his cap at the sudden gust.

I could see the main tower from where I sat,
and the wind in my face
gave me the feeling I could grasp
the tower like a cornstalk,   15

and snap it from its roots of rock.
The wind plays it like a flute,
this hollow shoot of rock.
The brim girded with barbwire   20
with a guard sitting there also,
listening intently to the sounds
as clouds cover the sun.

I thought of the day I was coming to prison,
in the back seat of a police car,   25
hands and ankles chained, the policeman pointed,
"See that big water tank? The big
silver one out there, sticking up?
That's the prison."

And here I am, I cannot believe it.   30
Sometimes it is such a dream, a dream,
where I stand up in the face of the wind,
like now, it blows at my jacket,
and my eyelids flick a little bit,
while I stare disbelieving. . . .   35

The third day of spring,
and four years later, I can tell you,
how a man can endure, how a man
can become so cruel, how he can die
or become so cold. I can tell you this,   40
I have seen it every day, every day,
and still I am strong enough to love you,
love myself and feel good;
even as the earth shakes and trembles,
and I have not a thing to my name,   45
I feel as if I have everything, everything.

[1979]

Joining the Conversation: Critical Thinking and Writing

1. In an interview in 1997, Baca noted that he wrote "Cloudy Day" in prison. How do the details of the poem's language bear witness to Baca's own experience of imprisonment? Do you think that a person who had never been imprisoned could write such a poem?
2. In the same interview, Baca was asked about this poem: "Was that written for a person?" He replied: "It was written for me." Baca did not say any more than that. What do you think he means? And how, specifically, is this meaning reflected in the poem?
3. In the final stanza, Baca recalls that he has now been in prison for four years. What has he learned about himself, and about the realities of prison, during this period of time?
4. Who is the "you" referred to in the final stanza? How do you interpret the last line? And why does Baca repeat the word "everything"?

CAROLYN FORCHÉ

Carolyn Forché was born in Detroit in 1950. After earning a bachelor's degree from Michigan State University and a master's degree from Bowling Green State University, she traveled widely in the Southwest, living among Pueblo Indians. Between 1978 and 1986 she made several visits to El Salvador, documenting human rights violations for Amnesty International. Her first book of poems, Gathering the Tribes, *won the Yale Younger Poets award in 1975. Forché is Director of the Lannan Center for Poetry and Poetics and holds the Lannan Chair in Poetry at Georgetown University in Washington, D.C. Her second book of poems,* The Country between Us *(1981), includes "The Colonel," which has been called a prose poem, i.e., a short work that looks like prose but that is highly rhythmical or rich in images, or both.*

The Colonel

What you have heard is true. I was in his house. His wife carried a tray of coffee and sugar. His daughter filed her nails, his son went out for the night. There were daily papers, pet dogs, a pistol on the cushion beside him. The moon swung bare on its black cord over the house. On the television was a cop show. It was in English. Broken bottles were embedded in the walls around the house to scoop the knee-caps from a man's legs or cut his hands to lace. On the windows there were gratings like those in liquor stores. We had dinner, rack of lamb, good wine, a gold bell was on the table for calling the maid. The maid brought green mangoes, salt, a type of bread. I was asked how I enjoyed the country. There was a brief commercial in Spanish. His wife took everything away. There was some talk then of how difficult it had become to govern. The parrot said hello on the terrace. The colonel told it to shutup, and pushed himself from the table. My friend said to me with his eyes: say nothing. The colonel returned with a sack used to bring groceries home. He spilled many human ears on the table. They were like dried peach halves. There is no other way to say this. He took one of them in his hands, shook it in our faces, dropped it into a water glass. It came alive there. I am tired of fooling around he said. As for the rights of anyone, tell your people they can go fuck themselves. He swept the ears to the floor with his arm and held the last of his wine in the air. Something for your poetry, no? he said. Some of the ears on the floor caught this scrap of his voice. Some of the ears on the floor were pressed to the ground.
May 1978

[1981]

Joining the Conversation: Critical Thinking and Writing

1. How would you characterize the colonel in a few sentences?
2. We are told that the colonel spoke of "how difficult it had become to govern." What do you suppose the colonel assumes is the purpose of government? What do you assume its purpose is?
3. How much do we know about the narrator? Can we guess the narrator's purpose in visiting the colonel? How would you characterize the narrator's tone? Do you believe the narrator?
4. What is your response to the last sentence?

PLAYS

BILLY GODA

Billy Goda, playwright and screenwriter, holds an MFA from Columbia University.
No Crime *was first published in* Best American Short Plays 1998–99. *His most recent
publication is* Dust *(2009), a thriller that ran in New York in 2008–09.*

No Crime

CHARACTERS

CAL ROBERTS, a good looking thirty-year-old man
JIM ABNER, a big, egotistical fifty-year-old man

CAL is in JIM ABNER's office. It is a large office with a great deal of room, light, and a
nice view. JIM has his cowboy boots up on his desk.

JIM: A time comes in a man's life when fifteen minutes can change his future,
change his life; these could be your fifteen minutes, Cal.

Pause as JIM *takes a tin of Skoal chewing tobacco out of his desk, packs it down,
and takes a dip. He will spit throughout the scene.*

You're one of three finalists for this position. Now it all depends upon your
interview. Whichever one of you has the best interview, that's the one I'll
hire. (*JIM SPITS*). Nasty habit. I've already met with the other two, so it's up to
you now, Cal. It's up to you. (*JIM SPITS.*) What do you have to say about that?

CAL: I look forward to the challenge . . .

JIM: Yeah, yeah, yeah, one of the others said that also. Every time we interview
I get that answer: "looking forward to something." You must get it out of a
book. Were you reading one of those "what to say in an interview" books?

CAL: I wasn't . . .

JIM: I hope not. We need original thinking here. This law firm's been around for   5
fifty-two years, and we've become so damn successful by original thinking; not
by memorizing some damn answers in a how to be interviewed book. Are you
aware of the success this firm has accomplished?

CAL: I am very aware of that . . .

JIM: We've been involved in some of the most important criminal cases in this
country, and you know what nearly every one of them have in common?
(*Pause.*) I'm asking what do these cases have in common? You said you know
about our firm . . .

CAL: That you've improved the situation of the defendant. You've either plea bargained for a much lesser charge or you've had your client acquitted.

JIM: That's good, very good. Dave told you to say that, didn't he? (*Laughing.*) That
s.o.b.'s ruining all my fun. That question usually scares the pants off the
applicant . . .

CAL: However, in 1988, the state versus Max Mainer, he received a life sentence.   10
In 1994, Tony Giovano received three consecutive life sentences for multiple murders, and I wonder if you shouldn't have gone with the insanity plea . . .

JIM: All right, Cal, you've done your homework; I don't need a history lesson. (*Pause.*) There is only one thing that matters when a client walks through that door. Do you know what that is?

CAL: That he can pay the bill for our legal services.

JIM: (*Laughing.*) Well, yes that too. Make that two things that matter. If he can pay our bill and if there is at least a slight chance of our improving his situation. If there is not that possibility we will reject the case no matter how much money they offer. If you lose cases you lose your reputation. We do not take kindly to losing cases here.

CAL: I understand.

JIM: When we went down with the Giovano fiasco, two very prestigious clients   15
walked out the door with his guilty verdict. (*JIM spits.*) How is Dave?

CAL: He's fine.

JIM: Dave speaks very highly of you.

CAL: Thank you.

JIM: I said Dave does, not me. I don't know you yet. That's one of the main reasons you're sitting in that chair right now—that crazy bastard's a very good friend of mine. At Harvard Law, he saved my butt more than once forcing me to study something other than women and beer. I never understood why he decided to become a professor, without a doubt he could have been one of the top litigaters in the country. We could have been partners. (*Pause.*) I have numerous applications with excellent resumes, but you have an ace in your pocket by the name of Dave Horowitz. That recommendation gives you the rail position. What do you have to say about that?

CAL: I think Dave's an excellent judge of character.   20

JIM: (*Laughing.*) I'm sure you do. He says you'll do whatever it takes to improve your situation—that's the feeling he gets from you. That's an important feeling, very important. What did Dave teach you, Cal? You better not give me a course title.

CAL: How to shoot a gun. How to aim and hit a target.

JIM: Well that's good, but I'm not interviewing you for our rifle team.

CAL: Everyone has a price, that becomes, that is, a weakness, and it's up to me, as a lawyer, as a thinking man, to find out what that is, and then, if need be, to use it. Ready, aim, fire, so to speak.

Long pause.
JIM *spits.*

JIM: A client walks into your office, sits down in your leather arm chair, Cal,   25
lights a cigar, and then tells you the truth of his case, let's say he cracked some lady on the head with a baseball bat splattering her brains all over the sidewalk . . . (*JIM spits.*) . . . and he played Mickey Mantle on her head because he was ordered to by his, let's call it a supervisor, and he did not question his supervisor's authority. What would you do? How would you feel, Cal? This client has confessed his guilt to you. He has confessed to this horrible, this heinous crime of an innocent lady's head being smashed open. What would you do in defending a client that was guilty, and your only hope of winning the case was by twisting the truth?

Long pause.

CAL: I cannot accurately answer that question.

JIM: Why not?

CAL: He is my client?

JIM: That's what I said . . .

CAL: He has already agreed to use our firm as his representation? 30

JIM: Correct . . .

CAL: He is not guilty.

JIM: Cal, he has confessed to you . . .

CAL: He is innocent . . . 35

JIM: He has told you about the murder . . .

CAL: He did not commit . . .

JIM: He bashed a lady's head in with a bat! Splattering her blood . . .

CAL: Blood on the sidewalk from someone else's bat . . .

JIM: Are you stupid, son?! What is wrong with you? I have told you, he has told you . . .

CAL: You say that my client is guilty, well I say that is impossible, Jim. It is impos 40 sible to say he is guilty. He is innocent until someone from the DA's office can persuade a jury of twelve to say he is not innocent. He is innocent until a verdict of guilty is returned. This is why I can not accurately answer your question; this is why your question becomes irrelevant. If he is my client then he is innocent, and it was someone else's bat. Who are the witnesses, Jim? Do you have eyewitnesses? Did he confess to the police? I don't think he confessed or he wouldn't be in my office. Only if he confessed to the police would I start with the idea of his guilt as a possibility. A possibility that I would evaluate and attempt to repudiate. Has our hypothetical client confessed to the police?

JIM: We'll say he has not.

CAL: Then he is not guilty. Then the only thing which can be proved is that some lady's head has been struck with a blunt object causing her death. What other evidence exists, Jim? Is there any other evidence?

JIM *spits.*

JIM: Your conscience.

CAL: My conscience is not on trial.

Pause.

JIM: Would you like a dip of tobacco? Green, Skoal, longcut. Dave's the idiot that 45 started me dipping; he thinks he's a Jewish cowboy from New York. I always chew tobacco when I think—that's as long as no women are around.

CAL: Yes, thank you.

JIM *passes the tin to* CAL. CAL *packs it down and places a dip in his mouth.*

JIM: I spit in this bronze cup. It was a present from my daughter. See that: "World's Greatest Dad."

CAL: That's a nice spit cup, sir.

JIM: I never hired a lawyer that dips tobacco.

CAL: It helps me think. 50

JIM: So your hypothetical client is not guilty?

CAL: No, he isn't.

JIM: I like that answer. I like the logic. The logic of truth not existing until it's been proven again.

CAL: And it can be a very difficult thing to prove.

Pause.
JIM *spits and then gives* CAL *an empty cup to spit in.*

JIM: My instincts seem to be the same as Dave's, and I go with my instincts, Cal. I'm betting you'll be a fine addition to this team.   55

CAL: Thank you. I'll do my best . . .

JIM: Is that another answer out of that damn book?

CAL: No, it's not.

JIM: When you start at this firm, you start on probation, so I can see if you have what it takes to succeed.

CAL: That's fine.   60

JIM: You'll do some leg work for me, gathering some background information. Let's see what questions you come up with, what possibilities you create. (*JIM spits.*) I ask everyone if they'd like a dip of tobacco. No one ever says yes. Most people think it's disgusting.

CAL: Maybe that's why we like it.

JIM: Yes, yes, maybe that is why. I want you to meet someone, Cal. (*JIM buzzes the secretary.*) Send him in.

A man enters the office.

Cal, this will be your first client. His name is John Stutts. He bashed an elderly lady's head in with a baseball bat.

Lights down.

[1998]

Joining the Conversation: Critical Thinking and Writing

1. At the very beginning of *No Crime* Cal is described as "good looking" and Jim is described as "big." What difference(s) might it make in seeing, reading, or viewing the play if Cal were "big" and Jim were "good looking"?

2. If you were asked to perform in this play, which role would you select? Please explain why.

3. Many people find it disgusting to watch someone chew—and spit—tobacco. *Why* are these people revolted by this practice? Why, in your view, did Goda give this habit to Jim, and why did Goda have Cal join Jim in chewing tobacco?

4. In an interview Goda said that he admired the film director Martin Scorcese because "There is always an edge to his work, always a feeling of danger and violence." Would you say that in *No Crime* there is "always an edge"? Please explain.

5. Cal's basic argument is that the job of a lawyer is to make the district attorney *prove* the guilt of a client who the defending lawyer *knows* is guilty. Thus, a guilty person should be vigorously defended and should go free if the guilt is not *proved*. As many lawyers say, "Cases are tried in a court of *law*, not a court of justice." Do you believe that it is immoral for a lawyer who thinks the evidence is inconclusive to argue on behalf of a person who he knows is guilty? Set forth your response in an essay of 250–500 words.

Jane Lapotaire in *Antigone*. National Theatre, London, 1984. (Donald Cooper/Photostage)

SOPHOCLES

One of the three great writers of tragedies in ancient Greece, Sophocles (496?–406 BCE) was born in Colonus, near Athens, into a well-to-do family. Well educated, he first won public acclaim as a tragic poet at the age of twenty-seven, in 468 BCE, when he defeated Aeschylus in a competition for writing a tragic play. He is said to have written some 120 plays, but only seven tragedies are extant; among them are Oedipus the King *(page 463),* Antigone, *and* Oedipus at Colonus. *He died, much honored, in his ninetieth year, in Athens, where he had lived his entire life.*

BACKGROUND TO THE STORY: Once King of Thebes, Oedipus was the father of two sons, Polynices and Eteocles, and of two daughters, Antigone and Ismene. Oedipus unwittingly killed his father, Laius, and married his own mother, Jocasta. When he learned what he had done, he blinded himself and left Thebes. Eteocles and Polynices quarreled, Polynices was driven out but returned to assault Thebes. In the battle, each brother killed the other; Creon (uncle of Oedipus's four children) became king and ordered that Polynices (whom Creon regards as a traitor because he invaded his own land) be left to rot on the battlefield unburied.

Antigone

*Translated by Michael Townsend**

CHARACTERS

ANTIGONE	HAEMON	EURYDICE
ISMENE	TEIRESIAS	SERVANT
CREON	BOY	CHORUS
GUARD	MESSENGER	

*Stage directions and footnotes have been added by the editors.

[*Enter* ANTIGONE *and* ISMENE.]

ANTIGONE: My darling sister Ismene, we have had
          A fine inheritance from Oedipus.
          God has gone through the whole range of sufferings
          And piled them all on us,—grief upon grief,
          Humiliation upon humiliation.   5
          And now this latest thing that our dictator
          Has just decreed . . . you heard of it? Or perhaps
          You haven't noticed our enemies at work.
ISMENE: No news, either good or bad, has come
          To me, Antigone: nothing since the day   10
          We were bereaved of our two brothers. No,
          Since the withdrawal of the Argive army
          Last night, I've heard nothing about our loved ones
          To make me glad or sad.
ANTIGONE: I thought as much.
          That's why I brought you out, outside the gate,   15
          So we could have a talk here undisturbed.
ISMENE: You've something on your mind. What is it then?
ANTIGONE: Only that our friend Creon has decided
          To discriminate between our brothers' corpses.
          Eteocles he buried with full honors   20
          To light his way to hell in a blaze of glory.
          But poor dear Polynices,—his remains
          Are not allowed a decent burial.
          He must be left unmourned, without a grave,
          A happy hunting ground for birds   25
          To peck for tidbits. This ukase applies
          To you,—and me of course. What's more, friend Creon
          Is on his way here now to supervise
          Its circulation in person. And don't imagine
          He isn't serious,—the penalty   30
          For disobedience is to be stoned to death.
          So, there you have it. You're of noble blood.
          Soon you must show your mettle,—if you've any.
ISMENE: Oh my fire-eating sister, what am I
          Supposed to do about it, if this is the case?   35
ANTIGONE: Just think it over—if you'll give a hand . . .
ISMENE: In doing what? What do you have in mind?
ANTIGONE: Just helping me do something for the corpse.
ISMENE: You don't intend to bury him? It's forbidden.
ANTIGONE: He is my brother, and yours. My mind's made up.   40
          You please yourself.
ISMENE: But Creon has forbidden. . . .
ANTIGONE: What Creon says is quite irrelevant.
          He is my brother. I will bury him.
ISMENE: Oh God.
          Have you forgotten how our father died,   45
          Despised and hated? How he turned
          Detective to discover his own crimes,
          Then stabbed his own eyes out with his own hands?

And then Jocasta, who was both together
His mother and his wife,   50
Hanged herself with a rope? Next, our two brothers
Became each other's murderers. We are left,
We two. How terrible if we as well
Are executed for disobeying
The lawful orders of the head of state.   55
Oh please remember,—we are women, aren't we?
We shouldn't take on men. In times of crisis
It is the strongest men who take control.
We must obey their orders, however harsh.
So, while apologizing to the dead,   60
Regretting that I act under constraint,
I will comply with my superior's orders.
Sticking one's neck out would be merely foolish.

ANTIGONE: Don't think I'm forcing you. In fact, I wouldn't
Have your assistance if you offered it.   65
You've made your bed; lie on it. I intend
To give my brother burial. I'll be glad
To die in the attempt,—if it's a crime,
Then it's a crime that God commands. I then
Could face my brother as a friend and look   70
Him in the eyes. Why shouldn't I make sure
I get on with the dead rather than with
The living? There is all eternity
To while away below. And as for you,
By all means be an atheist if you wish.   75

ISMENE: I'm not. I'm simply powerless to act
Against this city's laws.

ANTIGONE: That's your excuse.
Good-bye. I'm going now to make a grave
For our brother, whom I love.

ISMENE: Oh, dear.
I'm terribly afraid for you.

ANTIGONE: Don't make a fuss   80
On my account,—look after your own skin.

ISMENE: At least then promise me that you will tell
No one of this; and I'll keep quiet too.

ANTIGONE: For God's sake don't do that,—you're sure to be
Far more unpopular if you keep quiet.   85
No; blurt it out, please do.

ISMENE: You're very cheerful.

ANTIGONE: That is because I'm helping those I know
That I should help.

ISMENE: I only hope you can,
But it's impossible.

ANTIGONE: Must I hang back
From trying, just because you say I can't?   90

ISMENE: If it's impossible, you shouldn't try
At all.

ANTIGONE: If that's your line, you've earned my hatred
And that of our dead brother too, by rights.

Oh, kindly let me go my foolish way,
And take the consequences. I will suffer   95
Nothing worse than death in a good cause.

ISMENE: All right then, off you go. I'm bound to say
You're being very loyal, but very silly.

[*Exit* ANTIGONE *and* ISMENE, *separately. Enter* CHORUS.]

CHORUS: At last it has dawned, the day that sees
The force that rode from Argos driven   100
Back upon its road again
With headlong horses on a looser rein.

Roused by Polynices to aid his claim,
Like an eagle screaming,
With snow-tipped wings and bloody claws   105
And mouth agape, it wheeled about our fortress doors.

But Thebes, a hissing snake, fought back.
The god of fire could get no grip
Upon our crown of walls. That bird of prey,
Its beak balked of our blood, has turned away.   110

God hates presumption. When he saw
Those men in ostentatious force
And clash of gold advancing,
He singled out one man all set
To shout the victory cry upon the parapet,   115
And flung at him a lightning bolt, to curtail his prancing.

Covered in flame he dropped
Down like an empty balance and drummed the earth;
He who before had breathed
The winds of hate against us. In many a foray and rout, 120
War, a runaway horse, was hitting out.

Seven enemy kings at seven gates,
Fighting at equal odds,
Left their arms as trophies to Theban gods.

Elsewhere, the hated pair,   125
Sons of the same mother,
Crossed their swords in combat and killed each other.

But now that Victory has smiled on us,
Let us forget the war, and dance
At every temple all night long. And let   130
Bacchus be king in Thebes, until the strong earth reels.

Ah, here comes Creon, our ruler,—in haste.
Something new has developed.
He has something afoot . . .
Else why has he summoned us to council?   135

[*Enter* CREON.]

CREON: Well, friends, our city has passed through stormy weather.
        But now God has restored an even keel.
        Why have I summoned you? Because I know
        That you were at all times loyal to Laius.
        And afterwards, when Oedipus put things right,   140
        Then ruined them again, you showed
        Your steadiness throughout his sons' dispute.
        Well, now they're dead; and so, by due succession,
        The power of the crown passes to me.
        You cannot possibly judge a ruler's worth   145
        Until he exercises the power he's got.
        I've no time for the man who has full powers
        Yet doesn't use them to enact good measures,
        But adopts a timid policy of "do nothing."
        Those aren't my principles. I'm not the man   150
        To sit quietly by and watch my country
        Sliding towards the precipice of ruin.
        Nor can I be a friend to my country's foes.
        This I believe—and God may witness it—
        Our safety is bound up with that of our country. Therefore   155
        All other loyalties are subject to
        Our country's interests.
        By such measures I'll make this city great;—
        Measures like those that I have just enacted
        Concerning Oedipus' sons. That Eteocles   160
        Who died while fighting in his country's service,
        Is to be buried with ceremonial honors.
        But Polynices,—whose intention was
        To fight his way back from exile, burn to the ground
        His mother city and the temples of   165
        His family's gods, to slaughter out of hand
        And to enslave his fellow citizens—
        He's not to have a grave or any mourning.
        His corpse is to be left, a grim warning,
        Pecked at by birds and worried by the dogs.   170
        That is my policy. A malefactor mustn't
        Have the same treatment as the loyal man.
        I intend to see our country's friends rewarded
        When they are dead, as well as while they live.
CHORUS: We understand the attitude you take   175
        Towards these men. It's true your word is law,
        And you can legislate for living and dead. . . .
CREON: What do you think then of this new enactment?
CHORUS: If I were younger, I might criticize. . . .
CREON: No turning back. The guard is set on the corpse.   180
CHORUS: What are the penalties for disobeying?
CREON: The penalty is death. As simple as that.
CHORUS: That ought to stop them. Who'd be such a fool?
CREON: You'd be surprised. Men led astray by hopes
        Of gain will risk even their lives for money.   185

[*Enter* GUARD.]

GUARD: Sir, here I am. I can't pretend I'm puffed
          From running here with all possible speed.
          I kept changing my mind on the way.
          One moment I was thinking, "What's the hurry?
          You're bound to catch it when you get there." Then: 190
          "What are you dithering for? You'll get it hot
          And strong if Creon finds out from someone else."
          Torn by these doubts I seem to have taken my time.
          So what should be a short journey has become
          A long one. Anyway I have arrived.   195
          And now I'm going to tell you what I came
          To tell you, even if you've heard it. See,
          I've made up my mind to expect the worst.
          We can't avoid what's coming to us, can we?
CREON: Well then, what puts you in such deep despair?   200
GUARD: First I must make a statement—about myself.
          I didn't do it, and didn't see who did it.
          So I'm quite in the clear, you understand.
CREON: For God's sake tell me what it is, and then
          Get out.
GUARD: All right, all right. It amounts to this.   205
          Somebody's buried the body, thrown earth on it,
          And done the necessary purifications.
CREON: Someone has been a damn fool. Who was it?
GUARD: Dunno. There were no spade-marks in the earth.
          The ground was hard and dry, and so there was   210
          No sign of the intruder.
          See, when the man who had the first day watch
          Told us about it, we had the shock of our lives.
          The corpse had not been buried in a grave,
          But enough dust was thrown on to avoid   215
          The curse unburied bodies suffer from.
          There wasn't even a sign of any dog
          That might have come and scuffed the dust upon him.
          Then everyone started shouting. Each man blamed
          His mate. We very nearly came to blows.   220
          Everyone claimed that one of the others had done it,
          And tried to prove that he himself was blameless.
          To prove their innocence, some said they were
          Prepared to pick up red-hot coals or walk
          Through fire. While others swore on oath,   225
          By a catalog of gods, they didn't do it
          And weren't accomplices in any form.
          When our investigations made no progress,
          In the end one man came out with a sobering speech.
          We couldn't answer him, though what he said   230
          Was none too pleasant.
          He said we mustn't try to hush it up,
          But tell you everything. His view prevailed.
          Who was to bring the news? We tossed for it.
          I was the lucky person. I can tell you,   235

I don't like being the bearer of bad news.

CHORUS: I think I see the hand of God in this,
　　　　Bringing about the body's burial.

CREON: Shut up, before I lose my temper.
　　　　You may be old, try not to be foolish as well.　　　　240
　　　　How can you say God cares about this corpse?
　　　　Do you suppose God feels obliged to him
　　　　For coming to burn down his temples and
　　　　His statues, in defiance of his laws?
　　　　Ever noticed God being kind to evildoers?　　　　245
　　　　No. Certain hostile elements in the city
　　　　Who don't like discipline and resent my rule,
　　　　Are in on this. They've worked upon the guards
　　　　By bribes. There is no human institution
　　　　As evil as money. Money ruins nations,　　　　250
　　　　And makes men refugees. Money corrupts
　　　　The best of men into depravity.
　　　　The people who have done this thing for money
　　　　Will get what's coming to them. Listen here,
　　　　I swear to you by God who is my judge,　　　　255
　　　　That if you and your friends do not divulge
　　　　The name of him who did the burying
　　　　One hell won't be enough for you. You'll all
　　　　Be hanged up and flogged until you tell.
　　　　That ought to teach you to be more selective　　　　260
　　　　About what you get your money from.

GUARD:　　　　　　　　　　　　　　　Am I dismissed?
　　　　Or may I speak?

CREON:　　　　　　　　I thought I made it plain
　　　　I couldn't stand your talk.

GUARD:　　　　　　　　　　　Where does it hurt you,—
　　　　Your ears, or in your mind?

CREON:　　　　　　　　　　　What do you mean?
　　　　What does it matter where you give me pain?　　　　265

GUARD: The guilty party bothers you deep down.
　　　　But my offense is only at ear level.

CREON: My dear good man, you're much too talkative.

GUARD: I may be that, but I am not your culprit.

CREON: I think you are, and that you did it for money.　　　　270

GUARD: Oh God! I tell you your suspicions are wrong.

CREON: Suspicion he calls it! Look here, if you
　　　　Don't tell me who the culprits are, you'll find
　　　　That ill-gotten gains are not without their drawbacks. [*Exit* CREON.]

GUARD: Good luck to you, I hope you find the man.　　　　275
　　　　In any case I won't be in a hurry
　　　　To come back here again. I thank my stars
　　　　That I have saved my skin. I didn't expect to. [*Exit* GUARD.]

CHORUS: Many amazing things exist, and the most amazing is man.
　　　　He's the one, when the gale-force winds　　　　280
　　　　Blow and the big waves
　　　　Tower and topple on every side,
　　　　Cruises over the deep on the gray tide.

He's the one that to and fro
Over the clods year after year   285
Wends with his horses and ploughing gear,
Works to his will the untiring Earth, the greatest of gods.

He traps the nitwit birds, and the wild
Beasts in their lairs. The ocean's myriad clan
In woven nets he catches,—ingenious man.   290

He has devised himself shelter against
The rigors of frost and the pelting weather.
Speech and science he's taught himself,
And the city's political arts for living together.

For incurable diseases he has found a cure;   295
By his inventiveness defying
Every eventuality there can be,—except dying.

But the most brilliant gifts
Can be misapplied.
On his moral road   300
Man swerves from side to side.

God and the government ordain
Just laws; the citizen
Who rules his life by them
Is worthy of acclaim.   305

But he that presumes
To set the law at naught
Is like a stateless person,
Outlawed, beyond the pale.

With such a man I'd have   310
No dealings whatsoever.
In public and in private
He'd get the cold shoulder.

What's this? What on earth?
My God. Can it be? Yes, Antigone.   315
Your father before, now you!
Is it so, you were caught disobeying the law?
How could you have been so stupid?

    [Enter GUARD *with* ANTIGONE.]

GUARD: Here she is. She is the one,—the one that did it.
    We caught her in the act. Where's Creon gone?   320
CHORUS: There, by good luck he's coming out right now.

[Enter CREON.]

CREON: Soon as I leave the house, some trouble starts.
    What's happening?
GUARD: Well, well, I never thought
    That I'd be coming back here again so soon,

Considering how you swore at me just now. 325
But here I am, in spite of what I said.
I'm bringing in this girl. I caught her tending
The grave. I caught her, no one else. And so
I hand her over to you to stand her trial.
And now I reckon I'm entitled to beat it. 330

CREON: Give me full details, with the circumstances.

GUARD: This girl was burying him. As simple as that.

CREON: I trust you understand what you are saying.

GUARD: I saw her burying the corpse you said
Was not permitted to be buried. Clear enough? 335

CREON: Tell me precisely how you saw and caught her.

GUARD: It was like this. When we got back,
With your threats still smarting in our ears,
We swept all the dust from off the corpse,
And laid the moldering thing completely bare. 340
Then we went and sat on the high ground to windward,
To avoid the smell. And everyone gave hell
To the man who was on duty, to keep him up
To scratch. We watched till midday, when the sun
Is hottest. Suddenly a squall came on,— 345
A whirlwind with a thunderstorm; it ripped
The leaves from every tree in all the plain.
The air was full of it; we had to keep
Our eyes tight shut against the wrath of heaven.
At last, when all was over, there we see 350
The girl,—crying like a bird that finds
Its nest empty of chicks,—her having seen
The corpse uncovered. Then she started cursing
Whoever did it. Next she goes and fetches
Dust in her hands; and from a jug she pours 355
A set of three libations on the corpse.
When we saw that of course we jumped straight up
And grabbed the girl. She took it very calmly.
We charged her with this crime and the previous one,
And she admitted them. So I'm half glad, 360
Half sorry. Glad that I am out of danger,
But sorry someone that I like's in trouble.
However, main thing is that I'm all right.

CREON: You, with your eyes fixed on the ground.
Do you admit the charges or deny them? 365

ANTIGONE: I don't deny the charges. I admit them.

CREON: (*to* GUARD) All right, clear off. [*Exit* GUARD.] Consider yourself lucky
To be absolved of guilt.
(*to* ANTIGONE) Now tell me, briefly,—I don't want a speech.
You knew about my edict which forbade this? 370

ANTIGONE: Of course I knew. You made it plain enough.

CREON: You took it on yourself to disobey?

ANTIGONE: Sorry, who made this edict? Was it God?
Isn't a man's right to burial decreed
By divine justice? I don't consider your 375

Pronouncements so important that they can
Just . . . overrule the unwritten laws of heaven.
You are a man, remember.
These divine laws are not just temporary measures.
They stand forever. I would have to face   380
Them when I died. And I will die, without
Your troubling to arrange it. So, what matter
If I must die before my time? I'd welcome
An early death, living as I do now.
What I can't stand is passively submitting   385
To my own brother's body being unburied.
I dare say you think I'm being silly.
Perhaps you're not so very wise yourself.

CHORUS: She's difficult, just like her father was.
    She doesn't realize when to give in.   390

CREON: I know these rigid temperaments. They're the first
    To break. The hardest-tempered steel
    Will shatter at a blow. The highest-mettled
    Horses are broken in with a small bit.
    That's what is needed, discipline. This girl   395
    Knew damned well she was kicking over the traces,
    Breaking the law. And now when she has done it,
    She boasts about it, positively gloats.
    If she gets away with this behavior,
    Call me a woman and call her a man.   400
    I don't care if she is my sister's daughter.
    I don't care if she's closer to me than all
    My family. She and her sister won't get off.
    I'll execute them.
                Oh yes, her as well.
    She's in it too. Go get her. She's inside.   405
    I saw her in there muttering, half-balmy.
    It is her conscience. She can't hide her guilt.
    At least she doesn't try to justify it.

ANTIGONE: Won't my death be enough? Do you want more?
CREON: No, that will do, as far as I'm concerned.   410
ANTIGONE: Then why not do it now? Our wills conflict
    Head-on. No chance of reconciliation.
    I can't think of a finer reason for dying,—
    Guilty of having buried my own brother.
    These men are on my side. But they daren't say so.   415
CREON: That's where you're wrong. You're quite alone in this.
ANTIGONE: They're on my side. They're forced to cringe to you.
CREON: These men obey. But you and you alone
    Decide to disobey. Aren't you ashamed?
ANTIGONE: Ashamed? Ashamed of what? Ashamed of being   420
    Loyal to my own family, my own brother?
CREON: Eteocles was also your own brother.
ANTIGONE: Indeed he was. Of course he was my brother.
CREON: Then why were you so disloyal to him?
ANTIGONE: If he were living now, he'd back me up.   425

CREON: For treating his brother no differently from him!

ANTIGONE: It was his brother that died, not just some servant.

CREON: Died while commanding an invading force!
　　　But Eteocles died fighting for his country.

ANTIGONE: That doesn't affect the laws of burial.　　　　　　　　　430

CREON: You can't treat friend and enemy the same.

ANTIGONE: Who knows what the rules are among the dead?

CREON: Your enemy doesn't become your friend by dying.

ANTIGONE: If we must have these groupings, let me say
　　　I'll join anyone in loving, but not in hating.　　　　　　　435

CREON: All right then, die, and love them both in hell.
　　　I'm not here to be shoved around by a woman.

　　[*Enter* ISMENE, *guarded.*]

CHORUS: Oh, look, by the gate, here's Ismene.
　　　She's crying because of her sister.
　　　What a shame this heavy cloud of grief　　　　　　　　　440
　　　Should spoil her attractive appearance.

CREON: And now for you. You who've been skulking quiet,
　　　Injecting your slow poison like a viper.
　　　Imagine my not noticing,—I've been rearing
　　　Two furies in my house, ready to bite　　　　　　　　　　445
　　　The hand that fed them. Just you tell me now—
　　　Will you confess you were party to this burial,
　　　Or will you swear you had no knowledge of it?

ISMENE: I did it, if she did it. I'm involved.
　　　I'm in with her and bear my share of blame.　　　　　　　450

ANTIGONE: That's quite unjustified. You didn't want
　　　To help me, and I didn't let you join me.

ISMENE: You are in trouble. May I then not make
　　　Myself your comrade in adversity?

ANTIGONE: The dead know who it was that did the deed.　　　　455
　　　You took no action. Your speeches don't impress me.

ISMENE: How can you, being my sister, deny my wish
　　　To die with you for Polynices' sake?

ANTIGONE: Don't go and die as well as me, and don't
　　　Lay claim to what you haven't done. I'm going　　　　　460
　　　To die. One death's enough.

ISMENE: 　　　　　　　　　　　　Will life be worth
　　　Living to me, left all alone without you?

ANTIGONE: May I suggest an object of affection?
　　　Creon. He is your uncle, after all.

ISMENE: Why do you try to hurt me? What's the point?　　　　465

ANTIGONE: I may make fun of you, but I feel this deeply.

ISMENE: I only want to know how I can help you.

ANTIGONE: Well, save yourself then. I don't grudge you that.

ISMENE: I don't want that. I want to die with you.

ANTIGONE: You chose to live; I chose to die, remember?　　　470

ISMENE: I didn't express my innermost convictions.

ANTIGONE: You sounded pretty convinced at the time.

ISMENE: I still maintain that we two share the guilt.

ANTIGONE: Don't worry. You won't die. But I've already
　　　　Sacrificed my life to help the dead.   475
CREON: These girls! One of them's been mad all her life.
　　　　And now the other one's gone balmy too.
ISMENE: But, sir, however sensible one is,
　　　　Adversity is bound to affect one's judgment.
CREON: Well, it has yours! You join this criminal,   480
　　　　And identify yourself with her misdeeds . . .
ISMENE: There is no life left for me without her.
CREON: Forget about her. She's as good as dead.
ISMENE: So you would execute your own son's bride?
CREON: Plenty of other women in the world.   485
ISMENE: But they were so well suited to each other.
CREON: I won't have my son marrying a bitch.
ANTIGONE: Poor Haemon! See how much your father cares.
CREON: Oh, go to hell,—you and your marriage with you.
ISMENE: You really intend to take her from your son?   490
CREON: I won't stop the marriage. Death will stop it.
ISMENE: There's no way out? It is fixed that she dies?
CREON: Of course it's fixed. Stop wasting time.
　　　　You servants, take her in. It's very important
　　　　To keep women strictly disciplined.   495
　　　　That's the deterrent. Even the bravest people
　　　　Will step down quick when they see death loom up.

　　　　　　[*Exit* ISMENE, ANTIGONE, *and* GUARDS.]

CHORUS: Happy the man whose life is uneventful.
　　　　For once a family is cursed by God,
　　　　Disasters come like earthquake tremors, worse   500
　　　　With each succeeding generation.

　　　　It's like when the sea is running rough
　　　　Under stormy winds from Thrace.
　　　　The black ooze is stirred up from the sea-bed,
　　　　And louder and louder the waves crash on shore.   505

　　　　Look now at the last sunlight that sustains
　　　　The one surviving root of Oedipus' tree,—
　　　　The sword of death is drawn to hack it down.

　　　　And all through nothing more than intemperate language.
　　　　All through nothing more than hasty temper.   510

　　　　What power on earth can resist
　　　　Your strength, O God? You stand supreme,
　　　　Untouched by sleep that makes all else feel old,
　　　　Untired by the passing years that wear all else away.

　　　　I know one rule that has stood,   515
　　　　And will stand, forever.
　　　　That nothing in our life can be exempt
　　　　From the universal forces that make for ruin.

Hope, that tramps all roads, may help at times.
More often, it deludes weak-minded men.   520
They never notice, till they feel the fire.

It is a wise saying, that
When God is set against you,
You welcome the path to ruin,—but not for long.

Here comes Haemon, your youngest son.   525
I expect he's grieved about his bride,
And this sudden bar to his marriage.

[*Enter* HAEMON.]

CREON: There's one way of finding out for certain.
        My son, you've heard about this public decree.
        Have you come here in a spirit of indignation   530
        About your bride, or are you going to be
        Loyal to me whatever I'm involved in?
HAEMON: I am your son. So while your policies
        Are just, you have my full obedience.
        I certainly wouldn't consider any marriage   535
        As important as the right leadership by you.
CREON: Good, good. Your heart is in the right place. Nothing
        Should come before your loyalty to your father.
        Why else do fathers pray for well-behaved sons?
        They do things together. Work together against   540
        Their common enemy. Vie with each
        Other in being good friends to their friends.
        As for the man who brings up useless sons,
        He's got himself a load of trouble,—all
        His enemies laugh at them, a bad team.   545
        Never get carried away by a woman, son.
        Sex isn't everything. If she's a bitch,
        You'll feel a coldness as she lies beside you.
        Can there be anything worse than giving your love
        To a bitch that doesn't deserve it? No, reject her,   550
        And let her go and find a husband in hell.
        Now that I've caught her flagrantly disobeying
        When everybody else has toed the line,
        The eyes of the nation are on me. I must stay
        True to my principles. I must execute her.   555
        I don't give a damn for all her talk
        About family ties. If I allow
        My own relations to get out of control,
        That gives the cue to everybody else.
        People who are loyal members of their families   560
        Will be good citizens too. But if a person
        Sets himself up above the law and tries
        To tell his rulers what they ought to do,—
        You can't expect me to approve of that.
        Once a man has authority, he must be obeyed,—   565
        In big things and in small, in every act,

Whether just or not so just. I tell you this,
The well-disciplined man is good
At giving orders and taking them too.
In war, in a crisis, he's the sort of man   570
You like to have beside you. On the other hand,
There's nothing so disastrous as anarchy.
Anarchy means an ill-disciplined army,
A rabble that will break into a panic rout.
What follows? Plundered cities, homeless people.   575
A disciplined army loses few men;
Discipline pulls them through to victory.
We can't go about kowtowing to women.
If I must lose my throne, let it be a man
That takes it from me. I can't have people saying   580
My will has been defeated by a woman.

CHORUS: I think your observations very just,
          In general . . . though perhaps I'm old and silly.

HAEMON: Father, don't you agree,—
          Of all God's gifts, good sense is far the best.   585
          I'm sure I'd be the last person to deny
          That what you said is true. Yet there may be
          A lot of justice in the opposite view.
          I've one advantage over you,—I know
          Before you what the people think about you,   590
          Especially criticism. You're so held in awe
          That people dare not say things to your face.
          But I am able to hear their secret talk.
          The people feel sorry for Antigone.
          They say it isn't equitable she must die   595
          A horrible death for such a noble action.
          They say that she in fact deserves special
          Honor for refusing to allow
          The body of her brother to be left
          Unburied for dogs and birds to pull to pieces.   600
          That is their secret opinion, and it's gaining ground.
          Of course I want your rule to be a success.
          There's nothing more important to me than that.
          Such feeling is mutual, between father and son,—
          One's glad to see the other doing well.   605
          Don't be too single-minded, then. Don't think
          You have a complete monopoly of the truth.
          Isn't it true that people who refuse
          To see any other point of view but theirs
          Often get shown up and discredited?   610
          However acute one is, there's no disgrace
          In being able to learn, being flexible.
          In winter, when the streams turn into torrents,
          You can see the trees that try to resist the water
          Get rooted out and killed. But those that bend   615
          A little, manage to survive the flood.
          In a gale at sea if you cram on full sail,
          You'll soon have the waves breaking aboard

And bowling over all the furniture.
Why not relax and change your mind for once?   620
Perhaps at my age I should not express
An opinion, but I would like to say this:—
Not everyone can be right on every issue,
But the next best thing is to take notice of
And learn from the judicious thoughts of others.   625
CHORUS: Yes, everyone can learn. You, sir, can learn
    From him,—and he of course from you. There's much
    Of substance in the arguments on both sides.
CREON: Am I to stand here and be lectured to
    By a kid? A man of my experience!   630
HAEMON: I'm not suggesting anything illegal.
    I may be young, but judge me by the facts.
CREON: The facts are, you're encouraging my detractors.
HAEMON: I'm not encouraging anything that's wrong.
CREON: You seem to have caught Antigone's disease.   635
HAEMON: The people of Thebes don't call it a disease.
CREON: Must I ask their permission for everything?
HAEMON: You're talking like an adolescent now.
CREON: Am I the king of Thebes, or am I not?
HAEMON: It takes more than one person to make a nation.   640
CREON: But a nation is personified in its ruler.
HAEMON: In that case Thebes has got no population.
CREON: I take it you are siding with this woman.
HAEMON: It is your interests I have at heart.
CREON: You show it by arguing against me?   645
HAEMON: Because I think you're making a mistake.
CREON: Must I let my authority be undermined?
HAEMON: Yes, rather your authority than God's.
CREON: What character! Subservient to a woman
HAEMON: Subservient to what I think is right.   650
CREON: You've done nothing but back Antigone up.
HAEMON: Not only her, but God, and you as well.
CREON: Don't try to butter me up, you ladies' man.
HAEMON: You like to talk, but you're not prepared to listen.
CREON: This woman will not live to marry you.   655
HAEMON: Then she won't be the only one to die.
CREON: Oh, oh. Threats is it now? You've got a nerve.
HAEMON: I'm trying to show you that you're being perverse.
CREON: You will regret you tried to schoolmaster me.
HAEMON: If you weren't my father, I'd say you were deranged.   660
CREON: What's that? I've had enough of your abuse.
    By heaven, I swear I'll make you suffer for it.
    Take that hell-cat away. You'll watch her die.
    Ha, she will die in front of her bridegroom's nose.
HAEMON: I won't give you that satisfaction.   665
    I won't be around when she dies.
    You must find other friends to condone your madness.
    You will never set eyes on me again. [*Exit* HAEMON.]
CHORUS: He's rushed off in a really furious temper.
    He's young,—I fear he may do something rash.   670

CREON: Let him.
        Who does he think he is, God almighty?
        In any case, he won't save these girls from death.
CHORUS: You don't mean to execute them both?
CREON: No, no. You're right. Not her that wasn't involved.   675
CHORUS: What sort of execution do you intend?
CREON: I'll take her to a deserted spot
        And bury her alive in a trench.
        She'll have enough food to avoid the curse,—
        The people mustn't suffer because of her.   680
        There she can pray to the god she likes so much,—
        The god of death. Perhaps he'll save her life.
        Either that, or she'll find out too late
        That corpses are more trouble than they're worth.
CHORUS: What is it that nestles in   685
        The soft cheeks of a girl,
        And pervades the deep sea and the teeming earth,
        And persecutes god and man, a force
        Irresistible? We call it Love.
        A man possessed by Love loses control.   690
        Love drives the law-abiding into crime;
        And sets a family against itself.

        So here a lovely girl's appealing glance
        Has prevailed, and destroyed the bonds of blood.
        For Love makes mock of time-honored laws   695
        Ordaining loyalty from son to father.

        And grief also is irresistible.
        The tears come to my eyes,—I cannot stop them;
        Seeing Antigone go to such a bed,
        The bed that puts all mortal things to sleep.   700

ANTIGONE: Take a good look. With life still strong in me,
        I'm going on my last journey, seeing
        For the last time the bright rays of the sun.
        Unmarried, never having heard my wedding song,
        Death takes me to the dark riverbanks to be his bride.   705
CHORUS: You have one glorious consolation.
        By your own choice you go down to death
        Alive, not wasted by disease,
        Nor hacked by instruments of war.
ANTIGONE: I shall go to sleep like Niobe.°   710
        I know her story well. On Mount Sipylus
        The rock grew, like ivy, round her and weighed her down.
        And now the rain and snow
        Make tears that run across her stony face.
CHORUS: There's no comparison. For she was born   715
        Of divine parentage. You would be lucky
        To share the fate of mythical heroines.

710 Niobe Niobe boasted of her numerous children, provoking Apollo's mother to destroy them.
Niobe wept uncontrollably, and was turned into stone on Mount Sipylus, whose streams are her tears.

ANTIGONE: Are you getting at me? Wait till I'm dead.
　　　　　I'm going to die,—do I merit no respect?
　　　　　O my city, O my friends, rich householders,　　　　　720
　　　　　O river Dirce, with the sacred grove
　　　　　Of Thebes the Charioteer, I call you all
　　　　　To witness that I die with nobody
　　　　　To shed a tear for me, the victim
　　　　　Of an unjust law. Who'd like to go with me　　　　　725
　　　　　To an eerie heap of stones, a tomb that is no tomb,
　　　　　A no-man's land between the living and the dead?

CHORUS: You tried to do the right thing by your brother.
　　　　You stepped boldly towards the altar of Justice,
　　　　But somehow stumbled. I fear you must suffer　　　　　730
　　　　For your father's sins.

ANTIGONE: Don't speak of it again. It's only too well known,—
　　　　　My father's fate. To think how much
　　　　　Our family was admired, in generations past.
　　　　　Then came successive strokes of doom. My mother's　　　　　735
　　　　　Marriage to her son, the union
　　　　　From which I came, to end like this.
　　　　　My brother, dishonored, drags me down with him,
　　　　　And so I go to join my stricken family in hell.

CHORUS: We respect what you did for your brother.　　　　　740
　　　　But there's no question that the orders
　　　　Of those in authority must be obeyed.
　　　　You were self-willed. That has been your undoing.

ANTIGONE: I see I have no friends to say good-bye.
　　　　　No friends, no tears for me, no marriage to look back on.　　　　　745
　　　　　Never again to see the face of the sun.

CREON: If I don't stop this blubbering, we'll be here
　　　　All night. Stop wasting time. Take her away
　　　　As my instructions state, you are to place
　　　　Her in the vaulted trench, and brick it in.　　　　　750
　　　　It's up to her then,—either live or die.
　　　　My hands are clean in this. I've merely
　　　　Deprived her of all contact with the living.

ANTIGONE: This stone dugout, half tomb, half bridal-chamber,
　　　　　Will house me now for good. By this road　　　　　755
　　　　　I go below to Queen Persephone's kingdom,
　　　　　To see again so many of my family.
　　　　　As I am the latest recruit, so is my fate
　　　　　By far the cruelest. And I've not used
　　　　　My life's full span.　　　　　760
　　　　　At least I can look forward to a warm
　　　　　Welcome from my dear mother and father and
　　　　　My brother Eteocles. When they were dead,
　　　　　I washed them and prepared them for the grave
　　　　　With my own hands, and poured libations over them.　　　　　765
　　　　　But now, for doing the same to Polynices,
　　　　　This is my reward. Because Creon thinks
　　　　　I have committed an act of brazen defiance.

For this I'm being dragged off by force,
Deprived of my chance to marry and raise children.   770
I'm to be buried alive, not very pleasant. . . .
I just want to ask, what moral law
Have I disobeyed? But what's the point
Of appealing to God? Or asking
Help from my fellow humans? It appears   775
That virtue is to be repaid by malice.
If that is God's idea of what is right,
Then I apologize; I made a mistake.
But if Creon is wrong, I only hope
He isn't treated any better than me.   780

CHORUS: A hurricane of passionate conviction
Still sweeps her mind.

CREON: Don't stand about, you lot; or else . . .
Hurry, and off with her.

ANTIGONE: Oh, right before me now. Death.   785

CHORUS: If you had any hopes, I should forget them.
Your punishment is fixed. There's no appeal.

ANTIGONE: This is it. The time has come.
For doing what was right,
I'm dragged away to death.   790
And Thebes, city where I was born,
And you my friends, the rich people of Thebes,
Will you judge between us?
You might at least look and remember.

[*Exit* ANTIGONE *guarded*.]

CHORUS: My poor child, what must be   795
Must be. Console yourself,
Such things have happened before.

There's nothing that can win the fight
Against the force of destiny;
Not wealth, or military might,   800
Or city walls, or ships that breast the sea.

Lycurgus, king of Thrace, tried to stop
The bacchanal women and their torchlit orgies.
For his vindictive rage,
He lost his liberty with his temper, locked   805
By Bacchus in a mountain cave
To let his anger simmer down.

In Salmydessus on the Euxine Sea,
The two sons of Phineus lost their eyes.
In their stepmother's hand, a pointed shuttle . . .   810
And their blood on her nails cried out for vengeance.

But their mother was jailed in a cavern
Under a steep mountain far away.
She was Cleopatra, the North Wind's daughter.
A god's daughter, but fate weighed her down.   815

[*Enter* TEIRESIAS, *led by a boy.*]

TEIRESIAS: Councillors of Thebes, I have come,—
    A man with four eyes, half of them blind . . .
CREON: It's old Teiresias. What's up, old fellow?
TEIRESIAS: Listen, and I will tell you. I'm no liar . . .
CREON: I've never suggested that. Quite the reverse.   820
TEIRESIAS: By doing so, you were able to save Thebes.
CREON: True, I have found what you have said most useful.
TEIRESIAS: Listen to me. You're on the razor's edge.
CREON: What's wrong? The way you talk gives me a turn.
TEIRESIAS: You may think nothing's wrong. But my skill   825
    Says differently.
    I went to my accustomed place
    Of augury, where there's a wide view of
    The sky, to observe the birds. There I heard
    An unprecedented din of birds, barbarous,   830
    Confused, as though some madness stung them into
    Screaming. I heard them fighting with their claws;
    The noise was unmistakable, their wings
    Whirring . . . and I felt fear. Immediately
    I tried the burnt sacrifices, but   835
    They gave no flame. Only a damp vapor
    Smoldered and spat. The gall burst in the fire,
    Exposing the thighbones bare of fat.
    The boy saw all this and told it me.
    Thus I interpret. These signs portend evil   840
    For Thebes; and the trouble stems from your policy.
    Why? Because our altars are polluted
    By flesh brought by dogs and birds, pickings
    From Polynices' corpse. Small wonder that
    The gods won't accept our sacrifices.   845
    My son, I ask you to consider well
    What you are doing. We all make mistakes.
    The wise man, having made an error of judgment,
    Will seek a remedy, not keep grinding on.
    Obstinacy isn't far removed from folly.   850
    The man is dead. No need to persecute him.
    You can give way, with good grace, to a corpse.
    He has died once, why try to kill him again?
    I'm saying this because I wish you well.
    A bit of sound advice is always welcome.   855
CREON: Money! Must everyone set their cap at me
    Because of money? Even you augurers
    Have formed a corporation to exploit me.
    For years now I have been traded about
    By your gang in the open market like   860
    A piece of merchandise. All right, rake in
    The cash, pile up the wealth of Lydia
    And all the gold of India in bribes.
    You'll never persuade me to bury that corpse.
    Not even if the eagles of Zeus decide   865

To carry off its flesh in their claws
And place it right on their master's throne.
I refuse for the simple reason that
It's quite impossible for any man
To throw pollution on the gods. They are   870
Inviolate. But certain gifted men
That I could mention do not seem to mind
A little sharp practice, in the matter
Of telling a lie or two, strictly for cash.

TEIRESIAS: Well!   875
Can there exist a man who doesn't know . . .

CREON: Watch out, here comes another resounding cliché!

TEIRESIAS: . . . Good sense is a man's most precious attribute?

CREON: And bad judgment is a great encumbrance?

TEIRESIAS: It's an encumbrance you have plenty of.   880

CREON: . . . . No.
You started it, but I won't insult a "seer."

TEIRESIAS: You've done that already,—accused me of lying.

CREON: The whole lot of you seers are on the make.

TEIRESIAS: Kings also have been known to make their pile.   885

CREON: Are you implying some reflection on me?

TEIRESIAS: You wouldn't be king now, but for me.

CREON: You're good at your job. But you've gone crooked.

TEIRESIAS: Much more of this, and you'll make me reveal . . .

CREON: Reveal away. But straight, and not for bribes.   890

TEIRESIAS: You'll wish you had bribed me not to speak . . .

CREON: Don't try to pull the wool over my eyes.

TEIRESIAS: The sun won't run its course for many days
Before you have to repay a corpse of your own,
One of your own children as recompense.   895
One body that belongs to this world
You have locked up in a tomb. Another body
That rightly should be in the underworld
You have forcibly retained here on earth.
Because of this, the Furies have been waiting   900
To pay you back in your own coin. And so
It won't be long before your house is full
Of grief; I can see men and women crying.
Make up your own mind whether I've been bribed
To say this. Yes, it hurts. But you provoked me.   905
My boy, take me home. I'm not so young,—
I dare not be around when he explodes.
I only hope he learns from this to show
A little sense and keep a civil tongue. [*Exit* TEIRESIAS.]

CHORUS: That was a horrible prophecy.   910
I'm bound to say I've never known him wrong
In any of his predictions.

CREON: Yes, I know,
I know. I can't pretend that I'm not worried.
The consequences of giving in are terrible.
But if I hold out, I court disaster.   915

CHORUS: The right decision now is vitally important.
CREON: What should I do then? Tell me what to do.
CHORUS: You'll have to go and set Antigone free,
      And give the exposed corpse a burial.
CREON: Is that your real opinion? To give in?   920
CHORUS: And waste no time about it, for the wrath
      Of God will not be slow to catch you up.
CREON: Can't fight against what's destined. It is hard,
      But I'll change my mind. You servants,—
      Pick-axes, hurry, and come with me. I must   925
      Personally undo what I have done.
      I shouldn't have tried being unorthodox.
      I'll stick by the established laws in the future. [*Exit* CREON.]
CHORUS: We call on Bacchus, god of many names,
      And god of many places.   930
      You were once a little child
      In Thebes here, the darling of your mother's eye.
      Your father was Zeus, lord of the thundering sky;
      But your mother was Semele, a Theban girl.

      Are you among the rich cities   935
      Of Italy? Or presiding
      Over the cosmopolitan crowds
      That throng the Eleusinian Games?°

      Perhaps the firebrand lights your face
      Between the twin peaks of Mount Parnassus,   940
      Where the nymphs of Castaly°
      And Corycus walk free.

      Perhaps you hear the songs of poets
      Where the ivy wreathes the crags
      On Nysa, looking over green   945
      Vineyards clustering on the plain.

      But this is your home,—the oil-like waters
      Of Ismene River, and the fields
      Where the dragon's teeth were sown.

      This is your mother city, Thebes.   950
      This is the city you honor most.
      If ever you heard us before, come to us now.
      Our nation is in the grip of a dread disease.
      Hasten to help us, speed to doctor our pain
      Over the slopes of Parnes Hill or over the roaring seas.   955

    [*Enter* MESSENGER.]

MESSENGER: Citizens of Thebes, who knows how long
      Their luck will last? Whether you're up or down,
      It's all pure chance. You can't predict what's coming.
      Take Creon now. I thought he was doing well,—

938 Eleusis in ancient Greece was the site of celebrations for cults celebrating Demeter and
Persephone.   **941 Castaly** and **Corycus** are the names of springs.

The savior of his country, king of Thebes,   960
And the proud father of a lovely family.
He's lost the lot. Oh, yes, he's wealthy still;
But wealth can't buy you happiness. What's the use
Of money without the means of enjoying it?
His wealth's no more to him than a puff of smoke.   965
You can't say Creon lives; he's just a walking corpse.
CHORUS: About Creon's family, is there bad news then?
MESSENGER: They're dead. And those that live deserve to die.
CHORUS: How did they die? Who's dead? Why can't you tell me?
MESSENGER: Haemon is dead. Committed suicide.   970
CHORUS: He killed himself? His father didn't do it?
MESSENGER: Suicide, because Creon had murdered her.
CHORUS: Teiresias' prophecy was all too true.
MESSENGER: That's what has happened. Now it's up to you.

[*Enter* EURYDICE.]

CHORUS: Here is Eurydice, Creon's wife, poor woman.   975
          Why is she coming out? Perhaps she's heard. . . .
EURYDICE: As I was going out, I heard you talking.
          I was opening the door when I heard it,
          Some more bad news about my children. I fainted,
          But my maids held me up. Tell me about it.   980
          I am quite used to suffering.
MESSENGER: I'll tell you everything, my dear mistress.
          I was there, you know. No sense in glossing things over;
          You've got to hear it sometime.
          I went with my master, your husband, to the place   985
          Where Polynices' corpse was exposed,
          Cruelly torn by dogs. We said prayers
          Placating Hecate and Pluto; then we washed
          The body to purify it, gathered branches
          Of olive, and cremated him or what   990
          Was left of him. We piled him up a mound
          Of his mother-earth; then went to get
          Antigone. While we were on the way,
          Somebody heard a sound of crying coming
          From the stone chamber. He went up to Creon   995
          And told him of it. Creon hurried on.
          As we got near, the sound was all around us,—
          Impossible to tell whose it was.
          But Creon, in a voice breaking with grief,
          Said, "Dare I prophesy? These yards of ground   1000
          Will prove the bitterest journey of my life.
          It's faint, but it's my son's voice. Hurry, men,
          Get round the tomb, pull back the stones, and look
          Inside. Is it Haemon's voice, or do the gods
          Delude me?" At the far end of the tomb   1005
          We saw Antigone hanging by the neck
          In a noose of linen. He was hugging her
          And talking bitterly of their marriage and
          His father's action. Creon saw him and

Cried out and ran in, shouting, "Oh my son,   1010
What is this? What possessed you? Why are you trying
To kill yourself? Come out now, please, I beg you."
His son made no reply, just looked at him
Savagely with a look of deep contempt.
Then he suddenly drew his sword, evaded Creon,   1015
Held it out, and plunged the blade into his ribs.
He collapsed against Antigone's arms which were
Still warm, and hugged her. Then his blood came coughing,
And covered all her white cheeks with scarlet.
So now he lies, one corpse upon another;   1020
And thus their marriage is consummated,—in hell.
It only goes to show good sense is best,
When all this tragedy comes from one rash action.

[*Exit* EURYDICE *into palace.*]

CHORUS: What a strange thing. Eurydice has gone,
    Without saying a word.
MESSENGER: It is surprising.   1025
    I dare say she's too well-bred to go
    Showing her grief in public. I expect
    She's gone to have a good cry inside.
CHORUS: Perhaps. Noisy grief is a bad thing.
    But this extraordinary silence is ominous.   1030
MESSENGER: You're right. Let's go in then, and find out.
    She may have had her mind on something rash.
CHORUS: Who's coming? Creon with
    The body of his son.
    If truth be told, he is   1035
    Himself the murderer.

[*Enter* CREON *and* ATTENDANTS *carrying* HAEMON'S *body.*]

CREON: Wrong! How could I have been so wrong?
    And these deaths I caused—you have seen them—
    In my own family by my stubbornness.
    Oh my son, so young, to die so young,   1040
    And all because of me!
CHORUS: It's a bit late to find out you were wrong.
CREON: I know that. God has taken his revenge,
    Leapt on my head and beaten me
    And trampled on the only joy I had.   1045
    And all the years that I have labored—wasted.

[*Enter* SERVANT *from the palace.*]

SERVANT: My lord, what you see before your eyes,—
    It isn't all. You'd better come inside.
CREON: What fresh disaster could I suffer now?
SERVANT: Your wife, the mother of this corpse is dead.   1050
    Only a moment ago, she stabbed herself.
CREON: Oh death, can I never wash it away?
    Why are you destroying me? What
    Is your message now? Why stab me again?
    My wife dead too?   1055

[*The doors are opened, revealing* EURYDICE's *body.*]

SERVANT: See for yourself. They've brought the body out.
CREON: Oh.

Another blow. What else has fate in store?
My wife, my son.

SERVANT: Stabbed herself by the altar, and so passed on.   1060
But first she bewailed Megareus' death,
Her first son, that was; then Haemon's death.
And her last words were curses on your head.

CREON: Now I'm afraid. Why wasn't I killed?
Why didn't somebody kill me, stab me to death?   1065

SERVANT: Before she died she made a point of planting
The guilt of these two deaths squarely on you.

CREON: How did she die? How did she kill herself?

SERVANT: I told you. Stabbed herself. Under the heart.
Soon as she heard about her son's death.   1070

CREON: Nobody else to share the blame. Just me . . .
I killed you. I killed you, my dear.
Servants, carry me in, away from all this.
I wish I weren't alive.

CHORUS: Try to forget it. It is the only way.   1075

CREON: I invite Death. Do you only come uninvited?
Come and take me. I cannot bear to live.

CHORUS: No time for such thoughts now. You're still in charge.
You've got to see about these corpses, or
We'll all be polluted.

CREON: I meant what I said.   1080

CHORUS: No use in such prayers. You'll get what's destined.

CREON: Lead me away, a wreck, a useless wreck.
I'll keep out of the way. I killed them both.
Everything has crumbled. I feel
A huge weight on my head. [*Exit* CREON.]   1085

CHORUS: Who wants happiness? The main
Requirement is to be sensible.
This means not rebelling against
God's law, for that is arrogance.
The greater your arrogance, the heavier God's revenge.   1090
All old men have learned to be sensible;
But their juniors will not take the lesson as proved. [*Exit* CHORUS.]

[441 BCE]

Joining the Conversation: Critical Thinking and Writing

1. Would you argue that masks should be used for some (or all) of the characters in *Antigone*? If so, would they be masks that fully cover the face, Greek style, or some sort of half-masks? (A full mask enlarges the face, and conceivably the mouthpiece can amplify the voice, but only an exceptionally large theater might require such help. Perhaps half-masks are enough if the aim is chiefly to distance the actors from the audience and from daily reality, and to force the actors to develop resources other than facial gestures. One director, arguing in favor of

half-masks, has said that an actor who wears even a half-mask learns to act not with his eyes but with his neck.)

2. How would you costume the players? Would you dress them as the Greeks might have? Why? One argument sometimes used by those who hold that modern productions of Greek drama should use classical costumes is that Greek drama *ought* to be remote and ritualistic. Evaluate this view. What sort of modern dress might be effective?

3. If you were directing a college production of *Antigone,* how large a chorus would you use? (Sophocles is said to have used a chorus of fifteen.) Would you have the chorus recite (or chant) in unison, or would you assign lines to single speakers?

4. Although Sophocles called his play *Antigone,* many critics say that Creon is the real tragic hero, pointing out that Antigone is absent from the last third of the play. Argue for or against this view.

5. In some Greek tragedies, fate plays a great role in bringing about the downfall of the tragic hero. Though there are references to the curse on the House of Oedipus in *Antigone,* do we feel that Antigone goes to her death as a result of the workings of fate? Do we feel that fate is responsible for Creon's fall? Are both Antigone and Creon the creators of their own tragedy?

6. Are the words *hubris* (page 431) and *hamartia* (page 433) relevant to Antigone? To Creon? Argue your position.

7. Why does Creon, contrary to the Chorus's advice, bury the body of Polynices before he releases Antigone? Does his action show a zeal for piety as short-sighted as his earlier zeal for law? Is his action plausible, in view of the facts that Teiresias has dwelt on the wrong done to Polynices and that Antigone has ritual food to sustain her? Or are we not to worry about Creon's motive?

8. A *foil* is a character who, by contrast, sets off or helps define another character. To what extent is Ismene a foil to Antigone? Is she entirely without courage?

9. What function does Eurydice serve? How deeply do we feel about her fate?

Chapter Overview: Looking Backward/Looking Forward

1. Should a defense attorney defend a client whose guilt is obvious to everybody? If you were defending a client you believed to be innocent, but then discovered evidence of the client's guilt, would you tell the judge or keep this information to yourself?

2. During the civil rights campaigns of the 1950s and 1960s, Martin Luther King Jr. and many other activists frequently broke the law. What was their aim in doing so? Isn't it always wrong to break the law?

3. Often we say to ourselves or to someone else, "There should be a law against that." Is there an activity or specific form of behavior that you believe should be outlawed? Do you think that most people agree with you about this, or are you clearly in the minority? If your position on this issue became "the law," what would be the consequences?

4. Should a judge strictly abide by the letter of the law all the time? Can you imagine a situation when a judge knew a defendant to be guilty but nonetheless found him or her not guilty? Would such a decision make you respect the law more, or less?

5. Does the study of literature affect a person's attitude toward the law? Do you think that it makes a person more respectful of the law, or less? Which literary works have affected your own views about law and order?

6. Has the study of literature made you a better person? How would you prove this to someone?

CHAPTER 29

Worlds beyond Worlds

SHORT VIEWS

I consider it useless and tedious to represent what exists, because nothing that exists satisfies me. Nature is ugly, and I prefer the monsters of my fantasy to what is positively trivial.
Charles Baudelaire

Science fiction writers foresee the inevitable.
Isaac Asimov

The fancy that extraterrestrial life is by definition a higher order than our own is one that soothes all children, and many writers.
Joan Didion

There's no real objection to escapism, in the right places. . . . We all want to escape occasionally. But science fiction is often very far from escapism, in fact you might say that science fiction is escape into reality. . . . It's a fiction which does concern itself with real issues: the origin of man; our future. In fact I can't think of any form of literature which is more concerned with real issues, reality.
Arthur C. Clarke

It was agreed, that [in this book of poems written with the co-authorship of William Wordsworth], my endeavors should be directed to persons and characters supernatural, or at least romantic, yet so as to transfer from our inward nature a human interest and a semblance of truth sufficient to procure for these shadows of imagination that willing suspension of disbelief for the moment, which constitutes poetic faith.
Samuel Taylor Coleridge

All the works of man have their origin in creative fantasy. What right have we then to depreciate imagination?
Carl Jung

God creates lives; persons of imagination create fictional lives that may make a profound and, so to speak, more living impression on the world's memory.
Edmond and Jules de Goncourt

ESSAY

STEPHEN KING

Stephen King, with more than 100 million copies of his books in print, is one of America's most popular authors. King was born in Portland, Maine, in 1947. After graduating from the University of Maine he taught high school English until he was able to devote himself full-time to writing. In addition to writing stories and novels—some of which have been made into films—he has written Danse Macabre, *a book that, like the essay we reprint here, discusses the appeal of horror.*

Why We Crave Horror Movies

I think that we're all mentally ill; those of us outside the asylums only hide it a little better—and maybe not all that much better, after all. We've all known people who talk to themselves, people who sometimes squinch their faces into horrible grimaces when they believe no one is watching, people who have some hysterical fear—of snakes, the dark, the tight place, the long drop . . . and, of course, those final worms and grubs that are waiting so patiently underground.

When we pay our four or five bucks and seat ourselves at tenth-row center in a theater showing a horror movie, we are daring the nightmare.

Why? Some of the reasons are simple and obvious. To show that we can, that we are not afraid, that we can ride this roller coaster. Which is not to say that a really good horror movie may not surprise a scream out of us at some point, the way we may scream when the roller coaster twists through a complete 360 or plows through a lake at the bottom of the drop. And horror movies, like roller coasters, have always been the special province of the young; by the time one turns 40 or 50, one's appetite for double twists or 360-degree loops may be considerably depleted.

We also go to re-establish our feelings of essential normality; the horror movie is innately conservative, even reactionary. Freda Jackson as the horrible melting woman in *Die, Monster, Die!* confirms for us that no matter how far we may be removed from the beauty of a Robert Redford or a Diana Ross, we are still light-years from true ugliness.

5   And we go to have fun.

Ah, but this is where the ground starts to slope away, isn't it? Because this is a very peculiar sort of fun, indeed. The fun comes from seeing others menaced—sometimes killed. One critic has suggested that if pro football has become the voyeur's version of combat, then the horror film has become the modern version of the public lynching.

It is true that the mythic, "fairy-tale" horror film intends to take away the shades of gray. . . . It urges us to put away our more civilized and adult penchant for analysis and to become children again, seeing things in pure blacks and whites. It may be that horror movies provide psychic relief on this level because this invitation to lapse into simplicity, irrationality and even outright madness is extended so rarely. We are told we may allow our emotions a free rein . . . or no rein at all.

If we are all insane, then sanity becomes a matter of degree. If your insanity leads you to carve up women like Jack the Ripper or the Cleveland Torso Murderer, we clap you away in the funny farm (but neither of those two amateur-night surgeons was ever caught, heh-heh-heh); if, on the other hand, your insanity leads you only to talk to yourself when you're under stress or to pick your nose on your morning bus, then you are left alone to go about your business . . . though it is doubtful that you will ever be invited to the best parties.

The potential lyncher is in almost all of us (excluding saints, past and present; but then, most saints have been crazy in their own ways), and every now and then, he has to be let loose to scream and roll around in the grass. Our emotions and our fears form their own body, and we recognize that it demands its own exercise to maintain proper muscle tone. Certain of these emotional muscles are accepted—even exalted—in civilized society; they are, of course, the emotions that tend to maintain the status quo of civilization itself. Love, friendship, loyalty, kindness—these are all the emotions that we applaud, emotions that have been immortalized in the couplets of Hallmark cards[1] and in the verses (I don't dare call it poetry) of Leonard Nimoy.[2]

10   When we exhibit these emotions, society showers us with positive reinforcement; we learn this even before we get out of diapers. When, as children, we hug our rotten little puke of a sister and give her a kiss, all the aunts and uncles smile and twit and cry, "Isn't he the sweetest little thing?" Such coveted treats as chocolate-covered graham crackers often follow. But if we deliberately slam the rotten little puke of a sister's fingers in the door, sanctions follow—angry remonstrance from parents, aunts and uncles; instead of a chocolate-covered graham cracker, a spanking.

But anticivilization emotions don't go away, and they demand periodic exercise. We have such "sick" jokes as, "What's the difference between a truckload of bowling balls and a truckload of dead babies?" (You can't unload a truckload of bowling balls with a pitchfork . . . a joke, by the way, that I heard originally from a ten-year-old). Such a joke may surprise a laugh or a grin out of us even as we recoil, a possibility that confirms the thesis: If we share a brotherhood of man, then we also share an insanity of man. None of which is intended as a defense of either the sick joke or insanity but merely as an explanation of why the best horror films, like the best fairy tales, manage to be reactionary, anarchistic, and revolutionary all at the same time.

The mythic horror movie, like the sick joke, has a dirty job to do. It deliberately appeals to all that is worst in us. It is morbidity unchained, our most base instincts let free, our nastiest fantasies realized . . . and it all happens, fittingly enough, in the dark. For those reasons, good liberals often shy away from horror films. For myself, I like to see the most aggressive of them—*Dawn of the Dead*, for instance— as lifting a trap door in the civilized forebrain and throwing a basket of raw meat to the hungry alligators swimming around in that subterranean river beneath.

Why bother? Because it keeps them from getting out, man. It keeps them down there and me up here. It was Lennon and McCartney who said that all you need is love, and I would agree with that.

As long as you keep the gators fed.

[2009]

Joining the Conversation: Critical Thinking and Writing

1. In paragraph 6, King, paraphrasing an unnamed critic, suggests that "the horror film has become the modern version of the public lynching." In your opinion,

---

[1]**Hallmark cards** Hallmark is the largest manufacturer of greeting cards in the U.S.   [2]**Leonard Nimoy** (1931–), American actor, film director, poet, musician and photographer, best known as Dr. Spock on the Star Trek series.

why did some people find excitement in a lynching? Does the horror film offer somewhat similar excitement(s)?

2. King suggests in paragraph 11 that we have within us a stock of "anticivilization emotions [that] don't go away, and they demand periodic exercise." What, if any, evidence are you aware of that supports this view?

3. In paragraph 11, King tells a joke about dead babies. He suggests that jokes of this sort "may surprise a laugh or a grin out of us even as we recoil." Analyze your own response to the joke, or to similar jokes. Did you laugh or grin? Or was your response utterly different? If so, what was it?

4. In paragraphs 12 and 13, King says that horror movies serve a valuable social purpose. Do you think he has proved this point? What are the strengths (if any) and the weaknesses (if any) of his argument?

STORIES

GABRIEL GARCÍA MÁRQUEZ

Gabriel García Márquez was born in 1928 in Aracataca, a small village in Colombia. After being educated in Bogota, where he studied journalism and law, he worked as a journalist in Latin America, Europe, and the United States. He began writing fiction when he was in Paris, and at twenty-seven he published his first novel, La hojarasca *(Leaf Storm, 1955). During most of the 1960s he lived in Mexico, where he wrote film scripts and the novel that made him famous:* Cien años de soledad *(1967, translated in 1970 as* A Hundred Years of Solitude*). In 1982 García Márquez was awarded the Nobel Prize in Literature.*

In addition to writing stories and novels—often set in Macondo, a town modeled on Aracataca— García Márquez has written screenplays. A socialist, he now lives in Mexico because his presence is not welcome in Colombia.

A Very Old Man with Enormous Wings: A Tale for Children

Translated by Gregory Rabassa

On the third day of rain they had killed so many crabs inside the house that Pelayo had to cross his drenched courtyard and throw them into the sea, because the newborn child had a temperature all night and they thought it was due to the stench. The world had been sad since Tuesday. Sea and sky were a single ash-gray thing and the sands of the beach, which on March nights glimmered like powdered light, had become a stew of mud and rotten shellfish. The light was so weak at noon that when Pelayo was coming back to the house after throwing away the crabs, it was hard for him to see what it was that was moving and groaning in the rear of the courtyard. He had to go very close to see that it was an old man, a very old man, lying face down in the mud, who, in spite of his tremendous efforts, couldn't get up, impeded by his enormous wings.

Frightened by that nightmare, Pelayo ran to get Elisenda, his wife, who was putting compresses on the sick child, and he took her to the rear of the courtyard. They both looked at the fallen body with mute stupor. He was dressed like a rag-picker. There were only a few faded hairs left on his bald skull and very few teeth in his mouth, and his pitiful condition of a drenched great-grandfather had taken away any sense of grandeur he might have had. His huge buzzard wings, dirty and half-plucked, were forever entangled in the mud. They looked at him so long and so closely that Pelayo and Elisenda very soon overcame their surprise and in the end found him familiar. Then they dared speak to him, and he answered in an incomprehensible dialect with a strong sailor's voice. That was how they skipped over the inconvenience of the wings and quite intelligently concluded that he was a lonely castaway from some foreign ship wrecked by the storm. And yet, they called in a neighbor woman who knew everything about life and death to see him, and all she needed was one look to show them their mistake.

"He's an angel," she told them. "He must have been coming for the child, but the poor fellow is so old that the rain knocked him down."

On the following day everyone knew that a flesh-and-blood angel was held captive in Pelayo's house. Against the judgment of the wise neighbor woman, for whom angels in those times were the fugitive survivors of a celestial conspiracy, they did not have the heart to club him to death. Pelayo watched over him all afternoon from the kitchen, armed with his bailiff's club, and before going to bed he dragged him out of the mud and locked him up with the hens in the wire chicken coop. In the middle of the night, when the rain stopped, Pelayo and Elisenda were still killing crabs. A short time afterward the child woke up without a fever and with a desire to eat. Then they felt magnanimous and decided to put the angel on a raft with fresh water and provisions for three days and leave him to his fate on the high seas. But when they went out into the courtyard with the first light of dawn, they found the whole neighborhood in front of the chicken coop having fun with the angel, without the slightest reverence, tossing him things to eat through the openings in the wire as if he weren't a supernatural creature but a circus animal.

5   Father Gonzaga arrived before seven o'clock, alarmed at the strange news. By that time onlookers less frivolous than those at dawn had already arrived and they were making all kinds of conjectures concerning the captive's future. The simplest among them thought that he should be named mayor of the world. Others of sterner mind felt that he should be promoted to the rank of five-star general in order to win all wars. Some visionaries hoped that he could be put to stud in order to implant on earth a race of winged wise men who could take charge of the universe. But Father Gonzaga, before becoming a priest, had been a robust woodcutter. Standing by the wire, he reviewed his catechism in an instant and asked them to open the door so that he could take a close look at that pitiful man who looked more like a huge decrepit hen among the fascinated chickens. He was lying in a corner drying his open wings in the sunlight among the fruit peels and breakfast leftovers that the early risers had thrown him. Alien to the impertinences of the world, he only lifted his antiquarian eyes and murmured something in his dialect when Father Gonzaga went into the chicken coop and said good morning to him in Latin. The parish priest had his first suspicion of an imposter when he saw that he did not understand the language of God or know how to greet His ministers. Then he noticed that seen close up he was much too human: he had an unbearable smell of the outdoors, the back side of his wings was strewn with parasites and his main feathers had been mistreated by terrestrial winds, and nothing about him measured up to the proud dignity of angels. Then he came out of the chicken coop and in a brief sermon warned the curious against the risks of being ingenuous. He reminded them that the devil had the bad habit of making use of carnival tricks in order to confuse the unwary. He argued that if wings were not the essential element in determining the difference between a hawk and an airplane, they were

even less so in the recognition of angels. Nevertheless, he promised to write a letter to his bishop so that the latter would write to his primate so that the latter would write to the Supreme Pontiff in order to get the final verdict from the highest courts.

His prudence fell on sterile hearts. The news of the captive angel spread with such rapidity that after a few hours the courtyard had the bustle of a marketplace and they had to call in troops with fixed bayonets to disperse the mob that was about to knock the house down. Elisenda, her spine all twisted from sweeping up so much marketplace trash, then got the idea of fencing in the yard and charging five cents admission to see the angel.

The curious came from far away. A traveling carnival arrived with a flying acrobat who buzzed over the crowd several times, but no one paid any attention to him because his wings were not those of an angel but, rather, those of a sidereal bat. The most unfortunate invalids on earth came in search of health: a poor woman who since childhood had been counting her heartbeats and had run out of numbers; a Portuguese man who couldn't sleep because the noise of the stars disturbed him; a sleepwalker who got up at night to undo the things he had done while awake; and many others with less serious ailments. In the midst of that shipwreck disorder that made the earth tremble, Pelayo and Elisenda were happy with fatigue, for in less than a week they had crammed their rooms with money and the line of pilgrims waiting their turn to enter still reached beyond the horizon.

The angel was the only one who took no part in his own act. He spent his time trying to get comfortable in his borrowed nest, befuddled by the hellish heat of the oil lamps and sacramental candles that had been placed along the wire. At first they tried to make him eat some mothballs, which, according to the wisdom of the wise neighbor woman, were the food prescribed for angels. But he turned them down, just as he turned down the papal lunches that the penitents brought him, and they never found out whether it was because he was an angel or because he was an old man that in the end he ate nothing but eggplant mush. His only supernatural virtue seemed to be patience. Especially during the first days, when the hens pecked at him, searching for the stellar parasites that proliferated in his wings, and the cripples pulled out feathers to touch their defective parts with, and even the most merciful threw stones at him, trying to get him to rise so they could see him standing. The only time they succeeded in arousing him was when they burned his side with an iron for branding steers, for he had been motionless for so many hours that they thought he was dead. He awoke with a start, ranting in his hermetic language and with tears in his eyes, and he flapped his wings a couple of times, which brought on a whirlwind of chicken dung and lunar dust and a gale of panic that did not seem to be of this world. Although many thought that his reaction had been one not of rage but of pain, from then on they were careful not to annoy him, because the majority understood that his passivity was not that of a hero taking his ease but that of a cataclysm in repose.

Father Gonzaga held back the crowd's frivolity with formulas of maidservant inspiration while awaiting the arrival of a final judgment on the nature of the captive. But the mail from Rome showed no sense of urgency. They spent their time finding out if the prisoner had a navel, if his dialect had any connection with Aramaic, how many times he could fit on the head of a pin, or whether he wasn't just a Norwegian with wings. Those meager letters might have come and gone until the end of time if a providential event had not put an end to the priest's tribulations.

10   It so happened that during those days, among so many other carnival attractions, there arrived in town the traveling show of the woman who had been

changed into a spider for having disobeyed her parents. The admission to see her was not only less than the admission to see the angel, but people were permitted to ask her all manner of questions about her absurd state and to examine her up and down so that no one would ever doubt the truth of her horror. She was a frightful tarantula the size of a ram and with the head of a sad maiden. What was most heart-rending, however, was not her outlandish shape but the sincere affliction with which she recounted the details of her misfortune. While still practically a child she had sneaked out of her parents' house to go to a dance, and while she was coming back through the woods after having danced all night without permission, a fearful thunderclap rent the sky in two and through the crack came the lightning bolt of brimstone that changed her into a spider. Her only nourishment came from the meatballs that charitable souls chose to toss into her mouth. A spectacle like that, full of so much human truth and with such a fearful lesson, was bound to defeat without even trying that of a haughty angel who scarcely deigned to look at mortals. Besides, the few miracles attributed to the angel showed a certain mental disorder, like the blind man who didn't recover his sight but grew three new teeth, or the paralytic who didn't get to walk but almost won the lottery, and the leper whose sores sprouted sunflowers. Those consolation miracles, which were more like mocking fun, had already ruined the angel's reputation when the woman who had been changed into a spider finally crushed him completely. That was how Father Gonzaga was cured forever of his insomnia and Pelayo's courtyard went back to being as empty as during the time it had rained for three days and crabs walked through the bedrooms.

The owners of the house had no reason to lament. With the money they saved they built a two-story mansion with balconies and gardens and high netting so that crabs wouldn't get in during the winter, and with iron bars on the windows so that angels couldn't get in. Pelayo also set up a rabbit warren close to town and gave up his job as bailiff for good, and Elisenda bought some satin pumps with high heels and many dresses of iridescent silk, the kind worn on Sunday by the most desirable women in those times. The chicken coop was the only thing that didn't receive any attention. If they washed it down with creolin and burned tears of myrrh inside it every so often, it was not in homage to the angel but to drive away the dungheap stench that still hung everywhere like a ghost and was turning the new house into an old one. At first, when the child learned to walk, they were careful that he not get too close to the chicken coop. But then they began to lose their fears and got used to the smell, and before the child got his second teeth he'd gone inside the chicken coop to play, where the wires were falling apart. The angel was no less standoffish with him than with other mortals, but he tolerated the most ingenious infamies with the patience of a dog who had no illusions. They both came down with chicken pox at the same time. The doctor who took care of the child couldn't resist the temptation to listen to the angel's heart, and he found so much whistling in the heart and so many sounds in his kidneys that it seemed impossible for him to be alive. What surprised him most, however, was the logic of his wings. They seemed so natural on that completely human organism that he couldn't understand why other men didn't have them too.

When the child began school it had been some time since the sun and rain had caused the collapse of the chicken coop. The angel went dragging himself about here and there like a stray dying man. They would drive him out of the bedroom with a broom and a moment later find him in the kitchen. He seemed to be in so many places at the same time that they grew to think that he'd been duplicated, that he was reproducing himself all through the house, and the exasperated and unhinged Elisenda shouted that it was awful living in that hell full of angels. He could scarcely eat and his antiquarian eyes had also become so foggy that he went about bumping into posts. All he had left were the bare cannulae[1] of his last feathers. Pelayo threw a blanket over him and extended him the charity of letting him sleep in the shed, and only then did they notice that he had a temperature at night, and was delirious with the tongue twisters of an old Norwegian. That was one of the few times they became alarmed, for they thought he was going to die and not even the wise neighbor woman had been able to tell them what to do with dead angels.

And yet he not only survived his worst winter, but seemed improved with the first sunny days. He remained motionless for several days in the farthest corner of the courtyard, where no one would see him, and at the beginning of December some large, stiff feathers began to grow on his wings, the feathers of a scarecrow, which looked more like another misfortune of decrepitude. But he must have known the reason for those changes, for he was quite careful that no one should notice them, that no one should hear the sea chanteys that he sometimes sang under the stars. One morning Elisenda was cutting some bunches of onions for lunch when a wind that seemed to come from the high seas blew into the kitchen. Then she went to the window and caught the angel in his first attempts at flight. They were so clumsy that his fingernails opened a furrow in the vegetable patch and he was on the point of knocking the shed down with the ungainly flapping that slipped on the light and couldn't get a grip on the air. But he did manage to gain altitude. Elisenda let out a sigh of relief, for herself and for him, when she saw him pass over the last houses, holding himself up in some way with the risky flapping of a senile vulture. She kept watching him even when she was through cutting the onions and she kept on watching until it was no longer possible for her to see him, because then he was no longer an annoyance in her life but an imaginary dot on the horizon of the sea.

[1968]

---

[1]**cannulae** from a Latin word meaning small reed or pipe; a narrow tube for draining off fluid, introducing medication, etc.

Joining the Conversation: Critical Thinking and Writing

1. The subtitle is "A Tale for Children." Do you think that the story is more suited to children than to adults? What in the story do you think children would especially like, or dislike?
2. Is the story chiefly about the inability of adults to perceive and respect the miraculous world?
3. Characterize the narrator of the story.
4. Characterize Pelayo, Elisenda, their son, and the man with wings.

ARTHUR C. CLARKE

Arthur C. Clarke (1917–2008), an English writer of science fiction, is most widely known for his novel 2001: A Space Odyssey, *written with the film director Stanley Kubrick.*

During World War II, Clarke served in the Royal Air Force as a radar techni-cian and instructor. After the war, he earned a bachelor's degree, with honors, in mathematics and physics at King's College, London. In addition to writing science fiction, Clarke wrote several nonfiction books concerning rocketry and space flight, as well as a semiautobiographical novel, Glide Path *(1963). In 1958 he emigrated to Sri Lanka, apparently to pursue his interest in scuba diving. He lived the rest of his life there.*

The Nine Billion Names of God

"This is a slightly unusual request," said Dr. Wagner, with what he hoped was com-mendable restraint. "As far as I know, it's the first time anyone's been asked to supply a Tibetan monastery with an automatic sequence computer. I don't wish to be in-quisitive, but I should hardly have thought that your—ah—establishment had much use for such a machine. Could you explain just what you intend to do with it?"

"Gladly," replied the lama, readjusting his silk robe and carefully putting away the slide rule he had been using for currency conversions. "Your Mark V computer can carry out any routine mathematical operation involving up to ten digits. However, for our work we are interested in letters, not numbers. As we wish you to modify the output circuits, the machine will be printing words, not columns of figures."

"I don't understand . . ."

"This is a project on which we have been working for the last three centu-ries—since the lamasery was founded, in fact. It is somewhat alien to your way of thought, so I hope you will listen with an open mind while I explain it."

5   "Naturally."

"It is really quite simple. We have been compiling a list which shall contain all the possible names of God."

"I beg your pardon?"

"We have reason to believe," continued the lama imperturbably, "that all such names can be written with not more than nine letters in an alphabet we have devised."

"And you have been doing this for three centuries?"

10   "Yes. We expected it would take us about fifteen thousand years to complete the task."

"Oh." Dr. Wagner looked a little dazed. "Now I see why you wanted to hire one of our machines. But exactly what is the purpose of this project?"

The lama hesitated for a fraction of a second, and Wagner wondered if he had offended him. If so, there was no trace of annoyance in the reply.

"Call it ritual, if you like, but it's a fundamental part of our belief. All the many names of the Supreme Being—God, Jehovah, Allah, and so on—they are only man-made labels. There is a philosophical problem of some difficulty here, which I do not propose to discuss, but somewhere among all the possible combinations of letters, which can occur, are what one may call the real names of God. By sys-tematic permutation of letters, we have been trying to list them all."

"I see. You've been starting at AAAAAAAAA . . . and working up to ZZZZZZZZZ. . . ."

15   "Exactly—though we use a special alphabet of our own. Modifying the elec-tromatic typewriters to deal with this is, of course, trivial. A rather more interesting problem is that of devising suitable circuits to eliminate ridiculous combinations. For example, no letter must occur more than three times in succession."

"Three? Surely you mean two."

"Three is correct. I am afraid it would take too long to explain why, even if you understood our language."

"I'm sure it would," said Wagner hastily. "Go on."

"Luckily it will be a simple matter to adapt your automatic sequence computer for this work, since once it has been programmed properly it will permute each letter in turn and print the result. What would have taken us fifteen thousand years it will be able to do in a thousand days."

20   Dr. Wagner was scarcely conscious of the faint sounds from the Manhattan streets far below. He was in a different world, a world of natural, not man-made, mountains. High up in their remote aeries these monks had been patiently at work, generation after generation, compiling their lists of meaningless words. Was there any limit to the follies of mankind? Still, he must give no hint of his inner thoughts. The customer was always right . . .

"There's no doubt," replied the doctor, "that we can modify the Mark V to print lists of this nature. I'm much more worried about the problem of installation and maintenance. Getting out to Tibet, in these days, is not going to be easy."

"We can arrange that. The components are small enough to travel by air—that is one reason why we chose your machine. If you can get them to India, we will provide transport from there."

"And you want to hire two of our engineers?"

"Yes, for the three months which the project should occupy."

25   "I've no doubt that Personnel can manage that." Dr. Wagner scribbled a note on his desk pad. "There are just two other points—"

Before he could finish the sentence, the lama had produced a small slip of paper.

"This is my certified credit balance at the Asiatic Bank."

"Thank you. It appears to be—ah—adequate. The second matter is so trivial that I hesitate to mention it—but it's surprising how often the obvious gets overlooked. What source of electrical energy have you?"

"A diesel generator providing 50 kilowatts at 110 volts. It was installed about five years ago and is quite reliable. It's made life at the lamasery much more comfortable, but of course it was really installed to provide power for the motors driving the prayer wheels."

30   "Of course," echoed Dr. Wagner. "I should have thought of that."

* * *

The view from the parapet was vertiginous, but in time one gets used to anything. After three months George Hanley was not impressed by the two-thousand-foot swoop into the abyss or the remote checkerboard of fields in the valley below. He was leaning against the wind-smoothed stones and staring morosely at the distant mountains whose names he had never bothered to discover.

This, thought George, was the craziest thing that had ever happened to him. "Project Shangri-La," some wit at the labs had christened it. For weeks now, Mark V had been churning out acres of sheets covered with gibberish. Patiently, inexorably, the computer had been rearranging letters in all their possible combinations, exhausting each class before going on to the next. As the sheets had emerged from the electromatic typewriters, the monks had carefully cut them up and pasted them into enormous books. In another week, heaven be praised, they would have finished. Just what obscure calculations had convinced the monks that they needn't bother to go on to words of ten, twenty, or a hundred letters, George didn't know. One of his recurring nightmares was that there would be some change of plan and that the High Lama (whom they'd naturally called Sam Jaffe,[1] though he didn't look a bit like him) would suddenly announce that the project would be extended to approximately 2060 A.D. They were quite capable of it.

George heard the heavy wooden door slam in the wind as Chuck came out onto the parapet beside him. As usual, Chuck was smoking one of the cigars that made him so popular with the monks—who, it seemed, were quite willing to embrace all the minor and most of the major pleasures of life. That was one thing in their favor: they might be crazy, but they weren't bluenoses. Those frequent trips they took down to the village, for instance . . ." "Listen, George," said Chuck urgently. "I've learned something that means trouble."

"What's wrong? Isn't the machine behaving?" That was the worst contingency George could imagine. It might delay his return, than which nothing could be more horrible. The way he felt now, even the sight of a TV commercial would seem like manna from heaven. At least it would be some link from home.

35   "No—it's nothing like that." Chuck settled himself on the parapet, which was unusual, because normally he was scared of the drop.

"I've just found out what all this is about."

"What d'ya mean—I thought we knew."

"Sure—we know what the monks are trying to do. But we didn't know why. It's the craziest thing—"

"Tell me something new," growled George.

40   ". . . but old Sam's just come clean with me. You know the way he drops in every afternoon to watch the sheets roll out. Well, this time he seemed rather excited, or at least as near as he'll ever get to it. When I told him we were on the last cycle he asked me, in that cute English accent of his, if I'd ever wondered what they were trying to do. I said, 'Sure'—and he told me."

"Go on, I'll buy it."

"Well, they believe that when they have listed all His names—and they reckon that there are about nine billion of them—God's purpose will have been achieved. The human race will have finished what it was created to do, and there won't be any point in carrying on. Indeed, the very idea is something like blasphemy."

"Then what do they expect us to do? Commit suicide?"

"There's no need for that. When the list's completed, God steps in and simply winds things up . . . bingo!"

45   "Oh, I get it. When we finish our job, it will be the end of the world."

Chuck gave a nervous little laugh.

"That's just what I said to Sam. And do you know what happened? He looked at me in a very queer way, like I'd been stupid in class, and said, 'It's nothing as trivial as that.'"

George thought this over for a moment.

"That's what I call taking the Wide View," he said presently.

50   "But what d'ya suppose we should do about it? I don't see that it makes the slightest difference to us. After all, we already knew that they were crazy."

"Yes—but don't you see what may happen? When the list's complete and the Last Trump doesn't blow—or whatever it is that they expect—we may get the blame. It's our machine they've been using. I don't like the situation one little bit."

"I see," said George slowly. "You've got a point there. But this sort of thing's happened here before, you know. When I was a kid down in Louisiana we had a

[1]**Sam Jaffe** American film actor (1891–1984) who played the role of the High Lama in *Lost Horizon* (1937), a film set in the Himalayas.

crackpot preacher who said the world was going to end next Sunday. Hundreds of people believed him—even sold their homes. Yet nothing happened; they didn't turn nasty, as you'd expect. They just decided that he'd made a mistake in his calculations and went right on believing. I guess some of them still do."

"Well, this isn't Louisiana, in case you hadn't noticed. There are just two of us and hundreds of these monks. I like them, and I'll be sorry for old Sam when his lifework backfires on him. But all the same, I wish I was somewhere else."

"I've been wishing that for weeks. But there's nothing we can do until the contract's finished and the transport arrives to fly us out."

55   "Of course," said Chuck thoughtfully, "we could always try a bit of sabotage."

"Like hell we could! That would make things worse."

"Not the way I meant. Look at it like this. The machine will finish its run four days from now, on the present twenty-hours-a-day basis. The transport calls in a week. O.K., then all we need to do is to find something that wants replacing during one of the overhaul periods—something that will hold up the works for a couple of days. We'll fix it, of course, but not too quickly. If we time matters properly, we can be down at the airfield when the last name pops out of the register. They won't be able to catch us then."

"I don't like it," said George. "It will be the first time I ever walked out on a job. Besides, it would make them suspicious. No, I'll sit tight and take what comes."

"I still don't like it," he said seven days later, as the tough little mountain ponies carried them down the winding road. "And don't you think I'm running away because I'm afraid. I'm just sorry for those poor old guys up there, and I don't want to be around when they find what suckers they've been. Wonder how Sam will take it?"

60   "It's funny," replied Chuck, "but when I said goodbye I got the idea he knew we were walking out on him—and that he didn't care because he knew the machine was running smoothly and that the job would soon be finished. After that—well, of course, for him there just isn't any After That . . ."

George turned in his saddle and stared back up the mountain road. This was the last place from which one could get a clear view of the lamasery. The squat, angular buildings were silhouetted against the afterglow of the sunset; here and there lights gleamed like portholes in the sides of an ocean liner. Electric lights, of course, sharing the same circuit as the Mark V. How much longer would they share it? wondered George. Would the monks smash up the computer in their rage and disappointment? Or would they just sit down quietly and begin their calculations all over again?

He knew exactly what was happening up on the mountain at this very moment. The High Lama and his assistants would be sitting in their silk robes, inspecting the sheets as the junior monks carried them away from the typewriters and pasted them into the great volumes. No one would be saying anything. The only sound would be the incessant patter, the never-ending rainstorm, of the keys hitting the paper, for the Mark V itself was utterly silent as it flashed through its thousands of calculations a second. Three months of this, thought George, was enough to start anyone climbing up the wall.

"There she is!" called Chuck, pointing down into the valley. "Ain't she beautiful!"

She certainly was, thought George. The battered old DC-3 lay at the end of the runway like a tiny silver cross. In two hours she would be bearing them away to freedom and sanity. It was a thought worth savoring like a fine liqueur. George let it roll around in his mind as the pony trudged patiently down the slope.

65   The swift night of the high Himalayas was now almost upon them. Fortunately the road was very good, as roads went in this region, and they were both carrying torches. There was not the slightest danger, only a certain discomfort from the bitter cold. The sky overhead was perfectly clear and ablaze with the familiar, friendly stars. At least there would be no risk, thought George, of the pilot being unable to take off because of weather conditions. That had been his only remaining worry.

He began to sing but gave it up after a while. This vast arena of mountains, gleaming like whitely hooded ghosts on every side, did not encourage such ebullience. Presently George glanced at his watch.

"Should be there in an hour," he called back over his shoulder to Chuck. Then he added, in an afterthought, "Wonder if the computer's finished its run? It was due about now."

Chuck didn't reply, so George swung round in his saddle. He could just see Chuck's face, a white oval turned toward the sky.

"Look," whispered Chuck, and George lifted his eyes to heaven. (There is always a last time for everything.)

70   Overhead, without any fuss, the stars were going out.

[1953]

Joining the Conversation: Critical Thinking and Writing

1. How would you characterize the Caucasians whom we meet in "The Nine Billion Names of God"—Dr. Wagner, George Hanley, and Chuck? How would you characterize the lama?
2. Not until paragraphs 40–44 do we learn *why* the monks are engaged in the project. Do you think the story would have been more interesting if we had been told earlier? Why, or why not?
3. The lama explains that words such as "Supreme Being," "God," "Jehovah," and "Allah" are "only man-made labels," and they are *not* "the real names of God." Does this make sense to you? Please explain.
4. Many cultures have taboos on uttering or writing the name of God. Why do you suppose this is so?

POEMS

A Note on Ballads

Popular ballads, or **folk ballads,** such as "The Demon Lover," are anonymous stories told in song. They acquired their distinctive flavor by being passed down orally from generation to generation, each singer consciously or unconsciously modifying his or her inheritance. Most ballad singers were composers only by accident; they intended to transmit what they had heard, but their memories were sometimes faulty and their imaginations active. The modifications effected by oral transmission generally give a ballad three noticeable qualities:

1. It is impersonal; even when there is an "I" who sings the tale, this "I" is usually characterless.

2. The ballad—like other oral literature such as the nursery rhyme or the counting-out rhyme ("one potato, two potato")—is filled with repetition, sometimes of words, sometimes of phrases and even entire lines. Further, **stock epithets** (for instance, "my true true love," "far, far beyond the sea") are repeated from ballad to ballad.
3. Because the ballads were transmitted orally, residing in memory rather than on the printed page, weak stanzas were often dropped, leaving a series of sharp scenes, frequently with dialogue.

Popular ballads have been much imitated by professional poets, especially since the late eighteenth century. Two such **literary ballads** are John Keats's "La Belle Dame sans Merci" (page 1389) and A. E. Housman's "Is my team ploughing (page 1390)." In a literary ballad—the poem by Keats is a notable example—the story is sometimes infused with multiple meanings, with insistent symbolic implications. Ambiguity can be present in the popular ballad also, but it is of a different sort. Whether it is due to the loss of stanzas or to the creator's unconcern with some elements of the narrative, the ambiguity of the popular ballad commonly lies in the story itself rather than in the *significance* of the story.

ANONYMOUS

The Demon Lover

"O where have you been, my long, long love,
    This long seven years and mair?"°
"O I'm come to seek my former vows
    Ye granted me before."   4

"O hold your tongue of your former vows,
    For they will breed sad strife;
O hold your tongue of your former vows,
    For I am become a wife."   8

He turned him right and round about,
    And the tear blinded his ee:

2 mair more

"I wad never hae trodden On Irish ground,
   If it had not been for thee.   12

"I might hae had a king's daughter,
   Far, far beyond the sea;
I might have had a king's daughter,
   Had it not been for love o thee."   16

"If ye might have had a king's daughter,
   Yer sel ye had to blame;
Ye might have taken the king's daughter,
   For ye kend° that I was nane.   20

"If I was to leave my husband dear,
   And my two babes also,
O what have you to take me to,
   If with you I should go?"   24

"I hae seven ships upon the sea—
   The eighth brought me to land—
With four-and-twenty bold mariners,
   And music on every hand."   28

She has taken up her two little babes,
   Kissed them baith cheek and chin:
"O fair ye weel, my ain two babes,
   For I'll never see you again."   32

She set her foot upon the ship,
   No mariners could she behold;
But the sails were o the taffetie,°
   And the masts o the beaten gold.   36

They had not sailed a league, a league,
   A league but barely three,
With dismal grew his countenance,
   And drumlie° grew his ee.   40

They had not sailed a league, a league,
   A league but barely three,
Until she espied his cloven foot,
   And she wept right bitterlie.   44

"O hold your tongue of your weeping," says he,
   "Of your weeping now let me be;
I will show you how the lilies grow
   On the banks of Italy."   48

"O what hills are yon, yon pleasant hills,
   That the sun shines sweetly on?"
"O yon are the hills of heaven," he said.
   "Where you will never win."°   52

20 kend knew **35 taffetie** fabric used chiefly for women's clothing **40 drumlie** gloomy
52 win gain, get to

"O whaten mountain is you," she said,
 "All so dreary wi frost and snow?"
"O yon is the mountain of hell," he cried,
 "Where you and I will go."   56

He strack the tap-mast wi his hand,
 The fore-mast wi his knee,
And he brake that gallant ship in twain,
 And sank her in the sea.   60

Joining The Conversation: Critical Thinking and Writing

1. What takes place between lines 28 and 29 of "The Demon Lover"?
2. What is the first hint that supernatural forces ate at work?
3. What does the "cloven foot" (line 43) signify? Is the spirit motivated by malice?
   By love? By both?
4. In a paragraph, offer a character sketch of the wife. You may include a brief
   moral judgment, but devote most of your paragraph to describing her actions in
   such a way that they reveal a personality. This personality may, of course, be
   rather complex.

ANONYMOUS

The Wife of Usher's Well

There lived a wife at Usher's Well,
 And a wealthy wife was she;
She had three stout and stalwart sons,
 And sent them o'er the sea.   1

They hadna been a week from her,
 A week but barely ane,°
Whan word came to the carlin° wife
 That her three sons were gane.   8

They hadna been a week from her,
 A week but barely three,
Whan word came to the carlin wife
 That her sons she'd never see.   12

"I wish the wind may never cease,
 Nor [fashes°] in the flood,
Till my three sons come hame to me,
 In earthly flesh and blood."   16

It fell about the Martinmass,°
 When nights are lang and mirk,
The carlin wife's three sons came hame,
 And their hats were o' the birk.°   20

6 ane In Scottish and Middle English, used to mean a single unit or thing   **7 carlin** peasant
14 fashes troubles   **17 Martinmass** November 1   **20 birk** birch

It neither grew in syke° nor ditch,
   Nor yet in ony sheugh;°
But at the gates o Paradise,
   That birk grew fair eneugh.   24

"Blow up the fire, my maidens!
   Bring water from the well!
For a' my house shall feast this night,
   Since my three sons are well."   28

And she has made to them a bed,
   She's made it large and wide,
And she's ta'en her mantle her about,
   Sat down at the bed-side.   32

Up then crew the red, red cock,
   And up and crew the grey;
The eldest to the youngest said,
   "'Tis time we were away."   36

The cock he hadna craw'd but once,
   And clapp'd his wings at a',
When the youngest to the eldest said,
   "Brother, we must awa'.   40

"The cock doth craw, the day doth daw,
   The channerin° worm doth chide;
Gin° we be mist out o' our place,
   A sair° pain we maun° bide.   44

"Fare ye weel, my mother dear!
   Fareweel to barn and byre!°
And fare ye weel, the bonny lass
   That kindles my mother's fire!"   48

21 syke rivulet **22 sheugh** ditch **42 channerin** scolding **43 gin** If **44 sair** sore
maun must **46 byre** shed

Joining the Conversation: Critical Thinking and Writing

1. In a sentence or two, summarize the narrative of "The Wife of Usher's Well." That is, tell the story as briefly as possible.

2. Notice that the poem does not tell how the sons were lost. We are told in line 12 that the wife learns she will never see them again, and we are told in line 23 that the birch from which their hats are made grew at "the gates o Paradise." So we infer that they are dead, but the poet does not explicitly say so. Nor, for that matter, do we get any description of the appearance of any of the people, except for the lass in the last line, who is "bonny." Consider the mother. We are not told what she looked like or what her thoughts or feelings are. Yet we know her thoughts and feelings, and we can characterize her.

    In a sentence or two, characterize the mother. Then, in the first paragraph of an essay of 250 words, explain what your evidence is. Then try to explain the effect on the reader of the lack of explicit detail in the poem. In your final sentence or two, indicate whether you believe that the poem effectively sets the mother forth. (Most instructors in composition courses urge their students to give concrete details in their writing. Is it possible that additional details in this poem would not be useful?)

3. Medieval ghosts, for the most part, appear like ordinary mortals. They are not transparent, and they do not wear white sheets. Do you assume that the mother knows her sons are ghosts? At what point does she realize this?

4. In the last four stanzas, the sons talk about leaving, but there are no screams or tears. Do you assume they are glad to leave? Or, on the other hand, are they deeply regretful that they must leave? Exactly what, besides their mother, are they leaving? Indicate, without making excessive claims, what implications or associations may legitimately be found in the last stanza, especially in the last two lines.

JOHN KEATS

For a biographical note, see page 228.

La Belle Dame sans Merci°

O what can ail thee, knight at arms,
    Alone and palely loitering?
The sedge has withered from the lake,
    And no birds sing.   4

O what can ail thee, knight-at arms,
    So haggard and so woe-begone?
The squirrel's granary is full,
    And the harvest's done.   8

I see a lily on thy brow,
    With anguish moist and fever dew,
And on thy cheeks a fading rose
    Fast withereth too.   12

"I met a lady in the meads,
    Full beautiful—a faery's child,
Her hair was long, her foot was light,
    And her eyes were wild.   16

"I made a garland for her head,
    And bracelets too, and fragrant zone;°
She looked at me as she did love,
    And made sweet moan.   20

"I set her on my pacing steed,
    And nothing else saw all day long,
For sidelong would she bend and sing
    A faery's song.   24

°**La Belle Dame sans Merci** The beautiful pitiless lady   **18 fragrant zone** belt of flowers

"She found me roots of relish sweet,
    And honey wild, and manna dew,
And sure in language strange she said
    'I love thee true.'   28

"She took me to her elfin grot,
    And there she wept and sighed full sore,
And there I shut her wild wild eyes
    With kisses four.   32

"And there she lulléd me asleep,
    And there I dreamed—Ah! woe betide!
The latest dream I ever dreamt
    On the cold hill side.   36

"I saw pale kings and princes too,
    Pale warriors, death-pale were they all;
They cried, 'La Belle Dame sans Merci
    Thee hath in thrall!'   40

"I saw their starved lips in the gloam
    With horrid warning gapéd wide,
And I awoke, and found me here,
    On the cold hill's side.   44

"And this is why I sojourn here,
    Alone and palely loitering,
Though the sedge is withered from the lake,
    And no birds sing."   48

                    [1819]

Joining the Conversation: Critical Thinking and Writing

1. In the first three stanzas the speaker describes the knight as pale, haggard, and so forth. In the rest of the poem the knight recounts his experience. In a few sentences summarize the knight's experience, and indicate why it has caused him to appear as he now does.
2. The *femme fatale*—the dangerously seductive woman—appears in much literature. If you are familiar with one such work, compare it with Keats's poem.
3. What characteristics of the popular ballad (see the introductory note on page 1385) do you find in this poem? What characteristic does it *not* share with popular ballads? Set forth your response in an essay of 500 words.

A. E. HOUSMAN

For a biographical note, see page 682

Is my team ploughing

"Is my team ploughing,
    That I was used to drive

And hear the harness jingle
  When I was man alive?"   4

Ay, the horses trample,
  The harness jingles now;
No change though you lie under
  The land you used to plough.   8

"Is football playing
  Along the river shore,
With lads to chase the leather,
  Now I stand up no more?"   12

Ay, the ball is flying,
  The lads play heart and soul;
The goal stands up, the keeper
  Stands up to keep the goal.   16

"Is my girl happy,
  That I thought hard to leave,
And has she tired of weeping
  As she lies down at eve?"   20

Ay, she lies down lightly,
  She lies not down to weep;
Your girl is well contented.
  Be still, my lad, and sleep.   24

"Is my friend hearty,
  Now I am thin and pine,
And has he found to sleep in
  A better bed than mine?"   28

Yes, lad, I lie easy,
  I lie as lads would choose;
I cheer a dead man's sweetheart,
  Never ask me whose.   32

[1898]

Joining the Conversation: Critical Thinking and Writing

1. Characterize the speaker of the first, third, fifth, and seventh stanzas of "Is my team ploughing." Who is the speaker in the other stanzas?
2. How does the answer in the sixth stanza differ significantly from the answer in the second and fourth stanzas? How do you account for the difference?
3. List some of the characteristics of "Is my team ploughing" that show Housman's use of ballads. (On ballads, see page 1385.)

Looking Backward/Looking Forward

1. What is the strangest thing that has ever happened to you? Do you have an explanation for it?

2. What does the word "supernatural" mean? Have you ever had an experience of the supernatural?
3. If you were given the power to change the world in one way, and in one way only, what specific change would you make?
4. Do you believe in magic? What is the difference between magic and a miracle?
5. Do you think about the end of the world? In what ways?
6. In your view, is there another world or worlds beyond this one?
7. Many people believe in devils and demons, while many others do not. What is your view? Do you believe in angels?
8. Let's pretend that scientists have discovered the existence of another world, another form of civilization on a planet in outer space. Would you be eager to visit it? What would be the most important things about life on earth that you would want to communicate to this other civilization?
9. Often it is said that reading a good literary work transports us to "another world." What does this mean?
10. Has a work of art, a movie, or a TV show ever done for you what we say that literary works do—take you to another world?

Writing about Literature: An Overview of Critical Strategies

The Nature of Critical Writing

We have said that in everyday talk the commonest meaning of **criticism** is something like "finding fault," but that a critic can see excellences as well as faults. Because we turn to criticism with the hope that the critic has seen something we have missed, the most valuable criticism is not that which shakes its finger at faults but that which calls our attention to interesting things going on in the work of art. Here is a statement made by W. H. Auden in *The Dyer's Hand* (1963), suggesting that criticism is most useful when it calls our attention to things worth attending to:

> What is the function of a critic? So far as I am concerned, he can do me one or more of the following services:
>
> 1. Introduce me to authors or works of which I was hitherto unaware.
> 2. Convince me that I have undervalued an author or a work because I had not read them carefully enough.
> 3. Show me relations between works of different ages and cultures which I could never have seen for myself because I do not know enough and never shall.
> 4. Give a "reading" of a work which increases my understanding of it.
> 5. Throw light upon the process of artistic "Making."
> 6. Throw light upon the relation of art to life, science, economics, ethics, religion, etc. (8–9)

Auden does not neglect the delight we get from literature, but he extends (especially in his sixth point) the range of criticism to include topics beyond the literary work itself. Notice too the emphasis on observing, showing, and illuminating, which suggests that the function of critical writing is not very different from the commonest view of the function of imaginative writing.

Auden begins by saying that a critic can "introduce" him to an author. How would a critic introduce a reader to an author? It's not enough just to name the author; almost surely the advocate would give *reasons* why we should read the book. "It will really grip you"; "It's the funniest thing I've read in months"; "I was moved to tears." Auden lets the cat out of the bag in his next two assertions: the critic may "convince" him of something, or may "show" him something. Criticism is largely a matter of convincing and showing—really, showing and thereby convincing. We cannot just announce that we like or dislike something and expect people to agree; we have to point to evidence (that's the showing part) if we are going to convince.

We will return to the matter of evidence, but first let's hear another writer talk about criticism. In *Phoenix: The Posthumous Papers of D. H. Lawrence* (1936), the novelist D. H. Lawrence says this:

> Literary criticism can be no more than a reasoned account of the feeling produced upon the critic by the book he is criticizing. Criticism can never be a science: it is, in the first place, much too personal, and in the second, it is concerned with values that science ignores. (539)

We like Lawrence's assertion that criticism is *a reasoned account*—writing about literature is a rational activity, not a mere pouring out of emotion—but we equally like his assertion that it is rooted in *feeling*. As the chapters of this book have suggested, when we read we respond (perhaps with an intense interest, perhaps with a yawn). Our responses are worth examining. *Why* do we find this character memorable, or that character unbelievable?

As we examine our responses, and check the text to make sure that we have properly remembered it, we may find our responses changing, but finally we think we know what we think of the literary work, and we know *why* we think it. We are, in Lawrence's words, able to give "a reasoned account of the feeling produced . . . by the book."

Criticism as Argument:
Assumptions and Evidence

In this process of showing and convincing (Auden's words) and of offering a reasoned account (Lawrence's words), even when we are talking about a so-so movie or television show, what we say depends in large measure on certain conscious or unconscious assumptions that we make:

- "I liked it because the characters were very believable" (here the assumption is that characters ought to be believable);
- "I didn't like it; there was too much violence" (here the assumption is that violence ought not to be shown, or if it is shown it should be condemned);
- "I didn't like it; it was awfully slow" (here the assumption is probably that there ought to be a fair amount of physical action, perhaps even changes of scene, rather than characters just talking in the kitchen);
- "I didn't like it; I don't think topics of this sort should be discussed publicly" (here the assumption is a moral one, that it is indecent to present certain topics);
- "I liked it partly because it was refreshing to hear such frankness" (here again the assumption is moral, and more or less the reverse of the previous one).

In short, whether we realize it or not, our responses are rooted in assumptions. These assumptions, we may believe, are so self-evident that they do not need to be stated. Our readers, however, may disagree.

If we are to hold our readers' interest, and perhaps convince them to see things the way we do, we must recognize our assumptions and offer evidence—point to things in the work—that will convince the reader that our assumptions are reasonable. If we want to say that a short story ought to be realistic, we will call our reader's attention to unrealistic aspects in a particular story and, with this evidence in front of the reader, argue that the story is not worth much. Or, conversely, we might say that in a satiric story realism is not a valid criterion; what readers want is (as in a political caricature in a newspaper) exaggeration and humor, and in our critical study we will call attention to the delight that this or that bit of exaggeration offers.

In brief, as we suggested in Chapters 8 and 9 ("Arguing an Interpretation" and "Arguing an Evaluation"), argument consists of offering statements that are *reasons* for other statements ("The work means X *because* . . ."), and the words that follow "because" normally point to the evidence that we believe supports the earlier assertion.

Some Critical Strategies

Professional critics, like the ordinary moviegoer who recommends a movie to a friend, work from assumptions, but their assumptions are usually highly conscious, and the critics may define their assumptions at length. They regard themselves as, for instance, Freudians or Marxists or gay critics. They read all texts through the lens of a particular theory, and their focus enables them to see things that otherwise might go unnoticed. Most critics realize, however, that if a lens or a critical perspective or an interpretive strategy helps us to see certain things, it also limits our vision. They therefore regard their method not as an exclusive way of thinking but only as a useful tool.

What follows is a brief survey of the chief current approaches to literature. You may find, as you read these pages, that one or another approach sounds congenial, and you may want to make use of it in your reading and writing. On the other hand, it's important to remember that works of literature are highly varied, and we read them for various purposes—to kill time, to enjoy fanciful visions, to be amused, to learn about alien ways of feeling, and to learn about ourselves.

It may be best, therefore, to try to respond to each text in the way that the text seems to require rather than to read all texts according to a single formula. You'll find, of course, that some works will lead you to want to think about them from several angles. A play by Shakespeare may stimulate you to read a book about the Elizabethan playhouse, and another that offers a Marxist interpretation of the English Renaissance, and still another that offers a feminist analysis of Shakespeare's plays. All of these approaches, and others, may help to deepen your understanding of the literary works that you read.

Formalist Criticism (New Criticism)

Formalist criticism emphasizes the work as an independent creation, a self-contained unity, something to be studied in itself, not as part of some larger context, such as the author's life or a historical period. This kind of study is called formalist criticism because the emphasis is on the *form* of the work, the relationships between the parts—the construction of the plot, the contrasts between characters, the functions of rhymes, the point of view, and so on. Formalist critics explain how and why literary works—*these* words, in *this* order—constitute unique, complex structures that embody or set forth meanings.

Cleanth Brooks, who was perhaps America's most distinguished formalist critic, in an essay in the *Kenyon Review* (Winter 1951), set forth what he called his "articles of faith":

> That literary criticism is a description and an evaluation of its object.
>
> That the primary concern of criticism is with the problem of unity—the kind of whole which the literary work forms or fails to form, and the relation of the various parts to each other in building up this whole.

That the formal relations in a work of literature may include, but certainly exceed, those of logic.

That in a successful work, form and content cannot be separated.

That form is meaning.

Formalist criticism is, in essence, *intrinsic* rather than extrinsic criticism, for it concentrates on the work itself, independent of its writer and the writer's background—that is, independent of biography, psychology, sociology, and history. The discussions of a proverb ("A rolling stone") and of a short poem by Frost ("The Span of Life") on page 132–33 are brief examples.

In practice, of course, we usually bring outside knowledge to the work. For instance, a reader who is familiar with, say, *Hamlet* can hardly study some other tragedy by Shakespeare, such as *Romeo and Juliet,* without bringing to the second play some conception of what Shakespearean tragedy is or can be. A reader of Alice Walker's *The Color Purple* inevitably brings unforgettable outside material (perhaps the experience of being an African American, or some knowledge of the history of African Americans) to the literary work. It is hard to talk only about *Hamlet* or *The Color Purple* and not at the same time talk about, or at least have in mind, aspects of human experience.

Formalist criticism begins with a personal response to the literary work, but it goes on to try to account for that response by closely examining the work. It assumes that the author shaped the poem, play, or story so fully that the work guides the reader's responses.

The assumption that "meaning" is fully and completely presented within the text is not much in favor today, when many literary critics argue that the active or subjective reader (or even what Judith Fetterley, a feminist critic, has called "the resisting reader"), and not the author of the text, makes the "meaning." Still, even if we grant that the reader is active, not passive or coolly objective, we can hold with the formalists that the author is active too, constructing a text that in some measure controls the reader's responses.

Formalist criticism usually takes one of two forms, **explication** (the unfolding of meaning, line by line or even word by word) and **analysis** (the examination of the relations of parts). The essay on Yeats's "The Balloon of the Mind" (page 527) is an explication, a setting forth of the implicit meanings of the words. The essay on Kate Chopin's "The Story of an Hour" (page 69) is an analysis. The two essays on Frost's "Stopping by Woods on a Snowy Evening" (pages 215 and 219) are chiefly analyses but with some passages of explication.

Formalist criticism, also called the **New Criticism** (to distinguish it from the historical and biographical writing that in earlier decades had dominated literary study), began to achieve prominence in the late 1920s and was dominant from the late 1930s until about 1970, and even today it is widely considered the best way for a student to begin to study a work of literature. Formalist criticism empowers the student; that is, the student confronts the work immediately and is not told first to spend days or weeks or months in preparation—for instance, reading Freud and his followers in order to write a psychoanalytic essay or reading Marx and Marxists in order to write a Marxist essay, or doing research on "necessary historical background" in order to write a historical essay.

Deconstruction

Deconstruction, or deconstructive or poststructuralist criticism, can almost be characterized as the opposite of everything that formalist criticism stands for.

Deconstruction begins with the assumptions that language is unstable, elusive, unfaithful. (Language is all of these things because meaning is largely generated by opposition: *hot* means something in opposition to *cold,* but a hot day may be 90 degrees whereas a hot oven is at least 400 degrees, and a "hot item" may be of any temperature.) Deconstructionists seek to show that a literary work (usually called "a text" or "a discourse") is inevitably self-contradictory. Unlike formalist critics—who hold that an author constructs a coherent work with a stable meaning, and that competent readers can perceive this meaning—deconstructionists hold that a work has no coherent meaning at its center.

Despite the emphasis on indeterminacy, it is sometimes possible to detect in deconstructionist interpretations a view associated with Marxism. This is the idea that authors are "socially constructed" from the "discourses of power" or "signifying practices" that surround them. Thus, although authors may think they are individuals with independent minds, their works usually reveal—unknown to the authors—powerful social, cultural, or philosophic assumptions. Deconstructionists "interrogate" a text, and they reveal what the authors were unaware of or had thought they had kept safely out of sight. That is, deconstructionists often find a rather specific meaning—though this meaning is one that might surprise the author.

Deconstruction is valuable insofar as—like the New Criticism—it encourages close, rigorous attention to the text. The problem with deconstruction, however, is that too often it is reductive, telling the same story about every text—that here, yet again, and again, we see how a text is incoherent and heterogeneous.

Reader-Response Criticism

Probably all reading includes some sort of response—"This is terrific," "This is a bore," "I don't know what's going on here"—and almost all writing about literature begins with some such response, but specialists in literature disagree greatly about the role that response plays, or should play, in experiencing literature and in writing about it.

At one extreme are those who say that our response to a work of literature should be a purely aesthetic response—a response to a work of art—and not the response we would have to something comparable in real life. To take an obvious point: If in real life we heard someone plotting a murder, we would intervene, perhaps by calling the police or by attempting to warn the victim. But when we hear Macbeth and Lady Macbeth plot to kill King Duncan, we watch with deep *interest;* we hear their words with *pleasure,* and maybe with horror and fascination we even look forward to seeing the murder and to what the characters then will say and what will happen to the murderers.

When you think about it, the vast majority of works of literature do not have a close, obvious resemblance to the reader's life. Most readers of *Macbeth* are not Scots, and no readers are Scottish kings or queens. (It's not just a matter of older literature; no readers of Toni Morrison's *Beloved* are nineteenth-century African Americans.) The connections that readers make between themselves and the lives in most of the books they read are not, on the whole, connections based on ethnic or professional identities. Rather, they are connections with states of consciousness—for instance, a young person's sense of isolation from the family, or a young person's sense of guilt for initial sexual experiences.

Before we reject a work because it seems either too close to us ("I'm a man and I don't like the depiction of this man") or too far from our experience ("I'm not a woman, so how can I enjoy reading about these women?"), we should probably try to follow the advice of Virginia Woolf, who said, "Do not dictate to your author; try to become him." Nevertheless, some literary works of the past may today seem intolerable, at least in part. There are passages in Mark Twain's *Adventures of Huckleberry Finn,* where African Americans are stereotyped or called derogatory names, that deeply upset us today. We should, however, try to reconstruct the cultural assumptions of the age in which the work was written. If we do so, we may find that if in some ways it reflected its historical era, in other ways it challenged it.

Reader-response criticism, then, says that the "meaning" of a work is not merely something put into the work by the writer; rather, the "meaning" is an interpretation created or constructed or produced by the reader as well as the writer. Stanley Fish, an exponent of reader-response theory, in *Is There a Text in This Class?* (1980), puts it this way: "Interpretation is not the art of construing but of constructing. Interpreters do not decode poems; they make them" (327).

But does every reader see his or her individual image in each literary work? Even *Hamlet,* a play that has generated an enormous range of interpretation, is universally seen as a tragedy, a play that deals with painful realities. If someone were to tell us that *Hamlet* is a comedy, and that the end, with a pile of corpses, is especially funny, we would not say, "Oh, well, we all see things in our own way." We would conclude that we have just heard a misinterpretation.

Many people who subscribe to one version or another of a reader-response theory would agree that they are concerned not with all readers but with what they call *informed readers* or *competent readers.* Informed or competent readers are familiar with the conventions of literature and understand that in a play such as *Hamlet* the characters usually speak in verse. Such readers, then, do not express amazement that Hamlet often speaks metrically and sometimes uses rhyme. These readers understand that verse is the normal language for most of the characters in the play, and therefore such readers do not characterize Hamlet as a poet. Informed readers, in short, know the rules of the game.

There will still be plenty of room for differences of interpretation. Some people will find Hamlet not at all blameworthy, others will find him somewhat blameworthy, and still others may find him highly blameworthy. In short, we can say that a writer works against a background that is *shared* by readers. As readers, we are familiar with various kinds of literature, and we read or see *Hamlet* as a particular kind of literary work, a tragedy, a play that evokes (in Shakespeare's words) "woe or wonder," sadness and astonishment. Knowing (in a large degree) how we ought to respond, our responses are not merely private.

Archetypal Criticism (Myth Criticism)

Carl G. Jung, the Swiss psychiatrist, in *Contributions to Analytical Psychology* (1928) postulates the existence of a "collective unconscious," an inheritance in our brains consisting of "countless typical experiences [such as birth, escape from danger, selection of a mate] of our ancestors." Few people today believe in an inherited "collective unconscious," but many people agree that certain repeated experiences, such as going to sleep and hours later awakening, or the perception of the setting and of the rising sun, or of the annual death and rebirth of vegetation, manifest themselves in dreams, myths, and literature—in these instances, as stories of apparent death and rebirth. This archetypal plot of death and rebirth is said to be evident in Coleridge's *The Rime of the Ancient Mariner* (1798), for example. The ship suffers a deathlike calm and then is miraculously restored to motion, and, in a sort of parallel rebirth, the mariner moves from spiritual death to renewed perception of the holiness of life. Another archetypal plot is the quest, which usually involves the testing and initiation of a hero, and thus essentially represents the movement from innocence to experience.

In addition to archetypal plots there are archetypal characters, since an **archetype** is any recurring unit. Among archetypal characters are the scapegoat (as in Shirley Jackson's "The Lottery"), the hero (savior, deliverer), the terrible mother (witch, stepmother—even the wolf "grandmother" in the tale of Little Red Riding Hood), and the wise old man (father figure, magician).

Because, the theory holds, both writer and reader share unconscious memories, the tale an author tells (derived from the collective unconscious) may strangely move the reader, speaking to his or her collective unconscious. As Maud Bodkin puts it, in *Archetypal Patterns in Poetry* (1934), something within us "leaps in response to the effective presentation in poetry of an ancient theme" (4). But this emphasis on ancient (or repeated) themes has made archetypal criticism vulnerable to the charge that it is reductive. The critic looks for certain characters or patterns of action and values the work if the motifs are there, meanwhile overlooking what is unique, subtle, distinctive, and truly interesting about the work. That is, a work is regarded as good if it closely resembles other works, with the usual motifs and characters. A second weakness in some archetypal criticism is that in its search for the deepest meaning of a work the critic may crudely impose a pattern, seeing the quest in every walk down a street.

If archetypal criticism sometimes seems farfetched, it is nevertheless true that one of its strengths is that it invites us to use comparisons, and comparing is often an excellent way to see not only what a work shares with other works but what is distinctive in the work. The most successful practitioner of archetypal criticism was Northrop Frye (1912–91), whose numerous books help readers to see fascinating connections between works. For Frye's explicit comments about archetypal criticism, as well as for examples of such criticism in action, see especially his *Anatomy of Criticism* (1957) and *The Educated Imagination* (1964). On archetypes see also Chapter 16, "Archetypal Patterns," in Norman Friedman, *Form and Meaning in Fiction* (1975).

Historical Criticism

Historical criticism studies a work within its historical context. Thus, a student of *Julius Caesar, Hamlet,* or *Macbeth*—plays in which ghosts appear—may try to learn about Elizabethan attitudes toward ghosts. We may find that the Elizabethans took ghosts more seriously than we do, or, on the other hand, we may find that ghosts were explained in various ways—for instance, sometimes as figments of the imagination and sometimes as shapes taken by the devil in order to mislead the virtuous. Similarly, a historical essay concerned with *Othello* may be devoted to Elizabethan attitudes toward Moors, or to Elizabethan ideas of love, or, for that matter, to Elizabethan ideas of a daughter's obligations toward her father's wishes concerning her suitor.

The historical critic assumes (and the assumption can hardly be disputed) that writers, however individualistic, are shaped by the social contexts in which they live. Put another way, the goal of historical criticism is to understand how people in the past thought and felt. It assumes that such knowledge can enrich our understanding of a particular work. The assumption is, however, disputable because it may be argued that the artist may *not* have shared the age's view on this or that.

All of the half-dozen or so Moors in Elizabethan plays other than *Othello* are villainous or foolish, but this evidence does not prove that *therefore* Othello is villainous or foolish.

Biographical Criticism

One kind of historical research is the study of *biography,* which for our purposes includes not only biographies but also autobiographies, diaries, journals, letters, and so on. What experiences did Mark Twain undergo? Are some of the apparently sensational aspects of *Huckleberry Finn* in fact close to events that Twain experienced? If so, is he a "realist"? If not, is he writing in the tradition of the "tall tale"?

The really good biographies not only tell us about the life of the author—they enable us to return to the literary texts with a deeper understanding of how they came to be what they are. If, for example, you read Richard B. Sewall's biography of Emily Dickinson, you will find a wealth of material concerning her family and the world she moved in—for instance, the religious ideas that were part of her upbringing.

Biographical study may illuminate even the work of a contemporary author. If you are writing about the poetry of Adrienne Rich, for example, you may want to consider what she has told us in many essays about her life, in *On Lies, Secrets, and Silence* (1979) and *Blood, Bread, and Poetry* (1986), especially about her relations with her father and her husband.

Marxist Criticism

One form of historical criticism is **Marxist criticism**, named for Karl Marx (1818–83). Actually, to say "one form" is misleading because Marxist criticism today is varied, but essentially it sees history primarily as a struggle between socioeconomic classes, and it sees literature (and everything else, too) as the product of the economic forces of the period.

For Marxists, economics is the "base" or "infrastructure"; on this base rests a "superstructure" of ideology (law, politics, philosophy, religion, and the arts, including literature), reflecting the interests of the dominant class. Literature is a material product, produced—like bread or battleships—in order to be consumed in a given society. Marxist critics are concerned with Shakespeare's plays as part of a market economy: show *business,* the economics of the theater, including payments to authors and actors and revenue from audiences.

Few critics would disagree that works of art in some measure reflect the age that produced them, but most contemporary Marxist critics go further. First, they assert—in a repudiation of what has been called "vulgar Marxist theory"—that the deepest historical meaning of a literary work is to be found in what it does *not* say, what its ideology does not permit it to express. Second, Marxists take seriously Marx's famous comment that "the philosophers have only *interpreted* the world in various ways: the point is to *change* it." The critic's job is to change the world by revealing the economic basis of the arts. Not surprisingly, most Marxists are skeptical of such concepts as "genius" and "masterpiece." These concepts, they say, are part of the bourgeois myth that idealizes the individual and detaches art from its economic context. For an introduction to Marxist criticism, see Terry Eagleton, *Marxism and Literary Criticism* (1976).

New Historicist Criticism

A recent school of scholarship, called **New Historicism**, insists that there is no "history" in the sense of a narrative of indisputable past events. Rather, New

Historicism holds that there is only our version—our narrative, our representation—of the past. In this view, each age projects its own preconceptions on the past: Historians may think they are revealing the past, but they are revealing only their own historical situation and their personal preferences.

For example, in the nineteenth century and in the twentieth almost up to 1992, Columbus was represented as the heroic benefactor of humankind who discovered the New World. But even while plans were being made to celebrate the five-hundredth anniversary of his first voyage across the Atlantic, voices were raised in protest: Columbus did not "discover" a New World; after all, the indigenous people knew where they were, and it was Columbus who was lost because he thought he was in India. In short, people who wrote history in, say, 1900 projected onto the past their current views (colonialism was a good thing), and people who wrote history in 1992 projected onto that same period a very different set of views (colonialism was a bad thing).

Similarly, ancient Greece, once celebrated by historians as the source of democracy and rational thinking, is now more often regarded as a society that was built on slavery and on the oppression of women. And the Renaissance, once glorified as an age of enlightened thought, is now often seen as an age that tyrannized women, enslaved colonial people, and enslaved itself with its belief in witchcraft and astrology. Thinking about these changing views, we feel the truth of the witticism that the only thing more uncertain than the future is the past.

On the New Historicism, see H. Aram Veeser, ed., *The New Historicism* (1989), and Veeser, ed., *The New Historicism Reader* (1994).

Psychological or Psychoanalytic Criticism

One form that biographical study may take is **psychological criticism** or *psychoanalytic criticism,* which usually examines the author and the author's writings within the framework of Freudian psychology. A central doctrine of Sigmund Freud (1856–1939) is the Oedipus complex, the view that all males (Freud seems not to have made his mind up about females) unconsciously wish to displace their fathers and to sleep with their mothers. According to Freud, hatred for the father and love of the mother, normally repressed, may appear disguised in dreams. Works of art, like dreams, are disguised versions of repressed wishes.

In *Hamlet and Oedipus* (1949) Ernest Jones, amplifying some comments by Freud, argued that Hamlet delays killing Claudius because Claudius (who has killed Hamlet's father and married Hamlet's mother) has done exactly what Hamlet himself wanted to do. For Hamlet to kill Claudius, then, would be to kill himself.

If this approach interests you, take a look at Norman N. Holland's *Psychoanalysis and Shakespeare* (1966) or Frederick Crews's study of Hawthorne, *The Sins of the Fathers* (1966). Crews finds in Hawthorne's work evidence of unresolved Oedipal conflicts, and he accounts for the appeal of the fictions thus: The stories "rest on fantasy, but on the shared fantasy of mankind, and this makes for a more penetrating fiction than would any illusionistic slice of life" (263). For applications to other authors, consider Simon O. Lesser's *Fiction and the Unconscious* (1957), or an anthology of criticism, *Literature and Psychoanalysis,* edited by Edith Kurzweil and William Phillips (1983).

Psychological criticism can also turn from the author and the work to the reader, seeking to explain why we, as readers, respond in certain ways. Why is *Hamlet* so widely popular? A Freudian answer is that it is universal because it deals with a universal (Oedipal) impulse. We can, however, ask whether it appeals as strongly to women as to men (again, Freud was unsure about the Oedipus complex in women) and, if so, why it appeals to them. Or, more generally, we can ask if males and females read in the same way.

Gender Criticism (Feminist, and Lesbian and Gay Criticism)

This last question brings us to **gender criticism**. As we have seen, writing about literature usually seeks to answer questions. Historical scholarship, for instance, tries to answer such questions as "What did Shakespeare and his contemporaries believe about ghosts?" or "How did Victorian novelists and poets respond to Darwin's theory of evolution?" Gender criticism, too, asks questions. It is especially concerned with two issues, one about reading and one about writing: "Do men and women read in different ways?" and "Do they write in different ways?"

Feminist criticism can be traced back to the work of Virginia Woolf (1882–1941), but chiefly it grew out of the women's movement of the 1960s. The women's movement at first tended to hold that women are pretty much the same as men and therefore should be treated equally, but much recent feminist criticism has emphasized and explored the differences between women and men. Because the experiences of the sexes are different, the argument goes, their values and sensibilities are different, and their responses to literature are different. Further, literature written by women is different from literature written by men. Works written by women are seen by some feminist critics as embodying the experiences of a minority culture—a group marginalized by the dominant male culture. If you have read Susan Glaspell's *Trifles* (page 443) you'll recall that this literary work itself is largely concerned about the differing ways that males and females perceive the world. Not all women are feminist critics, and not all feminist critics are women; further, there are varieties of feminist criticism. For a good introduction, see *The New Feminist Criticism: Essays on Women, Literature, and Theory* (1985), edited by Elaine Showalter, and *Feminism: An Anthology of Literary Theory and Criticism,* edited by Robyn R. Warhol and Diane Price Herndl (1997). For the role of men in feminist criticism, see *Engendering Men,* edited by Joseph A. Boone and Michael Cadden (1990).

Feminist critics rightly point out that men have established the conventions of literature and that men have established the canon—that is, the body of literature that is said to be worth reading. Speaking a bit broadly, in this patriarchal or male-dominated body of literature, men are valued for being strong and active, whereas women are expected to be weak and passive. Thus, in the world of fairy tales, the admirable male is the energetic hero (Jack, the Giant-Killer) but the admirable female is the passive Sleeping Beauty. Active women such as the wicked stepmother —or a disguised form of the same thing, the witch—are generally villainous. (There are exceptions, such as Gretel in "Hansel and Gretel.") A woman hearing or reading the story of Sleeping Beauty or of Little Red Riding Hood (rescued by the powerful woodcutter), or any other work in which women seem to be trivialized, will respond differently than a man. For instance, a woman may be socially conditioned into admiring Sleeping Beauty, but only at great cost to her mental well-being. A more resistant female reader may recognize in herself no kinship with the beautiful, passive Sleeping Beauty and may respond to the story indignantly. Another way to put it is this: The male reader perceives a romantic story, but the resistant female reader perceives a story of oppression.

For discussions of the ways in which, it is argued, women *ought* to read, you may want to look at *Gender and Reading,* edited by Elizabeth A. Flynn and Patrocino Schweikart, and especially at Judith Fetterley's *The Resisting Reader* (1978). In her discussion of Faulkner's "A Rose for Emily," Fetterley contends that the society made Emily a "lady"—society dehumanized her by elevating her. Emily's father, seeking to shape her life, stood in the doorway of their house and drove away her suitors. So far as he was concerned, Emily was a nonperson, a creature whose own wishes were not to be regarded; he alone would shape her future. Because society (beginning with her father) made her a "lady"—a creature so elevated that she is not taken seriously as a passionate human being—she is able to kill Homer Barron and not be suspected.

Here is Fetterley speaking of the passage in which the townspeople crowd into her house when her death becomes known:

> When the would-be "suitors" finally get into her father's house, they discover the consequences of his oppression of her, for the violence contained in the rotted corpse of Homer Barron is the mirror image of the violence represented in the tableau, the back-flung front door flung back with a vengeance. (42)

("A Rose for Emily" appears on pages 249–56.)

Feminist criticism has been concerned not only with the depiction of women and men in a male-determined literary canon and with women's responses to these images but also with yet another topic: women's writing. Women have had fewer opportunities than men to become writers of fiction, poetry, and drama—for one thing, they have been less well educated in the things that the male patriarchy valued—but even when they *have* managed to write, men have sometimes neglected their work simply because it was written by a woman. Feminists have further argued that certain forms of writing have been especially the province of women—for instance journals, diaries, and letters; and predictably, these forms have not been given adequate space in the traditional, male-oriented canon.

In 1972, in an essay titled "When We Dead Awaken: Writing as Re-Vision," the poet and essayist Adrienne Rich effectively summed up the matter:

> A radical critique of literature, feminist in its impulse, would take the work first of all as a clue to how we live, how we have been living, how we have been led to imagine ourselves, how our language has trapped as well as liberated us: and how we can begin to see—and therefore live—afresh. . . . We need to know the writing of the past and know it differently than we have ever known it; not to pass on a tradition but to break its hold over us.

Much feminist criticism concerned with women writers has emphasized connections between the writer's biography and her work. Suzanne Juhasz, in her introduction to *Feminist Critics Read Emily Dickinson* (1983), puts it this way:

> The central assumption of feminist criticism is that gender informs the nature of art, the nature of biography, and the relation between them. Dickinson is a woman poet, and this fact is integral to her identity. Feminist criticism's sensitivity to the components of female experience in general and to Dickinson's identity as a woman generates essential insights about her. . . . Attention to the relationship between biography and art is a requisite of feminist criticism. To disregard it further strengthens those divisions continually created by traditional criticism, so that nothing about the woman writer can be seen whole. (1–5)

Feminist criticism has made many readers—men as well as women—increasingly aware of gender relationships within literary works.

Lesbian criticism and **gay criticism** have their roots in feminist criticism; that is, feminist criticism introduced many of the questions that these other, newer developments are now exploring.

Before turning to some of the questions that lesbian and gay critics address, it is necessary to say that lesbian criticism and gay criticism are not symmetrical, because lesbian and gay relationships themselves are not symmetrical. Straight society has traditionally been more tolerant of—or blinder to—lesbianism than male homosexuality. Further, lesbian literary theory has tended to see its affinities more with feminist theory than with gay theory: that is, the emphasis has been on gender (male/female) rather than on sexuality (homosexuality/bisexuality/heterosexuality). On the other hand, some gays and lesbians have been writing what is now being called queer theory.

These are some of the questions that this criticism addresses: (1) Do lesbians and gays read in ways that differ from the ways straight people read? (2) Do they write in ways that differ from those of straight people? (3) How have straight writers portrayed lesbians and gays, and how have lesbian and gay writers portrayed straight women and men? (4) What strategies did lesbian and gay writers use to make their work acceptable to a general public in an age when lesbian and gay behavior was unmentionable?

The examination of gender by gay and lesbian critics can help to illuminate literary works, but it should be added, too, that some—perhaps most—gay and lesbian critics write also as activists, reporting their findings not only to enable us to understand and to enjoy the works of (say) Whitman, but also to change society's view of sexuality. Thus, in *Disseminating Whitman* (1991), Michael Moon is impatient with earlier critical rhapsodies about Whitman's universalism. It used to be said that Whitman's celebration of the male body was a sexless celebration of brotherly love in a democracy, but Moon's view is that we must neither whitewash Whitman's poems with such high-minded talk nor reject them as indecent; rather, we must see exactly what Whitman is saying about a kind of experience to which society had shut its eyes, and we must take Whitman's view seriously.

One assumption in much lesbian and gay critical writing is that although gender greatly influences the ways in which we read, reading is a skill that can be learned, and therefore straight people—aided by lesbian and gay critics—can learn to read, with pleasure and profit, lesbian and gay writers. This assumption also underlies much feminist criticism, which often assumes that men must stop ignoring books by women and must learn (with the help of feminist critics) how to read them, and, in fact, how to read—with newly opened eyes—the sexist writings of men of the past and present.

In addition to the titles mentioned earlier concerning gay and lesbian criticism, consult Eve Kosofsky Sedgwick, *Between Men: English Literature and Male Homosocial Desire* (1985), and an essay by Sedgwick, "Gender Criticism," in *Redrawing the Boundaries,* edited by Stephen Greenblatt and Giles Gunn (1992).

Works that concern gay or lesbian experience include those by A. E. Housman, Gloria Naylor, Adrienne Rich, and Walt Whitman.

This appendix began by making the point that all readers, whether or not they consciously adopt a particular approach to literature, necessarily read through particular lenses. More precisely, a reader begins with a frame of interpretation and from within the frame selects one of the several competing methodologies. Critics often make great—even grandiose—claims for their approaches. For example,

Frederic Jameson, a Marxist, begins *The Political Unconscious: Narrative as a Socially Symbolic Act* (1981) thus:

> This book will argue the priority of the political interpretation of literary texts. It conceives of the political perspective not as some supplemental method, not as an optional auxiliary to other interpretive methods current today—the psychoanalytic or the myth-critical, the stylistic, the ethical, the structural—but rather as the absolute horizon of all reading and all interpretation. (7)

Readers who are interested in politics may be willing to assume "the priority of the political interpretation . . . as the absolute horizon of all reading and all interpretation," but other readers may respectfully decline to accept this assumption.

In talking about a critical approach, sometimes the point is made by saying that readers decode a text by applying a grid to it: the grid enables them to see certain things clearly. But what is sometimes forgotten is that a lens or a grid—an angle of vision or interpretive frame and a methodology—also prevents a reader from seeing certain other things. This is to be expected. What is important, then, is to remember this fact, and thus not to deceive ourselves by thinking that our keen tools enable us to see the whole. A psychoanalytic reading of *Hamlet* may be helpful, but it does not reveal all that is in *Hamlet,* and it does not refute the perceptions of another approach, let's say a historical study. Each approach may illuminate aspects neglected by others.

It is too much to expect a reader to apply all useful methods (or even several) at once—that would be rather like looking through a telescope with one eye and through a microscope with the other—but it is not too much to expect readers to be aware of the limitations of their methods. If you read much criticism, you will find two kinds of critics. There are, on the one hand, critics who methodically and mechanically peer through a lens or grid, and they find what can be easily predicted they will find. On the other hand, there are critics who (despite what may be inevitable class and gender biases) are relatively open-minded in their approach—critics who, one might say, do not at the outset of their reading believe that their method assures them that they have got the text's number and that by means of this method they will expose the text for what it is.

The philosopher Richard Rorty engagingly makes a distinction somewhat along these lines, in an essay he contributed to Umberto Eco's *Interpretation and Overinterpretation* (1992). There is a great difference, Rorty suggests,

> between knowing what you want to get out of a person or thing or text in advance and hoping that the person or thing or text will help you want something different—that he or she or it will help you to change your purposes, and thus to change your life. This distinction, I think, helps us highlight the difference between methodical and inspired readings of texts. (106)

Rorty goes on to say he has seen an anthology of readings on Conrad's *Heart of Darkness,* containing a psychoanalytic reading, a reader-response reading, and so on. "None of the readers had, as far as I could see," Rorty says,

> been enraptured or destabilized by *Heart of Darkness.* I got no sense that the book had made a big difference to them, that they cared much about Kurtz or Marlow or the woman "with helmeted head and tawny cheeks" whom Marlow sees on the bank of the river. These people, and that book, had no more changed these readers' purposes than the specimen under the microscope changes the purpose of the histologist. (107)

The kind of criticism that Rorty prefers he calls "unmethodical" criticism and "inspired" criticism. It is, for Rorty, the result of an "encounter" with some aspect of a work of art "which has made a difference to the critic's conception of who she is, what she is good for, what she wants to do with herself . . ." (107). This is not a matter of "respect" for the text, Rorty insists. Rather, he says "love" and "hate" are better words, "for a great love or a great loathing is the sort of thing that changes us by changing our purposes, changing the uses to which we shall put people and things and texts we encounter later" (107).

Your Turn: Putting Critical Strategies to Work

1. Which of the critical strategies described in this chapter do you find the most interesting? Which interests you the least?
2. In Chapter 3 we present two stories by Kate Chopin, "The Story of an Hour" and "The Storm." Which critical strategy do you think is the most rewarding for the study of this author? Explain why, using your favorite story of the two as a "case study" for your arguments.
3. Select a poem in this book that you especially enjoy, and explain why you value it so highly. Next, reread and think about this poem in relation to each of the critical strategies outlined in this chapter. In what ways do these strategies, one by one, enable you to respond to and understand the poem more deeply? Does one of them seem to you especially helpful? Are any of them unhelpful?
4. Imagine that you have been assigned to prepare a mini-anthology of three or four poems and two or three stories that are particularly suited to one of these critical strategies. List your selections, and then explain how your critical strategy gives a special insight into each one, and into the group of works as a whole.
5. Do you think that any of these critical strategies could be usefully combined with one or more of the others? Could, for example, reader-response criticism go hand-in-hand with gender criticism? Select a poem or a story to show how your combination of two or more strategies can be brought together effectively.
6. Do you find that some of these critical strategies are in conflict with one another? Can you, for instance, be a formalist critic and, say, a reader-response critic or a gender critic at the same time? Is it a problem if our interpretation of a literary work changes, depending on the critical strategy that we use?
7. As you review and think further about the critical strategies we have described, do you find anything missing? How would you respond to someone who says, "What really matters is our own interpretation of a literary work, not the interpretation that this or that critical strategy produces"?

The Basics of Manuscript Form

Basic Manuscript Form

Much of what follows is nothing more than common sense.

- Use good quality **8½″ × 11″** paper. Print out a second copy, in case the instructor's copy goes astray. Make sure also to back up the file on an external hard drive or CD, or in your e-mail account.
- If you write on a computer, **double-space,** and print on one side of the page only; set the printer for professional or best quality.
- Use **one-inch margins** on all sides.
- Put your last name and then the **page number** (in arabic numerals), so that the number is flush with the right-hand margin and one-half inch from the top margin.
- On the first page, below the top margin and flush with the left-hand margin, put your **full name,** your **instructor's name,** the **course number** (including the section), and the **date,** one item per line, double-spaced.
- Center the title of your essay. Remember that the title is important—it gives the readers their first glimpse of your essay. **Create your own title**—one that reflects your topic or thesis. For example, a paper on Charlotte Perkins Gilman's "The Yellow Wallpaper" should not be called "The Yellow Wallpaper" but might be called

> Disguised Tyranny in Gilman's "The Yellow Wallpaper"

or

> How to Drive a Woman Mad

These titles do at least a little in the way of rousing a reader's interest.

- **Capitalize the title thus:** Begin the first word of the title with a capital letter, and capitalize each subsequent word except articles (*a, an, the*), conjunctions (*and, but, if, when,* etc.), and prepositions (*in, on, with,* etc.):

> A Word on Behalf of Love

Notice that you do *not* enclose your title within quotation marks, and you do *not* italicize or underline it—though if it includes the title of a poem or a story, *that* title is enclosed within quotation marks, or if it includes the title of a novel or play, *that* title is set in italics, thus:

> Gilman's "The Yellow Wallpaper" and Medical Practice

and

> Gender Stereotypes in *Hamlet*

- **After writing your title, double-space,** indent one-half inch and begin your first sentence.

- Unless your instructor tells you otherwise, **use a staple** to hold the pages together. (Do not use a stiff binder; it will only add to the bulk of the instructor's stack of papers.)
- Extensive revisions should have been made in your drafts, but minor **last-minute revisions** may be made—neatly—on the finished copy if your instructor permits. Proofreading may catch some typographical errors, and you may notice some small weaknesses.

Quotations and Quotation Marks

First, a word about the *point* of using quotations. Don't use quotations to pad the length of a paper. Rather, give quotations from the work you are discussing so that your readers will see the material being considered and (especially in a research paper) so that your readers will know what some of the chief interpretations are and what your responses to them are.

Note: The next few paragraphs do *not* discuss how to include citations of sources, a topic taken up a little later in this appendix, under the heading "Documentation."

The Golden Rule: If you quote, *comment on* the quotation. Let the reader know what you make of it and why you quote it.

Additional principles:

1. **Identify the speaker or writer of the quotation** so that the reader is not left with a sense of uncertainty. Usually, in accordance with the principle of letting readers know where they are going, this identification precedes the quoted material, but occasionally it may follow the quotation, especially if it will provide something of a pleasant surprise. For instance, in a discussion of Flannery O'Connor's stories, you might quote a disparaging comment on one of the stories and then reveal that O'Connor herself was the speaker.

2. If the quotation is part of your own sentence, **be sure to fit the quotation grammatically and logically into your sentence.**

Incorrect: Holden Caulfield tells us very little about "what my lousy childhood was like."

Correct: Holden Caulfield tells us very little about what his "lousy childhood was like."

3. **Indicate any omissions or additions.** The quotation must be exact. Any material that you add—even one or two words—must be enclosed within square brackets, thus:

Hawthorne tells us that "owing doubtless to the depth of the gloom at that

particular spot [in the forest], neither the travellers nor their steeds were visible."

If you wish to omit material from within a quotation, indicate the ellipsis by three spaced periods. That is, at the point where you are omitting material, type a space, a period, a space, a period, a space, and a third period. If you are omitting material from the end of a quoted sentence, type a period (no space) immediately following the last word quoted, then a space, a period, a space, a third period, a space, and a final period to indicate the end of your sentence. The following example is based on a quotation from the sentences immediately above this one:

> The instructions say, "If you . . . omit material from within a quotation, [you
>
> must] indicate the ellipsis. . . . If you are omitting material from the end of a
>
> quoted sentence, type . . . a period to indicate the end. . . .

Notice that although material preceded "If you," an ellipsis is not needed to indicate the omission because "If you" began a sentence in the original. Customarily, initial and terminal omissions are indicated only when they are part of the sentence you are quoting. Even such omissions need not be indicated when the quoted material is obviously incomplete—when, for instance, it is a word or phrase.

4. **Distinguish between short and long quotations,** and treat each appropriately. **Short quotations** (usually defined as four or fewer lines of typed prose or up to three lines of poetry) are enclosed within quotation marks and run into the text (rather than being set off, without quotation marks), as in the following example:

> Hawthorne begins the story by telling us that "Young Goodman Brown came forth
>
> at sunset into the street at Salem village" (640), thus at the outset connecting the
>
> village with daylight. A few paragraphs later, when Hawthorne tells us that the
>
> road Brown takes was "darkened by all of the gloomiest trees of the forest" (640),
>
> he begins to associate the forest with darkness—and a very little later with evil.

If your short quotation is from a poem, be sure to follow the capitalization of the original, and use a slash mark (with a space before and after it) to indicate separate lines. Give the line numbers, if your source gives them, in parentheses, immediately after the closing quotation marks and before the closing punctuation, thus:

> In "Diving into the Wreck," Adrienne Rich's speaker says that she puts on
>
> "body-armor" (5). Obviously the journey is dangerous.

To set off a **long quotation** (more than four typed lines of prose or more than two lines of poetry), indent the entire quotation ten spaces or one inch from the left margin. Usually, a long quotation is introduced by a clause ending with a colon— for instance,

> The following passage will make this point clear:

or

> The closest we come to hearing an editorial voice is a long passage in the middle
>
> of the story:

Or some such lead-in. After typing your lead-in, double-space, and then type the quotation, indented and double-spaced.

5. **Commas and periods go inside the quotation marks.** If you are quoting material within a sentence of your own, and you need to use a comma or a period, these marks of punctuation go *before* the closing quotation mark, as in the following example, in which the author uses a comma after "trouble" and a period after "disease."

> Chopin tells us in the first sentence that "Mrs. Mallard was afflicted with
>
> heart trouble," and in the last sentence the doctors say that Mrs. Mallard
>
> "died of heart disease."

Exception: When the quotation is immediately followed by material in parentheses or in square brackets, close the quotation, then give the parenthetic or bracketed material, and then—after the closing parenthesis or bracket—insert the comma or period.

> Chopin tells us in the first sentence that "Mrs. Mallard was afflicted with
>
> heart trouble" (57), and in the last sentence the doctors say that Mrs.
>
> Mallard "died of heart disease" (58).

Semicolons, colons, and dashes go outside (after) the closing quotation mark.
Question marks and exclamation points go inside if they are part of the quotation, outside if they are your own.

In the following passage from a student's essay, notice the difference in the position of the question marks. The first question mark is part of the quotation, so it is enclosed within the quotation marks. The second question mark, however, is the student's, so it comes after the closing quotation mark.

> The older man says to Goodman Brown, "Sayest thou so?" Doesn't a reader
>
> become uneasy when the man immediately adds, "We are but a little way in
>
> the forest yet"?

Quotation Marks or Italics?

Use quotation marks around titles of short stories and other short works—that is, titles of chapters in books, essays, and poems that might not be published by themselves. Use italics for titles of books, periodicals, collections of essays, plays, and long poems such as *The Rime of the Ancient Mariner.*

A Note on the Possessive

It is awkward to use the possessive case for titles of literary works and secondary sources. Rather than "*The Great Gatsby*'s final chapter," write instead "the final chapter of *The Great Gatsby.*" Not "*The Oxford Companion to American Literature*'s entry on Emerson," but, instead, "the entry on Emerson in *The Oxford Companion to American Literature.*"

Documentation: Internal Parenthetical Citations and a List of Works Cited (MLA Format)

Documentation tells your reader exactly what your sources are. Here we describe how to create internal parenthetical citations and the Works Cited list.

Internal Parenthetical Citations

On page 1409 we distinguish between embedded quotations (which are short, are made part of your own sentence, and are enclosed in quotation marks) and quotations that are set off on the page and not enclosed in quotation marks (for example, three or more lines of poetry, five or more lines of typed prose).

For an embedded quotation, put the page reference in parentheses immediately after the closing quotation marks *without* any intervening punctuation. Then, after the parenthesis that follows the number, insert the necessary punctuation (for instance, a comma or a period):

> Brent Staples says that he "learned to smother the rage" he felt at "often being
>
> taken for a criminal" (337).

The period comes *after* the parenthetical citation. In the next example *no* punctuation comes after the first citation—because none is needed—and a comma comes *after* (not before or within) the second citation, because a comma is needed in the sentence:

> This is ironic because almost at the start of the story, in the second paragraph,
>
> Richards with the best of motives "hastened" (57) to bring his sad message; if he
>
> had at the start been "too late" (58), Mallard would have arrived at home first.

For a quotation that is not embedded within the text but is set off (by being indented ten spaces), put the parenthetical citation on the last line of the quotation, one space *after* the punctuation that ends the quoted sentence.

Four additional points:

- The abbreviations *p.*, *pg.*, and *pp.* are *not* used in citing pages.
- If a story is very short, perhaps running for only a page or two, your instructor may tell you there is no need to keep citing the page reference for each quotation. Simply include on your Works Cited list the story's page numbers, say, 205–206.
- If you are referring to a poem, your instructor may tell you to use parenthetical citations of line numbers rather than of page numbers. But, again, your Works Cited list will tell the reader where the poem can be found.
- If you are referring to a play with numbered lines, your instructor may prefer that in your parenthetical citations you give act, scene, and line, rather than page numbers. Use arabic (not roman) numerals, separating the act from the scene, and the scene from the line, by periods. Here, then, is how a reference to Act 3, Scene 2, line 105 would be given:

> When Hamlet says to Ophelia, "That's a fair thought to lie between maids'
>
> legs (3.2.105), she does not understand that he is making a lewd comment.

Parenthetical Citations and List of Works Cited

Parenthetical citations are clarified by means of a list, headed "Works Cited," that appears at the end of the essay. In this list you give alphabetically (last name first) the authors and titles that you have quoted or referred to in the essay, and full publication information.

Briefly, the idea is that the reader of your paper encounters an author's name and a parenthetical citation of pages. By checking the author's name in Works Cited, the reader can find the passage in the book. Suppose you are writing about Kate Chopin's "The Story of an Hour." Let's assume that you have already mentioned the author and the title of the story—that is, you have let the reader know the subject of the essay—and now you introduce a quotation from the story in a sentence such as this. (Notice the parenthetical citation of page numbers immediately after the quotation.)

> True, Mrs. Mallard at first expresses grief when she hears the news, but soon
>
> (unknown to her friends) she finds joy in it. So, Richards's "sad message" (57),
>
> though sad in Richards's eyes, is in fact a happy message.

Turning to Works Cited, the reader, knowing the quoted words are by Chopin, looks for Chopin and finds the following:

> Chopin, Kate. "The Story of an Hour." *Literature for Composition*.
>
> Ed. Sylvan Barnet, William Burto, and William E. Cain. 10th ed.
>
> New York: Pearson, 2014. 57-58. Print.

Thus the essayist informs the reader that the quoted words ("sad message") are to be found on page 57 of this anthology.

If you have not mentioned Chopin's name in some sort of lead-in, you will have to give her name within the parentheses so that the reader will know the author of the quoted words:

> What are we to make out of a story that ends by telling us that the leading
>
> character has died "of joy that kills" (Chopin 58)?

If you are referring to several works reprinted within one volume, instead of listing each item fully, it is acceptable in Works Cited to list each item simply by giving the author's name, the title of the work, then a period, a space, and the name of the anthologist, followed by the page numbers that the selection spans. Thus a reference to Chopin's "The Story of an Hour" would be followed only by: Barnet 57–58. This form requires that the anthology itself be cited under the name of the first-listed editor, thus:

> Barnet, Sylvan, William Burto, and William E. Cain., eds. *Literature*
>
> *for Composition*. 10th ed. New York: Pearson, 2014. Print.
>
> Chopin, Kate. "The Story of an Hour." Barnet 57-58.

If you are writing a research paper, you will use many sources. In the essay itself you will mention an author's name, quote or summarize from this author, and follow the quotation or summary with a parenthetical citation of the pages. In Works Cited you will give the full title, place of publication, and other bibliographic material.

Here are a few examples, all referring to an article by Joan Templeton, "The *Doll House* Backlash: Criticism, Feminism, and Ibsen." The article appeared in *PMLA* 104 (1989): 28–40, but this information is given only in Works Cited, not within the text of the student's essay.

If in the text of your essay you mention the author's name, the citation following a quotation (or a summary of a passage) will be merely a page number in parentheses, followed by a period, thus:

> In 1989 Joan Templeton argued that many critics, unhappy with recognizing
>
> Ibsen as a feminist, sought "to render Nora inconsequential" (29).

Or:

> In 1989 Joan Templeton noted that many critics, unhappy with recognizing
>
> Ibsen as a feminist, have sought to make Nora trivial (29).

If you don't mention the name of the author in a lead-in, you will have to give the name within the parenthetical citation:

> Many critics, attempting to argue that Ibsen was not a feminist, have tried to
>
> make Nora trivial (Templeton 29).

Notice in all of these examples that the final period comes after the parenthetical citation. *Exception:* When the quotation is longer than four lines and is therefore set off by being indented ten spaces from the left margin, end the quotation with the appropriate punctuation (period, question mark, or exclamation mark), hit the space bar, then type (in parentheses) the page number. In this case, do not put a period after the citation.

Another point: If your list of Works Cited includes more than one work by an author, in your essay when you quote or refer to one or the other you'll have to identify *which* work you are drawing on. You can provide the title in a lead-in, thus:

> In "The *Doll House* Backlash: Criticism, Feminism, and Ibsen," Templeton says,
>
> "Nora's detractors have often been, from the first, her husband's defenders" (30).

Or you can provide the information in the parenthetical citation, giving a shortened version of the title. This usually consists of the first word, unless it is *A, An,* or *The,* in which case including the second word is usually enough. Certain titles may require still another word or two, as in this example:

> According to Templeton, "Nora's detractors have often been, from the first, her
>
> husband's defenders" ("*Doll House* Backlash" 30).

Forms of Citation in Works Cited

In looking over the following sample entries in a Works Cited list, remember:

- The list of Works Cited appears at the end of the paper. It begins on a new page, and that page continues the numbering of the text pages.
- The list of Works Cited is arranged alphabetically by author (last name first).

- If a work is anonymous, list it under the first word of the title unless the first word is *A, An,* or *The,* in which case list it under the second word.
- If a work is by two authors, although the book is listed alphabetically under the first author's last name, the second author's name is given in the normal order, first name first.
- If you list two or more works by the same author, the author's name is not repeated after the first entry but is represented by three hyphens followed by a period and a space.
- Each item begins flush left; if an entry is longer than one line, subsequent lines in the entry are indented five spaces.

For details about preparing almost every imaginable kind of citation, consult the *MLA Handbook for Writers of Research Papers,* 7th ed. (New York: Modern Language Association, 2009). Here we give samples of the kinds of citations you are most likely to include in your list of Works Cited. (For citations of electronic sources, see pages 1419–1421.)

A book by one author:

Douglas, Ann. *The Feminization of American Culture.* New York: Knopf, 1977. Print.

Notice that the author's last name is given first, but otherwise the name is given as it appears on the title page. Do not substitute initials for names written out on the title page, but you may shorten the publisher's name—for example, from *Oxford University Press* to *Oxford UP.*

Take the title from the title page, not from the cover or the spine, and disregard unusual typography—for instance, the use of only capital letters or the use of & for *and.* Italicize both title and subtitle. The place of publication is indicated by the name of the city. If several cities have the same name (for instance, Cambridge, Massachusetts, and Cambridge, England) the name of the state or country may be added. If the title page lists several cities, give only the first one. For a print source, add the word "Print" at the end of the entry.

A book by two or three authors:

Gilbert, Sandra M., and Susan Gubar. *The Madwoman in the Attic: The Woman Writer and*

   the Nineteenth-Century Literary Imagination. New Haven: Yale UP, 1979. Print.

Notice that the book is listed under the last name of the first author (Gilbert) and that the second author's name is then given with first name (Susan) first. *If the book has more than three authors,* give the name of the first author only (last name first) and follow it with *et al.* (Latin for "and others").

A book by more than three authors:

Beidler, Peter G., et al. *A Reader's Companion to J. D. Salinger's* The Catcher in the Rye.

   Seattle: Coffeetown Press, 2009. Print.

A book in several volumes:

McQuade, Donald, et al., eds. *The Harper American Literature.* 2nd ed. 2 vols. New York:

   Harper, 1994. Print.

> Pope, Alexander. *The Correspondence of Alexander Pope*. Ed. George Sherburn. 5 vols.
>
> Oxford: Clarendon, 1955. Print.

The total number of volumes is given, regardless of the number that you have used.

If you have used more than one volume, within your essay you will parenthetically indicate a reference to, for instance, page 30 of volume 3 thus: (3: 30). If you have used only one volume of a multivolume work—let's say you used only volume 2 of McQuade's anthology—in your entry in Works Cited write, after the period following the date, Vol. 2. In your parenthetical citation within the essay you will therefore cite only the page reference (without the volume number) because the reader will (on consulting Works Cited) understand that in this example the reference is in volume 2.

If, instead of using the volumes as a whole, you used only an independent work within one volume—say, an essay in volume 2—in Works Cited omit the abbreviation *Vol.* Instead, give an arabic 2 (indicating volume 2) followed by a colon, a space, and the page numbers that encompass the selection you used:

> McPherson, James Alan. "Why I Like Country Music." *The Harper American Literature*. Ed.
>
> Donald McQuade et al. 2nd ed. 2 vols. New York: Longman, 1994. 2: 2304-15. Print.

Notice that this entry for McPherson specifies not only that the book consists of two volumes, but also that only one selection ("Why I Like Country Music," occupying pages 2304–2315 in volume 2) was used. If you use this sort of citation in Works Cited, in the body of your essay a documentary reference to this work will be only to the page; the volume number will *not* be added.

A book with a separate title in a set of volumes:

> Churchill, Winston. *The Age of Revolution*. Vol. 3 of *A History of the English-Speaking*
>
> *Peoples*. New York: Dodd, 1957. Print.
>
> Jonson, Ben. *The Complete Masques*. Ed. Stephen Orgel. Vol. 4 of *The Yale Ben Jonson*. New
>
> Haven: Yale UP, 1969. Print.

A revised edition of a book:

> Chaucer, Geoffrey. *The Riverside Chaucer*. Ed. Larry Benson. 3rd ed. Boston: Houghton,
>
> 1987. Print.
>
> Ellmann, Richard. *James Joyce*. Rev. ed. New York: Oxford UP, 1982. Print.

A reprint, such as a paperback version of an older hardcover book:

> Rourke, Constance. *American Humor*. 1931. Garden City: Doubleday, 1953. Print.

Notice that the entry cites the original date (1931) but indicates that the writer is using the Doubleday reprint of 1953.

An edited book other than an anthology:

> Keats, John. *The Letters of John Keats*. Ed. Hyder Edward Rollins. 2 vols. Cambridge:
>
> Harvard UP, 1958. Print.

An anthology: You can list an anthology either under the editor's name or under the title.

A work in a volume of works by one author:

> Sontag, Susan. "The Aesthetics of Silence." *Styles of Radical Will*. New York: Farrar, 1969.
>
> 3-34. Print.

This entry indicates that Sontag's essay "The Aesthetics of Silence" appears in a book of hers titled *Styles of Radical Will*. Notice that the page numbers of the short work are cited (not the page numbers that you may happen to refer to, but the page numbers of the entire piece).

A work in an anthology, that is, in a collection of works by several authors: Begin with the author and the title of the work you are citing, not with the name of the anthologist or the title of the anthology. The entry ends with the pages occupied by the selection you are citing:

> Ng, Fae Myenne. "A Red Sweater." *Charlie Chan Is Dead: An Anthology of Contemporary Asian*
>
> *American Fiction*. Ed. Jessica Hagedorn. New York: Penguin, 1993. 358-68. Print.

Normally, you will give the title of the work you are citing (probably an essay, short story, or poem) in quotation marks. If you are referring to a book-length work (for instance, a novel or a full-length play), italicize it. If the work is translated, after the period that follows the title, write *Trans.* and give the name of the translator, followed by a period and the name of the anthology.

If the collection is a multivolume work and you are using only one volume, in Works Cited you will specify the volume, as in the example (page 1415) of McPherson's essay. Because the list of Works Cited specifies the volume, your parenthetical documentary reference within your essay will specify (as mentioned earlier) only the page numbers, not the volume. Thus, although McPherson's essay appears on pages 2304–15 in the second volume of a two-volume work, a parenthetical citation will refer only to the page numbers because the citation in Works Cited specifies the volume.

Remember that the pages specified in the entry in your list of Works Cited are those of the *entire selection*, not simply the pages you refer to within your paper.

If you are referring to a *reprint of a scholarly article*, give details of the original publication:

> Mack, Maynard. "The World of Hamlet." *Yale Review* 41 (1952): 502-23. Rpt. in *Hamlet*.
>
> By William Shakespeare. Ed. Sylvan Barnet. New York: Penguin Putnam, 1998.
>
> 265-87. Print.

Two or more works in an anthology: If you are referring to more than one work in an anthology, in order to avoid repeating all the information about the anthology in each entry in Works Cited, under each author's name (in the appropriate alphabetical place) give the author and title of the work, then a period, a space, and the name of the anthologist, followed by the page numbers that the selection spans. A reference to Shakespeare's *Hamlet* would appear as

> Shakespeare, William. *Hamlet*. Barnet 878-980.

rather than by a full citation of Barnet's anthology. This form requires that the anthology itself also be listed, under Barnet.

Two or more works by the same author: Notice that the works are given in alphabetical order (*Fables* precedes *Fools*) and that the author's name is not repeated but is represented by three hyphens followed by a period and a space. If the author is the translator or editor of a volume, the three hyphens are followed not by a period but by a comma, then a space, then the appropriate abbreviation (*Trans.* or *Ed.*), then the title:

> Frye, Northrop. *Fables of Identity: Studies in Poetic Mythology.* New York: Harcourt, 1963.
>
> Print.
>
> ---. *Fools of Time: Studies in Shakespearean Tragedy.* Toronto: U of Toronto P, 1967. Print.

A translated book:

> Gogol, Nikolai. *Dead Souls.* Trans. Andrew McAndrew. New York: New American Library,
>
> 1961. Print.

If you are discussing the translation itself, as opposed to the book, list the work under the translator's name. Then put a comma, a space, and "trans." After the period following "trans," skip a space, then give the title of the book, a period, a space, and then "By" and the author's name, first name first. Continue with information about the place of publication, publisher, and date, as in any entry for a book.

An introduction, foreword, afterword, or other editorial apparatus:

> Fromm, Erich. Afterword. *1984.* By George Orwell. New York: New American Library, 1961.
>
> Print.

Usually a book with an introduction or comparable section is listed under the name of the author of the book rather than the name of the author of the editorial material (see the citation of Pope on page 1415). But if you are referring to the editor's apparatus rather than to the work itself, use the form just given.

Words such as *preface, introduction, afterword,* and *conclusion* are capitalized in the entry but are neither enclosed within quotation marks nor underlined.

A book review: First, here is an example of a review that does not have a title.

> Vendler, Helen. Rev. of *Essays on Style,* ed. Roger Fowler. *Essays in Criticism* 16 (1966):
>
> 457-63. Print.

If the review has a title, give the title after the period following the reviewer's name, before "Rev." If the review is unsigned, list it under the first word of the title, or the second word if the first word is *A, An,* or *The.* If an unsigned review has no title, begin the entry with "Rev. of" and alphabetize it under the title of the work being reviewed.

An encyclopedia: The first example is for a signed article, the second example is for an unsigned article.

Lang, Andrew. "Ballads." *Encyclopaedia Britannica*. 1910 ed. Print.

"Metaphor." *The New Encyclopaedia Britannica: Micropaedia*. 1974 ed. Print.

An article in a scholarly journal: Some journals are paginated consecutively; that is, the pagination of the second issue picks up where the first issue left off. Other journals begin each issue with a new page one. The forms of the citations in Works Cited differ slightly.

First, the citation of a *journal that uses continuous pagination:*

Burbick, Joan. "Emily Dickinson and the Economics of Desire." *American Literature* 58

(1986): 361-78. Print.

This article appeared in volume 58, which was published in 1986. (Notice that the volume number is followed by a space, then by the year in parentheses, and then by a colon, a space, and the page numbers of the entire article.) Although each volume consists of four issues, you do *not* specify the issue number when the journal is paginated continuously.

For a *journal that paginates each issue separately* (a quarterly journal will have four page ones each year), give the issue number directly after the volume number and a period, with no space before or after the period:

Spillers, Hortense J. "Martin Luther King and the Style of the Black Sermon." *The Black*

Scholar 3.1 (1971): 14-27. Print.

An article in a weekly, biweekly, or monthly publication:

McCabe, Bernard. "Taking Dickens Seriously." *Commonweal* 14 May 1965: 24. Print.

Notice that the volume number and the issue number are omitted for popular weeklies or monthlies such as *Time* and *Atlantic.*

An article in a newspaper: Because newspapers usually consist of several sections, a section number may precede the page number. The example indicates that an article begins on page 3 of section 2 and continues on a later page:

Wu, Jim. "Authors Praise New Forms." *New York Times* 8 Mar. 1996, late ed., sec. 2: 3+. Print.

You may have occasion to cite other than a printed source, for instance, a lecture. Here are the forms for the chief nonprint sources.

An interview:

Saretta, Howard. Personal interview. 3 Nov. 2011.

A lecture:

Heaney, Seamus. Tufts University, Medford, MA. 15 Oct. 1998. Lecture.

A television or radio program:

60 Minutes. CBS. WCBS, New York. 30 Jan. 1994. Television.

A film or video recording:

Modern Times. Dir. Charles Chaplin. United Artists, 1936. DVD.

A sound recording:

> Frost, Robert. "The Road Not Taken." *Robert Frost Reads His Poetry*. Caedmon, TC 1060,
>
> 1956. MP3.

A performance:

> *The Cherry Orchard*. By Anton Chekhov. Dir. Ron Daniels. American Repertory Theatre,
>
> Cambridge, MA. 3 Feb. 1994. Performance.

Citing Internet Sources

Many Web sites and pages are not prepared according to the style and form in which you want to cite them. Sometimes the name of the author is unknown, and other information may be missing or hard to find. Perhaps the main point to remember is that a source on the Internet is as much a source as is a book or article that you can track down and read in the library. If you have made use of it, you must acknowledge that you have done so and include the bibliographical information, as fully as you can, in your list of Works Cited.

The Wellesley College Library offers a valuable site for searching the Web and evaluating what you find there:

> http://new.wellesley.edu/lts/gettingstarted/startresearch

CHECKLIST: *Citing Sources on the Web*

Provide the following information:

☐ Author's name.
☐ Title of work in quotation marks, or in italics if a longer work or book title.
☐ Title of Web site in italics followed by a period.
☐ Publisher or sponsor of Web site followed by a comma. (Use *N.p.* if that information is not available.)
☐ Date of publication, followed by a period. (Use *n.d.* if that information is not available.)
☐ Publication medium—*Web*—followed by a period.
☐ Date of access when you accessed the site.
☐ Include the URL only when your reader cannot locate the source without it.

A short work within a scholarly project:

> Whitman, Walt. "Crossing Brooklyn Ferry." *The Walt Whitman Archive*. Ed. Kenneth M.
>
> Price and Ed Folson. The Walt Whitman Archive, 16 Mar. 1998. Web. 3 Apr. 2008.

1. Author's name
2. Title of work in quotation marks

3. Title of Web site in italics
4. Editors of Web site if available
5. Version or edition used
6. Publisher or sponsor of the site. If not available use *N.p.*
7. Date of publication
8. Medium of publication (*Web*)
9. Date of access (day, month, year)

A personal or professional site:

Winter, Mick. *How to Talk New Age*. The Well, 6 Jan. 2004. Web. 6 Apr. 2009.

An online book published independently:

Smith, Adam. *The Wealth of Nations*. New York: Methuen. 1904. *Bibliomania*, n.d. Web.

3 Mar. 2008.

1. Author's name
2. Title of work in italics
3. Edition used
4. City of publication, publisher, and year of publication
5. Title of the database or Web site in italics
6. Date of publication (use n.d. if unavailable)
7. Medium of publication (*Web*)
8. Date of access (day, month, year)

An online book within a scholarly project:

Whitman, Walt. *Leaves of Grass*. Philadelphia: McKay, 1891-92. *The Walt Whitman Archive*.

Ed. Kenneth M. Price and Ed Folson. The Walt Whitman Archive, 16 Mar. 1998. Web.

3 Apr. 2008.

An article in an online scholarly journal:

Jackson, Francis L. "Mexican Freedom: The Ideal of the Indigenous State." *Animus* 2.3

(1997): n. pag. Web. 4 Apr. 2009.

1. Author's name
2. Title of article in quotation marks
3. Name of the publication in italics
4. Volume number
5. Issue number if available
6. Date of publication
7. Inclusive page numbers if available (use *n. pag.* if no pages are cited)
8. Medium of publication (*Web*)
9. Date of access (day, month, year)

An article from a database:

Farley-Hills, David. "Hamlet's Account of the Pirates." *Review of English Studies* 50.199

(1999): 320-31. *JSTOR*. Web. 1 Apr. 2012.

An unsigned article in a newspaper or on a newswire:

"Drug Czar Wants to Sharpen Drug War." *TopNews* 6 Apr. 1998. Web. 6 Apr. 2012.

An unsigned article in a newspaper or on a Web site:

"Hiking: Richard W. DeKorte Park, Lyndhurst." *North Jersey.com*. North Jersey Media Group,

2 July 2009. Web. 10 July 2009.

An article in a magazine:

Pitta, Julie. "Un-Wired?" *Forbes.com*. Forbes, 20 Apr. 1998. Web. 6 Apr. 2012.

A review:

Beer, Francis A. Rev. of *Evolutionary Paradigms in the Social Sciences, Special Issue,*

International Studies Quarterly 40.3 (Sept. 1996). *Journal of Memetics* 1 (1997).

Web. 4 Jan. 2008.

An editorial or letter to the editor:

"The Net Escape Censorship? Ha!" Editorial. *Wired*. Wired, Sept. 1995. Web. 1 Apr. 2012.

E-mail:

Mendez, Michael R. "Re: Solar power." Message to Edgar V. Atamian. 11 Sept. 2012. E-mail.

Armstrong, David J. Message to the author. 30 Aug. 2012. E-mail.

An Online Posting: For online postings or synchronous communications, try to cite a version stored as a Web file, if one exists, as a courtesy to the reader. Label sources as needed (e.g., *Online posting, Online defense of dissertation*, and so forth, with neither underlining nor quotation marks). Follow these models as appropriate:

Listserv (electronic mailing list):

Kosten, A. "Major update of the WWWVL Migration and Ethnic Relations." 7 Apr. 1998.

Online posting. ERCOMER News. 7 May 1998.

A video accessed online:

The Poet's View: C. K. Williams. YouTube. The Academy of American Poets, 17 Mar. 2009.

Web. 1 Apr. 2012.

Photograph or painting accessed online:

Manet, Edouard. *Le Déjeuner sur l'herbe*. 1863. *Wikimedia Commons*. Wikimedia Foundation,

26 Nov. 2008. Web. 1 Apr. 2012.

How Much Do You Know about Citing Sources? A Quiz with Answers*

Taking this quiz will let you test yourself and will assist you in any discussion you have with your classmates about how to cite sources accurately and honestly.

QUIZ YOURSELF: HOW MUCH DO YOU KNOW ABOUT CITING SOURCES?

Section 1: Plagiarism and Academic Dishonesty

Which of the following examples describe violations of academic integrity? Check all the examples that are punishable under university rules.

_____ 1. You buy a term paper from a Web site and turn it in as your own work.

_____ 2. You ask a friend to write a paper for you.

_____ 3. You can't find the information you need, so you invent statistics, quotes, and sources that do not exist and cite them in your paper as if they were real.

_____ 4. Your professor requires you to use five sources, but you find one book written by one person that has all the information you need, so you cite that book as if it were information coming from other books and authors in order to make it look like you used five different sources.

_____ 5. Your history professor and your political science professor both assign a term paper. To save time, you write one paper that meets both requirements and hand it in to both professors.

_____ 6. You don't want to have too many quotes in your paper, so you do not put quotation marks around some sentences you copied from a source. You cite the source correctly at the end of the paragraph and in your Works Cited list.

_____ 7. You have copied a long passage from a book into your paper, and you changed some of the wording. You cite the source at the end of the passage and again in the Works Cited list.

---

*This quiz and the answers were written by Carmen Lowe, Director of the Tufts University Academic Resource Center. We are grateful to Ms. Lowe for permission to use her material.

_____ 8. While writing a long research paper, you come across an interesting hypothesis mentioned in a book, and you incorporate this hypothesis into your main argument. After you finish writing the paper, you can't remember where you initially found the hypothesis, so you don't bother to cite the source of your idea.

Section 2: Common Knowledge

Common knowledge is information that is widely known within a society or an intellectual community; therefore, if you include common knowledge in your paper, you do not need to cite the source where you found that information.

Answer *Yes* or *No* to the following questions:

_____ 1. In a high school class on American government, you learned about the checks-and-balances system of government, which separates power into the judicial, executive, and legislative branches. Now, you are writing a paper for an introductory political science class and you mention the concept of checks-and-balances you learned in high school. Should you cite your old high school textbook?

_____ 2. In writing a paper about pop culture in the 1980s, you want to include the year that President Ronald Reagan was shot but you cannot remember whether it was 1980 or 1981, so you look up the correct date in an encyclopedia. Do you have to include that encyclopedia as a source for the date on which Reagan was shot?

_____ 3. You do most of your research online and find lots of interesting Web sites from which you quote several passages. After you write the first draft, you ask your older and more experienced roommate if he knows how to cite Web sites. He says that Web sites are in the public domain and constitute common knowledge, and therefore they do not need to be cited. Is this true?

_____ 4. In writing a research paper on astrophysics, you come across something called the Eridanus Effect several times. You have never heard of this effect nor discussed it in your class, but after reading about it in six different astrophysics journal articles, you have a pretty clear idea of what it is and its most common characteristics. Is the Eridanus Effect common knowledge within astrophysics?

_____ 5. Your older sister works for a nonprofit organization that runs adult literacy programs in factories and unemployment centers in several major cities. During winter break, she tells you about the success of one of the programs in St. Louis and the innovative curricula it has designed. Several weeks into spring semester, you remember your conversation as you are writing an economics term paper on empowerment zones and unemployment in the inner city. If you include a description of the program, do you need to cite a source, even if it is just your sister?

_____ 6. You are writing a paper on Shakespeare's *Hamlet*. Your textbook's introduction to the play mentions that Shakespeare was born in 1564 in Stratford-upon-Avon. You mention these facts in your paper's introduction. Do you need to cite the introduction to your textbook?

_____ 7. You are writing a paper on Shakespeare's *Hamlet*. A footnote in your text-book mentions that some literary historians now believe that Shakespeare himself played the ghost when the play was first performed. If you mention Shakespeare's playing the ghost, do you need to cite this footnote in your textbook?

_____ 8. You are writing a paper on the assassination of Robert Kennedy. The three major biographies on him mention when he was killed and by whom. Do you have to cite all these biographies when you mention that date and the murderer's name?

_____ 9. You are writing a paper on the assassination of Robert Kennedy. The most influential biography on him mentions a controversial conspiracy theory first put forward in the early 1970s by a journalist for the *Washington Post*. When you mention this conspiracy theory, should you cite the biography?

Section 3: Quoting, Paraphrasing, and Summarizing Texts

Read the following passage excerpted from an online edition of a foreign policy magazine. Determine whether any of the sample sentences that follow improperly cite a source within the sentence or are plagiarized.

> The illegal trade in drugs, arms, intellectual property, people, and money is booming. Like the war on terrorism, the fight to control these illicit markets pits governments against agile, stateless, and resourceful networks empowered by globalization. Governments will continue to lose these wars until they adopt new strategies to deal with a larger, unprecedented struggle that now shapes the world as much as confrontations between nation-states once did.

—Moisés Naím, "The Five Wars of Globalization."
Foreign Policy Jan.-Feb. 2003: Online Edition.
<http://www.foreignpolicy.com>. January 13, 2003.

Read the following passages and mark **OK** if the passage is fine. If the passage is plagiarized, improperly paraphrased, or otherwise cited inadequately, mark it with **X**.

_____ 1. In his essay on "The Five Wars of Globalization," Moisés Naím argues that governments need to find new ways to handle the kinds of borderless illegal activity increasing under globalization.

_____ 2. In describing the "illegal trade in drugs, arms, intellectual property, people, and money" as "booming," Moisés Naím asserts that governments need to adopt new strategies to deal with this unprecedented struggle that now shapes the world (http://www.foreignpolicy.com).

_____ 3. Like the war on terror, the struggle to control illegal trade in drugs, arms, money, etc., pits governments against cunning, stateless, and enterprising networks empowered by globalization (Moises 2003).

_____ 4. Many experts believe that globalization is changing the face of foreign policy.

Read the following passage from a book on romance novels and soap operas, then read the statements that follow to determine whether any of them plagiarize or improperly cite material from the passage.

> The complexity of women's responses to romances has not been sufficiently acknowledged. Instead of exploring the possibility that romances, while serving to keep women in their place, may at the same time be concerned with real female problems, analysts of women's romances have generally seen the fantasy embodied in romantic fiction either as evidence of female "masochism" or as a simple reflection of the dominant masculine ideology. For instance, Germaine Greer, referring to the idealized males of women's popular novels, says, "This is the hero that women have chosen for themselves. The traits invented for him have been invented by women cherishing the chains of their bondage."[9] But this places too much blame on women, and assumes a freedom of choice which is not often in evidence—not in their lives and therefore certainly not in their popular arts.
>
> —Tania Modleski, *Loving with a Vengeance: Mass-Produced Fantasies for Women.* New York: Methuen, 1982. 37–38.

Read the following and mark **OK** if the statement is fine as is. If the statement is plagiarized in part or whole or is otherwise cited improperly, mark it with **X**.

_____ 1. Tania Modleski claims that Germaine Greer oversimplifies why women read romance novels (38).

_____ 2. Modleski states that although romance novels may keep women in their place, they also address real female problems (37).

_____ 3. Feminist critics see the fantasy embodied in romance novels either as evidence of female "masochism" or as a simple reflection of male chauvinism (Modleski 37–38).

_____ 4. One feminist writer, Germaine Greer, says that the idealized male featured in women's popular romance novels "is the hero that women have chosen for themselves. The traits invented for him have been invented by women cherishing the chains of their bondage."[9] (38).

_____ 5. Tania Modleski rejects the idea that the fantasies expressed in romance novels are merely a reflection of some innate masochism in women who, in the words of Germaine Greer, "cherish[. . .] the chains of their bondage" (37; Greer qtd. in Modleski, 38).

Section 4: Miscellaneous

_____ 1. **You read *Time* magazine every week and notice that the writers in the magazine never use footnotes or parenthetical citations. Why don't newswriters cite their sources?**
   a. Citing sources is required only of students, not professional writers.
   b. Professional publications are free to decide whether they will require footnotes or citations of any kind.
   c. By law, journalists are exempt from revealing their sources of information.
   d. Newspapers and magazines have limited space on the page, so they cut off the citations or footnotes to make room for more copy.

_____ 2. **Plagiarism is a violation of which of the following laws:**
   a. Copyright.
   b. Intellectual property.
   c. Both *a* and *b* above.
   d. None of the above; it is not a legal issue and is not punishable by law
       because it only pertains to students.

_____ 3. **If you use a quote found in a book of quotes or from an online
       compilation of quotes such as Bartlett's, how do you cite the quote?**
   a. You don't—quotes found in a collection of quotations (whether online
       or in a book) are considered well-known and in the public domain.
       Just include the name of the person to whom the quote is attributed.
       You can also add the date if it seems relevant.
   b. You should cite the original source of the quote followed by the biblio-
       graphic information from the quotation compilation, such as: Shakespeare,
       William. *A Midsummer Night's Dream.* Quoted in *Familiar Quotations:
       Being an Attempt to Trace to Their Sources Passages and Phrases in Common
       Use,* by John Bartlett (Boston: Little, Brown, 1886), 44.
   c. You should find the original source and cite that.
   d. All of the above: *a* is correct, and *b* and *c* are possible options if you
       want to be extra careful or if the quote is extremely important to your
       paper. Use your common sense in this situation.

Answer Key to Plagiarism Quiz

**The Plagiarism Quiz works best when the answers are discussed in class
or one-on-one with a student and professor.**

Section 1: Plagiarism and Academic Dishonesty

All eight incidents are forms of plagiarism or academic dishonesty. Many students
are confused about the last four incidents, so please discuss them with your
instructor if you need clarification.

Section 2: Common Knowledge

1. No; the basic facts about the checks-and-balances system are common
   knowledge and do not need to be cited.
2. No; even if you cannot remember the exact date of the assassination attempt on Reagan, it is common knowledge because the date is undisputed
   and can be found in a variety of sources.
3. No; writing on the Web is protected by copyright and must be cited, even
   if no author is listed.
4. Yes; it's common knowledge if it appears *undocumented* in five or more
   sources.
5. Yes; such a small program would not be widely known, so you should cite
   your sister as a source if you mention it. If you describe the program in
   more detail, it would make sense to research documents or newspaper
   descriptions and cite them rather than Big Sis.
6. No; the date and location of Shakespeare's birth is not in dispute and can be
   found in many sources, so it is common knowledge even if you did not know it.

7. Hmmm. This is a tricky situation. Since *some,* but not all, literary historians believe Shakespeare himself played the ghost, this is probably common knowledge among Shakespeare experts. You, however, are not a Shakespeare expert, so it would be wise to cite the footnote just to be safe. So the answer is, Yes—cite it!
8. No; undisputed dates are common knowledge.
9. Yes; conspiracy theories are controversial, and the details of such controversies need to be cited.

Section 3: Quoting, Paraphrasing, and Summarizing Texts

Illegal Trade Passage:

1. OK; an example of summary. The sentence gives the author and the title. (Remember, the Works Cited list will provide more publication information.)
2. X; two things are wrong: some of the language is too similar to the original, and the citation method is incorrect. Do not list the URL in your paper. The phrase "adopt new strategies to deal with this unprecedented struggle that now shapes the world" is too close to the source, in some places identical to it.
3. X; this paraphrase is too close to the original. The writer used a thesaurus to change key words, but the sentence structure is identical to the original. Plus, the author's last name (not first name) should appear in the parenthetical citation. (Also, using "etc." in the text is annoying!)
4. OK; This is common knowledge. The sentence is so general, it really has nothing to do with the passage from Moisés Naim, so there is no reason to cite him.

Romance Novel Passage:

1. OK; this summary is correct; the author's name appears in the sentence, so it does not need to appear in the parenthetical citation.
2. X; although the source is documented properly, some of the language is too close to the source, especially the phrases "keep women in their place" and "real female problems." These phrases need to be put into quotation marks or rewritten.
3. X; most of this sentence is copied directly from the source; it needs to be rewritten or partially enclosed in quotes.
4. X; the quote is properly attributed to Greer, but the page number refers to Modleski's book. Also, there's no need to copy the footnote number from the original.
5. OK; this example shows how to properly cite one writer quoted within the work of another. Also note how the ellipsis and brackets indicate how the "-ing" part of "cherish" was deleted to make the quote flow better. The ellipsis indicates that something was deleted; the brackets indicate that the ellipsis was not in the original source.

Section 4: Miscellaneous

1. c
2. c
3. d

Literary Credits

Photo Credits

Page 20: © Henry Martin/The New Yorker Collection/www.cartoonbank.com; 33: Maya portrait sculpture (mid-seventeenth century) Lord Pacal. Mayan Classic Period, mid-7th CE. Stucco. Height 16 7/8" (43 cm.). From the tomb at the Temple of the Inscriptions, Palenque. Location: Museo Nacional de Antropologia e Historia, Mexico City, D.F., Mexico. Scala/Art Resource, NY; 147: Dorothy Alexander; 188: Akg-images/Newscom; 194: Jose Armas; 200: Nancy Crampton; 205: Hulton Archive/Getty Images; 215: By permission of the Jones Library, Inc., Amherst, Massachusetts; 231: The Granger Collection; 233: Bettman/Corbis; 249t: B. Keating/Stock Photo/Black Star; 249b: Used with permission, Albert and Shirley Small Special Collections Library, University of Virginia; 251: Used with permission, Albert and Shirley Small Special Collections Library, University of Virginia; 252: Used with permission, Albert and Shirley Small Special Collections Library, University of Virginia; 256t: Used with permission, Albert and Shirley Small Special Collections Library, University of Virginia; 256b: Used with permission, Albert and Shirley Small Special Collections Library, University of Virginia; 258: Used with permission, Albert and Shirley Small Special Collections Library, University of Virginia; 259: Used with permission, Albert and Shirley Small Special Collections Library, University of Virginia; 260: Used with permission, Albert and Shirley Small Special Collections Library, University of Virginia; 261: Used with permission, Albert and Shirley Small Special Collections Library, University of Virginia; 318: Library of Congress Prints and Photographs Division [LC-USZ62-21207]; 321, 322: By permission of the Houghton Library, Harvard University; 323: Handcolored D.F. Barry photograph of Buffalo Bill on white horse, ca. 1912. Buffalo Bill Historical Center, Cody, Wyoming, U.S.A.; Original Buffalo Bill Museum Collection, Gift of Nina Osborne Batson, P.69.862; 343: © Nickolas Muray Photo Archives; 348: Authenticated News/Getty Images; 374: AP Images; 429: By permission of the Houghton Library, Harvard University; 443: AP Images; 444: The New York Public Library/Art Resource, NY; 462: Frederick Ayers/Photo Researchers, Inc.; 464: The John Vickers Theatre Collection/University of Bristol/ArenaPAL; 541: AP Images; 542: Bettmann/Corbis; 548: Nancy Crampton/AP Images; 551: Everett Collection Inc./Alamy; 624: Picture History/Newscom; 648: AP Photo; 654: Annie Valva; 664: Lebrecht Music and Arts Photo Library/Alamy; 673: Nancy Crampton; 677: Marion Ettlinger; 688: University of Georgia Photographic Services. All rights reserved; 693: UK History/Alamy; 705: Everett Collection Inc./Alamy; 713: Sophie Bassouls/Sygma/Corbis; 732: Bettmann/Corbis; 734: The Poetry Collection of the University Libraries, University at Buffalo, The State University of New York; 735: Robert Pack; 736: Nancy Crampton; 745: Bettmann/Corbis; 757: Bettmann/Corbis; 761: Bettmann/Corbis 763: © Imogen Cunningham Trust, 1959, 2012; 764: Nancy Crampton; 765: John Jonas Gruen/Hulton Archive/Getty Images; 766: Dorothy Alexander; 767: AP Photo/David Pickoff; 769: Everett Collection; 813: Photofest; 857: Infant Joy, from Songs of Innocence, published 1789 (coloured engraving), Blake, William (1757–1827)/Private Collection/The Bridgeman Art Library; 858: 'Infant Sorrow', plate 39 (Bentley 48) from 'Songs of Innocence and of Experience' (Bentley Copy L) 1789-94 (relief etching with pen & w/c), Blake, William (1757–1827)/Yale Center for British Art, Paul Mellon Collection, USA/The Bridgeman Art Library; 864: Dorothy Alexander; 867l: By permission of the Folger Shakespeare Library; 867r: Foto Marburg/Art Resource, NY; 869: Joe Cocks Studio Collection © Shakespeare Birthplace Trust; 870: Joe Cocks Studio Collection © Shakespeare Birthplace Trust; 871: Mark Douet/ArenaPal/The Image Works; 886: Martha Swope/The New York Public Library; 994: Jim West/Alamy; 1013: Bettmann/Corbis; 1026: Nancy Crampton; 1035: Pach Brothers/Corbis; 1042: Sam Garst; 1044: Inge Morath © The Inge Morath Foundation/Magnum Photos; 1046t: Lee J. Cobb in Death of a Salesman: Harry Ransom Humanities Research Center, The University of Texas at Austin; 1046b: Inge Morath © The Inge Morath Foundation/Magnum Photos; 1117: Frank Capri/Getty Images; 1125: AP Images/Noah Berger; 1134t: Joseph Bruchac; 1134b: Brown Brothers; 1135: © Linda Haas Photography;

Index of Authors, Titles, and First Lines of Poetry

Index of Terms